A Concordance to the Poems of

JONATHAN SWIFT

THE CORNELL CONCORDANCES

S. M. Parrish, *General Editor*

Supervisory Committee

M. H. Abrams
Donald D. Eddy
Ephim Fogel
Alain Seznec

POEMS OF MATTHEW ARNOLD, *edited by S. M. Parrish*
POEMS OF W. B. YEATS, *edited by S. M. Parrish*
POEMS OF EMILY DICKINSON, *edited by S. P. Rosenbaum*
WRITINGS OF WILLIAM BLAKE, *edited by David V. Erdman*
BYRON'S *DON JUAN, edited by Charles W. Hagelman, Jr., and Robert J. Barnes*
THÉÂTRE ET POÉSIES DE JEAN RACINE, *edited by Bryant C. Freeman*
BEOWULF, *edited by J. B. Bessinger, Jr.*
PLAYS OF W. B. YEATS, *edited by Eric Domville*
POEMS OF JONATHAN SWIFT, *edited by Michael Shinagel*

A Concordance to the Poems of

JONATHAN SWIFT

Edited by

MICHAEL SHINAGEL

Cornell University Press

ITHACA AND LONDON

International Standard Book Number 0–8014–0747–8
Library of Congress Catalog Card Number 72–4870

Printed in the United States of America by Vail-Ballou Press, Inc.

Librarians: Library of Congress cataloging information appears on the last page of the book.

In memory of
Cornell friends and colleagues

JOHN FINCH
GEORGE HEALEY
MARK ROWAN

CONTENTS

Preface   ix

Concordance to the Poems of Jonathan Swift   1

Appendix. Index Words in Order of Frequency   943

PREFACE

Doubtless Jonathan Swift would have dismissed a computerized concordance to his poetry as a mechanical operation of the spirit and consigned it to a basement room in the Grand Academy of Lagado. Yet, as more and more concordances to major authors become available, we gain an increasing appreciation of their value as reference tools. The case of Swift is no exception. Owing to his imaginative genius as a satirist and prose stylist, "the poems of Jonathan Swift," as Sir Harold Williams noted, "have been undeservedly overshadowed." The publication of this concordance will enable scholars to reconsider Swift's claims as a poet. As Swift himself recognized, he had "the Sin of Wit," and, as a glance at the list of Index Words in Order of Frequency will disclose, WIT is the most recurrent noun in his poetic vocabulary, appearing a total of 176 times. Significant word constellations reveal the extent to which Swift in his poetry stressed the intellect and the senses: KNOW (170), THINK (155), THOUGHT (109), MIND (95), KNOWN (43), SEE (243), EYES (87), SEEN (68), SIGHT (63), HEAR (82), EARS (48), NOSE (47), SMELL (17), TASTE (29). Similarly, his abiding concerns for such maters as age and health recur in his poems: OLD (169), YOUNG (44), TIME (118), SICK (50). In short, the information provided in this concordance will substantiate the truth of a remark made by Swift's first modern editor, F. Elrington Ball: "Without knowledge of his verse a true picture of Swift cannot be drawn. In his verse he sets forth his life as in a panorama, he shows more clearly than in his prose his peculiar turn of thought, and he reveals his character in all its phases."

Basic Text and Format

This concordance is based on the "definitive" three-volume edition of *The Poems of Jonathan Swift,* second edition, prepared by the late Sir Harold Williams for the Clarendon Press, Oxford, in 1958 (by permission of the Clarendon Press, Oxford). Although Williams did a monumental job in limiting and regularizing the corpus of Swift's poetry, his edition does not establish a clearly defined canon. Yet since this edition is the best and most comprehensive scholarly text we have available, I thought it best to follow

Williams's lead on matters of attribution, both for consistency and for accuracy, but at the same time to strike something of a scholarly compromise. After consulting authorities on Swift, I decided on the following editorial policy:

1. Include all poems supposedly by Swift that appear in the Williams edition (even when there is substantial doubt about Swift's authorship) and those poems in which he is believed to have had only a minor hand, but carry for all such poems (or lines from such poems) a capital letter "D" prefixed to all line entries in the concordance (see the section entitled "Doubtful Poems and Lines," below in this Preface, for further information).
2. Omit all verses placed by Williams at the end of Volume III under the rubric "Poems Attributed to Swift" (pp. 1055 *et seq.*).
3. Omit all poems not by Swift himself (for example, poems by Sheridan, Delany, and others).
4. Omit Swift's few Latin poems but include all foreign words and phrases from his English poems.

I have drawn on the informative notes provided by Sir Harold Williams to reconstruct many blank or incomplete words in the text of Swift's poems. Occasionally I have supplied a missing, obviously scatological, word to the text, as in the case of the celebrated concluding line to "Cassinus and Peter." All such reconstructed words are included in the concordance within brackets and are normally listed under an entry following all the unbracketed words.

The concordance provides a system of cross-referencing to help the reader locate words of interest. Generally, cross references are included when both the modern-spelling and the old-spelling variant exist and, in the concordance text, are farther apart than half a page (or more than about fifty lines apart), and when something more than the use of the apostrophe is responsible for the variant (e.g., EVERY and its variants are not cross-referenced). There is no cross-referencing for the second part of a name (e.g., FITZ-BAKER), but otherwise all second portions of hyphenated words, including even some nonsense words, are cross-referenced automatically to the whole word. The reader is advised, however, to be alert to the vagaries of Swift's orthography when consulting the concordance, for in some poems, such as "Merlin," Old English or pseudo–Old English variants occur. Similarly, as in the entries under SHERRY and SYLLABLE, some words are compounded from stuttered parts.

Swift's partiality to the octosyllabic couplet simplified the process of punching the IBM data cards for the computer, for in most cases one line of verse fitted neatly on each card, together with page and line numbers. The

few long lines that had to be divided can be recognized by the spaced periods that end the first portion of the line or begin the second. Refrain lines
carry REF in the line-number position, and are left unnumbered. One poem,
"A Cantata," had to be reconstructed from the text for special punching
and has no line references at all. Lines are automatically repeated as many
times as the index word occurs in the line. The concordance entries follow
Swift's punctuation, and sometimes single-stroke quotation marks are in-
distinguishable from apostrophes. The reader must also be attentive to the
computer's alphabetization. The hyphen, followed by the apostrophe, pre-
cedes the alphabet. For example, entries under the letter "A" run from A
(omitted word), to A-BED, A-BROACH, A-CLOCK, etc., to A's, then AB,
ABANDON'D, etc. Similarly, under "S," this sequence of entries illustrates the
rule: SEA, SEA-GOD, SEA-SICK, SEA's, SEAL, etc. One exception only to these
rules of alphabetization has been made to save the reader confusion: words
with initial apostrophe, like 'GAINST, or 'SPARAGRASS, have been moved to
the places they would occupy if their apostrophe were not present.

Great care has been taken to provide the reader with an accurate and
easily accessible text for the study of Swift's poetry, but with the scope and
complexity of a project such as this, it is almost inevitable that some
elusive errors will slip past even an Argus-eyed editor. For such failings I
cannot blame the computer or the programmer but only myself. Now that
my work is completed I find my feelings best expressed by a minor con-
temporary of Swift's, Charles Leslie, who in *A Defence of a book entituled:
The snake in the grass* (London, 1700) wrote: "I must trouble the reader to
correct the errata of the press, as he finds them. For I am quite tyr'd."

Abbreviated Titles

Title abbreviations for Swift's poems had to be streamlined to fit into the
fourteen columns available for them on the IBM cards. Such severe limita-
tions at times tested my ingenuity, especially when wrestling with some of
Swift's more prolix titles, but in most cases I have been able to devise abbreviations that correspond closely to the full title.

Listed below in alphabetical order are the abbreviated titles exactly
as they appear in the text of the concordance. After each abbreviation the
reader will find the full title of the poem and the page number on which
the poem begins in the Williams edition.

Abbreviation	Title	Page
A Quiet Life	A quiet Life, and a good Name	219
Advice Parson	Advice to a Parson. An Epigram	807
Aenigma	Aenigma	911
Ans to Crown	The Dean's Answer (to Sheridan's Upon stealing a Crown when the Dean was asleep)	1033

Abbreviation	Title	Page
Answer Delaney	The Answer (Swift to Dr. Delany)	366
Answer Fable	Answer to Dr. D—y's Fable of the Pheasant and the Lark	512
Answer Paulus	The Answer, by Dr. Swift (to Lindsay's Paulus)	432
Answer Rebus	The Answer (to A Rebus Written by a Lady, On The Rev. D—n S——t)	716
Apology Lady C	An Apology to the Lady C–R–T	375
Apollo	Apollo, To Dean Swift. By Himself	263
Apollo Outwit	Apollo Outwitted. To the Honourable Mrs. Finch, under her Name of Ardelia	119
Apples	Verses made for Women who cry Apples, &c.	951
Archbi Cashel	On the Archbishop of Cashel, and Bettesworth	818
Arch–Bish Dub	To his Grace the Arch-Bishop of Dublin, A Poem	339
Asparagus	Verses made for Women who cry Apples, &c.	952
Atlas	Atlas. writt. 1712 to the Earl of Oxford	160
Author Himself	The Author upon Himself	193
Authors Living	The Author's manner of Living	954
Ay and No	Ay and No. A Tale from Dublin	843
Ballyspellin	An Answer to the Ballyspellin Ballad	440
Bank Down	The Bank thrown down	286
Bauc & Phil 1	The Story of Baucis & Philemon	90
Bauc & Phil 2	Baucis and Philemon. Imitated, From the Eighth Book of Ovid	111
Beasts Confess	The Beasts Confession to the Priest, on Observing how most Men mistake their own Talents	601
Beau's Reply	The Beau's reply to the five Ladyes answer	428
Bec's B–Day	Bec's Birth–Day	760
Betty Grizette	To Betty the Grizette	522
Biddy Floyd	To Mrs. Biddy Floyd	118
Billet Players	Billet to the Company of Players	307
Birthday Song	Directions for a Birth–day Song	460
Bless Country	The Blessings of a Country Life	1036
Bro Protestant	On the Words—Brother Protestants, and Fellow Christians, so familiarly used by the Advocates for the Repeal of the Test Act in Ireland, 1733	811
Bubble	The Bubble	250
Burning Poem	On burning a dull Poem	469
By Dr. Swift	Verses written by Dr. Swift	611
Cadenus Vaness	Cadenus and Vanessa	686
Cantata	A Cantata	956
Carterets Arms	On Ld Carterets Arms given as the custom is, at every Inn where the Ld Lt. dines or lyes, with all the titles in a long Parchment (in Holyhead Journal Poems)	423
Cassinus Peter	Cassinus and Peter. A Tragical Elegy	593
Censure	On Censure	413
Charac Walpole	The Character of Sir Robert Walpole	540
City Shower	A Description of a City Shower	136
Clad in Brown	Clad all in Brown	786

Abbreviation	Title	Page
Collar Lap–Dog	On the Collar of Mrs. Dingley's Lap–Dog	763
Corinna	Corinna	149
Curate's Compl	Verses spoken extempore by Dean Swift on his Curate's Complaint of hard Duty	675
Dan J's Reply	Dan Jackson's Reply. Written by the Dean in the Name of Dan J—n	1003
Daphne	Daphne.	906
Day Judgement	The Day of Judgement	578
Dean and Duke	The Dean and Duke	678
Dean Hang Rape	An Excellent New Ballad: or, The true En—sh D——n to be hang'd for a R–pe	516
Dean Smedley	Dean Smedley Gone to seek his Fortune	455
Dean to Sherid	The Dean of St. Patrick's to Tho: Sheridan	975
Dean to Tho: S	The Dean to Tho: Sheridan	978
Dean's Reasons	The Dean's Reasons For not Building at Drapier's Hill	899
Death Daphne	Death and Daphne. To an agreeable young Lady, but extremely lean	903
Death of Swift	Verses on Death of Dr. Swift, D.S.P.D.	553
Descriptn Morn	A Description of the Morning	124
Desire Possess	Desire and Possession	411
Dialogue	A Dialogue between an eminent Lawyer and Dr. Swift Dean of St. Patrick's, being an allusion to the first Satire of the second book of Horace	489
Dial Rich Marb	A Pastoral Dialogue Between Richmond–Lodge and Marble–Hill	408
Dick, Maggot	Dick, A Maggot	785
Dick's Variety	Dick's Variety	787
Dicky Dolly	An Elegy on Dicky and Dolly	430
Dingley Brent	Dingley, and Brent. A Song	755
Discovery	The Discovery	62
Doctor Delaney	To Doctor D–L——Y, on the Libels Writ against him	500
Dog and Thief	The Dog and Thief	395
Dr. Helsham	To Dr. Helsham	1028
Dr. Rundle	On Dr. Rundle, Bishop of Derry	819
Dr. Sheridan	To Doctor Sheridan	1030
Drapier's Hill	Drapier's Hill	875
Earl of Oxford	To the Earl of Oxford, Late Lord Treasurer. Sent to him when he was in the Tower, before his Tryal	210
Earl of P–b–w	To the Earl of P—b—w	397
Elegy Boat	A quibbling Elegy on the Worshipful Judge Boat	284
Elegy on Demar	An Elegy On the Much lamented Death of Mr. Demar, the Famous rich Man, who died the 6th of this Inst. July, 1720	233
Elegy Patrige	An Elegy on Mr. Patrige, the Almanack–maker	98
Empty'ng Town	"In pity to the empty'ng Town"	122
Epigram 1	Epigrams (transcript by Stella)	327
Epigram 2	Epigrams (transcript by Stella)	328
Epigram 3	Epigrams (transcript by Stella)	328

Abbreviation	Title	Page
Epigr Fasting	Epigram on Fasting. From the French	949
Epigr Irish	Epigram (on Irish)	843
Epigr Kite	An Epigram, Inscribed to the Honourable Sergeant Kite	818
Epigr Prelate	Epigram. On seeing a worthy Prelate go out of Church in the Time of Divine Service, to wait on his Grace the D. of D....	809
Epigr Rundle	An Epigram (on Rundle)	822
Epigr Scolding	An Epigram on Scolding	949
Epigram Bust	Epigrams on the Busts in Richmond Hermitage	663
Epilogue	An Epilogue, To be spoke at the Theatre–Royal	274
Epist on Epist	An Epistle upon an Epistle	475
Epistle Lady	An Epistle To A Lady, Who desired the Author to make Verses on Her, in the Heroick Stile	629
Excellent Song	An Excellent new Song on a seditious Pamphlet	236
Fable Bitches	The Fable of the Bitches. Wrote in the Year 1715, on an attempt to repeal the Test Act	207
Fable of Midas	The Fable of Midas	156
Faggot	The Faggot. Written in the Year 1713, when the Queen's Ministers were quarrelling among themselves	189
First of April	The First of April: A Poem	320
Five Ladies	On the five Ladies at Sots–Hole, with the Doctor at their Head	425
Four Storyes	Upon four dismal Storyes in the Doctor's Letter, relating to four of my Friends	1037
From Catullus	From Catullus	679
Game Traffick	A Ballad on the Game of Traffick	74
Gift for Bec	A New–Year's–Gift for Bec	753
Grace's Answer	His Grace's Answer to Jonathan	361
Grand Question	The Grand Question debated. Whether Hamilton's Bawn should be turned into a Barrack or a Malt–House	866
Grub-Street	Advice to the Grub–street Verse–Writers	394
Harlyes Surgn	To Mr. Harlyes Surgeon	140
Heathen Christ	'The Heathen doth believe in Christ'	1036
Helter Skelter	Helter Skelter, or The Hue and Cry after the Attornies, going to ride the Circuit	573
Herrings	Verses made for Women who cry Apples, &c.	953
His Deafness	Written by the Reverend Dr. Swift. On his own Deafness	673
Hist V's House	The History of Vanbrug's House. 1706	86
Holyhead	Holyhead. Sept. 25. 1727 (in Holyhead Journal Poems)	420
Holyhead Journ	Poems from the Holyhead Journal. 1727	419
Horace 1, 7	Part of the Seventh Epistle of the First Book of Horace Imitated	170
Horace 1, 14	Horace. Book I. Ode XIV. Paraphrased and inscribed to Ir—d	770

Abbreviation	Title	Page
Horace 2, 1	The First Ode of the Second Book of Horace Para-phras'd: And Address'd to Richard St—le, Esq.	180
Horace 2, 6	Horace, Lib. 2. Sat. 6. Part of it imitated	198
Horace 4, 9	Part of the 9th Ode of the 4th Book of Horace, address'd to Doctor William King, late Lord Arch–Bishop of Dublin	242
Horrid Plot	Upon the horrid Plot discovered by Harlequin the B—— of R—'s French Dog	298
In Sickness	In Sickness. Written soon after the Author's coming to live in Ireland, upon the Queen's Death, October 1714	203
Ireld	Ireld (in Holyhead Journal Poems)	421
Irish Bishops	On the Irish Bishops. 1732	803
Irish–Club	On the Irish–Club	487
Irish–Feast	The Description of an Irish–Feast, translated almost literally out of the Original Irish	244
Jason Hassard	Mr. Jason Hassard, a Woollen–Drapier in Dublin, put up the Sign of the Golden Fleece, and desired a Motto in Verse	948
Journal	The Journal	278
Judas	Judas	806
Know Not What	Verses on I Know Not What	608
Lady Acheson	Lady A–S–N Weary of the Dean	859
Lady B– B–	Lady B– B– finding in the Authors Room some Verses Unfinished, underwrit a Stanza of her own, with Railery upon him, which gave Occasion to this Ballade	76
Lady's Dres Rm	The Lady's Dressing Room	525
Lady's Lament	My Lady's Lamentation and Complaint against the Dean	851
Lady Tablebook	Verses wrote in a Lady's Ivory Table–Book	60
Legion Club	A Character, Panegyric, and Description of the Legion Club	829
Letter	A Letter	940
Letter D. S–Y	A letter from D. S—t to D. S—y	371
Letter Dr Sh–n	A Letter to the Reverend Dr. Sh–n	988
Letter Sherid	A Left–handed Letter to Dr. Sheridan	967
Libel on D– D–	A Libel on D— D—. And a Certain Great Lord	480
Life of Swift	The Life and Genuine Character of Doctor Swift. Written by Himself	545
Little House	On the Little House by the Church Yard of Castle-knock	126
Love Song	A Love Song. In the Modern Taste	660
Magician's Rod	The Virtues of Sid Hamet the Magician's Rod	132
Manly Virtue	The Birth of Manly Virtue, from Callimachus	383
Mary to Sher	Mary the Cook–Maid's Letter to Dr. Sheridan	985
Merlin	A Famous Prediction of Merlin, the British Wizard	102

Abbreviation	Title	Page
Modern Lady	The Journal of a Modern Lady	444
Modern Poets	A Copy of Verses Upon two celebrated Modern Poets	393
Mr. Pulteney	On Mr. P—y being put out of the Council	537
Mrs Harris Pet	To Their Excellencies the Lords Justices of Ireland. The Humble Petition of Frances Harris	69
Mrs. Houghton	To Mrs. Houghton of Bormount, upon praising her Husband to Dr. Swift	947
Mullinex Dick	Tom Mullinex and Dick	784
Mullinix Tim	Mad Mullinix and Timothy	773
New Song	An Excellent New Song, Being the Intended Speech of a famous Orator against Peace	142
Noisy Tom	On Noisy Tom	825
Ode Athenian	Ode to the Athenian Society	16
Ode to King	Ode to the King. On his Irish Expedition	6
Ode Sancroft	Ode to Dr. William Sancroft, Late Lord Archbishop of Canterbury	34
Ode to Temple	Ode to the Honble Sir William Temple	26
Old Thorn	On Cutting down the Old Thorn at Market Hill	848
On Dreams	On Dreams. An Imitation of Petronius	363
On Old Glass	On a Very Old Glass	861
On Picture	On the foregoing Picture	993
On Poetry	On Poetry: A Rapsody	640
On the Union	Verses said to be written on the Union	96
Onyons	Verses made for Women who cry Apples, &c.	952
Oranges	Verses made for Women who cry Apples, &c.	953
Order of Bath	Verses on the Revival of the Order of Bath	389
Oysters	Verses made for Women who cry Apples, &c.	952
Paddy's Charac	On Paddy's Character of the Intelligencer	457
Panegyr Dean	A Panegyrick on the D—n, in the Person of a Lady in the North	887
Panegyr Swift	A Panegyric on the Reverend D—n S——t in Answer to the Libel on Dr. D—y, and a certain Great L—d	492
Parson's Case	The Parson's Case	676
Pastoral Dial	A Pastoral Dialogue	880
Peace Dunkirk	Peace and Dunkirk; Being an Excellent New Song upon the Surrender of Dunkirk to General Hill	168
Pethox	Pethox the Great	323
Place Damn'd	The Place of the Damn'd	575
Plague Country	The Plagues of a Country Life	1036
Portrait Life	A Portrait from the Life	955
Printer Newgat	On a Printer's being sent to Newgate, by —	824
Probatur Alit	Probatur Aliter	942
Problem	The Problem	65
Problem Solved	Apollo: or, A Problem solved	597
Prog Marriage	The Progress of Marriage	289
Prog of Beauty	The Progress of Beauty	226
Prog of Love	Phillis, Or, the Progress of Love	222
Prog of Poetry	The Progress of Poetry	230

Abbreviation	Title	Page
Prometheus	Prometheus, A Poem	344
Psyche	On Psyche	580
Receipt Youth	A Receipt to Restore Stella's Youth	759
Reply by Dean	Another Reply by the Dean in Dan Jackson's Name	1002
Rev Market–Hill	The Revolution at Market–Hill	883
Riddle 1	A Riddle. Written in the Year 1724	915
Riddle 2	Another (Riddle)	916
Riddle 3	Another (Riddle)	917
Riddle 4	Another (Riddle)	917
Riddle 5	Another (Riddle)	919
Riddle 6	Another (Riddle)	920
Riddle 7	Another (Riddle). The Gulph of all human Possessions	921
Riddle 8	Another (Riddle). Louisa to Strephon	924
Riddle 9	Another (Riddle). Written in the Year 1725	926
Riddle Answerd	[A Riddle by Doctor Delaney] Answered by Dean Swift	938
Robbin & Harry	Robbin and Harry	878
Run Bankers	The Run upon the Bankers	239
S–'s Ans Sh–d	D—n S—'s Answer to the Reverend Doctor Sh—n	972
Salamander	The Description of a Salamander	82
Satiric Elegy	A Satirical Elegy on the Death of a late Famous General	296
Scandal Poem 1	An Answer To a late scandalous Poem, wherein the Author most audaciously presumes to compare a Cloud to a Woman	617
Scandal Poem 2	An Answer To a Scandalous Poem, Wherein The Author most audaciously presumes to cast an Indignity upon their Highnesses the Clouds, by comparing them to a Woman	623
Scriblerus 1	Jeux D'Esprit of the Scriblerus Club. I	185
Scriblerus 3	Jeux D'Esprit of the Scriblerus Club. III	186
Scriblerus 6	Jeux D'Esprit of the Scriblerus Club. VI	188
Serious Poem	A Serious Poem upon William Wood	334
Servants Maxim	The Servants' Maxim	1035
Shall Repine	Shall I repine (in Holyhead Journal Poems)	419
Sher, A Goose	Sheridan, A Goose	982
Sheri Circles	To Mr. Thomas Sheridan, Upon his Verses written in Circles	1026
Sheridan Cavan	Sheridan at Cavan	1037
Sheridan's Sub	Sheridan's Submission. Written by the Dean	1004
Simile Silver	A Simile, On Our Want of Silver and the only Way to remedy it	354
St. Cecilia's	The Dean to himself on St. Cecilia's day	522
St. Pat's Well	Verses occasioned by the sudden drying up of St. Patrick's Well near Trinity College, Dublin, in 1726	789
Stel B–Day '18	On Stella's Birth–day Written AD. 1718–[19]	721
Stel B–day '20	Stella's Birth–day. Written AD. 1720–21	734
Stel B–day '21	To Stella on her Birth–day. Written AD. 1721–2	739

Abbreviation	Title	Page
Stel B–day 22	Stella's Birth–Day. A great Bottle of Wine, long buried, being that Day dug up	740
Stel B–day '24	Stella's Birth–Day (1724–5)	756
Stel B–day '26	Stella's Birth–Day. March 13. 1726–7	763
Stel Distress	Stella's Distress on the 3ᵈ fatal day of Octobʳ 1723	744
Stel Wood–Park	Stella at Wood–Park, A House of Charles Ford, Esq; eight Miles from Dublin	749
Stella '23	To Stella. March 13, M DCC XXIII–IV	754
Stella, Poems	To Stella, Who Collected and Transcribed his Poems	727
Stephen Duck	On Stephen Duck, the Thresher, and favourite Poet, A Quibbling Epigram	521
Storm	The Storm; Minerva's Petition	302
Strephon Chloe	Strephon and Chloe	584
Swift Ans Sher	Dr. Swift's Answer to Doctor Sheridan	1017
Swift to Pope	Dr. Sw— to Mr. P—e, While he was writing the Dunciad	405
Swift to Sheri	From Dr. Swift to Dr. Sheridan	1013
Temple Ill	Occasioned by Sir W– T–'s Late Illness and Recovery	51
Tho: Sheridan	To Tho: Sheridan	980
Tim and Fables	Tim and the Fables	782
To a Friend	To a Friend who had been much abused in many inveterate Libels	506
To Congreve	To Mr. Congreve	43
To Dean Swift	To Dean Swift. By Sir Arthur Acheson	876
To Ford	To Charles Ford Esqʳ. on his Birth–day Janʳʸ. 31ˢᵗ. for the Year 1722–3	311
To Janus	To Janus on New Year's Day	862
To Lord Harley	To Lord Harley, since Earl of Oxford, on his Marriage	176
To Mr. Delany	To Mr. Delany	215
To Mr. Gay	To Mr. Gay on his being Steward to the Duke of Queensberry	531
To Quilca	To Quilca, a Country House in no very good Repair, where the supposed Author, and some of his Friends, spent a Summer, in the Year 1725	1035
To Sheridan	Swift to Sheridan	1019
To Stella	To Stella, Visiting me in my Sickness	723
Toland's Invit	T—l—nd's Invitation to Dismal, to Dine with the Calves–Head Club	162
Tom Clinch	Clever Tom Clinch going to be hanged	399
Traulus 1	Traulus. The first Part. In a Dialogue Between Tom and Robin	795
Traulus 2	Traulus. The Second Part.	799
Upon His Grace	An Excellent New Song Upon His Grace Our good Lord Archbishop of Dublin	341
Upon Ladies	The Hardship put upon Ladies	662
Upright Judge 1	Verses on the upright Judge, who condemned the Drapier's Printer	349

Abbreviation	Title	Page
Upright Judge 2	Verses on the upright Judge, who condemned the Drapier's Printer	349
Upright Judge 3	Verses on the upright Judge, who condemned the Drapier's Printer	350
V's House	V——'s House Built from the Ruins of Whitehall that was Burnt	106
Vanbrug House	Vanbrug's House. An. 1703. Built from the burnt Ruins of Whitehall	79
Verses Vanessa	Verses to Vanessa	732
Verses Window	Verses left in a Window of Dublin Castle	368
Whitshed Motto	Whitshed's Motto on His Coach	348
Window Inns 1	On seeing Verses written upon Windows in Inns. I	400
Window Inns 2	On seeing Verses written upon Windows in Inns. II	401
Window Inns 3	On seeing Verses written upon Windows in Inns. III	401
Window Inns 4	On seeing Verses written upon Windows in Inns. IV	401
Windsor Proph	The W—ds—r Prophecy	147
Woman's Mind	The Furniture of a Woman's Mind	415
Wood Insect	Wood, an Insect	350
Wood Ironmongr	On Wood the Iron–monger	352
Wood's Brass	An Epigram on Woods's Brass–Money	338
Yahoo's	The Yahoo's Overthrow; or, The Kevan Bayl's New Ballad, upon Serjeant Kite's insulting the Dean	814
Young Nymph	A Beautiful Young Nymph Going to Bed	581
Young's Satire	On Reading Dr. Young's Satires, Called The Universal Passion	391

Doubtful Poems and Lines

Since this concordance is based on the edition of Swift's poems by Sir Harold Williams, I include a number of poems, and lines within poems, whose authorship is uncertain. My intention in including these readings is to be faithful to the Williams text and to be as comprehensive as possible in the preparation of the concordance. About each of the entries listed below, Williams expresses considerable doubt concerning attribution. Often Swift's part is "undetermined, and may be very slight," as in the "Epigrams against Carthy," or there is "no evidence to support Nichol's confident attribution," as in the "Ode to King William."

Listed below in alphabetical order are the abbreviated titles as they appear in the text of the concordance, followed by the full title and page references to the Williams edition. All entries based on these doubtful poems or lines have a capital letter "D" preceding the line reference.

Abbreviation	Title	Page
Aenigma Expl	The Aenigma in the last Mercury explain'd	912
Apollo's Edict	Apollo's Edict	269

Abbreviation	Title	Page
Ballad	A Ballad	840
Epig Carthy 1–25	Epigrams against Carthy	666–672 *seriatim*
Game Traffick	A Ballad on the Game of Traffick (ll. 25–28)	75
Horace 2, 6	Horace, Lib. 2. Sat. 6. (20 lines within brackets)	198–199
Nim–Dan–Dean 1	George Nim–Dan–Dean, Esq; to Mr. Sheridan, on his Verses, written July 15, 1721, at Ten in the Morning	1020–1022
Nim–Dan–Dean 2	George Nim–Dan–Dean's Invitation to Mr. Thomas Sheridan	1022–1024
Ode to William	Ode to King William, On His Successes in Ireland	11
On Poetry	On Poetry: A Rapsody	658–659
Riddle Answerd	Riddle Answered (ll. 6a–b)	939
Riddle 10–24	Riddles	927–937 *seriatim*
Scriblerus 4	Jeux D'Esprit of the Scriblerus Club. IV	186
Upstart	The Upstart	950
Widow and Cat	A Fable of the Widow and her Cat	153
Window Inns 5–11	On seeing Verses written upon Windows in Inns. V–XI	401–404 *seriatim*

Omitted Words

The precedents set by earlier Cornell concordances simplified the process of determining which words to omit from the indexing. Certain key homographs were checked closely in a preliminary computer printout to ensure that no significant words were omitted inadvertently. For example, since Swift used MIGHT only as a verb, the word was omitted completely, whereas since he used WILL both as a noun and as a verb, all the nouns were retained in the index and only the verbs omitted. Also omitted are Swift's ampersand, which occurs twenty-seven times in his poetry, and certain unreconstructable abbreviations, like C—N. Only the texts, not the titles, of Swift's poems are indexed.

Some common words of low frequency were included because they were thought to be of potential interest and did not contribute significantly to the bulk of the concordance. For the same reason some variant spellings of omitted words of high frequency (AGAIN, for example) were included (AG'EN, AGAYNE, AGEN).

Listed below are the 209 word-forms, together with their frequencies, omitted from the indexing.

A	3397	HE'S	57	SHE'LL	18
AGAIN	76	HER	934	SHE'S	23
ALSO	1	HERE	195	SHOU'D	66
ALTHO'	10	HERE'S	13	SHOULD	185
ALTHOUGH	17	HERS	2	SHOULDST	2
AM	61	HERSELF	8	SINCE	114
AN	305	HIM	436	SO	623
AND	4424	HIMSELF	42	SUCH	201
ANOTHER	47	HIS	1604	'T	3
ANOTHER'S	1	HOW	358	T'	29
ANOTHERS	1	I	1503	T'OTHER	1
ANOTHR	1	I'D	23	TH'	45
ARE	446	I'LL	76	THAN	221
AT	632	I'M	86	THAT	856
BE	793	I'VE	8	THAT'S	26
BECAUSE	68	IF	411	THE	5351
BEEN	82	IN	2230	THEE	125
BOTH	131	IN'T	8	THEIR	590
BUT	1123	INTO	89	THEIRS	12
BY	879	IS	770	THEM	190
CAN	398	IS'T	2	THEMSELVES	17
CAN'T	25	IT	729	THEN	367
CANNOT	47	IT'S	30	THERE	180
CANST	3	ITS	88	THERE'S	45
COU'D	74	ITSELF	4	THEREFORE	18
COULD	236	MAY	271	THESE	117
DID	115	ME	384	THEY	511
DIDST	1	MIGHT	97	THEY'D	3
DO	120	MUST	343	THEY'LL	13
DOES	58	MY	859	THEY'RE	10
DON'T	18	MYSELF	6	THEY'VE	4
DOST	3	NEITHER	37	THINE	12
DOTH	4	NO	518	THIS	479
EACH	107	NOR	326	THO	14
EITHER	33	NOT	585	THO'	136
'EM	75	NOW	409	THOSE	114
EVER	126	OF	2150	THOU	128
FOR	1258	ON	592	THOU'LT	7
FRO	2	OR	704	THOU'RT	5
FROM	657	OTHER	98	THOU'ST	3
HAD	286	OTHER'S	2	THOUGH	87
HADST	2	OTHERS	39	THOUR'T	3
HAS	172	OUR	377	THRO	6
HAST	17	OURS	5	THRO'	53
HATH	50	OURSELVES	2	THROUGH	46
HAVE	425	SHALL	242	THUS	213
HE	1119	SHALT	10	THY	335
HE'D	14	SHE	456	'TIL	1
HE'LL	30	SHE'D	11	'TILL	18

TILL	79	WER'T	4	WHO'D	2
'TIS	213	WERE	208	WHO'LL	2
T'IS	1	WERT	4	WHO'S	8
TIS	18	WHAT	463	WHOE'ER	5
TO	3436	WHAT'S	12	WHOE'RE	2
TOO	173	WHEN	635	WHOEVER	5
'TWAS	38	WHEN'ER	1	WHOM	96
TWAS	3	WHEN'RE	1	WHOSE	70
'TWERE	7	WHENE'ER	19	WHY	114
'TWILL	21	WHENE'RE	1	WILL (verb)	416
'TWOULD	9	WHENEVER	5	WITH	1232
TWOU'D	3	WHERE	225	WOU'D	108
UNLESS	21	WHER'ER	1	WOULD	303
UPON	103	WHERE-E'ER	4	YET	276
US	201	WHERE-EVER	1	YOU	1429
WAS	535	WHERE'E'ER	1	YOUR	934
WE	454	WHERE'ER	2	YOUR-SELF	1
WE'D	1	WHEREVER	6	YOURS	18
WE'LL	34	WHETHER	38	YOURSELF	10
WE'RE	1	WHICH	328	YOURSELVES	2
WE'VE	2	WHO	423		

As a convenience to the reader, these omitted words and their frequencies are included in the appropriate alphabetical places in the concordance, with variant forms occasionally combined (e.g., 'TIS, T'IS, and TIS), as they are in the appendix of frequencies.

Frequency List

In the appendix the reader will find in order of frequency the 13,660 index entries in the concordance, including the 209 omitted words. The range runs from a frequency of 5,351 for THE to a single entry for ZODIACK. Since this list is inclusive of all sorts of variant spellings, elisions, reconstructed words, doubtful poems and lines, and the like, we obviously cannot take the total as an accurate figure for Swift's poetic vocabulary. Even allowing for this inclusiveness, however, Swift's vocabulary is impressive for its scope and variety, especially when compared with the total of 10,097 in the concordance for Matthew Arnold and the total of 10,666 in the concordance for Yeats's poems.

When using the frequency list, the reader should remember that, following the computer's rules of alphabetization, bracketed words, and words that begin with an apostrophe, appear first, in that order, for each frequency. For example, the listing, under the frequency of 2, runs: [BURNET'S], [CARR], [CLEMENTS], [DILKS], [FARTS], [HARRISON], [SHIT], 'GAINST, 'PRENTICE, 'SCAP'T, A-CLOCK, A-DREAM'D, A-FOOT, A-WHILE, ABHOR'D, ABLER, and so on alphabetically to the final entry, YOURSELVES.

Acknowledgments

This concordance is the product of a number of years of work, during which I have been fortunate in securing the assistance and cooperation of a number of individuals and institutions. I am indebted to the Secretary of the Delegates of the Clarendon Press, Oxford, for permission to base my concordance on the Sir Harold Williams edition of Swift's poems. A grant from the National Endowment for the Humanities enabled me to get this project launched, and two timely grants from Union College (a Summer Research Grant and a Ford Humanities Research Grant) enabled me to sustain my efforts until the work was completed.

I have benefited from the counsel of Swift scholars during the early stages of my work. Professors Irvin Ehrenpreis, Maurice Johnson, and Louis A. Landa have been especially helpful in offering specific advice on matters of editorial policy. For their informed suggestions, interest, and encouragement, I am deeply grateful.

The onerous chores of checking the thousands of punched IBM data cards against the text of Swift's poems were shared with me, in part, by Ann M. Seemann and Scott M. Siegler. I appreciate their cheerful assistance. Audrey Werner and Marjorie Gleason supplied typing services as they were needed. Dr. Edwin K. Tolan and the staff of Schaffer Library, Union College, were most helpful in providing me with a study and with many professional services.

I would also like to thank James A. Painter, the computer programmer for the earlier Cornell Concordances, for again producing a distinctive and reliable program. I save for last my acknowledgment to Professor Stephen M. Parrish, the general editor of the Cornell Concordances, because my indebtedness to him is the greatest. He provided the necessary technical sophistication and steady support in making this concordance a reality. I gladly join the ranks of other Cornell concordance makers in expressing my admiration for his many talents as an editor, both in anticipating problems and in solving them.

MICHAEL SHINAGEL

Schenectady, New York

A Concordance to the Poems of
JONATHAN SWIFT

A   SEE NOW-A-DAYS,CAP-A-PEE,LACK-A-DAY   PAGE   TITLE   LINE
          3397   OMITTED WORD
A-BED
     When sober Folks are all a-bed.   . . . .   229 Prog of Beauty   104
     Or when a-bed, to let out Wind.   . . . .   590 Strephon Chloe   218
     What makes thee lie a-bed so late?   . . . .   594 Cassinus Peter   30
     I last get up, am first a-bed;   . . . .   918 Riddle 4   40
A-BROACH
     The Templer spruce, while ev'ry Spout's a-broach,   . .   138 City Shower   35
A-CLOCK
     As, "What's a-Clock?" And, "How's the Wind?   . . .   201 Horace 2, 6   69
     A frosty Morn--Past Four a-Clock.   . . . .   453 Modern Lady   283
A-DAY
     Read six hours a-day.   . . . .   855 Lady's Lament   132
A-DREAM'D
     So I was a-dream'd, methought,. .   70 Mrs Harris Pet   22
     And now my Dream's out: For I was a-dream'd   . . . .   868 Grand Question   49
A-FAR
     Like Light'ning dazzled from a-far: 352 Wood Ironmongr   14
A-FIRE
     The Moment I get one my Soul's all a-fire,   928 Riddle 11   D   11
A-FOOT
     For since we knew you walk a-foot, ...   622 Scandal Poem 1   175
     And since we find, you walk a-foot   . . . .   627 Scandal Poem 2   133
A-FRESH
     Again a-fresh to Cards they run, ...   453 Modern Lady   278
A-GROUND
     So the famous Tom Leigh, when quite run a-ground,   . .   968 Letter Sherid   19
A-GUE
     And I wish I may soon be not of an A-gue sick;   . . . 1030 Dr. Sheridan   3
A-KIN
     Are very near a-kin;   . . . .   401 Window Inns 4   2
A-LA-MAIN
     From Paris Gazette A-la-main, ...   398 Earl of P-b-w   10
A-NEW
     And will you venture both a-new?   . . . .   436 Answer Paulus   131
A-REEK
     A Messenger comes all a-reek, ...   398 Earl of P-b-w   13
A-RIGHT
     Who says, his numbers do not fadge a-right.   . . . .   988 Letter Dr Sh-n   20
A-THWART
     A Sable Cloud a-thwart the Welkin flings, ...   137 City Shower   14
A-TOP
     Grew Scrubby, dy'd a-top, was stunted: . . . . .   117 Bauc & Phil 2   177
A-WHILE
     With Caution us'd, may serve a-while.   . . . . . .   647 On Poetry   238
     Let me suppose thee for a Ship a-while, ...   770 Horace 1, 14   7
A'S
     An A's and B's your Malice vent, ...   645 On Poetry   159
AB
     Hannoniae qui primus ab oris.   . . . .   186 Scriblerus 4   D   6
     From us descended ab origine, ...   619 Scandal Poem 1   61
     From us descended ab origine;   . . . .   625 Scandal Poem 2   57
ABANDON'D
     On an abandon'd wretch by hopes forsook;   . . . .   54 Temple Ill   108
     Or Mason that abandon'd Bitch.   . . . .   299 Horrid Plot   23
     Abandon'd, stupid, slavish praters!   . . . . . .   436 Answer Paulus   134
ABASH'D
     "If Vice can ever be abash'd, ...   548 Life of Swift   117
ABASHT
     Abasht at what they saw and heard, ...   590 Strephon Chloe   195
ABATE
     Their noblest Use is to abate   . . . .   387 Manly Virtue   107
ABDICATES
     He fairly abdicates his Throne, ...   712 Cadenus Vaness   800
ABEL
     Except the Matchless Hero Abel.   . . . .   183 Horace 2, 1   86
ABETTING
     That Stella was helping, abetting and aiding, ...   264 Apollo   39
ABHOR
     Both Dukes and Lords abhor its Wood, ...   928 Riddle 12   D   7
ABHOR'D
     Had many Pendents, but abhor'd a Jack.   . . . . .   285 Elegy Boat   16
     Was more abhor'd, and scorn'd by those   . . . . .   775 Mullinix Tim   53
ABHORR'D
     "For he abhorr'd that senseless Tribe, ...   571 Death of Swift   465
ABIDE
     She can't abide to stay out late.   . . . .   293 Prog Marriage   98
ABJURATIONS
     Patents, Instalments, Abjurations, ...   174 Horace 1, 7   102
ABLE
     Able to lift it from the Ground;   . . . .   87 Hist V's House   30
     In short, he was an able Sculler.   . . . .   286 Elegy Boat   44
     Ye Pow'rs of Grub-street make me able, ...   346 Prometheus   57
     Was able Saturn to depose;   . . . .   461 Birthday Song   24
     In antient Times the Wise were able, ...   512 Answer Fable   1
     Than he's able to digest: . . . .   633 Epistle Lady   126
     Make you able upon Sight, ...   638 Epistle Lady   269
     Nor will be able with her shears   . . . .   760 Bec's B-Day   5
     Did not an able Statesman   . . . .   774 Mullinix Tim   17
     Whose able Heads support the Weight, ...   781 Mullinix Tim   257
     Some perhaps may think him able   . . . .   800 Traulus 2   45

ABLE   (CONTINUED)   PAGE   TITLE   LINE

The Servants amaz'd, are scarce ever able, ... 871 Grand Question   135
And now I find my Muse but ill able . . . . 989 Letter Dr Sh-n   30

ABLER
Nor, dares an abler Workman undertake . . . . 535 To Mr. Gay   133
We had a Hundred abler Men, ... 548 Life of Swift   99

ABODES
"Commodious to their own Abodes. . . . . 571 Death of Swift   454

ABOMINE
By topicks, which tho' I abomine 'em, ... 433 Answer Paulus   47

ABORTIVE
Sick lust of souls, and an abortive child; . . . . . . 47 To Congreve   124
To manage thy abortive Scheme; . . . . 696 Cadenus Vaness   299

ABOUND
Sin and the plague ever abound . . . . 37 Ode Sancroft   96
Wherever the Damn'd do Chiefly abound, ... 575 Place Damn'd   5

ABOUT
To buzz about the mighty Flame; . . . . 9 Ode to King   116
We join like Flyes, and Wasps, in buzzing about Wit. 18 Ode Athenian   75
About the Head crown'd with these Bays, ... 29 Ode to Temple   87
And rolls about her dreadful Eyes, ... 30 Ode to Temple   122
But sees thy meteor blaze about me shine, ... 54 Temple Ill   91
I keep in a Pocket ty'd about my Middle, next my Smock. 69 Mrs Harris Pet   7
Such a thing as this happen'd, just about the time of 71 Mrs Harris Pet   33
    Goosberries.
However, I was resolv'd to bring the Discourse slily 71 Mrs Harris Pet   36
    about,
Delivers Cards about, ... 74 Game Traffick   2
Would raise a House about two Storyes; . . . . . . 79 Vanbrug House   10
Then sheds about his Spawn, and dyes. . . . . . 80 Vanbrug House   38
And strole about, but hide their Quality, ... 90 Bauc & Phil 1   3
And got about a League from Land, ... 96 On the Union   18
And flies about the Candle-Light; . . . . . . 99 Elegy Patrige   52
Might raise a House about two Stories; . . . . . . 106 V's House   10
Thy House about thee like a Snail; . . . . . . 109 V's House   110
And strole about, but hide their Quality, ... 111 Bauc & Phil 2   3
About each Arm a Pudding-sleeve; . . . . . . 115 Bauc & Phil 2   120
All that you make this Stir about, ... 128 Little House   41
About a certain Magick Rod, ... 132 Magician's Rod   22
Now my new Benefactors have brought me about, ... 144 New Song   45
Should sink and fall about his Ears . . . . . . 160 Atlas   10
About some great Affair, at Two-- . . . . . . 200 Horace 2, 6   54
There flies about a strange Report . . . . . . 202 Horace 2, 6   89
Look round about how thick it lyes: . . . . . 254 Bubble   104
Without troubling his Head about Judgment or Wit: . . 263 Apollo   20
"Ye don't fall out about the Heir. . . . . . . 321 First of April   12
(For that's but a Sham Wood they carry about) . . . 336 Serious Poem   76
You may shew him about for a new Groaning Board. . . 336 Serious Poem   84
When ev'ry one turns round about, ... 341 Upon His Grace   8
To every Farmer twice a Week all round about the Yoke, 343 Upon His Grace   39
Whole Crouds about its Brazen Strings. . . . . . 345 Prometheus   30
About the grinding artick Pole; . . . . 362 Grace's Answer   34
The Captain walks about, and searches . . . . . . 377 Apology Lady C   61
Misled them many a League about. . . . . . . 412 Desire Possess   16
They croud about Preferment's Gate, ... 503 Doctor Delaney   93
Glad, that themselves cou'd walk about. . . . . . 546 Life of Swift   51
"I hear about two thousand Pound--- . . . . . . 547 Life of Swift   73
Say what you will about his reading, ... 548 Life of Swift   101
And, while they toss my Name about, ... 565 Death of Swift   303
Nor be concern'd about the Sale, ... 646 On Poetry   189
It whirls about for Want of Force, ... 688 Cadenus Vaness   54
With Pride wou'd drag about her Chain; . . . . . 693 Cadenus Vaness   233
About a Lady----- You know who; . . . . . . 696 Cadenus Vaness   321
Unheard she moves about my Bed. . . . . . . 727 To Stella   112
Is but to frisk about like you. . . . . 774 Mullinix Tim   28
He wildly flings his Filth about, ... 796 Traulus 1   26
Still swarm and buzz about his Nose? . . . . . 798 Traulus 1   87
About St. James's, cry, We Courtiers. . . . . . 812 Bro Protestant   22
Raise the Dirt about your Hole. . . . . . . 832 Legion Club   74
Prudes decay'd about may tack, ... 863 To Janus   21
The naughty boys about the village . . . . . . 902 Dean's Reasons   107
Old Batchelors about his Court: . . . . 903 Death Daphne   12
She ask't about her Friends below; . . . . . . 905 Death Daphne   73
He felt about his Heart a Damp, ... 905 Death Daphne   97
I'm up, and down, and round about, ... 929 Riddle 14   D 1
Like Milk 'tis cry'd about the Street, ... 929 Riddle 15   D 11
It wanders about, ... 939 Riddle Answerd   9
That I have nothing like my Nose about me. . . . . 1004 Dan J's Reply   24
That we walk all about, like a horse in a pound, . . . 1026 Sheri Circles   7
So about twelve at Night, the Punk . . . . . . 1033 Ans to Crown   1

ABOVE
Appear'd, above the Universal Main, ... 16 Ode Athenian   6
Far above all Reward, yet to which all is due, . . . 21 Ode Athenian   187
Woman seems now above all Vanity grown, ... 24 Ode Athenian   250
Look where the Pully's ty'd above! . . . . . . 29 Ode to Temple   102
To judge of things above by things below. . . . . 35 Ode Sancroft   38
Unless, perhaps, some stars above be so; . . . . . 39 Ode Sancroft   144
To be, as 'twas below, the brightest plant above; . . . 41 Ode Sancroft   229
There are degrees above I know . . . . 41 Ode Sancroft   231
And over and above, that I may have your Excellencies 73 Mrs Harris Pet   72
    Letter,

ABOVE	(CONTINUED)	PAGE	TITLE	LINE
Or whether it came from Above or Below.		77	Lady B- B-	18
As he himself could, when above.		101	Elegy Patrige	116
For Charms above and under Ground;		133	Magician's Rod	36
But seldom rose above a Sheet:		172	Horace 1, 7	42
Above a Thousand Pounds in Debt,		174	Horace 1, 7	115
She durst not look above your Wast;		222	Prog of Love	6
Her Hoop is hoist above his Nose,		292	Prog Marriage	79
But fasten'd to his Throne above;		345	Prometheus	32
When you're advanc'd above Dean Viz.		362	Grace's Answer	43
Rais'd high above his Birth by Knowledge,		384	Manly Virtue	33
The Man above, or under Ground.		393	Modern Poets	16
He left the Town above a Week.		398	Earl of P-b-w	15
Above two hundred miles from home?		403	Window Inns 10 D	4
Above the Door, at Country-fair,		457	Paddy's Charac	3
Above the Reach of Want is plac't:		483	Libel on D- D-	84
Attempt a Flight above a Haycock?		513	Answer Fable	22
And griev'd that a Tory should live above Ground.		518	Dean Hang Rape	34
Our Equal rais'd above our Size;		554	Death of Swift	14
Before, behind, above, below,		584	Strephon Chloe	13
No Vulgar Deity above		598	Problem Solved	21
Above a Term or two at most.		604	Beasts Confess	92
Above the Stars exalt your Stile,		657	On Poetry	471
She ne'er could shew her Face above.		689	Cadenus Vaness	82
Above her Wisdom to compose,		690	Cadenus Vaness	131
A Sweetness above all Perfumes;		691	Cadenus Vaness	161
Wisdom's above suspecting Wiles;		692	Cadenus Vaness	198
Wou'd meet with better Friends above.		695	Cadenus Vaness	269
A Project far above his Skill,		705	Cadenus Vaness	586
Led but a weary Life above.		712	Cadenus Vaness	829
Phoebus inspir'd me from above,		741	Stel B-day 22	25
There's not a Pow'r above will help you now:		771	Horace 1, 14	34
Or from above, or from below,		776	Mullinix Tim	84
Is divided above, but united below.		805	Irish Bishops	42
And a Hole above for peeping.		830	Legion Club	46
Above his Rent four Pounds a Year;		875	Drapier's Hill	4
Above our neighb'ring dull Divines!		888	Panegyr Dean	64
For whom she hang'd herself above?		905	Death Daphne	82
And revive above Ground,		939	Riddle Answerd	20
Fly, fly, above, above the Sky Rambling,		959	Cantata	
Fly, fly, above, above the Sky Rambling,		959	Cantata	
What he ripens above ground, he sours below it.		979	Dean to Tho: S	32
But above all I prefer Aeschylus,		988	Letter Dr Sh-n	28
Above a Song or two at most:		993	On Picture	24
. . .for Saunders already hath got above ten Jaunts.		1013	Swift to Sheri	6
ABROAD				
If <Guernsey> calls, send word you're gone abroad;		166	Toland's Invit	41
Abroad, was pester'd by the Boys,		221	A Quiet Life	50
My Lord's Abroad; my Lady too;		376	Apology Lady C	41
She went Abroad - - - She'd thought me mad.		377	Apology Lady C	52
Her Ladyship was gone Abroad;		377	Apology Lady C	80
When his speech came abroad, he paid him off clean,		816	Yahoo's	38
ABSENT				
And spare my absent Friends the Grief		204	In Sickness	25
Absent from whom all Clymes are curst		420	Holyhead	25
The Prudes condemn the absent Prudes;		449	Modern Lady	155
Luna was absent on Pretence		586	Strephon Chloe	65
He found her Thoughts would absent range,		704	Cadenus Vaness	566
An innocent and absent Friend;		765	Stel B-day '26	44
ABSENTEES				
Anothr act that absentees		422	Ireld	53
ABSOLUTION				
Repeat the Absolution loud;		222	Prog of Love	10
ABSTAINS				
Your Hand alone from Gold abstains,		243	Horace 4, 9	13
ABSTERSIVE				
There, many a Flow'r abstersive grew,		894	Panegyr Dean	249
ABSTRACTED				
And think all notions too abstracted		900	Dean's Reasons	63
ABSTRUSE				
Because the Diff'rence lyes abstruse		216	To Mr. Delany	47
With periods long, in terms abstruse!		434	Answer Paulus	82
ABSURD				
A Composition more absurd,		495	Panegyr Swift	62
And, so absurd, that could I raise up		607	Beasts Confess	199
Then soft Voice and Speech absurd,		696	Cadenus Vaness	328
When your speeches are absurd,		908	Daphne	61
ABSURDLY				
Absurdly bends his whole Designs.		641	On Poetry	24
ABUNDANCE				
And painted, lookt abundance better		93	Bauc & Phil 1	122
Now seem'd to look abundance better,		114	Bauc & Phil 2	97
ABUNDANTLY				
These Rhimers abundantly show it:		401	Window Inns 3	2
ABUS'D				
Enrag'd to see the World abus'd		64	Discovery	47
ABUSE				
Most fall at last to Interest, Folly, and Abuse.		24	Ode Athenian	277
He never meant the least Abuse--		172	Horace 1, 7	66
'Twixt Raillery and gross Abuse,		216	To Mr. Delany	48
Virtue or innocence abuse;		488	Irish-Club	26

		PAGE	TITLE	LINE
ABUSE	(CONTINUED)			
Except they know whom they abuse.		644	On Poetry	132
Your Gibes and all your foul Abuse, ...		1003	Dan J's Reply	14
I'm so full of Pity, I never abuse Sick;		1028	Dr. Helsham	2
ABUSIVE				
On Poets in all times abusive, ...		504	Doctor Delaney	133
ABYSS				
Beneath the vast abyss he plunges quick, ...		672	Epig Carthy 24 D	17
ACADEMICK				
So Academick dull Ale-drinkers		503	Doctor Delaney	97
ACCENTS				
His tongue with oily accents tipt, ...		951	Upstart D	28
ACCEPT				
Then (Sir,) accept this worthless Verse, ...		32	Ode to Temple	199
But, not a Soul his Office durst accept:		536	To Mr. Gay	153
Accept for once some serious Lines.		764	Stel B-day '26	14
Poor Tom, wilt thou never accept a Defiance, ...		1019	To Sheridan	1
ACCIDENT				
Mrs. Dukes, said I, here's an ugly Accident has happen'd out;		71	Mrs Harris Pet	37
ACCIDENTAL				
And will each accidental Glance		712	Cadenus Vaness	816
ACCIDENTS				
Which Time and Accidents will tarnish:		595	Cassinus Peter	52
They on no Accidents depend:		730	Stella, Poems	80
All accidents of life conspire		755	Stella '23	21
ACCOMPLISH'D				
Accomplish'd thus, his next Resort		385	Manly Virtue	63
Poultney deep, accomplish'd St. Johns, ...		635	Epistle Lady	175
In him, that's accomplish'd in Cringing and Canting: .		808	Advice Parson	6
ACCORDING				
According to my usuall habit, ...		311	To Ford	6
ACCOST				
Now, as a Jester, I accost you;		890	Panegyr Dean	113
ACCOSTING				
Accosting; said, Go shake your Cream.		897	Panegyr Dean	326
ACCOUNT				
And all his Grand Account to make?		241	Run Bankers	56
An account of my task.		855	Lady's Lament	138
And, should you call me to account, ...		899	Dean's Reasons	2
To you the sad Account I bring, ...		932	Riddle 19 D	23
ACCOUNTS				
Confounds Accounts, perplexes all Affairs;		536	To Mr. Gay	139
"Sir, our Accounts are diff'rent quite, ...		550	Life of Swift	194
By fair Accounts it would be found		606	Beasts Confess	173
Our whole Accounts of publick Debts.		774	Mullinix Tim	15
The House Accounts are daily rising		860	Lady Acheson	29
ACCOUTRED				
Him thus accoutred Peter found, ...		594	Cassinus Peter	25
ACCURST				
Yet, through Despair, of God and Man accurst, . . .		806	Judas	7
ACCUSATION				
They'll prove my Accusation just.		732	Stella, Poems	144
ACCUSE				
And I no more shall then Accuse		219	To Mr. Delany	109
I would accuse him to his Face		607	Beasts Confess	201
ACCUSER				
Of Brethren he's a false Accuser, ...		798	Traulus 1	79
Perjur'd Rebel, brib'd Accuser;		831	Legion Club	70
ACCUSES				
Accuses Chloe's tainted Breath;		449	Modern Lady	157
ACCUSING				
Accusing that false Creature, Man.		686	Cadenus Vaness	4
ACE				
She draws an Ace, and sees it red.		452	Modern Lady	233
Nor, of your Rank will bate an Ace, ...		888	Panegyr Dean	47
I thought an Ace you'd ne'er have bated, ...		1002	Reply by Dean	2
ACES				
If I had but a Pair of Aces, ...		75	Game Traffick	19
ACH SEE HEAD-ACH				
ACHELOUS				
That mixt with Achelous Spring, ...		293	Prog Marriage	109
ACHES				
Old Aches throb, your hollow Tooth will rage. . . .		137	City Shower	10
ACHILLES				
Our Prince has hit Him, like Achilles, in the Heel, .		10	Ode to King	142
ACHILLES'S				
Achilles's Scepter was of Wood, ...		134	Magician's Rod	59
ACHILOUS'				
To drink Achilous' Horn.		293	Prog Marriage	120
ACHING SEE AKEING				
With empty Purse, and aching Head, ...		453	Modern Lady	292
ACID				
Nothing but Acid left behind.		731	Stella, Poems	134
ACKNOWLEDGE				
Henceforth acknowledge, that a Nose		1002	Reply by Dean	4
ACONITE				
With Aconite anoint his Chops.		904	Death Daphne	42
ACQUAINTANCE				
Commence Acquaintance underneath a Shed.		138	City Shower	40
For old acquaintance bring him in.		468	Birthday Song	254

ACQUAINTANCE   (CONTINUED)   PAGE   TITLE   LINE

	PAGE	TITLE	LINE
ACQUAINTANCE (CONTINUED)			
Old Acquaintance, are you there?	835	Legion Club	150
ACQUAINTED			
So well acquainted with my Zeal	444	Modern Lady	3
Were but you and I acquainted,	839	Legion Club	221
. . .to have been acquainted with me, as she pretended.	1014	Swift to Sheri	11
ACQUIR'D			
With all acquir'd and nat'ral parts,	176	To Lord Harley	10
Her Knowledge, with such Pains acquir'd,	709	Cadenus Vaness	716
ACQUIT			
Of this, we'll grant you stand acquit,	154	Widow and Cat	D 36
ACRE			
"To grant me this and t' other Acre:	199	Horace 2, 6	D
ACROSS			
Darts weeping beams across heaven's wat'ry face;	52	Temple Ill	26
With a quill stuck across his nose.	983	Sher, A Goose	20
ACT			
Should heaven suspend to act but for a day;	53	Temple Ill	64
To raise a Roof with Act the Fift.	108	V's House	92
At Christnings well could act his Part,	115	Bauc & Phil 2	129
Can act as decently as they.	204	In Sickness	18
To act his Patience, and her chiding.	221	A Quiet Life	54
They seem to act an Ancient Tale,	239	Run Bankers	19
For leave to act in town? 'Tis plaguy dear.	308	Billet Players	18
Would he were here this night to act my part.	308	Billet Players	32
And, as a stroller, act in ev'ry play:	309	Billet Players	48
The next we act shall be as good as this.	309	Billet Players	58
But now I act as other Folk,	313	To Ford	55
Ennobling every Act, and Air,	385	Manly Virtue	61
An act for laying down the Plough,	422	Ireld	51
Anothr act that absentees	422	Ireld	53
But make an act secure and full	423	Ireld	57
To act such an opera once in a year	522	St. Cecilia's	5
To act with Infamy, or quit the Place.	535	To Mr. Gay	130
Have better learn'd to act their Parts.	562	Death of Swift	226
Sometimes to act the Parson's Part:	605	Beasts Confess	120
To act the Part of Tray, or Cupid;	607	Beasts Confess	208
The Graces wou'd act their Part,	692	Cadenus Vaness	172
Yet she wou'd act as best became	695	Cadenus Vaness	274
How shall I act? is not the Case,	724	To Stella	39
And should you act, a diff'rent Part,	776	Mullinix Tim	89
I know you love to act a Farce.	783	Tim and Fables	38
Command his attendance while you act your farce on,	818	Epigr Kite	6
We'll act as other Conqu'rors do;	886	Rev Market-Hill	91
None could ever act that part,	907	Daphne	23
That we both act the Part of the Clown and the Cow-dung	967	Letter Sherid	2
ACTAEON			
That you an Actaeon was, or are.	373	Letter D. S-y	63
ACTED			
On her Promise of yielding, she acted the Prude;	264	Apollo	46
How free we acted, and had no controller:	308	Billet Players	34
As Falstaff acted old King Harry:	475	Libel on D- D-	145
Was now convinc'd he acted wrong,	705	Cadenus Vaness	576
ACTING			
Thus, acting what he taught so well,	386	Manly Virtue	83
Should acting, die, nor leave behind	764	Stel B-day '26	29
ACTION			
Amaz'd Thy Action at the Boyne we see!	12	Ode to William	D 33
"Know no base action, at no guilt turn pale;	55	Temple Ill	142
I own, he hates an Action base,	484	Libel on D- D-	145
Had some heroick Action done,	554	Death of Swift	23
Upheld by each good Action past,	765	Stel B-day '26	63
In every Action thrusts his Nose	777	Mullinix Tim	119
ACTIONS			
You, Mighty Monarch, Nobler Actions Crown,	11	Ode to William	D 3
Their Thoughts, and Actions, Hopes, and Fears,	291	Prog Marriage	35
The Scenes and Actions of the Day before.	363	On Dreams	10
Heroick Actions early bred in,	398	Earl of P-b-w	34
My Actions with your Rules agree,	706	Cadenus Vaness	615
Your former Actions claim their Part,	765	Stel B-day '26	71
Bring all past Actions to thy Mind.	921	Riddle 7	4
ACTIVE			
His Body active as his Mind.	398	Earl of P-b-w	22
For, This was active, That was strong:	412	Desire Possess	14
Now the active young Attornies	573	Helter Skelter	1
So loitring, so active; so busy, so idle,	580	Psyche	3
ACTORS			
When Actors who at best are hardly Savers,	274	Epilogue	3
And then Comes in the Item of the Actors.	274	Epilogue	8
Item the Actors, freely gave a Day,	274	Epilogue	9
The public should bestow the actors six.	308	Billet Players	22
ACTS SEE RE-ACTS			
Before the play, or else between the acts:	47	To Congreve	126
Two Acts it cost him under Ground.	108	V's House	88
Two other Acts we may presume	108	V's House	89
Here, onely Nature acts her Part,	215	To Mr. Delany	21
Like Episodes between the Acts;	280	Journal	62
At Table now she acts her Part,	448	Modern Lady	100
They'll find his Life, and Acts, and Freedom,	494	Panegyr Swift	52
The Acts of Gods, and god-like Kings.	496	Panegyr Swift	103
But, the State-Emp'ric acts a safer Part;	534	To Mr. Gay	81

5

```
ACTS            (CONTINUED)                                          PAGE    TITLE            LINE
    Nor ever acts on private Views,      . . . . . . . .  607 Beasts Confess     185
ACUTE
    Of forward Face, and Ear acute,      . . . . . . . .   63 Discovery          26
    You, like some acute Philosopher,    . . . . . . . .  632 Epistle Lady       95
ACUTELY
    Yet Galen most acutely shews you,    . . . . . . . .  367 Answer Delaney     31
AD
    Quaedam quae attinent ad Scriblerum, . . . . . . .    186 Scriblerus 3        3
    Decree, that ad exemplum Regis,      . . . . . . . .  391 Young's Satire     24
    May serve, as arguments ad hominem.  . . . . . . .    433 Answer Paulus      48
    And so proceed ad infinitum: . . . . . . . . . .      651 On Poetry         340
ADAGE
    O tempora, O mores! as 'tis in the adage.  . . . . .  975 Dean to Sherid      2
ADAM
    More than your Predecessor, Adam, knew;  . . . . .     31 Ode to Temple     162
    As far up as Adam, . . . . . . . . . . . . .         247 Irish-Feast        83
    By Adam lighted walk up stairs:  . . . . . . . .     280 Journal            56
ADAMANTINE
    Arm'd in adamantine Chains,  . . . . . . . . .       661 Love Song          18
    To break that Adamantine Chain.  . . . . . . . .     702 Cadenus Vaness    487
ADAPT
    Adapt your Habit to your Phiz.   . . . . . . . .     779 Mullinix Tim      212
ADAPTED
    Adapted to a human Mind,  . . . . . . . . . .        659 On Poetry       D 410
ADAPTS
    To your Decays adapts my Sight,      . . . . . . . .  757 Stel B-day '24     44
ADD
    Add to the Victor's Happiness?   . . . . . . . .       6 Ode to King        11
    To add them in the next Edition; . . . . . . . .     418 Woman's Mind       62
    To add more Dignity and Light    . . . . . . .       497 Panegyr Swift     122
    Oh! would His Majesty but add a String.  . . . .     678 Dean and Duke      16
    "Or add some Grains of Folly more    . . . . . . .    714 Cadenus Vaness    874
    He will but add two Hundred Pound,   . . . . . . .    875 Drapier's Hill      6
    Add to them ten thousand more,   . . . . . . . .     931 Riddle 18       D  24
    Add another of royal Nature.     . . . . . . . .     940 Letter              6
ADDER
    An Adder of the sable Kind,  . . . . . . . . .       903 Death Daphne       27
ADDER'S
    Nor dread the Adder's Tooth, nor Scorpion's Sting.   .  792 St. Pat's Well     42
ADDICTED
    Addicted to no sort of Vice; . . . . . . . . .       171 Horace 1, 7        32
ADDING
    By adding largely to my Years:   . . . . . . . .     556 Death of Swift    106
ADDISON
    So Tickell mourn'd his Addison.  . . . . . . . .     271 Apollo's Edict  D  43
    Thus Addison by Lords Carest,    . . . . . . . .     482 Libel on D- D-     61
ADDISON'S
    Of Addison's immortal Page,  . . . . . . . .        496 Panegyr Swift     101
ADDITION
    A handsome Addition for Wine and good Chear, . . .   867 Grand Question     11
ADDRESS
    But find some new address, some fresh deceit,  . . . .   44 To Congreve        17
    Be Modest: nor Address your Betters  . . . . .       479 Epist on Epist    117
    And with Address each Genius held    . . . . .       701 Cadenus Vaness    450
    And thus address thee in the Sailor Stile.   . . . .  770 Horace 1, 14        8
    Mark my Address, and learn my Style, . . . . .       780 Mullinix Tim      235
    We'll teach him some better address to afford  . . . .   816 Yahoo's            53
    With such Address, and graceful Port,  . . . .       889 Panegyr Dean       83
ADDRESS'D
    When e'er my Viceroy is address'd,   . . . . . . . .  271 Apollo's Edict  D  50
    Poems address'd to great Men's Whores; . . . . . .   494 Panegyr Swift      35
ADDRESSES
    In all their Speeches, Votes, Addresses. . . . .     646 On Poetry         198
    In courtly style addresses Franck;   . . . . . . .    879 Robbin & Harry     50
ADDS
    But what adds to the Wonder more,    . . . . . . .    93 Bauc & Phil 1     129
ADDYD
    Seven and Ten addyd to nyne, . . . . . . . .        102 Merlin              1
ADEPTE
    Ah! Quanto rectius, Tu Adepte,   . . . . . . . .     476 Epist on Epist     29
ADEPTS
    When such Adepts as you, and I   . . . . . . . .     497 Panegyr Swift     146
ADHER'D
    Became a Clock, and still adher'd,   . . . . . . . .   94 Bauc & Phil 1     142
    Became a Clock, and still adher'd:   . . . . . . . .  113 Bauc & Phil 2      80
ADHERING
    Changing still, and still adhering,  . . . . . . .    799 Traulus 2          10
ADIEU
    And when thou'st bid adieu to Cares, . . . . .       181 Horace 2, 1        39
    And bid adieu to dear Champain:  . . . . . . .       311 To Ford            26
    All Happiness--and so adieu. . . . . . . . .        411 Dial Rich Marb    103
    So Nightingal and Lark adieu,    . . . . . . .       515 Answer Fable      105
    Adieu to ravishing Delights, . . . . . . . .        590 Strephon Chloe    197
    So, take my Secret, and adieu.   . . . . . . .       597 Cassinus Peter    116
    He came to take his last Adieu.  . . . . . . .       705 Cadenus Vaness    593
    Adieu bright Wit, and radiant Eyes;  . . . . . .      757 Stel B-day '24     27
ADJOURN'D
    Adjourn'd from tops and grammar to the inns; . . .    46 To Congreve        98
ADMINISTRATION
    And praise the whole Administration, . . . . . . .   658 On Poetry       D 190
```

	PAGE	TITLE	LINE

ADMIR'D
The Plan he much admir'd, and took . . . . 87 Hist V's House 19
And she admir'd as much at Him. . . . . 116 Bauc & Phil 2 148
Her Virtues fewer Swains admir'd: . . . . 700 Cadenus Vaness 441

ADMIRATION
Of Admiration and of Praise: . . . . . . 18 Ode Athenian 80
But fill'd with Admiration, stands, ... 227 Prog of Beauty 50
In Admiration at her Wit! . . . . 448 Modern Lady 115
"Nor Persons had in Admiration; . . . . 565 Death of Swift 326
And what will raise your Admiration, ... 927 Riddle 10 D 7

ADMIRE
And some shall admire his conyng Witt, ... 147 Windsor Proph 9
Approve thy Schemes, thy Wit admire, ... 182 Horace 2, 1 62
"What, they admire him for his Jokes-- . . . . . 202 Horace 2, 6 87
One Sex consenting to admire, ... 387 Manly Virtue 129
And, we admire the man, who saves . . . . 436 Answer Paulus 125
The Neighbours round admire his Shrewdness, ... 650 On Poetry 289
Why she likes him, admire not at her, ... 708 Cadenus Vaness 686
But all admire Inigo Jones: . . . . 727 Stella, Poems 4
Which, tho' with Trembling, all admire; . . . . . . 731 Stella, Poems 106
Admire to hear me speak so fine. . . . . . 891 Panegyr Dean 136
But, I admire your Patience most; . . . . 891 Panegyr Dean 147
See how the gaping crowd admire . . . . 950 Upstart D 15

ADMIRERS
Then catch Admirers while you may; . . . . . . 932 Riddle 19 D 19

ADMIRES
<Swift> much admires the Place and Air, ... 173 Horace 1, 7 83
Admires how modest Women can . . . . 417 Woman's Mind 47
Admires how Girls can talk with Fellows, ... 449 Modern Lady 163
I'll give her what she most admires, ... 702 Cadenus Vaness 500

ADMIRING
Admiring you, you pitying us. . . . . 755 Stella '23 38

ADMIT
Dear Harley, gen'rous Youth, admit . . . . . . 176 To Lord Harley 3
This every Pretender to Rhyme will admit, ... 263 Apollo 19
Will ne'er admit thee on the other. . . . . 671 Epig Carthy 22 D 6
She condescended to admit: . . . . 700 Cadenus Vaness 447
Nor would the Door admit her Hoop. . . . . . . 746 Stel Distress 30

ADMITS
An Evil, which admits no Cure: . . . . 413 Censure 2
Admits us in, to storm the Fortress; . . . . . . 885 Rev Market-Hill 70

ADMITTANCE
And found Admittance from the Dame. . . . . . . 222 Prog of Love 20

ADMITTED
Admitted private, when Superiors wait: . . . . . 194 Author Himself 30
I ne'er admitted Love a Guest. . . . . 728 Stella, Poems 14

ADO
She stole away with much ado, ... 292 Prog Marriage 94
With much ado, the Cheat he found; . . . . . . 346 Prometheus 48

ADONIS
Mourn'd Adonis, darling Youth: . . . . 660 Love Song 10
Thought him Adonis in his Bloom. . . . . 904 Death Daphne 58

ADOR'D
Why is a handsome Wife ador'd . . . . 592 Strephon Chloe 283
Ador'd the Clouds as Deityes. . . . . 619 Scandal Poem 1 80
Ador'd us Clouds as Deities; . . . . 626 Scandal Poem 2 78
Thus by the Nymphs and Swains ador'd, ... 694 Cadenus Vaness 246
A Shame to one so much ador'd . . . . 695 Cadenus Vaness 266
Be ador'd by the men . . . . 855 Lady's Lament 127

ADORATION
And into Adoration turns our Praise. . . . . . . 11 Ode to William D 8

ADORE
As Other Painters oft adore . . . . 227 Prog of Beauty 51
Enticing Coxcombs to adore, ... 292 Prog Marriage 75
Whom Paulus ever must adore, ... 433 Answer Paulus 23
With bended knees when they adore her . . . . . . 465 Birthday Song 157
Both to adore her and instruct her; . . . . 702 Cadenus Vaness 499
He must adore such God-like Men. . . . . . . 708 Cadenus Vaness 695
With what Devotion you adore 'um! . . . . 888 Panegyr Dean 52
And you adore him, because he adores you. . . . . 947 Mrs. Houghton 4
For you, by this Rule, must adore all Mankind. . . . . 947 Mrs. Houghton 6
Adore the Smoothness of thy Lines: . . . . . . 1020 Nim-Dan-Dean 1 D 4

ADORES
Robin adores that Spot of Earth, ... 314 To Ford 87
Adores her for the timely Aid. . . . . 729 Stella, Poems 38
And you adore him, because he adores you. . . . . . 947 Mrs. Houghton 4

ADORING
Who after you adoring fly, ... 499 Panegyr Swift 178

ADORN
But serve t' adorn the Baby-dress . . . . . . 6 Ode to King 14
The Under-wits adorn their Speech. . . . . . . 80 Vanbrug House 48
Adorn their Pails with Plate. . . . . . . 122 Empty'ng Town 8
Nor a new Star adorn the Skies: . . . . 271 Apollo's Edict D 37
Can Cowardice her Sex adorn, ... 725 To Stella 67
First, to adorn your Person well, ... 732 Verses Vanessa 3
Adorn our chrystal River's Banks: . . . . . . 896 Panegyr Dean 302

ADORN'D
Adorn'd with Golden Stars and Rays, ... 98 Elegy Patrige 28
Mambrino's Helm adorn'd his Head. . . . . . . 156 Fable of Midas 14
Which in old Times adorn'd the Fair; . . . . . . 692 Cadenus Vaness 179
Adorn'd by Nymphs with all their Care: . . . . . . 919 Riddle 5 4

7

ADORNS
The Lawrel, which adorns thy Head; . . . . 182 Horace 2, 1   66
His rural walks he ne'er adorns; . . . . 901 Dean's Reasons   91
ADOWN
If from adown the hopeful Chops . . . . 529 Lady's Dres Rm   103
ADRIFT
"Turn him adrift, and you shall find . . . . . . 304 Storm   33
ADULT'RATE
Apply'd to Wood's adult'rate Copper; . . . . . . 353 Wood Ironmongr   32
ADVANC'D
When you're advanc'd above Dean Viz. . . . . . 362 Grace's Answer   43
Advanc'd thy Fortune, and preserv'd thy Fame. . . . 531 To Mr. Gay   14
The Goat advanc'd with decent Pace; . . . . 603 Beasts Confess   59
As she advanc'd, that Womankind . . . . 694 Cadenus Vaness   236
Advanc'd like Atalanta's Star, ... 696 Cadenus Vaness   306
Declin'd in Health, advanc'd in Years. . . . . 703 Cadenus Vaness   529
ADVANC'T
Advanc't on tiptoe, lean'd his Head . . . . . . 63 Discovery   27
Thus far advanc't, he made a shift . . . . 108 V's House   91
ADVANCE
And solid Virtue does Your Name advance. . . . . . 11 Ode to William   D 4
E're we advance the Doctor higher . . . . 475 Epist on Epist   24
By his own Credit to advance the Sum; . . . . . . 533 To Mr. Gay   72
Interpret for a kind Advance. . . . . 712 Cadenus Vaness   817
And freely made the first Advance: . . . . 905 Death Daphne   68
If gravest Parsons here advance, ... 928 Riddle 12   D 17
ADVANCES
The Goddess made advances first, ... 178 To Lord Harley   67
Advances few, enriches none, ... 495 Panegyr Swift   73
Having thus overthrown all our further Advances. . . . 968 Letter Sherid   22
. . .she would have made Advances . . . . 1014 Swift to Sheri   11
ADVANCING
And now advancing to the Guard, ... 376 Apology Lady C   30
ADVANTAGE
Whilst all th' advantage by it got, ... 36 Ode Sancroft   71
I had my Advantage, and stood at Defiance, ... 144 New Song   31
'Tis true, but what advantage comes . . . . . . 899 Dean's Reasons   27
ADVENT'RER
The young Advent'rer o'er the Deep . . . . 252 Bubble   34
Where many a bold Advent'rer fell. . . . . 413 Desire Possess   44
ADVENT'RERS
Here all the bold Advent'rers came, ... 256 Bubble   138
ADVENTURES
But what Adventures more befell 'um . . . . . . 224 Prog of Love   85
Fam'd for a thousand bold adventures . . . . . . 619 Scandal Poem 1   60
Fam'd for a thousand bold Adventures; . . . . . . 625 Scandal Poem 2   56
ADVERTIZ'D
Are you to see it advertiz'd! . . . . 643 On Poetry   112
ADVICE
Which thou (such <Burnet's> shrewd Advice is) . . . 180 Horace 2, 1   5
Venture to give him some Advice. . . . . . . 218 To Mr. Delany   96
Then ventur'd to give him some sober Advice, ... 327 Epigram 1   5
Take this Advice then from your Friend. . . . . . 478 Epist on Epist   113
Take my advice; to make you safe, ... 487 Irish-Club   13
What's your advice? shall I give o're, ... 489 Dialogue   8
No longer my Advice regard: . . . . 501 Doctor Delaney   54
And give Advice before he gives the Pill. . . . . 534 To Mr. Gay   80
"But he would never take Advice: . . . . 558 Death of Swift   172
Advice in vain you would apply-- . . . . 595 Cassinus Peter   71
He freely gave the Poor Advice; . . . . 604 Beasts Confess   84
She thought it best to take Advice. . . . . . . 689 Cadenus Vaness   92
Ask no Advice, but think alone, ... 724 To Stella   37
I took Advice except my own, ... 775 Mullinix Tim   72
Dear Mullinix, your good Advice . . . . 779 Mullinix Tim   195
One gives Advice in Proverbs Old, ... 781 Mullinix Tim   271
As Moses, by divine Advice, ... 813 Bro Protestant   49
Then, prithee reflect, take a word of advice; . . . . 818 Archbi Cashel   7
Let me have your Advice in a weighty Affair. . . . 866 Grand Question   2
Never will I give advice . . . . 908 Daphne   79
I sometimes give Advice in Writing, ... 917 Riddle 3   9
Take wise Advice, and look behind, ... 921 Riddle 7   3
ADVIS'D
Tho' Delany advis'd you to plague me no longer, . . . 967 Letter Sherid   7
ADVISE
In vain then would the Muse the multitude advise, . . 37 Ode Sancroft   83
Either to govern or advise; . . . . 243 Horace 4, 9   8
Merely because her Friends advise; . . . . . . 294 Prog Marriage   134
For Will. to enter.--What shall I advise? . . . . . 538 Mr. Pulteney   0
Always to advise her wrong; . . . . 907 Daphne   36
But will never more advise thee. . . . . 907 Daphne   52
But let me advise you, when next I hear from you, . . 976 Dean to Sherid   9
ADVISER
Nor am that grave adviser which I meant; . . . . . 49 To Congreve   202
AENEAS
Before Aeneas durst aspire . . . . 619 Scandal Poem 1   65
Before Aeneas durst aspire . . . . 625 Scandal Poem 2   61
AEOLUS
Fierce Aeolus in Tempests roars. . . . . 924 Riddle 7   88
AEQUATOR
And 'twice a Year he'll cut th' Aequator, ... 98 Elegy Patrige   17

8

	PAGE	TITLE	LINE
AESCHYLUS			
But above all I prefer Aeschylus, ...	988	Letter Dr Sh-n	28
AESOP SEE ESOP			
A Pigeon wou'd, if shown by Aesop, ...	512	Answer Fable	9
AETATIS			
Aetatis suae fifty two	289	Prog Marriage	1
AETHER			
May breath your Bellies full of Aether.	361	Grace's Answer	24
"In wholesome Soil and Aether Pure;	476	Epist on Epist	50
AETHERIAL			
But, what alas! are Claps aetherial	618	Scandal Poem 1	23
But, what alas are Claps Aetherial, ...	624	Scandal Poem 2	17
AETNA			
The Gyants under Aetna ceas'd to groan, ...	9	Ode to King	96
AETNA'S			
And may compare to Aetna's Fire, ...	731	Stella, Poems	105
AFAR SEE A-FAR			
And now discovers from afar	17	Ode Athenian	34
AFFAIR			
About some great Affair, at Two--	200	Horace 2, 6	54
Let me have your Advice in a weighty Affair.	866	Grand Question	2
AFFAIRS SEE STATE-AFFAIRS			
And who in all profound Affairs	62	Discovery	11
And settled Europe's Grand Affairs, ...	181	Horace 2, 1	40
A hundred other Men's Affairs	200	Horace 2, 6	49
A Knave, who deep embroils his Lord's Affairs, . . .	535	To Mr. Gay	119
Confounds Accounts, perplexes all Affairs; . . .	536	To Mr. Gay	139
"Though trusted long in great Affairs, ...	565	Death of Swift	329
"What St. John's Skill in State Affairs, ...	567	Death of Swift	373
In all Affairs thou sole Director, ...	656	On Poetry	449
But Time, and Books, and State Affairs	703	Cadenus Vaness	544
In state affairs, or planting cale;	901	Dean's Reasons	76
I use to take in friends affairs, ...	901	Dean's Reasons	96
And, vext to see Affairs miscarry, ...	903	Death Daphne	9
AFFECT			
Affect ill-manner'd Pedantry, ...	27	Ode to Temple	45
Affect to take the upper hand, ...	546	Life of Swift	34
To affect me half an Hour;	636	Epistle Lady	192
But when her Tutor will affect	711	Cadenus Vaness	798
Nor let your Ills affect your Mind, ...	766	Stel B-day '26	81
AFFECTATION			
Onely by Affectation spoild, ...	216	To Mr. Delany	26
AFFECTED			
Of Nice, Coquet, Affected, Pert, and Vain. . . .	118	Biddy Floyd	10
Infallibly cures the Timber affected;	351	Wood Insect	26
Said, he affected Popularity:	606	Beasts Confess	160
In Florimel's affected Fears:	725	To Stella	70
Affected by each vulgar Dame;	887	Panegyr Dean	18
AFFECTING			
And calls, without affecting Airs, ...	605	Beasts Confess	131
AFFECTION			
And studied Affection came, ...	449	Modern Lady	132
No more--In mark of true Affection	779	Mullinix Tim	207
What truer Affection cou'd ever be shown, . . .	805	Irish Bishops	55
And, further to demonstrate his Affection, ...	825	Noisy Tom	3
AFFECTIONS			
How best to settle their Affections;	182	Horace 2, 1	56
Their kind Affections he has try'd;	606	Beasts Confess	163
AFFIRM			
Pliny shall prove what we affirm:	83	Salamander	26
But I affirm, 'tis false in Fact, ...	253	Bubble	57
Who dares affirm this is no pious age, ...	274	Epilogue	1
They contradict, affirm, dispute, ...	450	Modern Lady	176
By which he lost, he may affirm, ...	604	Beasts Confess	85
Affirm, can't glow to more Delight.	932	Riddle 19 D	10
AFFIRM'D			
Nay, 'twas affirm'd, he sometimes dealt in Rhime: . .	193	Author Himself	10
Affirm'd the Moon was sick, and fell	354	Simile Silver	7
AFFLICTED			
But o'er th' afflicted with a heavy pace	55	Temple Ill	121
AFFLICTIONS			
In wishing such afflictions less!	676	Parson's Case	18
AFFORD			
This made the Ancient Romans to afford	7	Ode to King	27
Nor can afford to buy gold Lace, ...	216	To Mr. Delany	43
My Lady says she can't afford one;	283	Journal	124
My Works he said, cou'd ne'er afford him Meat, . . .	670	Epig Carthy 20 D	3
Nor thy oppressing Lords afford thee Brass. . . .	793	St. Pat's Well	94
But we can afford you Six Traytors in Seven. . .	804	Irish Bishops	32
We'll teach him some better address to afford . . .	816	Yahoo's	53
AFFORDED			
Which has afforded thee much Chat, ...	181	Horace 2, 1	24
AFFORDS			
What meer Humanity affords, ...	204	In Sickness	14
And when 'tis foul, affords you Sport.	493	Panegyr Swift	20
Steel affords me present aid.	937	Riddle 24 D	42
AFFRONTS			
For those affronts they give him yearly.	463	Birthday Song	106
AFORESAID			
With an Order for the Chaplain aforesaid;.	73	Mrs Harris Pet	73
Whilst Stella aforesaid stood by with the Light; . . .	264	Apollo	36

	PAGE	TITLE	LINE
AFORESAID (CONTINUED)			
Which Crimes aforesaid (with her Leave)	687	Cadenus Vaness	15
AFRAID			
You're in the right, but be'n't afraid	92	Bauc & Phil 1	84
Good Folks, you need not be afraid,	112	Bauc & Phil 2	43
Take Courage, dear Comrades, and be not afraid,	400	Tom Clinch	19
"Of no Man's Greatness was afraid,	565	Death of Swift	327
What Mariner is not afraid,	703	Cadenus Vaness	532
As if they were afraid to lose 'em:	813	Bro Protestant	60
"Mister Curate, for all your grave Looks, I'm afraid,	872	Grand Question	147
As half asham'd, and half afraid,	922	Riddle 7	34
And is not afraid your Worship will grumble,	1027	Sheri Circles	26
AFRESH SEE A-FRESH			
But you have molded them afresh,	326	Pethox	77
AFRIC-MAPS			
So Geographers in Afric-Maps	645	On Poetry	177
AFTER			
So after th' Inundation of a War	16	Ode Athenian	11
The first of Plants after the Thunder, Storm, and Rain	16	Ode Athenian	28
After a mighty Light that leads her wandring Eye;	18	Ode Athenian	67
With promise of a mad Reversion after Death.	32	Ode to Temple	198
Oh but, said I, what if after all my Chaplain won't come to?	73	Mrs Harris Pet	68
After hard Throws of many a Day	81	Vanbrug House	73
The heavy Wall went clamb'ring after.	92	Bauc & Phil 1	94
Which after they have overthrown,	110	V's House	133
The heavy Wall climb'd slowly after.	112	Bauc & Phil 2	54
On Sundays, after Ev'ning Prayer.	116	Bauc & Phil 2	169
Leave hunting after Bribes, forget your Tropes:	162	Toland's Invit	6
Some few Days after Harley spies	172	Horace 1, 7	57
Had Bacchus after Daphne reel'd,	177	To Lord Harley	13
But, after sage Monitions from his Friends,	194	Author Himself	23
Thus after four important Hours	227	Prog of Beauty	53
After all their good Cheer,	246	Irish-Feast	58
And after many Days thou'lt find it,	255	Bubble	134
At Two or after we return all,	279	Journal	26
Till Supper comes, and after that,	280	Journal	53
Comes home a quarter after nine,	292	Prog Marriage	84
And so inglorious, after all!	296	Satiric Elegy	4
By Neno after he was drown'd.	299	Horrid Plot	38
'Tis now a Quarter after three	377	Apology Lady C	60
"And after all, to crown my Spleen,	380	Apology Lady C	157
Dick left a Pattern few will copy after,	430	Dicky Dolly	16
Wou'd strictly after Truth enquire	455	Dean Smedley	7
And after all he seldom Sped.	456	Dean Smedley	26
Where after he has fill'd his chest,	456	Dean Smedley	37
And after several Readings over,	475	Epist on Epist	13
Who after you adoring fly,	499	Panegyr Swift	178
But, after Marriage, practise more	588	Strephon Chloe	141
Consider well what may come after;	591	Strephon Chloe	232
Is after Marriage lost so soon,	591	Strephon Chloe	257
Says Grace before, and after Meat;	605	Beasts Confess	130
After venting all my Spight,	629	Epistle Lady	1
So, after toiling twenty Days,	642	On Poetry	65
And purify'd their mothers after.	675	Curate's Compl	8
And, after long computing, found	693	Cadenus Vaness	226
The Ladies walk'd till after Nine.	696	Cadenus Vaness	327
After a Week, a Month, a Quarter,	860	Lady Acheson	9
And Day succeeding after Day,	860	Lady Acheson	10
And after, me thought, I had lost my new Shoes;	868	Grand Question	51
First milk his cows, and after, pound:	902	Dean's Reasons	104
Not Phyllis after lying-in.	904	Death Daphne	38
And after all, I chiefly owe	927	Riddle 10 D	11
And after all you'll think it odd,	930	Riddle 15 D	21
After all you have writ,	939	Riddle Answerd	21
Nor after your Vittels ly sleeping supine	1017	Swift Ans Sher	16
AFTER-BIRTH			
For after-birth a Sooterkin;	504	Doctor Delaney	118
AFTER-DINNER			
Taking her After-dinner Nap:	895	Panegyr Dean	274
AFTER-TIMES			
A Monument to after-Times:	596	Cassinus Peter	76
Should be approv'd in After-times,	728	Stella, Poems	6
AFTERNOON			
And shall be chid this afternoon	292	Prog Marriage	95
At two Afternoon for our Psyche inquire,	580	Psyche	1
And make them ev'ry Afternoon	587	Strephon Chloe	117
AFTERNOONS			
Whole afternoons will sit beside her,	762	Bec's B-Day	49
AG'EN			
Presto be gone--Tis here ag'en,	251	Bubble	6
AGAIN SEE AGAYNE,AGEN			
76		OMITTED WORD	
AGAINST SEE 'GAINST			
Against all Logick and concluding Laws,	19	Ode Athenian	108
Against the proud usurpers of the pit;	46	To Congreve	110
Who may object against the Term,	83	Salamander	25
But up against the Steeple rear'd,	94	Bauc & Phil 1	141
But up against the Steeple rear'd,	113	Bauc & Phil 2	79
Against Dissenters wou'd repine,	115	Bauc & Phil 2	133
Shall hear Him harangue against Prior to Morrow.	143	New Song	6
And I'll Vote against Peace, with Spain, or without:	144	New Song	46

AGAINST   (CONTINUED)   PAGE   TITLE   LINE

	PAGE	TITLE		LINE
I'll Speech against Peace while Dismal's my Name,	145	New Song		53
Speak against Peace right many a Word;	147	Windsor Proph		8
"Must I, against all Right and Law,	154	Widow and Cat	D	21
He against Phebus Harp decreed,	156	Fable of Midas		27
Against whose Torrent while he Swims,	157	Fable of Midas		35
To Swim against this Pop'lar Tide,	158	Fable of Midas		74
A dang'rous Treatise writ against the Spleen;	195	Author Himself		48
If o'er against her you were plac't	222	Prog of Love		5
There out of my Sight, just against the North-Zone,	265	Apollo		85
Against the Phoenix I protest.	271	Apollo's Edict	D	51
Hither, though much against his Grain,	294	Prog Marriage		123
"As well against, as with the Tide,	304	Storm		36
Against an uncomplying Jury:	348	Whitshed Motto		14
Would guard your Nose against a Post.	367	Answer Delaney		48
Be here detained against my will?	403	Window Inns 10	D	2
Complaints against the Royal Butter.	410	Dial Rich Marb		54
Against the Side she would defend:	417	Woman's Mind		52
Just o'er against the Bell Inn	442	Ballyspellin		57
Against the Sex to write a Satyre,	445	Modern Lady		7
Because, though sore against her Will,	446	Modern Lady		40
But if she turn'd against his play,	456	Dean Smedley		29
We suffer sore against his Will;	485	Libel on D- D-		156
Why against Printers all this noise?	487	Irish-Club		9
And 'tis against poetic rules	488	Irish-Club		27
Must I commend against my conscience	490	Dialogue		37
She ne'er inspires against Conviction:	503	Doctor Delaney		106
Against all Rules to be a King:	513	Answer Fable		16
Against the Court is always blabbing,	514	Answer Fable		69
The Proverb says; No Fence against a Flayl.	521	Stephen Duck		2
But, Discontent against the Times;	549	Life of Swift		137
Against the Court to shew his Spight---.	550	Life of Swift		189
"Against the Craftsman and his Friend;	563	Death of Swift		274
"Against him lifting up their Heels.	569	Death of Swift		406
By reading Books against their Saviour;	592	Strephon Chloe		272
Against your greatest benefactor.	622	Scandal Poem 1		172
Nor, against my nat'ral Vein,	634	Epistle Lady		135
Against the harmless Alphabet;	645	On Poetry		158
Against our Sov'reign Lady's Peace,	687	Cadenus Vaness		17
Against the Statutes in that Case,	687	Cadenus Vaness		18
Against her Dignity and Crown:	687	Cadenus Vaness		19
Against Vanessa's Pow'r unite;	700	Cadenus Vaness		439
You caution'd me against their Charms,	706	Cadenus Vaness		620
Decreed the Cause against the Men.	713	Cadenus Vaness		853
Against Enslavers of Mankind!	725	To Stella		62
Its Force against your nearest Friends;	730	Stella, Poems		98
The Entry brusht against her Hoop,	751	Stel Wood-Park		50
And must against the warmer Days	759	Receipt Youth		25
Against us Ministers of State!	783	Tim and Fables		32
By bell'wing thus against the <Dean>?	795	Traulus 1		2
In vain, against the People's Fav'rite?	796	Traulus 1		10
Plac'd against the Church direct;	829	Legion Club		6
For the Court against the Nation.	836	Legion Club		172
To ease his Itch against the Stump,	849	Old Thorn		42
"Against that Assassin in Crape,	850	Old Thorn		67
The Spaniard, sore against his Will,	883	Rev Market-Hill		15
Against the Grain, a <Monarch's> Fist?	884	Rev Market-Hill		34
And fierce against the Whigs harangu'd?	884	Rev Market-Hill		39
To serve a friend against his will?	902	Dean's Reasons		114
Through me, though sore against my Will,	918	Riddle 4		11
And move it against Tyde and Wind.	934	Riddle 21	D	16

AGAYNE

	PAGE	TITLE	LINE
Yonge Symnele shall agayne miscarrye:	103	Merlin	11
And Norways pryd agayne shall marreye.	103	Merlin	12
Geryon shall have three Hedes agayne	103	Merlin	19

AGE

	PAGE	TITLE		LINE
The Wits, I mean the Atheists of the Age,	19	Ode Athenian		103
From ev'ry Age through which it pass't,	22	Ode Athenian		214
And all the contradictions of a poison'd age;	38	Ode Sancroft		118
Let not the outcasts of this outcast age	42	Ode Sancroft		261
Thus I look down with mercy on the age,	45	To Congreve		49
Lives pious witness of a better age;	52	Temple Ill		48
Just such an Insect of the Age	80	Vanbrug House		39
By Age and Claps grown cold as Snow,	84	Salamander		58
Who dares affirm this is no pious age,	274	Epilogue		1
Exact to what his Age amounts,	291	Prog Marriage		46
Of old age too, and in his bed!	296	Satiric Elegy		2
Griev'd at the Vices of the Age,	383	Manly Virtue		2
If you allow, the present Age	392	Young's Satire		33
The first perhaps may once an Age	462	Birthday Song		67
Who wisely thought my Age a Screen,	561	Death of Swift		221
"Because no Age could more deserve it.	571	Death of Swift		458
Then come old Age whene'er it will,	593	Strephon Chloe		311
Sweet Five and Twenty was his Age.	597	Problem Solved		6
Yet, such a lewd licentious Age	603	Beasts Confess		57
The Vandals of the present Age.	611	By Dr. Swift		12
Three Poets in an Age at most?	640	On Poetry		6
He sunk at length to wasting Age a Prey,	669	Epig Carthy 13	D	3
One of her tender Sex and Age.	705	Cadenus Vaness		579
Much less could his declining Age	706	Cadenus Vaness		636
Wherein his Dignity and Age	711	Cadenus Vaness		778

11

		PAGE	TITLE	LINE
AGE	(CONTINUED)			
No Age could furnish out a Pair		722	Stel B-Day '18	11
With such a stupid vicious Age,)		723	To Stella	8
When Age must print a furrow'd Trace		735	Stel B-day '20	49
Or at the Age of Forty three,		757	Stel B-day '24	25
Grief, Sickness, Poverty, and Age;		764	Stel B-day '26	32
You e'ry moment think an Age,		776	Mullinix Tim	107
To lash the Lewdness of the Age;		781	Mullinix Tim	254
Here, for an Age and more, improv'd their Vein,		793	St. Pat's Well	71
Regardful of your Age and Station,		889	Panegyr Dean	68
That golden Age, to Gold unknown;		894	Panegyr Dean	234
And Millions of the present Age.		922	Riddle 7	42
I Cannot but think that we live in a bad age,		975	Dean to Sherid	1
Make a Page of your own Age,		1013	Swift to Sheri	6
AGED SEE MIDDLE-AGED				
Thy Mast, which like some aged Patriot stood		770	Horace 1, 14	15
This aged, sickly, sapless Thorn		849	Old Thorn	21
The vig'rous Youth, and aged Sire:		922	Riddle 7	26
AGEN				
Next Day invited, comes agen;		173	Horace 1, 7	76
Insert it when you write agen:		485	Libel on D- D-	162
Yet he lives, and is ready to ravish agen,		519	Dean Hang Rape	52
Hey for Dublin Town agen!		574	Helter Skelter	56
"And were she to begin agen,		714	Cadenus Vaness	872
In various Forms appear agen		924	Riddle 7	93
AGES				
She seems a Medly of all Ages,		23	Ode Athenian	221
Besides, as they say, Service is no Inheritance in these Ages.		71	Mrs Harris Pet	41
The Poetry of Ages past,		81	Vanbrug House	90
The Poetry of Ages past,		110	V's House	132
But, in the chronicles of former ages,		308	Billet Players	29
For in those Ages Kings we find,		658	On Poetry	D 410
Those former Ages differ'd much from this:		806	Judas	9
Shall stand for Ages on Record,		848	Old Thorn	14
Sees the glorious Ages past.		862	To Janus	16
Philologers of future Ages,		1021	Nim-Dan-Dean 1	D 37
AGHNACLOY				
But we must go to Aghnacloy;		860	Lady Acheson	27
AGILITY				
All his Agility is gone;		885	Rev Market-Hill	80
AGITATE				
Will agitate the lazy Flood,		759	Receipt Youth	31
AGMONDISHAM				
For this I will not dine with Agmondisham,		1033	Ans to Crown	17
AGO				
What all the World knew long ago,		180	Horace 2, 1	8
That, long ago a Fortune-teller		223	Prog of Love	51
'Tis the Nymph that I courted some ten Years ago;		264	Apollo	44
"He dy'd a Year ago." The same.		563	Death of Swift	256
Phyllis, who but a Month ago		699	Cadenus Vaness	392
She must have long ago run out.		735	Stel B-day '20	32
By Food of twenty Years ago?		765	Stel B-day '26	56
But because the three former are long ago past,		967	Letter Sherid	11
And I love you so well, as I told you long ago,		979	Dean to Tho: S	17
For I heard, a month ago, that he was down there		1023	Nim-Dan-Dean 2	D 12
AGONY				
What Agony of Soul she feels		451	Modern Lady	226
AGREE				
And now they all agree, to name		67	Problem	51
Dick, we agree--all's true, thou'st said,		183	Horace 2, 1	99
You all agree, I make no doubt,		270	Apollo's Edict	D 23
And in his Robes, you must agree,		286	Elegy Boat	41
Was brib'd to make the Dean agree		294	Prog Marriage	130
(From whence Philosophers agree)		323	Pethox	9
But soft says the Herald, I cannot agree;		338	Serious Poem	119
In this the Dev'l in me agree;		401	Window Inns 2	4
Now, let me show how <Bob> and you agree.		532	To Mr. Gay	43
But, all agree, to give me over.		557	Death of Swift	134
My Actions with your Rules agree,		706	Cadenus Vaness	615
Because our Lawyers all agree,		821	Dr. Rundle	59
Yet all that know me will agree,		929	Riddle 15	D 3
AGREEABLY				
And, how agreeably surpriz'd		643	On Poetry	111
AGREED				
Suppose all Partyes now agreed,		222	Prog of Love	21
And, Chloe, 'tis by all agreed,		588	Strephon Chloe	157
Agreed. And yet, when Towzer snaps		797	Traulus 1	35
AGUE SEE A-GUE				
Friend Congreve a Feaver, Friend Howard an Ague,		1037	Four Storyes	2
AGUES				
Scatters strange agues o'er men's sickly minds,		52	Temple Ill	38
AH				
Ah, could You! could you hope a Poet for your Friend!		23	Ode Athenian	243
For You (ah, did I think I e'er should live to see		23	Ode Athenian	247
Ah, Britain, land of angels! which of all thy sins,		37	Ode Sancroft	92
But, ah, too much without a thorn.		37	Ode Sancroft	106
Ah, may no unkind earthquake of the State,		40	Ode Sancroft	190
Here would we sing--But, ah! you think I dream,		49	To Congreve	197
Ah, since our fears are fled, this insolent expel,		53	Temple Ill	55
Ah fav'rite youth, how happy is thy lot!--		53	Temple Ill	71

AH   (CONTINUED)

	PAGE	TITLE	LINE
Ah, should I tell a secret yet unknown,	54	Temple Ill	93
Ah! where must needy Poet seek for Aid,	138	City Shower	27
"Ah Doctor, how you love to jest?	202	Horace 2, 6	97
Ah Lovely Nymph be not too rash,	228	Prog of Beauty	67
Ah never lay thy Head to Rest!	361	Grace's Answer	14
Ah lovely Nymphs, remove your Fears,	445	Modern Lady	17
Ah! Quanto rectius, Tu Adepte,	476	Epist on Epist	29
Ah! dost thou not Envy the brave Colonel Chatres,	519	Dean Hang Rape	49
Ah! never to return Home;	573	Kelter Skelter	16
Ah! who in our degen'rate Days	895	Panegyr Dean	287
Ah, Strephon, how can you despise	924	Riddle 8	1
Ah, is not Love a pleasing Pain?	924	Riddle 8	12
Ah lovely Nymph, thou'rt in thy Prime!	932	Riddle 19	D 13
I much suspect you mean the latter, ah Sly-boot!	1003	Dan J's Reply	6

AID   SEE AYD

	PAGE	TITLE	LINE
Dar'd to suspend her unregarded aid,	43	To Congreve	4
Then call this verse, that speaks her largest aid,	44	To Congreve	27
"Learn to disdain their mercenary aid;	55	Temple Ill	140
Then call in Mercury for Aid,	99	Elegy Patrige	61
Attend when e'er I want their Aid,	120	Apollo Outwit	31
Ah! where must needy Poet seek for Aid,	138	City Shower	27
Descending to her Charge's aid,	177	To Lord Harley	44
Remov'd from kind Arbuthnot's Aid,	204	In Sickness	9
When he ask'd for my Aid, in the Forms that are usual:	265	Apollo	72
For foreign Aid what need they roam,	272	Apollo's Edict	D 62
Invoke not Citherea's Aid,	272	Apollo's Edict	D 72
Without your Aid, to read or spell;	325	Pethox	66
Have teiz'd, by calling to their Aid	371	Letter D. S-y	5
Beauty that needs no Aid of Art,	379	Apology Lady C	115
Inclines to aid a specious Lye;	414	Censure	14
Without whose aid you're all undone?	432	Answer Paulus	4
How can the Muse her Aid impart,	451	Modern Lady	220
Whose Councils aid the Sov'reign Pow'r,	548	Life of Swift	109
"Because he sought for no Man's Aid.	565	Death of Swift	328
Descend from Heav'n to Beauty's Aid;	590	Strephon Chloe	220
Did ever we desire his Aid:	657	On Poetry	492
His Mother's Aid no Youth invokes:	687	Cadenus Vaness	10
In a glad Hour Lucina's Aid	690	Cadenus Vaness	136
Then calls the Graces to her aid,	691	Cadenus Vaness	158
Where never Blush was call'd in Aid,	691	Cadenus Vaness	168
Searching in Books for Wisdom's Aid,	702	Cadenus Vaness	490
And shou'd Want or Desert stand in need of his Aid,	717	Answer Rebus	27
Adores her for the timely Aid.	729	Stella, Poems	38
And when I brag of Aid divine,	741	Stel B-day 22	29
And if the Muse deny her Aid	757	Stel B-day '24	33
Invited here to 'vengeful Morrough's Aid,	791	St. Pat's Well	23
Without my Aid, the best Divine	915	Riddle 1	29
Steel affords me present aid.	937	Riddle 24	D 42

AIDED

	PAGE	TITLE	LINE
But aided by the Wind, fought still for Life;	137	City Shower	24

AIDING

	PAGE	TITLE	LINE
That Stella was helping, abetting and aiding,	264	Apollo	39
Often aiding to impart	936	Riddle 24	D 25

AIL

	PAGE	TITLE	LINE
Pugh! said I, but that's not the Business that I ail.	70	Mrs Harris Pet	29

AIL'D

	PAGE	TITLE	LINE
He stop'd, and cou'd not tell what ail'd him.	376	Apology Lady C	34

AILMENTS

	PAGE	TITLE	LINE
From my Ailments give me Leisure,	632	Epistle Lady	87

AIM

	PAGE	TITLE	LINE
And every foolish Flye that dares to aim	9	Ode to King	115
That, missing Fire, or missing Aim	500	Doctor Delaney	23
Why will you aim to be preferr'd	501	Doctor Delaney	37
"And, if he often miss'd his Aim,	550	Life of Swift	198
"Yet, Malice never was his Aim;	571	Death of Swift	459
The Queen of Beauty lost her Aim.	700	Cadenus Vaness	433
Took Aim, and shot with all his Strength	703	Cadenus Vaness	516
But those who aim at Ridicule	707	Cadenus Vaness	664
Be these thy Arts; nor higher Aim	897	Panegyr Dean	341

AIM'D

	PAGE	TITLE	LINE
And all those flying Deaths that aim'd him from the Field,	8	Ode to King	67
Aim'd at the Head, but reach'd the Heart.	706	Cadenus Vaness	623

AIMS

	PAGE	TITLE	LINE
How endless are Ambition's Aims!	905	Death Daphne	90

AIR

	PAGE	TITLE	LINE
Whose Reason is weigh'd down by Popular air,	21	Ode Athenian	181
And seem (almost) transform'd to Water, Flame, and Air,	22	Ode Athenian	201
Or from the Sun, or from the Air, or from the Earth,	31	Ode to Temple	170
Leaving to Wits the spatious Air,	79	Vanbrug House	25
Till the Sun clears the Air; and then	84	Salamander	35
Leaving the Wits the Spacious Air	106	V's House	25
Breeding, and Wit, and Air, and decent Pride;	118	Biddy Floyd	8
Under pretence of Taking Air,	120	Apollo Outwit	23
Thrice mutter'd something to the Air.	120	Apollo Outwit	36
And step in Booths for Air.	122	Empty'ng Town	12
<Swift> much admires the Place and Air,	173	Horace 1, 7	83
He flatters with peculiar Air	216	To Mr. Delany	37
Through ev'ry Thread it lets in Air;	231	Prog of Poetry	36
The Witches left in open Air,	240	Run Bankers	34

13

AIR   (CONTINUED)   PAGE   TITLE   LINE
    While some build Castles in the Air, ...   257 Bubble   165
    And sent him up in Air to Hell.   . . . .   257 Bubble   184
    Suspended for a while in Air.   . . . .   258 Bubble   188
    When wretched Lovers live on Air, ...   270 Apollo's Edict   D 16
    "His ghostly Visage with an Air   . . . .   305 Storm   59
    And high in Air for ever ride; . . . .   347 Prometheus   74
    At Midnight, through the dark'ned Air;   . . . . .   354 Simile Silver   4
    And build a Castle in the Air.   . . . .   361 Grace's Answer   20
    But winding Walks and purer Air;   . . . .   378 Apology Lady C   100
    The scorching Sun, or chilling Air;   . . . .   379 Apology Lady C   122
    "The cooler Air, and dazzling Sun;   . . . .   380 Apology Lady C   142
    "The Awe of your Majestick Air?   . . . .   380 Apology Lady C   160
    Ennobling every Act, and Air, ...   385 Manly Virtue   61
    Scurrility with gibing Air;   . . . .   448 Modern Lady   127
    But, can you guess from womens air   . . . . . .   619 Scandal Poem 1   49
    Though Venus be as light as air, ...   621 Scandal Poem 1   115
    And gives himself a haughty air, ...   621 Scandal Poem 1   137
    But, can you guess from Woman's Air, ...   625 Scandal Poem 2   45
    Though Venus be as light as Air, ...   627 Scandal Poem 2   113
    And gives himself a haughty Air, ...   627 Scandal Poem 2   141
    It but reach'd the middle Air, ...   638 Epistle Lady   251
    Gives Judgment with decisive Air.   . . . .   649 On Poetry   266
    High up in Air he'll turn your Brains;   . . . .   666 Epig Carthy 2   D 6
    Expire, when first expos'd to open Air.   . . . . .   667 Epig Carthy 5   D 6
    Must strole in Air 'twixt Earth and Sky;   . . . .   689 Cadenus Vaness   86
    That gentle, soft, engaging Air, ...   692 Cadenus Vaness   178
    Corinna with that youthful Air, ...   699 Cadenus Vaness   388
    And what she spoke was in an Air, ...   707 Cadenus Vaness   662
    From wholesom Exercise and Air   . ˙. . . . . .   744 Stel Distress   5
    From wholsome Exercise and Air   . . . .   750 Stel Wood-Park   29
    Where Mirth, and Exercise, and Air, ...   759 Receipt Youth   27
    Thy graceful Steps, and Coll'nell's Air   . . . .   779 Mullinix Tim   205
    My Hat has much the nicer air, ...   780 Mullinix Tim   219
    From noxious Steams to purge the Air;   . . . . .   780 Mullinix Tim   250
    She fled and vanish'd into Air.   . . . .   850 Old Thorn   52
    "When thou, suspended high in Air, ...   851 Old Thorn   85
    Then flourishes thrice his Sword in the Air,   . . .   870 Grand Question   109
    To show my Face with scornful Air;   . . . . . .   887 Panegyr Dean   21
    Forbid in open Air to breath;   . . . .   894 Panegyr Dean   231
    None seek thee now in open Air;   . . . .   895 Panegyr Dean   281
    Despises exercise and air.   ˙. . . . .   901 Dean's Reasons   90
    In Youth exalted high in Air, ...   915 Riddle 1   1
    To fill the Earth, and Air, and Skies: . . . .   924 Riddle 7   92
    Where not a Chink let's in the Air;   . . . . . .   935 Riddle 23   D 15
    The dullest of Beasts and of Birds in the Air,   . . .   940 Letter   14
    No Bird in Air so swift can fly.   . . . .   942 Probatur Alit   26
    With what an air he mounts his coach!   . . . . .   951 Upstart   D 24
    I hasten'd down to Country Air, ...   1003 Dan J's Reply   2
    Air ripens not, nor Earth produces: . . . . . .   1035 To Quilca   6
AIRS   SEE AYRS,STATE-AIRS
    Now Moll had whirl'd her Mop with dext'rous Airs,   . .   124 Descriptn Morn   7
    And in the sneaking Parsons Airs   . . . .   292 Prog Marriage   68
    Thinks nothing gives one Airs so pretty;   . . . . .   417 Woman's Mind   41
    Assume a Dignitary's Airs, ...   495 Panegyr Swift   70
    When rapt in Heav'nly Airs, he sings   . . . . . .   496 Panegyr Swift   102
    Or swear it rotten; and with humble Airs, ...   534 To Mr. Gay   97
    "He gave himself no haughty Airs: . . . .   565 Death of Swift   330
    And calls, without affecting Airs, ...   605 Beasts Confess   131
    A Baby Face, no Life, no Airs, ...   699 Cadenus Vaness   414
    Had spoil'd his fashionable Airs;   . . . .   703 Cadenus Vaness   545
    And still encreasing in her Airs   . . . .   746 Stel Distress   34
    Each Moment rising in her Airs, ...   751 Stel Wood-Park   51
    Wno cou'd give the Looby such Airs?   . . . . . .   800 Traulus 2   25
    And not among Ladies to give themselves Airs.   . . .   868 Grand Question   38
    Give yourself ten thousand airs   . . . .   908 Daphne   77
AIRY
    And thus He did the Airy Goddess Court, ...   7 Ode to King   35
    Smooth as that airy nymph so subtly borne   . . . . . .   54 Temple Ill   117
    From Airy Garrets some descend, ...   279 Journal   29
    "He was too airy for a Dean---.   . . . .   547 Life of Swift   79
    On Airy Wings you take your Flight, ...   919 Riddle 5   25
    We are little airy Creatures, ...   930 Riddle 17   D 1
AJAX
    Thus Ajax, when with Rage possesst   . . . .   731 Stella, Poems   121
AKE
    Your Head, or Tooth, or Finger ake: . . . . . .   414 Censure   22
    The Bottle, till your Fingers ake: . . . .   892 Panegyr Dean   180
AKEING
    Set hoping, hoping, hoping hearts of Lovers akeing,   . . 959 Cantata
ALACK
    But Englond must cry alack and well a day, ...   147 Windsor Proph   13
    Nay, what's incredible, alack!   . . . .   674 His Deafness   7
ALARMS
    Now Finch alarms the Lords; he hears for certain,   . .   194 Author Himself   37
    Then as to War's Alarms I pray   . . . .   372 Letter D. S-y   38
ALAS
    And think, alas, to be by mortals writ, ...   20 Ode Athenian   126
    Because, alas, when we all dye   . . . .   21 Ode Athenian   162
    The Rebel Muse, alas, takes part   . . . .   23 Ode Athenian   238
    Alas, how fleeting, and how vain, ...   24 Ode Athenian   268

ALAS	(CONTINUED)	PAGE	TITLE	LINE
Alas, the occasions are so few:		38	Ode Sancroft	112
And those, alas, do show		39	Ode Sancroft	145
Why should the Sun, alas, be proud		41	Ode Sancroft	215
Alas, the Nymph would be undone.		226	Prog of Beauty	12
But these alas, are poor Supplyes		229	Prog of Beauty	115
Alas the Sexton is thy Banker now!		235	Elegy on Demar	38
Alas! all is not Gold that glisters;		254	Bubble	107
The Cause, alas, is quickly guesst,		293	Prog Marriage	101
Alas; they would not do you wrong;		414	Censure	15
Alas! I never thought		425	Five Ladies	9
Or how should I, alas! relate,		449	Modern Lady	140
In vain, alas! her Hope is fed;		452	Modern Lady	232
But there, alas! he could no Safety find;		538	Mr. Pulteney	21
Alas! that gives you small relief---!		546	Life of Swift	60
Who now, alas, no more is mist,		562	Death of Swift	247
The crystal Eye, alas, was miss't;		583	Young Nymph	61
But, what alas! are Claps aetherial		618	Scandal Poem 1	23
Alas! our Thunder soon goes out;		624	Scandal Poem 2	7
But, what alas are Claps Aetherial,		624	Scandal Poem 2	17
They lye, alas, too easy to be found,		772	Horace 1, 14	63
Which must alas no longer stand;		849	Old Thorn	22
For none, alas, by me can gain,		918	Riddle 4	15
Though I, alas! a Pris'ner be,		920	Riddle 6	1
It must be so; what else, alas,		1003	Dan J's Reply	7
Alas, Sir, I had no Design,		1005	Sheridan's Sub	17
And they, alas, yield small Relief,		1005	Sheridan's Sub	29
But, alas, the poor Dean neither Shudders nor burns,		1037	Four Storyes	5
ALASS				
Alass! a meer Chymerick Notion.		604	Beasts Confess	112
ALBION				
Yet pardon, native Albion, when I say		38	Ode Sancroft	128
Confessing Albion once her darling seat;		49	To Congreve	194
ALBION'S				
But Albion's cliffs are out at heel,		468	Birthday Song	244
ALCHYMISTS				
For when like stupid alchymists you try		49	To Congreve	207
ALCHYMY				
The Roguery of Alchymy,		27	Ode to Temple	25
ALCIDES				
Alcides, one of second Rate.		160	Atlas	18
Alcides held him in his Arms,		257	Bubble	183
Thou, like Alcides, shalt expire,		925	Riddle 8	38
ALDERMAN				
And, since the Alderman was mad you say,		350	Upright Judge 3	7
Rules, like an Alderman his Ward.		649	On Poetry	286
ALDERMEN				
Quakers and Aldermen, in State,		239	Run Bankers	14
Of Lord-May'r, Aldermen, and Shrieves,		494	Panegyr Swift	50
ALE				
We can but make it out in Ale.		92	Bauc & Phil 1	66
And here's to buy a Pot of Ale.		128	Little House	54
Now quaff of honest Ale a Quart,		184	Horace 2, 1	111
Like Porters o'er a Pot of Ale.		216	To Mr. Delany	50
His Credit out for Cheese and Ale;		231	Prog of Poetry	34
To brew her Ale, and raise her Paste:		282	Journal	90
He found he could purchase Two Tankards of Ale		288	Bank Down	37
The beer and the ale		402	Window Inns 8	D 7
Or, whether o'er a Pot of Ale,		412	Desire Possess	7
With muddy ale and mouldy bread		420	Holyhead	2
Like Hunters o'er their Evening Ale.		447	Modern Lady	79
When drunk with sour Election Ale,		450	Modern Lady	187
With ale and chops I'll treat who writes the best,		671	Epig Carthy 24	D 5
Condemn'd to Country Cottages and Ale;		793	St. Pat's Well	74
To strike him for a pot of ale?		899	Dean's Reasons	32
Not in philosophy, or ale,		901	Dean's Reasons	75
And charming when squeez'd in a Pot of brown Ale.		953	Oranges	2
Saunders said I, I would rather than a Quart of Ale,		987	Mary to Sher	31
ALE-DRINKERS				
So Academick dull Ale-drinkers		503	Doctor Delaney	97
ALE-HOUSE				
Would sit whole Ev'nings at the Ale-house:		352	Wood Ironmongr	6
And you durst not talk thus if I saw you at our ale-house		976	Dean to Sherid	32
ALE-HOUSE-BUSH				
Pull down an Ale-house-Bush, for Spite,		457	Paddy's Charac	8
ALECTO				
And there--behold Alecto stand,		596	Cassinus Peter	81
ALECTO'S				
Then, apply Alecto's Whip,		635	Epistle Lady	179
ALEHOUSE				
Still seen o'r'e many an Alehouse fire.		461	Birthday Song	38
ALERT				
Or should he pretend to be brisk and alert,		868	Grand Question	35
ALES				
To feast on Ales and Steaks.		425	Five Ladies	4
ALEXANDER				
. . .and your Man Alexander had not gone,		1013	Swift to Sheri	4
. . .to let Alexander know I was here,		1013	Swift to Sheri	4
. . .and send your Man Alexander to buy Corks,		1013	Swift to Sheri	6
I wish Alexander safe at St. Catherine's To-night,		1014	Swift to Sheri	9

```
                                                    PAGE    TITLE              LINE
ALEXANDRIAN
  With Alexandrian in the Close,      . . . . . . . . .  1022 Nim-Dan-Dean 1    D 53
ALEXANDRINE
  But enough of this Poetry Alexandrine    . . . . . .  1018 Swift Ans Sher      32
ALICANT
  And <Cuffe> grins for getting, the Alicant Plate.   . .  430 Dicky Dolly        21
ALIEN
  Which alien seems from Nature's Laws;    . . . . . .   923 Riddle 7            82
ALIGHT
  Was forc'd, for Safety, to alight,    . . . . . . .   127 Little House         32
ALIIS
  Cum Multis aliis (all his Foes)    . . . . . . . .   373 Letter D. S-y        71
ALIKE
  "All Motions are alike to him:   . . . . . . . . .   304 Storm                32
  Frighted alike at both Extremes,   . . . . . . . .   379 Apology Lady C      123
  Lovely alike, or heard or seen;  . . . . . . . . .   385 Manly Virtue         58
  Alike diffusing in his Flight   . . . . . . . . .   387 Manly Virtue        119
  Both alike; while neither mends.   . . . . . . . .   631 Epistle Lady         56
  Thus drest alike from Top to Toe,    . . . . . . .   780 Mullinix Tim        227
  And both alike diverting.   . . . . . . . . . . .   784 Mullinex Dick         6
  Are Christians alike; and it may be averr'd,    . . . .   816 Yahoo's             28
ALIVE
  Oft hovers where alive it haunted most;   . . . . . .    51 Temple Ill           8
  No Man alive has more Respect--    . . . . . . . .   173 Horace 1, 7          70
  And bring her back, alive or dead.   . . . . . . .   223 Prog of Love         36
  Will think his better Half alive.   . . . . . . .   235 Elegy on Demar       52
  Or swallow'd alive, or skilfully bruis'd.    . . . . .   351 Wood Insect         12
  To swallow Will. Wood either bruis'd or alive.    . . .   351 Wood Insect         14
  Where nature hardly seems alive.    . . . . . . . .   421 Holyhead            32
  One Bed while alive held both Doll and Dick    . . . .   430 Dicky Dolly         13
  And so might ev'ry Dunce alive.    . . . . . . . .   481 Libel on D- D-       48
  Which Homer never cou'd alive.   . . . . . . . . .   483 Libel on D- D-       86
  Must honour you alive and dead,    . . . . . . . .   490 Dialogue            50
  It must come out alive or dead.   . . . . . . . . .   527 Lady's Dres Rm       68
  "How is the Dean? He's just alive.   . . . . . . .   558 Death of Swift      148
  To keep Esteem and Love alive.   . . . . . . . . .   593 Strephon Chloe      310
  But let no Friend alive look into't.   . . . . . . .   643 On Poetry           108
  Employ your Muse on Kings alive;   . . . . . . . .   647 On Poetry           220
  Duke William, sweetest Prince alive.   . . . . . . .   656 On Poetry           440
  'Tis what no Man alive will say of you.   . . . . . .   670 Epig Carthy 18    D  2
  If such an Author were alive,   . . . . . . . . . .   709 Cadenus Vaness      700
  That I'm alive to tell you so.   . . . . . . . . .   766 Stel B-day '26       88
  Mount alive, and dead descend    . . . . . . . . .   801 Traulus 2           52
  Were Peter now alive, perhaps    . . . . . . . . .   821 Dr. Rundle          49
  And, sure as they're alive, at Night;    . . . . . .   891 Panegyr Dean       139
  No Lady alive can shew such a Skin.    . . . . . . .   928 Riddle 13         D  2
ALL
  (By all but Heaven and Me unseen,)    . . . . . . .     7 Ode to King         49
  And all those flying Deaths that aim'd him from the       8 Ode to King         67
     Field,
  (As those still do wh' have none at all)    . . . . .     8 Ode to King         84
  Your Presence all their Native Stubborness controuls,      9 Ode to King         90
  All lesser ones expire,   . . . . . . . . . . . .     9 Ode to King        112
  For all its boasted height,    . . . . . . . . . .    10 Ode to King        124
  For all its Plagiary Light,    . . . . . . . . . .    10 Ode to King        125
  And all Her boasted Influences are   . . . . . . .    10 Ode to King        138
  Nor is this all: As glorious is the Care    . . . . .    12 Ode to William    D 25
  An Arm on which all Europe's Hopes depend,    . . . ..    12 Ode to William    D 30
  The boundless Glory all Redounds to Thee,    . . . .    12 Ode to William    D 33
  The brave Attempt do's all our Foes disarm,    . . .    13 Ode to William    D 37
  Of glorious Deeds, that must all Tongues Employ:    . .    13 Ode to William    D 46
  That Mountain which was highest first of all    . . .    16 Ode Athenian         5
  When strait she sees the Countrey all around,    . . .    17 Ode Athenian        38
  An unknown Musick all around,    . . . . . . . . .    17 Ode Athenian        52
  And all we Fools, who are the greater part of it,    . .    18 Ode Athenian        71
  All Merit that transcends the humble Rules    . . . .    18 Ode Athenian        77
  Must e'en all herd with us their Kindred Fools,    . .    18 Ode Athenian        82
  The publick Stamp Heav'n sets on all that's Great and      18 Ode Athenian        93
     Good,
  By the new Modish System of reducing all to sense,    . .    19 Ode Athenian       107
  Against all Logick and concluding Laws,    . . . . .    19 Ode Athenian       108
  Of Solving all Appearances they please,    . . . . .    19 Ode Athenian       118
  And straight deny you to be Men, or any thing at all;   .    19 Ode Athenian       120
  That all the Praises it can give,    . . . . . . .    20 Ode Athenian       150
  Whom all the Charms of an Usurped Wife and State,    . .    20 Ode Athenian       154
  With all that Power unfelt, courts Mankind to be Great,     21 Ode Athenian       155
  Because, alas, when we all dye    . . . . . . . . .    21 Ode Athenian       162
  Far above all Reward, yet to which all is due,    . . .    21 Ode Athenian       187
  Far above all Reward, yet to which all is due,    . . .    21 Ode Athenian       187
  Impatient of all Answers, straight became    . . . .    22 Ode Athenian       191
  So well You answer all Phaenomenaes there;    . . . .    22 Ode Athenian       202
  With all that Factious or Enthusiastick Dotards dream,   .    22 Ode Athenian       204
  And all the incohaerent Jargon of the Schools,    . . .    22 Ode Athenian       205
  Tho' all the Fumes of Fear, Hope, Love, and Shame,    .    22 Ode Athenian       206
  She seems a Medly of all Ages,    . . . . . . . . .    23 Ode Athenian       221
  All of old Cut with a new Dye,    . . . . . . . . .    23 Ode Athenian       227
  And changes all to Beauty, and the Praise    . . . .    23 Ode Athenian       236
  May all the Blood, which shall by Womans scorn be shed     23 Ode Athenian       245
  Woman seems now above all Vanity grown,    . . . . .    24 Ode Athenian       250
  And 'spight of all that They or You can do,    . . . .    24 Ode Athenian       265
  It lost some mighty Pieces thro' all hands it past    . .    25 Ode Athenian       286
```

ALL   (CONTINUED)   PAGE   TITLE   LINE

The Body, tho' Gigantick, lyes all Cold and Dead.   .   25 Ode Athenian   291
And with blind Rage break all this peaceful Government;   25 Ode Athenian   300
And to all future Mankind shew   25 Ode Athenian   304
Virtue, the greatest of all Monarchies, ...   26 Ode to Temple   1
Spend all our present Stock in hopes of golden Rules. .   27 Ode to Temple   27
Our Knowledge is but mere Remembrance all,   27 Ode to Temple   30
We scrawl all o'er with old and empty Rules,   . . .   27 Ode to Temple   33
Think she there does all her Treasures hide,   . . .   27 Ode to Temple   37
As if they all were Spectres too, ...   27 Ode to Temple   41
(Which since has seiz'd on all the rest) . . . . .   28 Ode to Temple   54
That Knowledge forfeits all Humanity;   28 Ode to Temple   55
Yet at the last the Box sweeps all away.   29 Ode to Temple   80
Off fly the Vizards and discover all,   29 Ode to Temple   99
To drive all Virtue out, or look it dead!   30 Ode to Temple   123
Where all the fruitful Atoms lye, ...   32 Ode to Temple   171
And all her Jewels and her Plate,   32 Ode to Temple   182
'Tis all the Portion of my niggard Stars;   32 Ode to Temple   201
In vain all wholsome Herbs I sow,   33 Ode to Temple   208
Contriv'd to tire all patience out,   35 Ode Sancroft   15
Which all the mimic forms express, ...   35 Ode Sancroft   25
The figures all inverted shew,   35 Ode Sancroft   31
If all that our weak knowledge titles virtue, be   . . .   36 Ode Sancroft   45
Whilst all th' advantage by it got, ...   36 Ode Sancroft   71
Suppose the truth, like all the world, their own; . .   37 Ode Sancroft   80
Ah, Britain, land of angels! which of all thy sins, .   37 Ode Sancroft   92
'Tis all the angry slighted Muse can do   . . . .   38 Ode Sancroft   108
And all the contradictions of a poison'd age; . . . .   38 Ode Sancroft   118
Like all transcendent excellence below;   . . . . .   39 Ode Sancroft   146
And sheds, tho' all unseen, his sacred influence here. .   39 Ode Sancroft   153
Thinks heav'n has cancel'd all our sins, ...   40 Ode Sancroft   181
Cordials are in their talk, whilst all they mean   . .   42 Ode Sancroft   257
Stale forms of course, all mean deceivers use, ...   44 To Congreve   20
And by short views mistook for all their own; . . . .   45 To Congreve   60
Round all the circles of impertinence, ...   46 To Congreve   88
And court in prologues, all are country-bred; . . . .   46 To Congreve   96
O'er Nile, with all its wilderness of gods;   . . . .   46 To Congreve   104
Swore all the wits were his peculiar friends; . . . .   47 To Congreve   140
In pleasing all that's good among the great, ...   49 To Congreve   180
What poor regards would merit all below!   . . . . .   49 To Congreve   184
Yes; you are all malicious standers-by, ...   49 To Congreve   199
The subtil spirit all flies up in fume;   . . . . .   49 To Congreve   210
Thou universal cause of all my woes;   . . . . . .   53 Temple Ill   82
Is all the poor content delusion finds.--   . . . .   55 Temple Ill   150
Is in all Points the fittest Tool,   61 Lady Tablebook   28
And who in all profound Affairs   . . . .   62 Discovery   11
While all the rest stood gaping round   . . . . . .   63 Discovery   24
By all means to bring down the Rates, ...   64 Discovery   42
Bush smiling round on all, retreats   . . . . . .   64 Discovery   44
Whether all Passions, when in Ferment,   66 Problem   15
Beside all this, deep Scholars know,   66 Problem   21
And now the Ladys all are bent,   66 Problem   33
Spread all their Charms to catch a <Fart>;   . . . .   66 Problem   36
And now they all agree, to name   . . . . . .   67 Problem   51
Let's not fall out; We all have Share.   67 Problem   58
Therefore all the Money, I have, which, God knows,. . .   69 Mrs Harris Pet   6
So I tumbl'd and toss'd all Night,. . .   70 Mrs Harris Pet   20
Nay, said she, my Lord Collway's Folks are all very sad   70 Mrs Harris Pet   27
And in all the Places I liv'd, I never heard of such a   70 Mrs Harris Pet   31
   Thing.
(Now you must know, of all Things in the World,. .   . . 71 Mrs Harris Pet   35
 . . .as tho' I had call'd her all to naught; . . . .   71 Mrs Harris Pet   45
 . . .for a Conjurer in all my Life.   . . . . . .   72 Mrs Harris Pet   61
Oh but, said I, what if after all my Chaplain won't come   73 Mrs Harris Pet   68
   to?
Then all in the Place   . . . .   76 Lady B- B-   5
Not one of all the tunefull Throng   . . . . . .   79 Vanbrug House   15
And if they all had Power to build, ...   79 Vanbrug House   19
Throws all his Witt and Hours away   . . . . . .   80 Vanbrug House   43
(For all the Muses Geese are Swans)   . . . . . .   80 Vanbrug House   50
All stain'd with Infamy and Vice, ...   84 Salamander   39
All this we grant--why, then look yonder . . . . .   84 Salamander   45
With true Delight observed them all   . . . . . .   87 Hist V's House   17
There all the little School-boys run   87 Hist V's House   33
Having thro all the Village pass't, ...   91 Bauc & Phil 1   49
Makes you take all things in good Part: . . . . . .   94 Bauc & Phil 1   160
Tno' we all took it for a Jest: 98 Elegy Patrige   2
Not one of all his Crony Stars, ...   98 Elegy Patrige   7
But Patrige ended all Disputes, ...   99 Elegy Patrige   33
Weep all you Customers that use   . . . . . .   101 Elegy Patrige   107
Ripe fruit shall come, and all is wele.   . . . . . .   103 Merlin   14
Not one of all our tuneful Throng   106 V's House   15
So wide as to encompass all.   . . . .   108 V's House   82
Now Poets from all Quarters ran   108 V's House   95
Capacious House! 'tis own'd by all   109 V's House   115
Having thro' all the Village pass'd, ...   111 Bauc & Phil 2   17
And had the Service all by Heart;   . . . . . .   115 Bauc & Phil 2   130
He gathers all the Parish there;   . . . . . .   116 Bauc & Phil 2   170
Jove mix'd up all, and his best Clay imploy'd; . . .   118 Biddy Floyd   11
Let which I please of all the Nine   . . . .   120 Apollo Outwit   30
Reckoning Roof, Weather Cock and all, ...   126 Little House   7

ALL   (CONTINUED)   PAGE   TITLE   LINE

All that you make this Stir about, ...   128 Little House   41
More probably than all the rest;   . . . . . .   128 Little House   44
Now from all Parts the swelling Kennels flow, ...   139 City Shower   53
Filth of all Hues and Odours seem to tell   . . . . .   139 City Shower   55
Drown'd Puppies, stinking Sprats, all drench'd in Mud,   139 City Shower   62
I have heard all the Speech repeated by Hoppy.   . . .   143 New Song   9
The <Duke> shew'd me all his fine House; and the   143 New Song   15
    <Duchess>
Till all my Relations were put into Places.   . . . .   144 New Song   24
For why; I would fain have put all in a Flame,   . . .   144 New Song   43
And all my whole Family, Places by Dozens;   . . . .   144 New Song   48
But spight of the Harpy that crawls on all four, . . .   147 Windsor Proph   11
And all her Gestures were Lampoons.   . . . . .   150 Corinna   16
Miss came, and peep'd at all he had.   . . . . . .   150 Corinna   24
Her Common-Place-Book all gallant is, ...   150 Corinna   29
"Must I, against all Right and Law, ...   154 Widow and Cat   D   21
Midas, expos'd to all their Jears, ...   157 Fable of Midas   39
And there's the Jest, for Pan is All: . . . . .   157 Fable of Midas   58
Howe'er, 'tis all one in the Greek.   . . . . .   158 Fable of Midas   60
All Statesmen are in this Condition, ...   160 Atlas   15
And talk what Fools call Treason all the Night. . . .   163 Toland's Invit   16
My Province is, to see that all be right, ...   165 Toland's Invit   27
And the Whigs may all go Swing, ...   168 Peace Dunkirk   6
All their false deluded Hopes, ...   168 Peace Dunkirk   8
All Europe's Bus'ness in his Breast)   . . . . . .   170 Horace 1, 7   4
And Libell'd all the Junta round;   . . . . .   171 Horace 1, 7   38
And you the Tyrant o'er them all: . . . . .   173 Horace 1, 7   90
Suppose him gone through all Vexations, ...   174 Horace 1, 7   101
Now all the Doctor's Money's spent, ...   174 Horace 1, 7   107
Poor <Swift>, with all his Losses vext, ...   174 Horace 1, 7   113
With all acquir'd and nat'ral parts, ...   176 To Lord Harley   10
For such is all the sex's flight, ...   177 To Lord Harley   19
Which stupify'd them all to stocks.   . . . . .   178 To Lord Harley   46
Shew'd her the Virtues all combin'd, ...   178 To Lord Harley   51
Their looks are all by method set, ...   178 To Lord Harley   55
Round all the earth she casts her eyes;   . . . . .   178 To Lord Harley   61
What all the World knew long ago, ...   180 Horace 2, 1   8
And all its secret Causes trace, ...   180 Horace 2, 1   16
And dazzle all the Idol-Faces   . . . . .   182 Horace 2, 1   75
Now, now you carry all before ye, ...   183 Horace 2, 1   83
"On Popes, for all the Blood they've spilt, ...   183 Horace 2, 1   94
All this is foreign to thy Walk: . . . . . .   183 Horace 2, 1   102
That your Lordship would once let your Cares all alone   185 Scriblerus 1   3
A Pox of all Senders   . . . . . .   186 Scriblerus 4   D   1
And all his old Friends would rebuke   . . . . .   186 Scriblerus 4   D   9
Were much too strong for all their Hands.   . . . . .   189 Faggot   8
Though with united Strength they all pull, ...   191 Faggot   51
Humour, and Mirth, had Place in all he writ: . . . .   194 Author Himself   11
Well, now I have all this and more, ...   198 Horace 2, 6   7
All this is mine but till I die;   . . . . . .   198 Horace 2, 6   D
Remov'd from all th' ambitious Scene, ...   199 Horace 2, 6   D
I must by all means come to Town, ...   199 Horace 2, 6   13
Where all that passes, inter nos, ...   201 Horace 2, 6   79
I'm stopt by all the Fools I meet, ...   202 Horace 2, 6   91
By all the Dogs and Curs in Town;   . . . . .   207 Fable Bitches   2
Set all her Cubs at once upon her;   . . . . .   208 Fable Bitches   40
What Humor is, not all the Tribe   . . . . .   215 To Mr. Delany   19
And then fall foul on all the Town.   . . . . .   217 To Mr. Delany   56
All special Friends, and allways jarr.   . . . . .   217 To Mr. Delany   60
Thus all Society is lost, ...   217 To Mr. Delany   73
For all Buffoons have most in View   . . . . .   217 To Mr. Delany   77
All Subjects like Dan Jackson's Nose.   . . . . .   218 To Mr. Delany   102
To Rime all day without Offence;   . . . . .   219 To Mr. Delany   108
Suppose all Partyes now agreed, ...   222 Prog of Love   21
She ne'r before in all her Life   . . . . .   224 Prog of Love   65
One Argument she summ'd up all in, ...   224 Prog of Love   67
Fair Maidens all attend the Muse   . . . . .   224 Prog of Love   73
Till Phillis all her Trinkets pawn'd: . . . . .   224 Prog of Love   88
All Parallells exactly run;   . . . . .   226 Prog of Beauty   10
All reeking in a cloudy Steam, ...   226 Prog of Beauty   14
All her Complexions safe and sound, ...   226 Prog of Beauty   30
Gave Women all their Hearts could wish   . . . . .   227 Prog of Beauty   58
When the Materialls all are gone, ...   228 Prog of Beauty   78
For, all Astrologers maintain   . . . . .   228 Prog of Beauty   86
That Flamstead can with all his Skill   . . . . .   229 Prog of Beauty   99
When sober Folks are all a-bed, ...   229 Prog of Beauty   104
While the Parish, as she flies, ...   230 Prog of Poetry   15
When all his Drink is Hippocrene, ...   231 Prog of Poetry   32
While from below all Grub-street rings.   . . . . .   231 Prog of Poetry   46
Know all Men by these Presents, Death the Tamer   233 Elegy on Demar   1
His Heirs might well of all his Wealth possest, . . .   233 Elegy on Demar   5
Lords, Knights and Squires were all his humble Debtors.   234 Elegy on Demar   16
Nor all his Int'rest keep him from the Grave.   . . .   234 Elegy on Demar   22
Turns all again to barren Strand.   . . . . .   239 Run Bankers   4
Expos'd with all their Magick Ware.   . . . . .   240 Run Bankers   36
And all his Grand Account to make   . . . . .   241 Run Bankers   56
Produc'd with all their Bills and Gold, ...   241 Run Bankers   63
And all we poor Shopkeepers must our Horns pull in. .   237 Excellent Song   16
Within your Breast all Wisdom lyes, ...   243 Horace 4, 9   7
From snoring all Night.   . . . . . .   245 Irish-Feast   16

ALL	(CONTINUED)	PAGE	TITLE	LINE
The Floor is all wet		245	Irish-Feast	41
After all their good Cheer,		246	Irish-Feast	58
My Mannors all contig'ous round,		251	Bubble	19
Puts all upon a desp'rate Bett,		251	Bubble	22
He throws at all, and sweeps the Board.		253	Bubble	64
But Whale Directors eat up all.		253	Bubble	68
Alas! all is not Gold that glisters;		254	Bubble	107
All cover'd o'er with Slime and Mud.		255	Bubble	132
Here all the bold Advent'rers came,		256	Bubble	138
Computing all their Cost and Trouble,		259	Bubble	218
And taint all their Meat, and sour all their Drink.		263	Apollo	14
And taint all their Meat, and sour all their Drink.		263	Apollo	14
But her graceful black Locks, were all mingled with Grey		264	Apollo	42
Of all the fine Things he keeps in the Dark,		265	Apollo	61
I'll make it appear that they're all stol'n Ware:		265	Apollo	64
In all Parts of the Globe, where your Language is read;		265	Apollo	70
To believe all his Verses were written by me;		266	Apollo	100
Tho' she lives 'till she's Grey as a Badger all over.		266	Apollo	108
You all agree, I make no doubt,		270	Apollo's Edict D	23
Peers, Clergy, Gentry, all are Benefactors;		274	Epilogue	7
Are all resolv'd the Project to begin;		275	Epilogue	28
But Chints, Brocades, and Lace take all away,		275	Epilogue	33
And then all hands, Boys, to the Oar		279	Journal	18
All, Heteroclit Dan except,		279	Journal	19
At Two or after we return all,		279	Journal	26
Warn'd by the Bell, all Flocks come trembling,		279	Journal	28
Shews all her Secrets of House keeping,		282	Journal	87
On all Whig Papers, and Gazets:		282	Journal	100
Now all his hopes are in the Czar,		282	Journal	105
How transient all things are below:		283	Journal	116
For Clem gets all the dainty bits.		283	Journal	126
The Dams and the Weirs must all be your own,		287	Bank Down	6
You get all the Fish, and others get none,		287	Bank Down	7
All riding on Horseback to Hell and the Bank.		287	Bank Down	25
The Graces next, and all the Muses		290	Prog Marriage	9
But vow'd his Money all was spent;		294	Prog Marriage	126
Here, all Diversions of the Place		294	Prog Marriage	131
The Widow goes through all her Forms;		295	Prog Marriage	157
And so inglorious, after all!		296	Satiric Elegy	4
Come hither, all ye empty things,		296	Satiric Elegy	25
From all his ill-got honours flung,		297	Satiric Elegy	31
For, are not all Informers so?		298	Horrid Plot	6
Sir, you mistake me all this while:		298	Horrid Plot	16
That all the Noise they made was barking:		299	Horrid Plot	26
The Dean with all his best Endeavour		295	Horrid Plot	151
Was all decypher'd, and translated.		300	Horrid Plot	52
Then all this while have I been bubbled;		300	Horrid Plot	57
Your <Bishops> all are <Dogs> indeed.		301	Horrid Plot	76
"To drown him all Attempts are vain,		303	Storm	28
"All Motions are alike to him:		304	Storm	32
To speak to Elrington, and all the tribe,		307	Billet Players	6
I pity Elrington with all my heart;		308	Billet Players	31
All this and more, yet it would do no good.		308	Billet Players	42
Owns all your favours; here intends to stay,		309	Billet Players	47
To live and die all strollers for your sakes;		309	Billet Players	50
While We may search all Dublin o'er		315	To Ford	107
"Who is as good as all the Muses?		321	First of April	8
"For she belongs to all the Graces;		321	First of April	10
They dropp'd low Court'sies, One and All,		321	First of April	13
"We all shou'd march on this Occasion,		321	First of April	19
"'Tis all to save their Mother trouble;		321	First of April	24
Equal to all in Care and Love,		322	First of April	35
Which all deserve and all improve.		322	First of April	36
Which all deserve and all improve.		322	First of April	36
And seems all Feet, and Hands, and Eyes.		322	First of April	38
That all this Bus'ness was a Joke.		322	First of April	54
From Head to Foot, and all before;)		324	Pethox	16
Is all with precious Jewels strow'd.		324	Pethox	36
In all the various Colours seen,		325	Pethox	45
From thee our Youth all Virtues learn,		325	Pethox	59
With Patience, which all Ills supports,		325	Pethox	63
Found all the Realms before him waste;		326	Pethox	92
That he sent to all three a Challenge next morning.		327	Epigram 1	8
Yet we all should Rejoyce to be Hewers of Wood.		334	Serious Poem	4
And yet we all know much Gold it will bring,		334	Serious Poem	14
Is a Man of this World all true Flesh and Blood;		335	Serious Poem	50
I know you will say, this is all Heathen Greek;		337	Serious Poem	89
When Pow'r in all its Pomp appears,		340	Arch-Bish Dub	13
Struck all his Rage and Malice down;		340	Arch-Bish Dub	20
. . . who all in Money wallows,		342	Upon His Grace	15
And all the Rent I pay is scarce five Shillings in the Pound.		342	Upon His Grace	22
For fear my Lord should send it all into the poor Man's Box.		342	Upon His Grace	26
To every Farmer twice a Week all round about the Yoke,		343	Upon His Grace	39
His Baily Driving all my Cows into the Parish Pound.		343	Upon His Grace	4
On all the same Impression stuck.		344	Prometheus	10
All Parties and Religions joyn;		345	Prometheus	12
Do all in One Opinion jump;		345	Prometheus	18
Troops of all Tongues and Nations Muster:		345	Prometheus	28

ALL	(CONTINUED)	PAGE	TITLE	LINE
They say, all human Things depend:		345	Prometheus	34
Jove saw that all Devotion fail'd;		345	Prometheus	42
All ran to Pray'rs, both Priests and Laity,		353	Wood Ironmongr	21
Then what a huge Delight were all in,		353	Wood Ironmongr	25
And found his Copper all was base;		353	Wood Ironmongr	28
The Moon is Silver all this while.)		354	Simile Silver	16
So loud, till all the Nation hears;		354	Simile Silver	28
Where Wit in all its Glory shines;		361	Grace's Answer	2
Where Compliments with all their Pride		361	Grace's Answer	3
In her you'll center all your Joys,		362	Grace's Answer	47
But all are meer Productions of the Brain,		363	On Dreams	5
The Murd'rer dreams of all the Blood he spilt.		364	On Dreams	14
Because, among all human Race,		366	Answer Delaney	7
And that by all I e're did hear		372	Letter D. S-y	11
Cum Multis aliis (all his Foes)		373	Letter D. S-y	71
Thro' all the Rooms, and Courts, and Arches;		377	Apology Lady C	62
Examines all the Servants round,		377	Apology Lady C	63
All this was much beneath her Due,		379	Apology Lady C	118
Tho' seeming pleas'd at all she sees,		379	Apology Lady C	125
"And after all, to crown my Spleen,		380	Apology Lady C	157
Thus young, thus proof to all Temptations,		386	Manly Virtue	89
That will make all my Subjects with pride to obey.		389	Order of Bath	4
For this we know, all antient Sages		391	Young's Satire	23
Thro' all the Realm his Virtues run,		391	Young's Satire	25
If these be of all Crimes the worst,		392	Young's Satire	47
Get all your Verses printed fair,		394	Grub-Street	9
A Messenger comes all a-reek,		398	Earl of P-b-w	13
Shines in all Climates like a Star;		398	Earl of P-b-w	31
He swore from his Cart, it was all a damn'd Lye.		399	Tom Clinch	12
But I'll see you all damn'd before I will whittle.		399	Tom Clinch	16
By Satan taught, all Conj'rers know		401	Window Inns 2	1
They swear that they all by Love are inspir'd,		401	Window Inns 3	3
All this I have felt,		402	Window Inns 8	D 11
Put up your Wife, she's crosser than all four',		404	Window Inns 11	D 4
All Turns and Motion tries;		406	Swift to Pope	14
And all that He or They can say;		408	Dial Rich Marb	2
For, all the Courtly Madams round,		409	Dial Rich Marb	27
Lay all my fine Plantations waste,		410	Dial Rich Marb	69
Assist all Poets in Distresses,		411	Dial Rich Marb	94
All Happiness--and so adieu.		411	Dial Rich Marb	103
He strove to pick up all he found,		412	Desire Possess	25
But, all he took was just the same:		412	Desire Possess	32
And, gather'd all his Brother strow'd;		412	Desire Possess	36
All others who inferior sit,		414	Censure	8
But, all Appearances are strong.		414	Censure	16
While all she prates has nothing in it.		415	Woman's Mind	6
And take his Nonsense all for Wit:		416	Woman's Mind	8
On all Occasions, cut and dry.		416	Woman's Mind	14
She ravishes all Hearts to hear her.		416	Woman's Mind	36
All Christian vittals stink of fish		420	Holyhead	3
Absent from whom all Clymes are curst		420	Holyhead	25
Where all are fools, and all are knaves		421	Ireld	2
Where all are fools, and all are knaves		421	Ireld	2
In all employmts we can spare.		422	Ireld	48
To hang up all who smuggle wool.		423	Ireld	58
That all our wives should go in Chints.		423	Ireld	60
Exceeding all the fools of Totness.		423	Ireld	66
To move that all the Nation round		423	Ireld	67
Without whose aid you're all undone?		432	Answer Paulus	4
Soon licks up all unsav'ry steams;		432	Answer Paulus	8
And all for ten poor moidores fee!		434	Answer Paulus	80
Disclaim for ever all pretence		436	Answer Paulus	143
All other Nymphs expelling		441	Ballyspellin	51
Round all your Ballyspellin?		442	Ballyspellin	60
To all but one,		442	Ballyspellin	86
For all the Female Commonweal:		444	Modern Lady	4
To pitch on me, of all Mankind,		445	Modern Lady	6
On me, who think them all so fair,		445	Modern Lady	9
Of all the Satyre shall be mine.		445	Modern Lady	29
She sat all Night up at Quadrill.		446	Modern Lady	41
"I thank my Stars they are all light;		447	Modern Lady	68
Has all the Dinner-Cant by Heart:		448	Modern Lady	101
And while, with all this paultry Stuff,		448	Modern Lady	109
The Sum of all their senseless Prate,		449	Modern Lady	141
All mad to speak, and none to hearken,		450	Modern Lady	178
Now all alone poor Madam sits,		451	Modern Lady	198
"And such a Pain in all my Limbs!"		451	Modern Lady	209
And all the Gamester Ladies met,		451	Modern Lady	215
Our Madam can sit up all Night;		451	Modern Lady	217
Unskill'd in all the Terms of Art?		451	Modern Lady	221
All the Superfluous Whims relate,		451	Modern Lady	224
Most conscious that they all speak true,		453	Modern Lady	272
Now, all in haste they huddle on		453	Modern Lady	286
To all mankind a constant friend,		455	Dean Smedley	15
And after all he seldom Sped.		456	Dean Smedley	26
Ye Fates, when all he gets is Spent,		456	Dean Smedley	49
When all your list of Gods is out,		464	Birthday Song	143
But you may hook in all the rest.		465	Birthday Song	150
Bring all the Females of the Skyes:		465	Birthday Song	154
With genuin lustre all her own.		465	Birthday Song	174

ALL	(CONTINUED)	PAGE	TITLE	LINE
In vain are all attempts from Germany	. . . . .	467	Birthday Song	217
And turn it all to ridicule:	. . . .	468	Birthday Song	266
That sound Divine the Truth has spoke all	. .	469	Birthday Song	271
To warp the Sense of all Mankind:	. . . . .	475	Epist on Epist	22
But you must have Cascades, and all	. . . . .	476	Epist on Epist	37
All Pride) our Speaker for your Coxon:	. . . .	476	Epist on Epist	40
But you forsooth, your All must squander,	. . .	476	Epist on Epist	59
All by my Lady's kind Decision.	. . . .	478	Epist on Epist	100
You Forfeit all your Patròn's Grace,	. . . . .	480	Libel on D- D-	30
Let all his barren Lawrel's fade	. . . .	482	Libel on D- D-	67
Detesting all the Statesmen kind,	. . . . . .	482	Libel on D- D-	72
A Genius for all Stations fit,	. . . .	482	Libel on D- D-	79
To all their Journey-Men, than you,	. . . . .	483	Libel on D- D-	94
Why all this rage? Why these complaints?	. . .	487	Irish-Club	8
Why against Printers all this noise?	. . . . .	487	Irish-Club	9
And, to avoid all future ill, `.	. . . .	489	Dialogue	11
Shews all the malice of a Tory,	. . . .	489	Dialogue	26
Could all we little Folks that wait,	. . . . .	492	Panegyr Swift	1
And all Mankind as Fools, or Knaves;	. . . . .	493	Panegyr Swift	6
Would much compensate all we want.	. . . . . .	493	Panegyr Swift	8
It is to think all great Ones Elves,	. . . . .	493	Panegyr Swift	12
(And you of all Mankind should know)	. . . . .	493	Panegyr Swift	24
Most of his Virtues, all my Brains.	. . . . .	494	Panegyr Swift	57
That all the Loss your Purse sustain'd	. . . .	496	Panegyr Swift	88
The stinking Load of all the Crimes,	. . . . .	497	Panegyr Swift	116
But all the Filth both Spiss, and Sparse	. . .	497	Panegyr Swift	120
"Their Loads they all on Satan lay:	. . . . .	497	Panegyr Swift	134
Than all the Sins he ever bore.	. . . .	497	Panegyr Swift	141
That Humankind are all Yahoos.	. . . .	498	Panegyr Swift	168
Since you alone of all the Race	. . . .	498	Panegyr Swift	171
'Tis said, the Gods try'd all their Art,	. . .	501	Doctor Delaney	31
Make all true Patriots up to Shoe-boys	. . . .	501	Doctor Delaney	61
If all my Pains will earn a Crown.	. . . . . .	502	Doctor Delaney	68
Round all your Brethren cast your Eyes,	. . . .	502	Doctor Delaney	83
And press you down with all their Weight.	. . .	503	Doctor Delaney	94
Pronounce all Men of Wit, Free-thinkers.	. . .	503	Doctor Delaney	98
On Poets in all times abusive.	. . . .	504	Doctor Delaney	133
Suppose you had them all trepann'd	. . . . . .	505	Doctor Delaney	151
As if they all were of a Feather:	. . . . . .	513	Answer Fable	14
Against all Rules to be a King:	. . . .	513	Answer Fable	16
It frightens all the Village Boys.	. . . . . .	513	Answer Fable	26
And he of all Birds was a Pheasant.	. . . . .	513	Answer Fable	34
Cou'd read all Books were ever writ;	. . . . .	513	Answer Fable	36
Could read all Volumes up to Folio's,	. . . . .	513	Answer Fable	41
We all can find out whom he means,	. . . . . .	514	Answer Fable	65
And in all they do for us so kindly do mean,	.	516	Dean Hang Rape	2
'Twas what all his Life he had practis'd before.		517	Dean Hang Rape	22
Of drinking all Day, and whoring all Night.	. .	517	Dean Hang Rape	28
Of drinking all Day, and whoring all Night.	. .	517	Dean Hang Rape	28
To Hang him with <England> would lend him their Garters;		519	Dean Hang Rape	51
But, here was to pay the Devil and all.	. . .	519	Dean Hang Rape	58
For which all true Protestant Hearts should be glad;	.	520	Dean Hang Rape	68
His Poems, think them all not worth a Straw.	.	521	Stephen Duck	6
Suited to all Christian Fokes:	. . . .	523	Betty Grizette	18
Of all the Litter as it lay;	. . . .	526	Lady's Dres Rm	8
A nasty Compound of all Hues,	. . . .	527	Lady's Dres Rm	41
All varnish'd o'er with Snuff and Snot.	. . .	527	Lady's Dres Rm	50
He smelt it all the Time before.	. . . .	528	Lady's Dres Rm	82
Each Dame he sees with all her Stinks:	. . . .	529	Lady's Dres Rm	122
All Women his Description fits,	. . . .	529	Lady's Dres Rm	125
To all the Charms of Female Kind;	. . . . . .	530	Lady's Dres Rm	130
A bloated <Minister> in all his Geer,	. . . .	532	To Mr. Gay	33
Let all Domesticks feel your gentle Sway;	. . .	533	To Mr. Gay	55
And, with an Oath, assure him; all is well.	. .	534	To Mr. Gay	96
Hush-money sends to all the Neighbours round:	.	535	To Mr. Gay	108
Pays all the Cost, and gives the Villain Thanks.		535	To Mr. Gay	110
His Lordship would impute it all to Spight:	. .	535	To Mr. Gay	112
Confounds Accounts, perplexes all Affairs;	. .	536	To Mr. Gay	139
The subtle Knave had all the Plunder swept.	. .	536	To Mr. Gay	154
His Snot into the Mess; 'tis all his own.	. . .	536	To Mr. Gay	162
Who interrupted him in all his Leasings;	. . .	537	Mr. Pulteney	2
But, finding all his Artifices vain;	. . . . .	538	Mr. Pulteney	19
Behold a Foe more fierce than all the rest:	. .	538	Mr. Pulteney	32
Yet laugh our hearts out, one and all.	. . . .	545	Life of Swift	14
"Poor Man! he went, all on a sudden---!	. . .	547	Life of Swift	70
"And yet, I think, for all your Jokes,	. . . .	547	Life of Swift	93
Court, City, Camp, all one to him---.	. . . . .	548	Life of Swift	106
All scribbled in the worst of times,	. . . . .	550	Life of Swift	184
This Maxim more than all the rest	. . . . . .	553	Death of Swift	5
"In all Distresses of our Friends	. . . . . .	553	Death of Swift	7
We all behold with envious Eyes,	. . . .	554	Death of Swift	13
One, whom you love of all Mankind,	. . . . . .	554	Death of Swift	22
He'd wish his Rivals all in Hell.	. . . . . .	554	Death of Swift	34
'Tis all on me an Usurpation.	. . . .	555	Death of Swift	44
To all my Foes, dear Fortune, send	. . . . . .	555	Death of Swift	67
With all the Kindness they profess,	. . . . .	557	Death of Swift	121
But, all agree, to give me over.	. . . .	557	Death of Swift	134
Than all the Sniv'llers round my Bed.	. . . .	557	Death of Swift	142
",o, may we all for Death prepare!	. . . . . .	558	Death of Swift	153
"'Tis all bequeath'd to publick Uses.	. . . .	558	Death of Swift	156

ALL	(CONTINUED)	PAGE	TITLE	LINE
"He gave it all:--But first he dy'd.		558	Death of Swift	160
"And had the Dean, in all the Nation,		558	Death of Swift	161
Now Grub-Street Wits are all employ'd;		558	Death of Swift	165
Wisely on me lay all the Blame:		558	Death of Swift	170
"That all his vital Parts were sound.		559	Death of Swift	176
I'm sorry; but we all must dye.		561	Death of Swift	212
All Fortitude of Mind supplies:		561	Death of Swift	214
He searcheth all his Shop in vain;		563	Death of Swift	257
"It clearly shews that all Reflection		563	Death of Swift	275
"To all their Boroughs send them down:		564	Death of Swift	284
"The Courtiers have them all by Heart:		564	Death of Swift	286
"That all his Miracles were Cheats,		564	Death of Swift	295
"But, this I know, all People bought 'em;		565	Death of Swift	312
"But what he writ was all his own.		565	Death of Swift	318
"Spent all his Credit for his Friends:		565	Death of Swift	332
"Fair Liberty was all his Cry;		566	Death of Swift	347
"But, finding vain was all his Care,		567	Death of Swift	369
"Here ended all our golden Dreams.		567	Death of Swift	372
"Was all destroy'd by one Event.		568	Death of Swift	376
"Who long all Justice had discarded,		570	Death of Swift	421
"But what all Mortals may correct;		571	Death of Swift	464
"With all the Turns of Whigs and Tories:		572	Death of Swift	476
All to plunder, all to pillage;		574	Helter Skelter	40
All to plunder, all to pillage;		574	Helter Skelter	40
All to murder Equity,		574	Helter Skelter	49
Till the People all are quiet		574	Helter Skelter	51
All Folks who pretend to Religion and Grace,		575	Place Damn'd	1
Damn'd Time-Serving Priests all over the Nation;		576	Place Damn'd	12
Because she pays 'em all in Kind.		583	Young Nymph	56
Of Chloe all the Town has rung;		584	Strephon Chloe	1
Think what a Case all Men are now in,		585	Strephon Chloe	33
With loud Huzza's from all the Boys,		586	Strephon Chloe	69
Meer mortal Flesh was all he found:		586	Strephon Chloe	76
Will damp all Passion Sympathetick;		588	Strephon Chloe	134
One Blast will put out all his Fires.		588	Strephon Chloe	136
And, Chloe, 'tis by all agreed,		588	Strephon Chloe	157
They soon from all Constraint are freed;		590	Strephon Chloe	205
In her glitt'ring Birth-day Gear,		591	Strephon Chloe	228
While all the gross and filthy last.		591	Strephon Chloe	234
In all the Postures of her Face,		591	Strephon Chloe	239
More than from all the World beside.		591	Strephon Chloe	254
Unjustly all our Nymphs complain,		591	Strephon Chloe	255
And then throw all their Weapons down;		592	Strephon Chloe	262
All other Methods but the true.		592	Strephon Chloe	270
Is of all Wits the greatest Fool;		592	Strephon Chloe	278
A Crime that shocks all human Kind;		595	Cassinus Peter	68
A Crime to all her Sex unknown!)		596	Cassinus Peter	104
The blackest of all Female Deeds.		596	Cassinus Peter	106
Refin'd all Mettals with his Looks,		597	Problem Solved	3
Not all the Court of Heav'n could shew		597	Problem Solved	9
Inquire through all the Parish round		602	Beasts Confess	43
Were all the Schemes he had in View;		605	Beasts Confess	147
That all he did was for their Good;		606	Beasts Confess	162
More to my Praise than all my Volumes;		611	By Dr. Swift	10
From Jupiter took all dominion,		620	Scandal Poem 1	83
We govern all things there below.		620	Scandal Poem 1	88
O'er all your passions we preside:		620	Scandal Poem 1	90
We, to whom all the Gods give place.		620	Scandal Poem 1	96
And, in all clymates are at home:		621	Scandal Poem 1	128
Offensive to all pious ears.		622	Scandal Poem 1	168
From Jupiter took all Dominion,		626	Scandal Poem 2	81
We govern all Things there below.		626	Scandal Poem 2	86
O'er all your Passions we preside;		626	Scandal Poem 2	88
We, to whom all the Gods give Place:		626	Scandal Poem 2	94
And, in all Climates are at home;		627	Scandal Poem 2	122
After venting all my Spight,		629	Epistle Lady	1
Must, that all the World may know 'em,		631	Epistle Lady	47
Turning all to Ridicule:		631	Epistle Lady	52
Which, of all our modern Dames		631	Epistle Lady	67
All these Praises are your Due.		632	Epistle Lady	94
All your Virtues to my Sight.		633	Epistle Lady	98
Answer all domestick Ends,		633	Epistle Lady	101
Carve for all, yourself is starving.		633	Epistle Lady	124
Carve to all but just enuff.		633	Epistle Lady	129
I, as all the Parish knows,		634	Epistle Lady	137
All the Vices of a Court,		634	Epistle Lady	147
Could I not, thro' all his Ermin,		634	Epistle Lady	151
At whose Oars, like Slaves, they all pull:		635	Epistle Lady	160
All their Madness makes me merry:		635	Epistle Lady	164
What can all this Passion mean?		635	Epistle Lady	182
All your Eloquence will scarce		636	Epistle Lady	195
Sets the Spirits all a working.		636	Epistle Lady	206
But, to patch up all our Quarrels,		637	Epistle Lady	235
All my Fire would fall in Scraps,		638	Epistle Lady	263
All Human Race wou'd fain be Wits,		640	On Poetry	1
In modern Wit all printed Trash, is		643	On Poetry	93
Damns all your Thoughts as low and little,		644	On Poetry	121
You lose your Credit all at once;		644	On Poetry	137
Lay now aside all Thoughts of Fame,		646	On Poetry	183
In all their Speeches, Votes, Addresses.		646	On Poetry	198

ALL	(CONTINUED)	PAGE	TITLE	LINE
Of all the Virtues you can muster:	. . . . . .	647	On Poetry	222
Will smile, and think 'em all his own:	. . . . . .	647	On Poetry	226
All Virtues lodge in royal Ermine.	. . . . . .	647	On Poetry	228
In all our modern Criticks Jargon.)	. . . . . .	648	On Poetry	242
And at all Hazards boldly quote:	. . . . . .	648	On Poetry	248
Read all the Prefaces of Dryden,	. . . .	648	On Poetry	251
Thro' all the Lane, from End to End.	. . . . .	649	On Poetry	288
And all in due Subordination;	. . . . . .	650	On Poetry	314
And all their Brother Dunces lash,	. . . . . .	652	On Poetry	355
But, who can reach the Worst of all?	. . . . . .	653	On Poetry	388
Thro' all the Features of his Face;	. . . . . .	655	On Poetry	418
In all Affairs thou sole Director,	. . . . . .	656	On Poetry	449
On Lewis all his Bards bestow'd,	. . . . .	657	On Poetry	473
They could all Pow'r in Heaven divide,	. . . . . .	657	On Poetry	483
But now go search all Europe round	. . . . . .	659	On Poetry	D 410
I mean all Kings except our own,	. . . . . .	659	On Poetry	D 410
To find a King in all ye Crew,	. . . . .	659	On Poetry	D 410
Thus all are destin'd to obey	. . . . .	659	On Poetry	D 410
Thro' all the brutal Species ran,	. . . . . .	659	On Poetry	D 410
O! were they all but Nebuchadnazzars	. . . . . .	659	On Poetry	D 410
All coffers full except his own.	. . . . . .	659	On Poetry	D 416
All beneath yon flow'ry Rocks.	. . . .	660	Love Song	8
But all distinguish thy dull leaden Mass.	. . . . .	670	Epig Carthy 18	D 6
But all the rest shall club it I protest:---	. . . .	671	Epig Carthy 24	D 6
To all my Friends a Burthen grown,	. . . .	673	His Deafness	2
Saw all these mighty labours done,	. . . .	675	Curate's Compl	14
All this perform'd by Robert Hewit,	. . . . . .	675	Curate's Compl	16
Yet, all must own, thy wish is wise.	. . . . . .	676	Parson's Case	4
To shine, where all the gay resort,	. . . . . .	677	Parson's Case	27
Since all he got by Fraud, is lost by Stocks,	. . .	678	Dean and Duke	6
Yet, hang me, but for all her Art;	. . . . . .	679	From Catullus	3
With Impudence own'd all the Fact.	. . . . . .	687	Cadenus Vaness	24
Laid all the Fault on t' other Sex.	. . . . . .	687	Cadenus Vaness	26
From all the thousand Female Toys,	. . . . . .	688	Cadenus Vaness	47
On all Emergencies that rose.	. . . .	689	Cadenus Vaness	98
A Sweetness above all Perfumes;	. . . .	691	Cadenus Vaness	161
And all their Conduct wou'd be try'd	. . . . . .	694	Cadenus Vaness	238
She'd all undo, that she had done.	. . . . . .	694	Cadenus Vaness	255
Leave all Things to their Nat'ral Course.	. . . .	696	Cadenus Vaness	303
Watch'd all the Company she kept,	. . . .	696	Cadenus Vaness	309
In all she spoke, except to stare.	. . . . . .	698	Cadenus Vaness	357
Grew louder, all the Way up Stairs;	. . . . . .	698	Cadenus Vaness	369
With all her Wit, I wou'd not ask	. . . . . .	700	Cadenus Vaness	420
All humble Worth she strove to raise;	. . . . . .	701	Cadenus Vaness	456
On Pallas all Attempts are vain;	. . . . . .	701	Cadenus Vaness	468
The Boy made use of all his Craft,	. . . . . .	701	Cadenus Vaness	476
Cupid, tho' all his Darts were lost,	. . . . . .	702	Cadenus Vaness	492
Took Aim, and shot with all his Strength	. . . . .	703	Cadenus Vaness	516
To all he spoke, than e'er before;	. . . . . .	704	Cadenus Vaness	565
That all his Lectures were in vain?	. . . . . .	705	Cadenus Vaness	601
That all his Lessons were not lost.	. . . . . .	705	Cadenus Vaness	605
Appearances were all so strong,	. . . .	707	Cadenus Vaness	642
All that was witty, learn'd, and wise,	. . . . . .	708	Cadenus Vaness	697
How all wou'd for his Friendship strive;	. . . . .	709	Cadenus Vaness	701
Alone to fill up all her Wit;	. . . . . .	709	Cadenus Vaness	709
Thro' this she made all Objects pass,	. . . . . .	709	Cadenus Vaness	718
Will force all Nature to submit.	. . . . . .	709	Cadenus Vaness	725
She noted all she ever read,	. . . .	710	Cadenus Vaness	756
When 'tis a Compound of them all;	. . . .	711	Cadenus Vaness	773
In all their Equipages meet;	. . . .	711	Cadenus Vaness	775
A Truce with all sublime Conceits.	. . . . . .	711	Cadenus Vaness	793
All met, and Silence thrice proclaim'd,	. . . . . .	713	Cadenus Vaness	842
"She left all Business to her Son:	. . . . . .	714	Cadenus Vaness	881
Left all below at Six and Sev'n,	. . . . . .	714	Cadenus Vaness	888
The Corruption of Verse, for when all is done,	. . .	716	Answer Rebus	9
True Honour comprehends them all.	. . . .	724	To Stella	18
All Passions must be laid aside:	. . . . . .	724	To Stella	36
Drive all Objections from your Mind,	. . . . . .	724	To Stella	43
Nor calls up all the House at Night,	. . . . . .	725	To Stella	73
But all admire Inigo Jones:	. . . . . .	727	Stella, Poems	4
In all the Habitudes of Life,	. . . .	728	Stella, Poems	15
Counts all his Labours amply paid,	. . . . . .	729	Stella, Poems	37
And all the Fictions they pursue	. . . . . .	729	Stella, Poems	59
Had gone through all the Common-Places	. . . . .	730	Stella, Poems	75
Let Malice look with all her Eyes,	. . . . . .	730	Stella, Poems	81
Your Virtues, all suspended, wait	. . . . .	730	Stella, Poems	95
Which, tho' with Trembling, all admire;	. . . . .	731	Stella, Poems	106
Enriching all the Vales below.	. . . .	731	Stella, Poems	108
For Vices all have diff'rent Ends,	. . . . . .	733	Verses Vanessa	11
'Tis all her Thought and Art,	. . . .	733	Verses Vanessa	24
All Travellers at first incline	. . . . . .	734	Stel B-day '20	1
All Christian People to invite;	. . . .	735	Stel B-day '20	36
When Stella's Locks must all be grey	. . . . . .	735	Stel B-day '20	48
Though you and all your senceless Tribe	. . . . .	736	Stel B-day '20	51
All Men of Sense will pass your Dore	. . . . . .	736	Stel B-day '20	57
And all Your Virtues left unsung:	. . . . . .	739	Stel B-day '21	12
They'll call it all poetick Licence:	. . . . .	741	Stel B-day 22	28
I furnish Hints, and you should use all 'em,	. . . .	742	Stel B-day 22	38
She thought that all the world was Oatmeal:	. . .	745	Stel Distress	6
Got all things at the highest Price.	. . . . . .	745	Stel Distress	10

ALL	(CONTINUED)	PAGE	TITLE	LINE
When all the while you might remark Where all	. . . .	747	Stel Distress	47
When all the while you might remark Where all	. . . .	747	Stel Distress	47
When all her little Money spent,	. . . .	747	Stel Distress	54
Yet granting all I said were true,	. . . . . .	748	Stel Distress	75
Got all things at the highest Price.	. . . .	749	Stel Wood-Park	8
When all the while you might remark,	. . . . . .	751	Stel Wood-Park	63
When all her County-Savings gone,	. . . . . .	751	Stel Wood-Park	70
Bring all your Quilca cares to Dublin,	. . . .	753	Gift for Bec	24
And so take all upon your back.	. . . .	753	Gift for Bec	26
All accidents of life conspire	. . . .	755	Stella '23	21
And please all the rest,	. . . .	756	Dingley Brent	14
So long till all your Flesh is wasted,	. . . .	759	Receipt Youth	24
Round all your Body plump your Skin;	. . . . .	759	Receipt Youth	30
While all the Squires from nine Miles round,	. . .	760	Receipt Youth	42
But, if they can, by all their arts,	. . . . . .	761	Bec's B-Day	13
And all her bustling but supplies	. . . .	761	Bec's B-Day	27
Which can in spite of all Decays,	. . . .	764	Stel B-day '26	11
And by all Sages understood	. . . .	764	Stel B-day '26	27
For Vice in all its glitt'ring Dress:	. . . . . .	765	Stel B-day '26	48
That all Effects of Virtue end?	. . . .	765	Stel B-day '26	66
While all is Calm, his Arguments prevail,	. . . .	770	Horace 1, 14	27
'Till Pow'r, discharging all her stormy Bags,	. . .	771	Horace 1, 14	29
But prithee Tim, why all this Clutter?	. . . . .	773	Mullinix Tim	2
From all their Conduct this is plain,	. . . . .	773	Mullinix Tim	11
Whose Fleet, 'tis all our Friends Opinion,	. . . .	774	Mullinix Tim	23
While all the silly Wretch can do	. . . . . .	774	Mullinix Tim	27
But you when all the Show is past	. . . . . .	774	Mullinix Tim	41
When all the Bees are gone to settle,	. . . . .	775	Mullinix Tim	45
Of all thy Party through the Nation.	. . . . . .	775	Mullinix Tim	56
Thy Whisp'rings foisted in all Ears;	. . . . .	775	Mullinix Tim	62
Reviles all People in his Jargon,	. . . . . .	777	Mullinix Tim	113
While teizing all, by all he's teiz'd,	. . . . .	777	Mullinix Tim	125
While teizing all, by all he's teiz'd,	. . . . .	777	Mullinix Tim	125
Put all your Brother Puppets out,	. . . . .	777	Mullinix Tim	140
To interrupt all serious Matter,	. . . . . .	777	Mullinix Tim	144
They wou'd Consent, that all the Crew	. . . . .	778	Mullinix Tim	149
By all this Coyl what hast thou got?	. . . . .	778	Mullinix Tim	152
If Tories must have all the sport,	. . . . .	778	Mullinix Tim	153
Must all my <Dammee's>, <Bloods> and <Wounds>		779	Mullinix Tim	187
Use all the Talents of your mind.	. . . .	780	Mullinix Tim	232
The Children all our motions Aping.	. . . . .	780	Mullinix Tim	242
With what concerns all human kind,	. . . . . .	781	Mullinix Tim	264
And at the Gallows all deny'd;	. . . .	781	Mullinix Tim	274
The Beau in all his Ayrs exprest.	. . . . .	782	Tim and Fables	12
And Dick curse all the Tories.	. . . . .	784	Mullinex Dick	16
Tom was held by all the Town	. . . . . .	785	Mullinex Dick	27
In the House 'tis all he says;	. . . .	785	Mullinex Dick	39
All powder'd o'er from Tail to Chin;	. . . . .	785	Dick, Maggot	2
Thou must go naked all the Year.	. . . . . .	786	Clad in Brown	4
All outward and within is foul;	. . . .	787	Clad in Brown	14
When pelted all with Dirt they shine;	. . . .	787	Clad in Brown	20
Through all thy Land, in Armour, Fur and Lawn.	. .	792	St. Pat's Well	56
Drains all thy Lakes of Fish, of Fruits thy Land.	.	793	St. Pat's Well	64
And Blessings equally on all bestows.	. . . .	793	St. Pat's Well	68
Discourag'd Youths, now all their Hopes must fail,	. .	793	St. Pat's Well	73
Be all made Captives in their native Land;	. . .	793	St. Pat's Well	90
But all turn Leasers to that Mongril Breed,	. .	794	St. Pat's Well	95
While Traulus all his Ordure scatters.	. . . . .	796	Traulus 1	31
The Neighbours all cry, Shoot him dead,	. . . .	797	Traulus 1	39
He prates in Spight of all Impediment	. . . . .	797	Traulus 1	49
'Twas all for Love, and that's enough.	. . . . .	797	Traulus 1	62
The scrubest Cur in all the Pack	. . . . . .	798	Traulus 1	67
If that were all. But he's possess't:	. . . . .	798	Traulus 1	70
Wishes it were all unsaid.	. . . .	800	Traulus 2	22
A <Bishop> who rul'd all the rest of his Tribe;	. . .	803	Irish Bishops	2
And all Men believe he presides there incog.	. . .	804	Irish Bishops	15
If making Divisions was all their Intent,	. . . .	804	Irish Bishops	35
And have we not practis'd all Methods to gain you;	. .	805	Irish Bishops	57
Whose Perjury's the least of all their Crimes:	. . .	806	Judas	12
Drop from the Tree with all his Bowels burst;	. . .	806	Judas	.22
His Habitation let all Men forsake,	. . . . .	806	Judas	25
Uniting all, to shew their Amity,	. . . .	811	Bro Protestant	9
Thus all the Footmen, Shoe-boys, Porters,	. . .	812	Bro Protestant	21
And as our Sects, by all Decriptions,	. . . . .	813	Bro Protestant	51
Hath insulted us all by insulting the Dean.	. . .	814	Yahoo's	4
Hath met with returns of all sorts but applause;	. .	815	Yahoo's	17
Of all sizes and sorts, the Fanatical crew	. . .	815	Yahoo's	21
To the Dean of all Deans, tho' he wears not a sword.	.	816	Yahoo's	54
They shrewdly suspect it is all but a bite.	. . . .	818	Archbi Cashel	4
And say of the man what all honest men say.	. . . .	819	Archbi Cashel	10
Would offer all the Sands of Tagus;	. . . . . .	821	Dr. Rundle	42
But all his Gold could not avail	. . . . . .	821	Dr. Rundle	45
Because our Lawyers all agree,	. . . .	821	Dr. Rundle	59
Better we all were in our Graves	. . . . . .	824	Printer Newgat	1
All Mortals must be curious to enquire,	. . . .	825	Noisy Tom	5
Tear the Bible all to Pieces.	. . . .	831	Legion Club	66
All ye Gods, who rule the Soul	. . . . . .	832	Legion Club	83
Shews a Bribe in all his Hands:	. . . . . .	833	Legion Club	104
All involv'd in wild Disputes;	. . . .	833	Legion Club	114
Who are all grown reverend Preachers!	. . . . . .	838	Legion Club	204

ALL	(CONTINUED)	PAGE	TITLE	LINE
All in Arms prepare to back us:	. . . .	838	Legion Club	212
Send the Clergy all to graze;	. . . .	838	Legion Club	216
All the Soul in every Face.	. . . .	839	Legion Club	230
And Patricks' bell she was ringing all in muffles;	. .	840	Ballad	D 7
Those carters, and paviours, and footmen and all;	. . .	841	Ballad	D 17
The Lord of all the fruitful Plain,	. . . .	848	Old Thorn	10
Has canker'd all its Branches round;	. . . . . .	849	Old Thorn	18
And fled in Haste with all her Brood	. . . . . .	849	Old Thorn	39
All as she scrubb'd her meazly Rump.	. . . . . .	849	Old Thorn	44
(If all be true that Poets chant)	. . . .	849	Old Thorn	46
"Through all thy Empire I foresee,	. . . .	851	Old Thorn	78
Moving all like a pendulum;	. . . .	852	Lady's Lament	30
By the worst of all Squires,	. . . .	853	Lady's Lament	45
Let all the world judge.	. . . .	856	Lady's Lament	152
He's all the day saunt'ring,	. . . .	856	Lady's Lament	159
All dirty and wet:	. . . .	856	Lady's Lament	166
And all the day raves	. . . .	856	Lady's Lament	175
Shews all his gew-gaws,	. . . .	857	Lady's Lament	179
Where all goes to ruin	. . . .	857	Lady's Lament	193
His Horses too eat all our Hay.	. . . .	861	Lady Acheson	36
I'm all over dawb'd when I sit by the Dean.	. . .	868	Grand Question	30
But Hannah, who listen'd to all that was past,	. . .	868	Grand Question	41
For all the World, Captain, not half an Inch farther--	.	869	Grand Question	79
Tantara, tantara, while all the Boys hollow.	. . .	870	Grand Question	92
See, now comes the Captain all dawb'd with gold Lace:	.	870	Grand Question	93
To peep at the Captain, in all his fine Clo'es:	. . .	872	Grand Question	138
"Mister Curate, for all your grave Looks, I'm afraid,	.	872	Grand Question	147
And all his Handkerchiefs are rotten;	. . . . .	875	Drapier's Hill	16
No; not in all the British Court;	. . . . . .	876	To Dean Swift	7
All things gone on the same dull track,	. . . . .	877	To Dean Swift	31
All for Love, or the World well lost.	. . . . .	878	Robbin & Harry	20
Young Harry, as all Europe knows,	. . . . . .	879	Robbin & Harry	37
Old Robin, all his youth a sloven,	. . . . . .	879	Robbin & Harry	45
You sat and lows'd him all the Sun-shine Day.	. .	882	Pastoral Dial	34
And we of all our Hopes depriv'd;	. . . . . .	885	Rev Market-Hill	61
All his Agility is gone;	. . . .	885	Rev Market-Hill	80
Madam, whose Skill does all in Dress lye,	. . . .	886	Rev Market-Hill	99
As all your Politicians wise	. . . .	886	Rev Market-Hill	109
Thrice Rev'rend <Dean> for all I owe;	. . . . .	887	Panegyr Dean	2
But now in all our Sexes Name,	. . . .	887	Panegyr Dean	5
To all their weaker Sides are blind;	. . . . . .	887	Panegyr Dean	8
Ye Hawkers all, your Voices lift;	. . . . . .	887	Panegyr Dean	33
Nor, can he judge with all his Art	. . . . . .	889	Panegyr Dean	91
Whene'er you joke, 'tis all a Case;	. . . . . .	890	Panegyr Dean	121
Are largely paid for all your time.	. . . . . .	893	Panegyr Dean	196
Receives all Off'rings at her Shrine.	. . . . .	893	Panegyr Dean	206
And, O! may all who hither come,	. . . . . .	894	Panegyr Dean	223
Receiv'd the Gifts of all Mankind.	. . . . . .	894	Panegyr Dean	236
And Smedly, Flow'r of all Divines,	. . . . . .	897	Panegyr Dean	345
All risen since that flatt'ring time,	. . . . . .	899	Dean's Reasons	9
To me from all a us'rer's plumbs;	. . . . . .	899	Dean's Reasons	28
If all my rhetoric must fail	. . . .	899	Dean's Reasons	31
And think all notions too abstracted	. . . . .	900	Dean's Reasons	63
But now, let all his tenants round	. . . . . .	902	Dean's Reasons	103
Bequeathed to Pluto, Corps and all.	. . . . .	904	Death Daphne	32
All her spirits in a flame	. . . .	906	Daphne	19
And in dress place all your merit;	. . . . . .	908	Daphne	76
And clad my Body all in White:	. . . . . .	915	Riddle 1	4
All Languages I can command,	. . . .	915	Riddle 1	27
But see below me all Mankind.	. . . .	917	Riddle 3	4
The Vulgar all consult my Look.	. . . .	917	Riddle 3	8
By all the World I am oppress't,	. . . .	918	Riddle 4	9
Of whom all People make a Jest.	. . . .	918	Riddle 4	22
And all I get, I let it fly:	. . . .	918	Riddle 4	26
Sometimes run out of all I have;	. . . . . .	918	Riddle 4	32
And therefore, all that know me, say	. . . . .	918	Riddle 4	37
Adorn'd by Nymphs with all their Care:	. . . . .	919	Riddle 5	4
Contrives all Means the Gift to hide:	. . . . .	919	Riddle 5	22
And drive at last all Secrets out:	. . . . . .	920	Riddle 6	16
Vain Man, of all thy vain Pursuits.	. . . . . .	921	Riddle 7	2
Bring all past Actions to thy Mind.	. . . . . .	921	Riddle 7	4
How soon all human Pleasures pass.	. . . . . .	921	Riddle 7	6
When all the sad Reverse appears!	. . . . . .	921	Riddle 7	10
The last Result of all Designs:	. . . .	921	Riddle 7	12
All human Race must hither draw:	. . . . . .	922	Riddle 7	24
All prompted by the same Desire,	. . . . . .	922	Riddle 7	25
All make Oblations at this Shrine.	. . . . . .	922	Riddle 7	30
In at this Gulph all Off'rings pass,	. . . . .	922	Riddle 7	43
For which all Mortals leave their Home;	. . . . .	922	Riddle 7	52
And yet her Wealth was all her Guilt.	. . . . .	923	Riddle 7	66
All beauteous Offspring of one Womb,	. . . . .	923	Riddle 7	68
Or, whether op'ning all his Stores,	. . . . .	924	Riddle 7	87
They all were born from thy Embrace.	. . . . .	925	Riddle 8	24
And all my Kin, a num'rous Host,	. . . . . .	925	Riddle 8	28
All over naked I am seen,	. . . . .	926	Riddle 9	9
To their old Posts restor'd all Three,	. . . . .	926	Riddle 9	23
And after all, I chiefly owe	. . . .	927	Riddle 10	D 11
All Figures Heav'n or Earth can yield,	. . . . .	927	Riddle 10	D 16
Yet am not one of all you see.	. . . .	927	Riddle 10	D 18
But all I delight in is Pieces of Lead;	. . . . .	927	Riddle 11	D 6

ALL	(CONTINUED)	PAGE	TITLE	LINE
The Moment I get one my Soul's all a-fire,		928	Riddle 11	D 11
Yet all the World can't find me out,		929	Riddle 14	D 2
Yet all that know me will agree,		929	Riddle 15	D 3
And after all you'll think it odd,		930	Riddle 15	D 21
All devouring, all destroying,		930	Riddle 16	D 2
All devouring, all destroying,		930	Riddle 16	D 2
All of diff'rent Voice and Features,		930	Riddle 17	D 2
All of us in one you'll find,		931	Riddle 18	D 1
Yet among us all no Brother		931	Riddle 18	D 3
He's the Register of All		931	Riddle 18	D 9
Pierce us all with wounding Steel,		931	Riddle 18	D 21
One for all of us will feel.		931	Riddle 18	D 22
When all we see shall disappear.		932	Riddle 19	D 16
Join in all the Din of Battle.		933	Riddle 20	D 22
Jove, with all his loudest Thunder,		933	Riddle 20	D 23
In all Things false, yet always true,		935	Riddle 23	D 5
All Shapes and Features I can boast,		935	Riddle 23	D 10
All Colours, without Paint, put on,		935	Riddle 23	D 12
All Things on Earth I imitate,		935	Riddle 23	D 18
Of all inhabitants on earth,		936	Riddle 24	D 1
Are all my parents more than he:		936	Riddle 24	D 4
All the secrets of her heart.		936	Riddle 24	D 26
Like thyself I shine in all.		937	Riddle 24	D 38
Die like all that look on you.		937	Riddle 24	D 54
The Dead are all sound		939	Riddle Answerd	19
After all you have writ,		939	Riddle Answerd	21
Is that by which all Irishmen swear.		940	Letter	15
Is by all pious Christians thought,		942	Probatur Alit	5
I'd not look at all, unless I look't better.		943	Probatur Alit	38
For you, by this Rule, must adore all Mankind.		947	Mrs. Houghton	6
For all an example, for no one a pattern.		955	Portrait Life	8
Having thus overthrown all our further Advances.		968	Letter Sherid	22
Which is all at present from Dean of St. Patrick's.		977	Dean to Sherid	48
'Tis all you have for't; 'tis your best Magna Carta;		979	Dean to Tho: S	16
And you know all my geese are swans:		983	Sher, A Goose	12
. . . than you and all your kin:		985	Mary to Sher	8
And I don't care who knows it, 'tis all one to Mary.		986	Mary to Sher	22
I remember it was upon a Tuesday, of all Days in the Year.		986	Mary to Sher	26
But above all I prefer Aeschylus.		988	Letter Dr Sh-n	28
Which all may handle, none can flatter.		993	On Picture	18
For thee three Poets now are drudging all,		993	On Picture	25
To praise the Cheeks, Chin, Nose, the Bridge and all,		993	On Picture	26
And all that stuff of Toylet, Glass, and Box-comb?		1003	Dan J's Reply	9
Your Gibes and all your foul Abuse,		1003	Dan J's Reply	14
My Wounds Bleed all anew:		1005	Sheridan's Sub	31
. . .with all my Heart and Soul, upon my Word and Honour.		1014	Swift to Sheri	9
For all your colloguing,		1015	Swift to Sheri	45
I think you inspird by the Muses all nine		1017	Swift Ans Sher	4
And the worst of them all like a barn door did shine		1017	Swift Ans Sher	6
I'll tear all your Rules, and demolish your Pun Talk:		1019	To Sheridan	8
Then all must grant, your Lines are weighty,		1022	Nim-Dan-Dean 1	D 47
All must allow, your Numbers more,		1022	Nim-Dan-Dean 1	D 49
However, bring down yourself, and you bring down all;		1023	Nim-Dan-Dean 2	D 13
That we walk all about, like a horse in a pound,		1026	Sheri Circles	7
Which is all at present; and so I remain--		1027	Sheri Circles	28
Dean Cross, had he preach'd, would have made us all Pew-sick;		1029	Dr. Helsham	8
You may find they are all, by their yellow pale Hue, sick		1030	Dr. Helsham	27
Thro' all the Vallies, Hills, and Plains,		1035	To Quilca	9
All Servants at play.		1036	Plague Country	9
And doth all Christians hate;		1036	Heathen Christ	2
All people tease me,		1037	Sheridan Cavan	7
ALL-CONSOLING				
Thy want of all-consoling liquor,		676	Parson's Case	8
ALL-DEVOURING				
It grew an all-devouring Asp;		132	Magician's Rod	10
ALL-DIGESTING				
And, Ostrich-like, his all-digesting Maw.		532	To Mr. Gay	36
ALL-RULING				
All-ruling Tyrant of the Earth,		916	Riddle 2	1
ALL-SHAKING				
Unaw'd by Jove's all-shaking Nod.		466	Birthday Song	186
ALL'S				
Dick, we agree--all's true, thou'st said,		183	Horace 2, 1	99
ALLARM				
So, by the Kettles loud Allarm,		345	Prometheus	25
ALLAY				
Immortal Joy, that suffers no Allay from Fears,		6	Ode to King	2
ALLEDGE				
Since Men alledge they ne'er can find		691	Cadenus Vaness	142
ALLEDGES				
While ev'ry Fool his Claim alledges,		640	On Poetry	9
ALLEGIANCE				
They have no claim to Your allegiance,		620	Scandal Poem 1	97
Who better challenge your Allegiance,		626	Scandal Poem 2	95
\<ALLENS\>				
Those are \<Allens\>, Jack and Bob,		836	Legion Club	173

```
ALLEY   SEE CHANGE-ALLEY                             PAGE    TITLE          LINE
    Thro' ev'ry Alley to be found,   . . . . . . . .   651 On Poetry          315
ALLIANCE
    which plainly shews the near Alliance . . . . . .    98 Elegy Patrige      29
    And next Observe how this Alliance fits,            276 Epilogue           39
    Tho' I dare you to more than quadruple Alliance?   1019 To Sheridan         2
ALLIES
    "No Flatt'rers; no Allies in Blood;    . . . . .    566 Death of Swift     334
    Thorow stinking Lanes and Allies;    . . . . . .    574 Helter Skelter     42
ALLMOST
    Which backwards and forwards is allmost the same. . . .  148 Windsor Proph  24
ALLOT
    Yet to the Dean his Share allot;    . . . . . . .   406 Swift to Pope      17
ALLOW
    (We Poets oft our Bays allow,    . . . . . . . .      6 Ode to King         9
    If you allow, the present Age    . . . . . . . .   392 Young's Satire     33
    Allow your hatred strictly just;    . . . . . . .  498 Panegyr Swift     170
    Birds, as he says, and I allow,    . . . . . . .   513 Answer Fable       39
    "Perhaps I may allow, the Dean    . . . . . . .    571 Death of Swift    455
    Allow there's a Hell, but dispute of the Place;    575 Place Damn'd        2
    Which my very Foes allow me.    . . . . . . . .    631 Epistle Lady       64
    Madam, I allow 'tis true;    . . . . . . . . .     632 Epistle Lady       93
    Some Clergy too she wou'd allow,    . . . . . . .  701 Cadenus Vaness    460
    For Divines allow, that God    . . . . . . . .     830 Legion Club        31
    I allow the Pile may stand.    . . . . . . . . .   830 Legion Club        38
    Whom you allow a man of taste,    . . . . . . .    899 Dean's Reasons     22
    All must allow, your Numbers more,    . . . . .   1022 Nim-Dan-Dean 1   D 49
ALLOW'D
    Then, it must be allow'd, whenever I shine,        263 Apollo              7
    But thirdly and lastly, it must be allow'd,  . . . 263 \Apollo           15
    Because he ne'er one Thought allow'd               400 Window Inns 1       3
    As far as Modest Pride allow'd,    . . . . . .     482 Libel on D- D-     58
    Let due Reward to Merit be allow'd;    . . . . .   533 To Mr. Gay         57
    The Swine with contrite Heart allow'd,    . . .    602 Beasts Confess     37
    And yet, I hope 't will be allow'd,    . . . . .   622 Scandal Poem 1    151
    And yet, I hope, 'twill be allow'd,  . . . . .     628 Scandal Poem 2    155
    Since first the Court allow'd them Food.    . . .  652 On Poetry         366
    Let me be allow'd to tell    . . . . . . . . .     832 Legion Club        85
ALLOWANCE
    When the whole month's Allowance gone    . . . . . 747 Stel Distress
ALLOWED
    Was equally allowed to shine,    . . . . . . . .   455 Dean Smedley        3
ALLOWS
    For which Her <Majesty> allows him Grains.    . . . 521 Stephen Duck        4
    For Jupiter allows no more)    . . . . . . . . .   598 Problem Solved     18
    Though neither Foe nor Friend allows us.    . . .  603 Beasts Confess     78
    But this neither Reason nor Conscience allows;   . . 947 Mrs. Houghton     2
ALLUDING
    Whilst an alluding Hymn some Artist sings,    . . . 162 Toland's Invit    13
ALLUM
    Here Allum Flower to stop the Steams,    . . . . . 526 Lady's Dres Rm    27
ALLURE
    Allure the Cinder-picking Fair.   . . . . . . . .  779 Mullinix Tim      206
ALLUREMENTS
    When Love's Allurements long are past;    . . . .  711 Cadenus Vaness    783
ALLUSION
    And well, methinks, does this allusion fit    . .   45 To Congreve       75
    Can lend you an Allusion fitter,    . . . . . . .  485 Libel on D- D-    177
    To an Allusion so polite,    . . . . . . . . .     497 Panegyr Swift     123
    Now hear an Allusion!--A Mitre, you know,    . . . 805 Irish Bishops     41
ALLUSIONS
    But, Poets love profane allusions.   . . . . . . . 622 Scandal Poem 1    162
ALLWAYS
    All special Friends, and allways jarr.    . . . .  217 To Mr. Delany     60
    Not allways judges what is fit; . . . . . . . .    218 To Mr. Delany     92
    Than what it allways did before;    . . . . . .    255 Bubble           120
ALLY    SEE CHANGE-ALLY
    What Ally are they nestled in,    . . . . . . . .  505 Doctor Delaney   147
ALLY'D
    The Jack and Chimney near ally'd,    . . . . . .   113 Bauc & Phil 2     75
ALMA
    Alma Mater was thy Mother,    . . . . . . . . .    838 Legion Club      199
ALMANACK
    How by the Almanack 'tis clear,    . . . . . . .   781 Mullinix Tim     275
ALMANACKS
    Either for Almanacks or Shoes.    . . . . . . . .   99 Elegy Patrige     46
    His Pills, his Almanacks, or Shoes.   . . . . .    101 Elegy Patrige    108
ALMIGHTY
    And your Almighty Master, knew    . . . . . . .     38 Ode Sancroft     114
    To his undoubted Master, Heaven's Almighty Son.  . . 38 Ode Sancroft    134
    Preserve, Almighty Providence!    . . . . . . .    199 Horace 2, 6     D
    "While he obeys Almighty Will,    . . . . . . .    485 Libel on D- D-   167
    Almighty Anger to disarm?    . . . . . . . . .     949 Epigr Fasting      4
ALMIGHTY'S
    Th' Almighty's Orders to perform,    . . . . . .   496 Panegyr Swift     92
ALMOST
    The Battel almost by Great William's single Valour   8 Ode to King       64
        gain'd;
    Forgive a young and (almost) Virgin-muse,    . . .  18 Ode Athenian      62
    And seem (almost) transform'd to Water, Flame, and Air,  22 Ode Athenian 201
    And almost got priority of Sight,    . . . . . . .  30 Ode to Temple    130
```

```
ALMOST          (CONTINUED)                                  PAGE    TITLE              LINE
     And when I almost reach the Shore      . . . . . . .     32 Ode to Temple         194
     Finding the Mitre almost grown         . . . . . . .     40 Ode Sancroft         187
     The wooden Jack which had almost       . . . . . . .     93 Bauc & Phil 1        125
     A wooden Jack, which had almost        . . . . . . .    113 Bauc & Phil 2         65
     Till Fame and Eccho almost burst,      . . . . . . .    121 Apollo Outwit         59
     Your Rent is due almost a Week beside the Days of        343 Upon His Grace        44
        Grace.
     Are stronger, and almost as good.      . . . . . . .    367 Answer Delaney        50
     And Madam almost dress'd by Four;      . . . . . . .    447 Modern Lady           91
     For her Taste is almost as refin'd as her Wit.   . .    580 Psyche                10
     As Chloe's Skin, almost as bright.     . . . . . . .    589 Strephon Chloe       174
     To rhyme almost as ill as Duck;        . . . . . . .    658 On Poetry          D 186
     In Eyes with Reading almost blind;     . . . . . . .    703 Cadenus Vaness       527
     I almost wisht this Spud were in your Guts.      . .    882 Pastoral Dial         40
     That I have almost learn't to spell:   . . . . . . .    891 Panegyr Dean         134
     I almost sink with my own Weight,      . . . . . . .    917 Riddle 3              6
     I'm found almost in ev'ry Garden,      . . . . . . .    929 Riddle 14          D  5
ALMS
     He might be thought an Object fit for Alms.      . .    234 Elegy on Demar        12
ALOFT
     The Roof began to mount aloft          . . . . . . .     92 Bauc & Phil 1         92
     Aloft rose ev'ry Beam and Rafter,      . . . . . . .     92 Bauc & Phil 1         93
     The Roof began to mount aloft;         . . . . . . .    112 Bauc & Phil 2         52
     Aloft rose ev'ry Beam and Rafter,      . . . . . . .    112 Bauc & Phil 2         53
     There stuck aloft, in Publick View,    . . . . . . .    114 Bauc & Phil 2         87
     And, sits aloft on Pindus Head,        . . . . . . .    483 Libel on D- D-        87
     His Signs aloft no longer swing;       . . . . . . .    875 Drapier's Hill        14
ALONE
     The Jack would not be left alone       . . . . . . .     94 Bauc & Phil 1        140
     The Jack wou'd not be left alone,      . . . . . . .    113 Bauc & Phil 2         78
     To Pan alone rich Misers call,         . . . . . . .    157 Fable of Midas        57
     That your Lordship would once let your Cares all alone  185 Scriblerus 1           3
     Takes him to Windsor in his Coach, alone.     . . .    194 Author Himself        32
     But, why obscurely here alone?     . . . . . . . . .    203 In Sickness            3
     Your Hand alone from Gold abstains,    . . . . . . .    243 Horace 4, 9           13
     I alone can inspire the poetical Crowd;     . . . .    263 Apollo                16
     Simplicity alone can grace,        . . . . . . . . .    270 Apollo's Edict     D 29
     Then goes alone to take his Rest       . . . . . . .    292 Prog Marriage         89
     Simplicity alone is rare;  . . . . . . . . . . . . .    378 Apology Lady C       106
     Himself alone shou'd make him great.   . . . . . . .    384 Manly Virtue          36
     That he alone deserv'd Esteem,         . . . . . . .    386 Manly Virtue          75
     Confines his Faith to one alone;       . . . . . . .    387 Manly Virtue         132
     Mordanto gallops on alone,     . . . . . . . . . . .    398 Earl of P-b-w         19
     'I thought we were to Dine alone,      . . . . . . .    448 Modern Lady          102
     Nor do they trust their Tongue alone,  . . . . . . .    450 Modern Lady          188
     Now all alone poor Madam sits,     . . . . . . . . .    451 Modern Lady          198
     An Ass's Hoof alone can hold       . . . . . . . . .    469 Burning Poem           1
     Suppose my Lord and you alone;     . . . . . . . . .    480 Libel on D- D-        13
     He can alone the priesthood humble,    . . . . . . .    490 Dialogue              35
     Rightly you shew, that Wit alone       . . . . . . .    495 Panegyr Swift         72
     Since you alone of all the Race        . . . . . . .    498 Panegyr Swift        171
     "For her he boldly stood alone;        . . . . . . .    566 Death of Swift       349
     "On which alone, our Weal depended.    . . . . . . .    568 Death of Swift       378
     Alone, and by no Planter courted;      . . . . . . .    583 Young Nymph           46
     And could not let a Dunce alone:       . . . . . . .    602 Beasts Confess        24
     Nature alone must bear the Blame.      . . . . . . .    602 Beasts Confess        30
     That made him trust alone in Merit:    . . . . . . .    604 Beasts Confess       110
     Blackmore alone his Place supply'd:    . . . . . . .    652 On Poetry            372
     Who shines alone, without a Mate.      . . . . . . .    656 On Poetry            442
     Deaf, giddy, helpless, left alone,     . . . . . . .    673 His Deafness           1
     Alone distinguish'd Man from Brute:    . . . . . . .    697 Cadenus Vaness       345
     Alone to fill up all her Wit;      . . . . . . . . .    709 Cadenus Vaness       709
     A Lesson she alone can teach.      . . . . . . . . .    724 To Stella             34
     Ask no Advice, but think alone,        . . . . . . .    724 To Stella             37
     Courage to Man alone confin'd:         . . . . . . .    725 To Stella             66
     No: 'Twas for you alone he stole       . . . . . . .    726 To Stella             87
     Which might have conquer'd Troy;       . . . . . . .    731 Stella, Poems        124
     Yet seems to feel my pains alone,  . . . . . . . . .    754 Stella '23            17
     For thee alone they lye the Island round.     . . .    772 Horace 1, 14          64
     Henceforth depends alone on me.        . . . . . . .    776 Mullinix Tim          82
     One Traytor alone, and faithful Eleven;    . . . . .    804 Irish Bishops         31
     'Tis your gross panegyrics alone can bespatter.  . .    819 Archbi Cashel         14
     Now, said I, we are alone,     . . . . . . . . . . .    834 Legion Club          135
     When Saturn rul'd the Skies alone,     . . . . . . .    894 Panegyr Dean         233
     One of us alone can sleep,     . . . . . . . . . . .    931 Riddle 18          D 15
     Nor can I ever be alone;   . . . . . . . . . . . . .    935 Riddle 23          D 17
     To Man alone I owe my birth,       . . . . . . . . .    936 Riddle 24          D  2
     Like sots, alone I'm dull enough,      . . . . . . .    936 Riddle 24          D  9
     On rainy Days alone I dine,        . . . . . . . . .    954 Authors Living         1
     On rainy Days, I dine alone,       . . . . . . . . .    954 Authors Living         3
     In reading your Letter alone in my Hackny,    . . .    972 S-'s Ans Sh-d          1
ALONG
     Which in its dusky march along the plain,     . . .     40 Ode Sancroft         193
     Like an huge Snail along the Wall,     . . . . . . .    113 Bauc & Phil 2         86
     Along the high celestial Road;     . . . . . . . . .    231 Prog of Poetry        28
     Led with amazing Art along     . . . . . . . . . . .    386 Manly Virtue          85
     Along the plain like Lightning flew:   . . . . . . .    412 Desire Possess        22
     The rumbling words march fierce along,     . . . . .    461 Birthday Song         45
     He blew a Settlement along;    . . . . . . . . . . .    585 Strephon Chloe        40
     So fine a Coach along the Strand;      . . . . . . .    598 Problem Solved        14
```

28

```
ALONG          (CONTINUED)                          PAGE    TITLE        LINE
   For Food, along the barren Plain;     . . . . . .   759 Receipt Youth    6
   Only take this rule along,   . . . . . . . . . .    907 Daphne          35
ALOUD
   Will tell aloud your greatest Failing;   . . . . . 416 Woman's Mind     20
ALPHABET
   Against the harmless Alphabet;   . . . . . . . . . 645 On Poetry       158
ALREADY
   But she the Charm already try'd,   . . . . . . .   120 Apollo Outwit    38
   Your Foes already waiting stand   . . . . . . . .  258 Bubble          198
   I am too much reveng'd already by Time;   . . . .  266 Apollo          104
   Already dwindled to a Lath;   . . . . . . . .      293 Prog Marriage   105
   Who struts like any King already.   . . . . . . .  466 Birthday Song   188
   That you have got a Place already,   . . . . . . . 483 Libel on D- D-  104
   Their Work was half already done,   . . . . . . .  692 Cadenus Vaness  174
   Tho' she already can discern,   . . . . . . . . .  712 Cadenus Vaness  808
   I fancy already a Barrack contriv'd   . . . . . .  869 Grand Question   67
   Already have improv'd so well,   . . . . . . . .   891 Panegyr Dean    133
   . . .for Saunders already hath got above ten Jaunts.  1013 Swift to Sheri  6
ALSO      1                                              OMITTED WORD
ALT
   For he could reach to B. in alt:   . . . . . . .   598 Problem Solved   28
ALTAR
   He cut his Weazon at the Altar;   . . . . . . .    349 Upright Judge 1   3
   His Altar now no longer smokes,   . . . . . . .    687 Cadenus Vaness    9
ALTARS
   No Sacrifice on Altars blaz'd;   . . . . . . . .   346 Prometheus       44
   Make gilded spires and altars tumble.   . . . . .  490 Dialogue         36
   Why are thine Altars fix't beneath?   . . . . . .  894 Panegyr Dean    232
   Ten Thousand Altars smoaking round   . . . . . .   894 Panegyr Dean    237
   To thee no verdant Altars rear;   . . . . . . .    895 Panegyr Dean    282
   Your Altars near your Couches Side?   . . . . . .  896 Panegyr Dean    294
   Soon would their Altars Flame expire,   . . . . .  916 Riddle 2         13
ALTER'D
   But when I thought proper, I alter'd my Note;   . . . 144 New Song      39
ALTERATION
   A sudden Alteration feels,   . . . . . . . . . .    93 Bauc & Phil 1   127
   A sudden Alteration feels,   . . . . . . . . . .   113 Bauc & Phil 2    67
ALTERATIONS
   They talk of further Alterations,   . . . . . . .  283 Journal         129
ALTHO'     10                                            OMITTED WORD
ALTHOUGH   17                                            OMITTED WORD
ALTITUDE
   Your Altitude offends the Eyes,   . . . . . . .    414 Censure          11
   "How from his Altitude he stoops,   . . . . . . .  462 Birthday Song    73
ALWAYS   SEE ALLWAYS
   Who always loudest for Religion bawl,   . . . . .    8 Ode to King      83
   Yet wheresoe're you look you'll always find  . . .  18 Ode Athenian     74
   Which they have always ready, general and Cheap;  .  19 Ode Athenian    122
   But always with a stronger relish of the Last.   .  22 Ode Athenian    215
   Because he's always in my Chamber,. . . . . . . .   72 Mrs Harris Pet   51
   . . .and I always take his Part;   . . . . . . .    72 Mrs Harris Pet   51
   How I always pretended to be for the Tories:   . . 143 New Song         22
   Was like keeping her Monument always in sight.   . 144 New Song         38
   Is backwards and forwards always the same;   . . . 148 Windsor Proph    22
   And keep close to Thee always that Name,   . . . . 148 Windsor Proph    23
   Of Love shall always speak and write;   . . . . .  150 Corinna          10
   "Always together, tete a tete;   . . . . . . . .   202 Horace 2, 6      86
   Yet always wishing to retreat;   . . . . . . . .   202 Horace 2, 6     107
   Always together by the Ears;   . . . . . . . . .   216 To Mr. Delany    52
   ('Tis always done, Romances tell us,   . . . . .   223 Prog of Love     47
   This wicked Rogue Waters, who always is sinning,   238 Excellent Song   26
   We, humble strollers, always on the wing.   . . .  308 Billet Players   14
   To whom our country has been always dear,   . . .  309 Billet Players   45
   Because like a Watch it always cries Click:   . .  351 Wood Insect      21
   While he went always drunk to Bed.   . . . . . .   352 Wood Ironmongr    8
   Which made my Grand-Dame always stuff-her-Ears,  . 367 Answer Delaney   39
   Whose Conscience always was her care,   . . . . .  375 Apology Lady C    2
   'Tis come to what I always thought;   . . . . . .  409 Dial Rich Marb   29
   Before, I always found the wind   . . . . . . .    420 Holyhead         21
   Mean time the whig is always winner   . . . . . .  421 Ireld            11
   Have always been Apollo's friends;   . . . . . .   432 Answer Paulus    12
   I own his conscience always free,   . . . . . . .  434 Answer Paulus    55
   By clients always overwitted.   . . . . . . . .    434 Answer Paulus    60
   Always for saving their own bacon:   . . . . . .   434 Answer Paulus    65
   And Malice always judging worst;   . . . . . . .   448 Modern Lady     129
   "I always lose when you look on.   . . . . . . .   452 Modern Lady     245
   And lightning always in his Eyes:   . . . . . . .  461 Birthday Song    42
   A hanger on has always been,   . . . . . . . .     468 Birthday Song   253
   By Fate are always link'd together.   . . . . . .  501 Doctor Delaney   36
   Who in his Titles always lyes?   . . . . . . . .   505 Doctor Delaney  162
   Their Tales wou'd always justly suit   . . . . .   512 Answer Fable      3
   Against the Court is always blabbing,   . . . . .  514 Answer Fable     69
   Who thinks the Nation always err'd,   . . . . . .  514 Answer Fable     73
   Have Peter Waters always in your Mind;   . . . .   534 To Mr. Gay      101
   To see him always foremost stand,   . . . . . . .  546 Life of Swift    33
   "You know, I always fear'd the worst,   . . . . .  557 Death of Swift  129
   "Were always of the midling Kind:   . . . . . . .  570 Death of Swift  436
   Your Fancy then had always dwelt   . . . . . . .   591 Strephon Chloe  245
   Nine Muses always waiting round him,   . . . . .   598 Problem Solved   25
   His Conscience always was so nice,   . . . . . .   604 Beasts Confess   83
```

ALWAYS (CONTINUED)	PAGE	TITLE	LINE
By want of Skill, he always lost:	607	Beasts Confess	190
If I always seem too dull t'ye;	630	Epistle Lady	19
Give him always of the Prime,	633	Epistle Lady	127
(For my Friends have always thought	637	Epistle Lady	231
You rarely bite, are always bit:	651	On Poetry	330
Or they must always be at Odds.	695	Cadenus Vaness	263
She railly'd well, he always knew,	707	Cadenus Vaness	660
And swear it does not always follow,	741	Stel B-day 22	21
Have always been confin'd to Youth;	757	Stel B-day '24	16
For Nature, always in the Right,	757	Stel B-day '24	43
But always take a special care	762	Bec's B-Day	41
Could always bear to Strive with Man?	799	Traulus 1	96
His Spirit always strives with Slaves.	799	Traulus 1	100
Always various, always wrong:	800	Traulus 2	18
Always various, always wrong:	800	Traulus 2	18
Always firm in his Vocation,	836	Legion Club	171
The Captain, I'm sure, will always come here;	868	Grand Question	32
And, Madam, I always believ'd you so stout,	869	Grand Question	55
"But at Cuffs I was always the Cock of the School;	873	Grand Question	164
But, always carefull of the main,	878	Robbin & Harry	7
And, if he always be so thrifty,	878	Robbin & Harry	15
Always conquer'd, never yielding.	906	Daphne	8
Always peevisher and sillier:	906	Daphne	18
From a face that always smiles:	907	Daphne	22
Always to advise her wrong;	907	Daphne	36
Yet, though I always have my Will,	918	Riddle 4	19
I'm always by my Betters led;	918	Riddle 4	39
Yet, they always hope, our Favour.	934	Riddle 22	D 8
In all Things false, yet always true,	935	Riddle 23	D 5
Set it always in Motion.	939	Riddle Answer	14
You always are making a God of your Spouse,	947	Mrs. Houghton	1
I know the gander always goes	983	Sher, A Goose	19
And Saunders the Man says, you are always jesting and mocking,	986	Mary to Sher	27
AM 61		OMITTED WORD	
AMAIN			
He gave it me, and ever since I find I thrive amain.	342	Upon His Grace	30
AMALTHEA'S			
Come out with Amalthea's Horn.	464	Birthday Song	126
AMARANTHINE			
Drest up with Amaranthine Flow'rs.	590	Strephon Chloe	202
A Sprig of Amaranthine Flow'rs,	691	Cadenus Vaness	155
AMAZ'D			
Amaz'd Thy Action at the Boyne we see!	12	Ode to William	D 33
Sham'd and amaz'd, beholds the chatt'ring throng,	50	To Congreve	223
The good old Couple was amaz'd,	112	Bauc & Phil 2	35
Amaz'd to see Her look so Prim,	116	Bauc & Phil 2	147
They stand amaz'd, and think me grown	202	Horace 2, 6	103
Jove stood amaz'd, but looking round,	346	Prometheus	47
Amaz'd, confus'd, its Fate unknown,	579	Day Judgement	7
Cadenus was amaz'd to find	704	Cadenus Vaness	562
Her Hearers are amaz'd from whence	726	To Stella	79
The Servants amaz'd, are scarce ever able,	871	Grand Question	135
AMAZEMENT			
This put me the Fryar into an Amazement,	77	Lady B- B-	12
For, Baucis with Amazement found	92	Bauc & Phil 1	75
AMAZING			
When with amazing Joy she hears,	17	Ode Athenian	51
Led with amazing Art along	386	Manly Virtue	85
AMBASSADOR			
Revile His great ambassador,	38	Ode Sancroft	131
AMBIENT			
"Must in the Ambient Hedge be seen;	476	Epist on Epist	54
AMBITION			
And which our wild ambition foolishly compares	38	Ode Sancroft	126
Some whom ambition drives, seek Heaven's high Son	39	Ode Sancroft	166
Shews in the front the ambition of my wit;	44	To Congreve	36
From him let proud Ambition know,	386	Manly Virtue	99
To Your Ambition put an End.	478	Epist on Epist	114
Self-love, Ambition, Envy, Pride,	555	Death of Swift	41
But, since just Heav'n the Dukes ambition mocks	678	Dean and Duke	5
Ambition, Avarice, and Lust,	725	To Stella	45
AMBITION'S			
How endless are Ambition's Aims!	905	Death Daphne	90
AMBITIOUS			
Ambitious of a Regent's Heart	66	Problem	35
Suspend a while your vain ambitious Hopes,	162	Toland's Invit	5
Remov'd from all th' ambitious Scene,	199	Horace 2, 6	D
Carthy ambitious to retrieve his name,	671	Epig Carthy 24	D 1
But, stop ambitious Muse, in time;	896	Panegyr Dean	319
AMBITIOUSLY			
Some more ambitiously upwards fly,	32	Ode to Temple	173
AMBLE			
Or, with her Go-Cart amble Side by Side.	531	To Mr. Gay	12
AMBLING			
or Ambling or Sweet Canterbury,	957	Cantata	
AMBROSIA			
Exhal'd Ambrosia from within:	586	Strephon Chloe	88
AMBUSCADE			
Shall keep my Host in Ambuscade;	884	Rev Market-Hill	52

```
                                                            PAGE    TITLE          LINE
AMENDS
    Shall for my follies make amends:    . . . . . . .       755 Stella '23         36
    And, when this is over, we'll make him amends,  . . . .  817 Yahoo's           61
    You seem to praise to make amends,  . . . . . . . .     1003 Dan J's Reply      20
AMIDST
    My Lord, on Fire amidst the Dames,   . . . . . . . .      66 Problem           39
    They went by chance, amidst their Talk,   . . . . .      116 Bauc & Phil 2    153
    See Philip's Son amidst his Persian Guard;   . . . .     275 Epilogue          24
    Amidst a croud of hungry Bards cries out,   . . . . .    671 Epig Carthy 24  D  3
AMISS
    No wonder, then, we talk amiss  . . . . . . . .           35 Ode Sancroft      41
    For, take it kindly, or amiss,  . . . . . . . .          315 To Ford           99
    To shew she did not judge amiss,   . . . . . . .         713 Cadenus Vaness   855
    Why should my Shepherd take amiss  . . . . . . .         924 Riddle 8           9
AMITY
    Uniting all, to shew their Amity,                        811 Bro Protestant     9
AMONG
    Is fix't like Fate among the Stars,   . . . . . . .        6 Ode to King       20
    Among her Elder Sons the whole Estate?   . . . . .       32 Ode to Temple    181
    Among the noblest flow'rs a thousand pois'nous weeds,    37 Ode Sancroft     102
    Among thy stubborn sons there haunts that spirit of Jews, 38 Ode Sancroft     129
    Among proud Doctors and disputing Pharisees:   . . . .   39 Ode Sancroft     169
    In pleasing all that's good among the great,   . . . .   49 To Congreve      180
    To think what cattle she has got among;   . . . . .      50 To Congreve      224
    But still, tho' fixt among the Stars,   . . . . . .       66 Problem           27
    'Tis well.--But since we live among   . . . . . . .       83 Salamander        23
    That Thing, I mean, among the Kale,   . . . . . .        128 Little House      53
    Was lost among Pactolus Sands,   . . . . . . .          157 Fable of Midas    34
    For among good Friends, I love to be plain;   . . . .    168 Peace Dunkirk      7
    At Charing-Cross, among the Rout,   . . . . . . .        172 Horace 1, 7       59
    Among the numbers who employ  . . . . . . . .           176 To Lord Harley     1
    The chief among that glitt'ring crowd,   . . . . .       177 To Lord Harley    39
    Thou'lt tell of Leagues among the Great   . . . . .      181 Horace 2, 1       21
    "To justle here among a Crowd.   . . . . . . .           200 Horace 2, 6       34
    Where Jove a Seat among the Gods will give   . . . .     210 Earl of Oxford    13
    Say, which among the Heav'nly Pow'rs   . . . . .         227 Prog of Beauty    55
    Among his Brethren of the Quill:   . . . . . . .         231 Prog of Poetry    20
    Cryes out a Sage among the Croud,   . . . . . . .        253 Bubble            78
    To bath among the Belles and Beaux.   . . . . . .        294 Prog Marriage    144
    When we perform, look sharp among our crew,   . . . .    307 Billet Players    11
    I hear among Scholars there is a great Doubt   . . . .   334 Serious Poem      25
    Among a Crew of royst'ring Fellows   . . . . . . .       352 Wood Ironmongr     5
    Among the trembling Croud below.   . . . . . .          353 Wood Ironmongr    20
    Because, among all human Race,   . . . . . . .          366 Answer Delaney     7
    No Falshood now among the Great,   . . . . . . .        391 Young's Satire    14
    To sit among that <scoundrel> crew,   . . . . . . .      436 Answer Paulus    132
    No such among  . . . . . . . . . . .                    442 Ballyspellin      65
    That's but a trifle among Friends.   . . . . . . .       461 Birthday Song     28
    And when among Companions privy,   . . . . . . .        513 Answer Fable      37
    Picking Wit among Collegions,   . . . . . . .          523 Betty Grizette     23
    This, among Hibernian Asses,   . . . . . . .           523 Betty Grizette     33
    He pass'd his Hours among his Books;   . . . . .         604 Beasts Confess   105
    Among your femals make inquiryes:   . . . . . . .        619 Scandal Poem 1    73
    Among your Females make Inquiries;   . . . . . . .       625 Scandal Poem 2    71
    But search among the rhiming Race,   . . . . . .         651 On Poetry        327
    How wrong a Taste prevails among us;   . . . . . .       652 On Poetry        351
    Among ye savage Monsters crown'd   . . . . . . .        659 On Poetry      D 410
    Of either Sex, among the Crew,   . . . . . . .          689 Cadenus Vaness   102
    Which keeps the Peace among the Gods,   . . . . .        695 Cadenus Vaness   262
    Among those venerable Sires.   . . . . . . .           702 Cadenus Vaness   501
    Among their Brethren of the Skies,   . . . . . .         725 To Stella         53
    For, none among the upstart Race   . . . . . . .         739 Stel B-day '21    13
    You must have pass'd among the Crowd.   . . . .          742 Stel B-day 22     48
    When, among scholars, can we find   . . . . . .          755 Stella '23        19
    No, not among the Priests and Fryers.   . . . . .        773 Mullinix Tim       7
    And tho' perhaps among the Rout,   . . . . . . .         796 Traulus 1         25
    When you walk among your Books,   . . . . . . .          838 Legion Club      207
    Among his colleagues,   . . . . . . . .                856 Lady's Lament    161
    (Whom he brings in among us   . . . . . . .            856 Lady's Lament    163
    And not among Ladies to give themselves Airs.   . . .    868 Grand Question    38
    What, if among the courtly Tribe,   . . . . . . .        884 Rev Market-Hill   35
    Among our harmless Northern Swains;   . . . . . .        896 Panegyr Dean     300
    Had got Gallants among the Ghosts?   . . . . . .         905 Death Daphne      76
    So Jove pronounc'd among the Gods,   . . . . . .         924 Riddle 7          95
    There shou'd be Quarrels among Kings.   . . . . .        930 Riddle 15      D  20
    Yet among us all no Brother   . . . . . . . .           931 Riddle 18      D   3
    Among the Coals does often rattle.   . . . . . .         942 Probatur Alit      2
    For you can't but have heard of a trick among wizards,  . 976 Dean to Sherid   21
    You live among ill folks in a dunghill,   . . . . . .   1038 Sheridan Cavan    17
AMONGST
    Fall'n by mishap amongst a knot of beaux;   . . . .       50 To Congreve      216
AMORET
    Calls Amoret an arrant Jilt.   . . . . . . . .          450 Modern Lady      173
AMOROUS
    Repeating in his amorous Fits,   . . . . . . .          529 Lady's Dres Rm   117
    The Nymph who wrote this in an Amorous Fit,   . . .      716 Answer Rebus       1
    . . . and the soft soul of amorous Jemmy center.   . . . 1023 Nim-Dan-Dean 2 D 14
AMOUNT
    To what your lawful Perquisites amount.   . . . . .      533 To Mr. Gay        66
    Amount to just Nine thousand Souls.   . . . . . .        649 On Poetry        282
```

31

	PAGE	TITLE	LINE

AMOUNTING
  Amounting hardly to a Crown a Tribe;   . . . . . .   806 Judas   4
AMOUNTS
  Exact to what his Age amounts, ...   291 Prog Marriage   46
  The Diff'rence but amounts to this, ...   315 To Ford   100
AMOURS
  Could never prosper in amours.   . . . .   176 To Lord Harley   8
AMPHIBIOUS
  Th' amphibious Tyrant, with his rav'nous Band,   . .   793 St. Pat's Well   63
  Traulus of amphibious Breed, ...   799 Traulus 2   1
AMPLE
  Conceal'd behind that ample Screen, ...   354 Simile Silver   23
AMPLY
  Whom Fate has amply bless'd at home?   . . . . . .   272 Apollo's Edict   D   63
  How amply then does Pow'r provide   . . . .   493 Panegyr Swift   15
  Counts all his Labours amply paid, ...   729 Stella, Poems   37
AMUSE
  The mimick Animal amuse;   . . . .   885 Rev Market-Hill   77
AMUSEMENT
  A poor amusement for my scorn and hate;   . . . . .   53 Temple Ill   84
AN   305   OMITTED WORD
AN'ALL
  The Twist, the Squeeze, the Rump, the Fidge an'all,   .   783 Tim and Fables   17
AN'T
  For that, he said, (an't please your Excellencies). . .   73 Mrs Harris Pet   69
ANALOGY
  Some Wits have wondred what Analogy   . . . . . .   98 Elegy Patrige   19
ANARCHY
  Worse than the Anarchy at Sea, ...   824 Printer Newgat   3
ANCESTOR
  For their Ancestor trod Mortar;   . . . .   837 Legion Club   178
ANCESTORS
  Such as our Ancestors did use, ...   114 Bauc & Phil 2   103
  Tho' down from Ancestors Divine   . . . .   134 Magician's Rod   61
  How much our Ancestors out-sung us;   . . . . . .   652 On Poetry   352
ANCHOR
  At length, his Anchor fixt, and Canvas furl'd,   . . .   284 Elegy Boat   6
  I see the ship at anchor ride   . . . .   420 Holyhead   8
ANCIENT   SEE ANTIENT
  This made the Ancient Romans to afford   . . . . .   7 Ode to King   27
  We soon shall see them to their ancient Methods fall,   .   19 Ode Athenian   119
  They seem to act an Ancient Tale, ...   239 Run Bankers   19
  "'Tis a fair Trick, by ancient Rules--   . . . . . .   322 First of April   57
  Complain, as many an ancient Bard did, ...   652 On Poetry   349
  Degenerate from their ancient Brood, ...   652 On Poetry   365
  The witty Ancient enrobe, ...   670 Epig Carthy 21   D   2
  The Genius's of ancient Days!   . . . .   708 Cadenus Vaness   689
  Labours of many an ancient Sage, ...   922 Riddle 7   41
AND   4424   OMITTED WORD
ANDREW'S
  of St Andrew's the Green, and St George's the Blue   .   389 Order of Bath   2
ANEW   SEE A-NEW
  My Wounds Bleed all anew: . . . .   1005 Sheridan's Sub   31
  She mended at first, but now she's anew sick.   . . . .   1029 Dr. Helsham   6
ANGEL   SEE ARCH-ANGEL
  And, lo! where a Destroying Angel stands, ...   7 Ode to King   48
  The Angel (doubtless) kept th' Eternal Gate,   . . .   8 Ode to King   65
  Some angel say, what were the nation's crimes, ...   42 Ode Sancroft   245
  Howe'er it was civil in Angel or Elf, ...   77 Lady B- B-   19
  "An Angel sent by Heav'n's Command, ...   485 Libel on D- D-   166
  Resembling you as Angel Gods.   . . . .   499 Panegyr Swift   182
  Hangs a new Angel two doors from us   . . . . . .   734 Stel B-day '20   10
  I am bright as an Angel, and light as a Feather,   . .   928 Riddle 13   D   3
ANGEL-INN
  The Angel-Inn to ev'ry Friend: . . . .   734 Stel B-day '20   6
  To quit the true old Angel-Inn.   . . . .   734 Stel B-day '20   14
ANGEL'S
  An Angel's Face, a little crack't;   . . . .   734 Stel B-day '20   16
  In such a Form an Angel's Mind   . . . .   735 Stel B-day '20   20
ANGELS
  Whilst Angels tune the Voice, and God inspires the   17 Ode Athenian   56
    Tongue.
  Ah, Britain, land of angels! which of all thy sins,   . .   37 Ode Sancroft   92
  And They in Men and Angels Sight   . . . .   241 Run Bankers   62
  Are Angels, just as <Kings> are Gods.   . . . . . .   486 Libel on D- D-   198
  The Angels of your awful Nods, ...   499 Panegyr Swift   181
  How Angels look at thirty six)   . . . .   735 Stel B-day '20   18
ANGER
  Rather put on thy anger and thy spight, ...   37 Ode Sancroft   86
  (Free from our tyrant-passions, anger, scorn, or fear)   .   38 Ode Sancroft   116
  Work out, as Anger does in Vermin?   . . . .   66 Problem   16
  Not by Anger, but a Sneer: . . . .   637 Epistle Lady   228
  And, full of Anger, Shame, and Grief, ...   713 Cadenus Vaness   846
  And Anger sparkling in your Eyes, ...   731 Stella, Poems   114
  Makes Wit inflame, or Anger burn;   . . . .   731 Stella, Poems   118
  Or if these Lines your Anger fire, ...   732 Stella, Poems   141
  I had some Anger in my Wit.   . . . .   747 Stel Distress   68
  Sent in my Anger from the Land of Huns;   . . . . .   792 St. Pat's Well   60
  But if, still obdurate, your anger remains, ...   819 Archbi Cashel   11
  I will shew no anger needless.   . . . .   908 Daphne   60
  Almighty Anger to disarm?   . . . .   949 Epigr Fasting   4

	PAGE	TITLE	LINE

ANGER   (CONTINUED)
Hum--excellent good--your anger was stirr'd: . . . .   976 Dean to Sherid   7
Because my Master one Day in anger call'd you Goose.   .   985 Mary to Sher   12
ANGLE
"In either Angle shady Bowers: . . . .   476 Epist on Epist   52
ANGLESEY
When I saw you to-day, as I went with Lord Anglesey.   978 Dean to Tho: S   1
. . .with that great peer the Lord Anglesey.   . . . .   1022 Nim-Dan-Dean 2   D 6
ANGRY
'Tis all the angry slighted Muse can do   . . . . . .   38 Ode Sancroft   108
Check in thy satire, angry muse, ...   42 Ode Sancroft   259
Lord, said I, don't be angry,. . .   . .   72 Mrs Harris Pet   59
But the Cobler was angry, and swore he had rather   .   287 Bank Down   26
To pacify this angry Deity;   . . . .   353 Wood Ironmongr   22
Avoid the Rocks on Britain's angry Shore: . . . .   772 Horace 1, 14   62
Dear Tim, no more such angry Speeches, ...   783 Tim and Fables   35
ANGUISH
Or shew the Anguish, Toil, and Pain, ...   583 Young Nymph   69
She, with soft speech, my anguish chears, ...   754 Stella '23   13
ANIMAL
Provides each Animal it's Foe: . . . .   504 Doctor Delaney   128
How was the fearful Animal distress't!   . . . . . .   538 Mr. Pulteney   31
The mimick Animal amuse;   . . . .   885 Rev Market-Hill   77
ANIMALS
Near better animals, her father's sheep;   . . . . .   50 To Congreve   222
As Animals of largest Size   . . . .   81 Vanbrug House   81
As Animals of largest Size   . . . .   109 V's House   123
Were Animals of human kind, ...   658 On Poetry   D 410
ANIMATES
So Honour animates the Whole, ...   724 To Stella   13
ANIMATING
For when the animating Mind is fled, ...   25 Ode Athenian   288
<ANN>
When <Ann> for Heav'n resigns Her Throne.   . . . .   180 Horace 2, 1   12
ANN'ALL
The Muse her ann'all Tribute pays, ...   739 Stel B-day '21   2
ANNA'S
If Anna's happy Reign you praise, ...   271 Apollo's Edict   D 44
ANNALS
The Annals of a Female Day.   . . . .   445 Modern Lady   35
ANNE
To praise Queen Anne, nay more, defend her, ...   550 Life of Swift   186
True, Lady Anne no Danger fears, ...   885 Rev Market-Hill   57
By Lady Anne of Market-Hill.   . . . .   888 Panegyr Dean   36
ANNEXT
To pay the Penalty annext.   . . . .   501 Doctor Delaney   40
ANNO
That Semel'n anno ridet Apollo.   . . . .   741 Stel B-day 22   22
ANNOY'D
But with the odious smell and sight annoy'd, ...   50 To Congreve   225
ANNUAL
Was just one annual Hundred Pound.   . . . . . .   642 On Poetry   54
The Court with annual Birth-day Strains;   . . . . .   650 On Poetry   306
'Twere grafting on an annual Stock   . . . . . .   729 Stella, Poems   65
Resolv'd my annual Verse to pay   . . . .   740 Stel B-day 22   1
Your Annual Bard had rather chose   . . . . . .   756 Stel B-day '24   5
ANOINT
With Aconite anoint his Chops: . . . .   904 Death Daphne   42
ANOINTED
Must own it made by God's Anointed.   . . . . . .   821 Dr. Rundle   56
ANOINTS
With Spittle while she spins, anoints, ...   227 Prog of Beauty   42
ANON
. . .the Chaplain will be here anon.   . . . . . .   72 Mrs Harris Pet   49
And ever and anon with frightful Din   . . . . . .   139 City Shower   45
Anon in Beggar's Rags appear;   . . . .   935 Riddle 23   D 21
ANOTHER   47   OMITTED WORD
ANOTHER'S   1   OMITTED WORD
ANOTHERS   1   OMITTED WORD
ANOTHR   1   OMITTED WORD
ANSWER
I laugh at the grave Answer they will make, ...   19 Ode Athenian   121
So well You answer all Phaenomenaes there;   . . . .   22 Ode Athenian   202
Speak, for I wait thy answer, and expect   . . . .   53 Temple Ill   73
Pray take your Answer and be gone.   . . . . . .   91 Bauc & Phil 1   32
I answer; the Tories were in my good Graces, ...   144 New Song   23
Pretend to answer one Syl--lable, ...   183 Horace 2, 1   85
Unless i'th' Answer, of his Grace, ...   373 Letter D. S-y   59
Nor can it answer in the Event.   . . . .   478 Epist on Epist   104
"I answer, they may thank themselves;   . . . . .   548 Life of Swift   116
And Servants answer; Worse and Worse)   . . . . .   557 Death of Swift   124
Answer all domestick Ends, ...   633 Epistle Lady   101
I submit; and answer thus.   . . . .   636 Epistle Lady   188
To Bishop-Haters answer thus   . . . .   658 On Poetry   D 190
Then pray'd an Answer and sat down.   . . . . . .   687 Cadenus Vaness   20
He could not answer to his Fame   . . . .   702 Cadenus Vaness   494
But he must answer for her Faults.   . . . . . .   705 Cadenus Vaness   603
Will answer for the whole Arrear.   . . . . . .   740 Stel B-day '21   20
Return'd this Answer to a Tittle.   . . . . . .   742 Stel B-day 22   36
Herald lend the Muse an answer;   . . . .   800 Traulus 2   27
That he would answer both for Church and State;   . . .   825 Noisy Tom   2

	PAGE	TITLE	LINE
ANSWER (CONTINUED)			
How many to answer? One, two, three, four.	967	Letter Sherid	10
Three days for Answer I have waited,	1002	Reply by Dean	1
To read your Answer, and prepare Reply to't.	1003	Dan J's Reply	3
Must I make myself hoarse with demanding an Answer?	1019	To Sheridan	4
To answer your style without circumlocution.	1027	Sheri Circles	24
ANSWER'D			
He answer'd, that a Dog of late	298	Horrid Plot	3
These, she answer'd, are but Shadows,	833	Legion Club	100
ANSWERD			
'Twas answerd, she would not be seen.	290	Prog Marriage	8
ANSWERS			
Impatient of all Answers, straight became	22	Ode Athenian	191
His Answers were exceeding pretty	300	Horrid Plot	53
She answers in her usual Style,	447	Modern Lady	94
And I find it answers right:	634	Epistle Lady	145
Long Bills, and Answers, stuff'd with Lies,	690	Cadenus Vaness	121
Cadenus answers every End,	709	Cadenus Vaness	704
It answers Faith in Things divine.	723	To Stella	10
Her Ladyship answers, I'm just coming down;	873	Grand Question	181
Answers in decisive way,	906	Daphne	13
ANTAEUS			
Antaeus could by Magick Charms	257	Bubble	181
But we like Antaeus and Hercules fight,	968	Letter Sherid	29
ANTHONY			
And Anthony shall Court her in Ratteen.	275	Epilogue	20
ANTI-CHAMBER			
Now at the Anti-Chamber thrusting	788	Dick's Variety	33
ANTIC			
Like antic shapes in dreams, from waking eyes:	54	Temple Ill	100
Crouded round with antic Shapes;	832	Legion Club	88
ANTICK			
"Or shape the Yews to Antick Figure.	476	Epist on Epist	58
ANTIENT			
As antient nature's modern masters dream;	45	To Congreve	72
By antient Right are Builders too.	81	Vanbrug House	68
The Rubbish of an antient Pile.	81	Vanbrug House	84
In antient Time, as Story tells	90	Bauc & Phil 1	1
And mindfull of it's antient State,	93	Bauc & Phil 1	109
The Rubbish of an Antient Pile.	109	V's House	126
In antient Times, as Story tells,	111	Bauc & Phil 2	1
Which still their antient Nature keep;	114	Bauc & Phil 2	105
Atlas we read in antient Song	160	Atlas	1
For, if those antient Tales be true,	177	To Lord Harley	25
Sleep, or peruse some antient Book;	202	Horace 2, 6	110
The Founder of thy antient Race.	323	Pethox	4
But antient Philosophers wisely Remark,	334	Serious Poem	7
This Chain, as Antient Poets hold,	345	Prometheus	35
For this we know, all antient Sages	391	Young's Satire	23
With antient Mirmont at her Side.	410	Dial Rich Marb	64
In antient Times the Wise were able,	512	Answer Fable	1
"His Principles, of antient date,	549	Life of Swift	146
His antient Pipe in Sable dy'd,	594	Cassinus Peter	23
Go read in antient books enroll'd	619	Scandal Poem 1	51
Go read in antient Books enroll'd,	625	Scandal Poem 2	47
As what those antient Poets sing;	687	Cadenus Vaness	28
She nam'd the antient Heroes round,	697	Cadenus Vaness	350
Well may they boast that antient Blood, which runs	791	St. Pat's Well	17
As antient Judas by Transgression fell,	806	Judas	17
From antient Canons would not vary,	821	Dr. Rundle	39
By Chronicle of antient Date,	848	Old Thorn	2
The Ruin of her antient Seat;	849	Old Thorn	38
Would soon restore our antient Reign.	887	Panegyr Dean	10
I sigh to think of antient Days.	894	Panegyr Dean	226
ANTIENTLY			
Now hear an old Tale. There antiently stood	334	Serious Poem	17
ANTIQUATED			
Nor practise such an antiquated cheat;	44	To Congreve	18
"I keep no antiquated Stuff;	563	Death of Swift	267
ANTIQUE			
With antique Reliques of the Dead,	27	Ode to Temple	22
A Bed-sted in the antique mode	94	Bauc & Phil 1	147
A Bedstead of the Antique Mode,	114	Bauc & Phil 2	101
<ANTWERP>			
In <Antwerp> keep a frugal House,	183	Horace 2, 1	88
ANXIOUS			
Whose anxious Natives, Night and Day,	388	Manly Virtue	137
Or, ponder long with anxious Thought,	892	Panegyr Dean	161
ANY			
And straight deny you to be Men, or any thing at all;	19	Ode Athenian	120
Say Muse, for thou, if any, know'st	36	Ode Sancroft	43
So you know, what could I say to her any more,	71	Mrs Harris Pet	46
As any of the Caesars are.	100	Elegy Patrige	72
Thro' any Ears but of an Ass.	158	Fable of Midas	66
For any Pretenders	186	Scriblerus 4	D 2
By any Trick, or any Fault;	199	Horace 2, 6	D
By any Trick, or any Fault;	199	Horace 2, 6	D
Who I, for your Sake, have us'd better than any;	263	Apollo	26
The World in any Chain but Gold;	346	Prometheus	50
Glad to compound at any Rate;	378	Apology Lady C	94
For he'll be poor as any King:	409	Dial Rich Marb	40

```
ANY               (CONTINUED)                        PAGE   TITLE              LINE
   O yes! If any Man can find        . . . . . . . .   417  Woman's Mind         57
   At any rate,                      . . . . . . . .   441  Ballyspellin         50
   He waded without any shame,       . . . . . . . .   456  Dean Smedley         23
   (Says he) tho' swell'd like any porpus. . . . . .   456  Dean Smedley         32
   Who struts like any King already. . . . . . . . .   466  Birthday Song       188
   With so much beauty, shew me any maid . . . . . .   466  Birthday Song       189
   E'er enter any Mortal's Noddle.   . . . . . . . .   496  Panegyr Swift       105
   Looking big as any Gyants,        . . . . . . . .   573  Helter Skelter        3
   Drest like any Lady May'ress;     . . . . . . . .   630  Epistle Lady         36
   Never know I any Good in 'um,     . . . . . . . .   632  Epistle Lady         83
   Or any Brother-God in Heav'n:     . . . . . . . .   695  Cadenus Vaness      261
   To any speech but Tyger's barking. . . . . . . . .  762  Bec's B-Day          44
   Or hardy Scot, or any Land but this; . . . . . . .  793  St. Pat's Well       80
   Dare any of the mitred Host,      . . . . . . . .   820  Dr. Rundle            5
   And, in his house, if any body come, . . . . . . .  878  Robbin & Harry       23
   Come, will you have any;          . . . . . . . .   951  Apples                5
   Has this any likeness to good Madam Sheridan?       955  Portrait Life        10
   I despise any poet that truckled to Dan.  . . . .   976  Dean to Sherid       34
   For Spight I ne'er had any.       . . . . . . . .  1005  Sheridan's Sub       19
   If I write any more, it will make my poor Muse sick.  1030 Dr. Sheridan        1
APACE
   Her Petticoat transform'd apace,  . . . . . . . .   116  Bauc & Phil 2       141
   The Golden Spoils flew off apace, . . . . . . . .   158  Fable of Midas       75
   Poor Gentleman, he droops apace,  . . . . . . . .   556  Death of Swift       81
APART
   But Raillery, for once, apart,    . . . . . . . .    87  Hist V's House       43
   Cadenus, common Forms apart,      . . . . . . . .   703  Cadenus Vaness      540
   But Jest apart, restore, you Capon ye, . . . . . .  1033 Ans to Crown          7
APE
   As we say, Monsieur, to an Ape    . . . . . . . .    83  Salamander            5
   To ape the Thunder of the Skies;  . . . . . . . .   352  Wood Ironmongr       10
   The Daw a Thief, the Ape a Drole, . . . . . . . .   512  Answer Fable          7
   My Landlord was ready his <Deanship> to Ape  . . .  517  Lean Hang Rape       29
   The Mimick Ape began his Chatter, . . . . . . . .   602  Beasts Confess       47
   Teaching others how to ape ye;    . . . . . . . .   631  Epistle Lady         53
   A Dog, a Parrot, or an Ape,       . . . . . . . .   687  Cadenus Vaness       39
   She did her best to ape Woodpark. She strove in vain to   747  Stel Distress   48
      ape
   She did her best to ape Woodpark. She strove in vain to   747  Stel Distress   48
      ape
   She strove in vain to ape Wood-Park.  . . . . . .   751  Stel Wood-Park       64
APEING
   In apeing Lines from Cooper's Hill;  . . . . . . .  271  Apollo's Edict   D   47
APES
   Which worship'd cats, and sacrific'd to apes;  . .   46  To Congreve         106
APING
   The Children all our motions Aping.  . . . . . . .  780  Mullinix Tim        242
APOLLO
   This made him to Apollo pray      . . . . . . . .    81  Vanbrug House        69
   Soon knew Apollo by his looks,    . . . . . . . .   120  Apollo Outwit        15
   Apollo thought it vain to stay,   . . . . . . . .   121  Apollo Outwit        42
   Then full of Rage Apollo Spoke,   . . . . . . . .   121  Apollo Outwit        49
   Apollo play'd the Midwife's Part, . . . . . . . .   149  Corinna               2
   Now who but Delany can write like Apollo? . . . .   265  Apollo               88
   Apollo laugh'd till he was sick,  . . . . . . . .   321  First of April       15
   Since I'm Apollo stil'd by you,   . . . . . . . .   373  Letter D. S-y        51
   Your conqu'rer is become Apollo:  . . . . . . . .   462  Birthday Song        58
   That he's Apollo, is as plain, as . . . . . . . .   462  Birthday Song        59
   Then make this new Apollo sit     . . . . . . . .   462  Birthday Song        71
   You place the Muses and Apollo;   . . . . . . . .   477  Epist on Epist       80
   Fresh from the Tripod of Apollo,  . . . . . . . .   485  Libel on D- D-      181
   As from the tripod of Apollo      . . . . . . . .   490  Dialogue             47
   Where's now this Fav'rite of Apollo? . . . . . . .  562  Death of Swift      249
   Conducted by their Squire, Apollo:  . . . . . . .   585  Strephon Chloe       54
   Apollo, God of Light and Wit,     . . . . . . . .   597  Problem Solved        1
   In short; Apollo had no Beard.    . . . . . . . .   598  Problem Solved       32
   And, when Apollo struts on Pindus, . . . . . . . .  620  Scandal Poem 1      107
   Apollo stirs not out of dore      . . . . . . . .   621  Scandal Poem 1      121
   And when Apollo struts on Pindus, . . . . . . . .   626  Scandal Poem 2      105
   Apollo stirs not out of Door,     . . . . . . . .   627  Scandal Poem 2      115
   Bright Apollo lend thy Choir.     . . . . . . . .   661  Love Song            16
   That Semel'n anno ridet Apollo.   . . . . . . . .   741  Stel B-day 22        22
   Apollo having thought a little,   . . . . . . . .   742  Stel B-day 22        35
   Since it flies from Apollo.       . . . . . . . .   939  Riddle Answerd       24
APOLLO'S
   And drop his laurel at Apollo's feet.  . . . . . .   49  To Congreve         186
   Tho' the Thought be Apollo's, 'tis finely express'd;  266  Apollo             91
   Have always been Apollo's friends;  . . . . . . .   432  Answer Paulus        12
   Apollo's patron of the laws;  . . . . . . . . . .   433  Answer Paulus        22
   You'd know him by Apollo's Prints . . . . . . . .   462  Birthday Song        62
   You'd know him by Apollo's Cuts.  . . . . . . . .   462  Birthday Song        64
   You'd swear it is Apollo's Son;   . . . . . . . .   692  Cadenus Vaness      193
   I waited at Apollo's Shrine;      . . . . . . . .   741  Stel B-day 22        14
APOSTLE
   O! had I been Apostle to the Swiss,  . . . . . . .  793  St. Pat's Well       79
APOSTLES
   In a Dozen Apostles but one prov'd a Traytor!  . .  804  Irish Bishops        30
APOTHECARY'S
   He shuns Apothecary's Shops;  . . . . . . . . . .   605  Beasts Confess      133
```

35

	PAGE	TITLE	LINE
APPARITION			
He's with you like an Apparition.	398	Earl of P-b-w	30
APPEAL			
Th' appeal of dullness in the last resort:	53	Temple Ill	88
Then I'll appeal to each By-stander,	85	Salamander	69
"To morrow my Appeal comes on,	200	Horace 2, 6	51
To prove it I appeal to fact;	434	Answer Paulus	68
Till Prudence taught him to appeal	481	Libel on D- D-	43
. . .I appeal to your Friend Mr. Conna.	1014	Swift to Sheri	10
APPEALING			
Appealing to the Nation's Taste,	483	Libel on D- D-	83
APPEAR			
Or from thy private peaceful orb appear;	39	Ode Sancroft	155
What mortal change does in thy face appear,	52	Temple Ill	31
Late I beheld on every face appear;	52	Temple Ill	40
See Muse, what havock in these looks appear	55	Temple Ill	125
Why sure you won't appear in Town,	175	Horace 1, 7	123
Appear with slender Wands at Court:	189	Faggot	18
At Windsor <Swift> no sooner can appear,	194	Author Himself	33
But when He saw his Friend appear	220	A Quiet Life	5
If Celia should appear too soon	226	Prog of Beauty	11
I'll make it appear that they're all stol'n Ware:	265	Apollo	64
But if these Topicks should appear	311	To Ford	13
The greatest Lord, when you appear,	325	Pethox	43
Our Silver will appear again.	354	Simile Silver	32
What Dowdys they appear before her!	465	Birthday Song	158
To see some radiant Nymph appear	591	Strephon Chloe	227
Which I chose to make appear,	637	Epistle Lady	227
Wou'd seldom at the Park appear,	696	Cadenus Vaness	312
Where Pleasures mix'd with Pains appear,	711	Cadenus Vaness	776
When Goddesses appear below.	711	Cadenus Vaness	789
Come and appear, and save their Bail.	713	Cadenus Vaness	841
The Muse will at your Call appear,	743	Stel B-day 22	79
When first in publick we appear,	780	Mullinix Tim	229
Why in this Brown dost thou appear?	786	Clad in Brown	2
Could he but make his Gift appear	821	Dr. Rundle	51
But should a lordly Pike appear,	824	Printer Newgat	8
Where'er you appear:	855	Lady's Lament	118
How proud are we when you appear!	889	Panegyr Dean	82
In various Forms appear agen	924	Riddle 7	93
Anon in Beggar's Rags appear;	935	Riddle 23	D 21
Without it a Lady should never appear.	941	Letter	42
Dear Tom, this verse, which however the beginning may appear,. . .	1022	Nim-Dan-Dean 2	D 1
'Twill appear, to your cost, you are fairly trepann'd,	1027	Sheri Circles	15
APPEAR'D			
Or has he like some fearful Star appear'd?	10	Ode to King	130
Appear'd, above the Universal Main,	16	Ode Athenian	6
When to poetic view the Muse appear'd.	51	Temple Ill	16
No Meteor, no Eclipse appear'd!	98	Elegy Patrige	9
Gold ready Coin'd appear'd, instead	156	Fable of Midas	17
That the letters appear'd revers'd on the Pane,	264	Apollo	49
When it heard of a Bank appear'd to his Debtors,	288	Bank Down	42
Appear'd like one continu'd Spec'es,	344	Prometheus	8
And first a dirty Smock appear'd,	526	Lady's Dres Rm	11
Flew off, nor evermore appear'd.	590	Strephon Chloe	196
Forgiveness begg'd, that he appear'd	603	Beasts Confess	61
The Cause appear'd of so much Weight,	688	Cadenus Vaness	75
But since the Case appear'd so nice,	689	Cadenus Vaness	91
When Drapier's-hill appear'd in rhyme.	899	Dean's Reasons	10
APPEARANCE			
At the divine appearance of the Muse,	53	Temple Ill	76
No Heir, upon his first Appearance,	598	Problem Solved	11
APPEARANCES			
Of Solving all Appearances they please,	19	Ode Athenian	118
To solve appearances of sight	35	Ode Sancroft	28
But, all Appearances are strong.	414	Censure	16
Appearances were all so strong,	707	Cadenus Vaness	642
I own, Appearances are bad;	796	Traulus 1	21
APPEARING			
Appearing, show'd the Ruddy Morns Approach.	124	Descriptn Morn	2
And still appearing in Contrast.	529	Lady's Dres Rm	128
APPEARS			
Philosophy's exalted head appears;	16	Ode Athenian	15
Lo, it appears!	30	Ode to Temple	112
And holy Sancroft's motion quite irregular appears,	37	Ode Sancroft	81
Tho' fring'd with ev'ning gold the cloud appears so gay,	41	Ode Sancroft	217
Besides, it plainly now appears,	158	Fable of Midas	61
Her artificiall Face appears	226	Prog of Beauty	6
When e'er the bloody Bond appears,	240	Run Bankers	48
Where if the Dean by chance appears	294	Prog Marriage	139
Behold his funeral appears,	296	Satiric Elegy	17
When Pow'r in all its Pomp appears,	340	Arch-Bish Dub	13
. . . 'tis he that first appears,	341	Upon His Grace	3
And thus William Wood to my Fancy appears	350	Wood Insect	7
But no Contrivance yet appears,	367	Answer Delaney	53
For by old Proverbs it appears,	408	Dial Rich Marb	7
And, then their Tenderness appears,	556	Death of Swift	105
"Had he been rul'd, for ought appears,	559	Death of Swift	173
Yet beware of her Arts, for it plainly appears,	580	Psyche	13
So beautiful a Nymph appears	584	Strephon Chloe	3

APPEARS	(CONTINUED)	PAGE	TITLE	LINE
Such wicked insolence appears	. . . .	622	Scandal Poem 1	167
Cadenus now no more appears	. . . .	703	Cadenus Vaness	528
Appears a Hero to our Eyes;		710	Cadenus Vaness	733
She wonders where the Charm appears	. . . . . .	725	To Stella	69
Appears from Michaelmas to May;		759	Receipt Youth	4
Till he appears upon the Stage.	. . . .	776	Mullinix Tim	108
In your indignation what mercy appears,	. . . . . .	818	Epigr Kite	1
At Market Hill, as well appears	. . . . . .	848	Old Thorn	1
The Captain at Dinner appears in his Glory;		871	Grand Question	130
In you such Dignity appears;		888	Panegyr Dean	49
But, that which wonderful appears,	. . . .	915	Riddle 1	17
When all the sad Reverse appears!	. . . . . .	921	Riddle 7	10
Tho' so much of Heav'n appears in my Make,	. . . .	929	Riddle 13	D 7
Wasted he appears, and pale,	. . . . . .	936	Riddle 24	D 21
A school-boy knows this, for it plainly appears	. . . .	976	Dean to Sherid	19
APPENAGE				
That, Wealth should be the Appenage of Wit,	. . .	532	To Mr. Gay	26
APPETITE				
Will soon your Appetite repair.	. . . .	759	Receipt Youth	28
APPETITES				
For, as their Appetites to quench,	. . . . . .	480	Libel on D- D-	21
APPLAUD				
Repining, to applaud his Choice.	. . . .	387	Manly Virtue	134
APPLAUSE				
Then spoke with Censure, or Applause,	. . . . . .	697	Cadenus Vaness	352
Hath met with returns of all sorts but applause;	. . .	815	Yahoo's	17
And gapes for applause?	. . . .	857	Lady's Lament	180
APPLES				
Mingling with Apples in the Throng,	. . . . . .	811	Bro Protestant	12
See, Brother, how we Apples swim.	. . . . . .	811	Bro Protestant	14
Plumbs, Apples and Pears,	. . . .	951	Apples	2
APPLICATION				
Come to use, and Application:	. . . .	636	Epistle Lady	186
APPLIES				
Where every Fool his Mouth applies,	. . . . . .	158	Fable of Midas	63
And then to each applies a Plaister.	. . . . . .	582	Young Nymph	32
APPLY				
France do's in vain her feeble Arts apply	. . . .	13	Ode to William	D 41
And let my friend apply it as he please:	. . . . . .	49	To Congreve	204
Pliny shall prove, and we'll apply,	. . . . . .	83	Salamander	27
Again apply that <Swift> would be their Friend.	. . .	196	Author Himself	70
To me the good Fellows apply for Relief,	. . . . .	263	Apollo	9
Discreetly to apply this Fable.	. . . .	346	Prometheus	58
(To thee I apply great Smedley's Successor)	. . .	518	Dean Hang Rape	44
Advice in vain you would apply--	. . . . . .	595	Cassinus Peter	71
Apply the Tale, and you shall find	. . . . . .	603	Beasts Confess	73
Then, apply Alecto's Whip,	. . . .	635	Epistle Lady	179
You must apply to Mrs. Brent.	. . . .	742	Stel B-day 22	50
APPLY'D				
Apply'd at Bottom stops it's Course;	. . . . .	93	Bauc & Phil 1	102
Apply'd at Bottom, stops its Course,	. . . . .	113	Bauc & Phil 2	62
While He his utmost Strength apply'd,	. . . . .	158	Fable of Midas	73
This Tale may be apply'd in few Words	. . . . .	189	Faggot	15
"But, Pallas, you've apply'd too late,	. . . . .	304	Storm	37
Great, Good and Just was once apply'd	. . . . .	339	Arch-Bish Dub	1
Apply'd to Wood's adult'rate Copper;	. . . . .	353	Wood Ironmongr	32
Apply'd to Jove with fervent Prayer;	. . . . .	383	Manly Virtue	3
If well apply'd, can hardly miss:	. . . . .	463	Birthday Song	84
Must be apply'd directly wrong:	. . .	464	Birthday Song	118
Yet bears a Moral when apply'd to you	. . . . .	538	Mr. Pulteney	16
Apply'd to <George> exactly true is:	. . . . .	657	On Poetry	478
Or be so artfully apply'd,	. . . . .	709	Cadenus Vaness	728
I wish they had been well apply'd.	. . . . .	779	Mullinix Tim	210
And so apply'd to diff'rent Use.	. . . . . .	929	Riddle 15	D 12
APPLYD				
Nor are these Rules applyd to Her:	. . . . . .	733	Verses Vanessa	18
APPLYING				
Applying what we first Invent:	. . . .	215	To Mr. Delany	18
APPOINT				
Why then appoint him Son of Jove,	. . . . .	460	Birthday Song	15
APPOINTED				
Appointed sov'reign Judge to sit	. . . . .	655	On Poetry	427
APPOINTING				
Or, where appointing Lovers rove,	. . . . . .	894	Panegyr Dean	245
APPOLLO				
That I'm Befriended by Appollo,	. . . . . .	371	Letter D. S-y	10
APPREHEND				
She need no Rivals apprehend.	. . . . . .	702	Cadenus Vaness	507
APPROACH				
The Fair approach the speaking Part,	. . . . .	66	Problem	41
Before he durst the Nymph approach.	. . . . .	119	Apollo Outwit	8
Appearing, show'd the Ruddy Morns Approach.	. .	124	Descriptn Morn	2
Beck'ning the Doctor to approach.	. . . . .	172	Horace 1, 7	62
Nor let the Beaux approach too near.	. . . . .	228	Prog of Beauty	68
Nor to the Shore approach too nigh,	. . . . .	257	Bubble	174
The Learned met with free Approach,	. . . . .	701	Cadenus Vaness	458
He dare not venture to approach;	. . . . .	824	Printer Newgat	12
Let purse-proud C--n next approach,	. . . . .	951	Upstart	D 23
APPROACH'D				
When Death approach'd, to stand between:	. . . . .	561	Death of Swift	222

	PAGE	TITLE	LINE
APPROACHES			
"Winning my Way by slow Approaches, ...	380	Apology Lady C	151
APPROACHING			
Approaching joy at strife with parting woe.	51	Temple Ill	22
To help at my approaching End, ...	204	In Sickness	20
Approaching near the Town, he hears	338	Wood's Brass	5
The Ass approaching next, confess'd, ...	602	Beasts Confess	21
Nor think on our approaching Ills, ...	763	Stel B-day '26	5
This poor Isle's approaching Ruin?	862	To Janus	14
Approaching, finds it hard to part	922	Riddle 7	35
APPROBATION			
In Approbation of thy Tongue, ...	183	Horace 2, 1	81
By Dint of his sole Approbation.	475	Epist on Epist	20
To bespeak some Approbation, ...	833	Legion Club	111
APPROV'D			
Should be approv'd in After-times, ...	728	Stella, Poems	6
APPROVE			
You shall be coupled as you best approve, ...	165	Toland's Invit	31
Approve thy Schemes, thy Wit admire, ...	182	Horace 2, 1	62
The Council sit; approve the Doctor's Skill; . . .	534	To Mr. Gay	79
He now cou'd praise, esteem, approve, ...	703	Cadenus Vaness	546
APPROVES			
Approves his Foresight to the rest:	557	Death of Swift	128
As he approves, as he dislikes, ...	708	Cadenus Vaness	682
APRIL			
But we by gentle April showers	621	Scandal Poem 1	147
APRIL-FOOLS			
"The God has made us April-Fools.	322	First of April	58
APRON			
And Joe my Apron full of Bricks.	128	Little House	64
APT			
And honest Harry is too apt to stink.	166	Toland's Invit	38
Is apt to disoblige his Friends.	605	Beasts Confess	144
Her Scholar is not apt to learn;	712	Cadenus Vaness	809
Both are apt to be unruly, ...	835	Legion Club	155
We Sinners are too apt to slight.	942	Probatur Alit	20
APTLY			
Most aptly this Device explain:	393	Modern Poets	6
AQUILINE			
And Dan shall be with us with Nose aquiline	1018	Swift Ans Sher	27
AR'T			
And just began to cry;--What ar't!	112	Bauc & Phil 2	38
ARARAT			
On the high Top of peaceful Ararat;	16	Ode Athenian	26
ARBITERS			
Arbiters of Loss and Gain, ...	934	Riddle 22	D 2
ARBITRARY			
By arbitrary pow'r convey her	761	Bec's B-Day	23
ARBOR			
To his arbor for shelter, ...	857	Lady's Lament	192
ARBOUR			
Then Built, then took up with your Arbour, . . .	477	Epist on Epist	69
ARBUTHNOT			
No doubt, will prove a good Arbuthnot:	314	To Ford	76
Arbuthnot is no more my Friend, ...	555	Death of Swift	55
ARBUTHNOT'S			
Remov'd from kind Arbuthnot's Aid, ...	204	In Sickness	9
ARBUTHNOTT			
A Week; and Arbuthnott a Day, ...	561	Death of Swift	208
ARCADIANS			
Yet, kind Arcadians, on my Urn	595	Cassinus Peter	73
Mild Arcadians, ever blooming, ...	660	Love Song	5
ARCANA			
Some strange Arcana to unfold, ...	180	Horace 2, 1	2
ARCH			
Shrewd Fellows, and arch Wags, a Tribe	216	To Mr. Delany	53
You, o'er the high Triumphal Arch	326	Pethox	93
The wond'rous Arch behind you fell, ...	326	Pethox	95
Drives rattling o'er a brazen Arch:	353	Wood Ironmongr	18
You sprung an Arch, which in a Scurvy	477	Epist on Epist	71
ARCH-ANGEL			
Translated to arch-angel there.	42	Ode Sancroft	239
<ARCH-BISHOP>			
Why truly 'tis Satan, <Arch-bishop> of Hell: . . .	803	Irish Bishops	4
ARCH-PRELATE			
Chief of the mitred saints, and from arch-prelate here, .	42	Ode Sancroft	238
ARCHDEACON			
To Visits of Archdeacon Wall.	745	Stel Distress	20
To visits of <Archdeacon> <Wall>	750	Stel Wood-Park	40
ARCHER			
But grant her a Sieve, I can say something archer, . .	972	S-'s Ans Sh-d	9
ARCHES			
Thro' all the Rooms, and Courts, and Arches; . . .	377	Apology Lady C	62
To pluck her Brows in Arches round, ...	527	Lady's Dres Rm	56
ARCHIBALD			
Sir Archibald that val'rous Knight, ...	848	Old Thorn	9
(Sir Archibald whose fav'rite Name	848	Old Thorn	13
ARCHITECT			
To be his Architect at Blenheim.	87	Hist V's House	42
And make my Muse the Architect;	107	V's House	45
By the prudent Architect	829	Legion Club	5

ARCHITECTURE   PAGE   TITLE   LINE

		PAGE	TITLE	LINE
ARCHITECTURE				
Is hugely turnd to Architecture,	. . . .	86	Hist V's House	8
ARCHY				
A Spade let prudent Archy hold,	. . . .	743	Stel B-day 22	57
ARCHY'S				
Ten thousand Archy's arm'd with Spades		743	Stel B-day 22	73
ARDELIA				
But Wise Ardelia knew his Tricks.		120	Apollo Outwit	20
Were fair Ardelia not my Aunt,	. . . .	123	Empty'ng Town	19
ARDELIA'S				
To wait at Bright Ardelia's Side.	. . . . . .	120	Apollo Outwit	40
But Pallas owns Ardelia's Power,	. . . . . .	121	Apollo Outwit	47
ARDELIAH'S				
The Flashes of Ardeliah's Eyes.	. . . .	119	Apollo Outwit	12
ARDUOUS				
The Task is Arduous, Patrons find,	. . . . . .	475	Epist on Epist	21
ARE 446			OMITTED WORD	
ARETINE				
But were you as wicked as lewd Aretine	. . . . . .	1017	Swift Ans Sher	18
ARGO'S				
For thee they Argo's Hulk will Tax,	. . . . . .	100	Elegy Patrige	77
ARGU'D				
Thus argu'd my Lady, but argu'd in vain;	. . . . .	868	Grand Question	39
Thus argu'd my Lady, but argu'd in vain;	. . . . .	868	Grand Question	39
ARGUE				
They argue no corrupted Mind	. . . . . .	553	Death of Swift	3
Nor argue on the weaker Side;	. . . . . .	644	On Poetry	128
As Atheists argue, to entice,	. . . .	764	Stel B-day '26	21
When you furious argue wrong,	. . . .	908	Daphne	63
Must argue with calmness, or else will come short on't.		976	Dean to Sherid	12
Is this, that you argue like fools in a circle.	. . .	1026	Sheri Circles	4
ARGUMENT				
Or a weak argument by force maintain'd?	. . . . . .	34	Ode Sancroft	12
One Argument she summ'd up all in,	. . . . . .	224	Prog of Love	67
A weighty Argument indeed;	. . . .	298	Horrid Plot	13
And then your old Argument still will return:	. . . .	336	Serious Poem	63
ARGUMENT'S				
Your Argument's weak, and so you will find,	. . . .	947	Mrs. Houghton	5
ARGUMENTS				
Strong Arguments to keep You here,	. . . . . .	311	To Ford	14
You see, my Arguments are Strong;	. . . . . .	315	To Ford	109
Her Arguments directly tend	. . . . . .	417	Woman's Mind	51
His arguments convinc't the rest.	. . . . . .	423	Ireld	64
May serve, as arguments ad hominem.	. . . . . .	433	Answer Paulus	48
Brought weighty Arguments to prove	. . . . .	708	Cadenus Vaness	676
But tho' her Arguments were strong,	. . . . . .	710	Cadenus Vaness	746
While all is Calm, his Arguments prevail,	. . . . .	770	Horace 1, 14	27
Thick her arguments she lays on,	. . . .	906	Daphne	11
ARGUS				
And must be sung, like Argus, into ease	. . . . . .	8	Ode to King	76
ARIADNE				
Then Ariadne kindly Lends	. . . .	100	Elegy Patrige	79
ARIES				
He at fit Periods walks through Aries,	. . . . . .	98	Elegy Patrige	15
ARISE				
To see the Seeds of Vice arise,	. . . .	485	Libel on D- D-	176
ARISES				
"This mischief arises from witty Dean Swift."	. . .	843	Ay and No	6
ARISTOPHANES				
As Aristophanes declares;	. . . .	620	Scandal Poem 1	82
As Aristophanes declares:	. . . .	626	Scandal Poem 2	80
But as to Comic Aristophanes,	. . . .	988	Letter Dr Sh-n	5
ARISTOTLE'S				
Learn Aristotle's Rules by Rote,	. . . .	648	On Poetry	247
ARK				
With her World's fruitful System in her sacred Ark,	.	16	Ode Athenian	13
As never came from Noah's Ark:	. . . .	514	Answer Fable	54
ARM				
Your Arm has now Your Rightful Title show'd;	. . .	12	Ode to William D	29
An Arm on which all Europe's Hopes depend,	. . . .	12	Ode to William D	30
About each Arm a Pudding-sleeve;	. . . .	115	Bauc & Phil 2	120
His Hat for Show, beneath his Arm.	. . . .	410	Dial Rich Marb	66
Then from his Arm hoarse thunder rolls	. . . . .	461	Birthday Song	39
For thunder still his arm supplyes,	. . . .	461	Birthday Song	41
Two Rows of Teeth arm each devouring Jaw;	. . . .	532	To Mr. Gay	35
Her valiant Arm should force us back,	. . . . . .	885	Rev Market-Hill	60
ARM-PITS				
Beneath the Arm-pits well besmear'd.	. . . . . .	526	Lady's Dres Rm	12
Her Arm-pits would not stain her Gown:	. . . . . .	584	Strephon Chloe	22
ARM'D				
With Squibs and Crackers arm'd, to throw	. . . . .	353	Wood Ironmongr	19
Jove, arm'd with Terrors, burst the Skies,	. . . . .	578	Day Judgement	5
Arm'd in adamantine Chains,	. . . .	661	Love Song	18
Both Sexes, arm'd with Guilt and Spite,	. . . . .	700	Cadenus Vaness	438
Ten thousand Archy's arm'd with Spades	. . . . .	743	Stel B-day 22	73
ARMA				
Of Arma Virumque	. . . .	186	Scriblerus 4 D	5
ARMAGH				
Quoth Hugh of Armagh, "The mob is grown bold."	. . .	843	Ay and No	3
"But if I say the word--take care of Armagh!"	. . .	843	Ay and No	18

```
                                                          PAGE   TITLE              LINE
ARMED
    Conceal a fatal armed Force;        . . . . . . . .   209 Fable Bitches          44
ARMIS
    Is come up, vi & armis, to break the <Queen's> Peace.  .  142 New Song            4
    Then and there, Vi & Armis, with a certain Utensil,   .   264 Apollo             33
ARMOUR
    Through all thy Land, in Armour, Fur and Lawn.     . .   792 St. Pat's Well       56
    From gold brocade and shining armour, . . . . . . .   879 Robbin & Harry         41
ARMS
    How fond we are to court Her to our Arms!    . . . . .    23 Ode Athenian         232
    Or by Atchievments, Arms, Device      . . . . . . .    80 Vanbrug House          65
    Or by Atchievment, Arms, Device,      . . . . . . .   107 V's House              39
    By Law of Arms became your Prey,      . . . . . . .   154 Widow and Cat    D 34
    Into the Arms of Death would run,     . . . . . . .   243 Horace 4, 9            22
    Alcides held him in his Arms,         . . . . . . .   257 Bubble                183
    Your Arms, tho' both your Eyes were lost,    . . . . .   367 Answer Delaney       47
    His arms upon the booby's shoulders   . . . . . .   421 Ireld                  22
    These Titles and Arms                 . . . . . . .   424 Carterets Arms          7
    Dick Sigh'd for his Doll and his mournfull Arms       430 Dicky Dolly            7
        Cross'd,
    Hath mention'd arms on this side Sweden;     . . . . .   462 Birthday Song        52
    And paint a Coward fierce in arms.    . . . . . . .   464 Birthday Song         122
    To Arms by Thirst of Honour led,      . . . . . . .   500 Doctor Delaney          2
    "And gave them Arms to ward the Blow. . . . . . . .   569 Death of Swift         410
    And with rebellious Arms pretend      . . . . . . .   653 On Poetry             381
    Since Woolston gave us Arms to rout him.     . . . . .   657 On Poetry            494
    So bloom'd the Goddess in a Mortal's Arms.   . . . . .   669 Epig Carthy 13   D  2
    But never gave me equal Arms:         . . . . . . .   706 Cadenus Vaness         621
    Have dropt their Arms, and seiz'd the Plunder.    . .   775 Mullinix Tim          48
    Combin'd in Arms, they had their Foes defy'd,    . . .   793 St. Pat's Well       81
    All in Arms prepare to back us:       . . . . . . .   838 Legion Club           212
    My arms, like two props,              . . . . . . .   852 Lady's Lament          27
    Call forth our Cottagers to Arms;     . . . . . . .   884 Kev Market-Hill        44
ARMY'S
    "The Army's the only good School in the Nation;    . .   872 Grand Question       162
ARMYS
    Makes mighty Armys turn their Arses.  . . . . . .   461 Birthday Song           30
AROSE
    A Cloud arose and stopt the Light,    . . . . . . .   253 Bubble                 75
    And ev'ry Belle that since arose      . . . . . . .   311 To Ford                21
    The World from justling Seeds arose,  . . . . . . .   324 Pethox                 28
    When Questions on the Fact arose,     . . . . . . .   688 Cadenus Vaness         70
    When first this grand Debate arose    . . . . . . .   690 Cadenus Vaness        130
AROUND
    When strait she sees the Countrey all around,    . . .    17 Ode Athenian         38
    An unknown Musick all around,         . . . . . . .    17 Ode Athenian         52
    Thro' the Zodiack around, it shall quickly be spread, .   265 Apollo             69
    Orphans around his Bed the Lawyer sees,      . . . . .   364 On Dreams            23
    His Influence is diffus'd around;     . . . . . . .   385 Manly Virtue           38
    Let both around my Tomb be plac'd,    . . . . . . .   611 By Dr. Swift            5
    With Colonies might stock around      . . . . . . .   903 Death Daphne           17
    Sloth, Dirt, and Theft around her wait.      . . . . .  1035 To Quilca           12
ARRAH
    Arrah! who was him reading? 'twas a jauntleman in ruffles,   840 Ballad      D  6
ARRANT
    Calls Amoret an arrant Jilt.          . . . . . . .   450 Modern Lady           173
ARRAY'D
    Array'd in Lace, Brocades and Tissues.       . . . . .   525 Lady's Dres Rm        4
    Yet when we see thee thus array'd,    . . . . . . .   787 Clad in Brown          25
ARREAR
    Will answer for the whole Arrear.     . . . . . . .   740 Stel B-day '21        20
ARREARS
    And Parvisol discounts Arrears,       . . . . . . .   174 Horace 1, 7           111
ARRIAN
    An Arrian to usurp the Name!          . . . . . . .   819 Dr. Rundle              2
ARRIANS
    By coupling Orthodox with Arrians?    . . . . . . .   820 Dr. Rundle              8
ARRIV'D
    Of some Express arriv'd at Court;     . . . . . . .   202 Horace 2, 6            90
    Last Night arriv'd Clem and his Wife. . . . . . . .   283 Journal               118
    'Till <Hort> arriv'd ne'er kept a Wench;     . . . . .   303 Storm               18
    This Day arriv'd without his Train,   . . . . . . .   398 Earl of P-b-w          11
    Jason arriv'd two thousand Years before.     . . . . .   790 St. Pat's Well        8
    At Hamilton's Bawn, and the Troop is arriv'd. . . . .   869 Grand Question       68
ARRIVE
    "Behold the fatal Day arrive!         . . . . . . .   558 Death of Swift        147
ARRIVES
    Which still the sooner it arrives,    . . . . . . .    24 Ode Athenian          279
    He soon arrives at Harley's Gate;     . . . . . . .   174 Horace 1, 7           110
    When the True Wood arrives, as he soon will no doubt, .   336 Serious Poem        75
    Whoe'er arrives at Pow'r supreme,     . . . . . . .   592 Strephon Chloe        264
    Too soon arrives the dismal Day,      . . . . . . .   746 Stel Distress          25
    But now arrives the dismal Day:       . . . . . . .   751 Stel Wood-Park         45
ARROWS
    To poison'd Arrows from the Dark,     . . . . . . .   500 Doctor Delaney         28
ARRS
    Your effs and tees, and arrs, and esses?     . . . . .   487 Irish-Club          12
<ARSE>
    Once on a Time, was an <Arse> Gut,    . . . . . . .    66 Problem               23
    Does sympathize with Human <Arse>.    . . . . . . .    66 Problem               28
    Or a Kick on the <Arse>.              . . . . . . .   247 Irish-Feast            88
```

	PAGE	TITLE	LINE
<ARSE> (CONTINUED)			
Of e'ery Rogue that wears an <Arse>	497	Panegyr Swift	121
In every <Arse> you run your Snout, ...	774	Mullinix Tim	25
Tare out the Tale, and wipe your <Arse>	783	Tim and Fables	37
ARSES			
Makes mighty Armys turn their Arses.	461	Birthday Song	30
With their Tilters at their Arses, ...	573	Helter Skelter	6
He pierce the Clouds! he kiss our <arses>)	620	Scandal Poem 1	104
He pierce the Clouds! he kiss our <Arses>.)	626	Scandal Poem 2	102
Wipe our <Arses> with their <Votes>.	831	Legion Club	62
ART			
Of Nature and of Art, of deep Philosophy and Love, .	17	Ode Athenian	55
To be an Art as vain, as Bottling up of Wind:) . . .	21	Ode Athenian	185
And Poetry has lost the art to praise. . . .	38	Ode Sancroft	111
Say, whence it comes that thou art grown of late . . .	53	Temple Ill	83
Fools common-place thou art, their weak ensconcing fort,	53	Temple Ill	87
Now Poets find this Art is lost, ...	79	Vanbrug House	13
If this Rule holds in ev'ry Art, ...	87	Hist V's House	44
The Art of battring Walls, than building, ...	88	Hist V's House	46
Lost by Disuse the Art to roast	93	Bauc & Phil 1	126
Shews how the Art of Cobling bears	99	Elegy Patrige	39
Thus Patrige still shines in each Art, ...	100	Elegy Patrige	69
Turns to an Awl by Heav'nly Art;	100	Elegy Patrige	82
Now Poets feel this Art is lost:	106	V's House	14
Great Jove, he cry'd, the Art restore	107	V's House	43
Thou'rt well contriv'd, tho' thou art small;	109	V's House	116
Thy Mother burnt, art Born again;	109	V's House	120
Lost, by Disuse, the Art to Roast, ...	113	Bauc & Phil 2	66
To Cheat the God in his own Art.	120	Apollo Outwit	28
Deceitful Nymph I see thy Art, ...	121	Apollo Outwit	50
To be by Art prevented.	122	Empty'ng Town	4
And he endow'd her with his Art.	149	Corinna	4
Had lost his Art, and kept his Ears.	157	Fable of Midas	40
Renown'd for Skill in Faustus Art, ...	182	Horace 2, 1	50
Who knows his Art but not his Trade;	204	In Sickness	10
To you, by Art and Nature taught	215	To Mr. Delany	3
Unhelpt by Practice, Books, or Art.	215	To Mr. Delany	22
But, Art no longer can prevayl	228	Prog of Beauty	77
But Gadbury in Art profound	228	Prog of Beauty	93
We'll make a small one here by Art:	313	To Ford	58
And Secrecy, the Art of Courts.	325	Pethox	64
The Mixture thus by Chymick Art, ...	344	Prometheus	5
The busy Head with mimick Art runs o'er	363	On Dreams	9
Science and Art you say at stand are, ...	372	Letter D. S-y	41
Beauty that needs no Aid of Art, ...	379	Apology Lady C	115
Here, soon for every Art renown'd, ...	385	Manly Virtue	37
Led with amazing Art along	386	Manly Virtue	85
And where with Art to place a Patch.	416	Woman's Mind	32
Not for his boasted healing art;	432	Answer Paulus	17
Unskill'd in all the Terms of Art?	451	Modern Lady	221
"Thy Thanks and Verse, devoid of Art:	476	Epist on Epist	34
Shall be, when thou art left unsung;	494	Panegyr Swift	46
Laid out with no less Art than Pains, ...	494	Panegyr Swift	56
Is this the Art, good Doctor, say, ...	497	Panegyr Swift	142
'Tis said, the Gods try'd all their Art, ...	501	Doctor Delaney	31
Which tho' with Art you salt and beat, ...	528	Lady's Dres Rm	100
Thou art not half so nimble as a Hare:	539	Mr. Pulteney	40
Stuck on with Art on either Side, ...	581	Young Nymph	14
And when she once has got the Art, ...	588	Strephon Chloe	129
He scorns to make his Art a Trade;	605	Beasts Confess	135
Before you learn the Terms of Art:	647	On Poetry	240
Of Jobbers in the Poets Art, ...	650	On Poetry	312
Nature must give Way to Art.	660	Love Song	4
Well: but a Duke thou art; so pleasd the King . . .	678	Dean and Duke	15
Yet, hang me, but for all her Art; . . .	679	From Catullus	3
That Cupid now has lost his Art, ...	687	Cadenus Vaness	7
And shew'd but little of their Art;	692	Cadenus Vaness	173
Thro' Nature, and thro' Art she rang'd, ...	698	Cadenus Vaness	354
To scorn the Art of Female Tears.	705	Cadenus Vaness	597
And oft' the Dancing-Master's Art	710	Cadenus Vaness	740
For Stella never learn'd the Art, ...	725	To Stella	71
While Gracefulness its Art conceals, ...	726	To Stella	83
Nymph, would you learn the onely Art	732	Verses Vanessa	1
'Tis all her Thought and Art, ...	733	Verses Vanessa	24
Could Art or Time or Nature bribe	736	Stel B-day '20	52
To teach her ears the Art of list'ning, ...	762	Bec's B-Day	54
Unhappy Ship, thou art return'd in Vain:	770	Horace 1, 14	9
So thou art grown the Detestation	775	Mullinix Tim	55
This Graver understood his Art.	783	Tim and Fables	20
Thou now one Heap of Foulness art, ...	787	Clad in Brown	13
And yet they have learnt the chief Art of a Sov'reign,	805	Irish Bishops	47
Bless us, Morgan! Art thou there Man?	837	Legion Club	189
Bless mine Eyes! Art thou the Chairman?	837	Legion Club	190
Thou I hear, a pleasant Rogue art;	839	Legion Club	220
Nor, can he judge with all his Art	889	Panegyr Dean	91
Hard is the Toil, nor small the Art, ...	892	Panegyr Dean	181
The Grandeur or the Art of Building.	893	Panegyr Dean	200
Instructors ev'ry Art instill.	918	Riddle 4	12
If thou a real Being art;	919	Riddle 5	32
A new and wond'rous Art I show	920	Riddle 6	9
And still, the more I show my Art, ...	920	Riddle 6	17

ART   (CONTINUED)   PAGE   TITLE   LINE
    And so am I whilst thou art here;   . . . .   932 Riddle 19   D 14
    Now you write from your cellar,--I find out your art,   . 979 Dean to Tho: S   19
    And art thou forc'd to yield, ill-fated Poetaster?   .   1002 Reply by Dean   3
    So in the Kindred Painter's Art,   1021 Nim-Dan-Dean 1 D 35
    To encroach on his art by writing of bombas'; . . . .   1027 Sheri Circles   22
ARTFUL
    With artful Sigh and feigned Groan, ...   208 Fable Bitches   14
ARTFULLY
    Who artfully will pare and prune   . . . .   469 Birthday Song   277
    Or be so artfully apply'd, ...   709 Cadenus Vaness   728
    Stuck artfully a Parchment Case.   . . . .   904 Death Daphne   36
ARTHUR
    "Nor thou, Lord Arthur, shalt escape: . . . . . .   850 Old Thorn   65
    Sir Arthur begins, ...   851 Lady's Lament   6
    To 'scape them, Sir Arthur   . . . .   854 Lady's Lament   83
    Sir Arthur the Malster! how fine it will sound? . .   868 Grand Question   45
    Of this, to be sure, Sir Arthur has Warning, . . .   869 Grand Question   69
    Noble Captain, your Servant--Sir Arthur your Slave; .   869 Grand Question   72
    You must be obey'd--your Servant, Sir Arthur;   . . .   869 Grand Question   80
    No, Madam; 'tis only Sir Arthur a humming.   . . . .   871 Grand Question   128
    Sir Arthur too shall have his Will, ...   875 Drapier's Hill   9
    And so I bid Sir <Arthur> write.   . . . .   859 Lady Acheson   4
    Sir <Arthur>, since you set the Pattern, ...   888 Panegyr Dean   57
ARTHUR'S
    (I spare the Thistle for Sir Arthur's sake.)   . .   881 Pastoral Dial   18
    To drink Sir <Arthur's> Health and mine: . . . . .   890 Panegyr Dean   102
ARTICHOKES
    And steal my Artichokes no more;   . . . .   409 Dial Rich Marb   46
ARTICK
    About the grinding artick Pole;   . . . .   362 Grace's Answer   34
ARTICLE
    That ev'ry Article was true;   . . . .   688 Cadenus Vaness   71
    The Burial Article decrease;   . . . .   903 Death Daphne   8
ARTIFICERS
    Inclos'd Artificers to Choke.   . . . .   100 Elegy Patrige   94
ARTIFICES
    Well skill'd in Mid-wife Artifices;   . . . . . .   362 Grace's Answer   27
    But, finding all his Artifices vain;   . . . . . .   538 Mr. Pulteney   19
ARTIFICIAL
    To furnish artificial Ears.   . . . .   367 Answer Delaney   54
    Takes off her artificial Hair: . . . .   581 Young Nymph   10
ARTIFICIALL
    Her artificiall Face appears   . . . .   226 Prog of Beauty   6
    Assumes an artificiall Vigor;   . . . .   290 Prog Marriage   22
ARTILLERY
    Th' Artillery of the skies   . . . .   29 Ode to Temple   83
    In dagger-contests, and th' artillery of words,   . .   35 Ode Sancroft   13
ARTIST
    Whilst an alluding Hymn some Artist sings, ...   162 Toland's Invit   13
    Nor could the nicest Artist Paint, ...   480 Libel on D- D-   19
    In Flatt'ry an Artist, in Fawning a Slave, ...   807 Advice Parson   4
ARTISTS
    So when Cartesian artists try   . . . .   35 Ode Sancroft   27
ARTLESS
    "The Garden stor'd with artless Flowers, ...   476 Epist on Epist   51
    My artless Muse shall sing your Fame.   . . . . . .   887 Panegyr Dean   6
ARTS   SEE COLLEGE-ARTS
    Are Arts peculiar to dissembling France: . . . . .   11 Ode to William D   2
    France do's in vain her feeble Arts apply   . . . .   13 Ode to William D 41
    At once did Practice both these Arts: . . . . .   99 Elegy Patrige   48
    The God of Wit, and Light, and Arts, ...   176 To Lord Harley   9
    Terrestrial nymphs, by formal arts, ...   178 To Lord Harley   53
    The Arts new kindle into Life.   . . . .   385 Manly Virtue   46
    The Arts revive, the Vallies sing, ...   387 Manly Virtue   125
    "Fie, Madam, leave these little Arts.   . . . . .   452 Modern Lady   257
    "What Prodigys in Arts we drain   . . . .   462 Birthday Song   79
    Can half the Peerage by his Arts bewitch;   . . . .   535 To Mr. Gay   103
    Yet beware of her Arts, for it plainly appears, . .   580 Psyche   13
    But how shall I describe her Arts   . . . .   583 Young Nymph   67
    Those Arts by which at first they gain it, ...   592 Strephon Chloe   265
    They ply their former Arts below.   . . . .   647 On Poetry   210
    With pleasing Arts she could reduce   . . . . . .   700 Cadenus Vaness   448
    But, if they can, by all their arts, ...   761 Bec's B-Day   13
    To mend the World by useful Arts.   . . . .   780 Mullinix Tim   246
    Renown'd for Valour, Policy and Arts.   . . . . .   789 St. Pat's Well   6
    Here, from the neighbouring Nursery of Arts,   . . .   793 St. Pat's Well   69
    Be these thy Arts; nor higher Aim   . . . .   897 Panegyr Dean   341
AS
    (As those still do wh' have none at all)   . . . . .   8 Ode to King   84
    As in old Fabulous Hell, ...   9 Ode to King   92
    Her Sister Isles are Conquered too as well as She.   9 Ode to King   100
    Her Sister Isles are Conquered too as well as She.   9 Ode to King   100
    Just as the Sun puts out a Fire;   . . . .   9 Ode to King   114
    As if it meant to touch the Skies;   . . . . . .   10 Ode to King   123
    And end as it began, in Vapour, Stink, and Scum.   .   10 Ode to King   129
    And as a Mortal to his Vile Disease, ...   10 Ode to King   145
    Nor is this all: As glorious is the Care   . . . .   12 Ode to William D 25
    To preserve Conquests, as at first to gain: . . .   12 Ode to William D 26
    To which they look as to some Guardian God   . . .   12 Ode to William D 31
    As when the Deluge first began to fall, ...   16 Ode Athenian   1

AS　　　　　　　　(CONTINUED)　　　　　　　　　　　　PAGE　TITLE　　　　LINE

	PAGE	TITLE	LINE
It be as great as 'tis in Fame, ...	16	Ode Athenian	9
It be as great as 'tis in Fame, ...	16	Ode Athenian	9
And nigh to Heaven as is its Name.	16	Ode Athenian	10
As if the Universal Nile	17	Ode Athenian	42
Long wandring thro the Deep, as we are told . .	17	Ode Athenian	46
And Courts the wanton Echoes as they fly. . . .	17	Ode Athenian	59
Our Wit and Learning, narrow as our Trade; . . .	19	Ode Athenian	96
Who fain would rule the Pulpit, as they do the Stage, .	19	Ode Athenian	104
They're now, just now, as naturally born, . .	20	Ode Athenian	130
As from the Womb of Earth a field of Corn. . . .	20	Ode Athenian	131
But as for poor contented Me, ...	20	Ode Athenian	132
Which is perhaps as hard t' imagine right . . .	21	Ode Athenian	159
As to paint Eccho to the Sight:	21	Ode Athenian	160
To be an Art as vain, as Bottling up of Wind:) .	21	Ode Athenian	185
To be an Art as vain, as Bottling up of Wind:) .	21	Ode Athenian	185
Philosophy, as it before us lyes, ...	22	Ode Athenian	211
Our selves are rais'd as well as she, ...	24	Ode Athenian	264
Our selves are rais'd as well as she, ...	24	Ode Athenian	264
As at the closing an unhappy Scene	24	Ode Athenian	271
As if they all were Spectres too, ...	27	Ode to Temple	41
(As in a Theatre the Ignorant Fry, ...	29	Ode to Temple	94
And tho' as some ('tis said) for their Defence .	30	Ode to Temple	125
Resolv'd to give himself, as well as Country Peace.	30	Ode to Temple	134
Resolv'd to give himself, as well as Country Peace.	30	Ode to Temple	134
As loth to see the hated Court and Town, . . .	31	Ode to Temple	157
And murmurs as she glides away.	31	Ode to Temple	158
Since Heaven will claim its residence as well as birth,	35	Ode Sancroft	19
Since Heaven will claim its residence as well as birth,	35	Ode Sancroft	19
Disjointing shapes as in the fairy-land of dreams, .	35	Ode Sancroft	39
As if 'twould overshade the Royal Rose, ...	37	Ode Sancroft	104
A load as heavy as the Crown, ...	40	Ode Sancroft	188
A load as heavy as the Crown, ...	40	Ode Sancroft	188
Disturb the present Mitre, as that fearful storm of late,	40	Ode Sancroft	192
Swept up whole churches as it list, ...	40	Ode Sancroft	194
To be, as 'twas below, the brightest plant above; . . .	41	Ode Sancroft	229
As well as here below, ...	41	Ode Sancroft	232
As well as here below, ...	41	Ode Sancroft	232
First chid the zeal as unpoetic fire, ...	44	To Congreve	25
As antient nature's modern masters dream; . . .	45	To Congreve	72
A search, no doubt, as curious and as wise	46	To Congreve	93
A search, no doubt, as curious and as wise	46	To Congreve	93
As virtuosoes' in dissecting flies;	46	To Congreve	94
Last just as long as ev'ry cuckow's note: . . .	47	To Congreve	130
Last just as long as ev'ry cuckow's note: . . .	47	To Congreve	130
As a fresh miss, by fancy, face, and gown, ...	48	To Congreve	151
And let my friend apply it as he please:	49	To Congreve	204
Current like copper, and as often paid:	50	To Congreve	220
Faint inspiration sickens as she flies, ...	50	To Congreve	229
Such seem'd her eyes, as when an evening ray . .	51	Temple Ill	17
As when to scare th' ungrateful or the proud . .	52	Temple Ill	23
As parent earth, burst by imprison'd winds, ...	52	Temple Ill	37
As some fair pile, yet spar'd by zeal and rage, ...	52	Temple Ill	47
And shap'd my passion in such words as these.	53	Temple Ill	80
Smooth as that airy nymph so subtly borne . .	54	Temple Ill	117
Salutes the weary trav'ller as he walks;	55	Temple Ill	120
Nature's bare visage furrowed as he mows:	55	Temple Ill	124
As hard, as sensless, and as light:	60	Lady Tablebook	4
As hard, as sensless, and as light:	60	Lady Tablebook	4
As hard, as sensless, and as light:	60	Lady Tablebook	4
Is held as needfull as His Glyster	62	Discovery	12
Is held as needfull as His Glyster	62	Discovery	12
Work out, as Anger does in Vermin?	66	Problem	16
For, as when we a Gun discharge, ...	66	Problem	43
So when I went to put up my Purse, as God would have it,. . .	69	Mrs Harris Pet	8
. . .my Money was as safe as my Maidenhead.	69	Mrs Harris Pet	11
. . .my Money was as safe as my Maidenhead.	69	Mrs Harris Pet	11
. . .as you may very well think, ...	70	Mrs Harris Pet	20
Dame, said I, as loud as I could bawl,.	70	Mrs Harris Pet	26
Dame, said I, as loud as I could bawl,.	70	Mrs Harris Pet	26
Such a thing as this happen'd, just about the time of Goosberries.	71	Mrs Harris Pet	33
Besides, as they say, Service is no Inheritance in these Ages.	71	Mrs Harris Pet	41
. . .as tho' I had call'd her all to naught;	71	Mrs Harris Pet	45
I e'en left her, and came away as wise as I was before.	71	Mrs Harris Pet	47
I e'en left her, and came away as wise as I was before.	71	Mrs Harris Pet	47
So, as the Devil would have it,.	72	Mrs Harris Pet	52
If your Money be gone, as a Learned Divine says, d'ye see,	72	Mrs Harris Pet	56
. . .as who should say, ...	72	Mrs Harris Pet	62
. . .as in Duty bound, shall ever Pray.	73	Mrs Harris Pet	75
Once on a time, as old Stories reherse, ...	76	Lady B- B-	1
As Herald, he can in a Day	80	Vanbrug House	63
Just as the Mountain did the Mouse;	81	Vanbrug House	76
As Animals of largest Size	81	Vanbrug House	81
As Mastive Dogs in Modern Phrase are	82	Salamander	1
As Pies and Daws are often stil'd	82	Salamander	3
As we say, Monsieur, to an Ape	83	Salamander	5
Bestow'd as Hi'roglyphicks fit	83	Salamander	11

AS	(CONTINUED)	PAGE	TITLE	LINE
By Age and Claps grown cold as Snow,		84	Salamander	58
As from the Salamander's Spue;		85	Salamander	66
Five times at least as big as theirs,		87	Hist V's House	24
Five times at least as big as theirs,		87	Hist V's House	24
From such deep Rudiments as these		87	Hist V's House	35
In antient Time, as Story tells		90	Bauc & Phil 1	1
As Authors of the Legend write		90	Bauc & Phil 1	6
It rain'd as hard as it could pour,		90	Bauc & Phil 1	11
It rain'd as hard as it could pour,		90	Bauc & Phil 1	11
But bawl'd as loud as he could roar,		91	Bauc & Phil 1	35
But bawl'd as loud as he could roar,		91	Bauc & Phil 1	35
As if they ne're had drunk a drop.		92	Bauc & Phil 1	78
Such as our Grandfathers did use,		94	Bauc & Phil 1	149
The Cottage with such Feats as these		94	Bauc & Phil 1	153
As threadbare, and as full of Dust.		94	Bauc & Phil 1	170
As threadbare, and as full of Dust.		94	Bauc & Phil 1	170
As if a Man in making Posies		96	On the Union	9
Well, 'tis as Bickerstaff has guest,		98	Elegy Patrige	1
Just as if Patrige were not Dead,		98	Elegy Patrige	12
As if there had been no such Matter.		98	Elegy Patrige	18
As 'tis miscall'd, we know not who 'tis;		98	Elegy Patrige	32
And as the Boding Owl, or rather		99	Elegy Patrige	49
So Learned Patrige could as well		99	Elegy Patrige	53
And in his Fancy fly as far,		99	Elegy Patrige	55
And is Install'd as good a Star,		100	Elegy Patrige	71
As any of the Caesars are.		100	Elegy Patrige	72
Whate'er concerns you full as well,		101	Elegy Patrige	114
As he himself could, when above.		101	Elegy Patrige	116
And should they Build as fast as Write,		106	V's House	19
And should they Build as fast as Write,		106	V's House	19
As Herald, he can in a Day		107	V's House	37
And as a Poet, he has Skill		107	V's House	41
To build by Verse as heretofore,		107	V's House	44
Takes a French Play as lawful Prize,		107	V's House	58
Laughing as if he'd burst his Sides:		108	V's House	70
(As being Bricks at Second Hand,)		108	V's House	77
The Building, as the Poet Writ,		108	V's House	79
So wide as to encompass all.		108	V's House	82
The Plot as yet lay deep, and so		108	V's House	85
Like Bacchus Thou, as Poets feign,		109	V's House	119
As Animals of largest Size		109	V's House	123
In antient Times, as Story tells,		111	Bauc & Phil 2	1
As Authors of the Legend write;		111	Bauc & Phil 2	6
As if they ne'er had toucht a Drop.		112	Bauc & Phil 2	34
Such as our Ancestors did use,		114	Bauc & Phil 2	103
The Cottage by such Feats as these,		114	Bauc & Phil 2	107
As Thread-bare, and as full of Dust.		115	Bauc & Phil 2	124
As Thread-bare, and as full of Dust.		115	Bauc & Phil 2	124
And she admir'd as much at Him.		116	Bauc & Phil 2	148
It feels as if 'twere taking Root.		116	Bauc & Phil 2	162
As having Malice in her Heart,		120	Apollo Outwit	26
Howe'er such Verse as yours, I grant		123	Empty'ng Town	17
But soon as e'er he lay'd it down,		132	Magician's Rod	3
But when he lay'd it down, as quick		132	Magician's Rod	13
As ready was the Wand of Sid		133	Magician's Rod	27
Could scatter Opium full as well,		133	Magician's Rod	41
And drive as many Souls to Hell.		133	Magician's Rod	42
And made a Circle thrice as wide,		134	Magician's Rod	54
Came an Heir-loom, as Homer sings,		134	Magician's Rod	64
As Homer tells us o'er and o'er,		134	Magician's Rod	69
(Those Bully Greeks, who, as the Moderns do,		139	City Shower	49
And bear their Trophies with them as they go:		139	City Shower	54
They, as each Torrent drives, with rapid Force		139	City Shower	57
As t' other Midas did before?		157	Fable of Midas	50
Just as a Porter does his Pack		160	Atlas	4
But, as a Porter overpresst		160	Atlas	5
You shall be coupled as you best approve,		165	Toland's Invit	31
Will drink it now as well as Peers:		169	Peace Dunkirk	24
Will drink it now as well as Peers:		169	Peace Dunkirk	24
A spirit so inform'd as yours		176	To Lord Harley	7
Phoebus was beautiful as you:		177	To Lord Harley	26
From you, as from Latona's son.		177	To Lord Harley	32
(As fools are insolent and vain)		177	To Lord Harley	41
Thus Ca'ndish, as Aurora bright,		179	To Lord Harley	77
Dick, thour't resolv'd, as I am told,		180	Horace 2, 1	
Methinks I hear thee loud, as Trumpet,		182	Horace 2, 1	71
As Bagpipe shrill, or Oyster-Strumpet,		182	Horace 2, 1	72
As thro' the Hall thy Worship paces:		182	Horace 2, 1	76
As that my Muse is yet a Maid,		183	Horace 2, 1	100
But is for State-Affairs as fit,		183	Horace 2, 1	105
As mine for Politicks and Wit.		183	Horace 2, 1	106
So, Clowns on Scholars as on Wizards look,		193	Author Himself	7
Make Room; as if a Duke were passing by.		194	Author Himself	36
As thus, "Vouchsafe, Oh gracious Maker!		199	Horace 2, 6	D
Something in Verse as true as Prose;		199	Horace 2, 6	D
Something in Verse as true as Prose;		199	Horace 2, 6	D
As, "What's a-Clock?" And, "How's the Wind?		201	Horace 2, 6	69
My Lord and me as far as Stains,		201	Horace 2, 6	76
My Lord and me as far as Stains,		201	Horace 2, 6	76
As once a week we travel down		201	Horace 2, 6	77

	PAGE	TITLE		LINE
Faith Sir, you know as much as I.	202	Horace 2, 6		96
Faith Sir, you know as much as I.	202	Horace 2, 6		96
Can act as decently as they.	204	In Sickness		18
Can act as decently as they.	204	In Sickness		18
Since Death pursues the Coward as he flies.	210	Earl of Oxford		2
Just as the Rabble please to smile or frown.	210	Earl of Oxford		10
Which might as well have been in Prose;	215	To Mr. Delany		10
The last, as boundless as the Wind;	215	To Mr. Delany		15
The last, as boundless as the Wind;	215	To Mr. Delany		15
But as a poor pretending Beau	216	To Mr. Delany		41
Nay, Voiture is as like Tom Lee,	217	To Mr. Delany		63
As Rudeness is to Repartee.	217	To Mr. Delany		64
To make her Hair look black as Jet,	226	Prog of Beauty		18
As Other Painters oft adore	227	Prog of Beauty		51
Matter, as wise Logicians say,	228	Prog of Beauty		81
And Form, say I, as well as They,	228	Prog of Beauty		83
And Form, say I, as well as They,	228	Prog of Beauty		83
Yet as she wasts, she grows discreet,	229	Prog of Beauty		101
While all the Parish, as she flies,	230	Prog of Poetry		15
He us'd 'em full as kindly as himself.	234	Elegy on Demar		14
He us'd 'em full as kindly as himself.	234	Elegy on Demar		14
Old as he was, no vulgar known Disease	234	Elegy on Demar		29
But as his Gold he weigh'd, grim Death in spight,	234	Elegy on Demar		31
And as he saw his darling Money fail,	235	Elegy on Demar		33
As when a Conj'rer takes a Lease	240	Run Bankers		45
And as for the Dean,	238	Excellent Song		30
As great as they are,	247	Irish-Feast		79
As great as they are,	247	Irish-Feast		79
As far up as Adam,	247	Irish-Feast		83
As far up as Adam,	247	Irish-Feast		83
Here's ev'ry Piece as big as ten.	251	Bubble		8
Here's ev'ry Piece as big as ten.	251	Bubble		8
You shall observe as you are filling	251	Bubble		11
As Fishes on each other prey	253	Bubble		65
Directors fall as well as they,	253	Bubble		83
Directors fall as well as they,	253	Bubble		83
As Poets fein; but where's the Moral?	254	Bubble		94
But as a Guinnea will not pass	255	Bubble		117
A narrow Sound, though deep as Hell,	256	Bubble		139
For Fools will see as Wise men please.	257	Bubble		168
Run as they drink and drink and run.	257	Bubble		180
And as for their Works, when I please I may read 'em;	263	Apollo		22
And still as he writ, stood smiling and reading;	264	Apollo		40
That her Eyes were as bright as our self at Noon-Day;	264	Apollo		41
That her Eyes were as bright as our self at Noon-Day;	264	Apollo		41
But as for the Poem he writ on your Sash,	265	Apollo		65
To write a few Verses on you as my Friend;	265	Apollo		74
As I rode in my Chariot, a Thought to my Mind;	265	Apollo		76
Tho' she lives 'till she's Grey as a Badger all over.	266	Apollo		108
As Poet and as Patriot too?	270	Apollo's Edict	D	6
As Poet and as Patriot too?	270	Apollo's Edict	D	6
As glorious as Belinda's Hair?	271	Apollo's Edict	D	39
As glorious as Belinda's Hair?	271	Apollo's Edict	D	39
For Weavers now are just as poor as Wits;	276	Epilogue		40
For Weavers now are just as poor as Wits;	276	Epilogue		40
He was as hard, and pond'rous Wood at that:	285	Elegy Boat		20
As they did in old Times, make Money of Leather,	287	Bank Down		27
You raise Desire as well as Pride,	292	Prog Marriage		74
You raise Desire as well as Pride,	292	Prog Marriage		74
The horned Floud, as Poets sing:	293	Prog Marriage		110
Or in the cross-bath seeks as Heir	294	Prog Marriage		137
And, trust me, as the noise grows stronger,	296	Satiric Elegy		7
As by the news-papers we're told	296	Satiric Elegy		10
As Instinct leads them, in a Puddle;	294	Horrid Plot		148
As if he had thrown down a Dish.	299	Horrid Plot		34
Confess't as plain as he could bark;	300	Horrid Plot		55
Confess't as plain as he could bark;	300	Horrid Plot		55
"As well against, as with the Tide,	304	Storm		36
"As well against, as with the Tide,	304	Storm		36
"Or, as Fitzpatrick did before,	305	Storm		63
"If such a Sight as this can please ye,	305	Storm		69
And, as a stroller, act in ev'ry play:	309	Billet Players		48
The next we act shall be as good as this.	309	Billet Players		58
The next we act shall be as good as this.	309	Billet Players		58
Was full as hard to please as You,	313	To Ford		53
Was full as hard to please as You,	313	To Ford		53
But now I act as other Folk,	313	To Ford		55
And, Dawson street will serve as well	313	To Ford		61
To lead you thither, as Pell-mell,	313	To Ford		62
She's Now as handsom ev'ry bit,	313	To Ford		71
As fine as Hampton-court at least.	314	To Ford		90
As fine as Hampton-court at least.	314	To Ford		90
"Who is as good as all the Muses;	321	First of April		8
"Who is as good as all the Muses;	321	First of April		8
"A Wife as good as Heart cou'd wish one,	322	First of April		49
"A Wife as good as Heart cou'd wish one,	322	First of April		49
And, as a Proof, shew num'rous Scars	324	Pethox		13
Or whether, as the Learn'd contend,	324	Pethox		19
Whether, as Epicurus shows	324	Pethox		27
And, as an Instance of thy Pow'r,	325	Pethox		55

	PAGE	TITLE	LINE
AS (CONTINUED)			
And left a Chasm profound as Hell:	326	Pethox	96
A Siege as long as Troy endur'd.	326	Pethox	98
A Siege as long as Troy endur'd.	326	Pethox	98
As Thomas was cudgelld one day by his Wife, ...	327	Epigram 1	1
As Thorns were design'd to be from the Creation. .	334	Serious Poem	30
Just as when we say, the Devil's a Tinker	335	Serious Poem	54
When the True Wood arrives, as he soon will no doubt, .	336	Serious Poem	75
He'll Bellow as loud as the Dee'l in a Drum: . . .	336	Serious Poem	80
He'll Bellow as loud as the Dee'l in a Drum: . . .	336	Serious Poem	80
For fear the First Drop might as well be his Last: .	337	Serious Poem	112
His Firmness to the publick Good, as one that knows it Swore,	341	Upon His Grace	9
. . . and make him live as long	343	Upon His Grace	47
As did Methusalem of old, and so I end my Song. . .	343	Upon His Grace	48
This Chain, as Antient Poets hold, ...	345	Prometheus	35
As round as a Ball, without Head without Tail, . .	350	Wood Insect	5
As round as a Ball, without Head without Tail, . .	350	Wood Insect	5
For, as sure as a Gun they will give up the Ghost .	351	Wood Insect	23
For, as sure as a Gun they will give up the Ghost .	351	Wood Insect	23
Salmoneus, as the Grecian Tale is, ...	352	Wood Ironmongr	1
To make a Clatt'ring as they trod.	352	Wood Ironmongr	12
Which, as he scatter'd, we like Dolts, ...	353	Wood Ironmongr	33
As when of old, some Sorc'ress threw	354	Simile Silver	1
I hope to make you yet as clean, ...	361	Grace's Answer	5
As that same viz. St. <Patrick's> Dean.	361	Grace's Answer	6
As White as Snow, as bright as Day;	362	Grace's Answer	32
As White as Snow, as bright as Day;	362	Grace's Answer	32
As White as Snow, as bright as Day;	362	Grace's Answer	32
As White as Snow, as bright as Day;	362	Grace's Answer	32
As if he was awake, nods o'er his Text:	364	On Dreams	32
Be distant as one Head can bear;	366	Answer Delaney	30
That from each Ear, as he observes, ...	367	Answer Delaney	33
Both Right and Left, as Fellow-sufferers.	367	Answer Delaney	40
Are stronger, and almost as good.	367	Answer Delaney	50
And, as for Hands, there have been those, ...	367	Answer Delaney	51
But as to Ditto 't thro the Town, ...	372	Letter D. S-y	15
My Country's sav'd, as you have shown, ...	372	Letter D. S-y	17
On this, as upon other Isles, ...	372	Letter D. S-y	26
As you Dr. <Smedley> are, being sure	372	Letter D. S-y	33
As well as you, for a Midas:	372	Letter D. S-y	37
As well as you, for a Midas:	372	Letter D. S-y	37
Then as to War's Alarms I pray	372	Letter D. S-y	38
They are as once, and Idem still.	373	Letter D. S-y	50
As when Time serves, you more shall know.	373	Letter D. S-y	78
A Lady, Wise as well Fair, ...	375	Apology Lady C	1
Wou'd have the Text as well as Comment;	375	Apology Lady C	4
Wou'd have the Text as well as Comment;	375	Apology Lady C	4
So grave, as to be unpolite;	375	Apology Lady C	8
Nam'd me as plain as he cou'd speak:	376	Apology Lady C	47
Nam'd me as plain as he cou'd speak:	376	Apology Lady C	47
And much good Sense, as well as Breeding:	377	Apology Lady C	72
And much good Sense, as well as Breeding:	377	Apology Lady C	72
Now pale as Death, then blush'd and bow'd;	377	Apology Lady C	78
"As it was deem'd in former Days	384	Manly Virtue	5
And claim it as a Debt from Fate.	388	Manly Virtue	141
Tho as empty as Younge and as saucy as Sandes . .	389	Order of Bath	10
Tho as empty as Younge and as saucy as Sandes . .	389	Order of Bath	10
Tho as empty as Younge and as saucy as Sandes . .	389	Order of Bath	10
Tho as empty as Younge and as saucy as Sandes . .	389	Order of Bath	10
If this be Truth, as you attest, ...	391	Young's Satire	11
If possible, as good as He.	392	Young's Satire	30
If possible, as good as He.	392	Young's Satire	30
As will retrieve a lost Estate:	392	Young's Satire	44
That creeps as far to reach the Centre;	393	Modern Poets	8
Ye Rhimers, dead as soon as born, ...	394	Grub-Street	3
Ye Rhimers, dead as soon as born, ...	394	Grub-Street	3
His Body active as his Mind, ...	398	Earl of P-b-w	22
As clever Tom Clinch, while the Rabble was bawling,	399	Tom Clinch	1
But, as from the Windows the Ladies he spy'd, . .	399	Tom Clinch	9
And, you can do as much.	401	Window Inns 2	3
But dear as the <Devil>:	402	Window Inns 8	D 2
But, as for the dwellers.	403	Window Inns 9	D 4
Last Friday Night, as Neighbours use, ...	408	Dial Rich Marb	5
Pray God they now may find as true.	408	Dial Rich Marb	22
Was grown as wealthy as a Prince;	409	Dial Rich Marb	38
Was grown as wealthy as a Prince;	409	Dial Rich Marb	38
For he'll be poor as any King;	409	Dial Rich Marb	40
My Ice-house rob as heretofore, ...	409	Dial Rich Marb	45
And serve the Times as others do.	410	Dial Rich Marb	80
Beneath, a Chasm as deep as Hell, ...	413	Desire Possess	43
Beneath, a Chasm as deep as Hell, ...	413	Desire Possess	43
But, as he climb'd to grasp the Crown, ...	413	Desire Possess	47
And, as he now expiring lay, ...	413	Desire Possess	53
She gets a Cold as sure as Death;	417	Woman's Mind	45
She gets a Cold as sure as Death;	417	Woman's Mind	45
To use them as his truest friends	422	Ireld	46
His Ld ship as Wharton	423	Carterets Arms	6
As strong upon your back	428	Beau's Reply	3
As Tisdel smells of a sock:	428	Beau's Reply	4
Are soft and sweet as butter.	429	Beau's Reply	12

AS	(CONTINUED)	PAGE	TITLE	LINE
Such haggard lines as these	. . . .	429	Beau's Reply	14
As bad as Suffolk cheese.	. . . .	429	Beau's Reply	16
As bad as Suffolk cheese.	. . . .	429	Beau's Reply	16
As parent of the golden ore,	. . . .	433	Answer Paulus	24
'Tis wise, no doubt, as clients fat ye more,	. . .	433	Answer Paulus	41
May serve, as arguments ad hominem.	. . . . .	433	Answer Paulus	48
As ridden by a midnight hag:	. . . .	434	Answer Paulus	76
(As lucus comes a non lucendo)	. . . .	435	Answer Paulus	115
And wisely do as other men do.	. . . .	435	Answer Paulus	116
For, as the rabble daub, and rifle	. . . . . .	436	Answer Paulus	135
As well may I	. . . .	440	Ballyspellin	20
Now, as I live,	. . . .	442	Ballyspellin	73
Such Lyes as these	. . . .	442	Ballyspellin	80
As proper quite	. . . .	443	Ballyspellin	88
As those you write	. . . .	443	Ballyspellin	89
(As we shall shew you in the Sequel)	. . . . .	446	Modern Lady	37
An Hundred Tongues, as Poets use,	. . . . .	449	Modern Lady	137
"You have the Tale as cheap as I:	. . . . . .	449	Modern Lady	147
"You have the Tale as cheap as I:	. . . . . .	449	Modern Lady	147
That's not so bad as one that rubs	. . . . . .	452	Modern Lady	258
As if they had but just begun.	. . . . . .	453	Modern Lady	279
As Poet, Scholar and Divine.	. . . . . .	455	Dean Smedley	4
Return Him Beggar As He Went.	. . . . . .	456	Dean Smedley	50
As a Thorn-bush, or Oaken-bough,	. . . . . .	457	Paddy's Charac	1
And as ill Neighbours in the Night,	. . . .	457	Paddy's Charac	7
Next, as the Laws of Song require,	. . . . .	461	Birthday Song	21
For Jove, as every School-boy knows,	. . . . .	461	Birthday Song	23
As Overton has drawn his Sire	. . . . . .	461	Birthday Song	37
As loud as fifty mustard bowls;	. . . . .	461	Birthday Song	40
As loud as fifty mustard bowls;	. . . . .	461	Birthday Song	40
Tho fond of warlike Lyes as most men;	. . . .	462	Birthday Song	54
That he's Apollo, is as plain, as	. . . . .	462	Birthday Song	59
That he's Apollo, is as plain, as	. . . . .	462	Birthday Song	59
Old Phoebus is but half as bright,	. . . . .	462	Birthday Song	65
"As from the flowry Bed of Nile--	. . . . .	463	Birthday Song	81
Broad Innuendos, such as this,	. . . . . .	463	Birthday Song	83
And as he hears his Wit and Sence,	. . . . .	463	Birthday Song	91
As when they scarce have learn'd to spell.	. . .	463	Birthday Song	96
And write on paper black as Jet:	. . . . .	463	Birthday Song	114
As Julius, or the Youth of Pella,	. . . . .	464	Birthday Song	142
And as a Deity intrude,	. . . . . .	464	Birthday Song	145
When, who could think, tho' cold as Ice,	. . . .	470	Burning Poem	13
As Jove will not attend on less,	. . . . .	475	Epist on Epist	1
As Falstaff acted old King Harry:	. . . . .	475	Epist on Epist	10
And as he pass'd, so swell'd the Dee	. . . . .	476	Epist on Epist	45
Inrag'd, as Ern would do at thee.	. . . . .	476	Epist on Epist	46
Then to a Circle, as you were:	. . . . . .	477	Epist on Epist	74
As Fables: But you have refin'd	. . . . .	478	Epist on Epist	84
For, as their Appetites to quench,	. . . . .	480	Libel on D- D-	21
Himself, as rich as fifty Jews,	. . . . .	481	Libel on D- D-	39
Himself, as rich as fifty Jews,	. . . . .	481	Libel on D- D-	39
As far as Modest Pride allow'd,	. . . . .	482	Libel on D- D-	58
As far as Modest Pride allow'd,	. . . . .	482	Libel on D- D-	58
You, as a Critick, are so curious	. . . . .	483	Libel on D- D-	99
Through Courts and Senates as he goes;	. . . .	486	Libel on D- D-	190
Are Angels, just as <Kings> are Gods.	. . . .	486	Libel on D- D-	198
As from the tripod of Apollo	. . . .	490	Dialogue	47
And such as know what Greece has writ	. . .	491	Dialogue	51
Obtain such Privilege as you,	. . .	492	Panegyr Swift	3
And all Mankind as Fools, or Knaves;	. . . .	493	Panegyr Swift	6
Such Draughts as this, and then digest,	. . . .	495	Panegyr Swift	65
And 'tis as true, or Story lies,	. . . .	495	Panegyr Swift	74
To bless, as now you curse Mankind?	. . . .	496	Panegyr Swift	95
When such Adepts as you, and I	. . . .	497	Panegyr Swift	146
Resembling you as Angel Gods.	. . . .	499	Panegyr Swift	182
As some raw Youth in Country bred,	. . . .	500	Doctor Delaney	1
Fly Bullets now as thick as Hops,	. . . .	500	Doctor Delaney	9
Fly Bullets now as thick as Hops,	. . . .	500	Doctor Delaney	9
As if he heard Loud Thunders roul,	. . . .	500	Doctor Delaney	17
As fairest Fruits attract the Flyes.	. . . .	501	Doctor Delaney	42
Can sneer as learnedly as they,	. . . .	501	Doctor Delaney	49
Can sneer as learnedly as they,	. . . .	501	Doctor Delaney	49
For, as of old, Mathematicians	. . . .	503	Doctor Delaney	95
Wit, as the chief of Virtues's Friends,	. . . .	503	Doctor Delaney	99
Which, as the Nurse pursu'd to kill,	. . . .	504	Doctor Delaney	119
Dame Nature as the Learned show,	. . . .	504	Doctor Delaney	127
As if they all were of a Feather:	. . . .	513	Answer Fable	14
Birds, as he says, and I allow,	. . . .	513	Answer Fable	39
Were Scholars then, as we are now;	. . . .	513	Answer Fable	40
And as he wandred in his Park,	. . . .	513	Answer Fable	45
As never came from Noah's Ark:	. . . .	514	Answer Fable	54
By old Popish Cannons, as wise Men have Penn'd'em,	.	518	Dean Hang Rape	37
For Sodomy hang'd, as thou for a <Rape>.	.	518	Dean Hang Rape	48
That you who know musick no more than as ass	. . .	522	St. Ceciiia's	2
Of all the Litter as it lay;	. . . .	526	Lady's Dres Rm	8
As from within Pandora's Box,	. . . .	528	Lady's Dres Rm	83
As Mutton Cutlets, Prime of Meat,	. . . .	528	Lady's Dres Rm	99
As Laws of Cookery require,	. . . .	529	Lady's Dres Rm	101
You serve a potent Prince, as well as He.	. . . .	532	To Mr. Gay	44
You serve a potent Prince, as well as He.	. . . .	532	To Mr. Gay	44

AS	(CONTINUED)	PAGE	TITLE	LINE
And, as they robb'd the Father, rob the Son.		535	To Mr. Gay	118
Contrives, as he is hated, to be fear'd:		536	To Mr. Gay	138
Away they fled, and left him as they found him.		536	To Mr. Gay	160
Nor lets him sit as Justice on the Bench,		537	Mr. Pulteney	5
Thou art not half so nimble as a Hare:		539	Mr. Pulteney	40
"His Claim as good as other Folks---.		547	Life of Swift	94
"His Claim as good as other Folks---.		547	Life of Swift	94
"If he makes Mankind bad as Elves,		548	Life of Swift	115
"Which might as well, in his opinion,		550	Life of Swift	174
As never fav'ring the Pretender---:		550	Life of Swift	187
As Rochefoucault his Maxims drew		553	Death of Swift	1
I love my Friend as well as you,		554	Death of Swift	17
I love my Friend as well as you,		554	Death of Swift	17
His Brethren write as well as he?		554	Death of Swift	32
His Brethren write as well as he?		554	Death of Swift	32
St. John, as well as Pultney knows,		555	Death of Swift	59
St. John, as well as Pultney knows,		555	Death of Swift	59
"But now as Consort of the King,		560	Death of Swift	187
He'll treat me as he does my Betters.		561	Death of Swift	201
Which Pope must bear, as well as I.		561	Death of Swift	204
Which Pope must bear, as well as I.		561	Death of Swift	204
"He shews, as sure as God's in Gloc'ster,		564	Death of Swift	293
"He shews, as sure as God's in Gloc'ster,		564	Death of Swift	293
"Perform'd as Juglers do their Feats:		564	Death of Swift	296
"As for his Works in Verse and Prose,		565	Death of Swift	309
"As with a moral View design'd		565	Death of Swift	313
"As Numbers in their Hearts must own,		566	Death of Swift	337
"Two Kingdoms, just as Faction led,		566	Death of Swift	351
"As vile and profligate a Villain,		569	Death of Swift	419
"As modern Scroggs, or old Tressilian;		569	Death of Swift	420
Looking big as any Gyants,		573	Helter Skelter	3
As belonging to their betters:		573	Helter Skelter	24
And as very little Sence:		574	Helter Skelter	30
For her Taste is almost as refin'd as her Wit.		580	Psyche	10
For her Taste is almost as refin'd as her Wit.		580	Psyche	10
Like Iv'ry dry, and soft as Wax.		584	Strephon Chloe	26
For, as he view'd his Person round,		586	Strephon Chloe	75
(As in a Book he heard it read)		587	Strephon Chloe	101
How could a Nymph so chaste as Chloe,		588	Strephon Chloe	151
As Ships are toss't by Waves and Wind,		589	Strephon Chloe	170
Fair Utensil, as smooth and white		589	Strephon Chloe	173
As Chloe's Skin, almost as bright.		589	Strephon Chloe	174
As Chloe's Skin, almost as bright.		589	Strephon Chloe	174
As from a mossy Cliff distill,		589	Strephon Chloe	176
As sov'reign Med'cines for the Loins)		589	Strephon Chloe	182
As mortal as himself at least.		589	Strephon Chloe	186
As mortal as himself at least.		589	Strephon Chloe	186
And as he fill'd the reeking Vase,		590	Strephon Chloe	191
(As Pictures prove) with Garlands crown'd,		590	Strephon Chloe	194
As when you spy'd her on the Privy.		591	Strephon Chloe	248
Your Heart had been as whole as mine.		591	Strephon Chloe	250
Your Heart had been as whole as mine.		591	Strephon Chloe	250
Confering as they us'd to meet,		593	Cassinus Peter	3
He seem'd as just crept out of Bed;		594	Cassinus Peter	11
As well as Chymists by their Books:		597	Problem Solved	4
As well as Chymists by their Books:		597	Problem Solved	4
As handsome as my Lady's Page;		597	Problem Solved	5
As handsome as my Lady's Page;		597	Problem Solved	5
He left them Virgins as he found 'em.		598	Problem Solved	26
As much as now we find in Men.		601	Beasts Confess	4
As much as now we find in Men.		601	Beasts Confess	4
Not, as his Enemies object,		603	Beasts Confess	65
Of Chastity, as Monks do now;		603	Beasts Confess	70
As strictly too; as doth his Reverence.		603	Beasts Confess	72
As strictly too; as doth his Reverence.		603	Beasts Confess	72
As it hath long been his Desire,		606	Beasts Confess	172
As Esop would the World perswade;		607	Beasts Confess	211
As Trophies of a Muse deceas'd:		611	By Dr. Swift	6
As grating, or as loud as theirs?		617	Scandal Poem 1	6
As grating, or as loud as theirs?		617	Scandal Poem 1	6
As grating, or as loud as theirs?		617	Scandal Poem 1	6
What nymph on earth as fair as Iris?		619	Scandal Poem 1	74
Ador'd the Clouds as Deityes.		619	Scandal Poem 1	80
As Aristophanes declares;		620	Scandal Poem 1	82
As we think fit to smile or frown;		620	Scandal Poem 1	92
And, just as we dispose your brain,		620	Scandal Poem 1	93
In seas and woods, or low as hell		620	Scandal Poem 1	100
Though Venus be as light as air,		621	Scandal Poem 1	115
Though Venus be as light as air,		621	Scandal Poem 1	115
Provide you duly as we go		621	Scandal Poem 1	129
As if he made the weather fair.		621	Scandal Poem 1	138
So frequent or so loud as theirs?		624	Scandal Poem 2	6
What Nymph on Earth so fair as Iris?		625	Scandal Poem 2	72
Ador'd us Clouds as Deities;		626	Scandal Poem 2	78
As Aristophanes declares:		626	Scandal Poem 2	80
As we think fit to smile or frown:		626	Scandal Poem 2	90
And, just as we dispose your Brain,		626	Scandal Poem 2	91
In Seas, and Streams, or low as Hell:		626	Scandal Poem 2	98
Though Venus be as light as Air,		627	Scandal Poem 2	113
Though Venus be as light as Air,		627	Scandal Poem 2	113

AS	(CONTINUED)	PAGE	TITLE	LINE
With Care provide you as we go,		627	Scandal Poem 2	123
As you shall to your Sorrow know;		627	Scandal Poem 2	131
As if He made the Weather fair.		627	Scandal Poem 2	142
We, by Play, as Men by Drinking,		632	Epistle Lady	85
I, as all the Parish knows,		634	Epistle Lady	137
End, as it befits your Station;		636	Epistle Lady	185
This I must insist on. For, as		636	Epistle Lady	197
For your Sake, as well as mine,		637	Epistle Lady	217
For your Sake, as well as mine,		637	Epistle Lady	217
As my Method of Reforming,		637	Epistle Lady	229
As the Hirelings of St. <Stephens>.		637	Epistle Lady	244
As if it grew in common Hedges.		640	On Poetry	10
As how to strike the Muses Lyre.		641	On Poetry	32
As he, whom Phebus in his Ire		641	On Poetry	41
Now not so much as in Remainder		642	On Poetry	55
As learned Commentators view		643	On Poetry	103
As fresh as Farthings from the Mint:		644	On Poetry	114
As fresh as Farthings from the Mint:		644	On Poetry	114
Damns all your Thoughts as low and little,		644	On Poetry	121
Be silent as a Politician,		644	On Poetry	123
As Emblems of the sov'reign Pow'r,		646	On Poetry	193
As soon as you can hear his Knell,		646	On Poetry	205
As soon as you can hear his Knell,		646	On Poetry	205
And as they sail in Charon's Boat,		647	On Poetry	211
Who, as the Odours reach his Throne,		647	On Poetry	225
As to an Oracle submits.		649	On Poetry	268
And some as justly Fame extols		650	On Poetry	299
While others do as much for him.		651	On Poetry	334
Complain, as many an ancient Bard did,		652	On Poetry	349
The Rest pursue as thick as Hops:		654	On Poetry	400
The Rest pursue as thick as Hops:		654	On Poetry	400
And as their Heels elated rise,		654	On Poetry	403
By going on as he begun;		655	On Poetry	434
As long as Sun and Moon endure.		655	On Poetry	436
As long as Sun and Moon endure.		655	On Poetry	436
To rhyme almost as ill as Duck;		658	On Poetry	D 186
To rhyme almost as ill as Duck.		658	On Poetry	D 186
But Carthy, as from him thou learnest,		666	Epig Carthy 1	D 3
High as Longinus to the Stars ascends,		669	Epig Carthy 14	D 1
As pitiful as Tom MacLobe.		670	Epig Carthy 21	D 4
As pitiful as Tom MacLobe.		670	Epig Carthy 21	D 4
He'll make it muddy as a Bog.		671	Epig Carthy 21	D 8
Thy years as num'rous as thy days?		677	Parson's Case	36
Thy years as num'rous as thy days?		677	Parson's Case	36
Were (as he humbly did conceive)		687	Cadenus Vaness	16
As what those antient Poets sing;		687	Cadenus Vaness	28
As for Tibullus's Reports,		690	Cadenus Vaness	112
Infus'd, yet as it were by Stealth,		693	Cadenus Vaness	216
Of which, as she grew up, there stay'd		693	Cadenus Vaness	218
As she advanc'd, that Womankind		694	Cadenus Vaness	236
By her, as an unerring Guide.		694	Cadenus Vaness	239
Yet she wou'd act as best became		695	Cadenus Vaness	274
Thou hast, as thou shalt quickly see,		695	Cadenus Vaness	292
As who should say--she wants it here;		698	Cadenus Vaness	361
As came into her Fancy first,		698	Cadenus Vaness	382
Can do as soon as she is told.		700	Cadenus Vaness	425
Can do as soon as she is told.		700	Cadenus Vaness	425
As Years increase, she brighter shines,		703	Cadenus Vaness	536
Just as a Man sans Consequence.		707	Cadenus Vaness	659
As serious as a Tragick Play'r.		707	Cadenus Vaness	663
As serious as a Tragick Play'r.		707	Cadenus Vaness	663
As he approves, as he dislikes,		708	Cadenus Vaness	682
As he approves, as he dislikes,		708	Cadenus Vaness	682
As Rivers, tho' they bend and twine,		709	Cadenus Vaness	720
Or, as Philosophers, who find		709	Cadenus Vaness	722
For mean's her Design, and her Subject as mean,		716	Answer Rebus	5
As nat'ral Life the Body warms,		724	To Stella	11
Are not so sacred as her Word:		725	To Stella	56
As when a lofty Pile is rais'd,		727	Stella, Poems	1
As Tradesmen shew their Trash at first:)		728	Stella, Poems	22
As fine as Dawbers Hands can make it		734	Stel B-day '20	11
As fine as Dawbers Hands can make it		734	Stel B-day '20	11
Unless Delany as my Heir,		740	Stel B-day '21	19
Think Eusden's Right as good as mine.		741	Stel B-day 22	30
Think Eusden's Right as good as mine.		741	Stel B-day 22	30
You yearly sing as she grows old,		742	Stel B-day 22	39
For she, as Priestess, knows the Rites		743	Stel B-day 22	51
See! as you raise it from its Tomb,		743	Stel B-day 22	67
As the Coach stopp'd, she look'd & swore		746	Stel Distress	27
His Med'cine work as he design'd		746	Stel Distress	32
As the Coach stopp'd, she look'd & swore		746	Stel Distress	
His Malice work as he design'd:		750	Stel Wood-Park	24
As a matter they had no concern in.		756	Dingley Brent	12
As when a beauteous Nymph decays		756	Stel B-day '24	1
And as the Vegetables rise,		759	Receipt Youth	13
As rising from Medea's Kettle;		759	Receipt Youth	18
As, if the gout should seize the head,		761	Bec's B-Day	11
A goodly set as can be found		762	Bec's B-Day	51
Long Schemes of Life, as heretofore;		764	Stel B-day '26	16
As Atheists argue, to entice,		764	Stel B-day '26	21

AS (CONTINUED)

	PAGE	TITLE	LINE
To lead thee, as a Staff directs the Blind,	770	Horace 1, 14	17
As when some Writer in a public Cause,	770	Horace 1, 14	25
Such was Ierne's Claim, as just as thine,	771	Horace 1, 14	41
Such was Ierne's Claim, as just as thine,	771	Horace 1, 14	41
As those who long have stood the Storms of State,	772	Horace 1, 14	59
As Popish Craft? Did he not rail on't?	774	Mullinix Tim	19
Are Stale, and Worn as Troy-Town Story.	774	Mullinix Tim	36
Might want such noisy Fools as you;	774	Mullinix Tim	40
And, as that hateful hideous Grecian	775	Mullinix Tim	51
As if the Devil drove, they fly.	775	Mullinix Tim	68
And simple as I now stand here,	778	Mullinix Tim	157
Am, as you tell me, but their may-game,	778	Mullinix Tim	174
As Horace says, Optat ephippia.	779	Mullinix Tim	214
Be careful, as you walk behind,	780	Mullinix Tim	231
And found, as he the pages twirl'd,	782	Tim and Fables	7
Just as they lookt in the Original.	783	Tim and Fables	18
Such Jacobites as he deserve,--	783	Tim and Fables	33
Could roar as loud as Stenter,	785	Mullinex Dick	38
Could roar as loud as Stenter,	785	Mullinex Dick	38
As when rooting in a Bin,	785	Dick, Maggot	1
For, as he shakes his Wainscot Chops,	786	Dick, Maggot	11
Would then be not so brown as thou.	786	Clad in Brown	6
The Glass will seem as brown as those.	786	Clad in Brown	12
The Glass will seem as brown as those.	786	Clad in Brown	12
As shrivelled and as black as thine.	787	Clad in Brown	22
As shrivelled and as black as thine.	787	Clad in Brown	22
As shrivelled and as black as thine.	787	Clad in Brown	22
Could do such Feats as well as they.	788	Dick's Variety	18
Could do such Feats as well as they.	788	Dick's Variety	18
As you grew more degenerate and base,	792	St. Pat's Well	53
He barks as fast as he can utter.	797	Traulus 1	48
He barks as fast as he can utter.	797	Traulus 1	48
By <God> I'll bring you off as clean.	797	Traulus 1	60
They've done it, we thank 'em, but not as they meant;	804	Irish Bishops	36
As Machiavel taught 'em; divide and ye govern.	805	Irish Bishops	48
As antient Judas by Transgression fell,	806	Judas	17
Be as Pox'd and Profane as Fanatical <Hort>	808	Advice Parson	10
Be as Pox'd and Profane as Fanatical <Hort>	808	Advice Parson	10
As in a general Calamity.	811	Bro Protestant	10
As much as Hebrews and Philistines:	812	Bro Protestant	32
As much as Hebrews and Philistines:	812	Bro Protestant	32
As well may claim you for their Kin.	813	Bro Protestant	40
As Moses, by divine Advice,	813	Bro Protestant	49
And as our Sects, by all Descriptions,	813	Bro Protestant	51
As from the trodden Dust they spring,	813	Bro Protestant	53
As if they were afraid to lose 'em:	813	Bro Protestant	60
He's a Christian as good as the rest of the herd.	816	Yahoo's	29
He's a Christian as good as the rest of the herd.	816	Yahoo's	29
He kindled, as if the whole Satire had been	816	Yahoo's	41
He began as he bragg'd, with a rant and a roar;	816	Yahoo's	43
And Smithfield, as Rap was ne'er colted before;	817	Yahoo's	57
And, as your old wont is, change sides in a trice:	818	Archbi Cashel	8
As not the Handy-work of God;	821	Dr. Rundle	54
Is more secure as well as legal.	821	Dr. Rundle	58
Is more secure as well as legal.	821	Dr. Rundle	58
Where ev'ry Trout can make as high Rants	824	Printer Newgat	5
O'er his Inferiors as our Tyrants;	824	Printer Newgat	6
As I strole the City, oft I	829	Legion Club	1
Just as when he murther'd <Throp>.	835	Legion Club	144
Draw the Beasts as I describe 'em,	839	Legion Club	225
At Market Hill, as well appears	848	Old Thorn	1
All as she scrubb'd her mealzy Rump.	849	Old Thorn	44
And just as I handle 'em	852	Lady's Lament	29
And, as I am serious,	855	Lady's Lament	143
As soon as her Ladyship call'd to be drest,	868	Grand Question	43
As soon as her Ladyship call'd to be drest,	868	Grand Question	43
I hope you will use my House as your own.	869	Grand Question	82
As a Compliment due to a Lady so fair;	870	Grand Question	110
You're heartily welcome: But as for good Chear,	871	Grand Question	121
To keep off their Eyes, as they wait at the Table;	871	Grand Question	136
"You'll never want Parsons as long as you live;	872	Grand Question	142
"You'll never want Parsons as long as you live;	872	Grand Question	142
"But the Devil's as welcome wherever he goes:	872	Grand Question	144
"<God> <damn> me, he hobbles as bad as my Groom;	872	Grand Question	156
"<God> <damn> me, he hobbles as bad as my Groom;	872	Grand Question	156
As, who shou'd say, Now, am I Skinny and Lean?	873	Grand Question	176
But, he durst not so much as once open his Lips,	873	Grand Question	177
And sure, as monument of brass,	876	To Dean Swift	11
But, as of old, obscurely lain;	877	To Dean Swift	30
Runs out in tongue, as in estate;	878	Robbin & Harry	10
As Soldiers use, for love must marry,	878	Robbin & Harry	18
Young Harry, as all Europe knows,	879	Robbin & Harry	37
As at their Work they sate in counterview,	880	Pastoral Dial	5
Or crack such Lice as his betwixt your Nails?	882	Pastoral Dial	36
Attend him daily as their Chief,	883	Rev Market-Hill	23
Brave as the Upton Fan she wears:	885	Rev Market-Hill	58
She shall be caught as in a Noose,	885	Rev Market-Hill	64
And soon as we have got Possession,	886	Rev Market-Hill	90
We'll act as other Conqu'rors do;	886	Rev Market-Hill	91
As all your Politicians wise	886	Rev Market-Hill	109

	PAGE	TITLE		LINE
Nine more such Champions as the <Dean>,	887	Panegyr Dean		9
And, as you in Commission sit,	888	Panegyr Dean		41
To sing your Praise. And, first as <Dean>:	888	Panegyr Dean		44
As fits a Princess in Romance.	888	Panegyr Dean		54
Is seen, as when you mount our Pulpit.	889	Panegyr Dean		66
As well become St. <Patrick's> <Dean>;	889	Panegyr Dean		78
As clearly shows you bred at Court!	889	Panegyr Dean		84
Now, as a Jester, I accost you;	890	Panegyr Dean		113
To let me praise you as my Tutor.	891	Panegyr Dean		130
And, sure as they're alive, at Night;	891	Panegyr Dean		139
As soon as gone, will show their Spight:	891	Panegyr Dean		140
As soon as gone, will show their Spight:	891	Panegyr Dean		140
As if I were a darling Child.	891	Panegyr Dean		152
Now, enter as the Dairy Hand-maid:	892	Panegyr Dean		167
As who should say, to pluck a Rose.	893	Panegyr Dean		216
As if she ne'er could have enuff;	895	Panegyr Dean		261
As Nature prompts, his Off'ring pays?	895	Panegyr Dean		288
Sleek, <--> claims her as his Right:	897	Panegyr Dean		344
Nor can you tax me as unsteady,	899	Dean's Reasons		7
I am, as now too late I find,	899	Dean's Reasons		11
Their gifts, as misers do their gold;	900	Dean's Reasons		36
But, as for me, who ne'er could clamber high,	900	Dean's Reasons		51
Who send my mind (as I believe) less	900	Dean's Reasons		53
If when I talk, as talk I must,	901	Dean's Reasons		67
Fine as a Col'nel of the Guards,	904	Death Daphne		55
She, as she came into the Room,	904	Death Daphne		57
As just the Counterpart of his.	905	Death Daphne		66
As great as ever, at Quadrille?	905	Death Daphne		78
As great as ever, at Quadrille?	905	Death Daphne		78
Thy Hand as dry and cold as Lead,	905	Death Daphne		95
Thy Hand as dry and cold as Lead,	905	Death Daphne		95
That she throws away as foul;	907	Daphne		47
'Twill be just as I expect.	908	Daphne		82
Yet, as it oft attends the Great,	917	Riddle 3		5
And turn and wind me as they please.	920	Riddle 6		8
Distinctly seen as through a Glass:	920	Riddle 6		14
Here you may see, as in a Glass,	921	Riddle 7		5
As half asham'd, and half afraid,	922	Riddle 7		34
As fair and lovely as their Queen:	923	Riddle 7		70
As fair and lovely as their Queen:	923	Riddle 7		70
Olympus trembling as he nods,	924	Riddle 7		96
And of as noble Blood as you;	924	Riddle 8		4
And of as noble Blood as you;	924	Riddle 8		4
With Pleasure, as the Poet sings,	924	Riddle 8		15
I am bright as an Angel, and light as a Feather,	928	Riddle 13	D	3
I am bright as an Angel, and light as a Feather,	928	Riddle 13	D	3
I Am jet-Black, as you may see,	929	Riddle 15	D	1
In me you see them full as white,	932	Riddle 19	D	8
Then, since I shew as fine a Face,	932	Riddle 19	D	11
And as I please they're great and small;	934	Riddle 21	D	2
Again, as I'm dispos'd, the Foe	934	Riddle 21	D	5
And turn it as I have a Mind,	934	Riddle 21	D	15
As my thread of life is spun;	937	Riddle 24	D	44
Die like lovers as they gaze,	937	Riddle 24	D	49
And as for the Tragick	939	Riddle Answerd		15
As eels delight to creep in mud,	950	Upstart	D	7
But think it as sweet as her own.	952	Onyons		15
But think it as sweet as her own.	952	Onyons		15
Their Bellies are soft, and as white as a Custard.	953	Herrings		7
Their Bellies are soft, and as white as a Custard.	953	Herrings		7
Yet where He's not so rich as I;	954	Authors Living		9
As rude as a bear, no mule half so crabbed;	955	Portrait Life		5
As rude as a bear, no mule half so crabbed;	955	Portrait Life		5
Would, as he lay under, cry out, Sirrah, yield:	967	Letter Sherid		16
As a good quiet Soul, who no Mischief intends	968	Letter Sherid		27
And I'll use you as he did that overgrown Clown,	968	Letter Sherid		31
O tempora, O mores! as 'tis in the adage.	975	Dean to Sherid		2
And think of the sex as you please, I'd as lieve	976	Dean to Sherid		15
And think of the sex as you please, I'd as lieve	976	Dean to Sherid		15
You call them a riddle, as call them a sieve.	976	Dean to Sherid		16
But as for your threats, you may do what you can,	976	Dean to Sherid		33
As for your new rebus, or riddle, or crux,	977	Dean to Sherid		43
When I saw you to-day, as I went with Lord Anglesey.	978	Dean to Tho: S		1
And I love you so well, as I told you long ago,	979	Dean to Tho: S		17
You rhyme, as folks fence, in tierce and cart.	979	Dean to Tho: S		20
I gave, as you beg, your most humble respects:	979	Dean to Tho: S		24
For she never descends so low as the cellar;	979	Dean to Tho: S		26
For, as Helsham observes, there's nothing can chime	980	Tho: Sheridan		3
For he says, short as 'tis, it will give you a stool.	980	Tho: Sheridan		8
And thence, as fam'd John Bunyan sung,	983	Sher, A Goose		6
As for you're writing I am dead,	983	Sher, A Goose		25
But that's as much as to say, that my Master should die before ye,	986	Mary to Sher		19
But that's as much as to say, that my Master should die before ye,	986	Mary to Sher		19
Well, well, that's as God pleases,	986	Mary to Sher		20
Mary said he, (one Day, as I was mending my Master's Stocking,)	986	Mary to Sher		28
But as to Comic Aristophanes,	988	Letter Dr Sh-n		5
He and Cratinus used, as Horace says,	988	Letter Dr Sh-n		11

AS	(CONTINUED)	PAGE	TITLE	LINE	
For ought he knows, as bad as Thespis's.		988	Letter Dr Sh-n	23	
For ought he knows, as bad as Thespis's.		988	Letter Dr Sh-n	23	
Will you return as hard ones, if I call t'ye?		989	Letter Dr Sh-n	33	
I must confess that as to me, Sirs,		993	On Picture	13	
And future Poets, as they rise,		994	On Picture	31	
But be't as 'twill, this you must grant,		1003	Dan J's Reply	10	
As to your Spelling, let me see,		1004	Dan J's Reply	34	
Presents, as 'tis fitting,		1004	Sheridan's Sub	3	
In pard'ning, as in punishing,		1005	Sheridan's Sub	15	
. . .to have been acquainted with me, as she pretended.		1014	Swift to Sheri	11	
And I must confess as a Dean and Divine		1017	Swift Ans Sher	3	
Oh that Jove would give me such a talent as thine		1017	Swift Ans Sher	7	
But were you as wicked as lewd Aretine		1017	Swift Ans Sher	18	
But were you as wicked as lewd Aretine		1017	Swift Ans Sher	18	
As much as the Liffee's outdone by the Rhine		1018	Swift Ans Sher	26	
As much as the Liffee's outdone by the Rhine		1018	Swift Ans Sher	26	
Smooth as our Bason's gentle Flood,		1020	Nim-Dan-Dean 1	D	5
Close, as the Macedonian Phalanx:		1021	Nim-Dan-Dean 1	D	30
Where thirty weigh, as much as eighty.		1022	Nim-Dan-Dean 1	D	48
Where thirty weigh, as much as eighty.		1022	Nim-Dan-Dean 1	D	48
For, as for honest John, tho' I'm not sure on't,		1022	Nim-Dan-Dean 2	D	5
. . .and you'll believe me as sure as a gun, and own it;		1023	Nim-Dan-Dean 2	D	15
. . .and you'll believe me as sure as a gun, and own it;		1023	Nim-Dan-Dean 2	D	15
And so I conclude, with humble respects as usual, . . .		1024	Nim-Dan-Dean 2	D	18
And, as to the subject, our judgment mehercle		1026	Sheri Circles	3	
As his betters are us'd, shall be lash'd round the ring,		1027	Sheri Circles	19	
And, as fast as she could, to the Deanery flew sick.		1029	Dr. Helsham	11	
And, as fast as she could, to the Deanery flew sick.		1029	Dr. Helsham	11	
Could you but change a Crown as easy		1033	Ans to Crown	13	
As you can steal one, how 'twould please ye!		1033	Ans to Crown	14	
ASCEND					
Did Female Virtue e'er so high ascend,		531	To Mr. Gay	5	
ASCENDING					
Ascending make one Funeral-Blaze.		646	On Poetry	204	
ASCENDS					
From Hell a <Viceroy> Dev'l ascends,		486	Libel on D- D-	186	
High as Longinus to the Stars ascends,		669	Epig Carthy 14	D	1
ASCUE					
Who often has made me, by looking ascue, sick.		1030	Dr. Sheridan	5	
ASHAM'D					
And Harley, not asham'd his Choice to own,		194	Autnor Himself	31	
No Maid at Court is less asham'd,		590	Strephon Chloe	215	
Asham'd of them, than they of thee.		652	On Poetry	364	
The Graces half asham'd look'd down;		689	Cadenus Vaness	100	
Sure, you are not asham'd to stoop;		699	Cadenus Vaness	401	
Both of her self and Sex asham'd,		699	Cadenus Vaness	405	
For I'm asham'd to use a Glass;		758	Stel B-day '24	46	
I'm not asham'd to show my Face,		920	Riddle 6	24	
As half asham'd, and half afraid,		922	Riddle 7	34	
ASHES					
From the dead Ashes of a Flow'r		81	Vanbrug House	86	
A Pile shall from its Ashes rise		107	V's House	49	
From the dead Ashes of a Flow'r		109	V's House	128	
It burnt to Ashes in a Trice.		470	Burning Poem	14	
"You freely may forgive his Ashes.		550	Life of Swift	202	
Together both to Ashes turn.		687	Cadenus Vaness	34	
ASIDE					
And then the Toys are thrown aside.		6	Ode to King	18	
Then stept aside to fetch 'em Drink,		112	Bauc & Phil 2	29	
Then softly turn'd aside to view,		112	Bauc & Phil 2	39	
Will duck his Head, aside will start,		500	Doctor Delaney	5	
They glance aside without a Wound.		500	Doctor Delaney	30	
And made me throw my Pen aside;		555	Death of Swift	64	
"Would rather slip aside, and chuse		565	Death of Swift	321	
You who thro' Frailty step'd aside,		579	Day Judgement	13	
A Dog by Instinct turns aside,		640	On Poetry	17	
Lay now aside all Thoughts of Fame,		646	On Poetry	183	
All Passions must be laid aside:		724	To Stella	36	
Lord how this Frothy Coxcomb frets! (aside)		774	Mullinix Tim	16	
But turns aside like mad Ulysses:		796	Traulus 1	30	
Lay thy paltry Privilege aside,		832	Legion Club	71	
ASK					
To ask for what he fancy'd most.		94	Bauc & Phil 1	156	
To ask for what he fancy'd most:		115	Bauc & Phil 2	110	
I ask not to increase my Store,		198	Horace 2, 6	8	
Ask that of old Madam,		247	Irish-Feast	81	
Now ask me a Question. How came it to pass		336	Serious Poem	85	
To wait so long and have nothing to ask.		368	Verses Window	2	
I ask, if what you say be true,		392	Young's Satire	32	
Why should I ask of thee, my Muse,		449	Modern Lady	136	
Then, shou'd you dare to ask a Place,		480	Libel on D- D-	29	
To ask the judgement of a friend,		489	Dialogue	14	
I ask but for an Inch at most.		554	Death of Swift	20	
Dear Cassy, though to ask I dread,		595	Cassinus Peter	41	
Yet, ask I must. Is Caelia dead?		595	Cassinus Peter	42	
With all her Wit, I wou'd not ask		700	Cadenus Vaness	420	
Ask no Advice, but think alone,		724	To Stella	37	
Which you expect, but scorn to ask;		739	Stel B-day '21	4	
Nor do I ask for Stella's sake;		741	Stel B-day 22	31	
You perhaps will ask me, why so?		830	Legion Club	39	

52

ASK	(CONTINUED)	PAGE	TITLE	LINE
I shall ask, and you instruct me.		832	Legion Club	80
At breakfast he'll ask		855	Lady's Lament	137
We never ask to hear you twice.		889	Panegyr Dean	74
Yet never ask us once to play?		891	Panegyr Dean	146
Till you please to ask me thrice;		908	Daphne	80

ASK'D

		PAGE	TITLE	LINE
When he ask'd for my Aid, in the Forms that are usual:		265	Apollo	72
I Ask'd a Whig the other Night,		298	Horrid Plot	1
They ask'd her, how she lik'd the Play,		696	Cadenus Vaness	318
And gravely ask'd her what she thought,		698	Cadenus Vaness	379

ASK'T

She ask't about her Friends below;		905	Death Daphne	73

ASKS

		PAGE	TITLE	LINE
Asks of his Neighbor; Who is that?		63	Discovery	16
One asks the Watermen hard by,		109	V's House	99
But never asks, or asks in vain;		292	Prog Marriage	66
But never asks, or asks in vain;		292	Prog Marriage	66
And asks if it be time to rise;		446	Modern Lady	43
"Who only asks some pretty Cure,		476	Epist on Epist	49
Comes Dingley, and asks you, What was it?		756	Dingley Brent	15

ASKT

Askt me how our elections past.		422	Ireld	34

ASLEEP

		PAGE	TITLE	LINE
The Master Bawl'd out half asleep		90	Bauc & Phil 1	27
While the poor Child lay fast asleep.		150	Corinna	8
Whilst you're, like Baal, fast asleep.		403	Window Inns 10	D 10
Either drunk or asleep.		423	Carterets Arms	
His outward senses fast asleep;		900	Dean's Reasons	46

ASLOPE

While the first drizzling Show'r is born aslope,		137	City Shower	18

ASP

It grew an all-devouring Asp;		132	Magician's Rod	10

ASPECT

		PAGE	TITLE	LINE
When War her cloudy aspect just withdrew,		16	Ode Athenian	23
To Venus in Aspect Mali'n,		99	Elegy Patrige	60
Hither thy gentle Aspect bend,		101	Elegy Patrige	101
Tho' Candor and Truth in my Aspect I bear,		929	Riddle 13	D 5

ASPERSE

Unjustly Poets we asperse;		729	Stella, Poems	57

ASPERSION

		PAGE	TITLE	LINE
"Twas known, tho' he had born Aspersion;		606	Beasts Confess	151
'Tis a wrong, unjust Aspersion:		632	Epistle Lady	82

ASPIR'D

		PAGE	TITLE	LINE
Madly aspir'd to wear her chain:		177	To Lord Harley	42
To copy her, few Nymphs aspir'd;		700	Cadenus Vaness	440

ASPIRE

		PAGE	TITLE	LINE
Who think your Muse must first aspire;		475	Epist on Epist	23
I have no Title to aspire;		555	Death of Swift	45
Before Aeneas durst aspire		619	Scandal Poem 1	65
Before Aeneas durst aspire		625	Scandal Poem 2	61

ASPIRING

		PAGE	TITLE	LINE
Else what aspiring hero durst?		178	To Lord Harley	68
Rais'd up on Hope's aspiring Plumes,		252	Bubble	33
Aspiring, factious, fierce and loud		503	Doctor Delaney	87
Concannen, more aspiring Bard,		654	On Poetry	397
Aspiring, greedy, full of senseless Prate,		792	St. Pat's Well	51
Aspiring to exalt my Head:		897	Panegyr Dean	322

ASQUINT

Nor look Asquint on an old Friend.		101	Elegy Patrige	102

ASS

		PAGE	TITLE	LINE
Nor need the lion's skin conceal the ass;		48	To Congreve	172
Thro' any Ears but of an Ass.		158	Fable of Midas	66
An Ass was drinking at a Stream,		253	Bubble	74
An Ass hath swallow'd up the Moon,		253	Bubble	79
I'm not the Grandson of that Ass Quin;		350	Upright Judge 3	1
The Ass was dull, the Lyon brave,		512	Answer Fable	5
That you who know musick no more than as ass		522	St. Cecilia's	2
The Ass approaching next, confess'd,		602	Beasts Confess	21
The Ass was never known so stupid		607	Beasts Confess	207
Let Sir <Tom>, that rampant Ass,		831	Legion Club	63
Whereby you now confess your self to be a Goose or an Ass:		986	Mary to Sher	18

ASS'S

		PAGE	TITLE	LINE
An Ass's Hoof alone can hold		469	Burning Poem	1
No Vessel but an Ass's Head,		469	Burning Poem	4
While his own ass's Zaggs were more fit for the shears.		816	Yahoo's	49

ASSASSIN

		PAGE	TITLE	LINE
That Traitor, Assassin, Informer vile.		826	Noisy Tom	8
"Against that Assassin in Crape,		850	Old Thorn	67

ASSASSINE

They Assassine when young, and Poison when old.		148	Windsor Proph	20

ASSAULT

But, let us on our first Assault		885	Rev Market-Hill	83

ASSEMBLED

A Club assembled at the Rose;		565	Death of Swift	300

ASSEMBLIES

Such Assemblies, you might swear,		829	Legion Club	13

ASSEMBLING

From the four Elements assembling,		279	Journal	27

53

ASSEMBLING-GLASS
   When some rough hand breaks the assembling-glass. . . .   PAGE TITLE   LINE
   When some rough hand breaks the assembling-glass. . . .   45 To Congreve   64
ASSERT
   Assert that Hyde in writing story . . . .   489 Dialogue   25
   Why, then it was, I do assert, ...   547 Life of Swift   86
ASSES
   Clap't Asses Ears upon the Judge, ...   157 Fable of Midas   30
   Our Midas too has Asses Ears; . . . .   158 Fable of Midas   62
   With Asses Ears, and dirty Hands. . . . .   158 Fable of Midas   82
   To be your Asses Colts of State, ...   499 Panegyr Swift 180
   This, among Hibernian Asses, ...   523 Betty Grizette 33
   Hogs, Asses, Wolves, Baboons, & Goats . . . . . .   659 On Poetry   D 410
   To take his greatest Grandees for Asses. . . . . .   988 Letter Dr Sh-n 12
ASSESSORS
   Whom she or her Assessors knew. . . . .   689 Cadenus Vaness 103
ASSETS
   Your Assets fail, and Cash is wanting . . . . . .   477 Epist on Epist 63
ASSIGN
   Yet, some assign a diff'rent Reason; . . . .   588 Strephon Chloe 159
   While I assign my self a Task . . . .   739 Stel B-day '21   3
ASSIGN'D
   Assign'd for life to unremitting grief; . . . . . .   54 Temple Ill   110
   "And wish the Task had been assign'd . . . .   485 Libel on D- D- 169
   Three weighty Causes were assign'd, ...   598 Problem Solved 23
   What Reason can there be assign'd . . . .   640 On Poetry   11
   In Scripture, to the Dev'l assign'd: . . . .   798 Traulus 1   76
   This earthly Globe to thee assign'd, ...   894 Panegyr Dean 235
ASSIGNATION
   Keeps punctual to an Assignation; . . . .   724 To Stella   30
ASSIST
   Sent to assist an old unvanquish'd pride . . . . .   44 To Congreve   43
   Assist all Poets in Distresses, ...   411 Dial Rich Marb 94
   Come, assist me, Muse obedient, ...   832 Legion Club   75
ASSISTANCE
   Want your assistance now to clear 'em. . . . . .   186 Scriblerus 3   4
   She wants assistance more than I; . . . .   754 Stella '23   16
   By your Example and Assistance, ...   888 Panegyr Dean   55
ASSISTANT
   Who would not Write Verses with such an assistant. . .   77 Lady B- B-   REF
ASSISTERS
   We, Gentlemen, are Your Assisters, ...   254 Bubble   105
ASSISTS
   That Fortune still assists the bold, ...   588 Strephon Chloe 148
ASSIZES
   He'd have 'em try'd at the Assizes . . . .   788 Dick's Variety 21
ASSUAGE
   Which by Remembrance will assuage, ...   764 Stel B-day '26 31
ASSUAGES
   Our kindly help his fire assuages. . . . .   618 Scandal Poem 1 34
ASSUM'D
   And both assum'd a Sable Hue; . . . .   115 Bauc & Phil 2 122
ASSUME   SEE RE-ASSUME
   "<He> can assume more Forms than I, ...   303 Storm   29
   Assume a Dignitary's Airs, ...   495 Panegyr Swift   70
   Assume the Shapes of filthy Brutes. . . . .   670 Epig Carthy 19 D 2
   Of Poets dare assume my Place; . . . .   739 Stel B-day '21 14
ASSUMES
   An Eagle's Flight and State assumes, ...   252 Bubble   35
   Assumes an artificiall Vigor; . . . .   290 Prog Marriage   22
   From whence the tender Skin assumes . . . . . .   691 Cadenus Vaness 160
ASSUR'D
   And be assur'd, the Court will find him . . . . . .   190 Faggot   43
   Assur'd her he wou'd do his best: . . . .   302 Storm   10
   I have assur'd them twenty times, ...   741 Stel B-day 22   23
ASSURE
   Therefore I assure ye, ...   237 Excellent Song 22
   But Wood I assure you is no Heart of Oak; . . . .   336 Serious Poem   66
   And, with an Oath, assure him; all is well. . . .   534 To Mr. Gay   96
   Draw them like, for I assure you, ...   839 Legion Club 227
   If this be your practice, mean scrub, I assure Ye, . . 1019 To Sheridan   5
   Miss Morice was (I can assure you 'tis true) sick: . . 1029 Dr. Helsham   12
ASSURED
   At least, I'm well assured, that no Folk lays . . .   988 Letter Dr Sh-n 26
ASSWAGES
   Our kindly Help his Fire asswages; . . . .   624 Scandal Poem 2 32
ASTHMA
   And, wheezing Asthma, loth to stir: . . . . . .   895 Panegyr Dean 278
ASTONISH'D
   Astonish'd gave a dreadful Shriek; . . . .   849 Old Thorn   26
ASTORE
   Patrick astore, what news upon the town? . . . . .   840 Ballad   D 1
   Patrick astore, who was him made this law? . . . .   841 Ballad   D 11
ASTRAEA
   Nor when we see Astraea stand . . . .   433 Answer Paulus   31
ASTRAY
   We have too long been led astray, ...   27 Ode to Temple   17
   Our Horses astray, ... 1036 Plague Country   5
ASTRIDE
   She'll strain a Point, and sit astride, ...   100 Elegy Patrige   86
   And mounts astride upon the Dragon. . . . . . .   777 Mullinix Tim   116

	PAGE	TITLE	LINE
ASTROLOGER			
Strange, an Astrologer should Die,	98	Elegy Patrige	5
Which an Astrologer might use,	99	Elegy Patrige	45
ASTROLOGERS			
Astrologers and Lunaticks	101	Elegy Patrige	99
For, all Astrologers maintain	228	Prog of Beauty	86
ASTROLOGY			
There is 'twixt Cobling and Astrology;	98	Elegy Patrige	20
ASTRONOMERS			
Errors like this did old Astronomers misguide,	36	Ode Sancroft	65
ASUNDER			
If she like us would burst asunder!	'617	Scandal Poem 1	16
And burst asunder e'er he went to Hell;	806	Judas	18
AT 632		OMITTED WORD	
ATALANTA'S			
Advanc'd like Atalanta's Star,	696	Cadenus Vaness	306
ATAVUS			
From his Atavus and Grandsire;	800	Traulus 2	28
ATCHIEVE			
Nor could atchieve the promis'd Lawn,	495	Panegyr Swift	82
ATCHIEVING			
atchieving of nothing Still promising wonders	540	Charac Walpole	5
ATCHIEVMENTS			
Or by Atchievments, Arms, Device	80	Vanbrug House	65
ATCHIVEMENT			
Or by Atchivement, Arms, Device,	107	V's House	39
ATHEIST			
"Become an Atheist, or Socinian.	550	Life of Swift	175
ATHEIST'S			
And shakes the atheist's knees; such ghastly fear	52	Temple Ill	39
ATHEISTS			
The Wits, I mean the Atheists of the Age,	19	Ode Athenian	103
As Atheists argue, to entice,	764	Stel B-day '26	21
ATHERTON'S			
But I only behold thee in Atherton's Shape,	518	Dean Hang Rape	47
ATHWART			
They stick athwart my maw	429	Beau's Reply	15
ATLANTIS			
She pours it out in an Atlantis,	150	Corinna	31
ATLAS			
Atlas we read in antient Song	160	Atlas	1
So Atlas, lest the pondrous Sphears	160	Atlas	9
And Atlas is a Politician	160	Atlas	16
Suppose then Atlas ne'er so wise,	160	Atlas	19
This Atlas stands to prop the Court:	656	On Poetry	444
ATOM			
Each Atom by some other struck,	406	Swift to Pope	13
Down ev'ry mealy Atom drops	786	Dick, Maggot	12
ATOMS			
Is but a Crowd of Atoms justling in a heap,	20	Ode Athenian	127
Where all the fruitful Atoms lye,	32	Ode to Temple	171
And from contending Atoms came.	324	Pethox	32
Like Atoms are exempt from blows.	467	Birthday Song	238
The World shall in its Atoms end,	725	To Stella	57
ATRIDAE			
Hoc Ithacus velit, et magni mercentur Atridae.	980	Dean to Tho: S	38
ATROPHY			
Heart-sick of a high fever and consuming atrophy;	42	Ode Sancroft	252
ATTACK			
The Youth, in vain, would fly from Fate's Attack,	210	Earl of Oxford	3
Thou dar'st the greatest Prince attack,	325	Pethox	53
And now to attack her again hir prepares,	517	Dean Hang Rape	14
Resolv'd to make his first Attack:	588	Strephon Chloe	149
Which Malice must attack in vain;	693	Cadenus Vaness	209
Attack the Foe at Left and Right;	884	Rev Market-Hill	46
Then, least upon our first Attack	885	Rev Market-Hill	59
They tempted me t' attack your Highness,	1005	Sheridan's Sub	23
ATTACKING			
Attacking, when he took the Whim,	548	Life of Swift	105
ATTACKS			
Your Influence do's the vain Attacks defy	13	Ode to William	D 43
Attacks her in the milky Way:	228	Prog of Beauty	92
ATTAIN'D			
Attain'd by Flight the Muses Hill;	504	Doctor Delaney	120
ATTAINDER			
Since Cibber brought in an Attainder;	642	On Poetry	56
ATTEMPT			
The brave Attempt do's all our Foes disarm,	13	Ode to William	D 37
Attempt a 'Flight above a Haycock?	513	Answer Fable	22
And, should a Friend attempt to set him right,	535	To Mr. Gay	111
I attempt no higher Pitch.	635	Epistle Lady	172
Thus, Shou'd I attempt to climb,	638	Epistle Lady	257
A Bear will not attempt to fly:	640	On Poetry	14
Take Courage, and attempt a Third.	645	On Poetry	148
Their Heads attempt the nether Skies.	654	On Poetry	404
What Planter will attempt to yoke	703	Cadenus Vaness	534
ATTEMPTED			
His spite cannot wound, who attempted the Drapier.	818	Archbi Cashel	6
ATTEMPTER			
How shall a new Attempter learn	642	On Poetry	71

	PAGE	TITLE	LINE
ATTEMPTING			
Now you've done right, No Knight attempting	373	Letter D. S-y	75
ATTEMPTS			
On ev'ry Genius that attempts to rise;	193	Author Himself	4
"To drown him all Attempts are vain,	303	Storm	28
In vain are all attempts from Germany	467	Birthday Song	217
On Pallas all Attempts are vain;	701	Cadenus Vaness	468
ATTEND			
Attend when e'er I want their Aid,	120	Apollo Outwit	31
Attend thy Coach, and hear them shout	183	Horace 2, 1	80
Since Harley bid me first attend,	201	Horace 2, 6	65
Fair Maidens all attend the Muse	224	Prog of Love	73
Attend the progress of his herse.	296	Satiric Elegy	20
Thee to attend where-e'er thou go'st.	324	Pethox	38
As Jove will not attend on less,	475	Epist on Epist	1
The Vice-Roy, whom you now attend,	483	Libel on D- D-	113
"Madam, your Husband will attend	562	Death of Swift	233
To discourse, and to attend,	633	Epistle Lady	121
Proud to attend you at the Steerage.	656	On Poetry	456
Attend ye Popes, and Youngs, and Gays,	656	On Poetry	467
Tho' Foes to Love, attend the Session,	689	Cadenus Vaness	94
Whate'er Vexations Love attend,	702	Cadenus Vaness	506
He flies from his God, to attend on his Grace:	809	Epigr Prelate	4
That must attend the marry'd state;	879	Robbin & Harry	40
Attend him daily as their Chief,	883	Rev Market-Hill	23
ATTENDANCE			
And dance Attendance on the Great,	492	Panegyr Swift	2
Command his attendance while you act your farce on,	818	Epigr Kite	6
ATTENDED			
Juno attended at the Porch	290	Prog Marriage	11
Attended by her heavenly Race,	466	Birthday Song	184
Attended by a Brace of Curs,	760	Receipt Youth	43
Attended by the Sable-guard,	779	Mullinix Tim	202
ATTENDING			
Attending on a Royal Dame.	119	Apollo Outwit	4
Of Duns, attending at their Gate.	239	Run Bankers	16
Attending nightly round your Bed;	597	Cassinus Peter	114
Attending each his proper Station,	650	On Poetry	313
So, long attending at the Gate,	711	Cadenus Vaness	770
From Ford attending at her Call	745	Stel Distress	19
From Ford attending at her Call,	750	Stel Wood-Park	39
ATTENDS			
While the sly Mountebank attends his Trade,	364	On Dreams	33
Twice sev'n long Years the Court attends,	481	Libel on D- D-	54
Which oft attends that luke-warm Stream;	589	Strephon Chloe	180
Attends us first, and leaves us last:	708	Cadenus Vaness	685
Yet, as it oft attends the Great,	917	Riddle 3	5
ATTENTION			
And, with attention, read Tom Thumb;	900	Dean's Reasons	56
ATTEST			
If this be Truth, as you attest,	391	Young's Satire	11
Had Witness ready to attest,	688	Cadenus Vaness	68
ATTINENT			
Quaedam quae attinent ad Scriblerum,	186	Scriblerus 3	3
ATTON'D			
For which no Heads have yet atton'd!	181	Horace 2, 1	28
ATTONE			
For thou hast not a Groat to Attone for a \<Rape\>.	519	Dean Hang Rape	54
ATTORNEY			
In a Chancery Bill your Attorney engages,	288	Bank Down	46
ATTORNEY'S			
Or, for the Classicks read th' Attorney's Guide;	793	St. Pat's Well	77
ATTORNIES			
Now the active young Attornies	573	Helter Skelter	1
ATTRACT			
As fairest Fruits attract the Flyes.	501	Doctor Delaney	42
Attract the curious Trav'llers Eyes,	893	Panegyr Dean	202
ATTRIBUTE			
To Dunkin you attribute what I writ,	669	Epig Carthy 17	D 1
ATTRIBUTES			
First of God's darling attributes,	34	Ode Sancroft	5
AUDIENCE			
O! Cou'd I see this Audience Clad in Stuff,	275	Epilogue	31
Observe, the Audience is in Pain,	776	Mullinix Tim	93
AUDITORY			
There creeps two Auditory Nerves,	367	Answer Delaney	34
AUDOIN			
One shews how bravely Audoin Dy'd,	781	Mullinix Tim	273
AUGMENTATION			
Some augmentation Sr You know	422	Ireld	35
AUGRE-HOLE			
Bor'd a large Augre-hole in the Image's Breech;	336	Serious Poem	72
AUGURY			
She knew, by Augury Divine,	695	Cadenus Vaness	276
AUGUST			
Is sent to desire that, when your August vacation comes,	1022	Nim-Dan-Dean 2	D 2
AUGUSTA			
Spread thro' Augusta Trinobantum)	649	On Poetry	280
AUGUSTUS			
Perhaps you say Augustus shines	658	On Poetry	D 410

	PAGE	TITLE	LINE
AUKWARD			
Pickt the Demure, the Aukward, and the Coy;	118	Biddy Floyd	6
Through Modesty, or aukward Shame, ...	607	Beasts Confess	181
To Scandal next-----What aukward Thing	699	Cadenus Vaness	384
Nor quarrell'd at their aukward Bow.	701	Cadenus Vaness	461
AUKWARDNESS			
"Scoffing my College Aukwardness.	380	Apology Lady C	148
AUNT			
Were fair Ardelia not my Aunt, ...	123	Empty'ng Town	19
AUNT'S			
Her Aunt's my Gossip by my Father's Side:	882	Pastoral Dial	42
AUNTS			
While Mothers, Daughters, Aunts, ...	426	Five Ladies	30
AURA			
Aura, whose Tongue you hear a Mile hence, ...	450	Modern Lady	170
AURELIA'S			
Gilding my Aurelia's Brows, ...	661	Love Song	22
AURELIAN'S			
Carthy, no more insult Aurelian's Name, ...	668	Epig Carthy 10 D	1
AURORA			
Thus Ca'ndish, as Aurora bright, ...	179	To Lord Harley	77
Aurora usher'd in the Day, ...	270	Apollo's Edict D	21
Aurora with thy early Flute.	594	Cassinus Peter	34
So blush'd Aurora with coelestial Charms, ...	669	Epig Carthy 13 D	1
AURORA'S			
Then rising with Aurora's Light, ...	643	On Poetry	85
AUTH'RESS			
Turns Auth'ress, and is Curll's for Life.	150	Corinna	28
AUTHENTICK			
Th' Authentick mark of the Elect, ...	18	Ode Athenian	92
Then talk with more authentick Face, ...	648	On Poetry	243
AUTHOR			
First then, our Author has defin'd	83	Salamander	29
An Author thus who pants for Fame	500	Doctor Delaney	11
If such an Author were alive, ...	709	Cadenus Vaness	700
The Book, the Author, and the Friend.	709	Cadenus Vaness	705
The Nation scar'd, the Author doom'd to Death, . . .	771	Horace 1, 14	31
Every Greek and Roman Author.	838	Legion Club	214
(An Author, where I sometimes dip a Days)	988	Letter Dr Sh-n	18
A Friend of mine, that Author despises	988	Letter Dr Sh-n	21
AUTHOR'S			
"I must conceal my Author's Name, ...	449	Modern Lady	148
"The Rev'rend Author's good Intention, ...	564	Death of Swift	289
Our Author's Meaning, I presume, is	608	Beasts Confess	215
Pil'd in a Garret charm'd the Author's Sight. . . .	667	Epig Carthy 5 D	2
AUTHORITIES			
Authorities both old and recent	591	Strephon Chloe	251
AUTHORITY			
By his authority tis plain, ...	620	Scandal Poem 1	85
By his Authority, 'tis plain	626	Scandal Poem 2	83
Still their Authority was smaller.	690	Cadenus Vaness	115
AUTHORS			
No wonder, since wise Authors shew, ...	87	Hist V's House	39
As Authors of the Legend write	90	Bauc & Phil 1	6
As Authors of the Legend write;	111	Bauc & Phil 2	6
But Classick Authors--he ne'er miss'd 'em.	115	Bauc & Phil 2	136
Cheapning old Authors on a Stall.	170	Horace 1, 7	6
Some Authors say not quite so soon, ...	446	Modern Lady	39
By learned authors call'd Nubigenae.	619	Scandal Poem 1	62
By learned Authors call'd, Nubigenae.	625	Scandal Poem 2	58
(Those Authors he so oft had nam'd	708	Cadenus Vaness	690
AUTUMN			
Life's Autumn has no second Spring.	932	Riddle 19 D	24
AVAIL			
But, little could their Strength avail, ...	501	Doctor Delaney	33
'Twill not avail, when thy strong Sides are broke, . .	771	Horace 1, 14	37
To say he's mad will not avail:	797	Traulus 1	38
But all his Gold could not avail	821	Dr. Rundle	45
AVAILS			
Yet, what avails it to complain:	504	Doctor Delaney	135
AVARICE			
Led blindly on by avarice and pride, ...	39	Ode Sancroft	163
Pale Avarice and lurking Fraud	243	Horace 4, 9	11
Is he to Avarice inclin'd?	464	Birthday Song	123
"Meer Envy, Avarice, and Pride!	558	Death of Swift	159
Ambition, Avarice, and Lust, ...	725	To Stella	45
Is the same avarice of mind:	900	Dean's Reasons	38
AVAUNT			
Avaunt--ye cannot say 'twas I.	596	Cassinus Peter	88
AVE			
Without one Ave Mary.	245	Irish-Feast	36
AVERNUS			
Not the Stench of Lake Avernus, ...	834	Legion Club	125
AVERR'D			
Are Christians alike; and it may be averr'd, . . .	816	Yahoo's	28
AVERSION			
That, Standing Troops were his Aversion:	606	Beasts Confess	152
AVERSIONS			
The same Aversions, and Desires;	546	Life of Swift	44
AVERT			
T' avert th' impending judgments of my pen.	45	To Congreve	48

```
AVIGNION                                                        PAGE    TITLE            LINE
     Was then embarking at Avignion.    . . . . . . . .          774  Mullinix Tim        24
AVOID
     In haste she does th' offensive herd avoid. . . . . .        50  To Congreve        226
     (Take Notice, to avoid Offence      . . . . . . . .         486  Libel on D- D-     183
     And, to avoid all future ill,   . . . . . . .              489  Dialogue            11
     He scours away; and to avoid the Foe,   . . . . . .         538  Mr. Pulteney        23
     To avoid the publick Hatred;    . . . . . . . .            637  Epistle Lady       224
     That Stella may avoid Disgrace   . . . . . . . .           757  Stel B-day '24      13
     Avoid the Rocks on Britain's angry Shore:   . . . . .       772  Horace 1, 14        62
     However, to avoid Disgrace,   . . . . . . . .             917  Riddle 4             3
AW'D
     Stand in your sacred Presence aw'd;    . . . . . . .        243  Horace 4, 9         12
AWAKE
     When first he finds himself awake  . . . . . . .           241  Run Bankers         54
     As if he was awake, nods o'er his Text:   . . . . . .       364  On Dreams           32
     Am I awake, or do I dream?   . . . . . . . .              376  Apology Lady C      45
     Never speaking, still awake,   . . . . . . . .            933  Riddle 20        D   1
AWARE
     . . .before I was aware, out I blunder'd,   . . . . .        72  Mrs Harris Pet      52
     The gentle Pilgrims soon aware on't,   . . . . . .         112  Bauc & Phil 2       41
AWAY
     Before this Milk-white Heifer can be stole away,   . .        8  Ode to King         77
     But plumes her Silver Wings and flies away,   . . . .       16  Ode Athenian        17
     A Stealing Brook, and strove to creep away   . . . .        22  Ode Athenian       192
     Yet at the last the Box sweeps all away.   . . . . .        29  Ode to Temple       80
     Away the frighted Peasants fly,   . . . . . . .            30  Ode to Temple      109
     And murmurs as she glides away.   . . . . . . . .          31  Ode to Temple      158
     Or melts by the first show'r away.   . . . . . . .         39  Ode Sancroft       142
     However, she stole away my Garters,. . . . . . .           70  Mrs Harris Pet      19
     I e'en left her, and came away as wise as I was before.     71  Mrs Harris Pet      47
     Now you may go hang your self for me, and so went away.     72  Mrs Harris Pet      63
     Throws all his Witt and Hours away   . . . . . . .         80  Vanbrug House       43
     And call'd to take the Cards away.   . . . . . . .         86  Hist V's House       2
     But made his Leg and went away.   . . . . . . . .         121  Apollo Outwit       44
     They washt away the Chymick Power.   . . . . . . .        158  Fable of Midas      72
     Away upon his Errand goes,   . . . . . . . .             171  Horace 1, 7         24
     I hurry me in haste away,    . . . . . . . .             200  Horace 2, 6         25
     I'd send her far enough away--   . . . . . . . .          220  A Quiet Life        33
     When Daughters run away with Fellows)   . . . . . .        223  Prog of Love        48
     Away they rode in homely Sort   . . . . . . . .           224  Prog of Love        75
     But Chints, Brocades, and Lace take all away,   . . .       275  Epilogue            33
     Steals off to dose away his Beef,   . . . . . . .          279  Journal             40
     She stole away with much ado,   . . . . . . . .           292  Prog Marriage       94
     Away he trudges into Town;   . . . . . . . .             376  Apology Lady C      28
     Away he runs with zealous hotness   . . . . . . .         423  Ireld               65
     Away the God of Silence flew,   . . . . . . . .           448  Modern Lady        121
     "Twas you that threw the Game away;   . . . . . . .        452  Modern Lady        249
     Disgusted Strephon stole away   . . . . . . . .           529  Lady's Dres Rm     116
     Away they fled, and left him as they found him. . . . .     536  To Mr. Gay         160
     He scours away; and to avoid the Foe,   . . . . . .         538  Mr. Pulteney        23
     Away the Hare with double Swiftness fled.   . . . . .       538  Mr. Pulteney        28
     I'd have him throw away his Pen;   . . . . . . .           556  Death of Swift     103
     Draw their Swords and run away:   . . . . . . . .         574  Helter Skelter      48
     When Chloe stole your Heart away,   . . . . . . .         591  Strephon Chloe     236
     And Youth so swiftly glides away;   . . . . . . .         593  Strephon Chloe     304
     Except to pass an Hour away.   . . . . . . . .           607  Beasts Confess     188
     You need not throw your Pen away.   . . . . . . .         646  On Poetry          182
     Drawn by her Doves, away she flies,   . . . . . . .        692  Cadenus Vaness     186
     Away the fair Detractors went,   . . . . . . . .         699  Cadenus Vaness     408
     So the Wit that is lavishly thrown away here,   . . . .     716  Answer Rebus        17
     Away she will go   . . . . . . . .                      756  Dingley Brent       17
     The new-born Flesh will melt away;   . . . . . . .        760  Receipt Youth       52
     Away you see the Varlet scud,   . . . . . . . .          824  Printer Newgat       9
     In a Fright she crept away,   . . . . . . . .            834  Legion Club        131
     Away the frighted Spectre scuds,   . . . . . . .         905  Death Daphne        99
     That she throws away as foul;   . . . . . . . .          907  Daphne              47
     Nay give their very Souls away.   . . . . . . . .        930  Riddle 15        D  28
     For Time with Beauty flies away,   . . . . . . .         932  Riddle 19        D  21
     Our Boys run away,   . . . . . . . .                   1036  Plague Country       8
     Friend Pope overturnd by driving too fast away,   . . .    1037  Four Storyes         3
     And Robin at Sea had like to be cast away.   . . . .      1037  Four Storyes         4
AWE
     "Have kept Domestick Mice in awe,   . . . . . . .         154  Widow and Cat    D  24
     "The Awe of your Majestick Air?   . . . . . . . .        380  Apology Lady C     160
     "But never stood in Awe before 'em:   . . . . . . .       566  Death of Swift     340
     Stand in Awe without a Rod:   . . . . . . . .            633  Epistle Lady       104
     Was struck with Love, Esteem, and Awe,   . . . . .        708  Cadenus Vaness     692
     For the Captain, I warrant, will keep him in Awe;   . .     868  Grand Question      34
     Such reverential Awe express,   . . . . . . . .          889  Panegyr Dean        79
AWFUL
     Behold the awful Bench on which he sat,   . . . . .        285  Elegy Boat          19
     The Angels of your awful Nods,   . . . . . . . .         499  Panegyr Swift      181
AWFULLY
     But, awfully his Distance kept.   . . . . . . . .        587  Strephon Chloe     114
AWHILE    SEE A-WHILE
     For though with Loss or Victory awhile   . . . . . .       29  Ode to Temple       78
     That he might take his Rest awhile   . . . . . .          160  Atlas               12
AWKWARD    SEE AUKWARD
     Mean time a Pair of awkward Things   . . . . . . .         80  Vanbrug House       35
     A shambling awkward Gate he took,   . . . . . . .         95  Bauc & Phil 1      171
```

```
AWKWARD        (CONTINUED)                              PAGE   TITLE           LINE
    Are awkward when you try to flatter.  . . . . . . .  642 On Poetry          52
    Can personate an awkward Scorn  . . . . . . . . .    652 On Poetry         353
    Which when the Brute puts awkward on,  . . . . . .   885 Rev Market-Hill    79
    I hope to quit that awkward Shame . . . . . . . .    887 Panegyr Dean       17
AWKWARDLY
    Lord! said I, who's that parson? how awkwardly dangles he
                                                         978 Dean to Tho: S      2
AWL
    Turns to an Awl by Heav'nly Art;  . . . . . . .      100 Elegy Patrige      82
AXEL
    Were Silver, and the Axel Gold.  . . . . . . . .     598 Problem Solved     16
AY
    Ay, thought the God, are these your Tricks?  . . .   108 V's House          71
    Ay, this has some Savour:  . . . . . . . . . .       245 Irish-Feast        28
    "Ay,ay," quoth the Dean, "the cause is old gold."  . .  843 Ay and No        4
    "Ay,ay," quoth the Dean, "the cause is old gold."  . .  843 Ay and No        4
AY'S
    Dick with zealous No's and Ay's,  . . . . . . . .    785 Mullinex Dick      37
AYD
    He spake, and grudging, lent his Ayd;  . . . . . .   108 V's House          75
AYRS
    The Beau in all his Ayrs exprest.  . . . . . . .     782 Tim and Fables     12
AYSLABY
    <Walpole> and Ayslaby, to clear the Doubt,  . . .    195 Author Himself     41
AZURE
    On the smooth Ocean's azure Bed  . . . . . . . .     251 Bubble             27
    Vouchsafe to be an azure Knight,  . . . . . . . .    656 On Poetry         462
B
    Nor knew in law his A, B, C.  . . . . . . . . .      436 Answer Paulus     122
    For he could reach to B. in alt:  . . . . . . . .    598 Problem Solved     28
B'S
    An A's and B's your Malice vent,  . . . . . . .      645 On Poetry         159
B'Y'
    I pay my Club, and so God b'y'--.  . . . . . . .     954 Authors Living     10
BA-BA-BA-BANK
    And now he runs mad for a ba-ba-ba-Bank.  . . . .    287 Bank Down          20
BAAL
    Whilst you're, like Baal, fast asleep.  . . . . .    403 Window Inns 10  D  10
BABBY
    Or thrashing Babby in her new Stays.  . . . . . .    788 Dick's Variety     30
BABEL
    Confounded in that Babel of the pit;  . . . . . .     47 To Congreve       122
    Build Babel with their Tongues confounded.  . . . .  108 V's House          66
    "And make the Government a Babel:  . . . . . .       568 Death of Swift    384
    In the State to build a Babel:  . . . . . . . .      800 Traulus 2          37
    Like the Labourers of Babel.  . . . . . . . .        933 Riddle 20       D   8
BABES
    I dipp'd two babes in holy-water,  . . . . . . .     675 Curate's Compl      7
    Talk of their Milk for Babes of Grace;  . . . . .    892 Panegyr Dean      170
BABOON
    To expose the brisk Baboon?  . . . . . . . . .       634 Epistle Lady      154
    You'd swear it must be the Baboon of <Kilkenny>:  . . 803 Irish Bishops     10
BABOONS
    Hogs, Asses, Wolves, Baboons, & Goats  . . . . .     659 On Poetry       D 410
BABY
    A Baby Face, no Life, no Airs,  . . . . . . . .      699 Cadenus Vaness    414
BABY-DRESS
    But serve t' adorn the Baby-dress . . . . . . .        6 Ode to King        14
BABYES
    Besides a pair of princely Babyes,  . . . . . . .    465 Birthday Song     171
BACCHUS
    Like Bacchus Thou, as Poets feign,  . . . . . .      109 V's House         119
    Had Bacchus after Daphne reel'd,  . . . . . . .      177 To Lord Harley     13
    Presume to borrow Wit from Bacchus?  . . . . . .     671 Epig Carthy 22  D   2
    And Bacchus for the Poet's Use  . . . . . . . .      743 Stel B-day 22      65
BACK
    Flew dutifully back again,  . . . . . . . .           16 Ode Athenian       30
    Nor e'er call back again)  . . . . . . . . .          25 Ode Athenian      290
    Oft she looks back in vain,  . . . . . . . .          31 Ode to Temple     154
    Comes back with joy to its own seat at night;  . .    51 Temple Ill          6
    Grew to his Back instead of Wings;  . . . . . .       80 Vanbrug House      36
    Crawls back neglected to his Den.  . . . . . . .      84 Salamander         36
    'Twas never known to turn its back . . . . . . .      94 Bauc & Phil 1     136
    Here Five Foot deep lyes on his Back  . . . . .      101 Elegy Patrige     103
    He bore the Skyes upon his Back  . . . . . . .       160 Atlas               3
    With trembling Knees, and Terror at his Back;  . .   210 Earl of Oxford      4
    And bring her back, alive or dead.  . . . . . .      223 Prog of Love       38
    While George, and Dean, go back to Gammon.  . . .    280 Journal            42
    "But he'll come back the Knave he went."  . . . .    306 Storm              72
    . . . 'twould quickly break my Back.  . . . . .      343 Upon His Grace     46
    And promis'd to pay for it when he'd come back.  . .  399 Tom Clinch          4
    As strong upon your back  . . . . . . . . . .        428 Beau's Reply        3
    Will back be sent  . . . . . . . . . . . .           440 Ballyspellin       16
    'The Cook must keep it back a while;  . . . . .      447 Modern Lady        95
    Fail'd but an Inch to seize him by the Back.  . . .  538 Mr. Pulteney       34
    "The Nation stript go joyful back,  . . . . . .      571 Death of Swift    447
    But, Chloe drove him fiercely back.  . . . . . .     588 Strephon Chloe    150
    With Int'rest pays him back his own.  . . . . .      590 Strephon Chloe    214
    And grown so bold behind his Back  . . . . . . .     605 Beasts Confess    127
    And so take all upon your back.  . . . . . . . .     753 Gift for Bec       26
```

		PAGE	TITLE	LINE
BACK	(CONTINUED)			
Come back before you're out of Case;		760	Receipt Youth	50
Looks back with Joy where she has gone, ...		765	Stel B-day '26	75
Can <Fart> his Navy back again.		774	Mullinix Tim	32
Then sudden draws it back again, ...		776	Mullinix Tim	105
With powder'd Rump, and Back and Side, ...		785	Dick, Maggot	7
Fled to the Fountain back, from whence it came! . . .		793	St. Pat's Well	66
Can set the Mastiffs on your Back.		798	Traulus 1	68
A Rod should turn them back to Dust.		813	Bro Protestant	56
All in Arms prepare to meet us:		838	Legion Club	212
Strain their Necks with looking back:		863	To Janus	22
The <Dean>, to guard his Honour's Back, ...		883	Rev Market-Hill	13
Her valiant Arm should force us back, ...		885	Rev Market-Hill	60
Behind my Back, before my Nose, ...		887	Panegyr Dean	27
. . .I came back to sit with the Ladies this Night. .		1013	Swift to Sheri	3
. . .and come back from the Deanry, . . .		1013	Swift to Sheri	4
Come back t'us well freighted;		1014	Swift to Sheri	25
If you do not come back we shall weep out our eyn . .		1018	Swift Ans Sher	28
. . .and you shall go back in a fortnight, . . .		1023	Nim-Dan-Dean 2	D 8
BACK-DOOR				
Steal by the Back-door out, and leave him there; . . .		166	Toland's Invit	45
BACK-SIDE				
This Petticoat shall save thy dear Back-side; .		881	Pastoral Dial	22
BACK-WAY				
To try the Back-way to his Heart;		66	Problem	42
BACKS				
Than those with backs of silk and golden wings; .		46	To Congreve	92
Tormenting Fools behind their Backs;		240	Run Bankers	30
And lent them for Money the Backs of his Letters: .		288	Bank Down	43
Now Backs of Letters, though design'd		406	Swift to Pope	9
Her Milk-white Hands, both Palms and Backs, .		584	Strephon Chloe	25
And half the Chairs with broken backs.		746	Stel Distress	38
And half the Chairs with broken Backs:		751	Stel Wood-Park	56
And Sons of Whores--behind their Backs.		778	Mullinix Tim	164
To Hell on the Backs of the Clergy wou'd ride; . . .		804	Irish Bishops	18
BACKWARD				
May backward be perus'd, like Hebrew.		1021	Nim-Dan-Dean 1	D 42
BACKWARDS				
Is backwards and forwards always the same;		148	Windsor Proph	22
Which backwards and forwards is allmost the same. . . .		148	Windsor Proph	24
BACON				
A Flitch of Bacon off the Hook, ...		91	Bauc & Phil 1	58
A Flitch of Bacon off the Hook, ...		112	Bauc & Phil 2	26
May bring in Jeopardy thy Bacon, ...		181	Horace 2, 1	30
Always for saving their own bacon:		434	Answer Paulus	65
And make him crouch to save his bacon.		468	Birthday Song	250
If you had not took physick, I'd pay off your bacon, .		980	Tho: Sheridan	5
BACON-SLICE				
A Bacon-slice gives God Offence?		949	Epigr Fasting	2
BACON'S				
Dull Bacon's Essays, ...		855	Lady's Lament	148
BAD				
And the bad world may well believe the same;		49	To Congreve	198
Now you must know, because my Trunk has a very bad Lock,		69	Mrs Harris Pet	5
Their Vittells bad, their Lodging worse, ...		224	Prog of Love	79
To cut down fine Wood is a very bad Thing, ...		334	Serious Poem	13
To turn a Good Penny to Twenty Bad Ha'pence. . . .		335	Serious Poem	48
As bad as Suffolk cheese.		429	Beau's Reply	16
That's not so bad as one that rubs		452	Modern Lady	258
Nor, from your Lord his bad Condition hide;		534	To Mr. Gay	93
"If he makes Mankind bad as Elves, ...		548	Life of Swift	115
"It is not yet so bad with us."		557	Death of Swift	116
He sets the Stamp of Bad and Good, ...		649	On Poetry	273
From bad to worse, and worse they fall, ...		653	On Poetry	387
A mingled Mass of Good & Bad, ...		659	On Poetry	D 410
So Witches bent on bad Pursuits, ...		670	Epig Carthy 19	D 1
I own, Appearances are bad;		796	Traulus 1	21
By my soul there's bad news, for the gold she was pulled down,		840	Ballad	D 2
"<God> <damn> me, he hobbles as bad as my Groom; . . .		872	Grand Question	156
When too long, is bad at best.		940	Letter	9
I Cannot but think that we live in a bad age, ...		975	Dean to Sherid	1
For ought he knows, as bad as Thespis's.		988	Death Dr Sh-n	23
Though his Claret is bad, and he foots it on Stones, .		1037	Four Storyes	7
BADE				
Bade Goody Baucis mend the Fire		91	Bauc & Phil 1	56
BADGE				
This Badge of Honour in his Hair, ...		458	Paddy's Charac	20
BADGER				
Tho' she lives 'till she's Grey as a Badger all over. .		266	Apollo	108
BAFLING				
Who by that, vainly talks of bafling Death, ...		21	Ode Athenian	182
BAG				
Half sunk beneath his brief and bag, ...		434	Answer Paulus	75
Sent in a bag to Doctor Swift, ...		753	Gift for Bec	3
BAGNIO				
To <Dublin> he comes, to the Bagnio he goes, . . .		517	Dean Hang Rape	19
BAGPIPE				
As Bagpipe shrill, or Oyster-Strumpet, ...		182	Horace 2, 1	72
BAGS SEE MONEY-BAGS				
Thus Bankers o'er their Bills and Bags		240	Run Bankers	31

		PAGE	TITLE	LINE
BAGS	(CONTINUED)			
'Till Pow'r, discharging all her stormy Bags, . . .		771	Horace 1, 14	29
BAIL				
To cheat the World, become each other's Bail. . . .		668	Epig Carthy 8	D 4
Come and appear, and save their Bail.		713	Cadenus Vaness	841
In Spight to Justice, and refuse his Bail. . . .		826	Noisy Tom	20
BAILIFFS				
The watchful Bailiffs take their silent Stands, . . .		125	Descriptn Morn	17
He hated Bailiffs at his shoulder. . . .		455	Dean Smedley	10
BAILY				
His Baily Driving all my Cows into the Parish Pound.		343	Upon His Grace	4
Our Thatcher, Ditcher, Gard'ner, Baily.		891	Panegyr Dean	156
BAIT				
He caught his Fish, and sav'd his Bait. . . .		134	Magician's Rod	48
In short, the Gudgeon took the Bait:		173	Horace 1, 7	80
What has he else to bait his Traps, ...		484	Libel on D- D-	129
Meet when Butchers bait a Bear;		829	Legion Club	14
BAITED				
A baited Banker thus desponds, ...		241	Run Bankers	49
Like a Bear to be baited:		1014	Swift to Sheri	20
BAJAZET				
He trampled on this Haughty Bajazet, ...		7	Ode to King	42
BAKE				
To bake one Loaf, and keep one Dove in.		127	Little House	38
BALANCE				
In his own balance, false and light, ...		36	Ode Sancroft	55
With equal balance in her hand, ...		433	Answer Paulus	32
BALCONIES				
The Maids to the Doors and the Balconies ran, . . .		399	Tom Clinch	7
BALDNESS				
Spreads Leprosy and Baldness round.		84	Salamander	56
BALDWIN				
Dear Baldwin chaste, and witty Crosse, ...		821	Dr. Rundle	61
I'll chew you to Bullets, and puff you at Baldwin. . .		1019	To Sheridan	10
BALL SEE SNOW-BALL,TENNIS-BALL				
What do the Scepter, Crown and Ball, ...		6	Ode to King	12
And meets her hasting to the Ball, ...		292	Prog Marriage	85
As round as a Ball, without Head without Tail, . . .		350	Wood Insect	5
This ball of wax your ears will darken, ...		753	Gift for Bec	21
So, at a Ball, unthinking Fools delight		771	Horace 1, 14	49
A Ball of new-dropt Horse's Dung, ...		811	Bro Protestant	11
How oft a Week was kept a Ball		905	Death Daphne	83
BALLAD				
In making a Ballad, but was at a Stand, ...		77	Lady B- B-	23
He'll put you in a Ballad:		425	Five Ladies	12
BALLADS				
The Ballads pasted round the Wall, ...		93	Bauc & Phil 1	117
The Ballads pasted on the Wall, ...		114	Bauc & Phil 2	93
BALLANC'D				
His Merits ballanc'd you shall find, ...		654	On Poetry	395
BALLANCE				
In the same Ballance with our Tears, ...		24	Ode Athenian	257
Weigh'd in the Ballance, and found Light.		241	Run Bankers	64
BALLAST				
His Lading little, and his Ballast less.		284	Elegy Boat	4
BALLENTINE				
Are by Robert Ballentine lately brought over; . . .		236	Excellent Song	2
BALLS				
Two Balls of Glass may serve for Eyes, ...		229	Prog of Beauty	113
Balls, and Masquerades, and Shows, ...		631	Epistle Lady	41
For Visits, Ombre, Balls and Plays.)		700	Cadenus Vaness	431
BALLYSPELLIN				
You give to Ballyspellin.		440	Ballyspellin	6
When drank at Ballyspellin		440	Ballyspellin	12
From nasty Ballyspellin		440	Ballyspellin	18
To bring in Ballyspellin.		441	Ballyspellin	24
You met at Ballyspellin?		441	Ballyspellin	30
Than yours at Ballyspellin		441	Ballyspellin	36
At paltry Ballyspellin		441	Ballyspellin	42
Is found at Ballyspellin		441	Ballyspellin	48
Round all your Ballyspellin?		442	Ballyspellin	60
The Belles of Ballyspellin		442	Ballyspellin	66
Who lives at Ballyspellin		442	Ballyspellin	72
That leaks at Ballyspellin.		442	Ballyspellin	78
At dirty Ballyspellin		442	Ballyspellin	84
To force in Ballyspellin		443	Ballyspellin	90
BALLYSPELLING				
At lowsy Ballyspelling.		442	Ballyspellin	54
BAND				
Th' amphibious Tyrant, with his rav'nous Band, . .		793	St. Pat's Well	63
Both dress'd like divines, with band and face clean. .		843	Ay and No	2
"In mending your Cassock, and smoothing your Band: . .		872	Grand Question	150
So fine a Gown, a Band so clean, ...		889	Panegyr Dean	77
BANDS				
In the close bands of pleasing hymen.		675	Curate's Compl	6
With Bands of Fidlers to extend his Treyn. . . .		678	Dean and Duke	8
Shall scale the Rampart with your Bands.		884	Rev Market-Hill	54
BANDY				
Your bandy Leg, or crooked Nose.		416	Woman's Mind	22
BANE				
Malignant goddess! bane to my repose, ...		53	Temple Ill	81

BANE   (CONTINUED)

	PAGE	TITLE	LINE
"On Rural Squires, that Kingdom's Bane, ...	571	Death of Swift	443
BANGING			
Instead of your maiming, your shooting, or banging, . .	818	Epigr Kite	7
BANGOR			
You reply and rejoin like Hoadly of Bangor.	967	Letter Sherid	8
BANISH			
To banish Rats that haunt our Vault.	892	Panegyr Dean	162
BANISH'D			
Be ever banish'd from your Isle.	270	Apollo's Edict	D 15
Whence Gay was banish'd in Disgrace, ...	650	On Poetry	307
BANISH'T			
By Faction banish't here unite, ...	883	Rev Market-Hill	7
BANISHMENT			
I'm griev'd to hear your Banishment, ...	1002	Reply by Dean	14
BANISHT			
Till banisht by some Coxcombs Raillery;	294	Prog Marriage	142
Pray, what is this Bank of which the Town Rings? . .	287	Bank Down	1
To shut out the River by raising the Bank. . .	287	Bank Down	5
And Thanks to the Members that Kickt down the Bank. .	287	Bank Down	10
This Bank is to make us a New Paper Mill, ...	287	Bank Down	11
If nothing but Paper comes out of this Bank. . .	287	Bank Down	15
All riding on Horseback to Hell and the Bank. . .	287	Bank Down	25
With the Scrap of a Sole, and a Fig for the Bank. .	287	Bank Down	30
To turn to small Money a Bill on the Bank. . . .	288	Bank Down	35
With a Scrap of Bank Paper the Breadth of his Nail; .	288	Bank Down	38
And made him to Curse the poor innocent Bank. . .	288	Bank Down	40
When it heard of a Bank appear'd to his Debtors, . .	288	Bank Down	42
For old Nick gave the Papers the Mark of the Bank. .	288	Bank Down	45
By which they might Swimmingly land on a Bank. . .	288	Bank Down	50
For those are but Quacks, who mount on a Bank. . .	288	Bank Down	55
The Bank where last he set his Toe, ...	456	Dean Smedley	42
BANK SEE BA-BA-BA-BANK			
BANKER			
Alas the Sexton is thy Banker now!	235	Elegy on Demar	38
A dismal Banker must that Banker be, ...	235	Elegy on Demar	39
A dismal Banker must that Banker be, ...	235	Elegy on Demar	39
A baited Banker thus desponds, ...	241	Run Bankers	49
BANKER'S			
The Banker's ruin'd if he pays;	239	Run Bankers	18
So Pow'rful are a Banker's Bills	240	Run Bankers	37
BANKERS			
Breaking the Bankers and the Banks, ...	239	Run Bankers	7
Thus Bankers o'er their Bills and Bags	240	Run Bankers	31
Few Bankers will to Heav'n be Mounters:	241	Run Bankers	58
BANKRUPT			
Thus the deluded Bankrupt raves, ...	251	Bubble	21
BANKRUPTS			
Nor with Bankrupts fill Gazetts, ...	169	Peace Dunkirk	29
If Bankrupts, when they are undone, ...	392	Young's Satire	41
BANKS			
She, who on shady banks has joy'd to sleep	50	To Congreve	221
Breaking the Bankers and the Banks, ...	239	Run Bankers	7
The Banks of a River I know are good Things, . . .	287	Bank Down	2
But a Pox o' those Banks that choak up the Springs. .	287	Bank Down	3
"Fair Isis, and ye Banks of Cam, ...	462	Birthday Song	77
Adorn our chrystal River's Banks:	896	Panegyr Dean	302
How pleasant on the Banks of Styx, ...	905	Death Daphne	87
BANNERS			
But before you can put yourself under her banners, . .	979	Dean to Tho: S	27
BANQUET			
From ev'ry day a Lordly Banquet	745	Stel Distress	11
From ev'ry Day a lordly Banquet, ...	750	Stel Wood-Park	35
BANT'RING			
With labourers bant'ring, ...	856	Lady's Lament	160
BANTER			
You banter me, Madam, the Kingdom must grant-- . .	871	Grand Question	125
BAR SEE TEMPLE-BAR			
Then, from the bar, harangues the bench	434	Answer Paulus	77
Imagine <Lyndsay> at the bar:	435	Answer Paulus	107
No Pleader at the Bar could match	604	Beasts Confess	89
A Pick-purse at the Bar, or Bench;	645	On Poetry	165
Thus at the Bar that Booby Bettesworth, ...	812	Bro Protestant	25
More like to lampooning than pleading at bar. . . .	815	Yahoo's	14
BARBARIANS			
With Thieves, Fanatics, and Barbarians?	899	Dean's Reasons	18
BARBAROUS			
Descendents of the barbarous Huns, ...	326	Pethox	75
BARBAROUSLY			
Who barbarously think to 'scape reproach, ...	44	To Congreve	21
BARBER			
From the Barber and the Cutler, ...	574	Helter Skelter	33
And set the House to <Rupert> <Barber>.	477	Epist on Epist	70
BARBER'S			
I know she loves the Barber's Boy.	595	Cassinus Peter	62
He's powd'ring in a Barber's Shop;	788	Dick's Variety	32
BARD SEE CITY-BARD			
Now Birth-day Bard, with joy proceed	465	Birthday Song	151
That you, a low Hibernian Bard, ...	475	Epist on Epist	4
In some old Greek or Latian Bard, ...	479	Epist on Epist	120
Presumptuous Bard! How cou'd you dare	623	Scandal Poem 2	1
Poor starv'ling Bard, how small thy Gains! . . .	642	On Poetry	59

BARD   (CONTINUED)   PAGE   TITLE   LINE
     Complain, as many an ancient Bard did, ...   652 On Poetry   349
     Concannen, more aspiring Bard, ...   654 On Poetry   397
     Beware, O Bard, how you proceed.   . . . .   666 Epig Carthy 2   D 4
     Your Annual Bard had rather chose   . . . .   756 Stel B-day '24   5
     In what Figure can a Bard dress   . . . .   834 Legion Club   139
     Lives such a Bard on British plains?   . . . . . .   876 To Dean Swift   6
     The Bard, who humbly deigns to chuse   . . . .   887 Panegyr Dean   25
     Let the Love-sick Bard complain, ...   933 Riddle 20   D 13
BARDS
     Of that Bright God whom Bards invoke, ...   120 Apollo Outwit   14
     Two Bards that now in fashion reign, ...   393 Modern Poets   5
     A thousand Bards thy Right disown: . . . .   653 On Poetry   378
     On Lewis all his Bards bestow'd, ...   657 On Poetry   473
     Amidst a croud of hungry Bards cries out, ...   671 Epig Carthy 24   D 3
     By Scotish Bards of highest Fame, ...   848 Old Thorn   15
BARE   SEE THREAD-BARE, THREED-BARE
     Nature's bare visage furrowed as he mows: . . . . .   55 Temple Ill   124
     For neighb'ring Beaux to see it bare.   . . . . . .   222 Prog of Love   18
     His Two-Year's Coat so smooth and bare, ...   231 Prog of Poetry   35
     Bare Innocence is no Support, ...   413 Censure   5
     Scorcht were his Shins, his Legs were bare, ...   594 Cassinus Peter   17
     Bare Virtue could not live on Praise, ...   693 Death Daphne   213
     Bare, like a Carcase pick't by Crows, ...   904 Death Daphne   34
BARGAIN
     I throw into the Bargain, Jim: . . . . . .   314 To Ford   77
     And into the Bargain, I'll readily give you, ...   576 Place Damn'd   13
     And sells the King of Spain a Bargain.   . . . . .   777 Mullinix Tim   114
BARGAINS
     Of Bargains sold, or meanings double.   . . . . . .   469 Birthday Song   274
     Howe'er for selling Bargains fam'd, ...   590 Strephon Chloe   216
BARGES
     Your Vistos, Barges, and (A Pox on   . . . . . .   476 Epist on Epist   39
BARK
     Can howl, and bark, but never spoke.   . . . .   298 Horrid Plot   18
     Confess't as plain as he could bark;   . . . .   300 Horrid Plot   55
     The loud Cerberian tripple Bark.   . . . . . .   596 Cassinus Peter   80
     I can bark, or I can low, ...   933 Riddle 20   D 10
BARKING   SEE TRIPLE-BARKING
     That all the Noise they made was barking: . . . . .   299 Horrid Plot   26
     They set the very Lap-Dog barking;   . . . .   450 Modern Lady   179
     To any speech but Tyger's barking.   . . . .   762 Bec's B-Day   44
     Your barking Curs will seldom bite: . . . . . .   797 Traulus 1   46
     Than the barking of Towzer, or leap of a louse?   . . .   814 Yahoo's   9
BARKS
     He barks as fast as he can utter.   . . . .   797 Traulus 1   48
BARN
     In yonder Barn to keep us dry.   . . . .   90 Bauc & Phil 1   22
     To mend his Barn, cut Baucis down;   . . . .   117 Bauc & Phil 2   174
     "We'll to our Barn again repair."   . . . .   208 Fable Bitches   36
     O'erflow'd a Farmer's Barn and Stable, ...   811 Bro Protestant   2
     And the worst of them all like a barn door did shine . . 1017 Swift Ans Sher   6
BARN-DOOR
     Can scarce get o'er the Barn-Door Sill: . . . . .   230 Prog of Poetry   4
BAROMETRY
     A great Refinement in Barometry, ...   99 Elegy Patrige   42
BARON
     A word or two of Lord Chief Baron;   . . . .   282 Journal   98
BARONET
     Proud Baronet of Nova Scotia, ...   884 Rev Market-Hill   29
BARR'D   SEE FIVE-BARR'D
     Within our Breast be ev'ry Secret barr'd: . . . . .   210 Earl of Oxford   16
BARRACK
     "A Jayl or Barrack to repair;   . . . .   571 Death of Swift   452
     For a Barrack or Malt-House, we now must consider.   .   867 Grand Question   6
     If I make it a Barrack, the Crown is my Tenant.   .   867 Grand Question   19
     It must, and it shall be a Barrack, my Life.   .   867 Grand Question   26
     But, if you will give us a Barrack, my Dear, ...   868 Grand Question   31
     You might have a Barrack whenever you please: . . .   869 Grand Question   54
     Dear Madam, whene'er of a Barrack I think, ...   869 Grand Question   63
     I fancy already a Barrack contriv'd   . . . .   869 Grand Question   67
     Give me but a Barrack, a Fig for the Clergy.   . . .   873 Grand Question   190
BARREL
     Here from a barrel you may broach   . . . .   753 Gift for Bec   19
BARREN
     You strove to cultivate a barren Court in vain,   . . .   32 Ode to Temple   175
     Whate'er I plant (like Corn on barren Earth)   . . .   33 Ode to Temple   210
     And round the barren Common strays, ...   230 Prog of Poetry   10
     Turns all again to barren Strand.   . . . .   239 Run Bankers   4
     Let all his barren Lawrel's fade   . . . .   482 Libel on D- D-   67
     For Food, along the barren Plain;   . . . .   759 Receipt Youth   6
     Be she barren, be she old, ...   953 Oysters   13
BARRING-OUT
     Not School-boys at a Barring-out, ...   450 Modern Lady   182
BARTER
     And, Sixthly; for my Soul, to barter it   . . . . .   349 Whitshed Motto   21
BARTER'D
     Barter'd for Beauty, and for Gold;   . . . .   385 Manly Virtue   68
BASE
     Spend their base coin before the bashful maid,   . . .   50 To Congreve   219
     "Know no base action, at no guilt turn pale;   . . . .   55 Temple Ill   142

BASE   (CONTINUED)   PAGE   TITLE   LINE
    And found his Copper all was base;   . . . .   353 Wood Ironmongr   28
    I own, he hates an Action base, ...   484 Libel on D- D-   145
    oppressing true merit exalting the base   . . . . . .   540 Charac Walpole   7
    Is thought too base for human Breast;   . . . .   553 Death of Swift   6
    "Pursu'd by base envenom'd Pens, ...   568 Death of Swift   395
    He thought it base for Men in Stations, ...   606 Beasts Confess   177
    And, for her sake turn base detractor   . . . .   622 Scandal Poem 1   171
    But if you think this Trade too base, ...   647 On Poetry   233
    The Brave are worried by the Base.   . . . .   651 On Poetry   328
    Then from a Clay of Mixture base   . . . .   659 On Poetry   D   410
    Base Kings and Ministers of State, ...   725 To Stella   63
    Whatever base returns you find   . . . .   755 Stella '23   29
    Not so with thee thy base Invaders dealt; . . . .   791 St. Pat's Well   22
    As you grew more degenerate and base, ...   792 St. Pat's Well   53
    A fawning, base, trepaning Lyar, ...   798 Traulus 1   81
    Tom, for a goose you keep but base quills, ...   982 Sher, A Goose   1
    Dan's noble Mettle, Sherry base;   . . . .   1004 Dan J's Reply   31
    But I think it base in you to send a poor Fellow . . .   1014 Swift to Sheri   10
BASELY
    And selling basely by Retail, ...   19 Ode Athenian   102
BASER
    Shall they in baser Flames expire?   . . . .   732 Stella, Poems   142
BASEST
    But, I defy the basest Tongue   . . . .   602 Beasts Confess   17
BASHFUL
    Spend their base coin before the bashful maid, ...   50 To Congreve   219
    The bashful Dame, and loose'd her Tongue; . . . . .   386 Manly Virtue   86
    The bashful Muse will never bear   . . . . . .   583 Young Nymph   71
    The bashful Nymph no more withstands, ...   585 Strephon Chloe   43
    The bashful Maid, to hide her Blush, ...   893 Panegyr Dean   213
    For, while the bashful Sylvan Maid, ...   922 Riddle 7   33
    Emblem of the bashful dame, ...   936 Riddle 24   D   23
BASHFULL
    The Girl had such a Bashfull way.   . . . .   223 Prog of Love   32
BASILISK
    'Twas sure this Basilisk sent Temple thence, ...   30 Ode to Temple   124
BASIN
    Thus in a Basin drop a Shilling, ...   251 Bubble   9
    While you, from where the Basin stands, ...   884 Rev Market-Hill   53
BASIS
    Rais'd on a Basis unsecure?   . . . .   593 Strephon Chloe   300
    On Virtue's Basis fix'd to last, ...   711 Cadenus Vaness   782
BASKETS
    Whole Baskets full of Bits and Scraps, ...   208 Fable Bitches   19
BASON
    Hard by a filthy Bason stands, ...   526 Lady's Dres Rm   37
    The Bason takes whatever comes   . . . .   527 Lady's Dres Rm   39
BASON'S
    Smooth as our Bason's gentle Flood, ...   1020 Nim-Dan-Dean 1   D   5
BASTARD
    Nor Bastard of a Pedlar Scot;   . . . .   641 On Poetry   34
    A Bastard of your own begetting.   . . . .   644 On Poetry   116
BASTINGS
    What Bastings and Kicks!   . . . .   246 Irish-Feast   68
    Bastings heavy, dry, obtuse, ...   636 Epistle Lady   203
BAT
    The Bat, because her Wings are Leather, ...   99 Elegy Patrige   50
    The Owl, the Raven, and the Bat, ...   903 Death Daphne   29
BATCHELORS
    Old Batchelors about his Court: . . . . .   903 Death Daphne   12
BATE
    Nor, of your Rank will bate an Ace, ...   888 Panegyr Dean   47
BATED
    I thought an Ace you'd ne'er have bated, ...   1002 Reply by Dean   2
BATH   SEE CROSS-BATH
    A Shilling in the Bath You fling, ...   255 Bubble   113
    No other way but try the Bath: . . . .   293 Prog Marriage   106
    To bath among the Belles and Beaux.   . . . . . .   294 Prog Marriage   144
BATHING
    Or bathing in the Waters fair;   . . . .   915 Riddle 1   2
BATS
    They fly like Bats, on Parchment Wings, ...   239 Run Bankers   23
BATTEL
    The Battel almost by Great William's single Valour   8 Ode to King   64
        gain'd;
BATTER
    Which tosst up in a Pan with Batter, ...   91 Bauc & Phil 1   61
BATTER'D
    So have I seen a batter'd Beau   . . . . . .   84 Salamander   57
    So bright a batter'd, strolling Toast;   . . . . . .   581 Young Nymph   4
    This meagre Fop, that batter'd Beau: . . . . . .   905 Death Daphne   74
BATTERED
    In Phrases battered, stale, and trite, ...   448 Modern Lady   112
BATTLE
    How shall we search Thee in a battle gain'd, . . .   34 Ode Sancroft   11
    Whate'er you did in Battle slay, ...   154 Widow and Cat   D   33
    If in a Battle you should find, ...   554 Death of Swift   21
    Join in all the Din of Battle.   . . . . . .   933 Riddle 20   D   22
BATTLES
    Thou still with Battles stuff thy head full . . . .   462 Birthday Song   55

BATTLING
    His Virtues battling with his Place; . . . .   PAGE TITLE   LINE

His Virtues battling with his Place;   484 Libel on D- D- 146
BATTRING
    The Art of battring Walls, than building, ...   88 Hist V's House 46
BATTUS
    Where Battus from the Table-head, ...   649 On Poetry 264
BAUCIS
    Bade Goody Baucis mend the Fire . . . .   91 Bauc & Phil 1 56
    Quoth Baucis, this is wholsom Fare, ...   91 Bauc & Phil 1 63
    For, Baucis with Amazement found . . . .   92 Bauc & Phil 1 75
    Bid Goody Baucis mend the Fire; . . . .   111 Bauc & Phil 2 24
    Dame Baucis next, they play'd their Farce on: . .   115 Bauc & Phil 2 138
    When Baucis hastily cry'd out; . . . .   116 Bauc & Phil 2 155
    Here Baucis, there Philemon grew. . . . . . .   116 Bauc & Phil 2 172
    To mend his Barn, cut Baucis down; . . . . . .   117 Bauc & Phil 2 174
BAULK
    The most effectual Way to baulk . . . .   414 Censure 29
    Poor Tom has got a plaguy baulk---! . . . . . .   545 Life of Swift 22
BAVIUS
    Bavius in Wapping gains Renown, ...   650 On Poetry 301
BAWBLES
    Like other Bawbles of the Tow'r. . . . .   646 On Poetry 194
BAWD
    Were you drest like a bawd, and sold oysters at   979 Dean to Tho: S 10
    Billings-gate.
BAWDS
    Old carted Bawds such Garments wear, ...   787 Clad in Brown 19
BAWDY
    The Rogue's too Bawdy and too Prophane is. . . .   988 Letter Dr Sh-n 6
BAWL
    Who always loudest for Religion bawl, ...   8 Ode to King 83
    Dame, said I, as loud as I could bawl,. . . . . .   70 Mrs Harris Pet 26
    "Poets till they grow hoarse may bawl . . . . . .   321 First of April 21
    Let Lawyers bawl and strain their Throats, . . .   930 Riddle 15 D 25
BAWL'D
    The Master Bawl'd out half asleep . . . .   90 Bauc & Phil 1 27
    But bawl'd as loud as he could roar, ...   91 Bauc & Phil 1 35
    At sight of Will she bawl'd no more, ...   220 A Quiet Life 7
BAWLING
    As clever Tom Clinch, while the Rabble was bawling, .   399 Tom Clinch 1
BAWN
    This Hamilton's Bawn, while it sticks on my Hand, . .   866 Grand Question 3
    I'd rather the Bawn were sunk under Ground. . .   868 Grand Question 46
    At Hamilton's Bawn, and the Troop is arriv'd. . .   869 Grand Question 68
BAWTY
    Smooth Bawty did so far prevail; . . . .   208 Fable Bitches 16
    But Bawty, lost to Shame and Honour, ...   208 Fable Bitches 39
BAYES
    Take this short lesson from the god of bayes, . . .   49 To Congreve 203
BAYL
    Receives them while they wait for Bayl? . . . . .   504 Doctor Delaney 146
BAYLIFFS
    From Bayliffs claws thou scarce cou'd keep thy Bum free.   678 Dean and Duke 12
BAYS
    What can the Poet's humble Bays? . . . .   6 Ode to King 8
    (We Poets oft our Bays allow, ...   6 Ode to King 9
    By which our happy Prince carves out his Bays; . .   7 Ode to King 32
    About the Head crown'd with these Bays, ...   29 Ode to Temple 87
    Godlike the force of my young Congreve's bays, . .   44 To Congreve 41
    Of Wycherly, and you, and Mr. Bays; . . . . .   47 To Congreve 142
    And feeds upon imagin'd Bays . . . .   80 Vanbrug House 42
    But fenc'd his Head with his own Bays . . . . .   119 Apollo Outwit 7
    Nor will exchange His Plumbs for Bays: . . . . .   157 Fable of Midas 56
    So, Bays on Poets Brows have bin . . . .   457 Paddy's Charac 5
    And crown a Royal Dunce with Bays: . . . . . .   464 Birthday Song 120
    Foretell his Empire crown'd with Bays, ...   466 Birthday Song 195
    The Poet cannot claim his Bays; . . . .   505 Doctor Delaney 168
    He crown'd his youthful Head with Bays: . . . .   597 Problem Solved 8
    A Sprig of Bays in Fifty Years: . . . .   640 On Poetry 8
    And this, for Epicks claims the Bays, ...   650 On Poetry 295
    And tune your Harps, and strow your Bays. . . .   656 On Poetry 468
    In Nectar thrice infuses Bays, ...   691 Cadenus Vaness 156
    nor shall you twine the Crackling,Crackling Bays . .   958 Cantata
BE   793   OMITTED WORD
BE-DUK'D
    James is be-duk'd; : of course their friendshp ends .   678 Dean and Duke 2
BE'N'T
    You're in the right, but be'n't afraid . . . . .   92 Bauc & Phil 1 84
BE'ST
    But if thou be'st what thy mad vot'ries prate, . . .   54 Temple Ill 103
BE'T
    But be't as 'twill, this you must grant, ...   1003 Dan J's Reply 10
BEACH
    To leave you dry upon the Beach, ...   258 Bubble 196
BEAK
    With restless Beak thy blooming Fruit to spoil, . . .   792 St. Pat's Well 46
    And with her Beak gave many a Knock . . . . . .   849 Old Thorn 35
BEAM
    Crusts o'er the day, shadowing its parent beam . . . .   45 To Congreve 71
    Weak is the beam to dry up nature's tears, ...   51 Temple Ill 19
    Since one false beam of joy in sickly minds . . . . .   55 Temple Ill 149

BEAM	(CONTINUED)	PAGE	TITLE	LINE
A Song could draw a Stone or Beam,	. . . .	79	Vanbrug House	3
Aloft rose ev'ry Beam and Rafter,	. . . .	92	Bauc & Phil 1	93
A Verse could draw a Stone or Beam	. . . .	106	V's House	3
Aloft rose ev'ry Beam and Rafter,	. . . .	112	Bauc & Phil 2	53
Nor Chanticleer upon the Beam,	. . . .	153	Widow and Cat	D 13
Come down with that Beam,	. . . .	247	Irish-Feast	85
By intercepting ev'ry Beam;	. . . .	253	Bubble	76

BEAMING   SEE BRIGHT-BEAMING
BEAMS   SEE SUN-BEAMS

Like the sun's scatter'd beams which loosely pass,	. .	45	To Congreve	63
Darts weeping beams across heaven's wat'ry face;	. . .	52	Temple Ill	26
Shrouds her still beams; how should the stars be seen?	.	53	Temple Ill	58
If he displays, or hides his Beams;	. . . . . .	379	Apology Lady C	124
The influence of whose golden beams	. . . . . .	432	Answer Paulus	7
And darts her Beams or'e both our Isles,	. . . . .	466	Birthday Song	181
Florinda, dart their Heav'nly Beams,	. . . . . .	932	Riddle 19	D 2

BEANS

Forbidding his Disciples Beans)	. . . .	587	Strephon Chloe	126

BEAR

With heavenly peace of mind to bear	. . . .	38	Ode Sancroft	115
The Lyon, Eagle, Fox and Bear	. . . .	83	Salamander	9
And bear their Trophies with them as they go:	. . .	139	City Shower	54
Got Hercules to bear the Pile	. . . .	160	Atlas	11
I bear it for a quiet Life	. . . .	220	A Quiet Life	16
Are us'd like Dick, and bear the Blame.	. . . . . .	221	A Quiet Life	58
Nor Pegasus could bear the Load,	. . . .	231	Prog of Poetry	27
For know I cannot bear to hear,	. . . .	271	Apollo's Edict	D 48
Can You, my Friend, with Patience bear,	. . . . .	312	To Ford	36
From Realms that bear Vesputio's Name:	. . . . .	324	Pethox	24
I find you bear a good Report, and are an honest Man.	.	342	Upon His Grace	34
Be distant as one Head can bear;	. . . .	366	Answer Delaney	30
But yet, tho' seeming pleas'd, can't bear	. . . . .	379	Apology Lady C	121
"Consider what it is to bear	. . . .	380	Apology Lady C	145
"Or, if you are, be forc'd to bear	. . . .	380	Apology Lady C	159
A Loss that Dick thought, no Mortal cou'd bear.	. .	430	Dicky Dolly	6
Condemn'd to bear his client's purse;	. . . . . .	435	Answer Paulus	90
And bear the new Successor's frown;	. . . .	468	Birthday Song	259
Who for his Wine will bear his Jokes:	. . . . . .	556	Death of Swift	94
Which Pope must bear, as well as I.	. . . . . .	561	Death of Swift	204
"Six Deans they say must bear the Pall.	. . . . .	562	Death of Swift	231
The bashful Muse will never bear	. . . .	583	Young Nymph	71
Nature alone must bear the Blame;	. . . .	602	Beasts Confess	30
For our corrupted Times to bear;	. . . .	603	Beasts Confess	56
A Bear will not attempt to fly;	. . . .	640	On Poetry	14
And you must bear the whole Disgrace,	. . . . . .	644	On Poetry	141
Whose Virtues bear the strictest Test;	. . . . . .	655	On Poetry	412
But who can bear the Death's-Head in his Hand?	. . .	669	Epig Carthy 16	D 4
Who to yon rav'nous Isle thy Treasures bear,	. . .	794	St. Pat's Well	97
Could always bear to Strive with Man?	. . . . .	799	Traulus 1	96
Meet when Butchers bait a Bear;	. . . .	829	Legion Club	14
A pair of Brogues to bear thee dry to Mass!	. . .	882	Pastoral Dial	50
You, next to Dennis bear the Sway:	. . . .	889	Panegyr Dean	89
Yet Flow'rs I bear of ev'ry Kind;	. . . .	926	Riddle 9	2
A Man, a Woman, Lion, Bear,	. . . .	927	Riddle 10	D 14
Tho' Candor and Truth in my Aspect I bear,	. . . .	929	Riddle 13	D 5
It cannot bear Salt;	. . . .	939	Riddle Answerd	30
As rude as a bear, no mule half so crabbed;	. . . .	955	Portrait Life	5
To be call'd lean by a Skelton, who'd bear it?	. .	1003	Dan J's Reply	18
Like a Bear to be baited:	. . . .	1014	Swift to Sheri	20

BEARD

Long dreaded for his Bloody Tail and Fiery Beard,	.	10	Ode to King	131
No Comet with a Flaming Beard!	. . . .	98	Elegy Patrige	10
His prickled Beard, and hairy Breast!	. . . . . .	586	Strephon Chloe	92
In short; Apollo had no Beard.	. . . .	598	Problem Solved	32
('Twas Nature's Fault) without a Beard.	. . . . .	603	Beasts Confess	62
Before his downy Beard was grown!	. . . .	655	On Poetry	432
Nor, twice a week will shave his beard.	. . . . .	879	Robbin & Harry	44

BEARDED

A Peer, a scarcely bearded Youth,	. . . . . .	386	Manly Virtue	71

BEARING   SEE OVER-BEARING

Their Cow-boys bearing Cloaks before 'um,	. . . .	760	Receipt Youth	46

BEARS

Bears one, and but one branch of gold,	. . . . .	41	Ode Sancroft	226
There to surmount what bears me up, and sing	. . .	44	To Congreve	37
Shews how the Art of Cobling bears	. . . . .	99	Elegy Patrige	39
This Earth which bears his Body's Print,	. . . .	101	Elegy Patrige	111
Such is that Clan of boist'rous Bears	. . . . .	216	To Mr. Delany	51
Libertas bears a large Import:	. . . .	348	Whitshed Motto	11
Yet bears a Moral when apply'd to you	. . . . .	538	Mr. Pulteney	16
Our chilling Climate hardly bears	. . . . . .	640	On Poetry	7
Like Janus, bears a double Face;	. . . . . .	765	Stel B-day '26	74
Bears up his House, that's of his own contriving.	.	943	Probatur Alit	48

BEAST

No poys'nous Beast will in Her breed,	. . . . .	7	Ode to King	52
Out starts the little Beast, and mocks their idle Fears.		30	Ode to Temple	114
No Christian would turn out a Beast	. . . . . .	90	Bauc & Phil 1	19
Call'd him a Cuckold, Fool, and Beast,	. . . . .	221	A Quiet Life	48
Despis'd the Beast with many Heads,	. . . . .	498	Panegyr Swift	161
He grows a tyrant, dunce, or beast.	. . . . . .	658	On Poetry	D 204
Some Beast of Burthen or of Prey	. . . . . .	659	On Poetry	D 410

BEAST	(CONTINUED)	PAGE	TITLE	LINE
For here you see the Man, and there the Beast.	. . .	668	Epig Carthy 9	D 2
They call me Beast, and what Care I?	. . . . . .	778	Mullinix Tim	162
The dullest Beast, and Gentleman's Liquor,		940	Letter	1
The dullest Beast, and Swine's Delight	. . . . .	940	Letter	3
The dullest Beast when high in Stature,	. . . . .	940	Letter	5
The dullest Beast, and a Party distrest,	. . . . .	940	Letter	8
The dullest Beast, and the Saddle it wears,	. . . .	940	Letter	10
The dullest Beast and kind Voice of a Cat,	. . . .	940	Letter	12
The dullest Beast and fam'd College for Teagues		940	Letter	16
The dullest Beast and a Cobler's Tool,	. . . . .	941	Letter	18
The dullest Beast, and that which you kiss,	. . . .	941	Letter	21
The dullest Beast and Eggs unsound,	. . . . . .	941	Letter	25
The dullest Beast and what covers a House,	. . . .	941	Letter	27
The dullest Beast, and scandalous Vermin	. .	941	Letter	29
The dullest Beast, and what's cover'd with Crust,	. .	941	Letter	31
The dullest Beast mending Highways,	. . . . . .	941	Letter	33
The dullest Beast and a Hole in the Ground,	. . .	941	Letter	35
The dullest Beast, and what Doctors pretend	. .	941	Letter	37
The dullest Beast and Fish for Lent	. . . .	941	Letter	39
The dullest Beast and a shameful Jeer,	. . . . .	941	Letter	41
A Long-ear'd Beast, and a Field-house for Cattle,	.	942	Probatur Alit	1
A long-ear'd Beast, a Bird that prates,	. . . .	942	Probatur Alit	3
A long-ear'd Beast, and Woman of Endor,	. . .	942	Probatur Alit	7
With a long-ear'd Beast, and Med'cines Use,	. . .	942	Probatur Alit	9
A long-ear'd Beast and holy Fable,	. . . . .	942	Probatur Alit	11
A long-ear'd Beast, and Rhenish Wine,	. . . . .	942	Probatur Alit	13
A long-ear'd Beast and Flanders College,	. . .	942	Probatur Alit	15
A long-ear'd Beast, and Building Knight;	. . .	942	Probatur Alit	17
A long-ear'd Beast, and Bird of Night,	. . . .	942	Probatur Alit	19
A long-ear'd Beast, and shameful Vermin,	. . .	942	Probatur Alit	21
A long-ear'd Beast, and Irish Cart,	. . . .	942	Probatur Alit	23
A long-ear'd Beast, in Mud to lye,	. . . .	942	Probatur Alit	25
A long-ear'd Beast, and a sputt'ring old Whig,	. .	942	Probatur Alit	27
A long-ear'd Beast, and Liquor to write,	. . .	942	Probatur Alit	29
A long-ear'd Beast, and the Child of a Sheep,	. .	943	Probatur Alit	31
A Beast long-ear'd, and till Midnight you stay,	. .	943	Probatur Alit	33
A long-ear'd Beast, and the Drink you love best	. .	943	Probatur Alit	35
A long-ear'd Beast, and the sixteenth Letter,	. .	943	Probatur Alit	37
A long-ear'd Beast give me, and Eggs unsound,	. .	943	Probatur Alit	39
A long-ear'd Beast, another Name for Jeer,	. .	943	Probatur Alit	41
A long-ear'd Beast, and kind Noise of a Cat,	. .	943	Probatur Alit	43
A long-ear'd Beast, and what seasons your Beef,	. .	943	Probatur Alit	45
A long-ear'd Beast, a Thing that Force must drive in,		943	Probatur Alit	47
BEASTLY				
And, by the beastly way of Thinking,	. . . .	590	Strephon Chloe	209
BEASTS				
Whose harp could savage beasts enchant,	. . . . .	177	To Lord Harley	11
When Beasts could speak, (the Learned say	. . . . .	601	Beasts Confess	1
Beasts may degen'rate into Men.	. . . .	608	Beasts Confess	220
Draw the Beasts as I describe 'em,	. . . . . .	839	Legion Club	225
The Food of Worms, and Beasts obscene,	. . .	923	Riddle 7	59
The dullest of Beasts and of Birds in the Air,	. . .	940	Letter	14
BEAT				
Beat not the dirty paths where vulgar feet have trod,	.	49	To Congreve	205
What signify'd the French to beat?	. . . . . .	169	Peace Dunkirk	32
We sound a trumpet, or we beat a drum;	. . . . . .	308	Billet Players	37
Is destin'd to beat out his Brains.	. . . . . .	500	Doctor Delaney	16
Which tho' with Art you salt and beat,	. . . . .	528	Lady's Dres Rm	100
Or, with his fingers, beat the drum;	. . . . . .	900	Dean's Reasons	48
BEATEN SEE WEATHER-BEATEN				
These are the beaten methods of the stews,	. . . .	44	To Congreve	19
At trudging in a beaten Track,	. . . . .	183	Horace 2, 1	104
Nor beaten Paths be longer trac'd.	. . . . .	270	Apollo's Edict	D 11
Possession kept the beaten Road;	. . . . . .	412	Desire Possess	35
BEATING				
Forcing a wretched Trade by beating down the sale,	. .	19	Ode Athenian	101
The charming Silvia beating Flax,	. . . . . .	729	Stella, Poems	45
BEATS				
Who beats her Husband, who his Wife;	. . . . . .	781	Mullinix Tim	266
BEAU				
Become a General, Peer and Beau,	. . . . . .	84	Salamander	42
So have I seen a batter'd Beau	. . . . . .	84	Salamander	57
Box'd in a Chair the Beau impatient sits,	. . . .	139	City Shower	43
But as a poor pretending Beau	. . . . . .	216	To Mr. Delany	41
The glitt'ring Beau could hardly tell,	. . . . .	325	Pethox	65
Like a Beau in the Box, he bow'd low on each Side;	.	399	Tom Clinch	10
So nice and so compleat a Beau.	. . . .	597	Problem Solved	10
And Dido quickly smoak't the Beau.	. . . . . .	619	Scandal Poem 1	72
Nor souse to death a Birthday Beau;	. . . . .	622	Scandal Poem 1	178
And Dido quickly smoak'd the Beau.	. . . . .	625	Scandal Poem 2	70
From sloven Bernard to beau Dalacourt.	. . .	672	Epig Carthy 24	D 8
Was marry'd to the Tunbridge Beau,	. . . . .	699	Cadenus Vaness	393
And ev'ry Beau wou'd have his Jokes,	. . . . .	707	Cadenus Vaness	648
The Skill of ev'ry common Beau;	. . . . . .	712	Cadenus Vaness	813
The Beau in all his Ayrs exprest.	. . . . . .	782	Tim and Fables	12
Is doom'd to be a Beau for life:	. . . . . .	879	Robbin & Harry	52
Was call'd, to rig him out a Beau:	. . . . .	903	Death Daphne	20
This meagre Fop, that batter'd Beau:	. . . . .	905	Death Daphne	74
BEAU-SPELLING				
Here in Beau-spelling (tru tel deth)	. . . . . .	60	Lady Tablebook	9

		PAGE	TITLE	LINE
BEAU'S				
Yes, that beau's look, that voice, those critic ears,	•	48	To Congreve	173
BEAUS				
Those beds of dung, where schoolboys sprout up beaus	• •	46	To Congreve	99
Instead of powder'd Beaus,	• • • • • •	426	Five Ladies	31
More Beaus can kill	• • • • • • •	441	Ballyspellin	35
BEAUTEOUS				
This beauteous Queen by Heaven design'd	• • • • •	22	Ode Athenian	216
However beauteous for his Mother:	• • • • •	272	Apollo's Edict	D 57
"And beauteous Bess a diff'rent case is,	• • • • •	321	First of April	9
Behold three beauteous Vowels stand	• • • • •	467	Birthday Song	229
As when a beauteous Nymph decays	• • • • •	756	Stel B-day '24	1
All beauteous Offspring of one Womb,	• • • • •	923	Riddle 7	68
BEAUTIES				
"(Whose Beauties mortal Eyes escape,	• • • •	384	Manly Virtue	7
Those Beauties that might ever last.	• • • • •	595	Cassinus Peter	54
Those Beauties in a Female Mind,	• • • • •	691	Cadenus Vaness	143
BEAUTIFUL				
Phoebus was beautiful as you:	• • • • •	177	To Lord Harley	26
So beautiful a Nymph appears	• • • • •	584	Strephon Chloe	3
So beautiful to pass for Juno?	• • • • •	625	Scandal Poem 2	60
To witty, beautiful, and young.	• • • • •	887	Panegyr Dean	16
The Young, the Beautiful, and Brave,	• • • • •	923	Riddle 7	53
There's nought so beautiful in thee,	• • • • •	932	Riddle 19	D 5
BEAUTIFULL				
So beautifull to pass for Juno?	• • • • • •	619	Scandal Poem 1	64
BEAUTY				
And changes all to Beauty, and the Praise	• • • •	23	Ode Athenian	236
Render'd the topping beauty of the town,	• • • •	48	To Congreve	152
To form some Beauty by a new Receit,	• • • •	118	Biddy Floyd	2
Who with an English Beauty smitten	• • • •	293	Prog Marriage	111
From Venus born, thy Beauty shows,	• • • •	323	Pethox	1
Beauty that needs no Aid of Art,	• • • • •	379	Apology Lady C	115
Barter'd for Beauty, and for Gold;	• • • •	385	Manly Virtue	68
With so much beauty, shew me any maid	• • • •	466	Birthday Song	189
Queen of Wit and Beauty, Betty,	• • • •	522	Betty Grizette	1
And, thy Beauty thus dispatcht;	• • • • •	523	Betty Grizette	11
Not Love of Beauty less the Heart inflames	• • • •	532	To Mr. Gay	19
Though Beauty may beget Desire,	• • • • •	590	Strephon Chloe	221
For, Beauty, like supreme Dominion,	• • • • •	590	Strephon Chloe	223
Opinion falls, and Beauty dies.	• • • • •	591	Strephon Chloe	226
Since Beauty scarce endures a Day,	• • • • •	593	Strephon Chloe	303
Yet, with his Beauty, Wealth, and Parts,	• • • •	598	Problem Solved	19
His Shape and Beauty made him proud:	• • • •	602	Beasts Confess	38
With heav'nly beauty so endow'd;	• • • • •	619	Scandal Poem 1	75
Your Poets Chloe's beauty heightning	• • • •	621	Scandal Poem 1	149
With heav'nly Beauty so endow'd?	• • • •	625	Scandal Poem 2	73
Your Poets, Chloe's Beauty height'ning,	• • • •	628	Scandal Poem 2	153
The Child with native Beauty shone,	• • • •	692	Cadenus Vaness	175
By Beauty cou'd your Heart be won,	• • • •	692	Cadenus Vaness	192
The Queen of Beauty lost her Aim.	• • • •	700	Cadenus Vaness	433
Thy Beauty, Size, and Years, and Wit,	• • • •	722	Stel B-Day '18	10
And that her Beauty, soon or late,	• • • • •	723	To Stella	3
To this, the Beauty of your Frame.	• • • • •	726	To Stella	92
To Beauty, Dress, or Paint, or Youth,	• • • •	729	Stella, Poems	62
Beauty and Wit, too sad a Truth,	• • • • •	757	Stel B-day '24	15
With Youth and Beauty to enchant	• • • • •	759	Receipt Youth	19
I'll have Youth and Beauty still.	• • • • •	863	To Janus	30
With mutual Beauty smit, their Passion grew.	• • • •	880	Pastoral Dial	6
Was of her Beauty grown so vain,	• • • • •	905	Death Daphne	69
My Beauty to the Shades below.	• • • • •	927	Riddle 10	D 12
For Time with Beauty flies away,	• • • • •	932	Riddle 19	D 21
BEAUTY'S				
With Puppy Water, Beauty's Help	• • • •	526	Lady's Dres Rm	31
Descend from Heav'n to Beauty's Aid;	• • • •	590	Strephon Chloe	220
Oh Peter! Beauty's but a Varnish,	• • • •	595	Cassinus Peter	51
They celebrate her Beauty's Praise,	• • • •	697	Cadenus Vaness	331
To make you look like Beauty's Queen,	• • • •	736	Stel B-day '20	53
The God of Wit, and Beauty's Queen,	• • • •	757	Stel B-day '24	17
BEAUTYES				
Since mortal Beautyes drop so soon,	• • • • •	229	Prog of Beauty	118
BEAUX				
Fall'n by mishap amongst a knot of beaux;	• • • •	50	To Congreve	216
For neighb'ring Beaux to see it bare.	• • • •	222	Prog of Love	18
Nor let the Beaux approach too near.	• • • •	228	Prog of Beauty	68
To bath among the Belles and Beaux.	• • • •	294	Prog Marriage	144
Has her Cotemporary Beaux.	• • • •	311	To Ford	22
"Whose Owners set not up for Beaux.	• • • •	572	Death of Swift	468
Visits, Plays, and Powder'd Beaux.	• • • •	631	Epistle Lady	42
Pointed at Col'nels, Lords, and Beaux;	• • • •	701	Cadenus Vaness	478
Preferr'd before a Crowd of Beaux,	• • • •	710	Cadenus Vaness	751
Was long the quintessence of Beaux;	• • • •	879	Robbin & Harry	38
BEAVER				
His Beaver brush'd, his Shoes, and Gown,	• • • •	376	Apology Lady C	27
Looks up to your Window, and cocks up his Beaver.	• •	870	Grand Question	104
(His Beaver is cock'd; pray, Madam, mark that,	• •	870	Grand Question	105
BEC				
For Bec, a new supply of cares,	• • • • •	753	Gift for Bec	2
This day, dear Bec, is thy nativity,	• • • • •	760	Bec's B-Day	1
May Bec have many an evening nap	• • • • •	761	Bec's B-Day	39

BECAME | | PAGE | TITLE | LINE

		PAGE	TITLE	LINE
BECAME				
Impatient of all Answers, straight became	. . . . .	22	Ode Athenian	191
Became a Steeple with a Spire:	. . . .	92	Bauc & Phil 1	96
In it's old shape a Font became	. . . .	93	Bauc & Phil 1	112
Became a Clock, and still adher'd,	. . . .	94	Bauc & Phil 1	142
Became a Steeple with a Spire.	. . . .	113	Bauc & Phil 2	56
Became a Clock, and still adher'd:	. . . .	113	Bauc & Phil 2	80
Became Black Sattin, Flounc'd with Lace.	. . . .	116	Bauc & Phil 2	142
By Law of Arms became your Prey,	. . . .	154	Widow and Cat	D 34
Forgot at Home, became for Hire,	. . . .	482	Libel on D- D-	63
What Midas touch'd, became true Gold; but then,		668	Epig Carthy 12	D 1
Yet she wou'd act as best became	. . . .	695	Cadenus Vaness	274
If he was bolder than became	. . . .	705	Cadenus Vaness	588
BECAUSE 68			OMITTED WORD	
BECK'NING				
Beck'ning the Doctor to approach.		172	Horace 1, 7	62
Beck'ning to waft me o'er the Ferry.	. . . .	596	Cassinus Peter	84
BECKON'D				
First to a dapper Clerk she beckon'd,	. . . . .	690	Cadenus Vaness	108
BECOME				
. . .it might become you to be more civil:	. . . .	72	Mrs Harris Pet	55
Become a General, Peer and Beau,	. . . . . .	84	Salamander	42
Van is become by due Degrees	. . . .	87	Hist V's House	36
Would strait become a Golden Pippin:	. . . . .	156	Fable of Midas	6
Are each become a Harridan;	. . . .	311	To Ford	18
Your conqu'ror is become Apollo:	. . . .	462	Birthday Song	58
"Become an Atheist, or Socinian.	. . . . . .	550	Life of Swift	175
To cheat the World, become each other's Bail.	. .	668	Epig Carthy 8	D 4
Unites, and both become the same,	. . . . . .	687	Cadenus Vaness	32
As well become St. <Patrick's> <Dean>;	. . . .	889	Panegyr Dean	78
I now become your humble Suitor,	. . . . . .	891	Panegyr Dean	129
A cart would best become the knave,	. . . . .	951	Upstart	D 25
To leave off this passion which does not become you:	. .	976	Dean to Sherid	10
I am sure such Words does not become a Man of your Cloth,		985	Mary to Sher	3
BECOMES				
Grows a misfortune, or becomes a vice;	. . . . .	55	Temple Ill	136
Becomes his Brother's lawful Heir:	. . . . . .	366	Answer Delaney	14
Gold becomes Lead, touch'd lightly by thy Pen.	. . .	668	Epig Carthy 12	D 2
Becomes the Creature well enough.	. . . .	700	Cadenus Vaness	427
BECOMING				
Shirts becoming to the sight,	. . . .	573	Helter Skelter	22
BED SEE DEATH-BED, A-BED				
Then the Bell rung, and I went down to put my Lady to Bed,		69	Mrs Harris Pet	10
So Mary got me to Bed, and cover'd me up warm,	. . .	70	Mrs Harris Pet	18
And so went to Bed in a desperate Case.	. . . .	77	Lady B- B-	7
One Family was gone to bed;	. . . .	90	Bauc & Phil 1	26
The Sun has rose, and gone to Bed,	. . . . . .	98	Elegy Patrige	11
Now Betty from her Masters Bed had flown,	. . .	124	Descriptn Morn	3
She'd rather take you to her Bed	. . . . . .	222	Prog of Love	7
When first Diana leaves her Bed	. . . . . .	226	Prog of Beauty	1
So Celia went entire to bed,	. . . . . .	226	Prog of Beauty	29
Bring Straw for our Bed,	. . . .	246	Irish-Feast	49
On the smooth Ocean's azure Bed	. . . . . .	251	Bubble	27
His Candle out, and he a Bed.	. . . .	280	Journal	48
The Bed in which these Tyrants lie:	. . . . . .	283	Journal	122
In bed, where he can spare her best.	. . . . .	292	Prog Marriage	90
Of old age too, and in his bed!	. . . . . .	296	Satiric Elegy	2
While he went always drunk to Bed.	. . . . .	352	Wood Ironmongr	8
For, when in Bed we rest our weary Limbs,	. . .	363	On Dreams	7
Orphans around his Bed the Lawyer sees,	. . .	364	On Dreams	23
One Bed while alive held both Doll and Dick	. . .	430	Dicky Dolly	13
Steals to her sleeping Spouse to Bed.	. . . . .	453	Modern Lady	293
"As from the flowry Bed of Nile--	. . . . . .	463	Birthday Song	81
(His Name is up, he may in Bed lye)	. . . . .	476	Epist on Epist	48
"With lying on too hard a Bed;	. . . . . .	497	Panegyr Swift	133
Of Wit's fair Goddess brought to Bed,	. . . . .	504	Doctor Delaney	116
Than all the Sniv'llers round my Bed.	. . . . .	557	Death of Swift	142
But must, before she goes to Bed,	. . . . . .	582	Young Nymph	33
Took Col'nel Peleus to her Bed.	. . . .	587	Strephon Chloe	102
The Bride was put in Form to Bed;	. . . . . .	587	Strephon Chloe	112
That, e'er to Bed they venture up,	. . . . . .	587	Strephon Chloe	119
In Bed we left the married Pair;	. . . . . .	588	Strephon Chloe	145
And brings a Vessel into Bed;	. . . .	589	Strephon Chloe	172
He seem'd as just crept out of Bed;	. . . . . .	594	Cassinus Peter	11
Attending nightly round your Bed;	. . . . . .	597	Cassinus Peter	114
The Consort of his Throne and Bed,	. . . . .	655	On Poetry	425
Unheard she moves about my Bed.	. . . . . .	727	To Stella	112
Dorinda dreams of Dress a bed	. . . .	733	Verses Vanessa	23
Her bum upon a bed of nettles.	. . . . . .	901	Dean's Reasons	94
Fair Issue of the genial Bed,	. . . . . .	924	Riddle 8	5
A mushroom in a bed of dung;	. . . . . .	950	Upstart	D 4
A house-wife in bed, at table a slattern;	. . . .	955	Portrait Life	7
Well, but I must run and make the Bed, . . .		987	Mary to Sher	35
BED-STED				
A Bed-sted in the antique mode	. . . .	94	Bauc & Phil 1	147
BED-STEDS				
Stools, Tables, Chairs, and Bed-steds broke:	. . .	1035	To Quilca	4
BEDAUBS				
Bedaubs the guilty Great with nauseous Praise:	. . .	364	On Dreams	36

		PAGE	TITLE	LINE
BEDLAM				
So she roar'd like a Bedlam,.		71	Mrs Harris Pet	45
Yet many a Wretch in Bedlam, knows, ...		796	Traulus 1	23
BEDRAGGLED				
Bedraggled in my Walks so green:		409	Dial Rich Marb	48
BEDS				
Those beds of dung, where schoolboys sprout up beaus . .		46	To Congreve	99
On their Rushy Beds and Benches, ...		574	Helter Skelter	46
Between their Toylets and their Beds.		688	Cadenus Vaness	50
BEDSTEAD				
A Bedstead of the Antique Mode, ...		114	Bauc & Phil 2	101
BEE				
And yet the Cow, the Sheep, the Bee, ...		936	Riddle 24	D 3
BEECH				
And said: By my Shoul he's the Son of a Beech: . .		334	Serious Poem	28
BEEF				
With good Roast Beef his Belly full, ...		231	Prog of Poetry	21
Without whom they could get neither Claret nor Beef; .		263	Apollo	10
Steals off to dose away his Beef, ...		279	Journal	40
We'll make it firm with Beef and Claret.		760	Receipt Youth	56
A Stone and a quarter of Beef from my Sirloin. . .		867	Grand Question	18
Decant his Wine, and carve his Beef.		883	Rev Market-Hill	24
A long-ear'd Beast, and what seasons your Beef, . . .		943	Probatur Alit	45
Your Beef will on Thursday be salter than brine . .		1018	Swift Ans Sher	24
The Beef you have got, which I hear is a Chine . .		1018	Swift Ans Sher	30
BEELZEBUB'S				
And then at Beelzebub's Black-Hall, ...		486	Libel on D- D-	191
BEEN 82			OMITTED WORD	
BEER				
To a small Kilderkin of Beer		92	Bauc & Phil 1	67
In the Midst of their Beer:		246	Irish-Feast	60
The beer and the ale		402	Window Inns 8	D 7
Forbid your Daughters guzzling Beer;		587	Strephon Chloe	116
Small Beer, a Herring, and the Dean.		747	Stel Distress	56
Small Beer, a Herring, and the <Dean>.		751	Stel Wood-Park	72
BEES				
Like Bees, are humming in my Ears.		200	Horace 2, 6	50
The Bees are gather'd to a Swarm:		345	Prometheus	26
When all the Bees are gone to settle, ...		775	Mullinix Tim	45
BEETLE-BROWS				
His Beetle-brows and Eyes of Wall, ...		861	Lady Acheson	39
BEFALL				
What Fortune may befall his Nose.		993	On Picture	21
BEFELL				
Exactly said what now befell her, ...		223	Prog of Love	52
But what Adventures more befell 'um		224	Prog of Love	85
BEFITS				
Ill befits a lofty Stile.		634	Epistle Lady	140
End, as it befits your Station;		636	Epistle Lady	185
Thee best befits a lowly Style:		897	Panegyr Dean	329
Than what befits a rural Dame.		897	Panegyr Dean	342
BEFITTING				
Befitting Juno's fav'rite Maid.		626	Scandal Poem 2	76
BEFORE				
Before the Hero can commence a God.		7	Ode to King	30
Before this Milk-white Heifer can be stole away, . .		8	Ode to King	77
Philosophy, as it before us lyes, ...		22	Ode Athenian	211
And fling our Scraps before our Door.		28	Ode to Temple	57
Which we ne'er join'd before, but in Romances meet, . .		28	Ode to Temple	60
Ne'er sprang a youth from out this isle before		44	To Congreve	11
For never did poetic mine before		45	To Congreve	51
Before it grew a city butterfly;		46	To Congreve	90
Before the play, or else between the acts:		47	To Congreve	126
Spend their base coin before the bashful maid, ...		50	To Congreve	219
And from behind, and from before;		65	Problem	10
Some ply before, and some behind.		66	Problem	38
Before the Flame from Muzzle burst, ...		66	Problem	45
I e'en left her, and came away as wise as I was before. .		71	Mrs Harris Pet	47
. . .before I was aware, out I blunder'd, ...		72	Mrs Harris Pet	52
I was never taken for a Conjurer before,.		72	Mrs Harris Pet	58
Before one Soul would let 'em in.		90	Bauc & Phil 1	14
And grow a Church before your Eyes.		92	Bauc & Phil 1	90
Than a few Scrubby Trees before.		108	V's House	84
And grow a Church before your Eyes.		112	Bauc & Phil 2	50
Before he durst the Nymph approach.		119	Apollo Outwit	8
Where none e'er look'd for it before;		133	Magician's Rod	30
As t' other Midas did before?		157	Fable of Midas	50
Now, now you carry all before ye, ...		183	Horace 2, 1	83
"But rudely press before a Duke.		200	Horace 2, 6	39
Before his Credit or his Fee.		204	In Sickness	12
Plac'd me in Life too far before;		215	To Mr. Delany	8
She ne'r before in all her Life		224	Prog of Love	65
And before Corum Nobus so oft has been call'd, ...		238	Excellent Song	27
Than what it allways did before;		255	Bubble	120
I study'd a Fortnight, before I could find, ...		265	Apollo	75
Scarce run a Step before they part;		290	Prog Marriage	32
He made them weep before he dy'd.		296	Satiric Elegy	24
Before the secret wise Committee;		300	Horrid Plot	54
But Venus had been there before		302	Storm	11
"Or, as Fitzpatrick did before, ...		305	Storm	63
From Head to Foot, and all before;)		324	Pethox	16

BEFORE   (CONTINUED)   PAGE   TITLE   LINE
   Found all the Realms before him waste; . . . . . .   326 Pethox   92
   It falls before thy Rev'rend Years, ...   340 Arch-Bish Dub   14
   Come, you must take a Cup of Sack or two before you go. 342 Upon His Grace   24
   Before I'd touch his filthy Dross, than is Clandalkin   343 Upon His Grace   38
     Spire.
   To cut his Throat before he marry'd. . . . . 349 Upright Judge 2   4
   Before the Drapier shot a Letter, ... 353 Wood Ironmongr   35
   The Scenes and Actions of the Day before. . . . . . 363 On Dreams   10
   And stabs the Son before the Mother's Eyes. . . . . 364 On Dreams   16
   To one who sway'd some time before; . . . . 375 Apology Lady C   16
   But I'll see you all damn'd before I will whittle. . . . 399 Tom Clinch   16
   She spoke ten Thousand Times before. . . . . 416 Woman's Mind   12
   The Scandal of the Day before. . . . . 416 Woman's Mind   24
   I never was in hast before . . . . 420 Holyhead   19
   Before, I always found the wind . . . . 420 Holyhead   21
   Though he were drunk the night before, ... 434 Answer Paulus   72
   To fight our cause before the judge: . . . . 435 Answer Paulus   88
   "It must be One before we Sup.' . . . . 451 Modern Lady   213
   "Before my Lady call'd a King. . . . . 452 Modern Lady   253
   One thing he did before he went hence, ... 455 Dean Smedley   17
   (It must be read before 'tis warbled . . . . . . 463 Birthday Song   87
   We blacken what was white before. . . . . 463 Birthday Song   110
   Of whitening what before was black. . . . . 464 Birthday Song   116
   Than George and William claim'd before. . . . . . 464 Birthday Song   140
   What Dowdys they appear before her! . . . . 465 Birthday Song   158
   Before you Build and You Bestow, ... 479 Epist on Epist   116
   Before a Play, wou'd lose no Credit: . . . . . . 484 Libel on D- D-   142
   Before our Friends were gone to Pot, ... 498 Panegyr Swift   158
   In wit before the common Herd? . . . . 501 Doctor Delaney   38
   These they have often try'd before; . . . . 505 Doctor Delaney   155
   'Twas what all his Life he had practis'd before. . . . 517 Dean Hang Rape   22
   He smelt it all the Time before. . . . . 528 Lady's Dres Rm   82
   I place a <Statesman> full before my Sight. . . . . 532 To Mr. Gay   32
   At least, before your Master's Debts are paid. . . . 533 To Mr. Gay   62
   He lends my Lord, what was my Lord's before. . . . 533 To Mr. Gay   76
   And give Advice before he gives the Pill. . . . . . 534 To Mr. Gay   80
   Would love his Fav'rite better than before; . . . . 535 To Mr. Gay   113
   Nor can you go to Hell before you dye. . . . . . . 539 Mr. Pulteney   42
   But hold---: before we farther go, ... 545 Life of Swift   5
   Confounded Dull---, before he Dy'd---. . . . . . . 547 Life of Swift   89
   He told them fifty Times before. . . . . 556 Death of Swift   90
   "Before the Passing-Bell begun, ... 558 Death of Swift   151
   "But never stood in Awe before 'em: . . . . 566 Death of Swift   340
   But must, before she goes to Bed, ... 582 Young Nymph   33
   Before, behind, above, below, ... 584 Strephon Chloe   13
   Decorum than she did before; . . . . 588 Strephon Chloe   142
   The Nymph opprest before, behind, ... 589 Strephon Chloe   169
   To pass for Wits before a Rake! . . . . 592 Strephon Chloe   268
   E'er drove, before he sold his Land, ... 598 Problem Solved   13
   He'd shew his Face before the <King>: . . . . . . 602 Beasts Confess   34
   Says Grace before, and after Meat; . . . . 605 Beasts Confess   130
   Before Aeneas durst aspire . . . . 619 Scandal Poem 1   65
   Before Aeneas durst aspire . . . . 625 Scandal Poem 2   61
   I have often told before. . . . . 630 Epistle Lady   10
   Before he tries a five-barr'd Gate: . . . . 640 On Poetry   16
   Gone, where the Chickens went before. . . . . . . 642 On Poetry   70
   Before you learn the Terms of Art: . . . . 647 On Poetry   240
   Before his downy Beard was grown! . . . . 655 On Poetry   432
   Before one race of his was run; . . . . 675 Curate's Compl   15
   Pleading before the Cyprian Queen. . . . . 686 Cadenus Vaness   2
   To all he spoke, than e'er before; . . . . 704 Cadenus Vaness   565
   This Topick, never touch'd before, ... 709 Cadenus Vaness   714
   Preferr'd before a Crowd of Beaux, ... 710 Cadenus Vaness   751
   "To Women than they had before, ... 714 Cadenus Vaness   875
   And then before it grew too late, ... 722 Stel B-Day '18   15
   Before I could my Verses bring, ... 730 Stella, Poems   69
   Before he could his Poem close, ... 730 Stella, Poems   77
   Their Cow-boys bearing Cloaks before 'um, ... 760 Receipt Youth   46
   Come back before you're out of Case; . . . . . . 760 Receipt Youth   50
   But here, before the Frost can marr it, ... 760 Receipt Youth   55
   Those whom you dragg'd from Death before: . . . . . 764 Stel B-day '26   40
   Were hanged, before they'd part with you. . . . . . 778 Mullinix Tim   150
   Walk by my place, before my Betters. . . . . . . 778 Mullinix Tim   156
   Jason arriv'd two thousand Years before. . . . . . 790 St. Pat's Well   8
   He shot before your Foes were prim'd: . . . . . . 797 Traulus 1   58
   The <Dean> hath felt their Stings before; . . . . . 798 Traulus 1   85
   Before you condemn us, hear what we can say. . . . 805 Irish Bishops   54
   And Smithfield, I'll tell you, if not told before, . . 814 Yahoo's   2
   And Smithfield, as Rap was ne'er colted before; . . . 817 Yahoo's   57
   But before the Priest he fleeces . . . . 831 Legion Club   65
   Never durst a Muse before . . . . 834 Legion Club   119
   A spacious Thorn before the Gate. . . . . 848 Old Thorn   4
   Before he came here . . . . 852 Lady's Lament   15
   Consider, before . . . . 854 Lady's Lament   115
   Three Days before he was expected. . . . . 859 Lady Acheson   8
   Direct before her Lady's Face. . . . . 885 Rev Market-Hill   68
   They place before him Gloves and Shoes; . . . . . 885 Rev Market-Hill   78
   Behind my Back, before my Nose, ... 887 Panegyr Dean   27
   Will I ever tell before ye: . . . . 908 Daphne   66
   Though, if I rise before my Time, ... 918 Riddle 4   41

	PAGE	TITLE	LINE
BEFORE (CONTINUED)			
They cannot pass before they dance;	928	Riddle 12	D 18
But before you can put yourself under her banners, . .	979	Dean to Tho: S	27
But that's as much as to say, that my Master should die before ye,	986	Mary to Sher	19
. . .before my Master comes from Pray'rs, ...	987	Mary to Sher	35
And yet before your Stanza ends you flout me	1003	Dan J's Reply	21
And, before we find either, our noddles turn round. . .	1026	Sheri Circles	8
BEFRIEND			
Or in folly still befriend her, ...	907	Daphne	27
BEFRIENDED			
That I'm Befriended by Appollo, ...	371	Letter D. S-y	10
BEG			
For shame! two sturdy Rascalls beg;	91	Bauc & Phil 1	44
Truce, good My Lord, I beg a Truce!	175	Horace 1, 7	130
She'd beg with John from Door to Door:	224	Prog of Love	62
I beg you'll the Camelion spare.	270	Apollo's Edict	D 17
To beg his Favour is the Way new Favours still to win,	341	Upon His Grace	13
And once I was so bold to beg that I might see His Grace,	342	Upon His Grace	27
Thus, for a Tryal, let me beg of	366	Answer Delaney	15
Yet should this Blockhead beg a Place	423	Ireld	69
But, I beg, suspend a While, ...	631	Epistle Lady	49
With visits, or to beg a place;	677	Parson's Case	30
How should I beg of gentle Fate, ...	722	Stel B-Day '18	16
Don Carlos earnestly would beg, ...	746	Stel Distress	17
Don Carlos earnestly would beg, ...	750	Stel Wood-Park	15
I beg, you see the Case is Nice, ...	779	Mullinix Tim	196
Cringing comes to beg their Pardon;	800	Traulus 2	14
Their former Companions should beg at their Door. . .	804	Irish Bishops	28
And beg her a play-day.	858	Lady's Lament	218
Beg you would here continue still, ...	860	Lady Acheson	26
But, Madam, I beg you contrive and invent, ...	869	Grand Question	61
I gave, as you beg, your most humble respects:	979	Dean to Tho: S	24
BEG'D			
They beg'd Relief which none would grant;	90	Bauc & Phil 1	24
They beg'd from Door to Door in vain;	111	Bauc & Phil 2	12
Beg'd she'd forgive him; in Conclusion, ...	378	Apology Lady C	83
BEGAN			
And (I believe) began himself the Fight, ...	8	Ode to King	60
And end as it began, in Vapour, Stink, and Scum. . .	10	Ode to King	129
As when the Deluge first began to fall, ...	16	Ode Athenian	1
When the Bright Sun of Peace began to shine, . . .	16	Ode Athenian	24
In higher Strain than we began.	80	Vanbrug House	58
The Roof began to mount aloft	92	Bauc & Phil 1	92
The groaning Chair began to crawll	93	Bauc & Phil 1	105
In higher Strains than we began.	106	V's House	32
Till one in Raptures thus began	109	V's House	107
And just began to cry;--What ar't!	112	Bauc & Phil 2	38
The Roof began to mount aloft;	112	Bauc & Phil 2	52
The Groaning Chair began to crawl	113	Bauc & Phil 2	85
The Youth with Broomy Stumps began to trace . . .	124	Descriptn Morn	9
Duns at his Lordships Gate began to meet, ...	124	Descriptn Morn	13
And little Miss began to cry;	128	Little House	48
Phil cry'd, and John began to curse;	224	Prog of Love	80
Their Reign began with cruel Seizures;	283	Journal	120
He's gone, although his Friends began to hope	285	Elegy Boat	17
A rich Divine began to woo	289	Prog Marriage	2
The Masquerade began at two, ...	292	Prog Marriage	93
Till you began to change the Breed;	301	Horrid Plot	75
The Nymphs with whom You first began	311	To Ford	17
Thalia now began to smoke, ...	322	First of April	53
But when Wood's Brass began to sound, ...	338	Wood's Brass	7
"You spoke a Word began with H, ...	452	Modern Lady	254
I found my Head began to swim, ...	470	Burning Poem	9
There in the Soil began to root, ...	504	Doctor Delaney	121
The Mimick Ape began his Chatter, ...	602	Beasts Confess	47
The Council for the Fair began, ...	686	Cadenus Vaness	3
The Goddess soon began to see	689	Cadenus Vaness	104
Began, when I was but a Girl.	699	Cadenus Vaness	391
His Pride began to interpose, ...	710	Cadenus Vaness	750
By reading this Trifle, I quickly began	716	Answer Rebus	13
Don Carlos now began to find	746	Stel Distress	31
Began a thousand faults to spy	746	Stel Distress	36
Don Carlos now began to find	750	Stel Wood-Park	23
The Winter-Sky began to frown, ...	750	Stel Wood-Park	25
Began a Thousand Faults to spy;	751	Stel Wood-Park	53
He now began to storm and rave;	783	Tim and Fables	28
What Spirit since the World began, ...	799	Traulus 1	95
He began as he bragg'd, with a rant and a roar; . . .	816	Yahoo's	43
I began to rage and fret	832	Legion Club	94
Thus ended the Knight: Thus began his meek Wife: . .	867	Grand Question	25
BEGET			
Though Beauty may beget Desire, ...	590	Strephon Chloe	221
For talking may beget Suspicion:	644	On Poetry	124
His Person must Contempt beget.	706	Cadenus Vaness	639
May well be said Man did beget it.	812	Bro Protestant	38
BEGETS			
Begets a kinder Folly and Impertinence	18	Ode Athenian	79
Where Ignorance begets Disdain.	700	Cadenus Vaness	437

		PAGE	TITLE	LINE

BEGETTING
A Bastard of your own begetting. . . . . 644 On Poetry 116
BEGG'D
And begg'd like one both blind and lame; . . . . . . 207 Fable Bitches 8
His Pardon begg'd, but to be plain, ... 224 Prog of Love 57
To Neptune went, and begg'd in Form . . . . . . 302 Storm 3
Forgiveness begg'd, that he appear'd . . . . . . 603 Beasts Confess 61
His mother begg'd of us to dress him . . . . . . 619 Scandal Poem 1 67
His Mother begg'd of us to dress him, ... 625 Scandal Poem 2 63
We begg'd her but to patch her Face, ... 700 Cadenus Vaness 422
BEGGAR   SEE COUPLE-BEGGAR
Return Him Beggar As He Went. . . . . 456 Dean Smedley 50
A blind old Beggar from the Grave: . . . . . . 604 Beasts Confess 116
A Beggar there, and here a Queen. . . . . . . 911 Aenigma 8
BEGGAR'S
He comes to drain a Beggar's Purse: . . . . . . 484 Libel on D- D- 124
Not Beggar's Brat, on Bulk begot; . . . . . . 641 On Poetry 33
And make a Beggar's Brat a Peer. . . . . . . 916 Riddle 1 36
Anon in Beggar's Rags appear; . . . . 935 Riddle 23 D 21
The offspring of a beggar's brat. . . . . 950 Upstart D 6
BEGGAR'S-OP'RA
At Beggar's-Op'ra not so full Pit . . . . 889 Panegyr Dean 65
BEGGARS
Oh! then but to see how Beggars will Vapour, ... 287 Bank Down 21
For Beggars have Rags and Rags will make Paper, . . 287 Bank Down 22
Thus vagrant Beggars, to extort . . . . 667 Epig Carthy 6 D 1
Robin, to beggars, with a curse . . . . 878 Robbin & Harry 1
BEGGERS
So many Beggers pass this way, ... 90 Bauc & Phil 1 29
BEGGING
With Begging, Vain, Familiar Letters. . . . . . 479 Epist on Epist 118
BEGIN
I see the Fatal Fight begin; . . . . 7 Ode to King 47
Are all resolv'd the Project to begin; . . . . . . 275 Epilogue 28
Begin, my Muse, first from our Bowers, ... 278 Journal 7
And, when we found the Dog begin it, ... 300 Horrid Plot 69
Ten Thousand Cymbals now begin . . . . 354 Simile Silver 9
Unwilling Muse begin thy Lay, ... 445 Modern Lady 34
Quadrill's the Word, and so begin. . . . . . . 451 Modern Lady 219
And, if they begin a Fray, ... 574 Helter Skelter 47
"And were she to begin agen, ... 714 Cadenus Vaness 872
Your Ladyship smiles, and thus you begin; . . . . . 871 Grand Question 113
I thus begin. My grateful Muse . . . . 888 Panegyr Dean 37
From Heav'n I fall, tho' from Earth I begin, ... 928 Riddle 13 D 1
I shall, for Method Sake, begin with the last. . . . 967 Letter Sherid 12
A Woman's no Sieve (for with that you begin) . . . . 972 S-'s Ans Sh-d 5
BEGINNER
Instructing thus a young Beginner. . . . . . . 642 On Poetry 76
BEGINNING
But Wit and Weaving had the same beginning, ... 276 Epilogue 37
Dear Tom, this verse, which however the beginning may 1022 Nim-Dan-Dean 2 D 1
appear, . . .
BEGINS
To shew the Flood begins to cease, ... 16 Ode Athenian 20
This hopeful Sect, now it begins to see . . . . . . 19 Ode Athenian 111
When once he begins, he never will flinch, ... 143 New Song 7
When Charity begins to tread the Stage: . . . . . 274 Epilogue 2
And ev'ry one begins to find, ... 345 Prometheus 19
Then, furious he begins his March; . . . . . . 353 Wood Ironmongr 17
Begins the World with Fear and Shame, ... 500 Doctor Delaney 12
See, how the Dean begins to break: . . . . . . 556 Death of Swift 80
"His Stomach too begins to fail: . . . . 557 Death of Swift 111
And, thus the pious Wolf begins: . . . . 601 Beasts Confess 12
The Winter now begins to frown; . . . . 744 Stel Distress 1
Sir Arthur begins, ... 851 Lady's Lament 6
And give Satan his due Dan begins to refine . . . . 1017 Swift Ans Sher 10
BEGONE
Begone; unhand me, hellish Fry; . . . . 596 Cassinus Peter 87
BEGOT
Begot upon his grandame Earth; . . . . 433 Answer Paulus 26
Not Beggar's Brat, on Bulk begot; . . . . . . 641 On Poetry 33
BEGOTTEN
Begotten, and Born, and dying with Noise, ... 927 Riddle 11 D 1
BEGS
That begs the pow'rful blessing of thy pray'rs. . . . 42 Ode Sancroft 244
And begs, He would the other weigh. . . . . . . 63 Discovery 40
That, begs my Interest for a Place-- . . . . . . 200 Horace 2, 6 48
Begs leave to rail, but <damn> his Blood, ... 797 Traulus 1 55
BEGUILE
Fortune the gamesters does beguile, ... 29 Ode to Temple 79
Nor will my Lord so far Beguile . . . . 475 Epist on Epist 17
BEGUMM'D
Begumm'd, bematter'd, and beslim'd . . . . . . 527 Lady's Dres Rm 45
BEGUN
Which from Eternal Seeds begun, ... 20 Ode Athenian 128
I grieve, this Noble Work so happily begun, ... 24 Ode Athenian 275
No Conquest ever yet begun . . . . 25 Ode Athenian 283
No Simile shall be begun, ... 270 Apollo's Edict D 12
As if they had but just begun. . . . . 453 Modern Lady 279
"Before the Passing-Bell begun, ... 558 Death of Swift 151
By going on as he begun; . . . . 655 On Poetry 434

		PAGE	TITLE	LINE
BEGUN	**(CONTINUED)**			
And then stood where it first begun.		690	Cadenus Vaness	125
Thy greatest Evils yet are scarce begun.		793	St. Pat's Well	88
BEHAVE				
See, how behave his Friends profest,		545	Life of Swift	19
Now, see, when they meet, how their Honour's behave;		869	Grand Question	71
BEHAVIOUR				
Let <Prelates>, by their good behaviour,		488	Irish-Club	21
Who, had she known his vile Behaviour,		514	Answer Fable	77
Some try to learn polite Behaviour,		592	Strephon Chloe	271
BEHELD				
Late I beheld on every face appear;		52	Temple Ill	40
Trembling beheld the doubtful hand of fate;		52	Temple Ill	42
And thence Beheld a Lovely Maid		119	Apollo Outwit	3
When he beheld and smelt the Towels,		527	Lady's Dres Rm	44
"Beheld the dire destructive Scene:		568	Death of Swift	392
These Eyes, these Eyes beheld the Fact.		596	Cassinus Peter	98
St. George beheld thee with Delight,		656	On Poetry	461
The Nymphs with Scorn beheld their Foes:		687	Cadenus Vaness	21
BEHIND				
To lodge behind a golden cloud;		41	Ode Sancroft	216
More than a fade insipid mixture left behind.		50	To Congreve	212
That we the wretched, creeping far behind,		54	Temple Ill	115
And from behind, and from before;		65	Problem	10
Some ply before, and some behind.		66	Problem	38
He stood behind a Stall to lurk,		86	Hist V's House	15
Nor hid himself behind the Moon,		98	Elegy Patrige	13
The Epilogue behind, did frame		108	V's House	93
Observ'd the Roof behind the Grass;		127	Little House	24
This dang'rous Priest is got behind the Curtain:		194	Author Himself	38
"Whose Chariot's that we left behind?		201	Horace 2, 6	70
Yet swifter Fate will seize him from behind.		210	Earl of Oxford	6
Plac'd you in Life too far behind;		215	To Mr. Delany	6
In Church, secure behind her Fan		222	Prog of Love	11
What Papers Phil had left behind,		223	Prog of Love	44
Leaving the fiery red behind,		227	Prog of Beauty	35
To that dear Self he left behind;		235	Elegy on Demar	50
Tormenting Fools behind their Backs;		240	Run Bankers	30
The Moon lay safe behind the Cloud.		253	Bubble	80
Shall sink, and leave no mark behind it.		255	Bubble	136
Then fled, and left his Horn behind		293	Prog Marriage	115
He left behind so great a <stink>.		296	Satiric Elegy	16
The wond'rous Arch behind you fell,		326	Pethox	95
If you make the same Tryal, and Bore him Behind;		336	Serious Poem	78
Conceal'd behind that ample Screen,		354	Simile Silver	23
To lurk behind a mean Disguise;		386	Manly Virtue	78
Except some Leather lost behind.		398	Earl of P-b-w	24
Would halt behind him, were it bigger.		398	Earl of P-b-w	27
Though strong in Limbs, he lagg'd behind.		412	Desire Possess	38
Good Fortune peeping from behind;		452	Modern Lady	229
We left a little Duke behind;		466	Birthday Song	200
That safe behind the Wainscoat lyes.		504	Doctor Delaney	138
Who waited on his Eyes behind.		513	Answer Fable	30
That Hope at last remain'd behind;		528	Lady's Dres Rm	88
To him that looks behind the Scene,		530	Lady's Dres Rm	133
He left his Scut behind, and Half an Ear.		538	Mr. Pulteney	36
What Money was behind him found?		547	Life of Swift	72
What Writings had he left behind---?		550	Life of Swift	180
Before, behind, above, below,		584	Strephon Chloe	13
Since Husbands get behind the Scene,		588	Strephon Chloe	137
The Nymph opprest before, behind,		589	Strephon Chloe	169
Than she, to name her Parts behind,		590	Strephon Chloe	217
You'd think she utter'd from behind,		592	Strephon Chloe	281
Or strung on Pegs behind the Door;		592	Strephon Chloe	290
And grown so bold behind his Back		605	Beasts Confess	127
Is bit by him that comes behind;		651	On Poetry	342
That Feilding leaves him far behind.		654	On Poetry	396
So fast, his Lessons lagg'd behind:		704	Cadenus Vaness	557
Breaks like the Sun behind a Cloud,		726	To Stella	82
He flies, and leaves the Stars behind,		728	Stella, Poems	36
Nothing but Acid left behind.		731	Stella, Poems	134
It drags behind a spacious Womb,		743	Stel B-day 22	68
Should acting, die, nor leave behind		764	Stel B-day '26	29
That fly and leave no Marks behind?		765	Stel B-day '26	54
While Punch is hid behind the Scene,		776	Mullinix Tim	94
Shou'd Faustus, with the Devil behind him,		776	Mullinix Tim	101
And Sons of Whores--behind their Backs.		778	Mullinix Tim	164
Be careful, as you walk behind,		780	Mullinix Tim	231
Seen from behind a dirty Clout:		786	Clad in Brown	10
And have left us but Three out of Twenty behind 'em.		804	Irish Bishops	24
Half the best are still behind:		839	Legion Club	236
To leave something behind:		857	Lady's Lament	200
Give her half thy Face behind.		862	To Janus	8
Or, had only Eyes behind.--		862	To Janus	18
Thy Breeches torn behind, stand gaping wide;		881	Pastoral Dial	21
When you with Oonah stood behind a Ditch,		882	Pastoral Dial	37
Behind my Back, before my Nose,		887	Panegyr Dean	27
Shall creep no more behind a Bush;		893	Panegyr Dean	214
And leaves a lifeless corpse behind.		900	Dean's Reasons	50
In Line direct, hung down behind.		903	Death Daphne	28
I wisely chuse to walk behind;		917	Riddle 4	2

		PAGE	TITLE	LINE

BEHIND (CONTINUED)

	PAGE	TITLE	LINE
I'm forc'd to leave a Limb behind.	921	Riddle 6	36
Take wise Advice, and look behind,	921	Riddle 7	3
And leave behind their fruitless Wealth.	922	Riddle 7	32
Was bid to throw the Stones behind;	922	Riddle 7	46
So I'll leave him behind, for I certainly know it,	979	Dean to Tho: S	31
But that you left no Clap behind.	1033	Ans to Crown	6

BEHOLD

	PAGE	TITLE	LINE
With indignation I behold your wit	45	To Congreve	55
When, Behold the next Mornihg, a wonderful Riddle,	77	Lady B- B-	8
Behold, a Miracle was wroght	92	Bauc & Phil 1	74
She durst behold that Monster, Man:	222	Prog of Love	12
Ladyes, and Gentlemen, behold,	251	Bubble	7
Behold it mounting to the Top,	251	Bubble	14
Behold it swelling like a Sop.	251	Bubble	16
Behold the awful Bench on which he sat,	285	Elegy Boat	19
Behold his funeral appears,	296	Satiric Elegy	17
Come hither, and behold your fate.	296	Satiric Elegy	28
When you behold the milky Way	362	Grace's Answer	31
Behold him blooming, fresh, and fair,	384	Manly Virtue	17
Behold the Glory he has won,	385	Manly Virtue	41
Behold those Monarch-Oaks that rise,	393	Modern Poets	1
Behold a Poem rise!	406	Swift to Pope	16
Behold his glitt'ring Faulchion mow	461	Birthday Song	31
Behold three beauteous Vowels stand	467	Birthday Song	229
But I only behold thee in Atherton's Shape,	518	Dean Hang Rape	47
With hasty Zeal, behold, the Steward come,	533	To Mr. Gay	71
Behold a Foe more fierce than all the rest:	538	Mr. Pulteney	32
We all behold with envious Eyes,	554	Death of Swift	13
"Behold the fatal Day arrive!	558	Death of Swift	147
Behold the Ruins of the Night!	583	Young Nymph	58
Behold the Bridegroom and his Bride,	585	Strephon Chloe	57
And there--behold Alecto stand,	596	Cassinus Peter	81
Behold the Bottle, where it lies	743	Stel B-day 22	61
Behold a cage with sparrows fill'd,	753	Gift for Bec	11
Behold, it cracks by yon rough Eastern Wind.	770	Horace 1, 14	18
Behold! a proof of Irish sense!	843	Epigr Irish	1
Behold! the cruel Dean in Scorn	849	Old Thorn	23
Behold; a frothy Substance rise;	892	Panegyr Dean	183
Come hither and behold the Fruits,	921	Riddle 7	1
The wretched Purchase here behold	921	Riddle 7	17
Behold, the Coward, and the Brave,	922	Riddle 7	27
Wise and glorious to behold;	936	Riddle 24 D	20

BEHOLDER

	PAGE	TITLE	LINE
While every ignorant Beholder	63	Discovery	15

BEHOLDERS

	PAGE	TITLE	LINE
Or in the presence of beholders,	421	Ireld	21

BEHOLDS

	PAGE	TITLE	LINE
Sham'd and amaz'd, beholds the chatt'ring throng,	50	To Congreve	223
Beholds her from the Chaplain's Place	291	Prog Marriage	63

BEING

	PAGE	TITLE	LINE
Else where's the Gain in being Great?	6	Ode to King	5
Won't pay th' Impertinence of being known;	20	Ode Athenian	152
Thus fools, for being strong and num'rous known,	37	Ode Sancroft	79
That thou ne'er hadst a being of thy own,	54	Temple Ill	94
But being old continued just	94	Bauc & Phil 1	169
(As being Bricks at Second Hand,)	108	V's House	77
But being Old, continu'd	115	Bauc & Phil 2	123
Both Church and State, being still dependent.	372	Letter D. S-y	22
Being possitive there is no <P--st>	372	Letter D. S-y	31
As you Dr. <Smedley> are, being sure	372	Letter D. S-y	33
Lest my Mobb's Mouth, being seldom quiet	373	Letter D. S-y	66
And since I 'scap'd being made a Scoff,	377	Apology Lady C	55
For next to being Great our selves	493	Panegyr Swift	11
That Virtue, pleas'd by being shown,	706	Cadenus Vaness	608
"Since ev'ry Being loves its Like.	714	Cadenus Vaness	879
If thou a real Being art;	919	Riddle 5	32

BELABOR

	PAGE	TITLE	LINE
He saw Virago Nell belabor	220	A Quiet Life	21

BELATED

	PAGE	TITLE	LINE
Belated, seems on watch to lye,	583	Young Nymph	49
Your Man is belated,	1014	Swift to Sheri	21

BELFAST

	PAGE	TITLE	LINE
Then, without fail, we pack up for Belfast.	309	Billet Players	56

BELGICK

	PAGE	TITLE	LINE
To hear the Belgick Lyon roar.	468	Birthday Song	246

BELIEF

	PAGE	TITLE	LINE
Which to divulge might shake profane belief,	53	Temple Ill	77

BELIEV'D

	PAGE	TITLE	LINE
At which, 'tis hard to be believ'd,	117	Bauc & Phil 2	175
But who believ'd him when he said it:	220	A Quiet Life	38
Believ'd it best to condescend	306	Storm	75
Wise People, who believ'd with Reason	354	Simile Silver	5
Believ'd in God, and you in none.	495	Panegyr Swift	85
From Rogues who ne'er believ'd a God?	820	Dr. Rundle	30
And, Madam, I always believ'd you so stout,	869	Grand Question	55

BELIEVE

	PAGE	TITLE	LINE
And (I believe) began himself the Fight,	8	Ode to King	60
That I believe in much, I ne're can hope to see;	20	Ode Athenian	134
And when you find out these, believe true Fame is there.	21	Ode Athenian	186
Shall I believe a Spirit so divine	32	Ode to Temple	178

	PAGE	TITLE	LINE
BELIEVE (CONTINUED)			
Believe it firm, because perhaps the day is mild and still	37	Ode Sancroft	75
For, youth, believe, to you unseen, is fix'd	44	To Congreve	31
And the bad world may well believe the same;	49	To Congreve	198
He sees, yet hardly can believe,	115	Bauc & Phil 2	119
And hardly could believe his Eyes,	116	Bauc & Phil 2	146
I hope you don't believe me Jealous:	116	Bauc & Phil 2	158
Nor wou'd believe My Lord had sent;	172	Horace 1, 7	52
Believe me, what thou'st undertaken	181	Horace 2, 1	29
Give Hints, that Poets ne'er believe in God.	193	Author Himself	6
I dare believe that Four in Five	235	Elegy on Demar	51
Pray Gentlemen, believe your Eyes,	254	Bubble	102
To believe all his Verses were written by me;	266	Apollo	100
Believe me 'tis the Way to Rise.	361	Grace's Answer	12
Told him, she thought she might believe him;	378	Apology Lady C	86
Poor sweaty Paulus, who'd believe us ?	433	Answer Paulus	38
From many (and we may believe)	455	Dean Smedley	13
That Princes should believe in God:	468	Birthday Song	264
You can't, grave Sir, believe it hard,	475	Epist on Epist	3
Convince us they believe a Saviour;	488	Irish-Club	22
From Nature, I believe 'em true:	553	Death of Swift	2
"The Dean, if we believe Report,	565	Death of Swift	307
The Doctor, if you will believe him,	604	Beasts Confess	113
You, when it rains, like Fools believe,	627	Scandal Poem 2	125
What tho' they don't believe in Christ	658	On Poetry	D 190
But let me warn thee to believe	735	Stel B-day '20	45
I'll ne'er believe a Word they say.	757	Stel B-day '24	40
Believe me Stella, when you show	765	Stel B-day '26	67
And all Men believe he presides there incog.	804	Irish Bishops	15
Who send my mind (as I believe) less	900	Dean's Reasons	53
Who can believe with common Sense,	949	Epigr Fasting	1
. . . and I don't believe that's a true Story,	906	Mary to Sher	20
Oh! I forgot too, I believe there may be one more, . . .	1023	Nim-Dan-Dean 2	D 9
. . .and you'll believe me as sure as a gun, and own it; .	1023	Nim-Dan-Dean 2	D 15
The Heathen doth believe in Christ	1036	Heathen Christ	1
BELIEVES			
And scarce believes his Eyes, or Ears;	376	Apology Lady C	20
A Prelate who no God believes;	645	On Poetry	163
While none believes that what he said he meant:	797	Traulus 1	50
But his has the Odds, who believes and who trembles.	803	Irish Bishops	8
'Tis granted he believes a Deity.	820	Dr. Rundle	24
BELINDA'S			
As glorious as Belinda's Hair?	271	Apollo's Edict	D 39
BELL SEE PASSING-BELL			
Then the Bell rung, and I went down to put my Lady to Bed,	69	Mrs Harris Pet	10
Tis now no Kettle but a Bell.	93	Bauc & Phil 1	104
'Tis now no Kettle, but a Bell.	113	Bauc & Phil 2	64
Warn'd by the Bell, all Flocks come trembling,	279	Journal	28
Because he rang the Bell.	406	Swift to Pope	28
Just o'er against the Bell Inn	442	Ballyspellin	57
To hear, the other bore the Bell---?	546	Life of Swift	55
No more I hear my Church's Bell,	674	His Deafness	3
And Patricks' bell she was ringing all in muffles;	840	Ballad	D 7
BELL'WING			
By bell'wing thus against the <Dean>?	795	Traulus 1	2
BELLE			
And ev'ry Belle that since arose	311	To Ford	21
BELLES			
To bath among the Belles and Beaux.	294	Prog Marriage	144
The Belles of Ballyspellin	442	Ballyspellin	66
Of Belles and Toasts	442	Ballyspellin	83
BELLIES			
May breath your Bellies full of Aether.	361	Grace's Answer	24
Their Throats were cut, their Bellies ript,	923	Riddle 7	74
Their Bellies are soft, and as white as a Custard.	953	Herrings	7
BELLOW			
He'll Bellow as loud as the Dee'l in a Drum:	336	Serious Poem	80
BELLS			
The brazen Bells salute his Ears:	338	Wood's Brass	6
Guns, Trumpets, Drums, and Bells were drown'd.	338	Wood's Brass	8
BELLY			
Her Belly in the neighb'ring Pool:	230	Prog of Poetry	6
With good Roast Beef his Belly full,	231	Prog of Poetry	21
His Guts and Belly full of Wind;	231	Prog of Poetry	38
This Dragon had gotten two Sows in it's Belly;	337	Serious Poem	88
A Fox with Geese his Belly crams;	651	On Poetry	325
Her Belly burst, and slow her Pace:	895	Panegyr Dean	276
BELONGING			
As belonging to their betters:	573	Helter Skelter	24
BELONGS			
"For she belongs to all the Graces;	321	First of April	10
BELOV'D SEE BEST-BELOV'D			
Sing (belov'd Muse) the Pleasures of Retreat,	30	Ode to Temple	135
BELOVED			
For quitting her beloved London.	362	Grace's Answer	40
BELOW			
To judge of things above by things below.	35	Ode Sancroft	38
Of heav'n-born Truth below:	36	Ode Sancroft	53
Like all transcendent excellence below;	39	Ode Sancroft	146
The way which ev'ry wand'ring fool below	39	Ode Sancroft	157

BELOW   (CONTINUED)   PAGE   TITLE   LINE

Line	PAGE	TITLE	LINE
To be, as 'twas below, the brightest plant above;	41	Ode Sancroft	229
As well as here below,	41	Ode Sancroft	232
This bids some curious praters here below	45	To Congreve	73
What poor regards would merit all below!	49	To Congreve	184
Or whether it came from Above or Below.	77	Lady B- B-	18
It's Inclination for below;	92	Bauc & Phil 1	100
On Coblers Militant below,	100	Elegy Patrige	90
A Cellar next was dug below:	108	V's House	86
Its Inclinations for below:	113	Bauc & Phil 2	60
Her love on some bright youth below,	178	To Lord Harley	60
While from below all Grub-street rings.	231	Prog of Poetry	46
His faithful Steward, in the Shades below.	234	Elegy on Demar	8
Now bury'd in the Depth below,	256	Bubble	149
We are very ill us'd by us Mortals below;	263	Apollo	2
How transient all things are below:	283	Journal	116
Among the trembling Croud below.	353	Wood Ironmongr	20
Will make you scorn this World below.	362	Grace's Answer	30
The Height of Glory here below,	386	Manly Virtue	100
But just a Step below the Crown:	392	Young's Satire	38
With equal Longitude below:	393	Modern Poets	4
Madam, the Goldsmith waits below,	446	Modern Lady	56
Teaz'd by a Buzzing Wasp, Below,	458	Paddy's Charac	30
Below the Lash of Snarlers Jokes.	501	Doctor Delaney	46
The Dregs will serve to ripen Ore below;	532	To Mr. Gay	24
Descends for Shelter to the Shades below.	538	Mr. Pulteney	24
Before, behind, above, below,	584	Strephon Chloe	13
Inferior mortals there below.	617	Scandal Poem 1	4
We govern all things there below.	620	Scandal Poem 1	88
Inferior Mortals there below.	623	Scandal Poem 2	4
We govern all Things there below.	626	Scandal Poem 2	86
They ply their former Arts below.	647	On Poetry	210
'Tis only infinite below.	654	On Poetry	392
'Tis fifty thousand Times below it.	657	On Poetry	480
These Pleadings in the Courts below,	689	Cadenus Vaness	80
A Boy in yonder Isle below,	692	Cadenus Vaness	190
When Goddesses appear below.	711	Cadenus Vaness	789
Wherein his Genius was below	712	Cadenus Vaness	812
Left all below at Six and Sev'n,	714	Cadenus Vaness	888
Enriching all the Vales below.	731	Stella, Poems	108
That true Contempt for Things below,	765	Stel B-day '26	68
Or from above, or from below,	776	Mullinix Tim	84
Foulest Brute that stinks below,	786	Clad in Brown	1
Is divided above, but united below.	805	Irish Bishops	42
And, see, the Printer's Boy below:	887	Panegyr Dean	32
A Consult of Coquets below	903	Death Daphne	19
She ask't about her Friends below;	905	Death Daphne	73
But see below me all Mankind.	917	Riddle 3	4
Of raising Spirits from below;	920	Riddle 6	10
The Mysteries that lye below.	922	Riddle 7	50
My Beauty to the Shades below.	927	Riddle 10	D 12
What he ripens above ground, he sours below it.	979	Dean to Tho: S	32
BELYE			
Will he his Character belye?	445	Modern Lady	14
BELZEBUB			
With Belzebub in Black	426	Five Ladies	20
BEMATTER'D			
Begumm'd, bematter'd, and beslim'd	527	Lady's Dres Rm	45
BEMIR'D			
The loving Couple well bemir'd,	224	Prog of Love	77
BEMOAN			
(How would her Virgin Soul bemoan	596	Cassinus Peter	103
O, Grubstreet! how do I bemoan thee,	652	On Poetry	357
Retire, yet still bemoan their Country's Fate.	772	Horace 1, 14	60
BEN'T			
Whether this ben't a Salamander	85	Salamander	70
BENCH			
Behold the awful Bench on which he sat,	285	Elegy Boat	19
Since <Burnet's> Death, the <Bishop's> Bench,	303	Storm	17
Now, on the Bench fair Justice shines,	391	Young's Satire	15
Then, from the bar, harangues the bench	434	Answer Paulus	77
Nor lets him sit as Justice on the Bench,	537	Mr. Pulteney	5
"A wicked Monster on the Bench,	569	Death of Swift	417
A Pick-purse at the Bar, or Bench;	645	On Poetry	165
Extoll ye Bench of Bishops round,	658	On Poetry	D 190
Has got on the Bench many <Bishops> suffragan:	803	Irish Bishops	14
BENCHES			
Benches on Boats are plac't, not Boats on Benches.	285	Elegy Boat	12
Benches on Boats are plac't, not Boats on Benches.	285	Elegy Boat	12
On their Rushy Beds and Benches,	574	Helter Skelter	46
BEND			
Hither thy gentle Aspect bend,	101	Elegy Patrige	101
To bend where Golden Mines were hid;	133	Magician's Rod	28
With both his Hands to bend a Twig;	191	Faggot	50
Let courtly Slaves low bend the Knee	386	Manly Virtue	93
Now, bend thine Ear; since out it must:	596	Cassinus Peter	99
As Rivers, tho' they bend and twine,	709	Cadenus Vaness	720
And to the South my Squadrons bend:	884	Rev Market-Hill	50
For, I can break, but scorn to bend.	921	Piddle 6	38
How long shall mortals bend to gain?	950	Upstart	D 18
Wherever you bend, wherever you twine	1017	Swift Ans Sher	22

		PAGE	TITLE	LINE

BENDED
With bended knees when they adore her . . . . 465 Birthday Song 157
Here pay their Vows with bended Knees: . . . . 893 Panegyr Dean 208

BENDER
Swear they were with the Swedes at Bender, ... 788 Dick's Variety 23

BENDING
Which bow'd by evening-breeze with bending stalks, . . 54 Temple Ill 119
That, bending down it's Top, divines . . . . 133 Magician's Rod 23

BENDS
Absurdly bends his whole Designs. . . . . 641 On Poetry 24
And what is worse, your Passion bends . . . . . . 730 Stella, Poems 97

BENEATH
The herd beneath, who see the weathercock of state . . 37 Ode Sancroft 73
And wisely judge, no pow'r beneath divine . . . . . 44 To Congreve 29
Beneath (A new Receit for Paint) . . . . 60 Lady Tablebook 8
Decently hid beneath his Goun. . . . . 95 Bauc & Phil 1 176
Beneath, and mended Shoes in Hell. . . . . 100 Elegy Patrige 68
Beneath this verdant Hillock lies . . . . 235 Elegy on Demar 41
Beneath thy decent Steps, the Road . . . . 324 Pethox 35
Beneath whose ill Shade no Plant ever grew. . . . . 334 Serious Poem 32
The Butcher, feels the Lamb beneath his blade. . . . 364 On Dreams 18
All this was much beneath her Due, ... 379 Apology Lady C 118
(Happy beneath his righteous Sway) . . . . 388 Manly Virtue 138
She'll come no more beneath your Roof. . . . . . . 408 Dial Rich Marb 12
His Hat for Show, beneath his Arm. . . . . 410 Dial Rich Marb 66
If e'er I stoop beneath a crown'd Head: . . . . . 410 Dial Rich Marb 74
Beneath, a Chasm as deep as Hell, ... 413 Desire Possess 43
He sunk beneath the cumbrous Weight: . . . . . . 413 Desire Possess 52
Half sunk beneath his brief and bag, ... 434 Answer Paulus 75
Beneath a dry Canal there lies, ... 478 Epist on Epist 89
Beneath the Arm-pits well besmear'd. . . . . . . 526 Lady's Dres Rm 12
Which fell in Clouds beneath his Feet) . . . . . . 625 Scandal Poem 2 68
All beneath yon flow'ry Rocks. . . . . 660 Love Song 8
Beneath the vast abyss he plunges quick, ... 672 Epig Carthy 24 D 17
By gen'rous Wines beneath a Shade. . . . . 731 Stella, Poems 112
And think it far beneath your Due; . . . . 766 Stel B-day '26 86
And here, beneath the spreading Shade, ... 848 Old Thorn 7
Why are thine Altars fix't beneath? . . . . 894 Panegyr Dean 232
More than the Dirt beneath my Shoes, nor fear it. . . 1003 Dan J's Reply 15
'Bout latent Charms beneath my Cloaths; . . . . . . 1004 Dan J's Reply 22

BENEFACTOR
Against your greatest benefactor. . . . . 622 Scandal Poem 1 172

BENEFACTORS
Now my new Benefactors have brought me about, ... 144 New Song 45
Peers, Clergy, Gentry, all are Benefactors; . . . . 274 Epilogue 7

BENEFICE
Or some rich benefice provide, ... 676 Parson's Case 21

BENEFICIAL
More beneficial Ways than Rhime; . . . . 495 Panegyr Swift 67

BENEFIT
Will give a Night of Benefit to Weavers. . . . . . 274 Epilogue 4

BENT
To thee I owe that fatal bent of mind, ... 55 Temple Ill 131
And now the Ladys all are bent, ... 66 Problem 33
So bent on Gains, <Ju--ro> by <C--est> . . . . . 372 Letter D. S-y 32
"While Nature kindly bent to ease us, ... 554 Death of Swift 9
So Witches bent on bad Pursuits, ... 670 Epig Carthy 19 D 1
On whom the Queen of Love was bent . . . . 691 Cadenus Vaness 138
At last she spitefully was bent . . . . 697 Cadenus Vaness 338
When bent upon some smart Lampoon, ... 892 Panegyr Dean 189

BEQUEATH'D
Bequeath'd by Tripsy when she dy'd, ... 526 Lady's Dres Rm 30
"'Tis all bequeath'd to publick Uses. . . . . . . 558 Death of Swift 156

BEQUEATHED
Bequeathed to Pluto, Corps and all. . . . . 904 Death Daphne 32

BEREAVE
"The Pope would of our Faith bereave us, ... 549 Life of Swift 154

BERECYNTHIA
Thus Berecynthia takes her place, ... 466 Birthday Song 183

BERKELEY
"There's Berkeley in the same Condition; . . . . . 304 Storm 48
"We'll give you Berkeley for Bermudas. . . . . . . 305 Storm 52
But fearing Berkeley might be scar'd . . . . 306 Storm 77
When wise Ld <Berkeley> first came here, ... 62 Discovery 1

BERLIN
Is drawn by peacocks in her Berlin . . . . 621 Scandal Poem 1 124
Is drawn by Peacocks in her Berlin: . . . . 627 Scandal Poem 2 118

BERMUDAS
"We'll give you Berkeley for Bermudas. . . . . . . 305 Storm 52

BERNARD
From sloven Bernard to beau Dalacourt. . . . . . . 672 Epig Carthy 24 D 8

BERRIS
Nor shall grin Berris make up the Losse. . . . . . 103 Merlin 10

BESET
By this odious Crew beset, ... 832 Legion Club 93

BESIDE
That looks with scorn on half mankind beside; . . . 44 To Congreve 44
Beside all this, deep Scholars know, ... 66 Problem 21
Beside the getting of a Name? . . . . 83 Salamander 14
Beside, it Spues a filthy Froth, ... 84 Salamander 51
There are ten thousand Dicks beside; . . . . 221 A Quiet Life 56

		PAGE	TITLE	LINE
BESIDE	(CONTINUED)			
Hath she no other wants beside?		292	Prog Marriage	73
He own'd no Deity beside.		303	Storm	14
Your Rent is due almost a Week beside the Days of Grace.		343	Upon His Grace	44
A score of Goddesses beside.		460	Birthday Song	8
And griev'd your righteous Soul beside, ...		496	Panegyr Swift	91
With Int'rest, and a Praemium paid beside, ...		533	To Mr. Gay	69
More than from all the World beside.		591	Strephon Chloe	254
Whole afternoons will sit beside her, ...		762	Bec's B-Day	49
Beside a Brace of grave Divines;		1020	Nim-Dan-Dean 1	D 3
BESIDES				
. . .six Pence, besides Farthings, in Money, and Gold;		69	Mrs Harris Pet	2
Besides, as they say, Service is no Inheritance in these Ages.		71	Mrs Harris Pet	41
A Stock of tawdry Stuff besides,		80	Vanbrug House	46
Besides, that slow-pac'd Sign Bo-otes		98	Elegy Patrige	31
Besides, he could confound the Spheres, ...		99	Elegy Patrige	57
Besides, it plainly now appears, ...		158	Fable of Midas	61
Besides, this horrid Plot was found		299	Horrid Plot	37
"Besides, to me this seems a Bubble,		321	First of April	23
"With Virtue, Prudence, Wit besides;		322	First of April	48
And besides must be out of my Wits:		395	Dog and Thief	4
Besides, I'll hold a Groat, ...		425	Five Ladies	11
Besides you Songsters oft have shewn,		465	Birthday Song	163
Besides a pair of princely Babyes, ...		465	Birthday Song	171
Besides; your Patron may upbraid ye, ...		483	Libel on D- D-	103
Besides, his Memory decays, ...		556	Death of Swift	85
Besides, the Tale is false in Fact.		607	Beasts Confess	198
I have enough besides to spare, ...		692	Cadenus Vaness	196
Besides, she fear'd the Queen of Love		695	Cadenus Vaness	268
Besides, Dick forbid me, and call'd me a fool;		980	Tho: Sheridan	7
Besides, you found fault with our Vittles		986	Mary to Sher	25
BESIEGE				
And in their very Ports besiege, ...		463	Birthday Song	103
BESLIM'D				
Begumm'd, bematter'd, and beslim'd		527	Lady's Dres Rm	45
BESMEAR'D				
Beneath the Arm-pits well besmear'd.		526	Lady's Dres Rm	12
His Grazier's coat with dirt besmear'd, ...		879	Robbin & Harry	43
BESPATTER				
How evil Tongues his Life bespatter:		602	Beasts Confess	48
Whom never Faction cou'd bespatter, ...		655	On Poetry	413
'Tis your gross panegyrics alone can bespatter. . .		819	Archbi Cashel	14
Pray do they praise me or bespatter?		1003	Dan J's Reply	5
BESPEAK				
To bespeak some Approbation, ...		833	Legion Club	111
BESPEAKS				
You know, a cloudy sky bespeaks		618	Scandal Poem 1	29
You know a Cloudy Sky bespeaks		624	Scandal Poem 2	23
Whose Phiz bespeaks his diet water-gruel.		672	Epig Carthy 24	D 10
BESPOKE				
The Vicar and the Ring bespoke:		223	Prog of Love	23
BESS				
"And beauteous Bess a diff'rent case is,		321	First of April	9
Will cudgell's Bess, yet Will's a Cully		328	Epigram 3	2
Dye Ned and Bess; give Will to Joan, ...		328	Epigram 3	3
Dye Joan and Will; give Bess to Ned, ...		328	Epigram 3	5
That Gown was made for Old Queen Bess.		699	Cadenus Vaness	397
Big like Bess, and small like Sue;		936	Riddle 24	D 28
BEST				
'Tis the best Gemm in Royalty, ...		6	Ode to King	22
And His best Victory a Noble Death;		9	Ode to King	106
Take up at best with Lumber and the Leavings of a Fate:		32	Ode to Temple	184
(High Truth) the best resemblance of exalted Thee, .		36	Ode Sancroft	46
But foolish Man still judges what is best		36	Ode Sancroft	54
The best companion for the best of men:		52	Temple Ill	46
The best companion for the best of men:		52	Temple Ill	46
Names that would best their Natures suit:		83	Salamander	8
That best Foundations must be low.		87	Hist V's House	40
Does to his best look upward still.		101	Elegy Patrige	106
Told <Van> he knew his Talent best, ...		107	V's House	53
Jove saw the Cheat, but thought it best		108	V's House	67
Jove mix'd up all, and his best Clay imploy'd; . .		118	Biddy Floyd	11
And will quit my best Friends, while I'm Not in game.		144	New Song	26
He tore her lac'd Pinner;		153	Widow and Cat	D 12
You shall be coupled as you best approve, ...		165	Toland's Invit	31
Makes choice of him she fancies best, ...		178	To Lord Harley	63
How best to settle their Affections;		182	Horace 2, 1	56
Didst in thy calling do thy best.		182	Horace 2, 1	58
Yet Mum for that, hope still the best, ...		182	Horace 2, 1	69
Be satisfy'd, I'll do my best:--		201	Horace 2, 6	58
By reading those who teach it best.		219	To Mr. Delany	104
The best Mechanick Hand must fayl		228	Prog of Beauty	79
Is inactivity at best:		242	Horace 4, 9	2
Inform us, You that best can tell, ...		252	Bubble	49
South-Sea at best a mighty Bubble.		259	Bubble	220
Whom, when I with the best of my Talents endu'd, .		264	Apollo	45
When Actors who at best are hardly Savers, . . .		274	Epilogue	3
In bed, where he can spare her best.		292	Prog Marriage	90
The Dean with all his best Endeavour		295	Horrid Plot	151

BEST   (CONTINUED)   PAGE   TITLE   LINE

	PAGE	TITLE	LINE
Assur'd her he wou'd do his best:	302	Storm	10
Believ'd it best to condescend	306	Storm	75
I think the best Thing we can do is to scald him.	351	Wood Insect	34
The plainest Mails must be the best:	378	Apology Lady C	104
Is qualified best for a Dog in a String.	389	Order of Bath	12
What Lining best the Silk will suit;	416	Woman's Mind	30
Had the best wishes they cou'd give him.	455	Dean Smedley	14
He'll mount his Tub, and preach his best,	456	Dean Smedley	38
And fit your present Subject best.	460	Birthday Song	4
Of Gods I only quote the best,	465	Birthday Song	149
A hungry Vicarage at best;	484	Libel on D- D-	132
Whose Wit at best was next to none,	514	Answer Fable	67
On such a Point few Words are best,	526	Lady's Dres Rm	15
Then he who prophecy'd the best,	557	Death of Swift	127
Is best supported by Opinion;	590	Strephon Chloe	224
What Subject you can manage best;	642	On Poetry	80
The vilest Verse thrives best at Court.	646	On Poetry	186
The worst & best that could be had	659	On Poetry	D 410
That best ye regal Nature suit,	659	On Poetry	D 410
With ale and chops I'll treat who writes the best,	671	Epig Carthy 24	D 5
The Pleader having spoke his best,	688	Cadenus Vaness	67
She thought it best to take Advice.	689	Cadenus Vaness	92
Yet she wou'd act as best became	695	Cadenus Vaness	274
Whether the Red or Green were best,	698	Cadenus Vaness	380
She still determines what is best:	725	To Stella	60
Best Pattern of true Friends, beware;	727	To Stella	117
Take Comfort, that our own is best:	728	Stella, Poems	20
(The best we value by the worst,	728	Stella, Poems	21
She did her best to ape Woodpark. She strove in vain to ape	747	Stel Distress	48
My meaning will be best unravell'd,	782	Tim and Fables	1
But Dick the best at <farting>.	784	Mullinex Dick	8
But Tom was best at Borees:	784	Mullinex Dick	14
Or, grant him but a Drone at best:	798	Traulus 1	83
On his virtues hold forth; 'tis the very best way;	819	Archbi Cashel	9
Half the best are still behind:	839	Legion Club	236
Who makes the best figure,	856	Lady's Lament	169
And which is the best	856	Lady's Lament	171
But how to dispose of it to the best Bidder,	867	Grand Question	5
'Tis best to hang her on the Spot;	886	Rev Market-Hill	108
What Pints may best for Bottles pass,	889	Panegyr Dean	93
When proper to produce the best;	889	Panegyr Dean	95
Thee best befits a lowly Style:	897	Panegyr Dean	329
Without my Aid, the best Divine	915	Riddle 1	29
An humble Hanger-on at best;	918	Riddle 4	21
And shew where they can best confute.	930	Riddle 15	D 24
When too long, is bad at best.	940	Letter	9
A long-ear'd Beast, and the Drink you love best	943	Probatur Alit	35
A cart would best become the knave,	951	Upstart	D 25
'Tis all you have for't; 'tis your best Magna Carta;	979	Dean to Tho: S	16
So much, he swears the very best Piece is	988	Letter Dr Sh-n	22
But the loss of your Cough will be the best Sign	1017	Swift Ans Sher	14
BEST-BELOV'D			
In Virtue's best-belov'd Retreat;	385	Manly Virtue	50
BESTOW			
But, when a Goddess would bestow	178	To Lord Harley	59
Bestow to bury him one Iron Chest.	233	Elegy on Demar	6
The Sexton shall green Sods on thee bestow.	235	Elegy on Demar	37
The public should bestow the actors six.	308	Billet Players	22
It's Pity that he can't bestow you	476	Epist on Epist	41
Before you Build and You Bestow,	479	Epist on Epist	116
Bestow that Libeller a Lash,	515	Answer Fable	91
And shock our Sense, till we bestow.	667	Epig Carthy 6	D 4
Bestow my next I pray, to Pope or Swift.	669	Epig Carthy 17	D 4
With that Devotion we bestow,	711	Cadenus Vaness	788
Or how could she her Heart bestow	733	Verses Vanessa	21
BESTOW'D			
Bestow'd as Hi'roglyphicks fit	83	Salamander	11
His Heirs for Winding-Sheet bestow'd	235	Elegy on Demar	43
And the Gifts I bestow'd her, will find her a Lover,	266	Apollo	107
Proteus on you bestow'd the Boon	326	Pethox	81
And, Praise bestow'd in Grub-Street Rimes,	505	Doctor Delaney	165
Nor dare to use the gifts by heav'n bestow'd;	506	To a Friend	10
On Lewis all his Bards bestow'd,	657	On Poetry	473
Bestow'd her by nature,	854	Lady's Lament	98
Yet, some who ne'er bestow'd thee, boast	919	Riddle 5	29
BESTOWS			
To you the Muse this Verse bestows,	215	To Mr. Delany	9
To use the Gifts, that Heav'n bestows;	243	Horace 4, 9	18
"And with what Justice he bestows.	462	Birthday Song	76
And Blessings equally on all bestows.	793	St. Pat's Well	68
Who feels true Joys when he bestows thee.	920	Riddle 5	36
BESTRODE			
For if bestrode by you, Old <Nick>,	497	Panegyr Swift	138
BETIMES			
Her Talent she display'd betimes;	150	Corinna	13
Take care betimes to run him down:	171	Horace 1, 7	30
Next morn betimes the Bride was missing,	223	Prog of Love	26
And waits on the Captain betimes the next Morning.	869	Grand Question	70

		PAGE	TITLE	LINE
BETOKENS				
Betokens Entertainment there, ...		457	Paddy's Charac	4
BETRAY				
Nor bribe, insult, nor flatter, nor betray.		533	To Mr. Gay	56
You cannot bribe, betray, or plot.		641	On Poetry	48
They soon betray their native Place:		652	On Poetry	362
Betray, make Oath, impeach, inform, ...		778	Mullinix Tim	168
For those who rais'd me, I betray;		917	Riddle 3	12
BETRAY'D				
For, Stella has betray'd her Trust, ...		311	To Ford	2
My purest Passion has betray'd.		595	Cassinus Peter	58
Was, in the very Search, betray'd		702	Cadenus Vaness	491
The Town wou'd swear he had betray'd, ...		707	Cadenus Vaness	646
Those whom they could not conquer, they betray'd. . .		791	St. Pat's Well	24
When Christ was betray'd to Pilate, the Praetor, . .		804	Irish Bishops	29
BETRAYED				
Judas betrayed his Master with a Kiss:		806	Judas	10
BETRAYS				
He who betrays his Friend, shall never be		210	Earl of Oxford	17
A Villain, who his Friend betrays, ...		298	Horrid Plot	7
BETT				
Puts all upon a desp'rate Bett, ...		251	Bubble	22
Some Cully often wins a Bett		257	Bubble	162
BETTER				
Your Garden's better worth your noble Pain, ...		32	Ode to Temple	176
Here, on a better day, some druid dwelt, ...		49	To Congreve	191
Near better animals, her father's sheep;		50	To Congreve	222
Sprung from a better world, and chosen then		52	Temple Ill	45
Lives pious witness of a better age;		52	Temple Ill	48
. . .or instead of Him, a Better:		73	Mrs Harris Pet	73
And painted, lookt abundance better		93	Bauc & Phil 1	122
The better Half we had to say;		106	V's House	30
Now seem'd to look abundance better, ...		114	Bauc & Phil 2	97
Loves Mischief better than his Meat, ...		171	Horace 1, 7	14
To better Judgments willing to submit, ...		194	Author Himself	25
Will think his better Half alive.		235	Elegy on Demar	52
Since a living Dog better is than a dead Lyon, . . .		237	Excellent Song	13
Directors better know their Tools, ...		253	Bubble	58
Who I, for your Sake, have us'd better than any; . .		263	Apollo	26
No Boat was better deckt than He.		286	Elegy Boat	42
Rather than starve, a better man would strole. . . .		308	Billet Players	16
(Nor Jove himself could do it better)		353	Wood Ironmongr	36
Harangues the Rabble, and is better paid.		364	On Dreams	34
You see the better with the other:		366	Answer Delaney	22
None loves his King and Country better, ...		410	Dial Rich Marb	83
They may out-sell a better Thing;		418	Woman's Mind	63
Who kindly would leave thee no worse nor no better. .		424	Carterets Arms	20
But, shift him to a better scene, ...		435	Answer Paulus	117
Far better than a printed Book;		450	Modern Lady	191
Wou'd his own Temples better fit, ...		458	Paddy's Charac	22
With Capitals, the more the better.		469	Birthday Song	280
Their Offals, or their better Meat, ...		479	Epist on Epist	122
And place you in a better Station, ...		484	Libel on D- D-	119
Your Simile may better shine		486	Libel on D- D-	193
Your Industry no better throve, ...		495	Panegyr Swift	81
The Simile would better jump, ...		497	Panegyr Swift	136
To make their Trash the better sell.		505	Doctor Delaney	158
And better would give us, if better she had; . . .		520	Dean Hang Rape	70
And better would give us, if better she had; . . .		520	Dean Hang Rape	70
O may she better learn to keep		528	Lady's Dres Rm	97
Say, had the Court no better place to chuse		531	To Mr. Gay	7
Would love his Fav'rite better than before;		535	To Mr. Gay	113
He no where could have better pick'd;		545	Life of Swift	17
For much a better Man than You?		546	Life of Swift	36
And get the better of your Love;		546	Life of Swift	38
To make these Truths the better known, ...		547	Life of Swift	66
"And Preachers, find the better quarter, ...		549	Life of Swift	166
Wou'd please 'em better than to tell, ...		557	Death of Swift	125
Have better learn'd to act their Parts.		562	Death of Swift	226
"We hope he's in a better Place.		562	Death of Swift	242
"The Town hath got a better Taste:		563	Death of Swift	266
"I wish it soon may have a Better.		572	Death of Swift	484
'Twere better you had lickt her Leavings, ...		591	Strephon Chloe	242
A better Neighbour ne'er was found:		602	Beasts Confess	44
He better understands his Trade:		607	Beasts Confess	212
Tis sung. but we know better things.		621	Scandal Poem 1	142
The nettle never thrives the better.		621	Scandal Poem 1	146
Who better challenge your Allegiance, ...		626	Scandal Poem 2	95
'Tis sung, but we know better Things.		627	Scandal Poem 2	146
The Nettle never thrives the better;		628	Scandal Poem 2	150
We expect Employment better.		633	Epistle Lady	112
Switches better guide than Cudgels.		636	Epistle Lady	202
That they might some better Way tread, ...		637	Epistle Lady	223
A better than the Poet meant, ...		643	On Poetry	102
We now can better do without him, ...		657	On Poetry	493
Known by the Verse, yet better by the Notes. . . .		670	Epig Carthy 18	D 4
Far better than consulting Laws.		690	Cadenus Vaness	135
Wou'd meet with better Friends above.		695	Cadenus Vaness	269
In Flounces has a better Fancy.		700	Cadenus Vaness	419
To know the World a little better.		700	Cadenus Vaness	429
Cou'd better now the Cause decide.		713	Cadenus Vaness	837

		PAGE	TITLE	LINE
BETTER	(CONTINUED)			
To fill a Place, for want of better;		756	Stel B-day '24	10
While I can better hear than see;		758	Stel B-day '24	52
For better Game, and look for Grouse:		760	Receipt Youth	54
Companions that will please her better;		762	Bec's B-Day	48
A better and more pleasing Thought,		764	Stel B-day '26	10
And guide you to a better State.		766	Stel B-day '26	78
Which gets the better, Saint, or Snake.		777	Mullinix Tim	130
But Dick could better sputter.		784	Mullinex Dick	24
Dick knew better how to swing		785	Mullinex Dick	31
But Tom had better Learning.		785	Mullinex Dick	36
Not one Jot better looks the Sun		786	Clad in Brown	9
To better Judgments still submitting,		788	Dick's Variety	9
We'll teach him some better address to afford		816	Yahoo's	53
For who would not think it a much better choice,		818	Epigr Kite	3
Who shew'd a better Jus divinum?		820	Dr. Rundle	38
Your Title had been so much better.		821	Dr. Rundle	66
Poor rump, thou hadst been better sped,		822	Epigr Rundle	3
Better we all were in our Graves		824	Printer Newgat	1
We must give them better Quarter,		837	Legion Club	177
I was better for him,		853	Lady's Lament	57
'Twere better be blind,		856	Lady's Lament	153
Nor makes their conversation better,		900	Dean's Reasons	39
She has better learnt her creed:		907	Daphne	40
What fits it better than a Fan?		912	Aenigma Expl	D 10
But the sly Giver better knows thee;		920	Riddle 5	35
Will cover a House much better than Clay.		943	Probatur Alit	34
I'd not look at all, unless I look't better.		943	Probatur Alit	38
Better ne'er was try'd.		953	Herrings	5
She declares from her throne you must learn better manners		979	Dean to Tho: S	28
For a Parson, who shou'd know better Things,		985	Mary to Sher	6
...but my Sister Marget she writes better.		987	Mary to Sher	34
'Tis true no Nose could come in better,		993	On Picture	16
'Cause I call Dan my better half,		1004	Dan J's Reply	26
So Dan's the better, tho' the less,		1004	Dan J's Reply	32
Knew how to set you better Patterns;		1033	Ans to Crown	16
BETTERS				
Wher'er he went he never saw his Betters,		234	Elegy on Demar	15
The Ghost of old <Damer>, who left not his Betters,		288	Bank Down	41
And by the Orders of his Betters		373	Letter D. S-y	73
Be Modest: nor Address your Betters		479	Epist on Epist	117
With too much freedom treat my betters,		489	Dialogue	5
To treat our Betters like our Slaves,		493	Panegyr Swift	5
He shou'd have left them for his Betters;		548	Life of Swift	98
He'll treat me as he does my Betters.		561	Death of Swift	201
As belonging to their betters:		573	Helter Skelter	24
Thy Brother (far thy Betters) wore a Gown.		678	Dean and Duke	14
For Gods, their Betters, are too wise		689	Cadenus Vaness	83
Thus Tutors often treat their Betters.		705	Cadenus Vaness	591
Walk by my place, before my Betters,		778	Mullinix Tim	156
And, because he's their Betters, you carve for him first,		871	Grand Question	133
How dare you treat your Betters thus?		884	Rev Market-Hill	41
I'm always by my Betters led;		918	Riddle 4	39
When whip you trot up, without minding your betters,		978	Dean to Tho: S	3
By humble companions were sent to their betters:		1026	Sheri Circles	2
As his betters are us'd, shall be lash'd round the ring,		1027	Sheri Circles	19
Not seen by our Betters.		1036	Bless Country	3
BETTERTON				
He that has shone with Betterton and Weeks,		308	Billet Players	44
BETTESWORTH				
Thus at the Bar that Booby Bettesworth,		812	Bro Protestant	25
Bow <Bettesworth>, that booby, and <Scoundrel> in grain,		814	Yahoo's	3
BETTY				
Now Betty from her Masters Bed had flown,		124	Descriptn Morn	3
And Lady Betty soundly chides them.		279	Journal	34
Then to her Glass; and "Betty, pray		446	Modern Lady	48
"Here Betty, let me take my Drops,		451	Modern Lady	206
Queen of Wit and Beauty, Betty,		522	Betty Grizette	1
And Betty otherwise employ'd;		526	Lady's Dres Rm	6
Miss Betty, when she does a Fault,		694	Cadenus Vaness	242
Bid Lady Betty recollect her.		993	On Picture	10
Lady Betty presents you her service most humble,		1027	Sheri Circles	25
BETTY'S				
That I went to warm my self in Lady Betty's Chamber,.		69	Mrs Harris Pet	1
Nay, said I, I had it in Lady Betty's Chamber,...		70	Mrs Harris Pet	17
While Betty's buzzing at her Ear,		291	Prog Marriage	41
BETWEEN				
Confesses ignorance to judge between;		41	Ode Sancroft	208
Gets between them and my resentment's weight,		45	To Congreve	46
Born between whores and fops, by lewd compacts,		47	To Congreve	125
Before the play, or else between the acts:		47	To Congreve	126
To take thee kindly in between,		100	Elegy Patrige	87
Untouch't it pass't between his Grinders,		156	Fable of Midas	11
How should I thrust my self between?		200	Horace 2, 6	30
When Stock is high they come between,		253	Bubble	69
At Night between Cavan-street and College-Green:		264	Apollo	54
Between the Weavers and us Play-House Kings.		275	Epilogue	36
Like Episodes between the Acts;		280	Journal	62
Sure such Intelligence between		301	Horrid Plot	73
The Diff'rence is not much between		313	To Ford	59

BETWEEN   (CONTINUED)   PAGE   TITLE   LINE
    Between the <King> and Us but Brass, ...   346 Prometheus   68
    How shall we pass the Time between?   . . . . . .   451 Modern Lady   205
    When Death approach'd, to stand between: . . . . .   561 Death of Swift   222
    And then between two Blankets creeps.   . . . . .   582 Young Nymph   38
    Between his Legs, to spew or spit in.   . . . . .   594 Cassinus Peter   22
    No diff'rence could he find between   . . . . .   619 Scandal Poem 1   57
    No Diff'rence could he find between   . . . . .   625 Scandal Poem 2   53
    Then, squeeze it close between our Thumbs, ...   627 Scandal Poem 2   129
    Between their Toylets and their Beds.   . . . . . .   688 Cadenus Vaness   50
    Scarce knows what Diff'rence is between   . . . . .   700 Cadenus Vaness   416
    That rais'd between the Stones their daily Shoots;   . . .   880 Pastoral Dial   4
    Divide the Realm between us two.   . . . . . .   886 Rev Market-Hill   92
    Between the Scepter and the Spade.   . . . . . .   895 Panegyr Dean   290
BETWIXT
    A mighty gulph unpassable betwixt. . . . . . .   44 To Congreve   32
    Ragged, and not a Groat betwixt 'em.   . . . . . .   90 Bauc & Phil 1   10
    In trickling Streams betwixt her Joynts.   . . . . . .   227 Prog of Beauty   44
    No jarring consonant betwixt.   . . . . . .   467 Birthday Song   232
    Betwixt a true and spurious Merit;   . . . . . .   484 Libel on D- D-   148
    And let not Faction come betwixt.   . . . . . .   503 Doctor Delaney   108
    No Brush could force a way betwixt.   . . . . . .   526 Lady's Dres Rm   22
    For placing still some Book betwixt, ...   701 Cadenus Vaness   480
    Betwixt a State, and Vessel under Sail;   . . . . . .   770 Horace 1, 14   6
    Than strongest Weeds that grow these Stones betwixt: . .   880 Pastoral Dial   10
    Or crack such Lice as his betwixt your Nails?   .   882 Pastoral Dial   36
    The Knight triumphant reigns betwixt: . . . . . .   883 Rev Market-Hill   20
    Betwixt the Knight sublime and me?   . . . . . .   901 Dean's Reasons   66
BEVEL
    Think this Wall low, and that Wall bevel.   . . . . .   477 Epist on Epist   66
BEWARE
    Ovid had warn'd her to beware, ...   120 Apollo Outwit   21
    Beware of Carrots from Northumberlond.   . . . . . .   148 Windsor Proph   16
    Beware, nor over-bulky grow, ...   258 Bubble   193
    Beware of Subjects you call Trite, ...   371 Letter D. S-y   2
    Then, honest <Robin>, of thy Corps beware: . . . . .   539 Mr. Pulteney   39
    Yet beware of her Arts, for it plainly appears, ...   580 Psyche   13
    Beware, O Bard, how you proceed.   . . . . . .   666 Epig Carthy 2   D   4
    Best Pattern of true Friends, beware;   . . . . .   727 To Stella   117
    Beware, and when you hear the Surges roar, ...   772 Horace 1, 14   61
BEWEYLE
    Than shall the Fyshe beweyle his Bosse;   . . . . .   103 Merlin   9
BEWITCH
    Can half the Peerage by his Arts bewitch;   . . . . .   535 To Mr. Gay   103
BEYOND
    Happy beyond a private muse's fate, ...   49 To Congreve   179
    And sometimes walks beyond his Bounds.   . . . . . .   218 To Mr. Delany   94
    He gets to a Window beyond both the Tropicks;   . . . .   265 Apollo   84
    So Stars beyond a certain Height   . . . . . .   700 Cadenus Vaness   442
    For 'tis beyond the Pow'r of Meal, ...   786 Dick, Maggot   9
    Beyond the skies transports his mind, ...   900 Dean's Reasons   49
BIBLE
    Quotes from the Bible many a Sentence   . . . . .   605 Beasts Confess   121
    Tear the Bible all to Pieces.   . . . .   831 Legion Club   66
BICKERSTAFF
    Well, 'tis as Bickerstaff has guest, ...   98 Elegy Patrige   1
BID
    'Tis time to bid my friend a long farewell, ...   50 To Congreve   227
    Bid Goody Baucis mend the Fire;   . . . . . .   111 Bauc & Phil 2   24
    Then Madam bid the Chariot stand, ...   128 Little House   50
    And bid Friend Lewis go in quest   . . . . . .   171 Horace 1, 7   16
    And when thou'st bid adieu to Cares, ...   181 Horace 2, 1   39
    Since Harley bid me first attend, ...   201 Horace 2, 6   65
    Were bid in form, but sent Excuses: . . . . . .   290 Prog Marriage   10
    She bid me with a serious Face   . . . . .   311 To Ford   7
    And bid adieu to dear Champain: . . . . . .   311 To Ford   26
    She sent to bid him come and dine.   . . . . . .   375 Apology Lady C   6
    He long had bid the Court farwel, ...   375 Apology Lady C   13
    And fairly bid the <Devil> take   . . . . . .   400 Window Inns 1   7
    "But run to Tom, and bid him fix   . . . . .   446 Modern Lady   54
    Who at them rail bid God Confound: . . . . .   658 On Poetry   D 190
    Bid Povey secure him while you are haranguing.   818 Epigr Kite   8
    And so I bid Sir <Arthur> write.   . . . .   859 Lady Acheson   4
    Kit, run to your Master, and bid him come to us.   871 Grand Question   117
    "<God> <damn> me, they bid us reform and repent, . .   872 Grand Question   145
    Was bid to throw the Stones behind;   . . . . . .   922 Riddle 7   46
    Bid Lady Betty recollect her, ...   993 On Picture   10
BIDDER
    But how to dispose of it to the best Bidder, ...   867 Grand Question   5
BIDDY
    Which only pleased in Biddy Floyd: . . . . . .   272 Apollo's Edict   D   61
BIDS
    Bids us make Bricks, yet sends us to look out for Straw;   32 Ode to Temple   188
    This bids some curious praters here below   . . . . .   45 To Congreve   73
    And bids the ravish'd youth be bless'd.   . . . . .   178 To Lord Harley   64
    Then, bids the youngest of the Six, ...   189 Faggot   3
    Bids us to seek Peace and ensue it.   . . . . . .   220 A Quiet Life   18
    He bids me then to hold my Tongue, and up the Money
        locks,   342 Upon His Grace   25
    And bids him bless, and mend the Earth;   . . . . . .   384 Manly Virtue   16
    And Strephon bids us guess the rest;   . . . .   526 Lady's Dres Rm   16

		PAGE	TITLE	LINE
BIDS	(CONTINUED)			
He kindly bids me near him stand;		921	Riddle 6	29
BIENNIAL				
"Biennial Squires, to Market brought;		571	Death of Swift	445
BIG				
Five times at least as big as theirs, ...		87	Hist V's House	24
Tho' this Description looks so big, ...		134	Magician's Rod	65
Here's ev'ry Piece as big as ten.		251	Bubble	8
Looking big as any Gyants, ...		573	Helter Skelter	3
And with Hats so very big, Sir, ...		573	Helter Skelter	17
Some they do say, 'twas the big man of straw; . . .		841	Ballad	D 12
Just big enough to shelter two in;		878	Robbin & Harry	22
Big like Bess, and small like Sue;		936	Riddle 24	D 28
BIGGER				
Would halt behind him, were it bigger.		398	Earl of P-b-w	27
And thou, my dear, shalt have the bigger half.		881	Pastoral Dial	32
BILL				
And view it through a Jobber's Bill, ...		255	Bubble	122
To turn to small Money a Bill on the Bank.		288	Bank Down	35
In a Chancery Bill your Attorney engages, ...		288	Bank Down	46
To pass another Pop-ry bill		422	Ireld	44
The Bill might be with Costs dismist.		688	Cadenus Vaness	74
Or in your claw, or in your bill.		983	Sher, A Goose	22
BILLET				
Here, a Page fill'd with Billet Doux;		60	Lady Tablebook	13
BILLET-DOUX				
Knows how to write a Billet-doux, ...		325	Pethox	68
What Billet-doux, and clouded Cains!		585	Strephon Chloe	38
Or Billet-doux, or Lock of Hay:		893	Panegyr Dean	222
BILLETS				
By clapping Billets on your Door and Posts Sir. . .		1002	Reply by Dean	12
BILLING				
And Pigeons billing, Sparrows treading, ...		585	Strephon Chloe	51
BILLINGS-GATE				
Were you drest like a bawd, and sold oysters at Billings-gate.		979	Dean to Tho: S	10
BILLINGSGATE				
The Language Billingsgate excel, ...		496	Panegyr Swift	108
BILLS SEE QUACK-BILLS				
By Bills for Taxes and Repairs.		174	Horace 1, 7	112
Who gives no Bills, but of Mortality.		235	Elegy on Demar	40
Bills turn the Lenders into Debters, ...		240	Run Bankers	26
Thus Bankers o'er their Bills and Bags		240	Run Bankers	31
So pow'rful are a Banker's Bills		240	Run Bankers	37
Produc'd with all their Bills and Gold, ...		241	Run Bankers	63
Long Bills, and Answers, stuff'd with Lies, ...		690	Cadenus Vaness	121
And makes such reasonable Bills		735	Stel B-day '20	28
Scribble senseless Heads of Bills;		831	Legion Club	60
So much his Stay do's swell the Bills;		860	Lady Acheson	30
Presented him the weekly Bills		903	Death Daphne	5
Poor Miss Dingley oft hath felt its Bills.		941	Letter	24
BIN				
"Where most true Sons of Phoebus ha' bin.		320	First of April	4
So, Bays on Poets Brows have bin		457	Paddy's Charac	5
As when rooting in a Bin, ...		785	Dick, Maggot	1
BIND				
Prepar'd to leap o'er Sticks, or bind 'em.		190	Faggot	44
Or wou'd they but in Fetters bind, ...		515	Answer Fable	85
Tho' Peace with Olive bind his Hands, ...		655	On Poetry	419
Bind them fast, or from the Shelves		838	Legion Club	209
How firmly these Indentures bind.		1021	Nim-Dan-Dean 1	D 34
BINDS				
Some she binds 'Prentice to the Spade, ...		32	Ode to Temple	185
No common Ligament that binds		291	Prog Marriage	33
<BINGHAM>				
There observe the Tribe of <Bingham>, ...		836	Legion Club	163
BIPES				
A Creature bipes et implumis;		608	Beasts Confess	216
BIRCH				
Some say he's a Birch, a Thought very odd, ...		335	Serious Poem	33
Then leave him to his Birch;		426	Five Ladies	41
But Ferula and Birch;		1005	Sheridan's Sub	28
BIRD				
So men have got from Bird and Brute		83	Salamander	7
Then shall the tall black Daventry Bird		147	Windsor Proph	7
Swim where the Bird of Jove would sink, ...		253	Bubble	55
The Bird of Jove shall toil no more, ...		270	Apollo's Edict	D 25
The Bird of Pallas knows his Post, ...		324	Pethox	37
Flocks ev'ry ominous Bird of Prey;		413	Desire Possess	54
See the Bird of Juno stooping.		661	Love Song	31
Make up a Bird very swift of Flight.		940	Letter	4
A long-ear'd Beast, a Bird that prates, ...		942	Probatur Alit	3
A long-ear'd Beast, and Bird of Night, ...		942	Probatur Alit	19
No Bird in Air so swift can fly.		942	Probatur Alit	26
BIRDS				
The Birds are met to strip the Jays.		239	Run Bankers	20
My Groves, my Ecchoes, and my Birds, ...		411	Dial Rich Marb	91
He jumbles Men and Birds together, ...		513	Answer Fable	13
And he of all Birds was a Pheasant.		513	Answer Fable	34
Birds, as he says, and I allow, ...		513	Answer Fable	39
The strange Stupidity of Birds.		514	Answer Fable	60

		PAGE	TITLE	LINE
BIRDS	(CONTINUED)			
The dullest of Beasts and of Birds in the Air,	. . .	940	Letter	14
BIRTH	**SEE AFTER-BIRTH**			
When she sends forth such a malignant Birth,	. . . .	8	Ode to King	54
Took its first Growth and Birth	. . . . . .	10	Ode to King	126
The mighty Mountain labours with its birth,	. . .	30	Ode to Temple	108
Whence takes it its Increase, and whence its Birth,	.	31	Ode to Temple	169
Nature the hidden Spark did at my Birth infuse,	. . .	32	Ode to Temple	202
By an equivocal Birth	. . . .	33	Ode to Temple	211
Since Heaven will claim its residence as well as birth,		35	Ode Sancroft	19
Which gave them birth, can rob the world of day.	. . . .	46	To Congreve	82
How would you blush the shameful birth to hear	. . . .	46	To Congreve	85
Deals out to man the planet of his birth;	. . . . .	54	Temple Ill	90
His Birth he does from Phoebus raise,	. . . . . .	80	Vanbrug House	41
Of titles, birth, and fortune proud,	. . . .	177	To Lord Harley	40
Though French by Birth and Education:	. . . . .	300	Horrid Plot	50
And since her Birth the Ocean gave her,	. . . . .	303	Storm	23
That litt'rall Spot which gave him Birth,	. . . . .	314	To Ford	88
Jove grants the Prayer, gives Virtue Birth,	. . . .	384	Manly Virtue	15
Rais'd high above his Birth by Knowledge,	. . . .	384	Manly Virtue	33
By Phoebus (an incestuous birth)	. . . . . .	433	Answer Paulus	25
From the Planet of my Birth,	. . . .	634	Epistle Lady	141
Cou'd Horace give so sad a Monster Birth,	. . .	669	Epig Carthy 16	D 1
Fly to the Sea, my Place of Birth;	. . . . .	689	Cadenus Vaness	88
Did to it's wond'rous Birth conspire;	. . . . .	743	Stel B-day 22	64
To celebrate your Birth in Prose;	. . . . . .	756	Stel B-day '24	6
For whom, by Birth, I was design'd	. . . . . .	782	Mullinix Tim	281
To vilest Slaves I owe my Birth.	. . . . . .	916	Riddle 2	2
May justly claim their Birth from thee;	. . . .	919	Riddle 5	16
To Man alone I owe my birth,	. . . . . .	936	Riddle 24	D 2
BIRTH-DAY				
Sweet Poet, hir'd for birth-day Rimes,	. . . . .	462	Birthday Song	47
Now Birth-day Bard, with joy proceed	. . . . .	465	Birthday Song	151
"Here's Colley Cibber's Birth-day Poem.	. . . .	563	Death of Swift	270
In all her glitt'ring Birth-day Gear,	. . . . .	591	Strephon Chloe	228
The Court with annual Birth-day Strains;	. . . .	650	On Poetry	306
In the gay Trappings of a Birth-Day Night:	. . . .	771	Horace 1, 14	50
BIRTH-PLACE				
To be a fitter Birth-place for the God of Wit;	. . .	17	Ode Athenian	49
BIRTH-RIGHT				
A Birth-right for a mess of broth.	. . . . . .	879	Robbin & Harry	36
BIRTHDAY				
Nor souse to death a Birthday Beau.	. . . . . .	622	Scandal Poem 1	178
BISHOP	**SEE ARCH-BISHOP**			
He'll teaze you with King Charles and Bishop Laud,	.	166	Toland's Invit	42
A Bishop says the noble 'Squire, I hate the very Name,		342	Upon His Grace	17
You think you'll sooner be a Bishop:	. . . . .	478	Epist on Epist	102
Poor Bishop Judas, late repenting, dies;	. . . .	806	Judas	2
Make Rundle Bishop; fye for Shame!	. . . . .	819	Dr. Rundle	1
A Bishop in the Isle of Saints!	. . . . . .	819	Dr. Rundle	3
Rundle a Bishop! well he may;	. . . .	820	Dr. Rundle	19
A bishop that is no divine;	. . . .	876	To Dean Swift	21
The Bishop with his Foot may burn it;	. . . . .	892	Panegyr Dean	173
They'll make a sweet Bishop when Gentlefolks sup.	.	953	Oranges	4
A Dog and <Bishop> ne'er was seen,	. . . . .	301	Horrid Plot	74
Pleaded the <Bishop> lov'd a <Whore>,	. . . . .	302	Storm	12
"But, if you'll leave us <Bishop> Judas,	. . . .	305	Storm	51
A <Bishop> who rul'd all the rest of his Tribe;	. .	803	Irish Bishops	2
And who is this <Bishop>? And where does he dwell?	.	803	Irish Bishops	3
How nearly this <Bishop> our <Bishop> resembles!	. .	803	Irish Bishops	7
How nearly this <Bishop> our <Bishop> resembles!	. .	803	Irish Bishops	7
BISHOP-HATERS				
To Bishop-Haters answer thus	. . . .	658	On Poetry	D 190
BISHOP'S				
That only for the Bishop's Lease	. . .	343	Upon His Grace	46
What else are those thou seest in Bishop's Geer	. . .	792	St. Pat's Well	49
Our Bishop's Predecessor, Magus,	. . . . . .	821	Dr. Rundle	41
We guess't the <Bishop's> Foot was in it.	. . . .	300	Horrid Plot	70
Since <Burnet's> Death, the <Bishop's> Bench,	. . .	303	Storm	17
BISHOPRICK				
He lost his Bishoprick, and hang'd, or burst.	. . . .	806	Judas	8
And let his Bishoprick another take.	. . . . .	806	Judas	26
BISHOPRICKS				
Yet keep their Bishopricks, and 'scape the Cord.	. .	806	Judas	14
That Bishopricks are held in Fee.	. . . . . .	821	Dr. Rundle	60
BISHOPS				
To prove that Bishops were old Women.	. . . . .	455	Dean Smedley	20
Ye bishops far remov'd from saints;	. . . . .	487	Irish-Club	7
Extoll ye Bench of Bishops round,	. . . . .	658	On Poetry	D 190
Though ev'n the Bishops disappointed,	. . . . .	821	Dr. Rundle	55
Your <Bishops> all are <Dogs> indeed.	. . . . .	301	Horrid Plot	76
"In making <Bishops>, no one knows.	. . . . .	304	Storm	46
She sends us our <Bishops> and <Judges> and <Deans>,	.	520	Dean Hang Rape	69
Has got on the Bench many <Bishops> suffragan:	. .	803	Irish Bishops	14
Our <Bishops> puft up with Wealth and with Pride.	. .	804	Irish Bishops	17
And so may such <Bishops> for ever divide,	. . . .	805	Irish Bishops	37
The <Bishops> divide, but the Clergy unite.	. . .	805	Irish Bishops	44
Should the Bottom be split, our <Bishops> wou'd dread	.	805	Irish Bishops	45
But hold, cry the <Bishops>; and give us fair Play;	.	805	Irish Bishops	53
BIT				
And thou at Stockbridge wert not bit)	. . . . .	182	Horace 2, 1	60

		PAGE	TITLE	LINE
BIT	(CONTINUED)			
But mark what follow'd,--Faith she bit her.		208	Fable Bitches	18
And bit her Lips to make them red:		222	Prog of Love	14
Each Night a Bit drops off her Face		228	Prog of Beauty	87
She's Now as handsom ev'ry bit,		313	To Ford	71
And yet perhaps you may be bit.		445	Modern Lady	27
For that were not unjust a Bit,		497	Panegyr Swift	119
That bit your Neck but Yesterday,		504	Doctor Delaney	142
Thus, indulgent Chloe bit,		523	Betty Grizette	35
But, truly there the Dean was bit---.		547	Life of Swift	92
I damn such Fools!--Go, go, you're bit."		579	Day Judgement	22
To please you, she knows how to chuse a nice Bit;		580	Psyche	9
You rarely bite, are always bit:		651	On Poetry	330
Is bit by him that comes behind;		651	On Poetry	342
You thought that Satire Sir,--but you are bit.		669	Epig Carthy 17	D 2
Is thirty, and a Bit to spare.		699	Cadenus Vaness	389
Will condescend to take a Bit.		710	Cadenus Vaness	761
I bit my Nails, and scratch'd my Head,		740	Stel B-day 22	5
To nourish Vermin, may be bit.		813	Bro Protestant	64
But ne'er presume to eat a Bit;		897	Panegyr Dean	336
Wherein they need not lose a Bit,		1022	Nim-Dan-Dean 1	D 43
My worship is bit,		1037	Sheridan Cavan	9
BITCH SEE BEECH				
A Bitch that was full pregnant grown,		207	Fable Bitches	1
Or Mason that abandon'd Bitch:		299	Horrid Plot	23
I peept, and saw you kiss the dirty Bitch.		882	Pastoral Dial	38
For Whore and Rogue; and Dog and Bitch.		949	Epigr Scolding	4
BITE				
Would whisper to himself; A Bite,		107	V's House	62
The World shall feel her scratch and bite.		150	Corinna	12
And loudly cry'd--a Bite, a Bite.		208	Fable Bitches	42
And loudly cry'd--a Bite, a Bite.		208	Fable Bitches	42
Since you can teach dead Dogs to bite.		299	Horrid Plot	40
With Teeth or with Claws it will bite or will scratch,		351	Wood Insect	19
You quickly see the gudgeon bite,		421	Ireld	23
To bite his Pen, and drop a Tear.		561	Death of Swift	210
To scratch your Head, and bite your Nails.		643	On Poetry	90
You rarely bite, are always bit:		651	On Poetry	330
And these have smaller Fleas to bite 'em,		651	On Poetry	339
They burnish paper, or they bite a rogue:		672	Epig Carthy 25	D 2
Too rough to polish, and too blunt to bite.		672	Epig Carthy 25	D 4
'Tis just what Coxcombs call, a Bite.		708	Cadenus Vaness	673
Your barking Curs will seldom bite:		797	Traulus 1	46
They shrewdly suspect it is all but a bite.		818	Archbi Cashel	4
BITERS				
And God bless the Commons for Biting the Biters.		805	Irish Bishops	64
BITING				
In my own hum'rous biting Way?		555	Death of Swift	54
And God bless the Commons for Biting the Biters.		805	Irish Bishops	64
BITS				
Whole Baskets full of Bits and Scraps,		208	Fable Bitches	19
For Clem gets all the dainty bits.		283	Journal	126
And I'll give you these delicate Bits:		395	Dog and Thief	2
Your delicate Bits will not serve me a Meal,		395	Dog and Thief	5
Devour the Church's tiddest Bits,		498	Panegyr Swift	150
Presented with the choicest Bits:		745	Stel Distress	12
Presented with the nicest Bits:		750	Stel Wood-Park	10
BITTER				
The bitter cup is from him past:		40	Ode Sancroft	202
A bitter Whig, or Tory sow'r;		417	Woman's Mind	50
Though flatt'ring Knaves may call it bitter.		485	Libel on D- D-	178
"Both bitter Foes to Britain's Weal.		549	Life of Swift	153
He loves to be bitter at		854	Lady's Lament	89
To-morrow of a bitter Juice,		929	Riddle 15	D 10
BLAB				
Or if at last, I needs must blab it,		311	To Ford	5
But I'll tell you the Secret, and pray do not Blab,		335	Serious Poem	35
Nor blab it on the lonely Rocks,		597	Cassinus Peter	107
But if you blab, you are undone;		644	On Poetry	135
BLABBING				
Against the Court is always blabbing,		514	Answer Fable	69
BLACK SEE JET-BLACK				
And if so black the cloud, that heaven's bright queen		53	Temple Ill	57
Became Black Sattin, Flounc'd with Lace.		116	Bauc & Phil 2	142
When a holy black Suede, the Son of Bob,		147	Windsor Proph	1
Then shall the tall black Daventry Bird		147	Windsor Proph	7
To make her Hair look black as Jet,		226	Prog of Beauty	18
Three Colours, Black, and Red, and White,		226	Prog of Beauty	21
But when she rose, the black and red		226	Prog of Beauty	31
The Black, which would not be confin'd		227	Prog of Beauty	33
But her graceful black Locks, were all mingled with Grey		264	Apollo	42
Down the black Sea, and up the Streights,		282	Journal	107
With Belzebub in Black		426	Five Ladies	20
Why, how now dapper black		428	Beau's Reply	1
Our Ink is black, our Paper white;		463	Birthday Song	108
And write on paper black as Jet:		463	Birthday Song	114
Of whitening what before was black.		464	Birthday Song	116
That Club of Candidates in Black,		503	Doctor Delaney	85
But what's dy'd black will take no other hue.		670	Epig Carthy 18	D 8
As shrivelled and as black as thine.		787	Clad in Brown	22
And haunt thy holy Walls in white and black.		792	St. Pat's Well	48

```
BLACK            (CONTINUED)                            PAGE   TITLE          LINE
    Lorsha! and out of her shteeple there was hung a black  840 Ballad         D  9
       flag.
    Condemn'd to black gowns; . . . . . . . . . .      858 Lady's Lament      210
    In every point, like black and white: . . . . . . . 901 Dean's Reasons     72
    My Tongue is black, my Mouth is furr'd,            916 Riddle 1            39
    Captain Butler made some in the Church black and blue 1029 Dr. Helsham       7
       sick;
    Because no <--> But <Black?> Gown'd Foe,           373 Letter D. S-y       77
BLACK-GUARD
    Methinks I see a black-guard Rout . . . . .        183 Horace 2, 1         79
    Tom huzza'd the black-guard Boys, . . . . . . .    784 Mullinex Dick       19
BLACK-HALL
    And then at Beelzebub's Black-Hall,   . . . . .    486 Libel on D- D-     191
BLACK-SMITH
    This Thief and Black-Smith was so bold,   . . . . . 346 Prometheus         63
BLACKBIRD
    The Crib was down, the Blackbird caught.   . . . . . 127 Little House       30
BLACKEN
    We blacken what was white before. . . . . . . .    463 Birthday Song      110
BLACKEST
    The blackest of all Female Deeds.   . . . . . . .  596 Cassinus Peter     106
BLACKGUARD
    This summoning of blackguard boys? . . . . . . .   487 Irish-Club         10
BLACKMORE
    Blackmore alone his Place Supply'd:   . . . . . .  652 On Poetry         372
BLACKMORE'S
    When Death had finish'd Blackmore's Reign,   . . . . 653 On Poetry         374
BLADE
    The Butcher, feels the Lamb beneath his blade.   . . . 364 On Dreams        18
    While not a Blade of Grass, or Hay, . . . . . . .  759 Receipt Youth       3
    Shall rise one Blade of Grass, one Ear of Corn;   . . 793 St. Pat's Well     92
    Leave them not a Blade of Grass. . . . . . . . .   839 Legion Club       218
BLAM'D
    That Clouds are blam'd for giving Claps:   . . . . . 618 Scandal Poem 1     22
    That Clouds are blam'd for giving Claps; · . . . . . 624 Scandal Poem 2     16
BLAME
    Thus did the Muse severe unkindly blame . . . . .   44 To Congreve         23
    I came in without Danger; and was I to blame?   . .  144 New Song           33
    Yet still you think your Friend to blame.   . . . .  218 To Mr. Delany      82
    Are us'd like Dick, and bear the Blame.   . . . . . 221 A Quiet Life       58
    Who, loth to blame, or to incense,   . . . . . . .  377 Apology Lady C     73
    'Till Block-heads blame, and Judges praise,   . . .  505 Doctor Delany     167
    "If you resent it, who's to blame?   . . . . . . .  548 Life of Swift     121
    "The Praise is His, and Theirs the Blame.   . . . .  550 Life of Swift     200
    Wisely on me lay all the Blame:   . . . . . . . .  558 Death of Swift     170
    That, often I have been to blame:   . . . . . . .  602 Beasts Confess      14
    Nature alone must bear the Blame:   . . . . . . .  602 Beasts Confess      30
    (For which he owns himself to blame)   . . . . . .  607 Beasts Confess     182
    A Character to praise and blame,   . . . . . . . .  608 Know Not What       4
    For Fickleness how durst you blame us?   . . . . .  618 Scandal Poem 1     39
    For Fickleness how durst you blame us?   . . . . .  624 Scandal Poem 2     37
    We justly praise, or justly blame:   . . . . . . .  644 On Poetry         130
    Nor are the Men of Sense to blame,   . . . . . . .  688 Cadenus Vaness     63
    Mov'd with the lightest Touch of Blame,   . . . . .  730 Stella, Poems      88
    When she knows she's most to blame.   . . . . . . .  906 Daphne             20
    Nor can our Parson blame the Thing:   . . . . . . .  926 Riddle 9           14
BLAMELESS
    Tho' you lead a blameless Life,   . . . . . .      633 Epistle Lady       99
BLAMES
    A skilfull Critick justly blames   . . . . . . .   467 Birthday Song     209
BLANCH
    You cannot blanch his tawny Hide;   . . . . . . .  785 Dick, Maggot        8
BLANCHE
    And you and your cart shall give me carte blanche.   . . 979 Dean to Tho: S    14
BLAND
    The pliant bow, the forehead bland--   . . . . . . 951 Upstart           D 30
BLANK
    But Thanks to the House, the Projectors look blank,   .  287 Bank Down          9
BLANKETS
    And then between two Blankets creeps.   . . . . .  582 Young Nymph        38
BLASPHEME
    Poor Strephon, how would he blaspheme!   . . . . .  226 Prog of Beauty     16
    "You'll find him swear, blaspheme, and damn,   . .  305 Storm              57
    Hear him Blaspheme; and Swear, and Rayl,   . . . .  312 To Ford            45
BLASPHEMES
    (Who now so impiously blasphemes   . . . . . . .   530 Lady's Dres Rm    137
BLASPHEMING
    Nine Spirits of blaspheming Fops,   . . . . . . .  904 Death Daphne       41
BLASPHEMY
    Or if to Blasphemy it tends,   . . . . . . .      461 Birthday Song      27
    Such stupid blasphemy and nonsense?   . . . . . .  490 Dialogue           38
BLAST
    No Thunder e'er can blast,   . . . . . . . . .     29 Ode to Temple       82
    But when they find it turn with the first blast of fate,  37 Ode Sancroft      76
    Each line shall stab, shall blast, like daggers and like  37 Ode Sancroft      91
       fire;
    Puff'd by the people's spightful blast,   . . . . .  41 Ode Sancroft      220
    So, Modern Rhymers strive to blast   . . . . . .   81 Vanbrug House       89
    So Modern Rimers wisely Blast   . . . . . . . .   110 V's House         131
    Once, on a Time a Western Blast,   . . . . . . .  126 Little House        5
```

		PAGE	TITLE	LINE
BLAST	**(CONTINUED)**			
That, Death has overset him with a Blast.		285	Elegy Boat	22
One Blast will put out all his Fires.		588	Strephon Chloe	136
But, Caelia has contriv'd to blast		595	Cassinus Peter	53
BLASTED				
Hath blasted with poetick Fire.		641	On Poetry	42
BLASTS				
Tho' blasts from contrariety of winds,		41	Ode Sancroft	204
BLAZ'D				
No Sacrifice on Altars blaz'd;		346	Prometheus	44
BLAZE SEE FUNERAL-BLAZE				
But sees thy meteor blaze about me shine,		54	Temple Ill	91
Thy grate unconscious of a blaze,		676	Parson's Case	12
BLEAKY				
Else, rather on this bleaky shore		420	Holyhead	29
BLEAT				
I can bleat, or I can sing,		933	Riddle 20	D 11
BLED				
For Party he would scarce have Bled---:		549	Life of Swift	142
BLEED				
Shall on a day make sin and folly bleed;		47	To Congreve	134
Dear Cassy, thou must purge and bleed;		596	Cassinus Peter	89
In such a Cause would Cato bleed?		724	To Stella	41
My Wounds Bleed all anew:		1005	Sheridan's Sub	31
BLEEDING				
What Hampers full of bleeding Hearts!		585	Strephon Chloe	36
Of killing Eyes, or bleeding Hearts:		728	Stella, Poems	12
BLEMISH				
And, from the Spouse each Blemish hide		591	Strephon Chloe	253
BLEND				
Who blend it into folly's larger heap,		45	To Congreve	62
BLENHEIM				
To be his Architect at Blenheim.		87	Hist V's House	42
BLES'T				
How bles't am I by such a Man led!		890	Panegyr Dean	106
BLESS				
To bless the Primitive Sailer's weary sight,		16	Ode Athenian	7
Delude at once and Bless our Sight,		228	Prog of Beauty	70
Bless you late and early,		246	Irish-Feast	45
God Bless your Grace I then reply'd,		343	Upon His Grace	37
I mean His <Majesty>, God bless him.		346	Prometheus	62
And bids him bless, and mend the Earth;		384	Manly Virtue	16
To bless, is truly to be great!		386	Manly Virtue	102
And bless the Earth with genial Showers.		387	Manly Virtue	110
To bless him and to keep him there;		388	Manly Virtue	140
To bless, as now you curse Mankind?		496	Panegyr Swift	95
And bless his ravish't Sight to see		530	Lady's Dres Rm	142
And cursing <Bob>, forget to bless <the> <King>.		533	To Mr. Gay	52
To curse the Dean, or bless the Drapier.		558	Death of Swift	168
And happy Lovers bless my Reign----		694	Cadenus Vaness	248
I bless the Hand from whence they came,		727	To Stella	115
So God bless the Church, and three of our Mitres;		805	Irish Bishops	63
And God bless the Commons for Biting the Biters.		805	Irish Bishops	64
Bless us, Morgan! Art thou there Man?		837	Legion Club	189
Bless mine Eyes! Art thou the Chairman?		837	Legion Club	190
BLESS'D				
Where the bless'd spirit lodges like the dove,		41	Ode Sancroft	227
And bids the ravish'd youth be bless'd.		178	To Lord Harley	64
Whom Fate has amply bless'd at home?		272	Apollo's Edict	D 63
BLESSING				
That begs the pow'rful blessing of thy pray'rs.		42	Ode Sancroft	244
The Devil take me, said she, (blessing her self,)		71	Mrs Harris Pet	44
The Blessing of another Line:		272	Apollo's Edict	D 69
Then down I went upon my Knees, his Blessing to obtain,		342	Upon His Grace	29
Think what they wish so great a Blessing,		411	Desire Possess	3
A Blessing upon them, have sent us this Year,		516	Dean Hang Rape	3
Gives them a peny, and God's blessing		878	Robbin & Harry	6
BLESSINGS				
His Blessings down in fruitful Show'rs;		624	Scandal Poem 2	28
Display the blessings of the Nation,		658	On Poetry	D 190
And Blessings equally on all bestows.		793	St. Pat's Well	68
BLEST				
Whom were my Congreve blest to see and know,		49	To Congreve	183
Till the blest sun to give kind dawn of grace		52	Temple Ill	25
Blest Revolution, which creates		96	On the Union	5
How blest is he, who for his Country dies;		210	Earl of Oxford	1
What Land was ever half so blest?		391	Young's Satire	12
His Vassals easy, and the Owner blest;		533	To Mr. Gay	47
With favour & fortune fastidiously blest		540	Charac Walpole	1
If with such Talents Heav'n hath blest 'em		555	Death of Swift	65
Fair Britain in thy Monarch blest,		655	On Poetry	411
Or blest with such engaging Parts,		779	Mullinix Tim	199
How might then our Isle be blest?		830	Legion Club	30
How is the greatest Monarch blest,		916	Riddle 2	3
BLEW				
Blew out Love's Torch or chill'd the Flame:		85	Salamander	60
Chequer'd with Ribbons blew and green;		200	Horace 2, 6	29
Blew his last Breath to sink the lighter Scale.		235	Elegy on Demar	34
In blew shallon, shall Hanniball be Clad,		275	Epilogue	21
He blew a Settlement along:		585	Strephon Chloe	40

BLEW-EY'D
Nor borrow from the Blew-ey'd Maid, ... 272 Apollo's Edict D 73
BLIND
Whom blind and eager Curiosity . . . . 18 Ode Athenian 63
From us the Blind and thoughtless Croud, ... 18 Ode Athenian 87
And with blind Rage break all this peaceful Government; . 25 Ode Athenian 300
Foll'wing Opinion, dark, and blind, ... 36 Ode Sancroft 56
My Comrade's Blind, and I'm a Creeple . . . . . . 90 Bauc & Phil 1 16
You blind and lame! tis no such Thing . . . . . . 91 Bauc & Phil 1 42
And begg'd like one both blind and lame; . . . . . . 207 Fable Bitches 8
"Their Way--for now you see they're blind; . . . . . 208 Fable Bitches 34
Had not ill Fate, perverse and blind, ... 215 To Mr. Delany 5
Expos'd, to blind the Nation's Eyes, ... 354 Simile Silver 21
Say, foolish Females, Old and Blind, ... 449 Modern Lady 150
I pity wretched Strephon blind . . . . 530 Lady's Dres Rm 129
The God of Light could ne'er have been so blind, . . 532 To Mr. Gay 27
By Nature, Reason, Learning, blind; . . . . . . 579 Day Judgement 12
A blind old Beggar from the Grave: . . . . . . 604 Beasts Confess 116
In Eyes with Reading almost blind; . . . . . . 703 Cadenus Vaness 527
Say, Stella, was Prometheus blind, ... 726 To Stella 85
No Bloom of Youth can ever blind . . . . . . 736 Stel B-day '20 55
To lead thee, as a Staff directs the Blind, ... 770 Horace 1, 14 17
'Twere better be blind, ... 856 Lady's Lament 153
Happy Nation were we blind, ... 862 To Janus 17
To all their weaker Sides are blind; . . . . . . 887 Panegyr Dean 8
Because I am by Nature blind, ... 917 Riddle 4 1
Swans sing when dying, geese when blind. . . . . . 983 Sher, A Goose 14
BLINDED
But blinded by Resentment, seeks . . . . 731 Stella, Poems 125
BLINDFOLD
Say, why the Church is still led blindfold by the State? 40 Ode Sancroft 177
BLINDLY
Led blindly on by gross philosophy and pride, ... 36 Ode Sancroft 66
Led blindly on by avarice and pride, ... 39 Ode Sancroft 163
BLINDNESS
Either our blindness or our fate, ... 42 Ode Sancroft 241
BLINDS
Thus the deluding Muse oft blinds me to her Ways, . . 23 Ode Athenian 234
BLISS
See then what Mortals place their Bliss in! . . . . 223 Prog of Love 25
BLOATED
A bloated <Minister> in all his Geer, ... 532 To Mr. Gay 33
This bloated Harpy sprung from Hell, ... 895 Panegyr Dean 269
BLOCK   SEE WIG-BLOCK
Though he may be a Block-head, he is no real Block. . 335 Serious Poem 42
Your Block will fit it to a hair. . . . . 780 Mullinix Tim 220
BLOCK-HEAD
Though he may be a Block-head, he is no real Block. . 335 Serious Poem 42
BLOCK-HEADS
'Till Block-heads blame, and Judges praise, ... 505 Doctor Delaney 167
. . . Damn'd Block-heads, Damn'd Knaves, ... 576 Place Damn'd 7
BLOCKHEAD
Yet should this Blockhead beg a Place . . . . . 423 Ireld 69
'Till some fresh Blockhead takes your Place. . . . . 644 On Poetry 142
A Blockhead with melodious Voice . . . . 710 Cadenus Vaness 738
Except a Blockhead or a Rake . . . . 733 Verses Vanessa 20
The stupid blockhead and the liar. . . . . 950 Upstart D 16
BLOCKHEADS
I to such Blockheads set my Wit! . . . . 579 Day Judgement 21
BLOOD   SEE LIFE-BLOOD
The Great Distinguisher of Blood, ... 7 Ode to King 23
May all the Blood, which shall by Womans scorn be shed 23 Ode Athenian 245
Nor dipt in Blood, nor Widow's Tears, nor Orphan's   29 Ode to Temple 86
    Cries:
Sweepings from Butchers Stalls, Dung, Guts, and Blood   139 City Shower 61
The Wine, his Blood, our Predecessors shed: . . . . 162 Toland's Invit 12
We spent our Mony and our Blood, ... 169 Peace Dunkirk 33
"On Popes, for all the Blood they've spilt, ... 183 Horace 2, 1 94
For want of Milk, wou'd suck her Blood. . . . . . 208 Fable Bitches 22
Your Blood in ev'ry Noble Race! . . . . . . 325 Pethox 70
Is a Man of this World all true Flesh and Blood, . . 335 Serious Poem 50
To Blood and Quarrels, Brass unites: . . . . . . 345 Prometheus 22
I hug them till I squeeze their Blood. . . . . . 348 Whitshed Motto 10
The Murd'rer dreams of all the Blood he spilt. . . . 364 On Dreams 14
And sowrs the blood . . . . 440 Ballyspellin 11
"Forgetting his own Flesh and Blood? . . . . . . 558 Death of Swift 164
"No Flatt'rers; no Allies in Blood; . . . . . . 566 Death of Swift 334
"And reapt the profit, sought his Blood. . . . . . 569 Death of Swift 414
"Whose Fury Blood could never quench; . . . . . 569 Death of Swift 418
By Rapine, Theft, or Thirst of Blood. . . . . . 602 Beasts Confess 20
Without Respect to Friends, or Blood, ... 607 Beasts Confess 184
The Remnant of the royal Blood, ... 655 On Poetry 437
Choler preside, or Blood, or Phlegm, ... 724 To Stella 20
You think this Turbulence of Blood . . . . . . 731 Stella, Poems 127
And fill your Veins with sprightly Blood: . . . . . 759 Receipt Youth 32
Nor Flesh nor Blood will be the same, ... 759 Receipt Youth 33
By human Kind, but Flesh and Blood? . . . . . . 759 Receipt Youth 36
And if your Flesh and Blood be new, ... 760 Receipt Youth 37
It shou'd be yours. But <Damn> my Blood . . . . . 775 Mullinix Tim 73
Got? <Damn> my Blood I frank my Letters, ... 778 Mullinix Tim 155
And damns his Blood that in the Rear . . . . . 789 Dick's Variety 35

		PAGE	TITLE	LINE
BLOOD	(CONTINUED)			
Well may they boast that antient Blood, which runs	. .	791	St. Pat's Well	17
Begs leave to rail, but <damn> his Blood,	. . . . .	797	Traulus 1	55
From his Tenants vital Blood.	. . . .	800	Traulus 2	42
But is a Louse your Flesh and Blood?	. . . . .	812	Bro Protestant	36
How I tremble to think of the Blood it hath spilt!	.	871	Grand Question	111
"I never cou'd take to my Book for the Blood o'me,	.	873	Grand Question	165
<God> <damn> his Blood, and <Blood> and <Wounds>.	.	904	Death Daphne	44
By cruel Hands her Blood was spilt,	. . . . .	923	Riddle 7	65
And of as noble Blood as you;	. . . .	924	Riddle 8	4
Shall in thy dearest Blood be dy'd,	. . . . .	925	Riddle 8	43
They can't come near it for their Blood.	. . . .	928	Riddle 12	D 8
My Blood this Day is very sweet,	. . . . . .	929	Riddle 15	D 9
No Flesh, no Bones, no Blood --- no Ghost:	. . .	935	Riddle 23	D 11
To eels, we may compare his blood;	. . . . . .	950	Upstart	D 8
His blood delights in mud to run;	. . . . . .	950	Upstart	D 9
They make the Blood warmer,	. . . .	952	Onyons	4
<God> <damn> his Blood, and <Blood> and <Wounds>.	.	904	Death Daphne	44
BLOOD-HOUND				
Slow Vengeance, like a Blood-hound at his Heels.	.	210	Earl of Oxford	22
BLOODLESS				
I'll haunt thy Dreams, a bloodless Ghost;	. . . .	925	Riddle 8	27
<BLOODS>				
Must all my <Dammee's>, <Bloods> and <Wounds>	. . .	779	Mullinix Tim	187
BLOODY				
Long dreaded for his Bloody Tail and Fiery Beard,	.	10	Ode to King	131
Ready to fall Rome's bloody Sacrifice;	. . . . . .	12	Ode to William	D 22
Nor has it left the usual bloody Scar,	. . . . .	28	Ode to Temple	74
It is a bloody list we know)	. . . .	37	Ode Sancroft	94
When e'er the bloody Bond appears.	. . . .	240	Run Bankers	48
Observe where bloody Townshend stands	. . . . . .	312	To Ford	43
And still the bloody Field frequent,	. . . . . .	324	Pethox	17
Her Shoulders mark'd with bloody Tracks;	. . . . .	729	Stella, Poems	46
"Then bloody Caitiff think on me.	. . . .	851	Old Thorn	88
Who never fled the bloody Plains,	. . . .	925	Riddle 8	32
BLOOM				
His Virtues fade, his Vices bloom;	. . . . . .	646	On Poetry	200
When, lo! Vanessa in her Bloom,	. . . .	696	Cadenus Vaness	305
No Bloom of Youth can ever blind	. . . .	736	Stel B-day '20	55
Thought him Adonis in his Bloom.	. . . .	904	Death Daphne	58
They bloom in less than half an Hour:	. . . . .	926	Riddle 9	4
BLOOM'D				
So bloom'd the Goddess in a Mortal's Arms.	. . .	669	Epig Carthy 13	D 2
BLOOMING				
Fresh blooming, in young Harley's mind.	. . . . .	178	To Lord Harley	52
Behold him blooming, fresh, and fair,	. . . . . .	384	Manly Virtue	17
Mild Arcadians, ever blooming,	. . . .	660	Love Song	5
But for a blooming Nymph will pass,	. . . . . .	760	Receipt Youth	39
With restless Beak thy blooming Fruit to spoil,	. .	792	St. Pat's Well	46
BLOSSOM				
Nor Leaf, nor Fruit, nor Blossom bore.	. . . . .	134	Magician's Rod	70
No Fruit or Blossom to be seen,	. . . .	849	Old Thorn	19
BLOSUMS				
And from the Tree where Blosums fele,	. . . . . .	103	Merlin	13
BLOT				
When e're he please to blot it out;	. . . . . .	61	Lady Tablebook	22
I withdrew my Subscription by help of a Blot,	. .	144	New Song	29
These praises we blot out	. . . .	423	Carterets Arms	3
Blot out, correct, insert, refine,	. . . .	643	On Poetry	87
BLOTCHES				
Can Clouds give buboes, ulcers, blotches?	. . . . .	618	Scandal Poem 1	25
Can Clouds give Bubo's, Ulcers, Blotches,	. . . . .	624	Scandal Poem 2	19
BLOUNT				
Poor Patty Blount no more be seen	. . . .	409	Dial Rich Marb	47
BLOW				
A Blow on the Weam,	. . . .	247	Irish-Feast	87
Whole Squadrons with a single blow:	. . . . . .	461	Birthday Song	32
"And gave them Arms to ward the Blow.	. . . . . .	569	Death of Swift	410
The Roses blow, the Cowslip springs;	. . . . . .	621	Scandal Poem 1	141
The Roses blow, the Cowslip springs;	. . . . . .	627	Scandal Poem 2	145
And while this Vital Breath I blow,	. . . . . .	776	Mullinix Tim	83
Dame Nature, when she saw the Blow,	. . . . .	849	Old Thorn	25
"Nor, when I felt the dreadful Blow,	. . . . . .	850	Old Thorn	69
May give you a Blow you'll for ever repent.	. . .	941	Letter	40
Who, 'ere t' other gets up, demands the rising Blow.	.	967	Letter Sherid	14
BLOWN SEE OVER-BLOWN				
Like a fly blown Cake of Tallow,	. . . .	523	Betty Grizette	7
BLOWS SEE FLY-BLOWS				
Holland got Towns, and we got Blows,	. . . . .	168	Peace Dunkirk	3
Receiv'd a brace or two of Blows.	. . . .	220	A Quiet Life	24
Like Atoms are exempt from blows.	. . . .	467	Birthday Song	238
Cadenus warded off the Blows:	. . . .	701	Cadenus Vaness	479
Who turn with ev'ry Gale that blows from Court.	. .	771	Horace 1, 14	56
BLOWSE				
Of ev'ry Blowse	. . . .	442	Ballyspellin	71
BLUE				
Whether the Lights were burning blue.	. . . . .	112	Bauc & Phil 2	40
Take your blue Ribbin for a String.	. . . . . .	190	Faggot	38
They keep at Stains the old blue Boar,	. . . . .	225	Prog of Love	99
Of Red, and Yellow, Blue, and Green.	. . . . . .	325	Pethox	46
of St Andrew's the Green, and St George's the Blue	.	389	Order of Bath	2

90

```
BLUE              (CONTINUED)                               PAGE   TITLE           LINE
    Miss Moll the Jade will burn it blue:        . . . . . .  588 Strephon Chloe    128
    Our curtains blue on either side;        . . . . . . . .  621 Scandal Poem 1    134
    Our Curtains blue, from Side to Side:      . . . . . . .  627 Scandal Poem 2    138
    So green in different Lights may pass for blue,    . . .  670 Epig Carthy 18   D  7
    Red hat, and blue bonnet, and turbant's the same,  . . .  815 Yahoo's           23
    Captain Butler made some in the Church black and blue   1029 Dr. Helsham         7
          sick;
BLUE-BOYS
    Huzza their Brethren at the Blue-boys.     . . . . . .    501 Doctor Delaney     62
BLUFF                                                          ,
    I maul'd you when you look'd so bluff,     . . . . . .   1002 Reply by Dean      16
BLUNDER
    A Boat a Judge! yes, where's the Blunder?    . . . . .    286 Elegy Boat         39
    They laught at such an Irish Blunder,      . . . . . .    353 Wood Ironmongr     29
    Captain, I fear you've made some Blunder;    . . . . .    377 Apology Lady C     66
    When you blunder on, and blunder.    . . . . . . . .      908 Daphne             74
    When you blunder on, and blunder.    . . . . . . . .      908 Daphne             74
BLUNDER'D
    . . .before I was aware, out I blunder'd,    . . . . .     72 Mrs Harris Pet     52
    Blunder'd out a Thousand Times.    . . . . . . . .        523 Betty Grizette     20
BLUNDERS
    E'er a week pas't committing Blunders:     . . . . . .     62 Discovery           4
    by dint of experience improving in Blunders  . . . . .   540 Charac Walpole      6
    Nor for neglects or blunders chide her;    . . . . . .   762 Bec's B-Day        50
BLUNT
    Unpierc'd by the blunt Rays of Sight)                     31 Ode to Temple     167
    Too rough to polish, and too blunt to bite.  . . . . .   672 Epig Carthy 25   D  4
BLUNTED
    Or often blunted and recoil'd,   . . . . . . . . .       701 Cadenus Vaness    482
BLUNTER
    "With Hatchet blunter than thy Pate   . . . . . . .      851 Old Thorn          83
BLUNTS
    Or blunts the Point of ev'ry Dart;     . . . . . . .     687 Cadenus Vaness      8
BLURR'D
    The glass, by lovers nonsense blurr'd,     . . . . .     402 Window Inns 6    D  1
BLUSH
    How would you blush the shameful birth to hear   . . .    46 To Congreve        85
    How would they blush to hear it said,      . . . . . .   190 Faggot             31
    And teach her Cheeks again to blush.       . . . . . .   227 Prog of Beauty     48
    And blush to be so far out-done:     . . . . . . .       385 Manly Virtue       42
    Where never Blush was call'd in Aid,       . . . . . .   691 Cadenus Vaness    168
    They blush because they understand.      . . . . . .     692 Cadenus Vaness    171
    I've said enough to make him blush   . . . . . . .       860 Lady Acheson       13
    Nor need I blush, although you feel it wet;  . . . . .   881 Pastoral Dial      23
    The bashful Maid, to hide her Blush,       . . . . .     893 Panegyr Dean      213
    Blush for Ill-spelling, for Ill-lines,     . . . . . .  1002 Reply by Dean       7
BLUSH'D
    Now pale as Death, then blush'd and bow'd;   . . . . .   377 Apology Lady C     78
    So blush'd Aurora with coelestial Charms,    . . . . .   669 Epig Carthy 13   D  1
BLUSHES
    She blushes when by mortals seen;    . . . . . . . .     178 To Lord Harley     70
    Still blushes, and with speed retires,     . . . . . .   178 To Lord Harley     71
    And found in Blushes, Eloquence.     . . . . . . .       386 Manly Virtue       82
BLUSHING
    And Modesty with blushing Face;      . . . . . . . .     448 Modern Lady       123
BLUSTER
    So by the Brazen Trumpets Bluster,     . . . . . . .     345 Prometheus         27
BLUTRAKS
    "Your Noveds, and Blutraks, and Omurs and Stuff,    . .  872 Grand Question    159
BO
    "Can hardly tell how to cry Bo to a Goose;     . . . .   872 Grand Question    158
    Bo peep, bo peep, bo peep, bo peep, peep, bo bo peep.  . 961 Cantata
    Bo peep, bo peep, bo peep, bo peep, peep, bo bo peep.  . 961 Cantata
    Bo peep, bo peep, bo peep, bo peep, peep, bo bo peep.  . 961 Cantata
    Bo peep, bo peep, bo peep, bo peep, peep, bo bo peep.  . 961 Cantata
    Bo peep, bo peep, bo peep, bo peep, peep, bo bo peep.  . 961 Cantata
    Bo peep, bo peep, bo peep, bo peep, peep, bo bo peep.  . 961 Cantata
BO-OTES
    Besides, that slow-pac'd Sign Bo-otes      . . . . . .    98 Elegy Patrige      31
BOAR
    They keep at Stains the old blue Boar,     . . . . . .   225 Prog of Love       99
    Him the Boar in Silence creeping,      . . . . . . .     660 Love Song          11
    Like the tusk of a boar.   . . . . . . . . . . .        854 Lady's Lament      86
BOARD    SEE SIDE-BOARD,COUNCIL-BOARD
    He throws at all, and sweeps the Board.    . . . . .     253 Bubble             64
    You may shew him about for a new Groaning Board.   . .   336 Serious Poem       84
    Some who can perjure thro' a two-Inch Board,   . . . .   806 Judas              13
    No little scrub Joint shall come on my Board:      . .   867 Grand Question     14
    Let never at your Board be known   . . . . . . . .      897 Panegyr Dean      339
BOARD-WAGES
    No Scraps remain to save Board-wages.      . . . . . .   954 Authors Living      6
BOARDING-SCHOOLS
    In Boarding-Schools can have his Choice;     . . . . .   710 Cadenus Vaness    739
BOAST
    In vain, said He, does Utmost Thule boast    . . . .      7 Ode to King        51
    By which some fondly boast they shall for ever live,  . .20 Ode Athenian      151
    Altho' we boast our Winter-Sun looks bright,   . . . .    25 Ode Athenian      280
    Let not old Rome boast Fabius's Fate,      . . . . . .    28 Ode to Temple      70
    Those pow'rs the criticks, who may boast the odds  . . .  46 To Congreve       103
    To boast of favours that he never got;     . . . . . .    48 To Congreve       154
```

BOAST	(CONTINUED)		PAGE	TITLE	LINE
So Chymists boast they have a Power		. . . . . .	81	Vanbrug House	85
So Chymists boast they have a Pow'r		. . . . . .	109	V's House	127
On him could ever boast a Pow'r to seize;			234	Elegy on Demar	30
Byzantians boast, that on the Clod		. . . . . .	324	Pethox	39
The same thy Subjects boast of Thee.		. . . . .	324	Pethox	42
And therefore his witnesses justly may boast		. . . .	335	Serious Poem	39
The costly Boast of Regal Rooms,		. . . . . .	379	Apology Lady C	110
Thus, Pope, in vain you boast your Wit;		. . . .	406	Swift to Pope	21
God's Image, which was once their Boast.		. . . .	498	Panegyr Swift	166
Never did Covent Garden boast		. . . . . .	581	Young Nymph	3
Ne'er kept a Cause, he well may boast,		. . . . . .	604	Beasts Confess	91
Say Britain, cou'd you ever boast, --		. . . .	640	On Poetry	5
This I may boast, which few e'er cou'd,		. . . . . .	669	Epig Carthy 15	D 1
From knowing James, to boast he knows the Duke.		. .	678	Dean and Duke	4
Or when your Name and Family you boast,		. . . . .	771	Horace 1, 14	39
Well may they boast that antient Blood, which runs		. .	791	St. Pat's Well	17
The rest, who boast they have conferr'd it,		. . . .	820	Dr. Rundle	15
And at Hoath to boast his Fame,		. . . . . .	837	Legion Club	179
Yet, some who ne'er bestow'd thee, boast		. . . .	919	Riddle 5	29
All Shapes and Features I can boast,		. . . . . .	935	Riddle 23	D 10
Is the poison and dagger you boast in your jaws, trow?	.	979	Dean to Tho: S	5
Who from her Lover e'er could boast,		. . . . . .	993	On Picture	23
I mean, what no other mortal in the universe can boast of,		1024	Nim-Dan-Dean 2	D 16
	. . .				
BOASTED					
For all its boasted height,		. . . .	10	Ode to King	124
And all Her boasted Influences are		. . . . . .	10	Ode to King	138
Not for his boasted healing art;		.. . .	432	Answer Paulus	17
To others he boasted of knocking out brains,		. . . .	816	Yahoo's	47
DOASTER					
Thy Fame, thy Genius now declines, proud Boaster.		. .	1002	Reply by Dean	9
BOASTING					
Still boasting of Her Great Unknown;		. . . . . .	24	Ode Athenian	251
Then, boasting tell us where you din'd,		. . . . .	480	Libel on D- D-	5
BOASTS					
Our Letters say a Jesuite boasts		. . . .	422	Ireld	41
Who falsly boasts		. . . .	442	Ballyspellin	82
And boasts of his feats,		. . . .	856	Lady's Lament	177
BOAT					
Or in a Boat when e're thou wilt		. . . . . .	109	V's House	113
Each padling in his leaky Boat,		. . . .	256	Bubble	147
And how his Boat was over set,		. . . .	280	Journal	66
Since cruel Fate hath sunk our Justice Boat;		. . .	284	Elegy Boat	2
The common Death of many a stronger Boat.		. . . . .	284	Elegy Boat	10
And yet our Boat, how shall I reconcile it?		. . .	285	Elegy Boat	13
Was both a Boat, and in one Sense a Pilat.		. . .	285	Elegy Boat	14
Our Boat is now sail'd to the Stygian Ferry,		. . .	285	Elegy Boat	23
A Trade, our Boat had practic'd here so well.		. . .	285	Elegy Boat	26
We may place Boat in his old Post again.		. . .	285	Elegy Boat	30
We'll cry; look, here's our Boat, and there's the			285	Elegy Boat	36
Pendent.					
Here lies Judge Boat within a Coffin.		. . . . .	286	Elegy Boat	37
A Boat a Judge? yes, where's the Blunder?		. . . .	286	Elegy Boat	39
No Boat was better deckt than He.		. . . . . .	286	Elegy Boat	42
And as they sail in Charon's Boat,		. . . . . .	647	On Poetry	211
Chaff, straws, or fragments of some rotten boat,		. .	672	Epig Carthy 24	D 14
BOATS					
Benches on Boats are plac't, not Boats on Benches.		.	285	Elegy Boat	12
Benches on Boats are plac't, not Boats on Benches.		.	285	Elegy Boat	12
Should some imperious Neighbour sink the Boats,		. .	534	To Mr. Gay	89
BOB					
When a holy black Suede, the Son of Bob,		. . . . .	147	Windsor Proph	1
Full in his Face Bob shuts the Council Door:			537	Mr. Pulteney	4
(Cries Bob) "I'm Sorry for the News;		. . . . .	560	Death of Swift	192
Those are <Allens>, Jack and Bob,			836	Legion Club	173
"go tell your friend Bob and the other great folk,			843	Ay and No	13
Till <Bob>, the Poet's Foe, possess't her Ear.			531	To Mr. Gay	4
Now, let me show how <Bob> and you agree.		. . . .	532	To Mr. Gay	43
And cursing <Bob>, forget to bless <the> <King>.		. .	533	To Mr. Gay	52
Thus <Bob> shal't thou be mawl'd, fly where thou wil't:		538	Mr. Pulteney	38
BOB'S					
Bob's Spittle mix'd with Harry's <Turd>		. . . .	495	Panegyr Swift	63
BOBB					
The fittest Tools to work for Bobb.		. . . . . .	503	Doctor Delaney	90
BODICE					
Unlaces next her Steel-Rib'd Bodice;		. . . . .	582	Young Nymph	24
BODIES					
(When this huge Bodies Moisture was so great		. . . .	16	Ode Athenian	3
Such their exalted Bodies are,		. . . .	787	Clad in Brown	21
BODILESS					
Phantoms, bodiless and vain,		. . . .	833	Legion Club	101
BODING					
And as the Boding Owl, or rather		. . . . . .	99	Elegy Patrige	49
BODINGS SEE FORE-BODINGS					
BODY					
The Body, tho' Gigantick, lyes all Cold and Dead.			25	Ode Athenian	291
To keep that worthless clod, the body, in one place:	. .	36	Ode Sancroft	64
Now, Mrs. Dukes, you know, and every Body under-stands,		71	Mrs Harris Pet	42
But loathsom Spots his Body stain:		. . . . . .	83	Salamander	32
Her Body light, she tries her Wings,		. . . . .	230	Prog of Poetry	13

BODY	(CONTINUED)	PAGE	TITLE	LINE
With hungry Meals his Body pin'd,		231	Prog of Poetry	37
His Body active as his Mind,		398	Earl of P-b-w	22
Could from her taintless Body flow.		584	Strephon Chloe	14
We leave the body sweet and sound,		618	Scandal Poem 1	27
We leave the body sweet and sound;		624	Scandal Poem 2	21
He slew my Body, but you stab my Fame.		668	Epig Carthy 10	D 2
As nat'ral Life the Body warms,		724	To Stella	11
Round all your Body plump your Skin;		759	Receipt Youth	30
Does not the Body thrive and grow		765	Stel B-day '26	55
Like his Body, rank and foul:		800	Traulus 2	34
Lice from your Body suck their Food;		812	Bro Protestant	35
"Hist, Huzzy, I think I hear some Body coming--		871	Grand Question	127
And, in his house, if any body come,		878	Robbin & Harry	23
My spirits with my body progging,		900	Dean's Reasons	57
And clad my Body all in White:		915	Riddle 1	4
At Head and Foot my Body lopt:		915	Riddle 1	12
O'er Head and Body make a Rout,		920	Riddle 6	15
. . . than you have in your whole Body,		985	Mary to Sher	9
Every body knows, that I love to tell Truth and shame the Devil,		986	Mary to Sher	23
BODY'S				
. . .when a Body's plunder'd?		72	Mrs Harris Pet	53
'Twould grieve a Body's Heart to see't:		90	Bauc & Phil 1	18
This Earth which bears his Body's Print,		101	Elegy Patrige	111
Thy Body's cloathed like thy Soul.		787	Clad in Brown	16
BODYES				
And strip the Bodyes of the Dead.		256	Bubble	156
BOG				
He'll make it muddy as a Bog.		671	Epig Carthy 21	D 8
BOGS				
Thro' bogs and thro' briers,		853	Lady's Lament	46
BOIL SEE BOYL				
The God who made Scamander boil,		323	Pethox	7
Fire will not roast, nor Water boil.		1035	To Quilca	8
BOIL'D SEE BOYL'D				
Of roast or boil'd, to the Hungry is charming.		941	Letter	30
BOILEAU'S				
Translated from Boileau's Translation,		649	On Poetry	261
BOILING				
Was to a boiling Fountain turn'd,		293	Prog Marriage	118
BOIST'ROUS				
Such is that Clan of boist'rous Bears		216	To Mr. Delany	51
BOLD				
And like a Bold Romantick Knight		7	Ode to King	37
Thy just submission for this bold neglect.		53	Temple Ill	74
The bold Encroachers on the Deep,		239	Run Bankers	1
Here all the bold Advent'rers came,		256	Bubble	138
And once I was so bold to beg that I might see His Grace,		342	Upon His Grace	27
This Thief and Black-Smith was so bold,		346	Prometheus	63
In Senates bold, and fierce in War,		398	Earl of P-b-w	32
Where many a bold Advent'rer fell.		413	Desire Possess	44
That Fortune still assists the bold,		588	Strephon Chloe	148
And grown so bold behind his Back		605	Beasts Confess	127
Fam'd for a thousand bold adventures		619	Scandal Poem 1	60
From whence you draw such bold conclusions;		622	Scandal Poem 1	161
Fam'd for a thousand bold Adventures,		625	Scandal Poem 2	56
These Scriblers grow so bold of late,		783	Tim and Fables	31
Quoth Hugh of Armagh, "The mob is grown bold."		843	Ay and No	3
By your good Leave, my most profound and bold Sir,		1004	Dan J's Reply	30
BOLDER				
For Liberty no Champion bolder,		455	Dean Smedley	9
If he was bolder than became		705	Cadenus Vaness	588
BOLDLY				
Boldly we hence the brave Commencement Date		13	Ode to William	D 45
Instead of boldly sailing far to buy		19	Ode Athenian	97
And in Her own hearing I boldly did Vote,		144	New Song	40
And boldly Force the winged Quill		373	Letter D. S-y	53
Walks boldly home at dead of night;		435	Answer Paulus	92
Present it boldly on your knee,		469	Birthday Song	281
You then may boldly go in Quest		504	Doctor Delaney	143
Some, when an Heir succeeds; go boldly on,		535	To Mr. Gay	117
"For her he boldly stood alone;		566	Death of Swift	349
He boldly sent his Hand in quest,		589	Strephon Chloe	188
And at all Hazards boldly quote:		648	On Poetry	248
And boldly then invoke the Muse:		743	Stel B-day 22	76
Here unobserv'd, she boldly goes,		893	Panegyr Dean	215
Some enter boldly, some by Stealth,		922	Riddle 7	31
BOLDNESS				
Your gen'rous Boldness to defend		765	Stel B-day '26	43
BOLINGBROKE				
"Put my Lord Bolingbroke in Mind,		201	Horace 2, 6	55
When Bolingbroke with Pult'ney Dines.		483	Libel on D- D-	102
Provided Bolingbroke were dead.		560	Death of Swift	196
BOLSTERS				
The Bolsters that supply her Hips.		582	Young Nymph	28
BOLT				
The bolt discharg'd, the sky grows clear;		617	Scandal Poem 1	12
The Bolt discharg'd, the Sky grows clear:		624	Scandal Poem 2	12

```
                                                              PAGE    TITLE            LINE
BOLTER
    "A Boulter by name is no bolter of wit.  . . . . . .      843 Ay and No           10
BOLTON
    "In sending Bolton to Clonfert.  . . . . . . . .          304 Storm               42
    Or Bolton the wise  . . . . . . . .                       423 Carterets Arms
    For who but Lord Bolton was mitred for Merit?  . . .      808 Advice Parson        8
    <Montague> Learning, <Bolton> Eloquence:                  164 Toland's Invit      24
<BOLTON'S>
    Lord <Bolton's> good Grace, Lord <Carr>, and Lord        804 Irish Bishops       25
        <Howard>,
BOLTS    SEE THUNDER-BOLTS
BOLUS
    She takes a Bolus e'er she sleeps;  . . . . . . .         582 Young Nymph         37
BOMBAS'
    To encroach on his art by writing of bombas';  . . . .  1027 Sheri Circles       22
BOMBAST
    His rhet'ric, bombast, silly jests, are by far  . . . .  815 Yahoo's             13
BOND
    When e'er the bloody Bond appears.  . . . . . . .         240 Run Bankers         48
BONDAGE
    The Bondage and the Slavery of Years.                      24 Ode Athenian       259
    Some she does to Egyptian Bondage draw,  . . . . .        32 Ode to Temple      187
BONDS
    They have his Soul who have his Bonds,  . . . . . .      241 Run Bankers         51
BONE
    This breaks a Girth, and that a Bone.  . . . . . .       398 Earl of P-b-w       21
    And nothing left but Skin and Bone;  . . . . . .        759 Receipt Youth        8
    For, such a Shape of Skin and Bone  . . . . . .         904 Death Daphne        61
    He pick't my Marrow from the Bone.  . . . . . .         915 Riddle 1            14
    And pick my Chicken to the Bone:  . . . . . .           954 Authors Living       4
    Thou sorry Scare-crow of Skin and Bone,  . . . . .     1003 Dan J's Reply       17
BONES    SEE SHIN-BONES
    Within, his wife would break his Bones,  . . . . . .    221 A Quiet Life        51
    And strip the Bones, and melt the Oyl.  . . . . .       258 Bubble             204
    To Cudgel our Bones, and for Drink give us Verjuice;    335 Serious Poem        38
    And strip his Hyde, and pick his Bones,  . . . . .      413 Desire Possess      57
    Than if he heard you broke your Bones.  . . . . . .     546 Life of Swift       30
    No Flesh, no Bones, no Blood --- no Ghost:  . . . .     935 Riddle 23      D  11
    Yet he gets home at night with Health and whole Bones. 1037 Four Storyes         8
BONEY
    With skinny, boney, snip and lean,  . . . . . . .       861 Lady Acheson        42
BONNET
    Red hat, and blue bonnet, and turbant's the same,  . . . 815 Yahoo's            23
BONNY-CLABBER
    Of Parties o're our Bonny-Clabber.  . . . . . .         781 Mullinix Tim       260
BONY
    There's bony Jane  . . . . . . . . . . . .              442 Ballyspellin        55
    With two bony thumbs  . . . . . . . . . . . .           852 Lady's Lament       19
BOOBY
    And you like a Booby, the Bubble can swallow;  . . .    265 Apollo              87
    You see the Booby Husband sit  . . . . . . .            448 Modern Lady        114
    Thus at the Bar that Booby Bettesworth,  . . . . .      812 Bro Protestant      25
    Bow <Bettesworth>, that booby, and <Scoundrel> in grain, 814 Yahoo's            3
BOOBY'S
    His arms upon the booby's shoulders  . . . . . .        421 Ireld               22
BOOK    SEE TABLE-BOOK,PLAY-BOOK,PRAY'R-BOOK,COMMON-PLACE-BOOK
    The Name and Man, by whom the Book was writ,  . . .     21 Ode Athenian       166
    In that deep Grave a Book,  . . . . . . . . .            27 Ode to Temple       36
    In such a Book and such a Heart,  . . . . . . .          61 Lady Tablebook      26
    And take a Folio for a conj'ring Book.  . . . . .       193 Author Himself       8
    Sleep, or peruse some antient Book;  . . . . . .        202 Horace 2, 6        110
    When they saw the Dean's Book they were in a great Fury 237 Excellent Song      24
    (Consult his Book de Partium usu)  . . . . . . .        367 Answer Delaney      32
    The Dean sits plodding on a Book,  . . . . . .          405 Swift to Pope        7
    I know not in what Book or Page,  . . . . . .           412 Desire Possess       6
    Far better than a printed Book;  . . . . . . .          450 Modern Lady        191
    (As in a Book he heard it read)  . . . . . . .          587 Strephon Chloe     101
    A Paper Book is sent by Boyle,  . . . . . . .           611 By Dr. Swift         1
    Procure the Book for Love or Money,  . . . . . .        648 On Poetry          260
    Out skips a Book of Miscellanies.  . . . . . .          651 On Poetry          318
    But thy Book perish'd on its natal Day.  . . . . .      669 Epig Carthy 13  D   4
    Half of my Book at least is good.  . . . . . .          669 Epig Carthy 15  D   2
    While with the Fustian of thy Book  . . . . . .         670 Epig Carthy 21  D   1
    To turn to Ovid, the Book the Second;  . . . . .        690 Cadenus Vaness     109
    For placing still some Book betwixt,  . . . . . .       701 Cadenus Vaness     480
    And while the Book was in her Hand,  . . . . . .        702 Cadenus Vaness     514
    To see the Virgin mind her Book,  . . . . . .           704 Cadenus Vaness     551
    The Book, the Author, and the Friend.  . . . . . .      709 Cadenus Vaness     705
    No book for delight  . . . . . . . . . . .              855 Lady's Lament      145
    "I never cou'd take to my Book for the Blood o'me,  . . 873 Grand Question     165
    "But, the Sight of a Book makes me sick to this Day.  . 873 Grand Question     172
    When they surprize me at my Book!  . . . . . .          891 Panegyr Dean       138
    Instead of poring on a Book,  . . . . . . . .           892 Panegyr Dean       177
BOOKS    SEE LAW-BOOKS
    And rid her of her Lumber and Her Books,  . . . . .      23 Ode Athenian       229
    The Nymph who oft had read in Books,  . . . . . .       120 Apollo Outwit       13
    Unhelpt by Practice, Books, or Art.  . . . . . .        215 To Mr. Delany       22
    While He goes out to cheapen Books,  . . . . . .        291 Prog Marriage       39
    Our Parsons Read the Draper's Books, and make us        343 Upon His Grace      40
        honest Foke.
    Cou'd read all Books were ever writ;  . . . . . .       513 Answer Fable        36
```

```
BOOKS          (CONTINUED)                              PAGE    TITLE          LINE
  "I sent them with a Load of Books,       . . . . .    563 Death of Swift      259
  By reading Books against their Saviour;  . . . . .    592 Strephon Chloe      272
  On Love and Books in Rapture sweet;      . . . . .    593 Cassinus Peter        4
  As well as Chymists by their Books:      . . . . .    597 Problem Solved        4
  He pass'd his Hours among his Books;     . . . . .    604 Beasts Confess      105
  Go read in antient books enroll'd        . . . . . .  619 Scandal Poem 1       51
  Go read in antient Books enroll'd,       . . . . .    625 Scandal Poem 2       47
  And with Books my Mind embellish.        . . . . .    632 Epistle Lady         90
  And said she must consult her Books,     . . . . .    689 Cadenus Vaness      106
  That Scholars wou'd forsake their Books  . . . . .    694 Cadenus Vaness      234
  Well knowing from the Books she read     . . . . .    696 Cadenus Vaness      310
  Searching in Books for Wisdom's Aid,     . . . . .    702 Cadenus Vaness      490
  But Time, and Books, and State Affairs   . . . . .    703 Cadenus Vaness      544
  They temper Love and Books together;     . . . . .    712 Cadenus Vaness      825
  And Friend <Delany> at his Books,        . . . . .    756 Stel B-day '24       12
  When you walk among your Books,          . . . . . .  838 Legion Club         207
  A hater of books:         . . . . .                   854 Lady's Lament        94
  Wise books and reflection . . . . .                   854 Lady's Lament       101
  For, Cards we know, are Pluto's Books)   . . . . .    905 Death Daphne         80
BOON
  Proteus on you bestow'd the Boon         . . . . .    326 Pethox               81
  For you or I to crave a Boon;            . . . . .    371 Letter D. S-y         8
  A boon so small! But I may weep,         . . . . .    403 Window Inns 10   D    9
  This one, poor, humble Boon I want,      . . . . .    475 Epist on Epist        8
BOORS
  But for that Pack of churlish Boors      . . . . .     92 Bauc & Phil 1        86
  But, for that Pack of churlish Boors,    . . . . .    112 Bauc & Phil 2        46
BOOT    SEE SLY-BOOT
  Live on, and Stuff, to Boot, their Maws. . . . . .    479 Epist on Epist      126
BOOTH
  By Lovers spoke in Punch's Booth.        . . . . . .  650 On Poetry           298
  So at this Booth, which we call Dublin,  . . . . .    777 Mullinix Tim        137
BOOTHS
  And step in Booths for Air.  . . . . . . . .          122 Empty'ng Town        12
BOOTS
  He knew his Trade, and call'd it Boots.  . . . . .     99 Elegy Patrige        34
  And with Boots so very grazy     . . . . .            573 Helter Skelter       11
  With Jocky Boots, and Silver Spurs;      . . . . .    760 Receipt Youth        44
BOR'D
  Bor'd a large Augre-hole in the Image's Breech;  . .  336 Serious Poem         72
BORDER'D
  The Sleeves new border'd with a List     . . . . .     94 Bauc & Phil 1       167
  His Night-Cap border'd round with Lace   . . . . .    587 Strephon Chloe       93
BORDERING
  Two bordering Wits contend for Glory;    . . . . .    650 On Poetry           293
BORE
  Altho' the bore be ne'er so large,       . . . . . .   66 Problem              44
  Nor Leaf, nor Fruit, nor Blossom bore.   . . . . .    134 Magician's Rod       70
  So when Troy Chair-men bore the Wooden Steed,  . . .  139 City Shower          47
  He bore the Skyes upon his Back  . . . . . . .        160 Atlas                 3
  (Those honourable Wounds you bore        . . . . .    324 Pethox               15
  If you make the same Tryal, and Bore him Behind;  . . 336 Serious Poem         78
  And bore my Mother by a Prentice.        . . . . .    350 Upright Judge 3       4
  Suspected for the Love he bore   . . . . . . .        375 Apology Lady C       15
  Than all the Sins he ever bore.  . . . . . . .        497 Panegyr Swift       141
  Who bore for twice ten Years the publick Hate.  . . . 536 To Mr. Gay          144
  To hear, the other bore the Bell---?     . . . . . .  546 Life of Swift        55
  "He bore continual Persecution;          . . . . .    569 Death of Swift      400
  Where is the sacred Well, that bore my Name?  . . . . 793 St. Pat's Well       65
BOREES
  But Tom was best at Borees;      . . . . .            784 Mullinex Dick        14
BORN    SEE HEAV'N-BORN,LOW-BORN,CITY-BORN,STILL-BORN,FREE-BORN,HIGH-BORN,NEW-BORN
  They're now, just now, as naturally born,  . . . . .   20 Ode Athenian        130
  That Heaven's high Son was in a village born;  . . .   39 Ode Sancroft        172
  Born between whores and fops, by lewd compacts,  . .   47 To Congreve         125
  Born like a Phoenix from the Flame,      . . . . .     81 Vanbrug House        79
  Thy Mother burnt, art Born again;        . . . . .    109 V's House           120
  Born like a Phoenix from the Flame,      . . . . .    109 V's House           121
  While the first drizzling Show'r is born aslope,  . . 137 City Shower          18
  Born to retrieve her sex's fame.         . . . . .    177 To Lord Harley       38
  Chose, for her spouse, a mortal born:    . . . . .    178 To Lord Harley       66
  What Planet rul'd when you were born;    . . . . .    258 Bubble              191
  That since I was born, I hardly have spy'd it;  . . . 263 Apollo                6
  The sober Hen not born to swim   . . . . . . .        295 Horrid Plot         149
  That Mr. Ford was born to day:   . . . . . . .        311 To Ford               4
  Yet here were You and Ormonde born       . . . . .    314 To Ford              84
  From Venus born, thy Beauty shows,       . . . . .    323 Pethox                1
  A Kinder Wife was never born,    . . . . . . .        328 Epigram 2             3
  Ye Rhimers, dead as soon as born,        . . . . .    394 Grub-Street           3
  Had You and I been Courtiers born,       . . . . .    409 Dial Rich Marb       31
  Or, how this Evil can be born,   . . . . . . .        413 Censure               3
  Though born in Snow, it dy'd in Flame.   . . . . .    470 Burning Poem         16
  Which I was born to introduce,   . . . . . . .        555 Death of Swift       57
  Revive the Libels born to dye;   . . . . . . .        561 Death of Swift      203
  He was a Wit both born and bred;         . . . . .    602 Beasts Confess       28
  "Twas known, tho' he had born Aspersion;  . . . . .   606 Beasts Confess      151
  For those who are not Poets born:  . . . . . .        652 On Poetry           354
  A perfect Goddess born and bred. . . . . . . .        655 On Poetry           426
  To see a lovely Infant born:     . . . . .            692 Cadenus Vaness      189
  And, born directly to the Heart, . . . . . . .        703 Cadenus Vaness      522
```

BORN	(CONTINUED)	PAGE	TITLE	LINE
Tom a Foot-Boy bred and born,	. . . .	784	Mullinex Dick	11
When, for the Use of no Hibernian born,	. . . . .	793	St. Pat's Well	91
Were down the sudden Current born;	. . . . . .	811	Bro Protestant	4
Tho' born of human Filth and Sweat, it	. . . . . .	812	Bro Protestant	37
"Relentless Dean! to Mischief born,	. . . . . .	850	Old Thorn	58
Never since I was born did I hear so much Wit,	. .	873	Grand Question	173
Poor I, a Savage bred and born,	. . . .	891	Panegyr Dean	131
Twice were they bury'd, twice were born,	. . . . .	923	Riddle 7	75
They all were born from thy Embrace.	. . . . . .	925	Riddle 8	24
Begotten, and Born, and dying with Noise,	. . . .	927	Riddle 11	D 1
I ne'er was born, nor e'er can die,	. . . . . .	936	Riddle 23	D 26
You're so retrograde, sure you were born under Cancer:	.	1019	To Sheridan	3
BORNE				
Such were the storms good Sancroft long has borne;	. . .	40	Ode Sancroft	198
Smooth as that airy nymph so subtly borne	. . . .	54	Temple Ill	117
And borne on fancy's Pinions, thinks,	. . . . . .	80	Vanbrug House	51
To Fraunce, that evere he was borne.	. . . . . .	103	Merlin	8
Nor could have borne it half so long.	. . . . . .	160	Atlas	14
BORNEO'S				
Sly Hunters thus, in Borneo's Isle,	. . . . . .	885	Rev Market-Hill	75
BOROUGHS				
"To all their Boroughs send them down:	. . . . .	564	Death of Swift	284
BORROW				
Borrow from every one a Grace;	. . . .	28	Ode to Temple	64
Nor borrow from the Blew-ey'd Maid,	. . . . . .	272	Apollo's Edict	D 73
Presume to borrow Wit from Bacchus?	. . . . . .	671	Epig Carthy 22	D 2
BORROW'D				
Ne'er borrow'd more variety of Shapes	. . . . . .	22	Ode Athenian	199
Seems to have borrow'd some ungrateful tast	. . . .	22	Ode Athenian	212
With borrow'd Money in his Purse;	. . . . . .	173	Horace 1, 7	94
Her Splendor is but borrow'd light;	. . . . . .	465	Birthday Song	176
Bridles borrow'd for a Day,	. . . . . .	573	Helter Skelter	14
The trivial Turns, the borrow'd Wit,	. . . . . .	645	On Poetry	151
Borrow'd from the Mason Side:	. . . . . .	800	Traulus 2	44
I With borrow'd Silver shine,	. . . . . .	927	Riddle 10	D 1
BOSOM				
And heave her Bosom unaware	. . . .	222	Prog of Love	17
And deep transfix'd her Bosom too.	. . . . . .	703	Cadenus Vaness	519
Let Courtiers hug them in their Bosom,	. . . . .	813	Bro Protestant	59
If still your foul bosom more rancour contains;	. . .	819	Archbi Cashel	12
A Virgin in thy Bosom bred;	. . . . . .	924	Riddle 8	6
When on my Bosom thy bright Eyes,	. . . . . .	932	Riddle 19	D 1
BOSOMS				
For manly Bosoms chiefly fit,	. . . .	693	Cadenus Vaness	204
BOSSE				
Than shall the Fyshe beweyle his Bosse;	. . . . .	103	Merlin	9
BOSSU				
Wise Dennis, and profound Bossu.	. . . .	648	On Poetry	250
BOTARGO				
Botargo, Catsup, and Caveer.	. . . .	895	Panegyr Dean	268
BOTCH				
For want of which by way of Botch,	. . . . . .	96	On the Union	3
At last I'm fairly forc'd to botch for't.	. . . . .	993	On Picture	9
BOTH	131		OMITTED WORD	
BOTTLE				
He stopt at the George for a Bottle of Sack,	. . .	399	Tom Clinch	3
Behold the Bottle, where it lies	. . . . . .	743	Stel B-day 22	61
To stint me at Night to one Bottle of Wine;	. . . .	867	Grand Question	16
So well, what Bottle holds a Quart:	. . . . .	889	Panegyr Dean	92
Except a Bottle now and then,	. . . . . .	890	Panegyr Dean	99
The Bottle, till your Fingers ake:	. . . . . .	892	Panegyr Dean	180
Be cautious, or your Bottle flies.	. . . . . .	892	Panegyr Dean	184
We shall ne'er have one Bottle;	. . . .	1015	Swift to Sheri	40
BOTTLED				
. . .whether the Wine is to be bottled To-morrow, or no.		1013	Swift to Sheri	1
BOTTLES				
Two Bottles call'd for, (half her Store,	. . . . .	747	Stel Distress	49
Two Bottles call'd for, (half her Store;	. . . . .	751	Stel Wood-Park	65
What Pints may best for Bottles pass,	. . . . . .	889	Panegyr Dean	93
. . .for Corks to stop your Bottles, with a Vengeance.		1013	Swift to Sheri	5
BOTTLING				
To be an Art as vain, as Bottling up of Wind:)	. . .	21	Ode Athenian	185
With you and your bottling,	. . . .	1015	Swift to Sheri	38
The Verses you sent on the bottling your Wine	. . .	1017	Swift Ans Sher	1
BOTTOM				
And humbly at the bottom crawl.	. . . .	9	Ode to King	118
Apply'd at Bottom stops it's Course;	. . . . . .	93	Bauc & Phil 1	102
Apply'd at Bottom, stops its Course,	. . . . . .	113	Bauc & Phil 2	62
Light with its Bottom on the Ground.	. . . . . .	126	Little House	10
By their own Weight sunk to the Bottom;	. . . . .	158	Fable of Midas	79
The Bottom of the Pan to grope,	. . . . . .	528	Lady's Dres Rm	93
Should the Bottom be split, our <Bishops> wou'd dread	.	805	Irish Bishops	45
BOTTOM'D	SEE DOUBLE-BOTTOM'D			
BOUGH	SEE OAKEN-BOUGH			
(So Poets sing, with golden Bough	. . . . . .	896	Panegyr Dean	307
BOUGHS				
In Golden Boughs, and Golden Fruit,	. . . . . .	134	Magician's Rod	72
And on the Boughs her Garland hung,	. . . . . .	848	Old Thorn	6
BOUGHT				
You bought it at a cheaper Rate;	. . . . . .	28	Ode to Temple	73

```
BOUGHT              (CONTINUED)                              PAGE   TITLE          LINE
   I have Experience dearly bought,       . . . . . . . .    175 Horace 1, 7        133
   He that cou'd once have half a Kingdom bought,   . . .    234 Elegy on Demar      19
   Where Right, and Wrong, are bought and sold,    . . . .   385 Manly Virtue        67
   Where every knave & fool is bought . . . . . . . .        421 Ireld               3
   Nor sell what they so dearly bought,    . . . . . . .     488 Irish-Club          23
   And Kings, like private Folks, are bought and sold:  .    536 To Mr. Gay         136
   "But, this I know, all People bought 'em;   . . . . .     565 Death of Swift     312
   That Meat must be with Money bought;    . . . . . . .     693 Cadenus Vaness     214
   And, to be free, was dearly bought:     . . . . . . .     708 Cadenus Vaness     671
   By Thousands I am sold and bought,      . . . . . . .     918 Riddle 4            13
   If Wine's bought, or Victuals drest     . . . . . . .     931 Riddle 18        D  19
BOULT-HER
   The devil he may take her into hell and Boult-her!   . . 841 Ballad           D  14
BOULTER
   "A Boulter by name is no bolter of wit.  . . . . . .     843 Ay and No           10
BOULTER'S
   Had thou been join'd to Boulter's head.  . . . . . .     822 Epigr Rundle         4
BOUNC'D
   He bragg'd how he bounc'd, and he swore how he swore.  .  816 Yahoo's            44
BOUNC'T
   Out bounc't the Mastiff of the triple Head;   . . . .    538 Mr. Pulteney        27
BOUNCE
   They bounce from their Nest,   . . . . . . . . . .        245 Irish-Feast         33
BOUND    SEE HARD-BOUND,WELL-BOUND
   . . .as in Duty bound, shall ever Pray.  . . . . . .      73 Mrs Harris Pet       75
   With Wax the Father bound them fast,    . . . . . .       252 Bubble              38
   Conceive themselves in Conscience bound   . . . . .      414 Censure              9
   "By solemn League and Cov'nant bound,    . . . . . .     568 Death of Swift     381
   By Duty bound, on Stella's Day;    . . . . . . . .        740 Stel B-day 22        2
   While tortur'd Madam bound remains,     . . . . . .       885 Rev Market-Hill     71
   . . . since my Mother bound my Head,    . . . . . . .     985 Mary to Sher         1
   Truly I don't know who's bound to be sending . . . . .   1013 Swift to Sheri       5
BOUNDLESS
   The boundless Glory all Redounds to Thee,     . . . . .    12 Ode to William   D  35
   The last, as boundless as the Wind;    . . . . . . .      215 To Mr. Delany       15
BOUNDS
   Could leap the bounds which part your world and mine;  .   44 To Congreve         30
   And sometimes walks beyond his Bounds.   . . . . . . .    218 To Mr. Delany       94
   Unto the utmost Bounds of Skill,    . . . . . . . .       373 Letter D. S-y       54
BOUNTEOUS
   Unerring Heav'n, with bounteous Hand,   . . . . . . .     272 Apollo's Edict   D  64
   With open Heart and bounteous Hand:     . . . . . . .     693 Cadenus Vaness     210
   Thee bounteous Goddess Cloacine,    . . . . . . . .       894 Panegyr Dean       229
BOUNTY
   "On Learning how his Bounty flows,      . . . . . . .     462 Birthday Song       75
   "Content with what his Bounty gave,     . . . . . . .     476 Epist on Epist      35
   Living on the publick Bounty;      . . . . . . . .        574 Helter Skelter      38
'BOUT
   'Bout latent Charms beneath my Cloaths,    . . . . . .   1004 Dan J's Reply       22
BOW
   When soon the peaceful bow unstring'd is shown,   . . .    52 Temple Ill         27
   That the main String of Cupid's Bow,    . . . . . .       66 Problem             22
   Conclude the Bow relax'd again.    . . . . . . . .        66 Problem             32
   And, by a gentle Bow, divin'd    . . . . . . . .         133 Magician's Rod      31
   The faded Bow distilling Rain.     . . . . . . . .        290 Prog Marriage       14
   So like my own, without his Bow,    . . . . . . . .       692 Cadenus Vaness     191
   Nor quarrell'd at their aukward Bow.    . . . . . . .     701 Cadenus Vaness     461
   Where erst sate Cupid with his Bow;     . . . . . . .     757 Stel B-day '24      38
   Bow <Bettesworth>, that booby, and <Scoundrel> in grain,  814 Yahoo's             3
   Like the Bow that guards the Tartar,    . . . . . . .     927 Riddle 10        D   4
   The pliant bow, the forehead bland--    . . . . . . .     951 Upstart          D  30
BOW-SHOT
   Not a Bow-shot from the College,    . . . . . . . .       829 Legion Club          3
BOW-STRING
   Conclude Love's Bow-String at full Stretch;   . . .       66 Problem             30
BOW'D
   Which bow'd by evening-breeze with bending stalks,   . .   54 Temple Ill        119
   He mov'd, and bow'd and talk't with too much Grace;  . .  194 Author Himself      13
   So bow'd, was thankful for the Honour:   . . . . . .      376 Apology Lady C      25
   Now pale as Death, then blush'd and bow'd;    . . . .     377 Apology Lady C      78
   Like a Beau in the Box, he bow'd low on each Side;   .    399 Tom Clinch          10
BOW'R
   Four Stories climbing to her Bow'r;     . . . . . . .     581 Young Nymph          8
   He calls it a bow'r.    . . . . . . . . . . .             857 Lady's Lament      186
BOW'RS
   To silver Meads, and shady Bow'rs,      . . . . . . .     590 Strephon Chloe     201
   This said, she plucks in Heav'ns high Bow'rs    . . .     691 Cadenus Vaness     154
   The Bow'rs that hold those Nymphs divine;     . . . . .   729 Stella, Poems       42
BOWELS
   But oh! it turn'd poor Strephon's Bowels,     . . . . .   527 Lady's Dres Rm      43
   For how can stony Bowels melt,    . . . . . . . .         561 Death of Swift     215
   Drop from the Tree with all his Bowels burst;   . . .     806 Judas               22
BOWER
   Make me pollute the Muses' bower?      . . . . . . .      490 Dialogue            46
   The Shepherd in his Bower might sleep or sing,   . . .    792 St. Pat's Well      41
BOWERS
   Begin, my Muse, first from our Bowers,   . . . . . .      278 Journal              7
   "In either Angle shady Bowers:     . . . . . . . .        476 Epist on Epist      52
BOWING
   So, bowing, seemingly comply'd;   . . . . . . . . .       378 Apology Lady C      95
```

BOWL
    Fill the Bowl up again, ...   246 Irish-Feast   54
BOWLS
    As loud as fifty mustard bowls; . . . .   461 Birthday Song   40
    Nor plays at cards, or dice, or bowls; . . . . . .   901 Dean's Reasons   88
BOX   SEE SNUFF-BOX,CEDAR-BOX
    Yet at the last the Box sweeps all away. . . . . .   29 Ode to Temple   80
    And in a Corner of Mrs. Dukes's Box,. . .   70 Mrs Harris Pet   23
    Till then it was lock'd in my Box at Parnassus; . . .   265 Apollo   79
    For fear my Lord should send it all into the poor Man's   342 Upon His Grace   26
        Box.
    And up he mounts into the Box, ...   352 Wood Ironmongr   15
    Like a Beau in the Box, he bow'd low on each Side; . .   399 Tom Clinch   10
    Here a convenient Box you found, ...   477 Epist on Epist   67
    The fatal Box it self display'd, ...   494 Panegyr Swift   41
    Oh, wond'rous Box! my Lyre unstrung . . . . .   494 Panegyr Swift   45
    As from within Pandora's Box, ...   528 Lady's Dres Rm   83
    On Box of Cedar sits the Wife, ...   590 Strephon Chloe   207
    This box is cramm'd on ev'ry side . . . . . .   753 Gift for Bec   9
    With Snuff was fill'd his Ebon Box, ...   904 Death Daphne   39
    And the fourth a Box within, ...   931 Riddle 17   D   6
    Each groov'd, and Dove-tail'd, like a Box. . .   1021 Nim-Dan-Dean 1   D   26
BOX-COMB
    And all that stuff of Toylet, Glass, and Box-comb? .   1003 Dan J's Reply   9
BOX'D
    Box'd in a Chair the Beau impatient sits, ...   139 City Shower   43
BOXES
    With their pretty tinsel'd Boxes, ...   573 Helter Skelter   25
BOY   SEE SCHOOL-BOY,FOOT-BOY,POST-BOY
    From which Ingredients, First the dext'rous Boy . .   118 Biddy Floyd   5
    Boy, give us a Cup; . . . .   245 Irish-Feast   27
    And down the towring Boy is cast: . . . . . .   252 Bubble   40
    This is gratefully own'd by each Boy in the College, .   263 Apollo   17
    To tell what ev'ry School Boy knows: . . . . . .   281 Journal   82
    From a bo-bo-bo-Boy he pursues his old Hank, . .   287 Bank Down   19
    "Tho' there's a Boy whom a Lord chuses, ...   321 First of April   7
    "Or naughty Boy elopes from School, ...   497 Panegyr Swift   130
    I know she loves the Barber's Boy. . . . . . .   595 Cassinus Peter   62
    Nor Boy brought up to cleaning Shoes, ...   641 On Poetry   35
    A Boy in yonder Isle below, ...   692 Cadenus Vaness   190
    Mistakes Vanessa for a Boy; . . . .   693 Cadenus Vaness   201
    The Boy made use of all his Craft, ...   701 Cadenus Vaness   476
    Mean time the Boy in secret lurks, ...   702 Cadenus Vaness   513
    In School to hear the finest Boy. . . . . . .   704 Cadenus Vaness   553
    Knockt down the Boy, the Lanthorn broke; . . . .   781 Mullinix Tim   268
    At the Parsons, Tom, Halloo Boy, ...   831 Legion Club   67
    And, see, the Printer's Boy below: . . . . . .   887 Panegyr Dean   32
    The lowest boy in Martin's school . . . . . .   899 Dean's Reasons   13
    With a Boy that is only fit for School, ...   941 Letter   19
    You treat me like a Boy that knocks down his Foe, . .   967 Letter Sherid   13
    . . .and the Boy here had not been sent . . . . .   1013 Swift to Sheri   4
BOYL
    Unless, like the Dutch, you rather would boyl . . . .   352 Wood Insect   37
    <Sunderland>, <Orford>, <Boyl>, and <Richmond's> Grace   165 Toland's Invit   33
BOYL'D
    Your Onyons must be th'roughly boyl'd; . . . . . .   952 Onyons   9
BOYLE
    A Paper Book is sent by Boyle, ...   611 By Dr. Swift   1
BOYLS
    And boyls Potatoes for her Spouse, ...   878 Robbin & Harry   26
BOYNE
    Amaz'd Thy Action at the Boyne we see! . . . .   12 Ode to William   D   33
BOYS   SEE SCHOOL-BOYS,SHOE-BOYS,BLUE-BOYS,COW-BOYS
    But when he found the Boys at play, ...   86 Hist V's House   13
    Whom Roguish Boys in Stormy Nights . . . . .   100 Elegy Patrige   91
    Keep close then Boys, and never quarrel. . . . .   189 Faggot   13
    Abroad, was pester'd by the Boys, ...   221 A Quiet Life   50
    O'Rourk's jolly Boys . . . .   245 Irish-Feast   29
    And then all hands, Boys, to the Oar . . . . .   279 Journal   18
    And then again, Boys, to the Oar. . . . . . .   280 Journal   44
    And harmless Frolicks of her Boys; . . . . . .   322 First of April   34
    And get Ten thousand Girls and Boys. . . . . .   362 Grace's Answer   48
    Ten thousand Girls and Boys you'll get . . . . .   362 Grace's Answer   49
    So, Holla Boys; God save the King. . . . . .   418 Woman's Mind   64
    This summoning of blackguard boys? . . . . . .   487 Irish-Club   10
    It frightens all the Village Boys. . . . . . .   513 Answer Fable   26
    With loud Huzza's from all the Boys, ...   586 Strephon Chloe   69
    No little Boys and Girls to cry . . . .   778 Mullinix Tim   181
    Tom huzza'd the black-guard Boys, ...   784 Mullinex Dick   19
    Of Ideots roaring to the Boys. . . . . . .   788 Dick's Variety   8
    Let the Boys pelt him if they dare; . . . . . .   788 Dick's Variety   20
    Jolly boys of St. Kevans, St. Patrick's, Donore, .   814 Yahoo's   1
    Tantara, tantara, while all the Boys hollow. . . .   870 Grand Question   92
    The naughty boys about the village . . . . . .   902 Dean's Reasons   107
    The Terror of Women, and Pleasure of Boys, ...   927 Riddle 11   D   2
    And think your Boys may gather there-hence . . . . .   988 Letter Dr Sh-n   3
    Our Boys run away, ...   1036 Plague Country   8
BRAC'D
    Brac'd like a Drum her oily Skin; . . . .   895 Panegyr Dean   258
BRAC'T
    How monstrous Carthy looks to Flaccus brac't, . . .   668 Epig Carthy 9   D   1

	PAGE	TITLE	LINE
BRACE			
Receiv'd a brace or two of Blows.	220	A Quiet Life	24
None e'er was known to have a Brace.	366	Answer Delaney	8
Because he brib'd you with a Brace of Tench?	534	To Mr. Gay	92
Attended by a Brace of Curs,	760	Receipt Youth	43
His Brace of Puppies how they stuff,	861	Lady Acheson	33
Janus, since thou hast a Brace,	862	To Janus	6
Beside a Brace of grave Divines;	1020	Nim-Dan-Dean 1 D	3
BRACTONS			
The Lovers Fleta's, Bractóns, Cokes.	689	Cadenus Vaness	107
BRADLEY			
And Muggleton, Toland, and Bradley the taylor,	815	Yahoo's	27
BRAG			
It would be an Exploit to brag on,	281	Journal	69
Whate'er you brag,	441	Ballyspellin	47
And when I brag of Aid divine,	741	Stel B-day 22	29
Old Jason would have less to brag on.	948	Jason Hassard	6
BRAGG'D			
He began as he bragg'd, with a rant and a roar;	816	Yahoo's	43
He bragg'd how he bounc'd, and he swore how he swore.	816	Yahoo's	44
BRAGS			
"And thy confed'rate Dame, who brags	850	Old Thorn	61
BRAIDED			
Her Braided Hair to make thee Ends;	100	Elegy Patrige	80
BRAIN			
From broken scraps and filings of your brain.	45	To Congreve	58
But a wild form dependent on the brain,	54	Temple Ill	95
From some malicious Tory's Brain,	256	Bubble	158
He wonders what employs her Brain;	292	Prog Marriage	65
But all are meer Productions of the Brain,	363	On Dreams	5
While Ignorance, with Brain of Lead,	449	Modern Lady	134
I mean the Head without the Brain.	469	Burning Poem	6
And, just as we dispose your brain,	620	Scandal Poem 1	93
And, just as we dispose your Brain,	626	Scandal Poem 2	91
It but stupifies your Brain.	636	Epistle Lady	210
Entring warm your frigid Brain	638	Epistle Lady	268
You form'd this Project in your Brain,	695	Cadenus Vaness	289
A Thought came slowly from my Brain,	741	Stel B-day 22	8
The limbs are guided by the brain,	761	Bec's B-Day	20
A mere Contrivance of the Brain,	764	Stel B-day '26	20
Party and Spleen have turn'd his Brain,	796	Traulus 1	14
Empty Visions of the Brain.	833	Legion Club	102
For, if a new Crotchet comes into my Brain,	869	Grand Question	65
You toss and turn your Brain till Noon;	892	Panegyr Dean	190
Or, but a Creature of the Brain,	920	Riddle 5	33
Like Pallas from my Father's Brain.	927	Riddle 10 D	10
BRAINS			
Yet the same want of Brains produces each effect;	18	Ode Athenian	85
Whose maintenance requires no help from brains.	48	To Congreve	164
To think that your Brains Issue is	61	Lady Tablebook	19
Even so Master Doctor had Puzzled his Brains	77	Lady B- B-	22
And hot are their Brains,	246	Irish-Feast	62
While others wrack their busy Brains,	361	Grace's Answer	17
Not for inspiring poets brains	432	Answer Paulus	15
And then to cool her heated Brains,	446	Modern Lady	45
Most of his Virtues, all my Brains.	494	Panegyr Swift	57
Is destin'd to beat out his Brains.	500	Doctor Delaney	16
From threshing Corn, he turns to thresh his Brains;	521	Stephen Duck	3
Strephon had long perplex'd his Brains,	586	Strephon Chloe	72
High up in Air he'll turn your Brains;	666	Epig Carthy 2 D	6
A Sov'reign Medicine for the Brains.	743	Stel B-day 22	70
To others he boasted of knocking out brains,	816	Yahoo's	47
Many a Head that holds no Brains.	829	Legion Club	10
How cou'd these Chimeras get into your Brains?--	873	Grand Question	185
Your damnable Riddle, my poor Brains did rack nigh.	972	S-'s Ans Sh-d	2
BRAINSICK			
Brainsick Brute, they call a Peer.	837	Legion Club	176
BRAMBLE			
Here, by the sacred Bramble ting'd,	896	Panegyr Dean	313
BRANCH			
And pluckt a Laurel branch (for Laurel was the first that grew,	16	Ode Athenian	27
Bears one, and but one branch of gold,	41	Ode Sancroft	226
Depriv'd of Root, and Branch, and Rind,	926	Riddle 9	1
BRANCHES			
And form the Leaves, the Branches, and the Fruit.	32	Ode to Temple	174
With lofty Branches to the Skies,	393	Modern Poets	2
Has canker'd all its Branches round;	849	Old Thorn	18
The humble Branches of a Thorn.	896	Panegyr Dean	306
BRAND			
And brand me for a Woman-Hater?	445	Modern Lady	8
BRANDISH			
When I no more a Pen can brandish.	611	By Dr. Swift	4
BRANFORD			
By two such whisp'ring Kings of Branford.	64	Discovery	48
BRANGLING			
Drives out Brangling, and Contention,	637	Epistle Lady	215
These brangling jars of Whig and Tory,	774	Mullinix Tim	35
BRASS			
Wood got so much Copper? He got it by Brass;	336	Serious Poem	86
This Brass was a Dragon (observe what I tell ye)	337	Serious Poem	87

BRASS	(CONTINUED)	PAGE	TITLE	LINE
But when Wood's Brass began to sound,	. . . . . .	338	Wood's Brass	7
Smith's Dust, and Copper, Lead and Brass,	. . . .	344	Prometheus	4
To Blood and Quarrels, Brass unites:	. . . . . .	345	Prometheus	22
Then whips me on a Chain of Brass,	. . . .	345	Prometheus	39
Between the <King> and Us but Brass,	. . . . .	346	Prometheus	68
In Fillets of Brass roll'd up to his Ears:	. . . .	350	Wood Insect	8
And the Sound of his Brass we took for our Knell.	.	351	Wood Insect	32
With Brass two fiery Steeds he shod,	. . . . . .	352	Wood Ironmongr	11
Of polish't Brass, his flaming Car,	. . . . . .	352	Wood Ironmongr	13
To take the Noise of Brass for Thunder!	. . . .	353	Wood Ironmongr	30
If neither brass nor marble can withstand	. . . .	419	Shall Repine	1
And Impudence with Front of Brass;	. . . . . .	448	Modern Lady	131
Than my Friend Sir <Robert> <Brass>	. . . .	637	Epistle Lady	246
Nor thy oppressing Lords afford thee Brass.	. . .	793	St. Pat's Well	94
And sure, as monument of brass,	. . . .	876	To Dean Swift	11
An Ounce of Gold's worth ten of Brass, dull Pedant.	.	1004	Dan J's Reply	33
BRAT				
Not Beggar's Brat, on Bulk begot;	. . . . . .	641	On Poetry	33
And make a Beggar's Brat a Peer.	. . . . . .	916	Riddle 1	36
The offspring of a beggar's brat.	. . . .	950	Upstart	D 6
BRATS				
What gave her Brats and Pigs the Meazles,	. . . .	282	Journal	93
BRAVE				
The brave Attempt do's all our Foes disarm,	. . . .	13	Ode to William	D 37
Boldly we hence the brave Commencement Date	. . . .	13	Ode to William	D 45
How, by Brave Hands, the Royal Traytor fell;	. . .	162	Toland's Invit	10
By Force of Wine ev'n <Scarborough> is Brave,	. . .	163	Toland's Invit	21
The Brave, the Witty, and the Fair;	. . . . . .	216	To Mr. Delany	38
The Ass was dull, the Lyon brave,	. . . . . .	512	Answer Fable	5
Ah! dost thou not Envy the brave Colonel Chatres,	.	519	Dean Hang Rape	49
The Brave are worried by the Base.	. . . . . .	651	On Poetry	320
Brave as the Upton Fan she wears:	. . . . . .	885	Rev Market-Hill	58
Behold, the Coward, and the Brave,	. . . . . .	922	Riddle 7	27
The Young, the Beautiful, and Brave,	. . . . . .	923	Riddle 7	53
To you victorious and brave,	. . . .	1005	Sheridan's Sub	5
BRAVELY				
Did bravely snatch the lovely helpless Prize.	. . .	12	Ode to William	D 24
Which, what it bravely Won, do's well Maintain.	. .	12	Ode to William	D 28
Cry'd bravely, Patience, good my Dear.	. . . . .	220	A Quiet Life	6
And bravely Precox might oppose	. . . . . .	373	Letter D. S-y	70
Bravely despise Champagne at Court,	. . . . . .	488	Irish-Club	19
"By bravely running Priest-craft down:	. . . . .	564	Death of Swift	292
And, bravely drove his Rivals down	. . . . . .	585	Strephon Chloe	41
I bravely call the Tories Jacks,	. . . . . .	778	Mullinix Tim	163
One shews how bravely Audoin Dy'd,	. . . . . .	781	Mullinix Tim	273
And kept their Liberty, or bravely dy'd.	. . . .	793	St. Pat's Well	82
Bravely I resolved to stay.	. . . .	834	Legion Club	132
BRAWLER				
Who is that Hell-featur'd Brawler,	. . . . . .	834	Legion Club	137
BRAZEN				
"Be this thy sure defence, thy brazen wall,	. . . .	55	Temple Ill	141
First with the brazen Cannons Roar.	. . . . .	338	Wood's Brass	2
With brazen Trumps and brazen Drums.	. . . . .	338	Wood's Brass	4
With brazen Trumps and brazen Drums.	. . . . .	338	Wood's Brass	4
The brazen Bells salute his Ears:	. . . . . .	338	Wood's Brass	6
In Vain he brings his brazen Shield.	. . . . .	340	Arch-Bish Dub	24
With furious Din of Brazen Drums,	. . . . . .	340	Arch-Bish Dub	26
So by the Brazen Trumpets Bluster,	. . . . . .	345	Prometheus	27
Whole Crouds about its Brazen Strings.	. . . . .	345	Prometheus	30
Now while this Brazen Chain prevail'd,	. . . . .	345	Prometheus	41
And change it for a Brazen String.	. . . . . .	346	Prometheus	66
This Brazen Chain into a Rope;	. . . .	347	Prometheus	72
Drives rattling o'er a brazen Arch:	. . . . . .	353	Wood Ironmongr	18
To rend the Skies with brazen Din;	. . . . . .	354	Simile Silver	10
Join'd with a brazen Politician,	. . . . . .	354	Simile Silver	20
I knew a brazen Minister of State,	. . . . . .	536	To Mr. Gay	143
Brazen hilted lately burnish'd,	. . . .	573	Helter Skelter	7
His brazen Face, and fiery Nose:	. . . . . .	627	Scandal Poem 2	140
You Clutter still your Brazen Kettle.	. . . . .	775	Mullinix Tim	46
Of Brazen Knight they vainly sung:	. . . . . .	876	To Dean Swift	14
BREACH				
So vile Thy Breach of Trust is;	. . . .	154	Widow and Cat	D 42
A Breach of Liberty, 'tis own'd,	. . . . . .	181	Horace 2, 1	27
And factious Rage, and Breach of Trust,	. . . . .	725	To Stella	46
BREAD				
He chip't his Bread, the Pieces round	. . . . .	156	Fable of Midas	3
Of paultry Provender and Bread:	. . . . . .	156	Fable of Midas	18
Upon the Water cast thy Bread	. . . .	255	Bubble	133
His Wife and Children wanted Bread,	. . . . .	352	Wood Ironmongr	7
But my Master each Day gives me Bread;	. . . . .	395	Dog and Thief	6
To cry the Bread was stale, and mutter	. . . . .	410	Dial Rich Marb	53
No Butter sticks upon his Bread.	. . . . . .	410	Dial Rich Marb	56
With muddy ale and mouldy bread	. . . . . .	420	Holyhead	2
Try'd ev'ry sharping Trick for Bread,	. . . . .	456	Dean Smedley	25
Despising Slaves that cringe for Bread.	. . . . .	483	Libel on D- D-	88
A Slice of Bread, and Mutton-Chop,	. . . . . .	728	Stella, Poems	30
I Own 'tis not my Bread and Butter,	. . . . . .	773	Mullinix Tim	1
Instead of wholesome Bread and Cheese,	. . . . .	895	Panegyr Dean	265
Come, Six-pence a Dozen to get me some Bread,	. . .	953	Herrings	8

```
BREADTH                                               PAGE    TITLE         LINE
     With a Scrap of Bank Paper the Breadth of his Nail;    288 Bank Down         38
BREAK
     And with blind Rage break all this peaceful Government;  25 Ode Athenian     300
     To break thy Rod like naughty Lad?        . . . . . .  135 Magician's Rod     80
     Is come up, vi & armis, to break the <Queen's> Peace.  .  142 New Song         4
     But if he will break in, and walk up Stairs,   . . . .  166 Toland's Invit    44
     Try Lads, can you this Bundle break;      . . . . . .  189 Faggot             2
     And strove by Turns to break the Faggot:      . . . . .  189 Faggot            6
     Ods buds, why don't you break her Limbs:      . . . . .  220 A Quiet Life     28
     Within, his wife would break his Bones,   . . . . . .  221 A Quiet Life      51
     The Steed, oppress'd, would break his Girth,   . . . .  231 Prog of Poetry    29
     They break up Counters, Doors, and Tills,   . . . . .  240 Run Bankers       39
     Who gets a Cold, who break their Shins.   . . . . . .  280 Journal           64
     . . . 'twould quickly break my Back.      . . . . . .  343 Upon His Grace    46
     My Master Pope will break his Heart.      . . . . . .  410 Dial Rich Marb    72
     Break not his rest, nor hurt his lungs:   . . . . . .  433 Answer Paulus     54
     And write you must, or break a Vein:      . . . . . .  501 Doctor Delaney    52
     For, Sons of Phoebus never break their Trust.  . . . .  532 To Mr. Gay        18
     To drive a second, lest the whole should break.  . . .  535 To Mr. Gay       134
     See, how the Dean begins to break:        . . . . . .  556 Death of Swift    80
     Would break the Patience of a Job,        . . . . . .  604 Beasts Confess    88
     Did I ever break my Trust?       . . . . . . . . . . .  631 Epistle Lady      66
     To break that Adamantine Chain.       . . . . . . . .  702 Cadenus Vaness   487
     When out my brutish passions break,       . . . . . .  754 Stella '23        11
     Be grave and wise, 'twou'd break their Heart.  . . . .  776 Mullinix Tim      90
     And resolv'd to break their Pates,        . . . . . .  833 Legion Club       95
     But still, whene'er you Silence break,    . . . . . .  889 Panegyr Dean      71
     That with me shall break no squares.      . . . . . .  908 Daphne            78
     For, I can break, but scorn to bend.      . . . . . .  921 Riddle 6          38
     May break a Limb of Master or Miss.       . . . . . .  941 Letter            22
     To break open riddles with shears or with scissars.  .  976 Dean to Sherid    22
     Which fiercest Foes, cou'd break by no Means.  . . . . 1021 Nim-Dan-Dean 1  D 32
     Nor will they dare to break the Joints,   . . . . . . 1021 Nim-Dan-Dean 1  D 39
BREAKFAST
     Hawls him, and scolds us down to Breakfast.    . . . .  279 Journal           16
     To spunge a Breakfast once a Week;        . . . . . .  409 Dial Rich Marb    52
     But, when her breakfast gives her courage,   . . . . .  761 Bec's B-Day       35
     At breakfast he'll ask    . . . . . . . . . . . . . .  855 Lady's Lament    137
BREAKING
     Breaking the Bankers and the Banks,       . . . . . .  239 Run Bankers        7
     Or at her Mouth was breaking Wind.        . . . . . .  592 Strephon Chloe   282
BREAKS
     When some rough hand breaks the assembling-glass.  . .   45 To Congreve       64
     This breaks a Girth, and that a Bone.     . . . . . .  398 Earl of P-b-w     21
     Fair weather when the morning breaks,     . . . . . .  618 Scandal Poem 1    30
     Fair Weather, when the Morning breaks;    . . . . . .  624 Scandal Poem 2    24
     Sindges Hair, but breaks no Pates.        . . . . . .  638 Epistle Lady     256
     Set off with num'rous Breaks--and Dashes--   . . . . .  643 On Poetry         94
     'Tis ten to one, he breaks your Neck.     . . . . . .  666 Epig Carthy 2   D  8
     -----I'm sorry Mopsa breaks so fast;      . . . . . .  699 Cadenus Vaness   386
     Breaks like the Sun behind a Cloud,       . . . . . .  726 To Stella         82
     In doleful Scenes, that breaks our heart, . . . . . .  777 Mullinix Tim     121
BREAST
     And like that too, make every breast their home)  . .    8 Ode to King       70
     But ne'er since seated in one single Breast.   . . . .   26 Ode to Temple      7
     And left the Choice to his own Breast.    . . . . . .  107 V's House         54
     All Europe's Bus'ness in his Breast)      . . . . . .  170 Horace 1, 7        4
     Virtue conceal'd within our Breast        . . . . . .  210 Earl of Oxford    16
     Within your Breast all Wisdom lyes,       . . . . . .  242 Horace 4, 9        1
     Thy Breast unshaken can oppose    . . . . . . . . . .  243 Horace 4, 9        7
     Of Windows in his Breast;         . . . . . . . . . .  339 Arch-Bish Dub      9
     His Breast again would cover;     . . . . . . . . . .  400 Window Inns 1      2
     She slipt Spadillo in her Breast,         . . . . . .  400 Window Inns 1      6
     Securely, in the Thunderer's Breast,      . . . . . .  447 Modern Lady       74
     Is thought too base for human Breast;     . . . . . .  458 Paddy's Charac    32
     His prickled Beard, and hairy Breast!     . . . . . .  553 Death of Swift     6
     Impartial judge within your Breast        . . . . . .  586 Strephon Chloe    92
     When on thy Breast and Sides Herculean,   . . . . . .  642 On Poetry         79
     Thro' ev'ry Breast wou'd dart a Flame;    . . . . . .  656 On Poetry        463
     Stuck to the Point that pierc'd her Breast;   . . . . .  693 Cadenus Vaness  231
     Ne'er held Possession of his Breast;      . . . . . .  703 Cadenus Vaness   521
     By Honour seated in her Breast,   . . . . . . . . . .  711 Cadenus Vaness   769
     By Pallas breath'd into his Breast,       . . . . . .  725 To Stella         59
     Which had been latent in her breast.      . . . . . .  731 Stella, Poems    122
     Chloe, when on thy Breast I lye,          . . . . . .  755 Stella '23        24
                                                             925 Riddle 8          17
BREASTS
     True Friendship in two breasts requires   . . . . . .  546 Life of Swift     43
     In different Breasts together burn,       . . . . . .  687 Cadenus Vaness    33
     For Breasts incapable of Flame;   . . . . . . . . . .  688 Cadenus Vaness    64
     To Female Breasts, except her own;        . . . . . .  695 Cadenus Vaness   273
BREATH
     And hopes to lengthen Life by a Transfusion of Breath,   21 Ode Athenian    183
     Stays but to catch his utmost breath,     . . . . . .   24 Ode Athenian     274
     Whene'er I mourn, stops my complaining Breath,   . . .   32 Ode to Temple    197
     The Son of God pronounc'd by the same breath   . . . .   38 Ode Sancroft     119
     And since my essence on my breath depends,   . . . . .   55 Temple Ill       153
     Whose Breath or Touch, where e'er he came,   . . . . .   85 Salamander        59
     Blew his last Breath to sink the lighter Scale.  . . .  235 Elegy on Demar    34
     Ye bubbles rais'd by breath of Kings;     . . . . . .  296 Satiric Elegy     26
```

BREATH	(CONTINUED)	PAGE	TITLE	LINE
May breath your Bellies full of Aether.	. . . . . .	361	Grace's Answer	24
Can scarsely speak for want of Breath,	. . . . . .	379	Apology Lady C	127
And vows she scarce can fetch her Breath.	. . . . . .	417	Woman's Mind	46
Accuses Chloe's tainted Breath;	. . . .	449	Modern Lady	157
When now the flood invades his strugling breath,	. . .	672	Epig Carthy 24	D 12
With Honour, which no Breath can Stain,	. . . .	693	Cadenus Vaness	208
Who fondly put his Trust in pop'lar Breath.	. . . .	771	Horace 1, 14	32
And while this Vital Breath I blow,	. . . . . .	776	Mullinix Tim	83
I did but lose my precious Breath,	. . . .	778	Mullinix Tim	172
To lengthen my breath	. . . .	852	Lady's Lament	43
Forbid in open Air to breath;	. . . .	894	Panegyr Dean	231
For I hate a silent Breath,	. . . .	933	Riddle 20	D 29
The Breath of her Lover,	. . . .	952	Onyons	14

BREATH'D

"If you, who long have breath'd the Fumes	. . . . . .	380	Apology Lady C	139
By Pallas breath'd into his Breast,	. . . . . .	731	Stella, Poems	122

BREATHES

"He hardly breathes. The Dean is dead.	. . . . . .	558	Death of Swift	150

BREATHING

'No woman breathing takes up less;	. . . .	447	Modern Lady	97
And sure no Christian Poet breathing	. . . . . .	461	Birthday Song	25
Each breathing on her thrice, inspir'd	. . . .	692	Cadenus Vaness	177

BRED   SEE COUNTRY-BRED, HOME-BRED

Bred in my scene, and for the poet's sins	. . . . .	46	To Congreve	97
At length, a spark not too well bred	. . . . .	63	Discovery	25
There is a Worm by Phoebus bred	. . . .	79	Vanbrug House	29
Heroick Actions early bred in,	. . . .	398	Earl of P-b-w	34
As some raw Youth in Country bred,	. . . . . .	500	Doctor Delaney	1
He was a wit both born and bred;	. . . . .	602	Beasts Confess	28
Bred a Foundling, and an Heiress;	. . . . . .	630	Epistle Lady	35
Bred up in Ignorance and Sloth,	. . . . . .	655	On Poetry	409
A perfect Goddess born and bred.	. . . . . .	655	On Poetry	426
Tom a Foot-Boy bred and born,	. . . .	784	Mullinix Dick	11
That was bred to kill a Cow well:	. . . . . .	800	Traulus 2	30
As clearly shows you bred at Court!	. . . . .	889	Panegyr Dean	84
Poor I, a Savage bred and born,	. . . . .	891	Panegyr Dean	131
A Virgin in thy Bosom bred;	. . . .	924	Riddle 8	6
Nor have I bred a spurious Race;	. . . . .	925	Riddle 8	23
. . . I wonder where you were bred?	. . . . .	985	Mary to Sher	2

BREECH

Just at the Breech it flashes first:	. . . . . .	66	Problem	46
That, rais'd by Magick of her Breech,	. . . . .	132	Magician's Rod	17
And not a Rod for thy own Breech.	. . . . . .	135	Magician's Rod	84
Bor'd a large Augre-hole in the Image's Breech;	. . .	336	Serious Poem	72
Thus when you feel an hard-bound <Breech>	. . . .	66	Problem	29

BREECHES

Those Men who wore the Breeches least	. . . . .	221	A Quiet Life	47
His Waistcoat and Stockings, and Breeches were white,	. .	399	Tom Clinch	5
His Breeches torn exposing wide	. . . .	594	Cassinus Peter	15
Unbutton and let down your Breeches,	. . . . . .	783	Tim and Fables	36
Or darns his hose, or mends his Breeches,	. . . .	878	Robbin & Harry	27
Thy Breeches torn behind, stand gaping wide;	. . .	881	Pastoral Dial	21
Or, else be sure, your Broad-cloath Breeches,	. . .	1021	Nim-Dan-Dean 1	D 17

BREED

No poys'nous Beast will in Her breed,	. . . . . .	7	Ode to King	52
"To breed contempt where thou hast hop'd esteem."--	.	55	Temple Ill	146
Do not more differ in their Breed,	. . . . .	217	To Mr. Delany	62
Till you began to change the Breed;	. . . . .	301	Horrid Plot	75
To praise your Empress, and her Breed.	. . . . .	465	Birthday Song	152
But, how can I describe the rav'nous Breed?	. . . .	534	To Mr. Gay	83
"No Fools of Rank, a mungril Breed,	. . . . .	570	Death of Swift	437
Might breed Confusion in the State,	. . . . .	723	To Stella	4
Not like the Pastors of thy rav'nous Breed,	. . .	792	St. Pat's Well	31
But all turn Leasers to that Mongril Breed,	. . .	794	St. Pat's Well	95
Traulus of amphibious Breed,	. . . .	799	Traulus 2	1
In Mother Church to breed a Variance,	. . . . .	820	Dr. Rundle	7
To mend your Breed, the Murderer of a King.	. . . .	826	Noisy Tom	10
That Death should get a num'rous Breed;	. . . .	903	Death Daphne	14
Lest it may more quarrels breed	. . . .	907	Daphne	53

BREEDING   SEE COURT-BREEDING

Of common Breeding, common Sense,	. . . . . .	27	Ode to Temple	43
Brings his good parts and breeding in debate;	. . .	48	To Congreve	156
Breeding, and Wit, and Air, and decent Pride;	. . .	118	Biddy Floyd	8
And much good Sense, as well as Breeding:	. . . .	377	Apology Lady C	72
The rules of raillery and breeding,	. . . . .	489	Dialogue	4
You never can defend his Breeding!	. . . . .	548	Life of Swift	102
With Breeding, Humor, Wit, and Sense,	. . . . .	735	Stel B-day '20	25
To piddle like a Lady breeding.	. . . . . .	745	Stel Distress	8
To piddle like a Lady breeding:	. . . . . .	750	Stel Wood-Park	32
For breeding is a useful Creature.	. . . . .	940	Letter	7

BREEDS

Our British soil is over-rank, and breeds	. . .	37	Ode Sancroft	101
Thus censure seems that fiery froth which breeds	. . .	45	To Congreve	69
At the warm zeal that breeds this golden calf?	. . .	46	To Congreve	108
Which breeds at once both Hate and Scorn.	. . . .	413	Censure	4
Envy breeds in ev'ry Maid.	. . . .	522	Betty Grizette	6
She swills like a sow, and she breeds like a rabbit:	. .	955	Portrait Life	6

BREEZE   SEE EVENING-BREEZE

If a small Breeze obstructs the Course,	. . . . .	688	Cadenus Vaness	53

	PAGE	TITLE	LINE

BRENT
You must apply to Mrs. Brent, ... 742 Stel B-day 22 50
Dingley and Brent . . . . 755 Dingley Brent 1
BRENTS
If not, a thousand Mrs. Brents, ... 743 Stel B-day 22 72
BRETH
There in her own (far an el breth) . . . . 60 Lady Tablebook 10
BRETHREN
And our good Brethren of the Surly Sect . . . . 18 Ode Athenian 81
Sid's Brethren of the conj'ring Tribe . . . . . 134 Magician's Rod 49
Which made his Brethren of the Gown . . . . 171 Horace 1, 7 29
Among his Brethren of the Quill: . . . . . . 231 Prog of Poetry 20
He's just the same, his brethren are . . . . . 435 Answer Paulus 108
Huzza their Brethren at the Blue-boys. . . . . 501 Doctor Delaney 62
Round all your Brethren cast your Eyes, ... 502 Doctor Delaney 83
Because he did his Brethren good. . . . . . . 514 Answer Fable 62
Our Brethren of <England> who love us so dear, 516 Dean Hang Rape 1
Like other Brethren of his Gown, ... 549 Life of Swift 141
His Brethren write as well as he? . . . . . . 554 Death of Swift 32
For which his Brethren call him Fool: . . . . 603 Beasts Confess 82
Among their Brethren of the Skies, ... 725 To Stella 53
Of Brethren he's a false Accuser, ... 798 Traulus 1 79
Doctrine, or Discipline our Brethren, ... 812 Bro Protestant 30
Since Lice are Brethren to a <Scot>: . . . . 813 Bro Protestant 42
To call a Swarm of Lice his Brethren? . . . . 813 Bro Protestant 48
How will his Brethren make Complaints? . . . 819 Dr. Rundle 4
His Brethren find to take Offence; . . . . . . 820 Dr. Rundle 12
You might swear they both are Brethren: . . . 835 Legion Club 148
Brethren of a wond'rous Kind, ... 931 Riddle 18 D 2
We are little Brethren twain, ... 934 Riddle 22 D 1
BREVITY
For brevity I have retrench'd, ... 281 Journal 67
BREW
To brew her Ale, and raise her Paste: . . . . 282 Journal 90
Nor is old Nanny Shales, whene'er she does brew, sick. 1029 Dr. Helsham 16
BREW'D
Brew'd for the good time of the Year . . . . . . 92 Bauc & Phil 1 68
BREWING
Some Mischief is Brewing, the Project smells Rank, . 287 Bank Down 4
"Saw Mischief by a Faction brewing, ... 567 Death of Swift 367
If the Machinations brewing, ... 636 Epistle Lady 189
BRIAREUS
In the Porch Briareus stands, ... 833 Legion Club 103
Briareus the Secretary, ... 833 Legion Club 105
BRIB'D
Was brib'd to make the Dean agree . . . . . 294 Prog Marriage 130
(Venus was Brib'd to let it pass.) . . . . . 345 Prometheus 40
Because he brib'd you with a Brace of Tench? . . 534 To Mr. Gay 92
Damn'd Senators brib'd, Damn'd prostitute Slaves; . 576 Place Damn'd 8
Perjur'd Rebel, brib'd Accuser; . . . . 831 Legion Club 70
BRIBE
Him we persuaded with a mod'rate bribe, ... 307 Billet Players 5
They at a Pinch can bribe a Vote: . . . . . . 483 Libel on D- D- 96
Nor bribe, insult, nor flatter, nor betray. . . . 533 To Mr. Gay 56
You cannot bribe, betray, or plot. . . . . . . 641 On Poetry 48
Contrive to bribe the Judge's Vote. . . . . . 647 On Poetry 212
Lest you should take them for a Bribe, ... 730 Stella, Poems 84
Could Art or Time or Nature bribe . . . . . 736 Stel B-day '20 52
The Jews engag'd him with a paultry Bribe, . . . 806 Judas 3
Shews a Bribe in all his Hands; . . . . . . 833 Legion Club 104
You lost a Place, and sav'd a Bribe? . . . . . 884 Rev Market-Hill 36
BRIBER
of Juries & senates the bully & briber . . . . . 540 Charac Walpole 12
BRIBERY
Your Offers of Bribery cease; . . . . 396 Dog and Thief 14
BRIBES
By Pensions, Bribes, and three per Cent? . . . . 157 Fable of Midas 46
Commissions, Perquisites, and Bribes, ... 158 Fable of Midas 78
Leave hunting after Bribes, forget your Tropes: . . 162 Toland's Invit 6
Nor bribes my Lady's fav'rite Maid. . . . . . 605 Beasts Confess 136
And bribes with mundungus.) . . . . 856 Lady's Lament 164
The Lawyer's Fees, the Statesman's Bribes. . . . 922 Riddle 7 20
BRICKDUST
And Brickdust Moll had Scream'd through half the 124 Descriptn Morn 14
Street.
BRICKS
Bids us make Bricks, yet sends us to look out for Straw; 32 Ode to Temple 188
Why then, old Plays deserve old Bricks, . . . 108 V's House 72
Th' experienc't Bricks that knew their Trade, . . 108 V's House 76
(As being Bricks at Second Hand,) . . . . . 108 V's House 77
And Joe my Apron full of Bricks. . . . . . . 128 Little House 64
Thy Verse like Bricks, defy the Weather, . . . 1021 Nim-Dan-Dean 1 D 19
BRIDE
O'er the glad scene whence first she rose a bride: . 51 Temple Ill 12
Next morn betimes the Bride was missing, . . . 223 Prog of Love 26
And thought his Bride had sculk't for shame, . . 223 Prog of Love 30
Behold the Bridegroom and his Bride, ... 585 Strephon Chloe 57
The Bride was put in Form to Bed; . . . . . 587 Strephon Chloe 112
The Bride must either void or burst. . . . . . 589 Strephon Chloe 166
(Inspir'd with Courage from his Bride,) . . . . 589 Strephon Chloe 189
On House of Ease your future Bride, ... 591 Strephon Chloe 238

		PAGE	TITLE	LINE

BRIDEGROOM

No news of Phil. The Bridegroom came,	. . . . . .	223	Prog of Love	29
The Bridegroom dresst, to make a Figure,	. . . . .	290	Prog Marriage	21
With Bridegroom liquids hand in hand,	. . . . . .	467	Birthday Song	230
Behold the Bridegroom and his Bride,	. . . . . .	585	Strephon Chloe	57
Her Bridegroom in the Wedding-Sheets.	. . . . . .	588	Strephon Chloe	132

BRIDEGROOM'S

The Bridegroom's first Gift to their Mates,	. . . .	942	Probatur Alit	4

BRIDEWELL

Of Bridewell and the Compter dreams,	. . . . . .	582	Young Nymph	41
The Spawn of Bridewell, or the Stews;	. . . . . .	641	On Poetry	36

BRIDGE   SEE HOLBORN-BRIDGE

Or like a Bridge that joins a Marish	. . . . . .	645	On Poetry	173
To praise the Cheeks, Chin, Nose, the Bridge and all,		993	On Picture	26

BRIDLE

Which hath she most need of, a Spur or a Bridle?	. .	580	Psyche	4
For, the Right holds the Sword, and the Left holds the Bridle,)		870	Grand Question	108
A temper the Devil himself could not bridle,	. . . .	955	Portrait Life	3

BRIDLES

And with Bridles fine and gay,	. . . .	573	Helter Skelter	13
Bridles borrow'd for a Day,	. . . .	573	Helter Skelter	14
Bridles destin'd far to roam,	. . . .	573	Helter Skelter	15

BRIEF

Half sunk beneath his brief and bag,	. . . . . .	434	Answer Paulus	75
The Brief with weighty Crimes was charg'd,	. . . .	686	Cadenus Vaness	5
Directed them to mind their Brief;	. . . .	713	Cadenus Vaness	847

BRIEFS

For Cowley's Briefs, and Pleas of Waller,	. . . .	690	Cadenus Vaness	114

BRIERS

Thro' bogs and thro' briers,	. . . .	053	Lady's Lament	46
Pull down the fine briers,	. . . .	857	Lady's Lament	197

BRIGHT

When the Bright Sun of Peace began to shine,	. . .	16	Ode Athenian	24
Altho' we boast our Winter-Sun looks bright,	. . . .	25	Ode Athenian	280
Bright effluence of th' immortal ray,	. . . . .	34	Ode Sancroft	2
Since the bright essence fled, where haunts the reverend ghost?		36	Ode Sancroft	44
The Muse, like some bright country virgin, shows,	. .	50	To Congreve	215
And if so black the cloud, that heaven's bright queen	.	53	Temple Ill	57
Of that Bright God whom Bards invoke,	. . . . . .	120	Apollo Outwit	14
To wait at Bright Ardelia's Side.	. . . .	120	Apollo Outwit	40
Glasses and Linnen clean, and Pewter bright,	. . . .	165	Toland's Invit	28
Her love on some bright youth below,	. . . . . .	178	To Lord Harley	60
Thus the bright Empress of the Morn	. . . . . .	178	To Lord Harley	65
Thus Ca'ndish, as Aurora bright,	. . . .	179	To Lord Harley	77
That her Eyes were as bright as our self at Noon-Day;	.	264	Apollo	41
But in Stella's bright Eyes were plac'd right again;	.	264	Apollo	50
Your former Comrades, once so bright,	. . . . . .	311	To Ford	23
With Hermes, Son of Pleias bright.	. . . .	326	Pethox	86
As White as Snow, as bright as Day;	. . . . . .	362	Grace's Answer.	32
By Vulcan form'd so round and bright:	. . . . . .	433	Answer Paulus	28
Old Phoebus is but half as bright,	. . . .	462	Birthday Song	65
Poor Cynthia never shone so bright,	. . . . . .	465	Birthday Song	175
So bright a batter'd, strolling Toast;	. . . . .	581	Young Nymph	4
As Chloe's Skin, almost as bright.	. . . .	589	Strephon Chloe	174
Bright Goddesses, in Number five;	. . . .	656	On Poetry	439
Bright Apollo lend thy Choir.	. . . .	661	Love Song	16
To study bright Vanessa's Looks;	. . . .	694	Cadenus Vaness	235
So bright a Nymph to come unsought,	. . . . . .	710	Cadenus Vaness	752
Bright Phillis mending ragged Smocks,	. . . . . .	729	Stella, Poems	47
Adieu bright Wit, and radiant Eyes;	. . . . . .	757	Stel B-day '24	27
But, Cloacina Goddess bright,	. . . .	897	Panegyr Dean	343
My Genius piercing, sharp and bright,	. . . . . .	920	Riddle 6	5
I am bright as an Angel, and light as a Feather,	. .	928	Riddle 13	D 3
When on my Bosom thy bright Eyes,	. . . .	932	Riddle 19	D 1

BRIGHT-BEAMING

His Soul bright-beaming from his Eye,	. . . . . .	385	Manly Virtue	60

BRIGHTEN'D

By you were brighten'd and refin'd,	. . . . . .	326	Pethox	74

BRIGHTER

As Years increase, she brighter shines,	. . . . .	703	Cadenus Vaness	536
Truth shines the brighter, clad in Verse;	. . . .	729	Stella, Poems	58
In you, each Virtue brighter shines,	. . . . . .	739	Stel B-day '21	9
Dick was thought the brighter Wit,	. . . .	785	Mullinex Dick	35

BRIGHTEST

Be not the brightest pattern Earth can shew	. . .	36	Ode Sancroft	52
To be, as 'twas below, the brightest plant above;	. .	41	Ode Sancroft	229
Two brightest, brittlest earthly Things	. . . . .	227	Prog of Beauty	63
The brightest Virgin of the Green,	. . . .	721	Stel B-Day '18	6
Shew me the brightest Irish Toast,	. . . . . .	993	On Picture	22

BRIGHTNESS

The very Brightness of His Face	. . . .	9	Ode to King	94

BRILLIANT

Dear Smed I read thy Brilliant Lines,	. . . . .	361	Grace's Answer	1

BRIM

Then fill the Vessel to the Brim,	. . . . . .	251	Bubble	10
With mournful Note clocks round the Brim.	. . . .	295	Horrid Plot	150

BRIMSTONE

Both Pitch and Brimstone to fill up his Flaws;	. . .	285	Elegy Boat	28

	PAGE	TITLE	LINE

BRINE
Your Beef will on Thursday be salter than brine . . . — 1018 Swift Ans Sher 24

BRING
And too warm summers bring: . . . . — 37 Ode Sancroft 100
Unworthy the glad tidings which I bring, ... — 52 Temple Ill 35
By all means to bring down the Rates, ... — 64 Discovery 42
However, I was resolv'd to bring the Discourse slily about, — 71 Mrs Harris Pet 36
We'll bring on us no more Debts, ... — 169 Peace Dunkirk 28
May bring in Jeopardy thy Bacon, ... — 181 Horace 2, 1 30
Come trimming Harcourt; bring your Mace; . . . . — 190 Faggot 39
And bring her back, alive or dead. . . . . . — 223 Prog of Love 38
Bring Straw for our Bed, ... — 246 Irish-Feast 49
And yet we all know much Gold it will bring, ... — 334 Serious Poem 14
Then chuse which you please, and let each bring a Faggot, — 352 Wood Insect 39
'Tis true, a Glass will bring supplies . . . . . — 367 Answer Delaney 45
To bring in Ballyspellin. . . . . — 441 Ballyspellin 24
For which they bring a modern Pattern, ... — 460 Birthday Song 10
For when you bring your Song in print, ... — 463 Birthday Song 85
Bring all the Females of the Skyes; . . . . . . — 465 Birthday Song 154
For old acquaintance bring him in. . . . . . . — 468 Birthday Song 254
Lords keep a Pimp to bring a Wench; . . . . . — 480 Libel on D- D- 22
Or bring his Vermin in, but Scraps? . . . . . — 484 Libel on D- D- 130
You see him first the Peacock bring, ... — 513 Answer Fable 15
And orders the Landlord to bring him a Whore; . . . — 517 Dean Hang Rape 20
Will sure the Pretendr and Popery bring in. . . . . — 522 St. Cecilia's 8
The People with a Sigh their Taxes bring; . . . . — 533 To Mr. Gay 51
Bring from his Heart sincerer Groans, ... — 546 Life of Swift 29
"Prevail to bring him in convict. . . . . . . — 570 Death of Swift 430
Which could he to the Standard bring, ... — 602 Beasts Confess 33
Will never fail to bring in Pence; . . . . . . — 646 On Poetry 188
And bring in doubt their Pow'r divine; . . . . . — 687 Cadenus Vaness 12
Who bring the Lime, or place the Stones; . . . . — 727 Stella, Poems 3
Before I could my Verses bring, ... — 730 Stella, Poems 69
Bring all your Quilca cares to Dublin, ... — 753 Gift for Bec 24
To bring in (I could Cut his Throat) . . . . . . — 773 Mullinix Tim 14
But cou'd you bring me once to think, ... — 778 Mullinix Tim 165
By <God> I'll bring you off as clean. . . . . . — 797 Traulus 1 60
Though by the Female Side you proudly bring, . . . — 826 Noisy Tom 9
For he never fails to bring 'em; . . . . . . — 836 Legion Club 164
Bring our Dame a New-Year's Gift: . . . . . . — 862 To Janus 4
"Go, bring me my Smock, and leave off your Prate, . . — 870 Grand Question 83
A Purchase which will bring him clear, ... — 875 Drapier's Hill 3
Bring all past Actions to thy Mind. . . . . . — 921 Riddle 7 4
Who down direct our Lineage bring . . . . . . — 925 Riddle 8 29
To you the sad Account I bring, ... — 932 Riddle 19 D 23
Drums and Trumpets bring me out; . . . . . . — 933 Riddle 20 D 20
Nay, bring me here the tallest Man, ... — 934 Riddle 21 D 17
Or bring a tender Child and pliant, ... — 934 Riddle 21 D 19
But, however, if he be come, bring him down, . . . — 1023 Nim-Dan-Dean 2 D 8
Bring down Long Shanks Jim too, but now I think on't, . . . — 1023 Nim-Dan-Dean 2 D 11
However, bring down yourself, and you bring down all; . . . — 1023 Nim-Dan-Dean 2 D 13
However, bring down yourself, and you bring down all; . . . — 1023 Nim-Dan-Dean 2 D 13
I had forgot to desire you to bring down what I say you have,. . . — 1023 Nim-Dan-Dean 2 D 15

BRING'ST
Who, to pollute my shades, bring'st with thee down . . — 44 To Congreve 9

BRINGS
And now a Laurel wreath she brings from far, . . . — 16 Ode Athenian 18
And brings the dear Reward of Victory and Peace. . . — 16 Ode Athenian 21
Brings his good parts and breeding in debate; . . . — 48 To Congreve 156
Which brings a <Stink> from ev'ry Pore, ... — 65 Problem 9
Must fayl if Matter brings no Grist. . . . . . — 228 Prog of Beauty 84
Still brings us Hares when he can catch them: . . . — 281 Journal 74
Perhaps from what the Packet brings, ... — 282 Journal 109
Then if cutting down Wood brings Money good Store, . . — 334 Serious Poem 15
In Vain he brings his Brazen Shield. . . . . . — 340 Arch-Bish Dub 24
And so the Harp of Ireland brings, ... — 345 Prometheus 29
A packet though it brings in me. . . . . . . — 420 Holyhead 14
If fair, it brings you safe to Port, ... — 493 Panegyr Swift 19
A Nymph, that brings ten thousand Pound: . . . . — 545 Life of Swift 16
The smiling Cyprian Goddess brings . . . . . . — 585 Strephon Chloe 49
And brings a Vessel into Bed: . . . . — 589 Strephon Chloe 172
If Decency brings no Supplies, ... — 591 Strephon Chloe 225
Brings in Reason and Invention. . . . . . . — 637 Epistle Lady 216
First, this large parcel brings you tidings . . . . — 753 Gift for Bec 5
(Whom he brings in among us . . . . — 856 Lady's Lament 163

BRINK
And having fill'd it to the Brink, ... — 92 Bauc & Phil 1 71
Fill'd a large Jug up to the Brink; . . . . . . — 112 Bauc & Phil 2 30
So have I seen from Severn's Brink . . . . . . — 253 Bubble 53
So a poor wretch upon the brink of death, ... — 672 Epig Carthy 24 D 11
If Nayads swept them from the Brink) . . . . . — 894 Panegyr Dean 244

BRINKS
Or, near Fleet-Ditch's oozy Brinks, ... — 583 Young Nymph 47

BRISK
So highly courted by the brisk and gay? . . . . . — 54 Temple Ill 106
Brisk Susan whips her Linen from the Rope, ... — 137 City Shower 17
To expose the brisk Baboon? . . . . — 634 Epistle Lady 154
No other Monkey half so brisk; . . . . — 788 Dick's Variety 26

		PAGE	TITLE	LINE
BRISK (CONTINUED)				
Or should he pretend to be brisk and alert,		868	Grand Question	35
BRISKLY				
Briskly travel on their Journies,		573	Helter Skelter	2
BRISTLES				
Or on her Chin like Bristles grow.		527	Lady's Dres Rm	58
BRISTOW				
Windsor and Bristow then shall be		147	Windsor Proph	5
BRITAIN				
Ah, Britain, land of angels! which of all thy sins,		37	Ode Sancroft	92
On Britain Europes safety lyes		140	Harlyes Surgn	1
Poor Britain shall have Peace at last;		168	Peace Dunkirk	2
Hail Queen of Britain, Queen of Rhymes,		467	Birthday Song	221
Say Britain, cou'd you ever boast, --		640	On Poetry	5
Your Portion, taking Britain round,		642	On Poetry	53
Fair Britain in thy Monarch blest,		655	On Poetry	411
An Heir for Britain to secure		655	On Poetry	435
When haughty Britain was a Land unknown.		790	St. Pat's Well	10
Britain, by thee we fell, ungrateful Isle!		791	St. Pat's Well	25
Britain, with Shame confess, this Land of mine		791	St. Pat's Well	27
BRITAIN'S				
For ev'ry Wit in Britain's Isle		109	V's House	117
And Britain's lost if Harly dyes		140	Harlyes Surgn	2
"Both bitter Foes to Britain's Weal.		549	Life of Swift	153
Avoid the Rocks on Britain's angry Shore:		772	Horace 1, 14	62
BRITANNIA				
Britannia stript from her sole Guard the Laws,		12	Ode to William D	21
Britannia long will wear like steel		468	Birthday Song	243
BRITANNIA'S				
She saved Britannia's Right, and lost her own.		771	Horace 1, 14	46
BRITISH				
Our British soil is over-rank, and breeds		37	Ode Sancroft	101
Which, o'er a British Senate's Lids,		133	Magician's Rod	40
Of British Midas dirty Paws;		158	Fable of Midas	70
Resolv'd to save the British Nation,		300	Horrid Plot	49
That thy Descent is from the British Oak,		771	Horace 1, 14	38
Her Sons descended from the British Line;		771	Horace 1, 14	42
I sent the Magpye from the British Soil,		792	St. Pat's Well	45
Lives such a Bard on British plains?		876	To Dean Swift	6
No; not in all the British Court;		876	To Dean Swift	7
And, for our home-bred British Chear,		895	Panegyr Dean	267
Supporting half the British Crown;		919	Riddle 5	6
BRITONS				
The Britons, once a savage Kind,		326	Pethox	73
BRITTAIN				
Ran under Ground from Greece to Brittain,		293	Prog Marriage	112
T'is the Cur dog of Brittain & spaniel of Spain.		540	Charac Walpole	14
BRITTISH				
The Giddy Brittish Populace,		8	Ode to King	72
Rapt in the Vortex of the Brittish Star;		10	Ode to King	139
BRITTLEST				
Two brightest, brittlest earthly Things		227	Prog of Beauty	63
BROACH SEE A-BROACH				
Here from a barrel you may broach		753	Gift for Bec	19
BROAD				
Sweeps the broad scythe, and tramples on his face.		55	Temple Ill	122
Till entring on a broad High-way,		412	Desire Possess	23
Broad Innuendos, such as this,		463	Birthday Song	83
BROAD-CLOATH				
Or, else be sure, your Broad-cloath Breeches,		1021	Nim-Dan-Dean 1 D	17
BROCADE				
We dresst her in a gold Brocade,		619	Scandal Poem 1	77
We dress'd her in a Gold Brocade,		626	Scandal Poem 2	75
In her tarnish'd brocade?		855	Lady's Lament	122
From gold brocade and shining armour,		879	Robbin & Harry	41
BROCADES				
Hold up the prices of their Old Brocades.		275	Epilogue	16
But Chints, Brocades, and Lace take all away,		275	Epilogue	33
And Tradesmen, to compare Brocades.		291	Prog Marriage	54
In French brocades and Flanders Lace;		291	Prog Marriage	64
Array'd in Lace, Brocades and Tissues.		525	Lady's Dres Rm	4
From Fans, and Flounces, and Brocades,		688	Cadenus Vaness	45
They on the Gold Brocades and Satins rav'd,		771	Horace 1, 14	51
BROCADO'S				
Brocado's, and Damasks, and Tabbies, and Gawses,		236	Excellent Song	1
BROD'RICK				
Got the Great Seal, and turn out Brod'rick.		348	Whitshed Motto	18
BROGUE				
Teague made a good Pun by a Brogue in his Speech,		334	Serious Poem	27
BROGUES				
A pair of Brogues to bear thee dry to Mass!		882	Pastoral Dial	50
BROIL				
And forget to broil and riot,		574	Helter Skelter	52
BROKE				
Broke on his everlasting Shield.		8	Ode to King	71
It fell, and broke with its own Weight		26	Ode to Temple	4
There thy enchantment broke, and from this hour		55	Temple Ill	151
So from my Lord his Passion broke,		66	Problem	47
But, when th' enchanted Rod was broke,		134	Magician's Rod	57
Then, took and broke them one by one.		189	Faggot	10
So quickly broke if you divide.		189	Faggot	12

106

```
BROKE          (CONTINUED)                              PAGE   TITLE          LINE
    The Praetor broke the Consul's Head;       . . . . .    190 Faggot            32
    She stun'd, and then she broke his Pate.   . . . . .    221 A Quiet Life      44
    Guess how could such a Match be broke.     . . . . .    223 Prog of Love      24
    John wish't, that he had broke a Leg       . . . .      224 Prog of Love      83
    How oft she broke her marriage Vows        . . . . .    225 Prog of Love      89
    Conceive the whole Enchantment broke,      . . . . .    240 Run Bankers       33
    My Pipe it was broke,                      . . . . .    245 Irish-Feast       18
    An hundred Heads broke,                    . . . . . .  246 Irish-Feast       71
    This Grand Event half broke our Measures,  . . . . .    283 Journal          119
    Like Pris'ners when their Gall is broke.   . . . . .    313 To Ford           56
    The Omen is broke, the Danger is over;     . . . . .    351 Wood Insect       27
    Than if he heard you broke your Bones.     . . . . .    546 Life of Swift     30
    It happen'd when a Plague broke out,       . . . . . .  601 Beasts Confess     5
    Wretch that I was, I broke my Fast:        . . . . .    602 Beasts Confess    16
    I broke his Teeth, but where's the mighty harm?  . .    670 Epig Carthy 20  D  2
    And Pallas, if she broke the Laws,         . . . . .    695 Cadenus Vaness   264
    Hardly at length he Silence broke,         . . . . .    707 Cadenus Vaness   656
    When the strong Cords of Union once are Broke.  . .     770 Horace 1, 14      22
    'Twill not avail, when thy strong Sides are broke,  .   771 Horace 1, 14      37
    Knockt down the Boy, the Lanthorn broke;   . . . . .    781 Mullinix Tim     268
    "A Scholard, when just from his College broke loose,   872 Grand Question    157
    They part not till the Ring is broke.      . . . .      926 Riddle 9          16
    Stools, Tables, Chairs, and Bed-steds broke: . . . .  1035 To Quilca          4
BROKEN
    Upon a rubbish Heap of broken Laws         . . . . . .    9 Ode to King      102
    From broken scraps and filings of your brain.  . . .     45 To Congreve       58
    Whether in time, deduction's broken chain  . . . .       51 Temple Ill         3
    To a forlorn and broken Rake,              . . . . .    133 Magician's Rod    33
    For since old Sid has broken this,         . . . . .    135 Magician's Rod    85
    Take the three strongest of his broken Planks,  . . .   285 Elegy Boat        32
    Her Favors to some broken Ensign           . . . . .    295 Prog Marriage    160
    Or patch his broken Stocking Soals,        . . . . .    728 Stella, Poems     33
    And half the Chairs with broken backs.     . . . . .    746 Stel Distress     38
    And half the Chairs with broken Backs:     . . . . .    751 Stel Wood-Park    56
    Shall leave deciding broken Pates,         . . . . .    760 Receipt Youth     47
    To patch his broken fortunes, found        . . . . .    879 Robbin & Harry    31
    My broken Hose to patch and dern.          . . . . . .  890 Panegyr Dean     112
BROKER
    Some South Sea Broker from the City,       . . . . .    410 Dial Rich Marb    67
BROOD
    The Scots themselves, that Discontented Brood,  . . .     8 Ode to King       82
    For well she knew her num'rus Brood,       . . . . . .  208 Fable Bitches     21
    Degenerate from their ancient Brood,       . . . . .    652 On Poetry        365
    A nauseous Brood, that fills your Senate Walls,  . .    792 St. Pat's Well    57
    Just Heaven! to see the Dunghill dastard Brood  . .     826 Noisy Tom         17
    And fled in Haste with all her Brood       . . . . .    849 Old Thorn         39
BROODS
    Whence Broods of insect Poets rise.        . . . . . .   80 Vanbrug House     54
BROOK
    A Stealing Brook, and strove to creep away  . . . .      22 Ode Athenian     192
    There leaning near a gentle Brook,         . . . . .    202 Horace 2, 6      109
    One Night a Fool into a Brook              . . . . . .  255 Bubble           125
BROOM
    On their Crosiers to ride, like a Witch on a Broom.  .  804 Irish Bishops     22
BROOMS
    The Peaceful State of common Brooms.       . . . . .    132 Magician's Rod    20
BROOMSTICK
    Rides on a Broomstick for a Nag,           . . . . . .  132 Magician's Rod    16
BROOMY
    The Youth with Broomy Stumps began to trace  . . . .   124 Descriptn Morn     9
BROTH
    And Broth enough to fill her Paps,         . . . . . .  208 Fable Bitches     20
    A Birth-right for a mess of broth.         . . . . . .  879 Robbin & Harry    36
BROTHER
    To see the House of Brother <Van>:         . . . . . .  108 V's House         96
    Two Brother Hermits, Saints by Trade,      . . . . .    111 Bauc & Phil 2      7
    Tho' he's a younger Brother.               . . . . .    123 Empty'ng Town     24
    And Moynalta, his Brother,                 . . . . .    247 Irish-Feast       78
    Their Brother Quill-Men Workers for the Stage,  . .     276 Epilogue          41
    And to the God of Wealth his Brother       . . . . .    346 Prometheus        51
    With like Remorse his Brother of the Trade,  . . . .    364 On Dreams         17
    So, when an Eye hath lost it's Brother,    . . . . .    366 Answer Delaney    21
    And on the Brother Limb re-acts.           . . . . .    366 Answer Delaney    26
    Possession, and Desire, his Brother,       . . . . .    412 Desire Possess     9
    And, gather'd all his Brother strow'd;     . . . . .    412 Desire Possess    36
    And only with her Brother linkt            . . . .      465 Birthday Song    177
    With neither Spouse nor Brother near her,  . . . . .    466 Birthday Song    180
    And ev'ry virtuous Man his Brother:        . . . . .    606 Beasts Confess   180
    And all their Brother Dunces lash,         . . . . .    652 On Poetry        355
    Phoebus forbids thee one, his Brother      . . . . .    671 Epig Carthy 22  D  5
    Thy Brother (far thy Betters) wore a Gown.  . . . .     678 Dean and Duke     14
    Put all your Brother Puppets out,          . . . . .    777 Mullinix Tim     140
    See, Brother, how we Apples swim.          . . . . .    811 Bro Protestant    14
    Not for the World--we Doctors, Brother,    . . . . .    812 Bro Protestant    17
    Subscribes, Dear Sir, your Brother loving.  . . . .     812 Bro Protestant    20
    Calls Singleton his Brother Serjeant.      . . . . .    812 Bro Protestant    28
    Are Brother Protestants and Christians,    . . . .      812 Bro Protestant    31
    Employments for their Brother Vermin.      . . . . .    813 Bro Protestant    44
    Are his Brother Protestants, good men and true;  . .    815 Yahoo's           22
    When a Brother Thief is hanging.           . . . . . .  830 Legion Club       16
```

BROTHER   (CONTINUED)   PAGE   TITLE   LINE

    Son and Brother to a Queer,   837 Legion Club   175
    Every young Divine thy Brother.   838 Legion Club   200
    To welcome Brother Serving-men;   890 Panegyr Dean   100
    Yet among us all no Brother   931 Riddle 18   D   3
    Ev'ry Brother else reposes.   931 Riddle 18   D 18
BROTHER-GOD
    Or any Brother-God in Heav'n: 695 Cadenus Vaness   261
BROTHER-HERMITS
    Two Brother-Hermits, Saints by Trade   90 Bauc & Phil 1   7
BROTHER'S
    Becomes his Brother's lawful Heir: 366 Answer Delaney   14
BROTHERS
    Tho' the Court gives my Nephews, and Brothers, and   144 New Song   47
      Cousins,
    His Brothers fleece him when he's drunk.   607 Beasts Confess   196
BROTHR
    He tells his brothr fools at night   421 Ireld   24
BROUGHT
    You saw how near we were to Ruin brought,   12 Ode to William   D 17
    Yet how shall they be brought to know   21 Ode Athenian   167
    With Rules from musty Morals brought,   27 Ode to Temple   19
    Which in due time brought forth a House: 81 Vanbrug House   75
    From her Closet brought out a full Purse in her Clutche   143 New Song   16
    Now my new Benefactors have brought me about, 144 New Song   45
    The Nymph had soon been brought to yield: 177 To Lord Harley   14
    No sooner brought within the Walls,   209 Fable Bitches   45
    His Flesh brought down to Flying-Case: 231 Prog of Poetry   40
    Are by Robert Ballentine lately brought over; 236 Excellent Song   2
    In Pails was brought up,   244 Irish-Feast   10
    Now Water's brought, and Dinner done,   279 Journal   35
    The genial Virtue with him brought,   293 Prog Marriage   113
    Next Day another Message brought;   377 Apology Lady C   75
    Her Night-gown and her Slippers brought her,   446 Modern Lady   46
    Three Graces by Lucina brought her,   465 Birthday Song   165
    Of Wit's fair Goddess brought to Bed,   504 Doctor Delaney   116
    For why, they had both been brought up to the Trade   517 Dean Hang Rape   27
    "Nor Topicks brought to please the Crown,   570 Death of Swift   428
    "Biennial Squires, to Market brought;   571 Death of Swift   445
    Dame Juno brought a Priest demure.   586 Strephon Chloe   64
    Nor Boy brought up to cleaning Shoes,   641 On Poetry   35
    Since Cibber brought in an Attainder;   642 On Poetry   56
    And Horace brought ye tunefull Choir   658 On Poetry   D 410
    From Premisses erroneous brought,   695 Cadenus Vaness   280
    Shew'd Patterns just from India brought,   698 Cadenus Vaness   378
    Brought weighty Arguments to prove   708 Cadenus Vaness   676
    In vain; for see, your Friend hath brought   731 Stella, Poems   101
    Yet, since from Reason may be brought   764 Stel B-day '26   9
    From India's burning Clime I'm brought,   911 Aenigma   1
    From Colchos brought the Golden Fleece: 948 Jason Hassard   2
BROW
    Transplanted to the Hero's Brow)   6 Ode to King   10
    And seem'd to knit his Brow;   74 Game Traffick   6
    Stuck in an Irish Cabbin's Brow,   457 Paddy's Charac   2
    His Visage drops, he knits his Brow,   480 Libel on D- D-   15
    Put on the Critick's Brow, and sit   647 On Poetry   235
    Why, Stella, should you knit your Brow,   759 Receipt Youth   21
BROWN
    And thus the brown Meanders come   227 Prog of Beauty   43
    Why in this Brown dost thou appear?   786 Clad in Brown   2
    Would then be not so brown as thou.   786 Clad in Brown   6
    The Glass will seem as brown as those.   786 Clad in Brown   12
    Now brown and burnish'd like a nut,   937 Riddle 24   D 29
    And charming when squeez'd in a Pot of brown Ale.   953 Oranges   2
BROWS   SEE BEETLE-BROWS,EYE-BROWS
    That cloud the Brows   442 Ballyspellin   70
    So, Bays on Poets Brows have bin   457 Paddy's Charac   5
    To pluck her Brows in Arches round,   527 Lady's Dres Rm   56
    Gilding my Aurelia's Brows,   661 Love Song   22
    She shakes her Helm, she knits her Brows,   694 Cadenus Vaness   252
BRUGES
    James Bruges & the Dean had long been friends,   678 Dean and Duke   1
BRUIS'D
    Or swallow'd alive, or skilfully bruis'd.   351 Wood Insect   12
    To swallow Will. Wood either bruis'd or alive. 351 Wood Insect   14
BRUISE
    The hardest Bum will bruise with sitting squat.   881 Pastoral Dial   20
    My Footman came home from the Church, of a Bruise sick,   1029 Dr. Helsham   17
BRUNSWICK
    But George, and Brunswick are too rough.   467 Birthday Song   214
BRUSH
    By help of Pencil, Paint and Brush   227 Prog of Beauty   46
    Three times a Week to brush my Gown.   411 Dial Rich Marb   100
    No Brush could force a way betwixt.   526 Lady's Dres Rm   22
BRUSH'D
    His Beaver brush'd, his Shoes, and Gown,   376 Apology Lady C   27
BRUSHT
    The Entry brusht against her Hoop: 751 Stel Wood-Park   50
BRUTAL
    Thro' all the brutal Species ran,   659 On Poetry   D 410

		PAGE	TITLE	LINE
BRUTE				
So men have got from Bird and Brute		83	Salamander	7
You sawcy Brute,		440	Ballyspellin	2
The Characters of ev'ry Brute:		512	Answer Fable	4
Endow'd with Gifts from every Brute		659	On Poetry	D 410
Or some worse Brute in human Shape,		687	Cadenus Vaness	40
Alone distinguish'd Man from Brute:		697	Cadenus Vaness	345
Tho' I continue still a brute.		755	Stella '23	32
Foulest Brute that stinks below,		786	Clad in Brown	1
Towzer's the less offensive Brute.		797	Traulus 1	44
Brainsick Brute, they call a Peer.		837	Legion Club	176
Which when the Brute puts awkward on,		885	Rev Market-Hill	79
BRUTES				
The King of Brutes (to make it plain,		601	Beasts Confess	7
That he's the Nightingal of Brutes.		602	Beasts Confess	36
Brutes find out where their Talents lie:		640	On Poetry	13
Assume the Shapes of filthy Brutes.		670	Epig Carthy 19	D 2
When she saw three hundred Brutes,		833	Legion Club	113
The Joy of Man, the Pride of Brutes,		919	Riddle 5	1
Of Vegetables, Brutes, and Men.		924	Riddle 7	94
BRUTISH				
Permit a brutish Man to touch her?		588	Strephon Chloe	153
When out my brutish passions break,		754	Stella '23	11
BRUTUS				
But how would Brutus in my Place?		724	To Stella	40
BRY'R				
"And wound her Legs with ev'ry Bry'r.		850	Old Thorn	64
No more that Bry'r thy tender Leg shall rake:		881	Pastoral Dial	17
BUBBL'D				
Nor shall the bubbl'd virtuoso find		50	To Congreve	211
BUBBLE				
South-Sea at best a mighty Bubble.		259	Bubble	220
And you like a Booby, the Bubble can swallow;		265	Apollo	87
"Besides, to me this seems a Bubble,		321	First of April	23
Why will you make yourself a Bubble		593	Strephon Chloe	305
BUBBLED				
And we the bubbled Fools		27	Ode to Temple	26
Then all this while have I been bubbled;		300	Horrid Plot	57
Are bubbled thus by Prigs;		426	Five Ladies	35
BUBBLES				
Ye bubbles rais'd by breath of Kings;		296	Satiric Elegy	26
BUBBLING				
From purling Streams & Fountains bubbling		744	Stel Distress	3
From purling Streams and Fountains bubbling,		750	Stel Wood-Park	27
BUBO'S				
Can Clouds give Bubo's, Ulcers, Blotches,		624	Scandal Poem 2	19
BUBOES				
Can Clouds give buboes, ulcers, blotches?		618	Scandal Poem 1	25
BUCKET				
Think of a Bucket or a Pump.		83	Salamander	20
BUCKET-PLAY				
The Bucket-play 'twixt Whigs and Tories,		181	Horace 2, 1	17
BUCKETS				
Were now but leathern Buckets rang'd.		93	Bauc & Phil 1	116
Were now but Leathern Buckets rang'd.		114	Bauc & Phil 2	92
BUCKLES SEE HARNESS-BUCKLES				
BUCKLEY'S				
And with the help of Buckley's Pen		180	Horace 2, 1	3
BUCKS				
Leave John of Bucks, come here and laugh.		188	Scriblerus 6	4
BUDDING				
And re'ly Yours is budding too--		116	Bauc & Phil 2	160
BUDGET				
His Budget with Corruptions cramm'd,		486	Libel on D- D-	187
Complains his Budget was too small.		486	Libel on D- D-	192
BUDS				
Ods buds, why don't you break her Limbs:		220	A Quiet Life	28
BUFF				
Thy Soul, which through thy Hide of Buff,		787	Clad in Brown	17
BUFFOONS				
For all Buffoons have most in View		217	To Mr. Delany	77
BUGS				
Are swarms of Bugs and Hanoverians.		313	To Ford	50
BUILD				
Heroick Strains could build a Tower;		79	Vanbrug House	8
And if they all had Power to build,		79	Vanbrug House	19
With License to build Castles there;		79	Vanbrug House	26
In each Capacity to Build:		80	Vanbrug House	62
For Leave to build the Poet's Way.		81	Vanbrug House	70
They from it's Ruins build their own.		81	Vanbrug House	92
Raking up Mud to build a Wall;		87	Hist V's House	18
And so resolv'd a House to build;		87	Hist V's House	22
Heroick Strains could build a Tow'r;		106	V's House	8
And should they Build as fast as Write,		106	V's House	19
With Licence to build Castles there:		106	V's House	26
In both Capacities, to Build.		107	V's House	36
To build in Speculation still.		107	V's House	42
To build by Verse as heretofore,		107	V's House	44
Build Babel with their Tongues confounded.		108	V's House	66
They from its Ruins build their own.		110	V's House	134
Venture to build his Nest so low.		127	Little House	28

		PAGE	TITLE	LINE
BUILD	**(CONTINUED)**			
While some build Castles in the Air,		257	Bubble	165
Directors build 'em in the Seas;		257	Bubble	166
And build a Castle in the Air.		361	Grace's Answer	20
To raise the Stairs, or build the Cieling;		409	Dial Rich Marb	26
Before you Build and You Bestow,		479	Epist on Epist	116
"To build a House for Fools and Mad:		572	Death of Swift	480
To build on some Foundation sound;		592	Strephon Chloe	296
To build on Sand with Hay and Stubble?		593	Strephon Chloe	306
Since he no more can build, and plant, & revell,		678	Dean and Duke	9
In the State to build a Babel:		800	Traulus 2	46
We build a magazine.		843	Epigr Irish	4
To build a House five Hundred more.		875	Drapier's Hill	8
Must build a Castle at Drumlack:		883	Rev Market-Hill	14
I Will not build on yonder mount:		899	Dean's Reasons	1
BUILDER				
To praise the Pile, and Builder <Van>.		109	V's House	108
A Prudent Builder should forecast		592	Strephon Chloe	293
BUILDERS				
By antient Right are Builders too.		81	Vanbrug House	68
BUILDING				
Sole Patron of the building Trade,		79	Vanbrug House	24
For Building fam'd, and justly reckond		87	Hist V's House	37
The Art of battring Walls, than building,		88	Hist V's House	46
Sole Patron of the Building Trade,		106	V's House	24
Your Building shall be small enough.		108	V's House	74
The Building, as the Poet Writ,		108	V's House	79
Were spent in Building each a Room;		108	V's House	90
This Building was designed a Model,		127	Little House	36
But Building, Planning, and Devotion;		514	Answer Fable	56
Provided a Fund for building you Spittles:		805	Irish Bishops	59
Spy a Building large and lofty,		829	Legion Club	2
The Grandeur or the Art of Building.		893	Panegyr Dean	200
A long-ear'd Beast, and Building Knight;		942	Probatur Alit	17
BUILDING'S				
Could I from the Building's Top		830	Legion Club	21
BUILDINGS				
For farther Buildings, farther Planting.		477	Epist on Epist	64
BUILT				
He built up such a monstrous Pile,		87	Hist V's House	28
And first the Prologue built a Wall		108	V's House	81
My Father built Lusk,		246	Irish-Feast	74
My House was built but for a Show,		409	Dial Rich Marb	23
Plain Loyalty not built on Hope,		410	Dial Rich Marb	81
Then Built, then took up with your Arbour,		477	Epist on Epist	69
Nor, in a Palace built with Charge immense,		533	To Mr. Gay	63
Were built to thee, with Off'rings crown'd:		894	Panegyr Dean	238
BULK				
But neither Bulk nor Shape the same:		81	Vanbrug House	80
But neither Bulk, nor Shape the same:		109	V's House	122
It rises both in Bulk and Height,		251	Bubble	13
You'll ow Your Ruin to your Bulk;		258	Bubble	197
Too pond'rous is thy Bulk to mount the Sky;		539	Mr. Pulteney	41
Not Beggar's Brat, on Bulk begot;		641	On Poetry	33
In Bulk there are not more Degrees,		653	On Poetry	383
Various is my bulk and hue,		936	Riddle 24	D 27
BULKY	**SEE OVER-BULKY**			
That be my thought when some large bulky writ		44	To Congreve	35
BULL				
To thee the Bull will lend his Hide,		100	Elegy Patrige	75
BULLETS	**SEE LONG-BULLETS**			
The Bullets whistling round his Ears,		500	Doctor Delaney	4
Fly Bullets now as thick as Hops,		500	Doctor Delaney	9
I'll chew you to Bullets, and puff you at Baldwin.		1019	To Sheridan	10
BULLEY				
Or how the Bulley at a stroke		781	Mullinix Tim	267
BULLION				
The bullion stampt in your refining mind		45	To Congreve	53
BULLOCKS				
Fat Bullocks and Swine.		244	Irish-Feast	8
BULLY				
(Those Bully Greeks, who, as the Moderns do,		139	City Shower	49
"A Rake, a Bully, Pimp, or Spy.		303	Storm	30
Joan cudgell's Ned, yet Ned's a Bully		328	Epigram 3	1
of Juries & senates the bully & briber		540	Charac Walpole	12
Or, by a faithless Bully drawn,		582	Young Nymph	43
BUM				
A Bum so white		441	Ballyspellin	40
From Bayliffs claws thou scarce cou'd keep thy Bum free.		678	Dean and Duke	12
And first his Bum you see him Clap,		776	Mullinix Tim	109
The hardest Bum will bruise with sitting squat.		861	Pastoral Dial	20
Her bum upon a bed of nettles.		901	Dean's Reasons	94
BUMKINS				
And then we cry, to spur the bumkins on,		308	Billet Players	39
BUMM				
I'll hold you a Groat, when you wimble his Bumm,		336	Serious Poem	79
BUMP				
Friend Rundall fell with grievous bump,		822	Epigr Rundle	1
BUMS				
Strip their Bums; let Caleb hoyse 'em;		635	Epistle Lady	178
Then let us rise, and rest our weary Bums.		882	Pastoral Dial	52

	PAGE	TITLE	LINE
BUNDLE			
Should bundle Thistles up with Roses.	96	On the Union	10
Try Lads, can you this Bundle break;	189	Faggot	2
To make the Bundle strong and safe, ...	191	Faggot	45
Here in this bundle Janus sends	753	Gift for Bec	15
BUNGLER			
A Bungler thus, who scarce the Nail can hit, ...	535	To Mr. Gay	131
BUNGLING			
What bungling, rusty tools, are us'd by fate!	47	To Congreve	131
Some bungling Partner takes, ...	75	Game Traffick	10
BUNYAN			
And thence, as fam'd John Bunyan sung, ...	983	Sher, A Goose	6
BURDEN			
And is not this a grievous burden?	434	Answer Paulus	86
BURGUNDY			
I'll treat you with Burgundy. .·	426	Fíve Ladies	44
BURIAL			
The Burial Article decrease;	903	Death Daphne	8
BURLESQUE			
That same paultry Burlesque Stile:	631	Epistle Lady	50
BURN			
Warning the Cook-maid not to burn	94	Bauc & Phil 1	145
Warning the Cook-maid, not to burn	113	Bauc & Phil 2	83
It would Burn a whole Forest; nor was it a Fiction; .	334	Serious Poem	20
To burn an old Fryer, one Forrest by Name.	334	Serious Poem	22
Howe'er let us try him and see how he'll burn. . . .	336	Serious Poem	64
Tho' cold would burn, tho' dry would melt.	585	Strephon Chloe	28
Miss Moll the Jade will burn it blue:	588	Strephon Chloe	128
These Elegies and Sonnets burn, ...	595	Cassinus Peter	74
Like fire-works, she can burn in water.	618	Scandal Poem 1	38
Like Fire-works, she can burn in Water.	624	Scandal Poem 2	36
In different Breasts together burn, ...	687	Cadenus Vaness	33
But none will burn her for a Witch.	698	Cadenus Vaness	363
Which gently warms, but cannot burn;	711	Cadenus Vaness	784
Makes Wit inflame, or Anger burn; . . . ·. . . .	731	Stella, Poems	118
Whene'er they burn, if burn they must, ·.	732	Stella, Poems	143
Whene'er they burn, if burn they must, ...	732	Stella, Poems	143
The Bishop with his Foot may burn it;	892	Panegyr Dean	173
Nor warm the fair for whom I burn;	937	Riddle 24	D 52
BURN'D			
Thus Lamps, which burn'd in Tombs with silent Glare, .	667	Epig Carthy 5	D 5
BURND			
The Nymph who still with Passion burnd, ...	293	Prog Marriage	117
BURNET			
While Burnet in his deathless page	490	Dialogue	27
<BURNET'S>			
Which thou (such <Burnet's> shrewd Advice is) . . .	180	Horace 2, 1	5
Since <Burnet's> Death, the <Bishop's> Bench, . . .	303	Storm	17
BURNING			
Whether the Lights were burning blue.	112	Bauc & Phil 2	40
To have two thousand Pounds a Year, O 'tis a burning Shame!	342	Upon His Grace	18
A burning Shame, a crying Sin	659	On Poetry	D 410
From India's burning Clime I'm brought, ...	911	Aenigma	1
BURNISH			
Burnish and make a gaudy show, ...	84	Salamander	41
They burnish paper, or they bite a rogue:	672	Epig Carthy 25	D 2
BURNISH'D			
Brazen hilted lately burnish'd, ...	573	Helter Skelter	7
When, by you refin'd and burnish'd, ...	631	Epistle Lady	46
Now brown and burnish'd like a nut, ...	937	Riddle 24	D 29
BURNISHES			
Burnishes an old Year's Face.	863	To Janus	28
BURNS			
My Heart with Emulation burns	887	Panegyr Dean	29
But, alas, the poor Dean neither Shudders nor burns, .	1037	Four Storyes	5
BURNT			
Thy Mother burnt, art Born again;	109	V's House	120
So, the next Parson stub'd and burnt it.	117	Bauc & Phil 2	178
He burnt his candle to the snuff;	296	Satiric Elegy	14
It burnt to Ashes in a Trice.	470	Burning Poem	14
BURST			
As parent earth, burst by imprison'd winds, ...	52	Temple Ill	37
Before the Flame from Muzzle burst, ...	66	Problem	45
Laughing as if he'd burst his Sides:	108	V's House	70
Till Fame and Eccho almost burst, ...	121	Apollo Outwit	59
Did not burst with their stamping.	245	Irish-Feast	40
I thought my very Spleen would burst	313	To Ford	51
In Venom, till they burst their Lungs, ...	414	Censure	20
Rude Laughter seeming like to burst;	448	Modern Lady	128
Burst into her Chamber, and wou'd have Carest her, .	517	Dean Hang Rape	9
But, this with Envy makes me burst.	555	Death of Swift	70
Jove, arm'd with Terrors, burst the Skies, ...	578	Day Judgement	5
The Bride must either void or burst.	589	Strephon Chloe	166
To burst with Envy, Spite, and Rage, ...	611	By Dr. Swift	11
If she like us would burst asunder!	617	Scandal Poem 1	16
And, whisp'ring wisht, the Devil burst her	618	Scandal Poem 1	18
She ne'er was known to burst a lace.	618	Scandal Poem 1	20
I shou'd burst, and bursting drop.	638	Epistle Lady	262
Your Cable's burst, and you must quickly feel . . .	770	Horace 1, 14	19
Till, God knows why, at last it burst.	796	Traulus 1	18

			PAGE	TITLE	LINE
BURST	(CONTINUED)				
Those Splitters of Parsons in sunder shou'd burst?	. .		805	Irish Bishops	40
He lost his Bishoprick, and hang'd, or burst.	. . . .		806	Judas	8
And burst asunder e'er he went to Hell;	. . . . .		806	Judas	18
Drop from the Tree with all his Bowels burst;	. . .		806	Judas	22
The Parsons, for Envy, are ready to burst:	. . . .		871	Grand Question	134
You think your giddy Head will burst:	. . . . . .		893	Panegyr Dean	194
Her Belly burst, and slow her Pace:	. . . . . .		895	Panegyr Dean	276
We lye cramming ourselves, and are ready to burst,	. .		967	Letter Sherid	3
BURSTING					
Bursting into Pieces there:	. . . .		638	Epistle Lady	252
I shou'd burst, and bursting drop.	. . . .		638	Epistle Lady	262
BURTHEN					
My Life is now a Burthen grown	. . . . . .		204	In Sickness	21
And curse his wicked Burthen more	. . . . . .		497	Panegyr Swift	140
Some Beast of Burthen or of Prey	. . . . . .		659	On Poetry	D 410
To all my Friends a Burthen grown,	. . . . . .		673	His Deafness	2
BURTHENS					
What heavy burthens lawyers lay	. . . .		434	Answer Paulus	62
What burthens lawyers undergo	. . . .		434	Answer Paulus	70
BURY					
Bury those Carrots under a Hill.	. . . .		148	Windsor Proph	26
Bestow to bury him one Iron Chest.	. . . . . .		233	Elegy on Demar	6
You bury, on our Side the Channell	. . . . . .		315	To Ford	101
'To bury me is not so just	. . . .		663	Epigram Bust	1
BURY'D					
Now bury'd in the Depth below,	. . . .		256	Bubble	149
Here bury'd in one common Grave;	. . . . . .		923	Riddle 7	54
Twice were they bury'd, twice were born,	. . . . .		923	Riddle 7	75
BUS'NESS					
Let no pretence of Bus'ness make you stay,	. . . . .		166	Toland's Invit	39
All Europe's Bus'ness in his Breast)	. . . . .		170	Horace 1, 7	4
Her weighty Morning Bus'ness o'er	. . . . . .		291	Prog Marriage	55
Now to a word of bus'ness in our own.	. . . . .		309	Billet Players	54
That all this Bus'ness was a Joke.	. . . . . .		322	First of April	54
The Man of Bus'ness must retire.	. . . . . .		325	Pethox	48
The Bus'ness of the Nation stands.	. . . . . .		325	Pethox	52
Your bus'ness must be to provide	. . . . . .		460	Birthday Song	7
He cannot talk of Bus'ness now:	. . . . . .		480	Libel on D- D-	16
To Bus'ness snap'd the Poet's Quil,	. . . . .		482	Libel on D- D-	66
On weighty Bus'ness, to some neighb'ring Friend:	. . .		534	To Mr. Gay	86
Poor Ladies! though their Bus'ness be to play,	. . .		662	Upon Ladies	1
But, Death had Bus'ness to dispatch	. . . . .		904	Death Daphne	51
BUSH SEE THORN-BUSH,ALE-HOUSE-BUSH					
Now Enter Bush with new State-Airs,	. . . .		62	Discovery	9
Imagine now My <Lord> and Bush	. . . . . .		63	Discovery	21
My Ld, sd Bush, a Friend and I	. . . . . .		63	Discovery	33
Bush smiling round on all, retreats	. . . . . .		64	Discovery	44
Their Mattins chant in ev'ry Bush	. . . . . .		594	Cassinus Peter	32
Shall creep no more behind a Bush;	. . . . . .		893	Panegyr Dean	214
BUSINESS					
Pugh! said I, but that's not the Business that I ail.			70	Mrs Harris Pet	29
And Guest his Business e're he Spoke.	. . . . .		120	Apollo Outwit	16
"Your Business is to mind your Spinning.	. . . .		304	Storm	44
He says, his Business is to know	. . . . . .		446	Modern Lady	57
This Business of Importance o'er,	. . . . . .		447	Modern Lady	90
The World's mad Business now is o'er,	. . . . .		579	Day Judgement	19
Or, to compound the Business, whether	. . . . .		712	Cadenus Vaness	824
"She left all Business to her Son:	. . . . .		714	Cadenus Vaness	881
Domestic business never mind	. . . .		761	Bec's B-Day	33
Your hairy Business is a Muff.	. . . .		912	Aenigma Expl	D 4
BUST					
It is but prating to a bust.	. . . .		901	Dean's Reasons	68
BUSTLED					
She bustled and strugled, and made her Escape,	. . .		517	Dean Hang Rape	11
BUSTLING					
And all her bustling but supplies	. . . .		761	Bec's B-Day	27
BUSY					
And busy both with Hand and Eye	. . . .		86	Hist V's House	5
While others wrack their busy Brains,	. . . . .		361	Grace's Answer	17
The busy Head with mimick Art runs o'er	. . . .		363	On Dreams	9
So loitring, so active; so busy, so idle,	. . . . .		580	Psyche	3
Have my busy Muse employ'd,	. . . .		630	Epistle Lady	5
'Tis hard they must be busy Night and Day:	. . . .		662	Upon Ladies	2
Thy busy, drudging scene of life,	. . . . . .		676	Parson's Case	6
Thy busy never-meaning Face;	. . . .		775	Mullinix Tim	59
Of busy Mortals endless Toils:	. . . .		921	Riddle 7	14
Impertinent mixture of busy and idle.	. . . . . .		955	Portrait Life	4
BUT 1123				OMITTED WORD	
BUTCHER					
The Butcher, feels the Lamb beneath his blade.	. . .		364	On Dreams	18
Ev'n Lambs by Instinct fly the Butcher.	. . . . .		588	Strephon Chloe	154
Like a Butcher doom'd for Life,	. . . .		800	Traulus 2	39
BUTCHER'S					
Hence he learnt the Butcher's Guile,	. . . . . .		800	Traulus 2	37
BUTCHERS					
Sweepings from Butchers Stalls, Dung, Guts, and Blood			139	City Shower	61
Were they Masons, were they Butchers?	. . . . .		800	Traulus 2	26
Meet when Butchers bait a Bear;	. . . .		829	Legion Club	14
BUTLER					
The Butler with my Lady's Maid;	. . . .		150	Corinna	19

```
BUTLER      (CONTINUED)                              PAGE   TITLE           LINE
    I mean your Butler, Dawson, Car,        . . . . . . . .   217 To Mr. Delany       59
    Now, John the Butler must be sent       . . . . . . . .   223 Prog of Love       33
    <Dean>, Butler, Usher, Jester, Tutor;        . . . . .   888 Panegyr Dean       39
    Captain Butler made some in the Church black and blue   1029 Dr. Helsham         7
        sick;
BUTLER'S
    In Quality of Butler's Mate;        . . . . . . . . .     889 Panegyr Dean       88
BUTTER
    Complaints against the Royal Butter.    . . . . . .       410 Dial Rich Marb     54
    No Butter sticks upon his Bread.        . . . . . . .     410 Dial Rich Marb     56
    Are soft and sweet as butter.       . . . . . . . .       429 Beau's Reply       12
    I Own 'tis not my Bread and Butter,     . . . . . .       773 Mullinix Tim        1
    Such charming Butter never Man made.    . . . . . .       892 Panegyr Dean      168
    Thy Milk shall make us Tubs of Butter.  . . . . . .       892 Panegyr Dean      172
    Providing Butter for the Cook.      . . . . . . . .       892 Panegyr Dean      178
    The Butter from the Whey to part:   . . . . . . . .       892 Panegyr Dean      182
    The Butter comes; our Fears are ceas't;     . . . .       892 Panegyr Dean      185
    Come eat 'em with pure fresh Butter and Mustard,  . .     953 Herrings            6
BUTTER-WEIGHT
    I'll give my <Monarch> Butter-weight.   . . . . . .       657 On Poetry         488
BUTTERFLY
    Before it grew a city butterfly;        . . . . . . .      46 To Congreve        90
BUTTON
    His Cane upon a Button.     . . . . . . . . . . .         785 Mullinex Dick      32
BUXOM
    By buxom Lasses--Some repented      . . . . . . .        182 Horace 2, 1        52
BUY
    To purchase Kingdoms, and to buy Renown,    . . . .        11 Ode to William  D  1
    Instead of boldly sailing far to buy    . . . . . .       19 Ode Athenian       97
    And here's to buy a Pot of Ale.     . . . . . . . .      128 Little House       54
    Pretend to cheapen Goods, but nothing buy.  . . . .      138 City Shower        34
    Nor can afford to buy gold Lace.        . . . . . .      216 To Mr. Delany      43
    We'll buy English Silks for our Wives and our           237 Excellent Song    REF
        Daughters,
    Then we'll buy English Silks for our Wives and our      237 Excellent Song    REF
        Daughters,
    They would buy English Silks for their Wives. . .   . .  237 Excellent Song    REF
    Then we'll buy English Silks for our Wives and our      238 Excellent Song    REF
        Daughters,
    A Satyr, and the Gentry buy!        . . . . . . . .      502 Doctor Delaney     76
    And buy distinction at the dearest rate.    . . . .      506 To a Friend        12
    "Your Honour please to buy a Set?       . . . . . .      564 Death of Swift    280
    Her Judgment, how to buy a Mask.        . . . . . .      700 Cadenus Vaness    421
    Come buy my fine Wares,     . . . . . . . . . .          951 Apples              1
    My Masters come buy,    . . . . . . . . . . . .          952 Oysters             2
    Buy my Herring  . . . . . . . . . . . . . . .            953 Herrings            3
    Come, buy my fine Oranges, Sauce for your Veal,  . .     953 Oranges             1
    . . .and send your Man Alexander to buy Corks, . .  . . 1013 Swift to Sheri      6
BUYERS
    Both buyers and sellers, . . . . . . . . . . .           403 Window Inns 9   D  5
BUYING
    So because I had been buying things for my Lady last      69 Mrs Harris Pet      3
        Night,
BUZZ
    To buzz about the mighty Flame;     . . . . . . . .        9 Ode to King       116
    Still swarm and buzz about his Nose?    . . . . . .      798 Traulus 1          87
BUZZING
    We join like Flyes, and Wasps, in buzzing about Wit.  .   18 Ode Athenian       75
    While Betty's buzzing at her Ear,   . . . . . . .        291 Prog Marriage      41
    Teaz'd by a Buzzing Wasp, Below,    . . . . . . .        458 Paddy's Charac     30
BY    SEE STANDERS-BY,STANDER-BY                            OMITTED WORD
      879
BY-ROADS
    Through slipp'ry By-roads dark and deep,    . . . . .    412 Desire Possess     19
BY-STANDER
    Then I'll appeal to each By-stander,    . . . . . .       85 Salamander         69
    Her head is but a mere by-stander:      . . . . . . .    761 Bec's B-Day        26
BY'T
    And still the Truth he will Maintain, whate'er he loses  341 Upon His Grace      6
        by't.
    The Pedant gets a Mistress by't.        . . . . . . .    710 Cadenus Vaness    743
BYZANTIANS
    Byzantians boast, that on the Clod  . . . . . . .        324 Pethox             39
C
    Nor knew in law his A, B, C.    . . . . . . . .          436 Answer Paulus     122
CA'NDISH
    This character shall Ca'ndish claim,    . . . . . .      177 To Lord Harley     37
    Thus Ca'ndish, as Aurora bright,    . . . . . . .        179 To Lord Harley     77
CABBIN
    "Go, Sisters Nine, into that Cabbin;    . . . . . .      320 First of April      3
    And calls the Senate-House a Cabbin;    . . . . . .      514 Answer Fable       70
    Who held a Cabbin for ten Groats a Year;    . . . .      826 Noisy Tom          12
    A rotten Cabbin, dropping Rain;     . . . . . . .       1035 To Quilca           2
CABBIN'S
    Stuck in an Irish Cabbin's Brow,    . . . . . . .        457 Paddy's Charac      2
CABIN
    Repairs a cabin gone to ruin,   . . . . . . . . .        878 Robbin & Harry     21
CABINET
    A Cabinet to vulgar Eyes;   . . . . . . . . . .          528 Lady's Dres Rm     78
CABLE'S
    Your Cable's burst, and you must quickly feel   . . . .  770 Horace 1, 14       19
```

	PAGE	TITLE	LINE
CACKLE			
I'm sure you cackle like the sex.	983	Sher, A Goose	18
CACKLES			
Nor loudly cackles at the Door;	230	Prog of Poetry	7
CACKLING			
For Cackling shews the Goose is poor.	230	Prog of Poetry	8
CADENCE			
The Smallcoal-Man was heard with Cadence deep, . . .	124	Descriptn Morn	11
CADENUS			
Cadenus warded off the Blows:	701	Cadenus Vaness	479
Cadenus is a Subject fit, ...	702	Cadenus Vaness	502
Cadenus many things had writ;	702	Cadenus Vaness	510
Cadenus now no more appears	703	Cadenus Vaness	528
Cadenus with each Day declines, ...	703	Cadenus Vaness	537
Cadenus, common Forms apart, ...	703	Cadenus Vaness	540
Cadenus was amaz'd to find	704	Cadenus Vaness	562
Cadenus felt within him rise	706	Cadenus Vaness	624
Suppose Cadenus flourish'd then, ...	708	Cadenus Vaness	694
Cadenus answers every End, ...	709	Cadenus Vaness	704
Cadenus, who cou'd ne'er suspect	709	Cadenus Vaness	726
Cadenus, to his Grief and Shame, ...	710	Cadenus Vaness	744
So when Cadenus could not hide, ...	710	Cadenus Vaness	762
Forbid Cadenus to engage.	711	Cadenus Vaness	779
While thus Cadenus entertains	711	Cadenus Vaness	790
CADENUS'			
But this was for Cadenus' sake;	701	Cadenus Vaness	462
CADETS			
Poor we Cadets of Heav'n, not worth her Care, . . .	32	Ode to Temple	183
CAELIA			
Cry'd, Caelia! thrice, and sigh'd the rest.	595	Cassinus Peter	40
Yet, ask I must. Is Caelia dead?	595	Cassinus Peter	42
But, Caelia has contriv'd to blast	595	Cassinus Peter	53
"Here Cassy lies, by Caelia slain, ...	596	Cassinus Peter	77
Oh! Caelia, Caelia Caelia <shits>.	597	Cassinus Peter	118
Oh! Caelia, Caelia Caelia <shits>.	597	Cassinus Peter	118
Oh! Caelia, Caelia Caelia <shits>.	597	Cassinus Peter	118
CAELIA'S			
From Magazeen in Caelia's Eye.	272	Apollo's Edict D	59
And Caelia's horrid Fact relate;	596	Cassinus Peter	93
Discover Caelia's foul Disgrace.	597	Cassinus Peter	112
Thy Nose outshining Caelia's Eyes.	994	On Picture	33
CAESAR			
Call'd Pompey, Scipio and Caesar;	82	Salamander	2
CAESAR'S			
Unless I put in Caesar's Learning too, ...	28	Ode to Temple	67
In Caesar's court, or in Jerusalem;	39	Ode Sancroft	167
CAESARS			
As any of the Caesars are.	100	Elegy Patrige	72
CAGE			
Our Nightingal might fit a Cage, ...	515	Answer Fable	83
Behold a cage with sparrows fill'd, ...	753	Gift for Bec	11
CAINS			
What Billet-doux, and clouded Cains!	585	Strephon Chloe	38
CAITIFF			
How will the Caitiff Wretch be scar'd	241	Run Bankers	53
"Then bloody Caitiff think on me.	851	Old Thorn	88
CAKE			
Like a fly blown Cake of Tallow, ...	523	Betty Grizette	7
A maggot in a cake of fat, ...	950	Upstart D	5
CALAMITY			
As in a general Calamity.	811	Bro Protestant	10
CALE			
In state affairs, or planting cale;	901	Dean's Reasons	76
CALEB			
Strip their Bums; let Caleb hoyse 'em;	635	Epistle Lady	178
CALEDONIANS			
From thee, with Pride, the Caledonians trace . . .	790	St. Pat's Well	11
CALENTURE			
So, by a Calenture misled, ...	251	Bubble	25
CALF			
At the warm zeal that breeds this golden calf?	46	To Congreve	108
To see a wild calf	857	Lady's Lament	188
CALL			
Part of Your Merit Chance wou'd call her own, . . .	11	Ode to William D	11
Nor e'er call back again)	25	Ode Athenian	290
But what does our proud Ign'rance Learning call, . . .	27	Ode to Temple	28
Which we call deep Design and Politicks	29	Ode to Temple	93
What we call holy, and great, and just, and good, . . .	38	Ode Sancroft	124
Then call this verse, that speaks her largest aid, . . .	44	To Congreve	27
Call Titan sick, because their sight is so;	45	To Congreve	74
Call my Lord <Cutts> a Salamander.	83	Salamander	22
Lest he should call our Commonweal, ...	96	On the Union	15
Then call in Mercury for Aid, ...	99	Elegy Patrige	61
Methinks, I still wou'd call it mine:	115	Bauc & Phil 2	114
Obey my Call, and only mine.	120	Apollo Outwit	32
Thalia heard the Call and Flew	120	Apollo Outwit	39
Stays till 'tis fair, yet seems to call a Coach. . . .	138	City Shower	36
To Pan alone rich Misers call, ...	157	Fable of Midas	57
And talk what Fools call Treason all the Night. . .	163	Toland's Invit	16
Then order Squash to call a Hackney Chair. . . .	166	Toland's Invit	46
For in that Universall Call	241	Run Bankers	57

CALL	(CONTINUED)		PAGE	TITLE	LINE
To call nothing his, but the Rhyme and the Measure.	.		266	Apollo	102
Nor need you on the Graces call,	. . . .		272	Apollo's Edict	D 74
"And not a Muse will hear their Call:	. . . . . .		321	First of April	22
Some call him a Thorn, the Curse of a Nation,	. . .		334	Serious Poem	29
The first is an Insect they call a Wood-Louse,	. . .		350	Wood Insect	3
The Third is an Insect we call a Wood-Worm,	. . .		351	Wood Insect	17
Beware of Subjects you call Trite,	. . . .		371	Letter D. S-y	2
For, those we dext'rous Courtiers call,	. . . . .		409	Dial Rich Marb	33
Which modern Ladies call polite;	. . . .		448	Modern Lady	113
Her Chair to call the King of Clubs,	. . . . .		452	Modern Lady	259
Some call their Monarchs Sons of Saturn,	. . . . .		460	Birthday Song	9
Next call him Neptune with his Trident,	. . . . .		463	Birthday Song	97
His Learning none will call in doubt;	. . . . . .		484	Libel on D- D-	140
Though flatt'ring Knaves may call it bitter.	. . .		485	Libel on D- D-	178
And call the laws of wisdom fate,	. . . . . .		490	Dialogue	42
Refuse our Patron's Call to dine;	. . . . .		495	Panegyr Swift	68
Or call 'em Rogues, or get 'em kickt:	. . . . .		505	Doctor Delaney	154
He cannot call his Friends to Mind;	. . . . .		556	Death of Swift	87
"(I wish I knew what King to call.)	. . . . . .		562	Death of Swift	232
"Who call it Humour when they jibe:	. . . . .		571	Death of Swift	466
They learn to call a Spade, a Spade.	. . . . .		590	Strephon Chloe	204
Some call it witty to reflect	. . . . . .		592	Strephon Chloe	273
For which his Brethren call him Fool:	. . . . .		603	Beasts Confess	82
To call him Hypocrite and Quack.	. . . . .		605	Beasts Confess	128
Can you call me rude, or haughty?	. . . . .		631	Epistle Lady	70
Call it Tasting, and Imbibing:	. . . . .		633	Epistle Lady	116
I row by, and call them Names.	. . . . .		635	Epistle Lady	166
Call Dunces, Fools, and Sons of Whores,	. . . .		652	On Poetry	345
'Tis just what Coxcombs call, a Bite.	. . . . .		708	Cadenus Vaness	673
His Virtues she might call her own;	. . . . .		708	Cadenus Vaness	681
Love, why do we one Passion call?	. . . . .		711	Cadenus Vaness	772
And by such various Titles call,	. . . . . .		724	To Stella	17
What Stoicks call without our Power,	. . . .		729	Stella, Poems	63
Will call again and recommend	. . . . . .		734	Stel B-day '20	5
They'll call it all poetick Licence:	. . . . .		741	Stel B-day 22	28
The Muse will at your Call appear,	. . . .		743	Stel B-day 22	79
From Ford attending at her Call	. . . .		745	Stel Distress	19
From Ford attending at her Call,	. . . .		750	Stel Wood-Park	39
Call the Old Housekeeper, and get her	. . .		756	Stel B-day '24	9
A Nation thus, who oft Heav'ns Call neglects,	. .		771	Horace 1, 14	35
So at this Booth, which we call Dublin,	. . . .		777	Mullinix Tim	137
They call me Beast, and what Care I?	. . . .		778	Mullinix Tim	162
I bravely call the Tories Jacks,	. . . . .		778	Mullinix Tim	163
Why does he call him paultry Scribler,	. . . .		795	Traulus 1	3
To call a Swarm of Lice his Brethren?	. . . .		813	Bro Protestant	48
That serjeant at law, whom we call Kite the Second,	.		817	Yahoo's	67
Call for th' Orders of the House;	. . . . .		831	Legion Club	58
But we Mortals call him Cary.	. . . . . .		833	Legion Club	106
Brainsick Brute, they call a Peer.	. . . . .		837	Legion Club	176
Till she heard the Dean call, Will your Ladyship walk?	.		873	Grand Question	180
And call the Mansion Drapier's Hill;	. . . .		875	Drapier's Hill	10
The Rogue must call another day.	. . . . .		878	Robbin & Harry	4
Call forth our Cottagers to Arms;	. . . .		884	Rev Market-Hill	44
And, should you call me to account,	. . . .		899	Dean's Reasons	2
You call him a Sloven in earnest or jest.	. . .		943	Probatur Alit	36
You call them a riddle, as call them a sieve.	. .		976	Dean to Sherid	16
You call them a riddle, as call them a sieve.	. .		976	Dean to Sherid	16
Will you return as hard ones, if I call t'ye?	. .		989	Letter Dr Sh-n	33
'Cause I call Dan my better half,	. . . . . .		1004	Dan J's Reply	26
CALL'D					
The Muse was call'd in a poetic hour,	. . . .		43	To Congreve	2
. . .as tho' I had call'd her all to naught;	. . .		71	Mrs Harris Pet	45
(Now you must know, he hates to be call'd Parson,. . .			72	Mrs Harris Pet	54
Then my Lord call'd me; Harry, said my Lord, don't cry,			73	Mrs Harris Pet	66
Call'd Pompey, Scipio and Caesar;	. . . . .		82	Salamander	2
And call'd to take the Cards away,	. . . .		86	Hist V's House	2
They call'd at ev'ry Door; Good People,	. . .		90	Bauc & Phil 1	15
Call'd thereabouts Goodman Philemon;	. . . .		91	Bauc & Phil 1	52
He knew his Trade, and call'd it Boots.	. . .		99	Elegy Patrige	34
Call'd, in the Neighbourhood, Philemon.	. . .		111	Bauc & Phil 2	20
Then call'd the happy Composition, Floyd.	. . .		118	Biddy Floyd	12
Call'd to the Clerk in manner mild,	. . . .		128	Little House	51
He call'd for Drink, you saw him Sup	. . . .		156	Fable of Midas	7
Call'd him a Cuckold, Fool, and Beast,	. . .		221	A Quiet Life	48
And before Corum Nobus so oft has been call'd,	.		238	Excellent Song	27
Call'd, Love In A Tub, and Love In A Wood.	. .		337	Serious Poem	92
I'm sure he call'd me by my Name;	. . . . .		376	Apology Lady C	46
Call'd her good Nature to relieve him;	. . .		378	Apology Lady C	85
Call'd it unmanly and unwise	. . . . .		386	Manly Virtue	77
Call'd want of Shame, a want of Sense,	. . .		386	Manly Virtue	81
"Before my Lady call'd a King.	. . . . .		452	Modern Lady	253
On that poor Spot, call'd Del-Ville, yonder:	.		476	Epist on Epist	60
Call'd up at Mid-night, ran to save	. . . .		604	Beasts Confess	115
By learned authors call'd Nubigenae.	. . .		619	Scandal Poem 1	62
By learned Authors call'd, Nubigenae.	. . .		625	Scandal Poem 2	58
Where never Blush was call'd in Aid,	. . .		691	Cadenus Vaness	168
They call'd for Tea and Chocolate,	. . . .		698	Cadenus Vaness	374
And call'd for his Poetick Works;	. . . .		702	Cadenus Vaness	512
Call'd ev'ry Pow'r to ease my Pains,	. . .		726	To Stella	100
Two Bottles call'd for, (half her Store,	. .		747	Stel Distress	49

		PAGE	TITLE	LINE
CALL'D	**(CONTINUED)**			
Two Bottles call'd for, (half her Store;		751	Stel Wood-Park	65
Thee, happy Island, Pallas call'd her own,		790	St. Pat's Well	9
"To thee I often call'd in vain,		850	Old Thorn	66
As soon as her Ladyship call'd to be drest,		868	Grand Question	43
"My School-Master call'd me a Dunce and a Fool,		873	Grand Question	163
Was call'd, to rig him out a Beau;		903	Death Daphne	20
Besides, Dick forbid me, and call'd me a fool;		980	Tho: Sheridan	7
Suppose I call'd you goose, it is hard		983	Sher, A Goose	9
I call'd you goose instead of gander;		983	Sher, A Goose	16
Yes; you call'd my Master a Knave:		985	Mary to Sher	5
Because my Master one Day in anger call'd you Goose.		985	Mary to Sher	12
And he never call'd me worse than Sweet-heart drunk or sober:		985	Mary to Sher	14
To be call'd lean by a Skelton, who'd bear it?		1003	Dan J's Reply	18
By modern Poets, call'd Elision;		1021	Nim-Dan-Dean 1	D 12
CALLD				
And calld by Excellence, the Club:		217	To Mr. Delany	58
He calld my Dol a perfect toast.		422	Ireld	32
CALLING				
May'st still follow thy Calling there.		100	Elegy Patrige	74
Told 'em their Calling, and their Errant:		112	Bauc & Phil 2	42
Didst in thy calling do thy best.		182	Horace 2, 1	58
His Lineage, Calling, Shape or Sense		217	To Mr. Delany	69
By calling This your native Soyl;		311	To Ford	10
Have teiz'd, by calling to their Aid		371	Letter D. S-y	5
Rude stately through Holbourn, to die in his Calling;		399	Tom Clinch	2
No party-fool is calling names,		402	Window Inns 7	D 5
In calling Celia sweet and cleanly.		526	Lady's Dres Rm	18
CALLS				
From whence the neighbouring Farmer calls		127	Little House	17
If <Guernsey> calls, send word you're gone abroad;		166	Toland's Invit	41
Writes down my Conceits, and then calls them his own:		265	Apollo	86
Or calls a Council of her Maids		291	Prog Marriage	53
And calls the Family to Prayrs,		292	Prog Marriage	88
She calls it combing of his Head,		328	Epigram 2	2
Calls, Crach'rode, is the Doctor come?		377	Apology Lady C	58
Distress of Nations calls him hence,		387	Manly Virtue	113
She calls it witty to be rude;		416	Woman's Mind	18
Calls Lady Spade a hundred Cheats:		447	Modern Lady	73
Calls Amoret an arrant Jilt.		450	Modern Lady	173
And calls the Senate-House a Cabbin;		514	Answer Fable	70
And calls, without affecting Airs,		605	Beasts Confess	131
Then calls the Graces to her Aid,		691	Cadenus Vaness	158
Nor calls up all the House at Night,		725	To Stella	73
That Traulus calls for Vengeance on him?		796	Traulus 1	8
He calls you Rogue; There's nothing in it,		797	Traulus 1	53
Calls Singleton his Brother Serjeant.		812	Bro Protestant	28
He calls it a bow'r.		857	Lady's Lament	186
No longer calls me Snipe and Slattern;		888	Panegyr Dean	56
CALM				
My Conscience is clear, and my Spirits are calm,		400	Tom Clinch	21
While all is Calm, his Arguments prevail,		770	Horace 1, 14	27
CALMNESS				
Must argue with calmness, or else will come short on't.		976	Dean to Sherid	12
CALUMNY				
And calumny, by working under ground,		506	To a Friend	5
CALVES-HEAD				
To eat the Calves-Head with your trusty Friends.		162	Toland's Invit	4
CALVIN				
"The Pope, or Calvin he'd oppose,		549	Life of Swift	148
"By Calvin, than the Scarlet Whore:		549	Life of Swift	151
CAM				
"Fair Isis, and ye Banks of Cam,		462	Birthday Song	77
CAMBRAY				
To understand Malebranche or Cambray;		900	Dean's Reasons	52
CAMBRICK				
Cambrick Ruffles not their own;		573	Helter Skelter	20
CAMBRIDGE				
Two College Sophs of Cambridge Growth,		593	Cassinus Peter	1
Through Cambridge waft the direful Tale.		597	Cassinus Peter	110
CAME				
Whence came these Goths to overrun the pit?		46	To Congreve	84
When wise Ld <Berkeley> first came here,		62	Discovery	1
When Folks came thick to make their Court		62	Discovery	6
So when I came up again, I found my Pocket feel very light,		69	Mrs Harris Pet	12
Then my Dame Wadgar came,		70	Mrs Harris Pet	25
I e'en left her, and came away as wise as I was before.		71	Mrs Harris Pet	47
So the Chaplain came in; now the Servants say,		72	Mrs Harris Pet	50
That came through the Key-Hole, or in at the Casement,		77	Lady B- B-	14
Or whether it came from Above or Below.		77	Lady B- B-	18
Whose Breath or Touch, where e'er he came,		85	Salamander	59
Came to a Village hard by Rixham		90	Bauc & Phil 1	9
To a small Cottage came at last		91	Bauc & Phil 1	50
To a small Cottage came at last;		111	Bauc & Phil 2	18
Up to the Northern Tropick came,		119	Apollo Outwit	2
Which came with a prodigious Fall;		126	Little House	8
The Doctor's Family came by,		128	Little House	47
Came an Heir-loom, as Homer sings,		134	Magician's Rod	64
I came in without Danger; and was I to blame?		144	New Song	33

CAME   (CONTINUED)   PAGE   TITLE   LINE
    Miss came, and peep'd at all he had.   . . . .   150 Corinna   24
    Came sneaking to the Chariot-side, ...   172 Horace 1, 7   64
    Came early, and departed late: . . .   .   173 Horace 1, 7   79
    Down from her silver chariot came, ...   178 To Lord Harley   75
    Came up, and knock't the Praetor down. . . . . . .   190 Faggot   34
    At length to Musick's House she came, ...   207 Fable Bitches   7
    The Time pass'd on, and Musick came, ...   208 Fable Bitches   37
    That came together to be pleasd: . . . .   217 To Mr. Delany   76
    At length a lucky Lover came, ...   222 Prog of Love   19
    No news of Phil. The Bridegroom came, ...   223 Prog of Love   29
    Here all the bold Advent'rers came, ...   256 Bubble   138
    On Tuesday the Ninth, seditiously came, ...   263 Apollo   29
    To discover the Goods he came honestly by: . . . . .   264 Apollo   58
    Then Hebe came and took her Place   . . . . . .   290 Prog Marriage   15
    How came this wicked Plot to Light: . . . .   298 Horrid Plot   2
    "But how you came to interpose, ...   304 Storm   45
    Hearing the House was empty, came to town; . . . . .   307 Billet Players   2
    The high Descent from whence you came, ...   323 Pethox   12
    Whether thy Great Forefathers came . . . .   324 Pethox   23
    And from contending Atoms came.   . . . . . .   324 Pethox   32
    Tom's three dearest Friends came by in the Squabble, .   327 Epigram 1   3
    Now ask me a Question. How came it to pass . . . .   336 Serious Poem   85
    Ne'r came in sight . . . .   441 Ballyspellin   41
    She came from Eniskellin . . . .   442 Ballyspellin   63
    And studied Affection came, ...   449 Modern Lady   132
    "This Morning when the Parson came, ...   452 Modern Lady   238
    "This odious Chair how came I stuck in't, ...   452 Modern Lady   240
    As never came from Noah's Ark: . . . .   514 Answer Fable   54
    No Scruple came on him his Gown to expose, ...   517 Dean Hang Rape   21
    Pois'ning the Flesh from whence it came;   . . . .   529 Lady's Dres Rm   106
    He came to Court with Fortune clear, ...   606 Beasts Confess   165
    He never honestly came by 'em, ...   621 Scandal Poem 1   119
    Came early, out of pure Good-will, ...   698 Cadenus Vaness   366
    As came into her Fancy first, ...   698 Cadenus Vaness   382
    Although they came not in a Coach. .   . . . . .   701 Cadenus Vaness   459
    Ideas came into her Mind   . . . .   704 Cadenus Vaness   556
    He came to take his last Adieu. . . .   .   705 Cadenus Vaness   593
    Insensibly came on her Side;   . . .   .   709 Cadenus Vaness   729
    Howe'er it came, he cou'd not tell, ...   710 Cadenus Vaness   748
    I bless the Hand from whence they came, ...   727 To Stella   115
    A Thought came slowly from my Brain, ...   741 Stel B-day 22   8
    When both the Jacks and Robin came;   . . . . .   741 Stel B-day 22   18
    To thee, once fav'rite Isle, with Joy I came;   . . .   789 St. Pat's Well   2
    Confess the Soil from whence the Victors came. . .   791 St. Pat's Well   16
    Fled to the Fountain back, from whence it came! . .   793 St. Pat's Well   66
    They came of good Kindred, and cou'd not endure, .   804 Irish Bishops   27
    That he came from the Temple, his morals do show, .   815 Yahoo's   11
    What the De'el is't to him whence the Devil they came?   815 Yahoo's   24
    When his speech came abroad, he paid him off clean, .   816 Yahoo's   38
    Came but to plunder and enslave us;   . . . . .   820 Dr. Rundle   34
    Hither came every Village Maid . . . .   848 Old Thorn   5
    Before he came here . . . .   852 Lady's Lament   15
    His Majesty of Terrors came, ...   904 Death Daphne   54
    She, as he came into the Room, ...   904 Death Daphne   57
    Does he forget from whence he came?   . . . . .   950 Upstart   D 2
    . . .I came back to sit with the Ladies this Night.   1013 Swift to Sheri   3
    But how, Mr. Sheridan, came you to venture . . . .   1027 Sheri Circles   13
    My Footman came home from the Church, of a Bruise sick, 1029 Dr. Helsham   17
    This Night I came home with a very cold Dew sick, .   1030 Dr. Sheridan   2
CAMELEON
    And change like the Cameleon.   . . . .   935 Riddle 23   D 13
CAMELION
    I beg you'll the Camelion spare.   . . . .   270 Apollo's Edict   D 17
CAMP
    Court, City, Camp, all one to him---.   . . . . . .   548 Life of Swift   106
CAMPAIGNS
    Renown'd in Sieges and Campaigns, ...   925 Riddle 8   31
CAMPAINS
    On French Records for twenty long Campains; . . . .   771 Horace 1, 14   44
CAN   398   OMITTED WORD
CAN'ST
    Can'st hourly set him on the Rack, ...   325 Pethox   54
CAN'T   . 25   OMITTED WORD
CANAL
    Ierna's Lake, for your Canal, ...   476 Epist on Epist   38
    Beneath a dry Canal there lies, ...   478 Epist on Epist   89
CANALS
    In Whims, Parterres, Canals and Fences: . . . . .   477 Epist on Epist   62
CANCEL'D
    Thinks heav'n has cancel'd all our sins, ...   40 Ode Sancroft   181
CANCER
    That Cancer with his pois'nous Claws   . . . . .   228 Prog of Beauty   91
    You're so retrograde, sure you were born under Cancer: . 1019 To Sheridan   3
CANDIDATE
    Is now caress't by Candidate Divines;   . . . . . .   196 Author Himself   64
CANDIDATES
    That Club of Candidates in Black, ...   503 Doctor Delaney   85
    The Candidates observ'd his dirty Paws, ...   536 To Mr. Gay   157
CANDLE
    His Candle out, and he a Bed.   . . . .   280 Journal   48

CANDLE	(CONTINUED)	PAGE	TITLE	LINE
With farthing Candle for a Torch,	. . . .	290	Prog Marriage	12
He burnt his candle to the snuff;	. . . .	296	Satiric Elegy	14

CANDLE-LIGHT
And flies about the Candle-Light;	. . . .	99	Elegy Patrige	52
Through Candle-Light she view'd the Wine,	. . . . .	750	Stel Wood-Park	19
Thro candle-light she view'd the Wine	. . . . . .	746	Stel Distress	21

CANDLES
| For Candles, how she trucks her Driping; | . . . . . | 282 | Journal | 88 |

CANDOR
| Tho' Candor and Truth in my Aspect I bear, | . . . . | 929 | Riddle 13 | D 5 |

CANE
A flaxen wig, and clouded cane,	. . . .	619	Scandal Poem 1	70
A Flaxen Wig, and Clouded Cane.	. . . .	625	Scandal Poem 2	66
His Cane upon a Button.	. . . .	785	Mullinex Dick	32

CANKER-WORM
| Envy, a Canker-worm which tears | . . . . . | 458 | Paddy's Charac | 11 |

CANKER'D
| Has canker'd all its Branches round; | . . . . | 849 | Old Thorn | 18 |

CANN
| That you and he are Cup and Cann. | . . . . | 480 | Libel on D- D- | 10 |

CANNON'S
| He runs into a Cannon's Chops. | . . . . | 500 | Doctor Delaney | 10 |

CANNONS
| First with the brazen Cannons Roar. | . . . . | 338 | Wood's Brass | 2 |
| By old Popish Cannons, as wise Men have Penn'd'em, | . | 518 | Dean Hang Rape | 37 |

CANNOT 47 OMITTED WORD

CANON
And longs to be a Canon there;	. . . .	173	Horace 1, 7	84
A Canon! that's a Place too mean:	. . . .	173	Horace 1, 7	87
He claims it by a Canon;	. . . .	406	Swift to Pope	18

CANONS
Two Dozen Canons round your Stall,	. . . .	173	Horace 1, 7	89
From antient Canons would not vary,	. . . .	821	Dr. Rundle	39
Tho' ten thousand Canons roar,	. . . .	931	Riddle 18	D 23

CANST 3 OMITTED WORD

CANT   SEE DINNER-CANT
Thus in the Strolers usuall Cant	. . . .	90	Bauc & Phil 1	23
He in the old Celestial Cant,	. . . .	120	Apollo Outwit	17
Nor Shepherds use poetick Cant:	. . . .	270	Apollo's Edict	D 28
The Cant which ev'ry Fool repeats,	. . . .	645	On Poetry	153
Run o'er their Cant of stupid Lies,	. . . .	697	Cadenus Vaness	332

CANTERBURY
| or Ambling or Sweet Canterbury, | . . . . | 957 | Cantata | |

CANTING
Where, in the Strolers Canting Strain,	. . . . . .	111	Bauc & Phil 2	11
"For canting hypocrites to claim,	. . . .	550	Life of Swift	171
In him, that's accomplish'd in Cringing and Canting:	.	808	Advice Parson	6

CANVAS
| At length, his Anchor fixt, and Canvas furl'd, | . . . | 284 | Elegy Boat | 6 |

CAP   SEE NIGHT-CAP
His Cap had a new Cherry Ribbon to ty't.	. . . . .	399	Tom Clinch	6
In Velvet Cap his Head lies warm;	. . . .	410	Dial Rich Marb	65
First, lolling Sloth in Woollen Cap,	. . . . . .	895	Panegyr Dean	273

CAP-A-PEE
| Inclos'd Cap-a-pee in a strong Coat of Mail. | . . . . | 350 | Wood Insect | 6 |

CAPACIOUS
| Capacious House! 'tis own'd by all | . . . . . . | 109 | V's House | 115 |

CAPACITIES
| In both Capacities, to Build. | . . . . | 107 | V's House | 36 |

CAPACITY
In each Capacity to Build:	. . . .	80	Vanbrug House	62
Or wants Capacity to reach	. . . .	712	Cadenus Vaness	810
In each Capacity I mean	. . . .	888	Panegyr Dean	43

CAPE
| Nor would there be need of a strong Hempen Cape, | . . | 519 | Dean Hang Rape | 65 |

CAPERS
| Cutting Capers and Ramping, | . . . . | 245 | Irish-Feast | 38 |

CAPITALS
| With Capitals, the more the better. | . . . . | 469 | Birthday Song | 280 |
| But when in Capitals exprest, | . . . . | 643 | On Poetry | 99 |

CAPITOL
| You, in your Capitol secur'd, | . . . . | 326 | Pethox | 97 |

CAPON
| But Jest apart, restore, you Capon ye, | . . . . . | 1033 | Ans to Crown | 7 |

CAPRICE
| Where-e'er Caprice or Folly steers. | . . . . . | 687 | Cadenus Vaness | 38 |

CAPRICIOUS
| The Multitude's Capricious Pranks | . . . . . . | 239 | Run Bankers | 5 |
| Must laugh at her capricious Choice. | . . . . . . | 702 | Cadenus Vaness | 509 |

CAPS
| Twelve Commoners in Caps to Row you. | . . . . . | 476 | Epist on Epist | 42 |
| And with powder'd Caps and Wigs, Sir; | . . . . . | 573 | Helter Skelter | 18 |

CAPT
| Is Capt. Crach'rode here, pray?--No. | . . . . . | 376 | Apology Lady C | 43 |

CAPTAIN
Why certainly the Captain rav'd?	. . . . . .	376	Apology Lady C	36
The Captain walks about, and searches	. . . . .	377	Apology Lady C	61
Captain, I fear you've made some Blunder;	. . . . .	377	Apology Lady C	66
The Captain was a Man of Reading,	. . . . . .	377	Apology Lady C	71
The Captain too--he did not know	. . . . . .	377	Apology Lady C	81

CAPTAIN   (CONTINUED)   PAGE   TITLE   LINE

Text	PAGE	TITLE	LINE
The Captain swears the sea's too rough	420	Holyhead	9
The Captain, I'm sure, will always come here;	868	Grand Question	32
For the Captain, I warrant, will keep him in Awe;	868	Grand Question	34
And waits on the Captain betimes the next Morning.	869	Grand Question	70
Noble Captain, your Servant--Sir Arthur your Slave;	869	Grand Question	72
Good Morrow, good Captain,--I'll wait on you down,--	869	Grand Question	77
For all the World, Captain, not half an Inch farther--	869	Grand Question	79
Next Day, to be sure, the Captain will come,	870	Grand Question	87
See, now comes the Captain all dawb'd with gold Lace:	870	Grand Question	93
Drawn up in our Court; when the Captain cries, Stand.	870	Grand Question	100
The Captain, to shew he is proud of the Favour,	870	Grand Question	103
For, a Captain of Horse never takes off his Hat;	870	Grand Question	106
Pray, Captain, be pleas'd to light, and walk in:	871	Grand Question	114
The Captain salutes you with Congee profound;	871	Grand Question	115
And, Captain, you'll do us the Favour to stay,	871	Grand Question	119
You Officers, Captain, are so complaisant.	871	Grand Question	126
The Captain at Dinner appears in his Glory,	871	Grand Question	130
To peep at the Captain, in all his fine Clo'es:	872	Grand Question	138
That the Captain suppos'd he was Curate to Jenny.)	872	Grand Question	152
Captain Butler made some in the Church black and blue sick;	1029	Dr. Helsham	7

CAPTAIN'S
| For the Captain's entreated to sit by your Side; | 871 | Grand Question | 132 |

CAPTAINS
| By Captains and by Majors. | 426 | Five Ladies | 28 |

CAPTIVE
| Yet from an Empress, now a Captive grown, | 771 | Horace 1, 14 | 45 |

CAPTIVES
| Be all made Captives in their native Land; | 793 | St. Pat's Well | 90 |

CAR
And a Grim Slave to wait on his Triumphal Car.	7	Ode to King	44
I mean your Butler, Dawson, Car,	217	To Mr. Delany	59
Of polish't Brass, his flaming Car,	352	Wood Ironmongr	13
Tigellius plac'd in Phoebus' Car,	650	On Poetry	303
Or on a proud triumphal Car,	724	To Stella	26
But now let us hear what the Muse from your car says.	976	Dean to Sherid	6
By riding this morning too long in your car:	976	Dean to Sherid	28
And I wish your few friends, when they next see your car go,	976	Dean to Sherid	29

CAR'CATURA
| You will need no Car'catura; | 839 | Legion Club | 228 |

CARCASE
Her tainted Carcase to pursue,	85	Salamander	65
At once upon his Carcase light;	413	Desire Possess	56
What tho the royal Carcase must	467	Birthday Song	235
Bare, like a Carcase pick't by Crows,	904	Death Daphne	34

CARCASS
| Have put his Carcass in a Chest. | 235 | Elegy on Demar | 46 |
| To be cloath'd like a Carcass would make a Teague mad, | 237 | Excellent Song | 12 |

CARD
How Miss pickt ev'ry painted Card,	86	Hist V's House	4
"Well, if I ever touch a Card:	446	Modern Lady	51
She draws up Card by Card, to find	452	Modern Lady	228
She draws up Card by Card, to find	452	Modern Lady	228

CARDS
Delivers Cards about,	74	Game Traffick	2
And call'd to take the Cards away,	86	Hist V's House	2
Not a sham Thing of Clay or Cards.	87	Hist V's House	26
The Table, Cards, and Counters set,	451	Modern Lady	214
Again a-fresh to Cards they run,	453	Modern Lady	278
Think not Cards my chief Diversion,	632	Epistle Lady	81
The Men who slave at Cards from Morn to Night;	662	Upon Ladies	7
Nor plays at cards, or dice, or bowls;	901	Dean's Reasons	88
To visit where she sat at Cards;	904	Death Daphne	56
For, Cards we know, are Pluto's Books)	905	Death Daphne	80

CARE
Nor is this all: As glorious is the Care	12	Ode to William	D 25
Poor we Cadets of Heav'n, not worth her Care,	32	Ode to Temple	183
Take care betimes to run him down:	171	Horace 1, 7	30
From Dunns and Debts, and drown our Care;	184	Horace 2, 1	110
My State of Health none care to learn;	203	In Sickness	5
Let him, like you, observe with Care	218	To Mr. Delany	99
Ireland is now our royal Care,	269	Apollo's Edict	D 1
"Each take a Child into her Care,	321	First of April	5
"Divide the rest, but then take care,	321	First of April	11
Equal to all in Care and Love,	322	First of April	35
The Muses when they saw her care,	322	First of April	43
In thy great Care we place our Trust,	339	Arch-Bish Dub	7
Whose Conscience always was her care,	375	Apology Lady C	2
Now change the Scene; a nobler Care	387	Manly Virtue	111
And, Curl must have a special Care	394	Grub-Street	11
Your honest Care may fill; perhaps enlarge.	533	To Mr. Gay	46
"But, finding vain was all his Care,	567	Death of Swift	369
But ever with Prudence takes Care of the Main.	580	Psyche	8
Pulls off with Care, and first displays 'em,	581	Young Nymph	15
By Nature form'd with nicest Care,	584	Strephon Chloe	5
With Care provide you as we go,	627	Scandal Poem 2	123
Your Poem finish'd, next your Care	643	On Poetry	91
But first with Care imploy your Thoughts,	645	On Poetry	149
The Church is thy peculiar Care.	656	On Poetry	452

CARE	(CONTINUED)	PAGE	TITLE	LINE
And give him wholly to your Care.		692	Cadenus Vaness	197
She manag'd her Estate with Care,		693	Cadenus Vaness	220
It shew'd a true Paternal Care--		707	Cadenus Vaness	653
You pay too dearly for your Care;		727	To Stella	118
Then, who says care will kill a cat?		761	Bec's B-Day	7
For she, tho' over-run with care,		761	Bec's B-Day	9
The cat's nine lives and eke the care.		761	Bec's B-Day	30
But always take a special care		762	Bec's B-Day	41
You, to whose Care so oft I owe,		766	Stel B-day '26	87
They call me Beast, and what Care I?		778	Mullinix Tim	162
Some have the City in their Care,		780	Mullinix Tim	249
Our Care is to improve the mind,		781	Mullinix Tim	263
What care we how high runs his passion or pride?		817	Yahoo's	71
Poverty, and Grief, and Care,		832	Legion Club	89
"But if I say the word--take care of Armagh!"		843	Ay and No	18
The Thorn committed to her Care,		850	Old Thorn	50
Thus spoke to my Lady, the Knight full of Care;		866	Grand Question	1
Adorn'd by Nymphs with all their Care:		919	Riddle 5	4
For myself, I protest, I care not a fiddle		976	Dean to Sherid	13
. . . and you may go tell my Master; what care I?		986	Mary to Sher	21
And I don't care who knows it, 'tis all one to Mary.		986	Mary to Sher	22
. . .truly they don't care for your Wife's Company,		1013	Swift to Sheri	7
CAREFUL				
Careful Observers may fortel the Hour		136	City Shower	1
Be careful, as you walk behind,		780	Mullinix Tim	231
Under whose wise and careful Guardship,		890	Panegyr Dean	107
CAREFULL				
But, always carefull of the main,		878	Robbin & Harry	7
CAREFULLY				
Which when you have got, you so carefully hide it,		263	Apollo	5
And, carefully observe the Ground,		592	Strephon Chloe	295
CARELESS				
Careless and Ignorant Posterity,		21	Ode Athenian	163
Such is that Sprinkling which some careless Quean		137	City Shower	19
Look'd with an easie, careless Mien,		170	Horace 1, 7	9
If Molly happens to be careless,		417	Woman's Mind	43
That careless Wench! no Creature warn her		528	Lady's Dres Rm	71
For which you curse the careless Wench;		529	Lady's Dres Rm	108
Where not one careless Thought intrudes,		691	Cadenus Vaness	166
CARES				
To lose the providence of thy cares,		42	Ode Sancroft	242
And still it's Love to Houshold Cares		94	Bauc & Phil 1	143
And still its Love to Household Cares		113	Bauc & Phil 2	81
(His Mind with Publick Cares possest,		170	Horace 1, 7	3
And when thou'st bid adieu to Cares,		181	Horace 2, 1	39
Nor let such Cares disturb thy Rest.		182	Horace 2, 1	70
That your Lordship would once let your Cares all alone		185	Scriblerus 1	3
To your Friends who at least have no Cares but to please you		185	Scriblerus 1	5
Those Cares that haunt the Court and Town.		202	Horace 2, 6	112
His Mind is full of other Cares,		292	Prog Marriage	67
"What Ormond's Valour, Oxford's Cares,		567	Death of Swift	374
For Bec, a new supply of cares,		753	Gift for Bec	2
With six imagin'd cares to fright you.		753	Gift for Bec	14
To hold your cares for other folks.		753	Gift for Bec	18
Bring all your Quilca cares to Dublin,		753	Gift for Bec	24
Who drives her cares to hands and feet:		761	Bec's B-Day	18
Where there will be no cares to fright her.		762	Bec's B-Day	60
Now, for thy Safety Cares distract my Mind,		772	Horace 1, 14	58
But he cares not for it a Rush,		860	Lady Acheson	15
Those thankless and officious cares		901	Dean's Reasons	95
CARESS				
Now let's no more caress thy French,		373	Letter D. S-y	64
That Dido smitt, might more caress him		619	Scandal Poem 1	68
That Dido might the more caress him:		625	Scandal Poem 2	64
CARESS'D				
"Who saw this Factious Tribe caress'd,		549	Life of Swift	160
Caress'd by Ministers of State,		702	Cadenus Vaness	504
CARESS'T				
Is now caress't by Candidate Divines;		196	Author Himself	64
CARESSING				
Caressing Knaves and Dunces wooing,		484	Libel on D- D-	127
"So often seen caressing Chartres:		565	Death of Swift	324
CAREST				
Thus Addison by Lords Carest,		482	Libel on D- D-	61
Burst into her Chamber, and wou'd have Carest her,		517	Dean Hang Rape	9
The <Dean> was never so carest:		796	Traulus 1	16
CARK				
It would do your Heart good, to see how she will cark it.		580	Psyche	12
CARLE				
In spite of the Carle		186	Scriblerus 4	D 10
CARLETON				
Like Carleton cheap, or fam'd Duruel,		85	Salamander	62
CARLOS				
Don Carlos in a merry Spight		745	Stel Distress	1
Don Carlos made her sole Director.		745	Stel Distress	8
Don Carlos made her chief Director		745	Stel Distress	
Don Carlos earnestly would beg,		746	Stel Distress	17
Don Carlos now began to find		746	Stel Distress	31
You shew Don Carlos where to dwell,		748	Stel Distress	73

CARLOS   (CONTINUED)   PAGE   TITLE   LINE
    Don Carlos in a merry Spight, ...   749 Stel Wood-Park   1
    Don Carlos made her chief Director, ...   749 Stel Wood-Park   5
    Don Carlos earnestly would beg, ...   750 Stel Wood-Park   15
    Don Carlos now began to find   . . . .   750 Stel Wood-Park   23
CARMINA
    Yet, Neget quis Carmina Gallo.   . . . .   278 Journal   4
CARMINATIVE
    Carminative and Diuretick, ...   588 Strephon Chloe   133
CAROLINA
    But Carolina shines the clearer   . . . .   466 Birthday Song   179
CAROLINE
    Because it clinks to Caroline.   . . . .   467 Birthday Song   220
    May Caroline continue long, ...   467 Birthday Song   233
    Tho Caroline may fill your gaps   . . . .   467 Birthday Song   239
CARPS
    What Carps we met with for our pains: . . . . .   283 Journal   112
<CARR>
    You, Mullinex, and slobb'ring <Carr?>   . . . . . .   787 Dick's Variety   3
    Lord <Bolton's> good Grace, Lord <Carr>, and Lord   804 Irish Bishops   25
        <Howard>,
CARRICKDRUMRUSK
    And Carrickdrumrusk: . . . .   247 Irish-Feast   76
CARRIED
    So quickly, and so wonderfully carried on, ...   24 Ode Athenian   276
    And by one mighty Hero carried to it's height   . .   25 Ode Athenian   284
    One Coach oft' carried them when they were quick,   . .   430 Dicky Dolly   14
CARRIES
    But, carries Loads, and feeds on Thistles;   . . . .   607 Beasts Confess   214
CARRION
    And truck the Carrion for Tobacca, ...   220 A Quiet Life   32
    The veal is such carrion, ...   402 Window Inns 8   D   9
CARROT
    His carrot locks, and fiery nose;   . . . .   621 Scandal Poem 1   136
CARROTS
    Beware of Carrots from Northumberlond.   . . . . . .   148 Windsor Proph   16
    Carrots sown Thyn a deep root may get, ...   148 Windsor Proph   17
    Root out these Carrots, O Thou, whose Name   . . . .   148 Windsor Proph   21
    Bury those Carrots under a Hill.   . . . .   148 Windsor Proph   26
CARRY
    Or make you Fast, and carry you to Prayers: . . . .   166 Toland's Invit   43
    My Lord wou'd carry on the Jest, ...   173 Horace 1, 7   81
    Now, now you carry all before ye, ...   183 Horace 2, 1   83
    (For that's but a Sham Wood they carry about)   336 Serious Poem   76
    "Here, carry down those ten Pistoles   . . . . . .   447 Modern Lady   66
    And weekly carry out our Dust.   . . . .   787 Clad in Brown   28
    When Dick cries, Dust to carry out?   . . . . . .   787 Clad in Brown   30
CARRY'D
    Carry'd it to his Equalls high'r, ...   95 Bauc & Phil 1   179
    The Dean has carry'd Lady Jane   . . . .   294 Prog Marriage   124
    Why?--Virtues carry'd to Excess;   . . . .   603 Beasts Confess   76
CARRYD
    When Jests are carryd on too far, ...   218 To Mr. Delany   79
CARRYED
    They must be carryed through the Sky   . . . . .   620 Scandal Poem 1   112
CARS
    From rhyming in cars you may swing in a cart.   . . . . 976 Dean to Sherid   36
CART   SEE GO-CART
    Flirts from his Cart the Mud in <Walpole's> Face.   .   364 On Dreams   38
    He swore from his Cart, it was all a damn'd Lye.   . . 399 Tom Clinch   12
    Than at the Rumbling of a Cart: . . . .   674 His Deafness   6
    If thou wer't in a Cart, I fear   . . . .   787 Clad in Brown   23
    A long-ear'd Beast, and Irish Cart, ...   942 Probatur Alit   23
    A cart would best become the knave, ...   951 Upstart   D 25
    From rhyming in cars you may swing in a cart.   . . . . 976 Dean to Sherid   36
    Are you still in your cart with conviitia ex plaustro?   979 Dean to Tho: S   6
    But coach it or cart it, I'd have you know, Sirrah, .   979 Dean to Tho: S   11
    And you and your cart shall give me carte blanche.   .   979 Dean to Tho: S   14
    Since you write in a cart, keep it tecta et sarta,   .   979 Dean to Tho: S   15
    You rhyme, as folks fence, in tierce and cart.   . . . . 979 Dean to Tho: S   20
CART-AGO
    That I'll ne'er give my vote for Delenda Cart-ago.   979 Dean to Tho: S   18
CART'RET
    Cart'ret was welcom'd to the Shore   . . . .   338 Wood's Brass   1
CARTA
    'Tis all you have for't; 'tis your best Magna Carta; . 979 Dean to Tho: S   16
CARTE
    And you and your cart shall give me carte blanche.   . . 979 Dean to Tho: S   14
CARTED
    Old carted Bawds such Garments wear, ...   787 Clad in Brown   19
CARTERET
    For Fifty Times its Worth, to Carteret.   . . . .   349 Whitshed Motto   22
    When Carteret is gone . . . .   423 Carterets Arms   2
CARTERS
    Those carters, and paviours, and footmen and all;   . . 841 Ballad   D 17
CARTESIAN
    So when Cartesian artists try   . . . .   35 Ode Sancroft   27
CARTHY
    But Carthy, as from him thou learnest, ...   666 Epig Carthy 1   D   3
    What then must Carthy do in proper Season, ...   666 Epig Carthy 3   D   3
    Thy Labours, Carthy, long conceal'd from Light,   . .   667 Epig Carthy 5   D   1

	PAGE	TITLE	LINE

CARTHY (CONTINUED)

	PAGE	TITLE	LINE
Carthy, you say, writes well--his genius true.-- . . .	668	Epig Carthy 8	D 1
How monstrous Carthy looks to Flaccus brac't, . . .	668	Epig Carthy 9	D 1
Carthy, no more insult Aurelian's Name, ...	668	Epig Carthy 10	D 1
What Carthy publish'd needs no long Excuse, ...	668	Epig Carthy 11	D 1
So deeply Carthy to the Center tends.	669	Epig Carthy 14	D 2
Carthy ambitious to retrieve his name, ...	671	Epig Carthy 24	D 1

CARVE

To Flatter, Carve, and shew your Wit;	483	Libel on D- D-	106
We may carve for others thus;	633	Epistle Lady	119
And let others carve for us.	633	Epistle Lady	120
Carve for all, yourself is starving.	633	Epistle Lady	124
Carve to all but just enuff, ...	633	Epistle Lady	129
Let your Neighbours carve for you.	634	Epistle Lady	132
And, because he's their Betters, you carve for him first,	871	Grand Question	133
Decant his Wine, and carve his Beef.	883	Rev Market-Hill	24

CARVES

By which our happy Prince carves out his Bays; . . .	7	Ode to King	32

CARVING

Conversation is but carving, ...	633	Epistle Lady	123
At nicely carving show thy Wit;	897	Panegyr Dean	335

CARY

Says, says Cary, I have been a Servant.	70	Mrs Harris Pet	30
But we Mortals call him Cary.	833	Legion Club	106

CASCADES

But you must have Cascades, and all	476	Epist on Epist	37

CASE SEE FLYING-CASE

. . .that's a plain Case.	70	Mrs Harris Pet	17
And so went to Bed in a desperate Case.	77	Lady B- B-	7
For Jove consider'd well the Case, ...	79	Vanbrug House	17
For, Jove consider'd well the Case, ...	106	V's House	17
The Priest was pretty well in case, ...	170	Horace 1, 7	7
This, humbly offers me his Case--	200	Horace 2, 6	47
And what he thought the hardest Case, ...	221	A Quiet Life	45
And this is fair Diana's Case	228	Prog of Beauty	85
The Tenant's in a Dismal Case	240	Run Bankers	47
Are proper in my Lady's Case	294	Prog Marriage	132
May cost a crown or so; a common case:	308	Billet Players	26
"And beauteous Bess a diff'rent case is, ...	321	First of April	9
Another Case; the Sense of Hearing:	366	Answer Delaney	28
Now, should I own your case was grievous, ...	433	Answer Paulus	37
And should it be your Hero's case	460	Birthday Song	5
We rather should Lament his Case	485	Libel on D- D-	159
Your case consider'd, I must think	489	Dialogue	15
In either Case, an equal Chance is run:	535	To Mr. Gay	125
A strong Dilemma in a desp'rate Case!	535	To Mr. Gay	129
Let me suppose the Case my own.	547	Life of Swift	67
How glad the Case is not your own!	554	Death of Swift	30
In such a Case they talk in Tropes, ...	557	Death of Swift	117
"We must confess his Case was nice;	558	Death of Swift	171
Think what a Case all Men are now in, ...	585	Strephon Chloe	33
Which Nature gives in such a Case;	591	Strephon Chloe	240
Be easy, 'tis a common Case.	595	Cassinus Peter	50
Without Success; thus tells his Case:	604	Beasts Confess	94
Though hard to find in ev'ry Case	606	Beasts Confess	155
Observe the case: I state it thus:	622	Scandal Poem 1	157
Thus you have my Case at large, ...	631	Epistle Lady	43
(Which seldom is the Dunce's Case)	647	On Poetry	234
The Case is just the same with me:	679	From Catullus	6
Against the Statutes in that Case, ...	687	Cadenus Vaness	18
But since the Case appear'd so nice, ...	689	Cadenus Vaness	91
In Virgil (vide Dido's Case:)	690	Cadenus Vaness	111
And this she takes to be her Case.	709	Cadenus Vaness	703
But, in a weighty Case like this, ...	713	Cadenus Vaness	854
It makes no Diff'rence in the Case, ...	724	To Stella	21
How shall I act? is not the Case, ...	724	To Stella	39
Now, this is Stella's Case in Fact;	734	Stel B-day '20	15
We think you quite mistake the Case;	752	Stel Wood-Park	89
'Tis just the Case: For you have fasted	759	Receipt Youth	23
Come back before you're out of Case;	760	Receipt Youth	50
Grant this the Case, yet sure 'tis hard, ...	764	Stel B-day '26	25
I beg, you see the Case is Nice, ...	779	Mullinix Tim	196
Why Tom, I think the Case is plain, ...	796	Traulus 1	13
The smart-one replied, "There's no wit in the case; . . .	843	Ay and No	7
Whene'er you joke, 'tis all a Case;	890	Panegyr Dean	121
Here, when my Shoes are out of case, ...	896	Panegyr Dean	311
Stuck artfully a Parchment Case.	904	Death Daphne	36
Thus you have the case in view, ...	907	Daphne	49
But this I know, in either Case	918	Riddle 4	29
Although I'm often out of Case, ...	920	Riddle 6	23
And, 'tis your own Case, for you never can wound . . .	968	Letter Sherid	33
The Case, I have stated, ...	1014	Swift to Sheri	22

CASEMENT

Have worn a Casement o'er their Skin, ...	30	Ode to Temple	126
That came through the Key-Hole, or in at the Casement,	77	Lady B- B-	14

CASES

Quoth Herries, fairly putting Cases, ...	75	Game Traffick	17
By others us'd in the like Cases.	223	Prog of Love	50

CASH

Then said his Lordship with a Smile, I must have Lawful Cash,	342	Upon His Grace	35

122

	PAGE	TITLE	LINE
CASH (CONTINUED)			
Provided they had Cash to lend.	455	Dean Smedley	16
Your Assets fail, and Cash is wanting	477	Epist on Epist	63
CASHEL			
And, while at good Cashel you rail with such spite,	818	Archbi Cashel	3
CASHIER'D			
The ruling Rogue, who dreads to be cashier'd;	536	To Mr. Gay	137
CASSINUS			
Cassinus this, and t' other Peter)	594	Cassinus Peter	6
Friend Peter to Cassinus goes,	594	Cassinus Peter	7
CASSOCK			
His Wastcoat to a Cassock grew,	115	Bauc & Phil 2	121
It shames his Cassock and his Years	294	Prog Marriage	140
When my old cassock says a Welch divine	419	Shall Repine	5
I smell your gown and cassock	428	Beau's Reply	2
Thy thread-bare gown, thy cassock rent,	676	Parson's Case	9
"Thy Gown and Cassock oft be torn:	850	Old Thorn	60
"In mending your Cassock, and smoothing your Band:	872	Grand Question	150
"Whenever you see a Cassock and Gown,	872	Grand Question	153
CASSY			
Why, Cassy, thou wilt doze thy Pate:	594	Cassinus Peter	29
Dear Cassy, though to ask I dread,	595	Cassinus Peter	41
"Here Cassy lies, by Caelia slain,	596	Cassinus Peter	77
Dear Cassy, thou must purge and bleed;	596	Cassinus Peter	89
CAST SEE NEW-CAST			
Still cast it up and nauseate Company.	27	Ode to Temple	49
Was cast in the same Mold with mine?	32	Ode to Temple	179
Like a cast mistress to your wicked friend;	44	To Congreve	16
Where having cast his coat, and well pursu'd	46	To Congreve	117
Parson, said I, can you cast a Nativity,. ..	72	Mrs Harris Pet	53
Cast in his Dart which made three Moydores Light.	234	Elegy on Demar	32
And down the towring Boy is cast:	252	Bubble	40
So cast it in the Southern Seas,	255	Bubble	121
Upon the Water cast thy Bread	255	Bubble	133
Townshends cast Page or Walpole's groom	423	Ireld	72
Must in a diff'rent Mold be cast;	496	Panegyr Swift	107
Round all your Brethren cast your Eyes,	502	Doctor Delaney	83
When frighted Strephon cast his Eye on't	527	Lady's Dres Rm	61
"You cast a Sheep's Eye on her Ladyship's Maid;	872	Grand Question	148
But, now dismember'd here are cast,	923	Riddle 7	77
And Robin at Sea had like to be cast away.	1037	Four Storyes	4
CASTLE			
The Castle seldom frequents.	75	Game Traffick	16
The Castle of Slain,	247	Irish-Feast	75
And Castle roofs, and Steeple Spires.	257	Bubble	172
And build a Castle in the Air.	361	Grace's Answer	20
Passes the Lower Castle Yard,	376	Apology Lady C	29
Must build a Castle at Drumlack:	883	Rev Market-Hill	14
While in his lordly Castle fixt,	883	Rev Market-Hill	19
CASTLES			
With License to build Castles there;	79	Vanbrug House	26
With Licence to build Castles there:	106	V's House	26
While some build Castles in the Air,	257	Bubble	165
Earld Godwin's Castles overflown,	257	Bubble	171
CASTS			
Round all the earth she casts her eyes;	178	To Lord Harley	61
CAT SEE POLE-CAT			
While Rain depends, the pensive Cat gives o'er	136	City Shower	3
A Widow kept a Favourite Cat,	153	Widow and Cat	D 1
"I am a Cat of Honour--Stay,	154	Widow and Cat	D 31
Are Cat and Dog, and Rogue and Whore.	225	Prog of Love	100
Then, who says care will kill a cat?	761	Bec's B-Day	7
Or, like a Cat with Walnuts shod,	885	Rev Market-Hill	73
The dullest Beast and kind Voice of a Cat,	940	Letter	12
A long-ear'd Beast, and kind Noise of a Cat,	943	Probatur Alit	43
I pitied my Cat, whom I knew by her Mew sick;	1029	Dr. Helsham	5
CAT'S			
The cat's nine lives and eke the care.	761	Bec's B-Day	30
CATCH			
Stays but to catch his utmost breath,	24	Ode Athenian	274
And catch the living landscape thro' a scanty light,	35	Ode Sancroft	30
Spread all their Charms to catch a <Fart>;	66	Problem	36
A Lyrick Ode would Slate; a Catch	79	Vanbrug House	11
A Lyrick Ode would Slate; a Catch	106	V's House	11
Still brings us Hares when he can catch them:	281	Journal	74
For catch it nicely by the Head,	527	Lady's Dres Rm	67
To catch a Monkey by a Wile;	885	Rev Market-Hill	76
Then catch Admirers while you may;	932	Riddle 19	D 19
CATCHES			
In vain she catches at the empty Sound,	17	Ode Athenian	57
Tho' your lords, and your dogs, and your catches, me-thinks,	977	Dean to Sherid	45
CATCHING			
In public schemes, or catching flies,	901	Dean's Reasons	79
CATECHIS'D			
And catechis'd in ev'ry Street.	202	Horace 2, 6	92
CATERER			
Who's but my Caterer and Taster?	918	Riddle 4	18
CATH'RINES			
I thought the Lady at St. Cath'rines	1033	Ans to Crown	15

CATHARINE
    You would really on Thursday leave St Catharine   . .   1017 Swift Ans Sher   12
CATHEDRAL
    My foot was but just set out from my cathedral,   . . .   975 Dean to Sherid   3
CATHEDRALL
    Should lend your cathedrall to players and scrapers . .   522 St. Cecilia's   4
CATHERINE'S
    I wish Alexander safe at St. Catherine's To-night, . . 1014 Swift to Sheri   9

CATO
    Since Heaven and Cato both are pleas'd--   . . . .   42 Ode Sancroft   264
    In such a Cause would Cato bleed? . . . . . .   724 To Stella   41
CATS
    Which worship'd cats, and sacrific'd to apes; . . .   46 To Congreve   106
    Dead Cats and Turnip-Tops come tumbling down the Flood   139 City Shower   63
CATSUP
    Botargo, Catsup, and Caveer. . . . .   895 Panegyr Dean   268
CATTLE
    With other cattle to the city went; . . . .   46 To Congreve   116
    To think what cattle she has got among; . . . .   50 To Congreve   224
    Must let their Cattle range in vain . . . .   759 Receipt Youth   5
    A Long-ear'd Beast, and a Field-house for Cattle, .   942 Probatur Alit   1
CAUCASUS
    On Icy Caucasus to shiver, ...   346 Prometheus   55
CAUGHT
    And oft in contradiction's vortex caught,   . . .   36 Ode Sancroft   63
    The Crib was down, the Blackbird caught. . . , .   127 Little House   30
    He caught his Fish, and sav'd his Bait. . . .   154 Magician's Rod   48
    Much good may do 'em that have caught 'um. . .   158 Fable of Midas   80
    How Dan caught nothing in his Net, . . .   280 Journal   65
    Too cunning to be caught in Trapps. . . .   504 Doctor Delaney 126
    Then in a Net the Pheasant caught him, . . .   514 Answer Fable   49
    Her dearest Comrades never caught her . . .   584 Strephon Chloe   17
    For, if they keep not what they caught, . . .   591 Strephon Chloe 259
    He may be caught with sober Lies; . . . .   707 Cadenus Vaness 669
    And so obligingly am caught: . . . . . .   727 To Stella   114
    "He caught me one Morning coquetting his Wife, . .   873 Grand Question 167
    She shall be caught as in a Noose: . . . .   885 Rev Market-Hill 64
CAULDRON
    This Coyner of Raps in a Cauldron of Oyl. . .   352 Wood Insect   38
CAUSA
    Is, causa sine qua non. . . . .   406 Swift to Pope   20
CAUSE
    Without the Footing of a Cause; . . . . .   9 Ode to King   104
    Of which it is at once the Prophet and the Cause. . .   10 Ode to King   135
    And yet deny the Cause. . . . .   19 Ode Athenian   110
    Yet want your critics no just cause to rail, . .   45 To Congreve   65
    Thy looks, when every cause of grief is past! . .   52 Temple Ill   34
    Thou universal cause of all my woes; . . . .   53 Temple Ill   82
    But now, to solve the Nat'ral Cause . . . .   65 Problem   13
    The Philosophic Cause will shew. . . . .   126 Little House   4
    And Scholars give it for the Cause, ...   158 Fable of Midas   69
    To vamp the good Old Cause again, ...   180 Horace 2, 1   4
    "Without your Help the Cause is gone-- . . .   200 Horace 2, 6   52
    Could cause such wonderfull Effects. . . . .   227 Prog of Beauty 56
    While Partridge wisely shews the Cause . . .   228 Prog of Beauty 89
    But, let the Cause be what it will, ...   229 Prog of Beauty 97
    The Cause, alas, is quickly guesst, ...   293 Prog Marriage 101
    Who hate Your Person, and Your Cause, . . .   312 To Ford   30
    And, to defend the Whiggish Cause, ...   417 Woman's Mind   55
    But for a more substantial cause: . . . .   433 Answer Paulus   21
    To fight our cause before the judge: . . . .   435 Answer Paulus   88
    "Madam, you have no Cause to flounce, . . .   452 Modern Lady   262
    You've Cause to say he meant you well: . . .   475 Epist on Epist 25
    The point is plain: Remove the cause; . . .   487 Irish-Club   15
    Nor found it difficult to guess the Cause: . . .   536 To Mr. Gay   158
    "The Patrons of the good old Cause, ...   549 Life of Swift   162
    One quite indiff'rent in the Cause, ...   565 Death of Swift 305
    Or freely tell the secret Cause. . . . .   589 Strephon Chloe 162
    I here conjure thee, tell the Cause; . . . .   596 Cassinus Peter 92
    Ne'er kept a Cause, he well may boast, . . .   604 Beasts Confess 91
    Yet thou hast greater Cause to be . . . .   652 On Poetry   363
    (And why they were not, I can see no Cause;) . . .   662 Upon Ladies   6
    The Cause appear'd of so much Weight, . . .   688 Cadenus Vaness   75
    She'd hear the Cause another Day, ...   690 Cadenus Vaness 117
    For Sixteen Years the Cause was spun, . . .   690 Cadenus Vaness 124
    Wou'd shew the Merits of the Cause, ...   690 Cadenus Vaness 134
    Must yield her Foe the stronger Cause; . . .   695 Cadenus Vaness 265
    Cou'd better now the Cause decide. . . . .   713 Cadenus Vaness 837
    Decreed the Cause against the Men. . . . .   713 Cadenus Vaness 853
    In such a Cause would Cato bleed? . . . .   724 To Stella   41
    Or You without a Cause complain. . . . .   733 Verses Vanessa   16
    As when some Writer in a public Cause, . . .   770 Horace 1, 14   25
    How Solomon decides the Cause, ...   776 Mullinix Tim   98
    Then give those Rascals cause to laugh. . . .   778 Mullinix Tim   178
    "Ay,ay," quoth the Dean, "the cause is old gold." . .   843 Ay and No   4
    And make him soon give up the Cause. . . . .   861 Lady Acheson   40
    Good cause have I to sing and vapour, . . .   876 To Dean Swift   1
    Three Suff'rers in a ruin'd Cause. . . . .   883 Rev Market-Hill   6
    And seeks to learn the secret Cause, ...   923 Riddle 7   81

	PAGE	TITLE	LINE

CAUSELESS
    Causeless Joy, and true Despair; . . . .   832 Legion Club   90

CAUSES
    And all its secret Causes trace, ...   180 Horace 2, 1   16
    Which causes many Speculations. . . . .   283 Journal   130
    Nor let them taste what causes Wind; . . . .   587 Strephon Chloe   124
    Three weighty Causes were assign'd, ...   598 Problem Solved   23
    "No,no," quoth the Primate, "if causes we sift, ...   843 Ay and No   5
    I have a hundred causes ready: . . . .   899 Dean's Reasons   8

CAUTION
    But hid with Caution from the Wise. . . . .   60 Lady Tablebook   6
    With Caution us'd, may serve a-while. . . . .   647 On Poetry   238
    In a new World with Caution stept, ...   696 Cadenus Vaness   308
    And human Caution tries in vain . . . .   702 Cadenus Vaness   486
    With Caution drain it from the Lees) . . . .   743 Stel B-day 22   78

CAUTION'D
    You caution'd me against their Charms, ...   706 Cadenus Vaness   620

CAUTIOUS
    But wisely cautious of her Pence, ...   75 Game Traffick   15
    But Strephon cautious never meant . . . .   528 Lady's Dres Rm   92
    It so fell out, that cautious Harry . . . .   878 Robbin & Harry   17
    Be cautious, or your Bottle flies. . . . .   892 Panegyr Dean   184

CAVALCADE
    Nor its triumphal Cavalcade to grace . . . .   29 Ode to Temple   89

CAVALIERS
    And then the Jovial Cavaliers . . . .   926 Riddle 9   22

CAVAN
    I'll drive you to Cavan, from Cavan to Dundalk; . .   1019 To Sheridan   7
    I'll drive you to Cavan, from Cavan to Dundalk; . .   1019 To Sheridan   7
    You never have an old friend at Cavan. . . . . .   1038 Sheridan Cavan   18

CAVAN-STREET
    At Night between Cavan-street and College-Green: . .   264 Apollo   54

CAVE
    Here by a mountain's side, a reverend cave . . . . .   49 To Congreve   187
    This Cave within its Womb confines . . . .   921 Riddle 7   11

CAVE'S
    Why at this Cave's tremendous Mouth, ...   923 Riddle 7   83

CAVEER
    Botargo, Catsup, and Caveer. . . . .   895 Panegyr Dean   268

CAVERNS
    Whether the Winds in Caverns pent . . . .   923 Riddle 7   85

CAVES
    Of cradles and caves; . . . .   856 Lady's Lament   176

CAVILS
    And with cavils combats reason: . . . .   906 Daphne   12

CEADE
    Och ma ceade millia mollighart, on the feeders of swine!   841 Ballad   D 19

CEAS'D
    The Gyants under Aetna ceas'd to groan, ...   9 Ode to King   96
    Nor ceas'd the Faction to pursue, ...   494 Panegyr Swift   43

CEAS'T
    The Butter comes; our Fears are ceas't; . . . . .   892 Panegyr Dean   185

CEASE
    To shew the Flood begins to cease, ...   16 Ode Athenian   20
    Should come and make the Clatt'ring cease; . . . . .   189 Faggot   24
    For nothing else will make it cease,-- . . . . . .   220 A Quiet Life   13
    Your Offers of Bribery cease; . . . .   396 Dog and Thief   14
    Would Men of Genius cease to write, ...   502 Doctor Delaney   71
    Cease haughty Nymph; the Fates decree . . . . . .   905 Death Daphne   91

CEASED
    Their Virtues never ceased to sing, ...   445 Modern Lady   11
    His panegyrics then are ceased, ...   658 On Poetry   D 204

CEASELESS
    Weary the Gods with ceaseless Prayer, ...   388 Manly Virtue   139

CEASING
    My income ceasing. . . . .   1037 Sheridan Cavan   6

CEDAR
    On Box of Cedar sits the Wife, ...   590 Strephon Chloe   207

CEDAR-BOX
    Her Silver Vase in Cedar-Box. . . . .   896 Panegyr Dean   298

CEELING
    Would lift her Eyes up to the Ceeling, ...   222 Prog of Love   16

CEILING   SEE CIELING
    The Ceiling hardly six Foot high; . . . .   751 Stel Wood-Park   54

CELEBRATE
    They celebrate her Beauty's Praise, ...   697 Cadenus Vaness   331
    To celebrate some Suburb Trull; . . . .   730 Stella, Poems   72
    To celebrate your Birth in Prose; . . . .   756 Stel B-day '24   6
    You celebrate their Wit and Parts! . . . .   887 Panegyr Dean   12

CELESTIAL   SEE COELESTIAL
    He in the old Celestial Cant, ...   120 Apollo Outwit   17
    On Sight of this Celestial Prude, ...   121 Apollo Outwit   41
    For Pallas, with celestial light, ...   178 To Lord Harley   49
    Along the high celestial Road; . . . .   231 Prog of Poetry   28
    (Rais'd high like some celestial Fire . . . . . .   385 Manly Virtue   53
    Fair Decency, celestial Maid, ...   590 Strephon Chloe   219
    A Fire celestial, chaste, refin'd, ...   687 Cadenus Vaness   29
    Can in Celestial Language scold) . . . .   695 Cadenus Vaness   287

CELIA
    If Celia should appear too soon . . . .   226 Prog of Beauty   11
    So Celia went entire to bed, ...   226 Prog of Beauty   29

CELIA   (CONTINUED)   PAGE   TITLE   LINE
    But Celia can with ease reduce   . . . .   227 Prog of Beauty   45
    So rotting Celia stroles the Street   . . . .   229 Prog of Beauty   103
    Poor Celia, but of mortall Race   . . . .   229 Prog of Beauty   106
    By haughty Celia spent in Dressing;   . . . .   525 Lady's Dres Rm   2
    In calling Celia sweet and cleanly.   . . . .   526 Lady's Dres Rm   18
    Which Celia slept at least a Week in? . . . . 527 Lady's Dres Rm   54
    Oh! Celia, Celia, Celia shits!   . . . .   529 Lady's Dres Rm   118
    Oh! Celia, Celia, Celia shits!   . . . .   529 Lady's Dres Rm   118
    Oh! Celia, Celia, Celia shits!   . . . .   529 Lady's Dres Rm   118
    When Celia in her Glory shows, ...   530 Lady's Dres Rm   135
    Tis sung; wherever Celia treeds, ... 621 Scandal Poem 1   139
    'Tis sung, where-ever Celia treads, ...   627 Scandal Poem 2   143
    See, see, Celia, Celia Dies, ...   960 Cantata
    See, see, Celia, Celia Dies, ...   960 Cantata
CELIA'S
    Celia's the Wonder of her Sex;   . . . . 227 Prog of Beauty   54
    Of Celia's magnifying Glass.   . . . .   527 Lady's Dres Rm   60
    The smallest Worm in Celia's Nose, ... 527 Lady's Dres Rm   64
    Be once in Celia's Chamber seen!   . . . . 528 Lady's Dres Rm   96
    And oft in Celia's Tresses play.   . . . .   919 Riddle 5   12
CELL
    Far in this primitive cell might we pursue   . . . . . 49 To Congreve   195
    The muse retreats far in yon chrystal cell; . . . . . 50 To Congreve   228
    At least confine the tyrant to his cell.   . . . . . . 53 Temple Ill   56
    Consumes it self to weave a Cell.   . . . .   79 Vanbrug House   32
    Steals from her Private Cell by Night, ...   99 Elegy Patrige   51
    Creep in the Dark from Leathern Cell, ...   99 Elegy Patrige   54
    He hides within his darkest Cell.   . . . .   240 Run Bankers   44
    Retreating silent to his Cell;   . . . .   375 Apology Lady C   14
    Fix'd in a lonely, learned Cell, ...   385 Manly Virtue   48
    He drew dumb Merit from her Cell, ... 386 Manly Virtue   84
    Each within his proper Cell;   . . . .   830 Legion Club   44
    Confin'd Thee Goddess to a Cell: . . . . 895 Panegyr Dean   270
    Like a Monk in a cell.   . . . .   939 Riddle Answerd   D
CELLAR
    A Cellar next was dug below: . . . . 108 V's House   86
    To some snug Cellar let's repair   . . . . 184 Horace 2, 1   109
    Or Cellar, where they starve to Day. . . . .   505 Doctor Delaney   150
    No Cellar where on Tick to sup;   . . . . 581 Young Nymph   6
    In Saunder's Cellar on the Ground.   . . . . 743 Stel B-day 22   56
    The Cellar could contain but four)   . . . .   747 Stel Distress   50
    Now you write from your cellar,--I find out your art, . 979 Dean to Tho: S   19
    For she never descends so low as the cellar; . . .   979 Dean to Tho: S   26
    If once in your cellar my Phoebus should shine, . . . 979 Dean to Tho: S   29
CELLS
    The Saints would often leave their Cells   . . . . .   90 Bauc & Phil 1   2
    The Saints would often leave their Cells.   . . . . . 111 Bauc & Phil 2   2
    From Courts inclusive, down to Cells, ...   691 Cadenus Vaness   149
    In sep'rate Cells the He's and She's   . . . . 893 Panegyr Dean   207
    But, in their Cells and Vaults obscene   . . . . . . 895 Panegyr Dean   283
CEMENTED
    By Decency cemented round;   . . . . 593 Strephon Chloe   308
CEMENTS
    Love with White lead cements his Wings, ...   227 Prog of Beauty   61
CENS'RERS
    I'm too profuse some Cens'rers cry, ...   918 Riddle 4   25
CENS'RING
    Much of the cens'ring World complain'd, ...   603 Beasts Confess   49
CENSORIOUS
    Cries, "Lord, the World is so censorious!   . . . . . 450 Modern Lady   167
    Censorious People do in spight.   . . . .   942 Probatur Alit   18
CENSUR'D
    Is rightly censur'd by the Stagirite, ...   988 Letter Dr Sh-n   19
CENSURE
    To censure, to cry down, and rail, ...   19 Ode Athenian   114
    Censure, and Pedantry, and Pride, ...   25 Ode Athenian   296
    Thus censure seems that fiery froth which breeds . . . 45 To Congreve   69
    Tobacco, Censure, Coffee, Pride, and Port.   . . . . 194 Author Himself   22
    To censure Phillis for Perfumes;   . . . . 449 Modern Lady   159
    Thus, Fame and Censure with a Tether   . . . . . .   501 Doctor Delaney   35
    By censure frighted out of honour's road, ... 506 To a Friend   9
    Then spoke with Censure, or Applause, ...   697 Cadenus Vaness   352
    And, how would Censure glut her Spight?   . . . . .   726 To Stella   94
CENSURE'S
    But Censure's to be understood   . . . .   18 Ode Athenian   91
CENSURES
    Censures less, or less defames?   . . . . 631 Epistle Lady   68
    And gave, by turns, their Censures Vent.   . . . . . 699 Cadenus Vaness   409
CENSURING
    Of ev'ry censuring Privateer, ...   19 Ode Athenian   100
    Let Censuring Criticks then think what they list on't, 77 Lady B- B-   REF
CENT
    By Pensions, Bribes, and three per Cent?   . . . . . 157 Fable of Midas   46
    Yet our Stocks rise Cent. per Cent, ...   169 Peace Dunkirk   26
    Yet our Stocks rise Cent. per Cent, ...   169 Peace Dunkirk   26
    That a Pack of sly Knaves should get fifty per Cent, . 288 Bank Down   52
    To take, for Interest Cent. per Cent.   . . . . . .   446 Modern Lady   61
    To take, for Interest Cent. per Cent.   . . . . . .   446 Modern Lady   61
CENTAURS
    This Cloud produc'd a race of Centaurs   . . . . . . 619 Scandal Poem 1   59

	PAGE	TITLE	LINE
CENTAURS (CONTINUED)			
His Cloud produc'd a Race of Centaurs,	625	Scandal Poem 2	55
CENTER			
In her you'll center all your Joys,	362	Grace's Answer	47
In my Head and Heart they center;	630	Epistle Lady	33
So deeply Carthy to the Center tends.	669	Epig Carthy 14 D	2
. . . and the soft soul of amorous Jemmy center.	1023	Nim-Dan-Dean 2 D	14
George, Dan, Dean, and Nim to place in the center?	1027	Sheri Circles	14
CENTER'D			
In him is center'd and confin'd.	709	Cadenus Vaness	711
CENTRE			
That creeps as far to reach the Centre;	393	Modern Poets	8
Linkt perpendicular to the Centre:	654	On Poetry	402
CENTRY			
"From the first fierce cockaded Centry,	380	Apology Lady C	153
At North and South are posted Centry;	883	Rev Market-Hill	18
CENTURY			
But these are lost full many a Century.	988	Letter Dr Sh-n	14
CERBERIAN			
The loud Cerberian tripple Bark.	596	Cassinus Peter	80
CERBERUS			
And, Cerberus hath ready in his Paws,	285	Elegy Boat	27
There Cerberus lay watching in his Den,	538	Mr. Pulteney	25
To Cerberus they give a Sop,	647	On Poetry	213
CERTAIN			
About a certain Magick Rod,	132	Magician's Rod	22
To think upon a certain Leader,	157	Fable of Midas	42
Now Finch alarms the Lords; he hears for certain,	194	Author Himself	37
"A certain Doctor is observ'd of late,	195	Author Himself	43
"To haunt a certain Minister of State:	195	Author Himself	44
"You may for certain, if you please;	201	Horace 2, 6	60
With a certain false Traitress, one Stella by Name,	263	Apollo	30
Then and there, Vi & Armis, with a certain Utensil,	264	Apollo	33
A certain Goddess, God knows who,	587	Strephon Chloe	100
Her Fondness for a certain Earl	699	Cadenus Vaness	390
So Stars beyond a certain Height	700	Cadenus Vaness	442
Shou'd fix upon some certain Rule,	707	Cadenus Vaness	665
The Wrong is certain you were both in,	774	Mullinix Tim	37
CERTAINLY			
And by the Description I certainly know,	264	Apollo	43
If I light on a Thought, he will certainly steal it,	265	Apollo	59
Why certainly the Captain rav'd?	376	Apology Lady C	36
Most certainly there's the Hell to be found,	575	Place Damn'd	6
You certainly know, tho' so loudly you vapour,	818	Archbi Cashel	5
"Thou hast certainly gotten a Cup in thy Pate.	870	Grand Question	84
So I'll leave him behind, for I certainly know it,	979	Dean to Tho: S	31
CERULEAN			
He fixt the Star and String Cerulean.	656	On Poetry	464
CHACE			
Durst thou, ungrateful, from the <Senate> chace	826	Noisy Tom	15
CHAFF			
Chaff, straws, or fragments of some rotten boat,	672	Epig Carthy 24 D	14
Nothing but Chaff, and Straws, and Feathers;	688	Cadenus Vaness	56
Fools, Fops, and Rakes, for Chaff and Straws.	688	Cadenus Vaness	60
CHAIN			
Whether in time, deduction's broken chain	51	Temple Ill	3
Madly aspir'd to wear her chain:	177	To Lord Harley	42
There is a Chain let down from Jove,	345	Prometheus	31
This Chain, as Antient Poets hold,	345	Prometheus	35
Prometheus once this Chain purloin'd,	345	Prometheus	37
Then whips me on a Chain of Brass,	345	Prometheus	39
Now while this Brazen Chain prevail'd,	345	Prometheus	41
The World in any Chain but Gold;	346	Prometheus	50
Ty'd with the Chain himself had made;	346	Prometheus	54
He strove to steal that Chain of Gold,	346	Prometheus	64
Altho' the Chain will never crack,	346	Prometheus	69
This Brazen Chain into a Rope;	347	Prometheus	72
With Pride wou'd drag about her Chain;	693	Cadenus Vaness	233
To break that Adamantine Chain.	702	Cadenus Vaness	487
CHAINS			
These are the slaves whom reputation chains,	48	To Congreve	163
Which drags the slavish World in Chains.	243	Horace 4, 9	14
He comes to tye our Chains on faster,	484	Libel on D- D-	125
The chains which fetter free-born minds,	490	Dialogue	32
Arm'd in adamantine Chains,	661	Love Song	18
Omens, the Types of thy impending Chains.	792	St. Pat's Well	44
Like Montezume in golden Chains:	885	Rev Market-Hill	72
In Chains, thy Syllables are link'd.	1021	Nim-Dan-Dean 1 D	28
CHAIR SEE ELBOW-CHAIR			
And wedg'd in Corner of a Chair	75	Game Traffick	11
The groaning Chair began to crawll	93	Bauc & Phil 1	105
The Groaning Chair began to crawl	113	Bauc & Phil 2	85
Box'd in a Chair the Beau impatient sits,	139	City Shower	43
Then order Squash to call a Hackney Chair.	166	Toland's Invit	46
And <Harley> fill'd the Commons Chair)	180	Horace 2, 1	10
Keep up the Glasses of your Chair,	228	Prog of Beauty	74
To drive unseen her magick Chair,	354	Simile Silver	3
If he, who in the Chair presides,	391	Young's Satire	5
And doting in an easy chair;	401	Window Inns 5 D	4
"This odious Chair how came I stuck in't,	452	Modern Lady	240
Her Chair to call the King of Clubs,	452	Modern Lady	259

CHAIR   (CONTINUED)   PAGE   TITLE   LINE
    A Shilling to discharge his Chair, ...   481 Libel on D- D-   42
    Then, seated on a three-legg'd Chair, ...   581 Young Nymph   9
    She must have doves to draw her chair: . ·. . . .   621 Scandal Poem 1   116
    She must have Doves to draw her Chair.   . . . . . .   627 Scandal Poem 2   114
    Yet lik'd three Footmen to her Chair.   . . . . . .   693 Cadenus Vaness   221
    But rising from her Chair of State, ...   714 Cadenus Vaness   887
    To sossing in an elbow chair: . . . .   744 Stel Distress   6
    To sossing in an easy Chair;   . . . .   750 Stel Wood-Park   30
    She does not overset the chair;   . . . .   762 Bec's B-Day   42
    But, seated in an easy chair, ...   901 Dean's Reasons   89
CHAIR-MEN
    So when Troy Chair-men bore the Wooden Steed,   . . .   139 City Shower   47
    Instead of paying Chair-men, run them thro'.)   . . .   139 City Shower   50
    The Chair-Men are not to be found, ...   453 Modern Lady   284
CHAIRMAN
    Bless mine Eyes! Art thou the Chairman?   . . . . .   837 Legion Club   190
    Chairman to yon damn'd Committee!   . . . .   838 Legion Club   191
CHAIRMEN
    That no two Chairmen could be found   . . . .   87 Hist V's House   29
    Her Chairmen push him from the Wall: . . . . . .   292 Prog Marriage   86
CHAIRS
    Their Clamour 'lighting from their Chairs, ...   698 Cadenus Vaness   368
    And half the Chairs with broken backs.   . . . . . .   746 Stel Distress   38
    And half the Chairs with broken Backs: . . . . . .   751 Stel Wood-Park   56
    Stools, Tables, Chairs, and Bed-steds broke: . . .   1035 To Quilca   11
CHAISE
    Take Journies in it like a Chaise;   . . . . . .   109 V's House   112
    And that he may command the Chaise.   . . . .   860 Lady Acheson   20
CHALLENGE
    That he sent to all three a Challenge next morning.   . . 327 Epigram 1   8
    Who better challenge your Allegiance, ...   626 Scandal Poem 2   95
CHAMBER   SEE ANTI-CHAMBER
    That I went to warm my self in Lady Betty's Chamber,.   69 Mrs Harris Pet   1
    . .
    Nay, said I, I had it in Lady Betty's Chamber,. . .   70 Mrs Harris Pet   17
    Because he's always in my Chamber,. . . . .   72 Mrs Harris Pet   51
    And one small Chamber on a Floor.   . . . .   81 Vanbrug House   78
    The weary Dean goes to his Chamber, ...   280 Journal   57
    Burst into her Chamber, and wou'd have Carest her,   . . 517 Dean Hang Rape   9
    The Goddess from her Chamber issues, ...   525 Lady's Dres Rm   3
    Be once in Celia's Chamber seen!   . . . .   528 Lady's Dres Rm   96
CHAMBER-DAMSELS
    From you my Chamber-Damsels learn   . . . .   890 Panegyr Dean   111
CHAMBER-MAID
    That Moll the Chamber-maid can smoak, ...   890 Panegyr Dean   127
CHAMBERMAIDS
    And Chambermaids christen this Worm a Death-Watch: .   351 Wood Insect   20
CHAMBERS
    And if they find the Chambers neat, ...   734 Stel B-day '20   3
    And in the Chambers of your Viceroy crawls.   . . . .   792 St. Pat's Well   58
CHAMPAGNE
    Bravely despise Champagne at Court, ...   488 Irish-Club   19
CHAMPAIN
    And bid adieu to dear Champain: . . . .   311 To Ford   26
CHAMPION
    For Liberty no Champion bolder, ...   455 Dean Smedley   9
    Thou Champion for the Common-weal: . . . . . .   515 Answer Fable   88
    A Champion kill'd, or Trophy won;   . . . . . .   554 Death of Swift   24
    For Liberty a Champion stout, ...   820 Dr. Rundle   31
CHAMPIONS
    Platonick Champions, gain'd without one Female Wile,   .   24 Ode Athenian   252
    Nine more such Champions as the <Dean>, ...   887 Panegyr Dean   9
CHANC'D
    Whene'er he chanc'd his Hands to lay, ...   156 Fable of Midas   15
    Because it chanc'd, an old grave Don   . . . . . .   495 Panegyr Swift   84
    At an old stubborn Root I chanc'd to tug, ...   881 Pastoral Dial   25
CHANC'T
    He chanc't to spy a Clergy Lark;   . . . .   513 Answer Fable   46
CHANCE
    And thought too great ev'n for effects of Chance,   . .   8 Ode to King   63
    Has finish'd its short Race of Chance, ...   10 Ode to King   137
    Part of Your Merit Chance wou'd call her own, ...   11 Ode to William   D 11
    The Juggling Sea-god when by chance trepann'd   . . .   22 Ode Athenian   189
    They went by chance, amidst their Talk, ...   116 Bauc & Phil 2   153
    Where if the Dean by chance appears   . . . . . .   294 Prog Marriage   139
    But if by Chance I should deny it   . . . . . .   372 Letter D. S-y   19
    If chance a Mouse creeps in her Sight, ...   416 Woman's Mind   33
    And if you chance to come too late   . . . .   468 Birthday Song   257
    In either Case, an equal Chance is run: . . . . . .   535 To Mr. Gay   125
    But, if I chance to make a slip, ...   548 Life of Swift   119
    Or if she chance to close her Eyes, ...   582 Young Nymph   40
    From Chance, or natural Defect   . . . .   603 Beasts Confess   66
    Yet, merry Folks who want by chance   . . . . . .   756 Stel B-day '24   7
    In Lucass's by chance there lay   . . . .   782 Tim and Fables   3
    May'st dye like me by Chance; but not by Nature.   .   861 On Old Glass   2
    For, when by chance the meagre Shade   . . . . . .   905 Death Daphne   93
    For my part, it was by meer Chance . . . .   1013 Swift to Sheri   3
CHANCERY
    In a Chancery Bill your Attorney engages, ...   288 Bank Down   46

	PAGE	TITLE	LINE

CHANG'D
The Mortar onely chang'd it's Name,	93	Bauc & Phil 1	111
To a less noble Substance chang'd	93	Bauc & Phil 1	115
Chang'd in the Preface and the Text,	95	Bauc & Phil 1	178
He wisely chang'd their Element:	106	V's House	22
To a less Noble Substance chang'd,	114	Bauc & Phil 2	91
Though still in Sight, had chang'd their Ground.	226	Prog of Beauty	32
Chang'd for the worse in ev'ry Part,	410	Dial Rich Marb	71
But Things are strangely chang'd since then,	498	Panegyr Swift	163
And gracefully her Subject chang'd:	698	Cadenus Vaness	355

CHANGE
What mortal change does in thy face appear,	52	Temple Ill	31
By Change of Wind to Leeward Side	96	On the Union	19
And with small Change, a Pulpit grew.	114	Bauc & Phil 2	88
Thus, happy in their Change of Life,	116	Bauc & Phil 2	149
Who change Opinions with the changing Scene:	196	Author Himself	65
"Good Mr. Dean go change your Gown,	200	Horace 2, 6	23
If he shou'd now be cry'd down since his Change	235	Elegy on Demar	36
How prone to change in human life,	283	Journal	117
To mournful Ditties, Clio, change thy Note,	284	Elegy Boat	1
Till you began to change the Breed;	301	Horrid Plot	75
To change your Visage like the Moon,	326	Pethox	82
And change it for a Brazen String.	346	Prometheus	66
Now change the Scene; a nobler Care	387	Manly Virtue	111
You change a Circle to a Square,	477	Epist on Epist	73
That you Quadrata change Rotundis?	477	Epist on Epist	76
Or change his Comrades once a Quarter:	556	Death of Swift	96
How great a Change! how quickly made!	590	Strephon Chloe	203
Could change the Stock, or cog a Dye,	607	Beasts Confess	193
Change ev'ry feature ev'ry second.	618	Scandal Poem 1	46
Change ev'ry Feature, ev'ry Second.	625	Scandal Poem 2	42
Wou'd you have me change my Stile,	637	Epistle Lady	233
Change but their Names will do again.	647	On Poetry	232
But now a sudden Change was wrought,	704	Cadenus Vaness	560
Yet guess'd not whence could spring the Change.	704	Cadenus Vaness	567
If both shou'd now their Stations change.	712	Cadenus Vaness	805
Nor, change thy Course with ev'ry sudden Gust:	771	Horace 1, 14	54
Content, my good <Lords>; but let us change Hands;	805	Irish Bishops	61
And, as your old wont is, change sides in a trice:	818	Archbi Cashel	8
Nor can she change her Form so fast,	911	Aenigma	5
And change like the Cameleon.	935	Riddle 23	D 13
Could you but change a Crown as easy	1033	Ans to Crown	13

CHANGE-ALLEY
| The Stock-jobber thus, from Change-Alley goes down, | 396 | Dog and Thief | 9 |

CHANGE-ALLY
| Change-Ally is the dreadfull Name; | 256 | Bubble | 140 |

CHANGES
And changes all to Beauty, and the Praise	23	Ode Athenian	236
Dread from his Hand impending Changes.	655	On Poetry	422
The Changes which Faction has made in the State,	716	Answer Rebus	23
The fatal Changes Time hath made in thee.	792	St. Pat's Well	34

CHANGING
Who change Opinions with the changing Scene:	196	Author Himself	65
Changing still, and still adhering,	799	Traulus 2	10
Now, changing the scene,	854	Lady's Lament	87

CHANNEL
| Nor cross the Channel twice a Year, | 199 | Horace 2, 6 | 11 |

CHANNELL
| You bury, on our Side the Channell | 315 | To Ford | 101 |

CHANT
| Their Mattins chant in ev'ry Bush: | 594 | Cassinus Peter | 32 |
| (If all be true that Poets chant) | 849 | Old Thorn | 46 |

CHANTICLEER
| Nor Chanticleer upon the Beam, | 153 | Widow and Cat | D 13 |

CHAOS
In Chaos, kindled into Life;	324	Pethox	30
Earth must have been in Chaos swallow'd.	346	Prometheus	46
In Chaos made not such a Clatter:	450	Modern Lady	185

CHAPLAIN
. . .the Chaplain will be here anon.	72	Mrs Harris Pet	49
So the Chaplain came in; now the Servants say,. . .	72	Mrs Harris Pet	50
Oh but, said I, what if after all my Chaplain won't come to?	73	Mrs Harris Pet	68
With an Order for the Chaplain aforesaid;. .	73	Mrs Harris Pet	73
Or the Chaplain, (for 'tis his Trade). . .	73	Mrs Harris Pet	75
Looks like the Chaplain of the Household,	291	Prog Marriage	62
The Chaplain vows, he cannot fawn,	604	Beasts Confess	103

CHAPLAIN'S
| Beholds her from the Chaplain's Place | 291 | Prog Marriage | 63 |

CHAPLAINS
| Will tell him that Chaplains should not be so pert; | 868 | Grand Question | 36 |

CHAPLET
| And made an Humble Chaplet for the King. | 16 | Ode Athenian | 31 |

CHAPLETS
| With thy flow'ry Chaplets crown'd. | 661 | Love Song | 28 |

CHAPOON
| What's meant by Chapoon I can't guess | 373 | Letter D. S-y | 57 |

CHAPPEL
| Yet still St. Stephen's Chappel open lies | 538 | Mr. Pulteney | 7 |

CHAPS
| Spits in his mouth and stroaks his Chaps | 421 | Ireld | 14 |

```
CHAPS          (CONTINUED)                                   PAGE   TITLE            LINE
   At People's Heels with frothy Chaps;        . . . . . .   797 Traulus 1           36
   He might have found a Score of Chaps,       . . . . . .   821 Dr. Rundle          50
   With watry Chaps, and wagging Chin,         . . . . . .   895 Panegyr Dean       257
CHAPTER-TREATS
   First-Fruits and Tenths, and Chapter-Treats,     . . .   174 Horace 1, 7        103
CHARACTER
   This character shall Ca'ndish claim,        . . . . . .   177 To Lord Harley      37
   For, it would his Character Expose                        294 Prog Marriage      143
   Will he his Character belye?        . . . . . . . .        445 Modern Lady         14
   My Character impartial draws:       . . . . . . . .        565 Death of Swift     306
   A Character to praise and blame,    . . . . . . . .        608 Know Not What        4
CHARACTERS
   And Characters to Dedications:      . . . . . . . . .      484 Libel on D- D-     138
   The Characters of ev'ry Brute:                            512 Answer Fable         4
CHARG'D
   And, whisp'ring, charg'd me not to say      . . . . . .   311 To Ford              3
   The Brief with weighty Crimes was charg'd,  . . . . . .   686 Cadenus Vaness       5
CHARGE    SEE SCANDAL-CHARGE
   He Din'd and Sup'd at Charge of other Folk,               234 Elegy on Demar      10
   The Ducal Coffers, trusted to your Charge,  . . . . .     533 To Mr. Gay          45
   Next, hearken Gay, to what thy Charge requires,   . . .   533 To Mr. Gay          53
   Nor, in a Palace built with Charge immense,       . . .   533 To Mr. Gay          63
   "But who cou'd charge him, to his face,     . . . . . .   549 Life of Swift      144
   And may now perform your Charge.    . . . . . . . .        631 Epistle Lady        44
   I grow less equall to the Charge;                         739 Stel B-day '21       8
   For your Life, not a Word of the Matter, I charge ye:     873 Grand Question     109
   They dare not charge me to my Face:      . . . . . . .     918 Riddle 4            30
   You save the Charge of Lime and Trowels.    . . . . .    1021 Nim-Dan-Dean 1   D  24
CHARGE'S
   Descending to her Charge's aid,     . . . . . . . . .      177 To Lord Harley      44
CHARGES
   Or the vast Charges of a Smile;     . . . . . . . . .       24 Ode Athenian       253
   She'll pay the Charges to a Farthing:       . . . . . .    417 Woman's Mind        60
CHARING-CROSS
   At Charing-Cross, among the Rout,   . . . . . . . .        172 Horace 1, 7         59
   Might be proclaim'd at Charing-Cross.       . . . . . .    201 Horace 2, 6         80
CHARIOT
   Then Madam bid the Chariot stand,   . . . . . . . .        128 Little House        50
   Down from her silver chariot came,  . . . . . . . . .      178 To Lord Harley      75
   As I rode in my Chariot, a Thought to my Mind;            265 Apollo              76
   With chariot less for use than state;       . . . . . .    676 Parson's Case       24
   There's neither Chariot, Coach, or Mill,    . . . . .      929 Riddle 14        D   7
CHARIOT-SIDE
   Came sneaking to the Chariot-side,  . . . . . . . .        172 Horace 1, 7         64
CHARIOT'S
   "Whose Chariot's that we left behind?       . . . . . .    201 Horace 2, 6         70
CHARIOTS
   Come headlong tumbling from their mitred Chariots,   . .   806 Judas               20
CHARITY
   When Charity begins to tread the Stage:     . . . . .      274 Epilogue             2
   But whence this Wonderous Charity, in Play'rs,   . . .    275 Epilogue            11
   His Enemies, for want of Charity,   . . . . . . . .        606 Beasts Confess     159
   By Charity a mean Support,   . . . . . . . . . . .         667 Epig Carthy 6    D   2
CHARLES
   The dearest in Charles Mather's Shop,       . . . . . .    135 Magician's Rod      76
   He'll teaze you with King Charles and Bishop Laud,   .    166 Toland's Invit      42
   But by his Name-sake Charles of Sweden.          .        398 Earl of P-b-w       36
   "And well remembers Charles the Second.          .        556 Death of Swift     108
   But then, I'm sure, friend Charles, you want the spur.    671 Epig Carthy 23   D   2
CHARLEY
   How she cur'd Charley of the Chincough;     . . . . . .    282 Journal             92
CHARLOTTE
   Whilst Lady Charlotte, like a Stroller,     . . . . .      410 Dial Rich Marb      61
CHARLY
   For less than Charly Grattan's School:      . . . . .      478 Epist on Epist     111
CHARM    SEE COUNTER-CHARM
   But she the Charm already try'd,    . . . . . . . . .      120 Apollo Outwit       38
   She wonders where the Charm appears . . . . . . . .        725 To Stella           69
   It of every Charm.   . . . . . . . . . . . . . .           939 Riddle Answerd      32
   Or, how a Herring hath a Charm      . . . . . . . . .      949 Epigr Fasting        3
CHARM'D
   Our Prince has charm'd its many hundred Eyes;    . . .       8 Ode to King         78
   Pil'd in a Garret charm'd the Author's Sight.    . . .    667 Epig Carthy 5    D   2
   Charm'd by thy voice the 'Prentice drops    . . . . .      779 Mullinix Tim       203
   Charm'd with his Eyes and Chin and Snout,   . . . . .      904 Death Daphne        63
CHARMER
   Then, for a middle-aged Charmer,    . . . . . . . .        313 To Ford             69
   He, that of ev'ry ear's the charmer,        . . . . .      876 To Dean Swift        3
CHARMING
   Charming her greedy Ears   . . . . . . . . . . .            17 Ode Athenian        53
   Here you may read (Dear Charming Saint)     . . . . .       60 Lady Tablebook       7
   Nor Cindercola, charming Wench!     . . . . . . . . .      373 Letter D. S-y       65
   That could refuse this charming Ganymede,   . . . . .      466 Birthday Song      190
   The charming Couple now unites;     . . . . . . . . .      585 Strephon Chloe      45
   How that ungrateful charming Maid,  . . . . . . . .        595 Cassinus Peter      57
   The charming Silvia beating Flax,   . . . . . . . . .      729 Stella, Poems       45
   And from the Shelf a charming Crust I whipt:     . . .     881 Pastoral Dial       30
   Such charming Butter never Man made.        . . . . .      892 Panegyr Dean       168
   Of roast or boil'd, to the Hungry is charming.   . . .     941 Letter              30
   Charming Oysters I cry,      . . . . . . . . . . .         952 Oysters              1
```

		PAGE	TITLE	LINE
CHARMING (CONTINUED)				
And charming when squeez'd in a Pot of brown Ale. . . .		953	Oranges	2
CHARMS				
Whom all the Charms of an Usurped Wife and State,	.	20	Ode Athenian	154
How soon have You restor'd her Charms!		23	Ode Athenian	228
Spread all their Charms to catch a <Fart>;		66	Problem	36
For Charms above and under Ground;		133	Magician's Rod	36
Antaeus could by Magick Charms		257	Bubble	181
Will then lose their charms		424	Carterets Arms	8
Tries twenty Charms to mend her Luck.		452	Modern Lady	237
A squinting Monkey load with charms;		464	Birthday Song	121
Or, shall the charms of wealth and power		490	Dialogue	45
How thy Face charms ev'ry Shepherd, ...		522	Betty Grizette	3
To all the Charms of Female Kind;		530	Lady's Dres Rm	130
And, spight of Chloe's charms divine, ...		591	Strephon Chloe	249
So blush'd Aurora with coelestial Charms, ...		669	Epig Carthy 13	D 1
Imaginary Charms can find, ...		703	Cadenus Vaness	526
You caution'd me against their Charms, ...		706	Cadenus Vaness	620
'bout latent Charms beneath my Cloaths;		1004	Dan J's Reply	22
CHARNEL-HOUSE				
Sad Charnel-house! a dismal Dome, ...		922	Riddle 7	51
CHARON				
Charon in him will ferry Souls to Hell;		285	Elegy Boat	25
Lo, Charon from his leaky Wherry, ...		596	Cassinus Peter	83
CHARON'S				
There to supply old Charon's leaky Wherry:		285	Elegy Boat	24
And as they sail in Charon's Boat, ...		647	On Poetry	211
CHARTRES				
Now, Chartres at Sir Robert's Levee, ...		560	Death of Swift	189
"So often seen caressing Chartres:		565	Death of Swift	324
CHASE SEE CHIVY-CHASE				
CHASM				
And left a Chasm profound as Hell:		326	Pethox	96
Beneath, a Chasm as deep as Hell, ...		413	Desire Possess	43
And least a Chasm should intervene, ...		653	On Poetry	373
CHASTE				
Pallas, a Goddess chaste and wise, ...		302	Storm	1
How could a Nymph so chaste as Chloe, ...		588	Strephon Chloe	151
A Fire celestial, chaste, refin'd, ...		687	Cadenus Vaness	29
Dear Baldwin chaste, and witty Crosse, ...		821	Dr. Rundle	61
The chaste Diana's infant Face;		919	Riddle 5	8
CHASTER				
And chaster than the Queen of Night, ...		179	To Lord Harley	78
CHASTEST				
Diana thus, Heav'n's chastest queen, ...		178	To Lord Harley	73
CHASTISES				
When Margery chastises Ned		328	Epigram 2	1
CHASTITY				
Of Chastity, as Monks do now;		603	Beasts Confess	70
CHAT				
He deals, and Hears mysterious Chat;		63	Discovery	14
Which has afforded thee much Chat, ...		181	Horace 2, 1	24
Would take me in his Coach to chat, ...		201	Horace 2, 6	67
We sit an hour to drink and chat.		280	Journal	54
Fresh Matter for a World of Chat, ...		447	Modern Lady	82
I grow the Subject of their Chat:		565	Death of Swift	302
To chat a while, and warm his Nose:		594	Cassinus Peter	8
Scarce list'ning to their idle Chat;		697	Cadenus Vaness	335
And fell into their usual Chat, ...		698	Cadenus Vaness	375
CHATRES				
Ah! dost thou not Envy the brave Colonel Chatres, . .		519	Dean Hang Rape	49
To Chatres, Walpole, or a King, ...		622	Scandal Poem 1	165
CHATT'RING				
Sham'd and amaz'd, beholds the chatt'ring throng, . .		50	To Congreve	223
Nor to the chatt'ring feather'd Race, ...		597	Cassinus Peter	111
Spy the strutting chatt'ring Vermin?		634	Epistle Lady	152
Stood chatt'ring with incessant Din;		849	Old Thorn	34
In chatt'ring a magpie, in pride a jackdaw;		955	Portrait Life	2
CHATTER				
The Mimick Ape began his Chatter, ...		602	Beasts Confess	47
Devour the Church, and chatter to the State. . . .		792	St. Pat's Well	52
CHATTERING				
Their Chattering makes a louder Din		450	Modern Lady	180
CHEAP				
Which they have always ready, general and Cheap; . . .		19	Ode Athenian	122
Like Carleton cheap, or fam'd Duruel, ...		85	Salamander	62
I never sold so cheap a Fan.		447	Modern Lady	89
"You have the Tale as cheap as I:		449	Modern Lady	147
They both are cheap enough in Conscience, ...		461	Birthday Song	43
Then, why should the <Dean>, when Whores are so cheap,		518	Dean Hang Rape	41
You have cheap enough compounded.		637	Epistle Lady	240
That Herrings will be cheap this Year.		781	Mullinix Tim	276
CHEAPEN				
Pretend to cheapen Goods, but nothing buy.		138	City Shower	34
While He goes out to cheapen Books, ...		291	Prog Marriage	39
To cheapen Tea, and talk with Fops.		291	Prog Marriage	52
CHEAPER				
You bought it at a cheaper Rate;		28	Ode to Temple	73
And Paper makes Money, and what can be cheaper? . . .		287	Bank Down	23
CHEAPLY				
How cheaply had thy Liberty been sold, ...		531	To Mr. Gay	9

CHEAPNING | | PAGE | TITLE | LINE
Cheapning old Authors on a Stall. . . . . | 170 | Horace 1, 7 | 6
CHEAR
Then let old Englond make good Chear: . . . . | 147 | Windsor Proph | 4
With gen'rous Wines and costly Chear. . . . . | 749 | Stel Wood-Park | 4
From growing Riches with good Chear, ... | 750 | Stel Wood-Park | 43
A handsome Addition for Wine and good Chear, . . . | 867 | Grand Question | 11
You're heartily welcome: But as for good Chear, . . . | 871 | Grand Question | 121
And, for our home-bred British Chear, ... | 895 | Panegyr Dean | 267
To chear the solitary scenes: . . . . | 901 | Dean's Reasons | 84
CHEARFUL
"Was chearful to his dying Day, ... | 572 | Death of Swift | 477
With chearful Face, and inward Grief; . . . . . | 726 | To Stella | 102
CHEARFULL
With chearfull Looks, and honest Hearts. . . . . | 314 | To Ford | 82
CHEARFULLY
How chearfully the Hawkers cry . . . . | 502 | Doctor Delaney | 75
CHEARS
She, with soft speech, my anguish chears, ... | 754 | Stella '23 | 13
CHEAT
How shallow! and how gross the Cheat! . . . . | 29 | Ode to Temple | 101
In both, false mediums cheat our sight, ... | 39 | Ode Sancroft | 147
Nor practise such an antiquated cheat; . . . . | 44 | To Congreve | 18
I'll be my life but the dull cheat would pass, . . . | 48 | To Congreve | 171
Jove saw the Cheat, but thought it best . . . . | 108 | V's House | 67
To Cheat the God in his own Art. . . . . . . | 120 | Apollo Outwit | 28
Or do these Juglers cheat our Eyes? . . . . . | 250 | Bubble | 4
With much ado, the Cheat he found; . . . . . | 346 | Prometheus | 48
The Traders now no longer cheat; . . . . . . | 391 | Young's Satire | 13
To cheat and wrangle at Quadrille. . . . . . | 416 | Woman's Mind | 26
How oft they squabble, snarl and Cheat: . . . . | 453 | Modern Lady | 281
To the East Indies, there to cheat, ... | 456 | Dean Smedley | 35
"An infamous destructive Cheat. . . . . . . | 569 | Death of Swift | 408
To cheat the World, become each other's Bail. . . . | 668 | Epig Carthy 8 | D 4
Without her Privilege to cheat. . . . . | 1033 | Ans to Crown | 4
CHEATED
Still to be cheated, never to be pleas'd; . . . . | 55 | Temple Ill | 148
Be by a Parson cheated! . . . . | 426 | Five Ladies | 25
"How was she cheated by the Swains: . . . . . | 713 | Cadenus Vaness | 859
And me you have cheated. . . . . | 1014 | Swift to Sheri | 23
CHEATING
By vent'ring on the cheating Side, ... | 257 | Bubble | 163
CHEATS
Dues, Payments, Fees, Demands and Cheats, . . . | 174 | Horace 1, 7 | 104
The liquid Medium cheats your Sight, ... | 251 | Bubble | 15
Calls Lady Spade a hundred Cheats: . . . . . | 447 | Modern Lady | 73
"That all his Miracles were Cheats: . . . . . | 564 | Death of Swift | 295
He heard, there was a Club of Cheats . . . . . | 607 | Beasts Confess | 191
CHECK
Check in thy satire, angry muse, ... | 42 | Ode Sancroft | 259
"No Sheers to check her sprouting Vigour, ... | 476 | Epist on Epist | 57
And if you shou'd his Fury check, ... | 666 | Epig Carthy 2 | D 7
CHEEKS
And mingles in her muddy Cheeks. . . . . . | 227 | Prog of Beauty | 36
And teach her Cheeks again to blush. . . . . . | 227 | Prog of Beauty | 48
From her pale Cheeks pretends to show . . . . | 228 | Prog of Beauty | 94
If neither Cheeks, nor Lips be left. . . . . . | 229 | Prog of Beauty | 116
His ruddy Cheeks are no Disguise; . . . . . . | 291 | Prog Marriage | 49
But Elrington, tears falling from his cheeks, . . . | 308 | Billet Players | 43
The Roses of your Cheeks, I dare . . . . . . | 932 | Riddle 19 | D 9
To praise the Cheeks, Chin, Nose, the Bridge and all, | 993 | On Picture | 26
CHEER   SEE CHEAR
After all their good Cheer, ... | 246 | Irish-Feast | 58
From growing richer with good Cheer, ... | 745 | Stel Distress | 15
With richest Wines and costly Cheer: . . . . . | 745 | Stel Distress | 4
To spunge for good cheer, ... | 852 | Lady's Lament | 16
CHEESE
His Credit out for Cheese and Ale; . . . . . . | 231 | Prog of Poetry | 34
As bad as Suffolk cheese. . . . . | 429 | Beau's Reply | 16
In Cheese an individual Mite? . . . . | 504 | Doctor Delaney | 140
From Elephants to Mites in Cheese, ... | 653 | On Poetry | 384
One tells the Rise of Cheese, and Oat-meal, . . . | 781 | Mullinix Tim | 269
Instead of wholesome Bread and Cheese, ... | 895 | Panegyr Dean | 265
CHEQUER'D
Chequer'd with Ribbons blew and green; . . . . | 200 | Horace 2, 6 | 29
CHERRY
His Cap had a new Cherry Ribbon to ty't. . . . . | 399 | Tom Clinch | 6
CHERUB
Chief cherub, and chief lamp of that high sacred Seven, | 34 | Ode Sancroft | 3
CHEST
Bestow to bury him one Iron Chest. . . . . . | 233 | Elegy on Demar | 6
Have put his Carcass in a Chest. . . . . . . | 235 | Elegy on Demar | 46
The very Chest, in which they say . . . . . . | 235 | Elegy on Demar | 47
Or sick of Obstructions, and Pains in her Chest. . . | 351 | Wood Insect | 16
Where after he has fill'd his chest, ... | 456 | Dean Smedley | 37
And must you needs describe the Chest? . . . . | 527 | Lady's Dres Rm | 70
To view what in the Chest was hid. . . . . . | 528 | Lady's Dres Rm | 90
When plumpt into the reeking Chest; . . . . . | 529 | Lady's Dres Rm | 110
And Chest, that keeps my Lady's Tea, ... | 885 | Rev Market-Hill | 88
<CHESTER>
In his Journey to <Dublin>, he lighted at <Chester>, . | 517 | Dean Hang Rape | 7

	PAGE	TITLE	LINE
CHESTS			
And leave his emty Chests in View.	240	Run Bankers	40
CHEW			
I'll chew you to Bullets, and puff you at Baldwin. . .	1019	To Sheridan	10
So am I, when Tobacco, like Robin, I chew, sick. . .	1030	Dr. Helsham	28
CHICK			
Nor Chick, nor Duckling 'scapes, when Grim	153	Widow and Cat	D 14
The wing of a chick	853	Lady's Lament	63
Upon a Chick, and Pint of Wine.	954	Authors Living	2
CHICKEN			
Then, think on Stella's chicken porridge;	761	Bec's B-Day	36
With a tender Chicken.	952	Asparagus	5
And pick my Chicken to the Bone:	954	Authors Living	4
CHICKENS			
Tho' Chickens take a Month to fatten, ...	642	On Poetry	62
Gone, where the Chickens went before.	642	On Poetry	70
CHICKIN			
Thy Hints that Stella is no Chickin, ...	735	Stel B-day '20	42
CHID			
First chid the zeal as unpoetic fire, ...	44	To Congreve	25
The Mother scream'd, the Father chid, ...	223	Prog of Love	27
And shall be chid this afternoon	292	Prog Marriage	95
Will thus be by her Mother chid, ...	694	Cadenus Vaness	244
"Or chid the Dean, or pinch'd thy Spouse.	850	Old Thorn	70
Must I be every Moment chid	861	Lady Acheson	41
And have been often chid in vain:	901	Dean's Reasons	98
CHIDDEN			
To be chidden for explaining	908	Daphne	67
CHIDE			
Yet gave him not the Heart to chide;	704	Cadenus Vaness	571
Nor for neglects or blunders chide her;	762	Bec's B-Day	50
If Oonah once I kiss'd, forbear to chide:	882	Pastoral Dial	41
CHIDES			
And Lady Betty soundly chides them.	279	Journal	34
CHIDING			
To act his Patience, and her chiding.	221	A Quiet Life	54
CHIDINGS			
Of our good Dean's eternal chidings;	753	Gift for Bec	6
CHIEF			
Are the chief Heroes in the sacred List of Fame. . .	25	Ode Athenian	307
Chief cherub, and chief lamp of that high sacred Seven,	34	Ode Sancroft	3
Chief cherub, and chief lamp of that high sacred Seven,	34	Ode Sancroft	3
Chief of the mitred saints, and from arch-prelate here, .	42	Ode Sancroft	238
A Mousetrap-man chief Engineer.	88	Hist V's House	48
The chief among that glitt'ring crowd, ...	177	To Lord Harley	39
A word or two of Lord Chief Baron;	282	Journal	98
Could nothing but thy chief Reproach, ...	348	Whitshed Motto	3
Whose Godships are in chief request, ...	460	Birthday Song	3
Wit, as the chief of Virtues's Friends, ...	503	Doctor Delaney	99
To show the World his chief Reverse in you. . . .	532	To Mr. Gay	38
Think not Cards my chief Diversion, ...	632	Epistle Lady	81
Of Wit and Learning chief Protector;	656	On Poetry	450
Don Carlos made her chief Director	745	Stel Distress	
Don Carlos made her chief Director, ...	749	Stel Wood-Park	5
To be the chief of human Good, ...	764	Stel B-day '26	28
And yet they have learnt the chief Art of a Sov'reign,	805	Irish Bishops	47
"Thou chief Contriver of my Fall, ...	850	Old Thorn	57
Attend him daily as their Chief, ...	883	Rev Market-Hill	23
To dispute, her chief delight, ...	906	Daphne	9
And her chief Officers of State, ...	1035	To Quilca	11
CHIEFEST			
Their first and chiefest force	19	Ode Athenian	113
His Rival, for the Chiefest reckon'd, ...	546	Life of Swift	56
CHIEFLY			
And chiefly chuse to shine by Night.	228	Prog of Beauty	72
Fools chiefly float, the Wise are drown'd.	252	Bubble	52
Wherever the Damn'd do Chiefly abound, ...	575	Place Damn'd	5
For manly Bosoms chiefly fit, ...	693	Cadenus Vaness	204
That, Merit should be chiefly plac'd	697	Cadenus Vaness	342
To foul the Man he chiefly flatters.	796	Traulus 1	32
Chiefly where she nothing knows.	906	Daphne	16
To me he chiefly gives in Trust	915	Riddle 1	21
And after all, I chiefly owe	927	Riddle 10	D 11
I'm chiefly unruly, when strongest confin'd.	927	Riddle 11	D 4
CHIFTAN			
An herdie Chiftan, woe the morne	103	Merlin	7
CHILD			
Sick lust of souls, and an abortive child;	47	To Congreve	124
With Christian Nick-names like a Child;	82	Salamander	4
Vow'd it was pretty for a Child;	86	Hist V's House	10
Pray reach that Thing here to the Child, ...	128	Little House	52
While the poor Child lay fast asleep.	150	Corinna	8
"Each take a Child into her Care, ...	321	First of April	5
A Child may know it in the Dark:	453	Modern Lady	267
The Child with native Beauty shone, ...	692	Cadenus Vaness	175
But it shall ne'er be said, a Child	692	Cadenus Vaness	194
Wou'd use him like a younger Child;	693	Cadenus Vaness	225
A Father, and the Nymph his Child.	704	Cadenus Vaness	549
Come, be a good child:	855	Lady's Lament	124
As if I were a darling Child.	891	Panegyr Dean	152
Voluptuous Ease, the Child of Wealth, ...	895	Panegyr Dean	279

133

	PAGE	TITLE	LINE
CHILD (CONTINUED)			
Or bring a tender Child and pliant,	934	Riddle 21	D 19
A long-ear'd Beast, and the Child of a Sheep,	943	Probatur Alit	31
CHILD'S			
At Child's or Truby's never once had been;	194	Author Himself	18
CHILDLESS			
Where Childless Wives crowd ev'ry morn	293	Prog Marriage	119
CHILDREN			
The little Children in the Wood,	93	Bauc & Phil 1	120
The Little Children in the Wood:	114	Bauc & Phil 2	96
Wish'd Women might have Children fast,	115	Bauc & Phil 2	131
For Madmen, Children, Wits and Fools	181	Horace 2, 1	31
From Husband, Children, Wheel, or Spinnet.	322	First of April	42
His Wife and Children wanted Bread,	352	Wood Ironmongr	7
Tho' your Children by a Nod	633	Epistle Lady	103
Whose graceless Children scorn to own thee!	652	On Poetry	358
The Children all our motions Aping.	780	Mullinix Tim	242
The Mother-Kingdom left her Children free;	791	St. Pat's Well	20
Or sell his Children, House, and Lands,	821	Dr. Rundle	43
My Children are seven,	951	Apples	6
My children tattling.	1037	Sheridan Cavan	2
CHILDRENS			
Lye on you, and on your Childrens Head,	23	Ode Athenian	246
CHILL'D			
Blew out Love's Torch or chill'd the Flame:	85	Salamander	60
CHILLING			
The scorching Sun, or chilling Air;	379	Apology Lady C	122
The cold Conceits, the chilling Thoughts,	470	Burning Poem	7
Our chilling Climate hardly bears	640	On Poetry	7
CHIMAERA'S			
Or mere Chimaera's in the Mind,	765	Stel B-day '26	53
CHIME			
For, as Helsham observes, there's nothing can chime,	980	Tho: Sheridan	3
CHIMERAES			
How cou'd these Chimeraes get into your Brains?--	873	Grand Question	185
CHIMNEY			
While He from out of Chimney took	112	Bauc & Phil 2	25
The Chimney widen'd, and grew higher,	113	Bauc & Phil 2	55
The Jack and Chimney near ally'd,	113	Bauc & Phil 2	75
The Chimney to a Steeple grown,	113	Bauc & Phil 2	77
On a Chimney cut his Name.	837	Legion Club	180
CHIMNEY-SWEEP			
'Till drown'd in Shriller Notes of Chimney-Sweep,	124	Descriptn Morn	12
CHIMNIES			
Chimnies with Scorn rejecting Smoak;	1035	To Quilca	3
CHIMNY			
Whilst he from out the Chimny took	91	Bauc & Phil 1	57
The Chimny widen'd and grew high'r,	92	Bauc & Phil 1	95
Nor ever left the Chimny side.	94	Bauc & Phil 1	138
The Chimny to a Steeple grown,	94	Bauc & Phil 1	139
When Mrs Welch's Chimny smoks,	419	Holyhead Journ	1
CHIN			
Sits with his Knees up to his Chin;	127	Little House	20
With a Saint at his Chin, and a Seal in his Fob;	147	Windsor Proph	2
While at her Chin the Conflu'ents met.	227	Prog of Beauty	40
See but her Forehead and her Chin.	229	Prog of Beauty	100
We'll come and hold you by the Chin,	254	Bubble	106
'Tis Kindness to hold a Friend up by the Chin;	338	Serious Poem	118
To hold the Doctor by the Chin:	514	Answer Fable	64
Or on her Chin like Bristles grow.	527	Lady's Dres Rm	58
All powder'd o'er from Tail to Chin;	785	Dick, Maggot	2
But Maggots in your Nose and Chin,	813	Bro Protestant	39
And down my chin drops,	852	Lady's Lament	32
Grows down to my chin;	853	Lady's Lament	74
My chin will not stay,	853	Lady's Lament	75
With watry Chaps, and wagging Chin,	895	Panegyr Dean	257
Charm'd with his Eyes and Chin and Snout,	904	Death Daphne	63
To praise the Cheeks, Chin, Nose, the Bridge and all,	993	On Picture	26
CHINA			
A Lady's Face, and China ware.	227	Prog of Beauty	64
CHINCOUGH			
How she cur'd Charley of the Chincough;	282	Journal	92
CHINE			
The Beef you have got, which I hear is a Chine	1018	Swift Ans Sher	30
CHINESE			
From him the Tartar, and Chinese,	655	On Poetry	423
CHINK			
Or thro' a Chink convey their Smoke,	100	Elegy Patrige	93
In gaping Lines to fill a Chink;	645	On Poetry	168
Where not a Chink let's in the Air;	935	Riddle 23	D 15
CHINTS			
But Chints, Brocades, and Lace take all away,	275	Epilogue	33
That all our wives should go in Chints.	423	Ireld	60
CHIP'T			
He chip't his Bread, the Pieces round	156	Fable of Midas	3
CHIVY-CHASE			
Of Chivy-chase, and English Mall,	93	Bauc & Phil 1	118
CHLOE			
Thus, indulgent Chloe bit,	523	Betty Grizette	35
Of Chloe all the Town has rung;	584	Strephon Chloe	1
But, Chloe drove him fiercely back.	588	Strephon Chloe	150

		PAGE	TITLE	LINE
CHLOE	**(CONTINUED)**			
How could a Nymph so chaste as Chloe,		588	Strephon Chloe	151
And, Chloe, 'tis by all agreed,		588	Strephon Chloe	157
Can Chloe, heav'nly Chloe <piss>?		589	Strephon Chloe	178
Can Chloe, heav'nly Chloe <piss>?		589	Strephon Chloe	178
His Chloe in the homeli'st Strains;		590	Strephon Chloe	212
And, Chloe more experienc'd grown,		590	Strephon Chloe	213
When Chloe stole your Heart away,		591	Strephon Chloe	236
For Chloe, Sylvia, Phillis, Iris;		729	Stella, Poems	40
Fair Chloe would perhaps be found		729	Stella, Poems	43
If Chloe were a Sharper still,		905	Death Daphne	77
Chloe, when on thy Breast I lye,		925	Riddle 8	17
If Chloe o'er thy Heart prevails,		925	Riddle 8	19
CHLOE'S				
Accuses Chloe's tainted Breath;		449	Modern Lady	157
Chloe's of ev'ry Coxcomb jealous,		449	Modern Lady	162
By Lightning shot from Chloe's Eyes?		587	Strephon Chloe	110
As Chloe's Skin, almost as bright.		589	Strephon Chloe	174
And, spight of Chloe's Charms divine,		591	Strephon Chloe	249
Your Poets Chloe's beauty heightning		621	Scandal Poem 1	149
Your Poets, Chloe's Beauty height'ning,		628	Scandal Poem 2	153
CHLORIS				
Sonnets and Elegyes to Chloris		79	Vanbrug House	9
Sonnets, or Elogies to Chloris		106	V's House	9
CHOAK				
To Choak the Girls, or consume the Rabble;		283	Journal	114
But a Pox o' those Banks that choak up the Springs.		287	Bank Down	3
CHOAK'D				
Half choak'd with dust, half drown'd with rains;		403	Window Inns 10	D 6
CHOCOLATE				
They call'd for Tea and Chocolate,		698	Cadenus Vaness	374
CHOICE				
And left the Choice to his own Breast.		107	V's House	54
Makes choice of him she fancies best,		178	To Lord Harley	63
Their luckless Choice of Husbands--others,		182	Horace 2, 1	53
And Harley, not asham'd his Choice to own,		194	Author Himself	31
So odd a Choice, how could she make,		291	Prog Marriage	43
Repining, to applaud his Choice.		387	Manly Virtue	134
Now pray observe the Doctor's Choice,		513	Answer Fable	19
If Maidens are ravish't, it is their own Choice,		519	Dean Hang Rape	61
The World shall own, his Choice was wise and just,		532	To Mr. Gay	17
Must laugh at her capricious Choice.		702	Cadenus Vaness	509
In Boarding-Schools can have his Choice;		710	Cadenus Vaness	739
Choice Spirits, who employ their Parts,		780	Mullinix Tim	245
For who would not think it a much better choice,		818	Epigr Kite	3
CHOICEST				
My choicest Hours of Life are lost:		202	Horace 2, 6	106
Fill'd with the choicest common-places,		223	Prog of Love	49
'Tis grown the choicest Wit at Court,		468	Birthday Song	267
Presented with the choicest Bits:		745	Stel Distress	12
CHOIR				
Thus to his Choir of Muses spoke;		320	First of April	2
And sing like one of Milton's choir,		490	Dialogue	40
And Horace brought ye tunefull Choir		658	On Poetry	D 410
Bright Apollo lend thy Choir.		661	Love Song	16
CHOKE				
Inclos'd Artificers to Choke.		100	Elegy Patrige	94
CHOLER				
Choler preside, or Blood, or Phlegm,		724	To Stella	20
<CHOLMONDELEY>				
<Cholmondeley>, when Drunk, can never lose his Wand,		164	Toland's Invit	25
CHOOSE **SEE CHUSE,CHOUSE**				
To sing of Wars choose peaceful times.		462	Birthday Song	48
CHOP **SEE MUTTON-CHOP**				
CHOPP'D				
I chopp'd so fast, that few there minded.		675	Curate's Compl	12
CHOPS				
He runs into a Cannon's Chops.		500	Doctor Delaney	10
And Ointments good for scabby Chops.		526	Lady's Dres Rm	36
If from adown the hopeful Chops		529	Lady's Dres Rm	103
With ale and chops I'll treat who writes the best,		671	Epig Carthy 24	D 5
The Snow-ball destin'd at thy Chops;		779	Mullinix Tim	204
For, as he shakes his Wainscot Chops,		786	Dick, Maggot	11
When he opens his chops;		852	Lady's Lament	12
Supporting my chops,		852	Lady's Lament	28
With Aconite anoint his Chops:		904	Death Daphne	42
CHOQUE				
To choque your Sight, and raise your Malice)		313	To Ford	64
CHOSE				
And both chose Midas to decide;		156	Fable of Midas	26
Chose, for her spouse, a mortal born:		178	To Lord Harley	66
And chose me for an humble Friend;		201	Horace 2, 6	66
Who chose to leave his dearest pledges here,		309	Billet Players	46
He wou'd have chose a milder part;		485	Libel on D- D-	158
A Peacock chose for Flight and Voice:		513	Answer Fable	20
"And only chose the Wise and Good;		566	Death of Swift	333
That Strephon chose no proper Season.		588	Strephon Chloe	160
Which I chose to make appear,		637	Epistle Lady	227
He chose to justify his Pride;		710	Cadenus Vaness	763
Your Annual Bard had rather chose		756	Stel B-day '24	5
She chose a thread of greatest length		760	Bec's B-Day	3

135

		PAGE	TITLE	LINE
CHOSE	(CONTINUED)			
I chose these Rhymes out, for their Difficulty. . . .		989	Letter Dr Sh-n	32
CHOSEN				
Sprung from a better world, and chosen then		52	Temple Ill	45
For, few, a chosen few, must know, ...		922	Riddle 7	49
CHOUSE				
From London they come, silly People to chouse, . . .		396	Dog and Thief	17
CHRIST				
I mean, the way which leads to Christ:		39	Ode Sancroft	161
What tho' they don't believe in Christ		658	On Poetry	D 190
When Christ was betray'd to Pilate, the Praetor, . .		804	Irish Bishops	29
The Heathen doth believe in Christ		1036	Heathen Christ	1
CHRIST-CHURCH				
In Christ-Church cut his Throat for Jealousy. . . .		350	Upright Judge 3	6
CHRIST'NING				
Fresh from a wedding, or a christ'ning, ...		762	Bec's B-Day	53
CHRISTEN				
And Chambermaids christen this Worm a Death-Watch: .		351	Wood Insect	20
CHRISTIAN				
With Christian Nick-names like a Child;		82	Salamander	4
No Christian would turn out a Beast		90	Bauc & Phil 1	19
Not fitt to live on Christian Ground, ...		92	Bauc & Phil 1	87
Not fit to live on Christian Ground, ...		112	Bauc & Phil 2	47
"Of which the Christian World complain.		183	Horace 2, 1	98
In Christian Justice due to John.		225	Prog of Love	94
The Christian World his Deeds proclaim, ...		397	Earl of P-b-w	2
All Christian vittals stink of fish , ...		420	Holyhead	3
And sure no Christian Poet breathing		461	Birthday Song	25
And live like other christian fokes;		489	Dialogue	10
Suited to all Christian Fokes:		523	Betty Grizette	18
All Christian People to invite;		735	Stel B-day '20	36
The Christian Rites I introduc'd in vain:		792	St. Pat's Well	35
He's a Christian as good as the rest of the herd. . .		816	Yahoo's	29
He's still a Christian more than they.		820	Dr. Rundle	20
You say you will eat Grass on his Grave: a Christian eat Grass!		986	Mary to Sher	17
CHRISTIANS				
Are Brother Protestants and Christians, ...		812	Bro Protestant	31
Are Christians alike; and it may be averr'd, ...		816	Yahoo's	28
Is by all pious Christians thought, ...		942	Probatur Alit	5
And doth all Christians hate;		1036	Heathen Christ	2
CHRISTMAS				
By Christmas we shall see strange things.		282	Journal	110
CHRISTNINGS				
At Christnings well could act his Part, ...		115	Bauc & Phil 2	129
CHRONICAL				
Who pine us like a Chronical Disease;		9	Ode to King	88
CHRONICLE				
By Chronicle of antient Date, ...		848	Old Thorn	2
CHRONICLES				
But, in the chronicles of former ages, ...		308	Billet Players	29
CHRONOLOGY				
But lest Chronology should vary, ...		456	Dean Smedley	45
CHRYSTAL				
The muse retreats far in yon chrystal cell;		50	To Congreve	228
Such are the smiles where drops of chrystal show, . . .		51	Temple Ill	21
Troubling the chrystal fountain of the sight, ...		54	Temple Ill	97
Lead me to the Chrystal Mirrors, ...		661	Love Song	19
Adorn our chrystal River's Banks:		896	Panegyr Dean	302
CHURCH SEE CHRIST-CHURCH				
And think the Church itself does so;		37	Ode Sancroft	78
Say, why the Church is still led blindfold by the State?		40	Ode Sancroft	177
Of a declining Church, by Faction her worse foe opprest,		40	Ode Sancroft	186
And grow a Church before your Eyes.		92	Bauc & Phil 1	90
Grown to a Church by just Degrees, ...		94	Bauc & Phil 1	154
You've rais'd a Church here in a Minute, ...		94	Bauc & Phil 1	161
And grow a Church before your Eyes.		112	Bauc & Phil 2	50
Grown to a Church by just Degrees, ...		114	Bauc & Phil 2	108
In Church you heard her thro the Crowd		222	Prog of Love	9
In Church, secure behind her Fan		222	Prog of Love	11
With Church and King, the Lady's gone;		279	Journal	36
And drops him at the Church, to pray		292	Prog Marriage	81
(I forget in what Church) an Image of Wood;		334	Serious Poem	18
The Church I hate, and have good Reason:		349	Upright Judge 1	1
In Church your Grandsire cut his Throat;		349	Upright Judge 2	1
Both Church and State, being still dependent. . . .		372	Letter D. S-y	22
The Church and Clergy here, no doubt, ...		401	Window Inns 4	1
The Parson safe at Church, ...		426	Five Ladies	43
The Offals of a Church distress't, ...		484	Libel on D- D-	131
And go to Church, and say our Prayers.		495	Panegyr Swift	71
For the Good of our Church a true <English> <Dean>. .		516	Dean Hang Rape	4
In Church and in State was of Principles sound, . .		518	Dean Hang Rape	32
Our Church and our State dear <England> maintains, .		520	Dean Hang Rape	67
"That Church and State had suffer'd more		549	Life of Swift	150
"That Ruin'd Church and Monarch too.		549	Life of Swift	157
"And Lovers of the Church distress'd---:		549	Life of Swift	161
"More favour'd, than the Church by Law:		550	Life of Swift	169
"Destructive to the Church and King:		550	Life of Swift	173
"The Church had never such a Writer:		564	Death of Swift	297
"To rob the Church, their Tenants rack, ...		571	Death of Swift	448
In his own Church he keeps a Seat;		605	Beasts Confess	129

136

CHURCH	(CONTINUED)	PAGE	TITLE	LINE
To rise in Church, or Law, or State,		641	On Poetry	40
The Church is thy peculiar Care.		656	On Poetry	452
Devour the Church, and chatter to the State.		792	St. Pat's Well	52
So God bless the Church, and three of our Mitres;		805	Irish Bishops	63
Wou'd you rise in the Church, be Stupid and Dull,		807	Advice Parson	1
Lord Pam in the Church (cou'd you think it) kneel'd down		809	Epigr Prelate	1
While o'er the Church these Clouds are gathering,		813	Bro Protestant	47
In Mother Church to breed a Variance,		820	Dr. Rundle	7
That he would answer both for Church and State;		825	Noisy Tom	2
Plac'd against the Church direct;		829	Legion Club	6
Near the Church--you know the rest.		829	Legion Club	8
I mean the Church, the King, and Me.		926	Riddle 9	24
Went triumphant to Church, and sang stoutly Te Deum:		967	Letter Sherid	18
Captain Butler made some in the Church black and blue sick;		1029	Dr. Helsham	7
Lady Santry got out of the Church when she grew sick,		1029	Dr. Helsham	10
My Footman came home from the Church, of a Bruise sick,		1029	Dr. Helsham	17
A Church without Pews.		1036	Plague Country	4
CHURCH-YARD				
To the Church-yard, to take a walk;		116	Bauc & Phil 2	154
You see just by the Church-yard Stile;		127	Little House	14
CHURCH'S				
Hung loosely on the Church's pinnacle,		37	Ode Sancroft	74
Pity a miserable Church's tears,		42	Ode Sancroft	243
Devour the Church's tiddest Bits,		498	Panegyr Swift	150
No more I hear my Church's Bell,		674	His Deafness	3
CHURCHES				
Swept up whole churches as it list,		40	Ode Sancroft	194
CHURCHWARDEN				
Of a Churchwarden or a Tribe.		93	Bauc & Phil 1	124
CHURLE				
You Churle, I'll maintain		246	Irish-Feast	73
CHURLISH				
But for that Pack of churlish Boors		92	Bauc & Phil 1	86
But, for that Pack of churlish Boors,		112	Bauc & Phil 2	46
CHURN				
But, with his Hand, the <Dean> can churn it.		892	Panegyr Dean	174
CHUSE				
(But, surely such whom God did never for his People chuse)		8	Ode to King	86
Or a more worthy subject chuse:		42	Ode Sancroft	260
And chuse out wits who ne'er have seen his face;		48	To Congreve	170
None e'er chuse no modern Midas chuse,		157	Fable of Midas	51
Yet, wanting skill and pow'r to chuse,		178	To Lord Harley	57
And chiefly chuse to shine by Night.		228	Prog of Beauty	72
Then chuse which you please, and let each bring a Faggot,		352	Wood Insect	39
My Lady could not chuse but wonder:		377	Apology Lady C	65
Then diff'rent Studies chuse,		405	Swift to Pope	6
From Pulpits chuse Gallants.		426	Five Ladies	32
Chuse for Companions tete a tete,		480	Libel on D- D-	2
Nor ever chuse to Work with Tools		483	Libel on D- D-	91
And chuse to dine at home with Port:		488	Irish-Club	20
What's to be done? shall wit and learning chuse,		506	To a Friend	7
Say, had the Court no better place to chuse		531	To Mr. Gay	7
He'd rather chuse that I should dye,		557	Death of Swift	131
"Would rather slip aside, and chuse		565	Death of Swift	321
To please you, she knows how to chuse a nice Bit;		580	Psyche	9
For, ev'ry Nymph has Leave to chuse;		595	Cassinus Peter	64
When he hath Liberty to chuse.		607	Beasts Confess	186
Shou'd I lofty Numbers chuse,		638	Epistle Lady	260
You chuse to rule the Sable-flock.		656	On Poetry	454
Would chuse in Peace to drink my Coffee.		733	Verses Vanessa	30
I would rather chuse those;)		858	Lady's Lament	214
The Bard, who humbly deigns to chuse		887	Panegyr Dean	25
I wisely chuse to walk behind;		917	Riddle 4	2
But you learned Doctors can make whom you chuse sick.		1029	Dr. Helsham	19
Eat lean Meat, or chuse,		1036	Plague Country	3
CHUSES				
"Tho' there's a Boy whom a Lord chuses,		321	First of April	7
Whom Stella chuses for a Friend.		728	Stella, Poems	24
CHUSING				
In chusing Lace a Critick nice,		416	Woman's Mind	27
CHYMERICK				
Alass! a meer Chymerick Notion.		604	Beasts Confess	112
CHYMICK				
They washt away the Chymick Power.		158	Fable of Midas	72
The Mixture thus by Chymick Art,		344	Prometheus	5
(Note here, that in the Chymick Style,		354	Simile Silver	15
CHYMIST				
A Greater Chymist none, than I,		920	Riddle 6	19
CHYMISTS				
So Chymists boast they have a Power		81	Vanbrug House	85
So Chymists boast they have a Pow'r		109	V's House	127
For, first, I have often by Chymists been told,		263	Apollo	3
As well as Chymists by their Books:		597	Problem Solved	4
CIBBER				
Revis'd by Tibbalds, Moore, and Cibber.		561	Death of Swift	200
Since Cibber brought in an Attainder;		642	On Poetry	56
Harmonius Cibber entertains		650	On Poetry	305

	PAGE	TITLE	LINE
CIBBER'S			
"Here's Colley Cibber's Birth-day Poem.	563	Death of Swift	270
CICERO			
Cou'd quote you Cicero and Livy.	513	Answer Fable	38
CIELING			
To raise the Stairs, or build the Cieling;	409	Dial Rich Marb	26
The Cieling hardly six foot high	746	Stel Distress	36
CINDER			
The Fat upon a Cinder drops,	529	Lady's Dres Rm	104
CINDER-PICKING			
Allure the Cinder-picking Fair.	779	Mullinix Tim	206
CINDERCOLA			
Since Cindercola, first you Courted	372	Letter D. S-y	45
Nor Cindercola, charming Wench!	373	Letter D. S-y	65
CIRCLE SEE OPPOSITE-CIRCLE			
Or if thought's rolling globe her circle run,	51	Temple Ill	9
A Circle with their Rod describe,	134	Magician's Rod	50
And made a Circle thrice as wide,	134	Magician's Rod	54
Hemm'd by a triple Circle round,	200	Horace 2, 6	28
So when this Circle we have run,	280	Journal	59
You change a Circle to a Square,	477	Epist on Epist	73
Then to a Circle, as you were:	477	Epist on Epist	74
So large to grasp the Circle round;	641	On Poetry	30
And in its narrow Circle gathers	688	Cadenus Vaness	55
Let her describe a Circle round	743	Stel B-day 22	55
His Nose to get the Circle just in,	788	Dick's Variety	34
Is this, that you argue like fools in a circle.	1026	Sheri Circles	4
For the cord of your circle is now in their hand;	1027	Sheri Circles	16
CIRCLES			
Round all the circles of impertinence,	46	To Congreve	88
CIRCLING			
Or hunted fancy, by a circling flight,	51	Temple Ill	5
To whom the Tribe of circling Wits,	649	On Poetry	267
CIRCULAR			
It never was known that circular letters,	1026	Sheri Circles	1
CIRCULATION			
Unless a proper Circulation	239	Run Bankers	11
CIRCUMCISION			
Nor praise we less that Circumcision,	1021	Nim-Dan-Dean 1	D 11
CIRCUMFLEX			
Then with a Congee circumflex	64	Discovery	43
CIRCUMLOCUTION			
To answer your style without circumlocution.	1027	Sheri Circles	24
CIRCUMSTANCE			
Nor does thy essence fix'd depend on giddy circumstance	34	Ode Sancroft	7
"Points out some Circumstance to please us.	554	Death of Swift	10
Has ev'ry Circumstance to please us,	820	Dr. Rundle	25
CITHEREA'S			
Invoke not Citherea's Aid,	272	Apollo's Edict	D 72
CITIES			
O'er Cities, Rivers, Hills, and Seas:	627	Scandal Poem 2	120
CITIZEN			
Then vote a worthy Citizen to Jail,	826	Noisy Tom	19
CITRON			
Takes a large Dram of Citron Water.	446	Modern Lady	47
CITY			
Before it grew a city butterfly;	46	To Congreve	90
With other cattle to the city went;	46	To Congreve	116
Collects the City Filth in search of Gold.	364	On Dreams	22
"Of City Fogs and crowded Rooms,	380	Apology Lady C	140
Some South Sea Broker from the City,	410	Dial Rich Marb	67
Court, City, Camp, all one to him---.	548	Life of Swift	106
Court, City, Country want you not;	641	On Poetry	47
And in the Streets divert the City	780	Mullinix Tim	240
Some have the City in their Care,	780	Mullinix Tim	249
As I strole the City, oft I	829	Legion Club	1
How to plague and starve the City;	831	Legion Club	54
. . . I mean the city so smoaky,	1022	Nim-Dan-Dean 2	D 3
CITY-BARD			
In ev'ry Street a City-bard	649	On Poetry	285
CITY-BORN			
So much in mode, so very city-born;	44	To Congreve	14
CITYES			
If mountains sink to vales, if cityes dye	419	Shall Repine	3
O'er cityes, rivers, hills, and seas,	621	Scandal Poem 1	126
CIVIL			
. . .it might become you to be more civil:	72	Mrs Harris Pet	55
Howe'er it was civil in Angel or Elf,	77	Lady B- B-	19
In civil Terms,--"My Friend," says she,	208	Fable Bitches	25
My landlord is civil,	402	Window Inns 8	D 1
With feeding high, & Treatment civil,	746	Stel Distress	24
With feeding high, and Treatment civil,	750	Stel Wood-Park	22
(A civil Divine!	854	Lady's Lament	103
In civil Language, if he stays	860	Lady Acheson	18
. . . but I think Gentle folks should be civil.	986	Mary to Sher	24
And so I remain in a civil way, your Servant to command.	987	Mary to Sher	38
However, they own it is very civil in Mr. Sheridan,	1014	Swift to Sheri	8
CIVILIZE			
Did once their Land subdue and civilize:	790	St. Pat's Well	14
CLABBER SEE BONNY-CLABBER			

138

		PAGE	TITLE	LINE
CLACK				
	I hardly hear a Woman's Clack.	674	His Deafness	8
	To din thine Ears with unharmonious Clack, ...	792	St. Pat's Well	47
CLAD				
	Sit clad in lawn of purer woven day, ...	41	Ode Sancroft	235
	"T' expose thy soul, clad in this poor disguise; . . .	55	Temple Ill	144
	In England the Dead in Woollen are clad, ...	237	Excellent Song	10
	In blew shallon, shall Hanniball be Clad, ...	275	Epilogue	21
	O! Cou'd I see this Audience Clad in Stuff, . . .	275	Epilogue	31
	Indifference clad in Wisdom's Guise, ...	561	Death of Swift	213
	Truth shines the brighter, clad in Verse;	729	Stella, Poems	58
	Clad in a coat of Podesway, ...	879	Robbin & Harry	47
	So nicely clad from Head to Heel;	889	Panegyr Dean	76
	And clad my Body all in White:	915	Riddle 1	4
	A comely Dame once clad in white, ...	923	Riddle 7	63
	A Judge will eat, tho' clad in Ermin.	942	Probatur Alit	22
CLAIM				
	Who claim so many Titles to be Jews, ...	8	Ode to King	85
	Since Heaven will claim its residence as well as birth,	35	Ode Sancroft	19
	And whence we claim our shoeing horns, ...	99	Elegy Patrige	38
	This character shall Ca'ndish claim, ...	177	To Lord Harley	37
	Her Kennel once again to claim;	208	Fable Bitches	38
	Whether from War's stern God you claim	323	Pethox	11
	And claim it as a Debt from Fate, ...	388	Manly Virtue	141
	Is by my Promise what you claim;	445	Modern Lady	25
	What Claim have you to Place, or Pension? . . .	483	Libel on D- D-	109
	Can sometimes drop a Voter's Claim, ...	485	Libel on D- D-	149
	Thus, Envy pleads a nat'ral Claim	504	Doctor Delaney	131
	The Poet cannot claim his Bays;	505	Doctor Delaney	168
	"His Claim as good as other Folks---.	547	Life of Swift	94
	"For canting hypocrites to claim, ...	550	Life of Swift	171
	Is what our Maidens claim by Right:	588	Strephon Chloe	156
	They have no claim to Your allegiance	620	Scandal Poem 1	97
	While ev'ry Fool his Claim alledges, ...	640	On Poetry	9
	Your former Actions claim their Part, ...	765	Stel B-day '26	71
	Such was Ierne's Claim, as just as thine, ...	771	Horace 1, 14	41
	As well may claim you for their Kin.	813	Bro Protestant	40
	May justly claim their Birth from thee;	919	Riddle 5	16
CLAIM'D				
	And justly half the Merit claim'd	406	Swift to Pope	27
	Than George and William claim'd before.	464	Birthday Song	140
	While Montague, who claim'd the Station	481	Libel on D- D-	35
CLAIMS				
	In this Your Virtue claims a double share, ...	12	Ode to William D	27
	He claims it by a Canon;	406	Swift to Pope	18
	Can you put in higher Claims, ...	637	Epistle Lady	241
	And this, for Epicks claims the Bays, ...	650	On Poetry	295
	Sleek, <--> claims her as his Right:	897	Panegyr Dean	344
CLAM'ROUS				
	When frighted at the clam'rous Crew, ...	448	Modern Lady	120
CLAMB'RING				
	The heavy Wall went clamb'ring after.	92	Bauc & Phil 1	94
CLAMBER				
	And Nim and Dan to Garret clamber:	280	Journal	58
	But, as for me, who ne'er could clamber high, . . .	900	Dean's Reasons	51
CLAMOUR				
	Their Clamour 'lighting from their Chairs, ...	698	Cadenus Vaness	368
CLAMOURS				
	The clamours of ten thousand tongues	433	Answer Paulus	53
CLAN				
	Such is that Clan of boist'rous Bears	216	To Mr. Delany	51
	What think you of my fav'rite Clan, ...	314	To Ford	79
	I own, there may in ev'ry clan	435	Answer Paulus	103
	Are grown the Nuissance of your Clan, ...	777	Mullinix Tim	145
CLANDALKIN				
	Before I'd touch his filthy Dross, than is Clandalkin Spire.	343	Upon His Grace	38
CLANS				
	Surrounded with her Noisy Clans	448	Modern Lady	118
CLAP				
	Clap his own Nonsense in the place.	61	Lady Tablebook	24
	And got a good Clap, but committed no <Rape>. . .	517	Dean Hang Rape	24
	And first his Bum with Clap, ...	776	Mullinix Tim	109
	But that you left no Clap behind.	1033	Ans to Crown	6
CLAP'T				
	Clap't Asses Ears upon the Judge, ...	157	Fable of Midas	30
CLAPP'T				
	But hurry'd out, and clapp't the Dore.	220	A Quiet Life	8
CLAPPING				
	By clapping Billets on your Door and Posts Sir. . .	1002	Reply by Dean	12
CLAPS				
	By Age and Claps grown cold as Snow, ...	84	Salamander	56
	That Clouds are blam'd for giving Claps:	618	Scandal Poem 1	22
	But, what alas! are Claps aetherial	618	Scandal Poem 1	23
	That Clouds are blam'd for giving Claps;	624	Scandal Poem 2	16
	But, what alas are Claps Aetherial, ...	624	Scandal Poem 2	17
CLARET				
	Without whom they could get neither Claret nor Beef; .	263	Apollo	10
	We'll make it firm with Beef and Claret.	760	Receipt Youth	56
	Though his Claret is bad, and he foots it on Stones, .	1037	Four Storyes	7

		PAGE	TITLE	LINE
CLARK				
For since they talk'd with Doctor Clark,	• • • • •	468	Birthday Song	269
CLASH				
Then I clash and roar, and rattle,	• • • • • • •	933	Riddle 20	D 21
CLASS				
You are of a lower Class	• • • • • • • •	637	Epistle Lady	245
CLASSICK				
But Classick Authors--he ne'er miss'd 'em.	• • • •	115	Bauc & Phil 2	136
CLASSICKS				
Prize Classicks more than Sacred Writ:	• • • •	392	Young's Satire	40
Or, for the Classicks read th' Attorney's Guide;	•	793	St. Pat's Well	77
CLATT'RING				
While Spouts run clatt'ring o'er the Roof by Fits;	•	139	City Shower	44
Should come and make the Clatt'ring cease;	• • • • •	189	Faggot	24
What clatt'ring of Sticks,	• • • • • • • • •	246	Irish-Feast	66
To make a Clatt'ring as they trod.	• • • • • •	352	Wood Ironmongr	12
CLATTER				
And musical Clatter,	• • • • • • • •	245	Irish-Feast	32
In Chaos made not such a Clatter:	• • • • • • •	450	Modern Lady	185
Then, is not Female Clatter worse,	• • • • • • •	624	Scandal Poem 2	9
Intrude with Monkey grin, and clatter	• • • •	777	Mullinix Tim	143
CLATTRING				
And is not femal clattring worse,	• • • • • • •	617	Scandal Poem 1	9
CLAW				
"I! who so long with Tooth and Claw	• • • • • • •	154	Widow and Cat	D 23
Or in your claw, or in your bill.	• • • • • • • •	983	Sher, A Goose	22
CLAWS				
That Cancer with his pois'nous Claws	• • • •	228	Prog of Beauty	91
With Teeth or with Claws it will bite or will scratch,	•	351	Wood Insect	19
They might, unhurt by Envy's Claws;	• • • • • •	479	Epist on Epist	125
With Harpy Claws, and Pois'nous Tongue,	• • • •	504	Doctor Delaney	124
From Bayliffs claws thou scarce cou'd keep thy Bum free.	•	678	Dean and Duke	12
With harpy Claws it undermines the Ground,	• • • •	792	St. Pat's Well	61
CLAY				
Made up of iron mixt with clay,	• • • • • • • •	39	Ode Sancroft	139
And saw them dabling in their Clay,	• • • • • •	86	Hist V's House	14
Not a sham Thing of Clay or Cards.	• • • • • •	87	Hist V's House	26
Jove mix'd up all, and his best Clay imploy'd;	• • •	118	Biddy Floyd	11
While Dunces of the coarsest Clay,	• • • • • •	497	Panegyr Swift	148
Then from a Clay of Mixture base	• • • • • • •	659	On Poetry	D 410
He molded it with Female Clay:	• • • • • • •	726	To Stella	90
Will cover a House much better than Clay.	• • • •	943	Probatur Alit	34
CLEAN				
Flirts on you from her Mop, but not so clean.	• • • •	137	City Shower	20
Glasses and Linnen clean, and Pewter bright,	• • •	165	Toland's Invit	28
If the Printer will peach him, he'll scarce come off clean.		238	Excellent Song	32
I hope to make you yet as clean,	• • • • • • •	361	Grace's Answer	5
You hate to see ought that seems Clean	• • • • •	372	Letter D. S-y	44
She wipes it clean, and lays it by.	• • • • • •	581	Young Nymph	12
The Wife should study to be clean;	• • • • • •	588	Strephon Chloe	138
She's fair and clean, and that's the most;	• • • •	699	Cadenus Vaness	412
By <God> I'll bring you off as clean.	• • • • •	797	Traulus 1	60
When his speech came abroad, he paid him off clean,	• •	816	Yahoo's	38
Like a very foul mop, dirty more than they clean.	• •	819	Archbi Cashel	16
Both dress'd like divines, with band and face clean.	• •	843	Ay and No	2
With Parsons, what Lady can keep herself clean?	• • •	868	Grand Question	29
So fine a Gown, a Band so clean,	• • • • • • •	889	Panegyr Dean	77
To keep our Poultry sweet and clean;	• • • • • •	892	Panegyr Dean	164
. . . say is (tho' written somewhat at large) trim and clean;		1024	Nim-Dan-Dean 2	D 17
CLEANER				
Produce a richer vein or cleaner ore;	• • • • • •	45	To Congreve	52
CLEANING				
Nor Boy brought up to cleaning Shoes,	• • • • •	641	On Poetry	35
Some cleaning hollow Tubes, to spy	• • • • • •	780	Mullinix Tim	247
CLEANLINESS				
Such Cleanliness from Head to Heel:	• • • • • •	584	Strephon Chloe	10
From whence a Cleanliness remains,	• • • • • •	691	Cadenus Vaness	162
CLEANLY				
In calling Celia sweet and cleanly.	• • • • • •	526	Lady's Dres Rm	18
No cleanly Workman can endure the Stink.	• • • •	535	To Mr. Gay	128
Of cleanly Houses who will doubt,	• • • • • • •	787	Clad in Brown	29
CLEANLYNESS				
In utmost Cleanlyness excell	• • • • • • • •	732	Verses Vanessa	4
CLEANS'D				
These Venus cleans'd from ev'ry spurious Grain	• • •	118	Biddy Floyd	9
CLEAR				
She soars clear out of sight,	• • • • • • • •	31	Ode to Temple	144
Till Honesty and Conscience are clear out of sight.	•	36	Ode Sancroft	58
Wine can clear up <Godolphin's> cloudy Face,	• • • •	163	Toland's Invit	19
Want your assistance now to clear 'em.	• • • • •	186	Scriblerus 3	4
<Walpole> and Ayslaby, to clear the Doubt,	• • • •	195	Author Himself	41
I Often wish'd, that I had clear	• • • • • • •	198	Horace 2, 6	1
The Mimickry of deep yet clear.	• • • • • • • •	271	Apollo's Edict	D 49
The Wise pretend to make it clear,	• • • • • •	366	Answer Delaney	1
But, yet the Point is not so clear in	• • • • •	366	Answer Delaney	27
My Conscience is clear, and my Spirits are calm,	• •	400	Tom Clinch	21
But, when of smoak the room is clear,	• • • • •	419	Holyhead Journ	3
Whereof, to make the Matter clear,	• • • • • •	526	Lady's Dres Rm	9
You want a Hand to clear a filthy Sink;	• • • • •	535	To Mr. Gay	127

	PAGE	TITLE	LINE
CLEAR (CONTINUED)			
He came to Court with Fortune clear,	606	Beasts Confess	165
The bolt discharg'd, the sky grows clear;	617	Scandal Poem 1	12
The Bolt discharg'd, the Sky grows clear:	624	Scandal Poem 2	12
Clear your Looks, and smooth your Stile:	633	Epistle Lady	108
How shall his Innocence be clear?	707	Cadenus Vaness	641
How by the Almanack 'tis clear,	781	Mullinix Tim	275
His Guilt is clear the Proofs are pregnant,	798	Traulus 1	93
And swagger while the Coast is clear:	824	Printer Newgat	7
A Purchase which will bring him clear,	875	Drapier's Hill	3
Your style so clear, and so concise,	889	Panegyr Dean	73
CLEAR'D			
At last, the Point was fully clear'd;	598	Problem Solved	31
CLEARER			
But Carolina shines the clearer	466	Birthday Song	179
CLEAREST			
And toast them at the clearest Fire;	529	Lady's Dres Rm	102
CLEARLY			
Which now I clearly understand,	254	Bubble	99
"It clearly shews that all Reflection	563	Death of Swift	275
Hobbes clearly proves that ev'ry Creature	651	On Poetry	319
As clearly shows you bred at Court!	889	Panegyr Dean	84
CLEARS			
Till the Sun clears the Air; and then	84	Salamander	35
Her Spots are gone, her Visage clears.	226	Prog of Beauty	8
CLEAVINGS			
What a Clutter with Clippings, Dividings, and Cleavings!	804	Irish Bishops	33
CLEFT			
White Lead can plaister up a Cleft,	229	Prog of Beauty	114
CLEFTS			
Through Clefts oppugnant force a Vent;	923	Riddle 7	86
CLEM			
Last Night arriv'd Clem and his Wife.	283	Journal	118
For Clem gets all the dainty bits.	283	Journal	126
<CLEMENTS>			
There sit <Clements>, <Dilks>, and <Harrison>,	837	Legion Club	181
<Harrison>, and <Dilks>, and <Clements>,	837	Legion Club	185
CLERGY			
Peers, Clergy, Gentry, all are Benefactors;	274	Epilogue	7
The Church and Clergy here, no doubt,	401	Window Inns 4	1
He chanc't to spy a Clergy Lark;	513	Answer Fable	46
He hears the Clergy are offended;	605	Beasts Confess	126
Some Clergy too she wou'd allow,	701	Cadenus Vaness	460
To Hell on the Backs of the Clergy wou'd ride;	804	Irish Bishops	18
And the Clergy, forsooth, must take up with their Leavings.	804	Irish Bishops	34
The <Bishops> divide, but the Clergy unite.	805	Irish Bishops	44
He only the rights of the clergy debates,	816	Yahoo's	31
Send the Clergy all to graze;	838	Legion Club	216
Do but hear on the Clergy how glib his Tongue ran;	872	Grand Question	140
Give me but a Barrack, a Fig for the Clergy.	873	Grand Question	190
The Clergy keep me for their Ease,	920	Riddle 6	7
CLERGY-CLOTH			
Not sparing his own Clergy-Cloth,	548	Life of Swift	113
CLERGY-GOWN			
When they see a Clergy-Gown.	831	Legion Club	56
CLERGYMAN			
A Clergyman of special Note,	171	Horace 1, 7	27
CLERGYMEN			
To hinder Clergymen from thriving);	174	Horace 1, 7	106
If Clergymen, to shew their Wit,	392	Young's Satire	39
In Clergymen the greatest Fault.	942	Probatur Alit	6
CLERK			
Call'd to the Clerk in manner mild,	128	Little House	51
The Clerk said to her in a Heat,	128	Little House	55
For three thirteens and sixpence to the clerk.	308	Billet Players	20
First to a dapper Clerk she beckon'd,	690	Cadenus Vaness	108
Our Clerk, for he can read and write;	886	Rev Market-Hill	94
Where, to us unknown, a Clerk	931	Riddle 18 D	7
<CLEVELAND>			
Wine can give <Portland> Wit, and <Cleveland> Sense,	164	Toland's Invit	23
CLEVER			
I can't but think 'twould sound more clever,	198	Horace 2, 6 D	
As clever Tom Clinch, while the Rabble was bawling,	399	Tom Clinch	1
Then follow the Practice of clever Tom Clinch,	400	Tom Clinch	23
CLEW			
And I got thro' the Crowd, tho' not led by a Clew, sick	1029	Dr. Helsham	22
CLICK			
Because like a Watch it always cries Click:	351	Wood Insect	21
If the Maggot cries Click when it scratches the Post.	351	Wood Insect	24
CLIENT'S			
Condemn'd to bear his client's purse;	435	Answer Paulus	90
And, in his client's just defence,	435	Answer Paulus	111
CLIENTS			
By clients to her priests and trustees.	433	Answer Paulus	30
'Tis wise, no doubt, as clients fat ye more,	433	Answer Paulus	41
By clients always overwitted.	434	Answer Paulus	60
With early clients at his door,	434	Answer Paulus	71
On the Horses of their Clients;	573	Helter Skelter	4
And strip their Clients to their Coats;	930	Riddle 15 D	27

141

	PAGE	TITLE	LINE
CLIFF			
As from a mossy Cliff distill;	589	Strephon Chloe	176
CLIFFS			
But Albion's cliffs are out at heel, ...	468	Birthday Song	244
CLIFTS			
Mean time secure on Garr'way Clifts	256	Bubble	153
CLIMATE			
He damns the Climate, and complains of Spleen. . . .	137	City Shower	12
Our chilling Climate hardly bears	640	On Poetry	7
Whatever climate you were in.	899	Dean's Reasons	26
CLIMATES			
Shines in all Climates like a Star;	398	Earl of P-b-w	31
And, in all Climates are at home;	627	Scandal Poem 2	122
CLIMB			
To climb at Victory	9	Ode to King	103
And Climb the dark Stairs to your friends who have none:	185	Scriblerus 1	4
To climb to our Region, and thence to steal Fire; . .	266	Apollo	96
They often climb, and oftner creep.	412	Desire Possess	20
By Party-steps no Grandeur climb at, ...	503	Doctor Delaney	109
No higher climb than mount Olymp	620	Scandal Poem 1	102
No higher climb than Mount Olymp, ...	626	Scandal Poem 2	100
Thus, Shou'd I attempt to climb, ...	638	Epistle Lady	257
In vain to frisk or climb he tries;	885	Rev Market-Hill	81
CLIMB'D			
The heavy Wall climb'd slowly after.	112	Bauc & Phil 2	54
But, as he climb'd to grasp the Crown, ...	413	Desire Possess	47
CLIMBING			
Four Stories climbing to her Bow'r;	581	Young Nymph	8
CLIMBS			
Climbs downwards, deeper by a Yard:	654	On Poetry	398
Climbs from the Toe to touch the Heart.	710	Cadenus Vaness	741
CLIME			
To no one Clime shou'd be confin'd;	387	Manly Virtue	116
From India's burning Clime I'm brought, ...	911	Aenigma	1
CLIMES			
Those who in warmer Climes complain	731	Stella, Poems	109
CLINCH			
As clever Tom Clinch, while the Rabble was bawling, .	399	Tom Clinch	1
Then follow the Practice of clever Tom Clinch, . . .	400	Tom Clinch	23
CLINCHER			
One Clincher more, and I have done, ...	515	Answer Fable	101
CLING			
And, that they may the closer cling, ...	190	Faggot	37
CLINKER			
"A Protestant's a special Clinker;	550	Life of Swift	176
CLINKS			
Because it clinks to Caroline.	467	Birthday Song	220
CLIO			
To mournful Ditties, Clio, change thy Note, ...	284	Elegy Boat	1
Now, gentle Clio, sing or say, ...	690	Cadenus Vaness	126
Had not Clio in the Nick, ...	833	Legion Club	97
Clio, who had been so wise	833	Legion Club	109
Clio stifled with the Smell, ...	834	Legion Club	121
CLIPP'D			
Forc'd on me, crack'd, and clipp'd, and counterfeit, . .	45	To Congreve	56
CLIPP'T			
His wings are clipp't; he tryes no more in vain . . .	678	Dean and Duke	7
CLIPPINGS			
What a Clutter with Clippings, Dividings, and Cleavings!	804	Irish Bishops	33
CLO'ES			
To peep at the Captain, in all his fine Clo'es: . . .	872	Grand Question	136
CLOACINA			
But, Cloacina Goddess bright, ...	897	Panegyr Dean	343
CLOACINE			
Here, gentle Goddess Cloacine, ...	893	Panegyr Dean	205
Thee bounteous Goddess Cloacine, ...	894	Panegyr Dean	229
CLOAK			
He walk'd the Streets, and wore a Thread-bare Cloak; .	234	Elegy on Demar	9
I lost my new Cloak.	245	Irish-Feast	20
Sweetly snoring in his Cloak.	836	Legion Club	160
CLOAKS			
Their Hoods, their Cloaks, and get them gone: . . .	453	Modern Lady	287
Their Cow-boys bearing Cloaks before 'um, ...	760	Receipt Youth	46
CLOATH SEE BROAD-CLOATH			
CLOATH'D			
To be cloath'd like a Carcass would make a Teague mad,	237	Excellent Song	12
CLOATHED			
Thy Body's cloathed like thy Soul.	787	Clad in Brown	16
CLOATHS			
Incumbrances of Food and Cloaths;	231	Prog of Poetry	42
His odious Goun would soil her Cloaths, ...	292	Prog Marriage	80
And hire us out their scenes, and cloaths, and faces. .	307	Billet Players	8
'Bout latent Charms beneath my Cloaths;	1004	Dan J's Reply	22
CLOCK SEE A-CLOCK			
Became a Clock, and still adher'd, ...	94	Bauc & Phil 1	142
Became a Clock, and still adher'd:	113	Bauc & Phil 2	80
Like a clock without wheels;	852	Lady's Lament	34
CLOCKS			
With mournful Note clocks round the Brim.	295	Horrid Plot	150

	PAGE	TITLE	LINE
CLOD			
To keep that worthless clod, the body, in one place:	36	Ode Sancroft	64
Byzantians boast, that on the Clod	324	Pethox	39
CLOE			
Then Cloe, still go on to prate	735	Stel B-day '20	39
CLOE'S			
Or stop and light at Cloe's Head	735	Stel B-day '20	37
CLOG'D			
To Stomachs clog'd with costly Fare,	378	Apology Lady C	105
CLOGHER			
Smedley, thou Jonathan of Clogher,	476	Epist on Epist	31
CLOISTER'D			
To see her cloister'd like a Nun.	705	Cadenus Vaness	583
CLONFERT			
"In sending Bolton to Clonfert.	304	Storm	42
CLOSE			
Follow the model close, for so I'm sure they should,	40	Ode Sancroft	183
And keep close to Thee always that Name,	148	Windsor Proph	23
Keep close then Boys, and never quarrel.	189	Faggot	13
United close in ev'ry Part.	344	Prometheus	6
Yet link them close; in this they jump,	435	Answer Paulus	105
Or if she chance to close her Eyes,	582	Young Nymph	40
Then, squeeze it close between our Thumbs,	627	Scandal Poem 2	129
In the close bands of pleasing hymen.	675	Curate's Compl	6
Before he could his Poem close,	730	Stella, Poems	77
Because too close I hold my Purse.	918	Riddle 4	28
Close, as the Macedonian Phalanx:	1021	Nim-Dan-Dean 1	D 30
With Alexandrian in the Close,	1022	Nim-Dan-Dean 1	D 53
CLOSELY			
Fill'd up with Dirt so closely fixt,	526	Lady's Dres Rm	21
Thy Words so closely wedg'd, and short are,	1021	Nim-Dan-Dean 1	D 21
CLOSER			
And, that they may the closer cling,	190	Faggot	37
Embrac'd thee closer than a Wife;	924	Riddle 8	7
CLOSES			
But the Moment that he closes,	931	Riddle 18	D 17
CLOSEST			
The closest Mortal ever known.	202	Horace 2, 6	104
CLOSET			
From her Closet brought out a full Purse in her Clutche	143	New Song	16
Which made thy Closet much frequented	182	Horace 2, 1	51
To seek an old rag in the closet.	756	Dingley Brent	18
CLOSING			
As at the closing an unhappy Scene	24	Ode Athenian	271
CLOTH SEE CLERGY-CLOTH			
You know, I honour the Cloth,. .	72	Mrs Harris Pet	60
In painted Cloth we look for Fields,	122	Empty'ng Town	11
A Forehead Cloth with Oyl upon't	526	Lady's Dres Rm	25
I am sure such Words does not become a Man of your Cloth,	985	Mary to Sher	3
CLOUD			
He spake, and a dark Cloud flung o're his light,	8	Ode to King	58
Like the fam'd Hero in his Mother's Cloud,	18	Ode Athenian	88
To lodge behind a golden cloud;	41	Ode Sancroft	216
Tho' fring'd with ev'ning gold the cloud appears so gay,	41	Ode Sancroft	217
And if so black the cloud, that heaven's bright queen	53	Temple Ill	57
A Sable Cloud a-thwart the Welkin flings,	137	City Shower	14
A Cloud arose and stopt the Light,	253	Bubble	75
The Moon lay safe behind the Cloud.	253	Bubble	80
The Cloud, and drive the Hag to Hell:	354	Simile Silver	12
That cloud the Brows	442	Ballyspellin	70
A Cloud with Woman kind compare?	617	Scandal Poem 1	2
You'll see a Cloud in gentle weather	618	Scandal Poem 1	43
Jove dresst a Cloud in Juno's shape,	619	Scandal Poem 1	54
His Cloud, and Jove's imperiall Queen.	619	Scandal Poem 1	58
This Cloud produc'd a race of Centaurs	619	Scandal Poem 1	59
And yet her father is a Cloud:	619	Scandal Poem 1	76
No Lightning comes but from a Cloud.	622	Scandal Poem 1	152
A Woman with a Cloud compare?	623	Scandal Poem 2	2
A Cloud, in proper Seasons pours	624	Scandal Poem 2	27
You'll see a Cloud in gentle Weather	625	Scandal Poem 2	39
Jove drest a Cloud in Juno's Shape:	625	Scandal Poem 2	50
His Cloud, and Jove's Imperial Queen:	625	Scandal Poem 2	54
His Cloud produc'd a Race of Centaurs,	625	Scandal Poem 2	55
And yet her Father is a Cloud.	625	Scandal Poem 2	74
That Light'ning comes but from a Cloud.	628	Scandal Poem 2	156
Else she must interpose a Cloud:	689	Cadenus Vaness	78
Breaks like the Sun behind a Cloud,	726	Io Stella	82
A Fish, a Fowl, a Cloud, a Field,	927	Riddle 10	D 15
CLOUDED			
To weak, or old, or clouded Eyes.	367	Answer Delaney	46
What Billet-doux, and clouded Cains!	585	Strephon Chloe	38
A flaxen wig, and clouded cane,	619	Scandal Poem 1	70
A Flaxen Wig, and Clouded Cane.	625	Scandal Poem 2	66
Clouded if my face is seen,	937	Riddle 24	D 39
CLOUDS			
Raise envy's clouds to leave themselves in night,	45	To Congreve	79
With how undecent clouds are overcast	52	Temple Ill	33
If This to Clouds and Stars will venture,	393	Modern Poets	7
That Clouds are blam'd for giving Claps:	618	Scandal Poem 1	22
Can Clouds give buboes, ulcers, blotches?	618	Scandal Poem 1	25

CLOUDS   (CONTINUED)   PAGE   TITLE   LINE
    If Clouds were but like Femals fickle;   . . . . . .   618 Scandal Poem 1   42
    Ador'd the Clouds as Deityes.   . . . . .   619 Scandal Poem 1   80
    (Who makes you think the Clouds he pierces: . . . .   620 Scandal Poem 1   103
    He pierce the Clouds! he kiss our <arses>)   . . . .   620 Scandal Poem 1   104
    When you compare us Clouds to her: . . . . . .   622 Scandal Poem 1   160
    That Clouds are blam'd for giving Claps;   . . . . .   624 Scandal Poem 2   16
    Can Clouds give Bubo's, Ulcers, Blotches, ...   624 Scandal Poem 2   19
    Which fell in Clouds beneath his Feet)   . . . . .   625 Scandal Poem 2   68
    Ador'd us Clouds as Deities, ...   626 Scandal Poem 2   78
    (Who makes you think, the Clouds he pierces: . . . .   626 Scandal Poem 2   101
    He pierce the Clouds! He kiss their <Arses>.) . . .   626 Scandal Poem 2   102
    While o'er the Church these Clouds are gathering,   813 Bro Protestant   47
CLOUDY
    When War her cloudy aspect just withdrew, ...   16 Ode Athenian   23
    Wine can clear up <Godolphin's> cloudy Face, ...   163 Toland's Invit   19
    Sits on her cloudy wrinckled Face.   . . . .   226 Prog of Beauty   4
    All reeking in a cloudy Steam.   . . . .   226 Prog of Beauty   14
    The more she scolds, the more she's cloudy. . . . . .   617 Scandal Poem 1   14
    You know, a cloudy sky bespeaks   . . . .   618 Scandal Poem 1   29
    But, women in a cloudy plight   . . . . .   618 Scandal Poem 1   31
    The more she scolds, the more she's cloudy. . . . . .   624 Scandal Poem 2   14
    You know a Cloudy Sky bespeaks   . . . . .   624 Scandal Poem 2   23
    But, Women in a Cloudy Plight, ...   624 Scandal Poem 2   25
CLOUT   SEE DISH-CLOUT
    In power of Spittle and a Clout   . . . . . .   61 Lady Tablebook   21
    Her Washes, Slops, and every Clout, ...   530 Lady's Dres Rm   139
    Seen from behind a dirty Clout: . . . . . .   786 Clad in Brown   10
CLOVEN
    You may know by the Hand, it had no Cloven Foot.   . .   77 Lady B- B-   30
    And eke your cloven foot.   . . . . .   428 Beau's Reply   8
    That one cloven Tongue, ever sat on your Head; . . .   805 Irish Bishops   50
    If your Stockings were off, you cou'd show cloven Feet.   805 Irish Bishops   52
CLOWN
    One surly Clown lookt out, and said, ...   91 Bauc & Phil 1   37
    "Neal Gahagan, Hibernian Clown, ...   851 Old Thorn   82
    You shan't stir a Foot--You'll think me a Clown--   869 Grand Question   78
    "A Hundred to One, but it covers a Clown;   . . . .   872 Grand Question   154
    That we both act the Part of the Clown and the Cow-dung   967 Letter Sherid   2
    And I'll use you as he did that overgrown Clown,   . .   968 Letter Sherid   31
CLOWNISH
    His Money spent! a clownish Reason?   . . . .   294 Prog Marriage   127
CLOWNS
    So, Clowns on Scholars as on Wizards look, ...   193 Author Himself   7
CLOY'D
    With Women Compounds I am cloy'd, ...   272 Apollo's Edict   D 60
    With Elegies, the Town is cloy'd: . . . . .   558 Death of Swift   166
    Till the Company was cloy'd.   . . . . . .   630 Epistle Lady   6
CLOYING
    Ever eating, never cloying, ...   930 Riddle 16   D   1
CLUB
    From our Mysterious Club to keep out Spies, ...   165 Toland's Invit   29
    With which inspir'd we'll club each Night   . . . .   184 Horace 2, 1   113
    Let not the whigs our tory club rebuke;   . . . . . .   186 Scriblerus 3   1
    And calld by Excellence, the Club: . . . . .   217 To Mr. Delany   58
    But see, the Female Club disbands, ...   451 Modern Lady   196
    You may soon be of the Club.   . . . . .   502 Doctor Delaney   64
    That Club of Candidates in Black, ...   503 Doctor Delaney   85
    "My Lady Club wou'd take it ill, ...   562 Death of Swift   237
    A Club assembled at the Rose;   . . . . .   565 Death of Swift   300
    He heard, there was a Club of Cheats   . . . . . .   607 Beasts Confess   191
    But all the rest shall club it I protest:--- . . . .   671 Epig Carthy 24   D 6
    With the Name of Legion Club.   . . . . . .   829 Legion Club   12
    That the Club have Right to dwell   . . . . . .   830 Legion Club   43
    I pay my Club, and so God b'y'--.   . . . . . .   954 Authors Living   10
CLUB'D
    Club'd for a Feather to his Hat;   . . . .   903 Death Daphne   30
CLUBS
    Can in her Female Clubs dispute   . . . .   416 Woman's Mind   29
    Her Chair to call the King of Clubs, ...   452 Modern Lady   259
    But, never from Religious Clubs;   . . . .   583 Young Nymph   54
CLUD
    When Mother Clud had risen from Play, ...   86 Hist V's House   1
CLUMSY
    That clumsy outside of a Porter, ...   796 Traulus 1   19
    Hence the greazy clumsy Mien, ...   300 Traulus 2   31
CLUSTER
    With Prudence gath'ring up a Cluster   . . . .   647 On Poetry   221
CLUTCHES
    From her Closet brought out a full Purse in her Clutche   143 New Song   16
CLUTTER
    But then, to come and keep a Clutter   . . . . . .   314 To Ford   95
    That, a Rogue so Obscure should make such a Clutter, .   334 Serious Poem   6
    But prithee Tim, why all this Clutter?   . . . . . .   773 Mullinix Tim   2
    You Clutter still your Brazen Kettle.   . . . . .   775 Mullinix Tim   46
    What a Clutter with Clippings, Dividings, and   804 Irish Bishops   33
        Cleavings!
CLYENT
    He never squeez'd a needy Clyent: . . . .   603 Beasts Confess   80
CLYMATES
    And, in all clymates are at home: . . . .   621 Scandal Poem 1   128

144

```
CLYMES                                                             PAGE   TITLE           LINE
    Absent from whom all Clymes are curst      . . . . . . .       420  Holyhead              25
COACH   SEE HACKNEY-COACH
    Then lighted from his Glitt'ring Coach,        . . . . .       119  Apollo Outwit          6
    Stays till 'tis fair, yet seems to call a Coach.   . . .       138  City Shower           36
    He pull'd the String, and stopt his Coach,      . . . .        172  Horace 1, 7           61
    Attend thy Coach, and hear them shout     . . . . . . .        183  Horace 2, 1           80
    Takes him to Windsor in his Coach, alone.    . . . . . .       194  Author Himself        32
    Would take me in his Coach to chat,     . . . . . . .          201  Horace 2, 6           67
    A Coach and Six, and serv'd in Plate:                          251  Bubble                20
    If in her Coach she'll condescend    . . . . . . . . .         292  Prog Marriage         77
    Serve for a Motto on thy Coach?     . . . . . . . . .          348  Whtshed Motto          4
    One Coach oft' carried them when they were quick,    . .       430  Dicky Dolly           14
    With Coach and Six, and House in Town.      . . . . . .        585  Strephon Chloe        42
    So fine a Coach along the Strand,      . . . . . . .           598  Problem Solved        14
    I own, 'twas but a Coach and Four,      . . . . . . .          598  Problem Solved        17
    Without his taudry coach and four;      . . . . . . .          621  Scandal Poem 1       122
    Without his lacker'd Coach and Four,      . . . . . .          627  Scandal Poem 2       116
    Although they came not in a Coach.     . . . . . . .           701  Cadenus Vaness       459
    As the Coach stopp'd, she look'd & swore     . . . . .         746  Stel Distress         27
    As the Coach stopp'd, she look'd & swore     . . . . .         746  Stel Distress
    A peck of troubles for a coach.    . . . . . . . . .           753  Gift for Bec          20
    To live without a coach and six,    . . . . . . .             878  Robbin & Harry        30
    To troll it in a Coach and Six!     . . . . . . .             905  Death Daphne          88
    There's neither Chariot, Coach, or Mill,     . . . . .         929  Riddle 14         D   7
    With what an air he mounts his coach!    . . . . . .           951  Upstart           D  24
    To the very coach side, and threaten your letters.    . .      978  Dean to Tho: S         4
    But coach it or cart it, I'd have you know, Sirrah,   .        979  Dean to Tho: S        11
    No Sea overwhelms him, no Coach overturns;     . . . .        1037  Four Storyes           6
COACH-HIRE
    You'll spend in Coach-hire more than save in Wine.    . .      137  City Shower            8
COACH-MAN
    And, when the Coach-man comes for pay,     . . . . . .         878  Robbin & Harry         3
COACHES
    "Thro' Crowds of Coxcombs & of Coaches;     . . . . .          380  Apology Lady C       152
COACHMAN
    The Coachman stopt, she lookt, and swore     . . . . .         751  Stel Wood-Park        47
COADJUTOR
    And must have an old, or a young Coadjutor:     . . .          144  New Song              42
    Had fix'd on for her Coadjutor.    . . . . . . . .            701  Cadenus Vaness       465
    Robert and Darby's Coadjutor:     . . . . . . . . .          888  Panegyr Dean          40
COALS
    "My Husband left to pay for Coals:      . . . . . .           447  Modern Lady           67
    Computing by their Pecks of Coals,      . . . . . . .         649  On Poetry            281
    Or send him in a Peck of Coals;      . . . . . . .           728  Stella, Poems         34
    Among the Coals does often rattle.     . . . . . . .          942  Probatur Alit          2
COARSE
    he's loud in his laugh & he's coarse in his Jest    . . .     540  Charac Walpole         2
    While a coarse English Tongue will itch,     . . . . .        949  Epigr Scolding         3
COARSEST   SEE COURSEST
    While Dunces of the coarsest Clay,     . . . . . .           497  Panegyr Swift        148
COAST
    From Fleets triumphant o'er the Gallick Coast.    . . .        771  Horace 1, 14          40
    And swagger while the Coast is clear:     . . . . .           824  Printer Newgat         7
COASTERS
    The Coasters crowd to seise the Spoyl,     . . . . . .         258  Bubble               202
COASTS
    Of some Invasion on your coasts . . . . . . . . .             422  Ireld                 42
COAT    SEE WAST-COAT,TURN-COAT,SCARLET-COAT
    Where having cast his coat, and well pursu'd    . . .          46  To Congreve          117
    I never took one in Your Coat. .      . . . . . . .            72  Mrs Harris Pet        61
    With gawdy Coat, and shining Train,     . . . . . .            83  Salamander            31
    His Grazier's Coat reach down his Heels,     . . . . .         94  Bauc & Phil 1        166
    Like a rich Coat with Skirts of Frize:     . . . . .           96  On the Union           8
    His Grazier's Coat fall down his Heels;     . . . . .         115  Bauc & Phil 2        118
    When Dust and Rain at once his Coat invade;     . . .         138  City Shower           28
    His only Coat, where Dust confus'd with Rain,    . . .        138  City Shower           29
    For shunning those of his own Coat;     . . . . . .          171  Horace 1, 7           28
    With Coat embroider'd richly shine,     . . . . . .          182  Horace 2, 1           74
    His Two-Year's Coat so smooth and bare,     . . . . .         231  Prog of Poetry        35
    And only Coat of tarnish't Lace;      . . . . . . .          295  Prog Marriage        162
    Inclos'd Cap-a-pee in a strong Coat of Mail.    . . .         350  Wood Insect            6
    He had not learn'd to turn his Coat,     . . . . . .          604  Beasts Confess        97
    A Coat we gave him dy'd in grain     . . . . . . .           619  Scandal Poem 1        69
    A Coat we gave him, dy'd in Grain,     . . . . . .           625  Scandal Poem 2        65
    I have a Coat at home, that you may try,     . . . . .        780  Mullinix Tim         217
    'Tis not the Coat that looks so dun,     . . . . . .         786  Clad in Brown          7
    See they gently twitch his Coat,      . . . . . . .          836  Legion Club          169
    That Men of his Coat should be minding their Prayers.        868  Grand Question        37
    His Grazier's coat with dirt besmear'd,     . . . . .        879  Robbin & Harry        43
    Clad in a coat of Podesway,    . . . . . . . . .            879  Robbin & Harry        47
    His Coat, an Us'rer's Velvet Pall,     . . . . . .          904  Death Daphne          31
COATS   SEE JOCKEY-COATS
    Disguis'd in two old thredbare Coats     . . . . . .          63  Discovery             34
    And strip their Clients to their Coats;     . . . . .        930  Riddle 15         D  27
COAX
    You mistake; for a Slave, who will coax his superiors,   .    817  Yahoo's               68
COBBLE
    Nor pump to cobble wicked Verse;      . . . . . . .          181  Horace 2, 1           36
    For then he could Coyn and could Cobble together;    . .     287  Bank Down             28
```

145

	PAGE	TITLE	LINE

COBLER

A Cobler, Starmonger, and Quack, ... 101 Elegy Patrige 104
But the Cobler was angry, and swore he had rather . . 287 Bank Down 26

COBLER'S

The dullest Beast and a Cobler's Tool, ... 941 Letter 18

COBLERS

A List the Coblers Temples ties, ... 98 Elegy Patrige 23
On Coblers Militant below, ... 100 Elegy Patrige 90

COBLING

There is 'twixt Cobling and Astrology; . . . . . 98 Elegy Patrige 20
'Twixt Cobling and the Planet Science. . . . . . 98 Elegy Patrige 30
Shews how the Art of Cobling bears . . . . . . 99 Elegy Patrige 39
The Cobling and Star-gazing Part, ... 100 Elegy Patrige 70

COCK

Reckoning Roof, Weather Cock and all, ... 126 Little House 7
Dick would cock his Nose in scorn, ... 784 Mullinex Dick 9
"But at Cuffs I was always the Cock of the School; . 873 Grand Question 164

COCK'D

(His Beaver is cock'd; pray, Madam, mark that, . . . 870 Grand Question 105

COCK'T

He cock't his Hat, you would have said . . . . . 156 Fable of Midas 13

COCKADE

But like a Girl's Cockade, was ty'd . . . . . . 458 Paddy's Charac 17
And thinking this Cockade of Wit . . . . 458 Paddy's Charac 21

COCKADED

"From the first fierce cockaded Centry, ... 380 Apology Lady C 153

COCKER'D

Cocker'd by the Servants round, ... 631 Epistle Lady 37

COCKS

Looks up to your Window, and cocks up his Beaver. . . 870 Grand Question 104

COCKSCOMB

What senseless Cockscomb told you so, ... 505 Doctor Delaney 160

CODILL

"Four Mattadores, and lose Codill! . . . . . . 446 Modern Lady 52
Lord, Madam, you have lost Codill; . . . . . . 452 Modern Lady 246

CODLING

A Codling e'er it went his Lip in, ... 156 Fable of Midas 5
Where never yet a Codling ripen'd: . . . . . . 883 Rev Market-Hill 4

COELESTIAL

So blush'd Aurora with coelestial Charms, ... 669 Epig Carthy 13 D 1

COFFEE

Tobacco, Censure, Coffee, Pride, and Port. . . . 194 Author Himself 22
Her Spouse desires his Coffee soon, ... 291 Prog Marriage 37
Harmonious Coffee show thy Zeal, ... 515 Answer Fable 87
Would chuse in Peace to drink my Coffee. . . . . 733 Verses Vanessa 30
'Til coffee has her stomach lin'd; . . . . . . 761 Bec's B-Day 34
May fortune and her coffee get her . . . . . . 762 Bec's B-Day 47

COFFEE-HOUSE

Sauntering is Coffee-house in Dulman seen; . . . . 137 City Shower 11
Tho not a Coffee-house we read in . . . . 462 Birthday Song 51
Town-Jests, and Coffee-house Conceits; . . . . . 645 On Poetry 154

COFFEEHOUSE

At consort, coffeehouse, or court; . . . . . . 677 Parson's Case 28

COFFERS

His Coffers from the Coffin could not save, . . . 234 Elegy on Demar 21
With each a Million in his Coffers. . . . . . . 253 Bubble 72
The Ducal Coffers, trusted to your Charge, . . . 533 To Mr. Gay 45
To raise his Post, or fill his Coffers, ... 549 Life of Swift 139
All coffers full except his own. . . . . 659 On Poetry D 416

COFFIN

His Coffers from the Coffin could not save, . . . 234 Elegy on Demar 21
Here lies Judge Boat within a Coffin. . . . . . 286 Elegy Boat 37
Squeez'd in a Coffin turn to dust; . . . . . . 467 Birthday Song 236

COG

He never once wou'd cog the Dice, ... 456 Dean Smedley 28
Could change the Stock, or cog a Dye, ... 607 Beasts Confess 193

COIFS

Instead of Home-spun Coifs were seen, ... 115 Bauc & Phil 2 139
Pinning on Coifs and combing Hair; . . . . . . 321 First of April 30
Or greasy Coifs and Pinners reeking, ... 527 Lady's Dres Rm 53

COIN

Spend their base coin before the bashful maid, . . 50 To Congreve 219
Papists disarm'd, or Fall of Coin, ... 63 Discovery 31
So to confound, this hated Coin . . . . 345 Prometheus 11
If Wood's Coin should 'mongst Us pass . . . . . 372 Letter D. S-y 35
"But the lower the coin, the higher the mob. . . . 843 Ay and No 12
"That sinking the coin is a dangerous joke. . . . 843 Ay and No 14

COIN'D

Gold ready Coin'd appear'd, instead . . . . . . 156 Fable of Midas 17
Dissolv'd, and into Money Coin'd; . . . . 345 Prometheus 38

COKES

The Lovers Fleta's, Bractons, Cokes. . . . . . 689 Cadenus Vaness 107

COL'NEL

Took Col'nel Peleus to her Bed. . . . . 587 Strephon Chloe 102
Col'nel......may be your Debtor; . . . . 633 Epistle Lady 111
Fine as a Col'nel of the Guards, ... 904 Death Daphne 55

COL'NELS

Pointed at Col'nels, Lords, and Beaux; . . . . . 701 Cadenus Vaness 478

COLBERTEEN

Good Pinners edg'd with Colberteen: . . . . . . 115 Bauc & Phil 2 140
Rich Flanders Lace, and Colberteen. . . . . . . 700 Cadenus Vaness 417

		PAGE	TITLE	LINE
COLCHESTER				
No Colchester Oyster,	. . . .	953	Oysters	5
COLCHOS				
Hither from Colchos, with the fleecy Ore,	. . . . .	790	St. Pat's Well	7
From Colchos brought the Golden Fleece:	. . . . .	948	Jason Hassard	2
COLD				
The Body, tho' Gigantick, lyes all Cold and Dead.	.	25	Ode Athenian	291
. . . .because I was cold,	. . . .	69	Mrs Harris Pet	1
This Serpent is extreamly cold,	. . . .	84	Salamander	48
So cold, that put it in the Fire,	. . . .	84	Salamander	49
By Age and Claps grown cold as Snow,	. . . . .	84	Salamander	58
"I shall be starv'd with Cold and Hunger."	. . . .	208	Fable Bitches	30
Where for fear of the Cold, I never can pass;	. . . .	264	Apollo	32
Who gets a Cold, who break their Shins.	. . . . .	280	Journal	64
The persecution of cold Water.	. . . .	321	First of April	32
She gets a Cold as sure as Death;	. . . .	417	Woman's Mind	45
That pois'nous Juice which kills by Cold.	. . . . .	469	Burning Poem	2
The cold Conceits, the chilling Thoughts,	. . . . .	470	Burning Poem	7
When, who could think, tho' cold as Ice,	. . . . .	470	Burning Poem	13
Their Passions not more impotent and cold,	. . . .	532	To Mr. Gay	21
Tho' cold would burn, tho' dry would melt.	. . . .	585	Strephon Chloe	28
With Constitution cold and snowy,	. . . . . .	588	Strephon Chloe	152
Where hot and cold, where sharp and sweet,	. . . .	711	Cadenus Vaness	774
Or throw cold Water in her Face,	. . . . . .	725	To Stella	76
My quondam Friends are grown so Cold,	. . . . .	776	Mullinix Tim	78
Thy Hand as dry and cold as Lead,	. . . . . .	905	Death Daphne	95
And am at once both Hot and Cold:	. . . . . .	912	Aenigma	12
This Night I came home with a very cold Dew sick,	. .	1030	Dr. Sheridan	2
COLDLY				
But coldly said, Your Servant, Sir.	. . . . . .	172	Horace 1, 7	54
COLICK				
Think what can give the Colick Ease,	. . . . . .	589	Strephon Chloe	168
COLL'NELL				
Wish't him a Coll'nell for her Sake.	. . . . . .	291	Prog Marriage	44
COLL'NELL'S				
Thy graceful Steps, and Coll'nell's Aîr	. . . . .	779	Mullinix Tim	205
COLLEAGUES				
Among his colleagues,	. . . .	856	Lady's Lament	161
COLLECT				
Collect Excise, or wait upon the Tide.	. . . . . .	793	St. Pat's Well	78
COLLECTED				
Collected in that Infant's Mind.	. . . .	691	Cadenus Vaness	153
COLLECTION				
And that I may have a Share in next Sunday's Collection:		73	Mrs Harris Pet	71
With this let your Collection end	. . . .	608	Know Not What	2
COLLECTIONS				
In Curll's Collections, new and old,	. . . . . .	729	Stella, Poems	50
COLLECTS				
Collects the City Filth in search of Gold.	. . . .	364	On Dreams	22
COLLEDGE				
. . . in your Colledge.	. . . .	986	Mary to Sher	16
COLLEGE				
This is gratefully own'd by each Boy in the College,	.	263	Apollo	17
My Son shall never see a College.	. . . .	377	Apology Lady C	70
"Scoffing my College Aukwardness.	. . . . . .	380	Apology Lady C	148
He shines distinguish'd in a College,	. . . . . .	384	Manly Virtue	34
Two College Sophs of Cambridge Growth,	. . . . .	593	Cassinus Peter	1
A College Joke to cure the Dumps.	. . . . . .	594	Cassinus Peter	38
But Dick had seen a College.	. . . .	784	Mullinex Dick	4
Not a Bow-shot from the College,	. . . .	829	Legion Club	3
"A Scholard, when just from his College broke loose,	. .	872	Grand Question	157
The dullest Beast and fam'd College for Teagues	. .	940	Letter	16
A long-ear'd Beast and Flanders College,	. . . . .	942	Probatur Alit	15
COLLEGE-ARTS				
And by their college-arts methodically kill:	. . . .	42	Ode Sancroft	254
COLLEGE-GREEN				
At Night between Cavan-street and College-Green:	. .	264	Apollo	54
COLLEGES				
Confine her Walks to Colleges and Schools,	. . . .	27	Ode to Temple	39
Forg'd up in Colleges and Schools.	. . . . . .	483	Libel on D- D-	92
COLLEGIONS				
Picking Wit among Collegions,	. . . .	523	Betty Grizette	23
COLLEY				
"Here's Colley Cibber's Birth-day Poem.	. . . . .	563	Death of Swift	270
COLLINS				
Hobbes, Tindal, and Woolston, and Collins, and Nayler,		815	Yahoo's	26
COLLOGUING				
For all your colloguing,	. . . .	1015	Swift to Sheri	45
COLLWAY'S				
Nay, said she, my Lord Collway's Folks are all very sad		70	Mrs Harris Pet	27
COLONEL				
Ah! dost thou not Envy the brave Colonel Chatres,	. .	519	Dean Hang Rape	49
COLONELLING				
When you went Colonelling	. . . .	441	Ballyspellin	27
COLONIES				
With Colonies might stock around	. . . .	903	Death Daphne	17
COLONY				
A Conquest and a Colony from thee,	. . . . . .	791	St. Pat's Well	19
COLOUR				
Each Colour to it's Place and Use,	. . . .	227	Prog of Beauty	47

	PAGE	TITLE	LINE
COLOUR (CONTINUED)			
I must have another of Colour more gay	389	Order of Bath	3
For with one Colour I can paint;	930	Riddle 15	D 14
COLOUR'D			
A frouzy dirty colour'd red	226	Prog of Beauty	3
With Threads of diff'rent colour'd Yarn.	594	Cassinus Peter	14
COLOURS SEE WATER-COLOURS			
And colours of a faded hue;	35	Ode Sancroft	32
Three Colours, Black, and Red, and White,	226	Prog of Beauty	21
In all the various Colours seen,	325	Pethox	45
What Colours each Complexion match:	416	Woman's Mind	31
All Colours, without Paint, put on,	935	Riddle 23	D 12
COLT			
We'll colt him thro' Kevan, St. Patrick's, Donore,	817	Yahoo's	56
COLTED			
And Smithfield, as Rap was ne'er colted before;	817	Yahoo's	57
COLTS			
To be your Asses Colts of State,	499	Panegyr Swift	180
COLUMNS			
Be grav'd on either Side in Columns,	611	By Dr. Swift	9
COMB SEE BOX-COMB			
Equip our Kings, and Generalls at the Comb.	275	Epilogue	18
We comb the Wool, refine the Stuff,	948	Jason Hassard	3
COMB'D			
Whilst Mrs. Susan comb'd her Head:	698	Cadenus Vaness	373
COMBAT			
If a mind fix'd to combat fate	36	Ode Sancroft	47
The Combat of opposing Winds:	923	Riddle 7	80
COMBATS			
And with cavils combats reason:	906	Daphne	12
COMBIN'D			
The Farmers, spightfully combin'd,	174	Horace 1, 7	109
Shew'd her the Virtues all combin'd,	178	To Lord Harley	51
Combin'd in Arms, they had their Foes defy'd,	793	St. Pat's Well	81
COMBINE			
True Humor must with Wit combine,	216	To Mr. Delany	30
There's Mrs. Cut and she combine,	447	Modern Lady	76
And you and the Dean no more shall combine,	867	Grand Question	15
With Dennis you did ne'er combine,	890	Panegyr Dean	97
With Delany or Dan I would scorn to combine	1017	Swift Ans Sher	8
COMBING			
Pinning on Coifs and combing Hair;	321	First of April	30
She calls it combing of his Head,	328	Epigram 2	2
COMBS			
She combs his Head, and finds him Horn.	328	Epigram 2	4
And ev'ry day she combs his Head.	328	Epigram 3	6
And Rufa with her Combs of Lead,	450	Modern Lady	168
The various Combs for various Uses,	526	Lady's Dres Rm	20
COME			
(Th' impartial Deaths which come	8	Ode to King	68
Stay but a little while and down again 'twill come,	10	Ode to King	128
Shall (I foresee it) soon with Gothick Swarms come fort	25	Ode Athenian	298
Come from thy dear-lov'd Streams,	31	Ode to Temple	151
Whilst thus I write, vast shoals of critics come,	50	To Congreve	213
You that would grief describe, come here and trace	52	Temple Ill	51
. . . .this Five and Twenty Years, come Spring,	70	Mrs Harris Pet	30
Oh but, said I, what if after all my Chaplain won't come to?	73	Mrs Harris Pet	68
Because he could find no Word to come pat in.	76	Lady B- B-	4
You sha'n't come here nor get a Sous	91	Bauc & Phil 1	39
If I come down, I'll spoil your Trick	91	Bauc & Phil 1	45
No hurt shall come to You or Yours;	92	Bauc & Phil 1	85
Ripe fruit shall come, and all is wele.	103	Merlin	14
No Hurt shall come to You, or Yours;	112	Bauc & Phil 2	45
Dead Cats and Turnip-Tops come tumbling down the Flood	139	City Shower	63
Is come up, vi & armis, to break the <Queen's> Peace.	142	New Song	4
During Her Sacred Life, should never come over:	144	New Song	36
Will come; and <Hampden> shall have <Walpole's> Place.	165	Toland's Invit	34
If you'll be sure to come at Four,	173	Horace 1, 7	72
Must one Day come in competition,	182	Horace 2, 1	67
Come then, my lord, and take your part in	186	Scriblerus 3	7
Then come and take part in	186	Scriblerus 4	D 13
Leave John of Bucks, come here and laugh.	188	Scriblerus 6	4
Should come and make the Clatt'ring cease;	189	Faggot	24
Come Courtiers: Every Man his Stick:	190	Faggot	35
Come trimming Harcourt; bring your Mace;	190	Faggot	39
"The Peace is made, and Perkin must come over.	195	Author Himself	46
I must by all means come to Town,	199	Horace 2, 6	13
"Let my Lord know you're come to Town.	200	Horace 2, 6	24
Come with Petitions fairly pen'd,	200	Horace 2, 6	45
Finding her ripen'd Time was come,	207	Fable Bitches	3
For John was come of honest Kin:	224	Prog of Love	60
And thus the brown Meanders come	227	Prog of Beauty	43
If the Printer will peach him, he'll scarce come off clean.	238	Excellent Song	32
Come, Harper, strike up,	245	Irish-Feast	25
Come down with that Beam,	247	Irish-Feast	85
When Stock is high they come between,	253	Bubble	69
Come here their Losses to retrieve,	254	Bubble	90
We'll come and hold you by the Chin,	254	Bubble	106
Nor come within your Cullyes Reach,	258	Bubble	194

COME   (CONTINUED)   PAGE   TITLE   LINE

	PAGE	TITLE	LINE
Warn'd by the Bell, all Flocks come trembling, . . .	279	Journal	28
Her Ladyship is just come in, ...	292	Prog Marriage	92
New Lovers now will come in Swarms.	295	Prog Marriage	158
Come hither, all ye empty things, ...	296	Satiric Elegy	25
Come hither, and behold your fate.	296	Satiric Elegy	28
Come, help your lame Dog o'er the Style.	298	Horrid Plot	15
"But he'll come back the Knave he went."	306	Storm	72
Huzza! the school-boys roar, the play'rs are come!	308	Billet Players	38
Come, be content, since out it must, ...	311	To Ford	1
Nor shall I, when you hither come, ...	313	To Ford	67
But then, to come and keep a Clutter	314	To Ford	95
"When we come there we'll stand unseen, ...	321	First of April	27
For none but a Dunce would come under his Rod. . . .	335	Serious Poem	34
Then come the Poor and strip him so, they leave him not a Cross,	341	Upon His Grace	11
Come, you must take a Cup of Sack or two before you go.	342	Upon His Grace	24
She sent to bid him come and dine.	375	Apology Lady C	6
To dine with Her! and come at Three!	376	Apology Lady C	37
Calls, Crach'rode, is the Doctor come?	377	Apology Lady C	58
You'll fly when you get what you come here to steal, .	395	Dog and Thief	7
From London they come, silly People to chouse, . . .	396	Dog and Thief	17
And promis'd to pay for it when he'd come back. . .	399	Tom Clinch	4
Is this your justice, when I'm come	403	Window Inns 10 D	3
She'll come no more beneath your Roof.	408	Dial Rich Marb	12
'Tis come to what I always thought;	409	Dial Rich Marb	29
Then, let him come and take a Nap, ...	410	Dial Rich Marb	85
Till others come to help the pay	420	Holyhead	12
Should come in his place	424	Carterets Arms	10
How cou'd it come into your Mind, ...	445	Modern Lady	5
'This Company would come to Day--	448	Modern Lady	104
"Come, let us play the t'other Round.	453	Modern Lady	285
Because he dreaded to come nigh'r.	455	Dean Smedley	8
Come out with Amalthea's Horn.	464	Birthday Song	126
In Royal Robes they come by dozens	465	Birthday Song	169
And if you chance to come too late	468	Birthday Song	257
And let not Faction come betwixt.	503	Doctor Delaney	108
His Troubles and Sorrows now come in a Heap, . . .	519	Dean Hang Rape	59
It must come out alive or dead.	527	Lady's Dres Rm	68
With hasty Zeal, behold, the Steward come, . . .	533	To Mr. Gay	71
Come with a Purse of Guineas in your Hands. . . .	534	To Mr. Gay	100
Come, tell me truly, wou'd you take well, ...	546	Life of Swift	31
Yet, come in time to shew their Loves, ...	547	Life of Swift	64
The Day will come, when't shall be said, ...	547	Life of Swift	68
(When daily Howd'y's come of Course, ...	557	Death of Swift	123
"His Time was come, he ran his Race;	562	Death of Swift	241
And come to see each other damn'd;	579	Day Judgement	16
Come down to visit mortal Men:	587	Strephon Chloe	98
Consider well what may come after;	591	Strephon Chloe	232
Then come old Age whene'er it will, ...	593	Strephon Chloe	311
How? Not a Word come from thy lips?	594	Cassinus Peter	36
Come, tell us, has she play'd the Whore?	595	Cassinus Peter	45
I come, I come,--Medusa, see, ...	596	Cassinus Peter	85
I come, I come,--Medusa, see, ...	596	Cassinus Peter	85
Mr. Dean, You come too late:	630	Epistle Lady	28
Come to use, and Application:	636	Epistle Lady	186
Come out with some lampoon on D'Anvers.	658	On Poetry D	186
'Twou'd come to just Five Thousand Pound.	693	Cadenus Vaness	227
Mention'd a new Italian, come	696	Cadenus Vaness	322
And come in Crowds to see his Face:	709	Cadenus Vaness	702
So bright a Nymph to come unsought, ...	710	Cadenus Vaness	752
Come and appear, and save their Bail.	713	Cadenus Vaness	841
That, let what <Dean> soever come, ...	742	Stel B-day 22	45
Come back before you're out of Case;	760	Receipt Youth	50
And when the War is past you come	775	Mullinix Tim	49
But purely come to hear, and stare;	777	Mullinix Tim	128
Dick was come to high Renown	785	Mullinex Dick	25
Who come to fleece the Flocks, and not to feed. . .	792	St. Pat's Well	32
Whence come these inconsistent Fits?	796	Traulus 1	33
To grope for Words, and out they come.	797	Traulus 1	52
Come headlong tumbling from their mitred Chariots, . .	806	Judas	20
When told the Lieutenant was just come to Town, . . .	809	Epigr Prelate	2
Come, assist me, Muse obedient;	832	Legion Club	75
They'll come down to right themselves:	838	Legion Club	210
Would come and listen with Delight, ...	848	Old Thorn	11
You come to threescore.	854	Lady's Lament	116
Come, be a good child:	855	Lady's Lament	124
Must come in my sight;	855	Lady's Lament	146
Come, driven by heat, ...	857	Lady's Lament	189
Come flocking for pillage, ...	857	Lady's Lament	196
To come hither daily, ...	857	Lady's Lament	206
Come here out of pity, ...	858	Lady's Lament	216
No little scrub Joint shall come on my Board: . . .	867	Grand Question	14
The Captain, I'm sure, will always come here; . . .	868	Grand Question	32
But Madam, I guest there wou'd never come Good, . . .	868	Grand Question	47
And rather than come in the same Pair of Sheets . . .	869	Grand Question	59
Next Day, to be sure, the Captain will come, . . .	870	Grand Question	87
Kit, run to your Master, and bid him come to us. . .	871	Grand Question	117
You come in the very worst Time of the Year; . . .	871	Grand Question	122
Come hither, and take this old Gown for your Pains. .	873	Grand Question	186
But the Dean, if this Secret shou'd come to his Ears,	873	Grand Question	187

COME   (CONTINUED)

		PAGE	TITLE		LINE
And, in his house, if any body come,	. . . .	878	Robbin & Harry		23
And, then in surly Mode come here	. . . . . .	884	Rev Market-Hill		37
Come Spaniard, let us from our Farms	. . . .	884	Rev Market-Hill		43
Then, if our neighb'ring Friends come here,	. . . .	889	Panegyr Dean		81
The Neighbours who come here to dine,	. . . . .	891	Panegyr Dean		135
And, O! may all who hither come,	. . . . . .	894	Panegyr Dean		223
Come hither and behold the Fruits,	. . . . .	921	Riddle 7		1
They can't come near it for their Blood.	. . . .	928	Riddle 12	D	8
But soon will come the fatal Time,	. . . . .	932	Riddle 19	D	15
Will come, tho' not a Foot they go.	. . . . .	934	Riddle 21	D	6
Come dancing to me o'er the Plains.	. . . . .	934	Riddle 21	D	10
Swiftly I come, and enter there,	. . . . . .	935	Riddle 23	D	14
Come buy my fine Wares,	. . . .	951	Apples		1
Come, will you have any;	. . . .	951	Apples		5
Come, follow me by the Smell,	. . . . . .	952	Onyons		1
My Masters come buy,	. . . .	952	Oysters		2
Come eat 'em with pure fresh Butter and Mustard,	.	953	Herrings		6
Come, Six-pence a Dozen to get me some Bread,	. .	953	Herrings		8
Come, buy my fine Oranges, Sauce for your Veal,	. .	953	Oranges		1
Come sit by my side, while this picture I draw:	. .	955	Portrait Life		1
Must argue with calmness, or else will come short on't.	.	976	Dean to Sherid		12
You a Gentleman! marry come up,	. . . . . .	985	Mary to Sher		2
. . . to come out with such a Name.	. . . . .	985	Mary to Sher		6
He would come into our Kitchin,	. . .	987	Mary to Sher		32
'Tis true no Nose could come in better,	. . . . .	993	On Picture		16
. . .and come back from the Deanry,	. . .	1013	Swift to Sheri		4
Come back t'us well freighted;	. . . .	1014	Swift to Sheri		25
Till I come to a Drop;	. . . .	1015	Swift to Sheri		54
If you do not come back we shall weep out our eyn	. . .	1018	Swift Ans Sher		28
But if too many come your Madam will whine	. . . . .	1018	Swift Ans Sher		31
. . . come to town, but I don't know whether he be friend . . .		1023	Nim-Dan-Dean 2	D	7
But, however, if he be come, bring him down,	. . .	1023	Nim-Dan-Dean 2	D	8
. . . he's not come yet from Courtown, I fancy;	. . .	1023	Nim-Dan-Dean 2	D	11

COME-ROGUES
| Tho' you and your Come-rogues keep him out so late . . . | | 986 | Mary to Sher | | 16 |

COMEDIANS
| My Judgment of the old Comedians. | . . . . . . | 988 | Letter Dr Sh-n | | 16 |

COMEDIES
| These Comedies twain Friend Wood will contrive | . . . | 337 | Serious Poem | | 93 |

COMELY
| A comely Dame once clad in white, | . . . . | 923 | Riddle 7 | | 63 |

COMES
Let the vain sex dream on, their Empire comes from Us,		24	Ode Athenian		260
Yet so much sooner comes the long and gloomy Night.	. .	25	Ode Athenian		282
Comes back with joy to its own seat at night;	. . . .	51	Temple Ill		6
Say, whence it comes that thou art grown of late	. . .	53	Temple Ill		83
Till the kind <Looseness> comes, and then	. . . . .	66	Problem		31
For my Lord Dromedary comes a Tuesday without fail;	.	70	Mrs Harris Pet		28
To lodge in Garrats comes from thence.	. . . . . .	79	Vanbrug House		28
To lodge in Garrats, comes from thence.	. . . .	106	V's House		28
Where he comes ev'ry Week from Town;	. . . . .	128	Little House		57
Now in contiguous Drops the Flood comes down.	. . .	138	City Shower		31
But Cupid with a Satyr comes;	. . . .	150	Corinna		5
Next Day invited, comes agen;	. . . .	173	Horace 1, 7		76
By Harley <Swift> invited comes to Court.	. . . . .	194	Author Himself		28
But, St. John comes and whispers in his Ear;	. . . .	194	Author Himself		34
"To morrow my Appeal comes on,	. . . .	200	Horace 2, 6		51
But if a Sharper once comes in,	. . . . . .	253	Bubble		63
And then Comes in the Item of the Actors.	. . . .	274	Epilogue		8
At Ten, my Lady comes and Hectors,	. . . . .	278	Journal		13
Till Supper comes, and after that,	. . . . .	280	Journal		53
If nothing but Paper comes out of this Bank.	. . .	287	Bank Down		15
Comes home a quarter after nine,	. . . . .	292	Prog Marriage		84
To meet him next, the Soldier comes,	. . . . .	338	Wood's Brass		3
Tho' like the Cybel's Priest he comes,	. . . . .	340	Arch-Bish Dub		25
. . . yet still there comes a Season	. . . . . .	341	Upon His Grace		7
A Messenger comes all a-reek,	. . . .	398	Earl of P-b-w		13
So, sweetly screams if it comes near her,	. . . . .	416	Woman's Mind		35
(As lucus comes a non lucendo)	. . . . . .	435	Answer Paulus		115
Comes up with, "Madam, Dinner stays;	. . . . ● . .	447	Modern Lady		93
Now comes the gen'ral Scandal-Charge,	. . . . .	449	Modern Lady		144
"Whoever comes, I'm not within--	. . . .	451	Modern Lady		218
But now it comes into my mind,	. . . .	466	Birthday Song		199
He comes to drain a Beggar's Purse;	. . . . . .	484	Libel on D- D-		124
He comes to tye our Chains on faster,	. . . . .	484	Libel on D- D-		125
At last the Nightingal comes in,	. . . . . .	514	Answer Fable		63
To <Dublin> he comes, to the Bagnio he goes,	. . . .	517	Dean Hang Rape		19
Grave D. of St <Patrick> how comes it to pass	. . . .	522	St. Cecilia's		1
The Bason takes whatever comes	. . . . . .	527	Lady's Dres Rm		39
A Rival comes, and Tom---is nick'd---.	. . . . .	545	Life of Swift		18
A Set of Teeth completely comes,	. . . . . .	582	Young Nymph		20
Nor comes whene'er his Lady whistles;	. . . . .	607	Beasts Confess		213
He comes full gallop on his eagle;	. . . . .	620	Scandal Poem 1		114
No Lightning comes but from a Cloud.	. . . . .	622	Scandal Poem 1		152
He comes full gallop on his Eagle.	. . . . .	627	Scandal Poem 2		112
And shake it well, and down it comes.	. . . . .	627	Scandal Poem 2		130
That Light'ning comes but from a Cloud.	. . . . .	628	Scandal Poem 2		156
And here a Simile comes Pat in:	. . . .	642	On Poetry		61
Is bit by him that comes behind;	. . . .	651	On Poetry		342

```
COMES              (CONTINUED)                         PAGE    TITLE            LINE
    Comes pouring on me like a Flood.    . . . . . . .   655 On Poetry          438
    Down from Olympus comes with Joy,                    693 Cadenus Vaness     200
    Comes Dingley, and asks you, What was it?            756 Dingley Brent       15
    Punch comes, like you, and lets a <Fart>.   . . .   777 Mullinix Tim       122
    Perversely comes in evil Times,     . . . . . . .    798 Traulus 1           91
    Cringing comes to beg their Pardon;   . . . . . .    800 Traulus 2           14
    Talks whate'er comes in his Head,   . . . . . . .    800 Traulus 2           21
    He comes with his whims,   . . . . . . . . . .       852 Lady's Lament       39
    At last out it comes.                                854 Lady's Lament      110
    I'm grown a meer Mopus; no Company comes;   . . .    867 Grand Question      27
    For, if a new Crotchet comes into my Brain,          869 Grand Question      65
    See, now comes the Captain all dawb'd with gold Lace:  870 Grand Question    93
    At last comes the Troop, by the Word of Command   .  870 Grand Question      99
    "Observe how a Parson comes into a Room,             872 Grand Question     155
    And, when the Coach-man comes for pay,   . . . . .   878 Robbin & Harry       3
    But see, where Norah with the Sowins comes--  . . .  882 Pastoral Dial       51
    The Butter comes; our Fears are ceas't;              892 Panegyr Dean       185
    While nothing comes but Froth at first,   . . . . .  893 Panegyr Dean       193
    Comes fill'd with Rev'rence and Devotion.)           893 Panegyr Dean       212
    'Tis true, but what advantage comes   . . . . . .    899 Dean's Reasons      27
    To Ladies Skins there's nothing comes so near.       943 Probatur Alit       42
    Comes off by out-laughing the Company round.   . .   968 Letter Sherid       20
    When into my hands comes a letter from the droll. .  975 Dean to Sherid       4
    . . .before my Master comes from Pray'rs,   . . . .  987 Mary to Sher        35
    'Ere Vulcan comes to make him new.   . . . . . . .  1021 Nim-Dan-Dean 1    D  8
    Is sent to desire that, when your August vacation comes, 1022 Nim-Dan-Dean 2 D 2
        . . .
COMET
    No Comet with a Flaming Beard!   . . . . . . . .      98 Elegy Patrige       10
COMFORT
    Take Comfort, that our own is best:   . . . . . .    728 Stella, Poems       20
    (The only Comfort they propose,   . . . . . . . .    764 Stel B-day '26      23
COMFORTED
    He still was comforted to find   . . . . . . . . .   528 Lady's Dres Rm      87
COMIC
    But as to Comic Aristophanes,   . . . . . . . . .    988 Letter Dr Sh-n       5
COMING
    And timely on the coming Danger thought,   . . . .    12 Ode to William    D 19
    A coming Show'r your shooting Corns presage,   . . .  137 City Shower         9
    To t' other Ear I felt it coming on,   . . . . . .   367 Answer Delaney      43
    At coming in you saw her stoop;   . . . . . . . .    751 Stel Wood-Park      49
    Just Fifteen, coming Summer's Grass:                 760 Receipt Youth       40
    Give me Time when coming on:   . . . . . . . . .     863 To Janus            23
    "Hist, Huzzy, I think I hear some Body coming--      871 Grand Question     127
    Her Ladyship answers, I'm just coming down;   . . .  873 Grand Question     181
    And see now, it strikes ten, and I hear him coming up  987 Mary to Sher      36
        Stairs:
COMINGS
    My Goings out, and Comings in,   . . . . . . . .     918 Riddle 4            35
COMMAND
    You need but now give Orders and Command;            13 Ode to William    D 38
    <Helsham> does truly Wit command   . . . . . . .     373 Letter D. S-y       47
    "An Angel sent by Heav'n's Command,   . . . . . .    485 Libel on D- D-     166
    By Proclamation gave Command,   . . . . . . . .      601 Beasts Confess       9
    His Humour well our Laughter might command,   . . .  669 Epig Carthy 16    D  3
    Command his attendance while you act your farce on,  .  818 Epigr Kite        6
    "May that fell Dean, by whose Command                850 Old Thorn           73
    And that he may command the Chaise.   . . . . . .    860 Lady Acheson        20
    At last comes the Troop, by the Word of Command      870 Grand Question      99
    All Languages I can command,   . . . . . . . . .     915 Riddle 1            27
    I give Command to kill or save.   . . . . . . . .    916 Riddle 1            34
    A smile still ready at command,   . . . . . . . .    951 Upstart           D 29
    And so I remain in a civil way, your Servant to command.  987 Mary to Sher   38
COMMANDER   SEE LAND-COMMANDER
COMMANDS
    Thus my Subjects with pleasure will obey my Commands  .  389 Order of Bath    9
    Because her dear Papa commands.   . . . . . . . .    585 Strephon Chloe      44
    No Slave his Lord's Commands obeys,                  920 Riddle 6             3
COMMENC'D
    You never had commenc'd a Dean,                      495 Panegyr Swift       77
    Since he commenc'd Physician;   . . . . . . . . .    785 Mullinex Dick       26
COMMENCE
    Before the Hero can commence a God.   . . . . . .      7 Ode to King         30
    Commence Acquaintance underneath a Shed.   . . . .   138 City Shower         40
    Know'st thou not yet that Men commence   . . . . .   696 Cadenus Vaness     296
COMMENCEMENT
    Boldly we hence the brave Commencement Date          13 Ode to William    D 45
COMMEND
    If ev'ry Peer whom you commend,                      391 Young's Satire       9
    Commend the times, your thoughts correct   . . . .   489 Dialogue            23
    Must I commend against my conscience   . . . . . .   490 Dialogue            37
    Your Virtues safely I commend,   . . . . . . . .     730 Stella, Poems       79
COMMENDAM
    Elect of Cyprus in commendam.   . . . . . . . .      303 Storm               22
COMMENDS
    A Satyr where he most commends.   . . . . . . . .    216 To Mr. Delany       40
COMMENDUM
    For who wou'd have <Ferns> without a Commendum?   . . .  518 Dean Hang Rape   39
COMMENT
    Wou'd have the Text as well as Comment;   . . . . .  375 Apology Lady C       4
```

		PAGE	TITLE	LINE

COMMENTATORS
As learned Commentators view . . . . 643 On Poetry 103
COMMENTS
Of Comments and Disputes, ridiculous and vain, . . . 23 Ode Athenian 226
COMMISSION
"What need we open our Commission, ... 322 First of April 50
Hath joyn'd with himself two Hags in Commission: . . 336 Serious Poem 68
Take Notice, she has my Commission . . . . 418 Woman's Mind 61
And, as you in Commission sit, ... 888 Panegyr Dean 41
COMMISSIONS
By Places and Commissions sold, ... 157 Fable of Midas 47
Commissions, Perquisites, and Bribes, ... 158 Fable of Midas 78
COMMIT
The vilest Ruffian may commit a rape, ... 506 To a Friend 3
COMMITTED
The worst you can say, he committed a <Rape>. . . . . 516 Dean Hang Rape 6
And got a good Clap, but committed no <Rape>. . . . . 517 Dean Hang Rape 24
The Thorn committed to her Care, ... 850 Old Thorn 50
COMMITTEE
Before the secret wise Committee; . . . . 300 Horrid Plot 54
Let them form a grand Committee, ... 831 Legion Club 53
Chairman to yon damn'd Committee! . . . . 838 Legion Club 191
COMMITTING
E'er a week pas't committing Blunders: . . . . . . 62 Discovery 4
And this was no Time for committing a <Rape>. . . . 517 Dean Hang Rape 18
In ev'ry Debauch, but committing a <Rape>. . . . . 517 Dean Hang Rape 30
For no other Crime but committing a <Rape>. . . . . 518 Dean Hang Rape 36
And hang'd he must be for committing a <Rape>. . . . 519 Dean Hang Rape 60
Ty'd round the <Dean's> Neck, for committing a <Rape>. 519 Dean Hang Rape 66
COMMODE
A new Commode, a Top-knot, and a Ruff, ... 23 Ode Athenian 223
COMMODIOUS
"Commodious to their own Abodes. . . . . 571 Death of Swift 454
Thought no Method more commodious, ... 637 Epistle Lady 225
I wish I could find him out one more commodious. . . 803 Irish Bishops 12
COMMODORE
Make Gulliver his Commodore, ... 466 Birthday Song 206
COMMON
And had they common Generosity . . . . 24 Ode Athenian 261
Of common Breeding, common Sense, ... 27 Ode to Temple 43
Of common Breeding, common Sense, ... 27 Ode to Temple 43
Nought it contains is common or unclean, ... 50 To Congreve 233
From common Lightning of the Skies, ... 119 Apollo Outwit 10
The Peaceful State of common Brooms. . . . . 132 Magician's Rod 20
And round the barren Common strays, ... 230 Prog of Poetry 10
The common Death of many a stronger Boat. . . . . . 284 Elegy Boat 10
No common Ligament that binds . . . . 291 Prog Marriage 33
May cost a crown or so; a common case: . . . . . . 308 Billet Players 26
For Satyr now's so common grown . . . . 371 Letter D. S-y 3
Of common sense without a word in! . . . . 434 Answer Paulus 85
The lawyer is a common drudge, ... 435 Answer Paulus 87
Must deviate oft from common sense, ... 435 Answer Paulus 112
To common honesty and sense; . . . . 436 Answer Paulus 144
The common Slanders of the Times, ... 445 Modern Lady 31
"But now 'tis known to common Fame. . . . . 449 Modern Lady 149
It passes but for common Form; . . . . 453 Modern Lady 271
In wit before the common Herd? . . . . 501 Doctor Delaney 38
Must undergo the common Fate; . . . . 562 Death of Swift 251
Be easy, 'tis a common Case. . . . . 595 Cassinus Peter 50
As if it grew in common Hedges. . . . . 640 On Poetry 10
Cadenus, common Forms apart, ... 703 Cadenus Vaness 540
That common Forms were not design'd . . . . 706 Cadenus Vaness 612
The Skill of ev'ry common Beau; . . . . 712 Cadenus Vaness 813
"The Irish dear joys have enough common sense, . . . 843 Ay and No 15
To common law, or common sense; . . . . 876 To Dean Swift 20
To common law, or common sense; . . . . 876 To Dean Swift 20
And, what may serve a common Guest. . . . . 889 Panegyr Dean 96
Here bury'd in one common Grave; . . . . 923 Riddle 7 54
Who can believe with common Sense, ... 949 Epigr Fasting 1
Without a grain of common sense, ... 950 Upstart D 12
COMMON-PLACE
Fools common-place thou art, their weak ensconcing fort, 53 Temple Ill 87
COMMON-PLACE-BOOK
Her Common-Place-Book all gallant is, ... 150 Corinna 29
COMMON-PLACES
Fill'd with the choicest common-places, ... 223 Prog of Love 49
Had gone through all the Common-Places . . . . . . 730 Stella, Poems 75
COMMON-WEAL
And Wisdom for the Common-Weal. . . . . 391 Young's Satire 4
Thou Champion for the Common-weal: . . . . 515 Answer Fable 88
Duncenia to a Common-weal; . . . . 653 On Poetry 380
To serve my self and Common-weal, ... 778 Mullinix Tim 170
COMMONERS
And Commoners who love good Wine, ... 169 Peace Dunkirk 23
Twelve Commoners in Caps to Row you. . . . . 476 Epist on Epist 42
Yet Commoners with greatest Ease, ... 928 Riddle 12 D 11
COMMONLY
Commonly speaking, but a sad Jade is. . . . . . . 988 Letter Dr Sh-n 25
COMMONS
Likes both his Company and Commons; . . . . 173 Horace 1, 7 74
And <Harley> fill'd the Commons Chair) . . . . . 180 Horace 2, 1 10

	PAGE	TITLE	LINE
COMMONS (CONTINUED)			
Inform the Commons, that the Secret's out:	195	Author Himself	42
So the Commons unhors'd them, and this was their Doom,	804	Irish Bishops	21
And God bless the Commons for Biting the Biters.	805	Irish Bishops	64
COMMONWEAL			
Lest he should call our Commonweal,	96	On the Union	15
For all the Female Commonweal:	444	Modern Lady	4
COMMONWEALTHS			
Thus, Commonwealths receive a foreign Yoke,	770	Horace 1, 14	21
COMPACT			
Compact of Timber many a Load,	114	Bauc & Phil 2	102
COMPACTED SEE WELL-COMPACTED			
COMPACTS			
Born between whores and fops, by lewd compacts,	47	To Congreve	125
COMPAIR			
The Court had nothing to compair.	422	Ireld	30
COMPANION			
The best companion for the best of men:	52	Temple Ill	46
When that subtle Companion, in hopes to surpass us,	265	Apollo	80
A Companion with News,	1036	Plague Country	1
COMPANIONS			
Such high companions may delusion keep,	48	To Congreve	149
Surrounded with companions, fit	435	Answer Paulus	119
Chuse for Companions tete a tete,	480	Libel on D- D-	2
And when among Companions privy,	513	Answer Fable	37
My good Companions, never fear,	558	Death of Swift	143
Companions that will please her better;	762	Bec's B-Day	48
To have Companions in their Woes.)	764	Stel B-day '26	24
Their former Companions should beg at their Door.	804	Irish Bishops	28
Dear Companions hug and kiss,	835	Legion Club	151
By humble companions were sent to their betters:	1026	Sheri Circles	2
COMPANY			
Still cast it up and nauseate Company.	27	Ode to Temple	49
Kept Company with Men of Wit,	171	Horace 1, 7	39
Likes both his Company and Commons;	173	Horace 1, 7	74
And half the Company is teazd	217	To Mr. Delany	75
For leaving company so soon;	292	Prog Marriage	96
To let our company supply their places,	307	Billet Players	7
'This Company would come to Day--	448	Modern Lady	104
The Company to-morrow Night.	453	Modern Lady	289
But the Company stood in Defence of the Dame,	517	Dean Hang Rape	15
Till the Company was cloy'd.	630	Epistle Lady	6
Watch'd all the Company she kept,	696	Cadenus Vaness	309
She sent for Company to sup, She sends	747	Stel Distress	46
She sent for Company to sup;	751	Stel Wood-Park	62
I'm grown a meer Mopus; no Company comes;	867	Grand Question	27
The Company will fly the Room.	917	Riddle 4	8
Comes off by out-laughing the Company round.	968	Letter Sherid	20
. . .truly they don't care for your Wife's Company,	1013	Swift to Sheri	7
COMPAR'D			
You cannot be compar'd to one,	28	Ode to Temple	62
Compar'd for mischief, to Venereal?	618	Scandal Poem 1	24
What Drabs have been compar'd to Venus?	622	Scandal Poem 1	156
Compar'd for Mischief, to Venereal?	624	Scandal Poem 2	18
Each Drab has been compar'd to Venus:	628	Scandal Poem 2	160
Are you to be compar'd to Us?	884	Rev Market-Hill	42
Compar'd with which (and that's enough)	1021	Nim-Dan-Dean 1	D 9
COMPARE			
A Kingdom to a Ship compare;	96	On the Union	14
Could with this Rod of Sid compare.	135	Magician's Rod	78
And Tradesmen, to compare Brocades.	291	Prog Marriage	54
I must compare him to a Horse;	496	Panegyr Swift	113
A Cloud with Woman kind compare?	617	Scandal Poem 1	2
Compare us then to femal race!	620	Scandal Poem 1	95
Compare her radiant eyes to Lightning:	621	Scandal Poem 1	150
You may compare your Trull to us;	622	Scandal Poem 1	158
When you compare us Clouds to us:	622	Scandal Poem 1	160
Who knows how soon you will compare us	622	Scandal Poem 1	164
A Woman with a Cloud compare?	623	Scandal Poem 2	2
Compare Us then to Female Race!	626	Scandal Poem 2	93
Compare her radiant Eyes to Light'ning;	628	Scandal Poem 2	154
And may compare to Aetna's Fire,	731	Stella, Poems	105
If I compare you to the Cow?	759	Receipt Youth	22
The Lillies of thy Skin compare;	932	Riddle 19	D 7
To eels, we may compare his blood;	950	Upstart	D 8
COMPARES			
And which our wild ambition foolishly compares	38	Ode Sancroft	126
COMPARING			
Or else, comparing with the rest,	728	Stella, Poems	19
Ran to the Glass, and then comparing	783	Tim and Fables	14
COMPARISON			
Poor Satan will think the Comparison odious;	803	Irish Bishops	11
COMPARISONS			
But such Comparisons are odious.	622	Scandal Poem 1	180
But such Comparisons are odious.	628	Scandal Poem 2	162
COMPASS			
Nay, in the Compass of a Farthing.	929	Riddle 14	D 6
Will Hancock declares you are out of your compass,	1027	Sheri Circles	21
COMPASSION			
"Perhaps, may feel Compassion still,	485	Libel on D- D-	168
In Prudence and Compassion sent	849	Old Thorn	30

```
COMPELL'D                                                PAGE    TITLE          LINE
   Compell'd by you to tag in Rhimes   . . . . . . . .   445 Modern Lady          30
COMPELLING
   You thither are compelling    . . . . . . . . . .     440 Ballyspellin         15
COMPENSATE
   Would much compensate all we want.   . . . . . . . .  493 Panegyr Swift         8
COMPETENCE
   Just what you gave me, Competence:     . . . . . . .  199 Horace 2, 6          D
COMPETITION
   Must one Day come in competition,   . . . . . . . .   182 Horace 2, 1          67
COMPLAIN
   Oft 'gainst her Fountain does complain,   . . . . .    31 Ode to Temple       155
   The Dutch-hearted Whigs may rail and complain;        169 Peace Dunkirk        37
   "Of which the Christian World complain.    . . . . .  183 Horace 2, 1          98
   Of Rheumatism and Pox complain,   . . . . . . . .     311 To Ford              25
   Did Paulus e'er complain of sweat?    . . . . . .     432 Answer Paulus         5
   Since there are persons who complain                  489 Dialogue              1
   Yet, what avails it to complain:   . . . . . . . .    504 Doctor Delaney      135
   My Friend should have, when I complain,               546 Life of Swift        45
   "I know his nearest Friends complain,    . . . . .    547 Life of Swift        78
   Just in the Parts, where I complain;                  557 Death of Swift      136
   Unjustly all our Nymphs complain,   . . . . . . .     591 Strephon Chloe      255
   Nor, have I Reason to complain:   . . . . . . . .     595 Cassinus Peter       65
   Are witty, dull, rejoyce, complain.                   620 Scandal Poem 1       94
   Are witty, dull, rejoyce, complain.   . . . . . .     626 Scandal Poem 2       92
   Complain, as many an ancient Bard did,    . . . . .   652 On Poetry           349
   If 'tis with Reason they complain,                    691 Cadenus Vaness      146
   At last he ventur'd to complain:   . . . . . . . .    704 Cadenus Vaness      573
   Those who in warmer Climes complain    . . . . . .    731 Stella, Poems       109
   Or You without a Cause complain.                      733 Verses Vanessa       16
   Let me of partiall Fate complain;   . . . . . . .     739 Stel B-day '21        6
   Where stubborn Stoicks would complain.   . . . . .    765 Stel B-day '26       50
   Yet you of ev'ry Kiss complain;   . . . . . . . .     924 Riddle 8             11
   Let the Love-sick Bard complain,                      933 Riddle 20         D  13
   Nor shall they in the least complain,   . . . . . .   934 Riddle 21         D  21
COMPLAIN'D
   Himself complain'd of it to Juno.   . . . . . . .     513 Answer Fable         24
   Much of the cens'ring World complain'd,    . . . . .  603 Beasts Confess       49
COMPLAINING
   Whene'er I mourn, stops my complaining Breath,   . .   32 Ode to Temple       197
COMPLAINS
   He damns the Climate, and complains of Spleen.   . .  137 City Shower          12
   But here Mr. Wood complains that we Mock,    . . . .  335 Serious Poem         41
   Of Head-ach, and the Spleen complains;   . . . . .    446 Modern Lady          44
   Complains his Budget was too small.                   486 Libel on D- D-      192
   Wherein she grievously complains,   . . . . . . .     713 Cadenus Vaness      858
COMPLAINT
   But finding the Statue to make no Complaint,    . .   336 Serious Poem         73
COMPLAINTS
   Complaints against the Royal Butter.    . . . . . .   410 Dial Rich Marb       54
   At least, that such complaints are wise:    . . . .   433 Answer Paulus        40
   Why all this rage? Why these complaints?     . . . .  487 Irish-Club            8
   How will his Brethren make Complaints?    . . . . .   819 Dr. Rundle            4
COMPLAISANCE
   Interpreting her Complaisance,   . . . . . . . .      707 Cadenus Vaness      658
   Treat me with so much Complaisance,    . . . . . .    888 Panegyr Dean         53
COMPLAISANT
   You Officers, Captain, are so complaisant.            871 Grand Question      126
COMPLEAT
   And last, my Vengeance to Compleat,    . . . . . .    121 Apollo Outwit        61
   Suppose him, now, a Dean compleat,   . . . . . . .    174 Horace 1, 7          97
   Grandeur, by Goodness made compleat!    . . . . . .   386 Manly Virtue        101
   Request it of him to compleat your Stairs.    . . .   534 To Mr. Gay           98
   And with Jockey-Coats compleat;   . . . . . . . .     573 Helter Skelter       10
   So nice and so compleat a Beau.   . . . . . . . .     597 Problem Solved       10
   To compleat the Publick Ruin,   . . . . . . . .       636 Epistle Lady        190
   And, to compleat thy other curses,   . . . . . . .    676 Parson's Case        13
   But still the Work was not compleat,   . . . . . .    692 Cadenus Vaness      184
   Then to compleat it ev'ry way,   . . . . . . . .      726 To Stella            89
COMPLEATED
   Thus has our Prince compleated every Victory,    . .    9 Ode to King          98
COMPLEATLY
   Compleatly form'd in every Part,    . . . . . . . .   385 Manly Virtue         55
   The Monkey was compleatly drest,    . . . . . . . .   782 Tim and Fables       11
   To make a Work compleatly fine,    . . . . . . .     1022 Nim-Dan-Dean 1     D  45
COMPLEMENTALL
   Reply'd in complementall Style:    . . . . . . . .     94 Bauc & Phil 1       158
COMPLETELY
   A Set of Teeth completely comes.   . . . . . . .      582 Young Nymph          20
   Shews Sheba's Queen completely drest,    . . . . .    592 Strephon Chloe      287
COMPLEXION
   What Colours each Complexion match:    . . . . . .    416 Woman's Mind         31
   Nor is Complexion Honour's Place.   . . . . . . .     724 To Stella            22
   Will mend the complexion.   . . . . . . . . . .       854 Lady's Lament       102
   My complexion wan and green,   . . . . . . . . .      937 Riddle 24         D  40
COMPLEXIONS
   All her Complexions safe and sound,    . . . . . .    226 Prog of Beauty       30
COMPLICATED
   In vain: The complicated Wands   . . . . . . . .      189 Faggot                7
COMPLIMENT
   The greatest compliment she ever made,    . . . . .    44 To Congreve          28
```

		PAGE	TITLE	LINE
COMPLIMENT	**(CONTINUED)**			
And not my Compliment to spoyl	. . . .	311	To Ford	9
New Kings a compliment expect	. . . .	422	Ireld	37
One Compliment I had forgot,	. . . .	464	Birthday Song	129
A Compliment on Human-Kind:		608	Beasts Confess	218
As a Compliment due to a Lady so fair;	. . .	870	Grand Question	110
The rest of your compliment I dare not tell her,	. . .	979	Dean to Tho: S	25
COMPLIMENTAL				
A complimental Message sends:	. . . .	904	Death Daphne	48
COMPLIMENTS				
Where Compliments with all their Pride	. . . . . .	361	Grace's Answer	3
Can ready Compliments supply	. . . .	416	Woman's Mind	13
COMPLY'D				
So, bowing, seemingly comply'd;	. . . .	378	Apology Lady C	95
COMPLYES				
With which she patiently complyes,	. . . .	294	Prog Marriage	133
COMPOS'D				
Compos'd of Timber many a Load;	. . . .	94	Bauc & Phil 1	148
COMPOSE				
And let me in these Shades compose	. . . . . .	199	Horace 2, 6	D
Those Elements her name compose,	. . . .	467	Birthday Song	237
Above her Wisdom to compose,	. . . .	690	Cadenus Vaness	131
COMPOSITION				
The crazy composition shews,	. . . .	38	Ode Sancroft	137
Then call'd the happy Composition, Floyd.	. . .	118	Biddy Floyd	12
A Composition more absurd,	. . . .	495	Panegyr Swift	62
A Paste of Composition rare,	. . . .	526	Lady's Dres Rm	23
COMPOUND				
Glad to compound at any Rate;	. . . .	378	Apology Lady C	94
A nasty Compound of all Hues;	. . . .	527	Lady's Dres Rm	41
When 'tis a Compound of them all;	. . . . . .	711	Cadenus Vaness	773
Or, to compound the Business, whether	. . . . .	712	Cadenus Vaness	824
COMPOUNDED				
The Time was, when you'd have compounded	. . . . .	478	Epist on Epist	110
You have cheap enough compounded.	. . . .	637	Epistle Lady	240
COMPOUNDS				
With Women Compounds I am cloy'd,	. . . .	272	Apollo's Edict	D 60
COMPREHEND				
To comprehend a double Meaning.	. . . .	592	Strephon Chloe	276
Well comprehend their nat'ral Powers;	. . . . . .	607	Beasts Confess	204
COMPREHENDS				
True Honour comprehends them all.	. . . .	724	To Stella	18
COMPRISE				
If one short Volume cou'd comprise	. . . . . .	708	Cadenus Vaness	696
COMPTER				
Of Bridewell and the Compter dreams,	. . . . .	582	Young Nymph	41
COMPUTED				
Here I have computed the Profit will fall t'us.	. . .	867	Grand Question	8
COMPUTES				
Computes, that half a Parish Dues	. . . . . .	292	Prog Marriage	69
COMPUTING				
Computing all their Cost and Trouble,	. . . . .	259	Bubble	218
For nicely computing the Price by Retail,	. . . . .	288	Bank Down	36
Computing by their Pecks of Coals,	. . . . . .	649	On Poetry	281
And, after long computing, found	. . . . . .	693	Cadenus Vaness	226
Computing what I get and spend,	. . . .	918	Riddle 4	34
COMRADE				
But a Comrade of yours, that Traytor Delany,	. . .	263	Apollo	25
The <Dean>, and his Landlord, a jolly Comrade,	. . .	517	Dean Hang Rape	25
We see a Comrade get a fall,	. . . .	545	Life of Swift	13
However I wish, honest Comrade of mine	. . . . . .	1017	Swift Ans Sher	11
COMRADE'S				
My Comrade's Blind, and I'm a Creeple	. . . . .	90	Bauc & Phil 1	16
COMRADES				
Your former Comrades, once so bright,	. . . . . .	311	To Ford	23
Take Courage, dear Comrades, and be not afraid,	. . .	400	Tom Clinch	19
He grew, or else his Comrades ly'd,	. . . . .	547	Life of Swift	88
Or change his Comrades once a Quarter:	. . . . .	556	Death of Swift	96
Her dearest Comrades never caught her	. . . . . .	584	Strephon Chloe	17
COMYTH				
Then comyth foorthe, Ich understonde,	. . . . . .	102	Merlin	5
CON				
To state the question pro and con:	. . . .	435	Answer Paulus	100
CONCANNEN				
Concannen, more aspiring Bard,	. . . .	654	On Poetry	397
CONCEAL				
Nor need the lion's skin conceal the ass;	. . . . .	48	To Congreve	172
Conceal a fatal armed Force;	. . . .	209	Fable Bitches	44
Conceal, and cover us, Ye Counters.	. . . . . .	241	Run Bankers	60
Or suffer Envy to conceal	. . . .	243	Horace 4, 9	5
And when he has got it, finds Ways to conceal it;	. .	265	Apollo	60
Be sure conceal the Time and Place,	. . . . . .	311	To Ford	8
"I must conceal my Author's Name,	. . . .	449	Modern Lady	148
The Gypsey Visage to conceal:	. . . .	786	Dick, Maggot	10
How could it thus conceal a Courtier?	. . . . . .	796	Traulus 1	20
Conceal their talents from our eyes,	. . . . . .	900	Dean's Reasons	34
Conceal your Form with various Tricks;	. . . . . .	919	Riddle 5	27
CONCEAL'D				
Virtue conceal'd within our Breast	. . . .	242	Horace 4, 9	1
Conceal'd behind that ample Screen,	. . . . . .	354	Simile Silver	23
Or Libels yet conceal'd from sight---,	. . . . . .	550	Life of Swift	188

CONCEAL'D (CONTINUED) | PAGE TITLE | LINE

CONCEAL'D (CONTINUED)
Thy Labours, Carthy, long conceal'd from Light, . . 667 Epig Carthy 5 D 1
CONCEALS
While Gracefulness its Art conceals, ... 726 To Stella 83
CONCEIT
Of Dullness, Pride, Conceit, a medley, ... 455 Dean Smedley 2
The damnable the dear Conceit. . . . . 497 Panegyr Swift 127
CONCEITED
Here no conceited coxcombs pass, ... 402 Window Inns 7 D 3
If you think me too conceited, ... 630 Epistle Lady 15
Where petulant, conceited Fellows . . . . 777 Mullinix Tim 135
CONCEITS
Writes down my Conceits, and then calls them his own: . 265 Apollo 86
The cold Conceits, the chilling Thoughts, ... 470 Burning Poem 7
Town-Jests, and Coffee-house Conceits; . . . . . 645 On Poetry 154
A Truce with all sublime Conceits. . . . . . . 711 Cadenus Vaness 793
CONCEIV'D
And 'tis conceiv'd, their old Pretence . . . . 79 Vanbrug House 27
And 'tis conceiv'd, their old Pretence . . . . 106 V's House 27
Is well conceiv'd tho not defin'd; . . . . 215 To Mr. Delany 16
The Goddess, who conceiv'd an Hope, ... 306 Storm 73
Conceiv'd and kindled in the Mind, ... 687 Cadenus Vaness 30
Conceiv'd a Project in her Head, ... 690 Cadenus Vaness 132
CONCEIVE
Strange to conceive, how the same objects strike . . 51 Temple Ill 1
Conceive the Works of Midnight Hags, ... 240 Run Bankers 29
Conceive the whole Enchantment broke, ... 240 Run Bankers 33
Could not conceive what it should mean, ... 376 Apology Lady C 21
Conceive themselves in Conscience bound . . . . 414 Censure 9
Conceive the most invenom'd Dart, ... 595 Cassinus Peter 59
Wou'd not conceive a high disgrace . . . . . . 659 On Poetry D 410
Were (as he humbly did conceive) . . . . 687 Cadenus Vaness 16
CONCEIVES
Conceives a Lady standing by: . . . . 529 Lady's Dres Rm 124
CONCEPTIONS
Form'd by diseas'd conceptions, weak, and wild, . . . 47 To Congreve 123
CONCERN
My Life is here no Soul's Concern. . . . . . . 203 In Sickness 6
In high Concern for human Kind, ... 723 To Stella 5
As a matter they had no concern in. . . . . . . 756 Dingley Brent 12
Have no concern for Sabra's sake, ... 777 Mullinix Tim 129
It shall be no concern of mine. . . . . 902 Dean's Reasons 112
But have no concern to mend her. . . . . 907 Daphne 28
I hear with some Concern you roar, ... 1002 Reply by Dean 10
CONCERN'D
Nor be concern'd about the Sale, ... 646 On Poetry 189
Not that I know his Reverence was ever concern'd to my 986 Mary to Sher 15
knowledge,
CONCERNING
Concerning this Image there went a Prediction, . . . 334 Serious Poem 19
Like the Fiction of Poets concerning the Wind, . . . 927 Riddle 11 D 3
CONCERNS
Whate'er concerns you full as well, ... 101 Elegy Patrige 114
However, it concerns not you. . . . . 435 Answer Paulus 102
Concerns by thousands for your friends: . . . . . 753 Gift for Bec 16
With what concerns all human kind, ... 781 Mullinix Tim 264
CONCISE
Your style so clear, and so concise, ... 889 Panegyr Dean 73
CONCLUDE
And must, to human reasoning opposite, conclude . . 41 Ode Sancroft 209
Conclude Love's Bow-String at full Stretch; . . . 66 Problem 30
Conclude the Bow relax'd again. . . . . 66 Problem 32
And from thy painted Skin conclude. . . . . . 324 Pethox 26
May well conclude his Pow'r will never end. . . . 533 To Mr. Gay 74
To conclude this long Essay; . . . . 634 Epistle Lady 133
I conclude a Fortiori, ... 636 Epistle Lady 194
Hence we conclude, no Women's Hearts . . . . 688 Cadenus Vaness 61
And so I conclude, with humble respects as usual, . . . 1024 Nim-Dan-Dean 2 D 18
CONCLUDED
I concluded, looking round 'em, ... 839 Legion Club 241
CONCLUDING
Against all Logick and concluding Laws, ... 19 Ode Athenian 108
Concluding, that another Shot . . . . 500 Doctor Delaney 19
CONCLUSION
Beg'd she'd forgive him; in Conclusion, ... 378 Apology Lady C 83
CONCLUSIONS
To draw conclusions shall be left to you; . . . . 46 To Congreve 112
From whence you draw such bold conclusions; . . . 622 Scandal Poem 1 161
Her Foe's Conclusions were not sound, ... 695 Cadenus Vaness 279
CONCORD
In Concord here for ever fixt, ... 467 Birthday Song 231
CONCUBINE
Each Priest had a Concubine, jure Ecclesiae; . . . 518 Dean Hang Rape 38
CONDEMN
The Prudes condemn the absent Prudes; . . . . . 449 Modern Lady 155
Before you condemn us, hear what we can say. . . . 805 Irish Bishops 54
CONDEMN'D
The rest condemn'd, with rival Voice, ... 387 Manly Virtue 133
Condemn'd to bear his client's purse; . . . . . . 435 Answer Paulus 90
Condemn'd for thy Crime, at three score and ten? . . . 519 Dean Hang Rape 50
Condemn'd to Country Cottages and Ale; . . . . . 793 St. Pat's Well 74

	PAGE	TITLE	LINE
CONDEMN'D (CONTINUED)			
Condemn'd by Fate's supreme Decree,	849	Old Thorn	47
"That she condemn'd me to the Fire,	850	Old Thorn	62
Condemn'd to black gowns;	858	Lady's Lament	210
Condemn'd to live in Service hard;	883	Rev Market-Hill	11
Stabb'd to the Heart, condemn'd to Flame,	916	Riddle 2	7
Condemn'd by Female Hands to dye;	923	Riddle 7	62
CONDEMNS			
Some she condemns for Life to try	32	Ode to Temple	189
CONDENSED			
Condensed Filth in e'ry Part,	787	Clad in Brown	15
CONDESCEND			
If in her Coach she'll condescend	292	Prog Marriage	77
Believ'd it best to condescend	306	Storm	75
Cou'd never Condescend so low;	483	Libel on D- D-	112
Since you are pleas'd to condescend	489	Dialogue	13
Then pray, dear Doctor, condescend	493	Panegyr Swift	27
Will condescend to take a Bit.	710	Cadenus Vaness	761
CONDESCENDED			
She condescended to admit:	700	Cadenus Vaness	447
CONDESCENDS			
Now condescends to be my farmer,	876	To Dean Swift	4
CONDESCENSION			
His Excellency's condescension	421	Ireld	17
He overpays in Condescension.	483	Libel on D- D-	110
CONDITION			
All Statesmen are in this Condition,	160	Atlas	15
"There's Berkeley in the same Condition;	304	Storm	48
And what Condition can be worse?	484	Libel on D- D-	123
Nor, from your Lord his bad Condition hide;	534	To Mr. Gay	93
CONDITIONS			
Unite; but on Conditions cruel;	883	Rev Market-Hill	9
CONDUCT			
"By which wise Conduct they grow Friends	181	Horace 2, 1	47
How fam'd thy Conduct in the Fight,	326	Pethox	85
Your Conduct in this new Employ foretell.	532	To Mr. Gay	30
By Valour, Conduct, Fortune won;	641	On Poetry	26
And all their Conduct wou'd be try'd	694	Cadenus Vaness	238
His Conduct might have made him styl'd	704	Cadenus Vaness	548
Grown by Vanessa's Conduct wise.	712	Cadenus Vaness	831
Her hands and feet conduct her head,	761	Bec's B-Day	22
From all their Conduct this is plain,	773	Mullinix Tim	11
Thither, gentle Muse, conduct me,	832	Legion Club	79
CONDUCTED			
Conducted by their Squire, Apollo:	585	Strephon Chloe	54
CONDUIT			
Fall from the Conduit prone to Holborn-Bridge.	139	City Shower	60
CONFED'RATE			
"And thy confed'rate Dame, who brags	850	Old Thorn	61
CONFER			
To confer Notes with one another;	66	Problem	50
Confer on him the Holy Ghost;	820	Dr. Rundle	6
CONFERR'D			
The rest, who boast they have conferr'd it,	820	Dr. Rundle	15
CONFERRING			
Conferring as they us'd to meet,	593	Cassinus Peter	3
CONFESS			
Who must my Weakness and my Ignorance confess,	20	Ode Athenian	133
I must confess you've spoken once true.	349	Whitshed Motto	24
Which, I confess, is too long winded)	354	Simile Silver	18
"We must confess his Case was nice;	558	Death of Swift	171
Should to the Priest confess their Sins;	601	Beasts Confess	11
I must confess, on Friday last,	602	Beasts Confess	15
I Must confess,that I was somewhat Warm,	670	Epig Carthy 20	D 1
I must confess your Wine and Vittle	747	Stel Distress	65
I must confess, your Wine and Vittle	752	Stel Wood-Park	81
Confess the Soil from whence the Victors came.	791	St. Pat's Well	16
Britain, with Shame confess, this Land of mine	791	St. Pat's Well	27
Whereby you now confess your self to be a Goose or an Ass:	986	Mary to Sher	18
I must confess that as to me, Sirs,	993	On Picture	13
And I must confess as a Dean and Divine	1017	Swift Ans Sher	3
CONFESS'D			
"Those, who their Ignorance confess'd,	572	Death of Swift	471
The Ass approaching next, confess'd,	602	Beasts Confess	21
Confess'd a Sin, and God forgive him:	604	Beasts Confess	114
"And the Puppy confess'd, he expected no Good o'me.	873	Grand Question	166
CONFESS'T			
Confess't as plain as he could bark;	300	Horrid Plot	55
That might not be confess't;	400	Window Inns 1	4
Though 'tis confess't that those who ever saw	521	Stephen Duck	5
CONFESSES			
Confesses ignorance to judge between;	41	Ode Sancroft	208
CONFESSING			
Confessing Albion once her darling seat;	49	To Congreve	194
CONFEST			
Confest his Flame, and swore by Styx,	120	Apollo Outwit	18
Then must it truly be confest;	497	Panegyr Swift	144
Confest her of no mortal Race:	584	Strephon Chloe	8
Confest the conqu'ring Hero stands.	655	On Poetry	420

	PAGE	TITLE	LINE
CONFIDE			
And yet, I dare confide in you;	597	Cassinus Peter	115
For these our Criticks much confide in,	648	On Poetry	252
CONFIDENCE			
Of which, whoe'er lacks confidence to prate,	48	To Congreve	155
CONFIDENTLY			
But confidently they maintain,	366	Answer Delaney	9
CONFIDES			
In Ships decay'd no Mariner confides,	771	Horace 1, 14	47
CONFIN'D			
The Black, which would not be confin'd	227	Prog of Beauty	33
Have him confin'd in Iron Fetters;	373	Letter D. S-y	74
"If long confin'd to Fires and Screens,	380	Apology Lady C	137
"So shall the Eye, by Form confin'd,	384	Manly Virtue	11
To no one Clime shou'd be confin'd;	387	Manly Virtue	116
"His Friendship there to few confin'd,	570	Death of Swift	435
Keep them to wholsome Food confin'd,	587	Strephon Chloe	123
His Thoughts had wholly been confin'd	706	Cadenus Vaness	630
In him is center'd and confin'd.	709	Cadenus Vaness	711
Courage to Man alone confin'd:	725	To Stella	66
Have always been confin'd to Youth;	757	Stel B-day '24	16
Weary and Sea-sick when in thee confin'd,	772	Horace 1, 14	57
Than thus be confin'd.	856	Lady's Lament	154
Confin'd Thee Goddess to a Cell:	895	Panegyr Dean	270
Their knowledge, to themselves confin'd,	900	Dean's Reasons	37
I'm chiefly unruly, when strongest confin'd.	927	Riddle 11	D 4
CONFINE			
Confine her Walks to Colleges and Schools,	27	Ode to Temple	39
At least confine the tyrant to his cell.	53	Temple Ill	56
To Temples why do we confine?	894	Panegyr Dean	230
CONFINES			
Confines his Faith to one alone;	387	Manly Virtue	132
This Cave within its Womb confines	921	Riddle 7	11
CONFIRM'D			
Had been confirm'd by Fate's Decree;	694	Cadenus Vaness	258
CONFLAGRATION			
For ever--till the Conflagration.	466	Birthday Song	198
CONFLU'ENTS			
While at her Chin the Conflu'ents met.	227	Prog of Beauty	40
CONFLUENT			
And in huge Confluent join at Snow-Hill Ridge,	139	City Shower	59
CONFORMISTS			
Quakers, Conformists, Presbyterians,	345	Prometheus	14
CONFOUND			
Besides, he could confound the Spheres,	99	Elegy Patrige	57
So to confound, this hated Coin	345	Prometheus	11
We praise and confound	424	Carterets Arms	12
"To ruin, slaughter, and confound;	568	Death of Swift	382
Why, Plague confound her sandy Locks:	595	Cassinus Peter	47
Who at them rail bid God Confound:	658	On Poetry	D 190
To Teize, Perplex, Disturb, Confound,	777	Mullinix Tim	142
May their God, the Devil confound 'em.	839	Legion Club	242
Nought but one Thing can confound me,	933	Riddle 20	D 5
CONFOUNDED			
Confounded in that Babel of the pit;	47	To Congreve	122
Build Babel with their Tongues confounded.	108	V's House	66
"But, was it not confounded hard?	446	Modern Lady	50
He was a most confounded Tory---!	547	Life of Swift	83
Confounded Dull---, before he Dy'd---.	547	Life of Swift	89
CONFOUNDS			
Confounds Accounts, perplexes all Affairs;	536	To Mr. Gay	139
CONFUS'D			
Our Listner stood a while confus'd,	64	Discovery	45
His only Coat, where Dust confus'd with Rain,	138	City Shower	29
Amaz'd, confus'd, its Fate unknown,	579	Day Judgement	7
CONFUSION			
We toast Confusion to the Race of Kings:	162	Toland's Invit	14
Such Order from Confusion sprung,	530	Lady's Dres Rm	143
Might breed Confusion in the State,	723	To Stella	4
CONFUSIONS			
In short such dire Confusions follow'd,	346	Prometheus	45
CONFUSSION			
My Lady, pittying his Confussion,	378	Apology Lady C	84
CONFUTE			
And shew where they can best confute.	930	Riddle 15	D 24
CONFUTED			
Is Folly, at his Death confuted.	646	On Poetry	202
CONGEE			
Then with a Congee circumflex	64	Discovery	43
And well we know, The Congee Regal	821	Dr. Rundle	57
The Captain salutes you with Congee profound;	871	Grand Question	115
CONGENIAL			
Congenial Joy, and Life, and Light.	387	Manly Virtue	120
CONGREGATIONS			
I preached three congregations deaf,	675	Curate's Compl	10
CONGREVE			
By hopes my Congreve will reform the stage;	45	To Congreve	50
Whom were my Congreve blest to see and know,	49	To Congreve	183
Thus, Congreve spent, in writing Plays,	481	Libel on D- D-	33
And, crazy Congreve scarce cou'd spare	481	Libel on D- D-	41
Friend Congreve a Feaver, Friend Howard an Ague,	1037	Four Storyes	2

	PAGE	TITLE	LINE

CONGREVE'S
This off'ring long design'd to Congreve's fame; . . . 44 To Congreve 24
Godlike the force of my young Congreve's bays, . . . 44 To Congreve 41
But can no more obscure my Congreve's light . . . 45 To Congreve 80
Thus prostitute my Congreve's name is grown . . . 48 To Congreve 159
Should such a wretch usurp my Congreve's place, . . 48 To Congreve 169
In satire, to my Congreve's praises meant; . . . . . 48 To Congreve 176
Did Congreve's Wit inspire my Song: . . . . . . 496 Panegyr Swift 99
<CONINGSMARK>
Now, <Madam Coningsmark> her' Vengeance vows . . . . 195 Author Himself 53
CONJ'RER
As when a Conj'rer takes a Lease . . . . 240 Run Bankers 45
CONJ'RERS
And drive the Conj'rers to the Devil: . . . . . . 354 Simile Silver 30
By Satan taught, all Conj'rers know . . . . 401 Window Inns 2 1
CONJ'RING
Sid's Brethren of the conj'ring Tribe . . . . . . 134 Magician's Rod 49
And take a Folio for a conj'ring Book. . . . . . . 193 Author Himself 8
CONJECTORS
For so Conjectors would obtrude, ... 324 Pethox 25
CONJECTURE
I can't Conjecture, for Dr.<Dean> . . . . 372 Letter D. S-y 43
CONJECTURES
"And your Conjectures are not right; . . . . 550 Life of Swift 195
And first he modestly conjectures . . . . 704 Cadenus Vaness 568
CONJUGALL
He mark't the Conjugall Dispute, ... 219 A Quiet Life 3
CONJUNCTION
'Tis an unnatural Conjunction, ... 502 Doctor Delaney 81
CONJUR'D
Yet, when conjur'd by such a Friend-- . . . . . . 596 Cassinus Peter 96
CONJURE
I here conjure thee, tell the Cause; . . . . 596 Cassinus Peter 92
CONJURER
I was never taken for a Conjurer before,. . . . . . 72 Mrs Harris Pet 58
. . .for a Conjurer in all my Life. . . .. 72 Mrs Harris Pet 61
CONNA
. . .I appeal to your Friend Mr. Conna. . . . . . 1014 Swift to Sheri 10
CONNING
Conning old Topicks like a Parrot, ... 728 Stella, Poems 26
CONNS
Here conns his Notes, and takes a Whet, ... 127 Little House 21
CONOISSEUR
To get the Name of Conoisseur. . . . . 649 On Poetry 276
<CONOLLY>
To <Marshall>, <Conolly>, and <Dick> <Tighe>. . . . 436 Answer Paulus 146
CONQ'ROR
For you, my Conq'ror and my King, ... 1005 Sheridan's Sub 14
CONQU'RER
Your conqu'rer is become Apollo: . . . . 462 Birthday Song 58
CONQU'RING
Confest the conqu'ring Hero stands. . . . . 655 On Poetry 420
CONQU'RORS
Of some great King and Conqu'rors Death, ... 24 Ode Athenian 272
We'll act as other Conqu'rors do; . . . . 886 Rev Market-Hill 91
CONQUER
For something that will conquer Fire, ... 83 Salamander 18
To conquer Spain, and quell the Turk. . . . . . . 466 Birthday Song 194
Find him a Kingdom out to conquer; . . . . 466 Birthday Song 204
Those whom they could not conquer, they betray'd. . . . 791 St. Pat's Well 24
CONQUER'D
Which might alone have conquer'd Troy; . . . . . . 731 Stella, Poems 124
Always conquer'd, never yielding. . . . . 906 Daphne 8
CONQUERED
Her Sister Isles are Conquered too as well as She. . 9 Ode to King 100
CONQUERING
And spare the Labour of Your Conquering Hand. . . . 13 Ode to William D 40
CONQUEROUR
To Crown the happy Conquerour, ... 16 Ode Athenian 19
CONQUEST
No Conquest ever yet begun . . . . 25 Ode Athenian 283
Of Conquest in your your short and Happy Reign; . . 25 Ode Athenian 303
The Conquest and Discovery too: . . . . 26 Ode to Temple 10
A Conquest and a Colony from thee, ... 791 St. Pat's Well 19
CONQUEST'S
The mighty Conquest's left for you, ... 26 Ode to Temple 9
CONQUESTS
To preserve Conquests, as at first to gain: . . . . 12 Ode to William D 26
CONSCIENCE
And which they've now Conscience to way . . . . . 24 Ode Athenian 256
Till Honesty and Conscience are clear out of sight. . 36 Ode Sancroft 58
Necessity, thou tyrant conscience of the great, . . . 40 Ode Sancroft 176
Who has forty Years let out his Conscience to hire, . 142 New Song 2
Untill thou shalt have eas'd thy Conscience, . . . 181 Horace 2, 1 37
For I think in my Conscience he deals with Old Nick; . 265 Apollo 82
'Twas time in conscience he should die. . . . . . 296 Satiric Elegy 12
Whose Conscience always was her care, ... 375 Apology Lady C 2
My Conscience is clear, and my Spirits are calm, . . 400 Tom Clinch 21
Conceive themselves in Conscience bound . . . . . 414 Censure 9
I own his conscience always free, ... 434 Answer Paulus 55
They both are cheap enough in Conscience, ... 461 Birthday Song 43

```
CONSCIENCE       (CONTINUED)                         PAGE   TITLE            LINE
  Must I commend against my conscience  . . . . . .   490  Dialogue            37
  You then may soon your Conscience lull;  . . . . .  503  Doctor Delaney     112
  His Conscience always was so nice,  . . . . . . .   604  Beasts Confess      83
  Which, though his Conscience forc'd him to restore, . .  806  Judas           5
  But this neither Reason nor Conscience allows;  . .  947  Mrs. Houghton       2
  In Conscience too many,  . . . . . . . . . .        951  Apples              4
CONSCIOUS
  Or loves the muse to walk with conscious pride  . . . .   51  Temple Ill     11
  For, conscious of his Sheepish Gait,  . . . . . .   376  Apology Lady C     32
  Most conscious that they all speak true,  . . . . .  453  Modern Lady      272
  Nor shall the conscious Muse unfold.  . . . . . .   712  Cadenus Vaness    827
CONSENT
  Philemon by his Wife's consent  . . . . . . . . .    92  Bauc & Phil 1      69
  Her Parents and her Friends consent,  . . . . . .   290  Prog Marriage       5
  He for a while would not consent,  . . . . . . .    294  Prog Marriage     125
  "To Neptune speak, and he'll consent;  . . . . . .  306  Storm              71
  To this we freely shall consent,  . . . . . . . .   461  Birthday Song      17
  They wou'd Consent, that all the Crew  . . . . . .  778  Mullinix Tim      149
  And worry him out, 'till he gives his Consent.  . . .  869  Grand Question   62
CONSENTED
  Consented with the usuall Nod.  . . . . . . . .      81  Vanbrug House      72
CONSENTING
  Consenting with the usual Nod,  . . . . . . . . .   107  V's House          52
  One Sex consenting to admire,  . . . . . . . . .    387  Manly Virtue      129
CONSENTS
  You'll find it soon if Fate consents;  . . . . . .  743  Stel B-day 22      71
CONSEQUENCE
  Just as a Man sans Consequence.  . . . . . . . .    707  Cadenus Vaness    659
  See with what consequence he stalks,  . . . . . .   950  Upstart         D  13
CONSIDER
  Consider Humane Folly, and you'll quickly own,  . . .   20  Ode Athenian   149
  Consider where the Moon and Stars  . . . . . . .    100  Elegy Patrige      97
  "You ne'er consider whom you shove,  . . . . . . .  200  Horace 2, 6        38
  "Consider, 'tis my first Request.--  . . . . . . .  201  Horace 2, 6        57
  "Consider what it is to bear  . . . . . . . . . .   380  Apology Lady C    145
  Consider how much more is due  . . . . . . . . .    483  Libel on D- D-     93
  Consider well what may come after;  . . . . . . .   591  Strephon Chloe    232
  Consider what a Risk you run.  . . . . . . . . .    644  On Poetry         136
  But then, consider Dick, you'l find  . . . . . . .  788  Dick's Variety     13
  If this you consider, our Emblem is right;  . . . .  805  Irish Bishops      43
  Consider, before  . . . . . . . . . . . . . .       854  Lady's Lament     115
  For a Barrack or Malt-House, we now must consider. . .  867  Grand Question    6
  Consider now your Conversation;  . . . . . . . .    889  Panegyr Dean       67
  Consider, Strephon, what you do;  . . . . . . . .   925  Riddle 8           25
CONSIDER'D
  The Premises tenderly consider'd,. .                 73  Mrs Harris Pet     70
  For he wisely consider'd it must be a Sprite,  . . .   77  Lady B- B-        13
  For Jove consider'd well the Case,  . . . . . . .    79  Vanbrug House      17
  For, Jove consider'd well the Case,  . . . . . . .   106  V's House          17
  And that they ne'er consider'd yet.  . . . . . . .  200  Horace 2, 6        22
  But ne'er consider'd where they Slept.  . . . . . .  481  Libel on D- D-     38
  Your case consider'd, I must think  . . . . . . .   489  Dialogue           15
CONSIDERS
  She ne'er considers why, or where:  . . . . . . .   761  Bec's B-Day        24
CONSIGN
  Thus I consign you down to Fame,  . . . . . . . .   608  Know Not What       3
CONSIGN'D
  Not yet consign'd to Paste;  . . . . . . . . . .    394  Grub-Street         4
  Lyes there consign'd to endless Night;  . . . . . .  923  Riddle 7          64
CONSIGNE
  Whom you'd consigne to endless Fame?  . . . . . .   272  Apollo's Edict   D  71
CONSISTENCE
  The crude Consistence oft I tread.  . . . . . . .   896  Panegyr Dean      310
CONSISTS
  His Policy consists in setting Traps,  . . . . . .  535  To Mr. Gay        121
  The World consists of Puppet-shows;  . . . . . . .  777  Mullinix Tim      134
CONSOLING    SEE ALL-CONSOLING
CONSONANT
  No jarring consonant betwixt.  . . . . . . . . .    467  Birthday Song     232
CONSORT
  "But now as Consort of the King,  . . . . . . . .   560  Death of Swift    187
  The Consort of his Throne and Bed,  . . . . . . .   655  On Poetry         425
  At consort, coffeehouse, or court;  . . . . . . .   677  Parson's Case      28
CONSPICUOUS
  Fix them on high, conspicuous to be seen,  . . . .   285  Elegy Boat        33
CONSPIRE
  And You with fatal and Immortal Wit conspire  . . .   23  Ode Athenian     240
  To inflame both the Nations do plainly conspire;  . .  237  Excellent Song   19
  Did to it's wond'rous Birth conspire;  . . . . . .  743  Stel B-day 22      64
  All accidents of life conspire  . . . . . . . . .   755  Stella '23         21
  Let ev'ry cottager conspire  . . . . . . . . . .    902  Dean's Reasons    105
CONSQUENCE
  From whence the Consquence is plain,  . . . . . .   495  Panegyr Swift      76
CONSTABLE
  Or Constable with Staff of Peace,  . . . . . . .    189  Faggot             23
CONSTABLES
  On Watchmen, Constables and Duns,  . . . . . . .    583  Young Nymph        52
CONSTANCY
  Who for our Constancy are famous.  . . . . . . .    624  Scandal Poem 2     38
  My Constancy is still the same.  . . . . . . . .    916  Riddle 2            8
```

		PAGE	TITLE	LINE
CONSTANT				
Secure of constant peace within,	. . . .	434	Answer Paulus	57
To all mankind a constant friend,	. . . . . .	455	Dean Smedley	15
And, this he makes his constant Rule;	. . . .	603	Beasts Confess	81
Drop, for once, your constant Rule,	. . . . .	631	Epistle Lady	51
A constant, rational Delight,	. . . .	711	Cadenus Vaness	781
With such a constant, Loyal Zeal,	. . . . . .	778	Mullinix Tim	169
CONSTELLATION				
Shone ever such a Constellation.		656	On Poetry	466
CONSTELLATIONS				
The Glitt'ring Constellations Roll,	. . .	362	Grace's Answer	33
CONSTITUTION				
It still your Constitution hits.	. . . . . .	493	Panegyr Swift	18
With Constitution cold and snowy,	. . . . . .	588	Strephon Chloe	152
Not by his frigid Constitution;	. . . . . .	603	Beasts Confess	67
CONSTR'ING				
Constr'ing the Passion she had shown,	. . . . .	711	Cadenus Vaness	764
CONSTRAIN'D				
Had now constrain'd the Nymph to leak.	. . . .	589	Strephon Chloe	164
CONSTRAINT				
A Countenance with more Constraint.	. . . . . .	480	Libel on D- D-	20
They soon from all Constraint are freed;	. . . .	590	Strephon Chloe	205
CONSTRUE				
Now, since your Motto thus you construe,	. . . .	349	Whitshed Motto	23
CONSUL				
Or, Consul in his Purple Gown,	. . . .	190	Faggot	33
CONSUL'S				
The Consul's Fasces were unbound;	. . . . . .	190	Faggot	28
The Praetor broke the Consul's Head;	. . . . .	190	Faggot	32
CONSULT				
Consult his Peace, or Credit save?	. . . . . .	221	A Quiet Life	40
And Fools consult Interpreters in vain.	. . . .	363	On Dreams	6
(Consult his Book de Partium usu)	. . . . . .	367	Answer Delaney	32
Yet still you must consult the Maps,	. . . . .	467	Birthday Song	240
"We first consult our private Ends,	. . . . .	553	Death of Swift	8
Consult yourself, and if you find	. . . . .	642	On Poetry	77
And said she must consult her Books,	. . . . .	689	Cadenus Vaness	106
A Consult of Coquets below	. . . . .	903	Death Daphne	19
The Vulgar all consult my Look.	. . . . . .	917	Riddle 3	8
Consult the Stars, and thence foretell	. . . .	918	Riddle 4	43
Consult friend Whiteway.	. . . .	1038	Sheridan Cavan	12
CONSULTING				
Gravely consulting Ireland's Good,	. . . . . .	344	Prometheus	2
Far better than consulting Laws.	. . . . . .	690	Cadenus Vaness	135
Consulting with myself, I find,	. . . . . .	899	Dean's Reasons	3
And Lemnian God consulting strove,	. . . . . .	916	Riddle 2	10
CONSULTS				
She at the Glass consults her Looks	. . . . . .	291	Prog Marriage	40
CONSUME				
Consume, and perish from our sight,	. . . . . .	9	Ode to King	113
To Choak the Girls, or consume the Rabble;	. . .	283	Journal	114
Consume my Vitals they shall know,	. . . . . .	778	Mullinix Tim	175
CONSUMES				
Consumes it self to weave a Cell.	. . . . . .	79	Vanbrug House	32
CONSUMING				
Heart-sick of a high fever and consuming atrophy;	. . .	42	Ode Sancroft	252
See my weary Days consuming,	. . . .	660	Love Song	7
CONTAIN				
That swill'd more Liquor than it could contain,	. . .	137	City Shower	15
Such frigid Fustian could contain;	. . . . .	469	Burning Poem	5
You say, the Muse will not contain,	. . . . .	501	Doctor Delaney	51
The Cellar could contain but four)	. . . . .	747	Stel Distress	50
The Cupboard could contain but four;)	. . . . .	751	Stel Wood-Park	66
How will your Eyes contain their Tears,	. . . .	921	Riddle 7	9
CONTAINS				
Nought it contains is common or unclean,	. . . .	50	To Congreve	233
One Grave now contains them both Haec et Hic.	. . .	430	Dicky Dolly	15
With quaint Inscription, which contains,	. . . .	494	Panegyr Swift	55
The Lead yon Critick's Quill contains,	. . . .	500	Doctor Delaney	15
And in the spacious Womb contains	. . . . .	743	Stel B-day 22	69
If still your foul bosom more rancour contains;	. .	819	Archbi Cashel	12
Tell us, what this Pile contains?	. . . . . .	829	Legion Club	9
CONTEMNERS				
Contemners of thy Rites divine.	. . . .	895	Panegyr Dean	272
CONTEMNING				
Contemning Courts, at Courts unseen,	. . . . .	482	Libel on D- D-	73
CONTEMPLATION				
And for a while in heav'nly Contemplation sate	. . .	16	Ode Athenian	25
CONTEMPORARY				
And is Contemporary to Eternity.	. . . . . .	7	Ode to King	26
CONTEMPT				
"To breed contempt where thou hast hop'd esteem."--	. .	55	Temple Ill	146
His Person must Contempt beget.	. . . . . .	706	Cadenus Vaness	639
Love or Contempt, her Fancy strikes.	. . . . .	708	Cadenus Vaness	683
That true Contempt for Things below,	. . . . .	765	Stel B-day '26	68
CONTEND				
Or whether, as the Learn'd contend,	. . . . .	324	Pethox	19
Two bordering Wits contend for Glory;	. . . . .	650	On Poetry	293
CONTENDING				
His great contending Friends to reconcile.	. . . .	196	Author Himself	72
And from contending Atoms came.	. . . .	324	Pethox	32

	PAGE	TITLE	LINE
CONTENDING (CONTINUED)			
But with honest Wood's Love there is no contending, .	337	Serious Poem	105
Were seen contending in a Race;	412	Desire Possess	11
CONTENT			
Is all the poor content delusion finds.--	55	Temple Ill	150
But should be perfectly content, ...	199	Horace 2, 6	9
Come, be content, since out it must, ...	311	To Ford	1
Your Dressing-Plate, he'll be content	446	Modern Lady	60
"Content with what his Bounty gave, ...	476	Epist on Epist	35
Your Horace not content to quote, ...	494	Panegyr Swift	39
In ev'ry Turn of Life content, ...	602	Beasts Confess	41
Content yourself with humbler Place.	656	On Poetry	458
Say, Stella, feel you no Content, ...	764	Stel B-day '26	35
Content, my good <Lords>; but let us change Hands; .	805	Irish Bishops	61
Whatever they give me I must be content, ...	867	Grand Question	22
Hopes that will content you;	1014	Swift to Sheri	32
CONTENTED			
But as for poor contented Me, ...	20	Ode Athenian	132
Contented to be truly great, ...	385	Manly Virtue	49
Contented he, but Fate ordains	385	Manly Virtue	51
Contented rest; you have your due	608	Know Not What	6
Nor is contented with a Treat, ...	1033	Ans to Crown	3
CONTENTEDLY			
We often search contentedly the whole World round, . .	20	Ode Athenian	142
CONTENTION			
Drives out Brangling, and Contention, ...	637	Epistle Lady	215
CONTEST			
And 'twas a Folly to Contest:	175	Horace 1, 7	136
CONTESTS SEE DAGGER-CONTESTS			
CONTIG'OUS			
My Mannors all contig'ous round, ...	251	Bubble	19
CONTIGUOUS			
Now in contiguous Drops the Flood comes down. . . .	138	City Shower	31
CONTINU'D			
But being Old, continu'd just	115	Bauc & Phil 2	123
Appear'd like one continu'd Spec'es, ...	344	Prometheus	8
'Tis said, their Course continu'd long;	412	Desire Possess	13
Shou'd be one continu'd Play-Day:	631	Epistle Lady	40
CONTINUAL			
"He bore continual Persecution;	569	Death of Swift	400
CONTINUE			
And I would fain continue in it;	94	Bauc & Phil 1	162
And if his Heirs continue kind, ...	235	Elegy on Demar	49
May Caroline continue long, ...	467	Birthday Song	233
Your Friendship shall continue still:	593	Strephon Chloe	312
Tho' I continue still a brute.	755	Stella '23	32
So may we long continue thus, ...	755	Stella '23	37
Beg you would here continue still, ...	860	Lady Acheson	26
For, why should I continue still	902	Dean's Reasons	113
And continue special friends.	908	Daphne	84
CONTINUED			
But being old continued just	94	Bauc & Phil 1	169
And still continued by the last:	765	Stel B-day '26	64
CONTINUES			
And so continues 'till he dies.	646	On Poetry	196
While she continues in her Prime.	703	Cadenus Vaness	539
Continues healthy, fat, and fair.	761	Bec's B-Day	10
CONTRACTS			
Because, the Soul her Power contracts, ...	366	Answer Delaney	25
CONTRADICT			
They contradict, affirm, dispute, ...	450	Modern Lady	176
Lose not time to contradict her, ...	907	Daphne	29
I will never contradict you.	908	Daphne	58
CONTRADICTING			
And for a while unbends their contradicting Souls: . .	9	Ode to King	91
CONTRADICTION			
Into contradiction warm her, ...	907	Daphne	33
CONTRADICTION'S			
And oft in contradiction's vortex caught, ...	36	Ode Sancroft	63
CONTRADICTIONS			
And all the contradictions of a poison'd age; . . .	38	Ode Sancroft	118
CONTRARIETY			
Tho' blasts from contrariety of winds, ...	41	Ode Sancroft	204
CONTRARY			
And must have contrary Effects	695	Cadenus Vaness	282
Quite contrary Rebecca's led, ...	761	Bec's B-Day	21
CONTRAST			
And still appearing in Contrast.	529	Lady's Dres Rm	128
CONTRIBUTE			
To neither use thy tusks contribute right, ...	672	Epig Carthy 25	D 3
CONTRIBUTIONS			
The Contributions of the damn'd;	486	Libel on D- D-	188
CONTRITE			
The Swine with contrite Heart allow'd, ...	602	Beasts Confess	37
CONTRIV'D			
Contriv'd to tire all patience out, ...	35	Ode Sancroft	15
Thou'rt well contriv'd, tho' thou art small; . . .	109	V's House	116
Pulls out the Rags contriv'd to prop	582	Young Nymph	21
And, though contriv'd, we may suppose	589	Strephon Chloe	183
But, Caelia has contriv'd to blast	595	Cassinus Peter	53
Who had contriv'd a thousand Feats;	607	Beasts Confess	192

		PAGE	TITLE	LINE
CONTRIV'D	**(CONTINUED)**			
I fancy already a Barrack contriv'd		869	Grand Question	67
I have a Stratagem contriv'd;		885	Rev Market-Hill	62
So well contriv'd her Toes to pinch,		885	Rev Market-Hill	65
CONTRIVANCE				
But no Contrivance yet appears,		367	Answer Delaney	53
A mere Contrivance of the Brain,		764	Stel B-day '26	20
By this Contrivance Mr. <Dean>		797	Traulus 1	59
CONTRIVD				
Contrivd to preach his Sermon next		95	Bauc & Phil 1	177
CONTRIVE				
Contrive to shock your Minds, with many a sensless doubt,		'22	Ode Athenian	207
These Comedies twain Friend Wood will contrive		337	Serious Poem	93
And, let but our Mother Hibernia contrive		351	Wood Insect	13
With little Tom contrive		425	Five Ladies	3
Who wou'd not swear, when you contrive thus,		478	Epist on Epist	87
Contrive your Pile to last for Life;		593	Strephon Chloe	302
Contrive to bribe the Judge's Vote.		647	On Poetry	212
But, Madam, I beg you contrive and invent,		869	Grand Question	61
CONTRIVER				
I leave your Contriver, Pope:		410	Dial Rich Marb	82
"Thou chief Contriver of my Fall,		850	Old Thorn	57
CONTRIVES				
Contrives, as he is hated, to be fear'd:		536	To Mr. Gay	138
Contrives all Means the Gift to hide:		919	Riddle 5	22
CONTRIVING				
(The wicked Laity's contriving,		174	Horace 1, 7	105
Contriving for the Pot and Spit.		897	Panegyr Dean	332
Bears up his House, that's of his own contriving.		943	Probatur Alit	48
CONTROLLER				
How free we acted, and had no controller:		308	Billet Players	34
CONTROLLERS				
To Treasurers, Controllers, Stewards,		189	Faggot	16
CONTROULS				
Your Presence all their Native Stubborness controuls,		9	Ode to King	90
Your happy Frame at once controuls		28	Ode to Temple	68
CONVENIENT				
Here a convenient Box you found,		477	Epist on Epist	67
To make for Pigs convenient Styes:		892	Panegyr Dean	160
CONVERS'D				
But, having long convers'd with you,		325	Pethox	67
CONVERSATION				
Three Gifts for Conversation fit		215	To Mr. Delany	13
Our Conversation to refine		216	To Mr. Delany	29
Been for your Conversation fit,		406	Swift to Pope	23
For Conversation well endu'd;		416	Woman's Mind	17
How to shine in Conversation,		630	Epistle Lady	23
Conversation learn to relish,		632	Epistle Lady	89
Conversation is but carving,		633	Epistle Lady	123
Your Conversation to refine,		780	Mullinix Tim	243
Consider now your Conversation;		889	Panegyr Dean	67
Nor makes their conversation better,		900	Dean's Reasons	39
CONVERSE				
And, those with whom I now converse,		203	In Sickness	7
To know the Converse of Mankind.		696	Cadenus Vaness	315
His Converse is a System, fit		709	Cadenus Vaness	708
For want of your Converse,		1014	Swift to Sheri	35
CONVERSIBLE				
With so conversible a friend,		899	Dean's Reasons	24
CONVERSING				
Conversing with that rusty <Dean>!		891	Panegyr Dean	142
CONVERT				
But Jove will soon convert I hope,		347	Prometheus	71
Half convert me to a Stone.		838	Legion Club	196
CONVERTS				
Made your Sons Converts both to God and Sense:		792	St. Pat's Well	30
CONVEY				
Or thro' a Chink convey their Smoke,		100	Elegy Patrige	93
Convey a Libel in a Frown,		450	Modern Lady	192
Hither convey St. Patrick's Well;		478	Epist on Epist	92
Convey by Penny-Post to Lintot,		643	On Poetry	107
By arbitrary pow'r convey her		761	Bec's B-Day	23
So, those who here their Gifts convey,		922	Riddle 7	47
'Tis I that must the Lands convey,		930	Riddle 15	D 26
CONVEYING				
Who, under Tales conveying Truth,		482	Libel on D- D-	55
CONVEYS				
O'er Sea and Land conveys the Witch;		132	Magician's Rod	18
Conveys out my Paper of Hints by a Trick,		265	Apollo	81
CONVICT				
Convict of lyes is every sign,		420	Holyhead	5
"Prevail to bring him in convict.		570	Death of Swift	430
Nor endeavour to convict her.		907	Daphne	30
CONVICTION				
She ne'er inspires against Conviction:		503	Doctor Delaney	106
Conviction does but more incense;		730	Stella, Poems	91
CONVINC'D				
He would ne'er be convinc'd it was a True Saint:		336	Serious Poem	74
Was now convinc'd he acted wrong,		705	Cadenus Vaness	576
And soon convinc'd them by a Floud.		799	Traulus 1	98

	PAGE	TITLE	LINE
CONVINC'T			
But since you are convinc't at last	315	To Ford	111
His arguments convinc't the rest.	423	Ireld	64
But Tim Convinc't by your Perswasion, ...	774	Mullinix Tim	29
CONVINCE			
Convince us they believe a Saviour;	488	Irish-Club	22
To convince you, once endeavour.	908	Daphne	56
CONVINCING			
Transform'd by your convincing Tongue	887	Panegyr Dean	15
CONVITIA			
Are you still in your cart with convitia ex plaustro? .	979	Dean to Tho: S	6
CONVULSIONS			
So nature's craz'd convulsions make us dread	53	Temple Ill	65
CONYNG			
And some shall admire his conyng Witt, ...	147	Windsor Proph	9
CONYNGS			
Their Conyngs mark thou, for I have been told, . . .	148	Windsor Proph	19
COOK			
'The Cook must keep it back a while;	447	Modern Lady	95
Providing Butter for the Cook.	892	Panegyr Dean	178
COOK-MAID			
Warning the Cook-maid not to burn	94	Bauc & Phil 1	145
Warning the Cook-maid, not to burn	113	Bauc & Phil 2	83
The Cook-maid often hath by the End.	941	Letter	38
COOK'D			
Or dirty Offals cook'd with Herbage.	498	Panegyr Swift	153
COOK'RY			
Pish at his Cook'ry, damn his Wine;	495	Panegyr Swift	69
COOK'S			
For this is ev'ry Cook's Opinion, ...	952	Onyons	6
COOKERY			
As Laws of Cookery require, ...	529	Lady's Dres Rm	101
COOKS SEE PASTRY-COOKS			
Cooks make their Fowl look tight and spruce.	942	Probatur Alit	10
COOL			
And hardly waddles forth, to cool	230	Prog of Poetry	5
And then to cool her heated Brains, ...	446	Modern Lady	45
Shou'd cool your Heels a while, and wait	475	Epist on Epist	5
In Summer is very pleasant and cool.	941	Letter	20
COOLER			
"The cooler Air, and dazzling Sun;	380	Apology Lady C	142
COOLING			
With cooling Gales, like Zephirs fraught;	911	Aenigma	2
Your Engine fraught with cooling Gales, ...	912	Aenigma Expl D	5
COOPER'S			
In apeing Lines from Cooper's Hill;	271	Apollo's Edict D	47
And Drapier's vye with Cooper's Hill.	875	Drapier's Hill	20
COPPER			
Current like copper, and as often paid:	50	To Congreve	220
Takes up with Copper in the Place;	216	To Mr. Delany	44
Wood got so much Copper? He got it by Brass;	336	Serious Poem	86
Smith's Dust, and Copper, Lead and Brass, ...	344	Prometheus	4
Than the Liquor he deals in, his own melted Copper; . .	351	Wood Insect	36
And found his Copper all was base;	353	Wood Ironmongr	28
Apply'd to Wood's adult'rate Copper;	353	Wood Ironmongr	32
And ring Wood's Copper in our Ears	354	Simile Silver	27
"To treat gold reduc'd like Wood's copper pence. . . .	843	Ay and No	16
COPPER-SMITH			
Was a mad Copper-Smith of Elis:	352	Wood Ironmongr	2
COPPLE-CROWNS			
With spiral Tops, and Copple-Crowns:	896	Panegyr Dean	304
COPY			
And, mistakes to prevent, I have obtain'd a Copy. . .	143	New Song	10
Dick left a Pattern few will copy after, ...	430	Dicky Dolly	16
To copy her, few Nymphs aspir'd;	700	Cadenus Vaness	440
Say, Stella, when you copy next, ...	732	Stella, Poems	137
'Tis a true Copy, I'll say that for't, ...	783	Tim and Fables	21
COPY'S			
The copy's false, and sense is rack'd:	434	Answer Paulus	67
COQUET			
Of Nice, Coquet, Affected, Pert, and Vain.	118	Biddy Floyd	10
COQUETS			
Of Prudes, Coquets, and Harridans;	448	Modern Lady	119
That Women should be such Coquets:	450	Modern Lady	165
A Consult of Coquets below	903	Death Daphne	19
COQUETTE			
At twelve, a Wit and a Coquette;	150	Corinna	25
When to be prude, and when coquette;	178	To Lord Harley	56
The Swain is old, the Nymph Coquette.	290	Prog Marriage	30
Who neither was Coquette nor Prude.	702	Cadenus Vaness	497
COQUETTING			
I saw coquetting t' other Night	699	Cadenus Vaness	394
"He caught me one Morning coquetting his Wife, . . .	873	Grand Question	167
CORAL			
To search the Deep for Pearl and Coral.	254	Bubble	96
No Lips of Coral Teeth of Pearl.	272	Apollo's Edict D	55
CORAM			
Coram Regina prox' die Martis, ...	713	Cadenus Vaness	839
CORBET			
Corbet, though yet I know his Worth not, ...	314	To Ford	75

```
                                                                PAGE    TITLE            LINE
CORD
    Yet keep their Bishopricks, and 'scape the Cord.       .    .    806  Judas             14
    For the cord of your circle is now in their hand;      .  .  .   1027 Sheri Circles     16
    The cord, or the radius, it matters not whether,       .    .   1027 Sheri Circles     17
CORDIALS
    Cordials are in their talk, whilst all they mean      .  .  .     42  Ode Sancroft     257
    With Cordials in her Hands, and Eyes.     .   .   .   .   .   .   727  To Stella        110
CORDS
    Because the Cords escape their Eye       .   .   .   .   .   .    29  Ode to Temple      95
    When the strong Cords of Union once are Broke.    .    .    .    770  Horace 1, 14      22
CORINNA
    Into the World Corinna fell,       .   .   .   .   .   .   .   .   149  Corinna            3
    Corinna, Pride of Drury-Lane,        .   .   .   .   .   .   .    581  Young Nymph        1
    Corinna wakes. A dreadful Sight!      .   .   .   .   .   .   .    583  Young Nymph       57
    Corinna in the Morning dizen'd,        .   .   .   .   .   .   .   583  Young Nymph       73
    Corinna with that youthful Air,       .   .   .   .   .   .   .    699  Cadenus Vaness   388
CORKS
    . . .for Corks to stop your Bottles, with a Vengeance.       .   1013 Swift to Sheri     5
    . . .and send your Man Alexander to buy Corks, . .    .    .    1013 Swift to Sheri     6
CORN
    As from the Womb of Earth a field of Corn.     .   .   .   .     20  Ode Athenian      131
    Whate'er I plant (like Corn on barren Earth)     .   .   .   .    33  Ode to Temple     210
    With inoffensive feet o'er standing corn;      .   .   .   .   .   54  Temple Ill        118
    On Magazines of Corn or Hay,       .   .   .   .   .   .   .   .   156  Fable of Midas     16
    Grown fat with Corn and Sitting still,      .   .   .   .   .    230  Prog of Poetry     3
    England will send you corn enough.     .   .   .   .   .   .   .   422  Ireld             52
    And when we starve for want of Corn,      .   .   .   .   .   .    464  Birthday Song    125
    From threshing Corn, he turns to thresh his Brains;     .    521  Stephen Duck       3
    Except they tasted of the Corn:      .   .   .   .   .   .   .    746  Stel Distress     14
    Except they tasted of the Corn:      .   .   .   .   .   .   .    750  Stel Wood-Park    12
    Shall rise one Blade of Grass, one Ear of Corn;    .   .   .     793  St. Pat's Well    92
    Whole Ricks of Hay and Stacks of Corn,      .   .   .   .   .    811  Bro Protestant     3
CORNER
    Then to a Corner both withdrew.     .   .   .   .   .   .   .   .   63  Discovery         20
    And in a Corner of Mrs. Dukes's Box,. .     .   .   .   .   .     70  Mrs Harris Pet    23
    And wedg'd in Corner of a Chair      . . .   .   .   .   .   .    75  Game Traffick     11
    That, senseless, in a Corner stood,      .   .   .   .   .   .    132  Magician's Rod     8
    The Loyt'res quake, no Corner hides them,     .   .   .   .   .   279  Journal           33
    Twelvepence a Corner, if you dare.     .   .   .   .   .   .   .   315  To Ford          114
    To move it out from yonder Corner;      .   .   .   .   .   .    528  Lady's Dres Rm    72
CORNET'S
    "To be the strutting Cornet's Sport,      .   .   .   .   .   .   380  Apology Lady C   149
CORNS
    Whose Wideness kept their Toes from Corns,     .   .   .   .     99  Elegy Patrige     37
    A coming Show'r your shooting Corns presage,     .   .   .   .   137  City Shower        9
    Thus Lamb, renown'd for cutting Corns,      .   .   .   .   .    811  Bro Protestant    15
CORNUCOPIA
    Of Scandal now a Cornucopia;     .   .   .   .   .   .   .   .    150  Corinna           30
CORONATION-DAY
    Of one poor Coronation-day,      .   .   .   .   .   .   .   .      6  Ode to King       15
CORONETS
    Twelve Coronets, without thy leave!      .   .   .   .   .   .    181  Horace 2, 1       26
CORPS
    By Mortgage hath secur'd the Corps of Demar;     .   .   .      233  Elegy on Demar     2
    His meagre Corps, though full of Vigour,     .   .   .   .   .   398  Earl of P-b-w     26
    Then, honest <Robin>, of thy Corps beware:     .   .   .   .    539  Mr. Pulteney      39
    Bequeathed to Pluto, Corps and all.     .   .   .   .   .   .    904  Death Daphne      32
CORPSE
    And leaves a lifeless corpse behind.     .   .   .   .   .   .    900  Dean's Reasons    50
CORPSES
    See where those mangled Corpses lye;      .   .   .   .   .   .   923  Riddle 7          61
CORPUS
    Now sound in mind, and sound in corpus,     .   .   .   .   .    456  Dean Smedley      31
CORRECT
    He only stole Hints; the Verse is correct;     .   .   .   .    266  Apollo            90
    Then study to correct your Taste,     .   .   .   .   .   .   .   270  Apollo's Edict   D  10
    Commend the times, your thoughts correct .   .   .   .   .   .   489  Dialogue          23
    "But what all Mortals may correct;      .   .   .   .   .   .    571  Death of Swift   464
    Blot out, correct, insert, refine,     .   .   .   .   .   .   .   643  On Poetry         87
CORRECTION
    (Under Correction) with the thatcht,      .   .   .   .   .   .   313  To Ford           66
CORRECTLY
    Correctly fitted for the Press,      .   .   .   .   .   .   .    643  On Poetry        106
CORRESPONDENCE
    His Correspondence plainly dated,      .   .   .   .   .   .   .   300  Horrid Plot       51
CORRESPONDING
    Less corresponding than their Years.      .   .   .   .   .   .   291  Prog Marriage     36
CORRUPT
    Corrupt to Maggots Worms and Flyes.     .   .   .   .   .   .     81  Vanbrug House     82
    Corrupt to Maggots, Worms and Flyes.     .   .   .   .   .   .    109  V's House        124
    "Corrupt the Senate, rob the Crown;      .   .   .   .   .   .    568  Death of Swift   386
CORRUPTED
    What a corrupted Tast is ours      .   .   .   .   .   .   .   .   122  Empty'ng Town      5
    Oppress us in corrupted Times:       .   .   .   .   .   .   .    503  Doctor Delaney   102
    They argue no corrupted Mind      .   .   .   .   .   .   .   .    553  Death of Swift     3
    Damn'd Villians, Corrupted in every Station,     .   .   .   .   576  Place Damn'd      11
    For our corrupted Times to bear;      .   .   .   .   .   .   .   603  Beasts Confess    56
    Grown so corrupted in their Taste.      .   .   .   .   .   .    688  Cadenus Vaness    66
CORRUPTING
    And there corrupting to a Wound      .   .   .   .   .   .   .     84  Salamander        55
```

CORRUPTION
     PAGE   TITLE   LINE

		PAGE	TITLE	LINE
CORRUPTION				
See how Corruption grows,	. . . .	426	Five Ladies	29
The Corruption of Verse, for when all is done,	. . .	716	Answer Rebus	9
Say to Corruption--Thou'rt my Father.	. . . . .	813	Bro Protestant	62
CORRUPTIONS				
His Budget with Corruptions cramm'd,	. . . . .	486	Libel on D- D-	187
And, for Corruptions, how they weed 'em.	. . . . .	501	Doctor Delaney	58
But when they smelt such foul Corruptions round him;	. .	536	To Mr. Gay	159
On Corruptions running Riot.	. . . .	635	Epistle Lady	184
The foul Corruptions of Mankind.	. . . .	921	Riddle 7	16
CORRUPTS				
Corrupts and stagnates in the Veins,	. . . . . .	239	Run Bankers	10
CORUM				
And before Corum Nobus so oft has been call'd,	. . .	238	Excellent Song	27
COST				
To shew it cost its Price in War,	. . . . . .	28	Ode to Temple	75
Both to their own and Landlord's Cost;	. . . . .	79	Vanbrug House	14
But, to their own, or Landlord's Cost,	. . . . .	106	V's House	13
Two Acts it cost him under Ground.	. . . . .	108	V's House	88
Or let it cost Five hundred Pound,	. . . . .	199	Horace 2, 6	19
Men laugh at one another's Cost;	. . . . . .	217	To Mr. Delany	74
Computing all their Cost and Trouble,	. . . . .	259	Bubble	218
"Although 'tis hardly worth the Cost,	. . . . .	305	Storm	55
May cost a crown or so; a common case:	. . .	308	Billet Players	26
Pays all the Cost, and gives the Villain Thanks.	. .	535	To Mr. Gay	110
He fled to Earth, but first it cost him dear;	. . .	538	Mr. Pulteney	35
And, well he might; for to his Cost,	. . . .	607	Beasts Confess	189
If Lintot thinks 'twill quit the Cost,	. . . .	643	On Poetry	109
And what they cost? Vanessa guess'd,	. . . . .	698	Cadenus Vaness	381
Yet still resolv'd to spare no Cost;	. . . . .	702	Cadenus Vaness	493
She well remember'd to her Cost,	. . . . .	705	Cadenus Vaness	604
It cost me Lord knows how much Time	. . . . . .	741	Stel B-day 22	9
But, Men find it to their Cost,	. . . . . .	934	Riddle 22	D 5
The Critic to his Cost will find,	. . . . .	1021	Nim-Dan-Dean 1	D 33
'Twill appear, to your cost, you are fairly trepann'd,	.	1027	Sheri Circles	15
COSTLY				
Despis'd luxurious Wines, and costly Meat;	. . . .	194	Author Himself	15
To Stomachs clog'd with costly Fare,	. . . . .	378	Apology Lady C	105
The costly Boast of Regal Rooms,	. . . . . .	379	Apology Lady C	110
From gen'rous wines and costly fare,	. . . . .	401	Window Inns 5	D 3
"No gay Parterre with costly Green,	. . . . .	476	Epist on Epist	53
With richest Wines and costly Cheer:	. . . . .	745	Stel Distress	4
With gen'rous Wines and costly Chear.	. . . . .	749	Stel Wood-Park	4
COSTS				
The Bill might be with Costs dismist.	. . . . .	688	Cadenus Vaness	74
COTEMPORARY				
Has her Cotemporary Beaux.	. . . .	311	To Ford	22
COTTAGE				
To a small Cottage came at last	. . . . .	91	Bauc & Phil 1	50
Whilst You shall see your Cottage rise,	. . . . .	92	Bauc & Phil 1	89
The Cottage with such Feats as these	. . . . .	94	Bauc & Phil 1	153
To a small Cottage came at last;	. . . . .	111	Bauc & Phil 2	18
Whilst you shall see your Cottage rise,	. . . . .	112	Bauc & Phil 2	49
The Cottage by such Feats as these,	. . . . .	114	Bauc & Phil 2	107
A Cottage is Woodpark with You.	. . . . . .	748	Stel Distress	76
A Cottage is Wood-Park with you.	. . . . . .	752	Stel Wood-Park	92
COTTAGER				
Let ev'ry cottager conspire	. . . .	902	Dean's Reasons	105
COTTAGERS				
Call forth our Cottagers to Arms;	. . . . . .	884	Rev Market-Hill	44
COTTAGES				
Condemn'd to Country Cottages and Ale;	. . . . .	793	St. Pat's Well	74
COU'D 74	OMITTED WORD			
COU'D'ST				
Oh! cou'd'st thou, by some Magick Spell,	. . . . .	478	Epist on Epist	91
COUCH				
When on my sickly Couch I lay,	. . . .	726	To Stella	97
She at your sickly Couch will wait,	. . . . . .	766	Stel B-day '26	77
COUCHANT				
With couchant Cringe, and flattering Tale,	. . . .	208	Fable Bitches	15
COUCHES				
Your Altars near your Couches Side?	. . . . .	896	Panegyr Dean	294
COUGH				
But the loss of your Cough will be the best Sign	. . .	1017	Swift Ans Sher	14
COULD 236	OMITTED WORD			
COULD'ST				
Oh, could'st thou teach us how to zest	. . . . . .	495	Panegyr Swift	64
"Yet thou could'st tamely see me slain.	. . . . .	850	Old Thorn	68
COUNCEL				
Or calls a Councel of her Maids	. . . . . .	291	Prog Marriage	53
COUNCELLORS				
Damn'd Ignorant Prelates, and Councellors Privy.	. .	576	Place Damn'd	14
COUNCIL				
Too wise to take Council, too proud to take Warning,	.	327	Epigram 1	7
In ev'ry Council and Debate he stands for what is Right		341	Upon His Grace	5
Is to the Council , and the Court;	. . . . .	385	Manly Virtue	64
To get the name of council learned;	. . . .	435	Answer Paulus	114
The Council sit; approve the Doctor's Skill;	. . .	534	To Mr. Gay	79
Full in his Face Bob shuts the Council Door:	. . .	537	Mr. Pulteney	4
The Council for the Fair began,	. . . .	686	Cadenus Vaness	3
When the Defendant's Council rose,	. . . . . .	687	Cadenus Vaness	22

COUNCIL   (CONTINUED)   PAGE   TITLE   LINE
    Declar'd in Council, Death must marry: . . . . . .   903 Death Daphne   10
COUNCIL-BOARD
    For Wisdom, at Jove's Council-Board.   . . . . . .   695 Cadenus Vaness   267
COUNCILS
    Whose Councils aid the Sov'reign Pow'r, ...   548 Life of Swift   109
    We in frequent Councils are, ...   931 Riddle 18   D   5
COUNSEL
    Yet take one Word of Counsel by the way: . . . .   166 Toland's Invit   40
    I own, the Counsel were not wrong, ...   496 Panegyr Swift   98
    But now observe my Counsel (viz)   . . . .   779 Mullinix Tim   211
COUNSELLORS
    Like faithful Counsellors on either Side.   . . . .   770 Horace 1, 14   14
COUNT
    Hang up your Wife, and you'l count Four', ...   404 Window Inns 11   D   6
    Each Farmer in the Neighbourhood can count   . . . .   533 To Mr. Gay   65
COUNTED
    Pleas'd with an empty swelling to be counted great;   . . 36 Ode Sancroft   60
COUNTENANCE
    You keep Your Countenance for shame   . . . .   218 To Mr. Delany   81
    A Countenance with more Constraint.   . . . .   480 Libel on D- D-   20
    The Horse's Countenance Divine.   . . . .   498 Panegyr Swift   176
COUNTER-CHARM
    Oppose his Counter-Charm of Paper, ...   354 Simile Silver   26
COUNTER-SPELL
    To cure her by a Counter-spell: . . . .   354 Simile Silver   8
COUNTERFEIT
    Forc'd on me, crack'd, and clipp'd, and counterfeit, . .   45 To Congreve   56
    That's but a counterfeit sore Leg: . . . .   91 Bauc & Phil 1   43
    Can finely counterfeit a Fright;   . . . .   416 Woman's Mind   34
    With Rings and Hinges counterfeit   . . . .   528 Lady's Dres Rm   76
    Europa's counterfeit Gallant.   . . . .   759 Receipt Youth   20
COUNTERMAND
    To countermand his Orders by your own.   . . . . .   534 To Mr. Gay   88
COUNTERPART
    As just the Counterpart of his.   . . . .   905 Death Daphne   66
COUNTERS
    They break up Counters, Doors, and Tills, ...   240 Run Bankers   39
    Conceal, and cover us, Ye Counters.   . . . . . .   241 Run Bankers   60
    They lie open on Purpose, on Counters and Stalls, . .   263 Apollo   23
    The Table, Cards, and Counters set, ...   451 Modern Lady   214
    In ready Counters never pays, ...   452 Modern Lady   234
    Many to our Counters run, ...   934 Riddle 22   D   3
COUNTERVIEW
    As at their Work they sate in counterview, ...   880 Pastoral Dial   5
COUNTREE   SEE LCW-COUNTREE
COUNTREY
    When strait she sees the Countrey all around, ... 17 Ode Athenian   38
COUNTRY
    He sav'd his Country by Delays, ...   28 Ode to Temple   71
    Resolv'd to give himself, as well as Country Peace. .   30 Ode to Temple   134
    The Muse, like some bright country virgin, shows, . .   50 To Congreve   215
    To give the Town and Country Sport.   . . . . . .   62 Discovery   8
    Jove sent and found far in a Country Scene,   . . .   118 Biddy Floyd   3
    What? sell my Master's Country Seat?   . . . . .   128 Little House   56
    Out of Zeal for his Country, and want of a Place, .   142 New Song   3
    Where Town and Country Vicars flock in Tribes, . .   194 Author Himself   19
    Writ underneath the Country Signs;   . . . . . .   201 Horace 2, 6   72
    Oh, could I see my Country Seat.   . . . .   202 Horace 2, 6   108
    How blest is he, who for his Country dies;   . . .   210 Earl of Oxford   1
    With Life his Country, or his Friend.   . . . . .   243 Horace 4, 9   24
    To whom our country has been always dear,   . . .   309 Billet Players   45
    To One who for his Country died, ...   339 Arch-Bish Dub   2
    Our Country then can dread no Wrong: . . . . .   339 Arch-Bish Dub   6
    To find her in a country scene, ...   401 Window Inns 5   D   6
    None loves his King and Country better, ...   410 Dial Rich Marb   83
    And when their country lyse at stake   . . . . .   421 Ireld   7
    Trots to his country mansion down;   . . . . . .   435 Answer Paulus   94
    Be sometimes to your country true, ...   487 Irish-Club   17
    This country, now their own, for nought.   . . . .   488 Irish-Club   24
    As some raw Youth in Country bred, ...   500 Doctor Delaney   1
    and selling his Country to purchase his peace   . .   540 Charac Walpole   8
    Some Country Squire to Lintot goes, ...   562 Death of Swift   253
    "The Country Members, when in Town, ...   564 Death of Swift   283
    "To save their sinking Country lent, ...   568 Death of Swift   375
    At Country Dances, not a Nose   . . . .   584 Strephon Chloe   23
    His Country was his dearest Mother, ...   606 Beasts Confess   179
    Court, City, Country want you not;   . . . . . .   641 On Poetry   47
    Deny their Country like a Scot: . . . .   652 On Poetry   360
    But what she learnt at Country Fairs;   . . . . .   699 Cadenus Vaness   415
    A Pair to make a Country Dance, ...   756 Stel B-day '24   8
    And quite forgot their Country was enslav'd.   . . .   771 Horace 1, 14   52
    Condemn'd to Country Cottages and Ale;   . . . .   793 St. Pat's Well   74
    when wanted by his Country most;   . . . .   798 Traulus   90
    When the Rogues their Country fleece, ...   833 Legion Club   107
    Should in a country life delight, ...   901 Dean's Reasons   82
    Of Traytors who their Country sold.   . . . . . .   921 Riddle 7   18
    I hasten'd down to Country Air, ...   1003 Dan J's Reply   2
COUNTRY-BRED
    And court in prologues, all are country-bred;   . . . . 46 To Congreve   96

```
                                                           PAGE    TITLE            LINE
COUNTRY-FAIR
      Above the Door, at Country-fair,    . . . . . . . .  457 Paddy's Charac        3
COUNTRY-WENCHES
      Some to tumble Country-Wenches    . . . . . . .      574 Helter Skelter       45
COUNTRY'S
      But I sing of a Famous Lord, who seeks his Country's
        Good.                                              341 Upon His Grace        2
      My Country's sav'd, as you have shown,   . . . . . . 372 Letter D. S-y        17
      To perish for our Country's Good.   . . . . . . .    697 Cadenus Vaness      349
      The single Pillar for his Country's Good,            770 Horace 1, 14         16
      Retire, yet still bemoan their Country's Fate.   .   772 Horace 1, 14         60
COUNTS
      Then on her fingers Ends she counts                  291 Prog Marriage        45
      Counts all his Labours amply paid,   . . . . . .     729 Stella, Poems        37
COUNTY
      Into this and t' other County,   . . . . . . .       574 Helter Skelter       37
      Be gone down to the county of Wexford . . .         1022 Nim-Dan-Dean 2     D  6
COUNTY-SAVINGS
      When all her County-Savings gone,   . . . . . . .    751 Stel Wood-Park       70
COUP
      And of that dreadful coup d'eclat,   . . . . . . .   181 Horace 2, 1          23
COUPLE
      The good old Couple was amaz'd,    . . . . . . .     112 Bauc & Phil 2        35
      The loving Couple well bemir'd,    . . . . . . .     224 Prog of Love         77
      The Couple to the Temple went:     . . . . . . .     290 Prog Marriage         6
      This Couple met to talk of News.   . . . . . . .     408 Dial Rich Marb        6
      The charming Couple now unites;    . . . . . . .     585 Strephon Chloe       45
COUPLE-BEGGAR
      No Couple-Beggar in the Land    . . . . . . . .      926 Riddle 9             11
COUPLED    SEE ILL-COUPLED
      You shall be coupled as you best approve,    . . .   165 Toland's Invit       31
      By vicious Fancy coupled fast,     . . . . . . .     529 Lady's Dres Rm      127
COUPLET
      When he can in one Couplet fix                       555 Death of Swift       49
COUPLING
      By coupling Orthodox with Arrians?    . . . . . .    820 Dr. Rundle            8
COURAGE
      Your matchless Courage with Your Prudence joins       11 Ode to William    D  5
      Take Courage, dear Comrades, and be not afraid,      400 Tom Clinch           19
      And for his courage gets--a dinner.    . . . . . .   421 Ireld               12
      Low in Pocket, Cow'd in Courage,   . . . . . . .     574 Helter Skelter       53
      (Inspir'd with Courage from his Bride,)    . . . .   589 Strephon Chloe      189
      Take Courage, and attempt a Third.   . . . . . .     645 On Poetry           148
      Courage to Man alone confin'd:   . . . . . . . .     725 To Stella            66
      But, when her breakfast gives her courage,   . . .   761 Bec's B-Day          35
      That Courage which can make you just,    . . . . .   765 Stel B-day '26       45
      And therefore goes with Courage on.    . . . . .     765 Stel B-day '26       76
      But, Courage, my <Lords>, tho' it cannot be said  .  805 Irish Bishops        49
      Take Courage, Dan, this plainly shows                993 On Picture           19
COURSE
      To interrupt the Fortune of Your Course:   . . . .    13 Ode to William    D 42
      Will quickly take another course   . . . . . . .      19 Ode Athenian        116
      Runs violently o'er his usual Course.)   . . . . .    31 Ode to Temple       149
      Stale forms of course, all mean deceivers use,   .    44 To Congreve          20
      Apply'd at Bottom stops it's Course;   . . . . .      93 Bauc & Phil 1       102
      Apply'd at Bottom, stops its Course,   . . . . .     113 Bauc & Phil 2        62
      From Smithfield, or St. Pulchre's shape their Course, 139 City Shower         58
      That she stopt in her Course to look on them both; . 264 Apollo               38
      His Course of glorious Toil shou'd run,    . . . .   387 Manly Virtue        118
      'Tis said, their Course continu'd long;    . . . .   412 Desire Possess       13
      "But Nature freely takes her Course,   . . . . .     476 Epist on Epist       55
      To pay him Honour due, in Course   . . . . . .       496 Panegyr Swift       112
      Must by the Course of Nature dye:    . . . . . .     556 Death of Swift       74
      (When daily Howd'y's come of Course,   . . . . .     557 Death of Swift      123
      James is be-duk'd; : of course their friendshp ends . 678 Dean and Duke        2
      If a small Breeze obstructs the Course,    . . . .   688 Cadenus Vaness       53
      Leave all Things to their Nat'ral Course.    . . .   696 Cadenus Vaness      303
      Still to the Sea their Course incline;   . . . . .   709 Cadenus Vaness      721
      Lost are thy Oars that us'd thy Course to guide,     770 Horace 1, 14         13
      Nor, change thy Course with ev'ry sudden Gust:   . . 771 Horace 1, 14         54
      Not half thy Course of Misery is run,    . . . . .   793 St. Pat's Well       87
COURSEST
      So Goldsmiths say, the coursest Stuff,   . . . . .   345 Prometheus           23
COURT    SEE HAMPTON-COURT
      And thus He did the Airy Goddess Court,                7 Ode to King         35
      How fond we are to court Her to our Arms!              23 Ode Athenian       232
      As loth to see the hated Court and Town,   . . . .    31 Ode to Temple      157
      Whatever serves for innocent Emblems of the Court;    31 Ode to Temple      164
      You strove to cultivate a barren Court in vain,   .   32 Ode to Temple      175
      In Caesar's court, or in Jerusalem;    . . . . . .    39 Ode Sancroft       167
      And court in prologues, all are country-bred;    .    46 To Congreve         96
      When Folks came thick to make their Court    . . .    62 Discovery            6
      At Court, Vitruvius the second,    . . . . . . .      87 Hist V's House      38
      The Graces from the Court did next provide   . . .   118 Biddy Floyd          7
      He has vamp't an old Speech, and the Court to their
        sorrow,                                            143 New Song             5
      Tho' the Court gives my Nephews, and Brothers, and
        Cousins,                                           144 New Song            47
      Returning home one Day from Court,   . . . . . .     170 Horace 1, 7          2
      Appear with slender Wands at Court:    . . . . .     189 Faggot              18
      Which now disturbs the Queen and Court,    . . . .   190 Faggot              25
```

COURT	(CONTINUED)	PAGE	TITLE	LINE
And be assur'd, the Court will find him		190	Faggot	43
By Harley <Swift> invited comes to Court.		194	Author Himself	28
Of some Express arriv'd at Court;		202	Horace 2, 6	90
Those Cares that haunt the Court and Town.		202	Horace 2, 6	112
And Anthony shall Court her in Ratteen.		275	Epilogue	20
Must Imitate the Fashion of the Court.		275	Epilogue	30
To Lazy-Hill retiring from his Court,		284	Elegy Boat	7
First; how to swagger in a Court;		348	Whitshed Motto	12
He long had bid the Court farwel,		375	Apology Lady C	13
"To run the Gauntlet of the Court;		380	Apology Lady C	150
Is to the Council , and the Court;		385	Manly Virtue	64
When you are try'd in Scandal's Court.		413	Censure	6
The Court had nothing to compair.		422	Ireld	30
The wretch must be at court by nine;		434	Answer Paulus	74
To court their English German Cousins,		465	Birthday Song	170
'Tis grown the choicest Wit at Court,		468	Birthday Song	267
Twice sev'n long Years the Court attends,		481	Libel on D- D-	54
Bravely despise Champagne at Court,		488	Irish-Club	19
When <Jonathan> was great at Court,		498	Panegyr Swift	159
Against the Court is always blabbing,		514	Answer Fable	69
Say, had the Court no better place to chuse		531	To Mr. Gay	7
With these, the Court and Senate-house he plies,		532	To Mr. Gay	41
In ev'ry Court the Parallel will hold;		536	To Mr. Gay	135
The Court invited more than One, or Two;		536	To Mr. Gay	151
a prater at Court in the Stile of the Stews		540	Charac Walpole	10
"That he was well-receiv'd at Court---.		547	Life of Swift	85
Court, City, Camp, all one to him---.		548	Life of Swift	106
Against the Court to shew his Spight---.		550	Life of Swift	189
'Tis told at Court, the Dean is dead.		559	Death of Swift	178
"Was never ill receiv'd at Court:		565	Death of Swift	308
"He left the Court in meer Despair.		567	Death of Swift	370
To visit and to court them too;		587	Strephon Chloe	99
No Maid at Court is less asham'd,		590	Strephon Chloe	215
Not all the Court of Heav'n could shew		597	Problem Solved	9
He came to Court with Fortune clear,		606	Beasts Confess	165
To crowd the Court with their Relations:		606	Beasts Confess	178
To court her Majesty of Tyre		619	Scandal Poem 1	66
To court her Majesty of Tyre,		625	Scandal Poem 2	62
Court, nor Parli'ment, can 'scape ye;		631	Epistle Lady	54
All the Vices of a Court,		634	Epistle Lady	147
Court, City, Country want you not;		641	On Poetry	47
The vilest Verse thrives best at Court.		646	On Poetry	186
The Court with annual Birth-day Strains;		650	On Poetry	306
Since first the Court allow'd them Food.		652	On Poetry	366
This Atlas stands to prop the Court:		656	On Poetry	444
Each strait his service offers, pays his court,		672	Epig Carthy 24 D	7
At consort, coffeehouse, or court;		677	Parson's Case	28
She made a Speech in open Court;		713	Cadenus Vaness	857
The Court, so made his last O yes!		714	Cadenus Vaness	885
Who turn with ev'ry Gale that blows from Court.		771	Horace 1, 14	56
I feel you'll be disgrac'd at Court.		778	Mullinix Tim	154
To foreign Prelates make a slavish Court,		793	St. Pat's Well	75
The Jest of Wits, and to the Court unknown.		794	St. Pat's Well	100
To the Court it was fitter to pay his Devotion,		809	Epigr Prelate	5
Now twenty Years from Court exploded?		820	Dr. Rundle	28
For the Court against the Nation.		836	Legion Club	172
Or join with the Court in ev'ry Debate,		867	Grand Question	23
Drawn up in our Court; when the Captain cries, Stand.		870	Grand Question	100
No; not in all the British Court;		876	To Dean Swift	7
That court and courtiers have no taste:		877	To Dean Swift	28
Who wont to weed the Court of Gosford Knight,		880	Pastoral Dial	2
As clearly shows you bred at Court!		889	Panegyr Dean	84
At Pluto's Hall, his Court to pay:		903	Death Daphne	2
Old Batchelors about his Court,		903	Death Daphne	12
And scorn the Pleasures of a Court;		925	Riddle 8	34
That he's to have a Place at <Court>.		300	Horrid Plot	64
To serve a tastless <Court> twelve Years in vain?		531	To Mr. Gay	2
COURT-BREEDING				
What court-breeding this is?		853	Lady's Lament	69
COURT-LIKE				
Nor ever maid endur'd such court-like scorn,		44	To Congreve	13
COURT'S				
What Pamphlets in a Court's Defence		503	Doctor Delaney	103
COURT'SIES				
They dropp'd low Court'sies, One and All,		321	First of April	13
COURTED				
So highly courted by the brisk and gay?		54	Temple Ill	106
'Tis the Nymph that I courted some ten Years ago;		264	Apollo	44
Since Cindercola, first you Courted		372	Letter D. S-y	45
"He never courted Men in Station,		565	Death of Swift	325
Alone, and by no Planter courted;		583	Young Nymph	46
COURTESY				
"My House you've had on Courtesy;		208	Fable Bitches	26
COURTIER				
He can Lye like a Courtier, and think it no Scorn,		335	Serious Poem	45
I then will turn a Courtier too,		410	Dial Rich Marb	79
How could it thus conceal a Courtier?		796	Traulus 1	20
I am a Courtier in my Way;		917	Riddle 3	11
Thee, for a Gift, the Courtier sends		919	Riddle 5	19

		PAGE	TITLE	LINE

COURTIER'S
    "The powder'd Courtier's witty Sneer; . . . . 380 Apology Lady C 146
    Took up himself the Courtier's Trade, ... 482 Libel on D- D- 68
    Much I dread the Courtier's Fate, ... 933 Riddle 20 D 27
COURTIERS
    The Courtiers kept their Distance due, ... 63 Discovery 18
    Come Courtiers: Every Man his Stick: . . . . 190 Faggot 35
    Of Courtiers, each in their Degree . . . . 392 Young's Satire 29
    Had You and I been Courtiers born, ... 409 Dial Rich Marb 31
    For, those we dext'rous Courtiers call, ... 409 Dial Rich Marb 33
    The deepest Tricks of Courtiers knew. . . . . 494 Panegyr Swift 38
    "The Courtiers have them all by Heart: . . . . 564 Death of Swift 286
    (Like Courtiers, when they send a Note, ... 649 On Poetry 271
    About St. James's, cry, We Courtiers. . . . . 812 Bro Protestant 22
    Let Courtiers hug them in their Bosom, ... 813 Bro Protestant 59
    That court and courtiers have no taste: . . . . 877 To Dean Swift 28
COURTING
    Their courting a Retreat like you, ... 28 Ode to Temple 66
    . . . a courting Sly Nancy. . . . . 1023 Nim-Dan-Dean 2 D 12
COURTLY
    Thought it more courtly and discreet, ... 379 Apology Lady C 111
    Let courtly Slaves low bend the Knee . . . . 386 Manly Virtue 93
    For, all the Courtly Madams round, ... 409 Dial Rich Marb 27
    A Scholar to a Courtly Dame, ... 705 Cadenus Vaness 589
    In courtly style addresses Franck; . . . . 689 Cadenus Vaness 50
    What, if among the courtly Tribe, ... 884 Rev Market-Hill 35
    The courtly Dame, unmov'd by Fear, ... 922 Riddle 7 37
COURTOWN
    . . . he's not come yet from Courtown, I fancy; . . . 1023 Nim-Dan-Dean 2 D 11
COURTS
    And Courts the wanton Echoes as they fly. . . . . . 17 Ode Athenian 59
    With all that Power unfelt, courts Mankind to be Great, 21 Ode Athenian 155
    Still lurks in Palaces and Courts, ... 30 Ode to Temple 117
    And Secrecy, the Art of Courts. . . . . 325 Pethox 64
    Thro' all the Rooms, and Courts, and Arches; . . . . 377 Apology Lady C 62
    Pope walks, and courts the Muse. . . . . 405 Swift to Pope ' 8
    Contemning Courts, at Courts unseen, ... 482 Libel on D- D- 73
    Contemning Courts, at Courts unseen, ... 482 Libel on D- D- 73
    Who look on Courts with stricter Eyes, ... 485 Libel on D- D- 175
    Through Courts and Senates as he goes; . . . . 486 Libel on D- D- 190
    Mention Courts, you'll ne'er be quiet; . . . . 635 Epistle Lady 183
    These Pleadings in the Courts below, ... 689 Cadenus Vaness 80
    They never pass'd for Law in Courts; . . . . 690 Cadenus Vaness 113
    From Courts inclusive, down to Cells, ... 691 Cadenus Vaness 149
    How greater's his merit at four Courts or House, . . 814 Yahoo's 8
COURTSHIP
    Who pay'd his Courtship with the Croud, ... 482 Libel on D- D- 57
COUSINS
    Tho' the Court gives my Nephews, and Brothers, and
        Cousins, 144 New Song 47
    To court their English German Cousins, ... 465 Birthday Song 170
COV'NANT
    "By solemn League and Cov'nant bound, ... 568 Death of Swift 381
COV'TOUS
    You've taught the Cov'tous Wretches to o're-rate, . . 24 Ode Athenian 255
COVENT
    Never did Covent Garden boast . . . . 581 Young Nymph 3
COVER
    Conceal, and cover us, Ye Counters. . . . . . . 241 Run Bankers 60
    His Breast again would cover; . . . . 400 Window Inns 1 6
    The paper gilt, & Cover marbled) . . . . 463 Birthday Song 88
    It shines most in the Marble Cover. . . . . . . 475 Epist on Epist 14
    The Darts were in the Cover fix'd, ... 701 Cadenus Vaness 481
    Will cover a House much better than Clay. . . . . 943 Probatur Alit 34
COVER'D
    So Mary got me to Bed, and cover'd me up warm, . . 70 Mrs Harris Pet 18
    All cover'd o'er with Slime and Mud. . . . . . 255 Bubble 132
    The Nymph was cover'd with her Flammeum, ... 586 Strephon Chloe 61
    The dullest Beast, and what's cover'd with Crust, . . 941 Letter 31
COVERD
    Our Ocean's coverd o'er with Gold, ... 254 Bubble 103
COVERS
    "A Hundred to One, but it covers a Clown; . . . . 872 Grand Question 154
    The dullest Beast and what covers a House, . . . 941 Letter 27
COW
    The famish't Cow her Want supplies; . . . . . . 759 Receipt Youth 14
    If I compare you to the Cow? . . . . 759 Receipt Youth 22
    That was bred to kill a Cow well: . . . . . . 800 Traulus 2 30
    Where a cow would be startled, ... 853 Lady's Lament 47
    Now I am a Dog, or Cow, ... 933 Riddle 20 D 9
    And yet the Cow, the Sheep, the Bee, ... 936 Riddle 24 D 3
COW-BOYS
    Their Cow-boys bearing Cloaks before 'um, . . . 760 Receipt Youth 46
    That Cow-boys know you by your Dress! . . . . . 889 Panegyr Dean· 80
COW-DUNG
    That we both act the Part of the Clown and the Cow-dung 967 Letter Sherid 2
COW-<TURD>
    So prettily he pickt a Cow-<turd>: . . . . . . 514 Answer Fable 48
COW'D
    Low in Pocket, Cow'd in Courage, ... 574 Helter Skelter 53

		PAGE	TITLE	LINE
COWARD				
Since Death pursues the Coward as he flies.		210	Earl of Oxford	2
And paint a Coward fierce in arms.		464	Birthday Song	122
Fierce in Tongue, in Heart a Coward:		799	Traulus 2	12
Or hide his coward Snout in Mud.		824	Printer Newgat	10
Behold, the Coward, and the Brave,		922	Riddle 7	27
COWARDICE				
Can Cowardice her Sex adorn,		725	To Stella	67
Its Cowardice such,		939	Riddle Answerd	25
COWARDS				
(Cowards are Monarchs by that Title made)		11	Ode to William	D 10
COWLEY'S				
For Cowley's Briefs, and Pleas of Waller,		690	Cadenus Vaness	114
COWS				
His Baily Driving all my Cows into the Parish Pound.		343	Upon His Grace	4
In frosty Nights their starving Cows,		759	Receipt Youth	2
For stealing Cows, nor could he read the Psalter.		826	Noisy Tom	14
"Pigs and Faticks, Cows, and Teagues		851	Old Thorn	77
Where Goody Julia milks the Cows,		878	Robbin & Harry	25
First milk his cows, and after, pound:		902	Dean's Reasons	104
COWSLIP				
The Roses blow, the Cowslip springs;		621	Scandal Poem 1	141
The Roses blow, the Cowslip springs;		627	Scandal Poem 2	145
The Cowslip soft, and sweet Jonquil.		894	Panegyr Dean	252
COXCOMB				
And not the meanest coxcomb you can find,		48	To Congreve	157
But some gay coxcomb, or a rake.		177	To Lord Harley	22
Whole Hours can with a Coxcomb sit,		416	Woman's Mind	7
Chloe's of ev'ry Coxcomb jealous,		449	Modern Lady	162
For, ev'ry Coxcomb lends them Rods;		501	Doctor Delaney	48
By ev'ry Coxcomb, but her Lord?		592	Strephon Chloe	284
For a Coxcomb gaily dress'd?		632	Epistle Lady	76
Lord how this Frothy Coxcomb frets! (aside)		774	Mullinix Tim	16
Dick a Coxcomb, Tom was mad,		784	Mullinex Dick	5
Who could this Coxcomb be, and who his Sire?		825	Noisy Tom	6
Then which of us two is the quaint-er Coxcomb?		1003	Dan J's Reply	12
COXCOMB'S				
Expos'd to every Coxcomb's Eyes,		60	Lady Tablebook	5
Light on many a Coxcomb's Crown.		638	Epistle Lady	254
COXCOMBS				
Enticing Coxcombs to adore.		292	Prog Marriage	75
Till banist by some Coxcombs Raillery;		294	Prog Marriage	142
"Thro' Crowds of Coxcombs & of Coaches;		380	Apology Lady C	152
Here no conceited coxcombs pass,		402	Window Inns 7	D 3
'Tis just what Coxcombs call, a Bite.		708	Cadenus Vaness	673
And coxcombs in red ribbons shine:		876	To Dean Swift	22
COXON				
All Pride) our Speaker for your Coxon:		476	Epist on Epist	40
COY				
Pickt the Demure, the Aukward, and the Coy;		118	Biddy Floyd	6
Why, hang her, though she seem'd so coy,		595	Cassinus Peter	61
COYL				
By all this Coyl what hast thou got?		778	Mullinix Tim	152
COYN				
For then he could Coyn and could Cobble together;		287	Bank Down	28
Will sooner coyn a Thousand Lyes		503	Doctor Delaney	91
COYN'S				
The Coyn's Currant and Mettal Pure.		372	Letter D. S-y	34
COYNER				
This Coyner of Raps in a Cauldron of Oyl.		352	Wood Insect	38
CRAB				
He is an old Stump cut out of a Crab,		335	Serious Poem	36
And England has put this Crab to hard Use,		335	Serious Poem	37
CRABBED				
As rude as a bear, no mule half so crabbed;		955	Portrait Life	5
CRABS				
His crabs and sloes may freely pillage:		902	Dean's Reasons	108
CRACH'RODE				
Is Capt. Crach'rode here, pray?--No.		376	Apology Lady C	43
Calls, Crach'rode, is the Doctor come?		377	Apology Lady C	58
CRACK				
Was now dispos'd to a crack a Jest;		171	Horace 1, 7	15
Altho' the Chain will never crack,		346	Prometheus	69
Crack the Stones, and melt the Lead;		830	Legion Club	26
Let them, 'ere they crack a Louse,		831	Legion Club	57
Or crack such Lice as his betwixt your Nails?		882	Pastoral Dial	36
CRACK'D				
Forc'd on me, crack'd, and clipp'd, and counterfeit,		45	To Congreve	56
"And crack'd her tender Maidenhead		497	Panegyr Swift	132
CRACK'T				
An Angel's Face, a little crack't;		734	Stel B-day '20	16
CRACKERS				
With Squibs and Crackers arm'd, to throw		353	Wood Ironmongr	19
CRACKING				
At cracking a jest.		856	Lady's Lament	172
CRACKLING				
nor shall you twine the Crackling,Crackling Bays		958	Cantata	
nor shall you twine the Crackling,Crackling Bays		958	Cantata	
CRACKS				
The Paint by Perspiration cracks,		227	Prog of Beauty	37
The Cracks and Wrinkles of your Mind,		736	Stel B-day '20	56

```
CRACKS           (CONTINUED)                              PAGE   TITLE            LINE
     The smoaky Wainscot full of cracks      . . . . . .   746 Stel Distress       37
     The smutty Wainscot full of Cracks,     . . . . . .   751 Stel Wood-Park      55
     Behold, it cracks by yon rough Eastern Wind.  . . .   770 Horace 1, 14        18
CRACKT
     Crackt Lips, foul Teeth, and gummy Eyes,            226 Prog of Beauty        15
     We see the Nation's Credit crackt,      . . . . . .  253 Bubble               59
     Forgive him, Tom, his Head is crackt.               795 Traulus 1             6
     Are like the ravings of a crackt head;  . . . . .   900 Dean's Reasons       64
     And when with much Labour the Matter I crackt,  . . 972 S-'s Ans Sh-d         3
CRADLE
     Both softly to the Cradle creep:        . . . . . . 150 Corinna               6
CRADLES
     Of cradles and caves;   . . . . . . . . . . . . . . 856 Lady's Lament       176
CRAFT    SEE PRIEST-CRAFT
     The Boy made use of all his Craft,      . . . . . . 701 Cadenus Vaness      476
     As Popish Craft? Did he not rail on't?  . . . . .   774 Mullinix Tim         19
CRAFTSMAN
     "Against the Craftsman and his Friend;  . . . . . . 563 Death of Swift      274
CRAGS
     This Paper will soon make us richer than Crags.  .  287 Bank Down            18
CRAIGS
     From Sommers down to Craigs and Walpole.   . . . .  191 Faggot               52
CRAM
     And hates to cram the Sick with Slops:  . . . . .   605 Beasts Confess      134
     Taught harmless Man to cram and stuff.  . . . . .   895 Panegyr Dean        262
CRAMBO
     And ev'ry Crambo he could get;  . . . . . . . . .   730 Stella, Poems        74
CRAMM'D
     My long old-fashion'd Pocket, was presently cramm'd;  . 143 New Song         19
     And, if the Crosier could be cramm'd in,   . . . .  191 Faggot               47
     His Budget with Corruptions cramm'd,    . . . . .   486 Libel on D- D-      187
     This box is cramm'd on ev'ry side  . . . . . . .    753 Gift for Bec          9
CRAMMD
     Where I hear you are crammd evry day like a Swine   . 1017 Swift Ans Sher    13
CRAMMING
     We lye cramming ourselves, and are ready to burst,  . . 967 Letter Sherid     3
CRAMP
     Did very much his Genius cramp;  . . . . . . . .    172 Horace 1, 7          44
     Hard, tough, cramp, gutt'rall, harsh, stiff Names.  . . 467 Birthday Song   210
CRAMS
     A Fox with Geese his Belly crams;  . . . . . . .    651 On Poetry           325
CRANK
     Methinks I now see them so jovial and crank,   . . . 287 Bank Down           24
CRANNY
     Had you but through a Cranny spy'd  . . . . . . .   591 Strephon Chloe      237
CRANY
     Good Spelling, Master, your Crany has Lead on't.  . . 1004 Dan J's Reply     36
CRAPE
     With fifty Yards of Crape, shall sweep the Stage.   . . 275 Epilogue         26
     A holier Priest ne'er was wrapt up in Crape,   . . . . 516 Dean Hang Rape    5
     "Against that Assassin in Crape,  . . . . . . . .   850 Old Thorn            67
CRATINUS
     He and Cratinus used, as Horace says,   . . . . . . 988 Letter Dr Sh-n       11
CRAVE
     "I must a little longer crave;   . . . . . . . . .  208 Fable Bitches        32
     For you or I to crave a Boon;    . . . . . . . . .  371 Letter D. S-y         8
     "No larger Income dost thou Crave.      . . . . .   476 Epist on Epist       36
CRAWL
     And humbly at the bottom crawl.  . . . . . . . .      9 Ode to King        118
     The Groaning Chair began to crawl   . . . . . . .   113 Bauc & Phil 2        85
CRAWLL
     The groaning Chair began to crawll  . . . . . . .    93 Bauc & Phil 1       105
CRAWLS
     Crawls back neglected to his Den.   . . . . . . .    84 Salamander           36
     But spight of the Harpy that crawls on all four,  . . 147 Windsor Proph      11
     And in the Chambers of your Viceroy crawls.   . . . 792 St. Pat's Well       58
CRAZ'D
     So nature's craz'd convulsions make us dread   . . . 53 Temple Ill          65
CRAZY
     The crazy composition shews,  . . . . . . . . . .    38 Ode Sancroft       137
     Or crazy rules to make us wits by rote  . . . . .    47 To Congreve        129
     Our crazy double-bottom'd Realm.  . . . . . . . .    96 On the Union         22
     A Crazy Prelate, and a Royal Prude.     . . . . .   193 Author Himself        2
     And, crazy Congreve scarce cou'd spare  . . . . .   481 Libel on D- D-       41
CREAM
     He scratch'd her Maid, he stole the Cream,   . . .  153 Widow and Cat    D  11
     To make my Cream a Perquisite,   . . . . . . . .    154 Widow and Cat    D  39
     Now, loit'ring o'er her Tea and Cream,  . . . . .   447 Modern Lady          70
     Accosting; said, Go shake your Cream.   . . . . .   897 Panegyr Dean        326
CREAMS
     Her Ointments, Daubs, and Paints and Creams,   . .  530 Lady's Dres Rm      138
CREATE
     A female pow'r, loose-govern'd thoughts create;  . . 54 Temple Ill         104
     Faster than Nature can create;   . . . . . . . .    935 Riddle 23        D  19
CREATED
     Much Plague it created,  . . . . . . . . . . . .   1014 Swift to Sheri       15
CREATES
     Blest Revolution, which creates  . . . . . . . .     96 On the Union          5
     See, what Mirth the Sport creates;   . . . . . .    638 Epistle Lady        255
     Preserving what it first creates)   . . . . . . .   764 Stel B-day '26       42
```

```
                                                            PAGE    TITLE           LINE
CREATING
    At once creating Love and Pity.      . . . . . . . .    417 Woman's Mind          42
CREATION
    As Thorns were design'd to be from the Creation.   . .  334 Serious Poem          30
    In Time a new Creation springs.      . . . . . . . .    924 Riddle 7              90
    I am not one of God's Creation,      . . . . . . . .    927 Riddle 10        D     8
CREATURE   SEE FELLOW-CREATURE
    No Creature valu'd what they se'd:       . . . . . .     90 Bauc & Phil 1         25
    At first a gentle Creature;     . . . . . . . . . .     153 Widow and Cat    D     2
    There's not a creature here you ever knew.    . . . .   307 Billet Players        12
    No Creature in the Lane could sleep.      . . . . . .   352 Wood Ironmongr         4
    He cannot see one Creature dropping:     . . . . . .    500 Doctor Delaney        22
    That careless Wench! no Creature warn her     . . . .   528 Lady's Dres Rm        71
    You'd swear, that so divine a Creature    . . . . .     584 Strephon Chloe        19
    A Creature bipes et implumis;    . . . . . . . . .      608 Beasts Confess       216
    But Man we find the only Creature,    . . . . . . .     641 On Poetry             19
    Hobbes clearly proves that ev'ry Creature    . . . .    651 On Poetry            319
    Accusing that false Creature, Man.    . . . . . . .     686 Cadenus Vaness         4
    Becomes the Creature well enough.     . . . . . . .     700 Cadenus Vaness       427
    That scarce a Creature can be found,     . . . . .      776 Mullinix Tim          79
    We both are Mortal; but thou, frailer Creature,    .    861 On Old Glass           1
    To mortify the Creature more,    . . . . . . . . .      886 Rev Market-Hill      103
    I let no Creature see my Face.   . . . . . . . . .      917 Riddle 4               4
    Or, but a Creature of the Brain,    . . . . . . . .     920 Riddle 5              33
    For breeding is a useful Creature.    . . . . . . .     940 Letter                 7
CREATURES
    Creatures of ev'ry Kind but ours    . . . . . . .       607 Beasts Confess       203
    In Creatures of the rhiming Race.    . . . . . . .      653 On Poetry            386
    Yet many poor Creatures I help to ensnare.    . . .     929 Riddle 13        D     6
    We are little airy Creatures,    . . . . . . . .        930 Riddle 17        D     1
CREDIT
    But the Thing I stand upon, is the Credit of the House  71 Mrs Harris Pet        39
    Before his Credit or his Fee.    . . . . . . . .        204 In Sickness           12
    Dick suffer'd for his Peace and Credit,      . . . .    220 A Quiet Life          37
    Consult his Peace, or Credit save?    . . . . . .       221 A Quiet Life          40
    His Quiet small, his Credit less;    . . . . . . .      221 A Quiet Life          42
    His Credit out for Cheese and Ale;    . . . . . .       231 Prog of Poetry        34
    His Credit sunk, his Money spent,     . . . . . .       252 Bubble                47
    We see the Nation's Credit crackt,    . . . . . .       253 Bubble                59
    Before a Play, wou'd lose no Credit:     . . . . .      484 Libel on D- D-       142
    And spoils the Credit of the Function.    . . . . .     502 Doctor Delaney        82
    By his own Credit to advance the Sum;    . . . . .      533 To Mr. Gay            72
    "Spent all his Credit for his Friends:    . . . . .     565 Death of Swift       332
    And, with Credit fill my Station;    . . . . . . .      630 Epistle Lady          24
    You lose your Credit all at once;     . . . . . . .     644 On Poetry            137
    So two poor Knaves, who find their Credit fail,    .    668 Epig Carthy 8    D     3
    Thy credit sunk, thy money spent,    . . . . . . .      676 Parson's Case         10
    'Tis my own Credit lies at Stake.     . . . . . . .     741 Stel B-day 22         32
CREDIT'S
    Or kindly when his Credit's out,    . . . . . . .       728 Stella, Poems         31
CREDITORS
    When Creditors demand their Due;      . . . . . . .     240 Run Bankers           38
    And gave his Creditors the Slip.     . . . . . . .      456 Dean Smedley          44
CREECH
    Creech murder'd Horace in his senseless Rhymes,    .    666 Epig Carthy 3    D     1
CREED
    "Are taught to use them for their Creed.      . . .     564 Death of Swift       288
    She has better learnt her creed:     . . . . . . .      907 Daphne                40
CREEP
    A Stealing Brook, and strove to creep away    . . .      22 Ode Athenian         192
    Creep in the Dark from Leathern Cell,     . . . . .      99 Elegy Patrige         54
    Both softly to the Cradle creep:     . . . . . . .      150 Corinna                6
    Mark where the Sly Directors creep,      . . . . .      257 Bubble               173
    "Can creep, or run, can fly or swim,    . . . . . .     304 Storm                 31
    They often climb, and oftner creep.      . . . . .      412 Desire Possess        20
    With a Passage left to creep in,    . . . . . . .       830 Legion Club           45
    Shall creep no more behind a Bush;    . . . . . .       893 Panegyr Dean         214
    As eels delight to creep in mud,    . . . . . . .       950 Upstart          D     7
    Now Creep, Sweep, Sweep, Sweep the Deep,      . . .     960 Cantata
CREEPING
    That we the wretched, creeping far behind,    . . .      54 Temple Ill           115
    And saw the Parson creeping out;     . . . . . . .      127 Little House          26
    Him the Boar in Silence creeping,     . . . . . . .     660 Love Song             11
CREEPLE
    My Comrade's Blind, and I'm a Creeple    . . . . .       90 Bauc & Phil 1         16
CREEPS
    The Vicar once a Week creeps in,      . . . . . . .     127 Little House          19
    There creeps two Auditory Nerves,     . . . . . .       367 Answer Delaney        34
    That creeps as far to reach the Centre;      . . . .    393 Modern Poets           8
    If chance a Mouse creeps in her Sight,    . . . . .     416 Woman's Mind          33
    And then between two Blankets creeps.    . . . . .      582 Young Nymph           38
CREPT
    A Numbness crept through ev'ry Limb:     . . . . .      470 Burning Poem          10
    He follow'd, stript, and in he crept,    . . . . .      587 Strephon Chloe       113
    He seem'd as just crept out of Bed;      . . . . .      594 Cassinus Peter        11
    In a Fright she crept away,     . . . . . . . . .       834 Legion Club          131
CRETAN
    The Rashness of the Cretan Youth,     . . . . . . .     252 Bubble                42
CRETER
    And his Horse, the dear Creter, it prances and rears,  .  870 Grand Question      97
```

	PAGE	TITLE	LINE
CREW			
When we perform, look sharp among our crew,	307	Billet Players	11
And, in a crew, 'tis no injustice thought	308	Billet Players	27
And the whole crew this resolution takes,	309	Billet Players	49
Among a Crew of royst'ring Fellows	352	Wood Ironmongr	5
Got from his crew of <rogues> in grain;	435	Answer Paulus	118
To sit among that <scoundrel> crew,	436	Answer Paulus	132
When frighted at the clam'rous Crew,	448	Modern Lady	120
Too happy were the Poets Crew,	467	Birthday Song	223
A sudden universal Crew	528	Lady's Dres Rm	85
"Not so, the vile Fanatick Crew;	549	Life of Swift	156
A House of Peers, or Gaming Crew,	658	On Poetry	D 164
To find a King in all ye Crew;	659	On Poetry	D 410
Of either Sex, among the Crew,	689	Cadenus Vaness	102
They wou'd Consent, that all the Crew	778	Mullinix Tim	149
Of all sizes and sorts, the Fanatical crew	815	Yahoo's	21
By this odious Crew beset,	832	Legion Club	93
From the dire infectious Crew.	834	Legion Club	124
For, who would not be in that numerous Crew sick?	1029	Dr. Helsham	13
CRIB			
The Crib was down, the Blackbird caught.	127	Little House	30
CRIES			
Nor dipt in Blood, nor Widow's Tears, nor Orphan's Cries:	29	Ode to Temple	86
Because like a Watch it always cries Click:	351	Wood Insect	21
If the Maggot cries Click when it scratches the Post.	351	Wood Insect	24
The Soldier smiling hears the Widows Cries,	364	On Dreams	15
Cries, "Lord, the World is so censorious!	450	Modern Lady	167
Whene'er a flatt'ring Puppy cries	545	Life of Swift	25
Cries, "Is he gone? 'Tis time he shou'd.	559	Death of Swift	182
(Cries Bob) "I'm Sorry for the News;	560	Death of Swift	192
Who, when she loudly cries, Forbear,	641	On Poetry	21
Amidst a croud of hungry Bards cries out,	671	Epig Carthy 24	D 3
When Dick cries, Dust to carry out?	787	Clad in Brown	30
Drawn up in our Court; when the Captain cries, Stand.	870	Grand Question	100
It cries at a Touch,	939	Riddle Answerd	26
To a quarrelsome Fellow, cries, Let us be Friends.	968	Letter Sherid	28
CRIME			
Is in her Sex a Crime needs no excuse)	18	Ode Athenian	65
<Swift> had the Sin of Wit no venial Crime;	193	Author Himself	9
Forgive her, if it be a Crime,	224	Prog of Love	63
For no other Crime but committing a <Rape>.	518	Dean Hang Rape	36
Condemn'd for thy Crime, at three score and ten?	519	Dean Hang Rape	50
"In him was held a Crime of State.	569	Death of Swift	416
A Crime that shocks all human Kind;	595	Cassinus Peter	68
A Crime to all her Sex unknown!)	596	Cassinus Peter	104
His Crime he quickly understood;	604	Beasts Confess	99
CRIMES			
Some angel say, what were the nation's crimes,	42	Ode Sancroft	245
If these be of all Crimes the worst,	392	Young's Satire	47
The stinking Load of all the Crimes,	497	Panegyr Swift	116
Are ill excuses for a Servant's Crimes:	533	To Mr. Gay	68
He ow'd his Preservation to his Crimes.	536	To Mr. Gay	156
His Zeal was not to lash our Crimes,	549	Life of Swift	136
To palliate his Friend Oxford's Crimes;	550	Life of Swift	185
But hung himself to expiate his Crimes.	666	Epig Carthy 3	D 2
The Brief with weighty Crimes was charg'd,	686	Cadenus Vaness	5
Which Crimes aforesaid (with her Leave)	687	Cadenus Vaness	15
Where Virtues are imputed Crimes,	798	Traulus 1	92
Whose Perjury's the least of all their Crimes:	806	Judas	12
CRIMINAL			
Now, whereas the said Criminal seems past Repentance,	266	Apollo	93
"Or is he criminal that flies	380	Apology Lady C	165
CRIMSON			
"For Lands enrich'd by crimson Streams,	183	Horace 2, 1	96
CRING'D			
"That e'er he cring'd to Men in Place?	549	Life of Swift	145
Tho' he cring'd to his Deanship in very low strains,	816	Yahoo's	46
CRINGE			
With couchant Cringe, and flattering Tale,	208	Fable Bitches	15
Despising Slaves that cringe for Bread.	483	Libel on D- D-	88
CRINGING			
The cringing Knave who seeks a Place	604	Beasts Confess	93
Cringing comes to beg their Pardon;	800	Traulus 1	14
In him, that's accomplish'd in Cringing and Canting:	808	Advice Parson	6
CRIPPLE			
A Cripple with one Foot too short:	645	On Poetry	172
CRISIS			
Must furbish up and Nickname Crisis.	180	Horace 2, 1	6
CRITIC			
Yes, that beau's look, that voice, those critic ears,	48	To Congreve	173
The Critic to his Cost will find,	1021	Nim-Dan-Dean 1	D 33
CRITICIZE			
On you shall rail and criticize;	651	On Poetry	332
CRITICK			
And hence a Critick deep maintains,	156	Fable of Midas	21
In chusing Lace a Critick nice,	416	Woman's Mind	27
A skilfull Critick justly blames	467	Birthday Song	209
You, as a Critick, are so curious	483	Libel on D- D-	99
And looks a Critick in the Face.	500	Doctor Delaney	26
Whilst, ev'ry Critick can devour	502	Doctor Delaney	69

	PAGE	TITLE	LINE
CRITICK (CONTINUED)			
From hence the Critick Vermin sprung	504	Doctor Delaney	123
Some Critick may object, perhaps, ...	624	Scandal Poem 2	15
A forward Critick often dupes us	648	On Poetry	255
CRITICK'S			
The Lead yon Critick's Quill contains, ...	500	Doctor Delaney	15
Thy Labours, grown the Critick's Prey, ...	642	On Poetry	67
Put on the Critick's Brow, and sit	647	On Poetry	235
CRITICKS			
Those pow'rs the criticks, who may boast the odds .	46	To Congreve	103
Let Censuring Criticks then think what they list on't, . .	77	Lady B- B-	REF
However, if Criticks find Fault with the Phrase, . .	337	Serious Poem	101
"Nor, can I tell what Criticks thought 'em; . . .	565	Death of Swift	311
Damn'd Poets, Damn'd Criticks, . .	576	Place Damn'd	7
Some Criticks may object perhaps, ...	618	Scandal Poem 1	21
Lie Snug, and hear what Criticks say.	644	On Poetry	118
And Criticks have no partial Views, ...	644	On Poetry	131
Where Criticks mark'd your former Faults.	645	On Poetry	150
In all our modern Criticks Jargon.)	648	On Poetry	242
For these our Criticks much confide in, ...	648	On Poetry	252
Yet Criticks may object, why not?	813	Bro Protestant	41
CRITICS			
Yet want your critics no just cause to rail, ...	45	To Congreve	65
Whilst thus I write, vast shoals of critics come, . .	50	To Congreve	213
CROAKING			
By loud and unharmonious Croaking:	479	Epist on Epist	124
I sent you Millions of the croaking Race;	792	St. Pat's Well	54
CROCHETS			
To listen to minimms and quavers and Crochets . . .	522	St. Cecilia's	12
CROCODILE			
The Crocodile that lurking lyes, ...	257	Bubble	179
CROCUS			
The Crocus and the Daffodil, ...	894	Panegyr Dean	251
CROMWELLIAN			
A damn'd Cromwellian, knock'd me down.	926	Riddle 9	20
CRONIES			
Lords are a footboy's cronies in his sleep.	48	To Congreve	150
CRONY			
Not one of all his Crony Stars, ...	98	Elegy Patrige	7
To oblige your Crony <Swift>, ...	862	To Janus	3
CROOKED			
The crooked Paths of wandering Thames.	31	Ode to Temple	152
Your bandy Leg, or crooked Nose.	416	Woman's Mind	22
While crooked Cynthia swearing says, ...	449	Modern Lady	160
"He spar'd a Hump or crooked Nose, ...	572	Death of Swift	467
Are ten crooked sticks:	853	Lady's Lament	78
CROP			
The Groom was wisht to saddle Crop, ...	223	Prog of Love	35
Who crop the Nurseries of Learning here?	792	St. Pat's Well	50
We'll show him the way how to crop and to slit; . .	816	Yahoo's	52
CROP-SICK			
And crop-sick with unclub'd for wine, ...	434	Answer Paulus	73
CROPPING			
And slitting of noses, and cropping of ears, ...	816	Yahoo's	48
CROPT			
Would you not wish his Lawrels cropt?	554	Death of Swift	26
My Skin he flay'd, my Hair he cropt;	915	Riddle 1	11
CROSIER			
And, if the Crosier could be cramm'd in, ...	191	Faggot	47
By Faith and Prayer, this Crosier in my Hand, . . .	792	St. Pat's Well	39
CROSIERS			
How would it pollute their Crosiers and Rochets . .	522	St. Cecilia's	11
On their Crosiers to ride, like a Witch on a Broom. .	804	Irish Bishops	22
CROSS SEE CHARING-CROSS			
In vain I strive to cross this spacious Main, . . .	32	Ode to Temple	192
You need but cross the Irish Seas, ...	173	Horace 1, 7	91
Nor cross the Channel twice a Year, ...	199	Horace 2, 6	11
Then come the Poor and strip him so, they leave him not a Cross,	341	Upon His Grace	11
They cannot say the winds are cross	420	Holyhead	15
With such a cross Man, I wou'd lye in the Streets. .	869	Grand Question	60
And am his neighbour cross the way;	899	Dean's Reasons	30
Dean Cross, had he preach'd, would have made us all Pew-sick;	1029	Dr. Helsham	8
CROSS-BATH			
Or in the cross-bath seeks as Heir	294	Prog Marriage	137
CROSS'D			
Dick Sigh'd for his Doll and his mournfull Arms Cross'd,	430	Dicky Dolly	7
Pallas had cross'd her first Intent, ...	712	Cadenus Vaness	833
CROSSE			
Dear Baldwin chaste, and witty Crosse, ...	821	Dr. Rundle	61
CROSSER			
Put up your Wife, she's crosser than all four', . . .	404	Window Inns 11	D 4
CROSSES			
There hang three crosses at thy door:	404	Window Inns 11	D 1
'Fool, to put up four Crosses at your door, ...	404	Window Inns 11	D 3
'There are Three Crosses at your door--	404	Window Inns 11	D 5
CROSST			
And with his Dame the ocean crosst, ...	878	Robbin & Harry	19

CROST
                                                        PAGE   TITLE   LINE
     Then in his First Love why should he be crost?   .   .   .   337 Serious Poem   107
CROTCHET
     If Fortune should please to take such a Crotchet,   .   .   518 Dean Hang Rape   43
     For, if a new Crotchet comes into my Brain,   .   .   .   869 Grand Question   65
CROUCH
     And make him crouch to save his bacon.   .   .   .   .   .   .   468 Birthday Song   250
CROUCH'D
     Now lowly crouch'd, I cry Peccavi, ...   1005 Sheridan's Sub   11
CROUCHING
     The Tyrant Death lay crouching down, ...   7 Ode to King   39
CROUD
     From us the Blind and thoughtless Croud, ...   18 Ode Athenian   87
     Cryes out a Sage among the Croud, ...   253 Bubble   78
     Among the trembling Croud below.   .   .   .   .   .   .   353 Wood Ironmongr   20
     Who pay'd his Courtship with the Croud, ...   482 Libel on D- D-   57
     They croud about Preferment's Gate, ...   503 Doctor Delaney   93
     Amidst a croud of hungry Bards cries out,   .   .   .   671 Epig Carthy 24   D   3
     A Croud of fashionable Fops;   .   .   .   .   696 Cadenus Vaness   317
     Such a Croud their Ordure throws   .   .   .   .   .   830 Legion Club   19
CROUDED
     Crouded round with antic Shapes;   .   .   .   .   .   .   832 Legion Club   88
CROUDING
     Crouding the roads with naked feet.   .   .   .   .   .   401 Window Inns 5   D   10
CROUDS
     To Shops in Crouds the dagged Females fly,   .   .   .   138 City Shower   33
     Whole Crouds about its Brazen Strings.   .   .   .   .   345 Prometheus   30
     To keep good sense in crouds of fools;   .   .   .   .   436 Answer Paulus   124
     His honesty in crouds of knaves;   .   .   .   .   .   .   436 Answer Paulus   126
CROUN
     Demand a Croun a Quart for Stumm.   .   .   .   .   .   313 To Ford   68
CROW   SEE SCARE-CROW
     Was much surpriz'd to see a Crow   .   .   .   .   .   .   127 Little House   27
     H'as drop'd, and giv'n the Crow a Pudden!   .   .   .   547 Life of Swift   71
CROWD
     Is but a Crowd of Atoms justling in a heap,   .   .   .   20 Ode Athenian   127
     The chief among that glitt'ring crowd, ...   177 To Lord Harley   39
     "To justle here among a Crowd.   .   .   .   .   .   .   200 Horace 2, 6   34
     In Church you heard her thro the Crowd   .   .   .   .   222 Prog of Love   9
     The Coasters crowd to seise the Spoyl, ...   258 Bubble   202
     And Still the Madness of the Crowd.   .   .   .   .   .   258 Bubble   212
     I alone can inspire the poetical Crowd;   .   .   .   .   263 Apollo   16
     Where Childless wives crowd ev'ry morn   .   .   .   .   293 Prog Marriage   119
     Where numberless thy Vot'ries crowd: .   .   .   .   324 Pethox   22
     Is dress'd, and stealing thro' the Crowd,   .   .   .   377 Apology Lady C   77
     Nor, with your Kindred half the Palace crowd.   .   .   533 To Mr. Gay   58
     To crowd the Court with their Relations: .   .   .   606 Beasts Confess   178
     Who crowd the Press with hourly Trash.   .   .   .   .   652 On Poetry   356
     With Gifts superior to the Crowd, ...   700 Cadenus Vaness   445
     Preferr'd before a Crowd of Beaux, ...   710 Cadenus Vaness   751
     And crowd to Stella's at fourscore.   .   .   .   .   .   736 Stel B-day '20   58
     You must have pass'd among the Crowd.   .   .   .   .   742 Stel B-day 22   48
     And Sir I know you hate a Crowd.   .   .   .   .   .   .   860 Lady Acheson   24
     See how the gaping crowd admire   .   .   .   .   950 Upstart   D   15
     Are not you, in a Crowd, when you sweat and you stew,   1029 Dr. Helsham   9
        sick?
     And I got thro' the Crowd, tho' not led by a Clew, sick   1029 Dr. Helsham   22
CROWDED
     "Of City Fogs and crowded Rooms, ...   380 Apology Lady C   140
     "To pass to many crowded Stages, ...   380 Apology Lady C   155
     And Prints are crowded with his Name.   .   .   .   .   397 Earl of P-b-w   3
     Who wou'd not at a crowded Show, ...   554 Death of Swift   15
CROWDING
     Where tho' her elder sisters crowding throng,   .   .   49 To Congreve   181
     See, at her Levee crowding Swains   .   .   .   .   .   735 Stel B-day '20   23
CROWDS
     "Thro' Crowds of Coxcombs & of Coaches;   .   .   .   380 Apology Lady C   152
     And come in Crowds to see his Face: .   .   .   .   .   709 Cadenus Vaness   702
     So are Ladies in Crowds, when they squeeze and they   1030 Dr. Helsham   26
        screw, sick.
CROWN
     What do the Scepter, Crown and Ball, ...   6 Ode to King   12
     Spoil'd of his Leaden Crown: .   .   .   .   7 Ode to King   41
     You, Mighty Monarch, Nobler Actions Crown,   .   .   11 Ode to William   D   3
     Had You by dull Succession gain'd Your Crown,   .   .   11 Ode to William   D   9
     At once deserve a Crown, and gain it too.   .   .   .   12 Ode to William   D   16
     To Crown the happy Conquerour, ...   16 Ode Athenian   19
     A load as heavy as the Crown, ...   40 Ode Sancroft   188
     Nor hurricano from the Crown, ...   40 Ode Sancroft   191
     Was, like his Master's Crown, inwreath'd with thorn.   .   40 Ode Sancroft   200
     And if she can but win a Crown, ...   75 Game Traffick   23
     He wou'd not sell it for a Crown.   .   .   .   .   .   128 Little House   58
     Swore he'd rather lose a Crown, ...   168 Peace Dunkirk   19
     Thee with Immortal Honours crown, ...   182 Horace 2, 1   63
     'Tis for the Service of the Crown.   .   .   .   .   .   199 Horace 2, 6   14
     Virtue, to crown her Fav'rites, loves to try   .   .   .   210 Earl of Oxford   11
     And Silver Cynthia for a Crown;   .   .   .   .   .   .   255 Bubble   128
     And scarce a Crown is left to see the Play: .   .   .   275 Epilogue   34
     For sorry Stuff, can get a Crown a Page;   .   .   .   .   276 Epilogue   42
     May cost a crown or so; a common case: .   .   .   .   308 Billet Players   26
     Which lighting on th' Impostor's Crown, ...   353 Wood Ironmongr   37

```
CROWN          (CONTINUED)                              PAGE    TITLE              LINE
    "And after all, to crown my Spleen,     . . . . . . . .   380 Apology Lady C     157
    But just a Step below the Crown:        . . . . . . .     392 Young's Satire      38
    And, by his Crown will nothing get;     . . . . . . .     409 Dial Rich Marb      41
    A Crown and Scepter in her Hands;       . . . . . . .     413 Desire Possess      42
    But, as he climb'd to grasp the Crown,  . . . . . .       413 Desire Possess      47
    But Sr we must support the Crown.       . . . . . . . .   422 Ireld               40
    For here the Father kept his Crown.     . . . . . . .     460 Birthday Song       14
    And crown a Royal Dunce with Bays:      . . . . . . .     464 Birthday Song      120
    Here many a King his heart and Crown    . . . . . .       465 Birthday Song      167
    If all my Pains will earn a Crown.      . . . . . . .     502 Doctor Delaney      68
    "Corrupt the Senate, rob the Crown;     . . . . . . .     568 Death of Swift     386
    "Nor Topicks brought to please the Crown, . . . . .       570 Death of Swift     428
    That now the Pair must crown their Joys. . . . . .        586 Strephon Chloe      70
    They take Possession of the Crown,      . . . . . . .     592 Strephon Chloe     261
    Can <piss> upon his lawrel crown..      . . . . . . . .   620 'Scandal Poem 1    110
    Can <piss> upon his Lawrel Crown.       . . . . . . . .   626 Scandal Poem 2     108
    Shou'd a Monkey wear a Crown,           . . . . . . . .   634 Epistle Lady       149
    Light on many a Coxcomb's Crown.        . . . . . . . .   638 Epistle Lady       254
    The leaden Crown devolv'd to thee,      . . . . . . .     653 On Poetry          375
    Against her Dignity and Crown:          . . . . . . . .   687 Cadenus Vaness      19
    With Stella's Praise to crown the Year. . . . . . .       743 Stel B-day 22       80
    Amounting hardly to a Crown a Tribe;    . . . . . .       806 Judas               4
    Tho' Half a Crown o'er-pays his Sweat's Worth;   . .      812 Bro Protestant      26
    Tipping him with Half a Crown;          . . . . . . . .   834 Legion Club        134
    If I make it a Barrack, the Crown is my Tenant.  . .      867 Grand Question      19
    Supporting half the British Crown;      . . . . . . .     919 Riddle 5            6
    Could you but change a Crown as easy    . . . . . .      1033 Ans to Crown        13
CROWN'D
    Scatter'd with flowry Vales, with fruitful Gardens        17 Ode Athenian        40
        crown'd,
    About the Head crown'd with these Bays,  . . . . . .      29 Ode to Temple       87
    Thy fair indulgent Mother crown'd  . . . . . . .         324 Pethox              33
    If e'er I stoop beneath a crown'd Head:                  410 Dial Rich Marb      74
    Foretell his Empire crown'd with Bays,  . . . . . .      466 Birthday Song      195
    (As Pictures prove) with Garlands crown'd,              590 Strephon Chloe     194
    He crown'd his youthful Head with Bays.  . . . . .       597 Problem Solved       8
    A Prince the Moment he is crown'd,      . . . . . .      646 On Poetry          191
    Among ye savage Monsters crown'd        . . . . . .      659 On Poetry        D 410
    With thy flow'ry Chaplets crown'd.      . . . . . . .    661 Love Song           28
    Your jetty Locks with Garlands crown'd, . . . . . .      760 Receipt Youth       41
    Were built to thee, with Off'rings crown'd:   . . . .    894 Panegyr Dean       238
    If I treat you like <a> <crown'd> <Head>  . . . .        637 Epistle Lady       239
CROWNS   SEE COPPLE-CROWNS
    And therefore Crowns are now-a-days     . . . . . . .     98 Elegy Patrige       27
    Or dealing crowns to George and James.  . . . . . .      402 Window Inns 7    D   6
    Are most inclin'd to plunder Crowns.    . . . . . .     1033 Ans to Crown        12
CROWS
    You see the Crows feet round his Eyes.  . . . . . . .    291 Prog Marriage       50
    For want of Vultures, we have Crows.    . . . . . . .    347 Prometheus          76
    Which says, wou'd Crows in Silence eat  . . . . . .      479 Epist on Epist     121
    Are two iron crows,  . . . . . . . . . . . . .          853 Lady's Lament       80
    Bare, like a Carcase pick't by Crows,   . . . . . . .    904 Death Daphne        34
CRUDE
    The crude Consistence oft I tread.      . . . . . . .     896 Panegyr Dean      310
    These crude Materials once shall rise,  . . . . . .      924 Riddle 7            91
CRUEL
    Cruel Unknown! what is it You intend!   . . . . . .       23 Ode Athenian       242
    And should some Nymph who ne'er was cruel,  . . . .       85 Salamander          61
    Their Reign began with cruel Seizures;  . . . . . .      283 Journal            120
    Since cruel Fate hath sunk our Justice Boat;  . . .      284 Elegy Boat           2
    'Twas therefore cruel, hard, by Jove,   . . . . . .      495 Panegyr Swift       80
    No cruel Master could require  . . . . . . . . .         726 To Stella          105
    Behold! the cruel Dean in Scorn  . . . . . . . . .       849 Old Thorn           23
    Unite; but on Conditions cruel;  . . . . . . . . .       883 Rev Market-Hill      9
    By cruel Hands her Blood was spilt,     . . . . . . .    923 Riddle 7            65
    And I mourn the cruel Pain.  . . . . . . . . . .         933 Riddle 20        D  14
CRUELTY
    Have ev'n encreas't their Pride and Cruelty.  . . .       23 Ode Athenian       249
    Now Pride and Cruelty are flown,  . . . . . . . . .      391 Young's Satire      17
    Envy, and Cruelty, and Pride,  . . . . . . . . .         725 To Stella           49
CRUMBLE
    What House, when its Materials crumble,  . . . . .       593 Strephon Chloe     297
CRUMBLES
    This, crumbles into dust,  . . . . . . . . . . .          39 Ode Sancroft       140
CRUSHD
    The narrow Entry crushd her Hoop  . . . . . . . .        746 Stel Distress
CRUST
    And from the Shelf a charming Crust I whipt:   . . .     881 Pastoral Dial       30
    The dullest Beast, and what's cover'd with Crust,  . .   941 Letter              31
CRUSTS
    Crusts o'er the day, shadowing its parent beam . . . .    45 To Congreve         71
CRUX
    As for your new rebus, or riddle, or crux,  . . . . .    977 Dean to Sherid      43
CRY
    To censure, to cry down, and rail,  . . . . . . . .       19 Ode Athenian       114
    Then my Lord call'd me; Harry, said my Lord, don't cry,   73 Mrs Harris Pet      66
    And just began to cry;--What ar't!  . . . . . . .        112 Bauc & Phil 2       38
    And little Miss began to cry;  . . . . . . . . .         128 Little House        48
    But, some will cry, Turn-Coat, and rip up old Stories,   143 New Song            21
    But Englond must cry alack and well a day,  . . . . .    147 Windsor Proph       13
```

CRY	(CONTINUED)		PAGE	TITLE	LINE
	The Waiters stand in Ranks; the Yeomen cry,		194	Author Himself	35
	And tho men cry, they love a Jest,		218	To Mr. Delany	83
	The Neighbors round would cry out Shame.		220	A Quiet Life	36
	Then each transported Fop will cry,		228	Prog of Beauty	75
	They'll cry, Ye Shops, upon us fall		241	Run Bankers	59
	The Dean and his Printer then let us cry Fye on;		237	Excellent Song	11
	We'll cry; look, here's our Boat, and there's the Pendent.		285	Elegy Boat	36
	And then we cry, to spur the bumkins on,		308	Billet Players	39
	And when his last Speech the loud Hawkers did cry,		399	Tom Clinch	11
	To cry the Bread was stale, and mutter		410	Dial Rich Marb	53
	When at a Play to laugh, or cry,		415	Woman's Mind	3
	To cry, like statesmen, quanta patimur!		433	Answer Paulus	42
	Methinks I hear the Ladies cry,		445	Modern Lady	13
	Folks shrug, and cry, There's nothing in't.		475	Epist on Epist	12
	How chearfully the Hawkers cry		502	Doctor Delaney	75
	I cry, Pox take him, and his Wit.		555	Death of Swift	52
	The rest will give a Shrug and cry,		561	Death of Swift	211
	"Fair Liberty was all his Cry;		566	Death of Swift	347
	Now, methinks, I hear you cry;		632	Epistle Lady	91
	To cry it up, or run it down.		649	On Poetry	270
	No little Boys and Girls to cry		778	Mullinix Tim	181
	When thro' the streets I cry holloo?		779	Mullinix Tim	186
	The Neighbours all cry, Shoot him dead,		797	Traulus 1	39
	But hold, cry the <Bishops>; and give us fair Play;		805	Irish Bishops	53
	To cry; Lo, Judas, gone to his own Place:		806	Judas	24
	About St. James's, cry, We Courtiers.		812	Bro Protestant	22
	"Can hardly tell how to cry Bo to a Goose;		872	Grand Question	158
	I'm too profuse some Cens'rers cry,		918	Riddle 4	25
	Yet hyprocrite Fanaticks cry,		926	Riddle 9	17
	Charming Oysters I cry,		952	Oysters	1
	Would, as he lay under, cry out, Sirrah, yield:		967	Letter Sherid	16
	But pleas'd to find you do relent and cry on.		1002	Reply by Dean	15
	Now lowly crouch'd, I cry Peccavi.		1005	Sheridan's Sub	11
CRY'D					
	Lost youth, she cry'd, since first I met thee here!		52	Temple Ill	32
	But then his Honour cry'd, Godzooks!		74	Game Traffick	5
	Great Jove, he cry'd, the Art restore		107	V's House	43
	When Baucis hastily cry'd out;		116	Bauc & Phil 2	155
	Does he refuse me? Harley cry'd:		172	Horace 1, 7	55
	The Doctor in a Passion cry'd;		175	Horace 1, 7	131
	And loudly cry'd--a Bite, a Bite.		208	Fable Bitches	42
	Cry'd bravely, Patience, good my Dear.		220	A Quiet Life	6
	Phil cry'd, and John began to curse;		224	Prog of Love	80
	If he shou'd now be cry'd down since his Change		235	Elegy on Demar	36
	Thus loaded with Grief, Dick Sigh'd and he cry'd,		430	Dicky Dolly	10
	Cry'd out, ye Gods, what Sound is this?		589	Strephon Chloe	177
	Cry'd, Caelia! thrice, and sigh'd the rest.		595	Cassinus Peter	40
	Cry'd, Madam, why surely my Master's possest;		868	Grand Question	44
	Cry'd, Huzzy, why sure the Wench is gone mad:		873	Grand Question	184
	Like Milk 'tis cry'd about the Street,		929	Riddle 15	D 11
CRY'R					
	The Cry'r was order'd to dismiss		714	Cadenus Vaness	884
CRYES					
	Cryes out a Sage among the Croud,		253	Bubble	78
	Cryes, Lord have Mercy on his Soul,		500	Doctor Delaney	18
	Will you regard the Hawker's Cryes		505	Doctor Delaney	161
	Drown your Morals, Madam cryes;		863	To Janus	19
CRYING					
	A burning Shame, a crying Sin		659	On Poetry	D 410
CRYSTAL					
	Now, picking out a Crystal Eye,		581	Young Nymph	11
	The crystal Eye, alas, was miss't;		583	Young Nymph	61
CUBBARD					
	The Cubbard fasten'd with a Peg		746	Stel Distress	39
CUBBS					
	"That you wou'd with your Cubbs retire:		208	Fable Bitches	28
CUBIT					
	A Cubit at least		246	Irish-Feast	63
CUBS					
	"Stay till my tender Cubs can find,		208	Fable Bitches	33
	Set all her Cubs at once upon her;		208	Fable Bitches	40
CUCKOLD					
	Call'd him a Cuckold, Fool, and Beast,		221	A Quiet Life	48
	Some to Cuckold Farmers Spouses,		574	Helter Skelter	43
	By the horned Sun, he sure meant <Cuckold>,		373	Letter D. S-y	61
CUCKOLDS					
	Cuckolds, elopes, and runs in Debt		150	Corinna	27
CUCKOW'S					
	Last just as long as ev'ry cuckow's note:		47	To Congreve	130
CUD-GELLING					
	Deserves a good Cud-gelling		442	Ballyspellin	81
CUDGEL					
	To Cudgel our Bones, and for Drink give us Verjuice;		335	Serious Poem	38
CUDGELL'D					
	But the Tapster well Cudgell'd him both Side and Flank		288	Bank Down	39
	Went home, and was cudgell'd again by his Wife.		327	Epigram 1	10
	They Cudgell'd, and Cuft him, and kickt him down Stairs		517	Dean Hang Rape	16
CUDGELL'S					
	Joan cudgell's Ned, yet Ned's a Bully		328	Epigram 3	1

		PAGE	TITLE	LINE
CUDGELL'S (CONTINUED)				
Will cudgell's Bess, yet Will's a Cully		328	Epigram 3	2
CUDGELLD				
As Thomas was cudgelld one day by his Wife, ...		327	Epigram 1	1
CUDGELS				
With Cudgels of Oak, ...		246	Irish-Feast	69
If Cudgels are scarce, ...		247	Irish-Feast	86
Switches better guide than Cudgels.		636	Epistle Lady	202
CUE				
You hop'd to find many (for that was your Cue) sick; .		1029	Dr. Helsham	23
CUFF'D				
Who for his pains is cuff'd, and kick'd, ...		436	Answer Paulus	137
<CUFFE>				
And <Cuffe> grins for getting, the Alicant Plate. . .		430	Dicky Dolly	21
CUFFS				
"But at Cuffs I was always the Cock of the School; .		873	Grand Question	164
CUFT				
They Cudgell'd, and Cuft him, and kickt him down Stairs		517	Dean Hang Rape	16
CULLING				
Can mean my culling of a Face, ...		1003	Dan J's Reply	8
CULLY				
Some Cully often wins a Bett		257	Bubble	162
Will cudgell's Bess, yet Will's a Cully		328	Epigram 3	2
And snap some Cully passing by;		583	Young Nymph	50
The greatest cully of mankind:		899	Dean's Reasons	12
Steals from the Cully when he's drunk;		1033	Ans to Crown	2
CULLY'S				
How well a Cully's Purse was lin'd:		133	Magician's Rod	32
Fancies his Fingers in the Cully's Fob.		364	On Dreams	26
CULLYES				
Nor come within your Cullyes Reach, ...		258	Bubble	194
CULTIVATE				
You strove to cultivate a barren Court in vain, . . .		32	Ode to Temple	175
To form and cultivate her Mind.		706	Cadenus Vaness	631
CUM				
Cum Multis aliis (all his Foes)		373	Letter D. S-y	71
CUMBER'D				
This world he cumber'd long enough;		296	Satiric Elegy	13
CUMBROUS				
He sunk beneath the cumbrous Weight:		413	Desire Possess	52
CUNNING				
. . .to the Cunning Man;		72	Mrs Harris Pet	48
With Cunning that Defect supplies, ...		107	V's House	57
(This Lewis is a Cunning Shaver, ...		171	Horace 1, 7	17
But the Squire he was cunning and found what they meant,		288	Bank Down	51
You'll pardon me Sir, your Cunning I smoak, ...		336	Serious Poem	65
Had you been cunning Stagers, ...		426	Five Ladies	26
Too cunning to be caught in Trapps.		504	Doctor Delaney	126
She's too cunning, and too skilful, ...		907	Daphne	41
CUNNINGLY				
Then cunningly retire unseen, ...		253	Bubble	71
CUP				
The bitter cup is from him past:		40	Ode Sancroft	202
Potable Gold in Golden Cup.		156	Fable of Midas	8
And a Madder our Cup.		244	Irish-Feast	12
Boy, give us a Cup;		245	Irish-Feast	27
Come, you must take a Cup of Sack or two before you go.		342	Upon His Grace	24
If you'll redeem the Silver Cup		446	Modern Lady	58
Than Fish-Wives o'er a Cup of Gin:		450	Modern Lady	181
That you and he are Cup and Cann.		480	Libel on D- D-	10
To flourish o'er a Cup of Ginn?		505	Doctor Delaney	148
To take, his mornings Cup of Gin.		659	On Poetry	D 410
"Thou hast certainly gotten a Cup in thy Pate. . . .		870	Grand Question	84
Well roasted, with Sugar and Wine in a Cup, ...		953	Oranges	3
CUPBOARD				
The Cupboard could contain but four;)		751	Stel Wood-Park	66
CUPBOARDS				
Lock up from my Sight in Pantries and Cupboards: . .		263	Apollo	12
CUPID				
When Cupid did his Grandsire Jove intreat, ...		118	Biddy Floyd	1
But Cupid with a Satyr comes;		150	Corinna	5
Then Cupid thus: This little Maid		150	Corinna	9
Cupid shall ne'er mistake another		272	Apollo's Edict	D 56
A Cupid in his face and size, ...		466	Birthday Song	201
To act the Part of Tray, or Cupid;		607	Beasts Confess	208
Gentle Cupid o'er my Heart;		660	Love Song	2
That Cupid now has lost his Art, ...		687	Cadenus Vaness	7
But Cupid, full of Mischief, longs		701	Cadenus Vaness	466
And Cupid hop'd they wou'd improve		701	Cadenus Vaness	474
Cupid, tho' all his Darts were lost, ...		702	Cadenus Vaness	492
Where erst sate Cupid with his Bow;		757	Stel B-day '24	38
CUPID'S				
That the main String of Cupid's Bow, ...		66	Problem	22
Without one Word of Cupid's Darts, ...		728	Stella, Poems	11
That quite extinguish't Cupid's Lamp:		905	Death Daphne	98
CUPIDS				
The little Cupids hov'ring round, ...		590	Strephon Chloe	193
CUPS				
Twelve Cups of Tea, (with Grief I speak)		589	Strephon Chloe	163
CUR SEE CURR				
T'is the Cur dog of Brittain & spaniel of Spain. . .		540	Charac Walpole	14

		PAGE	TITLE	LINE
CUR	(CONTINUED)			
The scrubest Cur in all the Pack		798	Traulus 1	67
CUR'D				
How she cur'd Charley of the Chincough;		282	Journal	92
CURATE				
Thus to a Dean some Curate Sloven, ...		812	Bro Protestant	19
"Mister Curate, for all your grave Looks, I'm afraid,		872	Grand Question	147
That the Captain suppos'd he was Curate to Jenny.)	.	872	Grand Question	152
CURATE-SHIP				
And make thy curate-ship a dean;		676	Parson's Case	20
CURATE'S				
Thy curate's place, thy fruitful wife, ...		676	Parson's Case	5
CURCHYES				
And your Ladyship curchyes half way to the Ground!	. .	871	Grand Question	116
CURE				
And cure You both with a good Stick.		91	Bauc & Phil 1	46
And Cure the Wounds that Venus made.		99	Elegy Patrige	62
To cure her by a Counter-spell:		354	Simile Silver	8
An Evil, which admits no Cure:		413	Censure	2
To cure their Scabs		440	Ballyspellin	14
"Who only asks some pretty Cure, ...		476	Epist on Epist	49
Though not to cure, yet palliate each Disease. .		535	To Mr. Gay	124
"To cure the Vices of Mankind:		565	Death of Swift	314
A College Joke to cure the Dumps.		594	Cassinus Peter	38
And cure the Rank unsav'ry Smelling.		892	Panegyr Dean	166
That she'll own, or cure a fault.		907	Daphne	32
Of Spleen you cure the Female Sex.		919	Riddle 5	18
You cure with Ease and with Delight;		924	Riddle 8	14
CURES				
Infallibly cures the Timber affected;		351	Wood Insect	26
Or other Lap-Dog Cures for Sores.		494	Panegyr Swift	36
CURIOSITY				
Whom blind and eager Curiosity		18	Ode Athenian	63
(Yet Curiosity they say, ...		18	Ode Athenian	64
CURIOUS				
This bids some curious praters here below . . .		45	To Congreve	73
A search, no doubt, as curious and as wise . .		46	To Congreve	93
Then curious Hands this Texture take, ...		79	Vanbrug House	33
Whilst high, and nice, and curious Meats, . . .		378	Apology Lady C	107
You, as a Critick, are so curious		483	Libel on D- D-	99
Where, if the curious List to read 'em, ...		494	Panegyr Swift	51
Than what a curious Eye may trace		653	On Poetry	385
Still to be curious, never hearken.		753	Gift for Bec	22
And curious to know, ...		756	Dingley Brent	16
Still be she curious, never hearken		762	Bec's B-Day	43
All Mortals must be curious to enquire, ...		825	Noisy Tom	5
Attract the curious Trav'llers Eyes, ...		893	Panegyr Dean	202
Here, oft the Curious Trav'ller finds, ...		923	Riddle 7	79
CURL				
And, Curl must have a special Care		394	Grub-Street	11
Sell them to Curl for Fifty Pound, ...		395	Grub-Street	19
Now Curl his Shop from Rubbish drains;		560	Death of Swift	197
CURL'D				
Have it so formal, and so Curl'd, ...		780	Mullinix Tim	222
Which in the nicest Fashion curl'd, ...		903	Death Daphne	23
CURLL'S				
Turns Auth'ress, and is Curll's for Life. . . .		150	Corinna	28
In Curll's Collections, new and old, ...		729	Stella, Poems	50
CURMUDGEON				
Yet their Wine and their Victuals, those curmudgeon Lubbards		263	Apollo	11
CURR				
Whether Curr Plunket, or Whelp Skean, ...		298	Horrid Plot	20
Our Witness is a real Curr, ...		299	Horrid Plot	44
But, since it was a real Curr, ...		300	Horrid Plot	61
CURRANT				
He who so long was Currant 'twould be strange		235	Elegy on Demar	35
The Coyn's Currant and Mettal Pure.		372	Letter D. S-y	34
CURRENT				
Current like copper, and as often paid:		50	To Congreve	220
You hardly see the Current flow, ...		688	Cadenus Vaness	52
The Current of a Female Mind		688	Cadenus Vaness	57
Were down the sudden Current born;		811	Bro Protestant	4
CURRY				
'Tis true indeed, to curry Friends, ...		1003	Dan J's Reply	19
CURS				
By all the Dogs and Curs in Town;		207	Fable Bitches	2
Attended by a Brace of Curs, ...		760	Receipt Youth	43
Your barking Curs will seldom bite:		797	Traulus 1	46
CURS'D				
But I was fated to be curs'd.		595	Cassinus Peter	44
She curs'd the dark & winding Stairs		746	Stel Distress	33
CURSE				
To curse our greatest Enemy)		28	Ode to Temple	52
Phil cry'd, and John began to curse;		224	Prog of Love	80
And made him to Curse the poor innocent Bank. .		288	Bank Down	40
Some call him a Thorn, the Curse of a Nation, . .		334	Serious Poem	29
And, what is yet a greater curse, ...		435	Answer Paulus	89
To bless, as now you curse Mankind?		496	Panegyr Swift	95
And curse his wicked Burthen more		497	Panegyr Swift	140
For which you curse the careless Wench;		529	Lady's Dres Rm	108

	PAGE	TITLE	LINE
CURSE (CONTINUED)			
To curse the Dean, or bless the Drapier.	558	Death of Swift	168
Which drives you not to pray, but curse?	617	Scandal Poem 1	10
That drives you, not to pray, but curse?	624	Scandal Poem 2	10
And curse our modern Poetasters.	652	On Poetry	348
I curse her ev'ry hour sincerely;	679	From Catullus	7
And, what was yet a greater Curse,	741	Stel B-day 22	11
I'll Sputter, Swagger, Curse and Rail,	776	Mullinix Tim	85
And Dick curse all the Tories.	784	Mullinex Dick	16
Robin, to beggars, with a curse	878	Robbin & Harry	1
While others give me many a Curse,	918	Riddle 4	27
CURSED			
Where Whigs their cursed Trains had laid;	494	Panegyr Swift	42
The cursed Villain! now I see	783	Tim and Fables	29
CURSES			
I own, the curses of mankind	433	Answer Paulus	51
To pour down Curses on Mankind.	624	Scandal Poem 2	30
And, to compleat thy other curses,	676	Parson's Case	13
CURSING			
And cursing <Bob>, forget to bless <the> <King>.	533	To Mr. Gay	52
CURST			
Curst be the Wretch, nay doubly curst,	28	Ode to Temple	50
Curst be the Wretch, nay doubly curst,	28	Ode to Temple	50
What Land was ever half so curst?	392	Young's Satire	48
Absent from whom all Clymes are curst	420	Holyhead	25
Yet, though her spouse hath often curst her,	618	Scandal Poem 1	17
But, Woman is a curst inflamer;	618	Scandal Poem 1	35
But Woman is a curst Inflamer,	624	Scandal Poem 2	33
Thou'rt curst for Publishing, and he for not.	667	Epig Carthy 7 D	2
She curst the narrow winding Stairs:	751	Stel Wood-Park	52
Thou still with Tyrants in Succession curst,	793	St. Pat's Well	83
CURTAIN			
This dang'rous Priest is got behind the Curtain:	194	Author Himself	38
The Curtain falls, and we have done.	280	Journal	60
CURTAIN-LECTURE			
You need not fear a Curtain-Lecture.	362	Grace's Answer	38
CURTAINS			
Our curtains blue on either side;	621	Scandal Poem 1	134
Our Curtains blue, from Side to Side:	627	Scandal Poem 2	138
CUSHION-SIDE			
Stuck underneath his Cushion-side:	174	Horace 1, 7	100
CUSHOGUE			
And swears, Cushogue is to his Tast,	314	To Ford	89
CUSTARD			
Their Bellies are soft, and as white as a Custard.	953	Herrings	7
CUSTOM			
What hope of Custom in the Fair,	641	On Poetry	43
CUSTOMERS			
Weep all you Customers that use	101	Elegy Patrige	107
I can have Customers enough.	447	Modern Lady	85
CUSTOMS			
Of foreign Customs, Rites, and Laws;	697	Cadenus Vaness	353
CUT			
All of old Cut with a new Dye,	23	Ode Athenian	227
(In pieces cut, the Viper still did reunite)	30	Ode to Temple	132
Till on a Day cut out by Fate,	62	Discovery	5
And 'twice a Year he'll cut th' Aequator,	98	Elegy Patrige	17
Cut out large Slices to be fry'd:	112	Bauc & Phil 2	28
To mend his Barn, cut Baucis down;	117	Bauc & Phil 2	174
Our Merchant Ships may cut the Line,	168	Peace Dunkirk	21
To cut down fine Wood is a very bad Thing,	334	Serious Poem	13
Our Money to keep, let us Cut down One more.	334	Serious Poem	16
'Twas cut into Faggots, and put to the Flame,	334	Serious Poem	21
Some think him cut out from the Poisonous Yew,	334	Serious Poem	31
He is an old Stump cut out of a Crab,	335	Serious Poem	36
In Fillets roll'd, or cut in Pieces,	344	Prometheus	7
For, there my Grandsire cut his Weazon:	349	Upright Judge 1	2
He cut his Weazon at the Altar;	349	Upright Judge 1	3
In Church your Grandsire cut his Throat;	349	Upright Judge 2	1
To cut his Throat before he marry'd.	349	Upright Judge 2	4
In Christ-Church cut his Throat for Jealousy.	350	Upright Judge 3	6
'Tis true, say they, cut off the Head,	366	Answer Delaney	5
Your Rev'rence, but to cut one Leg off,	366	Answer Delaney	16
Cut off your Hand, and you may do	366	Answer Delaney	23
On all Occasions, cut and dry.	416	Woman's Mind	14
There's Mrs. Cut and she combine,	447	Modern Lady	76
The Deal, the Shuffle, and the Cut?	451	Modern Lady	223
Then him out a world of work,	466	Birthday Song	193
Sets of Phrases, cut and dry,	523	Betty Grizette	13
Descended, ready cut and dry:	591	Strephon Chloe	230
Doll never flies to cut her Lace,	725	To Stella	75
To cut it off these forty years.	760	Bec's B-Day	6
To bring in (I could Cut his Throat)	773	Mullinix Tim	14
Prefixt a Cut to ev'ry Tale.)	782	Tim and Fables	10
How to cut a Throat and smile:	800	Traulus 2	38
He had cut his own ears to be deaf to your nonsense.	818	Epigr Kite	10
On a Chimney cut his Name.	837	Legion Club	180
Cut down the Dock, 'twill sprout again: but O!	881	Pastoral Dial	15
To cut his hedges down for fire;	902	Dean's Reasons	106
Their Throats were cut, their Bellies ript,	923	Riddle 7	74
Cut from the Piece that made her Shift,	925	Riddle 8	42

CUT   (CONTINUED)   PAGE   TITLE   LINE
       Yet to cut the fatal thread . . . .   937 Riddle 24   D 45
       Who when I fought still cut me down, ...   1005 Sheridan's Sub   8
       And then to give me such a deadly Cut-- . . . . . .   1033 Ans to Crown   10
CUTLER
       From the Barber and the Cutler, ...   574 Helter Skelter   33
CUTLETS
       As Mutton Cutlets, Prime of Meat, ...   528 Lady's Dres Rm   99
CUTS
       What Stabs and what Cuts, ...   246 Irish-Feast   65
       You'd know him by Apollo's Cuts. . . . .   462 Birthday Song   64
       Cuts down with sacrilegious Hand. . . . .   849 Old Thorn   24
CUTT
       Cutt off large Slices to be fry'd; . . . .   91 Bauc & Phil 1   60
CUTTING
       Cutting Capers and Ramping, ...   245 Irish-Feast   38
       Then if cutting down Wood brings Money good Store, . .   334 Serious Poem   15
       By cutting of his Phrase, and trimming, ...   455 Dean Smedley   19
       Thus Lamb, renown'd for cutting Corns, ...   811 Bro Protestant   15
<CUTTS>
       Call my Lord <Cutts> a Salamander. . . . .   83 Salamander   22
CYBEL'S
       Tho' like the Cybel's Priest he comes, ...   340 Arch-Bish Dub   25
CYCLOPS'
       Emblem of the Cyclops' race; . . . .   936 Riddle 24   D 16
CYMBALS
       Ten Thousand Cymbals now begin . . . .   354 Simile Silver   9
       The Cymbals rattling Sounds dispell . . . .   354 Simile Silver   11
CYNTHIA   .
       And Silver Cynthia for a Crown; . . . .   255 Bubble   128
       While crooked Cynthia swearing says, ...   449 Modern Lady   160
       Poor Cynthia never shone so bright, ...   465 Birthday Song   175
       Cynthia, tune harmonious Numbers; . . . .   661 Love Song   13
CYPHERS
       And some, to be large cyphers in a state, ...   36 Ode Sancroft   59
CYPRESS
       His Lawrel now must only be a Cypress Wreath, . . .   9 Ode to King   105
       Mournful Cypress, verdant Willow, ...   661 Love Song   21
CYPRIAN
       They first invite the Cyprian Queen, ...   290 Prog Marriage   7
       The smiling Cyprian Goddess brings . . . .   585 Strephon Chloe   49
       Thus the Cyprian Goddess weeping, ...   660 Love Song   9
       Pleading before the Cyprian Queen. . . . .   686 Cadenus Vaness   2
CYPRUS
       Elect of Cyprus in commendam. . . . .   303 Storm   22
CZAR
       Now all his hopes are in the Czar, ...   282 Journal   105
D
       Grave D. of St <Patrick> how comes it to pass . . .   522 St. Cecilia's   1
D'ACQUIT
       To praise it, par maniere d'acquit; . . . .   379 Apology Lady C   120
D'ANVERS
       Leave to D'Anvers and his Mate, ...   635 Epistle Lady   173
       Come out with some lampoon on D'Anvers. . . . . .   658 On Poetry   D 186
D'ECLAT
       And of that dreadful coup d'eclat, ...   181 Horace 2, 1   23
<D'URFEY>
       And with Tom <D'urfey>, <Phillips>, <Dennis>, . . .   184 Horace 2, 1   115
D'YE
       Lord! Madam, says Mary, how d'ye do?. .. . . . .   70 Mrs Harris Pet   14
       If your Money be gone, as a Learned Divine says, d'ye
         see,   72 Mrs Harris Pet   56
       "D'ye hear the News---? the Dean is dead---! . . . .   547 Life of Swift   69
DABBLE
       Let them dabble in their Dung; . . . .   831 Legion Club   52
DABBLED
       Mean while the South rising with dabbled Wings, . . .   137 City Shower   13
DABLING
       And saw them dabling in their Clay, ...   86 Hist V's House   14
DAD
       They'll make you a Dad . . . .   953 Oysters   9
DAFFODIL
       The Crocus and the Daffodil, ...   894 Panegyr Dean   251
DAGGED
       To Shops in Crouds the dagged Females fly, ...   138 City Shower   33
DAGGER
       Is the poison and dagger you boast in your jaws, trow? .   979 Dean to Tho: S   5
DAGGER-CONTESTS
       In dagger-contests, and th' artillery of words, . . .   35 Ode Sancroft   13
DAGGERS
       Each line shall stab, shall blast, like daggers and like
         fire;   37 Ode Sancroft   91
DAGGL'D
       There live with daggl'd Mermaids pent, ...   689 Cadenus Vaness   89
DAGGLED
       'Till, daggled and tatter'd, ...   853 Lady's Lament   51
       Though daggled round, I scorn to fret: . . . . . .   890 Panegyr Dean   110
DAILY   SEE DAYLY
       'Tis but to say, that what we daily meet, ...   19 Ode Athenian   123
       Thou daily seest Him face to face, ...   34 Ode Sancroft   6
       Who daily vends seditious Trash: . . . .   515 Answer Fable   92

		PAGE	TITLE	LINE
DAILY	(CONTINUED)			
(When daily Howd'y's come of Course,		557	Death of Swift	123
Now Strephon daily entertains		590	Strephon Chloe	211
To us he made his daily Prayers,		626	Scandal Poem 2	79
From Slaves employ'd for daily Hire		726	To Stella	106
I'm daily stunn'd with such a Medley,		742	Stel B-day 22	43
For Virtue in her daily Race,		765	Stel B-day '26	73
Hence he draws his daily Food,		800	Traulus 2	41
Lash them daily, lash them duly,		835	Legion Club	156
To come hither daily,		857	Lady's Lament	206
The House Accounts are daily rising		860	Lady Acheson	29
That rais'd between the Stones their daily Shoots;		880	Pastoral Dial	4
Attend him daily as their Chief,		883	Rev Market-Hill	23
You merit new Employments daily:		891	Panegyr Dean	155
And here thy daily Vot'ries plac't		894	Panegyr Dean	239
DAINTILY				
On paper dribble daintily.		983	Sher, A Goose	8
DAINTY				
For Clem gets all the dainty bits.		283	Journal	126
Gotten from their dainty Doxies,		573	Helter Skelter	26
DAINTYES				
Ye Daintyes, I know nothing of ye,		733	Verses Vanessa	28
DAIRY				
To rule the Dairy next to Kit.		888	Panegyr Dean	42
Now, enter as the Dairy Hand-maid:		892	Panegyr Dean	167
DALACOURT				
From sloven Bernard to beau Dalacourt.		672	Epig Carthy 24	D 8
DAM				
By the Dam from Lordlings sprung,		799	Traulus 2	3
DAMASKS				
Brocado's, and Damasks, and Tabbies, and Gawses,		236	Excellent Song	1
DAME SEE GRAND-DAME				
Whom each one thought the happy Dame:		67	Problem	52
Then my Dame Wadgar came,		70	Mrs Harris Pet	25
Dame, said I, as loud as I could bawl,		70	Mrs Harris Pet	26
Dame Floyd looks out in grave Suspence		75	Game Traffick	13
Dame Baucis next, they play'd their Farce on:		115	Bauc & Phil 2	138
Attending on a Royal Dame.		119	Apollo Outwit	4
The Dame full wisely did Decree,		153	Widow and Cat	D 16
And found Admittance from the Dame.		222	Prog of Love	20
Soon make my Dame grow lank and spare:		230	Prog of Poetry	12
Then wou'd you paint a matchless Dame,		272	Apollo's Edict	D 70
"I'll warrant she's some flaunting Dame,		321	First of April	25
The gracious Dame, tho' well she knew		379	Apology Lady C	117
The bashful Dame, and loose'd her Tongue;		386	Manly Virtue	86
My Dame is hardly worth a Groat.		409	Dial Rich Marb	30
The Journal of a Modern Dame,		445	Modern Lady	24
The modern Dame is wak'd by Noon,		446	Modern Lady	38
When, to give ev'ry Dame her due,		449	Modern Lady	138
Dame Nature as the Learned show,		504	Doctor Delaney	127
But the Company stood in Defence of the Dame,		517	Dean Hang Rape	15
Each Dame he sees with all her Stinks:		529	Lady's Dres Rm	122
But princely Douglas, and his glorious Dame,		531	To Mr. Gay	13
Dame Juno brought a Priest demure.		586	Strephon Chloe	64
To kindle strife Dame Nature taught her,		618	Scandal Poem 1	37
She doubted not but such a Dame		693	Cadenus Vaness	230
The Triumphs of that stubborn Dame,		702	Cadenus Vaness	495
A Scholar to a Courtly Dame,		705	Cadenus Vaness	589
In half a week the Dame grew nice,		745	Stel Distress	9
In half a Week the Dame grew nice,		749	Stel Wood-Park	7
Dame Nature, when she saw the Blow,		849	Old Thorn	25
"And thy confed'rate Dame, who brags		850	Old Thorn	61
Bring our Dame a New-Year's Gift!		862	To Janus	4
And with his Dame the ocean crosst,		878	Robbin & Harry	19
Affected by each vulgar Dame:		887	Panegyr Dean	18
Than what befits a rural Dame.		897	Panegyr Dean	342
The courtly Dame, unmov'd by Fear,		922	Riddle 7	37
A comely Dame once clad in white,		923	Riddle 7	63
Emblem of the bashful dame,		936	Riddle 24	D 23
Is grown a Sad Dame,		1014	Swift to Sheri	34
DAME-NATURE				
To kindle Strife, Dame-Nature taught her:		624	Scandal Poem 2	35
<DAMER>				
The Ghost of old <Damer>, who left not his Betters,		288	Bank Down	41
DAMES				
My Lord, on Fire amidst the Dames,		66	Problem	39
Of Guardian Eunuchs to the Sultan Dames,		532	To Mr. Gay	20
Which, of all our modern Dames		631	Epistle Lady	67
A Party next of glitt'ring Dames,		698	Cadenus Vaness	364
What Lords and Dames of high Degree,		919	Riddle 5	15
DAMMEE				
Dammee, I say, they ought to starve.		783	Tim and Fables	34
<DAMMEE'S>				
Must all my <Dammee's>, <Bloods> and <Wounds>		779	Mullinix Tim	187
DAMN				
Damn her, why don't you Slit her Tongue?		220	A Quiet Life	12
"You'll find him swear, blaspheme, and damn,		305	Storm	57
Pish at his Cook'ry, damn his Wine;		495	Panegyr Swift	69
I damn such Fools!--Go, go, you're bit."		579	Day Judgement	22
'Twixt you and me <God> Damn the Lyers.		773	Mullinix Tim	8
And then-- <God> Damn the Lyars again.		773	Mullinix Tim	12

DAMN	(CONTINUED)	PAGE	TITLE	LINE
And when I damn my Soul to plague 'em,	. . . . . .	778	Mullinix Tim	173
It shou'd be yours. But <Damn> my Blood	. . . .	775	Mullinix Tim	73
Got? <Damn> my Blood I frank my Letters,	. . . .	778	Mullinix Tim	155
Got? <Damn> me, why I got my will!	. . . . . .	778	Mullinix Tim	159
<God> <damn> me Jack, she's wondrous fair.	. . . .	228	Prog of Beauty	76
<God> <damn> the Whigs and Tories too.	. . . . .	782	Mullinix Tim	284
Begs leave to rail, but <damn> his Blood,	. . . .	797	Traulus 1	55
"<God> <damn> me, they bid us reform and repent,	. .	872	Grand Question	145
"<God> <damn> me, he hobbles as bad as my Groom;	. .	872	Grand Question	156
<God> <damn> his Blood, and <Blood> and <Wounds>.	. .	904	Death Daphne	44
DAMN'D				
He swore from his Cart, it was all a damn'd Lye.	. .	399	Tom Clinch	12
But I'll see you all damn'd before I will whittle.	. .	399	Tom Clinch	16
The Contributions of the damn'd;	. . . .	486	Libel on D- D-	188
And damn'd the Mob, whom now he leads.	. . . . .	498	Panegyr Swift	162
The Place of the Damn'd,--I'll tell you my Mind.	. .	575	Place Damn'd	4
Wherever the Damn'd do Chiefly abound,	. . . . . .	575	Place Damn'd	5
Damn'd Poets, Damn'd Criticks,	. . . .	576	Place Damn'd	7
Damn'd Poets, Damn'd Criticks,	. . . .	576	Place Damn'd	7
. . . Damn'd Block-Heads, Damn'd Knaves,	. . . .	576	Place Damn'd	7
. . . Damn'd Block-Heads, Damn'd Knaves,	. . . .	576	Place Damn'd	7
Damn'd Senators brib'd, Damn'd prostitute Slaves;	. .	576	Place Damn'd	8
Damn'd Senators brib'd, Damn'd prostitute Slaves;	. .	576	Place Damn'd	8
Damn'd Lawyers and Judges, Damn'd Lords and Damn'd Squires,		576	Place Damn'd	9
Damn'd Lawyers and Judges, Damn'd Lords and Damn'd Squires,		576	Place Damn'd	9
Damn'd Lawyers and Judges, Damn'd Lords and Damn'd Squires,		576	Place Damn'd	9
Damn'd Spies and Informers, Damn'd Friends and Damn'd Lyars;		576	Place Damn'd	10
Damn'd Spies and Informers, Damn'd Friends and Damn'd Lyars;		576	Place Damn'd	10
Damn'd Spies and Informers, Damn'd Friends and Damn'd Lyars;		576	Place Damn'd	10
Damn'd Villians, Corrupted in every Station,	. . .	576	Place Damn'd	11
Damn'd Time-Serving Priests all over the Nation;	. . .	576	Place Damn'd	12
Damn'd Ignorant Prelates, and Councellors Privy.	. .	576	Place Damn'd	14
For We know by these Marks, the place of the Damn'd;	.	576	Place Damn'd	16
And come to see each other damn'd:	. . . .	579	Day Judgement	16
To find this Damn'd Pretender out,	. . . . .	774	Mullinix Tim	26
To thy own Side so Damn'd a Nuisance,	. . . . .	775	Mullinix Tim	73
Chairman to yon damn'd Committee!	. . . .	838	Legion Club	191
A damn'd Cromwellian, knock'd me down.	. . . . .	926	Riddle 9	20
'Twas the damn'd 'Squire with the hard Name,	. . .	1005	Sheridan's Sub	20
But we took our dividers, and found your <damn'd> metre,		1026	Sheri Circles	11
DAMNABLE				
And, the Devil's a damnable Poet.	. . . .	401	Window Inns 3	4
The damnable the dear Conceit.	. . . .	497	Panegyr Swift	127
His <Deanship> was now in a damnable Scrape,	. . . .	517	Dean Hang Rape	17
To this damnable Speaker had long ow'd a shame;	. . .	816	Yahoo's	37
Is a damnable Smell both Morning and Night.	. . . .	942	Probatur Alit	30
Your damnable Riddle, my poor Brains did rack nigh.	.	972	S-'s Ans Sh-d	2
DAMNABLY				
But swears how damnably the Men lie,	. . . . . .	526	Lady's Dres Rm	17
But think how damnably you err	. . . .	622	Scandal Poem 1	159
DAMNATION				
What Name for a Maid, was the first Man's Damnation?		973	S-'s Ans Sh-d	12
<DAMND>				
And sooner than Vote for a Peace I'll be <damnd>.	. .	143	New Song	20
DAMNING				
Damning to Hell the Jacobits?	. . . .	773	Mullinix Tim	4
Than saving your Souls, by damning our own?	. . . .	805	Irish Bishops	56
DAMNS				
He damns the Climate, and complains of Spleen.	. . .	137	City Shower	12
Damns all your Thoughts as low and little,	. . . .	644	On Poetry	121
And damns his Blood that in the Rear	. . . . . .	789	Dick's Variety	35
DAMON'S				
When Damon's Soul shall take its Flight,	. . . . .	270	Apollo's Edict	D 33
DAMP				
Will damp all Passion Sympathetick;	. . . . . .	588	Strephon Chloe	134
He felt about his Heart a Damp,	. . . .	905	Death Daphne	97
DAMPS				
Unwholsome Damps, offensive Dews:	. . . . . .	923	Riddle 7	56
DAMS				
The Dams and the Weirs must all be your own,	. . . .	287	Bank Down	6
DAMSEL				
And with the youthful Damsel sported.	. . . . . .	372	Letter D. S-y	46
DAMSELS SEE CHAMBER-DAMSELS				
DAN				
All Subjects like Dan Jackson's Nose.	. . . . . .	218	To Mr. Delany	102
How George, Nim, Dan, Dean pass their Days;	. . . .	278	Journal	2
All, Heteroclit Dan except,	. . . .	279	Journal	19
Dan leaves the Earthly Spade and Rake,	. . . . .	279	Journal	32
Dan growing drowsy like a Thief,	. . . .	279	Journal	39
And Nim and Dan to Garret clamber;	. . . . .	280	Journal	58
How Dan caught nothing in his Net,	. . . . .	280	Journal	65
How skilfully Dan mends his Nets,	. . . . .	281	Journal	75
Nim lost his Wig-block, Dan his Jordan,	. . . . .	283	Journal	123
Robin, and Jack, and Jack, and Dan?	. . . . . .	314	To Ford	80

		PAGE	TITLE	LINE
DAN	(CONTINUED)			
Now tell me, friend Thomas, Ford, Grattan, and merry Dan,		955	Portrait Life	9
I despise any poet that truckled to Dan.		976	Dean to Sherid	34
Let's quarrel no longer, since Dan and George Rochfort		979	Dean to Tho: S	35
Then George will rejoice, and Dan will sing high-day:		980	Dean to Tho: S	37
Take Courage, Dan, this plainly shows		993	On Picture	19
So far, dear Dan, that ev'ry Friend		993	On Picture	29
But ev'ry one that knows Dan, knows thy Master.		1002	Reply by Dean	6
'Cause I call Dan my better half,		1004	Dan J's Reply	26
To Dan the victorious,		1004	Sheridan's Sub	2
With Delany or Dan I would scorn to combine		1017	Swift Ans Sher	8
And give Satan his due Dan begins to refine		1017	Swift Ans Sher	10
And Dan shall be with us with Nose aquiline		1018	Swift Ans Sher	27
George, Dan, Dean, and Nim to place in the center?		1027	Sheri Circles	14
DAN'S				
Of Dan's large Nose, in modern Saphick,		993	On Picture	3
Dan's noble Mettle, Sherry base;		1004	Dan J's Reply	31
So Dan's the better, tho' the less,		1004	Dan J's Reply	32
Long, Long, Long, Long, like Dan's Long Nose.		1022	Nim-Dan-Dean 1	D 54
DANCE				
Two foolish guides in ev'ry sublunary dance:		34	Ode Sancroft	9
Lead them a Dance of many a Mile,		79	Vanbrug House	5
Lead 'em a Dance of many a Mile,		106	V's House	5
They dance in a Round,		245	Irish-Feast	37
By my Hand, you dance rarely,		246	Irish-Feast	47
And dance Attendance on the Great,		492	Panegyr Swift	2
And can no longer dance in Rhyme.		756	Stel B-day '24	4
A Pair to make a Country Dance,		756	Stel B-day '24	8
Dick could neatly dance a Jig,		784	Mullinex Dick	13
But Dick can <fart>, and dance and frisk,		788	Dick's Variety	25
They cannot pass before they dance;		928	Riddle 12	D 18
DANCES				
At Country Dances, not a Nose		584	Strephon Chloe	23
DANCING				
Here a Dog dancing on his Hamms		123	Empty'ng Town	13
We say, she's past her Dancing Days;		756	Stel B-day '24	2
Ever dancing round a Pole.		927	Riddle 10	D 6
Come dancing to me o'er the Plains.		934	Riddle 21	D 10
I wish he were in it a dancing a Jig.		942	Probatur Alit	28
DANCING-MASTER'S				
And oft' the Dancing-Master's Art		710	Cadenus Vaness	740
DANDRIFF				
Sweat, Dandriff, Powder, Lead and Hair;		526	Lady's Dres Rm	24
DANG'ROUS				
He turns to Politicks his dang'rous Wit,		194	Author Himself	26
This dang'rous Priest is got behind the Curtain:		194	Author Himself	38
A dang'rous Treatise writ against the Spleen;		195	Author Himself	48
Why in yon dang'rous Gulph profound		252	Bubble	50
I own it was a dang'rous Project;		300	Horrid Plot	71
How dang'rous Things were Men of Wit,		706	Cadenus Vaness	619
This dang'rous horrid motion Dish up?		774	Mullinix Tim	18
Some teach us in these dang'rous Days,		780	Mullinix Tim	251
A Patriot is a dang'rous Post		798	Traulus 1	89
DANGER				
And timely on the coming Danger thought,		12	Ode to William	D 19
I came in without Danger; and was I to blame?		144	New Song	33
The Toil, the Danger of the Seas;		199	Horace 2, 6	17
To keep out of Danger, a Doublet of Stone.		351	Wood Insect	10
The Omen is broke, the Danger is over;		351	Wood Insect	27
But now, the danger of a friend		420	Holyhead	23
No danger dreads upon the road;		435	Answer Paulus	96
The Danger past, takes Heart of Grace,		500	Doctor Delaney	25
But, now, your Danger to prevent,		742	Stel B-day 22	49
True, Lady Anne no Danger fears,		885	Rev Market-Hill	57
DANGEROUS				
His dangerous Excess of Heat,		387	Manly Virtue	108
"When up a dangerous Faction starts,		568	Death of Swift	379
What dangerous Paths young Virgins tread;		696	Cadenus Vaness	311
"That sinking the coin is a dangerous joke.		843	Ay and No	14
DANGERS				
Dangers with Prudence to discern;		325	Pethox	60
DANGLE				
And here no more will dangle Pope.		409	Dial Rich Marb	50
DANGLES				
Lord! said I, who's that parson? how awkwardly dangles he		978	Dean to Tho: S	2
DANIEL				
For Daniel was got from the Den of the Lions:		144	New Song	32
<Dean> <White>, <Dean> <Daniel>, and <Dean> <Smedley>		742	Stel B-day 22	44
Except to give <Dean> <Daniel> place.		888	Panegyr Dean	48
DANIEL'S				
Dull Daniel's whey-face;		858	Lady's Lament	224
DAPHNE				
Had Bacchus after Daphne reel'd,		177	To Lord Harley	13
Mark out the way where Daphne flew.		177	To Lord Harley	18
Yet Daphne never slack'd her pace,		177	To Lord Harley	27
Daphne knows, with equal ease,		906	Daphne	1
Daphne, 'twixt the Dean and you,		907	Daphne	50
Like Daphne sometimes in a Tree,		927	Riddle 10	D 17
DAPHNE'S				
And, hearing much of Daphne's Fame,		904	Death Daphne	53

DAPPER
　　Why, how now dapper black . . . . 428 Beau's Reply 1
　　First to a dapper Clerk she beckon'd, ... 690 Cadenus Vaness 108
DAR'D
　　Dar'd to suspend her unregarded aid; . . . . . . 43 To Congreve 4
　　Not dar'd to injure with our lowly song; . . . . 52 Temple Ill 44
　　Since Delany has dar'd, like Prometheus his Sire, . . 266 Apollo 95
　　Good Lord! I wondred how I dar'd to look him in the 342 Upon His Grace 28
　　　　Face.
DAR'ST
　　Thou dar'st the greatest Prince attack, ... 325 Pethox 53
DARBY
　　When I saw him so often with Darby and Wood. . . . 868 Grand Question 48
DARBY'S
　　Robert and Darby's Coadjutor: . . . . 888 Panegyr Dean 40
DARE
　　With what unhappy Men shall dare, ... 25 Ode Athenian 293
　　Who dare revile the integrity of verse: . . . . 53 Temple Ill 70
　　Henceforward let no Statesman dare, ... 96 On the Union 13
　　Yet hardly dare one Line Rehearse. . . . . . . 121 Apollo Outwit 60
　　This Day, (the Year I dare not tell,) . . . . . 149 Corinna 1
　　I dare believe that Four in Five . . . . 235 Elegy on Demar 51
　　And let them be seen by the World if he dare, . . 265 Apollo 63
　　No Son of mine shall dare to say, ... 270 Apollo's Edict D 20
　　Yet, this I dare foretel you from it, ... 299 Horrid Plot 35
　　Twelvepence a Corner, if you dare. . . . . . . 315 To Ford 114
　　Why Sirrah said the Noble 'Squire, how dare you see my 343 Upon His Grace 43
　　　　Face,
　　Dare you dispute, ... 440 Ballyspellin 1
　　Say what you dare, ... 441 Ballyspellin 32
　　Then, shou'd you dare to ask a Place, ... 480 Libel on D- D- 29
　　Nor Pope wou'd dare deny him Wit, ... 484 Libel on D- D- 143
　　Nor dare to use the gifts by heav'n bestow'd; . . 506 To a Friend 10
　　And yet, I dare confide in you; . . . . 597 Cassinus Peter 115
　　Presumptuous Poet, could you dare . . . . 617 Scandal Poem 1 1
　　Presumptuous Bard! How cou'd you dare . . . . . 623 Scandal Poem 2 1
　　Dare you, vile Murderer of Flaccus, ... 671 Epig Carthy 22 D 1
　　Knows nothing which it dare not own; . . . . . . 706 Cadenus Vaness 609
　　Nor dare distort my Face for shame. . . . . . . 727 To Stella 116
　　Dare you let these Reproaches stand, ... 732 Stella, Poems 139
　　Of Poets dare assume my Place; . . . . 739 Stel B-day '21 14
　　Though Dick, I dare presume to say, ... 788 Dick's Variety 17
　　Let the Boys pelt him if they dare; . . . . . . 788 Dick's Variety 20
　　Thy martial Sons, whom now they dare despise, . . 790 St. Pat's Well 13
　　Dare any of the mitred Host, ... 820 Dr. Rundle 5
　　He dare not venture to approach; . . . . 824 Printer Newgat 12
　　How dare you treat your Betters thus? . . . . . 884 Rev Market-Hill 41
　　Let others match it if they dare. . . . . 887 Panegyr Dean 22
　　They dare not charge me to my Face: . . . . . . 918 Riddle 4 30
　　The Roses of your Cheeks, I dare . . . . 932 Riddle 19 D 9
　　You'll dare not to question my minor or major. . . 976 Dean to Sherid 24
　　The rest of your compliment I dare not tell her, . 979 Dean to Tho: S 25
　　Tho' I dare you to more than quadruple Alliance? . 1019 To Sheridan 2
　　Nor will they dare to break the Joints, ... 1021 Nim-Dan-Dean 1 D 39
DARES
　　And every foolish Flye that dares to aim . . . . 9 Ode to King 115
　　Nor dares one Jacobite or Tory . . . . 183 Horace 2, 1 84
　　Who dares affirm this is no pious age, ... 274 Epilogue 1
　　She dares not say her Life's her own. . . . . . 328 Epigram 3 4
　　If Virtue dares not venture down, ... 392 Young's Satire 37
　　Who dares revile the Nation's Wisdom, ... 515 Answer Fable 93
　　That no Physician dares prescribe by Stealth: . . 533 To Mr. Gay 78
　　Nor, dares an abler Workman undertake . . . . . 535 To Mr. Gay 133
　　Who dares to Irony pretend; . . . . 555 Death of Swift 56
　　She dares not say the Poet lyes. . . . . 730 Stella, Poems 82
　　He dares defy both sense and wit. . . . . 876 To Dean Swift 16
　　What dares he not? He can, we know it, ... 876 To Dean Swift 17
　　Nor dares he, though he were a Duke, ... 888 Panegyr Dean 59
DARING
　　And what if daring Strephon dies . . . . 587 Strephon Chloe 109
DARK
　　He spake, and a dark Cloud flung o're his light, . 8 Ode to King 58
　　How shall we find Thee then in dark disputes? . . 34 Ode Sancroft 10
　　By dark reverted rays from its reflection made; . 35 Ode Sancroft 22
　　Foll'wing Opinion, dark, and blind, ... 36 Ode Sancroft 56
　　Thro' the dark mass, the dawn of so much sense, . 37 Ode Sancroft 88
　　Creep in the Dark from Leathern Cell, ... 99 Elegy Patrige 54
　　And Climb the dark Stairs to your friends who have none: 185 Scriblerus 1 4
　　Of all the fine Things he keeps in the Dark, . . 265 Apollo 61
　　That old rotten Wood will Shine in the Dark. . . 334 Serious Poem 8
　　Through slipp'ry By-roads dark and deep, ... 412 Desire Possess 19
　　A Child may know it in the Dark: . . . . 453 Modern Lady 267
　　They now can venture in the dark. . . . . 468 Birthday Song 270
　　To poison'd Arrows from the Dark, ... 500 Doctor Delaney 28
　　She curs'd the dark & winding Stairs . . . . . 746 Stel Distress 33
　　Sent from the Dark infernal Region . . . . . . 798 Traulus 1 77
　　But heavy, and dark, when you squeeze me together. . 928 Riddle 13 D 4
　　Sits, and takes them in the Dark. . . . . 931 Riddle 18 D 8
　　For a Riddle is dark, but a Woman is light. . . 972 S-'s Ans Sh-d 8
DARK'NED
　　At Midnight, through the dark'ned Air; . . . . . 354 Simile Silver 4

DARKEN
      This ball of wax your ears will darken, ...   753 Gift for Bec   21
DARKENS
      It darkens Reason's light.   . . . .   402 Window Inns 6   D   4
DARKEST
      He hides within his darkest Cell.   . . . .   240 Run Bankers   44
DARLING
      First of God's darling attributes, ...   34 Ode Sancroft   5
      Confessing Albion once her darling seat;   . . . .   49 To Congreve   194
      Where her own Temple was her darling theme;   . . .   51 Temple Ill   14
      And as he saw his darling Money fail, ...   235 Elegy on Demar   33
      Distill'd from Tripsy's darling Whelp;   . . . . .   526 Lady's Dres Rm   32
      Mourn'd Adonis, darling Youth;   . . . .   660 Love Song   10
      As if I were a darling Child.   . . . .   891 Panegyr Dean   152
DARMSTEDT
      Hesse Darmstedt makes too rough a sound, ...   467 Birthday Song   215
DARN
      The t' other he sat down to darn   . . . .   594 Cassinus Peter   13
DARNS
      Or darns his hose, or mends his Breeches, ...   878 Robbin & Harry   27
DART
      A sign God's dart is shot, and wrath o'erblown;   . . .   52 Temple Ill   28
      The Point of Sagittarius Dart, ...   100 Elegy Patrige   81
      Cast in his Dart which made three Moydores Light.   . .   234 Elegy on Demar   32
      Not for his skill to shoot the dart;   . . . . . .   432 Answer Paulus   18
      Conceive the most invenom'd Dart, ...   595 Cassinus Peter   59
      Or blunts the Point of ev'ry Dart;   . . . .   687 Cadenus Vaness   8
      Thro' ev'ry Breast wou'd dart a Flame;   . . . . .   693 Cadenus Vaness   231
      A Dart of such prodigious Length, ...   703 Cadenus Vaness   517
      And strongly shoot a radiant Dart, ...   764 Stel B-day '26   33
      Florinda, dart their Heav'nly Beams, ...   932 Riddle 19   D   2
DARTED
      She darted many a private Glance, ...   905 Death Daphne   67
DARTS
      The poys'nous Darts has made him reel, ...   10 Ode to King   143
      Darts weeping beams across heaven's wat'ry face;   . . .   52 Temple Ill   26
      Which darts on poets eyes a trembling light;   . . .   54 Temple Ill   98
      Nor shall his Darts at random fly   . . . .   272 Apollo's Edict   D 58
      And darts her Beams or'e both our Isles, ...   466 Birthday Song   181
      What powder'd Wigs! What Flames and Darts!   . . . .   585 Strephon Chloe   35
      The Darts were in the Cover fix'd, ...   701 Cadenus Vaness   481
      Cupid, tho' all his Darts were lost, ...   702 Cadenus Vaness   492
      Without one Word of Cupid's Darts, ...   728 Stella, Poems   11
DASHES
      Set off with num'rous Breaks--and Dashes--   . . . .   643 On Poetry   94
DASTARD
      Just Heaven! to see the Dunghill dastard Brood   . . .   826 Noisy Tom   17
DATE
      Boldly we hence the brave Commencement Date   . . . .   13 Ode to William   D 45
      In vain expects a longer Date   . . . .   229 Prog of Beauty   107
      "His Principles, of antient date, ...   549 Life of Swift   146
      And till they drove me out of Date, ...   555 Death of Swift   61
      His Kind of Wit is out of Date.   . . . .   562 Death of Swift   252
      Have put the Dean's Politicks quite out of Date;   . . .   716 Answer Rebus   24
      By Chronicle of antient Date, ...   848 Old Thorn   2
      When his Merit's out of Date, ...   933 Riddle 20   D 28
      Soon or late, my date is done, ...   937 Riddle 24   D 43
DATED
      His Correspondence plainly dated, ...   300 Horrid Plot   51
      Your Letter you'd dated, ...   1014 Swift to Sheri   14
DAUB
      For, as the rabble daub, and rifle   . . . .   436 Answer Paulus   135
DAUB'D
      On Paper daub'd so foul, ...   425 Five Ladies   14
DAUBS
      Her Ointments, Daubs, and Paints and Creams, ...   530 Lady's Dres Rm   138
DAUGHTER
      And was--His most obedient Daughter.   . . . . . .   224 Prog of Love   72
      Soft'ning with Songs to Son or Daughter, ...   321 First of April   31
      Just three; and every Grace a Daughter.   . . . . .   465 Birthday Song   166
      The Mother the Daughter, the Daughter the Mother.   .   929 Riddle 13   D 10
      The Mother the Daughter, the Daughter the Mother.   .   929 Riddle 13   D 10
DAUGHTERS
      When Daughters run away with Fellows)   . . . . .   223 Prog of Love   48
      We'll buy English Silks for our Wives and our
          Daughters,   237 Excellent Song   REF
      Then we'll buy English Silks for our Wives and our   237 Excellent Song   REF
          Daughters,
      . . .and their Daughters, ...   237 Excellent Song   REF
      Then we'll buy English Silks for our Wives and our   238 Excellent Song   REF
          Daughters,
      While Mothers, Daughters, Aunts, ...   426 Five Ladies   30
      Forbid your Daughters guzzling Beer;   . . . . . .   587 Strephon Chloe   116
      Offending Daughters oft wou'd hear   . . . . . .   694 Cadenus Vaness   240
DAUNCE
      Reaums shall daunce honde in honde, ...   103 Merlin   15
DAVENTRY
      Then shall the tall black Daventry Bird   . . . .   147 Windsor Proph   7
DAVID'S
      "He follow'd David's Lesson just, ...   566 Death of Swift   341

```
DAW                                                  PAGE    TITLE         LINE
     The Daw a Thief, the Ape a Drole,     . . . . . . .  512 Answer Fable      7
DAWB
     Less should I dawb it o're with transitory Praise,  . .   21 Ode Athenian    169
     That you're a Dawb, whilst I but paint,   . . . . .    1003 Dan J's Reply    11
DAWB'D
     I'm all over dawb'd when I sit by the Dean.   . . . .   868 Grand Question   30
     See, now comes the Captain all dawb'd with gold Lace:  .  870 Grand Question   93
DAWBERS
     As fine as Dawbers Hands can make it    . . . . . .   734 Stel B-day '20   11
DAWBS
     Rub off the Dawbs of white and Red;     . . . . . .   582 Young Nymph      34
DAWN   SEE MORNING-DAWN
     Thro' the dark mass, the dawn of so much sense,   . . .   37 Ode Sancroft    88
     Till the blest sun to give kind dawn of grace   . . . .   52 Temple Ill      25
     Ere Mornings dawn stole out to spy    . . . . . .     63 Discovery       35
DAWNS
     If hope e'er dawns the smallest of its rays.   . . . .   54 Temple Ill     112
DAWS
     As Pies and Daws are often stil'd     . . . . . . .    82 Salamander       3
DAWSON
     I mean your Butler, Dawson, Car,      . . . . . . .   217 To Mr. Delany    59
     And, Dawson street will serve as well   . . . . . .   313 To Ford         61
DAY   SEE CORONATION-DAY,TO-DAY,WEDDING-DAY,LACK-A-DAY,BIRTH-DAY,A-DAY,PLAY-DAY,HIGH-DAY
          LADY-DAY,NOON-DAY,LEVEE-DAY,YEARS-DAY
     Which guard the throne by night, and are its light by day:   34 Ode Sancroft      4
     Believe it firm, because perhaps the day is mild and still   37 Ode Sancroft     75
     Sit clad in lawn of purer woven day,  . . . . . . .    41 Ode Sancroft    235
     Crusts o'er the day, shadowing its parent beam   . . .    45 To Congreve     71
     Which gave them birth, can rob the world of day.   . . .   46 To Congreve     82
     Shall on a day make sin and folly bleed;   . . . . .    47 To Congreve    134
     Here, on a better day, some druid dwelt.   . . . . .    49 To Congreve    191
     Gives glad farewell to a tempestuous day;   . . . . .    51 Temple Ill      18
     Should heaven suspend to act but for a day;   . . . .    53 Temple Ill      64
     Till on a Day cut out by Fate,        . . . . . . .    62 Discovery        5
     And then your poor Petitioner, both Night and Day,   .    73 Mrs Harris Pet  74
     As Herald, he can in a Day            . . . . . . .    80 Vanbrug House    63
     After hard Throws of many a Day       . . . . . . .    81 Vanbrug House    73
     We can't be quiet Night nor day;      . . . . . . .    90 Bauc & Phil 1    30
     As Herald, he can in a Day            . . . . . . .   107 V's House        37
     When on a Day, which prov'd their last,   . . . . .   116 Bauc & Phil 2   151
     Which, from the fatal Day when first   . . . . . . .   134 Magician's Rod   67
     But repeats the same Note a whole Day, like a Finch.  .  143 New Song         8
     But England must cry alack and well a day,   . . . .   147 Windsor Proph    13
     This Day, (the Year I dare not tell,)   . . . . . .   149 Corinna          1
     Returning home one Day from Court.    . . . . . . .   170 Horace 1, 7      2
     I'd have him Dine with me to Day.     . . . . . . .   172 Horace 1, 7     50
     Next Day invited, comes agen;         . . . . . . .   173 Horace 1, 7     76
     Rides Day and Night at such a Rate,   . . . . . . .   174 Horace 1, 7    117
     Must one Day come in competition,     . . . . . . .   182 Horace 2, 1     67
     One day it will be no disgrace,       . . . . . . .   186 Scriblerus 3     5
     Or, "Have you nothing new to day      . . . . . . .   201 Horace 2, 6     73
     To Rime all day without Offence;      . . . . . . .   219 To Mr. Delany   108
     Like Peers, have Levees ev'ry Day     . . . ' . . .   239 Run Bankers     15
     The Day of Judgment will be soon,     . . . . . . .   253 Bubble          77
     Nine times a day it ebbs and flows,   . . . . . . .   256 Bubble         141
     Aurora usher'd in the Day,            . . . . . . .   270 Apollo's Edict  D 21
     Item the Actors, freely gave a Day,   . . . . . . .   274 Epilogue         9
     Now stinted in the short'ning Day,    . . . . . . .   280 Journal         51
     Is fifty, if he be a Day;             . . . . . . .   291 Prog Marriage   48
     He had those honours in his day.      . . . . . . .   296 Satiric Elegy   22
     That, every Dog must have his Day.    . . . . . . .   299 Horrid Plot     30
     That Mr. Ford was born to day:        . . . . . . .   311 To Ford          4
     And scarce a Day, can spare a Minute  . . . . . . .   322 First of April  41
     "Ye have forgot this Month and Day.--  . . . . . . .   322 First of April  56
     As Thomas was cudgelld one day by his Wife,   . . . .   327 Epigram 1        1
     And ev'ry day she combs his Head.     . . . . . . .   328 Epigram 3        6
     As White as Snow, as bright as Day;   . . . . . . .   362 Grace's Answer  32
     The Scenes and Actions of the Day before.   . . . . .   363 On Dreams       10
     For, ev'ry Day you shall be gaining   . . . . . . .   366 Answer Delaney  19
     Next Day another Message brought;     . . . . . . .   377 Apology Lady C  75
     Their Glory from the God of Day,      . . . . . . .   387 Manly Virtue   106
     Whose anxious Natives, night and Day,   . . . . . .   388 Manly Virtue   137
     But my Master each Day gives me Bread;   . . . . . .   395 Dog and Thief    6
     This Day arriv'd without his Train,   . . . . . . .   398 Earl of P-b-w   11
     Next Day the Post-boy winds his Horn,   . . . . . .   398 Earl of P-b-w   16
     The Scandal of the Day before.        . . . . . . .   416 Woman's Mind    24
     Here quiet they Lie, in hopes to rise one Day,   . . .   431 Dicky Dolly     22
     The Annals of a Female Day.           . . . . . . .   445 Modern Lady     35
     "Don't I look frightfully to Day?     . . . . . . .   446 Modern Lady     49
     'This Company would come to Day--     . . . . . . .   448 Modern Lady    104
     Talks half a Day in Praise of Silence;   . . . . . .   450 Modern Lady    171
     For yours can shine both day and night,   . . . . .   462 Birthday Song   66
     Your Phoebus royal, every day         . . . . . . .   462 Birthday Song   69
     Or Cellar, where they starve to Day.   . . . . . . .   505 Doctor Delaney 150
     Who spends his Day and Night in gall.   . . . . . .   515 Answer Fable   104
     Of drinking all Day, and whoring all Night.   . . . .   517 Dean Hang Rape  28
     Will send their Howd'ye's ev'ry day;   . . . . . . .   546 Life of Swift   59
     The Day will come, when't shall be said,   . . . . .   547 Life of Swift   68
     "Behold the fatal Day arrive!         . . . . . . .   558 Death of Swift 147
     A Week; and Arbuthnott a Day.         . . . . . . .   561 Death of Swift 208
```

DAY   (CONTINUED)   PAGE   TITLE   LINE

"Was chearful to his dying Day,   572 Death of Swift   477
Bridles borrow'd for a Day,   573 Helter Skelter   14
O Strephon, e'er that fatal Day   591 Strephon Chloe   235
Since Beauty scarce endures a Day,   593 Strephon Chloe   303
They still can do so every Day)   601 Beasts Confess   2
His Household twice a Day to Pray'rs.   605 Beasts Confess   132
Mistake our Talents ev'ry Day: 607 Beasts Confess   206
Be sure at Will's the following Day,   644 On Poetry   117
'Tis hard they must be busy Night and Day: 662 Upon Ladies   2
But forc'd from their Retirement into Day,   667 Epig Carthy 5   D   3
But thy Book perish'd on its natal Day.   669 Epig Carthy 13   D   4
She'd hear the Cause another Day,   690 Cadenus Vaness   117
Then told the Tattle of the Day,   696 Cadenus Vaness   319
Cadenus with each Day declines,   703 Cadenus Vaness   537
Stella this Day is thirty four,   721 Stel B-Day '18   1
Impatient both of Night and Day,   726 To Stella   98
That, should you live to see the Day   735 Stel B-day '20   47
By Duty bound, on Stella's Day;   740 Stel B-day 22   2
If Stella were unsung to Day;   741 Stel B-day 22   16
From ev'ry day a Lordly Banquet,   745 Stel Distress   11
To a sour Pint one day in twenty.   745 Stel Distress   14
Surpriz'd with ev'ry day a hot meal   745 Stel Distress   5
Too soon arrives the dismal Day,   746 Stel Distress   25
Her Quarter's out at Lady Day   746 Stel Distress   41
From ev'ry Day a lordly Banquet,   750 Stel Wood-Park   35
To half a Pint one Day in twenty.   750 Stel Wood-Park   38
But now arrives the dismal Day: 751 Stel Wood-Park   45
My verse on Stella's native day;   754 Stella '23   4
This day, dear Bec, is thy nativity,   760 Bec's B-Day   1
This Day, whate'er the Fates decree,   763 Stel B-day '26   1
This Day then, let us not be told,   763 Stel B-day '26   3
Who ev'ry Day and Hour the same are;   787 Dick's Variety   4
So teaz'd day and night   851 Lady's Lament   3
And pore ev'ry day on   856 Lady's Lament   149
He's all the day saunt'ring,   856 Lady's Lament   159
And all the day raves   856 Lady's Lament   175
And Day succeeding after Day,   860 Lady Acheson   10
And Day succeeding after Day,   860 Lady Acheson   10
And they must have three Meals a Day,   861 Lady Acheson   34
Three Dishes a Day, and three Hogsheads a Year.   867 Grand Question   12
Next Day, to be sure, the Captain will come,   870 Grand Question   87
"But, the Sight of a Book makes me sick to this Day. 873 Grand Question   172
The Rogue must call another day.   878 Robbin & Harry   4
And e'er a twelvemonth and a day   878 Robbin & Harry   11
You sat and lows'd him all the Sun-shine Day.   882 Pastoral Dial   34
How could she sit the live-long Day,   891 Panegyr Dean   145
Though I should see him twice a day,   899 Dean's Reasons   29
Death went upon a solemn Day,   903 Death Daphne   1
And fly unseen both Day and Night;   919 Riddle 5   26
I twice a Day a hunting go;   921 Riddle 6   31
Altho' 'tis open Night and Day,   928 Riddle 12   D   5
My Blood this Day is very sweet,   929 Riddle 15   D   9
Because my Master one Day in anger call'd you Goose. 985 Mary to Sher   12
   . . . one Day that you was here,   986 Mary to Sher   25
Mary said he, (one Day, as I was mending my Master's 986 Mary to Sher   28
   Stocking,)
Where I hear you are crammd evry day like a Swine   1017 Swift Ans Sher   13
DAYLY
To us he made his dayly pray'rs,   620 Scandal Poem 1   81
DAYS   SEE NOW-A-DAYS,DOG-DAYS
In the last wretched Remnant of his Days;   10 Ode to King   141
And water-colours of these Days,   21 Ode Athenian   170
These Days! where ev'n th' Extravagance of Poetry 21 Ode Athenian   171
In the pollution of these days;   38 Ode Sancroft   109
For, let heaven's wrath enlarge these weary days, 54 Temple Ill   111
I'm good for little at my days;   94 Bauc & Phil 1   163
Some few Days after Harley spies   172 Horace 1, 7   57
And after many Days thou'lt find it,   255 Bubble   134
When the Days are at shortest, to put it in Rhyme; 265 Apollo   78
Pray not a word of Halcyon Days.   271 Apollo's Edict   D   45
How George, Nim, Dan, Dean pass their Days;   278 Journal   2
Of Vigor in declining Days.   295 Horrid Plot   154
Your Rent is due almost a Week beside the Days of 343 Upon His Grace   44
   Grace.
The hireling Senator of modern Days,   364 On Dreams   35
"As it was deem'd in former Days   384 Manly Virtue   5
And golden Times, and Halcyon days,   466 Birthday Song   196
Thus Edgar proud, in Days of Yore,   476 Epist on Epist   43
And one poor Office, half his Days;   481 Libel on D- D-   34
So, after toiling twenty Days,   642 On Poetry   65
See my weary Days consuming,   660 Love Song   7
Thy week made up of fasting days,   676 Parson's Case   11
Thy years as num'rous as thy days?   677 Parson's Case   36
She knew in our degen'rate Days   693 Cadenus Vaness   212
The Genius's of ancient Days!   708 Cadenus Vaness   689
We say, she's past her Dancing Days;   756 Stel B-day '24   2
And must against the warmer Days   759 Receipt Youth   25
The gout that will prolong his days: 761 Bec's B-Day   16
Support a few remaining Days: 764 Stel B-day '26   12
Some teach us in these dang'rous Days,   780 Mullinix Tim   251

DAYS	(CONTINUED)	PAGE	TITLE	LINE
Three Days before he was expected.	. . . .	859	Lady Acheson	8
I sigh to think of antient Days.	. . . .	894	Panegyr Dean	226
Ah! who in our degen'rate Days	. . . .	895	Panegyr Dean	287
On rainy Days alone I dine,	. . . .	954	Authors Living	1
On rainy Days, I dine alone,	. . . .	954	Authors Living	3
I remember it was upon a Tuesday, of all Days in the Year.		986	Mary to Sher	26
Poets, in those Days, us'd to venture high,	. . . . .	988	Letter Dr Sh-n	13
(An Author, where I sometimes dip a Days)	. . . .	988	Letter Dr Sh-n	18
Three days for Answer I have waited,	. . . . . .	1002	Reply by Dean	1
DAZ'LING				
The daz'ling glory dimms their prostituted sight,	. . .	41	Ode Sancroft	221
DAZLED				
Of my own dazled, scanty Sense	. . . .	18	Ode Athenian	78
DAZLING				
With its own Light Your dazling Glory shines,	. . .	11	Ode to William	D 7
DAZZLE				
And dazzle all the Idol-Faces	. . . .	182	Horace 2, 1	75
DAZZLED				
Like Light'ning dazzled from a-far:	. . . . . .	352	Wood Ironmongr	14
DAZZLING				
"The cooler Air, and dazzling Sun;	. . . .	380	Apology Lady C	142
DE				
(Consult his Book de Partium usu)	. . . .	367	Answer Delaney	32
DE'EL				
The De'el take the Searcher.	. . . .	245	Irish-Feast	24
But this skip of a Lawyer, where the De'el did he grow?		814	Yahoo's	7
What the De'el is't to him whence the Devil they came?		815	Yahoo's	24
The De'el too that ow'd me a Shame,	. . . . . .	1005	Sheridan's Sub	21
DEAD				
The Body, tho' Gigantick, lyes all Cold and Dead.	.	25	Ode Athenian	291
With antique Reliques of the Dead,	. . . . . .	27	Ode to Temple	22
To drive all Virtue out, or look it dead!	. . . . .	30	Ode to Temple	123
Or whether dead imagination's ghost	. . . . . .	51	Temple Ill	7
That time is sick, or the world's mind is dead.--	. .	53	Temple Ill	66
For you freely must own you were at a Dead lift;	. . .	77	Lady B- B-	28
From the dead Ashes of a Flow'r	. . . .	81	Vanbrug House	86
Patrige is Dead, nay more, he dy'd	. . . . . .	98	Elegy Patrige	3
Just as if Patrige were not Dead;	. . . .	98	Elegy Patrige	12
When Philip King of Greece was Dead,	. . . . .	99	Elegy Patrige	64
From the dead Ashes of a Flow'r	. . . .	109	V's House	128
Dead Cats and Turnip-Tops come tumbling down the Flood	139	City Shower	63
If the Stick be taken from the dead Sea.	. . . . .	147	Windsor Proph	14
And bring her back, alive or dead.	. . . .	223	Prog of Love	38
In England the Dead in Woollen are clad,	. . . . .	237	Excellent Song	10
Since a living Dog better is than a dead Lyon,	. . .	237	Excellent Song	13
And strip the Bodyes of the Dead.	. . . .	256	Bubble	156
Is dead at last without evading.	. . . .	282	Journal	104
His Grace! impossible! what dead!	. . . .	296	Satiric Elegy	1
Since you can teach dead Dogs to bite.	. . . . .	299	Horrid Plot	40
Nor unsuccessful waits for dead Mens Shoes.	. . . .	364	On Dreams	30
And there's an End; the Man is dead;	. . . . . .	366	Answer Delaney	6
Ye Rhimers, dead as soon as born,	. . . .	394	Grub-Street	3
Walks boldly home at dead of night;	. . . . . .	435	Answer Paulus	92
Or pawing into dead mens paunches.	. . . . . .	461	Birthday Song	36
By Homer dead was taught to thrive,	. . . . . .	483	Libel on L- D-	85
Must honour you alive and dead,	. . . .	490	Dialogue	50
Will strike him dead upon the Spot:	. . . . . .	500	Doctor Delaney	20
It must come out alive or dead.	. . . .	527	Lady's Dres Rm	68
"D'ye hear the News---? the Dean is dead---!	. . . .	547	Life of Swift	69
I say no more---, because he's dead---.	. . . . .	549	Life of Swift	143
Will never leave him, till he's dead:	. . . . . .	556	Death of Swift	84
And more lament, when I was dead,	. . . . . .	557	Death of Swift	141
"He hardly breathes. The Dean is dead.	. . . . .	558	Death of Swift	150
'Tis told at Court, the Dean is dead.	. . . . . .	559	Death of Swift	178
"He's dead you say; why let him rot;	. . . . . .	559	Death of Swift	183
"Why, is he dead without his Shoes?	. . . . . .	560	Death of Swift	191
Provided Bolingbroke were dead.	. . . .	560	Death of Swift	196
"The Dean is dead, (and what is Trumps?)	. . . .	562	Death of Swift	228
Suppose me dead; and then suppose	. . . .	565	Death of Swift	299
I saw the Graves give up their Dead.	. . . . . .	578	Day Judgement	4
Yet, ask I must. Is Caelia dead?	. . . .	595	Cassinus Peter	42
Altho' the Writer long were dead?	. . . .	708	Cadenus Vaness	699
Doctors pronounce the patient dead;	. . . . . .	761	Bec's B-Day	12
Stella long dead, but first the Dean,	. . . . . .	762	Bec's B-Day	46
The Neighbours all cry, Shoot him dead,	. . . . .	797	Traulus 1	39
Mount alive, and dead descend	. . . .	801	Traulus 2	52
For I'd rather be dead,	. . . .	853	Lady's Lament	55
Whose names and works (tho' dead) are made	. . . .	876	To Dean Swift	9
Where each Supply of Dead, renews	. . . . . .	923	Riddle 7	55
I'm dead except I live in Light.	. . . .	929	Riddle 15	D 4
The Dead are all sound	. . . .	939	Riddle Answerd	19
Or, like my own Herrings, I soon shall be dead.	. .	953	Herrings	9
As for you're writing I am dead,	. . . .	983	Sher, A Goose	25
DEADLY				
Receive its last and deadly Wound,	. . . . . .	850	Old Thorn	51
And then to give me such a deadly Cut--	. . . . .	1033	Ans to Crown	10
DEAF				
When my Left Ear was deaf a Fortnight,	. . . . .	367	Answer Delaney	42
The Dean too deaf to hear.	. . . .	405	Swift to Pope	4

DEAF	(CONTINUED)	PAGE	TITLE	LINE
For, had our deaf Divine		406	Swift to Pope	22
Deaf, giddy, helpless, left alone,		673	His Deafness	1
I preached three congregations deaf,		675	Curate's Compl	10
But turn the deaf ear,		756	Dingley Brent	11
To make me deaf, and mend my Sight.		758	Stel B-day '24	54
He had cut his own ears to be deaf to your nonsense.		818	Epigr Kite	10

DEAFEN

| To deafen 'em with Puns and Rhime. | | 75 | Game Traffick | D 26 |

DEAL

My Lord to find out who must deal		74	Game Traffick	1
He had mixt little Wit with a great deal of Pains,		77	Lady B- B-	24
Thou must no longer deal in Farce,		181	Horace 2, 1	35
And deal in Vices of the graver Sort,		194	Author Himself	21
The Deal, the Shuffle, and the Cut?		451	Modern Lady	223
To deal it to the worst of Human-kind.		532	To Mr. Gay	28

DEALERS

| For dealers in Satyrick Wit: | | 463 | Birthday Song | 112 |

DEALING

| Or dealing crowns to George and James. | | 402 | Window Inns 7 | D 6 |

DEALS

Deals out to man the planet of his birth;		54	Temple Ill	90
He deals, and Hears mysterious Chat;		63	Discovery	14
For I think in my Conscience he deals with Old Nick;		265	Apollo	82
Than the Liquor he deals in, his own melted Copper;		351	Wood Insect	36

DEALT

| Nay, 'twas affirm'd, he sometimes dealt in Rhime: | | 193 | Author Himself | 10 |
| Not so with thee thy base Invaders dealt; | | 791 | St. Pat's Well | 22 |

DEAN   SEE NIM-DAN-DEAN

The Dean will give me Willow-Sticks,		128	Little House	63
No, Doctor, you shall be a Dean;		173	Horace 1, 7	88
Suppose him, now, a Dean compleat,		174	Horace 1, 7	97
Said Harley, Welcome Rev'rend Dean!		174	Horace 1, 7	121
The Doctor and Dean, Pope, Parnell and Gay		185	Scriblerus 1	1
Lord! how were they mistaken in the Dean!		196	Author Himself	66
"Lewis; the Dean will be of Use,		199	Horace 2, 6	15
"Good Mr. Dean go change your Gown,		200	Horace 2, 6	23
"And Mr. Dean, one Word from you--		201	Horace 2, 6	62
"How think you of our Friend the Dean?		202	Horace 2, 6	83
"You, Mr. Dean frequent the Great;		202	Horace 2, 6	93
Tho' a Printer and Dean		237	Excellent Song	5
The Dean and his Printer then let us cry Fye on;		237	Excellent Song	11
And as for the Dean,		238	Excellent Song	30
How George, Nim, Dan, Dean pass their Days;		278	Journal	2
At Seven, the Dean in Night-gown drest,		278	Journal	9
Go to the Dean to read Lucretius.		278	Journal	12
My Lord and Dean, the Fire forsake;		279	Journal	31
While George, and Dean, go back to Gammon.		280	Journal	42
George, Nim, and Dean, set out at Four,		280	Journal	43
The weary Dean goes to his Chamber,		280	Journal	57
How in the Lake the Dean was drench'd;		281	Journal	68
Or how the Dean delights to vex		281	Journal	77
I might have told how oft Dean <Percival>		281	Journal	79
The Dean must with his Quilt supply,		283	Journal	121
The Dean, she heard her Uncle say		291	Prog Marriage	47
The Dean, who us'd to dine at one,		291	Prog Marriage	59
The Dean has carry'd Lady Jane		294	Prog Marriage	124
Was brib'd to make the Dean agree		294	Prog Marriage	130
Where if the Dean by chance appears		294	Prog Marriage	139
The Dean with all his best Endeavour		295	Horrid Plot	151
The Dean and Sheridan, I hope,		313	To Ford	73
To humble that vexatious Dean.		348	Whitshed Motto	20
As that same viz. St. <Patrick's> Dean.		361	Grace's Answer	6
When you're advanc'd above Dean Viz.		362	Grace's Answer	43
Dear Dean, if e're again you Write,		371	Letter D. S-y	1
The Dean too deaf to hear.		405	Swift to Pope	4
The Dean sits plodding on a Book,		405	Swift to Pope	7
Yet to the Dean his Share allot;		406	Swift to Pope	17
No more the Dean, that grave Divine,		409	Dial Rich Marb	43
Here wont the Dean when he's to seek,		409	Dial Rich Marb	51
And thus the Dean is forc't to stay		420	Holyhead	11
The very Reverend Dean Smedley,		455	Dean Smedley	1
The Dean, Tom's honour'd Friend and Patron.		458	Paddy's Charac	28
You never had commenc'd a Dean,		495	Panegyr Swift	77
"D'ye hear the News---? the Dean is dead---!		547	Life of Swift	69
But, truly there the Dean was bit---.		547	Life of Swift	92
Thus did the Dean: his only scope		548	Life of Swift	130
See, how the Dean begins to break:		556	Death of Swift	80
"He was too airy for a Dean---.		547	Life of Swift	79
That, God be prais'd, the Dean is well.		557	Death of Swift	126
"How is the Dean? He's just alive.		558	Death of Swift	148
"He hardly breathes. The Dean is dead.		558	Death of Swift	150
"And had the Dean, in all the Nation,		558	Death of Swift	161
To curse the Dean, or bless the Drapier.		558	Death of Swift	168
'Tis told at Court, the Dean is dead.		559	Death of Swift	178
"The Dean is dead, (and what is Trumps?)		562	Death of Swift	228
"He lov'd the Dean. (I lead a Heart.)		562	Death of Swift	239
No further mention of the Dean;		562	Death of Swift	246
"The Dean was famous in his Time;		563	Death of Swift	263
"The Dean, if we believe Report,		565	Death of Swift	307
"With Horror, Grief, Despair the Dean		568	Death of Swift	391

DEAN	(CONTINUED)	PAGE	TITLE	LINE
"The Dean did by his Pen defeat		569	Death of Swift	407
"Vow'd on the Dean his Rage to vent,		570	Death of Swift	423
"Perhaps I may allow, the Dean		571	Death of Swift	455
Mr. Dean, You come too late:		630	Epistle Lady	28
Mr. Dean, you must reply.		632	Epistle Lady	92
Deuce is in you, Mr. Dean;		635	Epistle Lady	181
And make thy curate-ship a dean;		676	Parson's Case	20
James Bruges & the Dean had long been friends,		678	Dean and Duke	1
But, sure the Dean deserves a sharp Rebuke		678	Dean and Duke	3
The Duke and Dean seem near upon a levell.		678	Dean and Duke	10
A Duke to know a Dean! go smooth your Frown,		678	Dean and Duke	13
The First but a Rebus, the Last but a Dean.		716	Answer Rebus	6
To find her a great Witt, but the Dean a small Man.		716	Answer Rebus	14
To the poor Doings of the Dean:		745	Stel Distress	18
Small Beer, a Herring, and the Dean.		747	Stel Distress	56
Stella long dead, but first the Dean,		762	Bec's B-Day	46
Than the Dean storm, or Stella rattle.		762	Bec's B-Day	56
Thus to a Dean some Curate Sloven,		812	Bro Protestant	19
Hath insulted us all by insulting the Dean.		814	Yahoo's	4
The Dean and his merits we ev'ry one know,		814	Yahoo's	6
By leaving him under the pen of the Dean.		816	Yahoo's	39
To the Dean of all Deans, tho' he wears not a sword.		816	Yahoo's	54
To the Dean he shall go; they shall kiss, and be friends:		817	Yahoo's	62
But how? Why, the Dean shall to him disclose		817	Yahoo's	63
At Dublin's high feast sat Primate and Dean,		843	Ay and No	1
"Ay,ay," quoth the Dean, "the cause is old gold."		843	Ay and No	4
"This mischief arises from witty Dean Swift."		843	Ay and No	6
Behold! the cruel Dean in Scorn		849	Old Thorn	23
"Relentless Dean! to Mischief born,		850	Old Thorn	58
"Or chid the Dean, or pinch'd thy Spouse.		850	Old Thorn	70
"May that fell Dean, by whose Command		850	Old Thorn	73
By a Dean and a Knight;		851	Lady's Lament	4
Hallooing the Dean.		852	Lady's Lament	10
The Dean never stops,		852	Lady's Lament	11
But still to the Dean:		854	Lady's Lament	88
The Dean, you will swear,		856	Lady's Lament	157
The Dean or the digger;		856	Lady's Lament	170
The Dean has been doing.		857	Lady's Lament	194
The Dean wou'd visit Market-hill,		859	Lady Acheson	1
Or, Mr. Dean--I should with Joy		860	Lady Acheson	25
Of that insulting Tyrant Dean.		861	Lady Acheson	44
And you and the Dean no more shall combine,		867	Grand Question	15
I'm all over dawb'd when I sit by the Dean.		868	Grand Question	30
The Dean and the Doctor have humbled their Pride,		871	Grand Question	131
(For the Dean was so shabby and look'd like a Ninny,		872	Grand Question	151
So, then you look'd scornful, and snift at the Dean,		873	Grand Question	175
Till she heard the Dean call, Will your Ladyship walk?		873	Grand Question	180
But the Dean, if this Secret shou'd come to his Ears,		873	Grand Question	187
You never else had known the Dean,		877	To Dean Swift	29
When the Dean threw me this Tobacco-plug;		881	Pastoral Dial	26
Daphne, 'twixt the Dean and you,		907	Daphne	50
Which is all at present from Dean of St. Patrick's.		977	Dean to Sherid	48
And the Dean my Master is an honester Man . . .		985	Mary to Sher	8
And I must confess as a Dean and Divine		1017	Swift Ans Sher	3
George, Dan, Dean, and Nim to place in the center?		1027	Sheri Circles	14
Three fellows with whips, and the Dean holds the string.		1027	Sheri Circles	20
Dean Cross, had he preach'd, would have made us all		1029	Dr. Helsham	8
Pew-sick;				
But, alas, the poor Dean neither Shudders nor burns,		1037	Four Storyes	5
"I thought the <Dean> had been too proud,		200	Horace 2, 6	33
I can't Conjecture, for Dr.<Dean>		372	Letter D. S-y	43
To oppose the <Dean> your-self Exempting		373	Letter D. S-y	76
For the Good of our Church a true <English> <Dean>.		516	Dean Hang Rape	4
The <Dean> he pursu'd to recover his Game,		517	Dean Hang Rape	13
The <Dean>, and his Landlord, a jolly Comrade,		517	Dean Hang Rape	25
Then, why should the <Dean>, when Whores are so cheap,		518	Dean Hang Rape	41
The <Dean> he was vext that his Whores were so willing,		519	Dean Hang Rape	55
No Devil but <Dean> could Ravish 'em then,		519	Dean Hang Rape	64
When the good <English> <Dean> is hang'd up for a		520	Dean Hang Rape	72
<Rape>.				
<Dean> <White>, <Dean> <Daniel>, and <Dean> <Smedley>		742	Stel B-day 22	44
<Dean> <White>, <Dean> <Daniel>, and <Dean> <Smedley>		742	Stel B-day 22	44
<Dean> <White>, <Dean> <Daniel>, and <Dean> <Smedley>		742	Stel B-day 22	44
That, let what <Dean> soever come,		742	Stel B-day 22	45
To the poor Doings of the <Dean>.		750	Stel Wood-Park	42
Small Beer, a Herring, and the <Dean>.		751	Stel Wood-Park	72
Once more the <Dean> supplies their Place.		757	Stel B-day '24	14
By bell'wing thus against the <Dean>?		795	Traulus 1	2
What Mischief can the <Dean> have done him,		796	Traulus 1	7
Which gave the <Dean> the Name of Draper?		796	Traulus 1	12
The <Dean> was never so carest:		796	Traulus 1	16
By this Contrivance Mr. <Dean>		797	Traulus 1	59
The <Dean> hath felt their Stings before;		798	Traulus 1	85
Yet still the <Dean> on Freedom raves,		799	Traulus 1	99
By the <Dean> though gravely told,		863	To Janus	25
Our thriving <Dean> has purchas'd Land;		875	Drapier's Hill	2
A <Dean>, a Spaniard, and a Knight.		883	Rev Market-Hill	8
The <Dean> and Spaniard find it too well;		883	Rev Market-Hill	10
The <Dean>, to guard his Honour's Back,		883	Rev Market-Hill	13
The <Dean> and Spaniard must reproach ye;		884	Rev Market-Hill	30

```
DEAN            (CONTINUED)                              PAGE   TITLE            LINE
   Thrice Rev'rend <Dean> for all I owe;      . . . .    887  Panegyr Dean        2
   Nine more such Champions as the <Dean>,      . . .    887  Panegyr Dean        9
   A Panegyrick on <Dean> <Swift>.   . . . .   . . . .   887  Panegyr Dean       34
   Salutes the <Dean> in diff'rent Views;      . . . .   888  Panegyr Dean       38
   <Dean>, Butler, Usher, Jester, Tutor;       . . . .   888  Panegyr Dean       39
   To sing your Praise. And, first as <Dean>:  . . . .   888  Panegyr Dean       44
   Except to give <Dean> <Daniel> place.       . . . .   888  Panegyr Dean       48
   As well become St. <Patrick's> <Dean>;      . . . .   889  Panegyr Dean       78
   Now raise your Spirits, Mr. <Dean>:         . . . .   889  Panegyr Dean       85
   Conversing with that rusty <Dean>)!     . . . . .     891  Panegyr Dean      142
   Nor have you grumbled, rev'rend <Dean>,     . . . .   892  Panegyr Dean      163
   But, with his Hand, the <Dean> can churn it.  . .     892  Panegyr Dean      174
   Be not ungrateful to the <Dean>;        . . . . .     893  Panegyr Dean      218
   Shall sing the <Dean> in Smedly's Lines.    . . . .   897  Panegyr Dean      346
DEAN'RY
   To the Dean'ry House, and on the North Glass,   . . . 264  Apollo             31
DEAN'S
   When they saw the Dean's Book they were in a great Fury  237  Excellent Song  24
   "We shou'd indulge the Dean's disgust,    . . . . .   549  Life of Swift     159
   A Dean's but a Parson, and what is a Rebus?   . . .   716  Answer Rebus        7
   Have put the Dean's Politicks quite out of Date;  . . 716  Answer Rebus       24
   Of our good Dean's eternal chidings;    . . . . . .   753  Gift for Bec        6
   Ty'd round the <Dean's> Neck, for committing a <Rape>.  519  Dean Hang Rape   66
DEANERY
   Down to your Deanery repair   . . . . . . . .         361  Grace's Answer     19
   A Deanery you got, when in,   . . . . . . .           493  Panegyr Swift      21
   And, as fast as she could, to the Deanery flew sick.  . 1029  Dr. Helsham     11
DEANRY
   ..and come back from the Deanry, . . .   . . . . .    1013  Swift to Sheri     4
DEANRY-HOUSE
   The Deanry-house may well be match't    . . . . . .   313  To Ford            65
DEANS
   The Worst of disaffected Deans:       . . . . . .     514  Answer Fable       66
   "Six Deans they say must bear the Pall.     . . . .   562  Death of Swift    231
   On this Worrier of Deans whene'er we can hit,  . . .  816  Yahoo's            51
   To the Dean of all Deans, tho' he wears not a sword. . 816  Yahoo's           54
   A modus right fit for insulters of Deans.   . . . .   817  Yahoo's            59
   She sends us our <Bishops> and <Judges> and <Deans>, .  520  Dean Hang Rape   69
   Through the whole set of <Irish> <Deans>;   . . . .   742  Stel B-day 22      42
DEANSHIP
   In Spight of his Deanship and Journeyman Waters. . .  237  Excellent Song    REF
   In Spight of his Deanship and Journeyman Waters. . .  238  Excellent Song    REF
   Tho' he cring'd to his Deanship in very low strains, . 816  Yahoo's           46
   I then shall not value his Deanship a Straw,  . . .   868  Grand Question     33
   Your Deanship ought to recollect,   . . . . . . .     899  Dean's Reasons     20
   His <Deanship> was now in a damnable Scrape,  . . .   517  Dean Hang Rape     17
   My Landlord was ready his <Deanship> to Ape   . . .   517  Dean Hang Rape     29
   To see thy <Deanship> thus employ'd!    . . . . .     892  Panegyr Dean      176
DEAR
   And brings the dear Reward of Victory and Peace.  . .  16  Ode Athenian       21
   For a dear Ramble thro' Impertinence,       . . . .    18  Ode Athenian       69
   Then tell (dear fav'rite Muse)        . . . . .        30  Ode to Temple     115
   Here you may read (Dear Charming Saint)     . . . .    60  Lady Tablebook      7
   My Dear, I see your Forehead sprout:        . . . .   116  Bauc & Phil 2     156
   Dear Sid, then why wer't thou so mad    . . . .       135  Magician's Rod     79
   And dear Englond, if ought I understand,    . . . .   148  Windsor Proph      15
   Dear Harley, gen'rous Youth, admit      . . . . .     176  To Lord Harley      3
   How then, dear Harley, could I guess    . . . . .     177  To Lord Harley     23
   "My only Friend, my Dear," said she,    . . . . .     207  Fable Bitches       9
   Cry'd bravely, Patience, good my Dear.      . . . .   220  A Quiet Life        6
   Dear Will, I suffer this for Peace;     . . . . .     220  A Quiet Life       14
   Dear Will, but, what would People say?      . . . .   220  A Quiet Life       34
   To that dear Self he left behind;       . . . . .     235  Elegy on Demar     50
   For leave to act in town? 'Tis plaguy dear. . . . .   308  Billet Players     18
   To whom our country has been always dear,   . . . .   309  Billet Players     45
   And bid adieu to dear Champain.       . . . . . .     311  To Ford            26
   My dear Estate, how well I love it;     . . . . .     348  Whitshed Motto      7
   Dear Smed I read thy Brilliant Lines,       . . . .   361  Grace's Answer      1
   There your Dear Spouse and you together     . . . .   361  Grace's Answer     23
   Dear Dean, if e're again you Write,     . . . . .     371  Letter D. S-y       1
   Take Courage, dear Comrades, and be not afraid,  . .  400  Tom Clinch         19
   But dear as the <Devil>:    . . . . . . . .           402  Window Inns 8    D  2
   I pity you, dear Marble-Hill,   . . . . . . .         411  Dial Rich Marb    101
   Dick lost in Doll, a Wife Tender and Dear,  . . . .   430  Dicky Dolly         4
   Dear Madam, you are grown so hard,      . . . . .     447  Modern Lady        86
   'My Dear, for sure if I had known       . . . . .     448  Modern Lady       103
   Dear Madam, try to take a Nap--     . . . . . . .     451  Modern Lady       210
   Then pray, dear Doctor, condescend      . . . . .     493  Panegyr Swift      27
   The damnable the dear Conceit.      . . . . . .       497  Panegyr Swift     127
   Our Brethren of <England> who love us so dear,  . .   516  Dean Hang Rape      1
   Our Church and our State dear <England> maintains, .  520  Dean Hang Rape     67
   He fled to Earth, but first it cost him dear;  . . .  538  Mr. Pulteney       35
   Dear honest Ned is in the Gout,     . . . . . .       554  Death of Swift     27
   To all my Foes, dear Fortune, send      . . . . .     555  Death of Swift     67
   Dear Venus, hide this wond'rous Maid,       . . . .   585  Strephon Chloe     29
   Because her dear Papa commands.     . . . . . .       585  Strephon Chloe     44
   Now, Ponder well ye Parents dear;       . . . . .     587  Strephon Chloe    115
   Dear Cassy, though to ask I dread,      . . . . .     595  Cassinus Peter     41
   Dear Cassy, thou must purge and bleed;      . . . .   596  Cassinus Peter     89
   Dear Pallas, I have been this Morn      . . . . .     692  Cadenus Vaness    188
```

193

DEAR   (CONTINUED)   PAGE   TITLE   LINE
    Dear Madam, Let me set your Head: . . . . . .   699 Cadenus Vaness   398
    Dear Madam try this Pigeon's leg: . . . . 746 Stel Distress   18
    Dear Madam, try this Pigeon's Leg;   . . . . 750 Stel Wood-Park   16
    From me, Dear Stella, still be kind.   . . . . . .   755 Stella '23   30
    This day, dear Bec, is thy nativity, ... 760 Bec's B-Day   1
    Dear Vessel, still be to thy Steerage just, ...   771 Horace 1, 14   53
    No more my dear Delightful way tread, ... 779 Mullinix Tim   183
    Dear Mullinix, your good Advice   . . . . 779 Mullinix Tim   195
    Dear Mullinix, I now lament   . . . . 781 Mullinix Tim   277
    Dear Tim, no more such angry Speeches, ...   783 Tim and Fables   35
    Subscribes, Dear Sir, your Brother loving. . . . . .   812 Bro Protestant   20
    Dear Dick, prithee tell by what passion you move? . .   818 Archbi Cashel   1
    For thine, my dear Dick, give me leave to speak plain, . 819 Archbi Cashel   15
    Dear Baldwin chaste, and witty Crosse, ...   821 Dr. Rundle   61
    Dear Companions hug and kiss, ... 835 Legion Club   151
    "The Irish dear joys have enough common sense, . . .   843 Ay and No   15
    Dear friend, Doctor Jenny, ... 857 Lady's Lament   203
    My Dear, I have ponder'd again and again on't: . . .   867 Grand Question   20
    But, if you will give us a Barrack, my Dear, ...   868 Grand Question   31
    That I saw a huge Rat: O dear, how I scream'd! . . .   868 Grand Question   50
    Dear Madam, had you but the Spirit to teaze, ...   869 Grand Question   53
    Dear Madam, whene'er of a Barrack I think, ...   869 Grand Question   63
    And his Horse, the dear Creter, it prances and rears, . 870 Grand Question   97
    Dear Madam, be sure he's a fine spoken Man, ...   872 Grand Question   139
    This Petticoat shall save thy dear Back-side;   . . .   881 Pastoral Dial   22
    And thou, my dear, shalt have the bigger half. . . . .   881 Pastoral Dial   32
    But why shou'd we fight thus, my partner so dear, . .   979 Dean to Tho: S   33
    Dear Tom, I'm surpriz'd that your verse did not jingle;   980 Tho: Sheridan   1
    For that, dear Tom, ne'er fret and vex, ...   983 Sher, A Goose   17
    Thus you may see, dear Friend, ex pede hence   . . . .   988 Letter Dr Sh-n   15
    So far, dear Dan, that ev'ry Friend   . . . . 993 On Picture   29
    Dear Sheridan; a loving Pair   . . . . 1020 Nim-Dan-Dean 1   D   1
    Dear Tom, this verse, which however the beginning may   1022 Nim-Dan-Dean 2   D   1
        appear,. . .
DEAR-LOV'D
    Come from thy dear-lov'd Streams, ...   31 Ode to Temple   151
DEARER
    That Paper would quickly be dearer than Gold, . . .   288 Bank Down   32
DEAREST
    The dearest in Charles Mather's Shop, ...   135 Magician's Rod   76
    If, dearest Dismal, you for once can Dine . . . . .   162 Toland's Invit   1
    Who chose to leave his dearest pledges here, ...   309 Billet Players   46
    Tom's three dearest Friends came by in the Squabble, .   327 Epigram 1   3
    And buy distinction at the dearest rate.   . . . . . .   506 To a Friend   12
    "Disasters, to our Dearest Friends, ...   545 Life of Swift   8
    You are his Dearest Friend---; he lyes---:   . . . .   545 Life of Swift   26
    "But dearest Friends, they say, must part. . . . . .   562 Death of Swift   240
    Her dearest Comrades never caught her   . . . . . .   584 Strephon Chloe   17
    And makes it warm for Dearest Life.   . . . . . .   590 Strephon Chloe   208
    His Country was his dearest Mother, ...   606 Beasts Confess   179
    Ever dearest Friendship swearing;   . . . . 800 Traulus 2   16
    My dearest Life it is surprizing, ... 860 Lady Acheson   31
    This, dearest Sheelah, thou shalt share with me.   . .   881 Pastoral Dial   28
    Shall in thy dearest Blood be dy'd, ... 925 Riddle 8   43
DEARLY
    And for it does so dearly pay;   . . . .   28 Ode to Temple   77
    I have Experience dearly bought, ... 175 Horace 1, 7   133
    And made the Rascals pay him dearly   . . . . . .   463 Birthday Song   105
    Nor sell what they so dearly bought, ...   488 Irish-Club   23
    Yet, hang me, but I love her dearly.   . . . . . .   679 From Catullus   8
    And, to be free, was dearly bought: . . . . . .   708 Cadenus Vaness   671
    You pay too dearly for your Care;   . . . . 727 To Stella   118
DEARTH
    With War, and Pestilence, and Dearth, ...   10 Ode to King   134
DEATH   SEE DETH
    The Tyrant Death lay crouching down, ...   7 Ode to King   39
    And His best Victory a Noble Death;   . . . . . .   9 Ode to King   106
    Who by that, vainly talks of bafling Death, ...   21 Ode Athenian   182
    Of some great King and Conqu'rors Death, ...   24 Ode Athenian   272
    Make up its solemn Train with Death;   . . . . . .   29 Ode to Temple   90
    With promise of a mad Reversion after Death.   . . .   32 Ode to Temple   198
    Which strait pronounc'd his death;   . . . .   38 Ode Sancroft   120
    Is but the patient's death, and gain--   . . . . . .   42 Ode Sancroft   258
    Since Death pursues the Coward as he flies.   . . . .   210 Earl of Oxford   2
    Know all Men by these Presents, Death the Tamer   233 Elegy on Demar   1
    But as his Gold he weigh'd, grim Death in spight,   234 Elegy on Demar   31
    Into the Arms of Death would run, ...   243 Horace 4, 9   22
    The common Death of many a stronger Boat. . . . . .   284 Elegy Boat   10
    That, Death has overset him with a Blast. . . . . .   285 Elegy Boat   22
    Yet, spight of Death and Fate, I here maintain   . .   285 Elegy Boat   29
    Since <Burnet's> Death, the <Bishop's> Bench,   . .   303 Storm   17
    The Death of our Nation it seem'd to foretell,   . .   351 Wood Insect   31
    For our Fear's at an End with the Death of the Maggot.   352 Wood Insect   40
    Now pale as Death, then blush'd and bow'd; . . . . .   377 Apology Lady C   78
    In half a Walk fatigu'd to Death.   . . . . 379 Apology Lady C   128
    She gets a Cold as sure as Death;   . . . . 417 Woman's Mind   45
    Mopsa, who stinks her Spouse to Death, ...   449 Modern Lady   156
    Which way my Death can do them good;   . . . . . .   556 Death of Swift   78
    ",o, may we all for Death prepare!   . . . . 558 Death of Swift   153
    How those I love, my Death lament.   . . . . . .   561 Death of Swift   206

DEATH	(CONTINUED)	PAGE	TITLE	LINE
When Death approach'd, to stand between:	. . . . .	561	Death of Swift	222
Nor souse to death a Birthday Beau.	. . . .	622	Scandal Poem 1	178
Is Folly, at his Death confuted.	. . . . .	646	On Poetry	202
When Death had finish'd Blackmore's Reign,	. . . .	653	On Poetry	374
So a poor wretch upon the brink of death,	. . . . .	672	Epig Carthy 24	D 11
Late be her death, one gentle nod,	. . . .	762	Bec's B-Day	57
Those whom you dragg'd from Death before:	. . . .	764	Stel B-day '26	40
The Nation scar'd, the Author doom'd to Death,	. . .	771	Horace 1, 14	31
And fret the Tories Souls to Death,	. . . . .	778	Mullinix Tim	171
He tires me to death.	. . . .	852	Lady's Lament	44
Death went upon a solemn Day,	. . . .	903	Death Daphne	1
Declar'd in Council, Death must marry:	. . . . .	903	Death Daphne	10
That Death should get a num'rous Breed;	. . . .	903	Death Daphne	14
But, Death had Bus'ness to dispatch:	. . . . . .	904	Death Daphne	51
Death must not be a Spouse for thee:	. . . . . .	905	Death Daphne	92
Who scourg'd to Death that Scourge of Rome,	. . . .	925	Riddle 8	36
And a Whisper is my Death.	. . . . . .	933	Riddle 20	D 30
Seldom by the death of time;	. . . .	937	Riddle 24	D 48
DEATH-BED				
Religion now does on her death-bed lie,	. . . . . .	42	Ode Sancroft	251
DEATH-WATCH				
And Chambermaids christen this Worm a Death-Watch:	.	351	Wood Insect	20
DEATH'S				
Death's sting is swallow'd up in victory at last,	. . .	40	Ode Sancroft	201
DEATH'S-HEAD				
But who can bear the Death's-Head in his Hand?	. . .	669	Epig Carthy 16	D 4
DEATHLESS				
While Burnet in his deathless page	. . . . . .	490	Dialogue	27
DEATHLINGS				
Young Deathlings, who, by Practice made	. . . . .	903	Death Daphne	15
DEATHS				
And all those flying Deaths that aim'd him from the Field,		8	Ode to King	67
(Th' impartial Deaths which come	. . . . . .	8	Ode to King	68
DEBAS'D				
'Till Politicks debas'd my mind.	. . . .	782	Mullinix Tim	282
DEBASE				
Oh! let him not debase your Thoughts,	. . . . . .	465	Birthday Song	147
DEBATE				
Brings his good parts and breeding in debate;	. . . .	48	To Congreve	156
In ev'ry Council and Debate he stands for what is Right		341	Upon His Grace	5
The Doctor stood not to debate,	. . . .	378	Apology Lady C	93
A founder'd Horse will oft debate,	. . . . . .	640	On Poetry	15
When first this grand Debate arose	. . . . . .	690	Cadenus Vaness	130
While he sleeps the whole Debate,	. . . . . .	836	Legion Club	165
Or join with the Court in ev'ry Debate,	. . . . .	867	Grand Question	23
For we who debate on a subject important,	. . . . .	976	Dean to Sherid	11
DEBATED				
And thus debated with herself.	. . . .	691	Cadenus Vaness	141
DEBATES				
Nor highest Wisdom in Debates	. . . . . .	641	On Poetry	27
He only the rights of the clergy debates,	. . . . .	816	Yahoo's	31
DEBAUCH				
By prostituting her they first debauch.	. . . . . .	44	To Congreve	22
In ev'ry Debauch, but committing a <Rape>.	. . . .	517	Dean Hang Rape	30
DEBAUCH'D				
And since too oft debauch'd by Praise,	. . . . . .	33	Ode to Temple	204
DEBT				
Cuckolds, elopes, and runs in Debt	. . . . .	150	Corinna	27
Above a Thousand Pounds in Debt,	. . . .	174	Horace 1, 7	115
It is but so much more in Debt,	. . . .	200	Horace 2, 6	21
Dipt over head and Ears--in Debt.	. . . . . .	251	Bubble	24
And claim it as a Debt from Fate,	. . . .	388	Manly Virtue	141
But, like a King, to run in Debt.	. . . . . .	409	Dial Rich Marb	42
"Is not our Nation in his Debt?	. . . .	547	Life of Swift	96
Or in the Payment of a Debt	. . . .	724	To Stella	27
You, every Year the Debt enlarge,	. . . . . .	739	Stel B-day '21	7
I dying leave the Debt unpay'd,	. . . . . .	740	Stel B-day '21	18
Impatient to be out of Debt,	. . . . . .	887	Panegyr Dean	23
DEBTER				
And will be so much more your Debter	. . . . . .	463	Birthday Song	89
DEBTERS				
Bills turn the Lenders into Debters,	. . . . .	240	Run Bankers	26
DEBTOR				
Yet none was ever less their Debtor.	. . . . . .	410	Dial Rich Marb	84
Poor Kingdom thou wouldst be that Governor's debtor,	.	424	Carterets Arms	19
"That Kingdom he hath left his Debtor,	. . . . .	572	Death of Swift	483
Col'nel......may be your Debtor;	. . . . . .	633	Epistle Lady	111
For, had you made the <King> your debtor,	. . . . .	821	Dr. Rundle	65
DEBTORS				
Lords, Knights and Squires were all his humble Debtors.		234	Elegy on Demar	16
When it heard of a Bank appear'd to his Debtors,	. .	288	Bank Down	42
His Debtors they wonder'd to find him so frank,	. . .	288	Bank Down	44
Far from our Debtors,	. . . .	1036	Bless Country	1
DEBTS				
We'll bring on us no more Debts,	. . . . . .	169	Peace Dunkirk	28
From Dunns and Debts, and drown our Care;	. . . .	184	Horace 2, 1	110
At least, before your Master's Debts are paid.	. . .	533	To Mr. Gay	62
Intent the Publick Debts to pay,	. . . .	656	On Poetry	445
Our whole Accounts of publick Debts.	. . . . . .	774	Mullinix Tim	15

		PAGE	TITLE	LINE
DECANT				
Decant his Wine, and carve his Beef.		883	Rev Market-Hill	24
DECAY				
So would earth's face turn pale, and life decay,		53	Temple Ill	63
Repair a House gone to decay;		80	Vanbrug House	64
Repair a House gone to Decay,		107	V's House	38
Efficient of the Moon's Decay,		228	Prog of Beauty	90
The Tender Embryos half unknown decay,		667	Epig Carthy 5	D 4
DECAY'D				
His Fire is out, his Wit decay'd,		556	Death of Swift	101
To venture in a Ship decay'd?		703	Cadenus Vaness	533
Materials for an House decay'd.		727	To Stella	124
And thus, my Stock of Wit decay'd;		740	Stel B-day '21	17
In Ships decay'd no Mariner confides,		771	Horace 1, 14	47
Prudes decay'd about may tack,		863	To Janus	21
DECAYD				
And Mountague so far decayd,		311	To Ford	19
And though the Painting grows decayd		734	Stel B-day '20	7
DECAYS				
Besides, his Memory decays,		556	Death of Swift	85
As when a beauteous Nymph decays		756	Stel B-day '24	1
To your Decays adapts my Sight,		757	Stel B-day '24	44
Which can in spite of all Decays,		764	Stel B-day '26	11
DECEAS'D				
As Trophies of a Muse deceas'd:		611	By Dr. Swift	6
DECEIT				
How plain I see thro' the Deceit!		29	Ode to Temple	100
But find some new address, some fresh deceit,		44	To Congreve	17
"Stoop not to int'rest, flattery, or deceit;		55	Temple Ill	138
When Venus thought on a Deceit:		692	Cadenus Vaness	185
With much Deceit and little Wit;		695	Cadenus Vaness	291
DECEITFUL				
Deceitful Nymph I see thy Art,		121	Apollo Outwit	50
DECEIV'D				
But I'm deceiv'd, or thou regard'st me not;		53	Temple Ill	72
Deceiv'd thy self, instead of me;		695	Cadenus Vaness	293
DECEIVE				
And thus deceive the sharpest Eye:		607	Beasts Confess	194
E'er Stella can deceive a Friend.		725	To Stella	58
DECEIVERS				
Stale forms of course, all mean deceivers use,		44	To Congreve	20
DECEIVING				
Seduc'd by some deceiving Light,		412	Desire Possess	17
DECEMBER				
December in May.		1036	Plague Country	7
DECENCIES				
The thousand Decencies, that shone		384	Manly Virtue	27
DECENCY				
Fair Decency, celestial Maid,		590	Strephon Chloe	219
If Decency brings no Supplies,		591	Strephon Chloe	225
By Decency cemented round;		593	Strepnon Chloe	308
From whence that Decency of Mind,		691	Cadenus Vaness	164
Which Manners, Decency, and Pride,		730	Stella, Poems	99
DECENDS				
To whom from Midas down, decends		157	Fable of Midas	43
DECENT				
A Place not decent here to name.		108	V's House	94
Breeding, and Wit, and Air, and decent Pride;		118	Biddy Floyd	8
The Silver Virge, with decent Pride,		174	Horace 1, 7	99
Beneath thy decent Steps, the Road		324	Pethox	35
Direct that Women must be decent;		591	Strephon Chloe	252
The Goat advanc'd with decent Pace;		603	Beasts Confess	59
DECENTLY				
Decently hid beneath his Goun.		95	Bauc & Phil 1	176
What could he more, but decently retire?		196	Author Himself	74
Can act as decently as they.		204	In Sickness	18
DECIDE				
And both chose Midas to decide;		156	Fable of Midas	26
To decide of Wrong and Right?		638	Epistle Lady	270
Cou'd better now the Cause decide.		713	Cadenus Vaness	837
DECIDES				
How Solomon decides the Cause,		776	Mullinix Tim	98
DECIDING				
Shall leave deciding broken Pates,		760	Receipt Youth	47
DECISION				
All by my Lady's kind Decision.		478	Epist on Epist	100
DECISIVE				
Gives Judgment with decisive Air.		649	On Poetry	266
Answers in decisive way,		906	Daphne	13
DECK'D				
To see a Mortal Virgin deck'd		695	Cadenus Vaness	271
Like Flora, deck'd with fairest flowers;		937	Riddle 24	D 33
DECKT				
No Boat was better deckt than He.		286	Elegy Boat	42
DECLAIM'D				
"With what Impatience he declaim'd!		566	Death of Swift	346
DECLAR'D				
Declar'd in Council, Death must marry:		903	Death Daphne	10
DECLARE				
And, though I solemnly declare		202	Horace 2, 6	101
From me I declare you shall have no Denial,		336	Serious Poem	81

	PAGE	TITLE	LINE
DECLARE (CONTINUED)			
And our Marks of Things declare,	931	Riddle 18	D 6
DECLARES			
By a shrill Voice at noon declares,	94	Bauc & Phil 1	144
By a shrill Voice at Noon declares,	113	Bauc & Phil 2	82
As Aristophanes declares;	620	Scandal Poem 1	82
As Aristophanes declares:	626	Scandal Poem 2	80
She declares from her throne you must learn better manners	979	Dean to Tho: S	28
Will Hancock declares you are out of your compass,	1027	Sheri Circles	21
DECLIN'D			
To see her Empire thus declin'd,	690	Cadenus Vaness	129
Declin'd in Health, advanc'd in Years.	703	Cadenus Vaness	529
So little is thy Form declin'd	722	Stel B-Day '18	7
DECLINE			
The eager Muse took wing upon the Waves decline,	16	Ode Athenian	22
To see my Life so fast decline?	203	In Sickness	2
But much I fear he's in decline;	468	Birthday Song	256
I the lofty Stile decline.	637	Epistle Lady	218
DECLINES			
Cadenus with each Day declines,	703	Cadenus Vaness	537
But my Poetick Vein declines.	739	Stel B-day '21	10
Thy Fame, thy Genius now declines, proud Boaster.	1002	Reply by Dean	9
DECLINING			
Of a declining Church, by Faction her worse foe opprest,	40	Ode Sancroft	186
Of Vigor in declining Days.	295	Horrid Plot	154
"He spent his Life's declining Part;	570	Death of Swift	432
Much less could his declining Age	706	Cadenus Vaness	636
To shine through Life's declining Part.	764	Stel B-day '26	34
DECORUM			
"With Princes kept a due Decorum,	566	Death of Swift	339
Decorum than she did before;	588	Strephon Chloe	142
With Ladies what a strict Decorum!	888	Panegyr Dean	51
DECREASE			
The Burial Article decrease;	903	Death Daphne	8
DECREASING			
My school decreasing,	1037	Sheridan Cavan	5
DECREE			
The Dame full wisely did Decree,	153	Widow and Cat	D 16
Decree, that at exemplum Regis,	391	Young's Satire	24
Things were not ripe for a Decree,	689	Cadenus Vaness	105
Had been confirm'd by Fate's Decree;	694	Cadenus Vaness	258
But not prevent the Fates decree;	701	Cadenus Vaness	485
And, though by Heaven's severe Decree	726	To Stella	103
This Day, whate'er the Fates decree,	763	Stel B-day '26	1
Condemn'd by Fate's supreme Decree,	849	Old Thorn	47
Cease haughty Nymph; the Fates decree	905	Death Daphne	91
DECREED			
My hate, whose lash just heaven has long decreed	47	To Congreve	133
He against Phebus Harp decreed,	156	Fable of Midas	27
"For 'tis decreed by Jove and Fate,	304	Horrid Plot	38
But it was decreed by Fate---;	630	Epistle Lady	27
Decreed the Cause against the Men.	713	Cadenus Vaness	853
DECYPHER'D			
Was all decypher'd, and translated.	300	Horrid Plot	52
DEDICATIONS			
And Characters to Dedications:	484	Libel on D- D-	138
DEDUCTION'S			
Whether in time, deduction's broken chain	51	Temple Ill	3
DEDUCTIONS			
And therefore the Deductions nought,	695	Cadenus Vaness	281
DEE			
And as he pass'd, so swell'd the Dee	476	Epist on Epist	45
DEE'L			
He'll Bellow as loud as the Dee'l in a Drum:	336	Serious Poem	80
DEED			
"The <Devil> did the Deed, not they!	497	Panegyr Swift	135
Was Maid in Thought, and Word, and Deed,	588	Strephon Chloe	158
A Deed unknown to Female Race,	595	Cassinus Peter	69
DEEDS			
Of glorious Deeds, that must all Tongues Employ:	13	Ode to William	D 46
The Christian World his Deeds proclaim,	397	Earl of P-b-w	2
Men seldom by their Good Deeds rise:	495	Panegyr Swift	75
The blackest of all Female Deeds.	596	Cassinus Peter	106
DEEM'D			
"As it was deem'd in former Days	384	Manly Virtue	5
DEEP			
Has lull'd the Monster in a Deep	8	Ode to King	79
Long wandring thro the Deep, as we are told	17	Ode Athenian	46
Of Nature and of Art, of deep Philosophy and Love,	17	Ode Athenian	55
In that deep Grave a Book,	27	Ode to Temple	36
Which we call deep Design and Politicks	29	Ode to Temple	93
To dig the leaden Mines of deep Philosophy:	32	Ode to Temple	190
Beside all this, deep Scholars know,	66	Problem	21
From such deep Rudiments as these	87	Hist V's House	35
Here Five Foot deep lyes on his Back	101	Elegy Patrige	103
The Plot as yet lay deep, and so	108	V's House	85
The Smallcoal-Man was heard with Cadence deep,	124	Descriptn Morn	11
Carrots sown Thyn a deep root may get,	148	Windsor Proph	17
And hence a Critick deep maintains,	156	Fable of Midas	21
Deep sunk in Plenty, and Delight,	231	Prog of Poetry	23
The bold Encroachers on the Deep,	239	Run Bankers	1

DEEP	(CONTINUED)	PAGE	TITLE	LINE
The young Advent'rer o'er the Deep		252	Bubble	34
To search the Deep for Pearl and Coral.		254	Bubble	96
Here in the Deep to wash their Hands,		255	Bubble	110
A narrow Sound, though deep as Hell,		256	Bubble	139
The Monsters nestle in the Deep		257	Bubble	175
That Plague, Directors, to the Deep,		258	Bubble	207
The Mimickry of deep yet clear.		271	Apollo's Edict	D 49
But when the Sun goes to the Deep,		280	Journal	45
Through slipp'ry By-roads dark and deep,		412	Desire Possess	19
Beneath, a Chasm as deep as Hell,		413	Desire Possess	43
Or Grafton the deep		423	Carterets Arms	
But, they can smoak the deep Designs,		483	Libel on D- D-	101
"Those Secrets of the hoary deep!		528	Lady's Dres Rm	98
A Knave, who deep embroils his Lord's Affairs,		535	To Mr. Gay	119
Poultney deep, accomplish'd St. Johns,		635	Epistle Lady	175
Who sees the Ditch too deep and wide.		640	On Poetry	18
And deep transfix'd her Bosom too.		703	Cadenus Vaness	519
New Waves shall drive thee to the Deep again.		770	Horace 1, 14	10
And Tom for deep discerning;		785	Mullinex Dick	34
But where his deep law is, few mortals yet know:		815	Yahoo's	12
How deep and foul the Roads may grow,		860	Lady Acheson	19
Still rapt in speculations deep,		900	Dean's Reasons	45
Now Creep, Sweep, Sweep, Sweep the Deep,		960	Cantata	
DEEP-ROOTED				
Shall moving Delos now deep-rooted stand,		770	Horace 1, 14	3
DEEPER				
Climbs downwards, deeper by a Yard:		654	On Poetry	398
The deeper Politician.		785	Mullinex Dick	28
DEEPEST				
The deepest Tricks of Courtiers knew.		494	Panegyr Swift	38
DEEPLY				
"And, sure he must be deeply learn'd---!		547	Life of Swift	76
So deeply Carthy to the Center tends.		669	Epig Carthy 14	D 2
Tim, with his likeness deeply smitten,		783	Tim and Fables	25
His heart in poison deeply dipt,		951	Upstart	D 27
DEFAMES				
Censures less, or less defames?		631	Epistle Lady	68
DEFEAT				
Your Wisdom can with Ease Defeat.		340	Arch-Bish Dub	12
"The Dean did by his Pen defeat		569	Death of Swift	407
DEFEATED				
"And Foreign Foes defeated!		154	Widow and Cat	D 25
'Twas He defeated the Excise.		605	Beasts Confess	150
DEFECT				
With Cunning that Defect supplies,		107	V's House	57
"His Satyr points at no Defect,		571	Death of Swift	463
On ev'ry natural Defect;		592	Strephon Chloe	274
From Chance, or natural Defect		603	Beasts Confess	66
DEFECTS				
For those Defects he cannot mend;		217	To Mr. Delany	68
Supplying those defects by dress		879	Robbin & Harry	53
DEFENCE				
And tho' as some ('tis said) for their Defence		30	Ode to Temple	125
"Be this thy sure defence, thy brazen wall,		55	Temple Ill	141
To One who lives in its Defence,		339	Arch-Bish Dub	3
Said little in his own Defence:		377	Apology Lady C	74
And, in his client's just defence,		435	Answer Paulus	111
What Pamphlets in a Court's Defence		503	Doctor Delaney	103
But the Company stood in Defence of the Dame,		517	Dean Hang Rape	15
A Pamphlet in Sir Rob's Defence		646	On Poetry	187
Perverseness is your whole Defence:		730	Stella, Poems	92
When nothing's left, that's worth defence,		843	Epigr Irish	3
DEFEND				
That must their doubtful Liberty defend.		12	Ode to William	D 32
If he be innocent, defend him.		219	To Mr. Delany	112
That Man is ready to defend		243	Horace 4, 9	23
Against the Side she would defend:		417	Woman's Mind	52
And, to defend the Whiggish Cause,		417	Woman's Mind	55
Defend your liberties and laws.		487	Irish-Club	16
You never can defend his Breeding!		548	Life of Swift	102
To praise Queen Anne, nay more, defend her,		550	Life of Swift	186
Your gen'rous Boldness to defend		765	Stel B-day '26	43
DEFENDANT'S				
And takes the Plaintiff's and Defendant's Fees.		364	On Dreams	24
When the Defendant's Council rose,		687	Cadenus Vaness	22
DEFENDED				
"How oft have I defended?		154	Widow and Cat	D 27
DEFENDING				
And dy'd defending his opinion.		620	Scandal Poem 1	84
And dy'd defending his Opinion.		626	Scandal Poem 2	82
DEFENDS				
"But Heav'n his Innocence defends,		570	Death of Swift	425
DEFIANCE				
I had my Advantage, and stood at Defiance,		144	New Song	31
Poor Tom, wilt thou never accept a Defiance,		1019	To Sheridan	1
DEFILES				
But Gold defiles with frequent Touch,		158	Fable of Midas	67
DEFIN'D				
First then, our Author has defin'd		83	Salamander	29
Is well conceiv'd tho not defin'd;		215	To Mr. Delany	16

		PAGE	TITLE	LINE
DEFIN'D	(CONTINUED)			
But if Hell by Logical Rules be defin'd,	. . . . . .	575	Place Damn'd	3
DEFINE				
If Honour I would here define,	. . . .	723	To Stella	9
DEFLOWER'D				
No deflower'd eye can face the naked light:	. . . . .	41	Ode Sancroft	222
DEFY				
Your Influence do's the vain Attacks defy	. . . . .	13	Ode to William	D 43
You'll then defy the strongest Whig,	. . . .	191	Faggot	49
But, I defy the basest Tongue	. . . .	602	Beasts Confess	17
He dares defy both sense and wit.	. . . .	876	To Dean Swift	16
Thy Verse like Bricks, defy the Weather,	. . . . . .	1021	Nim-Dan-Dean 1	D 19
DEFY'D				
Combin'd in Arms, they had their Foes defy'd,	. . .	793	St. Pat's Well	81
DEFYES				
A Rat your utmost Rage defyes	. . . .	504	Doctor Delaney	137
DEGEN'RATE				
Beasts may degen'rate into Men.	. . . . . .	608	Beasts Confess	220
She knew in our degen'rate Days	. . . .	693	Cadenus Vaness	212
Ah! who in our degen'rate Days	. . . .	895	Panegyr Dean	287
DEGENERATE				
Degenerate from their ancient Brood,	. . . . . .	652	On Poetry	365
As you grew more degenerate and base,	. . . . .	792	St. Pat's Well	53
I scorn thy spurious and degenerate Line,	. . . . .	794	St. Pat's Well	101
DEGREE				
Well--tho' you've rais'd Her to this high Degree,	. .	24	Ode Athenian	263
What was his Name, of what Degree;	. . . .	171	Horace 1, 7	20
A serving-Man of low Degree:	. . . .	224	Prog of Love	54
And we order our Subjects, of every Degree,	. . . .	266	Apollo	99
To Wealth and Vice, in high Degree,	. . . . .	386	Manly Virtue	94
Of Courtiers, each in their Degree	. . . . . .	392	Young's Satire	29
To raise me to a high Degree:	. . . .	408	Dial Rich Marb	16
That Gods, of whatso'er Degree;	. . . .	694	Cadenus Vaness	259
What Lords and Dames of high Degree,	. . . . .	919	Riddle 5	15
DEGREES				
There are degrees above I know	. . . .	41	Ode Sancroft	231
Van is become by due Degrees	. . . .	87	Hist V's House	36
Grown to a Church by just Degrees,	. . . .	94	Bauc & Phil 1	154
Grown to a Church by just Degrees,	. . . .	114	Bauc & Phil 2	108
But by degrees when mounted high	. . . . . .	226	Prog of Beauty	5
Gain by Degrees huge Tracts of Land,	. . . . .	239	Run Bankers	2
With mean Degrees of Wit and Sense?	. . . . .	475	Epist on Epist	16
In Bulk there are not more Degrees,	. . . . .	653	On Poetry	383
Which thus fermenting, by Degrees	. . . .	731	Stella, Poems	129
DEIFI'D				
And Deifi'd in Verse;	. . . .	6	Ode to King	21
DEIGN				
Will deign your Livery to wear,	. . . .	325	Pethox	44
O, wou'd the Senate deign to show	. . . . . .	515	Answer Fable	81
DEIGNS				
The Bard, who humbly deigns to chuse	. . . . . .	887	Panegyr Dean	25
DEITIES				
Ador'd us Clouds as Deities;	. . . .	626	Scandal Poem 2	78
DEITY				
He own'd no Deity beside.	. . . .	303	Storm	14
To pacify this angry Deity;	. . . .	353	Wood Ironmongr	22
And as a Deity intrude,	. . . .	464	Birthday Song	145
Can such a Deity endure	. . . .	586	Strephon Chloe	89
No Vulgar Deity above	. . . .	598	Problem Solved	21
'Tis granted he believes a Deity.	. . . .	820	Dr. Rundle	24
DEITYES				
Ador'd the Clouds as Deityes.	. . . .	619	Scandal Poem 1	80
DEJECTED				
With a demure dejected Look.	. . . .	95	Bauc & Phil 1	172
But in a mild dejected Strain,	. . . .	704	Cadenus Vaness	572
DEL-VILLE				
On that poor Spot, call'd Del-Ville, yonder:	. . .	476	Epist on Epist	60
DELANY				
But a Comrade of yours, that Traytor Delany,	. . .	263	Apollo	25
Now who but Delany can write like Apollo?	. . .	265	Apollo	88
Since Delany has dar'd, like Prometheus his Sire,	. .	266	Apollo	95
Not Sheridan, but friend Delany.	. . . . . .	278	Journal	6
Delany sends a Silver Standish,	. . . .	611	By Dr. Swift	3
Unless Delany as my Heir,	. . . .	740	Stel B-day '21	19
Delany reports it, and he has a shrewd Tongue,	. .	967	Letter Sherid	1
Tho' Delany advis'd you to plague me no longer,	. .	967	Letter Sherid	7
The Devil and Delany;	. . . .	1005	Sheridan's Sub	22
With Delany or Dan I would scorn to combine	. . .	1017	Swift Ans Sher	8
. . . or foe, Delany;	. . . .	1023	Nim-Dan-Dean 2	D 7
And Friend <Delany> at his Books,	. . . . . .	756	Stel B-day '24	12
DELANY'S				
In thee Delany's spleen, John's mirth, Helsham's jokes,		1023	Nim-Dan-Dean 2	D 14
. . .				
DELAWERE				
Now, Delawere again familiar grows;	. . . . . .	196	Author Himself	67
DELAY				
Like prudent Fabius by Delay.	. . . .	656	On Poetry	446
What Venus meant by this Delay.	. . . .	690	Cadenus Vaness	127
DELAY'D				
Too long I have my Thanks delay'd;	. . . . . .	887	Panegyr Dean	3

DELAYING
   . . . .for I know there's no delaying ye. . . . . . .   PAGE   TITLE   LINE
    1023 Nim-Dan-Dean 2   D   8
DELAYS
    He sav'd his Country by Delays, ...   28 Ode to Temple   71
    by Sneaking Sniv'ling Round Delays. . . . . . .   958 Cantata
DELENDA
    That I'll ne'er give my vote for Delenda Cart-ago. .   979 Dean to Tho: S   18
DELF
    Five Nothings in five Plates of Delf. . . . . . .   747 Stel Distress   52
DELICATE
    And I'll give you these delicate Bits: . . . . . .   395 Dog and Thief   2
    Your delicate Bits will not serve me a Meal, ...   395 Dog and Thief   5
    Here's delicate Onyons to sell, ...   952 Onyons   2
    You hit it, you say,--you're a delicate hitter. . . .   977 Dean to Sherid   40
DELIGHT
    But the Delight of Doing Good . . . .   6 Ode to King   19
    With true Delight observed them all . . . .   87 Hist V's House   17
    That gives Surprise, and this Delight: . . . . . .   215 To Mr. Delany   24
    Deep sunk in Plenty, and Delight, ...   231 Prog of Poetry   23
    With what Delight, methinks, I trace . . . . . .   325 Pethox   69
    I wak'd with Delight, and not without Hope, ...   338 Serious Poem   115
    Then what a huge Delight were all in, ...   353 Wood Ironmongr   25
    With new Delight looks up and loves; . . . . . .   387 Manly Virtue   128
    Could give him more Delight. . . . . . .   395 Grub-Street   16
    And strangers delight to walk round 'em: . . . . .   403 Window Inns 9   D   3
    Their verses give delight . . . .   429 Beau's Reply   11
    Resolv'd for a Fortnight to Swim in Delight, ...   517 Dean Hang Rape   26
    St. George beheld thee with Delight, ...   656 On Poetry   461
    That innocent Delight he took . . . . . .   704 Cadenus Vaness   550
    In Learning let a Nymph delight, ...   710 Cadenus Vaness   742
    A constant, rational Delight, ...   711 Cadenus Vaness   781
    How would Ingratitude delight? . . . .   726 To Stella   93
    With Vigour and Delight perform'd. . . . . . .   726 To Stella   108
    So, at a Ball, unthinking Fools delight . . . . .   771 Horace 1, 14   49
    The Tories! you are their Delight. . . . . . .   776 Mullinix Tim   88
    Would come and listen with Delight, ...   848 Old Thorn   11
    I sat with delight, ...   852 Lady's Lament   17
    No book for delight . . . .   855 Lady's Lament   145
    Can you take Delight in viewing . . . . . .   862 To Janus   13
    Should in a country life delight, ...   901 Dean's Reasons   82
    Makes her sole delight to vex. . . . . . .   906 Daphne   4
    To dispute, her chief delight, ...   906 Daphne   9
    Nature to form me took Delight, ...   915 Riddle 1   3
    And my Delight is to expose . . . .   915 Riddle 1   25
    Of Mortals, and the Gods Delight. . . . . . .   916 Riddle 2   12
    Wherein the Men of Wit delight. . . . . . .   920 Riddle 6   6
    You cure with Ease and with Delight; . . . . .   924 Riddle 8   14
    But all I delight in is Pieces of Lead; . . . . .   927 Riddle 11   D   6
    Affirm, can't glow to more Delight. . . . . . .   932 Riddle 19   D   10
    The Delight of old and young, ...   933 Riddle 20   D   3
    The dullest Beast, and Swine's Delight . . . . .   940 Letter   3
    As eels delight to creep in mud, ...   950 Upstart   D   7
DELIGHTFUL
    On the delightful Strand, ...   17 Ode Athenian   37
    That this New, Noble, and Delightful Scene . . . .   20 Ode Athenian   136
    No more my dear Delightful way tread, ...   779 Mullinix Tim   183
    This is flatt'ring, and delightful; . . . .   907 Daphne   46
DELIGHTS
    Shew the Delights thy Sister Nature yields, ...   31 Ode to Temple   137
    Or how the Dean delights to vex . . . .   281 Journal   77
    For, though the Muse delights in Fiction, ...   503 Doctor Delaney   105
    Adieu to ravishing Delights, ...   590 Strephon Chloe   197
    When Miss delights in her Spinnet, ...   710 Cadenus Vaness   736
    Wherein the God of Earth delights. . . . . . .   743 Stel B-day 22   52
    His blood delights in mud to run; . . . .   950 Upstart   D   9
DELINQUENT
    Except to lash some grand Delinquent. . . . . .   190 Faggot   30
DELIVER'D
    Van was deliver'd of a Play, ...   81 Vanbrug House   74
    The Moon, deliver'd from her Pain, ...   354 Simile Silver   13
DELIVERS
    Delivers Cards about, ...   74 Game Traffick   2
DELOS
    Fam'd Delos did of old, ...   17 Ode Athenian   47
    Shall moving Delos now deep-rooted stand, ...   770 Horace 1, 14   3
DELPH
    Five Nothings in five Plates of Delph. . . . . .   751 Stel Wood-Park   68
DELPHICK
    Doubts, where the Delphick God . . . . . .   22 Ode Athenian   208
DELUDE
    Delude at once and Bless our Sight, ...   228 Prog of Beauty   70
    And with false flitting Shades our Minds delude, . .   363 On Dreams   2
DELUDED   SEE LONG-DELUDED
    All their false deluded Hopes, ...   168 Peace Dunkirk   8
    Thus the deluded Bankrupt raves, ...   251 Bubble   21
    Deluded Mortals, whom the Great . . . . . .   480 Libel on D- D-   1
    To keep her Spouse deluded still, ...   588 Strephon Chloe   143
DELUDES
    Thus every Fool her self deludes; . . . .   449 Modern Lady   154
DELUDING
    Thus the deluding Muse oft blinds me to her Ways, . .   23 Ode Athenian   234

		PAGE	TITLE	LINE

DELUGE
As when the Deluge first began to fall, ... 16 Ode Athenian 1
Threat'ning with Deluge this Devoted Town. . . . . . 138 City Shower 32
DELUSION
Such high companions may delusion keep, ... 48 To Congreve 149
Is all the poor content delusion finds.-- . . . . 55 Temple Ill 150
Thus with a puff the whole delusion ends. . . . . . 55 Temple Ill 154
DELUSIONS
Those who by wild delusion's entertain . . . . 45 To Congreve 77
Such gross Delusions could not pass, ... 158 Fable of Midas 65
DEMAND
When Creditors demand their Due; . . . . 240 Run Bankers 38
Demand a Croun a Quart for Stumm. . . . . 313 To Ford 68
"No Vermin can demand fair Play, ... 548 Life of Swift 126
DEMANDING
Must I make myself hoarse with demanding an Answer? . 1019 To Sheridan 4
DEMANDS
Dues, Payments, Fees, Demands and Cheats, ... 174 Horace 1, 7 104
Demands him in an higher Sphere; . . . . 387 Manly Virtue 112
While not a Soul demands your Ware? . . . . 641 On Poetry 44
The quarterly demands of nurses, ... 676 Parson's Case 14
Who, 'ere t' other gets up, demands the rising Blow. . 967 Letter Sherid 14
DEMAR
By Mortgage hath secur'd the Corps of Demar; . . . 233 Elegy on Demar 2
Demar the Wealthy, and the Wise. . . . . 235 Elegy on Demar 42
DEMEAN
Demean himself the Wedding-Night: . . . . 586 Strephon Chloe 74
Nor can Hyperbole's demean us, ... 622 Scandal Poem 1 155
Nor can Hyperboles demean us; . . . . 628 Scandal Poem 2 159
DEMOLISH
I'll tear all your Rules, and demolish your Pun Talk: 1019 To Sheridan 8
DEMOLISH'D
Which you demolish'd to the Ground: . . . . . . 477 Epist on Epist 68
DEMONIACS
These Demoniacs let me dub . . . . 829 Legion Club 11
DEMONSTRATE
And, further to demonstrate his Affection, ... 825 Noisy Tom 3
DEMONSTRATION
And thus by demonstration show, ... 434 Answer Paulus 69
DEMUR
Your Scholars want the whip,--I shan't demur;-- . . 671 Epig Carthy 23 D 1
Demur, Imparlance, and Essoign, ... 690 Cadenus Vaness 122
DEMURE
With a demure dejected Look. . . . . 95 Bauc & Phil 1 172
Pickt the Demure, the Aukward, and the Coy; . . . 118 Biddy Floyd 6
Dame Juno brought a Priest demure. . . . . . . 586 Strephon Chloe 64
DEN
Crawls back neglected to his Den. . . . . 84 Salamander 36
For Daniel was got from the Den of the Lions: . . . 144 New Song 32
There Cerberus lay watching in his Den, ... 538 Mr. Pulteney 25
A <Parliament>, or Den of Thieves. . . . . . . 645 On Poetry 164
While the Den of Thieves is full, ... 830 Legion Club 28
DENIAL
Howe'er she gave no flat Denial, ... 120 Apollo Outwit 25
From me I declare you shall have no Denial, ... 336 Serious Poem 81
DENIALS
That for twenty Denials you would not give out. . . . 869 Grand Question 56
DENIED
Tho' if he durst, he had denied. . . . . 378 Apology Lady C 96
DENIES
"And since unhappy distance thus denies . . . . . 55 Temple Ill 143
'Tis very true, and none denies, ... 433 Answer Paulus 39
DENNIS
Wise Dennis, and profound Bossu. . . . . 648 On Poetry 250
Dennis was out, and I got hither safe; . . . . . . 881 Pastoral Dial 31
The valiant Dennis you must fix on, ... 885 Rev Market-Hill 85
You, next to Dennis bear the Sway: . . . . 889 Panegyr Dean 89
With Dennis you did ne'er combine, ... 890 Panegyr Dean 97
Teach Dennis how to stir the Guile: . . . . 897 Panegyr Dean 330
And with Tom <D'urfey>, <Phillips>, <Dennis>, . . . 184 Horace 2, 1 115
DENOTES
And so a perjur'd Dog denotes . . . . 298 Horrid Plot 9
Thus think on Kings, ye Name denotes . . . . . . 659 On Poetry D 410
DENY
And yet deny the Cause. . . . . 19 Ode Athenian 110
And straight deny you to be Men, or any thing at all; . 19 Ode Athenian 120
"I'll dye, if you deny your Help. . . . . 207 Fable Bitches 12
Then can you deny it is Love in a Wood? . . . . . 337 Serious Poem 100
But if by Chance I should deny it . . . . 372 Letter D. S-y 19
Nor Pope wou'd dare deny him Wit, ... 484 Libel on D- D- 143
Deny their Country like a Scot: . . . . 652 On Poetry 360
Deny them Protestants--thou ly'st. . . . . 658 On Poetry D 190
And if the Muse deny her Aid . . . . 757 Stel B-day '24 33
I flatly deny it: . . . . 939 Riddle Answerd 8
. . .to make the Offer; and they cannot deny it. . . 1014 Swift to Sheri 8
DENY'D
'Tis not deny'd that when we write, ... 463 Birthday Song 107
Your Parts are good, 'tis not deny'd, ... 779 Mullinix Tim 209
And at the Gallows all deny'd; . . . . 781 Mullinix Tim 274
DEPART
Grief from Dorinda's face does ne'er depart . . . . 53 Temple Ill 53

		PAGE	TITLE	LINE
DEPARTED				
And drive departed Souls to Styx.		133	Magician's Rod	38
Came early, and departed late:		173	Horace 1, 7	79
Departed; and his Works must follow:		562	Death of Swift	250
In praise of long departed Wit,		611	By Dr. Swift	8
Whether some late departed Toasts		905	Death Daphne	75
DEPARTING				
"Now the departing Prayer is read:		558	Death of Swift	149
DEPARTS				
Poor <Swift> departs, and, what is worse,		173	Horace 1, 7	93
DEPARTURE				
Says not a Word of his Departure		860	Lady Acheson	11
DEPEND				
An Arm on which all Europe's Hopes depend,		12	Ode to William	D 30
Nor does thy essence fix'd depend on giddy circumstance		34	Ode Sancroft	7
They say, all human Things depend:		345	Prometheus	34
On whom my fears and hopes depend		420	Holyhead	24
"Depend upon't, I never will.		446	Modern Lady	53
Nor need depend upon his Pen---.		548	Life of Swift	100
Depend upon't their Judgment's right:		644	On Poetry	134
They on no Accidents depend:		730	Stella, Poems	80
. . . depend on't, in the end, he'll sham ye.		1023	Nim-Dan-Dean 2	D 10
DEPENDED				
"On which alone, our Weal depended.		568	Death of Swift	378
DEPENDENT				
But a wild form dependent on the brain,		54	Temple Ill	95
Both Church and State, being still dependent.		372	Letter D. S-y	22
DEPENDER				
I'm but a Meer Depender still:		918	Riddle 4	20
DEPENDS				
And since thy essence on my breath depends,		55	Temple Ill	153
While Rain depends, the pensive Cat gives o'er		136	City Shower	3
Harly depends upon your skill,		140	Harlyes Surgn	3
Henceforth depends alone on me.		776	Mullinix Tim	82
DEPONENTS				
Nor further those Deponents knew:		688	Cadenus Vaness	72
DEPOS'D				
Depos'd from off his Seat		26	Ode to Temple	3
My Sister has lately depos'd upon Oath,		264	Apollo	37
DEPOSE				
Was able Saturn to depose;		461	Birthday Song	24
Who shall depose it upon Oath.)		647	On Poetry	230
Who fairly could on Oath depose,		688	Cadenus Vaness	69
DEPOSITED				
Here lye deposited the Spoils		921	Riddle 7	13
DEPRAVITY				
(That Epidemick Error and Depravity		20	Ode Athenian	139
DEPRESS				
True Poets can depress and raise;		729	Stella, Poems	53
DEPRIV'D				
And we of all our Hopes depriv'd;		885	Rev Market-Hill	61
Depriv'd of Root, and Branch, and Rind,		926	Riddle 9	1
DEPTH				
Now bury'd in the Depth below,		256	Bubble	149
Tho' now your Depth must not be Sounded,		478	Epist on Epist	109
For, tho' in Nature Depth and Height		653	On Poetry	389
DERISION				
The Wealthy have you in Derision.		641	On Poetry	50
DERIVES				
That Princes wear derives from them;		98	Elegy Patrige	26
DERMOT				
A Nymph and Swain, Sheelah and Dermot hight,		880	Pastoral Dial	1
My Love for gentle Dermot faster grows		881	Pastoral Dial	13
Dermot, I vow, 'tis nothing else but Sweat.		881	Pastoral Dial	24
Dermot, how could you touch those nasty Sluts!		882	Pastoral Dial	39
Dermot, I swear, tho' Tady's Locks could hold		882	Pastoral Dial	45
Whether with Dermot, or His Grace:		890	Panegyr Dean	122
DERN				
My broken Hose to patch and dern.		890	Panegyr Dean	112
DERRY				
or with a down a high down derry,		957	Cantata	
DESCANT				
For Princes love you should descant		464	Birthday Song	127
DESCEND				
When Rains descend, and Tempests rise,		84	Salamander	34
May you Descend to take Renown,		121	Apollo Outwit	62
From Airy Garrets some descend,		279	Journal	29
You from the Neighb'ring Gaul descend;		324	Pethox	20
Descend from Heav'n to Beauty's Aid;		590	Strephon Chloe	220
An equal Priv'lege to descend.		653	On Poetry	382
Mount alive, and dead descend		801	Traulus 2	52
While I from Drapier's-Mount descend,		884	Rev Market-Hill	49
DESCENDED				
Descended from her sphere to find		179	To Lord Harley	79
Descended, ready cut and dry:		591	Strephon Chloe	230
From us descended ab origine,		619	Scandal Poem 1	61
From us descended ab origine,		625	Scandal Poem 2	57
Her Sons descended from the British Line;		771	Horace 1, 14	42
DESCENDENTS				
Descendents of the barbarous Huns,		326	Pethox	75

```
                                                           PAGE   TITLE            LINE
DESCENDING
   In this descending sheet you'll haply find      . . . . .    50 To Congreve       231
   Descending to her Charge's aid,            . . . . . . .     177 To Lord Harley     44
   And then, descending from the skies,        . . . . . .     178 To Lord Harley     62
   Descending lately from the Skies,          . . . . . . .    302 Storm               2
   Should but his Muse descending drop       . . . . . . .     728 Stella, Poems      29
DESCENDS
   Thus Venus to the Sea descends           . . . . . . . .     254 Bubble             93
   An equal Pow'r descends to thee.)         . . . . . . .     323 Pethox             10
   Descends for Shelter to the Shades below.   . . . . . .     538 Mr. Pulteney       24
   Or whether he at last descends           . . . . . . . .     712 Cadenus Vaness    822
   For she never descends so low as the cellar;  . . . .       979 Dean to Tho: S     26
DESCENT
   Thence, thro' a long Descent of Kings,      . . . . . . .    134 Magician's Rod     63
   The high Descent from whence you came,      . . . . . .     323 Pethox             12
   That thy Descent is from the British Oak:    . . . . .      771 Horace 1, 14       38
DESCRIB'D
   She thought he had himself describ'd,       . . . . . . .    708 Cadenus Vaness    678
DESCRIBE
   You that would grief describe, come here and trace  . .      52 Temple Ill         51
   Would you describe Turenne or Trump         . . . . . .      83 Salamander         19
   And now the Heraldry describe            . . . . . . . .      93 Bauc & Phil 1     123
   And nigh in Order plac'd, describe         . . . . . .      114 Bauc & Phil 2      99
   A Circle with their Rod describe,          . . . . . .      134 Magician's Rod     50
   Of Logick-mongers can describe;           . . . . . . .     215 To Mr. Delany      20
   Describe his Fall into the Main,          . . . . . . .     252 Bubble             43
   When you describe a lovely Girl,          . . . . . . .     272 Apollo's Edict  D  54
   'Tis needless to describe him fuller.       . . . . . .     286 Elegy Boat         43
   Describe the Lady and the Man.           . . . . . . .     450 Modern Lady       195
   And must you needs describe the Chest?      . . . . .       527 Lady's Dres Rm     70
   But, how can I describe the rav'nous Breed?   . . . .       534 To Mr. Gay         83
   But how shall I describe her Arts          . . . . . .     583 Young Nymph        67
   Of tedious Moralists describe,           . . . . . . .      724 To Stella          16
   Let her describe a Circle round          . . . . . . .      743 Stel B-day 22      55
   Old Latimer preaching did fairly describe    . . . . .     803 Irish Bishops       1
   Draw the Beasts as I describe 'em,        . . . . . . .     839 Legion Club       225
DESCRIBES
   And what She describes to be Merit is Treason:   . . .      716 Answer Rebus       22
DESCRIBING
   Scholars, when good Sense describing,       . . . . . .     633 Epistle Lady      115
DESCRIPTION
   And by a faint Description make them less.    . . . . .      21 Ode Athenian      174
   Description would but tire my Muse:        . . . . . .     116 Bauc & Phil 2     163
   Tho' this Description looks so big,        . . . . . . .    134 Magician's Rod     65
   And by the Description I certainly know,     . . . . .     264 Apollo             43
   All Women his Description fits,           . . . . . . .     529 Lady's Dres Rm    125
   To give us a Description graphick         . . . . . . .     993 On Picture          2
DESCRIPTIONS
   Nor ever since but in Descriptions found,    . . . . .      26 Ode to Temple      14
   Descriptions tedious, flat and dry,        . . . . . .     645 On Poetry         155
   And as our Sects, by all Descriptions,      . . . . .      813 Brd Protestant     51
DESCRY
   Although 'tis easy to descry            . . . . . . . . .    754 Stella '23         15
DESERT
   By Favour, or Desert preferr'd          . . . . . . . .      66 Problem            25
   Your Goodness more than my Desert         . . . . . . .      94 Bauc & Phil 1     159
   Their Goodness, more than his Desert---.     . . . . .     547 Life of Swift      87
   And shou'd Want or Desert stand in need of his Aid,  .     717 Answer Rebus       27
DESERTS
   To seek, in deserts, Fields Elysian?       . . . . . .     899 Dean's Reasons     16
DESERV'D
   That he alone deserv'd Esteem,          . . . . . . . .     386 Manly Virtue       75
DESERVE
   At once deserve a Crown, and gain it too.    . . . . .      12 Ode to William   D 16
   Why then, old Plays deserve old Bricks,     . . . . .      108 V's House          72
   Which all deserve and all improve.        . . . . . .      322 First of April     36
   "Because no Age could more deserve it.      . . . . .      571 Death of Swift    458
   Such Jacobites as he deserve,--         . . . . . . .      783 Tim and Fables     33
DESERVES
   The Way is thus; and well deserves your Thanks:  . .       285 Elegy Boat         31
   Deserves your Satire's keenest Rage;       . . . . . .     392 Young's Satire     34
   Deserves an Earl,               . . . . . . . . .         442 Ballyspellin       62
   Deserves a good Cud-gelling           . . . . . . . .     442 Ballyspellin       81
   And well deserves the Nation's Thanks.      . . . . .     515 Answer Fable       80
   But, sure the Dean deserves a sharp Rebuke    . . . .     678 Dean and Duke       3
   And either he deserves Disdain,          . . . . . . .     733 Verses Vanessa     15
DESERVING
   The least deserving of the Pack;         . . . . . . .     503 Doctor Delaney     86
   She loves a more deserving Swain.         . . . . . . .    595 Cassinus Peter     66
   And, from deserving friends, with-hold      . . . . .     900 Dean's Reasons     35
DESHABILLE
   To see the Girl in Deshabille.          . . . . . . .     698 Cadenus Vaness    367
DESIGN
   When Schonberg started at the Vast Design:    . . . .      12 Ode to William   D 34
   Which we call deep Design and Politicks     . . . . .      29 Ode to Temple      93
   One end in both, and the design the same;    . . . . .      42 Ode Sancroft      256
   'Tis with a foul design the muse you send,    . . . . .     44 To Congreve        15
   Nor tax the goddess of a mean design       . . . . . .      44 To Congreve        33
   To learn what Northern Kings design,       . . . . . .      63 Discovery          29
   . . .I design to be a Parson's Wife,       . . . . . .      72 Mrs Harris Pet     60
   Some part of what I here design          . . . . . . .     218 To Mr. Delany      89
```

DESIGN   (CONTINUED)   PAGE   TITLE   LINE
        And disappoint the sole Design, ...   481 Libel on D- D-   31
        Venus wou'd fail in her Design: . . . .   695 Cadenus Vaness   277
        Tho' her Design was not obtain'd, ...   713 Cadenus Vaness   834
        On so mean a Design, and a Subject so low.   . . .   716 Answer Rebus   4
        For mean's her Design, and her Subject as mean, . .   716 Answer Rebus   5
        But, that is with a good Design, ...   890 Panegyr Dean   101
        I never robb'd thee with Design: . . . .   896 Panegyr Dean   316
        Alas, Sir, I had no Design, ...   1005 Sheridan's Sub   17
        I know they have many a wicked Design . . . . . .   1017 Swift Ans Sher   9
DESIGN'D
        This Surly, Slipp'ry God, when He design'd   . . .   22 Ode Athenian   197
        This beauteous Queen by Heaven design'd   . . . .   22 Ode Athenian   216
        This off'ring long design'd to Congreve's fame; . . .   44 To Congreve   24
        My Lord--The Honour you design'd--   . . . . . .   173 Horace 1, 7   67
        As Thorns were design'd to be from the Creation.   334 Serious Poem   30
        Virtue was of this Sex design'd, ...   384 Manly Virtue   23
        Now Backs of Letters, though design'd . . . .   406 Swift to Pope   9
        These Stories were, of old, design'd   . . . . . .   478 Epist on Epist   83
        "Tis plain, his Writings were design'd   . . . . . .   550 Life of Swift   196
        "As with a moral View design'd   . . . .   565 Death of Swift   313
        Wherein the Moralist design'd   . . . .   608 Beasts Confess   217
        But, Woman was by Fate design'd   . . . .   624 Scandal Poem 2   29
        By flatt'ring <Kings> whom Heaven design'd   . . .   654 On Poetry   407
        That common Forms were not design'd   . . . .   706 Cadenus Vaness   612
        "A Model for her Sex design'd, ...   714 Cadenus Vaness   866
        She thinks that Nature ne'er design'd . . . .   725 To Stella   65
        His Med'cine work as he design'd . . . .   746 Stel Distress   32
        His Malice work as he design'd: . . . .   750 Stel Wood-Park   24
        For whom, by Birth, I was design'd   . . . .   782 Mullinix Tim   281
        Where friendship is by Fate design'd, ...   901 Dean's Reasons   69
DESIGNED
        This Building was designed a Model, ...   127 Little House   36
DESIGNING
        Who, with less designing Ends, ...   632 Epistle Lady   79
DESIGNS
        The Thoughts of Monarchs, and Designs of States, . .   30 Ode to Temple   105
        But, they can smoak the deep Designs, ...   483 Libel on D- D-   101
        No more of Jove's Designs than you)   . . . . . .   579 Day Judgement   18
        Absurdly bends his whole Designs. . . . .   641 On Poetry   24
        The Science she designs to teach: . . . . . .   712 Cadenus Vaness   811
        The last Result of all Designs: . . . .   921 Riddle 7   12
DESIR'D
        The holy Men desir'd their Host   . . . .   94 Bauc & Phil 1   155
        The Hermits then desir'd their Host   . . . . . .   115 Bauc & Phil 2   109
        Desir'd them not to talk so loud, ...   689 Cadenus Vaness   77
DESIRE
        But disappointed of his fond Desire   . . . .   22 Ode Athenian   195
        The muse and I no more revenge desire, ...   37 Ode Sancroft   90
        . . .I desire your Excellencies Protection, ...   73 Mrs Harris Pet   70
        What e're she would desire, to Grant, ...   120 Apollo Outwit   19
        Said Harley, I desire to know   . . . .   172 Horace 1, 7   47
        What I desire the World should know.   . . . . . .   200 Horace 2, 6   42
        "And now I earnestly desire, ...   208 Fable Bitches   27
        You raise Desire as well as Pride, ...   292 Prog Marriage   74
        Nor less the other to desire;   . . . .   387 Manly Virtue   130
        In Man, Possession, and Desire;   . . . .   411 Desire Possess   2
        Possession, and Desire, his Brother, ...   412 Desire Possess   9
        Desire, the swifter of the two, ...   412 Desire Possess   21
        Desire had now the Goal in Sight: . . . .   413 Desire Possess   39
        Desire, in Rapture gaz'd a while, ...   413 Desire Possess   45
        Though Beauty may beget Desire, ...   590 Strephon Chloe   221
        As it hath long been his Desire, ...   606 Beasts Confess   172
        Did ever we desire his Aid: . . . .   657 On Poetry   492
        With no desire to pray or preach; . . . .   677 Parson's Case   32
        And only know the gross Desire;   . . . .   687 Cadenus Vaness   36
        You have done what I desire: . . . .   839 Legion Club   232
        All prompted by the same Desire, ...   922 Riddle 7   25
        Is sent to desire that, when your August vacation comes, 1022 Nim-Dan-Dean 2   D 2
          . . .
        I had forgot to desire you to bring down what I say you 1023 Nim-Dan-Dean 2   D 15
          have,. . .
DESIRES
        Were my desires but heighten'd to my pow'r. . . . . .   44 To Congreve   40
        Desires some Friend to lend a Hand   . . . .   160 Atlas   8
        Her Spouse desires his Coffee soon, ...   291 Prog Marriage   37
        The same Aversions, and Desires; . . . .   546 Life of Swift   44
        The utmost her Desires will reach, ...   709 Cadenus Vaness   706
        Desires me singly   . . . .   1014 Swift to Sheri   30
DESIRING
        Desiring I would stand their Friend.   . . . . . .   200 Horace 2, 6   46
DESK
        Hear from my desk the words that follow; . . . . .   490 Dialogue   48
DESOLATION
        Still scatt'ring desolation where they go. . . . .   55 Temple Ill   130
DESP'RATE
        Puts all upon a desp'rate Bett, ...   251 Bubble   22
        A strong Dilemma in a desp'rate Case! . . . . . .   535 To Mr. Gay   129
        She'll tear me with her desp'rate Nails; . . . . .   925 Riddle 8   20
DESPAIR
        Despair and he lodge ever in its stead;   . . . . .   55 Temple Ill   128

	PAGE	TITLE	LINE
DESPAIR (CONTINUED)			
"Of Reprobation and Despair:	305	Storm	60
"He left the Court in meer Despair.	567	Death of Swift	370
"With Horror, Grief, Despair the Dean	568	Death of Swift	391
Then, leave me to despair and dye.	595	Cassinus Peter	72
Yet, through Despair, of God and Man accurst,	806	Judas	7
Causeless Joy, and true Despair;	832	Legion Club	90
DESPAIRING			
Despairing Wretches from the Grave;	764	Stel B-day '26	38
DESPERATE			
And so went to Bed in a desperate Case.	77	Lady B- B-	7
At Whist they will make a desperate Sweep.	943	Probatur Alit	32
DESPIS'D			
Despis'd luxurious Wines, and costly Meat;	194	Author Himself	15
Despis'd the Beast with many Heads,	498	Panegyr Swift	161
"Despis'd the Fools with Stars and Garters,	565	Death of Swift	323
Surer ways to be despis'd:	906	Daphne	6
DESPISE			
May'st thou despise a Poets Name.	121	Apollo Outwit	56
And teach her to despise thee more	292	Prog Marriage	76
And some thought modish to despise.	384	Manly Virtue	30
Nor will in you those Gifts despise,	484	Libel on D- D-	115
Bravely despise Champagne at Court,	488	Irish-Club	19
To value that which Men despise.	689	Cadenus Vaness	84
That I can vulgar Forms despise,	706	Cadenus Vaness	616
Which he had taught her to despise.	711	Cadenus Vaness	797
That vulgar Talent I despise	787	Dick's Variety	5
Thy martial Sons, whom now they dare despise,	790	St. Pat's Well	13
I now despise Fatigue and Hardship:	890	Panegyr Dean	108
Heav'n forbid he should despise thee;	907	Daphne	51
Ah, Strephon, how can you despise	924	Riddle 8	1
I despise any poet that truckled to Dan.	976	Dean to Sherid	34
DESPISES			
Despises rapparees, and rides	435	Answer Paulus	97
Tho' his soul he despises, he values his hide:	817	Yahoo's	72
Despises exercise and air.	901	Dean's Reasons	90
A Friend of mine, that Author despises	988	Letter Dr Sh-n	21
DESPISING			
Despising Slaves that cringe for Bread.	483	Libel on D- D-	88
His Station despising, unaw'd by the Place,	809	Epigr Prelate	3
DESPONDING			
Triumphant Tories, and desponding Whigs,	138	City Shower	41
Desponding Phillis was endu'd	222	Prog of Love	1
DESPONDS			
A baited Banker thus desponds,	241	Run Bankers	49
DESPOTICK			
The <Queen> (forsooth, Despotick) gave	181	Horace 2, 1	25
DESTIN'D			
Now destin'd, by the Powers divine,	272	Apollo's Edict	D 68
That <Hort> was destin'd to a Rope,	306	Storm	74
Is destin'd to beat out his Brains.	500	Doctor Delaney	16
Bridles destin'd far to roam,	573	Helter Skelter	15
Thus all are destin'd to obey	659	On Poetry	D 410
The Snow-ball destin'd at thy Chops;	779	Mullinix Tim	204
DESTROY			
"So, to destroy a guilty Land,	485	Libel on D- D-	165
To destroy the old Foundation,	801	Traulus 2	48
Quite destroy that Harpies Nest,	830	Legion Club	29
And with relentless Hands destroy	925	Riddle 8	21
DESTROY'D			
"That Ireland must be soon destroy'd,	304	Storm	39
"Was all destroy'd by one Event.	568	Death of Swift	376
(For Satire had destroy'd his little fame,)	671	Epig Carthy 24	D 2
DESTROYING			
And, lo! where a Destroying Angel stands,	7	Ode to King	48
All devouring, all destroying,	930	Riddle 16	D 2
DESTROYS			
A Wolf destroys a thousand Lambs.	651	On Poetry	326
DESTRUCTIVE SEE DYSTRUCTIVE			
"Destructive to the Church and King:	550	Life of Swift	173
"Beheld the dire destructive Scene:	568	Death of Swift	392
"An infamous destructive Cheat.	569	Death of Swift	408
DETAINED			
Be here detained against my will?	403	Window Inns 10	D 2
DETERMIN'D			
"And seem'd determin'd not to starve it,	571	Death of Swift	457
DETERMINE			
For Law and Gospel both determine	647	On Poetry	227
Which made our Swarm of Sects determine	813	Bro Protestant	43
DETERMINES			
She still determines what is best:	725	To Stella	60
DETEST			
Have I not Reason to detest 'em?	555	Death of Swift	66
How did the humbled Swain detest	586	Strephon Chloe	91
DETESTATION			
The Detestation you express	765	Stel B-day '26	47
So thou art grown the Detestation	775	Mullinix Tim	55
DETESTING			
Detesting all the Statesmen kind,	482	Libel on D- D-	72
DETH			
Here in Beau-spelling (tru tel deth)	60	Lady Tablebook	9

DETRACTING

	PAGE	TITLE	LINE
On what detracting People say?	414	Censure	18
Made use of by detracting foes.	433	Answer Paulus	50

DETRACTION

To leave one handle for Detraction.	608	Know Not What	8

DETRACTOR

And, for her sake turn base detractor	622	Scandal Poem 1	171

DETRACTORS

Detractors with an evil Tongue,	83	Salamander	24
Away the fair Detractors went,	699	Cadenus Vaness	408
In me, Detractors seek to find	918	Riddle 4	23

DEUCALION

Deucalion, to restore Mankind	922	Riddle 7	45

DEUCE

Deuce is in you, Mr. Dean;	635	Epistle Lady	181

DEUM

Went triumphant to Church, and sang stoutly Te Deum:	967	Letter Sherid	18

DEV'L

See here again the Dev'l to do;	223	Prog of Love	39
In this the Dev'l and you agree;	401	Window Inns 2	4
From Hell a <Viceroy> Dev'l ascends,	486	Libel on D- D-	186
In Scripture, to the Dev'l assign'd:	798	Traulus 1	76
I'll make the Dev'l a Saint this Hour,	930	Riddle 15	D 15

DEV'LISH

Why Dick, thy Wife has dev'lish Whims:	220	A Quiet Life	27

DEVIATE

Must deviate oft from common sense,	435	Answer Paulus	112

DEVICE

Or by Atchievments, Arms, Device,	80	Vanbrug House	65
Or by Atchievment, Arms, Device,	107	V's House	39
And you shall find by this Device,	366	Answer Delaney	17
Most aptly this Device explain:	393	Modern Poets	6
O, 'tis a quaint Device:	394	Grub-Street	6

DEVIL   SEE DE'EL,DEE'L,DEV'L

The Devil take me, said she, (blessing her self,)	71	Mrs Harris Pet	44
So, as the Devil would have it,	72	Mrs Harris Pet	52
. . .like the Devil.)	72	Mrs Harris Pet	54
Give us our earl, the devil take their duke.	186	Scriblerus 3	2
And the Devil may take their Duke.	186	Scriblerus 4	D 12
Their Gods were of Wood, but our Wood is the Devil:	334	Serious Poem	12
Unless by the Devil we mean Mr. Wood.	335	Serious Poem	56
But some will object, that the Devil oft spoke	335	Serious Poem	57
Perhaps you will say, 'tis the Devil that puts	335	Serious Poem	61
And instead of the Devil, this Son of Perdition	336	Serious Poem	67
And drive the Conj'rers to the Devil:	354	Simile Silver	30
That Love is the Devil, I'll prove when requir'd:	401	Window Inns 3	1
But, here was to pay the Devil and all.	519	Dean Hang Rape	58
No Devil nor <Dean> could Ravish 'em then,	519	Dean Hang Rape	64
And, whisp'ring wisht, the Devil burst her	618	Scandal Poem 1	18
This God on Earth turns Devil in Hell.	646	On Poetry	206
At last grown prouder than the Devil	746	Stel Distress	23
As if the Devil drove, they fly.	775	Mullinix Tim	68
Shou'd Faustus, with the Devil behind him,	776	Mullinix Tim	101
In vain--for the Devil a Parson wou'd stir.	804	Irish Bishops	20
In spite of the Devil would still be untoward.	804	Irish Bishops	26
What the De'el is't to him whence the Devil they came?	815	Yahoo's	24
While the Devil upon the Roof,	830	Legion Club	23
If the Devil be Thunder Proof,	830	Legion Club	24
Sometimes makes the Devil his Rod:	830	Legion Club	32
May their God, the Devil confound 'em.	839	Legion Club	242
The devil he may take her into hell and Boult-her!	841	Ballad	D 14
Next make a Devil of a Saint.	930	Riddle 15	D 16
A temper the Devil himself could not bridle,	955	Portrait Life	3
Every body knows, that I love to tell Truth and shame the Devil,	986	Mary to Sher	23
The Devil and Delany;	1005	Sheridan's Sub	22
And fairly bid the <Devil> take	400	Window Inns 1	7
But dear as the <Devil>:	402	Window Inns 8	D 2
The <Devil> ready stands, my <Swift>,	497	Panegyr Swift	124
"The <Devil> did the Deed, not they!	497	Panegyr Swift	135
At last grown prouder than the <Devil>,	750	Stel Wood-Park	21

DEVIL'S

Why Dick! the Devil's in thy Nell	220	A Quiet Life	9
Just as when we say, the Devil's a Tinker	335	Serious Poem	54
And, the Devil's a damnable Poet.	401	Window Inns 3	4
Methinks, or else the Devil's in't,	860	Lady Acheson	14
"But the Devil's as welcome wherever he goes:	872	Grand Question	144

DEVILS

(The Devils leaving the Possess't)	259	Bubble	215
Where Devils to a vale retreat	490	Dialogue	41

DEVIS'D

Never woman more devis'd	906	Daphne	5

DEVISE

This vap'ring Scab must needs devise	352	Wood Ironmongr	9
Can I devise poetic strains?	754	Stella '23	2

DEVOID

"Thy Thanks and Verse, devoid of Art:	476	Epist on Epist	34

DEVOLV'D

The leaden Crown devolv'd to thee,	653	On Poetry	375

DEVOTED

Threat'ning with Deluge this Devoted Town.	138	City Shower	32

```
DEVOTED        (CONTINUED)                          PAGE    TITLE         LINE
    To fix a Price on his devoted Head.    . . . . . . .   196 Author Himself   60
    Lets drive at Tom's devoted Noddle,    . . . . . . .   458 Paddy's Charac   24
DEVOTES
    To regal Rage devotes some Patriot's Head.   . . . .   364 On Dreams        12
DEVOTION
    "Nor with hir'd thoughts be thy devotion paid;   . . .    55 Temple Ill     139
    Jove saw that all Devotion fail'd;     . . . . . . .    345 Prometheus       42
    Yet Our Devotion may Grow Slack.       . . . . . . .    346 Prometheus       70
    To praise your Hero for Devotion:      . . . . . . .    468 Birthday Song   262
    Who have, to shew your great Devotion,   . . . . . .    495 Panegyr Swift    60
    But Building, Planning, and Devotion;    . . . . . .    514 Answer Fable     56
    With that Devotion we bestow,     . . . . . . .        711 Cadenus Vaness  788
    Devotion, Duty, and Respect,      . . . . . . .        711 Cadenus Vaness  799
    To the Court it was fitter to pay his Devotion,   . .   809 Epigr Prelate     5
    With what Devotion you adore 'um!      . . . . . . .    888 Panegyr Dean     52
    Comes fill'd with Rev'rence and Devotion.)   . . . .    893 Panegyr Dean    212
    Yet, some Devotion still remains   . . . . . . . .      896 Panegyr Dean    299
    Love, Joy, and Devotion   . . . . . . . . . . .        939 Riddle Answerd   13
DEVOUR
    Devour the Church's tiddest Bits,    . . . . . .       498 Panegyr Swift   150
    Whilst, ev'ry Critick can devour    . . . . . . .      502 Doctor Delaney   69
    Will more than half a Score devour.    . . . . .       642 On Poetry        64
    Devour the Church, and chatter to the State.   . . . . 792 St. Pat's Well   52
DEVOUR'D
    Devour'd the Lambs, the Fleeces sold,    . . . . .     153 Widow and Cat   D  9
DEVOURING    SEE ALL-DEVOURING,NEW-DEVOURING
    'Twas a devouring Serpent grown.   . . . . . . . .     132 Magician's Rod    4
    Till those devouring Swine run down,   . . . . . .     259 Bubble          214
    Two Rows of Teeth arm each devouring Jaw;   . . . .    532 To Mr. Gay       35
    All devouring, all destroying,    . . . . . . .        930 Riddle 16       D  2
DEVOURS
    Devours your Geese, the Wolf your Flocks:   . . . .    504 Doctor Delaney  130
DEVOUT
    (Which therefore made them more devout)   . . . . .    601 Beasts Confess    6
    In hopes to make you more devout;   .. . . . . . .     617 Scandal Poem 1    8
    And only makes you more devout.   . . . . . . . .      624 Scandal Poem 2    8
    'Though not so Gospel-ward devout.   . . . . . . .     820 Dr. Rundle       32
DEVOUTEST
    Have their devoutest Worshippers,   . . . . . . . .    100 Elegy Patrige    98
DEVOUTLY
    Devoutly lolling in his Seat;   . . . . . . . .        174 Horace 1, 7      98
    Thou'lt rail devoutly at the Peace,    . . . . . .     180 Horace 2, 1      15
    Or on the Matt devoutly kneeling    . . . . . . .      222 Prog of Love     15
DEW
    'Till Summer Show'rs and Ev'ning Dew,    . . . . .     759 Receipt Youth    11
    This Night I came home with a very cold Dew sick,  . . 1030 Dr. Sheridan     2
DEWS
    Unwholsome Damps, offensive Dews:   . . . . . .        923 Riddle 7         56
DEXT'ROUS
    From which Ingredients, First the dext'rous Boy   . .  118 Biddy Floyd       5
    Now Moll had whirl'd her Mop with dext'rous Airs,  . . 124 Descriptn Morn    7
    For, those we dext'rous Courtiers call,   . . . . .    409 Dial Rich Marb   33
    A Dext'rous Steward, when his Tricks are found,   . .  535 To Mr. Gay      107
    This was dext'rous at his Trowel,   . . . . . . .      800 Traulus 2        29
DEXT'ROUSLY
    Can dext'rously her Husband teize,    . . . . . .      416 Woman's Mind     37
DEXTERITY
    With such Dexterity you fit   . . . . . . .            890 Panegyr Dean    125
DEXTROUSLY
    Now dextrously her Plumpers draws,    . . . . . .      582 Young Nymph      17
DI'MOND
    The Di'mond and the Lover.   . . . . . . . .           400 Window Inns 1     8
DIADEM
    From whence 'tis plain the Diadem    . . . . . . .      98 Elegy Patrige    25
DIAMETER
    In each single verse, took up a diameter.   . . . .   1026 Sheri Circles    12
DIANA
    Diana thus, Heav'n's chastest queen,   . . . . . .     178 To Lord Harley   73
    When first Diana leaves her Bed    . . . . . . .       226 Prog of Beauty    1
DIANA'S
    And this is fair Diana's Case   . . . . . . .          228 Prog of Beauty   85
    The chaste Diana's infant Face;   . . . . . . .        919 Riddle 5          8
DICATES
    What friendship dicates more than wit.   . . . . .     176 To Lord Harley    4
DICE
    He never once wou'd cog the Dice,    . . . . . . .     456 Dean Smedley     28
    Nor plays at cards, or dice, or bowls;    . . . . .    901 Dean's Reasons   88
    To Lust and Luxury, and Dice:   . . . . . . .          917 Riddle 3         14
DICERES
    For scolding is just quasi diceres--school-din:   . .  979 Dean to Tho: S    8
DICK
    Dick, thour't resolv'd, as I am told,    . . . . .     180 Horace 2, 1       1
    When first I knew thee, Dick, thou wert    . . . .     182 Horace 2, 1      49
    Dick, we agree--all's true, thou'st said,   . . . .    183 Horace 2, 1      99
    Nell roar'd incessant, Dick sate mute:    . . . . .    219 A Quiet Life      4
    Why Dick! the Devil's in thy Nell    . . . . . .       220 A Quiet Life      9
    Will went again to visit Dick   . . . . . .           220 A Quiet Life     19
    Will drew out Dick to take a Quart,    . . . . . .     220 A Quiet Life     26
    Why Dick, thy Wife has dev'lish Whims:    . . . . .    220 A Quiet Life     27
    Dick suffer'd for his Peace and Credit,    . . . .     220 A Quiet Life     37
```

DICK	(CONTINUED)	PAGE	TITLE	LINE
Dick found it by his ill Success		221	A Quiet Life	41
Are us'd like Dick, and bear the Blame.		221	A Quiet Life	58
And Dick the Scavenger with equal Grace,		364	On Dreams	37
Doll dying first, Dick grew Melancholly,		430	Dicky Dolly	2
For Dick without Doll thought Living a Folly.		430	Dicky Dolly	3
Dick lost in Doll, a Wife Tender and Dear,		430	Dicky Dolly	4
But Dick lost by Doll, twelve hundred a Year,		430	Dicky Dolly	5
A Loss that Dick thought, no Mortal cou'd bear.		430	Dicky Dolly	6
Dick Sigh'd for his Doll and his mournfull Arms Cross'd,		430	Dicky Dolly	7
Thus loaded with Grief, Dick Sigh'd and he cry'd,		430	Dicky Dolly	10
One Bed while alive held both Doll and Dick		430	Dicky Dolly	13
Dick left a Pattern few will copy after,		430	Dicky Dolly	16
Tom and Dick had equal Fame,		784	Mullinex Dick	1
But Dick had seen a College.		784	Mullinex Dick	4
Dick a Coxcomb, Tom was mad,		784	Mullinex Dick	5
But Dick the best at <farting>.		784	Mullinex Dick	8
Dick would cock his Nose in scorn,		784	Mullinex Dick	9
But Dick was from an Oven.		784	Mullinex Dick	12
Dick could neatly dance a Jig,		784	Mullinex Dick	13
And Dick curse all the Tories.		784	Mullinex Dick	16
Dick would make a woful Noise,		784	Mullinex Dick	17
Dick nimbly skip the Gutter;		784	Mullinex Dick	22
But Dick could better sputter.		784	Mullinex Dick	24
Dick was come to high Renown		785	Mullinex Dick	25
Dick knew better how to swing		785	Mullinex Dick	31
Dick for Repartee was fit,		785	Mullinex Dick	33
Dick was thought the brighter Wit,		785	Mullinex Dick	35
Dick with zealous No's and Ay's,		785	Mullinex Dick	37
Forth issues wriggling Dick Drawcensir,		785	Dick, Maggot	6
When Dick cries, Dust to carry out?		787	Clad in Brown	30
But then, consider Dick, you'l find		788	Dick's Variety	13
Though Dick, I dare presume to say,		788	Dick's Variety	17
Dick I could venture every where,		788	Dick's Variety	19
But Dick can <fart>, and dance and frisk,		788	Dick's Variety	25
Dear Dick, prithee tell by what passion you move?		818	Archbi Cashel	1
For thine, my dear Dick, give me leave to speak plain,		819	Archbi Cashel	15
Dick Fitz-Baker, Dick the Player,		835	Legion Club	149
Dick Fitz-Baker, Dick the Player,		835	Legion Club	149
Besides, Dick forbid me, and call'd me a fool;		980	Tho: Sheridan	7
To <Marshall>, <Conolly>, and <Dick> <Tighe>.		436	Answer Paulus	146

DICK'S

| With Dick's own Staff his Peacefull Neighbor, | | 220 | A Quiet Life | 22 |

DICKS

| There are ten thousand Dicks beside; | | 221 | A Quiet Life | 56 |
| On the Puppy Pair of Dicks; | | 835 | Legion Club | 146 |

DICKY

| Under this Stone, lies Dicky and Dolly | | 430 | Dicky Dolly | 1 |

DICTATES

| But 'gainst the Dictates of your Mind, | | 496 | Panegyr Swift | 94 |

DID   115 | | | OMITTED WORD | |

DIDO

That Dido smitt, might more caress him		619	Scandal Poem 1	68
And Dido quickly smoak't the Beau.		619	Scandal Poem 1	72
That Dido might the more caress him:		625	Scandal Poem 2	64
And Dido quickly smoak'd the Beau.		625	Scandal Poem 2	70

DIDO'S

| In Virgil (vide Dido's Case:) | | 690 | Cadenus Vaness | 111 |

DIDST   1 | | | OMITTED WORD | |

DIE   SEE DYE

Strange, an Astrologer should Die,		98	Elegy Patrige	5
All this is mine but till I die;		198	Horace 2, 6	D
To those who die, for meriting to live.		210	Earl of Oxford	14
'Twas time in conscience he should die.		296	Satiric Elegy	12
To live and die all strollers for your sakes;		309	Billet Players	50
Rode stately through Holbourn, to die in his Calling;		399	Tom Clinch	2
"For her he stood prepar'd to die;		566	Death of Swift	348
How to live, and how to die.		630	Epistle Lady	26
Can wish to die, in strain heroick,		676	Parson's Case	2
Coram Regina prox' die Martis,		713	Cadenus Vaness	839
Die the next Year for want of Root:		730	Stella, Poems	68
Should acting, die, nor leave behind		764	Stel B-day '26	29
"It's a pity a Prelate should die without law;		843	Ay and No	17
Must die with her expiring Plant.		849	Old Thorn	48
I ne'er was born, nor e'er can die,		936	Riddle 23	D 26
Die like lovers as they gaze,		937	Riddle 24	D 49
Die for those I live to please;		937	Riddle 24	D 50
Die like all that look on you.		937	Riddle 24	D 54
But that's as much as to say, that my Master should die before ye,		986	Mary to Sher	19

DIED   SEE DY'D

| To One who for his Country died, | | 339 | Arch-Bish Dub | 2 |

DIES   SEE DYES

And needs must stink when e're it dies;		9	Ode to King	110
Shoots to the Earth and dies;		29	Ode to Temple	84
Like distant echo spent, the spirit dies.		50	To Congreve	230
How blest is he, who for his Country dies;		210	Earl of Oxford	1
And Discord, in his Presence, dies--		387	Manly Virtue	122
And what if daring Strephon dies		587	Strephon Chloe	109
Opinion falls, and Beauty dies.		591	Strephon Chloe	226

DIES	(CONTINUED)	PAGE	TITLE	LINE
And so continues 'till he dies.		646	On Poetry	196
Poor Bishop Judas, late repenting, dies;		806	Judas	2
Her, who, without thy Pity, dies?		924	Riddle 8	2
See, see, Celia, Celia Dies, ...		960	Cantata	
Dies, Dies, Dies, Dies, Dies, Dies, Dies, ...		960	Cantata	
Dies, Dies, Dies, Dies, Dies, Dies, Dies, ...		960	Cantata	
Dies, Dies, Dies, Dies, Dies, Dies, Dies, ...		960	Cantata	
Dies, Dies, Dies, Dies, Dies, Dies, Dies, ...		960	Cantata	
Dies, Dies, Dies, Dies, Dies, Dies, Dies, ...		960	Cantata	
Dies, Dies, Dies, Dies, Dies, Dies, Dies, ...		960	Cantata	
Dies, Dies, Dies, Dies, Dies, Dies, Dies, ...		960	Cantata	

DIET   SEE DYET

		PAGE	TITLE	LINE
Should them Ordain for Lenten Diet		373	Letter D. S-y	67
Whose Phiz bespeaks his diet water-gruel.		672	Epig Carthy 24	D 10
But, now to my diet, ...		853	Lady's Lament	59

DIFF'RENCE

Because the Diff'rence lyes abstruse		216	To Mr. Delany	47
The Diff'rence is not much between		313	To Ford	59
The Diff'rence but amounts to this, ...		315	To Ford	100
No diff'rence could he find between		619	Scandal Poem 1	57
No Diff'rence could he find between		625	Scandal Poem 2	53
Scarce knows what Diff'rence is between		700	Cadenus Vaness	416
It makes no Diff'rence in the Case, ...		724	To Stella	21
Here, Nature never Diff'rence made		895	Panegyr Dean	289
Nor can I the least Diff'rence find, ...		1033	Ans to Crown	5

DIFF'RENT

Each Number had it's diff'rent Power;		79	Vanbrug House	7
And each Part took a diff'rent Side;		99	Elegy Patrige	66
Each Number had it's diff'rent Pow'r;		106	V's House	7
Remove them to a diff'rent Light		226	Prog of Beauty	23
"And beauteous Bess a diff'rent case is, ...		321	First of April	9
Or take it in a diff'rent View;		392	Young's Satire	31
Then diff'rent Studies chuse, ...		405	Swift to Pope	6
'Tis strange, what diff'rent Thoughts inspire		411	Desire Possess	1
Whose Thoughts are of a diff'rent Mold, ...		485	Libel on D- D-	172
Must in a diff'rent Mold be cast;		496	Panegyr Swift	107
Our Friends are of a diff'rent mind;		546	Life of Swift	48
"I near, they're of a diff'rent kind:		550	Life of Swift	181
"Sir, our Accounts are diff'rent quite, ...		550	Life of Swift	194
Yet, some assign a diff'rent Reason;		588	Strephon Chloe	159
With Threads of diff'rent colour'd Yarn.		594	Cassinus Peter	14
Of diff'rent Spirits to discern, ...		642	On Poetry	72
To Moorlands of a diff'rent Parish.		645	On Poetry	174
Drag diff'rent Ways in miry Grounds.		645	On Poetry	176
A Gownman of a diff'rent Make.		701	Cadenus Vaness	463
One Passion, with a diff'rent Turn, ...		731	Stella, Poems	117
For Vices all have diff'rent Ends, ...		733	Verses Vanessa	11
And should you act, a diff'rent Part, ...		776	Mullinix Tim	89
Salutes our <Dean> in diff'rent Views;		888	Panegyr Dean	38
Two Vices of a diff'rent Kind:		918	Riddle 4	24
And so apply'd to diff'rent Use.		929	Riddle 15	D 12
All of diff'rent Voice and Features, ...		930	Riddle 17	D 2

DIFFER

Reformers and physicians differ but in name, ...		42	Ode Sancroft	255
For Wit and Humor differ quite, ...		215	To Mr. Delany	23
Do not more differ in their Breed, ...		217	To Mr. Delany	62
Can differ more than God and <Kings>		486	Libel on D- D-	196
Why Sir, I differ from you there, ...		547	Life of Swift	81
But, here I differ from the Knight		901	Dean's Reasons	71

DIFFER'D

Those former Ages differ'd much from this:		806	Judas	9

DIFFERENT

Tho' we be of two different Factions still, ...		18	Ode Athenian	72
Is but one thing under two different names;		41	Ode Sancroft	206
A different way their Fancy runs;		83	Salamander	16
We issue forth at different Hours;		278	Journal	8
Henceforth expect a different survey, ...		283	Journal	127
How different is this from Smedley?		476	Epist on Epist	47
"You know 'tis quite a different Thing.		560	Death of Swift	188
One Year is past; a different Scene.		562	Death of Swift	245
Shirts be wrought with different Letters, ...		573	Helter Skelter	23
You who in different Sects have shamm'd, ...		579	Day Judgement	15
How different from thine is Dunkin's Lot!		667	Epig Carthy 7	D 1
So green in different Lights may pass for blue, . . .		670	Epig Carthy 18	D 7
In different Breasts together burn, ...		687	Cadenus Vaness	33
So the Sun's Heat, with different Powers, ...		731	Stella, Poems	119
Can shew more different Hues than I;		911	Aenigma	4

DIFFICULT

Nor found it difficult to guess the Cause:		536	To Mr. Gay	158

DIFFICULTY

I can solve the Difficulty.		630	Epistle Lady	20
Remains a Difficulty still, ...		652	On Poetry	367
I chose these Rhymes out, for their Difficulty. . . .		989	Letter Dr Sh-n	32

DIFFUS'D

His Influence is diffus'd around;		385	Manly Virtue	38

DIFFUSING

Alike diffusing in his Flight		387	Manly Virtue	119

DIG

To dig the leaden Mines of deep Philosophy: . . .		32	Ode to Temple	190
These Raps he will honestly dig out with Shovels, . .		337	Serious Poem	97

		PAGE	TITLE	LINE
DIG	**(CONTINUED)**			
Or, from your noses dig out notches?	. . . .	618	Scandal Poem 1	26
Or from your Noses dig out Notches?	. . . .	624	Scandal Poem 2	20
And with Discretion dig the Mould:	. . . .	743	Stel B-day 22	58
May dig in vain in Pluto's Shades.	. . . . . .	743	Stel B-day 22	74
DIGEST				
Such Draughts as this, and then digest,	. . . . . .	495	Panegyr Swift	65
Than he's able to digest:	. . . .	633	Epistle Lady	126
DIGESTING	**SEE ALL-DIGESTING**			
DIGGER				
The Dean or the digger;	. . . .	856	Lady's Lament	170
DIGNIFY				
You dignify the noble Race,	. . . .	656	On Poetry	457
DIGNIFY'D				
Are by thy Numbers dignify'd.	. . . .	361	Grace's Answer	4
DIGNITARY'S				
Assume a Dignitary's Airs,	. . . .	495	Panegyr Swift	70
DIGNITY				
The Dignity of his Profession;	. . . .	375	Apology Lady C	10
To add more Dignity and Light	. . . .	497	Panegyr Swift	122
Against her Dignity and Crown:	. . . .	687	Cadenus Vaness	19
Wou'd still her Dignity maintain,	. . . .	705	Cadenus Vaness	595
Wherein his Dignity and Age	. . . .	711	Cadenus Vaness	778
In you such Dignity appears;	. . . .	888	Panegyr Dean	49
DILAPIDATIONS				
To mend dilapidations in the last?	. . . .	40	Ode Sancroft	179
DILATES				
Dilates, and makes the Vessel full:	. . . .	893	Panegyr Dean	192
DILEMMA				
A strong Dilemma in a desp'rate Case!	. . . . . .	535	To Mr. Gay	129
DILIGENCE				
His Diligence and quick Dispatch;	. . . .	604	Beasts Confess	90
\<DILKS\>				
There sit \<Clements\>, \<Dilks\>, and \<Harrison\>,	. . .	837	Legion Club	181
\<Harrison\>, and \<Dilks\>, and \<Clements\>,	. . . . .	837	Legion Club	185
DIMENSIONS				
Of thy Dimensions fit for Prose,	. . . .	1002	Reply by Dean	5
DIMINISH				
Enlarge, diminish, interline;	. . . .	643	On Poetry	88
DIMMISH				
My Eyes are somewhat dimmish grown;	. . . . . .	757	Stel B-day '24	42
DIMMS				
The daz'ling glory dimms their prostituted sight,	. . .	41	Ode Sancroft	221
DIMS				
Dims and obscures our sight:	. . . .	402	Window Inns 6	D 2
DIN	**SEE SCHOOL-DIN**			
Where Spirits throng'd with hideous Din,	. . . .	134	Magician's Rod	55
And ever and anon with frightful Din	. . . . .	139	City Shower	45
Nell scolded in so loud a Din	. . . .	219	A Quiet Life	1
At five the Footmen make a Din,	. . . .	292	Prog Marriage	91
With furious Din of Brazen Drums,	. . . .	340	Arch-Bish Dub	26
To rend the Skies with brazen Din:	. . . .	354	Simile Silver	10
Their Chattering makes a louder Din	. . . . . .	450	Modern Lady	180
To din thine Ears with unharmonious Clack,	. . .	792	St. Pat's Well	47
Stood chatt'ring with incessant Din;	. . . . . .	849	Old Thorn	34
Join in all the Din of Battle.	. . . .	933	Riddle 20	D 22
DIN'D				
Extremely proud--but I had din'd--	. . . .	173	Horace 1, 7	68
He Din'd and Sup'd at Charge of other Folk,	. . .	234	Elegy on Demar	10
Then, boasting tell us where you din'd,	. . . . .	480	Libel on D- D-	5
Forgets the Place where last he din'd:	. . . . . .	556	Death of Swift	88
DINE				
If you be wise, then go not far to Dine,	. . . .	137	City Shower	7
If, dearest Dismal, you for once can Dine	. . .	162	Toland's Invit	1
I'd have him Dine with me to Day.	. . . . . .	172	Horace 1, 7	50
We sup and we dine,	. . . .	244	Irish-Feast	6
The Dean, who us'd to dine at one,	. . . . . .	291	Prog Marriage	59
She sent to bid him come and dine.	. . . . . .	375	Apology Lady C	6
To dine with Her! and come at Three!	. . . . .	376	Apology Lady C	37
For I'm to dine with him at four	. . . .	423	Ireld	62
'I thought we were to Dine alone,	. . . .	448	Modern Lady	102
For which he summon'd you to Dine.	. . . . . .	481	Libel on D- D-	32
And chuse to dine at home with Port:	. . . . .	488	Irish-Club	20
Refuse our Patron's Call to dine;	. . . . . .	495	Panegyr Swift	68
Yet, when we dine without a Friend,	. . . . . .	886	Rev Market-Hill	97
The Neighbours who come here to dine,	. . . .	891	Panegyr Dean	135
Does he regard on what we dine?	. . . .	949	Epigr Fasting	6
On rainy Days alone I dine,	. . . .	954	Authors Living	1
On rainy Days, I dine alone,	. . . .	954	Authors Living	3
With me you'll no more have a Stomach to Dine	. .	1017	Swift Ans Sher	15
For this I will not dine with Agmondisham,	. . . .	1033	Ans to Crown	17
DINES				
When Bolingbroke with Pult'ney Dines.	. . . . . .	483	Libel on D- D-	102
DINGLEY				
To be directed here by Dingley.	. . . .	745	Stel Distress	10
Dingley and Brent	. . . .	755	Dingley Brent	1
Comes Dingley, and asks you, What was it?	. . . .	756	Dingley Brent	15
Poor Miss Dingley oft hath felt its Bills.	. . . .	941	Letter	24
Mrs. Dingley and Mrs. Johnson say,	. . .	1013	Swift to Sheri	7
Mrs. Dingley	. . . .	1014	Swift to Sheri	29

		PAGE	TITLE		LINE
DINGLEY'S					
Pray steal me not, I'm Mrs. Dingley's	. . . .	763	Collar Lap-Dog		1
DINGLY					
To be directed here by Dingly:	. . . .	750	Stel Wood-Park		34
DINING					
The Hour of Dining now is past;	. . . .	377	Apology Lady C		53
DINNER SEE AFTER-DINNER					
Invites the Fox to Dinner.	. . . .	153	Widow and Cat	D	15
Now Water's brought, and Dinner done,	. . . . .	279	Journal		35
Sits down to Dinner just at four;	. . . .	291	Prog Marriage		56
And for his courage gets--a dinner.	. . . . . .	421	Ireld		12
Comes up with, "Madam, Dinner stays;	. . . . .	447	Modern Lady		93
'I wish the Dinner at Old Nick."	. . . . . .	448	Modern Lady		99
And get a Dinner for your Hire,	. . . .	483	Libel on D- D-		108
Who, for a dinner, sell a vote;	. . . .	487	Irish-Club		4
And take a short Dinner here with us to-Day:	. . . .	871	Grand Question		120
The Captain at Dinner appears in his Glory;	. . .	871	Grand Question		130
Will dress a Dinner worth five Pound.	. . . . .	941	Letter		36
DINNER-CANT					
Has all the Dinner-Cant by Heart:	. . . .	448	Modern Lady		101
DINNER'S					
Yet, the plain Squire, when Dinner's done,	. . . .	920	Riddle 6		27
DINNERS					
Who at their Dinners, en famille	. . . .	480	Libel on D- D-		3
"And Madam, says he, if such Dinners you give,	. . .	872	Grand Question		141
DINT					
And plainly prove by dint of Text,	. . . . . .	456	Dean Smedley		39
By Dint of his sole Approbation.	. . . .	475	Epist on Epist		20
by dint of experience improving in Blunders	. . . . .	540	Charac Walpole		6
DIP					
And dip their Fins again to fly.	. . . .	254	Bubble		88
We only dip a Spunge in Water;	. . . .	627	Scandal Poem 2		128
(An Author, where I sometimes dip a Days)	. . . .	988	Letter Dr Sh-n		18
DIPP'D					
I dipp'd two babes in holy-water,	. . . .	675	Curate's Compl		7
DIPT					
Nor dipt in Blood, nor Widow's Tears, nor Orphan's Cries:		29	Ode to Temple		86
Dipt over head and Ears--in Debt.	. . . . . .	251	Bubble		24
His heart in poison deeply dipt,	. . . .	951	Upstart	D	27
DIRE					
Whate'er these dire fore-bodings meant,	. . . . . .	290	Prog Marriage		17
In short such dire Confusions follow'd,	. . . . . .	346	Prometheus		45
In Haste, with Imprecations dire,	. . . .	470	Burning Poem		11
"Beheld the dire destructive Scene:	. . . . . .	568	Death of Swift		392
Then, see the dire Effect of Pease,	. . . . . .	589	Strephon Chloe		167
From the dire infectious Crew.	. . . .	834	Legion Club		124
And by Exhalations dire,	. . . .	834	Legion Club		129
Sad Omens of the dire Event.	. . . .	849	Old Thorn		32
Shall on thee take a Vengeance dire;	. . . . . .	925	Riddle 8		37
DIRECT					
Our shallow Search and Judgment to direct.	. . . .	18	Ode Athenian		94
"Direct my Plow to find a Treasure:"	. . . . .	199	Horace 2, 6	D	
Direct to the North, where I never yet went;	. . . .	264	Apollo		48
"Direct, and fix the wandring Mind,	. . . . . .	384	Manly Virtue		12
I shall not offer to direct	. . . .	422	Ireld		38
Not to direct a Plague, or Storm,	. . . .	496	Panegyr Swift		93
And faithfully direct her Nail	. . . .	527	Lady's Dres Rm		65
Direct that Women must be decent;	. . . . . .	591	Strephon Chloe		252
Her Serpents hiss direct at me.	. . . .	596	Cassinus Peter		86
Direct the Zenith of the Sky;	. . . .	780	Mullinix Tim		248
Plac'd against the Church direct;	. . . .	829	Legion Club		6
Direct before her Lady's Face.	. . . .	885	Rev Market-Hill		68
In Line direct, hung down behind.	. . . . . .	903	Death Daphne		28
Who down direct our Lineage bring	. . . .	925	Riddle 8		29
And now I must go, and get Saunders to direct this Letter,		987	Mary to Sher		33
And tell who was it could direct her	. . . . . .	993	On Picture		11
DIRECTED					
Directed them to mind their Brief;	. . . . . .	713	Cadenus Vaness		847
To be directed here by Dingley.	. . . .	745	Stel Distress		10
To be directed here by Dingly:	. . . .	750	Stel Wood-Park		34
DIRECTING					
Directing ev'ry Vice we find	. . . .	798	Traulus 1		75
DIRECTION					
And yours to follow my Direction.	. . . . . .	932	Riddle 19	D	18
DIRECTIONS					
Receiv'd from thee profound Directions	. . . . .	182	Horace 2, 1		55
He gives Directions to the Town,	. . . . . .	649	On Poetry		269
DIRECTLY					
Her Arguments directly tend	. . . .	417	Woman's Mind		51
Must be apply'd directly wrong:	. . . .	464	Birthday Song		118
And, born directly to the Heart,	. . . .	703	Cadenus Vaness		522
DIRECTOR					
A Foot-boy to some Rogue Director?	. . . . . .	312	To Ford		40
In all Affairs thou sole Director,	. . . . . .	656	On Poetry		449
Don Carlos made her sole Director.	. . . . . .	745	Stel Distress		8
Don Carlos made her chief Director	. . . . . .	745	Stel Distress		
Don Carlos made her chief Director,	. . . . . .	749	Stel Wood-Park		5
DIRECTORS					
Directors better know their Tools,	. . . .	253	Bubble		58

211

		PAGE	TITLE	LINE
DIRECTORS	(CONTINUED)			
But Whale Directors eat up all.		253	Bubble	68
Directors fall as well as they,		253	Bubble	83
Thus by Directors we are told,		254	Bubble	101
For, where Directors get a Prize,		256	Bubble	159
Directors build 'em in the Seas;		257	Bubble	166
Mark where the Sly Directors creep,		257	Bubble	173
Directors thrown into the Sea		258	Bubble	185
Directors; for tis you I warn,		258	Bubble	189
That Plague, Directors, to the Deep,		258	Bubble	207
Directors Promises but Wind,		259	Bubble	219
Directors to a noble Mind.		706	Cadenus Vaness	613
DIRECTS				
My Lord seems pleas'd, but still directs		64	Discovery	41
To lead thee, as a Staff directs the Blind,		770	Horace 1, 14	17
DIREFUL				
Through Cambridge waft the direful Tale.		597	Cassinus Peter	110
DIRT				
Had par'd the Dirt, and Sprinkled round the Floor.		124	Descriptn Morn	6
A mingled Mass of Dirt and Sweat.		226	Prog of Beauty	20
Turn'd to that dirt from whence he sprung.		297	Satiric Elegy	32
Drawn through the dirt, his pockets pick'd;		436	Answer Paulus	138
Fill'd up with Dirt so closely fixt,		526	Lady's Dres Rm	21
With Dirt, and Sweat, and Ear-Wax grim'd.		527	Lady's Dres Rm	46
But, well embrown'd with Dirt and Hair.		594	Cassinus Peter	18
When pelted all with Dirt they shine;		787	Clad in Brown	20
He never muddles in the Dirt,		788	Dick's Variety	15
Raise the Dirt about your Hole.		832	Legion Club	74
His Grazier's coat with dirt besmear'd,		879	Robbin & Harry	43
Familiar grown to Dirt and Wet,		890	Panegyr Dean	109
More than the Dirt beneath my Shoes, nor fear it.		1003	Dan J's Reply	15
Sloth, Dirt, and Theft around her wait.		1035	To Quilca	12
DIRTY				
Beat not the dirty paths where vulgar feet have trod,		49	To Congreve	205
Of British Midas dirty Paws;		158	Fable of Midas	70
With Asses Ears, and dirty Hands.		158	Fable of Midas	82
But was so dirty, pale and thin,		174	Horace 1, 7	119
A frouzy dirty colour'd red		226	Prog of Beauty	3
At dirty Ballyspellin		442	Ballyspellin	84
Or dirty Offals cook'd with Herbage.		498	Panegyr Swift	153
And first a dirty Smock appear'd,		526	Lady's Dres Rm	11
The Candidates observ'd his dirty Paws,		536	To Mr. Gay	157
"To talk with Wits in dirty Shoes:		565	Death of Swift	322
Seen from behind a dirty Clout:		786	Clad in Brown	10
Like a very foul mop, dirty more than they clean.		819	Archbi Cashel	16
All dirty and wet:		856	Lady's Lament	166
I peept, and saw you kiss the dirty Bitch.		882	Pastoral Dial	38
A dirty parasite and slave;		951	Upstart	D 26
DISAFFECTED				
The Worst of disaffected Deans:		514	Answer Fable	66
Although I swear them Disaffected?		779	Mullinix Tim	190
DISAFFECTION				
"On Ministers, is disaffection.		563	Death of Swift	276
DISAPPEAR				
When all we see shall disappear.		932	Riddle 19	D 16
DISAPPOINT				
I'll disappoint its Nobler Part.		121	Apollo Outwit	52
And disappoint the sole Design,		481	Libel on D- D-	31
To disappoint Ixion's rape		619	Scandal Poem 1	53
To disappoint Ixion's Rape,		625	Scandal Poem 2	49
DISAPPOINTED				
But disappointed of his fond Desire		22	Ode Athenian	195
Since the Tories have thus disappointed my Hopes,		145	New Song	51
So disappointed when possessing.		411	Desire Possess	4
Though ev'n the Bishops disappointed,		821	Dr. Rundle	55
DISAPPOINTMENT				
Shame, Disappointment, Guilt, Surprize.		706	Cadenus Vaness	625
DISARM				
The brave Attempt do's all our Foes disarm,		13	Ode to William	D 37
And a Hair can disarm		939	Riddle Answerd	31
Almighty Anger to disarm?		949	Epigr Fasting	4
DISARM'D				
Papists disarm'd, or Fall of Coin,		63	Discovery	31
DISASTER				
Who sav'd thee from a great Disaster.		373	Letter D. S-y	56
Effects of many a sad Disaster;		582	Young Nymph	31
DISASTERS				
"Disasters, to our Dearest Friends,		545	Life of Swift	8
DISBANDS				
But see, the Female Club disbands,		451	Modern Lady	196
DISCARDED				
"Who long all Justice had discarded,		570	Death of Swift	421
DISCERN				
Dangers with Prudence to discern;		325	Pethox	60
Well I know, you can discern,		630	Epistle Lady	29
Of diff'rent Spirits to discern,		642	On Poetry	72
Tho' she already can discern,		712	Cadenus Vaness	808
DISCERN'D				
To make his Merit more discern'd,		384	Manly Virtue	31
That's more than ever I discern'd---;		547	Life of Swift	77

		PAGE	TITLE	LINE
DISCERNED				
And make his ignorance discerned,	. . . .	435	Answer Paulus	113
DISCERNING				
Nor wants a nice discerning Spirit,	. . . .	484	Libel on D- D-	147
And had a most discerning Head.	. . . .	710	Cadenus Vaness	757
And Tom for deep discerning;	. . . .	785	Mullinex Dick	34
DISCHARG'D				
The bolt discharg'd, the sky grows clear;	. . . . .	617	Scandal Poem 1	12
The Bolt discharg'd, the Sky grows clear:	. . . . .	624	Scandal Poem 2	12
DISCHARGE				
For, as when we a Gun discharge,	. . . .	66	Problem	43
For, let Mankind discharge their Tongues	. . . . .	414	Censure	19
A Shilling to discharge his Chair,	. . . .	481	Libel on D- D-	42
They may discharge it ev'ry Sup;	. . . .	587	Strephon Chloe	120
DISCHARGING				
In vain discharging many a Shaft,	. . . .	701	Cadenus Vaness	477
'Till Pow'r, discharging all her stormy Bags,	. . .	771	Horace 1, 14	29
DISCIPLES				
Forbidding his Disciples Beans)	. . . .	587	Strephon Chloe	126
Procure Disciples of your own..	. . . .	649	On Poetry	278
DISCIPLINE				
Doctrine, or Discipline our Brethren,	. . . . .	812	Bro Protestant	30
DISCLAIM				
Disclaim for ever all pretence	. . . .	436	Answer Paulus	143
Disclaim the Human Name, and Face,	. . . . . .	498	Panegyr Swift	172
DISCLOS'D				
He soon disclos'd his Nature.	. . . .	153	Widow and Cat	D 5
DISCLOSE				
A Glass that can to Sight disclose,	. . . . . .	527	Lady's Dres Rm	63
Can make us without Fear disclose	. . . .	706	Cadenus Vaness	610
But how? Why, the Dean shall to him disclose	. . . .	817	Yahoo's	63
DISCOMPOSE				
And softly stole to discompose her own.	. . . . . .	124	Descriptn Morn	4
DISCONTENT				
But, Discontent against the Times;	. . . .	549	Life of Swift	137
DISCONTENTED				
The Scots themselves, that Discontented Brood,	. . .	8	Ode to King	82
DISCORD				
And Discord, in his Presence, dies--	. . . . . .	387	Manly Virtue	122
Discord periwigg'd with Snakes,	. . . .	832	Legion Club	91
DISCOUNTS				
And Parvisol discounts Arrears,	. . . .	174	Horace 1, 7	111
DISCOURAG'D				
Discourag'd Youths, now all their Hopes must fail,	. .	793	St. Pat's Well	73
DISCOURSE				
However, I was resolv'd to bring the Discourse slily about,		71	Mrs Harris Pet	36
And if you had heard the Man discourse,	. . . . . .	375	Apology Lady C	11
Where from Discourse of this and that,	. . . . . .	565	Death of Swift	301
To discourse, and to attend,	. . . .	633	Epistle Lady	121
DISCOURSING				
Discoursing on old Stories past,	. . . .	116	Bauc & Phil 2	152
Discoursing with important Face,	. . . .	698	Cadenus Vaness	376
DISCOVER				
Off fly the Vizards and discover all,	. . . . . .	29	Ode to Temple	99
Seem to discover what they would have done	. . . . .	38	Ode Sancroft	132
And, by the most we can discover,	. . . .	67	Problem	59
And so might discover, or gain by the Plot:	. . . .	144	New Song	30
With wit and virtue to discover,	. . . .	177	To Lord Harley	35
"From whence, with half an Eye we may discover,	. . .	195	Author Himself	45
To discover the Goods he came honestly by:	. . . . .	264	Apollo	58
Discover Caelia's foul Disgrace.	. . . .	597	Cassinus Peter	112
She cannot discover	. . . .	952	Onyons	13
DISCOVER'D				
Those that dropt in the South-Sea discover'd this Plank		288	Bank Down	49
The Judge discover'd in her Face	. . . .	713	Cadenus Vaness	844
DISCOVERS				
And now discovers from afar	. . . .	17	Ode Athenian	34
Discovers Vulcan for thy Sire,	. . . .	323	Pethox	6
Discovers freedom without rage;	. . . .	490	Dialogue	28
It shews and discovers it self through a Trifle.	. . .	716	Answer Rebus	12
DISCOVERY				
To make some great Discovery,	. . . .	20	Ode Athenian	143
The Conquest and Discovery too:	. . . .	26	Ode to Temple	10
DISCREET				
Yet as she wasts, she grows discreet,	. . . . . .	229	Prog of Beauty	101
Thought it more courtly and discreet,	. . . . . .	379	Apology Lady C	111
DISCREETLY				
Discreetly to apply this Fable.	. . . .	346	Prometheus	58
Would so discreetly Things dispose,	. . . .	584	Strephon Chloe	15
DISCRETION				
Nor yields up virtue, at discretion,	. . . .	436	Answer Paulus	127
And fair Discretion left the Place,	. . . .	448	Modern Lady	122
Fair Discretion string the Lyre;	. . . .	661	Love Song	14
"And let him use it at Discretion.	. . . .	714	Cadenus Vaness	883
And with Discretion dig the Mould:	. . . .	743	Stel B-day 22	58
They must surrender at Discretion:	. . . .	885	Rev Market-Hill	89
DISDAIN				
"Learn to disdain their mercenary aid;	. . . . . .	55	Temple Ill	140
No sooner got, than with Disdain	. . . .	412	Desire Possess	27
Yet I disdain to offer those,	. . . .	433	Answer Paulus	49

		PAGE	TITLE	LINE
DISDAIN	**(CONTINUED)**			
That Mortals here disdain to love;	. . . .	689	Cadenus Vaness	81
Fill'd with Disdain, with Rage inflam'd,	. . . .	699	Cadenus Vaness	404
Where Ignorance begets Disdain.	. . . . . .	700	Cadenus Vaness	437
Vanessa, fill'd with just Disdain,	. . . . . .	705	Cadenus Vaness	594
And either he deserves Disdain,	. . . . . .	733	Verses Vanessa	15
Ye Great ones, why will ye disdain	. . . . .	896	Panegyr Dean	291
Treat not your Lovers with Disdain;	. . . . . .	932	Riddle 19	D 20
DISDAIN'D				
Disdain'd to enter in so late.	. . . .	711	Cadenus Vaness	771
DISDAINS				
Exalted Worth disdains to owe	. . . .	386	Manly Virtue	95
Disdains to serve ignoble Ends.	. . . .	503	Doctor Delaney	100
DISEAS'D				
Form'd by diseas'd conceptions, weak, and wild,	. . .	47	To Congreve	123
DISEASE				
Who pine us like a Chronical Disease;	. . . . .	9	Ode to King	88
And as a Mortal to his Vile Disease,	. . . . .	10	Ode to King	145
Who have well studied in the Worlds Disease,	. . . .	20	Ode Athenian	138
'Tis now grown an incurable Disease:	. . . . . .	33	Ode to Temple	205
Old as he was, no vulgar known Disease	. . . . .	234	Elegy on Demar	29
Though not to cure, yet palliate each Disease.	. . .	535	To Mr. Gay	124
Is to a Horse an evil Disease.	. . . .	941	Letter	34
DISEASES				
In return to her Scorn, I send her Diseases,	. . .	266	Apollo	105
DISENCUMBRED				
And, disencumbered of his load,	. . . .	435	Answer Paulus	95
DISGRAC'D				
I feel you'll be disgrac'd at Court.	. . . . . .	778	Mullinix Tim	154
DISGRACE				
And then to heighten the Disgrace	. . . .	61	Lady Tablebook	23
One day it will be no disgrace,	. . . .	186	Scriblerus 3	5
Vapors and Steams her Looks disgrace,	. . . . .	226	Prog of Beauty	2
You must expect the like disgrace,	. . . . . .	436	Answer Paulus	139
And leaves St. James's in Disgrace.	. . . . . .	482	Libel on D- D-	60
Lampoons on Whigs, when in Disgrace;	. . . . .	494	Panegyr Swift	33
How could you, Gay, disgrace the Muses Train,	. . .	531	To Mr. Gay	1
"Pervert the Law, disgrace the Gown,	. . . . .	568	Death of Swift	385
"He would have held it a Disgrace,	. . . . . .	571	Death of Swift	441
Discover Caelia's foul Disgrace.	. . . .	597	Cassinus Peter	112
And you must bear the whole Disgrace,	. . . . .	644	On Poetry	141
Whence Gay was banish'd in Disgrace,	. . . . .	650	On Poetry	307
Wou'd not conceive a high disgrace	. . . . . .	659	On Poetry	D 410
Resentments for her late Disgrace;	. . . . . .	713	Cadenus Vaness	845
That Stella may avoid Disgrace	. . . .	757	Stel B-day '24	13
But, lest you should my Skill disgrace,	. . . . .	760	Receipt Youth	49
May Whaley disgrace	. . . .	858	Lady's Lament	223
However, to avoid Disgrace,	. . . .	917	Riddle 4	3
And leave her votaries in disgrace?	. . . . . .	950	Upstart	D 20
DISGRACES				
Who, by Disgraces or ill Fortune sunk,	. . . . .	163	Toland's Invit	17
DISGUIS'D				
Disguis'd in two old threadbare Coats	. . . . .	63	Discovery	34
Disguis'd in tatter'd Habits, went	. . . . . .	111	Bauc & Phil 2	9
DISGUISE				
Which the disguise of greatness only served to hide;	. .	41	Ode Sancroft	214
"T' expose thy soul, clad in this poor disguise;	. . .	55	Temple Ill	144
And Tories (dress'd like Waiters) in Disguise.	. . .	165	Toland's Invit	30
His ruddy Cheeks are no Disguise;	. . . . . .	291	Prog Marriage	49
To lurk behind a mean Disguise;	. . . . . .	386	Manly Virtue	78
To make it seem in this Disguise,	. . . . . .	528	Lady's Dres Rm	77
And have no Secrets to disguise.	. . . . . .	706	Cadenus Vaness	617
To put on a Fool's Disguise,	. . . .	833	Legion Club	110
He oft employs me in Disguise,	. . . .	915	Riddle 1	19
DISGUISES				
For Priests and Jesuits in Disguises;	. . . . .	788	Dick's Variety	22
DISGUST				
"We shou'd indulge the Dean's disgust,	. . . . .	549	Life of Swift	159
DISGUSTED				
Disgusted Strephon stole away	. . . .	529	Lady's Dres Rm	116
DISH				
Upon a single Dish, and Tavern Wine,	. . . . .	162	Toland's Invit	2
White Lead, and Lusitanian Dish.	. . . . . .	227	Prog of Beauty	60
As if he had thrown down a Dish.	. . . . . .	299	Horrid Plot	34
Load our Plates from ev'ry Dish;	. . . . . .	633	Epistle Lady	109
Are swallow'd o'er a Dish of Tea;	. . . . . .	642	On Poetry	68
This dang'rous horrid motion Dish up?	. . . . .	774	Mullinix Tim	18
No sav'ry Dish without an Onyon;	. . . . . .	952	Onyons	7
And for his Victuals let a Ragman dish'em.	. . .	1033	Ans to Crown	18
DISH-CLOUT				
. . .and I would pin a Dish-clout to his Tail.	. . .	987	Mary to Sher	32
DISHES				
Three Dishes a Day, and three Hogsheads a Year.	. .	867	Grand Question	12
DISJOINTING				
Disjointing shapes as in the fairy-land of dreams,	. .	35	Ode Sancroft	39
DISLIKES				
As he approves, as he dislikes,	. . . .	708	Cadenus Vaness	682
DISMAL **SEE DOUBLE-DISMAL**				
A dismal shedding of her Locks	. . . .	85	Salamander	67
An Orator dismal of Nottinghamshire,	. . . . .	142	New Song	1
If, dearest Dismal, you for once can Dine	. . . . .	162	Toland's Invit	1

DISMAL   (CONTINUED)   PAGE   TITLE   LINE
    And Dismal double-Dismal looks;   . . . .   168 Peace Dunkirk   12
    A dismal Banker must that Banker be,   235 Elegy on Demar   39
    The Tenant's in a Dismal Case   . . . .   240 Run Bankers   47
    Too soon arrives the dismal Day, ...   746 Stel Distress   25
    But now arrives the dismal Day: . . . .   751 Stel Wood-Park   45
    But from the Root a dismal Groan   . . . .   850 Old Thorn   53
    Sad Charnel-house! a dismal Dome, ...   922 Riddle 7   51
DISMAL'S
    I'll Speech against Peace while Dismal's my Name,   .   145 New Song   53
DISMALLY
    And dismally was heard to whine . . . .   849 Old Thorn   43
DISMEMBER'D
    But, now dismember'd here are cast, ...   923 Riddle 7   77
DISMISS
    The Cry'r was order'd to dismiss   . . . .   714 Cadenus Vaness   884
DISMISSING
    Dismissing Mars, it next must follow   . . . . . .   462 Birthday Song   57
DISMIST
    The Bill might be with Costs dismist. . . . . . .   688 Cadenus Vaness   74
DISOBEDIENT
    Thou a disobedient Varlet, ...   838 Legion Club   201
DISOBEY
    "How Sons may safely disobey, ...   181 Horace 2, 1   45
    Pardon, if I disobey: . . . .   634 Epistle Lady   134
DISOBEY'D
    Once disobey'd him, Maid nor Wife.   . . . . . .   224 Prog of Love   66
DISOBLIGE
    But that he would not disoblige, ...   463 Birthday Song   104
    Is apt to disoblige his Friends.   . . . .   605 Beasts Confess   144
DISORDERLY
    In disorderly Sort, ...   245 Irish-Feast   15
DISOWN
    A thousand Bards thy Right disown: . . . . . .   653 On Poetry   378
DISPATCH
    For fear He shou'd dispatch more, ...   153 Widow and Cat   D   17
    Dispatch; or else that Rascal Northey, ...   190 Faggot   41
    His Diligence and quick Dispatch;   . . . .   604 Beasts Confess   90
    Dispatch the Rogues by whom they Rise. . . . . .   886 Rev Market-Hill   110
    But, Death had Bus'ness to dispatch: . . . . . .   904 Death Daphne   51
DISPATCHT
    And, thy Beauty thus dispatcht;   . . . .   523 Betty Grizette   11
DISPELL
    The Cymbals rattling Sounds dispell   . . . . . .   354 Simile Silver   11
DISPELLING
    The foggy mists dispelling   . . . .   442 Ballyspellin   69
DISPENSE
    And some kind pow'r for once dispense   37 Ode Sancroft   87
    That longer with Thee to Dispense, ...   154 Widow and Cat   D   43
    With Godliness cou'd well dispense, ...   455 Dean Smedley   5
    How cou'd so fine a Taste dispense   . . . .   475 Epist on Epist   15
DISPENSING
    Oh, may I see her soon dispensing   . . . .   295 Prog Marriage   159
DISPLAY
    Display their various nets for hearts: . . . . .   178 To Lord Harley   54
    Which, howsoever they display . . . .   387 Manly Virtue   105
    Display the blessings of the Nation, ...   658 On Poetry   D 190
    Wou'd you at once display your utmost Hate, . . .   667 Epig Cartny 4   D   3
DISPLAY'D
    Her Talent she display'd betimes;   . . . .   150 Corinna   13
    Yet more display'd, and rais'd his own.   . . . . .   386 Manly Virtue   88
    The fatal Box it self display'd, ...   494 Panegyr Swift   41
    And, thy freckled Neck display'd, ...   522 Betty Grizette   5
    Strephon, the Rogue, display'd it wide, ...   526 Lady's Dres Rm   13
    Display'd her Eloquence the more: . . . .   709 Cadenus Vaness   715
DISPLAYS
    Displays his Talent, sits till Ten, ...   173 Horace 1, 7   75
    Voiture in various Lights displays   . . . .   216 To Mr. Delany   33
    Displays his Pedantry unmerciful, ...   281 Journal   80
    Displays her Silver Face again.   . . . .   354 Simile Silver   14
    If he displays, or hides his Beams;   . . . . . .   379 Apology Lady C   124
    Pulls off with Care, and first displays 'em,   . . .   581 Young Nymph   15
    Who thus displays the New-year's-gift.   . . . . .   753 Gift for Bec   4
DISPLEASE
    His Vigilance might some displease;   . . . . . .   602 Beasts Confess   45
DISPLEASURE
    And under the Pain of our highest Displeasure,   . .   266 Apollo   101
    For your displeasure is their only shame.   . . .   309 Billet Players   52
DISPOS'D
    By lodging Folks dispos'd to sleep.   . . . . . .   94 Bauc & Phil 1   152
    By lodging Folks dispos'd to Sleep.   . . . . . .   114 Bauc & Phil 2   106
    Was now dispos'd to a crack a Jest;   . . . . . .   171 Horace 1, 7   15
    If still you be dispos'd to rhime, ...   645 On Poetry   145
    Again, as I'm dispos'd, the Foe   . . . .   934 Riddle 21   D   5
DISPOSE
    Would so discreetly Things dispose, ...   584 Strephon Chloe   15
    And, just as we dispose your brain, ...   620 Scandal Poem 1   93
    And, just as we dispose your Brain, ...   626 Scandal Poem 2   91
    But how to dispose of it to the best Bidder,   . . .   867 Grand Question   5
DISPUTE
    To overheare the grand Dispute.   . . . .   63 Discovery   28

	PAGE	TITLE	LINE
DISPUTE (CONTINUED)			
He mark't the Conjugall Dispute,	219	A Quiet Life	3
Can in her Female Clubs dispute	416	Woman's Mind	29
Dare you dispute,	440	Ballyspellin	1
They contradict, affirm, dispute,	450	Modern Lady	176
Allow there's a Hell, but dispute of the Place;	575	Place Damn'd	2
And these, she offer'd to dispute,	697	Cadenus Vaness	344
Vanessa finish'd the Dispute,	708	Cadenus Vaness	675
And taught Vanessa to dispute.	709	Cadenus Vaness	713
(We won't dispute a Year or more)	721	Stel B-Day '18	2
For of the two, without Dispute,	797	Traulus 1	43
To dispute, her chief delight,	906	Daphne	9
When learned Doctors will dispute,	930	Riddle 15	D 22
DISPUTES			
Of Comments and Disputes, ridiculous and vain,	23	Ode Athenian	226
How shall we find Thee then in dark disputes?	34	Ode Sancroft	10
But Patrige ended all Disputes,	99	Elegy Patrige	33
Then, for his Voice, there's none disputes	602	Beasts Confess	35
For long disputes will only weary us.	774	Mullinix Tim	34
All involv'd in wild Disputes;	833	Legion Club	114
Domestick Subject for Disputes,	919	Riddle 5	2
DISPUTING			
Among proud Doctors and disputing Pharisees:	39	Ode Sancroft	169
By disputing I will never	908	Daphne	55
DISQUALIFIED			
Are so disqualified by Fate	641	On Poetry	39
DISSECTING			
As virtuosoes' in dissecting flies;	46	To Congreve	94
DISSEMBLING			
Are Arts peculiar to dissembling France:	11	Ode to William	D 2
They mourn for me without dissembling.	561	Death of Swift	224
DISSENTERS			
Against Dissenters wou'd repine,	115	Bauc & Phil 2	133
And for dissenters he intends	422	Ireld	45
DISSOLV'D			
Dissolv'd, and into Money Coin'd;	345	Prometheus	38
DISSOLVES			
That a sieve dissolves riddles by help of the shears;	976	Dean to Sherid	20
DISTANCE			
Like sun-beams shot at too far distance from a glass;	35	Ode Sancroft	24
"And since unhappy distance thus denies	55	Temple Ill	143
The Courtiers kept their Distance due,	63	Discovery	18
He keeps his Distance in the Gallery	294	Prog Marriage	141
But, awfully his Distance kept.	587	Strephon Chloe	114
The Fellows learn to know their Distance.	888	Panegyr Dean	56
To be easy keep your distance;	907	Daphne	26
With Ease I make to keep their Distance,	934	Riddle 21	D 4
Of Serpent-Kind, and what at distance kills,	941	Letter	23
DISTANT			
Like distant echo spent, the spirit dies.	50	To Congreve	230
At distant hours the mind with forms so like!	51	Temple Ill	2
Be distant as one Head can bear;	366	Answer Delaney	30
By often shifting into distant Grounds;	538	Mr. Pulteney	18
From distant Regions, Fortune sends	883	Rev Market-Hill	1
Thro' distant Regions I can fly,	930	Riddle 15	D 17
DISTANTLY			
Does distantly my Pow'r obey.	934	Riddle 21	D 12
DISTILL			
As from a mossy Cliff distill;	589	Strephon Chloe	176
DISTILL'D			
Distill'd from Tripsy's darling Whelp;	526	Lady's Dres Rm	32
DISTILLING			
The faded Bow distilling Rain.	290	Prog Marriage	14
DISTILLS			
Her Heart, and from her Lips distills;	592	Strephon Chloe	280
DISTINCTION			
And buy distinction at the dearest rate.	506	To a Friend	12
DISTINCTLY			
Wherein she distinctly could read ev'ry Line,	264	Apollo	51
Are to the Life distinctly seen.	325	Pethox	72
Distinctly seen as through a Glass:	920	Riddle 6	14
DISTINGUISH			
And how distinguish, which is which,	642	On Poetry	73
But all distinguish thy dull leaden Mass.	670	Epig Carthy 18	D 6
How to distinguish Friends from Foes;	796	Traulus 1	24
DISTINGUISH'D			
He shines distinguish'd in a College;	384	Manly Virtue	34
Alone distinguish'd Man from Brute:	697	Cadenus Vaness	345
Distinguish'd ev'ry Feature in't;	783	Tim and Fables	16
DISTINGUISHER			
The Great Distinguisher of Blood,	7	Ode to King	23
DISTINGUISHING			
Without distinguishing her Face.	706	Cadenus Vaness	635
DISTORT			
Nor spoil your Shape, distort your Face,	414	Censure	23
Nor dare distort my Face for shame.	727	To Stella	116
DISTORTIONS			
Distortions, Groanings, Strainings, Heavings;	591	Strephon Chloe	241
DISTRACT			
Now, for thy Safety Cares distract my Mind,	772	Horace 1, 14	58

216

	PAGE	TITLE	LINE
DISTRACTED			
Such Marks of a distracted Mind;	704	Cadenus Vaness	563
DISTRESS			
You should have kiss'd it in your Distress,	135	Magician's Rod	81
Distress of Nations calls him hence,	387	Manly Virtue	113
"But succour'd Virtue in Distress,	566	Death of Swift	335
Had not her friends been in distress?	755	Stella '23	28
DISTRESS'D			
Thus thou, a Friend to the Distress'd,	182	Horace 2, 1	57
"And Lovers of the Church distress'd---:	549	Life of Swift	161
DISTRESS'T			
The Offals of a Church distress't,	484	Libel on D- D-	131
How was the fearful Animal distress't!	538	Mr. Pulteney	31
DISTRESSES			
Assist all Poets in Distresses,	411	Dial Rich Marb	94
"In all Distresses of our Friends	553	Death of Swift	7
DISTREST			
Was left in Foreign Lands distrest,	482	Libel on D- D-	62
The dullest Beast, and a Party distrest,	940	Letter	8
DISTRICTS			
These o'er their proper Districts govern,	649	On Poetry	283
DISTURB			
Disturb the present Mitre, as that fearful storm of late,	40	Ode Sancroft	192
Nor let such Cares disturb thy Rest.	182	Horace 2, 1	70
Not to disturb him in his Sleep;	280	Journal	46
To Teize, Perplex, Disturb, Confound,	777	Mullinix Tim	142
DISTURBS			
Which now disturbs the Queen and Court,	190	Faggot	25
DISUSE			
Lost by Disuse the Art to roast	93	Bauc & Phil 1	126
Lost, by Disuse, the Art to Roast,	113	Bauc & Phil 2	66
"Thro' long Disuse of Solitude;	379	Apology Lady C	136
DITCH			
Who sees the Ditch too deep and wide.	640	On Poetry	18
When you with Oonah stood behind a Ditch,	882	Pastoral Dial	37
DITCH'S SEE FLEET-DITCH'S			
DITCHER			
Our Thatcher, Ditcher, Gard'ner, Baily.	891	Panegyr Dean	156
DITCHES			
While Harry's fencing up his ditches.	878	Robbin & Harry	28
DITTIES			
To mournful Ditties, Clio, change thy Note,	284	Elegy Boat	1
DITTO			
But as to Ditto 't thro the Town,	372	Letter D. S-y	15
And <Wood's> ditto Pills do Swallow,	372	Letter D. S-y	30
DIU			
Et diu potuisse, et non potuisse refelli.	967	Letter Sherid	6
DIURETICK			
Carminative and Diuretick,	588	Strephon Chloe	133
DIVERSION			
Lose not your time, nor our diversion miss,	309	Billet Players	57
Think not Cards my chief Diversion,	632	Epistle Lady	81
Next, for his diversion,	853	Lady's Lament	67
DIVERSIONS			
Here, all Diversions of the Place	294	Prog Marriage	131
And take some small Diversions now and then?	662	Upon Ladies	4
DIVERT			
You still divert with merry Stories;	778	Mullinix Tim	148
And in the Streets divert the City	780	Mullinix Tim	240
DIVERTED			
Am more diverted with a quibble	900	Dean's Reasons	61
DIVERTING			
And both alike diverting,	784	Mullinex Dick	6
DIVIDE			
His Soul and Spirit did divide,	99	Elegy Patrige	65
So quickly broke if you divide.	189	Faggot	12
The Monster into Parts divide,	258	Bubble	203
"Divide the rest, but then take care,	321	First of April	11
Their Empire in our Hearts divide:	555	Death of Swift	42
They could all Pow'r in Heaven divide,	657	On Poetry	483
And so may such <Bishops> for ever divide,	805	Irish Bishops	37
The <Bishops> divide, the Clergy unite.	805	Irish Bishops	44
As Machiavel taught 'em; divide and ye govern.	805	Irish Bishops	48
Divide the Realm between us two.	886	Rev Market-Hill	92
DIVIDED			
Divided Hearts, united States.	96	On the Union	6
Is divided above, but united below.	805	Irish Bishops	42
DIVIDERS			
But we took our dividers, and found your <damn'd> metre,	1026	Sheri Circles	11
DIVIDINGS			
What a Clutter with Clippings, Dividings, and Cleavings!	804	Irish Bishops	33
DIVIN'D			
And, by a gentle Bow, divin'd	133	Magician's Rod	31
But, oh! how ill hast thou divin'd	595	Cassinus Peter	67
DIVIN'TY			
In the divin'ty of retreat,	36	Ode Sancroft	51
DIVINE			
Shall I believe a Spirit so divine	32	Ode to Temple	178
And divine Sancroft, weary with the weight	40	Ode Sancroft	185
Then with that grief we form in spirits divine,	43	To Congreve	5

DIVINE   (CONTINUED)   PAGE   TITLE   LINE
    And wisely judge, no pow'r beneath divine   . . . . .   44 To Congreve   29
    Such to unhallowed sight the Muse divine   . . . . .   52 Temple Ill   29
    At the divine appearance of the Muse, ...   53 Temple Ill   76
    If your Money be gone, as a Learned Divine says, d'ye   72 Mrs Harris Pet   56
        see,
    And stood up firm for Right Divine: . . . . .   115 Bauc & Phil 2   134
    For Vows Divine are kept by Fate.   . . . . . . 121 Apollo Outwit   48
    Tho' down from Ancestors Divine   . . . . . . 134 Magician's Rod   61
    Or, if it please the Powers Divine, ... 243 Horace 4, 9   19
    Now destin'd, by the Powers divine, ... 272 Apollo's Edict   D 68
    A rich Divine began to woo   . . .   289 Prog Marriage   2
    Canst thou imagine, dull Divine, ... 292 Prog Marriage   71
    He like an orderly Divine   . . . . . . 292 Prog Marriage   83
    The grave Divine with knotty Points perplext, ...   364 On Dreams   31
    So hearing of a grave Divine, ... 375 Apology Lady C   5
    For, had our deaf Divine   . . . . . . 406 Swift to Pope   22
    No more the Dean, that grave Divine, ... 409 Dial Rich Marb   43
    When my old cassock says a Welch divine   . . . .   419 Shall Repine   5
    To treat a dull Divine: . . . . . . 426 Five Ladies   24
    As Poet, Scholar and Divine.   . . . . .   455 Dean Smedley   4
    That sound Divine the Truth has spoke all   . . . . .   469 Birthday Song   271
    The Horse's Countenance Divine.   . . . . .   498 Panegyr Swift   176
    Far otherwise a great Divine, ... 513 Answer Fable   11
    For once to wet her Pen Divine: . . . . . . 515 Answer Fable   90
    This Protestant Zealot, this <English> Divine . . . . .   518 Dean Hang Rape   31
    You'd swear, that so divine a Creature   . . . . .   584 Strephon Chloe   19
    And, spight of Chloe's Charms divine, ...   591 Strephon Chloe   249
    Nor Eloquence Divine express, ... 595 Cassinus Peter   56
    For ever fixt by Right Divine, ... 642 On Poetry   57
    What Lineaments divine we trace   . . . . . . 655 On Poetry   417
    Our eldest Hope, divine Iulus, ... 655 On Poetry   429
    And bring in doubt their Pow'r divine;   . . . . .   687 Cadenus Vaness   12
    She knew, by Augury Divine, ... 695 Cadenus Vaness   276
    It answers Faith in Things divine.   . . . . .   723 To Stella   10
    The Bow'rs that hold those Nymphs divine;   . . . . .   729 Stella, Poems   42
    And when I brag of Aid divine, ... 741 Stel B-day 22   29
    First taught thee human Knowledge and divine; . . . .   791 St. Pat's Well   28
    As Moses, by divine Advice, ... 813 Bro Protestant   49
    Nor ever own'd a Pow'r Divine, ... 820 Dr. Rundle   35
    Every young Divine thy Brother.   . . . . .   838 Legion Club   200
    (A civil Divine!   . . . . . . 854 Lady's Lament   103
    Like a hearty divine;   . . . . . . 858 Lady's Lament   222
    A bishop that is no divine;   . . . . . . 876 To Dean Swift   21
    Contemners of thy Rites divine.   . . . . .   895 Panegyr Dean   272
    Be Witness for me, Nymph divine, ...   896 Panegyr Dean   315
    Without my Aid, the best Divine   . . . . .   915 Riddle 1   29
    Physician, Lawyer, and Divine, ...   922 Riddle 7   29
    Wrapt up in Majesty divine, ... 949 Epigr Fasting   5
    And I must confess as a Dean and Divine   . . . . .   1017 Swift Ans Sher   3
DIVINELY
    For Gulliver divinely shews, ... 498 Panegyr Swift   167
DIVINES
    That, bending down it's Top, divines   . . . . . . 133 Magician's Rod   23
    By dull Divines, who look with envious Eyes, ...   193 Author Himself   3
    Is now caress't by Candidate Divines: . . . . .   196 Author Himself   64
    From not the gravest of Divines, ... 764 Stel B-day '26   13
    For Divines allow, that God   . . . . . . 830 Legion Club   31
    Both dress'd like divines, with band and face clean. . .   843 Ay and No   2
    Above our neighb'ring dull Divines!   . . . . .   888 Panegyr Dean   64
    And Smedly, Flow'r of all Divines, ... 897 Panegyr Dean   345
    Beside a Brace of grave Divines;   . . . . . . 1020 Nim-Dan-Dean 1 D 3
DIVINITY
    Of Morals and Divinity, ...   19 Ode Athenian   106
    He reconcil'd Divinity and Wit.   . . . . .   194 Author Himself   12
DIVINUM
    Who shew'd a better Jus divinum?   . . . . . . 820 Dr. Rundle   38
DIVISIONS
    If making Divisions was all their Intent, ...   804 Irish Bishops   35
DIVULGE
    Which to divulge might shake profane belief, ...   53 Temple Ill   77
DIXON
    And, I'll engage with Peggy Dixon: . . . . . . 685 Rev Market-Hill   86
    With Peggy Dixon thoughtful sit, ... 897 Panegyr Dean   331
DIZEN'D
    Corinna in the Morning dizen'd, ...   583 Young Nymph   73
    (For sure, I had dizen'd you out like a Queen:) . . .   870 Grand Question   102
DO   120   OMITTED WORD
DO'S
    Which, what it bravely Won, do's well Maintain. . . .   12 Ode to William   D 28
    The brave Attempt do's all our Foes disarm, ...   13 Ode to William   D 37
    France do's in vain her feeble Arts apply   . . . . .   13 Ode to William   D 41
    Your Influence do's the vain Attacks defy   . . . . .   13 Ode to William   D 43
    So much his Stay do's swell the Bills;   . . . . .   860 Lady Acheson   30
DO'ST
    "When thou thy humble Lays do'st offer   . . . . .   476 Epist on Epist   32
DO'T
    And tho' some Malicious Young Spirit did do't, . . .   77 Lady B- B-   29
    She'd do't if 'twere to do again.   . . . . . . 224 Prog of Love   58
    She'll never do't another Time, ... 224 Prog of Love   64
    And, if Swearing can do't, shall be swingingly mawl'd: . 238 Excellent Song   29

		PAGE	TITLE	LINE
DO'T	(CONTINUED)			
Fine Ladyes never do't		428	Beau's Reply	6
"And this, or nothing else, wou'd do't.		714	Cadenus Vaness	877
DOAT				
Still wear, still doat on his Invisible Ring. . . .		21	Ode Athenian	157
DOATS				
And drain the Fish-ponds; while your Master doats; . .		534	To Mr. Gay	90
DOBSON				
Old Good-man Dobson of the Green		116	Bauc & Phil 2	165
DOCK				
Than yon tall Dock that rises to thy Nose.		881	Pastoral Dial	14
Cut down the Dock, 'twill sprout again: but O! . . .		881	Pastoral Dial	15
DOCTOR				
To find the Doctor out.		74	Game Traffick	4
Even so Master Doctor had Puzzled his Brains . . .		77	Lady B- B-	22
Step to the Doctor straight, and say, ...		172	Horace 1, 7	49
The Doctor fasten'd by the Eyes, ...		172	Horace 1, 7	58
Beck'ning the Doctor to approach.		172	Horace 1, 7	62
The Doctor now obeys the Summons, ...		173	Horace 1, 7	73
No, Doctor, you shall be a Dean;		173	Horace 1, 7	88
The Doctor in a Passion cry'd;		175	Horace 1, 7	131
The Doctor and Dean, Pope, Parnell and Gay		185	Scriblerus 1	1
"A certain Doctor is observ'd of late, ...		195	Author Himself	43
"Ah Doctor, how you love to jest?		202	Horace 2, 6	97
The Doctor with a double Fee ·		294	Prog Marriage	129
What must the unhappy Doctor do?		376	Apology Lady C	42
Calls, Crach'rode, is the Doctor come?		377	Apology Lady C	58
The Doctor frighten'd at his Fault, ...		377	Apology Lady C	76
The Doctor stood not to debate, ...		378	Apology Lady C	93
The Doctor takes his hint from hence, ...		379	Apology Lady C	129
I'd knock the Doctor down;		426	Five Ladies	38
Name honest Doctor Pelling;		440	Ballyspellin	21
For since they talk'd with Doctor Clark, ...		468	Birthday Song	269
E're he advance the Doctor higher		475	Epist on Epist	24
But, Rev'rend Doctor, you, we know, ...		483	Libel on D- D-	111
Then pray, dear Doctor, condescend . ·		493	Panegyr Swift	27
Is this the Art, good Doctor, say, ...		497	Panegyr Swift	142
And for his singing, Doctor, you know, ...		513	Answer Fable	23
The Doctor names but one at present, ...		513	Answer Fable	33
To hold the Doctor by the Chin:		514	Answer Fable	64
The Doctor, if you will believe him, ...		604	Beasts Confess	113
I find, says he, she wants a Doctor, ...		702	Cadenus Vaness	498
The Doctor might have fancy'd worse.--		707	Cadenus Vaness	655
Sent in a bag to Doctor Swift, ...		753	Gift for Bec	3
Dear friend, Doctor Jenny, ...		857	Lady's Lament	203
The Dean and the Doctor have humbled their Pride, . .		871	Grand Question	131
And, the Doctor was plaguily down in the Hips. . .		873	Grand Question	178
DOCTOR'S				
The Doctor's Family came by, ...		128	Little House	47
Now all the Doctor's Money's spent, ...		174	Horace 1, 7	107
In vain - - - no Doctor's to be found		377	Apology Lady C	64
Now pray observe the Doctor's Choice, ...		513	Answer Fable	19
The Council sit; approve the Doctor's Skill; . . .		534	To Mr. Gay	79
DOCTORS				
Among proud Doctors and disputing Pharisees:		39	Ode Sancroft	169
The Doctors tender of their Fame, ...		558	Death of Swift	169
Doctors pronounce the patient dead;		761	Bec's B-Day	12
Not for the World--we Doctors, Brother, ...		812	Bro Protestant	17
Of Doctors, Fevers, Plagues, and Pills.		903	Death Daphne	6
When learned Doctors will dispute, ...		930	Riddle 15	D 22
The dullest Beast, and what Doctors pretend		941	Letter	37
But you learned Doctors can make whom you chuse sick. .		1029	Dr. Helsham	19
DOCTRINE				
Doctrine, or Discipline our Brethren, ...		812	Bro Protestant	30
DOCTRINES				
His Doctrines when she first imbib'd;		708	Cadenus Vaness	679
DODDY				
. . . and not a spindle-shank'd hoddy doddy.		985	Mary to Sher	10
DOES 58			OMITTED WORD	
DOG SEE LAP-DOG				
Here a Dog dancing on his Hamms		123	Empty'ng Town	13
Are Cat and Dog, and Rogue and Whore.		225	Prog of Love	100
Since a living Dog better is than a dead Lyon, . . .		237	Excellent Song	13
He answer'd, that a Dog of late		298	Horrid Plot	3
And so a perjur'd Dog denotes		298	Horrid Plot	9
But you must know this Dog was lame.		298	Horrid Plot	12
Come, help your lame Dog o'er the Style.		298	Horrid Plot	15
I mean a Dog, without a Joke, ...		298	Horrid Plot	17
I'm still to seek which Dog you mean;		298	Horrid Plot	19
That, every Dog must have his Day.		299	Horrid Plot	30
Dog <Walpole> laid a Quart of Nog on't, ...		299	Horrid Plot	31
He'd either make a Hog or Dog on't, ...		299	Horrid Plot	32
A Dog of Spirit for his Years, ...		299	Horrid Plot	45
I thought it was a Dog in Doublet:		300	Horrid Plot	58
And not a Dog in Metaphor, ...		300	Horrid Plot	62
And, when we found the Dog begin it, ...		300	Horrid Plot	69
A Dog and <Bishop> ne'er was seen, ...		301	Horrid Plot	74
Is qualified best for a Dog in a String.		389	Order of Bath	12
Quoth the Thief to the Dog; let me into your Door, .		395	Dog and Thief	1
Quoth the Dog, I should then be more Villain than you're,		395	Dog and Thief	3

DOG	(CONTINUED)	PAGE	TITLE	LINE
A dog would be weary on.		402	Window Inns 8	D 10
In tipling at the Dog and Partridge;		411	Dial Rich Marb	98
T'is the Cur dog of Brittain & spaniel of Spain. .		540	Charac Walpole	14
A Dog by Instinct turns aside, ...		640	On Poetry	17
A Dog, a Parrot, or an Ape, ...		687	Cadenus Vaness	39
Now I am a Dog, or Cow, ...		933	Riddle 20	D 9
For Whore and Rogue; and Dog and Bitch.		949	Epigr Scolding	4
For, were you a Dog, I could not be rude t'ye.		968	Letter Sherid	26
I would not give such Language to a Dog, faith and troth		985	Mary to Sher	4
. . .when one would not turn out a Dog that one valued; .		1014	Swift to Sheri	10

DOG-DAYS
| Could in the Dog-Days smell her Toes. . . . . . . | | 584 | Strephon Chloe | 24 |

DOG-FISH
| A Pack of Dog-fish had him in the Wind: . . . . . | | 538 | Mr. Pulteney | 22 |

DOG-LOGICK
| And you have prov'd it by Dog-Logick. . . . . . | | 300 | Horrid Plot | 72 |

DOG-TRICKS
| For Statesmen never want Dog-tricks. . . . . . | | 300 | Horrid Plot | 60 |

DOGGREL
| Treat me not with Doggrel Rhime. . . . . | | 631 | Epistle Lady | 58 |
| The vilest Doggrel Grubstreet sends, ... | | 644 | On Poetry | 139 |

DOGS
As Mastive Dogs in Modern Phrase are		82	Salamander	1
By all the Dogs and Curs in Town;		207	Fable Bitches	2
Then, like the Dogs of Nile be wise, ...		257	Bubble	177
You pay them well; the Dogs have got		299	Horrid Plot	27
Since you can teach dead Dogs to bite.		299	Horrid Plot	40
Will none the Tory Dogs pursue, ...		779	Mullinix Tim	185
Tho' your lords, and your dogs, and your catches, me-thinks,		977	Dean to Sherid	45
Your <Bishops> all are <Dogs> indeed.		301	Horrid Plot	76

DOGS-HEADS
| Their Dogs-heads in a Porridge-pot: . . . . . . | | 299 | Horrid Plot | 28 |

DOING
Sure there's some Wondrous Joy in Doing Good; . . .		6	Ode to King	1
But the Delight of Doing Good		6	Ode to King	19
Nor, think your self secure in doing wrong, . . .		533	To Mr. Gay	59
"Envy hath own'd it was his doing, ...		569	Death of Swift	411
The Dean has been doing.		857	Lady's Lament	194

DOINGS
| To the poor Doings of the Dean: . . . . | | 745 | Stel Distress | 18 |
| To the poor Doings of the <Dean>. . . . . | | 750 | Stel Wood-Park | 42 |

DOL
| He calld my Dol a perfect toast. . . . . | | 422 | Ireld | 32 |

DOLEFUL
| Receive the News in doleful Dumps, ... | | 562 | Death of Swift | 227 |
| In doleful Scenes, that breaks our heart, ... | | 777 | Mullinix Tim | 121 |

DOLL
Doll dying first, Dick grew Melancholly, ...		430	Dicky Dolly	2
For Dick without Doll thought Living a Folly. . . .		430	Dicky Dolly	3
Dick lost in Doll, a Wife Tender and Dear, ...		430	Dicky Dolly	4
But Dick lost by Doll, twelve hundred a Year, . . .		430	Dicky Dolly	5
Dick Sigh'd for his Doll and his mournfull Arms Cross'd,		430	Dicky Dolly	7
Thought much of his Doll, and the Jointure he lost,		430	Dicky Dolly	8
One Bed while alive held both Doll and Dick		430	Dicky Dolly	13
Doll never flies to cut her Lace, ...		725	To Stella	75
When Doll hangs out a newer Face		735	Stel B-day '20	34

DOLLS
| Immortalize our Dolls and Jenneys. . . . . . | | 184 | Horace 2, 1 | 116 |

DOLLY
| Under this Stone, lies Dicky and Dolly . . . . . | | 430 | Dicky Dolly | 1 |

DOLTS
| Which, as he scatter'd, we like Dolts, ... | | 353 | Wood Ironmongr | 33 |

DOME
| A Flora does the Dome protect; . . . . | | 477 | Epist on Epist | 78 |
| Sad Charnel-house! a dismal Dome, ... | | 922 | Riddle 7 | 51 |

DOMES
| Yet, when your lofty Domes I praise, ... | | 894 | Panegyr Dean | 225 |

DOMESTIC
| Domestic business never mind . . . . | | 761 | Bec's B-Day | 33 |

DOMESTICK
"Have kept Domestick Mice in awe, ...		154	Widow and Cat	D 24
Soon grows Domestick, seldom fails		173	Horace 1, 7	77
Answer all domestick Ends, ...		633	Epistle Lady	101
Domestick Subject for Disputes, ...		919	Riddle 5	2

DOMESTICKS
| Let all Domesticks feel your gentle Sway; . . . . | | 533 | To Mr. Gay | 55 |

DOMINION
For, Beauty, like supreme Dominion, ...		590	Strephon Chloe	223
From Jupiter took all dominion, ...		620	Scandal Poem 1	83
From Jupiter took all Dominion, ...		626	Scandal Poem 2	81

DOMINIONS
| I a Slave in thy Dominions; . . . . | | 660 | Love Song | 3 |
| His large Dominions under Ground. . . . . . . | | 903 | Death Daphne | 18 |

DOMITIAN
| And, like Domitian, leap at Flyes. . . . . . . | | 824 | Printer Newgat | 14 |

DON
| That you're Don Quixote Redivivus? . . . . . . | | 478 | Epist on Epist | 88 |

DON	(CONTINUED)	PAGE	TITLE	LINE
Because it chanc'd, an old grave Don		495	Panegyr Swift	84
Don Carlos in a merry Spight		745	Stel Distress	1
Don Carlos made her Sole Director.		745	Stel Distress	8
Don Carlos made her chief Director		745	Stel Distress	
Don Carlos earnestly would beg,		746	Stel Distress	17
Don Carlos now began to find		746	Stel Distress	31
You shew Don Carlos where to dwell,		748	Stel Distress	73
Don Carlos in a merry Spight,		749	Stel Wood-Park	1
Don Carlos made her chief Director,		749	Stel Wood-Park	5
Don Carlos earnestly would beg,		750	Stel Wood-Park	15
Don Carlos now began to find		750	Stel Wood-Park	23

DON'T   18   OMITTED WORD

DONE   SEE UN-DONE,OUT-DONE

Seem to discover what they would have done		38	Ode Sancroft	132
But pray, Mary, can you tell what I have done with my Purse!		70	Mrs Harris Pet	15
Then since you now have done your worst,		175	Horace 1, 7	137
See, said the Sire, how soon 'tis done:		189	Faggot	9
But when she thought her Pains were done,		208	Fable Bitches	23
('Tis always done, Romances tell us,		223	Prog of Love	47
The Thing was done and past recalling:		224	Prog of Love	68
Without a Star this may be done,		271	Apollo's Edict	D 42
Now Water's brought, and Dinner done,		279	Journal	35
The Curtain falls, and we have done.		280	Journal	60
Minds nothing that is done or said,		291	Prog Marriage	57
Now you've done right, No Knight attempting		373	Letter D. S-y	75
Supposing now you Song is done,		469	Birthday Song	275
What's to be done? shall wit and learning chuse,		506	To a Friend	7
One Clincher more, and I have done,		515	Answer Fable	101
His Work is done, the Minister must out.		536	To Mr. Gay	150
Yet still I fear your Work is done but Half;		538	Mr. Pulteney	13
Had some heroick Action done,		554	Death of Swift	23
"What had the Publick done for him!		558	Death of Swift	158
"He never thought an Honour done him,		565	Death of Swift	319
Then think, what wonders will be done		655	On Poetry	433
Saw all these mighty labours done,		675	Curate's Compl	14
Their work was half already done,		692	Cadenus Vaness	174
She'd all undo, that she had done.		694	Cadenus Vaness	255
Pallas had done more Harm than Good;		700	Cadenus Vaness	435
"But now, repenting what was done,		714	Cadenus Vaness	880
The Corruption of Verse, for when all is done,		716	Answer Rebus	9
Not minding when the Song was done.		775	Mullinix Tim	44
What Mischief can the <Dean> have done him,		796	Traulus 1	7
They've done it, we thank 'em, but not as they meant;		804	Irish Bishops	36
You have done what I desire:		839	Legion Club	232
Will never have done with his Gibes and his Jeers:		873	Grand Question	188
Yet, the plain Squire, when Dinner's done,		920	Riddle 6	27
Soon or late, my date is done,		937	Riddle 24	D 43

DONEGAL

Take Qualities from Donegal.		272	Apollo's Edict	D 75

DONORE

Jolly boys of St. Kevans, St. Patrick's, Donore,		814	Yahoo's	1
We'll colt him thro' Kevan, St. Patrick's, Donore,		817	Yahoo's	56

DONOURS

Tho the Exchequer be drained by prodigal Donours		389	Order of Bath	5

DOOM

And on my verse pronounce their saucy doom;		50	To Congreve	214
Here (lovely Nymph pronounce my doom)		60	Lady Tablebook	11
The Goddess thus pronounc'd her Doom:		696	Cadenus Vaness	304
So the Commons unhors'd them, and this was their Doom,		804	Irish Bishops	21
From whom great Sylla round his Doom;		925	Riddle 8	35

DOOM'D

Doom'd ever in Suspence to dwell,		113	Bauc & Phil 2	63
There doom'd to whirl an endless Round.		413	Desire Possess	50
The Nation scar'd, the Author doom'd to Death,		771	Horace 1, 14	31
Like a Butcher doom'd for Life,		800	Traulus 2	39
Is doom'd to be a Beau for life:		879	Robbin & Harry	52
May I be doom'd for Life to weed in Rain.		882	Pastoral Dial	44

DOOMD

Doomd ever in suspense to dwell,		93	Bauc & Phil 1	103

DOOR   SEE BACK-DOOR,TEMPLE-DOOR,PANTRY-DOOR,BARN-DOOR

And fling our Scraps before our Door.		28	Ode to Temple	57
One Story high, one postern Door,		81	Vanbrug House	77
You're on the wrong side of the Door.		91	Bauc & Phil 1	36
They beg'd from Door to Door in vain;		111	Bauc & Phil 2	12
They beg'd from Door to Door in vain;		111	Bauc & Phil 2	12
The Slipshod Prentice from his Masters Door,		124	Descriptn Morn	5
She'd beg with John from Door to Door:		224	Prog of Love	62
She'd beg with John from Door to Door:		224	Prog of Love	62
Nor loudly cackles at the Door;		230	Prog of Poetry	7
Such a Worm was Will. Wood when he scratcht at the Door		351	Wood Insect	29
Quoth the Thief to the Dog; let me into your Door,		395	Dog and Thief	1
There hang three crosses at thy door:		404	Window Inns 11	D 1
'Fool, to put up four Crosses at your door,		404	Window Inns 11	D 3
'There are Three Crosses at your door--		404	Window Inns 11	D 5
With early clients at his door,		434	Answer Paulus	71
Above the Door, at Country-fair,		457	Paddy's Charac	3
Full in his Face Bob shuts the Council Door:		537	Mr. Pulteney	4
Or strung on Pegs behind the Door;		592	Strephon Chloe	290
Apollo stirs not out of Door,		627	Scandal Poem 2	115

DOOR	(CONTINUED)	PAGE	TITLE	LINE
The Rascal had mistook the Door:	. . . .	746	Stel Distress	28
Nor would the Door admit her Hoop.	. . . .	746	Stel Distress	30
The Rascal had mistook the Door	. . . .	746	Stel Distress	
The Rascal had mistook the Door:	. . . .	751	Stel Wood-Park	48
In at the door his monstrous Nose,		776	Mullinix Tim	104
Their former Companions should beg at their Door.	. .	804	Irish Bishops	28
Near the Door an entrance gapes,	. . . .	832	Legion Club	87
Enter that Infernal Door;	. . . .	834	Legion Club	120
By clapping Billets on your Door and Posts Sir.	. . .	1002	Reply by Dean	12
And the worst of them all like a barn door did shine	. .	1017	Swift Ans Sher	6

DOORE
| For I saw'd them reading upon the towlsel doore. | . . . . | 840 | Ballad | D 4 |

DOORS
They break up Counters, Doors, and Tills,	. . . . . .	240	Run Bankers	39
To turn her Naked out of Doors,	. . . .	295	Prog Marriage	163
The Maids to the Doors and the Balconies ran,	. . . . .	399	Tom Clinch	7
Lay Grubstreet at each others Doors:	. . . . . .	652	On Poetry	346
Hangs a new Angel two doors from us	. . . . . .	734	Stel B-day '20	10

DORE
They call'd at ev'ry Dore; Good People,	. . . . .	90	Bauc & Phil 1	15
But hurry'd out, and clapp't the Dore.	. . . . . .	220	A Quiet Life	8
Apollo stirs not out of dore	. . . .	621	Scandal Poem 1	121
All Men of Sense will pass your Dore	. . . . . .	736	Stel B-day '20	57

DORINDA
| Thus, when Dorinda wept, joy ev'ry face forsook, | . . . . | 53 | Temple Ill | 59 |
| Dorinda dreams of Dress a bed | . . . . | 733 | Verses Vanessa | 23 |

DORINDA'S
| It's watery footsteps in Dorinda's face; | . . . . . . | 52 | Temple Ill | 52 |
| Grief from Dorinda's face does ne'er depart | . . . . . | 53 | Temple Ill | 53 |

DORMANT
| Produce at last thy dormant Ducal Patent: | . . . . | 538 | Mr. Pulteney | 10 |

DORMOUSE
| Sleep like a Dormouse; | . . . . | 1035 | Servants Maxim | 2 |

DOROTHEA
| Mild Dorothea, peaceful, wise and great, | . . . . | 52 | Temple Ill | 41 |
| Mild Dorothea, whom we both have long | . . . . | 52 | Temple Ill | 43 |

DOROTHEA'S
| In the fair shrine of Dorothea's mind. | . . . . . . | 52 | Temple Ill | 50 |

DOS'D
| When dos'd with smoak, and smear'd with snuff: | . . . . | 936 | Riddle 24 | D 10 |

DOSE
| Steals off to dose away his Beef, | . . . . | 279 | Journal | 40 |

DOST 3 | | | OMITTED WORD | |

DOTARD
| Keeper, yon old Dotard smoke, | . . . . | 836 | Legion Club | 159 |

DOTARDS
| With all that Factious or Enthusiastick Dotards dream, | | 22 | Ode Athenian | 204 |

DOTH 4 | | | OMITTED WORD | |

DOTING
| And doting in an easy chair; | . . . . | 401 | Window Inns 5 | D 4 |

DOUBLE
In this Your Virtue claims a double share,		12	Ode to William	D 27
See how the double Nation lies;	. . . .	96	On the Union	7
A Vessel with a double Keel:	. . . .	96	On the Union	16
Strike your offended Sense with double Stink.	. . . . .	137	City Shower	6
When known, will save a double Sorrow.	. . . . . .	204	In Sickness	28
The Doctor with a double Fee	. . . .	294	Prog Marriage	129
Since t' other will in Strength be double;	. . . .	366	Answer Delaney	12
Their Meanings lewd, and double 'Entendres.	. . . .	449	Modern Lady	143
Of Bargains sold, or meanings double.	. . . . . .	469	Birthday Song	274
Thy Toil is lessen'd, and thy Profits double.	. . . . .	521	Stephen Duck	8
Away the Hare with double Swiftness fled.	. . . . .	538	Mr. Pulteney	28
And to take a double Fee;	. . . ., . .	574	Helter Skelter	50
To comprehend a double Meaning.	. . . .	592	Strephon Chloe	276
Like Janus, bears a double Face;	. . . .	765	Stel B-day '26	74
Lo, here I stand with double Face;	. . . .	917	Riddle 3	2
I with double lustre shine.	. . . .	936	Riddle 24	D 12
But your rhyme was not double, 'cause your sight was but single.		980	Tho: Sheridan	2

DOUBLE-BOTTOM'D
| Our crazy double-bottom'd Realm. | . . . . | 96 | On the Union | 22 |

DOUBLE-DISMAL
| And Dismal double-Dismal looks; | . . . . | 168 | Peace Dunkirk | 12 |

DOUBLED
| Although thy Size and Years arc doubled, | . . . . . | 721 | Stel B-Day '18 | 4 |

DOUBLET
| I thought it was a Dog in Doublet: | . . . . . . | 300 | Horrid Plot | 58 |
| To keep out of Danger, a Doublet of Stone. | . . . . . | 351 | Wood Insect | 10 |

DOUBLINGS
| Thy Turns and Doublings cannot save thee long. | . . . | 539 | Mr. Pulteney | 44 |

DOUBLY
Curst be the Wretch, nay doubly curst,	. . . . .	28	Ode to Temple	50
And doubly twisted it for strength;	. . . .	760	Bec's B-Day	4
My Petticoat is doubly fring'd.	. . . .	896	Panegyr Dean	314

DOUBT
Contrive to shock your Minds, with many a sensless doubt,		22	Ode Athenian	207
And not to satisfy the doubt;	. . . .	35	Ode Sancroft	16
A search, no doubt, as curious and as wise	. . . . .	46	To Congreve	93
I doubt your Heart is set on Pelf	. . . .	175	Horace 1, 7	125
<Walpole> and Ayslaby, to clear the Doubt,	. . . .	195	Author Himself	41

		PAGE	TITLE	LINE
DOUBT	(CONTINUED)			
"I doubt not, if his Lordship knew--		201	Horace 2, 6	61
The Point he could no longer doubt,		255	Bubble	129
You all agree, I make no doubt,		270	Apollo's Edict	D 23
But we doubt that our Purses will quickly grow lank,		287	Bank Down	14
She could not doubt her Uncle's Favour.		303	Storm	24
No doubt, will prove a good Arbuthnot:		314	To Ford	76
I hear among Scholars there is a great Doubt		334	Serious Poem	25
When the True Wood arrives, as he soon will no doubt,		336	Serious Poem	75
My Tenants, if you doubt, will prove it:		348	Whitshed Motto	8
The Church and Clergy here, no doubt,		401	Window Inns 4	1
Till Envy, Slander, Sloth, and Doubt,		412	Desire Possess	15
'Tis wise, no doubt, as clients fat ye more,		433	Answer Paulus	41
No doubt the text is here mistaken:		434	Answer Paulus	66
His Learning none will call in doubt;		484	Libel on D- D-	140
We thought, there now remain'd no room to doubt:		536	To Mr. Gay	149
Envy, I doubt, wou'd pow'rful prove,		546	Life of Swift	37
"And that, I doubt, is no good Sign.		557	Death of Swift	110
And bring in doubt their Pow'r divine;		687	Cadenus Vaness	12
And, had her Stock been less, no doubt		735	Stel B-day '20	31
Of cleanly Houses who will doubt,		787	Clad in Brown	29
The world is in doubt, whether hatred or love;		818	Archbi Cashel	2
'Though Fools may doubt his Faith in <Jesus>.		820	Dr. Rundle	26
Nor need we doubt the Fort to win;		885	Rev Market-Hill	55
A sieve keeps half in, and therefore, no doubt,		976	Dean to Sherid	25
But I doubt 'tis a Sham,		1015	Swift to Sheri	47
But I doubt the Oraculum,		1015	Swift to Sheri	55
DOUBTED				
She doubted not but such a Dame		693	Cadenus Vaness	230
She doubted not to win the Swain.		905	Death Daphne	70
DOUBTFUL				
That must their doubtful Liberty defend.		12	Ode to William	D 32
Trembling beheld the doubtful hand of fate;		52	Temple Ill	42
'Twas doubtful which was Rain, and which was Dust.		137	City Shower	26
And pausing o'er a Pipe, with doubtful Nod,		193	Author Himself	5
DOUBTLESS				
The Angel (doubtless) kept th' Eternal Gate,		8	Ode to King	65
DOUBTS				
Doubts, where the Delphick God . . .		22	Ode Athenian	208
Of Doubts, Impertinence, and Niceties,		22	Ode Athenian	213
To whom she might her Doubts propose		689	Cadenus Vaness	97
DOUGLAS				
But princely Douglas, and his glorious Dame,		531	To Mr. Gay	13
DOUN				
But with the upside doun to shew		92	Bauc & Phil 1	99
DOUX SEE BILLET-DOUX				
Here, a Page fill'd with Billet Doux;		60	Lady Tablebook	13
DOVE				
Where the bless'd spirit lodges like the dove,		41	Ode Sancroft	227
To bake one Loaf, and keep one Dove in.		127	Little House	38
DOVE-MUSE				
And the Dove-muse, will now no longer stay		16	Ode Athenian	16
And the Dove-muse is fled once more,		17	Ode Athenian	32
DOVE-TAIL'D				
Each groov'd, and Dove-tail'd, like a Box.		1021	Nim-Dan-Dean 1	D 26
DOVER				
And rides through Dover in the Morn:		398	Earl of P-b-w	17
DOVES				
And how her Doves were kill'd by Weezles:		282	Journal	94
She must have doves to draw her chair:		621	Scandal Poem 1	116
She must have Doves to draw her Chair.		627	Scandal Poem 2	114
Drawn by her Doves, away she flies,		692	Cadenus Vaness	186
Harness'd her Doves, and flew to Heav'n.		714	Cadenus Vaness	889
DOWDY				
But, ev'ry sublunary dowdy		617	Scandal Poem 1	13
But, ev'ry sublunary Dowdy,		624	Scandal Poem 2	13
DOWDYS				
What Dowdys they appear before her!		465	Birthday Song	158
DOWN				
The Tyrant Death lay crouching down,		7	Ode to King	39
Stay but a little while and down again 'twill come,		10	Ode to King	128
Giddy he grows, and down is hurl'd,		10	Ode to King	144
Forcing a wretched Trade by beating down the sale,		19	Ode Athenian	101
To censure, to cry down, and rail,		19	Ode Athenian	114
Whose Reason is weigh'd down by Popular air,		21	Ode Athenian	181
Which greedily they swallow down,		27	Ode to Temple	48
Down the ill-organ'd Engines fall;		29	Ode to Temple	98
And softly steals in many Windings down,		31	Ode to Temple	156
Ready to tumble down into the sky;		35	Ode Sancroft	36
And swallow'd them at last, or flung them down.		40	Ode Sancroft	197
Who, to pollute my shades, bring'st with thee down		44	To Congreve	9
Thus I look down with mercy on the age,		45	To Congreve	49
Return'd a finish'd spark this summer down,		47	To Congreve	119
And once drawn up, is ne'er let down again.		50	To Congreve	234
Down falls the summer's pride, and sadly shews		55	Temple Ill	123
By all means to bring down the Rates,		64	Discovery	42
And, instead of putting it into my Pocket, down it slipt:		69	Mrs Harris Pet	9
Then the Bell rung, and I went down to put my Lady to Bed,		69	Mrs Harris Pet	10
If I come down, I'll spoil your Trick		91	Bauc & Phil 1	45
His Grazier's Coat reach down his Heels,		94	Bauc & Phil 1	166

DOWN   (CONTINUED)   PAGE   TITLE   LINE

	PAGE	TITLE	LINE
But do not shed thy Influence down	100	Elegy Patrige	95
And, (like a Wag) sat down to Write,	107	V's House	61
Down from Olympus Top he Slides,	108	V's House	69
To a small Village down in Kent;	111	Bauc & Phil 2	10
But with the Upside down, to shew	113	Bauc & Phil 2	59
His Grazier's Coat fall down his Heels;	115	Bauc & Phil 2	118
Plain Goody would no longer down,	116	Bauc & Phil 2	143
To mend his Barn, cut Baucis down;	117	Bauc & Phil 2	174
The God laid down his Feeble Rays,	119	Apollo Outwit	5
When Nature would invite us down,	122	Empty'ng Town	3
The Crib was down, the Blackbird caught.	127	Little House	30
But soon as e'er he lay'd it down,	132	Magician's Rod	3
But when he lay'd it down, as quick	132	Magician's Rod	13
That, bending down it's Top, divines	133	Magician's Rod	23
Tho' down from Ancestors Divine	134	Magician's Rod	61
Now in contiguous Drops the Flood comes down.	138	City Shower	31
While Streams run down her oil'd Umbrella's Sides.	138	City Shower	38
Dead Cats and Turnip-Tops come tumbling down the Flood	139	City Shower	63
To whom from Midas down, decends	157	Fable of Midas	43
He must sink down, or find Up-holders	160	Atlas	22
Take care betimes to run him down:	171	Horace 1, 7	30
And down to Windsor takes his Guest.	173	Horace 1, 7	82
Down from her silver chariot came,	178	To Lord Harley	75
Came up, and knock't the Praetor down.	190	Faggot	34
From Sommers down to Craigs and Walpole.	191	Faggot	52
As once a week we travel down.	201	Horace 2, 6	77
Nor stoops to take the Staff, nor lays it down,	210	Earl of Oxford	9
Who first Run one another down,	217	To Mr. Delany	55
Down from her Window in the Sky,	226	Prog of Beauty	7
His Flesh brought down to Flying-Case:	231	Prog of Poetry	40
If he shou'd now be cry'd down since his Change	235	Elegy on Demar	36
Shake it down to the Feet,	246	Irish-Feast	50
Come down with that Beam,	247	Irish-Feast	85
And in he leaps, and down he sinks.	252	Bubble	32
And down the towring Boy is cast:	252	Bubble	40
A Flock of Geese jump down together,	253	Bubble	54
Sinks down at once, and there he lyes,	253	Bubble	82
Thus from a Hillock looking down,	255	Bubble	126
And justle one another down,	256	Bubble	146
Till those devouring Swine run down,	259	Bubble	214
Writes down my Conceits, and then calls them his own:	265	Apollo	86
Hawls him, and scolds us down to Breakfast.	279	Journal	16
Down the black Sea, and up the Streights,	282	Journal	107
And Thanks to the Members that Kickt down the Bank.	287	Bank Down	10
Sits down to Dinner just at four;	291	Prog Marriage	56
As if he had thrown down a Dish.	299	Horrid Plot	34
Our set of strollers, wand'ring up and down,	307	Billet Players	1
To cut down fine Wood is a very bad Thing,	334	Serious Poem	13
Then if cutting down Wood brings Money good Store,	334	Serious Poem	15
Our Money to keep, let us Cut down One more.	334	Serious Poem	16
Very soon to see Wood Drop down from a Rope.	338	Serious Poem	116
Struck all his Rage and Malice down;	340	Arch-Bish Dub	20
Then down I went upon my Knees, his Blessing to obtain,	342	Upon His Grace	29
There is a Chain let down from Jove,	345	Prometheus	31
With real Thunder knock't him down.	353	Wood Ironmongr	24
Like real Thunder knock't him down.	353	Wood Ironmongr	38
Down to your Deanery repair	361	Grace's Answer	19
You never did, for 'twould not down.	372	Letter D. S-y	16
If Virtue dares not venture down,	392	Young's Satire	37
Down from your Garrets haste,	394	Grub-Street	2
The Stock-jobber thus, from Change-Alley goes down,	396	Dog and Thief	9
The Hangman for Pardon fell down on his Knee;	399	Tom Clinch	13
And I can hardly get him down	411	Dial Rich Marb	99
She knock't him with the Scepter down.	413	Desire Possess	48
An act for laying down the Plough,	422	Ireld	51
I'd knock the Doctor down;	426	Five Ladies	38
Trots to his country mansion down;	435	Answer Paulus	94
"Here, carry down those ten Pistoles	447	Modern Lady	66
And wink a Reputation down;	450	Modern Lady	193
Pull down an Ale-house-Bush, for Spite,	457	Paddy's Charac	8
But this I think will not go down,	460	Birthday Song	13
Must venture down to entertain us.	465	Birthday Song	156
Shall at their snowy feet lay down:	465	Birthday Song	168
Or whom you once sung up, sing down.	468	Birthday Song	260
Went down like stupifying Draughts:	470	Burning Poem	8
Oft' swallow'd down a stronger Potion,	495	Panegyr Swift	61
Lye down obscure like other Folks	501	Doctor Delaney	45
Must ever keep it's Owner down:	502	Doctor Delaney	80
And press you down with all their Weight.	503	Doctor Delaney	94
From Homer down to Pope inclusive.	504	Doctor Delaney	134
They Cudgell'd, and Cuft him, and kickt him down Stairs	517	Dean Hang Rape	16
Perhaps he might have truckled down,	549	Life of Swift	140
"To all their Boroughs send them down:	564	Death of Swift	284
"By bravely running Priest-craft down:	564	Death of Swift	292
Her flabby Dugs and down they drop.	582	Young Nymph	22
Press down the Lumps, the Hollows fill,	582	Young Nymph	26
And, bravely drove his Rivals down	585	Strephon Chloe	41
Come down to visit mortal Men:	587	Strephon Chloe	98
And then throw all their Weapons down;	592	Strephon Chloe	262
The t' other he sat down to darn	594	Cassinus Peter	13

DOWN   (CONTINUED)   PAGE   TITLE   LINE

Sunk down her Nose, or seam'd her Face?   . . . . .   595 Cassinus Peter   49
Thus I consign you down to Fame, ... 608 Know Not What   3
Can raise them up, or sink them down, ... 620 Scandal Poem 1   91
Or, to Parnassus looking down, ...   620 Scandal Poem 1   109
His Blessings down in fruitful Show'rs;   . . . . . . 624 Scandal Poem 2   28
To pour down Curses on Mankind.   . . . . 624 Scandal Poem 2   30
Can raise them up, or sink them down, ... 626 Scandal Poem 2   89
Or, to Parnassus looking down, ...   626 Scandal Poem 2   107
And shake it well, and down it comes.   . . . . . . 627 Scandal Poem 2   130
Thousand Sparkles falling down   . . . . . . 638 Epistle Lady   253
The Muse invok'd, sit down to write;   . . . . .   643 On Poetry   86
Sit still, and swallow down your Spittle.   . . . . . . 644 On Poetry   122
And help yourself to run it down.   . . . . . . 644 On Poetry   126
To cry it up, or run it down.   . . . . 649 On Poetry   270
A Shole of Herrings down his Maw.   . . . . . . 651 On Poetry   324
From Flecknoe down to Howard's Time, ... 652 On Poetry   369
And ten to one drags down his feeble stick.   . . . . .   672 Epig Carthy 24   D 18
Then pray'd an Answer and sat down.   . . . . .   687 Cadenus Vaness   20
The Graces half asham'd look'd down;   . . . . . . 689 Cadenus Vaness   100
From Courts inclusive, down to Cells, ... 691 Cadenus Vaness   149
Down from Olympus comes with Joy, ... 693 Cadenus Vaness   200
When they grew pert, to pull them down.   . . . . . . 697 Cadenus Vaness   337
I gravely sat me down to think: . . . . 740 Stel B-day 22   4
And pull your haughty Stomach down, ... 748 Stel Distress   72
And pull your haughty Stomach down;   . . . . . . 752 Stel Wood-Park   88
Or melts my passions down with tears: . . . . . . 754 Stella '23   14
Be sent to Quilca down to graze;   . . . . 759 Receipt Youth   26
Knockt down the Boy, the Lanthorn broke;   . . . . .   781 Mullinix Tim   268
Unbutton and let down your Breeches, ... 783 Tim and Fables   36
Down ev'ry mealy Atom drops   . . . . 786 Dick, Maggot   12
Hang's down his Head, and drops his Tail, ...   797 Traulus 1   37
Lord Pam in the Church (cou'd you think it) kneel'd down   809 Epigr Prelate   1
Were down the sudden Current born;   . . . . . . 811 Bro Protestant   4
Knock him down, down, down, knock him down.   . . . . .   814 Yahoo's   REF
Knock him down, down, down, knock him down.   . . . . .   814 Yahoo's   REF
Knock him down, down, down, knock him down.   . . . . .   814 Yahoo's   REF
Knock him down, down, down, knock him down.   . . . . .   814 Yahoo's   REF
Knock him down, down, down, knock him down.   . . . . .   815 Yahoo's   REF
Knock him down, down, down, knock him down.   . . . . .   815 Yahoo's   REF
Knock him down, down, down, knock him down.   . . . . .   815 Yahoo's   REF
Knock him down, down, down, knock him down.   . . . . .   815 Yahoo's   REF
Knock him down, down, down, knock him down.   . . . . .   816 Yahoo's   REF
Knock him down, down, down, knock him down.   . . . . .   816 Yahoo's   REF
Knock him down, down, down, knock him down.   . . . . .   816 Yahoo's   REF
Knock him down, down, down, knock him down.   . . . . .   816 Yahoo's   REF
Knock him down, down, down, knock him down.   . . . . .   817 Yahoo's   REF
Knock him down, down, down, knock him down.   . . . . .   817 Yahoo's   REF
Knock him down, down, down, knock him down.   . . . . .   817 Yahoo's   REF
Knock him down, down, down, knock him down.   . . . . .   817 Yahoo's   REF
Knock him down, down, down,--keep him down.   . . . . .   817 Yahoo's   REF
Knock him down, down, down,--keep him down.   . . . . .   817 Yahoo's   REF
Knock him down, down, down,--keep him down.   . . . . .   817 Yahoo's   REF
Knock him down, down, down,--keep him down.   . . . . .   817 Yahoo's   REF
Drive them down on every Scull, ... 830 Legion Club   27
Whisper'd me, let down your Stick;   . . . . . . 833 Legion Club   98
They'll come down to right themselves: . . . . . . 838 Legion Club   210
By my soul there's bad news, for the gold she was pulled   840 Ballad   D   2
    down,
The gold she was pull'd down, of that I'm very sure,   .   840 Ballad   D   3
Cuts down with sacrilegious Hand.   . . . . . . 849 Old Thorn   24
"To hack my hallow'd Timber down;   . . . . . . 851 Old Thorn   84
And down my chin drops, ...   852 Lady's Lament   32
Grows down to my chin;   . . . . . . 853 Lady's Lament   74
Pull down the fine briers, ... 857 Lady's Lament   197
Good Morrow, good Captain,--I'll wait on you down,--   .   869 Grand Question   77
Then he low'rs down the Point, and kisses the Hilt.   .   871 Grand Question   112
And, the Doctor was plaguily down in the Hips.   .   873 Grand Question   178
Her Ladyship answers, I'm just coming down;   . . . .   873 Grand Question   181
Powder'd from shoulder down to flank, ... 879 Robbin & Harry   49
Cut down the Dock, 'twill sprout again: but O!   .   881 Pastoral Dial   15
Take down thy proudly swelling Sails, ... 897 Panegyr Dean   333
To cut his hedges down for fire;   . . . . . . 902 Dean's Reasons   106
In Line direct, hung down behind.   . . . . . . 903 Death Daphne   28
Who down direct our Lineage bring   . . . . . . 925 Riddle 8   29
A damn'd Cromwellian, knock'd down.   . . . . . . 926 Riddle 9   20
Why then I make pieces of Iron go down.   . . . . . . 927 Riddle 11   D   8
I'm up, and down, and round about, ... 929 Riddle 14   D   1
Yet endless Tears flow down in Streams.   . . . . . . 932 Riddle 19   D   4
or with a down a high down derry, ... 957 Cantata
or with a down a high down derry, ... 957 Cantata
You treat me like a Boy that knocks down his Foe,   . . 967 Letter Sherid   13
I'll first take you up, and then take you down: . . 968 Letter Sherid   32
Down in the Strand just where the new Pole is,   . . 988 Letter Dr Sh-n   8
I hasten'd down to Country Air, ... 1003 Dan J's Reply   2
Who when I fought still cut me down, ... 1005 Sheridan's Sub   8
Be gone down to the county of Wexford . . .   .   1022 Nim-Dan-Dean 2   D   6
But, however, if he be come, bring him down, ... 1023 Nim-Dan-Dean 2   D   8
Bring down Long Shanks Jim too, but now I think on't,   1023 Nim-Dan-Dean 2   D 11
    . . .
For I heard, a month ago, that he was down there . . . . 1023 Nim-Dan-Dean 2   D 12

```
DOWN              (CONTINUED)                                  PAGE    TITLE           LINE
     However, bring down yourself, and you bring down all; . . .   1023  Nim-Dan-Dean 2   D  13
     However, bring down yourself, and you bring down all; . . .   1023  Nim-Dan-Dean 2   D  13
     I had forgot to desire you to bring down what I say you       1023  Nim-Dan-Dean 2   D  15
         have,. . .
DOWNS
     Their ups and downs, with fifty Stories  . . . . . . .         181  Horace 2, 1          18
     And o'er unhabitable Downs  . . . . . . . . . .                646  On Poetry          179
     Nor seldom grace the flow'ry downs,  . . . . . . .             896  Panegyr Dean       303
DOWNWARD
     How some go downward to the Root,  . . . . . . . .              32  Ode to Temple      172
     Jove never sends us downward from the Skies,  . . . .          363  On Dreams            3
DOWNWARDS
     "Relaxing downwards in a <Stink>?  . . . . . . .               305  Storm               68
     Climbs downwards, deeper by a Yard:  . . . . . . .             654  On Poetry          398
DOWNY
     Before his downy Beard was grown!  . . . . . . . .             655  On Poetry          432
DOXIES
     Gotten from their dainty Doxies,  . . . . . . . .              573  Helter Skelter      26
DOZE
     Why, Cassy, thou wilt doze thy Pate:  . . . . .                594  Cassinus Peter      29
     But, to doze my Head, like Lodanum.  . . . . . . .             632  Epistle Lady        84
DOZEN
     Two Dozen Canons round your Stall,  . . . . . . .              173  Horace 1, 7         89
     In a Dozen Apostles but one prov'd a Traytor!  . . .           804  Irish Bishops       30
     With a Dozen large Vessels my Vault shall be stor'd,  .        867  Grand Question      13
     Come, Six-pence a Dozen to get me some Bread,  . . .           953  Herrings             8
     But, there were not a Dozen (to give 'em their Due) sick      1029  Dr. Helsham         24
DOZENS
     And all my whole Family, Places by Dozens;  . . . .            144  New Song            48
     In Royal Robes they come by dozens  . . . . . . .              465  Birthday Song      169
DR
     Then Good Dr. <Swift>  . . . . . . . .                          77  Lady B- B-          26
     The Rev'rend Dr. Raymond guess'd,  . . . . . . .               128  Little House        43
     Found out that it was Dr. <Swift>:  . . . . . .               171  Horace 1, 7         26
     As you Dr. <Smedley> are, being sure  . . . . . .             372  Letter D. S-y       33
     I can't Conjecture, for Dr.<Dean>  . . . . . . .              372  Letter D. S-y       43
     How much improv'd by Dr. <D.>  . . . . . . . .                779  Mullinix Tim       216
     Is Dr. <Tisdall> to my Knowledge.  . . . . . . .              942  Probatur Alit       16
DRAB
     Each Drab has been compar'd to Venus:  . . . . . .            628  Scandal Poem 2     160
DRABS
     To scratch their paultry drabs on glass;  . . . . .           402  Window Inns 7    D   4
     Those pocky Drabs  . . . . . . . . . .                         440  Ballyspellin        13
     What Drabs have been compar'd to Venus?  . . . .              622  Scandal Poem 1     156
DRAG
     To join, and drag you to the Ground.  . . . . . .             414  Censure             10
     Drag diff'rent Ways in miry Grounds.  . . . . . .             645  On Poetry          176
     With Pride wou'd drag about her Chain;  . . . . .             693  Cadenus Vaness     233
     I drag him upwards from his Hole.  . . . . . . .              921  Riddle 6            34
DRAG'D
     And drag'd me from my Mother's Side:  . . . . .               915  Riddle 1             8
DRAGG'D
     Half eat, and dragg'd it to his Hole.  . . . . .              583  Young Nymph         60
     Those whom you dragg'd from Death before:  . . . .            764  Stel B-day '26      40
DRAGON
     And He, the Dragon never sleeping,  . . . . . .               134  Magician's Rod      73
     O'er sees the Work, or Dragon rowes,  . . . . .               279  Journal             23
     How Valiant George rode o'er the Dragon;  . . . .            281  Journal             70
     This Brass was a Dragon (observe what I tell ye)  . .         337  Serious Poem        87
     This Dragon had gotten two Sows in it's Belly;  . .           337  Serious Poem        88
     And mounts astride upon the Dragon.  . . . . .               777  Mullinix Tim       116
     But this I am sure, the Most Rev'rend old Dragon,  .          803  Irish Bishops       13
     Oh! could we tame yon watchful Dragon,  . . . . .            948  Jason Hassard        5
DRAGS
     Which drags the slavish World in Chains.  . . . .            243  Horace 4, 9         14
     My Fancy drags this Monster to my View,  . . . .             532  To Mr. Gay          37
     And ten to one drags down his feeble stick.  . . .           672  Epig Carthy 24   D  18
     It drags behind a spacious Womb,  . . . . . . .              743  Stel B-day 22       68
DRAIN
     The Dutch from hence shall no more Millions drain;  . .       169  Peace Dunkirk       27
     The Swiss and Dutch whole Millions drain.  . . .             256  Bubble             160
     "What Prodigys in Arts we drain  . . . . . . .               462  Birthday Song       79
     He comes to drain a Beggar's Purse:  . . . . .               484  Libel on D- D-     124
     And drain the Fish-ponds; while your Master doats;  . .       534  To Mr. Gay          90
     With Caution drain it from the Lees)  . . . . .              743  Stel B-day 22       78
DRAIN'D
     So Maevius, when he drain'd his Skull  . . . . .             730  Stella, Poems       71
DRAINED
     Tho the Exchequer be drained by prodigal Donours  . .         389  Order of Bath        5
DRAINS
     Why shou'd I tell of Ponds and Drains,  . . . . .            283  Journal            111
     Now Curl his Shop from Rubbish drains;  . . . . .            560  Death of Swift     197
     Drains all thy Lakes of Fish, of Fruits thy Land.  .          793  St. Pat's Well      64
DRAM
     "And ev'ry Moment take a Dram,  . . . . . . .                305  Storm               58
     Takes a large Dram of Citron Water.  . . . . .               446  Modern Lady         47
     You won't give us a Dram.  . . . . . . . .                  1015  Swift to Sheri      48
DRANK
     And then he could pay for the Liquor he drank  . . .          287  Bank Down           29
     When drank at Ballyspellin  . . . . . . . . .                440  Ballyspellin        12
```

DRAPER | PAGE | TITLE | LINE
But, to this Parchment let the Draper . . . . . . | 354 | Simile Silver | 25
Which gave the <Dean> the Name of Draper? . . . . | 796 | Traulus 1 | 12
DRAPER'S
I Sing not of the Draper's Praise, nor yet of William | 341 | Upon His Grace | 1
Wood;
Our Parsons Read the Draper's Books, and make us | 343 | Upon His Grace | 40
honest Foke.
DRAPIER
But now, since the Drapier hath heartily maul'd him, . | 351 | Wood Insect | 33
Before the Drapier shot a Letter, ... | 353 | Wood Ironmongr | 35
"Must we the Drapier then forget? . . . . | 547 | Life of Swift | 95
To curse the Dean, or bless the Drapier. . . . | 558 | Death of Swift | 168
His spite cannot wound, who attempted the Drapier. . . | 818 | Archbi Cashel | 6
This Hill may keep the Name of Drapier: . . . . | 875 | Drapier's Hill | 18
For I am landlord to the Drapier: . . . . . . | 876 | To Dean Swift | 2
DRAPIER'S
And you on Drapier's Hill must lye, ... | 491 | Dialogue | 55
"Twas he that writ the Drapier's Letters---! . . . . | 548 | Life of Swift | 97
And call the Mansion Drapier's Hill; . . . . . . | 875 | Drapier's Hill | 10
When none the Drapier's Praise shall sing; . . . . | 875 | Drapier's Hill | 13
And Drapier's vye with Cooper's Hill. . . . . . | 875 | Drapier's Hill | 20
DRAPIER'S-HILL
And Drapier's-hill been still Drumlack; . . . . | 877 | To Dean Swift | 32
When Drapier's-hill appear'd in rhyme. . . . . . | 899 | Dean's Reasons | 10
DRAPIER'S-MOUNT
While I from Drapier's-Mount descend, ... | 884 | Rev Market-Hill | 49
DRAPIERS
That you who was found writing of Drapiers . . . . | 522 | St. Cecilia's | 3
DRAUGHT
When they had took a second Draught, ... | 92 | Bauc & Phil 1 | 73
And gave the Nymph a plenteous Draught; . . . . . | 293 | Prog Marriage | 114
I see her taste each nauseous Draught, ... | 727 | To Stella | 113
From thence a plenteous Draught infuse, ... | 743 | Stel B-day 22 | 75
DRAUGHTS   SEE MORNING-DRAUGHTS
Went down like stupifying Draughts: . . . . . . | 470 | Burning Poem | 8
Such Draughts as this, and then digest, ... | 495 | Panegyr Swift | 65
DRAW
I would not draw th' Idea from an empty Name; . . . | 21 | Ode Athenian | 161
Some she does to Egyptian Bondage draw, ... | 32 | Ode to Temple | 187
But wicked kings draw more examples than the good; . . | 40 | Ode Sancroft | 184
To draw conclusions shall be left to you; . . . . | 46 | To Congreve | 112
A Song could draw a Stone or Beam, ... | 79 | Vanbrug House | 3
A Verse could draw a Stone or Beam . . . . . | 106 | V's House | 3
Now, although to Draw Water is not very good, . . . | 334 | Serious Poem | 3
And draw like you my Patron's Face; . . . . . . | 496 | Panegyr Swift | 111
By Gnats, and draw the Nation's Dung, ... | 496 | Panegyr Swift | 115
Draw their Swords and run away: . . . . . . | 574 | Helter Skelter | 48
She must have doves to draw her chair: . . . . . | 621 | Scandal Poem 1 | 116
From whence you draw such bold conclusions; . . . . | 622 | Scandal Poem 1 | 161
She must have Doves to draw her Chair. . . . . . | 627 | Scandal Poem 2 | 114
A Whale of moderate Size will draw . . . . . . | 651 | On Poetry | 323
Draw the Beasts as I describe 'em, ... | 839 | Legion Club | 225
Draw them like, for I assure you, ... | 839 | Legion Club | 227
Draw them so that we may trace . . . . . . | 839 | Legion Club | 229
All human Race must hither draw: . . . . . . | 922 | Riddle 7 | 24
Come sit by my side, while this picture I draw: . . . | 955 | Portrait Life | 1
To draw the Face of such a Spectre. . . . . . | 993 | On Picture | 12
DRAWBACKS
In Poundage and Drawbacks, I lose half my Rent, . . | 867 | Grand Question | 21
DRAWCENSIR
Forth issues wriggling Dick Drawcensir, ... | 785 | Dick, Maggot | 6
DRAWERS
To be Hewers of Wood and Drawers of Water, ... | 334 | Serious Poem | 2
DRAWN
And once drawn up, is ne'er let down again. . . . . | 50 | To Congreve | 234
The Writings drawn, the Lawyer fee'd, ... | 222 | Prog of Love | 22
But by peculiar Whimseys drawn, ... | 279 | Journal | 21
Had drawn his Sword for Marius' Fall, ... | 340 | Arch-Bish Dub | 18
Drawn through the dirt, his pockets pick'd; . . . . | 436 | Answer Paulus | 138
As Overton has drawn his Sire . . . . . . | 461 | Birthday Song | 37
Or, by a faithless Bully drawn, ... | 582 | Young Nymph | 43
Is drawn by peacocks in her Berlin . . . . . | 621 | Scandal Poem 1 | 124
Is drawn by Peacocks in her Berlin: . . . . . | 627 | Scandal Poem 2 | 118
Ev'ry Fault have drawn a Gloss over: . . . . . | 632 | Epistle Lady | 96
Drawn by her Doves, away she flies, ... | 692 | Cadenus Vaness | 186
Like Hemp, which by a skilful Spinster drawn . . . | 806 | Judas | 15
Thus was I drawn in, ... | 855 | Lady's Lament | 135
Drawn up in our Court; when the Captain cries, Stand. | 870 | Grand Question | 100
But was unwarily drawn in; . . . . | 1005 | Sheridan's Sub | 18
DRAWS
Draws ev'ry rhyming, prating, dressing sot, ... | 48 | To Congreve | 153
With that he draws two Handfulls out, ... | 63 | Discovery | 37
Her Topicks from the Tories draws. . . . . . | 417 | Woman's Mind | 56
She draws up Card by Card, to find . . . . . . | 452 | Modern Lady | 228
She draws an Ace, and sees it red. . . . . . . | 452 | Modern Lady | 233
My Character impartial draws: . . . . | 565 | Death of Swift | 306
Now dextrously her Plumpers draws, ... | 582 | Young Nymph | 17
Thus whirling round, together draws . . . . . . | 688 | Cadenus Vaness | 59
His Pen to save a sinking Nation draws, ... | 770 | Horace 1, 14 | 26
Then sudden draws it back again, ... | 776 | Mullinix Tim | 105

DRAWS	(CONTINUED)	PAGE	TITLE	LINE

DRAWS   (CONTINUED)   PAGE TITLE   LINE
    Hence he draws his daily Food, ...   800 Traulus 2   41
    Hither the frantick Goddess draws . . . .   883 Rev Market-Hill   5
DREAD
    For, could you think? the fiercest foes you dread, . .   46 To Congreve   95
    So nature's craz'd convulsions make us dread . . . .   53 Temple Ill   65
    (By sure Prognosticks) when to dread a Show'r: 136 City Shower   2
    Our Country then can dread no Wrong: 339 Arch-Bish Dub   6
    Then how can we dread William Wood,   340 Arch-Bish Dub   21
    "You dread the waving of these Greens; . . . . . .   380 Apology Lady C   138
    Oppression hides, with guilty Dread, ...   387 Manly Virtue   123
    Must dread your pen, your person hate, ...   491 Dialogue   54
    Their Fellows, turn their Dread and Hate.   493 Panegyr Swift   14
    When first in Print, you see him dread . . . . . .   500 Doctor Delaney   13
    And dread no more the Rage of Grub, ...   502 Doctor Delaney   63
    What Spunging-House in dread of Jayl . . . .   504 Doctor Delaney   145
    "Then, since you dread no further Lashes, ... 550 Life of Swift   201
    Dear Cassy, though to ask I dread, ...   595 Cassinus Peter   41
    But, if you fail, my Spectre dread . . . .   597 Cassinus Peter   113
    Dread from his Hand impending Changes. . . . . . .   655 On Poetry   422
    Of half Mankind the Dread and Hate. . . . .   702 Cadenus Vaness   505
    Nor dread the Adder's Tooth, nor Scorpion's Sting. .   792 St. Pat's Well   42
    Should the Bottom be split, our <Bishops> wou'd dread . 805 Irish Bishops   45
    Much I dread the Courtier's Fate, ...   933 Riddle 20   D 27
DREADED
    Long dreaded for his Bloody Tail and Fiery Beard,   .   10 Ode to King   131
    Because he dreaded to come nigh'r. . . . .   455 Dean Smedley   8
DREADFUL
    And rolls about her dreadful Eyes, ...   30 Ode to Temple   122
    To make a dreadful Night at Noon: . . . .   98 Elegy Patrige   14
    And of that dreadful coup d'eclat, ...   181 Horace 2, 1   23
    A dreadful Interval of Spleen! . . . .   451 Modern Lady   204
    Corinna wakes. A dreadful Sight! . . . .   583 Young Nymph   57
    See the dreadful Strides she takes. . . . .   832 Legion Club   92
    Dreadful Sight! What learned Morgan . . . .   838 Legion Club   193
    Astonish'd gave a dreadful Shriek; . . . .   849 Old Thorn   26
    "Nor, when I felt the dreadful Blow, ...   850 Old Thorn   69
    And give him Words of dreadful Sounds, ...   904 Death Daphne   43
    Who regards the dreadful Sound. . . . .   931 Riddle 18   D 26
DREADFULL
    In such a dreadfull Night at least; . . . .   90 Bauc & Phil 1   20
    Change-Ally is the dreadfull Name; . . . .   256 Bubble   140
    Made trebly dreadfull in your Song. . . . .   461 Birthday Song   46
    For must a Hero not be dreadfull? . . . .   462 Birthday Song   56
DREADING
    "In dreading this vexatious Round? . . . .   380 Apology Lady C   162
    Dreading to be laid by th' Heels. . . . .   834 Legion Club   118
DREADS
    Nor dreads the Tyranny of Years, ...   6 Ode to King   3
    No danger dreads upon the road; . . . .   435 Answer Paulus   96
    The ruling Rogue, who dreads to be cashier'd; . . . .   536 To Mr. Gay   137
DREAM
    With all that Factious or Enthusiastick Dotards dream, .   22 Ode Athenian 204
    Let the vain sex dream on, their Empire comes from Us, .   24 Ode Athenian   260
    For, whate'er theologic lev'llers dream, ...   41 Ode Sancroft   230
    As antient nature's modern masters dream; . . . .   45 To Congreve   72
    Here would we sing--But, ah! you think I dream, . .   49 To Congreve   197
    Am I awake, or do I dream? . . . .   376 Apology Lady C   45
    He wak'd, and found it but a Dream; . . . .   705 Cadenus Vaness   585
    Me Phoebus in a midnight Dream . . . .   897 Panegyr Dean   325
DREAM'D   SEE A-DREAM'D
DREAM'S
    And now my Dream's out: For I was a-dream'd . . . .   868 Grand Question   49
DREAM'T
    Ne'er dream't of the Matter, ...   245 Irish-Feast   30
    I dream't Wood was told he should Dye by a Drop . .   337 Serious Poem   110
DREAMS
    Wake from thy wanton Dreams, ...   31 Ode to Temple   150
    Disjointing shapes as in the fairy-land of dreams, .   35 Ode Sancroft   39
    Thus are the lives of fools a sort of dreams, . . .   47 To Congreve   147
    Like antic shapes in dreams, from waking eyes: . .   54 Temple Ill   100
    She had with Dreams the other Night. . . . . . .   282 Journal   96
    But Dreams are like Oracles, hard to explain 'em, . .   337 Serious Poem   113
    Those Dreams that on the silent Night intrude, . .   363 On Dreams   1
    The Murd'rer dreams of all the Blood he spilt. . .   364 On Dreams   14
    And dreams of Forfeitures by Treason got. . . . .   364 On Dreams   20
    The Poets Mythologick Dreams, ...   478 Epist on Epist   85
    "Here ended all our golden Dreams. . . . .   567 Death of Swift   372
    Of Bridewell and the Compter dreams, ...   582 Young Nymph   41
    Or in the Iv'ry Gate of Dreams, ...   647 On Poetry   215
    Dreams of a Gown of forty-four; . . . .   703 Cadenus Vaness   525
    Dorinda dreams of Dress a bed . . . .   733 Verses Vanessa   23
    Than dreams of worlds intelligible; . . . .   900 Dean's Reasons   62
    I'll haunt thy Dreams, a bloodless Ghost; . . . .   925 Riddle 8   27
DREGS
    And sick with Dregs of Knowledge grown, ...   27 Ode to Temple   47
    Why near the dregs of youth perversely wilt thou stay, .   54 Temple Ill   105
    The Dregs will serve to ripen Ore below; . . . . .   532 To Mr. Gay   24
DRENCH
    We'll soundly drench your frize Sur-tout, ...   622 Scandal Poem 1   176

	PAGE	TITLE	LINE
DRENCH'D			
Drown'd Puppies, stinking Sprats, all drench'd in Mud,	139	City Shower	62
How in the Lake the Dean was drench'd;	281	Journal	68
DRESS			
For Man to dress and polish his Uncourtly Mind, . .	22	Ode Athenian	218
Tho' in strange uncouth postures, and uncomely dress; .	35	Ode Sancroft	26
Rally her dress, her language, and her gait;	50	To Congreve	218
Than let you see her dress her Head;	222	Prog of Love	8
We'll dress in Manufactures, made at home?	275	Epilogue	17
Lord, what a Dress these Parsons wear, ...	291	Prog Marriage	42
"To see th' important Men of Dress, ...	380	Apology Lady C	147
'I never can have Time to Dress, ...	447	Modern Lady	96
To dress a Thought, may toyl a Week;	502	Doctor Delaney	66
His mother begg'd of us to dress him	619	Scandal Poem 1	67
His Mother begg'd of us to dress him, ...	625	Scandal Poem 2	63
Set on Reading, than on Dress:	630	Epistle Lady	18
Your Poem in its modish Dress, ...	643	On Poetry	105
Than Titles, Figure, Shape, and Dress;	697	Cadenus Vaness	341
They railly'd next Vanessa's Dress;	699	Cadenus Vaness	396
To Beauty, Dress, or Paint, or Youth, ...	729	Stella, Poems	62
Dorinda dreams of Dress a bed	733	Verses Vanessa	23
Will not require Poetick Dress;	757	Stel B-day '24	32
For Vice in all its glitt'ring Dress:	765	Stel B-day '26	48
Just in this Dress the Painter drew it.	783	Tim and Fables	24
Their Dress, their Language, and the Scottish Name, .	791	St. Pat's Well	15
In his Dress and Figure seen:	800	Traulus 2	32
In what Figure can a Bard dress	834	Legion Club	139
Supplying those defects by dress	879	Robbin & Harry	53
Madam, whose Skill does all in Dress lye, ...	886	Rev Market-Hill	99
That Cow-boys know you by your Dress!	889	Panegyr Dean	80
To dress their Soupes and Fricassyes;	895	Panegyr Dean	266
Sits by this, to dress her soul.	907	Daphne	48
And in dress place all your merit;	908	Daphne	76
But, whatever be my dress, ...	937	Riddle 24 D	35
Will dress a Dinner worth five Pound.	941	Letter	36
DRESS'D			
Where high patrician souls dress'd heavenly gay, . . .	41	Ode Sancroft	234
And Tories (dress'd like Waiters) in Disguise. . .	165	Toland's Invit	30
Is dress'd, and stealing thro' the Crowd, ...	377	Apology Lady C	77
And Madam almost dress'd by Four;	447	Modern Lady	91
We dress'd her in a gold Brocade, ...	626	Scandal Poem 2	75
For a Coxcomb gaily dress'd?	632	Epistle Lady	76
Both dress'd like divines, with band and face clean. . .	843	Ay and No	2
DRESSING			
Draws ev'ry rhyming, prating, dressing sot, ...	48	To Congreve	153
The Poets Wits, than in the Players Dressing. . . .	276	Epilogue	46
By haughty Celia spent in Dressing;	525	Lady's Dres Rm	2
DRESSING-PLATE			
Your Dressing-Plate, he'll be content	446	Modern Lady	60
DRESST			
The Bridegroom dresst, to make a Figure, ...	290	Prog Marriage	21
Jove dresst a Cloud in Juno's shape, ...	619	Scandal Poem 1	54
We dresst her in a gold Brocade, ...	619	Scandal Poem 1	77
DREST			
Drest her again Genteel and Neat, ...	23	Ode Athenian	230
They rise ready drest, ...	245	Irish-Feast	35
So a Thief steals my Horse, and then gets him well drest	266	Apollo	92
In Drugget drest of Thirteen Pence a Yard, ...	275	Epilogue	23
At Seven, the Dean in Night-gown drest, ...	278	Journal	9
She by the tender Graces drest, ...	586	Strephon Chloe	59
Drest up with Amaranthine Flow'rs.	590	Strephon Chloe	202
Shews Sheba's Queen completely drest, ...	592	Strephon Chloe	287
Jove drest a Cloud in Juno's Shape:	625	Scandal Poem 2	50
Drest like any Lady May'ress;	630	Epistle Lady	36
Thus drest alike from Top to Toe, ...	780	Mullinix Tim	227
The Monkey was compleatly drest, ...	782	Tim and Fables	11
As soon as her Ladyship call'd to be drest, ...	868	Grand Question	43
When in my gaudy Liv'ry drest!	916	Riddle 2	4
In Royal Garments each was drest, ...	923	Riddle 7	71
If Wine's bought, or Victuals drest	931	Riddle 18 D	19
Were you drest like a bawd, and sold oysters at	979	Dean to Tho: S	10
Billings-gate.			
DREW			
Will drew out Dick to take a Quart, ...	220	A Quiet Life	26
She trembled when a Man drew near;	222	Prog of Love	3
He drew dumb Merit from his Cell, ...	386	Manly Virtue	84
This into gen'ral Odium drew him, ...	549	Life of Swift	132
As Rochefoucault his Maxims drew	553	Death of Swift	1
This drew us in at first to find	735	Stel B-day '20	19
The Duke of Lorrain drew his Sword, ...	776	Mullinix Tim	111
Just in this Dress the Painter drew it.	783	Tim and Fables	24
Her Pocket-Glass drew slily out;	904	Death Daphne	64
DRIBBLE			
On paper dribble daintily.	983	Sher, A Goose	8
DRIFT			
Which by the Style, the Matter, and the Drift, . . .	195	Author Himself	49
DRINK			
Invited both the Saints to Drink.	92	Bauc & Phil 1	72
Could Smoak, and Drink, and read the News;	95	Bauc & Phil 1	174
Then stept aside to fetch 'em Drink, ...	112	Bauc & Phil 2	29
He call'd for Drink, you saw him Sup	156	Fable of Midas	7

	PAGE	TITLE	LINE
DRINK (CONTINUED)			
But I love Elbow-room when're I drink, ...	166	Toland's Invit	37
Will drink it now as well as Peers:	169	Peace Dunkirk	24
When all his Drink is Hippocrene, ...	231	Prog of Poetry	32
Run as they drink and drink and run.	257	Bubble	180
Run as they drink and drink and run.	257	Bubble	180
And taint all their Meat, and sour all their Drink. .	263	Apollo	14
We sit an hour to drink and chat.	280	Journal	54
To drink Achilous' Horn.	293	Prog Marriage	120
To Cudgel our Bones, and for Drink give us Verjuice;	335	Serious Poem	38
He can Eat, Drink and Sleep; now and then for a Friend	335	Serious Poem	43
And here is a Guinea to drink.	396	Dog and Thief	12
Forbear their Tea, or drink it soon;	587	Strephon Chloe	118
On Embers plac'd, to drink it hot.	594	Cassinus Peter	28
Metaphorick Meat and Drink, ...	633	Epistle Lady	117
Would chuse in Peace to drink my Coffee.	733	Verses Vanessa	30
To drink Sir <Arthur's> Health and mine:	890	Panegyr Dean	102
A long-ear'd Beast, and the Drink you love best . .	943	Probatur Alit	35
Your ink is your drink, your pen is your pot. . .	979	Dean to Tho: S	22
. . .have it at their own House, to drink in quiet. . .	1013	Swift to Sheri	7
To eat my Meat, and drink my Medlicot, ...	1033	Ans to Crown	9
DRINKERS SEE ALE-DRINKERS			
DRINKING			
An Ass was drinking at a Stream, ...	253	Bubble	74
Of drinking all Day, and whoring all Night. . . .	517	Dean Hang Rape	28
We, by Play, as Men by Drinking, ...	632	Epistle Lady	85
The Students drinking, rais'd their Wit and Parts; .	793	St. Pat's Well	70
DRINKS			
"He hardly drinks a Pint of Wine;	557	Death of Swift	109
DRIPING			
For Candles, how she trucks her Driping;	282	Journal	88
DRIV'N			
Driv'n from the South-Sea to the Red.	258	Bubble	208
DRIVE			
To drive all Virtue out, or look it dead!	30	Ode to Temple	123
And drive departed Souls to Styx.	133	Magician's Rod	38
And drive as many Souls to Hell.	133	Magician's Rod	42
To drive unseen her magick Chair, ...	354	Simile Silver	3
The Cloud, and drive the Hag to Hell:	354	Simile Silver	12
And drive the Conj'rers to the Devil:	354	Simile Silver	30
Lets drive at Tom's devoted Noddle, ...	458	Paddy's Charac	24
To drive a second, lest the whole should break. . .	535	To Mr. Gay	134
Pass our Nights, to drive out thinking.	632	Epistle Lady	86
Drive me from my fav'rite Farce.	636	Epistle Lady	196
Drive all Objections from your Mind, ...	724	To Stella	43
New Waves shall drive thee to the Deep again. . .	770	Horace 1, 14	10
Drive them down on every Scull, ...	830	Legion Club	27
Honest Keeper, drive him further, ...	834	Legion Club	141
And drive at last all Secrets out:	920	Riddle 6	16
A long-ear'd Beast, a Thing that Force must drive in,	943	Probatur Alit	47
I'll drive you to Cavan, from Cavan to Dundalk; . .	1019	To Sheridan	7
DRIVEN			
Come, driven by heat, ...	857	Lady's Lament	189
DRIVES			
Some whom ambition drives, seek Heaven's high Son . .	39	Ode Sancroft	166
They, as each Torrent drives, with rapid Force . .	139	City Shower	57
While she drives on to see the Play.	292	Prog Marriage	82
Drives rattling o'er a brazen Arch:	353	Wood Ironmongr	18
Which drives you not to pray, but curse?	617	Scandal Poem 1	10
That drives you, not to pray, but curse?	624	Scandal Poem 2	10
Drives out Brangling, and Contention, ...	637	Epistle Lady	215
Who drives her cares to hands and feet:	761	Bec's B-Day	18
DRIVING			
His Baily Driving all my Cows into the Parish Pound.	343	Upon His Grace	4
With driving wrong, will make the Pannel split: . . .	535	To Mr. Gay	132
Friend Pope overturnd by driving too fast away, . .	1037	Four Storyes	3
DRIZZLING			
While the first drizzling Show'r is born aslope, . . .	137	City Shower	18
DROLE			
The Daw a Thief, the Ape a Drole, ...	512	Answer Fable	7
DROLL			
When into my hands comes a letter from the droll. . . .	975	Dean to Sherid	4
DROLS			
For lofty Lines in Smithfield Drols.	650	On Poetry	300
DROMEDARY			
For my Lord Dromedary comes a Tuesday without fail; .	70	Mrs Harris Pet	28
DRONE			
Presume not, Gay, unless you serve a Drone, . . .	534	To Mr. Gay	87
Or, grant him but a Drone at best:	798	Traulus 1	83
A Drone can raise a Hornet's Nest:	798	Traulus 1	84
DROOPING			
And Merit rears her drooping Head;	387	Manly Virtue	124
Thus when Philomela drooping, ...	661	Love Song	29
Oft' revives my drooping head:	937	Riddle 24	D 46
DROOPS			
"To raise up Virtue when she droops, ...	462	Birthday Song	74
Poor Gentleman, he droops apace, ...	556	Death of Swift	81
DROP			
And drop his laurel at Apollo's feet.	49	To Congreve	186
Time is no more when th' utmost drop is past; . . .	49	To Congreve	190
As if they ne're had drunk a drop.	92	Bauc & Phil 1	78

```
DROP           (CONTINUED)                              PAGE   TITLE            LINE
  As if they ne'er had toucht a Drop.    . . . . . . .  112 Bauc & Phil 2      34
  Since mortal Beautyes drop so soon,    . . . . . . .  229 Prog of Beauty    118
  Thus in a Basin drop a Shilling,       . . . . . . .  251 Bubble              9
  I dream't Wood was told he should Dye by a Drop  . . 337 Serious Poem      110
  For fear the First Drop might as well be his Last:  . 337 Serious Poem      112
  For it prov'd that he dy'd of a Drop at Killmainham:  . 337 Serious Poem    114
  Very soon to see Wood Drop down from a Rope.   . . .  338 Serious Poem      116
  The Inn has not one drop of wine       . . . . . . .  420 Holyhead            6
  Can sometimes drop a Voter's Claim,    . . . . . . .  485 Libel on D- D-    149
  To bite his Pen, and drop a Tear.      . . . . . . .  561 Death of Swift    210
  Her flabby Dugs and down they drop.    . . . . . . .  582 Young Nymph        22
  Drop, for once, your constant Rule,    . . . . . . .  631 Epistle Lady       51
  I shou'd burst, and bursting drop.     . . . . . . .  638 Epistle Lady      262
  Should but his Muse descending drop    . . . . . . .  728 Stella, Poems      29
  Drop from the Tree with all his Bowels burst;  . . .  806 Judas              22
  Hear the rattling Thunder drop.        . . . . . . .  830 Legion Club        22
  She would feel her Pinions drop,       . . . . . . .  834 Legion Club       128
  See the Scowling Visage drop,  . . . . . . . . . . .  835 Legion Club       143
  Grows drunk with a Drop.  . . . . . . . . . . . . .   939 Riddle Answerd     28
  Till I come to a Drop;  . . . . . . . . . . . . . . . 1015 Swift to Sheri    54
DROP'D
  H'as drop'd, and giv'n the Crow a Pudden!  . . . . .  547 Life of Swift      71
DROPP'D
  They dropp'd low Court'sies, One and All,   . . . .   321 First of April     13
DROPPING
  He cannot see one Creature dropping:   . . . . . . .  500 Doctor Delaney     22
  Should slip your Time of dropping Guineas;   . . . .  821 Dr. Rundle         64
  A rotten Cabbin, dropping Rain;   . . . . . . . . . . 1035 To Quilca           2
DROPS
  Such are the smiles where drops of chrystal show,  .  51 Temple Ill         21
  Now in contiguous Drops the Flood comes down.  . . .  138 City Shower        31
  Each Night a Bit drops off her Face    . . . . . . .  228 Prog of Beauty     87
  And drops him at the Church, to pray   . . . . . . .  292 Prog Marriage      81
  "Here Betty, let me take my Drops,     . . . . . . .  451 Modern Lady       206
  His Visage drops, he knits his Brow,   . . . . . . .  480 Libel on D- D-     15
  The Fat upon a Cinder drops,   . . . . . . . . . . .  529 Lady's Dres Rm    104
  Smart Jemmy Moor with Vigor drops,     . . . . . . .  654 On Poetry         399
  How soon thy vain Pretension drops;    . . . . . . .  671 Epig Carthy 22  D  3
  Charm'd by thy voice the 'Prentice drops  . . . . .   779 Mullinix Tim      203
  Down ev'ry mealy Atom drops   . . . . . . . . . . .   786 Dick, Maggot       12
  Hang's down his Head, and drops his Tail,   . . . .   797 Traulus 1          37
  And down my chin drops,  . . . . . . . . . . . . . .  852 Lady's Lament      32
DROPSY
  Pale Dropsy with a sallow Face,   . . . . . . . . .   895 Panegyr Dean      275
DROPT    SEE NEW-DROPT
  When dropt into the Southern Main,     . . . . . . .  250 Bubble              3
  Those that dropt in the South-Sea discover'd this Plank  288 Bank Down      49
  Nor Infants dropt, the spurious Pledges   . . . . .   641 On Poetry          37
  Have dropt their Arms, and seiz'd the Plunder.  . .   775 Mullinix Tim       48
  Like a fresh <Turd> just dropt on Snow.   . . . . .   786 Dick, Maggot       14
DROSS
  Through native dross your share is hardly known,  . . 45 To Congreve        59
  For he regards Ten thousand Pounds no more than Woods's  341 Upon His Grace 12
    Dross.
  Before I'd touch his filthy Dross, than is Clandalkin   343 Upon His Grace  38
    Spire.
DROUN'D
  They and their Village shall be droun'd,   . . . . .   92 Bauc & Phil 1      88
DROVE
  When Fortune hither drove me first;    . . . . . . .  313 To Ford            52
  And till they drove me out of Date,    . . . . . . .  555 Death of Swift     61
  And, bravely drove his Rivals down     . . . . . . .  585 Strephon Chloe     41
  But, Chloe drove him fiercely back.    . . . . . . .  588 Strephon Chloe    150
  E'er drove, before he sold his Land,   . . . . . . .  598 Problem Solved     13
  As if the Devil drove, they fly.  . . . . . . . . .   775 Mullinix Tim       68
  I drove the venom'd Serpent from thy Land;  . . . .   792 St. Pat's Well     40
  Old Saturn from his Empire drove;  . . . . . . . . .  894 Panegyr Dean      254
DROWN
  From Dunns and Debts, and drown our Care;   . . . .   184 Horace 2, 1       110
  And there in sweet Oblivion drown  . . . . . . . . .  202 Horace 2, 6       111
  And here they fish for Gold and drown:   . . . . . .  256 Bubble            148
  And headlong in the Waters drown.   . . . . . . . .   259 Bubble            216
  A Storm, to drown that Rascal <Hort>,  . . . . . . .  302 Storm               5
  Without a Mistress, hang or drown him.   . . . . . .  303 Storm              16
  "To drown him all Attempts are vain,   . . . . . . .  303 Storm              28
  "If one must drown, the other must;    . . . . . . .  304 Storm              50
  For me, you may hang 'em, or drown 'em.   . . . . .   403 Window Inns 9   D  6
  Hang, Drown, or knock him on the Head.   . . . . . .  797 Traulus 1          40
  Drown your Morals, Madam cryes;   . . . . . . . . .   863 To Janus           19
DROWN'D
  Had rather water'd it, than drown'd:   . . . . . . .   17 Ode Athenian       43
  They and their Houses shall be drown'd:   . . . . .   112 Bauc & Phil 2      48
  'Till drown'd in Shriller Notes of Chimney-Sweep,  .  124 Descriptn Morn     12
  Drown'd Puppies, stinking Sprats, all drench'd in Mud,  139 City Shower     62
  Fools chiefly float, the Wise are drown'd.   . . . .  252 Bubble             52
  We see you never can be drown'd:   . . . . . . . . .  258 Bubble            192
  Or t' other Puppy that was drown'd,    . . . . . . .  299 Horrid Plot        22
  By Neno after he was drown'd.  . . . . . . . . . . .  299 Horrid Plot        38
  Guns, Trumpets, Drums, and Bells were drown'd.  . .   338 Wood's Brass        8
  Half choak'd with dust, half drown'd with rains;  .   403 Window Inns 10  D  6
```

		PAGE	TITLE	LINE
DROWN'D (CONTINUED)				
With Eyes in Smoak and Weeping drown'd:	. . . . . .	594	Cassinus Peter	26
Who now in Vice and Slavery are drown'd.	. . . . . .	792	St. Pat's Well	38
DROWNDED				
In my own Thames may I be drownded,	. . . .	410	Dial Rich Marb	73
DROWSY				
Dan growing drowsy like a Thief,	. . . .	279	Journal	39
The drowsy Tyrant by his Minions led,	. . . . . .	364	On Dreams	11
DRUDGE				
Shou'd Young and Phillips drudge together.		393	Modern Poets	20
The lawyer is a common drudge,	. . . .	435	Answer Paulus	87
If I be not a drudge,	. . . .	856	Lady's Lament	151
DRUDGERY				
Some to the Drudgery of a Trade,	. . . .	32	Ode to Temple	186
DRUDGING				
Thy busy, drudging scene of life,	. . . .	676	Parson's Case	6
For thee three Poets now are drudging all,	. . . . .	993	On Picture	25
DRUGGET				
In Drugget drest of Thirteen Pence a Yard,	. . . .	275	Epilogue	23
DRUID				
Here, on a better day, some druid dwelt,	. . . . . .	49	To Congreve	191
Druid, a name she does with pride repeat,	. . . . . .	49	To Congreve	193
DRUM SEE HUM-DRUM,KETTLE-DRUM				
We sound a trumpet, or we beat a drum;	. . . . .	308	Billet Players	37
He'll Bellow as loud as the Dee'l in a Drum:	. . .	336	Serious Poem	80
Because she heard a sudden Drum,	. . .	726	To Stella	77
To rattle in their Ears your Drum.	. . .	775	Mullinix Tim	50
At the Head of his Troop, with Trumpet and Drum:	. .	870	Grand Question	88
Brac'd like a Drum her oily Skin:	. . . . . .	895	Panegyr Dean	258
Or, with his fingers, beat the drum;	. . . . . .	900	Dean's Reasons	48
DRUMLACK				
And Drapier's-hill been still Drumlack;	. . . . .	877	To Dean Swift	32
Must build a Castle at Drumlack:	. . . .	883	Rev Market-Hill	14
DRUMS				
With brazen Trumps and brazen Drums.	. . . . . .	338	Wood's Brass	4
Guns, Trumpets, Drums, and Bells were drown'd.	. . .	338	Wood's Brass	8
With furious Din of Brazen Drums,	. . . . . .	340	Arch-Bish Dub	26
Drums and Trumpets bring me out;	. . . .	933	Riddle 20	D 20
DRUNK				
As if they ne're had drunk a drop.	. . . . . .	92	Bauc & Phil 1	78
Feels not his Soul enliven'd when he's Drunk?	. . .	163	Toland's Invit	18
<Cholmondeley>, when Drunk, can never lose his Wand,	.	164	Toland's Invit	25
While he went always drunk to Bed.	. . . . . .	352	Wood Ironmongr	8
Either drunk or asleep.		423	Carterets Arms	
Though he were drunk the night before,	. . . . .	434	Answer Paulus	72
When drunk with sour Election Ale.	. . . . . .	450	Modern Lady	187
He had made himself Drunk with the Juice of the Grape,	.	517	Dean Hang Rape	23
His Brothers fleece him when he's drunk.	. . . . .	607	Beasts Confess	196
Grows drunk with a Drop.	. . . .	939	Riddle Answerd	28
And he never call'd me worse than Sweet-heart drunk or		985	Mary to Sher	14
sober:				
Steals from the Cully when he's drunk;	. . . . . .	1033	Ans to Crown	2
DRUNKARD				
And like a Drunkard gives it up again.	. . . . . .	137	City Shower	16
DRUNKEN				
At their Wits end like drunken Men.	. . . . . .	256	Bubble	152
No drunken Rake to pick her up,	. . . .	581	Young Nymph	5
The drunken Quarrels of a Rake,	. . . .	724	To Stella	24
DRURY-LANE				
For Drury-lane to shape thy Stile:	. . . . . .	181	Horace 2, 1	42
Corinna, Pride of Drury-Lane,	. . . .	581	Young Nymph	1
DRY				
Weak is the beam to dry up nature's tears,	. . . . .	51	Temple Ill	19
In yonder Barn to keep us dry.	. . . .	90	Bauc & Phil 1	22
Skilld in the Horse-laugh and dry Rub,	. . . . . .	217	To Mr. Delany	57
To leave you dry upon the Beach,	. . . .	258	Bubble	196
On all Occasions, cut and dry.	. . . .	416	Woman's Mind	14
And lessening rivers mourn their fountains dry	. . . .	419	Shall Repine	4
Beneath a dry Canal there lies,	. . . .	478	Epist on Epist	89
Sets of Phrases, cut and dry,	. . . .	523	Betty Grizette	13
For thee, than make a dry Nurse of thy Muse?	. . . .	531	To Mr. Gay	8
Like Iv'ry dry, and soft as Wax.	. . . .	584	Strephon Chloe	26
Tho' cold would burn, tho' dry would melt.	. . . . .	585	Strephon Chloe	28
Descended, ready cut and dry:	. . . .	591	Strephon Chloe	230
Bastings heavy, dry, obtuse,	. . . .	636	Epistle Lady	203
Descriptions tedious, flat and dry,	. . . .	645	On Poetry	155
But finding me so dull and dry since,	. . . . . .	741	Stel B-day 22	27
A pair of Brogues to bear thee dry to Mass!	. . . .	882	Pastoral Dial	50
Thy Hand as dry and cold as Lead,	. . . .	905	Death Daphne	95
Who from Materials hard and dry,	. . . .	920	Riddle 6	20
DRY'D				
By Phoebus newly Tann'd and Dry'd.	. . . . . .	100	Elegy Patrige	76
The Moysture dry'd they sink again,	. . . . . .	254	Bubble	87
Then, let them well be dry'd;	. . . .	394	Grub-Street	10
DRYDEN				
Read all the Prefaces of Dryden,	. . . .	648	On Poetry	251
DUB				
These Demoniacs let me dub	. . . .	829	Legion Club	11
Dub, dub, a-dub, dub. The Trumpeters follow,	. . . .	870	Grand Question	91
Dub, dub, a-dub, dub. The Trumpeters follow,	. . . .	870	Grand Question	91
Dub, dub, a-dub, dub. The Trumpeters follow,	. . . .	870	Grand Question	91

	PAGE	TITLE	LINE
DUBLIN			
Can you on Dublin look with Scorn?	314	To Ford	83
While We may search all Dublin o'er	315	To Ford	107
Lord William's Grace of Dublin Town,	341	Upon His Grace	3
In Dublin they'd be glad to see	420	Holyhead	13
From Dublin soon to London spread,	559	Death of Swift	177
Hey for Dublin Town agen!	574	Helter Skelter	56
To Liffy's filthy side in Dublin;	744	Stel Distress	4
To Liffy's stinking Tide in Dublin:	750	Stel Wood-Park	28
Bring all your Quilca cares to Dublin,	753	Gift for Bec	24
So at this Booth, which we call Dublin,	777	Mullinix Tim	137
No Dublin Letters,	1036	Bless Country	2
In his Journey to <Dublin>, he lighted at <Chester>,	517	Dean Hang Rape	7
To <Dublin> he comes, to the Bagnio he goes,	517	Dean Hang Rape	19
DUBLIN'S			
At Dublin's high feast sat Primate and Dean,	843	Ay and No	1
DUCAL			
The Ducal Coffers, trusted to your Charge,	533	To Mr. Gay	45
Shall he upon the Ducal Rights intrench,	534	To Mr. Gay	91
Produce at last thy dormant Ducal Patent:	538	Mr. Pulteney	10
DUCHESS			
A Duchess, or a Suburb-Wench.	645	On Poetry	166
The <Duke> shew'd me all his fine House; and the <Duchess>	143	New Song	15
DUCK			
Will duck his Head, aside will start,	500	Doctor Delaney	5
The Thresher Duck, could o'er the <Queen> prevail.	521	Stephen Duck	1
Thrice happy Duck, employ'd in threshing Stubble!	521	Stephen Duck	7
"By Stephen Duck, upon the Queen.	563	Death of Swift	272
To rhyme almost as ill as Duck;	658	On Poetry	D 186
DUCK-LANE			
"Sir you may find them in Duck-lane:	563	Death of Swift	258
DUCKING-STOOL			
No Parish Ducking-Stool can tame her:	624	Scandal Poem 2	34
No parish ducking-stool can tame her,	618	Scandal Poem 1	36
DUCKLING			
Nor Chick, nor Duckling 'scapes, when Grim	153	Widow and Cat	D 14
DUCKLINGS			
Young Ducklings, fostered by a Hen;	294	Prog Marriage	146
DUE			
What Trophies and what Triumphs are Your Due!	12	Ode to William	D 14
Far above all Reward, yet to which all is due,	21	Ode Athenian	187
The Courtiers kept their Distance due,	63	Discovery	18
And Poets if they had their Due,	81	Vanbrug House	67
Which in due time brought forth a House;	81	Vanbrug House	75
Van is become by due Degrees	87	Hist V's House	36
And now he thought to Seize his due,	120	Apollo Outwit	37
In Christian Justice due to John.	225	Prog of Love	94
When Creditors demand their Due;	240	Run Bankers	38
"With due Submission to the God,	321	First of April	17
Your Rent is due almost a Week beside the Days of Grace.	343	Upon His Grace	44
All this was much beneath her Due,	379	Apology Lady C	118
How to give ev'ry man his due:	433	Answer Paulus	34
When, to give ev'ry Dame her due,	449	Modern Lady	138
And give each other but their Due;	453	Modern Lady	273
To other sort of Folk was due:	478	Epist on Epist	106
Consider how much more is due	483	Libel on D- D-	93
To pay him Honour due, in Course	496	Panegyr Swift	112
Let due Reward to Merit be allow'd;	533	To Mr. Gay	57
"With Princes kept a due Decorum,	566	Death of Swift	339
Contented rest; you have your due	608	Know Not What	6
Due Regard for Men of Wit?	632	Epistle Lady	74
All these Praises are your Due.	632	Epistle Lady	94
And, that you may have your Due,	634	Epistle Lady	131
And all in due Subordination;	650	On Poetry	314
Because their Praises were his due	658	On Poetry	D 410
My Lines to him you give--to speak your due,	670	Epig Carthy 18	D 1
Due Vengeance, for her Patron's sake.	701	Cadenus Vaness	471
She gave due Notice, that both Parties,	713	Cadenus Vaness	838
And think it far beneath your Due;	766	Stel B-day '26	86
As a Compliment due to a Lady so fair;	870	Grand Question	110
When young is often due to the Vicar.	940	Letter	2
Perhaps you will say, 'tis in Gratitude due,	947	Mrs. Houghton	3
And give Satan his due Dan begins to refine	1017	Swift Ans Sher	10
But, there were not a Dozen (to give 'em their Due) sick	1029	Dr. Helsham	24
And due my rent is.	1037	Sheridan Cavan	4
DUEL			
A Duel fought last Night at Two,	696	Cadenus Vaness	320
DUELS			
Three Duels he fought, thrice ventur'd his Life	327	Epigram 1	9
DUES			
Talkt of his Off'rings, Tyths, and Dues,	95	Bauc & Phil 1	173
His Talk was now of Tythes and Dues,	115	Bauc & Phil 2	125
Dues, Payments, Fees, Demands and Cheats,	174	Horace 1, 7	104
Computes, that half a Parish Dues	292	Prog Marriage	69
DUG			
A Cellar next was dug below:	108	V's House	86
Dug out in an hour,	857	Lady's Lament	185
His meadows may be dug by swine,	902	Dean's Reasons	111

DUGS
    Her flabby Dugs and down they drop. . . . .

PAGE   TITLE   LINE

582 Young Nymph   22

DUK'D   SEE BE-DUK'D

DUKE
    And now the Duke has wisely ta'ne him . . . . .   87 Hist V's House   41
    Give us our earl, the devil take their duke. . . .   186 Scriblerus 3   2
    And the Devil may take their Duke. . . . .   186 Scriblerus 4   D 12
    Make Room; as if a Duke were passing by. . . . .   194 Author Himself   36
    "But rudely press before a Duke. . . . . .   200 Horace 2, 6   39
    The Duke expects my Lord and you, ...   200 Horace 2, 6   53
    How very mean a thing's a Duke; . . . . .   297 Satiric Elegy   30
    Or Shrewsbury's Duke . . . . .   423 Carterets Arms
    We left a little Duke behind; . . . . . .   466 Birthday Song   200
    "Because its Owner is a Duke? . . . . .   548 Life of Swift   124
    "Because a Duke was proud to own him: . .   565 Death of Swift   320
    With Lorraine's Duke, and Prince of Greece. .   592 Strephon Chloe   292
    Duke William, sweetest Prince alive. . .   656 On Poetry   440
    From knowing James, to boast he knows the Duke. . . 678 Dean and Duke   4
    The Duke and Dean seem near upon a levell. . . 678 Dean and Duke   10
    Oh! wer't thou not a Duke, my good Duke Humphry, . 678 Dean and Duke   11
    Oh! wer't thou not a Duke, my good Duke Humphry, . 678 Dean and Duke   11
    A Duke to know a Dean! go smooth your Frown, .   678 Dean and Duke   13
    Well: but a Duke thou art; so pleasd the King   678 Dean and Duke   15
    The Duke of Lorrain drew his Sword, . . .   776 Mullinix Tim   111
    Nor dares he, though he were a Duke, ... 888 Panegyr Dean   59
    The <Duke> shew'd me all his fine House; and the   143 New Song   15
        <Duchess>

DUKES
    Mrs. Dukes, said I, here's an ugly Accident has   71 Mrs Harris Pet   37
        happen'd out;
    Now, Mrs. Dukes, you know, and every Body under-stands,   71 Mrs Harris Pet   42
    But, since just Heav'n the Dukes ambition mocks . . 678 Dean and Duke   5
    Both Dukes and Lords abhor its Wood, ... 928 Riddle 12   D   7

DUKES'S
    And in a Corner of Mrs. Dukes's Box,. . . . . . 70 Mrs Harris Pet   23

DULL
    Had You by dull Succession gain'd Your Crown, . . 11 Ode to William   D   9
    I'll be my life but the dull cheat would pass, . . 48 To Congreve   171
    The dull, the noisy, and the lewd: . . . .   178 To Lord Harley   48
    In their dull hum-drum key . . . . .   186 Scriblerus 4   D   4
    By dull Divines, who look with envious Eyes, .   193 Author Himself   3
    Grown lazy, foggy, fat, and dull: . . . .   231 Prog of Poetry   22
    Canst thou imagine, dull Divine, ...   292 Prog Marriage   71
    But, Jacobites are strangely dull. . . . . 299 Horrid Plot   42
    Nor shall I dull in Silence sit; . . . .   411 Dial Rich Marb   89
    To treat a dull Divine: . . . . .   426 Five Ladies   24
    But dull Intregues . . . . . .   441 Ballyspellin   28
    So Academick dull Ale-drinkers . . .   503 Doctor Delaney   97
    First learn the Science to be dull, . . .   503 Doctor Delaney   111
    The Ass was dull, the Lyon brave, . . .   512 Answer Fable   5
    So dull, that but for Spleen and Spite, . .   514 Answer Fable   71
    Hear an old Fable, and a dull one too; . . 538 Mr. Pulteney   15
    Confounded Dull---, before he Dy'd---. . . 547 Life of Swift   89
    Are witty, dull, rejoyce, complain. . . . 620 Scandal Poem 1   94
    Are witty, dull, rejoyce, complain. . . . 626 Scandal Poem 2   92
    If I always seem too dull t'ye; . . . .   630 Epistle Lady   19
    But all distinguish thy dull leaden Mass. .   670 Epig Carthy 18   D   6
    In a dull Stream, which moving slow . . . 688 Cadenus Vaness   51
    And in dull Studies to engage . . . .   705 Cadenus Vaness   578
    This Racer wou'd prove but a dull founder'd Jade. . 717 Answer Rebus   28
    But finding me so dull and dry since, . .   741 Stel B-day 22   27
    Dull Uniformity in Fools . . . . .   787 Dick's Variety   1
    Wou'd you rise in the Church, be Stupid and Dull, . 807 Advice Parson   1
    Dull Bacon's Essays, ...   855 Lady's Lament   148
    Dull Daniel's whey-face; . . . . .   858 Lady's Lament   224
    But a Rabble of Tenants, and rusty dull Rumms; . 868 Grand Question   28
    All things gone on the same dull track, . . 877 To Dean Swift   31
    Above our neighb'ring dull Divines! . . .   888 Panegyr Dean   64
    Like sots, alone I'm dull enough, ... 936 Riddle 24   D   9
    An Ounce of Gold's worth ten of Brass, dull Pedant. . 1004 Dan J's Reply   33

DULLER
    That, when I'm duller than a Post, ... 891 Panegyr Dean   148

DULLEST
    The dullest Reader smoaks the Jest: . . . . . . 643 On Poetry   100
    --That Lady is the dullest Soul-- . . . .   698 Cadenus Vaness   359
    The dullest Beast, and Gentleman's Liquor, . . 940 Letter   1
    The dullest Beast, and Swine's Delight . . . 940 Letter   3
    The dullest Beast when high in Stature, . . 940 Letter   5
    The dullest Beast, and a Party distrest, . . 940 Letter   8
    The dullest Beast, and the Saddle it wears, . . 940 Letter   10
    The dullest Beast and kind Voice of a Cat, . . 940 Letter   12
    The dullest of Beasts and of Birds in the Air, . 940 Letter   14
    The dullest Beast and fam'd College for Teagues . 940 Letter   16
    The dullest Beast and a Cobler's Tool, . . . 941 Letter   18
    The dullest Beast, and that which you kiss, . . 941 Letter   21
    The dullest Beast and Eggs unsound, . . . 941 Letter   25
    The dullest Beast and what covers a House, . . 941 Letter   27
    The dullest Beast, and scandalous Vermin . .   941 Letter   29
    The dullest Beast, and what's cover'd with Crust, . 941 Letter   31
    The dullest Beast mending Highways, . . .   941 Letter   33
    The dullest Beast and a Hole in the Ground, . . 941 Letter   35

		PAGE	TITLE	LINE

DULLEST   (CONTINUED)
The dullest Beast, and what Doctors pretend   941 Letter   37
The dullest Beast and Fish for Lent   941 Letter   39
The dullest Beast and a shameful Jeer,   941 Letter   41

DULLNESS
Th' appeal of dullness in the last resort: 53 Temple Ill   88
Of Dullness, Pride, Conceit, a medley,   455 Dean Smedley   2

DULMAN
Sauntring in Coffee-house is Dulman seen;   137 City Shower   11

DULNESS
'Tis hard, where dulness over-rules,   436 Answer Paulus   123
"True genuine Dulness mov'd his Pity,   572 Death of Swift   469
Only Dulness can produce,   636 Epistle Lady   204
But to say truth, such Dulness reigns   742 Stel B-day 22   41

DULY
Duly let out a Nights to Steal for Fees.   125 Descriptn Morn   16
Were duly washt to keep 'em sweet;   586 Strephon Chloe   78
Provide you duly as we go   621 Scandal Poem 1   129
Nor, tho' his Priests be duly paid,   657 On Poetry   491
Lash them daily, lash them duly,   835 Legion Club   156
But, duly e'er you leave your Station,   893 Panegyr Dean   219

DUMB
Explaining strikes opposers Dumb;   281 Journal   84
Shall strike him dumb, and quell their Noise.   340 Arch-Bish Dub   28
He drew dumb Merit from her Cell,   386 Manly Virtue   84
But in the Praise of Virtue is dumb: 515 Answer Fable   94

DUMPS
Receive the News in doleful Dumps,   562 Death of Swift   227
A College Joke to cure the Dumps.   594 Cassinus Peter   38

DUN
"And hath she sent so soon to dun?   446 Modern Lady   65
'Tis not the Coat that looks so dun,   786 Clad in Brown   7

DUNCE
For none but a Dunce would come under his Rod.   335 Serious Poem   34
And crown a Royal Dunce with Bays: 464 Birthday Song   120
And so might ev'ry Dunce alive.   481 Libel on D- D-   48
And could not let a Dunce alone: 602 Beasts Confess   24
The Town will mark you for a Dunce: 644 On Poetry   138
He grows a tyrant, dunce, or beast.   658 On Poetry   D 204
He'll swear she's a dunce;   854 Lady's Lament   92
"My School-Master call'd me a Dunce and a Fool,   873 Grand Question   163
The worst Dunce in your School, 'till he's heav'd from   968 Letter Sherid   34
    the Ground

DUNCE'S
(Which seldom is the Dunce's Case)   647 On Poetry   234

DUNCENIA
Duncenia to a Common-weal;   653 On Poetry   380

DUNCES
So, the pert Dunces of Mankind   216 To Mr. Delany   45
Caressing Knaves and Dunces wooing,   484 Libel on D- D-   127
While Dunces of the coarsest Clay,   497 Panegyr Swift   148
On me, when Dunces are satyrick,   505 Doctor Delaney   169
Call Dunces, Fools, and Sons of Whores,   652 On Poetry   345
And all their Brother Dunces lash,   652 On Poetry   355

DUNCIAD
Immortal by the Dunciad;   876 To Dean Swift   10

DUNDALK
I'll drive you to Cavan, from Cavan to Dundalk;   1019 To Sheridan   7

DUNG   SEE COW-DUNG
Those beds of dung, where schoolboys sprout up beaus   46 To Congreve   99
Sweepings from Butchers Stalls, Dung, Guts, and Blood   139 City Shower   61
And turning Dung it self to Gold?   157 Fable of Midas   48
By Gnats, and draw the Nation's Dung,   496 Panegyr Swift   115
Such gaudy Tulips rais'd from Dung.   530 Lady's Dres Rm   144
By the Sire exhal'd from Dung: 799 Traulus 2   4
A Ball of new-dropt Horse's Dung,   811 Bro Protestant   11
Let them dabble in their Dung;   831 Legion Club   52
A mushroom in a bed of dung;   950 Upstart   D 4

DUNGHILL
Leap from the Dunghill in a trice,   84 Salamander   40
Just Heaven! to see the Dunghill dastard Brood   826 Noisy Tom   17
And on some Dunghill left to rot.   916 Riddle 1   42
You live among ill folks in a dunghill,   1038 Sheridan Cavan   17

DUNKIN
Dunkin has been for Latin fam'd--translate.   667 Epig Carthy 4   D 4
To Dunkin you attribute what I writ,   669 Epig Carthy 17   D 1

DUNKIN'S
How different from thine is Dunkin's Lot!   667 Epig Carthy 7   D 1

DUNKIRK
Dunkirk never shall be theirs,   169 Peace Dunkirk   36

DUNKIRK'S
But Dunkirk's ours, we'll hold it fast: 168 Peace Dunkirk   4

DUNNS
From Dunns and Debts, and drown our Care;   184 Horace 2, 1   110

DUNS
Duns at his Lordships Gate began to meet,   124 Descriptn Morn   13
Of Duns, attending at their Gate.   239 Run Bankers   16
On Watchmen, Constables and Duns,   583 Young Nymph   52

DUPE
a sharper in trifles a dupe in the main   540 Charac Walpole   4

235

		PAGE	TITLE	LINE
DUPES				
A forward Critick often dupes us	. . . .	648	On Poetry	255
DURING				
During Her Sacred Life, should never come over:	. .	144	New Song	36
DURST				
That I durst Pawn my Ears, 'twill tell	. . . . .	101	Elegy Patrige	113
Before he durst the Nymph approach.	. . . .	119	Apollo Outwit	8
Nor in her Presence durst be Rude,	. . . .	121	Apollo Outwit	43
Else what aspiring hero durst?	. . . .	178	To Lord Harley	68
The Scottish Nation, whom he durst offend,	. . .	196	Author Himself	69
That Will durst hardly venture in;	. . . . . .	219	A Quiet Life	2
She durst not look above your Wast;	. . . . . .	222	Prog of Love	6
She durst behold that Monster, Man:	. . . . . .	222	Prog of Love	12
Tho' if he durst, he had denied.	. . . .	378	Apology Lady C	96
Poor Envy durst not shew her Phiz,	. . . . .	456	Dean Smedley	21
Wou'd, if he durst, be more your Friend;	. . . .	483	Libel on D- D-	114
Which, if you durst but give it place,	. . . .	485	Libel on D- D-	179
Durst there show his right or most revnd face	. . .	522	St. Cecilia's	10
But, not a Soul his Office durst accept:	. . .	536	To Mr. Gay	153
For Fickleness how durst you blame us?	. . . . .	618	Scandal Poem 1	39
Before Aeneas durst aspire	. . . . .	619	Scandal Poem 1	65
For Fickleness how durst you blame us?	. . . . .	624	Scandal Poem 2	37
Before Aeneas durst aspire	. . . . .	625	Scandal Poem 2	61
To her, who durst not read Romances;	. . .	711	Cadenus Vaness	795
What honester folks never durst for their ears.	. .	815	Yahoo's	19
Durst thou, ungrateful, from the <Senate> chace	. . .	826	Noisy Tom	15
Never durst a Muse before	. . . . .	834	Legion Club	119
But, he durst not so much as once open his Lips,	. . .	873	Grand Question	177
And you durst not talk thus if I saw you at our ale-house	976	Dean to Sherid	32
DURUEL				
Like Carleton cheap, or fam'd Duruel,	. . . . . .	85	Salamander	62
DUSKY				
For this inferior world is but Heaven's dusky shade,	.	35	Ode Sancroft	21
Which in its dusky march along the plain,	. . . . .	40	Ode Sancroft	193
DUST				
This, crumbles into dust,	. . . .	39	Ode Sancroft	140
As threadbare, and as full of Dust.	. . . .	94	Bauc & Phil 1	170
As Thread-bare, and as full of Dust.	. . . . . .	115	Bauc & Phil 2	124
Not yet, the Dust had shun'd th' unequal Strife,	. .	137	City Shower	23
'Twas doubtful which was Rain, and which was Dust.	. .	137	City Shower	26
When Dust and Rain at once his Coat invade;	. . . .	138	City Shower	28
His only Coat, where Dust confus'd with Rain,	. . .	138	City Shower	29
Smith's Dust, and Copper, Lead and Brass,	. . . .	344	Prometheus	4
Half choak'd with dust, half drown'd with rains;	. .	403	Window Inns 10	D 6
Squeez'd in a Coffin turn to dust;	. . . .	467	Birthday Song	236
But, when thou seest me laid in Dust,	. . . . .	596	Cassinus Peter	100
I'm humbled e'er I meet the dust,'	. . . . . .	663	Epigram Bust	2
To Merit humbled in the Dust:	. . . . . .	765	Stel B-day '26	46
And weekly carry out our Dust.	. . . .	787	Clad in Brown	28
When Dick cries, Dust to carry out?	. . . . . .	787	Clad in Brown	30
In Egypt turn'd the Dust to Lice;	. . . .	813	Bro Protestant	50
As from the trodden Dust they spring,	. . . . . .	813	Bro Protestant	53
A Rod should turn them back to Dust.	. . . . . .	813	Bro Protestant	56
DUSTY				
O'er mountains steep, o'er dusty plains,	. . . . .	403	Window Inns 10	D 5
DUTCH				
Spight of Dutch Friends and English Foes,	. . .	168	Peace Dunkirk	1
The Dutch from hence shall no more Millions drain;	. .	169	Peace Dunkirk	27
The Swiss and Dutch whole Millions drain.	. . . .	256	Bubble	160
Unless, like the Dutch, you rather would boyl	. . . .	352	Wood Insect	37
DUTCH-HEARTED				
The Dutch-hearted Whigs may rail and complain;	. .	169	Peace Dunkirk	37
DUTCH-MEN				
To make the Dutch-men proud and great:	. . . . .	169	Peace Dunkirk	34
DUTCHESS				
A Dutchess or a Kitchen Girl.	. . . .	890	Panegyr Dean	124
Than where the haughty Dutchess Locks,	. . . . .	896	Panegyr Dean	297
DUTIFUL				
. . . Your most dutiful and obedient George Nim-Dan-Dean.	1024	Nim-Dan-Dean 2	D 18
DUTIFULLY				
Flew dutifully back again,	. . . .	16	Ode Athenian	30
DUTY				
. . .as in Duty bound, shall ever Pray.	. . . . .	73	Mrs Harris Pet	75
To pay their Duty at his Hearse!	. . . .	98	Elegy Patrige	8
A duty might be layd on linnen	. . . .	422	Ireld	50
Devotion, Duty, and Respect,	. . . .	711	Cadenus Vaness	799
By Duty bound, on Stella's Day;	. . . .	740	Stel B-day 22	2
'Twas to teach you in modester Language your Duty;	. .	968	Letter Sherid	25
DWELL				
Which unprovided where to dwell,	. . . .	79	Vanbrug House	31
Doomd ever in suspense to dwell,	. . . .	93	Bauc & Phil 1	103
Doom'd ever in Suspence to dwell,	. . . .	113	Bauc & Phil 2	63
Here would our Hero ever dwell,	. . . .	385	Manly Virtue	47
You find, the Gods in Homer dwell	. . . .	620	Scandal Poem 1	99
Because we dwell in higher Regions:	. . . . .	626	Scandal Poem 2	96
You find, the Gods in Homer dwell,	. . . . . .	626	Scandal Poem 2	97
But not to dwell on Things minute,	. . . . . .	708	Cadenus Vaness	674
You shew Don Carlos where to dwell,	. . . . . .	748	Stel Distress	73
And who is this <Bishop>? And where does he dwell?	. .	803	Irish Bishops	3
That the Club have Right to dwell	. . . .	830	Legion Club	43

	PAGE	TITLE	LINE
DWELL **(CONTINUED)**			
To sweep the Mansion-house they dwell in;	892	Panegyr Dean	165
Nor dwell on Subjects too sublime.	896	Panegyr Dean	320
Good Luck to those with whom I dwell.	918	Riddle 4	44
You're reported to dwell	939	Riddle Answerd	D
DWELLERS			
But, as for the dwellers,	403	Window Inns 9	D 4
DWELLING-PLACE			
Has given thee up a dwelling-place to fiends?	37	Ode Sancroft	95
DWELLS			
I'll search where ev'ry Virtue dwells,	691	Cadenus Vaness	148
The Nymph who dwells in every Tree,	849	Old Thorn	45
DWELT			
Here, on a better day, some druid dwelt,	49	To Congreve	191
Where dwelt a poor old honest Yeman	91	Bauc & Phil 1	51
Where dwelt a good old honest Yeoman,	111	Bauc & Phil 2	19
Your Fancy then had always dwelt	591	Strephon Chloe	245
With that which dwelt so near her Heart;	922	Riddle 7	36
DWINDLED			
Already dwindled to a Lath;	293	Prog Marriage	105
Now Love is dwindled to Intrigue,	687	Cadenus Vaness	13
DY'D			
That Men, who liv'd and dy'd without a Name,	25	Ode Athenian	306
And that her troubled Ghost still haunts there since she dy'd;	27	Ode to Temple	38
Patrige is Dead, nay more, he dy'd	98	Elegy Patrige	3
Grew Scrubby, dy'd a-top, was stunted:	117	Bauc & Phil 2	177
He made them weep before he dy'd.	296	Satiric Elegy	24
So Regulus in Torments dy'd.	325	Pethox	58
For it prov'd that he dy'd of a Drop at Killmainham:	337	Serious Poem	114
But lik'd neither loss and so quietly dy'd.	430	Dicky Dolly	12
Though born in Snow, it dy'd in Flame.	470	Burning Poem	16
Bequeath'd by Tripsy when she dy'd,	526	Lady's Dres Rm	30
While He went robbing on; old Master dy'd.	536	To Mr. Gay	148
Nor if you dy'd, wou'd fail to go	547	Life of Swift	62
Confounded Dull---, before he Dy'd---.	547	Life of Swift	89
"He gave it all:--But first he dy'd.	558	Death of Swift	160
"He dy'd a Year ago." The same.	563	Death of Swift	256
While she a Goddess dy'd in Grain	586	Strephon Chloe	85
By Thunder dy'd in Jove's Embrace;	587	Strephon Chloe	108
His antient Pipe in Sable dy'd,	594	Cassinus Peter	23
A Coat we gave him dy'd in grain	619	Scandal Poem 1	69
And dy'd defending his opinion.	620	Scandal Poem 1	84
A Coat we gave him, dy'd in Grain;	625	Scandal Poem 2	65
And dy'd defending his Opinion.	626	Scandal Poem 2	82
For when our high-born Howard dy'd,	652	On Poetry	371
But what's dy'd black will take no other hue.	670	Epig Carthy 18	D 8
It must a thousand Times have dy'd.	765	Stel B-day '26	58
One shews how bravely Audoin Dy'd,	781	Mullinix Tim	273
And kept their Liberty, or bravely dy'd.	793	St. Pat's Well	82
Shall in thy dearest Blood be dy'd,	925	Riddle 8	43
DY'ST			
"Dy'st on a more ignoble Tree,	851	Old Thorn	86
DYE			
Because, alas, when we all dye	21	Ode Athenian	162
All of old Cut with a new Dye,	23	Ode Athenian	227
(Madam, I dye without your Grace)	60	Lady Tablebook	15
'Twill just new dye the Lining.	75	Game Traffick	24
"I'll dye, if you deny your Help.	207	Fable Bitches	12
Dye Ned and Bess; give Will to Joan,	328	Epigram 3	3
Dye Joan and Will; give Bess to Ned,	328	Epigram 3	5
I dream't Wood was told he should Dye by a Drop	337	Serious Poem	110
The Maggot will dye, and the Sick will recover.	351	Wood Insect	28
Roses of richest Dye, that shone	379	Apology Lady C	113
If mountains sink to vales, if cityes dye	419	Shall Repine	3
Was left to starve, and dye in Wales.	481	Libel on D- D-	52
And there without a mitre dye.	491	Dialogue	56
The Rogues must dye for Want and Spight,	502	Doctor Delaney	72
Must dye for Want of Food and Rayment,	502	Doctor Delaney	73
Nor can you go to Hell before you dye.	539	Mr. Pulteney	42
Must by the Course of Nature dye:	556	Death of Swift	74
He'd rather chuse that I should dye,	557	Death of Swift	131
Revive the Libels born to dye;	561	Death of Swift	203
I'm sorry; but we all must dye.	561	Death of Swift	212
Why do we grieve that Friends should dye?	562	Death of Swift	243
Then, leave me to despair and dye.	595	Cassinus Peter	72
Could change the Stock, or cog a Dye,	607	Beasts Confess	193
May'st dye like me by Chance; but not by Nature.	861	On Old Glass	2
I dye unpity'd and forgot;	916	Riddle 1	41
Condemn'd by Female Hands to dye;	923	Riddle 7	62
For, should I dye for Love of you,	925	Riddle 8	26
DYES			
Then sheds about his Spaun, and dyes.	80	Vanbrug House	38
But scatt'ring round his Fly-blows, dyes;	80	Vanbrug House	53
And Britain's lost if Harlys dyes	140	Harlyes Surgn	2
He dyes, and leaves his mourning Mate	295	Prog Marriage	155
DYET			
In Dyet was perhaps too nice,	602	Beasts Confess	39
DYING **SEE NEVER-DYING**			
Who cou'd so well a dying Nation save,	12	Ode to William	D 15
Observe the dying Father speak:	189	Faggot	1

DYING   (CONTINUED)   PAGE TITLE   LINE
        Regardless of his dying Groans.   . . . .   413 Desire Possess   58
        Doll dying first, Dick grew Melancholly,   430 Dicky Dolly   2
        "Was chearful to his dying Day, ...   572 Death of Swift   477
        "And dying, never told his Pain.   . . . .   596 Cassinus Peter   78
        Hear me pay my dying Vows. . . . .   661 Love Song   24
        I dying leave the Debt unpay'd   740 Stel B-day '21   18
        Scarce glimmers, like a dying Snuff.   787 Clad in Brown   18
        Begotten, and Born, and dying with Noise,   . . .   927 Riddle 11   D   1
        Swans sing when dying, geese when blind. . . . . .   983 Sher, A Goose   14
DYSTRUCTIVE
        The mortal force of Time's dystructive hand   . . . . 419 Shall Repine   2
E'EN
        Must e'en all herd with us their Kindred Fools, . . . 18 Ode Athenian   82
        I e'en left her, and came away as wise as I was before. 71 Mrs Harris Pet   47
        Well then, I'll e'en go home, and fast; . . . . .   377 Apology Lady C   54
        E'en quit the House, for thou too long hast sat in't, . 538 Mr. Pulteney   9
E'ER   SEE WHERE-E'ER
        For You (ah, did I think I e'er should live to see .   23 Ode Athenian   247
        E'er flourish't under a Successor or a Son;   . . . .   25 Ode Athenian   285
        Nor e'er call back again) . . . .   25 Ode Athenian   290
        No Thunder e'er can blast, ...   29 Ode to Temple   82
        Shall e'er long grow into a Tree, ...   31 Ode to Temple   168
        None e'er but you, ...   38 Ode Sancroft   113
        Whom sin and want e'er furnish'd out a wit;   . . .   48 To Congreve   166
        If hope e'er dawns the smallest of its rays. . . .   54 Temple Ill   112
        E'er a week pas't committing Blunders: . . . . .   62 Discovery   4
        But e'er since Men invented Guns, ...   83 Salamander   15
        Whose Breath or Touch, where e'er he came, ... 85 Salamander   59
        E'er he could prove the good Squire ly'd.   . . . . 98 Elegy Patrige   4
        Attend when e'er I want their Aid, ...   120 Apollo Outwit   31
        Nor e'er expect another . . . .   123 Empty'ng Town   22
        But soon as e'er he lay'd it down, ...   132 Magician's Rod   3
        When e'er the Soil has Golden Mines;   . . . . . .   133 Magician's Rod   24
        Where none e'er look'd for it before;   . . . . . .   133 Magician's Rod   30
        A Codling e'er it went his Lip in, ...   156 Fable of Midas   5
        None e'er did modern Midas chuse, ...   157 Fable of Midas   51
        To others, e'er it be my own. . . . .   204 In Sickness   22
        What Poet e'er could take his Flight?   . . . . . .   231 Prog of Poetry   24
        What Poet e'er could sing a Note?   . . . .   231 Prog of Poetry   26
        Resume their own when e'er they please.   . . . . .   239 Run Bankers   8
        When e'er the bloody Bond appears. . . . .   240 Run Bankers   48
        When e'er my Viceroy is address'd, ...   271 Apollo's Edict   D 50
        At Sea, or Land, if e'er you found him, ...   303 Storm   15
        None e'er was known to have a Brace.   . . . . . .   366 Answer Delaney   8
        None e'er made Verses worse than he, ...   401 Window Inns 2   5
        If e'er I stoop beneath a crown'd Head: . . . . .   410 Dial Rich Marb   74
        Did Paulus e'er complain of sweat? . . . .   432 Answer Paulus   5
        Did Paulus e'er the sun forget?   . . . .   432 Answer Paulus   6
        E'er enter any Mortal's Noddle.   . . . .   496 Panegyr Swift   105
        Did Female Virtue e'er so high ascend, ...   531 To Mr. Gay   5
        "That e'er he cring'd to Men in Place? . . . . .   549 Life of Swift   145
        She takes a Bolus e'er she sleeps; . . . .   582 Young Nymph   37
        That, e'er to Bed they venture up, ...   587 Strephon Chloe   119
        But, e'er you sell your self to Laughter, ...   591 Strephon Chloe   231
        O Strephon, e'er that fatal Day   . . . .   591 Strephon Chloe   235
        Rash Mortals, e'er you take a Wife, ...   593 Strephon Chloe   301
        E'er drove, before he sold his Land, ...   598 Problem Solved   13
        And, if e'er he flyes is forc'd to tye em.   . . .   621 Scandal Poem 1   120
        Did I e'er my Mite withold . . . .   632 Epistle Lady   71
        E'er I reach'd Parnassus Top' . . . .   638 Epistle Lady   261
        I'm humbled e'er I meet the dust,' . . . .   663 Epigram Bust   2
        But e'er you mount his mettled Steed, ...   666 Epig Carthy 2   D   3
        This I may boast, which few e'er cou'd, ...   669 Epig Carthy 15   D   1
        What mortal else cou'd e'er go through it!   . . . 675 Curate's Compl   17
        To all he spoke, than e'er before; . . . .   704 Cadenus Vaness   565
        E'er Stella can deceive a Friend.   . . . .   725 To Stella   58
        Her firmness who could e'er have known, ...   755 Stella '23   25
        Then let him use you e'er so rough, ...   797 Traulus 1   61
        What e'er he speaks for Madness goes, ...   798 Traulus 1   65
        And burst asunder e'er he went to Hell; . . . . . .   806 Judas   18
        Than it e'er should be said . . . .   853 Lady's Lament   56
        And e'er a twelvemonth and a day   . . . .   878 Robbin & Harry   11
        But, duly e'er you leave your Station, ...   893 Panegyr Dean   219
        E'er join'd such Numbers Hand in Hand; . . . . . .   926 Riddle 9   12
        I ne'er was born, nor e'er can die, ...   936 Riddle 23   D 26
        Because she let's out more, than e'er she takes in. . . 972 S-'s Ans Sh-d   6
        Who from her Lover e'er could boast, ...   993 On Picture   23
E'ERY
        Of e'ery Rogue that wears an <Arse>   . . . . . .   497 Panegyr Swift   121
E'RE
        And needs must stink when e're it dies; . . . . . .   9 Ode to King   110
        I sigh when e're I think of it . . . .   24 Ode Athenian   270
        When e're he please to blot it out; . . . .   61 Lady Tablebook   22
        Or in a Boat when e're thou wilt   . . . .   109 V's House   113
        And Guest his Business e're he Spoke.   . . . . . .   120 Apollo Outwit   16
        What e're she would desire, to Grant, ...   120 Apollo Outwit   19
        Dear Dean, if e're again you Write, ...   371 Letter D. S-y   1
        And that by all I e're did hear   . . . .   372 Letter D. S-y   11
        When e're I 'gin, you should pursue . . . .   373 Letter D. S-y   52
        E're he advance the Doctor higher   . . . .   475 Epist on Epist   24

```
E'RE            (CONTINUED)                              PAGE   TITLE        LINE
   You e're return'd, or ever went?    . . . . . . . .  745 Stel Distress      22
E'REWHILE
   Where fatal Neptune rul'd e'rewhile, . . . . . . .   17 Ode Athenian       39
E'RY
   You e'ry moment think an Age,     . . . . . . . . .  776 Mullinix Tim      107
   Condensed Filth in e'ry Part,     . . . . . . . . .  787 Clad in Brown      15
EACH    107                                             OMITTED WORD
EAGER
   The eager Muse took wing upon the Waves decline,   . .  16 Ode Athenian     22
   Whom blind and eager Curiosity  . . . . . . . . .   18 Ode Athenian       63
   "So eager to express your Love,    . . . . . . . .  200 Horace 2, 6        37
   With eager Hast he longs to rove   . . . . . . . .  251 Bubble             29
   With eager hand he grasps the treacherous prey,   . .  672 Epig Carthy 24  D  15
EAGLE
   The Lyon, Eagle, Fox and Bear   . . . . . . .       83 Salamander          9
   The Eagle in the Tale, ye know,    . . . . . . .   458 Paddy's Charac      29
   Flyes like an Eagle or'e his head;    . . . . . .  461 Birthday Song       34
   He comes full gallop on his eagle: . . . . . . . . 620 Scandal Poem 1     114
   He comes full gallop on his Eagle.    . . . . . .  627 Scandal Poem 2     112
EAGLE'S
   Like the victorious wren perch'd on the eagle's wing; .  44 To Congreve    38
   An Eagle's Flight and State assumes,   . . . . . . .  252 Bubble           35
EAR
   Of forward Face, and Ear acute,    . . . . . . . .   63 Discovery         26
   But, St. John comes and whispers in his Ear;  . . . 194 Author Himself    34
   And thence into the Royal Ear instills.    . . . .  195 Author Himself    56
   And, in <Swift's> Ear thrusts half his powder'd Nose. 196 Author Himself   68
   Salute her, and she turn'd her Ear:    . . . . . .  222 Prog of Love        4
   While Betty's buzzing at her Ear,    . . . . . . .  291 Prog Marriage      41
   'Tis no great Loss to lose an Ear;    . . . . . . . 366 Answer Delaney      2
   For tho' the Place of either Ear,    . . . . . . .  366 Answer Delaney     29
   That from each Ear, as he observes,    . . . . . .  367 Answer Delaney     33
   One goes to this, and one to t' other Ear.   . . .  367 Answer Delaney     38
   When my Left Ear was deaf a Fortnight,   . . . . .  367 Answer Delaney     42
   To t' other Ear I felt it coming on,   . . . . . .  367 Answer Delaney     43
   But not to reach the Ear;    . . . . . . . . . . .  405 Swift to Pope       2
   And Guelph the strongest ear will wound.   . . . .  467 Birthday Song     216
   Is offensive to every true Protestant ear    . . . 522 St. Cecilia's       6
   Till <Bob>, the Poet's Foe, possess't her Ear.  . . 531 To Mr. Gay          4
   He left his Scut behind, and Half an Ear.   . . . . 538 Mr. Pulteney       36
   Offensive to a Loyal Ear---:    . . . . . . . . . . 550 Life of Swift     192
   Now, bend thine Ear; since out it must:   . . . . . 596 Cassinus Peter     99
   Vanessa's Praise rung in their Ear:    . . . . . .  694 Cadenus Vaness    241
   But turn the deaf ear,    . . . . . . . . . . . . . 756 Dingley Brent      11
   Shall rise one Blade of Grass, one Ear of Corn;  . . 793 St. Pat's Well    92
   Yet so tender is my Ear,    . . . . . . . . . . . . 933 Riddle 20       D  25
   Can shew a Nose, Eye, Tongue, or Ear,   . . . . . . 935 Riddle 23       D   8
EAR-WAX
   With Dirt, and Sweat, and Ear-Wax grim'd.   . . . . 527 Lady's Dres Rm     46
EAR'D    SEE LONG-EAR'D
EAR'S
   He, that of ev'ry ear's the charmer,   . . . . . .  876 To Dean Swift       3
EARL
   Give us our earl, the devil take their duke.  . . . 186 Scriblerus 3        2
   The Earl of Kildare,    . . . . . . . . . . . . .   247 Irish-Feast        77
   Nearly related to an Earl.    . . . . . . . . . .   289 Prog Marriage       4
   Deserves an Earl,    . . . . . . . . . . . . . . .  442 Ballyspellin       62
   Her Fondness for a certain Earl    . . . . . . . .  699 Cadenus Vaness    390
   Did not an Earl but lately Vote    . . . . . . . .  773 Mullinix Tim       13
   Proving the Earl a grand Offender,    . . . . . .   774 Mullinix Tim       21
   With Teague O'Murphy, or an Earl;    . . . . . . .  890 Panegyr Dean      123
EARLD
   Earld Godwin's Castles overflown,    . . . . . . .  257 Bubble            171
EARLE
   Give us but our Earle,    . . . . . . . . . . . .   186 Scriblerus 4    D  11
EARLIEST
   Vanessa's earliest Thoughts engage.   . . . . . . . 706 Cadenus Vaness    637
EARLY
   And the young Muse's early favour felt;   . . . . .  49 To Congreve       192
   Came early, and departed late:    . . . . . . . .   173 Horace 1, 7        79
   She knows her Early self no more,    . . . . . . .  227 Prog of Beauty     49
   Bless you late and early,    . . . . . . . . . . .  246 Irish-Feast        45
   Heroick Actions early bred in,    . . . . . . . .   398 Earl of P-b-w      34
   With early clients at his door,    . . . . . . . .  434 Answer Paulus      71
   And like his Father early wise.    . . . . . . . .  466 Birthday Song     192
   Aurora with thy early Flute.    . . . . . . . . .   594 Cassinus Peter     34
   What early Manhood has he shown,    . . . . . . .   655 On Poetry         431
   Came early, out of pure Good-will,    . . . . . .   698 Cadenus Vaness    366
   Those early Seeds by Venus sown,    . . . . . . .   701 Cadenus Vaness    472
   Instructed from her early Years    . . . . . . . .  705 Cadenus Vaness    596
EARN
   If all my Pains will earn a Crown.    . . . . . .   502 Doctor Delaney     68
   To earn a Stock of Pence and Praise,   . . . . . .  642 On Poetry          66
   O, could I earn for thee, my lovely Lass,   . . . . 882 Pastoral Dial      49
EARN'D
   Tom having earn'd a Twig of Lawrel,    . . . . . .  458 Paddy's Charac     14
EARNEST
   William's the Pledge and Earnest given by Fate   . . .  13 Ode to William D 47
   But half in Earnest, half in Jest;    . . . . . .   303 Storm              26
   With panting Heart, and earnest Eyes,   . . . . . . 452 Modern Lady       230
```

		PAGE	TITLE	LINE

EARNEST (CONTINUED)
	PAGE	TITLE	LINE
Has made the Man a Goose in earnest.	666	Epig Carthy 1	D 4
You call him a Sloven in earnest or jest.	943	Probatur Alit	36

EARNESTLY
	PAGE	TITLE	LINE
"And now I earnestly desire,	208	Fable Bitches	27
Don Carlos earnestly would beg,	746	Stel Distress	17
Don Carlos earnestly would beg,	750	Stel Wood-Park	15

EARS   SEE STUFF-HER-EARS
	PAGE	TITLE	LINE
Charming her greedy Ears	17	Ode Athenian	53
Yes, that beau's look, that voice, those critic ears,	48	To Congreve	173
And set the Planets by the Ears:	99	Elegy Patrige	58
That I durst Pawn mỹ Ears, 'twill tell	101	Elegy Patrige	113
Clap't Asses Ears upon the Judge,	157	Fable of Midas	30
Had lost his Art, and kept his Ears.	157	Fable of Midas	40
Our Midas too has Asses Ears;	158	Fable of Midas	62
Thro' any Ears but of an Ass.	158	Fable of Midas	66
With Asses Ears, and dirty Hands.	158	Fable of Midas	82
Should sink and fall about his Ears	160	Atlas	10
Like Bees, are humming in my Ears.	200	Horace 2, 6	50
Always together by the Ears;	216	To Mr. Delany	52
Dipt over head and Ears--in Debt.	251	Bubble	24
Has twice two Legs, two hanging Ears;	299	Horrid Plot	46
The brazen Bells salute his Ears:	338	Wood's Brass	6
In Fillets of Brass roll'd up to his Ears:	350	Wood Insect	8
And ring Wood's Copper in our Ears	354	Simile Silver	27
The lovely tingling in your Ears,	362	Grace's Answer	35
To furnish artificial Ears.	367	Answer Delaney	54
And scarce believes his Eyes, or Ears;	376	Apology Lady C	20
That Walls have Tongues, and Hedges, Ears.	408	Dial Rich Marb	8
Stunning her Royal Ears with talking;	410	Dial Rich Marb	59
Whose fingers itch for poets ears;	487	Irish-Club	6
The Bullets whistling round his Ears,	500	Doctor Delaney	4
She saves Half her Victuals, by feeding your Ears.	580	Psyche	14
To slip his Ears, yet struck his Nose:	589	Strephon Chloe	184
His Ears are half a Foot too short;	602	Beasts Confess	32
And is our thunder in your ears	617	Scandal Poem 1	5
Offensive to all pious ears.	622	Scandal Poem 1	168
And, is our Thunder in your Ears	624	Scandal Poem 2	5
To set Elysium by the Ears.	647	On Poetry	218
When vulgar Knaves would lose their Ears:	724	To Stella	32
This ball of wax your ears will darken,	753	Gift for Bec	21
To teach her ears the art of list'ning,	762	Bec's B-Day	54
To rattle in their Ears your Drum.	775	Mullinix Tim	50
Thy Whisp'rings foisted in all Ears;	775	Mullinix Tim	62
Now has the Speaker by the Ears,	788	Dick's Variety	27
To din thine Ears with unharmonious Clack,	792	St. Pat's Well	47
What honester folks never durst for their ears.	815	Yahoo's	19
And slitting of noses, and cropping of ears,	816	Yahoo's	48
A face for to kiss, without eyes, ears, or nose.	817	Yahoo's	64
While Jonathan's threaten'd with loss of his ears;	818	Epigr Kite	2
He had cut his own ears to be deaf to your nonsense.	818	Epigr Kite	10
First issuing, struck the Murd'rer's Ears;	850	Old Thorn	54
With Ribbins in Knots, at its Tail and its Ears:	870	Grand Question	98
But the Dean, if this Secret shou'd come to his Ears,	873	Grand Question	187
Sunk over head and ears in matter,	900	Dean's Reasons	59
I speak to Eyes and not to Ears.	915	Riddle 1	18

EARTH
	PAGE	TITLE	LINE
When Man himself's the Vermin of Her Earth;	8	Ode to King	55
From the worst Excrements of Earth;	10	Ode to King	127
Sent by just Heaven to threaten Earth	10	Ode to King	133
As from the Womb of Earth a field of Corn.	20	Ode Athenian	131
Shoots to the Earth and dies;	29	Ode to Temple	84
Expect some great gigantick Son of Earth;	30	Ode to Temple	111
Or from the Sun, or from the Air, or from the Earth,	31	Ode to Temple	170
Whate'er I plant (like Corn on barren Earth)	33	Ode to Temple	210
But where is ev'n thy Image on our earth?	35	Ode Sancroft	17
Be not the brightest pattern Earth can shew	36	Ode Sancroft	52
(Were his humanity on earth once more)	38	Ode Sancroft	133
As parent earth, burst by imprison'd winds,	52	Temple Ill	37
Heaven with a parent's eye regarding earth,	54	Temple Ill	89
The Earth would very soon be filld:	79	Vanbrug House	20
This Earth which bears his Body's Print,	101	Elegy Patrige	111
On Earth, the God of Wealth was made	106	V's House	23
Round all the earth she casts her eyes;	178	To Lord Harley	61
To raise the Lumber from the Earth.	231	Prog of Poetry	30
Because we wish the earth upon him Light,	234	Elegy on Demar	24
Robin adores that Spot of Earth,	314	To Ford	87
Earth must have been in Chaos swallow'd.	346	Prometheus	46
And bids him bless, and mend the Earth;	384	Manly Virtue	16
And bless the Earth with genial Showers.	387	Manly Virtue	110
Begot upon his grandame Earth;	433	Answer Paulus	26
Hunted from Earth, and Sea, and Hell, he flies	538	Mr. Pulteney	29
He fled to Earth, but first it cost him dear;	538	Mr. Pulteney	35
What nymph on earth so fair as Iris?	619	Scandal Poem 1	74
With which from earth to heav'n he springs;	621	Scandal Poem 1	118
What Nymph on Earth so fair as Iris?	625	Scandal Poem 2	72
This God on Earth turns Devil in Hell.	646	On Poetry	206
Must strole in Air 'twixt Earth and Sky;	689	Cadenus Vaness	86
Or else, shut out from Heaven and Earth,	689	Cadenus Vaness	87
Produc'd on Earth a wond'rous Maid,	690	Cadenus Vaness	137
"Her Name on Earth ----shall not be told.	692	Cadenus Vaness	183

EARTH	(CONTINUED)	PAGE	TITLE	LINE
Wherein the God of Earth delights.		743	Stel B-day 22	52
All-ruling Tyrant of the Earth,		916	Riddle 2	1
Superior none on Earth I find;		917	Riddle 3	3
To fill the Earth, and Air, and Skies:		924	Riddle 7	92
All Figures Heav'n or Earth can yield,		927	Riddle 10	D 16
That stands 'twixt Heav'n, and Earth, and Hell,		928	Riddle 12	D 2
From Heav'n I fall, tho' from Earth I begin,		928	Riddle 13	D 1
All Things on Earth I imitate,		935	Riddle 23	D 18
Of all inhabitants on earth,		936	Riddle 24	D 1
Air ripens not, nor Earth produces:		1035	To Quilca	6
EARTH'S				
Was but to light Earth's inconsiderable spot.		36	Ode Sancroft	72
So would earth's face turn pale, and life decay,		53	Temple Ill	63
EARTHEN				
And serv'd up in an earthen Platter;		91	Bauc & Phil 1	62
When from the homeliest Earthen Ware		896	Panegyr Dean	295
EARTHLY				
Howe'er our Earthly Motion varies,		98	Elegy Patrige	16
'Twixt earthly Femals and the Moon		226	Prog of Beauty	9
Two brightest, brittlest earthly Things		227	Prog of Beauty	63
Dan leaves the Earthly Spade and Rake,		279	Journal	32
But say, what earthly nymph do you know,		619	Scandal Poem 1	63
But say, what Earthly Nymph do you know,		625	Scandal Poem 2	59
An Instrument to earthly Love?		695	Cadenus Vaness	295
This earthly Globe to thee assign'd,		894	Panegyr Dean	235
EARTHQUAKE				
Ah, may no unkind earthquake of the State,		40	Ode Sancroft	190
Thus when an Earthquake lets in Light		240	Run Bankers	41
EARWIG				
Or found an Earwig in a Plum.		726	To Stella	78
EAS'D				
Untill thou shalt have eas'd thy Conscience,		181	Horace 2, 1	37
EASE				
And must be sung, like Argus, into ease		8	Ode to King	76
Till at last tir'd with loss of Time and Ease,		30	Ode to Temple	133
And kindled first with Indolence and Ease,		33	Ode to Temple	203
Talk'd with that saucy and familiar ease		47	To Congreve	141
Or Harness'd to a Nag, at ease		109	V's House	111
I'm Old, and fain wou'd live at Ease,		115	Bauc & Phil 2	115
To live in Plenty, Power and Ease.		173	Horace 1, 7	92
But Celia can with ease reduce		227	Prog of Beauty	45
Your Wisdom can with Ease Defeat.		340	Arch-Bish Dub	12
But ever ever live at Ease,		362	Grace's Answer	45
While he, at ease, secure and light,		435	Answer Paulus	91
"While Nature kindly bent to ease us,		554	Death of Swift	9
What gave me Ease, and how I slept?		557	Death of Swift	140
Think what can give the Colick Ease,		589	Strephon Chloe	168
On House of Ease your future Bride,		591	Strephon Chloe	238
To give him but a Writ of Ease,		606	Beasts Confess	170
Wou'dst thou not wish, in so much ease,		677	Parson's Case	35
Call'd ev'ry Pow'r to ease my Pains,		726	To Stella	100
What's next to be voted with ease you may guess.		816	Yahoo's	34
To ease his Itch against the Stump,		849	Old Thorn	42
To ease a poor Lady,		858	Lady's Lament	217
Voluptuous Ease, the Child of Wealth,		895	Panegyr Dean	279
Daphne knows, with equal ease,		906	Daphne	1
The Clergy keep me for their Ease,		920	Riddle 6	7
You cure with Ease and with Delight;		924	Riddle 8	14
Yet Commoners with greatest Ease,		928	Riddle 12	D 11
Yet we can, with greatest Ease,		931	Riddle 18	D 13
With Ease I make to keep their Distance;		934	Riddle 21	D 4
EASIE				
Look'd with an easie, careless Mien,		170	Horace 1, 7	9
EASIER				
I can easier scorn than hate:		634	Epistle Lady	144
EASILY				
And canst not easily retire,		181	Horace 2, 1	34
The foulest Impressions I easily take.		929	Riddle 13	D 8
EAST				
To the East Indies, there to cheat,		456	Dean Smedley	35
From East to west the world we roam,		621	Scandal Poem 1	127
From East to West, the World we roam;		627	Scandal Poem 2	121
EASTER				
A hundred Fees last Easter Term.		604	Beasts Confess	86
EASTERN				
Behold, it cracks by yon rough Eastern Wind.		770	Horace 1, 14	18
EASY				
In governments too easy, and too fruitful ground;		37	Ode Sancroft	97
And treads so soft, so easy, and so light,		54	Temple Ill	114
To find an easy Place to lay-her.		207	Fable Bitches	6
"Good Madam Pallas, pray be easy,		305	Storm	70
And doting in an easy chair;		401	Window Inns 5	D 4
Was easy, though they wanted Shoes;		481	Libel on D- D-	40
His Vassals easy, and the Owner blest;		533	To Mr. Gay	47
No Loss more easy to supply.		562	Death of Swift	244
And with Saddles eke so easy		573	Helter Skelter	12
Be easy, 'tis a common Case.		595	Cassinus Peter	50
(For you may easy be too far gone,		648	On Poetry	241
To sossing in an easy Chair;		750	Stel Wood-Park	30
Although 'tis easy to descry		754	Stella '23	15

241

EASY   (CONTINUED)   PAGE   TITLE   LINE
  They lye, alas, too easy to be found, ...   772 Horace 1, 14   63
  But, seated in an easy chair, ...   901 Dean's Reasons   89
  To be easy keep your distance; . . . .   907 Daphne   26
  Here, with an easy Search we find . . . .   921 Riddle 7   15
  Could you but change a Crown as easy . . . . . .   1033 Ans to Crown   13
EAT
  Eat, Honest Friends, and never spare, ...   91 Bauc & Phil 1   64
  To eat the Calves-Head with your trusty Friends. .   162 Toland's Invit   4
  But Whale Directors eat up all. . . . .   253 Bubble   68
  He can Eat, Drink and Sleep; now and then for a Friend 335 Serious Poem   43
  While Vultures eat his growing Liver: . . . . .   346 Prometheus   56
  But visit him, and eat some Fruit; . . . .   378 Apology Lady C   88
  Who often long'd to eat his Son: . . . .   460 Birthday Song   12
  Which says, wou'd Crows in Silence eat . . . . .   479 Epist on Epist   121
  Half eat, and dragg'd it to his Hole. . . . . . .   583 Young Nymph   60
  And Teeth are useless, where there's nought to eat. . 670 Epig Carthy 20   D 4
  His Horses too eat all our Hay. . . . .   861 Lady Acheson   36
  But ne'er presume to eat a Bit: . . . .   897 Panegyr Dean   336
  Till I eat the World at last. . . . .   930 Riddle 16   D 4
  A Judge will eat, tho' clad in Ermin. . . . . .   942 Probatur Alit   22
  Eat my Oysters, and lye near her, ...   953 Oysters   15
  Come eat 'em with pure fresh Butter and Mustard, . .   953 Herrings   6
  You say you will eat Grass on his Grave: a Christian   986 Mary to Sher   17
      eat Grass!
  You say you will eat Grass on his Grave: a Christian   986 Mary to Sher   17
      eat Grass!
  To eat my Meat, and drink my Medlicot, ...   1033 Ans to Crown   9
  Eat like a Turk, ...   1035 Servants Maxim   1
  Eat lean Meat, or chuse, ...   1036 Plague Country   3
EATING
  No eating in quiet, ...   853 Lady's Lament   60
  Ever eating, never cloying, ...   930 Riddle 16   D 1
EATS
  But, eats into it, like a Moth---! . . . .   548 Life of Swift   114
  How much he eats, how much he swills, ...   860 Lady Acheson   32
EBB
  That mighty Ebb never to flow again, ...   16 Ode Athenian   2
  At the first Ebb of Noise and Fears, ...   16 Ode Athenian   14
EBBS
  Nine times a day it ebbs and flows, ...   256 Bubble   141
EBON
  With Snuff was fill'd his Ebon Box, ...   904 Death Daphne   39
ECCENTRIC
  Many an eccentric and unthrifty motion make, ...   36 Ode Sancroft   69
ECCHO
  As to paint Eccho to the Sight: . . . .   21 Ode Athenian   160
  Till Fame and Eccho almost burst, ...   121 Apollo Outwit   59
  And serve to eccho ratling Nonsense; . . . . . .   461 Birthday Song   44
ECCHOES
  My Groves, my Ecchoes, and my Birds, ...   411 Dial Rich Marb   91
ECCLESIAE
  Each Priest had a Concubine, jure Ecclesiae; . . .   518 Dean Hang Rape   38
ECHO
  Like distant echo spent, the spirit dies. . . . .   50 To Congreve   230
  Where Echo sits, and list'ning mocks. . . . . .   597 Cassinus Peter   108
ECHOES
  And Courts the wanton Echoes as they fly. . . . .   17 Ode Athenian   59
ECLIPSE
  No Meteor, no Eclipse appear'd! . . . .   98 Elegy Patrige   9
  That this Eclipse was out of Season, ...   354 Simile Silver   6
EDG'D
  Good Pinners edg'd with Colberteen: . . . . . .   115 Bauc & Phil 2   140
  Shou'd never meddle with Edg'd Tools. . . . . .   181 Horace 2, 1   32
EDGAR
  Thus Edgar proud, in Days of Yore, ...   476 Epist on Epist   43
EDGE   SEE KENNEL-EDGE
  That all Effects of Virtue end? . . . .   765 Stel B-day '26   66
  Effects of its Magick, ...   939 Riddle Answerd   16
EDIFICE
  He saw the Edifice and smil'd, ...   86 Hist V's House   9
  What Edifice can long endure, ...   593 Strephon Chloe   299
EDITION
  To add them in the next Edition; . . . .   418 Woman's Mind   62
  "Here's Wolston's Tracts, the twelfth Edition; . . .   564 Death of Swift   281
EDUCATION
  Though French by Birth and Education: . . . . .   300 Horrid Plot   50
  "To give a young Gentleman right Education, ...   872 Grand Question   161
EELS
  As eels delight to creep in mud, ...   950 Upstart   D 7
  To eels, we may compare his blood; . . . .   950 Upstart   D 8
EFFECT
  Yet the same want of Brains produces each effect; . .   18 Ode Athenian   85
  If Rudeness be the Effect of Knowledge, ...   377 Apology Lady C   69
  So, to effect his <Monarch's> ends, ...   486 Libel on D- D-   185
  Then, see the dire Effect of Pease, ...   589 Strephon Chloe   167
  His Lessons wou'd have such Effect, ...   709 Cadenus Vaness   727
  With no Effect on Friends or Foes. . . . . . .   798 Traulus 1   66
EFFECTS
  And thought too great ev'n for effects of Chance, . .   8 Ode to King   63
  Do own th' Effects of Providence, ...   19 Ode Athenian   109

EFFECTS   (CONTINUED)   PAGE   TITLE   LINE
    She soon would find, the same Effects, ...   85 Salamander   64
    Could cause such wonderfull Effects.   . . . .   227 Prog of Beauty   56
    Effects of many a sad Disaster;   . . . .   582 Young Nymph   31
    And must have contrary Effects   . . . .   695 Cadenus Vaness   282
    That no Effects of Food remain?   . . . .   765 Stel B-day '26   60
EFFECTUAL
    The most effectual Way to baulk   . . . .   414 Censure   29
EFFICIENT
    Efficient of the Moon's Decay, ...   228 Prog of Beauty   90
EFFLUENCE
    Bright effluence of th' immortal ray, ...   34 Ode Sancroft   2
EFFS
    Your effs and tees, and arrs, and esses?   . . . . . .   487 Irish-Club   12
EGGS
    The dullest Beast and Eggs unsound, ...   941 Letter   25
    A long-ear'd Beast give me, and Eggs unsound,   . . .   943 Probatur Alit   39
EGYPT
    In Egypt turn'd the Dust to Lice;   . . . .   813 Bro Protestant   50
EGYPT'S
    We'll Rigg in Meath-Street, Egypt's hauty Queen,   .   275 Epilogue   19
EGYPTIAN
    Some she does to Egyptian Bondage draw, ...   32 Ode to Temple   187
EGYPTIANS
    Have Hearts more harden'd than Egyptians;   . . . . .   813 Bro Protestant   52
EIGHT
    In seventeen hundred eight and twenty, ...   456 Dean Smedley   47
    Of thirty six, and thirty eight;   . . . .   735 Stel B-day '20   40
EIGHTEEN-PENNY
    Where, in Eighteen-penny Gall'ry, ...   523 Betty Grizette   25
EIGHTEENPENCE
    And hardly pay Eighteenpence Tax in the Pound: . . .   144 New Song   50
EIGHTY
    Where thirty weigh, as much as eighty.   . . . . . .   1022 Nim-Dan-Dean 1   D   48
EITHER   33   OMITTED WORD
EJECT
    Eject it to th' extreamest parts, ...   761 Bec's B-Day   14
EJECTS
    Receive the Filth which he ejects, ...   85 Salamander   63
EKE
    And eke your cloven foot. . . . .   428 Beau's Reply   8
    And with Saddles eke so easy   . . . .   573 Helter Skelter   12
    Within an hour, and eke a half, ...   675 Curate's Compl   9
    The cat's nine lives and eke the care.   . . . . .   761 Bec's B-Day   30
EL
    There in her own (far an el breth)   . . . .   60 Lady Tablebook   10
ELATED
    And as their Heels elated rise, ...   654 On Poetry   403
    With Neck elated tow'rds the Skies!   . . . .   743 Stel B-day 22   62
ELBOW
    To sossing in an elbow chair: . . . .   744 Stel Distress   6
ELBOW-CHAIR
    Wedg'd in a spacious Elbow-Chair, ...   895 Panegyr Dean   259
    Reclining on his Elbow-chair, ...   649 On Poetry   265
ELBOW-ROOM
    But I love Elbow-room when're I drink, ...   166 Toland's Invit   37
ELBOWS
    Is out at elbows why should I repine?   . . . . . .   419 Shall Repine   6
    When my elbows he sees . . . .   852 Lady's Lament   25
    He swears my elbows . . . .   853 Lady's Lament   79
ELDER
    Among her Elder Sons the whole Estate?   . . . . .   32 Ode to Temple   181
    Where tho' her elder sisters crowding throng, ...   49 To Congreve   181
ELDEST
    Our eldest Hope, divine Iulus, ...   655 On Poetry   429
ELECT
    Th' Authentick mark of the Elect, ...   18 Ode Athenian   92
    Elect of Cyprus in commendam.   . . . .   303 Storm   22
ELECTED
    Shall Tory Rascals be Elected, ...   779 Mullinix Tim   189
ELECTION
    When drunk with sour Election Ale.   . . . .   450 Modern Lady   187
    And scold at an Election;   . . . .   784 Mullinex Dick   18
ELECTIONS
    Askt me how our elections past.   . . . .   422 Ireld   34
ELEGANCE
    For Grandeur, Elegance and Wit, ...   314 To Ford   93
ELEGIACK
    And that, for Elegiack Lays.   . . . .   650 On Poetry   296
ELEGIES
    With Elegies, the Town is cloy'd: . . . .   558 Death of Swift   166
    These Elegies and Sonnets burn, ...   595 Cassinus Peter   74
    To Elegies in mournful Tone, ...   643 On Poetry   83
ELEGYES
    Sonnets and Elegyes to Chloris   . . . .   79 Vanbrug House   9
ELEMENT
    He wisely chang'd their Element: . . . .   106 V's House   22
ELEMENTS
    From the four Elements assembling, ...   279 Journal   27
    Those Elements her name compose, ...   467 Birthday Song   237
    Here Elements have lost their Uses, ...   1035 To Quilca   5

		PAGE	TITLE	LINE
ELEPHANTS				
Place Elephants for want of Towns.	. . . .	646	On Poetry	180
From Elephants to Mites in Cheese,	. . . .	653	On Poetry	384
ELEVEN				
One Traytor alone, and faithful Eleven;	. . . . .	804	Irish Bishops	31
ELF				
Howe'er it was civil in Angel or Elf,	. . . . . .	77	Lady B- B-	19
A Giant now, and strait an Elf,	. . . .	935	Riddle 23	D 22
ELIJAH'S				
Elijah's Mantle's worn out.	. . . .	270	Apollo's Edict	D 24
ELIS				
Was a mad Copper-Smith of Elis:	. . . .	352	Wood Ironmongr	2
ELISION				
By modern Poets, call'd Elision;	. . . .	1021	Nim-Dan-Dean 1	D 12
ELL				
For, Holland not an Ell in	. . . .	441	Ballyspellin	45
Then Throttle thy self with an Ell of strong Tape,	.	519	Dean Hang Rape	53
ELOCUTION				
Finch, fam'd for tedious Elocution, proves	. . . . .	194	Author Himself	39
ELOGIES				
Sonnets, or Elogies to Chloris	. . . .	106	V's House	9
ELOPE				
Plump Johnny Gay will now elope;	. . . .	409	Dial Rich Marb	49
Never lets your Mind elope:	. . . .	636	Epistle Lady	214
ELOPES				
Cuckolds, elopes, and runs in Debt	. . . . . .	150	Corinna	27
"Or naughty Boy elopes from School,	. . . . . .	497	Panegyr Swift	130
ELOQUENCE				
<Montague> Learning, <Bolton> Eloquence:	. . .	164	Toland's Invit	24
Must feel thy Eloquence and Fire,	. . . .	182	Horace 2, 1	61
And found in Blushes, Eloquence.	. . . .	386	Manly Virtue	82
Nor Eloquence Divine express,	. . . .	595	Cassinus Peter	56
All your Eloquence will scarce	. . . .	636	Epistle Lady	195
On Learning, Eloquence and Wit.	. . . .	655	On Poetry	428
Display'd her Eloquence the more:	. . . .	709	Cadenus Vaness	715
ELOQUENTER				
But Tom is eloquenter.	. . . .	785	Mullinex Dick	40
ELRINGTON				
To speak to Elrington, and all the tribe,	. . . . .	307	Billet Players	6
I am not Elrington, nor Griffith he.	. . . . . .	307	Billet Players	10
I pity Elrington with all my heart;	. . . . . .	308	Billet Players	31
But Elrington, tears falling from his cheeks,	. . .	308	Billet Players	43
ELRINGTON'S				
A pox on Elrington's majestic tone!	. . . .	309	Billet Players	53
ELSE				
Else where's the Gain in being Great?	. . . . . .	6	Ode to King	5
Else why should the fam'd Lydian King,	. . . . . .	20	Ode Athenian	153
Before the play, or else between the acts:	. . . . .	47	To Congreve	126
And what is Parchment else but Leather?	. . . . .	99	Elegy Patrige	44
What else by Perquisites are meant,	. . . . . .	157	Fable of Midas	45
Else what aspiring hero durst?	. . . . . .	178	To Lord Harley	68
Dispatch; or else that Rascal Northey,	. . . . . .	190	Faggot	41
For nothing else will make it cease,--	. . . . .	220	A Quiet Life	13
Or else, that Mercury's her Foe.	. . . .	228	Prog of Beauty	96
"Or, else some hiding Hole he seeks,	. . . . . .	305	Storm	61
"Or, else he raves, and roars, and swears,	. . . . .	305	Storm	65
And sell them for Gold, or he can't shew his Love else,		337	Serious Poem	98
But sure if nothing else must pass,	. . . . . .	346	Prometheus	67
And may be something else withall.	. . . .	361	Grace's Answer	8
Or else the truest Maxim lyes:	. . . .	391	Young's Satire	22
Or else I may forfeit my Lease.	. . . .	396	Dog and Thief	16
Else, rather on this barren shore	. . . .	420	Holyhead	29
What has he else to bait his Traps,	. . . . . .	484	Libel on D- D-	129
He grew, or else his Comrades ly'd,	. . . . . .	547	Life of Swift	88
The Ladies else might think me shameless.)	. . . . .	586	Strephon Chloe	80
Horses thus, let Jockeys judge else,	. . . .	636	Epistle Lady	201
Or else perhaps he may invent	. . . .	643	On Poetry	101
What mortal else cou'd e'er go through it!	. . . . .	675	Curate's Compl	17
Else she must interpose a Cloud:	. . . .	689	Cadenus Vaness	78
Or else, shut out from Heaven and Earth,	. . . . .	689	Cadenus Vaness	87
Else he must enter his Protest:	. . . .	707	Cadenus Vaness	667
Which evil Tongues might else report,	. . . . . .	713	Cadenus Vaness	856
"And this, or nothing else, wou'd do't.	. . . . . .	714	Cadenus Vaness	877
Else you relapse to Human Kind.	. . . .	724	To Stella	44
Or else, comparing with the rest,	. . . .	728	Stella, Poems	19
Or else, to introduce the rest	. . . .	755	Stella '23	23
Or else poor Stella may be starv'd.	. . . . . .	761	Bec's B-Day	38
What else are those thou seest in Bishop's Geer	. . .	792	St. Pat's Well	49
Methinks, or else the Devil's in't,	. . . . . .	860	Lady Acheson	14
You never else had known the Dean,	. . . . . .	877	To Dean Swift	29
Dermot, I vow, 'tis nothing else but Sweat.	. . . .	881	Pastoral Dial	24
Ev'ry Brother else reposes.	. . . .	931	Riddle 18	D 18
Or else I will not ride one Inch of Ground.	. . . .	943	Probatur Alit	40
Or else you may spare	. . . .	952	Onyons	10
Must argue with calmness, or else will come short on't.		976	Dean to Sherid	12
They're fit for nothing else but pasquils.	. . . . .	982	Sher, A Goose	2
I've something else to do than watch.	. . . . . .	983	Sher, A Goose	24
It must be so; what else, alas,	. . . .	1003	Dan J's Reply	7
Or, else be sure, your Broad-cloath Breeches,	. . .	1021	Nim-Dan-Dean 1	D 17
Or else, to shew their learned Labour, you	. . . . .	1021	Nim-Dan-Dean 1	D 41

		PAGE	TITLE	LINE

ELVES
    It is to think all great Ones Elves, ... 493 Panegyr Swift 12
    "If he makes Mankind bad as Elves, ... 548 Life of Swift 115
ELYSIAN
    Wat'ring soft Elysian Plains. . . . . 661 Love Song 20
    Shall to Elysian fields invite her, ... 762 Bec's B-Day 59
    To seek, in deserts, Fields Elysian? . . . . . . 899 Dean's Reasons 16
    She fancy'd, those Elysian Shades . . . . 905 Death Daphne 85
ELYSIUM
    To set Elysium by the Ears. . . . . 647 On Poetry 218
ELYZIAN
    From Fields Elyzian, fabling Esop; . . . . 607 Beasts Confess 200
'EM   75   OMITTED WORD
EMBARGO
    For the sake of your senses wou'd lay an embargo. . . . 976 Dean to Sherid 30
EMBARK
    When Learnings little Houshold did embark . . . . . 16 Ode Athenian 12
EMBARKING
    Was then embarking at Avignion. . . . . 774 Mullinix Tim 24
EMBELLISH
    And with Books my Mind embellish. . . . . 632 Epistle Lady 90
EMBERS
    On Embers plac'd, to drink it hot. . . . . 594 Cassinus Peter 28
EMBLEM
    My Emblem, the laborious sun, ... 675 Curate's Compl 13
    Fair Freedom's Emblem once, which smoothly flows, . . 793 St. Pat's Well 67
    If this you consider, our Emblem is right; . . . . . 805 Irish Bishops 43
    Of Plenty thou the Emblem fair, ... 919 Riddle 5 3
    Emblem of the Fair am I, ... 936 Riddle 24 D 13
    Emblem of the Cyclops' race; . . . . 936 Riddle 24 D 16
    Emblem of a monarch old, ... 936 Riddle 24 D 19
    Emblem of the bashful dame, ... 936 Riddle 24 D 23
EMBLEMS
    Whatever serves for innocent Emblems of the Court; . . 31 Ode to Temple 164
    Fair Emblems of a fruitful Wedding. . . . . 585 Strephon Chloe 52
    As Emblems of the sov'reign Pow'r, ... 646 On Poetry 193
    Emblems of Insects vile, who spread their Spawn . . 792 St. Pat's Well 55
EMBRAC'D
    Embrac'd thee closer than a Wife; . . . . 924 Riddle 8 7
EMBRACE
    By Thunder dy'd in Jove's Embrace; . . . . 587 Strephon Chloe 108
    They all were born from thy Embrace. . . . . . . 925 Riddle 8 24
    Can you refuse a soft Embrace. . . . . 932 Riddle 19 D 12
EMBRACES
    From me; or my Embraces shun. . . . . 916 Riddle 2 6
EMBROIDER'D
    Or, had Embroider'd Mars pursu'd, ... 177 To Lord Harley 15
    With Coat embroider'd richly shine, ... 182 Horace 2, 1 74
    By these embroider'd high Heel Shoes, ... 885 Rev Market-Hill 63
EMBROILS
    A Knave, who deep embroils his Lord's Affairs, . . . 535 To Mr. Gay 119
    For, Vengeance more embroils, than Skill repairs. . . 536 To Mr. Gay 140
EMBROWN'D
    But, well embrown'd with Dirt and Hair. . . . . . 594 Cassinus Peter 18
EMBRYOS
    The Tender Embryos half unknown decay, ... 667 Epig Carthy 5 D 4
EMERGENCIES
    On all Emergencies that rose. . . . . 689 Cadenus Vaness 98
EMINENCE
    'Tis Eminence makes Envy rise, ... 501 Doctor Delaney 41
EMITS
    His Hide emits a Foulness out, ... 786 Clad in Brown 8
EMP'RIC   SEE STATE-EMP'RIC
EMP'ROR
    "Inform us, will the Emp'ror treat? . . . . 202 Horace 2, 6 94
EMPEROR
    Till its first Emperor rebellious Man . . . . . . 26 Ode to Temple 2
EMPIRE
    Let the vain sex dream on, their Empire comes from Us, 24 Ode Athenian 260
    And had enlarg'd her Empire wide, ... 303 Storm 13
    Foretell his Empire crown'd with Bays, ... 466 Birthday Song 195
    Their Empire in our Hearts divide: . . . . 555 Death of Swift 42
    Their Empire holds so short a Reign; . . . . . . 591 Strephon Chloe 256
    Not Empire to the Rising-Sun, ... 641 On Poetry 25
    To see her Empire thus declin'd, ... 690 Cadenus Vaness 129
    "Through all thy Empire I foresee, ... 851 Old Thorn 78
    Old Saturn from his Empire drove; . . . . 894 Panegyr Dean 254
EMPLOY   SEE IMPLOY
    Of glorious Deeds, that must all Tongues Employ: . . 13 Ode to William D 46
    Take, youth, these thoughts, large matter to employ . . 53 Temple Ill 67
    Or more employ the Female Sex? . . . . 65 Problem 2
    Among the numbers who employ . . . . 176 To Lord Harley 1
    His Talents to employ for nobler Ends; . . . . . . 194 Author Himself 24
    Your Conduct in this new Employ foretell. . . . . . 532 To Mr. Gay 30
    Employ your Muse on Kings alive; . . . . 647 On Poetry 220
    His Valour would no more employ; . . . . 731 Stella, Poems 123
    Choice Spirits, who employ their Parts, ... 780 Mullinix Tim 245
EMPLOY'D   SEE IMPLOY'D
    "And who but <Hort> can be employ'd? . . . . . . 304 Storm 40
    Thrice happy Duck, employ'd in threshing Stubble! . . 521 Stephen Duck 7
    And Betty otherwise employ'd; . . . . 526 Lady's Dres Rm 6

EMPLOY'D   (CONTINUED)   PAGE   TITLE   LINE
    Now Grub-Street Wits are all employ'd;   . . . . 558 Death of Swift   165
    Have my busy Muse employ'd, ...   630 Epistle Lady   5
    Had he employ'd his Time so long, ...   705 Cadenus Vaness   598
    From Slaves employ'd for daily Hire   . . . .   726 To Stella   106
    Your skilful Hand employ'd to save   . . . .   764 Stel B-day '26   37
    To see thy <Deanship> thus employ'd!   . . . .   892 Panegyr Dean   176
    Tho' hundreds have employ'd their Leisure, ...   929 Riddle 14   D   3
EMPLOYMENT
    We expect Employment better.   . . . .   633 Epistle Lady   112
EMPLOYMENTS
    Employments for their Brother Vermin.   . . . . . .   813 Bro Protestant   44
    You merit new Employments daily: . . . .   891 Panegyr Dean   155
EMPLOYMTS
    In all employmts we can spare.   . . . .   422 Ireld   48
EMPLOYS
    He wonders what employs her Brain;   . . . .   292 Prog Marriage   65
    His Money and her Time employs   . . . .   294 Prog Marriage   135
    From every Trifle that employs   . . . .   688 Cadenus Vaness   48
    He oft employs me in Disguise, ...   915 Riddle 1   19
EMPRESS
    Thus the bright Empress of the Morn   . . . .   178 To Lord Harley   65
    To praise your Empress, and her Breed.   . . . . .   465 Birthday Song   152
    Yet from an Empress, now a Captive grown, ...   771 Horace 1, 14   45
EMPTY
    A three Hours Scene of empty Pride, ...   6 Ode to King   17
    In vain she catches at the empty Sound, ...   17 Ode Athenian   57
    I would not draw th' Idea from an empty Name;   . . .   21 Ode Athenian   161
    And vanisht to an empty Title in the Last. . . . .   25 Ode Athenian   287
    We scrawl all o'er with old and empty Rules,   . . .   27 Ode to Temple   33
    Pleas'd with an empty swelling to be counted great; . .   36 Ode Sancroft   60
    His empty Paunch that he might fill, ...   156 Fable of Midas   9
    Come hither, all ye empty things, ...   296 Satiric Elegy   25
    Hearing the House was empty, came to town; . . . . .   307 Billet Players   2
    Tho as empty as Younge and as saucy as Sandes   . .   389 Order of Bath   10
    And empty both within. . . . .   401 Window Inns 4   4
    Your pockets grow empty, ...   402 Window Inns 8   D   3
    My Lady's empty Pockets know: . . . .   409 Dial Rich Marb   24
    With empty Purse, and aching Head, ...   453 Modern Lady   292
    Vain empty World farewel. But hark, ...   596 Cassinus Peter   79
    For which he sends this empty sack;   . . . .   753 Gift for Bec   25
    Must these like empty Shadows pass, ...   765 Stel B-day '26   51
    Pass only now for empty sounds? . . . .   779 Mullinix Tim   188
    Be empty of Learning, of Insolence full: . . . . .   807 Advice Parson   2
    Empty Visions of the Brain.   . . . .   833 Legion Club   102
    An empty Plate except your own. . . . .   897 Panegyr Dean   340
EMPTY'NG
    In pity to the empty'ng Town   . . . .   122 Empty'ng Town   1
EMTY
    And leave his emty Chests in View.   . . . .   240 Run Bankers   40
EMULATION
    Her End when Emulation misses, ...   554 Death of Swift   35
    My Heart with Emulation burns   . . . .   887 Panegyr Dean   29
EN
    Who at their Dinners, en famille   . . . .   480 Libel on D- D-   3
ENABLE
    They'll soon enable thee to spend, ...   183 Horace 2, 1   90
ENAGIN
    Laughlin O Enagin, ...   246 Irish-Feast   46
ENAMELL'D
    Enamell'd Fields, and verdant Trees;   . . . . . .   251 Bubble   28
ENAMOUR'D
    And, grew enamour'd with her Phiz, ...   905 Death Daphne   65
ENCHANT
    Whose harp could savage beasts enchant, ...   177 To Lord Harley   11
    With Youth and Beauty to enchant   . . . .   759 Receipt Youth   19
ENCHANTED
    But, when th' enchanted Rod was broke, ...   134 Magician's Rod   57
    It must be some enchanted Grove, ...   252 Bubble   31
ENCHANTMENT
    There thy enchantment broke, and from this hour   .   55 Temple Ill   151
    Conceive the whole Enchantment broke, ...   240 Run Bankers   33
ENCOMIUMS
    Thus your Encomiums, to be strong, ...   464 Birthday Song   117
ENCOMPASS
    So wide as to encompass all. . . . .   108 V's House   82
ENCOMPASS'D
    Out-number'd, half encompass'd round, ...   326 Pethox   87
    Half encompass'd by his Kin: . . . .   836 Legion Club   162
ENCOUNTER
    I encounter Vice with Mirth.   . . . .   634 Epistle Lady   142
ENCOUNTERS
    By fierce Encounters made in Wars;   . . . .   324 Pethox   14
ENCOURAGEMT
    Next for encouragemt of spinning, ...   422 Ireld   49
ENCREAS'T
    Have ev'n encreas't their Pride and Cruelty.   . .   23 Ode Athenian   249
    Encreas't by new intestin Wheels   . . . .   93 Bauc & Phil 1   128
ENCREASING
    And still encreasing in her Airs   . . . .   746 Stel Distress   34

	PAGE	TITLE	LINE

ENCROACH
To encroach on his art by writing of bombas';   . . . .   1027 Sheri Circles   22

ENCROACHERS
The bold Encroachers on the Deep, ...   239 Run Bankers   1

END   SEE RING'S-END
And end as it began, in Vapour, Stink, and Scum.   . .   10 Ode to King   129
One end in both, and the design the same;   . . . . .   42 Ode Sancroft   256
Upon St. James's End o' th' Town;   . . . .   100 Elegy Patrige   96
Will, or ought to end in Ropes;   . . . .   168 Peace Dunkirk   9
A River at my Garden's End, ...   198 Horace 2, 6   4
To help at my approaching End, ...   204 In Sickness   20
At their Wits end like drunken Men.   . . . .   256 Bubble   152
Some from the Lakes remotest end.   . . . .   279 Journal   30
And, when we view it thus, with Thief at End on't,   . .   285 Elegy Boat   35
To place him at the hinder End   . . . .   292 Prog Marriage   78
As did Methusalem of old, and so I end my Song.   . .   343 Upon His Grace   48
So strong, that from the lower End, ...   345 Prometheus   33
For our Fear's at an End with the Death of the Maggot.   . .   352 Wood Insect   40
And there's an End; the Man is dead;   . . . . . .   366 Answer Delaney   6
And if you should, we'd ne'er have end on't, ...   372 Letter D. S-y   21
To take his Iron by the End;   . . . .   393 Modern Poets   14
Must never our Misfortunes end?   . . . .   445 Modern Lady   15
To Your Ambition put an End.   . . . .   478 Epist on Epist   114
I end my labours with a Pun.   . . . .   515 Answer Fable   102
May well conclude his Pow'r will never end.   . . . .   533 To Mr. Gay   74
Her End when Emulation misses, ...   554 Death of Swift   35
With this let your Collection end   . . . .   608 Know Not What   2
End, as it befits your Station;   . . . .   636 Epistle Lady   185
Thro' all the Lane, from End to End.   . . . . . .   649 On Poetry   288
Thro' all the Lane, from End to End.   . . . . . .   649 On Poetry   288
Cadenus answers every End, ...   709 Cadenus Vaness   704
The Race of Lovers soon must end:)   . . . .   713 Cadenus Vaness   863
The World shall in its Atoms end, ...   725 To Stella   57
But his Pursuits are at an End, ...   728 Stella, Poems   23
That all Effects of Virtue end?   . . . .   765 Stel B-day '26   66
May he at his latter End   . . . .   801 Traulus 2   51
We'll place him at the lower End.   . . . .   886 Rev Market-Hill   98
But when the Year is at an End, ...   918 Riddle 4   33
I hourly wait some fatal End;   . . . .   921 Riddle 6   37
The Cook-maid often hath by the End.   . . . . . .   941 Letter   38
Tries who shall have it by the End.   . . . . . .   993 On Picture   30
And then you may kiss the low end of her Spine   . . .   1018 Swift Ans Sher   33
. . . depend on't, in the end, he'll sham ye.   . . . .   1023 Nim-Dan-Dean 2   D 10

END'S
. . .yet in the end's good metre, ...   1022 Nim-Dan-Dean 2   D 1

ENDANGER
My Life, it must endanger yours.   . . . .   727 To Stella   120

ENDEARMENTS
The soft Endearments of the Nymph and Swain.   . . .   880 Pastoral Dial   8

ENDEAVOUR
The Dean with all his best Endeavour   . . . . .   295 Horrid Plot   151
Nor endeavour to convict her.   . . . .   907 Daphne   30
To convince you, once endeavour.   . . . .   908 Daphne   56

ENDED
But Patrige ended all Disputes, ...   99 Elegy Patrige   33
When term is ended, leaves the town, ...   435 Answer Paulus   93
"Here ended all our golden Dreams.   . . . . . .   567 Death of Swift   372
"Too soon that precious Life was ended, ...   568 Death of Swift   377
Thus ended the Knight: Thus began his meek Wife: . .   867 Grand Question   25
No fault of mine, the scheme is ended: . . . . .   899 Dean's Reasons   6
. . .for you see plainly my Paper is ended.   . . . .   1014 Swift to Sheri   12

ENDLESS
With endless and with infinite;   . . . .   38 Ode Sancroft   127
Whom you'd consign to endless Fame?   . . . . . .   272 Apollo's Edict   D 71
There doom'd to whirl an endless Round.   . . . . .   413 Desire Possess   50
To scratch our endless Itch of Pow'r.   . . . . . .   493 Panegyr Swift   10
What endless Raptures must he find!   . . . . . .   587 Strephon Chloe   96
Where, in this Scene of endless Woe, ...   647 On Poetry   209
And from his endless hoarded Store, ...   875 Drapier's Hill   7
How endless are Ambition's Aims!   . . . .   905 Death Daphne   90
Of busy Mortals endless Toils: . . . .   921 Riddle 7   14
Lyes there consign'd to endless Night;   . . . . .   923 Riddle 7   64
Yet endless Tears flow down in Streams.   . . . . .   932 Riddle 19   D 4

ENDOR
Nor listen to the Witch of Endor;   . . . .   776 Mullinix Tim   100
A long-ear'd Beast, and Woman of Endor, ...   942 Probatur Alit   7

ENDOW
With some Gifts, at least endow me, ...   631 Epistle Lady   63
Yet should Swift endow the Schools   . . . . . .   830 Legion Club   35
If Gaffer Harry would endow her;   . . . .   879 Robbin & Harry   34

ENDOW'D
And he endow'd her with his Art.   . . . .   149 Corinna   4
Whom Jove endow'd with ev'ry Grace, ...   272 Apollo's Edict   D 66
With heav'nly beauty so endow'd;   . . . .   619 Scandal Poem 1   75
With heav'nly Beauty so endow'd?   . . . .   625 Scandal Poem 2   73
Endow'd with Gifts from every Brute   . . . . . .   659 On Poetry   D 410
To see Vanessa thus endow'd;   . . . .   693 Cadenus Vaness   229
Yet some of either Sex, endow'd   . . . .   700 Cadenus Vaness   444

ENDOWS
Wherewith our Vanity endows us, ...   603 Beasts Confess   77

		PAGE	TITLE	LINE
ENDS				
Nam'd ev'ry player on his fingers ends,		47	To Congreve	139
Thus with a puff the whole delusion ends.		55	Temple Ill	154
Her Braided Hair to make thee Ends;		100	Elegy Patrige	80
That Virtue in the Fingers ends:		157	Fable of Midas	44
"At last—and so the Story ends.		181	Horace 2, 1	48
Here ends the Fable and the Moral.		189	Faggot	14
His Talents to employ for nobler Ends;		194	Author Himself	24
To own the truth we have some private Ends.		275	Epilogue	14
And kisses George, and ends or Lectures:		278	Journal	14
Then on her fingers Ends she counts		291	Prog Marriage	45
The Godlike Ends for which he rose;		386	Manly Virtue	98
You see, when Folks have got their Ends,		408	Dial Rich Marb	19
True lawyers, for the wisest ends,		432	Answer Paulus	11
So, to effect his <Monarch's> ends,		486	Libel on D- D-	185
Disdains to serve ignoble Ends.		503	Doctor Delaney	100
Whose Malice, for the Worst of Ends,		515	Answer Fable	97
So, Robbers (and their Ends are just the same)		536	To Mr. Gay	141
"We first consult our private Ends,		553	Death of Swift	8
Will try to find their private Ends:		556	Death of Swift	76
"Without regarding private Ends,		565	Death of Swift	331
"Intent upon their private Ends;		569	Death of Swift	404
And, having no sinister Ends,		605	Beasts Confess	143
Who, with less designing Ends,		632	Epistle Lady	79
Answer all domestick Ends,		633	Epistle Lady	101
And have them at your Fingers Ends.		648	On Poetry	246
James is be-duk'd; : of course their friendshp ends		678	Dean and Duke	2
To work her Ends; which if it sped,		690	Cadenus Vaness	133
To like with less Seraphick Ends;		712	Cadenus Vaness	823
For nobler Ends by Nature meant.		731	Stella, Poems	116
For Vices all have diff'rent Ends,		733	Verses Vanessa	11
Whene'er it suits her private ends;		761	Bec's B-Day	32
Nor prize your Life for other Ends		765	Stel B-day '26	69
By nature meant for nobler Ends,		781	Mullinix Tim	279
To work whose Ends, his Madness pimps.		798	Traulus 1	72
Thus we both shall have our ends,		908	Daphne	83
And yet before your Stanza ends you flout me		1003	Dan J's Reply	21
ENDU'D				
Desponding Phillis was endu'd		222	Prog of Love	1
Whom, when I with the best of my Talents endu'd,		264	Apollo	45
And well thy Scholars are endu'd		325	Pethox	61
For Conversation well endu'd;		416	Woman's Mind	17
Thus, with Talents well endu'd		523	Betty Grizette	29
Her Soul was suddenly endu'd		693	Cadenus Vaness	206
ENDUR'D				
Nor ever maid endur'd such court-like scorn,		44	To Congreve	13
A Siege as long as Troy endur'd.		326	Pethox	98
ENDURE				
He fondly thought he might endure		119	Apollo Outwit	11
Unable to endure the Sight,		240	Run Bankers	43
But, never shall the Muse endure		242	Horace 4, 9	3
I ne'er could endure my Talent to smother,		336	Serious Poem	69
Ye Wise, instruct me to endure		413	Censure	1
And Patience can endure no more		468	Birthday Song	245
No cleanly Workman can endure the Stink.		535	To Mr. Gay	128
I tamely can endure the first,		555	Death of Swift	69
Can such a Deity endure		586	Strephon Chloe	89
What Edifice can long endure,		593	Strephon Chloe	299
As long as Sun and Moon endure.		655	On Poetry	436
Which raise a Flame that will endure		691	Cadenus Vaness	144
But how, my Friend, can I endure		778	Mullinix Tim	179
They came of good Kindred, and cou'd not endure,		804	Irish Bishops	27
And could not endure so vulgar a Taste,		868	Grand Question	42
ENDURES				
Since Beauty scarce endures a Day,		593	Strephon Chloe	303
If it both pleases and endures,		728	Stella, Poems	7
ENDYMION				
That Swain Endymion is not sound,		228	Prog of Beauty	95
ENDYMION'S				
Struck with Endymion's graceful mien,		178	To Lord Harley	74
ENEMIES				
What, tho' by Enemies 'tis said,		182	Horace 2, 1	65
This gave him Enemies in plenty,		549	Life of Swift	134
Not, as his Enemies object,		603	Beasts Confess	65
His Enemies, for want of Charity,		606	Beasts Confess	159
ENEMY				
How vainly (Sir) did Your fond Enemy try		9	Ode to King	101
To curse our greatest Enemy)		28	Ode to Temple	52
This Enemy of human Kind.		515	Answer Fable	86
No Enemy can match a Friend;		557	Death of Swift	120
ENEMYES				
I'm where my enemyes would wish		420	Holyhead	4
ENFLAMES				
What Pride a Female Heart enflames!		905	Death Daphne	89
ENGAG'D				
'Twas you engag'd me first to write,		445	Modern Lady	22
"And he's engag'd To-morrow Night!		562	Death of Swift	236
Engag'd him in a hundred Quarrels;		603	Beasts Confess	52
The Jews engag'd him with a paultry Bribe,		806	Judas	3
ENGAGE				
In scientific Strife engage;		385	Manly Virtue	44

		PAGE	TITLE	LINE
ENGAGE	(CONTINUED)			
Engage, and in the glorious Strife,		385	Manly Virtue	45
And in dull Studies to engage		705	Cadenus Vaness	578
Vanessa's earliest Thoughts engage.		706	Cadenus Vaness	637
Forbid Cadenus to engage.		711	Cadenus Vaness	779
But, (not in Wranglings to engage		723	To Stella	7
Some whose reforming Hands engage,		781	Mullinix Tim	253
And, I'll engage with Peggy Dixon:		885	Rev Market-Hill	86
ENGAGES				
In a Chancery Bill your Attorney engages,		288	Bank Down	46
ENGAGING				
That gentle, soft, engaging Air,		692	Cadenus Vaness	178
Or blest with such engaging Parts,		779	Mullinix Tim	199
ENGGED				
Tis pre engged and in his room		423	Ireld	71
ENGINE				
And by the forming Engine struck,		344	Prometheus	9
Your Engine fraught with cooling Gales,		912	Aenigma Expl	D 5
ENGINEER				
A Mousetrap-man chief Engineer.		88	Hist V's House	48
ENGINES				
Down the ill-organ'd Engines fall;		29	Ode to Temple	98
On what poor Engines move		29	Ode to Temple	104
ENGLAND				
Our true Irish Hearts from old England to wean;		237	Excellent Song	7
In England the Dead in Woollen are clad,		237	Excellent Song	10
Whoever our Trading with England would hinder,		237	Excellent Song	18
And England has put this Crab to hard Use,		335	Serious Poem	37
England will send you corn enough.		422	Ireld	52
And shew us, <England> is our Master:		484	Libel on D- D-	126
Our Brethren of <England> who love us so dear,		516	Dean Hang Rape	1
To Hang him all <England> would lend him their Garters;		519	Dean Hang Rape	51
Our Church and our State dear <England> maintains,		520	Dean Hang Rape	67
ENGLAND'S				
Of England's Glory, and her lasting Joy.		13	Ode to William	D 48
Tho' it would make you England's Primate:		503	Doctor Delaney	110
"To sacrifice old England's Glory,		568	Death of Swift	387
ENGLANDS				
If Englands friendship you would keep		422	Ireld	55
ENGLISH SEE ENTIRELY-ENGLISH				
Of Chivy-chase, and English Mall,		93	Bauc & Phil 1	118
Of Joan of France, and English Moll,		114	Bauc & Phil 2	94
His Rod was honest English Wood,		132	Magician's Rod	7
Here English Wits will be to seek,		158	Fable of Midas	59
Spight of Dutch Friends and English Foes,		168	Peace Dunkirk	1
But true English Men will fill,		169	Peace Dunkirk	38
We'll buy English Silks for our Wives and our Daughters,		237	Excellent Song	REF
Then we'll buy English Silks for our Wives and our Daughters,		237	Excellent Song	REF
They would buy English Silks for their Wives.		237	Excellent Song	REF
Then we'll buy English Silks for our Wives and our Daughters,		238	Excellent Song	REF
Of Value five Shillings, in English a Pencil;		264	Apollo	34
Who with an English Beauty smitten		293	Prog Marriage	111
An English or an Irish Hound;		299	Horrid Plot	21
Scotch, Irish, English, French unite		345	Prometheus	15
While English sharpers take the pay,		421	Ireld	9
In English vile, and viler French,		434	Answer Paulus	78
To court their English German Cousins,		465	Birthday Song	170
Wou'd have us lose our English Friends.		515	Answer Fable	98
But be they English, Irish, Scottish,		813	Bro Protestant	45
While a coarse English Tongue will itch,		949	Epigr Scolding	3
And look in English, French, and Scotch for't,		993	On Picture	8
. . .in plain English tell us so?		1013	Swift to Sheri	2
A Wretch! whom <English> Rogues to spite her,		302	Storm	7
For the Good of our Church a true <English> <Dean>.		516	Dean Hang Rape	4
This Protestant Zealot, this <English> Divine		518	Dean Hang Rape	31
When the good <English> <Dean> is hang'd up for a <Rape>.		520	Dean Hang Rape	72
ENGLOND SEE INGLONDE				
Then let old Englond make good Chear:		147	Windsor Proph	4
But Englond must cry alack and well a day,		147	Windsor Proph	13
And dear Englond, if ought I understand,		148	Windsor Proph	15
And Englond wouldst thou be happy still,		148	Windsor Proph	25
ENGRAV'D				
And the great Name engrav'd most fairly,		494	Panegyr Swift	53
ENGROSS				
Engross the Fancies of the Fair,		687	Cadenus Vaness	41
ENGROSSETH				
While she engrosseth ev'ry Swain,		585	Strephon Chloe	31
ENHANCE				
When to your Friends you would enhance		314	To Ford	91
ENHAUNCE				
How could I more enhaunce it's Fame?		470	Burning Poem	15
ENISKELLIN				
She came from Eniskellin		442	Ballyspellin	63
ENJOY				
But the Queen shall enjoy Her own again.		168	Peace Dunkirk	10
Than the Queen should enjoy Her own again.		168	Peace Dunkirk	20
And the Queen shall enjoy Her own again.		169	Peace Dunkirk	30

		PAGE	TITLE	LINE
ENJOY	**(CONTINUED)**			
And now you're out, enjoy your Grin.		493	Panegyr Swift	22
They pay a Trifle, and enjoy the rest.		533	To Mr. Gay	48
ENJOY'D				
Which when he had enjoy'd, he swore,		619	Scandal Poem 1	55
Which when he had enjoy'd, he swore		625	Scandal Poem 2	51
ENJOYS				
For the Queen now enjoys Her own again.		169	Peace Dunkirk	40
One enjoys them for the Rest.		931	Riddle 18 D	20
ENLARG'D				
Enlarg'd in Picture, Size and Letter		93	Bauc & Phil 1	121
And had enlarg'd her Empire wide,		303	Storm	13
On which the Pleader much enlarg'd;		686	Cadenus Vaness	6
ENLARGE				
For, let heaven's wrath enlarge these weary days,		54	Temple Ill	111
What some invent, the rest enlarge;		449	Modern Lady	145
Your honest Care may fill; perhaps enlarge.		533	To Mr. Gay	46
Enlarge, diminish, interline;		643	On Poetry	88
You, every Year the Debt enlarge,		739	Stel B-day '21	7
ENLIVEN'D				
Feels not his Soul enliven'd when he's Drunk?		163	Toland's Invit	18
ENNOBLING				
Ennobling every Act, and Air,		385	Manly Virtue	61
ENORMOUS				
He can punish Sins enormous.		830	Legion Club	34
ENOUGH SEE ENUFF				
'Tis Pride and Happiness enough to Me		24	Ode Athenian	266
Your Building shall be small enough.		108	V's House	74
And Broth enough to fill her Paps,		208	Fable Bitches	20
I'd send her far enough away--		220	A Quiet Life	33
Tho' Moneys scarce we shou'd have Trade enough;		275	Epilogue	32
This world he cumber'd long enough;		296	Satiric Elegy	13
Which few had learnt enough to prize,		384	Manly Virtue	29
He has not passengers enough.		420	Holyhead	10
England will send you corn enough.		422	Ireld	52
I know you well enough,		428	Beau's Reply	7
I can have Customers enough.		447	Modern Lady	85
'I wish ye may but have enough.'		448	Modern Lady	108
Not long enough to reach half round,		458	Paddy's Charac	16
They both are cheap enough in Conscience,		461	Birthday Song	43
But here's enough to shew your Style.		463	Birthday Song	82
Hanover may do well enough;		467	Birthday Song	213
I could give Instances Enough,		545	Life of Swift	23
"But, spick and span I have enough.		563	Death of Swift	268
Enough to win ten Thousand Hearts;		598	Problem Solved	20
You have cheap enough compounded.		637	Epistle Lady	240
I have enough besides to spare,		692	Cadenus Vaness	196
Becomes the Creature well enough.		700	Cadenus Vaness	427
Enough to read a Lady's Eyes;		712	Cadenus Vaness	815
Which others for Mantuas wou'd think fine enough;		716	Answer Rebus	16
To morrow will be Time enough		763	Stel B-day '26	7
'Twas all for Love, and that's enough.		797	Traulus	62
Keeper, I have seen enough,		839	Legion Club	239
"The Irish dear joys have enough common sense,		843	Ay and No	15
I guess well enough		854	Lady's Lament	107
I've said enough to make him blush		860	Lady Acheson	13
Yet never think they get enough;		861	Lady Acheson	35
Just big enough to shelter two in;		878	Robbin & Harry	22
Of their two Fames the World enough rings;		884	Rev Market-Hill	31
I have it now ---- 'Tis plain enough,		912	Aenigma Expl D	3
Like sots, alone I'm dull enough,		936	Riddle 24 D	9
For know, Prostration is enough to th' Lion.		1002	Reply by Dean	18
But enough of this Poetry Alexandrine		1018	Swift Ans Sher	32
Compar'd with which (and that's enough)		1021	Nim-Dan-Dean 1 D	9
ENQUIRE SEE INQUIRE				
To paint a Hero, we enquire		83	Salamander	17
Whoever pleaseth to enquire,		126	Little House	1
For, true or false, they'll ne'r enquire,		312	To Ford	33
Wou'd strictly after Truth enquire		455	Dean Smedley	7
Enquire what Regimen I kept;		557	Death of Swift	139
Nor are we studious to enquire,		781	Mullinix Tim	261
All Mortals must be curious to enquire,		825	Noisy Tom	5
ENQUIRES				
Another, of the Thames enquires,		109	V's House	101
Enquires for Swift in Verse and Prose:		562	Death of Swift	254
ENQUIRIES				
To 'scape Enquiries, leave the House in Flame.		536	To Mr. Gay	142
Or should a Porter make Enquiries		729	Stella, Poems	39
ENRAG'D SEE INRAG'D				
Enrag'd to see the World abus'd		64	Discovery	47
ENRAGES				
But this my Servants much enrages,		954	Authors Living	5
ENRICH				
With the Freight enrich themselves:		635	Epistle Lady	162
ENRICH'D				
"For Lands enrich'd by crimson Streams,		183	Horace 2, 1	96
ENRICHES				
Advances few, enriches none,		495	Panegyr Swift	73
ENRICHING				
Enriching all the Vales below.		731	Stella, Poems	108

```
                                                    PAGE   TITLE           LINE
ENROBE
    The witty Ancient you enrobe,      . . . . . . . . .   670 Epig Carthy 21    D  2
ENROLL'D
    Go read in antient books enroll'd   . . . . . . .     619 Scandal Poem 1      51
    Go read in antient Books enroll'd,  . . . . . . .     625 Scandal Poem 2      47
    "Vanessa, by the Gods enroll'd:     . . . . . . .     692 Cadenus Vaness     182
    By Honour only were enroll'd        . . . . . . .     725 To Stella           52
    These are the Goddesses enroll'd    . . . . . . .     729 Stella, Poems       49
ENSCONCING
    Fools common-place thou art, their weak ensconcing fort,   53 Temple Ill      87
ENSIGN
    Her Favors to some broken Ensign    . . . . . . . .   295 Prog Marriage      160
ENSLAV'D
    And quite forgot their Country was enslav'd.  . . . . 771 Horace 1, 14        52
    That when a Nation long enslav'd,   . . . . . . . .   875 Drapier's Hill      11
ENSLAVE
    Came but to plunder and enslave us;  . . . . . . .    820 Dr. Rundle          34
ENSLAVERS
    Against Enslavers of Mankind!       . . . . . . . .   725 To Stella           62
ENSNARE
    Yet many poor Creatures I help to ensnare.   . . . . 929 Riddle 13         D  6
ENSUE
    Bids us to seek Peace and ensue it.   . . . . . . .   220 A Quiet Life        18
    O, think what Evils must ensue;     . . . . . . .    588 Strephon Chloe     127
'ENTENDRES
    Their Meanings lewd, and double 'Entendres.   . . . . 449 Modern Lady       143
ENTER
    Now Enter Bush with new State-Airs,   . . . . . . .    62 Discovery           9
    Enter the Folks with Silks and Lace:  . . . . . . .  447 Modern Lady         81
    E'er enter any Mortal's Noddle.     . . . . . . . .   496 Panegyr Swift      105
    Or fearless enter in thro' virtue's gate,  . . . . . 506 To a Friend         11
    For Will. to enter.--What shall I advise?    . . . . 538 Mr. Pulteney         8
    Nor will let your Lessons enter.    . . . . . . .    630 Epistle Lady        34
    With Heads to Points the Gulph they enter,   . . . . 654 On Poetry          401
    Else he must enter his Protest:     . . . . . . . .   707 Cadenus Vaness     667
    Disdain'd to enter in so late.      . . . . . . . .   711 Cadenus Vaness     771
    Enter the Stage they never mind him;  . . . . . . .  776 Mullinix Tim       102
    Enter that Infernal Door;   . . . . . . . . . . .    834 Legion Club        120
    Now, enter as the Dairy Hand-maid:   . . . . . . .   892 Panegyr Dean       167
    And ev'ry Nymph must enter single;   . . . . . . .   893 Panegyr Dean       210
    Some enter boldly, some by Stealth,   . . . . . . .  922 Riddle 7            31
    But very few are found to enter;    . . . . . . . .   928 Riddle 12         D  4
    Swiftly I come, and enter there,    . . . . . . . .   935 Riddle 23         D 14
ENTER'D
    'Ere we enter'd at the Gates;   . . . . . . . . .    833 Legion Club         96
ENTERS
    He enters in, and walks up Stairs,   . . . . . . .   292 Prog Marriage       87
    She enters on her usual Theme;      . . . . . . .    447 Modern Lady         71
    Now enters over-weening Pride,      . . . . . . . .   448 Modern Lady        124
    The Man with the Kettle-drum enters the Gate;   . .  870 Grand Question      90
ENTERTAIN
    Those who by wild delusions entertain  . . . . . .    45 To Congreve         77
    Wou'd entertain without Expence,    . . . . . . . .   378 Apology Lady C     101
    Must venture down to entertain us.  . . . . . . . .   465 Birthday Song      156
    Nor entertain a thought so odd,     . . . . . . . .   468 Birthday Song      263
    With good sense to entertain us.    . . . . . . . .   633 Epistle Lady       114
    Yet cou'd such Notions entertain,   . . . . . . . .   705 Cadenus Vaness     600
    Than with her Wit to entertain him.  . . . . . . .   905 Death Daphne        72
ENTERTAIN'D
    He entertain'd her half a year      . . . . . . . .   745 Stel Distress        3
    He entertain'd her half a Year      . . . . . . . .   749 Stel Wood-Park       3
ENTERTAINMENT
    Betokens Entertainment there,       . . . . . . . .   457 Paddy's Charac       4
ENTERTAINS
    Such Tattle often entertains        . . . . . . . .   201 Horace 2, 6         75
    Now Strephon daily entertains       . . . . . . . .   590 Strephon Chloe     211
    Kindlier entertains her Friends?    . . . . . . . .   632 Epistle Lady        80
    Harmonius Cibber entertains   . . . . . . . . .      650 On Poetry          305
    While thus Cadenus entertains       . . . . . . . .   711 Cadenus Vaness     790
    Whom Stella freely entertains       . . . . . . . .   735 Stel B-day '20      24
    Who not one pleasure entertains     . . . . . . . .   901 Dean's Reasons      83
    No Muse harmonious Entertains,      . . . . . . . .   957 Cantata
ENTHRALL
    That force free virtue shou'd enthrall?   . . . . .   490 Dialogue            44
ENTHRON'D
    Enthron'd with Heav'nly Wit,    . . . . . . . . .     21 Ode Athenian       177
ENTHUSIASTICK
    With all that Factious or Enthusiastick Dotards dream,  22 Ode Athenian      204
ENTICE
    As Atheists argue, to entice    . . . . . . . . .    764 Stel B-day '26      21
    And some give out, that I entice    . . . . . . .    917 Riddle 3            13
ENTICING
    Enticing Coxcombs to adore,     . . . . . . . . .    292 Prog Marriage       75
ENTIRE    SEE INTIRE
    So Celia went entire to bed,    . . . . . . . . .    226 Prog of Beauty      29
ENTIRELY
    It is entirely their own Fault.     . . . . . . . .   591 Strephon Chloe     260
    Have my Soul entirely fill'd:   . . . . . . . . .    630 Epistle Lady        32
    Where the Nymph has entirely forsaken her Text:  . . 716 Answer Rebus        20
ENTIRELY-ENGLISH
    Of her entirely-English Heart,      . . . . . . . .    96 On the Union         2
```

ENTOMB'D

                                           PAGE   TITLE   LINE

Entry	Line text	PAGE	TITLE	LINE
ENTOMB'D	Expir'd To-day, entomb'd To-morrow,	204	In Sickness	27
ENTRANCE	At Entrance loudest, where they found	698	Cadenus Vaness	370
	Near the Door an entrance gapes,	832	Legion Club	87
	Can find an Entrance when they please.	928	Riddle 12	D 12
ENTREATED	Unless by you she was Entreated	372	Letter D. S-y	13
	For the Captain's entreated to sit by your Side;	871	Grand Question	132
ENTRENCHES	A Post so fill'd, on Nature's Laws entrenches;	285	Elegy Boat	11
ENTRING	And entring in the very nick,	220	A Quiet Life	20
	Till entring on a broad High-way,	412	Desire Possess	23
	Entring warm your frigid Brain	638	Epistle Lady	268
	At entring you might see her stoop	746	Stel Distress	29
	The Waves impetuous entring at your Keel.	770	Horace 1, 14	20
ENTRY	Prepar'd to Scrub the Entry and the Stairs.	124	Descriptn Morn	8
	The narrow Entry crushd her Hoop	746	Stel Distress	
	The Entry brusht against her Hoop:	751	Stel Wood-Park	50
ENUFF	Will serve for Sodder well enuff.	345	Prometheus	24
	Carve to all but just enuff.	633	Epistle Lady	129
	As if she ne'er could have enuff;	895	Panegyr Dean	261
	For modern Jasons that's enuff.	948	Jason Hassard	4
ENUR'D	For long enur'd to musty Rules,	493	Panegyr Swift	29
ENVELOPE	No Letter with an Envelope	395	Grub-Street	15
ENVENOM'D	"Pursu'd by base envenom'd Pens,	568	Death of Swift	395
	When his envenom'd Shirt he wore,	925	Riddle 8	39
ENVIOUS	By dull Divines, who look with envious Eyes,	193	Author Himself	3
	We all behold with envious Eyes,	554	Death of Swift	13
ENVIOUSLY	How enviously the Ladies look,	891	Panegyr Dean	137
ENVOYS	Perpetual Envoys too and fro;	781	Mullinix Tim	256
ENVY	Yet some I know with Envy swell,	202	Horace 2, 6	81
	Or suffer Envy to conceal	243	Horace 4, 9	5
	Pale Envy sickens--Errour flies--	387	Manly Virtue	121
	Till Envy, Slander, Sloth, and Doubt,	412	Desire Possess	15
	Poor Envy durst not shew her Phiz,	456	Dean Smedley	21
	Is by the Teeth of Envy torn,	458	Paddy's Charac	10
	Envy, a Canker-worm which tears	458	Paddy's Charac	11
	Yet envy not, that I repeat	497	Panegyr Swift	126
	Both Envy then and Malice must	498	Panegyr Swift	169
	'Tis Eminence makes Envy rise,	501	Doctor Delaney	41
	Thus, Envy pleads a nat'ral Claim	504	Doctor Delaney	131
	Ah! dost thou not Envy the brave Colonel Chatres,	519	Dean Hang Rape	49
	Envy breeds in ev'ry Maid.	522	Betty Grizette	6
	Envy, I doubt, wou'd pow'rful prove,	546	Life of Swift	37
	I envy not the Wits who write	548	Life of Swift	128
	She turns to Envy, Stings and Hisses:	554	Death of Swift	36
	Self-love, Ambition, Envy, Pride,	555	Death of Swift	41
	But, this with Envy makes me burst.	555	Death of Swift	70
	"Meer Envy, Avarice, and Pride!	558	Death of Swift	159
	"Envy hath own'd it was his doing,	569	Death of Swift	411
	To burst with Envy, Spite, and Rage,	611	By Dr. Swift	11
	That ev'ry Nymph with Envy own'd,	705	Cadenus Vaness	580
	I cannot but Envy the Pride of her Wit.	716	Answer Rebus	2
	Envy, and Cruelty, and Pride,	725	To Stella	49
	The Parsons, for Envy, are ready to burst:	871	Grand Question	134
	In Spight of Envy flourish still,	875	Drapier's Hill	19
	Envy must own, you understand your	888	Panegyr Dean	45
	Shall read with Envy and Surprize,	994	On Picture	32
ENVY'D	That might be envy'd by the Greeks;	893	Panegyr Dean	203
ENVY'S	Raise envy's clouds to leave themselves in night,	45	To Congreve	79
	They might, unhurt by Envy's Claws,	479	Epist on Epist	125
ENVYING	Envying to see themselves outdone.	87	Hist V's House	34
EPHESIANS	Like Paul's Ephesians, never heard it;	820	Dr. Rundle	16
EPHIPPIA	As Horace says, Optat ephippia.	779	Mullinix Tim	214
EPICKS	And this, for Epicks claims the Bays,	650	On Poetry	295
EPICURIUS	With Socratus and Epicurius.	891	Panegyr Dean	144
EPICURUS	Virgil and Epicurus will not do,	28	Ode to Temple	65
	Whether, as Epicurus shows	324	Pethox	27
EPIDEMICK	(That Epidemick Error and Depravity	20	Ode Athenian	139
EPIGRAM	Would Tile; an Epigram would Thatch.	79	Vanbrug House	12

	PAGE	TITLE	LINE
EPIGRAM (CONTINUED)			
Would Tile; an Epigram would Thatch.	106	V's House	12
EPIGRAMS			
Epistles, Riddles, Epigrams.	478	Epist on Epist	108
Satyrs and Epigrams in vain you write,	667	Epig Carthy 4	D 1
EPILOGUE			
The Epilogue behind, did frame	108	V's House	93
EPIMETHEUS			
When Epimetheus op'd the Locks,	528	Lady's Dres Rm	84
EPISCOPARI			
But thrice refus'd Episcopari.	821	Dr. Rundle	40
EPISODES			
Like Episodes between the Acts;	280	Journal	62
EPISTLES			
Epistles, Riddles, Epigrams.	478	Epist on Epist	108
EPITHALAMIUM			
And Phoebus sung th' Epithalamium.	586	Strephon Chloe	62
EPITHETS			
Those mighty Epithets, Learn'd, Good, and Great	28	Ode to Temple	59
Or oft when Epithets you link,	645	On Poetry	167
EQUAL			
Old Hay is equal to old Gold;	156	Fable of Midas	20
Equal to all in Care and Love;	322	First of April	35
An equal Pow'r descends to thee.)	323	Pethox	10
With equal Int'rest, equal Spight,	345	Prometheus	16
With equal Int'rest, equal Spight,	345	Prometheus	16
With equal Terrors, not with equal Guilt,	364	On Dreams	13
With equal Terrors, not with equal Guilt,	364	On Dreams	13
And Dick the Scavenger with equal Grace,	364	On Dreams	37
With equal Longitude below:	393	Modern Poets	4
And, kept at first an equal Pace:	412	Desire Possess	12
With equal balance in her hand,	433	Answer Paulus	32
Thus Families, like <Realms>, with equal Fate,	535	To Mr. Gay	115
In either Case, an equal Chance is run:	535	To Mr. Gay	125
Suppose your Friend and You, were Equal,	546	Life of Swift	32
"And thought they Both were equal Foes:	549	Life of Swift	149
Our Equal rais'd above our Size;	554	Death of Swift	14
An equal Priv'lege to descend.	653	On Poetry	382
Give <George> and Jove an equal Share.	657	On Poetry	486
Which having found an equal Flame,	687	Cadenus Vaness	31
But never gave me equal Arms:	706	Cadenus Vaness	621
"To put them on an equal Foot;	714	Cadenus Vaness	876
O, were I equal in Renown,	779	Mullinix Tim	197
Tom and Dick had equal Fame,	784	Mullinex Dick	1
And both had equal Knowledge;	784	Mullinex Dick	2
Daphne knows, with equal ease,	906	Daphne	1
EQUALL			
In London can you equall Him?	314	To Ford	78
I grow less equall to the Charge:	739	Stel B-day '21	8
EQUALLING			
In wholly equalling our sin and theirs,	38	Ode Sancroft	122
EQUALLS			
Carry'd it to his Equalls high'r,	95	Bauc & Phil 1	179
EQUALLY			
Was equally allowed to shine,	455	Dean Smedley	3
"Where Thousands equally were meant.	571	Death of Swift	462
Are equally held infinite,	653	On Poetry	390
And Blessings equally on all bestows.	793	St. Pat's Well	68
EQUIP			
Equip our Kings, and Generalls at the Comb.	275	Epilogue	18
You must no longer thus equip 'ye	779	Mullinix Tim	213
EQUIPAGE			
From Equipage and Park-Parades,	688	Cadenus Vaness	46
EQUIPAGES			
In all their Equipages meet;	711	Cadenus Vaness	775
EQUITY			
All to murder Equity,	574	Helter Skelter	49
EQUIVOCAL			
By an equivocal Birth	33	Ode to Temple	211
'ERE			
How Nim, no Hunter 'ere could match him,	281	Journal	73
Let them, 'ere they crack a Louse,	831	Legion Club	57
'Ere we enter'd at the Gates;	833	Legion Club	96
Who, 'ere t' other gets up, demands the rising Blow.	967	Letter Sherid	14
'Ere George had robb'd it of its Mud.	1020	Nim-Dan-Dean 1	D 6
'Ere Vulcan comes to make him new.	1021	Nim-Dan-Dean 1	D 8
ERE			
Ere Mornings dawn stole out to spy	63	Discovery	35
(Ere since Sir William <Gore> was May'r,	180	Horace 2, 1	9
To-morrow, ere the setting Sun,	694	Cadenus Vaness	254
ERECT			
Erect a new one in a Trice;	80	Vanbrug House	66
Erect a new one in a trice.	107	V's House	40
What Palaces shall we erect!	107	V's House	46
Proceeded to erect his Pile:	108	V's House	64
Where there are none, it stands erect,	133	Magician's Rod	25
A goodly pair, erect and wide,	157	Fable of Midas	31
To Fame a Temple you Erect,	477	Epist on Epist	77
ERMIN			
Could I not, thro' all his Ermin,	634	Epistle Lady	151
A Judge will eat, tho' clad in Ermin.	942	Probatur Alit	22

		PAGE	TITLE	LINE
ERMINE				
All Virtues lodge in royal Ermine.	. . . .	647	On Poetry	228
ERN				
Inrag'd, as Ern would do at thee.	. . . .	476	Epist on Epist	46
ERR				
But think how damnably you err	. . . .	622	Scandal Poem 1	159
You cannot err on Flatt'ry's Side.	. . . .	657	On Poetry	470
But here Vanessa cannot err,	. . . .	733	Verses Vanessa	17
ERR'D				
Who thinks the Nation always err'd,	. . . .	514	Answer Fable	73
ERRAND				
Away upon his Errand goes,	. . . .	171	Horace 1, 7	24
ERRANDS				
Than others do, on errands sleeveless;	. . . . . .	900	Dean's Reasons	54
ERRANT				
Told 'em their Calling, and their Errant:	. . . . .	112	Bauc & Phil 2	42
ERRING				
Each fond of erring with his guide:	. . . .	39	Ode Sancroft	165
ERRONEOUS				
From Premisses erroneous brought,	. . . .	695	Cadenus Vaness	280
ERROR				
(That Epidemick Error and Depravity	. . . .	20	Ode Athenian	139
Ev'ry Error I could find	. . . .	629	Epistle Lady	3
To shew you where your Error lies,	. . . .	730	Stella, Poems	90
Hither by luckless Error led,	. . . .	896	Panegyr Dean	309
ERRORS				
Errors like this did old Astronomers misguide,	. . . .	36	Ode Sancroft	65
And Errors of our Plenipoes.	. . . .	181	Horace 2, 1	20
One for truth, and one for errors:	. . . .	907	Daphne	44
ERROUR				
Pale Envy sickens--Errour flies--	. . . .	387	Manly Virtue	121
ERST				
Where erst sate Cupid with his Bow;	. . . .	757	Stel B-day '24	38
ESCAPE				
Because the Cords escape their Eye	. . . .	29	Ode to Temple	95
Whose well-compacted Forms escape the Light,	. . . .	31	Ode to Temple	166
"(Whose Beauties mortal Eyes escape,	. . . . . .	384	Manly Virtue	7
Yet safe from injured innocence escape:	. . . . .	506	To a Friend	4
She bustled and strugled, and made her Escape,	. . . .	517	Dean Hang Rape	11
"Nor thou, Lord Arthur, shalt escape:	. . . . .	850	Old Thorn	65
ESCAPES				
To furnish his Escapes,	. . . .	22	Ode Athenian	198
No Object Strephon's Eye escapes,	. . . .	527	Lady's Dres Rm	47
'Tis ten to one the Wit escapes;	. . . .	643	On Poetry	98
ESCHEW				
"Can it be strange if I eschew	. . . .	380	Apology Lady C	163
ESOP				
From Fields Elyzian, fabling Esop;	. . . .	607	Beasts Confess	200
As Esop would the World perswade;	. . . .	607	Beasts Confess	211
ESPOUS'D				
But, when espous'd, he ran the fate	. . . . . .	879	Robbin & Harry	39
ESPY'D				
Till me that Tyrant Man espy'd,	. . . .	915	Riddle 1	7
ESSAY				
To conclude this long Essay;	. . . .	634	Epistle Lady	133
But tho' you miss your third Essay,	. . . . . .	646	On Poetry	181
ESSAYS				
A Victim to the last Essays	. . . .	295	Horrid Plot	153
Pope's Essays upon some for Young's may pass,	. . .	670	Epig Carthy 18	D 5
Dull Bacon's Essays,	. . . .	855	Lady's Lament	148
ESSENCE				
Nor does thy essence fix'd depend on giddy circumstance .		34	Ode Sancroft	7
Since the bright essence fled, where haunts the reverend ghost?		36	Ode Sancroft	44
And since thy essence on my breath depends,	. . . . .	55	Temple Ill	153
ESSES				
Your effs and tees, and arrs, and esses?	. . . . .	487	Irish-Club	12
ESSOIGN				
Demur, Imparlance, and Essoign,	. . . .	690	Cadenus Vaness	122
ESTABLISH'T SEE HIGH-ESTABLISH'T				
ESTATE				
Among her Elder Sons the whole Estate?	. . . . .	32	Ode to Temple	181
I have in view a Lord's Estate,	. . . .	251	Bubble	18
(What could he less,) his whole Estate.	. . . . .	295	Prog Marriage	156
Natale Solum: My Estate:	. . . .	348	Whitshed Motto	6
My dear Estate, how well I love it;	. . . . .	348	Whitshed Motto	7
Resolv'd, nor Honour, nor Estate,	. . . . . .	384	Manly Virtue	35
As will retrieve a lost Estate:	. . . .	392	Young's Satire	44
The Son laughs that got, the hard gotten Estate,	. . .	430	Dicky Dolly	20
'Till he can purchase an Estate;	. . . .	456	Dean Smedley	36
She manag'd her Estate with Care,	. . . . . .	693	Cadenus Vaness	220
And rather than that, I would lose my Estate.	. . .	867	Grand Question	24
Runs out in tongue, as in estate;	. . . .	878	Robbin & Harry	10
ESTEEM				
"To breed contempt where thou hast hop'd esteem."--	. .	55	Temple Ill	146
That he alone deserv'd Esteem,	. . . .	386	Manly Virtue	75
To keep Esteem and Love alive.	. . . .	593	Strephon Chloe	310
When have I Esteem express'd	. . . .	632	Epistle Lady	75
He now cou'd praise, esteem, approve,	. . . . .	703	Cadenus Vaness	546
Was struck with Love, Esteem, and Awe,	. . . . .	708	Cadenus Vaness	692
With Gratitude, Respect, Esteem:	. . . . . .	711	Cadenus Vaness	787

		PAGE	TITLE	LINE
ESTEEM	(CONTINUED)			
With Friendship and Esteem possesst,		728	Stella, Poems	13
Esteem and Friendship to express,		757	Stel B-day '24	31
I have a great Esteem for Plautus;		988	Letter Dr Sh-n	2
ESTEEM'D				
I once esteem'd, and lov'd, and favour'd more,		44	To Congreve	12
Vanessa much esteem'd his Wit,		702	Cadenus Vaness	511
How wou'd it be esteem'd, and read,		708	Cadenus Vaness	698
ET				
One Grave now contains them both Haec et Hic.		430	Dicky Dolly	15
A Creature bipes et implumis;		608	Beasts Confess	216
Et diu potuisse, et non potuisse refelli.		967	Letter Sherid	6
Et diu potuisse, et non potuisse refelli.		967	Letter Sherid	6
Since you write in a cart, keep it tecta et sarta,		979	Dean to Tho: S	15
Hoc Ithacus velit, et magni mercentur Atridae.		980	Dean to Tho: S	38
ETC				
Sooner shall, etc.		445	Modern Lady	19
ETERNAL				
The Angel (doubtless) kept th' Eternal Gate,		8	Ode to King	65
And (I hope) an Eternal Sleep,		8	Ode to King	80
Which from Eternal Seeds begun,		20	Ode Athenian	128
Truth is eternal, and the Son of Heav'n,		34	Ode Sancroft	1
Eternal Objects of her Hate.		725	To Stella	64
Of our good Dean's eternal chidings;		753	Gift for Bec	6
So your eternal pen is still,		983	Sher, A Goose	21
ETERNITY				
And is Contemporary to Eternity.		7	Ode to King	26
ETERNIZE				
Yet if his Name you'd eternize		271	Apollo's Edict	D 40
EUNUCHS				
Of Guardian Eunuchs to the Sultan Dames,		532	To Mr. Gay	20
EUPOLIS				
I went in vain to look for Eupolis,		988	Letter Dr Sh-n	7
EURIPIDES				
Proceed to Tragicks, first Euripides		988	Letter Dr Sh-n	17
EUROPA'S				
Europa's counterfeit Gallant.		759	Receipt Youth	20
EUROPE				
But Europe mortify'd his Pride,		657	On Poetry	475
But now go search all Europe round		659	On Poetry	D 410
Young Harry, as all Europe knows,		879	Robbin & Harry	37
EUROPE'S				
An Arm on which all Europe's Hopes depend,		12	Ode to William	D 30
All Europe's Bus'ness in his Breast)		170	Horace 1, 7	4
And settled Europe's Grand Affairs,		181	Horace 2, 1	40
Knows ev'ry Prince in Europe's Face,		398	Earl of P-b-w	7
EUROPES				
On Britain Europes safety lyes		140	Harlyes Surgn	1
EUSDEN'S				
Think Eusden's Right as good as mine.		741	Stel B-day 22	30
EUSTACE				
Now scolding at my Lady Eustace,		788	Dick's Variety	29
EV'N				
And thought too great ev'n for effects of Chance,		8	Ode to King	63
These Days! where ev'n th' Extravagance of Poetry		21	Ode Athenian	171
And ev'n my very Thoughts transfers		23	Ode Athenian	235
Have ev'n encreas't their Pride and Cruelty.		23	Ode Athenian	249
But where is ev'n thy Image on our earth?		35	Ode Sancroft	17
By Force of Wine ev'n <Scarborough> is Brave,		163	Toland's Invit	21
Would prove ev'n Homer's Numbers flat.		467	Birthday Song	228
More precious far than ev'n the Gift		494	Panegyr Swift	47
"When, ev'n his own familiar Friends		569	Death of Swift	403
Ev'n Lambs by Instinct fly the Butcher.		588	Strephon Chloe	154
Ev'n Jove, and Mercury his pimp		620	Scandal Poem 1	101
Ev'n Jove, and Mercury his Pimp,		626	Scandal Poem 2	99
Though ev'n the Bishops disappointed,		821	Dr. Rundle	55
EV'NING				
Tho' fring'd with ev'ning gold the cloud appears so gay,		41	Ode Sancroft	217
On Sundays, after Ev'ning Prayer.		116	Bauc & Phil 2	169
Her ev'ning Work so fills her Head;		291	Prog Marriage	58
Our Madam o'er her Ev'ning Tea;		448	Modern Lady	117
That Ev'ning to a Puppet-Show---:		547	Life of Swift	63
'Till Summer Show'rs and Ev'ning Dew,		759	Receipt Youth	11
EV'NINGS				
Would sit whole Ev'nings at the Ale-house:		352	Wood Ironmongr	6
EV'RY				
Of ev'ry censuring Privateer,		19	Ode Athenian	100
From ev'ry Age through which it pass't,		22	Ode Athenian	214
Two foolish guides in ev'ry sublunary dance:		34	Ode Sancroft	9
And ev'ry stinking weed so lofty grows,		37	Ode Sancroft	103
The way which ev'ry wand'ring fool below		39	Ode Sancroft	157
Strip her of ev'ry ornament and grace,		42	Ode Sancroft	249
Last just as long as ev'ry cuckow's note:		47	To Congreve	130
Nam'd ev'ry player on his fingers ends,		47	To Congreve	139
Draws ev'ry rhyming, prating, dressing sot,		48	To Congreve	153
To ev'ry lew'd pretender of the town.		48	To Congreve	160
Still ev'ry tree the pendent sorrow wears;		51	Temple Ill	20
Thus, when Dorinda wept, joy ev'ry face forsook,		53	Temple Ill	59
Peruse my Leaves thro' ev'ry Part,		60	Lady Tablebook	1
Which brings a <Stink> from ev'ry Pore,		65	Problem	9
How Miss pickt ev'ry painted Card,		86	Hist V's House	4

255

EV'RY	(CONTINUED)	PAGE	TITLE	LINE
If this Rule holds in ev'ry Art,		87	Hist V's House	44
They call'd at ev'ry Dore; Good People,		90	Bauc & Phil 1	15
Aloft rose ev'ry Beam and Rafter,		92	Bauc & Phil 1	93
Steals thence his Plot, and ev'ry Joke,		107	V's House	59
For ev'ry Wit in Britain's Isle		109	V's House	117
Try'd ev'ry Tone might Pity win,		111	Bauc & Phil 2	13
Aloft rose ev'ry Beam and Rafter,		112	Bauc & Phil 2	53
The Heraldry of ev'ry Tribe.		114	Bauc & Phil 2	100
These Venus cleans'd from ev'ry spurious Grain		118	Biddy Floyd	9
With ev'ry Muse to Grace thy Song,		121	Apollo Outwit	55
Where he comes ev'ry Week from Town;		128	Little House	57
The Templer spruce, while ev'ry Spout's a-broach,		138	City Shower	35
Turn'd ev'ry thing he touch't to Gold:		156	Fable of Midas	2
His Works were hawk'd in ev'ry Street,		172	Horace 1, 7	41
I fancy'd ev'ry nymph would run		177	To Lord Harley	31
On ev'ry Genius that attempts to rise;		193	Author Himself	4
And catechis'd in ev'ry Street.		202	Horace 2, 6	92
Went here and there, and ev'ry where,		207	Fable Bitches	5
Within our Breast be ev'ry Secret barr'd:		210	Earl of Oxford	16
With ev'ry Talent of a Prude,		222	Prog of Love	2
Through ev'ry Thread it lets in Air;		231	Prog of Poetry	36
Like Peers, have Levees ev'ry Day		239	Run Bankers	15
Here's ev'ry Piece as big as ten.		251	Bubble	8
He melts his Wax at ev'ry Flame,		252	Bubble	46
By intercepting ev'ry Beam;		253	Bubble	76
Wherein she distinctly could read ev'ry Line,		264	Apollo	51
Whom Jove endow'd with ev'ry Grace,		272	Apollo's Edict D	66
To tell what ev'ry School Boy knows:		281	Journal	82
Tells ev'ry thing that you can think of,		282	Journal	91
Thinks ev'ry Syllable is true;		282	Journal	102
With ev'ry Wind he sail'd, and well could tack:		285	Elegy Boat	15
Where Childless wives crowd ev'ry morn		293	Prog Marriage	119
For, ev'ry Stander-by was marking		299	Horrid Plot	25
And that's a Name in ev'ry Plot:		300	Horrid Plot	48
"He knows to sail with ev'ry Wind;		304	Storm	34
"And ev'ry Moment take a Dram,		305	Storm	58
In ev'ry town we wait on Mr. May'r,		308	Billet Players	35
And, as a stroller, act in ev'ry play:		309	Billet Players	48
And ev'ry Belle that since arose		311	To Ford	21
She's Now as handsom ev'ry bit,		313	To Ford	71
A hundred Whores in ev'ry Street,		315	To Ford	106
With pungent Pains on ev'ry Side:		325	Pethox	57
Your Blood in ev'ry Noble Race!		325	Pethox	70
You strove for ev'ry Inch of Ground;		326	Pethox	88
And ev'ry day she combs his Head.		328	Epigram 3	6
'Tis a Metaphor known to ev'ry plain Thinker.		335	Serious Poem	53
In ev'ry Council and Debate he stands for what is Right		341	Upon His Grace	5
When ev'ry one turns round about,		341	Upon His Grace	8
United close in ev'ry Part.		344	Prometheus	6
And ev'ry one begins to find,		345	Prometheus	19
For, ev'ry Day you shall be gaining		366	Answer Delaney	19
That ev'ry <S--th>, and Type in Town		371	Letter D. S-y	4
Thro' ev'ry Sense to reach the Heart.		379	Apology Lady C	116
Like'd ev'ry Thing - - - at least thought fit		379	Apology Lady C	119
If ev'ry Peer whom you commend,		391	Young's Satire	9
It does its Office ev'ry Hour,		391	Young's Satire	20
With ev'ry Vice hath fill'd the Nation;		392	Young's Satire	36
Knows ev'ry Prince in Europe's Face,		398	Earl of P-b-w	7
His Window scrawl'd by ev'ry Rake,		400	Window Inns 1	5
And ev'ry where her footsteps trace,		401	Window Inns 5 D	7
And see her marks in ev'ry face:		401	Window Inns 5 D	8
Chang'd for the worse in ev'ry Part,		410	Dial Rich Marb	71
Flocks ev'ry ominous Bird of Prey;		413	Desire Possess	54
Has ev'ry Repartee in Store,		416	Woman's Mind	11
The humble whelp gives ev'ry vote.		421	Ireld	15
How to give ev'ry man his due:		433	Answer Paulus	34
I own, there may in ev'ry clan		435	Answer Paulus	103
Of ev'ry Blowse		442	Ballyspellin	71
Through ev'ry Game pursues her Tale,		447	Modern Lady	78
When, to give ev'ry Dame her due,		449	Modern Lady	138
Chloe's of ev'ry Coxcomb jealous,		449	Modern Lady	162
Try'd ev'ry sharping Trick for Bread,		456	Dean Smedley	25
A Numbness crept through ev'ry Limb:		470	Burning Poem	10
And so might ev'ry Dunce alive.		481	Libel on D- D-	48
A Soul with ev'ry Virtue fraught		482	Libel on D- D-	75
For, ev'ry Coxcomb lends them Rods;		501	Doctor Delaney	48
Whilst, ev'ry Critick can devour		502	Doctor Delaney	69
Can turn their Hands to ev'ry Jobb,		503	Doctor Delaney	89
The Characters of ev'ry Brute:		512	Answer Fable	4
Had Statesmen too of ev'ry Kind,		513	Answer Fable	29
In ev'ry Debauch, but committing a <Rape>.		517	Dean Hang Rape	30
How thy Face charms ev'ry Shepherd,		522	Betty Grizette	3
Envy breeds in ev'ry Maid.		522	Betty Grizette	6
In ev'ry Court the Parallel will hold;		536	To Mr. Gay	135
Will send their Howd'ye's ev'ry day:		546	Life of Swift	59
To save the Nation ev'ry hour?		548	Life of Swift	110
"But, ev'ry Hand may justly slay.		548	Life of Swift	127
"For ev'ry thing---, but what it should.		550	Life of Swift	179
A Lye, at ev'ry second word:		550	Life of Swift	191
Some Paragraph in ev'ry Paper,		558	Death of Swift	167

EV'RY   (CONTINUED)   PAGE   TITLE   LINE

"'Tis read by ev'ry Politician: 564   Death of Swift   282
To oblige a good Friend, she will trace ev'ry Market,   .   580   Psyche   11
Must ev'ry Morn her Limbs unite.   583   Young Nymph   66
By ev'ry size of Poets sung: 584   Strephon Chloe   2
While she engrosseth ev'ry Swain, ...   585   Strephon Chloe   31
And make them ev'ry Afternoon   587   Strephon Chloe   117
They may discharge it ev'ry Sup;   587   Strephon Chloe   120
On ev'ry natural Defect;   592   Strephon Chloe   274
By ev'ry Coxcomb, but her Lord?   592   Strephon Chloe   284
Their Mattins chant in ev'ry Bush: 594   Cassinus Peter   32
For, ev'ry Nymph has Leave to chuse;   595   Cassinus Peter   64
That ev'ry Subject in the Land   601   Beasts Confess   10
In ev'ry Turn of Life content, ...   602   Beasts Confess   41
His Practice was, in ev'ry Station   606   Beasts Confess   153
Though hard to find in ev'ry Case   606   Beasts Confess   155
And ev'ry virtuous Man his Brother: 606   Beasts Confess   180
Creatures of ev'ry Kind but ours   607   Beasts Confess   203
Mistake our Talents ev'ry Day: 607   Beasts Confess   206
But, ev'ry sublunary dowdy   617   Scandal Poem 1   13
Change ev'ry feature ev'ry second.   618   Scandal Poem 1   46
Change ev'ry feature ev'ry second.   618   Scandal Poem 1   46
But, ev'ry sublunary Dowdy, ...   624   Scandal Poem 2   13
Change ev'ry Feature, ev'ry Second.   625   Scandal Poem 2   42
Change ev'ry Feature, ev'ry Second.   625   Scandal Poem 2   42
Can ev'ry Spring produce you Flow'rs.   628   Scandal Poem 2   152
Ev'ry Error I could find   629   Epistle Lady   3
Thought the Life of ev'ry Lady   631   Epistle Lady   39
Not to publish ev'ry Trifle, ...   631   Epistle Lady   61
Ev'ry Fault have drawn a Gloss over: 632   Epistle Lady   96
Load our Plates from ev'ry Dish;   633   Epistle Lady   109
Give no more to ev'ry Guest, ...   633   Epistle Lady   125
While ev'ry Fool his Claim alledges, ...   640   On Poetry   9
The Cant which ev'ry Fool repeats, ...   645   On Poetry   153
Inherits ev'ry Virtue round, ...   646   On Poetry   192
In ev'ry Street a City-bard   649   On Poetry   285
Thro' ev'ry Alley to be found, ...   651   On Poetry   315
Hobbes clearly proves that ev'ry Creature   651   On Poetry   319
Thus ev'ry Poet in his Kind, ...   651   On Poetry   341
And ev'ry Vice that nurses both.   655   On Poetry   410
Thy Praises ev'ry Muse shall sing.   656   On Poetry   448
I curse her ev'ry hour sincerely;   679   From Catullus   7
Or blunts the Point of ev'ry Dart;   687   Cadenus Vaness   8
Stops thus, and turns with ev'ry Wind;   688   Cadenus Vaness   58
That ev'ry Article was true;   688   Cadenus Vaness   71
I'll search where ev'ry Virtue dwells, ...   691   Cadenus Vaness   148
Thro' ev'ry Breast wou'd dart a Flame;   693   Cadenus Vaness   231
That ev'ry rich and lordly Swain   693   Cadenus Vaness   232
With Nonsense ev'ry second Word, ...   696   Cadenus Vaness   329
That ev'ry Nymph with Envy own'd, ...   705   Cadenus Vaness   580
And ev'ry Shepherd was undone   705   Cadenus Vaness   582
And ev'ry Beau wou'd have his Jokes, ...   707   Cadenus Vaness   648
And faulter'd ev'ry Word he spoke;   707   Cadenus Vaness   657
While ev'ry Passion of her Mind   709   Cadenus Vaness   710
In ev'ry Point to make it fit, ...   709   Cadenus Vaness   724
The Skill of ev'ry common Beau;   712   Cadenus Vaness   813
She gather'd, under ev'ry Head, ...   713   Cadenus Vaness   850
"Since ev'ry Being loves its Like.   714   Cadenus Vaness   879
And yet through ev'ry Motion steals.   726   To Stella   84
Then to compleat it ev'ry way, ...   726   To Stella   89
Call'd ev'ry Pow'r to ease my Pains, ...   726   To Stella   100
And ev'ry Crambo he could get;   730   Stella, Poems   74
The Angel-Inn to ev'ry Friend: 734   Stel B-day '20   6
And ev'ry Virtue now supplyes   735   Stel B-day '20   21
On ev'ry Feature of her Face;   735   Stel B-day '20   50
From ev'ry day a Lordly Banquet   745   Stel Distress   11
Surpriz'd with ev'ry day a hot meal   745   Stel Distress   5
To see that ev'ry Glass was fine.   746   Stel Distress   22
To see that ev'ry Glass was fine.   750   Stel Wood-Park   20
From ev'ry Day a lordly Banquet, ...   750   Stel Wood-Park   35
From ev'ry Meal Pontack in plenty, ...   750   Stel Wood-Park   37
This box is cramm'd on ev'ry side   753   Gift for Bec   9
With gall in ev'ry word I speak, ...   754   Stella '23   12
Nor, change thy Course with ev'ry sudden Gust: . . .   771   Horace 1, 14   54
Who turn with ev'ry Gale that blows from Court. . . .   771   Horace 1, 14   56
The Tories are gone ev'ry Man over   773   Mullinix Tim   9
Prefixt a Cut to ev'ry Tale.)   782   Tim and Fables   10
Distinguish'd ev'ry Feature in't;   783   Tim and Fables   16
Tom would pray for ev'ry Whig, ...   784   Mullinex Dick   15
Down ev'ry mealy Atom drops   786   Dick, Maggot   12
Who ev'ry Day and Hour the same are;   787   Dick's Variety   4
Fill ev'ry Pipe, each Motion guide.   798   Traulus 1   74
Directing ev'ry Vice we find   798   Traulus 1   75
Think on ev'ry Vice in both, ...   799   Traulus 2   5
The Dean and his merits we ev'ry one know, ...   814   Yahoo's   6
Has ev'ry Circumstance to please us, ...   820   Dr. Rundle   25
Where ev'ry Trout can make as high Rants   824   Printer Newgat   5
"And wound her Legs with ev'ry Bry'r.   850   Old Thorn   64
Which spoils ev'ry feature   854   Lady's Lament   97
And pore ev'ry day on   856   Lady's Lament   149
Or join with the Court in ev'ry Debate, ...   867   Grand Question   23

EV'RY   (CONTINUED)   PAGE   TITLE   LINE
    He, that of ev'ry ear's the charmer, ...   876 To Dean Swift   3
    Ten thousand Lice, and ev'ry Louse was gold, ...   882 Pastoral Dial   46
    Stumbling at ev'ry Step she trod.   . . . .   885 Rev Market-Hill   74
    Watch ev'ry Syllable you speak: . . . .   889 Panegyr Dean   72
    Just to give ev'ry Man his Glass: . . . .   889 Panegyr Dean   94
    Of ev'ry Taste to know the Size;   . . . .   890 Panegyr Dean   118
    And Gaghagan take ev'ry Joke.   . . . .   890 Panegyr Dean   128
    By you instructed ev'ry Morn, ...   891 Panegyr Dean   132
    And ev'ry Nymph must enter single;   . . . .   893 Panegyr Dean   210
    Turn ev'ry Way thy watchful Eye;   . . . .   897 Panegyr Dean   337
    And ev'ry Guest be sure to ply: . . . .   897 Panegyr Dean   338
    Let ev'ry cottager conspire   . . . .   902 Dean's Reasons   105
    Instructors ev'ry Art instill.   . . . .   918 Riddle 4   12
    Yet you of ev'ry Kiss complain;   . . . .   924 Riddle 8   11
    A Pain which ev'ry happy Night   . . . .   924 Riddle 8   13
    Yet Flow'rs I bear of ev'ry Kind;   . . . .   926 Riddle 9   2
    I'm found almost in ev'ry Garden, ...   929 Riddle 14   D   5
    Ev'ry Brother else reposes.   . . . .   931 Riddle 18   D   18
    Yet ev'ry Thing that you can name;   . . . . . .   935 Riddle 23   D   2
    Yet ev'ry where I may be seen;   . . . .   935 Riddle 23   D   4
    I'm ev'ry one, but ne'er my self;   . . . .   935 Riddle 23   D   23
    For this is ev'ry Cook's Opinion, ...   952 Onyons   6
    In ev'ry vile Pamphlet you'll read the same Fancies,   968 Letter Sherid   21
    So far, dear Dan, that ev'ry Friend   . . . . .   993 On Picture   29
    But ev'ry one that knows Dan, knows thy Master. . .   1002 Reply by Dean   6
    For ev'ry Stroke goes to my Heart, ...   1005 Sheridan's Sub   32
EVADING
    Is dead at last without evading.   . . . .   282 Journal   104
EVEN
    Is even the nobler Man, our Learning and our Wit, . .   24 Ode Athenian   269
    And even the sharpest eye that has the prospect seen, . .   41 Ode Sancroft   207
    Even so Master Doctor had Puzzled his Brains   . . .   77 Lady B- B-   22
    Yet Manly Virtue even here   . . . .   385 Manly Virtue   69
    In vain; even there to spoil his Nod   . . . . . .   458 Paddy's Charac   33
    Not sparing even men of letters, ...   489 Dialogue   6
    But, out it flies, even when she meets   . . . . . .   588 Strephon Chloe   131
EVENING
    Such seem'd her eyes, as when an evening ray   . .   51 Temple Ill   17
    Like Hunters o'er their Evening Ale.   . . . . . .   447 Modern Lady   79
    May Bec have many an evening nap   . . . .   761 Bec's B-Day   39
EVENING-BREEZE
    Which bow'd by evening-breeze with bending stalks, . .   54 Temple Ill   119
EVENT
    Th' Impulse, the Fight, th' Event, were wholly Thine.   12 Ode to William   D 36
    This Grand Event half broke our Measures, ...   283 Journal   119
    A strange Event! whom Gold incites, ...   345 Prometheus   21
    Nor can it answer in the Event.   . . . .   478 Epist on Epist   104
    "Was all destroy'd by one Event.   . . . .   568 Death of Swift   376
    It was an unforeseen Event, ...   709 Cadenus Vaness   730
    For tho' by one perverse Event   . . . .   712 Cadenus Vaness   832
    Sad Omens of the dire Event.   . . . .   849 Old Thorn   32
EVER   SEE WHERE-EVER   126   OMITTED WORD
EVER-LAUGHING
    Like the ever-laughing Sage, ...   635 Epistle Lady   167
EVER-WAKING
    Sooth my ever-waking Slumbers: . . . .   661 Love Song   15
EVERE
    To Fraunce, that evere he was borne.   . . . . . .   103 Merlin   8
EVERLASTING
    Broke on his everlasting Shield.   . . . .   8 Ode to King   71
EVERMORE
    Evermore thy Tongue supply.   . . . .   523 Betty Grizette   14
    Flew off, nor evermore appear'd.   . . . .   590 Strephon Chloe   196
EVERY
    And stood 'twixt Him and every Fate: . . . . .   8 Ode to King   66
    And like that too, make every breast their home)   . . .   8 Ode to King   70
    Suspended every Horror of the Place, ...   9 Ode to King   95
    Thus has our Prince compleated every Victory,   . . .   9 Ode to King   98
    And every foolish Flye that dares to aim   . . . .   9 Ode to King   115
    Borrow from every one a Grace;   . . . .   28 Ode to Temple   64
    Search'd in the nest where every worm did lie   . . . .   46 To Congreve   89
    Thy looks, when every cause of grief is past!   . . . .   52 Temple Ill   34
    Late I beheld on every face appear;   . . . . . .   52 Temple Ill   40
    Expos'd to every Coxcomb's Eyes, ...   60 Lady Tablebook   5
    For every peeping Fop to Jear.   . . . .   60 Lady Tablebook   18
    While every ignorant Beholder   . . . .   63 Discovery   15
    Now, Mrs. Dukes, you know, and every Body under-stands,   71 Mrs Harris Pet   42
    We can not serve You every One, ...   91 Bauc & Phil 1   31
    Phoebus now shortning every Shade, ...   119 Apollo Outwit   1
    And every one was pleas'd, that heard it: . . . .   128 Little House   40
    Where every Fool his Mouth applies, ...   158 Fable of Midas   63
    Come Courtiers: Every Man his Stick: . . . . .   190 Faggot   35
    This every Pretender to Rhyme will admit, ...   263 Apollo   19
    And we order our Subjects, of every Degree,   . . .   266 Apollo   99
    That, every Dog must have his Day.   . . . . . .   299 Horrid Plot   30
    To every Farmer twice a Week all round about the Yoke,   343 Upon His Grace   39
    Here, soon for every Art renown'd, ...   385 Manly Virtue   37
    Compleatly form'd in every Part, ...   385 Manly Virtue   55
    Ennobling every Act, and Air, ...   385 Manly Virtue   61
    Convict of lyes is every sign, ...   420 Holyhead   5

EVERY   (CONTINUED)   PAGE   TITLE   LINE

Where every knave & fool is bought . . . .   421 Ireld   3
She sits tormenting every Guest, ...   448 Modern Lady   110
Thus every Fool her self deludes; . . . .   449 Modern Lady   154
For Jove, as every School-boy knows, ...   461 Birthday Song   23
Your Phoebus royal, every day . . . .   462 Birthday Song   69
Just three; and every Grace a Daughter. . . . . .   465 Birthday Song   166
And sees a Son in every God . . . .   466 Birthday Song   185
And, how you laugh'd at every Joke: . . . .   480 Libel on D- D-   8
Is offensive to every true Protestant ear . . . .   522 St. Cecilia's   6
And turn'd it round on every Side. . . . . . .   526 Lady's Dres Rm   14
Which waft a Stink round every Room. . . . . .   529 Lady's Dres Rm   114
Her Washes, Slops, and every Clout, ...   530 Lady's Dres Rm   139
In every Mouth the Question most in Vogue . . .   536 To Mr. Gay   145
"In every Jobb to have a Share, ...   571 Death of Swift   451
Damn'd Villians, Corrupted in every Station, . . .   576 Place Damn'd   11
They still can do so every Day) . . . .   601 Beasts Confess   2
Which now he runs out every Year; . . . . . .   606 Beasts Confess   166
With Vice polluting every Throne . . . .   659 On Poetry   D 410
Endow'd with Gifts from every Brute . . . . .   659 On Poetry   D 410
From every Trifle that employs . . . .   688 Cadenus Vaness   48
Which every Girl at five Years old . . . . . .   700 Cadenus Vaness   424
In every Scene had kept his Heart; . . . . . .   703 Cadenus Vaness   541
Cadenus answers every End, ...   709 Cadenus Vaness   704
You, every Year the Debt enlarge, ...   739 Stel B-day '21   7
From every Meal Pontack in plenty . . . . . .   745 Stel Distress   13
In every <Arse> you run your Snout, ...   774 Mullinix Tim   25
In every Action thrusts his Nose . . . .   777 Mullinix Tim   119
Dick I could venture every where, ...   788 Dick's Variety   19
Drive them down on every Scull, ...   830 Legion Club   27
First in every wicked Jobb, ...   836 Legion Club   174
Every Mischief in their Hearts, ...   837 Legion Club   187
Every young Divine thy Brother. . . . . . .   838 Legion Club   200
Every Greek and Roman Author. . . . . . .   838 Legion Club   214
Every Monster should be painted; . . . . . .   839 Legion Club   222
All the Soul in every Face. . . . .   839 Legion Club   230
Hither came every Village Maid . . . .   848 Old Thorn   5
The Nymph who dwells in every Tree, ...   849 Old Thorn   45
Haul'd up every hill; . . . .   853 Lady's Lament   50
Must I be every Moment chid . . . .   861 Lady Acheson   41
In every point, like black and white: . . . . .   901 Dean's Reasons   72
At every Motion undertook, ...   917 Riddle 3   7
The more they open every Heart. . . . . . .   920 Riddle 6   18
It of every Charm. . . . .   939 Riddle Answerd   32
For Pegasus runs, runs every Race . . . . . .   956 Cantata
Every body knows, that I love to tell Truth and shame 986 Mary to Sher   23
   the Devil,
For every one that knows me, knows . . . . . .   1004 Dan J's Reply   23
I nicely examind them every Line . . . .   1017 Swift Ans Sher   5
But turns at every Seam, an Inch in. . . . . .   1021 Nim-Dan-Dean 1 D 16
EVIDENCE
Your Evidence was lame. Proceed: . . . . . .   298 Horrid Plot   14
EVIL
'Twas in an evil hour to urge my hate, ...   47 To Congreve   132
Detractors with an evil Tongue, ...   83 Salamander   24
This Evil, therefore to prevent, ...   106 V's House   21
In good and evil Times the same. . . . . . .   243 Horace 4, 9   10
But this Idol Wood may do us great Evil, ...   334 Serious Poem   11
An Evil, which admits no Cure: . . . . . .   413 Censure   2
Or, how this Evil can be born, ...   413 Censure   3
What Scenes of Evil he unravels, ...   548 Life of Swift   111
"To save them from their evil Fate, ...   569 Death of Swift   415
If not; they must in evil Plight . . . . . .   587 Strephon Chloe   121
How evil Tongues his Life bespatter; . . . . .   602 Beasts Confess   48
Which evil Tongues might else report; . . . . .   713 Cadenus Vaness   856
But, Stella say, what evil Tongue . . . . . .   757 Stel B-day '24   35
Perversely comes in evil Times, ...   798 Traulus 1   91
Is to a Horse an evil Disease. . . . . . .   941 Letter   34
EVILS
Evils which a too gentle king, ...   37 Ode Sancroft   98
Of humane Evils upwards flew; . . . .   528 Lady's Dres Rm   86
O, think what Evils must ensue; . . . . . .   588 Strephon Chloe   127
Had she not evils of her own? . . . .   755 Stella '23   26
Thy greatest Evils yet are scarce begun. . . . .   793 St. Pat's Well   88
EVINCES
The kingly Prophet well evinces, ...   408 Dial Rich Marb   13
EVRY
Were in evry ones Judgment exceedingly fine, . . .   1017 Swift Ans Sher   2
Where I hear you are crammd evry day like a Swine . . 1017 Swift Ans Sher   13
EX
Then, I must be so too, ex traduce. . . . . . .   350 Upright Judge 3   8
Are you still in your cart with convitia ex plaustro? . 979 Dean to Tho: S   6
Thus you may see, dear Friend, ex pede hence . .   988 Letter Dr Sh-n   15
EX-CREMENTS
Souse them in their own Ex-crements. . . . . . .   837 Legion Club   186
EXACT
And with exact Poetick Justice: . . . .   225 Prog of Love   97
Exact to what his Age amounts, ...   291 Prog Marriage   46
I own, the Moral not exact; . . . .   607 Beasts Confess   197
Or fit more exact than one eye and one rhyme. . . .   980 Tho: Sheridan   4

```
                                                          PAGE    TITLE            LINE
EXACTING
    Since Waiting Women like Exacting Jades,      . . . .  275 Epilogue            15
EXACTLY
    Thought himself now exactly skill'd,   . . . . . . .    87 Hist V's House       21
    Exactly said what now befell her,    . . . . . . . .   223 Prog of Love         52
    All Parallells exactly run;   . . . . . . . . . . .    226 Prog of Beauty       10
    Punch is exactly of a Piece    . . . . . . . .        592 Strephon Chloe      291
    Apply'd to <George> exactly true is:   . . . . . . .   657 On Poetry           478
    Exactly true! Invidious Poet!   . . . . . . . .        657 On Poetry           479
    His Friendship was exactly tim'd,   . . . . . . . .    797 Traulus 1            57
EXALT
    And must exalt him to the Skies:     . . . . . . .     271 Apollo's Edict    D  41
    Above the Stars exalt your Stile,    . . . . . . .     657 On Poetry           471
    Aspiring to exalt my Head:    . . . . . . . . .        897 Panegyr Dean        322
EXALTATION
    Thus Sancroft, in the exaltation of retreat,   . . . .  41 Ode Sancroft        211
EXALTED    SEE FAR-EXALTED,HIGH-EXALTED
    (The Spirit of Exalted Poetry)     . . . . . . . .      7 Ode to King          46
    Philosophy's exalted head appears;   . . . . . . . .   16 Ode Athenian         15
    Is wonderfully mov'd by some exalted Men,    . . . .   20 Ode Athenian        137
    Look where exalted Vertue and Religion sit    . . .    21 Ode Athenian        176
    Still to be of the same exalted Sex with You.   . . .  24 Ode Athenian        267
    (High Truth) the best resemblance of exalted Thee,  . .  36 Ode Sancroft       46
    And far exalted objects lessen by their height:   . .  39 Ode Sancroft        148
    Now his exalted Spirit loaths    . . . . . . . .      231 Prog of Poetry       41
    When she's exalted in the Skies,     . . . . . . .    362 Grace's Answer       41
    Exalted Worth disdains to owe     . . . . . . . .     386 Manly Virtue         95
    Vanessa in exalted Strains,    . . . . . . . . .      711 Cadenus Vaness      791
    Exalted in his mighty Mind    . . . . . . . . .       728 Stella, Poems        35
    Such their exalted Bodies are,    . . : . . . . .     787 Clad in Brown        21
    From Market-Hill's exalted Head,     . . . . . . .    884 Rev Market-Hill      47
    To Works of more exalted Kind.    . . . . . . . .     893 Panegyr Dean        198
    In Youth exalted high in Air,     . . . . . . . .     915 Riddle 1              1
    By Fate exalted high in Place;    . . . . . . . .     917 Riddle 3              1
EXALTER
    Her Majesty never shall be my Exalter    . . . . .    664 Epigram Bust          3
EXALTING
    oppressing true merit exalting the base    . . . . .  540 Charac Walpole        7
EXALTS
    And, what exalts the Wonder more,     . . . . . . .   113 Bauc & Phil 2        69
    And Mercy here exalts her Throne;    . . . . . . .    391 Young's Satire       18
    Exalts the Spirits, sinks the Lees.    . . . . . .    731 Stella, Poems       130
EXAMIND
    I nicely examind them every Line    . . . . . . .    1017 Swift Ans Sher        5
EXAMINES
    Which yet whoe're examines right will find    . . .    21 Ode Athenian        184
    Examines all the Servants round,     . . . . . . .    377 Apology Lady C       63
EXAMPLE
    Let Stella's fair Example preach    . . . . . . .     724 To Stella            33
    By your Example and Assistance,    . . . . . . .      888 Panegyr Dean         55
    For all an example, for no one a pattern.    . . . .  955 Portrait Life         8
EXAMPLE'S
    For, such is good Example's Pow'r,    . . . . . . .   391 Young's Satire       19
EXAMPLES
    But wicked kings draw more examples than the good;  . .  40 Ode Sancroft      184
    For great Examples are but vain,     . . . . . . .    700 Cadenus Vaness      436
EXCEED
    Do far exceed your frisking Lambs    . . . . . . .    123 Empty'ng Town        15
    Whose Wisdom and whose Piety, do far exceed his Years. 341 Upon His Grace        4
    Where forty Lines, exceed fourscore.   . . . . . .   1022 Nim-Dan-Dean 1    D  50
EXCEEDING
    Was so exceeding tall and Strong,     . . . . . . .   160 Atlas                 2
    His Answers were exceeding pretty    . . . . . . .    300 Horrid Plot          53
    Exceeding all the fools of Totness.    . . . . . .    423 Ireld                66
    That I am often found exceeding    . . . . . . .      489 Dialogue              3
    Tho' I should be exceeding proud,    . . . . . . .    860 Lady Acheson         22
EXCEEDINGLY
    Were in evry ones Judgment exceedingly fine,   . . . . 1017 Swift Ans Sher      2
EXCEL
    The Language Billingsgate excel,     . . . . . . .    496 Panegyr Swift       108
    But rather than they should excel,     . . . . . .    554 Death of Swift       33
    In Harmony wou'd you Excel,    . . . . . . . . .      956 Cantata
EXCELL
    Wherein French Writers most excell:     . . . . . .   216 To Mr. Delany        32
    In utmost Cleanlyness excell    . . . . . . .         732 Verses Vanessa        4
EXCELL'D
    In gifts, wherein you both excell'd,     . . . . .    177 To Lord Harley       30
    But which excell'd was never found,     . . . . . .   393 Modern Poets         15
    To that wherein it most excell'd;    . . . . . . .    701 Cadenus Vaness      451
EXCELLENCE
    Like all transcendent excellence below;    . . . .    39 Ode Sancroft        146
    And calld by Excellence, the Club:    . . . . . . .   217 To Mr. Delany        58
    "Make thou its real Excellence    . . . . . . . .     384 Manly Virtue          9
    Either from Excellence or grace    . . . . . . .      423 Ireld                70
    I here except His Excellence.)     . . . . . . . .    486 Libel on D- D-      184
EXCELLENCIES
    For that, he said, (an't please your Excellencies). . .  73 Mrs Harris Pet     69
    . . .I desire your Excellencies Protection,   . . .    73 Mrs Harris Pet       70
    And over and above, that I may have your Excellencies   73 Mrs Harris Pet      72
        Letter,
```

	PAGE	TITLE	LINE
EXCELLENCY			
His Excellency too perhaps	421	Ireld	13
EXCELLENCY'S			
Putts This to's Excellency's Snout, ...	63	Discovery	39
His Excellency's condescension	421	Ireld	17
EXCELLENT			
Hum--excellent good--your anger was stirr'd:	976	Dean to Sherid	7
EXCELS			
Whose filial Piety excels	482	Libel on D- D-	77
Whoe'er excels in what we prize, ...	710	Cadenus Vaness	732
EXCEPT			
Except the Matchless Hero Abel.	183	Horace 2, 1	86
Except to lash some grand Delinquent.	190	Faggot	30
All, Heteroclit Dan except, ...	279	Journal	19
Except some Leather lost behind.	398	Earl of P-b-w	24
And yet I must except the Rhine, ...	410	Dial Rich Marb	75
And yet I must except the Rhine, ...	467	Birthday Song	219
I here except His Excellence.)	486	Libel on D- D-	184
But, why wou'd he, except he slobber'd, ...	548	Life of Swift	107
Except to pass an Hour away:	607	Beasts Confess	188
Except they know whom they abuse.	644	On Poetry	132
I mean all Kings except our own, ...	659	On Poetry	D 410
All coffers full except his own.	659	On Poetry	D 416
To Female Breasts, except her own;	695	Cadenus Vaness	273
In all she spoke, except to stare.	698	Cadenus Vaness	357
Except a Blockhead or a Rake	733	Verses Vanessa	20
Except where Wit and Virtue grew	733	Verses Vanessa	22
Except they tasted of the Corn:	746	Stel Distress	14
Except they tasted of the Corn:	750	Stel Wood-Park	12
I took Advice except my own, ...	775	Mullinix Tim	72
Except to give <Dean> <Daniel> place.	888	Panegyr Dean	48
Except a Bottle now and then, ...	890	Panegyr Dean	99
An empty Plate except your own.	897	Panegyr Dean	340
Was never seen, except her own:	904	Death Daphne	62
Except when I trade with a Ship or a Town, ...	927	Riddle 11	D 7
Can move an Inch except I will.	929	Riddle 14	D 8
I'm dead except I live in Light.	929	Riddle 15	D 4
EXCESS			
His dangerous Excess of Heat, ...	387	Manly Virtue	108
Why?--Virtues carry'd to Excess;	603	Beasts Confess	76
EXCHANGE			
Nor will exchange His Plumbs for Bays:	157	Fable of Midas	56
EXCHEQUER			
Tho the Exchequer be drained by prodigal Donours . .	389	Order of Bath	5
EXCISE			
'Twas He defeated the Excise.	605	Beasts Confess	150
Collect Excise, or wait upon the Tide.	793	St. Pat's Well	78
Project <Excise> and <South-Sea> <Schemes>: . . .	647	On Poetry	216
EXCITE			
Why then in vain he would excite our Mirth.	669	Epig Carthy 16	D 2
EXCREMENT			
Expos'd to th' Excrement of his, ...	61	Lady Tablebook	20
EXCREMENTAL			
Send up an excremental Smell	529	Lady's Dres Rm	111
EXCREMENTS SEE EX-CREMENTS			
From the worst Excrements of Earth;	10	Ode to King	127
EXCURSIONS			
The wild excursions of a youthful pen;	17	Ode Athenian	61
And by Excursions lost his Ground:	412	Desire Possess	26
EXCUS'D			
Grief that excus'd the tribute of my knees, ...	53	Temple Ill	79
And, first excus'd his youthful Face;	603	Beasts Confess	60
EXCUSE			
Is in her Sex a Crime needs no excuse)	18	Ode Athenian	65
And offer'd many a lame Excuse;	172	Horace 1, 7	65
"Send for him up, take no Excuse.	199	Horace 2, 6	16
She'd hear of no Excuse in Prose.	378	Apology Lady C	92
"Now strangely pleads in my Excuse:	379	Apology Lady C	132
"Learn hence t' excuse and pity me.	380	Apology Lady C	144
This Simile for his Excuse.	485	Libel on D- D-	164
Friend Peter, this I could excuse;	595	Cassinus Peter	63
Might well excuse a Stoick's Rage.	603	Beasts Confess	58
With each Fault, each Fault's Excuse:	631	Epistle Lady	60
What Carthy publish'd needs no long Excuse, ...	668	Epig Carthy 11	D 1
She might excuse a Man of Letters;	705	Cadenus Vaness	590
And now whereby I find you would fain make an Excuse,	985	Mary to Sher	11
And now I hope you'll excuse this rhyming, which I must . . .	1024	Nim-Dan-Dean 2	D 17
EXCUSES			
Were bid in form, but sent Excuses:	290	Prog Marriage	10
Are ill excuses for a Servant's Crimes:	533	To Mr. Gay	68
EXECUTE			
And when we execute our Plot, ...	886	Rev Market-Hill	107
EXEMPLIFIE			
And now to' exemplifie this Moral, ...	458	Paddy's Charac	13
EXEMPLUM			
Decree, that ad exemplum Regis, ...	391	Young's Satire	24
EXEMPT			
Like Atoms are exempt from blows.	467	Birthday Song	238
EXEMPTING			
To oppose the <Dean> your-self Exempting	373	Letter D. S-y	76

EXERCISE | | PAGE | TITLE | LINE
Hard Exercise, and harder Fare . . . . | 230 | Prog of Poetry | 11
For you to exercise your Spight. . . . . | 528 | Lady's Dres Rm | 74
From wholesom Exercise and Air . . . . | 744 | Stel Distress | 5
From wholsome Exercise and Air . . . . | 750 | Stel Wood-Park | 29
Where Mirth, and Exercise, and Air, ... | 759 | Receipt Youth | 27
The part of wholesome exercise: . . . . | 761 | Bec's B-Day | 28
Despises exercise and air. . . . . | 901 | Dean's Reasons | 90
EXERT
Or could my Muse exert the Rage . . . . | 496 | Panegyr Swift | 100
EXHAL'D
Exhal'd from sour unsavory Streams, ... | 526 | Lady's Dres Rm | 28
Exhal'd Ambrosia from within: . . . . | 586 | Strephon Chloe | 88
By the Sire exhal'd from Dung: . . . . | 799 | Traulus 2 | 4
EXHALATIONS
And by Exhalations dire, ... | 834 | Legion Club | 129
EXHALES
And up exhales a greasy Stench, ... | 529 | Lady's Dres Rm | 107
EXHAUSTED
Our King ne'er exhausted his fountain of Honours. . | 389 | Order of Bath | 6
EXHORTS
Scripture you know exhorts us to it, ... | 220 | A Quiet Life | 17
EXIL
Are now in Exil, or the Tower, ... | 311 | To Ford | 28
EXILE
"His Friends in Exile, or the Tower, ... | 568 | Death of Swift | 393
"In Exile with a steady Heart, ... | 570 | Death of Swift | 431
EXIST
Than if he never did exist. . . . . | 562 | Death of Swift | 248
EXPANDED
Expanded to invite a milder Gale. . . . . | 770 | Horace 1, 14 | 24
With Hoop expanded wide and light, ... | 897 | Panegyr Dean | 323
EXPANDS
The People's Voice expands his Paper Sail; . . . | 770 | Horace 1, 14 | 28
EXPANSE
Rapp'd through the wide expanse of thought, ... | 36 | Ode Sancroft | 62
EXPECT
Expect some great gigantick Son of Earth; . . . . | 30 | Ode to Temple | 111
Here we expect from you . . . . | 31 | Ode to Temple | 161
Speak, for I wait thy answer, and expect . . . . | 53 | Temple Ill | 73
We might expect to find next Year . . . . | 88 | Hist V's House | 47
Nor e'er expect another . . . . | 123 | Empty'ng Town | 22
Henceforth expect a different survey, ... | 283 | Journal | 127
Him twice a Week I here expect, ... | 411 | Dial Rich Marb | 95
New Kings a compliment expect . . . . | 422 | Ireld | 37
You must expect the like disgrace, ... | 436 | Answer Paulus | 139
"Shou'd Vice expect to 'scape rebuke, ... | 548 | Life of Swift | 123
We expect Employment better. . . . . | 633 | Epistle Lady | 112
Which you expect, but scorn to ask; . . . . . . | 739 | Stel B-day '21 | 4
Expect in time, to be a <Peer> . . . . | 778 | Mullinix Tim | 158
'Twill be just as I expect. . . . . | 908 | Daphne | 82
EXPECTATION
That must our Expectation mock, ... | 729 | Stella, Poems | 66
EXPECTED
We Irish Folks expected wonders, ... | 62 | Discovery | 2
From whom I once expected more; . . . . | 204 | In Sickness | 16
Three Days before he was expected. . . . . . . | 859 | Lady Acheson | 8
If I had expected so worthy a Guest:-- . . . . . | 871 | Grand Question | 123
"And the Puppy confess'd, he expected no Good o'me. . | 873 | Grand Question | 166
EXPECTING   SEE LONG-EXPECTING
EXPECTS
Whoe're expects to hold his part . . . . | 61 | Lady Tablebook | 25
The Duke expects my Lord and you, ... | 200 | Horace 2, 6 | 53
In vain expects a longer Date . . . . | 229 | Prog of Beauty | 107
To what her treach'rous Foe expects. . . . . . | 695 | Cadenus Vaness | 283
In Vain from injur'd Heav'n Relief expects. . . . | 771 | Horace 1, 14 | 36
EXPEDIENT
Let us try some new Expedient; . . . . | 832 | Legion Club | 76
EXPEDITION
So wonderful his Expedition, ... | 398 | Earl of P-b-w | 28
EXPEL
Ah, since our fears are fled, this insolent expel, . . | 53 | Temple Ill | 55
EXPELLING
To a Plot for expelling my Master K. James; . . . | 144 | New Song | 28
All other Nymphs expelling . . . . | 441 | Ballyspellin | 51
EXPENCE
They purchase Knowledge at the Expence . . . . . | 27 | Ode to Temple | 42
Can do it with a Small Expence. . . . . | 361 | Grace's Answer | 22
Wou'd entertain without Expence, ... | 378 | Apology Lady C | 101
Presume to treat him at his own Expence. . . . . | 533 | To Mr. Gay | 64
"She was at Lord knows what Expence . . . . . . | 713 | Cadenus Vaness | 864
And puts them to so small Expence, ... | 735 | Stel B-day '20 | 26
EXPENCES
And when you've been at vast Expences . . . . . | 477 | Epist on Epist | 61
If your Expences rise so high; . . . . | 478 | Epist on Epist | 95
EXPERIENC'D
And, Chloe more experienc'd grown, ... | 590 | Strephon Chloe | 213
Then hear an old experienc'd Sinner . . . . . . | 642 | On Poetry | 75
EXPERIENC'T
Th' experienc't Bricks that knew their Trade, . . . | 108 | V's House | 76

EXPERIENCE		PAGE	TITLE	LINE
I have Experience dearly bought,	. . . .	175	Horace 1, 7	133
By long Experience we have found	. . . .	258	Bubble	190
Where you have told us from Experience,	. . . .	313	To Ford	49
When by Experience one will do.	. . . .	366	Answer Delaney	4
by dint of experience improving in Blunders	. . . . .	540	Charac Walpole	6
Yet, by Experience, oft we find,	. . . .	546	Life of Swift	47
Let Reason and Experience prove.	. . . .	554	Death of Swift	12
Than from Experience find too late	. . . .	591	Strephon Chloe	243
And from your own experience know	. . . .	620	Scandal Poem 1	87
And from your own Experience know,	. . . .	626	Scandal Poem 2	85
And sad Experience taught their Use:	. . . .	705	Cadenus Vaness	607
Yet had she much Experience gain'd;	. . . .	713	Cadenus Vaness	835
By long Experience grown so wise,	. . . .	890	Panegyr Dean	117
EXPERIMENT				
To try the great Experiment;	. . . .	66	Problem	34
Thus, I find it by Experiment,	. . . .	636	Epistle Lady	207
To try a new Experiment:	. . . .	691	Cadenus Vaness	139
EXPIATE				
But hung himself to expiate his Crimes.	. . . . . .	666	Epig Carthy 3	D 2
EXPIR'D				
Expir'd To-day, entomb'd To-morrow,	. . . .	204	In Sickness	27
EXPIRE				
All lesser ones expire,	. . . .	9	Ode to King	112
'Twill make the very Flames expire,	. . . .	84	Salamander	50
Shall never but with Life expire.	. . . .	593	Strephon Chloe	314
Expire, when first expos'd to open Air.	. . . . .	667	Epig Carthy 5	D 6
Shall they in baser Flames expire?	. . . .	732	Stella, Poems	142
Though a Goddess must expire.	. . . .	834	Legion Club	130
Soon would their Altars Flame expire,	. . . . . .	916	Riddle 2	13
Thou, like Alcides, shalt expire,	. . . .	925	Riddle 8	38
And I roar out my Joy, and in Transport expire.	. .	928	Riddle 11	D 12
EXPIRING				
And, as he now expiring lay,	. . . .	413	Desire Possess	53
Expiring Shepherds at their Feet;	. . . . . .	590	Strephon Chloe	200
Must die with her expiring Plant.	. . . .	849	Old Thorn	48
EXPLAIN				
Ye wise Philosophers explain	. . . . . .	250	Bubble	1
A Moralist might here explain	. . . .	252	Bubble	41
But Dreams are like Oracles, hard to explain 'em,	.	337	Serious Poem	113
Most aptly this Device explain:	. . . .	393	Modern Poets	6
If your Worship will please to explain me this Rebus,	.	973	S-'s Ans Sh-d	13
I will either explain, or repay it by trucks;	. . . .	977	Dean to Sherid	44
Let me my Properties explain,	. . . .	1035	To Quilca	1
EXPLAIN'D				
Explain'd for what they were renown'd;	. . . . . .	697	Cadenus Vaness	351
EXPLAINING				
Explaining strikes opposers Dumb;	. . . .	281	Journal	84
Some shew they never want explaining,	. . . . . .	592	Strephon Chloe	275
To be chidden for explaining	. . . .	908	Daphne	67
EXPLODED				
With old Scraps from Plays exploded.	. . . . . .	523	Betty Grizette	16
With Fustian from exploded Plays,	. . . .	697	Cadenus Vaness	330
Now twenty Years from Court exploded?	. . . . . .	820	Dr. Rundle	28
EXPLOIT				
It would be an Exploit to brag on,	. . . . . .	281	Journal	69
EXPLORES				
With gentlest Touch, she next explores	. . . . . .	582	Young Nymph	29
EXPOS'D				
Expos'd to every Coxcomb's Eyes,	. . . .	60	Lady Tablebook	5
Expos'd to th' Excrement of his,	. . . .	61	Lady Tablebook	20
Midas, expos'd to all their Jears,	. . . .	157	Fable of Midas	39
Expos'd with all their Magick Ware.	. . . .	240	Run Bankers	36
Expos'd, to blind the Nation's Eyes,	. . . .	354	Simile Silver	21
"Expos'd the Fool, and lash'd the Knave:	. . . . .	565	Death of Swift	316
"For her he oft expos'd his own.	. . . .	566	Death of Swift	350
Expire, when first expos'd to open Air.	. . . . .	667	Epig Carthy 5	D 6
Expos'd to Want, and Wind, and Weather,	. . . . .	759	Receipt Youth	9
EXPOSE				
Methinks, when you expose the Scene,	. . . . . .	29	Ode to Temple	97
"T' expose thy soul, clad in this poor disguise;	. .	55	Temple Ill	144
For, it would his Character Expose	. . . .	294	Prog Marriage	143
Nor makes a Scruple to expose	. . . .	416	Woman's Mind	21
Nor ever fools or knaves expose	. . . .	489	Dialogue	9
No Scruple came on him his Gown to expose,	. . . .	517	Dean Hang Rape	21
The Stockings, why shou'd I expose,	. . . . . .	527	Lady's Dres Rm	51
To expose the brisk Baboon?	. . . .	634	Epistle Lady	154
I'll here expose your weaker Side.	. . . . . .	730	Stella, Poems	86
But, loth his Person to expose	. . . .	904	Death Daphne	33
And my Delight is to expose	. . . .	915	Riddle 1	25
EXPOSES				
Which most exposes ours to Scorn?	. . . .	725	To Stella	68
EXPOSING				
His Breeches torn exposing wide	. . . .	594	Cassinus Peter	15
EXPRESS				
Is at a loss for Figures to express	. . . . . .	21	Ode Athenian	172
Which all the mimic forms express,	. . . .	35	Ode Sancroft	25
Or from Whitehall some new Express,	. . . . . .	63	Discovery	30
T' express their Valor, Strength or Wit.	. . . . .	83	Salamander	12
"So eager to express your Love,	. . . .	200	Horace 2, 6	37
Of some Express arriv'd at Court;	. . . .	202	Horace 2, 6	90

EXPRESS	(CONTINUED)	PAGE	TITLE	LINE
For when you express a Friend's Love we are willing,	.	337	Serious Poem	103
Yet how shall I express in Words,	. . . . . .	514	Answer Fable	59
And, by their Fears express their Hopes:	. . . .	557	Death of Swift	118
Nor Eloquence Divine express,	. . . .	595	Cassinus Peter	56
And, O what virtue you express	. . . .	676	Parson's Case	17
Esteem and Friendship to express,	. . . . . .	757	Stel B-day '24	31
The Detestation you express	. . . .	765	Stel B-day '26	47
Such reverential Awe express,	. . . .	889	Panegyr Dean	79

EXPRESS'D

		PAGE	TITLE	LINE
Tho' the Thought be Apollo's, 'tis finely express'd;	.	266	Apollo	91
When have I Esteem express'd	. . . .	632	Epistle Lady	75

EXPREST

		PAGE	TITLE	LINE
So Things, which must not be exprest,	. . . . .	529	Lady's Dres Rm	109
But when in Capitals exprest,	. . . .	643	On Poetry	99
And yet her Words were so exprest,	. . . . . .	706	Cadenus Vaness	628
The Beau in all his Ayrs exprest.	. . . . .	782	Tim and Fables	12

EXTEND

		PAGE	TITLE	LINE
His indisputed Rights extend	. . . .	649	On Poetry	287
With Bands of Fidlers to extend his Treyn.	. .	678	Dean and Duke	8
Thy Nose's Length and Fame extend	. . . . .	993	On Picture	28

EXTENSIVE

		PAGE	TITLE	LINE
And, to a Genius so extensive,	. . . .	891	Panegyr Dean	157

EXTENT

		PAGE	TITLE	LINE
Like a just Map to tell the vast Extent	. . . .	25	Ode Athenian	302
To try their Wisdom's full Extent;	. . . . . .	697	Cadenus Vaness	339

EXTINCT

		PAGE	TITLE	LINE
Can shine, without him is extinct.	. . . . . .	465	Birthday Song	178

EXTINGUISH'T

		PAGE	TITLE	LINE
That quite extinguish't Cupid's Lamp:	. . . . .	905	Death Daphne	98

EXTOL

		PAGE	TITLE	LINE
Extol him for his generous mind:	. . . . .	464	Birthday Song	124
Extol the Greek and Roman Masters,	. . . . .	652	On Poetry	347

EXTOLL

		PAGE	TITLE	LINE
Extoll ye Bench of Bishops round,	. . . . .	658	On Poetry	D 190

EXTOLS

		PAGE	TITLE	LINE
And some as justly Fame extols	. . . .	650	On Poetry	299

EXTORT

		PAGE	TITLE	LINE
Thus vagrant Beggars, to extort	. . . . .	667	Epig Carthy 6	D 1

EXTRACT

		PAGE	TITLE	LINE
Have taught Men to extract with Skill,	. . . .	920	Riddle 6	21

EXTRAVAGANCE

		PAGE	TITLE	LINE
These Days! where ev'n th' Extravagance of Poetry	. .	21	Ode Athenian	171

EXTREAMEST

		PAGE	TITLE	LINE
Eject it to th' extreamest parts,	. . . .	761	Bec's B-Day	14

EXTREAMLY

		PAGE	TITLE	LINE
This Serpent is extreamly cold,	. . . .	84	Salamander	48

EXTREMELY

		PAGE	TITLE	LINE
Extremely proud--but I had din'd--	. . . . . .	173	Horace 1, 7	68
Last Night was so extremely fine,	. . . . . .	696	Cadenus Vaness	326

EXTREMES

		PAGE	TITLE	LINE
Fortune in both extremes,	. . . .	40	Ode Sancroft	203
Frighted alike at both Extremes,	. . . . . .	379	Apology Lady C	123

EY'D   SEE BLEW-EY'D

EYE

		PAGE	TITLE	LINE
In vain pursues the Musick with her longing Eye,	. .	17	Ode Athenian	58
After a mighty Light that leads her wandring Eye;	. .	18	Ode Athenian	67
Or in our Judgement or our Eye)	. . . . . .	20	Ode Athenian	140
Because the Cords escape their Eye	. . . .	29	Ode to Temple	95
In its reception to the eye,	. . . .	35	Ode Sancroft	29
To be observ'd by vulgar eye,	. . . .	39	Ode Sancroft	150
And even the sharpest eye that has the prospect seen,	.	41	Ode Sancroft	207
No deflower'd eye can face the naked light:	.	41	Ode Sancroft	222
Heaven with a parent's eye regarding earth,	. . . .	54	Temple Ill	89
And busy both with Hand and Eye	. . . . .	86	Hist V's House	5
You've some good Purchase in your Eye;	. . .	175	Horace 1, 7	128
"From whence, with half an Eye we may discover,	. . .	195	Author Himself	45
That I have an ill Eye, they wickedly think,	. . . .	263	Apollo	13
From Magazeen in Caelia's Eye.	. . . . . .	272	Apollo's Edict	D 59
So, when an Eye hath lost it's Brother,	. . . . .	366	Answer Delaney	21
"If his Majestick Eye you flee,	. . . . .	380	Apology Lady C	143
"So shall the Eye, by Form confin'd,	. . . . . .	384	Manly Virtue	11
His Soul bright-beaming from his Eye,	. . . . .	385	Manly Virtue	60
No Object Strephon's Eye escapes,	. . . . .	527	Lady's Dres Rm	47
When frighted Strephon cast his Eye on't	. . . .	527	Lady's Dres Rm	61
Now, picking out a Crystal Rye,	. . . . . .	581	Young Nymph	11
The crystal Eye, alas, was miss't;	. . . . .	583	Young Nymph	61
And thus deceive the sharpest Eye:	. . . . .	607	Beasts Confess	194
Than what a curious Eye may trace	. . . . .	653	On Poetry	385
Let Stella look with watchful Eye,	. . . . .	743	Stel B-day 22	59
That when they have you in their Eye,	. . . . .	775	Mullinix Tim	67
"You cast a Sheep's Eye on her Ladyship's Maid;	. .	872	Grand Question	148
Turn ev'ry Way thy watchful Eye;	. . . . .	897	Panegyr Dean	337
Observe me with revengeful Eye:	. . . . .	925	Riddle 8	18
Can shew a Nose, Eye, Tongue, or Ear,	. . . .	935	Riddle 23	D 8
Polish'd neck, and radient eye;	. . . . .	936	Riddle 24	D 14
In my eye my greatest grace,	. . . .	936	Riddle 24	D 15
With half an Eye	. . . .	938	Riddle Answerd	1
Or fit more exact than one eye and one rhyme.	. . .	980	Tho: Sheridan	4

EYE-BROWS

		PAGE	TITLE	LINE
Her Eye-Brows from a Mouse's Hyde,	. . . . .	581	Young Nymph	13

```
EYE-LIDS                                               PAGE    TITLE            LINE
     To sleep could Mortal Eye-lids fix    . . . . . .  133 Magician's Rod      37
EYES
     With Lightning in his Eyes, and Thunder in his Hands;   7 Ode to King       50
     Our Prince has charm'd its many hundred Eyes;    . . .   8 Ode to King      78
     And rolls about her dreadful Eyes,     . . . . . .  30 Ode to Temple      122
     And yet the world, whose eyes are on our mighty Prince,  40 Ode Sancroft   180
     Such seem'd her eyes, as when an evening ray    . .  51 Temple Ill         17
     Might seem, when first she rais'd her eyes to mine.  . .  52 Temple Ill     30
     Which darts on poets eyes a trembling light;   . . . .  54 Temple Ill       98
     Like antic shapes in dreams, from waking eyes:  . . . .  54 Temple Ill     100
     Expos'd to every Coxcomb's Eyes,     . . . . . . .  60 Lady Tablebook       5
     But hardly ever set my Eyes together, or slept a Wink.  70 Mrs Harris Pet   21
     And grow a Church before your Eyes.      . . . . .  92 Bauc & Phil 1       90
     To keep the Hair out of their Eyes;    . . . . . .  98 Elegy Patrige       24
     And grow a Church before your Eyes.      . . . . . 112 Bauc & Phil 2       50
     And hardly could believe his Eyes,     . . . . . . 116 Bauc & Phil 2      146
     The Flashes of Ardeliah's Eyes.      . . . . . . . 119 Apollo Outwit       12
     "I tore in Frolick; to your Eyes      . . . . . . 154 Widow and Cat    D  29
     The Doctor fasten'd by the Eyes,      . . . . . . 172 Horace 1, 7         58
     Round all the earth she casts her eyes;   . . . . . 178 To Lord Harley     61
     By dull Divines, who look with envious Eyes,   . . . . 193 Author Himself    3
     Would lift her Eyes up to the Ceeling,    . . . . . 222 Prog of Love       16
     Crackt Lips, foul Teeth, and gummy Eyes,   . . . . . 226 Prog of Beauty     15
     Two Balls of Glass may serve for Eyes,    . . . . . 229 Prog of Beauty    113
     Or do these Juglers cheat our Eyes?     . . . . . . 250 Bubble              4
     Pray Gentlemen, believe your Eyes,     . . . . . . 254 Bubble            102
     That her Eyes were as bright as our self at Noon-Day; 264 Apollo            41
     But in Stella's bright Eyes were plac'd right again;  . 264 Apollo           50
     You see the Crows feet round his Eyes.   . . . . . 291 Prog Marriage      50
     To look with Robin Grattan's Eyes:     . . . . . . 314 To Ford            86
     And seems all Feet, and Hands, and Eyes.   . . . . . 322 First of April     38
     Expos'd, to blind the Nation's Eyes,    . . . . . . 354 Simile Silver      21
     And stabs the Son before the Mother's Eyes.  . . . . 364 On Dreams          16
     To weak, or old, or clouded Eyes.      . . . . . . 367 Answer Delaney     46
     Your Arms, tho' both your Eyes were lost,   . . . . . 367 Answer Delaney    47
     And scarce believes his Eyes, or Ears:    . . . . . 376 Apology Lady C     20
     "The living Lusture of your Eyes?     . . . . . . 380 Apology Lady C    166
     "(Whose Beauties mortal Eyes escape,    . . . . . . 384 Manly Virtue        7
     Your Altitude offends the Eyes,      . . . . . . . 414 Censure            11
     She stretches, gapes, unglues her Eyes,   . . . . . 446 Modern Lady        42
     With panting Heart, and earnest Eyes,    . . . . . 452 Modern Lady       230
     And lightning always in his Eyes:     . . . . . . 461 Birthday Song      42
     And only wants to want his eyes.      . . . . . . 466 Birthday Song     202
     Who look on Courts with stricter Eyes,    . . . . . 485 Libel on D- D-    175
     Round all your Brethren cast your Eyes,   . . . . . 502 Doctor Delaney     83
     That in his Tail he wore his Eyes,     . . . . . . 513 Answer Fable       17
     Who waited on his Eyes behind.      . . . . . . . 513 Answer Fable       30
     A Cabinet to vulgar Eyes;    . . . . . . . . . . 528 Lady's Dres Rm     78
     We all behold with envious Eyes,      . . . . . . 554 Death of Swift     13
     Or if she chance to close her Eyes,    . . . . . . 582 Young Nymph        40
     By Lightning shot from Chloe's Eyes?    . . . . . . 587 Strephon Chloe    110
     With Eyes in Smoak and Weeping drown'd:   . . . . . 594 Cassinus Peter     26
     These Eyes, these Eyes beheld the Fact.   . . . . . 596 Cassinus Peter     98
     These Eyes, these Eyes beheld the Fact.   . . . . . 596 Cassinus Peter     98
     Preferment get, and spare his Eyes:    . . . . . . 604 Beasts Confess    108
     Compare her radiant eyes to Lightning:    . . . . . 621 Scandal Poem 1    150
     Compare her radiant Eyes to Light'ning;   . . . . . 628 Scandal Poem 2    154
     And tell the Murders of her Eyes.     . . . . . . 697 Cadenus Vaness    333
     She's not so handsome, in my Eyes:     . . . . . . 699 Cadenus Vaness    410
     In Eyes with Reading almost blind;     . . . . . . 703 Cadenus Vaness    527
     Appears a Hero to our Eyes;    . . . . . . . . . 710 Cadenus Vaness    733
     Enough to read a Lady's Eyes;     . . . . . . . . 712 Cadenus Vaness    815
     With half the Lustre of Your Eyes,     . . . . . . 722 Stel B-Day '18     13
     With Cordials in her Hands, and Eyes.   . . . . . . 727 To Stella         110
     Of killing Eyes, or bleeding Hearts:    . . . . . . 728 Stella, Poems      12
     Let Malice look with all her Eyes,     . . . . . . 730 Stella, Poems      81
     And Anger sparkling in your Eyes,     . . . . . . 731 Stella, Poems     114
     The fainting Rays of Stella's Eyes.    . . . . . . 735 Stel B-day '20     22
     Adieu bright Wit, and radiant Eyes;    . . . . . . 757 Stel B-day '24     27
     My Eyes are somewhat dimmish grown;    . . . . . . 757 Stel B-day '24     42
     And till I see them with these Eyes,    . . . . . . 758 Stel B-day '24     47
     Of pissing in the Rabble's Eyes.      . . . . . . 787 Dick's Variety      6
     Nor, in their Eyes at Random pisses,    . . . . . . 796 Traulus 1          29
     A face for to kiss, without eyes, ears, or nose.  . . 817 Yahoo's           64
     Bless mine Eyes! Art thou the Chairman?   . . . . . 837 Legion Club       190
     His Beetle-brows and Eyes of Wall,     . . . . . . 861 Lady Acheson       39
     Look not with your future Eyes:      . . . . . . . 862 To Janus           10
     Or, had only Eyes behind.--    . . . . . . . . . 862 To Janus           18
     I'll have none but forward Eyes:      . . . . . . 863 To Janus           20
     To keep off their Eyes, as they wait at the Table;  . 871 Grand Question   136
     Attract the curious Trav'llers Eyes,    . . . . . . 893 Panegyr Dean      202
     Conceal their talents from our eyes,    . . . . . . 900 Dean's Reasons     34
     Charm'd with his Eyes and Chin and Snout,   . . . . . 904 Death Daphne      63
     I speak to Eyes and not to Ears.      . . . . . . 915 Riddle 1           18
     How will your Eyes contain their Tears,   . . . . . 921 Riddle 7            9
     When on my Bosom thy bright Eyes,     . . . . . . 932 Riddle 19        D  1
     While true Lovers Eyes Weeping Sleep,    . . . . . 960 Cantata
     That inflammations in the eyes      . . . . . . . 982 Sher, A Goose       4
     Thy Nose outshining Caelia's Eyes.     . . . . . . 994 On Picture         33
```

```
EYN
     If you do not come back we shall weep out our eyn  . . .      1018 Swift Ans Sher     28
FABIUS
     Like prudent Fabius by Delay.  . . . . . . . .                 656 On Poetry         446
FABIUS'S
     Let not old Rome boast Fabius's Fate,   . . . . .              28 Ode to Temple       70
FABLE
     Here ends the Fable and the Moral.  . . . . . .               189 Faggot             14
     And from a Fable form a Truth:    . . . . . . .               252 Bubble             44
     Discreetly to apply this Fable.   . . . . . . .               346 Prometheus         58
     In proper Terms to write a Fable;   . . . . . .              512 Answer Fable         2
     Hear an old Fable, and a dull one too;  . . . . .            538 Mr. Pulteney        15
     "To turn Religion to a Fable,   . . . . . . . .              568 Death of Swift     383
     Read over here and there a Fable,   . . . . . . .            782 Tim and Fables       6
     An Inundation, says the Fable,    . . . . . . .              811 Bro Protestant       1
     A long-ear'd Beast and holy Fable,    . . . . .             942 Probatur Alit       11
FABLES
     As Fables: But you have refin'd   . . . . . . .              478 Epist on Epist      84
     Has learnt his Fables to refine;    . . . . . . .            513 Answer Fable        12
     The Fables writ by Mr. Gay,   . . . . . . . .                782 Tim and Fables       4
FABLING
     From Fields Elyzian, fabling Esop;   . . . . . .             607 Beasts Confess     200
FABRICK-ROOF
     And stepping o'er the Fabrick-roof,   . . . . .             127 Little House        33
FABULOUS
     As in old Fabulous Hell,   . . . . . . . . .                   9 Ode to King        92
FAC'D    SEE TWO-FAC'D
FACE    SEE WHEY-FACE
     The very Brightness of His Face   . . . . . .                  9 Ode to King        94
     Her Face patch't o'er with Modern Pedantry,   . . .          23 Ode Athenian      224
     I must, like him that painted Venus' Face,   . . .           28 Ode to Temple       63
     Thou daily seest Him face to face,   . . . . .               34 Ode Sancroft         6
     Thou daily seest Him face to face,   . . . . . .             34 Ode Sancroft         6
     No deflower'd eye can face the naked light:   . . .          41 Ode Sancroft       222
     To tear Religion's lovely face;   . . . . . .                42 Ode Sancroft       248
     O'er the sun's face, and from his heat proceeds,  . .        45 To Congreve         70
     Squander'd his noisy talents to my face;   . . .            47 To Congreve        138
     As a fresh miss, by fancy, face, and gown,   . . .           48 To Congreve        151
     And chuse out wits who ne'er have seen his face;   . .       48 To Congreve        170
     Darts weeping beams across heaven's wat'ry face;   . .       52 Temple Ill          26
     What mortal change does in thy face appear,   . . .          52 Temple Ill          31
     Late I beheld on every face appear;   . . . . .             52 Temple Ill          40
     It's watery footsteps in Dorinda's face;   . . .            52 Temple Ill          52
     Grief from Dorinda's face does ne'er depart   . . .          53 Temple Ill          53
     Thus, when Dorinda wept, joy ev'ry face forsook,  . .        53 Temple Ill          59
     So would earth's face turn pale, and life decay,  . .        53 Temple Ill          63
     Sweeps the broad scythe, and tramples on his face.  . .      55 Temple Ill         122
     Of forward Face, and Ear acute,   . . . . . .                63 Discovery           26
     Wine can clear up <Godolphin's> cloudy Face,   . . .        163 Toland's Invit      19
     And shew'd some Humour in his Face;   . . . . .             170 Horace 1, 7          8
     For wit and learning spoil'd his face.   . . . .            177 To Lord Harley      28
     Nor shew'd the Parson in his Gait or Face;   . . .          194 Author Himself      14
     The Parish jear'd him to his Face:    . . . . .             221 A Quiet Life        46
     Sits on her cloudy wrinckled Face.    . . . . .             226 Prog of Beauty       4
     Her artificiall Face appears    . . . . . . .               226 Prog of Beauty       6
     They form a frightfull hideous Face,    . . . .            226 Prog of Beauty      24
     A Lady's Face, and China ware.    . . . . . .              227 Prog of Beauty      64
     Each Night a Bit drops off her Face   . . . . .            228 Prog of Beauty      87
     To the Materialls of Her Face.    . . . . . .              229 Prog of Beauty     108
     But showed no more than half her Face   . . . .            290 Prog Marriage       16
     His ruddy, wrinckled, smirking Face,    . . . .            290 Prog Marriage       24
     Him let her Marry for his Face,    . . . . . .             295 Prog Marriage      161
     She bid me with a serious Face   . . . . . . .             311 To Ford              7
     So sometimes half a Face produce,    . . . . .             326 Pethox              83
     To Something Nobler in thy Face.    . . . . .              340 Arch-Bish Dub       16
     Good Lord! I wondred how I dar'd to look him in the         342 Upon His Grace      28
          Face.
     Why Sirrah said the Noble 'Squire, how dare you see my      343 Upon His Grace      43
          Face,
     O'er the Moon's Face a sable Hue,   . . . . . .            354 Simile Silver        2
     Displays her Silver Face again.   . . . . . .              354 Simile Silver       14
     Flirts from his Cart the Mud in <Walpole's> Face.   .       364 On Dreams           38
     Knows ev'ry Prince in Europe's Face,    . . . .            398 Earl of P-b-w        7
     And see her marks in ev'ry face;    . . . . . .          401 Window Inns 5    D   8
     He spurn'd them in his Rival's Face.    . . . .            412 Desire Possess      34
     Nor spoil your Shape, distort your Face,    . . .          414 Censure             23
     The sun, you say, his face has kist:    . . . .            432 Answer Paulus        9
     And Modesty with blushing Face;    . . . . . .             448 Modern Lady        123
     A Cupid in his face and size,    . . . . . . .             466 Birthday Song      201
     Would shew you many a Statesman's Face.   . . . .          485 Libel on D- D-     180
     And draw like you my Patron's Face;   . . . . .            496 Panegyr Swift      111
     Disclaim the Human Name, and Face,    . . . .              498 Panegyr Swift      172
     And looks a Critick in the Face.    . . . . .              500 Doctor Delaney      26
     Your Genius in your Face will fly.    . . . . .            503 Doctor Delaney     114
     Durst there show his right or most revnd face   . .        522 St. Cecilia's       10
     How thy Face charms ev'ry Shepherd,   . . . . .            522 Betty Grizette       3
     Full in his Face Bob shuts the Council Door:   . .          537 Mr. Pulteney         4
     "But who cou'd charge him, to his face,   . . . .          549 Life of Swift      144
     You plainly find it in his Face:    . . . . . .            556 Death of Swift      82
     "If such a Wretch had known his Face.   . . . .            571 Death of Swift     442
     Her graceful Mein, her Shape, and Face,   . . . .          584 Strephon Chloe       7
```

FACE	(CONTINUED)	PAGE	TITLE	LINE
Could give no Softness to his Face.		587	Strephon Chloe	94
Let fly a Rouzer in her Face.		590	Strephon Chloe	192
In all the Postures of her Face,		591	Strephon Chloe	239
Sunk down her Nose, or seam'd her Face?		595	Cassinus Peter	49
At which the Sun should hide his Face.		595	Cassinus Peter	70
He'd shew his Face before the <King>:		602	Beasts Confess	34
And, first excus'd his youthful Face;		603	Beasts Confess	60
I would accuse him to his Face		607	Beasts Confess	201
For hourly thundring in his face,		618	Scandal Poem 1	19
Keep the same face an hour together,		618	Scandal Poem 1	44
That Phebus ever shews his face;		621	Scandal Poem 1	132
Keep the same Face an Hour together:		625	Scandal Poem 2	40
That Phoebus ever shows his Face:		627	Scandal Poem 2	136
His brazen Face, and fiery Nose:		627	Scandal Poem 2	140
Then talk with more authentick Face,		648	On Poetry	243
Where Pope will never show his Face.		650	On Poetry	308
Thro' all the Features of his Face;		655	On Poetry	418
She ne'er could shew her Face above.		689	Cadenus Vaness	82
Discoursing with important Face,		698	Cadenus Vaness	376
I said her Face would never last.		699	Cadenus Vaness	387
A Baby Face, no Life, no Airs,		699	Cadenus Vaness	414
We begg'd her but to patch her Face,		700	Cadenus Vaness	422
Without distinguishing her Face.		706	Cadenus Vaness	635
And come in Crowds to see his Face:		709	Cadenus Vaness	702
The Judge discover'd in her Face		713	Cadenus Vaness	844
"She needs must tell them to their Face,		714	Cadenus Vaness	870
Or throw cold Water in her Face,		725	To Stella	76
With chearful Face, and inward Grief;		726	To Stella	102
Nor dare distort my Face for shame.		727	To Stella	116
An Angel's Face, a little crack't;		734	Stel B-day '20	16
When Doll hangs out a newer Face		735	Stel B-day '20	34
On ev'ry Feature of her Face;		735	Stel B-day '20	50
Like Janus, bears a double Face;		765	Stel B-day '26	74
Thy busy never-meaning Face;		775	Mullinix Tim	59
My very Face, at first I knew it,		783	Tim and Fables	23
Tom could talk with solemn Face,		784	Mullinex Dick	23
Who could forbear, that view'd each guilty Face,		806	Judas	23
A face for to kiss, without eyes, ears, or nose.		817	Yahoo's	64
All the Soul in every Face.		839	Legion Club	230
Both dress'd like divines, with band and face clean.		843	Ay and No	2
Thro' each line of her face		854	Lady's Lament	95
To the homeliest face:		854	Lady's Lament	100
His Tallow Face and Wainscot Paws,		861	Lady Acheson	38
She has got but half a Face;		862	To Janus	5
Give her half thy Face behind.		862	To Janus	8
Burnishes an old Year's Face.		863	To Janus	28
O law! the sweet Gentleman! look in his Face;		870	Grand Question	94
Direct before her Lady's Face.		885	Rev Market-Hill	68
To show my Face with scornful Air;		887	Panegyr Dean	21
Let others with Fanatick Face,		892	Panegyr Dean	169
Pale Dropsy with a sallow Face,		895	Panegyr Dean	275
A Lawyer o'er his Hands and Face,		904	Death Daphne	35
From a face that always smiles:		907	Daphne	22
Lo, here I stand with double Face;		917	Riddle 3	2
I let no Creature see my Face.		917	Riddle 4	4
They dare not charge me to my Face:		918	Riddle 4	30
The chaste Diana's infant Face;		919	Riddle 5	8
I'm not asham'd to show my Face,		920	Riddle 6	24
Then, since I shew as fine a Face,		932	Riddle 19	D 11
Clouded if my face is seen,		937	Riddle 24	D 39
How long shall virtue hide her face,		950	Upstart	D 19
To draw the Face of such a Spectre.		993	On Picture	12
Can mean my culling of a Face,		1003	Dan J's Reply	8
FACES SEE IDOL-FACES				
And hire us out their scenes, and cloaths, and faces.		307	Billet Players	8
Their Lands and their Faces unknown;		396	Dog and Thief	18
Where I shall see your Faces		425	Five Ladies	13
Worn out by Wits who rhyme on Faces;		730	Stella, Poems	76
FACETIOUS				
At Nine, grave Nim and George Facetious,		278	Journal	11
Swear, he's a most facetious Man,		480	Libel on D- D-	9
FACT				
But I affirm, 'tis false in Fact,		253	Bubble	57
To prove it I appeal to fact;		434	Answer Paulus	68
And Caelia's horrid Fact relate;		596	Cassinus Peter	93
These Eyes, these Eyes beheld the Fact.		596	Cassinus Peter	98
Besides, the Tale is false in Fact;		607	Beasts Confess	198
With Impudence own'd all the Fact.		687	Cadenus Vaness	24
When Questions on the Fact arose,		688	Cadenus Vaness	70
Now, this is Stella's Case in Fact;		734	Stel B-day '20	15
Yet cannot prove a single Fact.		795	Traulus 1	5
I found you mistaken in Matter of Fact.		972	S-'s Ans Sh-d	4
FACTION				
Of a declining Church, by Faction her worse foe opprest,		40	Ode Sancroft	186
So tossing Faction will o'erwhelm		96	On the Union	21
Had giv'n the Faction many a Wound,		171	Horace 1, 7	37
By Faction tir'd, with Grief he waits a while,		196	Author Himself	71
Nor ceas'd the Faction to pursue,		494	Panegyr Swift	43
Their Faction is five hundred Odds,		501	Doctor Delaney	47
And let not Faction come betwixt.		503	Doctor Delaney	108

	PAGE	TITLE	LINE
FACTION (CONTINUED)			
"Two Kingdoms, just as Faction led, ...	566	Death of Swift	351
"Saw Mischief by a Faction brewing, ...	567	Death of Swift	367
"When up a dangerous Faction starts, ...	568	Death of Swift	379
"Where, Folly, Pride, and Faction sway, ...	570	Death of Swift	433
Whom never Faction cou'd bespatter, ...	655	On Poetry	413
The Changes which Faction has made in the State, . .	716	Answer Rebus	23
Your Faction, when their Game was new, ...	774	Mullinix Tim	39
The Faction, (is it not Notorious?)	775	Mullinix Tim	75
By Faction banish't here unite, ...	883	Rev Market-Hill	7
FACTION'S			
While you in your Faction's Phrase	838	Legion Club	215
FACTIONS			
Tho' we be of two different Factions still, ...	18	Ode Athenian	72
FACTIOUS			
With all that Factious or Enthusiastick Dotards dream,	22	Ode Athenian	204
But these, you say, are factious Lyes	256	Bubble	157
Aspiring, factious, fierce and loud	503	Doctor Delaney	87
"Who saw this Factious Tribe caress'd, ...	549	Life of Swift	160
They plot to turn in factious Zeal, ...	653	On Poetry	379
And factious Rage, and Breach of Trust, ...	725	To Stella	46
Now to turn a Factious Tool!	838	Legion Club	198
FACTS			
I might have mention'd several facts, ...	280	Journal	61
FACULTY			
The Faculty, his humble Friends, ...	904	Death Daphne	47
FADE			
More than a fade insipid mixture left behind. . . .	50	To Congreve	212
Let all his barren Lawrel's fade	482	Libel on D- D-	67
His Virtues fade, his Vices bloom;	646	On Poetry	200
FADED			
And colours of a faded hue;	35	Ode Sancroft	32
The faded Bow distilling Rain.	290	Prog Marriage	14
FADGE			
Who says, his numbers do not fadge a-right.	988	Letter Dr Sh-n	20
FAGGOT			
And strove by Turns to break the Faggot:	189	Faggot	6
Then chuse which you please, and let each bring a Faggot,	352	Wood Insect	39
Shew Fire and Faggot in the Tail on't?	774	Mullinix Tim	20
FAGGOTS			
'Twas cut into Faggots, and put to the Flame, . . .	334	Serious Poem	21
FAH SEE FAYL			
The malice thou inspir'st I never fail	53	Temple Ill	85
For my Lord Dromedary comes a Tuesday without fail; .	70	Mrs Harris Pet	28
But the first Knave does seldom fail	74	Game Traffick	3
And if we find our Vittels fail	92	Bauc & Phil 1	65
Will hardly fail, and there is room for more: . . .	166	Toland's Invit	36
His Money spent, his Patrons fail, ...	231	Prog of Poetry	33
And as he saw his darling Money fail, ...	235	Elegy on Demar	33
Then, without fail, we pack up for Belfast.	309	Billet Players	56
And wou'd not fail to wait upon her.	376	Apology Lady C	26
Your Assets fail, and Cash is wanting	477	Epist on Epist	63
That you can't fail of more Provision, ...	478	Epist on Epist	99
Nor if you dy'd, wou'd fail to go	547	Life of Swift	62
"His Stomach too begins to fail:	557	Death of Swift	111
"If he shou'd fail her at Quadrill.	562	Death of Swift	238
But, if you fail, my Spectre dread	597	Cassinus Peter	113
Again you fail, yet Safe's the Word, ...	645	On Poetry	147
Will never fail to bring in Pence:	646	On Poetry	188
So two poor Knaves, who find their Credit fail, . .	668	Epig Carthy 8 D	3
Venus wou'd fail in her Design:	695	Cadenus Vaness	277
He never knew her Judgment fail, ...	710	Cadenus Vaness	755
Should at their Peril without fail	713	Cadenus Vaness	840
Discourag'd Youths, now all their Hopes must fail, .	793	St. Pat's Well	73
If they fail 'tis Want of Parts.	837	Legion Club	188
If all my rhetoric must fail	899	Dean's Reasons	31
Nor ever fail to seize my Foe;	921	Riddle 6	32
FAIL'D			
Jove saw that all Devotion fail'd;	345	Prometheus	42
His Spirits of a sudden fail'd him, ...	376	Apology Lady C	33
Fail'd but an Inch to seize him by the Back.	538	Mr. Pulteney	34
"And seldom fail'd of good Success;	566	Death of Swift	336
He fail'd, because he could not flatter:	604	Beasts Confess	96
FAILING SEE NEVER-FAILING			
Will tell aloud your greatest Failing;	416	Woman's Mind	20
But, thy Merit is thy Failing, ...	523	Betty Grizette	27
And to your Failing set your Hand?	732	Stella, Poems	140
FAILS			
Soon grows Domestick, seldom fails	173	Horace 1, 7	77
How Fortune fails him when he sets:	281	Journal	76
I guess the Hand, it seldom fails, ...	453	Modern Lady	268
Be mindful, when Invention fails, ...	643	On Poetry	89
To talk on me she never fails:	679	From Catullus	2
Tis Virtue fails in Him or You:	733	Verses Vanessa	14
For he never fails to seize 'em;	836	Legion Club	164
FAIN			
Who fain would rule the Pulpit, as they do the Stage,	19	Ode Athenian	104
Fain the fair Nymph would stay, ...	31	Ode to Temple	153
And I would fain continue in it;	94	Bauc & Phil 1	162
I'm Old, and fain wou'd live at Ease, ...	115	Bauc & Phil 2	115
For why; I would fain have put all in a Flame, . . .	144	New Song	43

FAIN   (CONTINUED)   PAGE   TITLE   LINE
    Because he fain would make a Show, ...   216 To Mr. Delany   42
    And fain wou'd hear it told again;   . . . .   376 Apology Lady C   22
    Fain would I think, our Female Friend sincere, . . .   531 To Mr. Gay   3
    "Who fain would pass for Lords indeed: . . . . .   570 Death of Swift   438
    All Human Race wou'd fain be Wits, ...   640 On Poetry   1
    Would fain be like us, ...   855 Lady's Lament   120
    I can't get it out, tho' I'd never so fain. . . . .   869 Grand Question   66
    And now whereby I find you would fain make an Excuse, .   985 Mary to Sher   11
FAINT
    And by a faint Description make them less.   21 Ode Athenian   174
    Faint inspiration sickens as she flies, ...   50 To Congreve   229
    Some faint Resemblance to produce, ...   81 Vanbrug House   87
    Some faint Resemblance to produce, ...   109 V's House   129
    Like the faint red upon a Pippin   . . . .   290 Prog Marriage   25
FAINTING
    The fainting Rays of Stella's Eyes: . . . . . .   735 Stel B-day '20   22
FAINTLY
    But oh! so faintly we pursue, ...   401 Window Inns 5   D 11
    And feels the Lash, and faintly screams; . . . . . .   582 Young Nymph   42
FAIR   SEE COUNTRY-FAIR,MAY-FAIR
    Nature's fair Table-book our tender Souls . . . . .   27 Ode to Temple   32
    Fain the fair Nymph would stay, ...   31 Ode to Temple   153
    As some fair pile, yet spar'd by zeal and rage, . . .   52 Temple Ill   47
    In the fair shrine of Dorothea's mind.   . . . . . .   52 Temple Ill   50
    The Fair approach the speaking Part, ...   66 Problem   41
    Scarce had they spoke when fair and soft . . . . . .   92 Bauc & Phil 1   91
    Fair Rosamond, and Robin Hood, ...   93 Bauc & Phil 1   119
    They scarce had Spoke; when, fair and soft, ...   112 Bauc & Phil 2   51
    Fair Rosamond, and Robin Hood, ...   114 Bauc & Phil 2   95
    Were fair Ardelia not my Aunt, ...   123 Empty'ng Town   19
    Guarded each fair Hesperian Pippin.   . . . . . .   134 Magician's Rod   74
    Stays till 'tis fair, yet seems to call a Coach. . .   138 City Shower   36
    The Brave, the Witty, and the Fair;   . . . . . .   216 To Mr. Delany   38
    Fair Maidens all attend the Muse   . . . .   224 Prog of Love   73
    <God> <damn> me Jack, she's wondrous fair. . . . .   228 Prog of Beauty   76
    And this is fair Diana's Case   . . . .   228 Prog of Beauty   85
    The Swain is rich, the Nymph is fair;   . . . . . .   290 Prog Marriage   28
    "'Tis a fair Trick, by ancient Rules--   . . . . . .   322 First of April   57
    Thy fair indulgent Mother crown'd   . . . .   324 Pethox   33
    The Weather's Fair, nay, that is true, ...   372 Letter D. S-y   23
    A Lady, Wise as well Fair, ...   375 Apology Lady C   1
    "O Jove, if Virtue be so fair   . . . .   383 Manly Virtue   4
    Behold him blooming, fresh, and fair, ...   384 Manly Virtue   17
    Now, on the Bench fair Justice shines, ...   391 Young's Satire   15
    Get all your Verses printed fair, ...   394 Grub-Street   9
    And then stand by to see fair play, ...   421 Ireld   10
    He sd our Ladyes were so fair   . . . .   422 Ireld   29
    Fair Ladies, Number five, ...   425 Five Ladies   1
    Our Lasses fair . . . .   441 Ballyspellin   31
    So fair so young, ...   442 Ballyspellin   64
    On me, who think them all so fair, ...   445 Modern Lady   9
    Than I turn Rebel to the Fair.   . . . .   445 Modern Lady   21
    And fair Discretion left the Place, ...   448 Modern Lady   122
    "Fair Isis, and ye Banks of Cam, ...   462 Birthday Song   77
    For ever fair and young--in Song.   . . . .   467 Birthday Song   234
    If fair, it brings you safe to Port, ...   493 Panegyr Swift   19
    Of Wit's fair Goddess brought to Bed, ...   504 Doctor Delaney   116
    "No Vermin can demand fair Play, ...   548 Life of Swift   126
    "Fair Liberty was all his Cry, ...   566 Death of Swift   347
    Fair Emblems of a fruitful Wedding.   . . . . . .   585 Strephon Chloe   52
    Say, fair ones, must I make a Pause?   . . . . . .   589 Strephon Chloe   161
    Fair Utensil, as smooth and white   . . . .   589 Strephon Chloe   173
    Fair Decency, celestial Maid, ...   590 Strephon Chloe   219
    By fair Accounts it would be found   . . . .   606 Beasts Confess   173
    Fair weather when the morning breaks, ...   618 Scandal Poem 1   30
    Of foul and fair we give you warning;   . . . . . .   619 Scandal Poem 1   48
    One minute whether foul or fair?   . . . .   619 Scandal Poem 1   50
    What nymph on earth so fair as Iris?   . . . . . .   619 Scandal Poem 1   74
    When Jove would some fair nymph inveigle . . . . . .   620 Scandal Poem 1   113
    As if he made the weather fair.   . . . .   621 Scandal Poem 1   138
    Fair Weather, when the Morning breaks;   . . . . . .   624 Scandal Poem 2   24
    Of Foul or Fair we give you warning;   . . . . . .   625 Scandal Poem 2   44
    One Minute, whether Foul or Fair?   . . . .   625 Scandal Poem 2   46
    What Nymph on Earth so fair as Iris?   . . . . . .   625 Scandal Poem 2   72
    When Jove would some fair Nymph inveigle, ...   627 Scandal Poem 2   111
    As if He made the Weather fair.   . . . .   627 Scandal Poem 2   142
    What hope of Custom in the Fair, ...   641 On Poetry   43
    Is needful, to transcribe it fair. . . . .   643 On Poetry   92
    Fair Britain in thy Monarch blest, ...   655 On Poetry   411
    Fair Discretion string the Lyre;   . . . .   661 Love Song   14
    To three fair virgins I did tie men   . . . . . .   675 Curate's Compl   5
    The Council for the Fair began, ...   686 Cadenus Vaness   3
    Engross the Fancies of the Fair, ...   687 Cadenus Vaness   41
    Which in old Times adorn'd the Fair;   . . . . . .   692 Cadenus Vaness   179
    Away the fair Detractors went, ...   699 Cadenus Vaness   408
    She's fair and clean, and that's the most; . . . .   699 Cadenus Vaness   412
    So tender of the Young and Fair?   . . . .   707 Cadenus Vaness   652
    Of Nymphs so gracefull, Wise and fair . . . . . .   722 Stel B-Day '18   12
    Let Stella's fair Example preach   . . . .   724 To Stella   33
    Fair Chloe would perhaps be found   . . . .   729 Stella, Poems   43

FAIR   (CONTINUED)   PAGE TITLE   LINE

    Continues healthy, fat, and fair. . . . .   761 Bec's B-Day   10
    Allure the Cinder-picking Fair. . . . .   779 Mullinix Tim   206
    Fair Freedom's Emblem once, which smoothly flows,   793 St. Pat's Well   67
    But hold, cry the <Bishops>; and give us fair Play; .   805 Irish Bishops   53
    As a Compliment due to a Lady so fair; . . . . . .   870 Grand Question   110
    And oft in Hand of Lady Fair;   912 Aenigma   10
    Or bathing in the Waters fair; . . . .   915 Riddle 1   2
    Of Plenty thou the Emblem fair, ...   919 Riddle 5   3
    As fair and lovely as their Queen: . . . .   923 Riddle 7   70
    Fair Issue of the genial Bed, ...   924 Riddle 8   5
    Make the fairest look more fair; . . . .   936 Riddle 24   D   6
    Emblem of the Fair am I, ...   936 Riddle 24   D   13
    Often fair, and soft, and tender, ...   937 Riddle 24   D   31
    Nor warm the fair for whom I burn; . . . . . .   937 Riddle 24   D   52
    But your fair Lines so grossly flatter, ... 1003 Dan J's Reply   4
FAIRER
    Fresh Objects fairer to his View; . . . . .   412 Desire Possess   30
    No new-flux't Rake shew'd fairer Skin; . . . . .   904 Death Daphne   37
    Growing old, grow still the fairer. . . . . . .   936 Riddle 24   D   8
FAIREST
    Though Splendor gives the fairest Mark   500 Doctor Delaney   27
    As fairest Fruits attract the Flyes. . . . . . .   501 Doctor Delaney   42
    Where'e'er they see the fairest Sign, ...   734 Stel B-day '20   2
    Make the fairest look more fair; . . . . . .   936 Riddle 24   D   6
    Like Flora, deck'd with fairest flowers; . . . . .   937 Riddle 24   D   33
FAIRLY
    Quoth Herries, fairly putting Cases, ...   75 Game Traffick   17
    And saw it fairly twice go round; . . . .   112 Bauc & Phil 2   31
    I hope you won it fairly. . . . .   154 Widow and Cat D   35
    Come with Petitions fairly pen'd, ...   200 Horace 2, 6   45
    Put in Your Money fairly told; . . . .   251 Bubble   5
    I think I'm very fairly off. . . . .   377 Apology Lady C   56
    And fairly bid the <Devil> take . . . .   400 Window Inns 1   7
    And the great Name engrav'd most fairly, ...   494 Panegyr Swift   53
    He ravish'd her fairly, and sav'd a good Shilling;   519 Dean Hang Rape   57
    Who fairly could on Oath depose, ...   688 Cadenus Vaness   69
    Which fairly hints they are in jest, ...   707 Cadenus Vaness   666
    He fairly abdicates his Throne, ...   712 Cadenus Vaness   800
    Old Latimer preaching did fairly describe . . . . . 803 Irish Bishops   1
    I join them fairly with a Ring, ...   926 Riddle 9   13
    And fairly shew a Reason, why . . . .   930 Riddle 15   D   19
    At last I'm fairly forc'd to botch for't. . . . .   993 On Picture   9
    'Twill appear, to your cost, you are fairly trepann'd, . 1027 Sheri Circles   15
FAIRS
    But what she learnt at Country Fairs; . . . . .   699 Cadenus Vaness   415
FAIRY-LAND
    Disjointing shapes as in the fairy-land of dreams, . . 35 Ode Sancroft   39
FAITH
    Their faith was so uncourtly when they said . . . .   39 Ode Sancroft   171
    Of Kingdoms, without Faith or Law. . . . . . .   96 On the Union   12
    Faith Sir, you know as much as I. . . . . . .   202 Horace 2, 6   96
    But mark what follow'd,--Faith she bit her. . . .   208 Fable Bitches   18
    That, Faith, I think, there scarce is Room   371 Letter D. S-y   7
    Confines his Faith to one alone; . . . . . .   387 Manly Virtue   132
    "The Pope would of our Faith bereave us, ...   549 Life of Swift   154
    Faith, he must make his Stories shorter, ...   556 Death of Swift   95
    It answers Faith in Things divine. . . . . .   723 To Stella   10
    By Faith and Prayer, this Crosier in my Hand, . .   792 St. Pat's Well   39
    'Though Fools may doubt his Faith in <Jesus>. . . .   820 Dr. Rundle   26
    I would not give such Language to a Dog, faith and troth 985 Mary to Sher   4
FAITHFUL
    Next, faithful Silence hath a sure Reward: . . . .   210 Earl of Oxford   15
    His faithful Steward, in the Shades below. . . . .   234 Elegy on Demar   8
    A faithful Treas'rer! What could he do more? . . .   533 To Mr. Gay   75
    Like faithful Counsellors on either Side. . . . .   770 Horace 1, 14   14
    One Traytor alone, and faithful Eleven; . . . . .   804 Irish Bishops   31
    The Shoes put on; our faithful Portress . . . .   885 Rev Market-Hill   69
FAITHFULLY
    And faithfully direct her Nail . . . .   527 Lady's Dres Rm   65
FAITHLESS
    Or, by a faithless Bully drawn, ...   582 Young Nymph   43
    Cannot be faithless if sure wou'd: . . . .   733 Verses Vanessa   10
FALL
    The wretched Insects singe their Wings, and fall, . . 9 Ode to King   117
    Ready to fall Rome's bloody Sacrifice; . . . . .   12 Ode to William D   22
    As when the Deluge first began to fall, ...   16 Ode Athenian   1
    We soon shall see them to their ancient Methods fall, 19 Ode Athenian   119
    In what Mock-habits have they put her, since the Fall! 22 Ode Athenian   219
    Most fall at last to Interest, Folly, and Abuse. .   24 Ode Athenian   277
    Down the ill-organ'd Engines fall; . . . . . .   29 Ode to Temple   98
    Papists disarm'd, or Fall of Coin, ...   63 Discovery   31
    Tho' on a Throne, wou'd fall to <shit>. . . . .   66 Problem   20
    Let's not fall out; We all had Share. . . . . .   67 Problem   58
    His Grazier's Coat fall down his Heels; . . . .   115 Bauc & Phil 2   118
    Which came with a prodigious Fall; . . . . . .   126 Little House   8
    Fall from the Conduit prone to Holborn-Bridge. .   139 City Shower   60
    Should sink and fall about his Ears . . . . . .   160 Atlas   10
    And then fall foul on all the Town; . . . . . .   217 To Mr. Delany   56
    From his own Hand foresees his Fall, ...   241 Run Bankers   50
    They'll cry, Ye Shops, upon us fall . . . . . .   241 Run Bankers   59

FALL	(CONTINUED)	PAGE	TITLE	LINE
Describe his Fall into the Main,	. . . .	252	Bubble	43
Directors fall as well as they,	. . . .	253	Bubble	83
Their Fall is but a Trick to rise:	. . . . . .	253	Bubble	84
And could that Mighty Warrior fall?	. . . . . .	296	Satiric Elegy	3
"Ye don't fall out about the Heir.	. . . . . .	321	First of April	12
Had drawn his Sword for Marius' Fall,	. . . . .	340	Arch-Bish Dub	18
Can rise upon their Master's Fall.	. . . . . .	409	Dial Rich Marb	34
Must fall, because our Masters rise.	. . . . . .	409	Dial Rich Marb	36
No more let fall those precious Tears.	. . . . .	445	Modern Lady	18
Lament upon their hapless fall	. . . .	490	Dialogue	43
Jove send, this Nightingal may fall,	. . . . . .	515	Answer Fable	103
We see a Comrade get a fall,	. . . .	545	Life of Swift	13
All my Fire would fall in Scraps,	. . . . . .	638	Epistle Lady	263
From bad to worse, and worse they fall,	. . . .	653	On Poetry	387
Lets fall her Knife, or spills the Salt,	. . . .	694	Cadenus Vaness	243
And he must fall a Prey to Time,	. . . .	703	Cadenus Vaness	538
Fall a Working like a Mole,	. . . .	832	Legion Club	73
"Thou chief Contriver of my Fall,	. . . . . .	850	Old Thorn	57
Here I have computed the Profit will fall t'us.	.	867	Grand Question	8
From Heav'n I fall, tho' from Earth I begin,	. .	928	Riddle 13	D 1
Most Things by me do rise and fall,	. . . . . .	934	Riddle 21	D 1
The oft'ner you fall, the oft'ner you write;	. .	968	Letter Sherid	30
Will quickly fall upon the tongue,	. . . . . .	983	Sher, A Goose	5
FALL'N				
Fall'n by mishap amongst a knot of beaux;	. . .	50	To Congreve	216
FALLING				
The Remnant of a falling Snuff,	. . . .	9	Ode to King	108
But Elrington, tears falling from his cheeks,	. .	308	Billet Players	43
Thousand Sparkles falling down	. . . .	638	Epistle Lady	253
Thy Muse from falling upon Pindar?	. . . . . .	666	Epig Carthy 2	D 2
A Sapling with a falling Oak?	. . . .	703	Cadenus Vaness	535
FALLOW				
And shou'd our Galls-town Wit grow fallow,		278	Journal	3
FALLS				
Falls sick in the Posteriors of the World.	. . .	10	Ode to King	146
Down falls the summer's pride, and sadly shews	. . .	55	Temple Ill	123
Then presently he falls to teize,	. . . . . .	201	Horace 2, 6	59
But Illium's lost, and Priam falls.	. . . . . .	209	Fable Bitches	46
Falls from her Tresses on her Front	. . . . . .	226	Prog of Beauty	19
And falls in Rivulets of Sweat,	. . . .	227	Prog of Beauty	38
The Time it falls, or when 'twill rise.	. . . .	256	Bubble	144
The Curtain falls, and we have done.	. . . . .	280	Journal	60
It falls before thy Rev'rend Years,	. . . . . .	340	Arch-Bish Dub	14
For she her self oft falls in Pieces.	. . . . .	362	Grace's Answer	28
Opinion falls, and Beauty dies.	. . . .	591	Strephon Chloe	226
Points out where each new Victim falls;	. . . .	923	Riddle 7	58
FALSE				
In his own balance, false and light,	. . . . . .	36	Ode Sancroft	55
In both, false mediums cheat our sight,	. . . .	39	Ode Sancroft	147
Once highly honour'd! False is the pretence	. . .	44	To Congreve	7
Since one false beam of joy in sickly minds	. . .	55	Temple Ill	149
That the false Wretch shou'd worry'd be:	. . .	153	Widow and Cat	D 18
All their false deluded Hopes,	. . . .	168	Peace Dunkirk	8
Made false Moves, and lost his Queen;	. . . . .	168	Peace Dunkirk	16
False Patience, and mistaken Pride!	. . . . . .	221	A Quiet Life	55
But I affirm, 'tis false in Fact,	. . . . . .	253	Bubble	57
With a certain false Traitress, one Stella by Name,	.	263	Apollo	30
For, true or false, they'll ne'r enquire,	. . . .	312	To Ford	33
For Metal on Metal is false Heraldry:	. . . . .	338	Serious Poem	120
And with false flitting Shades our Minds delude,	.	363	On Dreams	2
The copy's false, and sense is rack'd:	. . . . .	434	Answer Paulus	67
'Tis partly false, and partly true,	. . . . . .	464	Birthday Song	138
a Jobber of Stocks by retailing false news	. . . .	540	Charac Walpole	9
Besides, the Tale is false in Fact;	. . . . . .	607	Beasts Confess	198
Accusing that false Creature, Man.	. . . . . .	686	Cadenus Vaness	4
Regard not what is false or true,	. . . . . .	747	Stel Distress	60
Regard not whether false or true:	. . . . . .	751	Stel Wood-Park	76
Of Brethren he's a false Accuser,	. . . . . .	798	Traulus 1	79
In all Things false, yet always true,	. . . . .	935	Riddle 23	D 5
FALSHOOD				
No Falshood now among the Great,	. . . .	391	Young's Satire	14
Fill'd with Falshood, Spleen and Pride;	. . . . .	799	Traulus 2	8
FALSLY				
Did maliciously, falsly, and traiterously write,	. .	264	Apollo	35
Who falsly boasts	. . . .	442	Ballyspellin	82
FALSTAFF				
As Falstaff acted old King Harry:	. . . . . .	475	Epist on Epist	10
FAM'D				
Fam'd Delos did of old,	. . . .	17	Ode Athenian	47
Like the fam'd Hero in his Mother's Cloud,	. . .	18	Ode Athenian	88
Else why should the fam'd Lydian King,	. . . . .	20	Ode Athenian	153
Like Carleton cheap, or fam'd Duruel,	. . . . .	85	Salamander	62
For Building fam'd, and justly reckond	. . . . .	87	Hist V's House	37
Finch, fam'd for tedious Elocution, proves	. . .	194	Author Himself	39
How fam'd thy Conduct in the Fight,	. . . . . .	326	Pethox	85
Less to be fam'd, than to be fed,	. . . . . .	385	Manly Virtue	40
Of Prelate thus, for preaching fam'd,	. . . . .	406	Swift to Pope	25
Howe'er for selling Bargains fam'd,	. . . . . .	590	Strephon Chloe	216
Fam'd for a thousand bold adventures	. . . . .	619	Scandal Poem 1	60
Fam'd for a thousand bold Adventures;	. . . . .	625	Scandal Poem 2	56

FAM'D	(CONTINUED)	PAGE	TITLE	LINE
Dunkin has been for Latin fam'd--translate.		667	Epig Carthy 4	D 4
For Learning, Wit, and Wisdom fam'd;)		708	Cadenus Vaness	691
The dullest Beast and fam'd College for Teagues		940	Letter	16
And thence, as fam'd John Bunyan sung,		983	Sher, A Goose	6

FAME

		PAGE	TITLE	LINE
Parent of Valour and of Fame,		7	Ode to King	24
First, in the mighty List of Fame,		7	Ode to King	34
The glorious Structure of Your Fame to raise;		11	Ode to William	D 6
It be as great as 'tis in Fame,		16	Ode Athenian	9
Just so the Mighty Nile has suffer'd in it's Fame,		20	Ode Athenian	145
Were I to form a regular Thought of Fame,		21	Ode Athenian	158
Then tell us what is Fame? where shall we search for it?		21	Ode Athenian	175
And when you find out these, believe true Fame is there.		21	Ode Athenian	186
Are the chief Heroes in the sacred List of Fame.		25	Ode Athenian	307
This off'ring long design'd to Congreve's fame;		44	To Congreve	24
A walking vapor, like thy sister fame.		54	Temple Ill	102
For, what is understood by Fame		83	Salamander	13
And be thou Negligent of Fame,		121	Apollo Outwit	54
Till Fame and Eccho almost burst,		121	Apollo Outwit	59
Fame spreads the News, and People travel		157	Fable of Midas	37
Born to retrieve her sex's fame.		177	To Lord Harley	38
Whom you'd consigne to endless Fame?		272	Apollo's Edict	D 71
"Regardless of her House and Fame;		321	First of April	26
Fame now reports, the western Isle		387	Manly Virtue	135
Mordanto fills the Trump of Fame,		397	Earl of P-b-w	1
Each Limb, and Feature out of Fame;		449	Modern Lady	133
"But now 'tis known to common Fame.		449	Modern Lady	149
How could I more enhaunce it's Fame?		470	Burning Poem	15
To Fame a Temple you Erect,		477	Epist on Epist	77
And give up Party to his Fame.		485	Libel on D- D-	150
An Author thus who pants for Fame		500	Doctor Delaney	11
His Life is safe, I mean his Fame,		500	Doctor Delaney	24
Thus, Fame and Censure with a Tether		501	Doctor Delaney	35
To persecute the Muses Fame;		504	Doctor Delaney	132
To live obscure, and have no fame to lose?		506	To a Friend	8
Advanc'd thy Fortune, and preserv'd thy Fame.		531	To Mr. Gay	14
The Doctors tender of their Fame,		558	Death of Swift	169
Thus I consign you down to Fame,		608	Know Not What	3
Lay now aside all Thoughts of Fame,		646	On Poetry	183
And some as justly Fame extols		650	On Poetry	299
To purchase Fame by writing ill:		652	On Poetry	368
He slew my Body, but you stab my Fame.		668	Epig Carthy 10	D 2
(For Satire had destroy'd his little fame,)		671	Epig Carthy 24	D 2
"By which thou shalt be known to Fame:		692	Cadenus Vaness	181
A Goddess of unspotted Fame:		695	Cadenus Vaness	275
He could not answer to his Fame		702	Cadenus Vaness	494
Tom and Dick had equal Fame,		784	Mullinex Dick	1
By holy Zeal inspir'd, and led by Fame,		789	St. Pat's Well	1
And at Hoath to boast his Fame,		837	Legion Club	179
By Scotish Bards of highest Fame,		848	Old Thorn	15
Their fame to future times shall pass,		876	To Dean Swift	12
And wing'd with fame shall reach the skies.		877	To Dean Swift	34
My artless Muse shall sing your Fame.		887	Panegyr Dean	6
And, hearing much of Daphne's Fame,		904	Death Daphne	53
Thy Nose's Length and Fame extend		993	On Picture	28
Thy Fame, thy Genius now declines, proud Boaster.		1002	Reply by Dean	9

FAMED

		PAGE	TITLE	LINE
Some famed for Numbers soft and smooth,		650	On Poetry	297

FAMES

		PAGE	TITLE	LINE
Of their two Fames the World enough rings;		884	Rev Market-Hill	31

FAMILIAR

		PAGE	TITLE	LINE
Talk'd with that saucy and familiar ease		47	To Congreve	141
Now, Delaware again familiar grows;		196	Author Himself	67
Familiar in each Leader's Tent.		324	Pethox	18
With Begging, Vain, Familiar Letters.		479	Epist on Epist	118
"When, ev'n his own familiar Friends		569	Death of Swift	403
Then gave him some familiar Thumps,		594	Cassinus Peter	37
Familiar grown to Dirt and Wet,		890	Panegyr Dean	109
And where she is most familiar,		906	Daphne	17

FAMILIES

		PAGE	TITLE	LINE
Thus Families, like <Realms>, with equal Fate,		535	To Mr. Gay	115

FAMILLE

		PAGE	TITLE	LINE
Who at their Dinners, en famille		480	Libel on D- D-	3

FAMILY

		PAGE	TITLE	LINE
One Family was gone to bed;		90	Bauc & Phil 1	26
The Doctor's Family came by,		128	Little House	47
And all my whole Family, Places by Dozens;		144	New Song	48
And calls the Family to Prayrs,		292	Prog Marriage	88
Or when your Name and Family you boast,		771	Horace 1, 14	39

FAMISH'T

		PAGE	TITLE	LINE
The famish't Cow her Want supplies;		759	Receipt Youth	14

FAMOUS

		PAGE	TITLE	LINE
But I sing of a Famous Lord, who seeks his Country's Good.		341	Upon His Grace	2
"The Dean was famous in his Time;		563	Death of Swift	263
Who, for our Steddyness are famous		618	Scandal Poem 1	40
Who for our Constancy are famous.		624	Scandal Poem 2	38
His famous Letters made waste Paper;		875	Drapier's Hill	17
So the famous Tom Leigh, when quite run a-ground,		968	Letter Sherid	19

	PAGE	TITLE	LINE
FAN			
In Church, secure behind her Fan	222	Prog of Love	11
I never sold so cheap a Fan.	447	Modern Lady	89
Or by the tossing of the Fan,	450	Modern Lady	194
"Your Fan, a Moment, if you please.	452	Modern Lady	243
'Tis thou must fan the Lover's Fire;	590	Strephon Chloe	222
Brave as the Upton Fan she wears:	885	Rev Market-Hill	58
What fits it better than a Fan.	912	Aenigma Expl	D 10
FAN-TAIL			
With Fan-Tail and with Snake,	426	Five Ladies	34
FANATIC			
And thus Fanatic Saints, tho' neither in	812	Bro Protestant	29
FANATICAL			
Be as Pox'd and Profane as Fanatical <Hort>	808	Advice Parson	10
Of all sizes and sorts, the Fanatical crew	815	Yahoo's	21
FANATICK			
"Thought Popish and Fanatick Zeal,	549	Life of Swift	152
"Not so, the vile Fanatick Crew;	549	Life of Swift	156
Let others with Fanatick Face,	892	Panegyr Dean	169
Such Musick would make a Fanatick or Jew sick:	1029	Dr. Helsham	14
FANATICKS			
"Pigs and Fanaticks, Cows, and Teagues	851	Old Thorn	77
Yet hypocrite Fanaticks cry,	926	Riddle 9	17
FANATICS			
With Thieves, Fanatics, and Barbarians?	899	Dean's Reasons	18
FANCIED			
Once Horace fancied from a Man	666	Epig Carthy 1	D 1
FANCIES			
Makes choice of him she fancies best,	178	To Lord Harley	63
Fancies his Fingers in the Cully's Fob.	364	On Dreams	26
Engross the Fancies of the Fair,	687	Cadenus Vaness	41
She fancies Musick in his Tongue,	703	Cadenus Vaness	530
For why such Raptures, Flights, and Fancies,	711	Cadenus Vaness	794
In ev'ry vile Pamphlet you'll read the same Fancies,	968	Letter Sherid	21
FANCY			
As a fresh miss, by fancy, face, and gown,	48	To Congreve	151
But give the vigorous fancy room.	49	To Congreve	206
Or hunted fancy, by a circling flight,	51	Temple Ill	5
The fancy furnish'd by returning joy;	53	Temple Ill	68
Madness like this no fancy ever seiz'd,	55	Temple Ill	147
A different way their Fancy runs;	83	Salamander	16
And in his Fancy fly as far,	99	Elegy Patrige	55
No Thought, no Fancy, no Sublime,	215	To Mr. Delany	11
And Fools would fancy he intends	216	To Mr. Delany	39
And presently guess'd that the Fancy was mine;	264	Apollo	52
And thus William Wood to my Fancy appears	350	Wood Insect	7
Ever with some new Fancy struck,	452	Modern Lady	236
Yet be the Fancy old or new,	464	Birthday Song	137
Yet still you fancy you inherit	478	Epist on Epist	97
Your fancy with their pleasing fire,	489	Dialogue	20
To help our Fancy at a Lift;	497	Panegyr Swift	125
But raise your Fancy on the Wing;	501	Doctor Delaney	55
By vicious Fancy coupled fast,	529	Lady's Dres Rm	127
My Fancy drags this Monster to my View,	532	To Mr. Gay	37
I fancy, there is something in it.	545	Life of Swift	12
How does he fancy we can sit,	556	Death of Swift	91
His Fancy sunk, his Muse a Jade.	556	Death of Swift	102
"To fancy they cou'd live a Year!	563	Death of Swift	261
Or, struck with Fear, her Fancy runs	583	Young Nymph	51
And make him fancy what she will.	588	Strephon Chloe	144
Your Fancy then had always dwelt	591	Strephon Chloe	245
As came into her Fancy first,	698	Cadenus Vaness	382
In Flounces has a better Fancy.	700	Cadenus Vaness	419
Her Knowledge with her Fancy grew;	704	Cadenus Vaness	554
Love or Contempt, her Fancy strikes.	708	Cadenus Vaness	683
"This might their mutual Fancy strike,	714	Cadenus Vaness	878
But found my Wit and Fancy fled:	740	Stel B-day 22	6
Long-thinking made my Fancy worse.	741	Stel B-day 22	12
To fancy they can be unkind.	766	Stel B-day '26	82
If Punch, to spur their fancy, shews	776	Mullinix Tim	103
Some fancy this Promotion odd,	821	Dr. Rundle	53
I fancy already a Barrack contriv'd	869	Grand Question	67
Whether, your fruitful Fancy lies	892	Panegyr Dean	159
. . . he's not come yet from Courtown, I fancy;	1023	Nim-Dan-Dean 2	D 11
FANCY'D			
To ask for what he fancy'd most.	94	Bauc & Phil 1	156
To ask for what he fancy'd most:	115	Bauc & Phil 2	110
And People fancy'd he had Wit.	156	Fable of Midas	24
I fancy'd ev'ry nymph would run	177	To Lord Harley	31
The Doctor might have fancy'd worse.--	707	Cadenus Vaness	655
She fancy'd, those Elysian Shades	905	Death Daphne	85
FANCY'S			
And borne on fancy's Pinions, thinks,	80	Vanbrug House	51
FANN			
To fann th' unhappy Fire:	23	Ode Athenian	241
FANS			
And now he spreads his little Fans,	80	Vanbrug House	49
From Fans, and Flounces, and Brocades,	688	Cadenus Vaness	45
On Ribbons, Fans, and Gloves and Lace;	698	Cadenus Vaness	377
FANTASTIC			
Like that fantastic medley in the idol's toes,	38	Ode Sancroft	138

FANTASTICK

	PAGE	TITLE	LINE
In that fantastick Scene, and thinks	251	Bubble	30
Vain human Kind! Fantastick Race!	555	Death of Swift	39

FAR   SEE A-FAR

And now a Laurel wreath she brings from far,	16	Ode Athenian	18
Instead of boldly sailing far to buy	19	Ode Athenian	97
Far above all Reward, yet to which all is due,	21	Ode Athenian	187
Numberless Nations, stretching far and wide,	25	Ode Athenian	297
Like sun-beams shot at too far distance from a glass;	35	Ode Sancroft	24
And far exalted objects lessen by their height:	39	Ode Sancroft	148
Far sooner than the nobler mushroom grows:	46	To Congreve	100
Nor need I ramble far to force a rule,	46	To Congreve	113
Far in this primitive cell might we pursue	49	To Congreve	195
The muse retreats far in yon chrystal cell;	50	To Congreve	228
That we the wretched, creeping far behind,	54	Temple Ill	115
There in her own (far an el breth)	60	Lady Tablebook	10
And in his Fancy fly as far,	99	Elegy Patrige	55
Thus far advanc't, he made a shift	108	V's House	91
Jove sent and found far in a Country Scene,	118	Biddy Floyd	3
Do far exceed your frisking Lambs	123	Empty'ng Town	15
If you be wise, then go not far to Dine,	137	City Shower	7
From far, to gather golden Gravel;	157	Fable of Midas	38
My Lord and me as far as Stains,	201	Horace 2, 6	76
Smooth Bawty did so far prevail;	208	Fable Bitches	16
Plac'd you in Life too far behind;	215	To Mr. Delany	6
Plac'd me in Life too far before;	215	To Mr. Delany	8
When Jests are carryd on too far,	218	To Mr. Delany	79
I'd send her far enough away--	220	A Quiet Life	33
When you are seen, be seen from far,	228	Prog of Beauty	71
As far up as Adam,	247	Irish-Feast	83
But now, since I have gone so far on,	282	Journal	97
Why Muscovy is not so far,	282	Journal	106
And Mountague so far decayd,	311	To Ford	19
Whose Wisdom and whose Piety, do far exceed his Years.	341	Upon His Grace	4
Not saying, lest I go too far,	373	Letter D. S-y	62
And blush to be so far out-done:	385	Manly Virtue	42
That creeps as far to reach the Centre;	393	Modern Poets	8
Far less the Rabble roar and rail,	450	Modern Lady	186
Far better than a printed Book;	450	Modern Lady	191
Nor will my Lord so far Beguile	475	Epist on Epist	17
As far as Modest Pride allow'd,	482	Libel on D- D-	58
Ye bishops far remov'd from saints:	487	Irish-Club	7
More precious far than ev'n the Gift	494	Panegyr Swift	47
How far their Hearts from private Views,	501	Doctor Delaney	60
Far otherwise a great Divine,	513	Answer Fable	11
"Far to the Land of Slaves and Fens;	568	Death of Swift	396
Bridles destin'd far to roam,	573	Helter Skelter	15
(For you may easy be too far gone,	648	On Poetry	241
That Feilding leaves him far behind.	654	On Poetry	396
Thy Brother (far thy Betters) wore a Gown.	678	Dean and Duke	14
Far better than consulting Laws.	690	Cadenus Vaness	135
But rarely seen, and seen from far:	696	Cadenus Vaness	307
A Project far above his Skill,	705	Cadenus Vaness	586
Thus, far in jest. Though now I fear	751	Stel Wood-Park	73
And think it far beneath your Due;	766	Stel B-day '26	86
His rhet'ric, bombast, silly jests, are by far	815	Yahoo's	13
On a far less Villain's Nose.	830	Legion Club	20
Nay, he can make what's greater far,	876	To Dean Swift	23
How far to go, and when to spare:	890	Panegyr Dean	116
So far, dear Dan, that ev'ry Friend	993	On Picture	29
Far from our Debtors,	1036	Bless Country	1

FAR-EXALTED

| Pardon Ye great Unknown, and far-exalted Men, | 17 | Ode Athenian | 60 |

FARCE

So <Van> resolv'd to write a Farce,	107	V's House	55
Dame Baucis next, they play'd their Farce on:	115	Bauc & Phil 2	138
Thou must no longer deal in Farce,	181	Horace 2, 1	35
Fate put a Period to the Farce;	225	Prog of Love	96
Drive me from my fav'rite Farce.	636	Epistle Lady	196
And thus the Farce a fortnight went	747	Stel Distress	53
Thus for a week the Farce went on	747	Stel Distress	
Thus, for a Week the Farce went on;	751	Stel Wood-Park	69
I know you love to act a Farce.	783	Tim and Fables	38
Command his attendance while you act your farce on,	818	Epigr Kite	6

FARDINGAL

| With a huge Fardingal to swell her Fustian Stuff, | 23 | Ode Athenian | 222 |

FARE

And thus undoubtedly 'twill fare,	25	Ode Athenian	292
Quoth Baucis, this is wholsom Fare,	91	Bauc & Phil 1	63
Hard Exercise, and harder Fare	230	Prog of Poetry	11
O'Rourk's noble Fare	244	Irish-Feast	1
Why then fare them well,	245	Irish-Feast	23
To Stomachs clog'd with costly Fare,	378	Apology Lady C	105
From gen'rous wines and costly fare,	401	Window Inns 5	D 3

FARES

| So fares it in the Southern Sea | 253 | Bubble | 67 |

FAREWEL

| Vain empty World farewel. But hark, | 596 | Cassinus Peter | 79 |

FAREWELL

| 'Tis time to bid my friend a long farewell, | 50 | To Congreve | 227 |
| Gives glad farewell to a tempestuous day; | 51 | Temple Ill | 18 |

	PAGE	TITLE	LINE
FARMER			
From whence the neighbouring Farmer calls	127	Little House	17
By a Parliament Man when the Farmer was told,	288	Bank Down	31
To every Farmer twice a Week all round about the Yoke,	343	Upon His Grace	39
Each Farmer in the Neighbourhood can count	533	To Mr. Gay	65
Now condescends to be my farmer,	876	To Dean Swift	4
Was metamorphos'd to a farmer;	879	Robbin & Harry	42
You'll feed like a Farmer:	952	Onyons	5
FARMER'S			
The Farmer's Goose, who in the Stubble,	230	Prog of Poetry	1
O'erflow'd a Farmer's Barn and Stable;	811	Bro Protestant	2
FARMERS			
Hence we are by wise Farmers told,	156	Fable of Midas	19
The Farmers, spightfully combin'd,	174	Horace 1, 7	109
Some to Cuckold Farmers Spouses,	574	Helter Skelter	43
FARMS			
Come Spaniard, let us from our Farms	884	Rev Market-Hill	43
FARNHAM			
But lay the scene just here at Farnham school.	46	To Congreve	114
FARROW'D			
And thought whose Sow had farrow'd last:	115	Bauc & Phil 2	132
<FART>			
Spread all their Charms to catch a <Fart>;	66	Problem	36
His <Grace> swore by <God>, and her <Grace> let a <Fart>:	143	New Song	18
And you who ever <Fart> in vain,	774	Mullinix Tim	31
Can <Fart> his Navy back again.	774	Mullinix Tim	32
Punch comes, like you, and lets a <Fart>.	777	Mullinix Tim	122
I <Fart> with twenty Ladies by;	778	Mullinix Tim	161
By <God> says Tim (and let a <Fart>)	783	Tim and Fables	19
But Dick can <fart>, and dance and frisk,	788	Dick's Variety	25
<FARTED>			
He <farted> first, and then he spoke.	66	Problem	48
FARTHER			
Farther, we are by Pliny told	84	Salamander	47
Farther in haste the Poets throng,	109	V's House	105
For farther Buildings, farther Planting.	477	Epist on Epist	64
For farther Buildings, farther Planting.	477	Epist on Epist	64
But hold---: before we farther go,	545	Life of Swift	5
Is forc'd to lie farther,	854	Lady's Lament	84
For all the World, Captain, not half an Inch farther--	869	Grand Question	79
FARTHING			
Tho' in thy Walls he ne'er did Farthing spend,	234	Elegy on Demar	26
At Market for a Farthing more	255	Bubble	118
With farthing Candle for a Torch,	290	Prog Marriage	12
She'll pay the Charges to a Farthing:	417	Woman's Mind	60
Nay, in the Compass of a Farthing.	929	Riddle 14	D 6
Not a Farthing will gain 'em,	952	Apples	10
FARTHINGS			
. . .six Pence, besides Farthings, in Money, and Gold;	69	Mrs Harris Pet	2
As fresh as Farthings from the Mint:	644	On Poetry	114
<FARTING>			
But Dick the best at <farting>.	784	Mullinex Dick	8
<PARTS>			
<Parts> like a Laurel in the Flames.	66	Problem	40
FARWEL			
He long had bid the Court farwel,	375	Apology Lady C	13
FASCES			
The Consul's Fasces were unbound;	190	Faggot	28
FASHION SEE OUT-OF-FASHION			
The methods most in fashion to be lewd,	46	To Congreve	118
Must Imitate the Fashion of the Court.	275	Epilogue	30
Two Bards that now in fashion reign,	393	Modern Poets	5
Observe them but for fashion sake.	732	Verses Vanessa	6
Which in the nicest Fashion curl'd,	903	Death Daphne	23
FASHION'D SEE OLD-FASHION'D,OUT-OF-FASHION'D			
FASHIONABLE			
You find, to be the fashionable wit;	48	To Congreve	162
They, in their lewd and fashionable prate,	50	To Congreve	217
A Croud of fashionable Fops;	696	Cadenus Vaness	317
Had spoil'd his fashionable Airs;	703	Cadenus Vaness	545
FASHIONS			
And tho you must the Fashions take,	732	Verses Vanessa	5
FASND			
I'm fasnd both by wind and tide	420	Holyhead	7
FAST			
'Tis the world's wat'ry hour-glass streaming fast,	49	To Congreve	189
And should they Build as fast as Write,	106	V's House	19
Wish'd Women might have Children fast,	115	Bauc & Phil 2	131
While the poor Child lay fast asleep.	150	Corinna	8
Or make you Fast, and carry you to Prayers:	166	Toland's Invit	43
But Dunkirk's ours, we'll hold it fast:	168	Peace Dunkirk	4
To see my Life so fast decline?	203	In Sickness	2
With Wax the Father bound them fast,	252	Bubble	36
And when she has him by the Neck fast,	279	Journal	15
Well then, I'll e'en go home, and fast;	377	Apology Lady C	54
Whilst you're, like Baal, fast asleep.	403	Window Inns 10	D 10
By vicious Fancy coupled fast,	529	Lady's Dres Rm	127
Though your Prognosticks run too fast,	558	Death of Swift	145
For fine Ideas vanish fast,	591	Strephon Chloe	233
Wretch that I was, I broke my Fast:	602	Beasts Confess	16

FAST	(CONTINUED)	PAGE	TITLE	LINE
I chopp'd so fast, that few there minded.		675	Curate's Compl	12
-----I'm sorry Mopsa breaks so fast;		699	Cadenus Vaness	386
So fast, his Lessons lagg'd behind:		704	Cadenus Vaness	557
Self-Love, in Nature rooted fast,		708	Cadenus Vaness	684
Yet you, while Time is running fast,		764	Stel B-day '26	17
Nor sputter out your Oaths so fast,		780	Mullinix Tim	237
He barks as fast as he can utter.		797	Traulus 1	48
Tho' they gallop so fast; on the Road you may find 'em,		804	Irish Bishops	23
That the Mitre wou'd never stick fast on their Head,		805	Irish Bishops	46
Bind them fast, or from the Shelves		838	Legion Club	209
And fast out of spite:		853	Lady's Lament	54
His outward senses fast asleep;		900	Dean's Reasons	46
Nor can she change her Form so fast,		911	Aenigma	5
And, as fast as she could, to the Deanery flew sick.		1029	Dr. Helsham	11
Friend Pope overturnd by driving too fast away,		1037	Four Storyes	3
FAST'NED				
And there stood fast'ned to a Joist:		113	Bauc & Phil 2	58
FASTED				
'Tis just the Case: For you have fasted		759	Receipt Youth	23
FASTEN				
A Joyner to fasten a Saint in a Nitch,		336	Serious Poem	71
FASTEN'D				
The Doctor fasten'd by the Eyes,		172	Horace 1, 7	58
But fasten'd to his Throne above;		345	Prometheus	32
The Cubbard fasten'd with a Peg		746	Stel Distress	39
FASTER				
He comes to tye our Chains on faster,		484	Libel on D- D-	125
My Love for gentle Dermot faster grows		881	Pastoral Dial	13
Faster than Nature can create;		935	Riddle 23	D 19
FASTIDIOUSLY				
With favour & fortune fastidiously blest		540	Charac Walpole	1
FASTING				
Thy week made up of fasting days,		676	Parson's Case	11
Meager and lank with fasting grown,		759	Receipt Youth	7
FASTNED				
And there stood fastned to a Joyst,		92	Bauc & Phil 1	98
A Place was fastned to the Hook,		133	Magician's Rod	45
Both are fastned by the Tayl.		501	Doctor Delaney	34
FAT				
But when he was grown Sleek and Fat,		153	Widow and Cat	D 3
Grown fat with Corn and Sitting still,		230	Prog of Poetry	3
Grown lazy, foggy, fat, and dull:		231	Prog of Poetry	22
Fat Bullocks and Swine.		244	Irish-Feast	8
'Tis wise, no doubt, as clients fat ye more,		433	Answer Paulus	41
The Fat upon a Cinder drops,		529	Lady's Dres Rm	104
Continues healthy, fat, and fair.		761	Bec's B-Day	10
Will make a Horse go, though he be not fat.		940	Letter	13
A maggot in a cake of fat,		950	Upstart	D 5
. . . I mean that great fat joker, friend Helsham, he		1023	Nim-Dan-Dean 2	D 9
FATAL				
I see the Fatal Fight begin;		7	Ode to King	47
Where fatal Neptune rul'd e'rewhile,		17	Ode Athenian	39
And You with fatal and Immortal Wit conspire		23	Ode Athenian	240
The fatal Time when that cou'd be)		23	Ode Athenian	248
To thee I owe that fatal bent of mind,		55	Temple Ill	131
Which, from the fatal Day when first		134	Magician's Rod	67
Conceal a fatal armed Force;		209	Fable Bitches	44
The sleeping Hangman ties the fatal Noose,		364	On Dreams	29
Say, by what fatal Turn of Mind,		449	Modern Lady	151
The fatal Box it self display'd;		494	Panegyr Swift	41
"Is sentenc'd to the fatal Tree,		497	Panegyr Swift	129
"Behold the fatal Day arrive!		558	Death of Swift	147
O Strephon, e'er that fatal Day		591	Strephon Chloe	235
The fatal Changes Time hath made in thee.		792	St. Pat's Well	34
I hourly wait some fatal End;		921	Riddle 6	37
But soon will come the fatal Time,		932	Riddle 19	D 15
Yet to cut the fatal thread		937	Riddle 24	D 45
FATE				
Is fix't like Fate among the Stars,		6	Ode to King	20
And stood 'twixt Him and every Fate:		8	Ode to King	66
That Tennis-Ball of Fate;		10	Ode to King	121
William's the Pledge and Earnest given by Fate		13	Ode to William	D 47
Let not old Rome boast Fabius's Fate,		28	Ode to Temple	70
Take up at best with Lumber and the Leavings of a Fate:		32	Ode to Temple	184
If a mind fix'd to combat fate		36	Ode Sancroft	47
But when they find it turn with the first blast of fate,		37	Ode Sancroft	76
Either our blindness or our fate,		42	Ode Sancroft	241
A pride that well suspends poor mortals fate,		45	To Congreve	45
What bungling, rusty tools, are us'd by fate!		47	To Congreve	131
Happy beyond a private muse's fate,		49	To Congreve	179
Trembling beheld the doubtful hand of fate;		52	Temple Ill	42
Till on a Day cut out by Fate,		62	Discovery	5
For Vows Divine are kept by Fate.		121	Apollo Outwit	48
Yet, still so happy was his Fate,		134	Magician's Rod	47
Yet swifter Fate will seize him from behind.		210	Earl of Oxford	6
Had not ill Fate, perverse and blind,		215	To Mr. Delany	5
It was her Fate; must be forgiven;		224	Prog of Love	55
Fate put a Period to the Farce;		225	Prog of Love	96
For sure if this be Luna's Fate,		229	Prog of Beauty	105
Whom Fate has amply bless'd at home?		272	Apollo's Edict	D 63

FATE	(CONTINUED)	PAGE	TITLE	LINE
Since cruel Fate hath sunk our Justice Boat;	. . .	284	Elegy Boat	2
Yet, spight of Death and Fate, I here maintain	. . .	285	Elegy Boat	29
Come hither, and behold your fate.	. . .	296	Satiric Elegy	28
"For 'tis decreed by Jove and Fate,	. . . .	304	Storm	38
And while his Fate is in thy Hands,	. . . .	325	Pethox	51
Contented he, but Fate ordains	. . . .	385	Manly Virtue	51
And claim it as a Debt from Fate,	. . . .	388	Manly Virtue	141
When he goes out, you share his fate,	. . . . . .	468	Birthday Song	258
And call the laws of wisdom fate,	. . . .	490	Dialogue	42
By Fate are always link'd together.	. . . .	501	Doctor Delaney	36
Be that my Motto, and my Fate.	. . . .	505	Doctor Delaney	172
Thus Families, like <Realms>, with equal Fate,	. . .	535	To Mr. Gay	115
Must undergo the common Fate;	. . . .	562	Death of Swift	251
"To save them from their evil Fate,	. . . . . .	569	Death of Swift	415
Amaz'd, confus'd, its Fate unknown,	. . . .	579	Day Judgement	7
Thy Friend would gladly share thy Fate.	. . . .	596	Cassinus Peter	94
Fate never form'd the Gods to flye	. . . .	620	Scandal Poem 1	111
But, Woman was by Fate design'd	. . . . .	624	Scandal Poem 2	29
Fate never form'd the Gods to fly;	. . . . . .	626	Scandal Poem 2	109
But it was decreed by Fate---;	. . . .	630	Epistle Lady	27
Are so disqualified by Fate	. . . .	641	On Poetry	39
Melody resigns to Fate.	. . . .	661	Love Song	32
How should I beg of gentle Fate,	. . . .	722	Stel B-Day '18	16
Let me of partiall Fate complain;	. . . .	739	Stel B-day '21	6
You'll find it soon if Fate consents;	. . . . . .	743	Stel B-day 22	71
Our Fate in vain we would oppose,	. . . .	757	Stel B-day '24	29
Had fate a lucky'r one, she'd give it ye:	. . . . .	760	Bec's B-Day	2
Ordain'd by Fate to be the Land of Slaves:	. . . .	770	Horace 1, 14	2
Retire, yet still bemoan their Country's Fate.	. . .	772	Horace 1, 14	60
Nor fondly hope for some Reverse of Fate,	. . . .	793	St. Pat's Well	85
"And thou, the Wretch ordain'd by Fate,	. . . .	851	Old Thorn	81
But, when espous'd, he ran the fate	. . . . . .	879	Robbin & Harry	39
Such is the fate of Gosford's Knight	. . . . . .	900	Dean's Reasons	41
Where friendship is by Fate design'd,	. . . . . .	901	Dean's Reasons	69
I only hasten on my Fate.	. . . .	916	Riddle 1	38
By Fate exalted high in Place;	. . . .	917	Riddle 3	1
Much I dread the Courtier's Fate,	. . . .	933	Riddle 20	D 27
And swear by each Fate, and your new friends, each Fury,		1019	To Sheridan	6
FATE'S				
The Youth, in vain, would fly from Fate's Attack,	. .	210	Earl of Oxford	3
Had been confirm'd by Fate's Decree;	. . . . . .	694	Cadenus Vaness	258
Condemn'd by Fate's supreme Decree,	. . . . . .	849	Old Thorn	47
FATED SEE ILL-FATED				
But I was fated to be curs'd.	. . . .	595	Cassinus Peter	44
I think you are fated,	. . . .	1014	Swift to Sheri	19
FATES				
What petty Motives rule their Fates!	. . . . . .	30	Ode to Temple	106
O may the Fates thy Life prolong!	. . . .	339	Arch-Bish Dub	5
Ye Fates, when all he gets is Spent,	. . . . . .	456	Dean Smedley	49
But not prevent the Fates decree;	. . . .	701	Cadenus Vaness	485
This Day, whate'er the Fates decree,	. . . . . .	763	Stel B-day '26	1
Cease haughty Nymph; the Fates decree	. . . . .	905	Death Daphne	91
FATHER				
"The Son and Father, join to tell us,	. . . . . .	181	Horace 2, 1	44
Observe the dying Father speak:	. . . .	189	Faggot	1
The Mother scream'd, the Father chid,	. . . . .	223	Prog of Love	27
Because her Father us'd to say	. . . .	223	Prog of Love	31
To my much honor'd Father; These:	. . . . . .	223	Prog of Love	46
My Father built Lusk,	. . . .	246	Irish-Feast	74
With Wax the Father bound him fast,	. . . . . .	252	Bubble	38
And here the Father often gains	. . . .	293	Prog Marriage	121
But who thy Father, no Man knows,	. . . . . .	323	Pethox	2
He would not give a Groat to save his Father from the		342	Upon His Grace	16
Gallows.				
For here the Father kept his Crown.	. . . . . .	460	Birthday Song	14
And like his Father early wise.	. . . .	466	Birthday Song	192
And, as they robb'd the Father, rob the Son.	. . . .	535	To Mr. Gay	118
Good Father I must own with Shame,	. . . . . .	602	Beasts Confess	13
And yet her father is a Cloud:	. . . .	619	Scandal Poem 1	76
And yet her Father is a Cloud.	. . . .	625	Scandal Poem 2	74
A Father, and the Nymph his Child.	. . . . . .	704	Cadenus Vaness	549
Say to Corruption--Thou'rt my Father.	. . . . .	813	Bro Protestant	62
FATHER'D				
Who often father'd what he writ;	. . . .	171	Horace 1, 7	40
FATHER'S				
Near better animals, her father's sheep;	. . . . .	50	To Congreve	222
From his Father's scoundrel Race,	. . . . . .	800	Traulus 2	24
Her Aunt's my Gossip by my Father's Side:	. . . .	882	Pastoral Dial	42
Proficient in their Father's Trade,	. . . . . .	903	Death Daphne	74
Like Pallas from my Father's Brain.	. . . . . .	927	Riddle 10	D 10
FATHERS				
"And Fathers never shou'd say nay,	. . . . .	181	Horace 2, 1	46
Whose Scoundrel Fathers would not know 'em,	. . .	729	Stella, Poems	51
FATIGU'D				
In half a Walk fatigu'd to Death.	. . . . . .	379	Apology Lady C	128
FATIGUE				
I now despise Fatigue and Hardship:	. . . . . .	890	Panegyr Dean	108
FATIGUES				
And suffers numberless Fatigues.	. . . .	174	Horace 1, 7	96

		PAGE	TITLE	LINE
FATTEN				
Who fatten on poetick Scraps;		504	Doctor Delaney	125
Tho' Chickens take a Month to fatten, ...		642	On Poetry	62
FATTEST				
And freely from the fattest Side		91	Bauc & Phil 1	59
And freely from the fattest Side		112	Bauc & Phil 2	27
FATTYN				
From Toune of Stoffe to fattyn Londe		102	Merlin	6
FAU'T				
To publick Light your only Fau't;		731	Stella, Poems	102
FAULCHION				
Behold his glitt'ring Faulchion mow		461	Birthday Song	31
FAULT				
By any Trick, or any Fault;		199	Horace 2, 6	D
However, if Criticks find Fault with the Phrase, . .		337	Serious Poem	101
The Doctor frighten'd at his Fault, ...		377	Apology Lady C	76
In him; the Fault is in Mankind.		553	Death of Swift	4
It is entirely their own Fault.		591	Strephon Chloe	260
His Singing was another Fault;		598	Problem Solved	27
One Fault he hath, is sorry for't, ...		602	Beasts Confess	31
('Twas Nature's Fault) without a Beard.		603	Beasts Confess	62
His Fault is to be too Sincere;		605	Beasts Confess	142
Where a Fault shou'd move your Pity.		630	Epistle Lady	14
With each Fault, each Fault's Excuse:		631	Epistle Lady	60
Ev'ry Fault have drawn a Gloss over:		632	Epistle Lady	96
Tenderness my greatest Fault.)		637	Epistle Lady	232
Laid all the Fault on t' other Sex.		687	Cadenus Vaness	26
The Fault must on the Nymphs be plac'd, ...		688	Cadenus Vaness	65
Miss Betty, when she made a Fault, ...		694	Cadenus Vaness	242
And yet a Fault we often find		731	Stella, Poems	103
He's still finding fault, ...		853	Lady's Lament	61
No fault of mine, the scheme is ended:		899	Dean's Reasons	6
That she'll own, or cure a fault.		907	Daphne	32
Another great Fault, ...		939	Riddle Answerd	29
In Clergymen the greatest Fault.		942	Probatur Alit	6
Besides, you found fault with our Vittles		986	Mary to Sher	25
FAULT'S				
With each Fault, each Fault's Excuse:		631	Epistle Lady	60
FAULTER'D				
And faulter'd ev'ry Word he spoke;		707	Cadenus Vaness	657
FAULTLESS				
And, faultless to a single Hair.		584	Strephon Chloe	6
FAULTRING				
Panting - - - and faultring - - - Humm'd and Ha'd, . .		377	Apology Lady C	79
FAULTS				
Or name him, but to tell his Faults.		465	Birthday Song	148
The Servants Faults are on the Master laid.		533	To Mr. Gay	50
Some Faults we own: But, can you guess?		603	Beasts Confess	75
On your Faults no longer smile?		637	Epistle Lady	234
Where Criticks mark'd your former Faults.		645	On Poetry	150
But he must answer for her Faults.		705	Cadenus Vaness	603
Began a thousand faults to spy		746	Stel Distress	35
Began a Thousand Faults to spy;		751	Stel Wood-Park	53
FAULTY				
"And can I then be faulty found		380	Apology Lady C	161
In Good Manners, am I faulty?		631	Epistle Lady	69
FAUSTUS				
Renown'd for Skill in Faustus Art, ...		182	Horace 2, 1	50
Shou'd Faustus, with the Devil behind him, ...		776	Mullinix Tim	101
FAV'RING				
As never fav'ring the Pretender---:		550	Life of Swift	187
FAV'RITE				
Then tell (dear fav'rite Muse)		30	Ode to Temple	115
Ah fav'rite youth, how happy is thy lot!--		53	Temple Ill	71
None but the Fav'rite Nymph can smell it.		65	Problem	12
What think you of my fav'rite Clan, ...		314	To Ford	79
Would love his Fav'rite better than before;		535	To Mr. Gay	113
Where's now this Fav'rite of Apollo?		562	Death of Swift	249
Nor bribes my Lady's fav'rite Maid.		605	Beasts Confess	136
Befitting Juno's fav'rite Maid.		626	Scandal Poem 2	76
Drive me from my fav'rite Farce.		636	Epistle Lady	196
Some fav'rite System to their Mind, ...		709	Cadenus Vaness	723
To thee, once fav'rite Isle, with Joy I came; . . .		789	St. Pat's Well	2
In vain, against the People's Fav'rite?		796	Traulus 1	10
(Sir Archibald whose fav'rite Name		848	Old Thorn	13
Thy fav'rite Flow'rs of yellow Hue		894	Panegyr Dean	250
The fav'rite Messenger of Jove, ...		916	Riddle 2	9
FAV'RITES				
Virtue, to crown her Fav'rites, loves to try		210	Earl of Oxford	11
FAVOR				
His Favor, when his Passion's over.		224	Prog of Love	70
By losing their favor		424	Carterets Arms	18
FAVORITE				
Of a governing Statesman, or favorite Whore:		351	Wood Insect	30
FAVORS				
Her Favors to some broken Ensign		295	Prog Marriage	160
FAVOUR				
And the young Muse's early favour felt;		49	To Congreve	192
By Favour, or Desert preferr'd		66	Problem	25
And very much in Harley's Favour)		171	Horace 1, 7	18
In Favour grows with Ministers of State;		194	Author Himself	29

```
FAVOUR            (CONTINUED)                              PAGE    TITLE          LINE
   By Harley's Favour once again he shines;        . . . . .   196  Author Himself    63
   But first by your Favour,          . . . . . . . . . .       245  Irish-Feast       26
   She could not doubt her Uncle's Favour.   . . . . . .        303  Storm             24
   To beg his Favour is the Way new Favours still to win,      341  Upon His Grace    13
   To favour Wood and keep my Pension:  . . . . . . .           348  Whitshed Motto    16
   When'er the Wind of Favour sits,    . . . . . . . .          493  Panegyr Swift     17
   Would ne'er have shown him so much Favour;  . . . . .        514  Answer Fable      78
   To lose an Inch of Favour for a Friend?   . . . . .          531  To Mr. Gay         6
   With favour & fortune fastidiously blest  . . . . . .        540  Charac Walpole     1
   of favour & fortune unmerited vain  . . . . . . . .          540  Charac Walpole     3
   With Favour some, and some without;  . . . . . . .           565  Death of Swift   304
   Whose Favour she is sure to find,   . . . . . . . .          583  Young Nymph       55
   "She saw her Favour was misplac'd;   . . . . . . .           714  Cadenus Vaness   868
   The Captain, to shew he is proud of the Favour,            870  Grand Question   103
   And, Captain, you'll do us the Favour to stay,             871  Grand Question   119
   Yet, they always hope, our Favour.    . . . . . . . .        934  Riddle 22       D  8
FAVOUR'D
   I once esteem'd, and lov'd, and favour'd more,  . . . .      44  To Congreve       12
   The God, who favour'd her Request,   . . . . . . .           302  Storm              9
   When fortune favour'd, he was nice,   . . . . . . .          456  Dean Smedley      27
   "More favour'd, than the Church by Law:   . . . . .          550  Life of Swift    169
FAVOURITE
   A Widow kept a Favourite Cat,   . . . . . . . . .           153  Widow and Cat   D  1
   Your favourite Lord is none of those,    . . . . .          484  Libel on D- D-   136
FAVOURITES
   And still her favourites we meet,   . . . . . . . .          401  Window Inns 5   D  9
   With Paean's purest Fire his Favourites glow;   . . .       532  To Mr. Gay        23
FAVOURS
   To boast of favours that he never got;   . . . . . .        48  To Congreve      154
   Owns all your favours; here intends to stay,   . . . .      309  Billet Players    47
   To beg his Favour is the Way new Favours still to win,     341  Upon His Grace    13
   Your Favours left too long unpay'd;   . . . . . . .         887  Panegyr Dean       4
FAWN
   The Chaplain vows, he cannot fawn,   . . . . . . .          604  Beasts Confess   103
FAWND
   How Jonny wheadled, threatned, fawnd,   . . . . . .         224  Prog of Love      87
FAWNING
   With fawning Whine, and rueful Tone,   . . . . . .          208  Fable Bitches     13
   And swore the fawning Rascals ly'd:   . . . . . . .         657  On Poetry        476
   A fawning, base, trepaning Lyar,   . . . . . . . .          798  Traulus 1         81
   In Flatt'ry an Artist, in Fawning a Slave,   . . . .        807  Advice Parson      4
FAWNS
   He fawns upon you in a Minute.   . . . . . . . .            797  Traulus 1         54
FAYL
   The best Mechanick Hand must fayl   . . . . . . .           228  Prog of Beauty    79
   Must fayl if Matter brings no Grist.   . . . . . .          228  Prog of Beauty    84
FEAR
   We fondly stay at home in fear   . . . . . . . .            19  Ode Athenian      99
   Tho' all the Fumes of Fear, Hope, Love, and Shame,   .      22  Ode Athenian     206
   For of the person much I fear,   . . . . . . . .            35  Ode Sancroft      18
   (Free from our tyrant-passions, anger, scorn, or fear)     38  Ode Sancroft     116
   And which for ought I see, and much I fear,   . . .         39  Ode Sancroft     159
   Of those you so ignobly stoop to fear;   . . . . .          46  To Congreve       86
   And shakes the atheist's knees; such ghastly fear   .       52  Temple Ill        39
   And each imprison'd Hero quak'd for Fear.   . . . .         139  City Shower       52
   For fear He shou'd dispatch more,   . . . . . . .           153  Widow and Cat   D 17
   Though Fear should lend him Pinions like the Wind,         210  Earl of Oxford     5
   Where for fear of the Cold, I never can pass;   . .        264  Apollo            32
   "For Fear the rest shou'd say he squeeks;   . . . .        305  Storm             62
   For fear the First Drop might as well be his Last:   .     337  Serious Poem     112
   For fear my Lord should send it all into the poor Man's    342  Upon His Grace    26
     Box.
   You need not fear a Curtain-Lecture.   . . . . . .         362  Grace's Answer    38
   Captain, I fear you've made some Blunder;   . . . .        377  Apology Lady C    66
   I fear I shall be soon forgot.   . . . . . . . .            408  Dial Rich Marb    18
   But, now I fear it will be said,   . . . . . . . .          410  Dial Rich Marb    55
   But much I fear he's in decline;   . . . . . . . .          468  Birthday Song    256
   Begins the World with Fear and Shame,   . . . . .          500  Doctor Delaney    12
   To a Room full of Guests for fear of a <Rape>.   . .       517  Dean Hang Rape    12
   Yet still I fear your Work is done but Half;   . . .        538  Mr. Pulteney      13
   (Fear lent him Wings) for Safety to the Skies.   . .       538  Mr. Pulteney      30
   My good Companions, never fear,   . . . . . . . .          558  Death of Swift   143
   Are tortur'd with Suspence and Fear.   . . . . . .         561  Death of Swift   220
   Or, struck with Fear, her Fancy runs   . . . . . .         583  Young Nymph       51
   I fear thou wilt be mad indeed.   . . . . . . . .          596  Cassinus Peter    90
   You need not fear your Labour lost:   . . . . . .          643  On Poetry        110
   (For fear young Master shou'd be spoil'd,)   . . . .       693  Cadenus Vaness   224
   Can make us without Fear disclose   . . . . . . .          706  Cadenus Vaness   610
   Sorrow with Joy, and Hope with Fear.   . . . . . .         711  Cadenus Vaness   777
   And guilty Shame, and servile Fear,   . . . . . .          725  To Stella         48
   Thus, far in jest. Though now I fear   . . . . . .         751  Stel Wood-Park    73
   If thou wer't in a Cart, I fear   . . . . . . . .          787  Clad in Brown     23
   Then fear not his tongue, his sword, or his knife;   . .   817  Yahoo's           73
   The Silvan Pow'rs with Fear perplex'd   . . . . .          849  Old Thorn         29
   To live in fear, suspicion, variance,   . . . . . .        899  Dean's Reasons    17
   The courtly Dame, unmov'd by Fear,   . . . . . .           922  Riddle 7          37
   That the lowest Voice I fear;   . . . . . . . .            933  Riddle 20       D 26
   She'll be fruitful, never fear her.   . . . . . . .        953  Oysters           16
   But now I'll write short, for fear you're short taken.     980  Tho: Sheridan      6
   More than the Dirt beneath my Shoes, nor fear it.   . .   1003  Dan J's Reply     15
```

FEAR'D

	PAGE	TITLE	LINE
Contrives, as he is hated, to be fear'd:	536	To Mr. Gay	138
"You know, I always fear'd the worst, ...	557	Death of Swift	129
"Nor fear'd he God, nor Man regarded;	570	Death of Swift	422
Besides, she fear'd the Queen of Love	695	Cadenus Vaness	268

FEAR'S

| For our Fear's at an End with the Death of the Maggot. | 352 | Wood Insect | 40 |

FEARFUL

Or has he like some fearful Star appear'd?	10	Ode to King	130
Disturb the present Mitre, as that fearful storm of late,	40	Ode Sancroft	192
How was the fearful Animal distress't!	538	Mr. Pulteney	31

FEARING

| But fearing Berkeley might be scar'd . . . . . . | 306 | Storm | 77 |

FEARLESS

| Or fearless enter in thro' virtue's gate, ... | 506 | To a Friend | 11 |

FEARS

Immortal Joy, that suffers no Allay from Fears, . . .	6	Ode to King	2
At the first Ebb of Noise and Fears, ...	16	Ode Athenian	14
Out starts the little Beast, and mocks their idle Fears.	30	Ode to Temple	114
Ah, since our fears are fled, this insolent expel, . .	53	Temple Ill	55
Their Thoughts, and Actions, Hopes, and Fears, . . .	291	Prog Marriage	35
And then I shall be free from Fears, ...	410	Dial Rich Marb	77
On whom my fears and hopes depend	420	Holyhead	24
Ah lovely Nymphs, remove your Fears, ...	445	Modern Lady	17
"Nor fears from him ungrateful Force:	476	Epist on Epist	56
Redeems us from the slavish fears	490	Dialogue	33
And, by their Fears express their Hopes:	557	Death of Swift	118
In Florimel's affected Fears:	725	To Stella	70
True, Lady Anne no Danger fears, ...	885	Rev Market-Hill	57
The Butter comes; our Fears are ceas't;	892	Panegyr Dean	185

FEAST

To morrow We our Mystick Feast prepare, ...	162	Toland's Invit	7
Usquebagh to our Feast	244	Irish-Feast	9
They rise from their Feast, ...	246	Irish-Feast	61
Was too refin'd to give a Feast, ...	378	Apology Lady C	98
To feast on Ales and Steaks.	425	Five Ladies	4
'Twou'd please your Palate, like a feast, ...	546	Life of Swift	39
At Dublin's high feast sat Primate and Dean, . . .	843	Ay and No	1

FEASTS

| So to Her Midnight Feasts the Hag, ... | 132 | Magician's Rod | 15 |

FEATHER

And swimming never wet a Feather.	253	Bubble	56
As if they all were of a Feather:	513	Answer Fable	14
Club'd for a Feather to his Hat;	903	Death Daphne	30
I am bright as an Angel, and light as a Feather, . .	928	Riddle 13	D 3

FEATHER'D

| Or Song of feather'd Quire. . . . . | 123 | Empty'ng Town | 16 |
| Nor to the chatt'ring feather'd Race, ... | 597 | Cassinus Peter | 111 |

FEATHERS

| Nothing but Chaff, and Straws, and Feathers: . . . | 688 | Cadenus Vaness | 56 |

FEATS

The Cottage with such Feats as these	94	Bauc & Phil 1	153
The Cottage by such Feats as these, ...	114	Bauc & Phil 2	107
"Perform'd as Juglers do their Feats:	564	Death of Swift	296
Who had contriv'd a thousand Feats;	607	Beasts Confess	192
Could do such Feats as well as they.	788	Dick's Variety	18
And boasts of his feats, ...	856	Lady's Lament	177

FEATUR'D   SEE HELL-FEATUR'D

FEATURE

Or put one Feature out of Place;	414	Censure	24
Each Limb, and Feature out of Fame;	449	Modern Lady	133
Change ev'ry feature ev'ry second.	618	Scandal Poem 1	46
Change ev'ry Feature, ev'ry Second.	625	Scandal Poem 2	42
On ev'ry Feature of her Face;	735	Stel B-day '20	50
Distinguish'd ev'ry Feature in't;	783	Tim and Fables	16
Which spoils ev'ry feature	854	Lady's Lament	97

FEATURES

Scatt'ring loose features o'er the optic vein;	54	Temple Ill	96
In whom thy Features, Shape, and Mien, ...	325	Pethox	71
Thro' all the Features of his Face;	655	On Poetry	418
Form their Features, while I gibe them;	839	Legion Club	226
All of diff'rent Voice and Features, ...	930	Riddle 17	D 2
All Shapes and Features I can boast, ...	935	Riddle 23	D 10

FEAVER

| Gets not an Heir, but gets a Feaver; . . . . . . | 295 | Horrid Plot | 152 |
| Friend Congreve a Feaver, Friend Howard an Ague, . | 1037 | Four Storyes | 2 |

FEBRUARY

| Upon the Ides of February, ... | 456 | Dean Smedley | 46 |

FED

Let us (for shame) no more be fed	27	Ode to Temple	21
By Leaves of Mulberry is fed;	79	Vanbrug House	30
Has fed without Restraint, or Trouble;	230	Prog of Poetry	2
A savage Race by Shipwrecks fed, ...	256	Bubble	154
These Locusts whom our Fruits have fed, ...	258	Bubble	206
Less to be fam'd, than to be fed, ...	385	Manly Virtue	40
In vain, alas! her Hope is fed;	452	Modern Lady	232
And in his Palace fed and taught him.	514	Answer Fable	50
There to be stroak'd and fed with Pap;	607	Beasts Confess	210
With Scraps and Leavings to be fed.	735	Stel B-day '20	38

FEE

| Before his Credit or his Fee. . . . . | 204 | In Sickness | 12 |

FEE	(CONTINUED)	PAGE	TITLE	LINE
	The Doctor with a double Fee	294	Prog Marriage	129
	Tom gave him a Kick in the Guts for his Fee.	399	Tom Clinch	14
	(Provided he has got his fee.)	434	Answer Paulus	56
	And all for ten poor moidores fee!	434	Answer Paulus	80
	You'd swear, he never took a fee,	436	Answer Paulus	121
	And take a Guinea for your Fee.	469	Birthday Song	282
	And to take a double Fee;	574	Helter Skelter	50
	An offer'd Fee from Radcliff scorns;	811	Bro Protestant	16
	Must take no Fee of one another.	812	Bro Protestant	18
	That Bishopricks are held in Fee.	821	Dr. Rundle	60
FEE'D				
	The Writings drawn, the Lawyer fee'd,	222	Prog of Love	22
FEEBLE				
	France do's in vain her feeble Arts apply	13	Ode to William	D 41
	The God laid down his Feeble Rays,	119	Apollo Outwit	5
	And ten to one drags down his feeble stick.	672	Epig Carthy 24	D 18
	It pierc'd the feeble Volume thro',	703	Cadenus Vaness	518
	Flutters the feeble Pamphlet into Rags.	771	Horace 1, 14	30
FEED				
	To the lov'd Pasture where he us'd to feed,	31	Ode to Temple	148
	And yet to feed my Pride,	32	Ode to Temple	196
	Feed nothing in your lands but sheep	422	Ireld	56
	And feed on Fricassees and Olio's.	513	Answer Fable	42
	To feed his Luxury, or sooth his Pride.	534	To Mr. Gay	94
	Who come to fleece the Flocks, and not to feed.	792	St. Pat's Well	32
	Who from thee sprung, yet on thy Vitals feed;	794	St. Pat's Well	96
	You'll feed like a Farmer:	952	Onyons	5
FEEDERS				
	Their generous Feeders not provoking	479	Epist on Epist	123
	Och ma ceade millia mollighart, on the feeders of swine!	841	Ballad	D 19
FEEDING				
	She saves Half her Victuals, by feeding your Ears.	580	Psyche	14
	From stomach sharp, and hearty feeding	745	Stel Distress	7
	With feeding high, & Treatment civil,	746	Stel Distress	24
	With feeding high, and Treatment civil,	750	Stel Wood-Park	22
	From Stomach sharp and hearty feeding,	750	Stel Wood-Park	31
FEEDS				
	That feeds the huge unequal stream.	20	Ode Athenian	148
	And feeds upon imagin'd Bays:	80	Vanbrug House	42
	But, carries Loads, and feeds on Thistles;	607	Beasts Confess	214
	The Nutriment that feeds the Mind?	765	Stel B-day '26	62
	That in secret feeds her flame,	936	Riddle 24	D 24
FEEL				
	Her Tyrant too an unexpected Wound shall feel	10	Ode to King	140
	To make them understand, and feel me when I write;	37	Ode Sancroft	89
	Thus when you feel an hard-bound <Breech>	66	Problem	29
	So when I came up again, I found my Pocket feel very light,	69	Mrs Harris Pet	12
	Now Poets feel this Art is lost:	106	V's House	14
	But yet, methinks, I feel it true;	116	Bauc & Phil 2	159
	The World shall feel her scratch and bite.	150	Corinna	12
	Must feel thy Eloquence and Fire,	182	Horace 2, 1	61
	"And feel my Pulse, I know it stops:	451	Modern Lady	207
	"Perhaps, may feel Compassion still,	485	Libel on D- D-	168
	And feel a trembling at his Heart:	500	Doctor Delaney	6
	Let all Domesticks feel your gentle Sway;	533	To Mr. Gay	55
	Yet shou'd some Neighbour feel a Pain,	557	Death of Swift	135
	But Women now feel no such Fire,	687	Cadenus Vaness	35
	Yet seems to feel my pains alone,	754	Stella '23	17
	Say, Stella, feel you no Content,	764	Stel B-day '26	35
	Your Cable's burst, and you must quickly feel	770	Horace 1, 14	19
	I feel you'll be disgrac'd at Court.	778	Mullinix Tim	154
	She would feel her Pinions drop,	834	Legion Club	128
	But I feel my Spirits spent,	839	Legion Club	233
	Nor need I blush, although you feel it wet;	881	Pastoral Dial	23
	One for all of us will feel.	931	Riddle 18	D 22
	I feel not the least Love Surprize,	932	Riddle 19	D 3
	And at each Lash I feel the Smart	1005	Sheridan's Sub	33
FEELING	SEE FELLOW-FEELING			
FEELS				
	A sudden Alteration feels,	93	Bauc & Phil 1	127
	He spoke, and presently he feels	94	Bauc & Phil 1	165
	A sudden Alteration feels,	113	Bauc & Phil 2	67
	He spoke, and presently he feels,	115	Bauc & Phil 2	117
	It feels as if 'twere taking Root.	116	Bauc & Phil 2	162
	Feels not his Soul enliven'd when he's Drunk?	163	Toland's Invit	18
	And, though the Villain 'scape a while, he feels	210	Earl of Oxford	21
	The Butcher, feels the Lamb beneath his blade.	364	On Dreams	18
	What Agony of Soul she feels	451	Modern Lady	226
	"Like Renegadoes now he feels,	569	Death of Swift	405
	And feels the Lash, and faintly screams;	582	Young Nymph	42
	And when she feels an inward Motion,	893	Panegyr Dean	211
	Who feels true Joys when he bestows thee.	920	Riddle 5	36
	He feels at once both North and South:	923	Riddle 7	84
FEES				
	Duly let out a Nights to Steal for Fees.	125	Descriptn Morn	16
	Dues, Payments, Fees, Demands and Cheats,	174	Horace 1, 7	104
	And takes the Plaintiff's and Defendant's Fees.	364	On Dreams	24
	For licences shall pay no fees.	422	Ireld	54
	"And, keep the Peace, to pick up Fees:	571	Death of Swift	450

		PAGE	TITLE	LINE
FEES	(CONTINUED)			
A hundred Fees last Easter Term.		604	Beasts Confess	86
The Lawyer's Fees, the Statesman's Bribes.		922	Riddle 7	20
FEET				
Waiting for Orders at his Feet,		7	Ode to King	40
And drop his laurel at Apollo's feet.		49	To Congreve	186
Beat not the dirty paths where vulgar feet have trod,		49	To Congreve	205
With inoffensive feet o'er standing corn;		54	Temple Ill	118
The Fly'r, altho't had leaden Feet,		93	Bauc & Phil 1	131
The Flyer, tho't had Leaden Feet,		113	Bauc & Phil 2	71
Shake it down to the Feet,		246	Irish-Feast	50
You see the Crows feet round his Eyes.		291	Prog Marriage	50
And seems all Feet, and Hands, and Eyes.		322	First of April	38
To scatter Roses at her Feet;		379	Apology Lady C	112
Crouding the roads with naked feet.		401	Window Inns 5	D 10
Shall at their snowy feet lay down:		465	Birthday Song	168
His Hand, his Neck, his Mouth, and Feet		586	Strephon Chloe	77
Expiring Shepherds at their Feet;		590	Strephon Chloe	200
Which fell in Clouds beneath his Feet)		625	Scandal Poem 2	68
Lay humbly at your Monarch's Feet;		647	On Poetry	224
So, Poets lose their Feet by Time,		756	Stel B-day '24	3
Who drives her cares to hands and feet:		761	Bec's B-Day	18
Her hands and feet conduct her head,		761	Bec's B-Day	22
Her hands may meddle, feet may wander,		761	Bec's B-Day	25
If your Stockings were off, you cou'd show cloven Feet.		805	Irish Bishops	52
Without using my feet;		852	Lady's Lament	42
FEIGN				
Like Bacchus Thou, as Poets feign,		109	V's House	119
FEIGN'D				
Who said, his Gravity was feign'd:		603	Beasts Confess	50
FEIGNED				
With artful Sigh and feigned Groan,		208	Fable Bitches	14
FEILDING				
That Feilding leaves him far behind.		654	On Poetry	396
FEIN				
As Poets fein; but where's the Moral?		254	Bubble	94
FELE				
And from the Tree where Blosums fele,		103	Merlin	13
FELL				
It fell, and broke with its own Weight		26	Ode to Temple	4
Hence Mankind fell, and here must rise again.		32	Ode to Temple	177
So next Morning we told Whittle, and he fell a Swearing		70	Mrs Harris Pet	24
One rose a Star, the other fell		100	Elegy Patrige	67
It fell into its proper Station.		127	Little House	12
Into the World Corinna fell,		149	Corinna	3
Here fell a Pension, there a Place:		158	Fable of Midas	76
How, by Brave Hands, the Royal Traytor fell;		162	Toland's Invit	10
Where hundreds and where thousands fell,		252	Bubble	51
There is a Gulph where thousands fell,		256	Bubble	137
Recover Strength whene'er he fell,		257	Bubble	182
The wond'rous Arch behind you fell,		326	Pethox	95
Affirm'd the Moon was sick, and fell		354	Simile Silver	7
The Hangman for Pardon fell down on his Knee;		399	Tom Clinch	13
Where many a bold Advent'rer fell.		413	Desire Possess	44
To taint the Parts from whence they fell.		529	Lady's Dres Rm	112
And you who never fell--thro' Pride;		579	Day Judgement	14
Which fell in Clouds beneath his Feet)		625	Scandal Poem 2	68
Then fell to talking of the Weather;		696	Cadenus Vaness	325
And fell into their usual Chat,		698	Cadenus Vaness	375
She fell into her former Scene,		747	Stel Distress	55
She fell into her former Scene.		751	Stel Wood-Park	71
Britain, by thee we fell, ungrateful Isle!		791	St. Pat's Well	25
As antient Judas by Transgression fell,		806	Judas	17
Friend Rundall fell with grievous bump,		822	Epigr Rundle	1
Into Spleen and Vapours fell;		834	Legion Club	122
"May that fell Dean, by whose Command		850	Old Thorn	73
It so fell out, that cautious Harry		878	Robbin & Harry	17
That graceful on his Shoulders fell)		903	Death Daphne	26
FELLING				
Which is; Our Trees are felling;		443	Ballyspellin	87
FELLOW				
The gray old Fellow Poet Joe		126	Little House	3
Poh! Fellow keep not such a Pother		128	Little House	59
His Fellow Pick-Purse, watching for a job,		364	On Dreams	25
Should some obscure inferior fellow		464	Birthday Song	141
No matter what a Fellow sees.		699	Cadenus Vaness	403
Hail fellow, well met,		856	Lady's Lament	165
To a quarrelsome Fellow, cries, Let us be Friends.		968	Letter Sherid	28
But I think it base in you to send a poor Fellow		1014	Swift to Sheri	10
FELLOW-CREATURE				
Has made a Rat our Fellow-Creature.		812	Bro Protestant	34
FELLOW-FEELING				
A Fellow-feeling of my Pain.		546	Life of Swift	46
FELLOW-SUFFERERS				
Both Right and Left, as Fellow-sufferers.		367	Answer Delaney	40
FELLOWS				
You Fellows, what a Noise you keep!		90	Bauc & Phil 1	28
"To make a pair of Jolly Fellows,		181	Horace 2	43
Shrewd Fellows, and arch Wags, a Tribe		216	To Mr. Delany	53
When Daughters run away with Fellows)		223	Prog of Love	48
To me the good Fellows apply for Relief,		263	Apollo	9

	PAGE	TITLE	LINE
FELLOWS (CONTINUED)			
Fellows of modest Worth and Parts, ...	314	To Ford	81
Among a Crew of royst'ring Fellows	352	Wood Ironmongr	5
Admires how Girls can talk with Fellows, ...	449	Modern Lady	163
Their Fellows, turn their Dread and Hate.	493	Panegyr Swift	14
"The Fellows had a wretched Taste;	714	Cadenus Vaness	869
That Stella loves to talk with Fellows	735	Stel B-day '20	44
Where petulant, conceited Fellows	777	Mullinix Tim	135
The Fellows learn to know their Distance.	888	Panegyr Dean	56
Three fellows with whips, and the Dean holds the string.	1027	Sheri Circles	20
FELLS			
Now a new Misfortune fells, ...	′834	Legion Club	117
FELON			
Like the Felon from the Jailer, ...	574	Helter Skelter	36
FELONIOUS			
That some Verses were writ with felonious Intent, . .	264	Apollo	47
FELT			
And the young Muse's early favour felt;	49	To Congreve	192
To t' other Ear I felt it coming on, ...	367	Answer Delaney	43
All this I have felt, ...	402	Window Inns 8	D 11
In those who never Pity felt;	561	Death of Swift	216
Felt no Necessities of Nature.	584	Strephon Chloe	20
Her Hands the softest ever felt, ...	585	Strephon Chloe	27
Cadenus felt within him rise	706	Cadenus Vaness	624
From thee no Mark of Slavery they felt, ...	791	St. Pat's Well	21
The <Dean> hath felt their Stings before;	798	Traulus 1	85
"Nor, when I felt the dreadful Blow, ...	850	Old Thorn	69
How have I felt my Spirits rais'd, ...	887	Panegyr Dean	13
He felt about his Heart a Damp, ...	905	Death Daphne	97
Poor Miss Dingley oft hath felt its Bills.	941	Letter	24
FEMAL			
Undone at Play, the Femal Troops	254	Bubble	89
And is not femal clattring worse, ...	617	Scandal Poem 1	9
Compare us then to femal race!	620	Scandal Poem 1	95
FEMALE			
Platonick Champions, gain'd without one Female Wile, .	24	Ode Athenian	252
A female pow'r, loose-govern'd thoughts create; . . .	54	Temple Ill	104
Or more employ the Female Sex?	65	Problem	2
And how his Wife that Female Pedant, ...	282	Journal	85
Can in her Female Clubs dispute	416	Woman's Mind	29
For all the Female Commonweal:	444	Modern Lady	4
The Annals of a Female Day.	445	Modern Lady	35
Flew hov'ring o'er each Female Head.	449	Modern Lady	135
But see, the Female Club disbands, ...	451	Modern Lady	196
That fill a Female Gamester's Pate?	451	Modern Lady	225
To have both male & female Race, ...	460	Birthday Song	6
To all the Charms of Female Kind;	530	Lady's Dres Rm	130
Fain would I think, our Female Friend sincere, . . .	531	To Mr. Gay	3
Did Female Virtue e'er so high ascend, ...	531	To Mr. Gay	5
My female Friends, whose tender Hearts	562	Death of Swift	225
A Deed unknown to Female Race, ...	595	Cassinus Peter	69
The blackest of all Female Deeds.	596	Cassinus Peter	106
To Fondness for the Female Kind;	603	Beasts Confess	64
Then, is not Female Clatter worse, ...	624	Scandal Poem 2	9
Compare Us then to Female Race!	626	Scandal Poem 2	93
Do I, like the Female Tribe, ...	632	Epistle Lady	77
And Female Pleasures be to read and write.	662	Upon Ladies	8
From all the thousand Female Toys, ...	688	Cadenus Vaness	47
The Current of a Female Mind	688	Cadenus Vaness	57
Those Beauties in a Female Mind, ...	691	Cadenus Vaness	143
So lovely in the Female Kind, ...	691	Cadenus Vaness	165
To Female Breasts, except her own;	695	Cadenus Vaness	273
To scorn the Art of Female Tears.	705	Cadenus Vaness	597
He molded it with Female Clay:	726	To Stella	90
Female Vices most, or Male, ...	801	Traulus 2	54
Though by the Female Side you proudly bring, . . .	826	Noisy Tom	9
Indulgent you to Female Kind, ...	887	Panegyr Dean	7
What Pride a Female Heart enflames!	905	Death Daphne	89
Of Spleen you cure the Female Sex.	919	Riddle 5	18
Condemn'd by Female Hands to dye;	923	Riddle 7	62
FEMALES			
To Shops in Crouds the dagged Females fly, ...	138	City Shower	33
Say, foolish Females, Old and Blind, ...	449	Modern Lady	150
Bring all the Females of the Skyes:	465	Birthday Song	154
Like Females o'er their Morning Tea.	501	Doctor Delaney	50
What various Ways our Females take, ...	592	Strephon Chloe	267
Among your Females make Inquiries;	625	Scandal Poem 2	71
FEMALS			
'Twixt earthly Femals and the Moon	226	Prog of Beauty	9
If Clouds were but like Femals fickle;	618	Scandal Poem 1	42
Among your femals make inquiryes:	619	Scandal Poem 1	73
FEMININE			
When late a Feminine Magician, ...	354	Simile Silver	19
FENC'D			
But fenc'd his Head with his own Bays	119	Apollo Outwit	7
FENCE			
The Proverb says; No Fence against a Flayl. . . .	521	Stephen Duck	2
You rhyme, as folks fence, in tierce and cart.	979	Dean to Tho: S	20
FENCES			
In Whims, Parterres, Canals and Fences:	477	Epist on Epist	62

FENCING
While Harry's fencing up his ditches. . . . . . . 878 Robbin & Harry 28
FENS
"Far to the Land of Slaves and Fens; . . . . . . 568 Death of Swift 396
FERKS
And if provok'd, he soundly ferks his . . . . 463 Birthday Song 99
FERMENT
Whether all Passions, when in Ferment, ... 66 Problem 15
For should this Ferment last too long, ... 731 Stella, Poems 132
FERMENTING
Which thus fermenting, by Degrees . . . . 731 Stella, Poems 129
<FERNS>
For who wou'd have <Ferns> without a Commendum? . . . 518 Dean Hang Rape 39
FERRY
Our Boat is now sail'd to the Stygian Ferry, ... 285 Elegy Boat 23
Charon in him will ferry Souls to Hell; . . . . 285 Elegy Boat 25
Beck'ning to waft me o'er the Ferry. . . . . 596 Cassinus Peter 84
FERULA
But Ferula and Birch; . . . . 1005 Sheridan's Sub 28
FERVENT
Apply'd to Jove with fervent Prayer; . . . . . . 383 Manly Virtue 3
FETCH
Then stept aside to fetch 'em Drink, ... 112 Bauc & Phil 2 29
And vows she scarce can fetch her Breath. . . . . . 417 Woman's Mind 46
FETTER
The chains which fetter free-born minds, ... 490 Dialogue 32
FETTERS
Have him confin'd in Iron Fetters; . . . . . . 373 Letter D. S-y 74
Or wou'd they but in Fetters bind, ... 515 Answer Fable 85
FEVER   SEE FEAVER
Heart-sick of a high fever and consuming atrophy; . . . 42 Ode Sancroft 252
FEVERS
Of Doctors, Fevers, Plagues, and Pills. . . . . . 903 Death Daphne 6
FEW
Alas, the occasions are so few: . . . . 38 Ode Sancroft 112
"Since thy few ill-presented graces seem . . . . . . 55 Temple Ill 145
Than a few Scrubby Trees before. . . . . 108 V's House 84
Some few Days after Harley spies . . . . 172 Horace 1, 7 57
This Tale may be apply'd in few Words . . . . . . 189 Faggot 15
Few Hints from you will set him right, ... 218 To Mr. Delany 97
Few Bankers will to Heav'n be Mounters: . . . . . . 241 Run Bankers 58
To write a few Verses on you as my Friend; . . . . . 265 Apollo 74
Which few had learnt enough to prize, ... 384 Manly Virtue 29
Quoth King Robin, our Ribbands I see are too few . . 389 Order of Bath 1
Dick left a Pattern few will copy after, ... 430 Dicky Dolly 16
A few Grisetts . . . . 441 Ballyspellin 53
An Hundred Thousand were too few! . . . . . . 449 Modern Lady 139
Advances few, enriches none, ... 495 Panegyr Swift 73
On such a Point few Words are best, ... 526 Lady's Dres Rm 15
"A few, in Verse; but most, in Prose---. . . . . . 550 Life of Swift 182
"His Friendship there to few confin'd, ... 570 Death of Swift 435
Yet he was seconded by few: . . . . 605 Beasts Confess 148
And my few Perfections stifle. . . . . 631 Epistle Lady 62
How few have reach'd the low Sublime? . . . . . . 652 On Poetry 370
This I may boast, which few e'er cou'd, ... 669 Epig Carthy 15 D 1
I chopp'd so fast, that few there minded. . . . . . 675 Curate's Compl 12
The few soft Moments they can spare, ... 687 Cadenus Vaness 42
And 'twas observ'd, there were but few . . . . . . 689 Cadenus Vaness 101
To copy her, few Nymphs aspir'd; . . . . 700 Cadenus Vaness 440
Support a few remaining Days; . . . . 764 Stel B-day '26 12
But where his deep law is, few mortals yet know: . . . 815 Yahoo's 12
His guests are few, his visits rare, ... 901 Dean's Reasons 85
My Words are few, but spoke with Sense: . . . . . 917 Riddle 4 5
And few know how and where you fix. . . . . . . 919 Riddle 5 28
For, few, a chosen few, must know, ... 922 Riddle 7 49
For, few, a chosen few, must know, ... 922 Riddle 7 49
But very few are found to enter; . . . . 928 Riddle 12 D 4
Few are made, but Numbers lost. . . . . 934 Riddle 22 D 6
And I wish your few friends, when they next see your car 976 Dean to Sherid 29
go,
FEWDS
Forget their Fewds, and join to save their Wigs, . . 138 City Shower 42
FEWER
Her Virtues fewer Swains admir'd: . . . . 700 Cadenus Vaness 441
FICKLE
If Clouds were but like Femals fickle; . . . . . . 618 Scandal Poem 1 42
FICKLENESS
For Fickleness how durst you blame us? . . . . . 618 Scandal Poem 1 39
For Fickleness how durst you blame us? . . . . . 624 Scandal Poem 2 37
FICTION
It would Burn a whole Forest; nor was it a Fiction; . 334 Serious Poem 20
For, though the Muse delights in Fiction, ... 503 Doctor Delaney 105
Like the Fiction of Poets concerning the Wind, . . . 927 Riddle 11 D 3
FICTIONS
And all the Fictions they pursue . . . . 729 Stella, Poems 59
FIDDLE
Nor slowly move your Fiddle stick, ... 958 Cantata
For myself, I protest, I care not a fiddle . . . . 976 Dean to Sherid 13
FIDDLES
Nor yet, because he sweetly fiddles; . . . . . . 432 Answer Paulus 19
With trumpets and fiddles and organs and singing . . . 522 St. Cecilia's 7

PAGE TITLE LINE

```
                                                        PAGE    TITLE             LINE
FIDGE
   You Wrigle, Fidge, and make a Rout     . . . . . . .  777 Mullinix Tim        139
   The Twist, the Squeeze, the Rump, the Fidge an'all,   .  783 Tim and Fables     17
FIDLER
   A Fidler may a Fortune get;     . . . . . . . . .     710 Cadenus Vaness       737
FIDLERS
   With Bands of Fidlers to extend his Treyn.    . . . .  678 Dean and Duke        8
FIE    SEE FYE
   "Fie, Madam, leave these little Arts.     . . . . . .  452 Modern Lady         257
   . . . Fie Mr. Sheridan, 'tis a Shame   . . . . . .     985 Mary to Sher         5
FIELD
   For strait I saw the Field maintain'd,    . . . . . .    8 Ode to King         61
   And all those flying Deaths that aim'd from him from the   8 Ode to King       67
      Field,
   As from the Womb of Earth a field of Corn.    . . . .   20 Ode Athenian        131
   And still the bloody Field frequent,    . . . . . .    324 Pethox              17
   Where Wisdom stands to keep the Field,    . . . . . .  340 Arch-Bish Dub       23
   A Fish, a Fowl, a Cloud, a Field,     . . . . . . .    927 Riddle 10        D  15
   Yet I know a young Rogue, that thrown flat on the Field  967 Letter Sherid    15
FIELD-HOUSE
   A Long-ear'd Beast, and a Field-house for Cattle,    .  942 Probatur Alit      1
FIELDS
   Sing of thy Vales, sing of thy Woods, sing of thy      31 Ode to Temple      138
      Fields;
   Have in More Fields their Stations fix,    . . . . .   101 Elegy Patrige      100
   In painted Cloth we look for Fields,    . . . . . .    122 Empty'ng Town       11
   Enamell'd Fields, and verdant Trees;    . . . . . .    251 Bubble              28
   From Fields Elyzian, fabling Esop;    . . . . . . .    607 Beasts Confess     200
   Shall to Elysian fields invite her,    . . . . . .    762 Bec's B-Day         59
   To seek, in deserts, Fields Elysian?    . . . . . .    899 Dean's Reasons      16
FIENDS
   Has given thee up a dwelling-place to fiends?    . . .   37 Ode Sancroft       95
FIERCE
   Harry look'd fierce, and shook his ragged Mane:    . .  168 Peace Dunkirk      17
   By fierce Encounters made in Wars;    . . . . . . .    324 Pethox              14
   When once the fierce pursuing Gaul    . . . . . . .    340 Arch-Bish Dub       17
   "From the first fierce cockaded Centry,    . . . . .   380 Apology Lady C     153
   In Senates bold, and fierce in War,    . . . . . .    398 Earl of P-b-w       32
   The rumbling words march fierce along,    . . . . .   461 Birthday Song       45
   And paint a Coward fierce in arms.    . . . . . . .    464 Birthday Song      122
   Aspiring, factious, fierce and loud    . . . . . .    503 Doctor Delaney      87
   Behold a Foe more fierce than all the rest:    . . .   538 Mr. Pulteney       32
   Fierce in Tongue, in Heart a Coward:    . . . . . .    799 Traulus 2          12
   And fierce against the Whigs harangu'd?    . . . . .   884 Rev Market-Hill     39
   That looks hideous, fierce, and frightful;    . . . .  907 Daphne             45
   Fierce Aeolus in Tempests roars.    . . . . . . .     924 Riddle 7           88
FIERCELY
   Where Whig and Tory fiercely fight    . . . . . . .    421 Ireld               5
   But, Chloe drove him fiercely back.    . . . . . .    588 Strephon Chloe     150
FIERCEST
   For, could you think? the fiercest foes you dread,    . .   46 To Congreve     95
   Which fiercest Foes, cou'd break by no Means.    . . .  1021 Nim-Dan-Dean 1  D  32
FIERY
   Long dreaded for his Bloody Tail and Fiery Beard,    .   10 Ode to King       131
   Thus censure seems that fiery froth which breeds    . .   45 To Congreve       69
   Leaving the fiery red behind,    . . . . . . . .      227 Prog of Beauty      35
   With Brass two fiery Steeds he shod,    . . . . . .    352 Wood Ironmongr      11
   His carrot locks, and fiery nose;    . . . . . . .    621 Scandal Poem 1     136
   His brazen Face, and fiery Nose:    . . . . . . .     627 Scandal Poem 2     140
FIERY-RED
   Should with Poker fiery-red    . . . . . . . . .      830 Legion Club         25
FIFT
   To raise a Roof with Act the Fift.    . . . . . .     108 V's House           92
FIFTEEN
   Tho', like a virgin of fifteen,    . . . . . . . .    178 To Lord Harley      69
   What tho for fifteen years and more    . . . . . .    462 Birthday Song       49
   And hold for ever at fifteen.    . . . . . . . .      736 Stel B-day '20      54
   He Twenty one, and She Fifteen:    . . . . . . .      757 Stel B-day '24      18
   Just Fifteen, coming Summer's Grass:    . . . . . .    760 Receipt Youth       40
   To Fifteen Hundred Pounds a Year,    . . . . . .      884 Rev Market-Hill     38
FIFTH
   If the fifth you shou'd pursue    . . . . . . . .     931 Riddle 17        D   7
FIFTHLY
   And, Fifthly; you know whom I mean,    . . . . . .    348 Whitshed Motto      19
FIFTY
   Their ups and downs, with fifty Stories    . . . . .   181 Horace 2, 1        18
   With fifty Yards of Crape, shall sweep the Stage.    . .  275 Epilogue         26
   That a Pack of sly Knaves should get fifty per Cent,    .  288 Bank Down       52
   Aetatis suae fifty two    . . . . . . . . . . .       289 Prog Marriage       1
   Is fifty, if he be a Day,    . . . . . . . . .        291 Prog Marriage      48
   'Tis Fifty round Millions of Love, and a Mending.    .  337 Serious Poem      106
   For Fifty Times its Worth, to Carteret.    . . . . .   349 Whitshed Motto      22
   Sell them to Curl for Fifty Pound,    . . . . . .     395 Grub-Street         19
   For, he'll be Prince these fifty Years.    . . . . .   410 Dial Rich Marb      78
   As loud as fifty mustard bowls;    . . . . . . .      461 Birthday Song       40
   Your Heroine hardly fifty odd is.    . . . . . . .    465 Birthday Song      162
   Himself, as rich as fifty Jews,    . . . . . . .      481 Libel on D- D-      39
   He told them fifty Times before.    . . . . . . .     556 Death of Swift      90
   A Sprig of Bays in Fifty Years:    . . . . . . .      640 On Poetry           8
   'Tis fifty thousand Times below it.    . . . . . .    657 On Poetry          480
   At Fifty six, if this be true,    . . . . . . . .     757 Stel B-day '24      23
```

```
FIFTY          (CONTINUED)                              PAGE    TITLE              LINE
    But, some have kiss't the Gospel Fifty Times,    . . .   806 Judas               11
    His fund may last to five and fifty. . . . . . . .       878 Robbin & Harry      16
    At fifty two, when he grew loving, . . . . . . . .       879 Robbin & Harry      46
FIG
    A fig too for <Hanmer> . . . . . . . . . .              186 Scriblerus 4       D  7
    A Fig for Lechmere, King, and Hambden.   . . . . .      191 Faggot              48
    With the Scrap of a Sole, and a Fig for the Bank.    .  287 Bank Down           30
    A Fig for Partridges and Quails . . . . . . .          733 Verses Vanessa      27
    Give me but a Barrack, a Fig for the Clergy. . . .     873 Grand Question     190
    I tell you I'd not give a fig for your wine; . . . .   979 Dean to Tho: S      30
FIGHT
    He sought Her out in Fight, . . . . . . . . . .          7 Ode to King        36
    I see the Fatal Fight begin; . . . . . . . . . .         7 Ode to King        47
    And (I believe) began himself the Fight,  . . . .        8 Ode to King        60
    Th' Impulse, the Fight, th' Event, were wholly Thine.   12 Ode to William   D 36
    And tho' he oft renew'd the Fight,  . . . . . . .       30 Ode to Temple     129
    While, wise Men think they ought to fight . . . . .    189 Faggot             21
    For People to fight . . . . . . . . . . .             246 Irish-Feast        59
    How fam'd thy Conduct in the Fight, . . . . . . .      326 Pethox             85
    Where Whig and Tory fiercely fight . . . . . . .       421 Ireld              5
    They only fight for fighting sake, . . . . . . .       421 Ireld              8
    Had I a Heart to fight, . . . . . . . . .             426 Five Ladies        37
    To fight our cause before the judge: . . . . . .       435 Answer Paulus      88
    But we like Antaeus and Hercules fight, . . . . .     968 Letter Sherid      29
    But why shou'd we fight thus, my partner so dear,  .  979 Dean to Tho: S     33
FIGHTING
    They only fight for fighting sake, . . . . . . . .     421 Ireld              8
FIGHTS
    Who, led by Folly, fights with Nature;  . . . . .     641 On Poetry          20
FIGURE
    Resum'd the Figure of a Stick.  . . . . . .           132 Magician's Rod     14
    The Bridegroom dresst, to make a Figure,  . . . .     290 Prog Marriage      21
    A Skeleton in outward Figure,  . . . . . . .          398 Earl of P-b-w      25
    "Or shape the Yews to Antick Figure.   . . . . . .    476 Epist on Epist     58
    Observe our Figure in a Morning; . . . . . . . .      625 Scandal Poem 2     43
    I Shou'd make a Figure scurvy, . . . . . . .          637 Epistle Lady      219
    To represent in figure just . . . . . . . . .        659 On Poetry        D 410
    Than Titles, Figure, Shape, and Dress;  . . . . .     697 Cadenus Vaness    341
    The figure of Toope and Snake.  . . . . . . .         780 Mullinix Tim      226
    His own sweet Figure with the Print,  . . . . . .     783 Tim and Fables     15
    In his Dress and Figure seen: . . . . . . . .        800 Traulus 2          32
    In what Figure can a Bard dress . . . . . . .         834 Legion Club       139
    What a figure she made . . . . . . . .              855 Lady's Lament     121
    Who makes the best figure,  . . . . . . . .          856 Lady's Lament     169
FIGURES
    Is at a loss for Figures to express . . . . . . .      21 Ode Athenian      172
    The figures all inverted shew, . . . . . . . .        35 Ode Sancroft       31
    And will neither regard my Figures nor Tropes;   . .  145 New Song           52
    All Figures Heav'n or Earth can yield,   . . . . .    927 Riddle 10        D 16
FILIAL
    Whose filial Piety excels . . . . . . . .            482 Libel on D- D-     77
    Their filial Piety forgot,  . . . . . . . .          652 On Poetry         359
FILINGS
    From broken scraps and filings of your brain. . . .    45 To Congreve        58
FILL
    His empty Paunch that he might fill,  . . . . . .     156 Fable of Midas      9
    And fill <Jack Smith> with Hopes to keep his Place;  . 163 Toland's Invit     20
    Nor with Bankrupts fill Gazetts, . . . . . . .        169 Peace Dunkirk      29
    But true English Men will fill,  . . . . . . .        169 Peace Dunkirk      38
    Of Size that might a Pulpit fill,  . . . . . . .      170 Horace 1, 7        11
    And Broth enough to fill her Paps,  . . . . . .       208 Fable Bitches      20
    Fill the Bowl up again,  . . . . . . . .             246 Irish-Feast        54
    Then fill the Vessel to the Brim, . . . . . . .       251 Bubble             10
    Both Pitch and Brimstone to fill up his Flaws;   . .  285 Elegy Boat         28
    The whole Nations Pockets with Money will fill.  . .  287 Bank Down          13
    That fill a Female Gamester's Pate?  . . . . . .      451 Modern Lady       225
    Tho Caroline may fill your gaps . . . . . . .         467 Birthday Song     239
    Your honest Care may fill; perhaps enlarge.  . . .    533 To Mr. Gay         46
    To raise his Post, or fill his Coffers,  . . . . .    549 Life of Swift     139
    That serve to fill her hollow Jaws. . . . . . .       582 Young Nymph        18
    Press down the Lumps, the Hollows fill,  . . . . .    582 Young Nymph        26
    The fittest Man to fill a Place: . . . . . . .        606 Beasts Confess    156
    And, with Credit fill my Station; . . . . . . .       630 Epistle Lady       24
    If I can but fill my Nitch, . . . . . . . .          635 Epistle Lady      171
    In gaping Lines to fill a Chink; . . . . . . .        645 On Poetry         168
    With Savage-Pictures fill their Gaps;  . . . . .      645 On Poetry         178
    Alone to fill up all her Wit; . . . . . . . .        709 Cadenus Vaness    709
    To fill a Place, for want of better; . . . . . .      756 Stel B-day '24     10
    And fill your Veins with sprightly Blood: . . . .     759 Receipt Youth      32
    Fill ev'ry Pipe, each Motion guide.  . . . . . .      798 Traulus 1          74
    To fill the Earth, and Air, and Skies: . . . . .      924 Riddle 7           92
    If I can fill my Thimble,  . . . . . . . .          1015 Swift to Sheri     52
    Where less than forty, fill a Quart. . . . . . .    1022 Nim-Dan-Dean 1   D 52
FILL'D
    Here, a Page fill'd with Billet Doux; . . . . . .      60 Lady Tablebook     13
    He found it was strangely fill'd in the Middle.  .     77 Lady B- B-          9
    For he ne're could have fill'd it so well of himself. .77 Lady B- B-         20
    And having fill'd it to the Brink,  . . . . . .        92 Bauc & Phil 1      71
    Fill'd a large Jug up to the Brink; . . . . . .       112 Bauc & Phil 2      30
    Found his Head fill'd with many a System,  . . . .    115 Bauc & Phil 2     135
```

FILL'D   (CONTINUED)   PAGE   TITLE   LINE
    And <Harley> fill'd the Commons Chair)   . . . . .   180 Horace 2, 1   10
    Fill'd with the choicest common-places, ...   223 Prog of Love   49
    But fill'd with Admiration, stands, ...   227 Prog of Beauty   50
    With Water fill'd he could no longer float, ...   284 Elegy Boat   9
    A Post so fill'd, on Nature's Laws entrenches;   . . .   285 Elegy Boat   11
    With ev'ry Vice hath fill'd the Nation;   . . . . . .   392 Young's Satire   36
    When Pope has fill'd the Margins round, ...   395 Grub-Street   17
    Are fill'd with Hints, and interlin'd, ...   406 Swift to Pope   11
    Where after he has fill'd his chest, ...   456 Dean Smedley   37
    Fill'd up with Dirt so closely fixt, ...   526 Lady's Dres Rm   21
    Some fill'd with Washes, some with Paste, ...   526 Lady's Dres Rm   34
    And Shock her Tresses fill'd with Fleas.   . . . . .   583 Young Nymph   64
    While these Reflections fill'd his Head, ...   587 Strephon Chloe   111
    And as he fill'd the reeking Vase, ...   590 Strephon Chloe   191
    Have my Soul entirely fill'd: . . . .   630 Epistle Lady   32
    Fill'd with Disdain, with Rage inflam'd, ...   699 Cadenus Vaness   404
    Vanessa, fill'd with just Disdain, ...   705 Cadenus Vaness   594
    Behold a cage with sparrows fill'd, ...   753 Gift for Bec   11
    Fill'd with Falshood, Spleen and Pride, ...   799 Traulus 2   8
    Comes fill'd with Rev'rence and Devotion.)   . . . .   893 Panegyr Dean   212
    With Snuff was fill'd his Ebon Box, ...   904 Death Daphne   39
FILLD
    The Earth would very soon be filld: . . . .   79 Vanbrug House   20
FILLED
    A Minister so filled with Zeal, ...   391 Young's Satire   3
FILLETS
    In Fillets roll'd, or cut in Pieces, ...   344 Prometheus   7
    In Fillets of Brass roll'd up to his Ears: . . . .   350 Wood Insect   8
    And, over these Fillets he wisely has thrown,   . . .   351 Wood Insect   9
FILLING
    You shall observe as you are filling   . . . .   251 Bubble   11
    (Tho' meerly writ at first for filling   . . . . . .   648 On Poetry   253
FILLS
    From her red Locks her Mouth with Venom fills: . . .   195 Author Himself   55
    Her ev'ning Work so fills her Head;   . . . .   291 Prog Marriage   58
    Mordanto fills the Trump of Fame, ...   397 Earl of P-b-w   1
    It fills my Heart with Woe, ...   426 Five Ladies   21
    Whose rank Imagination fills, ...   592 Strephon Chloe   279
    Their Minds so plentifully fills, ...   735 Stel B-day '20   27
    A nauseous Brood, that fills your Senate Walls,   . .   792 St. Pat's Well   57
FILTH
    Receive the Filth which he ejects, ...   85 Salamander   63
    Filth of all Hues and Odours seem to tell   . . . .   139 City Shower   55
    Collects the City Filth in search of Gold.   . . . .   364 On Dreams   22
    But all the Filth both Spiss, and Sparse   . . . . .   497 Panegyr Swift   120
    Condensed Filth in e'ry Part, ...   787 Clad in Brown   15
    He wildly flings his Filth about, ...   796 Traulus 1   26
    Tho' born of human Filth and Sweat, it   . . . . .   812 Bro Protestant   37
FILTHY
    Beside, it Spues a filthy Froth, ...   84 Salamander   51
    Before I'd touch his filthy Dross, than is Clandalkin   343 Upon His Grace   38
        Spire.
    Hard by a filthy Bason stands, ...   526 Lady's Dres Rm   37
    You want a Hand to clear a filthy Sink;   . . . . .   535 To Mr. Gay   127
    While all the gross and filthy last.   . . . .   591 Strephon Chloe   234
    Your Goddess grown a filthy Mate.   . . . .   591 Strephon Chloe   244
    Assume the Shapes of filthy Brutes.   . . . .   670 Epig Carthy 19 D   2
    To Liffy's filthy side in Dublin;   . . . .   744 Stel Distress   D   4
    For why should you stay in that filthy hole, . . .   1022 Nim-Dan-Dean 2 D   3
FINCH
    But repeats the same Note a whole Day, like a Finch.   .   143 New Song   8
    Now Finch alarms the Lords; he hears for certain,   . .   194 Author Himself   37
    Finch, fam'd for tedious Elocution, proves   . . . .   194 Author Himself   39
    The Finch, the Linnet and the Thrush, ...   594 Cassinus Peter   31
FIND
    Yet wheresoe're you look you'll always find . . . . .   18 Ode Athenian   74
    Which yet whoe're examines right will find . . . . . .   21 Ode Athenian   184
    And when you find out these, believe true Fame is there. .   21 Ode Athenian   186
    We find in you at last united grown. . . . .   28 Ode to Temple   61
    How shall we find Thee then in dark disputes?   . . .   34 Ode Sancroft   10
    And God himself has said, He shall not find it here.   .   35 Ode Sancroft   20
    But when they find it turn with the first blast of fate,   37 Ode Sancroft   76
    But find some new address, some fresh deceit,   . . .   44 To Congreve   17
    And not the meanest coxcomb you can find, ...   48 To Congreve   157
    You find, to be the fashionable wit;   . . . . . .   48 To Congreve   162
    Nor shall the bubbl'd virtuoso find   . . . . . .   50 To Congreve   211
    In this descending sheet you'll haply find   . . . .   50 To Congreve   231
    Can scarce th' impression of his foot-steps find;   . . .   54 Temple Ill   116
    Nor thought to find so great a Peer   . . . . . .   62 Discovery   3
    You find his Passion by his Scent.   . . . .   66 Problem   18
    My Lord to find out who must deal   . . . .   74 Game Traffick   1
    To find the Doctor out.   . . . .   74 Game Traffick   4
    Because he could find no Word to come pat in.   . . .   76 Lady B- B-   4
    Now Poets find this Art is lost, ...   79 Vanbrug House   13
    Are these too low?--then find out grander, ...   83 Salamander   21
    She soon would find, the same Effects, ...   85 Salamander   64
    We might expect to find next Year   . . . .   88 Hist V's House   47
    And if we find our Vittels fail   . . . .   92 Bauc & Phil 1   65
    You'll find has so much Virtue in't, ...   101 Elegy Patrige   112
    He hop'd to find some lucky Hour, ...   121 Apollo Outwit   45

FIND	(CONTINUED)	PAGE	TITLE	LINE
Returning Home at Night, you'll find the Sink	. . .	137	City Shower	5
He must sink down, or find Up-holders	. . . . .	160	Atlas	22
Then where, said I, shall Harley find	. . . . . .	177	To Lord Harley	33
Descended from her sphere to find	. . . . . .	179	To Lord Harley	79
And be assur'd, the Court will find him	. . . . .	190	Faggot	43
"Direct my Plow to find a Treasure:"	.	199	Horace 2, 6	D
And find his Honour in a Pound,	. . . .	200	Horace 2, 6	27
To find an easy Place to lay-her.	. . . .	207	Fable Bitches	6
"Stay till my tender Cubs can find,	. . . . . .	208	Fable Bitches	33
He'll find the Secret out from thence	. . . . .	219	To Mr. Delany	107
But find her where so'er she fled,	. . . .	223	Prog of Love	37
Old Madam who went up to find	. . . .	223	Prog of Love	43
When first she taught them where to find	. . . .	227	Prog of Beauty	59
Then like Pactolus we should find	. . . . . .	255	Bubble	111
And after many Days thou'lt find it,	. . . . . .	255	Bubble	134
The Nation too too late will find	. . . .	259	Bubble	217
I study'd a Fortnight, before I could find,	. . . .	265	Apollo	75
And the Gifts I bestow'd her, will find her a Lover,	.	266	Apollo	107
Yet, when his Sand was out, we find at last,	. . .	285	Elegy Boat	21
His Debtors they wonder'd to find him so frank,	.	288	Bank Down	44
Will hardly find his Wife in Shoes.	. . . . . .	292	Prog Marriage	70
You find His Rev'rence past his Prime,	. . . .	293	Prog Marriage	104
For Husbands past their Youth to find;	. . . . .	293	Prog Marriage	116
"Turn him adrift, and you shall find	. . . . .	304	Storm	33
"You'll find him swear, blaspheme, and damn,	. . .	305	Storm	57
Find you but the Fryer, and I'll find the Wood.	. .	334	Serious Poem	24
Find you but the Fryer, and I'll find the Wood.	. .	334	Serious Poem	24
What Stuff he is made on you quickly may find,	.	336	Serious Poem	77
However, if Criticks find Fault with the Phrase,	.	337	Serious Poem	101
I hope he will find that no Love is lost.	.	337	Serious Poem	108
He gave it me, and ever since I find I thrive amain.	.	342	Upon His Grace	30
I find you bear a good Report, and are an honest Man.	.	342	Upon His Grace	34
And ev'ry one begins to find,	. . . . .	345	Prometheus	19
Where, if we find his Liver grows,	. . . . .	347	Prometheus	75
The Statesman rakes the Town to find a Plot,	. .	364	On Dreams	19
That, where we find the Members twain,	. . . . .	366	Answer Delaney	10
And you shall find by this Device,	. . . . .	366	Answer Delaney	17
But, Yet, you'll find by what will follow,	. . . . .	371	Letter D. S-y	9
To find her in a country scene,	. . . .	401	Window Inns 5	D 6
You'll find it soon by woful Proof,	. . . . . .	408	Dial Rich Marb	11
Pray God they now may find as true.	. . . . .	408	Dial Rich Marb	22
We soon shall find him full of Spleen,	. . . . .	410	Dial Rich Marb	57
Nor, will you find your Fortune sink,	. . . . .	414	Censure	25
O yes! If any Man can find	. . . . . .	417	Woman's Mind	57
She draws up Card by Card, to find	. . . . .	452	Modern Lady	228
Find him a Kingdom out to conquer;	. . . .	466	Birthday Song	204
To find out proper words for Harmony:	. . . . . .	467	Birthday Song	218
Find Rivers with harmonious names,	. . . . . .	468	Birthday Song	241
The Task is Arduous, Patrons find,	. . . . . .	475	Epist on Epist	21
They find an idle Hour to Prate.	. . . .	480	Libel on D- D-	28
To find a Verse in Virgil Spurious;	. . . . .	483	Libel on D- D-	100
They'll find his Life, and Acts, and Freedom,	. .	494	Panegyr Swift	52
You soon a Remedy may find;	. . . . . .	501	Doctor Delaney	44
Then, if you find the Terms too hard,	. . . . .	501	Doctor Delaney	53
If Scandal did not find them Payment.	. . . . .	502	Doctor Delaney	74
To find the Grub-Street Poet's Nest,	. . . . .	504	Doctor Delaney	144
Find the last Garrat where they lay,	. . . . .	505	Doctor Delaney	149
We all can find out whom he means,	. . . . . .	514	Answer Fable	65
He still was comforted to find	. . . . .	528	Lady's Dres Rm	87
But there, alas! he could no Safety find;	. . .	538	Mr. Pulteney	21
Yet, by Experience, oft we find,	. . . .	546	Life of Swift	47
"And Preachers, find the better quarter,	. . . . .	549	Life of Swift	166
If in a Battle you should find,	. . . . . .	554	Death of Swift	21
Will try to find their private Ends:	. . . . .	556	Death of Swift	76
You plainly find it in his Face:	. . . .	556	Death of Swift	82
He takes an Hour to find a Rhime:	. . . .	556	Death of Swift	100
"Sir you may find them in Duck-lane:	. . . . .	563	Death of Swift	258
"I find you're but a Stranger here.	. . . . . .	563	Death of Swift	262
Whose Favour she is sure to find,	. . . .	583	Young Nymph	55
What endless Raptures must he find!	. . . . .	587	Strephon Chloe	96
Find great Society in Stinking.	. . . . . .	590	Strephon Chloe	210
Than from Experience find too late	. . . .	591	Strephon Chloe	243
(Muse, find me Names to fix my Metre,	. . . .	594	Cassinus Peter	5
As much as now we find in Men.	. . . . .	601	Beasts Confess	4
Apply the Tale, and you shall find	. . . . .	603	Beasts Confess	73
You find it in his meagre Looks:	. . . . .	604	Beasts Confess	106
Though hard to find in ev'ry Case	. . . . . .	606	Beasts Confess	155
No diff'rence could he find between	. . . . .	619	Scandal Poem 1	57
You find, the Gods in Homer dwell	. . . . .	620	Scandal Poem 1	99
No Diff'rence could he find between	. . . . .	625	Scandal Poem 2	53
You find, the Gods in Homer dwell,	. . . . .	626	Scandal Poem 2	97
And since we find, you walk a-foot	. . . . . .	627	Scandal Poem 2	133
Ev'ry Error I could find	. . . .	629	Epistle Lady	3
And I find it answers right:	. . . .	634	Epistle Lady	145
Thus, I find it by Experiment,	. . . .	636	Epistle Lady	207
Brutes find out where their Talents lie:	. . . .	640	On Poetry	13
But Man we find the only Creature,	. . . . .	641	On Poetry	19
Consult yourself, and if you find	. . . . .	642	On Poetry	77
And if you find the general Vogue	. . . .	644	On Poetry	119
Or where we find your Fury set	. . . .	645	On Poetry	157

```
FIND           (CONTINUED)                              PAGE    TITLE            LINE

    His Merits ballanc'd you shall find,  . . . . . . .   654  On Poetry         395
    For in those Ages Kings we find,   . . . . . . . .    658  On Poetry       D 410
    To find a King in all ye Crew,   . . . . . . . .      659  On Poetry       D 410
    Each proper Quality to find  . . . . . . .            659  On Poetry       D 410
    So two poor Knaves, who find their Credit fail,       668  Epig Carthy 8   D   3
    I find that I have gain'd her Heart:   . . . . . .     679  From Catullus       4
    Since Men alledge they ne'er can find  . . . . .      691  Cadenus Vaness    142
    But in the Poets we may find,  . . . . . .            694  Cadenus Vaness    256
    I find, says he, she wants a Doctor,  . . . . . .     702  Cadenus Vaness    498
    Imaginary Charms can find,  . . . . . . .             703  Cadenus Vaness    526
    Cadenus was amaz'd to find  . . . . . . .             704  Cadenus Vaness    562
    Or, as Philosophers, who find  . . . . . . .          709  Cadenus Vaness    722
    "Who never cou'd one Lover find.  . . . . . . .       714  Cadenus Vaness    867
    To find her a great Witt, but the Dean a small Man.   716  Answer Rebus       14
    And yet a Fault we often find  . . . . . . . . .      731  Stella, Poems     103
    Yet when I find your Passions rise,  . . . . . . .    731  Stella, Poems     113
    By Time subsiding, you may find  . . . . . . .        731  Stella, Poems     133
    And if they find the Chambers neat,  . . . . . .      734  Stel B-day '20      3
    This drew us in at first to find  . . . . . . .       735  Stel B-day '20     19
    You'll find it soon if Fate consents;  . . . . .      743  Stel B-day 22      71
    Don Carlos now began to find  . . . . . . .           746  Stel Distress      31
    Don Carlos now began to find  . . . . . . .           750  Stel Wood-Park     23
    When, among scholars, can we find  . . . . . .        755  Stella '23         19
    Whatever base returns you find  . . . . . . .         755  Stella '23         29
    To find this Damn'd Pretender out,  . . . . . .       774  Mullinix Tim       26
    And now you find you fought for nothing.  . . . . .   774  Mullinix Tim       38
    You'll find it well prepar'd to take  . . . . . .     780  Mullinix Tim      225
    But then, consider Dick, you'l find  . . . . . .      788  Dick's Variety     13
    Directing ev'ry Vice we find  . . . . . . .           798  Traulus 1          75
    I wish I could find him out one more commodious.  . . . 803 Irish Bishops     12
    Tho' they gallop so fast; on the Road you may find 'em, 804 Irish Bishops     23
    His Brethren find to take Offence;  . . . . . .       820  Dr. Rundle         12
    Where to find on this Side Hell?  . . . . . . .       837  Legion Club       184
    Pray be patient, you shall find  . . . . . . .        839  Legion Club       235
    Find out, if you can,  . . . . . . . . .              856  Lady's Lament     167
    Yet I find, a New-Years Lace  . . . . . . .           863  To Janus           27
    The <Dean> and Spaniard find it too well;  . . . . .  883  Rev Market-Hill    10
    Consulting with myself, I find,  . . . . . . .        899  Dean's Reasons      3
    I am, as now too late I find,  . . . . . . .          899  Dean's Reasons     11
    But find the Rhime, and you're the Man.  . . . . .    912  Aenigma            14
    Superior none on Earth I find;  . . . . . . .         917  Riddle 3            3
    Because they find their Pockets pick't.  . . . . .    917  Riddle 3           16
    In me, Detractors seek to find  . . . . . . .         918  Riddle 4           23
    I cannot find I lose or win,  . . . . . . .           918  Riddle 4           36
    Here, with an easy Search we find  . . . . . .        921  Riddle 7           15
    And find a resting Place at last.  . . . . . .        923  Riddle 7           78
    Can find an Entrance when they please.  . . . . .     928  Riddle 12       D  12
    Yet all the World can't find me out,  . . . . . .     929  Riddle 14       D   2
    They never yet cou'd find my Measure.  . . . . . .    929  Riddle 14       D   4
    One of us you'll find in Jet,  . . . . . . .          930  Riddle 17       D   4
    All of us in one you'll find,  . . . . . . .          931  Riddle 18       D   1
    But you may find the same in me.  . . . . . .         932  Riddle 19       D   6
    But, Men find it to their Cost,  . . . . . . .        934  Riddle 22       D   5
    Your Argument's weak, and so you will find,  . . . .  947  Mrs. Houghton       5
    But keep a good tongue, or you'll find, to your smart, 976 Dean to Sherid    35
    Nay, hector and swagger, you'll still find me stanch, 979 Dean to Tho: S     13
    Now you write from your cellar,--I find out your art,  979 Dean to Tho: S     19
    Only one scurvy thing I find,  . . . . . . .          983  Sher, A Goose      13
    And now whereby I find you would fain make an Excuse,  985 Mary to Sher       11
    You will not find it in the Vatican.  . . . . . .     988  Letter Dr Sh-n     10
    And now I find my Muse but ill able  . . . . . .      989  Letter Dr Sh-n     30
    But when I would find Rhime for Rochfort,  . . . .    993  On Picture          7
    But pleas'd to find you do relent and cry on.  . . .  1002 Reply by Dean      15
    The Critic to his Cost will find,  . . . . . . .      1021 Nim-Dan-Dean 1  D 33
    And, before we find either, our noddles turn round. . 1026 Sheri Circles       8
    You hop'd to find many (for that was your Cue) sick;  1029 Dr. Helsham        23
    You may find they are all, by their yellow pale Hue, sick 1030 Dr. Helsham   27
    Nor can I the least Diff'rence find,  . . . . . .     1033 Ans to Crown        5
FINDERS   SEE GOLD-FINDERS
FINDING
    Finding the Mitre almost grown  . . . . . . .          40  Ode Sancroft      187
    Finding her ripen'd Time was come,  . . . . . .       207  Fable Bitches       3
    But finding the Statue to make no Complaint,  . . . . 336  Serious Poem       73
    In finding Ways and Means, and stopping Gaps:  . . .  535  To Mr. Gay        122
    But, finding all his Artifices vain;  . . . . . .     538  Mr. Pulteney       19
    "But, finding vain was all his Care,  . . . . . .     567  Death of Swift    369
    But finding me so dull and dry since,  . . . . . .    741  Stel B-day 22      27
    He's still finding fault,  . . . . . . . .            853  Lady's Lament      61
    Never finding full Repast,  . . . . . . . .           930  Riddle 16       D   3
FINDS
    Is all the poor content delusion finds.--  . . . . .   55  Temple Ill        150
    When first he finds himself awake  . . . . . . .      241  Run Bankers        54
    And when he has got it, finds Ways to conceal it;  . . 265 Apollo            60
    She combs his Head, and finds him Horn.  . . . . .    328  Epigram 2           4
    And finds out Pallas in the Skies:  . . . . . . .     692  Cadenus Vaness    187
    Approaching, finds it hard to part  . . . . . . .     922  Riddle 7           35
    Here, oft the Curious Trav'ller finds,  . . . . .     923  Riddle 7           79
FINE
    On Sundays to be fine in,  . . . . . . . .             75  Game Traffick      22
    And for themselves fine Garments make.  . . . . . .    79  Vanbrug House      34
```

FINE	(CONTINUED)		PAGE	TITLE	LINE
Then said; my House is grown so Fine,	. . . . .	.	115	Bauc & Phil 2	113
The <Duke> shew'd me all his fine House; and the <Duchess>			143	New Song	15
Methinks I see thee, spruce and fine,	. . . . .	.	182	Horace 2, 1	73
Of all the fine Things he keeps in the Dark,		. . .	265	Apollo	61
'Twill gain her Love to make her fine?	. . . .	.	292	Prog Marriage	72
As fine as Hampton-court at least.	. . . . . .		314	To Ford	90
To cut down fine Wood is a very bad Thing,	. . .		334	Serious Poem	13
Fine Words; I wonder where you stole 'um.	. . . .		348	Whitshed Motto	2
I'm sure a Man of your fine Sense	. . . . .	.	361	Grace's Answer	21
Lay all my fine Plantations waste,	. . . . . .		410	Dial Rich Marb	69
To think such Ladies fine,	. . . .		426	Five Ladies	22
Fine Ladyes never do't	. . . .		428	Beau's Reply	6
Fine Ladyes when they write,	. . . .		429	Beau's Reply	9
How cou'd so fine a Taste dispense	. . . . .		475	Epist on Epist	15
And with Bridles fine and gay,	. . . .		573	Helter Skelter	13
For fine Ideas vanish fast,	. . . .		591	Strephon Chloe	233
So fine a Coach along the Strand;	. . . . . .		598	Problem Solved	14
With haughty spouse in vesture fine,	. . . .		677	Parson's Case	33
Last Night was so extremely fine,	. . . . . .		696	Cadenus Vaness	326
Which others for Mantuas wou'd think fine enough;	. .		716	Answer Rebus	16
Her fine Panegyricks are quite out of Season,	. . .		716	Answer Rebus	21
As fine as Dawbers Hands can make it	. . . . .		734	Stel B-day '20	11
To see that ev'ry Glass was fine.	. . . . . .		746	Stel Distress	22
To see that ev'ry Glass was fine.	. . . . . .		750	Stel Wood-Park	20
Your Table neat, your Linnen fine;	. . . . . .		752	Stel Wood-Park	83
A fine occupation	. . . .		857	Lady's Lament	181
Pull down the fine briers,	. . . .		857	Lady's Lament	197
Sir Arthur the Malster! how fine it will sound?	. . .		868	Grand Question	45
'Twas a sad rainy Night--but the Morning is fine--	. .		869	Grand Question	74
With the fine flaming Sword that he holds in his Hand;			870	Grand Question	96
To peep at the Captain, in all his fine Clo'es:	. . .		872	Grand Question	138
Dear Madam, be sure he's a fine spoken Man,	. . . .		872	Grand Question	139
So fine a Gown, a Band so clean,	. . . . . .		889	Panegyr Dean	77
Admire to hear me speak so fine.	. . . . . .		891	Panegyr Dean	136
Fine as a Col'nel of the Guards,	. . . . . .		904	Death Daphne	55
Then, since I shew as fine a Face,	. . . . . .		932	Riddle 19	D 11
Lies in the Lap of Ladies fine.	. . . .		942	Probatur Alit	14
Come buy my fine Wares,	. . . .		951	Apples	1
Come, buy my fine Oranges, Sauce for your Veal,	. . .		953	Oranges	1
In Weather fine I nothing spend,	. . . . . .		954	Authors Living	7
Till she lent you her help, you were in a fine twitter:	.		977	Dean to Sherid	39
Were in evry ones Judgment exceedingly fine,	. . . .		1017	Swift Ans Sher	2
To make a Work compleatly fine,	. . . .		1022	Nim-Dan-Dean 1	D 45
FINE-LINEN					
Pray what is a Man? he's a fine-Linen Searcher.	. .		972	S-'s Ans Sh-d	10
FINELY					
Tho' the Thought be Apollo's, 'tis finely express'd;	.		266	Apollo	91
Stay--But let me see how finely will it Sound,	. . .		274	Epilogue	5
Can finely counterfeit a Fright;	. . . . . .		416	Woman's Mind	34
"Then, here's a Letter finely penn'd	. . . . . .		563	Death of Swift	273
FINER					
A finer House ten times than this,	. . . . . .		128	Little House	62
Great Folks are of a finer Mold;	. . . . . .		949	Epigr Scolding	1
FINEST					
The finest Miss	. . . .		442	Ballyspellin	77
In School to hear the finest Boy.	. . . . .		704	Cadenus Vaness	553
FINGER					
And with his Finger on his Thumb,	. . . . . .		281	Journal	83
Your Head, or Tooth, or Finger ake:	. . . . .		414	Censure	22
Nor lend a finger to the labour,	. . . . . .		434	Answer Paulus	64
Puts in his Finger and his Thumb,	. . . . .		797	Traulus 1	51
Upon thy Hand his Finger laid;	. . . . . .		905	Death Daphne	94
He has more Goodnes in his little Finger,	. . .		985	Mary to Sher	9
FINGERS					
Nam'd ev'ry player on his fingers ends,	. . . . .		47	To Congreve	139
That Virtue in the Fingers ends:	. . . . . .		157	Fable of Midas	44
Then on her fingers Ends she counts	. . . . .		291	Prog Marriage	45
Fancies his Fingers in the Cully's Fob.	. . . .		364	On Dreams	26
Whose fingers itch for poets ears;	. . . . . .		487	Irish-Club	6
And have them at your Fingers Ends.	. . . . .		648	On Poetry	246
My fingers, prolix,	. . . .		853	Lady's Lament	77
The Bottle, till your Fingers ake:	. . . . . .		892	Panegyr Dean	180
Or, with his fingers, beat the drum;	. . . . .		900	Dean's Reasons	48
Thy num'rous Fingers know their Way,	. . . . .		919	Riddle 5	11
FINISH'D					
Has finish'd its short Race of Chance,	. . . .		10	Ode to King	137
Return'd a finish'd spark this summer down,	. . . .		47	To Congreve	119
To form a just and finish'd piece,	. . . . . .		460	Birthday Song	1
Your Poem finish'd, next your Care	. . . . .		643	On Poetry	91
When Death had finish'd Blackmore's Reign,	. . . .		653	On Poetry	374
Vanessa finish'd the Dispute,	. . . .		708	Cadenus Vaness	675
FINISHING					
Thus finishing his grand Survey,	. . . . . .		529	Lady's Dres Rm	115
FINS					
And dip their Fins again to fly.	. . . . . .		254	Bubble	88
FIR'D					
And proud Roxana fir'd with jealous Rage,	. . . .		275	Epilogue	25
And fir'd with Indignation vows,	. . . . . .		694	Cadenus Vaness	253

```
FIRE   SEE A-FIRE                                          PAGE  TITLE            LINE
    Like Love, wrapt up in Fire;         . . . . . . . . .    8  Ode to King        69
    Just as the Sun puts out a Fire;     . . . . . . . .      9  Ode to King       114
    Would vanish in a Pyramid of Fire.   . . . . . . .       22  Ode Athenian      196
    To fann th' unhappy Fire:            . . . . . . . .     23  Ode Athenian      241
    Like Lambent Fire the Lightning plays;  . . . . . .     29  Ode to Temple      88
    In vain to quench this foolish Fire I try   . . . . .   33  Ode to Temple     206
    Each line shall stab, shall blast, like daggers and like 37  Ode Sancroft      91
        fire;
    First chid the zeal as unpoetic fire,  . . . . . . .    44  To Congreve        25
    Love's Fire, it seems, like inward Heat,  . . . . .     65  Problem            7
    My Lord, on Fire amidst the Dames,   . . . . . . .      66  Problem           39
    For something that will conquer Fire,  . . . . . .      83  Salamander        18
    So cold, that put it in the Fire,    . . . . . . . .    84  Salamander        49
    Bade Goody Baucis mend the Fire      . . . . . . .      91  Bauc & Phil 1     56
    Bid Goody Baucis mend the Fire;      . . . . . . .     111  Bauc & Phil 2     24
    And, since he could not spend his Fire,  . . . . .     172  Horace 1, 7       45
    But since thou'rt got into the Fire,  . . . . . . .    181  Horace 2, 1       33
    Must feel thy Eloquence and Fire,    . . . . . . .     182  Horace 2, 1       61
    Who full of Humor, Fire and Wit,     . . . . . . .     218  To Mr. Delany     91
    And Wool it is greasy, and quickly takes Fire.  . .    237  Excellent Song    21
    To climb to our Region, and thence to steal Fire;  .   266  Apollo            96
    My Lord and Dean, the Fire forsake;  . . . . . . .     279  Journal           31
    Whether thy Temper, full of Fire,    . . . . . . . .   323  Pethox            5
    (Rais'd high like some celestial Fire  . . . . . . .   385  Manly Virtue      53
    Still seen o'r'e many an Alehouse fire.  . . . . .     461  Birthday Song     38
    I threw the Volume in the Fire:      . . . . . . . .   470  Burning Poem      12
    From Paean's Fire to Party Zeal;     . . . . . . .     481  Libel on D- D-    44
    To snuff the Lights, and stir the Fire,  . . . . .     483  Libel on D- D-   107
    Your fancy with their pleasing fire, . . . . . . .     489  Dialogue          20
    That, missing Fire, or missing Aim   . . . . . . .     500  Doctor Delaney    23
    And toast them at the clearest Fire; . . . . . . .     529  Lady's Dres Rm   102
    With Paean's purest Fire his Favourites glow;  . .     532  To Mr. Gay        23
    His Fire is out, his Wit decay'd,    . . . . . . .     556  Death of Swift   101
    Her Tea-Kettle's on, and her Smock at the Fire:  .     580  Psyche            2
    'Tis thou must fan the Lover's Fire; . . . . . . .     590  Strephon Chloe   222
    And thus a mutual gentle Fire,       . . . . . . .     593  Strephon Chloe   313
    Our kindly help his fire assuages.   . . . . . . . .   618  Scandal Poem 1    34
    Our kindly Help his Fire asswages;   . . . . . . . .   624  Scandal Poem 2    32
    All my Fire would fall in Scraps,    . . . . . . . .   638  Epistle Lady     263
    Hath blasted with poetick Fire.      . . . . . . . .   641  On Poetry         42
    A Fire celestial, chaste, refin'd,   . . . . . . . .   687  Cadenus Vaness    29
    But Women now feel no such Fire,     . . . . . . . .   687  Cadenus Vaness    35
    The Fire that forms a manly Soul;    . . . . . . .     726  To Stella         88
    And may compare to Aetna's Fire,     . . . . . . .     731  Stella, Poems    105
    Or if these Lines your Anger fire,   . . . . . . .     732  Stella, Poems    141
    The God of Winds and God of Fire     . . . . . . .     743  Stel B-day 22     63
    Shew Fire and Faggot in the Tail on't?  . . . . .      774  Mullinix Tim      20
    "That she condemn'd me to the Fire,  . . . . . . .     850  Old Thorn         62
    To cut his hedges down for fire;     . . . . . . .     902  Dean's Reasons   106
    If I refus'd to lend them Fire.      . . . . . . . .   916  Riddle 2          14
    --Let indignation fire my strains,   . . . . . . . .   950  Upstart        D  21
    Fire will not roast, nor Water boil. . . . . . . .    1035  To Quilca         8
FIRE-WORKS
    Like fire-works, she can burn in water.  . . . . .     618  Scandal Poem 1    38
    Like Fire-works, she can burn in Water.  . . . . .     624  Scandal Poem 2    36
FIRES
    When Sol pursues her with his fires. . . . . . . .     178  To Lord Harley    72
    "If long confin'd to Fires and Screens,  . . . . .     380  Apology Lady C   137
    One Blast will put out all his Fires. . . . . . .      588  Strephon Chloe   136
    And thorns, to make fires;           . . . . . . .     857  Lady's Lament    198
FIRM
    Believe it firm, because perhaps the day is mild and still  37  Ode Sancroft   75
    Yet to firm heavenly minds,          . . . . . . . .    41  Ode Sancroft     205
    And stood up firm for Right Divine:  . . . . . . .     115  Bauc & Phil 2    134
    So soft, and yet so firm a mind?     . . . . . . .     755  Stella '23        20
    We'll make it firm with Beef and Claret.  . . . . .    760  Receipt Youth     56
    Always firm in his Vocation,         . . . . . . .     836  Legion Club      171
    And has taken just now a firm resolution  . . . . .   1027  Sheri Circles     23
FIRMLY
    Not firmly join'd to keep their Ground,  . . . . .     189  Faggot            19
    My Love to Sheelah is more firmly fixt  . . . . .      880  Pastoral Dial     9
    And yet I firmly stand my Ground:    . . . . . . .     926  Riddle 9          8
    How firmly these Indentures bind,    . . . . . . .    1021  Nim-Dan-Dean 1 D  34
FIRMNESS
    His Firmness to the publick Good, as one that knows it  341  Upon His Grace    9
        Swore,
    Her firmness who could e'er have known,  . . . . .     755  Stella '23        25
FIRST
    First, in the mighty List of Fame,   . . . . . . .       7  Ode to King       34
    Took its first Growth and Birth      . . . . . . .      10  Ode to King      126
    To preserve Conquests, as at first to gain:  . . .      12  Ode to William D  26
    As when the Deluge first began to fall,  . . . . .      16  Ode Athenian      1
    That Mountain which was highest first of all  . . .     16  Ode Athenian      5
    At the first Ebb of Noise and Fears, . . . . . . .      16  Ode Athenian     14
    And pluckt a Laurel branch (for Laurel was the first    16  Ode Athenian     27
        that grew,
    The first of Plants after the Thunder, Storm, and Rain  16  Ode Athenian     28
    In me, who am of the first Sect of these,  . . . .      18  Ode Athenian     76
    Their first and chiefest force       . . . . . . .      19  Ode Athenian    113
    Rather forgive what my first Transport said,  . . .     23  Ode Athenian    244
```

FIRST   (CONTINUED)   PAGE   TITLE   LINE

Till its first Emperor rebellious Man   . . . . . .   26 Ode to Temple   2
Who learnt himself that Heresy first   . . . . . .   28 Ode to Temple   53
And kindled first with Indolence and Ease, ...   33 Ode to Temple   203
First of God's darling attributes, ...   34 Ode Sancroft   5
But when they find it turn with the first blast of fate,   37 Ode Sancroft   76
Or melts by the first show'r away.   . . . . .   39 Ode Sancroft   142
Why should the first be ruin'd and laid waste, ...   40 Ode Sancroft   178
By prostituting her they first debauch.   . . . .   44 To Congreve   22
First chid the zeal as unpoetic fire, ...   44 To Congreve   25
Since thus I wander from my first intent, ...   49 To Congreve   201
O'er the glad scene whence first she rose a bride: . .   51 Temple Ill   12
There first the visionary sound was heard, ...   51 Temple Ill   15
Might seem, when first she rais'd her eyes to mine. . .   52 Temple Ill   30
Lost youth, she cry'd, since first I met thee here! . .   52 Temple Ill   32
When wise Ld <Berkeley> first came here, ...   62 Discovery   1
Watching the first unsav'ry Wind, ...   66 Problem   37
Just at the Breech it flashes first: . . . . . .   66 Problem   46
He <farted> first, and then he spoke.   . . . . . .   66 Problem   48
But the first Knave does seldom fail   . . . . .   74 Game Traffick   3
First then, our Author has defin'd   . . . . .   83 Salamander   29
Just in the Place where first it grew, ...   87 Hist V's House   32
And first the Prologue built a Wall   . . . . .   108 V's House   81
From which Ingredients, First the dext'rous Boy   . .   118 Biddy Floyd   5
Of Modest Poets thou be first, ... 121 Apollo Outwit   57
Which, from the fatal Day when first   . . . . .   134 Magician's Rod   67
While the first drizzling Show'r is born aslope, . . .   137 City Shower   18
At first a gentle Creature;   . . . . . . 153 Widow and Cat   D   2
Pray leave me where you found me first.   . . . . .   175 Horace 1, 7   138
The Goddess made advances first, ... 178 To Lord Harley   67
When first I knew thee, Dick, thou wert   . . . .   182 Horace 2, 1   49
"Consider, 'tis my first Request.--   . . . . .   201 Horace 2, 6   57
Since Harley bid me first attend, ... 201 Horace 2, 6   65
Applying what we first Invent: . . . . . . 215 To Mr. Delany   18
His Genius first found out the Rule   . . . . .   216 To Mr. Delany   35
Who first Run one another down, ... 217 To Mr. Delany   55
When first she ventur'd out with him.   . . . .   224 Prog of Love   82
When first for her he quitted Peg.   . . . . .   224 Prog of Love   84
When first Diana leaves her Bed   . . . . . . 226 Prog of Beauty   1
When first she taught them where to find   . . . .   227 Prog of Beauty   59
When first he finds himself awake   . . . . .   241 Run Bankers   54
But first by your Favour, ... 245 Irish-Feast   26
For, first, I have often by Chymists been told, . . .   263 Apollo   3
Pallas first taught us Poetry and Spinning;   . . . .   276 Epilogue   38
Begin, my Muse, first from our Bowers, ...   278 Journal   7
They first invite the Cyprian Queen, ...   290 Prog Marriage   7
First get a licence, then produce our ware: . . . .   308 Billet Players   36
The Nymphs with whom You first began   . . . . .   311 To Ford   17
When Fortune hither drove me first;   . . . . .   313 To Ford   52
First, Love In A Tub: 'Squire Wood has in Store   . .   337 Serious Poem   95
Then in his First Love why should he be crost? . . .   337 Serious Poem   107
For fear the First Drop might as well be his Last: .   337 Serious Poem   112
First with the brazen Cannons Roar.   . . . . .   338 Wood's Brass   2
. . . 'tis he that first appears, ... 341 Upon His Grace   3
When first the 'Squire, and Tinker Wood   . . . .   344 Prometheus   1
First; how to swagger in a Court;   . . . . . . 348 Whitshed Motto   12
The first is an Insect they call a Wood-Louse, . . .   350 Wood Insect   3
Mistook at first for Thunder-Bolts;   . . . . .   353 Wood Ironmongr   34
When first of Griz, you Grafton reated   . . . .   372 Letter D. S-y   14
Since Cindercola, first you Courted   . . . . .   372 Letter D. S-y   45
But first resolv'd, to shew his Taste   . . . . .   378 Apology Lady C   97
"From the first fierce cockaded Centry, ...   380 Apology Lady C   153
And, kept at first an equal Pace: . . . . . . 412 Desire Possess   12
Doll dying first, Dick grew Mellancholly, ...   430 Dicky Dolly   2
The first vex'd him much, but the other vex'd most. .   430 Dicky Dolly   9
By Phoebus First produc'd to light: . . . . .   433 Answer Paulus   27
Since first I learn'd to tune a String.   . . . .   445 Modern Lady   12
'Twas you engag'd me first to write, ...   445 Modern Lady   22
You pawn'd to him?-- "First shew him up.   . . . .   446 Modern Lady   59
But first, the Winner must invite   . . . . .   453 Modern Lady   288
The first perhaps may once an Age   . . . . .   462 Birthday Song   67
First, of the first. To vouch your Lyes   . . . .   465 Birthday Song   153
First, of the first. To vouch your Lyes   . . . .   465 Birthday Song   153
Who think your Muse must first aspire;   . . . .   475 Epist on Epist   23
When at a Skirmish first he hears   . . . . .   500 Doctor Delaney   3
When first in Print, you see him dread   . . . .   500 Doctor Delaney   .13
First learn the Science to be dull, ...   503 Doctor Delaney   111
Themselves would be the first to tell, ...   505 Doctor Delaney   157
You see him first the Peacock bring, ...   513 Answer Fable   15
And first a dirty Smock appear'd, ... 526 Lady's Dres Rm   11
And first: To make my Observation right, ...   532 To Mr. Gay   31
He fled to Earth, but first it cost him dear;   . . .   538 Mr. Pulteney   35
"We first consult our private Ends, ...   553 Death of Swift   8
Refin'd it first, and shew'd its Use.   . . . . .   555 Death of Swift   58
I tamely can endure the first, ... 555 Death of Swift   69
"And often told you so at first:"   . . . . .   557 Death of Swift   130
"He gave it all:--But first he dy'd.   . . . . .   558 Death of Swift   160
Pulls off with Care, and first displays 'em,   . . .   581 Young Nymph   15
Resolv'd to make his first Attack: . . . . .   588 Strephon Chloe   149
This Point must needs be settled first;   . . . . .   589 Strephon Chloe   165
Those Arts by which at first they gain it, ...   592 Strephon Chloe   265

FIRST	(CONTINUED)	PAGE	TITLE	LINE
No Heir, upon his first Appearance,	. . . .	598	Problem Solved	11
And, first excus'd his youthful Face;	. . . . . .	603	Beasts Confess	60
But first with Care imploy your Thoughts,	. . . . .	645	On Poetry	149
(Tho' meerly writ at first for filling	. . . . .	648	On Poetry	253
Since first the Court allow'd them Food.	. . . . .	652	On Poetry	366
Expire, when first expos'd to open Air.	. . . . . .	667	Epig Carthy 5	D 6
First to a dapper Clerk she beckon'd,	. . . . . .	690	Cadenus Vaness	108
And then stood where it first begun.	. . . .	690	Cadenus Vaness	125
When first this grand Debate arose	. . . .	690	Cadenus Vaness	130
First issu'd from Perfumers Shops	. . . .	696	Cadenus Vaness	316
As came into her Fancy first,	. . . .	698	Cadenus Vaness	382
And first he modestly conjectures	. . . .	704	Cadenus Vaness	568
His Doctrines when she first imbib'd;	. . . . . .	708	Cadenus Vaness	679
Attends us first, and leaves us last:	. . . . . .	708	Cadenus Vaness	685
Pallas had cross'd her first Intent,	. . . .	712	Cadenus Vaness	833
The First but a Rebus, the Last but a Dean.	. . . .	716	Answer Rebus	6
Since first I saw Thee at Sixteen	. . . .	721	Stel B-Day '18	5
When first for thee my Harp I strung:	. . . . . .	728	Stella, Poems	10
As Tradesmen shew their Trash at first:)	. . . . .	728	Stella, Poems	22
First, to adorn your Person well,	. . . .	732	Verses Vanessa	3
All Travellers at first incline	. . . .	734	Stel B-day '20	1
This drew us in at first to find	. . . .	735	Stel B-day '20	19
First, nine Ways looking, let her stand	. . . . . .	743	Stel B-day 22	53
(But first let Robert on his Knees	. . . .	743	Stel B-day 22	77
First, this large parcel brings you tidings	. . . . .	753	Gift for Bec	5
First to be fondled, then be kill'd.	. . . .	753	Gift for Bec	12
Stella long dead, but first the Dean,	. . . . . .	762	Bec's B-Day	46
Preserving what it first creates)	. . . .	764	Stel B-day '26	42
And first his Bum you see him Clap,	. . . . . .	776	Mullinix Tim	109
When first in publick we appear,	. . . .	780	Mullinix Tim	229
My very Face, at first I knew it,	. . . .	783	Tim and Fables	23
First taught thee human Knowledge and divine;	. . . .	791	St. Pat's Well	28
The last Invaders trampling on the first:	. . . . .	793	St. Pat's Well	84
So, Traulus when he first harangu'd,	. . . .	797	Traulus 1	41
How shou'd we rejoice, if, like Judas the first,	. . .	805	Irish Bishops	39
First take you our Tyths, and give us your Lands.	. .	805	Irish Bishops	62
Each modern Judas perish like the first;	. . . . .	806	Judas	21
First in every wicked Jobb,	. . . .	836	Legion Club	174
First issuing, struck the Murd'rer's Ears;	. . . . .	850	Old Thorn	54
First, let me suppose I make it a Malt-House:	. . . .	867	Grand Question	7
And, because he's their Betters, you carve for him first,	.	871	Grand Question	133
"The first Man I robb'd was a Parson by <God>.	. . .	873	Grand Question	170
Then, least upon our first Attack	. . . .	885	Rev Market-Hill	59
But, let us on our first Assault	. . . .	885	Rev Market-Hill	83
To sing your Praise. And, first as <Dean>:	. . . .	888	Panegyr Dean	44
While nothing comes but Froth at first,	. . . . .	893	Panegyr Dean	193
First, lolling Sloth in Woollen Cap,	. . . . . .	895	Panegyr Dean	273
First milk his cows, and after, pound:	. . . . . .	902	Dean's Reasons	104
And freely made the first Advance;	. . . .	905	Death Daphne	68
At first did put me to a stand;	. . . .	912	Aenigma Expl	D 2
I last get up, am first a-bed;	. . . .	918	Riddle 4	40
First I shew you but a Quarter,	. . . .	927	Riddle 10	D 3
The Bridegroom's first Gift to their Mates,	. . . . .	942	Probatur Alit	4
Yet still are no wiser than we were at first.	. . . .	967	Letter Sherid	4
I'll first take you up, and then take you down:	. . .	968	Letter Sherid	32
What Name for a Maid, was the first Man's Damnation?	. .	973	S-'s Ans Sh-d	12
Proceed to Tragicks, first Euripides	. . . . . .	988	Letter Dr Sh-n	17
She mended at first, but now she's anew sick.	. . . .	1029	Dr. Helsham	6
FIRST-FRUITS				
First-Fruits and Tenths, and Chapter-Treats,	. . .	174	Horace 1, 7	103
FISH	**SEE FYSHE, DOG-FISH**			
Which oft he us'd to fish withal:	. . . .	133	Magician's Rod	44
He caught his Fish, and sav'd his Bait.	. . . . .	134	Magician's Rod	48
And here they fish for Gold and drown:	. . . . . .	256	Bubble	148
You get all the Fish, and others get none,	. . . . .	287	Bank Down	7
All Christian vittals stink of fish	. . . . . .	420	Holyhead	3
For the more Livings you can fish up,	. . . . . .	478	Epist on Epist	101
And keep on Fish perpetual Lent.	. . . .	689	Cadenus Vaness	90
Drains all thy Lakes of Fish, of Fruits thy Land.	. .	793	St. Pat's Well	64
A Fish, a Fowl, a Cloud, a Field,	. . . .	927	Riddle 10	D 15
The dullest Beast and Fish for Lent	. . . . . .	941	Letter	39
FISH-PONDS				
And drain the Fish-ponds; while your Master doats;	. .	534	To Mr. Gay	90
FISH-WIVES				
Than Fish-Wives o'er a Cup of Gin:	. . . . . .	450	Modern Lady	181
FISHES				
As Fishes on each other prey	. . . .	253	Bubble	65
So Fishes rising from the Main	. . . .	254	Bubble	85
Where Fishes on each other prey;	. . . .	824	Printer Newgat	4
FIST				
By the meer Virtue of his Fist:	. . . .	132	Magician's Rod	12
It has; but then it greas'd his fist.	. . . . . .	432	Answer Paulus	10
Against the Grain, a <Monarch's> Fist?	. . . . .	884	Rev Market-Hill	34
His griesly Monarch's sooty Fist,	. . . .	903	Death Daphne	4
FIT				
And well, methinks, does this allusion fit	. . . . .	45	To Congreve	75
Van, (for 'tis fit the Reader know it)	. . . . .	80	Vanbrug House	59
Bestow'd as Hi'roglyphicks fit	. . . .	83	Salamander	11
He at fit Periods walks through Aries,	. . . . .	98	Elegy Patrige	15
<Van> (for 'tis fit the Reader know it)	. . . . .	107	V's House	33

FIT	(CONTINUED)	PAGE	TITLE	LINE
Fit to Invade or prop the Skies.	. . . .	107	V's House	50
Not fit to live on Christian Ground,	. . . . . .	112	Bauc & Phil 2	47
Tell me, Perfidious! Was it fit	. . . . .	154	Widow and Cat	D 38
But is for State-Affairs as fit,	. . . .	183	Horace 2, 1	105
Another in a surly Fit,	. . . .	200	Horace 2, 6	35
Three Gifts for Conversation fit	. . . .	215	To Mr. Delany	13
Not allways judges what is fit;	. . . .	218	To Mr. Delany	92
He might be thought an Object fit for Alms.	. . . . .	234	Elegy on Demar	12
We Phoebus think fit to proceed to his Sentence;	. . .	266	Apollo	94
Like'd ev'ry Thing - - - at least thought fit	. . .	379	Apology Lady C	119
Men of more Wit than Money, our Pensions will fit	. .	389	Order of Bath	7
Been for your Conversation fit,	. . . .	406	Swift to Pope	23
To fit them to his Vulgar Taste;	. . . . . .	410	Dial Rich Marb	70
Surrounded with companions, fit	. . . .	435	Answer Paulus	119
No Subject fit	. . . .	441	Ballyspellin	25
Wou'd his own Temples better fit,	. . . . . .	458	Paddy's Charac	22
And fit your present Subject best.	. . . . .	460	Birthday Song	4
I think this Practice only fit	. . . .	463	Birthday Song	111
But smooth your words to fit the tune,	. . . . . .	467	Birthday Song	212
A Genius for all Stations fit,	. . . .	482	Libel on D- D-	79
An Office for your Talents fit,	. . . .	483	Libel on D- D-	105
Our Nightingal might fit a Cage,	. . . .	515	Answer Fable	83
His meanest Work: For, had he thought it fit,	. . .	532	To Mr. Gay	25
'Tis fit the Maxim we should know.	. . . . . .	545	Life of Swift	6
It gives me such a jealous Fit,	. . . .	555	Death of Swift	51
As we think fit to smile or frown;	. . . .	620	Scandal Poem 1	92
As we think fit to smile or frown:	. . . .	626	Scandal Poem 2	90
The Similes that nothing fit;	. . . .	645	On Poetry	152
For manly Bosoms chiefly fit,	. . . .	693	Cadenus Vaness	204
A Project for thy Talents fit,	. . . . . .	695	Cadenus Vaness	290
Cadenus is a Subject fit,	. . . .	702	Cadenus Vaness	502
His Converse is a System, fit	. . . .	709	Cadenus Vaness	708
In ev'ry Point to make it fit,	. . . .	709	Cadenus Vaness	724
The Nymph who wrote this in an Amorous Fit,	. . . .	716	Answer Rebus	1
Was more than for her Sex was fit;	. . . .	723	To Stella	2
Am I a Poet fit for you?	. . . .	757	Stel B-day '24	24
Are you a Subject fit for me?	. . . .	757	Stel B-day '24	26
And fit their Proselytes for Vice;	. . . .	764	Stel B-day '26	22
Your Block will fit it to a hair.	. . . .	780	Mullinix Tim	220
Dick for Repartee was fit,	. . . .	785	Mullinex Dick	33
While his own ass's Zaggs were more fit for the shears.		816	Yahoo's	49
A modus right fit for insulters of Deans.	. . . . .	817	Yahoo's	59
A subject for their genius fit;	. . . .	876	To Dean Swift	15
With such Dexterity you fit	. . . .	890	Panegyr Dean	125
Do what is not fit to tell,	. . . .	931	Riddle 18	D 27
With a Boy that is only fit for School,	. . . . .	941	Letter	19
Fit for Lad or Lass,	. . . .	952	Asparagus	2
Or fit more exact than one eye and one rhyme.	. . . .	980	Tho: Sheridan	4
They're fit for nothing else but pasquils.	. . . . .	982	Sher, A Goose	2
Of thy Dimensions fit for Prose,	. . . .	1002	Reply by Dean	5

FITS

While Spouts run clatt'ring o'er the Roof by Fits;	.	139	City Shower	44
<Wharton> can only Swear by Fits,	. . . .	168	Peace Dunkirk	13
But only what my Station fits,	. . . .	199	Horace 2, 6	D
And next Observe how this Alliance fits,	. . . . .	276	Epilogue	39
By taking Fits whene'er she please:	. . . . . .	416	Woman's Mind	38
In Vapours and Hysterick Fits:	. . . .	451	Modern Lady	199
Her Spleen and Fits recover'd quite,	. . . .	451	Modern Lady	216
Repeating in his amorous Fits,	. . . .	529	Lady's Dres Rm	117
All Women his Description fits,	. . . .	529	Lady's Dres Rm	125
Ill it fits you to be witty,	. . . .	630	Epistle Lady	13
Why ever in these raging Fits,	. . . .	773	Mullinix Tim	3
Whence come these inconsistent Fits?	. . . .	796	Traulus 1	33
As fits a Princess in Romance.	. . . .	888	Panegyr Dean	54
What fits it better than a Fan.	. . . .	912	Aenigma Expl	D 10

FITT

Not fitt to live on Christian Ground,	. . . . . .	92	Bauc & Phil 1	87

FITTED

Correctly fitted for the Press,	. . . .	643	On Poetry	106

FITTER

To be a fitter Birth-place for the God of Wit;	. . .	17	Ode Athenian	49
Can lend you an Allusion fitter,	. . . . . .	485	Libel on D- D-	177
To the Court it was fitter to pay his Devotion,	. . .	809	Epigr Prelate	5

FITTEST

Is in all Points the fittest Tool,	. . . .	61	Lady Tablebook	28
The fittest Tools to work for Bobb.	. . . . . .	503	Doctor Delaney	90
The fittest Man to fill a Place:	. . . .	606	Beasts Confess	156

FITTING

His Jordan stood in Manner fitting	. . . . . .	594	Cassinus Peter	21
Presents, as 'tis fitting,	. . . .	1004	Sheridan's Sub	3

FITZ-BAKER

Dick Fitz-Baker, Dick the Player,	. . . . . .	835	Legion Club	149

FITZPATRICK

"Or, as Fitzpatrick did before,	. . . .	305	Storm	63

FIVE   SEE SIXTY-FIVE

. . .this Five and Twenty Years, come Spring,	. . .	70	Mrs Harris Pet	30
Five times at least as big as theirs,	. . . . . .	87	Hist V's House	24
Here Five Foot deep lyes on his Back	. . . . . .	101	Elegy Patrige	103
Or let it cost Five hundred Pound,	. . . .	199	Horace 2, 6	19
I dare believe that Four in Five	. . . .	235	Elegy on Demar	51

	PAGE	TITLE	LINE
FIVE (CONTINUED)			
Of Value five Shillings, in English a Pencil;	264	Apollo	34
At five the Footmen make a Din,	292	Prog Marriage	91
. . . and I to have but Five.	342	Upon His Grace	19
And all the Rent I pay is scarce five Shillings in the Pound.	342	Upon His Grace	22
Fair Ladies, Number five,	425	Five Ladies	1
Instead of Five you scor'd me Ten.	453	Modern Lady	265
That five years hence will both be Hebes.	465	Birthday Song	172
Five hundred Pound a Year's no Fool.	478	Epist on Epist	112
Their Faction is five hundred Odds,	501	Doctor Delaney	47
Five Hours, (and who can do it less in?)	525	Lady's Dres Rm	1
Sweet Five and Twenty was his Age.	597	Problem Solved	6
Bright Goddesses, in Number five;	656	On Poetry	439
'Twou'd come to just Five Thousand Pound.	693	Cadenus Vaness	227
Which every Girl at five Years old	700	Cadenus Vaness	424
Five thousand Guineas in her Purse?	707	Cadenus Vaness	654
Five Nothings in five Plates of Delf.	747	Stel Distress	52
Five Nothings in five Plates of Delf.	747	Stel Distress	52
Five Nothings in five Plates of Delph.	751	Stel Wood-Park	68
Five Nothings in five Plates of Delph.	751	Stel Wood-Park	68
To build a House five Hundred more.	875	Drapier's Hill	8
His fund may last to five and fifty.	878	Robbin & Harry	16
A Mistress worth five thousand pound;	879	Robbin & Harry	32
We'll take her Heels five Inches lower.	886	Rev Market-Hill	104
Will dress a Dinner worth five Pound.	941	Letter	36
FIVE-BARR'D			
Before he tries a five-barr'd Gate:	640	On Poetry	16
FIX			
To fix this nimble god,	49	To Congreve	208
Have in More Fields their Stations fix,	101	Elegy Patrige	100
To sleep could Mortal Eye-lids fix	133	Magician's Rod	37
To fix a Price on his devoted Head.	196	Author Himself	60
Fix them on high, conspicuous to be seen,	285	Elegy Boat	33
Three hundred pounds! Were I the price to fix,	308	Billet Players	21
"Direct, and fix the wandring Mind,	384	Manly Virtue	12
"But run to Tom, and bid him fix	446	Modern Lady	54
When he can in one Couplet fix	555	Death of Swift	49
(Muse, find me Names to fix my Metre,	594	Cassinus Peter	5
But once you fix him in a Tomb,	646	On Poetry	199
Shou'd fix upon some certain Rule,	707	Cadenus Vaness	665
(Could Poets or could Painters fix	735	Stel B-day '20	17
Keeper, shew me where to fix	835	Legion Club	145
Robin, who ne'r his mind could fix	878	Robbin & Harry	29
The valiant Dennis you must fix,	885	Rev Market-Hill	85
And few know how and where you fix.	919	Riddle 5	28
FIX'D			
Thus he has fix'd His Name	7	Ode to King	33
Nor does thy essence fix'd depend on giddy circumstance	34	Ode Sancroft	7
If a mind fix'd to combat fate	36	Ode Sancroft	47
Nothing is fix'd that mortals see or know,	39	Ode Sancroft	143
For, youth, believe, to you unseen, is fix'd	44	To Congreve	31
We lately fix'd our Viceroy there:	269	Apollo's Edict	D 2
Fix'd in a lonely, learned Cell,	385	Manly Virtue	48
Had fix'd on for her Coadjutor.	701	Cadenus Vaness	465
The Darts were in the Cover fix'd,	701	Cadenus Vaness	481
On Virtue's Basis fix'd to last,	711	Cadenus Vaness	782
FIX'T			
Is fix't like Fate among the Stars,	6	Ode to King	20
Why are thine Altars fix't beneath?	894	Panegyr Dean	232
FIXES			
With Obstinacy fixes there;	641	On Poetry	22
FIXT			
But still, tho' fixt among the Stars,	66	Problem	27
At length, his Anchor fixt, and Canvas furl'd,	284	Elegy Boat	6
In Concord here for ever fixt,	467	Birthday Song	231
Fill'd up with Dirt so closely fixt,	526	Lady's Dres Rm	21
For ever fixt by Right Divine,	642	On Poetry	57
He fixt the Star and String Cerulean.	656	On Poetry	464
Fixt Honour in her Infant Mind.	723	To Stella	6
Thou, fixt of old, be now the moving Land?	770	Horace 1, 14	4
My Love to Sheelah is more firmly fixt	880	Pastoral Dial	9
While in his lordly Castle fixt,	883	Rev Market-Hill	19
By which your jade Pegasus fixt in a tether,	1027	Sheri Circles	18
FLABBY			
Her flabby Dugs and down they drop.	582	Young Nymph	22
FLACCUS			
How monstrous Carthy looks to Flaccus brac't,	668	Epig Carthy 9	D 1
Dare you, vile Murderer of Flaccus,	671	Epig Carthy 22	D 1
Homer, Plutarch, Virgil, Flaccus,	838	Legion Club	211
FLAG			
Lorsha! and out of her shteeple there was hung a black flag.	840	Ballad	D 9
FLAGRANT			
So flagrant is Thy Insolence,	154	Widow and Cat	D 41
FLAIL SEE FLAYL			
The Tories Terror, Scourge and Flail.	776	Mullinix Tim	86
FLAM			
"Be witness if I tell a Flam:	462	Birthday Song	78
FLAM'D			
Then let us no longer by Parsons be Flam'd,	576	Place Damn'd	15

FLAME
    To buzz about the mighty Flame; . . . .   9 Ode to King 116
    And seem (almost) transform'd to Water, Flame, and Air, 22 Ode Athenian 201
    Before the Flame from Muzzle burst, ... 66 Problem 45
    Born like a Phoenix from the Flame, ... 81 Vanbrug House 79
    Blew out Love's Torch or chill'd the Flame: . . . . 85 Salamander 60
    Born like a Phoenix from the Flame, ... 109 V's House 121
    Confest his Flame, and swore by Styx, ... 120 Apollo Outwit 18
    For why; I would fain have put all in a Flame, . . . 144 New Song 43
    And to the Shepherd own'd her flame. . . . . 178 To Lord Harley 76
    Well harden'd in Flame, ... 246 Irish-Feast 70
    He melts his Wax at ev'ry Flame, ... 252 Bubble 46
    'Twas cut into Faggots, and put to the Flame, . . . 334 Serious Poem 21
    Though born in Snow, it dy'd in Flame. . . . . . . 470 Burning Poem 16
    To stinking Smoak it turns the Flame . . . . . . 529 Lady's Dres Rm 105
    To 'scape Enquiries, leave the House in Flame. . . . 536 To Mr. Gay 142
    Which having found an equal Flame, ... 687 Cadenus Vaness 31
    For Breasts incapable of Flame; . . . . 688 Cadenus Vaness 64
    Which raise a Flame that will endure . . . . . . 691 Cadenus Vaness 144
    Thro' ev'ry Breast wou'd dart a Flame; . . . . . . 693 Cadenus Vaness 231
    Cou'd scarce oppose Vanessa's Flame; . . . . . . 710 Cadenus Vaness 745
    To that you owe the nobler Flame. . . . . 726 To Stella 91
    Your Spirits kindle to a Flame, ... 730 Stella, Poems 87
    All her spirits in a flame . . . . . . 906 Daphne 19
    Stabb'd to the Heart, condemn'd to Flame, ... 916 Riddle 2 7
    Soon would their Altars Flame expire, ... 916 Riddle 2 13
    That in secret feeds her Flame, ... 936 Riddle 24 D 24
FLAMES
    <Parts> like a Laurel in the Flames.   66 Problem 40
    'Twill make the very Flames expire, ... 84 Salamander 50
    Lament his old Whitehall in Flames, ... 107 V's House 48
    "For Massacres, and Racks, and Flames, ... 183 Horace 2, 1 95
    What powder'd Wigs! What Flames and Darts! . . . . 585 Strephon Chloe 35
    Shall they in baser Flames expire? . . . . . . 732 Stella, Poems 142
FLAMING
    No Comet with a Flaming Beard! . . . . 98 Elegy Patrige 10
    Of polish't Brass, his flaming Car, ... 352 Wood Ironmongr 13
    Stood Hymen with a flaming Torch. . . . . . . 585 Strephon Chloe 48
    With the fine flaming Sword that he holds in his Hand; 870 Grand Question 96
FLAMMEUM
    The Nymph was cover'd with her Flammeum, ... 586 Strephon Chloe 61
FLAMSTEAD
    That Flamstead can with all his Skill . . . . . 229 Prog of Beauty 99
FLANDERS
    In French brocades and Flanders Lace; . . . . . 291 Prog Marriage 64
    Rich Flanders Lace, and Colberteen. . . . . . . 700 Cadenus Vaness 417
    A long-ear'd Beast and Flanders College, ... 942 Probatur Alit 15
FLANK
    But the Tapster well Cudgell'd him both Side and Flank 288 Bank Down 39
    From shoulder to flank . . . . 853 Lady's Lament 71
    Powder'd from shoulder down to flank, ... 879 Robbin & Harry 49
FLANNELL
    In Linnen, and on Yours, in Flannell. . . . . . 315 To Ford 102
FLASHES
    Just at the Breech it flashes first: . . . . . 66 Problem 46
    The Flashes of Ardeliah's Eyes. . . . . 119 Apollo Outwit 12
FLASHING
    But, when with squibbing, flashing, popping, ... 500 Doctor Delaney 21
FLAT
    Howe'er she gave no flat Denial, ... 120 Apollo Outwit 25
    Would prove ev'n Homer's Numbers flat. . . . . . 467 Birthday Song 228
    Descriptions tedious, flat and dry, ... 645 On Poetry 155
    Yet I know a young Rogue, that thrown flat on the Field 967 Letter Sherid 15
FLATLY
    I flatly deny it: . . . . 939 Riddle Answerd 8
FLATT'RERS
    "No Flatt'rers; no Allies in Blood; . . . . . . 566 Death of Swift 334
FLATT'RING
    Though flatt'ring Knaves may call it bitter. . . . . 485 Libel on D- D- 178
    Whene'er a flatt'ring Puppy cries . . . . 545 Life of Swift 25
    By flatt'ring <Kings> whom Heaven design'd . . . 654 On Poetry 407
    All risen since that flatt'ring time, ... 899 Dean's Reasons 9
    This is flatt'ring, and delightful; . . . . . . 907 Daphne 46
FLATT'RY
    And Flatt'ry tipt with nauseous Fleer, ... 725 To Stella 47
    In Flatt'ry an Artist, in Pawning a Slave, ... 807 Advice Parson 4
FLATT'RY'S
    You cannot err on Flatt'ry's Side. . . . . 657 On Poetry 470
FLATTER
    To Flatter, Carve, and shew your Wit; . . . . . 483 Libel on D- D- 106
    Nor bribe, insult, nor flatter, nor betray. . . . . 533 To Mr. Gay 56
    He fail'd, because he could not flatter: . . . . . 604 Beasts Confess 96
    To flatter Woman by a Metaphor! . . . . . . 622 Scandal Poem 1 169
    Are awkward when you try to flatter. . . . . . 642 On Poetry 52
    To flatter Knaves, or lose his Pension. . . . . . 650 On Poetry 310
    Nor Minister, nor Poet flatter. . . . . 655 On Poetry 414
    Of Wit, to flatter and seduce: . . . . 707 Cadenus Vaness 645
    Nor will in Panygyrick flatter. . . . . . . 729 Stella, Poems 56
    Say then more than they; nay, lavishly flatter, . . . 819 Archbi Cashel 13
    Which all may handle, none can flatter. . . . . . 993 On Picture 18
    But your fair Lines so grossly flatter, ... 1003 Dan J's Reply 4

          PAGE TITLE   LINE

	PAGE	TITLE	LINE
FLATTER (CONTINUED)			
Go flatter Kilmore.	1038	Sheridan Cavan	14
FLATTERING			
With couchant Cringe, and flattering Tale,	208	Fable Bitches	15
FLATTERS			
He flatters with peculiar Air	216	To Mr. Delany	37
To foul the Man he chiefly flatters.	796	Traulus 1	32
FLATTERY			
"Stoop not to int'rest, flattery, or deceit;	55	Temple Ill	138
Without reproach of flattery true	658	On Poetry	D 410
FLAUNTING			
"I'll warrant she's some flaunting Dame,	321	First of April	25
FLAWS			
Both Pitch and Brimstone to fill up his Flaws;	285	Elegy Boat	28
FLAX			
The charming Silvia beating Flax,	729	·Stella, Poems	45
Stuff his Guts with Flax and Grass;	831	Legion Club	64
FLAXEN			
A flaxen wig, and clouded cane,	619	Scandal Poem 1	70
A Flaxen Wig, and Clouded Cane.	625	Scandal Poem 2	66
A flaxen wig, and wast-coat gay,	879	Robbin & Harry	48
FLAY'D			
My Skin he flay'd, my Hair he cropt;	915	Riddle 1	11
FLAYL			
The Proverb says; No Fence against a Flayl.	521	Stephen Duck	2
FLEA			
Shew me the same numerick Flea,	504	Doctor Delaney	141
So, Nat'ralists observe, a Flea	651	On Poetry	337
FLEAS			
And Shock her Tresses fill'd with Fleas.	583	Young Nymph	64
Hath smaller Fleas that on him prey,	651	On Poetry	338
And these have smaller Fleas to bite 'em,	651	On Poetry	339
FLECKNOE			
From Flecknoe down to Howard's Time,	652	On Poetry	369
FLED			
And the Dove-muse is fled once more,	17	Ode Athenian	32
For when the animating Mind is fled,	25	Ode Athenian	288
Since the bright essence fled, where haunts the reverend ghost?	36	Ode Sancroft	44
Ah, since our fears are fled, this insolent expel,	53	Temple Ill	55
Since hope his last and greatest foe is fled,	55	Temple Ill	127
But find her where so'er she fled,	223	Prog of Love	37
Phillis, it seems, was fled with John.	223	Prog of Love	42
Then fled, and left his Horn behind	293	Prog Marriage	115
He took to the Street, and fled for his Life,	327	Epigram 1	2
Away they fled, and left him as they found him.	536	To Mr. Gay	160
Away the Hare with double Swiftness fled.	538	Mr. Pulteney	28
He fled to Earth, but first it cost him dear;	538	Mr. Pulteney	35
But found my Wit and Fancy fled:	740	Stel B-day 22	6
Fled to the Fountain back, from whence it came!	793	St. Pat's Well	66
And fled in Haste with all her Brood	849	Old Thorn	39
She fled and vanish'd into Air.	850	Old Thorn	52
His matrimonial Spirit fled;	905	Death Daphne	96
Who never fled the bloody Plains,	925	Riddle 8	32
And when I, vanquish'd, fled the Town,	1005	Sheridan's Sub	9
FLEE			
"If his Majestick Eye you fear,	380	Apology Lady C	143
"With Rapture, what they wont to flee.	384	Manly Virtue	14
FLEECE			
His Brothers fleece him when he's drunk.	607	Beasts Confess	196
Who come to fleece the Flocks, and not to feed.	792	St. Pat's Well	32
When the Rogues their Country fleece,	833	Legion Club	107
From Colchos brought the Golden Fleece:	948	Jason Hassard	2
FLEECES			
Devour'd the Lambs, the Fleeces sold,	153	Widow and Cat	D 9
But before the Priest he fleeces	831	Legion Club	65
FLEECY			
Hither from Colchos, with the fleecy Ore,	790	St. Pat's Well	7
And gaming Goats, and fleecy Flocks,	934	Riddle 21	D 8
FLEER			
Fleer, and gibe, and laugh, and flout;	523	Betty Grizette	32
Think it Wit to fleer, and gibe?	632	Epistle Lady	78
And Flatt'ry tipt with nauseous Fleer,	725	To Stella	47
How the hussies will fleer	855	Lady's Lament	117
I pass now where you fleer and laugh	1004	Dan J's Reply	25
FLEET			
Had not the Fleet gone out too late,	463	Birthday Song	102
Prepare a Fleet to waft him o'r'e,	466	Birthday Song	205
Whose Fleet, 'tis all our Friends Opinion,	774	Mullinix Tim	23
FLEET-DITCH'S			
Or, near Fleet-Ditch's oozy Brinks,	583	Young Nymph	47
FLEETING			
Alas, how fleeting, and how vain,	24	Ode Athenian	268
FLEETS			
From Fleets triumphant o'er the Gallick Coast.	771	Horace 1, 14	40
FLESH			
His Flesh brought down to Flying-Case:	231	Prog of Poetry	40
Remov'd the tough superfluous Flesh,	326	Pethox	78
Is a Man of this World all true Flesh and Blood;	335	Serious Poem	50
Pois'ning the Flesh from whence it came;	529	Lady's Dres Rm	106
"Forgetting his own Flesh and Blood?	558	Death of Swift	164

	PAGE	TITLE	LINE
FLESH (CONTINUED)			
Meer mortal Flesh was all he found:	586	Strephon Chloe	76
Without an Ounce of last Year's Flesh,	759	Receipt Youth	15
So long till all your Flesh is wasted,	759	Receipt Youth	24
Nor Flesh nor Blood will be the same,	759	Receipt Youth	33
By human Kind, but Flesh and Blood?	759	Receipt Youth	36
And if your Flesh and Blood be new,	759	Receipt Youth	37
The new-born Flesh will melt away;	760	Receipt Youth	52
But is a Louse your Flesh and Blood?	812	Bro Protestant	36
And Skin and Flesh in Pieces tore.	925	Riddle 8	40
No Flesh, no Bones, no Blood --- no Ghost:	935	Riddle 23 D	11
So sweet is their Flesh,	952	Oysters	4
FLETA'S			
The Lovers Fleta's, Bractons, Cokes.	689	Cadenus Vaness	107
FLEW			
Flew dutifully back again,	16	Ode Athenian	30
Thalia heard the Call and Flew	120	Apollo Outwit	39
The Golden Spoils flew off apace,	158	Fable of Midas	75
Mark out the way where Daphne flew.	177	To Lord Harley	18
Along the plain like Lightning flew:	412	Desire Possess	22
Away the God of Silence flew,	448	Modern Lady	121
Flew hov'ring o'er each Female Head.	449	Modern Lady	135
That ever screecht or ever flew.	515	Answer Fable	107
Of humane Evils upwards flew;	528	Lady's Dres Rm	86
The Vapours flew from out the Vent,	528	Lady's Dres Rm	91
Flew off, nor evermore appear'd.	590	Strephon Chloe	196
Harness'd her Doves, and flew to Heav'n.	714	Cadenus Vaness	889
By the Stygian Steams that flew,	834	Legion Club	123
And, as fast as she could, to the Deanery flew sick.	1029	Dr. Helsham	11
FLIES			
But plumes her Silver Wings and flies away,	16	Ode Athenian	17
As virtuosoes' in dissecting flies;	46	To Congreve	94
The subtil spirit all flies up in fume;	49	To Congreve	210
Faint inspiration sickens as she flies,	50	To Congreve	229
Kindled while reason sleeps, but quickly flies,	54	Temple Ill	99
Out from some Hole obscure he flies	84	Salamander	33
And flies about the Candle-Light;	99	Elegy Patrige	52
There flies about a strange Report	202	Horace 2, 6	89
Since Death pursues the Coward as he flies.	210	Earl of Oxford	2
While all the Parish, as she flies,	230	Prog of Poetry	15
He singing flies, and flying sings,	231	Prog of Poetry	45
To Kitchin, Parlour, Nurs'ry flies,	322	First of April	37
"Or is he criminal that flies	380	Apology Lady C	165
Pale Envy sickens--Errour flies--	387	Manly Virtue	121
Flies like a Squib from Place to Place,	398	Earl of P-b-w	8
Hunted from Earth, and Sea, and Hell, he flies	538	Mr. Pulteney	29
And Thunder roars, and Light'ning flies!	578	Day Judgement	6
But, out it flies, even when she meets	588	Strephon Chloe	131
Drawn by her Doves, away she flies,	692	Cadenus Vaness	186
Doll never flies to cut her Lace,	725	To Stella	75
He flies, and leaves the Stars behind,	728	Stella, Poems	36
He flies from his God, to attend on his Grace:	809	Epigr Prelate	4
Be cautious, or your Bottle flies.	892	Panegyr Dean	184
In public schemes, or catching flies,	901	Dean's Reasons	79
For Time with Beauty flies away,	932	Riddle 19 D	21
In vain from me the Sailor flies,	934	Riddle 21 D	13
Since it flies from Apollo.	939	Riddle Answerd	24
FLIGHT			
Take thy unwonted Flight,	30	Ode to Temple	118
Whene'er she takes this Flight	31	Ode to Temple	143
Or hunted fancy, by a circling flight,	51	Temple Ill	5
Time o'er the happy takes so swift a flight,	54	Temple Ill	113
For such is all the sex's flight,	177	To Lord Harley	19
While innocent, he scorns ignoble Flight;	196	Author Himself	61
What Poet e'er could take his Flight?	231	Prog of Poetry	24
An Eagle's Flight and State assumes,	252	Bubble	35
On Paper Wings he takes his Flight,	252	Bubble	37
When Damon's Soul shall take its Flight,	270	Apollo's Edict D	33
Alike diffusing in his Flight	387	Manly Virtue	119
Attain'd by Flight the Muses Hill;	504	Doctor Delaney	120
And fortune help the murd'rer in his flight;	506	To a Friend	2
A Peacock chose for Flight and Voice:	513	Answer Fable	20
Attempt a Flight above a Haycock?	513	Answer Fable	22
In vain I tempt too high a Flight.	897	Panegyr Dean	324
On Airy Wings you take your Flight,	919	Riddle 5	25
Make up a Bird very swift of Flight.	940	Letter	4
FLIGHTS			
High Raptures, and romantick Flights;	590	Strephon Chloe	198
At Poets flights to take offence:	622	Scandal Poem 1	154
At Poet's Flights to take Offence.	628	Scandal Poem 2	158
That when Platonick Flights were over,	707	Cadenus Vaness	650
For why such Raptures, Flights, and Fancies,	711	Cadenus Vaness	794
FLIM-FLAMS			
Rewards too great for your Flim-Flams,	478	Epist on Epist	107
FLINCH			
When once he begins, he never will flinch,	143	New Song	7
To show, I don't flinch,	246	Irish-Feast	53
Who hung like a Hero, and never would flinch.	400	Tom Clinch	24
FLING			
And fling our Scraps before our Door.	28	Ode to Temple	57
I'll fling the <Pisspot> on your head;	91	Bauc & Phil 1	38

	PAGE	TITLE	LINE
FLING (CONTINUED)			
A Shilling in the Bath You fling,	255	Bubble	113
I, who love to have a Fling,	637	Epistle Lady	221
FLINGS			
A Sable Cloud a-thwart the Welkin flings,	137	City Shower	14
He wildly flings his Filth about,	796	Traulus 1	26
FLIRTS			
Flirts on you from her Mop, but not so clean.	137	City Shower	20
The Flirts of his ill-mannerd Muse.	219	To Mr. Delany	110
Flirts from his Cart the Mud in <Walpole's> Face.	364	On Dreams	38
FLITCH			
A Flitch of Bacon off the Hook,	91	Bauc & Phil 1	58
A Flitch of Bacon off the Hook;	112	Bauc & Phil 2	26
FLITTING			
And with false flitting Shades our Minds delude,	363	On Dreams	2
FLOAT			
Fools chiefly float, the Wise are drown'd.	252	Bubble	52
Subscribers here by thousands float,	256	Bubble	145
With Water fill'd he could no longer float,	284	Elegy Boat	9
Who float upon the tide of state,	296	Satiric Elegy	27
If haply on the liquid surface float,	672	Epig Carthy 24	D 13
Together float with Tide and Wind;	811	Bro Protestant	6
FLOATING			
It seems some floating piece of Paradice,	17	Ode Athenian	44
Poor floating Isle, tost on ill Fortune's Waves,	770	Horace 1, 14	1
FLOCK SEE SABLE-FLOCK			
The Turnkey now his Flock returning sees,	125	Descriptn Morn	15
Till the small ragged Flock is met.	127	Little House	22
Where Town and Country Vicars flock in Tribes,	194	Author Himself	19
A Flock of Geese jump down together,	253	Bubble	54
With underlings thy flock to teach,	677	Parson's Case	31
FLOCKING			
Come flocking for pillage,	857	Lady's Lament	196
FLOCKS			
Warn'd by the Bell, all Flocks come trembling,	279	Journal	28
Flocks ev'ry ominous Bird of Prey;	413	Desire Possess	54
Devours your Geese, the Wolf your Flocks:	504	Doctor Delaney	130
Nightly nodding o'er your Flocks,	660	Love Song	6
Who come to fleece the Flocks, and not to feed.	792	St. Pat's Well	32
And gaming Goats, and fleecy Flocks,	934	Riddle 21	D 8
FLOOD			
To shew the Flood begins to cease,	16	Ode Athenian	20
Preserv'd by wonder from the Flood,	17	Ode Athenian	45
Now in contiguous Drops the Flood comes down.	138	City Shower	31
Dead Cats and Turnip-Tops come tumbling down the Flood	139	City Shower	63
He ran, he leapt into the Flood,	255	Bubble	130
And leave the Flood when he goes in it:	280	Journal	50
Of loud un-meaning Sounds, a rapid Flood	532	To Mr. Gay	39
Comes pouring on me like a Flood.	655	On Poetry	438
When now the flood invades his strugling breath,	672	Epig Carthy 24	D 12
From stagnating preserves the Flood;	731	Stella, Poems	128
Will agitate the lazy Flood,	759	Receipt Youth	31
Smooth as our Bason's gentle Flood,	1020	Nim-Dan-Dean 1	D 5
FLOOR			
And one small Chamber on a Floor.	81	Vanbrug House	78
Had par'd the Dirt, and Sprinkled round the Floor.	124	Descriptn Morn	6
The Floor is all wet	245	Irish-Feast	41
But, view them litter'd on the Floor,	592	Strephon Chloe	289
FLORA			
A Flora does the Dome protect;	477	Epist on Epist	78
And there neglected Flora settles	901	Dean's Reasons	93
Like Flora, deck'd with fairest flowers;	937	Riddle 24	D 33
FLORIMEL			
That Florimel wears Iron Stays:	449	Modern Lady	161
If Florimel had found her Love	905	Death Daphne	81
FLORIMEL'S			
In Florimel's affected Fears:	725	To Stella	70
FLORINDA			
Florinda, dart their Heav'nly Beams,	932	Riddle 19	D 2
FLOUD			
The horned Floud, as Poets sing:	293	Prog Marriage	110
And soon convinc'd them by a Floud.	799	Traulus 1	98
FLOUNC'D			
Became Black Sattin, Flounc'd with Lace.	116	Bauc & Phil 2	142
FLOUNCE			
Howe'er you flounce,	440	Ballyspellin	7
"Madam, you have no Cause to flounce,	452	Modern Lady	262
You neither fume, nor fret, nor flounce;	891	Panegyr Dean	150
FLOUNCES			
From Fans, and Flounces, and Brocades,	688	Cadenus Vaness	45
In Flounces has a better Fancy.	700	Cadenus Vaness	419
FLOURISH			
But, hope to see you flourish still.	411	Dial Rich Marb	102
To flourish o'er a Cup of Ginn?	505	Doctor Delaney	148
In Spight of Envy flourish still,	875	Drapier's Hill	19
FLOURISH'D			
And flourish'd by imputed Wit,	481	Libel on D- D-	50
Suppose Cadenus flourish'd then,	708	Cadenus Vaness	694
FLOURISH'T			
E'er flourish't under a Successor or a Son;	25	Ode Athenian	285

	PAGE	TITLE	LINE

FLOURISHES
Then flourishes thrice his Sword in the Air, ... 870 Grand Question 109
FLOURISHING
A Peaceful and a Flourishing Shore: . . . . . 17 Ode Athenian 35
Forever green and flourishing 'twill last, ... 29 Ode to Temple 85
Too flourishing a spring, ... 37 Ode Sancroft 99
FLOURISHT
A flourisht Night-cap on, to grace . . . . . . 290 Prog Marriage 23
FLOUT
Fleer, and gibe, and laugh, and flout; . . . . . 523 Betty Grizette 32
And yet before your Stanza ends you flout me . . . . 1003 Dan J's Reply 21
FLOW
That mighty Ebb never to flow again, ... 16 Ode Athenian 2
Now from all Parts the swelling Kennels flow, . . . 139 City Shower 53
Could from her taintless Body flow. . . . . . . 584 Strephon Chloe 14
You hardly see the Current flow, ... 688 Cadenus Vaness 52
Yet endless Tears flow down in Streams. . . . . . 932 Riddle 19 D 4
FLOW'R
From the dead Ashes of a Flow'r . . . . . . 81 Vanbrug House 86
From the dead Ashes of a Flow'r . . . . . . 109 V's House 128
There, many a Flow'r abstersive grew, ... 894 Panegyr Dean 249
And Smedly, Flow'r of all Divines, ... 897 Panegyr Dean 345
(With Flow'r of Sulphur powder'd well, ... 903 Death Daphne 25
FLOW'RS
Among the noblest flow'rs a thousand pois'nous weeds, . 37 Ode Sancroft 102
Of rip'ning fruits, and gilding flow'rs; . . . . . 432 Answer Paulus 14
Drest up with Amaranthine Flow'rs. . . . . . 590 Strephon Chloe 202
Can ev'ry Spring produce you Flow'rs. . . . . . 628 Scandal Poem 2 152
A Sprig of Amaranthine Flow'rs, ... 691 Cadenus Vaness 155
Thy fav'rite Flow'rs of yellow Hue . . . . . . 894 Panegyr Dean 250
Yet Flow'rs I bear of ev'ry Kind; . . . . . . 926 Riddle 9 2
FLOW'RY
All beneath yon flow'ry Rocks. . . . . . . 660 Love Song 8
With thy flow'ry Chaplets crown'd. . . . . . 661 Love Song 28
Or, offer'd in some flow'ry Vale, ... 894 Panegyr Dean 247
Nor seldom grace the flow'ry downs, ... 896 Panegyr Dean 303
FLOWER
Here Allum Flower to stop the Steams, ... 526 Lady's Dres Rm 27
"And Peerage is a wither'd Flower, ... 570 Death of Swift 440
FLOWERS
To shield the infant Fruits and Flowers, ... 387 Manly Virtue 109
"The Garden stor'd with artless Flowers, ... 476 Epist on Epist 51
Like Flora, deck'd with fairest flowers; . . . . . 937 Riddle 24 D 33
FLOWING
Sing heavenly Muse in sweetly flowing Strain, . . . 880 Pastoral Dial 7
FLOWN   SEE HIGH-FLOWN
Now Betty from her Masters Bed had flown, . . . 124 Descriptn Morn 3
Now Pride and Cruelty are flown, ... 391 Young's Satire 17
Had she flown but o'er the Top, ... 834 Legion Club 127
FLOWRS
Instead of Garlands made of Flowrs . . . . . 122 Empt'ng Town 7
Produce in May the sweetest flowrs. . . . . . 621 Scandal Poem 1 148
FLOWRY
Scatter'd with flowry Vales, with fruitful Gardens 17 Ode Athenian 40
crown'd,
"As from the flowry Bed of Nile-- . . . . . . 463 Birthday Song 81
FLOWS
Nine times a day it ebbs and flows, ... 256 Bubble 141
"On Learning how his Bounty flows, ... 462 Birthday Song 75
Fair Freedom's Emblem once, which smoothly flows, . 793 St. Pat's Well 67
FLOYD
Dame Floyd looks out in grave Suspence 75 Game Traffick 13
Then call'd the happy Composition, Floyd. . . . . 118 Biddy Floyd 12
Which only pleased in Biddy Floyd: . . . . . 272 Apollo's Edict D 61
FLUNG
He spake, and a dark Cloud flung o're his light, . . . 8 Ode to King 58
And swallow'd them at last, or flung them down. . . 40 Ode Sancroft 197
And grief flung sables on each menial look; . . . . 53 Temple Ill 60
From all his ill-got honours flung, ... 297 Satiric Elegy 31
FLUTE
Aurora with thy early Flute. . . . . 594 Cassinus Peter 34
FLUTT'RING
Flutt'ring spread thy purple Pinions, ... 660 Love Song 1
FLUTTERS
He flutters when he Thinks he flyes, ... 80 Vanbrug House 37
Flutters the feeble Pamphlet into Rags. . . . . 771 Horace 1, 14 30
FLUX'T   SEE NEW-FLUX'T
FLY
And Courts the wanton Echoes as they fly. . . . . 17 Ode Athenian 59
Wonder to see the Motions fly) . . . . . . 29 Ode to Temple 96
Off fly the Vizards and discover all, ... 29 Ode to Temple 99
Away the frighted Peasants fly, ... 30 Ode to Temple 109
Some more ambitiously upwards fly, ... 32 Ode to Temple 173
And in his Fancy fly as far, ... 99 Elegy Patrige 55
You fly, invoke the Gods; then turning, stop . . . 137 City Shower 21
To Shops in Crouds the dagged Females fly, ... 138 City Shower 33
<Swift>, who could neither fly nor hide, ... 172 Horace 1, 7 63
They fly from learning, wit, and light: . . . . . 177 To Lord Harley 20
They fly, and none can overtake . . . . . . 177 To Lord Harley 21
The Youth, in vain, would fly from Fate's Attack, . . 210 Earl of Oxford 3
Make Pinions for themselves to fly, ... 239 Run Bankers 22

		PAGE	TITLE	LINE
FLY	(CONTINUED)			
They fly like Bats, on Parchment Wings,		239	Run Bankers	23
And dip their Fins again to fly.		254	Bubble	88
Nor shall his Darts at random fly		272	Apollo's Edict	D 58
"Can creep, or run, can fly or swim,		304	Storm	31
You'll fly when you get what you come here to steal,		395	Dog and Thief	7
We fly from luxury and wealth,		401	Window Inns 5	D 1
Who after you adoring fly,		499	Panegyr Swift	178
Fly Bullets now as thick as Hops,		500	Doctor Delaney	9
Your Genius in your Face will fly.		503	Doctor Delaney	114
Fly from the Hawk, or pick his Pease up.		512	Answer Fable	10
Like a fly blown Cake of Tallow,		523	Betty Grizette	7
And, if unsav'ry Odours fly,		529	Lady's Dres Rm	123
Thus <Bob> shal't thou be mawl'd, fly where thou wil't:		538	Mr. Pulteney	38
Ev'n Lambs by Instinct fly the Butcher.		588	Strephon Chloe	154
Let fly a Rouzer in her Face.		590	Strephon Chloe	192
But, we can fly whene'er we please		621	Scandal Poem 1	125
Fate never form'd the Gods to fly;		626	Scandal Poem 2	109
But, we can fly where-e'er we please,		627	Scandal Poem 2	119
Have you seen a Rocket fly?		638	Epistle Lady	249
A Bear will not attempt to fly:		640	On Poetry	14
And fly for refuge to the grave:		676	Parson's Case	16
Fly to the Sea, my Place of Birth;		689	Cadenus Vaness	88
The Squires in Scorn will fly the House		760	Receipt Youth	53
That fly and leave no Marks behind?		765	Stel B-day '26	54
As if the Devil drove, they fly.		775	Mullinix Tim	68
The Company will fly the Room.		917	Riddle 4	8
And all I get, I let it fly:		918	Riddle 4	26
And fly unseen both Day and Night;		919	Riddle 5	26
Thro' distant Regions I can fly,		930	Riddle 15	D 17
It can never fly from you.		931	Riddle 17	D 8
No Bird in Air so swift can fly.		942	Probatur Alit	26
Fly, fly, above, above the Sky Rambling,		959	Cantata	
Fly, fly, above, above the Sky Rambling,		959	Cantata	
And fly with Hurry to Ramines;		1002	Reply by Dean	8
FLY-BLOWS				
But scatt'ring round his Fly-blows, dyes;		80	Vanbrug House	53
FLY'R				
The Fly'r, altho't had leaden Feet,		93	Bauc & Phil 1	131
FLYE				
And every foolish Flye that dares to aim		9	Ode to King	115
Fate never form'd the Gods to flye		620	Scandal Poem 1	111
FLYER				
The Flyer, tho't had Leaden Feet,		113	Bauc & Phil 2	71
FLYES				
This Gilded Meteor which flyes		10	Ode to King	122
We join like Flyes, and Wasps, in buzzing about Wit.		18	Ode Athenian	75
He flutters when he Thinks he flyes,		80	Vanbrug House	37
Corrupt to Maggots Worms and Flyes.		81	Vanbrug House	82
Corrupt to Maggots, Worms and Flyes.		109	V's House	124
With his Spanish flyes		423	Carterets Arms	
Flyes like an Eagle or'e his head;		461	Birthday Song	34
As fairest Fruits attract the Flyes.		501	Doctor Delaney	42
And, e'er he flyes is forc'd to tye em.		621	Scandal Poem 1	120
And, like Domitian, leap at Flyes.		824	Printer Newgat	14
FLYING				
And all those flying Deaths that aim'd him from the Field,		8	Ode to King	67
He singing flies, and flying sings,		231	Prog of Poetry	45
And flying think to quit the Score,		1002	Reply by Dean	11
FLYING-CASE				
His Flesh brought down to Flying-Case:		231	Prog of Poetry	40
FOB				
With a Saint at his Chin, and a Seal in his Fob;		147	Windsor Proph	2
Fancies his Fingers in the Cully's Fob.		364	On Dreams	26
FOE				
Of a declining Church, by Faction her worse foe opprest,		40	Ode Sancroft	186
Since hope his last and greatest foe is fled,		55	Temple Ill	127
If it were Friend or Foe,		77	Lady B- B-	17
And wafted with its Foe by violent Gust,		137	City Shower	25
Or else, that Mercury's her Foe.		228	Prog of Beauty	96
To spare a Foe, to save a Friend:		306	Storm	76
Because no <--> But <Black?> Gown'd Foe,		373	Letter D. S-y	77
Its Grandeur to its greatest Foe.		386	Manly Virtue	96
Provides each Animal it's Foe:		504	Doctor Delaney	128
Who does no Ill, can have no Foe,		514	Answer Fable	58
Resentment on this publick Foe;		515	Answer Fable	82
Till <Bob>, the Poet's Foe, possess't her Ear.		531	To Mr. Gay	4
He scours away; and to avoid the Foe,		538	Mr. Pulteney	23
Behold a Foe more fierce than all the rest:		538	Mr. Pulteney	32
Though neither Foe nor Friend allows us.		603	Beasts Confess	78
Must yield her Foe the stronger Cause;		695	Cadenus Vaness	265
To what her treach'rous Foe expects.		695	Cadenus Vaness	283
Since Fortune, my foe,		858	Lady's Lament	207
Attack the Foe at Left and Right;		884	Rev Market-Hill	46
Nor ever fail to seize my Foe;		921	Riddle 6	32
Again, as I'm dispos'd, the Foe		934	Riddle 21	D 5
You treat me like a Boy that knocks down his Foe,		967	Letter Sherid	13
. . . or foe, Delany;		1023	Nim-Dan-Dean 2	D 7
FOE'S				
Her Foe's Conclusions were not sound,		695	Cadenus Vaness	279

FOES

	PAGE	TITLE	LINE
The brave Attempt do's all our Foes disarm, ...	13	Ode to William	D 37
What northern hive pour'd out these foes to wit? . . .	46	To Congreve	83
For, could you think? the fiercest foes you dread, . .	46	To Congreve	95
"And Foreign Foes defeated!	154	Widow and Cat	D 25
Spight of Dutch Friends and English Foes, ...	168	Peace Dunkirk	1
Your Foes already waiting stand	258	Bubble	198
Your Foes, triumphant o'er the Laws, ...	312	To Ford	29
When Foes are o'ercome, we preserve them from Slaughter,	334	Serious Poem	1
Our Private and our Publick Foes, ...	339	Arch-Bish Dub	10
Cum Multis aliis (all his Foes)	373	Letter D. S-y	71
Made use of by detracting foes.	433	Answer Paulus	50
"And thought they Both were equal Foes:	549	Life of Swift	149
"Both bitter Foes to Britain's Weal.	549	Life of Swift	153
To all my Foes, dear Fortune, send	555	Death of Swift	67
"Who still were true, to please his Foes.	567	Death of Swift	364
"Whose Merits were, to be his Foes.	569	Death of Swift	402
Which my very Foes allow me.	631	Epistle Lady	64
Will pass for yours with Foes and Friends.	644	On Poetry	140
Their Foes superior by an Inch.	651	On Poetry	336
The Nymphs with Scorn beheld their Foes:	687	Cadenus Vaness	21
Tho' Foes to Love, attend the Session, ...	689	Cadenus Vaness	94
She'll prove the greatest of thy Foes:	696	Cadenus Vaness	300
Our inmost Secrets to our Foes:	706	Cadenus Vaness	611
With whom he serv'd, than by his Foes, ...	775	Mullinix Tim	54
Combin'd in Arms, they had their Foes defy'd, . . .	793	St. Pat's Well	81
How to distinguish Friends from Foes:	796	Traulus 1	24
He shot before your Foes were prim'd:	797	Traulus 1	58
With no Effect on Friends or Foes.	798	Traulus 1	66
But Ireland's Friends ne'er wanted Foes.	798	Traulus 1	88
His Follies to his greatest Foes.	915	Riddle 1	26
Invading Foes, without Resistance, ...	934	Riddle 21	D 3
Which fiercest Foes, cou'd break by no Means. . . .	1021	Nim-Dan-Dean 1	D 32

FOGGY

Grown lazy, foggy, fat, and dull:	231	Prog of Poetry	22
The foggy mists dispelling	442	Ballyspellin	69

FOGS

"Of City Fogs and crowded Rooms, ...	380	Apology Lady C	140

FOIL'D

But to scold is your trade, which I soon shou'd be foil'd in,	979	Dean to Tho: S	7

FOISTED

Thy Whisp'rings foisted in all Ears;	775	Mullinix Tim	62

FOKE

Our Parsons Read the Draper's Books, and make us honest Foke.	343	Upon His Grace	40

FOKES

And live like other christian fokes;	489	Dialogue	18
Suited to all Christian Fokes:	523	Betty Grizette	18
But he takes up with younger Fokes, ...	556	Death of Swift	93

FOLD

They Nightly slunk to rob the Fold, ...	153	Widow and Cat	D 8

FOLDS

That folds up itself in itself for a House:	350	Wood Insect	4

FOLIO

And take a Folio for a conj'ring Book.	193	Author Himself	8

FOLIO'S

Could read all Volumes up to Folio's, ...	513	Answer Fable	41

FOLK

He Din'd and Sup'd at Charge of other Folk, . . .	234	Elegy on Demar	10
With Pow'r no more than other Folk, ...	240	Run Bankers	35
But now I act as other Folk, ...	313	To Ford	55
To other sort of Folk was due:	478	Epist on Epist	106
We Mortals are strange kind of Folk.	545	Life of Swift	4
For if the Heav'nly Folk should know	689	Cadenus Vaness	79
"go tell your friend Bob and the other great folk, . .	843	Ay and No	13
At least, I'm well assured, that no Folk lays . . .	988	Letter Dr Sh-n	26

FOLKS SEE GENTLE-FOLKS

We Irish Folks expected wonders, ...	62	Discovery	2
When Folks came thick to make their Court	62	Discovery	6
. . .that we went and search'd the Folks round, . .	70	Mrs Harris Pet	22
Nay, said she, my Lord Collway's Folks are all very sad	70	Mrs Harris Pet	27
By lodging Folks dispos'd to sleep.	94	Bauc & Phil 1	152
Good Folks, you need not be afraid, ...	112	Bauc & Phil 2	43
By lodging Folks dispos'd to Sleep.	114	Bauc & Phil 2	106
And goes with Folks to shew the Sight:	116	Bauc & Phil 2	168
"See but the Fortune of some Folks!	202	Horace 2, 6	88
When sober Folks are all a-bed.	229	Prog of Beauty	104
And that's the reason, some folks think, ...	296	Satiric Elegy	15
The former folks were servants to the king, ...	308	Billet Players	13
You, happy Folks, are sure to meet	315	To Ford	105
You see, when Folks have got their Ends, ...	408	Dial Rich Marb	19
'Tis a sign she'll keep her folks, ...	419	Holyhead Journ	2
There are some prating folks in town, ...	422	Ireld	39
Enter the Folks with Silks and Lace:	447	Modern Lady	81
I wish some Folks would pare their Nails.	453	Modern Lady	269
Folks shrug, and cry, There's nothing in't.	475	Epist on Epist	12
Could all we little Folks that wait, ...	492	Panegyr Swift	1
Lye down obscure like other Folks	501	Doctor Delaney	45
And Kings, like private Folks, are bought and sold: .	536	To Mr. Gay	136
"His Claim as good as other Folks---.	547	Life of Swift	94

```
FOLKS          (CONTINUED)                                   PAGE    TITLE         LINE
    All Folks who pretend to Religion and Grace,      . . .   575  Place Damn'd       1
    (So some Folks told you, but they knew      . . . . . .   579  Day Judgement     17
    That Scholars were like other Folks:      . . . . . .     707  Cadenus Vaness   649
    To hold your cares for other folks.      . . . . . .      753  Gift for Bec      18
    Yet, merry Folks who want by chance      . . . . . .      756  Stel B-day '24     7
    To spare the Folks that gave him Ha'pence      . . . . .  796  Traulus 1         28
    Let Folks in high, or holy Stations,      . . . . . .     813  Bro Protestant    57
    What honester folks never durst for their ears.  . . .    815  Yahoo's           19
    Great Folks are of a finer Mold;      . . . . . . .       949  Epigr Scolding     1
    You rhyme, as folks fence, in tierce and cart.  . . . .   979  Dean to Tho: S    20
    . . . but I think Gentle folks should be civil.  . . .    986  Mary to Sher      24
    You live among ill folks in a dunghill,  . . . . . .    1038  Sheridan Cavan    17
FOLL'WERS
    The Roads are with his Foll'wers strown,      . . . .     398  Earl of P-b-w     20
FOLL'WING
    Foll'wing Opinion, dark, and blind,      . . . . . .       36  Ode Sancroft      56
FOLLIES
    Who both our Follies and Impertinencies see,      . . .    18  Ode Athenian      89
    Vext at their Follies, murmur'd in his Stream;  . . .      22  Ode Athenian     194
    In gath'ring follies from the wise;      . . . . . .       37  Ode Sancroft      85
    Thy various Follies, who can trace?      . . . . . .      555  Death of Swift    40
    Those, and twenty Follies more,      . . . . . . .        630  Epistle Lady       9
    Follies, from my Youth instill'd,      . . . . . . .      630  Epistle Lady      31
    Shall for my follies make amends:      . . . . . . .      755  Stella '23        36
    His Follies to his greatest Foes.      . . . . . .        915  Riddle 1          26
FOLLOW
    What mighty numbers follow them;      . . . . . .          39  Ode Sancroft     164
    Follow the model close, for so I'm sure they should,  .   40  Ode Sancroft     183
    May'st follow still thy Calling there.      . . . . .     100  Elegy Patrige     74
    And follow where he leads the Way:      . . . . . .       270  Apollo's Edict  D  9
    But, Yet, you'll find by what will follow,  . . . . .     371  Letter D. S-y      9
    Nor slip this Occasion to follow your Trade.  . . . .     400  Tom Clinch        20
    Then follow the Practice of clever Tom Clinch,  . . .     400  Tom Clinch        23
    Dismissing Mars, it next must follow      . . . . . .     462  Birthday Song     57
    But follow the securest rule,      . . . . . . .          468  Birthday Song    265
    I had it in the Words that follow.      . . . . . .       485  Libel on D- D-   182
    And follow the prevailing sect,      . . . . . . .        489  Dialogue          24
    Hear from my desk the words that follow;  . . . . . .     490  Dialogue          48
    Departed; and his Works must follow:      . . . . . .     562  Death of Swift   250
    The Muses next in Order follow,      . . . . . . .        585  Strephon Chloe    53
    You follow where we please to guide:      . . . . . .     620  Scandal Poem 1    89
    You follow where we please to guide;      . . . . . .     626  Scandal Poem 2    87
    And swear it does not always follow,      . . . . .       741  Stel B-day 22     21
    Dub, dub, a-dub, dub. The Trumpeters follow,  . . . .     870  Grand Question    91
    And yours to follow my Direction.      . . . . . .        932  Riddle 19       D 18
    Which plainly does follow,      . . . . . . . .           939  Riddle Answerd    23
    Come, follow me by the Smell,      . . . . . . .          952  Onyons             1
FOLLOW'D
    But mark what follow'd,--Faith she bit her.  . . . .      208  Fable Bitches     18
    In short such dire Confusions follow'd,      . . . . .    346  Prometheus        45
    There follow'd at his lying-in      . . . . . .           504  Doctor Delaney   117
    "He follow'd David's Lesson just,      . . . . . .        566  Death of Swift   341
    He follow'd, stript, and in he crept,      . . . . .      587  Strephon Chloe   113
FOLLOWERS
    Her Priests, her Train and Followers show      . . . .     27  Ode to Temple     40
FOLLOWING
    Related thus the following Tale.      . . . . . . .       412  Desire Possess     8
    Be sure at Will's the following Day,      . . . . .       644  On Poetry        117
    Your Garland in the following Reign,      . . . . .       647  On Poetry        231
FOLLOWS
    An Inventory follows here.      . . . . . . . .           526  Lady's Dres Rm    10
FOLLY
    Begets a kinder Folly and Impertinence      . . . . .      18  Ode Athenian      79
    Consider Humane Folly, and you'll quickly own,  . . .      20  Ode Athenian     149
    Men's Folly, Whimsyes, and Inconstancy,      . . . .       21  Ode Athenian     173
    Most fall at last to Interest, Folly, and Abuse.  . .      24  Ode Athenian     277
    Shall on a day make sin and folly bleed;  . . . . . .      47  To Congreve      134
    And 'twas a Folly to Contest:      . . . . . . .         175  Horace 1, 7      136
    Thus in a Sea of Folly tost,      . . . . . . .          202  Horace 2, 6      105
    For Dick without Doll thought Living a Folly.  . . .      430  Dicky Dolly        3
    "A servile Race in Folly nurs'd,      . . . . . .         568  Death of Swift   397
    "Where, Folly, Pride, and Faction sway,      . . . .      570  Death of Swift   433
    Who, led by Folly, fights with Nature;      . . . . .     641  On Poetry         20
    Is Folly, at his Death confuted.      . . . . . .         646  On Poetry        202
    Sloth, Folly, Rapine, Mischeif, Lust      . . . . .       659  On Poetry      D 410
    Where-e'er Caprice or Folly steers.      . . . . . .      687  Cadenus Vaness    38
    "Or add some Grains of Folly more      . . . . . .        714  Cadenus Vaness   874
    Her folly can trace;      . . . . . . . . .               854  Lady's Lament     96
    But, the folly of her sex      . . . . . . . .            906  Daphne             3
    Or in folly still befriend her,      . . . . . . .        907  Daphne            27
FOLLY'S
    Who blend it into folly's larger heap,      . . . . .      45  To Congreve       62
FOND
    How vainly (Sir) did Your fond Enemy try      . . . .      9  Ode to King      101
    And by a fond mistake      . . . . . . . . .              19  Ode Athenian     124
    But disappointed of his fond Desire      . . . . .        22  Ode Athenian     195
    How fond we are to court Her to our Arms!      . . .      23  Ode Athenian     232
    Each fond of erring with his guide:      . . . . .        39  Ode Sancroft     165
    While two fond lovers prate, the Muse and I.  . . .       49  To Congreve      200
    Why are we then so fond of two?  . . . . . . .          366  Answer Delaney     3
```

303

FOND   (CONTINUED)   PAGE   TITLE   LINE
    Tho fond of warlike Lyes as most men;   . . . . . .   462 Birthday Song   54
    And there he grew fond of another Man's Wife,   517 Dean Hang Rape   8
    Give up your fond paternal Pride, ...   644 On Poetry   127
    For he was fond of rural Strain.   . . . .   848 Old Thorn   12
    No Lady was ever more fond of a Spark;   . . . . . .   928 Riddle 11   D 10
    My Master is so fond of that Minister that keeps the   987 Mary to Sher   29
        School;
FONDLED
    First to be fondled, then be kill'd.   . . . .   753 Gift for Bec   12
FONDLING
    Bred a Fondling, and an Heiress;   . . . .   630 Epistle Lady   35
FONDLY
    We fondly stay at home in fear   . . . .   19 Ode Athenian   99
    By which some fondly boast they shall for ever live, . .   20 Ode Athenian   151
    He fondly thought he might endure   . . . .   119 Apollo Outwit   11
    Forgive me, when I fondly thought   . . . . . .   176 To Lord Harley   5
    Who fondly put his Trust in pop'lar Breath.   771 Horace 1, 14   32
    Nor fondly hope for some Reverse of Fate, ...   793 St. Pat's Well   85
FONDNESS
    To Fondness for the Female Kind;   . . . .   603 Beasts Confess   64
    Her Fondness for a certain Earl   . . . .   699 Cadenus Vaness   390
FONT
    In it's old shape a Font became   . . . .   93 Bauc & Phil 1   112
FOOD
    Still murmuring in their Wilderness for Food,   . . .   9 Ode to King   87
    Remembrance is our Treasure and our Food;   . . . .   27 Ode to Temple   31
    When Food and Rayment now grew scarce   . . . . .   225 Prog of Love   95
    Incumbrances of Food and Cloaths;   . . . . . .   231 Prog of Poetry   42
    Must dye for Want of Food and Rayment, ...   502 Doctor Delaney   73
    Keep them to wholsome Food confin'd, ...   587 Strephon Chloe   123
    Or ever went to seek my Food   . . . .   602 Beasts Confess   19
    Supports their Minds with heav'nly Food.   . . . .   605 Beasts Confess   124
    Since first the Court allow'd them Food.   . . . .   652 On Poetry   366
    That Vanity's the Food of Fools;   . . . .   710 Cadenus Vaness   759
    For Food, along the barren Plain;   . . . . . .   759 Receipt Youth   6
    By Food of twenty Years ago?   . . . .   765 Stel B-day '26   56
    That no Effects of Food remain?   . . . . . .   765 Stel B-day '26   60
    Hence he draws his daily Food, ...   800 Traulus 2   41
    Lice from your Body suck their Food;   . . . . .   812 Bro Protestant   35
    The Food of Worms, and Beasts obscene, ...   923 Riddle 7   59
FOOL   SEE PARTY-FOOL
    The way which ev'ry wand'ring fool below   . . . . .   39 Ode Sancroft   157
    What's that to her if mankind be a fool?   . . . . .   48 To Congreve   178
    If he be Wealthy and a Fool   . . . .   61 Lady Tablebook   27
    This Fool had got a lucky Hit, ...   156 Fable of Midas   23
    Where every Fool his Mouth applies, ...   158 Fable of Midas   63
    Call'd him a Cuckold, Fool, and Beast, ...   221 A Quiet Life   48
    One Fool may from another win, ...   253 Bubble   61
    One Night a Fool into a Brook   . . . .   255 Bubble   125
    'Fool, to put up four Crosses at your door,   . . .   404 Window Inns 11   D   3
    Where every knave & fool is bought   . . . . . .   421 Ireld   3
    The fool, who scrambles for a trifle;   . . . . .   436 Answer Paulus   136
    Thus every Fool her self deludes;   . . . . . .   449 Modern Lady   154
    Five hundred Pound a Year's no Fool.   . . . . .   478 Epist on Epist   112
    "Or pretty Miss has play'd the Fool, ...   497 Panegyr Swift   131
    "Expos'd the Fool, and lash'd the Knave: . . . .   565 Death of Swift   316
    Is of all Wits the greatest Fool;   . . . . . .   592 Strephon Chloe   278
    For which his Brethren call him Fool: . . . . .   603 Beasts Confess   82
    While ev'ry Fool his Claim alledges, ...   640 On Poetry   9
    The Cant which ev'ry Fool repeats, ...   645 On Poetry   153
    For such a Fool was never found, ...   727 To Stella   121
    "My School-Master call'd me a Dunce and a Fool,   .   873 Grand Question   163
    May turn and wind me like a fool.   . . . . . .   899 Dean's Reasons   14
    There's nobody but a Fool that would trust.   . . .   941 Letter   32
    Besides, Dick forbid me, and call'd me a fool;   . .   980 Tho: Sheridan   7
    . . .but that Man makes him a Fool.   . . . . . .   987 Mary to Sher   30
FOOL'S
    To put on a Fool's Disguise, ...   833 Legion Club   110
FOOLISH
    And every foolish Flye that dares to aim   . . . .   9 Ode to King   115
    In vain to quench this foolish Fire I try   . . . .   33 Ode to Temple   206
    Two foolish guides in ev'ry sublunary dance: . .   34 Ode Sancroft   9
    But foolish Man still judges what is best   . . . .   36 Ode Sancroft   54
    Say, foolish Females, Old and Blind, ...   449 Modern Lady   150
    Yet many a foolish thing he writ---;   . . . . .   547 Life of Swift   75
FOOLISHLY
    And foolishly are glad to see it at it's height   .   25 Ode Athenian   281
    And which our wild ambition foolishly compares . . . .   38 Ode Sancroft   126
FOOLS   SEE APRIL-FOOLS
    And all we Fools, who are the greater part of it,   18 Ode Athenian   71
    Must e'en all herd with us their Kindred Fools,   18 Ode Athenian   82
    Tho' Madmen and the Wits, Philosophers and Fools,   22 Ode Athenian   203
    More oft in Fools and Mad-mens hands than Sages   . .   23 Ode Athenian   220
    And we the bubbled Fools   . . . .   27 Ode to Temple   26
    And at once grow Scholars and Fools;   . . . . .   27 Ode to Temple   44
    Thus fools, for being strong and num'rous known,   37 Ode Sancroft   79
    Thus are the lives of fools a sort of dreams,   . . .   47 To Congreve   147
    Fools common-place thou art, their weak ensconcing fort, 53 Temple Ill   87
    That scorn of fools, by fools mistook for pride;   . .   55 Temple Ill   134
    That scorn of fools, by fools mistook for pride;   . .   55 Temple Ill   134

FOOLS	(CONTINUED)	PAGE	TITLE	LINE
And talk what Fools call Treason all the Night.		163	Toland's Invit	16
(As fools are insolent and vain)		177	To Lord Harley	41
For Madmen, Children, Wits and Fools		181	Horace 2, 1	31
And not like forty other Fools:		199	Horace 2, 6	D
When twenty Fools I never saw		200	Horace 2, 6	44
I'm stopt by all the Fools I meet,		202	Horace 2, 6	91
And Fools would fancy he intends		216	To Mr. Delany	39
Tormenting Fools behind their Backs;		240	Run Bankers	30
Fools chiefly float, the Wise are drown'd.		252	Bubble	52
Each Knave hath made a thousand Fools.		253	Bubble	60
For Fools will see as Wise men please.		257	Bubble	168
And Fools consult Interpreters in vain.		363	On Dreams	6
Where all are fools, and all are knaves		421	Ireld	2
He tells his brothr fools at night		421	Ireld	24
Exceeding all the fools of Totness.		423	Ireld	66
To keep good sense in crouds of fools;		436	Answer Paulus	124
To rail at men by nature fools:		488	Irish-Club	28
Nor ever fools or knaves expose		489	Dialogue	9
And all Mankind as Fools, or Knaves;		493	Panegyr Swift	6
Hated by Fools, and Fools to hate,		505	Doctor Delaney	171
Hated by Fools, and Fools to hate,		505	Doctor Delaney	171
The Fools, my Juniors by a Year,		561	Death of Swift	219
"Despis'd the Fools with Stars and Garters,		565	Death of Swift	323
"Taught Fools their Int'rest how to know;		569	Death of Swift	409
"No Fools of Rank, a mungril Breed,		570	Death of Swift	437
"To build a House for Fools and Mad:		572	Death of Swift	480
I damn such Fools!--Go, go, you're bit."		579	Day Judgement	22
You, when it rains, like Fools believe,		627	Scandal Poem 2	125
Into Knaves they turn their Fools:		635	Epistle Lady	158
Call Dunces, Fools, and Sons of Whores,		652	On Poetry	345
Fools, Fops, and Rakes, for Chaff and Straws.		688	Cadenus Vaness	60
That Vanity's the Food of Fools;		710	Cadenus Vaness	759
So, at a Ball, unthinking Fools delight		771	Horace 1, 14	49
Might want such noisy Fools as you;		774	Mullinix Tim	40
Dull Uniformity in Fools		787	Dick's Variety	1
'Though Fools may doubt his Faith in <Jesus>.		820	Dr. Rundle	26
For his Lunatics and Fools,		830	Legion Club	36
On this odious Group of Fools;		839	Legion Club	224
Is this, that you argue like fools in a circle.		1026	Sheri Circles	4
FOORTHE				
Then comyth foorthe, Ich understonde,		102	Merlin	5
FOOT SEE FORE-FOOT,FOUR-FOOT,A-FOOT				
You may know by the Hand, it had no Cloven Foot.		77	Lady B- B-	30
Here Five Foot deep lyes on his Back		101	Elegy Patrige	103
Nay, --now I cannot stir my Foot?		116	Bauc & Phil 2	161
We guess't the <Bishop's> Foot was in it.		300	Horrid Plot	70
From Head to Foot, and all before;)		324	Pethox	16
And eke your cloven foot.		428	Beau's Reply	8
And litter'd at Parnassus' Foot.		504	Doctor Delaney	122
In Regiments of Foot and Horse;		513	Answer Fable	28
His Ears are half a Foot too short;		602	Beasts Confess	32
A Cripple with one Foot too short:		645	On Poetry	172
"To put them on an equal Foot;		714	Cadenus Vaness	876
The Cieling hardly six foot high		746	Stel Distress	36
The Ceiling hardly six Foot high;		751	Stel Wood-Park	54
You shan't stir a Foot--You'll think me a Clown--		869	Grand Question	78
The Bishop with his Foot may burn it;		892	Panegyr Dean	173
At Head and Foot my Body lopt:		915	Riddle 1	12
Will come, tho' not a Foot they go.		934	Riddle 21	D 6
My foot was but just set out from my cathedral,		975	Dean to Sherid	3
FOOT-BOY				
A Foot-boy to some Rogue Director?		312	To Ford	40
Tom a Foot-Boy bred and born,		784	Mullinex Dick	11
FOOT-MAN'S				
But now they hear a Foot-Man's Rap:		451	Modern Lady	211
FOOT-STEPS				
Our predecessors foot-steps, still in view;		49	To Congreve	196
Can scarce th' impression of his foot-steps find;		54	Temple Ill	116
FOOTBOY'S				
Lords are a footboy's cronies in his sleep.		48	To Congreve	150
FOOTED SEE FOUR-FOOTED				
FOOTING				
Without the Footing of a Cause;		9	Ode to King	104
FOOTMAN				
The Footman in his usual Phrase,		447	Modern Lady	92
With whom a Footman out of Place		659	On Poetry	D 410
Footman, Traytor, vile Seducer,		831	Legion Club	69
My Footman came home from the Church, of a Bruise sick,		1029	Dr. Helsham	17
FOOTMEN				
At five the Footmen make a Din,		292	Prog Marriage	91
Yet lik'd three Footmen to her Chair.		693	Cadenus Vaness	221
With Footmen tippling under Ground,		729	Stella, Poems	44
Thus all the Footmen, Shoe-boys, Porters,		812	Bro Protestant	21
Those carters, and paviours, and footmen and all;		841	Ballad	D 17
FOOTS				
Though his Claret is bad, and he foots it on Stones,		1037	Four Storyes	7
FOOTSTEP				
Here a pale shape with upward footstep treads,		35	Ode Sancroft	33
FOOTSTEPS				
It's watery footsteps in Dorinda's face;		52	Temple Ill	52

```
FOOTSTEPS          (CONTINUED)                              PAGE   TITLE        LINE
    Ten thousand footsteps, full in view,    . . . . . . .  177 To Lord Harley    17
    And ev'ry where her footsteps trace,    . . . . . . .   401 Window Inns 5   D  7
FOOTSTOOL
    Made him his Footstool in the War,    . . . . . . . .     7 Ode to King       43
FOP
    For every peeping Fop to Jear.    . . . . . . . .        60 Lady Tablebook    18
    Then each transported Fop will cry,    . . . . . . .    228 Prog of Beauty    75
    This meagre Fop, that batter'd Beau:    . . . . . .     905 Death Daphne      74
FOPS
    Born between whores and fops, by lewd compacts,   . . .  47 To Congreve      125
    To cheapen Tea, and talk with Fops.   . . . . . . .     291 Prog Marriage     52
    Fools, Fops, and Rakes, for Chaff and Straws.   . . .   688 Cadenus Vaness    60
    A Croud of fashionable Fops;   . . . . . . . . .        696 Cadenus Vaness   317
    Nine Spirits of blaspheming Fops,   . . . . . . .       904 Death Daphne      41
FOR          1258
FOR'T                                                       OMITTED WORD
    But gath'ring spirits, wisely ran for't,   . . . . . .   64 Discovery        46
    And she wou'd kindly thank him for't.   . . . . . .     302 Storm             6
    One Fault he hath, is sorry for't,   . . . . . . .      602 Beasts Confess    31
    'Tis a true Copy, I'll say that for't,   . . . . . .    783 Tim and Fables    21
    'Tis all you have for't; 'tis your best Magna Carta;  . 979 Dean to Tho: S    16
    Will laugh in their sleeves: I can tell you they watch  979 Dean to Tho: S    36
        for't.
    And look in English, French, and Scotch for't,   . . . 993 On Picture        8
    At last I'm fairly forc'd to botch for't.   . . . . .   993 On Picture        9
FORBEAR
    And can you think the wise forbear to laugh   . . . .    46 To Congreve      107
    Ladys, quoth Levens, pray forbear,   . . . . . . .      67 Problem           57
    A third could not forbear his Mocks,   . . . . . .      91 Bauc & Phil 1     34
    Pray gentle-Folks forbear your Scoffing.   . . . .     286 Elegy Boat        38
    Forbear your poetry and jokes,   . . . . . . . .       489 Dialogue          17
    Himself could scarce forbear to kick,   . . . . . .    497 Panegyr Swift    139
    St. John himself will scarce forbear,   . . . . . .    561 Death of Swift   209
    Forbear their Tea, or drink it soon;   . . . . . .     587 Strephon Chloe   118
    Then cou'd I forbear to smile,   . . . . . . .         638 Epistle Lady     266
    Who, when she loudly cries, Forbear,   . . . . . .     641 On Poetry         21
    My good Friend Mullinix forbear,   . . . . . . .       775 Mullinix Tim      69
    Who could forbear, that view'd each guilty Face,   . . 806 Judas             23
    If Oonah once I kiss'd, forbear to chide:   . . . . .  882 Pastoral Dial     41
FORBID
    Forbid your Daughters guzzling Beer;   . . . . . .     587 Strephon Chloe   116
    Forbid Cadenus to engage.   . . . . . . . . .          711 Cadenus Vaness   779
    Forbid in open Air to breath;   . . . . . . . .        894 Panegyr Dean     231
    Heav'n forbid he should despise thee;   . . . . . .    907 Daphne            51
    Besides, Dick forbid me, and call'd me a fool;   . . . 980 Tho: Sheridan     7
FORBIDDING
    Forbidding his Disciples Beans)   . . . . . . .        587 Strephon Chloe   126
FORBIDS
    Phoebus forbids thee one, his Brother   . . . . . .    671 Epig Carthy 22   D  5
FORC'D
    Which soon her merit forc'd her to inspire;   . . . .   44 To Congreve       26
    Forc'd on me, crack'd, and clipp'd, and counterfeit,   45 To Congreve       56
    Was forc'd, for Safety, to alight,   . . . . . .       127 Little House      32
    Were forc'd to own to him their Obligation.   . . .    234 Elegy on Demar    18
    Was forc'd to send three Miles for Yest,   . . . .     282 Journal           89
    "Or, if you are, be forc'd to bear   . . . . . .       380 Apology Lady C   159
    Be often forc'd to rise at Night,   . . . . . .        587 Strephon Chloe   122
    And, e'er he flyes is forc'd to tye em.   . . . .      621 Scandal Poem 1   120
    But forc'd from their Retirement into Day,   . . .     667 Epig Carthy 5    D  3
    Which, though his Conscience forc'd him to restore,  . 806 Judas             5
    Is forc'd to lie farther,   . . . . . . . .            854 Lady's Lament     84
    I'm forc'd to leave a Limb behind.   . . . . . .       921 Riddle 6          36
    I'll write, tho' I'm forc'd to write in a wheelbarrow: 979 Dean to Tho: S    12
    At last I'm fairly forc'd to botch for't.   . . .      993 On Picture        9
    And art thou forc'd to yield, ill-fated Poetaster?   1002 Reply by Dean      3
FORC'T
    Has forc't to grope her uncouth way   . . . . . .       18 Ode Athenian      66
    Yet they were forc't to walk an Hour   . . . . . .      90 Bauc & Phil 1     12
    And thus the Dean is forc't to stay   . . . . . .      420 Holyhead          11
    Are forc't to look another Way;   . . . . . . .        922 Riddle 7          48
FORCE
    Of secret Malice, or of open Force.   . . . . . .       13 Ode to William   D 44
    Their first and chiefest force   . . . . . . . .        19 Ode Athenian     113
    Or a weak argument by force maintain'd?   . . . . .     34 Ode Sancroft      12
    Godlike the force of my young Congreve's bays,   . . .  44 To Congreve       41
    Nor need I ramble far to force a rule,   . . . . .      46 To Congreve      113
    In vain; for a superior Force   . . . . . . .          93 Bauc & Phil 1    101
    In vain; for a Superior Force   . . . . . . .         113 Bauc & Phil 2     61
    They, as each Torrent drives, with rapid Force   . . . 139 City Shower       57
    By Force of Wine ev'n <Scarborough> is Brave,   . . .  163 Toland's Invit    21
    Force him to take his Tythes in kind;   . . . . .      174 Horace 1, 7      110
    Conceal a fatal armed Force;   . . . . . . . .         209 Fable Bitches     44
    The Force of thy superior Voice   . . . . . . .        340 Arch-Bish Dub     27
    And boldly Force the winged Quill   . . . . . . .      373 Letter D. S-y     53
    The mortal force of Time's dystructive hand   . . .    419 Shall Repine       2
    To force in Ballyspellin   . . . . . . . . .           443 Ballyspellin      90
    "Nor fears from him ungrateful Force:   . . . . .      476 Epist on Epist    56
    That force free virtue shou'd enthrall?   . . . . .    490 Dialogue          44
    This Peacock kept a standing Force,   . . . . . .      513 Answer Fable      27
    No Brush could force a way betwixt.   . . . . . .      526 Lady's Dres Rm    22
```

	PAGE	TITLE	LINE
FORCE (CONTINUED)			
To force it out my Heart must rend;	596	Cassinus Peter	95
It whirls about for Want of Force,	688	Cadenus Vaness	54
But using neither Skill, nor Force,	696	Cadenus Vaness	302
Will force all Nature to submit.	709	Cadenus Vaness	725
Its Force against your nearest Friends;	730	Stella, Poems	98
Her valiant Arm should force us back,	885	Rev Market-Hill	60
I hardly now can force a Word.	916	Riddle 1	40
Through Clefts oppugnant force a Vent;	923	Riddle 7	86
A long-ear'd Beast, a Thing that Force must drive in,	943	Probatur Alit	47
FORCED			
Are forced to read the old gazettes.	⁴420	Holyhead	18
FORCES			
Our Forces let us both unite,	884	Rev Market-Hill	45
FORCING			
Forcing a wretched Trade by beating down the sale,	19	Ode Athenian	101
Then, turning to Hannah, and forcing a Frown,	873	Grand Question	182
FORD			
That Mr. Ford was born to day:	311	To Ford	4
How Ford would frown, how Jim would leer,	741	Stel B-day 22	19
Rebecca, Ford, and Grattons by.	743	Stel B-day 22	60
From Ford who thinks of nothing mean	745	Stel Distress	17
From Ford attending at her Call	745	Stel Distress	19
From Ford attending at her Call,	750	Stel Wood-Park	39
From Ford, who thinks of nothing mean,	750	Stel Wood-Park	41
Now tell me, friend Thomas, Ford, Grattan, and merry Dan,	955	Portrait Life	9
FORE-BODINGS			
Whate'er these dire fore-bodings meant,	290	Prog Marriage	17
FORE-FOOT			
Then with his Fore-foot set his Mark.	300	Horrid Plot	56
FORECAST			
A Prudent Builder should forecast	592	Strephon Chloe	293
FOREFATHERS			
Whether thy Great Forefathers came	324	Pethox	23
FOREHEAD			
My Dear, I see your Forehead sprout:	116	Bauc & Phil 2	156
See but her Forehead and her Chin.	229	Prog of Beauty	100
A Forehead Cloth with Oyl upon't	526	Lady's Dres Rm	25
Or Hairs that sink the Forehead low,	527	Lady's Dres Rm	57
Then tipt their Forehead in a Jeer,	698	Cadenus Vaness	360
The pliant bow, the forehead bland--	951	Upstart	D 30
FOREIGN			
"And Foreign Foes defeated!	154	Widow and Cat	D 25
All this is foreign to thy Walk;	183	Horace 2, 1	102
For foreign Aid what need they roam,	272	Apollo's Edict	D 62
Was left in Foreign Lands distrest,	482	Libel on D- D-	62
Of foreign Customs, Rites, and Laws;	697	Cadenus Vaness	353
Thus, Commonwealths receive a foreign Yoke,	770	Horace 1, 14	21
To foreign Prelates make a slavish Court,	793	St. Pat's Well	75
FOREMOST			
To see him always foremost stand,	546	Life of Swift	33
At Victuals foremost.	1035	Servants Maxim	4
FORESAW			
The Owl foresaw in pensive Mood	849	Old Thorn	37
FORESEE			
Shall (I foresee it) soon with Gothick Swarms come fort	25	Ode Athenian	298
When I foresee my special Friends,	556	Death of Swift	75
The Queen of Wisdom cow'd foresee,	701	Cadenus Vaness	484
The publick Safety I foresee,	776	Mullinix Tim	81
"Through all thy Empire I foresee,	851	Old Thorn	78
FORESEES			
From his own Hand foresees his Fall,	241	Run Bankers	50
FORESIGHT			
Approves his Foresight to the rest:	557	Death of Swift	128
FOREST SEE FORREST			
It left the Forest where 'twas nurst,	134	Magician's Rod	68
It would Burn a whole Forest; nor was it a Fiction;	334	Serious Poem	20
FORETEL SEE FORTEL			
Can like the Stars foretel the Weather;	99	Elegy Patrige	43
Yet, this I dare foretel you from it,	299	Horrid Plot	35
Foretel a Storm to last till Night.	624	Scandal Poem 2	26
FORETELL			
The Death of our Nation it seem'd to foretell,	351	Wood Insect	31
Foretell his Empire crown'd with Bays,	466	Birthday Song	195
Your Conduct in this new Employ foretell.	532	To Mr. Gay	30
Foretell a storm to last till night.	618	Scandal Poem 1	32
Consult the Stars, and thence foretell	918	Riddle 4	43
FORETELS			
Not one foretels I shall recover;	557	Death of Swift	133
FOREVER			
Forever green and flourishing 'twill last,	29	Ode to Temple	85
FORFEIT			
Or else I may forfeit my Lease.	396	Dog and Thief	16
You Forfeit all your Patron's Grace,	480	Libel on D- D-	30
FORFEITS			
That Knowledge forfeits all Humanity;	28	Ode to Temple	55
FORFEITURE			
He has a Forfeiture incurr'd,	712	Cadenus Vaness	802
FORFEITURES			
And dreams of Forfeitures by Treason got.	364	On Dreams	20

```
                                                              PAGE    TITLE            LINE
FORG'D
    Forg'd up in Colleges and Schools.      . . . . . . .      483  Libel on D- D-       92
FORGE
    Will Forge for thee a Paring-Knife,         . . . . . .    100  Elegy Patrige        84
    Up at his Forge by Morning-peep,      . . . . . . . .      352  Wood Ironmongr        3
    You at a Pinch could forge a Plot;          . . . . . .    494  Panegyr Swift        40
FORGET
    Forget their Fewds, and join to save their Wigs,          138  City Shower          42
    Leave hunting after Bribes, forget your Tropes:    . . .   162  Toland's Invit        6
    Forget he's like a Salamander.      . . . . . . . . .      270  Apollo's Edict    D 19
    But, which I gladly would forget,           . . . . . .    290  Prog Marriage        29
    (I forget in what Church) an Image of Wood;   . . . . .    334  Serious Poem         18
    Did Paulus e'er the sun forget?       . . . . . . . .      432  Answer Paulus         6
    Never may the Muse forget ye:       . . . . . . . . .      522  Betty Grizette        2
    And cursing <Bob>, forget to bless <the> <King>.   . . .   533  To Mr. Gay           52
    "Must we the Drapier then forget?      . . . . . . . .     547  Life of Swift        95
    And forget to broil and riot,       . . . . . . . . .      574  Helter Skelter       52
    In Silence, or forget with Pride.       . . . . . . .      726  To Stella            96
    O, may I never once forget      . . . . . . . . . . .      887  Panegyr Dean         24
    While I teach, and you forget;       . . . . . . . . .     908  Daphne               72
    The Lawyer must forget his Pleading,        . . . . . .    916  Riddle 1             31
    Does he forget from whence he came?      . . . . . . .     950  Upstart           D  2
    How could you forget so ungratefully a lass?    . . . .    977  Dean to Sherid       41
FORGETFUL
    Yet not forgetful of a Friend       . . . . . . . . .      183  Horace 2, 1          89
    Heedless, ignorant, forgetful?      . . . . . . . . .      630  Epistle Lady          8
FORGETS
    Forgets the Place where last he din'd:      . . . . . .    556  Death of Swift       88
    His manners forgets;          . . . . . . . . . . . .      855  Lady's Lament       142
    Forgets by whom it once was sav'd;   . . . . . . . .      875  Drapier's Hill       12
FORGETTING
    "Forgetting his own Flesh and Blood?      . . . . . .      558  Death of Swift      164
FORGIVE
    Forgive a young and (almost) Virgin-muse,     . . . .       18  Ode Athenian         62
    Rather forgive what my first Transport said,   . . . .     23  Ode Athenian        244
    Forgive (Original Mildness) this ill-govern'd zeal,        38  Ode Sancroft        107
    Forgive me, when I fondly thought      . . . . . . .      176  To Lord Harley        5
    Forgive her, if it be a Crime,      . . . . . . . . .     224  Prog of Love         63
    Beg'd she'd forgive him; in Conclusion,     . . . . .     378  Apology Lady C       83
    "You freely may forgive his Ashes.      . . . . . . .     550  Life of Swift       202
    Confess'd a Sin, and God forgive him:       . . . . .     604  Beasts Confess      114
    Good-natur'd Stella will forgive:       . . . . . . .     747  Stel Distress        58
    Forgive him, Tom, his Head is crackt.       . . . . .     795  Traulus 1             6
    Forgive me my sin.        . . . . . . . . . . . . . .     855  Lady's Lament       136
FORGIVEN
    It was her Fate; must be forgiven;      . . . . . . .     224  Prog of Love         55
FORGIVENESS
    Forgiveness begg'd, that he appear'd        . . . . .     603  Beasts Confess       61
FORGOT
    The <Queen> incens'd, his Services forgot,        . .     195  Author Himself       57
    Will ne'er be forgot,       . . . . . . . . . . . . .     244  Irish-Feast           2
    "Ye have forgot this Month and Day.--     . . . . .      322  First of April       56
    Tales here forgot, or yet unheard;      . . . . . . .     386  Manly Virtue         74
    I fear I shall be soon forgot.      . . . . . . . . .     408  Dial Rich Marb       18
    One Compliment I had forgot,        . . . . . . . . .     464  Birthday Song       129
    Forgot at Home, became for Hire,        . . . . . . .     482  Libel on D- D-       63
    Nor be the Handkerchiefs forgot     . . . . . . . . .     527  Lady's Dres Rm       49
    "I'm glad the Medals were forgot.       . . . . . . .     559  Death of Swift      184
    He quite forgot to say his Pray'rs.         . . . . .     605  Beasts Confess      118
    His Promises he ne'er forgot,       . . . . . . . . .     606  Beasts Confess      157
    Their filial Piety forgot,      . . . . . . . . . . .     652  On Poetry           359
    And quite forgot their Country was enslav'd.   . . . .    771  Horace 1, 14         52
    The generous Wheat forgot its Pride.        . . . . .     811  Bro Protestant        7
    I dye unpity'd and forgot;       . . . . . . . . . .      916  Riddle 1             41
    Has he forgot from whence he sprung?     . . . . . .      950  Upstart           D  3
    Oh! but I forgot, perhaps, by this time, you may have one
       . . .                                                 1023  Nim-Dan-Dean 2    D  7
    Oh! I forgot too, I believe there may be one more, . . . 1023  Nim-Dan-Dean 2    D  9
    I had forgot to desire you to bring down what I say you
       have,. . .                                            1023  Nim-Dan-Dean 2    D 15
FORGOTTEN
    His Medals and his Prints forgotten,        . . . . . .   875  Drapier's Hill       15
FORLORN
    To a forlorn and broken Rake,       . . . . . . . . .     133  Magician's Rod       33
    Ye Poets ragged and forlorn,        . . . . . . . . .     394  Grub-Street           1
    We should not thus have layn forlorn;       . . . . .     409  Dial Rich Marb       32
FORM
    Were I to form a regular Thought of Fame,     . . . .      21  Ode Athenian        158
    And form the Leaves, the Branches, and the Fruit.   . .    32  Ode to Temple       174
    Then with that grief we form in spirits divine,    . .     43  To Congreve           5
    But a wild form dependent on the brain,     . . . . .      54  Temple Ill           95
    I've seen a Snake in human Form,        . . . . . . .      84  Salamander           38
    To form some Beauty by a new Receit,        . . . . .     118  Biddy Floyd           2
    They form a frightfull hideous Face,        . . . . .     226  Prog of Beauty       24
    Cannot without a Form subsist,      . . . . . . . . .     228  Prog of Beauty       82
    And Form, say I, as well as They,       . . . . . . .     228  Prog of Beauty       83
    And from a Fable form a Truth:      . . . . . . . . .     252  Bubble               44
    Were bid in form, but sent Excuses:         . . . . .     290  Prog Marriage        10
    To Neptune went, and begg'd in Form         . . . . .     302  Storm                 3
    That lies in old Wood like a Hare in her Form;     . .    351  Wood Insect          18
    "So shall the Eye, by Form confin'd,        . . . . .     384  Manly Virtue         11
```

FORM   (CONTINUED)   PAGE   TITLE   LINE
    In manly Form to let them see   . . . .   384 Manly Virtue   25
    His outward Form, and Inward, vie, ...   385 Manly Virtue   59
    It passes but for common Form;   . . . .   453 Modern Lady   271
    To form a just and finish'd piece, ...   460 Birthday Song   1
    The Bride was put in Form to Bed;   . . . . . .   587 Strephon Chloe   112
    The outward Form no Help requir'd: . . . . . .   692 Cadenus Vaness   176
    Wou'd by her Model form their Mind, ...   694 Cadenus Vaness   237
    To form and cultivate her Mind.   . . . .   706 Cadenus Vaness   631
    "To form a Nymph of Wit and Sense;   . . . . .   713 Cadenus Vaness   865
    So little is thy Form declin'd   . . . .   722 Stel B-Day '18   7
    In such a Form an Angel's Mind   . . . .   735 Stel B-day '20   20
    Although we now can form no more   . . . . . .   764 Stel B-day '26   15
    Let them form a grand Committee, ...   831 Legion Club   53
    Form their Features, while I gibe them;   . . . .   839 Legion Club   226
    How could I form so wild a vision,.   . . . . .   899 Dean's Reasons   15
    Nor can she change her Form so fast, ...   911 Aenigma   5
    Nature to form me took Delight, ...   915 Riddle 1   3
    Conceal your Form with various Tricks;   . . . .   919 Riddle 5   27
    Lifeless, Life's perfect Form I wear, ...   935 Riddle 23   D   7
FORM'D
    A jargon form'd from the lost language, wit,   . . . 47 To Congreve   121
    Form'd by diseas'd conceptions, weak, and wild,   . . 47 To Congreve   123
    Jove ever form'd to make a <Stink>?   . . . . . .   65 Problem   4
    Has form'd a Model for your Land;   . . . .   272 Apollo's Edict   D 65
    Form'd like the Triple-Tree near Stephen's-Green;   . 285 Elegy Boat   34
    Compleatly form'd in every Part, ...   385 Manly Virtue   55
    By Vulcan form'd so round and bright: . . . . .   433 Answer Paulus   28
    To Virtue form'd a Princely Youth, ...   482 Libel on D- D-   56
    But form'd more perfect Gamester, you   . . . . .   494 Panegyr Swift   37
    But form'd by You, how should their Model   . . . . 496 Panegyr Swift   104
    By Nature form'd with nicest Care, ...   584 Strephon Chloe   5
    Fate never form'd the Gods to flye   . . . . . .   620 Scandal Poem 1   111
    Fate never form'd the Gods to fly;   . . . . . .   626 Scandal Poem 2   109
    Which form'd into a Garland sweet, ...   647 On Poetry   223
    You form'd this Project in your Brain, ...   695 Cadenus Vaness   289
    By something form'd, I nothing am, ...   935 Riddle 23   D   1
FORMAL
    Terrestrial nymphs, by formal arts, ...   178 To Lord Harley   53
    Some formal Visits, Looks, and Words, ...   204 In Sickness   13
    Ye formal Weepers for the Sick, ...   204 In Sickness   23
    Thy formal Nods; important Sneres;   . . . . . .   775 Mullinix Tim   61
    Have it so formal, and so Curl'd, ...   780 Mullinix Tim   222
    Tho' Lewd and Immoral, be Formal and Grave,   . . . 807 Advice Parson   3
FORMED
    "Was formed this Machi'villian Plot, ...   850 Old Thorn   74
FORMER
    Which yet their former Virtue keep, ...   94 Bauc & Phil 1   151
    The former folks were servants to the king,   . . . 308 Billet Players   13
    But, in the chronicles of former ages, ...   308 Billet Players   29
    Your former Comrades, once so bright, ...   311 To Ford   23
    "As it was deem'd in former Days   . . . .   384 Manly Virtue   5
    Where Criticks mark'd your former Faults.   . . . . 645 On Poetry   150
    They ply their former Arts below.   . . . . . .   647 On Poetry   210
    She fell into her former Scene, ...   747 Stel Distress   55
    She fell into her former Scene.   . . . .   751 Stel Wood-Park   71
    You'll be no more your former You;   . . . . . .   760 Receipt Youth   38
    Your former Actions claim their Part, ...   765 Stel B-day '26   71
    Their former Companions should beg at their Door.   . 804 Irish Bishops   28
    Those former Ages differ'd much from this: . . .   806 Judas   9
    But because the three former are long ago past,   . . 967 Letter Sherid   11
FORMERLY
    Went to one Griffith, formerly a play'r: . . . .   307 Billet Players   4
FORMING
    And by the forming Engine struck, ...   344 Prometheus   9
    Forming his Muse by <Smedley's> Modell, ...   458 Paddy's Charac   23
    Tis sung Prometheus forming Man   . . . .   659 On Poetry   D 410
    And forming you, mistook your Kind?   . . . . . .   726 To Stella   86
FORMS
    Whose well-compacted Forms escape the Light,   . . .   31 Ode to Temple   166
    Which all the mimic forms express, ...   35 Ode Sancroft   25
    Stale forms of course, all mean deceivers use,   . .   44 To Congreve   20
    At distant hours the mind with forms so like!   . .   51 Temple Ill   2
    Unknown the forms we the high-priesthood use   . . .   53 Temple Ill   75
    When he ask'd for my Aid, in the Forms that are usual: 265 Apollo   72
    The Widow goes through all her Forms;   . . . . .   295 Prog Marriage   157
    "<He> can assume more Forms than I, ...   303 Storm   29
    Cadenus, common Forms apart, ...   703 Cadenus Vaness   540
    That common Forms were not design'd   . . . . . .   706 Cadenus Vaness   612
    That I can vulgar Forms despise, ...   706 Cadenus Vaness   616
    The Fire that forms a manly Soul;   . . . . . .   726 To Stella   88
    Or Forms reflected from a Glass?   . . . .   765 Stel B-day '26   52
    It forms an union in the mind: . . . .   901 Dean's Reasons   70
    In various Forms appear agen   . . . .   924 Riddle 7   93
    Most wondrous Forms you see me wear   . . . . . .   927 Riddle 10   D 13
    By us forms his Laws, and Rules, ...   931 Riddle 18   D 11
FORREST
    To burn an old Fryer, one Forrest by Name.   . . .   334 Serious Poem   22
FORSAKE
    My Lord and Dean, the Fire forsake;   . . . . . .   279 Journal   31
    That Scholars wou'd forsake their Books   . . . .   694 Cadenus Vaness   234

		PAGE	TITLE	LINE
FORSAKE	(CONTINUED)			
For who could such a Nymph forsake	. . . .	733	Verses Vanessa	19
His Habitation let all Men forsake,	. . . .	806	Judas	25
FORSAKEN				
That those forsaken wretches who to-day	. . . . . .	38	Ode Sancroft	130
No longer shall forsaken Thames	. . . . . .	107	V's House	47
Where the Nymph has entirely forsaken her Text:	. . .	716	Answer Rebus	20
Forsaken by th' inspiring Nine,	. . . .	741	Stel B-day 22	13
FORSOOK				
Thus, when Dorinda wept, joy ev'ry face forsook,	. . .	53	Temple Ill	59
On an abandon'd wretch by hopes forsook;	. . .	54	Temple Ill	108
Forsook by hopes, ill fortune's last relief,	. . . .	54	Temple Ill	109
FORSOOTH				
The <Queen> (forsooth, Despotick) gave	. . . . . .	181	Horace 2, 1	25
But you forsooth, your All must squander,	. . . . .	476	Epist on Epist	59
And the Clergy, forsooth, must take up with their Leavings.		804	Irish Bishops	34
But at present, forsooth,	. . . .	852	Lady's Lament	23
FORSWEAR				
When Gold's to be got, to Forswear and Suborn.	. . .	335	Serious Poem	46
FORSWEARS				
(Who now again Quadrill forswears,)	. . . .	453	Modern Lady	291
FORT				
Rescu'd Her from the Giant's Fort:	. . . . .	7	Ode to King	38
Fools common-place thou art, their weak ensconcing fort,	.	53	Temple Ill	87
To Fort St. George a Pedlar went he.	. . . . . .	456	Dean Smedley	48
I well remember when I sat fort.	. . . .	783	Tim and Fables	22
Must raise a Fort at Market-Hill.	. . . .	883	Rev Market-Hill	16
Nor need we doubt the Fort to win;	. . . .	885	Rev Market-Hill	55
FORTEL				
Careful Observers may fortel the Hour	. . . . . .	136	City Shower	1
FORTH				
When she sends forth such a malignant Birth,	. . .	8	Ode to King	54
Shall (I foresee it) soon with Gothick Swarms come fort	.	25	Ode Athenian	298
Which in due time brought forth a House;	. . . .	81	Vanbrug House	75
And hardly waddles forth, to cool	. . . .	230	Prog of Poetry	5
Right Trusty, and so forth; We let you to know,	. . .	263	Apollo	1
We issue forth at different Hours;	. . . .	278	Journal	8
Forth issues wriggling Dick Drawcensir,	. . .	785	Dick, Maggot	6
On his virtues hold forth; 'tis the very best way;	. .	819	Archbi Cashel	9
Last trolled forth a gentle Swine	. . . .	849	Old Thorn	41
Call forth our Cottagers to Arms;	. . . .	884	Rev Market-Hill	44
Nature holds her forth two mirrors,	. . . .	907	Daphne	43
FORTIFY				
And join to fortify your Heart.	. . . .	765	Stel B-day '26	72
FORTIORI				
I conclude a Fortiori,	. . . .	636	Epistle Lady	194
FORTITUDE				
To point out which is moderation, which is fortitude.	.	41	Ode Sancroft	210
With Temp'rance, and with Fortitude;	. . . . . .	325	Pethox	62
All Fortitude of Mind supplies:	. . . .	561	Death of Swift	214
No real fortitude implies:	. . . .	676	Parson's Case	3
With Justice, Truth and Fortitude;	. . . .	693	Cadenus Vaness	207
FORTNIGHT				
I study'd a Fortnight, before I could find,	. . .	265	Apollo	75
When my Left Ear was deaf a Fortnight,	. . . . .	367	Answer Delaney	42
My Master scarce a Fortnight since,	. . . . .	409	Dial Rich Marb	37
Resolv'd for a Fortnight to Swim in Delight,	. . .	517	Dean Hang Rape	26
And thus the Farce a fortnight went	. . . . .	747	Stel Distress	53
. . .and you shall go back in a fortnight, ...		1023	Nim-Dan-Dean 2	D 8
FORTRESS				
Admits us in, to storm the Fortress;	. . . . .	885	Rev Market-Hill	70
FORTUNE				
To interrupt the Fortune of Your Course:	. . . . .	13	Ode to William	D 42
Fortune the gamesters does beguile,	. . . . .	29	Ode to Temple	79
Fortune in both extremes,	. . . . .	40	Ode Sancroft	203
Who, by Disgraces or ill Fortune sunk,	. . . . .	163	Toland's Invit	17
Of titles, birth, and fortune proud,	. . . . .	177	To Lord Harley	40
"See but the Fortune of some Folks!	. . . . . .	202	Horace 2, 6	88
Whose Fortune is not overgrown;	. . . . .	243	Horace 4, 9	16
How Fortune fails him when he sets;	. . . . .	281	Journal	76
When Fortune hither drove me first;	. . . . .	313	To Ford	52
Where, on the Summit Fortune stands;	. . . . .	413	Desire Possess	41
Nor, will you find your Fortune sink,	. . . . .	414	Censure	25
Good Fortune peeping from behind;		452	Modern Lady	229
When fortune favour'd, he was nice,	. . . . .	456	Dean Smedley	27
His Heart too Great, though Fortune little,	. . .	482	Libel on D- D-	81
And fortune help the murd'rer in his flight;	. . .	506	To a Friend	2
If Fortune should please to take such a Crotchet,	. .	518	Dean Hang Rape	43
Advanc'd thy Fortune, and preserv'd thy Fame.	. .	531	To Mr. Gay	14
With favour & fortune fastidiously blest	. . . . .	540	Charac Walpole	1
of favour & fortune unmerited vain	. . . . . .	540	Charac Walpole	3
He says, "Whenever Fortune sends	. . . . .	545	Life of Swift	7
To all my Foes, dear Fortune, send	. . . . .	555	Death of Swift	67
That Fortune still assists the bold,	. . . . .	588	Strephon Chloe	148
And meekly took what Fortune sent:	. . . . .	602	Beasts Confess	42
He came to Court with Fortune clear,	. . . . .	606	Beasts Confess	165
No Wonder how his Fortune sunk,	. . . . .	607	Beasts Confess	195
By Valour, Conduct, Fortune won;	. . . . .	641	On Poetry	26
But, now shou'd fortune shift the scene,	. . . . .	676	Parson's Case	19
A Fidler may a Fortune get;	. . . . . .	710	Cadenus Vaness	737

310

		PAGE	TITLE	LINE
FORTUNE	(CONTINUED)			
Oh, ne'er may Fortune shew her Spight,		758	Stel B-day '24	53
May fortune and her coffee get her		762	Bec's B-Day	47
Since Fortune, my foe,		858	Lady's Lament	207
From distant Regions, Fortune sends		883	Rev Market-Hill	1
O Fortune, 'tis a Scandal for thee		884	Rev Market-Hill	25
What Fortune may befall his Nose.		993	On Picture	21
FORTUNE-TELLER				
That, long ago a Fortune-teller		223	Prog of Love	51
FORTUNE'S				
Forsook by hopes, ill fortune's last relief,		54	Temple Ill	109
But, You, who till your Fortune's made		485	Libel on D- D-	153
You tell me, till my Fortune's made,		496	Panegyr Swift	96
Poor floating Isle, tost on ill Fortune's Waves,		770	Horace 1, 14	1
FORTUNES				
And you that did your Fortunes seek,		101	Elegy Patrige	109
Here various Kinds by various Fortunes led,		138	City Shower	39
The Fortunes of his latter Scene,		481	Libel on D- D-	46
To patch his broken fortunes, found		879	Robbin & Harry	31
FORTY SEE FOURTY				
Who has forty Years let out his Conscience to hire,		142	New Song	2
Should you live years forty more		187	Scriblerus 4	D 17
And not like forty other Fools:		199	Horace 2, 6	D
With Forty Things more: Now hear what the Law says,		236	Excellent Song	3
And forty others I could name--		298	Horrid Plot	11
He heys from hence at forty four,		456	Dean Smedley	33
With forty Pounds a Year at most.		484	Libel on D- D-	134
Or at the Age of Forty three,		757	Stel B-day '24	25
To cut it off these forty years.		760	Bec's B-Day	6
Where forty Lines, exceed fourscore.		1022	Nim-Dan-Dean 1	D 50
Where less than forty, fill a Quart.		1022	Nim-Dan-Dean 1	D 52
FORTY-FOUR				
Dreams of a Gown of forty-four;		703	Cadenus Vaness	525
FORWARD				
Of forward Face, and Ear acute,		63	Discovery	26
I forward the Grass, and ripen the Vine:		263	Apollo	8
And hasted forward to pursue		412	Desire Possess	29
A forward Critick often dupes us		648	On Poetry	255
What imports thy forward Sight?		862	To Janus	11
I'll have none but forward Eyes:		863	To Janus	20
FORWARDS				
Is backwards and forwards always the same;		148	Windsor Proph	22
Which backwards and forwards is allmost the same.		148	Windsor Proph	24
FOSTER'D				
And foster'd in a wretched inn.		40	Ode Sancroft	175
FOSTERED				
Young Ducklings, fostered by a Hen;		294	Prog Marriage	146
FOUGHT				
But aided by the Wind, fought still for Life;		137	City Shower	24
Three Duels he fought, thrice ventur'd his Life		327	Epigram 1	9
A Duel fought last Night at Two,		696	Cadenus Vaness	320
And now you find you fought for nothing.		774	Mullinix Tim	38
Who when I fought still cut me down,		1005	Sheridan's Sub	8
FOUL				
'Tis with a foul design the muse you send,		44	To Congreve	15
And then fall foul on all the Town;		217	To Mr. Delany	56
Crackt Lips, foul Teeth, and gummy Eyes,		226	Prog of Beauty	15
On Paper daub'd so foul,		425	Five Ladies	14
And when 'tis foul, affords you Sport.		493	Panegyr Swift	20
His foul Imagination links		529	Lady's Dres Rm	121
With which he makes so foul a Rout;)		530	Lady's Dres Rm	140
But when they smelt such foul Corruptions round him;		536	To Mr. Gay	159
Discover Caelia's foul Disgrace.		597	Cassinus Peter	112
Of foul and fair we give you warning;		619	Scandal Poem 1	48
One minute whether foul or fair?		619	Scandal Poem 1	50
Of Foul or Fair we give you warning;		625	Scandal Poem 2	44
One Minute, whether Foul or Fair?		625	Scandal Poem 2	46
All outward and within is foul;		787	Clad in Brown	14
To foul the Man he chiefly flatters.		796	Traulus 1	32
Like his Body, rank and foul:		800	Traulus 2	34
If still your foul bosom more rancour contains;		819	Archbi Cashel	12
Like a very foul mop, dirty more than they clean.		819	Archbi Cashel	16
And foul the green seat;		857	Lady's Lament	190
How deep and foul the Roads may grow,		860	Lady Acheson	19
That she throws away as foul;		907	Daphne	47
The foul Corruptions of Mankind.		921	Riddle 7	16
Your Gibes and all your foul Abuse,		1003	Dan J's Reply	14
FOULER				
For, would'st thou make a fouler Show,		786	Clad in Brown	3
FOULEST				
Foulest Brute that stinks below,		786	Clad in Brown	1
The foulest Impressions I easily take.		929	Riddle 13	D 8
FOULLY				
Your num'rous virtues foully stain'd;		436	Answer Paulus	142
FOULNESS				
His Hide emits a Foulness out,		786	Clad in Brown	8
Thou now one Heap of Foulness art,		787	Clad in Brown	13
FOULS				
There's nothing fouls the Hands so much:		158	Fable of Midas	68
FOUND				
And scorn it when 'tis found.		20	Ode Athenian	144

FOUND   (CONTINUED)   PAGE   TITLE   LINE

We've found a little inconsiderable Head   . . . . .   20 Ode Athenian   147
Nor ever since but in Descriptions found, ...   26 Ode to Temple   14
I'm sure I found them other kind of things   . . . . .   46 To Congreve   91
So when I came up again, I found my Pocket feel very   69 Mrs Harris Pet   12
    light,
. . .ty'd in a Rag, the Money was found.   . . . . .   70 Mrs Harris Pet   23
. . .and I found her full of Grief;   . . . . .   71 Mrs Harris Pet   34
He found it was strangely fill'd in the Middle. . . .   77 Lady B- B-   9
When he found a new Help from Invisible Hand. . . . .   77 Lady B- B-   25
But when he found the Boys at play, ...   86 Hist V's House   13
That no two Chairmen could be found   . . . . .   87 Hist V's House   29
For, Baucis with Amazement found   . . . . . .   92 Bauc & Phil 1   75
But this a Work so hard was found, ...   108 V's House   87
But no such House was to be found;   . . . . .   109 V's House   98
Yet (what is wonderful) they found, ...   112 Bauc & Phil 2   32
Found his Head fill'd with many a System, ...   115 Bauc & Phil 2   135
Jove sent and found far in a Country Scene, ...   118 Biddy Floyd   3
In Scottish Hills found precious Ore, ...   133 Magician's Rod   29
Yet since I know where a full Purse may be found, . .   144 New Song   49
Stole to the Pantry-Door, and found   . . . . .   150 Corinna   18
But found him thus their Merit Scan, ...   157 Fable of Midas   53
Found out that it was Dr. <Swift>:   . . . . .   171 Horace 1, 7   26
Pray leave me where you found me first.   . . . . .   175 Horace 1, 7   138
In History we never found   . . . . .   190 Faggot   27
No matter where the Money's found;   . . . . .   199 Horace 2, 6   20
His Genius first found out the Rule   . . . . .   216 To Mr. Delany   35
Dick found it by his ill Success   . . . . .   221 A Quiet Life   41
And found Admittance from the Dame.   . . . . .   222 Prog of Love   20
Weigh'd in the Ballance, and found Light.   . . . . .   241 Run Bankers   64
By long Experience we have found   . . . . .   258 Bubble   190
He found he could purchase Two Tankards of Ale . . .   288 Bank Down   37
But the Squire he was cunning and found what they meant,   288 Bank Down   51
Since others oft have found one there;   . . . . . .   294 Prog Marriage   138
Besides, this horrid Plot was found   . . . . .   299 Horrid Plot   37
And, when we found the Dog begin it, ...   300 Horrid Plot   69
At Sea, or Land, if e'er you found him, ...   303 Storm   15
"I found you did it by your Grinning;   . . . . .   304 Storm   43
Found all the Realms before him waste;   . . . . .   326 Pethox   92
And then I went to pay the 'Squire and in the Way I   343 Upon His Grace   41
    found,
With much ado, the Cheat he found;   . . . . .   346 Prometheus   48
And found his Copper all was base;   . . . . .   353 Wood Ironmongr   28
In vain - - - no Doctor's to be found   . . . . .   377 Apology Lady C   64
"And can I then be faulty found   . . . . .   380 Apology Lady C   161
And found in Blushes, Eloquence.   . . . . .   386 Manly Virtue   82
Too lately found! to lose him late!   . . . . .   388 Manly Virtue   142
But which excell'd was never found, ...   393 Modern Poets   15
He strove to pick up all he found, ...   412 Desire Possess   25
Before, I always found the wind   . . . . .   420 Holyhead   21
Perhaps be found one honest man: . . . . .   435 Answer Paulus   104
Is found at Ballyspellin   . . . . .   441 Ballyspellin   48
The Chair-Men are not to be found, ...   453 Modern Lady   284
(Which measur'd on his Head, was found   . . . . .   458 Paddy's Charac   15
I found my Head began to swim, ...   470 Burning Poem   9
Here a convenient Box you found, ...   477 Epist on Epist   67
A Passage may be found, I've heard, ...   479 Epist on Epist   119
That I am often found exceeding   . . . . .   489 Dialogue   3
That you who was found writing of Drapiers   . . . . .   522 St. Cecilia's   3
Strephon, who found the Room was void, ...   526 Lady's Dres Rm   3
A Pair of Tweezers next he found   . . . . .   527 Lady's Dres Rm   55
A Dext'rous Steward, when his Tricks are found, . . .   535 To Mr. Gay   107
Nor found it difficult to guess the Cause: . . . . .   536 To Mr. Gay   158
Away they fled, and left him as they found him. . . .   536 To Mr. Gay   160
What Money was behind him found?   . . . . .   547 Life of Swift   72
There must another Sett be found.   . . . . .   556 Death of Swift   98
"For when we open'd him we found, ...   559 Death of Swift   175
"But, not a Traytor cou'd be found, ...   567 Death of Swift   353
"Ingratitude he often found, ...   567 Death of Swift   359
Most certainly there's the Hell to be found, ...   575 Place Damn'd   6
Meer mortal Flesh was all he found: . . . . .   586 Strephon Chloe   76
He found her, while the Scent increas'd, ...   589 Strephon Chloe   185
On Sense and Wit your Passion found, ...   593 Strephon Chloe   307
Him thus accoutred Peter found, ...   594 Cassinus Peter   25
He left them Virgins as he found 'em.   . . . . .   598 Problem Solved   26
A better Neighbour ne'er was found: . . . . .   602 Beasts Confess   44
He found, his Virtues too severe   . . . . .   603 Beasts Confess   55
He found, the Ministers resent it, ...   604 Beasts Confess   101
By fair Accounts it would be found   . . . . .   606 Beasts Confess   173
He found the wisest Men he could, ...   607 Beasts Confess   183
None of these have Mercy found: . . . . .   638 Epistle Lady   247
When I found the tingling Pain, ...   638 Epistle Lady   267
Thro' ev'ry Alley to be found, ...   651 On Poetry   315
Which having found an equal Flame, ...   687 Cadenus Vaness   31
And, after long computing, found   . . . . .   693 Cadenus Vaness   226
Found out the Trick that Venus play'd, ...   694 Cadenus Vaness   251
She study'd well the Point, and found   . . . . .   695 Cadenus Vaness   278
At Entrance loudest, where they found   . . . . .   698 Cadenus Vaness   370
He found her Thoughts would absent range, ...   704 Cadenus Vaness   566
He wak'd, and found it but a Dream;   . . . . .   705 Cadenus Vaness   585
Your Lessons found the weakest Part, ...   706 Cadenus Vaness   622

FOUND   (CONTINUED)

	PAGE	TITLE	LINE
Or found an Earwig in a Plum.	726	To Stella	78
For such a Fool was never found,	727	To Stella	121
Fair Chloe would perhaps be found	729	Stella, Poems	43
But found my Wit and Fancy fled:	740	Stel B-day 22	6
A goodly set as can be found	762	Bec's B-Day	51
They lye, alas, too easy to be found,	772	Horace 1, 14	63
There's hardly twenty to be found;	773	Mullinix Tim	6
That scarce a Creature can be found,	776	Mullinix Tim	79
And found, as he the pages twirl'd,	782	Tim and Fables	7
Freedom and Virtue in thy Sons I found,	792	St. Pat's Well	37
He might have found a Score of Chaps,	821	Dr. Rundle	50
Thus, when the gentle Spina found	850	Old Thorn	49
No 'Squire to be found	858	Lady's Lament	211
To patch his broken fortunes, found	879	Robbin & Harry	31
If Florimel had found her Love	905	Death Daphne	81
From whom great Sylla found his Doom;	925	Riddle 8	35
But very few are found to enter;	928	Riddle 12	D 4
I'm found almost in ev'ry Garden,	929	Riddle 14	D 5
Yet but one of us is found	931	Riddle 18	D 25
I found you mistaken in Matter of Fact.	972	S-'s Ans Sh-d	4
You found out my rebus with very much modesty;	976	Dean to Sherid	37
Besides, you found fault with our Vittles	986	Mary to Sher	25
Is not a Penny often found	1004	Dan J's Reply	28
But we took our dividers, and found your <damn'd> metre,	1026	Sheri Circles	11
When I left you, I found myself of the Grape's Juice sick:	1028	Dr. Helsham	1

FOUNDATION

To build on some Foundation sound;	592	Strephon Chloe	296
To destroy the old Foundation,	801	Traulus 2	48

FOUNDATIONS

That best Foundations must be low.	87	Hist V's House	40

FOUNDER

The Founder of thy antient Race.	323	Pethox	4
The glorious Founder of their kingly Race:	790	St. Pat's Well	12

FOUNDER'D

A founder'd Horse will oft debate,	640	On Poetry	15
This Racer wou'd prove but a dull founder'd Jade.	717	Answer Rebus	28

FOUNDER'S

Thy Founder's Grandson and usurp his Place.	826	Noisy Tom	16

FOUNDERS

At his Ring's-End he founders in the Port.	284	Elegy Boat	8

FOUNDRED

Ly waiting for the foundred Skiffs,	256	Bubble	155
To tear you like a foundred Hulk	258	Bubble	199

FOUNT

Should stumble once into the Fount,	671	Epig Carthy 21	D 7

FOUNTAIN

Oft 'gainst her Fountain does complain,	31	Ode to Temple	155
Troubling the chrystal fountain of the sight,	54	Temple Ill	97
Was to a boiling Fountain turn'd,	293	Prog Marriage	118
Our King ne'er exhausted his fountain of Honours.	389	Order of Bath	6
Fled to the Fountain back, from whence it came!	793	St. Pat's Well	66

FOUNTAINS

And lessening rivers mourn their fountains dry	419	Shall Repine	4
From purling Streams & Fountains bubbling	744	Stel Distress	3
From purling Streams and Fountains bubbling,	750	Stel Wood-Park	27

FOUR   SEE FORTY-FOUR

And I had in a Purse, seven Pound, four Shillings and.	69	Mrs Harris Pet	2
'Tis true, seven Pound, four Shillings, and six Pence,.	71	Mrs Harris Pet	40
But spight of the Harpy that crawls on all four,	147	Windsor Proph	11
If you'll be sure to come at Four.	173	Horace 1, 7	72
(October next, it will be four)	201	Horace 2, 6	64
I meet perhaps from three or four,	204	In Sickness	15
Thus after four important Hours	227	Prog of Beauty	53
Nor can four hundred thousand sterling Pound	233	Elegy on Demar	3
I dare believe that Four in Five	235	Elegy on Demar	51
From the four Elements assembling,	279	Journal	27
George, Nim and Dean, set out at Four,	280	Journal	43
Sits down to Dinner just at four;	291	Prog Marriage	56
Hang up thy wife, and she'll make four.	404	Window Inns 11	D 2
'Fool, to put up four Crosses at your door,	404	Window Inns 11	D 3
Put up your Wife, she's crosser than all four',	404	Window Inns 11	D 4
Hang up your Wife, and you'l count Four',	404	Window Inns 11	D 6
Now pay four Shillings in the Pound.	409	Dial Rich Marb	28
For I'm to dine with him at four	423	Ireld	62
"Four Mattadores, and lose Codill!	446	Modern Lady	52
And Madam almost dress'd by Four;	447	Modern Lady	91
"When Lady Tricksy play'd a Four,	452	Modern Lady	250
A frosty Morn--Past Four a-Clock.	453	Modern Lady	283
He heys from hence at forty four,	456	Dean Smedley	33
Four Stories climbing to her Bow'r;	581	Young Nymph	8
I own, 'twas but a Coach and Four,	598	Problem Solved	17
Without his taudry coach and four:	621	Scandal Poem 1	122
Without his lacker'd Coach and Four,	627	Scandal Poem 2	116
I rode four more to great St. Mary;	675	Curate's Compl	3
Using four legs when two were weary.	675	Curate's Compl	4
Stella this Day is thirty four,	721	Stel B-Day '18	1
The Cellar could contain but four)	747	Stel Distress	50

	PAGE	TITLE	LINE
FOUR (CONTINUED)			
The Cupboard could contain but four;)	751	Stel Wood-Park	66
You are only to live four Years without Vittles!	805	Irish Bishops	60
How greater's his merit at four Courts or House,	814	Yahoo's	8
Of whom there are but four at most,	820	Dr. Rundle	13
Above his Rent four Pounds a Year;	875	Drapier's Hill	4
But, squeezing out four Lines in Rhime,	893	Panegyr Dean	195
How many to answer? One, two, three, four.	967	Letter Sherid	10
. . . four Years since October,	985	Mary to Sher	13
Here four of you got mischances to plague you,	1037	Four Storyes	1
FOUR-FOOT			
For libelling the Four-foot Race.	607	Beasts Confess	202
FOUR-FOOTED			
Whose Heart in this Four-footed Thing lies.	763	Collar Lap-Dog	2
FOURSCORE			
And crowd to Stella's at fourscore.	736	Stel B-day '20	58
Where forty Lines, exceed fourscore.	1022	Nim-Dan-Dean 1	D 50
FOURTH			
And the fourth a Box within,	931	Riddle 17	D 6
FOURTHLY			
And, Fourthly; 'tis to play an odd Trick,	348	Whitshed Motto	17
FOURTY			
That you are turning fourty two.	311	To Ford	12
Tis fourty to one	423	Carterets Arms	1
FOWL			
And fowl his Hands in Search of Hope.	528	Lady's Dres Rm	94
A Fish, a Fowl, a Cloud, a Field,	927	Riddle 10	D 15
Cooks make their Fowl look tight and spruce.	942	Probatur Alit	10
FOWL'D			
Fowl'd with the Scouring of her Hands;	526	Lady's Dres Rm	38
FOWLS			
Nor rides, nor walks, nor hunts, nor fowls,	901	Dean's Reasons	87
FOX			
The Lyon, Eagle, Fox and Bear	83	Salamander	9
The Fox and He were Friends of old,	153	Widow and Cat	D 6
Invites the Fox to Dinner.	153	Widow and Cat	D 15
Hounds hunt the Hare, the wily Fox	504	Doctor Delaney	129
The Stagg was swift, the Fox a Knave:	512	Answer Fable	6
A Fox with Geese his Belly crams;	651	On Poetry	325
FRAGMENTS			
Chaff, straws, or fragments of some rotten boat,	672	Epig Carthy 24	D 14
FRAGRANT			
And, Venus-like, her fragrant Skin	586	Strephon Chloe	87
FRAILER			
We both are Mortal; but thou, frailer Creature,	861	On Old Glass	1
FRAILTY			
You who thro' Frailty step'd aside,	579	Day Judgement	13
FRAME			
Your happy Frame at once controuls	28	Ode to Temple	68
The Epilogue behind, did frame	108	V's House	93
Your steady Soul preserves her Frame	243	Horace 4, 9	9
To this, the Beauty of your Frame.	726	To Stella	92
FRAMING			
For framing Laws to govern States;	641	On Poetry	28
FRANCE			
Howe're it be, the Pride of France	10	Ode to King	136
Are Arts peculiar to dissembling France:	11	Ode to William	D 2
France do's in vain her feeble Arts apply	13	Ode to William	D 41
Of Joan of France, and English Moll,	114	Bauc & Phil 2	94
The Praise of Italy or France	314	To Ford	92
FRANCK			
In courtly style addresses Franck;	879	Robbin & Harry	50
FRANK			
His Debtors they wonder'd to find him so frank,	288	Bank Down	44
Got? <Damn> my Blood I frank my Letters,	778	Mullinix Tim	155
FRANTICK			
Hither the frantick Goddess draws	883	Rev Market-Hill	5
FRAUD			
Pale Avarice and lurking Fraud	243	Horace 4, 9	11
Since all he got by Fraud, is lost by Stocks,	678	Dean and Duke	6
Fraud, Perjury, and Guilt are seen.	922	Riddle 7	22
FRAUDFUL			
(Give fraudful Vice the Mask and Screen,	386	Manly Virtue	79
FRAUGHT			
That Head so well by Wisdom fraught!	361	Grace's Answer	15
A Soul with ev'ry Virtue fraught	482	Libel on D- D-	75
With cooling Gales, like Zephirs fraught;	911	Aenigma	2
Your Engine fraught with cooling Gales,	912	Aenigma Expl	D 5
FRAUNCE			
Of Fraunce hir woe thys is the sygne,	102	Merlin	2
To Fraunce, that evere he was borne.	103	Merlin	8
FRAY			
And, if they begin a Fray,	574	Helter Skelter	47
FREAK			
To vex me more, he took a Freak,	915	Riddle 1	15
FREAKS			
Who in your merry Freaks,	425	Five Ladies	2
FRECKLED			
And, thy freckled Neck display'd,	522	Betty Grizette	5
FREDDY			
Now sing his little Highness Freddy,	466	Birthday Song	187

```
                                                              PAGE   TITLE            LINE
FREE
   (Free from our tyrant-passions, anger, scorn, or fear)   .     38 Ode Sancroft      116
   Then pray be free, and tell me which:  . . . . . . .         299 Horrid Plot        24
   How free we acted, and had no controller:   . . . . .       308 Billet Players     34
   A window here from scribbling free:   . . . . . . . .       402 Window Inns 7   D   2
   And then I shall be free from Fears,    . . . . . . .       410 Dial Rich Marb     77
   I own his conscience always free,  . . . . . . . . .        434 Answer Paulus      55
   Free Leave to play his Secretary,  . . . . . . . . .        475 Epist on Epist      9
   That force free virtue shou'd enthrall?  . . . . . .        490 Dialogue           44
   Thus was the Hare pursu'd, tho' free from Guilt;   . .      538 Mr. Pulteney       37
   From Bayliffs claws thou scarce cou'd keep thy Bum free.    678 Dean and Duke      12
   The Learned met with free Approach,   . . . . . . .         701 Cadenus Vaness    458
   And, to be free, was dearly bought;  . . . . . . . .        708 Cadenus Vaness    671
   The Mother-Kingdom left her Children free;   . . . .        791 St. Pat's Well     20
   My Trade is, Pris'ners to set free.   . . . . . . . .       920 Riddle 6            2
   Nay, further, the Moment you're free from your scalding,   1019 To Sheridan         9
FREE-BORN
   The chains which fetter free-born minds,  . . . . . .       490 Dialogue           32
FREE-THINKER
   "It serves for Sceptick, and Free-thinker,   . . . .        550 Life of Swift     177
FREE-THINKERS
   Pronounce all Men of Wit, Free-thinkers.  . . . . . .       503 Doctor Delaney     98
   This tempts Free-thinkers to refine,  . . . . . . .         687 Cadenus Vaness     11
FREED
   Pregnant with Greeks, impatient to be freed,   . . . .      139 City Shower        48
   They soon from all Constraint are freed;   . . . . .        590 Strephon Chloe    205
   From Passion you may then be freed,   . . . . . . .         731 Stella, Poems     135
FREEDOM
   But, if I may with freedom talk,   . . . . . . . .          183 Horace 2, 1       101
   These Gentlemen use me with Kindness and Freedom,   . .     263 Apollo             21
   I'd go in freedom to my grave,   . . . . . . . . .          421 Holyhead           33
   With too much freedom treat my betters,   . . . . . .       489 Dialogue            5
   Discovers freedom without rage;  . . . . . . . . .          490 Dialogue           28
   They'll find his Life, and Acts, and Freedom,   . . . .     494 Panegyr Swift      52
   How jealous of the Nation's Freedom,   . . . . . .          501 Doctor Delaney     57
   Might have her Freedom when she pleas'd:   . . . . .        704 Cadenus Vaness    575
   Now no one regards what he Utters with freedom,   . . .     717 Answer Rebus       25
   Freedom and Virtue in thy Sons I found,   . . . . . .       792 St. Pat's Well     37
   Yet still the <Dean> on Freedom raves,   . . . . .          799 Traulus 1          99
FREEDOM'S
   Fair Freedom's Emblem once, which smoothly flows,   . .     793 St. Pat's Well     67
FREELY
   For you freely must own you were at a Dead lift;   . . .     77 Lady B- B-         28
   And freely from the fattest Side   . . . . . . . .           91 Bauc & Phil 1      59
   And freely from the fattest Side   . . . . . . . .          112 Bauc & Phil 2      27
   Item the Actors, freely gave a Day,   . . . . . . .         274 Epilogue            9
   To this we freely shall consent,   . . . . . . . .          461 Birthday Song      17
   (I freely grant the Thought is old)   . . . . . . .         464 Birthday Song     131
   "But Nature freely takes her Course,   . . . . . . .        476 Epist on Epist     55
   "You freely may forgive his Ashes.   . . . . . . .          550 Life of Swift     202
   Or freely tell the secret Cause.   . . . . . . . .          589 Strephon Chloe    162
   He freely gave the Poor Advice;  . . . . . . . . .          604 Beasts Confess     84
   Whom Stella freely entertains   . . . . . . . . .           735 Stel B-day '20     24
   His crabs and sloes may freely pillage:  . . . . . .        902 Dean's Reasons    108
   And freely made the first Advance:   . . . . . . .          905 Death Daphne       68
   Pudet haec opprobria, I freely must tell ye,   . . . .      967 Letter Sherid       5
FREEMAN
   And tips you the Freeman a Wink;   . . . . . . . .          396 Dog and Thief      10
   Said the Freeman, your Guinea To-night would be spent,     396 Dog and Thief      13
FREIGHT
   With the Freight enrich themselves:   . . . . . . .         635 Epistle Lady      162
FREIGHTED
   Come back t'us well freighted;   . . . . . . . .           1014 Swift to Sheri     25
FRENCH
   Takes a French Play as lawful Prize,   . . . . . . .        107 V's House          58
   What signify'd the French to beat?   . . . . . . .          169 Peace Dunkirk      32
   Wherein French Writers most excell:   . . . . . . .         216 To Mr. Delany      32
   In French brocades and Flanders Lace;  . . . . . . .        291 Prog Marriage      64
   Though French by Birth and Education:  . . . . . . .        300 Horrid Plot        50
   Scotch, Irish, English, French unite   . . . . . . .        345 Prometheus         15
   Now let's no more caress thy French,   . . . . . . .        373 Letter D. S-y      64
   In English vile, and viler French,   . . . . . . .          434 Answer Paulus      78
   On French Records for twenty long Campains;   . . . .       771 Horace 1, 14       44
   So, the French, when our Generals soundly did pay 'em,     967 Letter Sherid      17
   And look in English, French, and Scotch for't,   . . .      993 On Picture          8
FREQUENT
   But Gold defiles with frequent Touch,   . . . . . .         158 Fable of Midas     67
   (By frequent observation taught)   . . . . . . . .          176 To Lord Harley      6
   "You, Mr. Dean frequent the Great;   . . . . . . .          202 Horace 2, 6        93
   And still the bloody Field frequent,   . . . . . . .        324 Pethox             17
   By frequent Practice learns the Trick   . . . . . .         416 Woman's Mind       39
   From whom she meets with frequent Rubs;  . . . . . .        583 Young Nymph        53
   So frequent or so loud as theirs?   . . . . . . . .         624 Scandal Poem 2      6
   The wits will frequent ye,   . . . . . . . . . .            855 Lady's Lament     133
   Ye who frequent this hallow'd Scene,   . . . . . . .        893 Panegyr Dean      217
   We in frequent Councils are,   . . . . . . . . .            931 Riddle 18       D   5
FREQUENTED
   Which made thy Closet much frequented   . . . . . .        182 Horace 2, 1        51
   Frequented Lords; saw those that saw the Queen;   . . .     194 Author Himself     17
FREQUENTS
   The Castle seldom frequents.   . . . . . . . . .             75 Game Traffick      16
```

```
FRESH    SEE A-FRESH                                      PAGE    TITLE              LINE
     But find some new address, some fresh deceit,   . . . .    44 To Congreve         17
     As a fresh miss, by fancy, face, and gown,   . . . . .     48 To Congreve        151
     Fresh blooming, in young Harley's mind. . . . . . .       178 To Lord Harley      52
     Such is the Poet, fresh in Pay,   . . . . . . . .         230 Prog of Poetry      17
     Behold him blooming, fresh, and fair,   . . . . . .       384 Manly Virtue        17
     Fresh Objects fairer to his View;   . . . . . . .         412 Desire Possess      30
     Fresh Matter for a World of Chat,   . . . . . . .         447 Modern Lady         82
     Fresh from the Tripod of Apollo,   . . . . . . .          485 Libel on D- D-     181
     As fresh as Farthings from the Mint:                      644 On Poetry          114
     'Till some fresh Blockhead takes your Place.   . . .      644 On Poetry          142
     Whate'er she gains is young and fresh;   . . . . . .      759 Receipt Youth       16
     Fresh from a wedding, or a christ'ning,   . . . . .       762 Bec's B-Day         53
     Like a fresh <Turd> just dropt on Snow.   . . . . .       786 Dick, Maggot        14
     Fresh from the Mud a wallowing Sow   . . . . . .          786 Clad in Brown        5
     So plump and so fresh,   . . . . . . . . . .             952 Oysters              3
     Fresh from Malahide;   . . . . . . . . .                 953 Herrings             4
     Come eat 'em with pure fresh Butter and Mustard,   . .   953 Herrings             6
FRESHEST
     Stock'd with the freshest gibberish of the town;   . . .  47 To Congreve        120
FRET
     Takes Horse, and in a mighty Fret   . . . . . .          174 Horace 1, 7        116
     Wou'd make him rage, and storm, and fret,   . . . . .    546 Life of Swift       28
     And fret the Tories Souls to Death,   . . . . . .        778 Mullinix Tim       171
     I began to rage and fret   . . . . . . . . .            832 Legion Club         94
     Though daggled round, I scorn to fret:   . . . . .       890 Panegyr Dean       110
     You neither fume, nor fret, nor flounce;   . . . . .     891 Panegyr Dean       150
     You no more at me shall fret,   . . . . . . .            908 Daphne              71
     Then I fret, and rave and gabble,   . . . . . .          933 Riddle 20       D   7
     For that, dear Tom, ne'er fret and vex,   . . . . .      983 Sher, A Goose       17
FRETFUL
     Are you positive and fretful?   . . . . . . . .          630 Epistle Lady         7
FRETS
     And full of Indignation frets   . . . . . . . .          450 Modern Lady        164
     Lord how this Frothy Coxcomb frets! (aside)   . . . .    774 Mullinix Tim        16
     He rages and frets,   . . . . . . . . . .              855 Lady's Lament      141
FRETT
     What Use in Life, to make Men frett?   . . . . . .       217 To Mr. Delany       71
FRETTS
     For want of matter swears and fretts,   . . . . . .      420 Holyhead            17
FRICASSEES
     And feed on Fricassees and Olio's.   . . . . . .         513 Answer Fable        42
FRICASSYES
     To dress their Soupes and Fricassyes;   . . . . . .      895 Panegyr Dean       266
FRIDAY
     Last Friday Night, as Neighbours use,   . . . . . .      408 Dial Rich Marb       5
     I must confess, on Friday last,   . . . . . . .          602 Beasts Confess      15
FRIEND
     Ah, could You! could you hope a Poet for your Friend!     23 Ode Athenian       243
     Like a cast mistress to your wicked friend;   . . . . .   44 To Congreve         16
     And let my friend apply it as he please:   . . . . .      49 To Congreve        204
     'Tis time to bid my friend a long farewell,   . . . . .   50 To Congreve        227
     My Ld, sd Bush, a Friend and I   . . . . . . .            63 Discovery           33
     If it were Friend or Foe,   . . . . . . . .               77 Lady B- B-          17
     A Friend in Turns and Windings try'd   . . . . . .        94 Bauc & Phil 1      137
     Nor look Asquint on an old Friend.   . . . . .           101 Elegy Patrige      102
     Desires some Friend to lend a Hand   . . . . . .         160 Atlas                8
     And bid Friend Lewis go in quest   . . . . . .           171 Horace 1, 7         16
     Thus trust us, a Friend to the Distress'd,   . . . . .   182 Horace 2, 1         57
     Yet not forgetful of a Friend   . . . . . .             183 Horace 2, 1         89
     For trust us, friend Mortimer   . . . . . . .            187 Scriblerus 4    D  16
     Again apply that <Swift> would be their Friend.   . . .  196 Author Himself      70
     A handsome House to lodge a Friend,   . . . . .          198 Horace 2, 6          3
     Desiring I would stand their Friend.   . . . . .         200 Horace 2, 6         46
     And chose me for an humble Friend;   . . . . .           201 Horace 2, 6         66
     "How think you of our Friend the Dean?   . . . . .       202 Horace 2, 6         83
     But, no obliging, tender Friend   . . . . . .            204 In Sickness         19
     "My only Friend, my Dear," said she,   . . . . .         207 Fable Bitches        9
     In civil Terms,--"My Friend," says she,   . . . . .      208 Fable Bitches       25
     The Guest reply'd,--"My Friend, your Leave,   . . . . .  208 Fable Bitches       31
     He who betrays his Friend, shall never be   . . . . .    210 Earl of Oxford      17
     Reproach not tho in jest, a Friend   . . . . . .         217 To Mr. Delany       67
     Yet still you think your Friend to blame.   . . . . .    218 To Mr. Delany       82
     Regards a Friend of yours and mine,   . . . . .          218 To Mr. Delany       90
     But when he saw his Friend appear   . . . . .            220 A Quiet Life         5
     Oh London Tavern! Thou hast lost a Friend,   . . . . .   234 Elegy on Demar      25
     With Life his Country, or his Friend.   . . . . .        243 Horace 4, 9         24
     To write a few Verses on you as my Friend;   . . . .     265 Apollo              74
     And will now be her Friend whenever she pleases;   . . . 266 Apollo             106
     Not Sheridan, but friend Delany.   . . . . . .           278 Journal              6
     A Villain, who his Friend betrays,   . . . . . .         298 Horrid Plot          7
     To spare a Foe, to save a Friend:   . . . . . .          306 Storm               76
     Can You, my Friend, with Patience bear,   . . . . .      312 To Ford             36
     He can Eat, Drink and Sleep; now and then for a Friend   335 Serious Poem        43
     These Comedies twain Friend Wood will contrive   . . .   337 Serious Poem        93
     'Tis Kindness to hold a Friend up by the Chin;   . . .   338 Serious Poem       118
     Then said my Lord, I'm very glad to see thee honest
          Friend,                                             342 Upon His Grace      31
     In Gold, Perhaps, my Friend you Wallow   . . . . .       372 Letter D. S-y       29
     To Worth and Learning is a Friend.   . . . . .           391 Young's Satire      10
     Who hir'd a subterraneous Friend,   . . . . . .          393 Modern Poets        13

                                      316
```

FRIEND   (CONTINUED)   PAGE   TITLE   LINE
  My honest Friend Wild, may he long hold his Place,   .   399 Tom Clinch   17
  But now, the danger of a friend . . . .   420 Holyhead   23
  And have we lost our only Friend? . . . .   445 Modern Lady   16
  To all mankind a constant friend, ...   455 Dean Smedley   15
  The Dean, Tom's honour'd Friend and Patron. . . .   458 Paddy's Charac   28
  Take this Advice then from your Friend, ...   478 Epist on Epist   113
  Wou'd, if he durst, be more your Friend; . . . . .   483 Libel on D- D-   114
  To ask the judgement of a friend, ...   489 Dialogue   14
  To teach the Science to your Friend. . . . .   493 Panegyr Swift   28
  Pain would I think, our Female Friend sincere, . . .   531 To Mr. Gay   3
  To lose an Inch of Favour for a Friend? . . . . .   531 To Mr. Gay   6
  Who, while th' unrighteous Mammon is his Friend, . .   533 To Mr. Gay   73
  On weighty Bus'ness, to some neighb'ring Friend: . .   534 To Mr. Gay   86
  And, should a Friend attempt to set him right, . . .   535 To Mr. Gay   111
  You are his Dearest Friend---; he lyes---: . . . .   545 Life of Swift   26
  Suppose your Friend and You, were Equal, ...   546 Life of Swift   32
  My Friend should have, when I complain, ...   546 Life of Swift   45
  To palliate his Friend Oxford's Crimes, ...   550 Life of Swift   185
  I love my Friend as well as you, ...   554 Death of Swift   17
  Arbuthnot is no more my Friend, ...   555 Death of Swift   55
  Thy Gifts, but never to my Friend: . . . .   555 Death of Swift   68
  No Enemy can match a Friend; . . . .   557 Death of Swift   120
  "No worthy Friend, no poor Relation? . . . . . .   558 Death of Swift   162
  And in his Place my good Friend Will; . . . .   560 Death of Swift   194
  "The Funeral of so good a Friend. . . . .   562 Death of Swift   234
  "Against the Craftsman and his Friend; . . . . . .   563 Death of Swift   274
  To oblige a good Friend, she will trace ev'ry Market, .   580 Psyche   11
  Friend Peter to Cassinus goes, ...   594 Cassinus Peter   7
  Friend Peter, this I could excuse; . . . .   595 Cassinus Peter   63
  Thy Friend would gladly share thy Fate. . . . . .   596 Cassinus Peter   94
  Yet, when conjur'd by such a Friend-- . . . . . .   596 Cassinus Peter   96
  Sometimes his Friend he would not spare, ...   602 Beasts Confess   25
  Though neither Foe nor Friend allows us. . . . . .   603 Beasts Confess   78
  Is to help yourself, and Friend. . . . .   633 Epistle Lady   122
  Than my Friend Sir <Robert> <Brass> . . . . . .   637 Epistle Lady   246
  But let no Friend alive look into't. . . . .   643 On Poetry   108
  But then, I'm sure, friend Charles, you want the spur.   671 Epig Carthy 23   D   2
  That you, friend Marcus, like a stoick . . . . . .   676 Parson's Case   1
  The Book, the Author, and the Friend. . . . . . .   709 Cadenus Vaness   705
  E'er Stella can deceive a Friend. . . . .   725 To Stella   58
  The Friend, the Mistress, and the Wife, ...   728 Stella, Poems   16
  Whom Stella chuses for a Friend. . . . .   728 Stella, Poems   24
  And when a Friend in Kindness tries . . . . . .   730 Stella, Poems   89
  In vain; for see, your Friend hath brought . . . .   731 Stella, Poems   101
  The Angel-Inn to ev'ry Friend: . . . .   734 Stel B-day '20   6
  And Friend <Delany> at his Books, ...   756 Stel B-day '24   12
  But I'll be still your Friend in Prose: . . . . . .   757 Stel B-day '24   30
  An innocent and absent Friend; . . . .   765 Stel B-day '26   44
  My good Friend Mullinix forbear. . . . .   775 Mullinix Tim   69
  But how, my Friend, can I endure . . . .   778 Mullinix Tim   179
  Friend Rundall fell with grievous bump, ...   822 Epigr Rundle   1
  "go tell your friend Bob and the other great folk, . .   843 Ay and No   13
  Dear friend, Doctor Jenny, ...   857 Lady's Lament   203
  Yet, when we dine without a Friend, ...   886 Rev Market-Hill   97
  Which never yet one Friend has lost you. . . . . .   890 Panegyr Dean   114
  With so conversible a friend, ...   899 Dean's Reasons   24
  To serve a friend against his will? . . . .   902 Dean's Reasons   114
  But often spunge upon a Friend: . . . .   954 Authors Living   8
  Now tell me, friend Thomas, Ford, Grattan, and merry   955 Portrait Life   9
    Dan,
  Friend Sheridan, when will you know your own Good? . .   968 Letter Sherid   24
  Thus you may see, dear Friend, ex pede hence . . .   980 Letter Dr Sh-n   15
  A Friend of mine, that Author despises . . . . . .   988 Letter Dr Sh-n   21
  So far, dear Dan, that ev'ry Friend . . . .   993 On Picture   29
  . . .I appeal to your Friend Mr. Conna. . . . . .   1014 Swift to Sheri   10
  When you have not one friend left in town, ...   1022 Nim-Dan-Dean 2   D   4
  . . . come to town, but I don't know whether he be friend 1023 Nim-Dan-Dean 2   D   7
    . .
  . . . I mean that great fat joker, friend Helsham, he .   1023 Nim-Dan-Dean 2   D   9
  Friend Congreve a Feaver, Friend Howard an Ague, . .   1037 Four Storyes   2
  Friend Congreve a Feaver, Friend Howard an Ague, . .   1037 Four Storyes   2
  Friend Pope overturnd by driving too fast away, . . .   1037 Four Storyes   3
  Consult friend Whiteway. . . . .   1038 Sheridan Cavan   12
  You never have an old friend at Cavan. . . . . .   1038 Sheridan Cavan   18
FRIEND'S
  For when you express a Friend's Love we are willing, .   337 Serious Poem   103
FRIENDLY
  And let the friendly Lines they writ . . . .   611 By Dr. Swift   7
  Of giddy Winds, but make some friendly Port. . . .   770 Horace 1, 14   12
  New-River-walk with friendly Shade. . . . .   884 Rev Market-Hill   51
FRIENDS
  Swore all the wits were his peculiar friends; . . . .   47 To Congreve   140
  Said, how a late report your friends had vex'd, . . .   47 To Congreve   143
  Eat, Honest Friends, and never spare, ...   91 Bauc & Phil 1   64
  And will quit my best Friends, while I'm Not in game.   144 New Song   26
  The Fox and He were Friends of old, ...   153 Widow and Cat   D   6
  To eat the Calves-Head with your trusty Friends. . . .   162 Toland's Invit   4
  Spight of Dutch Friends and English Foes, ...   168 Peace Dunkirk   1
  For among good Friends, I love to be plain; . . . .   168 Peace Dunkirk   7
  "By which wise Conduct they grow Friends . . . . .   181 Horace 2, 1   47

FRIENDS   (CONTINUED)   PAGE   TITLE   LINE
    And Climb the dark Stairs to your friends who have none: 185 Scriblerus 1   4
    To your Friends who at least have no Cares but to please   185 Scriblerus 1   5
        you
    And all his old Friends would rebuke . . . .   186 Scriblerus 4   D 9
    But, after sage Monitions from his Friends, ...   194 Author Himself   23
    His watchful Friends preserve him by a Sleight.   . . .   196 Author Himself   62
    His great contending Friends to reconcile. . . . . . .   196 Author Himself   72
    And spare my absent Friends the Grief . . . .   204 In Sickness   25
    All special Friends, and allways jarr.   . . . . . .   217 To Mr. Delany   60
    Under the Rose since here are none but friends;   . . .   275 Epilogue   13
    He's gone, although his Friends began to hope   . . . .   285 Elegy Boat   17
    Her Parents and her Friends consent, ...   290 Prog Marriage   5
    Merely because her Friends advise;   . . . .   294 Prog Marriage   134
    But what of that, his friends may say, ...   296 Satiric Elegy   21
    When to your Friends you would enhance   . . . . . .   314 To Ford   91
    Tom's three dearest Friends came by in the Squabble,   .   327 Epigram 1   3
    How quickly they neglect their Friends; . . . .   408 Dial Rich Marb   20
    To use them as his truest friends . . . .   422 Ireld   46
    Have always been Apollo's friends;   . . . .   432 Answer Paulus   12
    'To tell, when he invites his Friends: . . . . . .   448 Modern Lady   107
    That's but a trifle among Friends.   . . . . . .   461 Birthday Song   28
    Thus Gay, the Hare with many Friends, ...   481 Libel on D- D-   53
    Before our Friends were gone to Pot, ...   498 Panegyr Swift   158
    Wit, as the chief of Virtues's Friends, ...   503 Doctor Delaney   99
    Wou'd have us lose our English Friends.   . . . . . .   515 Answer Fable   98
    "Disasters, to our Dearest Friends, ...   545 Life of Swift   8
    See, how behave his Friends profest, ...   545 Life of Swift   19
    Our Friends are of a diff'rent mind;   . . . .   546 Life of Swift   48
    Let me suppose, two special Friends, ...   546 Life of Swift   52
    When you are Sick, your Friends, you say, ...   546 Life of Swift   58
    "I know his nearest Friends complain, ...   547 Life of Swift   78
    "In all Distresses of our Friends   . . . . . .   553 Death of Swift   7
    When I foresee my special Friends, ...   556 Death of Swift   75
    He cannot call his Friends to Mind;   . . . .   556 Death of Swift   87
    My female Friends, whose tender Hearts   . . . . . .   562 Death of Swift   225
    "But dearest Friends, they say, must part.   . . . . .   562 Death of Swift   240
    Why do we grieve that Friends should dye?   . . . . .   562 Death of Swift   243
    "Spent all his Credit for his Friends;   . . . . . .   565 Death of Swift   332
    "To reconcile his Friends in Power;   . . . .   567 Death of Swift   366
    "His Friends in Exile, or the Tower, ...   568 Death of Swift   393
    "When, ev'n his own familiar Friends . . . . . .   569 Death of Swift   403
    "The greatful People stand his Friends: . . . . . .   570 Death of Swift   426
    "And Friends would let him have his Way.   . . . . .   572 Death of Swift   478
    Damn'd Spies and Informers, Damn'd Friends and Damn'd   576 Place Damn'd   10
        Lyars;
    Is apt to disoblige his Friends.   . . . .   605 Beasts Confess   144
    Without Respect to Friends, or Blood, ...   607 Beasts Confess   184
    Treat the Publick, and your Friends, ...   631 Epistle Lady   55
    Kindlier entertains her Friends?   . . . .   632 Epistle Lady   80
    What is this to us your Friends?   . . . .   633 Epistle Lady   102
    (For my Friends have always thought   . . . . . .   637 Epistle Lady   231
    Will pass for yours with Foes and Friends.   . . . . .   644 On Poetry   140
    Get Scraps of Horace from your Friends, ...   648 On Poetry   245
    To all my Friends a Burthen grown, ...   673 His Deafness   2
    James Bruges & the Dean had long been friends,   . . .   678 Dean and Duke   1
    Wou'd meet with better Friends above.   . . . . . .   695 Cadenus Vaness   269
    Best Pattern of true Friends, beware;   . . . . . .   727 To Stella   117
    Its Force against your nearest Friends;   . . . . . .   730 Stella, Poems   98
    For Vengeance on his Friends the Greeks.   . . . . . .   731 Stella, Poems   126
    Concerns by thousands for your friends: . . . . . .   753 Gift for Bec   16
    Had not her friends been in distress?   . . . .   755 Stella '23   28
    Meantime your other juster friends . . . . . .   755 Stella '23   35
    Long may she live, and help her friends   . . . . .   761 Bec's B-Day   31
    Than merely to oblige your Friends;   . . . .   765 Stel B-day '26   70
    Take Pity on your pitying Friends;   . . . .   766 Stel B-day '26   80
    Whose Fleet, 'tis all our Friends Opinion, ...   774 Mullinix Tim   23
    My quondam Friends are grown so Cold, ...   776 Mullinix Tim   78
    I'll take you to some Friends of mine, ...   780 Mullinix Tim   244
    O, introduce me to your Friends!   . . . .   781 Mullinix Tim   280
    How to distinguish Friends from Foes;   . . . . . .   796 Traulus 1   24
    With no Effect on Friends or Foes.   . . . .   798 Traulus 1   66
    But Ireland's Friends ne'er wanted Foes.   . . . . .   798 Traulus 1   88
    When his Friends he most is hard on, ...   800 Traulus 2   13
    To the Dean he shall go; they shall kiss, and be friends: 817 Yahoo's   62
    Let you lie at friends houses.   . . . .   858 Lady's Lament   226
    This Winter to invite some Friends, ...   860 Lady Acheson   23
    An odd Triumvirate of Friends;   . . . .   883 Rev Market-Hill   2
    Then, if our neighb'ring Friends come here, ...   889 Panegyr Dean   81
    And, from deserving friends, with-hold   . . . . . .   900 Dean's Reasons   35
    I use to take in friends affairs;   . . . .   901 Dean's Reasons   96
    The Faculty, his humble Friends, ...   904 Death Daphne   47
    She ask't about her Friends below;   . . . .   905 Death Daphne   73
    And continue special friends.   . . . .   908 Daphne   84
    With Pleasure to his special Friends;   . . . . . .   919 Riddle 5   20
    To a quarrelsome Fellow, cries, Let us be Friends.   .   968 Letter Sherid   28
    And I wish your few friends, when they next see your car   976 Dean to Sherid   29
        go,
    'Tis true indeed, to curry Friends, ...   1003 Dan J's Reply   19
    And swear by each Fate, and your new friends, each Fury,   1019 To Sheridan   6
    . . . your friends you'd meet here. . . . .   1022 Nim-Dan-Dean 2   D 2

FRIENDSHIP

	PAGE	TITLE	LINE
What friendship dicates more than wit.	176	To Lord Harley	4
So strong you'll be, in Friendship ty'd;	189	Faggot	11
Performs what Friendship, Justice, Truth require:	196	Author Himself	73
Perhaps you wonder whence this Friendship Springs,	275	Epilogue	35
If Englands friendship you would keep	422	Ireld	55
And join in friendship, with a strict tye,	436	Answer Paulus	145
I do the most that Friendship can;	485	Libel on D- D-	151
That Human Friendship is but Stuff.	545	Life of Swift	24
'Tis true, we talk of Friendship much,	546	Life of Swift	41
True Friendship in two breasts requires	546	Life of Swift	43
The strongest Friendship yields to Pride,	554	Death of Swift	37
"His Friendship there to few confin'd,	570	Death of Swift	435
Your Friendship shall continue still:	593	Strephon Chloe	312
How all wou'd for his Friendship strive;	709	Cadenus Vaness	701
But Friendship in its greatest Height,	711	Cadenus Vaness	780
What Stella by her Friendship warm'd,	726	To Stella	107
With Friendship and Esteem possesst,	728	Stella, Poems	13
Esteem and Friendship to express,	757	Stel B-day '24	31
Such Friendship never Man profest,	796	Traulus 1	15
His Friendship was exactly tim'd,	797	Traulus 1	57
Ever dearest Friendship swearing;	800	Traulus 2	16
Where friendship is by Fate design'd,	901	Dean's Reasons	69

FRIENDSHIP'S

	PAGE	TITLE	LINE
But now, by Friendship's sacred Laws,	596	Cassinus Peter	91

FRIENDSHP

	PAGE	TITLE	LINE
James is be-duk'd; : of course their friendshp ends	678	Dean and Duke	2

FRIGHT

	PAGE	TITLE	LINE
We read of Kings, who in a Fright,	66	Problem	19
Put the old People in a Fright;	92	Bauc & Phil 1	80
How Jowler howl'd, and what a fright	282	Journal	95
"To put him in a plaguy Fright,	305	Storm	54
Can finely counterfeit a Fright;	416	Woman's Mind	34
With six imagin'd cares to fright you.	753	Gift for Bec	14
Where there will be no cares to fright her.	762	Bec's B-Day	60
In a Fright she crept away,	834	Legion Club	131
They rise, walk round, yet never fright.	920	Riddle 6	12

FRIGHTED

	PAGE	TITLE	LINE
(Glad of the Victory, yet frighted at the War)	17	Ode Athenian	33
Away the frighted Peasants fly,	30	Ode to Temple	109
For both were frighted to the Heart,	112	Bauc & Phil 2	37
Not frighted with an ignominious name,	309	Billet Players	51
Frighted alike at both Extremes,	379	Apology Lady C	123
When frighted at the clam'rous Crew,	448	Modern Lady	120
By censure frighted out of honour's road,	506	To a Friend	9
When frighted Strephon cast his Eye on't	527	Lady's Dres Rm	61
Away the frighted Spectre scuds,	905	Death Daphne	99

FRIGHTEN'D

	PAGE	TITLE	LINE
The Doctor frighten'd at his Fault,	377	Apology Lady C	76

FRIGHTENS

	PAGE	TITLE	LINE
It frightens all the Village Boys.	513	Answer Fable	26

FRIGHTFUL

	PAGE	TITLE	LINE
And ever and anon with frightful Din	139	City Shower	45
That looks hideous, fierce, and frightful;	907	Daphne	45

FRIGHTFULL

	PAGE	TITLE	LINE
They form a frightfull hideous Face,	226	Prog of Beauty	24

FRIGHTFULLY

	PAGE	TITLE	LINE
"Don't I look frightfully to Day?	446	Modern Lady	49

FRIGID

	PAGE	TITLE	LINE
Such frigid Fustian could contain;	469	Burning Poem	5
Not by his frigid Constitution;	603	Beasts Confess	67
Entring warm your frigid Brain	638	Epistle Lady	268

FRING'D

	PAGE	TITLE	LINE
Tho' fring'd with ev'ning gold the cloud appears so gay,	41	Ode Sancroft	217
My Petticoat is doubly fring'd.	896	Panegyr Dean	314

FRINGES

	PAGE	TITLE	LINE
On either Side with Fringes grac'd;	915	Riddle 1	6

FRISK

	PAGE	TITLE	LINE
Is but to frisk about like you.	774	Mullinix Tim	28
But Dick can <fart>, and dance and frisk,	788	Dick's Variety	25
In vain to frisk or climb he tries;	885	Rev Market-Hill	81

FRISKING

	PAGE	TITLE	LINE
Do far exceed your frisking Lambs	123	Empty'ng Town	15

FRIZE

	PAGE	TITLE	LINE
Like a rich Coat with Skirts of Frize:	96	On the Union	8
We'll soundly drench your frize Sur-tout,	622	Scandal Poem 1	176
We'll soundly souce your Frize Surtout.	627	Scandal Poem 2	134

FRO   2   OMITTED WORD

FROLICK

	PAGE	TITLE	LINE
"I tore in Frolick; to your Eyes	154	Widow and Cat	D 29

FROLICKS

	PAGE	TITLE	LINE
Her Frolicks, and pursues her Tail no more.	136	City Shower	4
And harmless Frolicks of her Boys;	322	First of April	34

FROM   657   OMITTED WORD

FRONT

	PAGE	TITLE	LINE
Shews in the front the ambition of my wit;	44	To Congreve	36
Falls from her Tresses on her Front	226	Prog of Beauty	19
And Impudence with Front of Brass;	448	Modern Lady	131
To smooth the Wrinkles on her Front;	526	Lady's Dres Rm	26
And smooth the Furrows in her Front,	582	Young Nymph	35
Thy Screw'd up front; thy State Grimace;	775	Mullinix Tim	60

FROST
    But here, before the Frost can marr it, ...   760 Receipt Youth   55
FROSTY
    A frosty Morn--Past Four a-Clock.   . . . . . .   453 Modern Lady   283
    In frosty Nights their starving Cows, ...   759 Receipt Youth   2
FROTH
    Thus censure seems that fiery froth which breeds   . . .   45 To Congreve   69
    Beside, it Spues a filthy Froth, ...   84 Salamander   51
    While nothing comes but Proth at first, ...   893 Panegyr Dean   193
FROTHY
    Lord how this Frothy Coxcomb frets! (aside)   . . . .   774 Mullinix Tim   16
    At People's Heels with frothy Chaps;   . . . . . .   797 Traulus 1   36
    Behold; a frothy Substance rise; . . . .   892 Panegyr Dean   183
FROUZY
    A frouzy dirty colour'd red . . . .   226 Prog of Beauty   3
FROWN
    Tempests long frown, and thunder threatens loud,   . . .   52 Temple Ill   24
    Whilst Patr'ot-like thou'lt strut and frown.   . . . .   182 Horace 2, 1   64
    Just as the Rabble please to smile or frown.   . . . .   210 Earl of Oxford   10
    The Godlike Hero with one frown   . . . .   340 Arch-Bish Dub   19
    Hypocrisy with Frown severe, ...   448 Modern Lady   126
    Convey a Libel in a Frown, ...   450 Modern Lady   192
    And bear the new Successor's frown;   . . . . . .   468 Birthday Song   259
    "Himself within the Frown of Power;   . . . . . .   568 Death of Swift   394
    "Not Strains of Law, nor Judges Frown, ...   570 Death of Swift   427
    As we think fit to smile or frown;   . . . . . .   620 Scandal Poem 1   92
    As we think fit to smile or frown;   . . . . . .   626 Scandal Poem 2   90
    Must I tremble at his Frown?   . . . .   634 Epistle Lady   150
    A Duke to know a Dean! go smooth your Frown,   . . .   678 Dean and Duke   13
    The Muses oft were seen to frown; . . . .   689 Cadenus Vaness   99
    Further than sometimes by a Frown, ...   697 Cadenus Vaness   336
    How Ford would frown, how Jim would leer, ...   741 Stel B-day 22   19
    The Winter now begins to frown; . . . .   744 Stel Distress   1
    The Winter-Sky began to frown, ...   750 Stel Wood-Park   25
    Let them stare and storm and frown, ...   831 Legion Club   55
    When I saw the Keeper frown, ...   834 Legion Club   133
    Then, turning to Hannah, and forcing a Frown,   . . .   873 Grand Question   182
FROWNS
    That I'm, by her frowns, ...   858 Lady's Lament   209
FROWZY
    Here Pettycoats in frowzy Heaps; . . . .   527 Lady's Dres Rm   48
    No Humours gross, or frowzy Steams, ...   584 Strephon Chloe   11
FROZEN   SEE Y-FROZEN
FRUGAL
    In <Antwerp> keep a frugal House, ...   183 Horace 2, 1   88
    Be frugal, Patt: pay what you owe, ...   479 Epist on Epist   115
FRUIT
    And form the Leaves, the Branches, and the Fruit.   . .   32 Ode to Temple   174
    Ripe fruit shall come, and all is wele.   . . .   103 Merlin   14
    Nor Leaf, nor Fruit, nor Blossom bore.   . . . . .   134 Magician's Rod   70
    In Golden Boughs, and Golden Fruit, ...   134 Magician's Rod   72
    But visit him, and eat some Fruit; . . . .   378 Apology Lady C   88
    In your own heart you'll reap the fruit, ...   755 Stella '23   31
    With restless Beak thy blooming Fruit to spoil,   . .   792 St. Pat's Well   46
    Motly Fruit of Mungril Seed: . . . .   799 Traulus 2   2
    No Fruit or Blossom to be seen, ...   849 Old Thorn   19
FRUITFUL
    With her World's fruitful System in her sacred Ark,   .   16 Ode Athenian   13
    Scatter'd with flowry Vales, with fruitful Gardens   17 Ode Athenian   40
      crown'd,
    Where all the fruitful Atoms lye, ...   32 Ode to Temple   171
    In governments too easy, and too fruitful ground;   . .   37 Ode Sancroft   97
    Fair Emblems of a fruitful Wedding.   . . . . . .   585 Strephon Chloe   52
    His Blessings down in fruitful Show'rs;   . . . . .   624 Scandal Poem 2   28
    Thy curate's place, thy fruitful wife, ...   676 Parson's Case   5
    The Lord of all the fruitful Plain, ...   848 Old Thorn   10
    Whether, your fruitful Fancy lies . . . .   892 Panegyr Dean   159
    She'll be fruitful, never fear her.   . . . . . .   953 Oysters   16
FRUITLESS
    "He labour'd many a fruitless Hour   . . . . . .   567 Death of Swift   365
    And in the fruitless Search pursue   . . . . . .   592 Strephon Chloe   269
    And leave behind their fruitless Wealth.   . . . .   922 Riddle 7   32
FRUITS   SEE FIRST-FRUITS
    These Locusts whom our Fruits have fed, ...   258 Bubble   206
    To shield the infant Fruits and Flowers, ...   387 Manly Virtue   109
    Of rip'ning fruits, and gilding flow'rs;   . . . .   432 Answer Paulus   14
    As fairest Fruits attract the Flyes.   . . . . .   501 Doctor Delaney   42
    Drains all thy Lakes of Fish, of Fruits thy Land.   . .   793 St. Pat's Well   64
    Come hither and behold the Fruits, ...   921 Riddle 7   1
FRY
    (As in a Theatre the Ignorant Fry, ...   29 Ode to Temple   94
    Begone; unhand me, hellish Fry;   . . . .   596 Cassinus Peter   87
FRY'D
    Cutt off large Slices to be fry'd;   . . . . . .   91 Bauc & Phil 1   60
    Cut out large Slices to be fry'd: . . . . . .   112 Bauc & Phil 2   28
FRYAR
    This put me the Fryar into an Amazement, ...   77 Lady B- B-   12
FRYER
    A Fryer would needs show his Talent in Latin;   . . .   76 Lady B- B-   2
    To burn an old Fryer, one Forrest by Name.   . . . .   334 Serious Poem   22
    Find you but the Fryer, and I'll find the Wood.   . .   334 Serious Poem   24

		PAGE	TITLE	LINE
FRYERS				
No, not among the Priests and Fryers.	. . . . . .	773	Mullinix Tim	7
FULL SEE MOON-FULL,SPOON-FULL				
Conclude Love's Bow-String at full Stretch;	. . .	66	Problem	30
. . .and I found her full of Grief;	. . . . .	71	Mrs Harris Pet	34
It still was full up to the Top	. . . . . .	92	Bauc & Phil 1	77
As threadbare, and as full of Dust.	. . . . . .	94	Bauc & Phil 1	170
Whate'er concerns you full as well,	. . . . . .	101	Elegy Patrige	114
As Thread-bare, and as full of Dust.	. . . . . .	115	Bauc & Phil 2	124
Then full of Rage Apollo Spoke,	. . . . . .	121	Apollo Outwit	49
And Joe my Apron full of Bricks.	. . . . . .	128	Little House	64
Could scatter Opium full as well,	. . . . . .	133	Magician's Rod	41
Sid's Scepter, full of Juice, did shoot	. . . .	134	Magician's Rod	71
From her Closet brought out a full Purse in her Clutche		143	New Song	16
Yet since I know where a full Purse may be found,	. .	144	New Song	49
The Dame full wisely did Decree,	. . . . . .	153	Widow and Cat	D 16
Old <Goldolphin> full of Spleen,	. . . . . .	168	Peace Dunkirk	15
Ten thousand footsteps, full in view,	. . . . . .	177	To Lord Harley	17
A Bitch that was full pregnant grown,	. . . . . .	207	Fable Bitches	1
Whole Baskets full of Bits and Scraps,	. . . . . .	208	Fable Bitches	19
Who full of Humor, Fire and Wit,	. . . . . .	218	To Mr. Delany	91
With good Roast Beef his Belly full,	. . . . . .	231	Prog of Poetry	21
His Guts and Belly full of Wind;	. . . . . .	231	Prog of Poetry	38
He us'd 'em full as kindly as himself.	. . . . . .	234	Elegy on Demar	14
His Mind is full of other Cares,	. . . . . .	292	Prog Marriage	67
I prov'd my Proposition full:	. . . . . .	299	Horrid Plot	41
Is not the truth the truth? Look full on me;	. . . .	307	Billet Players	9
Was full as hard to please as You,	. . . . . .	313	To Ford	53
Whether thy Temper, full of Fire,	. . . . . .	323	Pethox	5
May breath your Bellies full of Aether.	. . . . . .	361	Grace's Answer	24
His meagre Corps, though full of Vigour,	. . . . . .	398	Earl of P-b-w	26
We ne'er can have her full in view.	. . . . . .	401	Window Inns 5	D 12
Are full of renown,	. . . .	403	Window Inns 9	D 2
We soon shall find him full of Spleen,	. . . . . .	410	Dial Rich Marb	57
But make an act secure and full	. . . .	423	Ireld	57
To live without both full three Months .he try'd,	. .	430	Dicky Dolly	11
And full of Indignation frets	. . . . . .	450	Modern Lady	164
And Silvia full of inward Guilt,	. . . . . .	450	Modern Lady	172
Thou still with Battles stuff thy head full	. . . .	462	Birthday Song	55
To a Room full of Guests for fear of a <Rape>.	. . .	517	Dean Hang Rape	12
But leave it standing full in Sight	. . . . . .	528	Lady's Dres Rm	73
I place a <Statesman> full before my Sight.	. . . .	532	To Mr. Gay	32
Full in his Face Bob shuts the Council Door:	. . . .	537	Mr. Pulteney	4
What Hampers full of bleeding Hearts!	. . . . .	585	Strephon Chloe	36
He comes full gallop on his eagle:	. . . . . .	620	Scandal Poem 1	114
He comes full gallop on his Eagle.	. . . . . .	627	Scandal Poem 2	112
All coffers full except his own.	. . . . . .	659	On Poetry	D 416
To try their Wisdom's full Extent;	. . . . . .	697	Cadenus Vaness	339
But Cupid, full of Mischief, longs	. . . . . .	701	Cadenus Vaness	466
And, full of Anger, Shame, and Grief,	. . . . . .	713	Cadenus Vaness	846
Nail'd to her Window full in Sight	. . . . . .	735	Stel B-day '20	35
The smoaky Wainscot full of cracks	. . . . . .	746	Stel Distress	37
The smutty Wainscot full of Cracks,	. . . . . .	751	Stel Wood-Park	55
Grows plump and round, and full of Mettle,	. . . . .	759	Receipt Youth	17
Aspiring, greedy, full of senseless Prate,	. . . . .	792	St. Pat's Well	51
Be empty of Learning, of Insolence full:	. . . . .	807	Advice Parson	2
While the Den of Thieves is full,	. . . . . .	830	Legion Club	28
Thus spoke to my Lady, the Knight full of Care;	. .	866	Grand Question	1
Full Northward, let your Troops be led:	. . . .	884	Rev Market-Hill	48
At Beggar's-Op'ra not so full Pit	. . . . . .	889	Panegyr Dean	65
Dilates, and makes the Vessel full:	. . . . . .	893	Panegyr Dean	192
There is a Gate, we know full well,	. . . . . .	928	Riddle 12	D 1
Never finding full Repast,	. . . .	930	Riddle 16	D 3
In me you see them full as white,	. . . . . .	932	Riddle 19	D 8
But these are lost full many a Century.	. . . . .	988	Letter Dr Sh-n	14
I'm so full of Pity, I never abuse Sick;	. . . . .	1028	Dr. Helsham	2
FULLER				
'Tis needless to describe him fuller.	. . . .	286	Elegy Boat	43
FULLY				
At last, the Point was fully clear'd;	. . . . .	598	Problem Solved	31
And thus I am fully reveng'd for your late tricks,	. .	977	Dean to Sherid	47
FUME				
The subtil spirit all flies up in fume;	. . . . . .	49	To Congreve	210
Revile and slander, fume and storm,	. . . . . .	778	Mullinix Tim	167
You neither fume, nor fret, nor flounce;	. . . . . .	891	Panegyr Dean	150
FUMES				
Tho' all the Fumes of Fear, Hope, Love, and Shame,	.	22	Ode Athenian	206
"If you, who long have breath'd the Fumes	. . . . .	380	Apology Lady C	139
FUMETTE				
Unless it had the right Fumette:	. . . .	746	Stel Distress	16
Unless it had the right Fumette.	. . . .	750	Stel Wood-Park	14
FUMING				
Strephon who heard the fuming Rill	. . . .	589	Strephon Chloe	175
FUNCTION				
And spoils the Credit of the Function.	. . . . . .	502	Doctor Delaney	82
FUND				
Who can imagine whence the Fund is,	. . . . . .	477	Epist on Epist	75
A Fund of such Superior Merit,	. . . .	478	Epist on Epist	98
Proceeds that Fund of Wit and Sense;	. . . . . .	726	To Stella	80
Provided a Fund for building you Spittles:	. . . .	805	Irish Bishops	59
His fund may last to five and fifty.	. . . .	878	Robbin & Harry	16

FUNDAMENTALS   PAGE   TITLE   LINE

	PAGE	TITLE	LINE
FUNDAMENTALS			
The fundamentals of this tribe;	435	Answer Paulus	110
FUNERAL			
Behold his funeral appears,	296	Satiric Elegy	17
"The Funeral of so good a Friend.	562	Death of Swift	234
FUNERAL-BLAZE			
Ascending make one Funeral-Blaze.	646	On Poetry	204
FUR			
Through all thy Land, in Armour, Fur and Lawn.	792	St. Pat's Well	56
FURBISH			
Must furbish up and Nickname Crisis.	180	Horace 2, 1	6
FURBISH'D			
Thus having furbish'd up a Parson,	115	Bauc & Phil 2	137
FURIOUS			
With furious Din of Brazen Drums,	340	Arch-Bish Dub	26
Then, furious he begins his March;	353	Wood Ironmongr	17
In Party, furious to her Power;	417	Woman's Mind	49
When you furious argue wrong,	908	Daphne	63
FURL'D			
At length, his Anchor fixt, and Canvas furl'd,	284	Elegy Boat	6
FURNISH			
To furnish his Escapes,	22	Ode Athenian	198
Serves by retail to furnish half mankind.	45	To Congreve	54
To furnish artificial Ears.	367	Answer Delaney	54
Rich Ladies will furnish their Garrets with Stuff,	716	Answer Rebus	15
Might furnish a Second Rate Poet a Year:	716	Answer Rebus	18
No Age could furnish out a Pair	722	Stel B-Day '18	11
I furnish Hints, and you should use all 'em,	742	Stel B-day 22	38
FURNISH'D			
Whom sin and want e'er furnish'd out a wit;	48	To Congreve	166
That furnish'd spirit and motion through the whole;	53	Temple Ill	62
The fancy furnish'd by returning joy;	53	Temple Ill	68
And with Harness-Buckles furnish'd;	573	Helter Skelter	8
Those Materials I have furnish'd,	631	Epistle Lady	45
Furnish'd with Paper, Pens, and Ink,	740	Stel B-day 22	3
FURNISH'T			
Thus furnish't out, he sent his Train	904	Death Daphne	45
FURR			
And, lordly Gout wrapt up in Furr:	895	Panegyr Dean	277
FURR'D			
My Tongue is black, my Mouth is furr'd,	916	Riddle 1	39
FURROW'D			
When Age must print a furrow'd Trace	735	Stel B-day '20	49
FURROWED			
Nature's bare visage furrowed as he mows:	55	Temple Ill	124
FURROWS			
And smooth the Furrows in her Front,	582	Young Nymph	35
FURTHER			
Further than its own palace in her heart:	53	Temple Ill	54
They talk of further Alterations,	283	Journal	129
"Stand further Girl, or get you gone,	452	Modern Lady	244
"Then, since you dread no further Lashes,	550	Life of Swift	201
No further mention of the Dean;	562	Death of Swift	246
Proceed no further in your Part,	647	On Poetry	239
Nor further those Deponents knew:	688	Cadenus Vaness	72
Further than sometimes by a Frown,	697	Cadenus Vaness	336
Nor further looks, but thinks him young.	703	Cadenus Vaness	531
And, further to demonstrate his Affection,	825	Noisy Tom	3
Honest Keeper, drive him further,	834	Legion Club	141
Having thus overthrown all our further Advances.	968	Letter Sherid	22
Nay, further, the Moment you're free from your scalding,	1019	To Sheridan	9
FURY			
When they saw the Dean's Book they were in a great Fury	237	Excellent Song	24
And, secondly, to shew my Fury	348	Whitshed Motto	13
"Whose Fury Blood could never quench;	569	Death of Swift	418
Or where we find your Fury set	645	On Poetry	157
And if you shou'd his Fury check,	666	Epig Carthy 2 D	7
But a Fury in her heart.	907	Daphne	24
And swear by each Fate, and your new friends, each Fury,	1019	To Sheridan	6
FUSS			
Nor with Senates keep a Fuss,	636	Epistle Lady	187
FUSTIAN			
With a huge Fardingal to swell her Fustian Stuff,	23	Ode Athenian	222
Such frigid Fustian could contain;	469	Burning Poem	5
While with the Fustian of thy Book	670	Epig Carthy 21 D	1
With Fustian from exploded Plays,	697	Cadenus Vaness	330
FUTURE			
And to all future Mankind shew	25	Ode Athenian	304
And, to avoid all future ill,	489	Dialogue	11
On House of Ease your future Bride,	591	Strephon Chloe	238
Give future times the Satisfaction	608	Know Not What	7
Were future Happiness and Pain,	764	Stel B-day '26	19
Look not with your future Eyes:	862	To Janus	10
Their fame to future times shall pass,	876	To Dean Swift	12
And future Poets, as they rise,	994	On Picture	31
Philologers of future Ages,	1021	Nim-Dan-Dean 1 D	37
FYE			
The Dean and his Printer then let us cry Fye on;	237	Excellent Song	11
Make Rundle Bishop; fye for Shame!	819	Dr. Rundle	1
FYSHE			
Than shall the Fyshe beweyle his Bosse;	103	Merlin	9

		PAGE	TITLE	LINE
GABBLE				
Run to hear Jackpudding gabble;	. . . .	630	Legion Club	18
Then I fret, and rave and gabble,	. . . .	933	Riddle 20	D 7
GADBURY				
But Gadbury in Art profound	. . . .	228	Prog of Beauty	93
GAFFER				
If Gaffer Harry would endow her;	. . . .	879	Robbin & Harry	34
GAGHAGAN				
And Gaghagan take ev'ry Joke.	. . . .	890	Panegyr Dean	128
GAHAGAN				
"Neal Gahagan, Hibernian Clown,	. . . . . .	851	Old Thorn	82
GAILY				
For a Coxcomb gaily dress'd?	. . . .	632	Epistle Lady	76
GAIN				
Else where's the Gain in being Great?	. . . .	6	Ode to King	5
At once deserve a Crown, and gain it too.	. . .	12	Ode to William	D 16
To preserve Conquests, as at first to gain:	. . .	12	Ode to William	D 26
How mighty a Proselyte you gain!	. . . .	31	Ode to Temple	140
What could the Sages gain but unbelieving scorn;	. .	39	Ode Sancroft	170
Is but the patient's death, and gain--	. . . .	42	Ode Sancroft	258
So small the gain those from your wit do reap,	. . .	45	To Congreve	61
With those they rob, by what their trade does gain.	.	45	To Congreve	68
So, Men of old, to gain Renown, did	. . . .	108	V's House	65
And so might discover, or gain by the Plot:	. . . .	144	New Song	30
Gain by Degrees huge Tracts of Land,	. . . . .	239	Run Bankers	2
'Twill gain her Love to make her fine?	. . . .	292	Prog Marriage	72
Those Arts by which at first they gain it,	. . . . .	592	Strephon Chloe	265
You must learn, if you would gain us,	. . . . .	633	Epistle Lady	113
Thus we both should gain our Prize:	. . . .	638	Epistle Lady	273
And have we not practis'd all Methods to gain you;	.	805	Irish Bishops	57
Nothing she thought could sooner gain him,	. . .	905	Death Daphne	71
For none, alas, by me can gain,	. . . .	918	Riddle 4	15
Arbiters of Loss and Gain,	. . . . . .	934	Riddle 22	D 2
How long shall mortals bend to gain?	. . . . . .	950	Upstart	D 18
Not a Farthing will gain 'em,	. . . . . .	952	Apples	10
GAIN'D				
The Battel almost by Great William's single Valour		8	Ode to King	64
gain'd;				
Had You by dull Succession gain'd Your Crown,	.	11	Ode to William	D 9
Platonick Champions, gain'd without one Female Wile,	.	24	Ode Athenian	252
How shall we search Thee in a battle gain'd,	. . .	34	Ode Sancroft	11
Must lose the honour, you have gain'd,	. . . . .	436	Answer Paulus	141
By that rebuff your Virtue gain'd.	. . . . . .	496	Panegyr Swift	89
I find that I have gain'd her Heart:	. . . . .	679	From Catullus	4
Yet had she much Experience gain'd;	. . . . . .	713	Cadenus Vaness	835
GAINING				
For, ev'ry Day you shall be gaining	. . . . . .	366	Answer Delaney	19
GAINS				
And here the Father often gains	. . . .	293	Prog Marriage	121
So bent on Gains, <Ju--ro> by <C--est>	. . . .	372	Letter D. S-y	32
Poor starv'ling Bard, how small thy Gains!	. . .	642	On Poetry	59
Bavius in Wapping gains Renown,	. . . .	650	On Poetry	301
Whate'er she gains is young and fresh;	. . . . .	759	Receipt Youth	16
'GAINST				
Oft 'gainst her Fountain does complain,	. . . . .	31	Ode to Temple	155
But 'gainst the Dictates of your Mind,	. . . . .	496	Panegyr Swift	94
GAIT				
Rally her dress, her language, and her gait;	. . .	50	To Congreve	218
Nor shew'd the Parson in his Gait or Face;	. . . .	194	Author Himself	14
For, conscious of his Sheepish Gait,	. . . . . .	376	Apology Lady C	32
GALE				
Nor let the Zephyr's treach'rous Gale	. . . . .	597	Cassinus Peter	109
Expanded to invite a milder Gale.	. . . . . .	770	Horace 1, 14	24
Who turn with ev'ry Gale that blows from Court.	. .	771	Horace 1, 14	56
Were wafted by a gentle Gale.	. . . .	894	Panegyr Dean	248
GALEN				
Yet Galen most acutely shews you,	. . . .	367	Answer Delaney	31
GALES				
With cooling Gales, like Zephirs fraught;	. . . .	911	Aenigma	2
Your Engine fraught with cooling Gales,	. . . .	912	Aenigma Expl	D 5
GALL				
Like Pris'ners when their Gall is broke.	. . . .	313	To Ford	56
Who spends his Day and Night in gall.	. . . . .	515	Answer Fable	104
Can teaze, and gall, and give the Spleen;	. . . .	651	On Poetry	344
With gall in ev'ry word I speak,	. . . . . .	754	Stella '23	12
"My Kindred oft' thine Hide shall gall;	. . . . .	850	Old Thorn	59
GALL'RY				
Where, in Eighteen-penny Gall'ry,	. . . .	523	Betty Grizette	25
GALLANT				
Her Common-Place-Book all gallant is,	. . . .	150	Corinna	29
Was an unfortunate gallant.	. . . .	177	To Lord Harley	12
Europa's counterfeit Gallant.	. . . .	759	Receipt Youth	20
GALLANTS				
Now, here's a warrant; Gallants please to mark,	. . .	308	Billet Players	19
Gallants, by Tuesday next we must be gone.	. . .	308	Billet Players	40
Gallants, next Thursday night will be our last,	. .	309	Billet Players	55
My Grand-dame had Gallants by Twenties,	. . . .	350	Upright Judge 3	3
From Pulpits chuse Gallants.	. . . .	426	Five Ladies	32
Had got Gallants among the Ghosts?	. . . . . .	905	Death Daphne	76
GALLERY				
He keeps his Distance in the Gallery	. . . . . .	294	Prog Marriage	141

		PAGE	TITLE		LINE
GALLICK					
From Fleets triumphant o'er the Gallick Coast. . . .		771	Horace 1, 14		40
GALLIES					
Me she has to the Muse's Gallies ty'd, ...		32	Ode to Temple		191
GALLO					
Yet, Neget quis Carmina Gallo.		278	Journal		4
GALLOP					
He comes full gallop on his eagle:		620	Scandal Poem 1		114
He comes full gallop on his Eagle.		627	Scandal Poem 2		112
Tho' they gallop so fast; on the Road you may find 'em,		804	Irish Bishops		23
GALLOPING					
by Galloping high, or Level Pace, ...		957	Cantata		
Trolloping, Lolloping, Galloping, Trolloping		960	Cantata		
Lolloping, Galloping, Trollop, ...		960	Cantata		
Lolloping, Trolloping, Galloping, Lolloping, . . .		960	Cantata		
Trolloping, Galloping, Lollop, ...		960	Cantata		
GALLOPS					
Mordanto gallops on alone, ...		398	Earl of P-b-w		19
GALLOWS					
He would not give a Groat to save his Father from the Gallows.		342	Upon His Grace		16
And at the Gallows all deny'd;		781	Mullinix Tim		274
GALLS-TOWN					
And shou'd our Galls-town Wit grow fallow, ...		278	Journal		3
GALLUS					
Here (by the Way) by Gallus mean I, ...		278	Journal		5
GALLYPOTS					
Here Gallypots and Vials plac'd, ...		526	Lady's Dres Rm		33
GALSTOWN					
Of Galstown Lads (for so they are)		1020	Nim-Dan-Dean 1	D	2
GAMBLING					
Gambling, Rambling, Gambling.		959	Cantata		
Gambling, Rambling, Gambling.		959	Cantata		
GAME SEE MAY-GAME					
War! that mad Game, the World so loves to play, . . .		28	Ode to Temple		76
There should be a Peace, while I'm Not in game. . .		143	New Song		14
And will quit my best Friends, while I'm Not in game. .		144	New Song		26
For rather than hang, I would be Not in game. . . .		144	New Song		34
Because, fcr some Reasons, I was Not in game. . . .		144	New Song		44
And be a true Whig, while I am Not in game.		145	New Song		54
In hope to spring some nobler Game:		412	Desire Possess		31
Through ev'ry Game pursues her Tale, ...		447	Modern Lady		78
"I said I should not win a Game.		452	Modern Lady		239
"Twas you that threw the Game away;		452	Modern Lady		249
It never interrupts the Game, ...		453	Modern Lady		274
The <Dean> he pursu'd to recover his Game, ...		517	Dean Hang Rape		13
To spring more profitable Game.		646	On Poetry		184
For better Game, and look for Grouse:		760	Receipt Youth		54
Your Faction, when their Game was new, ...		774	Mullinix Tim		39
GAMESTER					
And all the Gamester Ladies met, ...		451	Modern Lady		215
But form'd more perfect Gamester, you		494	Panegyr Swift		37
GAMESTER'S					
That fill a Female Gamester's Pate?		451	Modern Lady		225
GAMESTERS					
Fortune the gamesters does beguile, ...		29	Ode to Temple		79
GAMING					
A House of Peers, or Gaming Crew, ...		658	On Poetry	D	164
And gaming Goats, and fleecy Flocks, ...		934	Riddle 21	D	8
GAMMON					
While George, and Dean, go back to Gammon.		280	Journal		42
GANDER					
I call'd you goose instead of gander;		983	Sher, A Goose		16
I know the gander always goes		983	Sher, A Goose		19
GANGES					
Hydaspes, Indus, and the Ganges, ...		655	On Poetry		421
GANYMEDE					
That could refuse this charming Ganymede, ...		466	Birthday Song		190
GAP					
Stands in the gap 'twixt me and wretched men, ...		45	To Congreve		47
GAPE					
But, Lord how the Rabble will stare and will gape, . .		520	Dean Hang Rape		71
I hate, who gape and sneer by Rules.		787	Dick's Variety		2
GAPES					
The Message told, he gapes--and stares, ...		376	Apology Lady C		19
She stretches, gapes, unglues her Eyes, ...		446	Modern Lady		42
Near the Door an entrance gapes, ...		832	Legion Club		87
And gapes for applause?		857	Lady's Lament		180
GAPING					
While all the rest stood gaping round		63	Discovery		24
And Scandal ever gaping wide, ...		448	Modern Lady		125
In gaping Lines to fill a Chink;		645	On Poetry		168
Like Martin Marrall, gaping on, ...		775	Mullinix Tim		43
The Ladies from the Windows gaping:		780	Mullinix Tim		241
Thy Breeches torn behind, stand gaping wide;		881	Pastoral Dial		21
See how the gaping crowd admire		950	Upstart	D	15
GAPS					
Tho Caroline may fill your gaps		467	Birthday Song		239
In finding Ways and Means, and stopping Gaps: . . .		535	To Mr. Gay		122
With Savage-Pictures fill their Gaps;		645	On Poetry		178

	PAGE	TITLE	LINE
GARBAGE			
And leave us nought but Guts and Garbage,	498	Panegyr Swift	152
GARD'NER			
Our Thatcher, Ditcher, Gard'ner, Baily.	891	Panegyr Dean	156
GARDEN			
Sits mounted on the Garden Roller.	410	Dial Rich Marb	62
"The Garden stor'd with artless Flowers,	476	Epist on Epist	51
Never did Covent Garden boast	581	Young Nymph	3
I'm found almost in ev'ry Garden,	929	Riddle 14	D 5
GARDEN'S			
Your Garden's better worth your noble Pain,	32	Ode to Temple	176
A River at my Garden's End,	198	Horace 2, 6	4
GARDENS			
Scatter'd with flowry Vales, with fruitful Gardens crown'd,	17	Ode Athenian	40
We Gardens, and you Wildernesses,	411	Dial Rich Marb	93
GARLAND			
Which form'd into a Garland sweet,	647	On Poetry	223
Your Garland in the following Reign,	647	On Poetry	231
And on the Boughs her Garland hung,	848	Old Thorn	6
GARLANDS			
Instead of Garlands made of Flowrs	122	Empty'ng Town	7
(As Pictures prove) with Garlands crown'd,	590	Strephon Chloe	194
Your jetty Locks with Garlands crown'd,	760	Receipt Youth	41
GARLICK			
For the Smell of them made me like Garlick and Rue sick	1029	Dr. Helsham	21
GARMENTS			
And for themselves fine Garments make.	79	Vanbrug House	34
Old carted Bawds such Garments wear,	787	Clad in Brown	19
In Royal Garments each was drest,	923	Riddle 7	71
I saw them of their Garments stript,	923	Riddle 7	73
GARR'WAY			
Mean time secure on Garr'way Clifts	256	Bubble	153
GARRAT			
Find the last Garrat where they lay,	505	Doctor Delaney	149
GARRATS			
To lodge in Garrats comes from thence.	79	Vanbrug House	28
To lodge in Garrats, comes from thence.	106	V's House	28
GARRET			
And Nim and Dan to Garret clamber:	280	Journal	58
Pil'd in a Garret charm'd the Author's Sight.	667	Epig Carthy 5	D 2
A Poet, starving in a Garret,	728	Stella, Poems	25
GARRETS			
From Airy Garrets some descend,	279	Journal	29
Down from your Garrets haste,	394	Grub-Street	2
In Garrets high, or under Ground:	651	On Poetry	316
Rich Ladies will furnish their Garrets with Stuff,	716	Answer Rebus	15
GARRISON			
How they swagger from their Garrison.	837	Legion Club	182
GARTERS			
However, she stole away my Garters,	70	Mrs Harris Pet	19
To Hang him all \<England\> would lend him their Garters;	519	Dean Hang Rape	51
"Despis'd the Fools with Stars and Garters,	565	Death of Swift	323
With handsome Garters at your Knees,	699	Cadenus Vaness	402
GATE SEE BILLINGS-GATE			
The Angel (doubtless) kept th' Eternal Gate,	8	Ode to King	65
A shambling awkward Gate he took,	95	Bauc & Phil 1	171
Duns at his Lordships Gate began to meet,	124	Descriptn Morn	13
He soon arrives at Harley's Gate;	174	Horace 1, 7	118
Of Duns, attending at their Gate.	239	Run Bankers	16
Unanswer'd at your Patron's Gate;	475	Epist on Epist	6
They croud about Preferment's Gate,	503	Doctor Delaney	93
Or fearless enter in thro' virtue's gate,	506	To a Friend	11
Before he tries a five-barr'd Gate:	640	On Poetry	16
Or in the Iv'ry Gate of Dreams,	647	On Poetry	215
So, long attending at the Gate,	711	Cadenus Vaness	770
Till Time hath open'd Reason's Gate:	730	Stella, Poems	96
My portly Motion, Mien, and Gate.	780	Mullinix Tim	234
See, the Muse unbars the Gate;	832	Legion Club	81
A spacious Thorn before the Gate.	848	Old Thorn	4
And so we saw him at our Gate	859	Lady Acheson	7
The Man with the Kettle-drum enters the Gate;	870	Grand Question	90
There is a Gate, we know full well,	928	Riddle 12	D 1
(Or they can never pass the Gate)	928	Riddle 12	D 14
GATES			
And in a Month he's at your Gates:	282	Journal	108
To kiss your Steps at Quilca Gates;	760	Receipt Youth	48
'Ere we enter'd at the Gates;	833	Legion Club	96
GATH'RING			
In gath'ring follies from the wise;	37	Ode Sancroft	85
But gath'ring spirits, wisely ran for't,	64	Discovery	46
Of gath'ring up herself again?	583	Young Nymph	70
With Prudence gath'ring up a Cluster	647	On Poetry	221
GATHER			
From far, to gather golden Gravel;	157	Fable of Midas	38
These I will gather and unite,	691	Cadenus Vaness	151
And think your Boys may gather there-hence	988	Letter Dr Sh-n	3
GATHER'D			
"But when we've gather'd Strength, I swear,	208	Fable Bitches	35
The Bees are gather'd to a Swarm:	345	Prometheus	26
And, gather'd all his Brother strow'd;	412	Desire Possess	36

GATHER'D   (CONTINUED)

	PAGE	TITLE	LINE
She gather'd, under ev'ry Head,	713	Cadenus Vaness	850

GATHERD

Widn'd and gatherd at his Wrist;	94	Bauc & Phil 1	168

GATHERING

while o'er the Church these Clouds are gathering,	813	Bro Protestant	47

GATHERS

He gathers all the Parish there;	116	Bauc & Phil 2	170
And in its narrow Circle gathers	688	Cadenus Vaness	55

GAUDY

Burnish and make a gaudy show,	84	Salamander	41
Such gaudy Tulips rais'd from Dung.	530	Lady's Dres Rm	144
These gaudy Shoes must Hannah place	885	Rev Market-Hill	67
When in my gaudy Liv'ry drest!	916	Riddle 2	4

GAUL

You from the Neighb'ring Gaul descend;	324	Pethox	20
When once the fierce pursuing Gaul	340	Arch-Bish Dub	17
Give up the phrase of haughty Gaul,	468	Birthday Song	247
From haughty Gaul to make Ragous.	895	Panegyr Dean	264

GAUNTLET

"To run the Gauntlet of the Court;	380	Apology Lady C	150

GAVE

Which gave them birth, can rob the world of day.	46	To Congreve	82
Howe'er she gave no flat Denial,	120	Apollo Outwit	25
The Walls in tumbling gave a Knock;	127	Little House	15
Then Mrs. Johnson gave her Verdict,	128	Little House	39
I talk'd of a Peace, and they both gave a start,	143	New Song	17
And gave it for Pan's oaten Reed:	156	Fable of Midas	28
The <Queen> (forsooth, Despotick) gave	181	Horace 2, 1	25
Just what you gave me, Competence:	199	Horace 2, 6	D
That Musick gave her Leave to litter,	208	Fable Bitches	17
Gave Women all their Hearts could wish	227	Prog of Beauty	58
He knows very well I ne'er gave a Refusal,	265	Apollo	71
Item the Actors, freely gave a Day,	274	Epilogue	9
What gave her Brats and Pigs the Meazles,	282	Journal	93
For old Nick gave the Papers the Mark of the Bank.	288	Bank Down	45
And gave the Nymph a plenteous Draught;	293	Prog Marriage	114
And since her Birth the Ocean gave her,	303	Storm	23
That litt'rall Spot which gave him Birth,	314	To Ford	88
He gave it me, and ever since I find I thrive amain.	342	Upon His Grace	30
Tom gave him a Kick in the Guts for his Fee.	399	Tom Clinch	14
Then gave the Subject out of Spite:	445	Modern Lady	23
And gave his Creditors the Slip.	456	Dean Smedley	44
"Content with what his Bounty gave,	476	Epist on Epist	35
Nor ever gave the Poor a Groat.	515	Answer Fable	100
This gave him Enemies in plenty,	549	Life of Swift	134
What gave me Ease, and how I slept?	557	Death of Swift	140
"He gave it all:--But first he dy'd.	558	Death of Swift	160
"He gave himself no haughty Airs:	565	Death of Swift	330
"And gave them Arms to ward the Blow.	569	Death of Swift	410
"He gave the little Wealth he had,	572	Death of Swift	479
Then gave him some familiar Thumps,	594	Cassinus Peter	37
By Proclamation gave Command,	601	Beasts Confess	9
He freely gave the Poor Advice;	604	Beasts Confess	84
A Coat we gave him dy'd in grain	619	Scandal Poem 1	69
A Coat we gave him, dy'd in Grain;	625	Scandal Poem 2	65
Since Woolston gave us Arms to rout him.	657	On Poetry	494
Gave Hints of who and who's together;	696	Cadenus Vaness	324
And gave, by turns, their Censures Vent.	699	Cadenus Vaness	409
Nor ever gave her Judgment wrong.	704	Cadenus Vaness	559
Yet gave him not the Heart to chide;	704	Cadenus Vaness	571
But never gave me equal Arms:	706	Cadenus Vaness	621
Which gave a Tincture o'er the Mass:	709	Cadenus Vaness	719
She gave due Notice, that both Parties,	713	Cadenus Vaness	838
Gave her own Reasons last; and then	713	Cadenus Vaness	852
Which gave the <Dean> the Name of Draper?	796	Traulus 1	12
To spare the Folks that gave him Ha'pence	796	Traulus 1	28
And, when they gave it, well 'tis known,	820	Dr. Rundle	17
They gave what never was their own.	820	Dr. Rundle	18
Astonish'd gave a dreadful Shriek;	849	Old Thorn	26
And with her Beak gave many a Knock	849	Old Thorn	35
'Till he gave me my Will, I wou'd give him no Rest:	869	Grand Question	58
I gave, as you beg, your most humble respects:	979	Dean to Tho: S	24

GAWDY

With gawdy Coat, and shining Train,	83	Salamander	31

GAWS   SEE GEW-GAWS

GAWSES

Brocado's, and Damasks, and Tabbies, and Gawses,	236	Excellent Song	1

GAY

To make the Pageant gay:	6	Ode to King	16
Tho' fring'd with ev'ning gold the cloud appears so gay,	41	Ode Sancroft	217
Where high patrician souls dress'd heavenly gay,	41	Ode Sancroft	234
So highly courted by the brisk and gay?	54	Temple Ill	106
But some gay coxcomb, or a rake.	177	To Lord Harley	22
The Doctor and Dean, Pope, Parnell and Gay	185	Scriblerus 1	1
"From Pope, from Parnel, or from Gay?	201	Horace 2, 6	74
Will half supply a Gay and Pope,	313	To Ford	74
I must have another of Colour more gay	389	Order of Bath	3
In Spight of Pope, in Spight of Gay,	408	Dial Rich Marb	1
Plump Johnny Gay will now elope;	409	Dial Rich Marb	49
"No gay Parterre with costly Green,	476	Epist on Epist	53

		PAGE	TITLE	LINE
GAY	(CONTINUED)			
	Thus Gay, the Hare with many Friends,	481	Libel on D- D-	53
	How could you, Gay, disgrace the Muses Train,	531	To Mr. Gay	1
	Next, hearken Gay, to what thy Charge requires,	533	To Mr. Gay	53
	Presume not, Gay, unless you serve a Drone,	534	To Mr. Gay	87
	Why must I be outdone by Gay,	555	Death of Swift	53
	Poor Pope will grieve a Month; and Gay	561	Death of Swift	207
	"Remote from St. John, Pope, and Gay.	570	Death of Swift	434
	And with Bridles fine and gay,	573	Helter Skelter	13
	Whence Gay was banish'd in Disgrace,	650	On Poetry	307
	To shine, where all the gay resort,	677	Parson's Case	27
	In the gay Trappings of a Birth-Day Night:	771	Horace 1, 14	50
	The Fables writ by Mr. Gay,	782	Tim and Fables	4
	A flaxen wig, and wast-coat gay,	879	Robbin & Harry	48
GAYS				
	Attend ye Popes, and Youngs, and Gays,	656	On Poetry	467
GAZ'D				
	And often on each other gaz'd;	112	Bauc & Phil 2	36
	Desire, in Rapture gaz'd a while,	413	Desire Possess	45
GAZE				
	And gaze in silent Wonder long,	109	V's House	106
	Die like lovers as they gaze,	937	Riddle 24	D 49
GAZETS				
	On all Whig Papers, and Gazets:	282	Journal	100
GAZETTE				
	From Paris Gazette A-la-màin,	398	Earl of P-b-w	10
GAZETTES				
	Are forced to read the old gazettes.	420	Holyhead	18
GAZETTS				
	Nor with Bankrupts fill Gazetts,	169	Peace Dunkirk	29
GAZING	SEE STAR-GAZING			
	By gazing upwards giddy grow,	37	Ode Sancroft	77
GEAR				
	In all her glitt'ring Birth-day Gear,	591	Strephon Chloe	228
GEER				
	A bloated <Minister> in all his Geer,	532	To Mr. Gay	33
	What else are those thou seest in Bishop's Geer	792	St. Pat's Well	49
GEESE				
	(For all the Muses Geese are Swans)	80	Vanbrug House	50
	And Geese their silver Plumes supply.	239	Run Bankers	24
	A Flock of Geese jump down together,	253	Bubble	54
	Devours your Geese, the Wolf your Flocks:	504	Doctor Delaney	130
	A Fox with Geese his Belly crams;	651	On Poetry	325
	And you know all my geese are swans:	983	Sher, A Goose	12
	Swans sing when dying, geese when blind.	983	Sher, A Goose	14
	Your geese are old,	1038	Sheridan Cavan	15
GEMM				
	'Tis the best Gemm in Royalty,	6	Ode to King	22
GEN'RAL				
	Thrice happy you have 'scap't this gen'ral Pest;	28	Ode to Temple	58
	A good Health to Gen'ral Hill,	169	Peace Dunkirk	39
	'Till Neptune with a Gen'ral Sweep	239	Run Bankers	3
	Now comes the gen'ral Scandal-Charge,	449	Modern Lady	144
	This into gen'ral Odium drew him,	549	Life of Swift	132
GEN'RAL'S				
	Great Ormonde lend thy Gen'ral's Staff:	191	Faggot	46
GEN'ROUS				
	Dear Harley, gen'rous Youth, admit	176	To Lord Harley	3
	From gen'rous wines and costly fare,	401	Window Inns 5	D 3
	Hail! happy Pope, whose gen'rous Mind,	482	Libel on D- D-	71
	Is gen'rous, valiant, just and wise,	646	On Poetry	195
	With plenteous meals, and gen'rous wine;	677	Parson's Case	34
	By gen'rous Wines beneath a Shade.	731	Stella, Poems	112
	With gen'rous Wines and costly Chear.	749	Stel Wood-Park	4
	Your gen'rous Boldness to defend	765	Stel B-day '26	43
	But, you have rais'd your gen'rous Mind	893	Panegyr Dean	197
	He gives; and with a gen'rous Pride,	919	Riddle 5	21
GENERAL				
	Which they have always ready, general and Cheap;	19	Ode Athenian	122
	Become a General, Peer and Beau,	84	Salamander	42
	And if you find the general Vogue	644	On Poetry	119
	As in a general Calamity.	811	Bro Protestant	10
GENERALLS				
	Equip our Kings, and Generalls at the Comb.	275	Epilogue	18
GENERALS				
	Like Roman Generals triumphant,	928	Riddle 12	D 15
	So, the French, when our Generals soundly did pay 'em,	967	Letter Sherid	17
GENEROSITY				
	And had they common Generosity	24	Ode Athenian	261
GENEROUS				
	With Just, and Generous, and Sincere.	385	Manly Virtue	62
	Extol him for his generous mind:	464	Birthday Song	124
	Their generous Feeders not provoking	479	Epist on Epist	123
	Mix'd in a noble generous Mind;	731	Stella, Poems	104
	The generous Wheat forgot its Pride,	811	Bro Protestant	7
GENIAL				
	The genial Virtue with him brought,	293	Prog Marriage	113
	And bless the Earth with genial Showers.	387	Manly Virtue	110
	Fair Issue of the genial Bed,	924	Riddle 8	5
GENIUS				
	When man's ill genius to my presence sent	47	To Congreve	135

GENIUS   (CONTINUED)

	PAGE	TITLE	LINE
Van's Genius without Thought or Lecture	86	Hist V's House	7
Did very much his Genius cramp;	172	Horace 1, 7	44
Thy Genius has perhaps a knack	183	Horace 2, 1	103
On ev'ry Genius that attempts to rise;	193	Author Himself	4
His Genius first found out the Rule	216	To Mr. Delany	35
A Genius for all Stations fit,	482	Libel on D- D-	79
That noble genius, who unbinds	490	Dialogue	31
Would Men of Genius cease to write,	502	Doctor Delaney	71
A Genius in the Rev'rend Gown,	502	Doctor Delaney	79
Your Genius in your Face will fly.	503	Doctor Delaney	114
And, where his Genius least inclines,	641	On Poetry	23
Whether your Genius most inclines	643	On Poetry	81
How Genius is no more rewarded;	652	On Poetry	350
Carthy, you say, writes well--his genius true.--	668	Epig Carthy 8	D 1
And with Address each Genius held	701	Cadenus Vaness	450
Wherein his Genius was below	712	Cadenus Vaness	812
But a Genius like her's no Subject can stifle,	716	Answer Rebus	11
His Genius of superior Kind;	788	Dick's Variety	14
A subject for their genius fit;	876	To Dean Swift	15
And, to a Genius so extensive,	891	Panegyr Dean	157
My Genius piercing, sharp and bright,	920	Riddle 6	5
Thy Fame, thy Genius now declines, proud Boaster.	1002	Reply by Dean	9

GENIUS'S

The Genius's of ancient Days!	708	Cadenus Vaness	689

GENTEEL

Drest her again Genteel and Neat,	23	Ode Athenian	230
And then, so nice, and so genteel;	584	Strephon Chloe	9
But then, a Parson so genteel,	889	Panegyr Dean	75

GENTEELER

Tom had the genteeler Swing,	785	Mullinex Dick	29

GENTLE

Evils which a too gentle king,	37	Ode Sancroft	98
Hither thy gentle Aspect bend,	101	Elegy Patrige	101
Jove Smil'd, and like a gentle God,	107	V's House	51
The gentle Pilgrims soon aware on't,	112	Bauc & Phil 2	41
And, by a gentle Bow, divin'd	133	Magician's Rod	31
At first a gentle Creature;	153	Widow and Cat	D 2
This Tale inclines the gentle Reader,	157	Fable of Midas	41
There leaning near a gentle Brook,	202	Horace 2, 6	109
So just, so gentle and so kind	422	Ireld	26
"To Spirits of less gentle kind.	485	Libel on D- D-	170
Let all Domesticks feel your gentle Sway;	533	To Mr. Gay	55
And thus a mutual gentle Fire,	593	Strephon Chloe	313
You'll see a Cloud in gentle weather	618	Scandal Poem 1	43
But we by gentle April showers	621	Scandal Poem 1	147
You'll see a Cloud in gentle Weather	625	Scandal Poem 2	39
While a little gentle Jerking	636	Epistle Lady	205
Give your Head some gentle Raps;	638	Epistle Lady	264
Gentle Cupid o'er my Heart;	660	Love Song	2
Now, gentle Clio, sing or say,	690	Cadenus Vaness	126
That gentle, soft, engaging Air,	692	Cadenus Vaness	178
How should I beg of gentle Fate,	722	Stel B-Day '18	16
Late be her death, one gentle nod,	762	Bec's B-Day	57
Thither, gentle Muse, conduct me,	832	Legion Club	79
Last trolled forth a gentle Swine	849	Old Thorn	41
Thus, when the gentle Spina found	850	Old Thorn	49
My Love for gentle Dermot faster grows	881	Pastoral Dial	13
So gentle in your whole Proceeding,	891	Panegyr Dean	153
Here, gentle Goddess Cloacine,	893	Panegyr Dean	205
Were wafted by a gentle Gale.	894	Panegyr Dean	248
. . . but I think Gentle folks should be civil.	986	Mary to Sher	24
Smooth as our Bason's gentle Flood,	1020	Nim-Dan-Dean 1	D 5

GENTLE-FOLKS

Pray gentle-Folks forbear your Scoffing.	286	Elegy Boat	38

GENTLEFOLKS

They'll make a sweet Bishop when Gentlefolks sup.	953	Oranges	4

GENTLEMAN   SEE JAUNTLEMAN

Poor Gentleman, he droops apace,	556	Death of Swift	81
O law! the sweet Gentleman! look in his Face;	870	Grand Question	94
"To give a young Gentleman right Education,	872	Grand Question	161
You a Gentleman! marry come up,	985	Mary to Sher	2

GENTLEMAN'S

The dullest Beast, and Gentleman's Liquor,	940	Letter	1

GENTLEMEN

Ladyes, and Gentlemen, behold,	251	Bubble	7
Pray Gentlemen, believe your Eyes,	254	Bubble	102
We, Gentlemen, are Your Assisters,	254	Bubble	105
These Gentlemen use me with Kindness and Freedom,	263	Apollo	21

GENTLEST

With gentlest Touch, she next explores	582	Young Nymph	29
But, what the gentlest Heart would vex,	687	Cadenus Vaness	25

GENTLY

Tho' ne'er so gently led	31	Ode to Temple	147
Which gently warms, but cannot burn;	711	Cadenus Vaness	784
See they gently twitch his Coat,	836	Legion Club	169

GENTRY

Peers, Clergy, Gentry, all are Benefactors;	274	Epilogue	7
"Quite thro' the Tribe of waiting Gentry;	380	Apology Lady C	154
A Satyr, and the Gentry buy!	502	Doctor Delaney	76
And thus, the Pair of humble Gentry,	883	Rev Market-Hill	17

		PAGE	TITLE	LINE

GENUIN
With genuin lustre all her own. . . . . — 465 Birthday Song — 174

GENUINE
The true, the genuine sweet'ning Lay? . . . . . — 497 Panegyr Swift — 143
That Rogue of genuine ministerial Kind: . . . . — 534 To Mr. Gay — 102
Three genuine Tomes of Swift's Remains. . . . . — 560 Death of Swift — 198
"True genuine Dulness mov'd his Pity, ... — 572 Death of Swift — 469

GEOGRAPHERS
So Geographers in Afric-Maps . . . . — 645 On Poetry — 177

GEOMETRY
A Scrap of Parchment hung by Geometry, ... — 99 Elegy Patrige — 41
'Tis just like this, which hangs by Geometry. . . . — 780 Mullinix Tim — 218

GEORGE
How George, Nim, Dan, Dean pass their Days; . . . — 278 Journal — 2
At Nine, grave Nim and George Facetious, ... — 278 Journal — 11
And kisses George, and ends or Lectures: . . . . — 278 Journal — 14
While George, and Dean, go back to Gammon. . . . — 280 Journal — 42
George, Nim and Dean, set out at Four, ... — 280 Journal — 43
How Valiant George rode o'er the Dragon; . . . . — 281 Journal — 70
George is half scar'd out of his Wits, ... — 283 Journal — 125
He stopt at the George for a Bottle of Sack, . . . — 399 Tom Clinch — 3
Or dealing crowns to George and James. . . . . — 402 Window Inns 7 — D 6
To Fort St. George a Pedlar went he. . . . . — 456 Dean Smedley — 48
Than George and William claim'd before. . . . . — 464 Birthday Song — 140
Tho George is gone a thousand miles. . . . . . — 466 Birthday Song — 182
But George, and Brunswick are too rough. . . . . — 467 Birthday Song — 214
St. George beheld thee with Delight, ... — 656 On Poetry — 461
St. George himself he plays the wag on, ... — 777 Mullinix Tim — 115
Let's quarrel no longer, since Dan and George Rochfort — 979 Dean to Tho: S — 35
Then George will rejoice, and Dan will sing high-day: . — 980 Dean to Tho: S — 37
'Ere George had robb'd it of its Mud. . . . . . — 1020 Nim-Dan-Dean 1 — D 6
. . . Your most dutiful and obedient George — 1024 Nim-Dan-Dean 2 — D 18
  Nim-Dan-Dean.
George, Dan, Dean, and Nim to place in the center? . — 1027 Sheri Circles — 14
Apply'd to <George> exactly true is: . . . . . — 657 On Poetry — 478
Give <George> and Jove an equal Share. . . . . — 657 On Poetry — 486

GEORGE'S
of St Andrew's the Green, and St George's the Blue . — 389 Order of Bath — 2
"From both your Streams in George's Reign! . . . . — 462 Birthday Song — 80

GERMAN
That we a German Prince must own . . . . . — 180 Horace 2, 1 — 11
To court their English German Cousins, ... — 465 Birthday Song — 170
But Mammon, and the <German> Line. . . . . . — 820 Dr. Rundle — 36

<GERMANS>
Or writing Libels on the <Germans>, ... — 993 On Picture — 5

GERMANY
In vain are all attempts from Germany . . . . . — 467 Birthday Song — 217

GERYON
Geryon shall have three Hedes agayne . . . . . — 103 Merlin — 19

GESTURES
And all her Gestures were Lampoons. . . . . . — 150 Corinna — 16
Has, with noise and odd gestures, been prating some years, — 815 Yahoo's — 18

GET
You sha'n't come here nor get a Sous . . . . . — 91 Bauc & Phil 1 — 39
Carrots sown Thyn a deep root may get, ... — 148 Windsor Proph — 17
I get a Whisper, and withdraw, ... — 200 Horace 2, 6 — 43
"To get my Warrant quickly signed: . . . . . — 201 Horace 2, 6 — 56
Lord! I should get so ill a Name, ... — 220 A Quiet Life — 35
Can scarce get o'er the Barn-Door Sill: . . . . — 230 Prog of Poetry — 4
And then get off with Money stor'd, ... — 253 Bubble — 62
For, where Directors get a Prize, ... — 256 Bubble — 159
Without whom they could get neither Claret nor Beef; . — 263 Apollo — 10
For sorry Stuff, can get a Crown a Page; . . . . — 276 Epilogue — 42
You get all the Fish, and others get none, . . . — 287 Bank Down — 7
You get all the Fish, and others get none, . . . — 287 Bank Down — 7
That a Pack of sly Knaves should get fifty per Cent, . — 288 Bank Down — 52
First get a licence, then produce our ware: . . . — 308 Billet Players — 36
If once they get you on the Spot . . . . . — 312 To Ford — 31
Sent Mercury to get another. . . . . . . — 346 Prometheus — 52
Get the Great Seal, and turn out Brod'rick. . . . — 348 Whitshed Motto — 18
And get Ten thousand Girls and Boys. . . . . — 362 Grace's Answer — 48
Ten thousand Girls and Boys you'll get . . . . — 362 Grace's Answer — 49
Get all your Verses printed fair, ... — 394 Grub-Street — 9
You'll fly when you get what you come here to steal, . — 395 Dog and Thief — 7
And, by his Crown will nothing get; . . . . . — 409 Dial Rich Marb — 41
And I can hardly get him down . . . . . . — 411 Dial Rich Marb — 99
To get the name of council learned; . . . . . — 435 Answer Paulus — 114
Scrambling with <rogues> to get a place: . . . . — 436 Answer Paulus — 140
"Stand further Girl, or get you gone, ... — 452 Modern Lady — 244
Their Hoods, their Cloaks, and get them gone: . . . — 453 Modern Lady — 287
Thro' thick and thin, to get a name. . . . . . — 456 Dean Smedley — 24
He'll get it read, and take the hint, ... — 463 Birthday Song — 86
But you some white-lead ink must get, ... — 463 Birthday Song — 113
Get Leave to sit whene'er you will; . . . . . — 480 Libel on D- D- — 4
And get a Dinner for your Hire, ... — 483 Libel on D- D- — 108
Or call 'em Rogues, or get 'em kickt: . . . . . — 505 Doctor Delaney — 154
We see a Comrade get a fall, ... — 545 Life of Swift — 13
And get the better of your Love; . . . . . . — 546 Life of Swift — 38
And get a Hatband, Scarf, and Gloves. . . . . — 547 Life of Swift — 65
Since Husbands get behind the Scene, ... — 588 Strephon Chloe — 137
Preferment get, and spare his Eyes: . . . . . — 604 Beasts Confess — 108

GET   (CONTINUED)   PAGE   TITLE   LINE

        What profit could you hope to get of her . . . . . .   622 Scandal Poem 1   170
        Get Scraps of Horace from your Friends,   648 On Poetry   245
        To get the Name of Conoisseur. . . .   649 On Poetry   276
        The Girl might pass, if we cou'd get her . . . . .   700 Cadenus Vaness   428
        A Fidler may a Fortune get;   . . . .   710 Cadenus Vaness   737
        And ev'ry Crambo he could get; . . . .   730 Stella, Poems   74
        Call the Old Housekeeper, and get her . . . . .   756 Stel B-day '24   9
        May fortune and her coffee get her . . . . . .   762 Bec's B-Day   47
        His Nose to get the Circle just in, ...   788 Dick's Variety   34
        Let them, when they once get in . . . . . .   831 Legion Club   47
        Yet never think they get enough; . . . . .   861 Lady Acheson   35
        I lose by the House what I get by the Land;   866 Grand Question   4
        I can't get it out, tho' I'd never so fain. . .   869 Grand Question   66
        How cou'd these Chimeraes get into your Brains?-- . .   873 Grand Question   185
        Swears, he could get her in an hour . . . . .   879 Robbin & Harry   33
        'Twill be our Int'rest to get rid of her: . . .   886 Rev Market-Hill   106
        And get the like Returns again. . . . . . .   890 Panegyr Dean   104
        That Death should get a num'rous Breed; . . .   903 Death Daphne   14
        And only to get others Wealth. . . . .   917 Riddle 3   18
        Who neither get, nor lose a Groat; . . . . . .   918 Riddle 4   14
        And all I get, I let it fly: . . . .   918 Riddle 4   26
        Computing what I get and spend, ...   918 Riddle 4   34
        I last get up, am first a-bed; . . . . . .   918 Riddle 4   40
        They get no Nourishment from me. . . . . .   926 Riddle 9   6
        The Moment I get one my Soul's all a-fire, ...   928 Riddle 11   D   11
        Come, Six-pence a Dozen to get me some Bread, . .   953 Herrings   8
        And I think I may say, you cou'd many good shillings get 979 Dean to Tho: S   9
        And now I must go, and get Saunders to direct this   987 Mary to Sher   33
                Letter,
        Would you get still more? . . . .   1038 Sheridan Cavan   13
GETS
        Gets between them and my resentment's weight, ...   45 To Congreve   46
        He gets to a Window beyond both the Tropicks; . . .   265 Apollo   84
        So a Thief steals my Horse, and then gets him well drest 266 Apollo   92
        Who gets a Cold, who break their Shins. . . . . .   280 Journal   64
        For Clem gets all the dainty bits. . . . . . .   283 Journal   126
        Gets not an Heir, but gets a Feaver; . . . . .   295 Horrid Plot   152
        Gets not an Heir, but gets a Feaver; . . . . .   295 Horrid Plot   152
        She gets a Cold as sure as Death; . . . . .   417 Woman's Mind   45
        And for his courage gets--a dinner. . . . . .   421 Ireld   12
        Because he gets . . . .   441 Ballyspellin   52
        Ye Fates, when all he gets is Spent, ...   456 Dean Smedley   49
        The Pedant gets a Mistress by't. . . . . . .   710 Cadenus Vaness   743
        So little gets for what she gives . . . . . .   735 Stel B-day '20   29
        He gets a thousand Thumps and Kicks . . . . .   777 Mullinix Tim   117
        Which gets the better, Saint, or Snake. . . . .   777 Mullinix Tim   130
        Who, 'ere t' other gets up, demands the rising Blow. . 967 Letter Sherid   14
        Yet he gets home at night with Health and whole Bones. 1037 Four Storyes   8
GETTING
        Beside the getting of a Name? . . . .   83 Salamander   14
        And <Cuffe> grins for getting, the Alicant Plate. . .   430 Dicky Dolly   21
GEW-GAWS
        Shews all his gew-gaws, ...   857 Lady's Lament   179
GHASTLY
        And shakes the atheist's knees; such ghastly fear . . . 52 Temple Ill   39
GHOST
        And that her troubled Ghost still haunts there since she 27 Ode to Temple   38
                dy'd;
        Since the bright essence fled, where haunts the reverend 36 Ode Sancroft   44
                ghost?
        Or whether dead imagination's ghost . . . . . .   51 Temple Ill   7
        And to his Pious Patron's Ghost. . . . . .   183 Horace 2, 1   92
        The Ghost of old <Damer>, who left not his Betters,   288 Bank Down   41
        For, as sure as a Gun they will give up the Ghost . .   351 Wood Insect   23
        Confer on him the Holy Ghost; . . . .   820 Dr. Rundle   6
        Who know there is an Holy Ghost: . . . . . .   820 Dr. Rundle   14
        I'll haunt thy Dreams, a bloodless Ghost; . . . .   925 Riddle 8   27
        No Flesh, no Bones, no Blood --- no Ghost: . . .   935 Riddle 23   D   11
GHOSTLY
        "His ghostly Visage with an Air . . . . . .   305 Storm   59
GHOSTS
        Had got Gallants among the Ghosts? . . . . .   905 Death Daphne   76
GIANT
        You'll see me stretch him to a Giant; . . . . .   934 Riddle 21   D   20
        A Giant now, and strait an Elf, ...   935 Riddle 23   D   22
GIANT'S
        Rescu'd Her from the Giant's Fort: . . . . .   7 Ode to King   38
GIBBERISH
        Stock'd with the freshest gibberish of the town; . . .   47 To Congreve   120
GIBE
        That meet for nothing but to gibe; . . . . . .   216 To Mr. Delany   54
        Fleer, and gibe, and laugh, and flout; . . . . .   523 Betty Grizette   32
        Think it Wit to fleer, and gibe? . . . . . .   632 Epistle Lady   78
        Form their Features, while I gibe them; . . . . .   839 Legion Club   226
GIBER
        of Virtue & worth by profession a giber . . . . .   540 Charac Walpole   11
GIBES
        Secur'd by Numbers from the Lay-men's Gibes; . . .   194 Author Himself   20
        Will never have done with his Gibes and his Jeers: . . 873 Grand Question   188
        Your Gibes and all your foul Abuse, ...   1003 Dan J's Reply   14

		PAGE	TITLE	LINE
GIBING				
	Scurrility with gibing Air;	448	Modern Lady	127
GIDDILY				
	Mistaken Ideots! see how giddily they run,	39	Ode Sancroft	162
GIDDINESS				
	My Head, with Giddiness, goes round;	926	Riddle 9	7
GIDDY				
	The Giddy Brittish Populace,	8	Ode to King	72
	Giddy he grows, and down is hurl'd,	10	Ode to King	144
	Nor does thy essence fix'd depend on giddy circumstance	34	Ode Sancroft	7
	By gazing upwards giddy grow,	37	Ode Sancroft	77
	The giddy turns of pop'lar rage,	38	Ode Sancroft	117
	Deaf, giddy, helpless, left alone,	673	His Deafness	1
	Of giddy Winds, but make some friendly Port.	770	Horace 1, 14	12
	You think your giddy Head will burst:	893	Panegyr Dean	194
GIFT	SEE NEW-YEAR'S-GIFT			
	Pay Thanks for the Gift,	77	Lady B- B-	27
	And tho' I can't my gift revoke,	121	Apollo Outwit	51
	More precious far than ev'n the Gift	494	Panegyr Swift	47
	The Gift (good Heav'ns preserve 't from Thieves)	494	Panegyr Swift	49
	Tho' he does not, I thank you for your Gift;	669	Epig Carthy 17	D 3
	For that one Gift to lay on Hands:	821	Dr. Rundle	44
	Could he but make his Gift appear	821	Dr. Rundle	51
	Bring our Dame a New-Year's Gift;	862	To Janus	4
	Thee, for a Gift, the Courtier sends	919	Riddle 5	19
	Contrives all Means the Gift to hide:	919	Riddle 5	22
	Whether he has the Gift or no.	919	Riddle 5	24
	Nor less that Shirt, my Rival's Gift,	925	Riddle 8	41
	The Bridegroom's first Gift to their Mates,	942	Probatur Alit	4
GIFTS				
	In gifts, wherein you both excell'd,	177	To Lord Harley	30
	Three Gifts for Conversation fit	215	To Mr. Delany	13
	To use the Gifts, that Heav'n bestows;	243	Horace 4, 9	18
	And the Gifts I bestow'd her, will find her a Lover,	266	Apollo	107
	Nor will in you those Gifts despise,	484	Libel on D- D-	115
	Nor dare to use the gifts by heav'n bestow'd;	506	To a Friend	10
	Nor, wilt thou of Gifts be sparing,	523	Betty Grizette	21
	Nor, will your nobler Gifts be misapply'd,	532	To Mr. Gay	15
	Thy Gifts, but never to my Friend:	555	Death of Swift	68
	With some Gifts, at least endow me,	631	Epistle Lady	63
	Endow'd with Gifts from every Brute	659	On Poetry	D 410
	With Gifts superior to the Crowd,	700	Cadenus Vaness	445
	Lastly, let his Gifts be try'd,	800	Traulus 2	43
	Receiv'd the Gifts of all Mankind.	894	Panegyr Dean	236
	Their gifts, as misers do their gold;	900	Dean's Reasons	36
	So, those who here their Gifts convey,	922	Riddle 7	47
GIGANTICK				
	The Body, tho' Gigantick, lyes all Cold and Dead.	25	Ode Athenian	291
	Expect some great gigantick Son of Earth;	30	Ode to Temple	111
GILD				
	Which he could neither Gild nor hide.	157	Fable of Midas	32
	Unweeting gild the tarnish'd Lace:	896	Panegyr Dean	312
GILDED				
	This Gilded Meteor which flyes	10	Ode to King	122
	If he has seen its gilded Spires.	109	V's House	102
	Like gilded Vapours to the Skies,	386	Manly Virtue	104
	Make gilded spires and altars tumble.	490	Dialogue	36
	Lur'd by the gilded Stern, and painted Sides.	771	Horace 1, 14	48
GILDING				
	Of rip'ning fruits, and gilding flow'rs;	432	Answer Paulus	14
	Gilding my Aurelia's Brows,	661	Love Song	22
	Or gilding in a sunny Morn	896	Panegyr Dean	305
GILT				
	The paper gilt, & Cover marbled)	463	Birthday Song	88
'GIN				
	When e're I 'gin, you should pursue	373	Letter D. S-y	52
GIN				
	Than Fish-Wives o'er a Cup of Gin:	450	Modern Lady	181
	To take, his mornings Cup of Gin.	659	On Poetry	D 410
GINN				
	To flourish o'er a Cup of Ginn?	505	Doctor Delaney	148
GIPSIES				
	Of Gipsies littering under Hedges,	641	On Poetry	38
GIRDLE				
	With that, he twisted his Girdle at me like a Rope,	72	Mrs Harris Pet	62
GIRL				
	The Girl had such a Bashfull way.	223	Prog of Love	32
	When you describe a lovely Girl,	272	Apollo's Edict	D 54
	A handsome young imperious Girl	289	Prog Marriage	3
	We have a Girl	442	Ballyspellin	61
	"Stand further Girl, or get you gone,	452	Modern Lady	244
	He long'd for a Girl that would struggle and squal,	519	Dean Hang Rape	56
	To squire a Royal Girl of two Years old!	531	To Mr. Gay	10
	To see the Girl in Deshabille.	698	Cadenus Vaness	367
	Began, when I was but a Girl.	699	Cadenus Vaness	391
	Which every Girl at five Years old	700	Cadenus Vaness	424
	The Girl might pass, if we cou'd get her	700	Cadenus Vaness	428
	Each Girl when pleas'd with what is taught,	710	Cadenus Vaness	734
	A Dutchess or a Kitchen Girl.	890	Panegyr Dean	124
GIRL'S				
	But like a Girl's Cockade, was ty'd	458	Paddy's Charac	17

331

GIRLS

	PAGE	TITLE	LINE
To Choak the Girls, or consume the Rabble;	283	Journal	114
And get Ten thousand Girls and Boys.	362	Grace's Answer	48
Ten thousand Girls and Boys you'll get	362	Grace's Answer	49
Admires how Girls can talk with Fellows,	449	Modern Lady	163
No little Boys and Girls to cry	778	Mullinix Tim	181
The girls of the village	857	Lady's Lament	195

GIRTH

	PAGE	TITLE	LINE
The Steed, oppress'd, would break his Girth,	231	Prog of Poetry	29
This breaks a Girth, and that a Bone.	398	Earl of P-b-w	21

GIV'N

	PAGE	TITLE	LINE
Had giv'n the Faction many a Wound,	171	Horace 1, 7	37
H'as drop'd, and giv'n the Crow a Pudden!	547	Life of Swift	71
Resume not what themselves have giv'n,	695	Cadenus Vaness	260

GIVE

	PAGE	TITLE	LINE
You need but now give Orders and Command;	13	Ode to William	D 38
That all the Praises it can give,	20	Ode Athenian	150
Resolv'd to give himself, as well as Country Peace.	30	Ode to Temple	134
But give the vigorous fancy room.	49	To Congreve	206
Till the blest sun to give kind dawn of grace	52	Temple Ill	25
To give the Town and Country Sport.	62	Discovery	8
I'll give something towards thy Loss;.	73	Mrs Harris Pet	67
And Houses would not give a Rent.	79	Vanbrug House	22
Give us but Straw, and let us Ly	90	Bauc & Phil 1	21
Give me that House in my own Hand;	128	Little House	49
The Dean will give me Willow-Sticks,	128	Little House	63
That Phebus must give Place to Pan;	157	Fable of Midas	54
And Scholars give it for the Cause,	158	Fable of Midas	69
Wine can give <Portland> Wit, and <Cleveland> Sense,	164	Toland's Invit	23
Their tongues and pens to give you joy,	176	To Lord Harley	2
Give us our earl, the devil take their duke.	186	Scriblerus 3	2
Give Hints, that Poets ne'er believe in God.	186	Scriblerus 4	D 11
To hear, yet give me no Relief;	193	Author Himself	6
Where Jove a Seat among the Gods will give	204	In Sickness	26
Venture to give him some Advice.	210	Earl of Oxford	13
Boy, give us a Cup;	218	To Mr. Delany	96
Then give us a Pinch	245	Irish-Feast	27
Will give a Night of Benefit to Weavers.	246	Irish-Feast	55
I give you Joy of the Report,	274	Epilogue	4
He'd give his Orders for a Storm;	300	Horrid Plot	63
"We'll give you Berkeley for Bermudas.	302	Storm	4
Good Manners must give Place to Profit.	305	Storm	52
Then ventur'd to give him some sober Advice,	311	To Ford	16
Dye Ned and Bess; give Will to Joan,	327	Epigram 1	5
Dye Joan and Will; give Bess to Ned,	328	Epigram 3	3
To Cudgel our Bones, and for Drink give us Verjuice;	328	Epigram 3	5
He makes no more to give ten Pounds than I to give a Pin.	335	Serious Poem	38
He makes no more to give ten Pounds than I to give a Pin.	341	Upon His Grace	14
He would not give a Groat to save his Father from the Gallows.	341	Upon His Grace	14
For, as sure as a Gun they will give up the Ghost	342	Upon His Grace	16
I'll give thee Surplice, Verge and Stall,	351	Wood Insect	23
Was too refin'd to give a Feast,	361	Grace's Answer	7
(Give fraudful Vice the Mask and Screen,	378	Apology Lady C	98
Could give him more Delight.	386	Manly Virtue	79
And I'll give you these delicate Bits:	395	Grub-Street	16
'Twill give you a scour:	395	Dog and Thief	2
And then he kindly give me hints	402	Window Inns 8	D 6
Their verses give delight	423	Ireld	59
How to give ev'ry man his due:	429	Beau's Reply	11
You give to Ballyspellin.	433	Answer Paulus	34
I would not give	440	Ballyspellin	6
And to each other give the Sign.	442	Ballyspellin	74
Now to another Scene give Place,	447	Modern Lady	77
When, to give ev'ry Dame her due,	447	Modern Lady	80
"Nay, Madam, give me leave to say	449	Modern Lady	138
And give each other but their Due;	452	Modern Lady	248
Had the best wishes they cou'd give him.	453	Modern Lady	273
For those affronts they give him yearly.	455	Dean Smedley	14
Give up the phrase of haughty Gaul,	463	Birthday Song	106
This will not give them half the trouble	468	Birthday Song	247
And give up Party to his Fame.	469	Birthday Song	2
Which, if you durst but give it place,	485	Libel on D- D-	150
What's your advice? shall I give o're,	485	Libel on D- D-	179
Thus, should I give your Humour place,	489	Dialogue	8
To give thee Lawn-Sleeves a Mitre and Rotchet,	496	Panegyr Swift	110
And better would give us, if better she had;	518	Dean Hang Rape	45
And give Advice before he gives the Pill.	520	Dean Hang Rape	70
I could give Instances Enough,	534	To Mr. Gay	80
Give others Riches, Power, and Station,	545	Life of Swift	23
But, all agree, to give me over.	555	Death of Swift	43
The rest will give a Shrug and cry,	557	Death of Swift	134
"Pray, do but give me leave to shew 'em;	561	Death of Swift	211
"Where Titles give no Right or Power,	563	Death of Swift	269
And into the Bargain, I'll readily give you,	570	Death of Swift	439
I saw the Graves give up their Dead.	576	Place Damn'd	13
Could give no Softness to his Face.	578	Day Judgement	4
Nor give the smallest Room to guess	587	Strephon Chloe	94
	588	Strephon Chloe	139

GIVE   (CONTINUED)   PAGE   TITLE   LINE

      Thin'k what can give the Colick Ease, ...   589 Strephon Chloe   168
      Would still the same Ideas give ye, ...   591 Strephon Chloe   247
      Nor for a Party give his Vote: . . . .   604 Beasts Confess   98
      To give him but a Writ of Ease, ...   606 Beasts Confess   170
      Give future times the Satisfaction   . . . . . .   608 Know Not What   7
      Can Clouds give buboes, ulcers, blotches?   . . . .   618 Scandal Poem 1   25
      Of foul and fair we give you warning;   . . . .   619 Scandal Poem 1   48
      We, to whom all the Gods give place.   . . . .   620 Scandal Poem 1   96
      Can Clouds give Bubo's, Ulcers, Blotches, ...   624 Scandal Poem 2   19
      Of Foul or Fair we give you warning;   . . . .   625 Scandal Poem 2   44
      We, to whom all the Gods give Place: . . . .   626 Scandal Poem 2   94
      From my Ailments give me Leisure, ...   632 Epistle Lady   87
      Give no more to ev'ry Guest, ...   633 Epistle Lady   125
      Give him always of the Prime, ...   633 Epistle Lady   127
      Give your Head some gentle Raps;   . . . .   638 Epistle Lady   264
      To Statesmen wou'd you give a Wipe, ...   643 On Poetry   95
      Give up your fond paternal Pride, ...   644 On Poetry   127
      To Cerberus they give a Sop, ...   647 On Poetry   213
      Can teaze, and gall, and give the Spleen;   . . . . .   651 On Poetry   344
      To Titles give the sole Pretence.   . . . .   656 On Poetry   460
      Give <George> and Jove an equal Share.   . . . . . .   657 On Poetry   486
      I'll give my <Monarch> Butter-weight.   . . . . . .   657 On Poetry   488
      Nature must give Way to Art.   . . . . . .   660 Love Song   4
      If you shou'd give him once the Reins, ...   666 Epig Carthy 2   D   5
      Cou'd Horace give so sad a Monster Birth, ...   669 Epig Carthy 16 D   1
      My Lines to him you give--to speak your due, ...   670 Epig Carthy 18 D   1
      And give him wholly to your Care.   . . . .   692 Cadenus Vaness   197
      Give Mortals neither Heat nor Light.   . . . . . .   700 Cadenus Vaness   443
      One way he knows to give her Pain: . . . .   701 Cadenus Vaness   469
      I'll give her what she most admires, ...   702 Cadenus Vaness   500
      Truth, Judgment, Wit, give Place to Spite, ...   730 Stella, Poems   93
      Had fate a lucky'r one, she'd give it ye: . . . . .   760 Bec's B-Day   2
      They give the sick man joy, and praise   . . . .   761 Bec's B-Day   15
      Or give my Scrap of Life to you, ...   766 Stel B-day '26   85
      Then give those Rascals cause to laugh.   . . . . . .   778 Mullinix Tim   178
      I give my self intire to you, ...   782 Mullinix Tim   283
      And, must their Malice ne'er give o'er?   . . . . . .   798 Traulus 1   86
      Who cou'd give the Looby such Airs?   . . . .   800 Traulus 2   25
      To give them by Turns an invisible Jog.   . . . . .   804 Irish Bishops   16
      But hold, cry the <Bishops>; and give us fair Play; . .   805 Irish Bishops   53
      First take you our Tyths, and give us your Lands. . .   805 Irish Bishops   62
      For thine, my dear Dick, give me leave to speak plain, .   819 Archbi Cashel   15
      Just to yawn, and give his Vote;   . . . .   836 Legion Club   170
      We must give them better Quarter, ...   837 Legion Club   177
      May Walmsley give wine, ...   858 Lady's Lament   221
      And make him soon give up the Cause.   . . . . . .   861 Lady Acheson   40
      Give her half thy Face behind.   . . . .   862 To Janus   8
      Give me Time when coming on: . . . .   863 To Janus   23
      Give me Velvet and Quadrille, ...   863 To Janus   29
      Whatever they give me I must be content, ...   867 Grand Question   22
      But, if you will give us a Barrack, my Dear, ...   868 Grand Question   31
      And not among Ladies to give themselves Airs. . . .   868 Grand Question   38
      That for twenty Denials you would not give out. . . .   869 Grand Question   56
      'Till he gave me my Will, I wou'd give him no Rest: . .   869 Grand Question   58
      "And Madam, says he, if such Dinners you give, . . .   872 Grand Question   141
      "To give a young Gentleman right Education, ...   872 Grand Question   161
      Give me but a Barrack, a Fig for the Clergy. . . . .   873 Grand Question   190
      We give the World to understand, ...   875 Drapier's Hill   1
      Except to give <Dean> <Daniel> place.   . . . . .   888 Panegyr Dean   48
      To give the least offensive Word;   . . . .   889 Panegyr Dean   70
      Just to give ev'ry Man his Glass: . . . .   889 Panegyr Dean   94
      And give him Words of dreadful Sounds, ...   904 Death Daphne   43
      Give yourself ten thousand airs   . . . .   908 Daphne   77
      Never will I give advice   . . . .   908 Daphne   79
      I give Command to kill or save.   . . . . .   916 Riddle 1   34
      I sometimes give Advice in Writing, ...   917 Riddle 3   9
      And some give out, that I entice   . . . .   917 Riddle 3   13
      By those who give me greatest Pain.   . . . .   918 Riddle 4   16
      While others give me many a Curse, ...   918 Riddle 4   27
      That they to others give thee most: . . . .   919 Riddle 5   30
      Nay their very Souls away.   . . . .   930 Riddle 15   D 28
      May give you a Blow you'll for ever repent.   . . . . .   941 Letter   40
      Can leave a Mark and give a Smart.   . . . . . .   942 Probatur Alit   24
      A long-ear'd Beast give me, and Eggs unsound, ...   943 Probatur Alit   39
      And you and your cart shall give me carte blanche. . .   979 Dean to Tho: S   14
      That I'll ne'er give my vote for Delenda Cart-ago. . .   979 Dean to Tho: S   18
      I tell you I'd not give a fig for your wine; . . . .   979 Dean to Tho: S   30
      For he says, short as 'tis, it will give you a stool. .   980 Tho: Sheridan   8
      I would not give such Language to a Dog, faith and troth   985 Mary to Sher   4
      To give us a Description graphick   . . . .   993 On Picture   2
      You won't give us a Dram.   . . . . . .   1015 Swift to Sheri   48
      Oh that Jove would give me such a talent as thine .   1017 Swift Ans Sher   7
      And give Satan his due Dan begins to refine   . . . . .   1017 Swift Ans Sher   10
      To give us your measures of lines by a quadrant. . . .   1026 Sheri Circles   10
      But, there were not a Dozen (to give 'em their Due) sick   1029 Dr. Helsham   24
      And then to give me such a deadly Cut--   . . . . . .   1033 Ans to Crown   10
GIVEN
      William's the Pledge and Earnest given by Fate . . .   13 Ode to William D 47
      Has given thee up a dwelling-place to fiends? . . . .   37 Ode Sancroft   95
      There some high spiritual throne to Sancroft shall be   42 Ode Sancroft   236
            given,

GIVEN   (CONTINUED)   PAGE   TITLE   LINE

	PAGE	TITLE	LINE
GIVEN (CONTINUED)			
A score of guineas, given under-hand,	308	Billet Players	23
GIVER			
But the sly Giver better knows thee;	920	Riddle 5	35
GIVES			
Gives murmuring passage to a lasting wave;	49	To Congreve	188
Gives glad farewell to a tempestuous day;	51	Temple Ill	18
This gives him Lodging, and provides	80	Vanbrug House	45
While Rain depends, the pensive Cat gives o'er	136	City Shower	3
And like a Drunkard gives it up again.	137	City Shower	16
Tho' the Court gives my Nephews, and Brothers, and Cousins,	144	New Song	47
And gives the Whigs and Rabble Sport.	190	Faggot	26
That gives Surprise, and this Delight;	215	To Mr. Delany	24
If nam'd with Scorn, gives just Offence.	217	To Mr. Delany	70
Who gives no Bills, but of Mortality.	235	Elegy on Demar	40
Or gives Relief to long-expecting Heirs.	364	On Dreams	28
Jove grants the Prayer, gives Virtue Birth,	384	Manly Virtue	15
But my Master each Day gives me Bread;	395	Dog and Thief	6
Talks Politicks, and gives the Toast.	398	Earl of P-b-w	6
Thinks nothing gives one Airs so pretty;	417	Woman's Mind	41
The humble whelp gives ev'ry vote.	421	Ireld	15
Nor gives her Tongue one Moment's Rest,	448	Modern Lady	111
And gives the Maids of Honor Sport.	468	Birthday Song	268
Though Splendor gives the fairest Mark	500	Doctor Delaney	27
And give Advice before he gives the Pill.	534	To Mr. Gay	80
Pays all the Cost, and gives the Villain Thanks.	535	To Mr. Gay	110
Alas! that gives you small relief---!	546	Life of Swift	60
It gives me such a jealous Fit;	555	Death of Swift	51
She gives you such Plenty, it puts you in Pain;	580	Psyche	7
Which Nature gives in such a Case;	591	Strephon Chloe	240
And gives himself a haughty air,	621	Scandal Poem 1	137
And gives himself a haughty Air,	627	Scandal Poem 2	141
Gives Imagination Scope,	636	Epistle Lady	213
Gives Judgment with decisive Air.	649	On Poetry	266
He gives Directions to the Town,	649	On Poetry	269
In vain, --- for soon the slender prop gives way;	672	Epig Carthy 24 D	16
So little gets for what she gives	735	Stel B-day '20	29
No Raillery gives just Offence	747	Stel Distress	61
Yet Raillery gives no Offence,	752	Stel Wood-Park	77
But, when her breakfast gives her courage,	761	Bec's B-Day	35
One gives Advice in Proverbs Old,	781	Mullinix Tim	271
And gives me a wipe	851	Lady's Lament	7
But sense gives a grace	854	Lady's Lament	99
And worry him out, 'till he gives his Consent.	869	Grand Question	62
Gives them a peny, and God's blessing	878	Robbin & Harry	6
To me he chiefly gives in Trust	915	Riddle 1	21
And yet my speaking gives Offence:	917	Riddle 4	6
And my Oppression gives them Rest.	918	Riddle 4	10
He gives; and with a gen'rous Pride,	919	Riddle 5	21
That gives imaginary Pain:	920	Riddle 5	34
Because my Magick gives no Pain.	934	Riddle 21 D	22
But gives it a Tweak;	939	Riddle Answerd	12
On such an Occasion the Law gives Relief.	943	Probatur Alit	46
A Bacon-slice gives God Offence?	949	Epigr Fasting	2
GIVING			
From giving Passage to a <Turd>.	66	Problem	26
That Clouds are blam'd for giving Claps:	618	Scandal Poem 1	22
That Clouds are blam'd for giving Claps;	624	Scandal Poem 2	16
GIZZARD			
One word shou'd stick thus in your gizzard.	983	Sher, A Goose	10
GLAD			
And glad Ierne now may see	9	Ode to King	99
(Glad of the Victory, yet frighted at the War)	17	Ode Athenian	33
And foolishly are glad to see it at it's height	25	Ode Athenian	281
O'er the glad scene whence first she rose a bride:	51	Temple Ill	12
Gives glad farewell to a tempestuous day;	51	Temple Ill	18
Unworthy the glad tidings which I bring,	52	Temple Ill	35
Then said my Lord, I'm very glad to see thee honest Friend,	342	Upon His Grace	31
What cou'd I've said? I'm mighty glad	377	Apology Lady C	51
Glad to compound at any Rate;	378	Apology Lady C	94
To win the Soul, and glad the Heart;	385	Manly Virtue	56
In Dublin they'd be glad to see	420	Holyhead	13
For which all true Protestant Hearts should be glad;	520	Dean Hang Rape	68
Glad, that themselves cou'd walk about.	546	Life of Swift	51
How glad the Case is not your own!	554	Death of Swift	30
"I'm glad the Medals were forgot.	559	Death of Swift	184
Safely glad to sup their Porridge,	574	Helter Skelter	54
In a glad Hour Lucina's Aid	690	Cadenus Vaness	136
Altho' it was plain, in her Heart she was glad,	873	Grand Question	183
Ne'er sad I mourn, ne'er glad rejoice,	936	Riddle 23 D	24
I'd be glad of a Knogging:	1015	Swift to Sheri	46
GLADDER			
True indeed, I should be gladder,	801	Traulus 2	49
GLADLY			
But, which I gladly would forget,	290	Prog Marriage	29
We gladly hear you, and submit:	314	To Ford	94
Thy Friend would gladly share thy Fate.	596	Cassinus Peter	94
He gladly offers in return:	711	Cadenus Vaness	785
Rebecca thus I gladly greet,	761	Bec's B-Day	17

		PAGE	TITLE	LINE

GLADLY (CONTINUED)
- Who gladly would your Suff'rings share; . . . . . . — 766 Stel B-day '26 — 84
- Yet would gladly see the Hunks . . . . — 836 Legion Club — 167

GLANCE
- They glance aside without a Wound. . . . . . . — 500 Doctor Delaney — 30
- And will each accidental Glance . . . . — 712 Cadenus Vaness — 816
- She darted many a private Glance, ... — 905 Death Daphne — 67

GLARE
- Thus Lamps, which burn'd in Tombs with silent Glare, . — 667 Epig Carthy 5 — D 5

GLASS SEE ASSEMBLING-GLASS,HOUR-GLASS,POCKET-GLASS
- Like sun-beams shot at too far distance from a glass; . — 35 Ode Sancroft — 24
- And in a Glass had made her see . . . . — 224 Prog of Love — 53
- Two Balls of Glass may serve for Eyes, ... — 229 Prog of Beauty — 113
- Shewn through a multiplying Glass . . . . — 255 Bubble — 119
- To the Dean'ry House, and on the North Glass, . . . — 264 Apollo — 31
- In talking ore a moderate Glass. . . . . — 279 Journal — 38
- She at the Glass consults her Looks . . . . . . — 291 Prog Marriage — 40
- (Not to be seen without a Glass) . . . . — 367 Answer Delaney — 35
- 'Tis true, a Glass will bring supplies . . . . . — 367 Answer Delaney — 45
- Your Mistress in a Glass to show, ... — 401 Window Inns 2 — 2
- The glass, by lovers nonsense blurr'd, ... — 402 Window Inns 6 — D 1
- To scratch their paultry drabs on glass; . . . . . — 402 Window Inns 7 — D 4
- Then to her Glass; and "Betty, pray . . . . . . — 446 Modern Lady — 48
- Of Celia's magnifying Glass. . . . . — 527 Lady's Dres Rm — 60
- A Glass that can to Sight disclose, ... — 527 Lady's Dres Rm — 63
- To see that ev'ry Glass was fine. . . . . — 746 Stel Distress — 22
- To see that ev'ry Glass was fine. . . . . — 750 Stel Wood-Park — 20
- For I'm asham'd to use a Glass; . . . . — 758 Stel B-day '24 — 46
- Or Forms reflected from a Glass? . . . . — 765 Stel B-day '26 — 52
- Ran to the Glass, and then comparing . . . . . . — 783 Tim and Fables — 14
- So <Turds> within a Glass inclose, ... — 786 Clad in Brown — 11
- The Glass will seem as brown as those. . . . . . — 786 Clad in Brown — 12
- Just to give ev'ry Man his Glass: . . . . — 889 Panegyr Dean — 94
- Distinctly seen as through a Glass: . . . . . . — 920 Riddle 6 — 14
- Here you may see, as in a Glass, ... — 921 Riddle 7 — 5
- One of us in Glass is set, ... — 930 Riddle 17 — D 3
- And all that stuff of Toylet, Glass, and Box-comb? . — 1003 Dan J's Reply — 9

GLASSES
- Glasses and Linnen clean, and Pewter bright, . . . — 165 Toland's Invit — 28
- Keep up the Glasses of your Chair, ... — 228 Prog of Beauty — 74
- Is strained thro' Glasses. . . . . — 938 Riddle Answerd — 6

GLEANINGS
- The Gleanings of Philosophy, ... — 27 Ode to Temple — 23

GLEBE
- Again the verdant Glebe renew; . . . . — 759 Receipt Youth — 12

GLEBES
- Mitres, and Glebes could scarce do more . . . . . — 493 Panegyr Swift — 9

GLEW
- And those to be sure, stuck together like Glew, sick. . — 1029 Dr. Helsham — 25

GLIB
- Do but hear on the Clergy how glib his Tongue ran; . . — 872 Grand Question — 140

GLIBBER
- And then to make them pass the glibber, ... — 561 Death of Swift — 199

GLIDES
- And murmurs as she glides away. . . . . — 31 Ode to Temple — 158
- And Youth so swiftly glides away; . . . . — 593 Strephon Chloe — 304

GLIMM'RINGS
- Short glimm'rings of the prelate glorify'd; . . . . — 41 Ode Sancroft — 213

GLIMMERS
- Scarce glimmers, like a dying Snuff. . . . . . . — 787 Clad in Brown — 18

GLISTERS
- Alas! all is not Gold that glisters; . . . . . . — 254 Bubble — 107

GLITT'RING
- In sum, a glitt'ring voice, a painted name, ... — 54 Temple Ill — 101
- Hung high and made a glitt'ring Show . . . . . . — 93 Bauc & Phil 1 — 114
- Hung high, and made a glitt'ring Show, ... — 114 Bauc & Phil 2 — 90
- Then lighted from his Glitt'ring Coach, ... — 119 Apollo Outwit — 6
- Or glitt'ring Tinsel of May-Fair, ... — 135 Magician's Rod — 77
- The chief among that glitt'ring crowd, ... — 177 To Lord Harley — 39
- The glitt'ring Beau could hardly tell, ... — 325 Pethox — 65
- The Glitt'ring Constellations Roll, ... — 362 Grace's Answer — 33
- Behold his glitt'ring Faulchion mow . . . . . . — 461 Birthday Song — 31
- In all her glitt'ring Birth-day Gear, ... — 591 Strephon Chloe — 228
- A Party out of glitt'ring Dames, ... — 698 Cadenus Vaness — 364
- For Vice in all its glitt'ring Dress: . . . . . . — 765 Stel B-day '26 — 48

GLITTER'D
- Glitter'd like Spangles on the Ground: . . . . . — 156 Fable of Midas — 4

GLOBE
- Or if thought's rolling globe her circle run, . . . — 51 Temple Ill — 9
- In all Parts of the Globe, where your Language is read; — 265 Apollo — 70
- Half the Globe from Sense and Knowledge. . . . . — 829 Legion Club — 4
- This earthly Globe to thee assign'd, ... — 894 Panegyr Dean — 235

GLOC'STER
- "He shews, as sure as God's in Gloc'ster, ... — 564 Death of Swift — 293

GLOOMY
- Yet so much sooner comes the long and gloomy Night. . . — 25 Ode Athenian — 282
- Gloomy Pluto, King of Terrors, ... — 661 Love Song — 17
- The Son of Pitch, and gloomy Night; . . . . . . — 929 Riddle 15 — D 2

GLORIA
- And here rest, Sic transit Gloria Mundi. . . . . . — 431 Dicky Dolly — 24

GLORIES
Did with new, unexperienc't Glories wait, ...   PAGE   TITLE   LINE

	PAGE	TITLE		LINE
Did with new, unexperienc't Glories wait,	21	Ode Athenian		156
GLORIFY'D				
Short glimm'rings of the prelate glorify'd;	41	Ode Sancroft		213
GLORIOUS				
The glorious Structure of Your Fame to raise;	11	Ode to William	D	6
Nor is this all: As glorious is the Care	12	Ode to William	D	25
Of glorious Deeds, that must all Tongues Employ:	13	Ode to William	D	46
As glorious as Belinda's Hair?	271	Apollo's Edict	D	39
Pontifick, made your glorious March;	326	Pethox		94
"A Scene so glorious and so new?	380	Apology Lady C		164
Engage, and in the glorious Strife,	385	Manly Virtue		45
His Course of glorious Toil shou'd run,	387	Manly Virtue		118
Are Seconds in this glorious Scheme;	391	Young's Satire		8
Nassau, who got the name of glorious	468	Birthday Song		251
But princely Douglas, and his glorious Dame,	531	To Mr. Gay		13
Smit with the glorious prize next struts in Sewel,	672	Epig Carthy 24	D	9
Keck at the Memory of Glorious.	775	Mullinix Tim		76
The glorious Founder of their kingly Race:	790	St. Pat's Well		12
Toast old Glorious in your Piss.	835	Legion Club		152
Sees the glorious Ages past.	862	To Janus		16
To make me glorious to the Sight	916	Riddle 2		11
Wise and glorious to behold;	936	Riddle 24	D	20
GLORY				
With its own Light Your dazling Glory shines,	11	Ode to William	D	7
The boundless Glory all Redounds to Thee,	12	Ode to William	D	35
Of England's Glory, and her lasting Joy.	13	Ode to William	D	48
The Royal Rose the glory of our morn,	37	Ode Sancroft		105
The daz'ling glory dimms their prostituted sight,	41	Ode Sancroft		221
The Glory of the Granard Race;	272	Apollo's Edict	D	67
Where Wit in all its Glory shines;	361	Grace's Answer		2
Behold the Glory he has won,	385	Manly Virtue		41
The Height of Glory here below,	386	Manly Virtue		100
Their Glory from the God of Day,	387	Manly Virtue		106
When Celia in her Glory shows,	530	Lady's Dres Rm		135
"To sacrifice old England's Glory,	568	Death of Swift		387
The Nation's Good, his Master's Glory,	605	Beasts Confess		145
Two bordering Wits contend for Glory;	650	On Poetry		293
The Captain at Dinner appears in his Glory;	871	Grand Question		130
GLOSS				
Ev'ry Fault have drawn a Gloss over:	632	Epistle Lady		96
GLOSSY				
With swelling scarf, and glossy gown,	676	Parson's Case		25
GLOVE				
And he and I were Hand in Glove.	741	Stel B-day 22		26
GLOVES SEE NIGHT-GLOVES				
And get a Hatband, Scarf, and Gloves.	547	Life of Swift		65
On Ribbons, Fans, and Gloves and Lace;	698	Cadenus Vaness		377
They place before him Gloves and Shoes;	885	Rev Market-Hill		78
GLOW				
With Paean's purest Fire his Favourites glow;	532	To Mr. Gay		23
The Heat that makes the Summit glow,	731	Stella, Poems		107
Affirm, can't glow to more Delight.	932	Riddle 19	D	10
GLUT				
And, how would Censure glut her Spight?	726	To Stella		94
GLUTTONY				
But Gluttony was ne'er his Vice:	602	Beasts Confess		40
Then Gluttony with greasy Paws,	894	Panegyr Dean		255
GLYSTER				
Is held as needfull as His Glyster	62	Discovery		12
GNATS				
Than swarms of gnats, that wanton in a ray	46	To Congreve		81
By Gnats, and draw the Nation's Dung,	496	Panegyr Swift		115
GO				
Go publish o'er the Plain	31	Ode to Temple		139
How some go downward to the Root,	32	Ode to Temple		172
Such are the ways ill-guided mortals go	35	Ode Sancroft		37
Still scatt'ring desolation where they go.	55	Temple Ill		130
That tho' 'tis hard to judge, yet Money can't go without Hands.	71	Mrs Harris Pet		43
Now you may go hang your self for me, and so went away.	72	Mrs Harris Pet		63
Can't you go work, or serve the King?	91	Bauc & Phil 1		41
And saw it fairly twice go round;	112	Bauc & Phil 2		31
If you be wise, then go not far to Dine,	137	City Shower		7
And bear their Trophies with them as they go:	139	City Shower		54
And the Whigs may all go Swing,	168	Peace Dunkirk		6
And bid Friend Lewis go in quest	171	Horace 1, 7		16
"Good Mr. Dean go change your Gown,	200	Horace 2, 6		23
Go to the Dean to read Lucretius.	278	Journal		12
While George, and Dean, go back to Gammon.	280	Journal		42
We go to Pray'rs, and then to play	280	Journal		52
"Go, Sisters Nine, into that Cabbin,	320	First of April		3
Come, you must take a Cup of Sack or two before you go.	342	Upon His Grace		24
Not saying, lest I go too far,	373	Letter D. S-y		62
Nay then 'tis time for me to go.	376	Apology Lady C		44
Well then, I'll e'en go home, and fast;	377	Apology Lady C		54
But pray. To morrow go at Ten,	377	Apology Lady C		67
Whether he ought to stay or go.	377	Apology Lady C		82
And thus I go off without Pray'r-Book or Psalm.	400	Tom Clinch		22
I'd go in freedom to my grave,	421	Holyhead		33
That all our wives should go in Chints.	423	Ireld		60

GO   (CONTINUED)

	PAGE	TITLE	LINE
"Go run, and light the Ladies up:	451	Modern Lady	212
But this I think will not go down,	460	Birthday Song	13
To rail, and go unpunish'd too;	492	Panegyr Swift	4
And go to Church, and say our Prayers.	495	Panegyr Swift	71
You then may boldly go in Quest	504	Doctor Delaney	143
Resolv'd to go thro' thick and thin;	528	Lady's Dres Rm	80
Some, when an Heir succeeds; go boldly on,	535	To Mr. Gay	117
Nor can you go to Hell before you dye.	539	Mr. Pulteney	42
But hold---: before we farther go,	545	Life of Swift	5
Nor if you dy'd, wou'd fail to go	547	Life of Swift	62
"The Nation stript go joyful back,	571	Death of Swift	447
"Go Snacks with Thieves and Rapparees,	571	Death of Swift	449
I damn such Fools!--Go, go, you're bit."	579	Day Judgement	22
I damn such Fools!--Go, go, you're bit."	579	Day Judgement	22
Why let it go, if I must tell it--	586	Strephon Chloe	83
Go read in antient books enroll'd	619	Scandal Poem 1	51
Provide you duly as we go	621	Scandal Poem 1	129
Go read in antient Books enroll'd,	625	Scandal Poem 2	47
With Care provide you as we go,	627	Scandal Poem 2	123
We'll watch your Steps where-e'er you go:	627	Scandal Poem 2	132
Go try your Hand a second Time.	645	On Poetry	146
But now go search all Europe round	659	On Poetry	D 410
What mortal else cou'd e'er go through it!	675	Curate's Compl	17
A Duke to know a Dean! go smooth your Frown,	678	Dean and Duke	13
Then Cloe, still go on to prate	735	Stel B-day '20	39
Away she will go	756	Dingley Brent	17
Some for the publick Service go,	781	Mullinix Tim	255
Thou must go naked all the Year.	786	Clad in Brown	4
To the Dean he shall go; they shall kiss, and be friends:	817	Yahoo's	62
"go tell your friend Bob and the other great folk,	843	Ay and No	13
But we must go to Aghnacloy;	860	Lady Acheson	27
"Go, bring me my Smock, and leave off your Prate,	870	Grand Question	83
How far to go, and when to spare:	890	Panegyr Dean	116
Accosting; said, Go shake your Cream.	897	Panegyr Dean	326
I twice a Day a hunting go;	921	Riddle 6	31
Why then I make pieces of Iron go down.	927	Riddle 11	D 8
What other Way they take to go,	928	Riddle 12	D 9
Will come, tho' not a Foot they go.	934	Riddle 21	D 6
Will go a Horse go, though he be not fat.	940	Letter	13
And I wish your few friends, when they next see your car go,	976	Dean to Sherid	29
. . .and you may go tell my Master; what care I?	986	Mary to Sher	21
And now I must go, and get Saunders to direct this Letter,	987	Mary to Sher	33
. . .and you shall go back in a fortnight,	1023	Nim-Dan-Dean 2	D 8
Go flatter Kilmore.	1038	Sheridan Cavan	14

GO-CART | | | |
| Or, with her Go-Cart amble Side by Side. | 531 | To Mr. Gay | 12 |
GO'ST | | | |
| Thee to attend where-e'er thou go'st. | 324 | Pethox | 38 |
GOAL | | | |
| Both from the Goal together start; | 290 | Prog Marriage | 31 |
| Desire had now the Goal in Sight: | 413 | Desire Possess | 39 |
GOAT | | | |
| The Goat advanc'd with decent Pace; | 603 | Beasts Confess | 59 |
GOATS | | | |
Hogs, Asses, Wolves, Baboons, & Goats	659	On Poetry	D 410
Your Works are like old Jacob's speckled Goats,	670	Epig Carthy 18	D 3
And gaming Goats, and fleecy Flocks,	934	Riddle 21	D 8
GOBBLED			
And Supper gobbled up in haste,	453	Modern Lady	277
GOD SEE SEA-GOD,BROTHER-GOD			
Before the Hero can commence a God.	7	Ode to King	30
(But, surely such whom God did never for his People chuse)	8	Ode to King	86
When some Patrician God wou'd visit the Immortal Jayl,	9	Ode to King	93
To which they look as to some Guardian God	12	Ode to William	D 31
To be a fitter Birth-place for the God of Wit;	17	Ode Athenian	49
Whilst Angels tune the Voice, and God inspires the Tongue.	17	Ode Athenian	56
This Surly, Slipp'ry God, when He design'd	22	Ode Athenian	197
Doubts, where the Delphick God	22	Ode Athenian	208
The God of Learning and of Light	22	Ode Athenian	209
Would want a God Himself to help him out.	22	Ode Athenian	210
Great God! (said I) what have I seen!	29	Ode to Temple	103
And God himself has said, He shall not find it here.	35	Ode Sancroft	20
The Son of God pronounc'd by the same breath	38	Ode Sancroft	119
To scribblers, and the god of light and wit;	45	To Congreve	76
Take this short lesson from the god of bayes,	49	To Congreve	203
To fix this nimble god,	49	To Congreve	208
Therefore all the Money, I have, which, God knows,	69	Mrs Harris Pet	6
So when I went to put up my Purse, as God would have it,.	69	Mrs Harris Pet	8
And, God knows, I thought.	69	Mrs Harris Pet	11
The God of Wealth was therefore made	79	Vanbrug House	23
His Pray'r was granted, for the God	81	Vanbrug House	71
On Earth, the God of Wealth was made	106	V's House	23
Jove Smil'd, and like a gentle God,	107	V's House	51
Ay, thought the God, are these your Tricks?	108	V's House	71
The God laid down his Feeble Rays,	119	Apollo Outwit	5

337

GOD	(CONTINUED)	PAGE	TITLE	LINE
Of that Bright God whom Bards invoke,		120	Apollo Outwit	14
To Cheat the God in his own Art.		120	Apollo Outwit	28
The God could not refuse her Prayer;		120	Apollo Outwit	34
Some May-Fair invented,		122	Empty'ng Town	2
The God of Wit to shew his Grudge.		157	Fable of Midas	29
The God of Wit, and Light, and Arts,		176	To Lord Harley	9
Give Hints, that Poets ne'er believe in God.		193	Author Himself	6
Thank God, 'twas neither Shame nor Sin,		224	Prog of Love	59
Pluto the god of Wealth, will joy to know		234	Elegy on Demar	7
Upon the god of Gold and Hell,		240	Run Bankers	42
The God, who favour'd her Request,		302	Storm	9
This morn the God of Wit and Joke,		320	First of April	1
"With due Submission to the God,		321	First of April	17
Wonder'd the God had sent them there.		322	First of April	44
"The God has made us April-Fools.		322	First of April	58
The God who made Scamander boil,		323	Pethox	7
Whether from War's stern God you claim		323	Pethox	11
God Bless your Grace I then reply'd,		343	Upon His Grace	37
Then God Preserve his Lordship's Grace,		343	Upon His Grace	47
And to the God of Wealth his Brother,		346	Prometheus	51
I mean His <Majesty>, God bless him.		346	Prometheus	62
Their Glory from the God of Day,		387	Manly Virtue	106
That had I been the God of Wit,		393	Modern Poets	18
But now He's grown a King, God wot,		408	Dial Rich Marb	17
Pray God they now may find as true.		408	Dial Rich Marb	22
So, Holla Boys; God save the King.		418	Woman's Mind	64
Away the God of Silence flew,		448	Modern Lady	121
The Spiteful Insect stung the God.		458	Paddy's Charac	34
Sole Patron, Judge, and God of Wit.		462	Birthday Song	72
And sees a Son in every God		466	Birthday Song	185
That Princes should believe in God:		468	Birthday Song	264
Can differ more than God and <Kings>		486	Libel on D- D-	196
Than those of Wit, or Trust in God.		495	Panegyr Swift	79
Believ'd in God, and you in none.		495	Panegyr Swift	85
For once there was a Time, God wot,		498	Panegyr Swift	157
The God of Light could ne'er have been so blind,		532	To Mr. Gay	27
That, God be prais'd, the Dean is well.		557	Death of Swift	126
Resigning to the Will of God.		561	Death of Swift	218
"Nor fear'd he God, nor Man regarded;		570	Death of Swift	422
A certain Goddess, God knows who,		587	Strephon Chloe	100
Apollo, God of Light and Wit,		597	Problem Solved	1
Confess'd a Sin, and God forgive him:		604	Beasts Confess	114
A Prelate who no God believes;		645	On Poetry	163
This God on Earth turns Devil in Hell.		646	On Poetry	206
Who at them rail bid God Confound:		658	On Poetry	D 190
Wherein the God of Earth delights.		743	Stel B-day 22	52
The God of Winds and God of Fire		743	Stel B-day 22	63
The God of Winds and God of Fire		743	Stel B-day 22	63
To half a Joynt, & God be thanked:		745	Stel Distress	12
To half a Joint, and God be thank it:		750	Stel Wood-Park	36
The God of Wit, and Beauty's Queen,		757	Stel B-day '24	17
Made your Sons Converts both to God and Sense:		792	St. Pat's Well	30
Till, God knows why, at last it burst.		796	Traulus 1	18
Which God pronounc'd he never wou'd,		799	Traulus 1	97
So God bless the Church, and three of our Mitres;		805	Irish Bishops	63
And God bless the Commons for Biting the Biters.		805	Irish Bishops	64
Yet, through Despair, of God and Man accurst,		806	Judas	7
He flies from his God, to attend on his Grace:		809	Epigr Prelate	4
Since God had no Hand in his Lordship's Promotion.		809	Epigr Prelate	6
From Rogues who ne'er believ'd a God?		820	Dr. Rundle	30
As not the Handy-work of God;		821	Dr. Rundle	54
For Divines allow, that God		830	Legion Club	31
May their God, the Devil confound 'em.		839	Legion Club	242
Two-fac'd Janus, God of Time,		862	To Janus	1
God of Time, if you be wise,		862	To Janus	9
And Lemnian God consulting strove,		916	Riddle 2	10
That I shou'd point the Word of God,		930	Riddle 15	D 23
You always are making a God of your Spouse,		947	Mrs. Houghton	1
A Bacon-slice gives God Offence?		949	Epigr Fasting	2
I pay my Club, and so God b'y'--.		954	Authors Living	10
Well, well, that's as God pleases,		986	Mary to Sher	20
You smell the <Stink>? by <God> you lye,		67	Problem	55
His <Grace> swore by <God>, and her <Grace> let a <Fart>:		143	New Song	18
<God> <damn> me Jack, she's wondrous fair.		228	Prog of Beauty	76
'Twixt you and me <God> Damn the Lyers.		773	Mullinix Tim	8
And then-- <God> Damn the Lyars again.		773	Mullinix Tim	12
I vow to <God> you're too severe.		775	Mullinix Tim	70
<God> <damn> the Whigs and Tories too.		782	Mullinix Tim	284
By <God> says Tim (and let a <Fart>)		783	Tim and Fables	19
By <God> I'll bring you off as clean.		797	Traulus 1	60
"<God> <damn> me, they bid us reform and repent,		872	Grand Question	145
"<God> <damn> me, he hobbles as bad as my Groom;		872	Grand Question	156
"By <God> they don't signify this Pinch of Snuff.		872	Grand Question	160
"The first Man I robb'd was a Parson by <God>.		873	Grand Question	170
<God> <damn> his Blood, and <Blood> and <Wounds>.		904	Death Daphne	44
GOD-LIKE				
The Acts of Gods, and god-like Kings.		496	Panegyr Swift	103
He must adore such God-like Men.		708	Cadenus Vaness	695

338

		PAGE	TITLE	LINE
GOD'S				
	First of God's darling attributes,	34	Ode Sancroft	5
	A sign God's dart is shot, and wrath o'erblown;	52	Temple Ill	28
	Of Stroling God's, whose usual Trade is,	120	Apollo Outwit	22
	To qualify him God's Vicegerent,	464	Birthday Song	134
	God's Image, which was once their Boast.	498	Panegyr Swift	166
	"He shews, as sure as God's in Gloc'ster,	564	Death of Swift	293
	Must own it made by God's Anointed.	821	Dr. Rundle	56
	Gives them a peny, and God's blessing	878	Robbin & Harry	6
	I am not one of God's Creation,	927	Riddle 10	D 8
GODDESS				
	And thus He did the Airy Goddess Court,	7	Ode to King	35
	(The goddess Muse herself has told me so)	41	Ode Sancroft	233
	Nor tax the goddess of a mean design	44	To Congreve	33
	Malignant goddess! bane to my repose,	53	Temple Ill	81
	But, when a Goddess would bestow	178	To Lord Harley	59
	The Goddess made advances first,	178	To Lord Harley	67
	Pallas, a Goddess chaste and wise,	302	Storm	1
	The Goddess, who conceiv'd an Hope,	306	Storm	73
	Pursue the Goddess Health in vain,	401	Window Inns 5	D 5
	And saw the treach'rous Goddess smile;	413	Desire Possess	46
	Six thousand years hath liv'd the Goddess,	465	Birthday Song	161
	Of Wit's fair Goddess brought to Bed,	504	Doctor Delaney	116
	The Goddess from her Chamber issues,	525	Lady's Dres Rm	3
	But Vengeance, Goddess never sleeping	529	Lady's Dres Rm	119
	Proceeding on, the lovely Goddess	582	Young Nymph	23
	The smiling Cyprian Goddess brings	585	Strephon Chloe	49
	And Hebe, Goddess ever young.	585	Strephon Chloe	56
	While she a Goddess dy'd in Grain	586	Strephon Chloe	85
	Yet, if the Goddess could be kind,	587	Strephon Chloe	95
	A certain Goddess, God knows who,	587	Strephon Chloe	100
	You think some Goddess from the Sky	591	Strephon Chloe	229
	Your Goddess grown a filthy Mate.	591	Strephon Chloe	244
	No Goddess could have pleas'd him more.	619	Scandal Poem 1	56
	A perfect Goddess born and bred.	655	On Poetry	426
	Thus the Cyprian Goddess weeping,	660	Love Song	9
	So bloom'd the Goddess in a Mortal's Arms.	669	Epig Carthy 13	D 2
	The Goddess soon began to see	689	Cadenus Vaness	104
	The Goddess much perplex'd in Mind,	690	Cadenus Vaness	128
	Like a young Heir, the thrifty Goddess	693	Cadenus Vaness	223
	A Goddess of unspotted Fame:	695	Cadenus Vaness	275
	Perfidious Goddess! but in vain	695	Cadenus Vaness	288
	The Goddess thus pronounc'd her Doom:	696	Cadenus Vaness	304
	The Goddess wou'd no longer wait;	714	Cadenus Vaness	886
	Though a Goddess must expire.	834	Legion Club	130
	Hither the frantick Goddess draws	883	Rev Market-Hill	5
	Here, gentle Goddess Cloacine	893	Panegyr Dean	205
	Thee bounteous Goddess Cloacine,	894	Panegyr Dean	229
	Confin'd Thee Goddess to a Cell:	895	Panegyr Dean	270
	But, Cloacina Goddess bright,	897	Panegyr Dean	343
	To my goddess Melpomene, pride of her sex,	979	Dean to Tho: S	23
	The Goddess Want in Triumph reigns;	1035	To Quilca	10
GODDESSES				
	A score of Goddesses beside.	460	Birthday Song	8
	And Goddesses have now and then	587	Strephon Chloe	97
	To Goddesses so heav'nly sweet,	590	Strephon Chloe	199
	Bright Goddesses, in Number five;	656	On Poetry	439
	When Goddesses appear below.	711	Cadenus Vaness	789
	These are the Goodesses enroll'd	729	Stella, Poems	49
GODHEAD				
	Which makes a Godhead of a Name,	7	Ode to King	25
GODLIKE				
	Godlike the force of my young Congreve's bays,	44	To Congreve	41
	The Godlike Hero with one frown	340	Arch-Bish Dub	19
	The Godlike Ends for which he rose;	386	Manly Virtue	98
	Such Godlike Virtues in the King,	391	Young's Satire	2
GODLINESS				
	With Godliness cou'd well dispense,	455	Dean Smedley	5
<GODOLPHIN>				
	Old <Godolphin> full of Spleen,	168	Peace Dunkirk	15
<GODOLPHIN'S>				
	Wine can clear up <Godolphin's> cloudy Face,	163	Toland's Invit	19
GODS				
	O'er Nile, with all its wilderness of gods;	46	To Congreve	104
	You fly, invoke the Gods; then turning, stop	137	City Shower	21
	Two Gods their Skill in Musick try'd,	156	Fable of Midas	25
	Where Jove a Seat among the Gods will give	210	Earl of Oxford	13
	The Heathens, we Read, had Gods made of Wood,	334	Serious Poem	9
	Their Gods were of Wood, but our Wood is the Devil:	334	Serious Poem	12
	Now made--ye Gods!--a Son and Heir,	384	Manly Virtue	18
	Weary the Gods with ceaseless Prayer,	388	Manly Virtue	139
	Take twenty Gods of Rome or Greece,	460	Birthday Song	2
	When all your list of Gods is out,	464	Birthday Song	143
	Of Gods I only quote the best,	465	Birthday Song	149
	To real Muses, Gods, and Streams.	478	Epist on Epist	86
	Are Angels, just as <Kings> are Gods.	486	Libel on D- D-	198
	The Acts of Gods, and god-like Kings.	496	Panegyr Swift	103
	Resembling you as Angel Gods.	499	Panegyr Swift	182
	'Tis said, the Gods try'd all their Art,	501	Doctor Delaney	31
	Cry'd out, ye Gods, what Sound is this?	589	Strephon Chloe	177
	You worship other Gods in vain	620	Scandal Poem 1	86
	We, to whom all the Gods give place.	620	Scandal Poem 1	96

```
GODS          (CONTINUED)                                    PAGE    TITLE          LINE
    You find, the Gods in Homer dwell      . . . . . .        620  Scandal Poem 1     99
    Fate never form'd the Gods to flye     . . . . . .        620  Scandal Poem 1    111
    You worship other Gods in vain:        . . . . . . .      626  Scandal Poem 2     84
    We, to whom all the Gods give Place:   . . . . . .        626  Scandal Poem 2     94
    You find, the Gods in Homer dwell,     . . . . . .        626  Scandal Poem 2     97
    Fate never form'd the Gods to fly;     . . . . . .        626  Scandal Poem 2    109
    But, Gods like us, have too much Sense . . . . .          628  Scandal Poem 2    157
    For Gods, their Betters, are too wise  . . . . .          689  Cadenus Vaness     83
    "Vanessa, by the Gods enroll'd:        . . . . . .        692  Cadenus Vaness    182
    That Gods, of whatso'er Degree,        . . . . . . .      694  Cadenus Vaness    259
    Which keeps the Peace among the Gods,  . . . . .          695  Cadenus Vaness    262
    (For Gods, we are by Homer told,       . . . . . .        695  Cadenus Vaness    286
    Oh, would it please the Gods to split  . . . . .          722  Stel B-Day '18      9
    All ye Gods, who rule the Soul         . . . . . .        832  Legion Club        83
    Of Mortals, and the Gods Delight.      . . . . .          916  Riddle 2           12
    So Jove pronounc'd among the Gods,     . . . . . .        924  Riddle 7           95
GODSHIP
    No Temple, to his Godship rais'd,      . . . . . .        346  Prometheus         43
    Only your Godship to implore,          . . . . . . .      403  Window Inns 10    D  7
GODSHIPS
    Whose Godships are in chief request,   . . . . . .        460  Birthday Song       3
GODWIN'S
    Earld Godwin's Castles overflown,      . . . . . .        257  Bubble            171
GODZOOKS
    But then his Honour cry'd, Godzooks!   . . . . .           74  Game Traffick       5
GOES
    And goes with Folks to shew the Sight: . . . . .          116  Bauc & Phil 2     168
    Away upon his Errand goes,             . . . . .          171  Horace 1, 7        24
    Goes round the House to wake the rest: . . . . .          278  Journal            10
    But when the Sun goes to the Deep,     . . . . .          280  Journal            45
    And leave the Flood when he goes in it: . . . . .         280  Journal            50
    The weary Dean goes to his Chamber,    . . . . .          280  Journal            57
    While He goes out to cheapen Books,    . . . . .          291  Prog Marriage      39
    Then goes alone to take his Rest       . . . . .          292  Prog Marriage      89
    The Widow goes through all her Forms;  . . . . .          295  Prog Marriage     157
    One goes to this, and one to t' other Ear. . . . .        367  Answer Delaney     38
    He goes to School! he reads! is learn'd! . . . . . .      384  Manly Virtue       32
    The Stock-jobber thus, from Change-Alley goes down,  .    396  Dog and Thief       9
    And thus it goes round  . . . . . . . . .                 424  Carterets Arms     11
    When he goes out, you share his fate,  . . . . . .        468  Birthday Song     258
    Through Courts and Senates as he goes; . . . . .          486  Libel on D- D-    190
    To <Dublin> he comes, to the Bagnio he goes,  . . . .     517  Dean Hang Rape     19
    Some Country Squire to Lintot goes,    . . . . .          562  Death of Swift    253
    Up goes her Hand, and off she slips    . . . . .          582  Young Nymph        27
    But must, before she goes to Bed,      . . . . . .        582  Young Nymph        33
    Friend Peter to Cassinus goes,         . . . . . .        594  Cassinus Peter      7
    Must, at the Rate that he goes on,     . . . . . .        606  Beasts Confess    167
    Alas! our Thunder soon goes out;       . . . . . .        624  Scandal Poem 2      7
    And therefore goes with Courage on.    . . . . . .        765  Stel B-day '26     76
    What e'er he speaks for Madness goes,  . . . . . .        798  Traulus 1          65
    Where all goes to ruin  . . . . . . . . .                 857  Lady's Lament     193
    "But the Devil's as welcome wherever he goes:  . . . .    872  Grand Question    144
    Here unobserv'd, she boldly goes,      . . . . . .        893  Panegyr Dean      215
    My Head, with Giddiness, goes round;   . . . . . .        926  Riddle 9            7
    I know the gander always goes          . . . . . .        983  Sher, A Goose      19
    For ev'ry Stroke goes to my Heart,     . . . . . .       1005  Sheridan's Sub     32
GOING
    By going on as he begun;  . . . . . . . . .              655  On Poetry         434
    At going in you saw her stoop  . . . . . . . .           746  Stel Distress
GOINGS
    My Goings out, and Comings in,  . . . . . . . .          918  Riddle 4           35
GOLD
    Tho' fring'd with ev'ning gold the cloud appears so gay,   41  Ode Sancroft      217
    Bears one, and but one branch of gold,  . . . . . .        41  Ode Sancroft      226
    He's a Gold Pencil tipt with Lead.     . . . . . .         61  Lady Tablebook     30
    . . .six Pence, besides Farthings, in Money, and Gold;     69  Mrs Harris Pet      2
    Turn'd ev'ry thing he touch't to Gold:  . . . . .         156  Fable of Midas      2
    Potable Gold in Golden Cup.            . . . . .          156  Fable of Midas      8
    Gold ready Coin'd appear'd, instead    . . . . .          156  Fable of Midas     17
    Old Hay is equal to old Gold;          . . . . .          156  Fable of Midas     20
    We learn't to weigh our Gold by Grains.  . . . . .        156  Fable of Midas     22
    And turning Dung it self to Gold?      . . . . . .        157  Fable of Midas     48
    But Gold defiles with frequent Touch,  . . . . .          158  Fable of Midas     67
    Nor can afford to buy gold Lace,       . . . . . .        216  To Mr. Delany      43
    But as his Gold he weigh'd, grim Death in spight,  .      234  Elegy on Demar     31
    Upon the god of Gold and Hell,         . . . . .          240  Run Bankers        42
    Produc'd with all their Bills and Gold,  . . . . .        241  Run Bankers        63
    Your Hand alone from Gold abstains,    . . . . . .        243  Horace 4, 9        13
    Our Ocean's coverd o'er with Gold,     . . . . .          254  Bubble            103
    Alas! all is not Gold that glisters;   . . . . . .        254  Bubble            107
    But Gold upon this Ocean spred         . . . . . .        255  Bubble            135
    And here they fish for Gold and drown:  . . . . .         256  Bubble            148
    Tho' I know nothing on't, 'tis I that make Gold;  . .     263  Apollo              4
    That Paper would quickly be dearer than Gold,  . .        288  Bank Down          32
    And yet we all know much Gold it will bring,  . . .       334  Serious Poem       14
    And sell them for Gold, or he can't shew his Love else,   337  Serious Poem       98
    A strange Event! whom Gold incites,    . . . . .          345  Prometheus         21
    When Jove was Young, was made of Gold.  . . . . .         345  Prometheus         36
    The World in any Chain but Gold;       . . . . . .        346  Prometheus         50
    He strove to steal that Chain of Gold,  . . . . .         346  Prometheus         64
```

GOLD (CONTINUED)	PAGE	TITLE	LINE	
Collects the City Filth in search of Gold.	364	On Dreams	22	
In Gold, Perhaps, my Friend you Wallow	372	Letter D. S-y	29	
Barter'd for Beauty, and for Gold;	385	Manly Virtue	68	
To weigh her priests, the lawyers, gold.	433	Answer Paulus	36	
Than those of Poets to the Lust of Gold.	532	To Mr. Gay	22	
Were Silver, and the Axel Gold.	598	Problem Solved	16	
We dresst her in a gold Brocade,	619	Scandal Poem 1	77	
We dress'd her in a Gold Brocade,	626	Scandal Poem 2	75	
What Midas touch'd, became true Gold; but then,	668	Epig Carthy 12	D	1
Gold becomes Lead, touch'd lightly by thy Pen.	668	Epig Carthy 12	D	2
They on the Gold Brocades and Satins rav'd,	771	Horace 1, 14	51	
But all his Gold could not avail	821	Dr. Rundle	45	
By my soul there's bad news, for the gold she was pulled down,	840	Ballad	D	2
The gold she was pull'd down, of that I'm very sure,	840	Ballad	D	3
"Ay,ay," quoth the Dean, "the cause is old gold."	843	Ay and No	4	
"To treat gold reduc'd like Wood's copper pence.	843	Ay and No	16	
See, now comes the Captain all dawb'd with gold Lace:	870	Grand Question	93	
From gold brocade and shining armour,	879	Robbin & Harry	41	
Ten thousand Lice, and ev'ry Louse was gold,	882	Pastoral Dial	46	
That golden Age, to Gold unknown;	894	Panegyr Dean	234	
Their gifts, as misers do their gold;	900	Dean's Reasons	36	
Each with a Gold and Purple Vest;	923	Riddle 7	72	
For Silver and Gold I don't trouble my Head,	927	Riddle 11	D	5
GOLD-FINDERS				
Or't had been happy for Gold-finders.	156	Fable of Midas	12	
GOLD'S				
When Gold's to be got, to Forswear and Suborn.	335	Serious Poem	46	
An Ounce of Gold's worth ten of Brass, dull Pedant.	1004	Dan J's Reply	33	
GOLDEN				
Spend all our present Stock in hopes of golden Rules.	27	Ode to Temple	27	
To lodge behind a golden cloud;	41	Ode Sancroft	216	
Than those with backs of silk and golden wings;	46	To Congreve	92	
At the warm zeal that breeds this golden calf?	46	To Congreve	108	
Adorn'd with Golden Stars and Rays,	98	Elegy Patrige	28	
When e'er the Soil has Golden Mines:	133	Magician's Rod	24	
To bend where Golden Mines were hid;	133	Magician's Rod	28	
In Golden Boughs, and Golden Fruit,	134	Magician's Rod	72	
In Golden Boughs, and Golden Fruit,	134	Magician's Rod	72	
"Your Golden Pippins, and your Pies,	154	Widow and Cat	D	26
Would strait become a Golden Pippin:	156	Fable of Midas	6	
Potable Gold in Golden Cup.	156	Fable of Midas	8	
The Golden Scurf peels off his Limbs:	157	Fable of Midas	36	
From far, to gather golden Gravel;	157	Fable of Midas	38	
The Golden Spoils flew off apace,	158	Fable of Midas	75	
A golden Monument would not be Right,	234	Elegy on Demar	23	
The Sea indeed had golden Sands.	255	Bubble	112	
The Golden Stars for Guinneas took,	255	Bubble	127	
The influence of whose golden beams	432	Answer Paulus	7	
As parent of the golden ore,	433	Answer Paulus	24	
And golden Times, and Halcyon days,	466	Birthday Song	196	
"Here ended all our golden Dreams.	567	Death of Swift	372	
Teaching by what Golden Rules	635	Epistle Lady	157	
Like Montezume in golden Chains:	885	Rev Market-Hill	72	
That golden Age, to Gold unknown;	894	Panegyr Dean	234	
Whose Off'rings plac't in golden Ranks,	896	Panegyr Dean	301	
(So Poets sing, with golden Bough	896	Panegyr Dean	307	
From Colchos brought the Golden Fleece:	948	Jason Hassard	2	
GOLDSMITH				
Madam, the Goldsmith waits below,	446	Modern Lady	56	
GOLDSMITHS				
So Goldsmiths say, the coursest Stuff,	345	Prometheus	23	
GONE				
Well: But then they would have had me gone.	72	Mrs Harris Pet	48	
If your Money be gone, as a Learned Divine says, d'ye see,	72	Mrs Harris Pet	56	
Repair a House gone to decay;	80	Vanbrug House	64	
One Family was gone to bed;	90	Bauc & Phil 1	26	
Pray take your Answer and be gone.	91	Bauc & Phil 1	32	
Although the Jug had twice gone round	92	Bauc & Phil 1	76	
The Sun has rose, and gone to Bed,	98	Elegy Patrige	11	
Repair a House gone to Decay,	107	V's House	38	
If <Guernsey> calls, send word you're gone abroad;	166	Toland's Invit	41	
Suppose him gone through all Vexations,	174	Horace 1, 7	101	
"Without your Help the Cause is gone--	200	Horace 2, 6	52	
And now 'twas high Time to be gone;	208	Fable Bitches	24	
The Horse and Pillion both were gone	223	Prog of Love	41	
To whom those Perquisites are gone	225	Prog of Love	93	
Her Spots are gone, her Visage clears.	226	Prog of Beauty	8	
When the Materialls all are gone,	228	Prog of Beauty	78	
Presto be gone--Tis here ag'en,	251	Bubble	6	
With Church and King, the Lady's gone;	279	Journal	36	
But now, since I have gone so far on,	282	Journal	97	
He's gone, although his Friends began to hope	285	Elegy Boat	17	
Is maukish, and his Stomach gone;	291	Prog Marriage	60	
Well, since he's gone, no matter how,	296	Satiric Elegy	5	
Gallants, by Tuesday next we must be gone.	308	Billet Players	40	
Her Ladyship was gone Abroad;	377	Apology Lady C	80	
When Carteret is gone	423	Carterets Arms	2	
My Rhimes are gone	442	Ballyspellin	85	

GONE   (CONTINUED)   PAGE   TITLE   LINE
    "Stand further Girl, or get you gone, ...   452 Modern Lady   244
    Their Hoods, their Cloaks, and get them gone: . . .   453 Modern Lady   287
    Had not the Fleet gone out too late, ...   463 Birthday Song   102
    Tho George is gone a thousand miles.   . . . . .   466 Birthday Song   182
    Before our Friends were gone to Pot, ...   498 Panegyr Swift   158
    And now that little next is gone.   . . . .   514 Answer Fable   68
    Cries, "Is he gone? 'Tis time he shou'd.   . . . . .   559 Death of Swift   182
    Gone, to be never heard of more, ...   642 On Poetry   69
    Gone, where the Chickens went before.   . . . .   642 On Poetry   70
    (For you may easy be too far gone, ...   648 On Poetry   241
    Had gone through all the Common-Places   . . . . . .   730 Stella, Poems   75
    When the whole month's Allowance gone   . . . . . .   747 Stel Distress
    When all her County-Savings gone, ...   751 Stel Wood-Park   70
    Looks back with Joy where she has gone, ...   765 Stel B-day '26   75
    The Tories are gone ev'ry Man over   . . . .   773 Mullinix Tim   9
    When all the Bees are gone to settle, ...   775 Mullinix Tim   45
    Presto be gone; with t' other Hop   . . . .   788 Dick's Variety   31
    To cry; Lo, Judas, gone to his own Place: . . . .   806 Judas   24
    Be gone: Thy Money perish with thee.   . . . . . .   821 Dr. Rundle   48
    Who regards him when he's gone? . . . .   863 To Janus   24
    Cry'd, Huzzy, why sure the Wench is gone mad: . . .   873 Grand Question   184
    All things gone on the same dull track, ...   877 To Dean Swift   31
    Repairs a cabin gone to ruin, ...   878 Robbin & Harry   21
    All his Agility is gone;   . . . .   885 Rev Market-Hill   80
    As soon as gone, will show their Spight: . . . . .   891 Panegyr Dean   140
    Like Thought I'm in a Moment gone, ...   935 Riddle 23   D 16
    . . .and your Man Alexander had not gone, . . .   1013 Swift to Sheri   4
    Be gone down to the county of Wexford . . .   . . .   1022 Nim-Dan-Dean 2   D 6
GOOD
    Sure there's some Wondrous Joy in Doing Good;   . . .   6 Ode to King   1
    But the Delight of Doing Good   . . . .   6 Ode to King   19
    And our good Brethren of the Surly Sect   . . . . .   18 Ode Athenian   81
    The publick Stamp Heav'n sets on all that's Great and   18 Ode Athenian   93
        Good,
    We odly Plato's Paradox make good, ...   27 Ode to Temple   29
    Those mighty Epithets, Learn'd, Good, and Great   28 Ode to Temple   59
    Sounds truly good, or truly great;   . . . .   36 Ode Sancroft   49
    Ill may I live, if the good Sancroft in his holy rest,   36 Ode Sancroft   50
    What we call holy, and great, and just, and good, . . . 38 Ode Sancroft   124
    But wicked kings draw more examples than the good; . .   40 Ode Sancroft   184
    Such were the storms good Sancroft long has borne; . .   40 Ode Sancroft   198
    Brings his good parts and breeding in debate; . . . .   48 To Congreve   156
    In pleasing all that's good among the great, ...   49 To Congreve   180
    Like good King Phys: and good King Ush: . . . . .   63 Discovery   23
    Like good King Phys: and good King Ush: . . . . .   63 Discovery   23
    Then Good Dr. <Swift>   . . . .   77 Lady B- B-   26
    They call'd at ev'ry Dore; Good People, ...   90 Bauc & Phil 1   15
    And cure You both with a good Stick.   . . . . . .   91 Bauc & Phil 1   46
    Brew'd for the good time of the Year   . . . . . .   92 Bauc & Phil 1   68
    Makes you take all things in good Part: . . . . .   94 Bauc & Phil 1   160
    I'm good for little at my days; . . . .   94 Bauc & Phil 1   163
    E'er he could ever prove the good Squire ly'd.   98 Elegy Patrige   4
    And is Install'd as good a Star, ...   100 Elegy Patrige   71
    To try good People's Hospitality.   . . . . . .   111 Bauc & Phil 2   4
    Where dwelt a good old honest Yeoman, ...   111 Bauc & Phil 2   19
    The good old Couple was amaz'd, ...   112 Bauc & Phil 2   35
    Good Folks, you need not be afraid, ...   112 Bauc & Phil 2   43
    Good Pinners edg'd with Colberteen: . . . . . .   115 Bauc & Phil 2   140
    Truth, Innocence, Good Nature, Look serene; . . . .   118 Biddy Floyd   4
    Like Sid's, but nothing near so good;   . . . . .   134 Magician's Rod   60
    I answer; the Tories were in my good Graces,   . . .   144 New Song   23
    Then let old Englond make good Chear: . . . . .   147 Windsor Proph   4
    For many good Groats his Tongue shall slitt: . . .   147 Windsor Proph   10
    Much good may do 'em that have caught 'um.   . . . .   158 Fable of Midas   80
    For among good Friends, I love to be plain; . . . .   168 Peace Dunkirk   7
    And Commoners who love good Wine, ...   169 Peace Dunkirk   23
    The Towns we took ne'er did us good, ...   169 Peace Dunkirk   31
    A good Health to Gen'ral Hill, ...   169 Peace Dunkirk   39
    You've some good Purchase in your Eye;   . . . . .   175 Horace 1, 7   128
    Truce, good My Lord, I beg a Truce!   . . . . . .   175 Horace 1, 7   130
    To vamp the good Old Cause again, ...   180 Horace 2, 1   4
    To a good honest Junta that never will teaze you.   185 Scriblerus 1   6
    "Good Mr. Dean go change your Gown, ...   200 Horace 2, 6   23
    Cry'd bravely, Patience, good my Dear.   . . . .   220 A Quiet Life   6
    Slaves to their Quiet and good Name, ...   221 A Quiet Life   57
    With good Roast Beef his Belly full, ...   231 Prog of Poetry   21
    In good and evil Times the same.   . . . . . .   243 Horace 4, 9   10
    Good Lord, what a Sight, ...   246 Irish-Feast   57
    After all their good Cheer, ...   246 Irish-Feast   58
    To me the good Fellows apply for Relief, ...   263 Apollo   9
    And of my meer Motion, and special good Grace,   . .   263 Apollo   27
    The Banks of a River I know are good Things,   . . .   287 Bank Down   2
    "Good Madam Pallas, pray be easy, ...   305 Storm   70
    And, with a licence from our good Lord May'r,   307 Billet Players   3
    For a good word or so, we understand.   . . . . .   308 Billet Players   24
    All this and more, yet it would do no good. . . . .   308 Billet Players   42
    The next we act shall be as good as this.   . . . .   309 Billet Players   58
    Good Manners must give Place to Profit.   . . . . .   311 To Ford   16
    No doubt, will prove a good Arbuthnot: . . . .   314 To Ford   76
    "Who is as good as all the Muses;   . . . .   321 First of April   8

"A Wife as good as Heart cou'd wish one, ...   322 First of April   49
Now, although to Draw Water is not very good,   . .   .   334 Serious Poem   3
Who could do them no Harm, if they did them no Good: .   334 Serious Poem   10
Then if cutting down Wood brings Money good Store,   .   334 Serious Poem   15
Teague made a good Pun by a Brogue in his Speech,   . .   334 Serious Poem   27
To turn a Good Penny to Twenty Bad Ha'pence.   . . . .   335 Serious Poem   48
Which cannot in Literal Sense be made Good, ...   335 Serious Poem   55
I often have seen two Plays very Good, ...   337 Serious Poem   91
Wood swears he will do it for Ireland's Good,   . . .   337 Serious Poem   99
I'll maintain with my Life, is Heraldry Good.   . . .   338 Serious Poem   122
Great, Good and Just was once apply'd   . . . . . .   339 Arch-Bish Dub   1
Because thour't Great, and Good, and Just.   . . . .   339 Arch-Bish Dub   8
But I sing of a Famous Lord, who seeks his Country's   341 Upon His Grace   2
   Good.
His Firmness to the publick Good, as one that knows it   341 Upon His Grace   9
   Swore,
Two thousand Pounds a Year, Good Lord! . .   . . . .   342 Upon His Grace   19
Good Lord! I wondred how I dar'd to look him in the   342 Upon His Grace   28
   Face.
I find you bear a good Report, and are an honest Man.   .   342 Upon His Grace   34
Gravely consulting Ireland's Good, ...   344 Prometheus   2
They swear I am so kind and good, ...   348 Whitshed Motto   9
You had good Reason when you stole 'um.   . . . . . .   349 Whitshed Motto   26
The Church I hate, and have good Reason: . . . . .   349 Upright Judge 1   1
And were you not so good a Writer   . . . .   361 Grace's Answer   9
Are stronger, and almost as good.   . . . .   367 Answer Delaney   50
My very good Lord, it's a very hard task   . . . .   368 Verses Window   1
Which if right ta'en, and but good Luck-hold   . . .   373 Letter D. S-y   60
And much good Sense, as well as Breeding: . . . . .   377 Apology Lady C   72
Call'd her good Nature to relieve him;   . . . . . .   378 Apology Lady C   85
For, such is good Example's Pow'r, ...   391 Young's Satire   19
Where Governors are good and wise;   . . . .   391 Young's Satire   21
If possible, as good as He.   . . . .   392 Young's Satire   30
They can do no good   . . . .   424 Carterets Arms   13
To keep good sense in crouds of fools;   . . . . . .   436 Answer Paulus   124
Deserves a good Cud-gelling   . . . .   442 Ballyspellin   81
Good Fortune peeping from behind;   . . . .   452 Modern Lady   229
"I think I never had good Luck in't.   . . . .   452 Modern Lady   241
Have once the public good in view: . . . .   487 Irish-Club   18
Let <Prelates>, by their good behaviour, ...   488 Irish-Club   21
The Gift (good Heav'ns preserve 't from Thieves)   .   494 Panegyr Swift   49
Men seldom by their Good Deeds rise: . . . . . .   495 Panegyr Swift   75
Is this the Art, good Doctor, say, ...   497 Panegyr Swift   142
How each the Publick Good pursues, ...   501 Doctor Delaney   59
Because he did his Brethren good.   . . . .   514 Answer Fable   62
For the Good of our Church a true <English> <Dean>.   516 Dean Hang Rape   4
And got a good Clap, but committed no <Rape>.   . . .   517 Dean Hang Rape   24
He ravish'd her fairly, and sav'd a good Shilling;   .   519 Dean Hang Rape   57
When the good <English> <Dean> is hang'd up for a   520 Dean Hang Rape   72
   <Rape>.
And Ointments good for scabby Chops.   . . . . . .   526 Lady's Dres Rm   36
"His Claim as good as other Folks---.   . . . . . .   547 Life of Swift   94
Which if he lik'd, much good may do him: . . . . .   549 Life of Swift   133
"The Patrons of the good old Cause, ...   549 Life of Swift   162
"Thought Protestant too Good a Name   . . . . . .   550 Life of Swift   170
Which way my Death can do them good;   . . . . . .   556 Death of Swift   78
"And that, I doubt, is no good Sign.   . . . . . .   557 Death of Swift   110
My good Companions, never fear, ...   558 Death of Swift   143
"So ready to do Strangers good, ...   558 Death of Swift   163
The Queen, so Gracious, Mild, and Good, ...   559 Death of Swift   181
And in his Place my good Friend Will;   . . . . . .   560 Death of Swift   194
"The Funeral of so good a Friend.   . . . .   562 Death of Swift   234
"The Rev'rend Author's good Intention, ...   564 Death of Swift   289
"And only chose the Wise and Good;   . . . . . .   566 Death of Swift   333
"And seldom fail'd of good Success;   . . . . . .   566 Death of Swift   336
To oblige a good Friend, she will trace ev'ry Market,   .   580 Psyche   11
It would do your Heart good, to see how she will cark it.   580 Psyche   12
Let Prudence with Good Nature strive, ...   593 Strephon Chloe   309
Good Father I must own with Shame, ...   602 Beasts Confess   13
Too zealous for the Nation's Good: . . . .   604 Beasts Confess   100
And, when his Med'cines do no good, ...   605 Beasts Confess   123
The Nation's Good, his Master's Glory, ...   605 Beasts Confess   145
That all he did was for their Good;   . . . . . .   606 Beasts Confess   162
Was too good to touch the Ground: . . . .   631 Epistle Lady   38
In Good Manners, am I faulty?   . . . .   631 Epistle Lady   69
Never know I any Good in 'um, ...   632 Epistle Lady   83
With good sense to entertain us.   . . . .   633 Epistle Lady   114
Scholars, when good Sense describing, ...   633 Epistle Lady   115
He sets the Stamp of Bad and Good, ...   649 On Poetry   273
And Reason good; for many a Year   . . . .   657 On Poetry   489
A mingled Mass of Good & Bad, ...   659 On Poetry   D 410
Half of my Book at least is good.   . . . .   669 Epig Carthy 15 D   2
Oh! wer't thou not a Duke, my good Duke Humphry,   .   678 Dean and Duke   11
To perish for our Country's Good.   . . . . . .   697 Cadenus Vaness   349
Pallas had done more Harm than Good;   . . . . . .   700 Cadenus Vaness   435
To such a Nymph the Wise and Good   . . . . . .   733 Verses Vanessa   9
Think Eusden's Right as good as mine.   . . . . . .   741 Stel B-day 22   30
From growing richer with good Cheer, ...   745 Stel Distress   15
From growing Riches with good Chear, ...   750 Stel Wood-Park   43
Of our good Dean's eternal chidings;   . . . . . .   753 Gift for Bec   6

GOOD	(CONTINUED)	PAGE	TITLE	LINE
I promise to be good again:		755	Stella '23	34
You tell a good jest,		756	Dingley Brent	13
To be the chief of human Good,		764	Stel B-day '26	28
Upheld by each good Action past,		765	Stel B-day '26	63
The single Pillar for his Country's Good,		770	Horace 1, 14	16
My good Friend Mullinix forbear.		775	Mullinix Tim	69
I must pursue the publick Good.		775	Mullinix Tim	74
Dear Mullinix, your good Advice		779	Mullinix Tim	195
Your Parts are good, 'tis not deny'd,		779	Mullinix Tim	209
He only meant it for your Good.		797	Traulus 1	56
Lord <Bolton's> good Grace, Lord <Carr>, and Lord <Howard>,		804	Irish Bishops	25
They came of good Kindred, and cou'd not endure,		804	Irish Bishops	27
Content, my good <Lords>; but let us change Hands;		805	Irish Bishops	61
Are his Brother Protestants, good men and true;		815	Yahoo's	22
He's a Christian as good as the rest of the herd.		816	Yahoo's	29
And, while at good Cashel you rail with such spite,		818	Archbi Cashel	3
Survive in thee, and make the Proverb good		826	Noisy Tom	18
Making good my Grandames Jest,		829	Legion Club	7
To spunge for good cheer,		852	Lady's Lament	16
Come, be a good child:		855	Lady's Lament	124
A handsome Addition for Wine and good Chear,		867	Grand Question	11
But Madam, I guest there wou'd never come Good,		868	Grand Question	47
Good Morrow, good Captain,--I'll wait on you down,--		869	Grand Question	77
Good Morrow, good Captain,--I'll wait on you down,--		869	Grand Question	77
You're heartily welcome: But as for good Chear,		871	Grand Question	121
"I ne'er knew a Parson without a good Nose,		872	Grand Question	143
"The Army's the only good School in the Nation;		872	Grand Question	162
"And the Puppy confess'd, he expected no Good o'me.		873	Grand Question	166
Good cause have I to sing and vapour,		876	To Dean Swift	1
But, that is with a good Design,		890	Panegyr Dean	101
Good Lord! what can my Lady mean,		891	Panegyr Dean	141
Good Luck to those with whom I dwell.		918	Riddle 4	44
Is good for Partridge, not for Hares.		940	Letter	11
Has this any likeness to good Madam Sheridan?		955	Portrait Life	10
Friend Sheridan, when will you know your own Good?		968	Letter Sherid	24
As a good quiet Soul, who no Mischief intends		968	Letter Sherid	27
Hum--excellent good--your anger was stirr'd:		976	Dean to Sherid	7
But keep a good tongue, or you'll find, to your smart,		976	Dean to Sherid	35
But thanks to the lady: I'm sure she's too good to ye;		976	Dean to Sherid	38
And I think I may say, you cou'd many good shillings get		979	Dean to Tho: S	9
By your good Leave, my most profound and bold Sir,		1004	Dan J's Reply	30
Good Spelling, Master, your Crany has Lead on't.		1004	Dan J's Reply	36
Or may your Gown never be good Lutherine		1018	Swift Ans Sher	29
. . .yet in the end's good metre,		1022	Nim-Dan-Dean 2	D 1
GOOD-MAN				
Old Good-man Dobson of the Green		116	Bauc & Phil 2	165
GOOD-NATUR'D				
Both the Good-natur'd and the Ill,		18	Ode Athenian	73
Still pleas'd with the good-natur'd Noise,		322	First of April	33
Good-natur'd Stella will forgive:		747	Stel Distress	58
GOOD-WILL				
Who to the Stars in pure Good-will,		101	Elegy Patrige	105
Came early, out of pure Good-will,		698	Cadenus Vaness	366
GOODLY				
Then rear 'em to goodly Pile,		79	Vanbrug House	6
Then rear 'em to a goodly Pile.		106	V's House	6
A goodly pair, erect and wide,		157	Fable of Midas	31
A goodly Sight to see her ride,		410	Dial Rich Marb	63
A goodly set as can be found		762	Bec's B-Day	51
GOODMAN				
Call'd thereabouts Goodman Philemon;		91	Bauc & Phil 1	52
GOODNES				
He has more Goodnes in his little Finger,		985	Mary to Sher	9
GOODNESS				
Your Goodness more than my Desert		94	Bauc & Phil 1	159
Grandeur, by Goodness made compleat!		386	Manly Virtue	101
Their Goodness, more than his Desert---.		547	Life of Swift	87
No Goodness could have pleas'd him more,		625	Scandal Poem 2	52
GOODS				
In Physick, Stolen Goods, or Love,		101	Elegy Patrige	115
Pretend to cheapen Goods, but nothing buy.		138	City Shower	34
To discover the Goods he came honestly by:		264	Apollo	58
GOODY				
Bade Goody Baucis mend the Fire		91	Bauc & Phil 1	56
Bid Goody Baucis mend the Fire;		111	Bauc & Phil 2	24
Plain Goody would no longer down,		116	Bauc & Phil 2	143
You'll never think of Goody Griz.		362	Grace's Answer	44
Where Goody Julia milks the Cows,		878	Robbin & Harry	25
GOOSBERRIES				
Such a thing as this happen'd, just about the time of Goosberries.		71	Mrs Harris Pet	33
GOOSE				
Or sell a Goose at the next Toun		95	Bauc & Phil 1	175
A Thing resembling a Goose Py,		109	V's House	104
The Farmer's Goose, who in the Stubble,		230	Prog of Poetry	1
For Cackling shews the Goose is poor.		230	Prog of Poetry	8
Has made the Man a Goose in earnest.		666	Epig Carthy 1	D 4
"Can hardly tell how to cry Bo to a Goose;		872	Grand Question	158

GOOSE   (CONTINUED)   PAGE TITLE   LINE

Tom, for a goose you keep but base quills, ...   982 Sher, A Goose   1
Suppose I call'd you goose, it is hard   . . . . . .   983 Sher, A Goose   9
You're my goose, and no other man's;   . . . .   983 Sher, A Goose   11
I call'd you goose instead of gander;   . . . .   983 Sher, A Goose   16
Because my Master one Day in anger call'd you Goose.   .   985 Mary to Sher   12
Whereby you now confess your self to be a Goose or an   986 Mary to Sher   18
     Ass:
GOR'D
Gor'd with unrelenting Tooth.   . . . .   660 Love Song   12
GORE
Or his sides they would gore . . . .   854 Lady's Lament   85
(Ere since Sir William <Gore> was May'r, ...   180 Horace 2, 1   9
GORGAN
Metamorphos'd to a Gorgan!   . . . .   838 Legion Club   194
GORGEOUS
No Hobby-horse, with gorgeous Top, ...   135 Magician's Rod   75
GOSFORD
Who wont to weed the Court of Gosford Knight,   . . .   880 Pastoral Dial   2
That, near the Knight of Gosford plac't, ...   899 Dean's Reasons   21
GOSFORD'S
Such is the fate of Gosford's Knight, ...   900 Dean's Reasons   41
GOSLING
Let them with their gosling Quills, ...   831 Legion Club   59
GOSPEL
And, though the gospel seems to say, ...   434 Answer Paulus   61
For Law and Gospel both determine   . . . .   647 On Poetry   227
But, some have kiss't the Gospel Fifty Times,   . . .   806 Judas   11
And the Gospel will inform us, ...   830 Legion Club   33
GOSPEL-WARD
'Though not so Gospel-ward devout.   . . . .   820 Dr. Rundle   32
GOSSIP
Her Aunt's my Gossip by my Father's Side: . . . .   882 Pastoral Dial   42
GOSSIPS
Still Groans while tatling Gossips prate.   93   Bauc & Phil 1   110
Of hearty gossips prating round;   . . . .   762 Bec's B-Day   52
GOT   SEE ILL-GOT
Only the Laurel got by Peace   29   Ode to Temple   81
And almost got priority of Sight, ...   30   Ode to Temple   130
Whilst all th' advantage by it got, ...   36   Ode Sancroft   71
To boast of favours that he never got;   48   To Congreve   154
To think what cattle she has got among;   50   To Congreve   224
So Mary got me to Bed, and cover'd me up warm,   . . .   70   Mrs Harris Pet   18
So men have got from Bird and Brute   83   Salamander   7
And got about a League from Land, ...   96   On the Union   18
And thus the Steeple got a Shock, ...   127 Little House   16
For Daniel was got from the Den of the Lions: . . .   144 New Song   32
This Fool had got a lucky Hit, ...   156 Fable of Midas   23
Got Hercules to bear the Pile   . . . .   160 Atlas   11
Holland got Towns, and we got Blows, ...   168 Peace Dunkirk   3
Holland got Towns, and we got Blows, ...   168 Peace Dunkirk   3
We have got it in a String, ...   168 Peace Dunkirk   5
But since thou'rt got into the Fire, ...   181 Horace 2, 1   33
This dang'rous Priest is got behind the Curtain: . .   194 Author Himself   38
If I ne'er got, or lost a groat, ...   199 Horace 2, 6   D
Tis never by Invention got, ...   216 To Mr. Delany   27
There sprawl'd a while, at last got out, ...   255 Bubble   131
Which when you have got, you so carefully hide it,   . .   263 Apollo   5
And when he has got it, finds Ways to conceal it;   . .   265 Apollo   60
I think I have now got him under my Lash;   . . . .   265 Apollo   66
You pay them well; the Dogs have got   . . . . . .   299 Horrid Plot   27
And look't since he has got his Wish, ...   299 Horrid Plot   33
When Gold's to be got, to Forswear and Suborn.   . . .   335 Serious Poem   46
Wood got so much Copper? He got it by Brass;   . . .   336 Serious Poem   86
Wood got so much Copper? He got it by Brass;   . . .   336 Serious Poem   86
And dreams of Forfeitures by Treason got.   . . . .   364 On Dreams   20
You see, where Folks have got their Ends, ...   408 Dial Rich Marb   19
No sooner got, than with Disdain   . . . .   412 Desire Possess   27
The truth will be got out   . . . .   423 Carterets Arms   4
The Son laughs that got, the hard gotten Estate,   . .   430 Dicky Dolly   20
(Provided he has got his fee.)   . . . .   434 Answer Paulus   56
Got from his crew of <rogues> in grain;   . . . . .   435 Answer Paulus   118
Spadillo here has got a Mark, ...   453 Modern Lady   266
Nassau, who got the name of glorious   . . . . . .   468 Birthday Song   251
That you have got a Place already, ...   483 Libel on D- D-   104
A Deanery you got, when in, ...   493 Panegyr Swift   21
Till you had got them in a Screw.   . . . .   494 Panegyr Swift   44
And got a good Clap, but committed no <Rape>.   . . .   517 Dean Hang Rape   24
Poor Tom has got a plaguy baulk---!   . . . . . .   545 Life of Swift   22
"The Town hath got a better Taste: . . . . . .   563 Death of Swift   266
"The Hawkers have not got 'em yet, ...   564 Death of Swift   279
"A Shame, he hath not got a Mitre!   . . . .   564 Death of Swift   298
And when she once has got the Art, ...   588 Strephon Chloe   129
Heaven send thou hast not got the Hypps.   . . . . .   594 Cassinus Peter   35
Since all he got by Fraud, is lost by Stocks,   . . .   678 Dean and Duke   6
Her Lace hath got within her Head   . . . . . .   733 Verses Vanessa   25
Got all things at the highest Price.   . . . . . .   745 Stel Distress   10
Got all things at the highest Price.   . . . . . .   749 Stel Wood-Park   8
By all this Coyl what hast thou got?   . . . . . .   778 Mullinix Tim   152
Got? <Damn> my Blood I frank my Letters, ...   778 Mullinix Tim   155

		PAGE	TITLE	LINE
GOT	(CONTINUED)			
Got? <Damn> me, why I got my will!		778	Mullinix Tim	159
Got? <Damn> me, why I got my will!		778	Mullinix Tim	159
Another when he got a hot Meal;		781	Mullinix Tim	270
Has got on the Bench many <Bishops> suffragan:		803	Irish Bishops	14
She has got but half a Face;		862	To Janus	5
Dennis was out, and I got hither safe;		881	Pastoral Dial	31
And soon as we have got Possession, ...		886	Rev Market-Hill	90
Had got Gallants among the Ghosts?		905	Death Daphne	76
No, no Victory, Victory he ever got, ...		957	Cantata	
Why sure, Mr. Poet, your head got a jar . . .		976	Dean to Sherid	27
. . .for Saunders already hath got above ten Jaunts. .		1013	Swift to Sheri	6
The Beef you have got, which I hear is a Chine .		1018	Swift Ans Sher	30
Lady Santry got out of the Church when she grew sick, .		1029	Dr. Helsham	10
And I got thro' the Crowd, tho' not led by a Clew, sick		1029	Dr. Helsham	22
Here four of you got mischances to plague you, ...		1037	Four Storyes	1
GOTH				
What Time the Goth, the Vandal, and the Hun, . . .		789	St. Pat's Well	3
GOTHICK				
Shall (I foresee it) soon with Gothick Swarms come fort		25	Ode Athenian	298
GOTHS				
Whence came these Goths to overrun the pit?		46	To Congreve	84
GOTTEN				
This Dragon had gotten two Sows in it's Belly; . . .		337	Serious Poem	88
<Meath> Smiles for the Joynture, though gotten, so late,		430	Dicky Dolly	19
The Son laughs that got, the hard gotten Estate, . .		430	Dicky Dolly	20
Gotten from their dainty Doxies, ...		573	Helter Skelter	26
"Thou hast certainly gotten a Cup in thy Pate. . . .		870	Grand Question	84
GOUN				
Decently hid beneath his Goun.		95	Bauc & Phil 1	176
In threed-bare Goun, would scarce a louse hold, . . .		291	Prog Marriage	61
His odious Goun would soil her Cloaths, ...		292	Prog Marriage	80
GOUT				
And, were I tortur'd with the Gout, ...		546	Life of Swift	49
Dear honest Ned is in the Gout, ...		554	Death of Swift	27
As, if the gout should seize the head, ...		761	Bec's B-Day	11
The gout that will prolong his days:		761	Bec's B-Day	16
And, lordly Gout wrapt up in Furr:		895	Panegyr Dean	277
GOVERN				
Either to govern or advise;		243	Horace 4, 9	8
"We govern here! where she presides		322	First of April	47
We govern all things there below.		620	Scandal Poem 1	88
We govern all Things there below.		626	Scandal Poem 2	86
For framing Laws to govern States;		641	On Poetry	28
These o'er their proper Districts govern, ...		649	On Poetry	283
As Machiavel taught 'em; divide and ye govern. .		805	Irish Bishops	48
GOVERN'D SEE ILL-GOVERN'D,LOOSE-GOVERN'D				
GOVERNING				
Of a governing Statesman, or favorite Whore:		351	Wood Insect	30
GOVERNMENT				
And with blind Rage break all this peaceful Government;		25	Ode Athenian	300
"And make the Government a Babel:		568	Death of Swift	384
The Government is now her own;		712	Cadenus Vaness	801
GOVERNMENTS				
In governments too easy, and too fruitful ground; . . .		37	Ode Sancroft	97
GOVERNOR'S				
How well the Governor's inclin'd.		422	Ireld	25
Poor Kingdom thou wouldst be that Governor's debtor, .		424	Carterets Arms	19
GOVERNORS				
Where Governors are good and wise;		391	Young's Satire	21
GOWN SEE GOUN, NIGHT-GOWN,CLERGY-GOWN				
As a fresh miss, by fancy, face, and gown, ...		48	To Congreve	151
But Weston has a new-cast Gown.		75	Game Traffick	21
'Twas Madam, in her Grogram Gown.		116	Bauc & Phil 2	144
A <Whig> and one that wears a Gown.		121	Apollo Outwit	64
Which made his Brethren of the Gown		171	Horace 1, 7	29
In that old Wig and rusty Gown!		175	Horace 1, 7	124
Or, Consul in his Purple Gown, ...		190	Faggot	33
"Good Mr. Dean go change your Gown, ...		200	Horace 2, 6	23
His Beaver brush'd, his Shoes, and Gown, ...		376	Apology Lady C	27
Three times a Week to brush my Gown.		411	Dial Rich Marb	100
Such Hatred to a Parson's Gown, ...		416	Woman's Mind	15
I'gad I'd wear a Gown.		426	Five Ladies	40
I smell your gown and cassock		428	Beau's Reply	2
A Genius in the Rev'rend Gown, ...		502	Doctor Delaney	79
No Scruple came on him his Gown to expose, . . .		517	Dean Hang Rape	21
The Pettycoats and Gown perfume, ...		529	Lady's Dres Rm	113
Like other Brethren of the Gown, ...		549	Life of Swift	141
"He doth an Honour to his Gown, ...		564	Death of Swift	291
"Pervert the Law, disgrace the Gown, ...		568	Death of Swift	385
Her Arm-pits would not stain her Gown:		584	Strephon Chloe	22
Thy thread-bare gown, thy cassock rent, ...		676	Parson's Case	9
With swelling scarf, and glossy gown, ...		676	Parson's Case	25
Thy Brother (far thy Betters) wore a Gown. . . .		678	Dean and Duke	14
That Gown was made for Old Queen Bess.		699	Cadenus Vaness	397
Dreams of a Gown of forty-four;		703	Cadenus Vaness	525
"Thy Gown and Cassock oft be torn:		850	Old Thorn	60
"Whenever you see a Cassock and gown, ...		872	Grand Question	153
Come hither, and take this old Gown for your Pains. .		873	Grand Question	186
So fine a Gown, a Band so clean, ...		889	Panegyr Dean	77
Their President, in Scarlet Gown, ...		904	Death Daphne	49

	PAGE	TITLE	LINE
GOWN (CONTINUED)			
Or may your Gown never be good Lutherine	1018	Swift Ans Sher	29
GOWN'D			
Because no <--> But <Black?> Gown'd Foe,	373	Letter D. S-y	77
GOWNMAN			
A Gownman of a diff'rent Make.	701	Cadenus Vaness	463
GOWNS			
Condemn'd to black gowns;	858	Lady's Lament	210
But 'tis observ'd, that Men in Gowns	1033	Ans to Crown	11
GRAC'D			
On either Side with Fringes grac'd;	915	Riddle 1	6
GRACE			
Borrow from every one a Grace;	28	Ode to Temple	64
Nor its triumphal Cavalcade to grace	29	Ode to Temple	89
Strip her of ev'ry ornament and grace,	42	Ode Sancroft	249
Who in his idiom vile, with Gray's-inn grace,	47	To Congreve	137
Till the blest sun to give kind dawn of grace	52	Temple Ill	25
(Madam, I dye without your Grace)	60	Lady Tablebook	15
Or if his Grace were no more skilld in	88	Hist V's House	45
With ev'ry Muse to Grace thy Song,	121	Apollo Outwit	55
<Sunderland>, <Orford>, <Boyl>, and <Richmond's> Grace	165	Toland's Invit	33
He mov'd, and bow'd and talk't with too much Grace;	194	Author Himself	13
And of my meer Motion, and special good Grace,	263	Apollo	27
Simplicity alone can grace,	270	Apollo's Edict D	29
Whom Jove endow'd with ev'ry Grace,	272	Apollo's Edict D	66
Imprimis: From his Grace a Hundred pound.	274	Epilogue	6
A flourisht Night-cap on, to grace	290	Prog Marriage	23
His Grace! impossible! what dead!	296	Satiric Elegy	1
Lord William's Grace of Dublin Town,	341	Upon His Grace	3
. . . and owns His Grace had Reason.	341	Upon His Grace	8
Has lost His Grace for Ten Years past . . .	341	Upon His Grace	10
Now from his Lordship's Grace I hold a little Piece of Ground,	342	Upon His Grace	21
And once I was so bold to beg that I might see His Grace,	342	Upon His Grace	27
God Bless your Grace I then reply'd, . .	343	Upon His Grace	37
Your Rent is due almost a Week beside the Days of Grace.	343	Upon His Grace	44
Then God Preserve his Lordship's Grace, . . .	343	Upon His Grace	47
And Dick the Scavenger with equal Grace,	364	On Dreams	37
Unless i'th' Answer, of his Grace,	373	Letter D. S-y	59
He lengthen'd my Life with a whole Year of Grace.	399	Tom Clinch	18
Either from Excellence or grace	423	Ireld	70
For If somebody's grace	424	Carterets Arms	9
Just three; and every Grace a Daughter.	465	Birthday Song	166
"To <Grafton's> Grace, with grateful Heart;	476	Epist on Epist	33
There shining 'midst his Train, to Grace	477	Epist on Epist	81
You Forfeit all your Patron's Grace,	480	Libel on D- D-	30
The Danger past, takes Heart of Grace,	500	Doctor Delaney	25
With Grace and Learning unendow'd,	503	Doctor Delaney	88
No Protestant Prelate, His Ldshp or Grace	522	St. Cecilia's	9
All Folks who pretend to Religion and Grace,	575	Place Damn'd	1
Says Grace before, and after Meat;	605	Beasts Confess	130
Tis but by our peculiar grace	621	Scandal Poem 1	131
'Tis but by our peculiar Grace,	627	Scandal Poem 2	135
And weekly persecute his grace	677	Parson's Case	29
Tom could move with lordly Grace,	784	Mullinex Dick	21
Cou'd you see his grim Grace, for a Pound to a Penny,	803	Irish Bishops	9
Lord <Bolton's> good Grace, Lord <Carr>, and Lord <Howard>,	804	Irish Bishops	25
He flies from his God, to attend on his Grace:	809	Epigr Prelate	4
"And nothing of that ever troubled your Grace.	843	Ay and No	8
But sense gives a grace	854	Lady's Lament	99
And grace my villa with his strains;	876	To Dean Swift	5
Whether with Dermot, or His Grace;	890	Panegyr Dean	122
Talk of their Milk for Babes of Grace;	892	Panegyr Dean	170
Nor seldom grace the flow'ry downs,	896	Panegyr Dean	303
I please the Young, I grace the Old,	912	Aenigma	11
And often have I seen thee grace	919	Riddle 5	7
In my eye my greatest grace,	936	Riddle 24 D	15
Wearied with saying Grace and Prayer,	1003	Dan J's Reply	1
For a Grace, if we smell it.	1015	Swift to Sheri	58
His <Grace> swore by <God>, and her <Grace> let a <Fart>:	143	New Song	18
His <Grace> swore by <God>, and her <Grace> let a <Fart>:	143	New Song	18
GRACEFUL			
Struck with Endymion's graceful mien,	178	To Lord Harley	74
But her graceful black Locks, were all mingled with Grey	264	Apollo	42
The powerful Voice, the graceful Mien,	385	Manly Virtue	57
Her graceful Mein, her Shape, and Face,	584	Strephon Chloe	7
You make the graceful Horace look	670	Epig Carthy 21 D	3
Thy graceful Steps, and Coll'nell's Air	779	Mullinix Tim	205
With such Address, and graceful Port,	889	Panegyr Dean	83
That graceful on his Shoulders fell)	903	Death Daphne	26
GRACEFULL			
So gracefull in their proper Place,	226	Prog of Beauty	22
Of Nymphs so gracefull, Wise and fair	722	Stel B-Day '18	12
GRACEFULLY			
And gracefully her Subject chang'd:	698	Cadenus Vaness	355

	PAGE	TITLE	LINE

GRACEFULNESS
While Gracefulness its Art conceals, ... 726 To Stella 83
GRACELESS
Whose graceless Children scorn to own thee! . . . . 652 On Poetry 358
GRACES
"Since thy few ill-presented graces seem . . . . . . 55 Temple Ill 145
The Graces from the Court did next provide . . . . 118 Biddy Floyd 7
I answer; the Tories were in my good Graces, ... 144 New Song 23
Nor need you on the Graces call, ... 272 Apollo's Edict D 74
The Graces next, and all the Muses . . . . . . 290 Prog Marriage 9
"For she belongs to all the Graces; . . . . . . 321 First of April 10
The Graces and the other Maid; . . . . . . 371 Letter D. S-y 6
They'll be no more like Graces, ... 425 Five Ladies 15
The Graces and their Mistress Venus . . . . . . 465 Birthday Song 155
That she hath Graces of her own: . . . . . . 465 Birthday Song 164
Three Graces by Lucina brought her, ... 465 Birthday Song 165
She by the tender Graces drest, ... 586 Strephon Chloe 59
In Order; on the Left, the Graces: . . . . . . 689 Cadenus Vaness 96
The Graces half asham'd look'd down; . . . . . . 689 Cadenus Vaness 100
Then calls the Graces to her Aid, ... 691 Cadenus Vaness 158
The Graces next wou'd act their Part, ... 692 Cadenus Vaness 172
With Graces, hitherto unknown . . . . . . 695 Cadenus Vaness 272
GRACIOUS
As thus, "Vouchsafe, Oh gracious Maker! . . . . . 199 Horace 2, 6 D
The gracious Dame, tho' well she knew . . . . . . 379 Apology Lady C 117
The Queen, so Gracious, Mild, and Good, ... 559 Death of Swift 181
GRAFTING
'Twere grafting on an annual Stock . . . . . . 729 Stella, Poems 65
GRAFTON
When first of Griz, you Grafton reated . . . . . . 372 Letter D. S-y 14
Or Grafton the deep . . . . . . 423 Carterets Arms
<GRAFTON'S>
"To <Grafton's> Grace, with grateful Heart; . . . . . 476 Epist on Epist 33
GRAIN
These Venus cleans'd from ev'ry spurious Grain . . . 118 Biddy Floyd 9
Hither, though much against his Grain, ... 294 Prog Marriage 123
Got from his crew of <rogues> in grain; . . . . . 435 Answer Paulus 118
While she a Goddess dy'd in Grain . . . . . . 586 Strephon Chloe 85
A Coat we gave him dy'd in grain . . . . . . 619 Scandal Poem 1 69
A Coat we gave him, dy'd in Grain; . . . . . . 625 Scandal Poem 2 65
Bow <Bettesworth>, that booby, and <Scoundrel> in grain, . 814 Yahoo's 3
There's nine Hundred Pounds for Labour and Grain, . . 867 Grand Question 9
Against the Grain, a <Monarch's> Fist? . . . . . 884 Rev Market-Hill 34
Without a grain of common sense, ... 950 Upstart D 12
GRAINS
We learn't to weigh our Gold by Grains. . . . . . 156 Fable of Midas 22
For which Her <Majesty> allows him Grains. . . . . 521 Stephen Duck 4
"Or add some Grains of Folly more . . . . . . 714 Cadenus Vaness 874
We'll oil him with kennel, and powd'r him with grains, . 817 Yahoo's 58
GRAMMAR
Adjourn'd from tops and grammar to the inns; . . . . 46 To Congreve 98
GRAMMER
Shew Reason, Grammer, Truth, or Sense? . . . . . 503 Doctor Delaney 104
GRANARD
The Glory of the Granard Race; . . . . . . 272 Apollo's Edict D 67
GRAND
To overheare the grand Dispute. . . . . . . 63 Discovery 28
And settled Europe's Grand Affairs, ... 181 Horace 2, 1 40
Who prates like his Grand mere . . . . . . 186 Scriblerus 4 D 8
Except to lash some grand Delinquent. . . . . . 190 Faggot 30
And all his Grand Account to make? . . . . . . 241 Run Bankers 56
Our noble Grand Jury, ... 237 Excellent Song 23
This Grand Event half broke our Measures, ... 283 Journal 119
Thus finishing his grand Survey, ... 529 Lady's Dres Rm 115
"That Jesus was a Grand Impostor: . . . . . . 564 Death of Swift 294
In State return'd the grand Parade; . . . . . . 586 Strephon Chloe 68
When first this grand Debate arose . . . . . . 690 Cadenus Vaness 130
Proving the Earl a grand Offender, ... 774 Mullinix Tim 21
Let them form a grand Committee, ... 831 Legion Club 53
GRAND-DAME
Which made my Grand-Dame always stuff-her-Ears, . . 367 Answer Delaney 39
My Grand-dame had Gallants by Twenties, ... 350 Upright Judge 3 3
GRAND-MONDE
How she might shine in the Grand-Monde, ... 705 Cadenus Vaness 581
GRANDAM
For Venus might be her great Grandam. . . . . . 465 Birthday Song 160
GRANDAME
Begot upon his grandame Earth; . . . . . . 433 Answer Paulus 26
GRANDAMES
Making good my Grandames Jest, ... 829 Legion Club 7
GRANDEES
To take his greatest Grandees for Asses. . . . . . 988 Letter Dr Sh-n 12
GRANDER
Are these too low?--then find out grander, ... 83 Salamander 21
And when you'd make an Heroe grander, ... 270 Apollo's Edict D 18
GRANDEUR
For Grandeur, Elegance and Wit, ... 314 To Ford 93
Its Grandeur to its greatest Foe. . . . . . . 386 Manly Virtue 96
Grandeur, by Goodness made compleat! . . . . . 386 Manly Virtue 101
By Party-steps no Grandeur climb at, ... 503 Doctor Delaney 109
Precedence, and support your Grandeur: . . . . . 888 Panegyr Dean 46

GRATIFY   (CONTINUED)   PAGE   TITLE   LINE
    Meerly to gratify their Spight;   . . . .   548 Life of Swift   129
GRATING
    As grating, or as loud as theirs?   . . . ·. . . .   617 Scandal Poem 1   6
GRATITUDE
    With Gratitude, Respect, Esteem;   . . . .   711 Cadenus Vaness   787
    He still has Gratitude and Sap'ence, ...   796 Traulus 1   27
    Resolv'd my Gratitude to show, ...   887 Panegyr Dean   1
    My Gratitude the World shall know: . . . .   887 Panegyr Dean   31
    Perhaps you will say, 'tis in Gratitude due, ...   947 Mrs. Houghton   3
GRATTAN
    Now tell me, friend Thomas, Ford, Grattan, and merry   955 Portrait Life   9
        Dan,
    While <Grattan>, <Sheridan>, and I, ...   499 Panegyr Swift   177
GRATTAN'S
    To look with Robin Grattan's Eyes: . . . .   314 To Ford   86
    For less than Charly Grattan's School: . . . . .   478 Epist on Epist   111
GRATTONS
    Rebecca, Ford, and Grattons by.   . . . .   743 Stel B-day 22   60
GRAV'D
    Be grav'd on either Side in Columns, ...   611 By Dr. Swift   9
GRAVE
    I laugh at the grave Answer they will make, ...   19 Ode Athenian   121
    In that deep Grave a Book, ...   27 Ode to Temple   36
    Nor am that grave adviser which I meant;   . . . . .   49 To Congreve   202
    Dame Floyd looks out in grave Suspence   . . . . . .   75 Game Traffick   13
    Step to this Grave but once a Week, ...   101 Elegy Patrige   110
    Hal -- grows more Pert, and <Somers> not so Grave: 163 Toland's Invit   22
    Nor all his Int'rest keep him from the Grave.   . . .   234 Elegy on Demar   22
    At Nine, grave Nim and George Facetious, ...   278 Journal   11
    The grave Divine with knotty Points perplext,   364 On Dreams   31
    So hearing of a grave Divine, ...   375 Apology Lady C   5
    So grave, as to be unpolite;   . . . .   375 Apology Lady C   8
    No more the Dean, that grave Divine, ...   409 Dial Rich Marb   43
    I'd go in freedom to my grave, ...   421 Holyhead   33
    One Grave now contains them both Haec et Hic.   . . .   430 Dicky Dolly   15
    You can't, grave Sir, believe it hard, ...   475 Epist on Epist   3
    Because it chanc'd, an old grave Don   . . . . . .   495 Panegyr Swift   84
    Grave D. of St <Patrick> how comes it to pass   522 St. Cecilia's   1
    "His Vein, ironically grave, ...   565 Death of Swift   315
    And on the Marble grave these Rhimes, ...   596 Cassinus Peter   75
    A blind old Beggar from the Grave: . . . .   604 Beasts Confess   116
    Hardly can be grave in Prose: . . . .   634 Epistle Lady   138
    And fly for refuge to the grave: . . . .   676 Parson's Case   16
    You must be grave, and I be wise.   . . . .   757 Stel B-day '24   28
    Despairing Wretches from the grave: . . . . . .   764 Stel B-day '26   38
    Be grave and wise, 'twou'd break their Heart.   . . .   776 Mullinix Tim   90
    The merry Tale with moral Grave.   . . . .   783 Tim and Fables   27
    Tho' Lewd and Immoral, be Formal and Grave,   807 Advice Parson   3
    In his Grave, and search his Trunks.   . . . . . .   836 Legion Club   168
    "Mister Curate, for all your grave Looks, I'm afraid,   872 Grand Question   147
    Grave Harry, when the poor are pressing   . . . . .   878 Pobbin & Harry   5
    Here bury'd in one common Grave;   . . . .   923 Riddle 7   54
    You say you will eat Grass on his Grave: a Christian   986 Mary to Sher   17
        eat Grass!
    Beside a Brace of grave Divines;   . . . .   1020 Nim-Dan-Dean 1   D   3
GRAVEL
    From far, to gather golden Gravel;   . . . . . .   157 Fable of Midas   38
GRAVELY
    Or gravely try to read the Lines   . . . . . .   201 Horace 2, 6   71
    So gravely, where the Subject's light. . . . . . .   218 To Mr. Delany   88
    Gravely consulting Ireland's Good, ...   344 Prometheus   2
    And, when he gravely has undone a Score, ...   535 To Mr. Gay   105
    The Queen of Learning gravely smiles, ...   692 Cadenus Vaness   199
    And gravely ask'd her what she thought, ...   698 Cadenus Vaness   379
    I gravely sat me down to think: . . . .   740 Stel B-day 22   4
    By the <Dean> though gravely told, ...   863 To Janus   25
GRAVER
    And deal in Vices of the graver Sort, ...   194 Author Himself   21
    This Graver understood his Art.   . . . .   783 Tim and Fables   20
GRAVES
    I saw the Graves give up their Dead.   . . . . . .   578 Day Judgement   4
    Better we all were in our Graves   . . . .   824 Printer Newgat   1
GRAVEST
    From not the gravest of Divines, ...   764 Stel B-day '26   13
    If gravest Parsons here advance, ...   928 Riddle 12   D   17
GRAVING
    You should try your graving Tools   . . . .   839 Legion Club   223
GRAVITATION
    For by the Laws of Gravitation, ...   127 Little House   11
GRAVITY
    Who said, his Gravity was feign'd: . . . .   603 Beasts Confess   50
GRAY
    The gray old Fellow Poet Joe   . . . .   126 Little House   3
    Lay by your White Staff & gray Habit, ...   187 Scriblerus 4   D   15
GRAY'S-INN
    Who in his idiom vile, with Gray's-inn grace,   . . .   47 To Congreve   137
GRAZE
    But when she must be turn'd to graze, ...   230 Prog of Poetry   9
    Be sent to Quilca down to graze;   . . . .   759 Receipt Youth   26
    Send the Clergy all to graze;   . . . .   838 Legion Club   216

GRAZERS   PAGE   TITLE   LINE
   What Herds of Kings would turn to Grazers.   . . . .   659 On Poetry   D 410
GRAZIER'S
   His Grazier's Coat reach down his Heels, ...   94 Bauc & Phil 1   166
   His Grazier's Coat fall down his Heels;   . . . . .   115 Bauc & Phil 2   118
   His Grazier's coat with dirt besmear'd, ... 879 Robbin & Harry   43
GRAZY
   And with Boots so very grazy   . . . .   573 Helter Skelter   11
GREAS'D
   It has; but then it greas'd his fist.   . . . .   432 Answer Paulus   10
GREASY   SEE GREAZY
   And Wool it is greasy, and quickly takes Fire.   . . .   237 Excellent Song   21
   Set up with greasy Linnen, ...   425 Five Ladies   7
   Or greasy Coifs and Pinners reeking, ...   527 Lady's Dres Rm   53
   And up exhales a greasy Stench, ...   529 Lady's Dres Rm   107
   With greasy Paper stuck upon't.   . . . .   582 Young Nymph   36
   One greasy Stocking round his Head, ...   594 Cassinus Peter   12
   Then Gluttony with greasy Paws, ...   894 Panegyr Dean   255
GREAT
   Else where's the Gain in being Great?   . . . . .   6 Ode to King   5
   The Great Distinguisher of Blood, ...   7 Ode to King   23
   And thought too great ev'n for effects of Chance,   .   8 Ode to King   63
   The Battel almost by Great William's single Valour   8 Ode to King   64
     gain'd;
   Is grown so impudently Great, ...   10 Ode to King   120
   (When this huge Bodies Moisture was so great   . . .   16 Ode Athenian   3
   It be as great as 'tis in Fame, ...   16 Ode Athenian   9
   Pardon Ye great Unknown, and far-exalted Men,   . . .   17 Ode Athenian   60
   The publick Stamp Heav'n sets on all that's Great and   18 Ode Athenian   93
     Good,
   To make some great Discovery, ...   20 Ode Athenian   143
   With all that Power unfelt, courts Mankind to be Great,   21 Ode Athenian   155
   And this Ye great Unknown, is only known in You.   . .   21 Ode Athenian   188
   To be the great Original   . . . .   22 Ode Athenian   217
   And rather Tite than Great, ...   23 Ode Athenian   231
   Still boasting of Her Great Unknown;   ` . . . . .   24 Ode Athenian   251
   Of some great King and Conqu'rors Death, ...   24 Ode Athenian   272
   To be Successors to these Great Unknown, ...   25 Ode Athenian   294
   Those mighty Epithets, Learn'd, Good, and Great   . .   28 Ode to Temple   59
   This great triumvirate of Souls.   . . . .   28 Ode to Temple   69
   Great God! (said I) what have I seen!   . . . . .   29 Ode to Temple   103
   Expect some great gigantick Son of Earth;   . . . .   30 Ode to Temple   111
   How noble a Reprisal on the Great!   . . . . . .   31 Ode to Temple   141
   Sounds truly good, or truly great;   . . . .   36 Ode Sancroft   49
   Pleas'd with an empty swelling to be counted great;   .   36 Ode Sancroft   60
   What we call holy, and great, and just, and good,   . .   38 Ode Sancroft   124
   Revile His great ambassador, ...   38 Ode Sancroft   131
   Necessity, thou tyrant conscience of the great,   . .   40 Ode Sancroft   176
   In pleasing all that's good among the great,   . . .   49 To Congreve   180
   Mild Dorothea, peaceful, wise and great, ...   52 Temple Ill   41
   Such were thy rules to be poetically great,   . . .   55 Temple Ill   137
   Nor thought to find so great a Peer   . . . . . .   62 Discovery   3
   To try the great Experiment;   . . . .   66 Problem   34
   . . .makes a great Hole in my Wages, ...   71 Mrs Harris Pet   40
   He had mixt little Wit with a great deal of Pains,   .   77 Lady B- B-   24
   A great Refinement in Barometry, ...   99 Elegy Patrige   42
   Great scholars have in Lucian Read, ...   99 Elegy Patrige   63
   Great Jove, he cry'd, the Art restore   . . . . .   107 V's House   43
   Philemon was in great Surprize, ...   116 Bauc & Phil 2   145
   Our great Magician, Hamet Sid, ...   132 Magician's Rod   5
   Whereas, Notwithstanding, I am in great Pain,   . . .   143 New Song   11
   But, most noble Senators, 'tis a great Shame   . . .   143 New Song   13
   That Her <Majesty> stood in great need of a Tutor,   . 144 New Song   41
   To make the Dutch-men proud and great: . . . .   169 Peace Dunkirk   34
   Harley, the Nation's great Support, ...   170 Horace 1, 7   1
   Thou'lt tell of Leagues among the Great   . . . .   181 Horace 2, 1   21
   Great Ormonde lend thy Gen'ral's Staff: . . . .   191 Faggot   46
   Yet, still was at the Tables of the Great.   . . . .   194 Author Himself   16
   His great contending Friends to reconcile.   . . .   196 Author Himself   72
   Great Ministers ne'er think of these;   . . . . .   199 Horace 2, 6   18
   About some great Affair, at Two--   . . . . . .   200 Horace 2, 6   54
   "My Lord and he are grown so great, ...   202 Horace 2, 6   85
   "You, Mr. Dean frequent the Great;   . . . . . .   202 Horace 2, 6   93
   When they saw the Dean's Book they were in a great Fury 237 Excellent Song   24
   As great as they are, ...   247 Irish-Feast   79
   The great ones swall'wing up the small   . . . .   253 Bubble   66
   He left behind so great a <stink>. . . . . . .   296 Satiric Elegy   16
   Said he-- "Great Sovereign of the Main, ...   303 Storm   27
   Your great Protectors, once in Power, ...   311 To Ford   27
   Whether thy Great Forefathers came   . . . . . .   324 Pethox   23
   But this Idol Wood may do us great Evil, ...   334 Serious Poem   11
   I hear among Scholars there is a great Doubt   . . .   334 Serious Poem   25
   Great, Good and Just was once apply'd   . . . . .   339 Arch-Bish Dub   1
   In thy great Care we place our Trust, ...   339 Arch-Bish Dub   7
   Because thour't Great, and Good, and Just.   . . .   339 Arch-Bish Dub   8
   Get the Great Seal, and turn out Brod'rick.   . . .   348 Whitshed Motto   18
   Bedaubs the guilty Great with nauseous Praise: . .   364 On Dreams   36
   'Tis no great Loss to lose an Ear;   . . . . . .   366 Answer Delaney   2
   Or if 'tis true, Great Phabus smiles   . . . . .   372 Letter D. S-y   25
   Who sav'd thee from a great Disaster.   . . . . .   373 Letter D. S-y   56
   Himself alone shou'd make him great.   . . . . . .   384 Manly Virtue   36

GREAT   (CONTINUED)   PAGE TITLE   LINE

	PAGE	TITLE	LINE
Contented to be truly great,	385	Manly Virtue	49
To bless, is truly to be great!	386	Manly Virtue	102
No Falshood now among the Great,	391	Young's Satire	14
Think what they wish so great a Blessing,	411	Desire Possess	3
Possession's Load was grown so great,	413	Desire Possess	51
For Venus might be her great Grandam.	465	Birthday Song	160
Rewards too great for your Flim-Flams,	478	Epist on Epist	107
Deluded Mortals, whom the Great	480	Libel on D- D-	1
His Heart too Great, though Fortune little,	482	Libel on D- D-	81
While most that are or would be great,	491	Dialogue	53
And dance Attendance on the Great,	492	Panegyr Swift	2
For next to being Great our selves	493	Panegyr Swift	11
It is to think all great Ones Elves,	493	Panegyr Swift	12
Poems address'd to great Men's Whores;	494	Panegyr Swift	35
And the great Name engrav'd most fairly,	494	Panegyr Swift	53
Who have, to shew your great Devotion,	495	Panegyr Swift	60
When <Jonathan> was great at Court,	498	Panegyr Swift	159
Far otherwise a great Divine,	513	Answer Fable	11
(To thee I apply great Smedley's Successor)	518	Dean Hang Rape	44
Offend our Patriot, Great Sir <Robert>,	548	Life of Swift	108
Some great Misfortune to portend,	557	Death of Swift	119
"Though trusted long in great Affairs,	565	Death of Swift	329
How great a Change! how quickly made!	590	Strephon Chloe	203
Find great Society in Stinking.	590	Strephon Chloe	210
You are not so great a Grievance	637	Epistle Lady	243
Great Poet of the Hollow-Tree.	653	On Poetry	376
Thou great Vicegerent of the King,	656	On Poetry	447
I rode four more to great St. Mary;	675	Curate's Compl	3
With labour small, and income great;	676	Parson's Case	23
For great Examples are but vain,	700	Cadenus Vaness	436
To find her a great Witt, but the Dean a small Man.	716	Answer Rebus	14
And shou'd he write Pamphlets, no Great Man wou'd read 'em:	717	Answer Rebus	26
May be proud to be licking a great man's posteriors.	817	Yahoo's	69
"go tell your friend Bob and the other great folk,	843	Ay and No	13
Ye Great ones, why will ye disdain	896	Panegyr Dean	291
As great as ever, at Quadrille?	905	Death Daphne	78
Yet, as it oft attends the Great,	917	Riddle 3	5
Though at the Tables of the Great,	920	Riddle 6	25
Too great for Mortals less than Kings.	924	Riddle 8	16
From whom great Sylla found his Doom;	925	Riddle 8	35
In our Ken, both great and small;	931	Riddle 18	D 10
And as I please they're great and small;	934	Riddle 21	D 2
Another great Fault,	939	Riddle Answerd	29
Great Folks are of a finer Mold;	949	Epigr Scolding	1
I have a great Esteem for Plautus;	988	Letter Dr Sh-n	2
...with that great peer the Lord Anglesey.	1022	Nim-Dan-Dean 2	D 6
...I mean that great fat joker, friend Helsham, he	1023	Nim-Dan-Dean 2	D 9
A great want of Shoes;	1036	Plague Country	2
GREATER			
And all we Fools, who are the greater part of it,	18	Ode Athenian	71
The greater half I had to say,	80	Vanbrug House	56
And, what is yet a greater curse,	435	Answer Paulus	89
He must be greater than his Sire:	461	Birthday Song	22
And take a Greater Patrick's Name.	478	Epist on Epist	94
Say, has the small or greater Pox	595	Cassinus Peter	48
Ridicule has greater Pow'r	636	Epistle Lady	199
The Greater for the Smallest watch,	651	On Poetry	321
Yet thou hast greater Cause to be	652	On Poetry	363
And, what was yet a greater Curse,	741	Stel B-day 22	11
Nay, he can make what's greater far,	876	To Dean Swift	23
A Greater Chymist none, than I,	920	Riddle 6	19
Greater be my size or less,	937	Riddle 24	D 36
To be much greater than a Pound?	1004	Dan J's Reply	29
GREATER'S			
How greater's his merit at four Courts or House,	814	Yahoo's	8
GREATEST			
The greatest scorn of Learned Vanity,	21	Ode Athenian	179
Virtue, the greatest of all Monarchies,	26	Ode to Temple	1
To curse our greatest Enemy)	28	Ode to Temple	52
The greatest compliment she ever made,	44	To Congreve	28
Since hope his last and greatest foe is fled,	55	Temple Ill	127
The greatest Lord, when you appear,	325	Pethox	43
Thou dar'st the greatest Prince attack,	325	Pethox	53
Its Grandeur to its greatest Foe.	386	Manly Virtue	96
Will tell aloud your greatest Failing;	416	Woman's Mind	20
Wherein yourselves have greatest Share?	449	Modern Lady	153
The greatest monarch may be stabb'd by night,	506	To a Friend	1
Can, unreveng'd, the greatest merit wound.	506	To a Friend	6
I see the greatest Owls in you,	515	Answer Fable	106
Is of all Wits the greatest Fool;	592	Strephon Chloe	278
Against your greatest benefactor.	622	Scandal Poem 1	172
Tenderness my greatest Fault.)	637	Epistle Lady	232
She'll prove the greatest of thy Foes:	696	Cadenus Vaness	300
But Friendship in its greatest Height,	711	Cadenus Vaness	780
She chose a thread of greatest length	760	Bec's B-Day	3
Thy greatest Evils yet are scarce begun.	793	St. Pat's Well	88
The greatest cully of mankind:	899	Dean's Reasons	12
His Follies to his greatest Foes.	915	Riddle 1	26
How is the greatest Monarch blest,	916	Riddle 2	3

```
GREATEST        (CONTINUED)                            PAGE   TITLE            LINE
  By those who give me greatest Pain.     . . . . . . .  918  Riddle 4            16
  Yet Commoners with greatest Ease,        . . . . . . . 928  Riddle 12        D  11
  Yet we can, with greatest Ease,          . . . . . . . 931  Riddle 18        D  13
  The greatest Whale, that swims the Sea   . . . . . . . 934  Riddle 21        D  11
  In my eye my greatest grace,    . . . . . . . . .      936  Riddle 24        D  15
  In Clergymen the greatest Fault.         . . . . . . . 942  Probatur Alit        6
  To take his greatest Grandees for Asses. . . . . . .   988  Letter Dr Sh-n      12
GREATFUL
  "The greatful People stand his Friends:  . . . . . .   570  Death of Swift     426
GREATNESS
  Which the disguise of greatness only served to hide; . .  41  Ode Sancroft     214
  "Of no Man's Greatness was afraid,       . . . . . .   565  Death of Swift     327
GREAZY
  Hence the greazy clumsy Mien,   . . . . . . . .        800  Traulus 2           31
GRECIAN
  Thus did the Grecian Wooden Horse,       . . . . . .   209  Fable Bitches       43
  Salmoneus, as the Grecian Tale is,       . . . . . . . 352  Wood Ironmongr       1
  Whatever Grecian Story tells:   . . . . . . . .        482  Libel on D- D-      78
  You shew you Skill in Grecian Story,     . . . . . .   483  Libel on D- D-      97
  And, as that hateful hideous Grecian     . . . . . .   775  Mullinix Tim        51
GREECE
  When Philip King of Greece was Dead,     . . . . . .    99  Elegy Patrige       64
  Ran under Ground from Greece to Brittain,  . . . .     293  Prog Marriage      112
  Take twenty Gods of Rome or Greece,      . . . . . .   460  Birthday Song        2
  And such as know what Greece has writ    . . . . . .   491  Dialogue            51
  With Lorraine's Duke, and Prince of Greece. . . . .    592  Strephon Chloe     292
  Jason, the valiant Prince of Greece,     . . . . . .   948  Jason Hassard        1
GREEDILY
  Which greedily they swallow down,     . . . . . . .     27  Ode to Temple       48
GREEDY
  Charming her greedy Ears   . . . . . . . . .            17  Ode Athenian        53
  Thus, when a greedy Sloven once has thrown  . . . . .  536  To Mr. Gay         161
  Aspiring, greedy, full of senseless Prate,  . . . . .  792  St. Pat's Well      51
GREEK
  Howe'er, 'tis all one in the Greek.   . . . . . .      158  Fable of Midas      60
  I know you will say, this is all Heathen Greek;  . . . 337  Serious Poem        89
  In some old Greek or Latian Bard,      . . . . . . .   479  Epist on Epist     120
  Then, lest with Greek he over-run ye,  . . . . . . .   648  On Poetry          259
  Extol the Greek and Roman Masters,     . . . . . . .   652  On Poetry          347
  Every Greek and Roman Author.   . . . . . . . .        838  Legion Club        214
GREEKS
  Pregnant with Greeks, impatient to be freed,  . . . .  139  City Shower         48
  (Those Bully Greeks, who, as the Moderns do,  . . . .  139  City Shower         49
  By Greeks and Romans understood,    . . . . . . .      697  Cadenus Vaness     348
  For Vengeance on his Friends the Greeks.  . . . . .    731  Stella, Poems      126
  That might be envy'd by the Greeks;   . . . . . .      893  Panegyr Dean       203
GREEN   SEE COLLEGE-GREEN,STEPHEN'S-GREEN
  Forever green and flourishing 'twill last,  . . . . .   29  Ode to Temple       85
  Old Good-man Dobson of the Green    . . . . . .        116  Bauc & Phil 2      165
  Chequer'd with Ribbons blew and green;  . . . . . .    200  Horace 2, 6         29
  The Sexton shall green Sods on thee bestow.  . . . .   235  Elegy on Demar      37
  St James's Park and Stephen's Green;   . . . . . . .   313  To Ford             60
  Of Red, and Yellow, Blue, and Green.   . . . . . .     325  Pethox              46
  of St Andrew's the Green, and St George's the Blue     389  Order of Bath        2
  Bedraggled in my Walks so green:    . . . . . .        409  Dial Rich Marb      48
  "No gay Parterre with costly Green,    . . . . . . .   476  Epist on Epist      53
  So green in different Lights may pass for blue,  . . . 670  Epig Carthy 18   D   7
  Whether the Red or Green were best,    . . . . . .     698  Cadenus Vaness     380
  The brightest Virgin of the Green,     . . . . . . .   721  Stel B-Day '18       6
  And foul the green seat;   . . . . . . . . .           857  Lady's Lament      190
  I here am Red, and there am Green,     . . . . . . .   911  Aenigma              7
  My complexion wan and green,    . . . . . . . . .      937  Riddle 24        D  40
GREENS
  "You dread the waving of these Greens;   . . . . . .   380  Apology Lady C     138
GREENWICH
  'Twas Greenwich. There he took a Ship,    . . . . .    456  Dean Smedley        43
GREET
  Rebecca thus I gladly greet,   . . . . . . . . .       761  Bec's B-Day         17
GREETING
  Petition and Greeting.   . . . . . . . . . .          1004  Sheridan's Sub       4
GREETS
  The Queen of Love, whom thus she greets,    . . . .    695  Cadenus Vaness     285
GREW
  And pluckt a Laurel branch (for Laurel was the first    16  Ode Athenian        27
    that grew,
  Before it grew a city butterfly;    . . . . . . .       46  To Congreve         90
  Grew to his Back instead of Wings;     . . . . . . .    80  Vanbrug House       36
  Just in the Place where first it grew,    . . . . .     87  Hist V's House      32
  The Chimny widen'd and grew high'r,    . . . . . . .    92  Bauc & Phil 1       95
  There stuck, and to a Pulpit grew,     . . . . . . .    93  Bauc & Phil 1      107
  Observ'd, they grew a num'rous Race.   . . . . . .     106  V's House           18
  The Chimney widen'd, and grew higher,     . . . . .    113  Bauc & Phil 2       55
  And with small Change, a Pulpit grew.     . . . . .    114  Bauc & Phil 2       88
  His Wastcoat to a Cassock grew,    . . . . . . .       115  Bauc & Phil 2      121
  Here Baucis, there Philemon grew.      . . . . . . .   116  Bauc & Pnil 2      172
  Grew Scrubby, dy'd a-top, was stunted:    . . . . .    117  Bauc & Phil 2      177
  It grew an all-devouring Asp;   . . . . . . . .        132  Magician's Rod      10
  And Puss grew Lion-hearted.    . . . . . . . .         153  Widow and Cat    D  10
  When Food and Rayment now grew scarce     . . . . .    225  Prog of Love        95
  Beneath whose ill Shade no Plant ever grew.  . . . .   334  Serious Poem        32
```

GREW	(CONTINUED)		PAGE	TITLE	LINE
	Doll dying first, Dick grew Melancholly,	. . . . .	430	Dicky Dolly	2
	By which he grew both rich and wise.	. . . .	513	Answer Fable	18
	And there he grew fond of another Man's Wife,	. . .	517	Dean Hang Rape	8
	He grew, or else his Comrades ly'd,	. . . .	547	Life of Swift	88
	As if it grew in common Hedges.	. . . . . .	640	On Poetry	10
	Of which, as she grew up, there stay'd	. . . . .	693	Cadenus Vaness	218
	When they grew pert, to pull them down.	. . . . .	697	Cadenus Vaness	337
	Grew louder, all the Way up Stairs;	. . . . . .	698	Cadenus Vaness	369
	Her Knowledge with her Fancy grew;	. . . . . .	704	Cadenus Vaness	554
	And since his Talk offensive grew,	. . . . . .	705	Cadenus Vaness	592
	By this new Passion grew inspir'd.	. . . . . .	709	Cadenus Vaness	717
	And then before it grew too late,	. . . .	722	Stel B-Day '18	15
	Except where Wit and Virtue grew	. . . .	733	Verses Vanessa	22
	In half a week the Dame grew nice,	. . . . . .	745	Stel Distress	9
	In half a Week the Dame grew nice,	. . . . . .	749	Stel Wood-Park	7
	As you grew more degenerate and base,	. . . . . .	792	St. Pat's Well	53
	At fifty two, when he grew loving,	. . . . . .	879	Robbin & Harry	46
	With mutual Beauty smit, their Passion grew.	. . . .	880	Pastoral Dial	6
	There, many a Flow'r abstersive grew,	. . . . .	894	Panegyr Dean	249
	And, grew enamour'd with her Phiz,	. . . . . .	905	Death Daphne	65
	Lady Santry got out of the Church when she grew sick,	.	1029	Dr. Helsham	10
GREY					
	But her graceful black Locks, were all mingled with Grey	264	Apollo	42
	Tho' she lives 'till she's Grey as a Badger all over.	.	266	Apollo	108
	When Stella's Locks must all be grey	. . . . .	735	Stel B-day '20	48
	That half your Locks are turn'd to Grey;	. . . . .	757	Stel B-day '24	39
GREYHOUND					
	Thus, a Greyhound out-runs the whole Pack in a Race,	.	580	Psyche	5
GRIEF					
	Then with that grief we form in spirits divine,	. . .	43	To Congreve	5
	Thy looks, when every cause of grief is past!	. . .	52	Temple Ill	34
	You that would grief describe, come here and trace	. .	52	Temple Ill	51
	Grief from Dorinda's face does ne'er depart	. . . .	53	Temple Ill	53
	And grief flung sables on each menial look;	. . . . .	53	Temple Ill	60
	And tell the irreligion of my grief;	. . . . .	53	Temple Ill	78
	Grief that excus'd the tribute of my knees,	. . . . .	53	Temple Ill	79
	Assign'd for life to unremitting grief;	. . . . .	54	Temple Ill	110
	. . .and I found her full of Grief;	. . . . .	71	Mrs Harris Pet	34
	By Faction tir'd, with Grief he waits a while,	. .	196	Author Himself	71
	And spare my absent Friends the Grief	. . . . .	204	In Sickness	25
	Thus loaded with Grief, Dick Sigh'd and he cry'd,	. .	430	Dicky Dolly	10
	Whene'er your Pride recals your Grief,	. . . . .	496	Panegyr Swift	87
	They send for Manners--; not for Grief---:	. . . .	546	Life of Swift	61
	"Whole Swarms of Sects, with grief, he saw	. . . .	550	Life of Swift	168
	"With Horror, Grief, Despair the Dean	. . . .	568	Death of Swift	391
	Twelve Cups of Tea, (with Grief I speak)	. . . .	589	Strephon Chloe	163
	The Swain at last, with Grief opprest,	. . . . .	595	Cassinus Peter	39
	And tho' she must with Grief reflect,	. . . . .	695	Cadenus Vaness	270
	Too late with Grief she understood,	. . . . . .	700	Cadenus Vaness	434
	Cadenus, to his Grief and Shame,	. . . . . .	710	Cadenus Vaness	744
	And, full of Anger, Shame, and Grief,	. . . . .	713	Cadenus Vaness	846
	With chearful Face, and inward Grief;	. . . . .	726	To Stella	102
	Grief, Sickness, Poverty, and Age;	. . . . . .	764	Stel B-day '26	32
	Wretched Ierne! with what Grief I see	. . . . .	792	St. Pat's Well	33
	Poverty, and Grief, and Care,	. . . . . .	832	Legion Club	89
	Both are welcome, Grief or Joy,	. . . . . .	933	Riddle 20	D 17
	Seem rather to renew my Grief,	. . . .	1005	Sheridan's Sub	30
GRIESLY					
	His griesly Monarch's sooty Fist,	. . . . . .	903	Death Daphne	4
GRIEV'D					
	How much the other Tree was griev'd,	. . . . .	117	Bauc & Phil 2	176
	Griev'd at the Vices of the Age,	. . . . . .	383	Manly Virtue	2
	And griev'd your righteous Soul beside,	. . . . .	496	Panegyr Swift	91
	And griev'd that a Tory should live above Ground.	. .	518	Dean Hang Rape	34
	He saw, and he was griev'd to see't,	. . . .	603	Beasts Confess	53
	I'm griev'd to hear your Banishment,	. . . . .	1002	Reply by Dean	14
GRIEVANCE					
	But here a Grievance seems to lie,	. . . . .	198	Horace 2, 6	D
	You are not so great a Grievance	. . . .	637	Epistle Lady	243
GRIEVE					
	I grieve, this Noble Work so happily begun,	. .	24	Ode Athenian	275
	'Twould grieve a Body's Heart to see't:	. .	90	Bauc & Phil 1	18
	He'll Grieve he did not raise you higher,	. . .	484	Libel on D- D-	118
	Shou'd stupid Libels grieve your Mind,	. . . .	501	Doctor Delaney	43
	"Although, we outwardly may Grieve,	. . . . .	545	Life of Swift	9
	What Poet would not grieve to see,	. . . . .	554	Death of Swift	31
	Poor Pope will grieve a Month; and Gay	. . . .	561	Death of Swift	207
	Why do we grieve that Friends should dye?	. . .	562	Death of Swift	243
	I grieve those Spirits should be spent,	. . . .	731	Stella, Poems	115
	A Truth for which thy Soul should grieve,	. . .	735	Stel B-day '20	46
	And grieve he ever left Pell-mell.	. . . . .	748	Stel Distress	74
	I grieve she ever saw the light.	. . . . .	754	Stella '23	6
	I will grieve, and hold my tongue.	. . . . .	908	Daphne	64
GRIEVES					
	If <Hort> must sink, she grieves to tell it,	. .	303	Storm	19
	For still you're short (which grieves your Spirit)	. .	475	Epist on Epist	27
GRIEVOUS					
	Now, should I own your case was grievous,	. . . . .	433	Answer Paulus	37
	And is not this a grievous burden?	. . . . . .	434	Answer Paulus	86
	Friend Rundall fell with grievous bump,	. . . . .	822	Epigr Rundle	1

		PAGE	TITLE	LINE
GRIEVOUS	(CONTINUED)			
No Work is grievous or offensive.		891	Panegyr Dean	158
GRIEVOUSLY				
Wherein she grievously complains,		713	Cadenus Vaness	858
GRIFFITH				
Went to one Griffith, formerly a play'r:		307	Billet Players	4
I am not Elrington, nor Griffith he.		307	Billet Players	10
GRIM				
And a Grim Slave to wait on his Triumphal Car.		7	Ode to King	44
Nor Chick, nor Duckling 'scapes, when Grim		153	Widow and Cat	D 14
But as his Gold he weigh'd, grim Death in spight,		234	Elegy on Demar	31
Cou'd you see his grim Grace, for a Pound to a Penny,		803	Irish Bishops	9
GRIM'D				
With Dirt, and Sweat, and Ear-Wax grim'd.		527	Lady's Dres Rm	46
GRIMACE				
Tho' by their Idiom and Grimace		652	On Poetry	361
Thy Screw'd up front; thy State Grimace;		775	Mullinix Tim	60
GRIN				
Nor shall grin Berris make up the Losse.		103	Merlin	10
How he and how we at each other should grin!		338	Serious Poem	117
And now you're out, enjoy your Grin.		493	Panegyr Swift	22
Intrude with Monkey grin, and clatter		777	Mullinix Tim	143
GRINAGIN				
Margery Grinagin.		246	Irish-Feast	48
GRINDERS				
Untouch't it pass't between his Grinders,		156	Fable of Midas	11
GRINDING				
About the grinding artick Pole;		362	Grace's Answer	34
GRINNING				
"I found you did it by your Grinning;		304	Storm	43
While he sits by a grinning,		425	Five Ladies	5
The Huntsmen seize the grinning Prize.		885	Rev Market-Hill	82
GRINS				
And <Cuffe> grins for getting, the Alicant Plate.		430	Dicky Dolly	21
GRIPING				
A griping Monarch, or a Jew.		658	On Poetry	D 164
GRISETTE				
In Lodgings like a poor Grisette.		746	Stel Distress	44
GRISETTS				
A few Grisetts		441	Ballyspellin	53
GRIST				
Must fayl if Matter brings no Grist.		228	Prog of Beauty	84
GRIZ				
You'll never think of Goody Griz.		362	Grace's Answer	44
When first of Griz, you Grafton reated		372	Letter D. S-y	14
GRIZETTE				
In Lodgings, like a poor Grizette,		751	Stel Wood-Park	59
GROAN				
The Gyants under Aetna ceas'd to groan,		9	Ode to King	96
With artful Sigh and feigned Groan,		208	Fable Bitches	14
How patiently you hear him groan!		554	Death of Swift	29
But from the Root a dismal Groan		850	Old Thorn	53
GROANING				
The groaning Chair began to crawll		93	Bauc & Phil 1	105
The Groaning Chair began to crawl		113	Bauc & Phil 2	85
You may shew him about for a new Groaning Board.		336	Serious Poem	84
GROANINGS				
Distortions, Groanings, Strainings, Heavings;		591	Strephon Chloe	241
GROANS				
Still Groans while tatling Gossips prate.		93	Bauc & Phil 1	110
Regardless of his dying Groans.		413	Desire Possess	58
Bring from his Heart sincerer Groans,		546	Life of Swift	29
GROAT				
Ragged, and not a Groat betwixt 'em.		90	Bauc & Phil 1	10
Not Rich, but ow'd no Man a Groat;		171	Horace 1, 7	34
You know I am not worth a Groat		175	Horace 1, 7	134
If I ne'er got, or lost a groat,		199	Horace 2, 6	D
In half a Minute is not worth one Groat;		234	Elegy on Demar	20
To ship a rogue, and pay him not a groat.		308	Billet Players	28
I'll hold you a Groat, when you wimble his Bumm,		336	Serious Poem	79
He would not give a Groat to save his Father from the Gallows.		342	Upon His Grace	16
My Dame is hardly worth a Groat.		409	Dial Rich Marb	30
Knows to a Groat the lowest Price;		416	Woman's Mind	28
Besides, I'll hold a Groat,		425	Five Ladies	11
Nor ever gave the Poor a Groat.		515	Answer Fable	100
For thou hast not a Groat to Attone for a <Rape>.		519	Dean Hang Rape	54
"And, Wealth he valu'd not a Groat:		567	Death of Swift	358
I'll hold you a Groat, and I wish I cou'd see't,		805	Irish Bishops	51
Who neither get, nor lose a Groat;		918	Riddle 4	14
GROATS				
For many good Groats his Tongue shall slitt:		147	Windsor Proph	10
Who held a Cabbin for ten Groats a Year;		826	Noisy Tom	12
GROGRAM				
'Twas Madam, in her Grogram Gown.		116	Bauc & Phil 2	144
GROOM				
The Groom was wisht to saddle Crop,		223	Prog of Love	35
Townshends cast Page or Walpole's groom		423	Ireld	72
"<God> <damn> me, he hobbles as bad as my Groom;		872	Grand Question	156
GROOV'D				
Each groov'd, and Dove-tail'd, like a Box.		1021	Nim-Dan-Dean 1	D 26

		PAGE	TITLE	LINE
GROPE				
Has forc't to grope her uncouth way		18	Ode Athenian	66
. . . would grope in Ignorance and Night,		22	Ode Athenian	208
The Bottom of the Pan to grope,		528	Lady's Dres Rm	93
To grope for Words, and out they come.		797	Traulus 1	52
GROSS				
How shallow! and how gross the Cheat!		29	Ode to Temple	101
Led blindly on by gross philosophy and pride,		36	Ode Sancroft	66
Such gross Delusions could not pass,		158	Fable of Midas	65
'Twixt Raillery and gross Abuse,		216	To Mr. Delany	48
No Humours gross, or frowzy Steams,		584	Strephon Chloe	11
While all the gross and filthy last.		591	Strephon Chloe	234
And only know the gross Desire;		687	Cadenus Vaness	36
'Tis your gross panegyrics alone can bespatter.		819	Archbi Cashel	14
GROSSLY				
But your fair Lines so grossly flatter,		1003	Dan J's Reply	4
GROTESQUE				
Humor is odd, grotesque, and wild,		216	To Mr. Delany	25
GROTTOS				
His grottos and seats;		856	Lady's Lament	178
GROUND SEE A-GROUND				
Search out this Utopian Ground,		26	Ode to Temple	11
In governments too easy, and too fruitful ground;		37	Ode Sancroft	97
Able to lift it from the Ground;		87	Hist V's House	30
Not fitt to live on Christian Ground,		92	Bauc & Phil 1	87
Two Acts it cost him under Ground.		108	V's House	88
Not fit to live on Christian Ground,		112	Bauc & Phil 2	47
Light with its Bottom on the Ground.		126	Little House	10
For Charms above and under Ground;.		133	Magician's Rod	36
Glitter'd like Spangles on the Ground:		156	Fable of Midas	4
Not firmly join'd to keep their Ground,		189	Faggot	19
Though still in Sight, had chang'd their Ground.		226	Prog of Beauty	32
And scorns the Ground, and upward springs,		230	Prog of Poetry	14
Redeem him from his Prison under Ground.		233	Elegy on Demar	4
A Mercy the Ground		245	Irish-Feast	39
Ran under Ground from Greece to Brittain,		293	Prog Marriage	112
And Virtue trampled on the Ground:		312	To Ford	42
You strove for ev'ry Inch of Ground;		326	Pethox	88
Now from his Lordship's Grace I hold a little Piece of Ground,		342	Upon His Grace	21
The Man above, or under Ground.		393	Modern Poets	16
And by Excursions lost his Ground:		412	Desire Possess	26
He threw them on the Ground again;		412	Desire Possess	28
To join, and drag you to the Ground.		414	Censure	10
Which you demolish'd to the Ground:		477	Epist on Epist	68
And calumny, by working under ground,		506	To a Friend	5
And griev'd that a Tory should live above Ground.		518	Dean Hang Rape	34
And, carefully observe the Ground,		592	Strephon Chloe	295
Was too good to touch the Ground:		631	Epistle Lady	38
In Garrets high, or under Ground:		651	On Poetry	316
Who pull'd a Palace to the Ground,		727	To Stella	122
With Footmen tippling under Ground,		729	Stella, Poems	44
In Saunder's Cellar on the Ground:		743	Stel B-day 22	56
With harpy Claws it undermines the Ground,		792	St. Pat's Well	61
Would needs have kept thee from the ground.		822	Epigr Rundle	6
Its Head reclining tow'rds the Ground.		849	Old Thorn	20
I'd rather the Bawn were sunk under Ground.		868	Grand Question	46
And your Ladyship curchyes half way to the Ground!		871	Grand Question	116
Provided, to improve the Ground,		875	Drapier's Hill	5
His large Dominions under Ground.		903	Death Daphne	18
And yet I firmly stand my Ground:		926	Riddle 9	8
And revive above Ground,		939	Riddle Answerd	20
Without it I rather would walk on the Ground.		941	Letter	26
The dullest Beast and a Hole in the Ground,		941	Letter	35
Or else I will not ride one Inch of Ground.		943	Probatur Alit	40
The worst Dunce in your School, 'till he's heav'd from the Ground		968	Letter Sherid	34
What he ripens above ground, he sours below it.		979	Dean to Tho: S	32
GROUNDS				
And longd to hunt upon my grounds		422	Ireld	28
By often shifting into distant Grounds;		538	Mr. Pulteney	18
Drag diff'rent Ways in miry Grounds.		645	On Poetry	176
GROUP				
On this odious Group of Fools;		839	Legion Club	224
GROUSE				
For better Game, and look for Grouse:		760	Receipt Youth	54
GROVE				
Or the much-talkt Oracular Grove		17	Ode Athenian	50
It must be some enchanted Grove,		252	Bubble	31
Who met his Mother in a grove;		460	Birthday Song	16
The Shelter of a shady Grove:		894	Panegyr Dean	246
GROVES				
My Groves, my Ecchoes, and my Birds,		411	Dial Rich Marb	91
GROW				
And at once grow Scholars and Fools;		27	Ode to Temple	44
Shall e'er long grow into a Tree,		31	Ode to Temple	168
Where nought but Weeds will grow.		33	Ode to Temple	209
By gazing upwards giddy grow,		37	Ode Sancroft	77
And grow a Church before your Eyes.		92	Bauc & Phil 1	90
And grow a Church before your Eyes.		112	Bauc & Phil 2	50
"By which wise Conduct they grow Friends		181	Horace 2, 1	47

GROW	(CONTINUED)	PAGE	TITLE	LINE
Then let us both in time grow wise,		184	Horace 2, 1	107
Soon make my Dame grow lank and spare:		230	Prog of Poetry	12
Our Wives they grow sullen		237	Excellent Song	14
Beware, nor over-bulky grow,		258	Bubble	193
And shou'd our Galls-town Wit grow fallow,		278	Journal	3
But we doubt that our Purses will quickly grow lank,		287	Bank Down	14
Yes, and a Place he will grow rich in;		300	Horrid Plot	65
"Poets till they grow hoarse may bawl		321	First of April	21
Yet Our Devotion may Grow Slack.		346	Prometheus	70
Have large proportion'd Roots that grow		393	Modern Poets	3
Your pockets grow empty,		402	Window Inns 8	D 3
And yet, grow mortify'd and vext		501	Doctor Delaney	39
Or on her Chin like Bristles grow.		527	Lady's Dres Rm	58
Will soon grow necessary to his Heirs.		535	To Mr. Gay	120
I grow the Subject of their Chat:		565	Death of Swift	302
I to laugh, and you grow wise.'		638	Epistle Lady	274
I grow less equall to the Charge:		739	Stel B-day '21	8
Does not the Body thrive and grow		765	Stel B-day '26	55
These Scriblers grow so bold of late,		783	Tim and Fables	31
But this skip of a Lawyer, Where the De'el did he grow?		814	Yahoo's	7
How deep and foul the Roads may grow,		860	Lady Acheson	19
Than strongest Weeds that grow these Stones betwixt:		880	Pastoral Dial	10
Love rooted out, again will never grow.		881	Pastoral Dial	16
And soon grow pert on Men of Sense;		887	Panegyr Dean	20
She may then grow wise for spight.		907	Daphne	38
Growing old, grow still the fairer.		936	Riddle 24	D 8
GROWING				
Dan growing drowsy like a Thief,		279	Journal	39
While Vultures eat his growing Liver:		346	Prometheus	56
From growing richer with good Cheer,		745	Stel Distress	15
From growing Riches with good Chear,		750	Stel Wood-Park	43
Growing old, grow still the fairer.		936	Riddle 24	D 8
GROWN				
Is grown so impudently Great,		10	Ode to King	120
Woman seems now above all Vanity grown,		24	Ode Athenian	250
And sick with Dregs of Knowledge grown,		27	Ode to Temple	47
We find in you at last united grown.		28	Ode to Temple	61
How is the Muse luxuriant grown.		31	Ode to Temple	142
'Tis now grown an incurable Disease:		33	Ode to Temple	205
Finding the Mitre almost grown		40	Ode Sancroft	187
Thus prostitute my Congreve's name is grown		48	To Congreve	159
Say, whence it comes that thou art grown of late		53	Temple Ill	83
By Age and Claps grown cold as Snow,		84	Salamander	58
The Chimny to a Steeple grown,		94	Bauc & Phil 1	139
Grown to a Church by just Degrees,		94	Bauc & Phil 1	154
The Chimney to a Steeple grown,		113	Bauc & Phil 2	77
Grown to a Church by just Degrees,		114	Bauc & Phil 2	108
Then said; my House is grown so Fine,		115	Bauc & Phil 2	113
'Twas a devouring Serpent grown.		132	Magician's Rod	4
But when he was grown Sleek and Fat,		153	Widow and Cat	D 3
"My Lord and he are grown so great,		202	Horace 2, 6	85
They stand amaz'd, and think me grown		202	Horace 2, 6	103
My Life is now a Burthen grown		204	In Sickness	21
A Bitch that was full pregnant grown,		207	Fable Bitches	1
Grown fat with Corn and Sitting still,		230	Prog of Poetry	3
Grown lazy, foggy, fat, and dull:		231	Prog of Poetry	22
And when the Sky is grown serene,		354	Simile Silver	31
For Satyr now's so common grown		371	Letter D. S-y	3
Your Mistress now is grown a Queen;		408	Dial Rich Marb	10
But now He's grown a King, God wot,		408	Dial Rich Marb	17
Was grown as wealthy as a Prince;		409	Dial Rich Marb	38
Possession's Load was grown so great,		413	Desire Possess	51
Dear Madam, you are grown so hard,		447	Modern Lady	86
'Tis grown the choicest Wit at Court,		468	Birthday Song	267
And grown a Minister of State,		482	Libel on D- D-	69
But I, in Politicks grown old,		485	Libel on D- D-	171
And, Chloe more experienc'd grown,		590	Strephon Chloe	213
Your Goddess grown a filthy Mate.		591	Strephon Chloe	244
And grown so bold behind his Back		605	Beasts Confess	127
Thy Labours, grown the Critick's Prey,		642	On Poetry	67
Before his downy Beard was grown!		655	On Poetry	432
To all my Friends a Burthen grown,		673	His Deafness	2
And Marriage grown a Money-League.		687	Cadenus Vaness	14
Grown so corrupted in their Taste.		688	Cadenus Vaness	66
In spight of Pallas, now were grown;		701	Cadenus Vaness	473
Grown old in Politicks and Wit;		702	Cadenus Vaness	503
What he had planted, now was grown;		708	Cadenus Vaness	680
Grown by Vanessa's Conduct wise.		712	Cadenus Vaness	831
At last grown prouder than the Devil		746	Stel Distress	23
At last grown prouder than the <Devil>,		750	Stel Wood-Park	21
But now, unable grown to write,		754	Stella '23	5
My Eyes are somewhat dimmish grown;		757	Stel B-day '24	42
Meager and lank with fasting grown,		759	Receipt Youth	7
That you are sick, and I grown old,		763	Stel B-day '26	4
Yet from an Empress, now a Captive grown,		771	Horace 1, 14	45
So thou art grown the Detestation		775	Mullinix Tim	55
My quondam Friends are grown so Cold,		776	Mullinix Tim	78
Are grown the Nuissance of your Clan,		777	Mullinix Tim	145
For Pride and Ignorance a Proverb grown,		794	St. Pat's Well	99
Who are all grown reverend Preachers!		838	Legion Club	204

GROWN   (CONTINUED)   PAGE   TITLE   LINE
    Quoth Hugh of Armagh, "The mob is grown bold."   . . .   843 Ay and No   3
    I'm grown a meer Mopus; no Company comes;   . . . . . .   867 Grand Question   27
    Familiar grown to Dirt and Wet, ...   890 Panegyr Dean   109
    By long Experience grown so wise, ...   890 Panegyr Dean   117
    She's grown so nice, and so penurious, ...   891 Panegyr Dean   143
    Was of her Beauty grown so vain, ...   905 Death Daphne   69
    Is grown a Sad Dame, ...   1014 Swift to Sheri   34
GROWS
    Giddy he grows, and down is hurl'd, ...   10 Ode to King   144
    And ev'ry stinking weed so lofty grows, ...   37 Ode Sancroft   103
    Far sooner than the nobler mushroom grows: . . . . .   46 To Congreve   100
    Grows a misfortune, or becomes a vice;   . . . . . .   55 Temple Ill   136
    Hal -- grows more Pert, and <Somers> not so Grave: . .   163 Toland's Invit   22
    Soon grows Domestick, seldom fails   . . . .   173 Horace 1, 7   77
    In Favour grows with Ministers of State;   . . . . . .   194 Author Himself   29
    Now, Delaware again familiar grows;   . . . .   196 Author Himself   67
    Yet as she wasts, she grows discreet, ...   229 Prog of Beauty   101
    And, trust me, as the noise grows stronger, ...   296 Satiric Elegy   7
    Grows neither Grass, nor Shrub, nor Tree;   . . . . .   324 Pethox   41
    Where, if we find his Liver grows, ...   347 Prometheus   75
    See how Corruption grows, ...   426 Five Ladies   29
    The bolt discharg'd, the sky grows clear;   . . . . .   617 Scandal Poem 1   12
    The Bolt discharg'd, the Sky grows clear;   . . . . .   624 Scandal Poem 2   12
    He grows a tyrant, dunce, or beast.   . . . .   658 On Poetry   D 204
    And though the Painting grows decayd   . . . . . .   734 Stel B-day '20   7
    You yearly sing as she grows old, ...   742 Stel B-day 22   39
    Grows plump and round, and full of Mettle, ...   759 Receipt Youth   17
    Grows down to my chin;   . . . .   853 Lady's Lament   74
    And then he grows mild;   . . . .   855 Lady's Lament   123
    My Love for gentle Dermot faster grows   . . . . .   881 Pastoral Dial   13
    Grows drunk with a Drop.   . . . .   939 Riddle Answerd   28
GROWTH
    And Rebel is the growth and manufacture of the Land.   .   8 Ode to King   57
    Took its first Growth and Birth   . . . .   10 Ode to King   126
    Two College Sophs of Cambridge Growth, ...   593 Cassinus Peter   1
    Look on him and see their Growth.   . . . .   799 Traulus 2   6
GRUB
    And dread no more the Rage of Grub, ...   502 Doctor Delaney   63
GRUB-STREET
    To find the Grub-Street Poet's Nest, ...   504 Doctor Delaney   144
    And, Praise bestow'd in Grub-Street Rimes, ...   505 Doctor Delaney   165
    Now Grub-Street Wits are all employ'd;   . . . . .   558 Death of Swift   165
    While from below all Grub-street rings.   . . . . .   231 Prog of Poetry   46
    Ye Pow'rs of Grub-street make me able, ...   346 Prometheus   57
GRUBSTREET
    (A Monarch's Right) on Grubstreet Line.   . . . . .   642 On Poetry   58
    The vilest Doggrel Grubstreet sends, ...   644 On Poetry   139
    Lay Grubstreet at each others Doors: . . . . . .   652 On Poetry   346
    O, Grubstreet! how do I bemoan thee, ...   652 On Poetry   357
GRUDGE
    The God of Wit to shew his Grudge.   . . . .   157 Fable of Midas   29
GRUDGING
    He spake, and grudging, lent his Ayd;   . . . . . .   108 V's House   75
GRUEL   SEE WATER-GRUEL
GRUMBLE
    And is not afraid your Worship will grumble, ...   1027 Sheri Circles   26
GRUMBLED
    Nor have you grumbled, rev'rend <Dean>, ...   892 Panegyr Dean   163
GUARD   SEE BLACK-GUARD,SABLE-GUARD,TYRANT-GUARD
    Britannia stript from her sole Guard the Laws,   . .   12 Ode to William   D 21
    Which guard the throne by night, and are its light by day: 34 Ode Sancroft   4
    See Philip's Son amidst his Persian Guard;   . . . .   275 Epilogue   24
    She left him Virtue for a Guard.   . . . .   306 Storm   78
    Would guard your Nose against a Post.   . . . . . .   367 Answer Delaney   48
    And now advancing to the Guard, ...   376 Apology Lady C   30
    Of Innocence, the surest Guard, ...   386 Manly Virtue   73
    Ye Muses guard your sacred Mount, ...   671 Epig Carthy 21   D 5
    On either Side his Honour's Guard: . . . . . .   883 Rev Market-Hill   12
    The <Dean>, to guard his Honour's Back, ...   883 Rev Market-Hill   13
GUARDED
    Guarded each fair Hesperian Pippin.   . . . .   134 Magician's Rod   74
GUARDIAN
    To which they look as to some Guardian God   . . . .   12 Ode to William   D 31
    But Pallas, guardian of the Maid, ...   177 To Lord Harley   43
    Of Guardian Eunuchs to the Sultan Dames, ...   532 To Mr. Gay   20
    Like Phoebus, guardian of the hours: . . . . . .   937 Riddle 24   D 34
GUARDS
    The Law so strictly guards the Monarch's Health,   . .   533 To Mr. Gay   77
    Fine as a Col'nel of the Guards, ...   904 Death Daphne   55
    Like the Bow that guards the Tartar, ...   927 Riddle 10   D 4
GUARDSHIP
    Under whose wise and careful Guardship, ...   890 Panegyr Dean   107
GUDGEON
    In short, the Gudgeon took the Bait: . . . . . .   173 Horace 1, 7   80
    You quickly see the gudgeon bite, ...   421 Ireld   23
    Thus, if a Gudgeon meet a Roach   . . . . . .   824 Printer Newgat   11
GUDGEONS
    And many Score of Gudgeons took;   . . . .   133 Magician's Rod   46
GUELPH
    And Guelph the strongest ear will wound.   . . . . .   467 Birthday Song   216

		PAGE	TITLE	LINE
<GUERNSEY>				
If <Guernsey> calls, send word you're gone abroad;		166	Toland's Invit	41
GUESS				
Methinks I'm satisfied to guess		20	Ode Athenian	135
How then, dear Harley, could I guess		177	To Lord Harley	23
Guess how could such a Match be broke.		223	Prog of Love	24
For Jove, it is not hard to guess him,		346	Prometheus	61
What's meant by Chapoon I can't guess		373	Letter D. S-y	57
I guess the Hand, it seldom fails,		453	Modern Lady	268
And Strephon bids us guess the rest;		526	Lady's Dres Rm	16
Nor found it difficult to guess the Cause:		536	To Mr. Gay	158
The Merit of a lucky Guess,		557	Death of Swift	122
Nor give the smallest Room to guess		588	Strephon Chloe	139
Nor can Imagination guess,		595	Cassinus Peter	55
Some Faults we own: But, can you guess?		603	Beasts Confess	75
But, can you guess from womens air		619	Scandal Poem 1	49
But, can you guess from Woman's Air,		625	Scandal Poem 2	45
Her kindness who could ever guess,		755	Stella '23	27
What's next to be voted with ease you may guess.		816	Yahoo's	34
I guess well enough		854	Lady's Lament	107
Which I must leave the world to guess.		879	Robbin & Harry	54
GUESS'D				
The Rev'rend Dr. Raymond guess'd,		128	Little House	43
And presently guess'd that the Fancy was mine;		264	Apollo	52
And what they cost? Vanessa guess'd,		698	Cadenus Vaness	381
Yet guess'd not whence could spring the Change.		704	Cadenus Vaness	567
GUESS'T				
We guess't the <Bishop's> Foot was in it.		300	Horrid Plot	70
GUESSER				
Whom would'st thou resemble? I leave thee a Guesser;		518	Dean Hang Rape	46
GUESSES				
Why so sagacious in your guesses?		487	Irish-Club	11
GUESST				
The Cause, alas, is quickly guesst,		293	Prog Marriage	101
GUEST				
Well, 'tis as Bickerstaff has guest,		98	Elegy Patrige	1
And Guest his Business e're he Spoke.		120	Apollo Outwit	16
And down to Windsor takes his Guest.		173	Horace 1, 7	82
The Guest reply'd,--"My Friend, your Leave,		208	Fable Bitches	31
For well he knew, to such a Guest,		378	Apology Lady C	103
She sits tormenting every Guest,		448	Modern Lady	110
Give no more to ev'ry Guest,		633	Epistle Lady	125
Love, hitherto a transient Guest,		711	Cadenus Vaness	768
I ne'er admitted Love a Guest.		728	Stella, Poems	14
But Madam, I guest there wou'd never come Good,		868	Grand Question	47
If I had expected so worthy a Guest:--		871	Grand Question	123
And, what may serve a common Guest.		889	Panegyr Dean	96
And ev'ry Guest be sure to ply:		897	Panegyr Dean	338
GUESTS				
To a Room full of Guests for fear of a <Rape>.		517	Dean Hang Rape	12
The Guests in less than half an Hour		642	On Poetry	63
His guests are few, his visits rare,		901	Dean's Reasons	85
GUIDE				
For, sure, we want some guide from Heav'n to show		39	Ode Sancroft	156
Each fond of erring with his guide:		39	Ode Sancroft	165
The Pilot knew not how to guide.		96	On the Union	20
In Leading strings her Infant-Steps to guide;		531	To Mr. Gay	11
You follow where we please to guide:		620	Scandal Poem 1	89
You follow where we please to guide;		626	Scandal Poem 2	87
Switches better guide than Cudgels.		636	Epistle Lady	202
By her, as an unerring Guide.		694	Cadenus Vaness	239
That Reason was her Guide in Love.		708	Cadenus Vaness	677
And guide you to a better State.		766	Stel B-day '26	78
Lost are the Oars that us'd thy Course to guide,		770	Horace 1, 14	13
Or, for the Classicks read th' Attorney's Guide;		793	St. Pat's Well	77
Fill ev'ry Pipe, each Motion guide.		798	Traulus 1	74
GUIDED SEE ILL-GUIDED				
The limbs are guided by the brain,		761	Bec's B-Day	20
GUIDES				
Two foolish guides in ev'ry sublunary dance:		34	Ode Sancroft	9
Your guides to true Simplicity.		270	Apollo's Edict	D 32
So steadily the Senate guides:		391	Young's Satire	6
GUILE				
Not by thy Valour, but superior Guile:		791	St. Pat's Well	26
Hence he learnt the Butcher's Guile,		800	Traulus 2	37
Teach Dennis how to stir the Guile:		897	Panegyr Dean	330
GUILT				
"Know no base action, at no guilt turn pale;		55	Temple Ill	142
With equal Terrors, not with equal Guilt,		364	On Dreams	13
He knows no guilt, who knows no sin.		434	Answer Paulus	58
Of modern Times, the Guilt is yours,		445	Modern Lady	32
And Silvia full of inward Guilt,		450	Modern Lady	172
Thus was the Hare pursu'd, tho' free from Guilt;		538	Mr. Pulteney	37
Too neatly guilt for me to soil.		611	By Dr. Swift	2
Both Sexes, arm'd with Guilt and Spite,		700	Cadenus Vaness	438
Shame, Disappointment, Guilt, Surprize.		706	Cadenus Vaness	625
His Guilt is clear the Proofs are pregnant,		798	Traulus 1	93
Fraud, Perjury, and Guilt are seen.		922	Riddle 7	22
And yet her Wealth was all her Guilt.		923	Riddle 7	66
GUILTY				
If he be Guilty, you must mend him,		219	To Mr. Delany	111

GUILTY   (CONTINUED)   PAGE   TITLE   LINE
    You must be guilty of the Plot, ...   312 To Ford   32
    Bedaubs the guilty Great with nauseous Praise: . .   364 On Dreams   36
    Oppression hides, with guilty Dread, ...   387 Manly Virtue   123
    "So, to destroy a guilty Land, ...   485 Libel on D- D-   165
    And guilty Shame, and servile Fear, ...   725 To Stella   48
    Who could forbear, that view'd each guilty Face,   . . .   806 Judas   23
GUINEA
    And here is a Guinea to drink.   . . . .   396 Dog and Thief   12
    Said the Freeman, your Guinea To-night would be spent,   396 Dog and Thief   13
    A Guinea shall reward your pains.   . . . .   463 Birthday Song   94
    And take a Guinea for your Fee. . . . .   469 Birthday Song   282
    To lose a Guinea at Picquet, ...   546 Life of Swift   27
GUINEAS
    A score of guineas, given under-hand, ...   308 Billet Players   23
    Come with a Purse of Guineas in your Hands. . . . .   534 To Mr. Gay   100
    Five thousand Guineas in her Purse?   . . . . . .   707 Cadenus Vaness   654
    Should slip your Time of dropping Guineas;   . . . .   821 Dr. Rundle   64
GUINNEA
    And seems a Guinnea to your View: . . . . . .   255 Bubble   116
    But as a Guinnea will not pass   . . . .   255 Bubble   117
    Your Guinnea's but a Guinnea still.   . . . . . .   255 Bubble   124
    Should pay a guinnea in the pound   . . . .   423 Ireld   68
GUINNEA'S
    Your Guinnea's but a Guinnea still.   . . . . . .   255 Bubble   124
GUINNEAS
    The Golden Stars for Guinneas took, ...   255 Bubble   127
GUISE
    Indifference clad in Wisdom's Guise, ...   561 Death of Swift   213
GULLET
    I keep my Gullet for the Halter.   . . . .   349 Upright Judge 1   4
GULLIVER
    Make Gulliver his Commodore, ...   466 Birthday Song   206
    For Gulliver divinely shews, ...   498 Panegyr Swift   167
GULPH
    A mighty gulph unpassable betwixt.   . . . .   44 To Congreve   32
    Why in yon dang'rous Gulph profound   . . . . .   252 Bubble   50
    There is a Gulph where thousands fell, ...   256 Bubble   137
    He tumbled in the Gulph profound;   . . . . . .   413 Desire Possess   49
    With Heads to Points the Gulph they enter, ...   654 On Poetry   401
    This Gulph insatiable imbibes   . . . .   922 Riddle 7   19
    In at this Gulph all Off'rings pass, ...   922 Riddle 7   43
GUMMY
    Crackt Lips, foul Teeth, and gummy Eyes, ...   226 Prog of Beauty   15
GUMS
    Both stroke her Hands, and rub her Gums, ...   150 Corinna   7
    The Scrapings of her Teeth and Gums, ...   527 Lady's Dres Rm   40
    Untwists a Wire; and from her Gums   . . . . .   582 Young Nymph   19
    Could rub my own gums, ...   852 Lady's Lament   20
GUN   SEE POT-GUN
    For, as when we a Gun discharge, ...   66 Problem   43
    For, as sure as a Gun they will give up the Ghost   .   351 Wood Insect   23
    . . .and you'll believe me as sure as a gun, and own it; . 1023 Nim-Dan-Dean 2 D 15
GUNS
    But e'er since Men invented Guns, ...   83 Salamander   15
    Guns, Trumpets, Drums, and Bells were drown'd.   . . .   338 Wood's Brass   8
GUST
    And wafted with its Foe by violent Gust, ...   137 City Shower   25
    Nor, change thy Course with ev'ry sudden Gust: . . .   771 Horace 1, 14   54
GUT
    Once on a Time, was an <Arse> Gut, ...   66 Problem   23
GUTS
    Sweepings from Butchers Stalls, Dung, Guts, and Blood   139 City Shower   61
    His Guts and Belly full of Wind;   . . . .   231 Prog of Poetry   38
    What Strokes on Guts, ...   246 Irish-Feast   67
    The Words in Wood's Mouth, or speaks from his Guts: .   335 Serious Poem   62
    Tom gave him a Kick in the Guts for his Fee.   .   399 Tom Clinch   14
    And leave us nought but Guts and Garbage, ...   498 Panegyr Swift   152
    Stuff his Guts with Flax and Grass;   . . . . .   831 Legion Club   64
    I almost wisht this Spud were in your Guts. . . . .   882 Pastoral Dial   40
GUTT'RALL
    Hard, tough, cramp, gutt'rall, harsh, stiff Names.   . .   467 Birthday Song   210
GUTTER
    For this, or that Side of a Gutter, ...   314 To Ford   96
    Dick nimbly skip the Gutter;   . . . .   784 Mullinex Dick   22
GUZZLING
    Forbid your Daughters guzzling Beer;   . . . . . .   587 Strephon Chloe   116
GYANT
    It shew'd the Visage of a Gyant.   . . . .   527 Lady's Dres Rm   62
GYANTS
    The Gyants under Aetna ceas'd to groan, ...   9 Ode to King   96
    Looking big as any Gyants, ...   573 Helter Skelter   3
GYPSEY
    The Gypsey Visage to conceal: . . . .   786 Dick, Maggot   10
H
    "You spoke a Word began with H, ...   452 Modern Lady   254
H'
    But H' thinks upon Jack How.   . . . .   74 Game Traffick   8
H'AS
    H'as drop'd, and giv'n the Crow a Pudden!   . . . . .   547 Life of Swift   71

	PAGE	TITLE	LINE
HA'			
"Where most true Sons of Phoebus ha' bin.	320	First of April	4
And said, "His Worship might ha' told us, ...	322	First of April	45
HA'D			
Panting - - - and faultring - - - Humm'd and Ha'd, . .	377	Apology Lady C	79
HA'PENCE			
To turn a Good Penny to Twenty Bad Ha'pence. . . .	335	Serious Poem	48
To spare the Folks that gave him Ha'pence	796	Traulus 1	28
HA'PENNY			
My twelve Thirteens and Six-pence ha'penny.	1033	Ans to Crown	8
HABIT			
Lay by your White Staff & gray Habit, ...	187	Scriblerus 4	D 15
According to my usuall habit, ...	311	To Ford	6
Adapt your Habit to your Phiz.	779	Mullinix Tim	212
HABITATION			
His Habitation let all Men forsake, ...	806	Judas	25
HABITS SEE MOCK-HABITS			
Disguis'd in tatter'd Habits, went	111	Bauc & Phil 2	9
HABITUDES			
In all the Habitudes of Life, ...	728	Stella, Poems	15
HACK			
"To hack my hallow'd Timber down;	851	Old Thorn	84
HACKNEY			
Then order Squash to call a Hackney Chair.	166	Toland's Invit	46
HACKNEY-COACH			
Now hardly here and there an Hackney-Coach	124	Descriptn Morn	1
HACKNY			
In reading your Letter alone in my Hackny, ...	972	S-'s Ans Sh-d	1
HAD 286		OMITTED WORD	
HADST 2		OMITTED WORD	
HAEC			
Haec olim meminisse juvabit.	187	Scriblerus 4	D 18
One Grave now contains them both Haec et Hic. . . .	430	Dicky Dolly	15
Pudet haec opprobria, I freely must tell ye, . . .	967	Letter Sherid	5
HAG			
So to Her Midnight Feasts the Hag, ...	132	Magician's Rod	15
The Cloud, and drive the Hag to Hell:	354	Simile Silver	12
As ridden by a midnight hag:	434	Answer Paulus	76
By an <old> <redhair'd> <murd'ring> <Hag> pursu'd, . .	193	Author Himself	1
HAGGARD			
Such haggard lines as these	429	Beau's Reply	14
HAGS			
Conceive the Works of Midnight Hags, ...	240	Run Bankers	29
Hath joyn'd with himself two Hags in Commission: . .	336	Serious Poem	68
HAIL			
Hail Queen of Britain, Queen of Rhymes, ...	467	Birthday Song	221
Hail! happy Pope, whose gen'rous Mind, ...	482	Libel on D- D-	71
With Sun-shine, rain, and hail, and snow.	621	Scandal Poem 1	130
With Sun-shine, Rain, and Hail, or Snow.	627	Scandal Poem 2	124
Hail fellow, well met, ...	856	Lady's Lament	165
HAIR			
To keep the Hair out of their Eyes;	98	Elegy Patrige	24
Her Braided Hair to make thee Ends;	100	Elegy Patrige	80
To make her Hair look black as Jet, ...	226	Prog of Beauty	18
As glorious as Belinda's Hair?	271	Apollo's Edict	D 30
Pinning on Coifs and combing Hair;	321	First of April	30
They rival Venus to a Hair;	445	Modern Lady	10
Whispers that Sappho's Hair is Red:	450	Modern Lady	169
This Badge of Honour in his Hair, ...	458	Paddy's Charac	20
Sweat, Dandriff, Powder, Lead and Hair;	526	Lady's Dres Rm	24
Takes off her artificial Hair:	581	Young Nymph	10
And, faultless to a single Hair.	584	Strephon Chloe	6
But, well embrown'd with Dirt and Hair.	594	Cassinus Peter	18
Sindges Hair, but breaks no Pates.	638	Epistle Lady	256
They'll teach you how to split a Hair, ...	657	On Poetry	485
Your Block will fit it to a hair.	780	Mullinix Tim	220
You judge so nicely to a Hair, ...	890	Panegyr Dean	115
I sometimes live in House of Hair, ...	912	Aenigma	9
Your House of Hair and Lady's Hand	912	Aenigma Expl	D 1
My Skin he flay'd, my Hair he cropt;	915	Riddle 1	11
And a Hair can disarm	939	Riddle Answerd	31
HAIR-LACE			
And but neglects to warm her Hair-Lace, ...	417	Woman's Mind	44
HAIRS			
Or Hairs that sink the Forehead low, ...	527	Lady's Dres Rm	57
HAIRY			
His prickled Beard, and hairy Breast!	586	Strephon Chloe	92
Your hairy Business is a Muff.	912	Aenigma Expl	D 4
HAL			
Hal -- grows more Pert, and <Somers> not so Grave: .	163	Toland's Invit	22
And strutting Hal-- is off the Hooks;	168	Peace Dunkirk	14
HALCYON			
Pray not a word of Halcyon Days.	271	Apollo's Edict	D 45
And golden Times, and Halcyon days, ...	466	Birthday Song	196
HALE			
"Last Year we thought him strong and hale;	557	Death of Swift	112
HALF			
And half Your Virtues had been lost in Shade. . .	11	Ode to William	D 12
That looks with scorn on half mankind beside; . . .	44	To Congreve	44
Serves by retail to furnish half mankind.	45	To Congreve	54
(Item, for half a Yard of Lace.)	60	Lady Tablebook	16

	PAGE	TITLE	LINE
The greater half I had to say,	80	Vanbrug House	56
The Master Bawl'd out half asleep	90	Bauc & Phil 1	27
The better Half we had to say;	106	V's House	30
And Brickdust Moll had Scream'd through half the Street.	124	Descriptn Morn	14
In half an Hour thou'lt make another.	128	Little House	60
Marries for Love, half Whore, half Wife;	150	Corinna	26
Marries for Love, half Whore, half Wife;	150	Corinna	26
Nor could have borne it half so long.	160	Atlas	14
"From whence, with half an Eye we may discover,	195	Author Himself	45
And, in <Swift's> Ear thrusts half his powder'd Nose.	196	Author Himself	68
A Terras Walk, and half a Rood	198	Horace 2, 6	5
And half the Company is teazd	217	To Mr. Delany	75
In half a Month she looks so thin	229	Prog of Beauty	98
He that cou'd once have half a Kingdom bought,	234	Elegy on Demar	19
In half a Minute is not worth one Groat;	234	Elegy on Demar	20
Will think his better Half alive.	235	Elegy on Demar	52
Not reckoning half an hour we pass,	279	Journal	37
This Grand Event half broke our Measures,	283	Journal	119
George is half scar'd out of his Wits,	283	Journal	125
But showed no more than half her Face	290	Prog Marriage	16
Half wither'd by a Winters keeping	290	Prog Marriage	26
Computes, that half a Parish Dues	292	Prog Marriage	69
But half in Earnest, half in Jest;	303	Storm	26
But half in Earnest, half in Jest;	303	Storm	26
With whom you toasted half the Night,	311	To Ford	24
Will half supply a Gay and Pope,	313	To Ford	74
And hardly hear of half a Score.	315	To Ford	108
With half a Word, when you require,	325	Pethox	47
So sometimes half a Face produce,	326	Pethox	83
Keep t' other Half for private Use.	326	Pethox	84
Out-number'd, half encompass'd round,	326	Pethox	87
In half a Walk fatigu'd to Death.	379	Apology Lady C	128
What Land was ever half so blest?	391	Young's Satire	12
What Land was ever half so curst?	392	Young's Satire	48
Half choak'd with dust, half drown'd with rains;	403	Window Inns 10	D 6
Half choak'd with dust, half drown'd with rains;	403	Window Inns 10	D 6
And justly half the Merit claim'd	406	Swift to Pope	27
But, half the Words pronouncing wrong;	416	Woman's Mind	10
Half sunk beneath his brief and bag,	434	Answer Paulus	75
Talks half a Day in Praise of Silence;	450	Modern Lady	171
To half the world a standing jest,	455	Dean Smedley	11
Not long enough to reach half round,	458	Paddy's Charac	16
Old Phoebus is but half as bright,	462	Birthday Song	65
This will not give them half the trouble	469	Birthday Song	273
And one poor Office, half his Days;	481	Libel on D- D-	34
I know a shorter way by half.	487	Irish-Club	14
My Work and me in half an Hour.	502	Doctor Delaney	70
Nor, with your Kindred half the Palace crowd.	533	To Mr. Gay	58
Nor, when a Mortgage lies on half his Lands,	534	To Mr. Gay	99
Can half the Peerage by his Arts bewitch;	535	To Mr. Gay	103
Yet still I fear your Work is done but Half;	538	Mr. Pulteney	13
He left his Scut behind, and Half an Ear.	538	Mr. Pulteney	36
Thou art not half so nimble as a Hare;	539	Mr. Pulteney	40
In half the Time, he talks them round;	556	Death of Swift	97
"The News thro' half the Town has run.	558	Death of Swift	152
She saves Half her Victuals, by feeding your Ears.	580	Psyche	14
Half eat, and dragg'd it to his Hole.	583	Young Nymph	60
You but o'er half the World can reign.	585	Strephon Chloe	32
And half unsmoakt, lay by his Side,	594	Cassinus Peter	24
His Ears are half a Foot too short;	602	Beasts Confess	32
To affect me half an Hour;	636	Epistle Lady	192
The Guests in less than half an Hour	642	On Poetry	63
Will more than half a Score devour.	642	On Poetry	64
The Tender Embryos half unknown decay,	667	Epig Carthy 5	D 4
Half of my Book at least is good.	669	Epig Carthy 15	D 2
Within an hour, and eke a half,	675	Curate's Compl	9
The Graces half asham'd look'd down;	689	Cadenus Vaness	100
Their Work was half already done,	692	Cadenus Vaness	174
Nam'd half the Rates, and lik'd the worst.	698	Cadenus Vaness	383
Of half Mankind the Dread and Hate.	702	Cadenus Vaness	505
With half the Lustre of Your Eyes,	722	Stel B-Day '18	13
With half thy Wit, thy Years and Size:	722	Stel B-Day '18	14
You'd leave her Virtues half untold.	742	Stel B-day 22	40
To half a Joynt, & God be thanked:	745	Stel Distress	12
He entertain'd her half a year	745	Stel Distress	3
In half a week the Dame grew nice,	745	Stel Distress	9
And half the Chairs with broken backs.	746	Stel Distress	38
Two Bottles call'd for, (half her Store,	747	Stel Distress	49
He entertain'd her half a Year	749	Stel Wood-Park	3
In half a Week the Dame grew nice,	749	Stel Wood-Park	7
To half a Joint, and God be thank it:	750	Stel Wood-Park	36
To half a Pint one Day in twenty.	750	Stel Wood-Park	38
And half the Chairs with broken Backs:	751	Stel Wood-Park	56
Two Bottles call'd for, (half her Store;	751	Stel Wood-Park	65
That half your Locks are turn'd to Grey;	757	Stel B-Day '24	39
I'd rather hang my self by half,	778	Mullinix Tim	177
No other Monkey half so brisk;	788	Dick's Variety	26
Not half thy Course of Misery is run,	793	St. Pat's Well	87
Tho' Half a Crown o'er-pays his Sweat's Worth;	812	Bro Protestant	26

		PAGE	TITLE	LINE
HALF	(CONTINUED)			
Half the Globe from Sense and Knowledge.		829	Legion Club	4
Shift the Scene for half an Hour,		832	Legion Club	77
Tipping him with Half a Crown;		834	Legion Club	134
Half encompass'd by his Kin:		836	Legion Club	162
Half convert me to a Stone.		838	Legion Club	196
Half the best are still behind:		839	Legion Club	236
But meets it half way;		853	Lady's Lament	76
She has got but half a Face;		862	To Janus	5
Give her half thy Face behind.		862	To Janus	8
In Poundage and Drawbacks, I lose half my Rent,		867	Grand Question	21
For all the World, Captain, not half an Inch farther--		869	Grand Question	79
And your Ladyship curchyes half way to the Ground!		871	Grand Question	116
And thou, my dear, shalt have the bigger half.		881	Pastoral Dial	32
Palladio was not half so skill'd in		893	Panegyr Dean	199
Supporting half the British Crown;		919	Riddle 5	6
As half asham'd, and half afraid,		922	Riddle 7	34
As half asham'd, and half afraid,		922	Riddle 7	34
They bloom in less than half an Hour:		926	Riddle 9	4
Then the Half, and then the Whole,		927	Riddle 10	D 5
With half an Eye		938	Riddle Answerd	1
Strengthens the Shoes of half the Rabble.		942	Probatur Alit	12
As rude as a bear, no mule half so crabbed;		955	Portrait Life	5
A sieve keeps half in, and therefore, no doubt,		976	Dean to Sherid	25
'Cause I call Dan my better half,		1004	Dan J's Reply	26
HALF-NOTHING				
On their tythes at half-nothing, their priesthood at less:		816	Yahoo's	33
HALF-P'ORTH				
A longer half-p'orth never did I see;		881	Pastoral Dial	27
HALL SEE BLACK-HALL				
As thro' the Hall thy Worship paces:		182	Horace 2, 1	76
At Pluto's Hall, his Court to pay:		903	Death Daphne	2
By Proserpine, at Pluto's Hall?		905	Death Daphne	84
HALLOO				
At the Parsons, Tom, Halloo Boy,		831	Legion Club	67
HALLOOING				
Hallooing the Dean.		852	Lady's Lament	10
HALLOW'D				
"To hack my hallow'd Timber down;		851	Old Thorn	84
Ye who frequent this hallow'd Scene,		893	Panegyr Dean	217
HALT				
Would halt behind him, were it bigger.		398	Earl of P-b-w	27
HALTER				
I keep my Gullet for the Halter.		349	Upright Judge 1	4
And yet she would raise me I know,--by a halter		664	Epigram Bust	4
Whose Master, Moore, preserv'd him from the Halter,		826	Noisy Tom	13
HALVES				
To spoil his work, and work by halves:		902	Dean's Reasons	110
HAMBDEN				
A Fig for Lechmere, King, and Hambden.		191	Faggot	48
HAMET				
Our great Magician, Hamet Sid,		132	Magician's Rod	5
HAMILTON'S				
This Hamilton's Bawn, while it sticks on my Hand,		866	Grand Question	3
At Hamilton's Bawn, and the Troop is arriv'd.		869	Grand Question	68
HAMMOND				
And this must pass for reading Hammond:		280	Journal	41
HAMMS				
Here a Dog dancing on his Hamms		123	Empty'ng Town	13
<HAMPDEN>				
Will come; and <Hampden> shall have <Walpole's> Place.		165	Toland's Invit	34
HAMPER				
Now to this hamper I invite you,		753	Gift for Bec	13
HAMPERS				
What Hampers full of bleeding Hearts!		585	Strephon Chloe	36
HAMPTON-COURT				
As fine as Hampton-court at least.		314	To Ford	90
HAMS				
Squat on her Hams, to make Maid's Water.		584	Strephon Chloe	18
HANCOCK				
Will Hancock declares you are out of your compass,		1027	Sheri Circles	21
HAND SEE UNDER-HAND, SECOND-HAND				
And spare the Labour of Your Conquering Hand.		13	Ode to William	D 40
When some rough hand breaks the assembling-glass.		45	To Congreve	64
Trembling beheld the doubtful hand of fate;		52	Temple Ill	42
When he found a new Help from Invisible Hand.		77	Lady B- B-	25
You may know by the Hand, it had no Cloven Foot.		77	Lady B- B-	30
And busy both with Hand and Eye		86	Hist V's House	5
(As being Bricks at Second Hand,)		108	V's House	77
Give me that House in my own Hand;		128	Little House	49
While Moses held it in his Hand,		132	Magician's Rod	2
Desires some Friend to lend a Hand		160	Atlas	8
The best Mechanick Hand must fayl		228	Prog of Beauty	79
And under Hand and Seal the Irish Nation		234	Elegy on Demar	17
The Hand that sign'd the Mortgage paid the Shot.		234	Elegy on Demar	28
From his own Hand foresees his Fall,		241	Run Bankers	50
Your Hand alone from Gold abstains,		243	Horace 4, 9	13
By my Hand, you dance rarely,		246	Irish Feast	47
Making by second hand their Offers,		253	Bubble	70
Unerring Heav'n, with bounteous Hand,		272	Apollo's Edict	D 64
Cut off your Hand, and you may do		366	Answer Delaney	23

363

HAND (CONTINUED)

		PAGE	TITLE		LINE
With t' other Hand the Work of two:		366	Answer Delaney		24
How that can be, when you at hand are,		372	Letter D. S-y		42
And surely Writes with slight of Hand		373	Letter D. S-y		48
The mortal force of Time's dystructive hand		419	Shall Repine		2
When my Ld shakes him by the hand		421	Ireld		20
With equal balance in her hand,		433	Answer Paulus		32
A Matadore is in her Hand.		452	Modern Lady		261
I guess the Hand, it seldom fails,		453	Modern Lady		268
With Bridegroom liquids hand in hand,		467	Birthday Song		230
With Bridegroom liquids hand in hand,		467	Birthday Song		230
Which with unsparing Hand, he strows		486	Libel on D- D-		189
With each a Libel in his Hand.		505	Doctor Delaney		152
You want a Hand to clear a filthy Sink;		535	To Mr. Gay		127
Affect to take the upper hand,		546	Life of Swift		34
"But, ev'ry Hand may justly slay.		548	Life of Swift		127
Up goes her Hand, and off she slips		582	Young Nymph		27
Walk Hand in Hand, and Side by Side;		585	Strephon Chloe		58
Walk Hand in Hand, and Side by Side;		585	Strephon Chloe		58
His Hand, his Neck, his Mouth, and Feet		586	Strephon Chloe		77
Steals out her Hand by Nature led,		589	Strephon Chloe		171
He boldly sent his Hand in quest,		589	Strephon Chloe		188
A Whip of Scorpions in her Hand.		596	Cassinus Peter		82
Or Prologue sent from Hand unknown.		643	On Poetry		84
Go try your Hand a second Time.		645	On Poetry		146
Dread from his Hand impending Changes.		655	On Poetry		422
But who can bear the Death's-Head in his Hand?		669	Epig Carthy 16	D	4
With eager hand he grasps the treacherous prey,		672	Epig Carthy 24	D	15
With zeal in heart, and notes in hand;		675	Curate's Compl		2
And on the Right Hand took their Places		689	Cadenus Vaness		95
With open Heart and bounteous Hand;		693	Cadenus Vaness		210
And while the Book was in her Hand,		702	Cadenus Vaness		514
I bless the Hand from whence they came,		727	To Stella		115
And to your Failing set your Hand?		732	Stella, Poems		140
And he and I were Hand in Glove.		741	Stel B-day 22		26
With an old Poker in her Hand;		743	Stel B-day 22		54
Your skilful Hand employ'd to save		764	Stel B-day '26		37
By Faith and Prayer, this Crosier in my Hand,		792	St. Pat's Well		39
Soon shall thy Sons, the Time is just at Hand,		793	St. Pat's Well		89
Since God had no Hand in his Lordship's Promotion.		809	Epigr Prelate		6
Cuts down with sacrilegious Hand.		849	Old Thorn		24
This Hamilton's Bawn, while it sticks on my Hand,		866	Grand Question		3
With the fine flaming Sword that he holds in his Hand;		870	Grand Question		96
Because he has never a Hand that is idle;		870	Grand Question		107
"I wish she wou'd lend you her pretty white Hand,		872	Grand Question		149
But, with his Hand, the <Dean> can churn it.		892	Panegyr Dean		174
Both hand in hand together jogging;		900	Dean's Reasons		58
Both hand in hand together jogging;		900	Dean's Reasons		58
Upon thy Hand his Finger laid;		905	Death Daphne		94
Thy Hand as dry and cold as Lead,		905	Death Daphne		95
And oft in Hand of Lady Fair;		912	Aenigma		10
Your House of Hair and Lady's Hand		912	Aenigma Expl	D	1
And often takes me by the Hand.		921	Riddle 6		30
E'er join'd such Numbers Hand in Hand;		926	Riddle 9		12
E'er join'd such Numbers Hand in Hand;		926	Riddle 9		12
. . .if I could write written hand,		987	Mary to Sher		37
For the cord of your circle is now in their hand;		1027	Sheri Circles		16

HAND-MAID

Now, enter as the Dairy Hand-maid:		892	Panegyr Dean		167

HANDFULLS

With that he draws two Handfulls out,		63	Discovery		37

HANDKERCHIEFS

Nor be the Handkerchiefs forgot		527	Lady's Dres Rm		49
And all his Handkerchiefs are rotten;		875	Drapier's Hill		16

HANDLE

I'd teach her how to handle Sticks:		220	A Quiet Life		30
To leave one handle for Detraction.		608	Know Not What		8
And just as I handle 'em		852	Lady's Lament		29
Which all may handle, none can flatter.		993	On Picture		18

HANDLED

Your Usher's Post must next be handled:		890	Panegyr Dean		105

HANDLING

You are no Text for my Handling, so take that from me:		72	Mrs Harris Pet		57

HANDS

With Lightning in his Eyes, and Thunder in his Hands;		7	Ode to King		50
More oft in Fools and Mad-mens hands than Sages		23	Ode Athenian		220
It lost some mighty Pieces thro' all hands it past		25	Ode Athenian		286
That tho' 'tis hard to judge, yet Money can't go without Hands.		71	Mrs Harris Pet		43
Then curious Hands this Texture take,		79	Vanbrug House		33
And School-Boys lag with Satchels in their Hands.		125	Descriptn Morn		18
Both stroke her Hands, and rub her Gums,		150	Corinna		7
Whene'er he chanc'd his Hands to lay,		156	Fable of Midas		15
And now the Virtue of his Hands,		157	Fable of Midas		33
There's nothing fouls the Hands so much:		158	Fable of Midas		68
With Asses Ears, and dirty Hands.		158	Fable of Midas		82
How, by Brave Hands, the Royal Traytor fell;		162	Toland's Invit		10
Were much too strong for all their Hands.		189	Faggot		8
With both his Hands to bend a Twig;		191	Faggot		50
The Workmanship of their own Hands.		227	Prog of Beauty		52
When Other Hands the Scales shall hold,		241	Run Bankers		61

HANDS   (CONTINUED)   PAGE   TITLE   LINE
  Here in the Deep to wash their Hands, ... 255 Bubble   110
  And then all hands, Boys, to the Oar   . . . . . 279 Journal   18
  With Informations in his Hands, ... 312 To Ford   44
  And seems all Feet, and Hands, and Eyes.   . . . . . 322 First of April   38
  And while his Fate is in thy Hands, ... 325 Pethox   51
  And, as for Hands, there have been those, ... 367 Answer Delaney   51
  A Crown and Scepter in her Hands;   . . . . . 413 Desire Possess   42
  Each twenty visits on her Hands.   . . . . 451 Modern Lady   197
  Can turn their Hands to ev'ry Jobb, ... 503 Doctor Delaney   89
  Fowl'd with the Scouring of her Hands;   . . . . . 526 Lady's Dres Rm   38
  And fowl his Hands in Search of Hope.   . . . . . 528 Lady's Dres Rm   94
  Come with a Purse of Guineas in your Hands. . . . .   534 To Mr. Gay   100
  Her Milk-white Hands, both Palms and Backs, ... 584 Strephon Chloe   25
  Her Hands the softest ever felt, ... 585 Strephon Chloe   27
  Tho' Peace with Olive bind his Hands, ... 655 On Poetry   419
  With Cordials in her Hands, and Eyes.   . . . . . 727 To Stella   110
  As fine as Dawbers Hands can make it   . . . . . 734 Stel B-day '20   11
  Who drives her cares to hands and feet: . . . . . 761 Bec's B-Day   18
  Her hands and feet conduct her head, ... 761 Bec's B-Day   22
  Her hands may meddle, feet may wander, ... 761 Bec's B-Day   25
  Some whose reforming Hands engage, ... 781 Mullinix Tim   253
  Content, my good <Lords>; but let us change Hands; .   805 Irish Bishops   61
  For that one Gift to lay on Hands: . . . .   821 Dr. Rundle   44
  Shews a Bribe in all his Hands: . . . .   833 Legion Club   104
  A Lawyer o'er his Hands and Face, ... 904 Death Daphne   35
  Condemn'd by Female Hands to dye;   . . . . . 923 Riddle 7   62
  By cruel Hands her Blood was spilt, ... 923 Riddle 7   65
  And with relentless Hands destroy   . . . . . 925 Riddle 8   21
  When into my hands comes a letter from the droll. . .   975 Dean to Sherid   4
HANDSOM
  She's Now as handsom ev'ry bit, ...   313 To Ford   71
  Would make at least a handsom show . . . .   422 Ireld   36
HANDSOME
  A handsome House to lodge a Friend, ...   198 Horace 2, 6   3
  A handsome young imperious Girl   . . . . . 289 Prog Marriage   3
  Why is a handsome Wife ador'd   . . . .   592 Strephon Chloe   283
  As handsome as my Lady's Page;   . . . . . 597 Problem Solved   5
  She may be handsome, young and rich, ... 698 Cadenus Vaness   362
  With handsome Garters at your Knees, ... 699 Cadenus Vaness   402
  She's not so handsome, in my Eyes: . . . . . 699 Cadenus Vaness   410
  Can ever be handsome.   . . . .   854 Lady's Lament   106
  A handsome Addition for Wine and good Chear,   . .   867 Grand Question   11
HANDY-WORK
  As not the Handy-work of God;   . . . .   821 Dr. Rundle   54
HANG
  Now you may go hang your self for me, and so went away. .   72 Mrs Harris Pet   63
  For rather than hang, I would be Not in game.   . . . 144 New Song   34
  Without a Mistress, hang or drown him.   . . . . . 303 Storm   16
  For me, you may hang 'em, or drown 'em.   . . . . . 403 Window Inns 9   D 6
  There hang three crosses at thy door: . . . .   404 Window Inns 11 D 1
  Hang up thy wife, and she'll make four.   . . . . . 404 Window Inns 11 D 2
  Hang up your Wife, and you'l count Four', ... 404 Window Inns 11 D 6
  To hang up all who smuggle wool.   . . . .   423 Ireld   58
  To Hang him all <England> would lend him their Garters; 519 Dean Hang Rape   51
  Why, hang her, though she seem'd so coy, ... 595 Cassinus Peter   61
  I would hang them if I cou'd:) . . . .   635 Epistle Lady   170
  Yet, hang me, but for all her Art;   . . . . . 679 From Catullus   3
  Yet, hang me, but I love her dearly.   . . . . . 679 From Catullus   8
  But what wou'd hang him if they cou'd.   . . . . . 777 Mullinix Tim   124
  I'd rather hang my self by half, ... 778 Mullinix Tim   177
  Hang, Drown, or knock him on the Head.   . . . . . 797 Traulus 1   40
  And let them rot, or hang, or stink.   . . . . . 799 Traulus 1   102
  'Tis best to hang her on the Spot;   . . . . . 886 Rev Market-Hill   108
HANG'D
  And I must be hang'd in your Stead.   . . . . . 395 Dog and Thief   8
  Shall a Subject so Loyal be hang'd by the Nape, . .   518 Dean Hang Rape   35
  For Sodomy hang'd, as thou for a <Rape>.   . . . . . 518 Dean Hang Rape   48
  And hang'd he must be for committing a <Rape>.   . .   519 Dean Hang Rape   60
  When the good <English> <Dean> is hang'd up for a
    <Rape>.   520 Dean Hang Rape   72
  Yet would rather be hang'd than he'd leave a warm Place. 580 Psyche   6
  I wonder why he was not hang'd;   . . . . . 797 Traulus 1   42
  He lost his Bishoprick, and hang'd, or burst.   . . . 806 Judas   8
  An I were to be hang'd, I can't sleep a Wink: . . . 869 Grand Question   64
  You never ventur'd to be hang'd.   . . . . . 884 Rev Market-Hill   40
  For whom she hang'd herself above? . . . .   905 Death Daphne   82
  . . .yet I'll be hang'd, less he . . . .   1022 Nim-Dan-Dean 2 D   5
HANG'S
  Hang's down his Head, and drops his Tail, ... 797 Traulus 1   37
HANGED
  Were hanged, before they'd part with you.   . . . . . 778 Mullinix Tim   150
HANGER
  A hanger on has always been, ...   468 Birthday Song   253
HANGER-ON
  An humble Hanger-on at best;   . . . .   918 Riddle 4   21
HANGING
  Has twice two Legs, two hanging Ears;   . . . . . 299 Horrid Plot   46
  . . . I'd see him hanging high'r, ...   343 Upon His Grace   37
  When a Brother Thief is hanging.   . . . .   830 Legion Club   16

		PAGE	TITLE	LINE
HANGMAN				
The sleeping Hangman ties the fatal Noose,	. . . .	364	On Dreams	29
The Hangman for Pardon fell down on his Knee;	. . .	399	Tom Clinch	13
HANGS				
While each pale Sinner hangs his Head,	. . . . . .	579	Day Judgement	9
Hangs a new Angel two doors from us	. . . . . .	734	Stel B-day '20	10
When Doll hangs out a newer Face	. . . . . .	735	Stel B-day '20	34
'Tis just like this, which hangs by Geometry.	. . .	780	Mullinix Tim	218
HANK				
From a bo-bo-bo-Boy he pursues his old Hank,	. . . .	287	Bank Down	19
HANKS				
Thy Words together ty'd in small Hanks,	. . . .	1021	Nim-Dan-Dean 1	D 29
<HANMER>				
A fig too for <Hanmer>	. . . .	186	Scriblerus 4	D 7
HANNAH				
But Hannah, who listen'd to all that was past,	. . .	868	Grand Question	41
Thus merciless Hannah ran on in her Talk,	. . .	873	Grand Question	179
Then, turning to Hannah, and forcing a Frown,	. . .	873	Grand Question	182
These gaudy Shoes must Hannah place	. . . . . .	885	Rev Market-Hill	67
For Hannah; when we have no need of her,	. . . .	886	Rev Market-Hill	105
Nor, will zealous Hannah pout	. . . . . .	896	Panegyr Dean	317
HANNIBALL				
In blew shallon, shall Hanniball be Clad,	. . . . .	275	Epilogue	21
HANNONIAE				
Hannoniae qui primus ab oris.	. . . .	186	Scriblerus 4	D 6
HANNOVERIANS				
Whigs, Tories, Trimmers, Hannoverians,	. . . . .	345	Prometheus	13
HANOVER				
Hanover may do well enough;	. . . .	467	Birthday Song	213
To our Illustrious House of Hanover.	. . . . . .	773	Mullinix Tim	10
I swore to the <Queen> that the <Prince> of <Hanover>		144	New Song	35
Was truer than Steele to the <Hanover> Line,	. . .	518	Dean Hang Rape	33
HANOVERIANS				
Are swarms of Bugs and Hanoverians.	. . . . . .	313	To Ford	50
HAPLESS				
(Say hapless Isle, altho'	. . . . . .	37	Ode Sancroft	93
Lament upon their hapless fall	. . . .	490	Dialogue	43
HAPLY				
Haply you judge these lines severely writ	. . . .	46	To Congreve	109
In this descending sheet you'll haply find	. . . .	50	To Congreve	231
If haply on the liquid surface float,	. . . . . .	672	Epig Carthy 24	D 13
HAPP'NING				
Which happ'ning on the Skin to light,	. . . . .	84	Salamander	54
HAPPEN'D				
Such a thing as this happen'd, just about the time of		71	Mrs Harris Pet	33
Goosberries.				
Mrs. Dukes, said I, here's an ugly Accident has		71	Mrs Harris Pet	37
happen'd out;				
It happen'd on a Winter's night,	. . . .	90	Bauc & Phil 1	5
It happen'd on a Winter Night,	. . . .	111	Bauc & Phil 2	5
A Juncture happen'd in his highest Pride:	. . . .	536	To Mr. Gay	147
It happen'd when a Plague broke out,	. . . . . .	601	Beasts Confess	5
HAPPENS				
If Molly happens to be careless,	. . . .	417	Woman's Mind	43
HAPPIER				
We speak it in a Happier Sense.	. . . .	339	Arch-Bish Dub	4
HAPPILY				
I grieve, this Noble Work so happily begun,	. . .	24	Ode Athenian	275
HAPPINESS				
Add to the Victor's Happiness?	. . . .	6	Ode to King	11
'Tis Pride and Happiness enough to Me	. . . . .	24	Ode Athenian	266
All Happiness--and so adieu.	. . . .	411	Dial Rich Marb	103
Were future Happiness and Pain,	. . . .	764	Stel B-day '26	19
HAPPY				
By which our happy Prince carves out his Bays;	. . .	7	Ode to King	32
To Crown the happy Conquerour,	. . . . .	16	Ode Athenian	19
Of Conquest in your your short and Happy Reign;	. .	25	Ode Athenian	303
Thrice happy you have 'scap't this gen'ral Pest;	. .	28	Ode to Temple	58
Your happy Frame at once controuls	. . . . . .	28	Ode to Temple	68
In this new happy Scene	. . . .	31	Ode to Temple	159
And that his subjects share his happy influence;	. .	40	Ode Sancroft	182
Since, happy Saint, since it has been of late	. . .	42	Ode Sancroft	240
Happy beyond a private muse's fate,	. . . . .	49	To Congreve	179
Ah fav'rite youth, how happy is thy lot!--	. . . .	53	Temple Ill	71
Time o'er the happy takes so swift a flight,	. . . .	54	Temple Ill	113
Whom each one thought the happy Dame:	. . . . .	67	Problem	52
Thrice happy Poet, who may trail	. . . . . .	109	V's House	109
Thus, happy in their Change of Life,	. . . . .	116	Bauc & Phil 2	149
Then call'd the happy Composition, Floyd.	. . . .	118	Biddy Floyd	12
Yet, still so happy was his Fate,	. . . . . .	134	Magician's Rod	47
And Englond wouldst thou be happy still,	. . . .	148	Windsor Proph	25
Or't had been happy for Gold-finders.	. . . . .	156	Fable of Midas	12
Him for an happy Man I own,	. . . .	243	Horace 4, 9	15
And, happy he, who wisely knows	. . . . . .	243	Horace 4, 9	17
If Anna's happy Reign you praise,	. . . . .	271	Apollo's Edict	D 44
'Tis happy to see the whole Kingdom in Rags,	. . .	287	Bank Down	16
And, thus set out this happy Pair,	. . . . .	290	Prog Marriage	27
You, happy Folks, are sure to meet	. . . . .	315	To Ford	105
(Happy beneath his righteous Sway)	. . . . .	388	Manly Virtue	138
With whom I'm happy in the worst	. . . . . .	420	Holyhead	26
Too happy were the Poets Crew,	. . . . . .	467	Birthday Song	223

		PAGE	TITLE	LINE
HAPPY	**(CONTINUED)**			
Not owing to his happy Vein		481	Libel on D- D-	45
Hail! happy Pope, whose gen'rous Mind, ...		482	Libel on D- D-	71
Thrice happy Duck, employ'd in threshing Stubble!		521	Stephen Duck	7
How happy for Us, that it is not at Home.		576	Place Damn'd	18
How happy I, were that the worst?		595	Cassinus Peter	43
And happy Lovers bless my Reign----		694	Cadenus Vaness	248
Was happy when he could prevail		746	Stel Distress	19
Was happy when he could prevail		750	Stel Wood-Park	17
Thee, happy Island, Pallas call'd her own, . . .		790	St. Pat's Well	9
Happy Nation were we blind, ...		862	To Janus	17
Happy, O Market-Hill! at least, ...		877	To Dean Swift	27
A Pain which ev'ry happy Night		924	Riddle 8	13
Let the happy Swain rejoice, ...		933	Riddle 20 D	15
HAPPYNESS				
If their own happyness they knew.		467	Birthday Song	224
HAPSBURGE				
Till Hapsburge makyth them but twayne.		103	Merlin	20
HARANGU'D				
So, Traulus when he first harangu'd, ...		797	Traulus 1	41
And fierce against the Whigs harangu'd?		884	Rev Market-Hill	39
Harangu'd, and welcom'd him to Town.		904	Death Daphne	50
HARANGUE				
Shall hear Him harangue against Prior to Morrow. . .		143	New Song	6
HARANGUES				
Harangues the Rabble, and is better paid.		364	On Dreams	34
Then, from the bar, harangues the bench		434	Answer Paulus	77
HARANGUING				
Bid Povey secure him while you are haranguing. .		818	Epigr Kite	8
Such a Noise, and such haranguing, ...		830	Legion Club	15
HARCOURT				
Come trimming Harcourt; bring your Mace;		190	Faggot	39
HARD				
Which is perhaps as hard t' imagine right		21	Ode Athenian	159
Who, like hard masters, taught the Sun		36	Ode Sancroft	67
As hard, as sensless, and as light:		60	Lady Tablebook	4
That tho' 'tis hard to judge, yet Money can't go without Hands.		71	Mrs Harris Pet	43
After hard Throws of many a Day		81	Vanbrug House	73
Came to a Village hard by Rixham		90	Bauc & Phil 1	9
It rain'd as hard as it could pour, ...		90	Bauc & Phil 1	11
But this a Work so hard was found, ...		108	V's House	87
One asks the Watermen hard by, ...		109	V's House	99
At which, 'tis hard to be believ'd, ...		117	Bauc & Phil 2	175
Whom to be hard on, whom to spare:		218	To Mr. Delany	100
Hard Exercise, and harder Fare		230	Prog of Poetry	11
He was as hard, and pond'rous Wood at that: . .		285	Elegy Boat	20
Was full as hard to please as You, ...		313	To Ford	53
And England has put this Crab to hard Use, . . .		335	Serious Poem	37
But Dreams are like Oracles, hard to explain 'em,		337	Serious Poem	113
I know the Times are something hard, but hope they soon will mend,		342	Upon His Grace	32
For Jove, it is not hard to guess him, ...		346	Prometheus	61
And thus I solve this hard Phaenomenon.		367	Answer Delaney	44
My very good Lord, it's a very hard task		368	Verses Window	1
The Son laughs that got, the hard gotten Estate,		430	Dicky Dolly	20
'Tis hard, where dulness over-rules, ...		436	Answer Paulus	123
So hard sometimes		441	Ballyspellin	22
"But, was it not confounded hard?		446	Modern Lady	50
Dear Madam, you are grown so hard, ...		447	Modern Lady	86
Hard, tough, cramp, gutt'ral, harsh, stiff Names.		467	Birthday Song	210
You can't, grave Sir, believe it hard, ...		475	Epist on Epist	3
'Twas therefore cruel, hard, by Jove, ...		495	Panegyr Swift	80
"With lying on too hard a Bed, ...		497	Panegyr Swift	133
Then, if you find the Terms too hard, ...		501	Doctor Delaney	53
Hard by a filthy Bason stands, ...		526	Lady's Dres Rm	37
Though hard to find in ev'ry Case		606	Beasts Confess	155
'Tis hard they must be busy Night and Day: . . .		662	Upon Ladies	2
A Nymph so hard to be subdu'd, ...		702	Cadenus Vaness	496
I was too hard upon--a little.		747	Stel Distress	66
I was too hard upon a little;		752	Stel Wood-Park	82
Grant this the Case, yet sure 'tis hard, ...		764	Stel B-day '26	25
That which is which, 'tis hard to know.		780	Mullinix Tim	228
When his Friends he most is hard on, ...		800	Traulus 2	13
If you say this is hard, on a man that is reckon'd		817	Yahoo's	66
Condemn'd to live in Service hard;		883	Rev Market-Hill	11
Hard is the Toil, nor small the Art, ...		892	Panegyr Dean	181
And then, with Heart more hard than Stone, . . .		915	Riddle 1	13
Who from Materials hard and dry, ...		920	Riddle 6	20
Approaching, finds it hard to part		922	Riddle 7	35
Suppose I call'd you goose, it is hard		983	Sher, A Goose	9
Will you return as hard ones, if I call t'ye? .		989	Letter Dr Sh-n	33
Pursu'd and laid me hard on.		1005	Sheridan's Sub	10
'Twas the damn'd 'Squire with the hard Name, . .		1005	Sheridan's Sub	20
HARD-BOUND				
Thus when you feel an hard-bound <Breech> . . .		66	Problem	29
HARD-LABOUR'D				
While my hard-labour'd Poem pines		502	Doctor Delaney	77
HARDEN'D				
Well harden'd in Flame, ...		246	Irish-Feast	70
Have Hearts more harden'd than Egyptians; . . .		813	Bro Protestant	52

	PAGE	TITLE	LINE
HARDER			
Hard Exercise, and harder Fare	230	Prog of Poetry	11
Are harder than ever were put by the Sphinx.	977	Dean to Sherid	46
HARDEST			
And what he thought the hardest Case, ...	221	A Quiet Life	45
But, still the hardest Part remains.	586	Strephon Chloe	71
The hardest Bum will bruise with sitting squat.	881	Pastoral Dial	20
How nice you split the hardest Text!	888	Panegyr Dean	62
HARDING			
Let them be sent to Mrs. Harding;	417	Woman's Mind	59
HARDLY			
Which hardly wants another puff, ...	9	Ode to King	109
Through native dross your share is hardly known, ...	45	To Congreve	59
But hardly ever set my Eyes together, or slept a Wink.	70	Mrs Harris Pet	21
Now hardly moves an Inch an Hour.	113	Bauc & Phil 2	74
He sees, yet hardly can believe, ...	115	Bauc & Phil 2	119
And hardly could believe his Eyes, ...	116	Bauc & Phil 2	146
Yet hardly dare one Line Rehearse.	121	Apollo Outwit	60
Now hardly here and there an Hackney-Coach	124	Descriptn Morn	1
And hardly pay Eighteenpence Tax in the Pound:	144	New Song	50
Will hardly fail, and there is room for more:	166	Toland's Invit	36
Old Read would hardly let him in.	174	Horace 1, 7	120
That Will durst hardly venture in;	219	A Quiet Life	2
And hardly waddles forth, to cool	230	Prog of Poetry	5
That since I was born, I hardly have spy'd it; . . .	263	Apollo	6
When Actors who at best are hardly Savers, ...	274	Epilogue	3
Will hardly find his Wife in Shoes.	292	Prog Marriage	70
"Although 'tis hardly worth the Cost, ...	305	Storm	55
We think, though You judge hardly of it, ...	311	To Ford	15
And hardly hear of half a Score.	315	To Ford	108
The glitt'ring Beau could hardly tell, ...	325	Pethox	65
Himself can hardly read 'em.	406	Swift to Pope	12
My Dame is hardly worth a Groat.	409	Dial Rich Marb	30
And I can hardly get him down	411	Dial Rich Marb	99
Where nature hardly seems alive.	421	Holyhead	32
In both, yet hardly save your stake.	436	Answer Paulus	130
If well apply'd, can hardly miss:	463	Birthday Song	84
Your Heroine hardly fifty odd is.	465	Birthday Song	162
Tho' it is hardly understood, ...	556	Death of Swift	77
"He hardly drinks a Pint of Wine;	557	Death of Swift	109
"He hardly breathes. The Dean is dead.	558	Death of Swift	150
It hardly holds the Honey-moon:	591	Strephon Chloe	258
We hardly thunder thrice a year:	617	Scandal Poem 1	11
We hardly Thunder thrice a Year;	624	Scandal Poem 2	11
Hardly can be grave in Prose:	634	Epistle Lady	138
Our chilling Climate hardly bears	640	On Poetry	7
I hardly hear a Woman's Clack.	674	His Deafness	8
You hardly see the Current flow, ...	688	Cadenus Vaness	52
He hardly knew, Till he was told, ...	706	Cadenus Vaness	632
Hardly at length he Silence broke, ...	707	Cadenus Vaness	656
At least, cou'd hardly wish them wrong.	710	Cadenus Vaness	747
The Cieling hardly six foot high	746	Stel Distress	36
The Ceiling hardly six Foot high, ...	751	Stel Wood-Park	54
There's hardly twenty to be found;	773	Mullinix Tim	6
Amounting hardly to a Crown a Tribe, ...	806	Judas	4
You have hardly seen a Score, ...	839	Legion Club	237
I hardly can pick, ...	853	Lady's Lament	64
"Can hardly tell how to cry Bo to a Goose;	872	Grand Question	158
I hardly now can force a Word.	916	Riddle 1	40
HARDNESS			
The Tenants poor, the Hardness of the Times, . . .	533	To Mr. Gay	67
HARDRESS			
Jack, the Grandson of Sir Hardress?	834	Legion Club	140
HARDSHIP			
I now despise Fatigue and Hardship:	890	Panegyr Dean	108
HARDSHIPS			
To hardships in pursuit of health;	401	Window Inns 5 D	2
HARDY			
Or hardy Scot, or any Land but this;	793	St. Pat's Well	80
HARE			
That lies in old Wood like a Hare in her Form; . . .	351	Wood Insect	18
The Hound be hunted by the Hare, ...	445	Modern Lady	20
Thus Gay, the Hare with many Friends, ...	481	Libel on D- D-	53
Hounds hunt the Hare, the wily Fox	504	Doctor Delaney	129
A Hare, who long had 'scap't pursuing Hounds, ...	538	Mr. Pulteney	17
(He had not seen a Hare the Lord knows when)	538	Mr. Pulteney	26
Away the Hare with double Swiftness fled.	538	Mr. Pulteney	28
Thus was the Hare pursu'd, tho' free from Guilt; . . .	538	Mr. Pulteney	37
Thou art not half so nimble as a Hare:	539	Mr. Pulteney	40
HARES			
Still brings us Hares when he can catch them:	281	Journal	74
Is good for Partridge, not for Hares.	940	Letter	11
HARK			
Vain empty World farewel. But hark, ...	596	Cassinus Peter	79
Hark, the Monkeys, how the prate!	832	Legion Club	82
HARK'EE			
But hark'ee, is it truly so, ...	493	Panegyr Swift	23
HARLEQUIN			
His Name is Harlequin, I wot, ...	300	Horrid Plot	47
HARLEY			
Harley, the Nation's great Support, ...	170	Horace 1, 7	1

		PAGE	TITLE	LINE
HARLEY	(CONTINUED)			
Said Harley, I desire to know		172	Horace 1, 7	47
Does he refuse me? Harley cry'd:		172	Horace 1, 7	55
Some few Days after Harley spies		172	Horace 1, 7	57
Said Harley, Welcome Rev'rend Dean!		174	Horace 1, 7	121
Dear Harley, gen'rous Youth, admit		176	To Lord Harley	3
How then, dear Harley, could I guess		177	To Lord Harley	23
Then where, said I, shall Harley find		177	To Lord Harley	33
By Harley <Swift> invited comes to Court. . . .		194	Author Himself	28
And Harley, not asham'd his Choice to own,		194	Author Himself	31
That <Swift> oils many a Spring which Harley moves.		194	Author Himself	40
Since Harley bid me first attend, ...		201	Horace 2, 6	65
Of him that Ireland sav'd, and Harley;		494	Panegyr Swift	54
And <Harley> fill'd the Commons Chair)		180	Horace 2, 1	10
HARLEY'S				
And very much in Harley's Favour)		171	Horace 1, 7	18
He soon arrives at Harley's Gate;		174	Horace 1, 7	118
Fresh blooming, in young Harley's mind. . . .		178	To Lord Harley	52
By Harley's Favour once again he shines; . . .		196	Author Himself	63
HARLOT				
Treat thy Mother like a Harlot!		838	Legion Club	202
HARLY				
And Britain's lost if Harly dyes		140	Harlyes Surgn	2
Harly depends upon your skill, ...		140	Harlyes Surgn	3
HARM				
. . .that I might do my self no Harm:		70	Mrs Harris Pet	19
"I never Harm intended.		154	Widow and Cat	D 30
Who could do them no Harm, if they did them no Good:		334	Serious Poem	10
And there can be no Harm in making a Tryal; . .		336	Serious Poem	82
I broke his Teeth, but where's the mighty harm? . . .		670	Epig Carthy 20	D 2
Pallas had done more Harm than Good;		700	Cadenus Vaness	435
HARMLESS				
The Rod was but a harmless Wand, ...		132	Magician's Rod	1
Poor York! the harmless Tool of others Hate; . .		195	Author Himself	51
And harmless Frolicks of her Boys;		322	First of April	34
Against the harmless Alphabet;		645	On Poetry	158
By Magick Spells, the harmless Maid;		707	Cadenus Vaness	647
Taught harmless Man to cram and stuff. . . .		895	Panegyr Dean	262
Among our harmless Northern Swains;		896	Panegyr Dean	300
HARMONIOUS				
Hear Sounds harmonious from the Skies. . . .		230	Prog of Poetry	16
Or in harmonious Numbers put		451	Modern Lady	222
Find Rivers with harmonious names, ...		468	Birthday Song	241
Harmonious Coffee show thy Zeal, ...		515	Answer Fable	87
Cynthia, tune harmonious Numbers;		661	Love Song	13
No Muse harmonious Entertains, ...		957	Cantata	
HARMONIUS				
Harmonius Cibber entertains		650	On Poetry	305
HARMONY				
To find out proper words for Harmony:		467	Birthday Song	218
In Harmony wou'd you Excel, ...		956	Cantata	
Or, of thy Harmony, or Wit.		1022	Nim-Dan-Dean 1	D 44
HARNESS-BUCKLES				
And with Harness-Buckles furnish'd;		573	Helter Skelter	8
HARNESS'D				
Or Harness'd to a Nag, at ease		109	V's House	111
Harness'd her Doves, and flew to Heav'n. . . .		714	Cadenus Vaness	889
HARP				
He against Phebus Harp decreed, ...		156	Fable of Midas	27
Whose harp could savage beasts enchant, . . .		177	To Lord Harley	11
And so the Harp of Ireland brings, ...		345	Prometheus	29
When first for thee my Harp I strung:		728	Stella, Poems	10
My Harp will soon in vain be strung, ...		739	Stel B-day '21	11
HARPER				
Come, Harper, strike up, ...		245	Irish-Feast	25
HARPIES				
Quite destroy that Harpies Nest, ...		830	Legion Club	29
HARPS				
And tune your Harps, and strow your Bays. . . .		656	On Poetry	468
HARPY				
But spight of the Harpy that crawls on all four, . . .		147	Windsor Proph	11
With Harpy Claws, and Pois'nous Tongue, ...		504	Doctor Delaney	124
With harpy Claws it undermines the Ground, . .		792	St. Pat's Well	61
This bloated Harpy sprung from Hell, ...		895	Panegyr Dean	269
HARRIDAN				
Are each become a Harridan;		311	To Ford	18
HARRIDANS				
Of Prudes, Coquets, and Harridans;		448	Modern Lady	119
<HARRISON>				
There sit <Clements>, <Dilks>, and <Harrison>, . .		837	Legion Club	181
<Harrison>, and <Dilks>, and <Clements>, ...		837	Legion Club	185
HARRY				
Then my Lord call'd me; Harry, said my Lord, don't cry,		73	Mrs Harris Pet	66
For honest Harry is no Witt, ...		123	Empty'ng Town	23
And honest Harry is too apt to stink.		166	Toland's Invit	38
Harry look'd fierce, and shook his ragged Mane:		168	Peace Dunkirk	17
As Falstaff acted old King Harry:		475	Epist on Epist	10
Grave Harry, when the poor are pressing		878	Robbin & Harry	5
It so fell out, that cautious Harry		878	Robbin & Harry	17
If Gaffer Harry would endow her;		879	Robbin & Harry	34
Young Harry, as all Europe knows, ...		879	Robbin & Harry	37

		PAGE	TITLE	LINE
HARRY'S				
Bob's Spittle mix'd with Harry's <Turd>		495	Panegyr Swift	63
Much talking is not Harry's vice, ...		878	Robbin & Harry	13
While Harry's fencing up his ditches.		878	Robbin & Harry	28
HARSH				
Hard, tough, cramp, gutt'rall, harsh, stiff Names. . .		467	Birthday Song	210
HARVESTS				
And waste in Luxury thy Harvests there;		794	St. Pat's Well	98
HAS 172			OMITTED WORD	
HAST 17			OMITTED WORD	
HASTE				
How proudly would he haste the joy to meet, ...		49	To Congreve	185
In haste she does th' offensive herd avoid.		50	To Congreve	226
Farther in haste the Poets throng, ...		109	V's House	105
I hurry me in haste away, ...		200	Horace 2, 6	25
Down from your Garrets haste, ...		394	Grub-Street	2
And Supper gobbled up in haste, ...		453	Modern Lady	277
Now, all in haste they huddle on		453	Modern Lady	286
In Haste, with Imprecations dire, ...		470	Burning Poem	11
And fled in Haste with all her Brood		849	Old Thorn	39
Their Sacrifice with Zeal and Haste:		894	Panegyr Dean	240
HASTED				
And hasted forward to pursue		412	Desire Possess	29
HASTEN				
I only hasten on my Fate.		916	Riddle 1	38
HASTEN'D				
I hasten'd down to Country Air, ...		1003	Dan J's Reply	2
HASTILY				
When Baucis hastily cry'd out;		116	Bauc & Phil 2	155
HASTING				
And meets her hasting to the Ball, ...		292	Prog Marriage	85
HASTY				
The tuck'd-up Sempstress walks with hasty Strides, . .		138	City Shower	37
With hasty Zeal, behold, the Steward come, ...		533	To Mr. Gay	71
HAT				
He cock't his Hat, you would have said		156	Fable of Midas	13
And sav'd his Oar, but lost his Hat.		281	Journal	72
His Hat for Show, beneath his Arm.		410	Dial Rich Marb	66
My Hat has much the nicer air, ...		780	Mullinix Tim	219
His Hat could nicely put on;		785	Mullinex Dick	30
Red hat, and blue bonnet, and turbant's the same, . . .		815	Yahoo's	23
For, a Captain of Horse never takes off his Hat; . .		870	Grand Question	106
Like Lorimer, to wear his Hat.		886	Rev Market-Hill	96
Club'd for a Feather to his Hat;		903	Death Daphne	30
HATBAND				
And get a Hatband, Scarf, and Gloves.		547	Life of Swift	65
HATCH				
But whether you can tread or hatch, ...		983	Sher, A Goose	23
HATCHET				
"With Hatchet blunter than thy Pate		851	Old Thorn	83
HATE				
'Twas in an evil hour to urge my hate, ...		47	To Congreve	132
My hate, whose lash just heaven has long decreed . . .		47	To Congreve	133
A poor amusement for my scorn and hate;		53	Temple Ill	84
. . .I hate a Thief.)		71	Mrs Harris Pet	35
Prevail'd on by the Thing you hate, ...		121	Apollo Outwit	63
Poor York! the harmless Tool of others Hate;		195	Author Himself	51
Who hate Your Person, and Your Cause, ...		312	To Ford	30
A Bishop says the noble 'Squire, I hate the very Name,		342	Upon His Grace	17
The Church I hate, and have good Reason:		349	Upright Judge 1	1
You hate to see ought that seems Clean		372	Letter D. S-y	44
Which breeds at once both Hate and Scorn.		413	Censure	4
A passage to the land I hate.		420	Holyhead	28
I hate the Vice-Roy, love the Man.		485	Libel on D- D-	152
Who, from my Soul, sincerely hate		485	Libel on D- D-	173
Must dread your pen, your person hate, ...		491	Dialogue	54
Their Fellows, turn their Dread and Hate.		493	Panegyr Swift	14
Could make you so sincerely hate		498	Panegyr Swift	155
Hated by Fools, and Fools to hate, ...		505	Doctor Delaney	171
Who bore for twice ten Years the publick Hate. . . .		536	To Mr. Gay	144
I can easier scorn than hate:		634	Epistle Lady	144
Wou'd you at once display your utmost Hate, ...		667	Epig Carthy 4	D 3
Of half Mankind the Dread and Hate.		702	Cadenus Vaness	505
Eternal Objects of her Hate.		725	To Stella	64
Who hate and scorn you, to a Man;		777	Mullinix Tim	146
I hate, who gape and snear by Rules.		787	Dick's Variety	2
And Sir I know you hate a Crowd.		860	Lady Acheson	24
To shorten my Tale, (for I hate a long Story,)		871	Grand Question	129
Ye who hate such inconsistence, ...		907	Daphne	25
For I hate a silent Breath, ...		933	Riddle 20	D 29
And doth all Christians hate;		1036	Heathen Christ	2
HATED				
As loth to see the hated Court and Town, ...		31	Ode to Temple	157
He hated <Wharton> like a Toad;		171	Horace 1, 7	36
So to confound, this hated Coin		345	Prometheus	11
He hated Bailiffs at his shoulder.		455	Dean Smedley	10
Hated by Fools, and Fools to hate, ...		505	Doctor Delaney	171
This Lark was hated in the Wood, ...		514	Answer Fable	61
Contrives, as he is hated, to be fear'd:		536	To Mr. Gay	138
'Tis true, he hated Sloth like Pease.		602	Beasts Confess	46
The Sharper swore he hated Play, ...		607	Beasts Confess	187

370

HATEFUL
    To reach that slavish hateful shore   . . . .   420 Holyhead   20
    And, as that hateful hideous Grecian   . . . . . .   775 Mullinix Tim   51
HATER   SEE WOMAN-HATER
    A hater of books: . . . .   854 Lady's Lament   94
HATERS   SEE BISHOP-HATERS
HATES
    (Now you must know, he hates to be call'd Parson,. . . .   72 Mrs Harris Pet   54
    I own, he hates an Action base, ...   484 Libel on D- D-   145
    And hates to cram the Sick with Slops: . . . . . .   605 Beasts Confess   134
    Where he loves, or where he hates.   . . . .   800 Traulus 2   20
HATH   50   OMITTED WORD
HATRED
    Such Hatred to a Parson's Gown, ...   416 Woman's Mind   15
    Allow your hatred strictly just;   . . . .   498 Panegyr Swift   170
    To avoid the publick Hatred;   . . . .   637 Epistle Lady   224
    Of keeping up a party hatred.   . . . .   779 Mullinix Tim   184
    The world is in doubt, whether hatred or love;   . . . .   818 Archbi Cashel   2
HATS
    And with Hats so very big, Sir, ...   573 Helter Skelter   17
HAUGHTILY
    How haughtily he lifts his Nose, ...   281 Journal   81
HAUGHTY
    He trampled on this Haughty Bajazet, ...   7 Ode to King   42
    The haughty Minister of State   . . . .   325 Pethox   49
    Give up the phrase of haughty Gaul, ...   468 Birthday Song   247
    By haughty Celia spent in Dressing;   . . . . . .   525 Lady's Dres Rm   2
    "He gave himself no haughty Airs: . . . .   565 Death of Swift   330
    And gives himself a haughty air, ...   621 Scandal Poem 1   137
    And gives himself a haughty Air, ...   627 Scandal Poem 2   141
    Can you call me rude, or haughty?   . . . .   631 Epistle Lady   70
    With haughty spouse in vesture fine, ...   677 Parson's Case   33
    And pull your haughty Stomach down, ...   748 Stel Distress   72
    And pull your haughty Stomach down, ...   752 Stel Wood-Park   88
    When haughty Britain was a Land unknown.   . . . . ˙.   790 St. Pat's Well   10
    From haughty Gaul to make Ragous.   . . . .   895 Panegyr Dean   264
    Than where the haughty Dutchess Locks, ...   896 Panegyr Dean   297
    Cease haughty Nymph; the Fates decree   . . . . . .   905 Death Daphne   91
    No haughty Nymph has Pow'r to run   . . . .   916 Riddle 2   5
    The haughty Prince, the humble Slave, ...   922 Riddle 7   28
HAUL'D
    Haul'd up every hill;   . . . .   853 Lady's Lament   50
HAUNCH
    A Haunch of Ven'son made her sweat   . . . . . .   746 Stel Distress   15
    A Haunch of Ven'son made her sweat, ...   750 Stel Wood-Park   13
HAUNCHES
    His milk-white Steed upon it's haunches, ...   461 Birthday Song   35
HAUNT
    "To haunt a certain Minister of State: . . . . .   195 Author Himself   44
    Those Cares that haunt the Court and Town.   . . . .   202 Horace 2, 6   112
    And haunt thy holy Walls in white and black.   . . . .   792 St. Pat's Well   48
    To banish Rats that haunt our Vault.   . . . . . .   892 Panegyr Dean   162
    I'll haunt thy Dreams, a bloodless Ghost;   . . . . .   925 Riddle 8   27
HAUNTED
    Oft hovers where alive it haunted most;   . . . . . .   51 Temple Ill   8
HAUNTS
    And that her troubled Ghost still haunts there since she
       dy'd;   27 Ode to Temple   38
    Since the bright essence fled, where haunts the reverend
       ghost?   36 Ode Sancroft   44
    Among thy stubborn sons there haunts that spirit of Jews,   38 Ode Sancroft   129
HAUTY
    We'll Rigg in Meath-Street, Egypt's hauty Queen,   .   275 Epilogue   19
HAVE   425   OMITTED WORD
HAVING
    Where having cast his coat, and well pursu'd   . . . .   46 To Congreve   117
    Which having wisely overthrown, ...   81 Vanbrug House   91
    Having thro all the Village pass't, ...   91 Bauc & Phil 1   49
    And having fill'd it to the Brink, ...   92 Bauc & Phil 1   71
    Philemon having paus'd a while   . . . .   94 Bauc & Phil 1   157
    Having thro' all the Village pass'd, ...   111 Bauc & Phil 2   17
    Philemon, having paus'd a while, ...   115 Bauc & Phil 2   111
    Thus having furbish'd up a Parson, ...   115 Bauc & Phil 2   137
    As having Malice in her Heart, ...   120 Apollo Outwit   26
    But, having long convers'd with you, ...   325 Pethox   67
    Tom having earn'd a Twig of Lawrel, ...   458 Paddy's Charac   14
    Having stolen from mine Hostess, ...   574 Helter Skelter   32
    And, having no sinister Ends, ...   605 Beasts Confess   143
    Which having found an equal Flame, ...   687 Cadenus Vaness   31
    The Pleader having spoke his best, ...   688 Cadenus Vaness   67
    Apollo having thought a little, ...   742 Stel B-day 22   35
    The Phantom, having humbly kiss't   . . . .   903 Death Daphne   3
    Having thus overthrown all our further Advances.   . . .   968 Letter Sherid   22
HAVOCK
    See Muse, what havock in these looks appear   . . . .   55 Temple Ill   125
HAWK
    Fly from the Hawk, or pick his Pease up.   . . . . .   512 Answer Fable   10
HAWK'D
    His Works were hawk'd in ev'ry Street, ...   172 Horace 1, 7   41
HAWKER
    The Hawker shews you one in Print, ...   644 On Poetry   113

HAWKER'S
    Will you regard the Hawker's Cryes . . . .   PAGE   TITLE   LINE

		PAGE	TITLE	LINE
HAWKER'S				
Will you regard the Hawker's Cryes		505	Doctor Delaney	161
HAWKERS				
And when his last Speech the loud Hawkers did cry,		399	Tom Clinch	11
How chearfully the Hawkers cry		502	Doctor Delaney	75
"The Hawkers have not got 'em yet,		564	Death of Swift	279
Ye Hawkers all, your Voices lift;		887	Panegyr Dean	33
HAWLS				
Hawls him, and scolds us down to Breakfast.		279	Journal	16
HAWS				
He haws and he hums,		854	Lady's Lament	109
HAWTHORNDEN				
Wise Hawthornden and Sterline's Lord.)		848	Old Thorn	16
HAY				
The one was Oats, the other Hay,		63	Discovery	38
On Magazines of Corn or Hay,		156	Fable of Midas	16
Old Hay is equal to old Gold;		156	Fable of Midas	20
"It serves for Stubble, Hay, and Wood,		550	Life of Swift	178
To build on Sand with Hay and Stubble?		593	Strephon Chloe	306
While not a Blade of Grass, or Hay,		759	Receipt Youth	3
Whole Ricks of Hay and Stacks of Corn,		811	Bro Protestant	3
His Horses too eat all our Hay.		861	Lady Acheson	36
Or Billet-doux, or Lock of Hay:		893	Panegyr Dean	222
No Straw, Oats, or Hay;		1036	Plague Country	6
HAYCOCK				
Attempt a Flight above a Haycock?		513	Answer Fable	22
HAZARDS				
And at all Hazards boldly quote:		648	On Poetry	248
HAZEL				
You know him by his hazel Snout:		785	Dick, Maggot	4
HE 1119			OMITTED WORD	
HE'D 14			OMITTED WORD	
HE'LL 30			OMITTED WORD	
HE'S 57			OMITTED WORD	
HEAD SEE BLOCK-HEAD,TABLE-HEAD,LATE-HEAD,CALVES-HEAD				
Philosophy's exalted head appears;		16	Ode Athenian	15
We've found a little inconsiderable Head		20	Ode Athenian	147
Lye on you, and on your Childrens Head,		23	Ode Athenian	246
About the Head crown'd with these Bays,		29	Ode to Temple	87
See how she rears her Head,		30	Ode to Temple	121
The Mitre, which his sacred head has worn,		40	Ode Sancroft	199
With Head reclining on his Shoulder,		63	Discovery	13
Advanc't on tiptoe, lean'd his Head		63	Discovery	27
I'll fling the <Pisspot> on your head;		91	Bauc & Phil 1	38
Found his Head fill'd with many a System,		115	Bauc & Phil 2	135
But fenc'd his Head with his own Bays		119	Apollo Outwit	7
He wav'd his Wreath Thrice o'er her Head,		120	Apollo Outwit	35
Mambrino's Helm adorn'd his Head.		156	Fable of Midas	14
The Meat shall represent the Tyrant's Head,		162	Toland's Invit	11
The Lawrel, which adorns thy Head;		182	Horace 2, 1	66
The Praetor broke the Consul's Head.		190	Faggot	32
To fix a Price on his devoted Head.		196	Author Himself	60
Than let you see her dress her Head;		222	Prog of Love	8
There practic'd how to place her Head,		222	Prog of Love	13
Till Midnight never shows her Head;		229	Prog of Beauty	102
Dipt over head and Ears--in Debt.		251	Bubble	24
Without troubling his Head about Judgment or Wit:		263	Apollo	20
And let the secret Head of Nile		270	Apollo's Edict	D 14
Or make a rumbling o'er his Head,		280	Journal	47
Her ev'ning Work so fills her Head;		291	Prog Marriage	58
From Head to Foot, and all before;)		324	Pethox	16
Thy Head with sparkling Rubies round;		324	Pethox	34
She calls it combing of his Head,		328	Epigram 2	2
She combs his Head, and finds him Horn.		328	Epigram 2	4
And ev'ry day she combs his Head.		328	Epigram 2	6
As round as a Ball, without Head without Tail,		350	Wood Insect	5
Ah never lay thy Head to Rest!		361	Grace's Answer	14
That Head so well by Wisdom fraught!		361	Grace's Answer	15
The busy Head with mimick Art runs o'er		363	On Dreams	9
To regal Rage devotes some Patriot's Head.		364	On Dreams	12
'Tis true, say they, cut off the Head,		366	Answer Delaney	5
Be distant as one Head can bear;		366	Answer Delaney	30
And Merit rears her drooping Head;		387	Manly Virtue	124
In Velvet Cap his Head lies warm;		410	Dial Rich Marb	65
If e'er I stoop beneath a crown'd Head:		410	Dial Rich Marb	74
Your Head, or Tooth, or Finger ake:		414	Censure	22
Lo here I sit at holy head		420	Holyhead	1
Flew hov'ring o'er each Female Head.		449	Modern Lady	135
"This Head of mine, Lord, how it Swims!		451	Modern Lady	208
With empty Purse, and aching Head,		453	Modern Lady	292
(Which measur'd on his Head, was found		458	Paddy's Charac	15
Flyes like an Eagle or'e his head;		461	Birthday Song	34
Thou still with Battles stuff thy head full		462	Birthday Song	55
No Vessel but an Ass's Head,		469	Burning Poem	4
I mean the Head without the Brain.		469	Burning Poem	6
I found my Head began to swim,		470	Burning Poem	9
And, sits aloft on Pindus Head,		483	Libel on D- D-	87
Will duck his Head, aside will start,		500	Doctor Delaney	5
Each Pot-gun levell'd at his Head:		500	Doctor Delaney	14
When Jove was, from his teeming Head,		504	Doctor Delaney	115
To squeeze it out from Head to Tail;		527	Lady's Dres Rm	66

HEAD   (CONTINUED)

	PAGE	TITLE	LINE
For catch it nicely by the Head,	527	Lady's Dres Rm	67
Out bounc't the Mastiff of the triple Head;	538	Mr. Pulteney	27
That old Vertigo in his Head,	556	Death of Swift	83
Or, had a Mitre on his Head	560	Death of Swift	195
"Had set a Price upon his Head;	566	Death of Swift	352
An horrid Vision seiz'd my Head,	578	Day Judgement	3
While each pale Sinner hangs his Head,	579	Day Judgement	9
Such Cleanliness from Head to Heel:	584	Strephon Chloe	10
While these Reflections fill'd his Head,	587	Strephon Chloe	111
One greasy Stocking round his Head,	594	Cassinus Peter	12
He crown'd his youthful Head with Bays:	597	Problem Solved	8
If my wand'ring Head be less	630	Epistle Lady	17
In my Head and Heart they center;	630	Epistle Lady	33
But, to doze my Head, like Lodanum.	632	Epistle Lady	84
And your Head turn Topsy-turvy.	637	Epistle Lady	220
Give your Head some gentle Raps;	638	Epistle Lady	264
To scratch your Head, and bite your Nails.	643	On Poetry	90
Conceiv'd a Project in her Head,	690	Cadenus Vaness	132
Whilst Mrs. Susan comb'd her Head:	698	Cadenus Vaness	373
Dear Madam, Let me set your Head:	699	Cadenus Vaness	398
Aim'd at the Head, but reach'd the Heart.	706	Cadenus Vaness	623
And had a most discerning Head.	710	Cadenus Vaness	757
She gather'd, under ev'ry Head,	713	Cadenus Vaness	850
Her Lace hath got within her Head	733	Verses Vanessa	25
Or stop and light at Cloe's Head	735	Stel B-day '20	37
I bit my Nails, and scratch'd my Head,	740	Stel B-day 22	5
How I should hide my Head for Shame,	741	Stel B-day 22	17
Now at the Table head she sits	745	Stel Distress	11
They ne'er troubled their head,	755	Dingley Brent	5
As, if the gout should seize the head,	761	Bec's B-Day	11
Her hands and feet conduct her head,	761	Bec's B-Day	22
Her head is but a mere by-stander:	761	Bec's B-Day	26
Forgive him, Tom, his Head is crackt.	795	Traulus 1	6
Hang's down his Head, and drops his Tail,	797	Traulus 1	37
Hang, Drown, or knock him on the Head.	797	Traulus 1	40
Talks whate'er comes in his Head,	800	Traulus 2	21
That the Mitre wou'd never stick fast on their Head,	805	Irish Bishops	46
That one cloven Tongue, ever sat on your Head;	805	Irish Bishops	50
Had thou been join'd to Boulter's head.	822	Epigr Rundle	4
An head so weighty and profound,	822	Epigr Rundle	5
Many a Head that holds no Brains.	829	Legion Club	10
Its Head reclining tow'rds the Ground.	849	Old Thorn	20
From my head to my heels,	852	Lady's Lament	33
You had like to have put it quite out of my Head.	870	Grand Question	86
At the Head of his Troop, with Trumpet and Drum:	870	Grand Question	88
From Market-Hill's exalted Head,	884	Rev Market-Hill	47
So nicely clad from Head to Heel:	889	Panegyr Dean	76
You think your giddy Head will burst:	893	Panegyr Dean	194
Aspiring to exalt my Head:	897	Panegyr Dean	322
Sunk over head and ears in matter,	900	Dean's Reasons	59
Are like the ravings of a crackt head;	900	Dean's Reasons	64
From her own Head, Megaera takes	903	Death Daphne	21
At Head and Foot my Body lopt:	915	Riddle 1	12
O'er Head and Body make a Rout,	920	Riddle 6	15
My Head, with Giddiness, goes round;	926	Riddle 9	7
For Silver and Gold I don't trouble my Head,	927	Riddle 11	D 5
Oft' revives my drooping head:	937	Riddle 24	D 46
Why sure, Mr. Poet, your head got a jar	976	Dean to Sherid	27
I leave it for the second head.	983	Sher, A Goose	26
. . . since my Mother bound my Head,	985	Mary to Sher	1
If I treat you like <a> <crown'd> <Head>	637	Epistle Lady	239

HEAD-ACH
| Of Head-ach, and the Spleen complains; | 446 | Modern Lady | 44 |

HEADLONG
| And headlong in the Waters drown. | 259 | Bubble | 216 |
| Come headlong tumbling from their mitred Chariots, | 806 | Judas | 20 |

HEADS   SEE HEDES, DOGS-HEADS,BLOCK-HEADS
And men seem walking on their heads;	35	Ode Sancroft	34
For which no Heads have yet atton'd!	181	Horace 2, 1	28
An hundred Heads broke,	246	Irish-Feast	71
Despis'd the Beast with many Heads,	498	Panegyr Swift	161
The Vi'lets ope their purple heads;	621	Scandal Poem 1	140
The Vi'lets ope their Purple Heads;	627	Scandal Poem 2	144
With Heads to Points the Gulph they enter,	654	On Poetry	401
Their Heads attempt the nether Skies.	654	On Poetry	404
The out or inside of their Heads,	688	Cadenus Vaness	49
Whose able Heads support the Weight,	781	Mullinix Tim	257
Scribble senseless Heads of Bills;	831	Legion Club	60

HEALING
| Not for his boasted healing art; | 432 | Answer Paulus | 17 |

HEALTH
A good Health to Gen'ral Hill,	169	Peace Dunkirk	39
My State of Health none care to learn;	203	In Sickness	5
To hardships in pursuit of health;	401	Window Inns 5	D 2
Pursue the Goddess Health in vain,	401	Window Inns 5	D 5
The Law so strictly guards the Monarch's Health,	533	To Mr. Gay	77
Declin'd in Health, advanc'd in Years.	703	Cadenus Vaness	529
To drink Sir <Arthur's> Health and mine:	890	Panegyr Dean	102
Preserve his health, his store increase;	902	Dean's Reasons	101
By riding Post I lose my Health;	917	Riddle 3	17

HEALTH	(CONTINUED)	PAGE	TITLE	LINE
Yet he gets home at night with Health and whole Bones.		1037	Four Storyes	8
HEALTHY				
Continues healthy, fat, and fair.		761	Bec's B-Day	10
HEAP				
Upon a rubbish Heap of broken Laws		9	Ode to King	102
His scrap of Life is but a Heap of Miseries, . . .		9	Ode to King	107
Is but a Crowd of Atoms justling in a heap, . . .		20	Ode Athenian	127
Who blend it into folly's larger heap, ...		45	To Congreve	62
Take up a well-bound Heap of Sticks.		189	Faggot	4
His Troubles and Sorrows now come in a Heap, . . .		519	Dean Hang Rape	59
Thou now one Heap of Foulness art, ...		787	Clad in Brown	13
HEAP'D				
Most think what has been heap'd on You, ...		478	Epist on Epist	105
HEAPS				
Here Pettycoats in frowzy Heaps;		527	Lady's Dres Rm	48
Huge Heaps of never-dying Works;		922	Riddle 7	40
HEAR				
How would you blush the shameful birth to hear		46	To Congreve	85
Hear my Request the Virgin said		120	Apollo Outwit	29
Shall hear Him harangue against Prior to Morrow. . .		143	New Song	6
To hear we are making a Peace without Spain;		143	New Song	12
Methinks I hear thee loud, as Trumpet, ...		182	Horace 2, 1	71
Attend thy Coach, and hear them shout		183	Horace 2, 1	80
How would they blush to hear it said, ...		190	Faggot	31
To hear, yet give me no Relief;		204	In Sickness	26
Hear Sounds harmonious from the Skies.		230	Prog of Poetry	16
With Forty Things more: Now hear what the Law says, .		236	Excellent Song	3
For know I cannot bear to hear, ...		271	Apollo's Edict	D 48
Hear him Blaspheme; and Swear, and Rayl, ...		312	To Ford	45
We gladly hear you, and submit:		314	To Ford	94
And hardly hear of half a Score.		315	To Ford	108
"And not a Muse will hear their Call:		321	First of April	22
Now hear an old Tale. There antiently stood		334	Serious Poem	17
I hear among Scholars there is a great Doubt		334	Serious Poem	25
Hear one Story more and then I will stop.		337	Serious Poem	109
And that by all I e're did hear		372	Letter D. S-y	11
And fain wou'd hear it told again;		376	Apology Lady C	22
She'd hear of no Excuse in Prose.		378	Apology Lady C	92
An Heir? and Stranger yet to hear, ...		384	Manly Virtue	19
The Dean too deaf to hear.		405	Swift to Pope	4
She ravishes all Hearts to hear her.		416	Woman's Mind	36
Methinks I hear the Ladies cry, ...		445	Modern Lady	13
Aura, whose Tongue you hear a Mile hence, ...		450	Modern Lady	170
But now they hear a Foot-Man's Rap:		451	Modern Lady	211
At last they hear the Watchman knock, ...		453	Modern Lady	282
To hear the Belgick Lyon roar.		468	Birthday Song	246
Hear from my desk the words that follow;		490	Dialogue	48
(May Heav'n Indulgent hear your Pray'r!)		498	Panegyr Swift	174
Hear an old Fable, and a dull one too;		538	Mr. Pulteney	15
To hear, the other bore the Bell---?		546	Life of Swift	55
"D'ye hear the News---? the Dean is dead---! . . .		547	Life of Swift	69
"I hear about two thousand Pound---		547	Life of Swift	73
"I hear, they're of a diff'rent kind:		550	Life of Swift	181
How patiently you hear him groan!		554	Death of Swift	29
Yet, thus methinks, I hear 'em speak;		556	Death of Swift	79
To hear his out-of-fashion'd Wit?		556	Death of Swift	92
"But laugh'd to hear an Idiot quote, ...		572	Death of Swift	473
Now, methinks, I hear you cry;		632	Epistle Lady	91
Then hear an old experienc'd Sinner		642	On Poetry	75
Lie Snug, and hear what Cricticks say.		644	On Poetry	118
As soon as you can hear his Knell, ...		646	On Poetry	205
At Wills you hear a Poem read, ...		649	On Poetry	263
Hear me pay my dying Vows.		661	Love Song	24
No more I hear my Church's Bell, ...		674	His Deafness	3
I hardly hear a Woman's Clack.		674	His Deafness	8
She'd hear the Cause another Day, ...		690	Cadenus Vaness	117
Offending Daughters oft wou'd hear		694	Cadenus Vaness	240
In School to hear the finest Boy.		704	Cadenus Vaness	553
We never hear the Workmen prais'd, ...		727	Stella, Poems	2
They never wou'd hear, ...		756	Dingley Brent	10
While I can better hear than see;		758	Stel B-day '24	52
And please her more to hear them tattle		762	Bec's B-Day	55
To hear such mortifying Stuff.		763	Stel B-day '26	8
Beware, and when you hear the Surges roar, ...		772	Horace 1, 14	61
But when they hear his rusty Voice, ...		776	Mullinix Tim	95
But purely come to hear, and stare;		777	Mullinix Tim	128
And, though you hear him Stut-tut-tut-ter, ...		797	Traulus 1	47
Now hear an Allusion!--A Mitre, you know, ...		805	Irish Bishops	41
Before you condemn us, hear what we can say.		805	Irish Bishops	54
For, let us hear the weak Pretence, ...		820	Dr. Rundle	11
Run to hear Jackpudding gabble;		830	Legion Club	18
Hear the rattling Thunder drop, ...		830	Legion Club	22
Thou I hear, a pleasant Rogue art;		839	Legion Club	220
And, Molly, she said, I should hear some ill News. .		868	Grand Question	52
"Hist, Huzzy, I think I hear some Body coming-- . .		871	Grand Question	127
Do but hear on the Clergy how glib his Tongue ran; . .		872	Grand Question	140
Never since I was born did I hear so much Wit, . . .		873	Grand Question	173
We never ask to hear you twice.		889	Panegyr Dean	74
Admire to hear me speak so fine.		891	Panegyr Dean	136
I will never hear you read.		907	Daphne	54

HEAR	(CONTINUED)	PAGE	TITLE	LINE
You shall never hear me thunder, ...		908	Daphne	73
Yet neither Smell, See, Taste, or Hear.		935	Riddle 23	D 9
But now let us hear what the Muse from your car says. .		976	Dean to Sherid	6
But let me advise you, when next I hear from you, . .		976	Dean to Sherid	9
And see now, it strikes ten, and I hear him coming up		987	Mary to Sher	36
Stairs:				
I hear with some Concern you roar, ...		1002	Reply by Dean	10
I'm griev'd to hear your Banishment, ...		1002	Reply by Dean	14
Where I hear you are crammd evry day like a Swine . .		1017	Swift Ans Sher	13
The Beef you have got, which I hear is a Chine . .		1018	Swift Ans Sher	30
HEARD				
Who heard you meant to write heroics next;		47	To Congreve	144
There first the visionary sound was heard, ...		51	Temple Ill	15
And in all the Places I liv'd, I never heard of such a		70	Mrs Harris Pet	31
Thing.				
Thalia heard the Call and Flew		120	Apollo Outwit	39
The Smallcoal-Man was heard with Cadence deep, . . .		124	Descriptn Morn	11
And every one was pleas'd, that heard it:		128	Little House	40
I have heard all the Speech repeated by Hoppy.		143	New Song	9
In Church you heard her thro the Crowd		222	Prog of Love	9
I heard it from my Grannam's Mouth, ...		254	Bubble	98
When it heard of a Bank appear'd to his Debtors, . . .		288	Bank Down	42
The Dean, she heard her Uncle say		291	Prog Marriage	47
Who ever heard of servants paying wages?		308	Billet Players	30
And if you had heard the Man discourse, ...		375	Apology Lady C	11
He had not heard of him--Pray see, ...		377	Apology Lady C	59
Lovely alike, or heard or seen;		385	Manly Virtue	58
He heard I kept a pack of hounds, ...		422	Ireld	27
Because they might have heard of one		460	Birthday Song	11
A Passage may be found, I've heard, ...		479	Epist on Epist	119
As if he heard Loud Thunders roul, ...		500	Doctor Delaney	17
Than if he heard you broke your Bones.		546	Life of Swift	30
For, I have heard another Story, ...		547	Life of Swift	82
Says Lintot, "I have heard the Name:		563	Death of Swift	255
(As in a Book he heard it read) . . :		587	Strephon Chloe	101
That, once he heard a School-boy tell, ...		587	Strephon Chloe	106
Strephon who heard the fuming Rill		589	Strephon Chloe	175
Abasht at what they saw and heard, ...		590	Strephon Chloe	195
And, I have heard thee oft salute		594	Cassinus Peter	33
He heard, there was a Club of Cheats		607	Beasts Confess	191
Gone, to be never heard of more, ...		642	On Poetry	69
She heard it--there she kept her Word;		690	Cadenus Vaness	119
Because she heard a sudden Drum, ...		726	To Stella	77
Like Paul's Ephesians, never heard it;		820	Dr. Rundle	16
What I heard in yonder Hell.		832	Legion Club	86
And dismally was heard to whine		849	Old Thorn	43
Till she heard the Dean call, Will your Ladyship walk?		873	Grand Question	180
For you can't but have heard of a trick among wizards, .		976	Dean to Sherid	21
I've often heard it from the wise, ...		982	Sher, A Goose	3
For I heard, a month ago, that he was down there . . .		1023	Nim-Dan-Dean 2	D 12
HEARERS				
In vain: her Hearers had no Share		698	Cadenus Vaness	356
Her Hearers are amaz'd from whence		726	To Stella	79
HEARING				
. . .and she, you know, is thick of Hearing;		70	Mrs Harris Pet	25
And in Her own hearing I boldly did Vote, ...		144	New Song	40
Hearing the House was empty, came to town;		307	Billet Players	2
Another Case; the Sense of Hearing:		366	Answer Delaney	28
So hearing of a grave Divine, ...		375	Apology Lady C	5
And, hearing much of Daphne's Fame, ...		904	Death Daphne	53
HEARKEN				
All mad to speak, and none to hearken, ...		450	Modern Lady	178
Next, hearken Gay, to what thy Charge requires, . . .		533	To Mr. Gay	53
Hearken, what my Lady says---:		630	Epistle Lady	11
Still to be curious, never hearken.		753	Gift for Bec	22
Still be she curious, never hearken		762	Bec's B-Day	43
HEARS				
When with amazing Joy she hears, ...		17	Ode Athenian	51
He deals, and Hears mysterious Chat;		63	Discovery	14
Now Finch alarms the Lords; he hears for certain, . .		194	Author Himself	37
Approaching near the Town, he hears		338	Wood's Brass	5
So loud, till all the Nation hears;		354	Simile Silver	28
The Soldier smiling hears the Widows Cries, ...		364	On Dreams	15
And as he hears his Wit and Sence, ...		463	Birthday Song	91
When at a Skirmish first he hears		500	Doctor Delaney	3
He hears the Clergy are offended;		605	Beasts Confess	126
This Prophecy he trembling hears.		850	Old Thorn	56
Never hears what you can say:		906	Daphne	14
HEARSE SEE HERSE				
To pay their Duty at his Hearse!		98	Elegy Patrige	8
HEART SEE SWEET-HEART				
But with my own Rebellious Heart, ...		23	Ode Athenian	239
Further than its own palace in her heart:		53	Temple Ill	54
And think thou seest my owners Heart, ...		60	Lady Tablebook	2
In such a Book and such a Heart, ...		61	Lady Tablebook	26
Ambitious of a Regent's Heart		66	Problem	35
To try the Back-way to his Heart;		66	Problem	42
'Twould grieve a Body's Heart to see't:		90	Bauc & Phil 1	18
Of her entirely-English Heart, ...		96	On the Union	2
For both were frighted to the Heart, ...		112	Bauc & Phil 2	37

	PAGE	TITLE	LINE
And had the Service all by Heart;	115	Bauc & Phil 2	130
As having Malice in her Heart,	120	Apollo Outwit	26
I doubt your Heart is set on Pelf	175	Horace 1, 7	125
Wont at such times each heart to pierce,	296	Satiric Elegy	19
I pity Elrington with all my heart;	308	Billet Players	31
If you have London still at heart	313	To Ford	57
"A Wife as good as Heart cou'd wish one,	322	First of April	49
But Wood I assure you is no Heart of Oak;	336	Serious Poem	66
Thro' ev'ry Sense to reach the Heart.	379	Apology Lady C	116
To win the Soul, and glad the Heart;	385	Manly Virtue	56
My Master Pope will break his Heart.	410	Dial Rich Marb	72
It fills my Heart with Woe,	426	Five Ladies	21
Had I a Heart to fight,	426	Five Ladies	37
In you, who ought to know my Heart,	444	Modern Lady	2
Has all the Dinner-Cant by Heart:	448	Modern Lady	101
With panting Heart, and earnest Eyes,	452	Modern Lady	230
Here many a King his heart and Crown	465	Birthday Song	167
"To <Grafton's> Grace, with grateful Heart;	476	Epist on Epist	33
His Heart too Great, though Fortune little,	482	Libel on D- D-	81
That, if we could but see his Heart,	485	Libel on D- D-	157
And feel a trembling at his Heart:	500	Doctor Delaney	6
The Danger past, takes Heart of Grace,	500	Doctor Delaney	25
His Heart is through his Libel seen,	514	Answer Fable	75
Not Love of Beauty less the Heart inflames	532	To Mr. Gay	19
And while he poisons, wins the Royal Heart.	534	To Mr. Gay	82
Bring from his Heart sincerer Groans,	546	Life of Swift	29
"He lov'd the Dean. (I lead a Heart.)	562	Death of Swift	239
"The Courtiers have them all by Heart:	564	Death of Swift	286
"In Exile with a steady Heart,	570	Death of Swift	431
It would do your Heart good, to see how she will cark it.	580	Psyche	12
She cannot help it for her Heart;	588	Strephon Chloe	130
When Chloe stole your Heart away,	591	Strephon Chloe	236
Your Heart had been as whole as mine.	591	Strephon Chloe	250
Her Heart, and from her Lips distills;	592	Strephon Chloe	280
To pierce an injur'd Lover's Heart.	595	Cassinus Peter	60
To force it out my Heart must rend;	596	Cassinus Peter	95
Not to the Nymph that keeps thy Heart;	596	Cassinus Peter	102
That in his Heart he lov'd a Jest;	602	Beasts Confess	22
The Swine with contrite Heart allow'd,	602	Beasts Confess	37
Yet could not for his Heart repent it.	604	Beasts Confess	102
He cannot help it for his Heart	605	Beasts Confess	119
In my Head and Heart they center;	630	Epistle Lady	33
Gentle Cupid o'er my Heart;	660	Love Song	2
With zeal in heart, and notes in hand;	675	Curate's Compl	2
I find that I have gain'd her Heart:	679	From Catullus	4
But, what the gentlest Heart would vex,	687	Cadenus Vaness	25
By Beauty cou'd your Heart be won,	692	Cadenus Vaness	192
With open Heart and bounteous Hand:	693	Cadenus Vaness	210
Vows, on Vanessa's Heart to take	701	Cadenus Vaness	470
And, born directly to the Heart,	703	Cadenus Vaness	522
In every Scene had kept his Heart;	703	Cadenus Vaness	541
Yet gave him not the Heart to chide;	704	Cadenus Vaness	571
Aim'd at the Head, but reach'd the Heart.	706	Cadenus Vaness	623
Climbs from the Toe to touch the Heart.	710	Cadenus Vaness	741
Will in your tainted Heart preside.	725	To Stella	50
To keep a worthy Lover's heart	732	Verses Vanessa	2
Or how could she her Heart bestow	733	Verses Vanessa	21
Her Stays stick to her Heart.	733	Verses Vanessa	26
In your own heart you'll reap the fruit,	755	Stella '23	31
Whose Heart in this Four-footed Thing lies.	763	Collar Lap-Dog	2
And join to fortify your Heart.	765	Stel B-day '26	72
Be grave and wise, 'twou'd break their Heart.	776	Mullinix Tim	90
In doleful Scenes, that breaks our heart,	777	Mullinix Tim	121
Fierce in Tongue, in Heart a Coward:	799	Traulus 2	12
I'm in spite of my heart led:	853	Lady's Lament	48
Altho' it was plain, in her Heart she was glad,	873	Grand Question	183
No Knife so keen to weed thee from my Heart.	881	Pastoral Dial	12
My Heart with Emulation burns	887	Panegyr Dean	29
Whose uncommunicative heart,	900	Dean's Reasons	43
And now her Heart with Pleasure jumps,	904	Death Daphne	59
What Pride a Female Heart enflames!	905	Death Daphne	89
He felt about his Heart a Damp,	905	Death Daphne	97
But a Fury in her heart.	907	Daphne	24
And then, with Heart more hard than Stone,	915	Riddle 1	13
Stabb'd to the Heart, condemn'd to Flame,	916	Riddle 2	7
The more they open every Heart.	920	Riddle 6	18
With that which dwelt so near her Heart;	922	Riddle 7	36
If Chloe o'er thy Heart prevails,	925	Riddle 8	19
All the secrets of her heart.	936	Riddle 24	D 26
His heart in poison deeply dipt,	951	Upstart	D 27
For ev'ry Stroke goes to my Heart,	1005	Sheridan's Sub	32
. . .with all my Heart and Soul, upon my Word and Honour.	1014	Swift to Sheri	9

HEART-SICK

| Heart-sick of a high fever and consuming atrophy; | 42 | Ode Sancroft | 252 |

HEARTED   SEE LION-HEARTED,DUTCH-HEARTED

HEARTILY

| But now, since the Drapier hath heartily maul'd him, | 351 | Wood Insect | 33 |
| You're heartily welcome: But as for good Chear, | 871 | Grand Question | 121 |

```
HEARTS                                                       PAGE  TITLE            LINE
     Divided Hearts, united States.        . . . . . . . .    96  On the Union        6
     Display their various nets for hearts:  . . . . . .     178  To Lord Harley     54
     Gave Women all their Hearts could wish  . . . . . .     227  Prog of Beauty     58
     Our true Irish Hearts from old England to wean;  . .    237  Excellent Song      7
     With chearfull Looks, and honest Hearts.               314  To Ford            82
     And when to the Joy of your Hearts he has Roar'd,  .   336  Serious Poem       83
     She ravishes all Hearts to hear her.  . . . . . .      416  Woman's Mind       36
     "Because you held the King of Hearts:  . . . . . .     452  Modern Lady       256
     How far their Hearts from private Views,  . . . . .    501  Doctor Delaney     60
     For which all true Protestant Hearts should be glad;  . 520  Dean Hang Rape    68
     Yet laugh our hearts out, one and all.  . . . . . .    545  Life of Swift      14
     Their Empire in our Hearts divide:                    555  Death of Swift     42
     The Screen remov'd, their Hearts are trembling,  .     561  Death of Swift    223
     My female Friends, whose tender Hearts  . . . . .     562  Death of Swift    225
     "As Numbers in their Hearts must own,  . . . . .      566  Death of Swift    337
     "With Wrath and Vengeance in their Hearts:  . . .     568  Death of Swift    380
     What Hampers full of bleeding Hearts!  . . . . . .     585  Strephon Chloe     36
     Enough to win ten Thousand Hearts;  . . . . . .       598  Problem Solved     20
     Hence we conclude, no Women's Hearts                  688  Cadenus Vaness     61
     Of killing Eyes, or bleeding Hearts:                  728  Stella, Poems      12
     To win the Truant School-Boys Hearts!  . . . . .      779  Mullinix Tim      200
     Have Hearts more harden'd than Egyptians;  . . .      813  Bro Protestant     52
     Every Mischief in their Hearts,  . . . . . . . .      837  Legion Club       187
     How well to win the Ladies Hearts,  . . . . . . .     887  Panegyr Dean       11
     Infecting thus our Hearts by Stealth;  . . . . .      895  Panegyr Dean      280
     Set hoping, hoping, hoping hearts of Lovers akeing,  . .  959  Cantata
HEARTY
     He should have had my hearty Vote,  . . . . . . .     349  Upright Judge 2     3
     What hearty Prayers that I should mend?  . . . . .     557  Death of Swift    138
     From stomach sharp, and hearty feeding  . . . . .      745  Stel Distress       7
     From Stomach sharp and hearty feeding,  . . . . .      750  Stel Wood-Park     31
     Of hearty gossips prating round;  . . . . . . . .      762  Bec's B-Day        52
     Like a hearty divine;  . . . . . . . . . .             858  Lady's Lament     222
HEAT
     It quite o'recame the vital Heat,)  . . . . . . .       16  Ode Athenian        4
     O'er the sun's face, and from his heat proceeds,  . .    45  To Congreve       70
     Love's Fire, it seems, like inward Heat,  . . . .        65  Problem            7
     The Clerk said to her in a Heat,  . . . . . . .        128  Little House       55
     Its Motion and its Heat maintains.  . . . . . . .      239  Run Bankers        12
     His dangerous Excess of Heat,  . . . . . . . .         387  Manly Virtue      108
     Give Mortals neither Heat nor Light.  . . . . . .      700  Cadenus Vaness    443
     The Heat that makes the Summit glow,  . . . . . .      731  Stella, Poems     107
     So the Sun's Heat, with different Powers,  . . . .     731  Stella, Poems     119
     Come, driven by heat,  . . . . . . . . . . .           857  Lady's Lament     189
HEATED
     And then to cool her heated Brains,  . . . . . . .     446  Modern Lady        45
     Or, to Passion quickly heated:  . . . . . . . .        630  Epistle Lady       16
HEATHEN
     I know you will say, this is all Heathen Greek;  . . .  337  Serious Poem       89
     Should be more scrup'lous than a Heathen.  . . . .     461  Birthday Song      26
     That no honest Heathen would be on their Side.  . .    805  Irish Bishops      38
     Yet, were he Heathen, Turk or Jew  . . . . . .         820  Dr. Rundle          9
     The Heathen doth believe in Christ  . . . . . . .     1036  Heathen Christ      1
HEATHENISH
     In Heathenish Times from the Trunk of an Oak:  . .     335  Serious Poem       58
     More Heathenish Times than those of our own;  . . .    335  Serious Poem       60
HEATHENS
     The Heathens, we Read, had Gods made of Wood,  . . .   334  Serious Poem        9
HEAV'D
     The worst Dunce in your School, 'till he's heav'd from 968  Letter Sherid      34
          the Ground
HEAV'N
     The publick Stamp Heav'n sets on all that's Great and   18  Ode Athenian       93
          Good,
     How much of Heav'n is in her naked looks.  . . . .     23  Ode Athenian      233
     Poor we Cadets of Heav'n, not worth her Care,  . .      32  Ode to Temple     183
     Truth is eternal, and the Son of Heav'n,  . . . .       34  Ode Sancroft        1
     For, sure, we want some guide from Heav'n to show  .    39  Ode Sancroft      156
     Thinks heav'n has cancel'd all our sins.  . . . .       40  Ode Sancroft      181
     When <Ann> for Heav'n resigns Her Throne.  . . . .     180  Horace 2, 1        12
     Few Bankers will to Heav'n be Mounters.  . . . .       241  Run Bankers        58
     To use the Gifts, that Heav'n bestows;  . . . . .      243  Horace 4, 9        18
     Now mounted up to Heav'n again,  . . . . . . .         256  Bubble            150
     Unerring Heav'n, with bounteous Hand,  . . . . .       272  Apollo's Edict  D  64
     (May Heav'n Indulgent hear your Pray'r!)  . . . .      498  Panegyr Swift     174
     Nor dare to use the gifts by heav'n bestow'd;  . .     506  To a Friend        10
     If with such Talents Heav'n hath blest 'em  . . .      555  Death of Swift     65
     "But Heav'n his Innocence defends,  . . . . . .        570  Death of Swift    425
     Descend from Heav'n to Beauty's Aid;  . . . . .        590  Strephon Chloe    220
     Not all the Court of Heav'n could shew  . . . . .      597  Problem Solved      9
     With which from earth to heav'n he springs;  . . .     621  Scandal Poem 1    118
     But, since just Heav'n the Dukes ambition mocks        678  Dean and Duke       5
     Or any Brother-God in Heav'n:  . . . . . . .           695  Cadenus Vaness    261
     Harness'd her Doves, and flew to Heav'n.  . . . .      714  Cadenus Vaness    889
     O then, whatever Heav'n intends,  . . . . . . .        766  Stel B-day '26     79
     In Vain from injur'd Heav'n Relief expects.  . . .     771  Horace 1, 14       36
     Heav'n forbid he should despise thee;  . . . . . .     907  Daphne             51
     All Figures Heav'n or Earth can yield,  . . . . .      927  Riddle 10       D  16
     That stands 'twixt Heav'n, and Earth, and Hell,  . .   928  Riddle 12       D   2
     From Heav'n I fall, tho' from Earth I begin,  . . .    928  Riddle 13       D   1
```

HEAV'N	(CONTINUED)	PAGE	TITLE	LINE
Tho' so much of Heav'n appears in my Make,	. . . .	929	Riddle 13	D 7
HEAV'N-BORN				
Of heav'n-born Truth below:		36	Ode Sancroft	53
HEAV'N'S				
Diana thus, Heav'n's chastest queen,	. . . .	178	To Lord Harley	73
"An Angel sent by Heav'n's Command,	. . . . .	485	Libel on D- D-	166
HEAV'NLY				
And for a while in heav'nly Contemplation sate	. . .	16	Ode Athenian	25
Enthron'd with Heav'nly Wit, ...		21	Ode Athenian	177
Turns to an Awl by Heav'nly Art;	. . . .	100	Elegy Patrige	82
Say, which among the Heav'nly Pow'rs	. . . .	227	Prog of Beauty	55
When rapt in Heav'nly Airs, he sings	. . . .	496	Panegyr Swift	102
By vent'ring on his heav'nly Wife?	. . . .	507	Strephon Chloe	104
Can Chloe, heav'nly Chloe <piss>?	. . . .	589	Strephon Chloe	178
To Goddesses so heav'nly sweet,	. . . . . .	590	Strephon Chloe	199
Supports their Minds with heav'nly Food.	. . .	605	Beasts Confess	124
With heav'nly beauty so endow'd;	. . . . .	619	Scandal Poem 1	75
With heav'nly Beauty so endow'd?		625	Scandal Poem 2	73
For if the Heav'nly Folk should know	. . . .	689	Cadenus Vaness	79
For how can Heav'nly Wisdom prove	. . . .	695	Cadenus Vaness	294
Florinda, dart their Heav'nly Beams, ...		932	Riddle 19	D 2
HEAV'NS				
The Gift (good Heav'ns preserve 't from Thieves)	. .	494	Panegyr Swift	49
Jove, nodding, shook the Heav'ns, and said,	. . . .	579	Day Judgement	10
This said, she plucks in Heav'ns high Bow'rs	. . .	691	Cadenus Vaness	154
A Nation thus, who oft Heav'ns Call neglects,	. . .	771	Horace 1, 14	35
HEAVE				
And heave her Bosom unaware		222	Prog of Love	17
HEAVEN				
(By all but Heaven and Me unseen,)	. . . . . .	7	Ode to King	49
Sent by just Heaven to threaten Earth	. . . . .	10	Ode to King	133
And nigh to Heaven as is its Name.		16	Ode Athenian	10
This beauteous Queen by Heaven design'd	. . .	22	Ode Athenian	216
Since Heaven will claim its residence as well as birth,		35	Ode Sancroft	19
In the metropolis of heaven;		42	Ode Sancroft	237
Since Heaven and Cato both are pleas'd--	. . .	42	Ode Sancroft	264
My hate, whose lash just heaven has long decreed	. . .	47	To Congreve	133
Should heaven suspend to act but for a day;		53	Temple Ill	64
Heaven with a parent's eye regarding earth;	. . .	54	Temple Ill	89
Lest with the Wicked, Heaven involve the Just?	. . .	210	Earl of Oxford	20
For Marriages are made in Heaven:		224	Prog of Love	56
Heaven send thou hast not got the Hypps.	. . .	594	Cassinus Peter	35
By flatt'ring <Kings> whom Heaven design'd	. . .	654	On Poetry	407
They could all Pow'r in Heaven divide, ...		657	On Poetry	483
Or else, shut out from Heaven and Earth,	. . .	689	Cadenus Vaness	87
Just Heaven! to see the Dunghill dastard Brood	. . .	826	Noisy Tom	17
I wish them in Heaven, ...		951	Apples	7
HEAVEN'S				
For this inferior world is but Heaven's dusky shade,	.	35	Ode Sancroft	21
To his undoubted Master, Heaven's Almighty Son.	.	38	Ode Sancroft	134
Some whom ambition drives, seek Heaven's high Son	. .	39	Ode Sancroft	166
That Heaven's high Son was in a village born;	. .	39	Ode Sancroft	172
Darts weeping beams across heaven's wat'ry face; . . .		52	Temple Ill	26
And if so black the cloud, that heaven's bright queen		53	Temple Ill	57
For, let heaven's wrath enlarge these weary days, .		54	Temple Ill	111
And, though by Heaven's severe Decree		726	To Stella	103
HEAVENLY				
With many a heavenly Song		17	Ode Athenian	54
With heavenly peace of mind to bear		38	Ode Sancroft	115
Wisely retreated to his heavenly rest.		40	Ode Sancroft	189
Yet to firm heavenly minds, ...		41	Ode Sancroft	205
And which (to heavenly soil transplanted) will improve, .		41	Ode Sancroft	228
Where high patrician souls dress'd heavenly gay, . . .		41	Ode Sancroft	234
Attended by her heavenly Race, ...		466	Birthday Song	184
Such heavenly Influence require, ...		641	On Poetry	31
Sing heavenly Muse in sweetly flowing Strain, ...		880	Pastoral Dial	7
HEAVINGS				
Distortions, Groanings, Strainings, Heavings; . . .		591	Strephon Chloe	241
HEAVN'LY				
Syrius, the swiftest of the heavn'ly Pack, ...		538	Mr. Pulteney	33
HEAVY				
A load as heavy as the Crown, ...		40	Ode Sancroft	188
But o'er th' afflicted with a heavy pace		55	Temple Ill	121
The heavy Wall went clamb'ring after.	. .	92	Bauc & Phil 1	94
The heavy Wall climb'd slowly after.	. . .	112	Bauc & Phil 2	54
What heavy burthens lawyers lay		434	Answer Paulus	62
You Travel with a heavy Load, ...		480	Libel on D-	11
Tells, with a Sneer, the Tidings heavy:		560	Death of Swift	190
Bastings heavy, dry, obtuse, ...		636	Epistle Lady	203
But heavy, and dark, when you squeeze me together. . .		928	Riddle 13	D 4
HEBE				
Then Hebe came and took her Place		290	Prog Marriage	15
And Hebe, Goddess ever young.		585	Strephon Chloe	56
HEBES				
That five years hence will both be Hebes.		465	Birthday Song	172
HEBREW				
May backward be perus'd, like Hebrew.		1021	Nim-Dan-Dean 1	D 42
HEBREWS				
As much as Hebrews and Philistines:		812	Bro Protestant	32

```
                                                              PAGE    TITLE              LINE
HECTOR
      To see a Scoundrel Strut and hector,      . . . . . .   312 To Ford               39
      Your Spouse shall there no longer hector  . . . . . .   362 Grace's Answer        37
      That she might o're the Servants hector   . . . . . .   745 Stel Distress          7
      She now can or'e the servants hector.     . . . . . .   745 Stel Distress
      That she might o'er the Servants hector.  . . . . . .   749 Stel Wood-Park         6
      Nay, hector and swagger, you'll still find me stanch,  .979 Dean to Tho: S        13
HECTORS
      At Ten, my Lady comes and Hectors,        . . . . . .   278 Journal               13
HEDES
      Geryon shall have three Hedes agayne      . . . . . .   103 Merlin                19
HEDGE
      "Must in the Ambient Hedge be seen;       . . . . . .   476 Epist on Epist        54
HEDGE-TAVERN
      At some Hedge-Tavern lies in Pawn;        . . . . . .   582 Young Nymph           44
HEDGES
      That Walls have Tongues, and Hedges, Ears. . . . . .    408 Dial Rich Marb         8
      As if it grew in common Hedges.           . . . . . .   640 On Poetry             10
      Of Gipsies littering under Hedges,        . . . . . .   641 On Poetry             38
      "To tear thy Hedges join in Leagues,      . . . . . .   851 Old Thorn             79
      To cut his hedges down for fire;          . . . . . .   902 Dean's Reasons       106
HEEDLESS
      Heedless, ignorant, forgetful?            . . . . . .   630 Epistle Lady           8
      When I talk, and you are heedless,        . . . . . .   908 Daphne                59
HEEL
      Our Prince has hit Him, like Achilles, in the Heel,     10 Ode to King          142
      But Albion's cliffs are out at heel,      . . . . . .   468 Birthday Song        244
      Such Cleanliness from Head to Heel:       . . . . . .   584 Strephon Chloe        10
      By these embroider'd high Heel Shoes,     . . . . . .   885 Rev Market-Hill       63
      So nicely clad from Head to Heel;         . . . . . .   889 Panegyr Dean          76
HEEL-PIECE
      Or like a Heel-piece to support           . . . . . .   645 On Poetry            171
HEELS
      His Grazier's Coat reach down his Heels,  . . . . . .    94 Bauc & Phil 1        166
      His Grazier's Coat fall down his Heels;   . . . . . .   115 Bauc & Phil 2        118
      Slow Vengeance, like a Blood-hound at his Heels.        210 Earl of Oxford        22
      To see a Knave's inverted Heels:          . . . . . .   451 Modern Lady          227
      Shou'd cool your Heels a while, and wait  . . . . . .   475 Epist on Epist         5
      "Against him lifting up their Heels.      . . . . . .   569 Death of Swift       406
      And as their Heels elated rise,           . . . . . .   654 On Poetry            403
      At People's Heels with frothy Chaps;      . . . . . .   797 Traulus 1             36
      Dreading to be laid by th' Heels.         . . . . . .   834 Legion Club          118
      From my head to my heels,                 . . . . . .   852 Lady's Lament         33
      We'll take her Heels five Inches lower.   . . . . . .   886 Rev Market-Hill      104
      In vain on lofty Heels I tread,           . . . . . .   897 Panegyr Dean         321
HEIFER
      Before this Milk-white Heifer can be stole away,  . .     8 Ode to King          77
HEIGHT
      For all its boasted height,               . . . . . .    10 Ode to King          124
      And 'twas perhaps Parnassus, if in height . . . . .      16 Ode Athenian           8
      And foolishly are glad to see it at it's height . . .    25 Ode Athenian         281
      And by one mighty Hero carried to it's height  . . .     25 Ode Athenian         284
      And far exalted objects lessen by their height:  . .     39 Ode Sancroft         148
      It rises both in Bulk and Height,         . . . . . .   251 Bubble                13
      The Wax is melted by the Height,          . . . . . .   252 Bubble                39
      The Height of Glory here below,           . . . . . .   386 Manly Virtue         100
      It was a Tow'r of monstrous Height,       . . . . . .   413 Desire Possess        40
      For, tho' in Nature Depth and Height      . . . . . .   653 On Poetry            389
      In Poetry the Height we know;             . . . . . .   654 On Poetry            391
      So Stars beyond a certain Height          . . . . . .   700 Cadenus Vaness       442
      But Friendship in its greatest Height,    . . . . . .   711 Cadenus Vaness       780
HEIGHT'NING
      Your Poets, Chloe's Beauty height'ning,   . . . . . .   628 Scandal Poem 2       153
HEIGHTEN
      And then to heighten the Disgrace         . . . . . .    61 Lady Tablebook        23
HEIGHTEN'D
      Were my desires but heighten'd to my pow'r. . . . .      44 To Congreve           40
HEIGHTNING
      Your Poets Chloe's beauty heightning      . . . . .     621 Scandal Poem 1       149
HEIR
      I made use of a Trope; that an Heir to invite,  . .     144 New Song              37
      Or in the cross-bath seeks as Heir        . . . . . .   294 Prog Marriage        137
      Gets not an Heir, but gets a Feaver;      . . . . . .   295 Horrid Plot          152
      "Ye don't fall out about the Heir.        . . . . . .   321 First of April        12
      Becomes his Brother's lawful Heir:        . . . . . .   366 Answer Delaney        14
      Now made--ye Gods!--a Son and Heir,       . . . . . .   384 Manly Virtue          18
      An Heir? and Stranger yet to hear,        . . . . . .   384 Manly Virtue          19
      An Heir, and Orphan of a Peer;            . . . . . .   384 Manly Virtue          20
      Some, when an Heir succeeds; go boldly on, . . . . .    535 To Mr. Gay           117
      "What has he left? And who's his Heir?    . . . . . .   558 Death of Swift       154
      No Heir, upon his first Appearance,       . . . . . .   598 Problem Solved        11
      An Heir for Britain to secure             . . . . . .   655 On Poetry            435
      Like a young Heir, the thrifty Goddess    . . . . .     693 Cadenus Vaness       223
      Unless Delany as my Heir,                 . . . . . .   740 Stel B-day '21        19
HEIR-LOOM
      Came an Heir-loom, as Homer sings,        . . . . . .   134 Magician's Rod        64
HEIRESS
      Bred a Fondling, and an Heiress;          . . . . . .   630 Epistle Lady          35
HEIRS
      To me and to my Heirs for ever.           . . . . . .   198 Horace 2, 6       D
      His Heirs might well of all his Wealth possest,  . .    233 Elegy on Demar         5
```

HEIRS	(CONTINUED)	PAGE	TITLE	LINE
His Heirs for Winding-Sheet bestow'd		235	Elegy on Demar	43
And if his Heirs continue kind,		235	Elegy on Demar	49
No Money left for squandring Heirs!		240	Run Bankers	25
Or gives Relief to long-expecting Heirs.		364	On Dreams	28
Will soon grow necessary to his Heirs.		535	To Mr. Gay	120

HELD

		PAGE	TITLE	LINE
Is held as needfull as His Glyster		62	Discovery	12
While Moses held it in his Hand,		132	Magician's Rod	2
And, since the same resemblance held		177	To Lord Harley	29
Held out Medusa's snaky locks,		178	To Lord Harley	45
And by his Looks, had he held out his Palms,		234	Elegy on Demar	11
Alcides held him in his Arms,		257	Bubble	183
While Mistress Iris held her Train,		290	Prog Marriage	13
I wonder you held out so long,		315	To Ford	110
One Bed while alive held both Doll and Dick		430	Dicky Dolly	13
"Because you held the King of Hearts:		452	Modern Lady	256
Held Monarchs labouring at the Oar;		476	Epist on Epist	44
Was, to be held a Misanthrope.		548	Life of Swift	131
"In him was held a Crime of State.		569	Death of Swift	416
"He would have held it a Disgrace,		571	Death of Swift	441
Are equally held infinite,		653	On Poetry	390
A Mastiff's teeth are justly held in vogue,		672	Epig Carthy 25	D 1
Vanessa held Montaigne, and read,		698	Cadenus Vaness	372
And with Address each Genius held		701	Cadenus Vaness	450
Ne'er held Possession of his Breast;		711	Cadenus Vaness	769
Tom was held the merrier Lad,		784	Mullinex Dick	7
And held them in subjection.		784	Mullinex Dick	20
Tom was held by all the Town		785	Mullinex Dick	27
That Bishopricks are held in Fee.		821	Dr. Rundle	60
Who held a Cabbin for ten Groats a Year;		826	Noisy Tom	12
Held up by my knees,		852	Lady's Lament	26

HELICON

		PAGE	TITLE	LINE
And Helicon; for if this Log		671	Epig Carthy 21	D 6

HELL

		PAGE	TITLE	LINE
As in old Fabulous Hell,		9	Ode to King	92
Beneath, and mended Shoes in Hell.		100	Elegy Patrige	68
And drive as many Souls to Hell.		133	Magician's Rod	42
Quoth Will; thy House is worse than Hell:		220	A Quiet Life	10
Upon the god of Gold and Hell,		240	Run Bankers	42
A narrow Sound, though deep as Hell,		256	Bubble	139
And sent him up in Air to Hell.		257	Bubble	184
Charon in him will ferry Souls to Hell;		285	Elegy Boat	25
All riding on Horseback to Hell and the Bank.		287	Bank Down	25
And left a Chasm profound as Hell:		326	Pethox	96
The Cloud, and drive the Hag to Hell:		354	Simile Silver	12
Beneath, a Chasm as deep as Hell,		413	Desire Possess	43
And pawn'd his word Hell is not local.		469	Birthday Song	272
From Hell a <Viceroy> Dev'l ascends,		486	Libel on D- D-	186
The Sentiments resemble Hell.		496	Panegyric Swift	109
Hunted from Earth, and Sea, and Hell, he flies		538	Mr. Pulteney	29
Nor can you go to Hell before you dye.		539	Mr. Pulteney	42
He'd wish his Rivals all in Hell.		554	Death of Swift	34
Allow there's a Hell, but dispute of the Place;		575	Place Damn'd	2
But if Hell by Logical Rules be defin'd,		575	Place Damn'd	3
Most certainly there's the Hell to be found,		575	Place Damn'd	6
And Hell to be sure is at Paris or Rome,		576	Place Damn'd	17
In seas and woods, or low as hell		620	Scandal Poem 1	100
In Seas, and Streams, or low as Hell:		626	Scandal Poem 2	98
This God on Earth turns Devil in Hell.		646	On Poetry	206
Damning to Hell the Jacobits?		773	Mullinix Tim	4
Human Race, or Imps of Hell.		801	Traulus 2	56
Why truly 'tis Satan, <Arch-bishop> of Hell:		803	Irish Bishops	4
To Hell on the Backs of the Clergy wou'd ride;		804	Irish Bishops	18
And burst asunder e'er he went to Hell;		806	Judas	18
Styx, through Hell whose Waters roll!		832	Legion Club	84
What I heard in yonder Hell.		832	Legion Club	86
In his Looks are Hell and Murther;		834	Legion Club	142
Where to find on this Side Hell?		837	Legion Club	184
The devil he may take her into hell and Boult-her!		841	Ballad	D 14
This bloated Harpy sprung from Hell,		895	Panegyr Dean	269
That stands 'twixt Heav'n, and Earth, and Hell,		928	Riddle 12	D 2

HELL-FEATUR'D

		PAGE	TITLE	LINE
Who is that Hell-featur'd Brawler,		834	Legion Club	137

HELLISH

		PAGE	TITLE	LINE
He squals in such a hellish Noise		513	Answer Fable	25
Begone; unhand me, hellish Fry;		596	Cassinus Peter	87

HELM

		PAGE	TITLE	LINE
And you whom Pluto's Helm does wisely shroud		18	Ode Athenian	86
Strait the Muse turns the Helm, and I launch out again;		32	Ode to Temple	195
Mambrino's Helm adorn'd his Head.		156	Fable of Midas	14
How the Helm is rul'd by <Walpole>		635	Epistle Lady	159
She shakes her Helm, she knits her Brows,		694	Cadenus Vaness	252

HELP

		PAGE	TITLE	LINE
Would want a God Himself to help him out.		22	Ode Athenian	210
Whose maintenance requires no help from brains.		48	To Congreve	164
Lord help me, said Mary, I never stirr'd out of this Place!		70	Mrs Harris Pet	16
When he found a new Help from Invisible Hand.		77	Lady B- B-	25
I withdrew my Subscription by help of a Blot,		144	New Song	29
And with the help of Buckley's Pen		180	Horace 2, 1	3

```
HELP           (CONTINUED)                             PAGE    TITLE              LINE
    "Without your Help the Cause is gone--      . . . . . .   200 Horace 2, 6         52
    To help at my approaching End,  . . . . . . . . .         204 In Sickness         20
    "I'll dye, if you deny your Help.  . . . . . . . .        207 Fable Bitches       12
    By help of Pencil, Paint and Brush  . . . . . .           227 Prog of Beauty      46
    This Paper they say, by the Help of a Quill,  . . .       287 Bank Down           12
    Come, help your lame Dog o'er the Style.  . . . . .       298 Horrid Plot         15
    To help an honest lad that's out of place,  . . . . .     308 Billet Players      25
    And speak without the Help of Lungs.  . . . . . . .       326 Pethox              80
    She'll help your Wife when she's in Labour.  . . . .      362 Grace's Answer      26
    Till others come to help the pay  . . . . . . . .         420 Holyhead            12
    To help our Fancy at a Lift;  . . . . . . . . .           497 Panegyr Swift      125
    And fortune help the murd'rer in his flight;  . . . .     506 To a Friend          2
    With Puppy Water, Beauty's Help  . . . . . . . .          526 Lady's Dres Rm      31
    She cannot help it for her Heart;  . . . . . . .          588 Strephon Chloe     130
    He cannot help it for his Heart.  . . . . . . . .         605 Beasts Confess     119
    Our kindly help his fire assuages.  . . . . . . .         618 Scandal Poem 1      34
    Our kindly Help his Fire asswages;  . . . . . . .         624 Scandal Poem 2      32
    Is to help yourself, and Friend.  . . . . . . . .         633 Epistle Lady       122
    And help yourself to run it down.  . . . . . . . .        644 On Poetry          126
    The outward Form no Help requir'd:  . . . . . . .         692 Cadenus Vaness     176
    Long may she live, and help her friends  . . . . . .      761 Bec's B-Day         31
    There's not a Pow'r above will help you now:  . . . .     771 Horace 1, 14        34
    (For Tonson had, to help the Sale,  . . . . . . .         782 Tim and Fables       9
    New Years help to make me old;  . . . . . . . .           863 To Janus            26
    Yet many poor Creatures I help to ensnare.  . . . . .     929 Riddle 13       D    6
    That a sieve dissolves riddles by help of the shears; .   976 Dean to Sherid      20
    Till she lent you her help, you were in a fine twitter: . 977 Dean to Sherid      39
    But help thee to be read with Points.  . . . . .         1021 Nim-Dan-Dean 1   D  40
HELP'D
    Which help'd to mortify his Pride,  . . . . . . .         704 Cadenus Vaness     570
    That Phoebus help'd me in my Rhymes,  . . . . . . .       741 Stel B-day 22       24
HELPING
    That Stella was helping, abetting and aiding,  . . . .    264 Apollo              39
    And I join my helping Voice;  . . . . . . . . .           933 Riddle 20       D   16
HELPLESS
    Did bravely snatch the lovely helpless Prize.  . . . .     12 Ode to William  D   24
    While you ly helpless on the Sand:  . . . . . .           258 Bubble             200
    "To save that helpless Land from Ruin,  . . . . . .       569 Death of Swift     412
    Deaf, giddy, helpless, left alone,  . . . . . . .         673 His Deafness         1
HELSHAM
    For, as Helsham observes, there's nothing can chime,  .   980 Tho: Sheridan        3
    . . . I mean that great fat joker, friend Helsham, he .  1023 Nim-Dan-Dean 2   D   9
    <Helsham> does truly Wit command  . . . . . . .          373 Letter D. S-y       47
HELSHAM'S
    In thee Delany's spleen, John's mirth, Helsham's jokes,  1023 Nim-Dan-Dean 2   D  14
       . . .
HELTER-SKELTER
    Or run helter-skelter  . . . . . . . . . . .             857 Lady's Lament      191
HEMM'D
    Hemm'd by a triple Circle round,  . . . . . . . .         200 Horace 2, 6         28
    Hemm'd in by a Thicket,  . . . . . . . . . .              938 Riddle Answerd       4
HEMP
    Like Hemp, which by a skilful Spinster drawn  . . . .     806 Judas               15
HEMPEN
    Smocks hempen wear;  . . . . . . . . . . . .              441 Ballyspellin        44
    Nor would there be need of a strong Hempen Cape,  . .     519 Dean Hang Rape      65
HEN
    Young Ducklings, fostered by a Hen;  . . . . . . .        294 Prog Marriage      146
    The sober Hen not born to swim  . . . . . . . .           295 Horrid Plot        149
HENCE    SEE THERE-HENCE
    Boldly we hence the brave Commencement Date  . . . .      13 Ode to William  D   45
    Hence Mankind fell, and here must rise again.  . . . .    32 Ode to Temple      177
    Last year, a lad hence by his parents sent  . . . .       46 To Congreve        115
    Hence we are by wise Farmers told,  . . . . . .          156 Fable of Midas      19
    And hence a Critick deep maintains,  . . . . . . .       156 Fable of Midas      21
    The Dutch from hence shall no more Millions drain;  . .  169 Peace Dunkirk       27
    The Doctor takes his hint from hence,  . . . . .         379 Apology Lady C     129
    "Learn hence t' excuse and pity me.  . . . . . .         380 Apology Lady C     144
    Distress of Nations calls him hence,  . . . . . .        387 Manly Virtue       113
    Aura, whose Tongue you hear a Mile hence,  . . . . .     450 Modern Lady        170
    One thing he did before he went hence,  . . . . .        455 Dean Smedley        17
    He heys from hence at forty four,  . . . . . . .         456 Dean Smedley        33
    That five years hence will both be Hebes.  . . . . .     465 Birthday Song      172
    From hence the Critick Vermin sprung  . . . . . .        504 Doctor Delaney     123
    Her Time was not till Nine Months hence.  . . . . .      586 Strephon Chloe      66
    Which he resolv'd to keep for ever hence,  . . . . .     603 Beasts Confess      71
    Hence we conclude, no Women's Hearts  . . . . . .        688 Cadenus Vaness      61
    My Prelates and my Students, sent from hence,  . . .     792 St. Pat's Well      29
    Hence the greazy clumsy Mien,  . . . . . . . .           800 Traulus 2           31
    Hence that mean and sordid Soul,  . . . . . . .          800 Traulus 2           33
    Hence that wild suspicious Peep,  . . . . . . .          800 Traulus 2           35
    Hence he learnt the Butcher's Guile,  . . . . . .        800 Traulus 2           37
    Hence he draws his daily Food,  . . . . . . . .          800 Traulus 2           41
    Send me hence ten thousand miles,  . . . . . . .         907 Daphne              21
    Thus you may see, dear Friend, ex pede hence  . . . .    988 Letter Dr Sh-n      15
HENCEFORTH
    Henceforth expect a different survey,  . . . . . .       283 Journal            127
    Henceforth depends alone on me.  . . . . . . .           776 Mullinix Tim        82
    Henceforth acknowledge, that a Nose  . . . . . .        1002 Reply by Dean        4
```

HENCEFORWARD
    Henceforward let no Statesman dare, ...   PAGE   TITLE   LINE
    Henceforward let no Statesman dare, ...   96 On the Union   13
    Henceforward shall print neither Pamphlets nor Linnen,   238 Excellent Song   28
    I swear from henceforward you shall be my Phoebus. . .   973 S-'s Ans Sh-d 14
HENDEL
    To Minheer Hendel next you run, ...   469 Birthday Song   276
HENLY'S
    "And Mr. Henly's last Oration: . . . .   563 Death of Swift   278
HER   SEE LAY-HER,STUFF-HER-EARS,BOULT-HER
        934   OMITTED WORD
HER'S
    No Thought of her's does ever roam, ...   322 First of April   39
    But a Genius like her's no Subject can stifle, . . .   716 Answer Rebus   11
HERALD
    Is both a Herald and a Poet; . . . .   80 Vanbrug House   60
    As Herald, he can in a Day . . . .   80 Vanbrug House   63
    Is both a Herald and a Poet, ...   107 V's House   34
    As Herald, he can in a Day . . . .   107 V's House   37
    Nor can the skilful Herald trace . . . .   323 Pethox   3
    But soft says the Herald, I cannot agree; . . . .   338 Serious Poem   119
    Herald lend the Muse an answer; . . . .   800 Traulus 2   27
HERALDRY
    And now the Heraldry describe . . . .   93 Bauc & Phil 1   123
    The Heraldry of ev'ry Tribe. . . . .   114 Bauc & Phil 2   100
    For Metal on Metal is false Heraldry: . . . . .   338 Serious Poem   120
    I'll maintain with my Life, is Heraldry Good.   338 Serious Poem   122
HERB
    Where neither herb nor tree will thrive, ...   421 Holyhead   31
HERBAGE
    Or dirty Offals cook'd with Herbage. . . . . . .   498 Panegyr Swift   153
HERBS
    In vain all wholsome Herbs I sow, ...   33 Ode to Temple   208
HERCULEAN
    When on thy Breast and Sides Herculean, ...   656 On Poetry   463
HERCULES
    Got Hercules to bear the Pile . . . .   160 Atlas   11
    Yet Hercules was not so strong, ...   160 Atlas   13
    But we like Antaeus and Hercules fight, ...   968 Letter Sherid   29
HERD
    Must e'en all herd with us their Kindred Fools, . . .   18 Ode Athenian   82
    The herd beneath, who see the weathercock of state   37 Ode Sancroft   73
    In haste she does th' offensive herd avoid. . . . . .   50 To Congreve   226
    In wit before the common Herd? . . . .   501 Doctor Delaney 38
    "The most malignant of the Herd, ...   549 Life of Swift   164
    He's a Christian as good as the rest of the herd.   816 Yahoo's   29
HERDIE
    An herdie Chiftan, woe the morne . . . .   103 Merlin   7
HERDS
    There whole herds suspended lie . . . .   35 Ode Sancroft   35
    What Herds of Kings would turn to Grazers. . . . .   659 On Poetry   D 410
    And lowing Herds, and piping Swains, ...   934 Riddle 21   D   9
HERE   195   OMITTED WORD
HERE'S   13   OMITTED WORD
HERESY
    Who learnt himself that Heresy first . . . .   28 Ode to Temple   53
HERETOFORE
    Were Hero's Titles heretofore, ...   83 Salamander   10
    The Horned Moon which heretofore . . . . . .   99 Elegy Patrige   35
    To build by Verse as heretofore, ...   107 V's House   44
    My Ice-house rob as heretofore, ...   409 Dial Rich Marb 45
    Long Schemes of Life, as heretofore; . . . . .   764 Stel B-day '26 16
HERMES
    The Rod of Hermes was renown'd . . . .   133 Magician's Rod 35
    With Hermes, Son of Pleias bright. . . . . . .   326 Pethox   86
    When Hermes, waiting with his rod, ...   762 Bec's B-Day   58
HERMITS   SEE BROTHER-HERMITS
    Two Brother Hermits, Saints by Trade, ...   111 Bauc & Phil 2   7
    We are but Saints, the Hermits said; . . . . . .   112 Bauc & Phil 2   44
    The Hermits then desir'd their Host . . . . . .   115 Bauc & Phil 2   109
HERO
    Before the Hero can commence a God. . . . . . .   7 Ode to King   30
    Like the fam'd Hero in his Mother's Cloud, ...   18 Ode Athenian   88
    And by one mighty Hero carried to it's height . . . .   25 Ode Athenian   284
    To paint a Hero, we enquire . . . .   83 Salamander   17
    And each imprison'd Hero quak'd for Fear. . . . .   139 City Shower   52
    Else what aspiring hero durst? . . . .   178 To Lord Harley 60
    Except the Matchless Hero Abel. . . . .   183 Horace 2   86
    The Godlike Hero with one frown . . . .   340 Arch-Bish Dub   19
    Here would our Hero ever dwell, ...   385 Manly Virtue   47
    Who hung like a Hero, and never would flinch. . . .   400 Tom Clinch   24
    Your Hero now another Mars is, ...   461 Birthday Song   29
    For must a Hero not be dreadfull? . . . .   462 Birthday Song   56
    Why then, your Hero must be told, ...   464 Birthday Song   132
    To praise your Hero for Devotion: . . . .   468 Birthday Song   262
    Confest the conqu'ring Hero stands. . . . . . .   655 On Poetry   420
    Appears a Hero to our Eyes; . . . .   710 Cadenus Vaness 733
HERO'S
    Transplanted to the Hero's Brow) . . . .   6 Ode to King   10
    Were Hero's Titles heretofore, ...   83 Salamander   10
    And should it be your Hero's case . . . .   460 Birthday Song   5
HEROE
    And when you'd make an Heroe grander, ...   270 Apollo's Edict D 18

HEROE   (CONTINUED)   PAGE   TITLE   LINE
  The Trojan Heroe paid his Vow.)   . . . . 896 Panegyr Dean   308
HEROES
  Are the chief Heroes in the sacred List of Fame.   . . 25 Ode Athenian   307
  Transmitted to the Heroes Line, ... 134 Magician's Rod   62
  Your tragick Heroes shall not rant, ...   270 Apollo's Edict   D 27
  She nam'd the antient Heroes round, ...   697 Cadenus Vaness   350
  Heroes and Heroins of old, ...   725 To Stella   51
  Name your Heroes one, by one. . . . .   834 Legion Club   136
HEROICK
  Heroick Strains could build a Tower;   . . . . . .   79 Vanbrug House   8
  Heroick Strains could build a Tow'r;   . . . . . .   106 V's House   8
  Heroick Actions early bred in, ...   398 Earl of P-b-w   34
  Had some heroick Action done, ...   554 Death of Swift   23
  Treat you in Heroick Strain. . . . .   634 Epistle Lady   136
  Can wish to die, in strain heroick, ...   676 Parson's Case   2
HEROICS
  Who heard you meant to write heroics next;   . . . .   47 To Congreve   144
HEROINE
  Your Heroine hardly fifty odd is.   . . . . 465 Birthday Song   162
HEROINS
  Heroes and Heroins of old, ...   725 To Stella   51
HERRIES
  Quoth Herries, fairly putting Cases, ...   75 Game Traffick   17
HERRING
  Small Beer, a Herring, and the Dean.   . . . . . .   747 Stel Distress   56
  Small Beer, a Herring, and the <Dean>.   . . . . .   751 Stel Wood-Park   72
  Or, how a Herring hath a Charm   . . . .   949 Epigr Fasting   3
  Buy my Herring   . . . .   953 Herrings   3
HERRINGS
  A Shole of Herrings down his Maw.   . . . .   651 On Poetry   324
  That Herrings will be cheap this Year.   . . . . .   781 Mullinix Tim   276
  Or, like my own Herrings, I soon shall be dead.   . . 953 Herrings   9
HERS   2   OMITTED WORD
HERSE
  Without a Tear will tend my Herse.   . . . .   203 In Sickness   8
  Attend the progress of his herse.   . . . . 296 Satiric Elegy   20
HERSELF   8   OMITTED WORD
HESPERIAN
  Guarded each fair Hesperian Pippin.   . . . . . .   134 Magician's Rod   74
HESSE
  Hesse Darmstedt makes too rough a sound, ...   467 Birthday Song   215
HETEROCLIT
  All, Heteroclit Dan except, ...   279 Journal   19
HETEROGENEOUS
  While Things of heterogeneous Kind, ...   811 Bro Protestant   5
HEWERS
  To be Hewers of Wood and Drawers of Water,   . . .   334 Serious Poem   2
  Yet we all should Rejoyce to be Hewers of Wood.   . . 334 Serious Poem   4
HEWIT
  All this perform'd by Robert Hewit, ...   675 Curate's Compl   16
HEWN
  From what Kind of Tree this Wood was Hewn out.   . . 334 Serious Poem   26
HEY
  How Markets went for Hey and Oats.   . . . . . .   63 Discovery   36
  Hey for Dublin Town agen!   . . . .   574 Helter Skelter   56
HEYS
  He heys from hence at forty four, ...   456 Dean Smedley   33
HI'ROGLYPHICKS
  Bestow'd as Hi'roglyphicks fit   . . . .   83 Salamander   11
HIBERNIA
  And, let but our Mother Hibernia contrive   . . . . 351 Wood Insect   13
HIBERNIAN
  That you, a low Hibernian Bard, ...   475 Epist on Epist   4
  This, among Hibernian Asses, ...   523 Betty Grizette   33
  When, for the Use of no Hibernian born, ...   793 St. Pat's Well   91
  "Neal Gahagan, Hibernian Clown, ...   851 Old Thorn   82
HIC
  One Grave now contains them both Haec et Hic.   . .   430 Dicky Dolly   15
HID
  And hid him from Poetick sight, ...   8 Ode to King   59
  But hid with Caution from the Wise.   . . . . . .   60 Lady Tablebook   6
  Decently hid beneath his Goun. . . . .   95 Bauc & Phil 1   176
  Nor hid himself behind the Moon, ...   98 Elegy Patrige   13
  To bend where Golden Mines were hid;   . . . . .   133 Magician's Rod   28
  Where can this idle Wench be hid?   . . . .   223 Prog of Love   28
  To view what in the Chest was hid.   . . . . . .   528 Lady's Dres Rm   90
  While Punch is hid behind the Scene, ...   776 Mullinix Tim   94
HIDDEN
  Nature the hidden Spark did at my Birth infuse,   . .   32 Ode to Temple   202
  But now stopt by some hidden Pow'rs   . . . . . .   93 Bauc & Phil 1   133
HIDE
  Think she there does all her Treasures hide,   . . .   27 Ode to Temple   37
  Which the disguise of greatness only served to hide; . . 41 Ode Sancroft 214
  To thee, what oft I vainly strive to hide, ...   55 Temple Ill   133
  And strole about, but hide their Quality, ...   90 Bauc & Phil 1   3
  To thee the Bull will lend his Hide, ...   100 Elegy Patrige   75
  And strole about, but hide their Quality, ...   111 Bauc & Phil 2   3
  Which he could neither Gild nor hide.   . . . . .   157 Fable of Midas   32
  <Swift>, who could neither fly nor hide, ... 172 Horace 1, 7   63
  Which when you have got, you so carefully hide it,   . . 263 Apollo   5

HIDE	(CONTINUED)	PAGE	TITLE	LINE
Nor shall you strive your Horns to hide,		362	Grace's Answer	53
There Night-gloves made of Tripsy's Hide,		526	Lady's Dres Rm	29
Nor, from your Lord his bad Condition hide;		534	To Mr. Gay	93
Dear Venus, hide this wond'rous Maid,		585	Strephon Chloe	29
And, from the Spouse each Blemish hide		591	Strephon Chloe	253
At which the Sun should hide his Face.		595	Cassinus Peter	70
To hide her from the World so long;		705	Cadenus Vaness	577
So when Cadenus could not hide,		710	Cadenus Vaness	762
If I should Stella's Kindness hide		726	To Stella	95
Have taught you from the World to hide:		730	Stella, Poems	100
How I should hide my Head for Shame,		741	Stel B-day 22	17
You cannot blanch his tawny Hide;		785	Dick, Maggot	8
His Hide emits a Foulness out,		786	Clad in Brown	8
Thy Soul, which through thy Hide of Buff,		787	Clad in Brown	17
Tho' his soul he despises, he values his hide:		817	Yahoo's	72
Or hide his coward Snout in Mud.		824	Printer Newgat	10
"My Kindred oft' thine Hide shall gall;		850	Old Thorn	59
The bashful Maid, to hide her Blush,		893	Panegyr Dean	213
From me no Secret he can hide;		915	Riddle 1	23
Contrives all Means the Gift to hide:		919	Riddle 5	22
How long shall virtue hide her face,		950	Upstart	D 19
HIDEOUS				
Where Spirits throng'd with hideous Din,		134	Magician's Rod	55
They form a frightfull hideous Face,		226	Prog of Beauty	24
And, as that hateful hideous Grecian		775	Mullinix Tim	51
That looks hideous, fierce, and frightful;		907	Daphne	45
HIDES				
He hides within his darkest Cell.		240	Run Bankers	44
The Loyt'res quake, no Corner hides them,		279	Journal	33
If he displays, or hides his Beams;		379	Apology Lady C	124
Oppression hides, with guilty Dread,		387	Manly Virtue	123
"Whose Protestation hides a Sting		550	Life of Swift	172
Who wisely hides his Wood and Wire;		592	Strephon Chloe	286
HIDING				
"Or, else some hiding Hole he seeks,		305	Storm	61
HIGH				
On the high Top of peaceful Ararat;		16	Ode Athenian	26
Well--tho' you've rais'd Her to this high Degree,		24	Ode Athenian	263
Chief cherub, and chief lamp of that high sacred Seven,		34	Ode Sancroft	3
(High Truth) the best resemblance of exalted Thee,		36	Ode Sancroft	46
Thus, primitive Sancroft moves too high		39	Ode Sancroft	149
Some whom ambition drives, seek Heaven's high Son		39	Ode Sancroft	166
That Heaven's high Son was in a village born;		39	Ode Sancroft	172
Yet does this high perfection well proceed		41	Ode Sancroft	223
Where high patrician souls dress'd heavenly gay,		41	Ode Sancroft	234
There some high spiritual throne to Sancroft shall be given,		42	Ode Sancroft	236
Heart-sick of a high fever and consuming atrophy;		42	Ode Sancroft	252
These pad on wit's high road, and suits maintain		45	To Congreve	67
Such high companions may delusion keep,		48	To Congreve	149
One Story high, one postern Door,		81	Vanbrug House	77
Soon reard a House two Storyes nigh;		86	Hist V's House	6
Hung high and made a glitt'ring Show		93	Bauc & Phil 1	114
Lookt high and low, walkt often round,		109	V's House	97
Hung high, and made a glitt'ring Show,		114	Bauc & Phil 2	90
And high in Order plac'd, describe		114	Bauc & Phil 2	99
But a Prince of high Renown,		168	Peace Dunkirk	18
What! I suppose now Stocks are high,		175	Horace 1, 7	127
And now 'twas high Time to be gone;		208	Fable Bitches	24
But by degrees when mounted high		226	Prog of Beauty	5
Along the high celestial Road;		231	Prog of Poetry	28
Supported high on Wings of Paper;		231	Prog of Poetry	44
When Stock is high they come between,		253	Bubble	69
Can soar with moistned Wings on high,		254	Bubble	86
High Treason by Statute! But here you object,		266	Apollo	89
Fix them on high, conspicuous to be seen,		285	Elegy Boat	33
But Six-pence a Letter is monstrous high Wages:		288	Bank Down	48
Threescore, I think, is pretty high;		296	Satiric Elegy	11
The high Descent from whence you came,		323	Pethox	12
You, o'er the high Triumphal Arch		326	Pethox	93
And high in Air for ever ride;		347	Prometheus	74
Whilst high, and nice, and curious Meats,		378	Apology Lady C	107
Rais'd high above his Birth by Knowledge,		384	Manly Virtue	33
(Rais'd high like some celestial Fire		385	Manly Virtue	53
(For, where high Honour is the Prize,		386	Manly Virtue	91
To Wealth and Vice, in high Degree,		386	Manly Virtue	94
Now rais'd on high, see, Virtue shews		386	Manly Virtue	97
High on a Length of prostrate Wood,		393	Modern Poets	12
To raise me to a high Degree:		408	Dial Rich Marb	16
Stand high in Honour, Wealth, or Wit;		414	Censure	7
Mounts, Walks, on high; and in a Hollow		477	Epist on Epist	79
If your Expences rise so high;		478	Epist on Epist	95
The Proof of your high Origine,		498	Panegyr Swift	175
If not, however seated high,		503	Doctor Delaney	113
Did Female Virtue e'er so high ascend,		531	To Mr. Gay	5
Stand high himself, keep others low?		554	Death of Swift	16
How with so high a Nymph he might		586	Strephon Chloe	73
High Raptures, and romantick Flights;		590	Strephon Chloe	198
How to relish Notions high;		630	Epistle Lady	25
In Garrets high, or under Ground:		651	On Poetry	316

HIGH	(CONTINUED)	PAGE	TITLE	LINE
Wou'd not conceive a high disgrace	. . . .	659	On Poetry	D 410
High up in Air he'll turn your Brains;	. . . . . .	666	Epig Carthy 2	D 6
High as Longinus to the Stars ascends,	. . .	669	Epig Carthy 14	D 1
This said, she plucks in Heav'ns high Bow'rs	.	691	Cadenus Vaness	154
Talks in a high Romantick Strain;	. . . . .	712	Cadenus Vaness	821
In high Concern for human Kind,	. . . .	723	To Stella	5
With feeding high, & Treatment civil,	. . . . . .	746	Stel Distress	24
The Cieling hardly six foot high	. . . . .	746	Stel Distress	36
With feeding high, and Treatment civil,	. . . . .	750	Stel Wood-Park	22
The Ceiling hardly six Foot high;	. . . . . .	751	Stel Wood-Park	54
Dick was come to high Renown	. . . .	785	Mullinex Dick	25
Let Folks in high, or holy Stations,	. . . .	813	Bro Protestant	57
What care we how high runs his passion or pride?	. . .	817	Yahoo's	71
Where ev'ry Trout can make as high Rants	. . . .	824	Printer Newgat	5
At Dublin's high feast sat Primate and Dean,	. . .	843	Ay and No	1
"When thou, suspended high in Air,	. . . . . .	851	Old Thorn	85
By these embroider'd high Heel Shoes,	. . . .	885	Rev Market-Hill	63
In vain I tempt too high a Flight.	. . . . . .	897	Panegyr Dean	324
But, as for me, who ne'er could clamber high,	. . .	900	Dean's Reasons	51
In Youth exalted high in Air,	. . . .	915	Riddle 1	1
By Fate exalted high in Place;	. . . .	917	Riddle 3	1
I saw thee rais'd to high Renown,	. . . . .	919	Riddle 5	5
What Lords and Dames of high Degree,	. . . .	919	Riddle 5	15
I'm but an Idol rais'd on high;	. . . . . .	926	Riddle 9	18
Sometimes in Panegyrick high,	. . . .	929	Riddle 15	D 5
The dullest Beast when high in Stature,	. . . . .	940	Letter	5
by Galloping high, or Level Pace,	. . . . . .	957	Cantata	
or with a down a high down derry,	. . . . . .	957	Cantata	
Poets, in those Days, us'd to venture high,	. . .	988	Letter Dr Sh-n	13
HIGH-BORN				
For when our high-born Howard dy'd,	. . . . . .	652	On Poetry	371
HIGH-DAY				
Then George will rejoice, and Dan will sing high-day:	.	980	Dean to Tho: S	37
HIGH-ESTABLISH'T				
On Learning's high-establish't Throne.	. . . . . .	25	Ode Athenian	295
HIGH-EXALTED				
Thou, high-exalted in thy Sphere,	. . . .	100	Elegy Patrige	73
HIGH-FLOWN				
Some high-flown Pamphlets, I suppose---:	. . . . .	550	Life of Swift	183
HIGH-PRIESTHOOD				
Unknown the forms we the high-priesthood use	. . .	53	Temple Ill	75
HIGH-WAY				
Till entring on a broad High-way,	. . . .	412	Desire Possess	23
HIGH'R				
The Chimny widen'd and grew high'r,	. . . . . .	92	Bauc & Phil 1	95
Carry'd it to his Equalls high'r,	. . . . . .	95	Bauc & Phil 1	179
. . . I'd see him hanging high'r,	. . . . . .	343	Upon His Grace	37
HIGHER				
In higher Strain than we began.	. . . . . .	80	Vanbrug House	58
In higher Strains than we began.	. . . . . .	106	V's House	32
The Chimney widen'd, and grew higher,	. . . . .	113	Bauc & Phil 2	55
Nor higher, than our Talents, rise,	. . . . .	184	Horace 2, 1	108
To shine the more still rising higher)	. . . . .	385	Manly Virtue	54
Demands him in an higher Sphere;	. . . . .	387	Manly Virtue	112
E're he advance the Doctor higher	. . . .	475	Epist on Epist	24
He'll Grieve he did not raise you higher,	. . . .	484	Libel on D- D-	118
Then let him have the higher Post;	. . . . .	554	Death of Swift	19
Yet, when you sink, I seem the higher.	. . . . .	555	Death of Swift	46
No higher climb than mount Olymp	. . . .	620	Scandal Poem 1	102
Because we dwell in higher Regions:	. . . .	626	Scandal Poem 2	96
No higher climb than Mount Olymp,	. . . . .	626	Scandal Poem 2	100
I attempt no higher Pitch.	. . . .	635	Epistle Lady	172
Can you put in higher Claims,	. . . .	637	Epistle Lady	241
To raise up Stella's virtue higher;	. . . . .	755	Stella '23	22
"But the lower the coin, the higher the mob.	. . .	843	Ay and No	12
Be these thy Arts; nor higher Aim	. . . . .	897	Panegyr Dean	341
HIGHEST				
That Mountain which was highest first of all	. . .	16	Ode Athenian	5
And under the Pain of our highest Displeasure,	. . .	266	Apollo	101
He rises to the highest Stations;	. . . . . .	386	Manly Virtue	90
My highest Progress in the Myst'ry	. . . . .	493	Panegyr Swift	31
(And this was thought the highest Post;	. . . . .	513	Answer Fable	31
A Juncture happen'd in his highest Pride:	. . . .	536	To Mr. Gay	147
Nor highest Wisdom in Debates	. . . . . .	641	On Poetry	27
But on the highest mount in Wales	. . . . .	733	Verses Vanessa	29
Got all things at the highest Price.	. . . . . .	745	Stel Distress	10
Got all things at the highest Price.	. . . . . .	749	Stel Wood-Park	8
By Scotish Bards of highest Fame,	. . . . .	848	Old Thorn	15
HIGHLY				
Once highly honour'd! False is the pretence	. . .	44	To Congreve	7
So highly courted by the brisk and gay?	. . . . .	54	Temple Ill	106
By you so oft, so highly prais'd!	. . . .	887	Panegyr Dean	14
HIGHNESS				
What tho' her Highness and her Spouse	. . . .	183	Horace 2, 1	87
His Rev'rence and her Highness walking:	. . . .	410	Dial Rich Marb	60
Now sing his little Highness Freddy,	. . . . .	466	Birthday Song	187
They tempted me t' attack your Highness,	. . . .	1005	Sheridan's Sub	23
HIGHT				
A Nymph and Swain, Sheelah and Dermot hight,	. . .	880	Pastoral Dial	1

HIGHWAYS   PAGE   TITLE   LINE
    The dullest Beast mending Highways, ...   941 Letter   33
HILL   SEE MARKET-HILL,DRAPIER'S-HILL,MARBLE-HILL,SNOW-HILL,LAZY-HILL
    Bury those Carrots under a Hill.   . . . .   148 Windsor Proph   26
    A good Health to Gen'ral Hill, ...   169 Peace Dunkirk   39
    In apeing Lines from Cooper's Hill;   . . . .   271 Apollo's Edict   D 47
    But, wisely left the Muses Hill, ...   482 Libel on D- D-   65
    And you on Drapier's Hill must lye, ...   491 Dialogue   55
    Attain'd by Flight the Muses Hill;   . . . .   504 Doctor Delaney   120
    Was Viceroy of a neighbouring Hill: . . . .   513 Answer Fable   44
    Parnassus' Hill has but two Tops, ... / . .   671 Epig Carthy 22   D   4
    At Market Hill, as well appears   . . . .   848 Old Thorn   1
    Haul'd up every hill;   . . . .   853 Lady's Lament   50
    And call the Mansion Drapier's Hill;   . . . .   875 Drapier's Hill   10
    This Hill may keep the Name of Drapier: . . . .   875 Drapier's Hill   18
    And Drapier's vye with Cooper's Hill.   . . . .   875 Drapier's Hill   20
HILL'S   SEE MARKET-HILL'S
HILLOCK
    Beneath this verdant Hillock lies   . . . .   235 Elegy on Demar   41
    Thus from a Hillock looking down, ...   255 Bubble   126
HILLS
    In Scottish Hills found precious Ore, ...   133 Magician's Rod   29
    O'er cityes, rivers, hills, and seas;   . . . . . .   621 Scandal Poem 1   126
    O'er Cities, Rivers, Hills, and Seas: . . . . . .   627 Scandal Poem 2   120
    Both Mountains, Woods, and Hills, and Rocks,   . . .   934 Riddle 21   D   7
    Thro' all the Vallies, Hills, and Plains, ...   1035 To Quilca   9
HILT
    Then he low'rs down the Point, and kisses the Hilt.   .   871 Grand Question   112
HILTED
    Brazen hilted lately burnish'd, ...   573 Helter Skelter   7
HIM   436   OMITTED WORD
HIMSELF   42   OMITTED WORD
HIMSELF'S
    When Man himself's the Vermin of Her Earth;   . . .   8 Ode to King   55
HINDER
    To hinder Clergymen from thriving);   . . . .   174 Horace 1, 7   106
    Whoever our Trading with England would hinder, . . .   237 Excellent Song   18
    To place him at the hinder End   . . . .   292 Prog Marriage   78
    Thou hast slain Horace, what shou'd hinder . . . . .   666 Epig Carthy 2   D   1
HINDS
    The Scottish Hinds too poor to house   . . . . . .   759 Receipt Youth   1
HINGES
    With Rings and Hinges counterfeit   . . . . . .   528 Lady's Dres Rm   76
HINT
    The Doctor takes his hint from hence, ...   379 Apology Lady C   129
    He'll get it read, and take the hint, ...   463 Birthday Song   86
    Hint the least Int'rest of your own;   . . . . . .   480 Libel on D- D-   14
    "To steal a Hint was never known, ...   565 Death of Swift   317
    We Poets when a Hint is new   . . . . . .   747 Stel Distress   59
    But Poets when a Hint is new   . . . .   751 Stel Wood-Park   75
    Nor for my Life will take the Hint.   . . . . . .   860 Lady Acheson   16
HINTS
    Give Hints, that Poets ne'er believe in God.   . . .   193 Author Himself   6
    Few Hints from you will set him right, ...   218 To Mr. Delany   97
    Conveys out my Paper of Hints by a Trick,   . . .   265 Apollo   81
    He only stole Hints; the Verse is correct; . . .   266 Apollo   90
    Are fill'd with Hints, and interlin'd, ...   406 Swift to Pope   11
    And then he kindly give me hints   . . . .   423 Ireld   59
    Their Inuendo's, Hints, and Slanders, ...   449 Modern Lady   142
    Gave Hints of who and who's together;   . . . . .   696 Cadenus Vaness   324
    Which fairly hints they are in jest, ...   707 Cadenus Vaness   666
    Thy Hints that Stella is no Chickin, ...   735 Stel B-day '20   42
    I furnish Hints, and you should use all 'em, . . .   742 Stel B-day 22   38
HIPPOCRENE
    When all his Drink is Hippocrene, ...   231 Prog of Poetry   32
    Their Phoebus I, my Spring their Hippocrene.   . . .   793 St. Pat's Well   72
HIPS
    The Bolsters that supply her Hips.   . . . . . .   582 Young Nymph   28
    And, the Doctor was plaguily down in the Hips. . .   873 Grand Question   178
HIR
    Of Fraunce hir woe thys is the sygne, ...   102 Merlin   2
HIR'D
    "Nor with hir'd thoughts be thy devotion paid; . . . .   55 Temple Ill   139
    Who hir'd a subterraneous Friend, ...   393 Modern Poets   13
    Sweet Poet, hir'd for birth-day Rimes, ...   462 Birthday Song   47
    "Nor Witness hir'd, nor Jury pick'd, ...   570 Death of Swift   429
HIRCINA
    Hircina rank with Sweat, presumes   . . . .   449 Modern Lady   158
HIRE   SEE COACH-HIRE
    Can hire a Lodging for a Song;   . . . .   79 Vanbrug House   16
    Who has forty Years let out his Conscience to hire, .   142 New Song   2
    And hire us out their scenes, and cloaths, and faces. .   307 Billet Players   8
    Forgot at Home, became for Hire, ...   482 Libel on D- D-   63
    And get a Dinner for your Hire, ...   483 Libel on D- D-   108
    Old Nurse-keepers would never hire   . . . . . .   605 Beasts Confess   137
    Or hire their Party-Pamphleteers, ...   647 On Poetry   217
    From Slaves employ'd for daily Hire   . . . . . .   726 To Stella   106
    Who votes for Mannors, who for Hire.   . . . . . .   781 Mullinix Tim   262
HIRELING
    The hireling Senator of modern Days, ...   364 On Dreams   35

```
                                                           PAGE    TITLE             LINE
HIRELINGS
    As the Hirelings of St. <Stephens>.        . . . . . .  637 Epistle Lady         244
HIS    1604                                                     OMITTED WORD
HISS
    Would hiss, and sting, and roll, and twist, . . . . .   132 Magician's Rod        11
    Her Serpents hiss direct at me.        . . . . . . . .  596 Cassinus Peter        86
HISSES
    She turns to Envy, Stings and Hisses:      . . . . . .  554 Death of Swift        36
HIST
    "Hist, Huzzy, I think I hear some Body coming--   . .   871 Grand Question       127
HIST'RY
    Is of short Sessions a long Hist'ry;      . . . . . .   493 Panegyr Swift         32
HISTORY
    The important history of Martin.       . . . . . . . .  186 Scriblerus 3           8
    In History we never found     . . . . . . . . . .      190 Faggot                27
HIT
    Our Prince has hit Him, like Achilles, in the Heel,    .  10 Ode to King         142
    This Fool had got a lucky Hit,     . . . . . . . . .    156 Fable of Midas        23
    But now the Senate (if things hit   . . . . . . .      182 Horace 2, 1           59
    The Moral is so plain to hit,    . . . . . . . . .      393 Modern Poets          17
    Our Thoughts, to hit your nicer Taste,    . . . . . .   496 Panegyr Swift        106
    A Bungler thus, who scarce the Nail can hit,    . . .   535 To Mr. Gay           131
    He hop'd to have a Lucky Hit,     . . . . . . . . .     547 Life of Swift         90
    She never hit one proper Place;    . . . . . . . . .    700 Cadenus Vaness       423
    On this Worrier of Deans whene'er we can hit,    . . .  816 Yahoo's               51
    You hit it, you say,--you're a delicate hitter.   . . . 977 Dean to Sherid        40
HITHER
    Hither thy gentle Aspect bend,     . . . . . . . .      101 Elegy Patrige        101
    Hither, though much against his Grain,    . . . . . .   294 Prog Marriage        123
    Come hither, all ye empty things,    . . . . . . . .    296 Satiric Elegy         25
    Come hither, and behold your fate.     . . . . . . .    296 Satiric Elegy         28
    When Fortune hither drove me first;    . . . . . . .    313 To Ford               52
    Nor shall I, when you hither come,     . . . . . . .    313 To Ford               67
    Hither convey St. Patrick's Well;    . . . . . . . .    478 Epist on Epist        92
    Hither from Colchos, with the fleecy Ore,    . . . . .  790 St. Pat's Well         7
    While others hither sent to save us,  ·. . . . . . .    820 Dr. Rundle            33
    Hither came every Village Maid     . . . . . . . .      848 Old Thorn              5
    To come hither daily,     . . . . . . . . . . .         857 Lady's Lament        206
    Come hither, and take this old Gown for your Pains.     873 Grand Question       186
    Dennis was out, and I got hither safe;     . . . . .    881 Pastoral Dial         31
    Hither the frantick Goddess draws      . . . . . . .    883 Rev Market-Hill        5
    And, O! may all who hither come,     . . . . . . . .    894 Panegyr Dean         223
    Hither by luckless Error led,      . . . . . . . .      896 Panegyr Dean         309
    Come hither and behold the Fruits,      . . . . . . .   921 Riddle 7               1
    All human Race must hither draw;      . . . . . . .     922 Riddle 7              24
    The poorest hither march in State,     . . . . . . .    928 Riddle 12         D   13
HITHERTO
    With Graces, hitherto unknown    . . . . . . . . .      695 Cadenus Vaness       272
    Love, hitherto a transient Guest,    . . . . . . . .    711 Cadenus Vaness       768
HITS
    It still your Constitution hits.      . . . . . . . .   493 Panegyr Swift         18
    And Millions miss, for one that hits.      . . . . .    640 On Poetry              2
HITT
    Then pray think this a lucky Hitt,     . . . . . . .    123 Empty'ng Town         21
HITTER
    You hit it, you say,--you're a delicate hitter.   . . . 977 Dean to Sherid        40
HIVE
    What northern hive pour'd out these foes to wit?   . . . 46 To Congreve          83
HOADLY
    You reply and rejoin like Hoadly of Bangor.    . . . .  967 Letter Sherid          8
HOARDED
    And from his endless hoarded Store,      . . . . . . .  875 Drapier's Hill         7
HOARSE
    "Poets till they grow hoarse may bawl  . . . . . . .    321 First of April        21
    Then from his Arm hoarse thunder rolls    . . . . . .   461 Birthday Song         39
    Must I make myself hoarse with demanding an Answer?    . 1019 To Sheridan          4
HOARY
    "Those Secrets of the hoary deep!     . . . . . . . .   528 Lady's Dres Rm        98
HOATH
    And at Hoath to boast his Fame,     . . . . . . . .     837 Legion Club          179
HOBBES
    Hobbes clearly proves that ev'ry Creature    . . . . .  651 On Poetry            319
    Hobbes, Tindal, and Woolston, and Collins, and Nayler, 815 Yahoo's               26
HOBBLES
    "<God> <damn> me, he hobbles as bad as my Groom;   . . . 872 Grand Question      156
HOBBY-HORSE
    No Hobby-horse, with gorgeous Top,      . . . . . . .   135 Magician's Rod        75
HOC
    Hoc Ithacus velit, et magni mercentur Atridae.    . .   980 Dean to Tho: S        38
HODDY
    . . . and not a spindle-shank'd hoddy doddy. . . . .    985 Mary to Sher          10
HOG
    He'd either make a Hog or Dog on't,     . . . . . . .   299 Horrid Plot           32
HOGART
    How I want thee, humorous Hogart?      . . . . . . .    839 Legion Club          219
HOGS
    Hogs, Asses, Wolves, Baboons, & Goats      . . . . .    659 On Poetry         D 410
HOGSHEADS
    Three Dishes a Day, and three Hogsheads a Year.   . .   867 Grand Question        12
HOH
    Sing, och, och, hoh, hoh. . . . . . . . . . . . .       840 Ballad            D REF
```

HOH   (CONTINUED)   PAGE   TITLE   LINE
   Sing, och, och, hoh, hoh. . . . .   840 Ballad   D REF
   Sing, och, och, hoh, hoh. . . . .   841 Ballad   D REF
   Sing, och, och, hoh, hoh. . . . .   841 Ballad   D REF
HOIST
   The Kettle to the Top was hoist   . . . .   92 Bauc & Phil 1   97
   The Kettle to the Top was hoist, ...   113 Bauc & Phil 2   57
   Her Hoop is hoist above his Nose, ...   292 Prog Marriage   79
HOLBORN-BRIDGE
   Fall from the Conduit prone to Holborn-Bridge. . . . 139 City Shower   60
HOLBOURN
   Rode stately through Holbourn, to die in his Calling; .   399 Tom Clinch   2
HOLD   SEE LUCK-HOLD,WITH-HOLD
   Whoe're expects to hold his part . . . .   61 Lady Tablebook   25
   But Dunkirk's ours, we'll hold it fast: . . . . .   168 Peace Dunkirk   4
   When Other Hands the Scales shall hold, ...   241 Run Bankers   61
   We'll come and hold you by the Chin, ...   254 Bubble   106
   No Phaeton to hold the Reins. . . . .   271 Apollo's Edict   D 53
   Hold up the prices of their Old Brocades. . . . .   275 Epilogue   16
   In threed-bare Goun, would scarce a louse hold, . . 291 Prog Marriage   61
   "This House don't want, nor will it hold us. . . .   322 First of April   46
   I'll hold you a Groat, when you wimble his Bumm, . . 336 Serious Poem   79
   'Tis Kindness to hold a Friend up by the Chin; . . . 338 Serious Poem   118
   Now from his Lordship's Grace I hold a little Piece of 342 Upon His Grace   21
    Ground,
   He bids me then to hold my Tongue, and up the Money   342 Upon His Grace   25
    locks,
   And Yet the Land I from him hold is set so on the Rack 343 Upon His Grace   45
   This Chain, as Antient Poets hold, ...   345 Prometheus   35
   'Twas plain he cou'd no longer hold . . . . . .   346 Prometheus   49
   My honest Friend Wild, may he long hold his Place, .   399 Tom Clinch   17
   Never to hold her Tongue a Minute; . . . .   415 Woman's Mind   5
   Besides, I'll hold a Groat, ...   425 Five Ladies   11
   Her scales you only see her hold . . . .   433 Answer Paulus   35
   An Ass's Hoof alone can hold . . . .   469 Burning Poem   1
   To hold the Doctor by the Chin: . . . .   514 Answer Fable   64
   In ev'ry Court the Parallel will hold; . . . . .   536 To Mr. Gay   135
   But hold---: before we farther go, ...   545 Life of Swift   5
   What right had he to hold the Whip? . . . . . .   548 Life of Swift   120
   "I wish he may hold out till Spring. . . . . . .   557 Death of Swift   114
   The Bow'rs that hold those Nymphs divine; . . . .   729 Stella, Poems   42
   And hold for ever at fifteen. . . . .   736 Stel B-day '20   54
   A Spade let prudent Archy hold, ...   743 Stel B-day 22   57
   To hold your cares for other folks. . . . . . .   753 Gift for Bec   18
   Ne're hold my peace, and ne'er stand still. . . .   778 Mullinix Tim   160
   I'll hold you a Groat, and I wish I cou'd see't, . . 805 Irish Bishops   51
   But hold, cry the <Bishops>; and give us fair Play; .   805 Irish Bishops   53
   On his virtues hold forth; 'tis the very best way; .   819 Archbi Cashel   9
   While they never hold their Tongue, ...   831 Legion Club   51
   Dermot, I swear, tho' Tady's Locks could hold . .   882 Pastoral Dial   45
   I hold Intelligence within. . . . .   885 Rev Market-Hill   56
   I will grieve, and hold my tongue. . . . .   908 Daphne   64
   Because too close I hold my Purse. . . . .   918 Riddle 4   28
   Think again of the sieve, and I'll hold you a wager, .   976 Dean to Sherid   23
   To hold out longer in Trysyllable. . . . .   989 Letter Dr Sh-n   31
   Tho' I ne'er saw her hold the Scissars, ...   993 On Picture   14
   Oh, there you think you have me safe! but hold Sir, .   1004 Dan J's Reply   27
   Will ne'er be smooth, nor hold the Stitches. . . .   1021 Nim-Dan-Dean 1   D 18
HOLDERS   SEE UP-HOLDERS
HOLDS
   Takes Snuff, and holds the Stakes. . . . .   75 Game Traffick   12
   If this Rule holds in ev'ry Art, ...   87 Hist V's House   44
   Their Empire holds so short a Reign; . . . . . .   591 Strephon Chloe   256
   It hardly holds the Honey-moon: . . . .   591 Strephon Chloe   258
   Many a Head that holds no Brains. . . . .   829 Legion Club   10
   With the fine flaming Sword that he holds in his Hand;   870 Grand Question   96
   For, the Right holds the Sword, and the Left holds the   870 Grand Question   108
    Bridle,)
   For, the Right holds the Sword, and the Left holds the   870 Grand Question   108
    Bridle,)
   So well, what Bottle holds a Quart: . . . . . .   889 Panegyr Dean   92
   Nature holds her forth two mirrors, ...   907 Daphne   43
   Three fellows with whips, and the Dean holds the string.   1027 Sheri Circles   20
HOLE   SEE AUGRE-HOLE,KEY-HOLE,SOTS-HOLE
   . . .makes a great Hole in my Wages, ...   71 Mrs Harris Pet   40
   Out from some Hole obscure he flies . . . . . .   84 Salamander   33
   Then shrink into it's Hole again. . . . .   84 Salamander   44
   "Or, else some hiding Hole he seeks, ...   305 Storm   61
   Both Solemnly put, in this hole on a Sunday, . . .   431 Dicky Dolly   23
   Half eat, and dragg'd it to his Hole. . . . . .   583 Young Nymph   60
   And a Hole above for peeping. . . . .   830 Legion Club   46
   Raise the Dirt about your Hole. . . . .   832 Legion Club   74
   A hole where a rabbit . . . .   857 Lady's Lament   183
   I drag him upwards from his Hole. . . . .   921 Riddle 6   34
   The dullest Beast and a Hole in the Ground, . . .   941 Letter   35
   For why should you stay in that filthy hole, . . .   1022 Nim-Dan-Dean 2   D 3
HOLIER
   A holier Priest ne'er was wrapt up in Crape, . . .   516 Dean Hang Rape   5
HOLLA
   So, Holla Boys; God save the King. . . . . . .   418 Woman's Mind   64

```
                                                            PAGE    TITLE          LINE
HOLLAND
    Holland got Towns, and we got Blows,        . . . . . .  168 Peace Dunkirk      3
    For, Holland not an Ell in    . . . . . . . . . .        441 Ballyspellin      45
    And with Holland Shirts so white,      . . . . . . .     573 Helter Skelter    21
HOLLOO
    When thro' the streets I cry holloo?    . . . . . . .    779 Mullinix Tim     186
HOLLOW
    Old Aches throb, your hollow Tooth will rage.   . . .    137 City Shower       10
    Mounts, Walks, on high; and in a Hollow      . . . . .   477 Epist on Epist    79
    That serve to fill her hollow Jaws.     . . . . . .      582 Young Nymph       18
    Some cleaning hollow Tubes, to spy      . . . . . .      780 Mullinix Tim     247
    Tantara, tantara, while all the Boys hollow.    . . . . 870 Grand Question    92
HOLLOW-TREE
    Great Poet of the Hollow-Tree.    . . . . . . . .        653 On Poetry        376
HOLLOWS
    Press down the Lumps, the Hollows fill,     . . . . .    582 Young Nymph       26
HOLY
    Ill may I live, if the good Sancroft in his holy rest,   36 Ode Sancroft       50
    And holy Sancroft's motion quite irregular appears,  . . 37 Ode Sancroft       81
    What we call holy, and great, and just, and good,  . . . 38 Ode Sancroft      124
    The holy Men desir'd their Host     . . . . . .          94 Bauc & Phil 1     155
    When a holy black Suede, the Son of Bob,    . . . . .    147 Windsor Proph      1
    Lo here I sit at holy head      . . . . . . . .          420 Holyhead           1
    For, he had made a holy Vow     . . . . . . . .          603 Beasts Confess    69
    By holy Zeal inspir'd, and led by Fame,     . . . . .    789 St. Pat's Well     1
    And haunt thy holy Walls in white and black.    . . . . 792 St. Pat's Well    48
    Let Folks in high, or holy Stations,    . . . . . .      813 Bro Protestant    57
    Confer on him the Holy Ghost;     . . . . . . .          820 Dr. Rundle         6
    Who know there is an Holy Ghost:     . . . . . .         820 Dr. Rundle        14
    A long-ear'd Beast and holy Fable,      . . . . . .      942 Probatur Alit     11
HOLY-WATER
    I dipp'd two babes in holy-water,    . . . . . . .       675 Curate's Compl     7
HOME
    And like that too, make every breast their home)   . . .  8 Ode to King       70
    We fondly stay at home in fear    . . . . . . . .         19 Ode Athenian      99
    Returning Home at Night, you'll find the Sink   . . . .  137 City Shower        5
    Returning home one Day from Court,      . . . . . .      170 Horace 1, 7        2
    At home, he was pursu'd with Noise,     . . . . . .      221 A Quiet Life      49
    Whom Fate has amply bless'd at home?    . . . . . .      272 Apollo's Edict  D 63
    We'll dress in Manufactures, made at home?  . . . . .    275 Epilogue          17
    Comes home a quarter after nine,    . . . . . . .        292 Prog Marriage     84
    But for her 'Squire when he's from home;    . . . . .    322 First of April    40
    Went home, and was cudgell'd again by his Wife. . . . .  327 Epigram 1         10
    Well then, I'll e'en go home, and fast;     . . . . .    377 Apology Lady C    54
    My Lady now returning home    . . . . . . . .            377 Apology Lady C    57
    Above two hundred miles from home?      . . . . . .      403 Window Inns 10  D  4
    Walks boldly home at dead of night;     . . . . . .      435 Answer Paulus     92
    Forgot at Home, became for Hire,    . . . . . . .        482 Libel on D- D-    63
    And chuse to dine at home with Port:    . . . . . .      488 Irish-Club        20
    Ah! never to return Home;     . . . . . . . .            573 Helter Skelter    16
    How happy for Us, that it is not at Home.   . . . . .    576 Place Damn'd      18
    And, in all clymates are at home:    . . . . . .         621 Scandal Poem 1   128
    And, in all Climates are at home,    . . . . . .         627 Scandal Poem 2   122
    And stays at home for want of Shoes:    . . . . . .      728 Stella, Poems     28
    My Orders are, I'm not at Home;     . . . . . .          742 Stel B-day 22     46
    I have a Coat at home, that you may try,    . . . . .    780 Mullinix Tim     217
    I return home at night,      . . . . . . . .             853 Lady's Lament     53
    With two pence left, walks home in rain.    . . . . .    878 Robbin & Harry     8
    For which all Mortals leave their Home;     . . . . .    922 Riddle 7          52
    My Footman came home from the Church, of a Bruise sick, 1029 Dr. Helsham      17
    This Night I came home with a very cold Dew sick,  . .  1030 Dr. Sheridan       2
    Yet he gets home at night with Health and whole Bones. 1037 Four Storyes       8
HOME-BRED
    And, for our home-bred British Chear,   . . . . . .      895 Panegyr Dean     267
HOME-SPUN
    Instead of Home-spun Coifs were seen,   . . . . . .      115 Bauc & Phil 2    139
HOMELI'ST
    His Chloe in the homeli'st Strains;     . . . . . .      590 Strephon Chloe   212
HOMELIEST
    To the homeliest face:    . . . . . . . .                854 Lady's Lament    100
    When from the homeliest Earthen Ware    . . . . . .      896 Panegyr Dean     295
HOMELY
    Return'd 'em Thanks in homely Stile;    . . . . . .      115 Bauc & Phil 2    112
    Away they rode in homely Sort    . . . . . .             224 Prog of Love      75
HOMER
    Came an Heir-loom, as Homer sings,      . . . . . .      134 Magician's Rod    64
    As Homer tells us o'er and o'er,     . . . . . . .       134 Magician's Rod    69
    By Homer dead was taught to thrive,     . . . . . .      483 Libel on D- D-    85
    Which Homer never cou'd alive.    . . . . . . .          483 Libel on D- D-    86
    From Homer down to Pope inclusive.      . . . . . .      504 Doctor Delaney   134
    You find, the Gods in Homer dwell    . . . . . .         620 Scandal Poem 1    99
    You find, the Gods in Homer dwell,      . . . . . .      626 Scandal Poem 2    97
    In Homer more than Homer knew.    . . . . . . .          643 On Poetry        104
    In Homer more than Homer knew.    . . . . . . .          643 On Poetry        104
    (For Gods, we are by Homer told,     . . . . . .         695 Cadenus Vaness   286
    Homer, Plutarch, Virgil, Flaccus,    . . . . . .         838 Legion Club      211
HOMER'S
    Would prove ev'n Homer's Numbers flat.      . . . . .    467 Birthday Song    228
HOMINEM
    May serve, as arguments ad hominem.     . . . . . .      433 Answer Paulus     48
```

HONDE
    Reaums shall daunce honde in honde, ... 103 Merlin   15
    Reaums shall daunce honde in honde, ... 103 Merlin   15
HONEST
    Where dwelt a poor old honest Yeman . . . . 91 Bauc & Phil 1   51
    Eat, Honest Friends, and never spare, ... 91 Bauc & Phil 1   64
    Where dwelt a good old honest Yeoman, ... 111 Bauc & Phil 2   19
    For honest Harry is no Witt, ... 123 Empty'ng Town   23
    His Rod was honest English Wood, ... 132 Magician's Rod   7
    And honest Harry is too apt to stink. . . . . . . 166 Toland's Invit   38
    Now quaff of honest Ale a Quart, ... 184 Horace 2, 1   111
    To a good honest Junta that never will teaze you. 185 Scriblerus 1   6
    For John was come of honest Kin: . . . . . 224 Prog of Love   60
    To help an honest lad that's out of place, ... 308 Billet Players   25
    With chearfull Looks, and honest Hearts. . . . . . 314 To Ford   82
    Then in Spight of your Sophistry, Honest Will. Wood 335 Serious Poem   49
    But with honest Wood's Love there is no contending, . 337 Serious Poem   105
    Then Master Steward takes my Rent, and tells me, honest 342 Upon His Grace   23
        Jo.
    Then said my Lord, I'm very glad to see thee honest 342 Upon His Grace   31
        Friend,
    I find you bear a good Report, and are an honest Man. . 342 Upon His Grace   34
    Our Parsons Read the Draper's Books, and make us 343 Upon His Grace   40
        honest Foke.
    My honest Friend Wild, may he long hold his Place, . 399 Tom Clinch   17
    And honest Paulus judges right. . . . . 432 Answer Paulus   2
    Perhaps be found one honest man: . . . . . 435 Answer Paulus   104
    Name honest Doctor Pelling; . . . . 440 Ballyspellin   21
    Your honest Care may fill; perhaps enlarge. . . . . 533 To Mr. Gay   46
    Then, honest <Robin>, of thy Corps beware: . . . . 539 Mr. Pulteney   39
    "He was an honest man I'll swear---: . . . . . . 547 Life of Swift   80
    Dear honest Ned is in the Gout, ... 554 Death of Swift   27
    That thou shouldst take an honest Trade, ... 787 Clad in Brown   27
    That no honest Heathen would be on their Side. . . 805 Irish Bishops   38
    And say of the man what all honest men say. . . . 819 Archbi Cashel   10
    Honest Keeper, drive him further, ... 834 Legion Club   141
    However I wish, honest Comrade of mine . . . . 1017 Swift Ans Sher   11
    For, as for honest John, tho' I'm not sure on't, . . . 1022 Nim-Dan-Dean 2 D 5
HONESTER
    What honester folks never durst for their ears. . . . 815 Yahoo's   19
    And the Dean my Master is an honester Man . . . 985 Mary to Sher   8
HONESTLY
    To discover the Goods he came honestly by: . . . 264 Apollo   58
    These Raps he will honestly dig out with Shovels, . . 337 Serious Poem   97
    He never honestly came by 'em, ... 621 Scandal Poem 1   119
HONESTY
    Till Honesty and Conscience are clear out of sight. . 36 Ode Sancroft   58
    His honesty in crouds of knaves; . . . . 436 Answer Paulus   126
    To common honesty and sense; . . . . 436 Answer Paulus   144
    And trust his Honesty just so much more. . . . . . 535 To Mr. Gay   114
HONEY-MOON
    It hardly holds the Honey-moon: . . . . 591 Strephon Chloe   258
HONOR
    But Tom is a Person of Honor so nice, ... 327 Epigram 1   6
    And gives the Maids of Honor Sport. . . . . . 468 Birthday Song   268
    To Virtue,--Honor, Sense, and Wit. . . . . . 732 Verses Vanessa   8
HONOR'D
    To my much honor'd Father; These: . . . . . . 223 Prog of Love   46
HONORS
    What honors we possesst of old. . . . . 619 Scandal Poem 1   52
HONOUR
    Provoke the honour of my Muse's rage, ... 42 Ode Sancroft   262
    You know, I honour the Cloth,. . . . . . . 72 Mrs Harris Pet   60
    But then his Honour cry'd, Godzooks! . . . . . 74 Game Traffick   5
    "I am a Cat of Honour--Stay, ... 154 Widow and Cat D 31
    My Lord--The Honour you design'd-- . . . . . . 173 Horace 1, 7   67
    And find his Honour in a Pound, ... 200 Horace 2, 6   27
    But Bawty, lost to Shame and Honour, ... 208 Fable Bitches   39
    But shall with unattainted Honour shine; . . . . . 210 Earl of Oxford   8
    So bow'd, was thankful for the Honour: . . . . . 376 Apology Lady C   25
    Resolv'd, nor Honour, nor Estate, ... 384 Manly Virtue   35
    (For, where high Honour is the Prize, ... 386 Manly Virtue   91
    Stand high in Honour, Wealth, or Wit; . . . . . . 414 Censure   7
    Must lose the honour, you have gain'd, ... 436 Answer Paulus   141
    This Badge of Honour in his Hair, ... 458 Paddy's Charac   20
    Must honour you alive and dead, ... 490 Dialogue   50
    Though Robin's Honour was in Pawn; . . . . . 495 Panegyr Swift   83
    To pay him Honour due, in Course . . . . . . 496 Panegyr Swift   112
    To Arms by Thirst of Honour led, ... 500 Doctor Delaney   2
    But she valu'd her Honour much more than her Life. . 517 Dean Hang Rape   10
    "Your Honour please to buy a Set? . . . . . . 564 Death of Swift   280
    "Those Maids of Honour (who can read) . . . . . 564 Death of Swift   287
    "He doth an Honour to his Gown, ... 564 Death of Swift   291
    "He never thought an Honour done him, ... 565 Death of Swift   319
    Truth and Honour how to prize; . . . . 630 Epistle Lady   22
    You raise the Honour of the Peerage, ... 656 On Poetry   455
    With Honour, which no Breath can Stain, ... 693 Cadenus Vaness   208
    Fixt Honour in her Infant Mind. . . . . 723 To Stella   6
    If Honour I would here define, ... 723 To Stella   9
    So Honour animates the Whole, ... 724 To Stella   13
    True Honour comprehends them all. . . . . 724 To Stella   18

		PAGE	TITLE	LINE
HONOUR	(CONTINUED)			
But, lest we should for Honour take		724	To Stella	23
In Points of Honour to be try'd,		724	To Stella	35
By Honour only were enroll'd		725	To Stella	52
By Honour seated in her Breast,		725	To Stella	59
Honour and Virtue, Sense and Wit,		758	Stel B-day '24	50
You honour me much--the Honour is mine,--		869	Grand Question	73
You honour me much--the Honour is mine,--		869	Grand Question	73
I'm sure he'll be proud of the Honour you do us;		871	Grand Question	118
Your Master's Honour to maintain;		890	Panegyr Dean	103
. . .with all my Heart and Soul, upon my Word and Honour.		10,14	Swift to Sheri	9
HONOUR'D				
Once highly honour'd! False is the pretence		44	To Congreve	7
Had lately honour'd with a <Mitre>.		302	Storm	8
The Dean, Tom's honour'd Friend and Patron.		458	Paddy's Charac	28
HONOUR'S				
By censure frighted out of honour's road,		506	To a Friend	9
Nor is Complexion Honour's Place.		724	To Stella	22
Now, see, when they meet, how their Honour's behave;		869	Grand Question	71
On either Side his Honour's Guard:		883	Rev Market-Hill	12
The <Dean>, to guard his Honour's Back,		883	Rev Market-Hill	13
HONOURABLE				
(Those honourable Wounds you bore		324	Pethox	15
HONOURS				
Thee with Immortal Honours crown,		182	Horace 2, 1	63
He had those honours in his day.		296	Satiric Elegy	22
From all his ill-got honours flung,		297	Satiric Elegy	31
He taught, how Men to Honours rise,		386	Manly Virtue	103
Our King ne'er exhausted his fountain of Honours.		389	Order of Bath	6
What Honours we possess'd of old!		625	Scandal Poem 2	48
HOOD				
Fair Rosamond, and Robin Hood,		93	Bauc & Phil 1	119
Fair Rosamond, and Robin Hood,		114	Bauc & Phil 2	95
HOODS				
Their Hoods, their Cloaks, and get them gone:		453	Modern Lady	287
HOOF				
His Horse had like to spoil his Hoof.		127	Little House	34
An Ass's Hoof alone can hold		469	Burning Poem	1
HOOK				
A Flitch of Bacon off the Hook,		91	Bauc & Phil 1	58
A Flitch of Bacon off the Hook;		112	Bauc & Phil 2	26
A Place was fastned to the Hook,		133	Magician's Rod	45
But you may hook in all the rest.		465	Birthday Song	150
HOOKS				
And strutting Hal-- is off the Hooks;		168	Peace Dunkirk	14
While <Sheridan> is off the hooks,		756	Stel B-day '24	11
HOOP				
Her Hoop is hoist above his Nose,		292	Prog Marriage	79
A Pettycoat without a Hoop!		699	Cadenus Vaness	400
Nor would the Door admit her Hoop.		746	Stel Distress	30
The narrow Entry crushd her Hoop		746	Stel Distress	
The Entry brusht against her Hoop:		751	Stel Wood-Park	50
With Hoop expanded wide and light,		897	Panegyr Dean	323
That she makes of your verses a hoop for Miss Tam,		1027	Sheri Circles	27
HOOPS				
Ride o'er the Waves in spacious Hoops,		254	Bubble	91
HOP				
Presto be gone; with t' other Hop		788	Dick's Variety	31
HOP'D				
"To breed contempt where thou hast hop'd esteem."--		55	Temple Ill	146
He hop'd to find some lucky Hour,		121	Apollo Outwit	45
And therefore hop'd she would recover		224	Prog of Love	69
Took Wing to Jove, and hop'd to rest		458	Paddy's Charac	31
He hop'd to have a Lucky Hit,		547	Life of Swift	90
So Venus hop'd, but hop'd in vain.		694	Cadenus Vaness	249
So Venus hop'd, but hop'd in vain.		694	Cadenus Vaness	249
And Cupid hop'd they wou'd improve		701	Cadenus Vaness	474
You hop'd to find many (for that was your Cue) sick;		1029	Dr. Helsham	23
HOPE				
And (I hope) an Eternal Sleep,		8	Ode to King	80
That I believe in much, I ne're can hope to see;		20	Ode Athenian	134
Tho' all the Fumes of Fear, Hope, Love, and Shame,		22	Ode Athenian	206
Ah, could You! could you hope a Poet for your Friend!		23	Ode Athenian	243
If hope e'er dawns the smallest of its rays.		54	Temple Ill	112
Since hope his last and greatest foe is fled,		55	Temple Ill	127
I hope you don't believe me Jealous:		116	Bauc & Phil 2	158
I hope you won it fairly.		154	Widow and Cat	D 35
Yet Mum for that, hope still the best,		182	Horace 2, 1	69
For who can hope to place one there,		271	Apollo's Edict	D 38
He's gone, although his Friends began to hope		285	Elegy Boat	17
The Goddess, who conceiv'd an Hope,		306	Storm	73
The Dean and Sheridan, I hope,		313	To Ford	73
So you are in Jest, and you will not I hope		335	Serious Poem	51
I hope you will own it is Love in a Maze;		337	Serious Poem	102
I hope he will find that no Love is lost.		337	Serious Poem	108
I wak'd with Delight, and not without Hope,		338	Serious Poem	115
I know the Times are something hard, but hope they soon will mend,		342	Upon His Grace	32
I hope you will not pay my Rent in that same Woods's Trash.		342	Upon His Grace	36

HOPE   (CONTINUED)   PAGE   TITLE   LINE

But Jove will soon convert I hope,   347 Prometheus   71
I hope to make you yet as clean,   361 Grace's Answer   5
Plain Loyalty not built on Hope,   410 Dial Rich Marb   81
But, hope to see you flourish still.   411 Dial Rich Marb   102
In hope to spring some nobler Game: 412 Desire Possess   31
In hope to see Spadillo rise;   452 Modern Lady   231
In vain, alas! her Hope is fed;   452 Modern Lady   232
That Hope at last remain'd behind;   528 Lady's Dres Rm   88
And fowl his Hands in Search of Hope.   528 Lady's Dres Rm   94
"We hope he's in a better Place.   562 Death of Swift   242
And yet, I hope 't will be allow'd,   622 Scandal Poem 1   151
What profit could you hope to get of her   622 Scandal Poem 1   170
And yet, I hope, 'twill be allow'd,   628 Scandal Poem 2   155
What hope of Custom in the Fair,   641 On Poetry   43
Our eldest Hope, divine Iulus,   655 On Poetry   429
He cou'd not hope she spoke in Jest.   706 Cadenus Vaness   629
Sorrow with Joy, and Hope with Fear.   711 Cadenus Vaness   777
Nor fondly hope for some Reverse of Fate,   793 St. Pat's Well   85
They may hope for Pence a Piece.   833 Legion Club   108
I hope you will use my House as your own.   869 Grand Question   82
I hope to quit that awkward Shame   887 Panegyr Dean   17
Yet, they always hope, our Favour.   934 Riddle 22   D   8
I hope you have swilld with new milk from the Kine   1018 Swift Ans Sher   25
I hope you will not think this a Pasquine   1018 Swift Ans Sher   34
And now I hope you'll excuse this rhyming, which I must   1024 Nim-Dan-Dean 2   D 17
  . . .
But, I hope I shall ne'er be, like you, of a Shrew sick 1030 Dr. Sheridan   4
HOPE'S
Rais'd up on Hope's aspiring Plumes,   252 Bubble   33
HOPEFUL
This hopeful Sect, now it begins to see   19 Ode Athenian   111
If from adown the hopeful Chops   529 Lady's Dres Rm   103
So hopeful, has by me been spoil'd;   692 Cadenus Vaness   195
HOPELESS
Though 'tis hopeless to reclaim them,   836 Legion Club   157
HOPES
An Arm on which all Europe's Hopes depend,   12 Ode to William   D 30
And hopes to lengthen Life by a Transfusion of Breath,   21 Ode Athenian   183
Spend all our present Stock in hopes of golden Rules.   27 Ode to Temple   27
By hopes my Congreve will reform the stage;   45 To Congreve   50
On an abandon'd wretch by hopes forsook;   54 Temple Ill   108
Forsook by hopes, ill fortune's last relief,   54 Temple Ill   109
Since the Tories have thus disappointed my Hopes,   145 New Song   51
Suspend a while your vain ambitious Hopes,   162 Toland's Invit   5
And fill <Jack Smith> with Hopes to keep his Place;   163 Toland's Invit   20
All their false deluded Hopes,   168 Peace Dunkirk   8
When that subtle Companion, in hopes to surpass us,   265 Apollo   80
Now all his hopes are in the Czar,   282 Journal   105
Their Thoughts, and Actions, Hopes, and Fears,   291 Prog Marriage   35
On whom my fears and hopes depend   420 Holyhead   24
Here quiet they Lie, in hopes to rise one Day,   431 Dicky Dolly   22
And, by their Fears express their Hopes;   557 Death of Swift   118
He owns, and hopes it is no Sin,   606 Beasts Confess   175
In hopes to make you more devout;   617 Scandal Poem 1   8
And hopes he will not think it strange   712 Cadenus Vaness   804
In hopes that Strangers may mistake it,   734 Stel B-day '20   12
Discourag'd Youths, now all their Hopes must fail,   793 St. Pat's Well   73
And we of all our Hopes depriv'd;   885 Rev Market-Hill   61
Hopes that will content you;   1014 Swift to Sheri   32
HOPING
Set hoping, hoping, hoping hearts of Lovers akeing,   959 Cantata
Set hoping, hoping, hoping hearts of Lovers akeing,   959 Cantata
Set hoping, hoping, hoping hearts of Lovers akeing,   959 Cantata
HOPPY
I have heard all the Speech repeated by Hoppy.   143 New Song   9
HOPS
Fly Bullets now as thick as Hops,   500 Doctor Delaney   9
The Rest pursue as thick as Hops: 654 On Poetry   400
HORACE
At Table you can Horace quote;   483 Libel on D- D-   95
Your Horace not content to quote,   494 Panegyr Swift   39
"A Verse from Horace, learn'd by Rote.   572 Death of Swift   474
It is well observ'd by Horace,   636 Epistle Lady   198
Get Scraps of Horace from your Friends,   648 On Poetry   245
And Horace brought ye tunefull Choir   658 On Poetry   D 410
Once Horace fancied from a Man   666 Epig Carthy 1   D   1
Thou hast slain Horace, what shou'd hinder   666 Epig Carthy 2   D   1
Creech murder'd Horace in his senseless Rhymes,   666 Epig Carthy 3   D   1
Who murder'd Horace without Rhyme or Reason?   666 Epig Carthy 3   D   4
Cou'd Horace give so sad a Monster Birth,   669 Epig Carthy 16   D   1
You make the graceful Horace look   670 Epig Carthy 21   D   3
As Horace says, Optat ephippia.   779 Mullinix Tim   214
He and Cratinus used, as Horace says,   988 Letter Dr Sh-n   11
Thus <Horace> in the House will prate,   812 Bro Protestant   23
HORN
Then fled, and left his Horn behind   293 Prog Marriage   115
To drink Achilous' Horn.   293 Prog Marriage   120
She combs his Head, and finds him Horn.   328 Epigram 2   4
Next Day the Post-boy winds his Horn,   398 Earl of P-b-w   16
Come out with Amalthea's Horn.   464 Birthday Song   126

```
                                                          PAGE    TITLE           LINE
HORNED
    The Horned Moon which heretofore    . . . . . . . .     99 Elegy Patrige       35
    The horned Floud, as Poets sing:    . . . . . . . .    293 Prog Marriage      110
    By the horned Sun, he sure meant <Cuckold>,   . . . .  373 Letter D. S-y       61
HORNET
    Humms, like a Hornet at his Nose,   . . . . . . .      458 Paddy's Charac      26
HORNET'S
    A Drone can raise a Hornet's Nest:  . . . . . . .      798 Traulus 1           84
HORNS
    And whence we claim our shbeing horns,   . . . . . .    99 Elegy Patrige       38
    And all we poor Shopkeepers must our Horns pull in.  . 237 Excellent Song      16
    Nor shall you strive your Horns to hide,   . . . . .  362 Grace's Answer      53
    For then your Horns will be your Pride.    . . . . .  362 Grace's Answer      54
HORRID
    Besides, this horrid Plot was found    . . . . . .     299 Horrid Plot         37
    An horrid Vision seiz'd my Head,    . . . . . . .      578 Day Judgement        3
    And Caelia's horrid Fact relate;   '  . . . . . . .   596 Cassinus Peter      93
    This dang'rous horrid motion Dish up?   . . . . . .    774 Mullinix Tim        18
    For thy horrid Looks, I own,    . . . . . . . .       838 Legion Club        195
HORROR
    Suspended every Horror of the Place,   . . . . . .       9 Ode to King         95
    "With Horror, Grief, Despair the Dean    . . . . .     568 Death of Swift     391
HORSE   SEE HOBBY-HORSE
    (The Pegasus, like an unruly Horse    . . . . . .      31 Ode to Temple      146
    His Horse had like to spoil his Hoof.    . . . . .     127 Little House        34
    Takes Horse, and in a mighty Fret    . . . . . .      174 Horace 1, 7        116
    Thus did the Grecian Wooden Horse,    . . . . . .     209 Fable Bitches       43
    The Horse and Pillion both were gone    . . . . .     223 Prog of Love        41
    The Horse and both the Riders tir'd:   . . . . . . .  224 Prog of Love        78
    So a Thief steals my Horse, and then gets him well drest 266 Apollo           92
    Where once their Sultan's Horse hath trod,    . . . . 324 Pethox              40
    I must compare him to a Horse;   . . . . . . . .      496 Panegyr Swift      113
    In Regiments of Foot and Horse;    . . . . . . . .    513 Answer Fable        28
    A founder'd Horse will oft debate,    . . . . . . .   640 On Poetry           15
    And his Horse, the dear Creter, it prances and rears,  . 870 Grand Question   97
    For, a Captain of Horse never takes off his Hat;   .  870 Grand Question     106
    Will make a Horse go, though he be not fat.    . . . . 940 Letter           13
    Is to a Horse an evil Disease.    . . . . . . .       941 Letter              34
    That we walk all about, like a horse in a pound,  . . 1026 Sheri Circles       7
HORSE-LAUGH
    Skilld in the Horse-laugh and dry Rub,    . . . . .    217 To Mr. Delany       57
HORSE'S
    The Horse's Countenance Divine.    . . . . . . .      498 Panegyr Swift      176
    A Ball of new-dropt Horse's Dung,    . . . . . .      811 Bro Protestant      11
HORSEBACK
    All riding on Horseback to Hell and the Bank.    . . . 287 Bank Down          25
HORSES
    On the Horses of their Clients;    . . . . . . . .    573 Helter Skelter       4
    Horses thus, let Jockeys judge else,   . . . . . . .  636 Epistle Lady       201
    His Horses too eat all our Hay.    . . . . . . . .    861 Lady Acheson        36
    Our Horses astray,   . . . . . . . . . . . . .      1036 Plague Country       5
<HORT>
    A Storm, to drown that Rascal <Hort>,    . . . . .    302 Storm                5
    'Till <Hort> arriv'd ne'er kept a Wench;   . . . . .  303 Storm               18
    If <Hort> must sink, she grieves to tell it,   . . .  303 Storm               19
    "And who but <Hort> can be employ'd?   . . . . . .    304 Storm               40
    That <Hort> was destin'd to a Rope,   . . . . . . .   306 Storm               74
    Be as Pox'd and Profane as Fanatical <Hort>    . . .  808 Advice Parson       10
HOSE
    Or spoils a Text, or mends his Hose.   . . . . . .    279 Journal             24
    Or darns his hose, or mends his Breeches,    . . . .  878 Robbin & Harry      27
    My broken Hose to patch and dern.    . . . . . . .    890 Panegyr Dean       112
HOSEN
    Walke sans wetynge Shoes ne hosen.    . . . . . .     102 Merlin               4
HOSPITABLE
    And then the hospitable Sire    . . . . . . . .        91 Bauc & Phil 1       55
    And then the Hospitable Sire    . . . . . . . .       111 Bauc & Phil 2       23
HOSPITALITY
    To try the People's Hospitality.    . . . . . . .      90 Bauc & Phil 1        4
    To try good People's Hospitality.   . . . . . . .     111 Bauc & Phil 2        4
HOST
    The holy Men desir'd their Host    . . . . . . .       94 Bauc & Phil 1      155
    The Hermits then desir'd their Host    . . . . . .    115 Bauc & Phil 2      109
    Sits up till Midnight with his Host,   . . . . . .    398 Earl of P-b-w        5
    Dare any of the mitred Host,    . . . . . . . .       820 Dr. Rundle           5
    Shall keep my Host in Ambuscade;    . . . . . . .     884 Rev Market-Hill     52
    And all my Kin, a num'rous Host,    . . . . . . .     925 Riddle 8            28
HOSTESS
    For John is Landlord, Phillis Hostess;   . . . . .    225 Prog of Love        98
    Having stolen from mine Hostess,    . . . . . . .     574 Helter Skelter      32
HOT
    And hot are their Brains,    . . . . . . . . .        246 Irish-Feast         62
    But a Kettle of scalding hot Water injected,    . . . 351 Wood Insect         25
    To Kensington, or hot St. James's;    . . . . . .     411 Dial Rich Marb      88
    The Weather and his Love were hot;    . . . . . .     586 Strephon Chloe      81
    On Embers plac'd, to drink it hot.    . . . . . .     594 Cassinus Peter      28
    Where hot and cold, where sharp and sweet,    . . . . 711 Cadenus Vaness     774
    Surpriz'd with ev'ry day a hot meal   . . . . . .     745 Stel Distress        5
    Another when he got a hot Meal;    . . . . . . .      781 Mullinix Tim       270
    And am at once both Hot and Cold:    . . . . . .      912 Aenigma             12
```

		PAGE	TITLE	LINE
HOTNESS				
Away he runs with zealous hotness	. . . .	423	Ireld	65
HOUND SEE BLOOD-HOUND				
An English or an Irish Hound;	. . . .	299	Horrid Plot	21
The Hound be hunted by the Hare,	. . . .	445	Modern Lady	20
The Hound wou'd scent, the Wolf would prole:	. . . .	512	Answer Fable	8
HOUNDS				
He heard I kept a pack of hounds,	. . . .	422	Ireld	27
Hounds hunt the Hare, the wily Fox	. . . .	504	Doctor Delaney	129
A Hare, who long had 'scap't pursuing Hounds,	. . .	538	Mr. Pulteney	17
So have I seen ill-coupled Hounds,	. . . .	645	On Poetry	175
HOUR				
The Muse was call'd in a poetic hour,	. . . . .	43	To Congreve	2
'Twas in an evil hour to urge my hate,	. . . . .	47	To Congreve	132
Perish the Muse's hour, thus vainly spent	. . .	48	To Congreve	175
There thy enchantment broke, and from this hour	. . .	55	Temple Ill	151
Yet they were forc't to walk an Hour	. . . . . .	90	Bauc & Phil 1	12
Now hardly moves an Inch an Hour.	. . . .	113	Bauc & Phil 2	74
He hop'd to find some lucky Hour,	. . . .	121	Apollo Outwit	45
In half an Hour thou'lt make another.	. . . . . .	128	Little House	60
Careful Observers may fortel the Hour	. . . .	136	City Shower	1
We squander there an Hour and more,	. . . . . .	279	Journal	17
Not reckoning half an hour we pass,	. . . . . .	279	Journal	37
We sit an hour to drink and chat.	. . . .	280	Journal	54
The Hour of Dining now is past;	. . . .	377	Apology Lady C	53
It does its Office ev'ry Hour,	. . . .	391	Young's Satire	20
They find an idle Hour to Prate.	. . . .	480	Libel on D- D-	28
My Work and me in half an Hour.	. . . .	502	Doctor Delaney	70
To save the Nation ev'ry hour?	. . . .	548	Life of Swift	110
He takes an Hour to find a Rhime:	. . . .	556	Death of Swift	100
"He labour'd many a fruitless Hour	. . . .	567	Death of Swift	365
Returning at the Midnight Hour;	. . . .	581	Young Nymph	7
Except to pass an Hour away:	. . . . . .	607	Beasts Confess	188
Keep the same face an hour together,	. . . . . .	618	Scandal Poem 1	44
Keep the same Face an Hour together:	. . . . . .	625	Scandal Poem 2	40
To affect me half an Hour;	. . . .	636	Epistle Lady	192
The Guests in less than half an Hour	. . . . . .	642	On Poetry	63
Within an hour, and eke a half,	. . . .	675	Curate's Compl	9
I curse her ev'ry hour sincerely;	. . . .	679	From Catullus	7
In a glad Hour Lucina's Aid	. . . . .	690	Cadenus Vaness	136
They could not be insur'd an Hour;	. . . . . .	729	Stella, Poems	64
Who ev'ry Day and Hour the same are;	. . . . . .	787	Dick's Variety	4
And from this Hour my Patronage resign.	. . . . .	794	St. Pat's Well	102
Shift the Scene for half an Hour,	. . . .	832	Legion Club	77
Dug out in an hour,	. . . .	857	Lady's Lament	185
Swears, he could get her in an hour	. . . . . .	879	Robbin & Harry	33
They bloom in less than half an Hour:	. . . . . .	926	Riddle 9	4
I'll make the Dev'l a Saint this Hour,	. . . . . .	930	Riddle 15	D 15
HOUR-GLASS				
'Tis the world's wat'ry hour-glass streaming fast,	. .	49	To Congreve	189
HOURLY				
Can'st hourly set him on the Rack,	. . . .	325	Pethox	54
Improving hourly in her Skill,	. . . .	416	Woman's Mind	25
For hourly thundring in his face,	. . . .	618	Scandal Poem 1	19
Who crowd the Press with hourly Trash.	. . . . . .	652	On Poetry	356
She hourly press'd for something new;	. . . . . .	704	Cadenus Vaness	555
She suffers hourly more than me,	. . . .	726	To Stella	104
I hourly wait some fatal End;	. . . .	921	Riddle 6	37
HOURS SEE MORNING-HOURS				
A three Hours Scene of empty Pride,	. . . . . .	6	Ode to King	17
At distant hours the mind with forms so like!	. . . .	51	Temple Ill	2
Throws all his Witt and Hours away	. . . .	80	Vanbrug House	43
Moves round but twice in twice twelve Hours	. . . .	93	Bauc & Phil 1	134
My choicest Hours of Life are lost:	. . . . . .	202	Horace 2, 6	106
Thus after four important Hours	. . . .	227	Prog of Beauty	53
We issue forth at different Hours;	. . . .	278	Journal	8
Whole Hours can with a Coxcomb sit,	. . . .	416	Woman's Mind	7
Five Hours, (and who can do it less in?)	. . . . .	525	Lady's Dres Rm	1
He pass'd his Hours among his Books;	. . . . . .	604	Beasts Confess	105
Read six hours a-day.	. . . .	855	Lady's Lament	132
Like Phoebus, guardian of the hours:	. . . . . .	937	Riddle 24	D 34
HOUSE SEE PIGEON-HOUSE,COFFEE-HOUSE,DEANRY-HOUSE,ALE-HOUSE,PARLIAMENT-HOUSE,ICE-HOUSE				
ALE-HOUSE-BUSH,SENATE-HOUSE,MANSION-HOUSE,CHARNEL-HOUSE,FIELD-HOUSE				
PLAY-HOUSE,SPUNGING-HOUSE,MAD-HOUSE,MALT-HOUSE				
But the Thing I stand upon, is the Credit of the House		71	Mrs Harris Pet	39
Would raise a House about two Storyes;	. . . . .	79	Vanbrug House	10
Sing Muse the House of Poet Van	. . . .	80	Vanbrug House	57
Repair a House gone to decay:	. . . .	80	Vanbrug House	64
Which in due time brought forth a House;	. . . . .	81	Vanbrug House	75
Soon reard a House two Storyes high;	. . . . . .	86	Hist V's House	6
And so resolv'd a House to build;	. . . .	87	Hist V's House	22
A reall House with Rooms and Stairs,	. . . . . .	87	Hist V's House	23
From House to House, wett to the Skin	. . . . .	90	Bauc & Phil 1	13
From House to House, wett to the Skin	. . . . .	90	Bauc & Phil 1	13
You look like Rogues would rob a House	. . . . .	91	Bauc & Phil 1	40
In his poor House to pass the Night;	. . . . . .	91	Bauc & Phil 1	54
Might raise a House about two Stories;	. . . . .	106	V's House	10
Sing Muse the House of Poet <Van>	. . . .	106	V's House	31
Repair a House gone to Decay,	. . . .	107	V's House	38
To see the House of Brother <Van>:	. . . . . .	108	V's House	96
But no such House was to be found;	. . . . . .	109	V's House	98

HOUSE	(CONTINUED)	PAGE	TITLE	LINE
Thy House about thee like a Snail;	. . . .	109	V's House	110
Capacious House! 'tis own'd by all	. . . .	109	V's House	115
Then said; my House is grown so Fine,	. . . . . .	115	Bauc & Phil 2	113
Give me that House in my own Hand;	. . . .	128	Little House	49
A finer House ten times than this,	. . . . . .	128	Little House	62
The <Duke> shew'd me all his fine House; and the <Duchess>		143	New Song	15
In <Antwerp> keep a frugal House,		183	Horace 2, 1	88
A handsome House to lodge a Friend,	. . . .	198	Horace 2, 6	3
At length to Musick's House she came,	. . . . . .	207	Fable Bitches	7
"Hath sent me to your House to whelp,	. . . . . .	207	Fable Bitches	11
"My House you've had on Courtesy;	. . . . . .	208	Fable Bitches	26
Quoth Will; thy House is worse than Hell:	. . . . . .	220	A Quiet Life	10
To the Dean'ry House, and on the North Glass,	. . . .	264	Apollo	31
Goes round the House to wake the rest:	. . . . . .	278	Journal	10
Shews all her Secrets of House keeping,	. . . . . .	282	Journal	87
This House will soon turn topsy turvey;	. . . .	283	Journal	128
But Thanks to the House, the Projectors look blank,	.	287	Bank Down	9
Hearing the House was empty, came to town;	. . . . .	307	Billet Players	2
"Regardless of her House and Fame;	. . . . . .	321	First of April	26
"This House don't want, nor will it hold us.	. . . .	322	First of April	46
That folds up itself in itself for a House,	. . .	350	Wood Insect	4
Then Woe be to those in the House who are sick:	. . .	351	Wood Insect	22
My House was built but for a Show,	. . . . . .	409	Dial Rich Marb	23
And set the House to <Rupert> <Barber>.	. . . . . .	477	Epist on Epist	70
To 'scape Enquiries, leave the House in Flame.	.	536	To Mr. Gay	142
E'en quit the House, for thou too long hast sat in't,	.	538	Mr. Pulteney	9
"To build a House for Fools and Mad:	. . . . . .	572	Death of Swift	480
With Coach and Six, and House in Town.	. . . . . .	585	Strephon Chloe	42
On House of Ease your future Bride,	. . . . . .	591	Strephon Chloe	238
What House, when its Materials crumble,	. . . . . .	593	Strephon Chloe	297
A House of Peers, or Gaming Crew,	. . . . . .	658	On Poetry	D 164
Nor calls up all the House at Night,	. . . . . .	725	To Stella	73
Materials for an House decay'd.	. . . . . .	727	To Stella	124
The House will never loose it's Trade;	. . . . . .	734	Stel B-day '20	8
Did Stella to his House invite;	. . . .	745	Stel Distress	2
Did Stella to his House invite:	. . . .	749	Stel Wood-Park	2
The Scottish Hinds too poor to house	. . . . . .	759	Receipt Youth	1
The Squires in Scorn will fly the House	. . . . .	760	Receipt Youth	53
To our Illustrious House of Hanover.	. . . . .	773	Mullinix Tim	10
In the House 'tis all he says;	. . . .	785	Mullinex Dick	39
Next Moment in the House of Peers,	. . . . . .	788	Dick's Variety	28
Thus <Horace> in the House will prate,	. . . . .	812	Bro Protestant	23
How greater's his merit at four Courts or House,	. .	814	Yahoo's	8
Or sell his Children, House, and Lands,	. . . . .	821	Dr. Rundle	43
Since the House is like to last,	. . . .	830	Legion Club	41
Call for th' Orders of the House;	. . . .	831	Legion Club	58
"An old Retainer to your House,	. . . .	850	Old Thorn	72
The House Accounts are daily rising	. . . . . .	860	Lady Acheson	29
I lose by the House what I get by the Land;	. . . .	866	Grand Question	4
I hope you will use my House as your own.	. . . . .	869	Grand Question	82
To build a House five Hundred more.	. . . . . .	875	Drapier's Hill	8
And, in his house, if any body come,	. . . . . .	878	Robbin & Harry	23
To take a House in Warwick Lane:	. . . .	904	Death Daphne	46
I sometimes live in House of Hair,	. . . . . .	912	Aenigma	9
Your House of Hair and Lady's Hand	. . . . . .	912	Aenigma Expl	D 1
The dullest Beast and what covers a House,	. . .	941	Letter	27
Will cover a House much better than Clay.	. . . .	943	Probatur Alit	34
Bears up his House, that's of his own contriving.	. .	943	Probatur Alit	48
. . .have it at their own House, to drink in quiet.	. .	1013	Swift to Sheri	7
HOUSE-WIFE				
A house-wife in bed, at table a slattern;	. . . . .	955	Portrait Life	7
HOUSEHOLD				
And still its Love to Household Cares	. . . . .	113	Bauc & Phil 2	81
Looks like the Chaplain of the Household,	. . . .	291	Prog Marriage	62
His Household twice a Day to Pray'rs.	. . . . . .	605	Beasts Confess	132
From ruling there the Household singly	. . . . . .	745	Stel Distress	9
From ruling there the Household singly,	. . . . . .	750	Stel Wood-Park	33
HOUSEKEEPER				
Call the Old Housekeeper, and get her	. . . . .	756	Stel B-day '24	9
HOUSES				
And Houses would not give a Rent.	. . . . . .	79	Vanbrug House	22
They and their Houses shall be drown'd:	. . . . .	112	Bauc & Phil 2	48
And make merry in their Houses;	. . . . . .	574	Helter Skelter	44
(While there are Houses to be let)	. . . . . .	746	Stel Distress	43
Of cleanly Houses who will doubt,	. . . .	787	Clad in Brown	29
Let you lie at friends houses.	. . . .	858	Lady's Lament	226
HOUSHOLD				
When Learnings little Houshold did embark	. . . .	16	Ode Athenian	12
And still it's Love to Houshold Cares	. . . . . .	94	Bauc & Phil 1	143
HOUSWIFE				
A Skillfull Houswife thus her Thumb	. . . . . .	227	Prog of Beauty	41
HOV'RING				
Flew hov'ring o'er each Female Head.	. . . . .	449	Modern Lady	135
The little Cupids hov'ring round,	. . . .	590	Strephon Chloe	193
Morpheus hov'ring o'er my Pillow,	. . . .	661	Love Song	23
HOVERS				
Oft hovers where alive it haunted most;	. . . . . .	51	Temple Ill	8
HOW	358		OMITTED WORD	

HOW'S   PAGE TITLE   LINE
 As, "What's a-Clock?" And, "How's the Wind? . . . 201 Horace 2, 6   69
HOWARD
 For when our high-born Howard dy'd, ... 652 On Poetry   371
 Friend Congreve a Feaver, Friend Howard an Ague,   . 1037 Four Storyes   2
 Lord <Bolton's> good Grace, Lord <Carr>, and Lord   804 Irish Bishops 25
  <Howard>,
HOWARD'S
 From Flecknoe down to Howard's Time, ... 652 On Poetry   369
HOWD'Y'S
 (When daily Howd'y's come of Course, ... 557 Death of Swift 123
HOWD'YE'S
 Will send their Howd'ye's ev'ry day: . . . . . . 546 Life of Swift   59
HOWE'ER
 Howe'er it was civil in Angel or Elf, ... 77 Lady B- B-   19
 Howe'er our Earthly Motion varies, ... 98 Elegy Patrige 16
 Howe'er she gave no flat Denial, ... 120 Apollo Outwit 25
 Howe'er such Verse as yours, I grant . . . 123 Empty'ng Town 17
 Howe'er, 'tis all one in the Greek. . . . 158 Fable of Midas 60
 Howe'er let us try him and see how he'll burn. . . 336 Serious Poem 64
 Howe'er you flounce, ... 440 Ballyspellin   7
 Howe'er for selling Bargains fam'd, ... 590 Strephon Chloe 216
 Howe'er it came, he cou'd not tell, ... 710 Cadenus Vaness 748
 Howe'er, to keep her Spirits up, ... 751 Stel Wood-Park 61
HOWE'RE
 Howe're it be, the Pride of France . . . . 10 Ode to King   136
 Howe're to keep her Spirits up Mean time to keep . . 747 Stel Distress 45
HOWEVER
 However, she stole away my Garters,. . . . . 70 Mrs Harris Pet 19
 However, I was resolv'd to bring the Discourse slily   71 Mrs Harris Pet 36
  about,
 However beauteous for his Mother: . . . . 272 Apollo's Edict D 57
 However, if Criticks find Fault with the Phrase, . . 337 Serious Poem 101
 However, it concerns not you. . . . . 435 Answer Paulus 102
 Be this however your Relief, ... 496 Panegyr Swift 86
 If not, however seated high, ... 503 Doctor Delaney 113
 At which, however well intended, ... 605 Beasts Confess 125
 However, we have too much sense . . . . 622 Scandal Poem 1 153
 However Stella, be not troubled, ... 721 Stel B-Day '18 3
 However, to avoid Disgrace, ... 917 Riddle 4   3
 However, they own it is very civil in Mr. Sheridan, . . 1014 Swift to Sheri 8
 However I wish, honest Comrade of mine . . . 1017 Swift Ans Sher 11
 Dear Tom, this verse, which however the beginning may 1022 Nim-Dan-Dean 2 D 1
  appear,. . .
 But, however, if he be come, bring him down, ... 1023 Nim-Dan-Dean 2 D 8
 However, bring down yourself, and you bring down all; . . . 1023 Nim-Dan-Dean 2 D 13
HOWL
 Can howl, and bark, but never spoke. . . . . 298 Horrid Plot   18
 Till they wriggle, howl, and skip. . . . . . 635 Epistle Lady 180
HOWL'D
 How Jowler howl'd, and what a fright . . . . 282 Journal   95
HOWSOEVER
 Which, howsoever they display . . . . . 387 Manly Virtue 105
HOYSE
 Strip their Bums; let Caleb hoyse 'em; . . . . 635 Epistle Lady 178
HUDDLE
 Now, all in haste they huddle on . . . . . 453 Modern Lady 286
HUE
 And colours of a faded hue. . . . . .   35 Ode Sancroft 32
 But kept it's Matter and it's Hue, . . .   93 Bauc & Phil 1 108
 And both assum'd a Sable Hue; . . . . 115 Bauc & Phil 2 122
 The Silver takes a nobler Hue, ... 255 Bubble   114
 O'er the Moon's Face a sable Hue, ... 354 Simile Silver   2
 But what's dy'd black will take no other hue. . . 670 Epig Carthy 18 D 8
 Thy fav'rite Flow'rs of yellow Hue. . . . 894 Panegyr Dean 250
 Your Thing of various Shape and Hue, . . . 912 Aenigma Expl D 7
 Various is my bulk and hue, ... 936 Riddle 24 D 27
 You may find they are all, by their yellow pale Hue, sick 1030 Dr. Helsham 27
HUES
 Filth of all Hues and Odours seem to tell . . . . 139 City Shower   55
 A nasty Compound of all Hues, ... 527 Lady's Dres Rm 41
 Can shew more different Hues than I; . . . 911 Aenigma   4
HUG
 I hug them till I squeeze their Blood. . . . 348 Whitshed Motto 10
 Then hug themselves, and reason thus; . . . . 557 Death of Swift 115
 Let Courtiers hug them in their Bosom, . . . 813 Bro Protestant 59
 Dear Companions hug and kiss, ... 835 Legion Club 151
HUGE
 (When this huge Bodies Moisture was so great . . 16 Ode Athenian   3
 That feeds the huge unequal stream. . . .   20 Ode Athenian 148
 With a huge Fardingal to swell her Fustian Stuff,   23 Ode Athenian 222
 Like a huge Insect up the Wall, ...   93 Bauc & Phil 1 106
 Like an huge Snail along the Wall; . . . 113 Bauc & Phil 2 86
 And in huge Confluent join at Snow-Hill Ridge, . 139 City Shower   59
 Gain by Degrees huge Tracts of Land, . . . 239 Run Bankers   2
 Then what a huge Delight were all in, . . . 353 Wood Ironmongr 25
 That I saw a huge Rat: O dear, how I scream'd! . . 868 Grand Question 50
 Huge Heaps of never-dying Works; . . . . 922 Riddle 7   40
HUGELY
 Is hugely turnd to Architecture, ... 86 Hist V's House 8

```
                                                          PAGE    TITLE              LINE
HUGH
     Quoth Hugh of Armagh, "The mob is grown bold."   .   .   .    843 Ay and No           3
HULK
     For thee they Argo's Hulk will Tax,          .   .   .   .   .  100 Elegy Patrige      77
     To tear you like a foundred Hulk    .   .   .   .   .   .   .  258 Bubble            199
HUM
     Who, while I talk, a song will hum,     .   .   .   .   .   .  900 Dean's Reasons     47
     Hum--excellent good--your anger was stirr'd:   .   .   .   .  976 Dean to Sherid      7
HUM-DRUM
     In their dull hum-drum key    .   .   .   .   .   .   .   .    186 Scriblerus 4     D  4
     Who is he? 'Tis hum-drum <Wynne>,    .   .   .   .   .   .    836 Legion Club       161
HUM'ROUS
     Either in verse or hum'rous prose,    .   .   .   .   .   .   489 Dialogue           10
     In my own hum'rous biting Way?   .   .   .   .   .   .   .    555 Death of Swift     54
     To Satire, Praise, or hum'rous Lines;   .   .   .   .   .    643 On Poetry          82
     Not a jest, or hum'rous story,    .   .   .   .   .   .   .   908 Daphne             65
HUMAN
     And must, to human reasoning opposite, conclude   .   .   .   41 Ode Sancroft      209
     Does sympathize with Human <Arse>.   .   .   .   .   .   .    66 Problem            28
     Without offence to Human Shape:   .   .   .   .   .   .   .    83 Salamander          6
     I've seen a Snake in human Form,   .   .   .   .   .   .   .   84 Salamander         38
     How prone to change in human life,   .   .   .   .   .   .   283 Journal           117
     They say, all human Things depend:   .   .   .   .   .   .   345 Prometheus         34
     Because, among all human Race.   .   .   .   .   .   .   .    366 Answer Delaney      7
     Thought human Learning wou'd not lessen    .   .   .   .   .  375 Apology Lady C      9
     "For once the Theme of human Sense.   .   .   .   .   .   .   384 Manly Virtue       10
     Disclaim the Human Name, and Face,    .   .   .   .   .   .   498 Panegyr Swift     172
     This Enemy of human Kind.   .   .   .   .   .   .   .   .   .  515 Answer Fable       86
     That Human Friendship is but Stuff.   .   .   .   .   .   .   545 Life of Swift      24
     Is thought too base for human Breast;   .   .   .   .   .    553 Death of Swift      6
     Vain human Kind! Fantastick Race!   .   .   .   .   .   .    555 Death of Swift     39
     "To merit well of human Kind:   .   .   .   .   .   .   .     567 Death of Swift    362
     "And, oh! how short are human Schemes!   .   .   .   .   .   567 Death of Swift    371
     "Offending Race of Human Kind,   .   .   .   .   .   .   .    579 Day Judgement      11
     A mortal human Touch impure?   .   .   .   .   .   .   .   .  586 Strephon Chloe     90
     A Crime that shocks all human Kind;   .   .   .   .   .   .   595 Cassinus Peter     68
     How just it suits with human Kind.   .   .   .   .   .   .    603 Beasts Confess     74
     All Human Race wou'd fain be Wits,   .   .   .   .   .   .    640 On Poetry           1
     Were Animals of human kind,   .   .   .   .   .   .   .   .   658 On Poetry       D 410
     Adapted to a human Mind,   .   .   .   .   .   .   .   .   .  659 On Poetry       D 410
     Or some worse Brute in human Shape,   .   .   .   .   .   .   687 Cadenus Vaness     40
     And human Caution tries in vain   .   .   .   .   .   .   .   702 Cadenus Vaness    486
     In high Concern for human Kind,   .   .   .   .   .   .   .   723 To Stella           5
     Else you relapse to Human Kind:   .   .   .   .   .   .   .   724 To Stella          44
     By human Kind, but Flesh and Blood?   .   .   .   .   .   .   759 Receipt Youth      36
     To be the chief of human Good,   .   .   .   .   .   .   .    764 Stel B-day '26     28
     With what concerns all human kind,   .   .   .   .   .   .    781 Mullinix Tim      264
     First taught thee human Knowledge and divine;   .   .   .    791 St. Pat's Well     28
     Human Race, or Imps of Hell.   .   .   .   .   .   .   .   .  801 Traulus 2          56
     Tho' born of human Filth and Sweat, it   .   .   .   .   .   812 Bro Protestant     37
     How soon all human Pleasures pass.   .   .   .   .   .   .    921 Riddle 7            6
     All human Race must hither draw:   .   .   .   .   .   .   .  922 Riddle 7           24
HUMAN-KIND
     A Compliment on Human-Kind:   .   .   .   .   .   .   .   .   608 Beasts Confess    218
     To deal it to the worst of Human-kind.   .   .   .   .   .    532 To Mr. Gay         28
HUMANE
     Consider Humane Folly, and you'll quickly own,   .   .   .    20 Ode Athenian      149
     Of humane Evils upwards flew;   .   .   .   .   .   .   .    528 Lady's Dres Rm     86
HUMANITY
     That Knowledge forfeits all Humanity;   .   .   .   .   .     28 Ode to Temple      55
     (Were his humanity on earth once more)   .   .   .   .   .    38 Ode Sancroft      133
     What meer Humanity affords,   .   .   .   .   .   .   .   .   204 In Sickness        14
HUMANKIND
     That Humankind are all Yahoos.   .   .   .   .   .   .   .    498 Panegyr Swift     168
HUMBLE
     What can the Poet's humble Praise?   .   .   .   .   .   .     6 Ode to King         7
     What can the Poet's humble Bays?   .   .   .   .   .   .   .    6 Ode to King         8
     And made an Humble Chaplet for the King.   .   .   .   .      16 Ode Athenian       31
     All Merit that transcends the humble Rules   .   .   .   .    18 Ode Athenian       77
     The Tribute of an humble Muse.   .   .   .   .   .   .   .     32 Ode to Temple     200
     The humble tribe mourn'd for the quick'ning soul,   .   .    53 Temple Ill         61
     And chose me for an humble Friend;   .   .   .   .   .   .   201 Horace 2, 6        66
     Lords, Knights and Squires were all his humble Debtors.     234 Elegy on Demar     16
     To teach the humble Wren to soar.   .   .   .   .   .   .    270 Apollo's Edict    D 26
     We, humble strollers, always on the wing.   .   .   .   .    308 Billet Players     14
     To the humble that vexatious Dean:   .   .   .   .   .   .   348 Whitshed Motto     20
     The humble whelp gives ev'ry vote.   .   .   .   .   .   .   421 Ireld             15
     This one, poor, humble Boon I want,   .   .   .   .   .   .   475 Epist on Epist      8
     "When thou thy humble Lays do'st offer   .   .   .   .   .   476 Epist on Epist     32
     He can alone the priesthood humble,   .   .   .   .   .   .   490 Dialogue           35
     Or swear it rotten; and with humble Airs,   .   .   .   .    534 To Mr. Gay         97
     Are an humble, prudent Wife;   .   .   .   .   .   .   .   .  633 Epistle Lady      100
     His humble Senate this professes,   .   .   .   .   .   .    646 On Poetry         197
     All humble Worth she strove to raise;   .   .   .   .   .    701 Cadenus Vaness    456
     She tends me, like an humble slave;   .   .   .   .   .   .   754 Stella '23          9
     While I, with humble Job, had rather,   .   .   .   .   .    813 Bro Protestant     61
     My humble Respects to my Lady unknown.--   .   .   .   .     869 Grand Question     81
     And thus, the Pair of humble Gentry,   .   .   .   .   .   .  883 Rev Market-Hill    17
     I now become your humble Suitor,   .   .   .   .   .   .   .  891 Panegyr Dean      129
     The humble Branches of a Thorn.   .   .   .   .   .   .   .   896 Panegyr Dean      306
     The Faculty, his humble Friends,   .   .   .   .   .   .   .  904 Death Daphne       47
```

HUMBLE   (CONTINUED)   PAGE   TITLE   LINE

    An humble Hanger-on at best;   . . . .   918 Riddle 4   21
    The haughty Prince, the humble Slave, ...   922 Riddle 7   28
    I gave, as you beg, your most humble respects: . . . .   979 Dean to Tho: S   24
    I would present my humble Service . . . .   1014 Swift to Sheri   11
    And so I conclude, with humble respects as usual, . . .   1024 Nim-Dan-Dean 2   D   18
    By humble companions were sent to their betters: 1026 Sheri Circles   2
    Lady Betty presents you her service most humble,   . . .   1027 Sheri Circles   25
HUMBLED
    How did the humbled Swain detest   . . . .   586 Strephon Chloe   91
    I'm humbled e'er I meet the dust,'   . . . .   663 Epigram Bust   2
    To Merit humbled in the Dust: . . . .   765 Stel B-day '26   46
    The Dean and the Doctor have humbled their Pride,   . .   871 Grand Question   131
HUMBLER
    An humbler Prospect only wait, ...   499 Panegyr Swift   179
    Content yourself with humbler Place.   . . . .   656 On Poetry   458
HUMBLY
    And humbly at the bottom crawl.   . . . .   9 Ode to King   118
    In manner submissive most humbly do pray, ...   185 Scriblerus 1   2
    This, humbly offers me his Case--   . . . .   200 Horace 2, 6   47
    Is humbly pray'd to ruin Twenty more. . . . .   535 To Mr. Gay   106
    Lay humbly at your Monarch's Feet;   . . . .   647 On Poetry   224
    Were (as he humbly did conceive)   . . . .   687 Cadenus Vaness   16
    Therefore he humbly would insist, ...   688 Cadenus Vaness   73
    On whose Petition (humbly shewing   . . . .   713 Cadenus Vaness   860
    The Bard, who humbly deigns to chuse   . . . .   887 Panegyr Dean   25
    Be humbly minded; know your Post;   . . . .   897 Panegyr Dean   327
    The Phantom, having humbly kiss't   . . . .   903 Death Daphne   3
    Most humbly sues for Pardon.   . . . .   1005 Sheridan's Sub   7
HUMDRUM
    Can listen to a tale humdrum, ...   900 Dean's Reasons   55
HUMILITY
    With those two pow'rful swords, Submission and Humility,   36 Ode Sancroft   48
HUMM'D
    Panting - - - and faultring - - - Humm'd and Ha'd,   . .   377 Apology Lady C   79
HUMMING
    Like Bees, are humming in my Ears.   . . . .   200 Horace 2, 6   50
    No, Madam; 'tis only Sir Arthur a humming.   . . . . .   871 Grand Question   128
HUMMS
    Humms, like a Hornet at his Nose, ...   458 Paddy's Charac   26
HUMOR
    Are Humor, Raillery and Witt: . . . .   215 To Mr. Delany   14
    What Humor is, not all the Tribe   . . . .   215 To Mr. Delany   19
    For Wit and Humor differ quite, ...   215 To Mr. Delany   23
    Humor is odd, grotesque, and wild, ...   216 To Mr. Delany   25
    True Humor must with Wit combine: . . . .   216 To Mr. Delany   30
    Part in worse humor than they met?   . . . .   217 To Mr. Delany   72
    Who full of Humor, Fire and Wit, ...   218 To Mr. Delany   91
    With Breeding, Humor, Wit, and Sense, ...   735 Stel B-day '20   25
HUMOROUS
    How I want thee, humorous Hogart?   . . . .   839 Legion Club   219
HUMOUR
    And shew'd some Humour in his Face;   . . . .   170 Horace 1, 7   8
    Lewis his Patron's Humour knows;   . . . .   171 Horace 1, 7   23
    Humour, and Mirth, had Place in all he writ: . . . .   194 Author Himself   11
    To taste his humour, and his wit;   . . . .   435 Answer Paulus   120
    Humour, you tumbled Topsy Turvy.   . . . .   477 Epist on Epist   72
    Thus, should I give your Humour place, ...   496 Panegyr Swift   110
    For sheer Wit, and Humour passes!   . . . .   523 Betty Grizette   34
    "Who call it Humour when they jibe: . . . .   571 Death of Swift   466
    Of Wit and Humour, Judges sov'reign.   . . . . . .   649 On Poetry   284
    His Humour well our Laughter might command, ...   669 Epig Carthy 16   D   3
    Nor shall I for his Humour, permit you to purloin   .   867 Grand Question   17
    More Wit and Humour than from Terence.   . . . . .   988 Letter Dr Sh-n   4
HUMOURS
    No Humours gross, or frowzy Steams, ...   584 Strephon Chloe   11
HUMP
    "He spar'd a Hump or crooked Nose, ...   572 Death of Swift   467
HUMPHRY
    Oh! wer't thou not a Duke, my good Duke Humphry,   . .   678 Dean and Duke   11
HUMS
    He haws and he hums, ...   854 Lady's Lament   109
HUN
    What Time the Goth, the Vandal, and the Hun,   . . .   789 St. Pat's Well   3
HUNDRED
    Our Prince has charm'd its many hundred Eyes;   . .   8 Ode to King   78
    Travels at least a Hundred Leagues, ...   174 Horace 1, 7   95
    For Life, six hundred Pounds a Year, ...   198 Horace 2, 6   2
    Or let it cost Five hundred Pound, ...   199 Horace 2, 6   19
    A hundred other Men's Affairs   . . . .   200 Horace 2, 6   49
    Nor can four hundred thousand sterling Pound   . . .   233 Elegy on Demar   3
    An Hundred at least, ...   244 Irish-Feast   11
    An hundred Heads broke, ...   246 Irish-Feast   71
    An hundred struck lame.   . . . .   246 Irish-Feast   72
    In Stock three hundred thousand Pounds;   . . . . .   251 Bubble   17
    Imprimis: From his Grace a Hundred pound.   . . . .   274 Epilogue   6
    Stay, let me see-- Three hundred pounds a year,   . .   308 Billet Players   17
    Three hundred pounds! Were I the price to fix,   . . .   308 Billet Players   21
    A hundred Whores in ev'ry Street, ...   315 To Ford   106
    Above two hundred miles from home?   . . . .   403 Window Inns 10   D   4
    Nor can ten Hundred Thousand Lyes, ...   414 Censure   27

HUNDRED   (CONTINUED)

		PAGE	TITLE	LINE
But Dick lost by Doll, twelve hundred a Year,	. . .	430	Dicky Dolly	5
Calls Lady Spade a hundred Cheats:	. . . .	447	Modern Lady	73
An Hundred Tongues, as Poets use,	. . . .	449	Modern Lady	137
An Hundred Thousand were too few!	. . . .	449	Modern Lady	139
In seventeen hundred eight and twenty,	. . . . . .	456	Dean Smedley	47
Be sung ten hundred thousand times.	. . . . . .	467	Birthday Song	222
Five hundred Pound a Year's no Fool.	. . . . .	478	Epist on Epist	112
From Lodging in a hundred Jayls,	. . . .	481	Libel on D- D-	51
Their Faction is five hundred Odds,	. . . . . .	501	Doctor Delaney	47
We had a Hundred abler Men,	. . . .	548	Life of Swift	99
"To sell him for Six Hundred Pound.	. . . . . .	567	Death of Swift	354
"He knew an hundred pleasant Stories,	. . . . .	572	Death of Swift	475
Surrounded with a Hundred Stinks,	. . . . . .	583	Young Nymph	48
Engag'd him in a hundred Quarrels,	. . . . . .	603	Beasts Confess	52
A hundred Fees last Easter Term.	. . . . . .	604	Beasts Confess	86
Was just one annual Hundred Pound.	. . . . . .	642	On Poetry	54
When she saw three hundred Brutes,	. . . . . .	833	Legion Club	113
I can shew two hundred more.	. . . .	839	Legion Club	238
There stood for many a hundred Years	. . . . .	848	Old Thorn	3
There's nine Hundred Pounds for Labour and Grain,	.	867	Grand Question	9
I increase it to Twelve, so three Hundred remain:	. .	867	Grand Question	10
"A Hundred to One, but it covers a Clown;	. . .	872	Grand Question	154
He will but add two Hundred Pound,	. . . . .	875	Drapier's Hill	6
To build a House five Hundred more.	. . . . .	875	Drapier's Hill	8
To Fifteen Hundred Pounds a Year,	. . . . . .	884	Rev Market-Hill	38
I have a hundred causes ready:	. . . .	899	Dean's Reasons	8
A hundred a Penny,	. . . .	951	Apples	3
With three hundred and sixty-five poems a year?	. . .	979	Dean to Tho: S	34

HUNDREDS

| Where hundreds and where thousands fell, | . . . . . . | 252 | Bubble | 51 |
| Tho' Hundreds have employ'd their Leisure, | . . . | 929 | Riddle 14 | D 3 |

HUNG

Hung loosely on the Church's pinnacle,		37	Ode Sancroft	74
Hung high and made a glitt'ring Show	. . . . . .	93	Bauc & Phil 1	114
A Scrap of Parchment hung by Geometry,		99	Elegy Patrige	41
Hung high, and made a glitt'ring Show,	. . . . .	114	Bauc & Phil 2	90
Where painted Monsters are hung out.	. . . . . .	172	Horace 1, 7	60
Which (in their Stile) is purely hung.	. . . . .	183	Horace 2, 1	82
Who hung like a Hero, and never would flinch.	. . . .	400	Tom Clinch	24
But hung himself to expiate his Crimes.	. . . . .	666	Epig Carthy 3	D 2
Lorsha! and out of her shteeple there was hung a black		840	Ballad	D 9
flag.				
And on the Boughs her Garland hung,	. . . . . .	848	Old Thorn	6
In Line direct, hung down behind.	. . . .	903	Death Daphne	28

HUNGER

| "I shall be starv'd with Cold and Hunger." | . . . . | 208 | Fable Bitches | 30 |

HUNGRY

With hungry Meals his Body pin'd,	. . . . . .	231	Prog of Poetry	37
A hungry Vicarage at best;	. . . .	484	Libel on D- D-	132
Amidst a croud of hungry Bards cries out,	. . . . .	671	Epig Carthy 24	D 3
Of roast or boil'd, to the Hungry is charming.	. . .	941	Letter	30

HUNKS

| Yet would gladly see the Hunks | . . . . | 836 | Legion Club | 167 |

HUNS

| Descendents of the barbarous Huns, | . . . . . . | 326 | Pethox | 75 |
| Sent in my Anger from the Land of Huns; | . . . . . | 792 | St. Pat's Well | 60 |

HUNT

| And longd to hunt upon my grounds | . . . . | 422 | Ireld | 28 |
| Hounds hunt the Hare, the wily Fox | . . . . . . | 504 | Doctor Delaney | 129 |

HUNTED

Or hunted fancy, by a circling flight,	. . . . . .	51	Temple Ill	5
The Hound be hunted by the Hare,	. . . .	445	Modern Lady	20
Hunted from Earth, and Sea, and Hell, he flies	. . .	538	Mr. Pulteney	29

HUNTER

| Supposing thou hast Tick with Hunter) | . . . . . | 182 | Horace 2, 1 | 78 |
| How Nim, no Hunter 'ere could match him, | . . . . | 281 | Journal | 73 |

HUNTERS

Like Hunters o'er their Evening Ale.	. . . . . .	447	Modern Lady	79
So keen thy Hunters, and thy Scent so strong;	. . .	539	Mr. Pulteney	43
Sly Hunters thus, in Borneo's Isle,	. . . . . .	885	Rev Market-Hill	75

HUNTING

| Leave hunting after Bribes, forget your Tropes: | . . . | 162 | Toland's Invit | 6 |
| I twice a Day a hunting go; | . . . . | 921 | Riddle 6 | 31 |

HUNTS

| Nor rides, nor walks, nor hunts, nor fowls, | . . . . . | 901 | Dean's Reasons | 87 |

HUNTSMEN

| The Huntsmen seize the grinning Prize. | . . . . . . | 885 | Rev Market-Hill | 82 |

HUPSOUS

| With sham Quotations Peri Hupsous: | . . . . . . | 648 | On Poetry | 256 |

HURL'D

| Giddy he grows, and down is hurl'd, | . . . . . . | 10 | Ode to King | 144 |

HURRICANO

| Nor hurricano from the Crown, | . . . . | 40 | Ode Sancroft | 191 |

HURRY

| I hurry me in haste away, | . . . . | 200 | Horace 2, 6 | 25 |
| And fly with Hurry to Ramines; | . . . . | 1002 | Reply by Dean | 8 |

HURRY'D

| But hurry'd out, and clapp't the Dore. | . . . . . | 220 | A Quiet Life | 8 |
| 'I'm hurry'd so, it makes me sick, | . . . . | 448 | Modern Lady | 98 |

HURT   PAGE   TITLE   LINE

		PAGE	TITLE	LINE
HURT				
	No hurt shall come to You or Yours;	92	Bauc & Phil 1	85
	No Hurt shall come to You, or Yours;	112	Bauc & Phil 2	45
	Break not his rest, nor hurt his lungs:	433	Answer Paulus	54
HUSBAND				
	From Husband, Children, Wheel, or Spinnet.	322	First of April	42
	Can dext'rously her Husband teize,	416	Woman's Mind	37
	"My Husband left to pay for Coals:	447	Modern Lady	67
	You see the Booby Husband sit	448	Modern Lady	114
	"Madam, your Husband will attend	562	Death of Swift	233
	Who beats her Husband, who his Wife;	781	Mullinix Tim	266
	If I had a Husband like him, I purtest,	869	Grand Question	57
HUSBAND'S				
	The kind Physician grants the Husband's Prayers,	364	On Dreams	27
	My Husband's a Sot,	952	Apples	8
HUSBANDS				
	Their luckless Choice of Husbands--others,	182	Horace 2, 1	53
	For Husbands past their Youth to find;	293	Prog Marriage	116
	Since Husbands get behind the Scene,	588	Strephon Chloe	137
HUSH-MONEY				
	Hush-money sends to all the Neighbours round:	535	To Mr. Gay	108
HUSSIES				
	How the hussies will fleer	855	Lady's Lament	117
HUT				
	In his Poor Hut to pass the Night;	111	Bauc & Phil 2	22
HUZZA				
	Huzza! the school-boys roar, the play'rs are come!	308	Billet Players	38
	Huzza their Brethren at the Blue-boys.	501	Doctor Delaney	62
HUZZA'D				
	Tom huzza'd the black-guard Boys,	784	Mullinex Dick	19
HUZZA'S				
	With loud Huzza's from all the Boys,	586	Strephon Chloe	69
HUZZY				
	"Hist, Huzzy, I think I hear some Body coming--	871	Grand Question	127
	Cry'd, Huzzy, why sure the Wench is gone mad:	873	Grand Question	184
HYDASPES				
	Hydaspes, Indus, and the Ganges,	655	On Poetry	421
HYDE				
	And strip his Hyde, and pick his Bones,	413	Desire Possess	57
	Assert that Hyde in writing story	489	Dialogue	25
	Her Eye-Brows from a Mouse's Hyde,	581	Young Nymph	13
	A ragged Shirt, and tawny Hyde.	594	Cassinus Peter	16
	And make thee tear thy tainted Hyde.	925	Riddle 8	44
HYMEN				
	Stood Hymen with a flaming Torch.	585	Strephon Chloe	48
	In the close bands of pleasing hymen.	675	Curate's Compl	6
HYMN				
	Whilst an alluding Hymn some Artist sings,	162	Toland's Invit	13
HYPERBOLE'S				
	Nor can Hyperbole's demean us,	622	Scandal Poem 1	155
HYPERBOLES				
	Nor can Hyperboles demean us;	628	Scandal Poem 2	159
HYPERBOLICK				
	Set out in Hyperbolick Strains,	463	Birthday Song	93
HYPOCRISY				
	Hypocrisy with Frown severe,	448	Modern Lady	126
HYPOCRITE				
	To call him Hypocrite and Quack.	605	Beasts Confess	128
HYPOCRITES				
	"For canting hypocrites to claim,	550	Life of Swift	171
HYPPS				
	Heaven send thou hast not got the Hypps.	594	Cassinus Peter	35
HYPROCRITE				
	Yet hyprocrite Fanaticks cry,	926	Riddle 9	17
HYSTERICK				
	In Vapours and Hysterick Fits:	451	Modern Lady	199
I	1503		OMITTED WORD	
I'D	23		OMITTED WORD	
I'GAD				
	I'gad I'd wear a Gown.	426	Five Ladies	40
I'LL	76		OMITTED WORD	
I'M	86		OMITTED WORD	
I'TH'				
	Unless i'th' Answer, of his Grace,	373	Letter D. S-y	59
I'VE	8		OMITTED WORD	
IBERIA				
	But proud Iberia soundly maul,	468	Birthday Song	248
ICE				
	When, who could think, tho' cold as Ice,	470	Burning Poem	13
ICE-HOUSE				
	My Ice-house rob as heretofore,	409	Dial Rich Marb	45
ICH				
	Then comyth foorthe, Ich understonde,	102	Merlin	5
ICY				
	On Icy Caucasus to shiver,	346	Prometheus	55
IDEA				
	I would not draw th' Idea from an empty Name;	21	Ode Athenian	161
IDEA'S				
	And both Idea's jump like Wits:	529	Lady's Dres Rm	126
IDEAS				
	For fine Ideas vanish fast,	591	Strephon Chloe	233

IDEAS   (CONTINUED)   PAGE   TITLE   LINE
     Would still the same Ideas give ye, ...   591 Strephon Chloe   247
     Ideas came into her Mind . . . .   704 Cadenus Vaness   556
IDEM
     They are as once, and Idem still. . . . .   373 Letter D. S-y   50
IDEOTS
     Mistaken Ideots! see how giddily they run, ...   39 Ode Sancroft   162
     And making -- some for Ideots pass   . . . .   373 Letter D. S-y   58
     Of Ideots roaring to the Boys.   . . . .   788 Dick's Variety   8
IDES
     Upon the Ides of February, ...   456 Dean Smedley   46
IDIOM
     Who in his idiom vile, with Gray's-inn grace, ...   47 To Congreve   137
     Tho' by their Idiom and Grimace   . . . .   652 On Poetry   361
IDIOT
     "But laugh'd to hear an Idiot quote, ...   572 Death of Swift   473
IDLE
     Out starts the little Beast, and mocks their idle Fears.   30 Ode to Temple   114
     Where can this idle Wench be hid?   . . . .   223 Prog of Love   28
     An idle Rogue, who spends his Quartridge   . . . . .   411 Dial Rich Marb   97
     They find an idle Hour to Prate.   . . . .   480 Libel on D- D-   28
     And idle Morals in the Schools   . . . .   493 Panegyr Swift   30
     So loitring, so active; so busy, so idle, ...   580 Psyche   3
     An idle Tale, 'tis no such Matter;   . . . .   627 Scandal Poem 2   127
     Scarce list'ning to their idle Chat;   . . . .   697 Cadenus Vaness   335
     Because he has never a Hand that is idle;   . . . . .   870 Grand Question   107
     Impertinent mixture of busy and idle.   . . . .   955 Portrait Life   4
IDOL
     But this Idol Wood may do us great Evil, ...   334 Serious Poem   11
     I'm but an Idol rais'd on high;   . . . .   926 Riddle 9   18
IDOL-FACES
     And dazzle all the Idol-Faces   . . . .   182 Horace 2, 1   75
IDOL'S
     Like that fantastic medley in the idol's toes, ...   38 Ode Sancroft   138
IERNA'S
     Ierna's Lake, for your Canal, ...   476 Epist on Epist   38
IERNE
     And glad Ierne now may see   . . . .   9 Ode to King   99
     Ierne, to the World's remotest Parts, ...   789 St. Pat's Well   5
     Wretched Ierne! with what Grief I see   . . . . . .   792 St. Pat's Well   33
IERNE'S
     Such was Ierne's Claim, as just as thine, ...   771 Horace 1, 14   41
IF   411   OMITTED WORD
IGN'RANCE
     But what does our proud Ign'rance Learning call,   . .   27 Ode to Temple   28
IGNOBLE
     While innocent, he scorns ignoble Flight;   . . . . .   196 Author Himself   61
     Disdains to serve ignoble Ends.   . . . .   503 Doctor Delaney   100
     "Dy'st'on a more ignoble Tree, ...   851 Old Thorn   86
IGNOBLY
     Of those you so ignobly stoop to fear;   . . . . . .   46 To Congreve   86
IGNOMINIOUS
     Not frighted with an ignominious name, ...   309 Billet Players   51
IGNORANCE
     Who must my Weakness and my Ignorance confess,   . . .   20 Ode Athenian   133
     . . . would grope in Ignorance and Night, ...   22 Ode Athenian   208
     (Methods in talk whereof our pride and ignorance make use) 38 Ode Sancroft   125
     Confesses ignorance to judge between;   . . . .   41 On Poetry   208
     And make his ignorance discerned, ...   435 Answer Paulus   113
     While Ignorance, with Brain of Lead, ...   449 Modern Lady   134
     "Those, who their Ignorance confess'd, ...   572 Death of Swift   471
     Bred up in Ignorance and Sloth, ...   655 On Poetry   409
     Where Ignorance begets Disdain.   . . . .   700 Cadenus Vaness   437
     For Pride and Ignorance a Proverb grown, ...   794 St. Pat's Well   99
IGNORANCE'S
     From Ignorance's Universal North, ...   25 Ode Athenian   299
IGNORANT
     Careless and Ignorant Posterity, ...   21 Ode Athenian   163
     (As in a Theatre the Ignorant Fry, ...   29 Ode to Temple   94
     But zeal is weak and ignorant, tho' wond'rous proud, . .   38 Ode Sancroft   135
     While every ignorant Beholder   . . . .   63 Discovery   15
     Damn'd Ignorant Prelates, and Councellors Privy.   . . . 576 Place Damn'd   14
     Heedless, ignorant, forgetful?   . . . .   630 Epistle Lady   8
     There's none so ignorant or weak   . . . .   890 Panegyr Dean   119
IGNORANTLY
     Others, ignorantly wise, ...   39 Ode Sancroft   168
ILL
     Both the Good-natur'd and the Ill, ...   18 Ode Athenian   73
     Ill may I live, if the good Sancroft in his holy rest,   36 Ode Sancroft   50
     And tho' I should but ill be understood   . . . . .   38 Ode Sancroft   121
     For, ill to them, long have I travell'd since   . . . .   46 To Congreve   87
     When man's ill genius to my presence sent   . . . . .   47 To Congreve   135
     In how ill season her resentments rule, ...   48 To Congreve   177
     Forsook by hopes, ill fortune's last relief, ...   54 Temple Ill   109
     Who, by Disgraces or ill Fortune sunk, ...   163 Toland's Invit   17
     Had not ill Fate, perverse and blind, ...   215 To Mr. Delany   5
     Lord! I should get so ill a Name, ...   220 A Quiet Life   35
     Dick found it by his ill Success   . . . .   221 A Quiet Life   41
     We are very ill us'd by you Mortals below;   . . . . .   263 Apollo   2
     That I have an ill Eye, they wickedly think, ...   263 Apollo   13
     Beneath whose ill Shade no Plant ever grew.   . . . .   334 Serious Poem   32

ILL   (CONTINUED)   PAGE   TITLE   LINE
     Her last Night's ill Success repeats, ...   447 Modern Lady   72
     I never saw you play so ill. . . . .   452 Modern Lady   247
     And as ill Neighbours in the Night, ...   457 Paddy's Charac   7
     Shou'd swear he never meant us ill;   . . . .   485 Libel on D- D-   155
     And, to avoid all future ill, ...   489 Dialogue   11
     Who does no Ill, can have no Foe, ...   514 Answer Fable   58
     Are ill excuses for a Servant's Crimes: . . . . .   533 To Mr. Gay   68
     "Ill suit with those profess'd of late: . . . . .   549 Life of Swift   147
     "My Lady Club wou'd take it ill, ...   562 Death of Swift   237
     "Was never ill receiv'd at Court: . . . .   565 Death of Swift   308
     But, oh! how ill hast thou divin'd . . . .   595 Cassinus Peter   67
     Ill it fits you to be witty, ...   630 Epistle Lady   13
     Ill befits a lofty Stile.   . . . .   634 Epistle Lady   140
     To purchase Fame by writing ill: . . . .   652 On Poetry   368
     To rhyme almost as ill as Duck.   . . . .   658 On Poetry   D 186
     Poor floating Isle, tost on ill Fortune's Waves,   . .   770 Horace 1, 14   1
     But, while in an ill tone, ...   856 Lady's Lament   155
     Or Mr. <Moor> will take it ill.   . . . .   860 Lady Acheson   28
     And, Molly, she said, I should hear some ill News. . .   868 Grand Question   52
     My Offers of Peace you ill understood.   . . . . . .   968 Letter Sherid   23
     And now I find my Muse but ill able   . . . .   989 Letter Dr Sh-n   30
     You live among ill folks in a dunghill, ...   1038 Sheridan Cavan   17
ILL-COUPLED
     So have I seen ill-coupled Hounds, ...   645 On Poetry   175
ILL-FATED
     And art thou forc'd to yield, ill-fated Poetaster?   . .   1002 Reply by Dean   3
ILL-GOT
     From all his ill-got honours flung, ...   297 Satiric Elegy   31
ILL-GOVERN'D
     Forgive (Original Mildness) this ill-govern'd zeal,   .   38 Ode Sancroft   107
ILL-GUIDED
     Such are the ways ill-guided mortals go   . . . . . .   35 Ode Sancroft   37
ILL-LINES
     Blush for Ill-spelling, for Ill-lines, ...   1002 Reply by Dean   7
ILL-MANNER'D
     Affect ill-manner'd Pedantry, ...   27 Ode to Temple   45
ILL-MANNERD
     The Flirts of his ill-mannerd Muse.   . . . . . .   219 To Mr. Delany   110
ILL-NATURE
     Rudeness, Ill-nature, Incivility, ...   27 Ode to Temple   46
ILL-ORGAN'D
     Down the ill-organ'd Engines fall;   . . . . . .   29 Ode to Temple   98
ILL-PRESENTED
     "Since thy few ill-presented graces seem . . . . . .   55 Temple Ill   145
ILL-SPELLING
     Blush for Ill-spelling, for Ill-lines, ...   1002 Reply by Dean   7
ILL-SPUN
     In twisting up an ill-spun Play: . . . .   80 Vanbrug House   44
ILLIT'RATE
     Thy insolent illit'rate vicar, ...   676 Parson's Case   7
ILLITERATE
     A lady illiterate;   . . . .   854 Lady's Lament   90
ILLIUM'S
     But Illium's lost, and Priam falls.   . . . . . .   209 Fable Bitches   46
ILLS
     With Patience, which all Ills supports, ...   325 Pethox   63
     Are ills you wisely wish to leave, ...   676 Parson's Case   15
     Nor think on our approaching Ills, ...   763 Stel B-day '26   5
     Nor let your Ills affect your Mind, ...   766 Stel B-day '26   81
ILLUSTRATE
     And, to Illustrate it, produce   . . . .   485 Libel on D- D-   163
ILLUSTRIOUS
     To our Illustrious House of Hanover.   . . . . . .   773 Mullinix Tim   10
IMAGE
     But where is ev'n thy Image on our earth?   . . . . .   35 Ode Sancroft   17
     (I forget in what Church) an Image of Wood;   . . . .   334 Serious Poem   18
     Concerning this Image there went a Prediction,   . . .   334 Serious Poem   19
     God's Image, which was once their Boast.   . . . . . .   498 Panegyr Swift   166
IMAGE'S
     Bor'd a large Augre-hole in the Image's Breech;   . .   336 Serious Poem   72
IMAGES
     Or images that sink in streams;   . . . .   35 Ode Sancroft   40
     Sit squeezing Images of Wax.   . . . .   240 Run Bankers   32
IMAGIN'D
     And the transported Muse imagin'd it   . . . . . .   17 Ode Athenian   48
     And feeds upon imagin'd Days: . . . .   80 Vanbrug House   42
     With six imagin'd cares to fright you.   . . . . . .   753 Gift for Bec   14
IMAGINABLE
     For, no imaginable things   . . . .   486 Libel on D- D-   195
IMAGINARY
     In striving to wash off th' imaginary paint: . . . .   42 Ode Sancroft   250
     Imaginary Charms can find, ...   703 Cadenus Vaness   526
     That gives imaginary Pain: . . . .   920 Riddle 5   34
IMAGINATION
     His foul Imagination links   . . . .   529 Lady's Dres Rm   121
     Whose rank Imagination fills, ...   592 Strephon Chloe   279
     Nor can Imagination guess, ...   595 Cassinus Peter   55
     Gives Imagination Scope, ...   636 Epistle Lady   213
IMAGINATION'S
     Or whether dead imagination's ghost   . . . .   51 Temple Ill   7

402

IMAGINE

	PAGE	TITLE	LINE
Perhaps imagine to be wondrous Wit	20	Ode Athenian	125
Which is perhaps as hard t' imagine right	21	Ode Athenian	159
Imagine now My <Lord> and Bush	63	Discovery	21
Canst thou imagine, dull Divine,	292	Prog Marriage	71
Imagine <Lyndsay> at the bar:	435	Answer Paulus	107
Who can imagine whence the Fund is,	477	Epist on Epist	75

IMAGINES

And <Lincoln> then imagines he has Land.	164	Toland's Invit	26

IMBIB'D

His Doctrines when she first imbib'd;	708	Cadenus Vaness	679

IMBIBE

Well taught by practice to imbibe	435	Answer Paulus	109

IMBIBES

The Torrent, merciless, imbibes	158	Fable of Midas	77
This Gulph insatiable imbibes	922	Riddle 7	19

IMBIBING

Call it Tasting, and Imbibing:	633	Epistle Lady	116

IMITATE

Must Imitate the Fashion of the Court.	275	Epilogue	30
Be studious well to imitate	780	Mullinix Tim	233
All Things on Earth I imitate,	935	Riddle 23	D 18

IMMENSE

Nor, in a Palace built with Charge immense,	533	To Mr. Gay	63

IMMORAL

Tho' Lewd and Immoral, be Formal and Grave,	807	Advice Parson	3

IMMORTAL

Immortal Joy, that suffers no Allay from Fears,	6	Ode to King	2
When some Patrician God wou'd visit the Immortal Jayl,	9	Ode to King	93
And You with fatal and Immortal Wit conspire	23	Ode Athenian	240
Bright effluence of th' immortal ray,	34	Ode Sancroft	2
Thee with Immortal Honours crown,	182	Horace 2, 1	63
Of Addison's immortal Page,	496	Panegyr Swift	101
Immortal made in Virgil's Lines,	658	On Poetry	D 410
Immortal by the Dunciad;	876	To Dean Swift	10

IMMORTALIZE

Immortalize our Dolls and Jenneys.	184	Horace 2, 1	116

IMPARLANCE

Demur, Imparlance, and Essoign,	690	Cadenus Vaness	122

IMPART

How can the Muse her Aid impart,	451	Modern Lady	220
The Secret thou shalt ne'er impart;	596	Cassinus Peter	101
Will scarce one precious word impart:	900	Dean's Reasons	44
Often aiding to impart	936	Riddle 24	D 25

IMPARTIAL

(Th' impartial Deaths which come	8	Ode to King	68
My Character impartial draws:	565	Death of Swift	306
Impartial judge within your Breast	642	On Poetry	79
To turn the true impartial Side!	921	Riddle 7	8

IMPATIENCE

"With what Impatience he declaim'd!	566	Death of Swift	346
With what Impatience they rejoice.	776	Mullinix Tim	96

IMPATIENT

Impatient of all Answers, straight became	22	Ode Athenian	191
Box'd in a Chair the Beau impatient sits,	139	City Shower	43
Pregnant with Greeks, impatient to be freed,	139	City Shower	48
Impatient to be like their Mothers,	182	Horace 2, 1	54
With rage impatient makes me wait	420	Holyhead	27
Impatient both of Night and Day,	726	To Stella	98
Impatient to be out of Debt,	887	Panegyr Dean	23

IMPEACH

Betray, make Oath, impeach, inform,	778	Mullinix Tim	168

IMPEDIMENT

He prates in Spight of all Impediment	797	Traulus 1	49

IMPENDING

T' avert th' impending judgments of my pen.	45	To Congreve	48
Dread from his Hand impending Changes.	655	On Poetry	422
Omens, the Types of thy impending Chains.	792	St. Pat's Well	44

IMPERFECT

Whence the weak shapes wild and imperfect pass,	35	Ode Sancroft	23

IMPERIAL

Retir'd to your Imperial Seat.	326	Pethox	90
His Cloud, and Jove's Imperial Queen:	625	Scandal Poem 2	54
Sometimes imperial Robes I wear,	935	Riddle 23	D 20

IMPERIALL

His Cloud, and Jove's imperiall Queen.	619	Scandal Poem 1	58

IMPERIOUS

A handsome young imperious Girl	289	Prog Marriage	3
Should some imperious Neighbour sink the Boats,	534	To Mr. Gay	89
Is very imperious.	855	Lady's Lament	144

IMPERTINENCE

For a dear Ramble thro' Impertinence,	18	Ode Athenian	69
Impertinence, the Scurvy of Mankind,	18	Ode Athenian	70
Begets a kinder Folly and Impertinence	18	Ode Athenian	79
Won't pay th' Impertinence of being known;	20	Ode Athenian	152
Of Doubts, Impertinence, and Niceties,	22	Ode Athenian	213
Round all the circles of impertinence,	46	To Congreve	88

IMPERTINENCIES

Who both our Follies and Impertinencies see,	18	Ode Athenian	89

IMPERTINENT

Impertinent mixture of busy and idle.	955	Portrait Life	4

IMPETUOUS

		PAGE	TITLE	LINE
You saw th' impetuous Torrent rolling on;	. . . . .	12	Ode to William	D 18
The Waves impetuous entring at your Keel.	. . . . .	770	Horace 1, 14	20

IMPIOUS

Sprung from her Womb that impious Line,	. . . . .	895	Panegyr Dean	271

IMPIOUSLY

(Who now so impiously blasphemes	. . . .	530	Lady's Dres Rm	137

IMPLIES

No real fortitude implies:	. . . .	676	Parson's Case	3

IMPLORE

Only your Godship to implore,	. . . .	403	Window Inns 10	D 7

IMPLOY

But first with Care imploy your Thoughts,	. . . . .	645	On Poetry	149

IMPLOY'D

Jove mix'd up all, and his best Clay imploy'd;	. . .	118	Biddy Floyd	11

IMPLUMIS

A Creature bipes et implumis;	. . . .	608	Beasts Confess	216

IMPORT

Libertas bears a large Import;	. . . .	348	Whitshed Motto	11

IMPORTANCE

This Business of Importance o'er,	. . . . . .	447	Modern Lady	90
When Things of more Importance press:	. . . . .	475	Epist on Epist	2
Their rights! their importance! We'll set on new rates	.	816	Yahoo's	32

IMPORTANT

The important history of Martin.	. . . . . .	186	Scriblerus 3	8
Thus after four important Hours	. . . .	227	Prog of Beauty	53
"To see th' important Men of Dress,	. . . . .	380	Apology Lady C	147
Discoursing with important Face,	. . . .	698	Cadenus Vaness	376
Thy formal Nods; important Sneres;	. . . . .	775	Mullinix Tim	61
For we who debate on a subject important,	. . . . .	976	Dean to Sherid	11

IMPORTS

What imports thy forward Sight?	. . . .	862	To Janus	11

IMPOSSIBLE

His Grace! impossible! what dead!	. . . .	296	Satiric Elegy	1
Impossible! it can't be me.	. . . .	376	Apology Lady C	38
Nothing impossible to Jove.	. . . .	384	Manly Virtue	22
For I'll prove it impossible they can be both.	. . .	976	Dean to Sherid	18
It is impossible to know by your Letter		1013	Swift to Sheri	1

IMPOSTOR

"That Jesus was a Grand Impostor:	. . . . . .	564	Death of Swift	294

IMPOSTOR'S

Which lighting on th' Impostor's Crown,	. . . . .	353	Wood Ironmongr	37

IMPOTENT

Their Passions not more impotent and cold,	. . . . .	532	To Mr. Gay	21
From the Impotent and Old?	. . . .	632	Epistle Lady	72

IMPRECATIONS

In Haste, with Imprecations dire,	. . . . . .	470	Burning Poem	11

IMPRESSION

Can scarce th' impression of his foot-steps find;	. . .	54	Temple Ill	116
On all the same Impression stuck.	. . . .	344	Prometheus	10
The same Impression on his Mind;	. . . . . .	345	Prometheus	20
It never makes the least Impression.	. . . . . .	798	Traulus 1	64

IMPRESSIONS

The foulest Impressions I easily take.	. . . . . .	929	Riddle 13	D 8

IMPRIMIS

Imprimis: From his Grace a Hundred pound.	. . . .	274	Epilogue	6
Imprimis, at the Temple Porch	. . . .	585	Strephon Chloe	47
But now for your verses; we tell you, imprimis,	. . .	1026	Sheri Circles	5

IMPRISON'D

As parent earth, burst by imprison'd winds,	. . . . .	52	Temple Ill	37
And each imprison'd Hero quak'd for Fear.	. . . . .	139	City Shower	52

IMPROV'D

Improv'd in Picture, Size, and Letter;	. . . . .	114	Bauc & Phil 2	98
How much improv'd by Dr. <D.>	. . . . .	779	Mullinix Tim	216
Here, for an Age and more, improv'd their Vein,	. . .	793	St. Pat's Well	71
Already have improv'd so well,	. . . .	891	Panegyr Dean	133

IMPROVE

And which (to heavenly soil transplanted) will improve,	.	41	Ode Sancroft	228
Which all deserve and all improve.	. . . .	322	First of April	36
Cou'd please them, and improve her own.	. . . . .	701	Cadenus Vaness	453
And Cupid hop'd they wou'd improve	. . . . . .	701	Cadenus Vaness	474
Our Care is to improve the mind,	. . . .	781	Mullinix Tim	263
Provided, to improve the Ground,	. . . .	875	Drapier's Hill	5

IMPROVING

Improving hourly in her Skill,	. . . .	416	Woman's Mind	25
by dint of experience improving in Blunders	. . . . .	540	Charac Walpole	6

IMPS

Transform'd to Imps, his Levee wait.	. . . . .	646	On Poetry	208
Incarnate with a thousand Imps,	. . . .	798	Traulus 1	71
Human Race, or Imps of Hell.	. . . .	801	Traulus 2	56

IMPUDENCE

And Impudence with Front of Brass;	. . . . . .	448	Modern Lady	131
Made up of Noise, and Impudence, and Lies.	. . . .	532	To Mr. Gay	42
With Impudence own'd all the Fact.	. . . . .	687	Cadenus Vaness	24
Yet still has Impudence to rise,	. . . .	824	Printer Newgat	13

IMPUDENTLY

Is grown so impudently Great,	. . . .	10	Ode to King	120

IMPULSE

Th' Impulse, the Fight, th' Event, were wholly Thine.		12	Ode to William	D 36
A powerful Impulse urge your Mind,	. . . . . .	642	On Poetry	78

	PAGE	TITLE	LINE
IMPURE			
A mortal human Touch impure?	586	Strephon Chloe	90
IMPUTE			
His Lordship would impute it all to Spight:	535	To Mr. Gay	112
IMPUTED			
And flourish'd by imputed Wit, ...	481	Libel on D- D-	50
And each Perfection wrong imputed	646	On Poetry	201
Where Virtues are imputed Crimes, ...	798	Traulus 1	92
IN SEE LYING-IN			
2230		OMITTED WORD	
IN'T 8		OMITTED WORD	
INACTIVITY			
Is inactivity at best:	242	Horace 4, 9	2
INCAPABLE			
For Breasts incapable of Flame;	688	Cadenus Vaness	64
Incapable of outward Stains;	691	Cadenus Vaness	163
INCARNATE			
Incarnate with a thousand Imps, ...	798	Traulus 1	71
INCENS'D			
The <Queen> incens'd, his Services forgot, ...	195	Author Himself	57
INCENSE			
Who, loth to blame, or to incense, ...	377	Apology Lady C	73
Of Incense many a thousand Load;	657	On Poetry	474
Conviction does but more incense;	730	Stella, Poems	91
INCENSED			
By the just Vengeance of incensed Skies, ...	806	Judas	1
INCESSANT			
Nell roar'd incessant, Dick sate mute:	219	A Quiet Life	4
Where loudest winds incessant roar	420	Holyhead	30
Rais'd ever such incessant Rout:	450	Modern Lady	183
Tormented with incessant pains, ...	754	Stella '23	1
Stood chatt'ring with incessant Din;	849	Old Thorn	34
INCESTUOUS			
By Phoebus (an incestuous birth)	433	Answer Paulus	25
INCH SEE TWO-INCH			
Now hardly moves an Inch an Hour.	113	Bauc & Phil 2	74
He wonder'd for how much an Inch 'twould be Sold: . .	288	Bank Down	33
You strove for ev'ry Inch of Ground;	326	Pethox	88
To lose an Inch of Favour for a Friend?	531	To Mr. Gay	6
Fail'd but an Inch to seize him by the Back.	538	Mr. Pulteney	34
I ask but for an Inch at most.	554	Death of Swift	20
Their Foes superior by an Inch.	651	On Poetry	336
For all the World, Captain, not half an Inch farther--	869	Grand Question	79
She'll not have Pow'r to stir an Inch;	885	Rev Market-Hill	66
Can move an Inch except I will.	929	Riddle 14	D 8
Or else I will not ride one Inch of Ground.	943	Probatur Alit	40
But turns at every Seam, an Inch in.	1021	Nim-Dan-Dean 1	D 16
INCHES			
At least twelve Inches overcast, ...	126	Little House	6
We'll take her Heels five Inches lower.	886	Rev Market-Hill	104
INCITES			
A strange Event! whom Gold incites, ...	345	Prometheus	21
INCIVILITY			
Rudeness, Ill-nature, Incivility, ...	27	Ode to Temple	46
INCLIN'D			
Still to unhappy restless thoughts inclin'd; . . .	55	Temple Ill	132
Is he to Avarice inclin'd?	464	Birthday Song	123
'Tis true, he was not much inclin'd	603	Beasts Confess	63
Yet not incurious, was inclin'd	696	Cadenus Vaness	314
If you are inclin'd	855	Lady's Lament	125
Are most inclin'd to plunder Crowns.	1033	Ans to Crown	12
INCLINATION			
It's Inclination for below;	92	Bauc & Phil 1	100
INCLINATIONS			
Its Inclinations for below;	113	Bauc & Phil 2	60
INCLIND			
How well the Governor's inclind.	422	Ireld	25
INCLINE			
Still to the Sea their Course incline;	709	Cadenus Vaness	721
All Travellers at first incline	734	Stel B-day '20	1
I wish you would tell me which way you incline . . .	1017	Swift Ans Sher	19
INCLINES			
This Tale inclines the gentle Reader, ...	157	Fable of Midas	41
Her Scale to neither Side inclines;	391	Young's Satire	16
Inclines to aid a specious Lye:	414	Censure	14
And, where his Genius most inclines, ...	641	On Poetry	23
Whether your Genius most inclines	643	On Poetry	81
INCLINING			
But more inclining to sit still.	170	Horace 1, 7	12
INCLOS'D			
Inclos'd Artificers to Choke.	100	Elegy Patrige	94
Inclos'd Cap-a-pee in a strong Coat of Mail. . . .	350	Wood Insect	6
INCLOSE			
Inclose him in a wooden Tow'r, ...	325	Pethox	56
So <Turds> within a Glass inclose, ...	786	Clad in Brown	11
INCLUSIVE			
From Homer down to Pope inclusive.	504	Doctor Delaney	134
From Courts inclusive, down to Cells, ...	691	Cadenus Vaness	149
INCOG			
And all Men believe he presides there incog. . . .	804	Irish Bishops	15
INCOGNITA			
Virtue's Terra Incognita, ...	26	Ode to Temple	12

                                                                    PAGE   TITLE   LINE
INCOHAERENT
    And all the incoherent Jargon of the Schools,   . . .   22 Ode Athenian   205
INCOHERENT
    And thousand incoherent journies take, ...   36 Ode Sancroft   70
INCOME
    "No larger Income dost thou Crave.   . . . .   476 Epist on Epist   36
    What Income can your Wants supply?   . . . .   478 Epist on Epist   96
    With labour small, and income great;   . . . .   676 Parson's Case   23
    My income ceasing.   . . . .   1037 Sheridan Cavan   6
INCONSIDERABLE
    We've found a little inconsiderable Head   . . . . .   20 Ode Athenian   147
    Was but to light Earth's inconsiderable spot.   . . . .   36 Ode Sancroft   72
INCONSISTENCE
    Ye who hate such inconsistence, ...   907 Daphne   25
INCONSISTENT
    Whence come these inconsistent Fits?   . . . .   796 Traulus 1   33
INCONSTANCY
    Men's Folly, Whimsyes, and Inconstancy, ...   21 Ode Athenian   173
INCREAS'D   SEE ENCREAS'T
    Increas'd by new Intestine Wheels: . . . .   113 Bauc & Phil 2   68
    He found her, while the Scent increas'd, ...   589 Strephon Chloe   185
    With Pains unknown increas'd her Smart.   . . . . .   703 Cadenus Vaness   523
INCREASE
    Whence takes it its Increase, and whence its Birth,   .   31 Ode to Temple   169
    I ask not to increase my Store, ...   198 Horace 2, 6   8
    As Years increase, she brighter shines, ...   703 Cadenus Vaness   536
    I increase it to Twelve, so three Hundred remain: . .   867 Grand Question   10
    Preserve his health, his store increase;   . . . . .   902 Dean's Reasons   101
INCREDIBLE
    Nay, what's incredible, alack!   . . . .   674 His Deafness   7
INCUMBRANCES
    Incumbrances of Food and Cloaths;   . . . .   231 Prog of Poetry   42
INCURABLE
    'Tis now grown an incurable Disease: . . . . . .   33 Ode to Temple   205
INCURIOUS
    Yet not incurious, was inclin'd   . . . .   696 Cadenus Vaness   314
INCURR'D
    He has a Forfeiture incurr'd, ...   712 Cadenus Vaness   802
INDECENTLY
    And, when indecently I rave, ...   754 Stella '23   10
INDEED
    Kings would indeed be Victims of the State;   . . . .   6 Ode to King   6
    . . .Indeed, says I, never worse;   . . . .   70 Mrs Harris Pet   14
    Of late indeed the Paper-Stamp   . . . .   172 Horace 1, 7   43
    The Sea indeed had golden Sands.   . . . .   255 Bubble   112
    And could he be indeed so old   . . . .   296 Satiric Elegy   9
    A weighty Argument indeed;   . . . .   298 Horrid Plot   13
    Your <Bishops> all are <Dogs> indeed.   . . . . . .   301 Horrid Plot   76
    But that indeed which pleasd me most   . . . . . .   422 Ireld   31
    "Who fain would pass for Lords indeed: . . . . .   570 Death of Swift   438
    I fear thou wilt be mad indeed.   . . .   596 Cassinus Peter   90
    Indeed, the Strictness of his Morals   . . . . . .   603 Beasts Confess   51
    True indeed, I should be gladder, ...   801 Traulus 2   49
    'Tis true, indeed, sometimes I save, ...   918 Riddle 4   31
    'Tis true indeed, to curry Friends, ...   1003 Dan J's Reply   19
INDENTURES
    How firmly these Indentures bind.   . . . .   1021 Nim-Dan-Dean 1   D 34
INDIA
    Shew'd Patterns just from India brought, ...   698 Cadenus Vaness   378
INDIA'S
    From India's burning Clime I'm brought, ...   911 Aenigma   1
INDIAN
    Right Indian this, right Macklin that;   . . . . . .   447 Modern Lady   83
    And painted like an Indian Queen.   . . . .   926 Riddle 9   10
INDIES
    To the East Indies, there to cheat, ...   456 Dean Smedley   35
INDIFF'RENT
    One quite indiff'rent in the Cause, ...   565 Death of Swift   305
INDIFFERENCE
    Indifference clad in Wisdom's Guise, ...   561 Death of Swift   213
    And if her Youth Indifference met, ...   706 Cadenus Vaness   638
INDIGINATION
    What indigination in her Mind   . . . .   725 To Stella   61
INDIGNATION
    With indignation I behold your wit   . . . .   45 To Congreve   55
    The Nymph, with indignation, view'd   . . . . . .   178 To Lord Harley   47
    And full of Indignation frets   . . . .   450 Modern Lady   164
    And fir'd with Indignation vows, ...   694 Cadenus Vaness   253
    In your indignation what mercy appears, ...   818 Epigr Kite   1
    --Let indignation fire my strains, ...   950 Upstart   D 21
INDIGNITY
    O, what Indignity and Shame   . . . .   654 On Poetry   405
INDISCREET
    His Zeal was sometimes indiscreet: . . . . . .   603 Beasts Confess   54
INDISCREETLY
    Nor indiscreetly to suppose   . . . .   218 To Mr. Delany   101
INDISPUTED
    His indisputed Rights extend   . . . .   649 On Poetry   287
INDITE
    Some tender Sonnet to indite, ...   184 Horace 2, 1   114

	PAGE	TITLE	LINE
INDITING			
But never of my own inditing.	917	Riddle 3	10
INDIVIDUAL			
In Cheese an individual Mite?	504	Doctor Delaney	140
"No Individual could resent,	571	Death of Swift	461
INDOLENCE			
And kindled first with Indolence and Ease,	33	Ode to Temple	203
INDULGE			
"We shou'd indulge the Dean's disgust,	549	Life of Swift	159
INDULGENT			
Venus, indulgent to her Kind	227	Prog of Beauty	57
Thy fair indulgent Mother crown'd	324	Pethox	33
(May Heav'n Indulgent hear your Pray'r!)	498	Panegyr Swift	174
Thus, indulgent Chloe bit,	523	Betty Grizette	35
Indulgent you to Female Kind,	887	Panegyr Dean	7
Are so indulgent, and so mild,	891	Panegyr Dean	151
INDUS			
Hydaspes, Indus, and the Ganges,	655	On Poetry	421
INDUSTRY			
Your Industry no better throve,	495	Panegyr Swift	81
INEPTE			
Qui nil moliris tam inepte?	476	Epist on Epist	30
INEVITABLY			
Must not inevitably tumble?	593	Strephon Chloe	298
Inevitably be undone.	606	Beasts Confess	168
INFALLIBLY			
Infallibly cures the Timber affected;	351	Wood Insect	26
INFAMOUS			
"And make her infamous in Story.	568	Death of Swift	388
"An infamous destructive Cheat.	569	Death of Swift	408
INFAMY			
All stain'd with Infamy and Vice,	84	Salamander	39
The Man, who Infamy to shun,	243	Horace 4, 9	21
To act with Infamy, or quit the Place.	535	To Mr. Gay	130
Are Lords of Infamy and Praise:	729	Stella, Poems	54
INFANT			
Rattles for Infant Royalty to play withal,	6	Ode to King	13
To shield the infant Fruits and Flowers,	387	Manly Virtue	109
Her infant Loves with purple Wings;	585	Strephon Chloe	50
This Infant shall restore my Reign.	691	Cadenus Vaness	147
To see a lovely Infant born:	692	Cadenus Vaness	189
Fixt Honour in her Infant Mind.	723	To Stella	6
The chaste Diana's infant Face;	919	Riddle 5	8
INFANT-STEPS			
In Leading strings her Infant-Steps to guide;	531	To Mr. Gay	11
INFANT'S			
Collected in that Infant's Mind.	691	Cadenus Vaness	153
INFANTS			
Nor Infants dropt, the spurious Pledges	641	On Poetry	37
INFECTING			
Infecting thus our Hearts by Stealth;	895	Panegyr Dean	280
INFECTIOUS			
Or no Infectious Weed,	7	Ode to King	53
From the dire infectious Crew.	834	Legion Club	124
INFERIOR			
For this inferior world is but Heaven's dusky shade,	35	Ode Sancroft	21
A more inferior Station seeks	227	Prog of Beauty	34
All others who inferior sit,	414	Censure	8
Should some obscure inferior fellow	464	Birthday Song	141
Or, some remote inferior Post,	484	Libel on D- D-	133
Ye <rascals> of inferior note,	487	Irish-Club	3
Inferior mortals there below.	617	Scandal Poem 1	4
Inferior Mortals there below.	623	Scandal Poem 2	4
Each Poet of inferior Size	651	On Poetry	331
INFERIORS			
O'er his Inferiors as our Tyrants;	824	Printer Newgat	6
INFERIOUR			
Th' inferiour Youth, to Learning led	385	Manly Virtue	39
INFERNAL			
Nor can they from infernal Mansions rise;	363	On Dreams	4
Sent from the Dark infernal Region	798	Traulus 1	77
Enter that Infernal Door;	834	Legion Club	120
INFEST			
And, turn'd to Lice, infest the King:	813	Bro Protestant	54
INFIDELITY			
Lo! Infidelity return'd again.	792	St. Pat's Well	36
INFINITE			
With endless and with infinite;	38	Ode Sancroft	127
Are equally held infinite,	653	On Poetry	390
'Tis only infinite below.	654	On Poetry	392
INFINITUM			
And so proceed ad infinitum:	651	On Poetry	340
INFINITY			
Make their minds travel o'er infinity of space,	36	Ode Sancroft	61
INFLAM'D			
Fill'd with Disdain, with Rage inflam'd,	699	Cadenus Vaness	404
INFLAME			
To inflame both the Nations do plainly conspire;	237	Excellent Song	19
Makes Wit inflame, or Anger burn;	731	Stella, Poems	118
INFLAME'D			
And now, inflame'd with rival Rage,	385	Manly Virtue	43

		PAGE	TITLE	LINE
INFLAMER				
But, Woman is a curst inflamer;	. . . .	618	Scandal Poem 1	35
But Woman is a curst Inflamer,	. . . .	624	Scandal Poem 2	33
INFLAMES SEE ENFLAMES				
Not Love of Beauty less the Heart inflames	. . . .	532	To Mr. Gay	19
INFLAMMATIONS				
That inflammations in the eyes	. . . .	982	Sher, A Goose	4
INFLICT				
What Punishment would you inflict?	. . . . . .	505	Doctor Delaney	153
Who Punishments on me inflict,	. . . .	917	Riddle 3	15
INFLUENCE				
Your Influence do's the vain Attacks defy	. . . . .	13	Ode to William	D 43
And sheds, tho' all unseen, his sacred influence here.	.	39	Ode Sancroft	153
Kind Star, still may'st thou shed thy sacred influence here,		39	Ode Sancroft	154
And that his subjects share his happy influence;	. . .	40	Ode Sancroft	182
But do not shed thy Influence down	. . . . . .	100	Elegy Patrige	95
His Influence is diffus'd around;	. . . .	385	Manly Virtue	38
The influence of whose golden beams	. . . . . .	432	Answer Paulus	7
Such heavenly Influence require,	. . . .	641	On Poetry	31
INFLUENCES				
And all Her boasted Influences are	. . . .	10	Ode to King	138
INFORM				
Inform the Commons, that the Secret's out:	. . . .	195	Author Himself	42
"Inform us, will the Emp'ror treat?	. . . . .	202	Horace 2, 6	94
Inform us, You that best can tell,	. . . .	252	Bubble	49
Betray, make Oath, impeach, inform,	. . . . . .	778	Mullinix Tim	168
And the Gospel will inform us,	. . . .	830	Legion Club	33
INFORM'D				
A spirit so inform'd as yours	. . . .	176	To Lord Harley	7
Inform'd a Minister of State.	. . . .	298	Horrid Plot	4
INFORMATIONS				
With Informations in his Hands,	. . . .	312	To Ford	44
INFORMER				
That Traitor, Assassin, Informer vile.	. . . . .	826	Noisy Tom	8
For never was Informer he,	. . . .	1036	Heathen Christ	3
INFORMERS				
For, are not all Informers so?	. . . .	298	Horrid Plot	6
Damn'd Spies and Informers, Damn'd Friends and Damn'd Lyars;		576	Place Damn'd	10
INFORMS				
And, Scholars teach, the Soul informs;	. . . . .	724	To Stella	12
INFUS'D				
Infus'd a strong prolifick Potion,	. . . .	293	Prog Marriage	108
Infus'd, yet as it were by Stealth,	. . . .	693	Cadenus Vaness	216
INFUSE				
Nature the hidden Spark did at my Birth infuse,	. . .	32	Ode to Temple	202
From thence a plenteous Draught infuse,	. . . . .	743	Stel B-day 22	75
INFUSES				
In Nectar thrice infuses Bays,	. . . .	691	Cadenus Vaness	156
INGLONDE				
And it shall by merye in olde Inglonde.	. . . . . .	103	Merlin	16
Then olde Inglonde shall be noe more.	. . . . .	103	Merlin	17
INGLORIOUS				
And so inglorious, after all!	. . . .	296	Satiric Elegy	4
Poor Sherry, inglorious,	. . . .	1004	Sheridan's Sub	1
INGRATITUDE				
"Ingratitude he often found,	. . . .	567	Death of Swift	359
How would Ingratitude delight?	. . . .	726	To Stella	93
INGREDIENTS				
From which Ingredients, First the dext'rous Boy	. .	118	Biddy Floyd	5
INHABIT				
Would scorn to inhabit,	. . . .	857	Lady's Lament	184
INHABITANTS				
Of all inhabitants on earth,	. . . .	936	Riddle 24	D 1
INHERENT				
In him such Virtues lye inherent,	. . . .	464	Birthday Song	133
INHERIT				
That with no Title to inherit,	. . . .	464	Birthday Song	135
Yet still you fancy you inherit	. . . .	478	Epist on Epist	97
INHERITANCE				
Besides, as they say, Service is no Inheritance in these Ages.		71	Mrs Harris Pet	41
INHERITS				
Inherits ev'ry Virtue round,	. . . .	646	On Poetry	192
INIGO				
But all admire Inigo Jones:	. . . .	727	Stella, Poems	4
INJECTED				
But a Kettle of scalding hot Water injected,	. . . .	351	Wood Insect	25
INJUR'D				
To pierce an injur'd Lover's Heart.	. . . .	595	Cassinus Peter	60
In Vain from injur'd Heav'n Relief expects.	. . . .	771	Horace 1, 14	36
To wash thy injur'd Off'rings out.	. . . .	896	Panegyr Dean	318
INJURE				
Not dar'd to injure with our lowly song;	. . . . .	52	Temple Ill	44
To injure the nation	. . . .	424	Carterets Arms	15
INJURED				
Yet safe from injured innocence escape:	. . . . .	506	To a Friend	4
INJUSTICE				
And, in a crew, 'tis no injustice thought	. . . . .	308	Billet Players	27

		PAGE	TITLE	LINE
INK				
Our Ink is black, our Paper white;		463	Birthday Song	108
But you some white-lead ink must get,		463	Birthday Song	113
You shou'd withdraw from pen and ink,		489	Dialogue	16
Or, on Parchment, Ink turn'd yellow:		523	Betty Grizette	8
Furnish'd with Paper, Pens, and Ink,		740	Stel B-day 22	3
'Tis Time at last to spare his Ink,		799	Traulus 1	101
Your ink is your poison, your pen is what not;		979	Dean to Tho: S	21
Your ink is your drink, your pen is your pot.		979	Dean to Tho: S	22
INMOST				
Our inmost Secrets to our Foes:		706	Cadenus Vaness	611
INN SEE GRAY'S-INN,ANGEL-INN				
And foster'd in a wretched inn.		40	Ode Sancroft	175
The Inn has not one drop of wine		420	Holyhead	6
Just o'er against the Bell Inn		442	Ballyspellin	57
INN'CENT				
She still is welcome with her inn'cent song;		49	To Congreve	182
INNOCENCE				
Made up of Virtue and transparent Innocence:		30	Ode to Temple	128
You make to truth, retreat, and innocence;		44	To Congreve	8
Truth, Innocence, Good Nature, Look serene;		118	Biddy Floyd	4
Of Innocence, the surest Guard,		386	Manly Virtue	73
Bare Innocence is no Support,		413	Censure	5
And me my Innocence secures.		445	Modern Lady	33
Virtue or innocence abuse;		488	Irish-Club	26
Yet safe from injured innocence escape:		506	To a Friend	4
"By Innocence and Resolution,		569	Death of Swift	399
"But Heav'n his Innocence defends,		570	Death of Swift	425
How shall his Innocence be clear?		707	Cadenus Vaness	641
INNOCENT				
Whatever serves for innocent Emblems of the Court;		31	Ode to Temple	164
While innocent, he scorns ignoble Flight;		196	Author Himself	61
If he be innocent, defend him.		219	To Mr. Delany	112
And made him to Curse the poor innocent Bank.		288	Bank Down	40
That innocent Delight he took		704	Cadenus Vaness	550
An innocent and absent Friend;		765	Stel B-day '26	44
He'll take his revenge on his innocent wife.		817	Yahoo's	74
INNS				
Adjourn'd from tops and grammar to the inns;		46	To Congreve	98
INNUENDO'S				
Your Innuendo's when you tell us		735	Stel B-day '20	43
INNUENDOS				
Broad Innuendos, such as this,		463	Birthday Song	83
INNUMERABLE				
Of Sparrows tam'd, of Nuts innumerable,		283	Journal	113
INOFFENSIVE				
With inoffensive feet o'er standing corn;		54	Temple Ill	118
INQUIRE SEE ENQUIRE				
At two Afternoon for our Psyche inquire,		580	Psyche	1
From yonder Puppet-Man inquire,		592	Strephon Chloe	285
Inquire through all the Parish round		602	Beasts Confess	43
INQUIRIES				
Among your Females make Inquiries;		625	Scandal Poem 2	71
INQUIRYES				
Among your femals make inquiryes:		619	Scandal Poem 1	73
INQUISITIONS				
"For Inquisitions taught by Spain,		183	Horace 2, 1	97
INRAG'D				
Inrag'd, as Ern would do at thee.		476	Epist on Epist	46
INSATIABLE				
This Gulph insatiable imbibes		922	Riddle 7	19
INSCRIPTION				
With quaint Inscription, which contains,		494	Panegyr Swift	55
INSECT				
Just such an Insect of the Age		80	Vanbrug House	39
Whence Broods of insect Poets rise.		80	Vanbrug House	54
Like a huge Insect up the Wall,		93	Bauc & Phil 1	106
The first is an Insect they call a Wood-Louse,		350	Wood Insect	3
The Third is an Insect we call a Wood-Worm,		351	Wood Insect	17
The Spiteful Insect stung the God.		458	Paddy's Charac	34
INSECTS				
The wretched Insects singe their Wings, and fall,		9	Ode to King	117
Emblems of Insects vile, who spread their Spawn		792	St. Pat's Well	55
INSENSIBLY				
Insensibly came on her Side;		709	Cadenus Vaness	729
INSERT				
Insert it when you write agen:		485	Libel on D- D-	162
Blot out, correct, insert, refine,		643	On Poetry	87
INSIDE				
The out or inside of their Heads,		688	Cadenus Vaness	49
INSINUATE				
Do but insinuate what is true.		729	Stella, Poems	60
INSINUATING				
With such insinuating Ways.		920	Riddle 6	4
INSIPID				
More than a fade insipid mixture left behind.		50	To Congreve	212
INSIST				
This I must insist on. For, as		636	Epistle Lady	197
Therefore he humbly would insist,		688	Cadenus Vaness	73
But still insist the Man is mad.		796	Traulus 1	22

INSOLENCE
    So flagrant is Thy Insolence, ... 154 Widow and Cat D 41
    He does, with Insolence and Pride. . . . . 172 Horace 1, 7 56
    Strange pride and insolence you shew, ... 617 Scandal Poem 1 3
    Such wicked insolence appears . . . . 622 Scandal Poem 1 167
    Strange Pride and Insolence you show, ... 623 Scandal Poem 2 3
    Be empty of Learning, of Insolence full: . . . . . 807 Advice Parson 2
    Puff'd up with pride and insolence, ... 950 Upstart D 11
INSOLENT
    Ah, since our fears are fled, this insolent expel, ... 53 Temple Ill 55
    (As fools are insolent and vain) . . . . 177 To Lord Harley 41
    Thy insolent illit'rate vicar, ... 676 Parson's Case 7
INSOLENTLY
    And insolently thrice, the slighted Maid . . . . . 43 To Congreve 3
INSPIR'D
    With which inspir'd we'll club each Night . . . . . 184 Horace 2, 1 113
    Till pious Love inspir'd her Son? . . . . 269 Apollo's Edict D 4
    They swear that they all by Love are inspir'd, ... 401 Window Inns 3 3
    (Inspir'd with Courage from his Bride,) . . . . . 589 Strephon Chloe 189
    Each breathing on her throne, inspir'd . . . . . 692 Cadenus Vaness 177
    By this new Passion grew inspir'd. . . . . . . 709 Cadenus Vaness 717
    Phoebus inspir'd me from above, ... 741 Stel B-day 22 25
    Nor ever Nymph inspir'd to Rhyme, ... 757 Stel B-day '24 21
    By holy Zeal inspir'd, and led by Fame, ... 789 St. Pat's Well 1
INSPIR'ST
    The malice thou inspir'st I never fail . . . . . . 53 Temple Ill 85
INSPIRATION
    Faint inspiration sickens as she flies, ... 50 To Congreve 229
INSPIRATIONS
    Our Inspirations to obey, ... 270 Apollo's Edict D 8
INSPIRD
    I think you inspird by the Muses all nine . . . . 1017 Swift Ans Sher 4
INSPIRE
    Which soon her merit forc'd her to inspire; . . . . 44 To Congreve 26
    I alone can inspire the poetical Crowd; . . . . . 263 Apollo 16
    Whom if I inspire, 'tis not to my Knowledge, ... 263 Apollo 18
    'Tis strange, what diff'rent Thoughts inspire . . . . 411 Desire Possess 1
    Inspire you with poetick Rage; . . . . 462 Birthday Song 68
    Not only can inspire, but pay. . . . . 462 Birthday Song 70
    Or, if the Muses must inspire . . . . 489 Dialogue 19
    Did Congreve's Wit inspire my Song; . . . . . . 496 Panegyr Swift 99
    Could Verse inspire, but seldom writ: . . . . . . 597 Problem Solved 2
    Love can with Speech inspire a Mute, ... 709 Cadenus Vaness 712
INSPIRES
    Whilst Angels tune the Voice, and God inspires the
      Tongue. 17 Ode Athenian 56
    She ne'er inspires against Conviction: . . . . . . 503 Doctor Delaney 106
INSPIRING
    Not for inspiring poets brains . . . . 432 Answer Paulus 15
    Forsaken by th' inspiring Nine, ... 741 Stel B-day 22 13
    Pour'd in a strong inspiring Juice: . . . . . . 743 Stel B-day 22 66
INSTALL'D
    And is Install'd as good a Star, ... 100 Elegy Patrige 71
INSTALMENTS
    Patents, Instalments, Abjurations, ... 174 Horace 1, 7 102
INSTANCE
    For instance; when the Lilly slipps . . . . . . 226 Prog of Beauty 25
    And, as an Instance of thy Pow'r, ... 325 Pethox 55
    For Instance: When you rashly think, ... 654 On Poetry 393
INSTANCES
    I could give Instances Enough, ... 545 Life of Swift 23
INSTEAD
    Instead of boldly sailing far to buy . . . . . . 19 Ode Athenian 97
    And, instead of putting it into my Pocket, down it slipt: . 69 Mrs Harris Pet 9
    . . .or instead of Him, a Better: . . . . 73 Mrs Harris Pet 73
    Grew to his Back instead of Wings; . . . . 80 Vanbrug House 36
    Instead of Home-spun Coifs were seen, ... 115 Bauc & Phil 2 139
    Instead of Garlands made of Flowrs . . . . . . 122 Empty'ng Town 7
    Instead of paying Chair-men, run them thro'.) . . . . 139 City Shower 50
    Gold ready Coin'd appear'd, instead . . . . . . 156 Fable of Midas 17
    With Quarter-staffs instead of White; . . . . . 189 Faggot 22
    And instead of the Devil, this Son of Perdition . . . 336 Serious Poem 67
    Instead of Spoils of Persian Looms, ... 379 Apology Lady C 109
    Will serve instead of place or pension . . . . . 421 Ireld 18
    Instead of powder'd Beaus, ... 426 Five Ladies 31
    Instead of Five you scor'd me Ten. . . . . . . 453 Modern Lady 265
    Deceiv'd thy self, instead of me; . . . . 695 Cadenus Vaness 293
    Instead of your maiming, your shooting, or banging, . . 818 Epigr Kite 7
    But, instead of new plays, ... 855 Lady's Lament 147
    Instead of poring on a Book, ... 892 Panegyr Dean 177
    Instead of wholesome Bread and Cheese, ... 895 Panegyr Dean 265
    I call'd you goose instead of gander; . . . . . . 983 Sher, A Goose 16
INSTILL
    Instructors ev'ry Art instill. . . . . 918 Riddle 4 12
INSTILL'D
    Follies, from my Youth instill'd, ... 630 Epistle Lady 31
INSTILLS
    And thence into the Royal Ear instills. . . . . 195 Author Himself 56
INSTINCT
    Who taught by Instinct how to shun . . . . . . 257 Bubble 178
    As Instinct leads them, in a Puddle; . . . . . . 294 Horrid Plot 148

INSTINCT (CONTINUED)	PAGE	TITLE	LINE
Ev'n Lambs by Instinct fly the Butcher.	588	Strephon Chloe	154
A Dog by Instinct turns aside,	640	On Poetry	17

INSTRUCT

Ye Wise, instruct me to endure	413	Censure	1
Both to adore her and instruct her;	702	Cadenus Vaness	499
I shall ask, and you instruct me.	832	Legion Club	80

INSTRUCTED

By some instructed Querist sleeping on the Sand,	22	Ode Athenian	190
Instructed from her early Years	705	Cadenus Vaness	596
By you instructed ev'ry Morn,	891	Panegyr Dean	132

INSTRUCTING

Instructing thus a young Beginner.	642	On Poetry	76
Instructing Members how to Vote.)	649	On Poetry	272

INSTRUCTORS

Instructors ev'ry Art instill.	918	Riddle 4	12

INSTRUCTS

Instructs us how to tame a Scold;	781	Mullinix Tim	272

INSTRUMENT

An Instrument to earthly Love?	695	Cadenus Vaness	295

INSULT

Nor bribe, insult, nor flatter, nor betray.	533	To Mr. Gay	56
Carthy, no more insult Aurelian's Name,	668	Epig Carthy 10	D 1

INSULTED

Hath insulted us all by insulting the Dean.	814	Yahoo's	4

INSULTERS

A modus right fit for insulters of Deans.	817	Yahoo's	59

INSULTING

Hath insulted us all by insulting the Dean.	814	Yahoo's	4
Of that insulting Tyrant Dean.	861	Lady Acheson	44

INSUR'D

They could not be insur'd an Hour;	729	Stella, Poems	64

INT'REST

"Stoop not to int'rest, flattery, or deceit;	55	Temple Ill	138
And now, the publick Int'rest to support,	194	Author Himself	27
Nor all his Int'rest keep him from the Grave.	234	Elegy on Demar	22
With equal Int'rest, equal Spight,	345	Prometheus	16
'Tis Virtue's Int'rest to be seen:)	386	Manly Virtue	80
Your Int'rest lyes to learn the knack	464	Birthday Song	115
Hint the least Int'rest of your own;	480	Libel on D- D-	14
With Int'rest, and a Praemium paid beside,	533	To Mr. Gay	69
"Taught Fools their Int'rest how to know;	569	Death of Swift	409
With Int'rest pays him back his own.	590	Strephon Chloe	214
'Twill be our Int'rest to get rid of her:	886	Rev Market-Hill	106
The Int'rest of his Realm had need	903	Death Daphne	13

INTEGRITY

Who dare revile the integrity of verse:	53	Temple Ill	70

INTELLIGENCE

Sure such Intelligence between	301	Horrid Plot	73
I hold Intelligence within.	885	Rev Market-Hill	56

INTELLIGIBLE

Than dreams of worlds intelligible;	900	Dean's Reasons	62

INTEND

Cruel Unknown! what is it You intend!	23	Ode Athenian	242
But the Secret is this; I did lately intend	265	Apollo	73
For to say Truth, she did intend him,	303	Storm	21
Don't you intend to put on Red?	699	Cadenus Vaness	399

INTENDED

"I never Harm intended.	154	Widow and Cat	D 30
He now intended to Retire.	172	Horace 1, 7	46
Intended in Time to succeed to your Place;	263	Apollo	28
At which, however well intended,	605	Beasts Confess	125
Whate'er I promised or intended,	899	Dean's Reasons	5

INTENDS

And Fools would fancy he intends	216	To Mr. Delany	39
It shews the Queen of Love intends	254	Bubble	95
Owns all your favours; here intends to stay,	309	Billet Players	47
And for dissenters he intends	422	Ireld	45
O then, whatever Heav'n intends,	766	Stel B-day '26	79
Or you may say--my Wife intends,	860	Lady Acheson	21
As a good quiet Soul, who no Mischief intends	968	Letter Sherid	27

INTENT

Since thus I wander from my first intent,	49	To Congreve	201
That some Verses were writ with felonious Intent,	264	Apollo	47
Of his Intent, you mean, your Merit.	475	Epist on Epist	28
That cou'd not be my Lord's Intent,	478	Epist on Epist	103
"Intent upon their private Ends;	569	Death of Swift	404
Intent the Publick Debts to pay,	656	On Poetry	445
Pallas had cross'd her first Intent,	712	Cadenus Vaness	833
If making Divisions was all their Intent,	804	Irish Bishops	35

INTENTION

"The Rev'rend Author's good Intention,	564	Death of Swift	289

INTER

Where all that passes, inter nos,	201	Horace 2, 6	79

INTERCEPTING

By intercepting ev'ry Beam;	253	Bubble	76

INTERCOURSE

What intercourse of minds can be	901	Dean's Reasons	65

INTEREST

Most fall at last to Interest, Folly, and Abuse.	24	Ode Athenian	277
That, begs my Interest for a Place--	200	Horace 2, 6	48

INTEREST	(CONTINUED)	PAGE	TITLE	LINE
And Interest the one Pursuit,		385	Manly Virtue	66
To take, for Interest Cent. per Cent.		446	Modern Lady	61
INTERFERE				
In such a Scene to interfere.		583	Young Nymph	72
INTERLIN'D				
Are fill'd with Hints, and interlin'd,		406	Swift to Pope	11
INTERLINE				
Enlarge, diminish, interline;		643	On Poetry	88
INTERMEDDL'D				
<Jove> never intermeddl'd here:		657	On Poetry	490
INTERPOSE				
Poor Will, who needs must interpose,		220	A Quiet Life	23
"But how you came to interpose,		304	Storm	45
But, here again you interpose;		484	Libel on D- D-	135
Else she must interpose a Cloud:		689	Cadenus Vaness	78
And yet I scorn to interpose,		696	Cadenus Vaness	301
His Pride began to interpose,		710	Cadenus Vaness	750
INTERPRET				
Interpret for a kind Advance.		712	Cadenus Vaness	817
INTERPRETATION				
Now tell me a Thing that wants Interpretation,		973	S-'s Ans Sh-d	11
INTERPRETERS				
And Fools consult Interpreters in vain.		363	On Dreams	6
INTERPRETING				
Interpreting her Complaisance,		707	Cadenus Vaness	658
INTERRUPT				
To interrupt the Fortune of Your Course:		13	Ode to William	D 42
To interrupt all serious Matter,		777	Mullinix Tim	144
May nothing interrupt his peace.		902	Dean's Reasons	102
INTERRUPTED				
Who interrupted him in all his Leasings;		537	Mr. Pulteney	2
INTERRUPTS				
It never interrupts the Game,		453	Modern Lady	274
INTERVAL				
A dreadful Interval of Spleen!		451	Modern Lady	204
INTERVALS				
Your intervals of time to spend		899	Dean's Reasons	23
INTERVENE				
And least a Chasm should intervene,		653	On Poetry	373
INTESTIN				
Encreas't by new intestin Wheels		93	Bauc & Phil 1	128
INTESTINE				
Increas'd by new Intestine Wheels:		113	Bauc & Phil 2	68
INTIRE				
I give my self intire to you,		782	Mullinix Tim	283
INTO 89			OMITTED WORD	
INTO'T				
But let no Friend alive look into't.		643	On Poetry	108
INTREAT				
When Cupid did his Grandsire Jove intreat,		118	Biddy Floyd	1
Short by the Knees intreat for Peace.		655	On Poetry	424
INTREATS				
The Nymph in sober Words intreats		711	Cadenus Vaness	792
INTREGUES				
But dull Intregues		441	Ballyspellin	28
INTRENCH				
Shall he upon the Ducal Rights intrench,		534	To Mr. Gay	91
INTRIGUE				
Now Love is dwindled to Intrigue,		687	Cadenus Vaness	13
INTRIGUES				
When weary'd with Intrigues of State,		480	Libel on D- D-	27
Is a Person very unfit for Intrigues.		940	Letter	17
INTRODUC'D				
And introduc'd the Lord knows why;		645	On Poetry	156
The Christian Rites I introduc'd in vain:		792	St. Pat's Well	35
INTRODUCE				
Which I was born to introduce,		555	Death of Swift	57
Or else, to introduce the rest		755	Stella '23	23
O, introduce me to your Friends!		781	Mullinix Tim	280
INTRUDE				
Those Dreams that on the silent Night intrude,		363	On Dreams	1
And as a Deity intrude,		464	Birthday Song	145
Intrude with Monkey grin, and clatter		777	Mullinix Tim	143
INTRUDES				
Where not one careless Thought intrudes,		691	Cadenus Vaness	166
INUENDO'S				
Their Inuendo's, Hints, and Slanders,		449	Modern Lady	142
INUNDATION				
So after th' Inundation of a War		16	Ode Athenian	11
An Inundation, says the Fable,		811	Bro Protestant	1
INVADE				
Fit to Invade or prop the Skies.		107	V's House	50
When Dust and Rain at once his Coat invade;		138	City Shower	28
INVADERS				
Not so with thee thy base Invaders dealt;		791	St. Pat's Well	22
The last Invaders trampling on the first:		793	St. Pat's Well	84
INVADES				
When now the flood invades his strugling breath,		672	Epig Carthy 24	D 12
INVADING				
Invading Foes, without Resistance,		934	Riddle 21	D 3

	PAGE	TITLE	LINE
INVASION			
Of some Invasion on your coasts	422	Ireld	42
I yield there might be an Invasion, ...	774	Mullinix Tim	30
INVEIGLE			
When Jove would some fair nymph inveigle	620	Scandal Poem 1	113
When Jove would some fair Nymph inveigle, ...	627	Scandal Poem 2	111
INVENOM'D			
Conceive the most invenom'd Dart, ...	595	Cassinus Peter	59
INVENT			
Applying what we first Invent:	215	To Mr. Delany	18
What some invent, the rest enlarge;	449	Modern Lady	145
Or else perhaps he may invent	643	On Poetry	101
But, Madam, I beg you contrive and invent, ...	869	Grand Question	61
INVENTED			
But e'er since Men invented Guns, ...	83	Salamander	15
Some God May-Fair invented, ...	122	Empty'ng Town	2
INVENTION			
Tis never by Invention got, ...	216	To Mr. Delany	27
And, Thirdly; 'tis a new Invention	348	Whitshed Motto	15
Brings in Reason and Invention.	637	Epistle Lady	216
Be mindful, when Invention fails, ...	643	On Poetry	89
Where <Young> must torture his Invention, ...	650	On Poetry	309
INVENTORY			
An Inventory follows here.	526	Lady's Dres Rm	10
INVERTED			
The figures all inverted shew, ...	35	Ode Sancroft	31
Inverted in May-Fair	122	Empty'ng Town	10
To see a Knave's inverted Heels:	451	Modern Lady	227
INVIDIOUS			
Exactly true! Invidious Poet!	657	On Poetry	479
INVISIBLE			
Still wear, still doat on his Invisible Ring. . . .	21	Ode Athenian	157
When he found a new Help from Invisible Hand. . . .	77	Lady B- B-	25
To give them by Turns an invisible Jog.	804	Irish Bishops	16
INVITATION			
<Toland> to you this Invitation sends, ...	162	Toland's Invit	3
Our Invitation was but slight	859	Lady Acheson	2
INVITE			
Who kindly did the Saints invite	91	Bauc & Phil 1	53
Who kindly did the Saints invite	111	Bauc & Phil 2	21
When Nature would invite us down, ...	122	Empty'ng Town	3
I made use of a Trope; that an Heir to invite, . . .	144	New Song	37
They first invite the Cyprian Queen, ...	290	Prog Marriage	7
But first, the Winner must invite	453	Modern Lady	288
All Christian People to invite;	735	Stel B-day '20	36
Did Stella to his House invite;	745	Stel Distress	2
Did Stella to his House invite:	749	Stel Wood-Park	2
Now to this hamper I invite you, ...	753	Gift for Bec	13
Shall to Elysian fields invite her, ...	762	Bec's B-Day	59
Expanded to invite a milder Gale.	770	Horace 1, 14	24
This Winter to invite some Friends, ...	860	Lady Acheson	23
INVITED			
Invited both the Saints to Drink.	92	Bauc & Phil 1	72
Next Day invited, comes agen;	173	Horace 1, 7	76
By Harley <Swift> invited comes to Court. . . .	194	Author Himself	28
The Court invited more than One, or Two;	536	To Mr. Gay	151
Invited here to 'vengeful Morrough's Aid, ...	791	St. Pat's Well	23
INVITES			
Invites the Fox to Dinner.	153	Widow and Cat	D 15
'To tell, when he invites his Friends:	448	Modern Lady	107
INVITING			
Would be but too inviting	123	Empty'ng Town	18
INVOCATION			
"And not leave one for Invocation.	321	First of April	20
INVOK'D			
The Muse invok'd, sit down to write;	643	On Poetry	86
INVOKE			
Of that Bright God whom Bards invoke, ...	120	Apollo Outwit	14
You fly, invoke the Gods; then turning, stop	137	City Shower	21
Invoke not Citherea's Aid, ...	272	Apollo's Edict	D 72
And boldly then invoke the Muse:	743	Stel B-day 22	76
INVOKES			
His Mother's Aid no Youth invokes:	687	Cadenus Vaness	10
Invokes his Mistress and his Muse, ...	728	Stella, Poems	27
INVOLV'D			
All involv'd in wild Disputes;	833	Legion Club	114
INVOLVE			
Lest with the Wicked, Heaven involve the Just? . . .	210	Earl of Oxford	20
INVULNERABLE			
By Love invulnerable thought, ...	702	Cadenus Vaness	489
INWARD			
Love's Fire, it seems, like inward Heat, ...	65	Problem	7
His outward Form, and Inward, vie, ...	385	Manly Virtue	59
And Silvia full of inward Guilt, ...	450	Modern Lady	172
With chearful Face, and inward Grief;	726	To Stella	102
And when she feels an inward Motion, ...	893	Panegyr Dean	211
INWREATH'D			
Was, like his Master's Crown, inwreath'd with thorn. .	40	Ode Sancroft	200
IRE			
As he, whom Phebus in his Ire	641	On Poetry	41

		PAGE	TITLE	LINE
IRELAND				
	Ireland is now our royal Care,	269	Apollo's Edict	D 1
	"That Ireland must be soon destroy'd,	304	Storm	39
	And so the Harp of Ireland brings,	345	Prometheus	29
	Of him that Ireland sav'd, and Harley;	494	Panegyr Swift	54
IRELAND'S				
	wood swears he will do it for Ireland's Good,	337	Serious Poem	99
	Gravely consulting Ireland's Good,	344	Prometheus	2
	But Ireland's Friends ne'er wanted Foes.	798	Traulus 1	88
IRIS				
	While Mistress Iris held her Train,	290	Prog Marriage	13
	Iris, for Scandal most notorious,	450	Modern Lady	166
	what nymph on earth so fair as Iris?	619	Scandal Poem 1	74
	What Nymph on Earth so fair as Iris?	625	Scandal Poem 2	72
	For Chloe, Sylvia, Phillis, Iris;	729	Stella, Poems	40
	And radiant Iris in the Pox.	729	Stella, Poems	48
	Not Iris, when she paints the Sky,	911	Aenigma	3
IRISH				
	We Irish Folks expected wonders,	62	Discovery	2
	You need but cross the Irish Seas,	173	Horace 1, 7	91
	And under Hand and Seal the Irish Nation	234	Elegy on Demar	17
	Our true Irish Hearts from old England to wean;	237	Excellent Song	7
	Because Irish Linen will soon turn to Tinder;	237	Excellent Song	20
	And Scipio, trail an Irish purple Plad.	275	Epilogue	22
	An English or an Irish Hound;	299	Horrid Plot	21
	Worse than a Pun, or Irish Phrase,	312	To Ford	38
	Scotch, Irish, English, French unite	345	Prometheus	15
	They laught at such an Irish Blunder,	353	Wood Ironmongr	29
	Stuck in an Irish Cabbin's Brow,	457	Paddy's Charac	2
	"So when poor Irish Rapparee,	497	Panegyr Swift	128
	The Irish Senate's Praises sing:	501	Doctor Delaney	56
	Irish Nymphs learn Irish Raillery:	523	Betty Grizette	26
	Irish Nymphs learn Irish Raillery:	523	Betty Grizette	26
	"The Irish Senate, if you nam'd,	566	Death of Swift	345
	But be they English, Irish, Scottish,	813	Bro Protestant	45
	"The Irish dear joys have enough common sense,	843	Ay and No	15
	Behold! a proof of Irish sense!	843	Epigr Irish	1
	Here Irish wit is seen	843	Epigr Irish	2
	A long-ear'd Beast, and Irish Cart,	942	Probatur Alit	23
	Shew me the brightest Irish Toast,	993	On Picture	22
	Through the whole set of <Irish> <Deans>;	742	Stel B-day 22	42
IRISHMEN				
	Is that by which all Irishmen swear.	940	Letter	15
IRON				
	Made up of iron mixt with clay,	39	Ode Sancroft	139
	Bestow to bury him one Iron Chest.	233	Elegy on Demar	6
	Have him confin'd in Iron Fetters;	373	Letter D. S-y	74
	To take his Iron by the End;	393	Modern Poets	14
	That Florimel wears Iron Stays:	449	Modern Lady	161
	But Time with Iron Teeth I ween	849	Old Thorn	17
	Are two iron crows,	853	Lady's Lament	80
	Why then I make pieces of Iron go down.	927	Riddle 11	D 8
	A Smoothing Iron, itself is rough.	1021	Nim-Dan-Dean 1	D 10
IRONICALLY				
	"His Vein, ironically grave,	565	Death of Swift	315
IRONY				
	That Irony which turns to Praise,	216	To Mr. Delany	34
	Must taste your irony and wit,	491	Dialogue	52
	Who dares to Irony pretend;	555	Death of Swift	56
IRREGULAR				
	And holy Sancroft's motion quite irregular appears,	37	Ode Sancroft	81
IRRELIGION				
	And tell the irreligion of my grief;	53	Temple Ill	78
IS 770				
IS'T 2		OMITTED WORD		
			OMITTED WORD	
ISCARIOTS				
	So, could we see a Set of new Iscariots,	806	Judas	19
ISIS				
	"Fair Isis, and ye Banks of Cam,	462	Birthday Song	77
ISLAND				
	For thee alone they lye the Island round.	772	Horace 1, 14	64
	Thee, happy Island, Pallas call'd her own,	790	St. Pat's Well	9
ISLE				
	(Say hapless Isle, altho'	37	Ode Sancroft	93
	Ne'er sprang a youth from out this isle before	44	To Congreve	11
	For ev'ry Wit in Britain's Isle	109	V's House	117
	But never shall our isle have Rest	259	Bubble	213
	Be ever banish'd from your Isle.	270	Apollo's Edict	D 15
	To live in this or t' other Isle,	315	To Ford	97
	Fame now reports, the western Isle	387	Manly Virtue	135
	Than Rule yon Isle and be a Slave.	421	Holyhead	34
	The Wise and Learned of our Isle;	475	Epist on Epist	18
	A Boy in yonder Isle below,	692	Cadenus Vaness	190
	Poor floating Isle, tost on ill Fortune's Waves,	770	Horace 1, 14	1
	To thee, once fav'rite Isle, with Joy I came;	789	St. Pat's Well	2
	Britain, by thee we fell, ungrateful Isle!	791	St. Pat's Well	25
	Who to yon rav'nous Isle thy Treasures bear,	794	St. Pat's Well	97
	A Bishop in the Isle of Saints!	819	Dr. Rundle	3
	What! thou the Spawn of him who sham'd our Isle,	826	Noisy Tom	7
	How might then our Isle be blest?	830	Legion Club	30
	Sly Hunters thus, in Borneo's Isle,	885	Rev Market-Hill	75

```
                                                        PAGE   TITLE            LINE
ISLE'S
    This poor Isle's approaching Ruin?      . . . . . . . 862 To Janus           14
ISLES
    Her Sister Isles are Conquered too as well as She.  .   9 Ode to King       100
    On this, as upon other Isles,    . . . . . . .       372 Letter D. S-y       26
    And darts her Beams or'e both our Isles,   . . . . . 466 Birthday Song      181
ISSU'D
    First issu'd from Perfumers Shops      . . . . .     696 Cadenus Vaness     316
ISSUE
    To think that your Brains Issue is     . . . . . .    61 Lady Tablebook      19
    We issue forth at different Hours;     . . . . . .   278 Journal              8
    The Parties ne'er could Issue join:    . . . . . .   690 Cadenus Vaness     123
    Fair Issue of the genial Bed,    . . . . . . . .     924 Riddle 8             5
ISSUE-PEAS
    A Pigeon pick'd her Issue-Peas;     . . . . . . .    583 Young Nymph         63
ISSUES
    The Goddess from her Chamber issues,      . . . .    525 Lady's Dres Rm       3
    Her Shankers, Issues, running Sores,      . . . .    582 Young Nymph         30
    Forth issues wriggling Dick Drawcensir,   . . . .    785 Dick, Maggot         6
ISSUING
    First issuing, struck the Murd'rer's Ears;   . . .   850 Old Thorn           54
IT      729                                              OMITTED WORD
IT'S    30                                               OMITTED WORD
ITALIAN
    Your words to some Italian Tune.   . . . . . . .     469 Birthday Song      278
    Mention'd a new Italian, come    . . . . . . . .     696 Cadenus Vaness     322
ITALICK
    You print it in Italick Type.    . . . . . . . .     643 On Poetry           96
ITALY
    The Praise of Italy or France    . . . . . . . .     314 To Ford             92
    Had my own native Italy o'er-run.   . . . . . . .    789 St. Pat's Well       4
ITCH
    Whose fingers itch for poets ears;   . . . . . . .   487 Irish-Club           6
    To scratch our endless Itch of Pow'r.   . . . . .    493 Panegyr Swift       10
    The Poet's Vein, or scribling Itch?      . . . . .   642 On Poetry           74
    To ease his Itch against the Stump,   . . . . . .    849 Old Thorn           42
    While a coarse English Tongue will itch,   . . . .   949 Epigr Scolding       3
ITEM
    (Item, for half a Yard of Lace.)    . . . . . . .     60 Lady Tablebook      16
    And then Comes in the Item of the Actors.   . . .    274 Epilogue             8
    Item the Actors, freely gave a Day,   . . . . . .    274 Epilogue             9
ITHACUS
    Hoc Ithacus velit, et magni mercentur Atridae.   . . 980 Dean to Tho: S      38
ITS     88                                               OMITTED WORD
ITSELF  4                                                OMITTED WORD
IULUS
    Our eldest Hope, divine Iulus,      . . . . . . .    655 On Poetry          429
IV'RY
    Like Iv'ry dry, and soft as Wax.    . . . . . . .    584 Strephon Chloe      26
    Or in the Iv'ry Gate of Dreams,     . . . . . . .    647 On Poetry          215
IXION'S
    To disappoint Ixion's rape    . . . . . . . .       619 Scandal Poem 1      53
    To disappoint Ixion's Rape,    . . . . . . . .      625 Scandal Poem 2      49
JABBER
    We scorn, for want of talk, to jabber   . . . . . . 781 Mullinix Tim       259
JACK
    But H' thinks upon Jack How.   . . . . . . . .       74 Game Traffick        8
    The wooden Jack which had almost    . . . . . . .     93 Bauc & Phil 1      125
    While in the Station of a Jack   . . . . . . . .     94 Bauc & Phil 1      135
    The Jack would not be left alone    . . . . . . .     94 Bauc & Phil 1      140
    A wooden Jack, which had almost     . . . . . . .    113 Bauc & Phil 2       65
    The Jack and Chimney near ally'd,   . . . . . . .    113 Bauc & Phil 2       75
    The Jack would not be left alone,   . . . . . . .    113 Bauc & Phil 2       78
    <God> <damn> me Jack, she's wondrous fair.   . . .   228 Prog of Beauty      76
    Had many Pendents, but abhor'd a Jack.    . . . .    285 Elegy Boat          16
    Robin, and Jack, and Jack, and Dan?    . . . . .    314 To Ford             80
    Robin, and Jack, and Jack, and Dan?    . . . . .    314 To Ford             80
    Jack, the Grandson of Sir Hardress?    . . . . .    834 Legion Club        140
    Those are <Allens>, Jack and Bob,   . . . . . .     836 Legion Club        173
    And fill <Jack Smith> with Hopes to keep his Place; . 163 Toland's Invit     20
JACKDAW
    In chatt'ring a magpie, in pride a jackdaw;   . . . 955 Portrait Life        2
JACKPUDDING
    Run to hear Jackpudding gabble;      . . . . . . .   830 Legion Club         18
JACKS
    When both the Jacks and Robin came;    . . . . . .  741 Stel B-day 22       18
    I bravely call the Tories Jacks,    . . . . . . .   778 Mullinix Tim       163
JACKSON'S
    All Subjects like Dan Jackson's Nose.    . . . . .  218 To Mr. Delany      102
JACOB'S
    Your Works are like old Jacob's speckled Goats,   . . 670 Epig Carthy 18   D  3
JACOBITE
    Nor dares one Jacobite or Tory   . . . . . . . .    183 Horace 2, 1         84
    Papist, and Jacobite, and Lib'ller?    . . . . . .  795 Traulus 1            4
JACOBITES
    But, Jacobites are strangely dull.   . . . . . . .  299 Horrid Plot         42
    With Plots; and Jacobites and Treason;    . . . .   775 Mullinix Tim        58
    Such Jacobites as he deserve,--   . . . . . . . .   783 Tim and Fables      33
JACOBITS
    Damning to Hell the Jacobits?    . . . . . . . .    773 Mullinix Tim         4
```

JADE

	PAGE	TITLE	LINE
At six Years old, the subtle Jade	150	Corinna	17
Why, what a Peal the Jade has rung,	220	A Quiet Life	11
His Fancy sunk, his Muse a Jade.	556	Death of Swift	102
Miss Moll the Jade will burn it blue:	588	Strephon Chloe	128
This Racer wou'd prove but a dull founder'd Jade.	717	Answer Rebus	28
Commonly speaking, but a sad Jade is.	988	Letter Dr Sh-n	25
By which your jade Pegasus fixt in a tether,	1027	Sheri Circles	18

JADES

Since Waiting Women like Exacting Jades,	275	Epilogue	15
'Twixt Jades and Teagues	441	Ballyspellin	29
The jades of sixteen,	855	Lady's Lament	130

JAIL

Then vote a worthy Citizen to Jail,	826	Noisy Tom	19

JAILER

Like the Felon from the Jailer,	574	Helter Skelter	36

JAMAICA

<Zounds> I would ship her for Jamaica	220	A Quiet Life	31
Or to Jamaica seems transported,	583	Young Nymph	45

JAMES

To a Plot for expelling my Master K. James;	144	New Song	28
Or dealing crowns to George and James.	402	Window Inns 7 D	6
James Bruges & the Dean had long been friends,	678	Dean and Duke	1
James is be-duk'd; : of course their friendshp ends	678	Dean and Duke	2
From knowing James, to boast he knows the Duke.	678	Dean and Duke	4
From round the Purlieus of St. James,	698	Cadenus Vaness	365
Than the Owners of St. <James>.	637	Epistle Lady	242

JAMES'S

Upon St. James's End o' th' Town;	100	Elegy Patrige	96
St James's Park and Stephen's Green;	313	To Ford	60
To Kensington, or hot St. James's;	411	Dial Rich Marb	88
And leaves St. James's in Disgrace.	482	Libel on D- D-	60
About St. James's, cry, We Courtiers.	812	Bro Protestant	22

JANE

The Dean has carry'd Lady Jane	294	Prog Marriage	124
There's bony Jane	442	Ballyspellin	55

JANUS

Janus hath lock'd his Temple-door?	462	Birthday Song	50
Returning Janus now prepares,	753	Gift for Bec	1
Here in this bundle Janus sends	753	Gift for Bec	15
Like Janus, bears a double Face;	765	Stel B-day '26	74
Two-fac'd Janus, God of Time,	862	To Janus	1
Janus, since thou hast a Brace,	862	To Janus	6

JAR

Why sure, Mr. Poet, your head got a jar	976	Dean to Sherid	27

JARGON

And all the incohaerent Jargon of the Schools,	22	Ode Athenian	205
A jargon form'd from the lost language, wit,	47	To Congreve	121
In all our modern Criticks Jargon.)	648	On Poetry	242
Reviles all People in his Jargon,	777	Mullinix Tim	113

JARR

All special Friends, and allways jarr.	217	To Mr. Delany	60

JARRING

No jarring consonant betwixt.	467	Birthday Song	232

JARS

These brangling jars of Whig and Tory,	774	Mullinix Tim	35

JASON

Jason arriv'd two thousand Years before.	790	St. Pat's Well	8
Jason, the valiant Prince of Greece,	948	Jason Hassard	1
Old Jason would have less to brag on.	948	Jason Hassard	6

JASONS

For modern Jasons that's enuff.	948	Jason Hassard	4

JAUNDICE

She need be no more with the Jaundice possess't;	351	Wood Insect	15

JAUNTLEMAN

Arrah! who was him reading? 'twas a jauntleman in ruffles,	840	Ballad D	6

JAUNTS

. . .for Saunders already hath got above ten Jaunts.	1013	Swift to Sheri	6

JAW

Two Rows of Teeth arm each devouring Jaw;	532	To Mr. Gay	35

JAWS

You strait stept in, and from the Monster's Jaws	12	Ode to William D	23
That serve to fill her hollow Jaws.	582	Young Nymph	18
By their lanthorn Jaws and Leathern,	835	Legion Club	147
Her Napkin pinn'd up to her Jaws,	894	Panegyr Dean	256
Is the poison and dagger you boast in your jaws, trow?	979	Dean to Tho: S	5

JAYL

When some Patrician God wou'd visit the Immortal Jayl,	9	Ode to King	93
Threatning the Pillory and Jayl.	312	To Ford	46
What Spunging-House in dread of Jayl	504	Doctor Delaney	145
"A Jayl or Barrack to repair;	571	Death of Swift	452

JAYLS

From Lodging in a hundred Jayls,	481	Libel on D- D-	51

JAYS

The Birds are met to strip the Jays.	239	Run Bankers	20

JEALOUS

I hope you don't believe me Jealous:	116	Bauc & Phil 2	158
And proud Roxana fir'd with jealous Rage,	275	Epilogue	25
Chloe's of ev'ry Coxcomb jealous,	449	Modern Lady	162
How jealous of the Nation's Freedom,	501	Doctor Delaney	57
It gives me such a jealous Fit,	555	Death of Swift	51

		PAGE	TITLE	LINE
JEALOUS	(CONTINUED)			
And, jealous Juno, ever snarling,	. . . .	621	Scandal Poem 1	123
And, jealous Juno, ever snarling,	. . . .	627	Scandal Poem 2	117
JEALOUSY				
In Christ-Church cut his Throat for Jealousy.	. . .	350	Upright Judge 3	6
JEAR				
For every peeping Fop to Jear.	. . . .	60	Lady Tablebook	18
JEAR'D				
The Parish jear'd him to his Face:	. . . .	221	A Quiet Life	46
JEARS				
Midas, expos'd to all their Jears,	. . . . . .	157	Fable of Midas	39
JEER				
Then tipt their Forehead in a Jeer,	. . . . . .	698	Cadenus Vaness	360
The dullest Beast and a shameful Jeer,	. . . . .	941	Letter	41
A long-ear'd Beast, another Name for Jeer,	. . . .	943	Probatur Alit	41
JEERS				
Will never have done with his Gibes and his Jeers:	. .	873	Grand Question	188
JEJUNE				
The Sense can ne're be too jejune,	. . . .	467	Birthday Song	211
JEMMY				
Smart Jemmy Moor with Vigor drops,	. . . . . .	654	On Poetry	399
. . . and the soft soul of amorous Jemmy center.	. . .	1023	Nim-Dan-Dean 2	D 14
JENNEYS				
Immortalize our Dolls and Jenneys.	. . . .	184	Horace 2, 1	116
JENNY				
Dear friend, Doctor Jenny,	. . . .	857	Lady's Lament	203
That the Captain suppos'd he was Curate to Jenny.)	.	872	Grand Question	152
JEOPARDY				
May bring in Jeopardy thy Bacon,	. . . .	181	Horace 2, 1	30
JERKING				
While a little gentle Jerking	. . . .	636	Epistle Lady	205
JERUSALEM				
In Caesar's court, or in Jerusalem;	. . . . . .	39	Ode Sancroft	167
JERVIS				
I think I have seen her Picture by Jervis.--	. . .	869	Grand Question	76
JEST				
Tho' we all took it for a Jest:	. . . .	98	Elegy Patrige	2
To turn the Matter to a Jest;	. . . .	108	V's House	68
And there's the Jest, for Pan is All:	. . . . . .	157	Fable of Midas	58
Was now dispos'd to a crack a Jest;	. . . . . .	171	Horace 1, 7	15
My Lord wou'd carry on the Jest,	. . . .	173	Horace 1, 7	81
But you resolv'd to have your Jest,	. . . . . .	175	Horace 1, 7	135
"Ah Doctor, how you love to jest?	. . . .	202	Horace 2, 6	97
Reproach not tho in jest, a Friend	. . . . . .	217	To Mr. Delany	67
And tho men cry, they love a Jest,	. . . . . .	218	To Mr. Delany	83
They love a Jest--when 'tis their own.	. . . . .	218	To Mr. Delany	86
To study the obliging Jest,	. . . .	219	To Mr. Delany	103
The Town has whisper'd round the Jest:	. . . . .	293	Prog Marriage	102
But half in Earnest, half in Jest;	. . . . . .	303	Storm	26
So you are in Jest, and you will not I hope	. . . .	335	Serious Poem	51
Why what a Jest shou'd I have been,	. . . . . .	377	Apology Lady C	49
This was the Speech, and here's the jest	. . . .	423	Ireld	63
Then thought to turn it to a Jest.	. . . . . .	447	Modern Lady	75
To half the world a standing jest,	. . . . . .	455	Dean Smedley	11
he's loud in his laugh & he's coarse in his Jest	. . .	540	Charac Walpole	2
They turn the Matter to a Jest;	. . . .	545	Life of Swift	20
"He ne'er offended with a Jest;	. . . .	572	Death of Swift	472
That in his Heart he lov'd a Jest:	. . . . . .	602	Beasts Confess	22
In a Jest I spend my Rage:	. . . .	635	Epistle Lady	168
The dullest Reader smoaks the Jest:	. . . . . .	643	On Poetry	100
He cou'd not hope she spoke in Jest.	. . . . . .	706	Cadenus Vaness	629
Which fairly hints they are in jest,	. . . . . .	707	Cadenus Vaness	666
Thus, far in jest. Though now I fear	. . . . . .	751	Stel Wood-Park	73
You tell a good jest,	. . . .	756	Dingley Brent	13
Provided Punch (for there's the Jest)	. . . . . .	777	Mullinix Tim	131
The Jest of Wits, and to the Court unknown.	. . . .	794	St. Pat's Well	100
I own, his Madness is a Jest,	. . . .	798	Traulus 1	69
Making good my Grandames Jest,	. . . .	829	Legion Club	7
At cracking a jest.	. . . .	856	Lady's Lament	172
Lord! Madam! your Ladyship sure is in jest;	. . . .	871	Grand Question	124
Not a jest, or hum'rous story,	. . . .	908	Daphne	65
Of whom all People make a Jest.	. . . .	918	Riddle 4	22
You call him a Sloven in earnest or jest.	. . . . .	943	Probatur Alit	36
But Jest apart, restore, you Capon ye,	. . . . .	1033	Ans to Crown	7
JESTER				
<Dean>, Butler, Usher, Jester, Tutor;	. . . . .	888	Panegyr Dean	39
Now, as a Jester, I accost you;	. . . .	890	Panegyr Dean	113
JESTING				
You think my jesting too severe:	. . . .	751	Stel Wood-Park	74
And Saunders the Man says, you are always jesting and		986	Mary to Sher	27
mocking,				
JESTS SEE TOWN-JESTS				
When Jests are carryd on too far,	. . . .	218	To Mr. Delany	79
His rhet'ric, bombast, silly jests, are by far	. . . .	815	Yahoo's	13
JESUITE				
Our Letters say a Jesuite boasts	. . . .	422	Ireld	41
JESUITS				
For Priests and Jesuits in Disguises;	. . . . . .	788	Dick's Variety	22
JESUS				
"That Jesus was a Grand Impostor:	. . . .	564	Death of Swift	294
'Though Fools may doubt his Faith in <Jesus>.	. . .	820	Dr. Rundle	26

```
                                                    PAGE    TITLE            LINE
JET
     To make her Hair look black as Jet,  . . . . . . .   226 Prog of Beauty    18
     And write on paper black as Jet:  . . . . . . . .    463 Birthday Song    114
     One of us you'll find in Jet,  . . . . . . . . .     930 Riddle 17       D  4
JET-BLACK
     I Am jet-Black, as you may see,  . . . . . . . .     929 Riddle 15       D  1
JETTY
     Your jetty Locks with Garlands crown'd,  . . . .     760 Receipt Youth     41
JEW
     A griping Monarch, or a Jew.  . . . . . . .          658 On Poetry       D 164
     Yet, were he Heathen, Turk or Jew,  . . . . . .      820 Dr. Rundle        9
     Such Musick would make a Fanatick or Jew sick:  . . 1029 Dr. Helsham      14
JEWELS
     And all her Jewels and her Plate,  . . . . . .        32 Ode to Temple   182
     Is all with precious Jewels strow'd.  . . . . . .    324 Pethox           36
     Surrounded with Jewels of Sulphur and Nitre.  . . . 003 Irish Bishops     6
JEWS
     Who claim so many Titles to be Jews,  . . . . . .      8 Ode to King      85
     Among thy stubborn sons there haunts that spirit of Jews,  38 Ode Sancroft  129
     Himself, as rich as fifty Jews,  . . . . . . . .     481 Libel on D- D-   39
     The Jews engag'd him with a paultry Bribe,  . . . .  806 Judas            3
JIBE
     "Who call it Humour when they jibe:  . . . . . .     571 Death of Swift  466
JIG
     Dick could neatly dance a Jig,  . . . . . . . .      784 Mullinex Dick    13
     I wish he were in it a dancing a Jig.  . . . . . .   942 Probatur Alit    28
JILT
     Calls Amoret an arrant Jilt.  . . . . . . . .        450 Modern Lady     173
JIM
     I throw into the Bargain, Jim:  . . . . . . .        314 To Ford          77
     How Ford would frown, how Jim would leer,  . . . .   741 Stel B-day 22    19
     Bring down Long Shanks Jim too, but now I think on't, 1023 Nim-Dan-Dean 2 D 11
       . . .
JINGLE
     Dear Tom, I'm surpriz'd that your verse did not jingle; 980 Tho: Sheridan  1
JO
     Then Master Steward takes my Rent, and tells me, honest  342 Upon His Grace  23
       Jo.
JOAN
     Of Joan of France, and English Moll,  . . . . .      114 Bauc & Phil 2    94
     Joan cudgell's Ned, yet Ned's a Bully  . . . . .     328 Epigram 3         1
     Dye Ned and Bess; give Will to Joan,  . . . . .      328 Epigram 3         3
     Dye Joan and Will; give Bess to Ned,  . . . . .      328 Epigram 3         5
JOB    SEE MONEY-JOB
     His Fellow Pick-Purse, watching for a job,  . . .    364 On Dreams        25
     Would break the Patience of a Job,  . . . . . .      604 Beasts Confess   88
     While I, with humble Job, had rather,  . . . . .     813 Bro Protestant   61
JOBB
     To do the Jobb too long he tarry'd,  . . . . . .     349 Upright Judge 2   2
     Can turn their Hands to ev'ry Jobb,  . . . . . .     503 Doctor Delaney   89
     "In every Jobb to have a Share,  . . . . . . .       571 Death of Swift  451
     First in every wicked Jobb,  . . . . . . . .         836 Legion Club     174
JOBBER    SEE STOCK-JOBBER
     a Jobber of Stocks by retailing false news  . . . .  540 Charac Walpole    9
     A Statesman, or a South-Sea Jobber.  . . . . . .     645 On Poetry       162
JOBBER'S
     And view it through a Jobber's Bill,  . . . . . .    255 Bubble          122
JOBBERS
     Of Jobbers in the Poets Art,  . . . . . . . .        650 On Poetry       312
JOCKEY
     And, like a Jockey for a Race,  . . . . . . . .      231 Prog of Poetry   39
JOCKEY-COATS
     And with Jockey-Coats compleat;  . . . . . . . .     573 Helter Skelter   10
JOCKEYS
     Horses thus, let Jockeys judge else,  . . . . . .    636 Epistle Lady    201
JOCKY
     With Jocky Boots, and Silver Spurs;  . . . . . .     760 Receipt Youth    44
JOE
     The gray old Fellow Poet Joe  . . . . . . . .        126 Little House      3
     And Joe my Apron full of Bricks.  . . . . . . .      128 Little House     64
JOG
     To give them by Turns an invisible Jog.  . . . . .   804 Irish Bishops    16
JOGGING
     And jogging my toes;  . . . . . . . . .              852 Lady's Lament    22
     Both hand in hand together jogging;  . . . . . .     900 Dean's Reasons   58
JOGLING
     by Jogling, Jogling, Jogling trot,  . . . . . .      957 Cantata
     by Jogling, Jogling, Jogling trot,  . . . . . .      957 Cantata
     by Jogling, Jogling, Jogling trot,  . . . . . .      957 Cantata
JOHN
     Leave John of Bucks, come here and laugh.  . . . .   188 Scriblerus 6      4
     But, St. John comes and whispers in his Ear;  . . . 194 Author Himself   34
     Now, John the Butler must be sent  . . . . . .       223 Prog of Love     33
     For John must neither light nor stop;  . . . . .     223 Prog of Love     36
     For truly John was missing too:  . . . . . .         223 Prog of Love     40
     Phillis, it seems, was fled with John.  . . . . .    223 Prog of Love     42
     For John was come of honest Kin:  . . . . . .        224 Prog of Love     60
     She'd beg with John from Door to Door:  . . . . .    224 Prog of Love     62
     Phil cry'd, and John began to curse;  . . . . . .    224 Prog of Love     80
     John wish't, that he had broke a Leg  . . . . . .    224 Prog of Love     83
     In Christian Justice due to John.  . . . . . . .     225 Prog of Love     94
```

JOHN	(CONTINUED)	PAGE	TITLE	LINE

JOHN   (CONTINUED)

	PAGE	TITLE	LINE
For John is Landlord, Phillis Hostess;	225	Prog of Love	98
St. John, as well as Pultney knows,	555	Death of Swift	59
St. John himself will scarce forbear,	561	Death of Swift	209
"Remote from St. John, Pope, and Gay.	570	Death of Swift	434
And thence, as fam'd John Bunyan sung,	983	Sher, A Goose	6
For, as for honest John, tho' I'm not sure on't, . . .	1022	Nim-Dan-Dean 2 D	5

JOHN'S

	PAGE	TITLE	LINE
"What St. John's Skill in State Affairs,	567	Death of Swift	373
In thee Delany's spleen, John's mirth, Helsham's jokes, . . .	1023	Nim-Dan-Dean 2 D	14

JOHNNY

	PAGE	TITLE	LINE
Plump Johnny Gay will now elope;	409	Dial Rich Marb	49

JOHNS

	PAGE	TITLE	LINE
Poultney deep, accomplish'd St. Johns,	635	Epistle Lady	175

JOHNSON

	PAGE	TITLE	LINE
Then Mrs. Johnson gave her Verdict,	128	Little House	39
Mrs. Dingley and Mrs. Johnson say, . . .	1013	Swift to Sheri	7
But Johnson Madam	1014	Swift to Sheri	33

JOIN   SEE JOYN

	PAGE	TITLE	LINE
We join like Flyes, and Wasps, in buzzing about Wit.	18	Ode Athenian	75
To shew his Skill, he Mars would join	99	Elegy Patrige	59
Forget their Fewds, and join to save their Wigs,	138	City Shower	42
And in huge Confluent join at Snow-Hill Ridge,	139	City Shower	59
"The Son and Father, join to tell us,	181	Horace 2, 1	44
To join, and drag you to the Ground.	414	Censure	10
And join in friendship, with a strict tye,	436	Answer Paulus	145
And when they join their Pericranies,	651	On Poetry	317
The Parties ne'er could Issue join:	690	Cadenus Vaness	123
And join to fortify your Heart.	765	Stel B-day '26	72
"To tear thy Hedges join in Leagues,	851	Old Thorn	79
Or join with the Court in ev'ry Debate,	867	Grand Question	23
I join them fairly with a Ring;	926	Riddle 9	13
And I join my helping Voice;	933	Riddle 20 D	16
Join in all the Din of Battle.	933	Riddle 20 D	22
Number, and Weight, and Measure join.	1022	Nim-Dan-Dean 1 D	46

JOIN'D   SEE JCYN'D,JOYNED

	PAGE	TITLE	LINE
Which we ne'er join'd before, but in Romances meet,	28	Ode to Temple	60
Not firmly join'd to keep their Ground,	189	Faggot	19
Join'd with a brazen Politician,	354	Simile Silver	20
Had thou been join'd to Boulter's head.	822	Epigr Rundle	4
E'er join'd such Numbers Hand in Hand.	926	Riddle 9	12

JOINING

	PAGE	TITLE	LINE
Many Voices joining round me;	933	Riddle 20 D	6

JOINS

	PAGE	TITLE	LINE
Your matchless Courage with Your Prudence joins	11	Ode to William D	5
(Salerno both together joins	589	Strephon Chloe	181
Or like a Bridge that joins a Marish	645	On Poetry	173

JOINT   SEE JOYNT

	PAGE	TITLE	LINE
To half a Joint, and God be thank it:	750	Stel Wood-Park	36
Put a word out of joint,	855	Lady's Lament	139
No little scrub Joint shall come on my Board:	867	Grand Question	14

JOINTS   SEE JOYNTS

	PAGE	TITLE	LINE
Nor will they dare to break the Joints,	1021	Nim-Dan-Dean 1 D	39

JOINTURE   SEE JOYNTURE

	PAGE	TITLE	LINE
Thought much of his Doll, and the Jointure he lost,	430	Dicky Dolly	8

JOIST   SEE JOYST

	PAGE	TITLE	LINE
And there stood fast'ned to a Joist:	113	Bauc & Phil 2	58

JOKE

	PAGE	TITLE	LINE
Steals thence his Plot, and ev'ry Joke,	107	V's House	59
'Twill not suffice, it was a Joke.	217	To Mr. Delany	66
I mean a Dog, without a Joke,	298	Horrid Plot	17
This morn the God of Wit and Joke,	320	First of April	1
That all this Bus'ness was a Joke.	322	First of April	54
And, how you laugh'd at every Joke:	480	Libel on D- D-	8
If, what he says be not a Joke,	545	Life of Swift	3
A College Joke to cure the Dumps.	594	Cassinus Peter	38
"That sinking the coin is a dangerous joke.	843	Ay and No	14
Whene'er you joke, 'tis all a Case;	890	Panegyr Dean	121
And Gaghagan take ev'ry Joke.	890	Panegyr Dean	128
. . . or at least not one that's witty, to joke w'ye? . .	1022	Nim-Dan-Dean 2 D	4

JOKER

	PAGE	TITLE	LINE
. . . I mean that great fat joker, friend Helsham, he	1023	Nim-Dan-Dean 2 D	9

JOKES

	PAGE	TITLE	LINE
"What, they admire him for his Jokes--	202	Horace 2, 6	87
Forbear your poetry and jokes,	489	Dialogue	17
Below the Lash of Snarlers Jokes.	501	Doctor Delaney	46
Stock't with Repartees and Jokes,	523	Betty Grizette	17
"And yet, I think, for all your Jokes,	547	Life of Swift	93
Who for his Wine will bear his Jokes:	556	Death of Swift	94
And ev'ry Beau wou'd have his Jokes,	707	Cadenus Vaness	648
I value not your Jokes of Noose,	1003	Dan J's Reply	13
In thee Delany's spleen, John's mirth, Helsham's jokes, . . .	1023	Nim-Dan-Dean 2 D	14

JOKING

	PAGE	TITLE	LINE
But laugh'd at their own silly joking.	755	Dingley Brent	6

JOLLY

	PAGE	TITLE	LINE
"To make a pair of Jolly Fellows,	181	Horace 2, 1	43
O'Rourk's jolly Boys	245	Irish-Feast	29
The <Dean>, and his Landlord, a jolly Comrade,	517	Dean Hang Rape	25
Jolly boys of St. Kevans, St. Patrick's, Donore,	814	Yahoo's	1

		PAGE	TITLE	LINE
JONATHAN				
Smedley, thou Jonathan of Clogher,	. . . .	476	Epist on Epist	31
When <Jonathan> was great at Court,	. . . .	498	Panegyr Swift	159
JONATHAN'S				
While Jonathan's threaten'd with loss of his ears;	. .	818	Epigr Kite	2
JONES				
But all admire Inigo Jones:	. . . .	727	Stella, Poems	4
JONNY				
How Jonny wheadled, threatned, fawnd,	. . . . . .	224	Prog of Love	87
JONQUIL				
The Cowslip soft, and sweet Jonquil.	. . . . . .	894	Panegyr Dean	252
JORDAN				
Nim lost his Wig-block, Dan his Jordan,	. . . . .	283	Journal	123
His Jordan stood in Manner fitting	. . . . . .	594	Cassinus Peter	21
JOT				
Not one Jot better looks the Sun	. . . . . .	786	Clad in Brown	9
JOULTER SEE JUG-JOULTER				
JOURNAL				
Or--but proceed we in our Journal,	. . . . . .	279	Journal	25
The Journal of a Modern Dame,	. . . .	445	Modern Lady	24
JOURNALS				
Nor London Journals, nor the Post-men,	. . . . .	462	Birthday Song	53
JOURNEY				
In his Journey to <Dublin>, he lighted at <Chester>,	.	517	Dean Hang Rape	7
JOURNEY-MEN				
To all their Journey-Men, than you,	. . . .	483	Libel on D- D-	94
JOURNEYMAN				
In Spight of his Deanship and Journeyman Waters.	. .	237	Excellent Song	REF
In Spight of his Deanship and Journeyman Waters.	. .	238	Excellent Song	REF
JOURNEYS				
In Journeys he out-rides the Post,	. . . .	398	Earl of P-b-w	4
JOURNIES				
And thousand incoherent journies take,	. . . . .	36	Ode Sancroft	70
Take Journies in it like a Chaise;	. . . . . .	109	V's House	112
Briskly travel on their Journies,	. . . .	573	Helter Skelter	2
Is useful in Journies, take Notice of that.	. . . .	943	Probatur Alit	44
JOURNY				
Their Journy long, their Money short;	. . . . .	224	Prog of Love	76
JOVE				
Jove ever form'd to make a <Stink>?	. . . . . .	65	Problem	4
For Jove consider'd well the Case,	. . . .	79	Vanbrug House	17
For, Jove consider'd well the Case,	. . . . . .	106	V's House	17
Great Jove, he cry'd, the Art restore	. . . . . .	107	V's House	43
Jove Smil'd, and like a gentle God,	. . . . . .	107	V's House	51
Not once suspecting, Jove would Smoak,	. . . . .	107	V's House	60
Jove saw the Cheat, but thought it best	. . . . .	108	V's House	67
When Cupid did his Grandsire Jove intreat,	. . . .	118	Biddy Floyd	1
Jove sent and found far in a Country Scene,	. . . .	118	Biddy Floyd	3
Jove mix'd up all, and his best Clay imploy'd;	. . .	118	Biddy Floyd	11
Where Jove a Seat among the Gods will give	. . . .	210	Earl of Oxford	13
Swim where the Bird of Jove would sink,	. . . . .	253	Bubble	55
The Bird of Jove shall toil no more,	. . . . . .	270	Apollo's Edict	D 25
Whom Jove endow'd with ev'ry Grace,	. . . . . .	272	Apollo's Edict	D 66
"For 'tis decreed by Jove and Fate,	. . . . . .	304	Storm	38
There is a Chain let down from Jove,	. . . . . .	345	Prometheus	31
When Jove was Young, was made of Gold.	. . . . .	345	Prometheus	36
Jove saw that all Devotion fail'd;	. . . .	345	Prometheus	42
Jove stood amaz'd, but looking round,	. . . . . .	346	Prometheus	47
For Jove, it is not hard to guess him,	. . . . .	346	Prometheus	61
But Jove will soon convert I hope,	. . . .	347	Prometheus	71
When Jove, in pity to the Town,	. . . .	353	Wood Ironmongr	23
(Nor Jove himself could do it better)	. . . . .	353	Wood Ironmongr	36
Jove never sends us downward from the Skies,	. . .	363	On Dreams	3
Apply'd to Jove with fervent Prayer;	. . . . . .	383	Manly Virtue	3
"O Jove, if Virtue be so fair	. . . .	383	Manly Virtue	4
Jove grants the Prayer, gives Virtue Birth,	. . . .	384	Manly Virtue	15
Nothing impossible to Jove.	. . . .	384	Manly Virtue	22
Took Wing to Jove, and hop'd to rest	. . . . . .	458	Paddy's Charac	31
Why then appoint him Son of Jove,	. . . .	460	Birthday Song	15
For Jove, as every School-boy knows,	. . . . . .	461	Birthday Song	23
As Jove will not attend on less,	. . . .	475	Epist on Epist	1
'Twas therefore cruel, hard, by Jove,	. . . . . .	495	Panegyr Swift	80
When Jove was, from his teeming Head,	. . . . . .	504	Doctor Delaney	115
Jove send, this Nightingal may fall,	. . . . . .	515	Answer Fable	103
Jove, arm'd with Terrors, burst the Skies,	. . . .	578	Day Judgement	5
Jove, nodding, shook the Heav'ns, and said,	. . . .	579	Day Judgement	10
Jove dresst a Cloud in Juno's shape,	. . . . . .	619	Scandal Poem 1	54
Ev'n Jove, and Mercury his pimp	. . . .	620	Scandal Poem 1	101
When Jove would some fair nymph inveigle	. . . . .	620	Scandal Poem 1	113
Jove drest a Cloud in Juno's Shape:	. . . . . .	625	Scandal Poem 2	50
Ev'n Jove, and Mercury his Pimp,	. . . .	626	Scandal Poem 2	99
When Jove would some fair Nymph inveigle,	. . . . .	627	Scandal Poem 2	111
Jove <pisses> on you through a Sieve;	. . . . .	627	Scandal Poem 2	126
Give <George> and Jove an equal Share.	. . . . .	657	On Poetry	486
But, when at last usurping Jove	. . . .	894	Panegyr Dean	253
The fav'rite Messenger of Jove,	. . . .	916	Riddle 2	9
So Jove pronounc'd among the Gods,	. . . . . .	924	Riddle 7	95
Jove, with all his loudest Thunder,	. . . . . .	933	Riddle 20	D 23
Oh that Jove would give me such a talent as thine	. .	1017	Swift Ans Sher	7
<Jove> never intermeddl'd here:	. . . .	657	On Poetry	490

JOVE'S
    Unaw'd by Jove's all-shaking Nod.   . . . . . . 466 Birthday Song 186
    No more of Jove's Designs than you) . . . . . . 579 Day Judgement 18
    By Thunder dy'd in Jove's Embrace; . . . . . . 587 Strephon Chloe 108
    His Cloud, and Jove's imperiall Queen. . . . . 619 Scandal Poem 1 58
    His Cloud, and Jove's Imperial Queen. . . . . 625 Scandal Poem 2 54
    For Wisdom, at Jove's Council-Board. . . . . 695 Cadenus Vaness 267
JOVIAL
    Methinks I now see them so jovial and crank, ... 287 Bank Down 24
    And then the Jovial Cavaliers . . . . 926 Riddle 9 22
JOWLER
    How Jowler howl'd, and what a fright . . . . . 282 Journal 95
JOY
    Sure there's some Wondrous Joy in Doing Good; . . . 6 Ode to King 1
    Immortal Joy, that suffers no Allay from Fears, . . 6 Ode to King 2
    Of England's Glory, and her lasting Joy. . . . . 13 Ode to William D 48
    When with amazing Joy she hears, ... 17 Ode Athenian 51
    How proudly would he haste the joy to meet, ... 49 To Congreve 185
    Comes back with joy to its own seat at night; . . 51 Temple Ill 6
    Approaching joy at strife with parting woe. . . 51 Temple Ill 22
    Thus, when Dorinda wept, joy ev'ry face forsook, . 53 Temple Ill 59
    The fancy furnish'd by returning joy; . . . . . 53 Temple Ill 68
    Since one false beam of joy in sickly minds . . . . 55 Temple Ill 149
    Their tongues and pens to give you joy, ... 176 To Lord Harley 2
    Pluto the god of Wealth, will joy to know . . . 234 Elegy on Demar 7
    I give you Joy of the Report, ... 300 Horrid Plot 63
    And when to the Joy of your Hearts he has Roar'd, . . 336 Serious Poem 83
    Congenial Joy, and Life, and Light. . . . . . 387 Manly Virtue 120
    Now Birth-day Bard, with joy proceed . . . . . 465 Birthday Song 151
    Down from Olympus comes with Joy, ... 693 Cadenus Vaness 200
    Was but the Master's secret Joy. . . . . . . 704 Cadenus Vaness 552
    Sorrow with Joy, and Hope with Fear. . . . . 711 Cadenus Vaness 777
    They give the sick man joy, and praise . . . . . 761 Bec's B-Day 15
    Shall still be kept with Joy by me: . . . . . 763 Stel B-day '26 2
    Can look with Joy on what is past. . . . . . 764 Stel B-day '26 18
    Looks back with Joy where she has gone, ... 765 Stel B-day '26 75
    To thee, once fav'rite Isle, with Joy I came; . . 789 St. Pat's Well 2
    Causeless Joy, and true Despair; . . . . . . 832 Legion Club 90
    Or, Mr. Dean--I should with Joy . . . . . . 860 Lady Acheson 25
    The Joy of Man, the Pride of Brutes, ... 919 Riddle 5 1
    The tender Pledges of our Joy. . . . . . . 925 Riddle 8 22
    And I roar out my Joy, and in Transport expire. . 928 Riddle 11 D 12
    Both are welcome, Grief or Joy, ... 933 Riddle 20 D 17
    Love, Joy, and Devotion . . . . 939 Riddle Answerd 13
JOY'D
    She, who on shady banks has joy'd to sleep . . . . 50 To Congreve 221
JOYFUL
    And thence with joyful, nimble Wing . . . . . 16 Ode Athenian 29
    "The Nation stript go joyful back, ... 571 Death of Swift 447
JOYN
    All Parties and Religions joyn; . . . . . . 345 Prometheus 12
JOYN'D
    Hath joyn'd with himself two Hags in Commission: . . 336 Serious Poem 68
JOYNED
    Joyned together in the Low-Countree. . . . . . 147 Windsor Proph 6
JOYNER
    A Joyner to fasten a Saint in a Nitch, ... 336 Serious Poem 71
JOYNT
    To half a Joynt, & God be thanked: . . . . . 745 Stel Distress 12
JOYNTS
    In trickling Streams betwixt her Joynts. . . . . 227 Prog of Beauty 44
JOYNTURE
    And spend her Joynture on his Whores: . . . . 295 Prog Marriage 164
    <Meath> Smiles for the Joynture, though gotten, so late, 430 Dicky Dolly 19
JOYS
    So are the Joys which Nature yields . . . . . 122 Empty'ng Town 9
    In her you'll center all your Joys, ... 362 Grace's Answer 47
    That now the Pair must crown their Joys. . . . 586 Strephon Chloe 70
    "The Irish dear joys have enough common sense, . 843 Ay and No 15
    Who feels true Joys when he bestows thee. . . . . 920 Riddle 5 36
JOYST
    And there stood fastned to a Joyst, ... 92 Bauc & Phil 1 98
JUDAS
    "But, if you'll leave us <Bishop> Judas, . . . 305 Storm 51
    How shou'd we rejoice, if, like Judas the first, . . 805 Irish Bishops 39
    Poor Bishop Judas, late repenting, dies; . . . 806 Judas 2
    Judas betrayed his Master with a Kiss: . . . . 806 Judas 10
    As antient Judas by Transgression fell, ... 806 Judas 17
    Each modern Judas perish like the first; . . . . 806 Judas 21
    To cry; Lo, Judas, gone to his own Place: . . . 806 Judas 24
JUDG'D
    And I'll be judg'd by standers-by. . . . . . 83 Salamander 28
JUDGE
    To judge of things above by things below. . . . . 35 Ode Sancroft 38
    Confesses ignorance to judge between; . . . . . 41 Ode Sancroft 208
    And wisely judge, no pow'r beneath divine . . . . 44 To Congreve 29
    Haply you judge these lines severely writ . . . . 46 To Congreve 109
    That tho' 'tis hard to judge, yet Money can't go without
      Hands. 71 Mrs Harris Pet 43
    Clap't Asses Ears upon the Judge, ... 157 Fable of Midas 30
    Here lies Judge Boat within a Coffin. . . . . . 286 Elegy Boat 37

```
JUDGE          (CONTINUED)                              PAGE   TITLE           LINE
     A Boat a Judge! yes, where's the Blunder?    . . . .   286  Elegy Boat        39
     A wooden Judge is no such Wonder.            . . . . .  286  Elegy Boat        40
     We think, though You judge hardly of it,              311  To Ford           15
     To fight our cause before the judge:         . . . . . 435  Answer Paulus     88
     Sole Patron, Judge, and God of Wit.          . . . . . 462  Birthday Song     72
     "I own my self no Judge of those:   . . . .            565  Death of Swift   310
     Horses thus, let Jockeys judge else,         . . . . . 636  Epistle Lady     201
     Impartial judge within your Breast                    642  On Poetry         79
     At Wills the puny Judge of Wit.              . . . . . 647  On Poetry        236
     Appointed sov'reign Judge to sit             . . . . . 655  On Poetry        427
     The Judge discover'd in her Face      . . . .          713  Cadenus Vaness   844
     To shew she did not judge amiss,             . . . . . 713  Cadenus Vaness   855
     Let all the world judge.    . . . .                    856  Lady's Lament    152
     A judge, without the least pretence          . . . . . 876  To Dean Swift     19
     Nor, can he judge with all his Art           . . . . . 889  Panegyr Dean      91
     You judge so nicely to a Hair,         .  .  .  .  .   890  Panegyr Dean     115
     A Judge will eat, tho' clad in Ermin.        . . . . . 942  Probatur Alit     22
JUDGE'S
     Contrive to bribe the Judge's Vote.          . . . . . 647  On Poetry        212
JUDGEMENT
     Or in our Judgement or our Eye)              . . . . .  20  Ode Athenian     140
     To ask the judgement of a friend,     . . . . . . .    489  Dialogue          14
     Judgement weak, and Passion strong,          . . . . . 800  Traulus 2         17
JUDGEMENT-SEAT
     That Venus, from the Judgement-Seat,         . . . . . 688  Cadenus Vaness    76
JUDGES
     But foolish Man still judges what is best    . . . . .  36  Ode Sancroft      54
     Not allways judges what is fit;    . . . . . . .       218  To Mr. Delany     92
     And honest Paulus judges right.    .  .   . . . . .    432  Answer Paulus      2
     'Till Block-heads blame, and Judges praise,  . . . . . 505  Doctor Delany    167
     "Not Strains of Law, nor Judges Frown,  . . . . .      570  Death of Swift   427
     Damn'd Lawyers and Judges, Damn'd Lords and Damn'd     576  Place Damn'd       9
       Squires,
     Of Wit and Humour, Judges sov'reign.   . . . . . .     649  On Poetry        284
     She sends us our <Bishops> and <Judges> and <Deans>,  .520  Dean Hang Rape    69
JUDGING
     And Malice always judging worst;   . . . . . . .       448  Modern Lady      129
JUDGMENT
     Our shallow Search and Judgment to direct.   . . . . .  18  Ode Athenian      94
     For Verse, (I speak my Judgment) Yours:      . . . . . 219  To Mr. Delany    106
     The Day of Judgment will be soon,     . . . . . . .    253  Bubble            77
     Without troubling his Head about Judgment or Wit:  . . 263  Apollo            20
     Or praise the Judgment of the Town,          . . . . . 644  On Poetry        125
     Gives Judgment with decisive Air.     . . . . . . .    649  On Poetry        266
     The Seeds of Knowledge, Judgment, Wit.       . . . . . 693  Cadenus Vaness   205
     In Judgment, Knowledge, Wit, and Taste;      . . . . . 697  Cadenus Vaness   343
     Their Judgment was upon the Whole,    . . . . . . .    698  Cadenus Vaness   358
     Her Judgment, how to buy a Mask.      . . . . . . .    700  Cadenus Vaness   421
     Nor ever gave her Judgment wrong.     . . . . . . .    704  Cadenus Vaness   559
     He never knew her Judgment fail,      . . . . . . .    710  Cadenus Vaness   755
     Truth, Judgment, Wit, give Place to Spite,   . . . . . 730  Stella, Poems     93
     My Judgment of the old Comedians.     . . . . . . .    988  Letter Dr Sh-n    16
     Were in evry ones Judgment exceedingly fine, . . . . .1017  Swift Ans Sher     2
     And, as to the subject, our judgment mehercle . . . .  1026 Sheri Circles      3
JUDGMENT'S
     Depend upon't their Judgment's right:        . . . . . 644  On Poetry        134
JUDGMENTS
     T' avert th' impending judgments of my pen.   . . . . . 45  To Congreve       48
     To better Judgments willing to submit,       . . . . . 194  Author Himself    25
     To better Judgments still submitting,        . . . . . 788  Dick's Variety     9
JUDICIOUS
     Judicious Rymer oft review:   . . . . . . .            648  On Poetry        249
     In her, a most judicious Taste.       . . . . . . .    711  Cadenus Vaness   767
JUG
     Step't with a Jug, and made a Vent;          . . . . .  92  Bauc & Phil 1     70
     Although the Jug had twice gone round        . . . . .  92  Bauc & Phil 1     76
     Fill'd a large Jug up to the Brink;          . . . . . 112  Bauc & Phil 2     30
JUG-JOULTER
     But others they do say, that it was Jug-Joulter,  . .  841  Ballad        D  13
JUGGLER'S
     The wily Shafts of State, those Juggler's Tricks   . .  29  Ode to Temple     92
JUGLERS
     Or do these Juglers cheat our Eyes?          . . . . . 250  Bubble             4
     "Perform'd as Juglers do their Feats:        . . . . . 564  Death of Swift   296
JUGLING
     The Jugling Sea-god when by chance trepann'd  . . . .   22  Ode Athenian     189
JUICE     SEE JUYCE
     But not the Virtue, Tast or Juice.    . . . . . .      109  V's House        130
     Sid's Scepter, full of Juice, did shoot      . . . . . 134  Magician's Rod    71
     That pois'nous Juice which kills by Cold.    . . . . . 469  Burning Poem       2
     He had made himself Drunk with the Juice of the Grape, 517  Dean Hang Rape    23
     Pour'd in a strong inspiring Juice:          . . . . . 743  Stel B-day 22     66
     More precious Juice than from a Still.       . . . . . 920  Riddle 6          22
     To-morrow of a bitter Juice,          . . . . . . .    929  Riddle 15     D  10
     When I left you, I found myself of the Grape's Juice   1028 Dr. Helsham        1
       sick:
JULIA
     Where Goody Julia milks the Cows,            . . . . . 878  Robbin & Harry    25
JULIUS
     As Julius, or the Youth of Pella,     . . . . . .      464  Birthday Song    142
```

```
                                                    PAGE   TITLE          LINE
JUMBLES
    He jumbles Men and Birds together,      . . . . . . .  513 Answer Fable      13
JUMBLING
    The Jumbling Particles of Matter        . . . . . . .  450 Modern Lady      184
JUMBLINGS
    Which, in its Jumblings round the Skull,  . . . . . .  893 Panegyr Dean     191
JUMP
    A Flock of Geese jump down together,    . . . . . . .  253 Bubble            54
    Do all in One Opinion jump;             . . .         345 Prometheus        18
    Yet link them close; in this they jump, . . . . . .   435 Answer Paulus    105
    The Simile would better jump,           . . . . . .   497 Panegyr Swift    136
    And both Idea's jump like Wits:         . . . . .     529 Lady's Dres Rm   126
    And then they take a Turn and jump on't. . . . . .    928 Riddle 12      D  16
JUMPS
    With Leaps and with Jumps,              . . . . . . .  245 Irish-Feast       42
    And now her Heart with Pleasure jumps,  . . . . . .   904 Death Daphne      59
JUNCTURE
    A Juncture happen'd in his highest Pride:  . . . . .  536 To Mr. Gay       147
JUNIORS
    The Fools, my Juniors by a Year,        . . . . . .   561 Death of Swift   219
JUNO
    Juno attended at the Porch              . . . . . .   290 Prog Marriage     11
    Himself complain'd of it to Juno.       . . . . . .   513 Answer Fable      24
    Dame Juno brought a Priest demure.      . . . . . .   586 Strephon Chloe    64
    So beautifull to pass for Juno?         . . . . . .   619 Scandal Poem 1    64
    And, jealous Juno, ever snarling,       . . . . . .   621 Scandal Poem 1   123
    So beautiful to pass for Juno?          . . . . . .   625 Scandal Poem 2    60
    And, jealous Juno, ever snarling,       . . . . . .   627 Scandal Poem 2   117
    See the Bird of Juno stooping.          . . . . . .   661 Love Song         31
JUNO'S
    Jove dresst a Cloud in Juno's shape,    . . . . . .   619 Scandal Poem 1    54
    To rigg her out for Juno's mayd.        . . . . . .   619 Scandal Poem 1    78
    Jove drest a Cloud in Juno's Shape:     . . . . . .   625 Scandal Poem 2    50
    Befitting Juno's fav'rite Maid.         . . . . . .   626 Scandal Poem 2    76
JUNTA
    And Libell'd all the Junta round;       . . . . .     171 Horace 1, 7       38
    To a good honest Junta that never will teaze you.  . .  185 Scriblerus 1     6
JUNTO
    Whisp'ring in Junto most profound,      . . . . . . .   63 Discovery         22
JUPITER
    For Jupiter allows no more)             . . . . . . .  598 Problem Solved    18
    From Jupiter took all dominion,         . . . . . .   620 Scandal Poem 1    83
    From Jupiter took all Dominion,         . . . . . .   626 Scandal Poem 2    81
JURE
    Each Priest had a Concubine, jure Ecclesiae;  . . .   518 Dean Hang Rape    38
JURIES
    of Juries & senates the bully & briber  . . . . . .   540 Charac Walpole    12
JURY
    Our noble Grand Jury,                   . . . . . . .  237 Excellent Song    23
    Against an uncomplying Jury:            . . . . . .   348 Whitshed Motto    14
    "Nor Witness hir'd, nor Jury pick'd,    . . . . . .   570 Death of Swift   429
JUS
    Who shew'd a better Jus divinum?        . . . . . . .  820 Dr. Rundle        38
JUST
    Just as the Sun puts out a Fire;        . . . . . . .    9 Ode to King      114
    Sent by just Heaven to threaten Earth   . . . . .      10 Ode to King      133
    But now Your Worth its just Reward shall have;  . . .  12 Ode to William  D 13
    When War her cloudy aspect just withdrew,  . . . .     16 Ode Athenian      23
    They're now, just now, as naturally born,  . . . .     20 Ode Athenian     130
    Just so the Mighty Nile has suffer'd in it's Fame,  .  20 Ode Athenian     145
    Like a just Map to tell the vast Extent . . . . .      25 Ode Athenian     302
    What we call holy, and great, and just, and good,  .   38 Ode Sancroft     124
    Yet want your critics no just cause to rail,  . . .    45 To Congreve       65
    But lay the scene just here at Farnham school.  . .    46 To Congreve      114
    Last just as long as ev'ry cuckow's note:  . . . . .   47 To Congreve      130
    My hate, whose lash just heaven has long decreed  . .  47 To Congreve      133
    Thy just submission for this bold neglect.  . . . .    53 Temple Ill        74
    Just at the Breech it flashes first:    . . . . . .    66 Problem           46
    Such a thing as this happen'd, just about the time of  71 Mrs Harris Pet    33
        Goosberries.
    'Twill just new dye the Lining.                        75 Game Traffick     24
    Just such an Insect of the Age          . . . . .      80 Vanbrug House     39
    Just as the Mountain did the Mouse;     . . . . .      81 Vanbrug House     76
    Just in the Place where first it grew,  . . . . .      87 Hist V's House    32
    Grown to a Church by just Degrees,      . . . . .      94 Bauc & Phil 1    154
    But being old continued just            . . . . .      94 Bauc & Phil 1    169
    Which just like ours, new rigg'd and man'd,  . . .     96 On the Union      17
    Just as if Patrige were not Dead;       . . . . .      98 Elegy Patrige     12
    And just began to cry;--What ar't!      . . . . . .   112 Bauc & Phil 2     38
    Grown to a Church by just Degrees,      . . . . .     114 Bauc & Phil 2    108
    But being Old, continu'd just           . . . . . .   115 Bauc & Phil 2    123
    You see just by the Church-yard Stile;  . . . . .     127 Little House      14
    That Rod was just a Type of Sid's,      . . . . . .   133 Magician's Rod    39
    Just as a Porter does his Pack          . . . . . .   160 Atlas              4
    Just what you gave me, Competence:      . . . . . .   199 Horace 2, 6    D
    Just as the Rabble please to smile or frown.  . . .   210 Earl of Oxford    10
    Lest with the Wicked, Heaven involve the Just?  . .   210 Earl of Oxford    20
    If nam'd with Scorn, gives just Offence.  . . . . .   217 To Mr. Delany     70
    There out of my Sight, just against the North-Zone,  .  265 Apollo           85
    And lastly for Stella, just out of her Prime,  . .    266 Apollo           103
    For Weavers now are just as poor as Wits;  . . . . .  276 Epilogue          40
```

JUST   (CONTINUED)   PAGE   TITLE   LINE

Text	PAGE	TITLE	LINE
Sits down to Dinner just at four;	291	Prog Marriage	56
Her Ladyship is just come in,	292	Prog Marriage	92
And 'twas but just; for, wise Men say,	299	Horrid Plot	29
"Look, there he stands, and 'tis but just	304	Storm	49
Just as when we say, the Devil's a Tinker	335	Serious Poem	54
Great, Good and Just was once apply'd	339	Arch-Bish Dub	1
Because thour't Great, and Good, and Just.	339	Arch-Bish Dub	8
With Just, and Generous, and Sincere.	385	Manly Virtue	62
But just a Step below the Crown:	392	Young's Satire	38
But, all he took was just the same:	412	Desire Possess	32
So just, so gentle and so kind	422	Ireld	26
He's just the same, his brethren are	435	Answer Paulus	108
And, in his client's just defence,	435	Answer Paulus	111
Just o'er against the Bell Inn	442	Ballyspellin	57
As if they had but just begun.	453	Modern Lady	279
To form a just and finish'd piece,	460	Birthday Song	1
Just three; and every Grace a Daughter.	465	Birthday Song	166
Are Angels, just as <Kings> are Gods.	486	Libel on D- D-	198
Allow your hatred strictly just;	498	Panegyr Swift	170
The World shall own, his Choice was wise and just,	532	To Mr. Gay	17
And trust his Honesty just so much more.	535	To Mr. Gay	114
So, Robbers (and their Ends are just the same)	536	To Mr. Gay	141
"Supposing these Reflections just;	549	Life of Swift	158
Just in the Parts, where I complain;	557	Death of Swift	136
"How is the Dean? He's just alive.	558	Death of Swift	148
"He follow'd David's Lesson just,	566	Death of Swift	341
"Two Kingdoms, just as Faction led,	566	Death of Swift	351
He seem'd as just crept out of Bed;	594	Cassinus Peter	11
How just it suits with human Kind.	603	Beasts Confess	74
And, just as we dispose your brain,	620	Scandal Poem 1	93
And, just as we dispose your Brain,	626	Scandal Poem 2	91
'Tis but just, you shou'd produce,	631	Epistle Lady	59
Carve to all but just enuff,	633	Epistle Lady	129
Was just one annual Hundred Pound.	642	On Poetry	54
Is gen'rous, valiant, just and wise,	646	On Poetry	195
Amount to just Nine thousand Souls.	649	On Poetry	282
To represent in figure just	659	On Poetry	D 410
'To bury me is not so just	663	Epigram Bust	1
But, since just Heav'n the Dukes ambition mocks	678	Dean and Duke	5
The Case is just the same with me:	679	From Catullus	6
'Twou'd come to just Five Thousand Pound.	693	Cadenus Vaness	227
Shew'd Patterns just from India brought,	698	Cadenus Vaness	378
Vanessa, fill'd with just Disdain,	705	Cadenus Vaness	594
Just as a Man sans Consequence.	707	Cadenus Vaness	659
'Tis just what Coxcombs call, a Bite.	708	Cadenus Vaness	673
They'll prove my Accusation just.	732	Stella, Poems	144
No Raillery gives just Offence	747	Stel Distress	61
They just keep Life and Soul together,	759	Receipt Youth	10
'Tis just the Case: For you have fasted	759	Receipt Youth	23
Just Fifteen, coming Summer's Grass:	760	Receipt Youth	40
That Courage which can make you just,	765	Stel B-day '26	45
Such was Ierne's Claim, as just as thine,	771	Horace 1, 14	41
Dear Vessel, still be to thy Steerage just,	771	Horace 1, 14	53
Thy Vertues meet their just Reward,	779	Mullinix Tim	201
'Tis just like this, which hangs by Geometry.	780	Mullinix Tim	218
Just as they lookt in the Original.	783	Tim and Fables	18
Just in this Dress the Painter drew it.	783	Tim and Fables	24
Like a fresh <Turd> just dropt on Snow.	786	Dick, Maggot	14
The Neighbours think it is but just	787	Clad in Brown	26
His Nose to get the Circle just in,	788	Dick's Variety	34
Soon shall thy Sons, the Time is just at Hand,	793	St. Pat's Well	89
By the just Vengeance of incensed Skies,	806	Judas	1
When told the Lieutenant was just come to Town,	809	Epigr Prelate	2
For Pity's Sake it would be just,	813	Bro Protestant	55
Just Heaven! to see the Dunghill dastard Brood	826	Noisy Tom	17
Just as when he murther'd <Throp>.	835	Legion Club	144
Just to yawn, and give his Vote;	836	Legion Club	170
And just as I handle 'em	852	Lady's Lament	29
"A Scholard, when just from his College broke loose,	872	Grand Question	157
Her Ladyship answers, I'm just coming down;	873	Grand Question	181
Just big enough to shelter two in;	878	Robbin & Harry	22
Just to give ev'ry Man his Glass:	889	Panegyr Dean	94
As just the Counterpart of his.	905	Death Daphne	66
'Twill be just as I expect.	908	Daphne	82
'Tis mine to make a just Reflection,	932	Riddle 19	D 17
My foot was but just set out from my cathedral,	975	Dean to Sherid	3
For scolding is just quasi diceres--school-din;	979	Dean to Tho: S	8
Down in the Strand just where the new Pole is,	988	Letter Dr Sh-n	8
And has taken just now a firm resolution	1027	Sheri Circles	23
JUSTER			
Meantime your other juster friends	755	Stella '23	35
JUSTICE			
Here, Towzer!--Do Him Justice.	154	Widow and Cat	D 45
Performs what Friendship, Justice, Truth require:	196	Author Himself	73
In Christian Justice due to John.	225	Prog of Love	94
And with exact Poetick Justice:	225	Prog of Love	97
Since cruel Fate hath sunk our Justice Boat;	284	Elegy Boat	2
Who talk'd of Justice, and of Truth,	386	Manly Virtue	72
Now, on the Bench fair Justice shines,	391	Young's Satire	15
Is this your justice, when I'm come	403	Window Inns 10	D 3

	PAGE	TITLE	LINE
JUSTICE (CONTINUED)			
Then offer'd at the throne of justice,	433	Answer Paulus	29
"And with what Justice he bestows.	462	Birthday Song	76
Nor lets him sit as Justice on the Bench,	537	Mr. Pulteney	5
"Who long all Justice had discarded,	570	Death of Swift	421
With some Law but little Justice,	574	Helter Skelter	31
What Justice in rewarding Merit?	655	On Poetry	415
With Justice, Truth and Fortitude;	693	Cadenus Vaness	207
In Spight to Justice, and refuse his Bail.	826	Noisy Tom	20
JUSTICES			
No less than Justices o' Quorum,	760	Receipt Youth	45
JUSTIFY			
He chose to justify his Pride;	710	Cadenus Vaness	763
JUSTLE			
"To justle here among a Crowd.	200	Horace 2, 6	34
And justle one another down,	256	Bubble	146
JUSTLING			
Is but a Crowd of Atoms justling in a heap,	20	Ode Athenian	127
Justling some thousand years till ripen'd by the Sun,	20	Ode Athenian	129
The World from justling Seeds arose,	324	Pethox	28
JUSTLY			
Of whom it may be justly said,	61	Lady Tablebook	29
For Building fam'd, and justly reckond	87	Hist V's House	37
And therefore his Witnesses justly may boast	335	Serious Poem	39
And justly half the Merit claim'd	406	Swift to Pope	27
I think they justly ought to share	422	Ireld	47
A skilfull Critick justly blames	467	Birthday Song	209
Their Tales wou'd always justly suit	512	Answer Fable	3
"But, ev'ry Hand may justly slay.	548	Life of Swift	127
We justly praise, or justly blame,	644	On Poetry	130
We justly praise, or justly blame:	644	On Poetry	130
And some as justly Fame extols	650	On Poetry	299
A Mastiff's teeth are justly held in vogue,	672	Epig Carthy 25	D 1
I justly keep the middle Way.	918	Riddle 4	38
May justly claim their Birth from thee;	919	Riddle 5	16
JUVABIT			
Haec olim meminisse juvabit.	187	Scriblerus 4	D 18
JUYCE			
But not the Virtue Tast nor Juyce.	81	Vanbrug House	88
K			
To a Plot for expelling my Master K. James;	144	New Song	28
KALE			
That Thing, I mean, among the Kale,	128	Little House	53
KECK			
Keck at the Memory of Glorious.	775	Mullinix Tim	76
KEEL			
A Vessel with a double Keel:	96	On the Union	16
The Waves impetuous entring at your Keel.	770	Horace 1, 14	20
KEEN			
So keen thy Hunters, and thy Scent so strong;	539	Mr. Pulteney	43
No Knife so keen to weed thee from my Heart.	881	Pastoral Dial	12
KEENEST			
Deserves your Satire's keenest kage;	392	Young's Satire	34
KEEP			
And keep Her for a Sacrifice.	8	Ode to King	75
To keep that worthless clod, the body, in one place:	36	Ode Sancroft	64
Such high companions may delusion keep,	48	To Congreve	149
I keep in a Pocket ty'd about my Middle, next my Smock.	69	Mrs Harris Pet	7
In yonder Barn to keep us dry.	90	Bauc & Phil 1	22
You Fellows, what a Noise you keep!	90	Bauc & Phil 1	28
Which yet their former Virtue keep,	94	Bauc & Phil 1	151
To keep the Hair out of their Eyes,	98	Elegy Patrige	24
Which still their antient Nature keep;	114	Bauc & Phil 2	105
To bake one Loaf, and keep one Dove in.	127	Little House	38
Poh! Fellow keep not such a Pother	128	Little House	59
To keep mischievous Spirits out:	134	Magician's Rod	52
And keep close to Thee always that Name,	148	Windsor Proph	23
And fill <Jack Smith> with Hopes to keep his Place;	163	Toland's Invit	20
From our Mysterious Club to keep out Spies,	165	Toland's Invit	29
But more than that, thou'lt keep a rout	180	Horace 2, 1	13
In <Antwerp> keep a frugal House,	183	Horace 2, 1	88
Keep close then Boys, and never quarrel.	189	Faggot	13
Not firmly join'd to keep their Ground,	189	Faggot	19
You keep Your Countenance for shame	218	To Mr. Delany	81
They keep at Stains the old blue Boar,	225	Prog of Love	99
Keep up the Glasses of your Chair,	228	Prog of Beauty	74
Nor all his Int'rest keep him from the Grave.	234	Elegy on Demar	22
His Revels to keep,	244	Irish-Feast	5
And scorns the middle Way to keep:	252	Bubble	36
Strong Arguments to keep You here,	311	To Ford	14
But then, to come and keep a Clutter	314	To Ford	95
Keep t' other Half for private Use.	326	Pethox	84
Our Money to keep, let us Cut down One more.	334	Serious Poem	16
Where Wisdom stands to keep the Field,	340	Arch-Bish Dub	23
To favour Wood and keep my Pension:	348	Whitshed Motto	16
I keep my Gullet for the Halter.	349	Upright Judge 1	4
To keep out of Danger, a Doublet of Stone.	351	Wood Insect	10
To bless him and to keep him there;	388	Manly Virtue	140
Shall keep the Key of my (no) Wine;	409	Dial Rich Marb	44
'Tis a sign she'll keep her folks,	419	Holyhead Journ	2
If Englands friendship you would keep	422	Ireld	55

KEEP   (CONTINUED)

	PAGE	TITLE	LINE
Nor scold, nor keep a splutter.	429	Beau's Reply	10
To keep good sense in crouds of fools;	436	Answer Paulus	124
'The Cook must keep it back a while;	447	Modern Lady	95
Lords keep a Pimp to bring a Wench;	480	Libel on D- D-	22
For keep him in, or turn him out,	484	Libel on D- D-	139
Must ever keep it's Owner down:	502	Doctor Delaney	80
Then keep your Virtue still unmixt,	503	Doctor Delaney	107
O may she better learn to keep	528	Lady's Dres Rm	97
For, keep, or turn him out, my Lord's undone.	535	To Mr. Gay	126
But, who are they that can keep touch---?	546	Life of Swift	42
Stand high himself, keep others low?	554	Death of Swift	16
"I keep no antiquated Stuff;	563	Death of Swift	267
"And, keep the Peace, to pick up Fees:	571	Death of Swift	450
Were duly washt to keep 'em sweet;	586	Strephon Chloe	78
Keep them to wholsome Food confin'd,	587	Strephon Chloe	123
To keep her Spouse deluded still,	588	Strephon Chloe	143
For, if they keep not what they caught,	591	Strephon Chloe	259
To keep Esteem and Love alive.	593	Strephon Chloe	310
Which he resolv'd to keep for ever hence,	603	Beasts Confess	71
Keep the same face an hour together,	618	Scandal Poem 1	44
But, we shall keep revenge in store	622	Scandal Poem 1	173
Keep the same Face an Hour together:	625	Scandal Poem 2	40
Nor with Senates keep a Fuss,	636	Epistle Lady	187
From Bayliffs claws thou scarce cou'd keep thy Bum free.	678	Dean and Duke	12
And keep on Fish perpetual Lent.	689	Cadenus Vaness	90
Will you keep strictly to the Text?	732	Stella, Poems	138
To keep a worthy Lover's heart	732	Verses Vanessa	2
Howe're to keep her Spirits up Mean time to keep	747	Stel Distress	45
Howe're to keep her Spirits up Mean time to keep	747	Stel Distress	45
Howe'er, to keep her Spirits up,	751	Stel Wood-Park	61
They just keep Life and Soul together,	759	Receipt Youth	10
I'll lead the Van, keep you the Rear.	780	Mullinix Tim	230
But keep your Swearing to the last.	780	Mullinix Tim	238
Yet keep their Bishopricks, and 'scape the Cord.	806	Judas	14
Knock him down, down, down,--keep him down.	817	Yahoo's	REF
With Parsons, what Lady can keep herself clean?	868	Grand Question	29
For the Captain, I warrant, will keep him in Awe;	868	Grand Question	34
To keep off their Eyes, as they wait at the Table;	871	Grand Question	136
"But, <Zounds>, by their Looks, they never keep Lent:	872	Grand Question	146
This Hill may keep the Name of Drapier;	875	Drapier's Hill	18
Shall keep my Host in Ambuscade;	884	Rev Market-Hill	52
To keep our Poultry sweet and clean;	892	Panegyr Dean	164
He still may keep a pack of knaves	902	Dean's Reasons	109
To be easy keep your distance;	907	Daphne	26
I justly keep the middle Way.	918	Riddle 4	38
The Clergy keep me for their Ease,	920	Riddle 6	7
Yet no Watch the rest will keep,	931	Riddle 18	D 16
When I'm vext, can't keep me under;	933	Riddle 20	D 24
With Ease I make to keep their Distance;	934	Riddle 21	D 4
But keep a good tongue, or you'll find, to your smart,	976	Dean to Sherid	35
Since you write in a cart, keep it tecta et sarta,	979	Dean to Tho: S	15
Tom, for a goose you keep but base quills,	982	Sher, A Goose	1
Tho' you and your Come-rogues keep him out so late	986	Mary to Sher	16
But now I'll secret keep your stuff;	1002	Reply by Dean	17
You keep such a twattling	1015	Swift to Sheri	37

KEEPER

When I saw the Keeper frown,	834	Legion Club	133
Honest Keeper, drive him further,	834	Legion Club	141
Keeper, shew me where to fix	835	Legion Club	145
Tye them Keeper in a Tether,	835	Legion Club	153
Keeper, yon old Dotard smoke,	836	Legion Club	159
Keeper, I must now retire,	839	Legion Club	231
Keeper, I have seen enough,	839	Legion Club	239

KEEPERS   SEE NURSE-KEEPERS

KEEPING

Was like keeping her Monument always in sight.	144	New Song	38
Shews all her Secrets of House keeping,	282	Journal	87
Half wither'd by a Winters keeping	290	Prog Marriage	26
Shrivel'd with a Winter's keeping.	523	Betty Grizette	10
Of keeping up a party hatred.	779	Mullinix Tim	184

KEEPS

It melts the Sword of War, yet keeps it in the Sheath.	29	Ode to Temple	91
Of all the fine Things he keeps in the Dark,	265	Apollo	61
He keeps his Distance in the Gallery	294	Prog Marriage	141
For while he keeps his Pen, you are not safe.	538	Mr. Pulteney	14
Not to the Nymph that keeps thy Heart;	596	Cassinus Peter	102
In his own Church he keeps a Seat;	605	Beasts Confess	129
Which keeps the Peace among the Gods,	695	Cadenus Vaness	262
Keeps punctual to an Assignation;	724	To Stella	30
And Chest, that keeps my Lady's Tea,	885	Rev Market-Hill	88
Who keeps his wisdom out of sight;	900	Dean's Reasons	42
A sieve keeps half in, and therefore, no doubt,	976	Dean to Sherid	25
Like a woman it keeps in less than it lets out.	976	Dean to Sherid	26
My Master is so fond of that Minister that keeps the School;	987	Mary to Sher	29

KEN

| In our Ken, both great and small; | 931 | Riddle 18 | D 10 |

KENNEL

| Her Kennel once again to claim; | 208 | Fable Bitches | 38 |
| We'll oil him with kennel, and powd'r him with grains, | 817 | Yahoo's | 58 |

KENNEL-EDGE
  The Kennel-Edge, where Wheels had worn the Place.   •   124 Descriptn Morn   10
KENNELS
  Now from all Parts the swelling Kennels flow,   •   •   •   139 City Shower   53
  In Streets where Kennels are too wide: •   •   •   •   •   645 On Poetry   170
KENSINGTON
  To Kensington, or hot St. James's;   •   •   •   •   •   411 Dial Rich Marb   88
KENT
  To a small Village down in Kent;   •   •   •   •   •   111 Bauc & Phil 2   10
  Unless the Men of Kent are Ly'rs,   •   •   •   •   •   257 Bubble   170
KENTISH-TOWN
  And Maevius reigns o'er Kentish-Town: •   •   •   •   650 On Poetry   302
KEPT
  The Angel (doubtless) kept th' Eternal Gate,   •   •   8 Ode to King   65
  The Courtiers kept their Distance due,   •   •   •   63 Discovery   18
  He kept the Model in his Mind.   •   •   •   •   86 Hist V's House   12
  But kept it's Matter and it's Hue,   •   •   •   93 Bauc & Phil 1   108
  Whose Wideness kept their Toes from Corns,   •   •   99 Elegy Patrige   37
  For Vows Divine are kept by Fate.   •   •   •   121 Apollo Outwit   48
  A Widow kept a Favourite Cat,   •   •   •   •   153 Widow and Cat   D   1
  "Have kept Domestick Mice in awe,   •   •   •   154 Widow and Cat   D   24
  Had lost his Art, and kept his Ears.   •   •   •   157 Fable of Midas   40
  Kept Company with Men of Wit,   •   •   •   •   171 Horace 1, 7   39
  And to be kept in my right wits.   •   •   •   •   199 Horace 2, 6   D
  Who neither time nor order kept.   •   •   •   •   279 Journal   20
  'Till <Hort> arriv'd ne'er kept a Wench;   •   •   303 Storm   18
  And, kept at first an equal Pace: •   •   •   412 Desire Possess   12
  Possession kept the beaten Road;   •   •   •   412 Desire Possess   35
  He heard I kept a pack of hounds,   •   •   •   422 Ireld   27
  For here the Father kept his Crown.   •   •   •   460 Birthday Song   14
  For Poets open Table kept,   •   •   •   •   481 Libel on D- D-   37
  This Peacock kept a standing Force,   •   •   •   513 Answer Fable   27
  Enquire what Regimen I kept;   •   •   •   •   557 Death of Swift   139
  "With Princes kept a due Decorum,   •   •   •   566 Death of Swift   339
  "But, kept the Tenor of his Mind,   •   •   •   567 Death of Swift   361
  But, awfully his Distance kept.   •   •   •   •   587 Strephon Chloe   114
  Ne'er kept a Cause, he well may boast,   •   •   604 Beasts Confess   91
  Your Secret kept, your Poem sunk,   •   •   •   644 On Poetry   143
  She heard it--there she kept her Word;   •   •   690 Cadenus Vaness   119
  Watch'd all the Company she kept,   •   •   •   696 Cadenus Vaness   309
  In every Scene had kept his Heart;   •   •   •   703 Cadenus Vaness   541
  Shall still be kept with Joy by me: •   •   •   763 Stel B-day '26   2
  And kept their Liberty, or bravely dy'd.   •   •   793 St. Pat's Well   82
  Would needs have kept thee from the ground.   •   •   822 Epigr Rundle   6
  How oft a Week was kept a Ball   •   •   •   •   905 Death Daphne   83
KERCHER
  Of Mantle and Kercher,   •   •   •   •   •   245 Irish-Feast   22
KERNEL
  (How that which we a Kernel see,   •   •   •   •   31 Ode to Temple   165
KETTLE
  The Kettle to the Top was hoist   •   •   •   •   92 Bauc & Phil 1   97
  Tis now no Kettle but a Bell.   •   •   •   •   •   93 Bauc & Phil 1   104
  The Kettle to the Top was hoist,   •   •   •   •   113 Bauc & Phil 2   57
  'Tis now no Kettle, but a Bell.   •   •   •   •   113 Bauc & Phil 2   64
  He'll not be too proud an old Kettle to mend;   •   •   335 Serious Poem   44
  But a Kettle of scalding hot Water injected,   •   •   351 Wood Insect   25
  As rising from Medea's Kettle;   •   •   •   •   759 Receipt Youth   18
  You Clutter still your Brazen Kettle.   •   •   •   775 Mullinix Tim   46
KETTLE-DRUM
  The Man with the Kettle-drum enters the Gate;   •   870 Grand Question   90
KETTLE'S   SEE TEA-KETTLE'S
KETTLES
  So, by the Kettles loud Allarm,   •   •   •   •   345 Prometheus   25
KEVAN
  We'll colt him thro' Kevan, St. Patrick's, Donore,   •   817 Yahoo's   56
KEVANS
  Jolly boys of St. Kevans, St. Patrick's, Donore,   •   814 Yahoo's   1
KEY   SEE ORMOND-KEY
  In their dull hum-drum key   •   •   •   •   •   186 Scriblerus 4   D   4
  Shall keep the Key of my (no) Wine;   •   •   •   409 Dial Rich Marb   44
  She must return to Ormond Key: •   •   •   •   751 Stel Wood-Park   46
  Then if we once can seize the Key,   •   •   •   885 Rev Market-Hill   87
  To you we often trust the Key: •   •   •   •   889 Panegyr Dean   90
KEY-HOLE
  That came through the Key-Hole, or in at the Casement,   77 Lady B- B-   14
KEYS
  But pawns her Snuff-Box, Rings, and Keys.   •   •   452 Modern Lady   235
KICK
  Or a Kick on the <Arse>.   •   •   •   •   •   247 Irish-Feast   88
  Tom gave him a Kick in the Guts for his Fee.   •   •   399 Tom Clinch   14
  Himself could scarce forbear to kick,   •   •   •   497 Panegyr Swift   139
KICK'D
  Who for his pains is cuff'd, and kick'd,   •   •   •   436 Answer Paulus   137
KICKS
  What Bastings and Kicks!   •   •   •   •   •   246 Irish-Feast   68
  He gets a thousand Thumps and Kicks   •   •   •   777 Mullinix Tim   117
KICKT
  And Thanks to the Members that Kickt down the Bank.   •   287 Bank Down   10
  Or call 'em Rogues, or get 'em kickt: •   •   •   505 Doctor Delaney   154
  They Cudgell'd, and Cuft him, and kickt him down Stairs   517 Dean Hang Rape   16

PAGE   TITLE   LINE

KILDARE
    The Earl of Kildare, ...
KILDERKIN

	PAGE	TITLE	LINE
The Earl of Kildare,	247	Irish-Feast	77

KILDERKIN
    To a small Kilderkin of Beer . . . .
<KILKENNY>
    You'd swear it must be the Baboon of <Kilkenny>:
KILL
    And by their college-arts methodically kill:
    Think what you save or what you kill
    More Beaus can kill
    Which, as the Nurse pursu'd to kill,
    May kill perhaps, but never wound. .
    We kill, 'tis true, but never wound;
    Then, who says care will kill a cat?
    That was bred to kill a Cow well:
    And kill with the spleen . .
    I give Command to kill or save.
    Which you say it can kill,
    Whose moving Touches, when they please, kill us. .

	PAGE	TITLE	LINE
To a small Kilderkin of Beer	92	Bauc & Phil 1	67
You'd swear it must be the Baboon of <Kilkenny>:	803	Irish Bishops	10
And by their college-arts methodically kill:	42	Ode Sancroft	254
Think what you save or what you kill	140	Harlyes Surgn	4
More Beaus can kill	441	Ballyspellin	35
Which, as the Nurse pursu'd to kill,	504	Doctor Delaney	119
May kill perhaps, but never wound.	618	Scandal Poem 1	28
We kill, 'tis true, but never wound;	624	Scandal Poem 2	22
Then, who says care will kill a cat?	761	Bec's B-Day	7
That was bred to kill a Cow well:	800	Traulus 2	30
And kill with the spleen	855	Lady's Lament	129
I give Command to kill or save.	916	Riddle 1	34
Which you say it can kill,	939	Riddle Answerd	17
Whose moving Touches, when they please, kill us.	988	Letter Dr Sh-n	29

KILL'D
    And how her Doves were kill'd by Weezles:
    A Champion kill'd, or Trophy won;
    First to be fondled, then be kill'd.

	PAGE	TITLE	LINE
And how her Doves were kill'd by Weezles:	282	Journal	94
A Champion kill'd, or Trophy won;	554	Death of Swift	24
First to be fondled, then be kill'd.	753	Gift for Bec	12

KILLING
    Of killing Eyes, or bleeding Hearts:

	PAGE	TITLE	LINE
Of killing Eyes, or bleeding Hearts:	728	Stella, Poems	12

KILLMAINHAM
    For it prov'd that he dy'd of a Drop at Killmainham:

	PAGE	TITLE	LINE
For it prov'd that he dy'd of a Drop at Killmainham:	337	Serious Poem	114

KILLS
    That pois'nous Juice which kills by Cold.
    Of Serpent-Kind, and what at distance kills,

	PAGE	TITLE	LINE
That pois'nous Juice which kills by Cold.	469	Burning Poem	2
Of Serpent-Kind, and what at distance kills,	941	Letter	23

KILMORE
    Go flatter Kilmore.

	PAGE	TITLE	LINE
Go flatter Kilmore.	1038	Sheridan Cavan	14

KIN   SEE A-KIN
    For John was come of honest Kin:
    That three little Vermin are kin to Will. Wood:
    He ne'er was partial to his Kin;
    As well may claim you for their Kin.
    Half encompass'd by his Kin:
    And all my Kin, a num'rous Host,
    . . . than you and all your kin:

	PAGE	TITLE	LINE
For John was come of honest Kin:	224	Prog of Love	60
That three little Vermin are kin to Will. Wood:	350	Wood Insect	2
He ne'er was partial to his Kin;	606	Beasts Confess	176
As well may claim you for their Kin.	813	Bro Protestant	40
Half encompass'd by his Kin:	836	Legion Club	162
And all my Kin, a num'rous Host,	925	Riddle 8	28
. . . than you and all your kin:	985	Mary to Sher	8

KIND   SEE WOMAN-KIND,HUMAN-KIND,SERPENT-KIND
    And some kind pow'r for once dispense
    Kind Star, still may'st thou shed thy sacred influence
       here,
    I'm sure I found them other kind of things
    But thanks his stars, that Phyllis has been kind;
    Till the blest sun to give kind dawn of grace
    Till the kind <Looseness> comes, and then
    This Reptil, of the Serpent kind,
    It was so perfect in its kind,
    Force him to take his Tythes in kind;
    A Mortal of superior kind.
    Remov'd from kind Arbuthnot's Aid,
    Venus, indulgent to her Kind
    And if his Heirs continue kind,
    Oh! would these Patriots be so kind
    The Britons, once a savage Kind,
    From what Kind of Tree this Wood was Hewn out.
    They swear I am so kind and good,
    The kind Physician grants the Husband's Prayers,
    For Models, made to mend our Kind,
    Kind Richmond-Lodge; the same to you.
    To me was most malicious kind
    So just, so gentle and so kind
    All by my Lady's kind Decision.
    And, how his Lordship was so kind;
    So, Men of Wit are but a kind
    Detesting all the Statesmen kind,
    "To Spirits of less gentle kind,
    Had Statesmen too of ev'ry Kind,
    This Enemy of human Kind.
    To all the Charms of Female Kind;
    That Rogue of genuine ministerial Kind:
    We Mortals are strange kind of Folk.
    "I hear, they're of a diff'rent kind:
    Vain human Kind! Fantastick Race!
    Kind Lady Suffolk in the Spleen,
    His Kind of Wit is out of Date.
    "And had a Kind of Knack at Rhyme:
    "To merit well of human Kind:
    "Were always of the midling Kind:
    "Offending Race of Human Kind,
    Because she pays 'em all in Kind.
    Yet, if the Goddess could be kind,
    A Crime that shocks all human Kind;
    Yet, kind Arcadians, on my Urn
    To Fondness for the Female Kind;
    How just it suits with human Kind.
    Their kind Affections he has try'd;
    Creatures of ev'ry Kind but ours
    A Cloud with Woman kind compare?

	PAGE	TITLE	LINE
And some kind pow'r for once dispense	37	Ode Sancroft	87
Kind Star, still may'st thou shed thy sacred influence here,	39	Ode Sancroft	154
I'm sure I found them other kind of things	46	To Congreve	91
But thanks his stars, that Phyllis has been kind;	48	To Congreve	158
Till the blest sun to give kind dawn of grace	52	Temple Ill	25
Till the kind <Looseness> comes, and then	66	Problem	31
This Reptil, of the Serpent kind,	83	Salamander	30
It was so perfect in its kind,	86	Hist V's House	11
Force him to take his Tythes in kind;	174	Horace 1, 7	110
A Mortal of superior kind.	179	To Lord Harley	80
Remov'd from kind Arbuthnot's Aid,	204	In Sickness	9
Venus, indulgent to her Kind	227	Prog of Beauty	57
And if his Heirs continue kind,	235	Elegy on Demar	49
Oh! would these Patriots be so kind	255	Bubble	109
The Britons, once a savage Kind,	326	Pethox	73
From what Kind of Tree this Wood was Hewn out.	334	Serious Poem	26
They swear I am so kind and good,	348	Whitshed Motto	9
The kind Physician grants the Husband's Prayers,	364	On Dreams	27
For Models, made to mend our Kind,	387	Manly Virtue	115
Kind Richmond-Lodge; the same to you.	411	Dial Rich Marb	104
To me was most malicious kind	420	Holyhead	22
So just, so gentle and so kind	422	Ireld	26
All by my Lady's kind Decision.	478	Epist on Epist	100
And, how his Lordship was so kind;	480	Libel on D- D-	6
So, Men of Wit are but a kind	480	Libel on D- D-	23
Detesting all the Statesmen kind,	482	Libel on D- D-	72
"To Spirits of less gentle kind,	485	Libel on D- D-	170
Had Statesmen too of ev'ry Kind,	513	Answer Fable	29
This Enemy of human Kind.	515	Answer Fable	86
To all the Charms of Female Kind;	530	Lady's Dres Rm	130
That Rogue of genuine ministerial Kind:	534	To Mr. Gay	102
We Mortals are strange kind of Folk.	545	Life of Swift	4
"I hear, they're of a diff'rent kind:	550	Life of Swift	181
Vain human Kind! Fantastick Race!	555	Death of Swift	39
Kind Lady Suffolk in the Spleen,	559	Death of Swift	179
His Kind of Wit is out of Date.	562	Death of Swift	252
"And had a Kind of Knack at Rhyme:	563	Death of Swift	264
"To merit well of human Kind:	567	Death of Swift	362
"Were always of the midling Kind:	570	Death of Swift	436
"Offending Race of Human Kind,	579	Day Judgement	11
Because she pays 'em all in Kind.	583	Young Nymph	56
Yet, if the Goddess could be kind,	587	Strephon Chloe	95
A Crime that shocks all human Kind;	595	Cassinus Peter	68
Yet, kind Arcadians, on my Urn	595	Cassinus Peter	73
To Fondness for the Female Kind;	603	Beasts Confess	64
How just it suits with human Kind.	603	Beasts Confess	74
Their kind Affections he has try'd;	606	Beasts Confess	163
Creatures of ev'ry Kind but ours	607	Beasts Confess	203
A Cloud with Woman kind compare?	617	Scandal Poem 1	2

```
KIND            (CONTINUED)                              PAGE   TITLE           LINE
    Thus ev'ry Poet in his Kind,        . . . . . . . .  651 On Poetry          341
    Were Animals of human kind,         . . . . . . . .  658 On Poetry        D 410
    So lovely in the Female Kind,       . . . . . . . .  691 Cadenus Vaness     165
    Interpret for a kind Advance.       . . . . . . . .  712 Cadenus Vaness     817
    In high Concern for human Kind,     . . . . . . . .  723 To Stella            5
    Else you relapse to Human Kind:     . . . . . . . .  724 To Stella           44
    And forming you, mistook your Kind? . . . . . . .    726 To Stella           86
    From me, Dear Stella, still be kind. . . . . . .     755 Stella '23          30
    By human Kind, but Flesh and Blood? . . . . . . .    759 Receipt Youth       36
    With what concerns all human kind,  . . . . . . .    781 Mullinix Tim       264
    But Tom was kind and loving;        . . . . . . .    784 Mullinex Dick       10
    His Genius of superior Kind;        . . . . . . .    788 Dick's Variety      14
    While Things of heterogeneous Kind, . . . . . . .    811 Bro Protestant       5
    But yet are so kind   . . . . . . . . . . . .        857 Lady's Lament      199
    To my Lady once be kind;  . . . . . . . . . .        862 To Janus             7
    Indulgent you to Female Kind,       . . . . . . .    887 Panegyr Dean         7
    To Works of more exalted Kind.      . . . . . . .    893 Panegyr Dean       198
    An Adder of the sable Kind,         . . . . . . .    903 Death Daphne        27
    Two Vices of a diff'rent Kind:      . . . . . . .    918 Riddle 4            24
    Though some are of so stubborn Kind, . . . . . .     921 Riddle 6            35
    Yet Flow'rs I bear of ev'ry Kind;   . . . . . . .    926 Riddle 9             9
    Brethren of a wond'rous Kind,       . . . . . . .    931 Riddle 18        D   2
    The dullest Beast and kind Voice of a Cat,  . . .    940 Letter              12
    A long-ear'd Beast, and kind Noise of a Cat, . . .   943 Probatur Alit       43
KINDER
    Begets a kinder Folly and Impertinence  . . . . .     18 Ode Athenian        79
    But Weavers will be Kinder to the Players, . . . .   276 Epilogue            43
    A Kinder Wife was never born,  . . . . . . . .       328 Epigram 2            3
KINDLE
    The Arts new kindle into Life.   . . . . . . . .     385 Manly Virtue        46
    To kindle strife Dame Nature taught her, . . . . .   618 Scandal Poem 1      37
    To kindle Strife, Dame-Nature taught her:  . . . .   624 Scandal Poem 2      35
    Your Spirits kindle to a Flame,  . . . . . . . .     730 Stella, Poems       87
KINDLED
    And kindled first with Indolence and Ease,  . . .     33 Ode to Temple      203
    'Tis but a low-born vapor kindled by a ray; . . . .   41 Ode Sancroft       218
    Kindled while reason sleeps, but quickly flies, . .   54 Temple Ill          99
    In Chaos, kindled into Life;  . . . . . . . .        324 Pethox              30
    Conceiv'd and kindled in the Mind,  . . . . . . .    687 Cadenus Vaness      30
    He kindled, as if the whole Satire had been . . .    816 Yahoo's             41
KINDLIER
    Kindlier entertains her Friends?  . . . . . . .      632 Epistle Lady        80
KINDLING
    Rip'ning, and kindling like the Sun.  . . . . . .    391 Young's Satire      26
KINDLLY
    Who kindlly did the Saints invite  . . . . . . .      91 Bauc & Phil 1       53
KINDLY
    Then Ariadne kindly Lends  . . . . . . .            100 Elegy Patrige       79
    To take thee kindly in between, . . . . . . . . .    100 Elegy Patrige       87
    Who kindly did the Saints invite  . . . . . . .      111 Bauc & Phil 2       21
    And take it kindly meant to show  . . . . . . .      200 Horace 2, 6         41
    He us'd 'em full as kindly as himself.  . . . . .    234 Elegy on Demar      14
    And she wou'd kindly thank him for't. . . . . . .    302 Storm                6
    For, take it kindly, or amiss,  . . . . . . . .      315 To Ford             99
    Yet kindly sells himself for nought  . . . . . .     421 Ireld                4
    And then he kindly give me hints  . . . . . . .      423 Ireld               59
    Who kindly would leave thee no worse nor no better. . .  424 Carterets Arms  20
    And in all they do for us so kindly do mean,  . . .  516 Dean Hang Rape       2
    "While Nature kindly bent to ease us,  . . . . .     554 Death of Swift       9
    Our kindly help his fire assuages.  . . . . . . .    618 Scandal Poem 1      34
    Our kindly Help his Fire assuages;  . . . . . . .    624 Scandal Poem 2      32
    Or kindly when his Credit's out,  . . . . . . .      728 Stella, Poems       31
    He kindly bids me near him stand;  . . . . . . .     921 Riddle 6            29
KINDNESS
    In kindness to maintain her Spouse;  . . . . . .     225 Prog of Love        90
    These Gentlemen use me with Kindness and Freedom, . .  263 Apollo           21
    'Tis Kindness to hold a Friend up by the Chin;  . .  338 Serious Poem       118
    With all the Kindness they profess,  . . . . . .     557 Death of Swift     121
    If I should Stella's Kindness hide  . . . . . .      726 To Stella           95
    And when a Friend in Kindness tries  . . . . . .     730 Stella, Poems       89
    Her kindness who could ever guess,  . . . . . . .    755 Stella '23          27
KINDRED
    Must e'en all herd with us their Kindred Fools, . .   18 Ode Athenian       82
    Nor, with your Kindred half the Palace crowd. . . .  533 To Mr. Gay         58
    They came of good Kindred, and cou'd not endure, . . 804 Irish Bishops      27
    "My Kindred oft' thine Hide shall gall;  . . . .     850 Old Thorn           59
    So in the Kindred Painter's Art,  . . . . . . .     1021 Nim-Dan-Dean 1   D 35
KINDS
    Should spring such short and transitory kinds,  . .   47 To Congreve       128
    Here various Kinds by various Fortunes led,  . . .   138 City Shower         39
KINE
    I hope you have swilld with new milk from the Kine  . . 1018 Swift Ans Sher 25
KING
    And made an Humble Chaplet for the King.  . . . .     16 Ode Athenian        31
    Else why should the fam'd Lydian King,  . . . . .     20 Ode Athenian       153
    Of some great King and Conqu'rors Death,  . . . .     24 Ode Athenian       272
    Evils which a too gentle king,  . . . . . . . .       37 Ode Sancroft        98
    Like good King Phys: and good King Ush:  . . . . .    63 Discovery           23
    Like good King Phys: and good King Ush:  . . . . .    63 Discovery           23
    Can't you go work, or serve the King?  . . . . .      91 Bauc & Phil 1       41
```

KING	(CONTINUED)	PAGE	TITLE	LINE
When Philip King of Greece was Dead,	. . . . .	99	Elegy Patrige	64
He'll teaze you with King Charles and Bishop Laud,		166	Toland's Invit	42
A Fig for Lechmere, King, and Hambden.	. . . . .	191	Faggot	48
With Church and King, the Lady's gone;	. . . .	279	Journal	36
And since he owns the King of Sweden	. .	282	Journal	103
The former folks were servants to the king,	. . . .	308	Billet Players	13
Which links the Subject to the King:	. . . . .	346	Prometheus	65
Quoth King Robin, our Ribbands I see are too few		389	Order of Bath	1
Our King ne'er exhausted his fountain of Honours.	. .	389	Order of Bath	6
And he who will leap over a Stick for the King	. .	389	Order of Bath	11
Such Godlike Virtues in the King,	. . . . .	391	Young's Satire	2
But now He's grown a King, God wot,	. .	408	Dial Rich Marb	17
For he'll be poor as any King:	. . . .	409	Dial Rich Marb	40
But, like a King, to run in Debt.	. . . . . .	409	Dial Rich Marb	42
None loves his King and Country better,	. . . .	410	Dial Rich Marb	83
So, Holla Boys; God save the King.	. . .	418	Woman's Mind	64
The King is ready when you will	. . . . .	422	Ireld	43
"Before my Lady call'd a King.	. . . . . .	452	Modern Lady	253
"Because you held the King of Hearts:	. . . .	452	Modern Lady	256
Her Chair to call the King of Clubs,	. . . .	452	Modern Lady	259
He must have been a King by Merit.	. . . . .	464	Birthday Song	136
Here many a King his heart and Crown	. . .	465	Birthday Song	167
Who struts like any King already.	. . . . . .	466	Birthday Song	188
As Falstaff acted old King Harry:	. . .	475	Epist on Epist	10
Against all Rules to be a King:	. . . . . .	513	Answer Fable	16
"Destructive to the Church and King:	. . . .	550	Life of Swift	173
"But now as Consort of the King,	. . . . .	560	Death of Swift	187
"(I wish I knew what King to call.)	. . . . .	562	Death of Swift	232
The King of Brutes (to make it plain,	. . . .	601	Beasts Confess	7
To serve the King, and please the Nation.	. .	606	Beasts Confess	154
To Chatres, Walpole, or a King,	. . . . .	622	Scandal Poem 1	165
Thou great Vicegerent of the King,	. . . . .	656	On Poetry	447
To find a King in all ye Crew,	. . . . .	659	On Poetry	D 410
He shap'd a King to rule ye Race	. . . . .	659	On Poetry	D 410
Gloomy Pluto, King of Terrors,	. . . . .	661	Love Song	17
Well: but a Duke thou art; so pleasd the King	. .	678	Dean and Duke	15
And sells the King of Spain a Bargain.	. . .	777	Mullinix Tim	114
And, turn'd to Lice, infest the King:	. . . .	813	Bro Protestant	54
To mend your Breed, the Murderer of a King.	. .	826	Noisy Tom	10
From Victors o'er the Memphian King;	. . . .	925	Riddle 8	30
I mean the Church, the King, and Me.	. . . .	926	Riddle 9	24
For you, my Conq'ror and my King,	. . .	1005	Sheridan's Sub	14
Between the <King> and Us but Brass,	. . . .	346	Prometheus	68
And cursing <Bob>, forget to bless <the> <King>.	. .	533	To Mr. Gay	52
He'd shew his Face before the <King>:	. . . .	602	Beasts Confess	34
Both at Senate-House, and <King>	. . . . .	637	Epistle Lady	222
For, had you made the <King> your debtor,	. .	821	Dr. Rundle	65
KING'S				
Whoe'er will not were them, is not the King's Lover.	.	236	Excellent Song	4
The Muses, by their King's Permission,	. . . . .	689	Cadenus Vaness	93
KINGDOM	**SEE MOTHER-KINGDOM**			
A Kingdom to a Ship compare;	. . . . . .	96	On the Union	14
He that cou'd once have half a Kingdom bought,	. .	234	Elegy on Demar	19
'Tis happy to see the whole Kingdom in Rags,	. . .	287	Bank Down	16
Poor Kingdom thou wouldst be that Governor's debtor,	.	424	Carterets Arms	19
Find him a Kingdom out to conquer;	. . . . .	466	Birthday Song	204
"That Kingdom he hath left his Debtor,	. . . .	572	Death of Swift	483
When, if you search the Kingdom round,	. . . .	773	Mullinix Tim	5
Would take the Kingdom into his Protection:	. .	825	Noisy Tom	4
You banter me, Madam, the Kingdom must grant--	. . .	871	Grand Question	125
KINGDOM'S				
"On Rural Squires, that Kingdom's Bane,	. . . .	571	Death of Swift	443
KINGDOMS				
To purchase Kingdoms, and to buy Renown,	. . . .	11	Ode to William	D 1
Of Kingdoms, without Faith or Law.	. . . . . .	96	On the Union	12
Yet when the Weight of Kingdoms lyes	. . . .	160	Atlas	20
"Two Kingdoms, just as Faction led,	. . . . .	566	Death of Swift	351
KINGLY				
The kingly Prophet well evinces,	. . . .	408	Dial Rich Marb	13
The glorious Founder of their kingly Race:	. . .	790	St. Pat's Well	12
KINGS				
Kings would indeed be Victims of the State;	. .	6	Ode to William	6
But wicked kings draw more examples than the good;	. .	40	Ode Sancroft	184
To learn what Northern kings design,	. . .	63	Discovery	29
By two such whisp'ring Kings of Branford.	. . . . .	64	Discovery	48
We read of Kings, who in a Fright,	. . . . .	66	Problem	19
Thence, thro' a long Descent of Kings,	. . . .	134	Magician's Rod	63
We toast Confusion to the Race of Kings:	. . . .	162	Toland's Invit	14
Equip our Kings, and Generalls at the Comb.	. .	275	Epilogue	18
In short our Kings and Princesses within,	. . . .	275	Epilogue	27
Between the Weavers and us Play-House Kings.	. .	275	Epilogue	36
Ye bubbles rais'd by breath of Kings;	. . . . .	296	Satiric Elegy	26
New Kings a compliment expect	. . . .	422	Ireld	37
The Acts of Gods, and god-like Kings.	. . . .	496	Panegyr Swift	103
And Kings are now no more than Men;	. . . .	498	Panegyr Swift	164
And Kings, like private Folks, are bought and sold:	.	536	To Mr. Gay	136
Employ your Muse on Kings alive;	. . . . .	647	On Poetry	220
For in those Ages Kings we find,	. . . . . .	658	On Poetry	D 410
I mean all Kings except our own,	. . . . .	659	On Poetry	D 410
Thus think on Kings, ye Name denotes	. . . . .	659	On Poetry	D 410

KINGS	(CONTINUED)	PAGE	TITLE	LINE
What Herds of Kings would turn to Grazers.	. . . .	659	On Poetry	D 410
Base Kings and Ministers of State,	. . . . . .	725	To Stella	63
Too great for Mortals less than Kings.	. . . . .	924	Riddle 8	16
There shou'd be Quarrels among Kings.	. . . .	930	Riddle 15	D 20
Both <Kings> and Ministers of State,	. . . .	485	Libel on D- D-	174
Can differ more than God and <Kings>	. . . .	486	Libel on D- D-	196
Are Angels, just as <Kings> are Gods.	. . . .	486	Libel on D- D-	198
Both <Kings> and Ministers of State.	. . . .	498	Panegyr Swift	156
By flatt'ring <Kings> whom Heaven design'd	. . . .	654	On Poetry	407

KISS

To let me kiss your other shore?	. . . .	403	Window Inns 10	D 8
To towse and kiss	. . . .	442	Ballyspellin	76
When We are lash'd, They kiss the Rod;	. . . .	561	Death of Swift	217
He pierce the Clouds! he kiss our <arses>)	. . .	620	Scandal Poem 1	104
He pierce the Clouds! He kiss their <Arses>.)	. .	626	Scandal Poem 2	102
To kiss your Steps at Quilca Gates;	. . . . .	760	Receipt Youth	48
Judas betrayed his Master with a Kiss:	. . . .	806	Judas	10
To the Dean he shall go; they shall kiss, and be friends:		817	Yahoo's	62
A face for to kiss, without eyes, ears, or nose.	. . .	817	Yahoo's	64
Dear Companions hug and kiss,	. . . . .	835	Legion Club	151
I peept, and saw you kiss the dirty Bitch.	. . .	882	Pastoral Dial	38
That oft I wake thee with a Kiss?	. . . . .	924	Riddle 8	10
Yet you of ev'ry Kiss complain;	. . . .	924	Riddle 8	11
The dullest Beast, and that which you kiss,	. . .	941	Letter	21
And then you may kiss the low end of her Spine	. . .	1018	Swift Ans Sher	33

KISS'D

You should have kiss'd it in your Distress,	. . . .	135	Magician's Rod	81
Was kiss'd and slobber'd by a Lad:	. . . . .	150	Corinna	22
If Oonah once I kiss'd, forbear to chide:	. . . .	882	Pastoral Dial	41

KISS'T

But, some have kiss't the Gospel Fifty Times,	. . .	806	Judas	11
What, if for nothing once you kiss't,	. . . . . .	884	Rev Market-Hill	33
The Phantom, having humbly kiss't	. . . .	903	Death Daphne	3

KISSES

And kisses George, and ends or Lectures:	. . . . .	278	Journal	14
Then he low'rs down the Point, and kisses the Hilt.	.	871	Grand Question	112

KISSING

But lest your Kissing should be spoyl'd,	. . . . .	952	Onyons	8

KIST

The sun, you say, his face has kist:	. . . .	432	Answer Paulus	9

KIT

Kit, run to your Master, and bid him come to us.	. . .	871	Grand Question	117
To rule the Dairy next to Kit.	. . . .	888	Panegyr Dean	42

KITCHEN

A Turn-spit in the <Royal> Kitchen.	. . . . .	300	Horrid Plot	66
We see him from our kitchen windows,	. . . . .	620	Scandal Poem 1	108
A Dutchess or a Kitchen Girl.	. . . . . .	890	Panegyr Dean	124

KITCHEN-WINDOWS

We see him from our Kitchen-windows:	. . . . . .	626	Scandal Poem 2	106

KITCHIN

To Kitchin, Parlour, Nurs'ry flies,	. . . . . .	322	First of April	37
He would come into our Kitchin, . . .	. . . . .	987	Mary to Sher	32

KITE

The Raven, Vulture, Owl, and Kite,	. . . . .	413	Desire Possess	55
That serjeant at law, whom we call Kite the Second,	.	817	Yahoo's	67

KNACK

Thy Genius has perhaps a knack	. . . .	183	Horace 2, 1	103
Your Int'rest lyes to learn the knack	. . . . .	464	Birthday Song	115
"And had a Kind of Knack at Rhyme:	. . . . .	563	Death of Swift	264

KNAVE

But the first Knave does seldom fail	. . . . .	74	Game Traffick	3
For on a Knave he never looks	. . . . . .	74	Game Traffick	7
Each Knave hath made a thousand Fools.	. . . .	253	Bubble	60
"But he'll come back the Knave he went."	. . . .	306	Storm	72
Un-man the poor Knave for sake of a Trope.	. . .	335	Serious Poem	52
Where every knave & fool is bought	. . . . .	421	Ireld	3
The Stagg was swift, the Fox a Knave:	. . . . .	512	Answer Fable	6
A Knave, who deep embroils his Lord's Affairs,	. . .	535	To Mr. Gay	119
The subtle Knave had all the Plunder swept.	. . .	536	To Mr. Gay	154
"Expos'd the Fool, and lash'd the Knave:	. . . .	565	Death of Swift	316
The cringing Knave who seeks a Place	. . . . .	604	Beasts Confess	93
A cart would best become the knave,	. . . . .	951	Upstart	D 25
Yes; you call'd my Master a Knave: . .	. . . .	985	Mary to Sher	5
Knave in your Teeth, Mr. Sheridan, . . .	. . .	985	Mary to Sher	7

KNAVE'S

To see a Knave's inverted Heels:	. . . .	451	Modern Lady	227

KNAVES

Since knaves are ne'er oblig'd for what they steal.	. .	45	To Congreve	66
That a Pack of sly Knaves should get fifty per Cent,	.	288	Bank Down	52
Where all are fools, and all are knaves	. . . .	421	Ireld	2
His honesty in crouds of knaves;	. . . . . .	436	Answer Paulus	126
Caressing Knaves and Dunces wooing,	. . . . .	484	Libel on D- D-	127
Though flatt'ring Knaves may call it bitter.	. . .	485	Libel on D- D-	178
Nor ever fools or knaves expose	. . . . . .	489	Dialogue	9
And all Mankind as Fools, or Knaves;	. . . .	493	Panegyr Swift	6
. . . Damn'd Block-Heads, Damn'd Knaves,	. . .	576	Place Damn'd	7
Into Knaves they turn their Fools:	. . . .	635	Epistle Lady	158
To flatter Knaves, or lose his Pension.	. . . .	650	On Poetry	310
So two poor Knaves, who find their Credit fail,	. .	668	Epig Carthy 8	D 3
When vulgar Knaves would lose their Ears:	. . . .	724	To Stella	32

		PAGE	TITLE	LINE
KNAVES	(CONTINUED)			
He still may keep a pack of knaves		902	Dean's Reasons	109
KNEE				
Let courtly Slaves low bend the Knee		386	Manly Virtue	93
The Hangman for Pardon fell down on his Knee; . . .		399	Tom Clinch	13
Present it boldly on your knee, ...		469	Birthday Song	281
KNEEL				
Nor could the nations kneel to viler shapes, ...		46	To Congreve	105
KNEEL'D				
Lord Pam in the Church (cou'd you think it) kneel'd down		809	Epigr Prelate	1
KNEELING				
Or on the Matt devoutly kneeling		222	Prog of Love	15
KNEES				
And shakes the atheist's knees; such ghastly fear . . .		52	Temple Ill	39
Grief that excus'd the tribute of my knees, ...		53	Temple Ill	79
Sits with his Knees up to his Chin;		127	Little House	20
With trembling Knees, and Terror at his Back;		210	Earl of Oxford	4
Then down I went upon my Knees, his Blessing to obtain,		342	Upon His Grace	29
With bended knees when they adore her		465	Birthday Song	157
Short by the Knees intreat for Peace.		655	On Poetry	424
With handsome Garters at your Knees, ...		699	Cadenus Vaness	402
(But first let Robert on his Knees		743	Stel B-day 22	77
Held up by my knees, ...		852	Lady's Lament	26
Here pay their Vows with bended Knees:		893	Panegyr Dean	208
KNELL				
And the Sound of his Brass we took for our Knell. . .		351	Wood Insect	32
As soon as you can hear his Knell, ...		646	On Poetry	205
Than if it rang out for my Knell:		674	His Deafness	4
KNEW				
More than your Predecessor, Adam, knew;		31	Ode to Temple	162
And your Almighty Master, knew		38	Ode Sancroft	114
For, tragedy, he knew, would lose you quite, ...		47	To Congreve	145
The Pilot knew not how to guide.		96	On the Union	20
He knew his Trade, and call'd it Boots.		99	Elegy Patrige	34
Told <Van> he knew his Talent best, ...		107	V's House	53
Th' experienc't Bricks that knew their Trade, ...		108	V's House	76
Knew how to preach old Sermons next.		115	Bauc & Phil 2	127
Soon knew Apollo by his looks, ...		120	Apollo Outwit	15
But Wise Ardelia knew his Tricks.		120	Apollo Outwit	20
What all the World knew long ago, ...		180	Horace 2, 1	8
When first I knew thee, Dick, thou wert		182	Horace 2, 1	49
"I doubt not, if his Lordship knew--		201	Horace 2, 6	61
For well he knew her num'rus Brood, ...		208	Fable Bitches	21
There's not a creature here you ever knew.		307	Billet Players	12
Or vex the Ladyes, when they knew		311	To Ford	11
Nor Persons Names, nor Places knew;		313	To Ford	54
This, when my Grandsire knew; they tell us he, . . .		350	Upright Judge 3	5
For well he knew, to such a Guest, ...		378	Apology Lady C	103
The gracious Dame, tho' well she knew		379	Apology Lady C	117
Nor knew in law his A, B, C.		436	Answer Paulus	122
He knew to stop a quater trois.		456	Dean Smedley	30
Because he never knew a letter.		463	Birthday Song	90
If their own happyness they knew.		467	Birthday Song	224
The deepest Tricks of Courtiers knew.		494	Panegyr Swift	38
I knew a brazen Minister of State, ...		536	To Mr. Gay	143
"He neither knew you, nor your Name;		548	Life of Swift	122
"(I wish I knew what King to call.)		562	Death of Swift	232
"He knew an hundred pleasant Stories, ...		572	Death of Swift	475
(So some Folks told you, but they knew		579	Day Judgement	17
For since we knew you walk a-foot, ...		622	Scandal Poem 1	175
In Homer more than Homer knew.		643	On Poetry	104
Nor further those Deponents knew:		688	Cadenus Vaness	72
Whom she or her Assessors knew.		689	Cadenus Vaness	103
She knew in our degen'rate Days		693	Cadenus Vaness	212
She knew, by Augury Divine, ...		695	Cadenus Vaness	276
I knew by what you said and writ, ...		706	Cadenus Vaness	618
He knew not how to reconcile		706	Cadenus Vaness	626
He hardly knew, Till he was told, ...		706	Cadenus Vaness	632
She railly'd well, he always knew, ...		707	Cadenus Vaness	660
He never knew her Judgment fail, ...		710	Cadenus Vaness	755
My very Face, at first I knew it, ...		783	Tim and Fables	23
Dick knew better how to swing		785	Mullinex Dick	31
"I ne'er was a Parson without a good Nose, ...		872	Grand Question	143
Than if they never knew a letter.		900	Dean's Reasons	40
Must be some painted Toy I knew;		912	Aenigma Expl	D 8
And the patientest Patient that ever you knew sick; . .		1028	Dr. Helsham	3
I pitied my Cat, whom I knew by her Mew sick; . . .		1029	Dr. Helsham	5
Knew how to set you better Patterns;		1033	Ans to Crown	16
KNIFE SEE WEEDING-KNIFE,PARING-KNIFE				
Lets fall her Knife, or spills the Salt, ...		694	Cadenus Vaness	243
In his Mouth to wear his Knife.		800	Traulus 2	40
Then fear not his tongue, his sword, or his knife; . .		817	Yahoo's	73
By your knife to be mangled than rack'd with your voice.		818	Epigr Kite	4
While each with stubbed Knife remov'd the Roots . . .		880	Pastoral Dial	3
No Knife so keen to weed thee from my Heart.		881	Pastoral Dial	12
KNIGHT				
And like a Bold Romantick Knight		7	Ode to King	37
Now you've done right, No Knight attempting		373	Letter D. S-y	75
Vouchsafe to be an azure Knight, ...		656	On Poetry	462
In publick with that odious Knight.		699	Cadenus Vaness	395
Sir Archibald that val'rous Knight, ...		848	Old Thorn	9

KNIGHT   (CONTINUED)   PAGE   TITLE   LINE

	PAGE	TITLE	LINE
By a Dean and a Knight;	851	Lady's Lament	4
Thus spoke to my Lady, the Knight full of Care;	866	Grand Question	1
Thus ended the Knight: Thus began his meek Wife:	867	Grand Question	25
The Knight his Opinion resolv'd to maintain.	868	Grand Question	40
Of Brazen Knight they vainly sung:	876	To Dean Swift	14
Who wont to weed the Court of Gosford Knight,	880	Pastoral Dial	2
A <Dean>, a Spaniard, and a Knight.	883	Rev Market-Hill	8
The Knight triumphant reigns betwixt:	883	Rev Market-Hill	20
Then, (let me see) we'll make the Knight	886	Rev Market-Hill	93
That, near the Knight of Gosford plac't,	899	Dean's Reasons	21
Such is the fate of Gosford's Knight,	900	Dean's Reasons	41
Betwixt the Knight sublime and me?	901	Dean's Reasons	66
But, here I differ from the Knight	901	Dean's Reasons	71
The neighbours wonder why the Knight	901	Dean's Reasons	81
At least in what regards the Knight.	902	Dean's Reasons	100
A long-ear'd Beast, and Building Knight;	942	Probatur Alit	17

KNIGHTS

	PAGE	TITLE	LINE
Lords, Knights and Squires were all his humble Debtors.	234	Elegy on Demar	16
That none are more properly Knights of the Post.	335	Serious Poem	40

KNIT

	PAGE	TITLE	LINE
And seem'd to knit his Brow;	74	Game Traffick	6
Why, Stella, should you knit your Brow,	759	Receipt Youth	21

KNITS

	PAGE	TITLE	LINE
His Visage drops, he knits his Brow,	480	Libel on D- D-	15
She shakes her Helm, she knits her Brows,	694	Cadenus Vaness	252

KNOCK

	PAGE	TITLE	LINE
The Walls in tumbling gave a Knock;	127	Little House	15
The Steeple, Knock, the Vicar, Walls.	127	Little House	18
I'd knock the Doctor down;	426	Five Ladies	38
At last they hear the Watchman knock,	453	Modern Lady	282
Hang, Drown, or knock him on the Head.	797	Traulus 1	40
Knock him down, down, down, knock him down.	814	Yahoo's	REF
Knock him down, down, down, knock him down.	814	Yahoo's	REF
Knock him down, down, down, knock him down.	815	Yahoo's	REF
Knock him down, down, down, knock him down.	815	Yahoo's	REF
Knock him down, down, down, knock him down.	816	Yahoo's	REF
Knock him down, down, down, knock him down.	816	Yahoo's	REF
Knock him down, down, down, knock him down.	817	Yahoo's	REF
Knock him down, down, down, knock him down.	817	Yahoo's	REF
Knock him down, down,--keep him down.	817	Yahoo's	REF
And with her Beak gave many a Knock	849	Old Thorn	35

KNOCK'D

	PAGE	TITLE	LINE
A damn'd Cromwellian, knock'd me down.	926	Riddle 9	20

KNOCK'T

	PAGE	TITLE	LINE
Came up, and knock't the Praetor down.	190	Faggot	34
With real Thunder knock't him down.	353	Wood Ironmongr	24
Like real Thunder knock't him down.	353	Wood Ironmongr	38
She knock't him with the Scepter down.	413	Desire Possess	48

KNOCKING

	PAGE	TITLE	LINE
To others he boasted of knocking out brains,	816	Yahoo's	47

KNOCKS

	PAGE	TITLE	LINE
You treat me like a Boy that knocks down his Foe,	967	Letter Sherid	13

KNOCKT

	PAGE	TITLE	LINE
Knockt down the Boy, the Lanthorn broke;	781	Mullinix Tim	268

KNOGGING

	PAGE	TITLE	LINE
I'd be glad of a Knogging:	1015	Swift to Sheri	46

KNOT   SEE TOP-KNOT

	PAGE	TITLE	LINE
Fall'n by mishap amongst a knot of beaux;	50	To Congreve	216

KNOTS   SEE SWORD-KNOTS

	PAGE	TITLE	LINE
With Ribbins in Knots, at its Tail and its Ears:	870	Grand Question	98

KNOTTY

	PAGE	TITLE	LINE
The grave Divine with knotty Points perplext,	364	On Dreams	31

KNOW

	PAGE	TITLE	LINE
Yet how shall they be brought to know	21	Ode Athenian	167
It is a bloody list we know)	37	Ode Sancroft	94
Nothing is fix'd that mortals see or know,	39	Ode Sancroft	143
Pretends so perfectly to know;	39	Ode Sancroft	158
There are degrees above I know	41	Ode Sancroft	231
Whom were my Congreve blest to see and know,	49	To Congreve	183
"Know no base action, at no guilt turn pale;	55	Temple Ill	142
Beside all this, deep Scholars know,	66	Problem	21
Now you must know, because my Trunk has a very bad Lock,	69	Mrs Harris Pet	5
. . .and she, you know, is thick of Hearing;	70	Mrs Harris Pet	25
. . .do you know what a Loss I have had?	70	Mrs Harris Pet	26
(Now you must know, of all Things in the World,.	71	Mrs Harris Pet	35
Now, Mrs. Dukes, you know, and every Body under-stands,	71	Mrs Harris Pet	42
So you know, what could I say to her any more,	71	Mrs Harris Pet	46
(Now you must know, he hates to be call'd Parson,. . .	72	Mrs Harris Pet	54
. . .I'd have you to know.	72	Mrs Harris Pet	58
You know, I honour the Cloth,. .	72	Mrs Harris Pet	60
Yet he did not know	77	Lady B- B-	16
You may know by the Hand, it had no Cloven Foot.	77	Lady B- B-	30
Van, (for 'tis fit the Reader know it)	80	Vanbrug House	59
As 'tis miscall'd, we know not who 'tis;	98	Elegy Patrige	32
<Van> (for 'tis fit the Reader know it)	107	V's House	33
Yet since I know where a full Purse may be found,	144	New Song	49
Said Harley, I desire to know.	172	Horace 1, 7	47
You know I am not worth a Groat:	175	Horace 1, 7	134
Thou pompously wilt let us know	180	Horace 2, 1	7
"Let my Lord know you're come to Town.	200	Horace 2, 6	24

KNOW   (CONTINUED)   PAGE   TITLE   LINE

What I desire the World should know.   . . . . . .   200 Horace 2, 6   42
Yet some I know with Envy swell, ... 202 Horace 2, 6   81
Faith Sir, you know as much as I.   . . . .   202 Horace 2, 6   96
I know no more than my Lord Mayor, ... 202 Horace 2, 6   102
Men have it when they know it not.   . . . .   216 To Mr. Delany   28
Scripture you know exhorts us to it, ...   220 A Quiet Life   17
Know all Men by these Presents, Death the Tamer . . .   233 Elegy on Demar   1
Pluto the god of Wealth, will joy to know   . . . . . .   234 Elegy on Demar   7
You know whom I mean, ...   238 Excellent Song   31
Directors better know their Tools, ...   253 Bubble   58
Right Trusty, and so forth; We let you to know, . . .   263 Apollo   1
Tho' I know nothing on't, 'tis I that make Gold; . . .   263 Apollo   4
And by the Description I certainly know, ...   264 Apollo   43
For know I cannot bear to hear, ...   271 Apollo's Edict   D 48
But you, who are a Scholar, know   . . . .   283 Journal   115
The Banks of a River I know are good Things, ...   287 Bank Down   2
Said I, from thence I nothing know;   . . . .   298 Horrid Plot   5
But you must know this Dog was lame.   . . . .   298 Horrid Plot   12
Corbet, though yet I know his Worth not, ...   314 To Ford   75
And yet we all know much Gold it will bring, ...   334 Serious Poem   14
I know you will say, this is all Heathen Greek; . . .   337 Serious Poem   89
I know the Times are something hard, but hope they soon   342 Upon His Grace   32
   will mend,
And, Fiftly; you know whom I mean, ...   348 Whitshed Motto   19
I know no Reason at this Time   . . . .   372 Letter D. S-y   27
As when Time serves, you more shall know.   . . . . .   373 Letter D. S-y   78
But you must know he was not quite   . . . .   375 Apology Lady C   7
The Captain too--he did not know   . . . .   377 Apology Lady C   81
From him let proud Ambition know, ...   386 Manly Virtue   99
For this we know, all antient Sages   . . . .   391 Young's Satire   23
I know a Trick to make you thrive;   . . . .   394 Grub-Street   5
By Satan taught, all Conj'rers know   . . . .   401 Window Inns 2   1
My Lady's empty Pockets know: . . . .   409 Dial Rich Marb   24
I know not in what Book or Page, ...   412 Desire Possess   6
Some augmentation Sr You know   . . . .   422 Ireld   35
I know you well enough, ...   428 Beau's Reply   7
<Lyndsay>, you know, what pains you take . . . . . .   436 Answer Paulus   129
In you, who ought to know my Heart, ...   444 Modern Lady   2
He says, his Business is to know   . . . .   446 Modern Lady   57
"And feel my Pulse, I know it stops: . . . .   451 Modern Lady   207
"And I know whom you mean to teach, ...   452 Modern Lady   255
And truly, Madam, I know when   . . . .   453 Modern Lady   264
A Child may know it in the Dark;   . . . .   453 Modern Lady   267
Lest that the reader shou'd not know, ...   456 Dean Smedley   41
The Eagle in the Tale, ye know, ...   458 Paddy's Charac   29
You'd know him by Apollo's Prints   . . . .   462 Birthday Song   62
You'd know him by Apollo's Cuts.   . . . .   462 Birthday Song   64
On Virtues which they know they want.   . . . . . .   464 Birthday Song   128
But, Rev'rend Doctor, you, we know, ...   483 Libel on D- D-   111
I know a shorter way by half.   . . . .   487 Irish-Club   14
And such as know what Greece has writ   . . . . . .   491 Dialogue   51
(And you of all Mankind should know)   . . . .   493 Panegyr Swift   24
That only know to preach and pray, ...   497 Panegyr Swift   149
Say, did you ever know by Sight   . . . .   504 Doctor Delaney   139
You have been Libell'd--Let us know   . . . .   505 Doctor Delaney   159
And for his singing, Doctor, you know, ...   513 Answer Fable   23
Tho' tis a Maxim you must know, ...   514 Answer Fable   57
We ne'er shou'd know that he could write: . . . . .   514 Answer Fable   72
That you who know musick no more than as ass   . . .   522 St. Cecilia's   2
Tho I name not the wretch you know who I mean   . . .   540 Charac Walpole   13
'Tis fit the Maxim we should know.   . . . .   545 Life of Swift   6
"I know his nearest Friends complain, ...   547 Life of Swift   78
"You know, I always fear'd the worst, ...   557 Death of Swift   129
"I know no more than what the News is, ...   558 Death of Swift   155
"You know 'tis quite a different Thing.   . . . . . .   560 Death of Swift   188
"But, this I know, all People bought 'em;   . . . . .   565 Death of Swift   312
"Taught Fools their Int'rest how to know;   . . . . .   569 Death of Swift   409
For We know by these Marks, the place of the Damn'd;   576 Place Damn'd   16
And should he struggle; I know what--   . . . . . .   586 Strephon Chloe   82
I know she loves the Barber's Boy.   . . . .   595 Cassinus Peter   62
You know, a cloudy sky bespeaks . . . .   618 Scandal Poem 1   29
But say, what earthly nymph do you know, ...   619 Scandal Poem 1   63
And from your own experience know   . . . .   620 Scandal Poem 1   87
Tis sung. But we know better things.   . . . .   621 Scandal Poem 1   142
You know a Cloudy Sky bespeaks   . . . .   624 Scandal Poem 2   23
But say, what Earthly Nymph do you know, ...   625 Scandal Poem 2   59
And from your own Experience know, ...   626 Scandal Poem 2   85
As you shall to your Sorrow know;   . . . .   627 Scandal Poem 2   131
'Tis sung, but we know better Things.   . . . . . .   627 Scandal Poem 2   146
Well I know, you can discern, ...   630 Epistle Lady   29
Must, that all the World may know 'em, ...   631 Epistle Lady   47
Never know I any Good in 'um, ...   632 Epistle Lady   83
Except they know whom they abuse.   . . . .   644 On Poetry   132
In Poetry the Height we know;   . . . .   654 On Poetry   391
And yet she would raise me I know,--by a halter   664 Epigram Bust   4
A Duke to know a Dean! go smooth your Frown,   . . .   678 Dean and Duke   13
And only know the gross Desire;   . . . .   687 Cadenus Vaness   36
For if the Heav'nly Folk should know   . . . . . .   689 Cadenus Vaness   79
To know the Converse of Mankind.   . . . .   696 Cadenus Vaness   315
About a Lady----- You know who;   . . . .   696 Cadenus Vaness   321

```
KNOW          (CONTINUED)                              PAGE    TITLE          LINE
  To know the World a little better.     . . . . . . . .    700 Cadenus Vaness   429
  (To know the World! a modern Phrase,   . . . . . .        700 Cadenus Vaness   430
  Whose Scoundrel Fathers would not know 'em,   . . .       729 Stella, Poems     51
  Ye Daintyes, I know nothing of ye,     . . . . . .        733 Verses Vanessa    28
  She'll have 'em know she scorns to stay   . . . . .       746 Stel Distress     42
  And you must know in what I writ   . . . . . .            747 Stel Distress     67
  And curious to know,   . . . . . . . .                    756 Dingley Brent     16
  Why, Tim, you have a Taste I know,   . . . . . . .        776 Mullinix Tim      91
  Consume my Vitals they shall know,   . . . . . . .        778 Mullinix Tim     175
  That which is which, 'tis hard to know.   . . . .         780 Mullinix Tim     228
  I know you love to act a Farce.   . . . . . . .           783 Tim and Fables    38
  You know him by his hazel Snout:   . . . . . . .          785 Dick, Maggot       4
  Now hear an Allusion!--A Mitre, you know,   . . . .       805 Irish Bishops     41
  The Dean and his merits we ev'ry one know,   . . . .      814 Yahoo's            6
  But where his deep law is, few mortals yet know:         815 Yahoo's           12
  You certainly know, tho' so loudly you vapour,   . .      818 Archbi Cashel      5
  Who know there is an Holy Ghost;   . . . . . . .          820 Dr. Rundle        14
  We know the Subject of their Quarrels;   . . . . .        820 Dr. Rundle        21
  And well we know, The Congee Regal   . . . . . .          821 Dr. Rundle        57
  Near the Church--you know the rest.   . . . . . .         829 Legion Club        8
  But you, my Life, may let him know,   . . . . . .         860 Lady Acheson      17
  And Sir I know you hate a Crowd.   . . . . . . .          860 Lady Acheson      24
  What dares he not? He can, we know it,   . . . . .        876 To Dean Swift     17
  My Gratitude the World shall know:   . . . . . .          887 Panegyr Dean      31
  The Fellows learn to know their Distance.   . . . .       888 Panegyr Dean      56
  That Cow-boys know you by your Dress!   . . . . .         889 Panegyr Dean      80
  Of ev'ry Taste to know the Size;   . . . . . .            890 Panegyr Dean     118
  Be humbly minded; know your Post;   . . . . . . .         897 Panegyr Dean     327
  For, Cards we know, are Pluto's Books)   . . . . .        905 Death Daphne      80
  In Learning would not know a Line:   . . . . . .          915 Riddle 1          30
  But this I know, in either Case   . . . . . . .           918 Riddle 4          29
  And therefore, all that know me, say   . . . . . .        918 Riddle 4          37
  Thy num'rous Fingers know their Way,   . . . . . .        919 Riddle 5          11
  Nor oft can the Receiver know   . . . . . . . .           919 Riddle 5          23
  And few know how and where you fix.   . . . . . .         919 Riddle 5          28
  For, few, a chosen few, must know,   . . . . . . .        922 Riddle 7          49
  There is a Gate, we know full well,   . . . . . .         928 Riddle 12      D   1
  Another Time I'll let you know.   . . . . . . .           928 Riddle 12      D  10
  Yet all that know me will agree,   . . . . . . .          929 Riddle 15      D   3
  Yet I know a young Rogue, that thrown flat on the Field   967 Letter Sherid     15
  Friend Sheridan, when will you know your own Good?   . .  968 Letter Sherid     24
  But coach it or cart it, I'd have you know, Sirrah,   .   979 Dean to Tho: S    11
  So I'll leave him behind, for I certainly know it,   .    979 Dean to Tho: S    31
  And you know all my geese are swans:   . . . . . .        983 Sher, A Goose     12
  I know the gander always goes   . . . . . . . .           983 Sher, A Goose     19
  For a Parson, who shou'd know better Things, . . . .      985 Mary to Sher       6
  Not that I know his Reverence was ever concern'd to my   986 Mary to Sher      15
      knowledge,
  For know, Prostration is enough to th' Lion.   . . . .  1002 Reply by Dean     18
  It is impossible to know by your Letter . . . . . .     1013 Swift to Sheri     1
  . . .to let Alexander know I was here, . . . . . .       1013 Swift to Sheri     4
  Truly I don't know who's bound to be sending . . . .     1013 Swift to Sheri     5
  I know they have many a wicked Design   . . . . . .      1017 Swift Ans Sher     9
  . . . come to town, but I don't know whether he be friend 1023 Nim-Dan-Dean 2 D  7
      . . .
  . . .for I know there's no delaying ye.   . . . . .      1023 Nim-Dan-Dean 2 D  8
KNOW'ST
  Say Muse, for thou, if any, know'st   . . . . . .          36 Ode Sancroft      43
  Know'st thou not yet that Men commence   . . . . .        696 Cadenus Vaness   296
KNOWING
  Not knowing What, or Where, or Who, You be,   . . .        19 Ode Athenian     115
  Not knowing how to spend his Time,   . . . . . .           75 Game Traffick  D  26
  Not knowing where to turn him next;   . . . . . .         174 Horace 1, 7      114
  Well knowing what the Poets meant:   . . . . . .          461 Birthday Song     18
  From knowing James, to boast he knows the Duke.   . . .   678 Dean and Duke      4
  Well knowing from the Books she read   . . . . . .        696 Cadenus Vaness   310
KNOWLEDGE
  Our Knowledge is but mere Remembrance all,   . . . .       27 Ode to Temple     30
  They purchase Knowledge at the Expence   . . . . .         27 Ode to Temple     42
  And sick with Dregs of Knowledge grown,   . . . . .        27 Ode to Temple     47
  That Knowledge forfeits all Humanity;   . . . . . .        28 Ode to Temple     55
  If all that our weak knowledge titles virtue, be   . .     36 Ode Sancroft      45
  Whose peevish knowledge thus perversely lies   . . . .     37 Ode Sancroft      84
  Whom if I inspire, 'tis not to my Knowledge;   . . . .    263 Apollo            18
  And to your knowledge there is often less in,   . . .     276 Epilogue          45
  If Rudeness be the Effect of Knowledge,   . . . . .       377 Apology Lady C    69
  Rais'd high above his Birth by Knowledge,   . . . . .     384 Manly Virtue      33
  The Seeds of Knowledge, Judgment, Wit.   . . . . .        693 Cadenus Vaness   205
  In Judgment, Knowledge, Wit, and Taste;   . . . . .       697 Cadenus Vaness   343
  With Virtue, Knowledge, Taste and Wit,   . . . . . .      700 Cadenus Vaness   446
  Her Knowledge with her Fancy grew;   . . . . . . .        704 Cadenus Vaness   554
  Her Knowledge, with such Pains acquir'd,   . . . . .      709 Cadenus Vaness   716
  And both had equal Knowledge;   . . . . . . . .           784 Mullinex Dick      2
  First taught thee human Knowledge and divine;   . . .     791 St. Pat's Well    28
  Half the Globe from Sense and Knowledge.   . . . . .      829 Legion Club        4
  Their knowledge, to themselves confin'd,   . . . . .      900 Dean's Reasons    37
  Is Dr. <Tisdall> to my Knowledge.   . . . . . . .         942 Probatur Alit     16
  Not that I know his Reverence was ever concern'd to my    986 Mary to Sher      15
      knowledge,
```

KNOWN

	PAGE	TITLE	LINE
Won't pay th' Impertinence of being known;	20	Ode Athenian	152
And this Ye great Unknown, is only known in You.	21	Ode Athenian	188
Thus fools, for being strong and num'rous known,	37	Ode Sancroft	79
Through native dross your share is hardly known,	45	To Congreve	59
'Twas never known to turn its back	94	Bauc & Phil 1	136
The closest Mortal ever known.	202	Horace 2, 6	104
Where I am neither lov'd nor known.	203	In Sickness	4
When known, will save a double Sorrow.	204	In Sickness	28
With shame, I have too lately known;	215	To Mr. Delany	2
For would you have their Meaning known?	218	To Mr. Delany	85
Old as he was, no vulgar known Disease	234	Elegy on Demar	29
That, they had never known their Letters.	240	Run Bankers	28
'Tis a Metaphor known to ev'ry plain Thinker.	335	Serious Poem	53
And, since we must grant, there never were known	335	Serious Poem	59
And under him no Tenant yet was ever known to thrive.	342	Upon His Grace	20
None e'er was known to have a Brace.	366	Answer Delaney	8
And whilst he made her Value known,	386	Manly Virtue	87
'My Dear, for sure if I had known	448	Modern Lady	103
"But now 'tis known to common Fame.	449	Modern Lady	149
Who, had she known his vile Behaviour,	514	Answer Fable	77
To make these Truths the better known,	547	Life of Swift	66
"To steal a Hint was never known,	565	Death of Swift	317
"If such a Wretch had known his Face.	571	Death of Swift	442
"Twas known, tho' he had born Aspersion;	606	Beasts Confess	151
The Ass was never known so stupid	607	Beasts Confess	207
She ne'er was known to burst a lace.	618	Scandal Poem 1	20
Tis known, that Socrates the wise	619	Scandal Poem 1	79
'Tis known, that Socrates the wise,	626	Scandal Poem 2	77
Was never known to spread so wide.	640	On Poetry	4
And when your Merits once are known,	649	On Poetry	277
Known by the Verse, yet better by the Notes.	670	Epig Carthy 18	D 4
"By which thou shalt be known to Fame:	692	Cadenus Vaness	181
Thus making others Wisdom known,	701	Cadenus Vaness	452
A Thing never known to the Muses or Phoebus:	716	Answer Rebus	8
Her firmness who could e'er have known,	755	Stella '23	25
'Tis true, but let it not be known,	757	Stel B-day '24	41
If it could ever yet be known	775	Mullinix Tim	71
And, when they gave it, well 'tis known,	820	Dr. Rundle	17
You never else had known the Dean,	877	To Dean Swift	29
You ne'er won, by Passion stir'd,	889	Panegyr Dean	69
Let never at your Board be known	897	Panegyr Dean	339
The Secret will never be known;	952	Onyons	12
It never was known that circular letters,	1026	Sheri Circles	1

KNOWS

	PAGE	TITLE	LINE
Therefore all the Money, I have, which, God knows,	69	Mrs Harris Pet	6
And, God knows, I thought.	69	Mrs Harris Pet	11
Lewis his Patron's Humour knows;	171	Horace 1, 7	23
Of Tricks, the Lord of <Oxford> knows,	181	Horace 2, 1	19
Who knows his Art but not his Trade;	204	In Sickness	10
Virtue repuls't, yet knows not to repine;	210	Earl of Oxford	7
She knows her Early self no more,	227	Prog of Beauty	49
And, happy he, who wisely knows	243	Horace 4, 9	17
She knows it is true,	247	Irish-Feast	84
Without a Pilot seldom knows	256	Bubble	143
He knows very well I ne'er gave a Refusal,	265	Apollo	71
To tell what ev'ry School Boy knows:	281	Journal	82
So for their Quack-Bills he knows whom to thank,	288	Bank Down	54
"He knows to sail with ev'ry Wind;	304	Storm	34
"In making <Bishops>, no one knows.	304	Storm	46
But who thy Father, no Man knows,	323	Pethox	2
The Bird of Pallas knows his Post,	324	Pethox	37
Knows how to write a Billet-doux.	325	Pethox	68
His Firmness to the publick Good, as one that knows it Swore,	341	Upon His Grace	9
Knows ev'ry Prince in Europe's Face,	398	Earl of P-b-w	7
Knows to a Groat the lowest Price;	416	Woman's Mind	28
He knows no guilt, who knows no sin.	434	Answer Paulus	58
He knows no guilt, who knows no sin.	434	Answer Paulus	58
For Jove, as every School-boy knows,	461	Birthday Song	23
That Scribbler lash, who neither knows,	515	Answer Fable	95
He knows a Thousand Tricks, whene'er he please,	535	To Mr. Gay	123
(He had not seen a Hare the Lord knows when)	538	Mr. Pulteney	26
St. John, as well as Pultney knows,	555	Death of Swift	59
To please you, she knows how to chuse a nice Bit;	580	Psyche	9
A certain Goddess, God knows who,	587	Strephon Chloe	100
Who knows how soon you will compare us	622	Scandal Poem 1	164
I, as all the Parish knows,	634	Epistle Lady	137
And introduc'd the Lord knows why;	645	On Poetry	156
From knowing James, to boast he knows the Duke.	678	Dean and Duke	4
Scarce knows what Diff'rence is between	700	Cadenus Vaness	416
One way he knows to give her Pain:	701	Cadenus Vaness	469
Knows nothing which it dare not own;	706	Cadenus Vaness	609
"She was at Lord knows what Expence,	713	Cadenus Vaness	864
It cost me Lord knows how much Time	741	Stel B-day 22	9
For she, as Priestess, knows the Rites	743	Stel B-day 22	51
The reason why no Mortal knows.	777	Mullinix Tim	120
Till, God knows why, at last it burst.	796	Traulus 1	18
Yet many a Wretch in Bedlam, knows,	796	Traulus 1	23
Who knows in Law, nor Text, nor Margent,	812	Bro Protestant	27
Young Harry, as all Europe knows,	679	Robbin & Harry	37

```
KNOWS          (CONTINUED)                                    PAGE    TITLE          LINE
    Daphne knows, with equal ease,                            906 Daphne              1
    Chiefly where she nothing knows.                          906 Daphne             16
    When she knows she's most to blame.                       906 Daphne             20
    But the sly Giver better knows thee;                      920 Riddle 5           35
    Knows one Tittle of the other;                            931 Riddle 18       D   4
    A school-boy knows this, for it plainly appears           976 Dean to Sherid     19
    And I don't care who knows it, 'tis all one to Mary.      986 Mary to Sher       22
    Every body knows, that I love to tell Truth and shame     986 Mary to Sher       23
        the Devil,
    For ought he knows, as bad as Thespis's.                  988 Letter Dr Sh-n     23
    That not the wisest Mortal knows                          993 On Picture         20
    But ev'ry one that knows Dan, knows thy Master.          1002 Reply by Dean       6
    But ev'ry one that knows Dan, knows thy Master.          1002 Reply by Dean       6
    For every one that knows me, knows                       1004 Dan J's Reply      23
    For every one that knows me, knows                       1004 Dan J's Reply      23
LABORIOUS
    My Emblem, the laborious sun,                             675 Curate's Compl     13
LABOUR
    And spare the Labour of Your Conquering Hand.              13 Ode to William  D  40
    She'll help your Wife when she's in Labour.               362 Grace's Answer     26
    Nor lend a finger to the labour,                          434 Answer Paulus      64
    You need not fear your Labour lost:                       643 On Poetry         110
    With labour small, and income great;                      676 Parson's Case      23
    There's nine Hundred Pounds for Labour and Grain,         867 Grand Question      9
    Nor is your Skill, or Labour less,                        892 Panegyr Dean      188
    And when with much Labour the Matter I crackt,            972 S-'s Ans Sh-d       3
    Or else, to shew their learned Labour, you               1021 Nim-Dan-Dean 1  D  41
LABOUR'D   SEE HARD-LABOUR'D
    "He labour'd many a fruitless Hour                        567 Death of Swift    365
    They mounted, and labour'd with Whip and with Spur,       804 Irish Bishops      19
LABOURERS
    With labourers bant'ring,                                 856 Lady's Lament     160
    Like the Labourers of Babel.                              933 Riddle 20       D   8
LABOURING
    Held Monarchs labouring at the Oar;                       476 Epist on Epist     44
LABOURS
    The mighty Mountain labours with its birth,                30 Ode to Temple    108
    Your Labours for the Publick Weal.                        243 Horace 4, 9         6
    I end my labours with a Pun.                              515 Answer Fable      102
    Thy Labours, grown the Critick's Prey,                    642 On Poetry          67
    Thy Labours, Carthy, long conceal'd from Light,           667 Epig Carthy 5   D   1
    Saw all these mighty labours done,                        675 Curate's Compl     14
    Counts all his Labours amply paid,                        729 Stella, Poems      37
    Labours of many an ancient Sage,                          922 Riddle 7           41
LAC'D
    He tore her best lac'd Pinner;                            153 Widow and Cat   D  12
    Yet, why should we be lac'd so straight;                  657 On Poetry         487
LACE   SEE HAIR-LACE
    (Item, for half a Yard of Lace.)                           60 Lady Tablebook     16
    Became Black Sattin, Flounc'd with Lace.                  116 Bauc & Phil 2     142
    Nor can afford to buy gold Lace,                          216 To Mr. Delany      43
    But Cnints, Brocades, and Lace take all away,             275 Epilogue           33
    In French brocades and Flanders Lace;                     291 Prog Marriage      64
    And only Coat of tarnish't Lace;                          295 Prog Marriage     162
    In chusing Lace a Critick nice,                           416 Woman's Mind       27
    Enter the Folks with Silks and Lace:                      447 Modern Lady        81
    This Lace is worth twelve Pounds a Yard;                  447 Modern Lady        87
    Array'd in Lace, Brocades and Tissues.                    525 Lady's Dres Rm      4
    His Night-Cap border'd round with Lace                    587 Strephon Chloe     93
    She ne'er was known to burst a lace.                      618 Scandal Poem 1     20
    On Ribbons, Fans, and Gloves and Lace;                    698 Cadenus Vaness    377
    Rich Flanders Lace, and Colberteen.                       700 Cadenus Vaness    417
    Doll never flies to cut her Lace,                         725 To Stella          75
    Her Lace hath got within her Head                         733 Verses Vanessa     25
    Yet I find, a New-Years Lace                              863 To Janus           27
    See, now comes the Captain all dawb'd with gold Lace:     870 Grand Question     93
    Unweeting gild the tarnish'd Lace:                        896 Panegyr Dean      312
LACK-A-DAY
    And said, lack-a-day! he's a proper young Man.            399 Tom Clinch          8
LACK'D
    And, what no Lawyer ever lack'd,                          687 Cadenus Vaness     23
LACKER'D
    Without his lacker'd Coach and Four,                      627 Scandal Poem 2    116
LACKS
    Of which, whoe'er lacks confidence to prate,               48 To Congreve      155
LACONICK
    He left us a Laconick Sentence,                           455 Dean Smedley       18
LAD
    Last year, a lad hence by his parents sent                 46 To Congreve      115
    To break thy Rod like naughty Lad?                        135 Magician's Rod      80
    Was kiss'd and slobber'd by a Lad:                        150 Corinna            22
    To help an honest lad that's out of place,                308 Billet Players     25
    The Lad lay swallow'd up in Spleen;                       594 Cassinus Peter     10
    Tom was held the merrier Lad,                             784 Mullinex Dick       7
    Fit for Lad or Lass,                                      952 Asparagus           2
    Of a Lass or a Lad;                                       953 Oysters            10
LADDER
    Cou'd he learn to mount a Ladder.                         801 Traulus 2          50
LADIES
    To pick up Sublunary Ladies.                              120 Apollo Outwit      24
```

LADIES   (CONTINUED)   PAGE   TITLE   LINE

But, as from the Windows the Ladies he spy'd,   . . .   399 Tom Clinch   9
Fair Ladies, Number five, ...   425 Five Ladies   1
To think such Ladies fine, ...   426 Five Ladies   22
Methinks I hear the Ladies cry, ...   445 Modern Lady   13
"The Ladies here to Night by Six."   . . . . . .   446 Modern Lady   55
Which modern Ladies call polite;   . . . . . .   448 Modern Lady   113
"Go run, and light the Ladies up: . . . . . .   451 Modern Lady   212
And all the Gamester Ladies met, ...   451 Modern Lady   215
"(Ladies I'll venture for the Vole.)   . . . . .   562 Death of Swift   230
The Ladies else might think me shameless.)   . . . .   586 Strephon Chloe   80
Poor Ladies! though their Bus'ness be to play, ...   662 Upon Ladies   1
The Ladies walk'd till after Nine.   . . . . . .   696 Cadenus Vaness   327
Rich Ladies will furnish their Garrets with Stuff,   .   716 Answer Rebus   15
I <Part> with twenty Ladies by;   . . . .   778 Mullinix Tim   161
The Ladies from the Windows gaping: . . . . .   700 Mullinix Tim   241
And not among Ladies to give themselves Airs.   . . .   868 Grand Question   38
How well to win the Ladies Hearts, ...   887 Panegyr Dean   11
With Ladies what a strict Decorum!   . . . . .   888 Panegyr Dean   51
How enviously the Ladies look, ...   891 Panegyr Dean   137
(The Ladies there must needs be Rooks, ...   905 Death Daphne   79
Lies in the Lap of Ladies fine.   . . . . . .   942 Probatur Alit   14
To Ladies Skins there's nothing comes so near.   . . .   943 Probatur Alit   42
. . .I came back to sit with the Ladies this Night.   .   1013 Swift to Sheri   3
Yet, Ladies are seldom at Ombre, or Lue, sick;   . . .   1029 Dr. Helsham   15
So are Ladies in Crowds, when they squeeze and they   1030 Dr. Helsham   26
    screw, sick.

LADING
His Lading little, and his Ballast less.   . . . . .   284 Elegy Boat   4

LADS
Try Lads, can you this Bundle break;   . . . . . .   189 Faggot   2
Of Galstown Lads (for so they are)   . . . . . .   1020 Nim-Dan-Dean 1   D 2

LADY
That I went to warm my self in Lady Betty's Chamber,.   69 Mrs Harris Pet   1
    . .
So because I had been buying things for my Lady last   69 Mrs Harris Pet   3
    Night,
Then the Bell rung, and I went down to put my Lady to   69 Mrs Harris Pet   10
    Bed,
Nay, said I, I had it in Lady Betty's Chamber,. . .   70 Mrs Harris Pet   17
. . .I remember when I was at my Lady Shrewsbury's,   .   71 Mrs Harris Pet   32
. . .and says my Lady, so will I.   73 Mrs Harris Pet   67
My Lady tho' she is no Player   . . . .   75 Game Traffick   9
At Ten, my Lady comes and Hectors, ...   278 Journal   13
And Lady Betty soundly chides them.   . . . . .   279 Journal   34
My Lady says she can't afford one;   . . . . . .   283 Journal   124
His Lady has twelve times miscarry'd, ...   293 Prog Marriage   100
The Dean has carry'd Lady Jane   . . . .   294 Prog Marriage   124
And, must my Lady slip her Season?   . . . . .   294 Prog Marriage   128
They peep'd, and saw a Lady there   . . . . . .   321 First of April   29
When Lady Luna is your Neighbour   . . . . . .   362 Grace's Answer   25
A Lady, Wise as well Fair, ...   375 Apology Lady C   1
My Lady--it must be my Lord.   . . . .   376 Apology Lady C   40
My Lord's Abroad; my Lady too;   . . . .   376 Apology Lady C   41
Had now my Lady been within.   . . . .   377 Apology Lady C   50
My Lady now returning home   . . . .   377 Apology Lady C   57
My Lady could not chuse but wonder: . . . . .   377 Apology Lady C   65
My Lady, pittying his Confussion, ...   378 Apology Lady C   84
Whilst Lady Charlotte, like a Stroller,   . . .   410 Dial Rich Marb   61
And, Madam, there's my Lady Spade   . . . . . .   446 Modern Lady   62
Calls Lady Spade a hundred Cheats: . . . . . .   447 Modern Lady   73
Describe the Lady and the Man.   . . . .   450 Modern Lady   195
"When Lady Tricksy play'd a Four, ...   452 Modern Lady   250
"Before my Lady call'd a King.   . . . .   452 Modern Lady   253
Conceives a Lady standing by: . . . .   529 Lady's Dres Rm   124
Kind Lady Suffolk in the Spleen, ...   559 Death of Swift   179
"My Lady Club wou'd take it ill, ...   562 Death of Swift   237
Nor comes whene'er his Lady whistles;   . . . .   607 Beasts Confess   213
Hearken, what my Lady says---:   . . . .   630 Epistle Lady   11
Drest like any Lady May'ress;   . . . .   630 Epistle Lady   36
Thought the Life of ev'ry Lady   . . . .   631 Epistle Lady   39
About a Lady----- You know who;   . . . .   696 Cadenus Vaness   321
--That Lady is the dullest Soul--   . . . . . .   698 Cadenus Vaness   359
To piddle like a Lady breeding, ...   745 Stel Distress   8
Her Quarter's out at Lady Day   . . . .   746 Stel Distress   41
To piddle like a Lady breeding;   . . . .   750 Stel Wood-Park   32
Now scolding at my Lady Eustace, ...   788 Dick's Variety   29
A lady illiterate;   . . . .   854 Lady's Lament   90
No Lady who wants them   . . . .   854 Lady's Lament   105
To ease a poor Lady, ...   858 Lady's Lament   217
To my Lady once be kind;   . . . .   862 To Janus   7
Thus spoke to my Lady, the Knight full of Care;   . .   866 Grand Question   1
With Parsons, what Lady can keep herself clean?   . .   868 Grand Question   29
Thus argu'd my Lady, but argu'd in vain;   . . .   868 Grand Question   39
Pray, how does my Lady?--My Wife's at your Service.--   869 Grand Question   75
My humble Respects to my Lady unknown.--   . . .   869 Grand Question   81
As a Compliment due to a Lady so fair;   . . . .   870 Grand Question   110
True, Lady Anne no Danger fears, ...   885 Rev Market-Hill   57
By Lady Anne of Market-Hill.   . . . .   888 Panegyr Dean   36
Good Lord! what can my Lady mean, ...   891 Panegyr Dean   141
But here my Lady will object;   . . . .   899 Dean's Reasons   19

LADY (CONTINUED)	PAGE	TITLE	LINE
And leaves my Lady in the Suds.	905	Death Daphne	100
And oft in Hand of Lady Fair;	912	Aenigma	10
No Lady was ever more fond of a Spark;	928	Riddle 11 D	10
No Lady alive can shew such a Skin.	928	Riddle 13 D	2
Tho' a Lady, I am stout,	933	Riddle 20 D	19
Without it a Lady should never appear.	941	Letter	42
But thanks to the lady: I'm sure she's too good to ye;	976	Dean to Sherid	38
Bid Lady Betty recollect her,	993	On Picture	10
. . .to my Lady Mountcashell: but, truly, I thought	1014	Swift to Sheri	11
Lady Betty presents you her service most humble,	1027	Sheri Circles	25
Lady Santry got out of the Church when she grew sick,	1029	Dr. Helsham	10
I thought the Lady at St. Cath'rines	1033	Ans to Crown	15
LADY-DAY			
Her Quarter's out at Lady-Day,	751	Stel Wood-Park	57
LADY'S			
The Butler with my Lady's Maid;	150	Corinna	19
A Lady's Face, and China ware.	227	Prog of Beauty	64
With Church and King, the Lady's gone;	279	Journal	36
Are proper in my Lady's Case	294	Prog Marriage	132
My Lady's empty Pockets know:	409	Dial Rich Marb	24
All by my Lady's kind Decision.	478	Epist on Epist	100
As handsome as my Lady's Page;	597	Problem Solved	5
Nor bribes my Lady's fav'rite Maid.	605	Beasts Confess	136
Against our Sov'reign Lady's Peace,	687	Cadenus Vaness	17
Enough to read a Lady's Eyes;	712	Cadenus Vaness	815
Direct before her Lady's Face.	885	Rev Market-Hill	68
And Chest, that keeps my Lady's Tea,	885	Rev Market-Hill	88
Your House of Hair and Lady's Hand	912	Aenigma Expl D	1
LADYES			
Ladyes, and Gentlemen, behold,	251	Bubble	7
Or vex the Ladyes, when they knew	311	To Ford	11
He sd our Ladyes were so fair	422	Ireld	29
Fine Ladyes never do't	428	Beau's Reply	6
Fine Ladyes when they write,	429	Beau's Reply	9
LADYS			
The Ladys vow, and swear they'll try,	65	Problem	5
And now the Ladys all are bent,	66	Problem	33
The Ladys vanish, in the Smother,	66	Problem	49
Ladys, quoth Levens, pray forbear,	67	Problem	57
The Ladys, or Lampoon the Sex.	281	Journal	78
LADYSHIP			
Her Ladyship is just come in,	292	Prog Marriage	92
Her Ladyship was gone Abroad;	377	Apology Lady C	80
As soon as her Ladyship call'd to be drest,	868	Grand Question	43
Your Ladyship lifts up the Sash to be seen,	870	Grand Question	101
Your Ladyship smiles, and thus you begin;	871	Grand Question	113
And your Ladyship curchyes half way to the Ground!	871	Grand Question	116
Lord! Madam! your Ladyship sure is in jest;	871	Grand Question	124
Till she heard the Dean call, Will your Ladyship walk?	873	Grand Question	180
Her Ladyship answers, I'm just coming down;	873	Grand Question	181
LADYSHIP'S			
"You cast a Sheep's Eye on her Ladyship's Maid;	872	Grand Question	148
LAG			
And School-Boys lag with Satchels in their Hands.	125	Descriptn Morn	18
LAGG'D			
Though strong in Limbs, he lagg'd behind.	412	Desire Possess	38
So fast, his Lessons lagg'd behind:	704	Cadenus Vaness	557
LAID SEE LAY'D,LAYD			
In a vile manger laid,	40	Ode Sancroft	174
Why should the first be ruin'd and laid waste,	40	Ode Sancroft	178
On t' other side (laid out for Shoes);	60	Lady Tablebook	14
The God laid down his Feeble Rays,	119	Apollo Outwit	5
Dog <Walpole> laid a Quart of Nog on't,	299	Horrid Plot	31
Prometheus on a Rock is laid,	346	Prometheus	53
Where Whigs their cursed Trains had laid;	494	Panegyr Swift	42
Laid out with no less Art than Pains,	494	Panegyr Swift	56
The Servants Faults are on the Master laid.	533	To Mr. Gay	50
But, when thou seest me laid in Dust,	596	Cassinus Peter	100
Laid all the Fault on t' other Sex.	687	Cadenus Vaness	26
All Passions must be laid aside:	724	To Stella	36
Dreading to be laid by th' Heels.	834	Legion Club	118
Upon thy Hand his Finger laid;	905	Death Daphne	94
Pursu'd and laid me hard on.	1005	Sheridan's Sub	10
Of Lash laid on by you.	1005	Sheridan's Sub	34
LAIN SEE LAYN			
When I have lain in it a Week!	780	Mullinix Tim	224
But, as of old, obscurely lain;	877	To Dean Swift	30
LAITY			
All ran to Pray'rs, both Priests and Laity,	353	Wood Ironmongr	21
LAITY'S			
(The wicked Laity's contriving,	174	Horace 1, 7	105
LAKE			
How in the Lake the Dean was drench'd;	281	Journal	68
Ierna's Lake, for your Canal,	476	Epist on Epist	38
Not the Stench of Lake Avernus.	834	Legion Club	125
LAKES			
Some from the Lakes remotest end.	279	Journal	30
Drains all thy Lakes of Fish, of Fruits thy Land.	793	St. Pat's Well	64
LAMB			
The Butcher, feels the Lamb beneath his blade.	364	On Dreams	18

	PAGE	TITLE	LINE
LAMB (CONTINUED)			
Thus Lamb, renown'd for cutting Corns,	811	Bro Protestant	15
LAMBENT			
Like Lambent Fire the Lightning plays;	29	Ode to Temple	88
LAMBETH			
York is from Lambeth sent, to shew the Queen	195	Author Himself	47
LAMBS			
Do far exceed your frisking Lambs	123	Empty'ng Town	15
Devour'd the Lambs, the Fleeces sold,	153	Widow and Cat	D 9
Ev'n Lambs by Instinct fly the Butcher.	588	Strephon Chloe	154
A Wolf destroys a thousand Lambs.	651	On Poetry	326
LAME			
You blind and lame! tis no such Thing	91	Bauc & Phil 1	42
And offer'd many a lame Excuse;	172	Horace 1, 7	65
And begg'd like one both blind and lame;	207	Fable Bitches	8
An hundred struck lame.	246	Irish-Feast	72
But you must know this Dog was lame.	298	Horrid Plot	12
Your Evidence was lame. Proceed:	298	Horrid Plot	14
Come, help your lame Dog o'er the Style.	298	Horrid Plot	15
LAMENT			
Lament his old Whitehall in Flames,	107	V's House	48
We rather should Lament his Case	485	Libel on D- D-	159
Lament upon their hapless fall	490	Dialogue	43
And more lament, when I was dead,	557	Death of Swift	141
How those I love, my Death lament.	561	Death of Swift	206
Dear Mullinix, I now lament	781	Mullinix Tim	277
How sorely I lament your Loss?	821	Dr. Rundle	62
LAMENTING			
Lamenting in unmanly Strains,	726	To Stella	99
LAMP			
Chief cherub, and chief lamp of that high sacred Seven,	34	Ode Sancroft	3
That quite extinguish't Cupid's Lamp:	905	Death Daphne	98
LAMPOON			
The Ladys, or Lampoon the Sex.	281	Journal	78
Safely write a smart Lampoon,	634	Epistle Lady	153
Come out with some lampoon on D'Anvers.	658	On Poetry	D 186
When bent upon some smart Lampoon,	892	Panegyr Dean	189
LAMPOONING			
More like to lampooning than pleading at bar.	815	Yahoo's	14
LAMPOONS			
And all her Gestures were Lampoons.	150	Corinna	16
Lampoons on Whigs, when in Disgrace;	494	Panegyr Swift	33
LAMPS			
Thus Lamps, which burn'd in Tombs with silent Glare,	667	Epig Carthy 5	D 5
LAND SEE LONDE, FAIRY-LAND			
And Rebel is the growth and manufacture of the Land.	8	Ode to King	57
No sooner does she land	17	Ode Athenian	36
'Tis you who must this Land subdue,	26	Ode to Temple	8
Ah, Britain, land of angels! which of all thy sins,	37	Ode Sancroft	92
And got about a League from Land,	96	On the Union	18
O'er Sea and Land conveys the Witch;	132	Magician's Rod	18
And <Lincoln> then imagines he has Land.	164	Toland's Invit	26
Of Land set out to plant a Wood.	198	Horace 2, 6	6
Gain by Degrees huge Tracts of Land,	239	Run Bankers	2
The Sea is richer than the Land,	254	Bubble	97
Has form'd a Model for your Land;	272	Apollo's Edict	D 65
By which they might Swimmingly land on a Bank.	288	Bank Down	50
At Sea, or Land, if e'er you found him,	303	Storm	15
On the Scene of this Land very soon to revive.	337	Serious Poem	94
And Yet the Land I from him hold is set so on the Rack	343	Upon His Grace	45
What Land was ever half so blest?	391	Young's Satire	12
What Land was ever half so curst?	392	Young's Satire	48
A passage to the land I hate.	420	Holyhead	28
Remove me from this Land of slaves	421	Ireld	1
"So, to destroy a guilty Land,	485	Libel on D- D-	165
"When such a Tempest shook the Land,	568	Death of Swift	389
"Far to the Land of Slaves and Fens;	568	Death of Swift	396
"To save that helpless Land from Ruin,	569	Death of Swift	412
E'er drove, before he sold his Land,	598	Problem Solved	13
That ev'ry Subject in the Land	601	Beasts Confess	10
Ordain'd by Fate to be the Land of Slaves:	770	Horace 1, 14	2
Thou, fixt of old, be now the moving Land?	770	Horace 1, 14	4
When haughty Britain was a Land unknown.	790	St. Pat's Well	10
Did once their Land subdue and civilize:	790	St. Pat's Well	14
Britain, with Shame confess, this Land of mine	791	St. Pat's Well	27
I drove the venom'd Serpent from thy Land;	792	St. Pat's Well	40
Through all thy Land, in Armour, Fur and Lawn.	792	St. Pat's Well	56
Sent in my Anger from the Land of Huns;	792	St. Pat's Well	60
Drains all thy Lakes of Fish, of Fruits thy Land.	793	St. Pat's Well	64
Or hardy Scot, or any Land but this;	793	St. Pat's Well	80
Be all made Captives in their native Land;	793	St. Pat's Well	90
With a Rood or two of Land,	830	Legion Club	37
"Not leave a Thistle on the Land;	850	Old Thorn	75
I lose by the House what I get by the Land;	866	Grand Question	4
And see how he rides like a Lord of the Land,	870	Grand Question	95
Our thriving <Dean> has purchas'd Land.	875	Drapier's Hill	2
No Couple-Beggar in the Land	926	Riddle 9	11
LAND-COMMANDER			
A Land-Commander, and a Tarr.	398	Earl of P-b-w	33
LANDED			
Mordanto's landed from Leghorn.	398	Earl of P-b-w	18

		PAGE	TITLE	LINE
LANDED-MEN				
Landed-Men shall have their Rent,		169	Peace Dunkirk	25
LANDLORD				
For John is Landlord, Phillis Hostess;		225	Prog of Love	98
Why, there's my Landlord now the 'Squire,		342	Upon His Grace	15
I'll vote for my Landlord to whom I pay Rent,		396	Dog and Thief	15
My landlord is civil,		402	Window Inns 8	D 1
And orders the Landlord to bring him a Whore;		517	Dean Hang Rape	20
The <Dean>, and his Landlord, a jolly Comrade,		517	Dean Hang Rape	25
My Landlord was ready his <Deanship> to Ape		517	Dean Hang Rape	29
For I am landlord to the Drapier:		876	To Dean Swift	2
LANDLORD'S				
Both to their own and Landlord's Cost;		79	Vanbrug House	14
But, to their own, or Landlord's Cost,		106	V's House	13
"(For thou shalt steal thy Landlord's Mare)		851	Old Thorn	87
LANDS				
"For Lands enrich'd by crimson Streams,		183	Horace 2, 1	96
Their Lands and their Faces unknown;		396	Dog and Thief	18
Feed nothing in your lands but sheep		422	Ireld	56
Was left in Foreign Lands distrest,		482	Libel on D- D-	62
Nor, when a Mortgage lies on half his Lands,		534	To Mr. Gay	99
First take you our Tyths, and give us your Lands.		805	Irish Bishops	62
Or sell his Children, House, and Lands,		821	Dr. Rundle	43
'Tis I that must the Lands convey,		930	Riddle 15	D 26
LANDSCAPE				
And catch the living landscape thro' a scanty light,		35	Ode Sancroft	30
LANE SEE DRURY-LANE,DUCK-LANE				
No Creature in the Lane could sleep.		352	Wood Ironmongr	4
In yonder lane		442	Ballyspellin	56
Thro' all the Lane, from End to End.		649	On Poetry	288
Be told the Lodging, Lane, and Sign,		729	Stella, Poems	41
To take a House in Warwick Lane:		904	Death Daphne	46
LANES				
Thorow stinking Lanes and Allies;		574	Helter Skelter	42
LANGUAGE				
A jargon form'd from the lost language, wit,		47	To Congreve	121
Rally her dress, her language, and her gait;		50	To Congreve	218
In all Parts of the Globe, where your Language is read;		265	Apollo	70
To speak a Language of their own;		450	Modern Lady	189
The Language Billingsgate excel,		496	Panegyr Swift	108
Can in Celestial Language scold)		695	Cadenus Vaness	287
Such Language, with her usual Style:		706	Cadenus Vaness	627
Their Dress, their Language, and the Scottish Name,		791	St. Pat's Well	15
In civil Language, if he stays		860	Lady Acheson	18
'Twas to teach you in modester Language your Duty;		968	Letter Sherid	25
I would not give such Language to a Dog, faith and troth		985	Mary to Sher	4
LANGUAGES				
All Languages I can command,		915	Riddle 1	27
LANGUID				
Languid like a love-sick maid,		937	Riddle 24	D 41
LANGUISH				
To languish in this odious Town,		748	Stel Distress	71
To languish in this odious Town,		752	Stel Wood-Park	87
LANGUISH'D				
Had sigh'd and languish'd, vow'd, and writ,		703	Cadenus Vaness	542
LANK				
Soon make my Dame grow lank and spare:		230	Prog of Poetry	12
But we doubt that our Purses will quickly grow lank,		287	Bank Down	14
Meager and lank with fasting grown,		759	Receipt Youth	7
I'm lean and am lank;		853	Lady's Lament	72
LANTHORN				
Knockt down the Boy, the Lanthorn broke;		781	Mullinix Tim	268
By their lanthorn Jaws and Leathern,		835	Legion Club	147
LAOCO'N				
Laoco'n struck the Outside with his Spear,		139	City Shower	51
LAP				
In Summer, on my verdant Lap:		410	Dial Rich Marb	86
Nor leaps upon his Master's Lap,		607	Beasts Confess	209
With Tyger slabb'ring in her lap;		761	Bec's B-Day	40
Upon the Queen of Sheba's lap.		776	Mullinix Tim	110
Him on my Lap you never more should see;		882	Pastoral Dial	47
Lies in the Lap of Ladies fine.		942	Probatur Alit	14
LAP-DOG				
They set the very Lap-Dog barking;		450	Modern Lady	179
Or other Lap-Dog Cures for Sores.		494	Panegyr Swift	36
LAPLAND				
Like Lapland Witches in a Sieve:		254	Bubble	92
LARDER				
Secure the Larder, and the Vault.		885	Rev Market-Hill	84
LARGE				
And some, to be large cyphers in a state,		36	Ode Sancroft	59
That be my thought when some large bulky writ		44	To Congreve	35
Take, youth, these thoughts, large matter to employ		53	Temple Ill	67
Altho' the bore be ne'er so large,		66	Problem	44
Cutt off large Slices to be fry'd:		91	Bauc & Phil 1	60
Cut out large Slices to be fry'd:		112	Bauc & Phil 2	28
Fill'd a large Jug up to the Brink;		112	Bauc & Phil 2	30
Bor'd a large Augre-hole in the Image's Breech;		336	Serious Poem	72
Libertas bears a large Import;		348	Whitshed Motto	11
Have large proportion'd Roots that grow		393	Modern Poets	3
Takes a large Dram of Citron Water.		446	Modern Lady	47

		PAGE	TITLE	LINE
LARGE	**(CONTINUED)**			
The Pleasure of so large a Grant	. . . .	493	Panegyr Swift	7
Thus you have my Case at large,	. . . .	631	Epistle Lady	43
So large to grasp the Circle round;	. . . . . .	641	On Poetry	30
First, this large parcel brings you tidings	. . . .	753	Gift for Bec	5
Spy a Building large and lofty,	. . . .	829	Legion Club	2
With a Dozen large Vessels my Vault shall be stor'd,	.	867	Grand Question	13
His large Dominions under Ground.	. . . . . .	903	Death Daphne	18
Of Dan's large Nose, in modern Saphick,	. . . . .	993	On Picture	3
. . . say is (tho' written somewhat at large) trim and clean;		1024	Nim-Dan-Dean 2	D 17
The segment so large 'twixt your reason and rhyme is,	.	1026	Sheri Circles	6
LARGELY				
By adding largely to my Years:	. . . .	556	Death of Swift	106
Must own, that Pain is largely paid	. . . . . .	731	Stella, Poems	111
Are largely paid for all your time.	. . . . . .	893	Panegyr Dean	196
LARGER				
Who blend it into folly's larger heap,	. . . . .	45	To Congreve	62
Sid's Rod was of a larger Stride,	. . . . . .	134	Magician's Rod	53
"No larger Income dost thou Crave.	. . . . . .	476	Epist on Epist	36
A larger Sacrifice in Vain you vow;	. . . . . .	771	Horace 1, 14	33
LARGEST				
Then call this verse, that speaks her largest aid,	. .	44	To Congreve	27
As Animals of largest Size	. . . .	81	Vanbrug House	81
As Animals of largest Size	. . . .	109	V's House	123
Then print it in the largest letter,	. . . . . .	469	Birthday Song	279
LARGLY				
Made up so largly in thy Mind.	. . . .	722	Stel B-Day '18	8
LARK				
He chanc't to spy a Clergy Lark;	. . . . . .	513	Answer Fable	46
Himself the Lark, my Lord the Pheasant:	. . . .	514	Answer Fable	52
A Lark he is, and such a Lark	. . . .	514	Answer Fable	53
A Lark he is, and such a Lark	. . . .	514	Answer Fable	53
This Lark was hated in the Wood,	. . . . . .	514	Answer Fable	61
So Nightingal and Lark adieu,	. . . .	515	Answer Fable	105
LARKS				
In roasting larks, or making laws:	. . . .	901	Dean's Reasons	78
LASH				
My hate, whose lash just heaven has long decreed	. . .	47	To Congreve	133
Except to lash some grand Delinquent.	. . . . .	190	Faggot	30
I think I have now got him under my Lash;	. . . .	265	Apollo	66
Below the Lash of Snarlers Jokes.	. . . . . .	501	Doctor Delaney	46
Bestow that Libeller a Lash.	. . . .	515	Answer Fable	91
That Scribbler lash, who neither knows,	. . . . .	515	Answer Fable	95
To punish Thieves, or lash a Suburb Wench.	. . . .	537	Mr. Pulteney	6
His Zeal was not to lash our Crimes,	. . . . .	549	Life of Swift	136
And feels the Lash, and faintly screams;	. . . .	582	Young Nymph	42
Still to lash, and lashing Smile,	. . . . . .	634	Epistle Lady	139
And all their Brother Dunces lash,	. . . . . .	652	On Poetry	355
To lash the Lewdness of the Age;	. . . . . .	781	Mullinix Tim	254
Lash them daily, lash them duly,	. . . . . .	835	Legion Club	156
Lash them daily, lash them duly,	. . . . . .	835	Legion Club	156
And at each Lash I feel the Smart	. . . . . .	1005	Sheridan's Sub	33
Of Lash laid on by you.	. . . .	1005	Sheridan's Sub	34
LASH'D				
"It must be Ridicul'd, or Lash'd.	. . . . . .	548	Life of Swift	118
When We are lash'd, They kiss the Rod;	. . . .	561	Death of Swift	217
"Expos'd the Fool, and lash'd the Knave:	. . . .	565	Death of Swift	316
"He lash'd the Vice but spar'd the Name.	. . . .	571	Death of Swift	460
I have laugh'd, and lash'd them round.	. . . . .	638	Epistle Lady	248
As his betters are us'd, shall be lash'd round the ring,		1027	Sheri Circles	19
LASHES				
"Then, since you dread no further Lashes,	. . . . .	550	Life of Swift	201
LASHING				
But lashing one another round:	. . . .	189	Faggot	20
Still to lash, and lashing Smile,	. . . . . .	634	Epistle Lady	139
LASS				
A Lass so sweet	. . . .	442	Ballyspellin	59
O, could I earn for thee, my lovely Lass,	. . . .	882	Pastoral Dial	49
Fit for Lad or Lass,	. . . .	952	Asparagus	2
Of a Lass or a Lad;	. . . .	953	Oysters	10
How could you forget so ungratefully a lass?	. . . .	977	Dean to Sherid	41
LASSES				
By buxom Lasses--Some repented	. . . .	182	Horace 2, 1	52
Our Lasses fair	. . . .	441	Ballyspellin	31
LAST				
And has at last redeem'd the Mighty Prize	. . . .	8	Ode to King	81
In the last wretched Remnant of his Days;	. . . .	10	Ode to King	141
But always with a stronger relish of the Last.	. . .	22	Ode Athenian	215
Most fall at last to Interest, Folly, and Abuse.	. . .	24	Ode Athenian	277
And vanisht to an empty Title in the Last.	. . .	25	Ode Athenian	287
We find in you at last united grown.	. . . . . .	28	Ode to Temple	61
Yet at the last the Box sweeps all away.	. . . .	29	Ode to Temple	80
Forever green and flourishing 'twill last,	. . .	29	Ode to Temple	85
Till at last tir'd with loss of Time and Ease,	. . .	30	Ode to Temple	133
To mend dilapidations in the last?	. . . . . .	40	Ode Sancroft	179
And swallow'd them at last, or flung them down.	. .	40	Ode Sancroft	197
Death's sting is swallow'd up in victory at last,	. .	40	Ode Sancroft	201
Last year, a Lad hence by his parents sent	. . .	46	To Congreve	115
Last just as long as ev'ry cuckow's note:	. . .	47	To Congreve	130
Th' appeal of dullness in the last resort:	. . . .	53	Temple Ill	88

LAST   (CONTINUED)   PAGE   TITLE   LINE

Forsook by hopes, ill fortune's last relief, ...   54 Temple Ill   109
Since hope his last and greatest foe is fled, ...   55 Temple Ill   127
So because I had been buying things for my Lady last   69 Mrs Harris Pet   3
  Night,
To a small Cottage came at last   . . . .   91 Bauc & Phil 1   50
To a small Cottage came at last;   . . . .   111 Bauc & Phil 2   18
And thought whose Sow had farrow'd last: . . . . .   115 Bauc & Phil 2   132
When on a Day, which prov'd their last, ...   116 Bauc & Phil 2   151
And last, my Vengeance to Compleat, ...   121 Apollo Outwit   61
Poor Britain shall have Peace at last;   . . . . . .   168 Peace Dunkirk   2
"At last--and so the Story ends.   181 Horace 2, 1   48
In your last Offices be quick: . . . .   204 In Sickness   24
The last, as boundless as the Wind;   . . . .   215 To Mr. Delany   15
Blew his last Breath to sink the lighter Scale. . . . .   235 Elegy on Demar   34
At the last Trumpet, unprepar'd, ...   241 Run Bankers   55
There sprawl'd a while, at last got out, ...   255 Bubble   131
My Sister transcrib'd it last Night, to his Sorrow,   265 Apollo   67
Is dead at last without evading.   . . . .   282 Journal   104
Last Night arriv'd Clem and his Wife.   283 Journal   118
Yet, when his Sand was out, we find at last, ...   285 Elegy Boat   21
A rooted Pox to last for ever.   . . . .   295 Prog Marriage   166
The last loud trump must wake him now: . . . . . .   296 Satiric Elegy   6
A Victim to the last Essays   . . . .   295 Horrid Plot   153
Gallants, next Thursday night will be our last, . . .   309 Billet Players   55
Or if at last, I needs must blab it, ...   311 To Ford   5
But since you are convinc't at last   . . . . . .   315 To Ford   111
For fear the First Drop might as well be his Last: . .   337 Serious Poem   112
And when his last Speech the loud Hawkers did cry, . .   399 Tom Clinch   11
Last Friday Night, as Neighbours use, ...   408 Dial Rich Marb   5
He whisprd publick things at last, ...   422 Ireld   33
Her last Night's ill Success repeats, ...   447 Modern Lady   72
At last they hear the Watchman knock, ...   453 Modern Lady   282
The Bank where last he set his Toe, ...   456 Dean Smedley   42
Find the last Garrat where they lay, ...   505 Doctor Delaney   149
At last the Nightingal comes in, ...   514 Answer Fable   63
That Hope at last remain'd behind;   . . . . . .   528 Lady's Dres Rm   88
Produce at last thy dormant Ducal Patent: . . . . .   538 Mr. Pulteney   10
Forgets the Place where last he din'd: . . . . .   556 Death of Swift   88
"Last Year we thought him strong and hale;   . . . . .   557 Death of Swift   112
They must be verify'd at last.   . . . .   558 Death of Swift   146
"Last Monday to the Pastry-cooks.   563 Death of Swift   260
"And Mr. Henly's last Oration: 563 Death of Swift   278
And, last to make the Matter sure, ...   586 Strephon Chloe   63
While all the gross and filthy last.   . . . . . .   591 Strephon Chloe   234
How long the Stuff is like to last;   . . . . . .   592 Strephon Chloe   294
Contrive your Pile to last for Life;   . . . . . .   593 Strephon Chloe   302
The Leavings of his last Night's Pot   . . . . . .   594 Cassinus Peter   27
The Swain at last, with Grief opprest, ...   595 Cassinus Peter   39
Those Beauties that might ever last.   . . . . . .   595 Cassinus Peter   54
At last, the Point was fully clear'd;   . . . . .   598 Problem Solved   31
I must confess, on Friday last, ...   602 Beasts Confess   15
A hundred Fees last Easter Term.   604 Beasts Confess   86
Foretell a storm to last till night.   . . . . . .   618 Scandal Poem 1   32
Foretel a Storm to last till Night.   . . . . . .   624 Scandal Poem 2   26
A Duel fought last Night at Two, ...   696 Cadenus Vaness   320
Last Night was so extremely fine, ...   696 Cadenus Vaness   326
At last she spitefully was bent   . . . . . .   697 Cadenus Vaness   338
Was that, last Sunday in the Ring?   . . . . . .   699 Cadenus Vaness   385
I said her Face would never last.   . . . . . .   699 Cadenus Vaness   387
At last he ventur'd to complain: . . . .   704 Cadenus Vaness   573
He came to take his last Adieu.   . . . .   705 Cadenus Vaness   593
Attends us first, and leaves us last: . . . . .   708 Cadenus Vaness   685
On Virtue's Basis fix'd to last, ...   711 Cadenus Vaness   782
Or whether he at last descends   . . . . . .   712 Cadenus Vaness   822
Gave her own Reasons last; and then   . . . . . .   713 Cadenus Vaness   852
The Court, so made his last O yes!   . . . . . .   714 Cadenus Vaness   885
The First but a Rebus, the Last but a Dean.   716 Answer Rebus   6
For should this Ferment last too long, ...   731 Stella, Poems   132
At last grown prouder than the Devil   . . . . . .   746 Stel Distress   23
At last grown prouder than the <Devil>, ...   750 Stel Wood-Park   21
Without an Ounce of last Year's Flesh, ...   759 Receipt Youth   15
And still continued by the last: . . . .   765 Stel B-day '26   64
Resolve to stand it out the last;   . . . . . .   774 Mullinix Tim   42
But keep your Swearing to the last.   . . . . . .   780 Mullinix Tim   238
The last Invaders trampling on the first: . . . . .   793 St. Pat's Well   84
Till, God knows why, at last it burst.   . . . . .   796 Traulus 1   18
'Tis Time at last to spare his Ink, ...   799 Traulus 1   101
Since the House is like to last, ...   830 Legion Club   41
Last trolled forth a gentle Swine   . . . . . .   849 Old Thorn   41
Receive its last and deadly Wound, ...   850 Old Thorn   51
At last out it comes.   . . . .   854 Lady's Lament   110
At last comes the Troop, by the Word of Command   870 Grand Question   99
Throws the last shilling in his purse, ...   878 Robbin & Harry   2
His fund may last to five and fifty.   . . . . . .   878 Robbin & Harry   16
But, when at last usurping Jove   894 Panegyr Dean   253
I last get up, am first a-bed;   . . . .   918 Riddle 4   40
And drive at last all Secrets out: . . . . . .   920 Riddle 6   16
The last Result of all Designs: . . . .   921 Riddle 7   12
And find a resting Place at last.   . . . . . .   923 Riddle 7   78
Till I eat the World at last.   . . . .   930 Riddle 16   D 4

```
LAST                (CONTINUED)                          PAGE    TITLE            LINE
      I shall, for Method Sake, begin with the last.    . . .    967 Letter Sherid      12
      Well, punners and rhymers must have the last word.  . .    976 Dean to Sherid      8
      At last I'm fairly forc'd to botch for't.    . . . . . .   993 On Picture          9
      Makes thy Verse smooth, and makes them last.   . . . .    1021 Nim-Dan-Dean 1   D 14
      Be last at Work,    . . . . . . . . . . . . . .          1035 Servants Maxim       3
LASTED
      Which lasted near two thousand years, . . . . . . .       490 Dialogue           34
LASTING
      Of England's Glory, and her lasting Joy.    . . . . .      13 Ode to William   D 48
      Gives murmuring passage to a lasting wave;   . . . . .     49 To Congreve        188
      While, Stella to your lasting Praise     . . . . . .      739 Stel B-day '21      1
      Some lasting Pleasure in the Mind,    . . . . . .        764 Stel B-day '26     30
      Like Walls, more lasting without Mortar:    . . . . .   1021 Nim-Dan-Dean 1   D 22
LASTLY
      But thirdly and lastly, it must be allow'd, . . . . .     263 Apollo             15
      And lastly for Stella, just out of her Prime,   . . .     266 Apollo            103
      Lastly, let his Gifts be try'd,    . . . . . . .          800 Traulus 2          43
LATE
      That Restless Tyrant, who of late    . . . . . .          10 Ode to King       119
      Which 'tis a shame to see how much of late    . . . .     24 Ode Athenian      254
      Disturb the present Mitre, as that fearful storm of late,  40 Ode Sancroft      192
      Since, happy Saint, since it has been of late    . . . .  42 Ode Sancroft      240
      Said, how a late report your friends had vex'd,   . . .   47 To Congreve       143
      Be what it will; late near yon whisp'ring stream,  . . .  51 Temple Ill         13
      Late I beheld on every face appear;    . . . . . .        52 Temple Ill         40
      Say, whence it comes that thou art grown of late   . . .  53 Temple Ill         83
      Of late indeed the Paper-Stamp    . . . . . . . .        172 Horace 1, 7        43
      Came early, and departed late:   . . . . . . . .        173 Horace 1, 7        79
      "A certain Doctor is observ'd of late,   . . . . . .     195 Author Himself     43
      He sues for Pardon, and repents too late.   . . . . .    195 Author Himself     52
      Bless you late and early,   . . . . . . . .              246 Irish-Feast        45
      The Nation too late will find    . . . . . . . .        259 Bubble            217
      'Tis late, the old and younger Pairs,    . . . . . .     280 Journal            55
      She can't abide to stay out late.   . . . . . . .        293 Prog Marriage      98
      He answer'd, that a Dog of late    . . . . . . .         298 Horrid Plot         3
      "But, Pallas, you've apply'd too late,   . . . . . .     304 Storm              37
      When late a Feminine Magician,    . . . . . . .         354 Simile Silver      19
      To vindicate his late Offence:   . . . . . . . .        379 Apology Lady C    130
      Too lately found! to lose him late!    . . . . . . .     388 Manly Virtue      142
      <Meath> Smiles for the Joynture, though gotten, so late,  430 Dicky Dolly        19
      Had not the Fleet gone out too late,   . . . . . . .     463 Birthday Song     102
      And if you chance to come too late   . . . . . .        468 Birthday Song     257
      "Ill suit with those profess'd of late:    . . . . .     549 Life of Swift     147
      Than from Experience find too late   . . . . . .        591 Strephon Chloe    243
      What makes thee lie a-bed so late?   . . . . . . .       594 Cassinus Peter     30
      Mr. Dean, You come too late:    . . . . . . . .         630 Epistle Lady       28
      (Late, very late, O, may he rule us.)   . . . . . .      655 On Poetry         430
      (Late, very late, O, may he rule us.)   . . . . . .      655 On Poetry         430
      Too late with Grief she understood,    . . . . . . .     700 Cadenus Vaness    434
      Disdain'd to enter in so late.   . . . . . . . .        711 Cadenus Vaness    771
      Resentments for her late Disgrace;    . . . . . . .      713 Cadenus Vaness    845
      And then before it grew too late,    . . . . . . .       722 Stel B-Day '18     15
      And that her Beauty, soon or late,    . . . . . . .      723 To Stella           3
      To which (though late) shall Stella rise.   . . . . .    725 To Stella          54
      Late be her death, one gentle nod,   . . . . . . .       762 Bec's B-Day        57
      These Scriblers grow so bold of late,   . . . . . .      783 Tim and Fables     31
      Virtue herself would now return too late.   . . . . .    793 St. Pat's Well     86
      Poor Bishop Judas, late repenting, dies;   . . . . .     806 Judas               2
      I am, as now too late I find,   . . . . . . . .         899 Dean's Reasons     11
      Whether some late departed Toasts    . . . . . . .       905 Death Daphne       75
      Soon or late, my date is done,    . . . . . . .         937 Riddle 24        D 43
      And thus I am fully reveng'd for your late tricks,   . .  977 Dean to Sherid     47
      Tho' you and your Come-rogues keep him out so late . . .  986 Mary to Sher       16
      . . .out so late at this Time of Year, . . . . . . .     1014 Swift to Sheri     10
LATE-HEAD
      I remember my late-head    . . . . . . . . .            1014 Swift to Sheri     26
LATELY
      The Queen has lately lost a Part    . . . . . . .         96 On the Union        1
      With shame, I have too lately known;   . . . . . .       215 To Mr. Delany       2
      Are by Robert Ballentine lately brought over;   . . . .  236 Excellent Song      2
      My Sister has lately depos'd upon Oath,   . . . . .      264 Apollo             37
      But the Secret is this; I did lately intend    . . . .   265 Apollo             73
      We lately fix'd our Viceroy there:   . . . . . .        269 Apollo's Edict   D  2
      Descending lately from the Skies,    . . . . . . .       302 Storm               2
      Had lately honour'd with a <Mitre>.   . . . . . .       302 Storm               8
      Too lately found! to lose him late!    . . . . . . .     388 Manly Virtue      142
      Than those on which you lately writ,   . . . . . .       489 Dialogue           22
      Brazen hilted lately burnish'd,   . . . . . . . .       573 Helter Skelter      7
      Lately taken out of Lim--    . . . . . . . .            574 Helter Skelter     28
      Did not an Earl but lately Vote    . . . . . . .         773 Mullinix Tim       13
LATENT
      The Latent Wiles, and Tricks of State,   . . . . . .     340 Arch-Bish Dub      11
      Which had been latent in her breast.    . . . . . .      755 Stella '23         24
      'Bout latent Charms beneath my Cloaths;   . . . . .     1004 Dan J's Reply      22
LATEST
      Where Thou, our latest Proselyte, shalt share:    . . .  162 Toland's Invit      8
      My latest tribute here I send    . . . . . . . .        608 Know Not What       1
LATH
      Already dwindled to a Lath;    . . . . . . . . .        293 Prog Marriage     105
```

```
                                                        PAGE   TITLE              LINE
LATIAN
    In some old Greek or Latian Bard,      . . . . . .  479 Epist on Epist        120
LATIMER
    Old Latimer preaching did fairly describe   . . . . 803 Irish Bishops          1
LATIN
    A Fryer would needs show his Talent in Latin;   . - .  76 Lady B- B-            2
    And Latin, vilest of the three:            . . . . 434 Answer Paulus          79
    Dunkin has been for Latin fam'd--translate.  . . . . 667 Epig Carthy 4    D    4
    There's Latin too that you may see  . . . . . . . 779 Mullinix Tim          215
LATONA'S
    From you, as from Latona's son.  . . . . . . .     177 To Lord Harley        32
LATTER
    The Fortunes of his latter Scene,    . . . . . . . 481 Libel on D- D-        46
    May he at his latter End . . . . . . . . . . .     801 Traulus 2             51
    I much suspect you mean the latter, ah Sly-boot!  . . . 1003 Dan J's Reply     6
LAUD
    He'll teaze you with King Charles and Bishop Laud,  . 166 Toland's Invit      42
LAUGH    SEE HORSE-LAUGH
    And what I us'd to laugh at in Romance,   . . . . .   8 Ode to King          62
    Do laugh perhaps at theirs, and pity mine and me. . . .  18 Ode Athenian       90
    I laugh at the grave Answer they will make,   . . . .  19 Ode Athenian      121
    And can you think the wise forbear to laugh  . . . . .  46 To Congreve       107
    She seem'd to laugh and squawl in Rhimes,  . . . . . 150 Corinna             15
    Leave John of Bucks, come here and laugh.  . . . . . 188 Scriblerus 6         4
    Men laugh at one another's Cost;   . . . . . . . . 217 To Mr. Delany         74
    And the loud Laugh proclaims the War;   . . . . . . 218 To Mr. Delany         80
    When at a Play to laugh, or cry,   . . . . . . . . 415 Woman's Mind           3
    Fleer, and gibe, and laugh, and flout;   . . . . . . 523 Betty Grizette       32
    he's loud in his laugh & he's coarse in his Jest  . . . 540 Charac Walpole      2
    Yet laugh our hearts out, one and all.   . . . . . . 545 Life of Swift       14
    They'd laugh, to see me make a rout,   . . . . . . 546 Life of Swift         50
    If I laugh at Whig and Tory;   . . . . . . . . . 636 Epistle Lady          193
    I to laugh, and you grow wise.  . . . . . . . . . 638 Epistle Lady          274
    Must laugh at her capricious Choice.   . . . . . . 702 Cadenus Vaness        509
    Since I must laugh, or cannot live,   . . . . . . . 747 Stel Distress         57
    Then give those Rascals cause to laugh.  . . . . . 778 Mullinix Tim          178
    But, Oh, how we laugh,   . . . . . . . . . . .     857 Lady's Lament         187
    Will laugh in their sleeves: I can tell you they watch  979 Dean to Tho: S     36
        for't.
    I pass now where you fleer and laugh  . . . . . . 1004 Dan J's Reply        25
LAUGH'D
    Apollo laugh'd till he was sick,   . . . . . . . 321 First of April         15
    And, how you laugh'd at every Joke:   . . . . . . 480 Libel on D- D-         8
    "But laugh'd to hear an Idiot quote,   . . . . . . 572 Death of Swift       473
    I have laugh'd, and lash'd them round.  . . . . . 638 Epistle Lady          248
    But laugh'd at their own silly joking.   . . . . . 755 Dingley Brent          6
    And, Madam, I laugh'd till I thought I shou'd split.  873 Grand Question      174
LAUGHING    SEE EVER-LAUGHING,OUT-LAUGHING
    Laughing as if he'd burst his Sides:   . . . . . . 108 V's House             70
    "We oft, are Laughing in our Sleeve.   . . . . . . 545 Life of Swift         10
    Runs laughing up to tell the Queen.   . . . . . . 559 Death of Swift        180
    Is by Laughing, not by Storming.   . . . . . . . 637 Epistle Lady          230
LAUGHLIN
    Laughlin O Enagin,    . . . . . . . . . . .       246 Irish-Feast           46
LAUGHS
    The Son laughs that got, the hard gotten Estate,  . . 430 Dicky Dolly         20
LAUGHT
    They laught at such an Irish Blunder,   . . . . . 353 Wood Ironmongr        29
LAUGHTER
    For so sad a Tale is no Subject of Laughter.  . . . 430 Dicky Dolly          18
    Rude Laughter seeming like to burst;   . . . . . . 448 Modern Lady          128
    But, e'er you sell your self to Laughter,  . . . . . 591 Strephon Chloe      231
    His Humour well our Laughter might command,  . . . . 669 Epig Carthy 16   D    3
LAUNCH
    Strait the Muse turns the Helm, and I launch out again;  32 Ode to Temple    195
LAUREAT
    A laureat make that is no poet;  . . . . . . . .   876 To Dean Swift         18
LAUREL
    And now a Laurel wreath she brings from far,  . . . .  16 Ode Athenian        18
    And pluckt a Laurel branch (for Laurel was the first   16 Ode Athenian        27
        that grew,
    And pluckt a Laurel branch (for Laurel was the first   16 Ode Athenian        27
        that grew,
    Only the Laurel got by Peace  . . . . . . .        29 Ode to Temple         81
    And drop his laurel at Apollo's feet.   . . . . . .  49 To Congreve         186
    <Farts> like a Laurel in the Flames.   . . . . . .  66 Problem              40
LAVISHLY
    So the Wit that is lavishly thrown away here,  . . . . 716 Answer Rebus        17
    Say then more than they; nay, lavishly flatter,   . . 819 Archbi Cashel       13
LAW
    Of Kingdoms, without Faith or Law.   . . . . . .    96 On the Union          12
    "Must I, against all Right and Law,   . . . . . . 154 Widow and Cat    D   21
    By Law of Arms became your Prey,   . . . . . . . 154 Widow and Cat    D   34
    With Forty Things more: Now hear what the Law says,  . 236 Excellent Song      3
    If Law be such a partial Whore,   . . . . . . . 392 Young's Satire        45
    Nor knew in law his A, B, C.   . . . . . . . .     436 Answer Paulus        122
    The Law so strictly guards the Monarch's Health,  . . 533 To Mr. Gay          77
    "More favour'd, than the Church by Law:   . . . . 550 Life of Swift        169
    "Pervert the Law, disgrace the Gown,   . . . . . . 568 Death of Swift       385
    "Not Strains of Law, nor Judges Frown,   . . . . . 570 Death of Swift       427
    With some Law but little Justice,   . . . . . . . 574 Helter Skelter       31
```

LAW   (CONTINUED)   PAGE   TITLE   LINE
      To rise in Church, or Law, or State, ...   641 On Poetry   40
      For Poets, Law makes no Provision: . . . .   641 On Poetry   49
      For Law and Gospel both determine   . . . .   647 On Poetry   227
      They never pass'd for Law in Courts;   . . . .   690 Cadenus Vaness   113
      A wholesome Law, Time out of mind, ...   694 Cadenus Vaness   257
      Who knows in Law, nor Text, nor Margent, ...   812 Bro Protestant   27
      But where his deep law is, few mortals yet know: . . .   815 Yahoo's   12
      That serjeant at law, whom we call Kite the Second,   . 817 Yahoo's   67
      Patrick astore, who was him made this law?   . . . . .   841 Ballad   D   11
      "It's a pity a Prelate should die without law;   . . .   843 Ay and No   17
      O law! the sweet Gentleman! look in his Face;   . .   870 Grand Question   94
      To common law, or common sense;   . . . .   876 To Dean Swift   20
      Necessity, the Tyrant's Law, ...   922 Riddle 7   23
      On such an Occasion the Law gives Relief.   . . . . .   943 Probatur Alit   46
LAW-BOOKS
      She threw her Law-books on the Shelf, ...   691 Cadenus Vaness   140
LAWFUL
      (If it may lawful be   . . . .   28 Ode to Temple   51
      Takes a French Play as lawful Prize, ...   107 V's House   58
      Then said his Lordship with a Smile, I must have
          Lawful Cash,   342 Upon His Grace   35
      Becomes his Brother's lawful Heir: . . . .   366 Answer Delaney   14
      To what your lawful Perquisites amount.   . . . . . .   533 To Mr. Gay   66
LAWN
      Sit clad in lawn of purer woven day, ...   41 Ode Sancroft   235
      Nor could atchieve the promis'd Lawn, ...   495 Panegyr Swift   82
      Though it would raise him to the Lawn: . . . . . .   604 Beasts Confess   104
      Through all thy Land, in Armour, Fur and Lawn.   . .   792 St. Pat's Well   56
      To slender Threads, may sometimes pass for Lawn.   . .   806 Judas   16
LAWN-SLEEVES
      To give thee Lawn-Sleeves a Mitre and Rotchet,   . .   518 Dean Hang Rape   45
LAWREL
      His Lawrel now must only be a Cypress Wreath,   . .   9 Ode to King   105
      The Lawrel, which adorns thy Head;   . . . .   182 Horace 2, 1   66
      The Lawrel so, by Poets worn, ...   458 Paddy's Charac   9
      Tom having earn'd a Twig of Lawrel, ...   458 Paddy's Charac   14
      Can <piss> upon his lawrel crown.   . . . .   620 Scandal Poem 1   110
      Can <piss> upon his lawrel Crown.   . . . .   626 Scandal Poem 2   108
LAWREL'S
      Let all his barren Lawrel's fade   . . . .   482 Libel on D- D-   67
LAWRELS
      Would you not wish his Lawrels cropt?   . . . . . .   554 Death of Swift   26
LAWS
      Upon a rubbish Heap of broken Laws   . . . .   9 Ode to King   102
      Transcending Nature's ordinary Laws, ...   10 Ode to King   132
      Britannia stript from her sole Guard the Laws,   . .   12 Ode to William   D   21
      Against all Logick and concluding Laws, ...   19 Ode Athenian   108
      By sober, Philosophick Laws, ...   65 Problem   14
      For by the Laws of Gravitation, ...   127 Little House   11
      May He whom Nature's Laws obey, ...   258 Bubble   209
      A Post so fill'd, on Nature's Laws entrenches;   . .   285 Elegy Boat   11
      Your Foes, triumphant o'er the Laws, ...   312 To Ford   29
      Apollo's patron of the laws;   . . . .   433 Answer Paulus   22
      Next, as the Laws of Song require, ...   461 Birthday Song   21
      Defend your liberties and laws.   . . . .   487 Irish-Club   16
      And call the laws of wisdom fate, ...   490 Dialogue   42
      As Laws of Cookery require, ...   529 Lady's Dres Rm   101
      "In Senates sit, at making Laws;   . . . .   549 Life of Swift   163
      But now, by Friendship's sacred Laws, ...   596 Cassinus Peter   91
      For framing Laws to govern States;   . . . .   641 On Poetry   28
      Had Women been the Makers of our Laws;   . . . . .   662 Upon Ladies   5
      Far better than consulting Laws.   . . . .   690 Cadenus Vaness   135
      And Pallas, if she broke the Laws, ...   695 Cadenus Vaness   264
      Of foreign Customs, Rites, and Laws;   . . . . . .   697 Cadenus Vaness   353
      This pedlar, at speaking and making of laws,   . . .   815 Yahoo's   16
      Let them rave of making Laws;   . . . .   831 Legion Club   50
      In roasting larks, or making laws: . . . .   901 Dean's Reasons   78
      Which alien seems from Nature's Laws;   . . . . . .   923 Riddle 8   11
      By us forms his Laws, and Rules, ...   931 Riddle 18   D   11
LAWYER
      The Writings drawn, the Lawyer fee'd, ...   222 Prog of Love   22
      Orphans around his Bed the Lawyer sees, ...   364 On Dreams   23
      The lawyer is a common drudge, ...   435 Answer Paulus   87
      The Lawyer swears, you may rely on't, ...   603 Beasts Confess   79
      And, what no Lawyer ever lack'd, ...   687 Cadenus Vaness   23
      One Lawyer to each Side was nam'd.   . . . .   713 Cadenus Vaness   843
      The Sum of what each Lawyer said;   . . . .   713 Cadenus Vaness   851
      But this skip of a Lawyer, where the De'el did he grow?   814 Yahoo's   7
      A Lawyer o'er his Hands and Face, ...   904 Death Daphne   35
      The Lawyer must forget his Pleading, ...   916 Riddle 1   31
      Physician, Lawyer, and Divine, ...   922 Riddle 7   29
LAWYER'S
      Sit light upon a lawyer's mind: . . . .   433 Answer Paulus   52
      You, who are skill'd in lawyer's lore, ...   489 Dialogue   7
      The Lawyer's Fees, the Statesman's Bribes.   . . . .   922 Riddle 7   20
LAWYERS
      True lawyers, for the wisest ends, ...   432 Answer Paulus   11
      To weigh her priests, the lawyers, gold.   . . . . .   433 Answer Paulus   36
      To prove, that lawyers are so wretched;   . . . . .   433 Answer Paulus   44
      What heavy burthens lawyers lay   . . . .   434 Answer Paulus   62

```
LAWYERS      (CONTINUED)                                    PAGE   TITLE            LINE
    What burthens lawyers undergo.  . . . . . . . .         434 Answer Paulus       70
    Damn'd Lawyers and Judges, Damn'd Lords and Damn'd      576 Place Damn'd         9
        Squires,
    Because our Lawyers all agree,  . . . . . . . .         821 Dr. Rundle          59
    Let Lawyers bawl and strain their Throats,  . . . .     930 Riddle 15        D  25
LAY
    The Tyrant Death lay crouching down,  . . . . . .         7 Ode to King        39
    And Sisiphus lay sleeping on his Stone.  . . . . .        9 Ode to King        97
    But lay the scene just here at Farnham school.  . . .    46 To Congreve       114
    These Men are Saints I'll lay my Life  . . . . .         92 Bauc & Phil 1      82
    The Plot as yet lay deep, and so  . . . . . .          108 V's House          85
    While the poor Child lay fast asleep.  . . . . .       150 Corinna             8
    Whene'er he chanc'd his Hands to lay,  . . . . .       156 Fable of Midas     15
    Lay by your White Staff & gray Habit,  . . . . .       187 Scriblerus 4     D 15
    His other Self, his Money lay.  . . . . . . .          235 Elegy on Demar     48
    The Moon lay safe behind the Cloud.  . . . . . .       253 Bubble             80
    "Sisters, said she, my Life I'll lay,  . . . . .       322 First of April     55
    Ah never lay thy Head to Rest!  . . . . . . .          361 Grace's Answer     14
    Lay all my fine Plantations waste,  . . . . . .        410 Dial Rich Marb     69
    Where Power and Titles scatter'd lay,  . . . . .       412 Desire Possess     24
    And, as he now expiring lay,  . . . . . . . .          413 Desire Possess     53
    Yet, whence proceeds this Weight we lay  . . . . .     414 Censure            17
    What heavy burthens lawyers lay  . . . . . . .         434 Answer Paulus      62
    Unwilling Muse begin thy Lay,  . . . . . . . .         445 Modern Lady        34
    "I'd lay my Life he never went:  . . . . . . .         451 Modern Lady       201
    Shall at their snowy feet lay down:  . . . . . .       465 Birthday Song     168
    "Their Loads they all on Satan lay:  . . . . . .       497 Panegyr Swift     134
    The true, the genuine sweet'ning Lay?  . . . . .       497 Panegyr Swift     143
    Find the last Garrat where they lay,  . . . . .        505 Doctor Delaney    149
    Of all the Litter as it lay;  . . . . . . .           526 Lady's Dres Rm      8
    There Cerberus lay watching in his Den,  . . . .       538 Mr. Pulteney       25
    Wisely on me lay all the Blame:  . . . . . . .         558 Death of Swift    170
    The Lad lay swallow'd up in Spleen;  . . . . . .       594 Cassinus Peter     10
    And half unsmoakt, lay by his Side,  . . . . . .       594 Cassinus Peter     24
    Lay now aside all Thoughts of Fame,  . . . . . .       646 On Poetry         183
    Lay humbly at your Monarch's Feet;  . . . . . .        647 On Poetry         224
    Lay Grubstreet at each others Doors:  . . . . .        652 On Poetry         346
    When on my sickly Couch I lay,  . . . . . . .          726 To Stella          97
    In Lucass's by chance there lay  . . . . . . .         782 Tim and Fables      3
    For that one Gift to lay on Hands:  . . . . . .        821 Dr. Rundle         44
    Lay thy paltry Priviledge aside,  . . . . . . .        832 Legion Club        71
    Or of his own, or Smedly's Lay,  . . . . . . .         893 Panegyr Dean      221
    I lay a Prisoner twenty Years;  . . . . . . .          926 Riddle 9           21
    Would, as he lay under, cry out, Sirrah, yield:  . .   967 Letter Sherid      16
    For the sake of your senses wou'd lay an embargo.  . . 976 Dean to Sherid     30
LAY-HER
    To find an easy Place to lay-her.  . . . . . . .       207 Fable Bitches       6
LAY-MEN'S
    Secur'd by Numbers from the Lay-men's Gibes;  . . .    194 Author Himself     20
LAY'D
    But soon as e'er he lay'd it down,  . . . . . . .      132 Magician's Rod      3
    But when he lay'd it down, as quick  . . . . . .       132 Magician's Rod     13
LAYD
    A duty might be layd on linnen  . . . . . . . .        422 Ireld              50
LAYING
    An act for laying down the Plough,  . . . . . . .      422 Ireld              51
LAYN
    We should not thus have layn forlorn;  . . . . . .     409 Dial Rich Marb     32
LAYS
    Nor stoops to take the Staff, nor lays it down,  . . . 210 Earl of Oxford      9
    Thalia, tell in sober Lays,  . . . . . . . .          278 Journal             1
    Your scurvey Lays,  . . . . . . . . . . . .           440 Ballyspellin        4
    "When thou thy humble Lays do'st offer  . . . . .     476 Epist on Epist     32
    She wipes it clean, and lays it by.  . . . . . .      581 Young Nymph        12
    Then in a Play-Book smoothly lays 'em.  . . . . .     581 Young Nymph        16
    And that, for Elegiack Lays.  . . . . . . . .         650 On Poetry         296
    Thick her arguments she lays on,  . . . . . . .       906 Daphne             11
    At least, I'm well assured, that no Folk lays  . . .  988 Letter Dr Sh-n     26
LAZY
    Grown lazy, foggy, fat, and dull:  . . . . . . .      231 Prog of Poetry     22
    Will agitate the lazy Flood,  . . . . . . . .         759 Receipt Youth      31
    Why will you place in lazy Pride  . . . . . . .       896 Panegyr Dean      293
    Witness his lazy, lousy son!  . . . . . . . .         950 Upstart          D 10
LAZY-HILL
    To Lazy-Hill retiring from his Court,  . . . . .      284 Elegy Boat          7
LD
    When wise Ld <Berkeley> first came here,  . . . .      62 Discovery           1
    My Ld, sd Bush, a Friend and I  . . . . . . .          63 Discovery          33
    When my Ld shakes him by the hand  . . . . . . .      421 Ireld              20
    His Ld ship as Wharton  . . . . . . . . . .           423 Carterets Arms      6
LDSHP
    No Protestant Prelate, His Ldshp or Grace  . . . .    522 St. Cecilia's       9
LE'PARD
    Spotted over like a Le'pard!  . . . . . . . .         522 Betty Grizette      4
LEAD     SEE WHITE-LEAD
    He's a Gold Pencil tipt with Lead.  . . . . . .        61 Lady Tablebook     30
    Lead them a Dance of many a Mile,  . . . . . .         79 Vanbrug House       5
    Lead 'em a Dance of many a Mile,  . . . . . . .       106 V's House           5
    White Lead, and Lusitanian Dish.  . . . . . .         227 Prog of Beauty     60
    Love with White lead cements his Wings,  . . . .      227 Prog of Beauty     61
```

447

LEAD	(CONTINUED)	PAGE	TITLE	LINE
White lead was sent us to repair	. . . .	227	Prog of Beauty	62
White Lead can plaister up a Cleft,	. . . . . .	229	Prog of Beauty	114
To lead you thither, as Pell-mell,	. . . . .	313	To Ford	62
Smith's Dust, and Copper, Lead and Brass,	. . .	344	Prometheus	4
While Ignorance, with Brain of Lead,	. . . . .	449	Modern Lady	134
And Rufa with her Combs of Lead,	. . . . . .	450	Modern Lady	168
The Lead yon Critick's Quill contains,	. . .	500	Doctor Delaney	15
Sweat, Dandriff, Powder, Lead and Hair;	. . . .	526	Lady's Dres Rm	24
"He lov'd the Dean. (I lead a Heart.)	. . . .	562	Death of Swift	239
Tho' you lead a blameless Life,	. . . .	633	Epistle Lady	99
Lead me to the Chrystal Mirrors,	. . . . . .	661	Love Song	19
Gold becomes Lead, touch'd lightly by thy Pen.	. . .	668	Epig Carthy 12	D 2
To lead thee, as a Staff directs the Blind,	. . . .	770	Horace 1, 14	17
I'll lead the Van, keep you the Rear.	. . . . .	780	Mullinix Tim	230
Crack the Stones, and melt the Lead;	. . . . .	830	Legion Club	26
I lead you to a nobler Scene;	. . . .	889	Panegyr Dean	86
Thy Hand as dry and cold as Lead,	. . . . . .	905	Death Daphne	95
But all I delight in is Pieces of Lead;	. . . .	927	Riddle 11	D 6
Good Spelling, Master, your Crany has Lead on't.	. . .	1004	Dan J's Reply	36
LEADEN				
Spoil'd his Leaden Crown;	. . . .	7	Ode to King	41
To dig the leaden Mines of deep Philosophy:	. . . .	32	Ode to Temple	190
The Fly'r, altho't had leaden Feet,	. . . . . .	93	Bauc & Phil 1	131
The Flyer, tho't had leaden Feet,	. . . . . .	113	Bauc & Phil 2	71
The leaden Crown devolv'd to thee,	. . . . . .	653	On Poetry	375
But all distinguish thy dull leaden Mass.	. . . . .	670	Epig Carthy 18	D 6
LEADER				
That vagrant leader of the mind,	. . . .	36	Ode Sancroft	57
To think upon a certain Leader,	. . . .	157	Fable of Midas	42
LEADER'S				
Familiar in each Leader's Tent.	. . . .	324	Pethox	18
LEADERS				
The Leaders whom you listed under,	. . . .	775	Mullinix Tim	47
LEADING				
In Leading strings her Infant-Steps to guide;	. . .	531	To Mr. Gay	11
LEADS				
After a mighty Light that leads her wandring Eye;	. .	18	Ode Athenian	67
I mean, the Way which leads to Christ:	. . . . . .	39	Ode Sancroft	161
And follow where he leads the Way:	. . . . . .	270	Apollo's Edict	D 9
As Instinct leads them, in a Puddle;	. . . . . .	294	Horrid Plot	148
And damn'd the Mob, whom now he leads.	. . . . .	498	Panegyr Swift	162
LEAF				
Nor Leaf, nor Fruit, nor Blossom bore.	. . . . .	134	Magician's Rod	70
LEAGUE SEE MONEY-LEAGUE				
And got about a League from Land,	. . . .	96	On the Union	18
Misled them many a League about.	. . . .	412	Desire Possess	16
"By solemn League and Cov'nant bound,	. . . . .	568	Death of Swift	381
LEAGUES				
Travels at least a Hundred Leagues,	. . . .	174	Horace 1, 7	95
Thou'lt tell of Leagues among the Great	. . . . .	181	Horace 2, 1	21
"To tear thy Hedges join in Leagues,	. . . . . .	851	Old Thorn	79
LEAK				
Had now constrain'd the Nymph to leak.	. . . . .	589	Strephon Chloe	164
LEAKS				
That leaks at Ballyspellin.	. . . .	442	Ballyspellin	78
LEAKY				
Each padling in his leaky Boat,	. . . .	256	Bubble	147
There to supply old Charon's leaky Wherry:	. . . .	285	Elegy Boat	24
Lo, Charon from his leaky Wherry,	. . . .	596	Cassinus Peter	83
LEAN				
What makes your Worship look so lean?	. . . . . .	174	Horace 1, 7	122
I'm lean and am lank;	. . . .	853	Lady's Lament	72
With skinny, boney, snip and lean,	. . . . . .	861	Lady Acheson	42
As, who shou'd say, Now, am I Skinny and Lean?	. .	873	Grand Question	176
To be call'd lean by a Skelton, who'd bear it?	. .	1003	Dan J's Reply	18
Eat lean Meat, or chuse,	. . . .	1036	Plague Country	3
LEAN'D				
Advanc't on tiptoe, lean'd his Head	. . . . . .	63	Discovery	27
LEANING				
There leaning near a gentle Brook,	. . . . . .	202	Horace 2, 6	109
LEAP				
Could leap the bounds which part your world and mine;	.	44	To Congreve	30
Leap from the Dunghill in a trice,	. . . . . .	84	Salamander	40
Prepar'd to leap o'er Sticks, or bind 'em.	. . . .	190	Faggot	44
And he who will leap over a Stick for the King	. .	389	Order of Bath	11
Than the barking of Towzer, or leap of a louse?	. .	814	Yahoo's	9
And, like Domitian, leap at Flyes.	. . . . . .	824	Printer Newgat	14
LEAPING				
Ten thousand sunk by leaping in.	. . . .	254	Bubble	108
LEAPS				
With Leaps and with Jumps,	. . . .	245	Irish-Feast	42
And in he leaps, and down he sinks.	. . . . . .	252	Bubble	32
Nor leaps upon his Master's Lap,	. . . .	607	Beasts Confess	209
LEAPT				
He ran, he leapt into the Flood,	. . . .	255	Bubble	130
To save his Life he leapt into the Main.	. . . . .	538	Mr. Pulteney	20
LEARN				
"Learn to disdain their mercenary aid;	. . . . .	55	Temple Ill	140
To learn what Northern Kings design,	. . . . . .	63	Discovery	29
If possible, to learn his Story,	. . . .	171	Horace 1, 7	21

LEARN	(CONTINUED)	PAGE	TITLE	LINE
My State of Health none care to learn;		203	In Sickness	5
From both, we learn to Railly well;		216	To Mr. Delany	31
To learn the Way that Phillis went,		223	Prog of Love	34
From thee our Youth all Virtues learn,		325	Pethox	59
"Learn hence t' excuse and pity me.		380	Apology Lady C	144
Your Int'rest lyes to learn the knack		464	Birthday Song	115
First learn the Science to be dull,		503	Doctor Delaney	111
Irish Nymphs learn Irish Raillery:		523	Betty Grizette	26
O may she better learn to keep		528	Lady's Dres Rm	97
He soon would learn to think like me,		530	Lady's Dres Rm	141
They learn to call a Spade, a Spade.		590	Strephon Chloe	204
Some try to learn polite Behaviour,		592	Strephon Chloe	271
I am now too old to learn:		630	Epistle Lady	30
Conversation learn to relish,		632	Epistle Lady	89
You must learn, if you would gain us,		633	Epistle Lady	113
Learn to relish Truth and Reason.		638	Epistle Lady	272
How shall a new Attempter learn		642	On Poetry	71
Before you learn the Terms of Art:		647	On Poetry	240
Learn Aristotle's Rules by Rote,		648	On Poetry	247
Is but to learn what he can teach,		709	Cadenus Vaness	707
Her Scholar is not apt to learn:		712	Cadenus Vaness	809
Nymph, would you learn the onely Art		732	Verses Vanessa	1
Mark my Address, and learn my Style,		780	Mullinix Tim	235
Cou'd he learn to mount a Ladder:		801	Traulus 2	50
The Fellows learn to know their Distance.		888	Panegyr Dean	56
From you my Chamber-Damsels learn		890	Panegyr Dean	111
And seeks to learn the secret Cause,		923	Riddle 7	81
She declares from her throne you must learn better manners		979	Dean to Tho: S	28
LEARN'D				
Those mighty Epithets, Learn'd, Good, and Great		28	Ode to Temple	59
Or whether, as the Learn'd contend,		324	Pethox	19
He goes to School! he reads! is learn'd!		384	Manly Virtue	32
Make you less virtous, learn'd, or wise.		414	Censure	28
Since first I learn'd to tune a String.		445	Modern Lady	12
As when they scarce have learn'd to spell.		463	Birthday Song	96
"And, sure he must be deeply learn'd---!		547	Life of Swift	76
Have better learn'd to act their Parts.		562	Death of Swift	226
"A Verse from Horace, learn'd by Rote.		572	Death of Swift	474
He had not learn'd to turn his Coat,		604	Beasts Confess	97
And, though you never learn'd to scan verse,		658	On Poetry	D 186
All that was witty, learn'd, and wise,		708	Cadenus Vaness	697
For Stella never learn'd the Art,		725	To Stella	71
The Learn'd in Sciences sublime,		918	Riddle 4	42
LEARN'T				
We learn't to weigh our Gold by Grains.		156	Fable of Midas	22
A Set of Phrases learn't by Rote;		415	Woman's Mind	1
That I have almost learn't to spell:		891	Panegyr Dean	134
LEARNED				
The greatest scorn of Learned Vanity,		21	Ode Athenian	179
Are nobler Subjects for your learned Pen;		31	Ode to Temple	160
If your Money be gone, as a Learned Divine says, d'ye see,		72	Mrs Harris Pet	56
So Learned Patrige could as well		99	Elegy Patrige	53
Fix'd in a lonely, learned Cell,		385	Manly Virtue	48
To get the name of council learned;		435	Answer Paulus	114
The Wise and Learned of our Isle;		475	Epist on Epist	18
Dame Nature as the Learned show,		504	Doctor Delaney	127
When Beasts could speak, (the Learned say		601	Beasts Confess	1
While others of the learned Robe		604	Beasts Confess	87
By learned authors call'd Nubigenae.		619	Scandal Poem 1	62
By learned Authors call'd, Nubigenae.		625	Scandal Poem 2	58
As learned Commentators view		643	On Poetry	103
The Learned met with free Approach,		701	Cadenus Vaness	458
Dreadful Sight! What learned Morgan		838	Legion Club	193
Thus, when the learned and the wise		900	Dean's Reasons	33
When learned Doctors will dispute,		930	Riddle 15	D 22
Or else, to shew their learned Labour, you		1021	Nim-Dan-Dean 1	D 41
But you learned Doctors can make whom you chuse sick.		1029	Dr. Helsham	19
LEARNEDLY				
Can sneer as learnedly as they,		501	Doctor Delaney	49
LEARNEST				
But Carthy, as from him thou learnest,		666	Epig Carthy 1	D 3
LEARNING				
Our Wit and Learning, narrow as our Trade;		19	Ode Athenian	96
Although they praise the Learning and the Wit,		21	Ode Athenian	164
The God of Learning and of Light		22	Ode Athenian	209
Is even the nobler Man, our Learning and our Wit,		24	Ode Athenian	269
But what does our proud Ign'rance Learning call,		27	Ode to Temple	28
Unless I put in Caesar's Learning too,		28	Ode to Temple	67
<Montague> Learning, <Bolton> Eloquence:		164	Toland's Invit	24
They fly from learning, wit, and light:		177	To Lord Harley	20
For wit and learning spoil'd his face.		177	To Lord Harley	28
You see my Learning; but to shorten it,		367	Answer Delaney	41
Thought human Learning wou'd not lessen		375	Apology Lady C	9
Th' inferiour Youth, to Learning led		385	Manly Virtue	39
To Worth and Learning is a Friend.		391	Young's Satire	10
Her Learning mounts to read a Song,		416	Woman's Mind	9
"On Learning how his Bounty flows,		462	Birthday Song	75
His Learning none will call in doubt;		484	Libel on D- D-	140
His Learning, though a Poet said it,		484	Libel on D- D-	141

LEARNING   (CONTINUED)   PAGE   TITLE   LINE
      For learning, probity and truth, ...   490 Dialogue   30
      With Grace and Learning unendow'd, ...   503 Doctor Delaney   88
      What's to be done? shall wit and learning chuse, . . .   506 To a Friend   7
      By Nature, Reason, Learning, blind;   . . . .   579 Day Judgement   12
      On Learning, Eloquence and Wit.   . . . .   655 On Poetry   428
      Of Wit and Learning chief Protector;   . . . .   656 On Poetry   450
      Now Learning, Valour, Virtue, Sense, ...   656 On Poetry   459
      The Queen of Learning gravely smiles, ...   692 Cadenus Vaness   199
      For Learning, Wit, and Wisdom fam'd;)   . . . .   708 Cadenus Vaness   691
      In Learning let a Nymph delight, ...   710 Cadenus Vaness   742
      And shew them his wit and his learning; . . . . . .   756 Dingley Brent   9
      But Tom had better Learning.   785 Mullinex Dick   36
      Who crop the Nurseries of Learning here? . . . . .   792 St. Pat's Well   50
      Be empty of Learning, of Insolence full: . . . . .   807 Advice Parson   2
      The Man has Learning, Sense and Morals.   . . . . .   820 Dr. Rundle   22
      How your superior Learning shines   . . . . .   888 Panegyr Dean   63
      In Learning would not know a Line: . . . . . .   915 Riddle 1   30
      A Treasure here of Learning lurks, ...   922 Riddle 7   39
LEARNING'S
      On Learning's high-establish't Throne.   . . . . . .   25 Ode Athenian   295
      For Learning's mighty Treasures look   . . . . .   27 Ode to Temple   35
LEARNINGS
      When Learnings little Houshold did embark . . . . .   16 Ode Athenian   12
LEARNS
      By frequent Practice learns the Trick   . . . . . .   416 Woman's Mind   39
LEARNT
      Who learnt himself that Heresy first   . . . . . .   28 Ode to Temple   53
      They learnt it not at Sermons or at pray'rs. . . . .   275 Epilogue   12
      Which few had learnt enough to prize, ...   384 Manly Virtue   29
      Has learnt his Fables to refine;   . . . . . .   513 Answer Fable   12
      Your Lesson learnt, you'll be secure   . . . . . .   649 On Poetry   275
      Altho' he never learnt to spell.   . . . . . .   650 On Poetry   292
      But what she learnt at Country Fairs;   . . . . .   699 Cadenus Vaness   415
      Hence he learnt the Butcher's Guile, ...   800 Traulus 2   37
      And yet they have learnt the chief Art of a Sov'reign,   805 Irish Bishops   47
      She has better learnt her creed: . . . . . .   907 Daphne   40
LEASE
      As when a Conj'rer takes a Lease   . . . . . .   240 Run Bankers   45
      That only for the Bishop's Lease . . .   .   343 Upon His Grace   46
      Or else I may forfeit my Lease.   . . . .   396 Dog and Thief   16
LEASERS
      But all turn Leasers to that Mongril Breed, ...   794 St. Pat's Well   95
LEASINGS
      Who interrupted him in all his Leasings;   . . . . .   537 Mr. Pulteney   2
      Of Nelly's pertness, Robin's leasings, ...   753 Gift for Bec   7
LEAST
      At least confine the tyrant to his cell.   . . . . .   53 Temple Ill   56
      Five times at least as big as theirs, ...   87 Hist V's House   24
      In such a dreadfull Night at least;   . . . . .   90 Bauc & Phil 1   20
      At least twelve Inches overcast, ...   126 Little House   6
      Scorning to show the least Respect.   . . . . .   133 Magician's Rod   26
      He never meant the least Abuse--   . . . . .   172 Horace 1, 7   66
      Travels at least a Hundred Leagues, ...   174 Horace 1, 7   95
      To your Friends who at least have no Cares but to please   185 Scriblerus 1   5
           you
      Those Men who wore the Breeches least   . . . . .   221 A Quiet Life   47
      An Hundred at least, ...   244 Irish-Feast   11
      A Cubit at least   . . . . .   246 Irish-Feast   63
      As fine as Hampton-court at least.   . . . . .   314 To Ford   90
      You are not in the least at Pains.   . . . . .   361 Grace's Answer   18
      Like'd ev'ry Thing - - - at least thought fit . . . .   379 Apology Lord C   119
      Where Virtue is in least Repute, ...   385 Manly Virtue   65
      When you have nam'd at least a Score   . . . . .   392 Young's Satire   28
      When you have not the least Suspicion, ...   398 Earl of P-b-w   29
      Would make at least a handsom show   . . . . .   422 Ireld   36
      At least, that such complaints are wise: . . . . .   433 Answer Paulus   40
      Hint the least Int'rest of your own;   . . . . .   480 Libel on D- D-   14
      The least deserving of the Pack;   . . . . .   503 Doctor Delaney   86
      Which Celia slept at least a Week in?   . . . . .   527 Lady's Dres Rm   54
      At least, before your Master's Debts are paid. . . .   533 To Mr. Gay   62
      To see him mortify'd at least---.   . . . . . .   546 Life of Swift   40
      As mortal as himself at least.   . . . . .   589 Strephon Chloe   186
      Are lofty'r by a mile at least.   . . . . .   620 Scandal Poem 1   106
      Are loftier by a Mile at least: . . . . .   626 Scandal Poem 2   104
      With some Gifts, at least endow me, ...   631 Epistle Lady   63
      And, where his Genius least inclines, ...   641 On Poetry   23
      And least a Chasm should intervene, ...   653 On Poetry   373
      Half of my Book at least is good.   . . . . .   669 Epig Carthy 15   D   2
      At least, cou'd hardly wish them wrong.   . . . . .   710 Cadenus Vaness   747
      Where Truth has not the least Pretence;   . . . . .   747 Stel Distress   62
      Where Truth has not the least Pretence;   . . . . .   752 Stel Wood-Park   78
      It never makes the least Impression.   . . . . .   798 Traulus 1   64
      Whose Perjury's the least of all their Crimes: . . .   806 Judas   12
      Least we should think ourselves neglected, ...   859 Lady Acheson   6
      A judge, without the least pretence   . . . . .   876 To Dean Swift   19
      Happy, O Market-Hill! at least, ...   877 To Dean Swift   27
      To smile on those who are least worthy.   . . . . .   884 Rev Market-Hill   26
      Then, least upon our first Attack   . . . . .   885 Rev Market-Hill   59
      Offend me with the least Rebuke.   . . . . .   888 Panegyr Dean   60
      To give the least offensive Word;   . . . . .   889 Panegyr Dean   70

LEAST	(CONTINUED)	PAGE	TITLE	LINE	
And, out you squeeze an Ounce at least.		892	Panegyr Dean	186	
At least in what regards the Knight.		902	Dean's Reasons	100	
I feel not the least Love Surprize,		932	Riddle 19	D	3
Nor shall they in the least complain,		934	Riddle 21	D	21
At least, I'm well assured, that no Folk lays		988	Letter Dr Sh-n	26	
. . . or at least not one that's witty, to joke w'ye?		1022	Nim-Dan-Dean 2	D	4
Nor can I the least Diff'rence find,		1033	Ans to Crown	5	

LEATHER

And what is Parchment else but Leather?		99	Elegy Patrige	44	
The Bat, because her Wings are Leather,		99	Elegy Patrige	50	
The Leather sounds, he trembles from within.		139	City Shower	46	
As they did in old Times, make Money of Leather,		287	Bank Down	27	
Except some Leather lost behind.		398	Earl of P-b-w	24	
When Shells and Leather shall for Money pass,		793	St. Pat's Well	93	

LEATHERN

Were now but leathern Buckets rang'd.		93	Bauc & Phil 1	116	
Creep in the Dark from Leathern Cell,		99	Elegy Patrige	54	
Were now but Leathern Buckets rang'd.		114	Bauc & Phil 2	92	
And here's a pair of leathern pokes,		753	Gift for Bec	17	
By their lanthorn Jaws and Leathern,		835	Legion Club	147	

LEAVE

Raise envy's clouds to leave themselves in night,		45	To Congreve	79	
For Leave to build the Poet's Way.		81	Vanbrug House	70	
The Saints would often leave their Cells		90	Bauc & Phil 1	2	
The Saints would often leave their Cells.		111	Bauc & Phil 2	2	
Roughen the Nap, and leave a mingled Stain.		138	City Shower	30	
Leave hunting after Bribes, forget your Tropes:		162	Toland's Invit	6	
Steal by the Back-door out, and leave him there;		166	Toland's Invit	45	
Pray leave me where you found me first.		175	Horace 1, 7	138	
Twelve Coronets, without thy leave!		181	Horace 2, 1	26	
Leave John of Bucks, come here and laugh.		188	Scriblerus 6	4	
That Musick gave her Leave to litter,		208	Fable Bitches	17	
The Guest reply'd,--"My Friend, your Leave,		208	Fable Bitches	31	
And leave his emty Chests in View.		240	Run Bankers	40	
Shall sink, and leave no mark behind it.		255	Bubble	136	
To leave you dry upon the Beach,		258	Bubble	196	
And leave the Flood when he goes in it:		280	Journal	50	
We look for a Salmon, you leave us a Stone.		287	Bank Down	8	
But for a parting Present leave her		295	Prog Marriage	165	
"But, if you'll leave us <Bishop> Judas,		305	Storm	51	
For leave to act in town? 'Tis plaguy dear.		308	Billet Players	18	
Who chose to leave his dearest pledges here,		309	Billet Players	46	
"And not leave one for Invocation.		321	First of April	20	
I own it, and therefore I leave you to seek.		337	Serious Poem	90	
Then come the Poor and strip him so, they leave him not a Cross,		341	Upon His Grace	11	
To leave the Margin wide.		394	Grub-Street	12	
I leave your Contriver, Pope:		410	Dial Rich Marb	82	
Who kindly would leave thee no worse nor no better.		424	Carterets Arms	20	
Then leave him to his Birch:		426	Five Ladies	41	
"Nay, Madam, give me leave to say		452	Modern Lady	248	
"Fie, Madam, leave these little Arts.		452	Modern Lady	257	
(But by his Leave he sinks a Score,)		456	Dean Smedley	34	
Free Leave to play his Secretary,		475	Epist on Epist	9	
Get Leave to sit whene'er you will;		480	Libel on D- D-	4	
And leave us nought but Guts and Garbage,		498	Panegyr Swift	152	
Whom would'st thou resemble? I leave thee a Guesser;		518	Dean Hang Rape	46	
But leave it standing full in Sight		528	Lady's Dres Rm	73	
To 'scape Enquiries, leave the House in Flame.		536	To Mr. Gay	142	
Cou'd never leave the World in quiet---;		548	Life of Swift	104	
"But, still our Monarchy wou'd leave us---.		549	Life of Swift	155	
Will never leave him, till he's dead:		556	Death of Swift	84	
"Pray, do but give me leave to shew 'em;		563	Death of Swift	269	
Yet would rather be hang'd than he'd leave a warm Place.		580	Psyche	6	
For, ev'ry Nymph has Leave to chuse;		595	Cassinus Peter	64	
Then, leave me to despair and dye.		595	Cassinus Peter	72	
To leave one handle for Detraction.		608	Know Not What	8	
We leave the body sweet and sound,		618	Scandal Poem 1	27	
We leave the Body sweet and sound;		624	Scandal Poem 2	21	
Leave to D'Anvers and his Mate,		635	Epistle Lady	173	
Are ills you wisely wish to leave,		676	Parson's Case	15	
Which Crimes aforesaid (with her Leave)		687	Cadenus Vaness	15	
Leave all Things to their Nat'ral Course.		696	Cadenus Vaness	303	
She ventures now to leave the Skies,		712	Cadenus Vaness	830	
I dying leave the Debt unpay'd,		740	Stel B-day '21	18	
You'd leave her Virtues half untold.		742	Stel B-day 22	40	
For when you sigh to leave Woodpark,		748	Stel Distress	69	
Yet, when you sigh to leave Wood-Park,		752	Stel Wood-Park	85	
Shall leave deciding broken Pates,		760	Receipt Youth	47	
Should acting, die, nor leave behind		764	Stel B-day '26	29	
That fly and leave no Marks behind?		765	Stel B-day '26	54	
Yet cannot leave his roguish Tricks;		777	Mullinix Tim	118	
Begs leave to rail, but <damn> his Blood,		797	Traulus 1	55	
For thine, my dear Dick, give me leave to speak plain,		819	Archbi Cashel	15	
Leave them not a Blade of Grass.		839	Legion Club	218	
"Not leave a Thistle on the Land;		850	Old Thorn	75	
To leave something behind:		857	Lady's Lament	200	
"Go, bring me my Smock, and leave off your Prate,		870	Grand Question	83	
Which I must leave the world to guess.		879	Robbin & Harry	54	
But, duly e'er you leave your Station,		893	Panegyr Dean	219	

		PAGE	TITLE	LINE
LEAVE	**(CONTINUED)**			
I'm forc'd to leave a Limb behind.		921	Riddle 6	36
And leave behind their fruitless Wealth.		922	Riddle 7	32
For which all Mortals leave their Home;		922	Riddle 7	52
When thee I leave, I leave my Life.		924	Riddle 8	8
When thee I leave, I leave my Life.		924	Riddle 8	8
Can leave a Mark and give a Smart.		942	Probatur Alit	24
And leave her votaries in disgrace?		950	Upstart	D 20
Leave off swearing		953	Herrings	2
To leave off this passion which does not become you:		976	Dean to Sherid	10
So I'll leave him behind, for I certainly know it,		979	Dean to Tho: S	31
I leave it for the second head.		983	Sher, A Goose	26
By your good Leave, my most profound and bold Sir,		1004	Dan J's Reply	30
You would really on Thursday leave St Catharine		1017	Swift Ans Sher	12
LEAVES				
And form the Leaves, the Branches, and the Fruit.		32	Ode to Temple	174
Peruse my Leaves thro' ev'ry Pait,		60	Lady Tablebook	1
By Leaves of Mulberry is fed;		79	Vanbrug House	30
Under those Sacred Leaves, Secure		119	Apollo Outwit	9
Leaves him a Victim to the vengeful Scot;		195	Author Himself	58
When first Diana leaves her Bed		226	Prog of Beauty	1
In Southern Seas he leaves his Name.		252	Bubble	48
Dan leaves the Earthly Spade and Rake,		279	Journal	32
He dyes, and leaves his mourning Mate		295	Prog Marriage	155
When term is ended, leaves the town,		435	Answer Paulus	93
Those Sacred Leaves that Lightning spares.		458	Paddy's Charac	12
And leaves St. James's in Disgrace.		482	Libel on D- D-	60
That Feilding leaves him far behind.		654	On Poetry	396
Attends us first, and leaves us last:		708	Cadenus Vaness	685
He flies, and leaves the Stars behind,		728	Stella, Poems	36
And leaves the Tartar Phiz, in show		786	Dick, Maggot	13
And leaves a lifeless corpse behind.		900	Dean's Reasons	50
And leaves my Lady in the Suds.		905	Death Daphne	100
LEAVING				
Leaving to Wits the spatious Air,		79	Vanbrug House	25
Leaving the Wits the Spacious Air		106	V's House	25
Leaving the Purple to the Nose.		226	Prog of Beauty	28
Leaving the fiery red behind,		227	Prog of Beauty	35
(The Devils leaving the Possess't)		259	Bubble	215
For leaving company so soon;		292	Prog Marriage	96
By leaving him under the pen of the Dean.		816	Yahoo's	39
By leaving out the needless Vowels,		1021	Nim-Dan-Dean 1	D 23
LEAVINGS				
Take up at best with Lumber and the Leavings of a Fate:		32	Ode to Temple	184
'Twere better you had lickt her Leavings,		591	Strephon Chloe	242
The Leavings of his last Night's Pot		594	Cassinus Peter	27
With Scraps and Leavings to be fed.		735	Stel B-day '20	38
And the Clergy, forsooth, must take up with their Leavings.		804	Irish Bishops	34
LECHMERE				
A Fig for Lechmere, King, and Hambden.		191	Faggot	48
Thus Speech'd it like a <Lechmere>.		153	Widow and Cat	D 20
LECTURE	**SEE CURTAIN-LECTURE**			
Van's Genius without Thought or Lecture		86	Hist V's House	7
LECTURES				
And kisses George, and ends or Lectures:		278	Journal	14
His Pupil might be tir'd with Lectures;		704	Cadenus Vaness	569
That all his Lectures were in vain?		705	Cadenus Vaness	601
LED				
Where none ever led the Way,		26	Ode to Temple	13
We have too long been led astray,		27	Ode to Temple	17
Tho' ne'er so gently led		31	Ode to Temple	147
Led blindly on by gross philosophy and pride,		36	Ode Sancroft	66
Led blindly on by avarice and pride,		39	Ode Sancroft	163
Say, why the Church is still led blindfold by the State?		40	Ode Sancroft	177
By Vow Oblig'd, By Passion led,		120	Apollo Outwit	33
Here various Kinds by various Fortunes led,		138	City Shower	39
The drowsy Tyrant by his Minions led,		364	On Dreams	11
Th' inferiour Youth, to Learning led		385	Manly Virtue	39
Led with amazing Art along		386	Manly Virtue	85
To Arms by Thirst of Honour led,		500	Doctor Delaney	2
"Two Kingdoms, just as Faction led,		566	Death of Swift	351
Steals out her Hand by Nature led,		589	Strephon Chloe	171
Who, led by Folly, fights with Nature;		641	On Poetry	20
Led but a weary Life above.		712	Cadenus Vaness	829
Quite contrary Rebecca's led,		761	Bec's B-Day	21
By holy Zeal inspir'd, and led by Fame,		789	St. Pat's Well	1
I'm in spite of my heart led:		853	Lady's Lament	48
Full Northward, let your Troops be led:		884	Rev Market-Hill	48
How bles't am I by such a Man led!		890	Panegyr Dean	106
Hither by luckless Error led,		896	Panegyr Dean	309
I'm always by my Betters led;		918	Riddle 4	39
And I got thro' the Crowd, tho' not led by a Clew, sick		1029	Dr. Helsham	22
LEE				
Nay, Voiture is as like Tom Lee,		217	To Mr. Delany	63
LEER				
With shameless Visage, and perfidious Leer,		532	To Mr. Gay	34
How Ford would frown, how Jim would leer,		741	Stel B-day 22	19
LEES				
Exalts the Spirits, sinks the Lees.		731	Stella, Poems	130
With Caution drain it from the Lees)		743	Stel B-day 22	76

LEEWARD

	PAGE	TITLE	LINE
By Change of Wind to Leeward Side	96	On the Union	19

LEFT

	PAGE	TITLE	LINE
The mighty Conquest's left for you,	26	Ode to Temple	9
Nor has it left the usual bloody Scar,	28	Ode to Temple	74
No province now is left her but to rail,	38	Ode Sancroft	110
To draw conclusions shall be left to you;	46	To Congreve	112
More than a fade insipid mixture left behind.	50	To Congreve	212
I e'en left her, and came away as wise as I was before.	71	Mrs Harris Pet	47
He left a void Space,	76	Lady B- B-	6
Nor ever left the Chimny side.	94	Bauc & Phil 1	138
The Jack would not be left alone	94	Bauc & Phil 1	140
And left the Choice to his own Breast.	107	V's House	54
Had never left each other's Side;	113	Bauc & Phil 2	76
The Jack wou'd not be left alone,	113	Bauc & Phil 2	78
It left the Forest where 'twas nurst,	134	Magician's Rod	68
"Whose Chariot's that we left behind?	201	Horace 2, 6	70
What Papers Phil had left behind,	223	Prog of Love	44
Where Nothing's left to work upon.	228	Prog of Beauty	80
If neither Cheeks, nor Lips be left.	229	Prog of Beauty	116
To that dear Self he left behind;	235	Elegy on Demar	50
No Money left for squandring Heirs!	240	Run Bankers	25
The Witches left in open Air,	240	Run Bankers	34
And scarce a Crown is left to see the Play:	275	Epilogue	34
The Ghost of old <Damer>, who left not his Betters,	288	Bank Down	41
Then fled, and left his Horn behind	293	Prog Marriage	115
He left behind so great a <stink>.	296	Satiric Elegy	16
She'll not have left one single Prelate:	303	Storm	20
She left him Virtue for a Guard.	306	Storm	78
And left a Chasm profound as Hell:	326	Pethox	96
Both Right and Left, as Fellow-sufferers.	367	Answer Delaney	40
When my Left Ear was deaf a Fortnight,	367	Answer Delaney	42
He left the Town above a Week.	398	Earl of P-b-w	15
Dick left a Pattern few will copy after,	430	Dicky Dolly	16
"My Husband left to pay for Coals:	447	Modern Lady	67
And fair Discretion left the Place,	448	Modern Lady	122
Unlucky Madam left in Tears,	453	Modern Lady	290
He left us a Laconick Sentence,	455	Dean Smedley	18
We left a little Duke behind;	466	Birthday Song	200
Was left to starve, and dye in Wales.	481	Libel on D- D-	52
Was left in Foreign Lands distrest,	482	Libel on D- D-	62
But, wisely left the Muses Hill,	482	Libel on D- D-	65
Shall be, when thou art left unsung;	494	Panegyr Swift	46
Away they fled, and left him as they found him.	536	To Mr. Gay	160
He left his Scut behind, and Half an Ear.	538	Mr. Pulteney	36
He shou'd have left them for his Betters;	548	Life of Swift	98
What Writings had he left behind---?	550	Life of Swift	180
"What has he left? And who's his Heir?	558	Death of Swift	154
"He left the Court in meer Despair.	567	Death of Swift	370
"That Kingdom he hath left his Debtor,	572	Death of Swift	483
In Bed we left the married Pair;	588	Strephon Chloe	145
He left them Virgins as he found 'em.	598	Problem Solved	26
Deaf, giddy, helpless, left alone,	673	His Deafness	1
In Order; on the Left, the Graces:	689	Cadenus Vaness	96
"She left all Business to her Son;	714	Cadenus Vaness	881
Left all below at Six and Sev'n,	714	Cadenus Vaness	888
Nothing but Acid left behind.	731	Stella, Poems	134
And all Your Virtues left unsung:	739	Stel B-day '21	12
And grieve he ever left Pell-mell.	748	Stel Distress	74
And nothing left but Skin and Bone;	759	Receipt Youth	8
The Mother-Kingdom left her Children free;	791	St. Pat's Well	20
And have left us but Three out of Twenty behind 'em.	804	Irish Bishops	24
With a Passage left to creep in,	830	Legion Club	45
When nothing's left, that's worth defence,	843	Epigr Irish	3
For, the Right holds the Sword, and the Left holds the Bridle,)	870	Grand Question	108
With two pence left, walks home in rain.	878	Robbin & Harry	8
Attack the Foe at Left and Right;	884	Rev Market-Hill	46
Your Favours left too long unpay'd;	887	Panegyr Dean	4
And on some Dunghill left to rot.	916	Riddle 1	42
They left me in the Lurch.	1005	Sheridan's Sub	25
I've nothing left to vent my Spleen	1005	Sheridan's Sub	27
When you have not one friend left in town,	1022	Nim-Dan-Dean 2	D 4
When I left you, I found myself of the Grape's Juice sick:	1028	Dr. Helsham	1
But that you left no Clap behind.	1033	Ans to Crown	6

LEG

	PAGE	TITLE	LINE
That's but a counterfeit sore Leg:	91	Bauc & Phil 1	43
But made his Leg and went away.	121	Apollo Outwit	44
John wish't, that he had broke a Leg	224	Prog of Love	83
Your Rev'rence, but to cut one Leg off,	366	Answer Delaney	16
New Vigour to the Leg remaining.	366	Answer Delaney	20
Your bandy Leg, or crooked Nose.	416	Woman's Mind	22
Dear Madam try this Pigeon's leg:	746	Stel Distress	18
The rusty Tongs have lost a Leg	746	Stel Distress	40
Dear Madam, try this Pigeon's Leg;	750	Stel Wood-Park	16
No more that Bry'r thy tender Leg shall rake:	881	Pastoral Dial	17

LEGAL

	PAGE	TITLE	LINE
Is more secure as well as legal.	821	Dr. Rundle	58

LEGEND

	PAGE	TITLE	LINE
As Authors of the Legend write	90	Bauc & Phil 1	6

LEGEND   (CONTINUED)   PAGE   TITLE   LINE
         As Authors of the Legend write;   . . . . 111 Bauc & Phil 2   6
LEGG'D   SEE THREE-LEGG'D
LEGHORN
         Mordanto's landed from Leghorn.   . . . .   398 Earl of P-b-w   18
LEGION
         In him they lodge, and make him Legion. . . . . . 798 Traulus 1   78
         With the Name of Legion Club.   . . . .   829 Legion Club   12
<LEGISLATORS>
         That pack of mimick <legislators>, ... 436 Answer Paulus   133
LEGS
         Has twice two Legs, two hanging Ears; . . . . . . 299 Horrid Plot   46
         Without your Legs, two Legs of Wood . . . . . .   367 Answer Delaney   49
         Without your Legs, two Legs of Wood . . . . . .   367 Answer Delaney   49
         Scorcht were his Shins, his Legs were bare, . . . 594 Cassinus Peter   17
         Between his Legs, to spew or spit in. . . . . .   594 Cassinus Peter   22
         Using four legs whon two were weary. . . . . . . 675 Curate's Compl   4
         "And wound her Legs with ev'ry Bry'r. . . . . .   850 Old Thorn   64
LEIGH
         So the famous Tom Leigh, when quite run a-ground, . . 968 Letter Sherid 19
LEISURE
         With Trembling must thy Leisure wait; . . . . . . 325 Pethox   50
         From my Ailments give me Leisure, ...   632 Epistle Lady   87
         Then at your leisure we'll be witty, ... 780 Mullinix Tim   239
         Tho' Hundreds have employ'd their Leisure, . . . 929 Riddle 14   D 3
LEMNIAN
         And Lemnian God consulting strove, ... 916 Riddle 2   10
LEND
         To thee the Bull will lend his Hide, ... 100 Elegy Patrige   75
         Desires some Friend to lend a Hand . . . . 160 Atlas   8
         Great Ormonde lend thy Gen'ral's Staff: . . . . . 191 Faggot   46
         Though Fear should lend him Pinions like the Wind, . . 210 Earl of Oxford 5
         Lend these to Paper-sparing Pope; . . . .   395 Grub-Street   13
         Nor lend a finger to the labour, ... 434 Answer Paulus   64
         Provided they had Cash to lend.   . . . . 455 Dean Smedley   16
         To Walpole you might lend a Line, ...   468 Birthday Song   255
         Can lend you an Allusion fitter, ... 485 Libel on D- D- 177
         To Hang him all <England> would lend him their Garters; 519 Dean Hang Rape 51
         Should lend your cathedrall to players and scrapers . . 522 St. Cecilia's 4
         Bright Apollo lend thy Choir.   . . . .   661 Love Song   16
         Herald lend the Muse an answer; . . . .   800 Traulus 2   27
         "I wish she wou'd lend you her pretty white Hand, . . 872 Grand Question 149
         If I refus'd to lend them Fire.   . . . . 916 Riddle 2   14
LENDERS
         Bills turn the Lenders into Debters, ... 240 Run Bankers   26
LENDS
         Then Ariadne kindly Lends   . . . .   100 Elegy Patrige   79
         For, ev'ry Coxcomb lends them Rods; . . . . 501 Doctor Delaney   48
         He lends my Lord, what was my Lord's before. . . . . 533 To Mr. Gay   76
LENGTH
         At length 'tis over-blown and past, ...   41 Ode Sancroft   219
         At length, a spark not too well bred . . . . . .   63 Discovery   25
         At length they in the Rubbish spy . . . .   109 V's House   103
         At length to Musick's House she came, ...   207 Fable Bitches   7
         At length a lucky Lover came, ... 222 Prog of Love   19
         The Length of their Skeans.   . . . .   246 Irish-Feast   64
         At length, his Anchor fixt, and Canvas furl'd, . . 284 Elegy Boat   6
         "To move this Walk's untoward Length . . . . . . 379 Apology Lady C 134
         High on a Length of prostrate Wood, ...   393 Modern Poets   12
         At length, presumes to vent his Satyr on . . . . 458 Paddy's Charac   27
         He sunk at length to wasting Age a Prey, ... 669 Epig Carthy 13 D 3
         A Dart of such prodigious Length, ...   703 Cadenus Vaness 517
         Hardly at length he Silence broke, ... 707 Cadenus Vaness 656
         No Length of Time can make you quit . . . . . .   758 Stel B-day '24   49
         She chose a thread of greatest length . . . . .   760 Bec's B-Day   3
         At length his Old Master (I need not him name) . . 816 Yahoo's   36
         Thy Nose's Length and Fame extend . . . .   993 On Picture   28
LENGTHEN
         And hopes to lengthen Life by a Transfusion of Breath,   21 Ode Athenian 183
         To lengthen my breath   . . . . 852 Lady's Lament   43
LENGTHEN'D
         He lengthen'd my Life with a whole Year of Grace. . . 399 Tom Clinch   18
LENT
         He spake, and grudging, lent his Ayd; . . . . . . 108 V's House   75
         And lent them for Money the Backs of his Letters: . . 288 Bank Down   43
         (Fear lent him Wings) for Safety to the Skies. . . . 538 Mr. Pulteney   30
         "To save their sinking Country lent, ... 568 Death of Swift 375
         And keep on Fish perpetual Lent.   . . . .   689 Cadenus Vaness   90
         "But, <Zounds>, by their Looks, they never keep Lent: 872 Grand Question 146
         The dullest Beast and Fish for Lent . . . . . .   941 Letter   39
         Till she lent you her help, you were in a fine twitter: . 977 Dean to Sherid 39
LENTEN
         Should them Ordain for Lenten Diet . . . . 373 Letter D. S-y   67
LEPROSY
         Spreads Leprosy and Baldness round. . . . .   84 Salamander   56
         And, if no Leprosy, a Pox.   . . . .   85 Salamander   68
LESBIA
         Lesbia for ever on me rails; . . . . 679 From Catullus   1
LESLIE
         May serve to wait on Mrs. Leslie: . . . .   886 Rev Market-Hill 100

```
                                                              PAGE   TITLE            LINE
LESS
    Less should I dawb it o're with transitory Praise,   . .   21 Ode Athenian        169
    And by a faint Decription make them less.    . . . . .     21 Ode Athenian        174
    For sure (thought He) it can't be less.    . . . . . .     63 Discovery           32
    To a less noble Substance chang'd   . . . . . . . .        93 Bauc & Phil 1       115
    To a less Noble Substance chang'd,    . . . . . . .       114 Bauc & Phil 2        91
    His Quiet small, his Credit less;    . . . . . . . .      221 A Quiet Life         42
    And to your knowledge there is often less in,    . .     276 Epilogue             45
    His Lading little, and his Ballast less.   . . . . .      284 Elegy Boat            4
    Less corresponding than their Years.   . . . . . .       291 Prog Marriage        36
    (What could he less,) his whole Estate.    . . . . .     295 Prog Marriage       156
    Nor less <Tom-T--d-Man> of true Statesman mold,          364 On Dreams            21
    Less to be fam'd, than to be fed,    . . . . . . . .      385 Manly Virtue         40
    Nor less the other to desire;    . . . . . . . . .        387 Manly Virtue        130
    Yet none was ever less their Debtor.   . . . . . . .      410 Dial Rich Marb       84
    Make you less virtous, learn'd, or wise.   . . . . .      414 Censure              28
    'No woman breathing takes up less;   . . . . . . .       447 Modern Lady          97
    Far less the Rabble roar and rail,   . . . . . . .       450 Modern Lady         186
    As Jove will not attend on less,    . . . . . . . .      475 Epist on Epist        1
    For less than Charly Grattan's School:   . . . . .       478 Epist on Epist      111
    "To Spirits of less gentle kind.    . . . . . . . .      485 Libel on D- D-      170
    Laid out with no less Art than Pains,    . . . . .       494 Panegyr Swift        56
    No less than Reasons of such Weight,   . . . . . .       498 Panegyr Swift       154
    Five Hours, (and who can do it less in?)   . . . .       525 Lady's Dres Rm        1
    Not Love of Beauty less the Heart inflames   . . .       532 To Mr. Gay           19
    No Maid at Court is less asham'd,    . . . . . . .       590 Strephon Chloe      215
    If my wand'ring Head be less    . . . . . . . . .        630 Epistle Lady         17
    Censures less, or less defames?    . . . . . . . .       631 Epistle Lady         68
    Censures less, or less defames?    . . . . . . . .       631 Epistle Lady         68
    Who, with less designing Ends,   . . . . . . . . .       632 Epistle Lady         79
    Scolding moves you less than Merriment.    . . . .       636 Epistle Lady        208
    The Guests in less than half an Hour   . . . . . .       642 On Poetry            63
    In wishing such afflictions less!    . . . . . . .       676 Parson's Case        18
    With chariot less for use than state;    . . . . .       676 Parson's Case        24
    Less modest than the Speech of Prudes;   . . . . .       691 Cadenus Vaness      167
    And said, she valu'd nothing less    . . . . . . .       697 Cadenus Vaness      340
    Much less could his declining Age    . . . . . . .       706 Cadenus Vaness      636
    To like with less Seraphick Ends;    . . . . . . .       712 Cadenus Vaness      823
    And, had her Stock been less, no doubt   . . . . .       735 Stel B-day '20       31
    I grow less equall to the Charge:    . . . . . . .       739 Stel B-day '21        8
    Lest you the town may have less trouble in,    . . .     753 Gift for Bec         23
    No less than Justices o' Quorum,   . . . . . . . .       760 Receipt Youth        45
    Towzer's the less offensive Brute.   . . . . . . .       797 Traulus 1            44
    On their tythes at half-nothing, their priesthood at less:  816 Yahoo's           33
    On a far less Villain's Nose.    . . . . . . . . .       830 Legion Club          20
    Nor is your Skill, or Labour less,   . . . . . . .       892 Panegyr Dean        188
    Who send my mind (as I believe) less   . . . . . .       900 Dean's Reasons       53
    Less useful is her Light than thine;   . . . . . .       919 Riddle 5             10
    Too great for Mortals less than Kings.   . . . . .       924 Riddle 8             16
    Nor less that Shirt, my Rival's Gift,    . . . . .       925 Riddle 8             41
    They bloom in less than half an Hour:    . . . . .       926 Riddle 9              4
    Greater be my size or less,    . . . . . . . . . .       937 Riddle 24         D  36
    Old Jason would have less to brag on.    . . . . .       948 Jason Hassard         6
    Like a woman it keeps in less than it lets out.    .     976 Dean to Sherid       26
    So Dan's the better, tho' the less,    . . . . . .      1004 Dan J's Reply        32
    Nor praise we less that Circumcision,    . . . . .      1021 Nim-Dan-Dean 1    D  11
    Where less than forty, fill a Quart.   . . . . . .      1022 Nim-Dan-Dean 1    D  52
    . . .yet I'll be hang'd, less he   . . . . . . . .      1022 Nim-Dan-Dean 2    D   5
LESSEN
    And far exalted objects lessen by their height:            39 Ode Sancroft       148
    Thought human Learning wou'd not lessen    . . . . .     375 Apology Lady C        9
LESSEN'D
    With lessen'd Lustre in their own;   . . . . . . .       384 Manly Virtue         28
    Thy Toil is lessen'd, and thy Profits double.    . .     521 Stephen Duck          8
LESSENING
    And lessening rivers mourn their fountains dry   . . .   419 Shall Repine          4
LESSENS
    Lessens the Terror of the Sound:   . . . . . . . .       500 Doctor Delaney        8
LESSER
    All lesser ones expire,    . . . . . . . . . . .           9 Ode to King         112
LESSON
    Take this short lesson from the god of bayes,    . . .    49 To Congreve         203
    "He follow'd David's Lesson just,    . . . . . . .       566 Death of Swift      341
    Your Lesson learnt, you'll be secure   . . . . . .       649 On Poetry           275
    A Lesson she alone can teach.    . . . . . . . . .       724 To Stella            34
LESSONS
    Nor will let your Lessons enter.   . . . . . . . .       630 Epistle Lady         34
    So fast, his Lessons lagg'd behind:    . . . . . .       704 Cadenus Vaness      557
    That all his Lessons were not lost.    . . . . . .       705 Cadenus Vaness      605
    Your Lessons found the weakest Part,   . . . . . .       706 Cadenus Vaness      622
    His Lessons wou'd have such Effect,    . . . . . .       709 Cadenus Vaness      727
LEST
    Lest here it live, when perish'd with his own;   . . .    48 To Congreve         168
    Lest he should call our Commonweal,    . . . . .          96 On the Union         15
    So Atlas, lest the pondrous Sphears    . . . . .         160 Atlas                 9
    Lest with the Wicked, Heaven involve the Just?   . .     210 Earl of Oxford       20
    Not saying, lest I go too far,   . . . . . . . .         373 Letter D. S-y        62
    Lest my Mobb's Mouth, being seldom quiet   . . . .       373 Letter D. S-y        66
    Lest that the reader shou'd not know,    . . . . .       456 Dean Smedley         41
    But lest Chronology should vary,   . . . . . . .         456 Dean Smedley         45
    To drive a second, lest the whole should break.    . .   535 To Mr. Gay          134
```

LEST   (CONTINUED)   PAGE   TITLE   LINE

   Then, lest with Greek he over-run ye, ...   648 On Poetry   259
   But lest he shou'd neglect his Studies   . . . . . .   693 Cadenus Vaness   222
   But, lest we should for Honour take   . . . . . .   724 To Stella   23
   Lest you should take them for a Bribe, ...   730 Stella, Poems   84
   Lest you the town may have less trouble in, ...   753 Gift for Bec   23
   But, lest you should my Skill disgrace, ...   760 Receipt Youth   49
   But, lest it might not be so proper, ... 886 Rev Market-Hill   101
   Lest it may more quarrels breed   . . . . 907 Daphne   53
   But lest your Kissing should be spoyl'd, ...   952 Onyons   8

LET

   Let the vain sex dream on, their Empire comes from Us,   24 Ode Athenian   260
   Let us (for shame) no more be fed   . . . . . .   27 Ode to Temple   21
   Let not old Rome boast Fabius's Fate, ...   28 Ode to Temple   70
   Let not the outcasts of this outcast age   . . . . . .   42 Ode Sancroft   261
   And let my friend apply it as he please: . . . . . .   49 To Congreve   204
   And once drawn up, is ne'er let down again.   . . . . . .   50 To Congreve   234
   For, let heaven's wrath enlarge these weary days, . . .   54 Temple Ill   111
   Let Censuring Criticks then think what they list on't,   77 Lady B- B-   REF
   Before one Soul would let 'em in.   . . . . . .   90 Bauc & Phil 1   14
   Give us but Straw, and let us Ly   . . . . . .   90 Bauc & Phil 1   21
   Henceforward let no Statesman dare, ...   96 On the Union   13
   But not a Soul would let them in.   . . . . . .   111 Bauc & Phil 2   14
   Let which I please of all the Nine   . . . . . .   120 Apollo Outwit   30
   Let Stubborn Pride Possess thee long, ...   121 Apollo Outwit   53
   Duly let out a Nights to Steal for Fees.   . . . . . .   125 Descriptn Morn   16
   Who has forty Years let out his Conscience to hire, .   142 New Song   2
   His <Grace> swore by <God>, and her <Grace> let a   143 New Song   18
      <Fart>:
   Then let old Englond make good Chear: . . . . . .   147 Windsor Proph   4
   Let no pretence of Bus'ness make you stay, ...   166 Toland's Invit   39
   Old Read would hardly let him in.   . . . . . .   174 Horace 1, 7   120
   Thou pompously wilt let us know   . . . . . .   180 Horace 2, 1   7
   Nor let such Cares disturb thy Rest.   . . . . . .   182 Horace 2, 1   70
   Then let us both in time grow wise, ...   184 Horace 2, 1   107
   That your Lordship would once let your Cares all alone   185 Scriblerus 1   3
   Let not the whigs our tory club rebuke;   . . . . . .   186 Scriblerus 3   1
   And let me in these Shades compose   . . . . . .   199 Horace 2, 6   D
   Or let it cost Five hundred Pound, ...   199 Horace 2, 6   19
   "Let my Lord know you're come to Town.   . . . . . .   200 Horace 2, 6   24
   'Tis (let me see) three Years and more, ...   201 Horace 2, 6   63
   Let him, like you, observe with Care   . . . . . .   218 To Mr. Delany   99
   Than let you see her dress her Head;   . . . . . .   222 Prog of Love   8
   Nor let the Beaux approach too near.   . . . . . .   228 Prog of Beauty   68
   But, let the Cause be what it will, ...   229 Prog of Beauty   97
   The Dean and his Printer then let us cry Fye on;   . . .   237 Excellent Song   11
   To let your Virtues lye obscure, ...   242 Horace 4, 9   4
   Tho not into the Secret let.   . . . . . .   257 Bubble   164
   Right Trusty, and so forth; We let you to know,   . . .   263 Apollo   1
   And let them be seen by the World if he dare, ...   265 Apollo   63
   Let his Success our Subjects sway   . . . . . .   270 Apollo's Edict   D   7
   And let the secret Head of Nile   . . . . . .   270 Apollo's Edict   D 14
   Nor let my Votaries show their Skill   . . . . . .   271 Apollo's Edict   D 46
   Stay--But let me see how finely will it Sound, ...   274 Epilogue   5
   But when let out, they run and muddle   . . . . . .   294 Prog Marriage   147
   Him let her Marry for his Face, ...   295 Prog Marriage   161
   Let pride be taught by this rebuke, ...   297 Satiric Elegy   29
   Now, let me tell you, plainly, Sir, ...   299 Horrid Plot   43
   To let our company supply their places, ...   307 Billet Players   7
   Stay, let me see-- Three hundred pounds a year, . . .   308 Billet Players   17
   So--let us now for Whisk prepare;   . . . . . .   315 To Ford   113
   Our Money to keep, let us Cut down One more. . . . . .   334 Serious Poem   16
   Howe'er let us try him and see how he'll burn.   . . . .   336 Serious Poem   64
   There is a Chain let down from Jove, ...   345 Prometheus   31
   (Venus was Brib'd to let it pass.)   . . . . . .   345 Prometheus   40
   But, let me now the Words translate: . . . . . .   348 Whitshed Motto   5
   And, let but our Mother Hibernia contrive   . . . . .   351 Wood Insect   13
   Then chuse which you please, and let each bring a Faggot,   352 Wood Insect   39
   But, to this Parchment let the Draper   . . . . . .   354 Simile Silver   25
   Thus, for a Tryal, let me beg of   . . . . . .   366 Answer Delaney   15
   In manly Form to let them see   . . . . . .   384 Manly Virtue   25
   Let courtly Slaves low bend the Knee   . . . . . .   386 Manly Virtue   93
   From him let proud Ambition know, ...   386 Manly Virtue   99
   Then, let them well be dry'd;   . . . . . .   394 Grub-Street   10
   Quoth the Thief to the Dog; let me into your Door, .   395 Dog and Thief   1
   Let me have but your Vote to serve for the Town, . .   396 Dog and Thief   11
   To let me kiss your other shore?   . . . . . .   403 Window Inns 10   D   8
   Then, let him come and take a Nap, ...   410 Dial Rich Marb   85
   For, let Mankind discharge their Tongues   . . . . .   414 Censure   19
   Their Malice, is--to let them talk.   . . . . . .   414 Censure   30
   Let them be sent to Mrs. Harding;   . . . . . .   417 Woman's Mind   59
   No more let fall those precious Tears.   . . . . . .   445 Modern Lady   18
   But let me now a while survey   . . . . . .   448 Modern Lady   116
   "Here Betty, let me take my Drops, ...   451 Modern Lady   206
   "Come, let us play the t'other Round.   . . . . . .   453 Modern Lady   285
   Oh! let him not debase your Thoughts, ...   465 Birthday Song   147
   Let all his barren Lawrel's fade   . . . . . .   482 Libel on D- D-   67
   Let <Prelates>, by their good behaviour, ...   488 Irish-Club   21
   And let not Faction come betwixt.   . . . . . .   503 Doctor Delaney   108
   You have been Libell'd--Let us know   . . . . .   505 Doctor Delaney   159
   There let him starve, and vent his Rage.   . . . . . .   515 Answer Fable   84

LET   (CONTINUED)   PAGE   TITLE   LINE

Let me praise thy Wit unmatcht. . . . .   523 Betty Grizette   12
The Virtues we must not let pass, ...   527 Lady's Dres Rm   59
But let me now, for I can do it well, ...   532 To Mr. Gay   29
Now, let me show how <Bob> and you agree. . . .   532 To Mr. Gay   43
Let all Domesticks feel your gentle Sway; . . . .   533 To Mr. Gay   55
Let due Reward to Merit be allow'd; . . . . .   533 To Mr. Gay   57
Then, let me now by Negatives proceed. . . . .   534 To Mr. Gay   84
Let Will. unheard by thee, his Thunder waste. . . .   538 Mr. Pulteney   12
Let me suppose, two special Friends, ...   546 Life of Swift   52
Let me suppose the Case my own. . . . . .   547 Life of Swift   67
Let Reason and Experience prove. . . . .   554 Death of Swift   12
Then let him have the higher Post; . . . . .   554 Death of Swift   19
"He's dead you say; why let him rot; . . . . .   559 Death of Swift   183
"And Friends would let him have his Way. . . . .   572 Death of Swift   478
Then let us no longer by Parsons be Flam'd, . . .   576 Place Damn'd   15
Nor let her loose to spoil your Trade. . . . .   585 Strephon Chloe   30
Why let it go, if I must tell it-- . . . . .   586 Strephon Chloe   83
Nor let them taste what causes Wind; . . . . .   587 Strephon Chloe   124
Let fly a Rouzer in her Face. . . . . .   590 Strephon Chloe   192
Or when a-bed, to let out Wind. . . . . .   590 Strephon Chloe   218
Let Prudence with Good Nature strive, ...   593 Strephon Chloe   309
Nor let the Zephyr's treach'rous Gale . . . . .   597 Cassinus Peter   109
And could not let a Dunce alone: . . . . .   602 Beasts Confess   24
With this let your Collection end . . . . .   608 Know Not What   2
Let both around my Tomb be plac'd, ...   611 By Dr. Swift   5
And let the friendly Lines they writ . . . . .   611 By Dr. Swift   7
If once we let you have your Swing. . . . .   622 Scandal Poem 1   166
Nor will let your Lessons enter. . . . . .   630 Epistle Lady   34
And let others carve for us. . . . . .   633 Epistle Lady   120
Let them neither starve, nor stuff: . . . . .   633 Epistle Lady   130
Let your Neighbours carve for you. . . . .   634 Epistle Lady   132
Let the Vessel split on Shelves, ...   635 Epistle Lady   161
Let me, tho' the Smell be Noisom, ...   635 Epistle Lady   177
Strip their Bums; let Caleb hoyse 'em; . . . .   635 Epistle Lady   178
Horses thus, let Jockeys judge else, ...   636 Epistle Lady   201
But let no Friend alive look into't. . . . .   643 On Poetry   108
Dear Madam, Let me set your Head: . . . . .   699 Cadenus Vaness   398
Now, said the Nymph, I'll let you see . . . . .   706 Cadenus Vaness   614
For, let a Man be ne'er so wise, ...   707 Cadenus Vaness   668
In Learning let a Nymph delight, ...   710 Cadenus Vaness   742
"And let him use it at Discretion. . . . .   714 Cadenus Vaness   883
Let Melancholy rule supreme, ...   724 To Stella   19
Let Stella's fair Example preach . . . . .   724 To Stella   33
Let Malice look with all her Eyes, ...   730 Stella, Poems   81
Dare you let these Reproaches stand, ...   732 Stella, Poems   139
But let me warn thee to believe . . . . .   735 Stel B-day '20   45
Let me of partiall Fate complain; . . . . .   739 Stel B-day '21   6
That, let what <Dean> soever come, ...   742 Stel B-day 22   45
First, nine Ways looking, let her stand . . . .   743 Stel B-day 22   53
Let her describe a Circle round . . . . .   743 Stel B-day 22   55
A Spade let prudent Archy hold, ...   743 Stel B-day 22   57
Let Stella look with watchful Eye, ...   743 Stel B-day 22   59
(But first let Robert on his Knees . . . . .   743 Stel B-day 22   77
(While there are Houses to be let) . . . . .   746 Stel Distress   43
'Tis true, but let it not be known, ...   757 Stel B-day '24   41
Must let their Cattle range in vain . . . . .   759 Receipt Youth   5
This Day then, let us not be told, ...   763 Stel B-day '26   3
Nor let your Ills affect your Mind, ...   766 Stel B-day '26   81
Let me suppose thee for a Ship a-while, ...   770 Horace 1, 14   7
By <God> says Tim (and let a <Fart>) . . . . .   783 Tim and Fables   19
Unbutton and let down your Breeches, ...   783 Tim and Fables   36
Let the Boys pelt him if they dare; . . . . .   788 Dick's Variety   20
Then let me use you e'er so rough, ...   797 Traulus 1   61
For let him sputter thro' a <Session>, ...   798 Traulus 1   63
And let them rot, or hang, or stink. . . . .   799 Traulus 1   102
Let me now the Vices trace, ...   800 Traulus 2   23
Lastly, let his Gifts be try'd, ...   800 Traulus 2   43
Content, my good <Lords>; but let us change Hands;   805 Irish Bishops   61
His Habitation let all Men forsake, ...   806 Judas   25
And let his Bishoprick another take. . . . .   806 Judas   26
Let Folks in high, or holy Stations, ...   813 Bro Protestant   57
Let Courtiers hug them in their Bosom, ...   813 Bro Protestant   59
For, let us hear the weak Pretence, ...   820 Dr. Rundle   11
These Demoniacs let me dub . . . . .   829 Legion Club   11
Let a royal Grant be pass'd, ...   830 Legion Club   42
Let them, when they once get in . . . . .   831 Legion Club   47
Let them rave of making Laws; . . . . .   831 Legion Club   50
Let them dabble in their Dung; . . . . .   831 Legion Club   52
Let them form a grand Committee, ...   831 Legion Club   53
Let them stare and storm and frown, ...   831 Legion Club   55
Let them, 'ere they crack a Louse, ...   831 Legion Club   57
Let them with their gosling Quills, ...   831 Legion Club   59
Let Sir <Tom>, that rampant Ass, ...   831 Legion Club   63
Let us try some new Expedient; . . . . .   832 Legion Club   76
Let me be allow'd to tell . . . . .   832 Legion Club   85
Whisper'd me, let down your Stick; . . . . .   833 Legion Club   98
Let them stare and stink together; . . . . .   835 Legion Club   154
Let all the world judge. . . . . .   856 Lady's Lament   152
Let you lie at friends houses. . . . . .   858 Lady's Lament   226
I said--why--Let him if he will, ...   859 Lady Acheson   3

```
LET                   (CONTINUED)                              PAGE  TITLE           LINE
     His Manners would not let him wait,     . . . . . . .    859 Lady Acheson         5
     But you, my Life, may let him know,     . . . . . . .    860 Lady Acheson        17
     Let me have your Advice in a weighty Affair.   . . . .   866 Grand Question       2
     First, let me suppose I make it a Malt-House:     . . . 867 Grand Question       7
     Then let us rise, and rest our weary Bums.  . . . . .    882 Pastoral Dial       52
     Come Spaniard, let us from our Farms     . . . . . .     884 Rev Market-Hill     43
     Our Forces let us both unite,     . . . . . . . . .      884 Rev Market-Hill     45
     Full Northward, let your Troops be led:      . . . . .   884 Rev Market-Hill     48
     But, let us on our first Assault     . . . . . . .       885 Rev Market-Hill     83
     Then, (let me see) we'll make the Knight     . . . .     886 Rev Market-Hill     93
     Let others match it if they dare.  . . . . . . . .       887 Panegyr Dean        22
     To let me praise you as my Tutor.    . . . . . . . .     891 Panegyr Dean       130
     Let others with Fanatick Face,     . . . . . . . . .     892 Panegyr Dean       169
     Let never at your Board be known     . . . . . . . .     897 Panegyr Dean       339
     But now, let all his tenants round     . . . . . . .     902 Dean's Reasons     103
     Let ev'ry cottager conspire  . . . . . . . . . .  .      902 Dean's Reasons     105
     I let no Creature see my Face.     . . . . . . . . .     917 Riddle 4             4
     And all I get, I let it fly:     . . . . . . . . .       918 Riddle 4            20
     Another Time I'll let you know.    . . . . . . . . .     928 Riddle 12       D   10
     Let Lawyers bawl and strain their Throats,     . . . .   930 Riddle 15       D   25
     Let the Love-sick Bard complain,   . . . . . . . .       933 Riddle 20       D   13
     Let the happy Swain rejoice,     . . . . . . . . .       933 Riddle 20       D   15
     --Let indignation fire my strains,   . . . . . . . .     950 Upstart         D   21
     Let purse-proud C--n next approach,     . . . . . . .    951 Upstart         D   23
     To a quarrelsome Fellow, cries, Let us be Friends.  .    968 Letter Sherid       28
     But now let us hear what the Muse from your car says.    976 Dean to Sherid       6
     But let me advise you, when next I hear from you,  .  .  976 Dean to Sherid       9
     As to your Spelling, let me see,     . . . . . . . .    1004 Dan J's Reply       34
     . . .to let Alexander know I was here, :  . . . . .     1013 Swift to Sheri       4
     And for his Victuals let a Ragman dish'em.   . . . .    1033 Ans to Crown        18
     Let me my Properties explain,    . . . . . . . . . .    1035 To Quilca            1
LET'S
     Let's not fall out; We all had Share.    . . . . . .      67 Problem             58
     To some snug Cellar let's repair   . . . . . . . .      184 Horace 2, 1        109
     Now let's no more caress thy French,     . . . . . .    373 Letter D. S-y       64
     Where not a Chink let's in the Air;    . . . . . . .    935 Riddle 23       D   15
     Because she let's out more, than e'er she takes in. . .  972 S-'s Ans Sh-d        6
     Let's quarrel no longer, since Dan and George Rochfort   979 Dean to Tho: S      35
LETS
     Through ev'ry Thread it lets in Air;     . . . . . .    231 Prog of Poetry      36
     Thus when an Earthquake lets in Light    . . . . . .    240 Run Bankers         41
     Lets drive at Tom's devoted Noddle,    . . . . . . .    458 Paddy's Charac      24
     Nor lets him sit as Justice on the Bench,    . . . .    537 Mr. Pulteney         5
     Never lets your Mind elope:  . . . . . . . . . .  .     636 Epistle Lady       214
     Lets fall her Knife, or spills the Salt,     . . . .    694 Cadenus Vaness     243
     Punch comes, like you, and lets a <Fart>.   . . . .     777 Mullinix Tim       122
     Like a woman it keeps in less than it lets out.  . .    976 Dean to Sherid      26
LETT
     While there are Lodgings to be lett.     . . . . . .    751 Stel Wood-Park      60
LETTER
     And over and above, that I may have your Excellencies
        Letter,                                               73 Mrs Harris Pet      72
     Enlarg'd in Picture, Size and Letter     . . . . . .     93 Bauc & Phil 1      121
     Improv'd in Picture, Size, and Letter;   . . . . . .    114 Bauc & Phil 2       98
     A Letter on the Toylet sees  . . . . . . . . . .  .     223 Prog of Love        45
     But Six-pence a Letter is monstrous high Wages:    . .  288 Bank Down           48
     Before the Drapier shot a Letter,    . . . . . . . .    353 Wood Ironmongr      35
     No Letter with an Envelope   . . . . . . . . . .  .     395 Grub-Street         15
     Hath sent this Letter by her Maid.     . . . . . . .    446 Modern Lady         63
     Because he never knew a letter.  . . . . . . . . .      463 Birthday Song       90
     Then print it in the largest letter,     . . . . . .    469 Birthday Song      279
     "Then, here's a Letter finely penn'd   . . . . . . .    563 Death of Swift     273
     Than if they never knew a letter.  . . . . . . . .      900 Dean's Reasons      40
     A long-ear'd Beast, and the sixteenth Letter,  . . .    943 Probatur Alit       37
     In reading your Letter alone in my Hackny,   . . . .    972 S-'s Ans Sh-d        1
     When into my hands comes a letter from the droll.  . .  975 Dean to Sherid       4
     And now I must go, and get Saunders to direct this
        Letter,                                              987 Mary to Sher        33
     It is impossible to know by your Letter  . . . . . .   1013 Swift to Sheri       1
     And, if they had not told me there was a Letter from you,
        . . .                                               1013 Swift to Sheri       4
     . . .I should have missed the Letter outright.     . .  1013 Swift to Sheri       4
     Your Letter you'd dated,   . . . . . . . . . .  .      1014 Swift to Sheri      14
     One Letter still another Locks;    . . . . . . . .     1021 Nim-Dan-Dean 1  D   25
LETTERS
     That, they had never known their Letters.    . . . .    240 Run Bankers         28
     That the letters appear'd revers'd on the Pane,  . .    264 Apollo              49
     And lent them for Money the Backs of his Letters:  . .  288 Bank Down           43
     Now Backs of Letters, though design'd    . . . . . .    406 Swift to Pope        9
     Our Letters say a Jesuite boasts   . . . . . . . .      422 Ireld               41
     With Begging, Vain, Familiar Letters.    . . . . . .    479 Epist on Epist     118
     Not sparing even men of letters,   . . . . . . . .      489 Dialogue             6
     "Twas he that writ the Drapier's Letters---!   . . .    548 Life of Swift       97
     Publish my Will, my Life, my Letters.    . . . . . .    561 Death of Swift     202
     Shirts be wrought with different Letters,    . . . .    573 Helter Skelter      23
     When Letters are in vulgar Shapes,   . . . . . . .      643 On Poetry           97
     She might excuse a Man of Letters;     . . . . . . .    705 Cadenus Vaness     590
     Got? <Damn> my Blood I frank my Letters,     . . . .    778 Mullinix Tim       155
     His famous Letters made waste Paper;     . . . . . .    875 Drapier's Hill      17
     To the very coach side, and threaten your letters. . .  978 Dean to Tho: S       4
```

		PAGE	TITLE	LINE
LETTERS	(CONTINUED)			
It never was known that circular letters,		1026	Sheri Circles	1
No Dublin Letters,		1036	Bless Country	2
LEV'LLERS				
For, whate'er theologic lev'llers dream,		41	Ode Sancroft	230
LEVEE				
Saw Poets at his Levee wait.		482	Libel on D- D-	70
Now, Chartres at Sir Robert's Levee,		560	Death of Swift	189
Transform'd to Imps, his Levee wait.		646	On Poetry	208
See, at her Levee crowding Swains		735	Stel B-day '20	23
LEVEE-DAY				
Not thinking it is Levee-Day;		200	Horace 2, 6	26
LEVEES				
Like Peers, have Levees ev'ry Day		239	Run Bankers	15
LEVEL				
No wonder when you raise and level,		477	Epist on Epist	65
by Galloping high, or Level Pace,		957	Cantata	
LEVELL				
The Duke and Dean seem near upon a levell.		678	Dean and Duke	10
LEVELL'D				
Each Pot-gun levell'd at his Head:		500	Doctor Delaney	14
LEVENS				
Ladys, quoth Levens, pray forbear,		67	Problem	57
LEVITY				
It was no levity of mind.		899	Dean's Reasons	4
LEW'D				
To ev'ry lew'd pretender of the town.		48	To Congreve	160
LEWD				
The methods most in fashion to be lewd,		46	To Congreve	118
Born between whores and fops, by lewd compacts,		47	To Congreve	125
They, in their lewd and fashionable prate,		50	To Congreve	217
The dull, the noisy, and the lewd:		178	To Lord Harley	48
Their Meanings lewd, and double 'Entendres.		449	Modern Lady	143
Yet, such a lewd licentious Age		603	Beasts Confess	57
Tho' Lewd and Immoral, be Formal and Grave,		807	Advice Parson	3
But were you as wicked as lewd Aretine		1017	Swift Ans Sher	18
LEWDNESS				
For songs of Loyalty and Lewdness.		650	On Poetry	290
To lash the Lewdness of the Age;		781	Mullinix Tim	254
LEWELLIN				
Lewellin! why?		440	Ballyspellin	19
LEWIS				
And bid Friend Lewis go in quest		171	Horace 1, 7	16
(This Lewis is a Cunning Shaver,		171	Horace 1, 7	17
Lewis his Patron's Humour knows;		171	Horace 1, 7	23
"Lewis; the Dean will be of Use,		199	Horace 2, 6	15
On Lewis all his Bards bestow'd,		657	On Poetry	473
Yet what the World refus'd to Lewis,		657	On Poetry	477
LIAR				
The stupid blockhead and the liar.		950	Upstart	D 16
LIB'LLER				
Papist, and Jacobite, and Lib'ller?		795	Traulus 1	4
LIBATION				
Offer to him a pure Libation;		893	Panegyr Dean	220
LIBEL				
Convey a Libel in a Frown,		450	Modern Lady	192
With each a Libel in his Hand,		505	Doctor Delaney	152
His Heart is through his Libel seen,		514	Answer Fable	75
This was a Libel meant at me;		783	Tim and Fables	30
LIBELL'D				
And Libell'd all the Junta round;		171	Horace 1, 7	38
You have been Libell'd--Let us know		505	Doctor Delaney	159
LIBELLER				
Bestow that Libeller a Lash,		515	Answer Fable	91
LIBELLING				
For libelling the Four-foot Race.		607	Beasts Confess	202
LIBELS				
Shou'd stupid Libels grieve your Mind,		501	Doctor Delaney	43
In Satyrs, Libels, lying Travels!		548	Life of Swift	112
Or Libels yet conceal'd from sight---,		550	Life of Swift	188
Revive the Libels born to dye;		561	Death of Swift	203
Or writing Libels on the <Germans>,		993	On Picture	5
LIBERTAS				
Libertas & natale Solum;		348	Whitshed Motto	1
Libertas bears a large Import;		348	Whitshed Motto	11
Libertas & natale Solum;		349	Whitshed Motto	25
LIBERTIES				
Defend your liberties and laws.		487	Irish-Club	16
LIBERTINE				
No Libertine, nor Over-nice,		171	Horace 1, 7	31
LIBERTY				
That must their doubtful Liberty defend.		12	Ode to William	D 32
A Breach of Liberty, 'tis own'd,		181	Horace 2, 1	27
For Liberty no Champion bolder,		455	Dean Smedley	9
How cheaply had thy Liberty been sold,		531	To Mr. Gay	9
"Fair Liberty was all his Cry;		566	Death of Swift	347
When he hath Liberty to chuse.		607	Beasts Confess	186
And kept their Liberty, or bravely dy'd.		793	St. Pat's Well	82
For Liberty a Champion stout,		820	Dr. Rundle	31
LICE				
Lice from your Body suck their Food;		812	Bro Protestant	35

LICE   (CONTINUED)   PAGE   TITLE   LINE
    Since Lice are Brethren to a <Scot>:   . . . . .   813 Bro Protestant   42
    To call a Swarm of Lice his Brethren?   . . . . .   813 Bro Protestant   48
    In Egypt turn'd the Dust to Lice;   . . . . . .   813 Bro Protestant   50
    And, turn'd to Lice, infest the King: 813 Bro Protestant   54
    Or crack such Lice as his betwixt your Nails?   882 Pastoral Dial   36
    Ten thousand Lice, and ev'ry Louse was gold, ... 882 Pastoral Dial   46
LICENCE
    With Licence to build Castles there: . . . . . .   106 V's House   26
    And, with a licence from our good Lord May'r, ...   307 Billet Players   3
    First get a licence, then produce our ware: . . . .   308 Billet Players   36
    Would grant him Licence to retire, ...   606 Beasts Confess   171
    They'll call it all poetick Licence: . . . . . .   741 Stel B-day 22   28
LICENCES
    For licences shall pay no fees. . . . .   422 Ireld   54
LICENSE
    With License to build Castles there;   . . . . . .   79 Vanbrug House   26
    And license to reside in town;   . . . .   676 Parson's Case   26
LICENTIOUS
    Yet, such a lewd licentious Age   . . . .   603 Beasts Confess   57
LICK
    To lick a Rascal Statesman's Spittle.   . . . . . .   482 Libel on D- D-   82
    To lick a Rascal Statesman's Spittle, ...   495 Panegyr Swift   59
LICKING
    May be proud to be licking a great man's posteriors. . . 817 Yahoo's   69
LICKS
    Soon licks up all unsav'ry steams; . . . .   432 Answer Paulus   8
LICKT
    'Twere better you had lickt her Leavings, ...   591 Strephon Chloe   242
LID
    He lifts the Lid, there needs no more, ...   528 Lady's Dres Rm   81
    So Strephon lifting up the Lid, ...   528 Lady's Dres Rm   89
LIDS   SEE EYE-LIDS
    Which, o'er a British Senate's Lids, ...   133 Magician's Rod   40
LIE   SEE LY,LYE
    There whole herds suspended lie . . . .   35 Ode Sancroft   35
    Religion now does on her death-bed lie, ...   42 Ode Sancroft   251
    Search'd in the nest where every worm did lie . . .   46 To Congreve   89
    But here a Grievance seems to lie, ...   198 Horace 2, 6   D
    They lie open on Purpose, on Counters and Stalls, .   263 Apollo   23
    The Bed in which these Tyrants lie: . . . . .   283 Journal   122
    Here quiet they Lie, in hopes to rise one Day, . . .   431 Dicky Dolly   22
    So long unbishoprick'd lie by, ...   497 Panegyr Swift   147
    But swears how damnably the Men lie, ...   526 Lady's Dres Rm   17
    What makes thee lie a-bed so late?   . . . . . .   594 Cassinus Peter   30
    Brutes find out where their Talents lie: . . . .   640 On Poetry   13
    Lie Snug, and hear what Criticks say.   . . . . . .   644 On Poetry   118
    Is forc'd to lie farther, ...   854 Lady's Lament   84
    Let you lie at friends houses.   . . . .   858 Lady's Lament   226
LIES   SEE LYES,LYSE.
    See where she lies! . . . .   30 Ode to Temple   120
    Whose peevish knowledge thus perversely lies   . . . .   37 Ode Sancroft   84
    See how the double Nation lies; . . . . . .   96 On the Union   7
    And whispers in a thousand Lies;   . . . .   158 Fable of Midas   64
    Beneath this verdant Hillock lies   . . . . . .   235 Elegy on Demar   41
    Here lies Judge Boat within a Coffin.   . . . . .   286 Elegy Boat   37
    That lies in old Wood like a Hare in her Form; . .   351 Wood Insect   18
    In Velvet Cap his Head lies warm;   . . . . . .   410 Dial Rich Marb   65
    Under this Stone, lies Dicky and Dolly   . . . . . .   430 Dicky Dolly   1
    Beneath a dry Canal there lies, ...   478 Epist on Epist   89
    And 'tis as true, or Story lies, ...   495 Panegyr Swift   74
    Made up of Noise, and Impudence, and Lies. . . .   532 To Mr. Gay   42
    Nor, when a Mortgage lies on half his Lands, . . .   534 To Mr. Gay   99
    Yet still St. Stephen's Chappel open lies: . . . .   538 Mr. Pulteney   7
    Lies rackt with Pain, and you without: . . . . . .   554 Death of Swift   28
    With Pains of Love tormented lies; . . . . . .   582 Young Nymph   39
    At some Hedge-Tavern lies in Pawn;   . . . . .   582 Young Nymph   44
    "Here Cassy lies, by Caelia slain, ...   596 Cassinus Peter   77
    Long Bills, and Answers, stuff'd with Lies, . . .   690 Cadenus Vaness   121
    Run o'er their Cant of stupid Lies, ...   697 Cadenus Vaness   332
    For Wit, I wonder where it lies.   . . . . . .   699 Cadenus Vaness   411
    He may be caught with sober Lies;   . . . . . .   707 Cadenus Vaness   669
    To shew you where your Error lies, ...   730 Stella, Poems   90
    'Tis my own Credit lies at Stake.   . . . . . .   741 Stel B-day 22   32
    Behold the Bottle, where it lies   . . . . . .   743 Stel B-day 22   61
    The Virtue lies not in the Place: . . . . . .   752 Stel Wood-Park   90
    Whose Heart in this Four-footed Thing lies.   .   763 Collar Lap-Dog   2
    Whether, your fruitful Fancy lies   . . . . . .   892 Panegyr Dean   159
    Lies in the Lap of Ladies fine. . . . . . .   942 Probatur Alit   14
    But now I smoak where lies the slander,-- . . . .   983 Sher, A Goose   15
LIEUTENANT
    Then, wo be to my Lord Lieutenant, ...   789 Dick's Variety   37
    When told the Lieutenant was just come to Town, . .   809 Epigr Prelate   2
LIEVE
    And think of the sex as you please, I'd as lieve   . . . 976 Dean to Sherid   15
LIFE
    His scrap of Life is but a Heap of Miseries,   . . .   9 Ode to King   107
    And hopes to lengthen Life by a Transfusion of Breath,   21 Ode Athenian   183
    Some she condemns for Life to try   . . . . . .   32 Ode to Temple   189
    I'll be my life but the dull cheat would pass, . . .   48 To Congreve   171
    So would earth's face turn pale, and life decay, . . . 53 Temple Ill   63

LIFE   (CONTINUED)   PAGE   TITLE   LINE
    Assign'd for life to unremitting grief;   54   Temple Ill   110
    . . .for a Conjurer in all my Life.   72   Mrs Harris Pet   61
    These Men are Saints I'll lay my Life   92   Bauc & Phil 1   82
    Thus, happy in their Change of Life, ...   116   Bauc & Phil 2   149
    But aided by the Wind, fought still for Life;   . . .   137   City Shower   24
    During Her Sacred Life, should never come over: . .   144   New Song   36
    Turns Auth'ress, and is Curll's for Life.   150   Corinna   28
    For Life, six hundred Pounds a Year, ... 198   Horace 2, 6   2
    My choicest Hours of Life are lost: 202   Horace 2, 6   106
    To see my Life so fast decline?   203   In Sickness   2
    My Life is here no Soul's Concern.   203   In Sickness   6
    My Life is now a Burthen grown   204   In Sickness   21
    Plac'd you in Life too far behind;   215   To Mr. Delany   6
    Plac'd me in Life too far before;   215   To Mr. Delany   8
    What Use in Life, to make Men frett?   217   To Mr. Delany   71
    I bear it for a quiet Life   220   A Quiet Life   16
    She ne'r before in all her Life   224   Prog of Love   65
    With Life his Country, or his Friend.   243   Horace 4, 9   24
    How prone to change in human life, ... 283   Journal   117
    "Sisters, said she, my Life I'll lay, ... 322   First of April   55
    In Chaos, kindled into Life;   324   Pethox   30
    Are to the Life distinctly seen.   325   Pethox   72
    He took to the Street, and fled for his Life,   . . .   327   Epigram 1   2
    Three Duels he fought, thrice ventur'd his Life   . .   327   Epigram 1   9
    I'll maintain with my Life, is Heraldry Good.   . . .   338   Serious Poem   122
    O may the Fates thy Life prolong!   339   Arch-Bish Dub   5
    The Arts new kindle into Life.   385   Manly Virtue   46
    Congenial Joy, and Life, and Light.   387   Manly Virtue   120
    He lengthen'd my Life with a whole Year of Grace.   . . 399   Tom Clinch   18
    "I'd lay my Life he never went: 451   Modern Lady   201
    They'll find his Life, and Acts, and Freedom,   . . .   494   Panegyr Swift   52
    His Life is safe, I mean his Fame, ... 500   Doctor Delaney   24
    But she valu'd her Honour much more than her Life.   . . 517   Dean Hang Rape   10
    'Twas what all his Life he had practis'd before.   . .   517   Dean Hang Rape   22
    To save his Life he leapt into the Main.   538   Mr. Pulteney   20
    Publish my Will, my Life, my Letters.   561   Death of Swift   202
    "Too soon that precious Life was ended, ... 568   Death of Swift   377
    But, what if he should lose his Life   587   Strephon Chloe   103
    And makes it warm for Dearest Life.   590   Strephon Chloe   208
    Contrive your Pile to last for Life;   593   Strephon Chloe   302
    Shall never but with Life expire.   593   Strephon Chloe   314
    In ev'ry Turn of Life content, ... 602   Beasts Confess   41
    How evil Tongues his Life bespatter: 602   Beasts Confess   48
    Thought the Life of ev'ry Lady   631   Epistle Lady   39
    Tho' you lead a blameless Life, ... 633   Epistle Lady   99
    For private Life, or publick Use?   641   On Poetry   46
    Thy busy, drudging scene of life, ... 676   Parson's Case   6
    A Baby Face, no Life, no Airs, ... 699   Cadenus Vaness   414
    Led but a weary Life above.   712   Cadenus Vaness   829
    As nat'ral Life the Body warms, ... 724   To Stella   11
    My Life, it must endanger yours.   727   To Stella   120
    In all the Habitudes of Life, ... 728   Stella, Poems   15
    All accidents of life conspire   755   Stella '23   21
    They just keep Life and Soul together, ... 759   Receipt Youth   10
    Long Schemes of Life, as heretofore;   764   Stel B-day '26   16
    Reflecting on a Life well spent?   764   Stel B-day '26   36
    Nor prize your Life for other Ends   765   Stel B-day '26   69
    Or give my Scrap of Life to you, ... 766   Stel B-day '26   85
    The various Scenes of mortal Life, ... 781   Mullinix Tim   265
    Like a Butcher doom'd for Life, ... 800   Traulus 2   39
    Nor for my Life will take the Hint.   860   Lady Acheson   16
    But you, my Life, may let him know, ... 860   Lady Acheson   17
    My dearest Life it is surprizing, ... 860   Lady Acheson   31
    It must, and it shall be a Barrack, my Life.   867   Grand Question   26
    "But he maul'd me, I ne'er was so maul'd in my Life; . 873   Grand Question   168
    For your Life, not a Word of the Matter, I charge ye: 873   Grand Question   189
    Is doom'd to be a Beau for life: 879   Robbin & Harry   52
    May I be doom'd for Life to weed in Rain.   882   Pastoral Dial   44
    That I could spend my Life in reading.   891   Panegyr Dean   154
    Should in a country life delight, ... 901   Dean's Reasons   82
    But, while I thus my Life relate, ... 916   Riddle 1   37
    When thee I leave, I leave my Life.   924   Riddle 8   8
    As my thread of life is spun;   937   Riddle 24   D 44
    They'll please to the Life;   953   Oysters   12
LIFE-BLOOD
    Money, the Life-blood of the Nation, ...   239   Run Bankers   9
LIFE'S
    She dares not say her Life's her own.   328   Epigram 3   4
    "He spent his Life's declining Part;   570   Death of Swift   432
    To shine through Life's declining Part.   764   Stel B-day '26   34
    Life's Autumn has no second Spring.   932   Riddle 19   D 24
    Lifeless, Life's perfect Form I wear, ... 935   Riddle 23   D   7
LIFELESS
    And leaves a lifeless corpse behind.   900   Dean's Reasons   50
    Lifeless, Life's perfect Form I wear, ... 935   Riddle 23   D   7
LIFFEE'S
    As much as the Liffee's outdone by the Rhine   1018   Swift Ans Sher   26
LIFFY'S
    To Liffy's filthy side in Dublin;   744   Stel Distress   4
    To Liffy's stinking Tide in Dublin: 750   Stel Wood-Park   28

```
LIFT                                                        PAGE    TITLE         LINE
     For you freely must own you were at a Dead lift;  . . .   77 Lady B- B-        28
     Able to lift it from the Ground;    . . . . . . . .       87 Hist V's House    30
     Would lift her Eyes up to the Ceeling,  . . . . . .      222 Prog of Love      16
     She ventures now to lift the Sash,   . . . . . . .       228 Prog of Beauty    65
     To help our Fancy at a Lift;    . . . . . . . . .        497 Panegyr Swift    125
     Ye Hawkers all, your Voices lift;    . . . . . . .       887 Panegyr Dean      33
LIFTED
     That he might yet be lifted by a Rope.   . . . . . .     285 Elegy Boat        18
LIFTING
     So Strephon lifting up the Lid,     . . . . . . . .      528 Lady's Dres Rm    89
     "Against him lifting up their Heels.   . . . . . . .     569 Death of Swift   406
LIFTS
     Who lifts the Poor, and sinks the Proud,   . . . . .     258 Bubble           210
     How haughtily he lifts his Nose,    . . . . . . .        281 Journal           81
     He lifts the Lid, there needs no more,    . . . . .      528 Lady's Dres Rm    81
     Your Ladyship lifts up the Sash to be seen,   . . . .    870 Grand Question   101
LIGAMENT
     No common Ligament that binds    . . . . . . . .         291 Prog Marriage     33
LIGHT   SEE CANDLE-LIGHT
     He spake, and a dark Cloud flung o're his light,  . . .    8 Ode to King       58
     Whilst at Your Victorious Light     . . . . . . . .        9 Ode to King      111
     For all its Plagiary Light,     . . . . . . . . .         10 Ode to King      125
     With its own Light Your dazling Glory shines,   . . .     11 Ode to William  D  7
     After a mighty Light that leads her wandring Eye;  . .    18 Ode Athenian      67
     The God of Learning and of Light    . . . . . . .         22 Ode Athenian     209
     And on the Terras light.    . . . . . . . . . .           30 Ode to Temple    119
     Whose well-compacted Forms escape the Light,  . . . .     31 Ode to Temple    166
     Which guard the throne by night, and are its light by day:  34 Ode Sancroft     4
     And catch the living landscape thro' a scanty light,  . .  35 Ode Sancroft    30
     In his own balance, false and light,    . . . . .         36 Ode Sancroft     55
     Was but to light Earth's inconsiderable spot.   . . .     36 Ode Sancroft     72
     No deflower'd eye can face the naked light:   . . . .     41 Ode Sancroft    222
     To scribblers, and the god of light and wit;   . . .     45 To Congreve       76
     But can no more obscure my Congreve's light   . . . .     45 To Congreve       80
     Which darts on poets eyes a trembling light;   . . . .    54 Temple Ill        98
     And treads so soft, so easy, and so light,   . . . . .    54 Temple Ill       114
     As hard, as sensless, and as light:    . . . . . .        60 Lady Tablebook     4
     So when I came up again, I found my Pocket feel very      69 Mrs Harris Pet    12
          light,
     Which happ'ning on the Skin to light,    . . . . . .      84 Salamander        54
     Light with its Bottom on the Ground.    . . . . .        126 Little House      10
     The God of Wit, and Light, and Arts,    . . . . .        176 To Lord Harley     9
     They fly from learning, wit, and light:   . . . . .      177 To Lord Harley    20
     For Pallas, with celestial light,   .  . . . . . .       178 To Lord Harley    49
     So gravely, where the Subject's light.    . . . . .      218 To Mr. Delany     88
     For John must neither light nor stop;    . . . . .       223 Prog of Love      36
     Remove them to a diff'rent Light    . . . . . . .        226 Prog of Beauty    23
     Her Body light, she tries her Wings,    . . . . .        230 Prog of Poetry    13
     Because we wish the Earth upon him Light,   . . . . .    234 Elegy on Demar    24
     Cast in his Dart which made three Moydores Light.  . .   234 Elegy on Demar    32
     Thus when an Earthquake lets in Light    . . . . .       240 Run Bankers       41
     Weigh'd in the Ballance, and found Light.   . . . . .    241 Run Bankers       64
     We rise with the Light,     . . . . . . . . . .          245 Irish-Feast       14
     A Cloud arose and stopt the Light,    . . . . . .        253 Bubble            75
     Whilst Stella aforesaid stood by with the Light;  . .    264 Apollo            36
     If I light on a Thought, he will certainly steal it,  .  265 Apollo            59
     They shall not see a Trail of Light:    . . . . .        270 Apollo's Edict  D 35
     How came this wicked Plot to Light:    . . . . . .       298 Horrid Plot        2
     Congenial Joy, and Life, and Light.    . . . . . .       387 Manly Virtue     120
     It darkens Reason's light.    . . . . . . . . .          402 Window Inns 6   D  4
     Seduc'd by some deceiving Light,    . . . . . . .        412 Desire Possess    17
     At once upon his Carcase light;     . . . . . . .        413 Desire Possess    56
     By Phoebus first produc'd to light:    . . . . . .       433 Answer Paulus     27
     Sit light upon a lawyer's mind:     . . . . . . .        433 Answer Paulus     52
     While he, at ease, secure and light,    . . . . .        435 Answer Paulus     91
     "I thank my Stars they are all light;    . . . . .       447 Modern Lady       68
     "Go run, and light the Ladies up:    . . . . . . .       451 Modern Lady      212
     Her Splendor is but borrow'd light;    . . . . . .       465 Birthday Song    176
     To add more Dignity and Light    . . . . . . . .         497 Panegyr Swift    122
     The God of Light could ne'er have been so blind,  . .    532 To Mr. Gay        27
     Apollo, God of Light and Wit,    . . . . . . . .         597 Problem Solved     1
     Though Venus be as light as air,    . . . . . . .        621 Scandal Poem 1   115
     Though Venus be as light as Air,    . . . . . . .        627 Scandal Poem 2   113
     Placing in the strongest Light,    . . . . . . .         633 Epistle Lady      97
     Light on many a Coxcomb's Crown.    . . . . . . .        638 Epistle Lady     254
     Then rising with Aurora's Light,    . . . . . . .        643 On Poetry         85
     Thy Labours, Carthy, long conceal'd from Light,   . .    667 Epig Carthy 5   D  1
     Give Mortals neither Heat nor Light.    . . . . .        700 Cadenus Vaness   443
     For, take it in its proper Light,    . . . . . . .       708 Cadenus Vaness   672
     To publick Light your only Fau't;    . . . . . . .       731 Stella, Poems    102
     Or stop and light at Cloe's Head    . . . . . . .        735 Stel B-day '20    37
     I grieve she ever saw the light.    . . . . . . .        754 Stella '23         6
     Pray, Captain, be pleas'd to light, and walk in:  . .    871 Grand Question   114
     With Hoop expanded wide and light,    . . . . . .        897 Panegyr Dean     323
     Less useful is her Light than thine;    . . . . .        919 Riddle 5          10
     I am bright as an Angel, and light as a Feather,  . .    928 Riddle 13       D  3
     I'm dead except I live in Light.    . . . . . . .        929 Riddle 15       D  4
     For a Riddle is dark, but a Woman is light.   . . .      972 S-'s Ans Sh-d      8
'LIGHTING
     Their Clamour 'lighting from their Chairs,   . . . .     698 Cadenus Vaness   368
```

```
                                                         PAGE    TITLE              LINE
LIGHT'NING
    Like Light'ning dazzled from a-far:     . . . . . .  352 Wood Ironmongr      14
    And Thunder roars, and Light'ning flies!   . . . . . 578 Day Judgement        6
    Compare her radiant Eyes to Light'ning;    . . . . . 628 Scandal Poem 2     154
    That Light'ning comes but from a Cloud.    . . . . . 628 Scandal Poem 2     156
LIGHTED
    Then lighted from his Glitt'ring Coach,    . . . . . 119 Apollo Outwit        6
    By Adam lighted walk up stairs:     . . . . . . . .  280 Journal             56
    In his Journey to <Dublin>, he lighted at <Chester>,  .  517 Dean Hang Rape   7
LIGHTER
    Blew his last Breath to sink the lighter Scale.   . . . 235 Elegy on Demar   34
LIGHTEST
    Mov'd with the lightest Touch of Blame,    . . . . . 730 Stella, Poems       88
LIGHTING
    Which lighting on th' Impostor's Crown,    . . . . . 353 Wood Ironmongr      37
    The Magpye, lighting on the Stock,     . . . . . . . 849 Old Thorn           33
LIGHTLY
    Gold becomes Lead, touch'd lightly by thy Pen.  . . .  668 Epig Carthy 12  D  2
LIGHTNING
    With Lightning in his Eyes, and Thunder in his Hands;   7 Ode to King        50
    Like Lambent Fire the Lightning plays;     . . . . .  29 Ode to Temple       88
    From common Lightning of the Skies,    . . . . . . . 119 Apollo Outwit       10
    Along the plain like Lightning flew:   . . . . . . . 412 Desire Possess      22
    Those Sacred Leaves that Lightning spares.    . . . . 458 Paddy's Charac      12
    And lightning always in his Eyes:   . . . . . . . .  461 Birthday Song       42
    By Lightning shot from Chloe's Eyes?   . . . . . . . 587 Strephon Chloe     110
    Compare her radiant eyes to Lightning:     . . . . . 621 Scandal Poem 1     150
    No Lightning comes but from a Cloud.   . . . . . . . 622 Scandal Poem 1     152
LIGHTS
    Torment, by pissing out their Lights;    . . . . . . 100 Elegy Patrige       92
    Whether the Lights were burning blue.    . . . . . . 112 Bauc & Phil 2       40
    Voiture in various Lights displays     . . . . . . . 216 To Mr. Delany       33
    To snuff the Lights, and stir the Fire,    . . . . . 483 Libel on D- D-     107
    So green in different Lights may pass for blue,  . . . 670 Epig Carthy 18  D  7
LIK'D
    But lik'd neither loss and so quietly dy'd.  . . . . . 430 Dicky Dolly      12
    Which if he lik'd, much good may do him:   . . . . . 549 Life of Swift      133
    Yet lik'd three Footmen to her Chair.  . . . . . . . 693 Cadenus Vaness     221
    They ask'd her, how she lik'd the Play,    . . . . . 696 Cadenus Vaness     318
    Nam'd half the Rates, and lik'd the worst.  . . . . . 698 Cadenus Vaness    383
LIKE   SEE COURT-LIKE,PATR'OT-LIKE,GOD-LIKE,OSTRICH-LIKE,VENUS-LIKE
    Is fix't like Fate among the Stars,      . . . . . .   6 Ode to King        20
    And like a Bold Romantick Knight     . . . . . . . .   7 Ode to King        37
    Like Love, wrapt up in Fire;    . . . . . . . . . .    8 Ode to King        69
    And like that too, make every breast their home)   . . .   8 Ode to King    70
    Who watch Her like a Prey,      . . . . . . . . . .    8 Ode to King        74
    And must be sung, like Argus, into ease    . . . . .   8 Ode to King        76
    Who pine us like a Chronical Disease:    . . . . . .   9 Ode to King        88
    Or has he like some fearful Star appear'd?   . . . . . 10 Ode to King      130
    Our Prince has hit Him, like Achilles, in the Heel,   . 10 Ode to King     142
    We join like Flyes, and Wasps, in buzzing about Wit.  . 18 Ode Athenian      75
    Like the fam'd Hero in his Mother's Cloud,   . . . . . 18 Ode Athenian      88
    Like a just Map to tell the vast Extent    . . . . . 25 Ode Athenian       302
    Like the Philosopher's Stone,   . . . . . . . . . .  26 Ode to Temple       15
    Taught us, like Spaniards, to be proud and poor,  . . . 28 Ode to Temple    56
    I must, like him that painted Venus' Face,   . . . . . 28 Ode to Temple     63
    Their courting a Retreat like you,     . . . . . . . 28 Ode to Temple       66
    Like Lambent Fire the Lightning plays;     . . . . . 29 Ode to Temple       88
    (The Pegasus, like an unruly Horse     . . . . . . . 31 Ode to Temple      146
    Whate'er I plant (like Corn on barren Earth)   . . . . 33 Ode to Temple    210
    Like sun-beams shot at too far distance from a glass;  . 35 Ode Sancroft    24
    Errors like this did old Astronomers misguide,   . . . 36 Ode Sancroft     65
    Who, like hard masters, taught the Sun   . . . . . . 36 Ode Sancroft       67
    Suppose the truth, like all the world, their own;  . . . 37 Ode Sancroft    80
    Each line shall stab, shall blast, like daggers and like  37 Ode Sancroft  91
        fire;
    Each line shall stab, shall blast, like daggers and like  37 Ode Sancroft  91
        fire;
    Like that fantastic medley in the idol's toes,  . . . .  38 Ode Sancroft   138
    Like all transcendent excellence below;    . . . . . 39 Ode Sancroft      146
    Like that prophetic tempest in the virgin reign,  . . . 40 Ode Sancroft    196
    Was, like his Master's Crown, inwreath'd with thorn.  . 40 Ode Sancroft    200
    This wilderness the world, like that poetic wood of old,  41 Ode Sancroft  225
    Where the bless'd spirit lodges like the dove,  . . . .  41 Ode Sancroft   227
    Like a cast mistress to your wicked friend;  . . . . . 44 To Congreve      16
    Like the victorious wren perch'd on the eagle's wing;  . 44 To Congreve    38
    Like the sun's scatter'd beams which loosely pass,  . . 45 To Congreve     63
    For when like stupid alchymists you try    . . . . . 49 To Congreve       207
    The Muse, like some bright country virgin, shows,  . . 50 To Congreve     215
    Current like copper, and as often paid:    . . . . . 50 To Congreve       220
    Like distant echo spent, the spirit dies.  . . . . . 50 To Congreve       230
    At distant hours the mind with forms so like!   . . . 51 Temple Ill         2
    Like antic shapes in dreams, from waking eyes:   . . . 54 Temple Ill      100
    A walking vapor, like thy sister fame.   . . . . . . 54 Temple Ill        102
    Madness like this no fancy ever seiz'd,    . . . . . 55 Temple Ill        147
    Like good King Phys: and good King Ush:    . . . . . 63 Discovery         23
    Love's Fire, it seems, like inward Heat,   . . . . . 65 Problem            7
    <Farts> like a Laurel in the Flames.   . . . . . . . 66 Problem           40
    So she roar'd like a Bedlam,. . . . . . . . . . . .  71 Mrs Harris Pet     45
    . . .like the Devil.)   . . . . . . . . . . . . . .  72 Mrs Harris Pet     54
    With that, he twisted his Girdle at me like a Rope,. . . 72 Mrs Harris Pet  62
```

LIKE (CONTINUED)

	PAGE	TITLE		LINE
Born like a Phoenix from the Flame,	81	Vanbrug House		79
With Christian Nick-names like a Child;	82	Salamander		4
Like Carleton cheap, or fam'd Duruel;	85	Salamander		62
You look like Rogues would rob a House	91	Bauc & Phil 1		40
Like a huge Insect up the Wall,	93	Bauc & Phil 1		106
Like a rich Coat with Skirts of Frize:	96	On the Union		8
Which just like ours, new rigg'd and man'd,	96	On the Union		17
Can like the Stars foretel the Weather;	99	Elegy Patrige		43
Jove Smil'd, and like a gentle God,	107	V's House		51
And, (like a Wag) sat down to Write,	107	V's House		61
Thy House about thee like a Snail;	109	V's House		110
Take Journies in it like a Chaise;	109	V's House		112
Like Bacchus Thou, as Poets feign,	109	V's House		119
Born like a Phoenix from the Flame,	109	V's House		121
Like an huge Snail along the Wall;	113	Bauc & Phil 2		86
His Horse had like to spoil his Hoof.	127	Little House		34
Stood without Motion, like a Stake.	133	Magician's Rod		34
Like Sid's, but nothing near so good;	134	Magician's Rod		60
To break thy Rod like naughty Lad?	135	Magician's Rod		80
And like a Drunkard gives it up again.	137	City Shower		16
But repeats the same Note a whole Day, like a Finch.	143	New Song		8
Was like keeping her Monument always in sight.	144	New Song		38
Thus Speech'd it like a <Lechmere>.	153	Widow and Cat	D	20
"Like Pole-Cat vile be treated?	154	Widow and Cat	D	22
Glitter'd like Spangles on the Ground:	156	Fable of Midas		4
And Tories (dress'd like Waiters) in Disguise.	165	Toland's Invit		30
He hated <Wharton> like a Toad;	171	Horace 1, 7		36
Tho', like a virgin of fifteen,	178	To Lord Harley		69
Impatient to be like their Mothers;	182	Horace 2, 1		54
Who prates like his Grand mere	186	Scriblerus 4	D	8
And not like forty other Fools:	199	Horace 2, 6	D	
Like Bees, are humming in my Ears.	200	Horace 2, 6		50
And begg'd like one both blind and lame;	207	Fable Bitches		8
Though Fear should lend him Pinions like the Wind,	210	Earl of Oxford		5
Slow Vengeance, like a Blood-hound at his Heels.	210	Earl of Oxford		22
Like Porters o'er a Pot of Ale.	216	To Mr. Delany		50
Nay, Voiture is as like Tom Lee,	217	To Mr. Delany		63
Let him, like you, observe with Care	218	To Mr. Delany		99
All Subjects like Dan Jackson's Nose.	218	To Mr. Delany		102
Are us'd like Dick, and bear the Blame.	221	A Quiet Life		58
By others us'd in the like Cases.	223	Prog of Love		50
And, like a Jockey for a Race,	231	Prog of Poetry		39
And up he rises like a Vapour,	231	Prog of Poetry		43
Like Peers, have Levees ev'ry Day	239	Run Bankers		15
They fly like Bats, on Parchment Wings,	239	Run Bankers		23
'Tis like the Writing on the Wall.	241	Run Bankers		52
To be cloath'd like a Carcass would make a Teague mad,	237	Excellent Song		12
Behold it swelling like a Sop.	251	Bubble		16
Like Lapland Witches in a Sieve:	254	Bubble		92
Then like Pactolus we should find	255	Bubble		111
At their Wits end like drunken Men.	256	Bubble		152
Then, like the Dogs of Nile be wise,	257	Bubble		177
To tear you like a foundred Hulk	258	Bubble		199
And you like a Booby, the Bubble can swallow;	265	Apollo		87
Now who but Delany can write like Apollo?	265	Apollo		88
Since Delany has dar'd, like Prometheus his Sire,	266	Apollo		95
Forget he's like a Salamander.	270	Apollo's Edict	D	19
Since Waiting Women like Exacting Jades,	275	Epilogue		15
Dan growing drowsy like a Thief,	279	Journal		39
Like Episodes between the Acts;	280	Journal		62
Form'd like the Triple-Tree near Stephen's-Green;	285	Elegy Boat		34
Like the faint red upon a Pippin	290	Prog Marriage		25
Looks like the Chaplain of the Household,	291	Prog Marriage		62
He like an orderly Divine	292	Prog Marriage		83
Like Pris'ners when their Gall is broke.	313	To Ford		56
To change your Visage like the Moon,	326	Pethox		82
He can Lye like a Courtier, and think it no Scorn,	335	Serious Poem		45
But Dreams are like Oracles, hard to explain 'em,	337	Serious Poem		113
Tho' like the Cybel's Priest he comes,	340	Arch-Bish Dub		25
Appear'd like one continu'd Spec'es,	344	Prometheus		8
That lies in old Wood like a Hare in her Form;	351	Wood Insect		18
Because like a Watch it always cries Click:	351	Wood Insect		21
Unless, like the Dutch, you rather would boyl	352	Wood Insect		37
Like Light'ning dazzled from a-far:	352	Wood Ironmongr		14
Which, as he scatter'd, we like Dolts,	353	Wood Ironmongr		33
Like real Thunder knock't him down.	353	Wood Ironmongr		38
And they like Stars shall Rise and Set.	362	Grace's Answer		50
With like Remorse his Brother of the Trade,	364	On Dreams		17
Or preach, you'd like him scarce the worse.	375	Apology Lady C		12
With native Lustre like her own;	379	Apology Lady C		114
(Rais'd high like some celestial Fire	385	Manly Virtue		53
Like gilded Vapours to the Skies,	386	Manly Virtue		104
And Manly Virtue, like the Sun,	387	Manly Virtue		117
Rip'ning, and kindling like the Sun.	391	Young's Satire		26
Flies like a Squib from Place to Place,	398	Earl of P-b-w		8
He's with you like an Apparition.	398	Earl of P-b-w		30
Shines in all Climates like a Star;	398	Earl of P-b-w		31
Like a Beau in the Box, he bow'd low on each Side;	399	Tom Clinch		10
Who hung like a Hero, and never would flinch.	400	Tom Clinch		24
Whilst you're, like Baal, fast asleep.	403	Window Inns 10	D	10

464

LIKE   (CONTINUED)   PAGE   TITLE   LINE

	PAGE	TITLE	LINE
But, like a King, to run in Debt.	409	Dial Rich Marb	42
Whilst Lady Charlotte, like a Stroller,	410	Dial Rich Marb	61
Along the plain like Lightning flew:	412	Desire Possess	22
Be so robustious like a Man.	417	Woman's Mind	48
They'll be no more like Graces,	425	Five Ladies	15
Than Venus like an Owl.	425	Five Ladies	16
To cry, like statesmen, quanta patimur!	433	Answer Paulus	42
You must expect the like disgrace,	436	Answer Paulus	139
Like Hunters o'er their Evening Ale.	447	Modern Lady	79
Rude Laughter seeming like to burst;	448	Modern Lady	128
(Says he) tho' swell'd like any porpus.	456	Dean Smedley	32
But like a Girl's Cockade, was ty'd	458	Paddy's Charac	17
Humms, like a Hornet at his Nose,	458	Paddy's Charac	26
Flyes like an Eagle or'e his head;	461	Birthday Song	34
Rebellious Waves with rods like Xerxes.	463	Birthday Song	100
Who struts like any King already.	466	Birthday Song	188
And like his Father early wise.	466	Birthday Song	192
Nine other tuneful words like that	467	Birthday Song	227
Like Atoms are exempt from blows.	467	Birthday Song	238
Britannia long will wear like steel	468	Birthday Song	243
Went down like stupifying Draughts:	470	Burning Poem	8
And live like other christian fokes;	489	Dialogue	18
And sing like one of Milton's choir,	490	Dialogue	40
To treat our Betters like our Slaves,	493	Panegyr Swift	5
And draw like you my Patron's Face;	496	Panegyr Swift	111
Lye down obscure like other Folks	501	Doctor Delaney	45
Like Females o'er their Morning Tea.	501	Doctor Delaney	50
Nor on a Theme like this repine,	515	Answer Fable	89
Spotted over like a Le'pard!	522	Betty Grizette	4
Like a fly blown Cake of Tallow,	523	Betty Grizette	7
Or on her Chin like Bristles grow.	527	Lady's Dres Rm	58
And both Idea's jump like Wits:	529	Lady's Dres Rm	126
He soon would learn to think like me,	530	Lady's Dres Rm	141
Thus Families, like <Realms>, with equal Fate,	535	To Mr. Gay	115
And Kings, like private Persons, are bought and sold:	536	To Mr. Gay	136
'Twou'd please your Palate, like a feast,	546	Life of Swift	39
But, eats into it, like a Moth---!	548	Life of Swift	114
Like other Brethren of his Gown,	549	Life of Swift	141
"He might have rose like other Men:	567	Death of Swift	356
"Like Renegadoes now he feels,	569	Death of Swift	405
Like so many little Mars's,	573	Helter Skelter	5
Like the soldier from the Sutler;	574	Helter Skelter	34
Like the Felon from the Jailer,	574	Helter Skelter	36
Like Iv'ry dry, and soft as Wax.	584	Strephon Chloe	26
But, soon with like Occasions prest,	589	Strephon Chloe	187
For, Beauty, like supreme Dominion,	590	Strephon Chloe	223
How long the Stuff is like to last;	592	Strephon Chloe	294
Such Singers are like Nicolini.	598	Problem Solved	30
'Tis true, he hated Sloth like Pease.	602	Beasts Confess	46
If she like us would burst asunder!	617	Scandal Poem 1	16
Like fire-works, she can burn in water.	618	Scandal Poem 1	38
If Clouds were but like Femals fickle;	618	Scandal Poem 1	42
Like Fire-works, she can burn in Water.	624	Scandal Poem 2	36
You, when it rains, like Fools believe,	627	Scandal Poem 2	125
But, Gods like us, have too much Sense	628	Scandal Poem 2	157
Drest like any Lady May'ress;	630	Epistle Lady	36
Do I, like the Female Tribe,	632	Epistle Lady	77
But, to doze my Head, like Lodanum.	632	Epistle Lady	84
You, like some acute Philosopher,	632	Epistle Lady	95
At whose Oars, like Slaves, they all pull:	635	Epistle Lady	160
Like the Watermen of Thames,	635	Epistle Lady	165
Like the ever-laughing Sage,	635	Epistle Lady	167
If I treat you like <a> <crown'd> <Head>	637	Epistle Lady	239
Like stepping Stones to save a Stride,	645	On Poetry	169
Or like a Heel-piece to support	645	On Poetry	171
Or like a Bridge that joins a Marish	645	On Poetry	173
Like other Bawbles of the Tow'r.	646	On Poetry	194
(Like Courtiers, when they send a Note,	649	On Poetry	271
Rules, like an Alderman his Ward.	649	On Poetry	286
Deny their Country like a Scot:	652	On Poetry	360
No Rhymer can like Welsted sink.	654	On Poetry	394
Comes pouring on me like a Flood.	655	On Poetry	438
Like prudent Fabius by Delay.	656	On Poetry	446
Your Works are like old Jacob's speckled Goats,	670	Epig Carthy 18 D	3
That you, friend Marcus, like a stoick	676	Parson's Case	1
So like my own, without his Bow,	692	Cadenus Vaness	191
Like a young Heir, the thrifty Goddess	693	Cadenus Vaness	223
Wou'd use him like a younger Child;	693	Cadenus Vaness	225
Advanc'd like Atalanta's Star,	696	Cadenus Vaness	306
To see her cloister'd like a Nun.	705	Cadenus Vaness	583
That Scholars were like other Folks:	707	Cadenus Vaness	649
To like with less Seraphick Ends;	712	Cadenus Vaness	823
But, in a weighty Case like this,	713	Cadenus Vaness	854
"Since ev'ry Being loves its Like.	714	Cadenus Vaness	879
But a Genius like her's no Subject can stifle,	716	Answer Rebus	11
Breaks like the Sun behind a Cloud,	726	To Stella	82
Conning old Topicks like a Parrot,	728	Stella, Poems	26
And like the Liquor and the Meat	734	Stel B-day '20	4
To make you look like Beauty's Queen	736	Stel B-day '20	53
Though you should live like old Methusalem,	742	Stel B-day 22	37

LIKE (CONTINUED)

	PAGE	TITLE		LINE
To piddle like a Lady breeding.	745	Stel Distress		8
In Lodgings like a poor Grisette.	746	Stel Distress		44
To piddle like a Lady breeding:	750	Stel Wood-Park		32
In Lodgings, like a poor Grizette,	751	Stel Wood-Park		59
She tends me, like an humble slave:	754	Stella '23		9
Unless he were like Phoebus, young;	757	Stel B-day '24		20
Unless, like Venus, in her Prime.	757	Stel B-day '24		22
Must these like empty Shadows pass,	765	Stel B-day '26		51
Like Janus, bears a double Face;	765	Stel B-day '26		74
Like faithful Counsellors on either Side.	770	Horace 1, 14		14
Thy Mast, which like some aged Patriot stood	770	Horace 1, 14		15
Like supple Patriots of the modern Sort,	771	Horace 1, 14		55
Is but to frisk about like you.	774	Mullinix Tim		28
Like Martin Marrall, gaping on,	775	Mullinix Tim		43
Punch comes, like you, and lets a <Fart>.	777	Mullinix Tim		122
Like thee, to please this thankless Town!	779	Mullinix Tim		198
'Tis just like this, which hangs by Geometry.	780	Mullinix Tim		218
Like a fresh <Turd> just dropt on Snow.	786	Dick, Maggot		14
Thy Body's cloathed like thy Soul.	787	Clad in Brown		16
Scarce glimmers, like a dying Snuff.	787	Clad in Brown		18
Not like the Pastors of the rav'nous Breed,	792	St. Pat's Well		31
But turns aside like mad Ulysses:	796	Traulus 1		30
Like his Body, rank and foul:	800	Traulus 2		34
Like a Rogue that steals a Sheep:	800	Traulus 2		36
Like a Butcher doom'd for Life,	800	Traulus 2		39
On their Crosiers to ride, like a Witch on a Broom.	804	Irish Bishops		22
How shou'd we rejoice, if, like Judas the first,	805	Irish Bishops		39
Like Hemp, which by a skilful Spinster drawn	806	Judas		15
Each modern Judas perish like the first;	806	Judas		21
More like to lampooning than pleading at bar.	815	Yahoo's		14
Like a very foul mop, dirty more than they clean.	819	Archbi Cashel		16
Like Paul's Ephesians, never heard it;	820	Dr. Rundle		16
And, like Domitian, leap at Flyes.	824	Printer Newgat		14
Since the House is like to last,	830	Legion Club		41
Fall a Working like a Mole,	832	Legion Club		73
Treat thy Mother like a Harlot!	838	Legion Club		202
Draw them like, for I assure you,	839	Legion Club		227
Both dress'd like divines, with band and face clean.	843	Ay and No		2
"To treat gold reduc'd like Wood's copper pence.	843	Ay and No		16
A wretch like poor Nancy,	851	Lady's Lament		2
My arms, like two props,	852	Lady's Lament		27
Moving all like a pendulum;	852	Lady's Lament		30
Like a clock without wheels;	852	Lady's Lament		34
Like the tusk of a boar.	854	Lady's Lament		86
Would fain be like us,	855	Lady's Lament		120
Like a hearty divine;	858	Lady's Lament		222
May'st dye like me by Chance; but not by Nature.	861	On Old Glass		2
If I had a Husband like him, I purtest,	869	Grand Question		57
You had like to have put it quite out of my Head.	870	Grand Question		86
And see how he rides like a Lord of the Land,	870	Grand Question		95
(For sure, I had dizen'd you out like a Queen:)	870	Grand Question		102
(For the Dean was so shabby and look'd like a Ninny,	872	Grand Question		151
Like Montezume in golden Chains:	885	Rev Market-Hill		72
Or, like a Cat with Walnuts shod,	885	Rev Market-Hill		73
Like Lorimer, to wear his Hat.	886	Rev Market-Hill		96
And get the like Returns again.	890	Panegyr Dean		104
Your Rev'rence thus, with like Success,	892	Panegyr Dean		187
Brac'd like a Drum her oily Skin;	895	Panegyr Dean		258
May turn and wind me like a fool.	899	Dean's Reasons		14
Are like the ravings of a crackt head;	900	Dean's Reasons		64
In every point, like black and white:	901	Dean's Reasons		72
Like Toupets of this upper World;	903	Death Daphne		24
Bare, like a Carcase pick't by Crows,	904	Death Daphne		34
With cooling Gales, like Zephirs fraught;	911	Aenigma		2
At once so like to Masts or Sails,	912	Aenigma Expl	D	6
Thou, like Alcides, shalt expire,	925	Riddle 8		38
And painted like an Indian Queen.	926	Riddle 9		10
Like the Bow that guards the Tartar,	927	Riddle 10	D	4
Like Pallas from my Father's Brain.	927	Riddle 10	D	10
Like Daphne sometimes in a Tree,	927	Riddle 10	D	17
Like the Fiction of Poets concerning the Wind,	927	Riddle 11	D	3
Like Roman Generals triumphant,	928	Riddle 12	D	15
Like lofty Pindar I can soar,	929	Riddle 15	D	6
Like Milk 'tis cry'd about the Street,	929	Riddle 15	D	11
Like the Labourers of the Babel.	933	Riddle 20	D	8
Like the Warblers of the Spring.	933	Riddle 20	D	12
And change like the Cameleon.	935	Riddle 23	D	13
Like Thought I'm in a Moment gone,	935	Riddle 23	D	16
Like sots, alone I'm dull enough,	936	Riddle 24	D	9
Metals I like them subdue,	936	Riddle 24	D	17
Slave like them to Vulcan too.	936	Riddle 24	D	18
Big like Bess, and small like Sue;	936	Riddle 24	D	28
Big like Bess, and small like Sue;	936	Riddle 24	D	28
Now brown and burnish'd like a nut,	937	Riddle 24	D	29
Like Flora, deck'd with fairest flowers;	937	Riddle 24	D	33
Like Phoebus, guardian of the hours:	937	Riddle 24	D	34
Like thyself I shine in all.	937	Riddle 24	D	38
Languid like a love-sick maid,	937	Riddle 24	D	41
Die like lovers as they gaze,	937	Riddle 24	D	49
Die like all that look on you.	937	Riddle 24	D	54

LIKE   (CONTINUED)   PAGE   TITLE   LINE

	PAGE	TITLE	LINE
Like a Monk in a cell.	939	Riddle Answerd	D
You'll feed like a Farmer:	952	Onyons	5
Or, like my own Herrings, I soon shall be dead.	953	Herrings	9
She swills like a sow, and she breeds like a rabbit:	955	Portrait Life	6
She swills like a sow, and she breeds like a rabbit:	955	Portrait Life	6
You reply and rejoin like Hoadly of Bangor.	967	Letter Sherid	8
You treat me like a Boy that knocks down his Foe,	967	Letter Sherid	13
But we like Antaeus and Hercules fight,	968	Letter Sherid	29
Like a woman it keeps in less than it lets out.	976	Dean to Sherid	26
Were you drest like a bawd, and sold oysters at Billings-gate.	979	Dean to Tho: S	10
i'm sure you cackle like the sex.	983	Sher, A Goose	18
That I have nothing like my Nose about me.	1004	Dan J's Reply	24
. . .although they like your Wine; but they had rather	1013	Swift to Sheri	7
Like a Bear to be baited:	1014	Swift to Sheri	20
And the worst of them all like a barn door did shine	1017	Swift Ans Sher	6
Where I hear you are crammd evry day like a Swine	1017	Swift Ans Sher	13
So I wish you were toothless like Lord Masserine	1017	Swift Ans Sher	17
Thy Verse like Bricks, defy the Weather,	1021	Nim-Dan-Dean 1	D 19
Like Walls, more lasting without Mortar:	1021	Nim-Dan-Dean 1	D 22
Each groov'd, and Dove-tail'd, like a Box.	1021	Nim-Dan-Dean 1	D 26
Or, like the Umbo of the Romans,	1021	Nim-Dan-Dean 1	D 31
May backward be perus'd, like Hebrew.	1021	Nim-Dan-Dean 1	D 42
Long, Long, Long, Long, like Dan's Long Nose.	1022	Nim-Dan-Dean 1	D 54
Is this, that you argue like fools in a circle.	1026	Sheri Circles	4
That we walk all about, like a horse in a pound,	1026	Sheri Circles	7
And look'd like a Rake, who was made in the Stews sick;	1029	Dr. Helsham	18
For the Smell of them made me like Garlick and Rue sick	1029	Dr. Helsham	21
And those to be sure, stuck together like Glew, sick.	1029	Dr. Helsham	25
So am I, when Tobacco, like Robin, I chew, sick.	1030	Dr. Helsham	28
But, I hope I shall ne'er be, like you, of a Shrew sick	1030	Dr. Sheridan	4
Eat like a Turk,	1035	Servants Maxim	1
Sleep like a Dormouse;	1035	Servants Maxim	2
And Robin at Sea had like to be cast away.	1037	Four Storyes	4
LIKE'D			
Like'd ev'ry Thing - - - at least thought fit	379	Apology Lady C	119
LIKENESS			
Tim, with his likeness deeply smitten,	783	Tim and Fables	25
Has this any likeness to good Madam Sheridan?	955	Portrait Life	10
LIKES			
Likes both his Company and Commons;	173	Horace 1, 7	74
Why she likes him, admire not at her,	708	Cadenus Vaness	686
LILLIES			
The Lillies of thy Skin compare;	932	Riddle 19	D 7
LILLIPUT			
Will soon subdue the Realm of Lilliput.	467	Birthday Song	208
LILLY			
For instance; when the Lilly slipps	226	Prog of Beauty	25
LIMB			
Phil wish't, that she had strained a Limb	224	Prog of Love	81
The Limb surviving, you may swear,	366	Answer Delaney	13
And on the Brother Limb re-acts.	366	Answer Delaney	26
Returning sound in Limb and Wind,	398	Earl of P-b-w	23
Each Limb, and Feature out of Fame;	449	Modern Lady	133
A Numbness crept through ev'ry Limb;	470	Burning Poem	10
And strive to tear you Limb from Limb,	651	On Poetry	333
And strive to tear you Limb from Limb,	651	On Poetry	333
In stomach or limb.	853	Lady's Lament	58
I'm forc'd to leave a Limb behind.	921	Riddle 6	36
May break a Limb of Master or Miss.	941	Letter	22
LIMBS			
The Golden Scurf peels off his Limbs:	157	Fable of Midas	36
Ods buds, why don't you break her Limbs:	220	A Quiet Life	28
With Limbs robust, and Voice that stuns;	326	Pethox	76
For, when in Bed we rest our weary Limbs,	363	On Dreams	7
Though strong in Limbs, he lagg'd behind.	412	Desire Possess	38
"And such a Pain in all my Limbs!"	451	Modern Lady	209
Must ev'ry Morn her Limbs unite.	583	Young Nymph	66
The limbs are guided by the brain,	761	Bec's B-Day	20
I must move my limbs;	852	Lady's Lament	40
LIME			
Who bring the Lime, or place the Stones;	727	Stella, Poems	3
You save the Charge of Lime and Trowels.	1021	Nim-Dan-Dean 1	D 24
<LINCOLN>			
And <Lincoln> then imagines he has Land.	164	Toland's Invit	26
LIN'D			
How well a Cully's Purse was lin'd:	133	Magician's Rod	32
'Til coffee has her stomach lin'd;	761	Bec's B-Day	34
LINE			
Each line shall stab, shall blast, like daggers and like fire;	37	Ode Sancroft	91
Yet hardly dare one Line Rehearse.	121	Apollo Outwit	60
Transmitted to the Heroes Line,	134	Magician's Rod	62
Our Merchant Ships may cut the Line,	168	Peace Dunkirk	21
Wherein she distinctly could read ev'ry Line,	264	Apollo	51
The Blessing of another Line:	272	Apollo's Edict	D 69
You had not writ a Line.	406	Swift to Pope	24
I but transcribe, for not a Line	445	Modern Lady	28
But swear his Line shall rule the Nation	466	Birthday Song	197

		PAGE	TITLE	LINE
LIPS				
And bit her Lips to make them red:	. . . .	222	Prog of Love	14
Crackt Lips, foul Teeth, and gummy Eyes,	. . . . .	226	Prog of Beauty	15
And takes Possession of the Lips,	. . . . .	226	Prog of Beauty	27
If neither Cheeks, nor Lips be left.	. . . . . .	229	Prog of Beauty	116
No Lips of Coral Teeth of Pearl.	. . . .	272	Apollo's Edict	D 55
Her Heart, and from her Lips distills;	. . . . . .	592	Strephon Chloe	280
How? Not a Word come from thy lips?	. . . . . .	594	Cassinus Peter	36
But, he durst not so much as once open his Lips,	. . .	873	Grand Question	177
But, if I ever touch her Lips again,	. . . . . .	882	Pastoral Dial	43
I move my Lips, but want a Voice;	. . . .	936	Riddle 23	D 25
LIQUID				
The liquid Medium cheats your Sight,	. . . . . .	251	Bubble	15
If haply on the liquid surface float,	. . . . . .	672	Epig Carthy 24	D 13
LIQUIDS				
With Bridegroom liquids hand in hand,	. . . . . .	467	Birthday Song	230
LIQUOR				
That swill'd more Liquor than it could contain,	. . .	137	City Shower	15
And then he could pay for the Liquor he drank	. . . .	287	Bank Down	29
So methought, he resolv'd no Liquor to taste,	. . . .	337	Serious Poem	111
Than the Liquor he deals in, his own melted Copper;	.	351	Wood Insect	36
Thy want of all-consoling liquor,	. . . .	676	Parson's Case	8
Ripens the Grape, the Liquor sours.	. . . . . .	731	Stella, Poems	120
And like the Liquor and the Meat	. . . .	734	Stel B-day '20	4
The dullest Beast, and Gentleman's Liquor,	. . . .	940	Letter	1
A long-ear'd Beast, and Liquor to write,	. . . . .	942	Probatur Alit	29
LIST				
First, in the mighty List of Fame,	. . . .	7	Ode to King	34
Are the chief Heroes in the sacred List of Fame.	. . .	25	Ode Athenian	307
It is a bloody list we know)	. . . .	37	Ode Sancroft	94
Swept up whole churches as it list,	. . . . . .	40	Ode Sancroft	194
Let Censuring Criticks then think what they list on't,	.	77	Lady B- B-	REF
The Sleeves new border'd with a List	. . . . .	94	Bauc & Phil 1	167
A List the Coblers Temples ties,	. . . .	98	Elegy Patrige	23
When all your list of Gods is out,	. . . .	464	Birthday Song	143
Where, if the curious List to read 'em,	. . . . . .	494	Panegyr Swift	51
LIST'NING				
Where Echo sits, and list'ning mocks.	. . . . . .	597	Cassinus Peter	108
Scarce list'ning to their idle Chat;	. . . . . .	697	Cadenus Vaness	335
To teach her ears the art of list'ning,	. . . . . .	762	Bec's B-Day	54
LISTED				
The Leaders whom you listed under,	. . . . . .	775	Mullinix Tim	47
LISTEN				
Listen while the muse thus teaches thee to sing:	. . .	52	Temple Ill	36
To listen to minimms and quavers and Crochets	. . . .	522	St. Cecilia's	12
Now listen while he next produces,	. . . .	526	Lady's Dres Rm	19
For tho' she seem'd to listen more	. . . .	704	Cadenus Vaness	564
Nor listen to the Witch of Endor;	. . . .	776	Mullinix Tim	100
And when I listen to the Noise,	. . . .	788	Dick's Variety	7
Would come and listen with Delight,	. . . . . .	848	Old Thorn	11
How could you, Sheelah, listen to his Tales,	. . . .	882	Pastoral Dial	35
Can listen to a tale humdrum,	. . . .	900	Dean's Reasons	55
LISTEN'D				
But Hannah, who listen'd to all that was past,	. . . .	868	Grand Question	41
LISTING				
And listing Troops for the Pretender.	. . . . . .	788	Dick's Variety	24
LISTNER				
Our Listner stood a while confus'd,	. . . .	64	Discovery	45
LITERAL				
Which cannot in Literal Sense be made Good,	. . . .	335	Serious Poem	55
LITERALLY				
It may be literally true.	. . . .	461	Birthday Song	20
LITT'RALL				
That litt'rall Spot which gave him Birth,	. . . . .	314	To Ford	88
LITTER				
Her Litter teeming from her Womb,	. . . .	207	Fable Bitches	4
That Musick gave her Leave to litter,	. . . . . .	208	Fable Bitches	17
Of all the Litter as it lay;	. . . .	526	Lady's Dres Rm	8
And sail'd with Litter Side by Side;	. . . . . .	811	Bro Protestant	8
LITTER'D				
And litter'd at Parnassus' Foot.	. . . .	504	Doctor Delaney	122
But, view them litter'd on the Floor,	. . . . . .	592	Strephon Chloe	289
The Room with Volumes litter'd round	. . . . . .	698	Cadenus Vaness	371
LITTERING				
Of Gipsies littering under Hedges,	. . . .	641	On Poetry	38
LITTLE				
Stay but a little while and down again 'twill come,	. .	10	Ode to King	128
When Learnings little Houshold did embark	. . . . .	16	Ode Athenian	12
How little, very little do prevail	. . . .	19	Ode Athenian	112
How little, very little do prevail	. . . .	19	Ode Athenian	112
We've found a little inconsiderable Head	. . . . . .	20	Ode Athenian	147
Out starts the little Beast, and mocks their idle Fears.		30	Ode to Temple	114
He had mixt little Wit with a great deal of Pains,	. .	77	Lady B- B-	24
And now he spreads his little Fans,	. . . .	80	Vanbrug House	49
There all the little School-boys run	. . . .	87	Hist V's House	33
The little Children in the Wood,	. . . .	93	Bauc & Phil 1	120
I'm good for little at my days;	. . . .	94	Bauc & Phil 1	163
The Little Children in the Wood:	. . . .	114	Bauc & Phil 2	96
This is the little strutting Pile,	. . . .	127	Little House	13
And little Miss began to cry;	. . . .	128	Little House	48
Then Cupid thus: This little Maid	. . . .	150	Corinna	9

LITTLE   (CONTINUED)   PAGE   TITLE   LINE
    She made a Song, how little Miss   . . . .   150 Corinna   21
    "I must a little longer crave;   . . . .   208 Fable Bitches   32
    And tell how little weight he sets, ...   282 Journal   99
    His Lading little, and his Ballast less.   . . . . . .   284 Elegy Boat   4
    He'd wish to sleep a little longer.   . . . .   296 Satiric Elegy   8
    Now from his Lordship's Grace I hold a little Piece of   342 Upon His Grace   21
        Ground,
    That three little Vermin are kin to Will. Wood: . .   350 Wood Insect   2
    Said little in his own Defence: . . . .   377 Apology Lady C   74
    Then said, I must speak to the People a little,   . . .   399 Tom Clinch   15
    With little Tom contrive   . . . .   425 Five Ladies   3
    "Fie, Madam, leave these little Arts.   . . . .   452 Modern Lady   257
    Now sing his little Highness Freddy, ...   466 Birthday Song   187
    We left a little Duke behind;   . . . .   466 Birthday Song   200
    His Heart too Great, though Fortune little, ...   482 Libel on D- D-   81
    Could all we little Folks that wait, ...   492 Panegyr Swift   1
    No Wonder you should think it little   . . . .   495 Panegyr Swift   58
    But, little could their Strength avail, ...   501 Doctor Delaney   33
    And now that little next is gone.   . . . .   514 Answer Fable   68
    "He gave the little Wealth he had, ...   572 Death of Swift   479
    Like so many little Mars's, ...   573 Helter Skelter   5
    And with very little Pence, ...   574 Helter Skelter   29
    And as very little Sence: . . . .   574 Helter Skelter   30
    With some Law but little Justice, ...   574 Helter Skelter   31
    The little Cupids hov'ring round, ...   590 Strephon Chloe   193
    And, if you now so little spare us, ...   622 Scandal Poem 1   163
    And, but little at a Time.   . . . .   633 Epistle Lady   128
    Safe within my little Wherry, ...   635 Epistle Lady   163
    While a little gentle Jerking   . . . ' . . . . .   636 Epistle Lady   205
    Damns all your Thoughts as low and little, ...   644 On Poetry   121
    Who, tho' too little to be seen, ...   651 On Poetry   343
    (For Satire had destroy'd his little fame,)   . . . . .   671 Epig Carthy 24   D   2
    And shew'd but little of their Art;   . . . .   692 Cadenus Vaness   173
    With much Deceit and little Wit;   . . . .   695 Cadenus Vaness   291
    I'll undertake my little Nancy   . . . .   700 Cadenus Vaness   418
    To know the World a little better.   . . . .   700 Cadenus Vaness   429
    So little is thy Form declin'd   . . . .   722 Stel B-Day '18   7
    An Angel's Face, a little crack't;   . . . .   734 Stel B-day '20   16
    So little gets for what she gives   . . . .   735 Stel B-day '20   29
    Apollo having thought a little, ...   742 Stel B-day 22   35
    When all her little Money spent, ...   747 Stel Distress   54
    I was too hard upon--a little.   . . . .   747 Stel Distress   66
    I was too hard upon a little;   . . . .   752 Stel Wood-Park   82
    No little Boys and Girls to cry   . . . .   778 Mullinix Tim   181
    I own I see but little Wit in: . . . .   788 Dick's Variety   10
    For he that has so little Wit, ...   813 Bro Protestant   63
    No little scrub Joint shall come on my Board: . . . .   867 Grand Question   14
    We are little airy Creatures, ...   930 Riddle 17   D   1
    I'll squeeze him to a little Span, ...   934 Riddle 21   D 18
    We are little Brethren twain, ...   934 Riddle 22   D   1
    He has more Goodnes in his little Finger, ...   985 Mary to Sher   9
LIV'D
    That Men, who liv'd and dy'd without a Name, ...   25 Ode Athenian   306
    And in all the Places I liv'd, I never heard of such a   70 Mrs Harris Pet   31
        Thing.
    Six thousand years hath liv'd the Goddess, ...   465 Birthday Song   161
    "He might have liv'd these Twenty Years: . . . . .   559 Death of Swift   174
LIV'RY
    When in my gaudy Liv'ry drest!   . . . .   916 Riddle 2   4
LIVE
    By which some fondly boast they shall for ever live,   . .   20 Ode Athenian   151
    For You (ah, did I think I e'er should live to see   .   23 Ode Athenian   247
    Ill may I live, if the good Sancroft in his hcly rest,   36 Ode Sancroft   50
    Lest here it live, when perish'd with his own;   . . .   48 To Congreve   168
    'Tis well.--But since we live among   . . . . . .   83 Salamander   23
    Not fitt to live on Christian Ground, ...   92 Bauc & Phil 1   87
    Not fit to live on Christian Ground, ...   112 Bauc & Phil 2   47
    I'm Old, and fain wou'd live at Ease, ...   115 Bauc & Phil 2   115
    To live in Plenty, Power and Ease.   . . . .   173 Horace 1, 7   92
    Should you live years forty more   . . . .   187 Scriblerus 4   D 17
    Could I but live on this side Trent;   . . . . . .   199 Horace 2, 6   10
    To those who die, for meriting to live.   . . . . .   210 Earl of Oxford   14
    And observe while you live, that no Man is shy   . .   264 Apollo   57
    And the Publick shall see't, if I live 'till to Morrow; .   265 Apollo   68
    When wretched Lovers live on Air, ...   270 Apollo's Edict   D 16
    To live and die all strollers for your sakes;   . . .   309 Billet Players   50
    To live in this or t' other Isle, ...   315 To Ford   97
    . . . and make him live as long   . . . .   343 Upon His Grace   47
    But ever ever live at Ease, ...   362 Grace's Answer   45
    For I live on a smelt.   . . . .   402 Window Inns 8   D 12
    To live without both full three Months he try'd,   . . .   430 Dicky Dolly   11
    Now, as I live, ...   442 Ballyspellin   73
    Live on, and Stuff, to Boot, their Maws.   . . . . .   479 Epist on Epist   126
    And live like other christian fokes;   . . . . . .   489 Dialogue   18
    To live obscure, and have no fame to lose?   . . . .   506 To a Friend   8
    And griev'd that a Tory should live above Ground.   .   518 Dean Hang Rape   34
    "To fancy they cou'd live a Year!   . . . .   563 Death of Swift   261
    Because they live in lower regions   . . . .   620 Scandal Poem 1   98
    How to live, and how to die.   . . . .   630 Epistle Lady   26
    There live with daggl'd Mermaids pent, ...   689 Cadenus Vaness   89

470

LIVE   (CONTINUED)   PAGE   TITLE   LINE
    Bare Virtue could not live on Praise, ...   693 Cadenus Vaness   213
    That, should you live to see the Day   . . . .   735 Stel B-day '20   47
    Though you should live like old Methusalem, ...   742 Stel B-day 22   37
    Since I must laugh, or cannot live, ...   747 Stel Distress   57
    Long may she live, and help her friends   . . . . . .   761 Bec's B-Day   31
    Once so renown'd to Live obscure?   . . . .   778 Mullinix Tim   180
    You are only to live four Years without Vittles!   . .   805 Irish Bishops   60
    Than live in Slavery to Slaves, ...   824 Printer Newgat   2
    "You'll never want Parsons as long as you live;   . .   872 Grand Question   142
    To live without a coach and six, ...   878 Robbin & Harry   30
    Condemn'd to live in Service hard;   . . . .   883 Rev Market-Hill   11
    To live in fear, suspicion, variance, ...   899 Dean's Reasons   17
    I sometimes live in House of Hair, ...   912 Aenigma   9
    I'm dead except I live in Light.   . . . . . .   929 Riddle 15   D 4
    Die for those I live to please;   . . . .   937 Riddle 24   D 50
    I Cannot but think that we live in a bad age,   . . .   975 Dean to Sherid   1
    You live among ill folks in a dunghill, ...   1038 Sheridan Cavan   17
LIVE-LONG
    How could she sit the live-long Day, ...   891 Panegyr Dean   145
LIVELY
    A lively Maggot sallies out, ...   785 Dick, Maggot   3
LIVER
    To prey on his Liver, but not to be seen: 266 Apollo   98
    While Vultures eat his growing Liver: . . . . . .   346 Prometheus   56
    Where, if we find his Liver grows, ...   347 Prometheus   75
LIVERY
    Will deign your Livery to wear, ...   325 Pethox   44
LIVES
    There is a Noon-tide in our Lives   . . . . . .   24 Ode Athenian   278
    Thus are the lives of fools a sort of dreams,   . . .   47 To Congreve   147
    Lives pious witness of a better age;   . . . .   52 Temple Ill   48
    Tho' she lives 'till she's Grey as a Badger all over. .   266 Apollo   108
    To One who lives in its Defence, ...   339 Arch-Bish Dub   3
    Who lives at Ballyspelling   . . . .   442 Ballyspellin   72
    Yet he lives, and is ready to ravish agen, ...   519 Dean Hang Rape   52
    Lives in a State of War by Nature.   . . . .   651 On Poetry   320
    We really wonder how she lives;   . . . .   735 Stel B-day '20   30
    The cat's nine lives and eke the care.   . . . .   761 Bec's B-Day   30
    Lives such a Bard on British plains?   . . . . . .   876 To Dean Swift   6
LIVING
    And catch the living landscape thro' a scanty light, . .   35 Ode Sancroft   30
    Since a living Dog better is than a dead Lyon,   . . .   237 Excellent Song   13
    "The living Lusture of your Eyes?   . . . . . .   380 Apology Lady C   166
    For Dick without Doll thought Living a Folly.   . . . .   430 Dicky Dolly   3
    "Past Six, and not a living Soul!   . . . .   451 Modern Lady   202
    Oh, were the Wretch but living still, ...   560 Death of Swift   193
    Living on the publick Bounty;   . . . .   574 Helter Skelter   38
LIVINGS
    For the more Livings you can fish up, ...   478 Epist on Epist   101
LIVY
    Cou'd quote you Cicero and Livy.   . . . .   513 Answer Fable   38
LO
    And, lo! where a Destroying Angel stands, ...   7 Ode to King   48
    Lo, it appears! . . . .   30 Ode to Temple   112
    Lo here I sit at holy head . . . .   420 Holyhead   1
    Lo, Charon from his leaky Wherry, ...   596 Cassinus Peter   83
    And lo, his Ministers of State, ...   646 On Poetry   207
    When, lo! Vanessa in her Bloom, ...   696 Cadenus Vaness   305
    Lo! Infidelity return'd again.   . . . .   792 St. Pat's Well   36
    To cry; Lo, Judas, gone to his own Place: . . . . . .   806 Judas   24
    Lo, here I stand with double Face;   . . . .   917 Riddle 3   2
    And lo! the Writing on the Walls   . . . .   923 Riddle 7   57
LOAD
    A load as heavy as the Crown, ...   40 Ode Sancroft   188
    Compos'd of Timber many a Load;   . . . .   94 Bauc & Phil 1   148
    Compact of Timber many a Load, ...   114 Bauc & Phil 2   102
    Nor Pegasus could bear the Load, ...   231 Prog of Poetry   27
    Possession's Load was grown so great, ...   413 Desire Possess   51
    And, disencumbred of his load, ...   435 Answer Paulus   95
    A squinting Monkey load with charms;   . . . .   464 Birthday Song   121
    You Travel with a heavy Load, ...   480 Libel on D- D-   11
    The stinking Load of all the Crimes, ...   497 Panegyr Swift   116
    "I sent them with a Load of Books, ...   563 Death of Swift   259
    Load our Plates from ev'ry Dish;   . . . .   633 Epistle Lady   109
    Of Incense many a thousand Load;   . . . .   657 On Poetry   474
LOADED
    Thus loaded with Grief, Dick Sigh'd and he cry'd,   . .   430 Dicky Dolly   10
    And, thy Memory is loaded . . . .   523 Betty Grizette   15
    But why shou'd he with that be loaded, ...   820 Dr. Rundle   27
LOADS
    "Their Loads they all on Satan lay: . . . .   497 Panegyr Swift   134
    Observe what Loads of stupid Rimes   . . . . . .   503 Doctor Delaney   101
    But, carries Loads, and feeds on Thistles;   . . . . .   607 Beasts Confess   214
    The Loads of Poems in his Praise, ...   646 On Poetry   203
LOAF
    To bake one Loaf, and keep one Dove in.   . . . . . .   127 Little House   38
LOAN
    Why, then recal your Loan;   . . . .   395 Grub-Street   18
LOATHS
    Now his exalted Spirit loaths   . . . .   231 Prog of Poetry   41

		PAGE	TITLE	LINE
LOATHSOM				
But loathsom Spots his Body stain:		83	Salamander	32
LOCAL				
And pawn'd his word Hell is not local.		469	Birthday Song	272
LOCK				
Now you must know, because my Trunk has a very bad Lock,		69	Mrs Harris Pet	5
Lock up from my Sight in Pantries and Cupboards:		263	Apollo	12
In my 'scritore lock up my quill?		489	Dialogue	12
Or Billet-doux, or Lock of Hay:		893	Panegyr Dean	222
LOCK'D				
Till then it was lock'd in my Box at Parnassus;		265	Apollo	79
Janus hath lock'd his Temple-door?		462	Birthday Song	50
LOCKS				
A dismal shedding of her Locks		85	Salamander	67
Held out Medusa's snaky locks,		178	To Lord Harley	45
From her red Locks her Mouth with Venom fills:		195	Author Himself	55
But her graceful black Locks, were all mingled with Grey		264	Apollo	42
He bids me then to hold my Tongue, and up the Money locks,		342	Upon His Grace	25
When Epimetheus op'd the Locks,		528	Lady's Dres Rm	84
Why, Plague confound her sandy Locks:		595	Cassinus Peter	47
His carrot locks, and fiery nose;		621	Scandal Poem 1	136
When Stella's Locks must all be grey		735	Stel B-day '20	48
That half your Locks are turn'd to Grey;		757	Stel B-day '24	39
Your jetty Locks with Garlands crown'd,		760	Receipt Youth	41
Dermot, I swear, tho' Tady's Locks could hold		882	Pastoral Dial	45
Than where the haughty Dutchess Locks,		896	Panegyr Dean	297
One Letter still another Locks;		1021	Nim-Dan-Dean 1	D 25
LOCUSTS				
These Locusts whom our Fruits have fed,		258	Bubble	206
LODANUM				
But, to doze my Head, like Lodanum.		632	Epistle Lady	84
LODGE SEE RICHMOND-LODGE				
To lodge behind a golden cloud;		41	Ode Sancroft	216
Despair and he lodge ever in its stead;		55	Temple Ill	128
To lodge in Garrats comes from thence.		79	Vanbrug House	28
To lodge in Garrats, comes from thence.		106	V's House	28
May lodge within thy Spacious Pile.		109	V's House	118
A handsome House to lodge a Friend,		198	Horace 2, 6	3
All Virtues lodge in royal Ermine.		647	On Poetry	228
In him they lodge, and make him Legion.		798	Traulus 1	78
LODGES				
Where the bless'd spirit lodges like the dove,		41	Ode Sancroft	227
LODGING				
Can hire a Lodging for a Song;		79	Vanbrug House	16
This gives him Lodging, and provides		80	Vanbrug House	45
By lodging Folks dispos'd to sleep.		94	Bauc & Phil 1	152
Can raise a Lodging for a Song.		106	V's House	16
By lodging Folks dispos'd to Sleep.		114	Bauc & Phil 2	106
Their Vittells bad, their Lodging worse,		224	Prog of Love	79
From Lodging in a hundred Jayls,		481	Libel on D- D-	51
Be told the Lodging, Lane, and Sign,		729	Stella, Poems	41
LODGINGS				
In Lodgings like a poor Grisette.		746	Stel Distress	44
In Lodgings, like a poor Grizette,		751	Stel Wood-Park	59
While there are Lodgings to be lett.		751	Stel Wood-Park	60
LOFTIER				
Are loftier by a Mile at least:		626	Scandal Poem 2	104
LOFTY				
And ev'ry stinking weed so lofty grows,		37	Ode Sancroft	103
With lofty Branches to the Skies,		393	Modern Poets	2
Ill befits a lofty Stile.		634	Epistle Lady	140
I the lofty Stile decline.		637	Epistle Lady	218
Shou'd I lofty Numbers chuse,		638	Epistle Lady	260
For lofty Lines in Smithfield Drols.		650	On Poetry	300
In lofty Style to make Replies,		711	Cadenus Vaness	796
As when a lofty Pile is rais'd,		727	Stella, Poems	1
Spy a Building large and lofty,		829	Legion Club	2
Yet, when your lofty Domes I praise,		894	Panegyr Dean	225
In vain on lofty Heels I tread,		897	Panegyr Dean	321
Like lofty Pindar I can soar,		929	Riddle 15	D 6
LOFTY'R				
Are lofty'r by a mile at least.		620	Scandal Poem 1	106
LOG				
And Helicon; for if this Log		671	Epig Carthy 21	D 6
LOGICAL				
But if Hell by Logical Rules be defin'd,		575	Place Damn'd	3
LOGICIANS				
Matter, as wise Logicians say,		228	Prog of Beauty	81
LOGICK SEE DOG-LOGICK				
Against all Logick and concluding Laws,		19	Ode Athenian	108
(The only Logick us'd by Us)		658	On Poetry	D 190
LOGICK-MONGERS				
Of Logick-mongers can describe;		215	To Mr. Delany	20
LOINS				
As sov'reign Med'cines for the Loins)		589	Strephon Chloe	182
LOIT'RING				
Now, loit'ring o'er her Tea and Cream,		447	Modern Lady	70
LOITRING				
So loitring, so active; so busy, so idle,		580	Psyche	3

472

	PAGE	TITLE	LINE
LOLL			
Loll out their Tongues, and thus they talk, ...	545	Life of Swift	21
LOLLING			
Devoutly lolling in his Seat;	174	Horace 1, 7	98
First, lolling Sloth in Woollen Cap, ...	895	Panegyr Dean	273
LOLLOP			
Trolloping, Galloping, Lollop, ...	960	Cantata	
LOLLOPING			
Trolloping, Lolloping, Galloping, Trolloping . . .	960	Cantata	
Lolloping, Galloping, Trollop, ...	960	Cantata	
Lolloping, Trolloping, Galloping, Lolloping, . . .	960	Cantata	
Lolloping, Trolloping, Galloping, Lolloping, . . .	960	Cantata	
LONDE			
From Toune of Stoffe to fattyn Londe	102	Merlin	6
LONDON			
Oh London Tavern! Thou hast lost a Friend, . . .	234	Elegy on Demar	25
In London! what would You do there?	312	To Ford	35
To London strait return again, ...	312	To Ford	48
If you have London still at heart	313	To Ford	57
In London can you equall Him?	314	To Ford	76
For quitting her beloved London.	362	Grace's Answer	40
From London they come, silly People to chouse, . .	396	Dog and Thief	17
Nor London Journals, nor the Post-men, ...	462	Birthday Song	53
From Dublin soon to London spread, ...	559	Death of Swift	177
LONELY			
Fix'd in a lonely, learned Cell, ...	385	Manly Virtue	48
Nor blab it on the lonely Rocks, ...	597	Cassinus Peter	107
LONG SEE LIVE-LONG			
Long dreaded for his Bloody Tail and Fiery Beard, .	10	Ode to King	131
Long wandring thro the Deep, as we are told . . .	17	Ode Athenian	46
With a long sweeping Train	23	Ode Athenian	225
Yet so much sooner comes the long and gloomy Night. .	25	Ode Athenian	282
We have too long been led astray, ...	27	Ode to Temple	17
Too long have our misguided Souls been taught . .	27	Ode to Temple	18
Shall e'er long grow into a Tree, ...	31	Ode to Temple	168
Such were the storms good Sancroft long has borne; .	40	Ode Sancroft	198
This off'ring long design'd to Congreve's fame; .	44	To Congreve	24
For, ill to them, long have I travell'd since . . .	46	To Congreve	87
Last just as long as ev'ry cuckow's note: . . .	47	To Congreve	130
My hate, whose lash just heaven has long decreed .	47	To Congreve	133
'Tis time to bid my friend a long farewell, . . .	50	To Congreve	227
Tempests long frown, and thunder threatens loud, .	52	Temple Ill	24
Mild Dorothea, whom we both have long	52	Temple Ill	43
And gaze in silent Wonder long, ...	109	V's House	106
Let Stubborn Pride Possess thee long, ...	121	Apollo Outwit	53
Thence, thro' a long Descent of Kings, ...	134	Magician's Rod	63
My long old-fashion'd Pocket, was presently cramm'd;	143	New Song	19
"I! who so long with Tooth and Claw	154	Widow and Cat	D 23
Nor could have borne it half so long.	160	Atlas	14
Too long upon his single Shoulders	160	Atlas	21
What all the World knew long ago, ...	180	Horace 2, 1	8
To be the Man I long have sought, ...	215	To Mr. Delany	4
That, long ago a Fortune-teller	223	Prog of Love	51
Their Journy long, their Money short;	224	Prog of Love	76
He who so long was Currant 'twould be strange . .	235	Elegy on Demar	35
By long Experience we have found	258	Bubble	190
This world he cumber'd long enough;	296	Satiric Elegy	13
I wonder you held out so long, ...	315	To Ford	110
But, having long convers'd with you, ...	325	Pethox	67
A Siege as long as Troy endur'd.	326	Pethox	98
. . . and make him live as long	343	Upon His Grace	47
To do the Jobb too long he tarry'd, ...	349	Upright Judge 2	2
By long Observation I have understood, ...	350	Wood Insect	1
Which, I confess, is too long winded)	354	Simile Silver	18
To wait so long and have nothing to ask. . . .	368	Verses Window	2
He long had bid the Court farwel, ...	375	Apology Lady C	13
"Thro' long Disuse of Solitude, ...	379	Apology Lady C	136
"If long confin'd to Fires and Screens, ...	380	Apology Lady C	137
"If you, who long have breath'd the Fumes . . .	380	Apology Lady C	139
My honest Friend Wild, may he long hold his Place, .	399	Tom Clinch	17
'Tis said, their Course continu'd long;	412	Desire Possess	13
With periods long, in terms abstruse!	434	Answer Paulus	82
Not long enough to reach half round, ...	458	Paddy's Charac	16
May Caroline continue long, ...	467	Birthday Song	233
Britannia long will wear like steel	468	Birthday Song	243
Twice sev'n long Years the Court attends, . . .	481	Libel on D- D-	54
For long enur'd to musty Rules, ...	493	Panegyr Swift	29
Is of short Sessions a long Hist'ry;	493	Panegyr Swift	32
So long unbishoprick'd lie by, ...	497	Panegyr Swift	147
E'en quit the House, for thou too long hast sat in't, .	538	Mr. Pulteney	9
A Hare, who long had 'scap't pursuing Hounds, . .	538	Mr. Pulteney	17
Thy Turns and Doublings cannot save thee long. . .	539	Mr. Pulteney	44
"Though trusted long in great Affairs, ...	565	Death of Swift	329
"Who long all Justice had discarded, ...	570	Death of Swift	421
Strephon had long perplex'd his Brains, ...	586	Strephon Chloe	72
How long the Stuff is like to last;	592	Strephon Chloe	294
What Edifice can long endure, ...	593	Strephon Chloe	299
As it hath long been his Desire, ...	606	Beasts Confess	172
In praise of long departed Wit, ...	611	By Dr. Swift	8
To conclude this long Essay;	634	Epistle Lady	133
As long as Sun and Moon endure.	655	On Poetry	436

LONG	(CONTINUED)		PAGE	TITLE		LINE
Thy Labours, Carthy, long conceal'd from Light,	. .		667	Epig Carthy 5	D	1
What Carthy publish'd needs no long Excuse,	. . . .		668	Epig Carthy 11	D	1
James Bruges & the Dean had long been friends,	. . .		678	Dean and Duke		1
Long Bills, and Answers, stuff'd with Lies,	. . . .		690	Cadenus Vaness		121
Seeds long unknown to Womankind,	. . . .		693	Cadenus Vaness		203
And, after long computing, found	. . . .		693	Cadenus Vaness		226
She reason'd, without plodding long,	. . . .		704	Cadenus Vaness		558
To hide her from the World so long;	. . . .		705	Cadenus Vaness		577
Had he employ'd his Time so long,	. . . .		705	Cadenus Vaness		598
Altho' the Writer long were dead?	. . . .		708	Cadenus Vaness		699
So, long attending at the Gate,	. . . .		711	Cadenus Vaness		770
When Love's Allurements long are past;	. . . . .		711	Cadenus Vaness		783
For should this Ferment last too long,	. . . . .		731	Stella, Poems		132
She must have long ago run out.	. . . .		735	Stel B-day '20		32
So may we long continue thus,	. . . .		755	Stella '23		37
So long till all your Flesh is wasted,	. . . . .		759	Receipt Youth		24
Long may she live, and help her friends	. . . . .		761	Bec's B-Day		31
Stella long dead, but first the Dean,	. . . . . .		762	Bec's B-Day		46
Long Schemes of Life, as heretofore;	. . . . . .		764	Stel B-day '26		16
On French Records for twenty long Campains;	. .		771	Horace 1, 14		44
As those who long have stood the Storms of State,	. .		772	Horace 1, 14		59
For long disputes will only weary us.	. . . . .		774	Mullinix Tim		34
My precious Time, so long mispent,	. . . . . .		781	Mullinix Tim		278
For Traulus long his Rancour nurst,	. . . . . .		796	Traulus 1		17
To this damnable Speaker had long ow'd a shame;	. . .		816	Yahoo's		37
Had this been your method to torture him, long since,	.		818	Epigr Kite		9
Hast thou been so long at School,	. . . .		838	Legion Club		197
My nose, long and thin,	. . . .		853	Lady's Lament		73
To shorten my Tale, (for I hate a long Story,)	. .		871	Grand Question		129
"You'll never want Parsons as long as you live;	. .		872	Grand Question		142
That when a Nation long enslav'd,	. . . .		875	Drapier's Hill		11
Was long the quintessence of Beaux;	. . . . . .		879	Robbin & Harry		38
Too long I have my Thanks delay'd;	. . . . . .		887	Panegyr Dean		3
Your Favours left too long unpay'd;	. . . . . .		887	Panegyr Dean		4
By long Experience grown so wise,	. . . .		890	Panegyr Dean		117
Or, ponder long with anxious Thought,	. . . . . .		892	Panegyr Dean		161
When too long, is bad at best.	. . . .		940	Letter		9
How long shall vice triumphant reign?	. . . . . .		950	Upstart	D	17
How long shall mortals bend to gain?	. . . . . .		950	Upstart	D	18
How long shall virtue hide her face,	. . . . . .		950	Upstart	D	19
But because the three former are long ago past,	. .		967	Letter Sherid		11
By riding this morning too long in your car:	. . .		976	Dean to Sherid		28
And I love you so well, as I told you long ago,	. .		979	Dean to Tho: S		17
For your Man, I long waited.	. . . .		1014	Swift to Sheri		18
The long and the short,	. . . .		1015	Swift to Sheri		41
Long, Long, Long, Long, like Dan's Long Nose.	. .		1022	Nim-Dan-Dean 1	D	54
Long, Long, Long, Long, like Dan's Long Nose.	. .		1022	Nim-Dan-Dean 1	D	54
Long, Long, Long, Long, like Dan's Long Nose.	. .		1022	Nim-Dan-Dean 1	D	54
Long, Long, Long, Long, like Dan's Long Nose.	. .		1022	Nim-Dan-Dean 1	D	54
Long, Long, Long, Long, like Dan's Long Nose.	. .		1022	Nim-Dan-Dean 1	D	54
Bring down Long Shanks Jim too, but now I think on't,			1023	Nim-Dan-Dean 2	D	11

LONG-BULLETS
| When you saw Tady at long-bullets play, | . . . . . . | | 882 | Pastoral Dial | | 33 |

LONG-DELUDED
| "And long-deluded Mortals see, | . . . . | | 384 | Manly Virtue | | 13 |

LONG-EAR'D
A Long-ear'd Beast, and a Field-house for Cattle,	.		942	Probatur Alit		1
A Long-ear'd Beast, a Bird that prates,	. . . . .		942	Probatur Alit		3
A long-ear'd Beast, and Woman of Endor,	. . . . .		942	Probatur Alit		7
With a long-ear'd Beast, and Med'cines Use,	. .		942	Probatur Alit		9
A long-ear'd Beast and holy Fable,	. . . .		942	Probatur Alit		11
A long-ear'd Beast, and Rhenish Wine,	. . . . .		942	Probatur Alit		13
A long-ear'd Beast and Flanders College,	. . . .		942	Probatur Alit		15
A long-ear'd Beast, and Building Knight;	. . . .		942	Probatur Alit		17
A long-ear'd Beast, and Bird of Night,	. . . . .		942	Probatur Alit		19
A long-ear'd Beast, and shameful Vermin,	. . . .		942	Probatur Alit		21
A long-ear'd Beast, and Irish Cart,	. . . . . .		942	Probatur Alit		23
A long-ear'd Beast, in Mud to lye,	. . . . . .		942	Probatur Alit		25
A long-ear'd Beast, and a sputt'ring old Whig,	. .		942	Probatur Alit		27
A long-ear'd Beast, and Liquor to write,	. . . .		942	Probatur Alit		29
A long-ear'd Beast, and the Child of a Sheep,	. .		943	Probatur Alit		31
A Beast long-ear'd, and till Midnight you stay,	. .		943	Probatur Alit		33
A long-ear'd Beast, and the Drink you love best	. .		943	Probatur Alit		35
A long-ear'd Beast, and the sixteenth Letter,	. .		943	Probatur Alit		37
A long-ear'd Beast give me, and Eggs unsound,	. .		943	Probatur Alit		39
A long-ear'd Beast, another Name for Jeer,	. . .		943	Probatur Alit		41
A long-ear'd Beast, and kind Noise of a Cat,	. .		943	Probatur Alit		43
A long-ear'd Beast, and what seasons your Beef	. .		943	Probatur Alit		45
A long-ear'd Beast, a Thing that Force must drive in,			943	Probatur Alit		47

LONG-EXPECTING
| Or gives Relief to long-expecting Heirs. | . . . . . | | 364 | On Dreams | | 28 |

LONG-THINKING
| Long-thinking made my Fancy worse. | . . . . . . | | 741 | Stel B-day 22 | | 12 |

LONG-WINDED
| Which, thundring out with lungs long-winded, | . . . . | | 675 | Curate's Compl | | 11 |

LONG'D
| Who often long'd to eat his Son: | . . . . | | 460 | Birthday Song | | 12 |
| He long'd for a Girl that would struggle and squal, | . . | | 519 | Dean Hang Rape | | 56 |

	PAGE	TITLE	LINE
LONGD			
And longd to hunt upon my grounds	422	Ireld	28
LONGER			
And the Dove-muse, will now no longer stay	16	Ode Athenian	16
No longer shall forsaken Thames	107	V's House	47
Plain Goody would no longer down, ...	116	Bauc & Phil 2	143
Quo' She, no longer parly;	154	Widow and Cat D	32
That longer with Thee to Dispense, ...	154	Widow and Cat D	43
Or when he can no longer stand	160	Atlas	7
Thou must no longer deal in Farce, ...	181	Horace 2, 1	35
"For shou'd you stay but one Week longer, ...	208	Fable Bitches	29
"I must a little longer crave;	208	Fable Bitches	32
But, Art no longer can prevayl	228	Prog of Beauty	77
In vain expects a longer Date	229	Prog of Beauty	107
No longer will tarry, ...	245	Irish-Feast	34
The Point he could no longer doubt, ...	255	Bubble	129
Nor beaten Paths be longer trac'd.	270	Apollo's Edict D	11
With Water fill'd he could no longer float, ...	284	Elegy Boat	8
He'd wish to sleep a little longer.	296	Satiric Elegy	8
The Matter now no longer sticks;	300	Horrid Plot	59
'Twas plain he cou'd no longer hold	346	Prometheus	49
Your Spouse shall there no longer hector	362	Grace's Answer	37
The Traders now no longer cheat;	391	Young's Satire	13
No longer my Advice regard:	501	Doctor Delaney	54
Then let us no longer by Parsons be Flam'd, ...	576	Place Damn'd	15
Why should he longer mince the Matter?	604	Beasts Confess	95
On your Faults no longer smile?	637	Epistle Lady	234
His Altar now no longer smokes, ...	687	Cadenus Vaness	9
She minds no longer what she taught.	704	Cadenus Vaness	561
Said, she shou'd be no longer teiz'd;	704	Cadenus Vaness	574
The Goddess wou'd no longer wait;	714	Cadenus Vaness	886
Thou Stella, wert no longer young, ...	728	Stella, Poems	9
She vows she will no longer stay, ...	751	Stel Wood-Park	58
And can no longer dance in Rhyme.	756	Stel B-day '24	4
Reports you are no longer young?	757	Stel B-day '24	36
You must no longer thus equip 'ye	779	Mullinix Tim	213
Which must alas no longer stand;	849	Old Thorn	22
His Signs aloft no longer swing;	875	Drapier's Hill	14
A longer half-p'orth never did I see;	881	Pastoral Dial	27
No longer calls me Snipe and Slattern;	888	Panegyr Dean	58
Vow'd, he no longer could support	903	Death Daphne	11
Tho' Delany advis'd you to plague me no longer, . . .	967	Letter Sherid	7
Let's quarrel no longer, since Dan and George Rochfort	979	Dean to Tho: S	35
To hold out longer in Trysyllable.	989	Letter Dr Sh-n	31
LONGING			
In vain pursues the Musick with her longing Eye, . . .	17	Ode Athenian	58
LONGINUS			
And if we have not read Longinus, ...	648	On Poetry	257
High as Longinus to the Stars ascends, ...	669	Epig Carthy 14 D	1
LONGITUDE			
With equal Longitude below:	393	Modern Poets	4
LONGS			
And longs to be a Canon there;	173	Horace 1, 7	84
With eager Hast he longs to rove	251	Bubble	29
But Cupid, full of Mischief, longs	701	Cadenus Vaness	466
LOOBY			
Who cou'd give the Looby such Airs?	800	Traulus 2	25
LOOK			
To which they look as to some Guardian God	12	Ode to William D	31
Yet wheresoe're you look you'll always find	18	Ode Athenian	74
Look where exalted Vertue and Religion sit	21	Ode Athenian	176
Look where you see	21	Ode Athenian	178
For Learning's mighty Treasures look	27	Ode to Temple	35
Look where the Pully's ty'd above!	29	Ode to Temple	102
To drive all Virtue out, or look it dead!	30	Ode to Temple	123
Bids us make Bricks, yet sends us to look out for Straw;	32	Ode to Temple	188
Thus I look down with mercy on the age, ...	45	To Congreve	49
Yes, that beau's look, that voice, those critic ears, .	48	To Congreve	173
And grief flung sables on each menial look;	53	Temple Ill	60
Wert thou right woman, thou shouldst scorn to look . .	54	Temple Ill	107
All this we grant--why, then look yonder	84	Salamander	45
You look like Rogues would rob a House	91	Bauc & Phil 1	40
With a demure dejected Look.	95	Bauc & Phil 1	172
Nor look Asquint on an old Friend.	101	Elegy Patrige	102
Does to his best look upward still.	101	Elegy Patrige	106
Now seem'd to look abundance better, ...	114	Bauc & Phil 2	97
Amaz'd to see Her look so Prim, ...	116	Bauc & Phil 2	147
Truth, Innocence, Good Nature, Look serene;	118	Biddy Floyd	4
In painted Cloth we look for Fields, ...	122	Empty'ng Town	11
What makes your Worship look so lean?	174	Horace 1, 7	122
By dull Divines, who look with envious Eyes, ...	193	Author Himself	3
So, Clowns on Scholars as on Wizards look, ...	193	Author Himself	7
She durst not look above your Wast;	222	Prog of Love	6
To make her Hair look black as Jet, ...	226	Prog of Beauty	18
Look round about how thick it lyes:	254	Bubble	104
That she stopt in her Course to look on them both; . .	264	Apollo	38
Peeps in the Ponds to look for Spawn:	279	Journal	22
We'll cry; look, here's our Boat, and there's the	285	Elegy Boat	36
Pendent.			
We look for a Salmon, you leave us a Stone.	287	Bank Down	8
But Thanks to the House, the Projectors look blank, .	287	Bank Down	9

LOOK	(CONTINUED)	PAGE	TITLE	LINE
"Look, there he stands, and 'tis but just		304	Storm	49
Is not the truth the truth? Look full on me;		307	Billet Players	9
When we perform, look sharp among our crew;		307	Billet Players	11
To look on Vice triumphant round,		312	To Ford	41
Can you on Dublin look with Scorn?		314	To Ford	83
To look with Robin Grattan's Eyes:		314	To Ford	86
Good Lord! I wondred how I dar'd to look him in the Face.		342	Upon His Grace	28
A while they on each other look,		405	Swift to Pope	5
"Don't I look frightfully to Day?		446	Modern Lady	49
But read a Nod, a Shrug, a Look,		450	Modern Lady	190
"I always lose when you look on.		452	Modern Lady	245
Who look on Courts with stricter Eyes;		485	Libel on D- D-	175
For Strephon ventur'd to look in,		528	Lady's Dres Rm	79
But let no Friend alive look into't.		643	On Poetry	108
You make the graceful Horace look		670	Epig Carthy 21	D 3
Let Malice look with all her Eyes,		730	Stella, Poems	81
How Angels look at thirty six)		735	Stel B-day '20	18
To make you look like Beauty's Queen		736	Stel B-day '20	53
Let Stella look with watchful Eye,		743	Stel B-day 22	59
For better Game, and look for Grouse:		760	Receipt Youth	54
Can look with Joy on what is past.		764	Stel B-day '26	18
Look to thy Self, and be no more the Sport		770	Horace 1, 14	11
When to look Scornful, when to Smile,		780	Mullinix Tim	236
Look on him and see their Growth.		799	Traulus 2	6
Yet I look on thee with Pity.		838	Legion Club	192
Look not with your future Eyes:		862	To Janus	10
O law! the sweet Gentleman! look in his Face;		870	Grand Question	94
How enviously the Ladies look,		891	Panegyr Dean	137
No Wonder now I look so thin;		915	Riddle 1	9
The Vulgar all consult my Look.		917	Riddle 3	8
Take wise Advice, and look behind,		921	Riddle 7	3
Are forc't to look another Way;		922	Riddle 7	48
Make the fairest look more fair;		936	Riddle 24	D 6
Die like all that look on you.		937	Riddle 24	D 54
Cooks make their Fowl look tight and spruce.		942	Probatur Alit	10
I'd not look at all, unless I look't better.		943	Probatur Alit	38
I went in vain to look for Eupolis,		988	Letter Dr Sh-n	7
And look in English, French, and Scotch for't,		993	On Picture	8
LOOK'D				
Where none e'er look'd for it before;		133	Magician's Rod	30
Harry look'd fierce, and shook his ragged Mane:		168	Peace Dunkirk	17
Look'd with an easie, careless Mien,		170	Horace 1, 7	9
The Graces half asham'd look'd down;		689	Cadenus Vaness	100
She look'd on Partridges with scorn		746	Stel Distress	13
As the Coach stopp'd, she look'd & swore		746	Stel Distress	27
As the Coach stopp'd, she look'd & swore		746	Stel Distress	
She look'd on Partridges with scorn,		750	Stel Wood-Park	11
(For the Dean was so shabby and look'd like a Ninny,		872	Grand Question	151
So, then you look'd scornful, and snift at the Dean,		873	Grand Question	175
I maul'd you when you look'd so bluff,		1002	Reply by Dean	16
And look'd like a Rake, who was made in the Stews sick;		1029	Dr. Helsham	18
LOOK'T				
And look't since he has got his Wish,		299	Horrid Plot	33
I'd not look at all, unless I look't better.		943	Probatur Alit	38
LOOKERS				
But then the Lookers on, the Tories		778	Mullinix Tim	147
LOOKING				
Thus from a Hillock looking down,		255	Bubble	126
Jove stood amaz'd, but looking round,		346	Prometheus	47
Looking big as any Gyants,		573	Helter Skelter	3
Or, to Parnassus looking down,		620	Scandal Poem 1	109
Or, to Parnassus looking down,		626	Scandal Poem 2	107
First, nine Ways looking, let her stand		743	Stel B-day 22	53
I concluded, looking round 'em,		839	Legion Club	241
Strain their Necks with looking back:		863	To Janus	22
Who often has made me, by looking ascue, sick.		1030	Dr. Sheridan	5
LOOKS				
How much of Heav'n is in her naked looks.		23	Ode Athenian	233
Altho' we boast our Winter-Sun looks bright,		25	Ode Athenian	280
Oft she looks back in vain,		31	Ode to Temple	154
That looks with scorn on half mankind beside;		44	To Congreve	44
Thy looks, when every cause of grief is past!		52	Temple Ill	34
See Muse, what havock in these looks appear		55	Temple Ill	125
For on a Knave he never looks		74	Game Traffick	7
Dame Floyd looks out in grave Suspence		75	Game Traffick	13
Soon knew Apollo by his looks,		120	Apollo Outwit	15
Tho' this Description looks so big,		134	Magician's Rod	65
And Dismal double-Dismal looks;		168	Peace Dunkirk	12
Their looks are all by method set,		178	To Lord Harley	55
Some formal Visits, Looks, and Words,		204	In Sickness	13
Vapors and Steams her Looks disgrace,		226	Prog of Beauty	2
In half a Month she looks so thin		229	Prog of Beauty	98
And by his Looks, had he held out his Palms,		234	Elegy on Demar	11
She at the Glass consults her Looks		291	Prog Marriage	40
Looks like the Chaplain of the Household,		291	Prog Marriage	62
With chearfull Looks, and honest Hearts.		314	To Ford	82
With new Delight looks up and loves;		387	Manly Virtue	128
And looks a Critick in the Face.		500	Doctor Delaney	26
To him that looks behind the Scene,		530	Lady's Dres Rm	133

LOOKS   (CONTINUED)   PAGE   TITLE   LINE

Tom for a wealthy Wife looks round, ...   545 Life of Swift   15
Refin'd all Mettals with his Looks, ...   597 Problem Solved   3
You find it in his meagre Looks: . . . .   604 Beasts Confess   106
Clear your Looks, and smooth your Stile: . . . . .   633 Epistle Lady   108
How monstrous Carthy looks to Flaccus brac't, ...   668 Epig Carthy 9   D   1
To study bright Vanessa's Looks: . . . . . .   694 Cadenus Vaness   235
Nor further looks, but thinks him young. . . . . . .   703 Cadenus Vaness   531
Looks back with Joy where she has gone, ...   765 Stel B-day '26   75
'Tis not the Coat that looks so dun, ...   786 Clad in Brown   7
Not one Jot better looks the Sun   . . . .   786 Clad in Brown   9
In his Looks are Hell and Murther;   . . . .   834 Legion Club   142
For thy horrid Looks, I own, ...   838 Legion Club   195
They reproach you with their Looks;   . . . .   838 Legion Club   208
Can tell by her looks   . . . .   854 Lady's Lament   93
Looks up to your Window, and cocks up his Beaver. . .   870 Grand Question   104
"But, <Zounds>, by their Looks, they never keep Lent: 872 Grand Question   146
"Mister Curate, for all your grave Looks, I'm afraid,   872 Grand Question   147
That looks hideous, fierce, and frightful; . . . . .   907 Daphne   45
And by a faint Description make them less. . . . .   21 Ode Athenian   174
One surly Clown lookt out, and said, ...   91 Bauc & Phil 1   37
And painted, lookt abundance better   . . . . . .   93 Bauc & Phil 1   122
Lookt high and low, walkt often round, ...   109 V's House   97
The Coachman stopt, she lookt and swore   . . . . .   751 Stel Wood-Park   47
Just as they lookt in the Original.   . . . . . .   783 Tim and Fables   18
LOOM   SEE HEIR-LOOM
LOOMS
Instead of Spoils of Persian Looms, ...   379 Apology Lady C   109
LOOSE
Scatt'ring loose features o'er the optic vein; . . . .   54 Temple Ill   96
Nor let her loose to spoil your Trade.   . . . . . .   585 Strephon Chloe   30
The House will never loose it's Trade.   . . . . . .   734 Stel B-day '20   8
"A Scholard, when just from his College broke loose,   872 Grand Question   157
Or may I loose my Weeding-knife--and Thee. . . . .   882 Pastoral Dial   48
LOOSE-GOVERN'D
A female pow'r, loose-govern'd thoughts create; . . .   54 Temple Ill   104
LOOSE'D
The bashful Dame, and loose'd her Tongue; . . . . .   386 Manly Virtue   86
LOOSELY
Hung loosely on the Church's pinnacle, ...   37 Ode Sancroft   74
Like the sun's scatter'd beams which loosely pass, . .   45 To Congreve   63
<LOOSENESS>
Till the kind <Looseness> comes, and then . . . . .   66 Problem   31
LOPT
At Head and Foot my Body lopt: . . . .   915 Riddle 1   12
LORD   SEE LD
By many a petty Lord possess'd, ...   26 Ode to Temple   6
My Lord seems pleas'd, but still directs   . . . . . .   64 Discovery   41
Works in my Lord by <Stool> and Sweat, ...   65 Problem   8
My Lord, on Fire amidst the Dames, ...   66 Problem   39
So from my Lord his Passion broke, ...   66 Problem   47
. . . . Lord! I thought I should have sunk outright: . .   69 Mrs Harris Pet   13
Lord! Madam, says Mary, how d'ye do?. . .   70 Mrs Harris Pet   14
Lord help me, said Mary, I never stirr'd out of this   70 Mrs Harris Pet   16
   Place!
Nay, said she, my Lord Collway's Folks are all very sad   70 Mrs Harris Pet   27
For my Lord Dromedary comes a Tuesday without fail; .   70 Mrs Harris Pet   28
Lord, said I, don't be angry, ...   72 Mrs Harris Pet   59
. . . .Lord, said I, what shall I do?   . . . . . .   73 Mrs Harris Pet   64
Then my Lord call'd me; Harry, said my Lord, don't cry,   73 Mrs Harris Pet   66
Then my Lord call'd me; Harry, said my Lord, don't cry,   73 Mrs Harris Pet   66
My Lord to find out who must deal   . . . .   74 Game Traffick   1
Call my Lord <Cutts> a Salamander.   . . . . . .   83 Salamander   22
But the Lord of Oxford swears, ...   169 Peace Dunkirk   35
My Lord, who (if a Man may say't)   . . . . . .   171 Horace 1, 7   13
Nor wou'd believe My Lord had sent;   . . . .   172 Horace 1, 7   52
My Lord--The Honour you design'd--   . . . .   173 Horace 1, 7   67
My Lord wou'd carry on the Jest, ...   173 Horace 1, 7   81
Truce, good My Lord, I beg a Truce!   . . . . . .   175 Horace 1, 7   130
Of Tricks, the Lord of <Oxford> knows, ...   181 Horace 2, 1   19
Come then, my Lord, and take your part in . . . . .   186 Scriblerus 3   7
Lord! how were they mistaken in the Dean! . . . . .   196 Author Himself   66
"Let my Lord know you're come to Town.   . . . . . .   200 Horace 2, 6   24
The Duke expects my Lord and you, ...   200 Horace 2, 6   53
"Put my Lord Bolingbroke in Mind, ...   201 Horace 2, 6   55
My Lord and me as far as Stains, ...   201 Horace 2, 6   76
"My Lord and he are grown so great, ...   202 Horace 2, 6   85
I know no more than my Lord Mayor, ...   202 Horace 2, 6   102
Lord! I should get so ill a Name, ...   220 A Quiet Life   35
Good Lord, what a Sight, ...   246 Irish-Feast   57
Thus when by Rooks a Lord is ply'd, ...   257 Bubble   161
My Lord and Dean, the Fire forsake;   . . . . . .   279 Journal   31
A word or two of Lord Chief Baron;   . . . . . .   282 Journal   98
Lord, what a Dress these Parsons wear, ...   291 Prog Marriage   42
And, with a licence from our good Lord May'r, ...   307 Billet Players   3
"Tho' there's a Boy whom a Lord chuses, ...   321 First of April   7
The greatest Lord, when you appear, ...   325 Pethox   43
But I sing of a Famous Lord, who seeks his Country's   341 Upon His Grace   2
   Good.
Lord William's Grace of Dublin Town, ...   341 Upon His Grace   3
Two thousand Pounds a Year, Good Lord! . .   . . . .   342 Upon His Grace   19

LORD (CONTINUED)   PAGE   TITLE   LINE

	PAGE	TITLE	LINE
For fear my Lord should send it all into the poor Man's Box.	342	Upon His Grace	26
Good Lord! I wondred how I dar'd to look him in the Face.	342	Upon His Grace	28
Then said my Lord, I'm very glad to see thee honest Friend,	342	Upon His Grace	31
My very good Lord, it's a very hard task	368	Verses Window	1
My Lady--it must be my Lord.	376	Apology Lady C	40
Cries, "Lord, the World is so censorious!	450	Modern Lady	167
"This Head of mine, Lord, how it Swims!	451	Modern Lady	208
Lord, Madam, you have lost Codill;	452	Modern Lady	246
And wou'd my Lord vouchsafe to grant	475	Epist on Epist	7
Nor will my Lord so far Beguile	475	Epist on Epist	17
Suppose my Lord and you alone;	480	Libel on D- D-	13
Your favourite Lord is none of those,	484	Libel on D- D-	136
Cryes, Lord have Mercy on his Soul,	500	Doctor Delaney	18
Himself the Lark, my Lord the Pheasant:	514	Answer Fable	52
A noble Lord hath told his Pranks,	515	Answer Fable	79
But, Lord how the Rabble will stare and will gape,	520	Dean Hang Rape	71
He lends my Lord, what was my Lord's before.	533	To Mr. Gay	76
Suppose your Lord a trusty Servant send,	534	To Mr. Gay	85
Nor, from your Lord his bad Condition hide;	534	To Mr. Gay	93
(He had not seen a Hare the Lord knows when)	538	Mr. Pulteney	26
"Then Lord have Mercy on his Soul.	562	Death of Swift	229
By ev'ry Coxcomb, but her Lord?	592	Strephon Chloe	284
And introduc'd the Lord knows why;	645	On Poetry	156
"She was at Lord knows what Expence,	713	Cadenus Vaness	864
It cost me Lord knows how much Time	741	Stel B-day 22	9
Lord how this Frothy Coxcomb frets! (aside)	774	Mullinix Tim	16
Then, wo be to my Lord Lieutenant,	789	Dick's Variety	37
Lord <Bolton's> good Grace, Lord <Carr>, and Lord <Howard>,	804	Irish Bishops	25
Lord <Bolton's> good Grace, Lord <Carr>, and Lord <Howard>,	804	Irish Bishops	25
Lord <Bolton's> good Grace, Lord <Carr>, and Lord <Howard>,	804	Irish Bishops	25
For who but Lord Bolton was mitred for Merit?	808	Advice Parson	8
Lord Pam in the Church (cou'd you think it) kneel'd down	809	Epigr Prelate	1
The Lord of all the fruitful Plain,	848	Old Thorn	10
Wise Hawthornden and Sterline's Lord.)	848	Old Thorn	16
"Nor thou, Lord Arthur, shalt escape:	850	Old Thorn	65
And see how he rides like a Lord of the Land,	870	Grand Question	95
Lord! Madam! your Ladyship sure is in jest;	871	Grand Question	124
Good Lord! what can my Lady mean,	891	Panegyr Dean	141
Lord! how politely they can scold;	949	Epigr Scolding	2
When I saw you to-day, as I went with Lord Anglesey.	978	Dean to Tho: S	1
Lord! said I, who's that parson? how awkwardly dangles he	978	Dean to Tho: S	2
So I wish you were toothless like Lord Masserine	1017	Swift Ans Sher	17
. . .with that great peer the Lord Anglesey.	1022	Nim-Dan-Dean 2	D 6
With this He putt up to My <Lord>	63	Discovery	17
Imagine now My <Lord> and Bush	63	Discovery	21

LORD-MAY'R

	PAGE	TITLE	LINE
Of Lord-May'r, Aldermen, and Shrieves,	494	Panegyr Swift	50

LORD-TREASURER

	PAGE	TITLE	LINE
Lord-Treasurer; for once be quick:	190	Faggot	36

LORD'S

	PAGE	TITLE	LINE
My Lord's an universal Lover.	67	Problem	60
I have in view a Lord's Estate,	251	Bubble	18
My Lord's Abroad; my Lady too;	376	Apology Lady C	41
That cou'd not be my Lord's Intent,	478	Epist on Epist	103
He lends my Lord, what was my Lord's before.	533	To Mr. Gay	76
A Knave, who deep embroils his Lord's Affairs,	535	To Mr. Gay	119
For, keep, or turn him out, my Lord's undone.	535	To Mr. Gay	126
No Slave his Lord's Commands obeys,	920	Riddle 6	3

LORDLINGS

	PAGE	TITLE	LINE
By the Dam from Lordlings sprung,	799	Traulus 2	3

LORDLY

	PAGE	TITLE	LINE
Because 'tis Lordly not to pay,	239	Run Bankers	13
That ev'ry rich and lordly Swain	693	Cadenus Vaness	232
From ev'ry day a Lordly Banquet	745	Stel Distress	11
From ev'ry Day a lordly Banquet,	750	Stel Wood-Park	35
Tom could move with lordly Grace,	784	Mullinex Dick	21
But should a lordly Pike appear,	824	Printer Newgat	8
While in his lordly Castle fixt,	883	Rev Market-Hill	19
And, lordly Gout wrapt up in Furr:	895	Panegyr Dean	277

LORDS

	PAGE	TITLE	LINE
These are the lords of the poetic schools,	46	To Congreve	101
Lords are a footboy's cronies in his sleep.	48	To Congreve	150
Frequented Lords; saw those that saw the Queen;	194	Author Himself	17
Now Finch alarms the Lords; he hears for certain,	194	Author Himself	37
Lords, Knights and Squires were all his humble Debtors.	234	Elegy on Demar	16
Lords keep a Pimp to bring a Wench;	480	Libel on D- D-	22
Thus Addison by Lords Carest,	482	Libel on D- D-	61
Starve twenty Lords to make one Scoundrel rich:	535	To Mr. Gay	104
"Who fain would pass for Lords indeed:	570	Death of Swift	438
Damn'd Lawyers and Judges, Damn'd Lords and Damn'd Squires,	576	Place Damn'd	9
Pointed at Col'nels, Lords, and Beaux;	701	Cadenus Vaness	478
Are Lords of Infamy and Praise:	729	Stella, Poems	54
Nor thy oppressing Lords afford thee Brass.	793	St. Pat's Well	94

LORDS   (CONTINUED)   PAGE   TITLE   LINE
    What Lords and Dames of high Degree, ...   919 Riddle 5   15
    Both Dukes and Lords abhor its Wood, ...   928 Riddle 12   D   7
    Tho' your lords, and your dogs, and your catches,   977 Dean to Sherid   45
        me-thinks,
    But, Courage, my <Lords>, tho' it cannot be said   805 Irish Bishops   49
    Content, my good <Lords>; but let us change Hands; . . 805 Irish Bishops   61
LORDSHIP   SEE LDSHIP
    That your Lordship would once let your Cares all alone 185 Scriblerus 1   3
    "I doubt not, if his Lordship knew-- . . . .   201 Horace 2, 6   61
    Then said his Lordship with a Smile, I must have   342 Upon His Grace   35
        Lawful Cash,
    And, how his Lordship was so kind;   . . . .   480 Libel on D- D-   6
    His Lordship would impute it all to Spight: . . . . 535 To Mr. Gay   112
    Or that on which his Lordship swears, ...   724 To Stella   31
LORDSHIP'S
    His Lordship's premier Ministre, ...   62 Discovery   10
    Now from his Lordship's Grace I hold a little Piece of 342 Upon His Grace   21
        Ground,
    Then God Preserve his Lordship's Grace, . . .   343 Upon His Grace   47
    Since God had no Hand in his Lordship's Promotion.   . 809 Epigr Prelate   6
LORDSHIPS
    Duns at his Lordships Gate began to meet, ...   124 Descriptn Morn   13
LORE
    You, who are skill'd in lawyer's lore, ...   489 Dialogue   7
LORIMER
    Like Lorimer, to wear his Hat.   . . . .   886 Rev Market-Hill   96
LORRAIN
    The Duke of Lorrain drew his Sword, ...   776 Mullinix Tim   111
LORRAINE'S
    With Lorraine's Duke, and Prince of Greece.   . . .   592 Strephon Chloe   292
LORSHA
    Lorsha! and out of her shteeple there was hung a black 840 Ballad   D   9
        flag.
LOSE
    To lose the providence of thy cares, ...   42 Ode Sancroft   242
    For, tragedy, he knew, would lose you quite, ...   47 To Congreve   145
    I have lost my Money, and shall lose my True-Love too.   73 Mrs Harris Pet   65
    <Cholmondeley>, when Drunk, can never lose his Wand, . 164 Toland's Invit   25
    Swore he'd rather lose a Crown, ...   168 Peace Dunkirk   19
    Lose not your time, nor our diversion miss, ... 309 Billet Players   57
    'Tis no great Loss to lose an Ear;   . . . . . .   366 Answer Delaney   2
    Too lately found! to lose him late!   . . . . . .   388 Manly Virtue   142
    Will then lose their charms   . . . . . .   424 Carterets Arms   8
    Must lose the honour, you have gain'd, ...   436 Answer Paulus   141
    "Four Mattadores, and lose Codill!   . . . . . .   446 Modern Lady   52
    "I always lose when you look on.   . . . . . .   452 Modern Lady   245
    Before a Play, wou'd lose no Credit: . . . . . .   484 Libel on D- D-   142
    Who must Obey, or lose his Place.   . . . . . .   485 Libel on D- D-   160
    To live obscure, and have no fame to lose?   . . . .   506 To a Friend   8
    wou'd have us lose our English Friends.   . . . . .   515 Answer Fable   98
    To lose an Inch of Favour for a Friend?   . . . . .   531 To Mr. Gay   6
    To lose a Guinea at Picquet, ...   546 Life of Swift   27
    But, what if he should lose his Life   . . . . . .   587 Strephon Chloe   103
    You lose your Credit all at once;   . . . . . .   644 On Poetry   137
    To flatter Knaves, or lose his Pension.   . . . . .   650 On Poetry   310
    We lose with Sharpers at Piquet;   . . . . . .   724 To Stella   28
    When vulgar Knaves would lose their Ears: . . . . . 724 To Stella   32
    So, Poets lose their Feet by Time, ...   756 Stel B-day '24   3
    I did but lose my precious Breath, ...   778 Mullinix Tim   172
    As if they were afraid to lose 'em: . . . . . .   813 Bro Protestant   60
    Well, if you could lose it quite.   . . . . . .   862 To Janus   12
    I lose by the House what I get by the Land;   . . . .   866 Grand Question   4
    In Poundage and Drawbacks, I lose half my Rent,   . . 867 Grand Question   21
    And rather than that, I would lose my Estate.   . . .   867 Grand Question   24
    Lose not time to contradict her, ...   907 Daphne   29
    By riding Post I lose my Health;   . . . .   917 Riddle 3   17
    Who neither get, nor lose a Groat;   . . . . . .   918 Riddle 4   14
    I cannot find I lose or win, ...   918 Riddle 4   36
    Wherein they need not lose a Bit, ...   1022 Nim-Dan-Dean 1 D 43
LOSES
    And tell who loses, and who wins, ...   280 Journal   63
    And still the Truth he will Maintain, whate'er he loses 341 Upon His Grace   6
        by't.
LOSING
    By losing their favor   . . . .   424 Carterets Arms   18
LOSS
    Is at a loss for Figures to express   . . . . . .   21 Ode Athenian   172
    For though with Loss or Victory awhile   . . . . .   29 Ode to Temple   78
    Till at last tir'd with loss of Time and Ease,   . . .   30 Ode to Temple   133
    . . .do you know what a Loss I have had?   . . . . .   70 Mrs Harris Pet   26
    I'll give something towards thy Loss;. . . . . .   73 Mrs Harris Pet   67
    'Tis no great Loss to lose an Ear;   . . . . . .   366 Answer Delaney   2
    The Loss of one is no such Trouble, ...   366 Answer Delaney   11
    Your Politicians at a loss   . . . . . .   420 Holyhead   16
    A Loss that Dick thought, no Mortal cou'd bear.   . .   430 Dicky Dolly   6
    But lik'd neither loss and so quietly dy'd.   . . . .   430 Dicky Dolly   12
    That all the Loss your Purse sustain'd   . . . . . .   496 Panegyr Swift   88
    No Loss more easy to supply.   . . . .   562 Death of Swift   244
    While Jonathan's threaten'd with loss of his ears; . . 818 Epigr Kite   2
    How sorely I lament your Loss?   . . . .   821 Dr. Rundle   62

		PAGE	TITLE	LINE
LOSS	(CONTINUED)			
Arbiters of Loss and Gain,	. . . .	934	Riddle 22	D 2
But the loss of your Cough will be the best Sign	. .	1017	Swift Ans Sher	14
LOSSE				
Nor shall grin Berris make up the Losse.	. . . . .	103	Merlin	10
LOSSES				
Poor <Swift>, with all his Losses vext,	. . . .	174	Horace 1, 7	113
Come here their Losses to retrieve,	. . . . . .	254	Bubble	90
LOST				
And half Your Virtues had been lost in Shade.	. . .	11	Ode to William	D 12
It lost some mighty Pieces thro' all hands it past	. .	25	Ode Athenian	286
And Poetry has lost the art to praise,	. . . . . .	38	Ode Sancroft	111
A jargon form'd from the lost language, wit,	. . .	47	To Congreve	121
Lost youth, she cry'd, since first I met thee here!	.	52	Temple Ill	32
I have lost my Money, and shall lose my True-Love too.		73	Mrs Harris Pet	65
Now Poets find this Art is lost,	. . . .	79	Vanbrug House	13
Lost by Disuse the Art to roast	. . . .	93	Bauc & Phil 1	126
The Queen has lately lost a Part	. . . .	96	On the Union	1
Now Poets feel this Art is lost:	. . . .	106	V's House	14
Lost, by Disuse, the Art to Roast,	. . . . . .	113	Bauc & Phil 2	66
A Third, who lost his Way by Night,	. . . . . .	127	Little House	31
And Britain's lost if Harly dyes	. . . .	140	Harlyes Surgn	2
Was lost among Pactolus Sands,	. . . .	157	Fable of Midas	34
Had lost his Art, and kept his Ears.	. . . . . .	157	Fable of Midas	40
Made false Moves, and lost his Queen;	. . . . . .	168	Peace Dunkirk	16
If I ne'er got, or lost a groat,	. . . .	199	Horace 2, 6	D
My choicest Hours of Life are lost:	. . . . . .	202	Horace 2, 6	106
But Bawty, lost to Shame and Honour,	. . . . . .	208	Fable Bitches	39
But Illium's lost, and Priam falls.	. . . . . .	209	Fable Bitches	46
Thus all Society is lost,	. . . .	217	To Mr. Delany	73
Oh London Tavern! Thou hast lost a Friend,	. . .	234	Elegy on Demar	25
I lost my new Cloak.	. . . .	245	Irish-Feast	20
Thus when a Whale hath lost the Tide	. . . . . .	258	Bubble	201
And sav'd his Oar, but lost his Hat.	. . . . . .	281	Journal	72
Nim lost his Wig-block, Dan his Jordan,	. . . . .	283	Journal	123
I hope he will find that no Love is lost.	. . . .	337	Serious Poem	108
Has lost His Grace for Ten Years past . . .	341	Upon His Grace	10
So, when an Eye hath lost it's Brother,	. . . . .	366	Answer Delaney	21
Your Arms, tho' both your Eyes were lost,	. . . .	367	Answer Delaney	47
As will retrieve a lost Estate:	. . . .	392	Young's Satire	44
Except some Leather lost behind.	. . . .	398	Earl of P-b-w	24
And by Excursions lost his Ground:	. . . . . .	412	Desire Possess	26
Dick lost in Doll, a Wife Tender and Dear,	. . .	430	Dicky Dolly	4
But Dick lost by Doll, twelve hundred a Year,	. .	430	Dicky Dolly	5
Thought much of his Doll, and the Jointure he lost,	.	430	Dicky Dolly	8
And have we lost our only Friend?	. . . . . .	445	Modern Lady	16
Lord, Madam, you have lost Codill;	. . . . . .	452	Modern Lady	246
From whence 'tis plain, they quite have lost	. . .	498	Panegyr Swift	165
Is after Marriage lost so soon,	. . . .	591	Strephon Chloe	257
Nor wonder how I lost my Wits;	. . . .	597	Cassinus Peter	117
By which he lost, he may affirm,	. . . .	604	Beasts Confess	85
No Love is lost on either Side.	. . . .	606	Beasts Confess	164
By want of Skill, he always lost:	. . . . . .	607	Beasts Confess	190
You need not fear your Labour lost:	. . . . . .	643	On Poetry	110
Since all he got by Fraud, is lost by Stocks,	. .	678	Dean and Duke	6
That Cupid now has lost his Art,	. . . .	687	Cadenus Vaness	7
The Queen of Beauty lost her Aim.	. . . . . .	700	Cadenus Vaness	433
Cupid, tho' all his Darts were lost,	. . . . . .	702	Cadenus Vaness	492
That all his Lessons were not lost.	. . . . . .	705	Cadenus Vaness	605
The lovely Nymph had lost her Nose.	. . . . . .	730	Stella, Poems	78
The rusty Tongs have lost a Leg	. . . .	746	Stel Distress	40
Lost are thy Oars that us'd thy Course to guide,	.	770	Horace 1, 14	13
She saved Britannia's Right, and lost her own.	. .	771	Horace 1, 14	46
Why Tom, the Man has lost his Wits!	. . . . . .	797	Traulus 1	34
He lost his Bishoprick, and hang'd, or burst.	. .	806	Judas	8
And after, me thought, I had lost my new Shoes;	. .	868	Grand Question	51
All for Love, or the World well lost.	. . . . .	878	Robbin & Harry	20
You lost a Place, and sav'd a Bribe?	. . . . .	884	Rev Market-Hill	36
Which never yet one Friend has lost you.	. . . .	890	Panegyr Dean	114
Few are made, but Numbers lost.	. . . .	934	Riddle 22	D 6
But these are lost full many a Century.	. . . .	988	Letter Dr Sh-n	14
Here Elements have lost their Uses,	. . . . . .	1035	To Quilca	5
LOT				
Ah fav'rite youth, how happy is thy lot!--	. . .	53	Temple Ill	71
How different from thine is Dunkin's Lot!	. . . .	667	Epig Carthy 7	D 1
LOTH				
As loth to see the hated Court and Town,	. . . .	31	Ode to Temple	157
Who, loth to blame, or to incense,	. . . . . .	377	Apology Lady C	73
And, wheezing Asthma, loth to stir:	. . . . . .	895	Panegyr Dean	278
But, loth his Person to expose	. . . .	904	Death Daphne	33
Yet still you are out (tho' to vex you I'm loth),	.	976	Dean to Sherid	17
LOUD				
Though very turbulent and very loud;	. . . . . .	38	Ode Sancroft	136
Tempests long frown, and thunder threatens loud,	. .	52	Temple Ill	24
Dame, said I, as loud as I could bawl,..	. .	70	Mrs Harris Pet	26
But bawl'd as loud as he could roar,	. . . . .	91	Bauc & Phil 1	35
Methinks I hear thee loud, as Trumpet,	. . . . .	182	Horace 2, 1	71
And the loud Laugh proclaims the War;	. . . . .	218	To Mr. Delany	80
Nell scolded in so loud a Din	. . . .	219	A Quiet Life	1
Repeat the Absolution loud;	. . . .	222	Prog of Love	10
The last loud trump must wake him now:	. . . . .	296	Satiric Elegy	6

	PAGE	TITLE	LINE
LOUD (CONTINUED)			
He'll Bellow as loud as the Dee'l in a Drum:	336	Serious Poem	80
So, by the Kettles loud Allarm,	345	Prometheus	25
So loud, till all the Nation hears;	354	Simile Silver	28
And when his last Speech the loud Hawkers did cry,	399	Tom Clinch	11
As loud as fifty mustard bowls:	461	Birthday Song	40
By loud and unharmonious Croaking,	479	Epist on Epist	124
As if he heard Loud Thunders roul,	500	Doctor Delaney	17
Aspiring, factious, fierce and loud	503	Doctor Delaney	87
Of loud un-meaning Sounds, a rapid Flood	532	To Mr. Gay	39
he's loud in his laugh & he's coarse in his Jest	540	Charac Walpole	2
But, Strephon sigh'd so loud and strong,	585	Strephon Chloe	39
With loud Huzza's from all the Boys,	586	Strephon Chloe	69
The loud Cerberian tripple Bark.	596	Cassinus Peter	80
As grating, or as loud as theirs?	617	Scandal Poem 1	6
So frequent or so loud as theirs?	624	Scandal Poem 2	6
Desir'd them not to talk so loud,	689	Cadenus Vaness	77
And if your Voice had not been loud,	742	Stel B-day 22	47
Could roar as loud as Stentor,	785	Mullinex Dick	38
LOUDER			
Their Chattering makes a louder Din	450	Modern Lady	180
Grew louder, all the Way up Stairs;	698	Cadenus Vaness	369
LOUDEST			
Who always loudest for Religion bawl,	8	Ode to King	83
His loudest Voice is low and weak,	405	Swift to Pope	3
Where loudest winds incessant roar	420	Holyhead	30
While each to be the loudest vies,	450	Modern Lady	175
At Entrance loudest, where they found	698	Cadenus Vaness	370
Jove, with all his loudest Thunder,	933	Riddle 20	D 23
LOUDLY			
And loudly cry'd--a Bite, a Bite.	208	Fable Bitches	42
Nor loudly cackles at the Door;	230	Prog of Poetry	7
Who, when she loudly cries, Forbear,	641	On Poetry	21
You certainly know, tho' so loudly you vapour,	818	Archbi Cashel	5
<LOUGHALL>			
And took their Progress tow'rds <Loughall>.	321	First of April	14
LOUSE SEE WOOD-LOUSE			
'Tis not that I value the Money three Skips of a Louse	71	Mrs Harris Pet	38
In threed-bare Goun, would scarce a louse hold,	291	Prog Marriage	61
The Louse of the Wood for a Med'cine is us'd,	351	Wood Insect	11
But is a Louse your Flesh and Blood?	812	Bro Protestant	36
Than the barking of Towzer, or leap of a louse?	814	Yahoo's	9
Let them, 'ere they crack a Louse,	831	Legion Club	57
Ten thousand Lice, and ev'ry Louse was gold,	882	Pastoral Dial	46
Without it a Writer is not worth a Louse.	941	Letter	28
LOUSY			
Witness his lazy, lousy son!	950	Upstart	D 10
LOV'D SEE DEAR-LOV'D			
To the lov'd Pasture where he us'd to feed,	31	Ode to Temple	148
I once esteem'd, and lov'd, and favour'd more,	44	To Congreve	12
Where I am neither lov'd nor known.	203	In Sickness	4
Pleaded the <Bishop> lov'd a <Whore>,	302	Storm	12
"He lov'd the Dean. (I lead a Heart.)	562	Death of Swift	239
That in his Heart he lov'd a Jest:	602	Beasts Confess	22
Would not be prais'd, yet lov'd to praise.	701	Cadenus Vaness	457
LOVE SEE SELF-LOVE,TRUE-LOVE			
Like Love, wrapt up in Fire;	8	Ode to King	69
Of Nature and of Art, of deep Philosophy and Love,	17	Ode Athenian	55
Tho' all the Fumes of Fear, Hope, Love, and Shame,	22	Ode Athenian	206
(Whether thro' Rage or Love, or both)	84	Salamander	52
And still it's Love to Houshold Cares	94	Bauc & Phil 1	143
In Physick, Stolen Goods, or Love,	101	Elegy Patrige	115
And still its Love to Household Cares	113	Bauc & Phil 2	81
Of Love shall always speak and write;	150	Corinna	10
Marries for Love, half Whore, half Wife;	150	Corinna	26
Seated at Table next the Men you love.	165	Toland's Invit	32
But I love Elbow-room when're I drink,	166	Toland's Invit	37
For among good Friends, I love to be plain;	168	Peace Dunkirk	7
And Commoners who love good Wine,	169	Peace Dunkirk	23
That you should meet, in love, success?	177	To Lord Harley	24
Her love on some bright youth below,	178	To Lord Harley	60
"So eager to express your Love,	200	Horace 2, 6	37
"Ah Doctor, how you love to jest?	202	Horace 2, 6	97
And tho men cry, they love a Jest,	218	To Mr. Delany	83
They love a Jest--when 'tis their own.	218	To Mr. Delany	86
Love never thinks of Rich and Poor,	224	Prog of Love	61
Love with White lead cements his Wings,	227	Prog of Beauty	61
Ye Pow'rs who over Love preside,	229	Prog of Beauty	117
It shews the Queen of Love intends	254	Bubble	95
Till pious Love inspir'd her Son?	269	Apollo's Edict	D 4
'Twill gain her Love to make her fine?	292	Prog Marriage	72
Equal to all in Care and Love,	322	First of April	35
'Tis Fifty round Millions of Love, and a Mending.	337	Serious Poem	106
Call'd, Love In A Tub, and Love In A Wood.	337	Serious Poem	92
Call'd, Love In A Tub, and Love In A Wood.	337	Serious Poem	92
First, Love In A Tub: 'Squire Wood has in Store	337	Serious Poem	95
And sell them for Gold, or he can't shew his Love else,	337	Serious Poem	98
Then can you deny it is Love in a Wood?	337	Serious Poem	100
I hope you will own it is Love in a Maze;	337	Serious Poem	102
For when you express a Friend's Love we are willing,	337	Serious Poem	103
We never say more than, your Love is a Million;	337	Serious Poem	104

LOVE   (CONTINUED)   PAGE   TITLE   LINE
    But with honest Wood's Love there is no contending,   .   337 Serious Poem   105
    Then in his First Love why should he be crost?   . . .   337 Serious Poem   107
    I hope he will find that no Love is lost.   . . . . .   337 Serious Poem   108
    My dear Estate, how well I love it;   . . . .   348 Whitshed Motto   7
    Suspected for the Love he bore   . . . .   375 Apology Lady C   15
    That Love is the Devil, I'll prove when requir'd: 401 Window Inns 3   1
    They swear that they all by Love are inspir'd,   . . .   401 Window Inns 3   3
    So when our passions Love hath stirr'd, ...   402 Window Inns 6   D 3
    At once creating Love and Pity.   417 Woman's Mind   42
    For Princes love you should descant   . . . . . .   464 Birthday Song   127
    I hate the Vice-Roy, love the Man.   485 Libel on D- D-   152
    Ye <senators>, who love to prate;   . . . . . .   487 Irish-Club   2
    Our Brethren of <England> who love us so dear,   516 Dean Hang Rape   1
    Should I the Queen of Love refuse, ...   530 Lady's Dres Rm   131
    Not Love of Beauty less the Heart inflames   . . . .   532 To Mr. Gay   19
    Would love his Fav'rite better than before;   . . . .   535 To Mr. Gay   113
    And get the better of your Love;   . . . .   546 Life of Swift   38
    I love my Friend as well as you, ...   554 Death of Swift   17
    One, whom you love of all Mankind, ...   554 Death of Swift   22
    How those I love, my Death lament.   . . . . . .   561 Death of Swift   206
    With Pains of Love tormented lies;   . . . . . .   582 Young Nymph   39
    The Weather and his Love were hot;   . . . . . .   586 Strephon Chloe   81
    And, Love such Nicety requires, ...   588 Strephon Chloe   135
    To keep Esteem and Love alive.   . . . . . .   593 Strephon Chloe   310
    On Love and Books in Rapture sweet;   . . . . . .   593 Cassinus Peter   4
    Was so unfortunate in Love.   . . . .   598 Problem Solved   22
    No Love is lost on either Side.   . . . . . .   606 Beasts Confess   164
    But, Poets love profane allusions.   . . . . . .   622 Scandal Poem 1   162
    Servants love you, and obey: . . . .   633 Epistle Lady   106
    I, who love to have a Fling, ...   637 Epistle Lady   221
    Procure the Book for Love or Money, ...   648 On Poetry   260
    Yet, hang me, but I love her dearly.   . . . . . .   679 From Catullus   8
    Now Love is dwindled to Intrigue, ...   687 Cadenus Vaness   13
    That modern Love is no such Thing   . . . . . .   687 Cadenus Vaness   27
    That Mortals here disdain to love;   . . . . . .   689 Cadenus Vaness   81
    Tho' Foes to Love, attend the Session, ...   689 Cadenus Vaness   94
    On whom the Queen of Love was bent   . . . . . .   691 Cadenus Vaness   138
    The Queen of Love was pleas'd, and proud, ...   693 Cadenus Vaness   228
    Besides, she fear'd the Queen of Love   . . . . . .   695 Cadenus Vaness   268
    The Queen of Love, whom thus she greets, ...   695 Cadenus Vaness   285
    An Instrument to earthly Love?   . . . . . .   695 Cadenus Vaness   295
    By Time, and ripen into Love.   . . . . . .   701 Cadenus Vaness   475
    By Love invulnerable thought, ...   702 Cadenus Vaness   489
    Whate'er Vexations Love attend, ...   702 Cadenus Vaness   506
    But understood not what was Love.   . . . . . .   703 Cadenus Vaness   547
    That Reason was her Guide in Love.   . . . . . .   708 Cadenus Vaness   677
    Love or Contempt, her Fancy strikes.   . . . . . .   708 Cadenus Vaness   683
    Was struck with Love, Esteem, and Awe, ...   708 Cadenus Vaness   692
    Love can with Speech inspire a Mute, ...   709 Cadenus Vaness   712
    Love, hitherto a transient Guest, ...   711 Cadenus Vaness   768
    Love, why do we one Passion call?   . . . . . .   711 Cadenus Vaness   772
    They temper Love and Books together;   . . . . . .   712 Cadenus Vaness   825
    Mean time the mournful Queen of Love   . . . . . .   712 Cadenus Vaness   828
    I ne'er admitted Love a Guest.   . . . . . .   728 Stella, Poems   14
    I know you love to act a Farce.   . . . . . .   783 Tim and Fables   38
    'Twas all for Love, and that's enough. . . . . . .   797 Traulus 1   62
    The world is in doubt, whether hatred or love;   . . .   818 Archbi Cashel   2
    As Soldiers use, for love must marry, ...   878 Robbin & Harry   18
    All for Love, or the World well lost.   . . . . . .   878 Robbin & Harry   20
    My Love to Sheelah is more firmly fixt . . . . . .   880 Pastoral Dial   9
    My Love for gentle Dermot faster grows . . . . . .   881 Pastoral Dial   13
    Love rooted out, again will never grow. . . . . . .   881 Pastoral Dial   16
    If Florimel had found his Love   . . . . . .   905 Death Daphne   81
    Ah, is not Love a pleasing Pain?   . . . . . .   924 Riddle 8   12
    For, should I dye for Love of you, ...   925 Riddle 8   26
    I feel not the least Love Surprize, ...   932 Riddle 19   D 3
    Love, Joy, and Devotion   . . . .   939 Riddle Answerd   13
    A long-ear'd Beast, and the Drink you love best   . . .   943 Probatur Alit   35
    And I love you so well, as I told you long ago,   . . .   979 Dean to Tho: S   17
    Every body knows, that I love to tell Truth and shame   986 Mary to Sher   23
        the Devil,
LOVE-SICK
    Let the Love-sick Bard complain, ...   933 Riddle 20   D 13
    Languid like a love-sick maid, ...   937 Riddle 24   D 41
LOVE'S
    Love's Fire, it seems, like inward Heat, ...   65 Problem   7
    Conclude Love's Bow-String at full Stretch;   . . .   66 Problem   30
    Blew out Love's Torch or chill'd the Flame: . . .   85 Salamander   60
    When Love's Allurements long are past; . . . . . .   711 Cadenus Vaness   783
LOVELINESS
    The Loveliness of Modesty, ...   384 Manly Virtue   26
LOVELY
    Did bravely snatch the lovely helpless Prize.   . . .   12 Ode to William   D 24
    To tear Religion's lovely face;   . . . .   42 Ode Sancroft   248
    Here (lovely Nymph pronounce my doom)   . . . . . .   60 Lady Tablebook   11
    And thence Beheld a Lovely Maid   . . . . . .   119 Apollo Outwit   3
    Ah Lovely Nymph be not too rash, ...   228 Prog of Beauty   67
    When you describe a lovely Girl, ...   272 Apollo's Edict   D 54
    The lovely tingling in your Ears, ...   362 Grace's Answer   35
    Lovely alike, or heard or seen;   . . . . . .   385 Manly Virtue   58

LOVELY	(CONTINUED)	PAGE	TITLE	LINE
Ah lovely Nymphs, remove your Fears,		445	Modern Lady	17
Proceeding on, the lovely Goddess		582	Young Nymph	23
So lovely in the Female Kind,		691	Cadenus Vaness	165
To see a lovely Infant born:		692	Cadenus Vaness	189
The lovely Nymph had lost her Nose.		730	Stella, Poems	78
O, could I earn for thee, my lovely Lass,		882	Pastoral Dial	49
As fair and lovely as their Queen:		923	Riddle 7	70
Ah lovely Nymph, thou'rt in thy Prime!		932	Riddle 19	D 13

LOVER

My Lord's an universal Lover.		67	Problem	60
And pay the merit of her Lover?		177	To Lord Harley	36
At length a lucky Lover came,		222	Prog of Love	19
Whoe'er will not were them, is not the King's Lover.		236	Excellent Song	4
And the Gifts I bestow'd her, will find her a Lover,		266	Apollo	107
The Di'mond and the Lover.		400	Window Inns 1	8
The Tutor turn'd a mortal Lover.		707	Cadenus Vaness	651
"Who never cou'd one Lover find.		714	Cadenus Vaness	867
And when your Lover is not true,		733	Verses Vanessa	13
The Breath of her Lover,		952	Onyons	14
Who from her Lover e'er could boast,		993	On Picture	23

LOVER'S

'Tis thou must fan the Lover's Fire;		590	Strephon Chloe	222
To pierce an injur'd Lover's Heart.		595	Cassinus Peter	60
To keep a worthy Lover's heart		732	Verses Vanessa	2

LOVERS

While two fond lovers prate, the Muse and I.		49	To Congreve	200
When wretched Lovers live on Air,		270	Apollo's Edict	D 16
New Lovers now will come in Swarms.		295	Prog Marriage	158
That now her Lovers must be payd;		311	To Ford	20
The glass, by lovers nonsense blurr'd,		402	Window Inns 6	D 1
"And Lovers of the Church distress'd---:		549	Life of Swift	161
Both special Wits, and Lovers both,		593	Cassinus Peter	2
By Lovers spoke in Punch's Booth.		650	On Poetry	298
On thy Margin Lovers wander,		661	Love Song	27
The Lovers Fleta's, Bractons, Cokes.		689	Cadenus Vaness	107
And happy Lovers bless my Reign----		694	Cadenus Vaness	248
The Race of Lovers soon must end:)		713	Cadenus Vaness	863
Or, where appointing Lovers rove,		894	Panegyr Dean	245
Treat not your Lovers with Disdain;		932	Riddle 19	D 20
Die like lovers as they gaze,		937	Riddle 24	D 49
Set hoping, hoping, hoping hearts of Lovers akeing,		959	Cantata	
While true Lovers Eyes Weeping Sleep,		960	Cantata	

LOVES

War! that mad Game, the World so loves to play,		28	Ode to Temple	76
Or loves the muse to walk with conscious pride		51	Temple Ill	11
Loves Mischief better than his Meat,		171	Horace 1, 7	14
Virtue, to crown her Fav'rites, loves to try		210	Earl of Oxford	11
But loves to take prodigious Rounds,		218	To Mr. Delany	93
With new Delight looks up and loves;		387	Manly Virtue	128
None loves his King and Country better,		410	Dial Rich Marb	83
Yet, come in time to shew their Loves,		547	Life of Swift	64
Her infant Loves with purple Wings;		585	Strephon Chloe	50
I know she loves the Barber's Boy.		595	Cassinus Peter	62
She loves a more deserving Swain.		595	Cassinus Peter	66
She loves herself, and taat's the Matter.		708	Cadenus Vaness	687
"Since ev'ry Being loves its Like,		714	Cadenus Vaness	879
That Stella loves to talk with Fellows		735	Stel B-day '20	44
Where he loves, or where he hates.		800	Traulus 2	20
He loves to be bitter at		854	Lady's Lament	89

LOVING

The loving Couple well bemir'd,		224	Prog of Love	77
But Tom was kind and loving;		784	Mullinex Dick	10
Subscribes, Dear Sir, your Brother loving.		812	Bro Protestant	20
At fifty two, when he grew loving,		879	Robbin & Harry	46
Dear Sheridan; a loving Pair		1020	Nim-Dan-Dean 1	D 1

LOW

Are these too low?--then find out grander,		83	Salamander	21
That best Foundations must be low.		87	Hist V's House	40
Lookt high and low, walkt often round,		109	V's House	97
Venture to build his Nest so low.		127	Little House	28
A serving-Man of low Degree:		224	Prog of Love	54
For if the Sea should sink so low		258	Bubble	195
They dropp'd low Court'sies, One and All,		321	First of April	13
Let courtly Slaves low bend the Knee		386	Manly Virtue	93
Like a Beau in the Box, he bow'd low on each Side;		399	Tom Clinch	10
His loudest Voice is low and weak,		405	Swift to Pope	3
Should be reduc'd so low,		426	Five Ladies	23
That you, a low Hibernian Bard,		475	Epist on Epist	4
Think this Wall low, and that Wall bevel.		477	Epist on Epist	66
Cou'd never Condescend so low;		483	Libel on D- D-	112
Or Hairs that sink the Forehead low,		527	Lady's Dres Rm	57
Stand high himself, keep others low?		554	Death of Swift	16
Low in Pocket, Cow'd in Courage,		574	Helter Skelter	53
In seas and woods, or low as hell		620	Scandal Poem 1	100
In Seas, and Streams, or low as Hell:		626	Scandal Poem 2	98
Damns all your Thoughts as low and little,		644	On Poetry	121
How few have reach'd the low Sublime?		652	On Poetry	370
You still are low ten thousand Mile.		657	On Poetry	472
On so mean a Design, and a Subject so low.		716	Answer Rebus	4
Tho' he cring'd to his Deanship in very low strains,		816	Yahoo's	46

LOW   (CONTINUED)   PAGE   TITLE   LINE
  I can bark, or I can low, ...   933 Riddle 20   D 10
  For she never descends so low as the cellar; . . . .   979 Dean to Tho: S   26
  And then you may kiss the low end of her Spine . . .   1018 Swift Ans Sher   33
LOW-BORN
  'Tis but a low-born vapor kindled by a ray; . . . . .   41 Ode Sancroft   218
LOW-COUNTREE
  Joyned together in the Low-Countree.   . . . . . .   147 Windsor Proph   6
LOW'RS
  Then he low'rs down the Point, and kisses the Hilt. .   871 Grand Question   112
LOWER
  So strong, that from the lower End, ...   345 Prometheus   33
  Passes the Lower Castle Yard, ...   376 Apology Lady C   29
  Because they live in lower regions . . . .   620 Scandal Poem 1   98
  You are of a lower Class   . . . .   637 Epistle Lady   245
  Their Passions move in lower Spheres, ...   687 Cadenus Vaness   37
  "But the lower the coin, the higher the mob. . . . .   843 Ay and No   12
  We'll place him at the lower End.   . . . .   886 Rev Market-Hill   98
  We'll take her Heels five Inches lower. . . . . .   886 Rev Market-Hill   104
LOWEST
  Knows to a Groat the lowest Price;   . . . .   416 Woman's Mind   28
  The lowest boy in Martin's school   . . . .   899 Dean's Reasons   13
  That the lowest Voice I fear;   . . . .   933 Riddle 20   D 26
LOWING
  And lowing Herds, and piping Swains, ...   934 Riddle 21   D 9
LOWLY
  Not dar'd to injure with our lowly song; . . . . .   52 Temple Ill   44
  Thee best befits a lowly Style: . . . .   897 Panegyr Dean   329
  Now lowly crouch'd, I cry Peccavi, ...   1005 Sheridan's Sub   11
LOWS'D
  You sat and lows'd him all the Sun-shine Day. . . .   882 Pastoral Dial   34
LOWSY
  At lowsy Ballyspelling.   . . . .   442 Ballyspellin   54
LOYAL
  Shall a Subject so Loyal be hang'd by the Nape, . .   518 Dean Hang Rape   35
  Offensive to a Loyal Ear---:   . . . .   550 Life of Swift   192
  With such a constant, Loyal Zeal, ...   778 Mullinix Tim   169
LOYALTY
  Plain Loyalty not built on Hope, ...   410 Dial Rich Marb   81
  For songs of Loyalty and Lewdness.   . . . .   650 On Poetry   290
LOYT'RES
  The Loyt'res quake, no Corner hides them, ...   279 Journal   33
LUBBARDS
  Yet their Wine and their Victuals, those curmudgeon   263 Apollo   11
    Lubbards
LUCAN
  From Virgil, Martial, Ovid, Lucan;   . . . .   657 On Poetry   482
LUCASS'S
  In Lucass's by chance there lay   . . . .   782 Tim and Fables   3
LUCENDO
  (As lucus comes a non lucendo)   . . . .   435 Answer Paulus   115
LUCIAN
  Great scholars have in Lucian Read, ...   99 Elegy Patrige   63
LUCINA
  Three Graces by Lucina brought her, ...   465 Birthday Song   165
LUCINA'S
  In a glad Hour Lucina's Aid   . . . .   690 Cadenus Vaness   136
LUCK
  Tries twenty Charms to mend her Luck.   . . . . .   452 Modern Lady   237
  "I think I never had good Luck in't.   . . . . . .   452 Modern Lady   241
  And may you ever have the luck   . . . .   658 On Poetry   D 186
  Good Luck to those with whom I dwell.   . . . . . .   918 Riddle 4   44
LUCK-HOLD
  Which if right ta'en, and but good Luck-hold . . .   373 Letter D. S-y   60
LUCKLESS
  Their luckless Choice of Husbands--others, ...   182 Horace 2, 1   53
  Hither by luckless Error led, ...   896 Panegyr Dean   309
LUCKY
  He hop'd to find some lucky Hour, ...   121 Apollo Outwit   45
  Then pray think this a lucky Hitt, ...   123 Empty'ng Town   21
  This Fool had got a lucky Hit, ...   156 Fable of Midas   23
  At length a lucky Lover came, ...   222 Prog of Love   19
  He hop'd to have a Lucky Hit, ...   547 Life of Swift   90
  The Merit of a lucky Guess, ...   557 Death of Swift   122
LUCKY'R
  Had fate a lucky'r one, she'd give it ye: . . . . .   760 Bec's B-Day   2
LUCRETIUS
  Go to the Dean to read Lucretius.   . . . .   278 Journal   12
LUCUS
  (As lucus comes a non lucendo)   . . . .   435 Answer Paulus   115
LUDGATE
  From Ludgate shines to Temple-bar.   . . . .   650 On Poetry   304
LUE
  Yet, Ladies are seldom at Ombre, or Lue, sick; . . .   1029 Dr. Helsham   15
LUKE-WARM
  Which oft attends that luke-warm Stream; . . . . .   539 Strephon Chloe   180
LULL
  You then may soon your Conscience lull; . . . . . .   503 Doctor Delaney   112
LULL'D
  Has lull'd the Monster in a Deep   . . . .   8 Ode to King   79

		PAGE	TITLE	LINE
LUMBER				
And rid her of her Lumber and Her Books,	. . . . .	23	Ode Athenian	229
Philosophy! the Lumber of the Schools,	. . . . . .	27	Ode to Temple	24
Take up at best with Lumber and the Leavings of a Fate:		32	Ode to Temple	184
To raise the Lumber from the Earth.	. . . .	231	Prog of Poetry	30
LUMP				
Together mingled in a Lump,	. . . .	345	Prometheus	17
Till in a Lump together stuck,	. . . .	406	Swift to Pope	15
To be but <rascals> in the lump.	. . . .	435	Answer Paulus	106
LUMPS				
Press down the Lumps, the Hollows fill,	. . . . .	582	Young Nymph	26
LUNA				
When Lady Luna is your Neighbour	. . . .	362	Grace's Answer	25
Luna was absent on Pretence	. . . .	586	Strephon Chloe	65
LUNA'S				
For sure if this be Luna's Fate,	. . . .	229	Prog of Beauty	105
LUNATICKS				
Astrologers and Lunaticks	. . . .	101	Elegy Patrige	99
LUNATICS				
For his Lunatics and Fools,	. . . .	830	Legion Club	36
LUNGS				
And speak without the Help of Lungs.	. . . . . .	326	Pethox	80
In Venom, till they burst their Lungs,	. . . . . .	414	Censure	20
Break not his rest, nor hurt his lungs:	. . . . .	433	Answer Paulus	54
Which, thundring out with lungs long-winded,	. . .	675	Curate's Compl	11
Roaring till their Lungs were spent,	. . . .	833	Legion Club	115
LUR'D				
Lur'd by the gilded Stern, and painted Sides.	. . .	771	Horace 1, 14	48
LURCH				
They left me in the Lurch.	. . . .	1005	Sheridan's Sub	25
LURK				
He stood behind a Stall to lurk,	. . . .	86	Hist V's House	15
To lurk behind a mean Disguise;	. . . .	386	Manly Virtue	78
LURKING				
Pale Avarice and lurking Fraud	. . . .	243	Horace 4, 9	11
The Crocodile that lurking lyes,	. . . .	257	Bubble	179
LURKS				
Still lurks in Palaces and Courts,	. . . .	30	Ode to Temple	117
Mean time the Boy in secret lurks,	. . . .	702	Cadenus Vaness	513
A Treasure here of Learning lurks,	. . . .	922	Riddle 7	39
LUSITANIAN				
White Lead, and Lusitanian Dish.	. . . .	227	Prog of Beauty	60
LUSK				
My Father built Lusk,	. . . .	246	Irish-Feast	74
LUST				
A lust of rhiming for a poet's vein,	. . . .	45	To Congreve	78
Sick lust of souls, and an abortive child;	. . . . .	47	To Congreve	124
To gratify their Lust of Pride,	. . . .	480	Libel on D- D-	26
Than those of Poets to the Lust of Gold.	. . . . .	532	To Mr. Gay	22
Sloth, Folly, Rapine, Mischeif, Lust	. . . . .	659	On Poetry	D 410
Ambition, Avarice, and Lust,	. . . .	725	To Stella	45
To please his Malice, or his Lust.	. . . . . .	915	Riddle 1	22
To Lust and Luxury, and Dice:	. . . .	917	Riddle 3	14
LUSTRE				
Shews lustre that was shaded in his seat;	. . . .	41	Ode Sancroft	212
With native Lustre like her own;	. . . .	379	Apology Lady C	114
With lessen'd Lustre in their own;	. . . .	384	Manly Virtue	28
With genuin lustre all her own.	. . . .	465	Birthday Song	174
With half the Lustre of Your Eyes,	. . . . . .	722	Stel B-Day '18	13
I with double lustre shine.	. . . .	936	Riddle 24	D 12
LUSTURE				
"The living Lusture of your Eyes?	. . . . . .	380	Apology Lady C	166
LUTHERINE				
Or may your Gown never be good Lutherine	. . . .	1018	Swift Ans Sher	29
LUXURIANT				
How is the Muse luxuriant grown,	. . . .	31	Ode to Temple	142
And making one luxuriant Shoot	. . . .	730	Stella, Poems	67
Who round the Vault luxuriant reign.	. . . . .	923	Riddle 7	60
LUXURIOUS				
Despis'd luxurious Wines, and costly Meat;	. . .	194	Author Himself	15
LUXURY				
We fly from luxury and wealth,	. . . .	401	Window Inns 5	D 1
To feed his Luxury, or sooth his Pride.	. . . .	534	To Mr. Gay	94
To pamper luxury and pride;	. . . .	676	Parson's Case	22
And waste in Luxury thy Harvests there;	. . .	794	St. Pat's Well	98
To Lust and Luxury, and Dice:	. . . .	917	Riddle 3	14
LY				
Here we ly starving in the Street	. . . . . .	90	Bauc & Phil 1	17
Give us but Straw, and let us Ly	. . . . . .	90	Bauc & Phil 1	21
Where may the Poets Palace ly?	. . . . . .	109	V's House	100
Ly waiting for the foundred Skiffs,	. . . . .	256	Bubble	155
While you ly helpless on the Sand:	. . . . .	258	Bubble	200
Nor after your Vittels ly sleeping supine	. . . .	1017	Swift Ans Sher	16
LY'D				
E'er he could prove the good Squire ly'd.	. . .	98	Elegy Patrige	4
For must you not have often ly'd,	. . . . . .	496	Panegyr Swift	90
He grew, or else his Comrades ly'd,	. . . . .	547	Life of Swift	88
And swore the fawning Rascals ly'd:	. . . . .	657	On Poetry	476
LY'RS				
Unless the Men of Kent are Ly'rs,	. . . . . .	257	Bubble	170

LY'ST
                                                            PAGE   TITLE   LINE

	PAGE	TITLE	LINE
LY'ST			
Deny them Protestants--thou ly'st.	658	On Poetry	D 190
LYAR			
A fawning, base, trepaning Lyar,	798	Traulus 1	81
LYARS			
Damn'd Spies and Informers, Damn'd Friends and Damn'd Lyars;	576	Place Damn'd	10
And then-- <God> Damn the Lyars again.	773	Mullinix Tim	12
LYDIAN			
Else why should the fam'd Lydian King,	20	Ode Athenian	153
LYE			
Lye on you, and on your Childrens Head,	23	Ode Athenian	246
Where all the fruitful Atoms lye,	32	Ode to Temple	171
Whether it be a Truth, or Lye.	65	Problem	6
You smell the <Stink>? by <God> you lye,	67	Problem	55
"Or do the Prints and Papers lye?	202	Horace 2, 6	95
To let your Virtues lye obscure,	242	Horace 4, 9	4
He can Lye like a Courtier, and think it no Scorn,	335	Serious Poem	45
He swore from his Cart, it was all a damn'd Lye.	399	Tom Clinch	12
Inclines to aid a specious Lye:	414	Censure	14
And, "Madam, if it be a Lye,	449	Modern Lady	146
In him such Virtues lye inherent,	464	Birthday Song	133
(His Name is up, he may in Bed lye)	476	Epist on Epist	48
And you on Drapier's Hill must lye,	491	Dialogue	55
Lye down obscure like other Folks	501	Doctor Delaney	45
If they would but lye quiet, and stifle their Voice,	519	Dean Hang Rape	63
A Lye, at ev'ry second word:	550	Life of Swift	191
Than his Prediction prove a Lye.	557	Death of Swift	132
Belated, seems on watch to lye,	583	Young Nymph	49
They lye, alas, too easy to be found,	772	Horace 1, 14	63
For thee alone they lye the Island round.	772	Horace 1, 14	64
So qualify'd to Swear and Lye,	779	Mullinix Tim	193
With such a cross Man, I wou'd lye in the Streets.	869	Grand Question	60
Madam, whose Skill does all in Dress lye,	886	Rev Market-Hill	99
Here lye deposited the Spoils	921	Riddle 7	13
And lye an undistinguish'd Mass.	922	Riddle 7	44
The Mysteries that lye below.	922	Riddle 7	50
See where those mangled Corpses lye;	923	Riddle 7	61
Chloe, when on thy Breast I lye,	925	Riddle 8	17
A long-ear'd Beast, in Mud to lye,	942	Probatur Alit	25
Eat my Oysters, and lye near her,	953	Oysters	15
We lye cramming ourselves, and are ready to burst,	967	Letter Sherid	3
LYERS			
'Twixt you and me <God> Damn the Lyers.	773	Mullinix Tim	8
LYES			
Philosophy, as it before us lyes,	22	Ode Athenian	211
The Body, tho' Gigantick, lyes all Cold and Dead.	25	Ode Athenian	291
Here Five Foot deep lyes on his Back	101	Elegy Patrige	103
On Britain Europes safety lyes	140	Harleys Surgn	1
Yet when the Weight of Kingdoms lyes	160	Atlas	20
Because the Diff'rence lyes abstruse	216	To Mr. Delany	47
Within your Breast all Wisdom lyes,	243	Horace 4, 9	7
Sinks down at once, and there he lyes,	253	Bubble	82
Look round about how thick it lyes:	254	Bubble	104
Yet He that on the Surface lyes	256	Bubble	142
But these, you say, are factious Lyes	256	Bubble	157
The Crocodile that lurking lyes,	257	Bubble	179
Or else the truest Maxim lyes:	391	Young's Satire	22
Nor can ten Hundred Thousand Lyes,	414	Censure	27
Convict of lyes is every sign,	420	Holyhead	5
Such Lyes as these	442	Ballyspellin	80
Tho fond of warlike Lyes as most men;	462	Birthday Song	54
Your Int'rest lyes to learn the knack	464	Birthday Song	115
First, of the first. To vouch your Lyes	465	Birthday Song	153
Will sooner coyn a Thousand Lyes	503	Doctor Delaney	91
That safe behind the Wainscoat lyes.	504	Doctor Delaney	138
Who in his Titles always lyes?	505	Doctor Delaney	162
You are his Dearest Friend---; he lyes---:	545	Life of Swift	26
Though some had spread a thousand Lyes;	605	Beasts Confess	149
She dares not say the Poet lyes.	730	Stella, Poems	82
Whoever says you have them, lyes.	758	Stel B-day '24	48
And makes me tell a Thousand Lyes:	915	Riddle 1	20
Lyes there consign'd to endless Night;	923	Riddle 7	64
LYING			
"With lying on too hard a Bed;	497	Panegyr Swift	133
In Satyrs, Libels, lying Travels!	548	Life of Swift	112
LYING-IN			
There follow'd at his lying-in	504	Doctor Delaney	117
Not Phyllis after lying-in.	904	Death Daphne	38
<LYNDSAY>			
<Lyndsay> mistakes the matter quite,	432	Answer Paulus	1
<Lyndsay>, 'tis you have set me on	435	Answer Paulus	99
Imagine <Lyndsay> at the bar:	435	Answer Paulus	107
<Lyndsay>, you know, what pains you take	436	Answer Paulus	129
<LYNDSAY'S>			
For Paulus' and for <Lyndsay's> sake	433	Answer Paulus	46
LYON			
The Lyon, Eagle, Fox and Bear	83	Salamander	9
Since a living Dog better is than a dead Lyon,	237	Excellent Song	13
To hear the Belgick Lyon roar.	468	Birthday Song	246
The Ass was dull, the Lyon brave,	512	Answer Fable	5

		PAGE	TITLE	LINE
LYRE				
	To such a subject tune my lyre	490	Dialogue	39
	Oh, wond'rous Box! my Lyre unstrung	494	Panegyr Swift	45
	As how to strike the Muses Lyre.	641	On Poetry	32
	To sing his Virtues on ye Lyre, ...	658	On Poetry	D 410
	Fair Discretion string the Lyre;	661	Love Song	14
LYRICK				
	A Lyrick Ode would Slate; a Catch	79	Vanbrug House	11
	A Lyrick Ode would Slate; a Catch	106	V's House	11
LYSE				
	And when their country lyse at stake	421	Ireld	7
MA				
	Och ma ceade millia mollighart, on the feeders of swine!	841	Ballad	D 19
	And prostrate, supplicate pour ma vie.	1005	Sheridan's Sub	12
<MACCARTNEY>				
	If to <Maccartney> thou wilt toast, ...	183	Horace 2, 1	91
MACE				
	Come trimming Harcourt; bring your Mace;	190	Faggot	39
MACEDONIAN				
	Close, as the Macedonian Phalanx:	1021	Nim-Dan-Dean 1	D 30
MACHI'VILLIAN				
	"Was formed this Machi'villian Plot, ...	850	Old Thorn	74
MACHIAVEL				
	As Machiavel taught 'em; divide and ye govern. . . .	805	Irish Bishops	48
MACHINATIONS				
	If the Machinations brewing, ...	636	Epistle Lady	189
MACHINE				
	O never may such vile Machine	528	Lady's Dres Rm	95
	An useless machine.	852	Lady's Lament	36
MACKLIN				
	Right Indian this, right Macklin that;	447	Modern Lady	83
MACLOBE				
	As pitiful as Tom MacLobe.	670	Epig Carthy 21	D 4
MAD				
	War! that mad Game, the World so loves to play, . . .	28	Ode to Temple	76
	With promise of a mad Reversion after Death.	32	Ode to Temple	198
	But if thou be'st what thy mad vot'ries prate, ...	54	Temple Ill	103
	Dear Sid, then why wer't thou so mad	135	Magician's Rod	79
	To be cloath'd like a Carcass would make a Teague mad,	237	Excellent Song	12
	And now he runs mad for a ba-ba-ba-Bank.	287	Bank Down	20
	And, since the Alderman was mad you say, ...	350	Upright Judge 3	7
	Was a mad Copper-Smith of Elis:	352	Wood Ironmongr	2
	She went Abroad - - - She'd thought me mad. . . .	377	Apology Lady C	52
	All mad to speak, and none to hearken, ...	450	Modern Lady	178
	"To build a House for Fools and Mad:	572	Death of Swift	480
	The World's mad Business now is o'er, ...	579	Day Judgement	19
	I fear thou wilt be mad indeed.	596	Cassinus Peter	90
	Dick a Coxcomb, Tom was mad, ...	784	Mullinex Dick	5
	But still insist the Man is mad.	796	Traulus 1	22
	But turns aside like mad Ulysses:	796	Traulus 1	30
	To say he's mad will not avail:	797	Traulus 1	38
	Cry'd, Huzzy, why sure the Wench is gone mad: . .	873	Grand Question	184
	Sufficient it were, one would think, in your mad rant, .	1026	Sheri Circles	9
MAD-HOUSE				
	What, said I, is this the Mad-House?	833	Legion Club	99
MAD-MEN'S				
	(For swords are madmen's tongues, and tongues are	35	Ode Sancroft	14
	mad-men's swords)			
MAD-MENS				
	More oft in Fools and Mad-mens hands than Sages . .	23	Ode Athenian	220
MADAM				
	(Madam, I dye without your Grace)	60	Lady Tablebook	15
	Lord! Madam, says Mary, how d'ye do?.	70	Mrs Harris Pet	14
	'Twas Madam, in her Grogram Gown.	116	Bauc & Phil 2	144
	Then Madam bid the Chariot stand, ...	128	Little House	50
	Old Madam who went up to find	223	Prog of Love	43
	Ask that of old Madam, ...	247	Irish-Feast	81
	"Good Madam Pallas, pray be easy, ...	305	Storm	70
	"Madam, the mighty Pow'r of Use	379	Apology Lady C	131
	Madam, the Goldsmith waits below, ...	446	Modern Lady	56
	And, Madam, there's my Lady Spade	446	Modern Lady	62
	Dear Madam, you are grown so hard, ...	447	Modern Lady	86
	Madam, if there be Truth in Man, ...	447	Modern Lady	88
	And Madam almost dress'd by Four;	447	Modern Lady	91
	Comes up with, "Madam, Dinner stays;	447	Modern Lady	93
	Our Madam o'er her Ev'ning Tea;	448	Modern Lady	117
	And, "Madam, if it be a Lye, ...	449	Modern Lady	146
	Now all alone poor Madam sits, ...	451	Modern Lady	198
	Dear Madam, try to take a Nap--	451	Modern Lady	210
	Our Madam can sit up all Night;	451	Modern Lady	217
	Lord, Madam, you have lost Codill;	452	Modern Lady	246
	"Nay, Madam, give me leave to say	452	Modern Lady	248
	"Fie, Madam, leave these little Arts.	452	Modern Lady	257
	"Madam, you have no Cause to flounce, ...	452	Modern Lady	262
	And truly, Madam, I know when	453	Modern Lady	264
	Unlucky Madam left in Tears, ...	453	Modern Lady	290
	"Madam, your Husband will attend	562	Death of Swift	233
	"No Madam, 'tis a shocking Sight, ...	562	Death of Swift	235
	Madam, I allow 'tis true;	632	Epistle Lady	93
	Dear Madam, Let me set your Head:	699	Cadenus Vaness	398
	Dear Madam try this Pigeon's leg:	746	Stel Distress	18

MADAM   (CONTINUED)   PAGE   TITLE   LINE

    Dear Madam, try this Pigeon's Leg; . . . . 750 Stel Wood-Park   16
    What, Madam? No walking, ... 854 Lady's Lament   111
    Drown your Morals, Madam cryes; . . . . 863 To Janus   19
    Cry'd, Madam, why surely my Master's possest; . . . 868 Grand Question   44
    But Madam, I guest there wou'd never come Good, . . 868 Grand Question   47
    Dear Madam, had you but the Spirit to teaze, ... 869 Grand Question   53
    And, Madam, I always believ'd you so stout, ... 869 Grand Question   55
    But, Madam, I beg you contrive and invent, ... 869 Grand Question   61
    Dear Madam, whene'er of a Barrack I think, ... 869 Grand Question   63
    Pray, Madam, be quiet; what was it I said?-- . . . 870 Grand Question   85
    Now, Madam, observe, how he marches in State: . . 870 Grand Question   89
    (His Beaver is cock'd; pray, Madam, mark that, . . 870 Grand Question   105
    Lord! Madam! your Ladyship sure is in jest; . . . . 871 Grand Question   124
    You banter me, Madam, the Kingdom must grant-- . . 871 Grand Question   125
    No, Madam; 'tis only Sir Arthur a humming. . . . 871 Grand Question   128
    Dear Madam, be sure he's a fine spoken Man, . . . 872 Grand Question   139
    "And Madam, says he, if such Dinners you give, . . 872 Grand Question   141
    "Now Madam, you'll think it a strange Thing to say, . 873 Grand Question   171
    And, Madam, I laugh'd till I thought I shou'd split. . 873 Grand Question   174
    While tortur'd Madam bound remains, ... 885 Rev Market-Hill   71
    Madam, whose Skill does all in Dress lye, ... 886 Rev Market-Hill   99
    And, Madam your Wife . . . . 953 Oysters   11
    Has this any likeness to good Madam Sheridan? . . 955 Portrait Life   10
    But Johnson Madam . . . . 1014 Swift to Sheri   33
    But if too many come your Madam will whine . . . 1018 Swift Ans Sher   31
    Now, <Madam Coningsmark> her Vengeance vows . . . 195 Author Himself   53
MADAMS
    For, all the Courtly Madams round, ... 409 Dial Rich Marb   27
MADDER
    And a Madder our Cup. . . . . 244 Irish-Feast   12
MADE
    This made the Ancient Romans to afford . . . . . 7 Ode to King   27
    Made him his Footstool in the War, ... 7 Ode to King   43
    The poys'nous Darts has made him reel, ... 10 Ode to King   143
    (Cowards are Monarchs by that Title made) . . . . 11 Ode to William   D 10
    And made an Humble Chaplet for the King. . . . . 16 Ode Athenian   31
    For tho' possess'd of present Vogue they've made . . 18 Ode Athenian   83
    The War methinks has made . . . . 19 Ode Athenian   95
    Made up of Virtue and transparent Innocence: . . 30 Ode to Temple   128
    By dark reverted rays from its reflection made; . . 35 Ode Sancroft   22
    Made up of iron mixt with clay, ... 39 Ode Sancroft   139
    The greatest compliment she ever made, ... 44 To Congreve   28
    The God of Wealth was therefore made . . . . . 79 Vanbrug House   23
    This made him to Apollo pray . . . . 81 Vanbrug House   69
    Till Peace hath made the Sky serene, ... 84 Salamander   43
    Step't with a Jug, and made a Vent; . . . . 92 Bauc & Phil 1   70
    Hung high and made a glitt'ring Show . . . . . . 93 Bauc & Phil 1   114
    How Patrige made his Opticks rise, ... 98 Elegy Patrige   21
    And Cure the Wounds that Venus made. . . . . . 99 Elegy Patrige   62
    On Earth, the God of Wealth was made . . . . . 106 V's House   23
    Thus far advanc't, he made a shift . . . . 108 V's House   91
    The Number made the Motion slow'r: . . . . . . 113 Bauc & Phil 2   70
    Hung high, and made a glitt'ring Show, ... 114 Bauc & Phil 2   90
    But made his Leg and went away. . . . . 121 Apollo Outwit   44
    Instead of Garlands made of Flowrs . . . . 122 Empty'ng Town   7
    And made a Circle thrice as wide, ... 134 Magician's Rod   54
    Or made it a Newmarket Switch, ... 135 Magician's Rod   83
    I made us of a Trope; that an Heir to invite, . . . 144 New Song   37
    She made a Song, how little Miss . . . . 150 Corinna   21
    Made false Moves, and lost his Queen; . . . . . 168 Peace Dunkirk   16
    Which made his Brethren of the Gown . . . . . . 171 Horace 1, 7   29
    The Goddess made advances first, ... 178 To Lord Harley   67
    Which made thy Closet much frequented . . . . . 182 Horace 2, 1   51
    "The Peace is made, and Perkin must come over. . . 195 Author Himself   46
    Made her retire, and quit her Right, ... 208 Fable Bitches   41
    And in a Glass had made her see . . . . 224 Prog of Love   53
    For Marriages are made in Heaven: . . . . 224 Prog of Love   56
    Cast in his Dart which made three Moydores Light. . 234 Elegy on Demar   32
    Each Knave hath made a thousand Fools. . . . . 253 Bubble   60
    The Poet had no more who made the Play. . . . . 274 Epilogue   10
    We'll dress in Manufactures, made at home? . . . 275 Epilogue   17
    And made him to Curse the poor innocent Bank. . . 288 Bank Down   40
    He made them weep before he dy'd. . . . . 296 Satiric Elegy   24
    That all the Noise they made was barking: . . . . 299 Horrid Plot   26
    "The God has made us April-Fools. . . . . 322 First of April   58
    The God who made Scamander boil, ... 323 Pethox   7
    By fierce Encounters made in Wars; . . . . 324 Pethox   14
    Pontifick, made your glorious March; . . . . . . 326 Pethox   94
    The Heathens, we Read, had Gods made of Wood, . . 334 Serious Poem   9
    Teague made a good Pun by a Brogue in his Speech, . 334 Serious Poem   27
    Which cannot in Literal Sense be made Good, . . . 335 Serious Poem   55
    What Stuff he is made on you quickly may find, . . 336 Serious Poem   77
    When Jove was Young, was made of Gold. . . . . 345 Prometheus   36
    Ty'd with the Chain himself had made; . . . . . 346 Prometheus   54
    Which made my Grand-Dame always stuff-her-Ears, . 367 Answer Delaney   39
    Which made it more surprizing how . . . . 376 Apology Lady C   17
    And since I 'scap'd being made a Scoff, ... 377 Apology Lady C   55
    Captain, I fear you've made some Blunder; . . . . 377 Apology Lady C   66
    Now made--ye Gods!--a Son and Heir, ... 384 Manly Virtue   18
    And whilst he made her Value known, ... 386 Manly Virtue   87

MADE (CONTINUED)

		PAGE	TITLE	LINE
Grandeur, by Goodness made compleat!	. . . . . .	386	Manly Virtue	101
For Models, made to mend our Kind,	. . . . .	387	Manly Virtue	115
Is made his Mansion for a while;	. . . . .	387	Manly Virtue	136
None e'er made Verses worse than he,	. . . . .	401	Window Inns 2	5
Made use of by detracting foes.	. . . .	433	Answer Paulus	50
In Chaos made not such a Clatter:	. . . .	450	Modern Lady	185
Made trebly dreadfull in your Song.	. . . . .	461	Birthday Song	46
To which he never made pretence,	. . . . .	463	Birthday Song	92
And made the Rascals pay' him dearly	. . . .	463	Birthday Song	105
But, You, who till your Fortune's made	. . . .	485	Libel on D- D-	153
You tell me, till my Fortune's made,	. . . . .	496	Panegyr Swift	96
The Ruin'd Party made his Sport,	. . . . . .	498	Panegyr Swift	160
She bustled and strugled, and made her Escape,	.	517	Dean Hang Rape	11
He had made himself Drunk with the Juice of the Grape,	.	517	Dean Hang Rape	23
There Night-gloves made of Tripsy's Hide,	. . . .	526	Lady's Dres Rm	29
Made up of Noise, and Impudence, and Lies.	. . .	532	To Mr. Gay	42
Made up of Malice, Truth, and Wit:	. . . . . .	545	Life of Swift	2
For, had We made him timely Offers,	. . . . .	549	Life of Swift	138
And made me throw my Pen aside;	. . . . .	555	Death of Swift	64
"Nor made a Sacrifice of those	. . . .	567	Death of Swift	363
How great a Change! how quickly made!	. . . .	590	Strephon Chloe	203
His Wig was made of sunny Rays,	. . . . .	597	Problem Solved	7
(Which therefore made them more devout)	. . . .	601	Beasts Confess	6
His Shape and Beauty made him proud:	. . . .	602	Beasts Confess	38
For, he had made a holy Vow	. . . . . .	603	Beasts Confess	69
That made him trust alone in Merit:	. . . . .	604	Beasts Confess	110
With which he made a tearing show:	. . . . .	619	Scandal Poem 1	71
To us he made his dayly pray'rs,	. . . . .	620	Scandal Poem 1	81
As if he made the weather fair.	. . . . .	621	Scandal Poem 1	138
With which he made a tearing Show:	. . . . .	625	Scandal Poem 2	69
To us he made his daily Prayers,	. . . . .	626	Scandal Poem 2	79
As if He made the Weather fair.	. . . . .	627	Scandal Poem 2	142
Immortal made in Virgil's Lines,	. . . . . .	658	On Poetry	D 410
Has made the Man a Goose in earnest.	. . . .	666	Epig Carthy 1	D 4
Thy week made up of fasting days,	. . , . . .	676	Parson's Case	11
That Gown was made for Old Queen Bess.	. . .	699	Cadenus Vaness	397
The Boy made use of all his Craft,	. . . . .	701	Cadenus Vaness	476
His Conduct might have made him styl'd	. . . .	704	Cadenus Vaness	548
Wou'd say, He made a treach'rous Use	. . . .	707	Cadenus Vaness	644
Thro' this she made all Objects pass,	. . . . .	709	Cadenus Vaness	718
She made a Speech in open Court;	. . . . .	713	Cadenus Vaness	857
The Court, so made his last O yes!	. . . . .	714	Cadenus Vaness	885
It is but a Paraphrase made on a Punn;	. . . .	716	Answer Rebus	10
The Changes which Faction has made in the State,	.	716	Answer Rebus	23
Made up so largly in thy Mind.	. . . . . .	722	Stel B-Day '18	8
Only to have the Ruins made	. . . . . .	727	To Stella	123
Long-thinking made my Fancy worse.	. . . .	741	Stel B-day 22	12
Don Carlos made her sole Director.	. . . . .	745	Stel Distress	8
Don Carlos made her chief Director	. . . . .	745	Stel Distress	
A Haunch of Ven'son made her sweat	. . . . .	746	Stel Distress	15
Don Carlos made her chief Director,	. . . . .	749	Stel Wood-Park	5
A Haunch of Ven'son made her sweat,	. . . . .	750	Stel Wood-Park	13
Have made thy Presence in a true Sence,	. . . .	775	Mullinix Tim	65
There's not a Puppet made of Wood,	. . . . .	777	Mullinix Tim	123
Made your Sons Converts both to God and Sense:	.	792	St. Pat's Well	30
The fatal Changes Time hath made in thee.	. . .	792	St. Pat's Well	34
Be all made Captives in their native Land;	. . .	793	St. Pat's Well	90
Has made a Rat our Fellow-Creature.	. . . .	812	Bro Protestant	34
Which make our Swarm of Sects determine	. . .	813	Bro Protestant	43
Must own it made by God's Anointed.	. . . . .	821	Dr. Rundle	56
For, had you made the <King> your debtor,	. . .	821	Dr. Rundle	65
Patrick astore, who was him made this law?	. . .	841	Ballad	D 11
What a figure she made	855	Lady's Lament	121
His famous Letters made waste Paper;	. . . .	875	Drapier's Hill	17
Whose names and works (tho' dead) are made	. . .	876	To Dean Swift	9
Such charming Butter never Man made.	. . . .	892	Panegyr Dean	168
Here, Nature never Diff'rence made	. . . . .	895	Panegyr Dean	289
Young Deathlings, who, by Practice made	. . . .	903	Death Daphne	15
And freely made the first Advance:	. . . . .	905	Death Daphne	68
To slit my Tongue, and made me speak:	. . . .	915	Riddle 1	16
Cut from the Piece that made her Shift,	. . . .	925	Riddle 8	42
Some are made, and some undone.	934	Riddle 22	D 4
Few are made, but Numbers lost.	934	Riddle 22	D 6
. . .she would have made Advances	1014	Swift to Sheri	11
Captain Butler made some in the Church black and blue sick;		1029	Dr. Helsham	7
Dean Cross, had he preach'd, would have made us all Pew-sick;		1029	Dr. Helsham	8
And look'd like a Rake, who was made in the Stews sick;		1029	Dr. Helsham	18
For the Smell of them made me like Garlick and Rue sick		1029	Dr. Helsham	21
Who often has made me, by looking ascue, sick.		1030	Dr. Sheridan	5

MADLY
| Madly aspir'd to wear her chain: | . . . . | 177 | To Lord Harley | 42 |

MADMEN
| Tho' Madmen and the Wits, Philosophers and Fools, | . | 22 | Ode Athenian | 203 |
| For Madmen, Children, Wits and Fools | . . . . . | 181 | Horace 2, 1 | 31 |

MADMEN'S
| (For swords are madmen's tongues, and tongues are mad-men's swords) | | 35 | Ode Sancroft | 14 |

MADNESS
    Madness like this no fancy ever seiz'd, ...   PAGE   TITLE   LINE

	PAGE	TITLE		LINE
Madness like this no fancy ever seiz'd,	55	Temple Ill		147
And Still the Madness of the Crowd.	258	Bubble		212
All their Madness makes me merry:	635	Epistle Lady		164
What e'er he speaks for Madness goes,	798	Traulus 1		65
I own, his Madness is a Jest,	798	Traulus 1		69
To work whose Ends, his Madness pimps.	798	Traulus 1		72

MADRID
| Mordanto at Madrid to seek: | 398 | Earl of P-b-w | | 14 |

MAECENAS
| To be Maecenas of the Nation, | 481 | Libel on D- D- | | 36 |

MAEVIUS
| And Maevius reigns o'er Kentish-Town: | 650 | On Poetry | | 302 |
| So Maevius, when he drain'd his Skull | 730 | Stella, Poems | | 71 |

MAGAZEEN
| From Magazeen in Caelia's Eye. | 272 | Apollo's Edict | D | 59 |

MAGAZINE
| We build a magazine. | 843 | Epigr Irish | | 4 |

MAGAZINES
| On Magazines of Corn or Hay, | 156 | Fable of Midas | | 16 |

MAGGOT
They thought it was an old Man's Maggot:	189	Faggot		5
If the Maggot cries Click when it scratches the Post.	351	Wood Insect		24
The Maggot will dye, and the Sick will recover.	351	Wood Insect		28
For our Fear's at an End with the Death of the Maggot.	352	Wood Insect		40
A lively Maggot sallies out,	785	Dick, Maggot		3
A maggot in a cake of fat,	950	Upstart	D	5

MAGGOTS
Corrupt to Maggots Worms and Flyes.	81	Vanbrug House		82
Corrupt to Maggots, Worms and Flyes.	109	V's House		124
But Maggots in your Nose and Chin,	813	Bro Protestant		39

MAGICAL
| Which proves a Magical Redoubt | 134 | Magician's Rod | | 51 |

MAGICIAN
| Our great Magician, Hamet Sid, | 132 | Magician's Rod | | 5 |
| When late a Feminine Magician, | 354 | Simile Silver | | 19 |

MAGICIANS
| Were by the Vulgar thought Magicians; | 503 | Doctor Delaney | | 96 |

MAGICK
That, rais'd by Magick of her Breech,	132	Magician's Rod		17
About a certain Magick Rod,	132	Magician's Rod		22
Expos'd with all their Magick Ware.	240	Run Bankers		36
What Magick makes our Money rise	250	Bubble		2
By Magick Virtue in the Spring,	255	Bubble		115
Antaeus could by Magick Charms	257	Bubble		181
To drive unseen her magick Chair,	354	Simile Silver		3
Oh! cou'd'st thou, by some Magick Spell,	478	Epist on Epist		91
By Magick Spells, the harmless Maid;	707	Cadenus Vaness		647
Most wond'rous is my Magick Power;	930	Riddle 15	D	13
Because my Magick gives no Pain.	934	Riddle 21	D	22
Effects of its Magick,	939	Riddle Answerd		16

MAGISTERIAL
| With Stella's magisterial pride. | 753 | Gift for Bec | | 10 |

MAGISTERIALLY
| Will magisterially out-shine us. | 648 | On Poetry | | 258 |

MAGNA
| 'Tis all you have for't; 'tis your best Magna Carta; | 979 | Dean to Tho: S | | 16 |

MAGNANIMITY
| What Magnanimity of Spirit? | 655 | On Poetry | | 416 |

MAGNI
| Hoc Ithacus velit, et magni mercentur Atridae. | 980 | Dean to Tho: S | | 38 |

MAGNIFICENCE
| Or Pride, or vain Magnificence; | 378 | Apology Lady C | | 102 |

MAGNIFICK
| Two Temples of magnifick Size, | 893 | Panegyr Dean | | 201 |

MAGNIFYING
| Of Celia's magnifying Glass. | 527 | Lady's Dres Rm | | 60 |

MAGPIE
| In chatt'ring a magpie, in pride a jackdaw; | 955 | Portrait Life | | 2 |

MAGPYE
| I sent the Magpye from the British Soil, | 792 | St. Pat's Well | | 45 |
| The Magpye, lighting on the Stock, | 849 | Old Thorn | | 33 |

MAGUS
| Our Bishop's Predecessor, Magus, | 821 | Dr. Rundle | | 41 |
| Said surly Peter, Magus, prithee | 821 | Dr. Rundle | | 47 |

MAID   SEE COOK-MAID,CHAMBER-MAID,HAND-MAID
And insolently thrice, the slighted Maid	43	To Congreve		3
Nor ever maid endur'd such court-like scorn,	44	To Congreve		13
Spend their base coin before the bashful maid,	50	To Congreve		219
And thence Beheld a Lovely Maid	119	Apollo Outwit		3
Then Cupid thus: This little Maid	150	Corinna		9
The Butler with my Lady's Maid;	150	Corinna		19
He scratch'd her Maid, he stole the Cream,	153	Widow and Cat	D	11
But Pallas, guardian of the Maid,	177	To Lord Harley		43
As that my Muse is yet a Maid,	183	Horace 2, 1		100
Once disobey'd him, Maid nor Wife.	224	Prog of Love		66
Nor borrow from the Blew-ey'd Maid,	272	Apollo's Edict	D	73
The Graces and the other Maid;	371	Letter D. S-y		6
Hath sent this Letter by her Maid.	446	Modern Lady		63
With so much beauty, shew me any maid	466	Birthday Song		189
Envy breeds in ev'ry Maid.	522	Betty Grizette		6

```
MAID          (CONTINUED)                        PAGE    TITLE            LINE
    Dear Venus, hide this wond'rous Maid,         585 Strephon Chloe       29
    Was Maid in Thought, and Word, and Deed,      588 Strephon Chloe      158
    No Maid at Court is less asham'd,             590 Strephon Chloe      215
    Fair Decency, celestial Maid,                 590 Strephon Chloe      219
    How that ungrateful charming Maid,            595 Cassinus Peter       57
    Nor bribes my Lady's fav'rite Maid.           605 Beasts Confess      136
    Befitting Juno's fav'rite Maid.               626 Scandal Poem 2       76
    Produc'd on Earth a wond'rous Maid,           690 Cadenus Vaness      137
    And sprinkles thrice the new-born Maid.       691 Cadenus Vaness      159
    That spurious Virtue in a Maid,               691 Cadenus Vaness      169
    A Tincture in the prudent Maid:               693 Cadenus Vaness      219
    For when in time the Martial Maid             694 Cadenus Vaness      250
    By Magick Spells, the harmless Maid;          707 Cadenus Vaness      647
    Hither came every Village Maid                848 Old Thorn             5
    "You cast a Sheep's Eye on her Ladyship's Maid; 872 Grand Question    148
    That her own Maid should overtop her;         886 Rev Market-Hill     102
    The bashful Maid, to hide her Blush,          893 Panegyr Dean        213
    For, while the bashful Sylvan Maid,           922 Riddle 7             33
    Languid like a love-sick maid,                937 Riddle 24        D   41
    What Name for a Maid, was the first Man's Damnation? 973 S-'s Ans Sh-d 12
MAID'S
    Squat on her Hams, to make Maid's Water.      584 Strephon Chloe       18
MAIDENHEAD
    . . .my Money was as safe as my Maidenhead.    69 Mrs Harris Pet       11
    "And crack'd her tender Maidenhead            497 Panegyr Swift       132
MAIDENS
    Fair Maidens all attend the Muse             224 Prog of Love         73
    If Maidens are ravish't, it is their own Choice, 519 Dean Hang Rape    61
    Is what our Maidens claim by Right:          588 Strephon Chloe      156
MAIDS    SEE MILK-MAIDS
    Or calls a Councel of her Maids              291 Prog Marriage        53
    The Maids to the Doors and the Balconies ran, 399 Tom Clinch           7
    And gives the Maids of Honor Sport.          468 Birthday Song       268
    "Those Maids of Honour (who can read)        564 Death of Swift      287
MAIL
    Inclos'd Cap-a-pee in a strong Coat of Mail.  350 Wood Insect          6
MAILS
    The plainest Mails must be the best:         378 Apology Lady C      104
MAIMING
    Instead of your maiming, your shooting, or banging, 818 Epigr Kite     7
MAIN    SEE A-LA-MAIN
    Appear'd, above the Universal Main,           16 Ode Athenian          6
    In vain I strive to cross this spacious Main,  32 Ode to Temple      192
    That the main String of Cupid's Bow,          66 Problem              22
    When dropt into the Southern Main,           250 Bubble                3
    Describe his Fall into the Main,             252 Bubble               43
    So Fishes rising from the Main               254 Bubble               85
    Said he-- "Great Sovereign of the Main,      303 Storm                27
    To save his Life he leapt into the Main.     538 Mr. Pulteney         20
    a sharper in trifles a dupe in the main      540 Charac Walpole        4
    But ever with Prudence takes Care of the Main. 580 Psyche              8
    But, always carefull of the main,            878 Robbin & Harry        7
MAINTAIN
    Which, what it bravely Won, do's well Maintain. 12 Ode to William  D  28
    By vile pretenders, who a stock maintain      45 To Congreve          57
    These pad on wit's high road, and suits maintain 45 To Congreve       67
    In kindness to maintain her Spouse,          225 Prog of Love         90
    For, all Astrologers maintain                228 Prog of Beauty       86
    You Churle, I'll maintain                    246 Irish-Feast          73
    Yet, spight of Death and Fate, I here maintain 285 Elegy Boat         29
    I'll maintain with my Life, is Heraldry Good. 338 Serious Poem       122
    And still the Truth he will Maintain, whate'er he loses 341 Upon His Grace 6
      by't.
    But confidently they maintain,               366 Answer Delaney        9
    From Principles the Whigs maintain;          417 Woman's Mind         54
    They still must practise to maintain it.     592 Strephon Chloe      266
    Wou'd still her Dignity maintain,            705 Cadenus Vaness      595
    For, tho' philosophers maintain              761 Bec's B-Day          19
    Then, who with Reason can maintain,          765 Stel B-day '26       59
    With the Tyth of the Tyth of the Tyth to maintain you; 805 Irish Bishops 58
    The Knight his Opinion resolv'd to maintain. 868 Grand Question       40
    Your Master's Honour to maintain;            890 Panegyr Dean        103
    But sprung (and I this Truth maintain)       927 Riddle 10        D    9
    And I must maintain 'em.                     952 Apples               11
MAINTAIN'D
    For strait I saw the Field maintain'd,         8 Ode to King          61
    Or a weak argument by force maintain'd?       34 Ode Sancroft         12
MAINTAINS
    And hence a Critick deep maintains,          156 Fable of Midas       21
    Its Motion and its Heat maintains.           239 Run Bankers          12
    Our Church and our State dear <England> maintains, 520 Dean Hang Rape 67
MAINTENANCE
    Whose maintenance requires no help from brains. 48 To Congreve       164
MAJESTIC
    A pox on Elrington's majestic tone!          309 Billet Players       53
MAJESTICK
    "If his Majestick Eye you flee,              380 Apology Lady C      143
    "The Awe of your Majestick Air?              380 Apology Lady C      160
    Observe with what majestick Port             656 On Poetry           443
```

MAJESTY

	PAGE	TITLE		LINE
Except her Majesty prevails	410	Dial Rich Marb		75
Where Majesty with Sweetness vyes,	466	Birthday Song		191
Oh! if his Majesty would please	606	Beasts Confess		169
To court her Majesty of Tyre	619	Scandal Poem 1		66
To court her Majesty of Tyre,	625	Scandal Poem 2		62
Her Majesty never shall be my Exalter	664	Epigram Bust		3
Oh! would His Majesty but add a String.	678	Dean and Duke		16
In majesty rise,	756	Dingley Brent		8
His Majesty of Terrors came,	904	Death Daphne		54
Wrapt up in Majesty divine,	949	Epigr Fasting		5
That Her <Majesty> stood in great need of a Tutor,	144	New Song		41
I mean His <Majesty>, God bless him.	346	Prometheus		62
For which Her <Majesty> allows him Grains.	521	Stephen Duck		4

MAJOR

	PAGE	TITLE		LINE
You'll dare not to question my minor or major.	976	Dean to Sherid		24

MAJORS

	PAGE	TITLE		LINE
By Captains and by Majors.	426	Five Ladies		20

MAKE

	PAGE	TITLE		LINE
To make the Pageant gay:	6	Ode to King		16
And like that too, make every breast their home)	8	Ode to King		70
I laugh at the grave Answer they will make,	19	Ode Athenian		121
To make some great Discovery,	20	Ode Athenian		143
And by a faint Description make them less.	21	Ode Athenian		174
We odly Plato's Paradox make good,	27	Ode to Temple		29
Make up its solemn Train with Death;	29	Ode to Temple		90
Bids us make Bricks, yet sends us to look out for Straw;	32	Ode to Temple		188
Make their minds travel o'er infinity of space,	36	Ode Sancroft		61
Many an eccentric and unthrifty motion make,	36	Ode Sancroft		69
To make them understand, and feel me when I write;	37	Ode Sancroft		89
(Methods in talk whereof our pride and ignorance make use)	38	Ode Sancroft		125
You make to truth, retreat, and innocence;	44	To Congreve		8
Or crazy rules to make us wits by rote	47	To Congreve		129
Shall on a day make sin and folly bleed;	47	To Congreve		134
So nature's craz'd convulsions make us dread	53	Temple Ill		65
When Folks came thick to make their Court	62	Discovery		6
Jove ever form'd to make a <Stink>?	65	Problem		4
Does make a wretched Shift,	75	Game Traffick	D	27
And for themselves fine Garments make.	79	Vanbrug House		34
Burnish and make a gaudy show,	84	Salamander		41
'Twill make the very Flames expire.	84	Salamander		50
We can but make it out in Ale.	92	Bauc & Phil 1		66
The Number make the Motion slower	93	Bauc & Phil 1		130
Make me the Parson if you please.	94	Bauc & Phil 1		164
To make a dreadful Night at Noon:	98	Elegy Patrige		14
Her Braided Hair to make thee Ends;	100	Elegy Patrige		80
Nor shall grin Berris make up the Losse.	103	Merlin		10
And make my Muse the Architect;	107	V's House		45
Canst make it serve thee for a Tilt.	109	V's House		114
Make me the Parson, if you please.	115	Bauc & Phil 2		116
All that you make this Stir about,	128	Little House		41
In half an Hour thou'lt make enough.	128	Little House		60
Says Nancy, I can make for Miss,	128	Little House		61
Then let old Englond make good Chear:	147	Windsor Proph		4
To make my Cream a Perquisite.	154	Widow and Cat	D	39
Let no pretence of Bus'ness make you stay,	166	Toland's Invit		39
Or make you Fast, and carry you to Prayers:	166	Toland's Invit		43
To make the Dutch-men proud and great:	169	Peace Dunkirk		34
"To make a pair of Jolly Fellows,	181	Horace 2, 1		43
Should come and make the Clatt'ring cease;	189	Faggot		24
To make the Bundle strong and safe,	191	Faggot		45
Make Room; as if a Duke were passing by.	194	Author Himself		36
Because he fain would make a Show,	216	To Mr. Delany		42
What Use in Life, to make Men frett?	217	To Mr. Delany		71
For nothing else will make it cease,--	220	A Quiet Life		13
But now, to make my Story Short	220	A Quiet Life		25
And bit her Lips to make them red:	222	Prog of Love		14
To make her Hair look black as Jet,	226	Prog of Beauty		18
Soon make my Dame grow lank and spare:	230	Prog of Poetry		12
Make Pinions for themselves to fly,	239	Run Bankers		22
And all his Grand Account to make?	241	Run Bankers		56
To be cloath'd like a Carcass would make a Teague mad,	237	Excellent Song		12
Tho' I know nothing on't, 'tis I that make Gold;	263	Apollo		4
I'll make it appear that they're all stol'n Ware:	265	Apollo		64
And when you'd make an Heroe grander,	270	Apollo's Edict	D	18
You all agree, I make no doubt,	270	Apollo's Edict	D	23
Or make a rumbling o'er his Head,	280	Journal		47
This Bank is to make us a New Paper Mill,	287	Bank Down		11
For Rags will make Paper, and Pa-ba-ba-brags,	287	Bank Down		17
This Paper will soon make us richer than Crags.	287	Bank Down		18
For Beggars have Rags and Rags will make Paper,	287	Bank Down		22
As they did in old Times, make Money of Leather,	287	Bank Down		27
The Bridegroom dresst, to make a Figure,	290	Prog Marriage		21
So odd a Choice, how could she make,	291	Prog Marriage		43
'Twill gain her Love to make her fine?	292	Prog Marriage		72
At five the Footmen make a Din,	292	Prog Marriage		91
Was brib'd to make the Dean agree	294	Prog Marriage		130
He'd either make a Hog or Dog on't,	299	Horrid Plot		32
We'll make a small one here by Art:	313	To Ford		58
That, a Rogue so Obscure should make such a Clutter,	334	Serious Poem		6
But finding the Statue to make no Complaint,	336	Serious Poem		73

MAKE   (CONTINUED)   PAGE   TITLE   LINE

	PAGE	TITLE	LINE
If you make the same Tryal, and Bore him Behind;	336	Serious Poem	78
Our Parsons Read the Draper's Books, and make us honest Foke.	343	Upon His Grace	40
. . . and make him live as long	343	Upon His Grace	47
Ye Pow'rs of Grub-street make me able,	346	Prometheus	57
To make a Clatt'ring as they trod.	352	Wood Ironmongr	12
That Sound will make the Parchment shrivel,	354	Simile Silver	29
I hope to make you yet as clean,	361	Grace's Answer	5
Will make you scorn this World below.	362	Grace's Answer	30
The Wise pretend to make it clear,	366	Answer Delaney	1
'Twere rude to make him tell it twice;	376	Apology Lady C	24
"Make thou its real Excellence	384	Manly Virtue	9
To make his Merit more discern'd,	384	Manly Virtue	31
Himself alone shou'd make him great.	384	Manly Virtue	36
That will make all my Subjects with pride to obey.	389	Order of Bath	4
If Others, whom you make your Theme,	391	Young's Satire	7
I know a Trick to make you thrive;	394	Grub-Street	5
Hang up thy wife, and she'll make four.	404	Window Inns 11	D 2
Their utmost Malice cannot make	414	Censure	21
Make you less virtous, learn'd, or wise.	414	Censure	28
Would make at least a handsom show	422	Ireld	36
But make an act secure and full	423	Ireld	57
And make his ignorance discerned,	435	Answer Paulus	113
Who Sowins make with Shelling	441	Ballyspellin	33
Then make this new Apollo sit	462	Birthday Song	71
Make some provision for the Yonker,	466	Birthday Song	203
Make Gulliver his Commodore,	466	Birthday Song	206
And make him crouch to save his bacon.	468	Birthday Song	250
To make it pass upon the Nation,	475	Epist on Epist	19
To make them work their own undoing.	484	Libel on D- D-	128
Take my advice; to make you safe,	487	Irish-Club	13
Make gilded spires and altars tumble.	490	Dialogue	36
Make me pollute the Muses' bower?	490	Dialogue	46
Could make you so sincerely hate	498	Panegyr Swift	155
Make all true Patriots up to Shoe-boys	501	Doctor Delaney	61
Tho' it would make you England's Primate:	503	Doctor Delaney	110
To make their Trash the better sell.	505	Doctor Delaney	158
Whereof, to make the Matter clear,	526	Lady's Dres Rm	9
To make it seem in this Disguise,	528	Lady's Dres Rm	77
For thee, than make a dry Nurse of thy Muse?	531	To Mr. Gay	8
And first: To make my Observation right,	532	To Mr. Gay	31
Be rich; but of your Wealth make no Parade;	533	To Mr. Gay	61
Starve twenty Lords to make one Scoundrel rich:	535	To Mr. Gay	104
With driving wrong, will make the Pannel split;	535	To Mr. Gay	132
Wou'd make him rage, and storm, and fret,	546	Life of Swift	28
They'd laugh, to see me make a rout,	546	Life of Swift	50
To make these Truths the better known,	547	Life of Swift	66
But, if I chance to make a slip,	548	Life of Swift	119
Faith, he must make his Stories shorter,	556	Death of Swift	95
And then to make them pass the glibber,	561	Death of Swift	199
"And, would you make him truly sower;	566	Death of Swift	343
"And make the Government a Babel:	568	Death of Swift	384
"And make her infamous in Story.	568	Death of Swift	388
"And make him of his Zeal repent;	570	Death of Swift	424
And make merry in their Houses;	574	Helter Skelter	44
Squat on her Hams, to make Maid's Water.	584	Strephon Chloe	18
And, last to make the Matter sure,	586	Strephon Chloe	63
And make them ev'ry Afternoon	587	Strephon Chloe	117
And make him fancy what she will.	588	Strephon Chloe	144
Resolv'd to make his first Attack;	588	Strephon Chloe	149
Say, fair ones, must I make a Pause?	589	Strephon Chloe	161
Why will you make yourself a Bubble	593	Strephon Chloe	305
The King of Brutes (to make it plain,	601	Beasts Confess	7
He scorns to make his Art a Trade;	605	Beasts Confess	135
In hopes to make you more devout;	617	Scandal Poem 1	8
Among your femals make inquiryes:	619	Scandal Poem 1	73
Among your Females make Inquiries;	625	Scandal Poem 2	71
Do but serve to make me Sport.	634	Epistle Lady	148
I Shou'd make a Figure scurvy,	637	Epistle Lady	219
Which I chose to make appear,	637	Epistle Lady	227
Only make it smart a while:	638	Epistle Lady	265
Make you able upon Sight,	638	Epistle Lady	269
Ascending make one Funeral-Blaze.	646	On Poetry	204
In vain you make ye strictest View	659	On Poetry	D 410
You make the graceful Horace look	670	Epig Carthy 21	D 3
He'll make it muddy as a Bog.	671	Epig Carthy 21	D 8
And make thy curate-ship a dean;	676	Parson's Case	20
A Gownman of a diff'rent Make.	701	Cadenus Vaness	463
Can make us without Fear disclose	706	Cadenus Vaness	610
In ev'ry Point to make it fit,	709	Cadenus Vaness	724
In lofty Style to make Replies,	711	Cadenus Vaness	796
Or should a Porter make Enquiries	729	Stella, Poems	39
As fine as Dawbers Hands can make it	734	Stel B-day '20	11
To make you look like Beauty's Queen	736	Stel B-day '20	53
To make Her only touch a Quail:	746	Stel Distress	20
To make her only touch a Quail.	750	Stel Wood-Park	18
Shall for my follies make amends:	755	Stella '23	36
A Pair to make a Country Dance,	756	Stel B-day '24	8
No Length of Time can make you quit	758	Stel B-day '24	49
To make me deaf, and mend my Sight.	758	Stel B-day '24	54

493

MAKE   (CONTINUED)   PAGE   TITLE   LINE

	PAGE	TITLE		LINE
We'll make it firm with Beef and Claret.	760	Receipt Youth		56
That Courage which can make you just,	765	Stel B-day '26		45
Of giddy Winds, but make some friendly Port.	770	Horace 1, 14		12
You Wrigle, Fidge, and make a Rout	777	Mullinix Tim		139
Betray, make Oath, impeach, inform,	778	Mullinix Tim		168
Dick would make a woful Noise,	784	Mullinex Dick		17
For, would'st thou make a fouler Show,	786	Clad in Brown		3
To foreign Prelates make a slavish Court,	793	St. Pat's Well		75
In him they lodge, and make him Legion.	798	Traulus 1		78
And, when this is over, we'll make him amends,	817	Yahoo's		61
Make Rundle Bishop; fye for Shame!	819	Dr. Rundle		1
How will his Brethren make Complaints?	819	Dr. Rundle		4
Could he but make his Gift appear	821	Dr. Rundle		51
Where ev'ry Trout can make as high Rants	824	Printer Newgat		5
Survive in thee, and make the Proverb good	826	Noisy Tom		18
And to make your Project pass,	839	Legion Club		217
Make use of your time.	854	Lady's Lament		114
And thorns, to make fires;	857	Lady's Lament		198
I've said enough to make him blush	860	Lady Acheson		13
And make him soon give up the Cause.	861	Lady Acheson		40
New Years help to make me old;	863	To Janus		26
First, let me suppose I make it a Malt-House:	867	Grand Question		7
If I make it a Barrack, the Crown is my Tenant.	867	Grand Question		19
A laureat make that is no poet;	876	To Dean Swift		18
Nay, he can make what's greater far,	876	To Dean Swift		23
Will make them welcome to his modicum:	878	Robbin & Harry		24
Then, (let me see) we'll make the Knight	886	Rev Market-Hill		93
To make you suitable Returns;	887	Panegyr Dean		30
To make for Pigs convenient Styes:	892	Panegyr Dean		160
Thy Milk shall make us Tubs of Butter.	892	Panegyr Dean		172
From haughty Gaul to make Ragous.	895	Panegyr Dean		264
And make a Beggar's Brat a Peer.	916	Riddle 1		36
To make me glorious to the Sight	916	Riddle 2		11
Of whom all People make a Jest.	918	Riddle 4		22
O'er Head and Body make a Rout,	920	Riddle 6		15
Is never pleas'd till I make one:	920	Riddle 6		28
All make Oblations at this Shrine.	922	Riddle 7		30
And make thee tear thy tainted Hyde.	925	Riddle 8		44
Why then I make pieces of Iron go down.	927	Riddle 11	D	8
Tho' so much of Heav'n appears in my Make,	929	Riddle 13	D	7
I'll make the Dev'l a Saint this Hour,	930	Riddle 15	D	15
Next make a Devil of a Saint.	930	Riddle 15	D	16
'Tis mine to make a just Reflection,	932	Riddle 19	D	17
With Ease I make to keep their Distance;	934	Riddle 21	D	4
Make the fairest look more fair;	936	Riddle 24	D	6
Make up a Bird very swift of Flight.	940	Letter		4
Will make a Horse go, though he be not fat.	940	Letter		13
Cooks make their Fowl look tight and spruce.	942	Probatur Alit		10
At Whist they will make a desperate Sweep.	943	Probatur Alit		32
To make their Water pass:	952	Asparagus		3
They make the Blood warmer,	952	Onyons		4
They'll make you a Dad	953	Oysters		9
They'll make a sweet Bishop when Gentlefolks sup.	953	Oranges		4
And now whereby I find you would fain make an Excuse,	985	Mary to Sher		11
Well, but I must run and make the Bed,	987	Mary to Sher		35
You seem to praise to make amends,	1003	Dan J's Reply		20
Make a Page of your own Age,	1013	Swift to Sheri		6
. . .to make the Offer; and they cannot deny it.	1014	Swift to Sheri		8
Must I make myself hoarse with demanding an Answer?	1019	To Sheridan		4
'Ere Vulcan comes to make him new.	1021	Nim-Dan-Dean 1	D	8
To make a Work compleatly fine,	1022	Nim-Dan-Dean 1	D	45
Such Musick would make a Fanatick or Jew sick:	1029	Dr. Helsham		14
But you learned Doctors can make whom you chuse sick.	1029	Dr. Helsham		19
If I write any more, it will make my poor Muse sick.	1030	Dr. Sheridan		1
In vain we make poor Sheelah toil,	1035	To Quilca		7

MAKER

	PAGE	TITLE		LINE
As thus, "Vouchsafe, Oh gracious Maker!	199	Horace 2, 6	D	

MAKERS

	PAGE	TITLE		LINE
Had Women been the Makers of our Laws;	662	Upon Ladies		5

MAKES

	PAGE	TITLE		LINE
Which makes a Godhead of a Name,	7	Ode to King		25
How the Mouse makes the mighty Mountain shake!	30	Ode to Temple		107
. . .makes a great Hole in my Wages,	71	Mrs Harris Pet		40
Makes take all things in good Part:	94	Bauc & Phil 1		160
What makes your Worship look so lean?	174	Horace 1, 7		122
Makes choice of him she fancies best,	178	To Lord Harley		63
Can he who makes himself a Slave	221	A Quiet Life		39
What Magick makes our Money rise	250	Bubble		2
And Paper makes Money, and what can be cheaper?	287	Bank Down		23
He makes no more to give ten Pounds than I to give a Pin.	341	Upon His Grace		14
Nor makes a Scruple to expose	416	Woman's Mind		21
With rage impatient makes me wait	420	Holyhead		27
'I'm hurry'd so, it makes me sick,	448	Modern Lady		98
Their Chattering makes a louder Din	450	Modern Lady		180
And makes her Part'ner understand	452	Modern Lady		260
Or makes 'em sensible of Shame.	453	Modern Lady		275
Makes mighty Armys turn their Arses.	461	Birthday Song		30
Hesse Darmstedt makes too rough a sound,	467	Birthday Song		215
'Tis Eminence makes Envy rise,	501	Doctor Delaney		41

```
MAKES              (CONTINUED)                          PAGE   TITLE            LINE
  With which he makes so foul a Rout;)      . . . . . . .   530  Lady's Dres Rm     140
  "If he makes Mankind bad as Elves,       . . . . . .     548  Life of Swift      115
  But, this with Envy makes me burst.      . . . . . .     555  Death of Swift      70
  And makes it warm for Dearest Life.      . . . . . .     590  Strephon Chloe     208
  What makes thee lie a-bed so late?       . . . . . . .   594  Cassinus Peter      30
  And, this he makes his constant Rule;    . . . . . .     603  Beasts Confess      81
  (Who makes you think the Clouds he pierces: . . . . .    620  Scandal Poem 1     103
  Though Mercury makes use of Wings        . . . . . . .   621  Scandal Poem 1     117
  Yet, though we grant she makes it wetter . . . . . .     621  Scandal Poem 1     145
  And only makes you more devout.          . . . . . . .   624  Scandal Poem 2       8
  (Who makes you think, the Clouds he pierces: . . . . .   626  Scandal Poem 2     101
  But, though we own, she makes it wetter, . . . . . .     628  Scandal Poem 2     149
  All their Madness makes me merry:        . . . . . . .   635  Epistle Lady       164
  For Poets, Law makes no Provision:       . . . . . . .   641  On Poetry           49
  It makes no Diff'rence in the Case,      . . . . . .     724  To Stella           21
  The Heat that makes the Summit glow,     . . . . . . .   731  Stella, Poems      107
  Makes Wit inflame, or Anger burn;        . . . . . . .   731  Stella, Poems      118
  And makes such reasonable Bills          . . . . . .     735  Stel B-day '20      28
  It never makes the least Impression.     . . . . . . .   798  Traulus 1           64
  Sometimes makes the Devil his Rod:       . . . . . . .   830  Legion Club         32
  Who makes the best figure,               . . . . . . .   856  Lady's Lament      169
  "But, the Sight of a Book makes me sick to this Day. .   873  Grand Question     172
  Dilates, and makes the Vessel full:      . . . . . . .   893  Panegyr Dean       192
  Nor makes their conversation better,     . . . . . . .   900  Dean's Reasons      39
  Makes her sole delight to vex.           . . . . . . .   906  Daphne               4
  And makes me tell a Thousand Lyes:       . . . . . . .   915  Riddle 1            20
  . . .but that Man makes him a Fool.      . . . . . . .   987  Mary to Sher        30
  If SHE makes sher, and RI makes ry,      . . . . . . .  1004  Dan J's Reply       35
  If SHE makes sher, and RI makes ry,      . . . . . . .  1004  Dan J's Reply       35
  Makes thy Verse smooth, and makes them last.   . . . .  1021  Nim-Dan-Dean 1  D 14
  Makes thy Verse smooth, and makes them last.   . . . .  1021  Nim-Dan-Dean 1  D 14
  That she makes of your verses a hoop for Miss Tam, . .  1027  Sheri Circles       27
MAKING
  In making a Ballad, but was at a Stand,  . . . . . .      77  Lady B- B-          23
  As if a Man in making Posies . . . . . . . .             96  On the Union         9
  To hear we are making a Peace without Spain; . . . .    143  New Song            12
  Making by second hand their Offers,      . . . . . .    253  Bubble              70
  "In making <Bishops>, no one knows.      . . . . . .    304  Storm               46
  And there can be no Harm in making a Tryal; . . . .     336  Serious Poem        82
  Talk not of making of thy Nest,          . . . . . .    361  Grace's Answer      13
  And making -- some for Ideots pass       . . . . . .    373  Letter D. S-y       58
  "In Senates sit, at making Laws;         . . . . . . .  549  Life of Swift      163
  Thus making others Wisdom known,         . . . . . . .  701  Cadenus Vaness     452
  And making one luxuriant Shoot           . . . . . . .  730  Stella, Poems       67
  If making Divisions was all their Intent, . . . . .     804  Irish Bishops       35
  This pedlar, at speaking and making of laws, . . . .    815  Yahoo's             16
  Making good my Grandames Jest,           . . . . . . .  829  Legion Club          7
  Let them rave of making Laws;            . . . . . . .  831  Legion Club         50
  In roasting larks, or making laws:       . . . . . .    901  Dean's Reasons      78
  You always are making a God of your Spouse, . . . .     947  Mrs. Houghton        1
  I spend my Time in making Sermons,       . . . . . .    993  On Picture           4
MAKYTH
  Till Hapsburge makyth them but twayne.   . . . . . .    103  Merlin              20
MALAHIDE
  Fresh from Malahide,   . . . . . . . . . .              953  Herrings             4
MALE
  To have both male & female Race,         . . . . . . .  460  Birthday Song        6
  Female Vices most, or Male,              . . . . . . .  801  Traulus 2           54
MALEBRANCHE
  To understand Malebranche or Cambray;    . . . . . .    900  Dean's Reasons      52
MALI'N
  To Venus in Aspect Mali'n,               . . . . . . .   99  Elegy Patrige       60
MALICE
  Of secret Malice, or of open Force.      . . . . . .     13  Ode to William   D 44
  Say what their senseless malice meant,   . . . . . .     42  Ode Sancroft       247
  The malice thou inspir'st I never fail   . . . . . .     53  Temple Ill          85
  As having Malice in her Heart,           . . . . . .    120  Apollo Outwit       26
  To choque your Sight, and raise your Malice) . . . .    313  To Ford             64
  Struck all his Rage and Malice down;     . . . . . .    340  Arch-Bish Dub       20
  Their utmost Malice cannot make          . . . . . .    414  Censure             21
  Their Malice, is--to let them talk.      . . . . . .    414  Censure             30
  And Malice always judging worst;         . . . . . .    448  Modern Lady        129
  Shews all the malice of a Tory,          . . . . . .    489  Dialogue            26
  Both Envy then and Malice must           . . . . . . .  498  Panegyr Swift      169
  Nor cou'd his Malice spare the <Queen>;  . . . . . .    514  Answer Fable        76
  Whose Malice, for the Worst of Ends,     . . . . . .    515  Answer Fable        97
  Made up of Malice, Truth, and Wit:       . . . . . .    545  Life of Swift        2
  "Yet, Malice never was his Aim;          . . . . . .    571  Death of Swift     459
  An A's and B's your Malice vent,         . . . . . .    645  On Poetry          159
  Which Malice must attack in vain;        . . . . . .    693  Cadenus Vaness     209
  Let Malice look with all her Eyes,       . . . . . .    730  Stella, Poems       81
  His Malice work as he design'd:          . . . . . .    750  Stel Wood-Park      24
  And, must their Malice ne'er give o'er?  . . . . . .    798  Traulus 1           86
  His malice is plain,   . . . . . . . . .                852  Lady's Lament        9
  To please his Malice, or his Lust.       . . . . . .    915  Riddle 1            22
MALICIOUS
  Yes; you are all malicious standers-by,  . . . . .       49  To Congreve        199
  And tho' some Malicious Young Spirit did do't, . .      77  Lady B- B-          29
  From some malicious Tory's Brain,        . . . . . .    256  Bubble             158
  To me was most malicious kind  . . . . . . .            420  Holyhead            22
```

495

```
                                                        PAGE  TITLE              LINE
MALICIOUSLY
     Did maliciously, falsly, and traiterously write,   .   .   .   264 Apollo           35
MALIGNANT
     When she sends forth such a malignant Birth,       .   .   .   .     8 Ode to King       54
     Malignant goddess! bane to my repose,  .  .  .  .  .  .  .  .    53 Temple Ill        81
     "The most malignant of the Herd,   .  .  .  .  .  .  .  .       549 Life of Swift    164
MALL
     Of Chivy-chase, and English Mall,   .  .  .  .  .  .  .          93 Bauc & Phil 1    118
MALSTER
     Sir Arthur the Malster! how fine it will sound?    .   .   .   868 Grand Question    45
MALT-HOUSE
     For a Barrack or Malt-House, we now must consider.    .        867 Grand Question     6
     First, let me suppose I make it a Malt-House:    .  .          867 Grand Question     7
MAMBRINO'S
     Mambrino's Helm adorn'd his Head.   .  .  .  .  .  .           156 Fable of Midas    14
MAMMON
     Who, while th' unrighteous Mammon is his Friend,   .   .      533 To Mr. Gay        73
     But Mammon, and the <German> Line.   .  .  .  .  .  .  .       820 Dr. Rundle        36
MAN   SEE MOUSETRAP-MAN,GOOD-MAN,UN-MAN,COACH-MAN,PUPPET-MAN,
      SERVING-MAN,SMALLCOAL-MAN
     When Man himself's the Vermin of Her Earth;    .  .  .          8 Ode to King       55
     The Name and Man, by whom the Book was writ,   .  .  .        21 Ode Athenian     166
     For Man to dress and polish his Uncourtly Mind,    .   .      22 Ode Athenian     218
     Is even the nobler Man, our Learning and our Wit,  .   .      24 Ode Athenian     269
     Till its first Emperor rebellious Man   .  .  .  .  .         26 Ode to Temple      2
     But foolish Man still judges what is best    .  .  .  .       36 Ode Sancroft      54
     And to mistaken man these truths rehearse,   .  .  .  .       53 Temple Ill        69
     Deals out to man the planet of his birth;    .  .  .  .       54 Temple Ill        90
     .  .  .to the Cunning Man;   .  .  .  .  .  .  .  .  .  .       72 Mrs Harris Pet    48
     As if a Man in making Posies   .  .  .  .  .  .  .            96 On the Union       9
     And no Man shall be sorie therefore.   .  .  .  .  .  .      103 Merlin            18
     Were several Years this Man and Wife,  .  .  .  .  .  .      116 Bauc & Phil 2    150
     Sprout, quoth the Man, What's this you tell us?    .  .      116 Bauc & Phil 2    157
     My Lord, who (if a Man may say't)    .  .  .  .  .  .        171 Horace 1, 7       13
     Not Rich, but ow'd no Man a Groat;   .  .  .  .  .  .  .      171 Horace 1, 7       34
     No Man alive has more Respect--   .  .  .  .  .  .  .  .      173 Horace 1, 7       70
     Come Courtiers: Every Man his Stick:   .  .  .  .  .  .      190 Faggot            35
     To be the Man I long have sought,    .  .  .  .  .  .  .      215 To Mr. Delany      4
     She trembled when a Man drew near;   .  .  .  .  .  .  .      222 Prog of Love       3
     She durst behold that Monster, Man:    .  .  .  .  .  .      222 Prog of Love      12
     Him for an happy Man I own,    .  .  .  .  .  .  .  .        243 Horace 4, 9       15
     The Man, who Infamy to shun,   .  .  .  .  .  .  .  .  .      243 Horace 4, 9       21
     That Man is ready to defend    .  .  .  .  .  .  .  .        243 Horace 4, 9       23
     And observe while you live, that no Man is shy     .  .      264 Apollo            57
     By a Parliament Man when the Farmer was told,   .  .        288 Bank Down         31
     Rather than starve, a better man would strole.  .  .        308 Billet Players    16
     But who thy Father, no Man knows,    .  .  .  .  .  .        323 Pethox             2
     The Man of Bus'ness must retire.   .  .  .  .  .  .          325 Pethox            48
     Is a Man of this World all true Flesh and Blood;   .  .      335 Serious Poem      50
     I find you bear a good Report, and are an honest Man.   .    342 Upon His Grace    34
     I'm sure a Man of your fine Sense    .  .  .  .  .  .        361 Grace's Answer    21
     And there's an End; the Man is dead;   .  .  .  .  .  .      366 Answer Delaney     6
     And if you had heard the Man discourse,    .  .  .  .        375 Apology Lady C    11
     The Captain was a Man of Reading,    .  .  .  .  .  .  .      377 Apology Lady C    71
     Who was the Man, he wish'd to seem;    .  .  .  .  .  .      386 Manly Virtue      76
     The Man above, or under Ground.    .  .  .  .  .  .  .      393 Modern Poets      16
     That would turn a Man out of his own?    .  .  .  .  .        396 Dog and Thief     20
     And said, lack-a-day! he's a proper young Man.  .  .        399 Tom Clinch         8
     In Man, Possession, and Desire;    .  .  .  .  .  .  .      411 Desire Possess     2
     Be so robustious like a Man.   .  .  .  .  .  .  .  .        417 Woman's Mind      48
     O yes! If any Man can find  .  .  .  .  .  .  .  .  .        417 Woman's Mind      57
     How to give ev'ry man his due:   .  .  .  .  .  .  .  .      433 Answer Paulus     34
     Perhaps be found one honest man:   .  .  .  .  .  .  .      435 Answer Paulus    104
     And, we admire the man, who saves    .  .  .  .  .  .        436 Answer Paulus    125
     Madam, if there be Truth in Man,   .  .  .  .  .  .  .      447 Modern Lady       88
     Describe the Lady and the Man.   .  .  .  .  .  .  .  .      450 Modern Lady      195
     Swear, he's a most facetious Man,    .  .  .  .  .  .        480 Libel on D- D-     9
     I hate the Vice-Roy, love the Man.   .  .  .  .  .  .        485 Libel on D- D-   152
     This Pheasant was a Man of Wit,    .  .  .  .  .  .  .      513 Answer Fable      35
     For much a better Man than You?    .  .  .  .  .  .  .      546 Life of Swift     36
     "Poor Man! he went, all on a sudden---!    .  .  .  .        547 Life of Swift     70
     "'tis own'd he was a Man of Wit---,    .  .  .  .  .  .      547 Life of Swift     74
     "He was an honest man I'll swear---:   .  .  .  .  .  .      547 Life of Swift     80
     "Nor fear'd he God, nor Man regarded;    .  .  .  .  .      570 Death of Swift   422
     Permit a brutish Man to touch her?   .  .  .  .  .  .        588 Strephon Chloe   153
     The fittest Man to fill a Place:   .  .  .  .  .  .  .      606 Beasts Confess   156
     And ev'ry virtuous Man his Brother:    .  .  .  .  .  .      606 Beasts Confess   180
     But Man we find the only Creature,   .  .  .  .  .  .        641 On Poetry         19
     Tis sung Prometheus forming Man    .  .  .  .  .  .  .      659 On Poetry      D 410
     Once Horace fancied from a Man   .  .  .  .  .  .  .  .      666 Epig Carthy 1   D  1
     Has made the Man a Goose in earnest.   .  .  .  .  .        666 Epig Carthy 1   D  4
     For here you see the Man, and there the Beast.  .  .        668 Epig Carthy 9   D  2
     'Tis what no Man alive will say of you.    .  .  .  .        670 Epig Carthy 18  D  2
     Accusing that false Creature, Man.   .  .  .  .  .  .        686 Cadenus Vaness     4
     Alone distinguish'd Man from Brute:    .  .  .  .  .  .      697 Cadenus Vaness   345
     She might excuse a Man of Letters;   .  .  .  .  .  .        705 Cadenus Vaness   590
     Just as a Man sans Consequence.    .  .  .  .  .  .  .      707 Cadenus Vaness   659
     For, let a Man be ne'er so wise,   .  .  .  .  .  .  .      707 Cadenus Vaness   668
     To find her a great Witt, but the Dean a small Man.    .    716 Answer Rebus      14
     And shou'd he write Pamphlets, no Great Man wou'd read      717 Answer Rebus      26
       'em:
```

MAN   (CONTINUED)   PAGE   TITLE   LINE
    Courage to Man alone confin'd: . . . .   725 To Stella   66
    They give the sick man joy, and praise . . . . . .   761 Bec's B-Day   15
    The Tories are gone ev'ry Man over . . . .   773 Mullinix Tim   9
    Who hate and scorn you, to a Man; . . . .   777 Mullinix Tim   146
    Such Friendship never Man profest, ...   796 Traulus 1   15
    But still insist the Man is mad. . . . .   796 Traulus 1   22
    To foul the Man he chiefly flatters. . . . . .   796 Traulus 1   32
    Why Tom, the Man has lost his Wits! . . . . . .   797 Traulus 1   34
    Could always bear to Strive with Man? . . . . . .   799 Traulus 1   96
    (And, Parsons tell us, no Man can do more) . . . .   806 Judas   6
    Yet, through Despair, of God and Man accurst, . . . 806 Judas   7
    May well be said Man did beget it. . . . .   812 Bro Protestant   38
    If you say this is hard, on a man that is reckon'd . 817 Yahoo's   66
    And say of the man what all honest men say. . . . . 819 Archbi Cashel   10
    The Man has Learning, Sense and Morals. . . . .   820 Dr. Rundle   22
    Bless us, Morgan! Art thou there Man? . . . . . .   837 Legion Club   189
    Some they do say, 'twas the big man of straw; . . . 841 Ballad   D 12
    Sure never did man see . . . .   851 Lady's Lament   1
    Whose master, whose man; . . . .   856 Lady's Lament   168
    With such a cross Man, I wou'd lye in the Streets. . 869 Grand Question   60
    The Man with the Kettle-drum enters the Gate; . . . 870 Grand Question   90
    Dear Madam, be sure he's a fine spoken Man, . . .   872 Grand Question   139
    "The first Man I robb'd was a Parson by <God>. . . . 873 Grand Question   170
    Just to give ev'ry Man his Glass: . . . .   889 Panegyr Dean   94
    How bles't am I by such a Man led! . . . .   890 Panegyr Dean   106
    Such charming Butter never Man made. . . . . . .   892 Panegyr Dean   168
    Taught harmless Man to cram and stuff. . . . . .   895 Panegyr Dean   262
    Whom you allow a man of taste, ...   899 Dean's Reasons   22
    But find the Rhime, and you're the Man. . . . . .   912 Aenigma   14
    And for the Rhime, to you're the Man, ...   912 Aenigma Expl   D   9
    Till me that Tyrant Man espy'd, ...   915 Riddle 1   7
    Nay; Man, my Master, is my Slave: . . . .   916 Riddle 1   33
    Shall Man presume to be my Master, ...   918 Riddle 4   17
    The Joy of Man, the Pride of Brutes, ...   919 Riddle 5   1
    The Soul of Man with Spleen you vex; . . . . . .   919 Riddle 5   17
    Vain Man, of all thy vain Pursuits. . . . . .   921 Riddle 7   2
    A Man, a Woman, Lion, Bear, ...   927 Riddle 10   D 14
    Nay, bring me here the tallest Man, ...   934 Riddle 21   D 17
    To Man alone I owe my birth, ...   936 Riddle 24   D   2
    Pray what is a Man? he's a fine-Linen Searcher. .   972 S-'s Ans Sh-d   10
    Well; if ever I saw such another Man . . . . .   985 Mary to Sher   1
    I am sure such Words does not become a Man of your   985 Mary to Sher   3
        Cloth,
    And the Dean my Master is an honester Man . . .   985 Mary to Sher   8
    My Master is a parsonable Man, ...   985 Mary to Sher   10
    And Saunders the Man says, you are always jesting and 986 Mary to Sher   27
        mocking,
    I thought my Master a wise Man, ...   987 Mary to Sher   30
    . . .but that Man makes him a Fool. . . . . . .   987 Mary to Sher   30
    . . .and your Man Alexander had not gone, . .   1013 Swift to Sheri   4
    . . .and send your Man Alexander to buy Corks, . . 1013 Swift to Sheri   6
    For your Man, I long waited. . . . .   1014 Swift to Sheri   18
    Your Man is belated, ...   1014 Swift to Sheri   21
    But no man pays me. . . . .   1037 Sheridan Cavan   8
MAN'D
    Which just like ours, new rigg'd and man'd, ...   96 On the Union   17
MAN'S   SEE FOOT-MAN'S
    When man's ill genius to my presence sent . . . . .   47 To Congreve   135
    They thought it was an old Man's Maggot. . . . . .   189 Faggot   5
    For fear my Lord should send it all into the poor Man's 342 Upon His Grace   26
        Box.
    And there he grew fond of another Man's Wife, . . . 517 Dean Hang Rape   8
    "Of no Man's Greatness was afraid, ...   565 Death of Swift   327
    "Because he sought for no Man's Aid. . . . . . .   565 Death of Swift   328
    May be proud to be licking a great man's posteriors. . 817 Yahoo's   69
    What Name for a Maid, was the first Man's Damnation? 973 S-'s Ans Sh-d   12
    You're my goose, and no other man's; . . . . . .   983 Sher, A Goose   11
MANAG'D
    She manag'd her Estate with Care, ...   693 Cadenus Vaness   220
MANAGE
    But, they can manage Whig and Tory: . . . .   483 Libel on D- D-   98
    What Subject you can manage best; . . . .   642 On Poetry   80
    To manage thy abortive Scheme; . . . .   696 Cadenus Vaness   299
MANAGEMENT
    "I" observe her Management within. . . . .   321 First of April   28
MANE
    Harry look'd fierce, and shook his ragged Mane: . . . 168 Peace Dunkirk   17
MANFULLY
    Now manfully thou'lt run a Tilt . . . .   183 Horace 2, 1   93
MANGER
    In a vile manger laid, ...   40 Ode Sancroft   174
MANGLED
    The Nymph, tho' in this mangled Plight, ...   583 Young Nymph   65
    By your knife to be mangled than rack'd with your voice. 818 Epigr Kite   4
    See where those mangled Corpses lye; . . . .   923 Riddle 7   61
MANHOOD
    What early Manhood has he shown, ...   655 On Poetry   431
MANIERE
    To praise it, par maniere d'acquit; . . . .   379 Apology Lady C   120

MANKIND

	PAGE	TITLE	LINE
Impertinence, the Scurvy of Mankind,	18	Ode Athenian	70
With all that Power unfelt, courts Mankind to be Great,	21	Ode Athenian	155
(And then how much a nothing is Mankind!	21	Ode Athenian	180
Than You to please and satisfie Mankind,	22	Ode Athenian	200
And to all future Mankind shew	25	Ode Athenian	304
Hence Mankind fell, and here must rise again.	32	Ode to Temple	177
That looks with scorn on half mankind beside;	44	To Congreve	44
Serves by retail to furnish half mankind.	45	To Congreve	54
What's that to her if mankind be a fool?	48	To Congreve	178
So, the pert Dunces of Mankind	216	To Mr. Delany	45
For, let Mankind discharge their Tongues	414	Censure	19
I own, the curses of mankind	433	Answer Paulus	51
To pitch on me, of all Mankind,	445	Modern Lady	6
To all mankind a constant friend,	455	Dean Smedley	15
To warp the Sense of all Mankind:	475	Epist on Epist	22
And all Mankind as Fools, or Knaves;	493	Panegyr Swift	6
(And you of all Mankind should know)	493	Panegyr Swift	24
To bless, as now you curse Mankind?	496	Panegyr Swift	95
"If he makes Mankind bad as Elves,	548	Life of Swift	115
"To please, and to reform Mankind;	550	Life of Swift	197
In him; the Fault is in Mankind.	553	Death of Swift	4
One, whom you love of all Mankind,	554	Death of Swift	22
"To cure the Vices of Mankind:	565	Death of Swift	314
To pour down Curses on Mankind.	624	Scandal Poem 2	30
The Plagues and Scourges of Mankind.	654	On Poetry	408
And represent them to Mankind	691	Cadenus Vaness	152
To know the Converse of Mankind.	696	Cadenus Vaness	315
Of half Mankind the Dread and Hate.	702	Cadenus Vaness	505
Must never to Mankind be told,	712	Cadenus Vaness	826
Against Enslavers of Mankind!	725	To Stella	62
And, is not Virtue in Mankind	765	Stel B-day '26	61
Receiv'd the Gifts of all Mankind.	894	Panegyr Dean	236
The greatest cully of mankind:	899	Dean's Reasons	12
But see below me all Mankind.	917	Riddle 3	4
The foul Corruptions of Mankind.	921	Riddle 7	16
Deucalion, to restore Mankind	922	Riddle 7	45
For you, by this Rule, must adore all Mankind.	947	Mrs. Houghton	6

MANLY

	PAGE	TITLE	LINE
In manly Form to let them see	384	Manly Virtue	25
Yet Manly Virtue even here	385	Manly Virtue	69
And Manly Virtue, like the Sun,	387	Manly Virtue	117
For manly Bosoms chiefly fit,	693	Cadenus Vaness	204
The Fire that forms a manly Soul;	726	To Stella	88

MANNER

	PAGE	TITLE		LINE
Call'd to the Clerk in manner mild,	128	Little House		51
But in a sawcy manner He	153	Widow and Cat	D	19
In manner submissive most humbly do pray,	185	Scriblerus 1		2
His Jordan stood in Manner fitting	594	Cassinus Peter		21
Her Manner now was something new;	707	Cadenus Vaness		661

MANNER'D   SEE ILL-MANNER'D
MANNERD   SEE ILL-MANNERD
MANNERS

	PAGE	TITLE		LINE
The Manners of the rural Race,	270	Apollo's Edict	D	30
Good Manners must give Place to Profit.	311	To Ford		16
I'll Try his Manners once again;	377	Apology Lady C		68
They send for Manners--; not for Grief---:	546	Life of Swift		61
In Good Manners, am I faulty?	631	Epistle Lady		69
Which Manners, Decency, and Pride,	730	Stella, Poems		99
His manners forgets;	855	Lady's Lament		142
His Manners would not let him wait,	859	Lady Acheson		5
She declares from her throne you must learn better manners	979	Dean to Tho: S		28

MANNORS

	PAGE	TITLE	LINE
My Mannors all contig'ous round,	251	Bubble	19
Who votes for Mannors, who for Hire.	781	Mullinix Tim	262

MANSION

	PAGE	TITLE	LINE
Is made his Mansion for a while;	387	Manly Virtue	136
Trots to his country mansion down;	435	Answer Paulus	94
And call the Mansion Drapier's Hill;	875	Drapier's Hill	10

MANSION-HOUSE

	PAGE	TITLE	LINE
To sweep the Mansion-house they dwell in;	892	Panegyr Dean	165

MANSIONS

	PAGE	TITLE	LINE
Nor can they from infernal Mansions rise;	363	On Dreams	4

MANTLE

	PAGE	TITLE	LINE
Of Mantle and Kercher,	245	Irish-Feast	22

MANTLE'S

	PAGE	TITLE		LINE
Elijah's Mantle's worn out.	270	Apollo's Edict	D	24

MANTUAS

	PAGE	TITLE	LINE
Which others for Mantuas wou'd think fine enough;	716	Answer Rebus	16

MANUFACTURE

	PAGE	TITLE	LINE
And Rebel is the growth and manufacture of the Land.	8	Ode to King	57

MANUFACTURES

	PAGE	TITLE	LINE
We'll dress in Manufactures, made at home?	275	Epilogue	17

MANY

	PAGE	TITLE	LINE
Our Prince has charm'd its many hundred Eyes;	8	Ode to King	78
Who claim so many Titles to be Jews,	8	Ode to King	85
And many a pleasant Wood,	17	Ode Athenian	41
With many a heavenly Song	17	Ode Athenian	54
Contrive to shock your Minds, with many a sensless doubt,	22	Ode Athenian	207
By many a petty Lord possess'd,	26	Ode to Temple	6
And softly steals in many Windings down,	31	Ode to Temple	156

MANY   (CONTINUED)   PAGE   TITLE   LINE
     Thro' many a needless sphere to run, ...   36 Ode Sancroft   68
     Many an eccentric and unthrifty motion make, ...   36 Ode Sancroft   69
     Lead them a Dance of many a Mile, ...   79 Vanbrug House   5
     After hard Throws of many a Day   . . . . . .   81 Vanbrug House   73
     So many Beggers pass this way, ...   90 Bauc & Phil 1   29
     Compos'd of Timber many a Load, ...   94 Bauc & Phil 1   148
     Lead 'em a Dance of many a Mile, ...   106 V's House   5
     Compact of Timber many a Load, ...   114 Bauc & Phil 2   102
     Found his Head fill'd with many a System, ...   115 Bauc & Phil 2   135
     And drive as many Souls to Hell.   . . . . . .   133 Magician's Rod   42
     And many Score of Gudgeons took;   . . . . . .   133 Magician's Rod   46
     Speak against Peace right many a Word;   . . . . . .   147 Windsor Proph   8
     For many good Groats his Tongue shall slitt: . . . .   147 Windsor Proph   10
     With many a Mouse, and many a Rat, ...   153 Widow and Cat   D   4
     With many a Mouse, and many a Rat, ...   153 Widow and Cat   D   4
     Had giv'n the Faction many a Wound, ...   171 Horace 1, 7   37
     And offer'd them many a lame Excuse;   . . . . .   172 Horace 1, 7   65
     That <Swift> oils many a Spring which Harley moves. .   194 Author Himself   40
     And after many Days thou'lt find it, ...   255 Bubble   134
     Which causes many Speculations.   . . . . . .   283 Journal   130
     The common Death of many a stronger Boat.   . . . . .   284 Elegy Boat   10
     Had many Pendents, but abhor'd a Jack.   . . . . . .   285 Elegy Boat   16
     For so many Six-pences, so many Pages, ...   288 Bank Down   47
     For so many Six-pences, so many Pages, ...   288 Bank Down   47
     "To pass to many crowded Stages, ...   380 Apology Lady C   155
     Misled them many a League about.   . . . . . .   412 Desire Possess   16
     Where many a bold Advent'rer fell.   . . . . . .   413 Desire Possess   44
     With many rebuke.   . . . .   423 Carterets Arms
     From many (and we may believe him)   . . . . . .   455 Dean Smedley   13
     Still seen o'r'e many an Alehouse fire.   . . . . . .   461 Birthday Song   38
     Here many a King his heart and Crown   . . . . .   465 Birthday Song   167
     How many pleasant Things he spoke, ...   480 Libel on D- D-   7
     Thus Gay, the Hare with many Friends, ...   481 Libel on D- D-   53
     Would shew you many a Statesman's Face.   . . . . .   485 Libel on D- D-   180
     Despis'd the Beast with many Heads, ...   498 Panegyr Swift   161
     Yet many a foolish thing he writ---;   . . . . . .   547 Life of Swift   75
     How many a Message would he send?   . . . . . .   557 Death of Swift   137
     "He labour'd many a fruitless Hour   . . . . . .   567 Death of Swift   365
     Like so many little Mars's, ...   573 Helter Skelter   5
     Effects of many a sad Disaster;   . . . . . .   582 Young Nymph   31
     Quotes from the Bible many a Sentence   . . . . .   605 Beasts Confess   121
     Light on many a Coxcomb's Crown.   . . . . . .   638 Epistle Lady   254
     Complain, as many an ancient Bard did, ...   652 On Poetry   349
     Of Incense many a thousand Load;   . . . . . .   657 On Poetry   474
     And Reason good; for many a Year   . . . . . .   657 On Poetry   489
     In vain discharging many a Shaft, ...   701 Cadenus Vaness   477
     Cadenus many things had writ;   . . . .   702 Cadenus Vaness   510
     May Bec have many an evening nap   . . . . . .   761 Bec's B-Day   39
     Yet many a Wretch in Bedlam, knows, ...   796 Traulus 1   23
     Has got on the Bench many <Bishops> suffragan: . .   803 Irish Bishops   14
     Many a Head that holds no Brains.   . . . . . .   829 Legion Club   10
     There stood for many a hundred Years   . . . . .   848 Old Thorn   3
     And with her Beak gave many a Knock   . . . . . .   849 Old Thorn   35
     There, many a Flow'r abstersive grew, ...   894 Panegyr Dean   249
     She darted many a private Glance, ...   905 Death Daphne   67
     While others give me many a Curse, ...   918 Riddle 4   27
     Labours of many an ancient Sage, ...   922 Riddle 7   41
     Where many for a Passage venture, ...   928 Riddle 12   D   3
     Yet many poor Creatures I help to ensnare.   . . . .   929 Riddle 13   D   6
     Many Voices joining round me;   . . . . . .   933 Riddle 20   D   6
     Many to our Counters run, ...   934 Riddle 22   D   3
     In Conscience too many, ...   951 Apples   4
     How many to answer? One, two, three, four.   . . . .   967 Letter Sherid   10
     And I think I may say, you cou'd many good shillings get 979 Dean to Tho: S   9
     But these are lost full many a Century.   . . . . .   988 Letter Dr Sh-n   14
     I know they have many a wicked Design   . . . . .   1017 Swift Ans Sher   9
     But if too many come your Madam will whine   . . . .   1018 Swift Ans Sher   31
     You hop'd to find many (for that was your Cue) sick; . 1029 Dr. Helsham   23
MAP
     Like a just Map to tell the vast Extent   . . . . .   25 Ode Athenian   302
MAPS   SEE AFRIC-MAPS
     Yet still you must consult the Maps, ...   467 Birthday Song   240
MARBLE
     If neither brass nor marble can withstand   . . . . .   419 Shall Repine   1
     It shines most in the Marble Cover.   . . . . . .   475 Epist on Epist   14
     And on the Marble grave these Rhimes, ...   596 Cassinus Peter   75
MARBLE-HILL
     Of Richmond-Lodge, and Marble-Hill.   . . . . . .   408 Dial Rich Marb   4
     Quoth Marble-Hill, right well I ween, ...   408 Dial Rich Marb   9
     I pity you, dear Marble-Hill;   . . . .   411 Dial Rich Marb   101
MARBLED
     The paper gilt, & Cover marbled)   . . . .   463 Birthday Song   88
MARCH
     Which in its dusky march along the plain, ...   40 Ode Sancroft   193
     March o'er the ruin'd plain with motion slow,   . . .   55 Temple Ill   129
     "We all shou'd march on this Occasion, ...   321 First of April   19
     Pontifick, made your glorious March;   . . . . . .   326 Pethox   94
     Then, furious he begins his March;   . . . . . .   353 Wood Ironmongr   17
     The rumbling words march fierce along, ...   461 Birthday Song   45
     The poorest hither march in State, ...   928 Riddle 12   D 13

	PAGE	TITLE	LINE
MARCH'D			
I March'd three miles thro' scorching sand,	675	Curate's Compl	1
MARCHES			
Now, Madam, observe, how he marches in State:	870	Grand Question	89
MARCUS			
That you, friend Marcus, like a stoick	676	Parson's Case	1
MARE			
"(For thou shalt steal thy Landlord's Mare)	851	Old Thorn	87
MARGENT			
Who knows in Law, nor Text, nor Margent,	812	Bro Protestant	27
MARGERY			
Margery Grinagin.	246	Irish-Feast	48
When Margery chastises Ned	328	Epigram 2	1
MARGET			
. . .but my Sister Marget she writes better.	987	Mary to Sher	34
MARGIN			
And round the Margin sindg'd his Soil,	323	Fethox	8
To leave the Margin wide.	394	Grub-Street	12
On thy Margin Lovers wander,	661	Love Song	27
The Margin of a purling Stream,	894	Panegyr Dean	241
MARGINS			
When Pope has fill'd the Margins round,	395	Grub-Street	17
MARINER			
The Mariner with Rapture sees	251	Bubble	26
What Mariner is not afraid,	703	Cadenus Vaness	532
In Ships decay'd no Mariner confides,	771	Horace 1, 14	47
MARINERS			
Thus oft by Mariners are shown,	257	Bubble	169
MARISH			
Or like a Bridge that joins a Marish	645	On Poetry	173
MARIUS'			
Had drawn his Sword for Marius' Fall,	340	Arch-Bish Dub	18
MARK			
Th' Authentick mark of the Elect,	18	Ode Athenian	92
And mark the Progress of their Work,	86	Hist V's House	16
Their Conyngs mark thou, for I have been told,	148	Windsor Proph	19
Mark out the way where Daphne flew.	177	To Lord Harley	18
But mark what follow'd,--Faith she bit her.	208	Fable Bitches	18
Shall sink, and leave no mark behind it.	255	Bubble	136
Mark where the Sly Directors creep,	257	Bubble	173
There's scarce one in ten, but what has my Mark;	265	Apollo	62
For old Nick gave the Papers the Mark of the Bank.	288	Bank Down	45
Then with his Fore-foot set his Mark.	300	Horrid Plot	56
Now, here's a warrant; Gallants please to mark,	308	Billet Players	19
Spadillo here has got a Mark,	453	Modern Lady	266
Though Splendor gives the fairest Mark	500	Doctor Delaney	27
The Town will mark you for a Dunce:	644	On Poetry	138
No more--In mark of true Affection	779	Mullinix Tim	207
Mark my Address, and learn my Style,	780	Mullinix Tim	235
From the no Mark of Slavery they felt,	791	St. Pat's Well	21
(His Beaver is cock'd; pray, Madam, mark that,	870	Grand Question	105
Can leave a Mark and give a Smart.	942	Probatur Alit	24
MARK'D			
Where Criticks mark'd your former Faults.	645	On Poetry	150
Her Shoulders mark'd with bloody Tracks;	729	Stella, Poems	46
MARK'T			
He mark't the Conjugall Dispute,	219	A Quiet Life	3
MARKET			
At Market for a Farthing more	255	Bubble	118
"Biennial Squires, to Market brought;	571	Death of Swift	445
To oblige a good Friend, she will trace ev'ry Market,	580	Psyche	11
At Market Hill, as well appears	848	Old Thorn	1
MARKET-HILL			
At Market-hill	441	Ballyspellin	34
The Dean wou'd visit Market-hill,	859	Lady Acheson	1
Happy, O Market-Hill! at least,	877	To Dean Swift	27
Must raise a Fort at Market-hill.	883	Rev Market-Hill	16
By Lady Anne of Market-Hill.	888	Panegyr Dean	36
MARKET-HILL'S			
From Market-Hill's exalted Head.	884	Rev Market-Hill	47
MARKETS			
How Markets went for Hey and Oats.	63	Discovery	36
MARKING			
For, ev'ry Stander-by was marking	299	Horrid Plot	25
MARKS			
And see her marks in ev'ry face;	401	Window Inns 5	D 8
Stain'd with the Marks of stinking Toes;	527	Lady's Dres Rm	52
For We know by these Marks, the place of the Damn'd;	576	Place Damn'd	16
Such Marks of a distracted Mind;	704	Cadenus Vaness	563
That fly and leave no Marks behind?	765	Stel B-day '26	54
The Marks peculiar of his Sire.	798	Traulus 1	82
And our Marks of Things declare,	931	Riddle 18	D 6
MARR			
But here, before the Frost can marr it,	760	Receipt Youth	55
MARRALL			
Like Martin Marrall, gaping on,	775	Mullinix Tim	43
MARREYE			
And Norways pryd agayne shall marreye.	103	Merlin	12
MARRIAGE			
How oft she broke her marriage Vows	225	Prog of Love	89
Proceed We to the Marriage Rites.	585	Strephon Chloe	46

	PAGE	TITLE	LINE
MARRIAGE (CONTINUED)			
But, after Marriage, practise more	588	Strephon Chloe	141
Is after Marriage lost so soon,	591	Strephon Chloe	257
And Marriage grown a Money-League.	687	Cadenus Vaness	14
And tho' no Marriage Words are spoke,	926	Riddle 9	15
MARRIAGES			
For Marriages are made in Heaven:	224	Prog of Love	56
MARRIED			
In Bed we left the married Pair;	588	Strephon Chloe	145
MARRIES			
Marries for Love, half Whore, half Wife;	150	Corinna	26
MARROW			
He pick't my Marrow from the Bone.	915	Riddle 1	14
MARRY			
Him let her Marry for his Face,	295	Prog Marriage	161
As Soldiers use, for love must marry,	878	Robbin & Harry	18
Declar'd in Council, Death must marry:	903	Death Daphne	10
You a Gentleman! marry come up,	985	Mary to Sher	2
MARRY'D			
But now, though scarce a twelvemonth marry'd,	293	Prog Marriage	99
To cut his Throat before he marry'd.	349	Upright Judge 2	4
Was marry'd to the Tunbridge Beau,	699	Cadenus Vaness	393
That must attend the marry'd state;	879	Robbin & Harry	40
MARS			
To shew his Skill, he Mars: would join	99	Elegy Patrige	59
Or, had Embroider'd Mars pursu'd,	177	To Lord Harley	15
Your Hero now another Mars is,	461	Birthday Song	29
Dismissing Mars, it next must follow	462	Birthday Song	57
But, he by Mars, in Scarlet Vest.	586	Strephon Chloe	60
MARS'S			
Like so many little Mars's,	573	Helter Skelter	5
<MARSHALL>			
To <Marshall>, <Conolly>, and <Dick> <Tighe>.	436	Answer Paulus	146
MARTIAL			
From Virgil, Martial, Ovid, Lucan;	657	On Poetry	482
For when in time the Martial Maid	694	Cadenus Vaness	250
Thy martial Sons, whom now they dare despise,	790	St. Pat's Well	13
MARTIN			
The important history of Martin.	186	Scriblerus 3	8
The Memoirs of Martin,	186	Scriblerus 4	D 14
Like Martin Marrall, gaping on,	775	Mullinix Tim	43
MARTIN'S			
The lowest boy in Martin's school	899	Dean's Reasons	13
MARTIS			
Coram Regina prox' die Martis,	713	Cadenus Vaness	839
MARTYR			
"For railing at the Royal Martyr.	549	Life of Swift	167
MARY			
Lord! Madam, says Mary, how d'ye do?.	70	Mrs Harris Pet	14
But pray, Mary, can you tell what I have done with my Purse!	70	Mrs Harris Pet	15
Lord help me, said Mary, I never stirr'd out of this Place!	70	Mrs Harris Pet	16
So Mary got me to Bed, and cover'd me up warm,	70	Mrs Harris Pet	18
Without one Ave Mary.	245	Irish-Feast	36
I rode four more to great St. Mary;	675	Curate's Compl	3
And I don't care who knows it, 'tis all one to Mary.	986	Mary to Sher	22
Mary said he, (one Day, as I was mending my Master's Stocking,)	986	Mary to Sher	28
MASK			
(Give fraudful Vice the Mask and Screen,	386	Manly Virtue	79
Her Judgment, how to buy a Mask.	700	Cadenus Vaness	421
MASON			
Or Mason that abandon'd Bitch:	299	Horrid Plot	23
Borrow'd from the Mason Side:	800	Traulus 2	44
MASONS			
Were they Masons, were they Butchers?	800	Traulus 2	26
MASQUERADE			
Taking their Tour in Masquerade	90	Bauc & Phil 1	8
Taking their Tour in Masquerade;	111	Bauc & Phil 2	8
The Masquerade began at two,	292	Prog Marriage	93
MASQUERADES			
Balls, and Masquerades, and Shows,	631	Epistle Lady	41
The sweetest Place for Masquerades:	905	Death Daphne	86
MASS			
Thro' the dark mass, the dawn of so much sense,	37	Ode Sancroft	88
A mingled Mass of Dirt and Sweat.	226	Prog of Beauty	20
Together mingl'd in a Mass	344	Prometheus	3
A mingled Mass of Good & Bad,	659	On Poetry	D 410
But all distinguish thy dull leaden Mass.	670	Epig Carthy 18	D 6
Which gave a Tincture o'er the Mass:	709	Cadenus Vaness	719
A pair of Brogues to bear thee dry to Mass!	882	Pastoral Dial	50
And lye an undistinguish'd Mass.	922	Riddle 7	44
Yet from this mingled Mass of Things,	924	Riddle 7	89
MASSACRES			
"For Massacres, and Racks, and Flames,	183	Horace 2, 1	95
MASSERINE			
So I wish you were toothless like Lord Masserine	1017	Swift Ans Sher	17
MAST			
Thy Mast, which like some aged Patriot stood	770	Horace 1, 14	15
I'm now a Sail, and now a Mast;	911	Aenigma	6

	PAGE	TITLE	LINE
MASTER SEE SCHOOL-MASTER			
And your Almighty Master, knew	38	Ode Sancroft	114
To his undoubted Master, Heaven's Almighty Son.	38	Ode Sancroft	134
Even so Master Doctor had Puzzled his Brains	77	Lady B- B-	22
The Master Bawl'd out half asleep	90	Bauc & Phil 1	27
To a Plot for expelling my Master K. James;	144	New Song	28
And how, when Master went to <piss>,	150	Corinna	23
Then Master Steward takes my Rent, and tells me, honest Jo.	342	Upon His Grace	23
And never turn upon thy Master	373	Letter D. S-y	55
But my Master each Day gives me Bread;	395	Dog and Thief	6
My Royal Master promis'd me	408	Dial Rich Marb	15
My Master scarce a Fortnight since,	409	Dial Rich Marb	37
My Master Pope will break his Heart.	410	Dial Rich Marb	72
And shew us, <England> is our Master:	484	Libel on D- D-	126
The Servants Faults are on the Master laid.	533	To Mr. Gay	50
And drain the Fish-ponds; while your Master doats;	534	To Mr. Gay	90
His Master, unsuspicious of his Pranks,	535	To Mr. Gay	109
While He went robbing on; old Master dy'd.	536	To Mr. Gay	148
(For fear young Master shou'd be spoil'd,)	693	Cadenus Vaness	224
No cruel Master could require	726	To Stella	105
Judas betrayed his Master with a Kiss:	806	Judas	10
At length his Old Master (I need not him name)	816	Yahoo's	36
Whose Master, Moore, preserv'd him from the Halter,	826	Noisy Tom	13
Whose master, whose man;	856	Lady's Lament	168
Kit, run to your Master, and bid him come to us.	871	Grand Question	117
Nay; Man, my Master, is my Slave:	916	Riddle 1	33
Shall Man presume to be my Master,	918	Riddle 4	17
He's our Master, we his Tools;	931	Riddle 18	D 12
May break a Limb of Master or Miss.	941	Letter	22
Yes; you call'd my Master a Knave:	985	Mary to Sher	5
And the Dean my Master is an honester Man	985	Mary to Sher	8
My Master is a parsonable Man,	985	Mary to Sher	10
Because my Master one Day in anger call'd you Goose.	985	Mary to Sher	12
But that's as much as to say, that my Master should die before ye,	986	Mary to Sher	19
. . . and you may go tell my Master; what care I?	986	Mary to Sher	21
My Master is so fond of that Minister that keeps the School;	987	Mary to Sher	29
I thought my Master a wise Man,	987	Mary to Sher	30
. . .before my Master comes from Pray'rs,	987	Mary to Sher	35
But ev'ry one that knows Dan, knows thy Master.	1002	Reply by Dean	6
Good Spelling, Master, your Crany has Lead on't.	1004	Dan J's Reply	36
MASTER'S SEE DANCING-MASTER'S			
Was, like his Master's Crown, inwreath'd with thorn.	40	Ode Sancroft	200
What? sell my Master's Country Seat?	128	Little House	56
Can rise upon their Master's Fall.	409	Dial Rich Marb	34
At least, before your Master's Debts are paid.	533	To Mr. Gay	62
The Master's pressing Wants must be supply'd;	533	To Mr. Gay	70
There, near thy Master's Throne in Shelter plac't,	538	Mr. Pulteney	11
The Nation's Good, his Master's Glory,	605	Beasts Confess	145
Nor leaps upon his Master's Lap,	607	Beasts Confess	209
Was but the Master's secret Joy	704	Cadenus Vaness	552
Cry'd, Madam, why surely my Master's possest;	868	Grand Question	44
Not you, to steal your Master's Wine;	890	Panegyr Dean	98
Your Master's Honour to maintain;	890	Panegyr Dean	103
Mary said he, (one Day, as I was mending my Master's Stocking,)	986	Mary to Sher	28
MASTERS			
Who, like hard masters, taught the Sun	36	Ode Sancroft	67
As antient nature's modern masters dream;	45	To Congreve	72
Now Betty from her Masters Bed had flown,	124	Descriptn Morn	3
The Slipshod Prentice from his Masters Door,	124	Descriptn Morn	5
Must fall, because our Masters rise.	409	Dial Rich Marb	36
Extol the Greek and Roman Masters,	652	On Poetry	347
My Masters come buy,	952	Oysters	2
MASTIFF			
Out bounc't the Mastiff of the triple Head;	538	Mr. Pulteney	27
MASTIFF'S			
A Mastiff's teeth are justly held in vogue,	672	Epig Carthy 25	D 1
MASTIFFS			
Can set the Mastiffs on your Back.	798	Traulus 1	68
MASTIVE			
As Mastive Dogs in Modern Phrase are	82	Salamander	1
MASTS			
At once so like to Masts or Sails,	912	Aenigma Expl	D 6
MATADORE			
"You took it with a Matadore;	452	Modern Lady	251
A Matadore is in her Hand.	452	Modern Lady	261
MATCH			
Guess how could such a Match be broke.	223	Prog of Love	24
How Nim, no Hunter 'ere could match him,	281	Journal	73
What Colours each Complexion match:	416	Woman's Mind	31
No Enemy can match a Friend;	557	Death of Swift	120
No Pleader at the Bar could match	604	Beasts Confess	89
But meddle seldom with their Match.	651	On Poetry	322
Let others match it if they dare.	887	Panegyr Dean	22
His Mind was running on his Match.	904	Death Daphne	52
MATCH'T			
The Deanry-house may well be match't	313	To Ford	65
Ne'er to be match't in modern Reading,	398	Earl of P-b-w	35

	PAGE	TITLE	LINE

MATCHLESS
- Your matchless Courage with Your Prudence joins · · — 11 Ode to William D 5
- Except the Matchless Hero Abel. · · · · · · — 183 Horace 2, 1 — 86
- Then wou'd you paint a matchless Dame, · · · — 272 Apollo's Edict D 70
- Her matchless Sons; whose Valour still remains · — 771 Horace 1, 14 — 43

MATE
- He dyes, and leaves his mourning Mate · · · · — 295 Prog Marriage — 155
- Your Goddess grown a filthy Mate. · · · · · — 591 Strephon Chloe — 244
- Leave to D'Anvers and his Mate, · · · · · · — 635 Epistle Lady — 173
- Who shines alone, without a Mate. · · · · · — 656 On Poetry — 442
- Softly seeks her silent Mate; · · · · · · · — 661 Love Song — 30
- In Quality of Butler's Mate; · · · · · · · — 889 Panegyr Dean — 88

MATER
- Alma Mater was thy Mother, · · · · · · · · — 838 Legion Club — 199

MATERIALLS
- When the Materialls all are gone, · · · · · — 228 Prog of Beauty — 78
- To the Materialls of Her Face. · · · · · · — 229 Prog of Beauty — 108

MATERIALS
- Materials would be quickly spent, · · · · · · — 79 Vanbrug House — 21
- What House, when its Materials crumble, · · · · — 593 Strephon Chloe — 297
- Those Materials I have furnish'd, · · · · · · — 631 Epistle Lady — 45
- Materials for an House decay'd. · · · · · · — 727 To Stella — 124
- Who from Materials hard and dry, · · · · · · — 920 Riddle 6 — 20
- These crude Materials once shall rise, · · · · — 924 Riddle 7 — 91

MATES
- The Bridegroom's first Gift to their Mates, · · · · — 942 Probatur Alit — 4

MATHEMATICIANS
- For, as of old, Mathematicians · · · · · · · — 503 Doctor Delaney — 95

MATHER'S
- The dearest in Charles Mather's Shop, · · · · · — 135 Magician's Rod — 76

MATRIMONIAL
- His matrimonial Spirit fled; · · · · · · · · — 905 Death Daphne — 96

MATT
- Or on the Matt devoutly kneeling · · · · · · · — 222 Prog of Love — 15
- Sharp are the Stones, take thou this rushy Matt; · · — 881 Pastoral Dial — 19

MATTADORES
- "Four Mattadores, and lose Codill! · · · · · · — 446 Modern Lady — 52

MATTER
- Take, youth, these thoughts, large matter to employ · · — 53 Temple Ill — 67
- Of Matter purulent and white · · · · · · · · — 84 Salamander — 53
- But kept it's Matter and it's Hue, · · · · · · — 93 Bauc & Phil 1 — 108
- As if there had been no such Matter. · · · · · — 98 Elegy Patrige — 18
- To turn the Matter to a Jest; · · · · · · · · — 108 V's House — 68
- And quickly did the Matter sift, · · · · · · · — 171 Horace 1, 7 — 25
- Which by the Style, the Matter, and the Drift, · · · — 195 Author Himself — 49
- No matter where the Money's found; · · · · · · — 199 Horace 2, 6 — 20
- Matter, as wise Logicians say, · · · · · · · — 228 Prog of Beauty — 81
- Must fayl if Matter brings no Grist. · · · · · — 228 Prog of Beauty — 84
- Ne'er dream't of the Matter, · · · · · · · · — 245 Irish-Feast — 30
- Well, since he's gone, no matter how, · · · · · — 296 Satiric Elegy — 5
- The Matter now no longer sticks; · · · · · · · — 300 Horrid Plot — 59
- For want of matter swears and fretts, · · · · · — 420 Holyhead — 17
- <Lyndsay> mistakes the matter quite, · · · · · — 432 Answer Paulus — 1
- Fresh Matter for a World of Chat, · · · · · · — 447 Modern Lady — 82
- The Jumbling Particles of Matter · · · · · · · — 450 Modern Lady — 184
- Whereof, to make the Matter clear, · · · · · · — 526 Lady's Dres Rm — 9
- They turn the Matter to a Jest; · · · · · · · — 545 Life of Swift — 20
- And, last to make the Matter sure, · · · · · · — 586 Strephon Chloe — 63
- Why should he longer mince the Matter? · · · · · — 604 Beasts Confess — 95
- An idle Tale, 'tis no such Matter; · · · · · · — 627 Scandal Poem 2 — 127
- She loves herself, and that's the Matter. · · · · — 699 Cadenus Vaness — 403
- As a matter they had no concern in. · · · · · · — 708 Cadenus Vaness — 687
- Tim, you mistake the Matter quite, · · · · · · — 756 Dingley Brent — 12
- To interrupt all serious Matter, · · · · · · · — 776 Mullinix Tim — 87
- Tom, you mistake the Matter quite; · · · · · · — 777 Mullinix Tim — 144
- "it's matter of weight, and a mere money-job; · · · — 797 Traulus 1 — 45
- For your Life, not a Word of the Matter, I charge ye: · — 843 Ay and No — 11
- And then, to mend the Matter still; · · · · · · — 873 Grand Question — 189
- Sunk over head and ears in matter, · · · · · · — 888 Panegyr Dean — 35
- And when with much Labour the Matter I crackt, · · · — 900 Dean's Reasons — 59
- I found you mistaken in Matter of Fact. · · · · · — 972 S—'s Ans Sh—d — 3
- 'Tis a vast Subject stuff'd with Matter, · · · · — 972 S—'s Ans Sh—d — 4
- · · · · · · · · · · · · · · · · · · · — 993 On Picture — 17

MATTERS
- The cord, or the radius, it matters not whether, · · · — 1027 Sheri Circles — 17

MATTINS
- Their Mattins chant in ev'ry Bush: · · · · · · — 594 Cassinus Peter — 32

MAUKINS
- Your Maukins there · · · · · · · · · · · · — 441 Ballyspellin — 43

MAUKISH
- Is maukish, and his Stomach gone; · · · · · · · — 291 Prog Marriage — 60

MAUL
- But proud Iberia soundly maul, · · · · · · · — 468 Birthday Song — 248
- Could maul a Minister of State: · · · · · · · — 555 Death of Swift — 62
- Musha! Why Parliament wouldn't you maul, · · · · — 841 Ballad D 16
- Oh! if I could, how I would maul · · · · · · · — 861 Lady Acheson — 37

MAUL'D
- But now, since the Drapier hath heartily maul'd him, · — 351 Wood Insect — 33
- "But he maul'd me, I ne'er was so maul'd in my Life; · — 873 Grand Question — 168
- "But he maul'd me, I ne'er was so maul'd in my Life; · — 873 Grand Question — 168
- I maul'd you when you look'd so bluff, · · · · · — 1002 Reply by Dean — 16

MAW
                                                 PAGE   TITLE   LINE

Entry	Page	Title	Line
They stick athwart my maw	429	Beau's Reply	15
And, Ostrich-like, his all-digesting Maw.	532	To Mr. Gay	36
A Shole of Herrings down his Maw.	651	On Poetry	324

MAWL'D
And, if Swearing can do't, shall be swingingly mawl'd:	238	Excellent Song	29
Thus <Bob> shal't thou be mawl'd, fly where thou wil't:	538	Mr. Pulteney	38
Be soundly mawl'd, and plagues the rest.	777	Mullinix Tim	132

MAWS
| Live on, and Stuff, to Boot, their Maws. | 479 | Epist on Epist | 126 |

MAXIM
Or else the truest Maxim lyes:	391	Young's Satire	22
Tho' tis a Maxim you must know,	514	Answer Fable	57
Wise Rochefoucault a Maxim writ,	545	Life of Swift	1
'Tis fit the Maxim we should know.	545	Life of Swift	6
This Maxim more than all the rest	553	Death of Swift	5
'Tis an old Maxim in the Schools,	710	Cadenus Vaness	758

MAXIMS
As Rochefoucault his Maxims drew	553	Death of Swift	1
Maxims wise, to rule the State.	635	Epistle Lady	174
Maxims teaching Wisdom's Use.	637	Epistle Lady	238
Two Maxims she could still produce,	705	Cadenus Vaness	606

MAY   271   OMITTED WORD

MAY-FAIR
Some God May-Fair invented,	122	Empty'ng Town	2
Inverted in May-Fair	122	Empty'ng Town	10
Or glitt'ring Tinsel of May-Fair,	135	Magician's Rod	77

MAY-GAME
| Am, as you tell me, but their may-game, | 778 | Mullinix Tim | 174 |

MAY'R   SEE LORD-MAY'R
(Ere since Sir William <Gore> was May'r,	180	Horace 2, 1	9
And, with a licence from our good Lord May'r,	307	Billet Players	3
In ev'ry town we wait on Mr. May'r,	308	Billet Players	35

MAY'RESS
| Drest like any Lady May'ress; | 630 | Epistle Lady | 36 |

MAY'ST
Kind Star, still may'st thou shed thy sacred influence here,	39	Ode Sancroft	154
May'st follow still thy Calling there.	100	Elegy Patrige	74
May'st thou despise a Poets Name.	121	Apollo Outwit	56
May'st dye like me by Chance; but not by Nature.	861	On Old Glass	2

MAYD
| To rigg her out for Juno's mayd. | 619 | Scandal Poem 1 | 78 |

MAYOR
| I know no more than my Lord Mayor, | 202 | Horace 2, 6 | 102 |

MAZE
| I hope you will own it is Love in a Maze; | 337 | Serious Poem | 102 |

MAZES
| Thro' the Mazes of your Mind, | 629 | Epistle Lady | 4 |

ME   384   OMITTED WORD

ME-THINKS
| Tho' your lords, and your dogs, and your catches, me-thinks, | 977 | Dean to Sherid | 45 |

MEADOWS
| His meadows may be dug by swine, | 902 | Dean's Reasons | 111 |

MEADS
| To silver Meads, and shady Bow'rs, | 590 | Strephon Chloe | 201 |

MEAGER
| Meager and lank with fasting grown, | 759 | Receipt Youth | 7 |

MEAGRE
His meagre Corps, though full of Vigour,	398	Earl of P-b-w	26
You find it in his meagre Looks:	604	Beasts Confess	106
This meagre Fop, that batter'd Beau:	905	Death Daphne	74
For, when by chance the meagre Shade	905	Death Daphne	93

MEAL   SEE OAT-MEAL
Your delicate Bits will not serve me a Meal,	395	Dog and Thief	5
From every Meal Pontack in plenty	745	Stel Distress	13
Surpriz'd with ev'ry day a hot meal	745	Stel Distress	5
From ev'ry Meal Pontack in plenty,	750	Stel Wood-Park	37
Another when he got a hot Meal;	781	Mullinix Tim	270
For 'tis beyond the Pow'r of Meal,	786	Dick, Maggot	9

MEALS
Either at Morning, or at Meals;	173	Horace 1, 7	78
With hungry Meals his Body pin'd,	231	Prog of Poetry	37
With plenteous meals, and gen'rous wine;	677	Parson's Case	34
And they must have three Meals a Day,	861	Lady Acheson	34

MEALY
| Down ev'ry mealy Atom drops | 786 | Dick, Maggot | 12 |

MEAN
The Wits, I mean the Atheists of the Age,	19	Ode Athenian	103
I mean, the way which leads to Christ:	39	Ode Sancroft	161
Cordials are in their talk, whilst all they mean	42	Ode Sancroft	257
Stale forms of course, all mean deceivers use,	44	To Congreve	20
Nor tax the goddess of a mean design	44	To Congreve	33
Mean time a Pair of awkward Things	80	Vanbrug House	35
That Thing, I mean, among the Kale,	128	Little House	53
Mean while the South rising with dabbled Wings,	137	City Shower	13
A Canon! that's a Place too mean:	173	Horace 1, 7	87
"I wonder what some People mean;	202	Horace 2, 6	84
I mean your Butler, Dawson, Car,	217	To Mr. Delany	59
Seditiously mean	237	Excellent Song	6

MEAN   (CONTINUED)   PAGE   TITLE   LINE
     You know whom I mean, ...   238 Excellent Song   31
     Mean time secure on Garr'way Clifts   . . . .   256 Bubble   153
     Here (by the Way) by Gallus mean I,   278 Journal   5
     How very mean a thing's a Duke;   . . . .   297 Satiric Elegy   30
     I mean a Dog, without a Joke, ...   298 Horrid Plot   17
     I'm still to seek which Dog you mean;   . . . . .   298 Horrid Plot   19
     Unless by the Devil we mean Mr. Wood.   . . . . .   335 Serious Poem   56
     I mean His <Majesty>, God bless him.   . . . . . .   346 Prometheus   62
     And, Fifthly; you know whom I mean, ...   348 Whitshed Motto   19
     Could not conceive what it should mean, ...   376 Apology Lady C   21
     To lurk behind a mean Disguise;   . . . .   386 Manly Virtue   78
     Or more to show the Thing I mean, ...   393 Modern Poets   9
     Mean time the whig is always winner   . . . . . .   421 Ireld   11
     "And I know whom you mean to teach, ...   452 Modern Lady   255
     I mean the Head without the Brain.   . . . .   469 Burning Poem   6
     With mean Degrees of Wit and Sense?   . . . . . .   475 Epist on Epist   16
     Of his Intent, you mean, your Merit.   . . . . .   475 Epist on Epist   28
     His Life is safe, I mean his Fame, ...   500 Doctor Delaney   24
     And in all they do for us so kindly do mean,   . .   516 Dean Hang Rape   2
     Tho I name not the wretch you know who I mean   .   540 Charac Walpole   13
     Of Quadrupeds I only mean)   . . . .   601 Beasts Confess   8
     What can all this Passion mean?   . . . .   635 Epistle Lady   182
     Then Poet, if you mean to thrive, ...   647 On Poetry   219
     (I mean the Oracles of Both, ...   647 On Poetry   229
     I mean all Kings except our own, ...   659 On Poetry   D 410
     By Charity a mean Support, ...   667 Epig Carthy 6   D 2
     Mean time the Boy in secret lurks, ...   702 Cadenus Vaness   513
     Mean time the mournful Queen of Love   . . . . .   712 Cadenus Vaness   828
     On so mean a Design, and a Subject so low.   . .   716 Answer Rebus   4
     For mean's her Design, and her Subject as mean,   .   716 Answer Rebus   5
     From Ford who thinks of nothing mean   . . . . .   745 Stel Distress   17
     Howe're to keep her Spirits up Mean time to keep   .   747 Stel Distress   45
     From Ford, who thinks of nothing mean, ...   750 Stel Wood-Park   41
     I mean when Tyger has been serv'd, ...   761 Bec's B-Day   37
     And by their Sweat procure a mean Support;   . . .   793 St. Pat's Well   76
     Say, Robin, what can Traulus mean   . . . .   795 Traulus 1   1
     Hence that mean and sordid Soul, ...   800 Traulus 2   33
     In each Capacity I mean   . . . .   888 Panegyr Dean   43
     Good Lord! what can my Lady mean, ...   891 Panegyr Dean   141
     Mean Time, the Wise a Question start, ...   919 Riddle 5   31
     I mean the Church, the King, and Me.   . . . . .   926 Riddle 9   24
     I much suspect you mean the latter, ah Sly-boot!   . 1003 Dan J's Reply   6
     Can mean my culling of a Face, ...   1003 Dan J's Reply   8
     If this be your practice, mean scrub, I assure Ye,   .1019 To Sheridan   5
     . . . I mean the city so smoaky, ...   1022 Nim-Dan-Dean 2   D 3
     . . . I mean that great fat joker, friend Helsham, he   .1023 Nim-Dan-Dean 2   D 9
     I mean, what no other mortal in the universe can boast of, 1024 Nim-Dan-Dean 2   D 16
          . . .
MEAN'S
     For mean's her Design, and her Subject as mean,   . . . 716 Answer Rebus   5
MEANDER
     Melancholly smooth Meander, ...   661 Love Song   25
MEANDERS
     And thus the brown Meanders come   . . . .   227 Prog of Beauty   43
MEANEST
     And not the meanest coxcomb you can find, ...   48 To Congreve   157
     Whose meanest Talent is his Wit: . . . .   482 Libel on D- D-   80
     His meanest Work: For, had he thought it fit,   . .   532 To Mr. Gay   25
MEANING   SEE UN-MEANING,NEVER-MEANING
     For would you have their Meaning known?   . . . . .   218 To Mr. Delany   85
     To comprehend a double Meaning.   . . . .   592 Strephon Chloe   276
     Our Author's Meaning, I presume, is   . . . . . .   608 Beasts Confess   215
     My meaning will be best unravell'd, ...   782 Tim and Fables   1
     I suppose meaning mine.)   . . . .   854 Lady's Lament   104
     When you quite mistake the meaning.   . . . . . .   908 Daphne   68
MEANINGS
     Their Meanings lewd, and double 'Entendres.   . . . . 449 Modern Lady   143
     Of Bargains sold, or meanings double.   . . . . .   469 Birthday Song   274
MEANNESS
     Be studious to practice true Meanness of Spirit;   . . 808 Advice Parson   7
MEANS
     By all means to bring down the Rates, ...   64 Discovery   42
     I must by all means come to Town, ...   199 Horace 2, 6   13
     And take it right, it means no more   . . . . . .   464 Birthday Song   139
     We all can find out whom he means, ...   514 Answer Fable   65
     In finding Ways and Means, and stopping Gaps: . .   535 To Mr. Gay   122
     ('Tis this the Sage of Samos means, ...   587 Strephon Chloe   125
     What he means by this stuff: . . . .   854 Lady's Lament   108
     Contrives all Means the Gift to hide: . . . . .   919 Riddle 5   22
     Which fiercest Foes, cou'd break by no Means.   . .   1021 Nim-Dan-Dean 1   D 32
MEANT
     As if it meant to touch the Skies;   . . . .   10 Ode to King   123
     Say what their senseless malice meant, ...   42 Ode Sancroft   247
     This wretch, to rouse my wrath, for ruin meant;   . .   47 To Congreve   136
     Who heard you meant to write heroics next;   . . . .   47 To Congreve   144
     In satire, to my Congreve's praises meant;   . . . .   48 To Congreve   176
     Nor am that grave adviser which I meant;   . . . .   49 To Congreve   202
     What else by Perquisites are meant, ...   157 Fable of Midas   45
     <Swift> seem'd to wonder what he meant, ...   172 Horace 1, 7   51
     He never meant the least Abuse--   . . . .   172 Horace 1, 7   66

MEANT	(CONTINUED)	PAGE	TITLE	LINE
And take it kindly meant to show		200	Horace 2, 6	41
For, sure, by Wit is onely meant		215	To Mr. Delany	17
For by the Sea she meant the South.		254	Bubble	100
But the Squire he was cunning and found what they meant,		288	Bank Down	51
Whate'er these dire fore-bodings meant.		290	Prog Marriage	17
What's meant by Chapoon I can't guess		373	Letter D. S-y	57
By the horned Sun, he sure meant <Cuckold>, ...		373	Letter D. S-y	61
Well knowing what the Poets meant:		461	Birthday Song	18
You've Cause to say he meant you well:		475	Epist on Epist	25
Shou'd swear he never meant us ill;		485	Libel on D- D-	155
But Strephon cautious never meant		528	Lady's Dres Rm	92
"And pity'd those who meant the Wound:		567	Death of Swift	360
"Where Thousands equally were meant.		571	Death of Swift	462
A better than the Poet meant, ...		643	On Poetry	102
While Readers wonder whom you meant.		645	On Poetry	160
What Venus meant by this Delay		690	Cadenus Vaness	127
Things took a Turn he never meant.		709	Cadenus Vaness	731
For nobler Ends by Nature meant.		731	Stella, Poems	116
By nature meant for nobler Ends, ...		781	Mullinix Tim	279
This was a Libel meant at me;		783	Tim and Fables	30
While none believes that what he said he meant: . . .		797	Traulus 1	50
He only meant it for your Good.		797	Traulus 1	56
They've done it, we thank 'em, but not as they meant; .		804	Irish Bishops	36
Thy Ruin, Tom, I never meant, ...		1002	Reply by Dean	13
MEANTIME				
Meantime your other juster friends		755	Stella '23	35
MEASUR'D				
(Which measur'd on his Head, was found		458	Paddy's Charac	15
MEASURE				
To call nothing his, but the Rhyme and the Measure. .		266	Apollo	102
But trash without measure		853	Lady's Lament	65
They never yet cou'd find my Measure.		929	Riddle 14	D 4
Number, and Weight, and Measure join.		1022	Nim-Dan-Dean 1	D 46
Nor can we think your Measure short, ...		1022	Nim-Dan-Dean 1	D 51
MEASURES				
This Grand Event half broke our Measures, ...		283	Journal	119
To give us your measures of lines by a quadrant. . .		1026	Sheri Circles	10
MEASURING				
And measuring by the scanty thread of wit		38	Ode Sancroft	123
MEAT **SEE ROAST-MEAT**				
The Meat shall represent the Tyrant's Head, ...		162	Toland's Invit	11
Loves Mischief better than his Meat, ...		171	Horace 1, 7	14
Despis'd luxurious Wines, and costly Meat;		194	Author Himself	15
And taint all their Meat, and sour all their Drink. .		263	Apollo	14
Their Offals, or their better Meat, ...		479	Epist on Epist	122
As Mutton Cutlets, Prime of Meat, ...		528	Lady's Dres Rm	99
Says Grace before, and after Meat;		605	Beasts Confess	130
Metaphorick Meat and Drink, ...		633	Epistle Lady	117
My Works he said, cou'd ne'er afford him Meat, . . .		670	Epig Carthy 20	D 3
That Meat must be with Money bought;		693	Cadenus Vaness	214
And like the Liquor and the Meat		734	Stel B-day '20	4
To eat my Meat, and drink my Medlicot, ...		1033	Ans to Crown	9
Eat lean Meat, or chuse, ...		1036	Plague Country	3
<MEATH>				
<Meath> Smiles for the Joynture, though gotten, so late,		430	Dicky Dolly	19
MEATH-STREET				
We'll Rigg in Meath-Street, Egypt's hauty Queen, .		275	Epilogue	19
MEATS				
Whilst high, and nice, and curious Meats, ...		378	Apology Lady C	107
MEAZLES				
What gave her Brats and Pigs the Meazles, ...		282	Journal	93
MEAZLY				
All as she scrubb'd her meazly Rump.		849	Old Thorn	44
MECAENAS				
That Robin Walpole is Mecaenas:		462	Birthday Song	60
MECHANICK				
The best Mechanick Hand must fayl		228	Prog of Beauty	79
A skill'd Mechanick that has stood, ...		393	Modern Poets	11
MED'CINE				
The Louse of the Wood for a Med'cine is us'd, . . .		351	Wood Insect	11
Your med'cine is repelling, ...		440	Ballyspellin	9
His Med'cine work as he design'd		746	Stel Distress	32
MED'CINES				
As sov'reign Med'cines for the Loins)		589	Strephon Chloe	182
And, when his Med'cines do no good, ...		605	Beasts Confess	123
With a long-ear'd Beast, and Med'cines use, . . .		942	Probatur Alit	9
MEDALS				
Some Medals sent him for his Wit;		547	Life of Swift	91
"I'm glad the Medals were forgot.		559	Death of Swift	184
His Medals and his Prints forgotten, ...		875	Drapier's Hill	15
MEDDLE				
Shou'd never meddle with Edg'd Tools.		181	Horace 2, 1	32
But meddle seldom with their Match.		651	On Poetry	322
Her hands may meddle, feet may wander, ...		761	Bec's B-Day	25
MEDEA'S				
As rising from Medea's Kettle;		759	Receipt Youth	18
MEDICINE				
A Sov'reign Medicine for the Brains.		743	Stel B-day 22	70
MEDIUM				
The liquid Medium cheats your Sight, ...		251	Bubble	15

```
                                                    PAGE    TITLE              LINE
MEDIUMS
   In both, false mediums cheat our sight,  . . . . . . .   39 Ode Sancroft      147
MEDLEY
   Like that fantastic medley in the idol's toes,  . . . .  38 Ode Sancroft      138
   Of Dullness, Pride, Conceit, a medley,  . . . . . . .   455 Dean Smedley        2
   I'm daily stunn'd with such a Medley,  . . . . . .      742 Stel B-day 22      43
MEDLICOT
   To eat my Meat, and drink my Medlicot,  . . . . . .    1033 Ans to Crown        9
MEDLY
   She seems a Medly of all Ages,  . . . . . . . .         23 Ode Athenian      221
MEDUSA
   I come, I come,--Medusa, see,  . . . . . . . .         596 Cassinus Peter     85
MEDUSA'S
   Held out Medusa's snaky locks,  . . . . . . . . .      178 To Lord Harley     45
MEDWAY
   Sabrina,Medway,and the Thames.  . . . . . . . .       468 Birthday Song     242
MEEK
   Thus ended the Knight: Thus began his meek Wife:  . .  867 Grand Question     25
MEEKLY
   And meekly took what Fortune sent:  . . . . . . .      602 Beasts Confess     42
MEER
   By the meer Virtue of his Fist:  . . . . . . . .       132 Magician's Rod     12
   What meer Humanity affords,  . . . . . . . . . .       204 In Sickness        14
   "You see 'tis meer Necessity,  . . . . . . . . .       207 Fable Bitches      10
   And of my meer Motion, and special good Grace,  . . .  263 Apollo             27
   But all are meer Productions of the Brain,  . . . .    363 On Dreams           5
   "Meer Envy, Avarice, and Pride!  . . . . . . . .       558 Death of Swift    159
   "He left the Court in meer Despair.  . . . . . .       567 Death of Swift    370
   Meer mortal Flesh was all he found:  . . . . . . .     586 Strephon Chloe     76
   Alass! a meer Chymerick Notion.  . . . . . . . .       604 Beasts Confess    112
   I'm grown a meer Mopus; no Company comes;  . . . .     867 Grand Question     27
   I'm but a Meer Depender still:  . . . . . . . .        918 Riddle 4           20
   For my part, it was by meer Chance . . .  . . .       1013 Swift to Sheri      3
MEERLY
   Meerly to gratify their Spight;  . . . . . . . .       548 Life of Swift     129
   (Tho' meerly writ at first for filling  . . . . . .    648 On Poetry         253
MEET
   'Tis but to say, that what we daily meet,  . . . . .    19 Ode Athenian      123
   Which we ne'er join'd before, but in Romances meet,  . . 28 Ode to Temple     60
   How proudly would he haste the joy to meet,  . . . . .  49 To Congreve       185
   Duns at his Lordships Gate began to meet,  . . . .     124 Descriptn Morn     13
   That you should meet, in love, success?  . . . . .     177 To Lord Harley     24
   I'm stopt by all the Fools I meet,  . . . . . . .      202 Horace 2, 6        91
   I meet perhaps from three or four,  . . . . . . .      204 In Sickness        15
   That meet for nothing but to gibe;  . . . . . . .      216 To Mr. Delany      54
   You, happy Folks, are sure to meet  . . . . . . .      315 To Ford           105
   To meet him next, the Soldier comes,  . . . . . .      338 Wood's Brass        8
   And still her favourites we meet,  . . . . . . . .     401 Window Inns 5    D  9
   Where can you meet  . . . . . . . . . .                442 Ballyspellin       58
   Three Syllables did never meet  . . . . . . . .        467 Birthday Song     225
   Resolv'd that Will. and he should meet no more;  . . . 537 Mr. Pulteney        3
   Conferring as they us'd to meet,  . . . . . . .        593 Cassinus Peter      3
   I'm humbled e'er I meet the dust,'  . . . . . . .      663 Epigram Bust        2
   Wou'd meet with better Friends above.  . . . . . .     695 Cadenus Vaness    269
   In all their Equipages meet;  . . . . . . . .          711 Cadenus Vaness    775
   If they should meet 'em in a Poem.  . . . . . .        729 Stella, Poems      52
   Thy Vertues meet their just Reward,  . . . . . .       779 Mullinix Tim      201
   Thus, if a Gudgeon meet a Roach  . . . . . . .         824 Printer Newgat     11
   Meet when Butchers bait a Bear;  . . . . . . .         829 Legion Club        14
   Now, see, when they meet, how their Honour's behave;  . 869 Grand Question     71
   . . . your friends you'd meet here. . . . . . . .     1022 Nim-Dan-Dean 2   D  2
MEETS
   Meets, and salutes her sister link again;  . . . . .    51 Temple Ill          4
   And meets her hasting to the Ball,  . . . . . .        292 Prog Marriage      85
   From whom she meets with frequent Rubs;  . . . . .     583 Young Nymph        53
   But, out it flies, even when she meets  . . . . .      588 Strephon Chloe    131
   In proper Season Pallas meets  . . . . . . . .         695 Cadenus Vaness    284
   But meets it half way;  . . . . . . . . .              853 Lady's Lament      76
MEGAERA
   From her own Head, Megaera takes  . . . . . . .        903 Death Daphne       21
MEHERCLE
   And, as to the subject, our judgment mehercle  . . .  1026 Sheri Circles       3
MEIN
   Her graceful Mein, her Shape, and Face,  . . . . .     584 Strephon Chloe      7
   Here, in their proper Shape and Mein,  . . . . .       922 Riddle 7           21
MELANCHOLLY
   Doll dying first, Dick grew Melancholly,  . . . . .    430 Dicky Dolly         2
   Melancholly smooth Meander,  . . . . . . . .           661 Love Song          25
MELANCHOLY
   When the sad, melancholy Muse  . . . . . . . .          24 Ode Athenian      273
   Let Melancholy rule supreme,  . . . . . . . .          724 To Stella          19
MELODIOUS
   We own, Your verses are melodious,  . . . . . .        622 Scandal Poem 1    179
   We own, your Verses are melodious;  . . . . . .        628 Scandal Poem 2    161
   A Blockhead with melodious Voice  . . . . . . .        710 Cadenus Vaness    738
MELODY
   Melody resigns to Fate.  . . . . . . . . .             661 Love Song          32
MELPOMENE
   To my goddess Melpomene, pride of her sex,  . . . .    979 Dean to Tho: S     23
MELT
   And strip the Bones, and melt the Oyl.  . . . . . .    258 Bubble            204
```

		PAGE	TITLE	LINE
MELT	**(CONTINUED)**			
For how can stony Bowels melt, ...		561	Death of Swift	215
Tho' cold would burn, tho' dry would melt.		585	Strephon Chloe	28
The new-born Flesh will melt away;		760	Receipt Youth	52
Crack the Stones, and melt the Lead;		830	Legion Club	26
MELTED				
The Wax is melted by the Height, ...		252	Bubble	39
Than the Liquor he deals in, his own melted Copper; .		351	Wood Insect	36
MELTS				
It melts the Sword of War, yet keeps it in the Sheath.		29	Ode to Temple	91
Or melts by the first show'r away.		39	Ode Sancroft	142
He melts his Wax at ev'ry Flame, ...		252	Bubble	46
Or melts my passions down with tears:		754	Stella '23	14
MEMBERS				
And Thanks to the Members that Kickt down the Bank. .		287	Bank Down	10
That, where we find the Members twain, ...		366	Answer Delaney	10
"The Country Members, when in Town, ...		564	Death of Swift	283
Instructing Members how to Vote.)		649	On Poetry	272
MEMINISSE				
Haec olim meminisse juvabit.		187	Scriblerus 4	D 18
hEMOIRS				
Or Memoirs of the New Utopia.		150	Corinna	32
The Memoirs of Martin, ...		186	Scriblerus 4	D 14
MEMORANDUMS				
Stale Memorandums of the Schools;		27	Ode to Temple	34
MEMORIALS				
But took Memorials on the Spot:		606	Beasts Confess	158
MEMORY				
And, thy Memory is loaded		523	Betty Grizette	15
Besides, his Memory decays, ...		556	Death of Swift	85
Keck at the Memory of Glorious.		775	Mullinix Tim	76
MEMPHIAN				
From Victors o'er the Memphian King;		925	Riddle 8	30
MEN	SEE CHAIR-MEN,DUTCH-MEN,POST-MEN,SERVING-MEN,JOURNEY-MEN,QUILL-MEN,LANDED-MEN			
Pardon Ye great Unknown, and far-exalted Men, . . .		17	Ode Athenian	60
And straight deny you to be Men, or any thing at all; .		19	Ode Athenian	120
Is wonderfully mov'd by some exalted Men, ...		20	Ode Athenian	137
With what unhappy Men shall dare, ...		25	Ode Athenian	293
That Men, who liv'd and dy'd without a Name, ...		25	Ode Athenian	306
And men seem walking on their heads;		35	Ode Sancroft	34
Stands in the gap 'twixt me and wretched men, ...		45	To Congreve	47
The best companion for the best of men:		52	Temple Ill	46
So men may see what once was womankind, ...		52	Temple Ill	49
So men have got from Bird and Brute		83	Salamander	7
But e'er since Men invented Guns, ...		83	Salamander	15
These Men are Saints I'll lay my Life		92	Bauc & Phil 1	82
The holy Men desir'd their Host		94	Bauc & Phil 1	155
So, Men of old, to gain Renown, did		108	V's House	65
Seated at Table next the Men you love.		165	Toland's Invit	32
But true English Men will fill, ...		169	Peace Dunkirk	38
Kept Company with Men of Wit, ...		171	Horace 1, 7	39
While, wise Men think they ought to fight		189	Faggot	21
Men have it when they know it not.		216	To Mr. Delany	28
What Use in Life, to make Men frett?		217	To Mr. Delany	71
Men laugh at one another's Cost;		217	To Mr. Delany	74
And tho men cry, they love a Jest, ...		218	To Mr. Delany	83
Those Men who wore the Breeches least		221	A Quiet Life	47
Know all Men by these Presents, Death the Tamer .		233	Elegy on Demar	1
And They in Men and Angels Sight		241	Run Bankers	62
At their Wits end like drunken Men.		256	Bubble	152
For Fools will see as Wise men please.		257	Bubble	168
Unless the Men of Kent are Ly'rs.		257	Bubble	170
And 'twas but just; for, wise Men say, ...		299	Horrid Plot	29
"To see th' important Men of Dress, ...		380	Apology Lady C	147
He taught, how Men to Honours rise, ...		386	Manly Virtue	103
Men of more Wit than Money, our Pensions will fit . .		389	Order of Bath	7
And this will suit Men of more Money than Wit. . .		389	Order of Bath	8
And wisely do as other men do.		435	Answer Paulus	116
Tho fond of warlike Lyes as most men;		462	Birthday Song	54
So, Men of Wit are but a kind		480	Libel on D- D-	23
To rail at men by nature fools:		488	Irish-Club	28
Not sparing even men of letters, ...		489	Dialogue	6
That Men of Wit can be no more		493	Panegyr Swift	25
Men seldom by their Good Deeds rise:		495	Panegyr Swift	75
And Kings are now no more than Men;		498	Panegyr Swift	164
Would Men of Genius cease to write, ...		502	Doctor Delaney	71
Point out the surest Men to rise, ...		502	Doctor Delaney	84
Than suffer Men of Parts to rise:		503	Doctor Delaney	92
Pronounce all Men of Wit, Free-thinkers.		503	Doctor Delaney	98
He jumbles Men and Birds together, ...		513	Answer Fable	13
By old Popish Cannons, as wise Men have Penn'd'em, .		518	Dean Hang Rape	37
Why are they so willful to struggle with Men? . . .		519	Dean Hang Rape	62
But swears how damnably the Men lie, ...		526	Lady's Dres Rm	17
We had a Hundred abler Men, ...		548	Life of Swift	99
"That e'er he cring'd to Men in Place?		549	Life of Swift	145
But there's no talking to some Men.		556	Death of Swift	104
"He never courted Men in Station.		565	Death of Swift	325
"He might have rose like other Men:		567	Death of Swift	356
Think what a Case all Men are now in, ...		585	Strephon Chloe	33
Come down to visit mortal Men.		587	Strephon Chloe	98
As much as now we find in Men.		601	Beasts Confess	4

```
MEN               (CONTINUED)                            PAGE   TITLE            LINE
    He thought it base for Men in Stations,      . . . . .   606 Beasts Confess    177
    He found the wisest Men he could,   . . . . . . . .      607 Beasts Confess    183
    Beasts may degen'rate into Men.     . . . . . . . .      608 Beasts Confess    220
    You men would be in wofull pickle   . . . . . . . .      618 Scandal Poem 1     41
    Due Regard for Men of Wit?          . . . . . . . . .    632 Epistle Lady       74
    We, by Play, as Men by Drinking,    . . . . . . .        632 Epistle Lady       85
    Why should they want the Privilege of Men,    . . . .    662 Upon Ladies         3
    The Men should slave at Cards from Morn to Night;   .    662 Upon Ladies         7
    To three fair virgins I did tie men . . . . . .          675 Curate's Compl      5
    Nor are the Men of Sense to blame,  . . . . . . .        688 Cadenus Vaness     63
    To value that which Men despise.    . . . . . . . .      689 Cadenus Vaness     84
    Since Men alledge they ne'er can find   . . . . .        691 Cadenus Vaness    142
    Know'st thou not yet that Men commence   . . . . .       696 Cadenus Vaness    296
    How dang'rous Things were Men of Wit,   . . . . . .      706 Cadenus Vaness    619
    He must adore such God-like Men.    . . . . . . .        708 Cadenus Vaness    695
    Yet now and then your Men of Wit    . . . . . . .        710 Cadenus Vaness    760
    Decreed the Cause against the Men.  . . . . . . .        713 Cadenus Vaness    853
    "She'd study to reform the Men;     . . . . . . .        714 Cadenus Vaness    873
    All Men of Sense will pass your Dore . . . . . .         736 Stel B-day '20     57
    And all Men believe he presides there incog.   . . .    804 Irish Bishops      15
    His Habitation let all Men forsake, . . . . . . .        806 Judas              25
    Are his Brother Protestants, good men and true; . .     815 Yahoo's            22
    And say of the man what all honest men say. . . . .      819 Archbi Casnel      10
    Be ador'd by the men      . . . . . . . . . .            855 Lady's Lament     127
    That Men of his Coat should be minding their Prayers.   868 Grand Question     37
    And soon grow pert on Men of Sense; . . . . . . .        887 Panegyr Dean       20
    Wherein the Men of Wit delight.     . . . . . . .        920 Riddle 6            6
    Have taught Men to extract with Skill,   . . . . .       920 Riddle 6           21
    Of Vegetables, Brutes, and Men.     . . . . . . .        924 Riddle 7           94
    But, Men find it to their Cost,     . . . . . . .        934 Riddle 22       D   5
    But 'tis observ'd, that Men in Gowns . . . . . .        1033 Ans to Crown       11
MEN'S   SEE MAD-MEN'S,LAY-MEN'S
    Men's Folly, Whimsyes, and Inconstancy,      . . . .     21 Ode Athenian       173
    Scatters strange agues o'er men's sickly minds,   . . . 52 Temple Ill          38
    A hundred other Men's Affairs  . . . . . . . . .        200 Horace 2, 6         49
    Poems address'd to great Men's Whores;   . . . . . .    494 Panegyr Swift       35
MEND
    To mend dilapidations in the last? . . . . . . . .       40 Ode Sancroft      179
    Bade Goody Baucis mend the Fire     . . . . . . .        91 Bauc & Phil 1      56
    Bid Goody Baucis mend the Fire;     . . . . . . .       111 Bauc & Phil 2      24
    To mend his Barn, cut Baucis down;  . . . . . . .       117 Bauc & Phil 2     174
    And Steal to mend your Wages?       . . . . . . . .     154 Widow and Cat   D  40
    For those Defects he cannot mend;   . . . . . . .       217 To Mr. Delany      68
    If he be Guilty, you must mend him, . . . . . . .       219 To Mr. Delany     111
    He'll not be too proud an old Kettle to mend;  . . .    335 Serious Poem       44
    I know the Times are something hard, but hope they soon 342 Upon His Grace     32
        will mend,
    And bids him bless, and mend the Earth;  . . . . .      384 Manly Virtue       16
    For Models, made to mend our Kind,  . . . . . . .       387 Manly Virtue      115
    Tries twenty Charms to mend her Luck.   . . . . . .     452 Modern Lady       237
    What hearty Prayers that I should mend?  . . . . .      557 Death of Swift    138
    And that unless the Sex would mend, . . . . . . .       713 Cadenus Vaness    862
    To make me deaf, and mend my Sight. . . . . . . .       758 Stel B-day '24     54
    To mend the World by useful Arts.   . . . . . . .       780 Mullinix Tim      246
    To mend your Breed, the Murderer of a King.  . . .      826 Noisy Tom          10
    Will mend the complexion.  . . . . . . . . . .          854 Lady's Lament     102
    And then, to mend the Matter still; . . . . . .         888 Panegyr Dean       35
    But have no concern to mend her.    . . . . . . .       907 Daphne             28
    If your Wife be a Scold, that will mend her.   . . .    942 Probatur Alit       8
MENDED
    Beneath, and mended Shoes in Hell.  . . . . . . .       100 Elegy Patrige      68
    She mended at first, but now she's anew sick.  . . .   1029 Dr. Helsham         6
MENDING
    'Tis Fifty round Millions of Love, and a Mending.  .    337 Serious Poem      106
    Bright Phillis mending ragged Smocks,   . . . . . .     729 Stella, Poems      47
    "In mending your Cassock, and smoothing your Band:  . . 872 Grand Question    150
    The dullest Beast mending Highways, . . . . . . .       941 Letter             33
    Mary said he, (one Day, as I was mending my Master's   986 Mary to Sher        28
        Stocking,)
MENDS
    Or spoils a Text, or mends his Hose. . . . . . .        279 Journal            24
    How skilfully Dan mends his Nets,   . . . . . . .       281 Journal            75
    Both alike; while neither mends.    . . . . . . .       631 Epistle Lady       56
    Or darns his hose, or mends his Breeches,    . . . .    878 Robbin & Harry     27
MENIAL
    And grief flung sables on each menial look;  . . . . .   53 Temple Ill         60
MENS   SEE MAD-MENS
    Nor unsuccessful waits for dead Mens Shoes.  . . .      364 On Dreams          30
    Or pawing into dead mens paunches.  . . . . . . . .     461 Birthday Song      36
    Mens Talents to their proper Use;   . . . . . . .       700 Cadenus Vaness    449
MENTION
    Or, mention but a vacant Post,      . . . . . . .       480 Libel on D- D-     17
    No further mention of the Dean;     . . . . . . .       562 Death of Swift    246
    Mention Courts, you'll ne'er be quiet;   . . . . .      635 Epistle Lady      183
MENTION'D
    I might have mention'd several facts,   . . . . . .     280 Journal            61
    Hath mention'd arms on this side Sweden;     . . . .    462 Birthday Song      52
    Mention'd a new Italian, come  . . . . . . . .          696 Cadenus Vaness    322
MERCENARY
    "Learn to disdain their mercenary aid;   . . . . . .     55 Temple Ill        140
```

MERCENTUR   PAGE   TITLE   LINE

	PAGE	TITLE	LINE
MERCENTUR			
Hoc Ithacus velit, et magni mercentur Atridae.	980	Dean to Tho: S	38
MERCHANT			
Our Merchant Ships may cut the Line,	168	Peace Dunkirk	21
MERCILESS			
The Torrent, merciless, imbibes	158	Fable of Midas	77
Thus merciless Hannah ran on in her Talk,	873	Grand Question	179
MERCURY			
This volatile mercury,	49	To Congreve	209
Then call in Mercury for Aid,	99	Elegy Patrige	61
When Mercury her Tresses mows	229	Prog of Beauty	109
Sent Mercury to get another.	346	Prometheus	52
Then Mercury with Silver Tongue,	585	Strephon Chloe	55
Ev'n Jove, and Mercury his pimp	620	Scandal Poem 1	101
Though Mercury makes use of Wings	621	Scandal Poem 1	117
Ev'n Jove, and Mercury his Pimp,	626	Scandal Poem 2	99
MERCURY'S			
Or else, that Mercury's her Foe.	228	Prog of Beauty	96
MERCY			
Thus I look down with mercy on the age,	45	To Congreve	49
A Mercy the Ground	245	Irish-Feast	39
And Mercy here exalts her Throne;	391	Young's Satire	18
A Tyrant for his Mercy praise,	464	Birthday Song	119
Cryes, Lord have Mercy on his Soul,	500	Doctor Delaney	18
"Then Lord have Mercy on his Soul.	562	Death of Swift	229
None of these have Mercy round:	638	Epistle Lady	247
In your indignation what mercy appears,	818	Epigr Kite	1
Your Mercy I rely on.	1005	Sheridan's Sub	13
MERE SEE MEER			
Our Knowledge is but mere Remembrance all,	27	Ode to Temple	30
Who prates like his Grand mere	186	Scriblerus 4 D	8
Her head is but a mere by-stander:	761	Bec's B-Day	26
A mere Contrivance of the Brain,	764	Stel B-day '26	20
Or mere Chimaera's in the Mind,	765	Stel B-day '26	53
"it's matter of weight, and a mere money-job;	843	Ay and No	11
MERELY SEE MEERLY			
Merely because her Friends advise;	294	Prog Marriage	134
Than merely to oblige your Friends;	765	Stel B-day '26	70
MERIT SEE PARTY-MERIT			
Part of Your Merit Chance wou'd call her own,	11	Ode to William D	11
All Merit that transcends the humble Rules	18	Ode Athenian	77
Which soon her merit forc'd her to inspire;	44	To Congreve	26
What poor regards would merit all below!	49	To Congreve	184
But found him thus their Merit Scan,	157	Fable of Midas	53
And pay the merit of her Lover?	177	To Lord Harley	36
To make his Merit more discern'd,	384	Manly Virtue	31
He drew dumb Merit from her Cell,	386	Manly Virtue	84
And Merit rears her drooping Head;	387	Manly Virtue	124
And justly half the Merit claim'd	406	Swift to Pope	27
Yet well they merit be pitied,	434	Answer Paulus	59
He must have been a King by Merit.	464	Birthday Song	136
Of his Intent, you mean, your Merit.	475	Epist on Epist	28
A Fund of such Superior Merit,	478	Epist on Epist	98
Betwixt a true and spurious Merit;	484	Libel on D- D-	148
Can, unreveng'd, the greatest merit wound.	506	To a Friend	6
But, thy Merit is thy Failing.	523	Betty Grizette	27
Let due Reward to Merit be allow'd;	533	To Mr. Gay	57
oppressing true merit exalting the base	540	Charac Walpole	7
The Merit of a lucky Guess,	557	Death of Swift	122
"To merit well of human Kind:	567	Death of Swift	362
That made him trust alone in Merit:	604	Beasts Confess	110
Would rise by Merit to Promotion;	604	Beasts Confess	111
What Justice in rewarding Merit?	655	On Poetry	415
That, Merit should be chiefly plac'd	697	Cadenus Vaness	342
Such Wonder by his Merit wrought;	710	Cadenus Vaness	753
'Tis Merit must with her prevail,	710	Cadenus Vaness	754
Nature in him had Merit plac'd,	711	Cadenus Vaness	766
And what She describes to be Merit is Treason:	716	Answer Rebus	22
The Merit and the Praise are yours.	728	Stella, Poems	8
To Merit humbled in the Dust:	765	Stel B-day '26	46
No Merit, no Science, no Virtue is wanting	808	Advice Parson	5
For who but Lord Bolton was mitred for Merit?	808	Advice Parson	8
How greater's his merit at four Courts or House,	814	Yahoo's	8
You merit new Employments daily:	891	Panegyr Dean	155
And in dress place all your merit;	908	Daphne	76
MERIT'S			
When his Merit's out of Date,	933	Riddle 20 D	28
MERITING			
To those who die, for meriting to live.	210	Earl of Oxford	14
MERITS			
"Whose Merits were, to be his Foes.	569	Death of Swift	402
And when your Merits once are known,	649	On Poetry	277
His Merits ballanc'd you shall find,	654	On Poetry	395
Wou'd shew the Merits of the Cause,	690	Cadenus Vaness	134
The Dean and his merits we ev'ry one know,	814	Yahoo's	6
Weigh but the Merits of the three,	884	Rev Market-Hill	27
MERMAIDS			
There live with daggl'd Mermaids pent,	689	Cadenus Vaness	89
MERRIER			
Tom was held the merrier Lad,	784	Mullinex Dick	7

MERRIMENT
   Scolding moves you less than Merriment. . . . . . .   PAGE   TITLE   LINE
   Scolding moves you less than Merriment. . . . . . .   636 Epistle Lady   208
MERRY
   Who in your merry Freaks, ...   425 Five Ladies   2
   And make merry in their Houses; . . . .   574 Helter Skelter   44
   All their Madness makes me merry: . . . .   635 Epistle Lady   164
   Don Carlos in a merry Spight . . . .   745 Stel Distress   1
   Don Carlos in a merry Spight, ...   749 Stel Wood-Park   1
   Yet, merry Folks who want by chance . . . . . .   756 Stel B-day '24   7
   You still divert with merry Stories; . . . . . .   778 Mullinix Tim   148
   The merry Tale with moral Grave. . . . .   783 Tim and Fables   27
   Now tell me, friend Thomas, Ford, Grattan, and merry   955 Portrait Life   9
     Dan,
   Whilst you three merry Poets traffick . . . . .   993 On Picture   1
MERYE
   And it shall by merye in olde Inglonde. . . . . . .   103 Merlin   16
MESS
   His Snot into the Mess; 'tis all his own. . . . .   536 To Mr. Gay   162
   A Birth-right for a mess of broth. . . . . . .   879 Robbin & Harry   36
MESSAGE
   The Message told, he gapes--and stares, ...   376 Apology Lady C   19
   What was the Message I receiv'd; . . . .   376 Apology Lady C   35
   Next Day another Message brought; . . . .   377 Apology Lady C   75
   How many a Message would he send? . . . .   557 Death of Swift   137
   A complimental Message sends: . . . .   904 Death Daphne   48
MESSENGER
   A Messenger comes all a-reek, ...   398 Earl of P-b-w   13
   The fav'rite Messenger of Jove, ...   916 Riddle 2   9
MET
   Lost youth, she cry'd, since first I met thee here! . .   52 Temple Ill   32
   Till the small ragged Flock is met. . . . . . .   127 Little House   22
   Part in worse humor than they met? . . . .   217 To Mr. Delany   72
   While at her Chin the Conflu'ents met. . . . . .   227 Prog of Beauty   40
   The Birds are met to strip the Jays. . . . . . .   239 Run Bankers   20
   What Carps we met with for our pains: . . . . .   283 Journal   112
   This Couple met to talk of News. . . . .   408 Dial Rich Marb   6
   Of Witches met together, ...   426 Five Ladies   19
   You met at Ballyspellin? . . . .   441 Ballyspellin   30
   And all the Gamester Ladies met, ...   451 Modern Lady   215
   Who met his Mother in a grove; . . . .   460 Birthday Song   16
   "You never met a Thing so smart, ...   564 Death of Swift   285
   The Learned met with free Approach, ...   701 Cadenus Vaness   458
   Had met her in a publick Place, ...   706 Cadenus Vaness   634
   And if her Youth Indifference met, ...   706 Cadenus Vaness   638
   But what Success Vanessa met, ...   712 Cadenus Vaness   818
   All met, and Silence thrice proclaim'd, ...   713 Cadenus Vaness   842
   Hath met with returns of all sorts but applause; . .   815 Yahoo's   17
   Hail fellow, well met, ...   856 Lady's Lament   165
   We both in one opinion met: . . . .   901 Dean's Reasons   74
METAL
   The pond'rous Metal seems to swim; . . . . . .   251 Bubble   12
   For Metal on Metal is false Heraldry: . . . . .   338 Serious Poem   120
   For Metal on Metal is false Heraldry: . . . . .   338 Serious Poem   120
METALS
   Metals I like them subdue, ...   936 Riddle 24   D   17
METAMORPHOS'D
   Was Metamorphos'd into Pews, ...   114 Bauc & Phil 2   104
   Till Metamorphos'd by his Grasp, ...   132 Magician's Rod   9
   Metamorphos'd to a Gorgan! . . . .   838 Legion Club   194
   Was metamorphos'd to a farmer; . . . .   879 Robbin & Harry   42
METAMORPHOS'T
   Was Metamorphos't into Pews; . . . .   94 Bauc & Phil 1   150
METAPHOR
   And not a Dog in Metaphor, ...   300 Horrid Plot   62
   'Tis a Metaphor known to ev'ry plain Thinker. . . .   335 Serious Poem   53
   To flatter Woman by a Metaphor! . . . .   622 Scandal Poem 1   169
   Altho' the Metaphor be worn and stale . . . . .   770 Horace 1, 14   5
METAPHORICK
   Metaphorick Meat and Drink, ...   633 Epistle Lady   117
METAPHYSICS
   Nor can of metaphysics smatter; . . . .   900 Dean's Reasons   60
METEOR
   This Gilded Meteor which flyes . . . .   10 Ode to King   122
   But sees thy meteor blaze about me shine, ...   54 Temple Ill   91
   No Meteor, no Eclipse appear'd! . . . .   98 Elegy Patrige   9
METHINKS   SEE ME-THINKS
   The War methinks has made . . . .   19 Ode Athenian   95
   Methinks I'm satisfied to guess . . . .   20 Ode Athenian   135
   Methinks, when you expose the Scene, ...   29 Ode to Temple   97
   And well, methinks, does this allusion fit . . . .   45 To Congreve   75
   Methinks, I still wou'd call it mine: . . . . . .   115 Bauc & Phil 2   114
   But yet, methinks, I feel it true; . . . .   116 Bauc & Phil 2   159
   Methinks I hear thee loud, as Trumpet, ...   182 Horace 2, 1   71
   Methinks I see thee, spruce and fine, ...   182 Horace 2, 1   73
   Methinks I see a black-guard Rout . . . .   183 Horace 2, 1   79
   Methinks I now see them so jovial and crank, . . .   287 Bank Down   24
   With what Delight, methinks, I trace . . . . .   325 Pethox   69
   Methinks I hear the Ladies cry, ...   445 Modern Lady   13
   Yet, thus methinks, I hear 'em speak; . . . . . .   556 Death of Swift   79
   Now, methinks, I hear you cry; . . . .   632 Epistle Lady   91
   Methinks, or else the Devil's in't, ...   860 Lady Acheson   14

```
METHOD                                                      PAGE      TITLE        LINE
    Their looks are all by method set,  . . . . . . .        178 To Lord Harley     55
    Thought no Method more commodious,   . . . . . . .       637 Epistle Lady      225
    As my Method of Reforming,   . . . . . . . . . .         637 Epistle Lady      229
    Had this been your method to torture him, long since,    818 Epigr Kite          9
    I shall, for Method Sake, begin with the last.   . . .   967 Letter Sherid      12
METHODICALLY
    And by their college-arts methodically kill:  . . . .     42 Ode Sancroft      254
METHODS
    We soon shall see them to their ancient Methods fall,  .  19 Ode Athenian      119
    (Methods in talk whereof our pride and ignorance make use) 38 Ode Sancroft     125
    These are the beaten methods of the stews,  . . . . .     44 To Congreve        19
    The methods most in fashion to be lewd,   . . . . . .     46 To Congreve       118
    All other Methods but the true.   . . . . . . . . .      592 Strephon Chloe    270
    And have we not practis'd all Methods to gain you;  . .  805 Irish Bishops      57
METHOUGHT
    So I was a-dream'd, methought,. . . . . . . . . . .       70 Mrs Harris Pet     22
    So methought, he resolv'd no Liquor to taste,  . . . .   337 Serious Poem      111
    Methought, when I this Poem read,  . . . . . . . . .     469 Burning Poem        3
METHUSALEM
    As did Methusalem of old, and so I end my Song.   . .    343 Upon His Grace     48
    Though you should live like old Methusalem,   . . . .    742 Stel B-day 22      37
METRE
    (Muse, find me Names to fix my Metre,   . . . . . .      594 Cassinus Peter      5
    . . .yet in the end's good metre,  . . . . . . . .      1022 Nim-Dan-Dean 2   D  1
    But we took our dividers, and found your <damn'd> metre, 1026 Sheri Circles     11
METROPOLIS
    In the metropolis of heaven;  . . . . . . . . . .        42 Ode Sancroft      237
    Of our Metropolis to <Swift>;  . . . . . . . . . .      494 Panegyr Swift      48
METTAL
    The Coyn's Currant and Mettal Pure.  . . . . . .        372 Letter D. S-y      34
METTALS
    Refin'd all Mettals with his Looks,  . . . . . . .      597 Problem Solved       3
METTLE
    Tis true; a Woman on her mettle   . . . . . . .         621 Scandal Poem 1    143
    'Tis true; a Woman on her Mettle,  . . . . . . .        628 Scandal Poem 2    147
    Set your Thoughts upon their Mettle:  . . . . . .       636 Epistle Lady      212
    Grows plump and round, and full of Mettle,  . . . .     759 Receipt Youth      17
    And rouse up your Mettle,   . . . . . . . . . .         953 Oysters             8
    Dan's noble Mettle, Sherry base;   . . . . . . .       1004 Dan J's Reply      31
METTLED
    The mettled and the vicious Steed  . . . . . . .        217 To Mr. Delany      61
    But e'er you mount his mettled Steed,  . . . . . .      666 Epig Carthy 2    D  3
MEW
    I pitied my Cat, whom I knew by her Mew sick;   . . .   1029 Dr. Helsham         5
MICE
    "Have kept Domestick Mice in awe,   . . . . . .         154 Widow and Cat    D 24
MICHAELMAS
    Appears from Michaelmas to May;   . . . . . . .         759 Receipt Youth       4
    For if to Michaelmas you stay,  . . . . . . . . .       760 Receipt Youth      51
MID-NIGHT
    Call'd up at Mid-night, ran to save   . . . . . .       604 Beasts Confess    115
MID-WIFE
    Well skill'd in Mid-wife Artifices;   . . . . . .       362 Grace's Answer     27
MIDAS
    Midas, we are in Story told,  . . . . . . . . .         156 Fable of Midas      1
    And both chose Midas to decide;   . . . . . . .         156 Fable of Midas     26
    Midas, expos'd to all their Jears,  . . . . . .         157 Fable of Midas     39
    To whom from Midas down, decends  . . . . . . .         157 Fable of Midas     43
    As t' other Midas did before?  . . . . . . . . .        157 Fable of Midas     50
    None e'er did modern Midas chuse,  . . . . . . .        157 Fable of Midas     51
    Our Midas too has Asses Ears,  . . . . . . . . .        158 Fable of Midas     62
    Of British Midas dirty Paws;   . . . . . . . .          158 Fable of Midas     70
    And Midas now neglected stands,   . . . . . . .         158 Fable of Midas     81
    As well as you, for a Midas:   . . . . . . . .          372 Letter D. S-y      37
    What Midas touch'd, became true Gold; but then,  . . .  668 Epig Carthy 12   D  1
MIDDLE
    I keep in a Pocket ty'd about my Middle, next my Smock.   69 Mrs Harris Pet      7
    He found it was strangely fill'd in the Middle.   . . .  77 Lady B- B-          9
    And scorns the middle Way to keep:  . . . . . . .       252 Bubble             36
    It but reach'd the middle Air,  . . . . . . . . .       638 Epistle Lady      251
    I justly keep the middle Way.  . . . . . . . . .        918 Riddle 4           38
MIDDLE-AGED
    Then, for a middle-aged Charmer,   . . . . . . .        313 To Ford            69
MIDDLE-STATE
    A middle-state 'twixt peace and war;  . . . . . .       876 To Dean Swift      24
MIDLING
    "Were always of the midling Kind:   . . . . . . .       570 Death of Swift    436
MIDNIGHT
    So to Her Midnight Feasts the Hag,   . . . . . .        132 Magician's Rod     15
    Till Midnight never shows her Head;  . . . . . .        229 Prog of Beauty    102
    Conceive the Works of Midnight Hags,  . . . . .         240 Run Bankers        29
    At Midnight, through the dark'ned Air;  . . . . .       354 Simile Silver       4
    Sits up till Midnight with his Host,  . . . . . .       398 Earl of P-b-w       5
    To be a Midnight Pack  . . . . . . . . . . . .          426 Five Ladies        18
    As ridden by a midnight hag:   . . . . . . . .          434 Answer Paulus      76
    Returning at the Midnight Hour;   . . . . . . .         581 Young Nymph         7
    Me Phoebus in a midnight Dream  . . . . . . . .         897 Panegyr Dean      325
    A Beast long-ear'd, and till Midnight you stay,  . . .  943 Probatur Alit      33
'MIDST
    There shining 'midst his Train, to Grace   . . . .      477 Epist on Epist     81
```

512

MIDST
                                                          PAGE   TITLE   LINE

	PAGE	TITLE		LINE
MIDST				
But was sorely put to't in the midst of a Verse,	76	Lady B- B-		3
By starving in the midst of Store,	157	Fable of Midas		49
In the Midst of their Beer:	246	Irish-Feast		60
But, in the midst of mirth and wine,	936	Riddle 24	D	11
MIDWIFE'S				
Apollo play'd the Midwife's Part,	149	Corinna		2
MIEN SEE MEIN				
Look'd with an easie, careless Mien,	170	Horace 1, 7		9
Struck with Endymion's graceful mien,	178	To Lord Harley		74
In whom thy Features, Shape, and Mien,	325	Pethox		71
The powerful Voice, the graceful Mien,	385	Manly Virtue		57
My portly Motion, Mien, and Gate.	780	Mullinix Tim		234
Hence the greazy clumsy Mien,	800	Traulus 2		31
MIGHT 97				
MIGHTY		OMITTED WORD		
First, in the mighty List of Fame,	7	Ode to King		34
And has at last redeem'd the Mighty Prize	8	Ode to King		81
To buzz about the mighty Flame;	9	Ode to King		116
You, Mighty Monarch, Nobler Actions Crown,	11	Ode to William	D	3
That mighty Ebb never to flow again,	16	Ode Athenian		2
After a mighty Light that leads her wandring Eye;	18	Ode Athenian		67
Just so the Mighty Nile has suffer'd in it's Fame,	20	Ode Athenian		145
And by one mighty Hero carried to it's height	25	Ode Athenian		284
It lost some mighty Pieces thro' all hands it past	25	Ode Athenian		286
The mighty Conquest's left for you,	26	Ode to Temple		9
For Learning's mighty Treasures look	27	Ode to Temple		35
Those mighty Epithets, Learn'd, Good, and Great	28	Ode to Temple		59
How the Mouse makes the mighty Mountain shake!	30	Ode to Temple		107
The mighty Mountain labours with its birth,	30	Ode to Temple		108
How mighty a Proselyte you gain!	31	Ode to Temple		140
What mighty numbers follow them;	39	Ode Sancroft		164
And yet the world, whose eyes are on our mighty Prince,	40	Ode Sancroft		180
Nor be thy mighty spirit rais'd,	42	Ode Sancroft		263
A mighty gulph unpassable betwixt.	44	To Congreve		32
Takes Horse, and in a mighty Fret	174	Horace 1, 7		116
South-Sea at best a mighty Bubble.	259	Bubble		220
And could that Mighty Warrior fall?	296	Satiric Elegy		3
What cou'd I've said? I'm mighty glad	377	Apology Lady C		51
"Madam, the mighty Pow'r of Use	379	Apology Lady C		131
Makes mighty Armys turn their Arses.	461	Birthday Song		30
I broke his Teeth, but where's the mighty harm?	670	Epig Carthy 20	D	12
Saw all these mighty labours done,	675	Curate's Compl		14
Exalted in his mighty Mind	728	Stella, Poems		35
MILD				
Believe it firm, because perhaps the day is mild and still	37	Ode Sancroft		75
Mild Dorothea, peaceful, wise and great,	52	Temple Ill		41
Mild Dorothea, whom we both have long	52	Temple Ill		43
Call'd to the Clerk in manner mild,	128	Little House		51
In mild Reproof to Woman-kind;	384	Manly Virtue		24
The Queen, so Gracious, Mild, and Good,	559	Death of Swift		181
Mild Arcadians, ever blooming,	660	Love Song		5
But in a mild dejected Strain,	704	Cadenus Vaness		572
And then he grows mild;	855	Lady's Lament		123
Are so indulgent, and so mild,	891	Panegyr Dean		151
--The rascal! that's too mild a name;	950	Upstart	D	1
MILDER				
He wou'd have chose a milder part;	485	Libel on D- D-		158
Expanded to invite a milder Gale.	770	Horace 1, 14		24
MILDNESS				
Forgive (Original Mildness) this ill-govern'd zeal,	38	Ode Sancroft		107
MILE				
Lead them a Dance of many a Mile,	79	Vanbrug House		5
Lead 'em a Dance of many a Mile,	106	V's House		5
Aura, whose Tongue you hear a Mile hence,	450	Modern Lady		170
Are lofty'r by a mile at least.	620	Scandal Poem 1		106
Are loftier by a Mile at least:	626	Scandal Poem 2		104
You still are low ten thousand Mile.	657	On Poetry		472
MILES				
Was forc'd to send three Miles for Yest,	282	Journal		89
Above two hundred miles from home?	403	Window Inns 10	D	4
Tho George is gone a thousand miles.	466	Birthday Song		182
I March'd three miles thro' scorching sand,	675	Curate's Compl		1
While all the Squires from nine Miles round,	760	Receipt Youth		42
Send me hence ten thousand miles,	907	Daphne		21
MILITANT				
On Coblers Militant below,	100	Elegy Patrige		90
MILK				
For want of Milk, wou'd suck her Blood.	208	Fable Bitches		22
Talk of their Milk for Babes of Grace;	892	Panegyr Dean		170
Thy Milk shall make us Tubs of Butter.	892	Panegyr Dean		172
First milk his cows, and after, pound:	902	Dean's Reasons		104
Like Milk 'tis cry'd about the Street,	929	Riddle 15	D	11
I hope you have swilld with new milk from the Kine	1018	Swift Ans Sher		25
MILK-MAIDS				
When Milk-maids in mock-state	122	Empty'ng Town		6
MILK-WHITE				
Before this Milk-white Heifer can be stole away,	8	Ode to King		77
His milk-white Steed upon it's haunches,	461	Birthday Song		35
Her Milk-white Hands, both Palms and Backs,	584	Strephon Chloe		25

		PAGE	TITLE	LINE
MILKS				
Where Goody Julia milks the Cows,	. . . .	878	Robbin & Harry	25
MILKSOP				
'Tis a perfect Milksop,	. . . .	939	Riddle Answerd	27
MILKY				
Attacks her in the milky Way:	. . . .	228	Prog of Beauty	92
Or ever name the milky Way.	. . . .	270	Apollo's Edict	D 22
When you behold the milky Way	. . . .	362	Grace's Answer	31
MILL				
This Bank is to make us a New Paper Mill,	. . . .	287	Bank Down	11
There's neither Chariot, Coach, or Mill,	. . . . .	929	Riddle 14	D 7
MILLIA				
Och ma ceade millia mollighart, on the feeders of swine!	841	Ballad	D 19
MILLION				
With each a Million in his Coffers.	. . . .	253	Bubble	72
We never say more than, your Love is a Million;	. . .	337	Serious Poem	104
MILLIONS				
The Dutch from hence shall no more Millions drain;	. .	169	Peace Dunkirk	27
The Swiss and Dutch whole Millions drain.	. . . .	256	Bubble	160
'Tis Fifty round Millions of Love, and a Mending.	. .	337	Serious Poem	106
And Millions miss, for one that hits.	. . . . . .	640	On Poetry	2
I sent you Millions of the croaking Race;	. . . . .	792	St. Pat's Well	54
And Millions of the present Age.	. . . .	922	Riddle 7	42
MILTON				
I murder poor Milton,	. . . .	856	Lady's Lament	156
MILTON'S				
And sing like one of Milton's choir,	. . . . . .	490	Dialogue	40
MIMIC				
Which all the mimic forms express,	. . . .	35	Ode Sancroft	25
MIMICK				
The busy Head with mimick Art runs o'er	. . . . .	363	On Dreams	9
That pack of mimick <legislators>,	. . . .	436	Answer Paulus	133
The Mimick Ape began his Chatter,	. . . .	602	Beasts Confess	47
The mimick Animal amuse;	. . . .	885	Rev Market-Hill	77
MIMICKRY				
The Mimickry of deep yet clear.	. . . .	271	Apollo's Edict	D 49
MINCE				
Why should he longer mince the Matter?	. . . . . .	604	Beasts Confess	95
MIND				
For Man to dress and polish his Uncourtly Mind,	. .	22	Ode Athenian	218
For when the animating Mind is fled,	. . . . . .	25	Ode Athenian	288
If a mind fix'd to combat fate	. . . .	36	Ode Sancroft	47
That vagrant leader of the mind,	. . . .	36	Ode Sancroft	57
With heavenly peace of mind to bear	. . . . . .	38	Ode Sancroft	115
The bullion stampt in your refining mind	. . . . .	45	To Congreve	53
Some short refreshment for your weary mind,	. . .	50	To Congreve	232
At distant hours the mind with forms so like!	. . .	51	Temple Ill	2
In the fair shrine of Dorothea's mind.	. . . . .	52	Temple Ill	50
That time is sick, or the world's mind is dead.--	. .	53	Temple Ill	66
To thee I owe that fatal bent of mind,	. . . . .	55	Temple Ill	131
He kept the Model in his Mind.	. . . .	86	Hist V's House	12
(His Mind with Publick Cares possest,	. . . . . .	170	Horace 1, 7	3
A virgin of superior mind,	. . . .	177	To Lord Harley	34
Fresh blooming, in young Harley's mind.	. . . . .	178	To Lord Harley	52
"Put my Lord Bolingbroke in Mind,	. . . . . .	201	Horace 2, 6	55
As I rode in my Chariot, a Thought to my Mind;	. .	265	Apollo	76
His Mind is full of other Cares,	. . . .	292	Prog Marriage	67
"Your Business is to mind your Spinning.	. . . .	304	Storm	44
The same Impression on his Mind;	. . . .	345	Prometheus	20
The Mind unburthen'd sports in various Whims,	. . .	363	On Dreams	8
"Direct, and fix the wandring Mind,	. . . . . .	384	Manly Virtue	12
His Body active as his Mind,	. . . .	398	Earl of P-b-w	22
More virtues in a Woman's Mind,	. . . .	417	Woman's Mind	58
Sit light upon a lawyer's mind:	. . . .	433	Answer Paulus	52
How cou'd it come into your Mind,	. . . .	445	Modern Lady	5
Say, by what fatal Turn of Mind,	. . . .	449	Modern Lady	151
Now sound in mind, and sound in corpus,	. . . . .	456	Dean Smedley	31
Extol him for his generous mind:	. . . .	464	Birthday Song	124
But now it comes into my mind,	. . . .	466	Birthday Song	199
Of Pandars to a vicious Mind,	. . . .	480	Libel on D- D-	24
Hail! happy Pope, whose gen'rous Mind,	. . . . .	482	Libel on D- D-	71
But 'gainst the Dictates of your Mind,	. . . . .	496	Panegyr Swift	94
Shou'd stupid Libels grieve your Mind,	. . . . .	501	Doctor Delaney	43
Have Peter Waters always in your Mind;	. . . . .	534	To Mr. Gay	101
Our Friends are of a diff'rent mind;	. . . . . .	546	Life of Swift	48
They argue no corrupted Mind,	. . . .	553	Death of Swift	3
He cannot call his Friends to Mind;	. . . . . .	556	Death of Swift	87
All Fortitude of Mind supplies:	. . . .	561	Death of Swift	214
"But, kept the Tenor of his Mind,	. . . . . .	567	Death of Swift	361
The Place of the Damn'd,--I'll tell you my Mind.	. .	575	Place Damn'd	4
Thro' the Mazes of your Mind,	. . . .	629	Epistle Lady	4
And with Books my Mind embellish.	. . . . . .	632	Epistle Lady	90
Never lets your Mind elope:	. . . .	636	Epistle Lady	214
For this Perverseness in the Mind?	. . . . . .	640	On Poetry	12
A powerful Impulse urge your Mind,	. . . . . .	642	On Poetry	78
Adapted to a human Mind,	. . . .	659	On Poetry	D 410
Conceiv'd and kindled in the Mind,	. . . . . .	687	Cadenus Vaness	30
The Current of a Female Mind,	. . . .	688	Cadenus Vaness	57
The Goddess much perplex'd in Mind,	. . . . . .	690	Cadenus Vaness	128
Those Beauties in a Female Mind,	. . . .	691	Cadenus Vaness	143
Collected in that Infant's Mind.	. . . .	691	Cadenus Vaness	153

```
MIND          (CONTINUED)                              PAGE   TITLE          LINE
   From whence that Decency of Mind,      . . . . . . . .   691 Cadenus Vaness   164
   Then sows within her tender Mind     . . . . . . . .     693 Cadenus Vaness   202
   Wou'd by her Model form their Mind,    . . . . . . .     694 Cadenus Vaness   237
   A wholesome Law, Time out of mind,   . . . . . . . .     694 Cadenus Vaness   257
   To see the Virgin mind her Book,    . . . . . . . .      704 Cadenus Vaness   551
   Ideas came into her Mind  . . . . . . . . . .            704 Cadenus Vaness   556
   Such Marks of a distracted Mind;    . . . . . . . .      704 Cadenus Vaness   563
   Directors to a noble Mind.    .  . . . . . . . .         706 Cadenus Vaness   613
   To form and cultivate her Mind.     . . . . . . . .      706 Cadenus Vaness   631
   While ev'ry Passion of her Mind     . . . . . . . .      709 Cadenus Vaness   710
   Some fav'rite System to their Mind,   . . . . . . .      709 Cadenus Vaness   723
   Directed them to mind their Brief;   . . . . . . . .     713 Cadenus Vaness   847
   Made up so largly in thy Mind.   . . . . . . . .         722 Stel B-Day '18     8
   Fixt Honour in her Infant Mind.     . . . . . . . .      723 To Stella          6
   Drive all Objections from your Mind,   . . . . . . .     724 To Stella         43
   What indignation in her Mind    . . . . . . . .          725 To Stella         61
   Exalted in his mighty Mind   . . . . . . . . .           728 Stella, Poems     35
   Mix'd in a noble generous Mind;     . . . . . . . .      731 Stella, Poems    104
   In such a Form an Angel's Mind     . . . . . . . .       735 Stel B-day '20    20
   The Cracks and Wrinckles of your Mind,   . . . . . .     736 Stel B-day '20    56
   So soft, and yet so firm a mind?    . . . . . . . .      755 Stella '23        20
   Domestic business never mind  . . . . . . . .            761 Bec's B-Day       33
   Some lasting Pleasure in the Mind,    . . . . . . .      764 Stel B-day '26    30
   Or mere Chimaera's in the Mind,     . . . . . . . .      765 Stel B-day '26    53
   The Nutriment that feeds the Mind?    . . . . . . .      765 Stel B-day '26    62
   Nor let your Ills affect your Mind,   . . . . . . .      766 Stel B-day '26    81
   Now, for thy Safety Cares distract my Mind,   . . . .    772 Horace 1, 14      58
   Enter the Stage they never mind him;   . . . . . . .     776 Mullinix Tim     102
   Will our own Party mind me not?    . . . . . . . .       779 Mullinix Tim     192
   Use all the Talents of your mind.    . . . . . . . .     780 Mullinix Tim     232
   Our Care is to improve the mind,    . . . . . . . .      781 Mullinix Tim     263
   'Till Politicks debas'd my mind.    . . . . . . . .      782 Mullinix Tim     282
   To polish your mind,     . . . . . . . .                 855 Lady's Lament    126
   Robin, who ne'r his mind could fix  . . . . . . . .      878 Robbin & Harry    29
   But, who have rais'd your gen'rous Mind    . . . . .     893 Panegyr Dean     197
   It was no levity of mind.  . . . . . .                   899 Dean's Reasons     4
   Is the same avarice of mind:   . . . . . . . .           900 Dean's Reasons    38
   Beyond the skies transports his mind,   . . . . . .      900 Dean's Reasons    49
   Who send my mind (as I believe) less   . . . . . .       900 Dean's Reasons    53
   It forms an union in the mind:    . . . . . . . .        901 Dean's Reasons    70
   His Mind was running on his Match.    . . . . . . .      904 Death Daphne      52
   Bring all past Actions to thy Mind.    . . . . . . .     921 Riddle 7           4
   And turn it as I have a Mind,    . . . . . . . .         934 Riddle 21     D   15
MINDED
   So, (if my Simile you minded,    . . . . . . . .         354 Simile Silver     17
   I chopp'd so fast, that few there minded.   . . . . .    675 Curate's Compl    12
   Ne'er minded a word that was spoken;    . . . . . . .    755 Dingley Brent      3
   Be humbly minded; know your Post;    . . . . . . . .     897 Panegyr Dean     327
MINDFUL
   Be mindful, when Invention fails,    . . . . . . . .     643 On Poetry         89
MINDFULL
   And mindfull of it's antient State,    . . . . . . .      93 Bauc & Phil 1    109
MINDING
   Not minding when the Song was done.     . . . . . .      775 Mullinix Tim      44
   That Men of his Coat should be minding their Prayers.    868 Grand Question    37
   When whip you trot up, without minding your betters,  .  978 Dean to Tho: S     3
MINDS
   Contrive to shock your Minds, with many a sensless doubt, 22 Ode Athenian     207
   Make their minds travel o'er infinity of space,   . . .   36 Ode Sancroft      61
   Yet to firm heavenly minds,  . . . . . . . . .            41 Ode Sancroft     205
   Nor wonder, if from such polluted minds   . . . . .       47 To Congreve      127
   Scatters strange agues o'er men's sickly minds,   . . .   52 Temple Ill        38
   Since one false beam of joy in sickly minds  . . . . .    55 Temple Ill       149
   The various Textures of their Minds,   . . . . . . .     291 Prog Marriage     34
   Minds nothing that is done or said,    . . . . . . .     291 Prog Marriage     57
   And with false flitting Shades our Minds delude,   . .   363 On Dreams          2
   The chains which fetter free-born minds,   . . . . .     490 Dialogue          32
   Supports their Minds with heav'nly Food.    . . . . .    605 Beasts Confess   124
   She minds no longer what he taught.    . . . . · . .     704 Cadenus Vaness   561
   Their Minds so plentifully fills,    . . . . . . . .     735 Stel B-day '20    27
   What intercourse of minds can be    . . . . . . . .      901 Dean's Reasons    65
MINE
   Do laugh perhaps at theirs, and pity mine and me.  . . .  18 Ode Athenian      90
   Was cast in the same Mold with mine?    . . . . . . .     32 Ode to Temple    179
   Pleads for her own neglect, and thus reproaches mine:    43 To Congreve        6
   Could leap the bounds which part your world and mine;  .  44 To Congreve       30
   To praise your parts by publishing of mine;   . . . . .   44 To Congreve       34
   For never did poetic mine before   . . . . . . . .       45 To Congreve       51
   Might seem, when first she rais'd her eyes to mine.  . .  52 Temple Ill        30
   And passing o'er, mistakes thee still for mine;   . . .   54 Temple Ill        92
   Methinks, I still wou'd call it mine:    . . . . . .     115 Bauc & Phil 2    114
   Obey my Call, and only mine.    . . . . . . . .          120 Apollo Outwit     32
   As mine for Politicks and Wit.     . . . . . . . .       183 Horace 2, 1      106
   All this is mine but till I die;    . . . . . . . .      198 Horace 2, 6     D
   Regards a Friend of yours and mine,    . . . . . .       218 To Mr. Delany     90
   If she were Mine, and had such Tricks,   . . . . . .     220 A Quiet Life      29
   And presently guess'd that the Fancy was mine;   . . .   264 Apollo            52
   No Son of mine shall dare to say,    . . . . . . . .     270 Apollo's Edict  D 20
   Of all the Satyre shall be mine.    . . . . . . . .      445 Modern Lady       29
   "This Head of mine, Lord, how it Swims!   . . . . . .    451 Modern Lady      208
```

		PAGE	TITLE	LINE
MINE	(CONTINUED)			
In Verse; but there is Truth in mine.		486	Libel on D- D-	194
But with a Sigh, I wish it mine:		555	Death of Swift	48
Having stolen from mine Hostess,		574	Helter Skelter	32
Your Heart had been as whole as mine.		591	Strephon Chloe	250
For your Sake, as well as mine,		637	Epistle Lady	217
Think Eusden's Right as good as mine.		741	Stel B-day 22	30
I'll take you to some Friends of mine;		780	Mullinix Tim	244
Britain, with Shame confess, this Land of mine		791	St. Pat's Well	27
Bless mine Eyes! Art thou the Chairman?		837	Legion Club	190
I suppose meaning mine.)		854	Lady's Lament	104
You honour me much--the Honour is mine,--		869	Grand Question	73
To drink Sir <Arthur's> Health and mine:		890	Panegyr Dean	102
No fault of mine, the scheme is ended:		899	Dean's Reasons	6
It shall be no concern of mine.		902	Dean's Reasons	112
What you see is none of mine,		927	Riddle 10	D 2
'Tis mine to make a just Reflection,		932	Riddle 19	D 17
A Friend of mine, that Author despises		988	Letter Dr Sh-n	21
However I wish, honest Comrade of mine		1017	Swift Ans Sher	11
MINERVA				
Minerva ne'er an Oath did Swear		372	Letter D. S-y	12
MINES				
To dig the leaden Mines of deep Philosophy:		32	Ode to Temple	190
When e'er the Soil has Golden Mines:		133	Magician's Rod	24
To bend where Golden Mines were hid;		133	Magician's Rod	28
MINGL'D				
Together mingl'd in a Mass		344	Prometheus	3
MINGLE				
(For, 'tis prophane when Sexes mingle;		893	Panegyr Dean	209
MINGLED				
Then, from the motly mingled Style		108	V's House	63
Roughen the Nap, and leave a mingled Stain.		138	City Shower	30
A mingled Mass of Dirt and Sweat.		226	Prog of Beauty	20
But her graceful black Locks, were all mingled with Grey		264	Apollo	42
Together mingled in a Lump,		345	Prometheus	17
Are mingled with stale.		402	Window Inns 8	D 8
A mingled Mass of Good & Bad,		659	On Poetry	D 410
Yet from this mingled Mass of Things,		924	Riddle 7	89
MINGLES				
And mingles in her muddy Cheeks.		227	Prog of Beauty	36
MINGLING				
Which mingling with prolifick Strife		324	Pethox	29
Mingling with Apples in the Throng,		811	Bro Protestant	12
MINHEER				
To Minheer Hendel next you run,		469	Birthday Song	276
MINIATURE				
And, though in Miniature, you shine,		752	Stel Wood-Park	84
MINIMMS				
To listen to minimms and quavers and Crochets		522	St. Cecilia's	12
MINIONS				
The drowsy Tyrant by his Minions led,		364	On Dreams	11
MINISTER				
A Premier Minister of State		160	Atlas	17
"To haunt a certain Minister of State:		195	Author Himself	44
Inform'd a Minister of State.		298	Horrid Plot	4
The haughty Minister of State		325	Pethox	49
A Minister so filled with Zeal,		391	Young's Satire	3
And grown a Minister of State,		482	Libel on D- D-	69
I knew a brazen Minister of State,		536	To Mr. Gay	143
His Work is done, the Minister must out.		536	To Mr. Gay	150
Could maul a Minister of State:		555	Death of Swift	62
Nor Minister, nor Poet flatter.		655	On Poetry	414
Now sing the Minister of State,		656	On Poetry	441
My Master is so fond of that Minister that keeps the School;		987	Mary to Sher	29
Nor Minister of State.		1036	Heathen Christ	4
A bloated <Minister> in all his Geer,		532	To Mr. Gay	33
MINISTERIAL				
That Rogue of genuine ministerial Kind:		534	To Mr. Gay	102
MINISTERS				
In Favour grows with Ministers of State;		194	Author Himself	29
Great Ministers ne'er think of these;		199	Horace 2, 6	18
Both <Kings> and Ministers of State,		485	Libel on D- D-	174
Our Ministers are void of Taste,		497	Panegyr Swift	145
Both <Kings> and Ministers of State.		498	Panegyr Swift	156
May sink by premier Ministers of State.		535	To Mr. Gay	116
"On Ministers, is disaffection.		563	Death of Swift	276
He found, the Ministers resent it,		604	Beasts Confess	101
Wicked Ministers of State		634	Epistle Lady	143
And lo, his Ministers of State,		646	On Poetry	207
Caress'd by Ministers of State,		702	Cadenus Vaness	504
Base Kings and Ministers of State,		725	To Stella	63
Against us Ministers of State!		783	Tim and Fables	32
Sir, we the Ministers of State.		812	Bro Protestant	24
Of twenty <Ministers> of State.		781	Mullinix Tim	258
MINISTRE				
His Lordship's premier Ministre,		62	Discovery	10
MINOR				
You'll dare not to question my minor or major.		976	Dean to Sherid	24
MINT				
As fresh as Farthings from the Mint:		644	On Poetry	114

	PAGE	TITLE	LINE
MINUTE			
You've rais'd a Church here in a Minute,	94	Bauc & Phil 1	161
In half a Minute is not worth one Groat;	234	Elegy on Demar	20
We watch his Motions to a Minute,	280	Journal	49
And scarce a Day, can spare a Minute	322	First of April	41
Never to hold her Tongue a Minute;	415	Woman's Mind	5
And, when I think upon't, this minute,	545	Life of Swift	11
One minute whether foul or fair?	619	Scandal Poem 1	50
One Minute, whether Foul or Fair?	625	Scandal Poem 2	46
But not to dwell on Things minute,	708	Cadenus Vaness	674
He fawns upon you in a Minute.	797	Traulus 1	54
MIRACLE			
Behold, a Miracle was wroght	92	Bauc & Phil 1	74
MIRACLES			
"That all his Miracles were Cheats,	564	Death of Swift	295
MIRMONT			
With antient Mirmont at her Side.	410	Dial Rich Marb	64
MIRRORS			
Lead me to the Chrystal Mirrors,	661	Love Song	19
Nature holds her forth two mirrors,	907	Daphne	43
MIRTH			
Humour, and Mirth, had Place in all he writ:	194	Author Himself	11
In Mirth the wedding-day was spent.	290	Prog Marriage	18
I encounter Vice with Mirth.	634	Epistle Lady	142
See, what Mirth the Sport creates;	638	Epistle Lady	255
Why then in vain he would excite our Mirth.	669	Epig Carthy 16	D 2
Where Mirth, and Exercise, and Air,	759	Receipt Youth	27
But, in the midst of mirth and wine,	936	Riddle 24	D 11
In thee Delany's spleen, John's mirth, Helsham's jokes,	1023	Nim-Dan-Dean 2	D 14
MIRY			
Drag diff'rent Ways in miry Grounds.	645	On Poetry	176
MISANTHROPE			
Was, to be held a Misanthrope.	548	Life of Swift	131
MISAPPLY'D			
Your Raillery is misapply'd:	175	Horace 1, 7	132
Nor, will your nobler Gifts be misapply'd,	532	To Mr. Gay	15
MISCALL'D			
As 'tis miscall'd, we know not who 'tis;	98	Elegy Patrige	32
MISCARRY			
And, vext to see Affairs miscarry,	903	Death Daphne	9
MISCARRY'D			
His Lady has twelve times miscarry'd,	293	Prog Marriage	100
MISCARRYE			
Yonge Symnele shall agayne miscarrye:	103	Merlin	11
MISCELLANIES			
Out skips a Book of Miscellanies.	651	On Poetry	318
MISCHANCES			
Here four of you got mischances to plague you,	1037	Four Storyes	1
MISCHEIF			
Sloth, Folly, Rapine, Mischeif, Lust	659	On Poetry	D 410
MISCHIEF			
Loves Mischief better than his Meat,	171	Horace 1, 7	14
Some Mischief is Brewing, the Project smells Rank,	287	Bank Down	4
"Saw Mischief by a Faction brewing,	567	Death of Swift	367
Compar'd for mischief, to Venereal?	618	Scandal Poem 1	24
Compar'd for Mischief, to Venereal?	624	Scandal Poem 2	18
But Cupid, full of Mischief, longs	701	Cadenus Vaness	466
What Mischief can the <Dean> have done him,	796	Traulus 1	7
Every Mischief in their Hearts,	837	Legion Club	187
"This mischief arises from witty Dean Swift."	843	Ay and No	6
"Relentless Dean! to Mischief bent,	850	Old Thorn	58
As a good quiet Soul, who no Mischief intends	968	Letter Sherid	27
MISCHIEVOUS			
To keep mischievous Spirits out:	134	Magician's Rod	52
MISERABLE			
Pity a miserable Church's tears,	42	Ode Sancroft	243
MISERIES			
His scrap of Life is but a Heap of Miseries,	9	Ode to King	107
MISERS			
To Pan alone rich Misers call,	157	Fable of Midas	57
Their gifts, as misers do their gold;	900	Dean's Reasons	36
MISERY			
Not half thy Course of Misery is run,	793	St. Pat's Well	87
MISFORTUNE			
Grows a misfortune, or becomes a vice;	55	Temple Ill	136
Some great Misfortune to portend,	557	Death of Swift	119
Now a new Misfortune fells,	834	Legion Club	117
MISFORTUNES			
Must never our Misfortunes end?	445	Modern Lady	15
MISGUIDE			
Errors like this did old Astronomers misguide,	36	Ode Sancroft	65
MISGUIDED			
Too long have our misguided Souls been taught	27	Ode to Temple	18
MISHAP			
Fall'n by mishap amongst a knot of beaux;	50	To Congreve	216
MISLED			
So, by a Calenture misled,	251	Bubble	25
Misled them many a League about.	412	Desire Possess	16
Some by philosophers misled,	490	Dialogue	49

MISPENT
    My precious Time, so long mispent, ...   PAGE TITLE   LINE
    My precious Time, so long mispent, ...   781 Mullinix Tim   276
MISPLAC'D
    "She saw her Favour was misplac'd; . . . .   714 Cadenus Vaness   868
MISS
    As a fresh miss, by fancy, face, and gown, ...   48 To Congreve   151
    How Miss pickt ev'ry painted Card, ...   86 Hist V's House   4
    And little Miss began to cry; . . . .   128 Little House   48
    Says Nancy, I can make for Miss, ...   128 Little House   61
    She made a Song, how little Miss . . . .   150 Corinna   21
    Miss came, and peep'd at all he had. . . . .   150 Corinna   24
    Lose not your time, nor our diversion miss, ...   309 Billet Players   57
    The finest Miss . . . . . .   442 Ballyspellin   77
    If well apply'd, can hardly miss: . . . .   463 Birthday Song   84
    "Or pretty Miss has play'd the Fool, ...   497 Panegyr Swift   131
    Miss Moll the Jade will burn it blue: . . . .   588 Strephon Chloe   128
    And Millions miss, for one that hits. . . . .   640 On Poetry   2
    But tho' you miss your third Essay, ...   646 On Poetry   181
    Miss Betty, when she does a Fault, ...   694 Cadenus Vaness   242
    When Miss delights in her Spinnet, ...   710 Cadenus Vaness   736
    Or miss but a point, ...   855 Lady's Lament   140
    May break a Limb of Master or Miss. . . . .   941 Letter   22
    Poor Miss Dingley oft hath felt its Bills. . . . .   941 Letter   24
    That she makes of your verses a hoop for Miss Tam, . . 1027 Sheri Circles   27
    Miss Morice was (I can assure you 'tis true) sick: . . 1029 Dr. Helsham   12
MISS'D
    The world has wholly miss'd; . . . .   39 Ode Sancroft   160
    But when I search'd, and miss'd my Purse,. . . . . .   69 Mrs Harris Pet   13
    But Classick Authors--he ne'er miss'd 'em. . . . .   115 Bauc & Phil 2   136
    "And, if he often miss'd his Aim,' . . . .   550 Life of Swift   198
MISS'T
    The crystal Eye, alas, was miss't; . . . .   583 Young Nymph   61
MISSE'S
    Taller than Misse's by two yards, ...   87 Hist V's House   25
MISSED
    . . .I should have missed the Letter outright. . . . 1013 Swift to Sheri   4
MISSES
    Her End when Emulation misses, ...   554 Death of Swift   35
MISSING
    Next morn betimes the Bride was missing, ...   223 Prog of Love   26
    For truly John was missing too: . . . .   223 Prog of Love   40
    That, missing Fire, or missing Aim . . . .   500 Doctor Delaney   23
    That, missing Fire, or missing Aim . . . .   500 Doctor Delaney   23
MIST
    Wrapp'd in a whirlwind and a mist; . . . .   40 Ode Sancroft   195
    Who now, alas, no more is mist, ...   562 Death of Swift   247
MISTAKE
    And by a fond mistake . . . .   19 Ode Athenian   124
    Cupid shall ne'er mistake another . . . .   272 Apollo's Edict D 56
    Sir, you mistake me all this while: . . . .   298 Horrid Plot   16
    And yet there must be some Mistake. . . . .   376 Apology Lady C   48
    And quite mistake Preferment's Road. . . . .   480 Libel on D- D-   12
    For though you may mistake a Year; . . . .   558 Death of Swift   144
    Mistake our Talents ev'ry Day: . . . .   607 Beasts Confess   206
    In hopes that Strangers may mistake it, ...   734 Stel B-day '20   12
    We think you quite mistake the Case; . . . .   752 Stel Wood-Park   89
    Tim, you mistake the matter quite, ...   776 Mullinix Tim   87
    Tom, you mistake the Matter quite; . . . .   797 Traulus 1   45
    You mistake; for a Slave, who will coax his superiors, .   817 Yahoo's   68
    When you quite mistake the meaning. . . . .   908 Daphne   68
MISTAKEN
    Mistaken Ideots! see how giddily they run, ...   39 Ode Sancroft   162
    And to mistaken man these truths rehearse, ...   53 Temple Ill   69
    Lord! how were they mistaken in the Dean! . . . . .   196 Author Himself   66
    False Patience, and mistaken Pride! . . . .   221 A Quiet Life   55
    No doubt the text is here mistaken: . . . .   434 Answer Paulus   66
    I found you mistaken in Matter of Fact. . . . . . .   972 S-'s Ans Sh-d   4
MISTAKES
    And passing o'er, mistakes thee still for mine: . .   54 Temple Ill   92
    And, mistakes to prevent, I have obtain'd a Copy. . .   143 New Song   10
    <Lyndsay> mistakes the matter quite, ...   432 Answer Paulus   1
    Mistakes Vanessa for a Boy; . . . .   693 Cadenus Vaness   201
MISTER   SEE MR
    "Mister Curate, for all your grave Looks, I'm afraid,   872 Grand Question   147
MISTOOK
    And by short views mistook for all their own; . . . .   45 To Congreve   60
    That scorn of fools, by fools mistook for pride; . . .   55 Temple Ill   134
    Mistook at first for Thunder-Bolts; . . . .   353 Wood Ironmongr   34
    Or may be I mistook the Word; . . . .   376 Apology Lady C   39
    And forming you, mistook your Kind? . . . .   726 To Stella   86
    The Rascal had mistook the Door: . . . .   746 Stel Distress   28
    The Rascal had mistook the Door . . . .   746 Stel Distress
    The Rascal had mistook the Door: . . . .   751 Stel Wood-Park   48
MISTRESS
    Like a cast mistress to your wicked friend; . . . .   44 To Congreve   16
    And then return'd it to your Mistress, ...   135 Magician's Rod   82
    While Mistress Iris held her Train, ...   290 Prog Marriage   13
    Without a Mistress, hang or drown him. . . . . . .   303 Storm   16
    Your Mistress in a Glass to show, ...   401 Window Inns 2   2
    Your Mistress now is grown a Queen; . . . .   408 Dial Rich Marb   10
    The Graces and their Mistress Venus . . . .   465 Birthday Song   155

	PAGE	TITLE	LINE
MISTRESS (CONTINUED)			
The Pedant gets a Mistress by't.	710	Cadenus Vaness	743
The Friend, the Mistress, and the Wife,	728	Stella, Poems	16
Invokes his Mistress and his Muse,	728	Stella, Poems	27
A Mistress worth five thousand pound;	879	Robbin & Harry	32
Your Mistress a Share,	952	Onyons	11
MISTS			
The foggy mists dispelling	442	Ballyspellin	69
MITE			
In Cheese an individual Mite?	504	Doctor Delaney	140
Did I e'er my Mite withold	632	Epistle Lady	71
MITES			
From Elephants to Mites in Cheese,	653	On Poetry	384
MITRE			
Finding the Mitre almost grown	40	Ode Sancroft	187
Disturb the present Mitre, as that fearful storm of late,	40	Ode Sancroft	192
The Mitre, which his sacred head has worn,	40	Ode Sancroft	199
I should present you with a Mitre.	361	Grace's Answer	10
And there without a mitre dye.	491	Dialogue	56
To give him Lawn-Sleeves a Mitre and Rotchet,	518	Dean Hang Rape	45
Or, had a Mitre on his Head	560	Death of Swift	195
"A Shame, he hath not got a Mitre!	564	Death of Swift	298
And He was a Primate, and He wore a Mitre,	803	Irish Bishops	5
Now hear an Allusion!--A Mitre, you know,	805	Irish Bishops	41
That the Mitre wou'd never stick fast on their Head,	805	Irish Bishops	46
Had lately honour'd with a <Mitre>.	302	Storm	8
MITRED			
Chief of the mitred saints, and from arch-prelate here,	42	Ode Sancroft	238
Come headlong tumbling from their mitred Chariots,	806	Judas	20
For who but Lord Bolton was mitred for Merit?	808	Advice Parson	8
Dare any of the mitred Host,	820	Dr. Rundle	5
MITRES			
Mitres, and Glebes could scarce do more	493	Panegyr Swift	9
So God bless the Church, and three of our Mitres;	805	Irish Bishops	63
MIX'D			
Jove mix'd up all, and his best Clay.imploy'd;	118	Biddy Floyd	11
Bob's Spittle mix'd with Harry's <Turd>	495	Panegyr Swift	63
Where Pleasures mix'd with Pains appear,	711	Cadenus Vaness	776
Mix'd in a noble generous Mind;	731	Stella, Poems	104
MIXT			
Made up of iron mixt with clay,	39	Ode Sancroft	139
He had mixt little Wit with a great deal of Pains,	77	Lady B- B-	24
That mixt with Achelous Spring,	293	Prog Marriage	109
O what a pleasure mixt with pain!	776	Mullinix Tim	106
MIXTURE			
More than a fade insipid mixture left behind.	50	To Congreve	212
The Mixture thus by Chymick Art,	344	Prometheus	5
Then from a Clay of Mixture base	659	On Poetry	D 410
Impertinent mixture of busy and idle.	955	Portrait Life	4
MOB			
And damn'd the Mob, whom now he leads.	498	Panegyr Swift	162
Quoth Hugh of Armagh, "The mob is grown bold."	843	Ay and No	3
"But the lower the coin, the higher the mob.	843	Ay and No	12
MOBB'S			
Lest my Mobb's Mouth, being seldom quiet	373	Letter D. S-y	66
MOCK			
But here Mr. Wood complains that we Mock,	335	Serious Poem	41
That must our Expectation mock,	729	Stella, Poems	66
MOCK-HABITS			
In what Mock-habits have they put her, since the Fall!	22	Ode Athenian	219
MOCK-STATE			
When Milk-maids in mock-state	122	Empty'ng Town	6
MOCKING			
And Saunders the Man says, you are always jesting and mocking,	986	Mary to Sher	27
MOCKS			
Out starts the little Beast, and mocks their idle Fears.	30	Ode to Temple	114
A third could not forbear his Mocks,	91	Bauc & Phil 1	34
Where Echo sits, and list'ning mocks.	597	Cassinus Peter	108
But, since just Heav'n the Dukes ambition mocks	678	Dean and Duke	5
MOD'RATE			
Him we persuaded with a mod'rate bribe,	307	Billet Players	5
MODE			
So much in mode, so very city-born;	44	To Congreve	14
A Bed-sted in the antique mode	94	Bauc & Phil 1	147
A Bedstead of the Antique mode,	114	Bauc & Phil 2	101
In State-Opinions a-la Mode,	171	Horace 1, 7	35
And, then in surly Mode come here	884	Rev Market-Hill	37
MODEL			
Follow the model close, for so I'm sure they should,	40	Ode Sancroft	183
He kept the Model in his Mind.	86	Hist V's House	12
The Model in his Table-book;	87	Hist V's House	20
This Building was designed a Model,	127	Little House	36
Has form'd a Model for your Land;	272	Apollo's Edict	D 65
But form'd by You, how should their Model	496	Panegyr Swift	104
Wou'd by her Model form their Mind,	694	Cadenus Vaness	237
"A Model for her Sex design'd,	714	Cadenus Vaness	866
MODELL			
Forming his Muse by <Smedley's> Modell,	458	Paddy's Charac	23
MODELS			
For Models, made to mend our Kind,	387	Manly Virtue	115

MODERATE | PAGE | TITLE | LINE
In talking ore a moderate Glass. | 279 | Journal | 38
A Whale of moderate Size will draw | 651 | On Poetry | 323
MODERATION
To point out which is moderation, which is fortitude. | 41 | Ode Sancroft | 210
MODERN
Her Face patch't o'er with Modern Pedantry, | 23 | Ode Athenian | 224
As antient nature's modern masters dream; | 45 | To Congreve | 72
Premising thus in Modern way | 80 | Vanbrug House | 55
A Type of Modern Witt and Style, | 81 | Vanbrug House | 83
So, Modern Rhymers strive to blast | 81 | Vanbrug House | 89
As Mastive Dogs in Modern Phrase are | 82 | Salamander | 1
Premising thus in Modern way | 106 | V's House | 29
A Type of Modern Wit and Style, | 109 | V's House | 125
So Modern Rimers wisely Blast | 110 | V's House | 131
None e'er did modern Midas chuse, | 157 | Fable of Midas | 51
The hireling Senator of modern Days, | 364 | On Dreams | 35
Ne'er to be match't in modern Reading, | 398 | Earl of P-b-w | 35
The Journal of a Modern Dame, | 445 | Modern Lady | 24
Of modern Times, the Guilt is yours, | 445 | Modern Lady | 32
The modern Dame is wak'd by Noon, | 446 | Modern Lady | 38
Which modern Ladies call polite; | 448 | Modern Lady | 113
For which they bring a modern Pattern, | 460 | Birthday Song | 10
And Nastiness of modern Times, | 497 | Panegyr Swift | 117
"As modern Scroggs, or old Tressilian; | 569 | Death of Swift | 420
Which, of all our modern Dames | 631 | Epistle Lady | 67
In modern Wit all printed Trash, is | 643 | On Poetry | 93
In all our modern Cricticks Jargon.) | 648 | On Poetry | 242
And curse our modern Poetasters. | 652 | On Poetry | 348
That modern Love is no such Thing | 687 | Cadenus Vaness | 27
(To know the World! a modern Phrase, | 700 | Cadenus Vaness | 430
Like supple Patriots of the modern Sort, | 771 | Horace 1, 14 | 55
Each modern Judas perish like the first; | 806 | Judas | 21
For modern Jasons that's enuff. | 948 | Jason Hassard | 4
Of Dan's large Nose, in modern Saphick, | 993 | On Picture | 3
By modern Poets, call'd Elision; | 1021 | Nim-Dan-Dean 1 | D 12
MODERNS
(Those Bully Greeks, who, as the Moderns do, | 139 | City Shower | 49
MODEST
Of Modest Poets thou be first, | 121 | Apollo Outwit | 57
Fellows of modest Worth and Parts, | 314 | To Ford | 81
Admires how modest Women can | 417 | Woman's Mind | 47
Be Modest: nor Address your Betters | 479 | Epist on Epist | 117
As far as Modest Pride allow'd, | 482 | Libel on D- D- | 58
Less modest than the Speech of Prudes; | 691 | Cadenus Vaness | 167
A modest Youth said something new, | 701 | Cadenus Vaness | 454
MODESTER
'Twas to teach you in modester Language your Duty; | 968 | Letter Sherid | 25
MODESTLY
And first he modestly conjectures | 704 | Cadenus Vaness | 568
MODESTY
The Loveliness of Modesty, | 384 | Manly Virtue | 26
And Modesty with blushing Face; | 448 | Modern Lady | 123
Through Modesty, or aukward Shame, | 607 | Beasts Confess | 181
Which though her Modesty would shroud, | 726 | To Stella | 81
To Modesty a weak Pretence; | 887 | Panegyr Dean | 19
You found out my rebus with very much modesty; | 976 | Dean to Sherid | 37
MODICUM
Will make them welcome to his modicum: | 878 | Robbin & Harry | 24
MODISH
By the new Modish System of reducing all to sense, | 19 | Ode Athenian | 107
And some thought modish to despise. | 384 | Manly Virtue | 30
Your Poem in its modish Dress, | 643 | On Poetry | 105
MODULATE
Taught them to modulate their Tongues, | 326 | Pethox | 79
MODUS
A modus right fit for insulters of Deans. | 817 | Yahoo's | 59
MOIDORES
And all for ten poor moidores fee! | 434 | Answer Paulus | 80
MOISTNED
Can soar with moistned Wings on high, | 254 | Bubble | 86
MOISTURE   SEE MOYSTURE
(When this huge Bodies Moisture was so great | 16 | Ode Athenian | 3
MOLD
Was cast in the same Mold with mine? | 32 | Ode to Temple | 179
Nor less <Tom-T--d-Man> of true Statesman mold, | 364 | On Dreams | 21
Whose Thoughts are of a diff'rent Mold, | 485 | Libel on D- D- | 172
Must in a diff'rent Mold be cast; | 496 | Panegyr Swift | 107
Great Folks are of a finer Mold; | 949 | Epigr Scolding | 1
MOLDED
But you have molded them afresh, | 326 | Pethox | 77
He molded it with Female Clay: | 726 | To Stella | 90
MOLE
Fall a Working like a Mole, | 832 | Legion Club | 73
MOLIRIS
Qui nil moliris tam inepte? | 476 | Epist on Epist | 30
MOLL
Of Joan of France, and English Moll, | 114 | Bauc & Phil 2 | 94
Now Moll had whirl'd her Mop with dext'rous Airs, | 124 | Descriptn Morn | 7
And Brickdust Moll had Scream'd through half the Street. | 124 | Descriptn Morn | 14

MOLL (CONTINUED)

	PAGE	TITLE	LINE
Miss Moll the Jade will burn it blue:	588	Strephon Chloe	128
That Moll the Chamber-maid can smoak,	890	Panegyr Dean	127

MOLLIGHART

Och ma ceade millia mollighart, on the feeders of swine!	841	Ballad	D 19

MOLLY

If Molly happens to be careless,	417	Woman's Mind	43
And, Molly, she said, I should hear some ill News.	868	Grand Question	52
And, Molly and I have thrust in our Nose,	872	Grand Question	137

MOMENT

"And ev'ry Moment take a Dram,	305	Storm	58
Thoughtful upon a Point of Moment:	375	Apology Lady C	3
No single Tongue one Moment mute;	450	Modern Lady	177
"Your Fan, a Moment, if you please.	452	Modern Lady	243
A Prince the Moment he is crown'd,	646	On Poetry	191
Each Moment rising in her Airs,	751	Stel Wood-Park	51
You e'ry moment think an Age,	776	Mullinix Tim	107
Next Moment in the House of Peers,	788	Dick's Variety	28
Must I be every Moment chid	861	Lady Acheson	41
The Moment I get one my Soul's all a-fire,	928	Riddle 11	D 11
But the Moment that he closes,	931	Riddle 18	D 17
Like Thought I'm in a Moment gone,	935	Riddle 23	D 16
Nay, further, the Moment you're free from your scalding,	1019	To Sheridan	9

MOMENT'S

Nor gives her Tongue one Moment's Rest,	448	Modern Lady	111

MOMENTS

The few soft Moments they can spare,	687	Cadenus Vaness	42

MONARCH

You, Mighty Monarch, Nobler Actions Crown,	11	Ode to William	D 3
Riches, the Wisest Monarch sings,	239	Run Bankers	21
The greatest monarch may be stabb'd by night,	506	To a Friend	1
"That Ruin'd Church and Monarch too.	549	Life of Swift	157
Fair Britain in thy Monarch blest,	655	On Poetry	411
A griping Monarch, or a Jew.	658	On Poetry	D 164
How is the greatest Monarch blest,	916	Riddle 2	3
Emblem of a monarch old,	936	Riddle 24	D 19
I'll give my <Monarch> Butter-weight.	657	On Poetry	488

MONARCH-OAKS

Behold those Monarch-Oaks that rise,	393	Modern Poets	1

MONARCH'S

The Law so strictly guards the Monarch's Health,	533	To Mr. Gay	77
(A Monarch's Right) on Grubstreet Line.	642	On Poetry	58
Lay humbly at your Monarch's Feet;	647	On Poetry	224
His griesly Monarch's sooty Fist,	903	Death Daphne	4
So, to effect his <Monarch's> ends,	486	Libel on D- D-	185
Against the Grain, a <Monarch's> Fist?	884	Rev Market-Hill	34

MONARCHIES

Virtue, the greatest of all Monarchies,	26	Ode to Temple	1

MONARCHS

(Cowards are Monarchs by that Title made)	11	Ode to William	D 10
The Thoughts of Monarchs, and Designs of States,	30	Ode to Temple	105
Some call their Monarchs Sons of Saturn,	460	Birthday Song	9
Held Monarchs labouring at the Oar;	476	Epist on Epist	44

MONARCHY

At Monarchy we nobly shew our Spight,	163	Toland's Invit	15
"But, still our Monarchy wou'd leave us---.	549	Life of Swift	155

MONDAY

"Last Monday to the Pastry-cooks.	563	Death of Swift	260

MONDE   SEE GRAND-MONDE

MONEY   SEE MONY, HUSH-MONEY

. . .six Pence, besides Farthings, in Money, and Gold;	69	Mrs Harris Pet	2
I was resolved to tell my Money, to see if it was right:	69	Mrs Harris Pet	4
Therefore all the Money, I have, which, God knows,. . .	69	Mrs Harris Pet	6
. . .my Money was as safe as my Maidenhead.	69	Mrs Harris Pet	11
. . .ty'd in a Rag, the Money was found.	70	Mrs Harris Pet	23
'Tis not that I value the Money three Skips of a Louse	71	Mrs Harris Pet	38
That tho' 'tis hard to judge, yet Money can't go without Hands.	71	Mrs Harris Pet	43
If your Money be gone, as a Learned Divine says, d'ye see,	72	Mrs Harris Pet	56
I have lost my Money, and shall lose my True-Love too.	73	Mrs Harris Pet	65
With borrow'd Money in his Purse;	173	Horace 1, 7	94
Or is your Money out at use?--	175	Horace 1, 7	129
Their Journy long, their Money short;	224	Prog of Love	76
His Money spent, his Patrons fail,	231	Prog of Poetry	33
And as he saw his darling Money fail,	235	Elegy on Demar	33
His other Self, his Money lay.	235	Elegy on Demar	48
Money, the Life-blood of the Nation,	239	Run Bankers	9
We want our Money on the Nail;	239	Run Bankers	17
No Money left for squandring Heirs!	240	Run Bankers	25
What Magick makes our Money rise	250	Bubble	2
Put in Your Money fairly told;	251	Bubble	5
His Credit sunk, his Money spent,	252	Bubble	47
And then get off with Money stor'd,	253	Bubble	62
The whole Nations Pockets with Money will fill.	287	Bank Down	13
And Paper makes Money, and what can be cheaper?	287	Bank Down	23
As they did in old Times, make Money of Leather,	287	Bank Down	27
To turn to small Money a Bill on the Bank.	288	Bank Down	35
And lent them for Money the Backs of his Letters:	288	Bank Down	43
But vow'd his Money all was spent;	294	Prog Marriage	126
His Money spent! a clownish Reason?	294	Prog Marriage	127

MONEY   (CONTINUED)   PAGE   TITLE   LINE
    His Money and her Time employs . . . .   294 Prog Marriage   135
    Then if cutting down Wood brings Money good Store,   .   334 Serious Poem   15
    Our Money to keep, let us Cut down One more.   . . .   334 Serious Poem   16
    . . . who all in Money wallows, ...   342 Upon His Grace   15
    He bids me then to hold my Tongue, and up the Money   342 Upon His Grace   25
      locks,
    Dissolv'd, and into Money Coin'd;   . . . . . .   345 Prometheus   38
    Men of more Wit than Money, our Pensions will fit   .   389 Order of Bath   7
    And this will suit Men of more Money than Wit.   . .   389 Order of Bath   8
    What Money was behind him found? . . . .   547 Life of Swift   72
    Procure the Book for Love or Money, ...   648 On Poetry   260
    Thy credit sunk, thy money spent, ...   676 Parson's Case   10
    That Meat must be with Money bought;   . . . . .   693 Cadenus Vaness   214
    When all her little Money spent, ...   747 Stel Distress   54
    When Shells and Leather shall for Money pass,   . .   793 St. Pat's Well   93
    Be gone: Thy Money perish with thee.   . . . . .   821 Dr. Rundle   48
    My money spent is, ...   1037 Sheridan Cavan   3
MONEY-BAGS
    His Money-Bags together sow'd.   235 Elegy on Demar   44
MONEY-JOB
    "it's matter of weight, and a mere money-job;   . . .   843 Ay and No   11
MONEY-LEAGUE
    And Marriage grown a Money-League.   . . . . . .   687 Cadenus Vaness   14
MONEY'S
    Now all the Doctor's Money's spent, ...   174 Horace 1, 7   107
    No matter where the Money's found;   . . . . . .   199 Horace 2, 6   20
MONEYS
    Tho' Moneys scarce we shou'd have Trade enough;   . . .   275 Epilogue   32
MONGERS   SEE LOGICK-MONGERS
MONGRIL   SEE MUNGRIL
    But all turn Leasers to that Mongril Breed,   . . .   794 St. Pat's Well   95
'MONGST
    If Wood's Coin should 'mongst Us pass   . . . . .   372 Letter D. S-y   35
MONITIONS
    But, after sage Monitions from his Friends,   . . .   194 Author Himself   23
MONK
    Like a Monk in a cell.   . . . .   939 Riddle Answerd   D
MONKEY
    A squinting Monkey load with charms;   . . . . .   464 Birthday Song   121
    Shou'd a Monkey wear a Crown, ...   634 Epistle Lady   149
    Intrude with Monkey grin, and clatter   . . . . .   777 Mullinix Tim   143
    The Monkey, who had seen the World.   . . . . .   782 Tim and Fables   8
    The Monkey was compleatly drest, ...   782 Tim and Fables   11
    No other Monkey half so brisk;   . . . .   788 Dick's Variety   26
    To catch a Monkey by a Wile;   . . . .   885 Rev Market-Hill   76
MONKEYS
    Hark, the Monkeys, how the prate!   . . . .   832 Legion Club   82
MONKS
    Of Chastity, as Monks do now;   . . . .   603 Beasts Confess   70
MONSIEUR
    As we say, Monsieur, to an Ape   . . . .   83 Salamander   5
MONSTER
    Has lull'd the Monster in a Deep   . . . . . .   8 Ode to King   79
    She durst behold that Monster, Man: . . . . .   222 Prog of Love   12
    The Monster into Parts divide, ...   258 Bubble   203
    My Fancy drags this Monster to my View, ...   532 To Mr. Gay   37
    "A wicked Monster on the Bench, ...   569 Death of Swift   417
    Cou'd Horace give so sad a Monster Birth,   . . .   669 Epig Carthy 16   D   1
    Every Monster should be painted;   . . . . . .   839 Legion Club   222
MONSTER'S
    You strait stept in, and from the Monster's Jaws   . .   12 Ode to William   D 23
MONSTERS
    Where painted Monsters are hung out.   . . . . .   172 Horace 1, 7   60
    The Monsters nestle in the Deep   . . . . . .   257 Bubble   175
    Among ye savage Monsters crown'd   . . . . . .   659 On Poetry   D 410
MONSTROUS
    He built up such a monstrous Pile, ...   87 Hist V's House   28
    But Six-pence a Letter is monstrous high Wages;   . .   288 Bank Down   48
    It was a Tow'r of monstrous Height, ...   413 Desire Possess   40
    How monstrous Carthy looks to Flaccus brac't,   . .   668 Epig Carthy 9   D   1
    In at the door his monstrous Nose, ...   776 Mullinix Tim   104
MONTAGUE
    While Montague, who claim'd the Station   . . . .   481 Libel on D- D-   35
    <Montague> Learning, <Bolton> Eloquence: . . . .   164 Toland's Invit   24
MONTAIGNE
    Vanessa held Montaigne, and read, ...   698 Cadenus Vaness   372
MONTEZUME
    Like Montezume in golden Chains: . . . . . .   885 Rev Market-Hill   72
MONTH
    In half a Month she looks so thin   . . . . . .   229 Prog of Beauty   98
    And in a Month he's at your Gates;   . . . . .   282 Journal   108
    "Ye have forgot this Month and Day.--   . . . . .   322 First of April   56
    Poor Pope will grieve a Month; and Gay   . . . .   561 Death of Swift   207
    Tho' Chickens take a Month to fatten, ...   642 On Poetry   62
    Phyllis, who but a Month ago . . . .   699 Cadenus Vaness   392
    After a Week, a Month, a Quarter, ...   860 Lady Acheson   9
    For I heard, a month ago, that he was down there . . .   1023 Nim-Dan-Dean 2   D 12
MONTH'S
    When the whole month's Allowance gone . . . . . .   747 Stel Distress

522

		PAGE	TITLE	LINE
MONTHS				
To spend six Months with Statesmen here.		199	Horace 2, 6	12
To live without both full three Months he try'd,		430	Dicky Dolly	11
Her Time was not till Nine Months hence.		586	Strephon Chloe	66
MONUMENT				
Was like keeping her Monument always in sight.		144	New Song	38
A golden Monument would not be Right,		234	Elegy on Demar	23
A Monument to after-Times:		596	Cassinus Peter	76
And sure, as monument of brass,		876	To Dean Swift	11
MONY				
We spent our Mony and our Blood,		169	Peace Dunkirk	33
MOOD				
The Owl foresaw in pensive Mood		849	Old Thorn	37
MOODY				
To rattle Moody for Neglect;		411	Dial Rich Marb	96
MOON SEE HONEY-MOON				
Nor hid himself behind the Moon,		98	Elegy Patrige	13
The Horned Moon which heretofore		99	Elegy Patrige	35
Consider where the Moon and Stars		100	Elegy Patrige	97
'Twixt earthly Femals and the Moon		226	Prog of Beauty	9
Send us new Nymphs with each new Moon.		229	Prog of Beauty	120
An Ass hath swallow'd up the Moon,		253	Bubble	79
The Moon lay safe behind the Cloud.		253	Bubble	80
To change your Visage like the Moon,		326	Pethox	82
Affirm'd the Moon was sick, and fell		354	Simile Silver	7
The Moon, deliver'd from her Pain,		354	Simile Silver	13
The Moon is Silver all this while.)		354	Simile Silver	16
Be a New Sun, and a New Moon.		362	Grace's Answer	52
As long as Sun and Moon endure.		655	On Poetry	436
MOON-FULL				
'Tis of Shine, a Mouth Moon-full,		1015	Swift to Sheri	49
MOON-SHINE				
So when upon a Moon-shine Night		253	Bubble	73
MOON'S				
Efficient of the Moon's Decay,		228	Prog of Beauty	90
O'er the Moon's Face a sable Hue,		354	Simile Silver	2
MOONS				
For in twice twelve revolving Moons,		150	Corinna	14
MOOR				
Smart Jemmy Moor with Vigor drops,		654	On Poetry	399
Or Mr. <Moor> will take it ill.		860	Lady Acheson	28
MOORE				
Revis'd by Tibbalds, Moore, and Cibber.		561	Death of Swift	200
Whose Master, Moore, preserv'd him from the Halter,		826	Noisy Tom	13
MOORLANDS				
To Moorlands of a diff'rent Parish.		645	On Poetry	174
MOP				
Now Moll had whirl'd her Mop with dext'rous Airs,		124	Descriptn Morn	7
Flirts on you from her Mop, but not so clean.		137	City Shower	20
To rail; she singing, still whirls on her Mop.		137	City Shower	22
Like a very foul mop, dirty more than they clean.		819	Archbi Cashel	16
MOPSA				
Mopsa, who stinks her Spouse to Death,		449	Modern Lady	156
-----I'm sorry Mopsa breaks so fast;		699	Cadenus Vaness	386
MOPUS				
I'm grown a meer Mopus; no Company comes;		867	Grand Question	27
MORAL				
Here ends the Fable and the Moral.		189	Faggot	14
As Poets fein; but where's the Moral?		254	Bubble	94
The Moral of this Tale is proper,		353	Wood Ironmongr	31
The Moral is so plain to hit,		393	Modern Poets	17
And now to' exemplifie this Moral,		458	Paddy's Charac	13
The Moral of the Tale is pleasant,		514	Answer Fable	51
Yet bears a Moral when apply'd to you		538	Mr. Pulteney	16
"As with a moral View design'd		565	Death of Swift	313
I own, the Moral not exact;		607	Beasts Confess	197
The merry Tale with moral Grave.		783	Tim and Fables	27
MORALIST				
A Moralist might here explain		252	Bubble	41
A Moralist profoundly sage,		412	Desire Possess	5
Wherein the Moralist design'd		608	Beasts Confess	217
MORALISTS				
Of tedious Moralists describe,		724	To Stella	16
MORALIZE				
And sweetly moralize a while.		894	Panegyr Dean	228
MORALS				
Of Morals and Divinity,		19	Ode Athenian	106
With Rules from musty Morals brought,		27	Ode to Temple	19
And idle Morals in the Schools		493	Panegyr Swift	30
Indeed, the Strictness of his Morals		603	Beasts Confess	51
Quote you Texts from Plutarch's Morals;		637	Epistle Lady	236
On Plutarch's Morals struck, were spoil'd.		701	Cadenus Vaness	483
That he came from the Temple, his morals do show,		815	Yahoo's	11
The Man has Learning, Sense and Morals.		820	Dr. Rundle	22
Drown your Morals, Madam cryes;		863	To Janus	19
MORDANTO				
Mordanto fills the Trump of Fame,		397	Earl of P-b-w	1
Mordanto in a Week from Spain.		398	Earl of P-b-w	12
Mordanto at Madrid to seek:		398	Earl of P-b-w	14
Mordanto gallops on alone,		398	Earl of P-b-w	19

MORDANTO'S
   Mordanto's landed from Leghorn. . . . .   398 Earl of P-b-w   18
MORE

	PAGE	TITLE		LINE
And the Dove-muse is fled once more,	17	Ode Athenian		32
Ne'er borrow'd more variety of Shapes	22	Ode Athenian		199
More oft in Fools and Mad-mens hands than Sages	23	Ode Athenian		220
Let us (for shame) no more be fed	27	Ode to Temple		21
More than your Predecessor, Adam, knew;	31	Ode to Temple		162
Some more ambitiously upwards fly,	32	Ode to Temple		173
The muse and I no more revenge desire,	37	Ode Sancroft		90
(Were his humanity on earth once more)	38	Ode Sancroft		133
But wicked kings draw more examples than the good;	40	Ode Sancroft		184
Or a more worthy subject chuse:	42	Ode Sancroft		260
I once esteem'd, and lov'd, and favour'd more,	44	To Congreve		12
But can no more obscure my Congreve's light	45	To Congreve		80
Time is no more when th' utmost drop is past;	49	To Congreve		190
More than a fade insipid mixture left behind.	50	To Congreve		212
Or more employ the Female Sex?	65	Problem		2
So you know, what could I say to her any more,	71	Mrs Harris Pet		46
. . .it might become you to be more civil:	72	Mrs Harris Pet		55
Or if his Grace were no more skilld in	88	Hist V's House		45
But what adds to the Wonder more,	93	Bauc & Phil 1		129
Your Goodness more than my Desert	94	Bauc & Phil 1		159
Patrige is Dead, nay more, he dy'd	98	Elegy Patrige		3
Have in More Fields their Stations fix,	101	Elegy Patrige		100
Then olde Inglonde shall be noe more.	103	Merlin		17
The Scene, a Wood, produc'd no more	108	V's House		83
And, what exalts the Wonder more,	113	Bauc & Phil 2		69
More probably than all the rest;	128	Little House		44
Her Frolicks, and pursues her Tail no more.	136	City Shower		4
You'll spend in Coach-hire more than save in Wine.	137	City Shower		8
That swill'd more Liquor than it could contain,	137	City Shower		15
There shall be Peace, pardie, and War no more.	147	Windsor Proph		12
For fear He shou'd dispatch more,	153	Widow and Cat	D	17
Hal -- grows more Pert, and <Somers> not so Grave:	163	Toland's Invit		22
Will hardly fail, and there is room for more:	166	Toland's Invit		36
The Dutch from hence shall no more Millions drain;	169	Peace Dunkirk		27
We'll bring on us no more Debts,	169	Peace Dunkirk		28
But more inclining to sit still.	170	Horace 1, 7		12
No Man alive has more Respect--	173	Horace 1, 7		70
Well, I shall think of that no more,	173	Horace 1, 7		71
What friendship dicates more than wit.	176	To Lord Harley		4
But more than that, thou'lt keep a rout	180	Horace 2, 1		13
Should you live years forty more	187	Scriblerus 4	D	17
What could he more, but decently retire?	196	Author Himself		74
Well, now I have all this and more,	198	Horace 2, 6		7
I can't but think 'twould sound more clever,	198	Horace 2, 6	D	
It is but so much more in Debt,	200	Horace 2, 6		21
Tells me i have more Zeal than Wit,	200	Horace 2, 6		36
'Tis (let me see) three Years and more,	201	Horace 2, 6		63
I know no more than my Lord Mayor,	202	Horace 2, 6		102
From whom I once expected more;	204	In Sickness		16
Or what I should repine at more,	215	To Mr. Delany		7
Do not more differ in their Breed,	217	To Mr. Delany		62
And I no more shall then Accuse	219	To Mr. Delany		109
At sight of Will she bawl'd no more,	220	A Quiet Life		7
But what Adventures more befell 'um	224	Prog of Beauty		85
A more inferior Station seeks	227	Prog of Beauty		34
She knows her Early self no more,	227	Prog of Beauty		49
With Pow'r no more than other Folk,	240	Run Bankers		35
With Forty Things more: Now hear what the Law says,	236	Excellent Song		3
At Market for a Farthing more	255	Bubble		118
The Bird of Jove shall toil no more,	270	Apollo's Edict	D	25
The Poet had no more who made the Play.	274	Epilogue		10
We squander there an Hour and more,	279	Journal		17
But now there need no more be said on't,	282	Journal		86
But showed no more than half her Face	290	Prog Marriage		16
And teach her to despise thee more	292	Prog Marriage		76
"<He> can assume more Forms than I,	303	Storm		29
All this and more, yet it would do no good.	308	Billet Players		42
"Can we do more than what she does.	322	First of April		52
Our Money to keep, let us Cut down One more.	334	Serious Poem		16
That none are more properly Knights of the Post.	335	Serious Poem		40
More Heathenish Times than those of our own!	335	Serious Poem		60
Strong Tubs for his Raps, Two thousand and more;	337	Serious Poem		96
We never say more than, your Love is a Million;	337	Serious Poem		104
Hear one Story more and then I will stop.	337	Serious Poem		109
. . . Ten thousand Pounds and more:	341	Upon His Grace		10
For he regards Ten thousand Pounds no more than Woods's Dross.	341	Upon His Grace		12
He makes no more to give ten Pounds than I to give a Pin.	341	Upon His Grace		14
She need be no more with the Jaundice possess't;	351	Wood Insect		15
For which Operation there's nothing more proper	351	Wood Insect		35
Now let's no more caress thy French,	373	Letter D. S-y		64
As when Time serves, you more shall know.	373	Letter D. S-y		78
Which made it more surprizing how	376	Apology Lady C		17
Thought it more courtly and discreet,	379	Apology Lady C		111
To make his Merit more discern'd,	384	Manly Virtue		31
To shine the more still rising higher)	385	Manly Virtue		54
Yet more display'd, and rais'd his own.	386	Manly Virtue		88

	PAGE	TITLE	LINE
I must have another of Colour more gay	389	Order of Bath	3
Men of more Wit than Money, our Pensions will fit	389	Order of Bath	7
And this will suit Men of more Money than Wit.	389	Order of Bath	8
If this be true, then how much more,	392	Young's Satire	27
Prize Classicks more than Sacred writ:	392	Young's Satire	40
Or more to show the Thing I mean,	393	Modern Poets	9
Could give him more Delight.	395	Grub-Street	16
Quoth the Dog, I should then be more Villain than you're,	395	Dog and Thief	3
For those who more will need 'em,	406	Swift to Pope	10
She'll come no more beneath your Roof.	408	Dial Rich Marb	12
No more the Dean, that grave Divine,	409	Dial Rich Marb	43
And steal my Artichokes no more;	409	Dial Rich Marb	46
Poor Patty Blount no more be seen	409	Dial Rich Marb	47
And here no more will dangle Pope.	409	Dial Rich Marb	50
More virtues in a Woman's Mind,	417	Woman's Mind	58
To morrow I shall tell you more,	423	Ireld	61
They'll be no more like Graces,	425	Five Ladies	15
But for a more substantial cause:	433	Answer Paulus	21
'Tis wise, no doubt, as clients fat ye more,	433	Answer Paulus	41
More Beaus can kill	441	Ballyspellin	35
No more let fall those precious Tears.	445	Modern Lady	18
Should be more scrup'lous than a Heathen.	461	Birthday Song	26
What tho for fifteen years and more	462	Birthday Song	49
And will be so much more your Debter	463	Birthday Song	89
And take it right, it means no more	464	Birthday Song	139
And Patience can endure no more	468	Birthday Song	245
With Capitals, the more the better.	469	Birthday Song	280
How could I more enhaunce it's Fame?	470	Burning Poem	15
When Things of more Importance press:	475	Epist on Epist	2
That you can't fail of more Provision,	478	Epist on Epist	99
For the more Livings you can fish up,	478	Epist on Epist	101
A Countenance with more Constraint.	480	Libel on D- D-	20
Consider how much more is due	483	Libel on D- D-	93
Wou'd, if he durst, be more your Friend;	483	Libel on D- D-	114
To <Walpole's> more than <Royal> Will..	484	Libel on D- D-	122
Can differ more than God and <Kings>	486	Libel on D- D-	196
Mitres, and Glebes could scarce do more	493	Panegyr Swift	9
That Men of Wit can be no more	493	Panegyr Swift	25
But form'd more perfect Gamester, you	494	Panegyr Swift	37
More precious far than ev'n the Gift	494	Panegyr Swift	47
A Composition more absurd,	495	Panegyr Swift	62
More beneficial Ways than Rhime;	495	Panegyr Swift	67
To add more Dignity and Light	497	Panegyr Swift	122
And curse his wicked Burthen more	497	Panegyr Swift	140
And Kings are now no more than Men;	498	Panegyr Swift	164
And dread no more the Rage of Grub,	502	Doctor Delaney	63
You but oblige 'em so much more:	505	Doctor Delaney	156
Would vex one more a thousand Times.	505	Doctor Delaney	166
One Clincher more, and I have done,	515	Answer Fable	101
But she valu'd her Honour much more than her Life.	517	Dean Hang Rape	10
That you who know musick no more than as ass	522	St. Cecilia's	2
He lifts the Lid, there needs no more,	528	Lady's Dres Rm	81
Their Passions not more impotent and cold,	532	To Mr. Gay	21
A faithful Treas'rer! What could he do more?	533	To Mr. Gay	75
Is humbly pray'd to ruin Twenty more.	535	To Mr. Gay	106
And trust his Honesty just so much more.	535	To Mr. Gay	114
For, Vengeance more embroils, than Skill repairs.	536	To Mr. Gay	140
The Court invited more than One, or Two;	536	To Mr. Gay	151
Resolv'd that Will. and he should meet no more;	537	Mr. Pulteney	3
Behold a Foe more fierce than all the rest.	538	Mr. Pulteney	32
That's more than ever I discern'd---;	547	Life of Swift	77
Their Goodness, more than his Desert---.	547	Life of Swift	87
I say no more---, because he's dead---.	549	Life of Swift	143
"That Church and State had suffer'd more	549	Life of Swift	150
"More favour'd, than the Church by Law:	550	Life of Swift	169
To praise Queen Anne, nay more, defend her,	550	Life of Swift	186
This Maxim more than all the rest	553	Death of Swift	5
More Sense than I can do in Six:	555	Death of Swift	50
Arbuthnot is no more my Friend,	555	Death of Swift	55
And more lament, when I was dead,	557	Death of Swift	141
"I know no more than what the News is,	558	Death of Swift	155
No Loss more easy to supply.	562	Death of Swift	244
Who now, alas, no more is mist,	562	Death of Swift	247
"Because no Age could more deserve it.	571	Death of Swift	458
No more of Jove's Designs than you)	579	Day Judgement	18
And I resent these Pranks no more.	579	Day Judgement	20
The bashful Nymph no more withstands,	585	Strephon Chloe	43
But, after Marriage, practise more	588	Strephon Chloe	141
And, Chloe more experienc'd grown,	590	Strephon Chloe	213
More than from all the World beside.	591	Strephon Chloe	254
Oh Peter, wou'd it were no more!	595	Cassinus Peter	46
She loves a more deserving Swain.	595	Cassinus Peter	66
For Jupiter allows no more)	598	Problem Solved	18
(Which therefore made them more devout)	601	Beasts Confess	6
When I no more a Pen can brandish.	611	By Dr. Swift	4
More to my Praise than all my Volumes;	611	By Dr. Swift	10
In hopes to make you more devout;	617	Scandal Poem 1	8
The more she scolds, the more she's cloudy.	617	Scandal Poem 1	14
The more she scolds, the more she's cloudy.	617	Scandal Poem 1	14

	PAGE	TITLE	LINE
No Goddess could have pleas'd him more.	619	Scandal Poem 1	56
That Dido smitt, might more caress him	619	Scandal Poem 1	68
If ever you provoke us more.	622	Scandal Poem 1	174
And only makes you more devout.	624	Scandal Poem 2	8
The more she scolds, the more she's cloudy.	624	Scandal Poem 2	14
The more she scolds, the more she's cloudy.	624	Scandal Poem 2	14
No Goodness could have pleas'd him more,	625	Scandal Poem 2	52
That Dido might the more caress him:	625	Scandal Poem 2	64
Those, and twenty Follies more,	630	Epistle Lady	9
Give no more to ev'ry Guest,	633	Epistle Lady	125
Scorn torments them more than Spight.	634	Epistle Lady	146
Thought no Method more commodious,	637	Epistle Lady	225
Will more than half a Score devour.	642	On Poetry	64
Gone, to be never heard of more,	642	On Poetry	69
In Homer more than Homer knew.	643	On Poetry	104
To spring more profitable Game.	646	On Poetry	184
Then talk with more authentick Face,	648	On Poetry	243
How Genius is no more rewarded;	652	On Poetry	350
In Bulk there are not more Degrees,	653	On Poetry	383
Concannen, more aspiring Bard,	654	On Poetry	397
Carthy, no more insult Aurelian's Name,	668	Epig Carthy 10	D 1
No more I hear my Church's Bell,	674	His Deafness	3
At Thunder now no more I start,	674	His Deafness	5
I rode four more to great St. Mary;	675	Curate's Compl	3
His wings are clipp't; he tryes no more in vain	678	Dean and Duke	7
Since he no more can build, and plant, & revell,	678	Dean and Duke	9
Pallas had done more Harm than Good;	700	Cadenus Vaness	435
Some Lines, more moving than the rest,	703	Cadenus Vaness	520
Cadenus now no more appears	703	Cadenus Vaness	528
For tho' she seem'd to listen more	704	Cadenus Vaness	564
Display'd her Eloquence the more:	709	Cadenus Vaness	715
Much to her Praise, more to his Own.	711	Cadenus Vaness	765
"Or add some Grains of Folly more	714	Cadenus Vaness	874
(We won't dispute a Year or more)	721	Stel B-Day '18	2
Was more than for her Sex was fit;	723	To Stella	2
She suffers hourly more than me,	726	To Stella	104
Conviction does but more incense;	730	Stella, Poems	91
His Valour would no more employ;	731	Stella, Poems	123
Or, if with more than usual Pain,	741	Stel B-day 22	7
Nor can be more securely plac't	747	Stel Distress	63
Nor can be more securely plac't	752	Stel Wood-Park	79
She wants assistance more than I;	754	Stella '23	16
Once more the <Dean> supplies their Place.	757	Stel B-day '24	14
You'll be no more your former You;	760	Receipt Youth	38
And please her more to hear them tattle	762	Bec's B-Day	55
A better and more pleasing Thought,	764	Stel B-day '26	10
Although we now can form no more	764	Stel B-day '26	15
Look to thy Self, and be no more the Sport	770	Horace 1, 14	11
Was more abhor'd, and scorn'd by those	775	Mullinix Tim	53
No more my dear Delightful way tread,	779	Mullinix Tim	183
No more--In mark of true Affection	779	Mullinix Tim	207
Dear Tim, no more such angry Speeches,	783	Tim and Fables	35
As you grew more degenerate and base,	792	St. Pat's Well	53
Here, for an Age and more, improv'd their Vein,	793	St. Pat's Well	71
I wish I could find him out one more commodious.	803	Irish Bishops	12
(And, Parsons tell us, no Man can do more)	806	Judas	6
Have Hearts more harden'd than Egyptians;	813	Bro Protestant	52
More like to lampooning than pleading at bar.	815	Yahoo's	14
While his own ass's Zaggs were more fit for the shears.	816	Yahoo's	49
If still your foul bosom more rancour contains;	819	Archbi Casnel	12
Say then more than they; nay, lavishly flatter,	819	Archbi Casnel	13
Like a very foul mop, dirty more than they clean.	819	Archbi Casnel	16
He's still a Christian more than they.	820	Dr. Rundle	20
There is a Reason still more weighty;	820	Dr. Rundle	23
Is more secure as well as legal.	821	Dr. Rundle	58
Could have more offended her Nose;	834	Legion Club	126
I can shew two hundred more.	839	Legion Club	238
To seek a more secure Retreat.	849	Old Thorn	40
"Dy'st on a more ignoble Tree,	851	Old Thorn	86
No more need be said on't,	857	Lady's Lament	201
No more in the spleen:	858	Lady's Lament	220
And you and the Dean no more shall combine,	867	Grand Question	15
To build a House five Hundred more.	875	Drapier's Hill	8
My Love to Sheelah is more firmly fixt	880	Pastoral Dial	9
No more that Bry'r thy tender Leg shall rake:	881	Pastoral Dial	17
Him on my Lap you never more should see;	882	Pastoral Dial	47
His Slaves have ten Times more than he.	884	Rev Market-Hill	28
To mortify the Creature more,	886	Rev Market-Hill	103
Nine such Champions as the <Dean>,	887	Panegyr Dean	9
To Works of more exalted Kind.	893	Panegyr Dean	198
Shall creep no more behind a Bush;	893	Panegyr Dean	214
Are sent up Off'rings more sincere	896	Panegyr Dean	296
Am more diverted with a quibble	900	Dean's Reasons	61
Never woman more devis'd	906	Daphne	5
But will never more advise thee.	907	Daphne	52
Lest it may more quarrels breed	907	Daphne	53
Never more will I suppose	908	Daphne	69
You no more at me shall fret,	908	Daphne	71
Can shew more different Hues than I;	911	Aenigma	4
And then, with Heart more hard than Stone,	915	Riddle 1	13

MORE	(CONTINUED)	PAGE	TITLE	LINE
To vex me more, he took a Freak,		915	Riddle 1	15
And still, the more I show my Art,		920	Riddle 6	17
The more they open every Heart.		920	Riddle 6	18
More precious Juice than from a Still.		920	Riddle 6	22
One Property more I would have you remark,		928	Riddle 11	D 9
No Lady was ever more fond of a Spark;		928	Riddle 11	D 10
Add to them ten thousand more,		931	Riddle 18	D 24
Affirm, can't glow to more Delight.		932	Riddle 19	D 10
Are all my parents more than he:		936	Riddle 24	D 4
Make the fairest look more fair;		936	Riddle 24	D 6
Because she let's out more, than e'er she takes in.		972	S-'s Ans Sh-d	6
Or fit more exact than one eye and one rhyme.		980	Tho: Sheridan	4
He has more Goodnes in his little Finger,		985	Mary to Sher	9
Whereof I cou'd say more to your Verses,		987	Mary to Sher	37
More Wit and Humour than from Terence.		988	Letter Dr Sh-n	4
More than the Dirt beneath my Shoes, nor fear it.		1003	Dan J's Reply	15
But now I can write no more,		1014	Swift to Sheri	12
With me you'll no more have a Stomach to Dine		1017	Swift Ans Sher	15
Tho' I dare you to more than quadruple Alliance?		1019	To Sheridan	2
Like Walls, more lasting without Mortar;		1021	Nim-Dan-Dean 1	D 22
All must allow, your Numbers more,		1022	Nim-Dan-Dean 1	D 49
Oh! I forgot too, I believe there may be one more,		1023	Nim-Dan-Dean 2	D 9
If I write any more, it will make my poor Muse sick.		1030	Dr. Sheridan	1
Would you get still more?		1038	Sheridan Cavan	13
MORE'S				
Will purchase me, the more's the Pity,		410	Dial Rich Marb	68
MORES				
O tempora, O mores! as 'tis in the adage.		975	Dean to Sherid	2
MORGAN				
Bless us, Morgan! Art thou there Man?		837	Legion Club	189
Dreadful Sight! What learned Morgan		838	Legion Club	193
Morgan! Would it not surprise one?		838	Legion Club	205
MORICE				
Miss Morice was (I can assure you 'tis true) sick:		1029	Dr. Helsham	12
MORN				
The Royal Rose the glory of our morn,		37	Ode Sancroft	105
Thus the bright Empress of the Morn		178	To Lord Harley	65
Next morn betimes the Bride was missing,		223	Prog of Love	26
Where Childless wives crowd ev'ry morn		293	Prog Marriage	119
This morn the God of Wit and Joke,		320	First of April	1
And rides through Dover in the Morn:		398	Earl of P-b-w	17
A frosty Morn--Past Four a-Clock.		453	Modern Lady	283
Must ev'ry Morn her Limbs unite.		583	Young Nymph	66
The Men should slave at Cards from Morn to Night;		662	Upon Ladies	7
Dear Pallas, I have been this Morn		692	Cadenus Vaness	188
In at the Pantry-door this Morn I slipt,		881	Pastoral Dial	29
By you instructed ev'ry Morn,		891	Panegyr Dean	132
Or gilding in a sunny Morn		896	Panegyr Dean	305
MORNE				
An herdie Chiftan, woe the morne		103	Merlin	7
MORNING				
So next Morning we told Whittle, and he fell a Swearing		70	Mrs Harris Pet	24
When, Behold the next Morning, a wonderful Riddle,		77	Lady B- B-	8
Either at Morning, or at Meals;		173	Horace 1, 7	78
Her weighty Morning Bus'ness o'er		291	Prog Marriage	55
That he sent to all three a Challenge next morning.		327	Epigram 1	8
Can, at her Morning Tea, run o'er		416	Woman's Mind	23
"And was not Tom this Morning sent?		451	Modern Lady	200
"This Morning when the Parson came,		452	Modern Lady	238
Like Females o'er their Morning Tea.		501	Doctor Delaney	50
Corinna in the Morning dizen'd,		583	Young Nymph	73
Fair weather when the morning breaks,		618	Scandal Poem 1	30
Observe our visage in a morning;		619	Scandal Poem 1	47
Fair Weather, when the Morning breaks;		624	Scandal Poem 2	24
Observe our Figure in a Morning;		625	Scandal Poem 2	43
From morning till night,		852	Lady's Lament	18
And waits on the Captain betimes the next Morning.		869	Grand Question	70
'Twas a sad rainy Night--but the Morning is fine--		869	Grand Question	74
"he caught me one Morning coquetting his Wife,		873	Grand Question	167
Is a damnable Smell both Morning and Night.		942	Probatur Alit	30
By riding this morning too long in your car:		976	Dean to Sherid	28
MORNING-DAWN				
But, with the Morning-Dawn, resumes		132	Magician's Rod	19
MORNING-DRAUGHTS				
His Morning-Draughts 'till Noon can swill,		231	Prog of Poetry	19
MORNING-HOURS				
Three Morning-Hours you toss and shake		892	Panegyr Dean	179
MORNING-PEEP				
Up at his Forge by Morning-peep,		352	Wood Ironmongr	3
MORNINGS				
Ere Mornings dawn stole out to spy		63	Discovery	35
To take, his mornings Cup of Gin.		659	On Poetry	D 410
MORNS				
Appearing, show'd the Ruddy Morns Approach.		124	Descriptn Morn	2
MORPHEUS				
Morpheus hov'ring o'er my Pillow,		661	Love Song	23
MORROUGH'S				
Invited here to 'vengeful Morrough's Aid,		791	St. Pat's Well	23
MORROW SEE TO-MORROW				
Shall hear Him harangue against Prior to Morrow.		143	New Song	6

MORROW	(CONTINUED)	PAGE	TITLE	LINE
To morrow We our Mystick Feast prepare,	. . . . .	162	Toland's Invit	7
"To morrow my Appeal comes on,	. . . . .	200	Horace 2, 6	51
And the Publick shall see't, if I live 'till to Morrow;		265	Apollo	68
But pray. To morrow go at Ten,	. . . . .	377	Apology Lady C	67
To morrow I shall tell you more,	. . . .	423	Ireld	61
To morrow will be Time enough	. . . .	763	Stel B-day '26	7
Good Morrow, good Captain,--I'll wait on you down,--	.	869	Grand Question	77

MORTAL

		PAGE	TITLE	LINE
And as a Mortal to his Vile Disease,	. . . . . .	10	Ode to King	145
How the physicians swarm to shew their mortal skill,	. .	42	Ode Sancroft	253
What mortal change does in thy face appear,	. . . .	52	Temple Ill	31
To sleep could Mortal Eye-lids fix	. . . .	133	Magician's Rod	37
Had purify'd her mortal sight;	. . . .	178	To Lord Harley	50
Chose, for her spouse, a mortal born:	. . . .	178	To Lord Harley	66
A Mortal of superior kind.	. . . .	179	To Lord Harley	80
The closest Mortal ever known.	. . . .	202	Horace 2, 6	104
Since mortal Beautyes drop so soon,	. . . . . .	229	Prog of Beauty	118
"(Whose Beauties mortal Eyes escape,	. . . . . .	384	Manly Virtue	7
The mortal force of Time's dystructive hand	. . . .	419	Shall Repine	2
A Loss that Dick thought, no Mortal cou'd bear.	. . .	430	Dicky Dolly	6
Presume to shew his mortal snout,	. . . .	464	Birthday Song	144
Did ever mortal see a Peacock	. . . .	513	Answer Fable	21
Confest her of no mortal Race:	. . . .	584	Strephon Chloe	8
Meer mortal Flesh was all he found:	. . . .	586	Strephon Chloe	76
A mortal human Touch impure?	. . . .	586	Strephon Chloe	90
Come down to visit mortal Men:	. . . .	587	Strephon Chloe	98
How Semele of mortal Race,	. . . .	587	Strephon Chloe	107
As mortal as himself at least.	. . . .	589	Strephon Chloe	186
What mortal else cou'd e'er go through it!	. . .	675	Curate's Compl	17
To see a Mortal Virgin deck'd	. . . .	695	Cadenus Vaness	271
The Tutor turn'd a mortal Lover.	. . . .	707	Cadenus Vaness	651
The reason why no Mortal knows.	. . . .	777	Mullinix Tim	120
The various Scenes of mortal Life,	. . . .	781	Mullinix Tim	265
We both are Mortal; but thou, frailer Creature,	. . .	861	On Old Glass	1
That not the wisest Mortal knows	. . . .	993	On Picture	20
I mean, what no other mortal in the universe can boast of,		1024	Nim-Dan-Dean 2	D 16

MORTAL'S

		PAGE	TITLE	LINE
E'er enter any Mortal's Noddle.	. . . .	496	Panegyr Swift	105
So bloom'd the Goddess in a Mortal's Arms.	. . .	669	Epig Carthy 13	D 2

MORTALITY

		PAGE	TITLE	LINE
Who gives no Bills, but of Mortality.	. . . . . .	235	Elegy on Demar	40

MORTALL

		PAGE	TITLE	LINE
Poor Celia, but of mortall Race	. . . .	229	Prog of Beauty	106

MORTALS

		PAGE	TITLE	LINE
And think, alas, to be by mortals writ,	. . . . .	20	Ode Athenian	126
Such are the ways ill-guided mortals go	. . . . .	35	Ode Sancroft	37
Nothing is fix'd that mortals see or know,	. . . .	39	Ode Sancroft	143
A pride that well suspends poor mortals fate,	. . .	45	To Congreve	45
She blushes when by mortals seen;	. . . . . .	178	To Lord Harley	70
See then what Mortals place their Bliss in!	. . . .	223	Prog of Love	25
When Mortals say she's in her Wain.	. . . . .	228	Prog of Beauty	88
We are very ill us'd by you Mortals below;	. . . .	263	Apollo	2
"And long-deluded Mortals see,	. . . .	384	Manly Virtue	13
Deluded Mortals, whom the Great	. . . . . .	480	Libel on D- D-	1
We Mortals are strange kind of Folk.	. . . . .	545	Life of Swift	4
"But wnat all Mortals may correct;	. . . . . .	571	Death of Swift	464
Rash Mortals, e'er you take a Wife,	. . . . . .	593	Strephon Chloe	301
Inferior mortals there below.	. . . .	617	Scandal Poem 1	4
Inferior Mortals there below.	. . . .	623	Scandal Poem 2	4
That Mortals here disdain to love;	. . . . . .	689	Cadenus Vaness	81
Give Mortals neither Heat nor Light.	. . . . .	700	Cadenus Vaness	443
(So Providence on Mortals waits,	. . . .	764	Stel B-day '26	41
But where his deep law is, few mortals yet know:	. . .	815	Yahoo's	12
All Mortals must be curious to enquire,	. . . . .	825	Noisy Tom	5
But we Mortals call him Cary.	. . . .	833	Legion Club	106
Of Mortals, and the Gods Delight.	. . . . . .	916	Riddle 2	12
Of busy Mortals endless Toils:	. . . .	921	Riddle 7	14
For which all Mortals leave their Home;	. . . . .	922	Riddle 7	52
Too great for Mortals less than Kings.	. . . . .	924	Riddle 8	16
How long shall mortals bend to gain?	. . . . . .	950	Upstart	D 18

MORTAR

		PAGE	TITLE	LINE
The Mortar onely chang'd it's Name,	. . . . . .	93	Bauc & Phil 1	111
For their Ancestor trod Mortar;	. . . .	837	Legion Club	178
Like Walls, more lasting without Mortar:	. . . .	1021	Nim-Dan-Dean 1	D 22

MORTGAGE

		PAGE	TITLE	LINE
By Mortgage hath secur'd the Corps of Demar;	. .	233	Elegy on Demar	2
The Hand that sign'd the Mortgage paid the Shot.	. .	234	Elegy on Demar	28
Nor, when a Mortgage lies on half his Lands,	. . .	534	To Mr. Gay	99

MORTIFY

		PAGE	TITLE	LINE
Which help'd to mortify his Pride,	. . . . . .	704	Cadenus Vaness	570
Resolv'd to mortify your Pride,	. . . .	730	Stella, Poems	85
To mortify the Creature more,	. . . .	886	Rev Market-Hill	103
How will it mortify thy Pride,	. . . .	921	Riddle 7	7

MORTIFY'D

		PAGE	TITLE	LINE
And yet, grow mortify'd and vext	. . . .	501	Doctor Delaney	39
To see him mortify'd at least---.	. . . . . .	546	Life of Swift	40
If they have mortify'd my Pride,	. . . .	555	Death of Swift	63
But Europe mortify'd his Pride,	. . . .	657	On Poetry	475

		PAGE	TITLE		LINE
MORTIFYING					
To hear such mortifying Stuff.		763	Stel B-day '26		8
MORTIMER					
For trust us, friend Mortimer		187	Scriblerus 4	D	16
MOSES					
While Moses held it in his Hand,		132	Magician's Rod		2
As Moses, by divine Advice,		813	Bro Protestant		49
MOSSY					
As from a mossy Cliff distill;		589	Strephon Chloe		176
MOST					
Most fall at last to Interest, Folly, and Abuse.		24	Ode Athenian		277
The most ungen'rous vices of the town;		44	To Congreve		10
The methods most in fashion to be lewd,		46	To Congreve		118
Oft hovers where alive it haunted most;		51	Temple Ill		8
Whisp'ring in Junto most profound,		63	Discovery		22
And, by the most we can discover,		67	Problem		59
To ask for what he fancy'd most.		94	Bauc & Phil 1		156
But most obsequious to the Squire.		95	Bauc & Phil 1		180
To ask for what he fancy'd most:		115	Bauc & Phil 2		110
But, most noble Senators, 'tis a great Shame		143	New Song		13
In manner submissive most humbly do pray,		185	Scriblerus 1		2
Wherein French Writers most excell:		216	To Mr. Delany		32
A Satyr where he most commends,		216	To Mr. Delany		40
For all Buffoons have most in View		217	To Mr. Delany		77
And was--His most obedient Daughter.		224	Prog of Love		72
"Where most true Sons of Phoebus ha' bin.		320	First of April		4
Yet Galen most acutely shews you,		367	Answer Delaney		31
Most aptly this Device explain:		393	Modern Poets		6
The most effectual Way to baulk		414	Censure		29
To me was most malicious kind		420	Holyhead		22
But that indeed which pleasd me most		422	Ireld		31
The first vex'd him much, but the other vex'd most.		430	Dicky Dolly		9
It was a most unfriendly Part		444	Modern Lady		1
Are you on Vices most severe		449	Modern Lady		152
Iris, for Scandal most notorious,		450	Modern Lady		166
Most conscious that they all speak true,		453	Modern Lady		272
Tho fond of warlike Lyes as most men;		462	Birthday Song		54
It shines most in the Marble Cover.		475	Epist on Epist		14
Most think what has been heap'd on You,		478	Epist on Epist		105
Swear, he's a most facetious Man,		480	Libel on D- D-		9
With forty Pounds a Year at most.		484	Libel on D- D-		134
I do the most that Friendship can;		485	Libel on D- D-		151
While most that are or would be great,		491	Dialogue		53
And the great Name engrav'd most fairly,		494	Panegyr Swift		53
Most of his Virtues, all my Brains.		494	Panegyr Swift		57
Durst there show his right or most revnd face		522	St. Cecilia's		10
In every Mouth the Question most in Vogue		536	To Mr. Gay		145
He was a most confounded Tory---!		547	Life of Swift		83
"The most malignant of the Herd,		549	Life of Swift		164
"A few, in Verse; but most, in Prose---.		550	Life of Swift		182
I ask but for an Inch at most.		554	Death of Swift		20
"Who truckle most, when treated worst.		568	Death of Swift		398
Most certainly there's the Hell to be found,		575	Place Damn'd		6
Which hath she most need of, a Spur or a Bridle?		580	Psyche		4
Conceive the most invenom'd Dart,		595	Cassinus Peter		59
Above a Term or two at most.		604	Beasts Confess		92
Three Poets in an Age at most?		640	On Poetry		6
Whether your Genius most inclines		643	On Poetry		81
She's fair and clean, and that's the most;		699	Cadenus Vaness		412
To that wherein it most excell'd;		701	Cadenus Vaness		451
I'll give her what she most admires,		702	Cadenus Vaness		500
And had a most discerning Head.		710	Cadenus Vaness		757
In her, a most judicious Taste.		711	Cadenus Vaness		767
Which most exposes ours to Scorn?		725	To Stella		68
Say, Stella, which you most repent		745	Stel Distress		21
Can please at most but once or twice.		788	Dick's Variety		12
When wanted by his Country most;		798	Traulus 1		90
When his Friends he most is hard on,		800	Traulus 2		13
Female Vices most, or Male,		801	Traulus 2		54
But this I am sure, the Most Rev'rend old Dragon,		803	Irish Bishops		13
Of whom there are but four at most,		820	Dr. Rundle		13
And, what the Wretches most resent,		883	Rev Market-Hill		21
But, I admire your Patience most;		891	Panegyr Dean		147
And where she is most familiar,		906	Daphne		17
When she knows she's most to blame.		906	Daphne		20
That they to others give thee most:		919	Riddle 5		30
Most wondrous Forms you see me wear		927	Riddle 10	D	13
Most wond'rous is my Magick Power;		930	Riddle 15	D	13
Pleasing most when most I speak,		933	Riddle 20	D	2
Pleasing most when most I speak,		933	Riddle 20	D	2
Most Things by me do rise and fall,		934	Riddle 21	D	1
I gave, as you beg, your most humble respects:		979	Dean to Tho: S		24
Above a Song or two at most:		993	On Picture		24
By your good Leave, my most profound and bold Sir,		1004	Dan J's Reply		30
Most humbly sues for Pardon.		1005	Sheridan's Sub		7
. . . Your most dutiful and obedient George Nim-Dan-Dean.		1024	Nim-Dan-Dean 2	D	18
Lady Betty presents you her service most humble,		1027	Sheri Circles		25
Are most inclin'd to plunder Crowns.		1033	Ans to Crown		12
MOTH					
But, eats into it, like a Moth---!		548	Life of Swift		114

MOTHER

	PAGE	TITLE	LINE
When Mother Clud had risen from Play,	86	Hist V's House	1
Thy Mother burnt, art Born again;	109	V's House	120
The Mother scream'd, the Father chid,	223	Prog of Love	27
I was nurs'd by their Mother.	247	Irish-Feast	80
However beauteous for his Mother:	272	Apollo's Edict D	57
"'Tis all to save their Mother trouble;	321	First of April	24
Thy fair indulgent Mother crown'd	324	Pethox	33
And bore my Mother by a Prentice.	350	Upright Judge 3	4
And, let but our Mother Hibernia contrive	351	Wood Insect	13
Who met his Mother in a grove;	460	Birthday Song	16
His Country was his dearest Mother,	606	Beasts Confess	179
His mother begg'd of us to dress him	619	Scandal Poem 1	67
His Mother begg'd of us to dress him,	625	Scandal Poem 2	63
Will thus be by her Mother chid,	694	Cadenus Vaness	244
Which the true Mother, which Pretender,	776	Mullinix Tim	99
In Mother Church to breed a Variance,	020	Dr. Rundle	7
Alma Mater was thy Mother,	838	Legion Club	199
Treat thy Mother like a Harlot!	838	Legion Club	202
And Mother Tellus trembled so	849	Old Thorn	27
The Mother the Daughter, the Daughter the Mother.	929	Riddle 13 D	10
The Mother the Daughter, the Daughter the Mother.	929	Riddle 13 D	10
. . . since my Mother bound my Head,	985	Mary to Sher	1

MOTHER-KINGDOM

	PAGE	TITLE	LINE
The Mother-Kingdom left her Children free;	791	St. Pat's Well	20

MOTHER'S

	PAGE	TITLE	LINE
Like the fam'd Hero in his Mother's Cloud,	18	Ode Athenian	88
And stabs the Son before the Mother's Eyes.	364	On Dreams	16
His Mother's Aid no Youth invokes:	687	Cadenus Vaness	10
To vindicate his Mother's Wrongs.	701	Cadenus Vaness	467
View him on the Mother's Side,	799	Traulus 2	7
And drag'd me from my Mother's Side:	915	Riddle 1	8

MOTHERS

	PAGE	TITLE	LINE
Impatient to be like their Mothers,	182	Horace 2, 1	54
While Mothers, Daughters, Aunts,	426	Five Ladies	30
And purify'd their mothers after.	675	Curate's Compl	8

MOTION

	PAGE	TITLE	LINE
Many an eccentric and unthrifty motion make,	36	Ode Sancroft	69
And holy Sancroft's motion quite irregular appears,	37	Ode Sancroft	81
That furnish'd spirit and motion through the whole;	53	Temple Ill	62
March o'er the ruin'd plain with motion slow,	55	Temple Ill	129
The Number make the Motion slower	93	Bauc & Phil 1	130
Howe'er our Earthly Motion varies,	98	Elegy Patrige	16
The Number made the Motion slow'r:	113	Bauc & Phil 2	70
Stood without Motion, like a Stake.	133	Magician's Rod	34
Its Motion and its Heat maintains.	239	Run Bankers	12
And of my meer Motion, and special good Grace,	263	Apollo	27
All Turns and Motion tries;	406	Swift to Pope	14
And yet through ev'ry Motion steals.	726	To Stella	84
This dang'rous horrid motion Dish up?	774	Mullinix Tim	18
Who in the motion have no share;	777	Mullinix Tim	127
My portly Motion, Mien, and Gate.	780	Mullinix Tim	234
Fill ev'ry Pipe, each Motion guide.	798	Traulus 1	74
And when she feels an inward Motion,	893	Panegyr Dean	211
At every Motion undertook,	917	Riddle 3	7
Set it always in Motion.	939	Riddle Answerd	14

MOTIONS

	PAGE	TITLE	LINE
Wonder to see the Motions fly)	29	Ode to Temple	96
We watch his Motions to a Minute,	280	Journal	49
"All Motions are alike to him:	304	Storm	32
The Children all our motions Aping.	780	Mullinix Tim	242

MOTIVES

	PAGE	TITLE	LINE
What petty Motives rule their Fates!	30	Ode to Temple	106

MOTLY

	PAGE	TITLE	LINE
Then, from the motly mingled Style	108	V's House	63
Motly Fruit of Mungril Seed:	799	Traulus 2	2

MOTTO

	PAGE	TITLE	LINE
Serve for a Motto on thy Coach?	348	Whitshed Motto	4
Now, since your Motto thus you construe,	349	Whitshed Motto	23
Be that my Motto, and my Fate.	505	Doctor Delaney	172

MOULD

	PAGE	TITLE	LINE
And with Discretion dig the Mould:	743	Stel B-day 22	58

MOULDERS

	PAGE	TITLE	LINE
That, moulders into rust,	39	Ode Sancroft	141

MOULDY

	PAGE	TITLE	LINE
With muddy ale and mouldy bread	420	Holyhead	2

MOUNT   SEE DRAPIER'S-MOUNT

	PAGE	TITLE	LINE
The Roof began to mount aloft	92	Bauc & Phil 1	92
The Roof began to mount aloft;	112	Bauc & Phil 2	52
For those are but Quacks, who mount on a Bank.	288	Bank Down	55
He'll mount his Tub, and preach his best,	456	Dean Smedley	38
Too pond'rous is thy Bulk to mount the Sky;	539	Mr. Pulteney	41
No higher climb than mount Olymp	620	Scandal Poem 1	102
No higher climb than Mount Olymp,	626	Scandal Poem 2	100
In Vehicles they mount the Sky:	626	Scandal Poem 2	110
But e'er you mount his mettled Steed,	666	Epig Carthy 2 D	3
Ye Muses guard your sacred Mount,	671	Epig Carthy 21 D	5
But on the highest mount in Wales	733	Verses Vanessa	29
Cou'd he learn to mount a Ladder.	801	Traulus 2	50
Mount alive, and dead descend	801	Traulus 2	52
Is seen, as when you mount our Pulpit.	889	Panegyr Dean	66

		PAGE	TITLE	LINE
MOUNT	(CONTINUED)			
I Will not build on yonder mount:		899	Dean's Reasons	1
MOUNTAGUE				
And Mountague so far decayd,		311	To Ford	19
MOUNTAIN				
That Mountain which was highest first of all		16	Ode Athenian	5
How the Mouse makes the mighty Mountain shake!		30	Ode to Temple	107
The mighty Mountain labours with its birth,		30	Ode to Temple	108
Just as the Mountain did the Mouse;		81	Vanbrug House	76
MOUNTAIN'S				
Here by a mountain's side, a reverend cave		49	To Congreve	187
MOUNTAINEER				
What was thy Grandsire but a Mountaineer,		826	Noisy Tom	11
MOUNTAINS				
O'er mountains steep, o'er dusty plains,		403	Window Inns 10	D 5
If mountains sink to vales, if cityes dye		419	Shall Repine	3
Safe through the Newry mountains sides.		435	Answer Paulus	98
Thorow Mountains thorow Vallies;		574	Helter Skelter	41
Both Mountains, Woods, and Hills, and Rocks,		934	Riddle 21	D 7
MOUNTCASHELL				
. . .to my Lady Mountcashell: but, truly, I thought		1014	Swift to Sheri	11
MOUNTEBANK				
While the sly Mountebank attends his Trade,		364	On Dreams	33
MOUNTED				
But by degrees when mounted high		226	Prog of Beauty	5
Now mounted up to Heav'n again,		256	Bubble	150
Sits mounted on the Garden Roller.		410	Dial Rich Marb	62
They mounted, and labour'd with Whip and with Spur,		804	Irish Bishops	19
MOUNTERS				
Few Bankers will to Heav'n be Mounters:		241	Run Bankers	58
MOUNTHARMAR				
Stella may vye with your Mountharmar:		313	To Ford	70
MOUNTING				
Behold it mounting to the Top,		251	Bubble	14
MOUNTS				
And up he mounts into the Box,		352	Wood Ironmongr	15
Her Learning mounts to read a Song,		416	Woman's Mind	9
Mounts, Walks, on high; and in a Hollow		477	Epist on Epist	79
And mounts astride upon the Dragon.		777	Mullinix Tim	116
With what an air he mounts his coach!		951	Upstart	D 24
MOURN				
Whene'er I mourn, stops my complaining Breath,		32	Ode to Temple	197
And lessening rivers mourn their fountains dry		419	Shall Repine	4
They mourn for me without dissembling.		561	Death of Swift	224
And I mourn the cruel Pain;		933	Riddle 20	D 14
Ne'er sad I mourn, ne'er glad rejoice,		936	Riddle 23	D 24
MOURN'D				
The humble tribe mourn'd for the quick'ning soul,		53	Temple Ill	61
So Tickell mourn'd his Addison.		271	Apollo's Edict	D 43
Mourn'd Adonis, darling Youth:		660	Love Song	10
MOURNFUL				
To mournful Ditties, Clio, change thy Note,		284	Elegy Boat	1
With mournful Note clocks round the Brim.		295	Horrid Plot	150
To Elegies in mournful Tone,		643	On Poetry	83
Mournful Cypress, verdant Willow,		661	Love Song	21
Mean time the mournful Queen of Love		712	Cadenus Vaness	828
MOURNFULL				
Dick Sigh'd for his Doll and his mournfull Arms Cross'd,		430	Dicky Dolly	7
MOURNING				
He dyes, and leaves his mourning Mate		295	Prog Marriage	155
MOUSE				
How the Mouse makes the mighty Mountain shake!		30	Ode to Temple	107
Just as the Mountain did the Mouse;		81	Vanbrug House	76
With many a Mouse, and many a Rat,		153	Widow and Cat	D 4
If chance a Mouse creeps in her Sight,		416	Woman's Mind	33
MOUSE'S				
Her Eye-Brows from a Mouse's Hyde,		581	Young Nymph	13
MOUSETRAP-MAN				
A Mousetrap-man chief Engineer.		88	Hist V's House	48
MOUTH				
Where every Fool his Mouth applies,		158	Fable of Midas	63
From his own Mouth, if this be so?		172	Horace 1, 7	48
From her red Locks her Mouth with Venom fills:		195	Author Himself	55
I heard it from my Grannam's Mouth,		254	Bubble	98
The Words in Wood's Mouth, or speaks from his Guts:		335	Serious Poem	62
Lest my Mobb's Mouth, being seldom quiet		373	Letter D. S-y	66
Spits in his mouth and stroaks his Chaps		421	Ireld	14
Rolls from his Mouth in plenteous Streams of Mud;		532	To Mr. Gay	40
In every Mouth the Question most in Vogue		536	To Mr. Gay	145
His Hand, his Neck, his Mouth, and Feet		586	Strephon Chloe	77
Or at her Mouth was breaking Wind.		592	Strephon Chloe	282
His triple-barking Mouth to Stop:		647	On Poetry	214
In his Mouth to wear his Knife.		800	Traulus 2	40
My Tongue is black, my Mouth is furr'd,		916	Riddle 1	39
In at each Mouth the Spirits pass,		920	Riddle 6	13
Why at this Cave's tremendous Mouth,		923	Riddle 7	83
'Tis of Shine, a Mouth Moon-full,		1015	Swift to Sheri	49
MOV'D				
Is wonderfully mov'd by some exalted Men,		20	Ode Athenian	137
And Puppets mov'd by Wire		123	Empty'ng Town	14

MOV'D   (CONTINUED)   PAGE   TITLE   LINE

He mov'd, and bow'd and talk't with too much Grace;   . .   194 Author Himself   13
"True genuine Dulness mov'd his Pity, ...   572 Death of Swift   469
That mov'd the Nymphs to be unkind.   598 Problem Solved   24
Mov'd with the lightest Touch of Blame, ...   730 Stella, Poems   88

MOVE
On what poor Engines move   . . . .   29 Ode to Temple   104
Now move, and now in Order Stand.   . . . . . .   108 V's House   78
"To move this Walk's untoward Length   . . . . . .   379 Apology Lady C   134
To move that all the Nation round   . . . .   423 Ireld   67
To move it out from yonder Corner;   . . . . . .   528 Lady's Dres Rm   72
If this perhaps your Patience move   . . . . . .   554 Death of Swift   11
Where a Fault shou'd move your Pity.   . . . . .   630 Epistle Lady   14
Their Passions move in lower Spheres, ...   687 Cadenus Vaness   37
Tom could move with lordly Grace, ...   784 Mullinex Dick   21
Dear Dick, prithee tell by what passion you move?   . .   818 Archbi Cashel   1
I must move my limbs;   . . . .   852 Lady's Lament   40
Can move an Inch except I will.   . . . . . .   929 Riddle 14   D 8
And move it against Tyde and Wind.   . . . . . .   934 Riddle 21   D 16
I move my Lips, but want a Voice, ...   936 Riddle 23   D 25
Nor slowly move your Fiddle stick, ...   958 Cantata

MOVES
Whatever moves our Wonder or our Sport, ...   31 Ode to Temple   163
Thus, primitive Sancroft moves too high   . . . . .   39 Ode Sancroft   149
Moves round but twice in twice twelve Hours   93 Bauc & Phil 1   134
Now hardly moves an Inch an Hour.   . . . . .   113 Bauc & Phil 2   74
Made false Moves, and lost his Queen;   . . . . .   168 Peace Dunkirk   16
That <Swift> oils many a Spring which Harley moves.   .   194 Author Himself   40
The wondring World, where'er he moves, ...   387 Manly Virtue   127
That moves his Patients to Repentance: . . . . .   605 Beasts Confess   122
Scolding moves you less than Merriment.   . . . . .   636 Epistle Lady   208
Unheard she moves about my Bed.   . . . . . .   727 To Stella   112

MOVING
Thence to the Neck; and moving thorow there;   . . . .   367 Answer Delaney   37
In a dull Stream, which moving slow   . .   . . . .   688 Cadenus Vaness   51
Some Lines, more moving than the rest, ...   703 Cadenus Vaness   520
Shall moving Delos now deep-rooted stand, ...   770 Horace 1, 14   3
Thou, fixt of old, be now the moving Land?   . . . . .   770 Horace 1, 14   4
Moving all like a pendulum;   . . . . . .   852 Lady's Lament   30
Whose moving Touches, when they please, kill us.   . . .   988 Letter Dr Sh-n   29

MOW
Behold his glitt'ring Faulchion mow   . . . . 461 Birthday Song   31
That Time sits with his Scythe to mow   . . . . . .   757 Stel B-day '24   37

MOWS
Nature's bare visage furrowed as he mows: . . . . .   55 Temple Ill   124
When Mercury her Tresses mows   . . . . . .   229 Prog of Beauty   109

MOYDORES
Cast in his Dart which made three Moydores Light.   . .   234 Elegy on Demar   32

MOYNALTA
And Moynalta, his Brother, ...   247 Irish-Feast   78

MOYSTER
Is sweeter and moyster, ...   953 Oysters   6

MOYSTURE
The Moysture dry'd they sink again, ... 254 Bubble   87

MR   SEE MISTER
Of Wycherly, and you, and Mr. Bays;   . . . . .   47 To Congreve   142
"Good Mr. Dean go change your Gown, ...   200 Horace 2, 6   23
"And Mr. Dean, one Word from you--   . . . .   201 Horace 2, 6   62
"You, Mr. Dean frequent the Great;   . . . . .   202 Horace 2, 6   93
In ev'ry town we wait on Mr. May'r, ...   308 Billet Players   35
That Mr. Ford was born to day: . . . . .   311 To Ford   4
But here Mr. Wood complains that we Mock, ...   335 Serious Poem   41
Unless by the Devil we mean Mr. Wood.   . . . . .   335 Serious Poem   56
Nor can you prove it, Mr. Pasquin.   . . . . .   350 Upright Judge 3   2
"And Mr. Henly's last Oration: . . . . .   563 Death of Swift   278
Mr. Dean, You come too late: . . . .   630 Epistle Lady   28
Mr. Dean, you must reply.   . . . .   632 Epistle Lady   92
Deuce is in you, Mr. Dean;   . . . .   635 Epistle Lady   181
The Fables writ by Mr. Gay, ...   782 Tim and Fables   4
By this Contrivance Mr. <Dean>   . . . . .   797 Traulus 1   59
Or, Mr. Dean--I should with Joy   . . . . .   860 Lady Acheson   25
Or Mr. <Moor> will take it ill.   . . . . . .   860 Lady Acheson   28
Now raise your Spirits, Mr. <Dean>:   . . . . .   889 Panegyr Dean   85
Why sure, Mr. Poet, your head got a jar   976 Dean to Sherid   27
. . . Fie Mr. Sheridan, 'tis a Shame   . . . . .   985 Mary to Sher   5
Knave in your Teeth, Mr. Sheridan, . . .   985 Mary to Sher   7
However, they own it is very civil in Mr. Sheridan, . . . 1014 Swift to Sheri   8
. . .I appeal to your Friend Mr. Conna.   . . . .   1014 Swift to Sheri   10
But how, Mr. Sheridan, came you to venture   1027 Sheri Circles   13

MRS
And in a Corner of Mrs. Dukes's Box,. .   . . . . .   70 Mrs Harris Pet   23
Mrs. Dukes, said I, here's an ugly Accident has
   happen'd out;   71 Mrs Harris Pet   37
Now, Mrs. Dukes, you know, and every Body under-stands,   71 Mrs Harris Pet   42
Truly, says he, Mrs. Nab,. .   . . .   72 Mrs Harris Pet   55
Then Mrs. Johnson gave her Verdict, ...   128 Little House   39
Let them be sent to Mrs. Harding;   . . . . .   417 Woman's Mind   59
When Mrs Welch's Chimny smoks, ...   419 Holyhead Journ   1
There's Mrs. Cut and she combine, ...   447 Modern Lady   76
Whilst Mrs. Susan comb'd her Head: . . . . .   698 Cadenus Vaness   373
You must apply to Mrs. Brent, ...   742 Stel B-day 22   50

MRS	(CONTINUED)	PAGE	TITLE	LINE
If not, a thousand Mrs. Brents,	. . . .	743	Stel B-day 22	72
Pray steal me not, I'm Mrs. Dingley's	. . . . . .	763	Collar Lap-Dog	1
May serve to wait on Mrs. Leslie.	. . . .	886	Rev Market-Hill	100
Mrs. Dingley and Mrs. Johnson say,	. . .	1013	Swift to Sheri	7
Mrs. Dingley and Mrs. Johnson say,	. . .	1013	Swift to Sheri	7
Mrs. Dingley	. . . .	1014	Swift to Sheri	29

MUCH

		PAGE	TITLE	LINE
That I believe in much, I ne're can hope to see;	. .	20	Ode Athenian	134
(And then how much a nothing is Mankind!	. . . . .	21	Ode Athenian	180
How much of Heav'n is in her naked looks.	. . . . .	23	Ode Athenian	233
Which 'tis a shame to see how much of late	. . . . .	24	Ode Athenian	254
Yet so much sooner comes the long and gloomy Night.	. .	25	Ode Athenian	282
For of the person much I fear,	. . . . . .	35	Ode Sancroft	18
Thro' the dark mass, the dawn of so much sense,	. . . .	37	Ode Sancroft	88
But, ah, too much without a thorn.	. . . .	37	Ode Sancroft	106
And which for ought I see, and much I fear,	. . . .	39	Ode Sancroft	159
So much in mode, so very city-born;	. . . . . .	44	To Congreve	14
The Plan he much admir'd, and took	. . . .	87	Hist V's House	19
You'll find has so much Virtue in't,	. . . . .	101	Elegy Patrige	112
And she admir'd as much at Him.	. . . .	116	Bauc & Phil 2	148
How much the other Tree was griev'd,	. . . . .	117	Bauc & Phil 2	176
Was much surpriz'd to see a Crow	. . . . . .	127	Little House	27
There's nothing fouls the Hands so much:	. . . . .	158	Fable of Midas	68
Much good may do 'em that have caught 'um.	. . . . .	158	Fable of Midas	80
And very much in Harley's Favour)	. . . . .	171	Horace 1, 7	18
Did very much his Genius cramp;	. . . . . .	172	Horace 1, 7	44
<Swift> much admires the Place and Air,	. . . .	173	Horace 1, 7	83
So much, that you neglect your Self.	. . . . .	175	Horace 1, 7	126
Which has afforded thee much Chat,	. . . . .	181	Horace 2, 1	24
Which made thy Closet much frequented	. . . . .	182	Horace 2, 1	51
Were much too strong for all their Hands.	. . . . .	189	Faggot	8
He mov'd, and bow'd and talk't with too much Grace;	. . .	194	Author Himself	13
It is but so much more in Debt,	. . . .	200	Horace 2, 6	21
Faith Sir, you know as much as I.	. . . . . .	202	Horace 2, 6	96
To my much honor'd Father; These:	. . . .	223	Prog of Love	46
I am too much reveng'd already by Time;	. . . . .	266	Apollo	104
He wonder'd for how much an Inch 'twould be Sold:	. . .	288	Bank Down	33
She stole away with much ado,	. . . . . .	292	Prog Marriage	94
Hither, though much against his Grain,	. . . . .	294	Prog Marriage	123
The Diff'rence is not much between	. . . .	313	To Ford	59
And yet we all know much Gold it will bring,	. . . .	334	Serious Poem	14
Wood got so much Copper? He got it by Brass;	. . . .	336	Serious Poem	86
With much ado, the Cheat he found;	. . . . .	346	Prometheus	48
And much good Sense, as well as Breeding:	. . .	377	Apology Lady C	72
All this was much beneath her Due,	. . . . .	379	Apology Lady C	118
If this be true, then how much more,	. . . . . .	392	Young's Satire	27
And, you can do as much:	. . . .	401	Window Inns 2	3
Thought much of his Doll, and the Jointure he lost,	. .	430	Dicky Dolly	8
The first vex'd him much, but the other vex'd most.	.	430	Dicky Dolly	9
And will be so much more your Debter	. . . .	463	Birthday Song	89
With so much beauty, shew me any maid	. . .	466	Birthday Song	189
But much I fear he's in decline.	. . . . . .	468	Birthday Song	256
Consider how much more is due	. . . . . .	483	Libel on D- D-	93
There's too much satire in my vein,	. . . .	489	Dialogue	2
With too much freedom treat my betters,	. . . . .	489	Dialogue	5
Would much compensate all we want.	. . . . .	493	Panegyr Swift	8
You but oblige 'em so much more:	. . . . . .	505	Doctor Delaney	156
Would ne'er have shown him so much Favour;	. . . .	514	Answer Fable	78
But she valu'd her Honour much more than her Life.	. .	517	Dean Hang Rape	10
And trust his Honesty just so much more.	. . . . .	535	To Mr. Gay	114
For much a better Man than You?	. . . . .	546	Life of Swift	36
'Tis true, we talk of Friendship much,	. . . . .	546	Life of Swift	41
Which if he lik'd, much good may do him:	. . . .	549	Life of Swift	133
Thus much may serve by way of Proem,	. . . . .	555	Death of Swift	71
"Had too much Satyr in his Vein;	. . . . .	571	Death of Swift	456
"No Nation wanted it so much:	. . . . . .	572	Death of Swift	482
As much as now we find in Men.	. . . . .	601	Beasts Confess	4
Much of the cens'ring World complain'd,	. . . .	603	Beasts Confess	49
'Tis true, he was not much inclin'd	. . . .	603	Beasts Confess	63
However, we have too much sense	. . . . .	622	Scandal Poem 1	153
But, Gods like us, have too much Sense	. . . .	628	Scandal Poem 2	157
Now not so much as in Remainder	. . . . .	642	On Poetry	55
For these our Criticks much confide in,	. . . .	648	On Poetry	252
While others do as much for him.	. . . . . .	651	On Poetry	334
How much our Ancestors out-sung us;	. . . . .	652	On Poetry	352
Wou'dst thou not wish, in so much ease,	. . . . .	677	Parson's Case	35
On which the Pleader much enlarg'd;	. . . . .	686	Cadenus Vaness	6
The Cause appear'd of so much Weight,	. . . . .	688	Cadenus Vaness	75
There was on both Sides much to say:	. . . . .	690	Cadenus Vaness	116
The Goddess much perplex'd in Mind,	. . . . .	690	Cadenus Vaness	128
A Shame to one so much ador'd	. . . . . .	695	Cadenus Vaness	266
With much Deceit and little Wit;	. . . . . .	695	Cadenus Vaness	291
Vanessa much esteem'd his Wit,	. . . . . .	702	Cadenus Vaness	511
Much less could his declining Age	. . . . .	706	Cadenus Vaness	636
Much to her Praise, more to his Own.	. . . . .	711	Cadenus Vaness	765
Yet had she much Experience gain'd;	. . . . .	713	Cadenus Vaness	835
Thus much for the Verse, we proceed to the next,	. .	716	Answer Rebus	19
It cost me Lord knows how much Time	. . . . .	741	Stel B-day 22	9
How much improv'd by Dr. <D.>	. . . .	779	Mullinix Tim	216
My Hat has much the nicer air,	. . . .	780	Mullinix Tim	219

533

		PAGE	TITLE	LINE	
MUCH	(CONTINUED)				
Those former Ages differ'd much from this:		806	Judas	9	
As much as Hebrews and Philistines:		812	Bro Protestant	32	
For who would not think it a much better choice,		818	Epigr Kite	3	
Your Title had been so much better.		821	Dr. Rundle	66	
So much his Stay do's swell the Bills;		860	Lady Acheson	30	
How much he eats, how much he swills,		860	Lady Acheson	32	
How much he eats, how much he swills,		860	Lady Acheson	32	
You honour me much--the Honour is mine,--		869	Grand Question	73	
Never since I was born did I hear so much Wit,		873	Grand Question	173	
But, he durst not so much as once open his Lips,		873	Grand Question	177	
Much talking is not Harry's vice,		878	Robbin & Harry	13	
Treat me with so much Complaisance,		888	Panegyr Dean	53	
And, hearing much of Daphne's Fame,		904	Death Daphne	53	
Tho' so much of Heav'n appears in my Make,		929	Riddle 13	D	7
Much I dread the Courtier's Fate,		933	Riddle 20	D	27
Will cover a House much better than Clay.		943	Probatur Alit	34	
But this my Servants much enrages,		954	Authors Living	5	
And when with much Labour the Matter I crackt,		972	S-'s Ans Sh-d	3	
You found out my rebus with very much modesty;		976	Dean to Sherid	37	
But that's as much as to say, that my Master should die before ye,		986	Mary to Sher	19	
So much, he swears the very best Piece is		988	Letter Dr Sh-n	22	
I much suspect you mean the latter, ah Sly-boot!		1003	Dan J's Reply	6	
To be much greater than a Pound?		1004	Dan J's Reply	29	
Much Plague it created,		1014	Swift to Sheri	15	
My Soul it much grated,		1014	Swift to Sheri	17	
As much as the Liffee's outdone by the Rhine		1018	Swift Ans Sher	26	
Where thirty weigh, as much as eighty.		1022	Nim-Dan-Dean 1	D	48
MUCH-TALKT					
Or the much-talkt Oracular Grove		17	Ode Athenian	50	
MUD					
Raking up Mud to build a Wall;		87	Hist V's House	18	
Drown'd Puppies, stinking Sprats, all drench'd in Mud,		139	City Shower	62	
All cover'd o'er with Slime and Mud.		255	Bubble	132	
Flirts from his Cart the Mud in <Walpole's> Face.		364	On Dreams	38	
Your water's mud,		440	Ballyspellin	10	
Rolls from his Mouth in plenteous Streams of Mud;		532	To Mr. Gay	40	
Fresh from the Mud a wallowing Sow		786	Clad in Brown	5	
Or hide his coward Snout in Mud.		824	Printer Newgat	10	
A long-ear'd Beast, in Mud to lye,		942	Probatur Alit	25	
As eels delight to creep in mud,		950	Upstart	D	7
His blood delights in mud to run;		950	Upstart	D	9
'Ere George had robb'd it of its Mud.		1020	Nim-Dan-Dean 1	D	6
MUDDLE					
But when let out, they run and muddle		294	Prog Marriage	147	
MUDDLES					
He never muddles in the Dirt,		788	Dick's Variety	15	
MUDDY					
And mingles in her muddy Cheeks.		227	Prog of Beauty	36	
With muddy ale and mouldy bread		420	Holyhead	2	
He'll make it muddy as a Bog.		671	Epig Carthy 21	D	8
MUFF					
Your hairy Business is a Muff.		912	Aenigma Expl	D	4
MUFFLES					
And Patricks' bell she was ringing all in muffles;		840	Ballad	D	7
MUGGLETON					
And Muggleton, Toland, and Bradley the taylor,		815	Yahoo's	27	
MUGGS					
And neither Muggs nor Pots whole.		425	Five Ladies	8	
MULBERRY					
By Leaves of Mulberry is fed;		79	Vanbrug House	30	
MULE					
As rude as a bear, no mule half so crabbed;		955	Portrait Life	5	
MULLINEX					
You, Mullinex, and slobb'ring <Carr?>		787	Dick's Variety	3	
MULLINIX					
My good Friend Mullinix forbear.		775	Mullinix Tim	69	
Dear Mullinix, your good Advice		779	Mullinix Tim	195	
Dear Mullinix, I now lament		781	Mullinix Tim	277	
MULTIPLYING					
Shewn through a multiplying Glass		255	Bubble	119	
MULTIS					
Cum Multis aliis (all his Foes)		373	Letter D. S-y	71	
MULTITUDE					
In vain then would the Muse the multitude advise,		37	Ode Sancroft	83	
MULTITUDE'S					
The Multitude's Capricious Pranks		239	Run Bankers	5	
MUM					
Yet Mum for that, hope still the best,		182	Horace 2, 1	69	
MUNDI					
And here rest, Sic transit Gloria Mundi.		431	Dicky Dolly	24	
MUNDUNGUS					
And bribes with mundungus.)		856	Lady's Lament	164	
MUNGRIL					
"No Fools of Rank, a mungril Breed,		570	Death of Swift	437	
Motly Fruit of Mungril Seed:		799	Traulus 2	2	
MURD'RER					
The Murd'rer dreams of all the Blood he spilt.		364	On Dreams	14	
And fortune help the murd'rer in his flight;		506	To a Friend	2	

```
MURD'RER'S                                               PAGE    TITLE              LINE
    First issuing, struck the Murd'rer's Ears;   . . . .  850 Old Thorn             54
<MURD'RING>
    By an <old> <redhair'd> <murd'ring> <Hag> pursu'd, . .  193 Author Himself       1
MURDER
    All to murder Equity,  . . . . . . . . . . . . .       574 Helter Skelter       49
    I murder poor Milton,  . . . . . . . . . . . .         856 Lady's Lament       156
MURDER'D
    Creech murder'd Horace in his senseless Rhymes, . .    666 Epig Carthy 3    D   1
    Who murder'd Horace without Rhyme or Reason?  . . .    666 Epig Carthy 3    D   4
<MURDERED>
    On <Swift's> Reproaches for her <murdered> <spouse>  .  195 Author Himself      54
MURDERER
    Dare you, vile Murderer of Flaccus,  . . . . . . .     671 Epig Carthy 22   D   1
    To mend your Breed, the Murderer of a King.  . . . .   826 Noisy Tom            10
MURDERS
    And tell the Murders of her Eyes.  . . . . . . .       697 Cadenus Vaness      333
MURMUR'D
    Vext at their Follies, murmur'd in his Stream; . . .    22 Ode Athenian        194
MURMURING
    Still murmuring in their Wilderness for Food,  . . .     9 Ode to King          87
    Gives murmuring passage to a lasting wave; . . . . .    49 To Congreve         188
    Or murmuring at Whigs Preferments.  . . . . . . .      993 On Picture            6
MURMURS
    And murmurs as she glides away. . . . . . . . .        31 Ode to Temple        158
MURTHER
    In his Looks are Hell and Murther;  . . . . . . .      834 Legion Club         142
MURTHER'D
    Just as when he murther'd <Throp>. . . . . . . .       835 Legion Club         144
MUSCOVY
    Why Muscovy is not so far,  . . . . . . . . . .        282 Journal             106
    Either from Muscovy or Rome;  . . . . . . . . .        696 Cadenus Vaness      323
MUSE    SEE DOVE-MUSE,VIRGIN-MUSE
    The eager Muse took wing upon the Waves decline,  . .   16 Ode Athenian         22
    And the transported Muse imagin'd it  . . . . . . .     17 Ode Athenian         48
    Thus the deluding Muse oft blinds me to her Ways,  . .  23 Ode Athenian        234
    The Rebel Muse, alas, takes part  . . . . . . . .      23 Ode Athenian        238
    When the sad, melancholy Muse  . . . . . . . . .       24 Ode Athenian        273
    Then tell (dear fav'rite Muse)  . . . . . . . . .      30 Ode to Temple       115
    Sing (belov'd Muse) the Pleasures of Retreat,  . . .   30 Ode to Temple       135
    How is the Muse luxuriant grown,  . . . . . . . .      31 Ode to Temple       142
    Strait the Muse turns the Helm, and I launch out again;  32 Ode to Temple     195
    The Tribute of an humble Muse,  . . . . . . . . .      32 Ode to Temple       200
    Say Muse, for thou, if any, know'st  . . . . . . .     36 Ode Sancroft         43
    In vain then would the Muse the multitude advise,  . .  37 Ode Sancroft        83
    The muse and I no more revenge desire,  . . . . .      37 Ode Sancroft         90
    'Tis all the angry slighted Muse can do  . . . . .     38 Ode Sancroft        108
    (The goddess Muse herself has told me so)  . . . .     41 Ode Sancroft        233
    Check in thy satire, angry muse,  . . . . . . . .      42 Ode Sancroft        259
    The Muse was call'd in a poetic hour,  . . . . . .     43 To Congreve           2
    'Tis with a foul design the muse you send,  . . . .    44 To Congreve          15
    Thus did the Muse severe unkindly blame  . . . . .     44 To Congreve          23
    While two fond lovers prate, the Muse and I.  . . .    49 To Congreve         200
    The Muse, like some bright country virgin, shows,  . .  50 To Congreve        215
    The muse retreats far in yon chrystal cell;  . . . .   50 To Congreve         228
    Or loves the muse to walk with conscious pride  . .    51 Temple Ill           11
    When to poetic view the Muse appear'd.  . . . . .      51 Temple Ill           16
    Such to unhallowed sight the Muse divine  . . . .      52 Temple Ill           29
    Listen while the muse thus teaches thee to sing:  . .   52 Temple Ill          36
    At the divine appearance of the Muse,  . . . . .      53 Temple Ill           76
    See Muse, what havock in these looks appear  . . . .   55 Temple Ill          125
    Sing Muse the House of Poet Van  . . . . . . . .       80 Vanbruq House        57
    Sing Muse the House of Poet <Van>  . . . . . . . .    106 V's House            31
    And make my Muse the Architect;  . . . . . . . .      107 V's House            45
    Description would but tire my Muse:  . . . . . . .    116 Bauc & Phil 2       163
    With ev'ry Muse to Grace thy Song,  . . . . . . .     121 Apollo Outwit        55
    Subject or Patron of his Muse,  . . . . . . . .       157 Fable of Midas       52
    As that my Muse is yet a Maid,  . . . . . . . .       183 Horace 2, 1         100
    To you the Muse this Verse bestows,  . . . . . . .    215 To Mr. Delany         9
    The Flirts of his ill-manner'd Muse.  . . . . . .     219 To Mr. Delany       110
    Fair Maidens all attend the Muse  . . . . . . . .     224 Prog of Love         73
    The Muse has now not time to tell 'um.  . . . . .     224 Prog of Love         86
    But, never shall the Muse endure  . . . . . . . .     242 Horace 4, 9           3
    Begin, my Muse, first from our Bowers,  . . . . .     278 Journal               7
    "And not a Muse will hear their Call:  . . . . . .    321 First of April       22
    Pope walks, and courts the Muse.  . . . . . . .       405 Swift to Pope         8
    Unwilling Muse begin thy Lay,  . . . . . . . . .      445 Modern Lady          34
    Why should I ask of thee, my Muse,  . . . . . . .     449 Modern Lady         136
    How can the Muse her Aid impart,  . . . . . . . .     451 Modern Lady         220
    Forming his Muse by <Smedley's> Modell,  . . . . .    458 Paddy's Charac       23
    Who think your Muse must first aspire;  . . . . .     475 Epist on Epist       23
    Ne'er did a true satyric muse  . . . . . . . . .      488 Irish-Club           25
    Or could my Muse exert the Rage  . . . . . . . .      496 Panegyr Swift       100
    You say, the Muse will not contain,  . . . . . . .    501 Doctor Delaney       51
    For, though the Muse delights in Fiction,  . . . .    503 Doctor Delaney      105
    Never may the Muse forget ye:  . . . . . . . . .      522 Betty Grizette        2
    For thee, than make a dry Nurse of thy Muse?  . . .   531 To Mr. Gay            8
    His Fancy sunk, his Muse a Jade.  . . . . . . . .     556 Death of Swift      102
    The bashful Muse will never bear  . . . . . . . .     583 Young Nymph          71
    (Muse, find me Names to fix my Metre,  . . . . . .    594 Cassinus Peter        5
    As Trophies of a Muse deceas'd:  . . . . . . . .      611 By Dr. Swift          6
```

MUSE   (CONTINUED)   PAGE   TITLE   LINE
      Have my busy Muse employ'd, ...   630 Epistle Lady   5
      When my Muse officious ventures   . . . .   635 Epistle Lady   155
      Such a Rocket is my Muse, ...   638 Epistle Lady   259
      The Muse invok'd, sit down to write;   . . . . . .   643 On Poetry   86
      Employ your Muse on Kings alive;   . . . .   647 On Poetry   220
      Thy Praises ev'ry Muse shall sing.   . . . . . .   656 On Poetry   448
      Thy Muse from falling upon Pindar?   . . . . . .   666 Epig Carthy 2   D   2
      Nor shall the conscious Muse unfold.   . . . . .   712 Cadenus Vaness   827
      Invokes his Mistress and his Muse, ...   728 Stella, Poems   27
      Should but his Muse descending drop   . . . . . .   728 Stella, Poems   29
      The Muse her ann'all Tribute pays, ...   739 Stel B-day '21   2
      And boldly then invoke the Muse: . . . .   743 Stel B-day 22   76
      The Muse will at your Call appear, ...   743 Stel B-day 22   79
      And if the Muse deny her Aid   . . . .   757 Stel B-day '24   33
      Herald lend the Muse an answer;   . . . .   800 Traulus 2   27
      Come, assist me, Muse obedient, ...   832 Legion Club   75
      Thither, gentle Muse, conduct me, ...   832 Legion Club   79
      See, the Muse unbars the Gate;   . . . .   832 Legion Club   81
      Never durst a Muse before   . . . .   834 Legion Club   119
      Sing heavenly Muse in sweetly flowing Strain,   . . 880 Pastoral Dial   7
      My artless Muse shall sing your Fame.   . . . . .   887 Panegyr Dean   6
      Me for the Subject of his Muse.   . . . .   887 Panegyr Dean   26
      I thus begin. My grateful Muse   . . . .   888 Panegyr Dean   37
      But, stop ambitious Muse, in time;   . . . . . .   896 Panegyr Dean   319
      No Muse harmonious Entertains, ...   957 Cantata
      But now let us hear what the Muse from your car says. 976 Dean to Sherid   6
      And now I find my Muse but ill able   . . . . . .   989 Letter Dr Sh-n   30
      Thy Muse is tuck'd up, and succinct;   . . . . .   1021 Nim-Dan-Dean 1   D 27
      If I write any more, it will make my poor Muse sick.   1030 Dr. Sheridan   1
MUSE'S
      Me she has to the Muse's Gallies ty'd, ...   32 Ode to Temple   191
      Provoke the honour of my Muse's rage, ...   42 Ode Sancroft   262
      Soft'ning the muse's thunder into praise: . . .   44 To Congreve   42
      Perish the Muse's hour, thus vainly spent   . . .   48 To Congreve   175
      Happy beyond a private muse's fate, ...   49 To Congreve   179
      And the young Muse's early favour felt;   . . . .   49 To Congreve   192
      To prostitute the Muse's Name, ...   654 On Poetry   406
MUSES
      (For all the Muses Geese are Swans)   . . . . .   80 Vanbrug House   50
      When on their Queen the Muses wait;   . . . . . .   121 Apollo Outwit   46
      The Graces next, and all the Muses   . . . . . .   290 Prog Marriage   9
      Thus to his Choir of Muses spoke;   . . . . . .   320 First of April   2
      "Who is as good as all the Muses;   . . . . . .   321 First of April   8
      The Muses when they saw her care, ...   322 First of April   43
      You place the Muses and Apollo;   . . . .   477 Epist on Epist   80
      To real Muses, Gods, and Streams.   . . . . . .   478 Epist on Epist   86
      But, wisely left the Muses Hill, ...   482 Libel on D- D-   65
      Or, if the Muses must inspire   . . . .   489 Dialogue   19
      Attain'd by Flight the Muses Hill;   . . . . . .   504 Doctor Delaney   120
      To persecute the Muses Fame;   . . . .   504 Doctor Delaney   132
      How could you, Gay, disgrace the Muses Train,   . . 531 To Mr. Gay   1
      The Muses next in Order follow, ...   585 Strephon Chloe   53
      Nine Muses always waiting round him, ...   598 Problem Solved   25
      As how to strike the Muses Lyre.   . . . .   641 On Poetry   32
      Ye Muses guard your sacred Mount, ...   671 Epig Carthy 21   D   5
      The Muses, by their King's Permission, ...   689 Cadenus Vaness   93
      The Muses oft were seen to frown;   . . . . . .   689 Cadenus Vaness   99
      A Thing never known to the Muses or Phoebus: . .   716 Answer Rebus   8
      I think you inspird by the Muses all nine   . . .   1017 Swift Ans Sher   4
MUSES'
      Make me pollute the Muses' bower?   . . . .   490 Dialogue   46
MUSHA
      Musha! Why Parliament wouldn't you maul, ...   841 Ballad   D 16
MUSHROOM
      Far sooner than the nobler mushroom grows: . . .   46 To Congreve   100
      A mushroom in a bed of dung;   . . . .   950 Upstart   D   4
MUSICAL
      And musical Clatter, ...   245 Irish-Feast   32
MUSICK
      An unknown Musick all around, ...   17 Ode Athenian   52
      In vain pursues the Musick with her longing Eye,   . . 17 Ode Athenian   58
      Two Gods their Skill in Musick try'd, ...   156 Fable of Midas   25
      That Musick gave her Leave to litter, ...   208 Fable Bitches   17
      The Time pass'd on, and Musick came, ...   208 Fable Bitches   37
      In musick, Raffling-rooms, and Toys, ...   294 Prog Marriage   136
      Wrought by the Musick of the Spheres - - -   . . .   362 Grace's Answer   36
      That you who know musick no more than as ass   . .   522 St. Cecilia's   2
      She fancies Musick in his Tongue, ...   703 Cadenus Vaness   530
      Suit your Words to your Musick well, ...   956 Cantata
      Musick well, Musick well, ...   956 Cantata
      Musick well, Musick well, ...   956 Cantata
      Suit your Words to your Musick well, ...   956 Cantata
      Suit your Words to your Musick well, ...   956 Cantata
      Such Musick would make a Fanatick or Jew sick: . . 1029 Dr. Helsham   14
MUSICK'S
      At length to Musick's House she came, ...   207 Fable Bitches   7
MUST   343   OMITTED WORD
MUSTARD
      As loud as fifty mustard bowls;   . . . .   461 Birthday Song   40
      Come eat 'em with pure fresh Butter and Mustard,   . . 953 Herrings   6

		PAGE	TITLE	LINE
MUSTER				
Troops of all Tongues and Nations Muster:	. . . . .	345	Prometheus	28
Of all the Virtues you can muster:	. . . .	647	On Poetry	222
MUSTY				
With Rules from musty Morals brought,	. . . . . .	27	Ode to Temple	19
For long enur'd to musty Rules,	. . . .	493	Panegyr Swift	29
MUTE				
Nell roar'd incessant, Dick sate mute:	. . . . .	219	A Quiet Life	4
No single Tongue one Moment mute;	. . . . . .	450	Modern Lady	177
Love can with Speech inspire a Mute,	. . . . .	709	Cadenus Vaness	712
MUTTER				
I own it hath often provok'd me to Mutter,	. . . . .	334	Serious Poem	5
To cry the Bread was stale, and mutter	. . . . .	410	Dial Rich Marb	53
MUTTER'D				
Thrice mutter'd something to the Air.	. . . . . .	120	Apollo Outwit	36
MUTTON				
She'll never think of Mutton Pies.	. . . . . .	362	Grace's Answer	42
As Mutton Cutlets, Prime of Meat,	. . . . . .	528	Lady's Dres Rm	99
MUTTON-CHOP				
A Slice of Bread, and Mutton-Chop,	. . . . . .	728	Stella, Poems	30
MUTUAL				
And thus a mutual gentle Fire,	. . . .	593	Strephon Chloe	313
"This might their mutual Fancy strike,	. . . . .	714	Cadenus Vaness	878
With mutual Beauty smit, their Passion grew.	. . . .	880	Pastoral Dial	6
MUZZLE				
Before the Flame from Muzzle burst,	. . . . . .	66	Problem	45
MY 859			OMITTED WORD	
MYSELF 6			OMITTED WORD	
MYST'RY				
My highest Progress in the Myst'ry	. . . . . .	493	Panegyr Swift	31
MYSTERIES				
The Mysteries that lye below.	. . . .	922	Riddle 7	50
MYSTERIOUS				
He deals, and Hears mysterious Chat;	. . . . .	63	Discovery	14
From our Mysterious Club to keep out Spies,	. . . .	165	Toland's Invit	29
MYSTERY				
Out slipp't a Mystery of State	. . . .	62	Discovery	7
MYSTICK				
To morrow We our Mystick Feast prepare,	. . . . .	162	Toland's Invit	7
MYTHOLOGICK				
The Poets Mythologick Dreams,	. . . .	478	Epist on Epist	85
NAB				
Truly, says he, Mrs. Nab, . . .	. . . .	72	Mrs Harris Pet	55
NAG				
Or Harness'd to a Nag, at ease	. . . .	109	V's House	111
Rides on a Broomstick for a Nag,	. . . .	132	Magician's Rod	16
NAIL				
We want our Money on the Nail;	. . . .	239	Run Bankers	17
With a Scrap of Bank Paper the Breadth of his Nail;	. . . .	288	Bank Down	38
And faithfully direct her Nail	. . . .	527	Lady's Dres Rm	65
A Bungler thus, who scarce the Nail can hit,	. . . .	535	To Mr. Gay	131
He pays his Workmen on the Nail.	. . . .	646	On Poetry	190
NAIL'D				
Nail'd to her Window full in Sight	. . . . . .	735	Stel B-day '20	35
NAILS				
I wish some Folks would pare their Nails.	. . . .	453	Modern Lady	269
To scratch your Head, and bite your Nails.	. . . .	643	On Poetry	90
I bit my Nails, and scratch'd my Head,	. . . .	740	Stel B-day 22	5
Or crack such Lice as his betwixt your Nails?	. . . .	882	Pastoral Dial	36
And rub thy Teeth, and pair thy Nails.	. . . . .	897	Panegyr Dean	334
She'll tear me with her desp'rate Nails;	. . . .	925	Riddle 8	20
NAKED				
How much of Heav'n is in her naked looks.	. . . .	23	Ode Athenian	233
No deflower'd eye can face the naked light:	. . . .	41	Ode Sancroft	222
To turn her Naked out of Doors,	. . . .	295	Prog Marriage	163
Crouding the roads with naked feet.	. . . . . .	401	Window Inns 5	D 10
Thou must go naked all the Year.	. . . . . .	786	Clad in Brown	4
All over naked I am seen,	. . . .	926	Riddle 9	9
NAM'D				
Nam'd ev'ry player on his fingers ends,	. . . . .	47	To Congreve	139
If nam'd with Scorn, gives just Offence.	. . . .	217	To Mr. Delany	70
Nam'd me as plain as he cou'd speak:	. . . . .	376	Apology Lady C	47
When you have nam'd at least a Score	. . . . .	392	Young's Satire	28
"The Irish Senate, if you nam'd,	. . . . . .	566	Death of Swift	345
She nam'd the antient Heroes round,	. . . . .	697	Cadenus Vaness	350
Nam'd half the Rates, and lik'd the worst.	. . . .	698	Cadenus Vaness	383
(Those Authors he so oft had nam'd.	. . . . .	708	Cadenus Vaness	690
One Lawyer to each Side was nam'd.	. . . . .	713	Cadenus Vaness	843
NAME				
Which makes a Godhead of a Name,	. . . . . .	7	Ode to King	25
Thus he has fix'd His Name	. . . .	7	Ode to King	33
And solid Virtue does Your Name advance.	. . . .	11	Ode to William	D 4
Your Name shall the remaining Work perform,	. . .	13	Ode to William	D 39
And nigh to Heaven as is its Name.	. . . . . .	16	Ode Athenian	10
I would not draw th' Idea from an empty Name;	. . .	21	Ode Athenian	161
The Name and Man, by whom the Book was writ,	. . .	21	Ode Athenian	166
Whether that very Name was He, or You, or I?	. . .	21	Ode Athenian	168
That Men, who liv'd and dy'd without a Name,	. . .	25	Ode Athenian	306
Reformers and physicians differ but in name,	. . .	42	Ode Sancroft	255
Thus prostitute my Congreve's name is grown	. . .	48	To Congreve	159
Whose name must not within my lines be shewn,	. . .	48	To Congreve	167

537

NAME	(CONTINUED)	PAGE	TITLE		LINE
Druid, a name she does with pride repeat,		49	To Congreve		193
In sum, a glitt'ring voice, a painted name,		54	Temple Ill		101
And now they all agree, to name		67	Problem		51
Beside the getting of a Name?		83	Salamander		14
The Mortar onely chang'd it's Name,		93	Bauc & Phil 1		111
A Place not decent here to name.		108	V's House		94
May'st thou despise a Poets Name.		121	Apollo Outwit		56
I'll Speech against Peace while Dismal's my Name,		145	New Song		53
Root out these Carrots, O Thou, whose Name		148	Windsor Proph		21
And keep close to Thee always that Name,		148	Windsor Proph		23
What was his Name, of what Degree;		171	Horace 1, 7		20
Lord! I should get so ill a Name,		220	A Quiet Life		35
Slaves to their Quiet and good Name,		221	A Quiet Life		57
In Southern Seas he leaves his Name.		252	Bubble		48
Change-Ally is the dreadfull Name;		256	Bubble		140
With a certain false Traitress, one Stella by Name,		263	Apollo		30
Or ever name the milky Way.		270	Apollo's Edict	D	22
Yet if his Name you'd eternize		271	Apollo's Edict	D	40
And forty others I could name--		298	Horrid Plot		11
His Name is Harlequin, I wot,		300	Horrid Plot		47
And that's a Name in ev'ry Plot:		300	Horrid Plot		48
Not frighted with an ignominious name,		309	Billet Players		51
From Realms that bear Vesputio's Name:		324	Pethox		24
To burn an old Fryer, one Forrest by Name.		334	Serious Poem		22
A Bishop says the noble 'Squire, I hate the very Name,		342	Upon His Grace		17
I'm sure he call'd me by my Name;		376	Apology Lady C		46
And Prints are crowded with his Name.		397	Earl of P-b-w		3
To get the name of council learned;		435	Answer Paulus		114
Name honest Doctor Pelling;		440	Ballyspellin		21
"I must conceal my Author's Name,		449	Modern Lady		148
Thro' thick and thin, to get a name.		456	Dean Smedley		24
Or name him, but to tell his Faults.		465	Birthday Song		148
Those Elements her name compose,		467	Birthday Song		237
Nassau, who got the name of glorious		468	Birthday Song		251
(His Name is up, he may in Bed lye)		476	Epist on Epist		48
And take a Greater Patrick's Name.		478	Epist on Epist		94
He'll turn it off with; Name your Toast.		480	Libel on D- D-		18
And the great Name engrav'd most fairly,		494	Panegyr Swift		53
Disclaim the Human Name, and Face,		498	Panegyr Swift		172
Tho I name not the wretch you know who I mean		540	Charac Walpole		13
"He neither knew you, nor your Name;		548	Life of Swift		122
"Thought Protestant too Good a Name		550	Life of Swift		170
Says Lintot, "I have heard the Name:		563	Death of Swift		255
And, while they toss my Name about,		565	Death of Swift		303
"He lash'd the Vice but spar'd the Name.		571	Death of Swift		460
Than she, to name her Parts behind,		590	Strephon Chloe		217
Which others, whom he will not name,		605	Beasts Confess		139
For Poems read without a Name		644	On Poetry		129
To get the Name of Conoisseur.		649	On Poetry		276
To prostitute the Muse's Name,		654	On Poetry		406
Thus think on Kings, ye Name denotes		659	On Poetry	D	410
Carthy, no more insult Aurelian's Name,		668	Epig Carthy 10	D	1
Carthy ambitious to retrieve his name,		671	Epig Carthy 24	D	1
And said, "Vanessa is the Name,		692	Cadenus Vaness		180
"Her Name on Earth ----shall not be told.		692	Cadenus Vaness		183
Nor ought of Stella, but the Name;		759	Receipt Youth		34
Or when your Name and Family you boast,		771	Horace 1, 14		39
Tom cou'd write and spell his Name,		784	Mullinex Dick		3
Their Dress, their Language, and the Scottish Name,		791	St. Pat's Well		15
Where is the sacred Well, that bore my Name?		793	St. Pat's Well		65
Which gave the <Dean> the Name of Draper?		796	Traulus 1		12
At length his Old Master (I need not him name)		816	Yahoo's		36
An Arrian to usurp the Name!		819	Dr. Rundle		2
With the Name of Legion Club.		829	Legion Club		12
Name your Heroes one, by one.		834	Legion Club		136
On a Chimney cut his Name.		837	Legion Club		180
"A Boulter by name is no bolter of wit.		843	Ay and No		10
(Sir Archibald whose fav'rite Name		848	Old Thorn		13
This Hill may keep the Name of Drapier:		875	Drapier's Hill		18
But now your name with Penshurst vies,		877	To Dean Swift		33
But now in all our Sexes Name,		887	Panegyr Dean		5
Yet ev'ry Thing that you can name,		935	Riddle 23	D	2
A long-ear'd Beast, another Name for Jeer,		943	Probatur Alit		41
--The rascal! that's too mild a name;		950	Upstart	D	1
What Name for a Maid, was the first Man's Damnation?		973	S-'s Ans Sh-d		12
. . . to come out with such a Name.		985	Mary to Sher		6
'Twas the damn'd 'Squire with the hard Name,		1005	Sheridan's Sub		20
NAME-SAKE					
But by his Name-sake Charles of Sweden.		398	Earl of P-b-w		36
NAMELESS					
(With other Parts that shall be nameless,		586	Strephon Chloe		79
NAMES SEE NICK-NAMES					
Is but one thing under two different names;		41	Ode Sancroft		206
Rend'ring shades, things, and substances of names;		47	To Congreve		146
Names that would best their Natures suit:		83	Salamander		8
When I and some others subscribed our Names		144	New Song		27
Nor Persons Names, nor Places knew;		313	To Ford		54
No party-fool is calling names,		402	Window Inns 7	D	5
Hard, tough, cramp, gutt'rall, harsh, stiff Names.		467	Birthday Song		210
Find Rivers with harmonious names,		468	Birthday Song		241

NAMES	(CONTINUED)	PAGE	TITLE	LINE
The Doctor names but one at present,		513	Answer Fable	33
(Muse, find me Names to fix my Metre,		594	Cassinus Peter	5
I row by, and call them Names.		635	Epistle Lady	166
Change but their Names will do again.		647	On Poetry	232
Whose names and works (tho' dead) are made		876	To Dean Swift	9

NANCY

Says Nancy, I can make for Miss,		128	Little House	61
I'll undertake my little Nancy		700	Cadenus Vaness	418
A wretch like poor Nancy,		851	Lady's Lament	2
. . . a courting Sly Nancy,		1023	Nim-Dan-Dean 2	D 12

NANNY

Nor is old Nanny Shales, whene'er she does brew, sick.		1029	Dr. Helsham	16

NAP

Roughen the Nap, and leave a mingled Stain.		138	City Shower	30
Then, let him come and take a Nap,		410	Dial Rich Marb	85
Dear Madam, try to take a Nap--		451	Modern Lady	210
May Bec have many an evening nap		761	Bec's B-Day	39
Taking her After-dinner Nap:		895	Panegyr Dean	274

NAPE

Shall a Subject so Loyal be hang'd by the Nape,		518	Dean Hang Rape	35

NAPKIN

Her Napkin pinn'd up to her Jaws,		894	Panegyr Dean	256

NARROW

No wonder then she quits the narrow Path of Sense		18	Ode Athenian	68
Our Wit and Learning, narrow as our Trade;		19	Ode Athenian	96
A narrow Sound, though deep as Hell,		256	Bubble	139
And in its narrow Circle gathers		688	Cadenus Vaness	55
The narrow Entry crushd her Hoop		746	Stel Distress	
She curst the narrow winding Stairs:		751	Stel Wood-Park	52

NASSAU

Nassau, who got the name of glorious		468	Birthday Song	251

NASTINESS

And Nastiness of modern Times,		497	Panegyr Swift	117

NASTY

From nasty Ballyspellin		440	Ballyspellin	18
A nasty Compound of all Hues,		527	Lady's Dres Rm	41
That nasty Pantheon.		856	Lady's Lament	150
Dermot, how could you touch those nasty Sluts!		882	Pastoral Dial	39

NAT'RAL

But now, to solve the Nat'ral Cause		65	Problem	13
With all acquir'd and nat'ral parts,		176	To Lord Harley	10
Thus, Envy pleads a nat'ral Claim		504	Doctor Delaney	131
Well comprehend their nat'ral Powers;		607	Beasts Confess	204
Nor, against my nat'ral Vein,		634	Epistle Lady	135
Leave all Things to their Nat'ral Course.		696	Cadenus Vaness	303
As nat'ral Life the Body warms,		724	To Stella	11

NAT'RALISTS

So, Nat'ralists observe, a Flea		651	On Poetry	337

NATAL

But thy Book perish'd on its natal Day.		669	Epig Carthy 13	D 4

NATALE

Libertas & natale Solum;		348	Whitshed Motto	1
Natale Solum: My Estate:		348	Whitshed Motto	6
Libertas & natale Solum;		349	Whitshed Motto	25

NATION

Who cou'd so well a dying Nation save,		12	Ode to William	D 15
See how the double Nation lies;		96	On the Union	7
The Scottish Nation, whom he durst offend,		196	Author Himself	69
And under Hand and Seal the Irish Nation		234	Elegy on Demar	17
Money, the Life-blood of the Nation,		239	Run Bankers	9
The Nation too too late will find		259	Bubble	217
Resolv'd to save the British Nation,		300	Horrid Plot	49
The Bus'ness of the Nation stands.		325	Pethox	52
Some call him a Thorn, the Curse of a Nation,		334	Serious Poem	29
The Death of our Nation it seem'd to foretell,		351	Wood Insect	31
So loud, till all the Nation hears;		354	Simile Silver	28
With ev'ry Vice hath fill'd the Nation;		392	Young's Satire	36
To move that all the Nation round		423	Ireld	67
To injure the nation		424	Carterets Arms	15
But swear his Line shall rule the Nation		466	Birthday Song	197
To make it pass upon the Nation,		475	Epist on Epist	19
To be Maecenas of the Nation,		481	Libel on D- D-	36
Although it might have pleas'd the Nation.		484	Libel on D- D-	120
Who thinks the Nation always err'd,		514	Answer Fable	73
"Is not our Nation in his Debt?		547	Life of Swift	96
To save the Nation ev'ry hour?		548	Life of Swift	110
"And had the Dean, in all the Nation,		558	Death of Swift	161
"The Nation stript go joyful back,		571	Death of Swift	447
"No Nation wanted it so much:		572	Death of Swift	482
Damn'd Time-Serving Priests all over the Nation;		576	Place Damn'd	12
To serve the King, and please the Nation.		606	Beasts Confess	154
Say, Poet, in what other Nation,		656	On Poetry	465
Display the blessings of the Nation,		658	On Poetry	D 190
His Pen to save a sinking Nation draws,		770	Horace 1, 14	26
The Nation scar'd, the Author doom'd to Death,		771	Horace 1, 14	31
A Nation thus, who oft Heav'ns Call neglects,		771	Horace 1, 14	35
Of all thy Party through the Nation.		775	Mullinix Tim	56
Sell the Nation for a Pin;		831	Legion Club	48
For the Court against the Nation.		836	Legion Club	172
Happy Nation were we blind,		862	To Janus	17

```
NATION       (CONTINUED)                                       PAGE  TITLE            LINE
    "The Army's the only good School in the Nation;      . .   872 Grand Question     162
    That when a Nation long enslav'd, . . . . . . . .         875 Drapier's Hill       11
NATION-SAVING
    Revile that Nation-saving Paper,  . . . . . . . .         796 Traulus 1            11
NATION'S
    Some angel say, what were the nation's crimes, . . . .     42 Ode Sancroft        245
    Harley, the Nation's great Support, . . . . . . .         170 Horace 1, 7           1
    We see the Nation's Credit crackt, . . . . . .           253 Bubble               59
    Expos'd, to blind the Nation's Eyes, . . . . . .         354 Simile Silver        21
    Appealing to the Nation's Taste, . . . . . . . .         483 Libel on D- D-       83
    By Gnats, and draw the Nation's Dung, . . . . .          496 Panegyr Swift       115
    How jealous of the Nation's Freedom, . . . . . .         501 Doctor Delaney       57
    And well deserves the Nation's Thanks. . . . . .         515 Answer Fable         80
    Who dares revile the Nation's Wisdom, . . . . .          515 Answer Fable         93
    Not so a Nation's Revenues are paid: . . . . . .         533 To Mr. Gay           49
    Too zealous for the Nation's Good: . . . . . . .         604 Beasts Confess      100
    The Nation's Good, his Master's Glory, . . . . .         605 Beasts Confess      145
    On the Nation's Representers; . . . . . . . .            635 Epistle Lady        156
NATIONS
    Numberless Nations, stretching far and wide, . . . .      25 Ode Athenian        297
    Nor could the nations kneel to viler shapes, . . . .      46 To Congreve         105
    To inflame both the Nations do plainly conspire; . .    237 Excellent Song       19
    The whole Nations Pockets with Money will fill. . .     287 Bank Down            13
    Troops of all Tongues and Nations Muster: . . . .       345 Prometheus           28
    Distress of Nations calls him hence, . . . . . .        387 Manly Virtue        113
NATIVE
    Your Presence all their Native Stubborness controuls,     9 Ode to King          90
    Into his Native Sea, . . . . . .                         22 Ode Athenian        193
    Yet pardon, native Albion, when I say . . . . .          38 Ode Sancroft        128
    From strength of its own native seed, . . . . . .        41 Ode Sancroft        224
    Through native dross your share is hardly known, . .     45 To Congreve          59
    By calling This your native Soyl; . . . . . .           311 To Ford              10
    With native Lustre like her own; . . . . . .           379 Apology Lady C      114
    They soon betray their native Place: . . . . . .        652 On Poetry           362
    The Child with native Beauty shone, . . . . . .         692 Cadenus Vaness      175
    My verse on Stella's native day: . . . . . .           754 Stella '23            4
    Had my own native Italy o'er-run. . . . . .            789 St. Pat's Well        4
    Be all made Captives in their native Land; . . . .      793 St. Pat's Well       90
NATIVES
    Whose anxious Natives, Night and Day, . . . . .         388 Manly Virtue        137
NATIVITY
    Parson, said I, can you cast a Nativity,. . . .          72 Mrs Harris Pet       53
    This day, dear Bec, is thy nativity, . . . . .         760 Bec's B-Day           1
NATUR'D    SEE GOOD-NATUR'D
NATURAL    SEE NAT'RAL
    On ev'ry natural Defect; . . . . . . . .               592 Strephon Chloe      274
    From Chance, or natural Defect . . . . . . .           603 Beasts Confess       66
NATURALLY
    They're now, just now, as naturally born, . . . .       20 Ode Athenian        130
NATURE    SEE ILL-NATURE,DAME-NATURE
    Of Nature and of Art, of deep Philosophy and Love, .    17 Ode Athenian         55
    (Which Nature never can retain, . . . . .               25 Ode Athenian        289
    Shew the Delights thy Sister Nature yields, . . .        31 Ode to Temple       137
    Why then does Nature so unjustly share . . . .          32 Ode to Temple       180
    Nature the hidden Spark did at my Birth infuse, . .      32 Ode to Temple       202
    Which still their antient Nature keep; . . . .         114 Bauc & Phil 2       105
    Truth, Innocence, Good Nature, Look serene; . . .      118 Biddy Floyd           4
    When Nature would invite us down, . . . . . . .        122 Empty'ng Town         3
    So are the Joys which Nature yields . . . . .          122 Empty'ng Town         9
    He soon disclos'd his Nature. . . . . . . .            153 Widow and Cat     D   5
    To you, by Art and Nature taught . . . . . .           215 To Mr. Delany         3
    Here, onely Nature acts her Part, . . . . . .          215 To Mr. Delany        21
    Call'd her good Nature to relieve him; . . . .         378 Apology Lady C       85
    Where nature hardly seems alive. . . . . . .           421 Holyhead             32
    By Nature turn'd to play the Rake-well, . . . .        446 Modern Lady          36
    "But Nature freely takes her Course, . . . . .         476 Epist on Epist       55
    To rail at men by nature fools: . . . . . .            488 Irish-Club           28
    Dame Nature as the Learned show, . . . . . .           504 Doctor Delaney      127
    From Nature, I believe 'em true: . . . . . .           553 Death of Swift        2
    "While Nature kindly bent to ease us, . . . . .        554 Death of Swift        9
    Must by the Course of Nature dye: . . . . . .          556 Death of Swift       74
    By Nature, Reason, Learning, blind; . . . . .          579 Day Judgement        12
    By Nature form'd with nicest Care, . . . . . .         584 Strephon Chloe        5
    Felt no Necessities of Nature. . . . . . .             584 Strephon Chloe       20
    The Time when Wants of Nature press; . . . . .         588 Strephon Chloe      140
    Steals out her Hand by Nature led, . . . . .           589 Strephon Chloe      171
    Which Nature gives in such a Case; . . . . .           591 Strephon Chloe      240
    Let Prudence with Good Nature strive, . . . .          593 Strephon Chloe      309
    Nature alone must bear the Blame: . . . . .            602 Beasts Confess       30
    To kindle strife Dame Nature taught her, . . .         618 Scandal Poem 1       37
    Who, led by Folly, fights with Nature; . . . .         641 On Poetry            20
    Lives in a State of War by Nature. . . . . .           651 On Poetry           320
    For, tho' in Nature Depth and Height . . . .           653 On Poetry           389
    That best ye regal Nature suit, . . . . . .            659 On Poetry         D 410
    Nature must give Way to Art. . . . . . .               660 Love Song             4
    Thro' Nature, and thro' Art she rang'd, . . .          698 Cadenus Vaness      354
    For Nature must be Nature still. . . . . . .           705 Cadenus Vaness      587
    For Nature must be Nature still. . . . . . .           705 Cadenus Vaness      587
    Self-Love, in Nature rooted fast, . . . . .            708 Cadenus Vaness      684
    Will force all Nature to submit. . . . . . .           709 Cadenus Vaness      725
```

		PAGE	TITLE	LINE

NATURE   (CONTINUED)
Nature in him had Merit plac'd, ... 711 Cadenus Vaness 766
She thinks that Nature ne'er design'd   . . . . . . 725 To Stella 65
For nobler Ends by Nature meant.   . . . . 731 Stella, Poems 116
Could Art or Time or Nature bribe   . . . . 736 Stel B-day '20 52
For Nature, always in the Right, ... 757 Stel B-day '24 43
Thus, nature hath resolv'd to pay her   . . . . . . 761 Bec's B-Day 29
By nature meant for nobler Ends, ... 781 Mullinix Tim 279
But in no other Sense, than Nature   . . . . 812 Bro Protestant 33
Dame Nature, when she saw the Blow, ... 849 Old Thorn 25
Bestow'd her by nature, ... 854 Lady's Lament 98
May'st dye like me by Chance; but not by Nature.   . 861 On Old Glass 2
As Nature prompts, his Off'ring pays?   . . . . . . 895 Panegyr Dean 288
Here, Nature never Diff'rence made   . . . . . . 895 Panegyr Dean 289
Nature holds her forth two mirrors, ... 907 Daphne 43
Nature to form me took Delight, ... 915 Riddle 1 3
Because I am by Nature blind, ... 917 Riddle 4 1
Faster than Nature can create;   . . . . 935 Riddle 23 D 19
Add another of royal Nature.   . . . . 940 Letter 6
NATURE'S
Transcending Nature's ordinary Laws, ... 10 Ode to King 132
Nature's fair Table-book our tender Souls   . . . . 27 Ode to Temple 32
As antient nature's modern masters dream;   . . . . 45 To Congreve 72
Weak is the beam to dry up nature's tears, ... 51 Temple Ill 19
So nature's craz'd convulsions make us dread   . . . 53 Temple Ill 65
Nature's bare visage furrowed as he mows: . . . . 55 Temple Ill 124
May He whom Nature's Laws obey, ... 258 Bubble 209
A Post so fill'd, on Nature's Laws entrenches;   . . 285 Elegy Boat 11
('Twas Nature's Fault) without a Beard.   . . . . . 603 Beasts Confess 62
Which alien seems from Nature's Laws;   . . . . . . 923 Riddle 7 82
NATURES
Names that would best their Natures suit: . . . . 83 Salamander 8
NAUGHT
. . .as tho' I had call'd her all to naught;   . . . 71 Mrs Harris Pet 45
"Who sell their Souls and Votes for Naught;   . . . . 571 Death of Swift 446
NAUGHTY
To break thy Rod like naughty Lad?   . . . . 135 Magician's Rod 80
"Or naughty Boy elopes from School, ... 497 Panegyr Swift 130
The naughty boys about the village . . . . 902 Dean's Reasons 107
NAUSEATE
Still cast it up and nauseate Company.   . . . . . 27 Ode to Temple 49
NAUSEOUS
Bedaubs the guilty Great with nauseous Praise: . . . 364 On Dreams 36
And Flatt'ry tipt with nauseous Fleer, ... 725 To Stella 47
I see her taste each nauseous Draught, ... 727 To Stella 113
A nauseous Brood, that fills your Senate Walls,   . . 792 St. Pat's Well 57
NAVY
Can <Fart> his Navy back again.   . . . . 774 Mullinix Tim 32
NAY
Curst be the Wretch, nay doubly curst, ... 28 Ode to Temple 50
Nay, said I, I had it in Lady Betty's Chamber,. . . . 70 Mrs Harris Pet 17
Nay, said she, my Lord Collway's Folks are all very sad 70 Mrs Harris Pet 27
Patrige is Dead, nay more, he dy'd   . . . . . . 98 Elegy Patrige 3
Nay, --now I cannot stir my Foot: . . . . . . 116 Bauc & Phil 2 161
"And Fathers never shou'd say nay, ... 181 Horace 2, 1 46
Nay, 'twas affirm'd, he sometimes dealt in Rhime;   . . 193 Author Himself 10
Nay, Voiture is as like Tom Lee, ... 217 To Mr. Delany 63
Nay would it not Your Passion raise   . . . . . . 312 To Ford 37
The Weather's Fair, nay, that is true, ... 372 Letter D. S-y 23
Nay then 'tis time for me to go.   . . . . 376 Apology Lady C 44
"Nay, Madam, give me leave to say . . . . 452 Modern Lady 248
To praise Queen Anne, nay more, defend her,   . . . 550 Life of Swift 186
Nay, what's incredible, alack! . . . . 674 His Deafness 7
Nay, though the treach'rous Rascal Thomas   . . . . 734 Stel B-day '20 9
Say then more than they; nay, lavishly flatter,   . . 819 Archbi Cashel 13
Nay, he can make what's greater far, ... 876 To Dean Swift 23
Nay; Man, my Master, is my Slave!   . . . . . . 916 Riddle 1 33
Nay give their very Souls away.   . . . . . . 929 Riddle 14 D 6
Nay, in the Compass of a Farthing.   . . . . . . 930 Riddle 15 D 28
Nay, bring me here the tallest Man, ... 934 Riddle 21 D 17
Nay, hector and swagger, you'll still find me stanch,   . 979 Dean to Tho: S 13
Nay, further, the Moment you're free from your scalding,   1019 To Sheridan 9
NAYADS
If Nayads swept them from the Brink)   . . . . . . 894 Panegyr Dean 244
NAYLER
Hobbes, Tindal, and Woolston, and Collins, and Nayler,   815 Yahoo's 26
NE
Walke sans wetynge Shoes ne hosen.   . . . . 102 Merlin 4
NE'ER
Ne'er borrow'd more variety of Shapes   . . . . . 22 Ode Athenian 199
But ne'er since seated in one single Breast.   . . . . 26 Ode to Temple 7
Which we ne'er join'd before, but in Romances meet,   . . 28 Ode to Temple 60
He ne'er could overcome her quite, ... 30 Ode to Temple 131
Tho' ne'er so gently led . . . . 31 Ode to Temple 147
Ne'er sprang a youth from out this isle before   . . 44 To Congreve 11
Since knaves are ne'er oblig'd for what they steal.   . . 45 To Congreve 66
And chuse out wits who ne'er have seen his face;   . . 48 To Congreve 170
And once drawn up, is ne'er let down again.   . . . . 50 To Congreve 234
Grief from Dorinda's face does ne'er depart   . . . . 53 Temple Ill 53
That thou ne'er hadst a being of thy own, ... 54 Temple Ill 94
Altho' the bore be ne'er so large, ... 66 Problem 44

NE'ER   (CONTINUED)   PAGE   TITLE   LINE

And should some Nymph who ne'er was cruel, ...   85 Salamander   61
As if they ne'er had toucht a Drop.   . . . .   112 Bauc & Phil 2   34
But Classick Authors--he ne'er miss'd 'em.   . . . .   115 Bauc & Phil 2   136
Suppose then Atlas ne'er so wise, ...   160 Atlas   19
The Towns we took ne'er did us good, ...   169 Peace Dunkirk   31
The Nymph would ne'er have been a prude.   . . . .   177 To Lord Harley   16
Give Hints, that Poets ne'er believe in God.   . . .   193 Author Himself   6
If I ne'er got, or lost a groat, ...   199 Horace 2, 6   D
Great Ministers ne'er think of these;   . . . .   199 Horace 2, 6   18
And that they ne'er consider'd yet.   . . . . . .   200 Horace 2, 6   22
"You ne'er consider whom you shove, ...   200 Horace 2, 6   38
Tho' in thy Walls he ne'er did Farthing spend,   . . .   234 Elegy on Demar   26
Will ne'er be forgot, ...   244 Irish-Feast   2
Ne'er dream't of the Matter, ...   245 Irish-Feast   30
He knows very well I ne'er gave a Refusal, ...   265 Apollo   71
Cupid shall ne'er mistake another   . . . .   272 Apollo's Edict   D 56
A Dog and <Bishop> ne'er was seen, ...   301 Horrid Plot   74
'Till <Hort> arriv'd ne'er kept a Wench;   . . . . . .   303 Storm   18
I ne'er could endure my Talent to smother, ...   336 Serious Poem   69
He would ne'er be convinc'd it was a True Saint: . .   336 Serious Poem   74
Minerva ne'er an Oath did Swear   . . . .   372 Letter D. S-y   12
And if you should, we'd ne'er have end on't, ...   372 Letter D. S-y   21
Our King ne'er exhausted his fountain of Honours.   . .   389 Order of Bath   6
Ne'er to be match't in modern Reading, ...   398 Earl of P-b-w   35
Because he ne'er one Thought allow'd   . . . . . .   400 Window Inns 1   3
We ne'er can have her full in view.   . . . .   401 Window Inns 5   D 12
But ne'er consider'd where they Slept.   . . . . . .   481 Libel on D- D-   38
Ne'er did a true satyric muse   . . . .   488 Irish-Club   25
She ne'er inspires against Conviction: . . . . .   503 Doctor Delaney   106
We ne'er shou'd know that he could write: . . . . .   514 Answer Fable   72
Would ne'er have shown him so much Favour: . . . . .   514 Answer Fable   78
A holier Priest ne'er was wrapt up in Crape,   . . .   516 Dean Hang Rape   5
Which can ne'er be worse for wearing.   . . . . . .   523 Betty Grizette   22
The God of Light could ne'er have been so blind,   . .   532 To Mr. Gay   27
"He ne'er offended with a Jest;   . . . .   572 Death of Swift   472
The Secret thou shalt ne'er impart;   . . . .   596 Cassinus Peter   101
But Gluttony was ne'er his Vice: . . . .   602 Beasts Confess   40
A better Neighbour ne'er was found: . . . .   602 Beasts Confess   44
Ne'er kept a Cause, he well may boast, ...   604 Beasts Confess   91
His Promises he ne'er forgot, ...   606 Beasts Confess   157
He ne'er was partial to his Kin;   . . . .   606 Beasts Confess   176
She ne'er was known to burst a lace.   . . . . . .   618 Scandal Poem 1   20
Mention Courts, you'll ne'er be quiet;   . . . . . .   635 Epistle Lady   183
And since you ne'er provok'd their Spight, ...   644 On Poetry   133
My Works he said, cou'd ne'er afford him Meat,   . . .   670 Epig Carthy 20   D 3
Will ne'er admit thee on the other.   . . . .   671 Epig Carthy 22   D 6
She ne'er could shew her Face above.   . . . . . .   689 Cadenus Vaness   82
The Parties ne'er could Issue join: . . . .   690 Cadenus Vaness   123
Since Men alledge they ne'er can find   . . . . . .   691 Cadenus Vaness   142
But it shall ne'er be said, a Child   . . . . . .   692 Cadenus Vaness   194
For, let a Man be ne'er so wise, ...   707 Cadenus Vaness   668
Cadenus, who cou'd ne'er suspect   . . . .   709 Cadenus Vaness   726
Ne'er held Possession of his Breast;   . . . . . .   711 Cadenus Vaness   769
She thinks that Nature ne'er design'd   . . . . . .   725 To Stella   65
I ne'er admitted Love a Guest.   . . . .   728 Stella, Poems   14
Ne'er minded a word that was spoken;   . . . . . .   755 Dingley Brent   3
They ne'er troubled their head, ...   755 Dingley Brent   5
I'll ne'er believe a Word they say.   . . . .   757 Stel B-day '24   40
Oh, ne'er may Fortune shew her Spight, ...   758 Stel B-day '24   53
She ne'er considers why, or where: . . . .   761 Bec's B-Day   24
Ne're hold my peace, and ne'er stand still.   . . . .   778 Mullinix Tim   160
And, must their Malice ne'er give o'er?   . . . . . .   798 Traulus 1   86
But Ireland's Friends ne'er wanted Foes.   . . . . .   798 Traulus 1   88
And Smithfield, as Rap was ne'er colted before;   . . .   817 Yahoo's   57
From Rogues who ne'er believ'd a God?   . . . . . .   820 Dr. Rundle   30
"I ne'er knew a Parson without a good Nose, ...   872 Grand Question   143
"But he maul'd me, I ne'er was so maul'd in my Life;   .   873 Grand Question   168
You ne'er was known, by Passion stir'd, ...   889 Panegyr Dean   69
With Dennis you did ne'er combine, ...   890 Panegyr Dean   97
As if she ne'er could have enuff: . . . .   895 Panegyr Dean   261
But ne'er presume to eat a Bit: . . . .   897 Panegyr Dean   336
But, as for me, who ne'er could clamber high,   . . .   900 Dean's Reasons   51
His rural walks he ne'er adorns;   . . . .   901 Dean's Reasons   91
No--that scheme will ne'er succeed, ...   907 Daphne   39
I will ne'er object a word.   . . . .   908 Daphne   62
Yet, some who ne'er bestow'd thee, boast   . . . . . .   919 Riddle 5   29
I'm ev'ry one, but ne'er my self;   . . . .   935 Riddle 23   D 23
Ne'er sad I mourn, ne'er glad rejoice, ...   936 Riddle 23   D 24
Ne'er sad I mourn, ne'er glad rejoice, ...   936 Riddle 23   D 24
I ne'er was born, nor e'er can die, ...   936 Riddle 23   D 26
Better ne'er was try'd.   . . . .   953 Herrings   5
That I'll ne'er give my vote for Delenda Cart-ago.   . .   979 Dean to Tho: S   18
For that, dear Tom, ne'er fret and vex, ...   983 Sher, A Goose   17
Tho' I ne'er saw her hold the Scissars, ...   993 On Picture   14
I thought an Ace you'd ne'er have bated, ...   1002 Reply by Dean   2
For Spight I ne'er had any.   . . . .   1005 Sheridan's Sub   19
We shall ne'er have one Bottle;   . . . .   1015 Swift to Sheri   40
Will ne'er be smooth, nor hold the Stitches.   . . . .   1021 Nim-Dan-Dean 1   D 18
But, I hope I shall ne'er be, like you, of a Shrew sick   1030 Dr. Sheridan   4

	PAGE	TITLE	LINE

NE'R
She ne'r before in all her Life . . . . 224 Prog of Love 65
For, true or false, they'll ne'r enquire, ... 312 To Ford 33
You, for the News are ne'r to seek, ... 315 To Ford 103
Ne'r came in sight . . . . 441 Ballyspellin 41
Robin, who ne'r his mind could fix . . . . 878 Robbin & Harry 29

NE'RE
That I believe in much, I ne're can hope to see; . . 20 Ode Athenian 134
For he ne're could have fill'd it so well of himself. . 77 Lady B- B- 20
As if they ne're had drunk a drop. . . . . 92 Bauc & Phil 1 78
The Sense can ne're be too jejune, ... 467 Birthday Song 211
Ne're hold my peace, and ne'er stand still. . . . . . 778 Mullinix Tim 160

NEAL
Quoth Neal, whate'er the rest may think, ... 67 Problem 53
"Neal Gahagan, Hibernian Clown, ... 851 Old Thorn 82

NEAR
You saw how near we were to Ruin brought, ... 12 Ode to William D 17
Near better animals, her father's sheep; . . . . . 50 To Congreve 222
Be what it will; late near yon whisp'ring stream, . . . 51 Temple Ill 13
Why near the dregs of youth perversely wilt thou stay, . 54 Temple Ill 105
which plainly shews the near Alliance . . . . 98 Elegy Patrige 29
A near Resemblance to the Spheres. . . . . 99 Elegy Patrige 40
The Jack and Chimney near ally'd, ... 113 Bauc & Phil 2 75
Like Sid's, but nothing near so good; . . . . 134 Magician's Rod 60
Observ'd a Parson near Whitehall, ... 170 Horace 1, 7 5
There leaning near a gentle Brook, ... 202 Horace 2, 6 109
She trembled when a Man drew near; . . . . 222 Prog of Love 3
Nor let the Beaux approach too near. . . . . 228 Prog of Beauty 68
How near was she to be undone, ... 269 Apollo's Edict D 3
Form'd like the Triple-Tree near Stephen's-Green; . . 285 Elegy Boat 34
Approaching near the Town, he hears . . . . 338 Wood's Brass 5
Which near the Os Petrosum pass; . . . . 367 Answer Delaney 36
Are very near a-kin; . . . . 401 Window Inns 4 2
So, sweetly screams if it comes near her, ... 416 Woman's Mind 35
With neither Spouse nor Brother near her, ... 466 Birthday Song 180
Which lasted near two thousand years, ... 490 Dialogue 34
There, near thy Master's Throne in Shelter plac't, . . 538 Mr. Pulteney 11
Or, near Fleet-Ditch's oozy Brinks, ... 583 Young Nymph 47
The Duke and Dean seem near upon a levell. . . . . . 678 Dean and Duke 10
Near the Church--you know the rest. . . . . 829 Legion Club 8
Near the Door an entrance gapes, ... 832 Legion Club 87
And be thought a near Relation; . . . . 833 Legion Club 112
Your Altars near your Couches Side? . . . . 896 Panegyr Dean 294
That, near the Knight of Gosford plac't, ... 899 Dean's Reasons 21
I near the Side-board take my Seat; . . . . 920 Riddle 6 26
He kindly bids me near him stand; . . . . 921 Riddle 6 29
With that which dwelt so near her Heart; . . . . . . 922 Riddle 7 36
They can't come near it for their Blood. . . . . . 928 Riddle 12 D 8
To Ladies Skins there's nothing comes so near. . . . 943 Probatur Alit 42
Eat my Oysters, and lye near her, ... 953 Oysters 15

NEAREST
"I know his nearest Friends complain, ... 547 Life of Swift 78
Its Force against your nearest Friends; . . . . . . 730 Stella, Poems 98

NEARLY
Nearly related to an Earl. . . . . 289 Prog Marriage 4
How nearly this <Bishop> our <Bishop> resembles! . . 803 Irish Bishops 7

NEAT
Drest her again Genteel and Neat, ... 23 Ode Athenian 230
And with Whips and Spurs so neat, ... 573 Helter Skelter 9
And if they find the Chambers neat, ... 734 Stel B-day '20 3
Your Table neat, your Linnen fine; . . . . 752 Stel Wood-Park 83

NEATLY
Too neatly guilt for me to soil. . . . . 611 By Dr. Swift 2
Dick could neatly dance a Jig, ... 784 Mullinex Dick 13

NEBUCHADNAZZARS
O! were they all but Nebuchadnazzars . . . . 659 On Poetry D 410

NECESSARY
Will soon grow necessary to his Heirs. . . . . . . 535 To Mr. Gay 120

NECESSITIES
Felt no Necessities of Nature. . . . . 584 Strephon Chloe 20

NECESSITY
Necessity, thou tyrant conscience of the great, . . . 40 Ode Sancroft 176
"You see 'tis meer Necessity, ... 207 Fable Bitches 10
Necessity, the Tyrant's Law, ... 922 Riddle 7 23

NECK
And when she has him by the Neck fast, ... 279 Journal 15
Thence to the Neck; and moving thorow there; . . . . 367 Answer Delaney 37
That bit your Neck but Yesterday, ... 504 Doctor Delaney 142
Ty'd round the <Dean's> Neck, for committing a <Rape>. 519 Dean Hang Rape 66
And, thy freckled Neck display'd, ... 522 Betty Grizette 5
His Hand, his Neck, his Mouth, and Feet . . . . . . 586 Strephon Chloe 77
'Tis ten to one, he breaks your Neck. . . . . 666 Epig Carthy 2 D 8
With Neck elated tow'rds the Skies! . . . . 743 Stel B-day 22 62
Polish'd neck, and radient eye; . . . . 936 Riddle 24 D 14

NECKS
Strain their Necks with looking back: . . . . . . 863 To Janus 22

NECTAR
In Nectar thrice infuses Bays, ... 691 Cadenus Vaness 156

NED
When Margery chastises Ned . . . . 328 Epigram 2 1
Joan cudgell's Ned, yet Ned's a Bully . . . . . . 328 Epigram 3 1

NED	(CONTINUED)	PAGE	TITLE	LINE
Dye Ned and Bess; give Will to Joan,		328	Epigram 3	3
Dye Joan and Will; give Bess to Ned,		328	Epigram 3	5
Dear honest Ned is in the Gout,		554	Death of Swift	27

NED'S
| Joan cudgell's Ned, yet Ned's a Bully | | 328 | Epigram 3 | 1 |

NEED
You need but now give Orders and Command;		13	Ode to William	D 38
Nor need I ramble far to force a rule,		46	To Congreve	113
Nor need the lion's skin conceal the ass;		48	To Congreve	172
Good Folks, you need not be afraid,		112	Bauc & Phil 2	43
That Her <Majesty> stood in great need of a Tutor,		144	New Song	41
You need but cross the Irish Seas,		173	Horace 1, 7	91
For foreign Aid what need they roam,		272	Apollo's Edict	D 62
Nor need you on the Graces call,		272	Apollo's Edict	D 74
But now there need no more be said on't,		282	Journal	86
"You need not then have been so pert,		304	Storm	41
"What need we open our Commission,		322	First of April	50
She need be no more with the Jaundice possess't;		351	Wood Insect	15
You need not fear a Curtain-Lecture.		362	Grace's Answer	38
Snarlerus next, I'm sure has need		373	Letter D. S-y	68
For those who more will need 'em,		406	Swift to Pope	10
Nor would there be need of a strong Hempen Cape,		519	Dean Hang Rape	65
Nor need depend upon his Pen---.		548	Life of Swift	100
Which hath she most need of, a Spur or a Bridle?		580	Psyche	4
Can see each other do their Need.		590	Strephon Chloe	206
You need not fear your Labour lost:		643	On Poetry	110
You need not throw your Pen away.		646	On Poetry	182
She need no Rivals apprehend.		702	Cadenus Vaness	507
And shou'd Want or Desert stand in need of his Aid,		717	Answer Rebus	27
'Tis true, nor need I to be told,		776	Mullinix Tim	77
At length his Old Master (I need not him name)		816	Yahoo's	36
You will need no Car'catura;		839	Legion Club	228
No more need be said on't,		857	Lady's Lament	201
He need not tell a Story twice,		878	Robbin & Harry	14
Nor need I blush, although you feel it wet;		881	Pastoral Dial	23
Nor need we doubt the Fort to win;		885	Rev Market-Hill	55
For Hannah; when we have no need of her,		886	Rev Market-Hill	105
The Int'rest of his Realm had need		903	Death Daphne	13
Wherein they need not lose a Bit,		1022	Nim-Dan-Dean 1	D 43

NEEDFUL
| Is needful, to transcribe it fair. | | 643 | On Poetry | 92 |

NEEDFULL
| Is held as needfull as His Glyster | | 62 | Discovery | 12 |

NEEDLESS
Thro' many a needless sphere to run,		36	Ode Sancroft	68
'Tis needless to describe him fuller.		286	Elegy Boat	43
I will shew no anger needless.		908	Daphne	60
By leaving out the needless Vowels,		1021	Nim-Dan-Dean 1	D 23

NEEDS
And needs must stink when e're it dies;		9	Ode to King	110
Is in her Sex a Crime needs no excuse)		18	Ode Athenian	65
Must needs be right, so well resembling theirs.		48	To Congreve	174
A Fryer would needs show his Talent in Latin;		76	Lady B- B-	2
And it needs must be one that could both Read and Write:		77	Lady B- B-	15
Poor Will, who needs must interpose,		220	A Quiet Life	23
Or if at last, I needs must blab it,		311	To Ford	5
This vap'ring Scab must needs devise		352	Wood Ironmongr	9
And Skin's yet whole, I needs must own,		372	Letter D. S-y	18
Beauty that needs no Aid of Art,		379	Apology Lady C	115
But, since the truth must needs be stretched		433	Answer Paulus	43
And must you needs describe the Chest?		527	Lady's Dres Rm	70
He lifts the Lid, there needs no more,		528	Lady's Dres Rm	81
This Point must needs be settled first;		589	Strephon Chloe	165
A Wag he was, he needs must own,		602	Beasts Confess	23
What Carthy publish'd needs no long Excuse,		668	Epig Carthy 11	D 1
"She needs must tell them to their Face,		714	Cadenus Vaness	870
Would needs have kept thee from the ground.		822	Epigr Rundle	6
Will needs have it so,		858	Lady's Lament	208
(The Ladies there must needs be Rooks,		905	Death Daphne	79

NEEDY
| Ah! where must needy Poet seek for Aid, | | 138 | City Shower | 27 |
| He never squeez'd a needy Clyent: | | 603 | Beasts Confess | 80 |

NEGATIVES
| Then, let me now by Negatives proceed. | | 534 | To Mr. Gay | 84 |

NEGET
| Yet, Neget quis Carmina Gallo. | | 278 | Journal | 4 |

NEGLECT
Pleads for her own neglect, and thus reproaches mine:		43	To Congreve	6
Thy just submission for this bold neglect.		53	Temple Ill	74
I'm sure I never shou'd neglect--		173	Horace 1, 7	69
So much, that you neglect your Self.		175	Horace 1, 7	126
How quickly they neglect their Friends;		408	Dial Rich Marb	20
To rattle Moody for Neglect;		411	Dial Rich Marb	96
But lest he shou'd neglect his Studies		693	Cadenus Vaness	222

NEGLECTED
Crawls back neglected to his Den.		84	Salamander	36
And Midas now neglected stands,		158	Fable of Midas	81
Least we should think ourselves neglected,		859	Lady Acheson	6
And there neglected Flora settles		901	Dean's Reasons	93

		PAGE	TITLE	LINE
NEGLECTS				
And but neglects to warm her Hair-Lace,		417	Woman's Mind	44
Nor for neglects or blunders chide her;		762	Bec's B-Day	50
A Nation thus, who oft Heav'ns Call neglects,		771	Horace 1, 14	35
NEGLIGENT				
And be thou Negligent of Fame,		121	Apollo Outwit	54
NEIGHB'RING				
For neighb'ring Beaux to see it bare.		222	Prog of Love	18
Her Belly in the neighb'ring Pool:		230	Prog of Poetry	6
You from the Neighb'ring Gaul descend;		324	Pethox	20
With Servants, Tenants, and the neighb'ring Squires.		533	To Mr. Gay	54
On weighty Bus'ness, to some neighb'ring Friend:		534	To Mr. Gay	86
Above our neighb'ring dull Divines!		888	Panegyr Dean	64
Then, if our neighb'ring Friends come here,		889	Panegyr Dean	81
NEIGHBOR				
Asks of his Neighbor; who is that?		63	Discovery	16
With Dick's own Staff his Peacefull Neighbor,		220	A Quiet Life	22
NEIGHBORS				
The Neighbors round would cry out Shame.		220	A Quiet Life	36
NEIGHBOUR				
When Lady Luna is your Neighbour		362	Grace's Answer	25
Upon the shoulders of their neighbour,		434	Answer Paulus	63
Should some imperious Neighbour sink the Boats,		534	To Mr. Gay	89
Yet shou'd some Neighbour feel a Pain,		557	Death of Swift	135
To prove I did my Neighbour wrong;		602	Beasts Confess	18
A better Neighbour ne'er was found:		602	Beasts Confess	44
And am his neighbour cross the way;		899	Dean's Reasons	30
NEIGHBOURHOOD				
Call'd, in the Neighbourhood, Philemon.		111	Bauc & Phil 2	20
Each Farmer in the Neighbourhood can count		533	To Mr. Gay	65
The neighbourhood round,		858	Lady's Lament	212
NEIGHBOURING				
From whence the neighbouring Farmer calls		127	Little House	17
Was Viceroy of a neighbouring Hill:		513	Answer Fable	44
Here, from the neighbouring Nursery of Arts,		793	St. Pat's Well	69
NEIGHBOURS				
Last Friday Night, as Neighbours use,		408	Dial Rich Marb	5
And as ill Neighbours in the Night,		457	Paddy's Charac	7
Hush-money sends to all the Neighbours round:		535	To Mr. Gay	108
Let your Neighbours carve for you.		634	Epistle Lady	132
The Neighbours round admire his Shrewdness,		650	On Poetry	289
The Neighbours think it is but just		787	Clad in Brown	26
The Neighbours all cry, Shoot him dead,		797	Traulus 1	39
The Neighbours who come here to dine,		891	Panegyr Dean	135
The neighbours wonder why the Knight		901	Dean's Reasons	81
NEITHER	37		OMITTED WORD	
NELL				
Nell scolded in so loud a Din		219	A Quiet Life	1
Nell roar'd incessant, Dick sate mute:		219	A Quiet Life	4
Why Dick! the Devil's in thy Nell		220	A Quiet Life	9
He saw Virago Nell belabor		220	A Quiet Life	21
Nell serv'd him at the usu'll Rate		221	A Quiet Life	43
I'm rifled, quoth Nell,		245	Irish-Feast	21
NELLY'S				
Of Nelly's pertness, Robin's leasings,		753	Gift for Bec	7
NENO				
By Neno after he was drown'd.		299	Horrid Plot	38
NEPHEWS				
Tho' the Court gives my Nephews, and Brothers, and Cousins,		144	New Song	47
NEPTUNE				
Where fatal Neptune rul'd e'rewhile,		17	Ode Athenian	39
'Till Neptune with a Gen'ral Sweep		239	Run Bankers	3
To Neptune went, and begg'd in Form		302	Storm	3
"To Neptune speak, and he'll consent;		306	Storm	71
O Neptune! Neptune! must I still		403	Window Inns 10	D 1
O Neptune! Neptune! must I still		403	Window Inns 10	D 1
Next call him Neptune with his Trident,		463	Birthday Song	97
NERO				
The Wish of Nero now is Theirs,		240	Run Bankers	27
NERVES				
There creeps two Auditory Nerves,		367	Answer Delaney	34
NESBITT				
By that rogue Nesbitt,		1037	Sheridan Cavan	10
NEST				
Search'd in the nest where every worm did lie		46	To Congreve	89
Venture to build his Nest so low.		127	Little House	28
They bounce from their Nest,		245	Irish-Feast	33
Talk not of making of thy Nest,		361	Grace's Answer	13
To find the Grub-Street Poet's Nest,		504	Doctor Delaney	144
A Drone can raise a Hornet's Nest:		798	Traulus 1	84
Quite destroy that Harpies Nest,		830	Legion Club	29
NESTLE				
The Monsters nestle in the Deep		257	Bubble	175
NESTLED				
What Ally are they nestled in,		505	Doctor Delaney	147
NET				
How Dan caught nothing in his Net,		280	Journal	65
Then in a Net the Pheasant caught him,		514	Answer Fable	49
NETHER				
Their Heads attempt the nether Skies.		654	On Poetry	404

NETS | PAGE | TITLE | LINE
Display their various nets for hearts: . . . . | 178 | To Lord Harley | 54
How skilfully Dan mends his Nets, ... | 281 | Journal | 75
NETTLE
Will often <piss> upon a nettle; . . . . | 621 | Scandal Poem 1 | 144
The nettle never thrives the better. . . . . | 621 | Scandal Poem 1 | 146
Will often <piss> upon a Nettle; . . . . | 628 | Scandal Poem 2 | 148
The Nettle never thrives the better; . . . . | 628 | Scandal Poem 2 | 150
But, with Raillery to nettle, ... | 636 | Epistle Lady | 211
NETTLES
My Spud these Nettles from the Stones can part, . . | 881 | Pastoral Dial | 11
Her bum upon a bed of nettles. . . . . | 901 | Dean's Reasons | 94
NEVER
(But, surely such whom God did never for his People | 8 | Ode to King | 86
  chuse)
That mighty Ebb never to flow again, ... | 16 | Ode Athenian | 2
(Which Nature never can retain, ... | 25 | Ode Athenian | 289
For never did poetic mine before . . . . | 45 | To Congreve | 51
To boast of favours that he never got; . . . . . . | 48 | To Congreve | 154
The malice thou inspir'st I never fail . . . . . . | 53 | Temple Ill | 85
Still to be cheated, never to be pleas'd; . . . . . | 55 | Temple Ill | 148
. . .Indeed, says I, never worse; . . . . | 70 | Mrs Harris Pet | 14
Lord help me, said Mary, I never stirr'd out of this | 70 | Mrs Harris Pet | 16
  Place!
And in all the Places I liv'd, I never heard of such a | 70 | Mrs Harris Pet | 31
  Thing.
I was never taken for a Conjurer before,. . . . . . | 72 | Mrs Harris Pet | 58
. . .I'm sure I never thought you so; . . . . . . | 72 | Mrs Harris Pet | 59
I never took one in Your Coat. . . . . | 72 | Mrs Harris Pet | 61
For on a Knave he never looks . . . . | 74 | Game Traffick | 7
Eat, Honest Friends, and never spare, ... | 91 | Bauc & Phil 1 | 64
'Twas never known to turn its back . . . . . . | 94 | Bauc & Phil 1 | 136
Had never left each other's Side; . . . . . . | 113 | Bauc & Phil 2 | 76
And He, the Dragon never sleeping, ... | 134 | Magician's Rod | 73
When once he begins, he never will flinch, ... | 143 | New Song | 7
During Her Sacred Life, should never come over: . . | 144 | New Song | 8
"I never Harm intended. . . . . | 154 | Widow and Cat D | 30
<Cholmondeley>, when Drunk, can never lose his Wand, . | 164 | Toland's Invit | 25
Dunkirk never shall be theirs, ... | 169 | Peace Dunkirk | 36
So never offer'd once to stir, ... | 172 | Horace 1, 7 | 53
He never meant the least Abuse-- . . . . . . | 172 | Horace 1, 7 | 66
I'm sure I never shou'd neglect-- . . . . . . | 173 | Horace 1, 7 | 69
In Winter--never to reside. . . . . | 173 | Horace 1, 7 | 86
Could never prosper in amours. . . . . | 176 | To Lord Harley | 8
Yet Daphne never slack'd her pace, ... | 177 | To Lord Harley | 27
Shou'd never meddle with Edg'd Tools. . . . . . | 181 | Horace 2, 1 | 32
"And Fathers never shou'd say nay, ... | 181 | Horace 2, 1 | 46
To a good honest Junta that never will teaze you. . . | 185 | Scriblerus 1 | 6
Keep close then Boys, and never quarrel. . . . . | 189 | Faggot | 13
In History we never found . . . . | 190 | Faggot | 27
At Child's or Truby's never once had been; . . . . | 194 | Author Himself | 18
When twenty Fools I never saw . . . . . . | 200 | Horace 2, 6 | 44
He who betrays his Friend, shall never be . . . . | 210 | Earl of Oxford | 17
Tis never by Invention got, ... | 216 | To Mr. Delany | 27
I never quarrell with my Wife, ... | 220 | A Quiet Life | 15
Love never thinks of Rich and Poor, ... | 224 | Prog of Love | 61
She'll never do't another Time, ... | 224 | Prog of Love | 64
Till Midnight never shows her Head; . . . . . . | 229 | Prog of Beauty | 102
Wher'er he went he never saw his Betters, ... | 234 | Elegy on Demar | 15
That, they had never known their Letters. . . . . | 240 | Run Bankers | 28
But, never shall the Muse endure . . . . . . | 242 | Horace 4, 9 | 3
And swimming never wet a Feather. . . . . . | 253 | Bubble | 56
We see you never can be drown'd: . . . . . . | 258 | Bubble | 192
But never shall our isle have Rest . . . . . | 259 | Bubble | 213
Where for fear of the Cold, I never can pass;) . . . | 264 | Apollo | 32
Direct to the North, where I never yet went; . . . . | 264 | Apollo | 48
But never asks, or asks in vain; . . . . . . | 292 | Prog Marriage | 66
Can howl, and bark, but never spoke. . . . . . . | 298 | Horrid Plot | 18
For Statesmen never want Dog-tricks. . . . . | 300 | Horrid Plot | 60
A Kinder Wife was never born, ... | 328 | Epigram 2 | 3
And, since we must grant, there never were known . . | 335 | Serious Poem | 59
We never say more than, your Love is a Million; . . . | 337 | Serious Poem | 104
Pray never press your self for Rent, but pay me when you | 342 | Upon His Grace | 33
  can,
Altho' the Chain will never crack, ... | 346 | Prometheus | 69
Ah never lay thy Head to Rest! . . . . | 361 | Grace's Answer | 14
She'll never think of Mutton Pies. . . . . . | 362 | Grace's Answer | 42
You'll never think of Goody Griz. . . . . . . | 362 | Grace's Answer | 44
Jove never sends us downward from the Skies, . . . | 363 | On Dreams | 3
You never did, for 'twould not down. . . . . . | 372 | Letter D. S-y | 16
And never turn upon thy Master . . . . | 373 | Letter D. S-y | 55
My Son shall never see a College. . . . . . . | 377 | Apology Lady C | 70
But which excell'd was never found, ... | 393 | Modern Poets | 15
Who hung like a Hero, and never would flinch. . . . | 400 | Tom Clinch | 24
Never to hold her Tongue a Minute; . . . . | 415 | Woman's Mind | 5
I never was in hast before . . . . | 420 | Holyhead | 19
Alas! I never thought . . . . | 425 | Five Ladies | 9
Fine Ladyes never do't . . . . | 428 | Beau's Reply | 6
But, Satan never saw . . . . | 429 | Beau's Reply | 13
You'd swear, he never took a fee, ... | 436 | Answer Paulus | 121
Their Virtues never ceased to sing, ... | 445 | Modern Lady | 11

Must never our Misfortunes end? . . . .   445 Modern Lady   15
"Depend upon't, I never will. . . . .   446 Modern Lady   53
I never sold so cheap a Fan. . . . .   447 Modern Lady   89
'I never can have Time to Dress, ...   447 Modern Lady   96
'He's so unkind, he never sends . . . .   448 Modern Lady   106
"I'd lay my Life he never went: . . . .   451 Modern Lady   201
In ready Counters never pays, ...   452 Modern Lady   234
"I think I never had good Luck in't. . . . .   452 Modern Lady   241
I never saw you play so ill. . . . .   452 Modern Lady   247
It never interrupts the Game, ...   453 Modern Lady   274
He never once wou'd cog the Dice, ...   456 Dean Smedley   28
Because he never knew a letter. . . . .   463 Birthday Song   90
To which he never made pretence, ...   463 Birthday Song   92
For Patrons never pay so well, ...   463 Birthday Song   95
Poor Cynthia never shone so bright, ...   465 Birthday Song   175
Three Syllables did never meet . . . .   467 Birthday Song   225
Because he never was victorious, ...   468 Birthday Song   252
Which Homer never cou'd alive. . . . .   483 Libel on D- D-   86
Cou'd never Condescend so low; . . . .   483 Libel on D- D-   112
Shou'd swear he never meant us ill; . . . .   485 Libel on D- D-   155
You never had commenc'd a Dean, ...   495 Panegyr Swift   77
As never came from Noah's Ark: . . . .   514 Answer Fable   54
Who never had one publick Thought, ...   515 Answer Fable   99
Never may the Muse forget ye: . . . .   522 Betty Grizette   2
But Strephon cautious never meant . . . .   528 Lady's Dres Rm   92
O never may such vile Machine . . . .   528 Lady's Dres Rm   95
But Vengeance, Goddess never sleeping . . . .   529 Lady's Dres Rm   119
For, Sons of Phoebus never break their Trust. . . . .   532 To Mr. Gay   18
May well conclude his Pow'r will never end. . . . . .   533 To Mr. Gay   74
You never can defend his Breeding! . . . .   548 Life of Swift   102
Cou'd never leave the World in quiet---; . . . . . .   548 Life of Swift   104
As never fav'ring the Pretender---: . . . .   550 Life of Swift   187
Thy Gifts, but never to my Friend; . . . .   555 Death of Swift   68
Will never leave him, till he's dead: . . . .   556 Death of Swift   84
My good Companions, never fear, ...   558 Death of Swift   143
"But he would never take Advice: . . . .   558 Death of Swift   172
In those who never Pity felt; . . . .   561 Death of Swift   216
Than if he never did exist. . . . .   562 Death of Swift   248
"This Ode you never yet have seen, ...   563 Death of Swift   271
"You never met a Thing so smart; . . . .   564 Death of Swift   285
"The Church had never such a Writer: . . . .   564 Death of Swift   297
"Was never ill receiv'd at Court: . . . .   565 Death of Swift   308
"To steal a Hint was never known, ...   565 Death of Swift   317
"He never thought an Honour done him, ...   565 Death of Swift   319
"He never courted Men in Station, ...   565 Death of Swift   325
"But never stood in Awe before 'em: . . . .   566 Death of Swift   340
"In Princes never put thy Trust. . . . .   566 Death of Swift   342
"But, Power was never in his Thought; . . . .   567 Death of Swift   357
"Whose Fury Blood could never quench; . . . .   569 Death of Swift   418
"Yet, Malice never was his Aim; . . . .   571 Death of Swift   459
Ah! never to return Home; . . . .   573 Helter Skelter   16
And you who never fell--thro' Pride; . . . .   579 Day Judgement   14
Never did Covent Garden boast . . . .   581 Young Nymph   3
But, never from Religious Clubs; . . . .   583 Young Nymph   54
The bashful Muse will never bear . . . .   583 Young Nymph   71
Her dearest Comrades never caught her . . . .   584 Strephon Chloe   17
Some shew they never want explaining, ...   592 Strephon Chloe   275
Shall never but with Life expire. . . . .   593 Strephon Chloe   314
But, such a Sight was never seen, ...   594 Cassinus Peter   9
"And dying, never told his Pain. . . . .   596 Cassinus Peter   78
He never squeez'd a needy Clyent: . . . .   603 Beasts Confess   80
Old Nurse-keepers would never hire . . . .   605 Beasts Confess   137
The Ass was never known so stupid . . . .   607 Beasts Confess   207
May kill perhaps, but never wound. . . . .   618 Scandal Poem 1   28
Fate never form'd the Gods to flye . . . .   620 Scandal Poem 1   111
He never honestly came by 'em, ...   621 Scandal Poem 1   119
The nettle never thrives the better. . . . .   621 Scandal Poem 1   146
Or may we never thunder throw, ...   622 Scandal Poem 1   177
We kill, 'tis true, but never wound; . . . .   624 Scandal Poem 2   22
Fate never form'd the Gods to fly; . . . .   626 Scandal Poem 2   109
The Nettle never thrives the better; . . . .   628 Scandal Poem 2   150
Never know I any Good in 'um, ...   632 Epistle Lady   83
Never once cou'd have the Pow'r . . . .   636 Epistle Lady   191
Never lets your Mind elope: . . . .   636 Epistle Lady   214
Was never known to spread so wide. . . . .   640 On Poetry   4
Gone, to be never heard of more, ...   642 On Poetry   69
Will never fail to bring in Pence; . . . .   646 On Poetry   188
Our Poets (you can never want 'em, ...   649 On Poetry   279
Altho' he never learnt to spell. . . . .   650 On Poetry   292
Where Pope will never show his Face; . . . .   650 On Poetry   308
Whom never Faction cou'd bespatter, ...   655 On Poetry   413
<Jove> never intermeddl'd here . . . .   657 On Poetry   490
And, though you never learn'd to scan verse, ...   658 On Poetry   D 186
Her Majesty never shall be my Exalter . . . .   664 Epigram Bust   3
To talk on me she never fails: . . . .   679 From Catullus   2
They never pass'd for Law in Courts; . . . .   690 Cadenus Vaness   113
Where never Blush was call'd in Aid, ...   691 Cadenus Vaness   168
"'Tis what Vanessa never did. . . . .   694 Cadenus Vaness   245
I said her Face would never last. . . . .   699 Cadenus Vaness   387
She never hit one proper Place; . . . .   700 Cadenus Vaness   423

NEVER   (CONTINUED)   PAGE   TITLE   LINE

But never gave me equal Arms: 706 Cadenus Vaness   621
A Science which he never taught,   708 Cadenus Vaness   670
For Persons whom he never saw.   708 Cadenus Vaness   693
This Topick, never touch'd before,   709 Cadenus Vaness   714
Things took a Turn he never meant.   709 Cadenus Vaness   731
But, sure, she never talk'd so well.   710 Cadenus Vaness   749
He never knew her Judgment fail,   710 Cadenus Vaness   755
Must never to Mankind be told,   712 Cadenus Vaness   826
"Who never cou'd one Lover find.   714 Cadenus Vaness   867
A Thing never known to the Muses or Phoebus: 716 Answer Rebus   8
For Stella never learn'd the Art,   725 To Stella   71
Doll never flies to cut her Lace,   725 To Stella   75
For such a Fool was never found,   727 To Stella   121
We never hear the Workmen prais'd,   727 Stella, Poems   2
The House will never loose it's Trade;   734 Stel B-day '20   8
Still to be curious, never hearken.   753 Gift for Bec   22
They never would hear,   756 Dingley Brent   10
Domestic business never mind   761 Bec's B-Day   33
Still be she curious, never hearken   762 Bec's B-Day   43
Enter the Stage they never mind him;   776 Mullinix Tim   102
He never muddles in the Dirt,   788 Dick's Variety   15
Such Friendship never Man profest,   796 Traulus 1   15
The <Dean> was never so carest;   796 Traulus 1   16
It never makes the least Impression.   798 Traulus 1   64
Which God pronounc'd he never wou'd,   799 Traulus 1   97
Provocation never waits,   800 Traulus 2   19
That the Mitre wou'd never stick fast on their Head,   805 Irish Bishops   46
What honester folks never durst for their ears.   815 Yahoo's   19
Like Paul's Ephesians, never heard it;   820 Dr. Rundle   16
They gave what never was their own.   820 Dr. Rundle   18
While they never hold their Tongue,   831 Legion Club   51
Never durst a Muse before   834 Legion Club   119
For he never fails to bring 'em;   836 Legion Club   164
Sure never did man see   851 Lady's Lament   1
The Dean never stops,   852 Lady's Lament   11
I should never sit still: 852 Lady's Lament   38
Yet never think they get enough;   861 Lady Acheson   35
But Madam, I guest there wou'd never come Good,   868 Grand Question   47
I can't get it out, tho' I'd never so fain.   869 Grand Question   66
For, a Captain of Horse never takes off his Hat;   870 Grand Question   106
Because he has never a Hand that is idle;   870 Grand Question   107
"You'll never want Parsons as long as you live;   872 Grand Question   142
"But, <Zounds>, by their Looks, they never keep Lent: 872 Grand Question   146
"I never cou'd take to my Book for the Blood o'me,   873 Grand Question   165
Never since I was born did I hear so much Wit,   873 Grand Question   173
Will never have done with his Gibes and his Jeers: 873 Grand Question   188
You never else had known the Dean,   877 To Dean Swift   29
Love rooted out, again will never grow.   881 Pastoral Dial   16
A longer half-p'orth never did I see;   881 Pastoral Dial   27
Him on my Lap you never more should see;   882 Pastoral Dial   47
Where never yet a Codling ripen'd: 883 Rev Market-Hill   4
You never ventur'd to be hang'd.   884 Rev Market-Hill   40
O, may I never once forget   887 Panegyr Dean   24
We never ask to hear you twice.   889 Panegyr Dean   74
Which never yet one Friend has lost you.   890 Panegyr Dean   114
Yet never ask us once to play?   891 Panegyr Dean   146
Such charming Butter never Man made.   892 Panegyr Dean   168
Here, Nature never Diff'rence made   895 Panegyr Dean   289
I never robb'd thee with Design: 896 Panegyr Dean   316
Let never at your Board be known   897 Panegyr Dean   339
Than if they never knew a letter.   900 Dean's Reasons   40
From which I never could refrain,   901 Dean's Reasons   97
Was never seen, except her own: 904 Death Daphne   62
Never woman more devis'd   906 Daphne   5
Always conquer'd, never yielding.   906 Daphne   8
Never hears what you can say: 906 Daphne   14
Never take it in your thought,   907 Daphne   31
But will never more advise thee.   907 Daphne   52
I will never hear you read.   907 Daphne   54
By disputing I will never   908 Daphne   55
I will never contradict you.   908 Daphne   58
Never more will I suppose   908 Daphne   69
You shall never hear me thunder,   908 Daphne   73
Never will I give advice   908 Daphne   79
But never of my own inditing.   917 Riddle 3   10
They rise, walk round, yet never fright.   920 Riddle 6   12
Is never pleas'd till I make one: 920 Riddle 6   28
Who never fled the bloody Plains,   925 Riddle 8   32
(Or they can never pass the Gate)   928 Riddle 12   D   14
They never yet cou'd find my Measure.   929 Riddle 14   D   4
Ever eating, never cloying,   930 Riddle 16   D   1
Never finding full Repast,   930 Riddle 16   D   3
It can never fly from you.   931 Riddle 17   D   8
Never speaking, still awake,   933 Riddle 20   D   1
Without it a Lady should never appear.   941 Letter   42
The Secret will never be known;   952 Onyons   12
She'll be fruitful, never fear her.   953 Oysters   16
And, 'tis your own Case, for you never can wound   968 Letter Sherid   33
And that she's a Riddle, can never be right,   972 S-'s Ans Sh-d   7
For she never descends so low as the cellar;   979 Dean to Tho: S   26

NEVER   (CONTINUED)   PAGE   TITLE   LINE
   And he never call'd me worse than Sweet-heart drunk or   985 Mary to Sher   14
     sober:
   Thy Ruin, Tom, I never meant, ...   1002 Reply by Dean   13
   Or may your Gown never be good Lutherine   . . . . .   1018 Swift Ans Sher   29
   Poor Tom, wilt thou never accept a Defiance, ...   1019 To Sheridan   1
   It never was known that circular letters, ...   1026 Sheri Circles   1
   I'm so full of Pity, I never abuse Sick;   1028 Dr. Helsham   2
   For never was Informer he, ...   1036 Heathen Christ   3
   You never have an old friend at Cavan.   . . . . . .   1038 Sheridan Cavan   18
NEVER-DYING
   Huge Heaps of never-dying Works;   . . . .   922 Riddle 7   40
NEVER-FAILING
   And by their never-failing ways . . . .   19 Ode Athenian   117
NEVER-MEANING
   Thy busy never-meaning Face;   . . . .   775 Mullinix Tim   59
NEW   SEE A-NEW
   By the new Modish System of reducing all to sense,   19 Ode Athenian   107
   That this New, Noble, and Delightful Scene   . . . .   20 Ode Athenian   136
   Did with new, unexperienc't Glories wait, ...   21 Ode Athenian   156
   A new Commode, a Top-knot, and a Ruff, ...   23 Ode Athenian   223
   All of old Cut with a new Dye, ...   23 Ode Athenian   227
   In this new happy Scene   . . . .   31 Ode to Temple   159
   But find some new address, some fresh deceit,   44 To Congreve   17
   Beneath (A new Receit for Paint)   . . . . . .   60 Lady Tablebook   8
   Now Enter Bush with new State-Airs, ...   62 Discovery   9
   Or from Whitehall some new Express, ...   63 Discovery   30
   'Twill just new dye the Lining.   . . . .   75 Game Traffick   24
   When he found a new Help from Invisible Hand. . . .   77 Lady B- B-   25
   Erect a new one in a Trice;   . . . .   80 Vanbrug House   66
   Encreas't by new intestin Wheels   . . . . . .   93 Bauc & Phil 1   128
   The Sleeves new border'd with a List   . . . . . .   94 Bauc & Phil 1   167
   Which just like ours, new rigg'd and man'd, ...   96 On the Union   17
   Erect a new one in a trice.   . . . .   107 V's House   40
   Increas'd by new Intestine Wheels: . . . . . .   113 Bauc & Phil 2   68
   To form some Beauty by a new Receit,   ` . . . . .   118 Biddy Floyd   2
   Now my new Benefactors have brought me about, ...   144 New Song   45
   Shall not see one New Years-Day in that Year, ...   147 Windsor Proph   3
   Or Memoirs of the New Utopia.   . . . .   150 Corinna   32
   Or, "Have you nothing new to day   . . . . . ; . .   201 Horace 2, 6   73
   Some new unbeaten Passage to the Sky;   . . . . . .   210 Earl of Oxford   12
   Send us new Nymphs with each new Moon.   . . . . .   229 Prog of Beauty   120
   Send us new Nymphs with each new Moon.   . . . . .   229 Prog of Beauty   120
   I lost my new Cloak.   . . . .   245 Irish-Feast   20
   Nor a new Star adorn the Skies: . . . .   271 Apollo's Edict D 37
   This Bank is to make us a New Paper Mill,   287 Bank Down   11
   New Lovers now will come in Swarms.   . . . . . .   295 Prog Marriage   158
   You may shew him about for a new Groaning Board. . . .   336 Serious Poem   84
   To beg his Favour is the Way new Favours still to win,   341 Upon His Grace   13
   And, Thirdly; 'tis a new Invention   . . . . . .   348 Whitshed Motto   15
   Be a New Sun, and a New Moon.   . . . .   362 Grace's Answer   52
   Be a New Sun, and a New Moon.   . . . .   362 Grace's Answer   52
   New Vigour to the Leg remaining.   . . . . . .   366 Answer Delaney   20
   "A Scene so glorious and so new?   . . . .   380 Apology Lady C   164
   The Arts new kindle into Life.   . . . .   385 Manly Virtue   46
   With new Delight looks up and loves;   . . . . . .   387 Manly Virtue   128
   His Cap had a new Cherry Ribbon to ty't.   . . . .   399 Tom Clinch   6
   New Kings a compliment expect   . . . . . .   422 Ireld   37
   Ever with some new Fancy struck, ...   452 Modern Lady   236
   Then make this new Apollo sit   . . . . . .   462 Birthday Song   71
   Yet be the Fancy old or new, ...   464 Birthday Song   137
   And bear the new Successor's frown;   . . . . . .   468 Birthday Song   259
   Your Conduct in this new Employ foretell.   . . . . .   532 To Mr. Gay   30
   How shall a new Attempter learn   . . . . . .   642 On Poetry   71
   To try a new Experiment: . . . .   691 Cadenus Vaness   139
   In a new World with Caution stept, ...   696 Cadenus Vaness   308
   Mention'd a new Italian, come   . . . . . .   696 Cadenus Vaness   322
   A modest Youth said something new, ...   701 Cadenus Vaness   454
   She hourly press'd for something new;   . . . . . .   704 Cadenus Vaness   555
   Her Manner now was something new;   . . . . . .   707 Cadenus Vaness   661
   By this new Passion grew inspir'd.   . . . . . .   709 Cadenus Vaness   717
   In Pleasure seek for something new: . . . . . .   728 Stella, Poems   18
   In Curll's Collections, new and old, ...   729 Stella, Poems   50
   Hangs a new Angel two doors from us   . . . . .   734 Stel B-day '20   10
   We Poets when a Hint is new   . . . .   747 Stel Distress   59
   But Poets when a Hint is new   . . . .   751 Stel Wood-Park   75
   For Bec, a new supply of cares, ...   753 Gift for Bec   2
   And if your Flesh and Blood be new, ...   760 Receipt Youth   37
   New Waves shall drive thee to the Deep again. . . .   770 Horace 1, 14   10
   Your Faction, when their Game was new, ...   774 Mullinix Tim   39
   Or thrashing Babby in her new Stays.   . . . . .   788 Dick's Variety   30
   So, could we see a Set of new Iscariots, ...   806 Judas   19
   Their rights! their importance! We'll set on new rates . 816 Yahoo's   32
   What is there in it strange or new?   . . . . . .   820 Dr. Rundle   10
   Let us try some new Expedient;   . . . .   832 Legion Club   76
   Now a new Misfortune fells, ...   834 Legion Club   117
   But, instead of new plays, ...   855 Lady's Lament   147
   New Years help to make me old;   . . . .   863 To Janus   26
   And after, me thought, I had lost my new Shoes;   . . .   868 Grand Question   51
   For, if a new Crotchet comes into my Brain, ...   869 Grand Question   65
   Will not have one new thing to say.   . . . .   878 Robbin & Harry   12

NEW   (CONTINUED)   PAGE   TITLE   LINE

    Down in the Strand just where the new Pole is,   . . .   988 Letter Dr Sh-n   8
    I hope you have swilld with new milk from the Kine   1018 Swift Ans Sher   25
    And swear by each Fate, and your new friends, each Fury, 1019 To Sheridan   6
    'Ere Vulcan comes to make him new.   . . . .   1021 Nim-Dan-Dean 1   D   8
NEW-BORN
    And sprinkles thrice the new-born Maid.   . . . . . .   691 Cadenus Vaness   159
    The new-born Flesh will melt away;   . . . .   760 Receipt Youth   52
NEW-CAST
    But Weston has a new-cast Gown   . . . .   75 Game Traffick   21
NEW-DEVOURING
    See, where the new-devouring Vermin runs, ...   792 St. Pat's Well   59
NEW-DROPT
    A Ball of new-dropt Horse's Dung, ...   811 Bro Protestant   11
NEW-FLUX'T
    No new-flux't Rake shew'd fairer Skin;   904 Death Daphne   37
    You merit new Employments daily: . . . .   891 Panegyr Dean   155
    A new and wond'rous Art I show   920 Riddle 6   9
    Points out where each new Victim falls;   . . . . .   923 Riddle 7   58
    In Time a new Creation springs.   924 Riddle 7   90
    I'm still the same --- but ever new.   . . . . . .   935 Riddle 23   D   6
    As for your new rebus, or riddle, or crux, ...   977 Dean to Sherid   43
NEW-RIVER-WALK
    New-River-walk with friendly Shade, ...   884 Rev Market-Hill   51
NEW-YEAR'S
    Bring our Dame a New-Year's Gift: . . . .   862 To Janus   4
NEW-YEAR'S-GIFT
    Who thus displays the New-year's-gift.   . . . . .   753 Gift for Bec   4
NEW-YEARS
    Yet I find, a New-Years Lace   . . . .   863 To Janus   27
NEWER
    When Doll hangs out a newer Face   . . . .   735 Stel B-day '20   34
NEWLY
    By Phoebus newly Tann'd and Dry'd.   . . . .   100 Elegy Patrige   76
NEWMARKET
    Or made it a Newmarket Switch, ...   135 Magician's Rod   83
NEWRY
    Safe through the Newry mountains sides.   . . . . . .   435 Answer Paulus   98
NEWS
    Could Smoak, and Drink, and read the News;   95 Bauc & Phil 1   174
    Cou'd smoak his Pipe, and read the News;   . . . . .   115 Bauc & Phil 2   126
    Fame spreads the News, and People travel   . . . . .   157 Fable of Midas   37
    No news of Phil. The Bridegroom came, ...   223 Prog of Love   29
    You, for the News are ne'r to seek, ...   315 To Ford   103
    This Couple met to talk of News.   . . . .   408 Dial Rich Marb   6
    a Jobber of Stocks by retailing false news   . . . .   540 Charac Walpole   9
    "D'ye hear the News---? the Dean is dead---!   . . .   547 Life of Swift   69
    "The News thro' half the Town has run.   . . . . .   558 Death of Swift   152
    "I know no more than what the News is, ...   558 Death of Swift   155
    (Cries Bob) "I'm Sorry for the News;   . . . . .   560 Death of Swift   192
    Receive the News in doleful Dumps, ...   562 Death of Swift   227
    Patrick astore, what news upon the town?   . . . .   840 Ballad   D   1
    By my soul there's bad news, for the gold she was pulled 840 Ballad   D   2
        down,
    And, Molly, she said, I should hear some ill News.   .   868 Grand Question   52
    A Companion with News, ...   1036 Plague Country   1
NEWS-PAPERS
    As by the news-papers we're told?   . . . .   296 Satiric Elegy   10
NEXT
    Who heard you meant to write heroics next;   . . . .   47 To Congreve   144
    I keep in a Pocket ty'd about my Middle, next my Smock.   69 Mrs Harris Pet   7
    So next Morning we told Whittle, and he fell a Swearing   70 Mrs Harris Pet   24
    And that I may have a Share in next Sunday's   73 Mrs Harris Pet   71
        Collection:
    When, Behold the next Morning, a wonderful Riddle,   .   77 Lady B- B-   8
    We might expect to find next Year   . . . .   88 Hist V's House   47
    Or sell a Goose at the next Toun   . . . .   95 Bauc & Phil 1   175
    Contrivd to preach his Sermon next   . . . . . .   95 Bauc & Phil 1   177
    A Cellar next was dug below: . . . .   108 V's House   86
    Knew how to preach old Sermons next, ...   115 Bauc & Phil 2   127
    Dame Baucis next, they play'd their Farce on: . . .   115 Bauc & Phil 2   138
    So, the next Parson stub'd and burnt it.   . . . .   117 Bauc & Phil 2   178
    The Graces from the Court did next provide   . . . .   118 Biddy Floyd   7
    His next will be a Rod in Piss.   . . . .   135 Magician's Rod   86
    Seated at Table next the Men you love.   . . . . .   165 Toland's Invit   32
    Next Day invited, comes agen;   . . . .   173 Horace 1, 7   76
    Not knowing where to turn him next;   . . . . . .   174 Horace 1, 7   114
    And smiling, whispers to the next,   . . . · . . .   200 Horace 2, 6   32
    (October next, it will be four)   . . . .   201 Horace 2, 6   64
    Next, faithful Silence hath a sure Reward: . . . .   210 Earl of Oxford   15
    Next morn betimes the Bride was missing, ...   223 Prog of Love   26
    And resolv'd the next Winter, for that is the Time,   265 Apollo   77
    And next Observe how this Alliance fits, ...   276 Epilogue   39
    The Graces next, and all the Muses   . . . .   290 Prog Marriage   9
    Gallants, by Tuesday next we must be gone.   . . . .   308 Billet Players   40
    Gallants, next Thursday night will be our last,   . .   309 Billet Players   55
    The next we act shall be as good as this.   . . . .   309 Billet Players   58
    That he sent to all three a Challenge next morning. .   327 Epigram 1   8
    To meet him next, the Soldier comes, ...   338 Wood's Brass   3
    Snarlerus next, I'm sure has need   . . . .   373 Letter D. S-y   68
    Next Day another Message brought;   . . . .   377 Apology Lady C   75

NEXT	(CONTINUED)	PAGE	TITLE	LINE
Accomplish'd thus, his next Resort		385	Manly Virtue	63
Next Day the Post-boy winds his Horn,		398	Earl of P-b-w	16
To add them in the next Edition;		418	Woman's Mind	62
Next for encouragemt of spinning,		422	Ireld	49
This World is his, and theirs the next.		456	Dean Smedley	40
Next, as the Laws of Song require,		461	Birthday Song	21
Dismissing Mars, it next must follow		462	Birthday Song	57
Next call him Neptune with his Trident,		463	Birthday Song	97
To Minheer Hendel next you run,		469	Birthday Song	276
For next to being Great our selves		493	Panegyr Swift	11
Whose Wit at best was next to none,		514	Answer Fable	67
And now that little next is gone.		514	Answer Fable	68
Now listen while he next produces,		526	Lady's Dres Rm	19
A Pair of Tweezers next he found		527	Lady's Dres Rm	55
Next, hearken Gay, to what thy Charge requires,		533	To Mr. Gay	53
"Next, here's Sir Robert's Vindication,		563	Death of Swift	277
Unlaces next her Steel-Rib'd Bodice;		582	Young Nymph	24
With gentlest Touch, she next explores		582	Young Nymph	29
The Muses next in Order follow,		585	Strephon Chloe	53
The Ass approaching next, confess'd,		602	Beasts Confess	21
Your Poem finish'd, next your Care		643	On Poetry	91
Bestow my next I pray, to Pope or Swift.		669	Epig Carthy 17	D 4
Smit with the glorious prize next struts in Sewel,		672	Epig Carthy 24	D 9
The Graces next wou'd act their Part,		692	Cadenus Vaness	172
A Party next of glitt'ring Dames,		698	Cadenus Vaness	364
To Scandal next-----What aukward Thing		699	Cadenus Vaness	384
They railly'd next Vanessa's Dress;		699	Cadenus Vaness	396
Thus much for the Verse, we proceed to the next,		716	Answer Rebus	19
Die the next Year for want of Root:		730	Stella, Poems	68
Say, Stella, when you copy next,		732	Stella, Poems	137
Next Moment in the House of Peers,		788	Dick's Variety	28
What's next to be voted with ease you may guess.		816	Yahoo's	34
(For none could tell whose Turn was next)		849	Old Thorn	31
Next, for his diversion,		853	Lady's Lament	67
And waits on the Captain betimes the next Morning.		869	Grand Question	70
Next Day, to be sure, the Captain will come,		870	Grand Question	87
To rule the Dairy next to Kit.		888	Panegyr Dean	42
Proceed we to your preaching next:		888	Panegyr Dean	61
You, next to Dennis bear the Sway:		889	Panegyr Dean	89
Your Usher's Post must next be handled:		890	Panegyr Dean	105
Next make a Devil of a Saint.		930	Riddle 15	D 16
Let purse-proud C--n next approach,		951	Upstart	D 23
But let me advise you, when next I hear from you,		976	Dean to Sherid	9
And I wish your few friends, when they next see your car go,		976	Dean to Sherid	29

NICE   SEE OVER-NICE

		PAGE	TITLE	LINE
Of Nice, Coquet, Affected, Pert, and Vain.		118	Biddy Floyd	10
You must, although the Point be nice,		218	To Mr. Delany	95
But Tom is a Person of Honor so nice,		327	Epigram 1	6
But then the 'Squire so trim and nice,		376	Apology Lady C	23
Whilst high, and nice, and curious Meats,		378	Apology Lady C	107
In chusing Lace a Critick nice,		416	Woman's Mind	27
When fortune favour'd, he was nice,		456	Dean Smedley	27
Nor wants a nice discerning Spirit,		484	Libel on D- D-	147
"We must confess his Case was nice;		558	Death of Swift	171
To please you, she knows how to chuse a nice Bit;		580	Psyche	9
And then, so nice, and so genteel;		584	Strephon Chloe	9
So nice and so compleat a Beau.		597	Problem Solved	10
In Dyet was perhaps too nice,		602	Beasts Confess	39
His Conscience always was so nice,		604	Beasts Confess	83
But since the Case appear'd so nice,		689	Cadenus Vaness	91
In half a week the Dame grew nice,		745	Stel Distress	9
In half a Week the Dame grew nice,		749	Stel Wood-Park	7
I beg, you see the Case is Nice,		779	Mullinix Tim	196
Such Pastimes, when our Taste is nice,		788	Dick's Variety	11
How nice you split the hardest Text!		888	Panegyr Dean	62
She's grown so nice, and so penurious,		891	Panegyr Dean	143

NICELY

		PAGE	TITLE	LINE
No wonder then, if nicely skill'd		80	Vanbrug House	61
No wonder then, if nicely skill'd		107	V's House	35
For nicely computing the Price by Retail,		288	Bank Down	36
For catch it nicely by the Head,		527	Lady's Dres Rm	67
His Hat could nicely put on;		765	Mullinex Dick	30
So nicely clad from Head to Heel;		889	Panegyr Dean	76
You judge so nicely to a Hair,		890	Panegyr Dean	115
At nicely carving show thy Wit;		897	Panegyr Dean	335
I nicely examind them every Line		1017	Swift Ans Sher	5

NICER

		PAGE	TITLE	LINE
Our Thoughts, to hit your nicer Taste,		496	Panegyr Swift	106
My Hat has much the nicer air,		780	Mullinix Tim	219
Offensive to thy nicer Nose.		895	Panegyr Dean	286

NICEST

		PAGE	TITLE	LINE
Nor could the nicest Artist Paint,		480	Libel on D- D-	19
By Nature form'd with nicest Care,		584	Strephon Chloe	5
Presented with the nicest Bits:		750	Stel Wood-Park	10
Which in the nicest Fashion curl'd,		903	Death Daphne	23
The Short'ning is the nicest Part.		1021	Nim-Dan-Dean 1	D 36

NICETIES

		PAGE	TITLE	LINE
Of Doubts, Impertinence, and Niceties,		22	Ode Athenian	213

NICETY
    And, Love such Nicety requires, ...   588 Strephon Chloe   135

	PAGE	TITLE	LINE

NICK
    And entring in the very nick, ...   220 A Quiet Life   20
    For I think in my Conscience he deals with Old Nick;   265 Apollo   82
    For old Nick gave the Papers the Mark of the Bank. .   288 Bank Down   45
    'I wish the Dinner at Old Nick." . . . .   448 Modern Lady   99
    Had not Clio in the Nick, ...   833 Legion Club   97
    For if bestrode by you, Old <Nick>, ...   497 Panegyr Swift   138
NICK-NAMES
    With Christian Nick-names like a Child; . . . . .   82 Salamander   4
NICK'D
    A Rival comes, and Tom---is nick'd---. . . . . . .   545 Life of Swift   18
NICKNAME
    Must furbish up and Nickname Crisis. . . . . .   180 Horace 2, 1   6
NICOLINI
    Such Singers are like Nicolini. . . . .   598 Problem Solved   30
NIGGARD
    'Tis all the Portion of my niggard Stars; . . . . .   32 Ode to Temple   201
NIGH
    And nigh to Heaven as is its Name. . . . . . .   16 Ode Athenian   10
    Nor to the Shore approach too nigh, ...   257 Bubble   174
    Your damnable Riddle, my poor Brains did rack nigh. .   972 S-'s Ans Sh-d   2
NIGH'R
    Because he dreaded to come nigh'r. . . . . . .   455 Dean Smedley   8
NIGHT   SEE TO-NIGHT,MID-NIGHT,WEDDING-NIGHT
    . . . would grope in Ignorance and Night, ...   22 Ode Athenian   208
    Yet so much sooner comes the long and gloomy Night. . .   25 Ode Athenian   282
    Which guard the throne by night, and are its light by day: 34 Ode Sancroft   4
    Raise envy's clouds to leave themselves in night, . . .   45 To Congreve   79
    And told you so at Will's but t' other night. . . . .   47 To Congreve   146
    Comes back with joy to its own seat at night; . . . .   51 Temple Ill   6
    So because I had been buying things for my Lady last   69 Mrs Harris Pet   3
        Night,
    So I tumbl'd and toss'd all Night,. . . . .   70 Mrs Harris Pet   20
    And then your poor Petitioner, both Night and Day, .   73 Mrs Harris Pet   74
    It happen'd on a Winter's night, ...   90 Bauc & Phil 1   5
    In such a dreadfull Night at least; . . . . . .   90 Bauc & Phil 1   20
    We can't be quiet Night nor day; . . . .   90 Bauc & Phil 1   30
    In his poor House to pass the Night; . . . . . .   91 Bauc & Phil 1   54
    To make a dreadful Night at Noon: . . . . . .   98 Elegy Patrige   14
    Steals from her Private Cell by Night, ...   99 Elegy Patrige   51
    It happen'd on a Winter Night, ...   111 Bauc & Phil 2   5
    In his Poor Hut to pass the Night; . . . . . .   111 Bauc & Phil 2   22
    He'll talk of them from Noon till Night, ...   116 Bauc & Phil 2   167
    A Third, who lost his Way by Night, ...   127 Little House   31
    Returning Home at Night, you'll find the Sink . . .   137 City Shower   5
    And talk what Fools call Treason all the Night. . .   163 Toland's Invit   16
    Rides Day and Night at such a Rate, ...   174 Horace 1, 7   117
    And chaster than the Queen of Night, ...   179 To Lord Harley   78
    With which inspir'd we'll club each Night . . . .   184 Horace 2, 1   113
    And chiefly chuse to shine by Night. . . . . . .   228 Prog of Beauty   72
    Each Night a Bit drops off her Face . . . . . .   228 Prog of Beauty   87
    From snoring all Night. . . . .   245 Irish-Feast   16
    So when upon a Moon-shine Night . . . .   253 Bubble   73
    One Night a Fool into a Brook . . . .   255 Bubble   125
    At Night between Cavan-street and College-Green: . .   264 Apollo   54
    My Sister transcrib'd it last Night, to his Sorrow, .   265 Apollo   67
    Will give a Night of Benefit to Weavers. . . . .   274 Epilogue   4
    She had with Dreams the other Night. . . . . .   282 Journal   96
    Last Night arriv'd Clem and his Wife. . . . . .   283 Journal   118
    I promise nothing for the Night; . . . .   290 Prog Marriage   20
    I Ask'd a Whig the other Night, ...   298 Horrid Plot   1
    Would he were here this night to act my part. . . .   308 Billet Players   32
    Gallants, next Thursday night will be our last, . .   309 Billet Players   55
    With whom you toasted half the Night, ...   311 To Ford   24
    Those Dreams that on the silent Night intrude, . . .   363 On Dreams   1
    Whose anxious Natives, Night and Day, ...   388 Manly Virtue   137
    Last Friday Night, as Neighbours use, ...   408 Dial Rich Marb   5
    He tells his brothr fools at night . . . .   421 Ireld   24
    Though he were drunk the night before, ...   434 Answer Paulus   72
    Walks boldly home at dead of night; . . . . . .   435 Answer Paulus   92
    She sat all Night up at Quadrill. . . . . . .   446 Modern Lady   41
    "The Ladies here to Night by Six." . . . . . .   446 Modern Lady   55
    "And I may have Revenge to Night." . . . . . .   447 Modern Lady   69
    Our Madam can sit up all Night; . . . .   451 Modern Lady   217
    The Company to-morrow Night. . . . .   453 Modern Lady   289
    And as ill Neighbours in the Night, ...   457 Paddy's Charac   7
    For yours can shine both day and night, ...   462 Birthday Song   66
    The greatest monarch may be stabb'd by night, . . .   506 To a Friend   1
    Who spends his Day and Night in gall. . . . . .   515 Answer Fable   104
    Of drinking all Day, and whoring all Night. . . .   517 Dean Hang Rape   28
    "And he's engag'd To-morrow Night! . . . . . .   562 Death of Swift   236
    Behold the Ruins of the Night! . . . .   583 Young Nymph   58
    Be often forc'd to rise at Night, ...   587 Strephon Chloe   122
    Foretell a storm to last till night. . . . . . .   618 Scandal Poem 1   32
    Foretel a Storm to last till Night. . . . . . .   624 Scandal Poem 2   26
    'Tis hard they must be busy Night and Day: . . . .   662 Upon Ladies   2
    The Men should slave at Cards from Morn to Night; .   662 Upon Ladies   7
    A Duel fought last Night at Two, ...   696 Cadenus Vaness   320
    Last Night was so extremely fine, ...   696 Cadenus Vaness   326

NIGHT	(CONTINUED)	PAGE	TITLE	LINE
I saw coquetting t' other Night		699	Cadenus Vaness	394
Nor calls up all the House at Night,		725	To Stella	73
Impatient both of Night and Day,		726	To Stella	98
In the gay Trappings of a Birth-Day Night:		771	Horace 1, 14	50
So teaz'd day and night		851	Lady's Lament	3
From morning till night,		852	Lady's Lament	18
I return home at night,		853	Lady's Lament	53
To stint me at Night to one Bottle of Wine;		867	Grand Question	16
'Twas a sad rainy Night--but the Morning is fine--		869	Grand Question	74
Robin from noon to night will prate,		878	Robbin & Harry	9
And, sure as they're alive, at Night;		891	Panegyr Dean	139
And fly unseen both Day and Night;		919	Riddle 5	26
Lyes there consign'd to endless Night;		923	Riddle 7	64
A Pain which ev'ry happy Night		924	Riddle 8	13
Altho' 'tis open Night and Day,		928	Riddle 12	D 5
The Son of Pitch, and gloomy Night;		929	Riddle 15	D 2
A long-ear'd Beast, and Bird of Night,		942	Probatur Alit	19
Is a damnable Smell both Morning and Night.		942	Probatur Alit	30
. . .I came back to sit with the Ladies this Night.		1013	Swift to Sheri	3
This Night I came home with a very cold Dew sick,		1030	Dr. Sheridan	2
So about twelve at Night, the Punk		1033	Ans to Crown	1
Yet he gets home at night with Health and whole Bones.		1037	Four Storyes	8
NIGHT-CAP				
His Night-Cap border'd round with Lace		587	Strephon Chloe	93
A flourisht Night-cap on, to grace		290	Prog Marriage	23
NIGHT-GLOVES				
There Night-gloves made of Tripsy's Hide,		526	Lady's Dres Rm	29
NIGHT-GOWN				
At Seven, the Dean in Night-gown drest,		278	Journal	9
Her Night-gown and her Slippers brought her,		446	Modern Lady	46
A Rug; for Night-gown he had none.		594	Cassinus Peter	20
NIGHT'S				
(The third Night's Profits of his Play;)		230	Prog of Poetry	18
Her last Night's ill Success repeats,		447	Modern Lady	72
The Leavings of his last Night's Pot		594	Cassinus Peter	27
NIGHTINGAL				
At last the Nightingal comes in,		514	Answer Fable	63
Our Nightingal might fit a Cage,		515	Answer Fable	83
Jove send, this Nightingal may fall,		515	Answer Fable	103
So Nightingal and Lark adieu,		515	Answer Fable	105
That he's the Nightingal of Brutes.		602	Beasts Confess	36
NIGHTLY				
They Nightly slunk to rob the Fold,		153	Widow and Cat	D 8
Attending nightly round your Bed;		597	Cassinus Peter	114
Nightly nodding o'er your Flocks,		660	Love Song	6
NIGHTS				
Whom Roguish Boys in Stormy Nights		100	Elegy Patrige	91
Duly let out a Nights to Steal for Fees.		125	Descriptn Morn	16
Pass our Nights, to drive out thinking.		632	Epistle Lady	86
In frosty Nights their starving Cows,		759	Receipt Youth	2
NIL				
Qui nil moliris tam inepte?		476	Epist on Epist	30
NILE				
As if the Universal Nile		17	Ode Athenian	42
Just so the Mighty Nile has suffer'd in it's Fame,		20	Ode Athenian	145
O'er Nile, with all its wilderness of gods;		46	To Congreve	104
Then, like the Dogs of Nile be wise,		257	Bubble	177
And let the secret Head of Nile		270	Apollo's Edict	D 14
"As from the flowry Bed of Nile--		463	Birthday Song	81
NIM				
How George, Nim, Dan, Dean pass their Days;		278	Journal	2
At Nine, grave Nim and George Facetious,		278	Journal	11
George, Nim and Dean, set out at Four,		280	Journal	43
And Nim and Dan to Garret clamber:		280	Journal	58
How Nim, no Hunter 'ere could match him,		281	Journal	73
Nim lost his Wig-block, Dan his Jordan,		283	Journal	123
George, Dan, Dean, and Nim to place in the center?		1027	Sheri Circles	14
NIM-DAN-DEAN				
. . . Your most dutiful and obedient George		1024	Nim-Dan-Dean 2	D 18
Nim-Dan-Dean.				
NIMBLE				
And thence with joyful, nimble Wing		16	Ode Athenian	29
To fix this nimble god,		49	To Congreve	208
Thou art not half so nimble as a Hare:		539	Mr. Pulteney	40
There's Nimble Tim a passing by.		778	Mullinix Tim	182
And I must be nimble,		1015	Swift to Sheri	51
NIMBLY				
Dick nimbly skip the Gutter;		784	Mullinex Dick	22
NINE SEE NYNE				
Let which I please of all the Nine		120	Apollo Outwit	30
Nine times a day it ebbs and flows,		256	Bubble	141
At Nine, grave Nim and George Facetious,		278	Journal	11
Comes home a quarter after nine,		292	Prog Marriage	84
"Go, Sisters Nine, into that Cabbin,		320	First of April	3
The wretch must be at court by nine:		434	Answer Paulus	74
Nine other tuneful words like that		467	Birthday Song	227
Her Time was not till Nine Months hence.		586	Strephon Chloe	66
Nine Muses always waiting round him,		598	Problem Solved	25
Amount to just Nine thousand Souls.		649	On Poetry	282
The Ladies walk'd till after Nine.		696	Cadenus Vaness	327

NINE	(CONTINUED)	PAGE	TITLE	LINE
Forsaken by th' inspiring Nine,		741	Stel B-day 22	13
First, nine Ways looking, let her stand		743	Stel B-day 22	53
While all the Squires from nine Miles round,		760	Receipt Youth	42
The Cat's nine lives and eke the care.		761	Bec's B-Day	30
There's nine Hundred Pounds for Labour and Grain,		867	Grand Question	9
Nine more such Champions as the <Dean>,		887	Panegyr Dean	9
Nine Spirits of blaspheming Fops,		904	Death Daphne	41
I think you inspir'd by the Muses all nine		1017	Swift Ans Sher	4

NINETEEN

| Throughout two Realms nineteen in twenty. | | 549 | Life of Swift | 135 |

NINNIES

| That such a pair of wealthy Ninnies | | 821 | Dr. Rundle | 63 |

NINNY

| (For the Dean was so shabby and look'd like a Ninny, | | 872 | Grand Question | 151 |

NINTH

| On Tuesday the Ninth, seditiously came, | | 263 | Apollo | 29 |

NITCH

| A Joyner to fasten a Saint in a Nitch, | | 336 | Serious Poem | 71 |
| If I can but fill my Nitch, | | 635 | Epistle Lady | 171 |

NITRE

| Surrounded with Jewels of Sulphur and Nitre. | | 803 | Irish Bishops | 6 |

NO   518

NO'S   OMITTED WORD

| Dick with zealous No's and Ay's, | | 785 | Mullinex Dick | 37 |

NOAH'S

| As never came from Noah's Ark: | | 514 | Answer Fable | 54 |

NOBLE

And His best Victory a Noble Death;		9	Ode to King	106
That this New, Noble, and Delightful Scene		20	Ode Athenian	136
I grieve, this Noble Work so happily begun,		24	Ode Athenian	275
How noble a Reprisal on the Great!		31	Ode to Temple	141
Your Garden's better worth your noble Pain,		32	Ode to Temple	176
To a less noble Substance chang'd		93	Bauc & Phil 1	115
To a less Noble Substance chang'd,		114	Bauc & Phil 2	91
But, most noble Senators, 'tis a great Shame		143	New Song	13
Our noble Grand Jury,		237	Excellent Song	23
O'Rourk's noble Fare		244	Irish-Feast	1
Your Blood in ev'ry Noble Race!		325	Pethox	70
A Bishop says the noble 'Squire, I hate the very Name,		342	Upon His Grace	17
Why Sirrah said the Noble 'Squire, how dare you see my Face,		343	Upon His Grace	43
That noble genius, who unbinds		490	Dialogue	31
A noble Lord hath told his Pranks,		515	Answer Fable	79
You dignify the noble Race,		656	On Poetry	457
Directors to a noble Mind.		706	Cadenus Vaness	613
Mix'd in a noble generous Mind;		731	Stella, Poems	104
Noble Captain, your Servant--Sir Arthur your Slave;		869	Grand Question	72
And of as noble Blood as you;		924	Riddle 8	4
Dan's noble Mettle, Sherry base;		1004	Dan J's Reply	31

NOBLER

You, Mighty Monarch, Nobler Actions Crown,		11	Ode to William	D 3
Is even the nobler Man, our Learning and our Wit,		24	Ode Athenian	269
Are nobler Subjects for your learned Pen;		31	Ode to Temple	160
Far sooner than the nobler mushroom grows:		46	To Congreve	100
Now to a nobler Office put,		66	Problem	24
I'll disappoint its Nobler Part.		121	Apollo Outwit	52
His Talents to employ for nobler Ends;		194	Author Himself	24
The Silver takes a nobler Hue,		255	Bubble	114
To Something Nobler in thy Face.		340	Arch-Bish Dub	16
He now shall shine in nobler Scenes:		385	Manly Virtue	52
Now change the Scene; a nobler Care		387	Manly Virtue	111
In hope to spring some nobler Game:		412	Desire Possess	31
Nor, will your nobler Gifts be misapply'd,		532	To Mr. Gay	15
To that you owe the nobler Flame.		726	To Stella	91
For nobler Ends by Nature meant.		731	Stella, Poems	116
By nature meant for nobler Ends,		781	Mullinix Tim	279
I lead you to a nobler Scene;		889	Panegyr Dean	86

NOBLEST

Among the noblest flow'rs a thousand pois'nous weeds,		37	Ode Sancroft	102
Their noblest Use is to abate		387	Manly Virtue	107
To Virtue, in the Noblest Sense,		697	Cadenus Vaness	347

NOBLY

| At Monarchy we nobly shew our Spight, | | 163 | Toland's Invit | 15 |

NOBODY

| There's nobody but a Fool that would trust. | | 941 | Letter | 32 |

NOBUS

| And before Corum Nobus so oft has been call'd, | | 238 | Excellent Song | 27 |

NOD

Consented with the usuall Nod.		81	Vanbrug House	72
Consenting with the usual Nod,		107	V's House	52
And pausing o'er a Pipe, with doubtful Nod,		193	Author Himself	5
But read a Nod, a Shrug, a Look,		450	Modern Lady	190
In vain; even there to spoil his Nod		458	Paddy's Charac	33
Unaw'd by Jove's all-shaking Nod.		466	Birthday Song	186
Tho' your Children by a Nod		633	Epistle Lady	103
A Nod, a Shrug, a scornful Smile,		647	On Poetry	237
Late be her death, one gentle nod,		762	Bec's B-Day	57

NODDING

| Jove, nodding, shook the Heav'ns, and said, | | 579 | Day Judgement | 10 |
| Nightly nodding o'er your Flocks, | | 660 | Love Song | 6 |

		PAGE	TITLE	LINE
NODDLE				
Warburton took it in his Noddle,	. . . .	127	Little House	35
Lets drive at Tom's devoted Noddle,	. . . .	458	Paddy's Charac	24
E'er enter any Mortal's Noddle.	. . . .	496	Panegyr Swift	105
NODDLES				
And, before we find either, our noddles turn round.	. .	1026	Sheri Circles	8
NODS				
As if he was awake, nods o'er his Text:	. . . . . .	364	On Dreams	32
The Angels of your awful Nods,	. . . .	499	Panegyr Swift	181
Thy formal Nods; important Sneres;	. . . .	775	Mullinix Tim	61
Olympus trembling as he nods.	. . . .	924	Riddle 7	96
NOE				
Then olde Inglonde shall be noe more.	. . . . . .	103	Merlin	17
NOG				
Dog <Walpole> laid a Quart of Nog on't,	. . . . .	299	Horrid Plot	31
NOISE				
At the first Ebb of Noise and Fears,	. . . .	16	Ode Athenian	14
You Fellows, what a Noise you keep!	. . . .	90	Bauc & Phil 1	28
At home, he was pursu'd with Noise,	. . . .	221	A Quiet Life	49
Till rowz'd by the Noise,	. . . .	245	Irish-Feast	31
And, trust me, as the noise grows stronger,	. . . . .	296	Satiric Elegy	7
That all the Noise they made was barking:	. . . . .	299	Horrid Plot	26
Still pleas'd with the good-natur'd Noise,	. . . . .	322	First of April	33
Shall strike him dumb, and quell their Noise.	. . . .	340	Arch-Bish Dub	28
To take the Noise of Brass for Thunder!	. . . . . .	353	Wood Ironmongr	30
Why against Printers all this noise?	. . . .	487	Irish-Club	9
He squals in such a hellisn Noise	. . . .	513	Answer Fable	25
Made up of Noise, and Impudence, and Lies.	. . . . .	532	To Mr. Gay	42
Dick would make a woful Noise,	. . . .	784	Mullinex Dick	17
And when I listen to the Noise,	. . . .	788	Dick's Variety	7
Has, with noise and odd gestures, been prating some years,	.	815	Yahoo's	18
Such a Noise, and such haranguing,	. . . .	830	Legion Club	15
With the Noise, the Sight, the Scent.	. . . .	839	Legion Club	234
Begotten, and Born, and dying with Noise,	. . . . .	927	Riddle 11	D 1
A long-ear'd Beast, and kind Noise of a Cat,	. . .	943	Probatur Alit	43
NOISOM				
No noisom Whiffs, or sweaty Streams,	'	584	Strephon Chloe	12
Let me, tho' the Smell be Noisom,	. . . .	635	Epistle Lady	177
NOISY				
Squander'd his noisy talents to my face;	. . . . . .	47	To Congreve	138
The dull, the noisy, and the lewd:	. . . .	178	To Lord Harley	48
Surrounded with her Noisy Clans	. . . .	448	Modern Lady	118
Whate'er the noisy Scoundrel says	. . . .	505	Doctor Delaney	163
Might want such noisy Fools as you;	. . . .	774	Mullinix Tim	40
If noisy <Tom> should in the <Senate> prate,	. . . .	825	Noisy Tom	1
NON				
Is, causa sine qua non.	. . . .	406	Swift to Pope	20
(As lucus comes a non lucendo)	. . . .	435	Answer Paulus	115
Et diu potuisse, et non potuisse refelli.	. . . . . .	967	Letter Sherid	6
NONE				
By none but its Possessors to be understood:	. . . .	6	Ode to King	4
(As those still do wh' have none at all)	. . . . . .	8	Ode to King	84
Where none ever led the Way,	. . . .	26	Ode to Temple	13
With Rules to search it, yet obtain'd by none.	. . . .	26	Ode to Temple	16
None e'er but you,	. . . .	38	Ode Sancroft	113
None but the Fav'rite Nymph can smell it.	. . . . .	65	Problem	12
They beg'd Relief which none would grant;	. . . . .	90	Bauc & Phil 1	24
Where there are none, it stands erect,	. . . . . .	133	Magician's Rod	25
Where none e'er look'd for it before;	. . . .	133	Magician's Rod	30
None e'er did modern Midas chuse,	. . . .	157	Fable of Midas	51
They fly, and none can overtake	. . . .	177	To Lord Harley	21
And Climb the dark Stairs to your friends who have none:	.	185	Scriblerus 1	4
'Tis thought could be the Work of none but <Swift>	. .	195	Author Himself	50
My State of Health none care to learn;	. . . . . .	203	In Sickness	5
The Reason is plain, they are none of his own;	. . . .	264	Apollo	56
Under the Rose since here are none but friends;	. . . .	275	Epilogue	13
You get all the Fish, and others get none,	. . . . .	287	Bank Down	7
For none but a Dunce would come under his Rod.	. . .	335	Serious Poem	34
That none are more properly Knights of the Post.	. . .	335	Serious Poem	40
None e'er was known to have a Brace.	. . . . . .	366	Answer Delaney	8
None e'er made Verses worse than he,	. . . .	401	Window Inns 2	5
None loves his King and Country better,	. . . . . .	410	Dial Rich Marb	83
Yet none was ever less their Debtor.	. . . .	410	Dial Rich Marb	84
'Tis very true, and none denies,	. . . .	433	Answer Paulus	39
All mad to speak, and none to hearken,	. . . . . .	450	Modern Lady	178
Your favourite Lord is none of those,	. . . . . .	484	Libel on D- D-	136
His Learning none will call in doubt;	. . . . . .	484	Libel on D- D-	140
Advances few, enriches none,	. . . .	495	Panegyr Swift	73
Believ'd in God, and you in none.	. . . .	495	Panegyr Swift	85
Whose Wit at best was next to none,	. . . .	514	Answer Fable	67
None ever saw her pluck a Rose.	. . . .	584	Strephon Chloe	16
A Rug; for Night-gown he had none.	. . . .	594	Cassinus Peter	20
Then, for his Voice, there's none disputes	. . . . .	602	Beasts Confess	35
None of these have Mercy found:	. . . .	638	Epistle Lady	247
Out-done by none in Rhyming well,	. . . .	650	On Poetry	291
But none will burn her for a Witch.	. . . .	698	Cadenus Vaness	363
For, none among the upstart Race	. . . .	739	Stel B-day '21	13
Will none the Tory Dogs pursue	. . . .	779	Mullinix Tim	185
While none believes that what he said he meant:	. . . .	797	Traulus 1	50
(For none could tell whose Turn was next)	. . . . .	849	Old Thorn	31
I'll have none but forward Eyes:	. . . .	863	To Janus	20

NONE (CONTINUED)

	PAGE	TITLE	LINE
When none the Drapier's Praise shall sing;	875	Drapier's Hill	13
For none but witlings there resort,	876	To Dean Swift	8
There's none so ignorant or weak	890	Panegyr Dean	119
None seek thee now in open Air;	895	Panegyr Dean	281
For, none can say that ever yet	901	Dean's Reasons	73
None could ever act that part,	907	Daphne	23
Superior none on Earth I find;	917	Riddle 3	3
For none, alas, by me can gain,	918	Riddle 4	15
A Greater Chymist none, than I,	920	Riddle 6	19
What you see is none of mine,	927	Riddle 10	D 2
Which all may handle, none can flatter.	993	On Picture	18

NONSENCE

Clap his own Nonsence in the place.	61	Lady Tablebook	24
And serve to eccho ratling Nonsence;	461	Birthday Song	44
But Nonsence wrapt up in a Stink)	775	Mullinix Tim	64

NONSENSE

Of Spleen, of Politicks and Nonsense,	181	Horace 2, 1	38
The glass, by lovers nonsense blurr'd,	402	Window Inns 6	D 1
And take his Nonsense all for Wit:	416	Woman's Mind	8
Such stupid blasphemy and nonsense?	490	Dialogue	38
With Nonsense ev'ry second Word,	696	Cadenus Vaness	329
He had cut his own ears to be deaf to your nonsense.	818	Epigr Kite	10
From Tubs their snuffling Nonsense utter:	892	Panegyr Dean	171

NOON

By a shrill Voice at noon declares,	94	Bauc & Phil 1	144
To make a dreadful Night at Noon;	98	Elegy Patrige	14
By a shrill Voice at Noon declares,	113	Bauc & Phil 2	82
He'll talk of them from Noon till Night,	116	Bauc & Phil 2	167
His Morning-Draughts 'till Noon can swill,	231	Prog of Poetry	19
She rises to her Tea at noon.	291	Prog Marriage	38
The modern Dame is wak'd by Noon,	446	Modern Lady	38
Robin from noon to night will prate,	878	Robbin & Harry	9
You toss and turn your Brain till Noon;	892	Panegyr Dean	190

NOON-DAY

| That her Eyes were as bright as our self at Noon-Day; | 264 | Apollo | 41 |

NOON-TIDE

| There is a Noon-tide in our Lives | 24 | Ode Athenian | 278 |

NOOSE

The sleeping Hangman ties the fatal Noose,	364	On Dreams	29
She shall be caught as in a Noose:	885	Rev Market-Hill	64
I value not your Jokes of Noose,	1003	Dan J's Reply	13

NOR   326

NORAH   OMITTED WORD

| But see, where Norah with the Sowins comes-- | 882 | Pastoral Dial | 51 |

NORTH

From Ignorance's Universal North,	25	Ode Athenian	299
To the Dean'ry House, and on the North Glass,	264	Apollo	31
Direct to the North, where I never yet went;	264	Apollo	48
At North and South are posted Centry;	883	Rev Market-Hill	18
He feels at once both North and South:	923	Riddle 7	84

NORTH-ZONE

| There out of my Sight, just against the North-Zone, | 265 | Apollo | 85 |

NORTHERN

What northern hive pour'd out these foes to wit?	46	To Congreve	83
To learn what Northern Kings design,	63	Discovery	29
Up to the Northern Tropick came,	119	Apollo Outwit	2
Among our harmless Northern Swains;	896	Panegyr Dean	300

NORTHEY

| Dispatch; or else that Rascal Northey, | 190 | Faggot | 41 |

NORTHUMBERLOND

| Beware of Carrots from Northumberlond. | 148 | Windsor Proph | 16 |

NORTHWARD

| Full Northward, let your Troops be led: | 884 | Rev Market-Hill | 48 |

NORWAYS

| And Norways pryd agayne shall marreye. | 103 | Merlin | 12 |

NOS

| Where all that passes, inter nos, | 201 | Horace 2, 6 | 79 |

NOSE

And, in <Swift's> Ear thrusts half his powder'd Nose.	196	Author Himself	68
All Subjects like Dan Jackson's Nose.	218	To Mr. Delany	102
Leaving the Purple to the Nose.	226	Prog of Beauty	28
No Painting can restore a Nose,	229	Prog of Beauty	111
How haughtily he lifts his Nose,	281	Journal	81
Her Hoop is hoist above his Nose,	292	Prog Marriage	79
Would guard your Nose against a Post.	367	Answer Delaney	48
When they're to pull him by the Nose,	373	Letter D. S-y	72
Your bandy Leg, or crooked Nose.	416	Woman's Mind	22
Humms, like a Hornet at his Nose,	458	Paddy's Charac	26
The smallest Worm in Celia's Nose,	527	Lady's Dres Rm	64
If Strephon would but stop his Nose;	530	Lady's Dres Rm	136
"He spar'd a Hump or crooked Nose,	572	Death of Swift	467
At Country Dances, not a Nose	584	Strephon Chloe	23
To slip his Ears, yet struck his Nose:	589	Strephon Chloe	184
To chat a while, and warm his Nose:	594	Cassinus Peter	8
Sunk down her Nose, or seam'd her Face?	595	Cassinus Peter	49
His carrot locks, and fiery nose;	621	Scandal Poem 1	136
His brazen Face, and fiery Nose:	627	Scandal Poem 2	140
The lovely Nymph had lost her Nose.	730	Stella, Poems	78
In at the door his monstrous Nose,	776	Mullinix Tim	104
In every Action thrusts his Nose	777	Mullinix Tim	119

NOSE   (CONTINUED)   PAGE   TITLE   LINE
      Dick would cock his Nose in scorn, ...   784 Mullinex Dick   9
      His Nose to get the Circle just in, ...   788 Dick's Variety   34
      Still swarm and buzz about his Nose?   . . . .   798 Traulus 1   87
      But Maggots in your Nose and Chin, ...   813 Bro Protestant   39
      A face for to kiss, without eyes, ears, or nose. . .   817 Yahoo's   64
      On a far less Villain's Nose.   . . . .   830 Legion Club   20
      Could have more offended her Nose;   . . . .   834 Legion Club   126
      Or scratching my nose, ... 852 Lady's Lament   21
      My nose, long and thin, ... 853 Lady's Lament   73
      And, Molly and I have thrust in our Nose, ...   872 Grand Question   137
      "I ne'er knew a Parson without a good Nose, ...   872 Grand Question   143
      Than yon tall Dock that rises to thy Nose. . . . .   881 Pastoral Dial   14
      Behind my Back, before my Nose, ...   887 Panegyr Dean   27
      Offensive to thy nicer Nose.   . . . . 895 Panegyr Dean   286
      Can shew a Nose, Eye, Tongue, or Ear, ...   935 Riddle 23   D   8
      With a quill stuck across his nose.   . . . .   983 Sher, A Goose   20
      Of Dan's large Nose, in modern Saphick, ...   993 On Picture   3
      'Tis true no Nose could come in better, ...   993 On Picture   16
      What Fortune may befall his Nose.   . . . . . .   993 On Picture   21
      To praise the Cheeks, Chin, Nose, the Bridge and all,   993 On Picture   26
      Thy Nose outshining Caelia's Eyes.   . . . . . .   994 On Picture   33
      Henceforth acknowledge, that a Nose   . . . . . .   1002 Reply by Dean   4
      That I have nothing like my Nose about me. . . . .   1004 Dan J's Reply   24
      And Dan shall be with us with Nose aquiline . . .   1018 Swift Ans Sher   27
      Long, Long, Long, Long, like Dan's Long Nose. . .   1022 Nim-Dan-Dean 1 D   54
NOSE'S
      Thy Nose's Length and Fame extend   . . . . . .   993 On Picture   28
NOSES
      By telling Noses with a Party strong.   . . . . . .   533 To Mr. Gay   60
      Or, from your noses dig out notches?   . . . . . .   618 Scandal Poem 1   26
      Or from your Noses dig out Notches?   . . . . . .   624 Scandal Poem 2   20
      And slitting of noses, and cropping of ears, ...   816 Yahoo's   48
NOT   585   OMITTED WORD
NOTCHES
      Or, from your noses dig out notches?   . . . .   618 Scandal Poem 1   26
      Or from your Noses dig out Notches?   . . . .   624 Scandal Poem 2   20
NOTE
      Last just as long as ev'ry cuckow's note: . . . . . .   47 To Congreve   130
      But repeats the same Note a whole Day, like a Finch. .   143 New Song   8
      But when I thought proper, I alter'd my Note; . . .   144 New Song   39
      A Clergyman of special Note, ...   171 Horace 1, 7   27
      What Poet e'er could sing a Note?   . . . . . .   231 Prog of Poetry   26
      To mournful Ditties, Clio, change thy Note, ...   284 Elegy Boat   1
      With mournful Note clocks round the Brim. . . . . . .   295 Horrid Plot   150
      (Note here, that in the Chymick Style, ...   354 Simile Silver   15
      Ye <rascals> of inferior note, ...   487 Irish-Club   3
      (Like Courtiers, when they send a Note, ...   649 On Poetry   271
NOTED
      She noted all she ever read, ... 710 Cadenus Vaness   756
NOTES
      To confer Notes with one another;   . . . .   66 Problem   50
      'Till drown'd in Shriller Notes of Chimney-Sweep, . .   124 Descriptn Morn   12
      Here conns his Notes, and takes a Whet, ...   127 Little House   21
      Known by the Verse, yet better by the Notes. . . . .   670 Epig Carthy 18 D   4
      With zeal in heart, and notes in hand;   . . . . . .   675 Curate's Compl   2
NOTHING   SEE HALF-NOTHING
      (And then how much a nothing is Mankind! . . . . .   21 Ode Athenian   180
      Nothing is fix'd that mortals see or know, ...   39 Ode Sancroft   143
      Like Sid's, but nothing near so good;   . . . . . .   134 Magician's Rod   60
      Pretend to cheapen Goods, but nothing buy. . . . . .   138 City Shower   34
      There's nothing fouls the Hands so much: . . . . . .   158 Fable of Midas   68
      Or, "Have you nothing new to day   . . . .   201 Horace 2, 6   73
      That meet for nothing but to gibe;   . . . .   216 To Mr. Delany   54
      For nothing else will make it cease,--   . . . . . .   220 A Quiet Life   13
      Tho' I know nothing on't, 'tis I that make Gold; . .   263 Apollo   4
      To call nothing his, but the Rhyme and the Measure. .   266 Apollo   102
      How Dan caught nothing in his Net, ...   280 Journal   65
      Why should he sink where nothing seem'd to press? . . .   284 Elegy Boat   3
      If nothing but Paper comes out of this Bank. . . .   287 Bank Down   15
      I promise nothing for the Night: . . . . . .   290 Prog Marriage   20
      Minds nothing that is done or said, ...   291 Prog Marriage   57
      Said I, from thence I nothing know;   . . . .   298 Horrid Plot   5
      But sure if nothing else must pass, ...   346 Prometheus   67
      Could nothing but thy chief Reproach, ...   348 Whitshed Motto   3
      For which Operation there's nothing more proper . . .   351 Wood Insect   35
      To wait so long and have nothing to ask. . . . . . .   368 Verses Window   2
      He'd treat with nothing that was Rare, ...   378 Apology Lady C   99
      Nothing impossible to Jove.   . . . .   384 Manly Virtue   22
      With nothing to tempt ye: . . . .   402 Window Inns 8   D   4
      And, by his Crown will nothing get;   . . . . . .   409 Dial Rich Marb   41
      While all she prates has nothing in it.   . . . . . .   415 Woman's Mind   6
      Thinks nothing gives one Airs so pretty; . . . . . .   417 Woman's Mind   41
      The Court had nothing to compair.   . . . .   422 Ireld   30
      Feed nothing in your lands but sheep   . . . .   422 Ireld   56
      Folks shrug, and cry, There's nothing in't. . . . . .   475 Epist on Epist   12
      atchieving of nothing Still promising wonders . . . .   540 Charac Walpole   5
      Have I nothing then to praise?   . . . .   630 Epistle Lady   12
      Where you have nothing to produce   . . . .   641 On Poetry   45
      The Similes that nothing fit;   . . . . 645 On Poetry   152
      Nothing but Chaff, and Straws, and Feathers: . . . .   688 Cadenus Vaness   56

NOTHING	(CONTINUED)	PAGE	TITLE	LINE
And said, she valu'd nothing less		697	Cadenus Vaness	340
Knows nothing which it dare not own;		706	Cadenus Vaness	609
"And this, or nothing else, wou'd do't.		714	Cadenus Vaness	877
Nothing but Acid left behind.		731	Stella, Poems	134
Ye Daintyes, I know nothing of ye, ...		733	Verses Vanessa	28
From Ford who thinks of nothing mean		745	Stel Distress	17
From Ford, who thinks of nothing mean, ...		750	Stel Wood-Park	41
And nothing left but Skin and Bone;		759	Receipt Youth	8
And now you find you fought for nothing.		774	Mullinix Tim	38
He calls you Rogue; There's nothing in it, . . .		797	Traulus 1	53
"And nothing of that ever troubled your Grace. . . .		843	Ay and No	8
Dermot, I vow, 'tis nothing else but Sweat. . . .		881	Pastoral Dial	24
What, if for nothing once you kiss't, ...		884	Rev Market-Hill	33
While nothing comes but Froth at first, ...		893	Panegyr Dean	193
May nothing interrupt his peace.		902	Dean's Reasons	102
Nothing she thought could sooner gain him, ...		905	Death Daphne	71
Chiefly where she nothing knows.		906	Daphne	16
By something form'd, I nothing am, ...		935	Riddle 23	D 1
To Ladies Skins there's nothing comes so near. . . .		943	Probatur Alit	42
In Weather fine I nothing spend, ...		954	Authors Living	7
For, as Helsham observes, there's nothing can chime, .		980	Tho: Sheridan	3
They're fit for nothing else but pasquils.		982	Sher, A Goose	2
That I have nothing like my Nose about me.		1004	Dan J's Reply	24
I've nothing left to vent my Spleen		1005	Sheridan's Sub	27
NOTHING'S				
Where Nothing's left to work upon.		228	Prog of Beauty	80
When nothing's left, that's worth defence, ...		843	Epigr Irish	3
NOTHINGS				
Five Nothings in five Plates of Delf.		747	Stel Distress	52
Five Nothings in five Plates of Delph.		751	Stel Wood-Park	68
NOTICE				
Take Notice, she has my Commission		418	Woman's Mind	61
(Take Notice, to avoid Offence		486	Libel on D- D-	183
She gave due Notice, that both Parties, ...		713	Cadenus Vaness	838
Is useful in Journies, take Notice of that.		943	Probatur Alit	44
NOTION				
Reject with scorn that stupid Notion		468	Birthday Song	261
And though he had no other Notion, ...		514	Answer Fable	55
Alass! a meer Chymerick Notion.		604	Beasts Confess	112
NOTIONS				
How to relish Notions high;		630	Epistle Lady	25
Yet cou'd such Notions entertain, ...		705	Cadenus Vaness	600
"Though with your state-sieve your own notions you split,		843	Ay and No	9
And think all notions too abstracted		900	Dean's Reasons	63
NOTORIOUS				
Iris, for Scandal most notorious, ...		450	Modern Lady	166
The Faction, (is it not Notorious?)		775	Mullinix Tim	75
NOTTINGHAMSHIRE				
An Orator dismal of Nottinghamshire, ...		142	New Song	1
NOTWITHSTANDING				
Whereas, Notwithstanding, I am in great Pain, . . .		143	New Song	11
NOUGHT				
Where nought but Weeds will grow.		33	Ode to Temple	209
Nought it contains is common or unclean, ...		50	To Congreve	233
Yet kindly sells himself for nought		421	Ireld	4
This country, now their own, for nought.		488	Irish-Club	24
And leave us nought but Guts and Garbage, ...		498	Panegyr Swift	152
And Teeth are useless, where there's nought to eat. . .		670	Epig Carthy 20	D 4
And therefore the Deductions nought, ...		695	Cadenus Vaness	281
There's nought so beautiful in thee, ...		932	Riddle 19	D 5
Nought but one Thing can confound me, ...		933	Riddle 20	D 5
NOURISH				
To nourish Vermin, may be bit.		813	Bro Protestant	64
NOURISHMENT				
Turn thy Nourishment to Poison!		838	Legion Club	206
They get no Nourishment from me.		926	Riddle 9	6
NOVA				
Proud Baronet of Nova Scotia, ...		884	Rev Market-Hill	29
NOVEDS				
"Your Noveds, and Blutraks, and Omurs and Stuff, . .		872	Grand Question	159
NOW 409				OMITTED WORD
NOW-A-DAYS				
And therefore Crowns are now-a-days		98	Elegy Patrige	27
NOW'S				
For Satyr now's so common grown		371	Letter D. S-y	3
NOXIOUS				
From noxious Steams to purge the Air;		780	Mullinix Tim	250
NOYSOM				
But, when he smelt a noysom Steam		589	Strephon Chloe	179
NUBIGENAE				
By learned authors call'd Nubigenae.		619	Scandal Poem 1	62
By learned Authors call'd, Nubigenae.		625	Scandal Poem 2	58
NUISANCE				
To thy own Side so Damn'd a Nuisance, ...		775	Mullinix Tim	66
NUISSANCE				
A perfect Nuissance to the rest.		455	Dean Smedley	12
Are grown the Nuissance of your Clan, ...		777	Mullinix Tim	145
NUM'ROUS				
Thus fools, for being strong and num'rous known, . . .		37	Ode Sancroft	79
Observ'd, they grew a num'rous Race.		106	V's House	18

NUM'ROUS	(CONTINUED)	PAGE	TITLE	LINE
And, as a Proof, shew num'rous Scars		324	Pethox	13
Your num'rous virtues foully stain'd;		436	Answer Paulus	142
Set off with num'rous Breaks--and Dashes--		643	On Poetry	94
Thy years as num'rous as thy days?		677	Parson's Case	36
Those num'rous Virtues which the Tribe		724	To Stella	15
That Death should get a num'rous Breed;		903	Death Daphne	14
Thy num'rous Fingers know their Way,		919	Riddle 5	11
And all my Kin, a num'rous Host,		925	Riddle 8	28

NUM'RUS

| For well she knew her num'rus Brood, | | 208 | Fable Bitches | 21 |

NUMBER

Each Number had it's diff'rent Power;		79	Vanbrug House	7
The Number make the Motion slower		93	Bauc & Phil 1	130
Each Number had it's diff'rent Pow'r;		106	V's House	7
The Number made the Motion slow'r:		113	Bauc & Phil 2	70
Fair Ladies, Number five,		425	Five Ladies	1
Bright Goddesses, in Number five;		656	On Poetry	439
Number, and Weight, and Measure join.		1022	Nim-Dan-Dean 1	D 46

NUMBER'D   SEE OUT-NUMBER'D

NUMBERLESS

Numberless Nations, stretching far and wide,		25	Ode Athenian	297
And suffers numberless Fatigues.		174	Horace 1, 7	96
Where numberless thy Vot'ries crowd:		324	Pethox	22

NUMBERS

What mighty numbers follow them;		39	Ode Sancroft	164
Among the numbers who employ		176	To Lord Harley	1
Secur'd by Numbers from the Lay-men's Gibes;		194	Author Himself	20
Are by thy Numbers dignify'd.		361	Grace's Answer	4
Or in harmonious Numbers put		451	Modern Lady	222
Would prove ev'n Homer's Numbers flat.		467	Birthday Song	228
"As Numbers in their Hearts must own,		566	Death of Swift	337
"While Numbers to Preferment rose;		569	Death of Swift	401
Shou'd I lofty Numbers chuse,		638	Epistle Lady	260
Some famed for Numbers soft and smooth,		650	On Poetry	297
Cynthia, tune harmonious Numbers;		661	Love Song	13
E'er join'd such Numbers Hand in Hand;		926	Riddle 9	12
Few are made, but Numbers lost.		934	Riddle 22	D 6
Who says, his numbers do not fadge a-right.		988	Letter Dr Sh-n	20
All must allow, your Numbers more,		1022	Nim-Dan-Dean 1	D 49

NUMBNESS

| A Numbness crept through ev'ry Limb: | | 470 | Burning Poem | 10 |

NUMERICK

| Shew me the same numerick Flea, | | 504 | Doctor Delaney | 141 |

NUMEROUS

That Poets were a numerous Race,		79	Vanbrug House	18
And sudden spreads a numerous Offspring round;		792	St. Pat's Well	62
For, who would not be in that numerous Crew sick?		1029	Dr. Helsham	13

NUN

| To see her cloister'd like a Nun. | | 705 | Cadenus Vaness | 583 |

NURS'D

| I was nurs'd by their Mother. | | 247 | Irish-Feast | 80 |
| "A servile Race in Folly nurs'd, | | 568 | Death of Swift | 397 |

NURS'RY

| To Kitchin, Parlour, Nurs'ry flies, | | 322 | First of April | 37 |

NURSE

| Which, as the Nurse pursu'd to kill, | | 504 | Doctor Delaney | 119 |
| For thee, than make a dry Nurse of thy Muse? | | 531 | To Mr. Gay | 8 |

NURSE-KEEPERS

| Old Nurse-keepers would never hire | | 605 | Beasts Confess | 137 |

NURSERIES

| Who crop the Nurseries of Learning here? | | 792 | St. Pat's Well | 50 |

NURSERY

| Here, from the neighbouring Nursery of Arts, | | 793 | St. Pat's Well | 69 |

NURSES

| And ev'ry Vice that nurses both. | | 655 | On Poetry | 410 |
| The quarterly demands of nurses, | | 676 | Parson's Case | 14 |

NURST

| It left the Forest where 'twas nurst, | | 134 | Magician's Rod | 68 |
| For Traulus long his Rancour nurst, | | 796 | Traulus 1 | 17 |

NUT

| Now brown and burnish'd like a nut, | | 937 | Riddle 24 | D 29 |

NUTRIMENT

| The Nutriment will from within | | 759 | Receipt Youth | 29 |
| The Nutriment that feeds the Mind? | | 765 | Stel B-day '26 | 62 |

NUTS

| Of Sparrows tam'd, of Nuts innumerable, | | 283 | Journal | 113 |

NYMPH

Fain the fair Nymph would stay,		31	Ode to Temple	153
Smooth as that airy nymph so subtly borne		54	Temple Ill	117
Here (lovely Nymph pronounce my doom)		60	Lady Tablebook	11
None but the Fav'rite Nymph can smell it.		65	Problem	12
And should some Nymph who ne'er was cruel,		85	Salamander	61
Before he durst the Nymph approach.		119	Apollo Outwit	8
The Nymph who oft had read in Books,		120	Apollo Outwit	13
Deceitful Nymph I see thy Art,		121	Apollo Outwit	50
The Nymph had soon been brought to yield;		177	To Lord Harley	14
The Nymph would ne'er have been a prude.		177	To Lord Harley	16
I fancy'd ev'ry nymph would run		177	To Lord Harley	31
The Nymph, with indignation, view'd		178	To Lord Harley	47
Alas, the Nymph would be undone.		226	Prog of Beauty	12

NYMPH   (CONTINUED)   PAGE   TITLE   LINE
     Ah Lovely Nymph be not too rash, ...   228 Prog of Beauty   67
     'Tis the Nymph that I courted some ten Years ago;   . .   264 Apollo   44
     The Swain is rich, the Nymph is fair;   . . . . .   290 Prog Marriage   28
     The Swain is old, the Nymph Coquette.   . . . . .   290 Prog Marriage   30
     And gave the Nymph a plenteous Draught;   . . . . .   293 Prog Marriage   114
     The Nymph who still with Passion burnd, ...   293 Prog Marriage   117
     A Nymph, that brings ten thousand Pound: . . . . .   545 Life of Swift   16
     The Nymph, tho' in this mangled Plight, ...   583 Young Nymph   65
     So beautiful a Nymph appears   . . . .   584 Strephon Chloe   3
     The bashful Nymph no more withstands, ...   585 Strephon Chloe   43
     The Nymph was cover'd with her Flammeum, ...   586 Strephon Chloe   61
     How with so high a Nymph he might   . . . .   586 Strephon Chloe   73
     He'll sweat, and then the Nymph may smell it.   . . .   586 Strephon Chloe   84
     How could a Nymph so chaste as Chloe, ...   588 Strephon Chloe   151
     Had now constrain'd the Nymph to leak.   . . . . .   589 Strephon Chloe   164
     The Nymph opprest before, behind, ...   589 Strephon Chloe   169
     To see some radiant Nymph appear   . . . .   591 Strephon Chloe   227
     For, ev'ry Nymph has Leave to chuse;   . . . . .   595 Cassinus Peter   64
     Not to the Nymph that keeps thy Heart;   . . . . .   596 Cassinus Peter   102
     But say, what earthly nymph do you know, ...   619 Scandal Poem 1   63
     What nymph on earth so fair as Iris?   . . . . .   619 Scandal Poem 1   74
     When Jove would some fair nymph inveigle   . . . . .   620 Scandal Poem 1   113
     But say, what Earthly Nymph do you know, ...   625 Scandal Poem 2   59
     What Nymph on Earth so fair as Iris?   . . . . .   625 Scandal Poem 2   72
     When Jove would some fair Nymph inveigle, ...   627 Scandal Poem 2   111
     The Nymph stood silent out of spight, ...   699 Cadenus Vaness   406
     A Nymph so hard to be subdu'd, ...   702 Cadenus Vaness   496
     A Father, and the Nymph his Child.   . . . .   704 Cadenus Vaness   549
     That ev'ry Nymph with Envy own'd, ...   705 Cadenus Vaness   580
     Now, let the Nymph, I'll let you see   . . . . .   706 Cadenus Vaness   614
     Whether the Nymph were Young or Old;   . . . . .   706 Cadenus Vaness   633
     In Learning let a Nymph delight, ...   710 Cadenus Vaness   742
     So bright a Nymph to come unsought, ...   710 Cadenus Vaness   752
     The Nymph in sober Words intreats   . . . .   711 Cadenus Vaness   792
     The Nymph will have her Turn, to be . . . .   712 Cadenus Vaness   806
     Whether the Nymph, to please her Swain, ...   712 Cadenus Vaness   820
     "To form a Nymph of Wit and Sense, ...   713 Cadenus Vaness   865
     The Nymph who wrote this in an Amorous Fit,   . . .   716 Answer Rebus   1
     Where the Nymph has entirely forsaken her Text: . . . 716 Answer Rebus   20
     (That either Nymph might have her Swain,) . . . . .   722 Stel B-Day '18 D 17
     The lovely Nymph had lost her Nose. . . . .   730 Stella, Poems   78
     Nymph, would you learn the onely Art . . . .   732 Verses Vanessa   1
     To such a Nymph the Wise and Good   . . . .   733 Verses Vanessa   9
     For who could such a Nymph forsake   . . . .   733 Verses Vanessa   19
     Than on a Nymph of Stella's Tast.   . . . .   747 Stel Distress   64
     Than on a Nymph of Stella's Taste.   . . . .   752 Stel Wood-Park   80
     As when a beauteous Nymph decays   . . . .   756 Stel B-day '24   1
     Nor ever Nymph inspir'd to Rhyme, ...   757 Stel B-day '24   21
     But for a blooming Nymph will pass, ...   760 Receipt Youth   39
     To rouse and warn the Nymph within. . . . .   849 Old Thorn   36
     The Nymph who dwells in every Tree, ...   849 Old Thorn   45
     A Nymph and Swain, Sheelah and Dermot hight, ...   880 Pastoral Dial   1
     The soft Endearments of the Nymph and Swain.   . . . .   880 Pastoral Dial   8
     And ev'ry Nymph must enter single;   . . . .   893 Panegyr Dean   210
     Be Witness for me, Nymph divine, ...   896 Panegyr Dean   315
     Cease haughty Nymph; the Fates decree   . . . . .   905 Death Daphne   91
     No haughty Nymph has Pow'r to run   . . . .   916 Riddle 2   5
     Ah lovely Nymph, thou'rt in thy Prime!   . . . . . .   932 Riddle 19   D 13
NYMPHS
     Terrestrial nymphs, by formal arts, ...   178 To Lord Harley   53
     Send us new Nymphs with each new Moon.   . . . . .   229 Prog of Beauty   120
     The Nymphs with whom You first began   . . . . . .   311 To Ford   17
     All other Nymphs expelling   . . . .   441 Ballyspellin   51
     Ah lovely Nymphs, remove your Fears, ...   445 Modern Lady   17
     Irish Nymphs learn Irish Raillery: . . . .   523 Betty Grizette   26
     Unjustly all our Nymphs complain, ...   591 Strephon Chloe   255
     That mov'd the Nymphs to be unkind.   . . . .   598 Problem Solved   24
     The Shepherds and the Nymphs were seen   . . . . .   686 Cadenus Vaness   1
     The Nymphs with Scorn beheld their Foes: . . . . .   687 Cadenus Vaness   21
     The Fault must on the Nymphs be plac'd, ...   688 Cadenus Vaness   65
     Thus by the Nymphs and Swains ador'd, ...   694 Cadenus Vaness   246
     To copy her, few Nymphs aspir'd;   . . . .   700 Cadenus Vaness   440
     Of Nymphs so gracefull, Wise and fair   . . . . .   722 Stel B-Day '18   12
     The Bow'rs that hold those Nymphs divine; . . . . .   729 Stella, Poems   42
     Adorn'd by Nymphs with all their Care: . . . . .   919 Riddle 5   4
NYNE
     Seven and Ten addyd to nyne, ...   102 Merlin   1
O
     Root out these Carrots, O Thou, whose Name   . . .   148 Windsor Proph   21
     O there is the Sport   . . . .   245 Irish-Feast   13
     O how was I trick't, ...   245 Irish-Feast   17
     Laughlin O Enagin, ...   246 Irish-Feast   46
     O! Cou'd I see this Audience Clad in Stuff,   . . .   275 Epilogue   31
     O may the Fates thy Life prolong!   . . . .   339 Arch-Bish Dub   5
     To have two thousand Pounds a Year, O 'tis a burning   342 Upon His Grace   18
          Shame!
     "O Jove, if Virtue be so fair   . . . .   383 Manly Virtue   4
     O, 'tis a quaint Device: . . . .   394 Grub-Street   6
     O Neptune! Neptune! must I still   . . . .   403 Window Inns 10 D   1
     O yes! If any Man can find   . . . .   417 Woman's Mind   57

O

		(CONTINUED)	PAGE	TITLE	LINE

O, wou'd the Senate deign to show . . . . 515 Answer Fable 81
O never may such vile Machine . . . . 528 Lady's Dres Rm 95
O may she better learn to keep . . . . 528 Lady's Dres Rm 97
",o, may we all for Death prepare! . . . . 558 Death of Swift 153
O, think what Evils must ensue; . . . . 588 Strephon Chloe 127
O Strephon, e'er that fatal Day . . . . 591 Strephon Chloe 235
O, Grubstreet! how do I bemoan thee, ... 652 On Poetry 357
O, what Indignity and Shame . . . . 654 On Poetry 405
(Late, very late, O, may he rule us.) . . . . . 655 On Poetry 430
O! were they all but Nebuchadnazzars . . . . . . 659 On Poetry D 410
Beware, O Bard, how you proceed. . . . . 666 Epig Carthy 2 D 4
And, O what virtue you express . . . . 676 Parson's Case 17
The Court, so made his last O yes! . . . . 714 Cadenus Vaness 885
O then, whatever Heav'n intends, ... 766 Stel B-day '26 79
O what a pleasure mixt with pain! . . . . 776 Mullinix Tim 106
O, were I equal in Renown, ... 779 Mullinix Tim 197
O, introduce me to your Friends! . . . . 781 Mullinix Tim 280
O! had I been Apostle to the Swiss, ... 793 St. Pat's Well 79
That I saw a huge Rat: O dear, how I scream'd! . 868 Grand Question 50
O law! the sweet Gentleman! look in his Face; . 870 Grand Question 94
Happy, O Market-Hill! at least, ... 877 To Dean Swift 27
Cut down the Dock, 'twill sprout again: but O! . 881 Pastoral Dial 15
O, could I earn for thee, my lovely Lass, . . . 882 Pastoral Dial 49
O Fortune, 'tis a Scandal for thee . . . . . . 884 Rev Market-Hill 25
O, may I never once forget ' . . . . 887 Panegyr Dean 24
And, O! may all who hither come, ... 894 Panegyr Dean 223
O, 'tis pretty Picking . . . . 952 Asparagus 4
O tempora, O mores! as 'tis in the adage. . . . 975 Dean to Sherid 2
O tempora, O mores! as 'tis in the adage. . . . 975 Dean to Sherid 2

O'

Upon St. James's End o' th' Town; . . . . 100 Elegy Patrige 96
But a Pox o' those Banks that choak up the Springs. . 287 Bank Down 3
No less than Justices o' Quorum. . . . . 760 Receipt Youth 45

O'ER   SEE O'RE,OR'E

Her Face patch't o'er with Modern Pedantry, ... 23 Ode Athenian 224
We scrawl all o'er with old and empty Rules, . . . 27 Ode to Temple 33
Have worn a Casement o'er their Skin, ... 30 Ode to Temple 126
Go publish o'er the Plain . . . . 31 Ode to Temple 139
Runs violently o'er his usual Course.) . . . . . 31 Ode to Temple 149
Make their minds travel o'er infinity of space, . 36 Ode Sancroft 61
This could i do, and proudly o'er him tow'r, . . 44 To Congreve 39
O'er the sun's face, and from his heat proceeds, . 45 To Congreve 70
Crusts o'er the day, shadowing its parent beam . 45 To Congreve 71
O'er Nile, with all its wilderness of gods; . . 46 To Congreve 104
O'er the glad scene whence first she rose a bride: . 51 Temple Ill 12
Scatters strange agues o'er men's sickly minds, . 52 Temple Ill 38
And passing o'er, mistakes thee still for mine. . 54 Temple Ill 92
Scatt'ring loose features o'er the optic vein; . 54 Temple Ill 96
Time o'er the happy takes so swift a flight, . . 54 Temple Ill 113
With inoffensive feet o'er standing corn; . . . 54 Temple Ill 118
But o'er th' afflicted with a heavy pace . . . 55 Temple Ill 121
March o'er the ruin'd plain with motion slow, . 55 Temple Ill 129
Scrawl'd o'er with Trifles thus, and quite . . . 60 Lady Tablebook 3
He wav'd his Wreath Thrice o'er her Head, . . . 120 Apollo Outwit 35
And stepping o'er the Fabrick-roof, ... 127 Little House 33
O'er Sea and Land conveys the Witch; . . . . . 132 Magician's Rod 18
Which, o'er a British Senate's Lids, ... 133 Magician's Rod 40
As Homer tells us o'er and o'er, ... 134 Magician's Rod 69
As Homer tells us o'er and o'er, ... 134 Magician's Rod 69
While Rain depends, the pensive Cat gives o'er . 136 City Shower 3
While Spouts run clatt'ring o'er the Roof by Fits; . 139 City Shower 44
And you the Tyrant o'er them all: . . . . 173 Horace 1, 7 90
Prepar'd to leap o'er Sticks, or bind 'em. . . 190 Faggot 44
And pausing o'er a Pipe, with doubtful Nod, . . 193 Author Himself 5
Like Porters o'er a Pot of Ale. . . . . 216 To Mr. Delany 50
If o'er against her you were plac't . . . . . . 222 Prog of Love 5
Can scarce get o'er the Barn-Door Sill; . . . . 230 Prog of Poetry 4
Thus Bankers o'er their Bills and Bags . . . . 240 Run Bankers 31
The young Advent'rer o'er the Deep . . . . . . 252 Bubble 34
Ride o'er the Waves in spacious Hoops, ... 254 Bubble 91
Our Ocean's coverd o'er with Gold, ... 254 Bubble 103
All cover'd o'er with Slime and Mud. . . . . . 255 Bubble 132
O'er sees the Work, or Dragon rowes, ... 279 Journal 23
Or make a rumbling o'er his Head, ... 280 Journal 47
How Valiant George rode o'er the Dragon; . . . 281 Journal 70
Her weighty Morning Bus'ness o'er . . . . 291 Prog Marriage 55
Come, help your lame Dog o'er the Style. . . . 298 Horrid Plot 15
Your Foes, triumphant o'er the Laws, ... 312 To Ford 29
While We may search all Dublin o'er . . . . . . 315 To Ford 107
You, o'er the high Triumphal Arch . . . . 326 Pethox 93
Drives rattling o'er a brazen Arch: . . . . . . 353 Wood Ironmongr 18
O'er the Moon's Face a sable Hue, ... 354 Simile Silver 2
The busy Head with mimick Art runs o'er . . . . 363 On Dreams 9
As if he was awake, nods o'er his Text: . . . . 364 On Dreams 32
Have you not o'er a Sawpit seen, ... 393 Modern Poets 10
O'er mountains steep, o'er dusty plains, ... 403 Window Inns 10 D 5
O'er mountains steep, o'er dusty plains, ... 403 Window Inns 10 D 5
Or, whether o'er a Pot of Ale, ... 412 Desire Possess 7
Can, at her Morning Tea, run o'er . . . . 416 Woman's Mind 23
Just o'er against the Bell Inn . . . . 442 Ballyspellin 57

561

O'ER   (CONTINUED)

	PAGE	TITLE	LINE
Now, loit'ring o'er her Tea and Cream,	447	Modern Lady	70
Like Hunters o'er their Evening Ale.	447	Modern Lady	79
This Business of Importance o'er,	447	Modern Lady	90
Our Madam o'er her Ev'ning Tea;	448	Modern Lady	117
Flew hov'ring o'er each Female Head.	449	Modern Lady	135
Than Fish-Wives o'er a Cup of Gin:	450	Modern Lady	181
Like Females o'er their Morning Tea.	501	Doctor Delaney	50
To flourish o'er a Cup of Ginn?	505	Doctor Delaney	148
The Thresher Duck, could o'er the <Queen> prevail.	521	Stephen Duck	1
All varnish'd o'er with Snuff and Snot.	527	Lady's Dres Rm	50
When o'er your Patron's Treasure you preside,	532	To Mr. Gay	16
Plyes you with Stories o'er and o'er,	556	Death of Swift	89
Plyes you with Stories o'er and o'er,	556	Death of Swift	89
The World's mad Business now is o'er,	579	Day Judgement	19
You but o'er half the World can reign.	585	Strephon Chloe	32
A Rug was o'er his Shoulders thrown;	594	Cassinus Peter	19
Beck'ning to waft me o'er the Ferry.	596	Cassinus Peter	84
When Syrius o'er the welkin rages,	618	Scandal Poem 1	33
O'er all your passions we preside:	620	Scandal Poem 1	90
While we, o'er Tenariffa plac't,	620	Scandal Poem 1	105
O'er cityes, rivers, hills, and seas,	621	Scandal Poem 1	126
When Syrius o'er the Welkin rages,	624	Scandal Poem 2	31
O'er all your Passions we preside;	626	Scandal Poem 2	88
While we, o'er Tenariffa plac't,	626	Scandal Poem 2	103
O'er Cities, Rivers, Hills, and Seas:	627	Scandal Poem 2	120
Are swallow'd o'er a Dish of Tea;	642	On Poetry	68
And o'er unhabitable Downs	646	On Poetry	179
These o'er their proper Districts govern,	649	On Poetry	283
And Maevius reigns o'er Kentish-Town;	650	On Poetry	302
Gentle Cupid o'er my Heart;	660	Love Song	2
Nightly nodding o'er your Flocks,	660	Love Song	6
Morpheus hov'ring o'er my Pillow,	661	Love Song	23
Run o'er their Cant of stupid Lies,	697	Cadenus Vaness	332
Which gave a Tincture o'er the Mass:	709	Cadenus Vaness	719
That she might o'er the Servants hector.	749	Stel Wood-Park	6
From Fleets triumphant o'er the Gallick Coast.	771	Horace 1, 14	40
All powder'd o'er from Tail to Chin;	785	Dick, Maggot	2
Who o'er each String and Wire preside,	798	Traulus 1	73
And, must their Malice ne'er give o'er?	798	Traulus 1	86
While o'er the Church these Clouds are gathering,	813	Bro Protestant	47
O'er his Inferiors as our Tyrants;	824	Printer Newgat	6
Had she flown but o'er the Top,	834	Legion Club	127
A Lawyer o'er his Hands and Face,	904	Death Daphne	35
O'er Head and Body make a Rout,	920	Riddle 6	15
If Chloe o'er thy Heart prevails,	925	Riddle 8	19
From Victors o'er the Memphian King;	925	Riddle 8	30
Come dancing to me o'er the Plains.	934	Riddle 21	D 10

O'ER-PAYS
| Tho' Half a Crown o'er-pays his Sweat's Worth; | 812 | Bro Protestant | 26 |

O'ER-RUN
| Had my own native Italy o'er-run. | 789 | St. Pat's Well | 4 |

O'ERBLOWN
| A sign God's dart is shot, and wrath o'erblown; | 52 | Temple Ill | 28 |

O'ERCOME
| When Foes are o'ercome, we preserve them from Slaughter, | 334 | Serious Poem | 1 |

O'ERFLOW'D
| O'erflow'd a Farmer's Barn and Stable; | 811 | Bro Protestant | 2 |

O'ERWHELM
| So tossing Faction will o'erwhelm | 96 | On the Union | 21 |

O'ME
| "I never cou'd take to my Book for the Blood o'me, | 873 | Grand Question | 165 |
| "And the Puppy confess'd, he expected no Good o'me. | 873 | Grand Question | 166 |

O'MURPHY
| With Teague O'Murphy, or an Earl; | 890 | Panegyr Dean | 123 |

O'R'E
Still seen o'r'e many an Alehouse fire.	461	Birthday Song	38
And when we scrawl our Paper o'r'e,	463	Birthday Song	109
Prepare a Fleet to waft him o'r'e,	466	Birthday Song	205

O'RE
He spake, and a dark Cloud flung o're his light,	8	Ode to King	58
Less should I dawb it o're with transitory Praise,	21	Ode Athenian	169
What's your advice? shall I give o're,	489	Dialogue	8
That she might o're the Servants hector	745	Stel Distress	7
Of Parties o're our Bonny-Clabber.	781	Mullinix Tim	260

O'RE-RATE
| You've taught the Cov'tous Wretches to o're-rate, | 24 | Ode Athenian | 255 |

O'RECAME
| It quite o'recame the vital Heat,) | 16 | Ode Athenian | 4 |

O'ROURK'S
| O'Rourk's noble Fare | 244 | Irish-Feast | 1 |
| O'Rourk's jolly Boys | 245 | Irish-Feast | 29 |

OAK
With Cudgels of Oak,	246	Irish-Feast	69
In Heathenish Times from the Trunk of an Oak:	335	Serious Poem	58
But Wood I assure you is no Heart of Oak;	336	Serious Poem	66
A Sapling with a falling Oak?	703	Cadenus Vaness	535
That thy Descent is from the British Oak:	771	Horace 1, 14	38

OAKEN-BOUGH
| As a Thorn-bush, or Oaken-bough, | 457 | Paddy's Charac | 1 |

```
OAKS   SEE MONARCH-OAKS                              PAGE    TITLE            LINE
OAR
    In vain I tug and pull the Oar,       . . . . . . .    32 Ode to Temple      193
    And then all hands, Boys, to the Oar  . . . . . .     279 Journal            18
    And then again, Boys, to the Oar.     . . . . . . .   280 Journal            44
    And sav'd his Oar, but lost his Hat.  . . . . . . .   281 Journal            72
    Held Monarchs labouring at the Oar;   . . . . . . .   476 Epist on Epist     44
OARS
    At whose Oars, like Slaves, they all pull:  . . . .   635 Epistle Lady      160
    Lost are thy Oars that us'd thy Course to guide,  . .  770 Horace 1, 14      13
OAT-MEAL
    One tells the Rise of Cheese, and Oat-meal,  . . . .  781 Mullinix Tim      269
OATEN
    And gave it for Pan's oaten Reed:     . . . . . . .   156 Fable of Midas     28
OATES
    Porter, and Prendergast, and Oates.   . . . . . . .   298 Horrid Plot        10
OATH
    My Sister has lately depos'd upon Oath,  . . . . . .  264 Apollo             37
    Minerva ne'er an Oath did Swear       . . . . . . .   372 Letter D. S-y      12
    And, with an Oath, assure him; all is well.  . . . .  534 To Mr. Gay         96
    Who shall depose it upon Oath.)       . . . . . . .   647 On Poetry         230
    Who fairly could on Oath depose,      . . . . . . .   688 Cadenus Vaness     69
    Betray, make Oath, impeach, inform,   . . . . . . .   778 Mullinix Tim      168
OATHS
    Ten thousand Oaths upon Record,       . . . . . . .   725 To Stella          55
    Nor sputter out your Oaths so fast,   . . . . . . .   780 Mullinix Tim      237
OATMEAL
    She thought that all the world was Oatmeal:  . . . .  745 Stel Distress       6
OATS
    How Markets went for Hey and Oats.    . . . . . . .    63 Discovery          36
    The one was Oats, the other Hay,      . . . . . . .    63 Discovery          38
    No Straw, Oats, or Hay;               . . . . . . .  1036 Plague Country      6
OBDURATE
    But if, still obdurate, your anger remains,  . . . .  819 Archbi Cashel      11
OBEDIENT
    And was--His most obedient Daughter.  . . . . . . .   224 Prog of Love       72
    Come, assist me, Muse obedient,       . . . . . . .   832 Legion Club        75
    . . . Your most dutiful and obedient George         1024 Nim-Dan-Dean 2   D  18
        Nim-Dan-Dean.
OBEY
    Obey my Call, and only mine.          . . . . . . .   120 Apollo Outwit      32
    May He whom Nature's Laws obey,       . . . . . . .   258 Bubble            209
    Our Inspirations to obey,             . . . . . . .   270 Apollo's Edict   D  8
    That will make all my Subjects with pride to obey.  . 389 Order of Bath       4
    Thus my Subjects with pleasure will obey my Commands. 389 Order of Bath       9
    Who must Obey, or lose his Place.     . . . . . . .   485 Libel on D- D-    160
    Servants love you, and obey:          . . . . . . .   633 Epistle Lady      106
    Thus all are destin'd to obey         . . . . . . .   659 On Poetry        D 410
    Does distantly my Pow'r obey.         . . . . . . .   934 Riddle 21        D  12
OBEY'D
    You must be obey'd--your Servant, Sir Arthur;  . . .  869 Grand Question     80
OBEYS
    The Doctor now obeys the Summons,     . . . . . . .   173 Horace 1, 7        73
    "While he obeys Almighty Will,        . . . . . . .   485 Libel on D- D-    167
    No Slave his Lord's Commands obeys,   . . . . . . .   920 Riddle 6           3
OBJECT
    Who may object against the Term,      . . . . . . .    83 Salamander         25
    He might be thought an Object fit for Alms.  . . . .  234 Elegy on Demar     12
    High Treason by Statute! But here you object,  . . .  266 Apollo             89
    But some will object, that the Devil oft spoke  . .   335 Serious Poem       57
    No Object Strephon's Eye escapes,     . . . . . . .   527 Lady's Dres Rm     47
    Not, as his Enemies object,           . . . . . . .   603 Beasts Confess     65
    Some Criticks may object perhaps,     . . . . . . .   618 Scandal Poem 1     21
    Some Critick may object, perhaps,     . . . . . . .   624 Scandal Poem 2     15
    Yet Criticks may object, why not?     . . . . . . .   813 Bro Protestant     41
    But here my Lady will object;         . . . . . . .   899 Dean's Reasons     19
    I will ne'er object a word.           . . . . . . .   908 Daphne             62
OBJECTION
    And, is not this Objection odd        . . . . . . .   820 Dr. Rundle         29
OBJECTIONS
    Drive all Objections from your Mind,  . . . . . . .   724 To Stella          43
OBJECTS
    And far exalted objects lessen by their height:  . .   39 Ode Sancroft      148
    Strange to conceive, how the same objects strike  . .  51 Temple Ill          1
    Turns up old objects to the soul her sun;  . . . . .   51 Temple Ill         10
    Fresh Objects fairer to his View;     . . . . . . .   412 Desire Possess     30
    Who proper Objects must provide       . . . . . . .   480 Libel on D- D-     25
    Thro' this she made all Objects pass,  . . . . . . .  709 Cadenus Vaness    718
    Eternal Objects of her Hate.          . . . . . . .   725 To Stella          64
OBLATIONS
    All make Oblations at this Shrine.    . . . . . . .   922 Riddle 7           30
OBLIG'D
    Since knaves are ne'er oblig'd for what they steal.  .  45 To Congreve       66
    By Vow Oblig'd, By Passion led,       . . . . . . .   120 Apollo Outwit      33
OBLIGATION
    Were forc'd to own to him their Obligation.  . . . .  234 Elegy on Demar     18
OBLIGE
    You but oblige 'em so much more:      . . . . . . .   505 Doctor Delaney    156
    To oblige a good Friend, she will trace ev'ry Market,  . 580 Psyche          11
    Than merely to oblige your Friends;   . . . . . . .   765 Stel B-day '26     70
    To oblige your Crony <Swift>,         . . . . . . .   862 To Janus            3
```

	PAGE	TITLE	LINE
OBLIGING			
But, no obliging, tender Friend	204	In Sickness	19
For an obliging Ridicule:	216	To Mr. Delany	36
To study the obliging Jest,	219	To Mr. Delany	103
Tho' by your obliging Sway	633	Epistle Lady	105
OBLIGINGLY			
And so obligingly am caught:	727	To Stella	114
OBLIVION			
And there in sweet Oblivion drown	202	Horace 2, 6	111
OBLOQUY			
Railing a Rule of Wit, and Obloquy a Trade,	18	Ode Athenian	84
OBSCENE			
But, in their Cells and Vaults obscene	895	Panegyr Dean	283
The Food of Worms, and Beasts obscene,	923	Riddle 7	59
OBSCURE			
But can no more obscure my Congreve's light	45	To Congreve	80
Out from some Hole obscure he flies	84	Salamander	33
To let your Virtues lye obscure,	242	Horace 4, 9	4
That, a Rogue so Obscure should make such a Clutter,	334	Serious Poem	6
Should some obscure inferior fellow	464	Birthday Song	141
Lye down obscure like other Folks	501	Doctor Delaney	45
To live obscure, and have no fame to lose?	506	To a Friend	8
Once so renown'd to Live obscure?	778	Mullinix Tim	180
OBSCURELY			
But, why obscurely here alone?	203	In Sickness	3
But, as of old, obscurely lain;	877	To Dean Swift	30
OBSCURES			
Dims and obscures our sight:	402	Window Inns 6	D 2
OBSEQUIOUS			
But most obsequious to the Squire.	95	Bauc & Phil 1	180
OBSERV'D			
To be observ'd by vulgar eye,	39	Ode Sancroft	150
Observ'd, they grew a num'rous Race.	106	V's House	18
Observ'd the Roof behind the Grass;	127	Little House	24
Observ'd a Parson near Whitehall,	170	Horace 1, 7	5
"A certain Doctor is observ'd of late,	195	Author Himself	43
The Candidates observ'd his dirty Paws,	536	To Mr. Gay	157
It is well observ'd by Horace,	636	Epistle Lady	198
And 'twas observ'd, there were but few	689	Cadenus Vaness	101
But 'tis observ'd, that Men in Gowns	1033	Ans to Crown	11
OBSERVATION			
(By frequent observation taught)	176	To Lord Harley	6
By long Observation I have understood,	350	Wood Insect	1
And first: To make my Observation right,	532	To Mr. Gay	31
OBSERVE			
Observe the dying Father speak:	189	Faggot	1
Let him, like you, observe with Care	218	To Mr. Delany	99
You shall observe as you are filling	251	Bubble	11
And observe while you live, that no Man is shy	264	Apollo	57
And next Observe how this Alliance fits,	276	Epilogue	39
Observe where bloody Townshend stands	312	To Ford	43
"T' observe her Management within.	321	First of April	28
This Brass was a Dragon (observe what I tell ye)	337	Serious Poem	87
Observe this Pattern; there's a Stuff,	447	Modern Lady	84
Observe what Loads of stupid Rimes	503	Doctor Delaney	101
Now pray observe the Doctor's Choice,	513	Answer Fable	19
And, carefully observe the Ground,	592	Strephon Chloe	295
Observe our visage in a morning;	619	Scandal Poem 1	47
Observe the case: I state it thus:	622	Scandal Poem 1	157
Observe our Figure in a Morning;	625	Scandal Poem 2	43
So, Nat'ralists observe, a Flea	651	On Poetry	337
Observe with what majestick Port	656	On Poetry	443
Observe them but for fashion sake.	732	Verses Vanessa	6
Observe, the Audience is in Pain,	776	Mullinix Tim	93
But now observe my Counsel (viz)	779	Mullinix Tim	211
There observe the Tribe of <Bingham>,	836	Legion Club	163
Now, Madam, observe, how he marches in State:	870	Grand Question	89
"Observe how a Parson comes into a Room,	872	Grand Question	155
Observe me with revengeful Eye:	925	Riddle 8	18
I observe your Wicket	938	Riddle Answerd	3
OBSERVED			
With true Delight observed them all	87	Hist V's House	17
OBSERVERS			
Careful Observers may fortel the Hour	136	City Shower	1
OBSERVES			
Some Waq observes me thus perplext,	200	Horace 2, 6	31
That from each Ear, as he observes,	367	Answer Delaney	33
For, as Helsham observes, there's nothing can chime,	980	Tho: Sheridan	3
OBSERVING			
Pallas observing Stella's Wit	723	To Stella	1
Pluto observing, since the Peace,	903	Death Daphne	7
OBSTINACY			
With Obstinacy fixes there;	641	On Poetry	22
OBSTRUCTIONS			
Or sick of Obstructions, and Pains in her Chest.	351	Wood Insect	16
OBSTRUCTS			
If a small Breeze obstructs the Course,	688	Cadenus Vaness	53
OBTAIN			
Then down I went upon my Knees, his Blessing to obtain,	342	Upon His Grace	29
Obtain such Privilege as you,	492	Panegyr Swift	3

OBTAIN'D

	PAGE	TITLE	LINE
With Rules to search it, yet obtain'd by none.	26	Ode to Temple	16
And, mistakes to prevent, I have obtain'd a Copy.	143	New Song	10
Tho' her Design was not obtain'd,	713	Cadenus Vaness	834

OBTRUDE

	PAGE	TITLE	LINE
For so Conjectors would obtrude,	324	Pethox	25

OBTUSE

	PAGE	TITLE	LINE
Bastings heavy, dry, obtuse,	636	Epistle Lady	203

OBVIATE

	PAGE	TITLE	LINE
Which we cou'd neither obviate, nor shun.	12	Ode to William	D 20

OCCASION

	PAGE	TITLE	LINE
We had Occasion for a Plot;	300	Horrid Plot	68
"We all shou'd march on this Occasion,	321	First of April	19
"There's no occasion here for us,	322	First of April	51
Nor slip this Occasion to follow your Trade.	400	Tom Clinch	20
On such an Occasion the Law gives Relief.	943	Probatur Alit	46

OCCASIONS

	PAGE	TITLE	LINE
Alas, the occasions are so few:	38	Ode Sancroft	112
On all Occasions, cut and dry.	416	Woman's Mind	14
But, soon with like Occasions prest,	589	Strephon Chloe	187

OCCUPATION

	PAGE	TITLE	LINE
A fine occupation	857	Lady's Lament	181

OCEAN

	PAGE	TITLE	LINE
But Gold upon this Ocean spred	255	Bubble	135
For Venus rising from the Ocean	293	Prog Marriage	107
And since her Birth the Ocean gave her,	303	Storm	23
And with his Dame the ocean crosst,	878	Robbin & Harry	19

OCEAN'S

	PAGE	TITLE	LINE
On the smooth Ocean's azure Bed	251	Bubble	27
Our Ocean's coverd o'er with Gold,	254	Bubble	103

OCH

	PAGE	TITLE	LINE
Sing, och, och, hoh, hoh.	840	Ballad	D REF
Sing, och, och, hoh, hoh.	840	Ballad	D REF
Sing, och, och, hoh, hoh.	841	Ballad	D REF
Sing, och, och, hoh, hoh.	841	Ballad	D REF
Och ma ceade millia mollighart, on the feeders of swine!	841	Ballad	D 19

OCTOBER

	PAGE	TITLE	LINE
(October next, it will be four)	201	Horace 2, 6	64
. . . four Years since October,	985	Mary to Sher	13

ODD

	PAGE	TITLE	LINE
They tell us something strange and odd,	132	Magician's Rod	21
Humor is odd, grotesque, and wild,	216	To Mr. Delany	25
So odd a Choice, how could she make,	291	Prog Marriage	43
"Thalia said, 'tis somewhat odd,	321	First of April	18
Some say he's a Birch, a Thought very odd,	335	Serious Poem	33
And, Fourthly; 'tis to play an odd Trick,	348	Whitshed Motto	17
Your Heroine hardly fifty odd is.	465	Birthday Song	162
Nor entertain a thought so odd,	468	Birthday Song	263
Has, with noise and odd gestures, been prating some years,	815	Yahoo's	18
And, is not this Objection odd	820	Dr. Rundle	29
Some fancy this Promotion odd,	821	Dr. Rundle	53
"So, I took to the Road, and what's very odd,	873	Grand Question	169
An odd Triumvirate of Friends;	883	Rev Market-Hill	2
Still her odd perverseness shows	906	Daphne	15
And after all you'll think it odd,	930	Riddle 15	D 21

ODDS

	PAGE	TITLE	LINE
Those pow'rs the criticks, who may boast the odds	46	To Congreve	103
And, Statesmen by ten thousand odds	486	Libel on D- D-	197
Their Faction is five hundred Odds,	501	Doctor Delaney	47
Unless the Odds be on our Side.	554	Death of Swift	38
Or they must always be at Odds.	695	Cadenus Vaness	263
But his has the Odds, who believes and who trembles.	803	Irish Bishops	8

ODE

	PAGE	TITLE	LINE
A Lyrick Ode would Slate; a Catch	79	Vanbrug House	11
A Lyrick Ode would Slate; a Catch	106	V's House	11
"This Ode you never yet have seen,	563	Death of Swift	271

ODIOUS

	PAGE	TITLE	LINE
But with the odious smell and sight annoy'd,	50	To Congreve	225
His odious Goun would soil her Cloaths,	292	Prog Marriage	80
"This odious Chair how came I stuck in't,	452	Modern Lady	240
Was, When will They turn out this odious Rogue?	536	To Mr. Gay	146
But such Comparisons are odious.	622	Scandal Poem 1	180
But such Comparisons are odious.	628	Scandal Poem 2	162
Than to shew their Vices odious:	637	Epistle Lady	226
In publick with that odious Knight.	699	Cadenus Vaness	395
To languish in this odious Town,	748	Stel Distress	71
To languish in this odious Town,	752	Stel Wood-Park	87
Poor Satan will think the Comparison odious;	803	Irish Bishops	11
By this odious Crew beset,	832	Legion Club	93
On this odious Group of Fools;	839	Legion Club	224

ODIUM

	PAGE	TITLE	LINE
This into gen'ral Odium drew him,	549	Life of Swift	132

ODLY

	PAGE	TITLE	LINE
We odly Plato's Paradox make good,	27	Ode to Temple	29

ODOURS

	PAGE	TITLE	LINE
Filth of all Hues and Odours seem to tell	139	City Shower	55
And, if unsav'ry Odours fly,	529	Lady's Dres Rm	123
Who, as the Odours reach his Throne,	647	On Poetry	225

ODS

	PAGE	TITLE	LINE
Ods buds, why don't you break her Limbs:	220	A Quiet Life	28

OF   SEE UNHEARD-OF,OUT-OF-FASHION'D,OUT-OF-FASHION   PAGE   TITLE   LINE
    2150   OMITTED WORD

OFF
    Depos'd from off his Seat   26 Ode to Temple   3
    Off fly the Vizards and discover all,   29 Ode to Temple   99
    In striving to wash off th' imaginary paint: 42 Ode Sancroft   250
    A Flitch of Bacon off the Hook,   91 Bauc & Phil 1   58
    Cutt off large Slices to be fry'd;   91 Bauc & Phil 1   60
    A Flitch of Bacon off the Hook;   112 Bauc & Phil 2   26
    The Golden Scurf peels off his Limbs: 157 Fable of Midas   36
    The Golden Spoils flew off apace,   158 Fable of Midas   75
    And strutting Hal-- is off the Hooks;   168 Peace Dunkirk   14
    Each Night a Bit drops off her Face   228 Prog of Beauty   87
    If the Printer will peach him, he'll scarce come off 238 Excellent Song   32
        clean.
    And then get off with Money stor'd,   253 Bubble   62
    Steals off to dose away his Beef,   279 Journal   40
    'Tis true, say they, cut off the Head,   366 Answer Delaney   5
    Your Rev'rence, but to cut one Leg off,   366 Answer Delaney 16
    Cut off your Hand, and you may do   366 Answer Delaney 23
    I think I'm very fairly off.   377 Apology Lady C 56
    And thus I go off without Pray'r-Book or Psalm. 400 Tom Clinch   22
    He'll turn it off with; Name your Toast.   480 Libel on D- D- 18
    Takes off her artificial Hair: 581 Young Nymph   10
    Pulls off with Care, and first displays 'em, 581 Young Nymph   15
    Up goes her Hand, and off she slips   582 Young Nymph   27
    Rub off the Dawbs of White and Red;   582 Young Nymph   34
    Flew off, nor evermore appear'd.   590 Strephon Chloe 196
    Set off with num'rous Breaks--and Dashes--   643 On Poetry   94
    Cadenus warded off the Blows: 701 Cadenus Vaness 479
    Poor Stella must pack off to Town.   744 Stel Distress   2
    Poor Stella must pack off to Town.   750 Stel Wood-Park 26
    While <Sheridan> is off the hooks,   756 Stel B-day '24 11
    To cut it off these forty years.   760 Bec's B-Day   6
    By <God> I'll bring you off as clean.   797 Traulus 1   60
    If your Stockings were off, you cou'd show cloven Feet. 805 Irish Bishops 52
    When his speech came abroad, he paid him off clean, 816 Yahoo's   38
    "Go, bring me my Smock, and leave off your Prate, 870 Grand Question 83
    For, a Captain of Horse never takes off his Hat; 870 Grand Question 106
    To keep off their Eyes, as they wait at the Table; 871 Grand Question 136
    Leave off swearing   953 Herrings   2
    I must now, at one Sitting, pay off my old Score: 967 Letter Sherid   9
    Comes off by out-laughing the Company round. 968 Letter Sherid 20
    To leave off this passion which does not become you: 976 Dean to Sherid 10
    If you had not took physick, I'd pay off your bacon, 980 Tho: Sheridan   5
OFF'RING
    This off'ring long design'd to Congreve's fame;   44 To Congreve   24
    As Nature prompts, his Off'ring pays?   895 Panegyr Dean 288
OFF'RINGS
    Talkt of his Off'rings, Tyths, and Dues,   95 Bauc & Phil 1 173
    Receives all Off'rings at her Shrine.   893 Panegyr Dean 206
    Were built to thee, with Off'rings crown'd: 894 Panegyr Dean 238
    Are sent up Off'rings more sincere   896 Panegyr Dean 296
    Whose Off'rings plac't in golden Ranks,   896 Panegyr Dean 301
    To wash thy injur'd Off'rings out.   896 Panegyr Dean 318
    Profusely pours her Off'rings here.   922 Riddle 7   38
    In at this Gulph all Off'rings pass,   922 Riddle 7   43
OFFALS
    Their Offals, or their better Meat,   479 Epist on Epist 122
    The Offals of a Church distress't,   484 Libel on D- D- 131
    Or dirty Offals cook'd with Herbage.   498 Panegyr Swift 153
OFFENCE
    Without offence to Human Shape: 83 Salamander   6
    If nam'd with Scorn, gives just Offence.   217 To Mr. Delany 70
    To Rime all day without Offence;   219 To Mr. Delany 108
    To vindicate his late Offence: 379 Apology Lady C 130
    (Take Notice, to avoid Offence   486 Libel on D- D- 183
    At Poets flights to take offence: 622 Scandal Poem 1 154
    At Poet's Flights to take Offence.   628 Scandal Poem 2 158
    No Raillery gives just Offence   747 Stel Distress 61
    Yet Raillery gives no Offence,   752 Stel Wood-Park 77
    His Brethren find to take Offence;   820 Dr. Rundle   12
    To take Offence at what you speak.   890 Panegyr Dean 120
    And yet my speaking gives Offence: 917 Riddle 4   6
    A Bacon-slice gives God Offence?   949 Epigr Fasting   2
OFFEND
    The Scottish Nation, whom he durst offend,   196 Author Himself 69
    My satire may offend, 'tis true: 435 Answer Paulus 101
    Offend our Patriot, Great Sir <Robert>,   548 Life of Swift 108
    Offend me with the least Rebuke.   888 Panegyr Dean   60
OFFENDED
    Strike your offended Sense with double Stink. 137 City Shower   6
    "He ne'er offended with a Jest;   572 Death of Swift 472
    He hears the Clergy are offended;   605 Beasts Confess 126
    Could have more offended her Nose;   834 Legion Club   126
OFFENDER
    Proving the Earl a grand Offender,   774 Mullinix Tim   21
OFFENDING
    "Offending Race of Human Kind,   579 Day Judgement 11
    Offending Daughters oft wou'd hear   694 Cadenus Vaness 240
OFFENDS
    Your Altitude offends the Eyes,   414 Censure   11

```
                                                      PAGE   TITLE           LINE
OFFENSIVE
   In haste she does th' offensive herd avoid. . . . . .    50 To Congreve      226
   Is offensive to every true Protestant ear   . . . . .   522 St. Cecilia's      6
   Offensive to a Loyal Ear---:   . . . . . . . . .        550 Life of Swift    192
   Offensive to all pious ears. . . . . . . . . .          622 Scandal Poem 1   168
   And since his Talk offensive grew,   . . . . . . .      705 Cadenus Vaness   592
   Towzer's the less offensive Brute.   . . . . . .        797 Traulus 1         44
   To give the least offensive Word;   . . . . . . .       889 Panegyr Dean      70
   No Work is grievous or offensive.   . . . . . . .       891 Panegyr Dean     158
   Offensive to thy nicer Nose.   . . . . . . . .          895 Panegyr Dean     286
   Unwholsome Damps, offensive Dews:   . . . . . . .       923 Riddle 7          56
OFFER
   I shall not offer to direct   . . . . . . . . .         422 Ireld             38
   Yet I disdain to offer those,   . . . . . . . .         433 Answer Paulus     49
   "When thou thy humble Lays do'st offer   . . . . .      476 Epist on Epist    32
   Would offer all the Sands of Tagus;   . . . . . .       821 Dr. Rundle        42
   Offer to him a pure Libation;   . . . . . . . .         893 Panegyr Dean     220
   . . .to make the Offer; and they cannot deny it. . . .  1014 Swift to Sheri     8
OFFER'D
   So never offer'd once to stir,   . . . . . . . .        172 Horace 1, 7       53
   And offer'd many a lame Excuse;   . . . . . . . .       172 Horace 1, 7       65
   Then offer'd at the throne of justice,   . . . . .      433 Answer Paulus     29
   "Unless it offer'd to be witty,   . . . . . . . .       572 Death of Swift   470
   And these, she offer'd to dispute,   . . . . . . .      697 Cadenus Vaness   344
   An offer'd Fee from Radcliff scorns;   . . . . . .      811 Bro Protestant    16
   Or, offer'd in some flow'ry Vale,   . . . . . . .       894 Panegyr Dean     247
OFFERS
   This, humbly offers me his Case--   . . . . . . .       200 Horace 2, 6       47
   Making by second hand their Offers,   . . . . . .       253 Bubble            70
   Your Offers of Bribery cease;   . . . . . . . .         396 Dog and Thief     14
   For, had We made him timely Offers,   . . . . . .       549 Life of Swift    138
   Each strait his service offers, pays his court,  . .    672 Epig Carthy 24   D  7
   He gladly offers in return:   . . . . . . . .           711 Cadenus Vaness   785
   My Offers of Peace you ill understood.   . . . . .      968 Letter Sherid     23
OFFICE
   Now to a nobler Office put,   . . . . . . . . .          66 Problem           24
   It does its Office ev'ry Hour,   . . . . . . . .        391 Young's Satire    20
   And one poor Office, half his Days;   . . . . . .       481 Libel on D- D-    34
   An Office for your Talents fit,   . . . . . . .         483 Libel on D- D-   105
   But, not a Soul his Office durst accept:   . . . .      536 To Mr. Gay       153
OFFICERS
   You Officers, Captain, are so complaisant.   . . . .    871 Grand Question   126
   And her chief Officers of State,   . . . . . . .       1035 To Quilca         11
OFFICES
   In your last Offices be quick:   . . . . . . . .        204 In Sickness       24
OFFICIOUS
   When my Muse officious ventures   . . . . . . .         635 Epistle Lady     155
   Those thankless and officious cares   . . . . . .       901 Dean's Reasons    95
OFFSPRING
   And sudden spreads a numerous Offspring round;  . . .   792 St. Pat's Well    62
   Worthy Offspring of a Shoeboy,   . . . . . . .          831 Legion Club       68
   All beauteous Offspring of one Womb,   . . . . .        923 Riddle 7          68
   The offspring of a beggar's brat.   . . . . . . .       950 Upstart          D  6
OFT
   (We Poets oft our Bays allow,   . . . . . . . .           6 Ode to King        9
   More oft in Fools and Mad-mens hands than Sages  . .     23 Ode Athenian     220
   Thus the deluding Muse oft blinds me to her Ways, . .    23 Ode Athenian     234
   And tho' he oft renew'd the Fight,   . . . . . .         30 Ode to Temple    129
   Oft she looks back in vain.   . . . . . . . .            31 Ode to Temple    154
   Oft 'gainst her Fountain does complain,   . . . .        31 Ode to Temple    155
   And since too oft debauch'd by Praise,   . . . . .       33 Ode to Temple    204
   And oft in contradiction's vortex caught,   . . . .      36 Ode Sancroft      63
   Oft hovers where alive it haunted most;   . . . .        51 Temple Ill         8
   To thee, what oft I vainly strive to hide,   . . . .     55 Temple Ill       133
   The Nymph who oft had read in Books,   . . . . .        120 Apollo Outwit     13
   Which oft he us'd to fish withal:   . . . . . .         133 Magician's Rod    44
   "How oft have I defended?   . . . . . . . . .           154 Widow and Cat    D 27
   How oft she broke her marriage Vows   . . . . . .       225 Prog of Love      89
   As Other Painters oft adore   . . . . . . . .           227 Prog of Beauty    51
   And before Corum Nobus so oft has been call'd,  . . .   238 Excellent Song    27
   Thus oft by Mariners are shown,   . . . . . . .         257 Bubble           169
   She can swear to the Person, whom oft she has seen, . . 264 Apollo            53
   I might have told how oft Dean <Percival>   . . . .     281 Journal           79
   Since others oft have found one there;   . . . . .      294 Prog Marriage    138
   But some will object, that the Devil oft spoke  . . .   335 Serious Poem      57
   For she her self oft falls in Pieces.   . . . . .       362 Grace's Answer    28
   Must deviate oft from common sense,   . . . . . .       435 Answer Paulus    112
   How oft they squabble, snarl and Cheat:   . . . .       453 Modern Lady      281
   Besides you Songsters oft have shewn,   . . . . .       465 Birthday Song    163
   Then shew, how Statesmen oft are stung   . . . . .      496 Panegyr Swift    114
   Till, scaping oft without a Wound,   . . . . . .        500 Doctor Delaney     7
   "We oft, are Laughing in our Sleeve.   . . . . .        545 Life of Swift     10
   Yet, by Experience, oft we find,   . . . . . . .        546 Life of Swift     47
   "For her he oft expos'd his own.   . . . . . . .        566 Death of Swift   350
   "He vented oft his Wrath in vain:   . . . . . .         571 Death of Swift   444
   Which oft attends that luke-warm Stream;   . . . .      589 Strephon Chloe   180
   And, I have heard thee oft salute   . . . . . . .       594 Cassinus Peter    33
   A founder'd Horse will oft debate   . . . . . . .       640 On Poetry         15
   Or oft when Epithets you link,   . . . . . . .          645 On Poetry        167
   Judicious Rymer oft review:   . . . . . . . .           648 On Poetry        249
   The Muses oft were seen to frown;   . . . . . . .       689 Cadenus Vaness    99
```

OFT   (CONTINUED)   PAGE   TITLE   LINE
    Offending Daughters oft wou'd hear   . . . .   694 Cadenus Vaness   240
    (Those Authors he so oft had nam'd   708 Cadenus Vaness   690
    You, to whose Care so oft I owe, ...   766 Stel B-day '26   87
    A Nation thus, who oft Heav'ns Call neglects,   . . .   771 Horace 1, 14   35
    With Omens oft I strove to warn thy Swains,   . . .   792 St. Pat's Well   43
    As I strole the City, oft I   . . . .   829 Legion Club   1
    "Thy Gown and Cassock oft be torn: . . . .   850 Old Thorn   60
    By you so oft, so highly prais'd!   . . . .   887 Panegyr Dean   14
    The crude Consistence oft I tread.   . . . .   896 Panegyr Dean   310
    How oft a Week was kept a Ball   . . . .   905 Death Daphne   83
    And oft in Hand of Lady Fair;   . . . .   912 Aenigma   10
    He oft employs me in Disguise, ...   915 Riddle 1   19
    Yet, as it oft attends the Great, ...   917 Riddle 3   5
    And oft in Celia's Tresses play.   . . . .   919 Riddle 5   12
    Nor oft can the Receiver know   . . . .   919 Riddle 5   23
    Oft in the Train of Venus seen, ...   923 Riddle 7   69
    Here, oft the Curious Trav'ller finds, ...   923 Riddle 7   79
    That oft I wake thee with a Kiss?   . . . . ✎ . .   924 Riddle 8   10
    Poor Miss Dingley oft hath felt its Bills. . . . .   941 Letter   24
OFT'
    One Coach oft' carried them when they were quick,   . .   430 Dicky Dolly   14
    Oft' swallow'd down a stronger Potion, ...   495 Panegyr Swift   61
    How oft' am I for Rime to seek?   . . . .   502 Doctor Delaney   65
    And oft' the Dancing-Master's Art   . . . . . .   710 Cadenus Vaness   740
    "My Kindred oft' thine Hide shall gall;   . . . . .   850 Old Thorn   59
    Oft' revives my drooping head: . . . . . .   937 Riddle 24   D 46
OFT'NER
    The oft'ner you fall, the oft'ner you write; . . . .   968 Letter Sherid   30
    The oft'ner you fall, the oft'ner you write; . . . .   968 Letter Sherid   30
OFTEN
    We often search contentedly the whole World round,   . .   20 Ode Athenian   142
    Current like copper, and as often paid: . . . . . .   50 To Congreve   220
    As Pies and Daws are often stil'd   . . . . . .   82 Salamander   3
    The Saints would often leave their Cells   . . . . . .   90 Bauc & Phil 1   2
    Lookt high and low, walkt often round, ...   109 V's House   97
    The Saints would often leave their Cells.   . . . . . .   111 Bauc & Phil 2   2
    And often on each other gaz'd;   . . . .   112 Bauc & Phil 2   36
    Who often father'd what he writ;   . . . .   171 Horace 1, 7   40
    I Often wish'd, that I had clear   . . . .   198 Horace 2, 6   1
    Such Tattle often entertains   . . . .   201 Horace 2, 6   75
    Some Cully often wins a Bett   . . . .   257 Bubble   162
    For, first, I have often by Chymists been told, . . .   263 Apollo   3
    And to your knowledge there is often less in, ...   276 Epilogue   45
    And here the Father often gains   . . . . . .   293 Prog Marriage   121
    I own it hath often provok'd me to Mutter, ...   334 Serious Poem   5
    I often have seen two Plays very Good, ...   337 Serious Poem   91
    They often climb, and oftner creep.   . . . . . .   412 Desire Possess   20
    Who often long'd to eat his Son: . . . .   460 Birthday Song   12
    That I am often found exceeding   . . . .   489 Dialogue   3
    For must you not have often ly'd, ...   496 Panegyr Swift   90
    These they have often try'd before;   . . . . . .   505 Doctor Delaney   155
    By often shifting into distant Grounds;   . . . . . .   538 Mr. Pulteney   18
    "And, if he often miss'd his Aim, ...   550 Life of Swift   198
    "And often told you so at first:"   . . . .   557 Death of Swift   130
    "So often seen caressing Chartres"   . . . .   565 Death of Swift   324
    "Ingratitude he often found, ...   567 Death of Swift   359
    Be often forc'd to rise at Night, ...   587 Strephon Chloe   122
    Strephon, who had been often told, ...   588 Strephon Chloe   147
    That, often I have been to blame: . . . .   602 Beasts Confess   14
    Have often practis'd to their Shame.   . . . . . .   605 Beasts Confess   140
    Yet, though her spouse hath often curst her, ...   618 Scandal Poem 1   17
    Will often <piss> upon a nettle;   . . . .   621 Scandal Poem 1   144
    Will often <piss> upon a Nettle;   . . . .   628 Scandal Poem 2   148
    I have often told before.   . . . .   630 Epistle Lady   10
    A forward Critick often dupes us   . . . . . .   648 On Poetry   255
    Or often blunted and recoil'd, ...   701 Cadenus Vaness   482
    Thus Tutors often treat their Betters.   . . . . . .   705 Cadenus Vaness   591
    And yet a Fault we often find   . . . . . .   731 Stella, Poems   103
    And often see a Puppet-show.   . . . . . .   776 Mullinix Tim   92
    "To thee I often call'd in vain, ...   850 Old Thorn   66
    When I saw him so often with Darby and Wood. . . . .   868 Grand Question   48
    To you we often trust the Key: . . . . . .   889 Panegyr Dean   90
    And have been often chid in vain: . . . . . .   901 Dean's Reasons   98
    And often have I seen thee grace   . . . . . .   919 Riddle 5   7
    Although I'm often out of Case, ...   920 Riddle 6   23
    And often takes me by the Hand.   . . . . . .   921 Riddle 6   30
    Often aiding to impart   . . . . . .   936 Riddle 24   D 25
    Often fair, and soft, and tender, ...   937 Riddle 24   D 31
    When young is often due to the Vicar.   . . . . . .   940 Letter   2
    The Cook-maid often hath by the End.   . . . . . .   941 Letter   38
    Among the Coals does often rattle.   . . . .   942 Probatur Alit   2
    But often spunge upon a Friend.   . . . .   954 Authors Living   8
    I've often heard it from the wise, ...   982 Sher, A Goose   3
    Is not a Penny often found   . . . .   1004 Dan J's Reply   28
    Who often has made me, by looking ascue, sick. . . . .   1030 Dr. Sheridan   5
OFTNER
    They often climb, and oftner creep.   . . . .   412 Desire Possess   20
OGLING
    What ogling, sighing, toasting, vowing!   . . . . . .   585 Strephon Chloe   34

		PAGE	TITLE	LINE
Oh but, said I, what if after all my Chaplain won't come to?		73	Mrs Harris Pet	68
As thus, "Vouchsafe, Oh gracious Maker!		199	Horace 2, 6	D
Oh, could I see my Country Seat.		202	Horace 2, 6	108
Oh London Tavern! Thou hast lost a Friend,		234	Elegy on Demar	25
Oh! would these Patriots be so kind		255	Bubble	109
Oh, may some Western Tempest sweep		258	Bubble	205
Oh! then but to see how Beggars will Vapour,		287	Bank Down	21
Oh, may I see her soon dispensing		295	Prog Marriage	159
Oh, were but You and I so wise		314	To Ford	85
But oh! so faintly we pursue,		401	Window Inns 5	D 11
Oh! let him not debase your Thoughts,		465	Birthday Song	147
Oh! cou'd'st thou, by some Magick Spell,		478	Epist on Epist	91
Oh, wond'rous Box! my Lyre unstrung		494	Panegyr Swift	45
Oh, could'st thou teach us how to zest		495	Panegyr Swift	64
But oh! it turn'd poor Strephon's Bowels,		527	Lady's Dres Rm	43
Oh! Celia, Celia, Celia shits!		529	Lady's Dres Rm	118
Oh, were the Wretch but living still,		560	Death of Swift	193
"And, oh! how short are human Schemes!		567	Death of Swift	371
Oh Peter, wou'd it were no more!		595	Cassinus Peter	46
Oh Peter! Beauty's but a Varnish,		595	Cassinus Peter	51
But, oh! how ill hast thou divin'd		595	Cassinus Peter	67
Oh! Caelia, Caelia Caelia <shits>.		597	Cassinus Peter	118
Oh! if his Majesty would please		606	Beasts Confess	169
But, oh, how unsecure thy Throne!		653	On Poetry	377
Oh! wer't thou not a Duke, my good Duke Humphry,		678	Dean and Duke	11
Oh! would His Majesty but add a String.		678	Dean and Duke	16
Oh, would it please the Gods to split		722	Stel B-Day '18	9
Oh, ne'er may Fortune shew her Spight,		758	Stel B-day '24	53
But, Oh, how we laugh,		857	Lady's Lament	187
Oh! if I could, how I would maul		861	Lady Acheson	37
Oh! that I could but once be rid		861	Lady Acheson	43
Oh! could we tame yon watchful Dragon,		948	Jason Hassard	5
Oh, there you think you have me safe! but hold Sir,		1004	Dan J's Reply	27
Oh that Jove would give me such a talent as thine		1017	Swift Ans Sher	7
Oh! but I forgot, perhaps, by this time, you may have one		1023	Nim-Dan-Dean 2	D 7
Oh! I forgot too, I believe there may be one more,		1023	Nim-Dan-Dean 2	D 9
OIL SEE OYL				
We'll oil him with kennel, and powd'r him with grains,		817	Yahoo's	58
OIL'D				
While Streams run down her oil'd Umbrella's Sides.		138	City Shower	38
OILS				
That <Swift> oils many a Spring which Harley moves.		194	Author Himself	40
OILY SEE OYLY				
Brac'd like a Drum her oily Skin;		895	Panegyr Dean	258
His tongue with oily accents tipt,		951	Upstart	D 28
OINTMENTS				
And Ointments good for scabby Chops.		526	Lady's Dres Rm	36
Her Ointments, Daubs, and Paints and Creams,		530	Lady's Dres Rm	138
OLD				
As in old Fabulous Hell,		9	Ode to King	92
Fam'd Delos did of old,		17	Ode Athenian	47
All of old Cut with a new Dye,		23	Ode Athenian	227
We scrawl all o'er with old and empty Rules,		27	Ode to Temple	33
Let not old Rome boast Fabius's Fate,		28	Ode to Temple	70
Errors like this did old Astronomers misguide,		36	Ode Sancroft	65
This wilderness the world, like that poetic wood of old,		41	Ode Sancroft	225
Sent to assist an old unvanquish'd pride		44	To Congreve	43
Turns up old objects to the soul her sun;		51	Temple Ill	10
Disguis'd in two old threadbare Coats		63	Discovery	34
Once on a time, as old Stories reherse,		76	Lady B- B-	1
In times of old, when Time was young,		79	Vanbrug House	1
And 'tis conceiv'd, their old Pretence		79	Vanbrug House	27
Where dwelt a poor old honest Yeman		91	Bauc & Phil 1	51
Put the old People in a Fright;		92	Bauc & Phil 1	80
In it's old shape a Font became		93	Bauc & Phil 1	112
But being old continued just		94	Bauc & Phil 1	169
Nor look Asquint on an old Friend.		101	Elegy Patrige	102
In Times of Old, when Time was Young,		106	V's House	1
And 'tis conceiv'd, their old Pretence		106	V's House	27
Lament his old Whitehall in Flames,		107	V's House	48
So, Men of old, to gain Renown, did		108	V's House	65
Why then, old Plays deserve old Bricks,		108	V's House	72
Why then, old Plays deserve old Bricks,		108	V's House	72
Where dwelt a good old honest Yeoman,		111	Bauc & Phil 2	19
The good old Couple was amaz'd,		112	Bauc & Phil 2	35
I'm Old, and fain wou'd live at Ease,		115	Bauc & Phil 2	115
But being Old, continu'd just		115	Bauc & Phil 2	123
Knew how to preach old Sermons next,		115	Bauc & Phil 2	127
Discoursing on old Stories past,		116	Bauc & Phil 2	152
Old Good-man Dobson of the Green		116	Bauc & Phil 2	165
He in the old Celestial Cant,		120	Apollo Outwit	17
The gray old Fellow Poet Joe		126	Little House	3
For since old Sid has broken this,		135	Magician's Rod	85
Old Aches throb, your hollow Tooth will rage.		137	City Shower	10
He has vamp't an old Speech, and the Court to their sorrow,		143	New Song	5
But, some will cry, Turn-Coat, and rip up old Stories,		143	New Song	21
And must have an old, or a young Coadjutor:		144	New Song	42

OLD   (CONTINUED)   PAGE   TITLE   LINE
      Then let old England make good Chear: . . . . . .   147 Windsor Proph   4
      They Assassine when young, and Poison when old. . . . .   148 Windsor Proph   20
      At six Years old, the subtle Jade   . . . .   150 Corinna   17
      The Fox and He were Friends of old, ...   153 Widow and Cat   D   6
      Old Hay is equal to old Gold;   . . . .   156 Fable of Midas   20
      Old Hay is equal to old Gold;   . . . .   156 Fable of Midas   20
      Old <Goldolphin> full of Spleen, ...   168 Peace Dunkirk   15
      Cheapning old Authors on a Stall.   . . . .   170 Horace 1, 7   6
      Old Read would hardly let him in.   . . . .   174 Horace 1, 7   120
      In that old Wig and rusty Gown!   . . . .   175 Horace 1, 7   124
      To vamp the good Old Cause again, ...   180 Horace 2, 1   4
      And all his old Friends would rebuke   . . . .   186 Scriblerus 4   D   4
      They thought it was an old Man's Maggot: . . . . .   189 Faggot   5
      Old Madam who went up to find   . . . .   223 Prog of Love   43
      They keep at Stains the old blue Boar, ...   225 Prog of Love   99
      Old as he was, no vulgar known Disease   . . . . . .   234 Elegy on Demar   29
      Our true Irish Hearts from old England to wean;   . .   237 Excellent Song   7
      Ask that of old Madam, ...   247 Irish-Feast   81
      For I think in my Conscience he deals with Old Nick;   265 Apollo   82
      Hold up the prices of their Old Brocades.   . . . . .   275 Epilogue   16
      'Tis late, the old and younger Pairs, ...   280 Journal   55
      There to supply old Charon's leaky Wherry: . . . .   285 Elegy Boat   24
      We may place Boat in his old Post again.   . . . . .   285 Elegy Boat   30
      From a bo-bo-bo-Boy he pursues his old Hank, ...   287 Bank Down   19
      As they did in old Times, make Money of Leather,   . .   287 Bank Down   27
      The Ghost of old <Damer>, who left not his Betters,   .   288 Bank Down   41
      For old Nick gave the Papers the Mark of the Bank.   .   288 Bank Down   45
      The Swain is old, the Nymph Coquette.   . . . . . .   290 Prog Marriage   30
      Of old age too, and in his bed!   . . . .   296 Satiric Elegy   2
      And could he indeed so old   . . . .   296 Satiric Elegy   9
      That old rotten Wood will Shine in the Dark.   . . .   334 Serious Poem   8
      Now hear an old Tale. There antiently stood   . . . .   334 Serious Poem   17
      To burn an old Fryer, one Forrest by Name.   . . . .   334 Serious Poem   22
      He is an old Stump cut out of a Crab, ...   335 Serious Poem   36
      He'll not be too proud an old Kettle to mend;   . . .   335 Serious Poem   44
      And then your old Argument still will return: . . .   336 Serious Poem   63
      As did Methusalem of old, and so I end my Song.   . .   343 Upon His Grace   48
      By that old Thief Prometheus? Wood   . . . .   346 Prometheus   60
      That lies in old Wood like a Hare in her Form;   . . .   351 Wood Insect   18
      As when of old, some Sorc'ress threw   . . . .   354 Simile Silver   4
      To weak, or old, or clouded Eyes.   . . . .   367 Answer Delaney   46
      I'm sure Old <Jour--> you'd not stand by it;   . . .   372 Letter D. S-y   20
      For by old Proverbs it appears, ...   408 Dial Rich Marb   7
      When my old cassock says a Welch divine   . . . . .   419 Shall Repine   5
      Are forced to read the old gazettes.   . . . .   420 Holyhead   18
      'I wish the Dinner at Old Nick."   . . . .   448 Modern Lady   99
      Say, foolish Females, Old and Blind, ...   449 Modern Lady   150
      To prove that Bishops were old Women.   . . . . . .   455 Dean Smedley   20
      Old Phoebus is but half as bright, ...   462 Birthday Song   65
      (I freely grant the Thought is old)   . . . .   464 Birthday Song   131
      Yet be the Fancy old or new, ...   464 Birthday Song   137
      For old acquaintance bring him in.   . . . .   468 Birthday Song   254
      As Falstaff acted old King Harry: . . . .   475 Epist on Epist   10
      These Stories were, of old, design'd   . . . .   478 Epist on Epist   83
      In some old Greek or Latian Bard, ...   479 Epist on Epist   120
      But I, in Politicks grown old, ...   485 Libel on D-   171
      Because it chanc'd, an old grave Don   . . . .   495 Panegyr Swift   84
      For if bestrode by you, Old <Nick>, ...   497 Panegyr Swift   138
      For, as of old, Mathematicians   . . . .   503 Doctor Delaney   95
      By old Popish Cannons, as wise Men have Penn'd'em,   .   518 Dean Hang Rape   37
      With old Scraps from Plays exploded.   . . . . . .   523 Betty Grizette   16
      To squire a Royal Girl of two Years old!   . . . . .   531 To Mr. Gay   10
      While He went robbing on; old Master dy'd.   . . . .   536 To Mr. Gay   148
      Hear an old Fable, and a dull one too;   . . . . . .   538 Mr. Pulteney   15
      "The Patrons of the good old Cause, ...   549 Life of Swift   162
      That old Vertigo in his Head, ...   556 Death of Swift   83
      "To sacrifice old England's Glory, ...   568 Death of Swift   387
      "As modern Scroggs, or old Tressilian;   . . . . . .   569 Death of Swift   420
      Authorities both old and recent   . . . .   591 Strephon Chloe   251
      Then come old Age whene'er it will, ...   593 Strephon Chloe   311
      A blind old Beggar from the Grave: . . . .   604 Beasts Confess   116
      Old Nurse-keepers would never hire   . . . .   605 Beasts Confess   137
      What honors we possesst of old.   . . . .   619 Scandal Poem 1   52
      What Honours we possess'd of old!   . . . .   625 Scandal Poem 2   48
      I am now too old to learn: . . . .   630 Epistle Lady   30
      From the Impotent and Old?   . . . .   632 Epistle Lady   72
      Then hear an old experienc'd Sinner   . . . .   642 On Poetry   75
      Your Works are like old Jacob's speckled Goats,   . .   670 Epig Carthy 18   D   3
      Which in old Times adorn'd the Fair;   . . . . . .   692 Cadenus Vaness   179
      That Gown was made for Old Queen Bess.   . . . . .   699 Cadenus Vaness   397
      Which every Girl at five Years old   . . . .   700 Cadenus Vaness   424
      Grown old in Politicks and Wit;   . . . .   702 Cadenus Vaness   503
      Whether the Nymph were Young or Old;   . . . . . .   706 Cadenus Vaness   633
      'Tis an old Maxim in the Schools, ...   710 Cadenus Vaness   758
      Heroes and Heroins of old, ...   725 To Stella   51
      Conning old Topicks like a Parrot, ...   728 Stella, Poems   26
      In Curll's Collections, new and old, ...   729 Stella, Poems   50
      To quit the true old Angel-Inn.   . . . .   734 Stel B-day '20   14
      Though you should live like old Methusalem, ...   742 Stel B-day 22   37
      You yearly sing as she grows old, ...   742 Stel B-day 22   39

OLD	(CONTINUED)	PAGE	TITLE	LINE
With an old Poker in her Hand;		743	Stel B-day 22	54
To seek an old rag in the closet.		756	Dingley Brent	18
Call the Old Housekeeper, and get her		756	Stel B-day '24	9
That you are sick, and I grown old,		763	Stel B-day '26	4
Thou, fixt of old, be now the moving Land?		770	Horace 1, 14	4
One gives Advice in Proverbs Old,		781	Mullinix Tim	271
Old carted Bawds such Garments wear,		787	Clad in Brown	19
To destroy the old Foundation,		801	Traulus 2	48
Old Latimer preaching did fairly describe		803	Irish Bishops	1
But this I am sure, the Most Rev'rend old Dragon,		803	Irish Bishops	13
At length his Old Master (I need not him name)		816	Yahoo's	36
And, as your old wont is, change sides in a trice:		818	Archbi Cashel	8
Old Acquaintance, are you there?		835	Legion Club	150
Toast Old Glorious in your Piss.		835	Legion Club	152
Keeper, yon old Dotard smoke,		836	Legion Club	159
"Ay,ay," quoth the Dean, "the cause is old gold."		843	Ay and No	4
"An old Retainer to your House,		850	Old Thorn	72
That silly old puss		855	Lady's Lament	119
New Years help to make me old;		863	To Janus	26
Burnishes an old Year's Face.		863	To Janus	28
Come hither, and take this old Gown for your Pains.		873	Grand Question	186
But, as of old, obscurely lain;		877	To Dean Swift	30
Old Robin, all his youth a sloven,		879	Robbin & Harry	45
At an old stubborn Root I chanc'd to tug,		881	Pastoral Dial	25
Old Saturn from his Empire drove;		894	Panegyr Dean	254
Old Batchelors about his Court:		903	Death Daphne	12
I please the Young, I grace the Old,		912	Aenigma	11
To their old Posts restor'd all Three,		926	Riddle 9	23
The Delight of old and young,		933	Riddle 20	D 3
Growing old, grow still the fairer.		936	Riddle 24	D 8
Emblem of a monarch old,		936	Riddle 24	D 19
A long-ear'd Beast, and a sputt'ring old Whig,		942	Probatur Alit	27
Old Jason would have less to brag on.		948	Jason Hassard	6
Be she barren, be she old,		953	Oysters	13
I must now, at one Sitting, pay off my old Score:		967	Letter Sherid	9
My Judgment of the old Comedians.		988	Letter Dr Sh-n	16
Smoother than Pegasus' old Shoe,		1021	Nim-Dan-Dean 1	D 7
Nor is old Nanny Shales, whene'er she does brew, sick.		1029	Dr. Helsham	16
Your geese are old,		1038	Sheridan Cavan	15
You never have an old friend at Cavan.		1038	Sheridan Cavan	18
By an <old> <redhair'd> <murd'ring> <Hag> pursu'd,		193	Author Himself	1
OLD-FASHION'D				
My long old-fashion'd Pocket, was presently cramm'd;		143	New Song	19
OLDE				
And it shall by merye in olde Inglonde.		103	Merlin	16
Then olde Inglonde shall be noe more.		103	Merlin	17
OLDER				
"He's older than he would be reckon'd		556	Death of Swift	107
Twice ten years older than his wife		879	Robbin & Harry	51
OLIM				
Haec olim meminisse juvabit.		187	Scriblerus 4	D 18
OLIO'S				
And feed on Fricassees and Olio's.		513	Answer Fable	42
OLIVE				
Tho' Peace with Olive bind his Hands,		655	On Poetry	419
OLYMP				
No higher climb than mount Olymp		620	Scandal Poem 1	102
No higher climb than Mount Olymp,		626	Scandal Poem 2	100
OLYMPUS				
Down from Olympus Top he Slides,		108	V's House	69
Down from Olympus comes with Joy,		693	Cadenus Vaness	200
Olympus trembling as he nods.		924	Riddle 7	96
OMBRE				
For Visits, Ombre, Balls and Plays.)		700	Cadenus Vaness	431
Yet, Ladies are seldom at Ombre, or Lue, sick;		1029	Dr. Helsham	15
OMEN				
The Omen is broke, the Danger is over;		351	Wood Insect	27
OMENS				
With Omens oft I strove to warn thy Swains,		792	St. Pat's Well	43
Omens, the Types of thy impending Chains.		792	St. Pat's Well	44
Sad Omens of the dire Event.		849	Old Thorn	32
OMINOUS				
Flocks ev'ry ominous Bird of Prey;		413	Desire Possess	54
OMIT				
But Songsters must omit it not.		464	Birthday Song	130
When did ever I omit		632	Epistle Lady	73
OMNIPOTENCE				
And one would think 'twere past Omnipotence to please;		9	Ode to King	89
OMURS				
"Your Noveds, and Blutraks, and Omurs and Stuff,		872	Grand Question	159
ON SEE HANGER-ON				
592			OMITTED WORD	
ON'T				
Let Censuring Criticks then think what they list on't,		77	Lady B- B-	REF
The gentle Pilgrims soon aware on't,		112	Bauc & Phil 2	41
Those Romans were too wise to think on't,		190	Faggot	29
Tho' I know nothing on't, 'tis I that make Gold;		263	Apollo	4
But now there need no more be said on't,		282	Journal	86
And, when we view it thus, with Thief at End on't,		285	Elegy Boat	35
Dog <Walpole> laid a Quart of Nog on't,		299	Horrid Plot	31
He'd either make a Hog or Dog on't,		299	Horrid Plot	32

ON'T   (CONTINUED)   PAGE   TITLE   LINE
  And if you should, we'd ne'er have end on't, ...   372 Letter D. S-y   21
  When frighted Strephon cast his Eye on't   . . . . .   527 Lady's Dres Rm   61
  The Lawyer swears, you may rely on't, ...   603 Beasts Confess   79
  As Popish Craft? Did he not rail on't?   774 Mullinix Tim   19
  Shew Fire and Faggot in the Tail on't?   774 Mullinix Tim   20
  Again he'll tell him, and again on't. . . . .   789 Dick's Variety   38
  No more need be said on't, ...   857 Lady's Lament   201
  I smell when I tread on't.   . . . .   857 Lady's Lament   202
  My Dear, I have ponder'd again and again on't: . . .   867 Grand Question   20
  And then they take a Turn and jump on't.   . . . . .   928 Riddle 12   D 16
  Must argue with calmness, or else will come short on't.   976 Dean to Sherid   12
  Good Spelling, Master, your Crany has Lead on't.   . .   1004 Dan J's Reply   36
  For, as for honest John, tho' I'm not sure on't, . . .   1022 Nim-Dan-Dean 2   D   5
  . . . depend on't, in the end, he'll sham ye.   . . .   1023 Nim-Dan-Dean 2   D 10
  Bring down Long Shanks Jim too, but now I think on't,   1023 Nim-Dan-Dean 2   D 11
    . . .

ONCE
  Of which it is at once the Prophet and the Cause.   . .   10 Ode to King   135
  At once deserve a Crown, and gain it too.   . . . . .   12 Ode to William   D 16
  And the Dove-muse is fled once more, ...   17 Ode Athenian   32
  And at once grow Scholars and Fools;   . . . . . .   27 Ode to Temple   44
  Your happy Frame at once controuls   . . . . . .   28 Ode to Temple   68
  And some kind pow'r for once dispense . . . .   37 Ode Sancroft   87
  (Were his humanity on earth once more)   . . . . .   38 Ode Sancroft   133
  Once highly honour'd! False is the pretence   . . . .   44 To Congreve   7
  I once esteem'd, and lov'd, and favour'd more,   . . .   44 To Congreve   12
  Confessing Albion once her darling seat;   . . . . .   49 To Congreve   194
  And once drawn up, is ne'er let down again. . . . . .   50 To Congreve   234
  So men may see what once was womankind, ...   52 Temple Ill   49
  Once on a Time, was an <Arse> Gut, ...   66 Problem   23
  Once on a time, as old Stories reherse, ...   76 Lady B- B-   1
  But Raillery, for once, apart, ...   87 Hist V's House   43
  At once did Practice both these Arts: . . . . . .   99 Elegy Patrige   48
  Step to this Grave but once a Week, ...   101 Elegy Patrige   110
  Not once suspecting, Jove would Smoak, ...   107 V's House   60
  Till once, a Parson of our Town, ...   117 Bauc & Phil 2   173
  Once, on a Time a Western Blast, ...   126 Little House   5
  The Vicar once a Week creeps in, ...   127 Little House   19
  When Dust and Rain at once his Coat invade;   . . . .   138 City Shower   28
  When once he begins, he never will flinch, ...   143 New Song   7
  If, dearest Dismal, you for once can Dine   . . . . .   162 Toland's Invit   1
  So never offer'd once to stir, ...   172 Horace 1, 7   53
  That your Lordship would once let your Cares all alone   185 Scriblerus 1   3
  Lord-Treasurer; for once be quick: . . . . . .   190 Faggot   36
  At Child's or Truby's never once had been;   . . . .   194 Author Himself   18
  By Harley's Favour once again he shines;   . . . . .   196 Author Himself   63
  As once a week we travel down   . . . .   201 Horace 2, 6   77
  From whom I once expected more;   . . . .   204 In Sickness   16
  Her Kennel once again to claim;   . . . .   208 Fable Bitches   38
  Set all her Cubs at once upon her;   . . . . . .   208 Fable Bitches   40
  Once disobey'd him, Maid nor Wife.   . . . . . .   224 Prog of Love   66
  Delude at once and Bless our Sight, ...   228 Prog of Beauty   70
  He that cou'd once have half a Kingdom bought,   . . .   234 Elegy on Demar   19
  But if a Sharper once comes in, ...   253 Bubble   63
  Sinks down at once, and there he lyes, ...   253 Bubble   82
  Your former Comrades, once so bright, ...   311 To Ford   23
  Your great Protectors, once in Power, ...   311 To Ford   27
  If once they get you on the Spot   . . . .   312 To Ford   31
  Where once their Sultan's Horse hath trod, ...   324 Pethox   40
  The Britons, once a savage Kind, ...   326 Pethox   73
  And sav'd him at once from the Shrew and the Rabble;   327 Epigram 1   4
  Great, Good and Just was once apply'd   . . . . .   339 Arch-Bish Dub   1
  When once the fierce pursuing Gaul   . . . . . .   340 Arch-Bish Dub   17
  And once I was so bold to beg that I might see His   342 Upon His Grace   27
    Grace,
  Prometheus once this Chain purloin'd, ...   345 Prometheus   37
  I must confess you've spoken once true.   . . . . . .   349 Whitshed Motto   24
  They are as once, and Idem still.   . . . .   373 Letter D. S-y   50
  I'll Try his Manners once again;   . . . .   377 Apology Lady C   68
  Once on a Time, a righteous Sage, ...   383 Manly Virtue   1
  "For once the Theme of human Sense.   . . . . . .   384 Manly Virtue   10
  Thanks to my Stars, I once can see   . . . . . .   402 Window Inns 7   D   1
  To spunge a Breakfast once a Week;   . . . . . .   409 Dial Rich Marb   52
  At once upon his Carcase light;   . . . .   413 Desire Possess   56
  Which breeds at once both Hate and Scorn.   . . . . .   413 Censure   4
  At once creating Love and Pity.   . . . .   417 Woman's Mind   42
  He never once wou'd cog the Dice, ...   456 Dean Smedley   28
  The first perhaps may once an Age   . . . . . .   462 Birthday Song   67
  Or whom you once sung up, sing down.   . . . . .   468 Birthday Song   260
  Have once the public good in view: . . . .   487 Irish-Club   18
  For once there was a Time, God wot, ...   498 Panegyr Swift   157
  God's Image, which was once their Boast.   . . . . .   498 Panegyr Swift   166
  For once to wet thy Pen Divine: . . . .   515 Answer Fable   90
  To act such an opera once in a year   . . . . . .   522 St. Cecilia's   5
  Be once in Celia's Chamber seen!   . . . .   528 Lady's Dres Rm   96
  Thus, when a greedy Sloven once has thrown   . . . .   536 To Mr. Gay   161
  Or change his Comrades once a Quarter;   . . . . .   556 Death of Swift   96
  But once in Twenty Thousand Years.   . . . . . .   584 Strephon Chloe   4
  That, once he heard a School-boy tell, ...   587 Strephon Chloe   106
  And when she once has got the Art, ...   588 Strephon Chloe   129

```
ONCE          (CONTINUED)                          PAGE  TITLE           LINE
     If once we let you have your Swing.      . . . 622  Scandal Poem 1    166
     Drop, for once, your constant Rule,      . . . 631  Epistle Lady       51
     Never once cou'd have the Pow'r          . . . 636  Epistle Lady      191
     You lose your Credit all at once;        . . . 644  On Poetry         137
     But once you fix him in a Tomb,          . . . 646  On Poetry         199
     And when your Merits once are known,     . . . 649  On Poetry         277
     Once Horace fancied from a Man               . 666  Epig Carthy 1    D   1
     If he shou'd give him once the Reins,    . . . 666  Epig Carthy 2    D   5
     Wou'd you at once display your utmost Hate,  . 667  Epig Carthy 4    D   3
     Should stumble once into the Fount,      . . . 671  Epig Carthy 21   D   7
     Whom Pallas, once Vanessa's Tutor,       . . . 701  Cadenus Vaness    464
     Stella, for once you reason wrong;       . . . 731  Stella, Poems     131
     But when I once am out of pain,          . . . 755  Stella '23         33
     Once more the <Dean> supplies their Place.   . 757  Stel B-day '24     14
     Accept for once some serious Lines.      . . . 764  Stel B-day '26     14
     When the strong Cords of Union once are Broke. 770  Horace 1, 14       22
     But cou'd you bring me once to think,    . . . 778  Mullinix Tim      165
     Once so renown'd to Live obscure?        . . . 778  Mullinix Tim      180
     Can please at most but once or twice.    . . . 788  Dick's Variety     12
     To thee, once fav'rite Isle, with Joy I came; . 789  St. Pat's Well     2
     Did once their Land subdue and civilize:     . 790  St. Pat's Well     14
     Fair Freedom's Emblem once, which smoothly flows, 793 St. Pat's Well   67
     Let them, when they once get in . . . . . . .  831  Legion Club        47
     If he sees her but once,                 . . . 854  Lady's Lament      91
     Oh! that I could but once be rid         . . . 861  Lady Acheson       43
     To my Lady once be kind;                 . . . 862  To Janus            7
     But, he durst not so much as once open his Lips, . 873  Grand Question  177
     Forgets by whom it once was sav'd;       . . . 875  Drapier's Hill     12
     If Oonah once I kiss'd, forbear to chide:    . 882  Pastoral Dial      41
     What, if for nothing once you kiss't,    . . . 884  Rev Market-Hill    33
     Then if we once can seize the Key,       . . . 885  Rev Market-Hill    87
     O, may I never once forget               . . . 887  Panegyr Dean       24
     Yet never ask us once to play?           . . . 891  Panegyr Dean      146
     To convince you, once endeavour.         . . . 908  Daphne             56
     And am at once both Hot and Cold:        . : . . 912  Aenigma           12
     At once so like to Masts or Sails,       . . . 912  Aenigma Expl     D   6
     A comely Dame once clad in white,        . . . 923  Riddle 7           63
     He feels at once both North and South:   . . . 923  Riddle 7           84
     These crude Materials once shall rise,   . . . 924  Riddle 7           91
     And once a Weaver in our Town,           . . . 926  Riddle 9           19
     If once in your cellar my Phoebus should shine, . 979  Dean to Tho: S   29
ONE   SEE SMART-ONE
     Of one poor Coronation-day,              . . . .   6  Ode to King       15
     And one would think 'twere past Omnipotence to please; .  9  Ode to King  89
     Platonick Champions, gain'd without one Female Wile, .  24  Ode Athenian  252
     And by one mighty Hero carried to it's height . . .  25  Ode Athenian   284
     But ne'er since seated in one single Breast. . . .  26  Ode to Temple    7
     You cannot be compar'd to one,           . . . .  28  Ode to Temple    62
     Borrow from every one a Grace;           . . . .  28  Ode to Temple    64
     To keep that worthless clod, the body, in one place: .  36  Ode Sancroft  64
     Is but one thing under two different names; . . .  41  Ode Sancroft    206
     Bears one, and but one branch of gold,   . . . .  41  Ode Sancroft    226
     Bears one, and but one branch of gold,   . . . .  41  Ode Sancroft    226
     One end in both, and the design the same;    .  42  Ode Sancroft       256
     Since one false beam of joy in sickly minds . . .  55  Temple Ill      149
     The one was Oats, the other Hay,         . . . .  63  Discovery         38
     To confer Notes with one another;        . . . .  66  Problem           50
     Whom each one thought the happy Dame:    . . . .  67  Problem           52
     I never took one in Your Coat.           . . . .  72  Mrs Harris Pet    61
     And it needs must be one that could both Read and Write: .  77  Lady B- B-  15
     Not one of all the tunefull Throng       . . . .  79  Vanbrug House     15
     Erect a new one in a Trice;              . . . .  80  Vanbrug House     66
     One Story high, one postern Door,        . . . .  81  Vanbrug House     77
     One Story high, one postern Door,        . . . .  81  Vanbrug House     77
     And one small Chamber on a Floor.        . . . .  81  Vanbrug House     78
     Before one Soul would let 'em in.        . . . .  90  Bauc & Phil 1     14
     One Family was gone to bed;              . . . .  90  Bauc & Phil 1     26
     We can not serve You every One,          . . . .  91  Bauc & Phil 1     31
     One swore he'd send 'em to the Stocks,   . . . .  91  Bauc & Phil 1     33
     One surly Clown lookt out, and said,     . . . .  91  Bauc & Phil 1     37
     Without one Wonder in the Sky;           . . . .  98  Elegy Patrige      6
     Not one of all his Crony Stars,          . . . .  98  Elegy Patrige      7
     One rose a Star, the other fell          . . . .  100  Elegy Patrige    67
     Not one of all our tuneful Throng        . . . .  106  V's House         15
     Erect a new one in a trice.              . . . .  107  V's House         40
     One asks the Watermen hard by,           . . . .  109  V's House         99
     Till one in Raptures thus began          . . . .  109  V's House        107
     Yet hardly dare one Line Rehearse.       . . . .  121  Apollo Outwit     60
     A <Whig> and one that wears a Gown.      . . . .  121  Apollo Outwit     64
     To bake one Loaf, and keep one Dove in.  . . . .  127  Little House      38
     To bake one Loaf, and keep one Dove in.  . . . .  127  Little House      38
     And every one was pleas'd, that heard it: . . .  128  Little House      40
     Shall not see one New Years-Day in that Year, . .  147  Windsor Proph     3
     Howe'er, 'tis all one in the Greek.      . . . .  158  Fable of Midas    60
     Alcides, one of second Rate.             . . . .  160  Atlas             18
     Yet take one Word of Counsel by the way: . . . .  166  Toland's Invit    40
     Returning home one Day from Court,       . . . .  170  Horace 1, 7        2
     Must one Day come in competition,        . . . .  182  Horace 2, 1       67
     Nor dares one Jacobite or Tory           . . . .  183  Horace 2, 1       84
     Pretend to answer one Syl--lable,        . . . .  183  Horace 2, 1       85
```

ONE	(CONTINUED)	PAGE	TITLE	LINE
One day it will be no disgrace,		186	Scriblerus 3	5
Then, took and broke them one by one.		189	Faggot	10
Then, took and broke them one by one.		189	Faggot	10
But lashing one another round:		189	Faggot	20
"And Mr. Dean, one Word from you--		201	Horace 2, 6	62
'Tis one to me.--"Then, tell us, pray		202	Horace 2, 6	99
And begg'd like one both blind and lame;		207	Fable Bitches	8
"For shou'd you stay but one Week longer,		208	Fable Bitches	29
Under one Roof, or in one Ship with me.		210	Earl of Oxford	18
Under one Roof, or in one Ship with me.		210	Earl of Oxford	18
Who first Run one another down,		217	To Mr. Delany	55
Men laugh at one another's Cost;		217	To Mr. Delany	74
One Argument she summ'd up all in,		224	Prog of Love	67
Bestow to bury him one Iron Chest.		233	Elegy on Demar	6
In half a Minute is not worth one Groat;		234	Elegy on Demar	20
Without one Ave Mary.		245	Irish-Feast	36
One Fool may from another win,		253	Bubble	61
One Night a Fool into a Brook		255	Bubble	125
And justle one another down,		256	Bubble	146
With a certain false Traitress, one Stella by Name,		263	Apollo	30
There's scarce one in ten, but what has my Mark;		265	Apollo	62
For who can hope to place one there,		271	Apollo's Edict D	38
My Lady says she can't afford one;		283	Journal	124
Was both a Boat, and in one Sense a Pilat.		285	Elegy Boat	14
At one she rambles to the Shops		291	Prog Marriage	51
The Dean, who us'd to dine at one,		291	Prog Marriage	59
Since others oft have found one there;		294	Prog Marriage	138
She'll not have left one single Prelate:		303	Storm	20
"In making <Bishops>, no one knows.		304	Storm	46
"If one must drown, the other must;		304	Storm	50
Went to one Griffith, formerly a play'r:		307	Billet Players	4
We'll make a small one here by Art:		313	To Ford	58
"There's one for each and one to spare:		321	First of April	6
"There's one for each and one to spare:		321	First of April	6
They dropp'd low Court'sies, One and All,		321	First of April	13
"And not leave one for Invocation.		321	First of April	20
"A Wife as good as Heart cou'd wish one,		322	First of April	49
As Thomas was cudgelld one day by his Wife,		327	Epigram 1	1
Our Money to keep, let us Cut down One more.		334	Serious Poem	16
To burn an old Fryer, one Forrest by Name.		334	Serious Poem	22
My Tale is a wise one if well understood,		334	Serious Poem	23
I told you one Tale, I will tell you another.		336	Serious Poem	70
Hear one Story more and then I will stop.		337	Serious Poem	109
To One who for his Country died,		339	Arch-Bish Dub	2
To One who lives in its Defence.		339	Arch-Bish Dub	3
The Godlike Hero with one frown		340	Arch-Bish Dub	19
When ev'ry one turns round about,		341	Upon His Grace	8
His Firmness to the publick Good, as one that knows it Swore,		341	Upon His Grace	9
Appear'd like one continu'd Spec'es,		344	Prometheus	8
Do all in One Opinion jump;		345	Prometheus	18
And ev'ry one begins to find,		345	Prometheus	19
When by Experience one will do.		366	Answer Delaney	4
The Loss of one is no such Trouble,		366	Answer Delaney	11
Your Rev'rence, but to cut one Leg off,		366	Answer Delaney	16
Be distant as one Head can bear;		366	Answer Delaney	30
One goes to this, and one to t' other Ear.		367	Answer Delaney	38
One goes to this, and one to t' other Ear.		367	Answer Delaney	38
To one who sway'd some time before;		375	Apology Lady C	16
And Interest the one Pursuit,		385	Manly Virtue	66
To no one Clime shou'd be confin'd;		387	Manly Virtue	116
One Sex consenting to admire,		387	Manly Virtue	129
Confines his Faith to one alone;		387	Manly Virtue	132
Because he ne'er one Thought allow'd		400	Window Inns 1	3
Or put one Feature out of Place;		414	Censure	24
Thinks nothing gives one Airs so pretty;		417	Woman's Mind	41
The Inn has not one drop of wine		420	Holyhead	6
Tis fourty to one		423	Carterets Arms	1
One Bed while alive held both Doll and Dick		430	Dicky Dolly	13
One Coach oft' carried them when they were quick,		430	Dicky Dolly	14
One Grave now contains them both Haec et Hic.		430	Dicky Dolly	15
Here quiet they Lie, in hopes to rise one Day,		431	Dicky Dolly	22
Perhaps be found one honest man:		435	Answer Paulus	104
To all but one,		442	Ballyspellin	86
Nor gives her Tongue one Moment's Rest,		446	Modern Lady	111
No single Tongue one Moment mute;		450	Modern Lady	177
"It must be One before we Sup.'		451	Modern Lady	213
That's not so bad as one that rubs		452	Modern Lady	258
One thing he did before he went hence,		455	Dean Smedley	17
Because they might have heard of one		460	Birthday Song	11
One Compliment I had forgot,		464	Birthday Song	129
This one, poor, humble Boon I want,		475	Epist on Epist	8
And one poor Office, half his Days;		481	Libel on D- D-	34
And sing like one of Milton's choir,		490	Dialogue	40
He cannot see one Creature dropping:		500	Doctor Delaney	22
Would vex one more a thousand Times.		505	Doctor Delaney	166
The Doctor names but one at present,		513	Answer Fable	33
Who never had one publick Thought,		515	Answer Fable	99
One Clincher more, and I have done,		515	Answer Fable	101
Starve twenty Lords to make one Scoundrel rich:		535	To Mr. Gay	104

ONE   (CONTINUED)   PAGE   TITLE   LINE

The Court invited more than One, or Two;   . . . . . .   536 To Mr. Gay   151
Hear an old Fable, and a dull one too;   . . . . . .   538 Mr. Pulteney   15
Yet laugh our hearts out, one and all.   . . . . . .   545 Life of Swift   14
Court, City, Camp, all one to him---.   . . . . . .   548 Life of Swift   106
But---not one Sermon, you may swear---.   . . . . . .   550 Life of Swift   193
One, whom you love of all Mankind, ... 554 Death of Swift   22
When he can in one Couplet fix   . . . .   555 Death of Swift   49
Not one foretels I shall recover;   . . . .   557 Death of Swift   133
One Year is past; a different Scene;   . . . . . .   562 Death of Swift   245
One quite indiff'rent in the Cause, ...   565 Death of Swift   305
"Was all destroy'd by one Event.   . . . .   568 Death of Swift   376
"And shew'd by one satyric Touch, ...   572 Death of Swift   481
One Blast will put out all his Fires.   . . . . .   588 Strephon Chloe   136
One greasy Stocking round his Head, ...   594 Cassinus Peter   12
One Fault he hath, is sorry for't, ...   602 Beasts Confess   31
To leave one handle for Detraction.   . . . . . .   608 Know Not What   8
One minute whether foul or fair?   . . . .   619 Scandal Poem 1   50
One Minute, whether Foul or Fair?   . . . .   625 Scandal Poem 2   46
Shou'd be one continu'd Play-Day: . . . .   631 Epistle Lady   40
And Millions miss, for one that hits.   . . . . .   640 On Poetry   2
Was just one annual Hundred Pound.   . . . . . .   642 On Poetry   54
'Tis ten to one the Wit escapes;   . . . .   643 On Poetry   98
The Hawker shews you one in Print, ...   644 On Poetry   113
A Cripple with one Foot too short;   . . . . . .   645 On Poetry   172
Ascending make one Funeral-Blaze.   . . . .   646 On Poetry   204
And one is Whig, and one is Tory.   . . . .   650 On Poetry   294
And one is Whig, and one is Tory.   . . . .   650 On Poetry   294
'Tis ten to one, he breaks your Neck.   . . . . .   666 Epig Carthy 2   D   8
Phoebus forbids thee one, his Brother   . . . . .   671 Epig Carthy 22   D   5
And ten to one drags down his feeble stick.   . .   672 Epig Carthy 24   D 18
Before one race of his was run;   . . . .   675 Curate's Compl   15
Where not one careless Thought intrudes,   . . .   691 Cadenus Vaness   166
A Shame to one so much ador'd   . . . .   695 Cadenus Vaness   266
She never hit one proper Place;   . . . .   700 Cadenus Vaness   423
One way ne knows to give her Pain: . . . . . .   701 Cadenus Vaness   469
One of her tender Sex and Age.   . . . .   705 Cadenus Vaness   579
If one short Volume cou'd comprise   . . . . . .   708 Cadenus Vaness   696
Love, why do we one Passion call?   . . . .   711 Cadenus Vaness   772
For tho' by one perverse Event   . . . .   712 Cadenus Vaness   832
One Lawyer to each Side was nam'd.   . . . . . .   713 Cadenus Vaness   843
"Who never cou'd one Lover find.   . . . .   714 Cadenus Vaness   867
Now no one regards what he Utters with freedom,   . . .   717 Answer Rebus   25
Without one Word of Cupid's Darts, ...   728 Stella, Poems   11
And making one luxuriant Shoot   . . . .   730 Stella, Poems   67
One Passion, with a diff'rent Turn, ...   731 Stella, Poems   117
To a sour Pint one day in twenty.   . . . .   745 Stel Distress   14
To half a Pint one Day in twenty, ...   750 Stel Wood-Park   38
He Twenty one, and She Fifteen: . . . .   757 Stel B-day '24   18
Had fate a lucky'r one, she'd give it ye: . . . .   760 Bec's B-Day   2
Late be her death, one gentle nod, ...   762 Bec's B-Day   57
One tells the Rise of Cheese, and Oat-meal,   . . .   781 Mullinix Tim   269
One gives Advice in Proverbs Old, ...   781 Mullinix Tim   271
One shews how bravely Audoin Dy'd, ...   781 Mullinix Tim   273
Not one Jot better looks the Sun   . . . .   786 Clad in Brown   9
Thou now one Heap of Foulness art, ...   787 Clad in Brown   13
He sees one single Tory there: . . . .   789 Dick's Variety   36
Shall rise one Blade of Grass, one Ear of Corn;   . . .   793 St. Pat's Well   92
Shall rise one Blade of Grass, one Ear of Corn;   . . .   793 St. Pat's Well   92
I wish I could find him out one more commodious.   . . .   803 Irish Bishops   12
In a Dozen Apostles but one prov'd a Traytor!   . . . .   804 Irish Bishops   30
One Traytor alone, and faithful Eleven;   . . . .   804 Irish Bishops   31
That one cloven Tongue, ever sat on your Head;   . . . .   805 Irish Bishops   50
Must take no Fee of one another.   . . . .   812 Bro Protestant   18
The Dean and his merits we ev'ry one know, ...   814 Yahoo's   6
For that one Gift to lay on Hands;   . . . . . .   821 Dr. Rundle   44
Name your Heroes one, by one.   . . . .   834 Legion Club   136
Name your Heroes one, by one.   . . . .   834 Legion Club   136
Morgan! Would it not surprise one?   . . . . . .   838 Legion Club   205
For one of his station!   . . . .   857 Lady's Lament   182
To stint me at Night to one Bottle of Wine;   . . . .   867 Grand Question   16
"A Hundred to One, but it covers a Clown, ...   872 Grand Question   154
"He caught me one Morning coquetting his Wife,   . . .   873 Grand Question   167
Will not have one new thing to say.   . . . . . .   878 Robbin & Harry   12
Which never yet one Friend has lost you.   . . . .   890 Panegyr Dean   114
Will scarce one precious word impart: . . . . .   900 Dean's Reasons   44
We both in one opinion met: . . . .   901 Dean's Reasons   74
Who not one pleasure entertains   . . . .   901 Dean's Reasons   83
With not one opinion right: . . . .   906 Daphne   10
One for truth, and one for errors: . . . . . .   907 Daphne   44
One for truth, and one for errors: . . . . . .   907 Daphne   44
Is never pleas'd till I make one: . . . .   920 Riddle 6   28
Here bury'd in one common Grave;   . . . .   923 Riddle 7   54
All beauteous Offspring of one Womb, ...   923 Riddle 7   68
I am not one of God's Creation, ...   927 Riddle 10   D   8
Yet am not one of all you see.   . . . .   927 Riddle 10   D 18
One Property more I would have you remark, ...   928 Riddle 11   D   9
The Moment I get one my Soul's all a-fire, ...   928 Riddle 11   D 11
My Parent and I produce one another, ...   929 Riddle 13   D   9
For with one Colour I can paint;   . . . .   930 Riddle 15   D 14
One of us in Glass is set, ...   930 Riddle 17   D   3

575

ONE   (CONTINUED)   PAGE   TITLE   LINE
    One of us you'll find in Jet, ...   930 Riddle 17   D 4
    All of us in one you'll find, ...   931 Riddle 18   D 1
    Knows one Tittle of the other; . . . .   931 Riddle 18   D 4
    One of us alone can sleep, ...   931 Riddle 18   D 15
    One enjoys them for the Rest. . . . . . .   931 Riddle 18   D 20
    One for all of us will feel. . . . .   931 Riddle 18   D 22
    Yet but one of us is found . . . .   931 Riddle 18   D 25
    There's but one of us can smell. . . . . .   931 Riddle 18   D 28
    Nought but one Thing can confound me, . . .   933 Riddle 20   D 5
    I'm ev'ry one, but ne'er my self; . . . . .   935 Riddle 23   D 23
    Or else I will not ride one Inch of Ground. . . 943 Probatur Alit   40
    For all an example, for no one a pattern. .   955 Portrait Life   8
    I must now, at one Sitting, pay off my old Score: 967 Letter Sherid   9
    How many to answer? One, two, three, four. . . . 967 Letter Sherid   10
    Or fit more exact than one eye and one rhyme.   980 Tho: Sheridan   4
    Or fit more exact than one eye and one rhyme.   980 Tho: Sheridan   4
    One word shou'd stick thus in your gizzard. . . . 983 Sher, A Goose   10
    Only one scurvy thing I find, ...   983 Sher, A Goose   13
    Because my Master one Day in anger call'd you Goose. 985 Mary to Sher   12
    And I don't care who knows it, 'tis all one to Mary. 986 Mary to Sher   22
    . . . one Day that you was here, ...   986 Mary to Sher   25
    Mary said he, (one Day, as I was mending my Master's
      Stocking,)   986 Mary to Sher   28
    For I can tell you one Thing, that I can, ... 988 Letter Dr Sh-n   9
    But ev'ry one that knows Dan, knows thy Master. . . . 1002 Reply by Dean   6
    Yet one thing vexes me, I own, ...   1003 Dan J's Reply   16
    For every one that knows me, knows . . . . 1004 Dan J's Reply   23
    . . .when one would not turn out a Dog that one valued; . 1014 Swift to Sheri 10
    . . .when one would not turn out a Dog that one valued; . 1014 Swift to Sheri 10
    And cannot send one Verse. . . . .   1014 Swift to Sheri   36
    We shall ne'er have one Bottle. . . . . . .   1015 Swift to Sheri   40
    One Letter still another Locks; . . . .   1021 Nim-Dan-Dean 1   D 25
    When you have not one friend left in town, . . 1022 Nim-Dan-Dean 2   D 4
    . . . or at least not one that's witty, to joke w'ye? . 1022 Nim-Dan-Dean 2   D 4
    Oh! but I forgot, perhaps, by this time, you may have one 1023 Nim-Dan-Dean 2   D 7
    Oh! I forgot too, I believe there may be one more, . . . 1023 Nim-Dan-Dean 2   D 9
    Sufficient it were, one would think, in your mad rant, . 1026 Sheri Circles   9
    As you can steal one, how 'twould please ye! . . . . 1033 Ans to Crown   14
ONELY
    The Mortar onely chang'd it's Name, ...   93 Bauc & Phil 1   111
    For, sure, by Wit is onely meant . . . .   215 To Mr. Delany   17
    Here, onely Nature acts her Part, ...   215 To Mr. Delany   21
    Onely by Affectation spoild, ...   216 To Mr. Delany   26
    We onely send our Thunder out . . . .   617 Scandal Poem 1   7
    Nymph, would you learn the onely Art . . . . . .   732 Verses Vanessa   1
ONES
    All lesser ones expire, ...   9 Ode to King   112
    The great ones swall'wing up the small . . . . . 253 Bubble   66
    It is to think all great Ones Elves, ... 493 Panegyr Swift   12
    Say, fair ones, must I make a Pause? . . . . . .   589 Strephon Chloe   161
    Ye Great ones, why will ye disdain . . . .   896 Panegyr Dean   291
    Will you return as hard ones, if I call t'ye? . . . 989 Letter Dr Sh-n   33
    Were in evry ones Judgment exceedingly fine, . . . 1017 Swift Ans Sher   2
ONLY
    His Lawrel now must only be a Cypress Wreath, . . . 9 Ode to King   105
    That what surprises us can only please: . . . . . 20 Ode Athenian   141
    Because 'tis said (and perhaps only said) . . . . 20 Ode Athenian   146
    And this Ye great Unknown, is only known in You. . 21 Ode Athenian   188
    Only the Laurel got by Peace . . . .   29 Ode to Temple   81
    Which the disguise of greatness only served to hide; . 41 Ode Sancroft   214
    Obey my Call, and only mine. . . . .   120 Apollo Outwit   32
    His only Coat, where Dust confus'd with Rain, . . 138 City Shower   29
    <Wharton> can only Swear by Fits, ...   168 Peace Dunkirk   13
    Their only pride is to refuse. . . . .   178 To Lord Harley   58
    But only what my Station fits, ...   199 Horace 2, 6   D
    "My only Friend, my Dear," said she, ...   207 Fable Bitches   9
    He stole Hints; the Verse is correct; . . . . .   266 Apollo   90
    Which only pleased in Biddy Floyd; . . . . . .   272 Apollo's Edict   D 61
    And only Coat of tarnish't Lace; . . . .   295 Prog Marriage   162
    For your displeasure is their only shame. . . . . 309 Billet Players   52
    That only for the Bishop's Lease . . . .   343 Upon His Grace   46
    And wou'd not only grant his Suit. . . . . . .   378 Apology Lady C   87
    "Only for want of outward Shape) . . . .   384 Manly Virtue   8
    Only your Godship to implore, ...   403 Window Inns 10   D 7
    They only fight for fighting sake, ...   421 Ireld   8
    Her scales you only see her hold . . . .   433 Answer Paulus   35
    And have we lost our only Friend? . . . .   445 Modern Lady   16
    Not only can inspire, but pay. . . . .   462 Birthday Song   70
    I think this Practice only fit . . . .   463 Birthday Song   111
    Of Gods I only quote the best, ...   465 Birthday Song   149
    And only with her Brother linkt . . . .   465 Birthday Song   177
    And only wants to want his eyes. . . . .   466 Birthday Song   202
    "Who only asks some pretty Cure, ...   476 Epist on Epist   49
    Which only Winter's Rain supplies. . . . . . .   478 Epist on Epist   90
    True Politicians only Pay . . . .   483 Libel on D- D-   89
    Not only what themselves have <shit> . . . . . .   497 Panegyr Swift   118
    That only know to preach and pray, ...   497 Panegyr Swift   149

```
ONLY           (CONTINUED)                              PAGE    TITLE            LINE
    An humbler Prospect only wait,  . . . . . . . .      499  Panegyr Swift       179
    But I only behold thee in Atherton's Shape,   . . . . 518  Dean Hang Rape       47
    Himself, pass only for the Second---?   . . . . . .   546  Life of Swift        57
    Thus did the Dean: his only scope   . . . . . . .     548  Life of Swift       130
    "I only was the Princess then;   . . . . . . . . .    559  Death of Swift      186
    "And only chose the Wise and Good;   . . . . . . .    566  Death of Swift      333
    Of Quadrupeds I only mean)   . . . . . . . .          601  Beasts Confess        8
    And only makes you more devout.  . . . . . . . .      624  Scandal Poem 2        8
    We only dip a Spunge in Water;   . . . . . . . .      627  Scandal Poem 2      128
    Only Dulness can produce,   . . . . . . . . .         636  Epistle Lady        204
    Only make it smart a while:  . . . . . . . .          638  Epistle Lady        265
    But Man we find the only Creature,   . . . . . .      641  On Poetry            19
    The Vermin only teaze and pinch   . . . . . . .       651  On Poetry           335
    'Tis only infinite below.  . . . . . . . . .          654  On Poetry           392
    (The only Logick us'd by Us)   . . . . . . . .        658  On Poetry         D 190
    He only publish'd for my private Use.   . . . . .     668  Epig Carthy 11    D   2
    And only know the gross Desire;   . . . . . . .       687  Cadenus Vaness       36
    By Honour only were enroll'd   . . . . . . . .        725  To Stella            52
    Only to have the Ruins made  . . . . . . . . .        727  To Stella           123
    To publick Light your only Fau't;   . . . . . .       731  Stella, Poems       102
    Can only be a Stander-by.  . . . . . . . . .          741  Stel B-day 22        34
    To make Her only touch a Quail:  . . . . . . .        746  Stel Distress        20
    To make her only touch a Quail.  . . . . . . .        750  Stel Wood-Park       18
    (The only Comfort they propose,  . . . . . . .        764  Stel B-day '26       23
    For long disputes will only weary us.   . . . . .     774  Mullinix Tim         34
    Pass only now for empty sounds?  . . . . . . . .      779  Mullinix Tim        188
    He only meant it for your Good.  . . . . . . .        797  Traulus 1            56
    You are only to live four Years without Vittles!     805  Irish Bishops        60
    He only the rights of the clergy debates,   . . . .   816  Yahoo's              31
    Or, had only Eyes behind.--   . . . . . . . .         862  To Janus             18
    No, Madam; 'tis only Sir Arthur a humming.   . .      871  Grand Question      128
    "The Army's the only good School in the Nation;  . .  872  Grand Question      162
    Only take this rule along,   . . . . . . . . .        907  Daphne               35
    I only hasten on my Fate.  . . . . . . . . .          916  Riddle 1             38
    And only to get others Wealth.   . . . . . . .        917  Riddle 3             18
    With a Boy that is only fit for School,   . . . .     941  Letter               19
    Only one scurvy thing I find,  . . . . . . . .        983  Sher, A Goose        13
ONYON
    No sav'ry Dish without an Onyon;  . . . . . . .       952  Onyons                7
ONYONS
    Here's delicate Onyons to sell,  . . . . . . .        952  Onyons                2
    Your Onyons must be th'roughly boyl'd;   . . . . .    952  Onyons                9
OONAH
    When you with Oonah stood behind a Ditch,   . . . .   882  Pastoral Dial        37
    If Oonah once I kiss'd, forbear to chide:   . . . .   882  Pastoral Dial        41
OOZE
    Because she rose from stinking Ooze?   . . . . . .    530  Lady's Dres Rm      132
OOZY
    Or, near Fleet-Ditch's oozy Brinks,   . . . . .       583  Young Nymph          47
OP'D
    When Epimetheus op'd the Locks,  . . . . . . .        528  Lady's Dres Rm       84
OP'NING
    Or, whether op'ning all his Stores,   . . . . . .     924  Riddle 7             87
OP'RA     SEE BEGGAR'S-OP'RA
OPE
    The Vi'lets ope their purple heads,   . . . . .       621  Scandal Poem 1      140
    The Vi'lets ope their Purple Heads;   . . . . .       627  Scandal Poem 2      144
OPEN
    Of secret Malice, or of open Force.   . . . . .        13  Ode to William    D  44
    The Witches left in open Air,  . . . . . . . .        240  Run Bankers          34
    They lie open on Purpose, on Counters and Stalls,    263  Apollo               23
    "What need we open our Commission,   . . . . . .      322  First of April       50
    For Poets open Table kept,   . . . . . . . .          481  Libel on D- D-       37
    Yet still St. Stephen's Chappel open lies   . . .     538  Mr. Pulteney          7
    For when we please, we open wide   . . . . . . .      621  Scandal Poem 1      133
    For, when we please, we open wide   . . . . . .       627  Scandal Poem 2      137
    Expire, when first expos'd to open Air.   . . . .     667  Epig Carthy 5     D   6
    With open Heart and bounteous Hand:   . . . . .       693  Cadenus Vaness      210
    She made a Speech in open Court;  . . . . . . .       713  Cadenus Vaness      857
    But, he durst not so much as once open his Lips,     873  Grand Question      177
    Forbid in open Air to breath;  . . . . . . . .        894  Panegyr Dean        231
    None seek thee now in open Air;  . . . . . . .        895  Panegyr Dean        281
    The more they open every Heart.  . . . . . . .        920  Riddle 6             18
    Altho' 'tis open Night and Day,  . . . . . . .        928  Riddle 12         D   5
    To break open riddles with shears or with scissars. . . 976  Dean to Sherid    22
OPEN'D
    "For when we open'd him we found,   . . . . . . .     559  Death of Swift      175
    Till Time hath open'd Reason's Gate:   . . . . .      730  Stella, Poems        96
OPENS
    When he opens his chops;   . . . . . . . . .          852  Lady's Lament        12
OPERA     SEE OP'RA
    To act such an opera once in a year   . . . . .       522  St. Cecilia's         5
OPERATION
    For which Operation there's nothing more proper  . . 351  Wood Insect          35
OPERATOR'S
    Which by the Operator's Skill,   . . . . . . .        582  Young Nymph          25
OPINION
    Foll'wing Opinion, dark, and blind,   . . . . .        36  Ode Sancroft         56
    Do all in One Opinion jump;  . . . . . . . . .        345  Prometheus           18
    "Which might as well, in his opinion,   . . . . .     550  Life of Swift       174


                              577
```

OPINION	(CONTINUED)	PAGE	TITLE	LINE
Is best supported by Opinion;	. . . .	590	Strephon Chloe	224
Opinion falls, and Beauty dies.	. . . .	591	Strephon Chloe	226
And dy'd defending his opinion.	. . . . . .	620	Scandal Poem 1	84
And dy'd defending his Opinion.	. . . . . .	626	Scandal Poem 2	82
Whose Fleet, 'tis all our Friends Opinion,	. . .	774	Mullinix Tim	23
The Knight his Opinion resolv'd to maintain.	. .	868	Grand Question	40
We both in one opinion met:	. . . .	901	Dean's Reasons	74
With not one opinion right:	. . . .	906	Daphne	10
For this is ev'ry Cook's Opinion,	. . . . .	952	Onyons	6
OPINIONS	SEE STATE-OPINIONS			
Who change Opinions with the changing Scene:	. . . .	196	Author Himself	65
OPIUM				
Could scatter Opium full as well,	. . . .	133	Magician's Rod	41
OPPOSE				
Thy Breast unshaken can oppose	. . . . .	339	Arch-Bish Dub	9
Oppose his Counter-Charm of Paper,	. . . . .	354	Simile Silver	26
And bravely Precox might oppose	. . . . .	373	Letter D. S-y	70
To oppose the <Dean> your-self Exempting	. . . .	373	Letter D. S-y	76
'Twas to no purpose to oppose,	. . . .	378	Apology Lady C	91
"The Pope, or Calvin he'd oppose,	. . . . .	549	Life of Swift	148
Cou'd scarce oppose Vanessa's Flame;	. . . .	710	Cadenus Vaness	745
Our Fate in vain we would oppose,	. . . . . .	757	Stel B-day '24	29
OPPOSERS				
Explaining strikes opposers Dumb;	. . . .	281	Journal	84
OPPOSING				
The Combat of opposing Winds:	. . . . . .	923	Riddle 7	80
OPPOSITE				
Because 'tis opposite to theirs.		37	Ode Sancroft	82
And must, to human reasoning opposite, conclude	. .	41	Ode Sancroft	209
OPPOSITE-CIRCLE				
In Square or in Opposite-Circle or Trine	. . . .	1018	Swift Ans Sher	23
OPPRESS				
Oppress us in corrupted Times:	. . . .	503	Doctor Delaney	102
OPPRESS'D				
The Steed, oppress'd, would break his Girth,	. . .	231	Prog of Poetry	29
With a Whirl of Thought oppress'd,	. . . . . .	578	Day Judgement	1
OPPRESS'T				
By all the World I am oppress't,	. . . .	918	Riddle 4	9
OPPRESSING				
oppressing true merit exalting the base	. . . . . .	540	Charac Walpole	7
Nor thy oppressing Lords afford thee Brass.	. . . .	793	St. Pat's Well	94
OPPRESSION				
Oppression hides, with guilty Dread,	. . . . . .	387	Manly Virtue	123
The oppression of Virtue, not wages of Sin:	. . . .	816	Yahoo's	42
And my Oppression gives them Rest.	. . . . . .	918	Riddle 4	10
OPPREST				
Of a declining Church, by Faction her worse foe opprest,		40	Ode Sancroft	186
The Nymph opprest before, behind,	. . . . . .	589	Strephon Chloe	169
The Swain at last, with Grief opprest,	. . . . .	595	Cassinus Peter	39
OPPROBRIA				
Pudet haec opprobria, I freely must tell ye,	. . . .	967	Letter Sherid	5
OPPUGNANT				
Through Clefts oppugnant force a Vent;	. . . . . .	923	Riddle 7	86
OPTAT				
As Horace says, Optat ephippia.	. . . .	779	Mullinix Tim	214
OPTIC				
Scatt'ring loose features o'er the optic vein;	. . . .	54	Temple Ill	96
OPTICKS				
How Patrige made his Opticks rise,	. . . . . .	98	Elegy Patrige	21
OR	704		OMITTED WORD	
OR'E				
Flyes like an Eagle or'e his head;	. . . . . .	461	Birthday Song	34
And darts her Beams or'e both our Isles,	. . . .	466	Birthday Song	181
She now can or'e the servants hector.		745	Stel Distress	
OR'T				
Or't had been happy for Gold-finders.	. . . . .	156	Fable of Midas	12
ORACLE				
As to an Oracle submits.		649	On Poetry	268
ORACLES				
But Dreams are like Oracles, hard to explain 'em,	. .	337	Serious Poem	113
(I mean the Oracles of Both,	. . . .	647	On Poetry	229
ORACULAR				
Or the much-talkt Oracular Grove	. . . . . .	17	Ode Athenian	50
ORACULUM				
But I doubt the Oraculum,	. . . .	1015	Swift to Sheri	55
ORANGES				
Come, buy my fine Oranges, Sauce for your Veal,	. .	953	Oranges	1
ORATION				
"And Mr. Henly's last Oration:	. . . . . .	563	Death of Swift	278
ORATOR				
An Orator dismal of Nottinghamshire,	. . . . . .	142	New Song	1
ORB				
Or from thy private peaceful orb appear;	. . . . .	39	Ode Sancroft	155
ORDAIN				
Should them Ordain for Lenten Diet	. . . . .	373	Letter D. S-y	67
ORDAIN'D				
Ordain'd by Fate to be the Land of Slaves:	. . . .	770	Horace 1, 14	2
"And thou, the Wretch ordain'd by Fate,	. . . .	851	Old Thorn	81
ORDAINS				
Contented he, but Fate ordains	. . . .	385	Manly Virtue	51

	PAGE	TITLE	LINE
ORDER			
With an Order for the Chaplain aforesaid;	73	Mrs Harris Pet	73
Now move, and now in Order Stand.	108	V's House	78
And high in Order plac'd, describe	114	Bauc & Phil 2	99
Then order Squash to call a Hackney Chair.	166	Toland's Invit	46
We order a Vulture, in Snape of the Spleen,	266	Apollo	97
And we order our Subjects, of every Degree,	266	Apollo	99
Who neither time nor order kept.	279	Journal	20
Such Order from Confusion sprung,	530	Lady's Dres Rm	143
The Muses next in Order follow,	585	Strephon Chloe	53
In Order; on the Left, the Graces:	689	Cadenus Vaness	96
His Similes in Order set,	730	Stella, Poems	73
ORDER'D			
The Cry'r was order'd to dismiss	714	Cadenus Vaness	884
ORDERLY			
He like an orderly Divine	292	Prog Marriage	83
ORDERS			
Waiting for Orders at his Feet,	7	Ode to King	40
You need but now give Orders and Command;	13	Ode to William D	38
He'd give his Orders for a Storm,	302	Storm	4
And by the Orders of his Betters	373	Letter D. S-y	73
Th' Almighty's Orders to perform,	496	Panegyr Swift	92
And orders the Landlord to bring him a Whore;	517	Dean Hang Rape	20
To countermand his Orders by your own.	534	To Mr. Gay	88
My Orders are, I'm not at Home;	742	Stel B-day 22	46
Call for th' Orders of the House;	831	Legion Club	58
ORDINARY			
Transcending Nature's ordinary Laws,	10	Ode to King	132
ORDURE			
While Traulus all his Ordure scatters.	796	Traulus 1	31
Such a Croud their Ordure throws	830	Legion Club	19
ORE			
Produce a richer vein or cleaner ore;	45	To Congreve	52
In Scottish Hills found precious Ore,	133	Magician's Rod	29
In talking ore a moderate Glass.	279	Journal	38
As parent of the golden ore,	433	Answer Paulus	24
The Dregs will serve to ripen Ore below;	532	To Mr. Gay	24
Hither from Colchos, with the fleecy Ore,	790	St. Pat's Well	7
<ORFORD>			
<Sunderland>, <Orford>, <Boyl>, and <Richmond's> Grace	165	Toland's Invit	33
ORGAN'D SEE ILL-ORGAN'D			
ORGANS			
With trumpets and fiddles and organs and singing	522	St. Cecilia's	7
ORIGINAL			
To be the great Original	22	Ode Athenian	217
Forgive (Original Mildness) this ill-govern'd zeal,	38	Ode Sancroft	107
Just as they lookt in the Original.	783	Tim and Fables	18
Both of the Picture and Original.	993	On Picture	27
ORIGINE			
The Proof of your high Origine,	498	Panegyr Swift	175
From us descended ab origine,	619	Scandal Poem 1	61
From us descended ab origine;	625	Scandal Poem 2	57
ORIS			
Hannoniae qui primus ab oris.	186	Scriblerus 4 D	6
ORMOND			
She must return to Ormond Key:	751	Stel Wood-Park	46
ORMOND-KEY			
She must return to Ormond-Key.	746	Stel Distress	26
ORMOND'S			
"What Ormond's Valour, Oxford's Cares,	567	Death of Swift	374
ORMONDE			
Great Ormonde lend thy Gen'ral's Staff:	191	Faggot	46
Yet here were You and Ormonde born	314	To Ford	84
ORNAMENT			
Strip her of ev'ry ornament and grace,	42	Ode Sancroft	249
ORPHAN			
An Heir, and Orphan of a Peer;	384	Manly Virtue	20
ORPHAN'S			
Nor dipt in Blood, nor Widow's Tears, nor Orphan's Cries:	29	Ode to Temple	86
Nor widow's sighs, nor orphan's tears,	296	Satiric Elegy	18
ORPHANS			
Orphans around his Bed the Lawyer sees,	364	On Dreams	23
ORTHODOX			
By coupling Orthodox with Arrians?	820	Dr. Rundle	8
OS			
Which near the Os Petrosum pass;	367	Answer Delaney	36
OSTRICH-LIKE			
And, Ostrich-like, his all-digesting Maw.	532	To Mr. Gay	36
OTHER 98		OMITTED WORD	
OTHER'S 2		OMITTED WORD	
OTHERS 39		OMITTED WORD	
OTHERWISE			
Far otherwise a great Divine,	513	Answer Fable	11
And Betty otherwise employ'd;	526	Lady's Dres Rm	6
OUGHT			
And which for ought I see, and much I fear,	39	Ode Sancroft	159
And dear Englond, if ought I understond,	148	Windsor Proph	15
Will, or ought to end in Ropes;	168	Peace Dunkirk	9
While, wise Men think they ought to fight	189	Faggot	21
(Who ought for Peace and Plenty Pray.)	372	Letter D. S-y	40

		PAGE	TITLE	LINE
OUGHT	(CONTINUED)			
You hate to see ought that seems Clean		372	Letter D. S-y	44
Whether he ought to stay or go.		377	Apology Lady C	82
I think they justly ought to share		422	Ireld	47
In you, who ought to know my Heart, ...		444	Modern Lady	2
"Had he been rul'd, for ought appears, ...		559	Death of Swift	173
While We, whom Reason ought to sway, ...		607	Beasts Confess	205
Nor ought of Stella, but the Name;		759	Receipt Youth	34
Me, surely me, you ought to spare, ...		766	Stel B-day '26	83
Dammee, I say, they ought to starve.		783	Tim and Fables	34
Your Deanship ought to recollect, ...		899	Dean's Reasons	20
For ought he knows, as bad as Thespis's.		988	Letter Dr Sh-n	23
OUNCE				
Without an Ounce of last Year's Flesh, ...		759	Receipt Youth	15
And, out you squeeze an Ounce at least.		892	Panegyr Dean	186
An Ounce of Gold's worth ten of Brass, dull Pedant. .		1004	Dan J's Reply	33
OUR	377		OMITTED WORD	
OURS	5		OMITTED WORD	
OURSELVES	2		OMITTED WORD	
OUT	SEE BARRING-OUT			
By which our happy Prince carves out his Bays; . . .		7	Ode to King	32
He sought Her out in Fight, ...		7	Ode to King	36
Just as the Sun puts out a Fire;		9	Ode to King	114
And when you find out these, believe true Fame is there.		21	Ode Athenian	186
Would want a God Himself to help him out.		22	Ode Athenian	210
Search out this Utopian Ground, ...		26	Ode to Temple	11
Out starts the little Beast, and mocks their idle Fears.		30	Ode to Temple	114
To drive all Virtue out, or look it dead!		30	Ode to Temple	123
She soars clear out of sight, ...		31	Ode to Temple	144
Bids us make Bricks, yet sends us to look out for Straw;		32	Ode to Temple	188
Strait the Muse turns the Helm, and I launch out again;		32	Ode to Temple	195
Contriv'd to tire all patience out, ...		35	Ode Sancroft	15
Till Honesty and Conscience are clear out of sight. .		36	Ode Sancroft	58
To point out which is moderation, which is fortitude. .		41	Ode Sancroft	210
Ne'er sprang a youth from out this isle before . . .		44	To Congreve	11
What northern hive pour'd out these foes to wit? . . .		46	To Congreve	83
Whom sin and want e'er furnish'd out a wit;		48	To Congreve	166
And chuse out wits who ne'er have seen his face; . . .		48	To Congreve	170
Deals out to man the planet of his birth;		54	Temple Ill	90
On t' other side (laid out for Shoes);		60	Lady Tablebook	14
When e're he please to blot it out;		61	Lady Tablebook	22
Till on a Day cut out by Fate, ...		62	Discovery	5
Out slipp't a Mystery of State		62	Discovery	7
Ere Mornings dawn stole out to spy		63	Discovery	35
With that he draws two Handfulls out, ...		63	Discovery	37
Work out, as Anger does in Vermin?		66	Problem	16
Let's not fall out; We all had Share.		67	Problem	58
Lord help me, said Mary, I never stirr'd out of this Place!		70	Mrs Harris Pet	16
Mrs. Dukes, said I, here's an ugly Accident has happen'd out;		71	Mrs Harris Pet	37
. . .before I was aware, out I blunder'd, ...		72	Mrs Harris Pet	52
My Lord to find out who must deal		74	Game Traffick	1
To find the Doctor out.		74	Game Traffick	4
Dame Floyd looks out in grave Suspence		75	Game Traffick	13
Are these too low?--then find out grander, ...		83	Salamander	21
Out from some Hole obscure he flies		84	Salamander	33
Blew out Love's Torch or chill'd the Flame:		85	Salamander	60
No Christian would turn out a Beast		90	Bauc & Phil 1	19
The Master Bawl'd out half asleep		90	Bauc & Phil 1	27
One surly Clown lookt out, and said, ...		91	Bauc & Phil 1	37
Whilst he from out the Chimny took		91	Bauc & Phil 1	57
We can but make it out in Ale.		92	Bauc & Phil 1	66
To keep the Hair out of their Eyes;		98	Elegy Patrige	24
Torment, by pissing out their Lights;		100	Elegy Patrige	92
While He from out of Chimney took		112	Bauc & Phil 2	25
Cut out large Slices to be fry'd;		112	Bauc & Phil 2	28
When Baucis hastily cry'd out;		116	Bauc & Phil 2	155
Points out the Place of either Yew;		116	Bauc & Phil 2	171
Duly let out a Nights to Steal for Fees.		125	Descriptn Morn	16
And saw the Parson creeping out;		127	Little House	26
To keep mischievous Spirits out;		134	Magician's Rod	52
Who has forty Years let out his Conscience to hire, .		142	New Song	2
Out of Zeal for his Country, and want of a Place, . .		142	New Song	3
From her Closet brought out a full Purse in her Clutche		143	New Song	16
Root out these Carrots, O Thou, whose Name		148	Windsor Proph	21
She pours it out in an Atlantis.		150	Corinna	31
From our Mysterious Club to keep out Spies, ...		165	Toland's Invit	29
Steal by the Back-door out, and leave him there; . .		166	Toland's Invit	45
<Sunderland's> run out of his Wits, ...		168	Peace Dunkirk	11
Found out that it was Dr. <Swift>:		171	Horace 1, 7	26
Where painted Monsters are hung out.		172	Horace 1, 7	60
Or is your Money out at use?--		175	Horace 1, 7	129
Mark out the way where Daphne flew.		177	To Lord Harley	18
Held out Medusa's snaky locks, ...		178	To Lord Harley	45
With--who is in--and who is out, ...		180	Horace 2, 1	14
Inform the Commons, that the Secret's out:		195	Author Himself	42
Of Land set out to plant a Wood.		198	Horace 2, 6	6
His Genius first found out the Rule		216	To Mr. Delany	35
He'll find the Secret out from thence		219	To Mr. Delany	107
But hurry'd out, and clapp't the Dore.		220	A Quiet Life	8

OUT   (CONTINUED)

	PAGE	TITLE	LINE
Will drew out Dick to take a Quart,	220	A Quiet Life	26
The Neighbors round would cry out Shame.	220	A Quiet Life	36
When first she ventur'd out with him.	224	Prog of Love	82
His Credit out for Cheese and Ale;	231	Prog of Poetry	34
And by his Looks, had he held out his Palms,	234	Elegy on Demar	11
Cryes out a Sage among the Croud,	253	Bubble	78
There sprawl'd a while, at last got out,	255	Bubble	131
Conveys out my Paper of Hints by a Trick,	265	Apollo	81
There out of my Sight, just against the North-Zone,	265	Apollo	85
And lastly for Stella, just out of her Prime,	266	Apollo	103
Elijah's Mantle's worn out.	270	Apollo's Edict	D 24
George, Nim and Dean, set out at Four,	280	Journal	43
His Candle out, and he a Bed.	280	Journal	48
George is half scar'd out of his Wits,	283	Journal	125
Yet, when his Sand was out, we find at last,	285	Elegy Boat	21
To shut out the River by raising the Bank.	287	Bank Down	5
If nothing but Paper comes out of this Bank.	287	Bank Down	15
And, thus set out this happy Pair,	290	Prog Marriage	27
While He goes out to cheapen Books,	291	Prog Marriage	39
She can't abide to stay out late.	293	Prog Marriage	98
But when let out, they run and muddle	294	Prog Marriage	147
To turn her Naked out of Doors,	295	Prog Marriage	163
And hire us out their scenes, and cloaths, and faces.	307	Billet Players	8
To help an honest lad that's out of place,	308	Billet Players	25
Come, be content, since out it must,	311	To Ford	1
I wonder you held out so long,	315	To Ford	110
"Ye don't fall out about the Heir.	321	First of April	12
From what Kind of Tree this Wood was Hewn out.	334	Serious Poem	26
Some think him cut out from the Poisonous Yew,	334	Serious Poem	31
He is an old Stump cut out of a Crab,	335	Serious Poem	36
These Raps he will honestly dig out with Shovels,	337	Serious Poem	97
Get the Great Seal, and turn out Brod'rick.	348	Whitshed Motto	18
To keep out of Danger, a Doublet of Stone.	351	Wood Insect	10
That this Eclipse was out of Season,	354	Simile Silver	6
And besides must be out of my Wits:	395	Dog and Thief	4
That would turn a Man out of his own?	396	Dog and Thief	20
But overcharg'd, and out of Wind,	412	Desire Possess	37
Or put one Feature out of Place;	414	Censure	24
Is out at elbows why should I repine?	419	Shall Repine	6
These praises we blot out	423	Carterets Arms	3
The truth will be got out	423	Carterets Arms	4
Then gave the Subject out of Spite:	445	Modern Lady	23
Each Limb, and Feature out of Fame;	449	Modern Lady	133
Set out in Hyperbolick Strains,	463	Birthday Song	93
Had not the Fleet gone out too late,	463	Birthday Song	102
Come out with Amalthea's Horn.	464	Birthday Song	126
When all your list of Gods is out,	464	Birthday Song	143
Then cut him out a world of work,	466	Birthday Song	193
Find him a Kingdom out to conquer;	466	Birthday Song	204
To find out proper words for Harmony:	467	Birthday Song	218
But Albion's cliffs are out at heel,	468	Birthday Song	244
When he goes out, you share his fate,	468	Birthday Song	258
For keep him in, or turn him out,	484	Libel on D- D-	139
And now you're out, enjoy your Grin.	493	Panegyr Swift	22
Laid out with no less Art than Pains,	494	Panegyr Swift	56
Is destin'd to beat out his Brains.	500	Doctor Delaney	16
Point out the surest Men to rise,	502	Doctor Delaney	84
By censure frighted out of honour's road,	506	To a Friend	9
We all can find out whom he means,	514	Answer Fable	65
Blunder'd out a Thousand Times.	523	Betty Grizette	20
To squeeze it out from Head to Tail;	527	Lady's Dres Rm	66
It must come out alive or dead.	527	Lady's Dres Rm	68
To move it out from yonder Corner;	528	Lady's Dres Rm	72
The Vapours flew from out the Vent,	528	Lady's Dres Rm	91
For, keep, or turn him out, my Lord's undone.	535	To Mr. Gay	126
Was, when will They turn out this odious Rogue?	536	To Mr. Gay	146
His Work is done, the Minister must out.	536	To Mr. Gay	150
Out bounc't the Mastiff of the triple Head;	538	Mr. Pulteney	27
Yet laugh our hearts out, one and all.	545	Life of Swift	14
Loll out their Tongues, and thus they talk,	545	Life of Swift	21
"Points out some Circumstance to please us.	554	Death of Swift	10
And till they drove me out of Date,	555	Death of Swift	61
His Fire is out, his Wit decay'd,	556	Death of Swift	101
"I wish he may hold out till Spring.	557	Death of Swift	114
His Kind of Wit is out of Date.	562	Death of Swift	252
Lately taken out of Lim--	574	Helter Skelter	28
Now, picking out a Crystal Eye,	581	Young Nymph	11
Pulls out the Rags contriv'd to prop	582	Young Nymph	21
But, out it flies, even when she meets	588	Strephon Chloe	131
One Blast will put out all his Fires.	588	Strephon Chloe	136
Steals out her Hand by Nature led,	589	Strephon Chloe	171
Cry'd out, ye Gods, what Sound is this?	589	Strephon Chloe	177
Or when a-bed, to let out Wind.	590	Strephon Chloe	218
But, sure a Tell-tale out of School	592	Strephon Chloe	277
He seem'd as just crept out of Bed;	594	Cassinus Peter	11
To force it out my Heart must rend;	596	Cassinus Peter	95
Now, bend thine Ear; since out it must:	596	Cassinus Peter	99
It happen'd when a Plague broke out,	601	Beasts Confess	5
Which now he runs out every Year;	606	Beasts Confess	166
We onely send our Thunder out	617	Scandal Poem 1	7

	PAGE	TITLE		LINE
Or, from your noses dig out notches?	618	Scandal Poem 1		26
To rigg her out for Juno's mayd.	619	Scandal Poem 1		78
Apollo stirs not out of dore .	621	Scandal Poem 1		121
Alas! our Thunder soon goes out;	624	Scandal Poem 2		7
Or from your Noses dig out Notches?	624	Scandal Poem 2		20
Apollo stirs not out of Door,	627	Scandal Poem 2		115
Pass our Nights, to drive out thinking.	632	Epistle Lady		86
Drives out Brangling, and Contention,	637	Epistle Lady		215
Brutes find out where their Talents lie:	640	On Poetry		13
Blot out, correct, insert, refine,	643	On Poetry		87
Out skips a Book of Miscellanies.	651	On Poetry		318
Come out with some lampoon on D'Anvers.	658	On Poetry	D	186
With whom a Footman out of Place	659	On Poetry	D	410
Amidst a croud of hungry Bards cries out,	671	Epig Carthy 24	D	3
Than if it rang out for my Knell:	674	His Deafness		4
Which, thundring out with lungs long-winded,	675	Curate's Compl		11
The out or inside of their Heads,	688	Cadenus Vaness		49
Or else, shut out from Heaven and Earth,	689	Cadenus Vaness		87
And finds out Pallas in the Skies:	692	Cadenus Vaness		187
Found out the Trick that Venus play'd,	694	Cadenus Vaness		251
A wholesome Law, Time out of mind,	694	Cadenus Vaness		257
Came early, out of pure Good-will,	698	Cadenus Vaness		366
The Nymph stood silent out of spight,	699	Cadenus Vaness		406
Her fine Panegyricks are quite out of Season,	716	Answer Rebus		21
Have put the Dean's Politicks quite out of Date;	716	Answer Rebus		24
No Age could furnish out a Pair	722	Stel B-Day '18		11
Or kindly when his Credit's out,	728	Stella, Poems		31
Worn out by Wits who rhyme on Faces;	730	Stella, Poems		76
She must have long ago run out.	735	Stel B-day '20		32
When Doll hangs out a newer Face	735	Stel B-day '20		34
And yet run out by starving here:	745	Stel Distress		16
Her Quarter's out at Lady Day	746	Stel Distress		41
To running out by starving here.	750	Stel Wood-Park		44
Her Quarter's out at Lady-Day,	751	Stel Wood-Park		57
When out my brutish passions break,	754	Stella '23		11
But when I once am out of pain,	755	Stella '23		33
Come back before you're out of Case;	760	Receipt Youth		50
Rebecca shews they're out in that.	761	Bec's B-Day		8
To find this Damn'd Pretender out,	774	Mullinix Tim		26
Resolve to stand it out the last;	774	Mullinix Tim		42
Put all your Brother Puppets out,	777	Mullinix Tim		140
Nor sputter out your Oaths so fast,	780	Mullinix Tim		237
Tare out the Tale, and wipe your <Arse>	783	Tim and Fables		37
A lively Maggot sallies out,	785	Dick, Maggot		3
His Hide emits a Foulness out,	786	Clad in Brown		8
And weekly carry out our Dust.	787	Clad in Brown		28
When Dick cries, Dust to carry out?	787	Clad in Brown		30
To grope for Words, and out they come.	797	Traulus 1		52
I wish I could find him out one more commodious.	803	Irish Bishops		12
And have left us but Three out of Twenty behind 'em.	804	Irish Bishops		24
To others he boasted of knocking out brains,	816	Yahoo's		47
Lorsha! and out of her shteeple there was hung a black	840	Ballad	D	9
flag.				
And fast out of spite:	853	Lady's Lament		54
And wear out my smocks:	854	Lady's Lament		82
At last out it comes.	854	Lady's Lament		110
Put a word out of joint,	855	Lady's Lament		139
Find out, if you can,	856	Lady's Lament		167
Dug out in an hour,	857	Lady's Lament		185
Come here out of pity,	858	Lady's Lament		216
And now my Dream's out: For I was a-dream'd	868	Grand Question		49
That for twenty Denials you would not give out.	869	Grand Question		56
And worry him out, 'till he gives his Consent.	869	Grand Question		62
I can't get it out, tho' I'd never so fain.	869	Grand Question		66
You had like to have put it quite out of my Head.	870	Grand Question		86
(For sure, I had dizen'd you out like a Queen:)	870	Grand Question		102
Runs out in tongue, as in estate:	878	Robbin & Harry		10
It so fell out, that cautious Harry	878	Robbin & Harry		17
Love rooted out, again will never grow.	881	Pastoral Dial		16
Dennis was out, and I got hither safe;	881	Pastoral Dial		31
Impatient to be out of Debt,	887	Panegyr Dean		23
And, out you squeeze an Ounce at least.	892	Panegyr Dean		186
But, squeezing out four Lines in Rhime,	893	Panegyr Dean		195
Here, when my Shoes are out of case,	896	Panegyr Dean		311
To wash thy injur'd Off'rings out.	896	Panegyr Dean		318
Who keeps his wisdom out of sight;	900	Dean's Reasons		42
Was call'd, to rig him out a Beau	903	Death Daphne		20
Thus furnish't out, he sent his Train	904	Death Daphne		45
Her Pocket-Glass drew slily out;	904	Death Daphne		64
And some give out, that I entice	917	Riddle 3		13
Sometimes run out of all I have;	918	Riddle 4		32
My Goings out, and Comings in,	918	Riddle 4		35
And drive at last all Secrets out:	920	Riddle 6		16
Although I'm often out of Case,	920	Riddle 6		23
Points out where each new Victim falls;	923	Riddle 7		58
And I roar out my Joy, and in Transport expire.	928	Riddle 11	D	12
Yet all the World can't find me out,	929	Riddle 14	D	2
Drums and Trumpets bring me out;	933	Riddle 20	D	20
When his Merit's out of Date,	933	Riddle 20	D	28
Without stirring out,	939	Riddle Answerd		10

		PAGE	TITLE	LINE
OUT	(CONTINUED)			
Would, as he lay under, cry out, Sirrah, yield: . . .		967	Letter Sherid	16
Because she let's out more, than e'er she takes in. . .		972	S-'s Ans Sh-d	6
My foot was but just set out from my cathedral,		975	Dean to Sherid	3
Yet still you are out (tho' to vex you I'm loth),		976	Dean to Sherid	17
Like a woman it keeps in less than it lets out.		976	Dean to Sherid	26
You found out my rebus with very much modesty;		976	Dean to Sherid	37
Now you write from your cellar,--I find out your art, .		979	Dean to Tho: S	19
From out the pen will presently		983	Sher, A Goose	7
. . . to come out with such a Name.		985	Mary to Sher	6
Tho' you and your Come-rogues keep him out so late . .		986	Mary to Sher	16
To hold out longer in Trysyllable.		989	Letter Dr Sh-n	31
I chose these Rhymes out, for their Difficulty.		989	Letter Dr Sh-n	32
. . .out so late at this Time of Year, ...		1014	Swift to Sheri	10
. . .when one would not turn out a Dog that one valued; .		1014	Swift to Sheri	10
If you do not come back we shall weep out our eyn . . .		1018	Swift Ans Sher	28
By leaving out the needless Vowels, ...		1021	Nim-Dan-Dean 1	D 23
Will Hancock declares you are out of your compass, . .		1027	Sheri Circles	21
Lady Santry got out of the Church when she grew sick, .		1029	Dr. Helsham	10
OUT-DONE				
And blush to be so far out-done:		385	Manly Virtue	42
Out-done by none in Rhyming well,		650	On Poetry	291
OUT-LAUGHING				
Comes off by out-laughing the Company round.		968	Letter Sherid	20
OUT-NUMBER'D				
Out-number'd, half encompass'd round, ...		326	Pethox	87
OUT-OF-FASHION				
I own, that out-of-fashion Stuff		700	Cadenus Vaness	426
OUT-OF-FASHION'D				
To hear his out-of-fashion'd Wit?		556	Death of Swift	92
OUT-RIDES				
In Journeys he out-rides the Post, ...		398	Earl of P-b-w	4
OUT-RUNS				
Thus, a Greyhound out-runs the whole Pack in a Race, .		580	Psyche	5
OUT-SELL				
They may out-sell a better Thing;		418	Woman's Mind	63
OUT-SHINE				
Will magisterially out-shine us.		648	On Poetry	258
OUT-SUNG				
How much our Ancestors out-sung us;		652	On Poetry	352
OUTCAST				
Let not the outcasts of this outcast age		42	Ode Sancroft	261
OUTCASTS				
Let not the outcasts of this outcast age		42	Ode Sancroft	261
OUTDONE				
Envying to see themselves outdone.		87	Hist V's House	34
Why must I be outdone by Gay, ...		555	Death of Swift	53
As much as the Liffee's outdone by the Rhine		1018	Swift Ans Sher	26
OUTRAGES				
But not of your Outrages:		154	Widow and Cat	D 37
OUTRIGHT				
. . . Lord! I thought I should have sunk outright: . .		69	Mrs Harris Pet	13
. . .I should have missed the Letter outright. . . .		1013	Swift to Sheri	4
OUTSHINING				
Thy Nose outshining Caelia's Eyes.		994	On Picture	33
OUTSIDE				
Laoco'n struck the Outside with his Spear, ...		139	City Shower	51
That clumsy outside of a Porter, ...		796	Traulus 1	19
OUTSPREAD				
While Victory, with Wings outspread, ...		461	Birthday Song	33
OUTWARD				
"Only for want of outward Shape)		384	Manly Virtue	8
His outward Form, and Inward, vie, ...		385	Manly Virtue	59
A Skeleton in outward Figure, ...		398	Earl of P-b-w	25
Was taken with his Person outward, ...		514	Answer Fable	47
Incapable of outward Stains;		691	Cadenus Vaness	163
The outward Form no Help requir'd:		692	Cadenus Vaness	176
All outward and within is foul;		787	Clad in Brown	14
His outward senses fast asleep;		900	Dean's Reasons	46
OUTWARDLY				
"Although, we outwardly may Grieve, ...		545	Life of Swift	9
OVEN				
Or of a Pigeon-house, or Oven, ...		127	Little House	37
But Dick was from an Oven.		784	Mullinex Dick	12
OVER				
And over and above, that I may have your Excellencies Letter,		73	Mrs Harris Pet	72
During Her Sacred Life, should never come over: . .		144	New Song	36
"The Peace is made, and Perkin must come over. . . .		195	Author Himself	46
His Favor, when his Passion's over.		224	Prog of Love	70
Ye Pow'rs who over Love preside, ...		229	Prog of Beauty	117
Are by Robert Ballentine lately brought over; . . .		236	Excellent Song	2
Then over us spread, ...		246	Irish-Feast	51
Dipt over head and Ears--in Debt.		251	Bubble	24
Tho' she lives 'till she's Grey as a Badger all over. .		266	Apollo	108
And how his Boat was over set, ...		280	Journal	66
And, over these Fillets he wisely has thrown, . . .		351	Wood Insect	9
The Omen is broke, the Danger is over;		351	Wood Insect	27
And he who will leap over a Stick for the King		389	Order of Bath	11
Now Voices over Voices rise;		450	Modern Lady	174

OVER   (CONTINUED)   PAGE   TITLE   LINE

    And after several Readings over, ...   475 Epist on Epist 13
    Spotted over like a Le'pard! . . . .   522 Betty Grizette 4
    But, all agree, to give me over. . . . .   557 Death of Swift 134
    And Vacation's over--then . . . .   574 Helter Skelter 55
    Damn'd Time-Serving Priests all over the Nation;   576 Place Damn'd 12
    Ev'ry Fault have drawn a Gloss over: . . . . .   632 Epistle Lady 96
    That when Platonick Flights were over, ...   707 Cadenus Vaness 650
    The Tories are gone ev'ry Man over . . . . . .   773 Mullinix Tim 9
    Read over here and there a Fable, ...   782 Tim and Fables 6
    And, when this is over, we'll make him amends, .   817 Yahoo's 61
    I'm all over dawb'd when I sit by the Dean. . .   868 Grand Question 30
    Sunk over head and ears in matter, ...   900 Dean's Reasons 59
    All over naked I am seen, ...   926 Riddle 9 9
OVER-BEARING
    Positive and over-bearing, ...   799 Traulus 2 9
OVER-BLOWN
    At length 'tis over-blown and past, ...   41 Ode Sancroft 219
OVER-BULKY
    Beware, nor over-bulky grow, ...   258 Bubble 193
OVER-NICE
    No Libertine, nor Over-nice, ...   171 Horace 1, 7 31
OVER-RANK
    Our British soil is over-rank, and breeds . . .   37 Ode Sancroft 101
OVER-RULES
    'Tis hard, where dulness over-rules, ...   436 Answer Paulus 123
OVER-RUN
    Then, lest with Greek he over-run ye, ...   648 On Poetry 259
    For she, tho' over-run with care, ...   761 Bec's B-Day 9
    I'm quite over-run . . . .   852 Lady's Lament 13
OVER-TOPT
    Rather than thus be over-topt, ...   554 Death of Swift 25
OVER-WEENING
    Now enters over-weening Pride, ...   448 Modern Lady 124
OVERBOARD
    "Or, throw him overboard, he'll ride . . . . .   304 Storm 35
OVERCAST
    With how undecent clouds are overcast . . . .   52 Temple Ill 33
    At least twelve Inches overcast, ...   126 Little House 6
OVERCHARG'D
    But overcharg'd, and out of Wind, ...   412 Desire Possess 37
OVERCOME
    He ne'er could overcome her quite, ...   30 Ode to Temple 131
OVERFLOWN
    Earld Godwin's Castles overflown, ...   257 Bubble 171
OVERGROWN
    Whose Fortune is not overgrown; . . . .   243 Horace 4, 9 16
    And I'll use you as he did that overgrown Clown, .   968 Letter Sherid 31
OVERHEARD
    The Strangers overheard, and said, ...   92 Bauc & Phil 1 83
OVERHEARE
    To overheare the grand Dispute. . . . .   63 Discovery 28
OVERJOY'D
    How are the Servants overjoy'd . . . .   892 Panegyr Dean 175
OVERLOAD
    That now would overload a Team, ...   79 Vanbrug House 4
    That now would overload a Team; . . . .   106 V's House 4
OVERPAYS
    He overpays in Condescension. . . . .   483 Libel on D- D- 110
OVERPRESST
    But, as a Porter overpresst . . . .   160 Atlas 5
OVERRUN
    Whence came these Goths to overrun the pit? . . .   46 To Congreve 84
OVERSET
    That, Death has overset him with a Blast. . . .   285 Elegy Boat 22
    She does not overset the chair; . . . .   762 Bec's B-Day 42
OVERSHADE
    As if 'twould overshade the Royal Rose, ...   37 Ode Sancroft 104
OVERTAKE
    They fly, and none can overtake . . . .   177 To Lord Harley 21
OVERTHROWN
    Which having wisely overthrown, ...   81 Vanbrug House 91
    Which after they have overthrown, ...   110 V's House 133
    Having thus overthrown all our further Advances. .   968 Letter Sherid 22
OVERTON
    As Overton has drawn his Sire . . . .   461 Birthday Song 37
OVERTOP
    That her own Maid should overtop her; . . . .   886 Rev Market-Hill 102
OVERTURND
    Friend Pope overturnd by driving too fast away, .   1037 Four Storyes 3
OVERTURNS
    No Sea overwhelms him, no Coach overturns; . . .   1037 Four Storyes 6
OVERWHELMS
    No Sea overwhelms him, no Coach overturns; . . .   1037 Four Storyes 6
OVERWITTED
    By clients always overwitted. . . . .   434 Answer Paulus 60
OVID
    Ovid had warn'd her to beware, ...   120 Apollo Outwit 21
    The Spokes, we are by Ovid told, ...   598 Problem Solved 15
    From Virgil, Martial, Ovid, Lucan; . . . . . .   657 On Poetry 482
    To turn to Ovid, Book the Second; . . . . . .   690 Cadenus Vaness 109

```
                                                 PAGE    TITLE           LINE
OW                                               258 Bubble             197
    You'll ow Your Ruin to your Bulk;     . . . . . . . .
OW'D
    Not Rich, but ow'd no Man a Groat;    . . . . .   171 Horace 1, 7     34
    He ow'd his Preservation to his Crimes.   . . .   536 To Mr. Gay     156
    To this damnable Speaker had long ow'd a shame;  816 Yahoo's         37
    The De'el too that ow'd me a Shame,  . . . . .  1005 Sheridan's Sub   21
OWE
    To thee I owe that fatal bent of mind,   . . . .  55 Temple Ill     131
    Exalted Worth disdains to owe   . . .            386 Manly Virtue    95
    Be frugal, Patt: pay what you owe,   . . . . .   479 Epist on Epist 115
    Who owe their Virtues to their Stations,        484 Libel on D- D-  137
    To that you owe the nobler Flame.   . . . . . .  726 To Stella       91
    Now should my Praises owe their Truth           729 Stella, Poems   61
    Ungrateful; since to her I owe   . . . . . . .   754 Stella '23       7
    You, to whose Care so oft I owe,   . . . . . .   766 Stel B-day '26  87
    Thrice Rev'rend <Dean> for all I owe;           887 Panegyr Dean     2
    To vilest Slaves I owe my Birth.   . . . . . .   916 Riddle 2         2
    And after all, I chiefly owe   . . . . . . . .   927 Riddle 10     D 11
    To Man alone I owe my birth,   . . . . . . . .   936 Riddle 24     D  2
OWES
    For, 'tis to me he owes his Wit;   . . . . . .   411 Dial Rich Marb  90
OWING
    Not owing to his happy Vein   . . . . . . . .    481 Libel on D- D-  45
OWL
    And as the Boding Owl, or rather   . . . . . .    99 Elegy Patrige   49
    The Raven, Vulture, Owl, and Kite,   . . . . .   413 Desire Possess  55
    Than Venus like an Owl.   . . . . . . . .        425 Five Ladies     16
    The Owl foresaw in pensive Mood                  849 Old Thorn       37
    The Owl, the Raven, and the Bat,   . . . . .     903 Death Daphne    29
OWLS
    I see the greatest Owls in you,   . . . . . . .  515 Answer Fable   106
OWN
    With its own Light Your dazling Glory shines,     11 Ode to William D  7
    Part of Your Merit Chance wou'd call her own,     11 Ode to William D 11
    Of my own dazled, scanty Sense   . . . . . .      18 Ode Athenian    78
    Do own th' Effects of Providence,   . . . . .     19 Ode Athenian   109
    Consider Humane Folly, and you'll quickly own,    20 Ode Athenian   149
    But with my own Rebellious Heart,   . . . . .     23 Ode Athenian   239
    It fell, and broke with its own Weight           26 Ode to Temple    4
    These are the Paradises of her own;   . . . .     31 Ode to Temple  145
    In his own balance, false and light,   . . . .    36 Ode Sancroft    55
    Suppose the truth, like all the world, their own;  37 Ode Sancroft   80
    On his own secret regular sphere,   . . . . .     39 Ode Sancroft   152
    From strength of its own native seed,            41 Ode Sancroft   224
    Pleads for her own neglect, and thus reproaches mine:  43 To Congreve   6
    And by short views mistook for all their own;  . . .  45 To Congreve  60
    Lest here it live, when perish'd with his own;        48 To Congreve 168
    Comes back with joy to its own seat at night;  . . .   51 Temple Ill    6
    Where her own Temple was her darling theme;          51 Temple Ill   14
    Further than its own palace in her heart:  . . . .    53 Temple Ill   54
    That thou ne'er hadst a being of thy own,            54 Temple Ill   94
    There in her own (far an el breth)  . . . . . .       60 Lady Tablebook  10
    Clap his own Nonsense in the place.   . . . . .       61 Lady Tablebook  24
    For you freely must own you were at a Dead lift;      77 Lady B- B-      28
    And Poets their own Verses sung,   . . . . . .        79 Vanbrug House    2
    Both to their own and Landlord's Cost;   . . . .      79 Vanbrug House   14
    They from it's Ruins build their own.  . . . . .      81 Vanbrug House   92
    And Poets their own Verse Sung,   . . . . . .        106 V's House        2
    But, to their own, or Landlord's Cost,   . . . .     106 V's House       13
    And left the Choice to his own Breast.  . . . .      107 V's House       54
    They from its Ruins build their own.  . . . . .      110 V's House      134
    But fenc'd his Head with his own Bays   . . . .      119 Apollo Outwit    7
    To Cheat the God in his own Art.   . . . . . .       120 Apollo Outwit   28
    And softly stole to discompose her own.  . . .       124 Descriptn Morn   4
    Give me that House in my own Hand;   . . . . .       128 Little House    49
    And not a Rod for thy own Breech.   . . . . .        135 Magician's Rod  84
    And in Her own hearing I boldly did Vote,            144 New Song        40
    By their own Weight sunk to the Bottom;   . . .      158 Fable of Midas  79
    But the Queen shall enjoy Her own again.  . . .      168 Peace Dunkirk   10
    Than the Queen should enjoy Her own again.  . .      168 Peace Dunkirk   20
    And the Queen shall enjoy Her own again.  . . .      169 Peace Dunkirk   30
    For the Queen now enjoys Her own again.   . . .      169 Peace Dunkirk   40
    For shunning those of his own Coat;   . . . . .      171 Horace 1, 7     28
    From his own Mouth, if this be so?   . . . . .       172 Horace 1, 7     48
    That we a German Prince must own                     180 Horace 2, 1     11
    And Harley, not asham'd his Choice to own,           194 Author Himself  31
    I own, I'm pleas'd with this Rebuke,  . . . . .      200 Horace 2, 6     40
    To others, e'er it be my own.   . . . . . . .        204 In Sickness     22
    To You, whose Virtues I must own                     215 To Mr. Delany    1
    They love a Jest--when 'tis their own.  . . . .      218 To Mr. Delany   86
    With Dick's own Staff his Peacefull Neighbor,        220 A Quiet Life    22
    The Workmanship of their own Hands.  . . . . .       227 Prog of Beauty  52
    Were forc'd to own to him their Obligation.          234 Elegy on Demar  18
    Resume their own when e'er they please.  . . . .     239 Run Bankers      8
    From his own Hand foresees his Fall,   . . . . .     241 Run Bankers     50
    Him for an happy Man I own                           243 Horace 4, 9     15
    The Reason is plain, they are none of his own;  . .  264 Apollo          56
    And from my own Stock, provided with Topicks,        265 Apollo          83
    Writes down my Conceits, and then calls them his own:  265 Apollo        86
    To own the truth we have some private Ends.  . . . . 275 Epilogue        14
```

OWN   (CONTINUED)   PAGE   TITLE   LINE

	PAGE	TITLE	LINE
The Dams and the Weirs must all be your own,	287	Bank Down	6
He'll soon return to his own Vomit.	299	Horrid Plot	36
I own it was a dang'rous Project;	300	Horrid Plot	71
Now to a word of bus'ness in our own.	309	Billet Players	54
She dares not say her Life's her own.	328	Epigram 3	4
I own it hath often provok'd me to Mutter,	334	Serious Poem	5
He can Rap his own Raps, and has the true Sapience	335	Serious Poem	47
More Heathenish Times than those of our own;	335	Serious Poem	60
I own it, and therefore I leave you to seek.	337	Serious Poem	90
I hope you will own it is Love in a Maze;	337	Serious Poem	102
Than the Liquor he deals in, his own melted Copper;	351	Wood Insect	36
And Skin's yet whole, I needs must own,	372	Letter D. S-y	18
Said little in his own Defence:	377	Apology Lady C	74
With native Lustre like her own;	379	Apology Lady C	114
With lessen'd Lustre in their own;	384	Manly Virtue	28
Yet more display'd, and rais'd his own.	386	Manly Virtue	88
And swear they are your own.	395	Grub-Street	20
That would turn a Man out of his own?	396	Dog and Thief	20
In my own Thames may I be drownded,	410	Dial Rich Marb	73
Now, should I own your case was grievous,	433	Answer Paulus	37
I own, the curses of mankind	433	Answer Paulus	51
I own his conscience always free,	434	Answer Paulus	55
Always for saving their own. bacon:	434	Answer Paulus	65
I own, there may in ev'ry clan	435	Answer Paulus	103
To villains of his own profession.	436	Answer Paulus	128
To speak a Language of their own;	450	Modern Lady	189
Wou'd his own Temples better fit,	458	Paddy's Charac	22
That she hath Graces all her own;	465	Birthday Song	164
With genuin lustre all her own.	465	Birthday Song	174
If their own happyness they knew.	467	Birthday Song	224
Hint the least Int'rest of your own;	480	Libel on D- D-	14
To make them work their own undoing.	484	Libel on D- D-	128
I own, he hates an Action base,	484	Libel on D- D-	145
This country, now their own, for nought.	488	Irish-Club	24
I own, the Counsel were not wrong,	496	Panegyr Swift	98
If Maidens are ravish't, it is their own Choice,	519	Dean Hang Rape	61
The World shall own, his Choice was wise and just,	532	To Mr. Gay	17
Presume to treat him at his own Expence.	533	To Mr. Gay	64
By his own Credit to advance the Sum;	533	To Mr. Gay	72
To countermand his Orders by your own.	534	To Mr. Gay	88
His Snot into the Mess; 'tis all his own.	536	To Mr. Gay	162
Let me suppose the Case my own.	547	Life of Swift	67
Not sparing his own Clergy-Cloth,	548	Life of Swift	113
"The World must own it, to their Shame;	550	Life of Swift	199
How glad the Case is not your own!	554	Death of Swift	30
In my own hum'rous biting Way?	555	Death of Swift	54
"Forgetting his own Flesh and Blood?	558	Death of Swift	164
"I promis'd them, I own; but when?	559	Death of Swift	185
"I own my self no Judge of those:	565	Death of Swift	310
"But what he writ was all his own.	565	Death of Swift	318
"Because a Duke was proud to own him:	565	Death of Swift	320
"As Numbers in their Hearts must own,	566	Death of Swift	337
"For her he oft expos'd his own.	566	Death of Swift	350
"When, ev'n his own familiar Friends	569	Death of Swift	403
"Commodious to their own Abodes.	571	Death of Swift	454
Cambrick Ruffles not their own;	573	Helter Skelter	20
With Int'rest pays him back his own.	590	Strephon Chloe	214
It is entirely their own Fault.	591	Strephon Chloe	260
I own, 'twas but a Coach and Four,	598	Problem Solved	17
Good Father I must own with Shame,	602	Beasts Confess	13
A Wag he was, he needs must own,	602	Beasts Confess	23
Some Faults we own: But, can you guess?	603	Beasts Confess	75
In his own Church he keeps a Seat;	605	Beasts Confess	129
I own, the Moral not exact;	607	Beasts Confess	197
And from your own experience know	620	Scandal Poem 1	87
We own, Your verses are melodious,	622	Scandal Poem 1	179
And from your own Experience know,	626	Scandal Poem 2	85
But, though we own, she makes it wetter,	628	Scandal Poem 2	149
We own, your Verses are melodious;	628	Scandal Poem 2	161
A Bastard of your own begetting.	644	On Poetry	116
Will smile, and think 'em all his own:	647	On Poetry	226
Procure Disciples of your own.	649	On Poetry	278
Whose graceless Children scorn to own thee!	652	On Poetry	358
I mean all Kings except your own,	659	On Poetry	D 410
All coffers full except his own.	659	On Poetry	D 416
Yet, all must own, thy wish is wise.	676	Parson's Case	4
So like my own, without his Bow,	692	Cadenus Vaness	191
To Female Breasts, except her own;	695	Cadenus Vaness	273
I own, that out-of-fashion Stuff	700	Cadenus Vaness	426
Cou'd please them, and improve her own.	701	Cadenus Vaness	453
Knows nothing which it dare not own;	706	Cadenus Vaness	609
His Virtues she might call her own;	708	Cadenus Vaness	681
Much to her Praise, more to his Own.	711	Cadenus Vaness	765
The Government is now her own;	712	Cadenus Vaness	801
Gave her own Reasons last; and then	713	Cadenus Vaness	852
Suppose the Question not your own:	724	To Stella	38
Take Comfort, that our own is best:	728	Stella, Poems	20
Must own, that Pain is largely paid	731	Stella, Poems	111
They must have Stella's of their own;	739	Stel B-day '21	16
'Tis my own Credit lies at Stake.	741	Stel B-day 22	32

	PAGE	TITLE	LINE
And is a Stoic in her own.	754	Stella '23	18
Had she not evils of her own?	755	Stella '23	26
In your own heart you'll reap the fruit,	755	Stella '23	31
But laugh'd at their own silly joking.	755	Dingley Brent	6
That Virtue, stil'd its own Reward,	764	Stel B-day '26	26
She saved Britannia's Right, and lost her own.	771	Horace 1, 14	46
I Own 'tis not my Bread and Butter,	773	Mullinix Tim	1
To thy own Side so Damn'd a Nuisance,	775	Mullinix Tim	66
I took Advice except my own,	775	Mullinix Tim	72
Will our own Party mind me not?	779	Mullinix Tim	192
His own sweet Figure with the Print,	783	Tim and Fables	15
I own I see but little Wit in:	788	Dick's Variety	10
Had my own native Italy o'er-run,	789	St. Pat's Well	4
Thee, happy Island, Pallas call'd her own,	790	St. Pat's Well	9
I own, Appearances are bad;	796	Traulus 1	21
I own, his Madness is a Jest,	798	Traulus 1	69
Than saving your Souls, by damning our own?	805	Irish Bishops	56
To cry; Lo, Judas, gone to his own Place:	806	Judas	24
While his own ass's Zaggs were more fit for the shears.	816	Yahoo's	49
He had cut his own ears to be deaf to your nonsense.	818	Epigr Kite	10
They gave what never was their own.	820	Dr. Rundle	18
Must own it made by God's Anointed.	821	Dr. Rundle	56
Souse them in their own Ex-crements.	837	Legion Club	186
For thy horrid Looks, I own,	838	Legion Club	195
"Though with your state-sieve your own notions you split,	843	Ay and No	9
"Then who will own thee for a Scot?	850	Old Thorn	76
Could rub my own gums,	852	Lady's Lament	20
I hope you will use my House as your own.	869	Grand Question	82
That her own Maid should overtop her;	886	Rev Market-Hill	102
Envy must own, you understand your	888	Panegyr Dean	45
Or of his own, or Smedly's Lay,	893	Panegyr Dean	221
An empty Plate except your own.	897	Panegyr Dean	340
From her own Head, Megaera takes	903	Death Daphne	21
Was never seen, except her own:	904	Death Daphne	62
That she'll own, or cure a fault.	907	Daphne	32
I almost sink with my own Weight;	917	Riddle 3	6
But never of my own inditing.	917	Riddle 3	10
Bears up his House, that's of his own contriving.	943	Probatur Alit	48
But think it as sweet as her own.	952	Onyons	15
Or, like my own Herrings, I soon shall be dead.	953	Herrings	9
Friend Sheridan, when will you know your own Good?	968	Letter Sherid	24
And, 'tis your own Case, for you never can wound	968	Letter Sherid	33
Yet one thing vexes me, I own,	1003	Dan J's Reply	16
Make a Page of your own Age,	1013	Swift to Sheri	6
. . .have it at their own House, to drink in quiet.	1013	Swift to Sheri	7
However, they own it is very civil in Mr. Sheridan,	1014	Swift to Sheri	8
. . .and you'll believe me as sure as a gun, and own it;	1023	Nim-Dan-Dean 2	D 15
. . . your own spirit of pun, and own wit.	1024	Nim-Dan-Dean 2	D 16
. . . your own spirit of pun, and own wit.	1024	Nim-Dan-Dean 2	D 16

OWN'D

Capacious House! 'tis own'd by all	109	V's House	115
And to the Shepherd own'd her flame.	178	To Lord Harley	76
A Breach of Liberty, 'tis own'd,	181	Horace 2, 1	27
This is gratefully own'd by each Boy in the College,	263	Apollo	17
He own'd no Deity beside.	303	Storm	14
Thus, Steel who own'd what other writ,	481	Libel on D- D-	49
"'tis own'd he was a Man of Wit---,	547	Life of Swift	74
"Envy hath own'd it was his doing,	569	Death of Swift	411
But own'd, he had a stubborn Spirit	604	Beasts Confess	109
With Impudence own'd all the Fact.	687	Cadenus Vaness	24
That ev'ry Nymph with Envy own'd,	705	Cadenus Vaness	580
She own'd the wand'ring of her Thoughts,	705	Cadenus Vaness	602
Nor ever own'd a Pow'r Divine,	820	Dr. Rundle	35

OWNER

Must ever keep it's Owner down:	502	Doctor Delaney	80
His Vassals easy, and the Owner blest;	533	To Mr. Gay	47
"Because its Owner is a Duke?	548	Life of Swift	124

OWNERS

And think thou seest my owners Heart,	60	Lady Tablebook	2
"Whose Owners set not up for Beaux.	572	Death of Swift	468
Than the Owners of St. <James>.	637	Epistle Lady	242

OWNING

| Be proud of owning such Relations; | 813 | Bro Protestant | 58 |

OWNS

But Pallas owns Ardelia's Power,	121	Apollo Outwit	47
And since he owns the King of Sweden	282	Journal	103
Owns all your favours; here intends to stay,	309	Billet Players	47
. . . and owns His Grace had Reason.	341	Upon His Grace	8
He owns, and hopes it is no Sin,	606	Beasts Confess	175
(For which he owns himself to blame)	607	Beasts Confess	182
For, here he owns, that now and then	608	Beasts Confess	219

OXFORD

| But the Lord of Oxford Swears, | 169 | Peace Dunkirk | 35 |
| Of Tricks, the Lord of <Oxford> knows, | 181 | Horace 2, 1 | 19 |

OXFORD'S

| To palliate his Friend Oxford's Crimes, | 550 | Life of Swift | 185 |
| "What Ormond's Valour, Oxford's Cares, | 567 | Death of Swift | 374 |

OYL

| To think of Oyl and Soot, is vain, | 229 | Prog of Beauty | 110 |
| And strip the Bones, and melt the Oyl. | 258 | Bubble | 204 |

OYL   (CONTINUED)   PAGE   TITLE   LINE
     This Coyner of Raps in a Cauldron of Oyl.   . . . .   352 Wood Insect   38
     A Forehead Cloth with Oyl upon't   . . . .   526 Lady's Dres Rm   25
OYLY
     'Twill be so oyly, and so sleek . . . .   780 Mullinix Tim   223
OYSTER
     No Colchester Oyster, ...   953 Oysters   5
OYSTER-STRUMPET
     As Bagpipe shrill, or Oyster-Strumpet, ...   182 Horace 2, 1   72
OYSTERS
     Charming Oysters I cry, ...   952 Oysters   1
     Eat my Oysters, and lye near her, ...   953 Oysters   15
     Were you drest like a bawd, and sold oysters at   979 Dean to Tho: S   10
         Billings-gate.
PAC'D   SEE SLOW-PAC'D
PACE
     But o'er th' afflicted with a heavy pace . . . . . .   55 Temple Ill   121
     Yet Daphne never slack'd her pace, ...   177 To Lord Harley   27
     And, kept at first an equal Pace: . . . .   412 Desire Possess   12
     Too scornful now to stop his Pace, ...   412 Desire Possess   33
     The Goat advanc'd with decent Pace;   . . . .   603 Beasts Confess   59
     Her Belly burst, and slow her Pace: . . . .   895 Panegyr Dean   276
     by Galloping high, or Level Pace, ...   957 Cantata
PACES
     As thro' the Hall thy Worship paces: . . . .   182 Horace 2, 1   76
PACIFY
     To pacify this angry Deity;   . . . .   353 Wood Ironmongr   22
     And sell, to pacify his wrath, ...   879 Robbin & Harry   35
PACK
     But for that Pack of churlish Boors   . . . .   92 Bauc & Phil 1   86
     But, for that Pack of churlish Boors, ...   112 Bauc & Phil 2   46
     Just as a Porter does his Pack   . . . .   160 Atlas   4
     That a Pack of sly Knaves should get fifty per Cent,   288 Bank Down   52
     Then, without fail, we pack up for Belfast.   . . . .   309 Billet Players   56
     He heard I kept a pack of hounds, ...   422 Ireld   27
     To be a Midnight Pack   426 Five Ladies   18
     That pack of mimick <legislators>, ...   436 Answer Paulus   133
     Ye pack of pensionary <Peers>, ...   487 Irish-Club   5
     The least deserving of the Pack;   . . . .   503 Doctor Delaney   86
     A Pack of Dog-fish had him in the Wind: . . . . .   538 Mr. Pulteney   22
     Syrius, the swiftest of the heavn'ly Pack, ...   538 Mr. Pulteney   33
     Thus, a Greyhound out-runs the whole Pack in a Race, . 580 Psyche   5
     Poor Stella must pack off to Town.   . . . .   744 Stel Distress   2
     Poor Stella must pack off to Town.   . . . .   750 Stel Wood-Park   26
     The scrubest Cur in all the Pack   . . . .   798 Traulus   67
     He still may keep a pack of knaves   . . . .   902 Dean's Reasons   109
PACKET
     Perhaps from what the Packet brings, ...   282 Journal   109
     A packet though it brings in me.   . . . .   420 Holyhead   14
PACTOLUS
     Was lost among Pactolus Sands, ...   157 Fable of Midas   34
     Then like Pactolus we should find   . . . .   255 Bubble   111
PAD
     These pad on wit's high road, and suits maintain   . . . 45 To Congreve   67
PADDY
     Paddy repin'd to see him wear   . . . .   458 Paddy's Charac   19
PADLING
     Each padling in his leaky Boat, ...   256 Bubble   147
PAEAN'S
     From Paean's Fire to Party Zeal;   . . . .   481 Libel on D- D-   44
     With Paean's purest Fire his Favourites glow;   . . .   532 To Mr. Gay   23
PAGE
     Here, a Page fill'd with Billet Doux;   . . . .   60 Lady Tablebook   13
     For sorry Stuff, can get a Crown a Page;   . . . . .   276 Epilogue   42
     I know not in what Book or Page, ...   412 Desire Possess   6
     Townshends cast Page or Walpole's groom   . . . . .   423 Ireld   72
     While Burnet in his deathless page . . . .   490 Dialogue   27
     Of Addison's immortal Page, ...   496 Panegyr Swift   101
     As handsome as my Lady's Page;   . . . .   597 Problem Solved   5
     Make a Page of your own Age, ...   1013 Swift to Sheri   6
PAGEANT
     To make the Pageant gay: . . . .   6 Ode to King   16
PAGES
     For so many Six-pences, so many Pages, ...   288 Bank Down   47
     "And stand the Staring of your Pages;   . . . . . .   380 Apology Lady C   156
     And found, as he the pages twirl'd, ...   782 Tim and Fables   7
     How will they pore upon thy Pages?   . . . . . .   1021 Nim-Dan-Dean 1 D 38
PAID   SEE PAY'D,PAYD
     Current like copper, and as often paid: . . . . .   50 To Congreve   220
     "Nor with hir'd thoughts be thy devotion paid;   . . .   55 Temple Ill   139
     For now the Surgeon must be paid;   . . . .   225 Prog of Love   92
     The Hand that sign'd the Mortgage paid the Shot.   . .   234 Elegy on Demar   28
     Harangues the Rabble, and is better paid.   . . . .   364 On Dreams   34
     Not so a Nation's Revenues are paid: . . . . . .   364 On Dreams   34
     At least, before your Master's Debts are paid.   . . .   533 To Mr. Gay   49
     With Int'rest, and a Praemium paid beside,   . . .   533 To Mr. Gay   62
     The Rites perform'd, the Parson paid, ...   533 To Mr. Gay   69
     Nor, tho' his Priests be duly paid, ...   586 Strephon Chloe   67
     Counts all his Labours amply paid, ...   657 On Poetry   491
     Must own, that Pain is largely paid . . . . . .   729 Stella, Poems   37
     When his speech came abroad, he paid him off clean, . . 731 Stella, Poems   111
                                                              816 Yahoo's   38

PAID	(CONTINUED)	PAGE	TITLE	LINE
	Are largely paid for all your time.	893	Panegyr Dean	196
	The Trojan Heroe paid his Vow.)	896	Panegyr Dean	308
PAILS				
	Adorn their Pails with Plate.	122	Empty'ng Town	8
	In Pails was brought up, ...	244	Irish-Feast	10
PAIN				
	Your Garden's better worth your noble Pain, . . .	32	Ode to Temple	176
	Whereas, Notwithstanding, I am in great Pain, . . .	143	New Song	11
	And under the Pain of our highest Displeasure, . . .	266	Apollo	101
	The Moon, deliver'd from her Pain, ...	354	Simile Silver	13
	"And such a Pain in all my Limbs!"	451	Modern Lady	209
	How, Pain they might from Pleasure part:	501	Doctor Delaney	32
	A Fellow-feeling of my Pain.	546	Life of Swift	46
	Lies rackt with Pain, and you without:	554	Death of Swift	28
	Yet shou'd some Neighbour feel a Pain, ...	557	Death of Swift	135
	She gives you such Plenty, it puts you in Pain; . .	580	Psyche	7
	Or shew the Anguish, Toil, and Pain, ...	583	Young Nymph	69
	"And dying, never told his Pain.	596	Cassinus Peter	78
	When I found the tingling Pain, ...	638	Epistle Lady	267
	One way he knows to give her Pain:	701	Cadenus Vaness	469
	From Phoebus Rays they suffer Pain, ...	731	Stella, Poems	110
	Must own, that Pain is largely paid	731	Stella, Poems	111
	If I perform this Task with Pain	739	Stel B-day '21	5
	Or, if with more than usual Pain, ...	741	Stel B-day 22	7
	But when I once am out of pain, ...	755	Stella '23	33
	Were future Happiness and Pain, ...	764	Stel B-day '26	19
	That Patience under tort'ring Pain, ...	765	Stel B-day '26	49
	Observe, the Audience is in Pain, ...	776	Mullinix Tim	93
	O what a pleasure mixt with pain!	776	Mullinix Tim	106
	By those who give me greatest Pain.	918	Riddle 4	16
	That gives imaginary Pain:	920	Riddle 5	34
	Ah, is not Love a pleasing Pain?	924	Riddle 8	12
	A Pain which ev'ry happy Night	924	Riddle 8	13
	And I mourn the cruel Pain;	933	Riddle 20	D 14
	Because my Magick gives no Pain.	934	Riddle 21	D 22
PAINS				
	He had mixt little Wit with a great deal of Pains, . .	77	Lady B- B-	24
	But when she thought her Pains were done, ...	208	Fable Bitches	23
	What Carps we met with for our pains:	283	Journal	112
	That Title by anothers Pains.	293	Prog Marriage	122
	With pungent Pains on ev'ry Side:	325	Pethox	57
	Or sick of Obstructions, and Pains in her Chest. . .	351	Wood Insect	16
	You are not in the least at Pains.	361	Grace's Answer	18
	What pains he takes to be prolix!	434	Answer Paulus	83
	<Lyndsay>, you know, what pains you take	436	Answer Paulus	129
	Who for his pains is cuff'd, and kick'd, ...	436	Answer Paulus	137
	A Guinea shall reward your pains.	463	Birthday Song	94
	Laid out with no less Art than Pains, ...	494	Panegyr Swift	56
	If all my Pains will earn a Crown.	502	Doctor Delaney	68
	With Pains of Love tormented lies;	582	Young Nymph	39
	How unproportion'd to thy Pains!	642	On Poetry	60
	With Pains unknown increas'd her Smart.	703	Cadenus Vaness	523
	Her Knowledge, with such Pains acquir'd, ...	709	Cadenus Vaness	716
	Where Pleasures mix'd with Pains appear, ...	711	Cadenus Vaness	776
	Call'd ev'ry Pow'r to ease my Pains, ...	726	To Stella	100
	Tormented with incessant pains, ...	754	Stella '23	1
	That I these pains can undergo.	754	Stella '23	8
	Yet seems to feel my pains alone, ...	754	Stella '23	17
	Come hither, and take this old Gown for your Pains. .	873	Grand Question	186
PAINT				
	As to paint Eccho to the Sight:	21	Ode Athenian	160
	In striving to wash off th' imaginary paint: . . .	42	Ode Sancroft	250
	Beneath (A new Receit for Paint)	60	Lady Tablebook	8
	To paint a Hero, we enquire	83	Salamander	17
	The Paint by Perspiration cracks, ...	227	Prog of Beauty	37
	By help of Pencil, Paint and Brush	227	Prog of Beauty	46
	Then wou'd you paint a matchless Dame, ...	272	Apollo's Edict	D 70
	And paint a Coward fierce in arms.	464	Birthday Song	62
	Nor could the nicest Artist Paint, ...	480	Libel on D- D-	19
	To Beauty, Dress, or Paint, or Youth;	729	Stella, Poems	14
	For with one Colour I can paint;	930	Riddle 15	D 14
	All Colours, without Paint, put on, ...	935	Riddle 23	D 12
	That you're a Dawb, whilst I but paint, ...	1003	Dan J's Reply	11
PAINTED				
	I must, like him that painted Venus' Face, ...	28	Ode to Temple	63
	In sum, a glitt'ring voice, a painted name, ...	54	Temple Ill	101
	How Miss pickt ev'ry painted Card, ...	86	Hist V's House	4
	And painted, lookt abundance better	93	Bauc & Phil 1	122
	In painted Cloth we look for Fields, ...	122	Empty'ng Town	11
	Where painted Monsters are hung out.	172	Horace 1, 7	60
	And from thy painted Skin conclude.	324	Pethox	26
	Lur'd by the gilded Stern, and painted Sides. . . .	771	Horace 1, 14	48
	Every Monster should be painted;	839	Legion Club	222
	Must be some painted Toy I knew;	912	Aenigma Expl	D 8
	And painted like an Indian Queen.	926	Riddle 9	10
PAINTER				
	Just in this Dress the Painter drew it.	783	Tim and Fables	24
PAINTER'S				
	So in the Kindred Painter's Art, ...	1021	Nim-Dan-Dean 1	D 35

	PAGE	TITLE	LINE
PAINTERS			
As Other Painters oft adore	227	Prog of Beauty	51
(Could Poets or could Painters fix	735	Stel B-day '20	17
PAINTING			
No Painting can restore a Nose, ...	229	Prog of Beauty	111
And though the Painting grows decayd	734	Stel B-day '20	7
PAINTS			
Some with Pomatum, Paints and Slops, ...	526	Lady's Dres Rm	35
Her Ointments, Daubs, and Paints and Creams, . . .	530	Lady's Dres Rm	138
Not Iris, when she paints the Sky, ...	911	Aenigma	3
PAIR			
If I had but a Pair of Aces, ...	75	Game Traffick	19
Mean time a Pair of awkward Things	80	Vanbrug House	35
A goodly pair, erect and wide, ...	157	Fable of Midas	31
"To make a pair of Jolly Fellows, ...	181	Horace 2, 1	43
Who now the wandring Pair pursues:	224	Prog of Love	74
And, thus set out this happy Pair, ...	290	Prog Marriage	27
Besides a pair of princely Babyes, ...	465	Birthday Song	171
A Pair of Tweezers next he found	527	Lady's Dres Rm	55
That now the Pair must crown their Joys.	586	Strephon Chloe	70
In Bed we left the married Pair;	588	Strephon Chloe	145
No Age could furnish out a Pair	722	Stel B-Day '18	11
And here's a pair of leathern pokes, ...	753	Gift for Bec	17
A Pair to make a Country Dance, ...	756	Stel B-day '24	8
That such a pair of wealthy Ninnies	821	Dr. Rundle	63
On the Puppy Pair of Dicks;	835	Legion Club	146
And rather than come in the same Pair of Sheets . .	869	Grand Question	59
A pair of Brogues to bear thee dry to Mass! . . .	882	Pastoral Dial	50
And thus, the Pair of humble Gentry, ...	883	Rev Market-Hill	17
And rub thy Teeth, and pair thy Nails.	897	Panegyr Dean	334
Dear Sheridan; a loving Pair	1020	Nim-Dan-Dean 1 D	1
PAIR-ROYALS			
For Pair-royals and Sequents;	75	Game Traffick	14
PAIRS			
'Tis late, the old and younger Pairs, ...	280	Journal	55
PALACE			
Further than its own palace in her heart:	53	Temple Ill	54
Where may the Poets Palace ly?	109	V's House	100
(Without your passing thro the Palace	313	To Ford	63
And in his Palace fed and taught him.	514	Answer Fable	50
Nor, with your Kindred half the Palace crowd. . . .	533	To Mr. Gay	58
Nor, in a Palace built with Charge immense, . . .	533	To Mr. Gay	63
Who pull'd a Palace to the Ground, ...	727	To Stella	122
PALACES			
Still lurks in Palaces and Courts, ...	30	Ode to Temple	117
What Palaces shall we erect!	107	V's House	46
PALATE			
A Priest would please your Palate;	425	Five Ladies	10
'Twou'd please your Palate, like a feast, ...	546	Life of Swift	39
PALE			
Here a pale shape with upward footstep treads, . . .	35	Ode Sancroft	33
So would earth's face turn pale, and life decay, . .	53	Temple Ill	63
"Know no base action, at no guilt turn pale; . . .	55	Temple Ill	142
But was so dirty, pale and thin, ...	174	Horace 1, 7	119
From her pale Cheeks pretends to show	228	Prog of Beauty	94
Pale Avarice and lurking Fraud	243	Horace 4, 9	11
Now pale as Death, then blush'd and bow'd;	377	Apology Lady C	78
Pale Envy sickens--Errour flies--	387	Manly Virtue	121
While each pale Sinner hangs his Head, ...	579	Day Judgement	9
Pale Dropsy with a sallow Face, ...	895	Panegyr Dean	275
Wasted he appears, and pale, ...	936	Riddle 24 D	21
You may find they are all, by their yellow pale Hue, sick	1030	Dr. Helsham	27
PALL			
"Six Deans they say must bear the Pall.	562	Death of Swift	231
His Coat, an Us'rer's Velvet Pall, ...	904	Death Daphne	31
PALLADIO			
Palladio was not half so skill'd in	893	Panegyr Dean	199
PALLAS			
But Pallas owns Ardelia's Power, ...	121	Apollo Outwit	47
But Pallas, guardian of the Maid, ...	177	To Lord Harley	43
For Pallas, with celestial light, ...	178	To Lord Harley	49
Pallas first taught us Poetry and Spinning; . . .	276	Epilogue	38
Pallas, a Goddess chaste and wise, ...	302	Storm	1
"But, Pallas, you've apply'd too late, ...	304	Storm	37
"Good Madam Pallas, pray be easy, ...	305	Storm	70
The Bird of Pallas knows his Post, ...	324	Pethox	37
And finds out Pallas in the Skies:	692	Cadenus Vaness	187
Dear Pallas, I have been this Morn	692	Cadenus Vaness	188
But Pallas here was at a Stand;	693	Cadenus Vaness	211
And Pallas, if she broke the Laws, ...	695	Cadenus Vaness	264
In proper Season Pallas meets	695	Cadenus Vaness	284
Pallas had done more Harm than Good;	700	Cadenus Vaness	435
Whom Pallas, once Vanessa's Tutor, ...	701	Cadenus Vaness	464
On Pallas all Attempts are vain;	701	Cadenus Vaness	468
In spight of Pallas, now were grown;	701	Cadenus Vaness	473
Vanessa, tho' by Pallas taught, ...	702	Cadenus Vaness	488
Pallas had cross'd her first Intent, ...	712	Cadenus Vaness	833
Pallas observing Stella's Wit	723	To Stella	1
By Pallas breath'd into his Breast, ...	731	Stella, Poems	122
Thee, happy Island, Pallas call'd her own, . . .	790	St. Pat's Well	9
Like Pallas from my Father's Brain.	927	Riddle 10 D	10

		PAGE	TITLE	LINE
PALLAS	(CONTINUED)			
And if you be my Phoebus, pray who was your Pallas? .		977	Dean to Sherid	42
PALLIATE				
Though not to cure, yet palliate each Disease. . . .		535	To Mr. Gay	124
To palliate his Friend Oxford's Crimes, ...		550	Life of Swift	185
PALMS				
And by his Looks, had he held out his Palms, ...		234	Elegy on Demar	11
Her Milk-white Hands, both Palms and Backs, ...		584	Strephon Chloe	25
PALTRY SEE PAULTRY				
At paltry Ballyspellin '		441	Ballyspellin	42
Lay thy paltry Priviledge aside, ...		832	Legion Club	71
PAM				
Lord Pam in the Church (cou'd you think it) kneel'd down		809	Epigr Prelate	1
PAMPER				
To pamper luxury and pride;		676	Parson's Case	22
PAMPHLET				
A Pamphlet in Sir Rob's Defence		646	On Poetry	187
Flutters the feeble Pamphlet into Rags.		771	Horace 1, 14	30
In ev'ry vile Pamphlet you'll read the same Fancies, .		968	Letter Sherid	21
PAMPHLETEER SEE PARTY-PAMPHLETEER				
PAMPHLETS				
Henceforward shall print neither Pamphlets nor Linnen,		238	Excellent Song	28
What Pamphlets in a Court's Defence		503	Doctor Delaney	103
Some high-flown Pamphlets, I suppose---:		550	Life of Swift	183
And shou'd he write Pamphlets, no Great Man wou'd read 'em:		717	Answer Rebus	26
PAN				
Which tosst up in a Pan with Batter, ...		91	Bauc & Phil 1	61
That Phebus must give Place to Pan:		157	Fable of Midas	54
To Pan alone rich Misers call, ...		157	Fable of Midas	57
And there's the Jest, for Pan is All:		157	Fable of Midas	58
The Bottom of the Pan to grope, ...		528	Lady's Dres Rm	93
PAN'S				
And gave it for Pan's oaten Reed:		156	Fable of Midas	28
PANDARS				
Of Pandars to a vicious Mind, . . . ·.		480	Libel on D- D-	24
PANDORA'S				
As from within Pandora's Box, ...		528	Lady's Dres Rm	83
PANE				
That the letters appear'd revers'd on the Pane, . . .		264	Apollo	49
PANEGYRICK				
I take it for a Panegyrick.		505	Doctor Delaney	170
Who'll write my Panegyrick?---come, be stout: . . .		671	Epig Carthy 24	D 4
A Panegyrick on <Dean> <Swift>.		887	Panegyr Dean	34
Sometimes in Panegyrick high, ...		929	Riddle 15	D 5
PANEGYRICKS				
Your Panegyricks here provide, ...		657	On Poetry	469
Her fine Panegyricks are quite out of Season, . . .		716	Answer Rebus	21
PANEGYRICS				
His panegyrics then are ceased, ...		658	On Poetry	D 204
'Tis your gross panegyrics alone can bespatter. . . .		819	Archbi Cashel	14
PANNEL				
With driving wrong, will make the Pannel split: . . .		535	To Mr. Gay	132
PANT				
And with the Virtues pant to wear		498	Panegyr Swift	173
PANTHEON				
That nasty Pantheon.		856	Lady's Lament	150
PANTING				
Panting - - - and faultring - - - Humm'd and Ha'd, . .		377	Apology Lady C	79
With panting Heart, and earnest Eyes, ...		452	Modern Lady	230
PANTRIES				
Lock up from my Sight in Pantries and Cupboards: . .		263	Apollo	12
PANTRY-DOOR				
Stole to the Pantry-Door, and found		150	Corinna	18
In at the Pantry-door this Morn I slipt, ...		881	Pastoral Dial	29
PANTS				
An Author thus who pants for Fame		500	Doctor Delaney	11
PANYGYRICK				
Nor will in Panygyrick flatter.		729	Stella, Poems	56
PAP				
There to be stroak'd and fed with Pap;		607	Beasts Confess	210
PAPA				
Because her dear Papa commands.		585	Strephon Chloe	44
PAPER				
Supported high on Wings of Paper;		231	Prog of Poetry	44
On Paper Wings he takes his Flight, ...		252	Bubble	37
Conveys out my Paper of Hints by a Trick, ...		265	Apollo	81
This Bank is to make us a New Paper Mill, ...		287	Bank Down	11
This Paper they say, by the Help of a Quill, . . .		287	Bank Down	12
If nothing but Paper comes out of this Bank. . . .		287	Bank Down	15
For Rags will make Paper, and Pa-ba-ba-brags, . . .		287	Bank Down	17
This Paper will soon make us richer than Crags. . .		287	Bank Down	18
For Beggars have Rags and Rags will make Paper, . .		287	Bank Down	22
And Paper makes Money, and what can be cheaper? . .		287	Bank Down	23
That Paper would quickly be dearer than Gold, . . .		288	Bank Down	32
With a Scrap of Bank Paper the Breadth of his Nail; . .		288	Bank Down	38
While his Tenants in Paper must pay him his Rent: . .		288	Bank Down	53
Oppose his Counter-Charm of Paper, ...		354	Simile Silver	26
On Paper daub'd so foul, ...		425	Five Ladies	14
Of paper how is he profuse, ...		434	Answer Paulus	81
The paper gilt, & Cover marbled)		463	Birthday Song	88

591

PAPER	(CONTINUED)	PAGE	TITLE	LINE
Our Ink is black, our Paper white;		463	Birthday Song	108
And when we scrawl our Paper o'r'e,		463	Birthday Song	109
And write on paper black as Jet:		463	Birthday Song	114
Some Paragraph in ev'ry Paper,		558	Death of Swift	167
With greasy Paper stuck upon't.		582	Young Nymph	36
A Paper Book is sent by Boyle,		611	By Dr. Swift	1
They burnish paper, or they bite a rogue:		672	Epig Carthy 25	D 2
Furnish'd with Paper, Pens, and Ink,		740	Stel B-day 22	3
The People's Voice expands his Paper Sail;		770	Horace 1, 14	28
Revile that Nation-saving Paper,		796	Traulus 1	11
His famous Letters made waste Paper;		875	Drapier's Hill	17
Provide me but with Paper Wings,		930	Riddle 15	D 18
On paper dribble daintily.		983	Sher, A Goose	8
. . .for you see plainly my Paper is ended.		1014	Swift to Sheri	12
PAPER-SPARING				
Lend these to Paper-sparing Pope;		395	Grub-Street	13
PAPER-STAMP				
Of late indeed the Paper-Stamp		172	Horace 1, 7	43
PAPERS SEE NEWS-PAPERS				
"Or do the Prints and Papers lye?		202	Horace 2, 6	95
What Papers Phil had left behind,		223	Prog of Love	44
On all Whig Papers, and Gazets:		282	Journal	100
For old Nick gave the Papers the Mark of the Bank.		288	Bank Down	45
PAPIST				
Papist, and Jacobite, and Lib'ller?		795	Traulus 1	4
PAPISTS				
Papists disarm'd, or Fall of Coin,		63	Discovery	31
Sprung from Papists and a Regicide;		832	Legion Club	72
PAPS				
And Broth enough to fill her Paps,		208	Fable Bitches	20
PAR				
To praise it, par maniere d'acquit;		379	Apology Lady C	120
PAR'D				
Had par'd the Dirt, and Sprinkled round the Floor.		124	Descriptn Morn	6
PARADE				
Be rich; but of your Wealth make no Parade;		533	To Mr. Gay	61
In State return'd the grand Parade;		586	Strephon Chloe	68
PARADES SEE PARK-PARADES				
PARADICE				
It seems some floating piece of Paradice,		17	Ode Athenian	44
PARADISES				
These are the Paradises of her own;		31	Ode to Temple	145
PARADOX				
How strange a Paradox is true,		25	Ode Athenian	305
We odly Plato's Paradox make good,		27	Ode to Temple	29
When a paradox you stick to,		908	Daphne	57
PARADOXES				
Paradoxes weakly wielding,		906	Daphne	7
PARAGRAPH				
Some Paragraph in ev'ry Paper,		558	Death of Swift	167
PARALLEL				
In ev'ry Court the Parallel will hold;		536	To Mr. Gay	135
PARALLELLS				
All Parallells exactly run;		226	Prog of Beauty	10
PARAPHRASE				
It is but a Paraphrase made on a Punn;		716	Answer Rebus	10
PARASITE				
A dirty parasite and slave;		951	Upstart	D 26
PARCEL				
First, this large parcel brings you tidings		753	Gift for Bec	5
A parcel of Teagues,		856	Lady's Lament	162
PARCHMENT				
A Scrap of Parchment hung by Geometry,		99	Elegy Patrige	41
And what is Parchment else but Leather?		99	Elegy Patrige	44
They fly like Bats, on Parchment Wings,		239	Run Bankers	23
A Parchment of prodigious Size;		354	Simile Silver	22
But, to this Parchment let the Draper		354	Simile Silver	25
That Sound will make the Parchment shrivel,		354	Simile Silver	29
Or, on Parchment, Ink turn'd yellow:		523	Betty Grizette	8
Stuck artfully a Parchment Case.		904	Death Daphne	36
PARD'NING				
In pard'ning, as in punishing,		1005	Sheridan's Sub	15
PARDIE				
There shall be Peace, pardie, and War no more.		147	Windsor Proph	12
PARDON				
Pardon Ye great Unknown, and far-exalted Men,		17	Ode Athenian	60
Yet pardon, native Albion, when I say		38	Ode Sancroft	128
He sues for Pardon, and repents too late.		195	Author Himself	52
His Pardon begg'd, but to be plain,		224	Prog of Love	57
We'll pardon you for what is past.		315	To Ford	112
You'll pardon me Sir, your Cunning I smoak,		336	Serious Poem	65
The Hangman for Pardon fell down on his Knee;		399	Tom Clinch	13
Pardon, if I disobey:		634	Epistle Lady	134
Cringing comes to beg their Pardon;		800	Traulus 2	14
Most humbly sues for Pardon.		1005	Sheridan's Sub	7
PARE				
I wish some Folks would pare their Nails.		453	Modern Lady	269
Who artfully will pare and prune		469	Birthday Song	277
PARENT				
Parent of Valour and of Fame,		7	Ode to King	24

PARENT   (CONTINUED)   PAGE   TITLE   LINE
   Crusts o'er the day, shadowing its parent beam . . . .   45 To Congreve   71
   As parent earth, burst by imprison'd winds, ...   52 Temple Ill   37
   As parent of the golden ore, ...   433 Answer Paulus   24
   My Parent and I produce one another, ...   929 Riddle 13   D 9
PARENT'S
   Heaven with a parent's eye regarding earth, ...   54 Temple Ill   89
PARENTS
   Last year, a lad hence by his parents sent . . . . .   46 To Congreve   115
   Her Parents and her Friends consent, ...   290 Prog Marriage   5
   Now, Ponder well ye Parents dear; . . . .   587 Strephon Chloe   115
   Are all my parents more than he: . . . .   936 Riddle 24   D 4
PARING-KNIFE
   Will Forge for thee a Paring-Knife, ...   100 Elegy Patrige   84
PARIS
   From Paris Gazette A-la-main, ...   398 Earl of P-b-w   10
   And Hell to be sure is at Paris or Rome, ...   576 Place Damn'd   17
PARISH
   He gathers all the Parish there; . . . .   116 Bauc & Phil 2   170
   The Parish jear'd him to his Face; . . . .   221 A Quiet Life   46
   While all the Parish, as she flies, ...   230 Prog of Poetry   15
   Computes, that half a Parish Dues . . . .   292 Prog Marriage   69
   His Baily Driving all my Cows into the Parish Pound.   343 Upon His Grace   4
   Inquire through all the Parish round . . . .   602 Beasts Confess   43
   No parish ducking-stool can tame her, ...   618 Scandal Poem 1   36
   No Parish Ducking-Stool can tame her: . . . . . .   624 Scandal Poem 2   34
   I, as all the Parish knows, ...   634 Epistle Lady   137
   To Moorlands of a diff'rent Parish. . . . .   645 On Poetry   174
PARK   SEE WOOD-PARK
   In Summer round the Park to ride, ...   173 Horace 1, 7   85
   St James's Park and Stephen's Green; . . . .   313 To Ford   60
   And as he wandred in his Park, ...   513 Answer Fable   45
   Wou'd seldom at the Park appear, ...   696 Cadenus Vaness   312
PARK-PARADES
   From Equipage and Park-Parades, ...   688 Cadenus Vaness   46
PARLI'MENT
   Court, nor Parli'ment, can 'scape ye; . . . . . .   631 Epistle Lady   54
PARLIAMENT
   By a Parliament Man when the Farmer was told, . . .   288 Bank Down   31
   Musha! Why Parliament wouldn't you maul, ...   841 Ballad   D 16
   A <Parliament>, or Den of Thieves. . . . . . .   645 On Poetry   164
   <Privilege> of <Parliament>, ...   833 Legion Club   116
PARLIAMENT-HOUSE
   Who d vote a Rogue into the Parliament-house, . . .   396 Dog and Thief   19
PARLIAMENTS
   In parliaments, or pudding-pies. . . . .   901 Dean's Reasons   80
PARLOUR
   To Kitchin, Parlour, Nurs'ry flies, ...   322 First of April   37
PARLY
   Quo' She, no longer parly; . . . .   154 Widow and Cat D 32
PARNASSUS
   And 'twas perhaps Parnassus, if in height . . . .   16 Ode Athenian   8
   Till then it was lock'd in my Box at Parnassus; . .   265 Apollo   79
   Or, to Parnassus looking down, ...   620 Scandal Poem 1   109
   Or, to Parnassus looking down, ...   626 Scandal Poem 2   107
   E'er I reach'd Parnassus Top . . . .   638 Epistle Lady   261
PARNASSUS'
   And litter'd at Parnassus' Foot. . . . .   504 Doctor Delaney   122
   If, on Parnassus' Top you sit, ...   651 On Poetry   329
   Parnassus' Hill has but two Tops, ...   671 Epig Carthy 22 D 4
PARNEL
   "From Pope, from Parnel, or from Gay? . . . . . .   201 Horace 2, 6   74
PARNELL
   The Doctor and Dean, Pope, Parnell and Gay   185 Scriblerus 1   1
PARODOX
   This parodox I'll undertake . . . .   433 Answer Paulus   45
PARROT
   A Dog, a Parrot, or an Ape, ...   687 Cadenus Vaness   39
   Conning old Topicks like a Parrot, ...   728 Stella, Poems   26
PARSON
   Parson, said I, can you cast a Nativity, . . .   72 Mrs Harris Pet   53
   (Now you must know, he hates to be call'd Parson, . . . 72 Mrs Harris Pet   54
   With these is Parson Swift, ...   75 Game Traffick D 25
   Make me the Parson if you please. . . . .   94 Bauc & Phil 1   164
   Make me the Parson, if you please. . . . .   115 Bauc & Phil 2   116
   Thus having furbish'd up a Parson, ...   115 Bauc & Phil 2   137
   Till once, a Parson of our Town, ...   117 Bauc & Phil 2   173
   So, the next Parson stub'd and burnt it. . . . .   117 Bauc & Phil 2   178
   And saw the Parson creeping out; . . . .   127 Little House   26
   Observ'd a Parson near Whitehall, ...   170 Horace 1, 7   5
   In quest, who might this Parson be, ...   171 Horace 1, 7   19
   Nor shew'd the Parson in his Gait or Face; . . .   194 Author Himself   14
   Be by a Parson cheated! . . . .   426 Five Ladies   25
   The Parson safe at Church, ...   426 Five Ladies   43
   "This Morning when the Parson came, ...   452 Modern Lady   238
   The Rites perform'd, the Parson paid, ...   586 Strephon Chloe   67
   A Dean's but a Parson, and what is a Rebus? . . .   716 Answer Rebus   7
   In vain--for the Devil a Parson wou'd stir. . . .   804 Irish Bishops   20
   If truly you would be reveng'd on the parson, . . .   818 Epigr Kite   5
   "I ne'er knew a Parson without a good Nose, . . .   872 Grand Question   143
   "Observe how a Parson comes into a Room, ...   872 Grand Question   155

	PAGE	TITLE	LINE	
PARSON (CONTINUED)				
"The first Man I robb'd was a Parson by <God>.	873	Grand Question	170	
But then, a Parson so genteel,	889	Panegyr Dean	75	
Nor can our Parson blame the Thing:	926	Riddle 9	14	
Lord! said I, who's that parson? how awkwardly dangles he	978	Dean to Tho: S	2	
For a Parson, who shou'd know better Things,	985	Mary to Sher	6	
PARSON'S				
. . .I design to be a Parson's Wife,	72	Mrs Harris Pet	60	
Such Hatred to a Parson's Gown,	416	Woman's Mind	15	
Sometimes to act the Parson's Part:	605	Beasts Confess	120	
PARSONABLE				
My Master is a parsonable Man,	985	Mary to Sher	10	
PARSONS				
Lord, what a Dress these Parsons wear,	291	Prog Marriage	42	
And in the sneaking Parsons Airs	292	Prog Marriage	68	
Our Parsons Read the Draper's Books, and make us honest Foke.	343	Upon His Grace	40	
Then let us no longer by Parsons be Flam'd,	576	Place Damn'd	15	
Those Splitters of Parsons in sunder shou'd burst?	805	Irish Bishops	40	
(And, Parsons tell us, no Man can do more)	806	Judas	6	
At the Parsons, Tom, Halloo Boy,	831	Legion Club	67	
With Parsons, what Lady can keep herself clean?	868	Grand Question	29	
The Parsons, for Envy, are ready to burst:	871	Grand Question	134	
"You'll never want Parsons as long as you live;	872	Grand Question	142	
If gravest Parsons here advance,	928	Riddle 12	D 17	
PART				
Part of Your Merit Chance wou'd call her own,	11	Ode to William	D 11	
And all we Fools, who are the greater part of it,	18	Ode Athenian	71	
The Rebel Muse, alas, takes part	23	Ode Athenian	238	
Could leap the bounds which part your world and mine;	44	To Congreve	30	
Peruse my Leaves thro' ev'ry Part,	60	Lady Tablebook	1	
Whoe're expects to hold his part	61	Lady Tablebook	25	
The Fair approach the speaking Part,	66	Problem	41	
. . .and I always take his Part;	72	Mrs Harris Pet	51	
Makes you take all things in good Part:	94	Bauc & Phil 1	160	
The Queen has lately lost a Part	96	On the Union	1	
And each Part took a diff'rent Side;	99	Elegy Patrige	66	
The Cobling and Star-gazing Part,	100	Elegy Patrige	70	
At Christnings well could act his Part,	115	Bauc & Phil 2	129	
I'll disappoint its Nobler Part.	121	Apollo Outwit	52	
Apollo play'd the Midwife's Part,	149	Corinna	2	
Come then, my lord, and take your part in	186	Scriblerus 3	7	
Then come and take part in	186	Scriblerus 4	D 13	
Here, onely Nature acts her Part,	215	To Mr. Delany	21	
Part in worse humor than they met?	217	To Mr. Delany	72	
Some part of what I here design	218	To Mr. Delany	89	
Scarce run a Step before they part;	290	Prog Marriage	32	
Now, for my part, I think upon the whole,	308	Billet Players	15	
Would he were here this night to act my part.	308	Billet Players	32	
United close in ev'ry Part.	344	Prometheus	6	
Compleatly form'd in every Part,	385	Manly Virtue	55	
Chang'd for the worse in ev'ry Part,	410	Dial Rich Marb	71	
It was a most unfriendly Part	444	Modern Lady	1	
At Table now she acts her Part,	448	Modern Lady	100	
He wou'd have chose a milder part;	485	Libel on D- D-	158	
How, Pain they might from Pleasure part:	501	Doctor Delaney	32	
But, the State-Emp'ric acts a safer Part;	534	To Mr. Gay	81	
Perhaps, his Travels, Part the Third;	550	Life of Swift	190	
"But dearest Friends, they say, must part.	562	Death of Swift	240	
"He spent his Life's declining Part;	570	Death of Swift	432	
But, still the hardest Part remains.	586	Strephon Chloe	71	
Sometimes to act the Parson's Part:	605	Beasts Confess	120	
To act the Part of Tray, or Cupid;	607	Beasts Confess	208	
Proceed no further in your Part,	647	On Poetry	239	
But these are not a thousandth Part	650	On Poetry	311	
The Graces next wou'd act their Part,	692	Cadenus Vaness	172	
Your Lessons found the weakest Part,	706	Cadenus Vaness	622	
The part of wholesome exercise:	761	Bec's B-Day	28	
To shine through Life's declining Part.	764	Stel B-day '26	34	
Your former Actions claim their Part,	765	Stel B-day '26	71	
And should you act, a diff'rent Part,	776	Mullinix Tim	89	
Perform the part of Punchinelloes;	777	Mullinix Tim	136	
Were hanged, before they'd part with you.	778	Mullinix Tim	150	
Condensed Filth in e'ry Part,	787	Clad in Brown	15	
My Spud these Nettles from the Stones can part,	881	Pastoral Dial	11	
The Butter from the Whey to part:	892	Panegyr Dean	182	
None could ever act that part,	907	Daphne	23	
Approaching, finds it hard to part	922	Riddle 7	35	
They part not till the Ring is broke.	926	Riddle 9	16	
That we both act the Part of the Clown and the Cow-dung	967	Letter Sherid	2	
For my part, it was by meer Chance	1013	Swift to Sheri	3	
You won't part with a Spoon-full,	1015	Swift to Sheri	50	
The Short'ning is the nicest Part.	1021	Nim-Dan-Dean 1	D 36	
PART'NER				
And makes her Part'ner understand	452	Modern Lady	260	
PARTED				
Nor cou'd they now be parted;	153	Widow and Cat	D 7	
PARTERRE				
"No gay Parterre with costly Green,	476	Epist on Epist	53	
PARTERRES				
In Whims, Parterres, Canals and Fences:	477	Epist on Epist	62	

	PAGE	TITLE	LINE
PARTHENOPE			
Or from Parthenope the proud,	324	Pethox	21
PARTIAL			
If Law be such a partial Whore,	392	Young's Satire	45
He ne'er was partial to his Kin;	606	Beasts Confess	176
And Criticks have no partial Views,	644	On Poetry	131
PARTIALL			
Let me of partiall Fate complain;	739	Stel B-day '21	6
PARTICLES			
The Jumbling Particles of Matter	450	Modern Lady	184
PARTIES			
All Parties and Religions joyn;	345	Prometheus	12
The Parties ne'er could Issue join:	690	Cadenus Vaness	123
She gave due Notice, that both Parties,	713	Cadenus Vaness	838
Of Parties o're our Bonny-Clabber.	781	Mullinix Tim	260
PARTING			
Approaching joy at strife with parting woe.	51	Temple Ill	22
But for a parting Present leave her	295	Prog Marriage	165
PARTIUM			
(Consult his Book de Partium usu)	367	Answer Delaney	32
PARTLY			
'Tis partly false, and partly true,	464	Birthday Song	138
'Tis partly false, and partly true,	464	Birthday Song	138
PARTNER			
Some bungling Partner takes,	75	Game Traffick	10
But why shou'd we fight thus, my partner so dear,	979	Dean to Tho: S	33
PARTRIDGE			
While Partridge wisely shews the Cause	228	Prog of Beauty	89
In tipling at the Dog and Partridge;	411	Dial Rich Marb	98
Is good for Partridge, not for Hares.	940	Letter	11
PARTRIDGES			
A Fig for Partridges and Quails	733	Verses Vanessa	27
She look'd on Partridges with scorn	746	Stel Distress	13
She look'd on Partridges with scorn,	750	Stel Wood-Park	11
PARTS			
To praise your parts by publishing of mine;	44	To Congreve	34
Brings his good parts and breeding in debate;	48	To Congreve	156
Thus Patrige, by his Wit and Parts,	99	Elegy Patrige	47
Now from all Parts the swelling Kennels flow,	139	City Shower	53
With all acquir'd and nat'ral parts,	176	To Lord Harley	10
To show their Parts, will scold and rail,	216	To Mr. Delany	49
The Monster into Parts divide,	258	Bubble	203
In all Parts of the Globe, where your Language is read;	265	Apollo	70
Fellows of modest Worth and Parts,	314	To Ford	81
Than suffer Men of Parts to rise:	503	Doctor Delaney	92
To taint the Parts from whence they fell.	529	Lady's Dres Rm	112
Just in the Parts, where I complain;	557	Death of Swift	136
"That all his vital Parts were sound.	559	Death of Swift	176
Have better learn'd to act their Parts.	562	Death of Swift	226
To recollect the scatter'd Parts?	583	Young Nymph	68
(With other Parts that shall be nameless,	586	Strephon Chloe	79
Than she, to name her Parts behind,	590	Strephon Chloe	217
Yet, with his Beauty, Wealth, and Parts,	598	Problem Solved	19
Are won by Virtue, Wit, and Parts;	688	Cadenus Vaness	62
Eject it to th' extreamest parts,	761	Bec's B-Day	14
Or blest with such engaging Parts,	779	Mullinix Tim	199
Your Parts are good, 'tis not deny'd,	779	Mullinix Tim	209
Choice Spirits, who employ their Parts,	780	Mullinix Tim	245
Ierne, to the World's remotest Parts,	789	St. Pat's Well	5
The Students drinking, rais'd their Wit and Parts;	793	St. Pat's Well	70
If they fail 'tis Want of Parts.	837	Legion Club	188
You celebrate their Wit and Parts!	887	Panegyr Dean	12
PARTY			
So I went to the Party suspected,	71	Mrs Harris Pet	34
In Party, furious to her Power;	417	Woman's Mind	49
From Paean's Fire to Party Zeal;	481	Libel on D- D-	44
And give up Party to his Fame.	485	Libel on D- D-	150
The Ruin'd Party made his Sport,	498	Panegyr Swift	160
By telling Noses with a Party strong.	533	To Mr. Gay	60
For Party he would scarce have Bled---:	549	Life of Swift	142
Nor for a Party give his Vote:	604	Beasts Confess	98
A Party next of glitt'ring Dames,	698	Cadenus Vaness	364
Of all thy Party through the Nation.	775	Mullinix Tim	56
Of keeping up a party hatred.	779	Mullinix Tim	184
Will our own Party mind me not?	779	Mullinix Tim	192
Party and Spleen have turn'd his Brain,	796	Traulus 1	14
The dullest Beast, and a Party distrest,	940	Letter	8
PARTY-FOOL			
No party-fool is calling names,	402	Window Inns 7	D 5
PARTY-MERIT			
From Party-Merit seek Support;	646	On Poetry	185
PARTY-PAMPHLETEER			
Or hire their Party-Pamphleteers,	647	On Poetry	217
PARTY-STEPS			
By Party-steps no Grandeur climb at,	503	Doctor Delaney	109
PARTYES			
Suppose all Partyes now agreed,	222	Prog of Love	21
PARVISOL			
And Parvisol discounts Arrears,	174	Horace 1, 7	111
PAS'T			
E'er a week pas't committing Blunders:	62	Discovery	4

```
                                                      PAGE   TITLE           LINE
PASQUILS
     They're fit for nothing else but pasquils.  . . . . .   982 Sher, A Goose      2
PASQUIN
     Nor can you prove it, Mr. Pasquin.  . . . . . . .       350 Upright Judge 3    2
PASQUINE
     I hope you will not think this a Pasquine  . . . . .   1018 Swift Ans Sher    34
PASS
     Whence the weak shapes wild and imperfect pass,  . . .    35 Ode Sancroft      23
     Like the sun's scatter'd beams which loosely pass,  . .   45 To Congreve       63
     I'll be my life but the dull cheat would pass,  . . . .   48 To Congreve      171
     So many Beggers pass this way, . . . . . . . .            90 Bauc & Phil 1     29
     In his poor House to pass the Night; . . . . . . .        91 Bauc & Phil 1     54
     In his Poor Hut to pass the Night;  . . . . . . .        111 Bauc & Phil 2     22
     A Traveller, who by did pass,  . . . . . . . .           127 Little House      23
     Such gross Delusions could not pass, . . . . . . .       158 Fable of Midas    65
     But as a Guinnea will not pass . . . . . . . .           255 Bubble           117
     Where for fear of the Cold, I never can pass;  . . . .   264 Apollo            32
     How George, Nim, Dan, Dean pass their Days;  . . . .     278 Journal            2
     Not reckoning half an hour we pass,  . . . . . . .       279 Journal           37
     And this must pass for reading Hammond: . . . . .        280 Journal           41
     Now ask me a Question. How came it to pass  . . . .      336 Serious Poem      85
     (Venus was Brib'd to let it pass.) . . . . . . .         345 Prometheus        40
     But sure if nothing else must pass, . . . . . . .        346 Prometheus        67
     Which near the Os Petrosum pass; . . . . . . .           367 Answer Delaney    36
     If Wood's Coin should 'mongst Us pass  . . . . . .       372 Letter D. S-y     35
     Tho' now I'm poor I them might pass  . . . . . . .       372 Letter D. S-y     36
     And making -- some for Ideots pass . . . . . . .         373 Letter D. S-y     58
     "To pass to many crowded Stages,  . . . . . . .          380 Apology Lady C   155
     Here no conceited coxcombs pass, . . . . . . . .         402 Window Inns 7    D 3
     To pass another Pop-ry bill  . . . . . . . .             422 Ireld             44
     How shall we pass the Time between?  . . . . . .         451 Modern Lady      205
     To make it pass upon the Nation,  . . . . . . .          475 Epist on Epist    19
     Grave D. of St <Patrick> how comes it to pass  . . .     522 St. Cecilia's      1
     The Virtues we must not let pass,  . . . . . . .         527 Lady's Dres Rm    59
     And strive to pass, in publick view,? . . . . . .        546 Life of Swift     35
     Himself, pass only for the Second---? . . . . . .        546 Life of Swift     57
     And then to make them pass the glibber,  . . . . .       561 Death of Swift   199
     "Who fain would pass for Lords indeed:  . . . . .        570 Death of Swift   438
     To pass for Wits before a Rake!  . . . . . . .           592 Strephon Chloe   268
     Except to pass an Hour away:  . . . . . . . .            607 Beasts Confess   188
     And, if the whole may pass for true, . . . . . . .       608 Know Not What      5
     So beautifull to pass for Juno?  . . . . . . .           619 Scandal Poem 1    64
     So beautiful to pass for Juno? . . . . . . . .           625 Scandal Poem 2    60
     Pass our Nights, to drive out thinking.  . . . . .       632 Epistle Lady      86
     Will pass for yours with Foes and Friends.  . . . .      644 On Poetry        140
     Pope's Essays upon some for Young's may pass,  . . .     670 Epig Carthy 18   D 5
     So green in different Lights may pass for blue,  . .     670 Epig Carthy 18   D 7
     The Girl might pass, if we cou'd get her . . . . .       700 Cadenus Vaness   428
     Thro' this she made all Objects pass,  . . . . .         709 Cadenus Vaness   718
     All Men of Sense will pass your Dore  . . . . .          736 Stel B-day '20    57
     And Wrinkles undistinguish'd pass, . . . . . . .         758 Stel B-day '24    45
     But for a blooming Nymph will pass,  . . . . . .         760 Receipt Youth     39
     Must these like empty Shadows pass, . . . . . . .        765 Stel B-day '26    51
     Pass only now for empty sounds?  . . . . . . .           779 Mullinix Tim     188
     When Shells and Leather shall for Money pass,  . . .     793 St. Pat's Well    93
     To slender Threads, may sometimes pass for Lawn. . . .   806 Judas             16
     And to make your Project pass, . . . . . . . .           839 Legion Club      217
     Their fame to future times shall pass, . . . . .         876 To Dean Swift     12
     What Pints may best for Bottles pass,  . . . . .         889 Panegyr Dean      93
     In at each Mouth the Spirits pass, . . . . . . .         920 Riddle 6          13
     How soon all human Pleasures pass. . . . . . . .         921 Riddle 7           6
     In at this Gulph all Off'rings pass, . . . . . .         922 Riddle 7          43
     (Or they can never pass the Gate)  . . . . . . .         928 Riddle 12        D 14
     They cannot pass before they dance;  . . . . . .         928 Riddle 12        D 18
     To make their Water pass:  . . . . . . . .               952 Asparagus          3
     I pass now where you fleer and laugh  . . . . .         1004 Dan J's Reply     25
PASS'D
     Having thro' all the Village pass'd, . . . . . .         111 Bauc & Phil 2     17
     The Time pass'd on, and Musick came,  . . . . . .        208 Fable Bitches     37
     And as he pass'd, so swell'd the Dee . . . . . .         476 Epist on Epist    45
     He pass'd his Hours among his Books; . . . . . .         604 Beasts Confess   105
     They never pass'd for Law in Courts; . . . . . .         690 Cadenus Vaness   113
     You must have pass'd among the Crowd. . . . . .          742 Stel B-day 22     48
     Let a royal Grant be pass'd, . . . . . . . .             830 Legion Club       42
PASS'T
     From ev'ry Age through which it pass't, . . . . .         22 Ode Athenian     214
     Having thro all the Village pass't,  . . . . . .          91 Bauc & Phil 1     49
     Untouch't it pass't between his Grinders,  . . . .       156 Fable of Midas    11
PASSAGE
     Gives murmuring passage to a lasting wave; . . . .        49 To Congreve      188
     From giving Passage to a <Turd>. . . . . . . .            66 Problem           26
     Some new unbeaten Passage to the Sky;  . . . . .         210 Earl of Oxford    12
     A passage to the land I hate.  . . . . . . .             420 Holyhead          28
     A Passage may be found, I've heard,  . . . . . .         479 Epist on Epist   119
     With a Passage left to creep in, . . . . . . .           830 Legion Club       45
     Where many for a Passage venture,  . . . . . .           928 Riddle 12        D 3
PASSENGERS
     He has not passengers enough.  . . . . . . . .           420 Holyhead          10
PASSES
     Where all that passes, inter nos,  . . . . . . .         201 Horace 2, 6       79
     Passes the Lower Castle Yard,  . . . . . . . .           376 Apology Lady C    29
```

                                  596

		PAGE	TITLE	LINE
PASSES	(CONTINUED)			
It passes but for common Form;		453	Modern Lady	271
For sheer Wit, and Humour passes!		523	Betty Grizette	34
And whatever passes		938	Riddle Answer'd	5
PASSING				
And passing o'er, mistakes thee still for mine:		54	Temple Ill	92
Make Room; as if a Duke were passing by.		194	Author Himself	36
In the Pell-mell when passing by,		228	Prog of Beauty	73
To seise you in your passing by:		257	Bubble	176
(Without your passing thro the Palace		313	To Ford	63
And snap some Cully passing by;		583	Young Nymph	50
There's Nimble Tim a passing by.		778	Mullinix Tim	182
PASSING-BELL				
"Before the Passing-Bell begun,		558	Death of Swift	151
PASSION				
And shap'd my passion in such words as these.		53	Temple Ill	80
So sweet a Passion who cou'd think,		65	Problem	3
You find his Passion by his Scent.		66	Problem	18
So from my Lord his Passion broke,		66	Problem	47
By Vow Oblig'd, By Passion led,		120	Apollo Outwit	33
The Doctor in a Passion cry'd;		175	Horace 1, 7	131
The Nymph who still with Passion burnd,		293	Prog Marriage	117
Nay would it not Your Passion raise		312	To Ford	37
If that same Universal Passion		392	Young's Satire	35
A Passion for a Scarlet-Coat;		415	Woman's Mind	2
Will damp all Passion Sympathetick;		588	Strephon Chloe	134
On Sense and Wit your Passion found,		593	Strephon Chloe	307
My purest Passion has betray'd.		595	Cassinus Peter	58
Or, to Passion quickly heated;		630	Epistle Lady	16
What can all this Passion mean?		635	Epistle Lady	182
Young's universal Passion, Pride,		640	On Poetry	3
Or grant her Passion be sincere,		707	Cadenus Vaness	640
While ev'ry Passion of her Mind		709	Cadenus Vaness	710
By this new Passion grew inspir'd.		709	Cadenus Vaness	717
Constr'ing the Passion she had shown,		711	Cadenus Vaness	764
Love, why do we one Passion call?		711	Cadenus Vaness	772
His Want of Passion will redeem,		711	Cadenus Vaness	786
And what is worse, your Passion bends		730	Stella, Poems	97
One Passion, with a diff'rent Turn,		731	Stella, Poems	117
From Passion you may then be freed,		731	Stella, Poems	135
Judgement weak, and Passion strong,		800	Traulus 2	17
What care we how high runs his passion or pride?		817	Yahoo's	71
Dear Dick, prithee tell by what passion you move?		818	Archbi Cashel	1
With mutual Beauty smit, their Passion grew.		880	Pastoral Dial	6
You ne'er was known, by Passion stir'd,		889	Panegyr Dean	69
To leave off this passion which does not become you:		976	Dean to Sherid	10
PASSION'S				
His Favor, when his Passion's over.		224	Prog of Love	70
PASSIONS SEE TYRANT-PASSIONS				
Whether all Passions, when in Ferment,		66	Problem	15
So when our passions Love hath stirr'd,		402	Window Inns 6	D 3
Their Passions not more impotent and cold,		532	To Mr. Gay	21
O'er all your passions we preside:		620	Scandal Poem 1	90
O'er all your passions we preside:		626	Scandal Poem 2	88
Their Passions move in lower Spheres,		687	Cadenus Vaness	37
All Passions must be laid aside:		724	To Stella	36
Yet when I find your Passions rise,		731	Stella, Poems	113
When out my brutish passions break,		754	Stella '23	11
Or melts my passions down with tears:		754	Stella '23	14
No Passions so weak		939	Riddle Answer'd	11
PAST				
And one would think 'twere past Omnipotence to please;		9	Ode to King	89
It lost some mighty Pieces thro' all hands it past		25	Ode Athenian	286
The bitter cup is from him past:		40	Ode Sancroft	202
At length 'tis over-blown and past,		41	Ode Sancroft	219
Time is no more when th' utmost drop is past;		49	To Congreve	190
Thy looks, when every cause of grief is past!		52	Temple Ill	34
The Poetry of Ages past,		81	Vanbrug House	90
The Poetry of Ages past,		110	V's House	132
Discoursing on old Stories past,		116	Bauc & Phil 2	152
The Thing was done and past recalling:		224	Prog of Love	68
Now, whereas the said Criminal seems past Repentance,		266	Apollo	93
You find his Rev'rence past his Prime,		293	Prog Marriage	104
For Husbands past their Youth to find;		293	Prog Marriage	116
We'll pardon you for what is past.		315	To Ford	112
Has lost His Grace for Ten Years past .		341	Upon His Grace	10
The Hour of Dining now is past;		377	Apology Lady C	53
Askt me how our elections past.		422	Ireld	34
My Word is past, I must submit,		445	Modern Lady	26
"Past Six, and not a living Soul!		451	Modern Lady	202
A frosty Morn--Past Four a-Clock.		453	Modern Lady	283
The Danger past, takes Heart of Grace,		500	Doctor Delaney	25
For Poetry, he's past his Prime,		556	Death of Swift	99
One Year is past; a different Scene;		562	Death of Swift	245
"His way of Writing now is past;		563	Death of Swift	265
When Love's Allurements long are past;		711	Cadenus Vaness	783
We say, she's past her Dancing Days;		756	Stel B-day '24	2
Can look with Joy on what is past.		764	Stel B-day '26	18
Upheld by each good Action past,		765	Stel B-day '26	63
But you when all the Show is past		774	Mullinix Tim	41
And when the War is past you come		775	Mullinix Tim	49

```
PAST              (CONTINUED)                        PAGE   TITLE              LINE
    Sees the glorious Ages past.       . . . . . . . .    862  To Janus             16
    But Hannah, who listen'd to all that was past,   . .  868  Grand Question       41
    Bring all past Actions to thy Mind.      . . . .      921  Riddle 7              4
    But because the three former are long ago past,  . .  967  Letter Sherid        11
PASTE
    To brew her Ale, and raise her Paste:     . . . . .   282  Journal              90
    Not yet consign'd to Paste;      . . . . . . . . . .  394  Grub-Street           4
    A Paste of Composition rare,     . . . . . . . .      526  Lady's Dres Rm       23
    Some fill'd with Washes, some with Paste,   . . . .   526  Lady's Dres Rm       34
PASTED
    The Ballads pasted round the Wall,    . . . . . . .    93  Bauc & Phil 1       117
    The Ballads pasted on the Wall,   . . . . . . .       114  Bauc & Phil 2        93
PASTIME
    For Pastime, or to shew his Wit;      . . . . . . .   703  Cadenus Vaness      543
PASTIMES
    Such Pastimes, when our Taste is nice,    . . . . .   788  Dick's Variety       11
PASTORS
    Not like the Pastors of thy rav'nous Breed,   . . .  792  St. Pat's Well       31
PASTRY-COOKS
    "Last Monday to the Pastry-cooks.     . . . . . .    563  Death of Swift      260
PASTURE
    To the lov'd Pasture where he us'd to feed,   . . .   31  Ode to Temple       148
PAT
    Because he could find no Word to come pat in.  . . .  76  Lady B- B-            4
    And here a Simile comes Pat in:   . . . . . . . .    642  On Poetry            61
PATCH
    And where with Art to place a Patch.     . . . . .   416  Woman's Mind         32
    But, to patch up all our Quarrels,    . . . . . . .  637  Epistle Lady        235
    We begg'd her but to patch her Face,     . . . . .   700  Cadenus Vaness      422
    Or patch his broken Stocking Soals,      . . . . .   728  Stella, Poems        33
    To patch his broken fortunes, found      . . . . .   879  Robbin & Harry       31
    My broken Hose to patch and dern.     . . . . . . .  890  Panegyr Dean        112
PATCH'T
    Her Face patch't o'er with Modern Pedantry,   . . .   23  Ode Athenian        224
PATE
    She stun'd, and then she broke his Pate.    . . . .  221  A Quiet Life         44
    That fill a Female Gamester's Pate?      . . . . .   451  Modern Lady         225
    Why, Cassy, thou wilt doze thy Pate:     . . . . .   594  Cassinus Peter       29
    "With Hatchet blunter than thy Pate      . . . . .   851  Old Thorn            83
    "Thou hast certainly gotten a Cup in thy Pate.  . .  870  Grand Question       84
PATENT
    Produce at last thy dormant Ducal Patent:    . . .   538  Mr. Pulteney         10
PATENTS
    Patents, Instalments, Abjurations,    . . . . . . .  174  Horace 1, 7         102
PATERNAL
    Give up your fond paternal Pride,     . . . . . . .  644  On Poetry           127
    It shew'd a true Paternal Care--      . . . . . . .  707  Cadenus Vaness      653
PATERNALL
    His Wings are his Paternall Rent,     . . . . . . .  252  Bubble               45
PATES
    Sindges Hair, but breaks no Pates,    . . . . . . .  638  Epistle Lady        256
    Shall leave deciding broken Pates,    . . . . . . .  760  Receipt Youth        47
    And resolv'd to break their Pates,    . . . . . . .  833  Legion Club          95
PATH
    No wonder then she quits the narrow Path of Sense . .  18  Ode Athenian        68
PATHS
    To shew the Paths of both must be together trod,  . .  7  Ode to King         29
    The crooked Paths of wandering Thames.   . . . . . .  31  Ode to Temple      152
    Beat not the dirty paths where vulgar feet have trod, .  49  To Congreve      205
    Nor beaten Paths be longer trac'd.    . . . . . . .  270  Apollo's Edict    D 11
    What dangerous Paths young Virgins tread;   . . . .  696  Cadenus Vaness      311
PATIENCE
    Contriv'd to tire all patience out,   . . . . . . .   35  Ode Sancroft         15
    Cry'd bravely, Patience, good my Dear.   . . . . .   220  A Quiet Life          6
    To act his Patience, and her chiding.    . . . . .   221  A Quiet Life         54
    False Patience, and mistaken Pride!      . . . . .   221  A Quiet Life         55
    Can You, my Friend, with Patience bear,     . . . .  312  To Ford              36
    With Patience, which all Ills supports,     . . . .  325  Pethox               63
    And Patience can endure no more       . . . . . .    468  Birthday Song       245
    If this perhaps your Patience move    . . . . . . .  554  Death of Swift       11
    Would break the Patience of a Job,    . . . . . . .  604  Beasts Confess       88
    That Patience under tort'ring Pain,   . . . . . . .  765  Stel B-day '26       49
    But, I admire your Patience most;     . . . . . . .  891  Panegyr Dean        147
PATIENT
    Doctors pronounce the patient dead;   . . . . . . .  761  Bec's B-Day          12
    Pray be patient, you shall find   . . . . . . . . .  839  Legion Club         235
    And the patientest Patient that ever you knew sick; . . 1028  Dr. Helsham        3
PATIENT'S
    Is but the patient's death, and gain--   . . . . .    42  Ode Sancroft        258
PATIENTEST
    And the patientest Patient that ever you knew sick; . . 1028  Dr. Helsham        3
PATIENTLY
    With which she patiently complyes,    . . . . . . .  294  Prog Marriage       133
    How patiently you hear him groan!     . . . . . . .  554  Death of Swift       29
PATIENTS
    That moves his Patients to Repentance:   . . . . .   605  Beasts Confess      122
PATIMUR
    To cry, like statesmen, quanta patimur!     . . . .  433  Answer Paulus        42
PATR'OT-LIKE
    Whilst Patr'ot-like thou'lt strut and frown.  . . .  182  Horace 2, 1          64
```

	PAGE	TITLE	LINE
PATRICIAN			
When some Patrician God wou'd visit the Immortal Jayl,	9	Ode to King	93
Where high patrician souls dress'd heavenly gay, . . .	41	Ode Sancroft	234
PATRICK			
Patrick astore, what news upon the town?	840	Ballad	D 1
Patrick astore, who was him made this law?	841	Ballad	D 11
Grave D. of St <Patrick> how comes it to pass . . .	522	St. Cecilia's	1
PATRICK'S			
Hither convey St. Patrick's Well;	478	Epist on Epist	92
And take a Greater Patrick's Name.	478	Epist on Epist	94
Jolly boys of St. Kevans, St. Patrick's, Donore, .	814	Yahoo's	1
We'll colt him thro' Kevan, St. Patrick's, Donore, .	817	Yahoo's	56
Which is all at present from Dean of St. Patrick's.	977	Dean to Sherid	48
As that same viz. St. <Patrick's> Dean.	361	Grace's Answer	6
As well become St. <Patrick's> <Dean>;	889	Panegyr Dean	78
PATRICKS'			
And Patricks' bell she was ringing all in muffles; . .	840	Ballad	D 7
PATRIGE			
Patrige is Dead, nay more, he dy'd	98	Elegy Patrige	3
Just as if Patrige were not Dead;	98	Elegy Patrige	12
How Patrige made his Opticks rise, ...	98	Elegy Patrige	21
But Patrige ended all Disputes, ...	99	Elegy Patrige	33
Thus Patrige, by his Wit and Parts, ...	99	Elegy Patrige	47
So Learned Patrige could as well	99	Elegy Patrige	53
Thus Patrige still shines in each Art, ...	100	Elegy Patrige	69
PATRIOT			
As Poet and as Patriot too?	270	Apollo's Edict	D 6
Offend our Patriot, Great Sir <Robert>, ...	548	Life of Swift	108
Thy Mast, which like some aged Patriot stood . . .	770	Horace 1, 14	15
A Patriot is a dang'rous Post	798	Traulus 1	89
PATRIOT'S			
To regal Rage devotes some Patriot's Head.	364	On Dreams	12
PATRIOTS			
Oh! would these Patriots be so kind	255	Bubble	109
Make all true Patriots up to Shoe-boys	501	Doctor Delaney	61
Like supple Patriots of the modern Sort, ...	771	Horace 1, 14	55
PATRON			
Sole Patron of the building Trade, ...	79	Vanbrug House	24
Sole Patron of the Building Trade, ...	106	V's House	24
Subject or Patron of his Muse, ...	157	Fable of Midas	52
Apollo's patron of the laws;	433	Answer Paulus	22
The Dean, Tom's honour'd Friend and Patron. . . .	458	Paddy's Charac	28
Sole Patron, Judge, and God of Wit.	462	Birthday Song	72
Besides; your Patron may upbraid ye, ...	483	Libel on D- D-	103
PATRON'S			
Lewis his Patron's Humour knows;	171	Horace 1, 7	23
And to his Pious Patron's Ghost.	183	Horace 2, 1	92
Unanswer'd at your Patron's Gate;	475	Epist on Epist	6
You Forfeit all your Patron's Grace, ...	480	Libel on D- D-	30
Refuse our Patron's Call to dine;	495	Panegyr Swift	68
And draw like you my Patron's Face;	496	Panegyr Swift	111
When o'er your Patron's Treasure you preside, . . .	532	To Mr. Gay	16
Due Vengeance, for her Patron's sake.	701	Cadenus Vaness	471
PATRONAGE			
And from this Hour my Patronage resign.	794	St. Pat's Well	102
PATRONS			
His Money spent, his Patrons fail, ...	231	Prog of Poetry	33
For Patrons never pay so well, ...	463	Birthday Song	95
The Task is Arduous, Patrons find, ...	475	Epist on Epist	21
"The Patrons of the good old Cause, ...	549	Life of Swift	162
PATT			
Be frugal, Patt: pay what you owe, ...	479	Epist on Epist	115
PATTERN			
Be not the brightest pattern Earth can shew . . .	36	Ode Sancroft	52
Take Pattern by your Sister Star, ...	228	Prog of Beauty	69
Dick left a Pattern few will copy after, ...	430	Dicky Dolly	16
Observe this Pattern; there's a Stuff, ...	447	Modern Lady	84
For which they bring a modern Pattern, ...	460	Birthday Song	10
Best Pattern of true Friends, beware;	727	To Stella	117
Sir <Arthur>, since you set the Pattern, ...	888	Panegyr Dean	57
For all an example, for no one a pattern.	955	Portrait Life	8
PATTERNS			
Shew'd Patterns just from India brought, ...	698	Cadenus Vaness	378
Knew how to set you behind Patterns;	1033	Ans to Crown	16
PATTY			
Poor Patty Blount no more be seen	409	Dial Rich Marb	47
PAUL'S			
Like Paul's Ephesians, never heard it;	820	Dr. Rundle	16
PAULTRY			
Of paultry Provender and Bread:	156	Fable of Midas	18
To scratch their paultry drabs on glass;	402	Window Inns 7	D 4
And while, with all this paultry Stuff, ...	448	Modern Lady	109
Ye paultry underlings of state, ...	487	Irish-Club	1
That same paultry Burlesque Stile:	631	Epistle Lady	50
Why does he call him paultry Scribler;	795	Traulus 1	3
The Jews engag'd him with a paultry Bribe, ...	806	Judas	3
PAULUS			
And honest Paulus judges right.	432	Answer Paulus	2
Did Paulus e'er complain of sweat?	432	Answer Paulus	5
Did Paulus e'er the sun forget?	432	Answer Paulus	6
Whom Paulus ever must adore, ...	433	Answer Paulus	23

PAULUS   (CONTINUED)   PAGE   TITLE   LINE

	PAGE	TITLE	LINE
PAULUS (CONTINUED)			
Poor sweaty Paulus, who'd believe us ?	433	Answer Paulus	38
PAULUS'			
For Paulus' and for <Lyndsay's> sake	433	Answer Paulus	46
PAUNCH			
His empty Paunch that he might fill,	156	Fable of Midas	9
PAUNCHES			
Or pawing into dead mens paunches.	461	Birthday Song	36
PAUS'D			
Philemon having paus'd a while	94	Bauc & Phil 1	157
Philemon, having paus'd a while,	115	Bauc & Phil 2	111
PAUSE			
Say, fair ones, must I make a Pause?	589	Strephon Chloe	161
PAUSING			
And pausing o'er a Pipe, with doubtful Nod,	193	Author Himself	5
PAVIOURS			
Those carters, and paviours, and footmen and all;	841	Ballad	D 17
Those rascally paviours who did us undermine,	841	Ballad	D 18
PAWING			
Or pawing into dead mens paunches.	461	Birthday Song	36
PAWN			
That I durst Pawn my Ears, 'twill tell	101	Elegy Patrige	113
Though Robin's Honour was in Pawn,	495	Panegyr Swift	83
At some Hedge-Tavern lies in Pawn;	582	Young Nymph	44
You pawn your Word for him--who'll vouch for you?	668	Epig Carthy 8	D 2
PAWN'D			
Till Phillis all her Trinkets pawn'd:	224	Prog of Love	88
You pawn'd to him?-- "First shew him up.	446	Modern Lady	59
And pawn'd his word Hell is not local.	469	Birthday Song	272
PAWNS			
But pawns her Snuff-Box, Rings, and Keys.	452	Modern Lady	235
PAWS			
Of British Midas dirty Paws;	158	Fable of Midas	70
And, Cerberus hath ready in his Paws,	285	Elegy Boat	27
The Candidates observ'd his dirty Paws,	536	To Mr. Gay	157
His Tallow Face and Wainscot Paws,	861	Lady Acheson	38
Then Gluttony with greasy Paws,	894	Panegyr Dean	255
PAY			
Won't pay th' Impertinence of being known;	20	Ode Athenian	152
And with such Scanty Wages pay	24	Ode Athenian	258
And for it does so dearly pay;	28	Ode to Temple	77
Pay Thanks for the Gift,	77	Lady B- B-	27
To pay their Duty at his Hearse!	98	Elegy Patrige	8
And hardly pay Eighteenpence Tax in the Pound:	144	New Song	50
And pay the merit of her Lover?	177	To Lord Harley	36
"When are the Troops to have their Pay?	202	Horace 2, 6	100
Which those who tend the Sick for pay	204	In Sickness	17
Such is the Poet, fresh in Pay,	230	Prog of Poetry	17
Because 'tis Lordly not to pay,	239	Run Bankers	13
And then he could pay for the Liquor he drank	287	Bank Down	29
While his Tenants in Paper must pay him his Rent:	288	Bank Down	53
You pay them well; the Dogs have got	299	Horrid Plot	27
To ship a rogue, and pay him scarce a groat.	308	Billet Players	28
And all the Rent I pay is scarce five Shillings in the Pound.	342	Upon His Grace	22
Pray never press your self for Rent, but pay me when you can,	342	Upon His Grace	33
I hope you will not pay my Rent in that same Woods's Trash.	342	Upon His Grace	36
And then I went to pay the 'Squire and in the Way I found,	343	Upon His Grace	41
I'll vote for my Landlord to whom I pay Rent,	396	Dog and Thief	15
And promis'd to pay for it when he'd come back.	399	Tom Clinch	4
Now pay four Shillings in the Pound.	409	Dial Rich Marb	28
She'll pay the Charges to a Farthing:	417	Woman's Mind	60
Till others come to help the pay	420	Holyhead	12
While English sharpers take the pay,	421	Ireld	9
For licences shall pay no fees.	422	Ireld	54
Should pay a guinnea in the pound	423	Ireld	68
"My Husband left to pay for Coals:	447	Modern Lady	67
Not only can inspire, but pay.	462	Birthday Song	70
For Patrons never pay so well,	463	Birthday Song	95
And made the Rascals pay him dearly	463	Birthday Song	105
Be frugal, Patt: pay what you owe,	479	Epist on Epist	115
True Politicians only Pay	483	Libel on D- D-	89
To pay him Honour due, in Course	496	Panegyr Swift	112
To pay the Penalty annext.	501	Doctor Delaney	40
But, here was to pay the Devil and all.	519	Dean Hang Rape	58
They pay a Trifle, and enjoy the rest.	533	To Mr. Gay	48
Intent the Publick Debts to pay,	656	On Poetry	445
Hear me pay my dying Vows.	661	Love Song	24
From Visits to receive and pay,	688	Cadenus Vaness	43
You pay too dearly for your Care;	727	To Stella	118
Resolv'd my annual Verse to pay	740	Stel B-day 22	1
Time was, when I could yearly pay	754	Stella '23	3
Thus, nature hath resolv'd to pay her	761	Bec's B-Day	29
To the Court it was fitter to pay his Devotion,	809	Epigr Prelate	5
And, when the Coach-man comes for pay,	878	Robbin & Harry	3
To be his Slaves must pay him Rent;	883	Rev Market-Hill	22
Here pay their Vows with bended Knees:	893	Panegyr Dean	208
To pay your Tribute on the Plain?	896	Panegyr Dean	292

```
PAY              (CONTINUED)                                 PAGE    TITLE              LINE
    At Pluto's Hall, his Court to pay:        . . . . . . .   903 Death Daphne           2
    But strips himself to pay the Porter.      . . . . . .    928 Riddle 12          D   20
    I pay my Club, and so God b'y'--.                         954 Authors Living        10
    I must now, at one Sitting, pay off my old Score:    .    967 Letter Sherid         9
    So, the French, when our Generals soundly did pay 'em,    967 Letter Sherid        17
    If you had not took physick, I'd pay off your bacon.  .   980 Tho: Sheridan         5
    On Thursday I'll pay my Respects at your Shrine    . . .  1017 Swift Ans Sher       21
PAY'D
    Who pay'd his Courtship with the Croud,    . . . . .      482 Libel on D- D-       57
PAYD
    That now her Lovers must be payd;   . . . . . . . .       311 To Ford              20
PAYING
    Instead of paying Chair-men, run them thro'.)   . . . .   139 City Shower          50
    Who ever heard of servants paying wages?  . . . . . .     308 Billet Players       30
PAYMENT
    If Scandal did not find them Payment.      . . . . . .    502 Doctor Delaney       74
    Or in the Payment of a Debt    . . . . . . . .            724 To Stella            27
PAYMENTS
    Dues, Payments, Fees, Demands and Cheats,   . . . . . .   174 Horace 1, 7         104
PAYS    SEE O'ER-PAYS
    The Banker's ruin'd if he pays;    . . . . . . . .        239 Run Bankers          18
    In ready Counters never pays,       . . . . . . . .       452 Modern Lady         234
    Pays all the Cost, and gives the Villain Thanks.   .      535 To Mr. Gay          110
    Because she pays 'em all in Kind. . . . . . . . .         583 Young Nymph          56
    With Int'rest pays him back his own.  . . . . . . .       590 Strephon Chloe      214
    He pays his Workmen on the Nail.   . . . . . . . .        646 On Poetry           190
    Each strait his service offers, pays his court,    .      672 Epig Carthy 24    D   7
    The Muse her ann'all Tribute pays,    . . . . . . .       739 Stel B-day '21        2
    Where Phoebus pays a scanty Stipend,   . . . . . .        883 Rev Market-Hill       3
    As Nature prompts, his Off'ring pays?   . . . . . .       895 Panegyr Dean        288
    But no man pays me. . . . . . . . . . . . . . .           1037 Sheridan Cavan       8
PEACE
    That Tyrant-Guard on Peace,       . . . . . . . .           8 Ode to King          73
    And brings the dear Reward of Victory and Peace.    .      16 Ode Athenian         21
    When the Bright Sun of Peace began to shine,     . . .     16 Ode Athenian         24
    But you by Peace,     . . . . . . . . . . . .              28 Ode to Temple        72
    Only the Laurel got by Peace     . . . . . . . . .         29 Ode to Temple        81
    Resolv'd to give himself, as well as Country Peace.        30 Ode to Temple       134
    With heavenly peace of mind to bear     . . . . . .        38 Ode Sancroft        115
    Till Peace hath made the Sky serene,       . . . . .       84 Salamander           43
    Is come up, vi & armis, to break the <Queen's> Peace.  .  142 New Song              4
    To hear we are making a Peace without Spain;     . . . .  143 New Song             12
    There should be a Peace, while I'm Not in game.    .      143 New Song             14
    I talk'd of a Peace, and they both gave a start,    . . . 143 New Song             17
    And sooner than Vote for a Peace I'll be <damnd>.     .   143 New Song             20
    And I'll Vote against Peace, with Spain, or without:      144 New Song             46
    I'll Speech against Peace while Dismal's my Name,    .    145 New Song             53
    Speak against Peace right many a Word;    . . . . . .     147 Windsor Proph         8
    There shall be Peace, pardie, and War no more.     .     147 Windsor Proph        12
    Poor Britain shall have Peace at last;    . . . . . .     168 Peace Dunkirk         2
    Thou'lt rail devoutly at the Peace,      . . . . . . .    180 Horace 2, 1          15
    Or Constable with Staff of Peace,      . . . . . . .      189 Faggot               23
    "The Peace is made, and Perkin must come over.    .      195 Author Himself       46
    Dear Will, I suffer this for Peace;     . . . . . . .     220 A Quiet Life         14
    Bids us to seek Peace and ensue it.      . . . . . . .    220 A Quiet Life         18
    Dick suffer'd for his Peace and Credit,    . . . . . .    220 A Quiet Life         37
    Consult his Peace, or Credit save?      . . . . . . .     221 A Quiet Life         40
    (Who ought for Peace and Plenty Pray.)     . . . . . .    372 Letter D. S-y        40
    Secure of constant peace within,       . . . . . . .     434 Answer Paulus        57
    and selling his Country to purchase his peace     .      540 Charac Walpole        8
    "And, keep the Peace, to pick up Fees:    . . . . . .    571 Death of Swift      450
    Tho' Peace with Olive bind his Hands,     . . . . . .    655 On Poetry           419
    Short by the Knees intreat for Peace.      . . . . . .    655 On Poetry           424
    Against our Sov'reign Lady's Peace,      . . . . . .     687 Cadenus Vaness       17
    Which keeps the Peace among the Gods,      . . . . . .    695 Cadenus Vaness      262
    Would chuse in Peace to drink my Coffee.     . . . . .    733 Verses Vanessa       30
    Ne're hold my peace, and ne'er stand still.    . .       778 Mullinix Tim        160
    A middle-state 'twixt peace and war;      . . . . . .    876 To Dean Swift        24
    Be peace and war, and both, and neither.     . . . .     876 To Dean Swift        26
    May nothing interrupt his peace.       . . . . . . .     902 Dean's Reasons      102
    Pluto observing, since the Peace,      . . . . . . .     903 Death Daphne          7
    My Offers of Peace you ill understood.     . . . . . .   968 Letter Sherid        23
PEACEFUL
    On the high Top of peaceful Ararat;       . . . . . . .    16 Ode Athenian         26
    A Peaceful and a Flourishing Shore;       . . . . . . .    17 Ode Athenian         35
    And with blind Rage break all this peaceful Government;    25 Ode Athenian        300
    Or from thy private peaceful orb appear;     . . . . .     39 Ode Sancroft        155
    When soon the peaceful bow unstring'd is shown,           52 Temple Ill           27
    Mild Dorothea, peaceful, wise and great,     . . . .      52 Temple Ill           41
    The Peaceful State of common Brooms.      . . . . . .     132 Magician's Rod       20
    To sing of Wars choose peaceful times.     . . . . . .    462 Birthday Song        48
PEACEFULL
    With Dick's own Staff his Peacefull Neighbor,     . . .   220 A Quiet Life         22
PEACH
    If the Printer will peach him, he'll scarce come off      238 Excellent Song       32
        clean.
PEACOCK
    You see him first the Peacock bring,      . . . . . . .   513 Answer Fable         15
    A Peacock chose for Flight and Voice:      . . . . . .    513 Answer Fable         20
    Did ever mortal see a Peacock     . . . . . . . . .       513 Answer Fable         21


                                 601
```

```
PEACOCK          (CONTINUED)                          PAGE    TITLE            LINE
   This Peacock kept a standing Force,     . . . . . . .   513 Answer Fable        27
PEACOCK'S
   This Pheasant by the Peacock's Will,       . . . . . .  513 Answer Fable        43
PEACOCKS
   Is drawn by peacocks in her Berlin       . . . . . .    621 Scandal Poem 1     124
   Is drawn by Peacocks in her Berlin:      . . . . . .    627 Scandal Poem 2     118
PEAL
   Why, what a Peal the Jade has rung,     . . . . . .     220 A Quiet Life        11
PEARL
   To search the Deep for Pearl and Coral.    . . . . .    254 Bubble              96
   No Lips of Coral Teeth of Pearl.     . . . . . . .      272 Apollo's Edict    D 55
PEARS
   Plumbs, Apples and Pears,      . . . . . . . . .        951 Apples               2
PEAS    SEE ISSUE-PEAS
PEASANTS
   Away the frighted Peasants fly,      . . . . . . . .     30 Ode to Temple      109
PEASE
   Fly from the Hawk, or pick his Pease up.    . . . . .   512 Answer Fable        10
   Then, see the dire Effect of Pease,     . . . . . . .   589 Strephon Chloe     167
   'Tis true, he hated Sloth like Pease.     . . . . . .   602 Beasts Confess      46
PECCAVI
   Now lowly crouch'd, I cry Peccavi,     . . . . . . .   1005 Sheridan's Sub      11
PECK
   Or send him in a Peck of Coals;      . . . . . . .      728 Stella, Poems       34
   A peck of troubles for a coach.    . . . . . . . .      753 Gift for Bec        20
PECKS
   Computing by their Pecks of Coals,     . . . . . . .    649 On Poetry          281
PECULIAR
   Are Arts peculiar to dissembling France:     . . . .     11 Ode to William    D  2
   Swore all the wits were his peculiar friends;    . . .   47 To Congreve        140
   He flatters with peculiar Air      . . . . . . . .      216 To Mr. Delany       37
   But by peculiar Whimseys drawn,      . . . . . . .      279 Journal             21
   Tis but by our peculiar grace      . . . . . . . .      621 Scandal Poem 1     131
   'Tis but by our peculiar Grace,      . . . . . . .      627 Scandal Poem 2     135
   The Church is thy peculiar Care.     . . . . . . .      656 On Poetry          452
   The Marks peculiar of his Sire.      . . . . . . .      798 Traulus 1           82
PEDANT
   And how his Wife that Female Pedant,     . . . . . .    282 Journal             85
   The Pedant gets a Mistress by't.     . . . . . . . .    710 Cadenus Vaness     743
   An Ounce of Gold's worth ten of Brass, dull Pedant.  . 1004 Dan J's Reply       33
PEDANTRY
   Her Face patch't o'er with Modern Pedantry,     . . .    23 Ode Athenian       224
   Censure, and Pedantry, and Pride,      . . . . . . .     25 Ode Athenian       296
   Affect ill-manner'd Pedantry,      . . . . . . . .       27 Ode to Temple       45
   Who preach the saucy pedantry of rules;     . . . . .    46 To Congreve        102
   Displays his Pedantry unmerciful,     . . . . . . .     281 Journal             80
PEDE
   Thus you may see, dear Friend, ex pede hence     . . .  988 Letter Dr Sh-n      15
PEDLAR
   To Fort St. George a Pedlar went he.     . . . . . .    456 Dean Smedley        48
   Nor Bastard of a Pedlar Scot;      . . . . . . . .      641 On Poetry           34
   This pedlar, at speaking and making of laws,     . . .  815 Yahoo's             16
PEELS
   The Golden Scurf peels off his Limbs:     . . . . . .   157 Fable of Midas      36
PEEP    SEE MORNING-PEEP
   To peep upon a twinkling Star.     . . . . . . . .       99 Elegy Patrige       56
   Hence that wild suspicious Peep,     . . . . . . . .    800 Traulus 2           35
   To peep at the Captain, in all his fine Clo'es:    . .  872 Grand Question     138
   Bo peep, bo peep, bo peep, bo peep, peep, bo bo peep.  . 961 Cantata
   Bo peep, bo peep, bo peep, bo peep, peep, bo bo peep.  . 961 Cantata
   Bo peep, bo peep, bo peep, bo peep, peep, bo bo peep.  . 961 Cantata
   Bo peep, bo peep, bo peep, bo peep, peep, bo bo peep.  . 961 Cantata
   Bo peep, bo peep, bo peep, bo peep, peep, bo bo peep.  . 961 Cantata
   Bo peep, bo peep, bo peep, bo peep, peep, bo bo peep.  . 961 Cantata
PEEP'D
   Miss came, and peep'd at all he had.     . . . . . .    150 Corinna             24
   They peep'd, and saw a Lady there    . . . . . . .      321 First of April      29
PEEPING
   For every peeping Fop to Jear.     . . . . . . . .       60 Lady Tablebook      18
   Good Fortune peeping from behind;      . . . . . . .    452 Modern Lady        229
   Soon punish'd Strephon for his Peeping;     . . . . .   529 Lady's Dres Rm     120
   And a Hole above for peeping.      . . . . . . . .      830 Legion Club         46
PEEPS
   Peeps in the Ponds to look for Spawn:     . . . . . .   279 Journal             22
PEEPT
   I peept, and saw you kiss the dirty Bitch.    . . . .   882 Pastoral Dial       38
PEER
   Nor thought to find so great a Peer    . . . . . . .     62 Discovery            3
   Become a General, Peer and Beau,     . . . . . . .      84 Salamander          42
   An Heir, and Orphan of a Peer;     . . . . . . . .      384 Manly Virtue        20
   Pleas'd in the Person of a Peer;     . . . . . . .      385 Manly Virtue        70
   A Peer, a scarcely bearded Youth,    . . . . . . .      386 Manly Virtue        71
   If ev'ry Peer whom you commend,      . . . . . . .      391 Young's Satire       9
   Brainsick Brute, they call a Peer.     . . . . . . .    837 Legion Club        176
   And make a Beggar's Brat a Peer.     . . . . . . .      916 Riddle 1            36
   . . .with that great peer the Lord Anglesey.    . . .  1022 Nim-Dan-Dean 2    D  6
   Expect in time, to be a <Peer>     . . . . . . . .      778 Mullinix Tim       158
PEERAGE
   Can half the Peerage by his Arts bewitch;     . . . .   535 To Mr. Gay         103
   "And Peerage is a wither'd Flower,     . . . . . . .    570 Death of Swift     440
```

		PAGE	TITLE	LINE
PEERAGE	**(CONTINUED)**			
	You raise the Honour of the Peerage, ...	656	On Poetry	455
PEERS				
	Will drink it now as well as Peers:	169	Peace Dunkirk	24
	Like Peers, have Levees ev'ry Day	239	Run Bankers	15
	Peers, Clergy, Gentry, all are Benefactors;	274	Epilogue	7
	A House of Peers, or Gaming Crew, ...	658	On Poetry	D 164
	Next Moment in the House of Peers, ...	788	Dick's Variety	28
	Ye pack of pensionary <Peers>, ...	487	Irish-Club	5
PEEVISH				
	Whose peevish knowledge thus perversely lies . . .	37	Ode Sancroft	84
	Thy peevish, and perpetual teizing, ...	775	Mullinix Tim	57
	Spightful, peevish, rude, untoward;	799	Traulus 2	11
PEEVISHER				
	Always peevisher and sillier:	906	Daphne	18
PEEVISHNESS				
	When Peevishness and Spleen succeed.	731	Stella, Poems	136
PEG				
	When first for her he quitted Peg.	224	Prog of Love	84
	The Cubbard fasten'd with a Peg	746	Stel Distress	39
PEGASUS				
	(The Pegasus, like an unruly Horse	31	Ode to Temple	146
	Nor Pegasus could bear the Load, ...	231	Prog of Poetry	27
	For Pegasus runs, runs every Race	956	Cantata	
	By which your jade Pegasus fixt in a tether, . . .	1027	Sheri Circles	18
PEGASUS'				
	Smoother than Pegasus' old Shoe, ...	1021	Nim-Dan-Dean 1	D 7
PEGGY				
	And, I'll engage with Peggy Dixon:	885	Rev Market-Hill	86
	With Peggy Dixon thoughtful sit, ...	897	Panegyr Dean	331
PEGS				
	Or strung on Pegs behind the Door;	592	Strephon Chloe	290
PELEUS				
	Took Col'nel Peleus to her Bed.	587	Strephon Chloe	102
PELF				
	I doubt your Heart is set on Pelf	175	Horace 1, 7	125
	So to the Poor if he refus'd his Pelf, ...	234	Elegy on Demar	13
PELL-MELL				
	In the Pell-mell when passing by, ...	228	Prog of Beauty	73
	To lead you thither, as Pell-mell, ...	313	To Ford	62
	And grieve he ever left Pell-mell.	748	Stel Distress	74
PELLA				
	As Julius, or the Youth of Pella, ...	464	Birthday Song	142
PELLING				
	Name honest Doctor Pelling;	440	Ballyspellin	21
PELT				
	Let the Boys pelt him if they dare;	788	Dick's Variety	20
PELTED				
	Without, they pelted him with Stones, ...	221	A Quiet Life	52
	When pelted all with Dirt they shine;	787	Clad in Brown	20
	Thou would'st be pelted worse than they're. . . .	787	Clad in Brown	24
PELTS				
	Pelts him by Turns with Verse and Prose, ...	458	Paddy's Charac	25
PEN				
	The wild excursions of a youthful pen;	17	Ode Athenian	61
	Are nobler Subjects for your learned Pen;	31	Ode to Temple	160
	T' avert th' impending judgments of my pen. . . .	45	To Congreve	48
	And with the help of Buckley's Pen	180	Horace 2, 1	3
	So have I seen within a Pen	294	Prog Marriage	145
	Since this Reflection slipt your Pen, ...	485	Libel on D- D-	161
	You shou'd withdraw from pen and ink, ...	489	Dialogue	16
	Must dread your pen, your person hate, ...	491	Dialogue	54
	For once to wet thy Pen Divine:	515	Answer Fable	90
	For while he keeps his Pen, you are not safe. . . .	538	Mr. Pulteney	14
	Nor need depend upon his Pen---.	548	Life of Swift	100
	And made me throw my Pen aside;	555	Death of Swift	64
	I'd have him throw away his Pen;	556	Death of Swift	103
	To bite his Pen, and drop a Tear.	561	Death of Swift	210
	"Had he but spar'd his Tongue and Pen, ...	567	Death of Swift	355
	"The Dean did by his Pen defeat	569	Death of Swift	407
	When I no more a Pen can brandish.	611	By Dr. Swift	4
	You need not throw your Pen away.	646	On Poetry	182
	Gold becomes Lead, touch'd lightly by thy Pen. . .	668	Epig Carthy 12	D 2
	His Pen to save a sinking Nation draws, ...	770	Horace 1, 14	26
	By leaving him under the pen of the Dean.	816	Yahoo's	39
	Your ink is your poison, your pen is what not; . .	979	Dean to Tho: S	21
	Your ink is your drink, your pen is your pot. . .	979	Dean to Tho: S	22
	From out the pen will presently	983	Sher, A Goose	7
	So your eternal pen is still, ...	983	Sher, A Goose	21
PEN'D				
	Come with Petitions fairly pen'd, ...	200	Horace 2, 6	45
PENALTY				
	To pay the Penalty annext.	501	Doctor Delaney	40
PENCE	**SEE SIX-PENCE**			
	. . .six Pence, besides Farthings, in Money, and Gold;	69	Mrs Harris Pet	2
	'Tis true, seven Pound, four Shillings, and six Pence,. . .	71	Mrs Harris Pet	40
	But wisely cautious of her Pence, ...	75	Game Traffick	15
	He touch'd the Pence when others touch'd the Pot; . .	234	Elegy on Demar	27
	In Drugget drest of Thirteen Pence a Yard, . . .	275	Epilogue	23
	And Sell for Twenty Pence a Yard of theirs; . . .	276	Epilogue	44

PENCE	(CONTINUED)	PAGE	TITLE	LINE
And with very little Pence,	. . . .	574	Helter Skelter	29
To earn a Stock of Pence and Praise,	. . . . . .	642	On Poetry	66
Will never fail to bring in Pence;	. . . . . .	646	On Poetry	188
They may hope for Pence a Piece.	. . . . .	833	Legion Club	108
"To treat gold reduc'd like Wood's copper pence.	. . .	843	Ay and No	16
With two pence left, walks home in rain.		878	Robbin & Harry	8

PENCES SEE SIX-PENCES

PENCIL

He's a Gold Pencil tipt with Lead.	. . . . . .	61	Lady Tablebook	30
By help of Pencil, Paint and Brush	. . . . .	227	Prog of Beauty	46
Of Value five Shillings, in English a Pencil;	. .	264	Apollo	34

PENDENT

Still ev'ry tree the pendent sorrow wears;	. . . . .	51	Temple Ill	20
We'll cry; look, here's our Boat, and there's the Pendent.		285	Elegy Boat	36

PENDENTS

Had many Pendents, but abhor'd a Jack.	. . . . . .	285	Elegy Boat	16

PENDULUM

Moving all like a pendulum;	. . . .	852	Lady's Lament	30

PENN'D

"Then, here's a Letter finely penn'd	. . . . . .	563	Death of Swift	273
By old Popish Cannons, as wise Men have Penn'd 'em,	.	518	Dean Hang Rape	37

PENNY SEE EIGHTEEN-PENNY

To turn a Good Penny to Twenty Bad Ha'pence.	. . .	335	Serious Poem	48
Cou'd you see his grim Grace, for a Pound to a Penny,		803	Irish Bishops	9
A hundred a Penny,	. . . .	951	Apples	3
Is not a Penny often found	. . . .	1004	Dan J's Reply	28

PENNY-POST

Convey by Penny-Post to Lintot,	. . . .	643	On Poetry	107

PENNYLESS

With pennyless and starv'ling strains;	. . . . . .	432	Answer Paulus	16

PENS

Their tongues and pens to give you joy,	. . . . .	176	To Lord Harley	2
"Pursu'd by base envenom'd Pens,	. . . . . .	568	Death of Swift	395
Furnish'd with Paper, Pens, and Ink,	. . . . . .	740	Stel B-day 22	3

PENSHURST

But now your name with Penshurst vies,	. . . . . .	877	To Dean Swift	33

PENSION

Here fell a Pension, there a Place:	. . . . .	158	Fable of Midas	76
To favour Wood and keep my Pension:	. . . . . .	348	Whitshed Motto	16
Will serve instead of place or pension	. . . . .	421	Ireld	18
What Claim have you to Place, or Pension?	. . . .	483	Libel on D- D-	109
"Hath been rewarded with a Pension:	. . . .	564	Death of Swift	290
To flatter Knaves, or lose his Pension.	. . . . .	650	On Poetry	310

PENSIONARY

Ye pack of pensionary <Peers>,	. . . .	487	Irish-Club	5

PENSIONS

By Pensions, Bribes, and three per Cent?	. . . . .	157	Fable of Midas	46
Men of more Wit than Money, our Pensions will fit	. .	389	Order of Bath	7

PENSIVE

While Rain depends, the pensive Cat gives o'er	. . .	136	City Shower	3
The Owl foresaw in pensive Mood	. . . . . .	849	Old Thorn	37

PENT

There live with daggl'd Mermaids pent,	. . . . .	689	Cadenus Vaness	89
Whether the Winds in Caverns pent	. . . . . .	923	Riddle 7	85

PENURIOUS

She's grown so nice, and so penurious,	. . . . .	891	Panegyr Dean	143

PENY

Gives them a peny, and God's blessing	. . . . .	878	Robbin & Harry	6

PEOPLE

(But, surely such whom God did never for his People chuse)		8	Ode to King	86
They call'd at ev'ry Dore; Good People,	. . . . .	90	Bauc & Phil 1	15
Put the old People in a Fright;	. . . . .	92	Bauc & Phil 1	80
And People fancy'd he had Wit:	. . . . .	156	Fable of Midas	24
Fame spreads the News, and People travel	. . . . .	157	Fable of Midas	37
"I wonder what some People mean;	. . . . .	202	Horace 2, 6	84
Dear Will, but, what would People say?	. . . . .	220	A Quiet Life	34
For People to fight	. . . .	246	Irish-Feast	59
Wise People, who believ'd with Reason	. . . . .	354	Simile Silver	5
From London they come, silly People to chouse,	. .	396	Dog and Thief	17
Then said, I must speak to the People a little,	. .	399	Tom Clinch	15
On what detracting People say?	. . . . .	414	Censure	18
The People with a Sigh their Taxes bring;	. . . .	533	To Mr. Gay	51
"But, this I know, all People bought 'em;	. . . .	565	Death of Swift	312
"The greatful People stand his Friends;	. . . . .	570	Death of Swift	426
Till the People all are quiet	. . . .	574	Helter Skelter	51
'Tis true, the People understood,	. . . . .	606	Beasts Confess	161
All Christian People to invite;	. . . . .	735	Stel B-day '20	36
Reviles all People in his Jargon,	. . . . .	777	Mullinix Tim	113
Of whom all People make a Jest.	. . . . .	918	Riddle 4	22
Censorious People do in spight.	. . . . .	942	Probatur Alit	18
All people tease me,	. . . .	1037	Sheridan Cavan	7

PEOPLE'S

Puff'd by the people's spightful blast,	. . . . .	41	Ode Sancroft	220
To try the People's Hospitality.	. . . . .	90	Bauc & Phil 1	4
To try good People's Hospitality.	. . . . .	111	Bauc & Phil 2	4
The People's Voice expands his Paper Sail;	. . . .	770	Horace 1, 14	28
In vain, against the People's Fav'rite?	. . . . .	796	Traulus 1	10
At People's Heels with frothy Chaps;	. . . . .	797	Traulus 1	36

PER

	PAGE	TITLE	LINE
By Pensions, Bribes, and three per Cent?	157	Fable of Midas	46
Yet our Stocks rise Cent. per Cent,	169	Peace Dunkirk	26
That a Pack of sly Knaves should get fifty per Cent,	288	Bank Down	52
To take, for Interest Cent. per Cent.	446	Modern Lady	61

PERCEIVING

But well perceiving Wit was scarce,	107	V's House	56

PERCH'D

Like the victorious wren perch'd on the eagle's wing;	44	To Congreve	38

<PERCIVAL>

I might have told how oft Dean <Percival>	281	Journal	79

PERDITION

And instead of the Devil, this Son of Perdition	336	Serious Poem	67

PERFECT

It was so perfect in its kind,	86	Hist V's House	11
A perfect Stranger to the Spleen;	170	Horace 1, 7	10
He calld my Dol a perfect toast.	422	Irel d	32
A perfect Nuissance to the rest.	455	Dean Smedley	12
But form'd more perfect Gamester, you	494	Panegyr Swift	37
"To publick Use! A perfect Whim!	558	Death of Swift	157
A perfect Goddess born and bred.	655	On Poetry	426
Lifeless, Life's perfect Form I wear,	935	Riddle 23	D 7
'Tis a perfect Milksop,	939	Riddle Answerd	27

PERFECTION

Yet does this high perfection well proceed	41	Ode Sancroft	223
And each Perfection wrong imputed	646	On Poetry	201

PERFECTIONS

And my few Perfections stifle.	631	Epistle Lady	62

PERFECTLY

Pretends so perfectly to know;	39	Ode Sancroft	158
But should be perfectly content,	199	Horace 2, 6	9

PERFIDIOUS

Tell me, Perfidious! Was it fit	154	Widow and Cat	D 38
With shameless Visage, and perfidious Leer,	532	To Mr. Gay	34
Perfidious Goddess! but in vain	695	Cadenus Vaness	288

PERFORM

Your Name shall the remaining Work perform,	13	Ode to William	D 39
When we perform, look sharp among our crew,	307	Billet Players	11
Th' Almighty's Orders to perform,	496	Panegyr Swift	92
And may now perform your Charge.	631	Epistle Lady	44
If I perform this Task with Pain	739	Stel B-day '21	5
Perform the part of Punchinelloes;	777	Mullinix Tim	136

PERFORM'D

"Perform'd as Juglers do their Feats:	564	Death of Swift	296
The Rites perform'd, the Parson paid,	586	Strephon Chloe	67
All this perform'd by Robert Hewit,	675	Curate's Compl	16
With Vigour and Delight perform'd.	726	To Stella	108

PERFORMS

Performs what Friendship, Justice, Truth require:	196	Author Himself	73

PERFUME

There (A safe way to use Perfume)	60	Lady Tablebook	12
The Pettycoats and Gown perfume,	529	Lady's Dres Rm	113

PERFUMERS

First issu'd from Perfumers Shops	696	Cadenus Vaness	316

PERFUMES

To censure Phillis for Perfumes;	449	Modern Lady	159
A Sweetness above all Perfumes;	691	Cadenus Vaness	161

PERHAPS

And 'twas perhaps Parnassus, if in height	16	Ode Athenian	8
Do laugh perhaps at theirs, and pity mine and me.	18	Ode Athenian	90
Perhaps imagine to be wondrous Wit	20	Ode Athenian	125
Because 'tis said (and perhaps only said)	20	Ode Athenian	146
Which is perhaps as hard t' imagine right	21	Ode Athenian	159
Believe it firm, because perhaps the day is mild and still	37	Ode Sancroft	75
Unless, perhaps, some stars above be so;	39	Ode Sancroft	144
'Twill then, perhaps, be worth thy while	181	Horace 2, 1	41
Thy Genius has perhaps a knack	183	Horace 2, 1	103
I meet perhaps from three or four,	204	In Sickness	15
Perhaps you wonder whence this Friendship Springs,	275	Epilogue	35
Perhaps from what the Packet brings,	282	Journal	109
While We perhaps must wait a Week:	315	To Ford	104
Perhaps you will say, 'tis the Devil that puts	335	Serious Poem	61
In Gold, Perhaps, my Friend you Wallow	372	Letter D. S-y	29
His Excellency too perhaps	421	Irel d	13
Perhaps be found one honest man:	435	Answer Paulus	104
And yet perhaps you may be bit.	445	Modern Lady	27
The first perhaps may once an Age	462	Birthday Song	67
"Perhaps, may feel Compassion still,	485	Libel on D- D-	168
Your honest Care may fill; perhaps enlarge.	533	To Mr. Gay	46
Perhaps he might have truckled down,	549	Life of Swift	140
Perhaps, his Travels, Part the Third;	550	Life of Swift	190
If this perhaps your Patience move	554	Death of Swift	11
"Perhaps I may allow, the Dean	571	Death of Swift	455
And might perhaps be too severe:	602	Beasts Confess	26
In Dyet was perhaps too nice,	602	Beasts Confess	39
Some Criticks may object perhaps,	618	Scandal Poem 1	21
May kill perhaps, but never wound.	618	Scandal Poem 1	28
Some Critick may object, perhaps,	624	Scandal Poem 2	15
Or else perhaps he may invent	643	On Poetry	101
Perhaps you say Augustus shines	658	On Poetry	D 410
Fair Chloe would perhaps be found	729	Stella, Poems	43

PERHAPS   (CONTINUED)   PAGE   TITLE   LINE
    Perhaps you're quite another Thing.   .   .   .   .   .   .   730 Stella, Poems   70
    And tho' perhaps among the Rout, ...   796 Traulus 1   25
    Some perhaps may think him able   .   .   .   .   800 Traulus 2   45
    Were Peter now alive, perhaps   .   .   .   .   821 Dr. Rundle   49
    You perhaps will ask me, why so?   .   .   .   .   830 Legion Club   39
    Scorpion Rods perhaps may tame them.   .   .   .   .   .   836 Legion Club   158
    Then, perhaps, you may reform her: .   .   .   .   .   .   907 Daphne   34
    Perhaps you will say, 'tis in Gratitude due, ...   947 Mrs. Houghton   3
    Tho' perhaps you may tell it   .   .   .   .   1015 Swift to Sheri   57
    Oh! but I forgot, perhaps, by this time, you may have one   1023 Nim-Dan-Dean 2   D   7
      . . .
PERI
    With sham Quotations Peri Hupsous: .   .   .   .   648 On Poetry   256
PERICRANIES
    And when they join their Pericranies, ...   651 On Poetry   317
PERIL
    Be put to the Peril, and Toyl of a <Rape>?   .   .   .   .   518 Dean Hang Rape   42
    Should at their Peril without fail   .   .   .   .   713 Cadenus Vaness   840
PERIOD
    Fate put a Period to the Farce;   .   .   .   .   225 Prog of Love   96
PERIODS
    He at fit Periods walks through Aries, ...   98 Elegy Patrige   15
    With periods long, in terms abstruse!   .   .   .   .   .   .   434 Answer Paulus   82
PERISH
    Consume, and perish from our sight, ...   9 Ode to King   113
    Perish the Muse's hour, thus vainly spent   .   .   .   .   48 To Congreve   175
    "Resolve to perish with his <Whore>;   .   .   .   .   .   .   305 Storm   64
    To perish for our Country's Good.   .   .   .   .   697 Cadenus Vaness   349
    Each modern Judas perish like the first;   .   .   .   .   .   806 Judas   21
    Be gone: Thy Money perish with thee.   .   .   .   .   .   821 Dr. Rundle   48
    Yet I perish in my prime, ...   937 Riddle 24   D 47
PERISH'D
    Lest here it live, when perish'd with his own;   .   .   .   .   48 To Congreve   168
    But thy Book perish'd on its natal Day.   .   .   .   .   .   669 Epig Carthy 13   D   4
PERIWIGG'D
    Discord periwigg'd with Snakes, ...   832 Legion Club   91
PERJUR'D
    And so a perjur'd Dog denotes   .   .   .   .   298 Horrid Plot   9
    Perjur'd Rebel, brib'd Accuser;   .   .   .   .   831 Legion Club   70
PERJURE
    Some who can perjure thro' a two-Inch Board;   .   .   .   806 Judas   13
PERJURY
    Fraud, Perjury, and Guilt are seen.   .   .   .   .   922 Riddle 7   22
PERJURY'S
    Whose Perjury's the least of all their Crimes: .   .   .   .   806 Judas   12
PERKIN
    "The Peace is made, and Perkin must come over.   .   .   195 Author Himself   46
PERMISSION
    The Muses, by their King's Permission, ...   689 Cadenus Vaness   93
PERMIT
    Permit a brutish Man to touch her?   .   .   .   .   588 Strephon Chloe   153
    If your wives will permit ye, ...   858 Lady's Lament   215
    Nor shall I for his Humour, permit you to purloin   .   .   .   867 Grand Question   17
    Permit me then to raise my Style, ...   894 Panegyr Dean   227
PERMITTED
    Permitted so by Providence: .   .   .   .   387 Manly Virtue   114
PERPENDICULAR
    Linkt perpendicular to the Centre: .   .   .   .   654 On Poetry   402
PERPETUAL
    And keep on Fish perpetual Lent.   .   .   .   .   689 Cadenus Vaness   90
    Thus, to the World's perpetual Shame, ...   700 Cadenus Vaness   432
    And Sheridan's perpetual teazings.   .   .   .   .   .   .   753 Gift for Bec   8
    Thy peevish, and perpetual teizing, ...   775 Mullinix Tim   57
    Run on in a perpetual Round, ...   777 Mullinix Tim   141
    Perpetual Envoys too and fro;   .   .   .   .   781 Mullinix Tim   256
PERPLEX
    Did ever Problem thus perplex, ...   65 Problem   1
    To Teize, Perplex, Disturb, Confound, ...   777 Mullinix Tim   142
PERPLEX'D
    Strephon had long perplex'd his Brains, ...   586 Strephon Chloe   72
    The Goddess much perplex'd in Mind, ...   690 Cadenus Vaness   128
    The Silvan Pow'rs with Fear perplex'd   .   .   .   .   .   849 Old Thorn   29
PERPLEXES
    Confounds Accounts, perplexes all Affairs;   .   .   .   .   536 To Mr. Gay   139
PERPLEXT
    Some Wag observes me thus perplext, ...   200 Horace 2, 6   31
    The grave Divine with knotty Points perplext,   .   .   .   364 On Dreams   31
PERQUISITE
    To make my Cream a Perquisite, ...   154 Widow and Cat   D 39
PERQUISITES
    What else by Perquisites are meant, ...   157 Fable of Midas   45
    Commissions, Perquisites, and Bribes, ...   158 Fable of Midas   78
    To whom those Perquisites are gone   .   .   .   .   .   .   225 Prog of Love   93
    The Perquisites of Pimps and Wits.   .   .   .   .   .   .   498 Panegyr Swift   151
    To what your lawful Perquisites amount.   .   .   .   .   .   533 To Mr. Gay   66
PERRIWIG
    A Perriwig of twisted Snakes;   .   .   .   .   903 Death Daphne   22
PERSECUTE
    To persecute the Muses Fame;   .   .   .   .   504 Doctor Delaney   132
    And weekly persecute his grace   .   .   .   .   677 Parson's Case   29

PERSECUTION   PAGE   TITLE   LINE

	PAGE	TITLE	LINE
PERSECUTION			
The persecution of cold Water.	321	First of April	32
"He bore continual Persecution;	569	Death of Swift	400
PERSIAN			
See Philip's Son amidst his Persian Guard;	275	Epilogue	24
Instead of Spoils of Persian Looms,	379	Apology Lady C	109
PERSON			
When Treason there in Person seems to stand,	8	Ode to King	56
For of the person much I fear,	35	Ode Sancroft	18
She can swear to the Person, whom oft she has seen,	264	Apollo	53
Who hate Your Person, and Your Cause,	312	To Ford	30
But Tom is a Person of Honor so nice,	327	Epigram 1	6
Pleas'd in the Person of a Peer;	385	Manly Virtue	70
Must dread your pen, your person hate,	491	Dialogue	54
Was taken with his Person outward,	514	Answer Fable	47
For, as he view'd his Person round,	586	Strephon Chloe	75
His Person must Contempt beget.	706	Cadenus Vaness	639
First, to adorn your Person well,	732	Verses Vanessa	3
He rails at my person:	853	Lady's Lament	68
But, loth his Person to expose	904	Death Daphne	33
My Person tall, and slender Waste,	915	Riddle 1	5
Is a Person very unfit for Intrigues.	940	Letter	17
PERSONATE			
Can personate an awkward Scorn	652	On Poetry	353
PERSONS			
Nor Persons Names, nor Places knew;	313	To Ford	54
Since there are persons who complain	489	Dialogue	1
"Nor Persons had in Admiration;	565	Death of Swift	326
For Persons whom he never saw.	708	Cadenus Vaness	693
PERSPIRATION			
The Paint by Perspiration cracks,	227	Prog of Beauty	37
PERSUADED			
Him we persuaded with a mod'rate bribe,	307	Billet Players	5
PERSWADE			
As Esop would the World perswade;	607	Beasts Confess	211
PERSWASION			
But Tim Convinc't by your Perswasion,	774	Mullinix Tim	29
PERT			
Of Nice, Coquet, Affected, Pert, and Vain.	118	Biddy Floyd	10
Hal -- grows more Pert, and <Somers> not so Grave:	163	Toland's Invit	22
So, the pert Dunces of Mankind	216	To Mr. Delany	45
"You need not then have been so pert,	304	Storm	41
When they grew pert, to pull them down.	697	Cadenus Vaness	337
Will tell him that Chaplains should not be so pert;	868	Grand Question	36
And soon grow pert on Men of Sense;	887	Panegyr Dean	20
PERTLY			
When you pertly raise your Snout,	523	Betty Grizette	31
PERTNESS			
Of Nelly's pertness, Robin's leasings,	753	Gift for Bec	7
PERUS'D			
May backward be perus'd, like Hebrew.	1021	Nim-Dan-Dean 1	D 42
PERUSE			
Peruse my Leaves thro' ev'ry Part,	60	Lady Tablebook	1
Sleep, or peruse some antient Book;	202	Horace 2, 6	110
PERVERSE			
Had not ill Fate, perverse and blind,	215	To Mr. Delany	5
For tho' by one perverse Event	712	Cadenus Vaness	832
PERVERSELY			
Whose peevish knowledge thus perversely lies	37	Ode Sancroft	84
Why near the dregs of youth perversely wilt thou stay,	54	Temple Ill	105
Perversely comes in evil Times,	798	Traulus 1	91
PERVERSENESS			
For this Perverseness in the Mind?	640	On Poetry	12
Perverseness is your whole Defence:	730	Stella, Poems	92
Still her odd perverseness shows	906	Daphne	15
PERVERT			
"Pervert the Law, disgrace the Gown,	568	Death of Swift	385
PEST			
Thrice happy you have 'scap't this gen'ral Pest;	28	Ode to Temple	58
PESTER'D			
Abroad, was pester'd by the Boys,	221	A Quiet Life	50
PESTILENCE			
With War, and Pestilence, and Dearth,	10	Ode to King	134
PETER			
Have Peter Waters always in your Mind;	534	To Mr. Gay	101
Cassinus this, and t' other Peter)	594	Cassinus Peter	6
Friend Peter to Cassinus goes,	594	Cassinus Peter	7
Him thus accoutred Peter found,	594	Cassinus Peter	25
Oh Peter, wou'd it were no more!	595	Cassinus Peter	46
Oh Peter! Beauty's but a Varnish,	595	Cassinus Peter	51
Friend Peter, this I could excuse;	595	Cassinus Peter	63
Think, Peter, how my Soul is rack'd.	596	Cassinus Peter	97
Said surly Peter, Magus, prithee	821	Dr. Rundle	47
Were Peter now alive, perhaps	821	Dr. Rundle	49
PETITION			
. . .I must Petition You.	73	Mrs Harris Pet	69
By vertue of some sly Petition:	182	Horace 2, 1	68
"And if you must have your Petition,	304	Storm	47
On whose Petition (humbly shewing	713	Cadenus Vaness	860
Petition and Greeting.	1004	Sheridan's Sub	4

	PAGE	TITLE	LINE
PETITIONER			
And then your poor Petitioner, both Night and Day,	73	Mrs Harris Pet	74
PETITIONS			
Come with Petitions fairly pen'd,	200	Horace 2, 6	45
PETROSUM			
Which near the Os Petrosum pass;	367	Answer Delaney	36
PETTICOAT			
Her Petticoat transform'd apace,	116	Bauc & Phil 2	141
This Petticoat shall save thy dear Back-side;	881	Pastoral Dial	22
My Petticoat is doubly fring'd.	896	Panegyr Dean	314
PETTICOATS			
"Shall rent her Petticoats to Rags,	850	Old Thorn	63
PETTY			
By many a petty Lord possess'd,	26	Ode to Temple	6
What petty Motives rule their Fates!	30	Ode to Temple	106
PETTYCOAT			
A Pettycoat without a Hoop!	699	Cadenus Vaness	400
PETTYCOATS			
Here Pettycoats in frowzy Heaps;	527	Lady's Dres Rm	48
The Pettycoats and Gown perfume,	529	Lady's Dres Rm	113
PETULANT			
Where petulant, conceited Fellows	777	Mullinix Tim	135
PEW-SICK			
Dean Cross, had he preach'd, would have made us all Pew-sick;	1029	Dr. Helsham	8
PEWS			
Was Metamorphos't into Pews;	94	Bauc & Phil 1	150
Was Metamorphos'd into Pews;	114	Bauc & Phil 2	104
A Church without Pews.	1036	Plague Country	4
PEWTER			
Glasses and Linnen clean, and Pewter bright,	165	Toland's Invit	28
PHABUS			
Or if 'tis true, Great Phabus smiles	372	Letter D. S-y	25
PHAENOMENAES			
So well You answer all Phaenomenaes there;	22	Ode Athenian	202
PHAENOMENON			
And thus I solve this hard Phaenomenon.	367	Answer Delaney	44
PHAETON			
No Phaeton to hold the Reins.	271	Apollo's Edict	D 53
PHALANX			
Close, as the Macedonian Phalanx:	1021	Nim-Dan-Dean 1	D 30
PHANTOM			
The Phantom, having humbly kiss't	903	Death Daphne	3
PHANTOMS			
Phantoms, bodiless and vain,	833	Legion Club	101
PHARISEES			
Among proud Doctors and disputing Pharisees:	39	Ode Sancroft	169
PHEASANT			
And he of all Birds was a Pheasant.	513	Answer Fable	34
This Pheasant was a Man of Wit,	513	Answer Fable	35
This Pheasant by the Peacock's Will,	513	Answer Fable	43
Then in a Net the Pheasant caught him,	514	Answer Fable	49
Himself the Lark, my Lord the Pheasant:	514	Answer Fable	52
PHEBUS			
He against Phebus Harp decreed,	156	Fable of Midas	27
That Phebus must give Place to Pan:	157	Fable of Midas	54
That Phebus ever shews his face;	621	Scandal Poem 1	132
As he, whom Phebus in his Ire	641	On Poetry	41
PHIL			
No news of Phil. The Bridegroom came,	223	Prog of Love	29
What Papers Phil had left behind,	223	Prog of Love	44
Phil cry'd, and John began to curse;	224	Prog of Love	80
Phil wish't, that she had strained a Limb	224	Prog of Love	81
PHILEMON			
Call'd thereabouts Goodman Philemon;	91	Bauc & Phil 1	52
Philemon by his Wife's consent	92	Bauc & Phil 1	69
Philemon whisper'd to his Wife,	92	Bauc & Phil 1	81
Philemon having paus'd a while	94	Bauc & Phil 1	157
Call'd, in the Neighbourhood, Philemon.	111	Bauc & Phil 2	20
Philemon, having paus'd a while,	115	Bauc & Phil 2	111
Philemon was in great Surprize,	116	Bauc & Phil 2	145
Here Baucis, there Philemon grew.	116	Bauc & Phil 2	172
PHILIP			
When Philip King of Greece was Dead,	99	Elegy Patrige	64
Restore the Ships by Philip taken,	468	Birthday Song	249
PHILIP'S			
See Philip's Son amidst his Persian Guard;	275	Epilogue	24
PHILIPS			
Theocritus and Philips be,	270	Apollo's Edict	D 31
Although to Praise it Philips Writ.	484	Libel on D- D-	144
PHILISTINES			
As much as Hebrews and Philistines:	812	Bro Protestant	32
PHILLIPS			
Shou'd Young and Phillips drudge together.	393	Modern Poets	20
And with Tom <D'urfey>, <Phillips>, <Dennis>,	184	Horace 2, 1	115
PHILLIS			
Desponding Phillis was endu'd	222	Prog of Love	1
To learn the Way that Phillis went;	223	Prog of Love	34
Phillis, it seems, was fled with John.	223	Prog of Love	42
Till Phillis all her Trinkets pawn'd:	224	Prog of Love	88
For John is Landlord, Phillis Hostess;	225	Prog of Love	98

PHILLIS   (CONTINUED)   PAGE   TITLE   LINE
    To censure Phillis for Perfumes;   . . . .   449 Modern Lady   159
    For Chloe, Sylvia, Phillis, Iris;   . . . .   729 Stella, Poems   40
    Bright Phillis mending ragged Smocks, ...   729 Stella, Poems   47
PHILOLOGERS
    Philologers of future Ages, ...   1021 Nim-Dan-Dean 1   D   37
PHILOMELA
    Thus when Philomela drooping, ...   661 Love Song   29
PHILOSOPHER
    You, like some acute Phil'osopher, ...   632 Epistle Lady   95
PHILOSOPHER'S
    Like the Philosopher's Stone, ...   26 Ode to Temple   15
PHILOSOPHERS
    Tho' Madmen and the Wits, Philosophers and Fools,   .   22 Ode Athenian   203
    Ye wise Philosophers explain   . . . .   250 Bubble   1
    (From whence Philosophers agree, ...   323 Pethox   9
    But antient Philosophers wisely Remark, ...   334 Serious Poem   7
    Some by philosophers misled, ...   490 Dialogue   49
    Or, as Philosophers, who find   . . . .   709 Cadenus Vaness   722
    For, tho' philosophers maintain . . . .   761 Bec's B-Day   19
    Thus Tim, Philosophers suppose, ...   777 Mullinix Tim   133
PHILOSOPHIC
    The Philosophic Cause will shew.   . . . .   126 Little House   4
PHILOSOPHICK
    By sober, Philosophick Laws, ...   65 Problem   14
PHILOSOPHY
    Of Nature and of Art, of deep Philosophy and Love,   17 Ode Athenian   55
    A Stock of Wisdom and Philosophy, ...   19 Ode Athenian   98
    Wondrous Refiners of Philosophy, ...   19 Ode Athenian   105
    Philosophy, as it before us lyes, ...   22 Ode Athenian   211
    The Gleanings of Philosophy, ...   27 Ode to Temple   23
    Philosophy! the Lumber of the Schools, ...   27 Ode to Temple   24
    To dig the leaden Mines of deep Philosophy: . . .   32 Ode to Temple   190
    In Wisdom and Philosophy;   . . . .   33 Ode to Temple   207
    Led blindly on by gross philosophy and pride,   .   36 Ode Sancroft   66
    Not in philosophy, or ale, ...   901 Dean's Reasons   75
PHILOSOPHY'S
    Philosophy's exalted head appears;   . . . . . .   16 Ode Athenian   15
PHIZ
    Poor Envy durst not shew her Phiz, ...   456 Dean Smedley   21
    Whose Phiz bespeaks his diet water-gruel.   . . .   672 Epig Carthy 24   D   10
    Adapt your Habit to your Phiz. . . . .   779 Mullinix Tim   212
    And leaves the Tartar Phiz, in show   . . . . .   786 Dick, Maggot   13
    And, grew enamour'd with her Phiz, ...   905 Death Daphne   65
PHLEGM
    Or stuff'd with Phlegm up to the Throat   . . . .   231 Prog of Poetry   25
    Choler preside, or Blood, or Phlegm, ...   724 To Stella   20
PHOEBUS   SEE PHEBUS,PHABUS
    There is a Worm by Phoebus bred, ...   79 Vanbrug House   29
    His Birth he does from Phoebus raise, ...   80 Vanbrug House   41
    By Phoebus newly Tann'd and Dry'd. . . . . .   100 Elegy Patrige   76
    Phoebus now shortning every Shade, ...   119 Apollo Outwit   1
    Phoebus was beautiful as you: . . . .   177 To Lord Harley   26
    We Phoebus think fit to proceed to his Sentence;   . .   266 Apollo   94
    "Where most true Sons of Phoebus ha' bin.   . . . .   320 First of April   4
    By Phoebus (an incestuous birth)   . . . . .   433 Answer Paulus   25
    By Phoebus first produc'd to light: . . . . .   433 Answer Paulus   27
    Old Phoebus is but half as bright, ...   462 Birthday Song   65
    Your Phoebus royal, every day   . . . .   462 Birthday Song   69
    For, Sons of Phoebus never break their Trust.   . .   532 To Mr. Gay   18
    And Phoebus sung th' Epithalamium. . . . . .   586 Strephon Chloe   62
    That Phoebus ever shows his Face;   . . . . .   627 Scandal Poem 2   136
    Phoebus forbids thee one, his Brother   . . . .   671 Epig Carthy 22   D   5
    A Thing never known to the Muses or Phoebus: . . .   716 Answer Rebus   8
    From Phoebus Rays they suffer Pain, ...   731 Stella, Poems   110
    That Phoebus help'd me in my Rhymes, ...   741 Stel B-day 22   24
    Phoebus inspir'd me from above, ...   741 Stel B-day 22   25
    Unless he were like Phoebus, young;   . . . . .   757 Stel B-day '24   20
    Their Phoebus I, my Spring their Hippocrene.   . .   793 St. Pat's Well   72
    Be my Phoebus while I rhime.   . . . .   862 To Janus   2
    Where Phoebus pays a scanty Stipend, ...   883 Rev Market-Hill   3
    Me Phoebus in a midnight Dream . . . .   897 Panegyr Dean   325
    Like Phoebus, guardian of the hours: . . . . .   937 Riddle 24   D   34
    I swear from henceforward you shall be my Phoebus.   .   973 S-'s Ans Sh-d   14
    And if you be my Phoebus, pray who was your Pallas?   977 Dean to Sherid   42
    If once in your cellar my Phoebus should shine,   . . .   979 Dean to Tho: S   29
PHOEBUS'
    Tigellius plac'd in Phoebus' Car, ...   650 On Poetry   303
PHOENIX
    Born like a Phoenix from the Flame, ...   81 Vanbrug House   79
    Born like a Pnoenix from the Flame, ...   109 V's House   121
    Against the Phoenix I protest. . . . .   271 Apollo's Edict   D   51
PHRASE
    As Mastive Dogs in Modern Phrase are   . . . . .   82 Salamander   1
    We style him by no other Phrase;   . . . .   298 Horrid Plot   8
    Worse than a Pun, or Irish Phrase, ...   312 To Ford   38
    However, if Criticks find Fault with the Phrase,   .   337 Serious Poem   101
    The Footman in his usual Phrase, ...   447 Modern Lady   92
    By cutting of his Phrase, and trimming, ...   455 Dean Smedley   19
    Give up the phrase of haughty Gaul, ...   468 Birthday Song   247
    (To know the World! a modern Phrase, ...   700 Cadenus Vaness   430

	PAGE	TITLE	LINE
PHRASE (CONTINUED)			
While you in your Faction's Phrase	838	Legion Club	215
PHRASES			
A Set of Phrases learn't by Rote;	415	Woman's Mind	1
In Phrases battered, stale, and trite, . . .	448	Modern Lady	112
Sets of Phrases, cut and dry, ...	523	Betty Grizette	13
PHYLLIS			
But thanks his stars, that Phyllis has been kind; . .	48	To Congreve	158
Phyllis, who but a Month ago	699	Cadenus Vaness	392
Not Phyllis after lying-in.	904	Death Daphne	38
PHYS			
Like good King Phys: and good King Ush:	63	Discovery	23
PHYSICIAN			
The kind Physician grants the Husband's Prayers, . .	364	On Dreams	27
That no Physician dares prescribe by Stealth: . . .	533	To Mr. Gay	78
Since he commenc'd Physician;	785	Mullinex Dick	26
Physician, Lawyer, and Divine, ...	922	Riddle 7	29
PHYSICIANS			
How the physicians swarm to shew their mortal skill, . .	42	Ode Sancroft	253
Reformers and physicians differ but in name, ...	42	Ode Sancroft	255
PHYSICK			
In Physick, Stolen Goods, or Love, ...	101	Elegy Patrige	115
If you had not took physick, I'd pay off your bacon, .	980	Tho: Sheridan	5
PICK			
And could pick up a Third.	75	Game Traffick	20
To pick up Sublunary Ladies.	120	Apollo Outwit	24
He strove to pick up all he found, ...	412	Desire Possess	25
And strip his Hyde, and pick his Bones, ...	413	Desire Possess	57
Fly from the Hawk, or pick his Pease up.	512	Answer Fable	10
"And, keep the Peace, to pick up Fees:	571	Death of Swift	450
No drunken Rake to pick her up, ...	581	Young Nymph	5
I hardly can pick, ...	853	Lady's Lament	64
And pick my Chicken to the Bone:	954	Authors Living	4
PICK-PURSE			
His Fellow Pick-Purse, watching for a job, ...	364	On Dreams	25
A Pick-purse at the Bar, or Bench;	645	On Poetry	165
PICK'D			
Drawn through the dirt, his pockets pick'd;	436	Answer Paulus	138
He no where could have better pick'd;	545	Life of Swift	17
"Nor Witness hir'd, nor Jury pick'd, ...	570	Death of Swift	429
A Pigeon pick'd her Issue-Peas;	583	Young Nymph	63
PICK'T			
My Pocket was pick't, ...	245	Irish-Feast	19
Bare, like a Carcase pick't by Crows, ...	904	Death Daphne	34
He pick't my Marrow from the Bone.	915	Riddle 1	14
Because they find their Pockets pick't.	917	Riddle 3	16
PICKING SEE CINDER-PICKING			
Picking Wit among Collegions, ...	523	Betty Grizette	23
Now, picking out a Crystal Eye, ...	581	Young Nymph	11
Pursue thy Trade of Scandall picking, ...	735	Stel B-day '20	41
While they sit a picking Straws	831	Legion Club	49
In rhetoric, or picking straws;	901	Dean's Reasons	77
O, 'tis pretty Picking	952	Asparagus	4
PICKLE			
You men would be in wofull pickle	618	Scandal Poem 1	41
PICKT			
How Miss pickt ev'ry painted Card, ...	86	Hist V's House	4
Pickt the Demure, the Aukward, and the Coy; . . .	118	Biddy Floyd	6
So prettily he pickt a Cow-<turd>:	514	Answer Fable	48
PICQUET			
To lose a Guinea at Picquet, ...	546	Life of Swift	27
PICTURE			
Enlarg'd in Picture, Size and Letter	93	Bauc & Phil 1	121
Improv'd in Picture, Size, and Letter;	114	Bauc & Phil 2	98
I think I have seen her Picture by Jervis.-- . . .	869	Grand Question	76
Come sit by my side, while this picture I draw: . .	955	Portrait Life	1
Both of the Picture and Original.	993	On Picture	27
PICTURES SEE SAVAGE-PICTURES			
(As Pictures prove) with Garlands crown'd, ...	590	Strephon Chloe	194
PIDDLE			
To piddle like a Lady breeding.	745	Stel Distress	8
To piddle like a Lady breeding:	750	Stel Wood-Park	32
PIEC'D			
She piec'd it up again with Scotch.	96	On the Union	4
PIECE SEE HEEL-PIECE			
It seems some floating piece of Paradice, ...	17	Ode Athenian	44
Here's ev'ry Piece as big as ten.	251	Bubble	8
Now from his Lordship's Grace I hold a little Piece of Ground,	342	Upon His Grace	21
To form a just and finish'd piece, ...	460	Birthday Song	1
Punch is exactly of a Piece	592	Strephon Chloe	291
They may hope for Pence a Piece.	833	Legion Club	108
Cut from the Piece that made her Shift, ...	925	Riddle 8	42
So much, he swears the very best Piece is . . .	988	Letter Dr Sh-n	22
PIECES			
It lost some mighty Pieces thro' all hands it past . .	25	Ode Athenian	286
(In pieces cut, the Viper still did reunite) . . .	30	Ode to Temple	132
He chip't his Bread, the Pieces round	156	Fable of Midas	3
In Fillets roll'd, or cut in Pieces, ...	344	Prometheus	7
For she her self oft falls in Pieces.	362	Grace's Answer	28
Bursting into Pieces there:	638	Epistle Lady	252

		PAGE	TITLE	LINE
PIECES (CONTINUED)				
Tear the Bible all to Pieces.		831	Legion Club	66
He takes me to pieces.		853	Lady's Lament	70
And Skin and Flesh in Pieces tore.		925	Riddle 8	40
But all I delight in is Pieces of Lead;		927	Riddle 11	D 6
Why then I make pieces of Iron go down.		927	Riddle 11	D 8
PIERC'D				
You would swear it pierc'd the Sky;		638	Epistle Lady	250
It pierc'd the feeble Volume thro',		703	Cadenus Vaness	518
Stuck to the Point that pierc'd her Breast;		703	Cadenus Vaness	521
PIERCE				
Wont at such times each heart to pierce,		296	Satiric Elegy	19
To pierce an injur'd Lover's Heart.		595	Cassinus Peter	60
He pierce the Clouds! he kiss our <arses>)		620	Scandal Poem 1	104
He pierce the Clouds! He kiss their <Arses>.)		626	Scandal Poem 2	102
Pierce us all with wounding Steel,		931	Riddle 18	D 21
PIERCES				
(Who makes you think the Clouds he pierces:		620	Scandal Poem 1	103
(Who makes you think, the Clouds he pierces:		626	Scandal Poem 2	101
PIERCING				
My Genius piercing, sharp and bright,		920	Riddle 6	5
PIES SEE PUDDING-PIES				
As Pies and Daws are often stil'd		82	Salamander	3
"Your Golden Pippins, and your Pies,		154	Widow and Cat	D 26
She'll never think of Mutton Pies.		362	Grace's Answer	42
PIETY				
Whose Wisdom and whose Piety, do far exceed his Years.		341	Upon His Grace	4
Whose filial Piety excels		482	Libel on D- D-	77
Their filial Piety forgot,		652	On Poetry	359
PIGEON				
A Pigeon wou'd, if shown by Aesop,		512	Answer Fable	9
A Pigeon pick'd her Issue-Peas;		583	Young Nymph	63
PIGEON-HOUSE				
Or of a Pigeon-house, or Oven,		127	Little House	37
PIGEON'S				
Dear Madam try this Pigeon's leg:		746	Stel Distress	18
Dear Madam, try this Pigeon's Leg;		750	Stel Wood-Park	16
PIGEONS				
And Pigeons billing, Sparrows treading,		585	Strephon Chloe	51
PIGMY'S				
It might have been a Pigmy's Tomb.		128	Little House	46
PIGS				
What gave her Brats and Pigs the Meazles,		282	Journal	93
"Pigs and Fanaticks, Cows, and Teagues		851	Old Thorn	77
To make for Pigs convenient Styes:		892	Panegyr Dean	160
PIKE				
But should a lordly Pike appear,		824	Printer Newgat	8
PIL'D				
Pil'd in a Garret charm'd the Author's Sight.		667	Epig Carthy 5	D 2
PILAT				
Was both a Boat, and in one Sense a Pilat.		285	Elegy Boat	14
PILATE				
When Christ was betray'd to Pilate, the Praetor,		804	Irish Bishops	29
PILE				
As some fair pile, yet spar'd by zeal and rage,		52	Temple Ill	47
Then rear 'em to goodly Pile,		79	Vanbrug House	6
The Rubbish of an antient Pile.		81	Vanbrug House	84
He built up such a monstrous Pile,		87	Hist V's House	28
Then rear 'em to a goodly Pile.		106	V's House	6
A Pile shall from its Ashes rise		107	V's House	49
Proceeded to erect his Pile:		108	V's House	64
To praise the Pile, and Builder <Van>.		109	V's House	108
May lodge within thy Spacious Pile.		109	V's House	118
The Rubbish of an Antient Pile.		109	V's House	126
This is the little strutting Pile,		127	Little House	13
Got Hercules to bear the Pile		160	Atlas	11
Contrive your Pile to last for Life;		593	Strephon Chloe	302
As when a lofty Pile is rais'd,		727	Stella, Poems	1
So if this Pile of scatter'd Rhymes		728	Stella, Poems	5
Tell us, what this Pile contains?		829	Legion Club	9
I allow the Pile may stand.		830	Legion Club	38
PILGRIMS				
The gentle Pilgrims soon aware on't,		112	Bauc & Phil 2	41
PILL				
And give Advice before he gives the Pill.		534	To Mr. Gay	80
PILLAGE				
All to plunder, all to pillage;		574	Helter Skelter	40
Come flocking for pillage,		857	Lady's Lament	196
His crabs and sloes may freely pillage:		902	Dean's Reasons	108
PILLAR				
The single Pillar for his Country's Good,		770	Horace 1, 14	16
PILLION				
The Horse and Pillion both were gone		223	Prog of Love	41
PILLORY				
Threatning the Pillory and Jayl.		312	To Ford	46
PILLOW				
To see her from her Pillow rise		226	Prog of Beauty	13
Morpheus hov'ring o'er my Pillow,		661	Love Song	23
PILLS				
His Pills, his Almanacks, or Shoes.		101	Elegy Patrige	108
And <Wood's> ditto Pills do Swallow,		372	Letter D. S-y	30

PILLS	(CONTINUED)	PAGE	TITLE	LINE
And talk of Spectacles and Pills;	. . . .	763	Stel B-day '26	6
Of Doctors, Fevers, Plagues, and Pills.	. . . . . .	903	Death Daphne	6
PILOT				
The Pilot knew not how to guide.	. . . .	96	On the Union	20
Without a Pilot seldom knows	. . . .	256	Bubble	143
PIMP				
"A Rake, a Bully, Pimp, or Spy.	. . . .	303	Storm	30
Lords keep a Pimp to bring a Wench;	. . . .	480	Libel on D- D-	22
Ev'n Jove, and Mercury his pimp	. . . .	620	Scandal Poem 1	101
Ev'n Jove, and Mercury his Pimp,	. . . .	626	Scandal Poem 2	99
PIMPS				
Than Pimps to Wickedness in Pow'r?	. . . .	493	Panegyr Swift	26
The Perquisites of Pimps and Wits.	. . . .	498	Panegyr Swift	151
To work whose Ends, his Madness pimps.	. . . . . .	798	Traulus 1	72
PIN				
He makes no more to give ten Pounds than I to give a Pin.		341	Upon His Grace	14
Sell the Nation for a Pin;	. . . .	831	Legion Club	48
It would not signify a pin	. . . .	899	Dean's Reasons	25
. . .and I would pin a Dish-clout to his Tail.	. . .	987	Mary to Sher	32
PIN'D				
With hungry Meals his Body pin'd,	. . . . . .	231	Prog of Poetry	37
PINCH				
Then give us a Pinch	. . . .	246	Irish-Feast	55
They at a Pinch can bribe a Vote:	. . . . . .	483	Libel on D- D-	96
You at a Pinch could forge a Plot;	. . . . . .	494	Panegyr Swift	40
The Vermin only teaze and pinch	. . . . . .	651	On Poetry	335
Taking then a Pinch of Snuff;	. . . . . .	839	Legion Club	240
"By <God> they don't signify this Pinch of Snuff.	. .	872	Grand Question	160
So well contriv'd her Toes to pinch,	. . . . . .	885	Rev Market-Hill	65
PINCH'D				
"Or chid the Dean, or pinch'd thy Spouse.	. . . . .	850	Old Thorn	70
PINCHING				
Thus a wise Taylor is not pinching,	. . . . . .	1021	Nim-Dan-Dean 1	D 15
PINDAR				
Thy Muse from falling upon Pindar?	. . . . . .	666	Epig Carthy 2	D 2
Like lofty Pindar I can soar,	. . . .	929	Riddle 15	D 6
PINDUS				
And, sits aloft on Pindus Head,	. . . . . .	483	Libel on D- D-	87
And, when Apollo struts on Pindus,	. . . . . .	620	Scandal Poem 1	107
And when Apollo struts on Pindus,	. . . . . .	626	Scandal Poem 2	105
PINE				
Who pine us like a Chronical Disease;	. . . . .	9	Ode to King	88
Pine unpitied to my urn,	. . . .	937	Riddle 24	D 51
PINES				
While my hard-labour'd Poem pines	. . . . .	502	Doctor Delaney	77
PINIONS				
And borne on fancy's Pinions, thinks,	. . . . .	80	Vanbrug House	51
Though Fear should lend him Pinions like the Wind,	.	210	Earl of Oxford	5
Make Pinions for themselves to fly,	. . . . .	239	Run Bankers	22
Flutt'ring spread thy purple Pinions,	. . . . .	660	Love Song	1
She would feel her Pinions drop,	. . . . . .	834	Legion Club	128
PINN'D				
Her Napkin pinn'd up to her Jaws,	. . . . .	894	Panegyr Dean	256
PINNACLE				
Hung loosely on the Church's pinnacle,	. . . . .	37	Ode Sancroft	74
PINNER				
He tore her best lac'd Pinner;	. . . .	153	Widow and Cat	D 12
"'Tis true, the Pinner which you prize	. . . . .	154	Widow and Cat	D 28
PINNERS				
Good Pinners edg'd with Colberteen:	. . . . .	115	Bauc & Phil 2	140
Or greasy Coifs and Pinners reeking,	. . . . .	527	Lady's Dres Rm	53
PINNING				
Pinning on Coifs and combing Hair;	. . . . .	321	First of April	30
PINT				
Now venture at a Pint of Port,	. . . . . .	184	Horace 2, 1	112
"He hardly drinks a Pint of Wine;	. . . . .	557	Death of Swift	109
Surprize him with a Pint of Stout,	. . . . .	728	Stella, Poems	32
To a sour Pint one day in twenty.	. . . . .	745	Stel Distress	14
To half a Pint one Day in twenty.	. . . . .	750	Stel Wood-Park	38
Upon a Chick, and Pint of Wine.	. . . . .	954	Authors Living	2
That we may have a Pint.	. . . .	1015	Swift to Sheri	44
PINTS				
What Pints may best for Bottles pass,	. . . . .	889	Panegyr Dean	93
PIOUS				
Lives pious witness of a better age;	. . . . .	52	Temple Ill	48
And to his Pious Patron's Ghost.	. . . . .	183	Horace 2, 1	92
Till pious Love inspir'd her Son?	. . . . .	269	Apollo's Edict	D 4
Who dares affirm this is no pious age,	. . . . .	274	Epilogue	1
And, thus the pious Wolf begins:	. . . . .	601	Beasts Confess	12
But, through a pious Resolution;	. . . . .	603	Beasts Confess	68
Offensive to all pious ears.	. . . . . .	622	Scandal Poem 1	168
Of pious Prelates what a Stock	. . . . .	656	On Poetry	453
Is by all pious Christians thought,	. . . . .	942	Probatur Alit	5
PIPE				
Cou'd smoak his Pipe, and read the News;	. . . .	115	Bauc & Phil 2	126
And pausing o'er a Pipe, with doubtful Nod,	. . .	193	Author Himself	5
My Pipe it was broke,	. . . .	245	Irish-Feast	18
His antient Pipe in Sable dy'd,	. . . . .	594	Cassinus Peter	23
Fill ev'ry Pipe, each Motion guide.	. . . . .	798	Traulus 1	74

		PAGE	TITLE	LINE	
PIPE	(CONTINUED)				
With his Pipe and his Pot,		952	Apples		9
PIPING					
And lowing Herds, and piping Swains,		934	Riddle 21	D	9
PIPPIN					
Guarded each fair Hesperian Pippin.		134	Magician's Rod		74
Would strait become a Golden Pippin:		156	Fable of Midas		6
Like the faint red upon a Pippin		290	Prog Marriage		25
Or, a tawny speckled Pippin,		523	Betty Grizette		9
Said to the Pippin, plump, and prim,		811	Bro Protestant		13
PIPPINS					
"Your Golden Pippins, and your Pies,		154	Widow and Cat	D	26
PIQUET					
We lose with Sharpers at Piquet;		724	To Stella		28
PISH					
Pish at his Cook'ry, damn his Wine;		495	Panegyr Swift		69
PISS					
His next will be a Rod in Piss.		135	Magician's Rod		86
Toast old Glorious in your Piss.		835	Legion Club		152
And how, when Master went to <piss>,		150	Corinna		23
Can Chloe, heav'nly Chloe <piss>?		589	Strephon Chloe		178
Can <piss> upon his lawrel crown.		620	Scandal Poem 1		110
Will often <piss> upon a nettle;		621	Scandal Poem 1		144
Can <piss> upon his Lawrel Crown.		626	Scandal Poem 2		108
Will often <piss> upon a Nettle;		628	Scandal Poem 2		148
PISSES					
Nor, in their Eyes at Random pisses,		796	Traulus 1		29
Jove <pisses> on you through a Sieve;		627	Scandal Poem 2		126
PISSING					
Torment, by pissing out their Lights;		100	Elegy Patrige		92
Of pissing in the Rabble's Eyes.		787	Dick's Variety		6
<PISSPOT>					
I'll fling the <Pisspot> on your head;		91	Bauc & Phil 1		38
<PISST>					
And Puss had on her Plumpers <pisst>.		583	Young Nymph		62
PISTOLES					
"Here, carry down those ten Pistoles		447	Modern Lady		66
PIT					
Whence came these Goths to overrun the pit?		46	To Congreve		84
Against the proud usurpers of the pit;		46	To Congreve		110
Confounded in that Babel of the pit;		47	To Congreve		122
For, should the vilest scribbler to the pit,		48	To Congreve		165
At Beggar's-Op'ra not so full Pit		889	Panegyr Dean		65
PITCH					
Both Pitch and Brimstone to fill up his Flaws;		285	Elegy Boat		28
To pitch on me, of all Mankind,		445	Modern Lady		6
I attempt no higher Pitch.		635	Epistle Lady		172
The Son of Pitch, and gloomy Night;		929	Riddle 15	D	2
PITCHY					
And scrape her Pitchy Sides for Wax.		100	Elegy Patrige		78
PITIED					
Yet well they merit be pitied,		434	Answer Paulus		59
I pitied my Cat, whom I knew by her Mew sick;		1029	Dr. Helsham		5
PITIFUL					
As pitiful as Tom MacLobe.		670	Epig Carthy 21	D	4
PITS SEE ARM-PITS					
PITTYING					
My Lady, pittying his Confussion,		378	Apology Lady C		84
PITY					
Do laugh perhaps at theirs, and pity mine and me.		18	Ode Athenian		90
Pity a miserable Church's tears,		42	Ode Sancroft		243
'Troth I could pity you; but this is it,		48	To Congreve		161
Triumphant Star! Some Pity show		100	Elegy Patrige		89
Try'd ev'ry Tone might Pity win,		111	Bauc & Phil 2		13
In pity to the empty'ng Town		122	Empty'ng Town		1
I pity Elrington with all my heart;		308	Billet Players		31
When Jove, in pity to the Town,		353	Wood Ironmongr		23
"Learn hence t' excuse and pity me.		380	Apology Lady C		144
Will purchase me, the more's the Pity,		410	Dial Rich Marb		68
I pity you, dear Marble-Hill;		411	Dial Rich Marb		101
At once creating Love and Pity.		417	Woman's Mind		42
It's Pity that he can't bestow you		476	Epist on Epist		41
I pity wretched Strephon blind		530	Lady's Dres Rm		129
In those who never Pity felt;		561	Death of Swift		216
"True genuine Dulness mov'd his Pity,		572	Death of Swift		469
Where a Fault shou'd move your Pity.		630	Epistle Lady		14
Take Pity on your pitying Friends;		766	Stel B-day '26		80
Yet I look on thee with Pity.		838	Legion Club		192
"It's a pity a Prelate should die without law;		843	Ay and No		17
Come here out of pity,		858	Lady's Lament		216
Her, who, without thy Pity, dies?		924	Riddle 8		2
I'm so full of Pity, I never abuse Sick;		1028	Dr. Helsham		2
PITY'D					
"And pity'd those who meant the Wound:		567	Death of Swift		360
PITY'S					
For Pity's Sake it would be just,		813	Bro Protestant		55
PITYING					
Admiring you, you pitying us.		755	Stella '23		38
Take Pity on your pitying Friends;		766	Stel B-day '26		80
PLAC'D					
And high in Order plac'd, describe		114	Bauc & Phil 2		99

PLAC'D   (CONTINUED)

	PAGE	TITLE	LINE
Plac'd you in Life too far behind;	215	To Mr. Delany	6
Plac'd me in Life too far before;	215	To Mr. Delany	8
But in Stella's bright Eyes were plac'd right again;	264	Apollo	50
Were you but plac'd on Satan's Rump;	497	Panegyr Swift	137
Here Gallypots and Vials plac'd,	526	Lady's Dres Rm	33
On Embers plac'd, to drink it hot.	594	Cassinus Peter	28
Let both around my Tomb be plac'd,	611	By Dr. Swift	5
Tigellius plac'd in Phoebus' Car,	650	On Poetry	303
The Fault must on the Nymphs be plac'd,	688	Cadenus Vaness	65
That, Merit should be chiefly plac'd	697	Cadenus Vaness	342
She plac'd it in the strongest View.	701	Cadenus Vaness	455
Nature in him had Merit plac'd,	711	Cadenus Vaness	766
Plac'd against the Church direct;	829	Legion Club	6
Which in its proper Station plac'd,	1021	Nim-Dan-Dean 1	D 13

PLAC'T

	PAGE	TITLE	LINE
If o'er against her you were plac't	222	Prog of Love	5
Benches on Boats are plac't, not Boats on Benches.	285	Elegy Boat	12
Above the Reach of Want is plac't:	483	Libel on D- D-	84
There, near thy Master's Throne in Shelter plac't,	538	Mr. Pulteney	11
While we, o'er Tenariffa plac't,	620	Scandal Poem 1	105
While we, o'er Tenariffa plac't,	626	Scandal Poem 2	103
Nor can be more securely plac't	747	Stel Distress	63
Nor can be more securely plac't	752	Stel Wood-Park	79
And here thy daily Vot'ries plac't	894	Panegyr Dean	239
Whose Off'rings plac't in golden Ranks,	896	Panegyr Dean	301
That, near the Knight of Gosford plac't,	899	Dean's Reasons	21

PLACE   SEE BIRTH-PLACE,DWELLING-PLACE,COMMON-PLACE

	PAGE	TITLE	LINE
Suspended every Horror of the Place,	9	Ode to King	95
Of time or place,	34	Ode Sancroft	8
To keep that worthless clod, the body, in one place:	36	Ode Sancroft	64
Should such a wretch usurp my Congreve's place,	48	To Congreve	169
Who that had Wit would place it here,	60	Lady Tablebook	17
Clap his own Nonsence in the place.	61	Lady Tablebook	24
Lord help me, said Mary, I never stirr'd out of this Place!	70	Mrs Harris Pet	16
Then all in the Place	76	Lady B- B-	5
Just in the Place where first it grew,	87	Hist V's House	32
A Place not decent here to name.	108	V's House	94
Points out the Place of either Yew;	116	Bauc & Phil 2	171
The Kennel-Edge, where Wheels had worn the Place.	124	Descriptn Morn	10
A Place was fastned to the Hook,	133	Magician's Rod	45
Out of Zeal for his Country, and want of a Place,	142	New Song	3
That Phebus must give Place to Pan:	157	Fable of Midas	54
Here fell a Pension, there a Place:	158	Fable of Midas	76
And fill <Jack Smith> with Hopes to keep his Place;	163	Toland's Invit	20
Will come; and <Hampden> shall have <Walpole's> Place.	165	Toland's Invit	34
<Swift> much admires the Place and Air,	173	Horace 1, 7	83
A Canon! that's a Place too mean:	173	Horace 1, 7	87
In Scribler to have had a place.	186	Scriblerus 3	6
And squeeze it in, or quit your Place:	190	Faggot	40
Humour, and Mirth, had Place in all he writ:	194	Author Himself	11
That, begs my Interest for a Place--	200	Horace 2, 6	48
To find an easy Place to lay-her.	207	Fable Bitches	6
Takes up with Copper in the Place;	216	To Mr. Delany	44
There practic'd how to place her Head,	222	Prog of Love	13
See then what Mortals place their Bliss in!	223	Prog of Love	25
So gracefull in their proper Place,	226	Prog of Beauty	22
Each Colour to it's Place and Use,	227	Prog of Beauty	47
Intended in Time to succeed to your Place;	263	Apollo	28
For who can hope to place one there,	271	Apollo's Edict	D 38
We may place Boat in his old Post again.	285	Elegy Boat	30
Then Hebe came and took her Place	290	Prog Marriage	15
Beholds her from the Chaplain's Place	291	Prog Marriage	63
To place him at the hinder End	292	Prog Marriage	78
Here, all Diversions of the Place	294	Prog Marriage	131
That he's to have a Place at <Court>.	300	Horrid Plot	64
Yes, and a Place he will grow rich in;	300	Horrid Plot	65
To help an honest lad that's out of place,	308	Billet Players	25
Be sure conceal the Time and Place,	311	To Ford	8
Good Manners must give Place to Profit.	311	To Ford	16
In thy great Care we place our Trust,	339	Arch-Bish Dub	7
And willingly resigns its Place	340	Arch-Bish Dub	15
They search't his Pockets on the Place,	353	Wood Ironmongr	27
For tho' the Place of either Ear,	366	Answer Delaney	29
Flies like a Squib from Place to Place,	398	Earl of P-b-w	8
Flies like a Squib from Place to Place,	398	Earl of P-b-w	8
My honest Friend Wild, may he long hold his Place,	399	Tom Clinch	17
To place me with the Prince of Wales.	410	Dial Rich Marb	76
Or put one Feature out of Place;	414	Censure	24
And where with Art to place a Patch.	416	Woman's Mind	32
Will serve instead of place or pension	421	Ireld	18
Yet should this Blockhead beg a Place	423	Ireld	69
Should come in his place	424	Carterets Arms	10
Scrambling with <rogues> to get a place:	436	Answer Paulus	140
Now to another Scene give Place,	447	Modern Lady	80
And fair Discretion left the Place,	448	Modern Lady	122
Thus Berecynthia takes her place,	466	Birthday Song	183
You place the Muses and Apollo;	477	Epist on Epist	80
Your Whimsical, Poetick Place.	477	Epist on Epist	82
Then, shou'd you dare to ask a Place,	480	Libel on D- D-	29

PLACE   (CONTINUED)   PAGE TITLE   LINE

Rejects a servile Usher's Place, ...   482 Libel on D- D-   59
That you have got a Place already, ...   483 Libel on D- D-   104
What Claim have you to Place, or Pension?   . . . .   483 Libel on D- D-   109
And place you in a better Station, ...   484 Libel on D- D-   119
His Virtues battling with his Place;   . . . .   484 Libel on D- D-   146
Who must Obey, or lose his Place.   . . . .   485 Libel on D- D-   160
Which, if you durst but give it place, ...   485 Libel on D- D-   179
Or vile Submissions, when in Place;   . . . .   494 Panegyr Swift   34
Thus, should I give your Humour place, ...   496 Panegyr Swift   110
Say, had the Court no better place to chuse   . . . .   531 To Mr. Gay   7
I place a <Statesman> full before my Sight.   . . . .   532 To Mr. Gay   32
To act with Infamy, or quit the Place. . . . .   535 To Mr. Gay   130
"That e'er he cring'd to Men in Place? . . . .   549 Life of Swift   145
Forgets the Place where last he din'd: . . . .   556 Death of Swift   88
And in his Place my good Friend Will;   . . . .   560 Death of Swift   194
"We hope he's in a better Place.   . . . .   562 Death of Swift   242
Allow there's a Hell, but dispute of the Place;   . .   575 Place Damn'd   2
The Place of the Damn'd,--I'll tell you my Mind.   . .   575 Place Damn'd   4
For We know by these Marks, the place of the Damn'd;   .   576 Place Damn'd   16
Yet would rather be hang'd than he'd leave a warm Place.   580 Psyche   6
The cringing Knave who seeks a Place   . . . .   604 Beasts Confess   93
The fittest Man to fill a Place: . . . .   606 Beasts Confess   156
We, to whom all the Gods give place.   . . . .   620 Scandal Poem 1   96
We, to whom all the Gods give place.   . . . .   626 Scandal Poem 2   94
'Till some fresh Blockhead takes your Place.   . . . .   644 On Poetry   142
Place Elephants for want of Towns.   . . . .   646 On Poetry   180
Of Unities, in Time and Place.   . . . .   648 On Poetry   244
They soon betray their native Place: . . . .   652 On Poetry   362
Blackmore alone his Place supply'd: . . . .   652 On Poetry   372
Content yourself with humbler Place.   . . . .   656 On Poetry   458
With whom a Footman out of Place   . . . .   659 On Poetry   D 410
Thy curate's place, thy fruitful wife, ...   676 Parson's Case   5
With visits, or to beg a place; . . . .   677 Parson's Case   30
Fly to the Sea, my Place of Birth;   . . . .   689 Cadenus Vaness   88
She then referr'd them to a Place   . . . .   690 Cadenus Vaness   110
She never hit one proper Place;   . . . .   700 Cadenus Vaness   423
Had met her in a publick Place, ...   706 Cadenus Vaness   634
Nor is Complexion Honour's Place.   . . . .   724 To Stella   22
But how would Brutus in my Place?   . . . .   724 To Stella   40
Who bring the Lime, or place the Stones;   . . . . .   727 Stella, Poems   3
Truth, Judgment, Wit, give Place to Spite, ...   730 Stella, Poems   93
Then, who can think we'll quit the Place   . . . . .   735 Stel B-day '20   33
Of Poets dare assume my Place;   . . . .   739 Stel B-day '21   14
The Place, the Welcome, and the Spark, ...   748 Stel Distress   70
The Virtue lies not in the Place: . . . .   752 Stel Wood-Park   90
To fill a Place, for want of better;   . . . .   756 Stel B-day '24   10
Once more the <Dean> supplies their Place.   . . . .   757 Stel B-day '24   14
Walk by my place, before my Betters, ...   778 Mullinix Tim   156
Cou'd we place him in a Station, ...   801 Traulus 2   47
To cry; Lo, Judas, gone to his own Place: . . . .   806 Judas   24
His Station despising, unaw'd by the Place, ...   809 Epigr Prelate   3
Thy Founder's Grandson and usurp his Place.   . . . .   826 Noisy Tom   16
Time and Place are in thy Power.   . . . .   832 Legion Club   78
You lost a Place, and sav'd a Bribe?   . . . .   884 Rev Market-Hill   36
These gaudy Shoes must Hannah place   . . . .   885 Rev Market-Hill   67
They place before him Gloves and Shoes; . . . .   885 Rev Market-Hill   78
We'll place him at the lower End.   . . . .   886 Rev Market-Hill   98
Except to give <Dean> <Daniel> place.   . . . .   888 Panegyr Dean   48
Why will you place in lazy Pride   . . . .   896 Panegyr Dean   293
The sweetest Place for Masquerades: . . . .   905 Death Daphne   86
And in dress place all your merit;   . . . .   908 Daphne   76
By Fate exalted high in Place;   . . . .   917 Riddle 3   1
To place them in another View, ...   919 Riddle 5   13
And find a resting Place at last.   . . . .   923 Riddle 7   78
In no Place have I ever been, ...   935 Riddle 23   D 3
George, Dan, Dean, and Nim to place in the center?   1027 Sheri Circles   14
PLACES   SEE COMMON-PLACES
And in all the Places I liv'd, I never heard of such a   70 Mrs Harris Pet   31
    Thing.
Till all my Relations were put into Places.   . . . .   144 New Song   24
And all my whole Family, Places by Dozens;   . . . .   144 New Song   48
By Places and Commissions sold, ...   157 Fable of Midas   47
To let our company supply their places, ...   307 Billet Players   7
Nor Persons Names, nor Places knew;   . . . . . .   313 To Ford   54
And on the Right Hand took their Places   689 Cadenus Vaness   95
PLACING
And, placing Raillery in Railing, ...   416 Woman's Mind   19
Placing in the strongest Light, ...   633 Epistle Lady   97
For placing still some Book betwixt, ...   701 Cadenus Vaness   480
PLAD
And Scipio, trail an Irish purple Plad.   . . . . .   275 Epilogue   22
PLAGIARY
For all its Plagiary Light, ...   10 Ode to King   125
PLAGUE
Sin and the plague ever abound   . . . .   37 Ode Sancroft   96
That Plague, Directors, to the Deep, ...   258 Bubble   207
To spare the Rich, and plague the Poor; . . . .   392 Young's Satire   46
Not to direct a Plague, or Storm, ...   496 Panegyr Swift   93
Why, Plague confound her sandy Locks: . . . . . .   595 Cassinus Peter   47
It happen'd when a Plague broke out, ...   601 Beasts Confess   5

```
PLAGUE          (CONTINUED)                              PAGE    TITLE           LINE
     And when I damn my Soul to plague 'em,      . . . . . .   778 Mullinix Tim        173
     How to plague and starve the City;       . . . . . . .   831 Legion Club          54
     Tho' Delany advis'd you to plague me no longer,   . . .   967 Letter Sherid         7
     Much Plague it created,       . . . . . . . . . .       1014 Swift to Sheri       15
     Here four of you got mischances to plague you,   . . . .  1037 Four Storyes          1
PLAGUES
     The Plagues and Scourges of Mankind.      . . . . . .    654 On Poetry           408
     Be soundly mawl'd, and plagues the rest.    . . . . . .  777 Mullinix Tim        132
     Of Doctors, Fevers, Plagues, and Pills.     . . . . .    903 Death Daphne          6
PLAGUILY
     And, the Doctor was plaguily down in the Hips.   . . .   873 Grand Question      178
PLAGUY
     "To put him in a plaguy Fright,      . . . . . . . .     305 Storm                54
     For leave to act in town? 'Tis plaguy dear.    . . . .   308 Billet Players       18
     Poor Tom has got a plaguy baulk---!      . . . . . . .   545 Life of Swift        22
PLAIN
     How plain I see thro' the Deceit!      . . . . . . .      29 Ode to Temple       100
     Go publish o'er the Plain       . . . . . . . . . .       31 Ode to Temple       139
     Which in its dusky march along the plain,     . . . .     40 Ode Sancroft        193
     March o'er the ruin'd plain with motion slow,     . . .   55 Temple Ill          129
     . . .that's a plain Case.      . . . . . . . . . . .      70 Mrs Harris Pet       17
     From whence 'tis plain the Diadem      . . . . . . .      98 Elegy Patrige        25
     Plain Goody would no longer down,      . . . . . . . .   116 Bauc & Phil 2       143
     For among good Friends, I love to be plain;    . . . .   168 Peace Dunkirk         7
     His Pardon begg'd, but to be plain,      . . . . . .     224 Prog of Love         57
     The Reason is plain, they are none of his own;    . . .  264 Apollo               56
     Confess't as plain as he could bark;     . . . . . .     300 Horrid Plot          55
     Sir, to be plain, I tell you what;      . . . . . . .    300 Horrid Plot          67
     'Tis a Metaphor known to ev'ry plain Thinker.    . . .   335 Serious Poem         53
     'Twas plain he cou'd no longer hold      . . . . . . .   346 Prometheus           49
     Nam'd me as plain as he cou'd speak:     . . . . . . .   376 Apology Lady C       47
     The Moral is so plain to hit,      . . . . . . . .       393 Modern Poets         17
     Plain Loyalty not built on Hope,      . . . . . . . .    410 Dial Rich Marb       81
     Along the plain like Lightning flew:     . . . . . .     412 Desire Possess       22
     Will prove herself a Tory plain,     . . . . . . . .     417 Woman's Mind         53
     That he's Apollo, is as plain, as     . . . . . . .      462 Birthday Song        59
     The point is plain: Remove the cause;     . . . . . .    487 Irish-Club           15
     From whence the Consequence is plain,     . . . . . .    495 Panegyr Swift        76
     From whence 'tis plain, they quite have lost    . . . .  498 Panegyr Swift       165
     "Tis plain, his Writings were design'd    . . . . . .    550 Life of Swift       196
     The King of Brutes (to make it plain,    . . . . . .     601 Beasts Confess        7
     By his authority tis plain,      . . . . . . . . .       620 Scandal Poem 1       85
     By his Authority, 'tis plain       . . . . . . . .       626 Scandal Poem 2       83
     For Food, along the barren Plain;      . . . . . . .     759 Receipt Youth         6
     From all their Conduct this is plain,     . . . . . .    773 Mullinix Tim         11
     Why Tom, I think the Case is plain,      . . . . . .     796 Traulus 1            13
     For thine, my dear Dick, give me leave to speak plain,  . 819 Archbi Cashel      15
     The Lord of all the fruitful Plain,      . . . . . .     848 Old Thorn            10
     His malice is plain,      . . . . . . . . . . . .        852 Lady's Lament         9
     Altho' it was plain, in her Heart she was glad,   . . .  873 Grand Question      183
     To pay your Tribute on the Plain?      . . . . . .       896 Panegyr Dean        292
     I have it now ---- 'Tis plain enough,     . . . . . .    912 Aenigma Expl    D    3
     Yet, the plain Squire, when Dinner's done,    . . . .    920 Riddle 6             27
     . . .in plain English tell us so?      . . . . . . .    1013 Swift to Sheri        2
PLAINEST
     The plainest Mails must be the best:     . . . . . . .   378 Apology Lady C      104
     Nor can the plainest Word pronounce      . . . . . .     891 Panegyr Dean        149
PLAINLY
     which plainly shews the near Alliance    . . . . . .      98 Elegy Patrige        29
     Besides, it plainly now appears,      . . . . . . . .    158 Fable of Midas       61
     To inflame both the Nations do plainly conspire;    . .  237 Excellent Song       19
     Subscribers plainly see 'um there,      . . . . . . .    257 Bubble              167
     Now, let me tell you, plainly, Sir,      . . . . . .     299 Horrid Plot          43
     His Correspondence plainly dated,      . . . . . . .     300 Horrid Plot          51
     And plainly prove by dint of Text,     . . . . . . .     456 Dean Smedley         39
     You plainly find it in his Face:      . . . . . . . .    556 Death of Swift       82
     Yet beware of her Arts, for it plainly appears,    . .   580 Psyche               13
     My proof is thus: I plainly see      . . . . . . . .     679 From Catullus         5
     Yet Standers-by may plainly see      . . . . . . . .     926 Riddle 9              5
     Which plainly does follow,      . . . . . . . . . .      939 Riddle Answerd       23
     A school-boy knows this, for it plainly appears    . .   976 Dean to Sherid       19
     Take Courage, Dan, this plainly shows     . . . . . .    993 On Picture           19
     . . .for you see plainly my Paper is ended.    . . . .  1014 Swift to Sheri       12
PLAINS
     O'er mountains steep, o'er dusty plains,    . . . . .    403 Window Inns 10  D    5
     Wat'ring soft Elysian Plains.      . . . . . . . . .     661 Love Song            20
     Lives such a Bard on British plains?     . . . . . .     876 To Dean Swift         6
     Who never fled the bloody Plains,      . . . . . . . .   925 Riddle 8             32
     Come dancing to me o'er the Plains.      . . . . . .     934 Riddle 21       D   10
     Thro' all the Vallies, Hills, and Plains,     . . . .   1035 To Quilca             9
PLAINTIFF'S
     And takes the Plaintiff's and Defendant's Fees.    . .   364 On Dreams            24
PLAISTER
     White Lead can plaister up a Cleft,      . . . . . .     229 Prog of Beauty      114
     And then to each applies a Plaister.     . . . . . .     582 Young Nymph          32
     A wicked Rat her Plaister stole,      . . . . . . . .    583 Young Nymph          59
PLAN
     The Plan he much admir'd, and took     . . . . . . .      87 Hist V's House       19
PLANET
     Deals out to man the planet of his birth;     . . . .     54 Temple Ill           90
```

		PAGE	TITLE	LINE
PLANET	**(CONTINUED)**			
	'Twixt Cobling and the Planet Science.	98	Elegy Patrige	30
	What Planet rul'd when you were born;	258	Bubble	191
	From the Planet of my Birth, ...	634	Epistle Lady	141
PLANETS				
	And set the Planets by the Ears:	99	Elegy Patrige	58
PLANK				
	Those that dropt in the South-Sea discover'd this Plank	288	Bank Down	49
PLANKS				
	Take the three strongest of his broken Planks, . . .	285	Elegy Boat	32
PLANNING				
	But Building, Planning, and Devotion;	514	Answer Fable	56
PLANT				
	Whate'er I plant (like Corn on barren Earth) . . .	33	Ode to Temple	210
	To be, as 'twas below, the brightest plant above; . . .	41	Ode Sancroft	229
	Of Land set out to plant a Wood.	198	Horace 2, 6	6
	Beneath whose ill Shade no Plant ever grew. . . .	334	Serious Poem	32
	Since he no more can build, and plant, & revell, . . .	678	Dean and Duke	9
	Must die with her expiring Plant.	849	Old Thorn	48
PLANTATIONS				
	Lay all my fine Plantations waste, ...	410	Dial Rich Marb	69
PLANTED				
	What he had planted, now was grown;	708	Cadenus Vaness	680
PLANTER				
	Alone, and by no Planter courted;	583	Young Nymph	46
	What Planter will attempt to yoke	703	Cadenus Vaness	534
PLANTING				
	For farther Buildings, farther Planting.	477	Epist on Epist	64
	In state affairs, or planting cale;	901	Dean's Reasons	76
PLANTS				
	The first of Plants after the Thunder, Storm, and Rain	16	Ode Athenian	28
PLATE	**SEE DRESSING-PLATE**			
	And all her Jewels and her Plate, ...	32	Ode to Temple	182
	Adorn their Pails with Plate.	122	Empty'ng Town	8
	A Coach and Six, and serv'd in Plate:	251	Bubble	20
	And <Cuffe> grins for getting, the Alicant Plate. .	430	Dicky Dolly	21
	He would have seiz'd the Spanish Plate, ...	463	Birthday Song	101
	And on her Plate a treble Share, ...	895	Panegyr Dean	260
	An empty Plate except your own.	897	Panegyr Dean	340
PLATES				
	Load our Plates from ev'ry Dish;	633	Epistle Lady	109
	Five Nothings in five Plates of Delf.	747	Stel Distress	52
	Five Nothings in five Plates of Delph.	751	Stel Wood-Park	68
PLATO				
	"By Plato, and by Socrates, ...	384	Manly Virtue	6
PLATO'S				
	We odly Plato's Paradox make good, ...	27	Ode to Temple	29
PLATONICK				
	Platonick Champions, gain'd without one Female Wile, .	24	Ode Athenian	252
	That when Platonick Flights were over, ...	707	Cadenus Vaness	650
PLATTER				
	And serv'd up in an earthen Platter;	91	Bauc & Phil 1	62
PLAUSTRO				
	Are you still in your cart with convitia ex plaustro? .	979	Dean to Tho: S	6
PLAUTUS				
	I have a great Esteem for Plautus;	988	Letter Dr Sh-n	2
PLAY	**SEE BUCKET-PLAY**			
	Rattles for Infant Royalty to play withal, . . .	6	Ode to King	13
	War! that mad Game, the World so loves to play, . .	28	Ode to Temple	76
	Before the play, or else between the acts:	47	To Congreve	126
	In twisting up an ill-spun Play:	80	Vanbrug House	44
	Van was deliver'd of a Play, ...	81	Vanbrug House	74
	When Mother Clud had risen from Play, ...	86	Hist V's House	1
	But when he found the Boys at play, ...	86	Hist V's House	13
	Takes a French Play as lawful Prize, ...	107	V's House	58
	(The third Night's Profits of his Play;)	230	Prog of Poetry	18
	Undone at Play, the Femal Troops	254	Bubble	89
	The Poet had no more who made the Play.	274	Epilogue	10
	And scarce a Crown is left to see the Play:	275	Epilogue	34
	We go to Pray'rs, and then to play	280	Journal	52
	While she drives on to see the Play.	292	Prog Marriage	82
	And, as a stroller, act in ev'ry play:	309	Billet Players	48
	And, Fourthly; 'tis to play an odd Trick, ...	348	Whitshed Motto	17
	When at a Play to laugh, or cry, ...	415	Woman's Mind	3
	And then stand by to see fair play, ...	421	Ireld	10
	By Nature turn'd to play the Rake-well, ...	446	Modern Lady	36
	I never saw you play so ill.	452	Modern Lady	247
	"Come, let us play the t'other Round.	453	Modern Lady	285
	But if she turn'd against his play, ...	456	Dean Smedley	29
	Free Leave to play his Secretary, ...	475	Epist on Epist	9
	For solid Work, but not for Play;	483	Libel on D- D-	90
	Before a Play, wou'd lose no Credit:	484	Libel on D- D-	142
	"No Vermin can demand fair Play, ...	548	Life of Swift	126
	The Sharper swore he hated Play, ...	607	Beasts Confess	187
	We, by Play, as Men by Drinking, ...	632	Epistle Lady	85
	Poor Ladies! though their Bus'ness be to play, . . .	662	Upon Ladies	1
	From Scandal, Politicks, and Play, ...	688	Cadenus Vaness	44
	They ask'd her, how she lik'd the Play, ...	696	Cadenus Vaness	318
	But hold, cry the <Bishops>; and give us fair Play; .	805	Irish Bishops	53
	When you saw Tady at long-bullets play, ...	882	Pastoral Dial	33
	Yet never ask us once to play?	891	Panegyr Dean	146

PLAY   (CONTINUED)   PAGE   TITLE   LINE

	PAGE	TITLE	LINE
And oft in Celia's Tresses play.	919	Riddle 5	12
Tho' we play them Tricks for ever,	934	Riddle 22	D 7
All Servants at play.	1036	Plague Country	9
PLAY-BOOK			
Then in a Play-Book smoothly lays 'em.	581	Young Nymph	16
PLAY-DAY			
Shou'd be one continu'd Play-Day:	631	Epistle Lady	40
And beg her a play-day.	858	Lady's Lament	218
PLAY-HOUSE			
Between the Weavers and us Play-House Kings.	275	Epilogue	36
In the Play-House upper Regions;	523	Betty Grizette	24
Nor saw the Play-House twice a Year;	696	Cadenus Vaness	313
PLAY'D			
Dame Baucis next, they play'd their Farce on:	115	Bauc & Phil 2	138
Apollo play'd the Midwife's Part,	149	Corinna	2
"When Lady Tricksy play'd a Four,	452	Modern Lady	250
"Or pretty Miss has play'd the Fool,	497	Panegyr Swift	131
Come, tell us, has she play'd the Whore?	595	Cassinus Peter	45
Found out the Trick that Venus play'd,	694	Cadenus Vaness	251
PLAY'R			
Went to one Griffith, formerly a play'r:	307	Billet Players	4
As serious as a Tragick Play'r.	707	Cadenus Vaness	663
PLAY'RS			
But whence this Wonderous Charity, in Play'rs,	275	Epilogue	11
Huzza! the school-boys roar, the play'rs are come!	308	Billet Players	38
PLAYER			
Nam'd ev'ry player on his fingers ends,	47	To Congreve	139
My Lady tho' she is no Player	75	Game Traffick	9
Dick Fitz-Baker, Dick the Player,	835	Legion Club	149
PLAYERS			
But Weavers will be Kinder to the Players,	276	Epilogue	43
The Poets Wits, than in the Players Dressing.	276	Epilogue	46
Should lend your cathedrall to players and scrapers	522	St. Cecilia's	4
PLAYS			
Like Lambent Fire the Lightning plays;	29	Ode to Temple	88
Why then, old Plays deserve old Bricks,	108	V's House	72
I often have seen two Plays very Good,	337	Serious Poem	91
Thus, Congreve spent, in writing Plays,	481	Libel on D- D-	33
With old Scraps from Plays exploded.	523	Betty Grizette	16
Visits, Plays, and Powder'd Beaux.	631	Epistle Lady	42
With Fustian from exploded Plays,	697	Cadenus Vaness	330
For Visits, Ombre, Balls and Plays.)	700	Cadenus Vaness	431
St. George himself he plays the wag on,	777	Mullinix Tim	115
But, instead of new plays,	855	Lady's Lament	147
Nor plays at cards, or dice, or bowls;	901	Dean's Reasons	88
PLEADED			
Pleaded the <Bishop> lov'd a <Whore>,	302	Storm	12
PLEADER			
No Pleader at the Bar could match	604	Beasts Confess	89
On which the Pleader much enlarg'd;	686	Cadenus Vaness	6
The Pleader having spoke his best,	688	Cadenus Vaness	67
PLEADING			
Pleading before the Cyprian Queen.	686	Cadenus Vaness	2
More like to lampooning than pleading at bar.	815	Yahoo's	14
The Lawyer must forget his Pleading,	916	Riddle 1	31
PLEADINGS			
These Pleadings in the Courts below,	689	Cadenus Vaness	80
PLEADS			
Pleads for her own neglect, and thus reproaches mine:	43	To Congreve	6
"Now strangely pleads in my Excuse:	379	Apology Lady C	132
Thus, Envy pleads a nat'ral Claim	504	Doctor Delaney	131
PLEAS			
For Cowley's Briefs, and Pleas of Waller,	690	Cadenus Vaness	114
PLEAS'D			
Pleas'd with an empty swelling to be counted great;	36	Ode Sancroft	60
Since Heaven and Cato both are pleas'd--	42	Ode Sancroft	264
Still to be cheated, never to be pleas'd;	55	Temple Ill	148
My Lord seems pleas'd, but still directs	64	Discovery	41
And every one was pleas'd, that heard it:	128	Little House	40
Went where he pleas'd, said what he thought,	171	Horace 1, 7	33
I own, I'm pleas'd with this Rebuke,	200	Horace 2, 6	40
Still pleas'd with the good-natur'd Noise,	322	First of April	33
But yet, tho' seeming pleas'd, can't bear	379	Apology Lady C	121
Tho' seeming pleas'd at all she sees,	379	Apology Lady C	125
Pleas'd in the Person of a Peer;	385	Manly Virtue	70
Although it might have pleas'd the Nation.	484	Libel on D- D-	120
Since you are pleas'd to condescend	489	Dialogue	13
No Goddess could have pleas'd him more.	619	Scandal Poem 1	56
No Goodness could have pleas'd him more,	625	Scandal Poem 2	52
The Queen of Love was pleas'd, and proud,	693	Cadenus Vaness	228
Might have her Freedom when she pleas'd:	704	Cadenus Vaness	575
That Virtue, pleas'd by being shown,	706	Cadenus Vaness	608
Each Girl when pleas'd with what is taught,	710	Cadenus Vaness	734
How well are the Spectators pleas'd!	777	Mullinix Tim	126
Pray, Captain, be pleas'd to light, and walk in:	871	Grand Question	114
(Though sometimes thou wer't pleas'd to wink,	894	Panegyr Dean	243
Is never pleas'd till I make one:	920	Riddle 6	28
But pleas'd to find you do relent and cry on.	1002	Reply by Dean	15
PLEASANT			
And many a pleasant Wood,	17	Ode Athenian	41

PLEASANT   (CONTINUED)

	PAGE	TITLE	LINE
How many pleasant Things he spoke,	480	Libel on D- D-	7
The Moral of the Tale is pleasant,	514	Answer Fable	51
"He knew an hundred pleasant Stories,	572	Death of Swift	475
Thou I hear, a pleasant Rogue art;	839	Legion Club	220
How pleasant on the Banks of Styx,	905	Death Daphne	87
In Summer is very pleasant and cool.	941	Letter	20

PLEASD

	PAGE	TITLE	LINE
That came together to be pleasd:	217	To Mr. Delany	76
But that indeed which pleasd me most	422	Ireld	31
Well: but a Duke thou art; so pleasd the King	678	Dean and Duke	15

PLEASE

	PAGE	TITLE	LINE
And one would think 'twere past Omnipotence to please;	9	Ode to King	89
Of Solving all Appearances they please,	19	Ode Athenian	118
That what surprises us can only please:	20	Ode Athenian	141
Than You to please and satisfie Mankind,	22	Ode Athenian	200
And let my friend apply it as he please:	49	To Congreve	204
When e're he please to blot it out;	61	Lady Tablebook	22
For that, he said, (an't please your Excellencies)...	73	Mrs Harris Pet	69
Make me the Parson if you please.	94	Bauc & Phil 1	164
Make me the Parson, if you please.	115	Bauc & Phil 2	116
Let which I please of all the Nine	120	Apollo Outwit	30
To your Friends who at least have no Cares but to please you	185	Scriblerus 1	5
"You may for certain, if you please;	201	Horace 2, 6	60
Just as the Rabble please to smile or frown.	210	Earl of Oxford	10
To please themselves by vexing You	217	To Mr. Delany	78
Resume their own when e'er they please.	239	Run Bankers	8
Or, if it please the Powers Divine,	243	Horace 4, 9	19
Put on what Spectacles You please,	255	Bubble	123
For Fools will see as Wise men please.	257	Bubble	168
And as for their Works, when I please I may read 'em;	263	Apollo	22
"If such a Sight as this can please ye,	305	Storm	69
Now, here's a warrant; Gallants please to mark,	308	Billet Players	19
Was full as hard to please as You,	313	To Ford	53
Then chuse which you please, and let each bring a Fagyot,	352	Wood Insect	39
And strive, and strive, your Wife to please.	362	Grace's Answer	46
By taking Fits whene'er she please:	416	Woman's Mind	38
A Priest would please your Palate;	425	Five Ladies	10
"Your Fan, a Moment, if you please.	452	Modern Lady	243
And Precedents we can produce, if it please ye,	518	Dean Hang Rape	40
If Fortune should please to take such a Crotchet,	518	Dean Hang Rape	43
He knows a Thousand Tricks, whene'er he please,	535	To Mr. Gay	123
'Twou'd please your Palate, like a feast,	546	Life of Swift	39
"To please, and to reform Mankind;	550	Life of Swift	197
"Points out some Circumstance to please us.	554	Death of Swift	10
Wou'd please 'em better than to tell,	557	Death of Swift	125
"Your Honour please to buy a Set?	564	Death of Swift	280
"Who still were true, to please his Foes.	567	Death of Swift	364
"Nor Topicks brought to please the Crown,	570	Death of Swift	428
To please you, she knows how to chuse a nice Bit;	580	Psyche	9
To serve the King, and please the Nation.	606	Beasts Confess	154
Oh! if his Majesty would please	606	Beasts Confess	169
You follow where we please to guide:	620	Scandal Poem 1	89
But, we can fly whene'er we please	621	Scandal Poem 1	125
For when we please, we open wide	621	Scandal Poem 1	133
You follow where we please to guide:	626	Scandal Poem 2	87
But, we can fly where-e'er we please,	627	Scandal Poem 2	119
For, when we please, we open wide	627	Scandal Poem 2	137
Talk with Sense, whate'er you please on,	638	Epistle Lady	271
Cou'd please them, and improve her own.	701	Cadenus Vaness	453
Whether the Nymph, to please her Swain,	712	Cadenus Vaness	820
Oh, would it please the Gods to split	722	Stel B-Day '18	9
And please all the rest,	756	Dingley Brent	14
Companions that will please her better;	762	Bec's B-Day	48
And please her more to hear them tattle	762	Bec's B-Day	55
Like thee, to please this thankless Town!	779	Mullinix Tim	198
Can please at most but once or twice.	788	Dick's Variety	12
Has ev'ry Circumstance to please us,	820	Dr. Rundle	25
You might have a Barrack whenever you please:	869	Grand Question	54
How to vex and how to please;	906	Daphne	2
Till you please to ask me thrice;	908	Daphne	80
I please the Young, I grace the Old,	912	Aenigma	11
To please his Malice, or his Lust.	915	Riddle 1	22
And whenso're you please to shine,	919	Riddle 5	9
And turn and wind me as they please.	920	Riddle 6	8
Can find an Entrance when they please.	928	Riddle 12	D 12
Turn and wind him where we please.	931	Riddle 18	D 14
And as I please they're great and small;	934	Riddle 21	D 2
Die for those I live to please;	937	Riddle 24	D 50
They'll please to the Life;	953	Oysters	12
If your Worship will please to explain me this Rebus,	973	S-'s Ans Sh-d	13
And think of the sex as you please, I'd as lieve	976	Dean to Sherid	15
Whose moving Touches, when they please, kill us.	988	Letter Dr Sh-n	29
As you can steal one, how 'twould please ye!	1033	Ans to Crown	14

PLEASED

	PAGE	TITLE	LINE
Which only pleased in Biddy Floyd:	272	Apollo's Edict	D 61

PLEASES

	PAGE	TITLE	LINE
And will now be her Friend whenever she pleases;	266	Apollo	106
If it both pleases and endures,	728	Stella, Poems	7
Well, well, that's as God pleases, ...	986	Mary to Sher	20

619

PLEASETH
    Whoever pleaseth to enquire, ...   126 Little House   1
PLEASING
    In pleasing all that's good among the great, ...   49 To Congreve   180
    If this you think a pleasing Scene . . . .   312 To Ford   47
    Your fancy with their pleasing fire, ...   489 Dialogue   20
    In the close bands of pleasing hymen. . . . . . .   675 Curate's Compl   6
    With pleasing Arts she could reduce . . . . . .   700 Cadenus Vaness   448
    A better and more pleasing Thought, ...   764 Stel B-day '26   10
    Ah, is not Love a pleasing Pain? . . . .   924 Riddle 8   12
    Pleasing most when most I speak, ...   933 Riddle 20   D   2
PLEASURE
    "Or if it be thy Will and Pleasure . . . . . .   199 Horace 2, 6   D
    Thus my Subjects with pleasure will obey my Commands .   389 Order of Bath   9
    The Pleasure of so large a Grant . . . .   493 Panegyr Swift   7
    How, Pain they might from Pleasure part: . . . .   501 Doctor Delaney   32
    I shall read and think with Pleasure: . . . . .   632 Epistle Lady   88
    In Pleasure seek for something new: . . . . . .   728 Stella, Poems   18
    Some lasting Pleasure in the Mind, ...   764 Stel B-day '26   30
    O what a pleasure mixt with pain! . . . .   776 Mullinix Tim   106
    Tim with surprize and pleasure staring, ...   783 Tim and Fables   13
    I swallow with pleasure. . . . .   853 Lady's Lament   66
    Who not one pleasure entertains . . . .   901 Dean's Reasons   83
    And now her Heart with Pleasure jumps, ...   904 Death Daphne   59
    With Pleasure to his special Friends: . . . . .   919 Riddle 5   20
    With Pleasure, as the Poet sings, ...   924 Riddle 8   15
    The Terror of Women, and Pleasure of Boys, ...   927 Riddle 11   D   2
PLEASURES
    Sing (belov'd Muse) the Pleasures of Retreat, . . .   30 Ode to Temple   135
    And Female Pleasures be to read and write. . . . .   662 Upon Ladies   8
    Where Pleasures mix'd with Pains appear, ...   711 Cadenus Vaness   776
    How soon all human Pleasures pass. . . . .   921 Riddle 7   6
    And scorn the Pleasures of a Court; . . . . . .   925 Riddle 8   34
PLEDGE
    William's the Pledge and Earnest given by Fate . . .   13 Ode to William   D 47
PLEDGES
    Who chose to leave his dearest pledges here, ...   309 Billet Players   46
    Nor Infants dropt, the spurious Pledges . . . . .   641 On Poetry   37
    The tender Pledges of our Joy. . . . .   925 Riddle 8   22
PLEIAS
    With Hermes, Son of Pleias bright. . . . .   326 Pethox   86
PLENIPOES
    And Errors of our Plenipoes. . . . .   181 Horace 2, 1   20
PLENTEOUS
    And gave the Nymph a plenteous Draught; . . . . .   293 Prog Marriage   114
    Rolls from his Mouth in plenteous Streams of Mud; . .   532 To Mr. Gay   40
    With plenteous meals, and gen'rous wine; . . . . .   677 Parson's Case   34
    From thence a plenteous Draught infuse, ...   743 Stel B-day 22   75
PLENTIFULLY
    Their Minds so plentifully fills, ...   735 Stel B-day '20   27
PLENTY
    To live in Plenty, Power and Ease. . . . .   173 Horace 1, 7   92
    Deep sunk in Plenty, and Delight, ...   231 Prog of Poetry   23
    (Who ought for Peace and Plenty Pray.) . . . . .   372 Letter D. S-y   40
    This gave him Enemies in plenty, ...   549 Life of Swift   134
    She gives you such Plenty, it puts you in Pain; . . .   580 Psyche   7
    From every Meal Pontack in plenty . . . .   745 Stel Distress   13
    From ev'ry Meal Pontack in plenty, ...   750 Stel Wood-Park   37
    Of Plenty thou the Emblem fair, ...   919 Riddle 5   3
PLIANT
    Or bring a tender Child and pliant, ...   934 Riddle 21   D 19
    The pliant bow, the forehead bland-- . . . . . .   951 Upstart   D 30
PLIES
    With these, the Court and Senate-house he plies, . .   532 To Mr. Gay   41
PLIGHT
    The Nymph, tho' in this mangled Plight, ...   583 Young Nymph   65
    If not; they must in evil Plight . . . .   587 Strephon Chloe   121
    But, women in a cloudy plight . . . .   618 Scandal Poem 1   31
    But, Women in a Cloudy Plight, ...   624 Scandal Poem 2   25
PLINY
    Pliny shall prove what we affirm: . . . .   83 Salamander   26
    Pliny shall prove, and we'll apply, ...   83 Salamander   27
    Farther, we are by Pliny told . . . .   84 Salamander   47
    And, by the Sentiments of Pliny, ...   598 Problem Solved   29
PLODDING
    Then Plodding, he thought on a whimsical Prank . . .   288 Bank Down   34
    The Dean sits plodding on a Book, ...   405 Swift to Pope   7
    She reason'd, without plodding long, ...   704 Cadenus Vaness   558
PLOT
    Steals thence his Plot, and ev'ry Joke, ...   107 V's House   59
    The Plot as yet lay deep, and so . . . .   108 V's House   85
    To a Plot for expelling my Master K. James; . . . .   144 New Song   28
    And so might discover, or gain by the Plot: . . . .   144 New Song   30
    How came this wicked Plot to Light: . . . .   298 Horrid Plot   2
    Besides, this horrid Plot was found . . . . . .   299 Horrid Plot   37
    And that's a Name in ev'ry Plot: . . . .   300 Horrid Plot   48
    We had Occasion for a Plot; . . . .   300 Horrid Plot   68
    You must be guilty of the Plot, ...   312 To Ford   32
    The Statesman rakes the Town to find a Plot, ...   364 On Dreams   19
    You at a Pinch could forge a Plot; . . . .   494 Panegyr Swift   40
    You cannot bribe, betray, or plot. . . . .   641 On Poetry   48

```
PLOT         (CONTINUED)                              PAGE    TITLE         LINE
     They plot to turn in factious Zeal,     . . . . . . .   653 On Poetry        379
     And in a Plot for the Pretender?        . . . . . . .   774 Mullinix Tim      22
     And when I roar a Plot, a Plot,         . . . . . . .   779 Mullinix Tim     191
     And when I roar a Plot, a Plot,         . . . . . . .   779 Mullinix Tim     191
     "Was formed this Machi'villian Plot,                    850 Old Thorn         74
     And when we execute our Plot,      . . . . . . . . .    886 Rev Market-Hill  107
PLOTS
     With Plots; and Jacobites and Treason;     . . . . .    775 Mullinix Tim      58
PLOUGH
     An act for laying down the Plough,     . . . . . . .    422 Ireld            51
PLOW
     "Direct my Plow to find a Treasure:"     . . . . . .    199 Horace 2, 6       D
PLUCK
     To pluck her Brows in Arches round,     . . . . . . .   527 Lady's Dres Rm    56
     None ever saw her pluck a Rose.     . . . . . . . .     584 Strephon Chloe    16
     As who should say, to pluck a Rose.     . . . . . . .   893 Panegyr Dean     216
PLUCKS
     This said, she plucks in Heav'ns high Bow'rs     . . . . 691 Cadenus Vaness   154
PLUCKT
     And pluckt a Laurel branch (for Laurel was the first    16 Ode Athenian       27
          that grew,
PLUG     SEE TOBACCO-PLUG
PLUM
     Or found an Earwig in a Plum.     . . . . . . . . . .   726 To Stella         78
PLUMBS
     Nor will exchange His Plumbs for Bays:     . . . . .    157 Fable of Midas    56
     To me from all a us'rer's plumbs;     . . . . . . . .   899 Dean's Reasons    28
     Plumbs, Apples and Pears,     . . . . . . . . . .      951 Apples             2
PLUMES
     But plumes her Silver Wings and flies away,     . . . .  16 Ode Athenian      17
     And Geese their silver Plumes supply.     . . . . . .   239 Run Bankers       24
     Rais'd up on Hope's aspiring Plumes,     . . . . . .    252 Bubble            33
PLUMP
     Plump Johnny Gay will now elope;     . . . . . . . .    409 Dial Rich Marb    49
     Grows plump and round, and full of Mettle,     . . . .  759 Receipt Youth     17
     Round all your Body plump your Skin;  '     . . . . .   759 Receipt Youth     30
     Said to the Pippin, plump, and prim,     . . . . . .    811 Bro Protestant    13
     So plump and so fresh,     . . . . . . . . . . .       952 Oysters            3
PLUMPERS
     Now dextrously her Plumpers draws,     . . . . . . .    582 Young Nymph       17
     And Puss had on her Plumpers <pisst>.     . . . . . .   583 Young Nymph       62
PLUMPT
     When plumpt into the reeking Chest;     . . . . . . .   529 Lady's Dres Rm   110
PLUNDER
     The subtle Knave had all the Plunder swept.     . . . .  536 To Mr. Gay       154
     All to plunder, all to pillage;     . . . . . . . .    574 Helter Skelter    40
     Have dropt their Arms, and seiz'd the Plunder.     . . . 775 Mullinix Tim     48
     Came but to plunder and enslave us;     . . . . . . .   820 Dr. Rundle        34
     Are most inclin'd to plunder Crowns.     . . . . . . .  1033 Ans to Crown     12
PLUNDER'D
     . . .when a Body's plunder'd?     . . . . . . . . .     72 Mrs Harris Pet     53
PLUNGES
     Then plunges in the Southern Waves,     . . . . . . .   251 Bubble            23
     Beneath the vast abyss he plunges quick,     . . . . .  672 Epig Carthy 24    D  17
PLUNKET
     Whether Curr Plunket, or Whelp Skean,     . . . . . .   298 Horrid Plot       20
PLUTARCH
     Homer, Plutarch, Virgil, Flaccus,     . . . . . . . .   838 Legion Club      211
PLUTARCH'S
     Quote you Texts from Plutarch's Morals;     . . . . .   637 Epistle Lady     236
     On Plutarch's Morals struck, were spoil'd.     . . . .  701 Cadenus Vaness   483
PLUTO
     Pluto the god of Wealth, will joy to know     . . . .   234 Elegy on Demar     7
     Gloomy Pluto, King of Terrors,     . . . . . . . . .    661 Love Song         17
     Pluto observing, since the Peace,     . . . . . . . .   903 Death Daphne       7
     Bequeathed to Pluto, Corps and all.     . . . . . . .   904 Death Daphne      32
PLUTO'S
     And you whom Pluto's Helm does wisely shroud     . . . . 18 Ode Athenian      86
     May dig in vain in Pluto's Shades.     . . . . . . .    743 Stel B-day 22     74
     At Pluto's Hall, his Court to pay:     . . . . . . .    903 Death Daphne       2
     For, Cards we know, are Pluto's Books)     . . . . .    905 Death Daphne      80
     By Proserpine, at Pluto's Hall?     . . . . . . . .     905 Death Daphne      84
PLY
     Some ply before, and some behind.     . . . . . . . .    66 Problem           38
     They ply their former Arts below.     . . . . . . . .   647 On Poetry        210
     And ev'ry Guest be sure to ply:     . . . . . . . .     897 Panegyr Dean     338
PLY'D
     Thus when by Rooks a Lord is ply'd,     . . . . . . .   257 Bubble           161
PLYES
     Plyes you with Stories o'er and o'er,     . . . . . .   556 Death of Swift    89
POCKET
     I keep in a Pocket ty'd about my Middle, next my Smock.  69 Mrs Harris Pet     7
     And, instead of putting it into my Pocket, down it slipt: 69 Mrs Harris Pet    9
     So when I came up again, I found my Pocket feel very     69 Mrs Harris Pet    12
          light,
     My long old-fashion'd Pocket, was presently cramm'd;  .  143 New Song         19
     My Pocket was pick't,     . . . . . . . . . . .        245 Irish-Feast       19
     Into whose pocket valiant Willy put,     . . . . . .    467 Birthday Song    207
     Low in Pocket, Cow'd in Courage,     . . . . . . . .    574 Helter Skelter    53
```

		PAGE	TITLE	LINE
POCKET-GLASS				
And Vanity with Pocket-Glass;		448	Modern Lady	130
Her Pocket-Glass drew slily out;		904	Death Daphne	64
POCKETS				
The whole Nations Pockets with Money will fill.		287	Bank Down	13
They search't his Pockets on the Place,		353	Wood Ironmongr	27
Your pockets grow empty,		402	Window Inns 8	D 3
My Lady's empty Pockets know:		409	Dial Rich Marb	24
Drawn through the dirt, his pockets pick'd;		436	Answer Paulus	138
Because they find their Pockets pick't.		917	Riddle 3	16
POCKY				
Those pocky Drabs		440	Ballyspellin	13
Satira's but some pocky Quean.		530	Lady's Dres Rm	134
Or sink her to a pocky Whore.		929	Riddle 15	D 8
PODESWAY				
Clad in a coat of Podesway,		879	Robbin & Harry	47
POEM				
But as for the Poem he writ on your Sash,		265	Apollo	65
Behold a Poem rise!		406	Swift to Pope	16
Methought, when I this Poem read,		469	Burning Poem	3
While my hard-labour'd Poem pines		502	Doctor Delaney	77
Proceed we therefore to our Poem.		555	Death of Swift	72
"Here's Colley Cibber's Birth-day Poem.		563	Death of Swift	270
Be reduc'd into a Poem.		631	Epistle Lady	48
Your Poem finish'd, next your Care		643	On Poetry	91
Your Poem in its modish Dress,		643	On Poetry	105
Your Secret kept, your Poem sunk,		644	On Poetry	143
At Wills you hear a Poem read,		649	On Poetry	263
If they should meet 'em in a Poem.		729	Stella, Poems	52
Before he could his Poem close,		730	Stella, Poems	77
POEMS				
Your still-born Poems shall revive,		394	Grub-Street	7
Poems address'd to great Men's Whores;		494	Panegyr Swift	35
His Poems, think them all not worth a Straw.		521	Stephen Duck	6
For Poems read without a Name		644	On Poetry	129
The Loads of Poems in his Praise,		646	On Poetry	203
With three hundred and sixty-five poems a year?		979	Dean to Tho: S	34
POET				
Ah, could You! could you hope a Poet for your Friend!		23	Ode Athenian	243
Sing Muse the House of Poet Van		80	Vanbrug House	57
Is both a Herald and a Poet;		80	Vanbrug House	60
Sing Muse the House of Poet <Van>		106	V's House	31
Is both a Herald and a Poet,		107	V's House	34
And as a Poet, he has Skill		107	V's House	41
The Building, as the Poet Writ,		108	V's House	79
Thrice happy Poet, who may trail		109	V's House	109
The gray old Fellow Poet Joe		126	Little House	3
Ah! where must needy Poet seek for Aid,		138	City Shower	27
Such is the Poet, fresh in Pay,		230	Prog of Poetry	17
What Poet e'er could take his Flight?		231	Prog of Poetry	24
What Poet e'er could sing a Note?		231	Prog of Poetry	26
As Poet and as Patriot too?		270	Apollo's Edict	D 6
The Poet had no more who made the Play.		274	Epilogue	10
And, the Devil's a damnable Poet.		401	Window Inns 3	4
As Poet, Scholar and Divine.		455	Dean Smedley	4
And sure no Christian Poet breathing		461	Birthday Song	25
Sweet Poet, hir'd for birth-day Rimes,		462	Birthday Song	47
His Learning, though a Poet said it,		484	Libel on D- D-	141
The Poet cannot claim his Bays;		505	Doctor Delaney	168
Wou'd either Poet take it well,		546	Life of Swift	54
What Poet would not grieve to see,		554	Death of Swift	31
Presumptuous Poet, could you dare		617	Scandal Poem 1	1
A better than the Poet meant,		643	On Poetry	102
Then Poet, if you mean to thrive,		647	On Poetry	219
Each Poet of inferior Size		651	On Poetry	331
Thus ev'ry Poet in his Kind,		651	On Poetry	341
Great Poet of the Hollow-Tree.		653	On Poetry	376
Nor Minister, nor Poet flatter.		655	On Poetry	414
Say, Poet, in what other Nation,		656	On Poetry	465
Exactly true! Invidious Poet!		657	On Poetry	479
Might furnish a Second Rate Poet a Year:		716	Answer Rebus	18
A Poet, starving in a Garret,		728	Stella, Poems	25
She dares not say the Poet lyes.		730	Stella, Poems	82
No Poet ever sweetly sung,		757	Stel B-day '24	19
Am I a Poet fit for you?		757	Stel B-day '24	24
A laureat make that is no poet;		876	To Dean Swift	18
With Pleasure, as the Poet sings,		924	Riddle 8	15
Why sure, Mr. Poet, your head got a jar		976	Dean to Sherid	27
I despise any poet that truckled to Dan.		976	Dean to Sherid	34
POET'S				
What can the Poet's humble Praise?		6	Ode to King	7
What can the Poet's humble Bays?		6	Ode to King	8
A lust of rhiming for a poet's vein,		45	To Congreve	78
Bred in my scene, and for the poet's sins		46	To Congreve	97
For Leave to build the Poet's Way.		81	Vanbrug House	70
He values not the Poet's Praise,		157	Fable of Midas	55
To Bus'ness shap'd the Poet's Quil,		482	Libel on D- D-	66
To find the Grub-Street Poet's Nest,		504	Doctor Delaney	144
Till <Bob>, the Poet's Foe, possess't her Ear.		531	To Mr. Gay	4
At Poet's Flights to take Offence.		628	Scandal Poem 2	158
The Poet's Vein, or scribling Itch?		642	On Poetry	74

```
POET'S              (CONTINUED)              PAGE    TITLE              LINE
   And Bacchus for the Poet's Use        . . . . . . .    743 Stel B-day 22       65
POETASTER
   And art thou forc'd to yield, ill-fated Poetaster?    . .   1002 Reply by Dean       3
POETASTERS
   And curse our modern Poetasters.      . . . . . . . .    652 On Poetry         348
POETIC
   This wilderness the world, like that poetic wood of old,     41 Ode Sancroft      225
   The Muse was call'd in a poetic hour,     . . . . . .     43 To Congreve         2
   For never did poetic mine before      . . . . . . . .     45 To Congreve        51
   These are the lords of the poetic schools,    . . . . .     46 To Congreve       101
   When to poetic view the Muse appear'd.    . . . . . .     51 Temple Ill         16
   And 'tis against poetic rules         . . . . . . . .    488 Irish-Club         27
   What Sword-knots! What Poetic Strains!    . . . . . .    585 Strephon Chloe     37
   Can I devise poetic strains?      . . . . . . . .    754 Stella '23          2
POETICAL
   I alone can inspire the poetical Crowd;    . . . . . .    263 Apollo            16
POETICALLY
   Such were thy rules to be poetically great,   . . . . .     55 Temple Ill        137
POETICK
   And hid him from Poetick sight,       . . . . . . . .      8 Ode to King        59
   And with exact Poetick Justice:       . . . . . . . .    225 Prog of Poesy      97
   Nor Shepherds use poetick Cant:       . . . . . . . .    270 Apollo's Edict  D  28
   Have taught him his poetick Words.    . . . . . . . .    411 Dial Rich Marb     92
   Inspire you with poetick Rage;        . . . . . . . .    462 Birthday Song      68
   Your Whimsical, Poetick Place.        . . . . . . . .    477 Epist on Epist     82
   Who fatten on poetick Scraps;         . . . . . . . .    504 Doctor Delaney    125
   Hath blasted with poetick Fire.       . . . . . . . .    641 On Poetry          42
   And call'd for his Poetick Works;     . . . . . . . .    702 Cadenus Vaness    512
   But my Poetick Vein declines.         . . . . . . . .    739 Stel B-day '21     10
   They'll call it all poetick Licence:  . . . . . . . .    741 Stel B-day 22      28
   Will not require Poetick Dress;       . . . . . . . .    757 Stel B-day '24     32
POETRY
   (The Spirit of Exalted Poetry)        . . . . . . . .      7 Ode to King        46
   These Days! where ev'n th' Extravagance of Poetry   . .     21 Ode Athenian     171
   Seeds and runs up to Poetry.          . . . . . . . .     33 Ode to Temple     212
   And Poetry has lost the art to praise,    . . . . . .     38 Ode Sancroft      111
   The Poetry of Ages past,              . . . . . . . .     81 Vanbrug House      90
   The Poetry of Ages past,              . . . . . . . .    110 V's House         132
   Pallas first taught us Poetry and Spinning;   . . . . .    276 Epilogue          38
   Forbear your poetry and jokes,        . . . . . . . .    489 Dialogue           17
   And, each to Poetry pretends:         . . . . . . . .    546 Life of Swift      53
   For Poetry, he's past his Prime,      . . . . . . . .    556 Death of Swift     99
   In Poetry the Height we know;         . . . . . . . .    654 On Poetry         391
   But enough of this Poetry Alexandrine     . . . . . .   1018 Swift Ans Sher     32
POETS
   (We Poets oft our Bays allow,         . . . . . . . .      6 Ode to King         9
   Which darts on poets eyes a trembling light;  . . . . .     54 Temple Ill        98
   And Poets their own Verses sung,      . . . . . . . .     79 Vanbrug House       2
   Now Poets find this Art is lost,      . . . . . . . .     79 Vanbrug House      13
   That Poets were a numerous Race,      . . . . . . . .     79 Vanbrug House      18
   Whence Broods of insect Poets rise.   . . . . . . . .     80 Vanbrug House      54
   And Poets if they had their Due,      . . . . . . . .     81 Vanbrug House      67
   And Poets their own Verses Sung,      . . . . . . . .    106 V's House           2
   Now Poets feel this Art is lost:      . . . . . . . .    106 V's House          14
   Now Poets from all Quarters ran       . . . . . . . .    108 V's House          95
   Where may the Poets Palace ly?        . . . . . . . .    109 V's House         100
   Farther in haste the Poets throng,    . . . . . . . .    109 V's House         105
   Like Bacchus Thou, as Poets feign,    . . . . . . . .    109 V's House         119
   May'st thou despise a Poets Name.     . . . . . . . .    121 Apollo Outwit      56
   Of Modest Poets thou be first,        . . . . . . . .    121 Apollo Outwit      57
   Give Hints, that Poets ne'er believe in God.  . . . . .    193 Author Himself      6
   As Poets fein; but where's the Moral?     . . . . . .    254 Bubble             94
   Tho' Poets have the second Sight,     . . . . . . . .    270 Apollo's Edict  D  34
   When Poets soar in youthful Strains,  . . . . . . . .    271 Apollo's Edict  D  52
   The Poets Wits, than in the Players Dressing.   . . .    276 Epilogue           46
   The horned Floud, as Poets sing:      . . . . . . . .    293 Prog Marriage     110
   "Poets till they grow hoarse may bawl     . . . . . .    321 First of April     21
   This Chain, as Antient Poets hold,    . . . . . . . .    345 Prometheus         35
   Ye Poets ragged and forlorn,          . . . . . . . .    394 Grub-Street         1
   Assist all Poets in Distresses,       . . . . . . . .    411 Dial Rich Marb     94
   Not for inspiring poets brains        . . . . . . . .    432 Answer Paulus      15
   An Hundred Tongues, as Poets use,     . . . . . . . .    449 Modern Lady       137
   So, Bays on Poets Brows have bin      . . . . . . . .    457 Paddy's Charac      5
   The Lawrel so, by Poets worn,         . . . . . . . .    458 Paddy's Charac      9
   Well knowing what the Poets meant:    . . . . . . . .    461 Birthday Song      18
   Too happy were the Poets Crew,        . . . . . . . .    467 Birthday Song     223
   The Poets Mythologick Dreams,         . . . . . . . .    478 Epist on Epist     85
   For Poets open Table kept,        . . . . . . . .    481 Libel on D- D-     37
   Saw Poets at his Levee wait.      . . . . . . . .    482 Libel on D- D-     70
   By Sages, Priests, or Poets taught;   . . . . . . . .    482 Libel on D- D-     76
   Whose fingers itch for poets ears;    . . . . . . . .    487 Irish-Club          6
   On Poets in all times abusive,        . . . . . . . .    504 Doctor Delaney    133
   Than those of Poets to the Lust of Gold.  . . . . . .    532 To Mr. Gay         22
   Damn'd Poets, Damn'd Criticks,    . .    . . . . . . .    576 Place Damn'd        7
   By ev'ry size of Poets sung:          . . . . . . . .    584 Strephon Chloe      2
   Your Poets Chloe's beauty heightning      . . . . . .    621 Scandal Poem 1    149
   At Poets flights to take offence:     . . . . . . . .    622 Scandal Poem 1    154
   But, Poets love profane allusions.    . . . . . . . .    622 Scandal Poem 1    162
   Your Poets, Chloe's Beauty height'ning,   . . . . . .    628 Scandal Poem 2    153
   Three Poets in an Age at most?        . . . . . . . .    640 On Poetry           6
```

```
POETS          (CONTINUED)                                PAGE   TITLE              LINE
     For Poets, Law makes no Provision:        . . . . . . .   641  On Poetry            49
     Our Poets (you can never want 'em,        . . . . . . .   649  On Poetry           279
     Of Jobbers in the Poets Art,              . . . . . . .   650  On Poetry           312
     For those who are not Poets born:         . . . . . . .   652  On Poetry           354
     As what those antient Poets sing;         . . . . . . .   687  Cadenus Vaness       28
     But in the Poets we may find,             . . . . . . .   694  Cadenus Vaness      256
     True Poets can depress and raise;         . . . . . . .   729  Stella, Poems        53
     Unjustly Poets we asperse;                . . . . . . .   729  Stella, Poems        57
     (Could Poets or could Painters fix        . . . . . . .   735  Stel B-day '20       17
     Of Poets dare assume my Place;            . . . . . . .   739  Stel B-day '21       14
     We Poets when a Hint is new               . . . . . . .   747  Stel Distress        59
     But Poets when a Hint is new              . . . . . . .   751  Stel Wood-Park       75
     So, Poets lose their Feet by Time,        . . . . . . .   756  Stel B-day '24        3
     (If all be true that Poets chant)         . . . . . . .   849  Old Thorn            46
     (So Poets sing, with golden Bough         . . . . . . .   896  Panegyr Dean        307
     Like the Fiction of Poets concerning the Wind,  . . . .   927  Riddle 11        D   3
     Poets, in those Days, us'd to venture high,     . . . .   988  Letter Dr Sh-n       13
     Whilst you three merry Poets traffick     . . . . . . .   993  On Picture            1
     For thee three Poets now are drudging all, . . . . . .    993  On Picture           25
     And future Poets, as they rise,           . . . . . . .   994  On Picture           31
     By modern Poets, call'd Elision;          . . . . . . .  1021  Nim-Dan-Dean 1   D  12
POH
     Poh! Fellow keep not such a Pother        . . . . . . .   128  Little House         59
POINT
     To point out which is moderation, which is fortitude.  .   41  Ode Sancroft        210
     The Point of Sagittarius Dart,            . . . . . . .   100  Elegy Patrige        81
     She'll strain a Point, and sit astride,   . . . . . .     100  Elegy Patrige        86
     You must, although the Point be nice,     . . . . . .     218  To Mr. Delany        95
     The Point he could no longer doubt,       . . . . . .     255  Bubble              129
     But, yet the Point is not so clear in     . . . . . .     366  Answer Delaney       27
     Thoughtful upon a Point of Moment:        . . . . . . .   375  Apology Lady C        3
     The point is plain: Remove the cause;     . . . . . .     487  Irish-Club           15
     Point out the surest Men to rise,         . . . . . . .   502  Doctor Delany        84
     On such a Point few Words are best,       . . . . . .     526  Lady's Dres Rm       15
     This Point must needs be settled first;   . . . . . .     589  Strephon Chloe      165
     At last, the Point was fully clear'd;     . . . . . .     598  Problem Solved       31
     Or blunts the Point of ev'ry Dart;        . . . . . .     687  Cadenus Vaness        8
     She study'd well the Point, and found     . . . . . .     695  Cadenus Vaness      278
     Stuck to the Point that pierc'd her Breast; . . . . .     703  Cadenus Vaness      521
     In ev'ry Point to make it fit,            . . . . . .     709  Cadenus Vaness      724
     Or miss but a point,                      . . . . . . .   855  Lady's Lament       140
     Then he low'rs down the Point, and kisses the Hilt. .     871  Grand Question      112
     In every point, like black and white:     . . . . . .     901  Dean's Reasons       72
     That I shou'd point the Word of God,      . . . . . .     930  Riddle 15        D  23
POINTED
     Pointed at Col'nels, Lords, and Beaux;    . . . . . .     701  Cadenus Vaness      478
     Or sharp pointed rocks,                   . . . . . . .   854  Lady's Lament        81
POINTS
     Is in all Points the fittest Tool,        . . . . . . .    61  Lady Tablebook       28
     Points out the Place of either Yew;       . . . . . . .   116  Bauc & Phil 2       171
     The grave Divine with knotty Points perplext,   . . .     364  On Dreams            31
     "Points out some Circumstance to please us.  . . . .      554  Death of Swift       10
     "His Satyr points at no Defect,           . . . . . . .   571  Death of Swift      463
     With Heads to Points the Gulph they enter, . . . . .      654  On Poetry           401
     In Points of Honour to be try'd,          . . . . . .     724  To Stella            35
     Points out where each new Victim falls;   . . . . . .     923  Riddle 7             58
     But help thee to be read with Points.     . . . . . .    1021  Nim-Dan-Dean 1   D  40
POIS'NING
     Pois'ning the Flesh from whence it came;  . . . . . .     529  Lady's Dres Rm      106
POIS'NOUS
     Among the noblest flow'rs a thousand pois'nous weeds,  .   37  Ode Sancroft        102
     That Cancer with his pois'nous Claws      . . . . . .     228  Prog of Beauty       91
     That pois'nous Juice which kills by Cold. . . . . . .     469  Burning Poem          2
     With Harpy Claws, and Pois'nous Tongue,   . . . . . .     504  Doctor Delaney      124
POISON
     They Assassine when young, and Poison when old.  . . .    148  Windsor Proph        20
     Turn thy Nourishment to Poison!           . . . . . . .   838  Legion Club         206
     His heart in poison deeply dipt,          . . . . . .     951  Upstart          D  27
     Is the poison and dagger you boast in your jaws, trow? .   979  Dean to Tho: S        5
     Your ink is your poison, your pen is what not; . . . .    979  Dean to Tho: S       21
POISON'D
     And all the contradictions of a poison'd age;  . . . .    38  Ode Sancroft        118
     To poison'd Arrows from the Dark,         . . . . . .     500  Doctor Delaney       28
     Who sees, will spew; who smells, be poison'd. . . . .     583  Young Nymph          74
POISONOUS    SEE POYS'NOUS
     Some think him cut out from the Poisonous Yew,  . . .     334  Serious Poem         31
POISONS
     And while he poisons, wins the Royal Heart.  . . . .      534  To Mr. Gay           82
POKER
     With an old Poker in her Hand;            . . . . . . .   743  Stel B-day 22        54
     Should with Poker fiery-red               . . . . . . .   830  Legion Club          25
POKES
     And here's a pair of leathern pokes,      . . . . . . .   753  Gift for Bec         17
POLE
     About the grinding artick Pole;           . . . . . . .   362  Grace's Answer       34
     And, when I have him by the Pole,         . . . . . .     921  Riddle 6             33
     Ever dancing round a Pole.                . . . . . . .   927  Riddle 10        D   6
     Down in the Strand just where the new Pole is,  . . .     988  Letter Dr Sh-n        8
POLE-CAT
     "Like Pole-Cat vile be treated?           . . . . . . .   154  Widow and Cat    D  22
```

	PAGE	TITLE	LINE
POLICY			
His Policy consists in setting Traps,	535	To Mr. Gay	121
Renown'd for Valour, Policy and Arts.	789	St. Pat's Well	6
POLISH			
For Man to dress and polish his Uncourtly Mind,	22	Ode Athenian	218
Too rough to polish, and too blunt to bite.	672	Epig Carthy 25	D 4
To polish your mind,	855	Lady's Lament	126
POLISH'D			
Polish'd neck, and radient eye;	936	Riddle 24	D 14
POLISH'T			
Of polish't Brass, his flaming Car,	352	Wood Ironmongr	13
POLITE			
And teach him how to be polite.	218	To Mr. Delany	98
Which modern Ladies call polite;	448	Modern Lady	113
To an Allusion so polite,	497	Panegyr Swift	123
Some try to learn polite Behaviour,	592	Strephon Chloe	271
POLITELY			
Lord! how politely they can scold;	949	Epigr Scolding	2
POLITICIAN			
And Atlas is a Politician	160	Atlas	16
Join'd with a brazen Politician,	354	Simile Silver	20
"'Tis read by ev'ry Politician:	564	Death of Swift	282
Be silent as a Politician,	644	On Poetry	123
The deeper Politician.	785	Mullinex Dick	28
POLITICIANS			
Your Politicians at a loss	420	Holyhead	16
True Politicians only Pay	483	Libel on D- D-	89
Though by the Politicians Scheme	592	Strephon Chloe	263
As all your Politicians wise	886	Rev Market-Hill	109
POLITICKS			
Which we call deep Design and Politicks	29	Ode to Temple	93
Of Spleen, of Politicks and Nonsense,	181	Horace 2, 1	38
As mine for Politicks and Wit.	193	Horace 2, 1	106
He turns to Politicks his dang'rous Wit,	194	Author Himself	26
But for the Politicks of Pue,	282	Journal	101
Talks Politicks, and gives the Toast.	398	Earl of P-b-w	6
But I, in Politicks grown old,	485	Libel on D- D-	171
From Scandal, Politicks, and Play,	688	Cadenus Vaness	44
Grown old in Politicks and Wit,	702	Cadenus Vaness	503
Have put the Dean's Politicks quite out of Date;	716	Answer Rebus	24
'Till Politicks debas'd my mind.	782	Mullinix Tim	282
POLLUTE			
Who, to pollute my shades, bring'st with thee down	44	To Congreve	9
Make me pollute the Muses' bower?	490	Dialogue	46
How would it pollute their Crosiers and Rochets	522	St. Cecilia's	11
POLLUTED			
Nor wonder, if from such polluted minds	47	To Congreve	127
POLLUTING			
With Vice polluting every Throne	659	On Poetry	D 410
POLLUTION			
In the pollution of these days;	38	Ode Sancroft	109
POMATUM			
Some with Pomatum, Paints and Slops,	526	Lady's Dres Rm	35
POMONA			
Here poor Pomona sits on thorns:	901	Dean's Reasons	92
POMP			
When Pow'r in all its Pomp appears,	340	Arch-Bish Dub	13
POMPEY			
Call'd Pompey, Scipio and Caesar;	82	Salamander	2
POMPOSITY			
With what pomposity he talks;	950	Upstart	D 14
POMPOUSLY			
Thou pompously wilt let us know	180	Horace 2, 1	7
POND'ROUS			
The pond'rous Metal seems to swim;	251	Bubble	12
He was as hard, and pond'rous Wood at that:	285	Elegy Boat	20
Too pond'rous is thy Bulk to mount the Sky;	539	Mr. Pulteney	41
PONDER			
Now, Ponder well ye Parents dear;	587	Strephon Chloe	115
Or, ponder long with anxious Thought,	892	Panegyr Dean	161
PONDER'D			
My Dear, I have ponder'd again and again on't:	867	Grand Question	20
PONDROUS			
So Atlas, lest the pondrous Sphears	160	Atlas	9
PONDS SEE FISH-PONDS			
Peeps in the Ponds to look for Spawn:	279	Journal	22
Why shou'd I tell of Ponds and Drains,	283	Journal	111
PONTACK			
From every Meal Pontack in plenty	745	Stel Distress	13
From ev'ry Meal Pontack in plenty,	750	Stel Wood-Park	37
PONTIFICK			
Pontifick, made your glorious March;	326	Pethox	94
POOL			
Her Belly in the neighb'ring Pool:	230	Prog of Poetry	6
POOR			
Of one poor Coronation-day,	6	Ode to King	15
But as for poor contented Me,	20	Ode Athenian	132
Taught us, like Spaniards, to be proud and poor,	28	Ode to Temple	56
On what poor Engines move	29	Ode to Temple	104
Poor we Cadets of Heav'n, not worth her Care,	32	Ode to Temple	183
A pride that well suspends poor mortals fate,	45	To Congreve	45

POOR   (CONTINUED)

	PAGE	TITLE	LINE
What poor regards would merit all below!	49	To Congreve	184
A poor amusement for my scorn and hate;	53	Temple Ill	84
"I' expose thy soul, clad in this poor disguise;	55	Temple Ill	144
Is all the poor content delusion finds.--	55	Temple Ill	150
And then your poor Petitioner, both Night and Day,	73	Mrs Harris Pet	74
Where dwelt a poor old honest Yeman	91	Bauc & Phil 1	51
In his poor House to pass the Night;	91	Bauc & Phil 1	54
In his Poor Hut to pass the Night;	111	Bauc & Phil 2	22
While the poor Child lay fast asleep.	150	Corinna	8
Poor Britain shall have Peace at last;	168	Peace Dunkirk	2
Poor <Swift> departs, and, what is worse,	173	Horace 1, 7	93
Poor <Swift>, with all his Losses vext,	174	Horace 1, 7	113
Poor York! the harmless Tool of others Hate;	195	Author Himself	51
But as a poor pretending Beau	216	To Dr. Delany	41
Poor Will, who needs must interpose,	220	A Quiet Life	23
Love never thinks of Rich and Poor,	224	Prog of Love	61
Poor Strephon, how would he blaspheme!	226	Prog of Beauty	16
Poor Celia, but of mortall Race	229	Prog of Beauty	106
But these alas, are poor Supplyes	229	Prog of Beauty	115
For Cackling shews the Goose is poor.	230	Prog of Poetry	8
So to the Poor if he refus'd his Pelf,	234	Elegy on Demar	13
And all we poor Shopkeepers must our Horns pull in.	237	Excellent Song	16
Each poor Subscriber to the Sea	253	Bubble	81
Who lifts the Poor, and sinks the Proud,	258	Bubble	210
For Weavers now are just as poor as Wits;	276	Epilogue	40
And made him to Curse the poor innocent Bank.	288	Bank Down	40
Un-man the poor Knave for sake of a Trope.	335	Serious Poem	52
Then come the Poor and strip him so, they leave him not a Cross,	341	Upon His Grace	11
For fear my Lord should send it all into the poor Man's Box.	342	Upon His Grace	26
Tho' now I'm poor I them might pass	372	Letter D. S-y	36
To spare the Rich, and plague the Poor;	392	Young's Satire	46
For he'll be poor as any King:	409	Dial Rich Marb	40
Poor Patty Blount no more be seen	409	Dial Rich Marb	47
Poor Kingdom thou wouldst be that Governor's debtor,	424	Carterets Arms	19
Poor sweaty Paulus, who'd believe us ?	433	Answer Paulus	38
And all for ten poor moidores fee!	434	Answer Paulus	80
Now all alone poor Madam sits,	451	Modern Lady	198
Poor Envy durst not shew her Phiz,	456	Dean Smedley	21
Poor Cynthia never shone so bright,	465	Birthday Song	175
This one, poor, humble Boon I want,	475	Epist on Epist	8
On that poor Spot, call'd Del-Ville, yonder:	476	Epist on Epist	60
And one poor Office, half his Days;	481	Libel on D- D-	34
"So when poor Irish Rapparee,	497	Panegyr Swift	128
Nor ever gave the Poor a Groat.	515	Answer Fable	100
But oh! it turn'd poor Strephon's Bowels,	527	Lady's Dres Rm	43
The Tenants poor, the Hardness of the Times,	533	To Mr. Gay	67
Poor Tom got a plaguy baulk---!	545	Life of Swift	22
"Poor Man! he went, all on a sudden---!	547	Life of Swift	70
Poor Gentleman, he droops apace,	556	Death of Swift	81
"No worthy Friend, no poor Relation?	558	Death of .Swift	162
Poor Pope will grieve a Month; and Gay	561	Death of Swift	207
He freely gave the Poor Advice;	604	Beasts Confess	84
Poor starv'ling Bard, how small thy Gains!	642	On Poetry	59
Poor Ladies! though their Bus'ness be to play,	662	Upon Ladies	1
So two poor Knaves, who find their Credit fail,	668	Epig Carthy 8 D	3
So a poor wretch upon the brink of death,	672	Epig Carthy 24 D	11
Poor Stella must pack off to Town.	744	Stel Distress	2
To the poor Doings of the Dean:	745	Stel Distress	18
In Lodgings like a poor Grisette.	746	Stel Distress	44
Poor Stella must pack off to Town.	750	Stel Wood-Park	26
To the poor Doings of the <Dean>.	750	Stel Wood-Park	42
In Lodgings, like a poor Grizette.	751	Stel Wood-Park	59
The Scottish Hinds too poor to house	759	Receipt Youth	1
Or else poor Stella may be starv'd.	761	Bec's B-Day	38
Poor floating Isle, tost on ill Fortune's Waves,	770	Horace 1, 14	1
Poor Satan will think the Comparison odious;	803	Irish Bishops	11
Poor Bishop Judas, late repenting, dies;	806	Judas	2
Poor rump, thou hadst been better sped,	822	Epigr Rundle	3
A wretch like poor Nancy,	851	Lady's Lament	2
I murder poor Milton,	856	Lady's Lament	156
To ease a poor Lady,	858	Lady's Lament	217
This poor Isle's approaching Ruin?	862	To Janus	14
Grave Harry, when the poor are pressing	878	Robbin & Harry	5
Poor I, a Savage bred and born,	891	Panegyr Dean	131
Here poor Pomona sits on thorns:	901	Dean's Reasons	92
Yet many poor Creatures I help to ensnare.	929	Riddle 13 D	6
Poor Miss Dingley oft hath felt his Bills.	941	Letter	24
Your damnable Riddle, my poor Brains did rack nigh.	972	S-'s Ans Sh-d	2
I am but a poor Servant,	986	Mary to Sher	24
Poor Sherry, inglorious,	1004	Sheridan's Sub	1
But I think it base in you to send a poor Fellow	1014	Swift to Sheri	10
Is a poor Supernaculum;	1015	Swift to Sheri	56
Poor Tom, wilt thou never accept a Defiance,	1019	To Sheridan	1
Poor I myself I was, when I withdrew, sick,	1029	Dr. Helsham	20
If I write any more, it will make my poor Muse sick.	1030	Dr. Sheridan	1
In vain we make poor Sheelah toil,	1035	To Quilca	7
But, alas, the poor Dean neither Shudders nor burns,	1037	Four Storyes	5

		PAGE	TITLE	LINE

PORTER (CONTINUED)
Porter, and Prendergast, and Oates. . . . . 298 Horrid Plot 10
Or should a Porter make Enquiries . . . . 729 Stella, Poems 39
That clumsy outside of a Porter, ... 796 Traulus 1 19
But strips himself to pay the Porter. . . . . . . 928 Riddle 12 D 20
PORTERS
Like Porters o'er a Pot of Ale. . . . . 216 To Mr. Delany 50
Thus all the Footmen, Shoe-boys, Porters, ... 812 Bro Protestant 21
PORTION
'Tis all the Portion of my niggard Stars; . . . . . 32 Ode to Temple 201
Your Portion, taking Britain round, ... 642 On Poetry 53
\<PORTLAND\>
Wine can give \<Portland\> Wit, and \<Cleveland\> Sense, 164 Toland's Invit 23
PORTLY
My portly Motion, Mien, and Gate. . . . . . . 780 Mullinix Tim 234
PORTRESS
The Shoes put on; our faithful Portress . . . . . 885 Rev Market-Hill 69
PORTS
And in their very Ports besiege, ... 463 Birthday Song 103
POSIES
As if a Man in making Posies . . . . 96 On the Union 9
POSITIVE
Are you positive and fretful? . . . . 630 Epistle Lady 7
Positive and over-bearing, ... 799 Traulus 2 9
POSSESS
Let Stubborn Pride Possess thee long, ... 121 Apollo Outwit 53
POSSESS'D
For tho' possess'd of present Vogue they've made . . . 18 Ode Athenian 83
By many a petty Lord possess'd, ... 26 Ode to Temple 6
What Honours we possess'd of old! . . . . 625 Scandal Poem 2 48
POSSESS'T
(The Devils leaving the Possess't) . . . . 259 Bubble 215
She need be no more with the Jaundice possess't; . . . 351 Wood Insect 15
Till \<Bob\>, the Poet's Foe, possess't her Ear. . . . . 531 To Mr. Gay 4
If that were all. But he's possess't: . . . . . 798 Traulus 1 70
POSSESSING
So disappointed when possessing. . . . . 411 Desire Possess 4
POSSESSION
And takes Possession of the Lips, ... 226 Prog of Beauty 27
In Man, Possession, and Desire; . . . . 411 Desire Possess 2
Possession, and Desire, his Brother, ... 412 Desire Possess 9
Possession kept the beaten Road; . . . . 412 Desire Possess 35
They take Possession of the Crown, ... 592 Strephon Chloe 261
Ne'er held Possession of his Breast; . . . . . . 711 Cadenus Vaness 769
"She puts the World in his Possession, ... 714 Cadenus Vaness 882
And soon as we have got Possession, ... 886 Rev Market-Hill 90
POSSESSION'S
Possession's Load was grown so great, ... 413 Desire Possess 51
POSSESSORS
By none but its Possessors to be understood: . . . . 6 Ode to King 4
POSSESST
What honors we possesst of old. . . . . . . 619 Scandal Poem 1 52
With Friendship and Esteem possesst, ... 728 Stella, Poems 13
Thus Ajax, when with Rage possesst . . . . . . 731 Stella, Poems 121
POSSEST
(His Mind with Publick Cares possest, ... 170 Horace 1, 7 3
His Heirs might well of all his Wealth possest, . . . 233 Elegy on Demar 5
Cry'd, Madam, why surely my Master's possest; . . . 868 Grand Question 44
POSSIBLE
If possible, to learn his Story, ... 171 Horace 1, 7 21
If possible, as good as He. . . . . 392 Young's Satire 30
POSSITIVE
Being possitive there is no \<P--st\> . . . . . . 372 Letter D. S-y 31
POST SEE PENNY-POST
A Post so fill'd, on Nature's Laws entrenches; . . . 285 Elegy Boat 11
We may place Boat in this old Post again. . . . . . 285 Elegy Boat 30
The Bird of Pallas knows his Post, ... 324 Pethox 37
That none are more properly Knights of the Post. . . 335 Serious Poem 40
If the Maggot cries Click when it scratches the Post. . 351 Wood Insect 24
Would guard your Nose against a Post. . . . . . 367 Answer Delaney 48
In Journeys he out-rides the Post, ... 398 Earl of P-b-w 4
Or, mention but a vacant Post, ... 480 Libel on D- D- 17
Or, some remote inferior Post, ... 484 Libel on D- D- 133
(And this was thought the highest Post; . . . . . 513 Answer Fable 31
To raise his Post, or fill his Coffers, ... 549 Life of Swift 139
Then let him have the higher Post; . . . . . . 554 Death of Swift 19
A Patriot is a dang'rous Post . . . . 798 Traulus 1 89
Your Usher's Post must next be handled: . . . . . 890 Panegyr Dean 105
That, when I'm duller than a Post, ... 891 Panegyr Dean 148
Be humbly minded; know your Post; . . . . . . 897 Panegyr Dean 327
By riding Post I lose my Health; . . . . 917 Riddle 3 17
POST-BOY
Next Day the Post-boy winds his Horn, ... 398 Earl of P-b-w 16
POST-MEN
Nor London Journals, nor the Post-men, ... 462 Birthday Song 53
POSTED
At North and South are posted Centry; . . . . . 883 Rev Market-Hill 18
POSTERIORS
Falls sick in the Posteriors of the World. . . . . 10 Ode to King 146
May be proud to be licking a great man's posteriors. . . 817 Yahoo's 69

```
                                                           PAGE    TITLE              LINE
POSTERITY
    Careless and Ignorant Posterity,      . . . . . . . .    21 Ode Athenian          163
POSTERN
    One Story high, one postern Door,       . . . . . .      81 Vanbrug House          77
POSTS
    To their old Posts restor'd all Three,    . . . . . .   926 Riddle 9               23
    By clapping Billets on your Door and Posts Sir.   . . . 1002 Reply by Dean         12
POSTURES
    Tho' in strange uncouth postures, and uncomely dress;  .  35 Ode Sancroft          26
    In all the Postures of her Face,    . . . . . . .       591 Strephon Chloe        239
POT    SEE PORRIDGE-POT
    And here's to buy a Pot of Ale.      . . . . . . .      128 Little House           54
    Like Porters o'er a Pot of Ale.     . . . . . . .       216 To Mr. Delany          50
    He touch'd the Pence when others touch'd the Pot;   . . 234 Elegy on Demar         27
    Or, whether o'er a Pot of Ale,     . . . . . . . .      412 Desire Possess          7
    Before our Friends were gone to Pot,     . . . . . .    498 Panegyr Swift         158
    To reach the Pot on t' other Side.     . . . . . .      589 Strephon Chloe        190
    The Leavings of his last Night's Pot      . . . . .     594 Cassinus Peter         27
    Contriving for the Pot and Spit.      . . . . . .       897 Panegyr Dean          332
    To strike him for a pot of ale?   . . . . . . . .       899 Dean's Reasons         32
    With his Pipe and his Pot,     . . . . . . . .          952 Apples                  9
    And charming when squeez'd in a Pot of brown Ale.  . .  953 Oranges                 2
    Your ink is your drink, your pen is your pot.   . . .   979 Dean to Tho: S         22
POT-GUN
    Each Pot-gun levell'd at his Head:      . . . . . .     500 Doctor Delaney         14
POTABLE
    Potable Gold in Golden Cup.     . . . . . . . .         156 Fable of Midas          8
POTATOES
    And boyls Potatoes for her Spouse,      . . . . . .     878 Robbin & Harry         26
POTENT
    You serve a potent Prince, as well as He.    . . . . .  532 To Mr. Gay             44
POTHER
    Poh! Fellow keep not such a Pother    . . . . . .       128 Little House           59
POTION
    Infus'd a strong prolifick Potion,     . . . . . . .    293 Prog Marriage         108
    Oft' swallow'd down a stronger Potion,    . . . . . .   495 Panegyr Swift          61
POTS
    And neither Muggs nor Pots whole.     . . . . . .       425 Five Ladies             6
POTUISSE
    Et diu potuisse, et non potuisse refelli.    . . . . .  967 Letter Sherid           6
    Et diu potuisse, et non potuisse refelli.    . . . . .  967 Letter Sherid           6
POULTNEY
    Poultney deep, accomplish'd St. Johns,    . . . . . .   635 Epistle Lady          175
POULTRY
    To keep our Poultry sweet and clean;   . . . . . . .    892 Panegyr Dean          164
POUND
    And I had in a Purse, seven Pound, four Snillings and.   69 Mrs Harris Pet          2
        . .
    'Tis true, seven Pound, four Shillings, and six Pence,.  71 Mrs Harris Pet         40
        . .
    And hardly pay Eighteenpence Tax in the Pound:   . . .  144 New Song               50
    Or let it cost Five hundred Pound,     . . . . . . .    199 Horace 2, 6            19
    And find his Honour in a Pound,     . . . . . . .       200 Horace 2, 6            27
    Nor can four hundred thousand sterling Pound   . . . .  233 Elegy on Demar          3
    Imprimis: From his Grace a Hundred pound.    . . . . .  274 Epilogue                6
    And all the Rent I pay is scarce five Shillings in the  342 Upon His Grace         22
        Pound.
    His Baily Driving all my Cows into the Parish Pound.    343 Upon His Grace          4
    Sell them to Curl for Fifty Pound,     . . . . . . .    395 Grub-Street            19
    Now pay four Shillings in the Pound.     . . . . . .    409 Dial Rich Marb         28
    Should pay a guinnea in the pound . . . . . . . .       423 Ireld                  68
    Five hundred Pound a Year's no Fool.      . . . . .     478 Epist on Epist        112
    A Nymph, that brings ten thousand Pound:     . . . . .  545 Life of Swift          16
    "I hear about two thousand Pound---    . . . . . .      547 Life of Swift          73
    "To sell him for Six Hundred Pound.     . . . . . .     567 Death of Swift        354
    He's poorer by ten thousand Pound.     . . . . . .      606 Beasts Confess        174
    Was just one annual Hundred Pound.     . . . . . .      642 On Poetry              54
    'Twou'd come to just Five Thousand Pound.    . . . . .  693 Cadenus Vaness        227
    Cou'd you see his grim Grace, for a Pound to a Penny,   803 Irish Bishops           9
    He will but add two Hundred Pound,     . . . . . . .    875 Drapier's Hill          6
    A Mistress worth five thousand pound;     . . . . . .   879 Robbin & Harry         32
    First milk his cows, and after, pound:    . . . . . .   902 Dean's Reasons        104
    Will dress a Dinner worth five Pound.     . . . . . .   941 Letter                 36
    To be much greater than a Pound?    . . . . . . .      1004 Dan J's Reply          29
    That we walk all about, like a horse in a pound,   . . 1026 Sheri Circles           7
POUNDAGE
    In Poundage and Drawbacks, I lose half my Rent,     . . 867 Grand Question         21
POUNDS
    Above a Thousand Pounds in Debt,     . . . . . . . .    174 Horace 1, 7           115
    For Life, six hundred Pounds a Year,     . . . . . .    198 Horace 2, 6             2
    In Stock three hundred thousand Pounds;    . . . . . .  251 Bubble                 17
    Stay, let me see-- Three hundred pounds a year,   . . . 308 Billet Players         17
    Three hundred pounds! Were I the price to fix,   . . .  308 Billet Players         21
    . . . Ten thousand Pounds and more:    . . . . . .     341 Upon His Grace         10
    For he regards Ten thousand Pounds no more than Woods's 341 Upon His Grace         12
        Dross.
    He makes no more to give ten Pounds than I to give a    341 Upon His Grace         14
        Pin.
    To have two thousand Pounds a Year, O 'tis a burning    342 Upon His Grace         18
        Shame!
    Two thousand Pounds a Year, Good Lord! . .    . . . .   342 Upon His Grace         19
```

```
POUNDS          (CONTINUED)                          PAGE    TITLE            LINE
    This Lace is worth twelve Pounds a Yard:    . . . . .   447 Modern Lady        87
    With forty Pounds a Year at most.      . . . . . . .    484 Libel on D- D-     134
    With Twenty Thousand Pounds a Year Rents,              598 Problem Solved      12
    In Rents three thousand Pounds a Year.     . . . . .   821 Dr. Rundle          52
    There's nine Hundred Pounds for Labour and Grain,   .  867 Grand Question       9
    Above his Rent four Pounds a Year;    . . . . . .      875 Drapier's Hill       4
    To Fifteen Hundred Pounds a Year,     . . . . . . .    884 Rev Market-Hill     38
    Can grant ten Thousand Pounds a Year,    . . . . .     916 Riddle 1            35
POUR
    It rain'd as hard as it could pour,                    90 Bauc & Phil 1        11
    To pour down Curses on Mankind.    . . . . . . . .    624 Scandal Poem 2       30
    And prostrate, supplicate pour ma vie.   . . . . .   1005 Sheridan's Sub       12
POUR'D
    What northern hive your pour'd out these foes to wit?  . . .   46 To Congreve    83
    Pour'd in a strong inspiring Juice:    . . . . . . .   743 Stel B-day 22       66
POURING
    Comes pouring on me like a Flood.    . . . . . . .     655 On Poetry          438
POURS
    She pours it out in an Atlantis,      . . . . . . .    150 Corinna             31
    A Cloud, in proper Seasons pours    . . . . . . .     624 Scandal Poem 2       27
    Profusely pours her Off'rings here.    . . . . . .     922 Riddle 7            38
POUT
    Nor, will zealous Hannah pout     . . . . . . . .      896 Panegyr Dean       317
POVERTY
    Grief, Sickness, Poverty, and Age;     . . . . . .     764 Stel B-day '26      32
    Poverty, and Grief, and Care,     . . . . . . . .     832 Legion Club         89
    Shew your poverty of spirit, . . . . . . . . . .       908 Daphne              75
POVEY
    Bid Povey secure him while you are haranguing.    . .  818 Epigr Kite           8
POW'R
    And some kind pow'r for once dispense . . . . . .      37 Ode Sancroft         87
    Thrice, with a prophet's voice and prophet's pow'r,  . .   43 To Congreve       1
    And wisely judge, no pow'r beneath divine   . . . .   44 To Congreve          29
    Were my desires but heighten'd to my pow'r.  . . . .  44 To Congreve          40
    A female pow'r, loose-govern'd thoughts create;   .   54 Temple Ill          104
    I here renounce thy visionary pow'r;    . . . . .     55 Temple Ill          152
    Each Number had it's diff'rent Pow'r;    . . . . .    106 V's House            7
    So Chymists boast they have a Pow'r    . . . . . .    109 V's House          127
    Were want of Pow'r, or want of Sense:   . . . . .     154 Widow and Cat    D  44
    Yet, wanting skill and pow'r to chuse,    . . . .     178 To Lord Harley      57
    On him could ever boast a Pow'r to seize;   . . .     234 Elegy on Demar      30
    With Pow'r no more than other Folk,    . . . . . .    240 Run Bankers         35
    An equal Pow'r descends to thee.)   . . . . . . .     323 Pethox              10
    And, as an Instance of thy Pow'r,    . . . . . .      325 Pethox              55
    When Pow'r in all its Pomp appears,    . . . . . .    340 Arch-Bish Dub       13
    "Madam, the mighty Pow'r of Use     . . . . . . .     379 Apology Lady C     131
    For, such is good Example's Pow'r,    . . . . . .     391 Young's Satire      19
    Of those who want the Pow'r to rise.   . . . . . .    414 Censure             12
    To scratch our endless Itch of Pow'r.   . . . . .     493 Panegyr Swift       10
    How amply then does Pow'r provide   . . . . . . .     493 Panegyr Swift       15
    Than Pimps to Wickedness in Pow'r?    . . . . . .     493 Panegyr Swift       26
    May well conclude his Pow'r will never end.   . . .   533 To Mr. Gay          74
    Whose Councils aid the Sov'reign Pow'r,   . . . .     548 Life of Swift      109
    Whoe'er arrives at Pow'r supreme,    . . . . . .      592 Strephon Chloe     264
    Never once cou'd have the Pow'r     . . . . . . .     636 Epistle Lady       191
    Ridicule has greater Pow'r    . . . . . . . . .       636 Epistle Lady       199
    As Emblems of the sov'reign Pow'r,    . . . . . .     646 On Poetry          193
    They could in doubt their Pow'r in Heaven divide,     657 On Poetry          483
    And bring in doubt their Pow'r divine;   . . . . .    687 Cadenus Vaness      12
    My Pow'r shall be again restor'd,    . . . . . .      694 Cadenus Vaness     247
    Against Vanessa's Pow'r unite;     . . . . . . .      700 Cadenus Vaness     439
    Call'd ev'ry Pow'r to ease my Pains,    . . . . .     726 To Stella          100
    By arbitrary pow'r convey her     . . . . . . .       761 Bec's B-day         23
    'Till Pow'r, discharging all her stormy Bags,   . .   771 Horace 1, 14        29
    There's not a Pow'r above will help you now:   . . .  771 Horace 1, 14        34
    For 'tis beyond the Pow'r of Meal,    . . . . . .     786 Dick, Maggot         9
    Nor ever own'd a Pow'r Divine,     . . . . . . .      820 Dr. Rundle          35
    She'll not have Pow'r to stir an Inch;   . . . . .    885 Rev Market-Hill     66
    No haughty Nymph has Pow'r to run    . . . . . .      916 Riddle 2             5
    And such is my prolific Pow'r,     . . . . . . .      926 Riddle 9             3
    Does distantly my Pow'r obey.     . . . . . . . .     934 Riddle 21        D  12
POW'RFUL
    With those two pow'rful swords, Submission and Humility,   36 Ode Sancroft   48
    That begs the pow'rful blessing of thy pray'rs.   . . .   42 Ode Sancroft    244
    So Pow'rful are a Banker's Bills    . . . . . . .     240 Run Bankers         37
    Envy, I doubt, wou'd pow'rful prove,   . . . . . .    546 Life of Swift       37
POW'RS
    Those pow'rs the criticks, who may boast the odds  . . .   46 To Congreve    103
    But now stopt by some hidden Pow'rs   . . . . . .     93 Bauc & Phil 1      133
    Say, which among the Heav'nly Pow'rs   . . . . . .    227 Prog of Beauty      55
    Ye Pow'rs who over Love preside,    . . . . . . .     229 Prog of Beauty     117
    Ye Pow'rs of Grub-street make me able,   . . . .      346 Prometheus          57
    The Silvan Pow'rs with Fear perplex'd    . . . . .    849 Old Thorn           29
POWD'R
    We'll oil him with kennel, and powd'r him with grains,  .  817 Yahoo's         58
POWD'RING
    He's powd'ring in a Barber's Shop;    . . . . . . .   788 Dick's Variety      32
POWDER
    The Soot or Powder which was wont    . . . . . . .    226 Prog of Beauty      17
    Sweat, Dandriff, Powder, Lead and Hair;   . . . . .   526 Lady's Dres Rm      24
```

	PAGE	TITLE	LINE
POWDER'D			
And, in <Swift's> Ear thrusts half his powder'd Nose.	196	Author Himself	68
"The powder'd Courtier's witty Sneer;	380	Apology Lady C	146
Instead of powder'd Beaus,	426	Five Ladies	31
And with powder'd Caps and Wigs, Sir;	573	Helter Skelter	18
What powder'd Wigs! What Flames and Darts!	585	Strephon Chloe	35
(The Wig was powder'd round with Sleet,	625	Scandal Poem 2	67
Visits, Plays, and Powder'd Beaux.	631	Epistle Lady	42
All powder'd o'er from Tail to Chin;	785	Dick, Maggot	2
With powder'd Rump, and Back and Side,	785	Dick, Maggot	7
Powder'd from shoulder down to flank,	,879	Robbin & Harry	49
(With Flow'r of Sulphur powder'd well,	903	Death Daphne	25
POWER			
With all that Power unfelt, courts Mankind to be Great,	21	Ode Athenian	155
In power of Spittle and a Clout	61	Lady Tablebook	21
Each Number had it's diff'rent Power;	79	Vanbrug House	7
And if they all had Power to build,	79	Vanbrug House	19
So Chymists boast they have a Power	81	Vanbrug House	85
But slacken'd by some secret Power,	113	Bauc & Phil 2	73
But Pallas owns Ardelia's Power,	121	Apollo Outwit	47
They washt away the Chymick Power.	158	Fable of Midas	72
To live in Plenty, Power and Ease.	173	Horace 1, 7	92
Your great Protectors, once in Power,	311	To Ford	27
Because, the Soul her Power contracts,	366	Answer Delaney	25
Where Power and Titles scatter'd lay,	412	Desire Possess	24
In Party, furious to her Power;	417	Woman's Mind	49
Or, shall the charms of wealth and power	490	Dialogue	45
Give others Riches, Power, and Station,	555	Death of Swift	43
"Provoke him with a slave in Power:	566	Death of Swift	344
"But, Power was never in his Thought;	567	Death of Swift	357
"To reconcile his Friends in Power;	567	Death of Swift	366
"Himself within the Frown of Power,	568	Death of Swift	394
"Where Titles give no Right or Power,	570	Death of Swift	439
What Stoicks call without our Power,	729	Stella, Poems	63
Time and Place are in thy Power.	832	Legion Club	78
Most wond'rous is my Magick Power;	930	Riddle 15	D 13
POWERFUL			
The powerful Voice, the graceful Mien,	385	Manly Virtue	57
A powerful Impulse urge your Mind,	642	On Poetry	78
POWERS			
Or, if it please the Powers Divine,	243	Horace 4, 9	19
Now destin'd, by the Powers divine,	272	Apollo's Edict	D 68
Not for his superficial powers	432	Answer Paulus	13
Well comprehend their nat'ral Powers;	607	Beasts Confess	204
So the Sun's Heat, with different Powers,	731	Stella, Poems	119
POX			
And, if no Leprosy, a Pox.	85	Salamander	68
A Pox of all Senders	186	Scriblerus 4	D 1
But a Pox o' those Banks that choak up the Springs.	287	Bank Down	3
A rooted Pox to last for ever.	295	Prog Marriage	166
A pox on Elrington's majestic tone!	309	Billet Players	53
Of Rheumatism and Pox complain,	311	To Ford	25
And He must thunder, with a Pox.	352	Wood Ironmongr	16
Your Vistos, Barges, and (A Pox on	476	Epist on Epist	39
I cry, Pox take him, and his Wit.	555	Death of Swift	52
Say, has the small or greater Pox	595	Cassinus Peter	48
And radiant Iris in the Pox.	729	Stella, Poems	48
Of Shin-Bones rotted by the Pox.	904	Death Daphne	40
POX'D			
Be as Pox'd and Profane as Fanatical <Hort>	808	Advice Parson	10
POYS'NOUS			
No poys'nous Beast will in Her breed,	7	Ode to King	52
The poys'nous Darts has made him reel,	10	Ode to King	143
PRACTIC'D			
There practic'd how to place her Head,	222	Prog of Love	13
A Trade, our Boat had practic'd here so well.	285	Elegy Boat	26
PRACTICE			
At once did Practice both these Arts:	99	Elegy Patrige	48
Unhelpt by Practice, Books, or Art.	215	To Mr. Delany	22
Then follow the Practice of clever Tom Clinch,	400	Tom Clinch	23
By frequent Practice learns the Trick	416	Woman's Mind	39
Well taught by practice to imbibe	435	Answer Paulus	109
I think this Practice only fit	463	Birthday Song	111
His Practice was, in ev'ry Station	606	Beasts Confess	153
Be studious to practice true Meanness of Spirit;	808	Advice Parson	7
Young Deathlings, who, by Practice made	903	Death Daphne	15
If this be your practice, mean scrub, I assure Ye,	1019	To Sheridan	5
PRACTIS'D			
'Twas what all his Life he had practis'd before.	517	Dean Hang Rape	22
Have often practis'd to their Shame.	605	Beasts Confess	140
And have we not practis'd all Methods to gain you;	805	Irish Bishops	57
PRACTISE			
Nor practise such an antiquated cheat;	44	To Congreve	18
But, after Marriage, practise more	588	Strephon Chloe	141
They still must practise to maintain it.	592	Strephon Chloe	266
PRAEMIUM			
With Int'rest, and a Praemium paid beside,	533	To Mr. Gay	69
PRAETOR			
The Praetor broke the Consul's Head;	190	Faggot	32
Came up, and knock't the Praetor down.	190	Faggot	34
When Christ was betray'd to Pilate, the Praetor,	804	Irish Bishops	29

PRAIS'D   PAGE   TITLE   LINE

	PAGE	TITLE	LINE
PRAIS'D			
That, God be prais'd, the Dean is well.	557	Death of Swift	126
Would not be prais'd, yet lov'd to praise.	701	Cadenus Vaness	457
We never hear the Workmen prais'd,	727	Stella, Poems	2
By you so oft, so highly prais'd!	887	Panegyr Dean	14
PRAISE			
What can the Poet's humble Praise?	6	Ode to King	7
And into Adoration turns our Praise.	11	Ode to William	D 8
Of Admiration and of Praise:	18	Ode Athenian	80
Although they praise the Learning and the Wit,	21	Ode Athenian	164
Less should I dawb it o're with transitory Praise,	21	Ode Athenian	169
And changes all to Beauty, and the Praise	23	Ode Athenian	236
And since too oft debauch'd by Praise,	33	Ode to Temple	204
And Poetry has lost the art to praise,	38	Ode Sancroft	111
To praise your parts by publishing of mine;	44	To Congreve	34
Soft'ning the muse's thunder into praise;	44	To Congreve	42
To praise the Pile, and Builder <Van>.	109	V's House	108
He values not the Poet's Praise,	157	Fable of Midas	55
That Irony which turns to Praise,	216	To Mr. Delany	34
If Anna's happy Reign you praise,	271	Apollo's Edict	D 44
The Praise of Italy or France	314	To Ford	92
I Sing not of the Draper's Praise, nor yet of William Wood;	341	Upon His Grace	1
Bedaubs the guilty Great with nauseous Praise:	364	On Dreams	36
To praise it, par maniere d'acquit;	379	Apology Lady C	120
We praise and confound	424	Carterets Arms	12
And senseless praise	440	Ballyspellin	5
Talks half a Day in Praise of Silence;	450	Modern Lady	171
A Tyrant for his Mercy praise,	464	Birthday Song	119
To praise your Empress, and her Breed.	465	Birthday Song	152
To praise your Hero for Devotion:	468	Birthday Song	262
Although to Praise it Philips Writ.	484	Libel on D- D-	144
It might be something in your Praise:	505	Doctor Delaney	164
And, Praise bestow'd in Grub-Street Rimes,	505	Doctor Delaney	165
'Till Block-heads blame, and Judges praise,	505	Doctor Delaney	167
But in the Praise of Virtue is dumb:	515	Answer Fable	94
Let me praise thy Wit unmatcht.	523	Betty Grizette	12
To praise Queen Anne, nay more, defend her,	550	Life of Swift	186
"The Praise is His, and Theirs the Blame.	550	Life of Swift	200
A Character to praise and blame,	608	Know Not What	4
In praise of long departed Wit,	611	By Dr. Swift	8
More to my Praise than all my Volumes;	611	By Dr. Swift	10
Have I nothing then to praise?	630	Epistle Lady	12
Sing my Praise in Strain sublime:	631	Epistle Lady	57
To earn a Stock of Pence and Praise,	642	On Poetry	66
To Satire, Praise, or hum'rous Lines;	643	On Poetry	82
Or praise the Judgment of the Town,	644	On Poetry	125
We justly praise, or justly blame:	644	On Poetry	130
The Loads of Poems in his Praise,	646	On Poetry	203
And praise the whole Administration,	658	On Poetry	D 190
Bare Virtue could not live on Praise,	693	Cadenus Vaness	213
Vanessa's Praise rung in their Ear:	694	Cadenus Vaness	241
They celebrate her Beauty's Praise,	697	Cadenus Vaness	331
Would not be prais'd, yet lov'd to praise.	701	Cadenus Vaness	457
He now cou'd praise, esteem, approve,	703	Cadenus Vaness	546
How was her Tutor wont to praise	708	Cadenus Vaness	688
Much to her Praise, more to his Own.	711	Cadenus Vaness	765
The Merit and the Praise are yours.	728	Stella, Poems	8
Are Lords of Infamy and Praise:	729	Stella, Poems	54
While, Stella to your lasting Praise	739	Stel B-day '21	1
With Stella's Praise to crown the Year.	743	Stel B-day 22	80
They give the sick man joy, and praise	761	Bec's B-Day	15
When none the Drapier's Praise shall sing;	875	Drapier's Hill	13
He sounds my Praise in Verse and Prose.	887	Panegyr Dean	28
To sing your Praise. And, first as <Dean>:	888	Panegyr Dean	44
To let me praise you as my Tutor.	891	Panegyr Dean	130
Yet, when your lofty Domes I praise,	894	Panegyr Dean	225
To praise the Cheeks, Chin, Nose, the Bridge and all,	993	On Picture	26
Pray do they praise me or bespatter?	1003	Dan J's Reply	5
You seem to praise to make amends,	1003	Dan J's Reply	20
Nor praise we less that Circumcision,	1021	Nim-Dan-Dean 1	D 11
PRAISES			
That all the Praises it can give,	20	Ode Athenian	150
In satire, to my Congreve's praises meant;	48	To Congreve	176
These praises we blot out	423	Carterets Arms	3
The Irish Senate's Praises sing:	501	Doctor Delaney	56
All these Praises are your Due.	632	Epistle Lady	94
Thy Praises ev'ry Muse shall sing.	656	On Poetry	448
Because their Praises were his due	658	On Poetry	D 410
Now should my Praises owe their Truth	729	Stella, Poems	61
PRANCE			
To Prance with me the Statue round.	776	Mullinix Tim	80
PRANCES			
And his Horse, the dear Creter, it prances and rears,	870	Grand Question	97
PRANK			
Then Plodding, he thought on a whimsical Prank	288	Bank Down	34
PRANKS			
The Multitude's Capricious Pranks	239	Run Bankers	5
A noble Lord hath told his Pranks,	515	Answer Fable	79
His Master, unsuspicious of his Pranks,	535	To Mr. Gay	109
And I resent these Pranks no more.	579	Day Judgement	20

	PAGE	TITLE	LINE
PRATE			
Of which, whoe'er lacks confidence to prate, ...	48	To Congreve	155
While two fond lovers prate, the Muse and I.	49	To Congreve	200
They, in their lewd and fashionable prate, ...	50	To Congreve	217
But if thou be'st what thy mad vot'ries prate, ...	54	Temple Ill	103
Still Groans while tatling Gossips prate.	93	Bauc & Phil 1	110
But, Tom will prate	441	Ballyspellin	49
The Sum of all their senseless Prate, ...	449	Modern Lady	141
They find an idle Hour to Prate.	480	Libel on D- D-	28
Ye <senators>, who love to prate;	487	Irish-Club	2
Then Cloe, still go on to prate	735	Stel B-day '20	39
Aspiring, greedy, full of senseless Prate, ...	792	St. Pat's Well	51
Thus <Horace> in the House will prate, ...	812	Bro Protestant	23
If noisy <Tom> should in the <Senate> prate, ...	825	Noisy Tom	1
Hark, the Monkeys, how the prate!	832	Legion Club	82
"Go, bring me my Smock, and leave off your Prate, . .	870	Grand Question	83
Robin from noon to night will prate, ...	878	Robbin & Harry	9
PRATED			
I wish when you prated, ...	1014	Swift to Sheri	13
PRATER			
a prater at Court in the Stile of the Stews	540	Charac Walpole	10
PRATERS			
This bids some curious praters here below	45	To Congreve	73
Abandon'd, stupid, slavish praters!	436	Answer Paulus	134
PRATES			
Who prates like his Grand mere	186	Scriblerus 4	D 8
While all she prates has nothing in it.	415	Woman's Mind	6
He prates in Spight of all Impediment	797	Traulus 1	49
A long-ear'd Beast, a Bird that prates, ...	942	Probatur Alit	3
PRATING			
Draws ev'ry rhyming, prating, dressing sot, ...	48	To Congreve	153
There are some prating folks in town, ...	422	Ireld	39
Of hearty gossips prating round;	762	Bec's B-Day	52
Has, with noise and odd gestures, been prating some years,	815	Yahoo's	18
It is but prating to a bust.	901	Dean's Reasons	68
PRAY			
Ladys, quoth Levens, pray forbear, ...	67	Problem	57
But pray, Mary, can you tell what I have done with my Purse!	70	Mrs Harris Pet	15
. . .as in Duty bound, shall ever Pray.	73	Mrs Harris Pet	75
This made him to Apollo pray	81	Vanbrug House	69
Pray take your Answer and be gone.	91	Bauc & Phil 1	32
Then pray think this a lucky Hitt, ...	123	Empty'ng Town	21
Pray reach that Thing here to the Child, ...	128	Little House	52
Pray leave me where you found me first.	175	Horace 1, 7	138
In manner submissive most humbly do pray, ...	185	Scriblerus 1	2
And if I pray by Reason's rules, ...	199	Horace 2, 6	D
'Tis one to me.--"Then, tell us, pray	202	Horace 2, 6	99
Pray Gentlemen, believe your Eyes, ...	254	Bubble	102
Pray not a word of Halcyon Days.	271	Apollo's Edict	D 45
Pray gentle-Folks forbear your Scoffing.	286	Elegy Boat	38
Pray, what is this Bank of which the Town Rings? . . .	287	Bank Down	1
And drops him at the Church, to pray	292	Prog Marriage	81
Then pray be free, and tell me which:	299	Horrid Plot	24
"Good Madam Pallas, pray be easy, ...	305	Storm	70
But I'll tell you the Secret, and pray do not Blab, .	335	Serious Poem	35
Pray never press your self for Rent, but pay me when you can,	342	Upon His Grace	33
Then as to War's Alarms I pray	372	Letter D. S-y	38
(Who ought for Peace and Plenty Pray.)	372	Letter D. S-y	40
Is Capt. Crach'rode here, pray?--No.	376	Apology Lady C	43
He had not heard of him--Pray see, ...	377	Apology Lady C	59
But pray. To morrow go at Ten, ...	377	Apology Lady C	67
Pray God they now may find as true.	408	Dial Rich Marb	22
Then Reader pray shed some tears of Salt Water, . . .	430	Dicky Dolly	17
Then to her Glass; and "Betty, pray	446	Modern Lady	48
Then pray, dear Doctor, condescend	493	Panegyr Swift	27
That only know to preach and pray, ...	497	Panegyr Swift	149
Now pray observe the Doctor's Choice, ...	513	Answer Fable	19
"Pray, do but give me leave to shew 'em;	563	Death of Swift	269
Which drives you not to pray, but curse!	617	Scandal Poem 1	10
That drives you, not to pray, but curse?	624	Scandal Poem 2	10
Bestow my next I pray, to Pope or Swift.	669	Epig Carthy 17	D 4
With no desire to pray or preach;	677	Parson's Case	32
Pray steal me not, I'm Mrs. Dingley's	763	Collar Lap-Dog	1
Tom would pray for ev'ry Whig, ...	784	Mullinex Dick	15
Pray be patient, you shall find	839	Legion Club	235
Pray, how does my Lady?--My Wife's at your Service.--	869	Grand Question	75
Pray, Madam, be quiet; what was it I said?-- . . .	870	Grand Question	85
(His Beaver is cock'd; pray, Madam, mark that, . . .	870	Grand Question	105
Pray, Captain, be pleas'd to light, and walk in: . .	871	Grand Question	114
Pray what is a Man? he's a fine-Linen Searcher. . .	972	S-'s Ans Sh-d	10
I can't pray in quiet for you and your verses,-- .	976	Dean to Sherid	5
And if you be my Phoebus, pray who was your Pallas? .	977	Dean to Sherid	42
Pray do they praise me or bespatter?	1003	Dan J's Reply	5
PRAY'D			
Is humbly pray'd to ruin Twenty more.	535	To Mr. Gay	106
Then pray'd an Answer and sat down.	687	Cadenus Vaness	20
PRAY'R			
His Pray'r was granted, for the God	81	Vanbrug House	71
(May Heav'n Indulgent hear your Pray'r!)	498	Panegyr Swift	174

	PAGE	TITLE	LINE

PRAY'R   (CONTINUED)

Is at study or pray'r.   856   Lady's Lament   158

PRAY'R-BOOK

And thus I go off without Pray'r-Book or Psalm.   . .   400   Tom Clinch   22

PRAY'RS

That begs the pow'rful blessing of thy pray'rs.   . . .   42   Ode Sancroft   244
They learnt it not at Sermons or at pray'rs.   275   Epilogue   12
We go to Pray'rs, and then to play   280   Journal   52
"And, but for Shame, wou'd say his Pray'rs.   305   Storm   66
All ran to Pray'rs, both Priests and Laity, ...   353   Wood Ironmongr   21
He quite forgot to say his Pray'rs.   605   Beasts Confess   118
His Household twice a Day to Pray'rs.   605   Beasts Confess   132
To us he made his dayly pray'rs, ...   620   Scandal Poem 1   81
. . .before my Master comes from Pray'rs, ...   987   Mary to Sher   35

PRAYER

On Sundays, after Ev'ning Prayer.   116   Bauc & Phil 2   169
The God could not refuse her Prayer;   120   Apollo Outwit   34
Apply'd to Jove with fervent Prayer;   383   Manly Virtue   3
Jove grants the Prayer, gives Virtue Birth,   . . .   384   Manly Virtue   15
Weary the Gods with ceaseless Prayer, ...   388   Manly Virtue   139
"Now the departing Prayer is read: 558   Death of Swift   149
By Faith and Prayer, this Crosier in my Hand,   . .   792   St. Pat's Well   39
Wearied with saying Grace and Prayer, ...   1003   Dan J's Reply   1

PRAYERS

Or make you Fast, and carry you to Prayers: 166   Toland's Invit   43
The kind Physician grants the Husband's Prayers,   . .   364   On Dreams   27
Of Prayers, that he might well succeed, ...   373   Letter D. S-y   69
And go to Church, and say our Prayers.   495   Panegyr Swift   71
What hearty Prayers that I should mend?   557   Death of Swift   138
To us he made his daily Prayers, ...   626   Scandal Poem 2   79
That Men of his Coat should be minding their Prayers.   .   868   Grand Question   37

PRAYRS

And calls the Family to Prayrs, ...   292   Prog Marriage   88

PRE

Tis pre engged and in his room   423   Ireld   71

PREACH

Who preach the saucy pedantry of rules;   46   To Congreve   102
Contrivd to preach his Sermon next   95   Bauc & Phil 1   177
Knew how to preach old Sermons next, ...   115   Bauc & Phil 2   127
Or preach, you'd like him scarce the worse.   375   Apology Lady C   12
He'll mount his Tub, and preach his best, ...   456   Dean Smedley   38
That only know to preach and pray, ...   497   Panegyr Swift   149
With no desire to pray or preach;   677   Parson's Case   32
Let Stella's fair Example preach   724   To Stella   33

PREACH'D

Dean Cross, had he preach'd, would have made us all   1029   Dr. Helsham   8
        Pew-sick;

PREACHED

I preached three congregations deaf, ...   675   Curate's Compl   10

PREACHERS

"And Preachers, find the better quarter, ...   549   Life of Swift   166
What Preachers talk, or Sages write, ...   691   Cadenus Vaness   150
Who are all grown reverend Preachers!   838   Legion Club   204

PREACHING

Of Prelate thus, for preaching fam'd, ...   406   Swift to Pope   25
Old Latimer preaching did fairly describe   803   Irish Bishops   1
Proceed we to your preaching next: 888   Panegyr Dean   61

PRECEDENCE

Precedence, and support your Grandeur: 888   Panegyr Dean   46

PRECEDENTS

And Precedents we can produce, if it please ye,   . . .   518   Dean Hang Rape   40

PRECINCTS

Into the Precincts of the Rose, ...   226   Prog of Beauty   26

PRECIOUS

In Scottish Hills found precious Ore, ...   133   Magician's Rod   29
Is all with precious Jewels strow'd.   324   Pethox   36
No more let fall those precious Tears.   445   Modern Lady   18
The Time too precious now to waste, ...   453   Modern Lady   276
More precious far than ev'n the Gift   494   Panegyr Swift   47
"Too soon that precious Life was ended, ...   568   Death of Swift   377
I did but lose my precious Breath, ...   778   Mullinix Tim   172
My precious Time, so long mispent, ...   781   Mullinix Tim   278
Will scarce one precious word impart: 900   Dean's Reasons   44
More precious Juice than from a Still.   920   Riddle 6   22

PRECOX

And bravely Precox might oppose   373   Letter D. S-y   70

PREDECESSOR

More than your Predecessor, Adam, knew;   31   Ode to Temple   162
Our Bishop's Predecessor, Magus, ...   821   Dr. Rundle   41

PREDECESSORS

Our predecessors foot-steps, still in view;   49   To Congreve   196
The Wine, his Blood, our Predecessors shed: . . .   162   Toland's Invit   12
Whate'er your Predecessors taught us, ...   988   Letter Dr Sh-n   1

PREDICTION

Concerning this Image there went a Prediction,   . . .   334   Serious Poem   19
Than his Prediction prove a Lye.   557   Death of Swift   132

PREFACE

Chang'd in the Preface and the Text: 95   Bauc & Phil 1   178
Vampt in the Preface and the Text;   115   Bauc & Phil 2   128

PREFACES

Read all the Prefaces of Dryden, ...   648   On Poetry   251

		PAGE	TITLE	LINE
PREFER				
Prefer our Villaes where the Thames is,	. . . . .	411	Dial Rich Marb	87
But above all I prefer Aeschylus,	. . . . . .	988	Letter Dr Sh-n	28
PREFERMENT				
"While Numbers to Preferment rose;	. . . .	569	Death of Swift	401
Preferment get, and spare his Eyes:	. . . .	604	Beasts Confess	108
PREFERMENT'S				
And quite mistake Preferment's Road.	. . . . .	480	Libel on D- D-	12
They croud about Preferment's Gate,	. . . . .	503	Doctor Delaney	93
PREFERMENTS				
Or murmuring at Whigs Preferments.	. . . . . .	993	On Picture	6
PREFERR'D				
By Favour, or Desert preferr'd	. . . .	66	Problem	25
Why will you aim to be preferr'd	. . . .	501	Doctor Delaney	37
Because himself is not preferr'd;	. . . .	514	Answer Fable	74
"In surest way to be preferr'd---;	. . . .	549	Life of Swift	165
Preferr'd before a Crowd of Beaux,	. . . . . .	710	Cadenus Vaness	751
PREFERRING				
Preferring his Regard for me	. . . .	204	In Sickness	11
PREFIXT				
Prefixt a Cut to ev'ry Tale.)	. . . .	782	Tim and Fables	10
PREGNANT				
Pregnant with Greeks, impatient to be freed,	. . . .	139	City Shower	48
A Bitch that was full pregnant grown,	. . . . . .	207	Fable Bitches	1
His Guilt is clear the Proofs are pregnant,	. . . .	798	Traulus 1	93
PRELATE SEE ARCH-PRELATE				
Short glimm'rings of the prelate glorify'd;	. . . . .	41	Ode Sancroft	213
A Crazy Prelate, and a Royal Prude.	. . . . .	193	Author Himself	2
She'll not have left one single Prelate:	. . . . .	303	Storm	20
Of Prelate thus, for preaching fam'd,	. . . . . .	406	Swift to Pope	25
No Protestant Prelate, His Ldshp or Grace	. . . .	522	St. Cecilia's	9
A Prelate who no God believes,	. . . . . .	645	On Poetry	163
"It's a pity a Prelate should die without law;	. . .	843	Ay and No	17
PRELATES				
Damn'd Ignorant Prelates, and Councellors Privy.	. .	576	Place Damn'd	14
Of pious Prelates what a Stock	. . . . . .	656	On Poetry	453
My Prelates and my Students, sent from hence,	. .	792	St. Pat's Well	29
To foreign Prelates make a slavish Court,	. . . .	793	St. Pat's Well	75
Let <Prelates>, by their good behaviour,	. . . .	488	Irish-Club	21
PREMIER				
His Lordship's premier Ministre,	. . . .	62	Discovery	10
A Premier Minister of State	. . . . . .	160	Atlas	17
May sink by premier Ministers of State.	. . . .	535	To Mr. Gay	116
PREMISE				
When I premise, that Tim has Travell'd.	. . . .	782	Tim and Fables	2
PREMISES				
The Premises tenderly consider'd,.	73	Mrs Harris Pet	70
PREMISING				
Premising thus in Modern way	. . . . . .	80	Vanbrug House	55
Premising thus in Modern way	. . . . . .	106	V's House	29
PREMISSES				
From Premisses erroneous brought,	. . . . . .	695	Cadenus Vaness	280
PRENDERGAST				
Porter, and Prendergast, and Oates.	. . . . .	298	Horrid Plot	10
'PRENTICE				
Some she binds 'Prentice to the Spade,	. . . .	32	Ode to Temple	185
Charm'd by thy voice the 'Prentice drops	. . .	779	Mullinix Tim	203
PRENTICE				
The Slipshod Prentice from his Masters Door,	. .	124	Descriptn Morn	5
And bore my Mother by a Prentice.	. . . . .	350	Upright Judge 3	4
PRENTICES				
The Prentices procur'd a Riding	. . . . .	221	A Quiet Life	53
PREPAR'D				
Prepar'd to Scrub the Entry and the Stairs.	. .	124	Descriptn Morn	8
Prepar'd to leap o'er Sticks, or bind 'em.	. . .	190	Faggot	44
"For her he stood prepar'd to die;	. . . . . .	566	Death of Swift	348
You'll find it well prepar'd to take	. . . . . .	780	Mullinix Tim	225
PREPARE				
To morrow We our Mystick Feast prepare,	. . .	162	Toland's Invit	7
So--let us now for Whisk prepare;	. . . . . .	315	To Ford	113
Prepare a Fleet to waft him o'r'e,	. . . . . .	466	Birthday Song	205
",o, may we all for Death prepare!	. . . . . .	558	Death of Swift	153
All in Arms prepare to back us:	. . . . . .	838	Legion Club	212
To read your Answer, and prepare Reply to't.	. .	1003	Dan J's Reply	3
PREPARES				
And now to attack her again he prepares,	. . . .	517	Dean Hang Rape	14
Returning Janus now prepares,	. . . .	753	Gift for Bec	1
PRESAGE				
A coming Show'r your shooting Corns presage,	. . .	137	City Shower	9
PRESBYTERIANS				
Quakers, Conformists, Presbyterians,	. . . . .	345	Prometheus	14
PRESCRIBE				
That no Physician dares prescribe by Stealth:	. . .	533	To Mr. Gay	78
PRESENCE				
Your Presence all their Native Stubborness controuls,		9	Ode to King	90
When man's ill genius to my presence sent	. . . .	47	To Congreve	135
Nor in her Presence durst be Rude,	. . . . .	121	Apollo Outwit	43
Stand in your sacred Presence aw'd;	. . . . .	243	Horace 4, 9	12
If by thy Presence he's withstood?	. . . . .	340	Arch-Bish Dub	22
And Discord, in his Presence, dies--	. . . . .	387	Manly Virtue	122
Or in the presence of beholders,	. . . . . .	421	Ireld	21

PRESENCE   (CONTINUED)   PAGE   TITLE   LINE
      Have made thy Presence in a true Sence, ... 775 Mullinix Tim   65
PRESENT
      For tho' possess'd of present Vogue they've made . . .   18 Ode Athenian   83
      Spend all our present Stock in hopes of golden Rules. .   27 Ode to Temple   27
      Disturb the present Mitre, as that fearful storm of late,   40 Ode Sancroft   192
      But for a parting Present leave her   . . . . .   295 Prog Marriage   165
      I should present you with a Mitre.   . . . .   361 Grace's Answer   10
      If you allow, the present Age   . . . .   392 Young's Satire   33
      And fit your present Subject best.   . . . .   460 Birthday Song   4
      Present it boldly on your knee, ...   469 Birthday Song   281
      The Doctor names but one at present, ...   513 Answer Fable   33
      The Vandals of the present Age.   . . . .   611 By Dr. Swift   12
      That, present Times have no Pretence   . . . . .   697 Cadenus Vaness   346
      But at present, forsooth, ...   852 Lady's Lament   23
      Present a Sacrifice unclean;   . . . . . .   895 Panegyr Dean   284
      And Millions of the present Age.   . . . .   922 Riddle 7   42
      Steel affords me present aid.   . . . .   937 Riddle 24   D 42
      Which is all at present from Dean of St. Patrick's. .   977 Dean to Sherid   48
      I would present my humble Service . . . .   1014 Swift to Sheri   11
      Her Service to present you, ...   1014 Swift to Sheri   31
      Which is all at present; and so I remain-- . . . . . 1027 Sheri Circles   28
PRESENTED   SEE ILL-PRESENTED
      Presented with the choicest Bits: . . . .   745 Stel Distress   12
      Presented with the nicest Bits: . . . .   750 Stel Wood-Park   10
      Presented him the weekly Bills . . . .   903 Death Daphne   5
PRESENTLY
      He spoke, and presently he feels   . . . .   94 Bauc & Phil 1   165
      He spoke, and presently he feels, ...   115 Bauc & Phil 2   117
      My long old-fashion'd Pocket, was presently cramm'd; . 143 New Song   19
      Then presently he falls to teize, ...   201 Horace 2, 6   59
      And presently guess'd that the Fancy was mine; . . .   264 Apollo   52
      From out the pen will presently . . . .   983 Sher, A Goose   7
PRESENTS
      Know all Men by these Presents, Death the Tamer   . .   233 Elegy on Demar   1
      Presents, as 'tis fitting, ...   1004 Sheridan's Sub   3
      Lady Betty presents you her service most humble, . . . 1027 Sheri Circles   25
PRESERV'D
      Preserv'd by wonder from the Flood, ...   17 Ode Athenian   45
      Advanc'd thy Fortune, and preserv'd thy Fame. . . .   531 To Mr. Gay   14
      Whose Master, Moore, preserv'd him from the Halter, .   826 Noisy Tom   13
PRESERVATION
      He ow'd his Preservation to his Crimes.   . . . . .   536 To Mr. Gay   156
PRESERVE
      To preserve Conquests, as at first to gain: . . .   12 Ode to William D 26
      His watchful Friends preserve him by a Sleight. . . .   196 Author Himself   62
      Preserve, Almighty Providence!   . . . .   199 Horace 2, 6   D
      When Foes are o'ercome, we preserve them from Slaughter, 334 Serious Poem   1
      Then God Preserve his Lordship's Grace, . . .   343 Upon His Grace   47
      The Gift (good Heav'ns preserve 't from Thieves) . .   494 Panegyr Swift   49
      Preserve his health, his store increase; . . . . . .   902 Dean's Reasons   101
PRESERVES
      Your steady Soul preserves her Frame   . . . . . .   243 Horace 4, 9   9
      From stagnating preserves the Flood;   . . . . . .   731 Stella, Poems   128
PRESERVING
      Preserving what it first creates)   . . . .   764 Stel B-day '26   42
PRESIDE
      Ye Pow'rs who over Love preside, ...   229 Prog of Beauty   117
      When o'er your Patron's Treasure you preside, ...   532 To Mr. Gay   16
      O'er all your passions we preside: . . . .   620 Scandal Poem 1   90
      O'er all your Passions we preside;   . . . .   626 Scandal Poem 2   88
      Choler preside, or Blood, or Phlegm, ...   724 To Stella   20
      Will in your tainted Heart preside.   . . . .   725 To Stella   50
      Who o'er each String and Wire preside, ...   798 Traulus 1   73
PRESIDENT
      Their President, in Scarlet Gown, ...   904 Death Daphne   49
PRESIDES
      "We govern here! where she presides   . . . .   322 First of April   47
      If he, who in the Chair presides, ...   391 Young's Satire   5
      And all Men believe he presides there incog. . . . .   804 Irish Bishops   15
PRESS
      "But rudely press before a Duke.   . . . .   200 Horace 2, 6   39
      Why should he sink where nothing seem'd to press? . . . 284 Elegy Boat   3
      Pray never press your self for Rent, but pay me when you 342 Upon His Grace   33
         can,
      When Things of more Importance press: . . . .   475 Epist on Epist   2
      And press you down with all their Weight. . . . . .   503 Doctor Delaney   94
      Press down the Lumps, the Hollows fill, ...   582 Young Nymph   26
      The Time when Wants of Nature press;   . . . .   588 Strephon Chloe   140
      Correctly fitted for the Press, ...   643 On Poetry   106
      Who crowd the Press with hourly Trash.   . . . . . .   652 On Poetry   356
PRESS'D
      She hourly press'd for something new;   . . . . . .   704 Cadenus Vaness   555
PRESSING
      The Master's pressing Wants must be supply'd; . . . .   533 To Mr. Gay   70
      Grave Harry, when the poor are pressing . . . . . .   878 Robbin & Harry   5
PREST
      But, soon with like Occasions prest, ...   589 Strephon Chloe   187
PRESTO
      Presto be gone--Tis here ag'en, ...   251 Bubble   6
      Presto be gone; with t' other Hop   . . . .   788 Dick's Variety   31

	PAGE	TITLE	LINE
PRESUME			
Two other Acts we may presume	108	V's House	89
Presume to shew his mortal snout, ...	464	Birthday Song	144
Presume to treat him at his own Expence.	533	To Mr. Gay	64
Presume not, Gay, unless you serve a Drone, . . .	534	To Mr. Gay	87
Our Author's Meaning, I presume, is	608	Beasts Confess	215
Presume to borrow Wit from Bacchus?	671	Epig Carthy 22 D	2
Though Dick, I dare presume to say, ...	788	Dick's Variety	17
But ne'er presume to eat a Bit:	897	Panegyr Dean	336
Or, if to whisper I presume, ...	917	Riddle 4	7
Shall Man presume to be my Master, ...	918	Riddle 4	17
PRESUMES			
Hircina rank with Sweat, presumes	449	Modern Lady	158
At length, presumes to vent his Satyr on . . .	458	Paddy's Charac	27
PRESUMPTUOUS			
Presumptuous Poet, could you dare	617	Scandal Poem 1	1
Presumptuous Bard! How cou'd you dare	623	Scandal Poem 2	1
PRETENCE			
Once highly honour'd! False is the pretence	44	To Congreve	7
And 'tis conceiv'd, their old Pretence	79	Vanbrug House	27
And 'tis conceiv'd, their old Pretence	106	V's House	27
Under pretence of Taking Air, ...	120	Apollo Outwit	23
Let no pretence of Bus'ness make you stay, ...	166	Toland's Invit	39
Disclaim for ever all pretence	436	Answer Paulus	143
To which he never made pretence, ...	463	Birthday Song	92
Luna was absent on Pretence	586	Strephon Chloe	65
To Titles give the sole Pretence.	656	On Poetry	460
That, present Times have no Pretence	697	Cadenus Vaness	346
Where Truth has not the least Pretence;	747	Stel Distress	62
Where Truth has not the least Pretence;	752	Stel Wood-Park	78
For, let us hear the weak Pretence, ...	820	Dr. Rundle	11
A judge, without the least pretence	876	To Dean Swift	19
To Modesty a weak Pretence;	887	Panegyr Dean	19
PRETEND			
Pretend to cheapen Goods, but nothing buy.	138	City Shower	34
Pretend to answer one Syl--lable, ...	183	Horace 2, 1	85
The Wise pretend to make it clear, ...	366	Answer Delaney	1
Who dares to Irony pretend;	555	Death of Swift	56
All Folks who pretend to Religion and Grace, . . .	575	Place Damn'd	1
And with rebellious Arms pretend	653	On Poetry	381
Then, who with Reason can pretend, ...	765	Stel B-day '26	65
Or should he pretend to be brisk and alert, ...	868	Grand Question	35
The dullest Beast, and what Doctors pretend	941	Letter	37
PRETENDED			
How I always pretended to be for the Tories:	143	New Song	22
. . .to have been acquainted with me, as she pretended. .	1014	Swift to Sheri	11
PRETENDER			
To ev'ry lew'd pretender of the town.	48	To Congreve	160
This every Pretender to Rhyme will admit, ...	263	Apollo	19
As never fav'ring the Pretender---:	550	Life of Swift	187
And in a Plot for the Pretender?	774	Mullinix Tim	22
To find this Damn'd Pretender out, ...	774	Mullinix Tim	26
Which the true Mother, which Pretender, ...	776	Mullinix Tim	99
And listing Troops for the Pretender.	788	Dick's Variety	24
PRETENDERS			
By vile pretenders, who a stock maintain	45	To Congreve	57
For any Pretenders	186	Scriblerus 4 D	2
PRETENDING			
But as a poor pretending Beau	216	To Mr. Delany	41
PRETENDR			
Will sure the Pretendr and Popery bring in.	522	St. Cecilia's	8
PRETENDS			
Pretends so perfectly to know;	39	Ode Sancroft	158
From her pale Cheeks pretends to show	228	Prog of Beauty	94
And, each to Poetry pretends:	546	Life of Swift	53
PRETENSION			
How soon thy vain Pretension drops;	671	Epig Carthy 22 D	3
PRETTILY			
So prettily he pickt a Cow-<turd>:	514	Answer Fable	48
PRETTY			
Vow'd it was pretty for a Child;	86	Hist V's House	10
The Priest was pretty well in case, ...	170	Horace 1, 7	7
Threescore, I think, is pretty high;	296	Satiric Elegy	11
His Answers were exceeding pretty	300	Horrid Pretty	53
Thinks nothing gives one Airs so pretty;	417	Woman's Mind	41
"Who only asks some pretty Cure, ...	476	Epist on Epist	49
"Or pretty Miss has play'd the Fool, ...	497	Panegyr Swift	131
With their pretty tinsel'd Boxes, ...	573	Helter Skelter	25
"I wish she wou'd lend you her pretty white Hand, . .	872	Grand Question	149
O, 'tis pretty Picking	952	Asparagus	4
PREVAIL			
How little, very little do prevail	19	Ode Athenian	112
Smooth Bawty did so far prevail;	208	Fable Bitches	16
The Thresher Duck, could o'er the <Queen> prevail. .	521	Stephen Duck	1
"Prevail to bring him in convict.	570	Death of Swift	430
'Tis Merit must with her prevail, ...	710	Cadenus Vaness	754
Was happy when he could prevail	746	Stel Distress	19
Was happy when he could prevail	750	Stel Wood-Park	17
While all is Calm, his Arguments prevail, ...	770	Horace 1, 14	27
In him, tell me which prevail, ...	801	Traulus 2	53

```
PREVAIL'D                                         PAGE   TITLE          LINE
    Prevail'd on by the Thing you hate,     . . . . . . .   121 Apollo Outwit    63
    Now while this Brazen Chain prevail'd,  . . . . . . .   345 Prometheus       41
PREVAILING
    And follow the prevailing sect,   . . . . . . . . .     489 Dialogue         24
PREVAILS
    Except her Majesty prevails   . . . . . . . . .         410 Dial Rich Marb   75
    How wrong a Taste prevails among us;   . . . . . . .    652 On Poetry       351
    If Chloe o'er thy Heart prevails,   . . . . . . .       925 Riddle 8         19
PREVAYL
    But, Art no longer can prevayl   . . . . . . . . .      228 Prog of Beauty   77
PREVENT
    This Evil, therefore to prevent,   . . . . . . . .      106 V's House        21
    And, mistakes to prevent, I have obtain'd a Copy.  . .  143 New Song         10
    But not prevent the Fates decree;   . . . . . . . .     701 Cadenus Vaness  485
    But, now, your Danger to prevent,   . . . . . . . .     742 Stel B-day 22    49
PREVENTED
    To be by Art prevented.   . . . . . . . . . . .         122 Empty'ng Town     4
    <Wharton>, unless prevented by a Whore,   . . . . .     166 Toland's Invit   35
PREY
    Who watch Her like a Prey,   . . . . . . . . .            8 Ode to King      74
    By Law of Arms became your Prey,   . . . . . . .        154 Widow and Cat  D 34
    As Fishes on each other prey   . . . . . . . .          253 Bubble           65
    To prey on his Liver, but not to be seen:   . . . . .   266 Apollo           98
    Flocks ev'ry ominous Bird of Prey;   . . . . . .        413 Desire Possess   54
    Thy Labours, grown the Critick's Prey,   . . . . .      642 On Poetry        67
    Hath smaller Pleas that on him prey,   . . . . . .      651 On Poetry       338
    Some Beast of Burthen or of Prey   . . . . . . .        659 On Poetry      D 410
    He sunk at length to wasting Age a Prey,   . . . . .    669 Epig Carthy 13 D  3
    With eager hand he grasps the treacherous prey,   . .   672 Epig Carthy 24 D 15
    And he must fall a Prey to Time,   . . . . . . .        703 Cadenus Vaness  538
    Where Fishes on each other prey;   . . . . . . .        824 Printer Newgat    4
PRI'R
    But use You ten times worse than Pri'r.   . . . . .     312 To Ford          34
PRIAM
    But Illium's lost, and Priam falls.   . . . . . . .     209 Fable Bitches    46
PRICE
    To shew it cost its Price in War,   . . . . . . .        28 Ode to Temple    75
    To fix a Price on his devoted Head.   . . . . . .       196 Author Himself   60
    For nicely computing the Price by Retail,   . . . . .   288 Bank Down        36
    Three hundred pounds! Were I the price to fix,   . . .  308 Billet Players   21
    Knows to a Groat the lowest Price;   . . . . . .        416 Woman's Mind     28
    "Had set a Price upon his Head;   . . . . . . . .       566 Death of Swift  352
    To raise the Volume's Price, a Shilling.)   . . . .     648 On Poetry       254
    Got all things at the highest Price.   . . . . . .      745 Stel Distress    10
    Got all things at the highest Price.   . . . . . .      749 Stel Wood-Park    8
PRICES
    Hold up the prices of their Old Brocades.   . . . . .   275 Epilogue         16
PRICKLED
    His prickled Beard, and hairy Breast!   . . . . . .     586 Strephon Chloe   92
PRIDE    SEE PRYD
    A three Hours Scene of empty Pride,   . . . . . .         6 Ode to King      17
    Howe're it be, the Pride of France   . . . . . .        10 Ode to King     136
    Have ev'n encreas't their Pride and Cruelty.   . . .    23 Ode Athenian    249
    'Tis Pride and Happiness enough to Me   . . . . .       24 Ode Athenian    266
    Censure, and Pedantry, and Pride,   . . . . . . .       25 Ode Athenian    296
    And yet to feed my Pride,   . . . . . . . . .           32 Ode to Temple   196
    Led blindly on by gross philosophy and pride,   . . .   36 Ode Sancroft     66
    (Methods in talk whereof our pride and ignorance make use)  38 Ode Sancroft 125
    Led blindly on by avarice and pride,   . . . . .        39 Ode Sancroft    163
    Sent to assist an old unvanquish'd pride   . . . .      44 To Congreve      43
    A pride that well suspends poor mortals fate,   . . .   45 To Congreve      45
    Druid, a name she does with pride repeat,   . . . .     49 To Congreve     193
    Or loves the muse to walk with conscious pride   . .    51 Temple Ill       11
    Down falls the summer's pride, and sadly shews   . .    55 Temple Ill      123
    That scorn of fools, by fools mistook for pride;   . .  55 Temple Ill      134
    Breeding, and Wit, and Air, and decent Pride,   . . .  118 Biddy Floyd       8
    Let Stubborn Pride Possess thee long,   . . . . .      121 Apollo Outwit    53
    He does, with Insolence and Pride.   . . . . . .       172 Horace 1, 7      56
    The Silver Virge, with decent Pride,   . . . . .       174 Horace 1, 7      99
    Their only pride is to refuse.   . . . . . . . .       178 To Lord Harley   58
    Tobacco, Censure, Coffee, Pride, and Port.   . . .     194 Author Himself   22
    Nor puff'd by Pride, nor sunk by Spleen.   . . . . .   199 Horace 2, 6    D
    False Patience, and mistaken Pride!   . . . . . .      221 A Quiet Life     55
    You raise Desire as well as Pride,   . . . . . .       292 Prog Marriage    74
    True to his profit and his pride,   . . . . . . .      296 Satiric Elegy    23
    Let pride be taught by this rebuke,   . . . . .        297 Satiric Elegy    29
    Where Compliments with all their Pride   . . . . .     361 Grace's Answer    3
    For then your Horns will be your Pride.   . . . .      362 Grace's Answer   54
    Or Pride, or vain Magnificence;   . . . . . . .        378 Apology Lady C  102
    That will make all my Subjects with pride to obey.  .  389 Order of Bath     4
    Now Pride and Cruelty are flown,   . . . . . .         391 Young's Satire   17
    Now enters over-weening Pride,   . . . . . . . .       448 Modern Lady     124
    Of Dullness, Pride, Conceit, a medley,   . . . . .     455 Dean Smedley      2
    All Pride) our Speaker for your Coxon:   . . . .       476 Epist on Epist   40
    To gratify their Lust of Pride,   . . . . . . . .      480 Libel on D- D-   26
    As far as Modest Pride allow'd,   . . . . . . .        482 Libel on D- D-   58
    For you to gratify your Pride?   . . . . . . . .       493 Panegyr Swift    16
    Whene'er your Pride recals your Grief,   . . . . .     496 Panegyr Swift    87
    To feed his Luxury, or sooth his Pride.   . . . . .    534 To Mr. Gay       94
    A Juncture happen'd in his highest Pride:   . . . .    536 To Mr. Gay      147
```

PRIDE   (CONTINUED)   PAGE   TITLE   LINE
       The strongest Friendship yields to Pride, ...   554 Death of Swift   37
       Self-love, Ambition, Envy, Pride, ...   555 Death of Swift   41
       If they have mortify'd my Pride, ...   555 Death of Swift   63
       "Meer Envy, Avarice, and Pride!   . . . .   558 Death of Swift   159
       "Where, Folly, Pride, and Faction sway, ...   570 Death of Swift   433
       And you who never fell--thro' Pride;   . . . .   579 Day Judgement   14
       Corinna, Pride of Drury-Lane, ...   581 Young Nymph   1
       Strange pride and insolence you shew, ...   617 Scandal Poem 1   3
       Strange Pride and Insolence you show, ...   623 Scandal Poem 2   3
       Young's universal Passion, Pride, ...   640 On Poetry   3
       Give up your fond paternal Pride, ...   644 On Poetry   127
       But Europe mortify'd his Pride, ...   657 On Poetry   475
       To pamper luxury and pride;   . . . .   676 Parson's Case   22
       With Pride wou'd drag about her Chain;   . . . . . .   693 Cadenus Vaness   233
       Which help'd to mortify his Pride, ...   704 Cadenus Vaness   570
       His Pride began to interpose, ...   710 Cadenus Vaness   750
       He chose to justify his Pride;   . . . .   710 Cadenus Vaness   763
       I cannot but Envy the Pride of her Wit.   . . . . . .   716 Answer Rebus   2
       Envy, and Cruelty, and Pride, ...   725 To Stella   49
       In Silence, or forget with Pride.   . . . .   726 To Stella   96
       Resolv'd to mortify your Pride, ...   730 Stella, Poems   85
       Which Manners, Decency, and Pride, ...   730 Stella, Poems   99
       With Stella's magisterial pride.   . . . .   753 Gift for Bec   10
       From thee, with Pride, the Caledonians trace   . . .   790 St. Pat's Well   11
       For Pride and Ignorance a Proverb grown, ...   794 St. Pat's Well   99
       Fill'd with Falshood, Spleen and Pride;   . . . . .   799 Traulus 2   8
       Our <Bishops> puft up with Wealth and with Pride.   . .   804 Irish Bishops   17
       The generous Wheat forgot its Pride, ...   811 Bro Protestant   7
       What care we how high runs his passion or pride?   . .   817 Yahoo's   71
       The Dean and the Doctor have humbled their Pride,   . .   871 Grand Question   131
       Why will you place in lazy Pride   . . . .   896 Panegyr Dean   293
       What Pride a Female Heart enflames!   . . . . .   905 Death Daphne   89
       I see his Vanity and Pride: . . . .   915 Riddle 1   24
       The Joy of Man, the Pride of Brutes, ...   919 Riddle 5   1
       He gives; and with a gen'rous Pride,   , ...   919 Riddle 5   21
       How will it mortify thy Pride, ...   921 Riddle 7   7
       Puff'd up with pride and insolence, ...   950 Upstart   D 11
       In chatt'ring like a magpie, in pride a jackdaw;   . .   955 Portrait Life   2
       To my goddess Melpomene, pride of her sex, ...   979 Dean to Tho: S   23
PRIEST
       The Priest was pretty well in case, ...   170 Horace 1, 7   7
       This dang'rous Priest is got behind the Curtain: . .   194 Author Himself   38
       Tho' like the Cybel's Priest he comes, ...   340 Arch-Bish Dub   25
       A Priest would please your Palate;   . . . .   425 Five Ladies   10
       A holier Priest ne'er was wrapt up in Crape,   . . .   516 Dean Hang Rape   5
       Each Priest had a Concubine, jure Ecclesiae;   . . .   518 Dean Hang Rape   38
       Dame Juno brought a Priest demure.   . . . . .   586 Strephon Chloe   64
       Should to the Priest confess their Sins;   . . . . .   601 Beasts Confess   11
       But before the Priest he fleeces   . . . .   831 Legion Club   65
PRIEST-CRAFT
       "By bravely running Priest-craft down: . . . . . .   564 Death of Swift   292
PRIESTESS
       For she, as Priestess, knows the Rites   . . . . . .   743 Stel B-day 22   51
PRIESTHOOD   SEE HIGH-PRIESTHOOD
       He can alone the priesthood humble, ...   490 Dialogue   35
       On their tythes at half-nothing, their priesthood at less: 816 Yahoo's   33
PRIESTS
       Her Priests, her Train and Followers show   . . . .   27 Ode to Temple   40
       All ran to Pray'rs, both Priests and Laity,   . . .   353 Wood Ironmongr   21
       By clients to her priests and trustees.   . . . . .   433 Answer Paulus   30
       To weigh her priests, the lawyers, gold.   . . . . .   433 Answer Paulus   36
       By Sages, Priests, or Poets taught;   . . . . . .   482 Libel on D- D-   76
       Damn'd Time-Serving Priests all over the Nation;   . .   576 Place Damn'd   12
       Nor, tho' his Priests be duly paid, ...   657 On Poetry   491
       No, not among the Priests and Fryers.   . . . . .   773 Mullinix Tim   7
       For Priests and Jesuits in Disguises;   . . . . . .   788 Dick's Variety   22
       She sent her Priests in Wooden Shoes   . . . . . .   895 Panegyr Dean   263
PRIGS
       Are bubbled thus by Prigs;   . . . .   426 Five Ladies   35
PRIM
       Amaz'd to see Her look so Prim, ...   116 Bauc & Phil 2   147
       Said to the Pippin, plump, and prim, ...   811 Bro Protestant   13
PRIM'D
       He shot before your Foes were prim'd: . . . . . .   797 Traulus 1   58
PRIMATE
       Tho' it would make you England's Primate: . . . .   503 Doctor Delaney   110
       And He was a Primate, and He wore a Mitre, ...   803 Irish Bishops   5
       At Dublin's high feast sat Primate and Dean,   . . .   843 Ay and No   1
       "No,no," quoth the Primate, "if causes we sift,   . . .   843 Ay and No   5
PRIME
       And lastly for Stella, just out of her Prime,   . . .   266 Apollo   103
       You find His Rev'rence past his Prime, ...   293 Prog Marriage   104
       As Mutton Cutlets, Prime of Meat, ...   528 Lady's Dres Rm   99
       For Poetry, he's past his Prime, ...   556 Death of Swift   99
       Give him always of the Prime, ...   633 Epistle Lady   127
       While she continues in her Prime.   . . . . .   703 Cadenus Vaness   539
       Unless, like Venus, in her Prime.   . . . . .   757 Stel B-day '24   22
       You're now in your prime, ...   854 Lady's Lament   113
       Ah lovely Nymph, thou'rt in thy Prime!   . . . . .   932 Riddle 19   D 13
       Yet I perish in my prime, ...   937 Riddle 24   D 47

PRIMITIVE

	PAGE	TITLE	LINE
To bless the Primitive Sailer's weary sight, ...	16	Ode Athenian	7
Thus, primitive Sancroft moves too high	39	Ode Sancroft	149
Far in this primitive cell might we pursue	49	To Congreve	195

PRIMUS

Hannoniae qui primus ab oris.	186	Scriblerus 4	D 6

PRINCE

By which our happy Prince carves out his Bays; . . .	7	Ode to King	32
Our Prince has charm'd its many hundred Eyes; . . .	8	Ode to King	78
Thus has our Prince compleated every Victory, . . .	9	Ode to King	98
Our Prince has hit Him, like Achilles, in the Heel, .	10	Ode to King	142
And yet the world, whose eyes are on our mighty Prince,	40	Ode Sancroft	180
But a Prince of high Renown, ...	168	Peace Dunkirk	18
That we a German Prince must own	180	Horace 2, 1	11
Thou dar'st the greatest Prince attack, ...	325	Pethox	53
Knows ev'ry Prince in Europe's Face, ...	398	Earl of P-b-w	7
Was grown as wealthy as a Prince;	409	Dial Rich Marb	38
To place me with the Prince of Wales.	410	Dial Rich Marb	76
For, he'll be Prince these fifty Years.	410	Dial Rich Marb	78
You serve a potent Prince, as well as He.	532	To Mr. Gay	44
With Lorraine's Duke, and Prince of Greece.	592	Strephon Chloe	292
A Prince the Moment he is crown'd, ...	646	On Poetry	191
Duke William, sweetest Prince alive.	656	On Poetry	440
The haughty Prince, the humble Slave, ...	922	Riddle 7	28
Jason, the valiant Prince of Greece, ...	948	Jason Hassard	1
I swore to the <Queen> that the <Prince> of <Hanover>	144	New Song	35

PRINCELY

Besides a pair of princely Babyes, ...	465	Birthday Song	171
To Virtue form'd a Princely Youth, ...	482	Libel on D- D-	56
But princely Douglas, and his glorious Dame, ...	531	To Mr. Gay	13

PRINCES

That Princes wear derives from them;	98	Elegy Patrige	26
That we should put no Trust in Princes;	408	Dial Rich Marb	14
For Princes love you should descant	464	Birthday Song	127
That Princes should believe in God:	468	Birthday Song	264
"With Princes kept a due Decorum, ...	566	Death of Swift	339
"In Princes never put thy Trust.	566	Death of Swift	342

PRINCESS

"I only was the Princess then;	559	Death of Swift	186
As fits a Princess in Romance.	888	Panegyr Dean	54

PRINCESSES

In short our Kings and Princesses within, ...	275	Epilogue	27

PRINCIPALITIES

Into small States and Principalities, ...	26	Ode to Temple	5

PRINCIPLE

But still I'm in Principle ever the same, ...	144	New Song	25

PRINCIPLES

From Principles the Whigs maintain;	417	Woman's Mind	54
Took proper Principles to thrive;	481	Libel on D- D-	47
In Church and in State was of Principles sound, . .	518	Dean Hang Rape	32
"His Principles, of antient date, ...	549	Life of Swift	146

PRINT

This Earth which bears his Body's Print, ...	101	Elegy Patrige	111
Henceforward shall print neither Pamphlets nor Linnen,	238	Excellent Song	28
For when you bring your Song in print, ...	463	Birthday Song	85
Then print it in the largest letter, ...	469	Birthday Song	279
I'd tell of yours in Rhyme and Print:	475	Epist on Epist	11
When first in Print, you see him dread	500	Doctor Delaney	13
You print it in Italick Type.	643	On Poetry	96
The Hawker shews you one in Print, ...	644	On Poetry	113
When Age must print a furrow'd Trace	735	Stel B-day '20	49
His own sweet Figure with the Print, ...	783	Tim and Fables	15

PRINTED

Get all your Verses printed fair, ...	394	Grub-Street	9
Far better than a printed Book;	450	Modern Lady	191
In modern Wit all printed Trash, is	643	On Poetry	93

PRINTER

Tho' a Printer and Dean	237	Excellent Song	5
The Dean and his Printer then let us cry Fye on; . .	237	Excellent Song	11
If the Printer will peach him, he'll scarce come off clean.	238	Excellent Song	32

PRINTER'S

Unsold upon the Printer's Lines.	502	Doctor Delaney	78
And, see, the Printer's Boy below:	887	Panegyr Dean	32

PRINTERS

Why against Printers all this noise?	407	Irish-Club	9

PRINTS

"Or do the Prints and Papers lye?	202	Horace 2, 6	95
And Prints are crowded with his Name.	397	Earl of P-b-w	3
You'd know him by Apollo's Prints.	462	Birthday Song	62
His Medals and his Prints forgotten, ...	875	Drapier's Hill	15

PRIOR

Shall hear Him harangue against Prior to Morrow. . .	143	New Song	6

PRIORITY

And almost got priority of Sight, ...	30	Ode to Temple	130

PRIS'NER

Though I, alas! a Pris'ner be, ...	920	Riddle 6	1

PRIS'NERS

Like Pris'ners when their Gall is broke.	313	To Ford	56
My Trade is, Pris'ners to set free.	920	Riddle 6	2

```
PRISON                                                         PAGE   TITLE            LINE
    Redeem him from his Prison under Ground.    .  .  .  .  .   233 Elegy on Demar       4
PRISONER
    I lay a Prisoner twenty Years;              .  .  .  .  .   926 Riddle 9            21
PRITHEE
    But prithee Tim, why all this Clutter?      .  .  .  .  .   773 Mullinix Tim         2
    Dear Dick, prithee tell by what passion you move?   .  .   818 Archbi Cashel        1
    Then, prithee reflect, take a word of advice;   .  .  .    818 Archbi Cashel        7
    Said surly Peter, Magus, prithee  .  .  .  .  .  .  .      821 Dr. Rundle          47
PRIV'LEGE
    An equal Priv'lege to descend.    .  .  .  .  .  .  .  .   653 On Poetry          382
PRIVATE
    Or from thy private peaceful orb appear;    .  .  .  .  .    39 Ode Sancroft       155
    Happy beyond a private muse's fate,         .  .  .  .  .    49 To Congreve        179
    Steals from her Private Cell by Night,         .  .  .  .    99 Elegy Patrige       51
    Admitted private, when Superiors wait:         .  .  .  .   194 Author Himself      30
    To own the truth we have some private Ends.   .  .  .  .    275 Epilogue           14
    Keep t' other Half for private Use.         .  .  .  .  .   326 Pethox              84
    Our Private and our Publick Foes,           .  .  .  .  .   339 Arch-Bish Dub       10
    How far their Hearts from private Views,    .  .  .  .  .   501 Doctor Delaney      60
    And Kings, like private Folks, are bought and sold:       536 To Mr. Gay         136
    "We first consult our private Ends,         .  .  .  .  .   553 Death of Swift       8
    Will try to find their private Ends:        .  .  .  .  .   556 Death of Swift      76
    "Without regarding private Ends,            .  .  .  .  .   565 Death of Swift     331
    "Intent upon their private Ends;            .  .  .  .  .   569 Death of Swift     404
    Nor ever acts on private Views,             .  .  .  .  .   607 Beasts Confess     185
    For private Life, or publick Use?           .  .  .  .  .   641 On Poetry           46
    A publick, or a private Robber;             .  .  .  .  .   645 On Poetry          161
    He only publish'd for my private Use.       .  .  .  .  .   668 Epig Carthy 11   D   2
    The Urchin from his private Stand           .  .  .  .  .   702 Cadenus Vaness     515
    Whene'er it suits her private ends;         .  .  .  .  .   761 Bec's B-Day         32
    She darted many a private Glance,           .  .  .  .  .   905 Death Daphne        67
PRIVATEER
    Of ev'ry censuring Privateer,       .  .  .  .  .  .  .  .    19 Ode Athenian       100
PRIVATEERS
    And not be snapt by Privateers,       .  .  .  .  .  .  .   168 Peace Dunkirk       22
PRIVILEDGE
    Lay thy paltry Priviledge aside,       .  .  .  .  .  .  .   832 Legion Club         71
PRIVILEGE
    Obtain such Privilege as you,       .  .  .  .  .  .  .  .   492 Panegyr Swift        3
    Why should they want the Privilege of Men,   .  .  .  .    662 Upon Ladies          3
    Without her Privilege to cheat.       .  .  .  .  .  .  .  1033 Ans to Crown         4
    <Privilege> of <Parliament>,       .  .  .  .  .  .  .  .   833 Legion Club        116
PRIVY
    And when among Companions privy,       .  .  .  .  .  .    513 Answer Fable        37
    Damn'd Ignorant Prelates, and Councellors Privy.   .  .    576 Place Damn'd        14
    As when you spy'd her on the Privy.   .  .  .  .  .  .  .   591 Strephon Chloe     248
PRIZE
    And has at last redeem'd the Mighty Prize   .  .  .  .  .     8 Ode to King         81
    Did bravely snatch the lovely helpless Prize.   .  .  .     12 Ode to William   D  24
    Takes a French Play as lawful Prize,   .  .  .  .  .  .    107 V's House           58
    "'Tis true, the Pinner which you prize   .  .  .  .  .  .   154 Widow and Cat    D  28
    For, where Directors get a Prize,   .  .  .  .  .  .  .  .   256 Bubble             159
    Which few had learnt enough to prize,   .  .  .  .  .  .    384 Manly Virtue        29
    (For, where high Honour is the Prize,   .  .  .  .  .  .    386 Manly Virtue        91
    Prize Classicks more than Sacred Writ:   .  .  .  .  .  .   392 Young's Satire      40
    Truth and Honour how to prize;   .  .  .  .  .  .  .  .  .   630 Epistle Lady        22
    Thus we both should gain our Prize:   .  .  .  .  .  .  .   638 Epistle Lady       273
    Smit with the glorious prize next struts in Sewel,   .  .   672 Epig Carthy 24   D   9
    Whoe'er excels in what we prize,   .  .  .  .  .  .  .  .    710 Cadenus Vaness     732
    Nor prize your Life for other Ends   .  .  .  .  .  .  .    765 Stel B-day '26      69
    The Huntsmen seize the grinning Prize.   .  .  .  .  .  .   885 Rev Market-Hill     82
PRO
    To state the question pro and con:   .  .  .  .  .  .  .    435 Answer Paulus      100
PROBABLY
    More probably than all the rest;   .  .  .  .  .  .  .  .    128 Little House        44
PROBITY
    For learning, probity and truth,   .  .  .  .  .  .  .  .    490 Dialogue            30
PROBLEM
    Did ever Problem thus perplex,   .  .  .  .  .  .  .  .  .    65 Problem              1
PROCEED
    Yet does this high perfection well proceed   .  .  .  .     41 Ode Sancroft       223
    We Phoebus think fit to proceed to his Sentence;   .  .    266 Apollo              94
    Or--but proceed we in our Journal,   .  .  .  .  .  .  .    279 Journal             25
    Your Evidence was lame. Proceed:   .  .  .  .  .  .  .  .    298 Horrid Plot         14
    Now Birth-day Bard, with joy proceed   .  .  .  .  .  .    465 Birthday Song      151
    Then, let me now by Negatives proceed.   .  .  .  .  .  .   534 To Mr. Gay          84
    Proceed we therefore to our Poem.   .  .  .  .  .  .  .  .   555 Death of Swift      72
    Proceed we to the Marriage Rites.   .  .  .  .  .  .  .  .   585 Strephon Chloe      46
    Proceed no further in your Part,   .  .  .  .  .  .  .  .    647 On Poetry          239
    And so proceed ad infinitum:  .  .  .  .  .  .  .  .  .  .   651 On Poetry          340
    Beware, O Bard, how you proceed.   .  .  .  .  .  .  .  .    666 Epig Carthy 2    D   4
    Thus much for the Verse, we proceed to the next,   .  .    716 Answer Rebus        19
    And how would Socrates proceed?   .  .  .  .  .  .  .  .    724 To Stella           42
    Proceed we to your preaching next:   .  .  .  .  .  .  .    888 Panegyr Dean        61
    Proceed to Tragicks, first Euripides   .  .  .  .  .  .    988 Letter Dr Sh-n      17
PROCEEDED
    Proceeded to erect his Pile:   .  .  .  .  .  .  .  .  .  .   108 V's House           64
PROCEEDING
    Proceeding on, the lovely Goddess   .  .  .  .  .  .  .  .   582 Young Nymph         23
    She'd have a summary Proceeding.   .  .  .  .  .  .  .  .    713 Cadenus Vaness     849
```

	PAGE	TITLE	LINE
PROCEEDING (CONTINUED)			
So gentle in your whole Proceeding,	891	Panegyr Dean	153
PROCEEDS			
O'er the sun's face, and from his heat proceeds,	45	To Congreve	70
Yet, whence proceeds this Weight we lay	414	Censure	17
Proceeds that Fund of Wit and Sense;	726	To Stella	80
PROCLAIM			
The Christian World his Deeds proclaim,	397	Earl of P-b-w	2
But why proclaim her for a Toast?	699	Cadenus Vaness	413
PROCLAIM'D			
Might be proclaim'd at Charing-Cross.	201	Horace 2, 6	80
All met, and Silence thrice proclaim'd,	713	Cadenus Vaness	842
PROCLAIMS			
And the loud Laugh proclaims the War;	218	To Mr. Delany	80
PROCLAMATION			
Now, through the Realm a Proclamation spread,	196	Author Himself	59
By Proclamation gave Command,	601	Beasts Confess	9
PROCUR'D			
The Prentices procur'd a Riding	221	A Quiet Life	53
PROCURE			
Procure the Book for Love or Money,	648	On Poetry	260
Procure Disciples of your own.	649	On Poetry	278
And by their Sweat procure a mean Support;	793	St. Pat's Well	76
PRODIGAL			
Tho the Exchequer be drained by prodigal Donours	389	Order of Bath	5
PRODIGIES			
But Prodigies are wrought to prove	384	Manly Virtue	21
PRODIGIOUS			
Which came with a prodigious Fall;	126	Little House	8
But loves to take prodigious Rounds,	218	To Mr. Delany	93
A Parchment of prodigious Size;	354	Simile Silver	22
A Dart of such prodigious Length,	703	Cadenus Vaness	517
PRODIGY			
Scar'd at th' unheard-of Prodigy,	30	Ode to Temple	110
PRODIGYS			
"What Prodigys in Arts we drain	462	Birthday Song	79
PRODUC'D			
The Scene, a Wood, produc'd no more	108	V's House	83
Produc'd with all their Bills and Gold,	241	Run Bankers	63
By Phoebus first produc'd to light:	433	Answer Paulus	27
This Cloud produc'd a race of Centaurs	619	Scandal Poem 1	59
His Cloud produc'd a Race of Centaurs,	625	Scandal Poem 2	55
Produc'd on Earth a wond'rous Maid,	690	Cadenus Vaness	137
What produc'd them, can you tell?	801	Traulus 2	55
PRODUCE			
Produce a richer vein or cleaner ore;	45	To Congreve	52
Some faint Resemblance to produce,	81	Vanbrug House	87
Some faint Resemblance to produce,	109	V's House	129
First get a licence, then produce our ware:	308	Billet Players	36
So sometimes half a Face produce,	326	Pethox	83
And, to Illustrate it, produce	485	Libel on D- D-	163
And Precedents we can produce, if it please ye,	518	Dean Hang Rape	40
Produce at last thy dormant Ducal Patent:	538	Mr. Pulteney	10
Produce in May the sweetest flowrs.	621	Scandal Poem 1	148
Can ev'ry Spring produce you Flow'rs.	628	Scandal Poem 2	152
'Tis but just, you shou'd produce,	631	Epistle Lady	59
Only Dulness can produce,	636	Epistle Lady	204
Or from Solomon produce	637	Epistle Lady	237
Where you have nothing to produce	641	On Poetry	45
Two Maxims she could still produce,	705	Cadenus Vaness	606
When proper to produce the best;	889	Panegyr Dean	95
My Parent and I produce one another,	929	Riddle 13	D 9
PRODUCES			
Yet the same want of Brains produces each effect;	18	Ode Athenian	85
Now listen while he next produces,	526	Lady's Dres Rm	19
Air ripens not, nor Earth produces:	1035	To Quilca	6
PRODUCT			
The Product of your Toil and Sweating;	644	On Poetry	115
PRODUCTION			
So your Production was the same,	324	Pethox	31
PRODUCTIONS			
But all are meer Productions of the Brain,	363	On Dreams	5
PROEM			
Thus much may serve by way of Proem,	555	Death of Swift	71
PROFANE SEE PROPHANE			
Which to divulge might shake profane belief,	53	Temple Ill	77
But, Poets love profane allusions.	622	Scandal Poem 1	162
Be as Pox'd and Profane as Fanatical <Hort>	808	Advice Parson	10
PROFESS			
With all the Kindness they profess,	557	Death of Swift	121
PROFESS'D			
"Ill suit with those profess'd of late:	549	Life of Swift	147
PROFESSES			
His humble Senate this professes,	646	On Poetry	197
PROFESSION			
The Dignity of his Profession;	375	Apology Lady C	10
To villains of his own profession.	436	Answer Paulus	128
of Virtue & worth by profession a giber	540	Charac Walpole	11
PROFEST			
See, how behave his Friends profest,	545	Life of Swift	19
Such Friendship never Man profest,	796	Traulus 1	15

PROFICIENT
    Proficient in their Father's Trade, ...   903 Death Daphne   16

PROFIT
    True to his profit and his pride, ...   296 Satiric Elegy   23
    Good Manners must give Place to Profit. . . . . .   311 To Ford   16
    "And reapt the profit, sought his Blood. . . . .   569 Death of Swift   414
    What profit could you hope to get of her . . . . . .   622 Scandal Poem 1   170
    Here I have computed the Profit will fall t'us. . . .   867 Grand Question   8

PROFITABLE
    To spring more profitable Game. . . . .   646 On Poetry   184

PROFITS
    (The third Night's Profits of his Play;) . . . . .   230 Prog of Poetry   18
    Thy Toil is lessen'd, and thy Profits double. . .   521 Stephen Duck   8

PROFLIGATE
    "As vile and profligate a Villain, ...   569 Death of Swift   419

PROFOUND
    And who in all profound Affairs . . . .   62 Discovery   11
    Whisp'ring in Junto most profound, ...   63 Discovery   22
    Receiv'd from thee profound Directions . . . . . .   182 Horace 2, 1   55
    But Gadbury in Art profound . . . .   228 Prog of Beauty   93
    Why in yon dang'rous Gulph profound . . . .   252 Bubble   50
    And left a Chasm profound as Hell: . . . .   326 Pethox   96
    He tumbled in the Gulph profound; . . . .   413 Desire Possess   49
    Nor Skill in Sciences profound, ...   641 On Poetry   29
    Wise Dennis, and profound Bossu. . . . .   648 On Poetry   250
    An head so weighty and profound, ...   822 Epigr Rundle   5
    The Captain salutes you with Congee profound; . .   871 Grand Question   115
    By your good Leave, my most profound and bold Sir, . .   1004 Dan J's Reply   30

PROFOUNDLY
    A Moralist profoundly sage, ...   412 Desire Possess   5

PROFUSE
    Of paper how is he profuse, ...   434 Answer Paulus   81
    I'm too profuse some Cens'rers cry, ...   918 Riddle 4   25

PROFUSELY
    Which thus she will Venture profusely to throw, . . .   716 Answer Rebus   3
    Profusely pours her Off'rings here. . . . .   922 Riddle 7   38

PROGGING
    My spirits with my body progging, ...   900 Dean's Reasons   57

PROGNOSTICKS
    (By sure Prognosticks) when to dread a Show'r: . . .   136 City Shower   2
    Though your Prognosticks run too fast, ...   558 Death of Swift   145

PROGRESS
    And mark the Progress of their Work, ...   86 Hist V's House   16
    Attend the progress of his herse. . . . .   296 Satiric Elegy   20
    And took their Progress tow'rds <Loughall>. . . . .   321 First of April   14
    My highest Progress in the Myst'ry . . . .   493 Panegyr Swift   31

PROJECT
    Are all resolv'd the Project to begin: . . . . . .   275 Epilogue   28
    Some Mischief is Brewing, the Project smells Rank, .   287 Bank Down   4
    I own it was a dang'rous Project; . . . .   300 Horrid Plot   71
    Project <Excise> and <South-Sea> <Schemes>: . . .   647 On Poetry   216
    Conceiv'd a Project in her Head, ...   690 Cadenus Vaness   132
    You form'd this Project in your Brain, ...   695 Cadenus Vaness   289
    A Project for thy Talents fit, ...   695 Cadenus Vaness   290
    A Project far above his Skill, ...   705 Cadenus Vaness   586
    And, by the Project vainly try'd, ...   713 Cadenus Vaness   836
    And to make your Project pass, ...   839 Legion Club   217

PROJECTORS
    But Thanks to the House, the Projectors look blank, .   287 Bank Down   9

PROLE
    The Hound wou'd scent, the Wolf would prole: . . . .   512 Answer Fable   8

PROLIFIC
    And such is my prolific Pow'r, ...   926 Riddle 9   3

PROLIFICK
    Infus'd a strong prolifick Potion, ...   293 Prog Marriage   108
    Which mingling with prolifick Strife . . . .   324 Pethox   29
    While we, by soft prolifick Show'rs, ...   628 Scandal Poem 2   151

PROLIX
    What pains he takes to be prolix! . . . .   434 Answer Paulus   83
    My fingers, prolix, ...   853 Lady's Lament   77

PROLOGUE
    And first the Prologue built a Wall . . . . . .   108 V's House   81
    Or Prologue sent from Hand unknown. . . . .   643 On Poetry   84
    That wrote the Prologue, and if you stay with him, . .   1023 Nim-Dan-Dean 2   D 10

PROLOGUES
    And court in prologues, all are country-bred; . . .   46 To Congreve   96

PROLONG
    O may the Fates thy Life prolong! . . . .   339 Arch-Bish Dub   5
    The gout that will prolong his days: . . . .   761 Bec's B-Day   16

PROMETHEUS
    Since Delany has dar'd, like Prometheus his Sire, . .   266 Apollo   95
    Prometheus once this Chain purloin'd, ...   345 Prometheus   37
    Prometheus on a Rock is laid, ...   346 Prometheus   53
    By that old Thief Prometheus? Wood . . . .   346 Prometheus   60
    With which Prometheus shall be ty'd, ...   347 Prometheus   73
    Tis sung Prometheus forming Man . . . .   659 On Poetry   D 410
    Say, Stella, was Prometheus blind, ...   726 To Stella   85

PROMIS'D
    And promis'd to pay for it when he'd come back. . . .   399 Tom Clinch   4
    My Royal Master promis'd me . . . .   408 Dial Rich Marb   15
    Nor could atchieve the promis'd Lawn, ...   495 Panegyr Swift   82

		PAGE	TITLE	LINE
PROMIS'D	(CONTINUED)			
	"I promis'd them, I own; but when?	559	Death of Swift	185
PROMISE				
	With promise of a mad Reversion after Death. . . .	32	Ode to Temple	198
	On her Promise of yielding, she acted the Prude; . . .	264	Apollo	46
	I promise nothing for the Night:	290	Prog Marriage	20
	Is by my Promise what you claim;	445	Modern Lady	25
	I promise to be good again:	755	Stella '23	34
	I promise to use you well.	952	Onyons	3
PROMISED				
	Whate'er I promised or intended, ...	899	Dean's Reasons	5
PROMISES				
	Directors Promises but Wind, ...	259	Bubble	219
	His Promises he ne'er forgot, ...	606	Beasts Confess	157
PROMISING				
	atchieving of nothing Still promising wonders	540	Charac Walpole	5
PROMOTION				
	Would rise by Merit to Promotion;	604	Beasts Confess	111
	Since God had no Hand in his Lordship's Promotion. .	809	Epigr Prelate	6
	Some fancy this Promotion odd, ...	821	Dr. Rundle	53
PROMPTED				
	All prompted by the same Desire, ...	922	Riddle 7	25
PROMPTS				
	As Nature prompts, his Off'ring pays?	895	Panegyr Dean	288
PRONE				
	Fall from the Conduit prone to Holborn-Bridge. . . .	139	City Shower	60
	How prone to change in human life, ...	283	Journal	117
PRONOUNC'D				
	The Son of God pronounc'd by the same breath . . .	38	Ode Sancroft	119
	Which strait pronounc'd his death;	38	Ode Sancroft	120
	The Goddess thus pronounc'd her Doom:	696	Cadenus Vaness	304
	Which God pronounc'd he never wou'd, ...	799	Traulus 1	97
	So Jove pronounc'd among the Gods, ...	924	Riddle 7	95
PRONOUNCE				
	And on my verse pronounce their saucy doom;	50	To Congreve	214
	Here (lovely Nymph pronounce my doom)	60	Lady Tablebook	11
	And I pronounce, (the Satyr said)	150	Corinna	11
	I here pronounce	440	Ballyspellin	8
	Pronounce all Men of Wit, Free-thinkers.	503	Doctor Delaney	98
	Doctors pronounce the patient dead;	761	Bec's B-Day	12
	Nor can the plainest Word pronounce, ...	891	Panegyr Dean	149
PRONOUNCES				
	Pronounces you a stupid Rogue;	644	On Poetry	120
PRONOUNCING				
	But, half the Words pronouncing wrong;	416	Woman's Mind	10
PROOF				
	And, as a Proof, shew num'rous Scars	324	Pethox	13
	Thus young, thus proof to all Temptations, ...	386	Manly Virtue	89
	You'll find it soon by woful Proof, ...	408	Dial Rich Marb	11
	The Proof of your high Origine, ...	498	Panegyr Swift	175
	My proof is thus: I plainly see	679	From Catullus	5
	If the Devil be Thunder Proof, ...	830	Legion Club	24
	Behold! a proof of Irish sense!	843	Epigr Irish	1
PROOFS				
	His Guilt is clear the Proofs are pregnant, ...	798	Traulus 1	93
PROP				
	Fit to Invade or prop the Skies.	107	V's House	50
	Pulls out the Rags contriv'd to prop	582	Young Nymph	21
	This Atlas stands to prop the Court:	656	On Poetry	444
	In vain, --- for soon the slender prop gives way; . . .	672	Epig Carthy 24	D 16
PROPER				
	It fell into its proper Station.	127	Little House	12
	But when I thought proper, I alter'd my Note; . . .	144	New Song	39
	When We, by proper Signs and Symbols tell, ...	162	Toland's Invit	9
	So gracefull in their proper Place, ...	226	Prog of Beauty	22
	The Window is her proper Sphear;	228	Prog of Beauty	66
	Unless a proper Circulation	239	Run Bankers	11
	Are proper in my Lady's Case	294	Frog Marriage	132
	For which Operation there's nothing more proper . . .	351	Wood Insect	35
	The Moral of this Tale is proper, ...	353	Wood Ironmongr	31
	Provided, at a proper Time;	378	Apology Lady C	89
	And said, lack-a-day! he's a proper young Man. . . .	399	Tom Clinch	8
	At proper Seasons to be sick;	416	Woman's Mind	40
	As proper quite	443	Ballyspellin	88
	To find out proper words for Harmony:	467	Birthday Song	218
	Who proper Objects must provide	480	Libel on D- D-	25
	Took proper Principles to thrive;	481	Libel on D- D-	47
	In proper Terms to write a Fable;	512	Answer Fable	2
	That Strephon chose no proper Season.	588	Strephon Chloe	160
	A Cloud, in proper Seasons pours	624	Scandal Poem 2	27
	These o'er their proper Districts govern, ...	649	On Poetry	283
	Attending each his proper Station, ...	650	On Poetry	313
	Each proper Quality to find	659	On Poetry	D 410
	What then must Carthy do in proper Season, ...	666	Epig Carthy 3	D 3
	In proper Season Pallas meets	695	Cadenus Vaness	284
	She never hit one proper Place;	700	Cadenus Vaness	423
	Mens Talents to their proper Use;	700	Cadenus Vaness	449
	For, take it in its proper Light, ...	708	Cadenus Vaness	672
	At proper Times to scream and start;	725	To Stella	72
	Each within his proper Cell;	830	Legion Club	44
	But, lest it might not be so proper, ...	886	Rev Market-Hill	101

PROPER	(CONTINUED)	PAGE	TITLE	LINE
When proper to produce the best;		889	Panegyr Dean	95
Here, in their proper Shape and Mein, ...		922	Riddle 7	21
Which in its proper Station plac'd, ...		1021	Nim-Dan-Dean 1	D 13
PROPERLY				
That none are more properly Knights of the Post. . .		335	Serious Poem	40
PROPERTIES				
Let me my Properties explain, ...		1035	To Quilca	1
PROPERTY				
One Property more I would have you remark, ...		928	Riddle 11	D 9
PROPHANE				
(For, 'tis prophane when Sexes mingle;		893	Panegyr Dean	209
The Rogue's too Bawdy and too Prophane is.		988	Letter Dr Sh-n	6
PROPHECIES				
Nor for his prophecies in riddles:		432	Answer Paulus	20
PROPHECY				
This Prophecy he trembling hears.		850	Old Thorn	56
PROPHECY'D				
Then he who prophecy'd the best, ...		557	Death of Swift	127
PROPHET				
Of which it is at once the Prophet and the Cause. . .		10	Ode to King	135
Reverses what the Prophet did;		132	Magician's Rod	6
The kingly Prophet well evinces, ...		408	Dial Rich Marb	13
PROPHET'S				
Thrice, with a prophet's voice and prophet's pow'r, . .		43	To Congreve	1
Thrice, with a prophet's voice and prophet's pow'r, . .		43	To Congreve	1
PROPHETIC				
Like that prophetic tempest in the virgin reign, . . .		40	Ode Sancroft	196
PROPORTION				
Rose in proportion to his Wit:		108	V's House	80
PROPORTION'D				
Have large proportion'd Roots that grow		393	Modern Poets	3
PROPOSE				
To whom she might her Doubts propose		689	Cadenus Vaness	97
(The only Comfort they propose, ...		764	Stel B-day '26	23
PROPOSITION				
I prov'd my Proposition full:		299	Horrid Plot	41
PROPS				
My arms, like two props, ...		852	Lady's Lament	27
He trips up my props, ...		852	Lady's Lament	31
PROSE				
Something in Verse as true as Prose;		199	Horace 2, 6	D
Which might as well have been in Prose;		215	To Mr. Delany	10
For Prose, I recommend Voiture's, ...		219	To Mr. Delany	105
She'd hear of no Excuse in Prose.		378	Apology Lady C	92
Pelts him by Turns with Verse and Prose, ...		458	Paddy's Charac	25
Either in verse or hum'rous prose, ...		489	Dialogue	10
The Turn of Verse, nor Stile of Prose;		515	Answer Fable	96
"A few, in Verse; but most, in Prose---.		550	Life of Swift	182
That I had some repute for Prose;		555	Death of Swift	60
Enquires for Swift in Verse and Prose:		562	Death of Swift	254
"As for his Works in Verse and Prose, ...		565	Death of Swift	309
Hardly can be grave in Prose:		634	Epistle Lady	138
To celebrate your Birth in Prose;		756	Stel B-day '24	6
But I'll be still your Friend in Prose:		757	Stel B-day '24	30
He sounds my Praise in Verse and Prose.		887	Panegyr Dean	28
You can taste my verse or prose:		908	Daphne	70
Of thy Dimensions fit for Prose, ...		1002	Reply by Dean	5
PROSELYTE				
How mighty a Proselyte you gain!		31	Ode to Temple	140
Where Thou, our latest Proselyte, shalt share: . . .		162	Toland's Invit	8
PROSELYTES				
And fit their Proselytes for Vice;		764	Stel B-day '26	22
PROSERPINE				
By Proserpine, at Pluto's Hall?		905	Death Daphne	84
PROSPECT				
And even the sharpest eye that has the prospect seen, .		41	Ode Sancroft	207
An humbler Prospect only wait, ...		499	Panegyr Swift	179
PROSPER				
Could never prosper in amours.		176	To Lord Harley	8
PROSTITUTE				
Thus prostitute my Congreve's name is grown . . .		48	To Congreve	159
Damn'd Senators brib'd, Damn'd prostitute Slaves; . .		576	Place Damn'd	8
To prostitute the Muse's Name, ...		654	On Poetry	406
PROSTITUTED				
The daz'ling glory dimms their prostituted sight, . .		41	Ode Sancroft	221
PROSTITUTING				
By prostituting her they first debauch.		44	To Congreve	22
PROSTRATE				
High on a Length of prostrate Wood, ...		393	Modern Poets	12
And prostrate, supplicate pour ma vie.		1005	Sheridan's Sub	12
PROSTRATION				
For know, Prostration is enough to th' Lion. . . .		1002	Reply by Dean	18
PROTECT				
A Flora does the Dome protect;		477	Epist on Epist	78
PROTECTION				
. . .I desire your Excellencies Protection, ...		73	Mrs Harris Pet	70
I take thee under my Protection.		779	Mullinix Tim	208
Would take the Kingdom into his Protection:		825	Noisy Tom	4
PROTECTOR				
Of Wit and Learning chief Protector;		656	On Poetry	450

```
                                                           PAGE     TITLE          LINE
PROTECTORS
    Your great Protectors, once in Power,      . . . . . .  311 To Ford             27
PROTEST    SEE PURTEST
    "'Tis now no Secret--I protest    . . . . . . .         202 Horace 2, 6         98
    Against the Phoenix I protest.    . . . . . . . .       271 Apollo's Edict   D  51
    But all the rest shall club it I protest:---  . .       671 Epig Carthy 24   D   6
    Else he must enter his Protest:   . . . . . . .         707 Cadenus Vaness     667
    For myself, I protest, I care not a fiddle  . . . .     976 Dean to Sherid      13
PROTESTANT
    This Protestant Zealot, this <English> Divine  . . .    518 Dean Hang Rape      31
    For which all true Protestant Hearts should be glad;    520 Dean Hang Rape      68
    Is offensive to every true Protestant ear   . . . .     522 St. Cecilia's        6
    No Protestant Prelate, His Ldshp or Grace   . . . .     522 St. Cecilia's        9
    "Thought Protestant too Good a Name  . . . . . .        550 Life of Swift      170
    What Protestant can be so sottish,    . . . . . .       813 Bro Protestant      46
PROTESTANT'S
    "A Protestant's a special Clinker;    . . . . . .       550 Life of Swift      176
PROTESTANTS
    Deny them Protestants--thou ly'st.    . . . . . . .     658 On Poetry        D 190
    Are Brother Protestants and Christians,   . . . . .     812 Bro Protestant      31
    Are his Brother Protestants, good men and true;   . .   815 Yahoo's             22
PROTESTATION
    "Whose Protestation hides a Sting    . . . . . . .      550 Life of Swift      172
PROTEUS
    Then Proteus urg'd the same Request,    . . . . . .     303 Storm               25
    Proteus on you bestow'd the Boon    . . . . . . .       326 Pethox              81
PROUD    SEE PURSE-PROUD
    Of that proud Tyrant Sex of Hers.    . . . . . .        23 Ode Athenian        237
    But what does our proud Ign'rance Learning call,  . .   27 Ode to Temple        28
    Taught us, like Spaniards, to be proud and poor,  . .   28 Ode to Temple        56
    But zeal is weak and ignorant, tho' wond'rous proud, . . 38 Ode Sancroft       135
    Among proud Doctors and disputing Pharisees:  . . . .   39 Ode Sancroft       169
    Why should the Sun, alas, be proud    . . . . . .       41 Ode Sancroft       215
    Against the proud usurpers of the pit;    . . . . .     46 To Congreve        110
    As when to scare th' ungrateful or the proud   . . . .  52 Temple Ill          23
    To make the Dutch-men proud and great:    . . . . .     169 Peace Dunkirk       34
    Extremely proud--but I had din'd--    . . . . . . .     173 Horace 1, 7         68
    Of titles, birth, and fortune proud,    . . . . . .     177 To Lord Harley      40
    "I thought the <Dean> had been too proud,   . . . .     200 Horace 2, 6         33
    Who lifts the Poor, and sinks the Proud,    . . . . .   258 Bubble             210
    And proud Roxana fir'd with jealous Rage,   . . . .     275 Epilogue            25
    Or from Parthenope the proud,    . . . . . . .          324 Pethox              21
    Too wise to take Council, too proud to take Warning, .  327 Epigram 1            7
    He'll not be too proud an old Kettle to mend;   . . .   335 Serious Poem        44
    From him let proud Ambition know,    . . . . . .        386 Manly Virtue        99
    The Sage, who said he should be proud    . . . . .      400 Window Inns 1        1
    But proud Iberia soundly maul,    . . . . . . .         468 Birthday Song      248
    Thus Edgar proud, in Days of Yore,    . . . . . .       476 Epist on Epist      43
    "Because a Duke was proud to own him:    . . . . .      565 Death of Swift     320
    His Shape and Beauty made him proud:    . . . . .       602 Beasts Confess      38
    Am I spightful, proud, unjust?    . . . . . . . .       631 Epistle Lady        65
    Proud to attend you at the Steerage.    . . . . . .     656 On Poetry          456
    The Queen of Love was pleas'd, and proud,   . . . .     693 Cadenus Vaness     228
    Or on a proud triumphal Car,    . . . . . . .           724 To Stella           26
    Be proud of owning such Relations;    . . . . . .       813 Bro Protestant      58
    May be proud to be licking a great man's posteriors. .  817 Yahoo's             69
    Tho' I should be exceeding proud,    . . . . . . .      860 Lady Acheson        22
    The Captain, to shew he is proud of the Favour,   . .   870 Grand Question     103
    I'm sure he'll be proud of the Honour you do us;  . .   871 Grand Question     118
    Proud Baronet of Nova Scotia,    . . . . . . .          884 Rev Market-Hill     29
    How proud are we when you appear!    . . . . . .        889 Panegyr Dean        82
    Thy Fame, thy Genius now declines, proud Boaster.  . .  1002 Reply by Dean       9
PROUDER
    At last grown prouder than the Devil    . . . . . .     746 Stel Distress       23
    At last grown prouder than the <Devil>,   . . . . .     750 Stel Wood-Park      21
PROUDLY
    This could i do, and proudly o'er him tow'r,   . . .    44 To Congreve         39
    How proudly would he haste the joy to meet,   . . . .   49 To Congreve        185
    Though by the Female Side you proudly bring,   . . . .  826 Noisy Tom            9
    How proudly he talks    . . . . . . . . .              856 Lady's Lament      173
    Take down thy proudly swelling Sails,    . . . . . .    897 Panegyr Dean       333
PROV'D
    When on a Day, which prov'd their last,    . . . . .    116 Bauc & Phil 2      151
    I prov'd my Proposition full:    . . . . . . .          299 Horrid Plot         41
    And you have prov'd it by Dog-Logick.    . . . . . .    300 Horrid Plot         72
    For it prov'd that he dy'd of a Drop at Killmainham:    337 Serious Poem       114
    In a Dozen Apostles but one prov'd a Traytor!   . . .   804 Irish Bishops       30
PROVE
    Pliny shall prove what we affirm:    . . . . . .        83 Salamander          26
    Pliny shall prove, and we'll apply,    . . . . . .      83 Salamander          27
    E'er he could prove the good Squire ly'd.   . . . .     98 Elegy Patrige        4
    No doubt, will prove a good Arbuthnot:    . . . . .     314 To Ford             76
    My Tenants, if you doubt, will prove it:    . . . . .   348 Whitshed Motto       8
    Nor can you prove it, Mr. Pasquin.    . . . . . .       350 Upright Judge 3      2
    But Prodigies are wrought to prove    . . . . . .       384 Manly Virtue        21
    That Love is the Devil, I'll prove when requir'd:  . .  401 Window Inns 3        1
    Will prove herself a Tory plain,    . . . . . . .       417 Woman's Mind        53
    To prove, that lawyers are so wretched;   . . . . .     433 Answer Paulus       44
    To prove it I appeal to fact;    . . . . . . .          434 Answer Paulus       68
    To prove that Bishops were old Women.    . . . . .      455 Dean Smedley        20
    And plainly prove by dint of Text,    . . . . . .       456 Dean Smedley        39
```

		PAGE	TITLE	LINE
PROVE	(CONTINUED)			
Would prove ev'n Homer's Numbers flat.		467	Birthday Song	228
Envy, I doubt, wou'd pow'rful prove,		546	Life of Swift	37
Let Reason and Experience prove.		554	Death of Swift	12
Than his Prediction prove a Lye.		557	Death of Swift	132
(As Pictures prove) with Garlands crown'd,		590	Strephon Chloe	194
To prove I did my Neighbour wrong;		602	Beasts Confess	18
For how can Heav'nly Wisdom prove		695	Cadenus Vaness	294
She'll prove the greatest of thy Foes:		696	Cadenus Vaness	300
Brought weighty Arguments to prove		708	Cadenus Vaness	676
This Racer wou'd prove but a dull founder'd Jade.		717	Answer Rebus	28
They'll prove my Accusation just.		732	Stella, Poems	144
Yet cannot prove a single Fact.		795	Traulus 1	5
For I'll prove it impossible they can be both.		976	Dean to Sherid	18
PROVENDER				
Of paultry Provender and Bread:		156	Fable of Midas	18
PROVERB				
Why then the Proverb is not right,		299	Horrid Plot	39
The Proverb says; No Fence against a Flayl.		521	Stephen Duck	2
For Pride and Ignorance a Proverb grown,		794	St. Pat's Well	99
Survive in thee, and make the Proverb good		826	Noisy Tom	18
PROVERBS				
For by old Proverbs it appears,		408	Dial Rich Marb	7
One gives Advice in Proverbs Old,		781	Mullinix Tim	271
PROVES				
Which proves a Magical Redoubt		134	Magician's Rod	51
Finch, fam'd for tedious Elocution, proves		194	Author Himself	39
Hobbes clearly proves that ev'ry Creature		651	On Poetry	319
PROVIDE				
The Graces from the Court did next provide		118	Biddy Floyd	7
Your bus'ness must be to provide		460	Birthday Song	7
Who proper Objects must provide		480	Libel on D- D-	25
How amply then does Pow'r provide		493	Panegyr Swift	15
Provide you duly as we go		621	Scandal Poem 1	129
With Care provide you as we go,		627	Scandal Poem 2	123
Your Panegyricks here provide,		657	On Poetry	469
Or some rich benefice provide,		676	Parson's Case	21
Provide me but with Paper Wings,		930	Riddle 15	D 18
PROVIDED				
And from my own Stock, provided with Topicks,		265	Apollo	83
Provided, at a proper Time;		378	Apology Lady C	89
(Provided he has got his fee.)		434	Answer Paulus	56
Provided they had Cash to lend.		455	Dean Smedley	16
Provided Bolingbroke were dead.		560	Death of Swift	196
Provided Punch (for there's the Jest)		777	Mullinix Tim	131
Provided a Fund for building you Spittles:		805	Irish Bishops	59
Provided, to improve the Ground,		875	Drapier's Hill	5
PROVIDENCE				
Do own th' Effects of Providence,		19	Ode Athenian	109
To lose the providence of thy cares,		42	Ode Sancroft	242
Preserve, Almighty Providence!		199	Horace 2, 6	D
Permitted so by Providence:		387	Manly Virtue	114
(So Providence on Mortals waits,		764	Stel B-day '26	41
PROVIDES				
This gives him Lodging, and provides		80	Vanbrug House	45
Provides each Animal it's Foe:		504	Doctor Delaney	128
PROVIDING				
Providing Butter for the Cook.		892	Panegyr Dean	178
PROVINCE				
No province now is left her but to rail,		38	Ode Sancroft	110
My Province is, to see that all be right,		165	Toland's Invit	27
PROVING				
Proving the Earl a grand Offender,		774	Mullinix Tim	21
PROVISION				
Make some provision for the Yonker,		466	Birthday Song	203
That you can't fail of more Provision,		478	Epist on Epist	99
For Poets, Law makes no Provision:		641	On Poetry	49
PROVISO				
But it is with this Proviso,		830	Legion Club	40
PROVOCATION				
Provocation never waits,		800	Traulus 2	19
PROVOK'D				
I own it hath often provok'd me to Mutter,		334	Serious Poem	5
And if provok'd, he soundly ferks his		463	Birthday Song	99
And since you ne'er provok'd their Spight,		644	On Poetry	133
PROVOKE				
Provoke the honour of my Muse's rage,		42	Ode Sancroft	262
"Provoke him with a slave in Power:		566	Death of Swift	344
If ever you provoke us more.		622	Scandal Poem 1	174
PROVOKING				
Their generous Feeders not provoking		479	Epist on Epist	123
PROX'				
Coram Regina prox' die Martis,		713	Cadenus Vaness	839
PRUDE				
On Sight of this Celestial Prude,		121	Apollo Outwit	41
The Nymph would ne'er have been a prude.		177	To Lord Harley	16
When to be prude, and when coquette;		178	To Lord Harley	56
A Crazy Prelate, and a Royal Prude.		193	Author Himself	2
With ev'ry Talent of a Prude,		222	Prog of Love	2
On her Promise of yielding, she acted the Prude;		264	Apollo	46
Who neither was Coquette nor Prude.		702	Cadenus Vaness	497

		PAGE	TITLE		LINE
PRUDENCE					
Your matchless Courage with Your Prudence joins	. .	11	Ode to William	D	5
"With Virtue, Prudence, Wit besides;	. . . . . .	322	First of April		48
Dangers with Prudence to discern;	. . . .	325	Pethox		60
Till Prudence taught him to appeal	. . . . . .	481	Libel on D- D-		43
But ever with Prudence takes Care of the Main.	.	580	Psyche		8
Let Prudence with Good Nature strive,	. . . .	593	Strephon Chloe		309
With Prudence gath'ring up a Cluster	. . . . .	647	On Poetry		221
In Prudence and Compassion sent	. . . .	849	Old Thorn		30
PRUDENT					
A Prudent Builder should forecast	. . . . .	592	Strephon Chloe		293
Are an humble, prudent Wife;	. . . .	633	Epistle Lady		100
Like prudent Fabius by Delay.	. . . .	656	On Poetry		446
A Tincture in the prudent Maid:	. . . . . .	693	Cadenus Vaness		219
A Spade let prudent Archy hold,	. . . . . .	743	Stel B-day 22		57
By the prudent Architect	. . . .	829	Legion Club		5
PRUDES					
That he had serv'd the Prudes a Trick.	. . . .	321	First of April		16
Of Prudes, Coquets, and Harridans;	. . . . .	448	Modern Lady		119
The Prudes condemn the absent Prudes;	. . . . .	449	Modern Lady		155
The Prudes condemn the absent Prudes;	. . . . .	449	Modern Lady		155
Less modest than the Speech of Prudes;	. . . .	691	Cadenus Vaness		167
Prudes decay'd about may tack,	. . . .	863	To Janus		21
PRUNE					
Who artfully will pare and prune	. . . . . .	469	Birthday Song		277
PRYD					
And Norways pryd agayne shall marreye.	. . . .	103	Merlin		12
PRYTHEE					
Then prythee tell me what am I.	. . . . . .	936	Riddle 23	D	27
PSALM					
And thus I go off without Pray'r-Book or Psalm.	. .	400	Tom Clinch		22
PSALTER					
For stealing Cows, nor could he read the Psalter.	. .	826	Noisy Tom		14
PSYCHE					
At two Afternoon for our Psyche inquire,	. . . . .	580	Psyche		1
PUBLIC					
The public should bestow the actors six.	. . . . .	308	Billet Players		22
Have once the public good in view:	. . . .	487	Irish-Club		18
As when some Writer in a public Cause,	. . . . .	770	Horace 1, 14		25
In public schemes, or catching flies,	. . . . .	901	Dean's Reasons		79
Watching for the public weal.	. . . .	936	Riddle 24	D	22
PUBLICK					
The publick Stamp Heav'n sets on all that's Great and Good,		18	Ode Athenian		93
There stuck aloft, in Publick View,	. . . . . .	114	Bauc & Phil 2		87
(His Mind with Publick Cares possest,	. . . . .	170	Horace 1, 7		3
And now, the publick Int'rest to support,	. . . .	194	Author Himself		27
Your Labours for the Publick Weal.	. . . . . .	243	Horace 4, 9		6
And the Publick shall see't, if I live 'till to Morrow;		265	Apollo		68
Our Private and our Publick Foes,	. . . . . .	339	Arch-Bish Dub		10
His Firmness to the publick Good, as one that knows it Swore,		341	Upon His Grace		9
He whisprd publick things at last,	. . . . . .	422	Ireld		33
How each the Publick Good pursues,	. . . . . .	501	Doctor Delaney		59
Resentment on this publick Foe;	. . . .	515	Answer Fable		82
Who never had one publick Thought,	. . . . . .	515	Answer Fable		99
Who bore for twice ten Years the publick Hate.	. .	536	To Mr. Gay		144
And strive to pass, in publick view,	. . . . .	546	Life of Swift		35
"'Tis all bequeath'd to publick Uses.	. . . . .	558	Death of Swift		156
"To publick Use! A perfect Whim!	. . . . . .	558	Death of Swift		157
"What had the Publick done for him!	. . . . . .	558	Death of Swift		158
"And turn the Tax for publick Roads	. . . . . .	571	Death of Swift		453
Living on the publick Bounty;	. . . .	574	Helter Skelter		38
Treat the Publick, and your Friends,	. . . . .	631	Epistle Lady		55
To compleat the Publick Ruin,	. . . .	636	Epistle Lady		190
To avoid the publick Hatred;	. . . .	637	Epistle Lady		224
For private Life, or publick Use?	. . . . . .	641	On Poetry		46
A publick, or a private Robber;	. . . .	645	On Poetry		161
Intent the Publick Debts to pay,	. . . . . .	656	On Poetry		445
How well his publick Thrift is shewn?	. . . . .	659	On Poetry	D	416
In publick with that odious Knight.	. . . . .	699	Cadenus Vaness		395
Had met her in a publick Place,	. . . . . .	706	Cadenus Vaness		634
To publick Light your only Fau't;	. . . . . .	731	Stella, Poems		102
Our whole Accounts of publick Debts.	. . . . .	774	Mullinix Tim		15
I must pursue the publick Good.	. . . .	775	Mullinix Tim		74
The publick Safety I foresee,	. . . .	776	Mullinix Tim		81
When first in publick we appear,	. . . . . .	780	Mullinix Tim		229
Some for the publick Service go,	. . . . . .	781	Mullinix Tim		255
PUBLISH					
Go publish o'er the Plain	. . . .	31	Ode to Temple		139
Publish my Will, my Life, my Letters.	. . . . .	561	Death of Swift		202
Not to publish ev'ry Trifle,	. . . .	631	Epistle Lady		61
PUBLISH'D					
What Carthy publish'd needs no long Excuse,	. . . .	668	Epig Carthy 11	D	1
He only publish'd for my private Use.	. . . . .	668	Epig Carthy 11	D	2
PUBLISHING					
To praise your parts by publishing of mine;	. . . .	44	To Congreve		34
Thou'rt curst for Publishing, and he for not.	. . .	667	Epig Carthy 7	D	2
PUDDEN					
H'as drop'd, and giv'n the Crow a Pudden!	. . . .	547	Life of Swift		71

	PAGE	TITLE	LINE
PUDDING-PIES			
In parliaments, or pudding-pies.	901	Dean's Reasons	80
PUDDING-SLEEVE			
About each Arm a Pudding-sleeve;	115	Bauc & Phil 2	120
PUDDLE			
As Instinct leads them, in a Puddle;	294	Horrid Plot	148
PUDET			
Pudet haec opprobria, I freely must tell ye,	967	Letter Sherid	5
PUE			
But for the Politicks of Pue,	282	Journal	101
PUFF			
Which hardly wants another puff,	' 9	Ode to King	109
Thus with a puff the whole delusion ends.	55	Temple Ill	154
I'll chew you to Bullets, and puff you at Baldwin.	1019	To Sheridan	10
PUFF'D			
Puff'd by the people's spightful blast,	41	Ode Sancroft	220
Nor puff'd by Pride, nor sunk by Spleen.	199	Horace 2, 6	D
Puff'd up with pride and insolence,	950	Upstart	D 11
PUFT			
Our <Bishops> puft up with Wealth and with Pride.	804	Irish Bishops	17
PUGH			
Pugh! said I, but that's not the Business that I ail.	70	Mrs Harris Pet	29
PULCHRE'S			
From Smithfield, or St. Pulchre's shape their Course,	139	City Shower	58
PULL			
In vain I tug and pull the Oar,	32	Ode to Temple	193
Though with united Strength they all pull,	191	Faggot	51
And all we poor Shopkeepers must our Horns pull in.	237	Excellent Song	16
When they're to pull him by the Nose,	373	Letter D. S-y	72
Pull down an Ale-house-Bush, for Spite,	457	Paddy's Charac	8
At whose Oars, like Slaves, they all pull:	635	Epistle Lady	160
When they grew pert, to pull them down.	697	Cadenus Vaness	337
And pull your haughty Stomach down,	748	Stel Distress	72
And pull your haughty Stomach down;	752	Stel Wood-Park	88
Pull down the fine briers,	857	Lady's Lament	197
PULL'D			
He pull'd the String, and stopt his Coach,	172	Horace 1, 7	61
Who pull'd a Palace to the Ground,	727	To Stella	122
The gold she was pull'd down, of that I'm very sure,	840	Ballad	D 3
PULLED			
By my soul there's bad news, for the gold she was pulled down,	840	Ballad	D 2
PULLS			
Pulls off with Care, and first displays 'em,	581	Young Nymph	15
Pulls out the Rags contriv'd to prop	582	Young Nymph	21
PULLY'S			
Look where the Pully's ty'd above!	29	Ode to Temple	102
PULPIT			
Who fain would rule the Pulpit, as they do the Stage,	19	Ode Athenian	104
And with small Change, a Pulpit grew.	114	Bauc & Phil 2	88
Of Size that might a Pulpit fill,	170	Horace 1, 7	11
Is seen, as when you mount our Pulpit.	889	Panegyr Dean	66
PULPITS			
From Pulpits chuse Gallants.	426	Five Ladies	32
PULPITT			
There stuck, and to a Pulpitt grew,	93	Bauc & Phil 1	107
PULSE			
"And feel my Pulse, I know it stops:	451	Modern Lady	207
PULT'NEY			
When Bolingbroke with Pult'ney Dines.	483	Libel on D- D-	102
<PULTENEY'S>			
Sir <Robert> weary'd by Will. <Pulteney's> Teazings,	537	Mr. Pulteney	1
PULTNEY			
St. John, as well as Pultney knows,	555	Death of Swift	59
PUMP			
Think of a Bucket or a Pump.	83	Salamander	20
Nor pump to cobble wicked Verse;	181	Horace 2, 1	36
PUMPS			
Splish, splash in their pumps.	245	Irish-Feast	44
PUN			
Worse than a Pun, or Irish Phrase,	312	To Ford	38
Teague made a good Pun by a Brogue in his Speech,	334	Serious Poem	27
I end my labours with a Pun.	515	Answer Fable	102
With rebus and pun.	852	Lady's Lament	14
I'll tear all your Rules, and demolish your Pun Talk:	1019	To Sheridan	8
. . . your own spirit of pun, and own wit.	1024	Nim-Dan-Dean 2	D 16
PUNCH			
Punch is exactly of a Piece	592	Strephon Chloe	291
While Punch is hid behind the Scene,	776	Mullinix Tim	94
If Punch, to spur their fancy, shews	776	Mullinix Tim	103
Punch roaring ran, and running roar'd.	776	Mullinix Tim	112
Punch comes, like you, and lets a <Fart>.	777	Mullinix Tim	122
Provided Punch (for there's the Jest)	777	Mullinix Tim	131
Tim thour't the Punch to stir up trouble in;	777	Mullinix Tim	138
PUNCH'S			
By Lovers spoke in Punch's Booth.	650	On Poetry	298
PUNCHINELLOES			
Perform the part of Punchinelloes;	777	Mullinix Tim	136
PUNCTUAL			
Keeps punctual to an Assignation;	724	To Stella	30

		PAGE	TITLE	LINE
PUNGENT				
With pungent Pains on ev'ry Side:		325	Pethox	57
PUNISH				
To punish Thieves, or lash a Suburb Wench.		537	Mr. Pulteney	6
He can punish Sins enormous.		830	Legion Club	34
To punish my sins, ...		851	Lady's Lament	5
PUNISH'D				
Soon punish'd Strephon for his Peeping;		529	Lady's Dres Rm	120
PUNISHING				
In pard'ning, as in punishing, ...		1005	Sheridan's Sub	15
PUNISHMENT				
What Punishment would you inflict?		505	Doctor Delaney	153
PUNISHMENTS				
Who Punishments on me inflict, ...		917	Riddle 3	15
PUNK				
So about twelve at Night, the Punk		1033	Ans to Crown	1
PUNN				
It is but a Paraphrase made on a Punn;		716	Answer Rebus	10
PUNNERS				
Well, punners and rhymers must have the last word. . .		976	Dean to Sherid	8
PUNS				
To deafen 'em with Puns and Rhime.		75	Game Traffick	D 28
PUNY				
At Wills the puny Judge of Wit.		647	On Poetry	236
PUPIL				
His Pupil might be tir'd with Lectures;		704	Cadenus Vaness	569
The Tutor; and the Pupil, he:		712	Cadenus Vaness	807
PUPPET				
There's not a Puppet made of Wood, ·		777	Mullinix Tim	123
PUPPET-MAN				
From yonder Puppet-Man inquire, ...		592	Strephon Chloe	285
PUPPET-SHOW---				
That Ev'ning to a Puppet-Show---:		547	Life of Swift	63
And often see a Puppet-show.		776	Mullinix Tim	92
PUPPET-SHOWS				
The World consists of Puppet-shows;		777	Mullinix Tim	134
PUPPETS				
And Puppets mov'd by Wire		123	Empty'ng Town	14
Put all your Brother Puppets out, ...		777	Mullinix Tim	140
PUPPIES				
Drown'd Puppies, stinking Sprats, all drench'd in Mud,		139	City Shower	62
His Brace of Puppies how they stuff, ...		861	Lady Acheson	33
PUPPY				
Or t' other Puppy that was drown'd, ...		299	Horrid Plot	22
With Puppy Water, Beauty's Help		526	Lady's Dres Rm	31
Whene'er a flatt'ring Puppy cries		545	Life of Swift	25
On the Puppy Pair of Dicks;		835	Legion Club	146
"And the Puppy confess'd, he expected no Good o'me. .		873	Grand Question	166
PURCHAS'D				
Our thriving <Dean> has purchas'd Land;		875	Drapier's Hill	2
PURCHASE				
To purchase Kingdoms, and to buy Renown, ...		11	Ode to William	D 1
They purchase Knowledge at the Expence		27	Ode to Temple	42
You've some good Purchase in your Eye;		175	Horace 1, 7	128
He found he could purchase Two Tankards of Ale . . .		288	Bank Down	37
Will purchase me, the more's the Pity, ...		410	Dial Rich Marb	68
'Till he can purchase an Estate;		456	Dean Smedley	36
and selling his Country to purchase his peace		540	Charac Walpole	8
To purchase Fame by writing ill:		652	On Poetry	368
A Purchase which will bring him clear, ...		875	Drapier's Hill	3
The wretched Purchase here behold		921	Riddle 7	17
PURE				
Who to the Stars in pure Good-will, ...		101	Elegy Patrige	105
The Coyn's Currant and Mettal Pure.		372	Letter D. S-y	34
"In wholesome Soil and Aether Pure;		476	Epist on Epist	50
For ever, uncorrupt and pure;		691	Cadenus Vaness	145
Came early, out of pure Good-will, ...		698	Cadenus Vaness	366
Offer to him a pure Libation;		893	Panegyr Dean	220
Come eat 'em with pure fresh Butter and Mustard, . .		953	Herrings	6
PURELY				
Which (in their Stile) is purely hung.		183	Horace 2, 1	82
But purely come to hear, and stare;		777	Mullinix Tim	128
PURER				
Sit clad in lawn of purer woven day, ...		41	Ode Sancroft	235
But winding Walks and purer Air;		378	Apology Lady C	100
PUREST				
With Paean's purest Fire his Favourites glow; . . .		532	To Mr. Gay	23
My purest Passion has betray'd.		595	Cassinus Peter	58
PURGE				
Dear Cassy, thou must purge and bleed;		596	Cassinus Peter	89
From noxious Steams to purge the Air;		780	Mullinix Tim	250
PURGE-SICK				
Both when I am Purge-sick, and when I am Spew-sick. .		1028	Dr. Helsham	4
PURIFY'D				
Had purify'd her mortal sight;		178	To Lord Harley	50
And purify'd their mothers after.		675	Curate's Compl	8
PURLIEUS				
From round the Purlieus of St. James, ...		698	Cadenus Vaness	365
PURLING				
Swiftly purling in a Round, ...		661	Love Song	26
From purling Streams & Fountains bubbling		744	Stel Distress	3

		PAGE	TITLE	LINE
PURLING	(CONTINUED)			
From purling Streams and Fountains bubbling,	. . . .	750	Stel Wood-Park	27
The Margin of a purling Stream,	. . . .	894	Panegyr Dean	241
PURLOIN				
Nor shall I for his Humour, permit you to purloin	. .	867	Grand Question	17
PURLOIN'D				
Prometheus once this Chain purloin'd,	. . . . . .	345	Prometheus	37
PURPLE				
Or, Consul in his Purple Gown,	. . . .	190	Faggot	33
Leaving the Purple to the·Nose.	. . . .	226	Prog of Beauty	28
And Scipio, trail an Irish purple Plad.	. . . . .	275	Epilogue	22
Her infant Loves with purple Wings;	. . . . . .	585	Strephon Chloe	50
The Vi'lets ope their purple heads,	. . . . . .	621	Scandal Poem 1	140
The Vi'lets ope their Purple Heads;	. . . . . .	627	Scandal Poem 2	144
Flutt'ring spread thy purple Pinions,	. . . . . .	660	Love Song	1
Each with a Gold and Purple Vest;	. . . .	923	Riddle 7	72
PURPOSE				
They lie open on Purpose, on Counters and Stalls,	. .	263	Apollo	23
'Twas to no purpose to oppose,	. . . .	378	Apology Lady C	91
PURSE SEE PICK-PURSE				
And I had in a Purse, seven Pound, four Shillings and.		69	Mrs Harris Pet	2
. .				
So when I went to put up my Purse, as God would have		69	Mrs Harris Pet	8
it,. . .				
But when I search'd, and miss'd my Purse,. .	. . . .	69	Mrs Harris Pet	13
But pray, Mary, can you tell what I have done with my		70	Mrs Harris Pet	15
Purse!				
How well a Cully's Purse was lin'd:	. . . . . .	133	Magician's Rod	32
From her Closet brought out a full Purse in her Clutche		143	New Song	16
Yet since I know where a full Purse may be found,	. .	144	New Song	49
With borrow'd Money in his Purse;	. . . .	173	Horace 1, 7	94
Condemn'd to bear his client's purse;	. . . . . .	435	Answer Paulus	90
With empty Purse, and aching Head,	. . . . . .	453	Modern Lady	292
He comes to drain a Beggar's Purse:	. . . . . .	484	Libel on D- D-	124
That all the Loss your Purse sustain'd	. . . . .	496	Panegyr Swift	88
Come with a Purse of Guineas in your Hands.	. . . .	534	To Mr. Gay	100
Five thousand Guineas in her Purse?	. . . . . .	707	Cadenus Vaness	654
Throws the last shilling in his purse,	. . . . . .	878	Robbin & Harry	2
Because too close I hold my Purse.	. . . . . .	918	Riddle 4	28
PURSE-PROUD				
Let purse-proud C--n next approach,	. . . . . .	951	Upstart	D 23
PURSES				
But we doubt that our Purses will quickly grow lank,	.	287	Bank Down	14
PURSU'D				
Where having cast his coat, and well pursu'd	. . . .	46	To Congreve	117
Or, had Embroider'd Mars pursu'd,	. . . . .	177	To Lord Harley	15
By an ‹old› ‹redhair'd› ‹murd'ring› ‹Hag› pursu'd,	. .	193	Author Himself	1
At home, he was pursu'd with Noise,	. . . . . .	221	A Quiet Life	49
Which, as the Nurse pursu'd to kill,	. . . . . .	504	Doctor Delaney	119
The ‹Dean› he pursu'd to recover his Game,	. . .	517	Dean Hang Rape	13
Thus was the Hare pursu'd, tho' free from Guilt;	. .	538	Mr. Pulteney	37
"While they pursu'd each others Ruin.	. . . . . .	567	Death of Swift	368
"Pursu'd by base envenom'd Pens,	. . . . . .	568	Death of Swift	395
Pursu'd and laid me hard on.	. . . .	1005	Sheridan's Sub	10
PURSUE				
Far in this primitive cell might we pursue	. . . . .	49	To Congreve	195
Her tainted Carcase to pursue,	. . . .	85	Salamander	65
When e're I 'gin, you should pursue	. . . . . .	373	Letter D. S-y	52
Pursue the Goddess Health in vain,	. . . . .	401	Window Inns 5	D 5
But oh! so faintly we pursue,	. . . .	401	Window Inns 5	D 11
And hasted forward to pursue .	. . . .	412	Desire Possess	29
Nor ceas'd the Faction to pursue	. . . .	494	Panegyr Swift	43
And in the fruitless Search pursue	. . . . . .	592	Strephon Chloe	269
The Rest pursue as thick as Hops:	. . . . . .	654	On Poetry	400
Variety we still Pursue,	. . . .	728	Stella, Poems	17
And all the Fictions they pursue	. . . .	729	Stella, Poems	59
Pursue thy Trade of Scandall picking,	. . . . . .	735	Stel B-day '20	41
I must pursue the publick Good.	. . . .	775	Mullinix Tim	74
Will none the Tory Dogs pursue,	. . . . . .	779	Mullinix Tim	185
If the fifth you shou'd pursue	. . . .	931	Riddle 17	D 7
PURSUES				
In vain pursues the Musick with her longing Eye,	. .	17	Ode Athenian	58
Her Frolicks, and pursues her Tail no more.	. . .	136	City Shower	4
When Sol pursues her with his fires.	. . . . .	178	To Lord Harley	72
Since Death pursues the Coward as he flies.	. . .	210	Earl of Oxford	2
Who now the wandring Pair pursues:	. . . . . .	224	Prog of Love	74
From a bo-bo-bo-Boy he pursues his old Hank,	. . .	287	Bank Down	19
Through ev'ry Game pursues her Tale,	. . . . .	447	Modern Lady	78
How each the Publick Good pursues,	. . . . . .	501	Doctor Delaney	59
PURSUING				
When once the fierce pursuing Gaul	. . . . . .	340	Arch-Bish Dub	17
A Hare, who long had 'scap't pursuing Hounds,	. ·	538	Mr. Pulteney	17
PURSUIT				
And Interest the one Pursuit,	. . . .	385	Manly Virtue	66
To hardships in pursuit of health;	. . . . . .	401	Window Inns 5	D 2
PURSUITS				
So Witches bent on bad Pursuits,	. . . . . .	670	Epig Carthy 19	D 1
But his Pursuits are at an End,	. . . .	728	Stella, Poems	23
Vain Man, of all thy vain Pursuits.	. . . . . .	921	Riddle 7	2
PURTEST				
If I had a Husband like him, I purtest,	. . . . .	869	Grand Question	57

PURULENT   PAGE TITLE   LINE

	PAGE	TITLE		LINE
PURULENT				
Of Matter purulent and white	84	Salamander		53
PUSH				
Her Chairmen push him from the Wall:	292	Prog Marriage		86
PUSS				
And Puss grew Lion-hearted.	153	Widow and Cat	D	10
And Puss had on her Plumpers <pisst>.	583	Young Nymph		62
That silly old puss	855	Lady's Lament		119
PUT				
In what Mock-habits have they put her, since the Fall!	22	Ode Athenian		219
'Tis you must put us in the Way;	27	Ode to Temple		20
Unless I put in Caesar's Learning too,	28	Ode to Temple		67
Rather put on thy anger and thy spight,	37	Ode Sancroft		86
Now to a nobler Office put,	66	Problem		24
So when I went to put up my Purse, as God would have it,...	69	Mrs Harris Pet		8
Then the Bell rung, and I went down to put my Lady to Bed,	69	Mrs Harris Pet		10
But was sorely put to't in the midst of a Verse,	76	Lady B- B-		3
This put me the Fryar into an Amazement,	77	Lady B- B-		12
So cold, that put it in the Fire,	84	Salamander		49
Put the old People in a Fright,	92	Bauc & Phil 1		80
Till all my Relations were put into Places.	144	New Song		24
For why; I would fain have put all in a Flame,	144	New Song		43
"Put my Lord Bolingbroke in Mind,	201	Horace 2, 6		55
Fate put a Period to the Farce;	225	Prog of Love		96
Have put his Carcass in a Chest.	235	Elegy on Demar		46
Put in Your Money fairly told;	251	Bubble		5
Put on what Spectacles You please,	255	Bubble		123
When the Days are at shortest, to put it in Rhyme;	265	Apollo		78
"To put him in a plaguy Fright,	305	Storm		54
'Twas cut into Faggots, and put to the Flame,	334	Serious Poem		21
And England has put this Crab to hard Use,	335	Serious Poem		37
'Fool, to put up four Crosses at your door,	404	Window Inns 11	D	3
Put up your Wife, she's crosser than all four',	404	Window Inns 11	D	4
That we should put no Trust in Princes;	408	Dial Rich Marb		14
Or put one Feature out of Place;	414	Censure		24
The Sight will put her in a Swown.	416	Woman's Mind		16
To put the question strains his throat.	421	Ireld		16
He'll put you in a Ballad:	425	Five Ladies		12
Both Solemnly put, in this hole on a Sunday,	431	Dicky Dolly		23
Or in harmonious Numbers put	451	Modern Lady		222
Into whose pocket valiant Willy put,	467	Birthday Song		207
To Your Ambition put an End.	478	Epist on Epist		114
Be put to the Peril, and Toyl of a <Rape>?	518	Dean Hang Rape		42
"In Princes never put thy Trust.	566	Death of Swift		342
The Bride was put in Form to Bed;	587	Strephon Chloe		112
One Blast will put out all his Fires.	588	Strephon Chloe		136
Can you put in higher Claims,	637	Epistle Lady		241
Put on the Critick's Brow, and sit	647	On Poetry		235
Don't you intend to put on Red?	699	Cadenus Vaness		399
"To put them on an equal Foot;	714	Cadenus Vaness		876
Have put the Dean's Politicks quite out of Date;	716	Answer Rebus		24
Who fondly put his Trust in pop'lar Breath.	771	Horace 1, 14		32
Put all your Brother Puppets out,	777	Mullinix Tim		140
His Hat could nicely put on;	785	Mullinex Dick		30
To put on a Fool's Disguise,	833	Legion Club		110
Soon repent, or put to Slaughter	838	Legion Club		213
Put a word out of joint,	855	Lady's Lament		139
You had like to have put it quite out of my Head.	870	Grand Question		86
The Shoes put on; our faithful Portress	885	Rev Market-Hill		69
At first did put me to a stand;	912	Aenigma Expl	D	2
All Colours, without Paint, put on,	935	Riddle 23	D	12
Are harder than ever were put by the Sphinx.	977	Dean to Sherid		46
But before you can put yourself under her banners,	979	Dean to Tho: S		27
PUTRID				
Their Sores and putrid Ulcers show,	667	Epig Carthy 6	D	3
PUTS				
Just as the Sun puts out a Fire;	9	Ode to King		114
Puts all upon a desp'rate Bett,	251	Bubble		22
Perhaps you will say, 'tis the Devil that puts	335	Serious Poem		61
She gives you such Plenty, it puts you in Pain;	580	Psyche		7
"She puts the World in his Possession,	714	Cadenus Vaness		882
And puts them to so small Expence,	735	Stel B-day '20		26
Puts in his Finger and his Thumb,	797	Traulus 1		51
Which when the Brute puts awkward on,	885	Rev Market-Hill		79
PUTT				
With this He putt up to My <Lord>	63	Discovery		17
PUTTING				
And, instead of putting it into my Pocket, down it slipt:	69	Mrs Harris Pet		9
Quoth Herries, fairly putting Cases,	75	Game Traffick		17
PUTTS				
Putts This to's Excellency's Snout,	63	Discovery		39
PUZZLED				
Even so Master Doctor had Puzzled his Brains	77	Lady B- B-		22
PY				
A Thing resembling a Goose Py,	109	V's House		104
PYRAMID				
Would vanish in a Pyramid of Fire.	22	Ode Athenian		196
QUA				
Is, causa sine qua non.	406	Swift to Pope		20

		PAGE	TITLE	LINE
QUACK				
A Cobler, Starmonger, and Quack,	. . . . . .	101	Elegy Patrige	104
To call him Hypocrite and Quack.	. . . .	605	Beasts Confess	128
QUACK-BILLS				
So for their Quack-Bills he knows whom to thank,	. .	288	Bank Down	54
QUACKS				
For those are but Quacks, who mount on a Bank.	. . .	288	Bank Down	55
QUADRANT				
To give us your measures of lines by a quadrant.	. . .	1026	Sheri Circles	10
QUADRATA				
That you Quadrata change Rotundis?	. . . . . .	477	Epist on Epist	76
QUADRILL				
She sat all Night up at Quadrill.	. . . .	446	Modern Lady	41
(Who now again Quadrill forswears,)	. . . .	453	Modern Lady	291
"If he shou'd fail her at Quadrill.	. . . .	562	Death of Swift	238
QUADRILL'S				
Quadrill's the Word, and so begin.	. . . .	451	Modern Lady	219
QUADRILLE				
To cheat and wrangle at Quadrille.	. . . .	416	Woman's Mind	26
Give me Velvet and Quadrille,	. . . .	863	To Janus	29
As great as ever, at Quadrille?	. . . .	905	Death Daphne	78
QUADRUPEDS				
Of Quadrupeds I only mean)	. . . .	601	Beasts Confess	8
QUADRUPLE				
Tho' I dare you to more than quadruple Alliance?	. .	1019	To Sheridan	2
QUAE				
Quaedam quae attinent ad Scriblerum,	. . . .	186	Scriblerus 3	3
QUAEDAM				
Quaedam quae attinent ad Scriblerum,	. . . .	186	Scriblerus 3	3
QUAFF				
Now quaff of honest Ale a Quart,	. . . .	184	Horace 2, 1	111
QUAIL				
To make Her only touch a Quail:	. . . .	746	Stel Distress	20
To make her only touch a Quail.	. . . .	750	Stel Wood-Park	18
QUAILS				
A Fig for Partridges and Quails	. . . .	733	Verses Vanessa	27
QUAINT				
O, 'tis a quaint Device:	. . . .	394	Grub-Street	6
With quaint Inscription, which contains,	. . . . . .	494	Panegyr Swift	55
QUAINT-ER				
Then which of us two is the quaint-er Coxcomb?	. . .	1003	Dan J's Reply	12
QUAK'D				
And each imprison'd Hero quak'd for Fear.	. . . . .	139	City Shower	52
QUAKE				
See, how they tremble! how they quake!	. . . .	30	Ode to Temple	113
The Loyt'res quake, no Corner hides them,	. . . . .	279	Journal	33
QUAKERS				
Quakers and Aldermen, in State,	. . . .	239	Run Bankers	14
Quakers, Conformists, Presbyterians,	. . . . . .	345	Prometheus	14
QUAKING				
now trembling Shiv'ring Quiv'ring Quaking,		959	Cantata	
QUALIFIED				
Is qualified best for a Dog in a String.	. . . . .	389	Order of Bath	12
QUALIFY				
To qualify him God's Vicegerent,	. . . .	464	Birthday Song	134
QUALIFY'D				
So qualify'd to Swear and Lye,	. . . .	779	Mullinix Tim	193
QUALITIES				
Take Qualities from Donegal.	. . . .	272	Apollo's Edict	D 75
QUALITY				
And strole about, but hide their Quality,	. . . . .	90	Bauc & Phil 1	3
And strole about, but hide their Quality,	. . . . .	111	Bauc & Phil 2	3
Each proper Quality to find	. . . .	659	On Poetry	D 410
In Quality of Butler's Mate;	. . . .	889	Panegyr Dean	88
QUANTA				
To cry, like statesmen, quanta patimur!	. . . . . .	433	Answer Paulus	42
QUANTO				
Ah! Quanto rectius, Tu Adepte,	. . . .	476	Epist on Epist	29
QUARREL				
Keep close then Boys, and never quarrel.	. . . . .	189	Faggot	13
Let's quarrel no longer, since Dan and George Rochfort		979	Dean to Tho: S	35
QUARRELL				
I never quarrell with my Wife,	. . . .	220	A Quiet Life	15
QUARRELL'D				
Nor quarrell'd at their aukward Bow.	. . . .	701	Cadenus Vaness	461
QUARRELS				
To Blood and Quarrels, Brass unites:	. . . .	345	Prometheus	22
Then, why these quarrels to the sun,	. . . .	432	Answer Paulus	3
Engag'd him in a hundred Quarrels:	. . . .	603	Beasts Confess	52
But, to patch up all our Quarrels,	. . . .	637	Epistle Lady	235
The drunken Quarrels of a Rake,	. . . .	724	To Stella	24
We know the Subject of their Quarrels;	. . . . . .	820	Dr. Rundle	21
Lest it may more quarrels breed	. . . .	907	Daphne	53
There shou'd be Quarrels among Kings.	. . . . . .	930	Riddle 15	D 20
QUARRELSOME				
To a quarrelsome Fellow, cries, Let us be Friends.	.	968	Letter Sherid	28
QUART				
Now quaff of honest Ale a Quart,	. . . .	184	Horace 2, 1	111
Will drew out Dick to take a Quart,	. . . .	220	A Quiet Life	26
Dog <Walpole> laid a Quart of Nog on't,	. . . . .	299	Horrid Plot	31
Demand a Croun a Quart for Stumm.	. . . .	313	To Ford	68

```
QUART          (CONTINUED)                                   PAGE    TITLE          LINE
     So well, what Bottle holds a Quart:      . . . . . .      889  Panegyr Dean       92
     Saunders said I, I would rather than a Quart of Ale,      987  Mary to Sher       31
     We shall not have a Quart.                               1015  Swift to Sheri     42
     Where less than forty, fill a Quart.  . . . . . . .      1022  Nim-Dan-Dean 1  D  52
QUARTER
     Comes home a quarter after nine,       . . . . . . .      292  Prog Marriage      84
     'Tis now a Quarter after three        . . . . . . .       377  Apology Lady C     60
     "And Preachers, find the better quarter,    . . . .       549  Life of Swift     166
     Or change his Comrades once a Quarter:      . . . .       556  Death of Swift     96
     We must give them better Quarter,     . . . . . . .       837  Legion Club       177
     After a Week, a Month, a Quarter,     . . . . . . .       860  Lady Acheson        9
     A Stone and a quarter of Beef from my Sirloin.            867  Grand Question     18
     First I shew you but a Quarter,       . . . . . . .       927  Riddle 10       D   3
QUARTER-STAFFS
     With Quarter-staffs instead of White;      . . . . .      189  Faggot            22
QUARTER'S
     Her Quarter's out at Lady Day         . . . . . . .       746  Stel Distress     41
     Her Quarter's out at Lady-Day,        . . . . . . .       751  Stel Wood-Park    57
QUARTERLY
     The quarterly demands of nurses,      . . . . . . .       676  Parson's Case     14
QUARTERS
     Now Poets from all Quarters ran       . . . . . . .       108  V's House         95
QUARTRIDGE
     An idle Rogue, who spends his Quartridge    . . . . .     411  Dial Rich Marb    97
QUASI
     For scolding is just quasi diceres--school-din:  . . .    979  Dean to Tho: S     8
QUATER
     He knew to stop a quater trois.  . . . . . . . . .        456  Dean Smedley      30
QUAVERS
     To listen to minimms and quavers and Crochets  . . . .    522  St. Cecilia's     12
QUEAN
     Such is that Sprinkling which some careless Quean  . .    137  City Shower       19
     Satira's but some pocky Quean.  . . . . . . . .           530  Lady's Dres Rm   134
QUEEN
     This beauteous Queen by Heaven design'd    . . . . .       22  Ode Athenian     216
     And if so black the cloud, that heaven's bright queen  .   53  Temple Ill        57
     The Queen has lately lost a Part  . . . . . . . .          96  On the Union       1
     When on their Queen the Muses wait;   . . . . . . .       121  Apollo Outwit     46
     But the Queen shall enjoy Her own again.    . . . .       168  Peace Dunkirk     10
     Made false Moves, and lost his Queen.       . . . .       168  Peace Dunkirk     16
     Than the Queen should enjoy Her own again.  . . . .       168  Peace Dunkirk     20
     And the Queen shall enjoy Her own again.    . . . .       169  Peace Dunkirk     30
     For the Queen now enjoys Her own again.     . . . .       169  Peace Dunkirk     40
     Diana thus, Heav'n's chastest queen,  . . . . . . .       178  To Lord Harley    73
     And chaster than the Queen of Night,  . . . . . . .       179  To Lord Harley    78
     Which now disturbs the Queen and Court,    . . . .        190  Faggot            25
     Frequented Lords; saw those that saw the Queen;  . .      194  Author Himself    17
     York is from Lambeth sent, to shew the Queen  . . .       195  Author Himself    47
     It shews the Queen of Love intends    . . . . . . .       254  Bubble            95
     We'll Rigg in Meath-Street, Egypt's hauty Queen,         275  Epilogue          19
     They first invite the Cyprian Queen,  . . . . . .         290  Prog Marriage      7
     Your Mistress now is grown a Queen;   . . . . . . .       408  Dial Rich Marb    10
     For want of tattling to the Queen;    . . . . . . .       410  Dial Rich Marb    58
     Hail Queen of Britain, Queen of Rhymes,    . . . .        467  Birthday Song    221
     Hail Queen of Britain, Queen of Rhymes,    . . . .        467  Birthday Song    221
     Refus'd the Visits of a Queen;        . . . . . . .       482  Libel on D- D-    74
     Queen of Wit and Beauty, Betty,       . . . . . . .       522  Betty Grizette     1
     Should I the Queen of Love refuse,    . . . . . . .       530  Lady's Dres Rm   131
     To praise Queen Anne, nay more, defend her,   . . .       550  Life of Swift    186
     Runs laughing up to tell the Queen.   . . . . . . .       559  Death of Swift   180
     The Queen, so Gracious, Mild, and Good,    . . . .        559  Death of Swift   181
     "By Stephen Duck, upon the Queen.     . . . . . . .       563  Death of Swift   272
     Shews Sheba's Queen completely drest,  . . . . . .        592  Strephon Chloe   287
     His Cloud, and Jove's imperiall Queen.     . . . .        619  Scandal Poem 1    58
     His Cloud, and Jove's Imperial Queen:      . . . .        625  Scandal Poem 2    54
     Pleading before the Cyprian Queen.    . . . . . . .       686  Cadenus Vaness     2
     On whom the Queen of Love was bent    . . . . . . .       691  Cadenus Vaness   138
     The Queen of Learning gravely smiles,  . . . . . .        692  Cadenus Vaness   199
     The Queen of Love was pleas'd, and proud,  . . . .        693  Cadenus Vaness   228
     Besides, she fear'd the Queen of Love  . . . . . .        695  Cadenus Vaness   268
     The Queen of Love, whom thus she greets,   . . . .        695  Cadenus Vaness   285
     That Gown was made for Old Queen Bess.     . . . .        699  Cadenus Vaness   397
     The Queen of Beauty lost her Aim.     . . . . . . .       700  Cadenus Vaness   433
     The Queen of Wisdom cou'd foresee,    . . . . . . .       701  Cadenus Vaness   484
     Mean time the mournful Queen of Love  . . . . . . .       712  Cadenus Vaness   828
     To make you look like Beauty's Queen  . . . . . . .       736  Stel B-day '20    53
     The God of Wit, and Beauty's Queen,   . . . . . . .       757  Stel B-day '24    17
     Upon the Queen of Sheba's lap.  . . . . . . . .           776  Mullinix Tim     110
     (For sure, I had dizen'd you out like a Queen:)   . . .   870  Grand Question   102
     A Beggar there, and here a Queen.     . . . . . . .       911  Aenigma            8
     As fair and lovely as their Queen:    . . . . . . .       923  Riddle 7          70
     And painted like an Indian Queen.     . . . . . . .       926  Riddle 9          10
     I swore to the <Queen> that the <Prince> of <Hanover>    144  New Song          35
     The <Queen> (forsooth, Despotick) gave     . . . . .     181  Horace 2, 1       25
     The <Queen> incens'd, his Services forgot,  . . . .      195  Author Himself    57
     Nor cou'd his Malice spare the <Queen>;     . . . .      514  Answer Fable      76
     The Thresher Duck, could o'er the <Queen> prevail.   .   521  Stephen Duck       1
<QUEEN'S>
     Is come up, vi & armis, to break the <Queen's> Peace.  .  142  New Song           4
```

	PAGE	TITLE	LINE
QUEER			
Son and Brother to a Queer,	837	Legion Club	175
QUELL			
Shall strike him dumb, and quell their Noise.	340	Arch-Bish Dub	28
To conquer Spain, and quell the Turk.	466	Birthday Song	194
QUENCH			
In vain to quench this foolish Fire I try	33	Ode to Temple	206
For, as their Appetites to quench,	480	Libel on D- D-	21
"Whose Fury Blood could never quench;	569	Death of Swift	418
QUERIST			
By some instructed Querist sleeping on the Sand,	22	Ode Athenian	190
QUEST			
And bid Friend Lewis go in quest	171	Horace 1, 7	16
In quest, who might this Parson be,	171	Horace 1, 7	19
You then may boldly go in Quest	504	Doctor Delaney	143
He boldly sent his Hand in quest,	589	Strephon Chloe	188
QUESTION			
And question me of this and that;	201	Horace 2, 6	68
Now ask me a Question. How came it to pass	336	Serious Poem	85
To put the question strains his throat.	421	Ireld	16
To state the question pro and con:	435	Answer Paulus	100
In every Mouth the Question most in Vogue	536	To Mr. Gay	145
Suppose the Question not your own:	724	To Stella	38
Mean Time, the Wise a Question start,	919	Riddle 5	31
You'll dare not to question my minor or major.	976	Dean to Sherid	24
QUESTIONS			
When Questions on the Fact arose,	688	Cadenus Vaness	70
QUI			
Hannoniae qui primus ab oris.	186	Scriblerus 4	D 6
Qui nil moliris tam inepte?	476	Epist on Epist	30
QUIBBLE			
Am more diverted with a quibble	900	Dean's Reasons	61
QUIBBLES			
For Sherry's Quibbles, and thy Skill	373	Letter D. S-y	49
QUICK			
Would turn so quick you scarce could see't	93	Bauc & Phil 1	132
Turn'd round so quick, you scarce cou'd see't;	113	Bauc & Phil 2	72
But when he lay'd it down, as quick	132	Magician's Rod	13
Lord-Treasurer; for once be quick:	190	Faggot	36
In your last Offices be quick:	204	In Sickness	24
One Coach oft' carried them when they were quick,	430	Dicky Dolly	14
His Diligence and quick Dispatch;	604	Beasts Confess	90
Beneath the vast abyss he plunges quick,	672	Epig Carthy 24	D 17
Now, tan-tan-tan-tan-tan-ti-vi quick quick,	958	Cantata	
Now, tan-tan-tan-tan-tan-ti-vi quick quick,	958	Cantata	
QUICK'NING			
The humble tribe mourn'd for the quick'ning soul,	53	Temple Ill	61
QUICKEST			
The quickest Ship I can surprize,	934	Riddle 21	D 14
QUICKLY			
Will quickly take another course	19	Ode Athenian	116
Consider Humane Folly, and you'll quickly own,	20	Ode Athenian	149
So quickly, and so wonderfully carried on,	24	Ode Athenian	276
Kindled while reason sleeps, but quickly flies,	54	Temple Ill	99
Materials would be quickly spent,	79	Vanbrug House	21
And quickly did the Matter sift,	171	Horace 1, 7	25
So quickly broke if you divide.	189	Faggot	12
"To get my Warrant quickly signed:	201	Horace 2, 6	56
And Wool it is greasy, and quickly takes Fire.	237	Excellent Song	21
Thro' the Zodiack around, it shall quickly be spread,	265	Apollo	69
But we doubt that our Purses will quickly grow lank,	287	Bank Down	14
That Paper would quickly be dearer than Gold,	288	Bank Down	32
The Cause, alas, is quickly guesst,	293	Prog Marriage	101
What Stuff he is made on you quickly may find,	336	Serious Poem	77
. . . 'twould quickly break my Back.	343	Upon His Grace	46
How quickly they neglect their Friends;	408	Dial Rich Marb	20
You quickly see the gudgeon bite,	421	Ireld	23
How great a Change! how quickly made!	590	Strephon Chloe	203
His Crime he quickly understood;	604	Beasts Confess	99
And Dido quickly smoak't the Beau.	619	Scandal Poem 1	72
And Dido quickly smoak'd the Beau.	625	Scandal Poem 2	70
Or, to Passion quickly heated:	630	Epistle Lady	16
Thou hast, as thou shalt quickly see,	695	Cadenus Vaness	292
By reading this Trifle, I quickly began	716	Answer Rebus	13
Your Cable's burst, and you must quickly feel	770	Horace 1, 14	19
Will quickly fall upon the tongue,	983	Sher, A Goose	5
QUIET			
We can't be quiet Night nor day;	90	Bauc & Phil 1	30
I bear it for a quiet Life	220	A Quiet Life	16
His Quiet small, his Credit less;	221	A Quiet Life	42
Slaves to their Quiet and good Name,	221	A Quiet Life	57
Quiet the Raging of the Sea,	258	Bubble	211
Lest my Mobb's Mouth, being seldom quiet	373	Letter D. S-y	66
Here quiet they Lie, in hopes to rise one Day,	431	Dicky Dolly	22
If they would but lye quiet, and stifle their Voice,	519	Dean Hang Rape	63
Cou'd never leave the World in quiet---;	548	Life of Swift	104
Till the People all are quiet	574	Helter Skelter	51
Mention Courts, you'll ne'er be quiet;	635	Epistle Lady	183
No eating in quiet,	853	Lady's Lament	60
Pray, Madam, be quiet; what was it I said?--	870	Grand Question	85
You say it is quiet,	939	Riddle Answerd	7

	PAGE	TITLE	LINE
QUIET (CONTINUED)			
As a good quiet Soul, who no Mischief intends . . .	968	Letter Sherid	27
I can't pray in quiet for you and your verses,-- . . .	976	Dean to Sherid	5
. . .have it at their own House, to drink in quiet. . .	1013	Swift to Sheri	7
QUIETLY			
But lik'd neither loss and so quietly dy'd.	430	Dicky Dolly	12
QUIL			
To Bus'ness shap'd the Poet's Quil, ...	482	Libel on D- D-	66
QUILCA			
Bring all your Quilca cares to Dublin, ...	753	Gift for Bec	24
Be sent to Quilca down to graze;	759	Receipt Youth	26
To kiss your Steps at Quilca Gates;	760	Receipt Youth	48
QUILL			
He suck't his Vittels thro' a Quill;	156	Fable of Midas	10
Among his Brethren of the Quill:	231	Prog of Poetry	20
This Paper they say, by the Help of a Quill, . . .	287	Bank Down	12
And boldly Force the winged Quill	373	Letter D. S-y	53
In my 'scritore lock up my quill?	489	Dialogue	12
The Lead yon Critick's Quill contains, ...	500	Doctor Delaney	15
With a quill stuck across his nose.	983	Sher, A Goose	20
QUILL-MEN			
Their Brother Quill-Men Workers for the Stage, . .	276	Epilogue	41
QUILLS			
Let them with their gosling Quills, ...	831	Legion Club	59
Tom, for a goose you keep but base quills, ...	982	Sher, A Goose	1
QUILT			
The Dean must with his Quilt supply, ...	283	Journal	121
QUIN			
I'm not the Grandson of that Ass Quin;	350	Upright Judge 3	1
QUINTESSENCE			
Was long the quintessence of Beaux;	879	Robbin & Harry	38
QUIRE			
Or Song of feather'd Quire.	123	Empty'ng Town	16
QUIRES			
And sent in Quires to line a Trunk;	644	On Poetry	144
QUIS			
Yet, Neget quis Carmina Gallo.	278	Journal	4
QUIT			
And will quit my best Friends, while I'm Not in game.	144	New Song	26
And squeeze it in, or quit your Place:	190	Faggot	40
Made her retire, and quit her Right, ...	208	Fable Bitches	41
To act with Infamy, or quit the Place.	535	To Mr. Gay	130
E'en quit the House, for thou too long hast sat in't, .	538	Mr. Pulteney	9
If Lintot thinks 'twill quit the Cost, ...	643	On Poetry	109
To quit the true old Angel-Inn.	734	Stel B-day '20	14
Then, who can think we'll quit the Place	735	Stel B-day '20	33
No Length of Time can make you quit	758	Stel B-day '24	49
I hope to quit that awkward Shame	887	Panegyr Dean	17
And flying think to quit the Score, ...	1002	Reply by Dean	11
QUITE			
It quite o'recame the vital Heat,)	16	Ode Athenian	4
He ne'er could overcome her quite, ...	30	Ode to Temple	131
And holy Sancroft's motion quite irregular appears, .	37	Ode Sancroft	81
For, tragedy, he knew, would lose you quite, . . .	47	To Congreve	145
Scrawl'd o'er with Trifles thus, and quite	60	Lady Tablebook	3
'Twould ruin Undertakers quite.	106	V's House	20
For Wit and Humor differ quite, ...	215	To Mr. Delany	23
But you must know he was not quite	375	Apology Lady C	7
"Quite thro' the Tribe of waiting Gentry;	380	Apology Lady C	154
<Lyndsay> mistakes the matter quite, ...	432	Answer Paulus	1
As proper quite	443	Ballyspellin	88
Some Authors say not quite so soon, ...	446	Modern Lady	39
Her Spleen and Fits recover'd quite, ...	451	Modern Lady	216
And quite mistake Preferment's Road.	480	Libel on D- D-	12
From whence 'tis plain, they quite have lost . . .	498	Panegyr Swift	165
"Sir, our Accounts are diff'rent quite, ...	550	Life of Swift	194
"But now, he's quite another Thing;	557	Death of Swift	113
"You know 'tis quite a different Thing.	560	Death of Swift	188
One quite indiff'rent in the Cause, ...	565	Death of Swift	305
He quite forgot to say his Pray'rs.	605	Beasts Confess	118
Her fine Panegyricks are quite out of Season, . . .	716	Answer Rebus	21
Have put the Dean's Politicks quite out of Date; . .	716	Answer Rebus	24
Perhaps you're quite another Thing.	730	Stella, Poems	70
We think you quite mistake the Case;	752	Stel Wood-Park	89
Quite contrary Rebecca's led, ...	761	Bec's B-Day	21
And quite forgot their Country was enslav'd. . . .	771	Horace 1, 14	52
Tim, you mistake the matter quite, ...	776	Mullinix Tim	87
Tom, you mistake the Matter quite;	797	Traulus 1	45
Quite destroy that Harpies Nest, ...	830	Legion Club	29
I'm quite over-run	852	Lady's Lament	13
My spirit's quite shatter'd, ...	853	Lady's Lament	52
Well, if you could lose it quite.	862	To Janus	12
You had like to have put it quite out of my Head. . .	870	Grand Question	86
From these I am recover'd quite, ...	902	Dean's Reasons	99
That quite extinguish't Cupid's Lamp:	905	Death Daphne	98
When you quite mistake the meaning.	908	Daphne	68
So the famous Tom Leigh, when quite run a-ground, . .	968	Letter Sherid	19
QUITS			
No wonder then she quits the narrow Path of Sense . .	18	Ode Athenian	68
QUITTED			
When first for her he quitted Peg.	224	Prog of Love	84

	PAGE	TITLE	LINE
QUITTING			
For quitting her beloved London.	362	Grace's Answer	40
QUIV'RING			
now trembling Shiv'ring Quiv'ring Quaking,	959	Cantata	
QUIXOTE			
That you're Don Quixote Redivivus?	478	Epist on Epist	88
QUO'			
Quo' She, no longer parly;	154	Widow and Cat	D 32
QUONDAM			
My quondam Friends are grown so Cold,	776	Mullinix Tim	78
QUORUM			
No less than Justices o' Quorum,	760	Receipt Youth	45
QUOTATION			
And quote Quotation on Quotation.	649	On Poetry	262
And quote Quotation on Quotation.	649	On Poetry	262
QUOTATIONS			
With sham Quotations Peri Hupsous:	648	On Poetry	256
QUOTE			
We should them Quote, unless for Rhime.	372	Letter D. S-y	28
Of Gods I only quote the best,	465	Birthday Song	149
At Table you can Horace quote;	483	Libel on D- D-	95
Your Horace not content to quote,	494	Panegyr Swift	39
Cou'd quote you Cicero and Livy.	513	Answer Fable	38
"But laugh'd to hear an Idiot quote,	572	Death of Swift	473
Quote you Texts from Plutarch's Morals;	637	Epistle Lady	236
And at all Hazards boldly quote:	648	On Poetry	248
And quote Quotation on Quotation.	649	On Poetry	262
QUOTES			
Quotes from the Bible many a Sentence	605	Beasts Confess	121
QUOTH			
Quoth Neal, whate'er the rest may think,	67	Problem	53
Quoth Ross, for, I'll be sworn, 'twas I.	67	Problem	56
Ladys, quoth Levens, pray forbear,	67	Problem	57
Quoth Herries, fairly putting Cases,	75	Game Traffick	17
Quoth Baucis, this is wholsom Fare,	91	Bauc & Phil 1	63
Sprout, quoth the Man, What's this you tell us?	116	Bauc & Phil 2	157
Quoth Will; thy House is worse than Hell:	220	A Quiet Life	10
I'm rifled, quoth Nell,	245	Irish-Feast	21
Quoth King Robin, our Ribbands I see are too few	389	Order of Bath	1
Quoth the Thief to the Dog; let me into your Door,	395	Dog and Thief	1
Quoth the Dog, I should then be more Villain than you're,	395	Dog and Thief	3
Quoth Marble-Hill, right well I ween,	408	Dial Rich Marb	9
Quoth Hugh of Armagh, "The mob is grown bold."	843	Ay and No	3
"Ay,ay," quoth the Dean, "the cause is old gold."	843	Ay and No	4
"No,no," quoth the Primate, "if causes we sift,	843	Ay and No	5
RABBIT			
A hole where a rabbit	857	Lady's Lament	183
She swills like a sow, and she breeds like a rabbit:	955	Portrait Life	6
RABBLE			
And gives the Whigs and Rabble Sport.	190	Faggot	26
Just as the Rabble please to smile or frown.	210	Earl of Oxford	10
To Choak the Girls, or consume the Rabble;	283	Journal	114
And sav'd him at once from the Shrew and the Rabble;	327	Epigram 1	4
Harangues the Rabble, and is better paid.	364	On Dreams	34
As clever Tom Clinch, while the Rabble was bawling,	399	Tom Clinch	1
For, as the rabble daub, and rifle	436	Answer Paulus	135
Far less the Rabble roar and rail,	450	Modern Lady	186
But, Lord how the Rabble will stare and will gape,	520	Dean Hang Rape	71
Such a Rout and such a Rabble	830	Legion Club	17
But a Rabble of Tenants, and rusty dull Rumms;	868	Grand Question	28
Strengthens the Shoes of half the Rabble.	942	Probatur Alit	12
RABBLE'S			
Of pissing in the Rabble's Eyes.	787	Dick's Variety	6
RACE			
Has finish'd its short Race of Chance,	10	Ode to King	137
That Poets were a numerous Race,	79	Vanbrug House	18
Observ'd, they grew a num'rous Race.	106	V's House	18
We toast Confusion to the Race of Kings:	162	Toland's Invit	14
Poor Celia, but of mortall Race	229	Prog of Beauty	106
And, like a Jockey for a Race,	231	Prog of Poetry	39
A savage Race by Shipwrecks fed,	256	Bubble	154
The Manners of the rural Race,	270	Apollo's Edict	D 30
The Glory of the Granard Race;	272	Apollo's Edict	D 67
The Founder of thy antient Race.	323	Pethox	4
Your Blood in ev'ry Noble Race!	325	Pethox	70
Because, among all human Race,	366	Answer Delaney	7
And Travels not, but runs a Race.	398	Earl of P-b-w	9
Were seen contending in a Race;	412	Desire Possess	11
To have both male & female Race,	460	Birthday Song	6
Attended by her heavenly Race,	466	Birthday Song	184
Since you alone of all the Race	498	Panegyr Swift	171
Vain human Kind! Fantastick Race!	555	Death of Swift	39
"His Time was come, he ran his Race;	562	Death of Swift	241
"A servile Race in Folly nurs'd,	568	Death of Swift	397
"Offending Race of Human Kind,	579	Day Judgement	11
Thus, a Greyhound out-runs the whole Pack in a Race,	580	Psyche	5
Confest her of no mortal Race:	584	Strephon Chloe	8
How Semele of mortal Race,	587	Strephon Chloe	107
A Deed unknown to Female Race,	595	Cassinus Peter	69
Nor to the chatt'ring feather'd Race,	597	Cassinus Peter	111

RACE	(CONTINUED)		PAGE	TITLE	LINE
	For libelling the Four-foot Race.		607	Beasts Confess	202
	This Cloud produc'd a race of Centaurs		619	Scandal Poem 1	59
	Compare us then to femal race!		620	Scandal Poem 1	95
	His Cloud produc'd a Race of Centaurs,		625	Scandal Poem 2	55
	Compare Us then to Female Race!		626	Scandal Poem 2	93
	All Human Race wou'd fain be Wits,		640	On Poetry	1
	But search among the rhiming Race,		651	On Poetry	327
	In Creatures of the rhiming Race.		653	On Poetry	386
	You dignify the noble Race,		656	On Poetry	457
	He shap'd a King to rule ye Race		659	On Poetry	D 410
	Before one race of his was run;		675	Curate's Compl	15
	The Race of Lovers soon must end:)		713	Cadenus Vaness	863
	"They were a senseless, stupid Race:		714	Cadenus Vaness	871
	For, none among the upstart Race		739	Stel B-day '21	13
	For Virtue in her daily Race,		765	Stel B-day '26	73
	The glorious Founder of their kingly Race:		790	St. Pat's Well	12
	I sent you Millions of the croaking Race;		792	St. Pat's Well	54
	From his Father's scoundrel Race,		800	Traulus 2	24
	Human Race, or Imps of Hell.		801	Traulus 2	56
	All human Race must hither draw:		922	Riddle 7	24
	Nor have I bred a spurious Race;		925	Riddle 8	23
	Emblem of the Cyclops' race;		936	Riddle 24	D 16
	For Pegasus runs, runs every Race		956	Cantata	
RACER					
	This Racer wou'd prove but a dull founder'd Jade.		717	Answer Rebus	28
RACK					
	Can'st hourly set him on the Rack,		325	Pethox	54
	And Yet the Land I from him hold is set so on the Rack		343	Upon His Grace	45
	"To rob the Church, their Tenants rack,		571	Death of Swift	448
	Your damnable Riddle, my poor Brains did rack nigh.		972	S-'s Ans Sh-d	2
RACK'D					
	The copy's false, and sense is rack'd:		434	Answer Paulus	67
	Think, Peter, how my Soul is rack'd.		596	Cassinus Peter	97
	By your knife to be mangled than rack'd with your voice.		818	Epigr Kite	4
RACKS					
	"For Massacres, and Racks, and Flames,		183	Horace 2, 1	95
RACKT					
	Lies rackt with Pain, and you without:		554	Death of Swift	28
RADCLIFF					
	An offer'd Fee from Radcliff scorns;		811	Bro Protestant	16
RADIANT					
	To see some radiant Nymph appear		591	Strephon Chloe	227
	Compare her radiant eyes to Lightning:		621	Scandal Poem 1	150
	Compare her radiant Eyes to Light'ning;		628	Scandal Poem 2	154
	And radiant Iris in the Pox.		729	Stella, Poems	48
	Adieu bright Wit, and radiant Eyes;		757	Stel B-day '24	27
	And strongly shoot a radiant Dart,		764	Stel B-day '26	33
RADIENT					
	Polish'd neck, and radient eye;		936	Riddle 24	D 14
RADIUS					
	The cord, or the radius, it matters not whether,		1027	Sheri Circles	17
RAFFLING-ROOMS					
	In musick, Raffling-rooms, and Toys,		294	Prog Marriage	136
RAFTER					
	Aloft rose ev'ry Beam and Rafter,		92	Bauc & Phil 1	93
	Aloft rose ev'ry Beam and Rafter,		112	Bauc & Phil 2	53
RAG					
	. . .ty'd in a Rag, the Money was found.		70	Mrs Harris Pet	23
	No, not a rag,		441	Ballyspellin	46
	To seek an old rag in the closet.		756	Dingley Brent	18
	She was ringing very sorry, her tongue tied up with rag;		840	Ballad	D 8
RAGE					
	And with blind Rage break all this peaceful Government;		25	Ode Athenian	300
	The giddy turns of pop'lar rage,		38	Ode Sancroft	117
	Provoke the honour of my Muse's rage,		42	Ode Sancroft	262
	As some fair pile, yet spar'd by zeal and rage,		52	Temple Ill	47
	(Whether thro' Rage or Love, or both)		84	Salamander	52
	Then full of Rage Apollo Spoke,		121	Apollo Outwit	49
	Old Aches throb, your hollow Tooth will rage.		137	City Shower	10
	And proud Roxana fir'd with jealous Rage,		275	Epilogue	25
	Struck all his Rage and Malice down;		340	Arch-Bish Dub	20
	To regal Rage devotes some Patriot's Head.		364	On Dreams	12
	And now, inflame'd with rival Rage,		385	Manly Virtue	43
	Deserves your Satire's keenest Rage;		392	Young's Satire	34
	With rage impatient makes me wait		420	Holyhead	27
	Inspire you with poetick Rage;		462	Birthday Song	68
	Why all this rage? Why these complaints?		487	Irish-Club	8
	Discovers freedom without rage;		490	Dialogue	28
	Or could my Muse exert the Rage		496	Panegyr Swift	100
	And dread no more the Rage of Grub,		502	Doctor Delaney	63
	A Rat your utmost Rage defyes		504	Doctor Delaney	137
	There let him starve, and vent his Rage.		515	Answer Fable	84
	Wou'd make him rage, and storm, and fret,		546	Life of Swift	28
	"Vow'd on the Dean his Rage to vent,		570	Death of Swift	423
	Might well excuse a Stoick's Rage.		603	Beasts Confess	58
	To burst with Envy, Spite, and Rage,		611	By Dr. Swift	11
	In a Jest I spend my Rage:		635	Epistle Lady	168
	I may storm and rage in vain;		636	Epistle Lady	209
	Fill'd with Disdain, with Rage inflam'd,		699	Cadenus Vaness	404
	And factious Rage, and Breach of Trust,		725	To Stella	46

```
RAGE              (CONTINUED)                          PAGE   TITLE           LINE
    Thus Ajax, when with Rage possesst     . . . . . . . .   731 Stella, Poems     121
    I began to rage and fret      . . . . . . . . . .        832 Legion Club        94
RAGES
    When Syrius o'er the welkin rages,     . . . . . . . .   618 Scandal Poem 1     33
    When Syrius o'er the Welkin rages      . . . . . . . .   624 Scandal Poem 2     31
    He rages and frets,  . . . . . . . . . . .              855 Lady's Lament      141
RAGGED
    Ragged, and not a Groat betwixt 'em.   . . . . . . . .    90 Bauc & Phil 1     10
    Till the small ragged Flock is met.    . . . . . . . .   127 Little House       22
    Harry look'd fierce, and shook his ragged Mane:  . . .  168 Peace Dunkirk      17
    Ye Poets ragged and forlorn,    . . . . . . . .         394 Grub-Street         1
    A ragged Shirt, and tawny Hyde.    . . . . . .          594 Cassinus Peter     16
    Bright Phillis mending ragged Smocks,  . . . . . . .    729 Stella, Poems      47
RAGING
    Quiet the Raging of the Sea,    . . . . . . . . .       258 Bubble            211
    Why ever in these raging Fits,  . . . . . . . . .       773 Mullinix Tim        3
RAGMAN
    And for his Victuals let a Ragman dish'em.   . . . . . 1033 Ans to Crown       18
RAGOUS
    From haughty Gaul to make Ragous.   . . . . . . .       895 Panegyr Dean      264
RAGS
    'Tis happy to see the whole Kingdom in Rags,   . . . .  287 Bank Down          16
    For Rags will make Paper, and Pa-ba-ba-brags,  . . .    287 Bank Down          17
    For Beggars have Rags and Rags will make Paper,  . .    287 Bank Down          22
    For Beggars have Rags and Rags will make Paper,  . .    287 Bank Down          22
    Pulls out the Rags contriv'd to prop   . . . . . . .    582 Young Nymph        21
    Flutters the feeble Pamphlet into Rags.    . . . .      771 Horace 1, 14       30
    "Shall rent her Petticoats to Rags,    . . . . . . .    850 Old Thorn          63
    Anon in Beggar's Rags appear;   . . . . . . . . .       935 Riddle 23        D 21
RAIL    SEE RAYL
    To censure, to cry down, and rail,  . . . . . .          19 Ode Athenian      114
    No province now is left her but to rail,   . . . . .     38 Ode Sancroft      110
    Yet want your critics no just cause to rail,   . . . .    45 To Congreve        65
    On thee to wreak the tribute when I rail;  . . . . .     53 Temple Ill         86
    To rail; she singing, still whirls on her Mop.   . . .  137 City Shower        22
    The Dutch-hearted Whigs may rail and complain;   . . .  169 Peace Dunkirk      37
    Thou'lt rail devoutly at the Peace,    . . . . . . .    180 Horace 2, 1        15
    To show their Parts, will scold and rail,  . . . . .    216 To Mr. Delany      49
    Far less the Rabble roar and rail,     . . . . . . .    450 Modern Lady       186
    While thus they rail, and scold, and storm,  . . . .    453 Modern Lady       270
    To rail at men by nature fools:    . . . . . . .        488 Irish-Club         28
    To rail, and go unpunish'd too;    . . . . . . . .      492 Panegyr Swift       4
    On you shall rail and criticize;   . . . . . . .        651 On Poetry         332
    Who at them rail bid God Confound:     . . . . . . .    658 On Poetry        D 190
    As Popish Craft? Did he not rail on't?     . . . . .    774 Mullinix Tim       19
    I'll Sputter, Swagger, Curse and Rail,     . . . . .    776 Mullinix Tim       85
    Begs leave to rail, but <damn> his Blood,  . . . . .    797 Traulus 1          55
    And, while at good Cashel you rail with such spite,  . 818 Archbi Cashel       3
RAILING
    Railing a Rule of Wit, and Obloquy a Trade,    . . .     18 Ode Athenian       84
    And, placing Raillery in Railing,  . . . . . . . .      416 Woman's Mind       19
    And, thy Raillery is Railing.   . . . . . . . . .       523 Betty Grizette     28
    "For railing at the Royal Martyr.  . . . . . . .       549 Life of Swift     167
RAILLERY
    But Raillery, for once, apart,  . . . . . . . . .        87 Hist V's House     43
    Your Raillery is misapply'd:    . . . . . . . . .       175 Horace 1, 7       132
    Are Humor, Raillery and Witt:   . . . . . . . . .       215 To Mr. Delany      14
    'Twixt Raillery and gross Abuse,   . . . . . . .        216 To Mr. Delany      48
    Till banist by some Coxcombs Raillery;     . . . . .    294 Prog Marriage     142
    And, placing Raillery in Railing,  . . . . . . . .      416 Woman's Mind       19
    The rules of raillery and breeding,    . . . . . .      489 Dialogue            4
    Irish Nymphs learn Irish Raillery:     . . . . . .      523 Betty Grizette     26
    And, thy Raillery is Railing.   . . . . . . . . .       523 Betty Grizette     28
    But, with Raillery to nettle,   . . . . . . . . .       636 Epistle Lady      211
    No Raillery gives just Offence  . . . . . . . . .       747 Stel Distress      61
    Yet Raillery gives no Offence,  . . . . . . . . .       752 Stel Wood-Park     77
    For though my Raillery were true,  . . . . . . .        752 Stel Wood-Park     91
RAILLY
    From both, we learn to Railly well;    . . . . . . .    216 To Mr. Delany      31
RAILLY'D
    They railly'd next Vanessa's Dress;    . . . . . . .    699 Cadenus Vaness    396
    She railly'd well, he always knew,     . . . . . . .    707 Cadenus Vaness    660
RAILS
    Lesbia for ever on me rails;    . . . . . . . . .       679 From Catullus       1
    He rails at my person:  . . . . . . . . . . .          853 Lady's Lament      68
RAIN
    The first of Plants after the Thunder, Storm, and Rain  16 Ode Athenian       28
    While Rain depends, the pensive Cat gives o'er   . . .  136 City Shower         3
    'Twas doubtful which was Rain, and which was Dust.  .   137 City Shower        26
    When Dust and Rain at once his Coat invade;  . . . .    138 City Shower        28
    His only Coat, where Dust confus'd with Rain,  . . .    138 City Shower        29
    The faded Bow distilling Rain.  . . . . . . . .         290 Prog Marriage      14
    Which only Winter's Rain supplies.     . . . . . .      478 Epist on Epist     90
    With Sun-shine, rain, and hail, and snow.  . . . .      621 Scandal Poem 1    130
    With Sun-shine, Rain, and Hail, or Snow.   . . . .      627 Scandal Poem 2    124
    With two pence left, walks home in rain.   . . . . .    878 Robbin & Harry      8
    May I be doom'd for Life to weed in Rain.  . . . .      882 Pastoral Dial      44
    A rotten Cabbin, dropping Rain;    . . . . . . .       1035 To Quilca           2
RAIN'D
    It rain'd as hard as it could pour,    . . . . . . .     90 Bauc & Phil 1     11
```

RAINS

	PAGE	TITLE	LINE
When Rains descend, and Tempests rise,	84	Salamander	34
Half choak'd with dust, half drown'd with rains;	403	Window Inns 10 D	6
You, when it rains, like Fools believe,	627	Scandal Poem 2	125

RAINY

	PAGE	TITLE	LINE
'Twas a sad rainy Night--but the Morning is fine--	869	Grand Question	74
On rainy Days alone I dine,	954	Authors Living	1
On rainy Days, I dine alone,	954	Authors Living	3

RAIS'D

	PAGE	TITLE	LINE
Well--tho' you've rais'd Her to this high Degree,	24	Ode Athenian	263
Our selves are rais'd as well as she,	24	Ode Athenian	264
Nor be thy mighty spirit rais'd,	42	Ode Sancroft	263
Might seem, when first she rais'd her eyes to mine.	52	Temple Ill	30
So when the War has rais'd a Storm	84	Salamander	37
You've rais'd a Church here in a Minute,	94	Bauc & Phil 1	161
That, rais'd by Magick of her Breech,	132	Magician's Rod	17
Rais'd up on Hope's aspiring Plumes,	252	Bubble	33
Ye bubbles rais'd by breath of Kings;	296	Satiric Elegy	26
No Temple, to his Godship rais'd,	346	Prometheus	43
Rais'd high above his Birth by Knowledge,	384	Manly Virtue	33
(Rais'd high like some celestial Fire	385	Manly Virtue	53
Yet more display'd, and rais'd his own.	386	Manly Virtue	88
Now rais'd on high, see, Virtue shews	386	Manly Virtue	97
Rais'd ever such incessant Rout:	450	Modern Lady	183
Such gaudy Tulips rais'd from Dung.	530	Lady's Dres Rm	144
Our Equal rais'd above our Size;	554	Death of Swift	14
Rais'd on a Basis unsecure?	593	Strephon Chloe	300
As when a lofty Pile is rais'd,	727	Stella, Poems	1
The Students drinking, rais'd their Wit and Parts;	793	St. Pat's Well	70
That rais'd between the Stones their daily Shoots;	880	Pastoral Dial	4
How have I felt my Spirits rais'd,	887	Panegyr Dean	13
But, you have rais'd your gen'rous Mind	893	Panegyr Dean	197
Rais'd up by you in twenty Weeks:	893	Panegyr Dean	204
For those who rais'd me, I betray;	917	Riddle 3	12
I saw thee rais'd to high Renown,	919	Riddle 5	5
I'm but an Idol rais'd on high;	926	Riddle 9	18

RAISE

	PAGE	TITLE	LINE
The glorious Structure of Your Fame to raise;	11	Ode to William D	6
Raise envy's clouds to leave themselves in night,	45	To Congreve	79
Would raise a House about two Storyes;	79	Vanbrug House	10
His Birth he does from Phoebus raise;	80	Vanbrug House	41
Might raise a House about two Stories;	106	V's House	10
Can raise a Lodging for a Song.	106	V's House	16
To raise a Roof with Act the Fift.	108	V's House	92
To raise the Lumber from the Earth.	231	Prog of Poetry	30
To brew her Ale, and raise her Paste:	282	Journal	90
You raise Desire as well as Pride,	292	Prog Marriage	74
Nay would it not Your Passion raise	312	To Ford	37
To choque your Sight, and raise your Malice)	313	To Ford	64
To raise me to a high Degree:	408	Dial Rich Marb	16
To raise the Stairs, or build the Cieling;	409	Dial Rich Marb	26
Whoe'er will raise	442	Ballyspellin	79
"To raise up Virtue when she droops,	462	Birthday Song	74
No wonder when you raise and level,	477	Epist on Epist	65
He'll Grieve he did not raise you higher,	484	Libel on D- D-	118
But raise your Fancy on the Wing;	501	Doctor Delaney	55
When you pertly raise your Snout,	523	Betty Grizette	31
To raise his Post, or fill his Coffers,	549	Life of Swift	139
Though it would raise him to the Lawn:	604	Beasts Confess	104
And, so absurd, that could I raise up	607	Beasts Confess	199
Can raise them up, or sink them down,	620	Scandal Poem 1	91
Can raise them up, or sink them down,	626	Scandal Poem 2	89
To raise the Volume's Price, a Shilling.)	648	On Poetry	254
You raise the Honour of the Peerage,	656	On Poetry	455
And yet she would raise me I know,--by a halter	664	Epigram Bust	4
Which raise a Flame that will endure	691	Cadenus Vaness	144
All humble Worth she strove to raise;	701	Cadenus Vaness	456
True Poets can depress and raise;	729	Stella, Poems	53
See! as you raise it from its Tomb,	743	Stel B-day 22	67
To raise up Stella's virtue higher;	755	Stella '23	22
A Drone can raise a Hornet's Nest.	798	Traulus 1	84
Raise the Dirt about your Hole.	832	Legion Club	74
Must raise a Fort at Market-Hill.	883	Rev Market-Hill	16
Now raise your Spirits, Mr. <Dean>:	889	Panegyr Dean	85
Permit me then to raise my Style,	894	Panegyr Dean	227
And what will raise your Admiration,	927	Riddle 10 D	7
And raise a Virgin to the Sky,	929	Riddle 15 D	7

RAISING

	PAGE	TITLE	LINE
To shut out the River by raising the Bank.	287	Bank Down	5
Of raising Spirits from below;	920	Riddle 6	10

RAKE

	PAGE	TITLE	LINE
To a forlorn and broken Rake,	133	Magician's Rod	33
But some gay coxcomb, or a rake.	177	To Lord Harley	22
Dan leaves the Earthly Spade and Rake,	279	Journal	32
"A Rake, a Bully, Pimp, or Spy.	303	Storm	30
His Window scrawl'd by ev'ry Rake,	400	Window Inns 1	5
<Zounds> who wou'd be a Rake?	426	Five Ladies	36
Wou'd be a Rake, but wanted Sense.	455	Dean Smedley	6
No drunken Rake to pick her up,	581	Young Nymph	5
To pass for Wits before a Rake!	592	Strephon Chloe	268
The drunken Quarrels of a Rake,	724	To Stella	24

		PAGE	TITLE	LINE
RAKE	(CONTINUED)			
Except a Blockhead or a Rake		733	Verses Vanessa	20
No more that Bry'r thy tender Leg shall rake: . . .		881	Pastoral Dial	17
No new-flux't Rake shew'd fairer Skin;		904	Death Daphne	37
And look'd like a Rake, who was made in the Stews sick;		1029	Dr. Helsham	18
RAKE-WELL				
By Nature turn'd to play the Rake-well, ...		446	Modern Lady	36
RAKES				
The Statesman rakes the Town to find a Plot, . . .		364	On Dreams	19
Fools, Fops, and Rakes, for Chaff and Straws. . . .		688	Cadenus Vaness	60
RAKING				
Raking up Mud to build a Wall;		87	Hist V's House	18
RALLY				
Rally her dress, her language, and her gait;		50	To Congreve	218
RAMBLE				
For a dear Ramble thro' Impertinence, ...		18	Ode Athenian	69
Nor need I ramble far to force a rule, ...		46	To Congreve	113
RAMBLES				
At one she rambles to the Shops		291	Prog Marriage	51
RAMBLING				
Fly, fly, above, above the Sky Rambling, ...		959	Cantata	
Gambling, Rambling, Gambling.		959	Cantata	
RAMINES				
And fly with Hurry to Ramines;		1002	Reply by Dean	8
RAMPANT				
Let Sir <Tom>, that rampant Ass, ...		831	Legion Club	63
RAMPART				
Shall scale the Rampart with your Bands.		884	Rev Market-Hill	54
RAMPING				
Cutting Capers and Ramping, ...		245	Irish-Feast	38
RAN				
But gath'ring spirits, wisely ran for't, ...		64	Discovery	46
Now Poets from all Quarters ran		108	V's House	95
A School-boy ran unto't and thought, ...		127	Little House	29
He ran, he leapt into the Flood, ...		255	Bubble	130
Ran under Ground from Greece to Brittain, ...		293	Prog Marriage	112
All ran to Pray'rs, both Priests and Laity, ...		353	Wood Ironmongr	21
The Maids to the Doors and the Balconies ran, . . .		399	Tom Clinch	7
"His Time was come, he ran his Race;		562	Death of Swift	241
Call'd up at Mid-night, ran to save		604	Beasts Confess	115
Thro' all the brutal Species ran, ...		659	On Poetry	D 410
Then Stella ran to my Relief		726	To Stella	101
Punch roaring ran, and running roar'd.		776	Mullinix Tim	112
Ran to the Glass, and then comparing		783	Tim and Fables	14
Do but hear on the Clergy how glib his Tongue ran; .		872	Grand Question	140
Thus merciless Hannah ran on in her Talk, ...		873	Grand Question	179
But, when espous'd, he ran the fate		879	Robbin & Harry	39
RANCOUR				
For Traulus long his Rancour nurst, ...		796	Traulus 1	17
If still your foul bosom more rancour contains; . .		819	Archbi Cashel	12
RANDOM				
Nor shall his Darts at random fly		272	Apollo's Edict	D 58
Nor shall we think you talk at random, ...		465	Birthday Song	159
Nor, in their Eyes at Random pisses, ...		796	Traulus 1	29
RANG				
Because he rang the Bell.		406	Swift to Pope	28
Than if it rang out for my Knell:		674	His Deafness	4
RANG'D				
Were now but leathern Buckets rang'd.		93	Bauc & Phil 1	116
Were now but Leathern Buckets rang'd.		114	Bauc & Phil 2	92
Thro' Nature, and thro' Art she rang'd, ...		698	Cadenus Vaness	354
RANGE				
He found her Thoughts would absent range, ...		704	Cadenus Vaness	566
Must let their Cattle range in vain		759	Receipt Youth	5
RANK SEE OVER-RANK				
Some Mischief is Brewing, the Project smells Rank, .		287	Bank Down	4
Hircina rank with Sweat, presumes		449	Modern Lady	158
"No Fools of Rank, a mungril Breed, ...		570	Death of Swift	437
Whose rank Imagination fills, ...		592	Strephon Chloe	279
Like his Body, rank and foul:		800	Traulus 2	34
Nor, of your Rank will bate an Ace, ...		888	Panegyr Dean	47
And cure the Rank unsav'ry Smelling.		892	Panegyr Dean	166
RANKS				
The Waiters stand in Ranks; the Yeomen cry, . . .		194	Author Himself	35
Whose Off'rings plac't in golden Ranks, ...		896	Panegyr Dean	301
RANT				
Your tragick Heroes shall not rant, ...		270	Apollo's Edict	D 27
He began as he bragg'd, with a rant and a roar; . .		816	Yahoo's	43
Sufficient it were, one would think, in your mad rant, .		1026	Sheri Circles	9
RANTS				
Where ev'ry Trout can make as high Rants		824	Printer Newgat	5
RAP				
He can Rap his own Raps, and has the true Sapience .		335	Serious Poem	47
But now they hear a Foot-Man's Rap:		451	Modern Lady	211
And Smithfield, as Rap was ne'er colted before; . .		817	Yahoo's	57
RAPE				
The vilest Ruffian may commit a rape, ...		506	To a Friend	3
To disappoint Ixion's rape		619	Scandal Poem 1	53
To disappoint Ixion's Rape, ...		625	Scandal Poem 2	49
The worst you can say, he committed a <Rape>. . . .		516	Dean Hang Rape	6
To a Room full of Guests for fear of a <Rape>. . . .		517	Dean Hang Rape	12

		PAGE	TITLE	LINE

RAPE (CONTINUED)

And this was no Time for committing a <Rape>. . . . 517 Dean Hang Rape 18
And got a good Clap, but committed no <Rape>. . . . 517 Dean Hang Rape 24
In ev'ry Debauch, but committing a <Rape>. . . . 517 Dean Hang Rape 30
For no other Crime but committing a <Rape>. . . . 518 Dean Hang Rape 36
Be put to the Peril, and Toyl of a <Rape>? . . . 518 Dean Hang Rape 42
For Sodomy hang'd, as thou for a <Rape>. . . . . 518 Dean Hang Rape 48
For thou hast not a Groat to Attone for a <Rape>. . 519 Dean Hang Rape 54
And hang'd he must be for committing a <Rape>. . . 519 Dean Hang Rape 60
Ty'd round the <Dean's> Neck, for committing a <Rape>. 519 Dean Hang Rape 66
When the good <English> <Dean> is hang'd up for a
  <Rape>. 520 Dean Hang Rape 72

RAPID

They, as each Torrent drives, with rapid Force . . . 139 City Shower 57
Of loud un-meaning Sounds, a rapid Flood . . . . . 532 To Mr. Gay 39

RAPINE

By Rapine, Theft, or Thirst of Blood. . . . . . . 602 Beasts Confess 20
Sloth, Folly, Rapine, Mischeif, Lust . . . . . . 659 On Poetry D 410

RAPP'D

Rapp'd through the wide expanse of thought, ... 36 Ode Sancroft 62

RAPPAREE

"So when poor Irish Rapparee, ... 497 Panegyr Swift 128

RAPPAREES

Despises rapparees, and rides . . . . 435 Answer Paulus 97
"Go Snacks with Thieves and Rapparees, ... 571 Death of Swift 449

RAPS

He can Rap his own Raps, and has the true Sapience . 335 Serious Poem 47
Strong Tubs for his Raps, Two thousand and more; . . 337 Serious Poem 96
These Raps he will honestly dig out with Shovels, . 337 Serious Poem 97
This Coyner of Raps in a Cauldron of Oyl. . . . . 352 Wood Insect 38
Give your Head some gentle Raps; . . . . 638 Epistle Lady 264

RAPT

Rapt in the Vortex of the Brittish Star; . . . . . 10 Ode to King 139
When rapt in Heav'nly Airs, he sings . . . . . 496 Panegyr Swift 102
Still rapt in speculations deep, ... 900 Dean's Reasons 45

RAPTURE

The Mariner with Rapture sees . . . . . 251 Bubble 26
"With Rapture, what they wont to flee. . . . . 384 Manly Virtue 14
Desire, in Rapture gaz'd a while, ... 413 Desire Possess 45
On Love and Books in Rapture sweet; . . . . . . 593 Cassinus Peter 4

RAPTURES

Till one in Raptures thus began . . . . 109 V's House 107
What endless Raptures must he find! . . . . . . 587 Strephon Chloe 96
High Raptures, and romantick Flights; . . . . . 590 Strephon Chloe 198
For why such Raptures, Flights, and Fancies, . . . 711 Cadenus Vaness 794

RARE

He'd treat with nothing that was Rare, ... 378 Apology Lady C 99
Simplicity alone is rare; . . . . 378 Apology Lady C 106
A Paste of Composition rare, ... 526 Lady's Dres Rm 23
His guests are few, his visits rare, ... 901 Dean's Reasons 85
I, a virtue strange and rare, ... 936 Riddle 24 D 5

RARELY

By my Hand, you dance rarely, ... 246 Irish-Feast 47
You rarely bite, are always bit: . . . . 651 On Poetry 330
But rarely seen, and seen from far: . . . . . . 696 Cadenus Vaness 307

RARER

And myself, which yet is rarer, ... 936 Riddle 24 D 7

RARY-SHOW

There you shall see a Rary-Show . . . . 362 Grace's Answer 29

RASCAL

Dispatch; or else that Rascal Northey, ... 190 Faggot 41
A Storm, to drown that Rascal <Hort>, ... 302 Storm 5
To lick a Rascal Statesman's Spittle. . . . . . 482 Libel on D- D- 82
To lick a Rascal Statesman's Spittle, ... 495 Panegyr Swift 59
Nay, though the treach'rous Rascal Thomas . . . . 734 Stel B-day '20 9
The Rascal had mistook the Door: . . . . 746 Stel Distress 28
The Rascal had mistook the Door . . . . 746 Stel Distress
The Rascal had mistook the Door: . . . . 751 Stel Wood-Park 48
--The rascal! that's too mild a name; . . . . . 950 Upstart D 1

RASCALLS

For shame! two sturdy Rascalls beg; . . . . . . 91 Bauc & Phil 1 44

RASCALLY

Those rascally paviours who did us undermine, . . . 841 Ballad D 18

RASCALS

And made the Rascals pay him dearly . . . . . . 463 Birthday Song 105
And swore the fawning Rascals ly'd: . . . . . . 657 On Poetry 476
Then give those Rascals cause to laugh. . . . . . 778 Mullinix Tim 178
Shall Tory Rascals be Elected, ... 779 Mullinix Tim 189
To be but <rascals> in the lump. . . . . 435 Answer Paulus 106
Ye <rascals> of inferior note, ... 487 Irish-Club 3

RASH

Ah Lovely Nymph be not too rash, ... 228 Prog of Beauty 67
Rash Mortals, e'er you take a Wife, ... 593 Strephon Chloe 301

RASHLY

For Instance: When you rashly think, ... 654 On Poetry 393

RASHNESS

The Rashness of the Cretan Youth, ... 252 Bubble 42

RAT

With many a Mouse, and many a Rat, ... 153 Widow and Cat D 4
A Rat your utmost Rage defyes . . . . 504 Doctor Delaney 137
A wicked Rat her Plaister stole, ... 583 Young Nymph 59

RAT	(CONTINUED)		PAGE	TITLE	LINE
	Has made a Rat our Fellow-Creature.	. . . . . .	812	Bro Protestant	34
	That I saw a huge Rat: O dear, how I scream'd!	. .	868	Grand Question	50
RATE	SEE O'RE-RATE				
	You bought it at a cheaper Rate;	. . . .	28	Ode to Temple	73
	Treated at this ungodly Rate	. . . .	91	Bauc & Phil 1	48
	Treated at this ungodly Rate,	. . . .	111	Bauc & Phil 2	16
	Alcides, one of second Rate.	. . . .	160	Atlas	18
	Rides Day and Night at such a Rate,	. . . . .	174	Horace 1, 7	117
	Nell serv'd him at the usu'll Rate	. . . . . .	221	A Quiet Life	43
	Glad to compound at any Rate;	. . . . . .	378	Apology Lady C	94
	And sell their Votes at such a Rate,	. . . . . .	392	Young's Satire	43
	At any rate,	. . . .	441	Ballyspellin	50
	And buy distinction at the dearest rate.	. . . .	506	To a Friend	12
	Nor, at an under Rate his Timber sell;	. . . . .	534	To Mr. Gay	95
	Must, at the Rate that he goes on,	. . . . . .	606	Beasts Confess	167
	Might furnish a Second Rate Poet a Year:	. . . .	716	Answer Rebus	18
RATED					
	I scolded and rated;	. . . .	1014	Swift to Sheri	16
RATES					
	By all means to bring down the Rates,	. . . . . .	64	Discovery	42
	Nam'd half the Rates, and lik'd the worst.	. . . . . .	698	Cadenus Vaness	383
	Their rights! their importance! We'll set on new rates	.	816	Yahoo's	32
RATHER					
	Had rather water'd it, than drown'd:	. . . .	17	Ode Athenian	43
	And rather Tite than Great;	. . . .	23	Ode Athenian	231
	Rather forgive what my first Transport said,	. . .	23	Ode Athenian	244
	Rather put on thy anger and thy spight,	. . . .	37	Ode Sancroft	86
	And as the Boding Owl, or rather	. . . .	99	Elegy Patrige	49
	For rather than hang, I would be Not in game.	. .	144	New Song	34
	Swore he'd rather lose a Crown,	. . . .	168	Peace Dunkirk	19
	She'd rather take you to her Bed	. . . . .	222	Prog of Love	7
	But the Cobler was angry, and swore he had rather	. .	287	Bank Down	26
	Rather than starve, a better man would strole.	. . . .	308	Billet Players	16
	Unless, like the Dutch, you rather would boyl	. . .	352	Wood Insect	37
	Else, rather on this bleaky shore	. . ·	420	Holyhead	29
	And we shall take you rather	. . . .	426	Five Ladies	17
	We rather should Lament his Case	. . . .	485	Libel on D- D-	159
	Rather than thus be over-topt,	. . . .	554	Death of Swift	25
	But rather than they should excel,	. . . .	554	Death of Swift	33
	He'd rather chuse that I should dye,	. . . . . .	557	Death of Swift	131
	"Would rather slip aside, and chuse	. . . .	565	Death of Swift	321
	Yet would rather be hang'd than he'd leave a warm Place.		580	Psyche	6
	Your Annual Bard had rather chose	. . . . . .	756	Stel B-day '24	5
	I'd rather hang my self by half,	. . . .	778	Mullinix Tim	177
	While I, with humble Job, had rather,	. . . . .	813	Bro Protestant	61
	For I'd rather be dead,	. . . .	853	Lady's Lament	55
	I would rather chuse those:)	. . . .	858	Lady's Lament	214
	And rather than that, I would lose my Estate.	. . .	867	Grand Question	24
	I'd rather the Bawn were sunk under Ground.	. . . .	868	Grand Question	46
	And rather than come in the same Pair of Sheets	. .	869	Grand Question	59
	Without it I rather would walk on the Ground.	. . .	941	Letter	26
	Saunders said I, I would rather than a Quart of Ale,	.	987	Mary to Sher	31
	Seem rather to renew my Grief,	. . . .	1005	Sheridan's Sub	30
	. . .although they like your Wine; but they had rather	. .	1013	Swift to Sheri	7
RATIONAL					
	A constant, rational Delight,	. . . .	711	Cadenus Vaness	781
RATLING					
	And serve to eccho ratling Nonsense;	. . . . . .	461	Birthday Song	44
RATS					
	To banish Rats that haunt our Vault.	. . . . . .	892	Panegyr Dean	162
RATTEEN					
	And Anthony shall Court her in Ratteen.	. . . . .	275	Epilogue	20
RATTLE					
	To rattle Moody for Neglect;	. . . .	411	Dial Rich Marb	96
	Than the Dean storm, or Stella rattle.	. . . . . .	762	Bec's B-Day	56
	To rattle in their Ears your Drum.	. . . .	775	Mullinix Tim	50
	Then I clash and roar, and rattle,	. . . . . .	933	Riddle 20	D 21
	Among the Coals does often rattle.	. . . . . .	942	Probatur Alit	2
RATTLES					
	Rattles for Infant Royalty to play withal,	. . . .	6	Ode to King	13
RATTLING					
	Drives rattling o'er a brazen Arch:	. . . . . .	353	Wood Ironmongr	18
	The Cymbals rattling Sounds dispell	. . . . . .	354	Simile Silver	11
	Hear the rattling Thunder drop,	. . . .	830	Legion Club	22
	My wife a rattling,	. . . .	1037	Sheridan Cavan	1
RAV'D					
	Why certainly the Captain rav'd?	. . . .	376	Apology Lady C	36
	They on the Gold Brocades and Satins rav'd,	. . . .	771	Horace 1, 14	51
RAV'NOUS					
	But, how can I describe the rav'nous Breed?	. . . .	534	To Mr. Gay	83
	Not like the Pastors of thy rav'nous Breed,	. . . .	792	St. Pat's Well	31
	Th' amphibious Tyrant, with his rav'nous Band,	. . .	793	St. Pat's Well	63
	Who to yon rav'nous Isle thy Treasures bear,	. . . .	794	St. Pat's Well	97
RAVE					
	And, when indecently I rave,	. . . .	754	Stella '23	10
	He now began to storm and rave;	. . . .	783	Tim and Fables	28
	Let them rave of making Laws;	. . . .	831	Legion Club	50
	Then I fret, and rave and gabble,	. . . .	933	Riddle 20	D 7

	PAGE	TITLE	LINE
RAVEN			
The Raven, Vulture, Owl, and Kite, ...	413	Desire Possess	55
The Owl, the Raven, and the Bat, ...	903	Death Daphne	29
RAVES			
Thus the deluded Bankrupt raves, ...	251	Bubble	21
"Or, else he raves, and roars, and swears, ...	305	Storm	65
Yet still the \<Dean\> on Freedom raves, ...	799	Traulus 1	99
And all the day raves	856	Lady's Lament	175
RAVINGS			
Are like the ravings of a crackt head;	900	Dean's Reasons	64
RAVISH			
Yet he lives, and is ready to ravish agen, ...	519	Dean Hang Rape	52
No Devil nor \<Dean\> could Ravish 'em then, ...	519	Dean Hang Rape	64
RAVISH'D			
And bids the ravish'd youth be bless'd.	178	To Lord Harley	64
He ravish'd her fairly, and sav'd a good Shilling; . .	519	Dean Hang Rape	57
RAVISH'T			
If Maidens are ravish't, it is their own Choice, . .	519	Dean Hang Rape	61
RAVISHES			
She ravishes all Hearts to hear her.	416	Woman's Mind	36
RAVISHING			
Adieu to ravishing Delights, ...	590	Strephon Chloe	197
RAVISHT			
And bless his ravisht Sight to see	530	Lady's Dres Rm	142
RAW			
As some raw Youth in Country bred, ...	500	Doctor Delaney	1
RAY			
Bright effluence of th' immortal ray, ...	34	Ode Sancroft	2
'Tis but a low-born vapor kindled by a ray;	41	Ode Sancroft	218
Than swarms of gnats, that wanton in a ray	46	To Congreve	81
Such seem'd her eyes, as when an evening ray . . .	51	Temple Ill	17
RAYL			
Hear him Blaspheme; and Swear, and Rayl, ...	312	To Ford	45
RAYMENT			
When Food and Rayment now grew scarce	225	Prog of Love	95
Must dye for Want of Food and Rayment, ...	502	Doctor Delaney	73
RAYMOND			
The Rev'rend Dr. Raymond guess'd, ...	128	Little House	43
RAYS			
Unpierc'd by the blunt Rays of Sight)	31	Ode to Temple	167
By dark reverted rays from its reflection made; . . .	35	Ode Sancroft	22
If hope e'er dawns the smallest of its rays, ...	54	Temple Ill	112
Adorn'd with Golden Stars and Rays, ...	98	Elegy Patrige	28
The God laid down his Feeble Rays, ...	119	Apollo Outwit	5
His Wig was made of sunny Rays, ...	597	Problem Solved	7
Three times refin'd in Titan's Rays:	691	Cadenus Vaness	157
From Phoebus Rays they suffer Pain, ...	731	Stella, Poems	110
The fainting Rays of Stella's Eyes:	735	Stel B-day '20	22
RE-ACTS			
And on the Brother Limb re-acts.	366	Answer Delaney	26
RE-ASSUME			
Here may it re-assume its Stream, ...	478	Epist on Epist	93
RE'LY			
And re'ly Yours is budding too--	116	Bauc & Phil 2	160
REACH			
And when I almost reach the Shore	32	Ode to Temple	194
His Grazier's Coat reach down his Heels, ...	94	Bauc & Phil 1	166
From a Shoe Sole to reach the Skies;	98	Elegy Patrige	22
Pray reach that Thing here to the Child, ...	128	Little House	52
Nor come within your Cullyes Reach, ...	258	Bubble	194
Thro' ev'ry Sense to reach the Heart.	379	Apology Lady C	116
That creeps as far to reach the Centre;	393	Modern Poets	8
But not to reach the Ear;	405	Swift to Pope	2
To reach that slavish hateful shore	420	Holyhead	20
Not long enough to reach half round, ...	458	Paddy's Charac	16
Above the Reach of Want is plac't:	483	Libel on D- D-	84
To reach the Pot on t' other Side.	589	Strephon Chloe	190
For he could reach to B. in alt:	598	Problem Solved	28
Who, as the Odours reach his Throne, ...	647	On Poetry	225
But, who can reach the Worst of all?	653	On Poetry	388
The utmost her Desires will reach, ...	709	Cadenus Vaness	706
Or wants Capacity to reach	712	Cadenus Vaness	810
And wing'd with fame shall reach the skies.	877	To Dean Swift	34
REACH'D			
It but reach'd the middle Air, ...	638	Epistle Lady	251
E'er I reach'd Parnassus Top	638	Epistle Lady	261
How few have reach'd the low Sublime?	652	On Poetry	370
Aim'd at the Head, but reach'd the Heart.	706	Cadenus Vaness	623
READ			
Here you may read (Dear Charming Saint)	60	Lady Tablebook	7
We read of Kings, who in a Fright, ...	66	Problem	19
And it needs must be one that could both Read and Write:	77	Lady B- B-	15
Could Smoak, and Drink, and read the News;	95	Bauc & Phil 1	174
Great scholars have in Lucian Read, ...	99	Elegy Patrige	63
Cou'd smoak his Pipe, and read the News;	115	Bauc & Phil 2	126
The Nymph who oft had read in Books, ...	120	Apollo Outwit	13
Atlas we read in antient Song	160	Atlas	1
Old Read would hardly let him in.	174	Horace 1, 7	120
Or gravely try to read the Lines	201	Horace 2, 6	71
And as for their Works, when I please I may read 'em;	263	Apollo	22
Wherein she distinctly could read ev'ry Line, ...	264	Apollo	51

READY   (CONTINUED)   PAGE   TITLE   LINE
    Gold ready Coin'd appear'd, instead   . . . .   156 Fable of Midas   17
    That Man is ready to defend   . . . .   243 Horace 4, 9   23
    They rise ready drest, ...   245 Irish-Feast   35
    And, Cerberus hath ready in his Paws, ...   285 Elegy Boat   27
    Can ready Compliments supply   . . . .   416 Woman's Mind   13
    The King is ready when you will   . . . .   422 Ireld   43
    In ready Counters never pays, ...   452 Modern Lady   234
    The <Devil> ready stands, my <Swift>, ...   497 Panegyr Swift   124
    My Landlord was ready his <Deanship> to Ape   . .   517 Dean Hang Rape   29
    Yet he lives, and is ready to ravish agen,   . . .   519 Dean Hang Rape   52
    "So ready to do Strangers good, ...   558 Death of Swift   163
    Descended, ready cut and dry;   . . . .   591 Strephon Chloe   230
    Had Witness ready to attest, ...   688 Cadenus Vaness   68
    The Parsons, for Envy, are ready to burst: . . .   871 Grand Question   134
    I have a hundred causes ready: . . . .   899 Dean's Reasons   8
    A smile still ready at command, ...   951 Upstart   D 29
    We lye cramming ourselves, and are ready to burst, .   967 Letter Sherid   3
REAL
    Our Witness is a real Curr, ...   299 Horrid Plot   44
    But, since it was a real Curr, ...   300 Horrid Plot   61
    Though he may be a Block-head, he is no real Block.   335 Serious Poem   42
    With real Thunder knock't him down.   . . . . . .   353 Wood Ironmongr   24
    Like real Thunder knock't him down.   . . . . . .   353 Wood Ironmongr   38
    He told the real Truth in Rhime.   . . . .   378 Apology Lady C   90
    "Make thou its real Excellence   . . . .   384 Manly Virtue   9
    To real Muses, Gods, and Streams.   . . . .   478 Epist on Epist   86
    No real fortitude implies: . . . .   676 Parson's Case   3
    If thou a real Being art;   . . . .   919 Riddle 5   32
REALL
    A reall House with Rooms and Stairs, ...   87 Hist V's House   23
REALLY
    Are really but Vulgar Treats: . . . .   378 Apology Lady C   108
    'But really 'tis my Spouse's Way;   . . . .   448 Modern Lady   105
    We really wonder how she lives;   . . . .   735 Stel B-day '20   30
    You would really on Thursday leave St Catharine   . . 1017 Swift Ans Sher   12
REALM
    Our crazy double-bottom'd Realm.   . . . .   96 On the Union   22
    Now, through the Realm a Proclamation spread,   .   196 Author Himself   59
    Thro' all the Realm his Virtues run, ...   391 Young's Satire   25
    Will soon subdue the Realm of Lilliput.   . . . .   467 Birthday Song   208
    Divide the Realm between us two.   . . . .   886 Rev Market-Hill   92
    The Int'rest of his Realm had need   . . . . . .   903 Death Daphne   13
REALMS
    From Realms that bear Vesputio's Name: . . . .   324 Pethox   24
    Found all the Realms before him waste;   . . . .   326 Pethox   92
    Throughout two Realms nineteen in twenty.   . . .   549 Life of Swift   135
    Thus Families, like <Realms>, with equal Fate,   . . 535 To Mr. Gay   115
REAP
    So small the gain those from your wit do reap,   .   45 To Congreve   61
    In your own heart you'll reap the fruit, ...   755 Stella '23   31
REAPT
    "And reapt the profit, sought his Blood.   . . .   569 Death of Swift   414
REAR
    Then rear 'em to goodly Pile, ...   79 Vanbrug House   6
    Then rear 'em to a goodly Pile.   . . . .   106 V's House   6
    I'll lead the Van, keep you the Rear.   . . . . .   780 Mullinix Tim   230
    And damns his Blood that in the Rear   . . . . .   789 Dick's Variety   35
    To thee no verdant Altars rear;   . . . .   895 Panegyr Dean   282
REAR'D
    But up against the Steeple rear'd, ...   94 Bauc & Phil 1   141
    But up against the Steeple rear'd, ...   113 Bauc & Phil 2   79
    On Tiptoe stood and rear'd his Snout, ...   127 Little House   25
REARD
    Soon reard a House two Storyes high;   . . . . .   86 Hist V's House   6
REARS
    See how she rears her Head, ...   30 Ode to Temple   121
    And Merit rears her drooping Head;   . . . .   387 Manly Virtue   124
    And his Horse, the dear Creter, it prances and rears, . 870 Grand Question   97
REASON
    Whose Reason is weigh'd down by Popular air,   . . .   21 Ode Athenian   181
    Kindled while reason sleeps, but quickly flies,   . . . 54 Temple Ill   99
    The Reason is plain, they are none of his own;   . .   264 Apollo   56
    His Money spent! a clownish Reason?   . . . . . .   294 Prog Marriage   127
    And that's the reason, some folks think, ...   296 Satiric Elegy   15
    . . . and owns His Grace good Reason.   . . . . . .   341 Upon His Grace   8
    You had good Reason when you stole 'um.   . . . . .   349 Whitshed Motto   26
    The Church I hate, and have good Reason: . . . .   349 Upright Judge 1   1
    Wise People, who believ'd with Reason   . . . . .   354 Simile Silver   5
    I know no Reason at this Time   . . . .   372 Letter D. S-y   27
    Yet cannot tell the Reason why: . . . .   415 Woman's Mind   4
    Shew Reason, Grammer, Truth, or Sense?   . . . . .   503 Doctor Delaney   104
    Let Reason and Experience prove.   . . . .   554 Death of Swift   12
    Have I not Reason to detest 'em?   . . . .   555 Death of Swift   66
    Then hug themselves, and reason thus;   . . . . . .   557 Death of Swift   115
    By Nature, Reason, Learning, blind;   . . . . . .   579 Day Judgement   12
    Yet, some assign a diff'rent Reason;   . . . . . .   588 Strephon Chloe   159
    Nor, have I Reason to complain: . . . .   595 Cassinus Peter   65
    While We, whom Reason ought to sway, ...   607 Beasts Confess   205
    Brings in Reason and Invention.   . . . .   637 Epistle Lady   216
    Learn to relish Truth and Reason.   . . . .   638 Epistle Lady   272

REASON	(CONTINUED)	PAGE	TITLE	LINE
What Reason can there be assign'd		640	On Poetry	11
And Reason good; for many a Year		657	On Poetry	489
Who murder'd Horace without Rhyme or Reason?		666	Epig Carthy 3	D 4
If 'tis with Reason they complain,		691	Cadenus Vaness	146
That Reason was her Guide in Love.		708	Cadenus Vaness	677
Stella, for once you reason wrong;		731	Stella, Poems	131
The strongest Reason will submit		732	Verses Vanessa	7
Yet, since from Reason may be brought		764	Stel B-day '26	9
Then, who with Reason can maintain,		765	Stel B-day '26	59
Then, who with Reason can pretend,		765	Stel B-day '26	65
The reason why no Mortal knows.		777	Mullinix Tim	120
There is a Reason still more weighty;		820	Dr. Rundle	23
And with cavils combats reason:		906	Daphne	12
They for that Reason shun this Way:		928	Riddle 12	D 6
And fairly shew a Reason, why		930	Riddle 15	D 19
But this neither Reason nor Conscience allows;		947	Mrs. Houghton	2
The segment so large 'twixt your reason and rhyme is,		1026	Sheri Circles	6
REASON'D				
The Sexton reason'd well,		406	Swift to Pope	26
She reason'd, without plodding long,		704	Cadenus Vaness	558
REASON'S				
And if I pray by Reason's rules,		199	Horace 2, 6	D
It darkens Reason's light.		402	Window Inns 6	D 4
Till Time hath open'd Reason's Gate:		730	Stella, Poems	96
REASONABLE				
And makes such reasonable Bills		735	Stel B-day '20	28
REASONING				
And must, to human reasoning opposite, conclude		41	Ode Sancroft	209
REASONS				
Because, for some Reasons, I was Not in game.		144	New Song	44
No less than Reasons of such Weight,		498	Panegyr Swift	154
Gave her own Reasons last; and then		713	Cadenus Vaness	852
REATED				
When first of Griz, you Grafton reated		372	Letter D. S-y	14
REAUMS				
Reaums shall daunce honde in honde,		103	Merlin	15
REBECCA				
Rebecca, Ford, and Grattons by.		743	Stel B-day 22	60
Rebecca shews they're out in that.		761	Bec's B-Day	8
Rebecca thus I gladly greet,		761	Bec's B-Day	17
REBECCA'S				
Quite contrary Rebecca's led,		761	Bec's B-Day	21
REBEL				
And Rebel is the growth and manufacture of the Land.		8	Ode to King	57
The Rebel Muse, alas, takes part		23	Ode Athenian	238
Than I turn Rebel to the Fair.		445	Modern Lady	21
Perjur'd Rebel, brib'd Accuser;		831	Legion Club	70
REBELLIOUS				
But with my own Rebellious Heart,		23	Ode Athenian	239
Till its first Emperor rebellious Man		26	Ode to Temple	2
Rebellious Waves with rods like Xerxes.		463	Birthday Song	100
And with rebellious Arms pretend		653	On Poetry	381
REBUFF				
By that rebuff your Virtue gain'd.		496	Panegyr Swift	89
REBUKE				
Let not the whigs our tory club rebuke;		186	Scriblerus 3	1
And all his old Friends would rebuke		186	Scriblerus 4	D 9
I own, I'm pleas'd with this Rebuke,		200	Horace 2, 6	40
Let pride be taught by this rebuke,		297	Satiric Elegy	29
with many rebuke.		423	Carterets Arms	
"Shou'd Vice expect to 'scape rebuke,		548	Life of Swift	123
But, sure the Dean deserves a sharp Rebuke		678	Dean and Duke	3
Offend me with the least Rebuke.		888	Panegyr Dean	60
REBUS				
The First but a Rebus, the Last but a Dean.		716	Answer Rebus	6
A Dean's but a Parson, and what is a Rebus?		716	Answer Rebus	7
With rebus and pun.		852	Lady's Lament	14
If your Worship will please to explain me this Rebus,		973	S-'s Ans Sh-d	13
You found out my rebus with very much modesty;		976	Dean to Sherid	37
As for your new rebus, or riddle, or crux,		977	Dean to Sherid	43
RECAL				
Why, then recal your Loan;		395	Grub-Street	18
RECALLING				
The Thing was done and past recalling:		224	Prog of Love	68
RECALS				
Whene'er your Pride recals your Grief,		496	Panegyr Swift	87
RECEIT				
Beneath (A new Receit for Paint)		60	Lady Tablebook	8
To form some Beauty by a new Receit,		118	Biddy Floyd	2
RECEIV'D SEE WELL-RECEIV'D				
Receiv'd from thee profound Directions		182	Horace 2, 1	55
Receiv'd a brace or two of Blows.		220	A Quiet Life	24
What was the Message I receiv'd;		376	Apology Lady C	35
"Was never ill receiv'd at Court:		565	Death of Swift	308
Receiv'd the Gifts of all Mankind.		894	Panegyr Dean	236
RECEIVE				
Receive the Filth which he ejects,		85	Salamander	63
Receive the News in doleful Dumps,		562	Death of Swift	227
From Visits to receive and pay,		688	Cadenus Vaness	43
Thus, Commonwealths receive a foreign Yoke,		770	Horace 1, 14	21

	PAGE	TITLE	LINE
RECEIVE (CONTINUED)			
Receive its last and deadly Wound, ...	850	Old Thorn	51
RECEIVER			
Nor oft can the Receiver know	919	Riddle 5	23
RECEIVES			
Receives them while they wait for Bayl?	504	Doctor Delaney	146
Receives all Off'rings at her Shrine.	893	Panegyr Dean	206
RECENT			
Authorities both old and recent	591	Strephon Chloe	251
RECEPTION			
In its reception to the eye, ...	35	Ode Sancroft	29
RECKON'D			
His Rival, for the Chiefest reckon'd, ...	546	Life of Swift	56
"He's older than he would be reckon'd	556	Death of Swift	107
While Women, if it could be reckon'd	618	Scandal Poem 1	45
While Women, if it could be reckon'd, ...	625	Scandal Poem 2	41
If you say this is hard, on a man that is reckon'd . .	817	Yahoo's	66
RECKOND			
For Building fam'd, and justly reckond	87	Hist V's House	37
RECKONING			
Reckoning Roof, Weather Cock and all, ...	126	Little House	7
Not reckoning half an hour we pass, ...	279	Journal	37
RECLAIM			
Though 'tis hopeless to reclaim them, ...	836	Legion Club	157
RECLINING			
With Head reclining on his Shoulder, ...	63	Discovery	13
Reclining on his Elbow-chair, ...	649	On Poetry	265
Its Head reclining tow'rds the Ground.	849	Old Thorn	20
RECOIL'D			
Or often blunted and recoil'd, ...	701	Cadenus Vaness	482
RECOLLECT			
To recollect the scatter'd Parts?	583	Young Nymph	68
Your Deanship ought to recollect, ...	899	Dean's Reasons	20
Bid Lady Betty recollect her, ...	993	On Picture	10
RECOLLECTS			
He recollects not what he says;	556	Death of Swift	86
RECOMMEND			
For Prose, I recommend Voiture's, ...	219	To Mr. Delany	105
To Woolston recommend our youth	490	Dialogue	29
To recommend him to the Squire;	605	Beasts Confess	138
Will call again and recommend	734	Stel B-day '20	5
RECOMMENDATION			
Is recommendation	424	Carterets Arms	16
RECONCIL'D			
He reconcil'd Divinity and Wit.	194	Author Himself	12
RECONCILE			
His great contending Friends to reconcile.	196	Author Himself	72
And yet our Boat, how shall I reconcile it?	285	Elegy Boat	13
"To reconcile his Friends in Power;	567	Death of Swift	366
He knew not how to reconcile	706	Cadenus Vaness	626
RECORD			
Ten thousand Oaths upon Record, ...	725	To Stella	55
Shall stand for Ages on Record, ...	848	Old Thorn	14
RECORDS			
On French Records for twenty long Campains; . . .	771	Horace 1, 14	44
RECOVER			
And therefore hop'd she would recover	224	Prog of Love	69
Recover Strength whene'er he fell, ...	257	Bubble	182
Recover Strength and Vigor there, ...	258	Bubble	186
The Maggot will dye, and the Sick will recover. . . .	351	Wood Insect	28
The <Dean> he pursu'd to recover his Game, ...	517	Dean Hang Rape	13
Not one foretels I shall recover;	557	Death of Swift	133
RECOVER'D			
Her Spleen and Fits recover'd quite, ...	451	Modern Lady	216
She scarce recover'd in a Week.	849	Old Thorn	28
From these I am recover'd quite, ...	902	Dean's Reasons	99
RECTIUS			
Ah! Quanto rectius, Tu Adepte, ...	476	Epist on Epist	29
RED SEE FIERY-RED			
From her red Locks her Mouth with Venom fills: . . .	195	Author Himself	55
And bit her Lips to make them red:	222	Prog of Love	14
A frouzy dirty colour'd red	226	Prog of Beauty	3
Three Colours, Black, and Red, and White, ...	226	Prog of Beauty	21
But when she rose, the black and red	226	Prog of Beauty	31
Leaving the fiery red behind, ...	227	Prog of Beauty	35
Driv'n from the South-Sea to the Red.	258	Bubble	208
Like the faint red upon a Pippin	290	Prog Marriage	25
Of Red, and Yellow, Blue, and Green.	325	Pethox	46
Whispers that Sappho's Hair is Red:	450	Modern Lady	169
She draws an Ace, and sees it red.	452	Modern Lady	233
Rub off the Dawbs of White and Red, ...	582	Young Nymph	34
Whether the Red or Green were best, ...	698	Cadenus Vaness	380
Don't you intend to put on Red?	699	Cadenus Vaness	399
Red hat, and blue bonnet, and turbant's the same, . .	815	Yahoo's	23
And coxcombs in red ribbons shine:	876	To Dean Swift	22
I here am Red, and there am Green, ...	911	Aenigma	7
REDEEM			
Redeem him from his Prison under Ground.	233	Elegy on Demar	4
If you'll redeem the Silver Cup	446	Modern Lady	58
His Want of Passion will redeem, ...	711	Cadenus Vaness	786

	PAGE	TITLE	LINE

REDEEM'D
And has at last redeem'd the Mighty Prize . . . . . 8 Ode to King 81
REDEEMS
Redeems us from the slavish fears . . . . 490 Dialogue 33
<REDHAIR'D>
By an <old> <redhair'd> <murd'ring> <Hag> pursu'd, . . 193 Author Himself 1
REDIVIVUS
That you're Don Quixote Redivivus? . . . . 478 Epist on Epist 88
REDOUBT
Which proves a Magical Redoubt . . . . 134 Magician's Rod 51
REDOUNDS
The boundless Glory all Redounds to Thee, ... 12 Ode to William D 35
REDUC'D
Should be reduc'd so low, ... 426 Five Ladies 23
Be reduc'd into a Poem. . . . . 631 Epistle Lady 48
"To treat gold reduc'd like Wood's copper pence. . . . 843 Ay and No 16
REDUCE
But Celia can with ease reduce . . . . 227 Prog of Beauty 45
With pleasing Arts she could reduce . . . . . . 700 Cadenus Vaness 448
REDUCING
By the new Modish System of reducing all to sense, . . 19 Ode Athenian 107
REED
And gave it for Pan's oaten Reed: . . . . . . 156 Fable of Midas 28
REEDS
Nor whisper to the tattling Reeds, ... 596 Cassinus Peter 105
REEK   SEE A-REEK
REEKING
All reeking in a cloudy Steam, ... 226 Prog of Beauty 14
Or greasy Coifs and Pinners reeking, ... 527 Lady's Dres Rm 53
When plumpt into the reeking Chest; . . . . . 529 Lady's Dres Rm 110
And as he fill'd the reeking Vase, ... 590 Strephon Chloe 191
REEL
The poys'nous Darts has made him reel, ... 10 Ode to King 143
They reel and stagger too and fro, ... 256 Bubble 151
REEL'D
Had Bacchus after Daphne reel'd, ... 177 To Lord Harley 13
REFELLI
Et diu potuisse, et non potuisse refelli. . . . . 967 Letter Sherid 6
REFELLING
And think there's no refelling . . . . 440 Ballyspellin 3
REFERR'D
She then referr'd them to a Place . . . . . . 690 Cadenus Vaness 110
REFIN'D
Whene're they would be thought refin'd . . . . . 216 To Mr. Delany 46
By you were brighten'd and refin'd, ... 326 Pethox 74
Was too refin'd to give a Feast, ... 378 Apology Lady C 98
As Fables: But you have refin'd . . . . . . 478 Epist on Epist 84
Refin'd it first, and shew'd its Use. . . . . . 555 Death of Swift 58
For her Taste is almost as refin'd as her Wit. . . . 580 Psyche 10
Refin'd all Mettals with his Looks, ... 597 Problem Solved 3
When, by you refin'd and burnish'd, ... 631 Epistle Lady 46
A Fire celestial, chaste, refin'd, ... 687 Cadenus Vaness 29
Three times refin'd in Titan's Rays: . . . . . 691 Cadenus Vaness 157
REFINE
Our Conversation to refine . . . . 216 To Mr. Delany 29
Has learnt his Fables to refine; . . . . . . 513 Answer Fable 12
Blot out, correct, insert, refine, ... 643 On Poetry 87
This tempts Free-thinkers to refine, ... 687 Cadenus Vaness 11
Your Conversation to refine, ... 780 Mullinix Tim 243
We comb the Wool, refine the Stuff, ... 948 Jason Hassard 3
And give Satan his due Dan begins to refine . . . . 1017 Swift Ans Sher 10
REFINEMENT
A great Refinement in Barometry, ... 99 Elegy Patrige 42
REFINERS
Wondrous Refiners of Philosophy, ... 19 Ode Athenian 105
REFINING
The bullion stampt in your refining mind . . . . . 45 To Congreve 53
REFLECT
Some call it witty to reflect . . . . 592 Strephon Chloe 273
And tho' she must with Grief reflect, ... 695 Cadenus Vaness 270
Then, prithee reflect, take a word of advice; . . . . 818 Archbi Cashel 7
REFLECTED
Or Forms reflected from a Glass? . . . . . . 765 Stel B-day '26 52
REFLECTING
Reflecting on a Life well spent? . . . . . . 764 Stel B-day '26 36
REFLECTION
By dark reverted rays from its reflection made; . . . 35 Ode Sancroft 22
Since this Reflection slipt your Pen, ... 485 Libel on D- D- 161
"It clearly shews that all Reflection . . . . . 563 Death of Swift 275
Wise books and reflection . . . . 854 Lady's Lament 101
'Tis mine to make a just Reflection, ... 932 Riddle 19 D 17
REFLECTIONS
"Supposing these Reflections just; . . . . . 549 Life of Swift 158
While these Reflections fill'd his Head, ... 587 Strephon Chloe 111
REFORM
By hopes my Congreve will reform the stage; . . . 45 To Congreve 50
"To please, and to reform Mankind; . . . . . 550 Life of Swift 197
To reform the World, than Sour. . . . . . . 636 Epistle Lady 200
"She'd study to reform the Men; . . . . . . 714 Cadenus Vaness 873
"<God> <damn> me, they bid us reform and repent, . . . 872 Grand Question 145
Then, perhaps, you may reform her: . . . . . . 907 Daphne 34

		PAGE	TITLE	LINE
REFORMERS				
	That sent these wild reformers to our times;	42	Ode Sancroft	246
	Reformers and physicians differ but in name, ...	42	Ode Sancroft	255
REFORMING				
	As my Method of Reforming, ...	637	Epistle Lady	229
	Some whose reforming Hands engage, ...	781	Mullinix Tim	253
REFRAIN				
	From which I never could refrain, ...	901	Dean's Reasons	97
REFRESHMENT				
	Some short refreshment for your weary mind, ...	50	To Congreve	232
REFUGE				
	And fly for refuge to the grave:	676	Parson's Case	16
REFUS'D				
	So to the Poor if he refus'd his Pelf, ...	234	Elegy on Demar	13
	Refus'd the Visits of a Queen;	482	Libel on D- D-	74
	Yet what the World refus'd to Lewis, ...	657	On Poetry	477
	But thrice refus'd Episcopari.	821	Dr. Rundle	40
	If I refus'd to lend them Fire.	916	Riddle 2	14
REFUSAL				
	He knows very well I ne'er gave a Refusal, ...	265	Apollo	71
REFUSE				
	The God could not refuse her Prayer;	120	Apollo Outwit	34
	Does he refuse me? Harley cry'd:	172	Horace 1, 7	55
	Their only pride is to refuse.	178	To Lord Harley	58
	That could refuse this charming Ganymede, ...	466	Birthday Song	190
	Refuse our Patron's Call to dine;	495	Panegyr Swift	68
	Should I the Queen of Love refuse, ...	530	Lady's Dres Rm	131
	In Spight to Justice, and refuse his Bail.	826	Noisy Tom	20
	Can you refuse a soft Embrace.	932	Riddle 19	D 12
REGAL				
	To regal Rage devotes some Patriot's Head.	364	On Dreams	12
	The costly Boast of Regal Rooms, ...	379	Apology Lady C	110
	That best ye regal Nature suit, ...	659	On Poetry	D 410
	And well we know, The Congee Regal	821	Dr. Rundle	57
REGARD				
	Van saw, but seemd not to regard, ...	86	Hist V's House	3
	And will neither regard my Figures nor Tropes;	145	New Song	52
	Preferring his Regard for me	204	In Sickness	11
	No longer my Advice regard:	501	Doctor Delaney	54
	Will you regard the Hawker's Cryes	505	Doctor Delaney	161
	Without Regard to Whig or Tory, ...	605	Beasts Confess	146
	Due Regard for Men of Wit?	632	Epistle Lady	74
	Some small Regard for State and Wealth:	693	Cadenus Vaness	217
	Regard not what is false or true;	747	Stel Distress	60
	Regard not whether false or true:	751	Stel Wood-Park	76
	Does he regard on what we dine?	949	Epigr Fasting	6
REGARD'ST				
	But I'm deceiv'd, or thou regard'st me not;	53	Temple Ill	72
REGARDED				
	"Nor fear'd he God, nor Man regarded;	570	Death of Swift	422
REGARDFUL				
	Regardful of your Age and Station, ...	889	Panegyr Dean	68
REGARDING				
	Heaven with a parent's eye regarding earth, ...	54	Temple Ill	89
	"Without regarding private Ends, ...	565	Death of Swift	331
REGARDLESS				
	"Regardless of her House and Fame;	321	First of April	26
	Regardless of his dying Groans.	413	Desire Possess	58
	Regardless both of Wrong and Right.	730	Stella, Poems	94
REGARDS				
	What poor regards would merit all below!	49	To Congreve	184
	Regards a Friend of yours and mine, ...	218	To Mr. Delany	90
	For he regards Ten thousand Pounds no more than Woods's	341	Upon His Grace	12
	Dross.			
	Now no one regards what he Utters with freedom, . . .	717	Answer Rebus	25
	Who regards him when he's gone?	863	To Janus	24
	At least in what regards the Knight.	902	Dean's Reasons	100
	Who regards the dreadful Sound.	931	Riddle 18	D 26
REGENT'S				
	Ambitious of a Regent's Heart	66	Problem	35
REGICIDE				
	Sprung from Papists and a Regicide;	832	Legion Club	72
REGIMEN				
	Enquire what Regimen I kept;	557	Death of Swift	139
REGIMENTS				
	In Regiments of Foot and Horse;	513	Answer Fable	28
REGINA				
	Coram Regina prox' die Martis, ...	713	Cadenus Vaness	839
REGION				
	To climb to our Region, and thence to steal Fire; . . .	266	Apollo	96
	Sent from the Dark infernal Region	798	Traulus 1	77
REGIONS				
	In the Play-House upper Regions;	523	Betty Grizette	24
	Because they live in lower regions	620	Scandal Poem 1	98
	Because we dwell in higher Regions:	626	Scandal Poem 2	96
	From distant Regions, Fortune sends	883	Rev Market-Hill	1
	Thro' distant Regions I can fly, ...	930	Riddle 15	D 17
REGIS				
	Decree, that ad exemplum Regis, ...	391	Young's Satire	24
REGISTER				
	He's the Register of All	931	Riddle 18	D 9

	PAGE	TITLE	LINE
REGNANT			
A Traytor to the Vices regnant.	798	Traulus 1	94
REGULAR			
Were I to form a regular Thought of Fame,	21	Ode Athenian	158
On his own secret regular sphere,	39	Ode Sancroft	152
REGULUS			
So Regulus in Torments dy'd.	325	Pethox	58
REHEARSE			
And to mistaken man these truths rehearse,	53	Temple Ill	69
Yet hardly dare one Line Rehearse.	121	Apollo Outwit	60
REHERSE			
Once on a time, as old Stories reherse,	76	Lady B- B-	1
REIGN			
Of Conquest in your your short and Happy Reign;	25	Ode Athenian	303
Like that prophetic tempest in the virgin reign,	40	Ode Sancroft	196
If Anna's happy Reign you praise,	271	Apollo's Edict D	44
Their Reign began with cruel Seizures;	283	Journal	120
Two Bards that now in fashion reign,	393	Modern Poets	5
"From both your Streams in George's Reign!	462	Birthday Song	80
You but o'er half the World can reign.	585	Strephon Chloe	32
Their Empire holds so short a Reign;	591	Strephon Chloe	256
Your Garland in the following Reign,	647	On Poetry	231
When Death had finish'd Blackmore's Reign,	653	On Poetry	374
This Infant shall restore my Reign.	691	Cadenus Vaness	147
And happy Lovers bless my Reign----	694	Cadenus Vaness	248
Would soon restore our antient Reign.	887	Panegyr Dean	10
Who round the Vault luxuriant reign.	923	Riddle 7	60
How long shall vice triumphant reign?	950	Upstart D	17
REIGNS			
And Maevius reigns o'er Kentish-Town:	650	On Poetry	302
But to say truth, such Dulness reigns	742	Stel B-day 22	41
The Knight triumphant reigns betwixt:	883	Rev Market-Hill	20
The Goddess Want in Triumph reigns:	1035	To Quilca	10
REINS			
No Phaeton to hold the Reins.	271	Apollo's Edict D	53
If you shou'd give him once the Reins,	666	Epig Carthy 2 D	5
REJECT			
Reject with scorn that stupid Notion	468	Birthday Song	261
Which, if you in scorn reject,	908	Daphne	81
REJECTING			
Chimnies with Scorn rejecting Smoak;	1035	To Quilca	3
REJECTS			
Rejects a servile Usher's Place,	482	Libel on D- D-	59
REJOICE			
With what Impatience they rejoice.	776	Mullinix Tim	96
How shou'd we rejoice, if, like Judas the first,	805	Irish Bishops	39
Let the happy Swain rejoice,	933	Riddle 20 D	15
Ne'er sad I mourn, ne'er glad rejoice,	936	Riddle 23 D	24
Then George will rejoice, and Dan will sing high-day:	980	Dean to Tho: S	37
REJOIN			
You reply and rejoin like Hoadly of Bangor.	967	Letter Sherid	8
REJOINDERS			
But with Rejoinders and Replies,	690	Cadenus Vaness	120
REJOYCE			
Yet we all should Rejoyce to be Hewers of Wood.	334	Serious Poem	4
Are witty, dull, rejoyce, complain.	620	Scandal Poem 1	94
Are witty, dull, rejoyce, complain.	626	Scandal Poem 2	92
RELAPSE			
Else you relapse to Human Kind:	724	To Stella	44
RELATE			
Or how should I, alas! relate,	449	Modern Lady	140
All the Superfluous Whims relate,	451	Modern Lady	224
And Caelia's horrid Fact relate;	596	Cassinus Peter	93
But, while I thus my Life relate,	916	Riddle 1	37
RELATED			
Nearly related to an Earl.	289	Prog Marriage	4
Related thus the following Tale.	412	Desire Possess	8
RELATION			
"No worthy Friend, no poor Relation?	558	Death of Swift	162
Thersites (he was your Relation)	775	Mullinix Tim	52
And be thought a near Relation;	833	Legion Club	112
RELATIONS			
Till all my Relations were put into Places.	144	New Song	24
To crowd the Court with their Relations:	606	Beasts Confess	178
Be proud of owning such Relations;	813	Bro Protestant	58
RELAX'D			
Conclude the Bow relax'd again.	66	Problem	32
RELAXING			
"Relaxing downwards in a <Stink>?	305	Storm	68
RELENT			
But pleas'd to find you do relent and cry on.	1002	Reply by Dean	15
RELENTLESS			
"Relentless Dean! to Mischief born,	850	Old Thorn	58
And with relentless Hands destroy	925	Riddle 8	21
RELIEF			
Forsook by hopes, ill fortune's last relief,	54	Temple Ill	109
They beg'd Relief which none would grant;	90	Bauc & Phil 1	24
To hear, yet give me no Relief;	204	In Sickness	26
To me the good Fellows apply for Relief,	263	Apollo	9
Or gives Relief to long-expecting Heirs.	364	On Dreams	28
Be this however your Relief,	496	Panegyr Swift	86

```
RELIEF            (CONTINUED)                                  PAGE    TITLE            LINE
    Alas! that gives you small relief---!  . . . . . . . .      546  Life of Swift       60
    Then Stella ran to my Relief  . . . . . . . . . .          726  To Stella          101
    In Vain from injur'd Heav'n Relief expects.   . . . .      771  Horace 1, 14        36
    On such an Occasion the Law gives Relief.     . . . .      943  Probatur Alit       46
    And they, alas, yield small Relief,  . . . . . . .        1005  Sheridan's Sub      29
RELIEVE
    Call'd her good Nature to relieve him;  . . . . . .        378  Apology Lady C      85
RELIGION
    Who always loudest for Religion bawl,   . . . . . .          8  Ode to King         83
    Look where exalted Vertue and Religion sit    . . . .       21  Ode Athenian       176
    Religion now does on her death-bed lie,       . . . .       42  Ode Sancroft       251
    "To turn Religion to a Fable,   . . . . . . . .            568  Death of Swift     383
    All Folks who pretend to Religion and Grace,              575  Place Damn'd         1
    It seems, they had Religion then,   . . . . . . . .        601  Beasts Confess       3
RELIGION'S
    To tear Religion's lovely face;   . . . . . . . .          42  Ode Sancroft       248
RELIGIONS
    All Parties and Religions joyn;   . . . . . . . .         345  Prometheus          12
RELIGIOUS
    But, never from Religious Clubs;  . . . . . . . .         583  Young Nymph         54
RELIQUES
    With antique Reliques of the Dead,    . . . . . . .        27  Ode to Temple       22
RELISH
    But always with a stronger relish of the Last.   . . .     22  Ode Athenian       215
    How to relish Notions high;   . . . . . . . . .           630  Epistle Lady        25
    Conversation learn to relish,   . . . . . . . . .         632  Epistle Lady        89
    Learn to relish Truth and Reason.   . . . . . . . .       638  Epistle Lady       272
RELY
    The Lawyer swears, you may rely on't,               603  Beasts Confess      79
    Your Mercy I rely on.   . . . . . . . . . .              1005  Sheridan's Sub      13
REMAIN
    Yet shall these Traces of your Wit remain   . . . . .      25  Ode Athenian       301
    That no Effects of Food remain?    . . . . . . . .        765  Stel B-day '26      60
    I increase it to Twelve, so three Hundred remain:        867  Grand Question      10
    No Scraps remain to save Board-wages.   . . . . . .       954  Authors Living       6
    And so I remain in a civil way, your Servant to command.  987  Mary to Sher        38
    Which is all at present; and so I remain--   . . . . .   1027  Sheri Circles       28
REMAIN'D
    That Hope at last remain'd behind;   . . . . . . .        528  Lady's Dres Rm      88
    We thought, there now remain'd no room to doubt:  . . .   536  To Mr. Gay         149
REMAINDER
    Now not so much as in Remainder   . . . . . . . .         642  On Poetry           55
REMAINING
    Your Name shall the remaining Work perform,   . . . .      13  Ode to William    D 39
    New Vigour to the Leg remaining.   . . . . . . . .        366  Answer Delaney      20
    Support a few remaining Days:  . . . . . . . . .          764  Stel B-day '26      12
REMAINS
    Three genuine Tomes of Swift's Remains.   . . . . .       560  Death of Swift     198
    But, still the hardest Part remains.   . . . . . . .      586  Strephon Chloe      71
    Remains a Difficulty still,  . . . . . . . . .            652  On Poetry          367
    From whence a Cleanliness remains,   . . . . . . .        691  Cadenus Vaness     162
    Her matchless Sons; whose Valour still remains   . . .    771  Horace 1, 14        43
    But if, still obdurate, your anger remains,   . . . .     819  Archbi Cashel       11
    While tortur'd Madam bound remains,   . . . . . . .       885  Rev Market-Hill     71
    Yet, some Devotion still remains  . . . . . . . .         896  Panegyr Dean       299
    Another villain yet remains--   . . . . . . . .           950  Upstart           D 22
REMARK
    But antient Philosophers wisely Remark,   . . . . . .     334  Serious Poem         7
    When all the while you might remark Where all   . . . .   747  Stel Distress       47
    When all the while you might remark,   . . . . . . .      751  Stel Wood-Park      63
    One Property more I would have you remark,    . . . .     928  Riddle 11         D  9
REMEDY
    Think on some Remedy in time   . . . . . . . .           293  Prog Marriage      103
    You soon a Remedy may find;  . . . . . . . . .            501  Doctor Delaney      44
REMEMBER
    . . .I remember when I was at my Lady Shrewsbury's,   .    71  Mrs Harris Pet      32
    "Well, I remember what she won;   . . . . . . . .         446  Modern Lady         64
    For Strephon could remember well,   . . . . . . .         587  Strephon Chloe     105
    I well remember when I sat fort.   . . . . . . .          783  Tim and Fables      22
    I remember it was upon a Tuesday, of all Days in the      986  Mary to Sher        26
        Year.
    I remember my late-head   . . . . . . . . . . .          1014  Swift to Sheri      26
REMEMBER'D
    She well remember'd to her Cost,   . . . . . . .          705  Cadenus Vaness     604
REMEMBERS
    Remembers he the Trees has seen;   . . . . . . .         116  Bauc & Phil 2      166
    "And well remembers Charles the Second.   . . . . .       556  Death of Swift     108
    She scarce remembers what is Trumps.   . . . . . .        904  Death Daphne        60
REMEMBRANCE
    Our Knowledge is but mere Remembrance all,    . . . .      27  Ode to Temple       30
    Remembrance is our Treasure and our Food;    . . . .      27  Ode to Temple       31
    Which by Remembrance will assuage,   . . . . . .         764  Stel B-day '26      31
REMNANT
    The Remnant of a falling Snuff,   . . . . . . . .          9  Ode to King        108
    In the last wretched Remnant of his Days;    . . . .      10  Ode to King        141
    The Remnant of the royal Blood,   . . . . . . . .        655  On Poetry          437
REMORSE
    With like Remorse his Brother of the Trade,   . . . .     364  On Dreams           17
REMOTE
    Or, some remote inferior Post,   . . . . . . . . .        484  Libel on D- D-     133
```

```
REMOTE          (CONTINUED)                      PAGE   TITLE            LINE
   The Time is not remote, when I      . . . . . . . .   556 Death of Swift    73
   "Remote from St. John, Pope, and Gay.    . . . . .   570 Death of Swift   434
REMOTEST
   Some from the Lakes remotest end.   . . . . . . . .   279 Journal          30
   Ierne, to the World's remotest Parts,    . . . . . .   789 St. Pat's Well    5
REMOV'D
   Remov'd from all th' ambitious Scene,    . . . . .   199 Horace 2, 6     D
   Remov'd from kind Arbuthnot's Aid,  . . . . . . .   204 In Sickness       9
   Remov'd the tough superfluous Flesh,     . . . . . .   326 Pethox          78
   Ye bishops far remov'd from saints;      . . . . . . .   487 Irish-Club        7
   The Screen remov'd, their Hearts are trembling,  . . .   561 Death of Swift   223
   While each with stubbed Knife remov'd the Roots  . . .   880 Pastoral Dial     3
REMOVE
   Remove them to a diff'rent Light    . . . . . . . .   226 Prog of Beauty   23
   Remove me from this land of slaves  . . . . . . . .   421 Ireld            1
   Ah lovely Nymphs, remove your Fears,     . . . . . .   445 Modern Lady      17
   The point is plain: Remove the cause;    . . . . . .   487 Irish-Club       15
REND
   To rend the Skies with brazen Din;  . . . . . . .   354 Simile Silver    10
   To force it out my Heart must rend;      . . . . . .   596 Cassinus Peter   95
REND'RING
   Rend'ring shades, things, and substances of names;  . .    47 To Congreve     148
RENDER'D
   Render'd the topping beauty of the town, . . . . . .    48 To Congreve     152
RENEGADOES
   "Like Renegadoes now he feels,      . . . . . . . .   569 Death of Swift   405
RENEW
   Again the verdant Glebe renew;      . . . . . . . .   759 Receipt Youth    12
   Seem rather to renew my Grief,      . . . . . . . .  1005 Sheridan's Sub   30
RENEW'D
   And tho' he oft renew'd the Fight,       . . . . . .    30 Ode to Temple   129
RENEWS
   Where each Supply of Dead, renews   . . . . . . .   923 Riddle 7         55
RENOUNCE
   I here renounce thy visionary pow'r;     . . . . . .    55 Temple Ill      152
   "I swear I saw you thrice renounce.      . . . . . . .   452 Modern Lady     263
RENOWN
   To purchase Kingdoms, and to buy Renown,     . . . .    11 Ode to William  D   1
   So, Men of old, to gain Renown, did      . . . . . .   108 V's House        65
   May you Descend to take Renown,     . . . . . . . .   121 Apollo Outwit    62
   But a Prince of high Renown,        . . . . . . . . .   168 Peace Dunkirk    18
   Are full of renown,  . . . . . . . . . . . . . .   403 Window Inns 9   D   2
   Bavius in Wapping gains Renown,     . . . . . . . .   650 On Poetry       301
   O, were I equal in Renown,   . . . . . . . . . . .   779 Mullinix Tim    197
   Dick was come to high Renown        . . . . . . . . .   785 Mullinex Dick    25
   I saw thee rais'd to high Renown,   . . . . . . . .   919 Riddle 5          5
RENOWN'D
   The Rod of Hermes was renown'd      . . . . . . . .   133 Magician's Rod   35
   Renown'd for Skill in Faustus Art,  . . . . . . . .   182 Horace 2, 1      50
   Here, soon for every Art renown'd,  . . . . . . . .   385 Manly Virtue     37
   Explain'd for what they were renown'd;   . . . . . .   697 Cadenus Vaness  351
   Once so renown'd to Live obscure?   . . . . . . . .   778 Mullinix Tim    180
   Renown'd for Valour, Policy and Arts.    . . . . . .   789 St. Pat's Well    6
   Thus Lamb, renown'd for cutting Corns,   . . . . . .   811 Bro Protestant   15
   Renown'd in Sieges and Campaigns,   . . . . . . .   925 Riddle 8         31
RENT
   And Houses would not give a Rent.   . . . . . . . .    79 Vanbrug House    22
   Landed-Men shall have their Rent,   . . . . . . . .   169 Peace Dunkirk    25
   His Tenants wrong him in his Rent;  . . . . . . . .   174 Horace 1, 7     108
   His Wings are his Paternall Rent,   . . . . . . . .   252 Bubble           45
   While his Tenants in Paper must pay him his Rent:  . .   288 Bank Down        53
   And all the Rent I pay is scarce five Shillings in the   342 Upon His Grace   22
      Pound.
   Then Master Steward takes my Rent, and tells me, honest  342 Upon His Grace   23
      Jo.
   Pray never press your self for Rent, but pay me when you 342 Upon His Grace   33
      can,
   I hope you will not pay my Rent in that same Woods's     342 Upon His Grace   36
      Trash.
   Your Rent is due almost a Week beside the Days of        343 Upon His Grace   44
      Grace.
   I'll vote for my Landlord to whom I pay Rent,    . . .   396 Dog and Thief    15
   Thy thread-bare gown, thy cassock rent,  . . . . . .   676 Parson's Case     9
   "Shall rent her Petticoats to Rags,      . . . . . . .   850 Old Thorn        63
   In Poundage and Drawbacks, I lose half my Rent,  . . .   867 Grand Question   21
   Above his Rent four Pounds a Year;       . . . . . . .   875 Drapier's Hill    4
   To be his Slaves must pay him Rent;      . . . . . . .   883 Rev Market-Hill  22
   And due my rent is.  . . . . . . . . . . . . . .  1037 Sheridan Cavan    4
RENTS
   With Twenty Thousand Pounds a Year Rents,    . . . .   598 Problem Solved   12
   In Rents three thousand Pounds a Year.   . . . . . .   821 Dr. Rundle       52
REPAIR
   Repair a House gone to decay;       . . . . . . . .    80 Vanbrug House    64
   Repair a House to Decay,     . . . . . . . . . . .   107 V's House        38
   To some snug Cellar let's repair    . . . . . . . .   184 Horace 2, 1     109
   "We'll to our Barn again repair."   . . . . . . . .   208 Fable Bitches    36
   White lead was sent us to repair    . . . . . . . .   227 Prog of Beauty   62
   Down to your Deanery repair  . . . . . . . . . . .   361 Grace's Answer   19
   "A Jayl or Barrack to repair;       . . . . . . . .   571 Death of Swift   452
   Will soon your Appetite repair.     . . . . . . . .   759 Receipt Youth    28
```

REPAIRS   PAGE   TITLE   LINE
   By Bills for Taxes and Repairs.   . . . .   174 Horace 1, 7   112
   For, Vengeance more embroils, than Skill repairs.   . . .   536 To Mr. Gay   140
   Repairs a cabin gone to ruin, ...   878 Robbin & Harry   21
REPARTEE
   As Rudeness is to Repartee.   . . . .   217 To Mr. Delany   64
   Has ev'ry Repartee in Store, ...   416 Woman's Mind   11
   Dick for Repartee was fit, ...   785 Mullinex Dick   33
REPARTEES
   Stock't with Repartees and Jokes, ...   523 Betty Grizette   17
REPAST
   Never finding full Repast, ...   930 Riddle 16   D   3
REPAY
   I will either explain, or repay it by trucks;   . . . .   977 Dean to Sherid   44
REPEAT
   Druid, a name she does with pride repeat, ...   49 To Congreve   193
   To silent Shades repeat thy Verse, ...   121 Apollo Outwit   58
   Repeat the Absolution loud: . . . .   222 Prog of Love   10
   Yet shall I not again repeat   . . . .   453 Modern Lady   280
   Yet envy not, that I repeat   . . . .   497 Panegyr Swift   126
REPEATED
   I have heard all the Speech repeated by Hoppy.   . . .   143 New Song   9
REPEATING
   Repeating in his amorous Fits, ...   529 Lady's Dres Rm   117
REPEATS
   But repeats the same Note a whole Day, like a Finch.   .   143 New Song   8
   Her last Night's ill Success repeats, ...   447 Modern Lady   72
   The Cant which ev'ry Fool repeats, ...   645 On Poetry   153
REPELLING
   Your med'cine is repelling, ...   440 Ballyspellin   9
REPENT
   "And make him of his Zeal repent;   . . . .   570 Death of Swift   424
   Yet could not for his Heart repent it.   . . . . .   604 Beasts Confess   102
   Say, Stella, which you most repent   . . . . . .   745 Stel Distress   21
   Soon repent, or put to Slaughter   . . . .   838 Legion Club   213
   "<God> <damn> me, they bid us reform and repent, ...   872 Grand Question   145
   May give you a Blow you'll for ever repent.   . . .   941 Letter   40
REPENTANCE
   Now, whereas the said Criminal seems past Repentance,   .   266 Apollo   93
   That moves his Patients to Repentance: . . . . . .   605 Beasts Confess   122
REPENTED
   By buxom Lasses--Some repented   . . . .   182 Horace 2, 1   52
REPENTING
   "But now, repenting what was done, ...   714 Cadenus Vaness   880
   Poor Bishop Judas, late repenting, dies;   . . . . .   806 Judas   2
REPENTS
   He sues for Pardon, and repents too late.   . . . . .   195 Author Himself   52
REPIN'D
   Paddy repin'd to see him wear   . . . .   458 Paddy's Charac   19
REPINE
   Against Dissenters wou'd repine, ...   115 Bauc & Phil 2   133
   'Tis true,--then why should I repine, ...   203 In Sickness   1
   Virtue repuls't, yet knows not to repine;   . . . . .   210 Earl of Oxford   7
   Or what I should repine at more, ...   215 To Mr. Delany   7
   Can suffer Want, and not repine.   . . . .   243 Horace 4, 9   20
   Is out at elbows why should I repine?   . . . . .   419 Shall Repine   6
   Nor on a Theme like this repine, ...   515 Answer Fable   89
REPINING
   Repining, to applaud his Choice.   . . . .   387 Manly Virtue   134
REPLENISHED
   'Twas still replenished to the Top, ...   112 Bauc & Phil 2   33
REPLIED
   The smart-one replied, "There's no wit in the case;   . .   843 Ay and No   7
REPLIES
   But with Rejoinders and Replies, ...   690 Cadenus Vaness   120
   In lofty Style to make Replies, ...   711 Cadenus Vaness   796
REPLY
   Mr. Dean, you must reply.   . . . .   632 Epistle Lady   92
   You reply and rejoin like Hoadly of Bangor.   . . . .   967 Letter Sherid   8
   To read your Answer, and prepare Reply to't.   . . . .   1003 Dan J's Reply   3
REPLY'D
   Reply'd in complementall Style: . . . .   94 Bauc & Phil 1   158
   The Guest reply'd,--"My Friend, your Leave,   . . .   208 Fable Bitches   31
   God Bless your Grace I then reply'd, ...   343 Upon His Grace   37
REPORT
   Said, how a late report your friends had vex'd,   . . .   47 To Congreve   143
   There flies about a strange Report   . . . . . .   202 Horace 2, 6   89
   I give you Joy of the Report, ...   300 Horrid Plot   63
   I find you bear a good Report, and are an honest Man.   .   342 Upon His Grace   34
   "Yet here we had a strong report, ...   547 Life of Swift   84
   "The Dean, if we believe Report, ...   565 Death of Swift   307
   Which evil Tongues might else report, ...   713 Cadenus Vaness   856
REPORTED
   You're reported to dwell   . . . .   939 Riddle Answerd   D
REPORTS
   Fame now reports, the western Isle   . . . . . .   387 Manly Virtue   135
   As for Tibullus's Reports, ...   690 Cadenus Vaness   112
   Reports you are no longer young?   . . . .   757 Stel B-day '24   36
   Delany reports it, and he has a shrewd Tongue,   . . .   967 Letter Sherid   1
REPOSE
   Malignant goddess! bane to my repose, ...   53 Temple Ill   81

```
                                                        PAGE    TITLE           LINE
REPOSES
  Ev'ry Brother else reposes.  . . . . . . . . . .      931 Riddle 18          D 18
REPRESENT
  The Meat shall represent the Tyrant's Head,           162 Toland's Invit       11
  Are said to represent the Seas,    . . . . . . .      239 Run Bankers           6
  Here shift the Scene, to represent                    561 Death of Swift      205
  To represent in figure just   . . . . . . . .         659 On Poetry          D 410
  And represent them to Mankind  . . . . . . . .        691 Cadenus Vaness      152
REPRESENTERS
  On the Nation's Representers;  . . . . . . . .         635 Epistle Lady        156
REPRISAL
  How noble a Reprisal on the Great!  . . . . .          31 Ode to Temple        141
REPROACH
  Who barbarously think to 'scape reproach,             44 To Congreve           21
  Reproach not tho in jest, a Friend   . . . . . .      217 To Mr. Delany        67
  Could nothing but thy chief Reproach,  . . . . .      348 Whitshed Motto        3
  Without reproach of flattery true  . . . . . . .      658 On Poetry          D 410
  They reproach you with their Looks;  . . . . .        838 Legion Club         208
  The <Dean> and Spaniard must reproach ye;  . . .      884 Rev Market-Hill      30
REPROACHES
  Pleads for her own neglect, and thus reproaches mine: .   43 To Congreve        6
  On <Swift's> Reproaches for her <murdered> <spouse>  .   195 Author Himself    54
  Dare you let these Reproaches stand,  . . . . . .      732 Stella, Poems       139
REPROBATION
  "Of Reprobation and Despair:   . . . . . . .          305 Storm                60
REPROOF
  In mild Reproof to Woman-kind;   . . . . . .          384 Manly Virtue         24
REPROVE
  And reprove her when she's right;  . . . . . . .      907 Daphne               37
REPTIL
  This Reptil, of the Serpent kind,   . . . . . .        83 Salamander           30
REPULS'T
  Virtue repuls't, yet knows not to repine;  . . .      210 Earl of Oxford        7
REPUTATION
  These are the slaves whom reputation chains,  . . . .  48 To Congreve         163
  And wink a Reputation down;  . . . . . . . . .        450 Modern Lady         193
  Reputation ever tearing, . . . . . . . . . . .        800 Traulus 2            15
REPUTE
  Where Virtue is in least Repute,   . . . . . . .      385 Manly Virtue         65
  That I had some repute for Prose;  . . . . . .        555 Death of Swift       60
REQUEST
  Hear my Request the Virgin said   . . . . . . .       120 Apollo Outwit        29
  "Consider, 'tis my first Request.--  . . . . . .      201 Horace 2, 6          57
  The God, who favour'd her Request,   . . . . . .      302 Storm                 9
  Then Proteus urg'd the same Request,   . . . . .      303 Storm                25
  Whose Godships are in chief request,   . . . . .      460 Birthday Song         3
  Request it of him to compleat your Stairs.  . . . .   534 To Mr. Gay           98
REQUIR'D
  That Love is the Devil, I'll prove when requir'd:  . .   401 Window Inns 3      1
  The outward Form no Help requir'd:   . . . . . .      692 Cadenus Vaness      176
REQUIRE
  Performs what Friendship, Justice, Truth require:  . .   196 Author Himself    73
  With half a Word, when you require,  . . . . . .      325 Pethox               47
  Next, as the Laws of Song require,   . . . . . .      461 Birthday Song        21
  As Laws of Cookery require,  . . . . . . . . .        529 Lady's Dres Rm      101
  Such heavenly Influence require,  . . . . . . .       641 On Poetry            31
  No cruel Master could require  . . . . . . . .        726 To Stella           105
  Will not require Poetick Dress;   . . . . . .         757 Stel B-day '24       32
REQUIRES
  Whose maintenance requires no help from brains.  . .   48 To Congreve        164
  Next, hearken Gay, to what thy Charge requires,  . . .   533 To Mr. Gay        53
  True Friendship in two breasts requires  . . . . .    546 Life of Swift        43
  And, Love such Nicety requires,   . . . . . .         588 Strephon Chloe      135
RESCU'D
  Rescu'd Her from the Giant's Fort:   . . . . . .        7 Ode to King          38
RESEMBLANCE
  (High Truth) the best resemblance of exalted Thee,  .   36 Ode Sancroft       46
  Some faint Resemblance to produce,   . . . . .         81 Vanbrug House        87
  A near Resemblance to the Spheres.   . . . . . .       99 Elegy Patrige        40
  Some faint Resemblance to produce.   . . . . . .      109 V's House           129
  And, since the same resemblance held  . . . . . .     177 To Lord Harley       29
RESEMBLE
  The Sentiments resemble Hell.  . . . . . . . . .      496 Panegyr Swift       109
  Whom would'st thou resemble? I leave thee a Guesser;  .   518 Dean Hang Rape  46
RESEMBLES
  How nearly this <Bishop> our <Bishop> resembles!  . .   803 Irish Bishops      7
RESEMBLING
  Must needs be right, so well resembling theirs.  . . .   48 To Congreve      174
  A Thing resembling a Goose Py,   . . . . . .          109 V's House           104
  Resembling you as Angel Gods.  . . . . . . . .        499 Panegyr Swift       182
RESENT
  "If you resent it, who's to blame?  . . . . . . .     548 Life of Swift       121
  "No Individual could resent,   . . . . . . . .        571 Death of Swift      461
  And I resent these Pranks no more.   . . . . . .      579 Day Judgement        20
  He found, the Ministers resent it,   . . . . . .      604 Beasts Confess      101
  And, what the Wretches most resent,  . . . . . .      883 Rev Market-Hill      21
RESENTMENT
  Resentment on this publick Foe;  . . . . . . .        515 Answer Fable         82
  But blinded by Resentment, seeks   . . . . . . .      731 Stella, Poems       125
RESENTMENT'S
  Gets between them and my resentment's weight,  . . .   45 To Congreve         46
```

	PAGE	TITLE	LINE
RESENTMENTS			
In how ill season her resentments rule, ...	48	To Congreve	177
Resentments for her late Disgrace;	713	Cadenus Vaness	845
RESIDE			
In Winter--never to reside.	173	Horace 1, 7	86
And license to reside in town;	676	Parson's Case	26
RESIDENCE			
Since Heaven will claim its residence as well as birth,	35	Ode Sancroft	19
RESIGN			
And from this Hour my Patronage resign.	794	St. Pat's Well	102
RESIGNING			
Resigning to the Will of God.	561	Death of Swift	218
RESIGNS			
When <Ann> for Heav'n resigns Her Throne. . . .	180	Horace 2, 1	12
And willingly resigns its Place	340	Arch-Bish Dub	15
Melody resigns to Fate.	661	Love Song	32
RESISTANCE			
Resistance on the Wedding-Night	588	Strephon Chloe	155
Invading Foes, without Resistance, ...	934	Riddle 21	D 3
RESOLUTION			
And the whole crew this resolution takes, ...	309	Billet Players	49
"By Innocence and Resolution, ...	569	Death of Swift	399
But, through a pious Resolution;	603	Beasts Confess	68
And has taken just now a firm resolution	1027	Sheri Circles	23
RESOLV'D			
Resolv'd to give himself, as well as Country Peace. .	30	Ode to Temple	134
However, I was resolv'd to bring the Discourse slily about,	71	Mrs Harris Pet	36
And so resolv'd a House to build;	87	Hist V's House	22
So <Van> resolv'd to write a Farce, ...	107	V's House	55
And was resolv'd upon a Tryal, ...	120	Apollo Outwit	27
But you resolv'd to have your Jest, ...	175	Horace 1, 7	135
Dick, thou'rt resolv'd, as I am told, ...	180	Horace 2, 1	1
And resolv'd the next Winter, for that is the Time, .	265	Apollo	77
Are all resolv'd the Project to begin;	275	Epilogue	28
Resolv'd to save the British Nation, ...	300	Horrid Plot	49
So methought, he resolv'd no Liquor to taste, . . .	337	Serious Poem	111
But first resolv'd, to shew his Taste	378	Apology Lady C	97
Resolv'd, nor Honour, nor Estate, ...	384	Manly Virtue	35
Resolv'd for a Fortnight to Swim in Delight, . . .	517	Dean Hang Rape	26
Resolv'd to go thro' thick and thin;	528	Lady's Dres Rm	80
Resolv'd that Will. and he should meet no more; . .	537	Mr. Pulteney	3
Resolv'd to make his first Attack:	588	Strephon Chloe	149
Which he resolv'd to keep for ever hence, ...	603	Beasts Confess	71
Yet still resolv'd to spare no Cost;	702	Cadenus Vaness	493
Resolv'd to mortify your Pride, ...	730	Stella, Poems	85
Resolv'd my annual Verse to pay	740	Stel B-day 22	1
Thus, nature hath resolv'd to pay her	761	Bec's B-Day	29
And resolv'd to break their Pates, ...	833	Legion Club	95
The Knight his Opinion resolv'd to maintain. . . .	868	Grand Question	40
Resolv'd my Gratitude to show, ...	887	Panegyr Dean	1
RESOLVE			
"Resolve to perish with his <Whore>;	305	Storm	64
Resolve to stand it out the last;	774	Mullinix Tim	42
RESOLVED			
I was resolved to tell my Money, to see if it was right:	69	Mrs Harris Pet	4
Bravely I resolved to stay.	834	Legion Club	132
RESORT			
Th' appeal of dullness in the last resort:	53	Temple Ill	88
And you, our Subjects, when you here resort, . . .	275	Epilogue	29
Accomplish'd thus, his next Resort	385	Manly Virtue	63
To shine, where all the gay resort, ...	677	Parson's Case	27
For none but witlings there resort, ...	876	To Dean Swift	8
There's not a Soul, that does resort here, ...	928	Riddle 12	D 19
RESORTS			
What Serpent's that which still resorts, ...	30	Ode to Temple	116
RESPECT			
Scorning to show the least Respect.	133	Magician's Rod	26
No Man alive has more Respect--	173	Horace 1, 7	70
Without Respect to Friends, or Blood, ...	607	Beasts Confess	184
With Gratitude, Respect, Esteem:	711	Cadenus Vaness	787
Devotion, Duty, and Respect, ...	711	Cadenus Vaness	799
RESPECTS			
My humble Respects to my Lady unknown.--	869	Grand Question	81
I gave, as you beg, your most humble respects: . . .	979	Dean to Tho: S	24
On Thursday I'll pay my Respects at your Shrine . .	1017	Swift Ans Sher	21
And so I conclude, with humble respects as usual, . . .	1024	Nim-Dan-Dean 2	D 18
REST			
(Which since has seiz'd on all the rest)	28	Ode to Temple	54
Ill may I live, if the good Sancroft in his holy rest,	36	Ode Sancroft	50
Wisely retreated to his heavenly rest.	40	Ode Sancroft	189
While all the rest stood gaping round	63	Discovery	24
Quoth Neal, whate'er the rest may think, ...	67	Problem	53
More probably than all the rest;	128	Little House	44
Unloads upon a Stall to rest	160	Atlas	6
That he might take his Rest awhile	160	Atlas	12
Nor let such Cares disturb thy Rest.	182	Horace 2, 1	70
And that he might securely Rest, ...	235	Elegy on Demar	45
But never shall our isle have Rest	259	Bubble	213
Goes round the House to wake the rest:	278	Journal	10
Then goes alone to take his Rest	292	Prog Marriage	89

REST	(CONTINUED)	PAGE	TITLE	LINE
"For Fear the rest shou'd say he squeeks;		305	Storm	62
"Divide the rest, but then take care,		321	First of April	11
Ah never lay thy Head to Rest!		361	Grace's Answer	14
For, when in Bed we rest our weary Limbs,		363	On Dreams	7
The rest condemn'd, with rival Voice,		387	Manly Virtue	133
His arguments convinc't the rest.		423	Ireld	64
And here rest, Sic transit Gloria Mundi.		431	Dicky Dolly	24
Break not his rest, nor hurt his lungs:		433	Answer Paulus	54
Nor gives her Tongue one Moment's Rest,		448	Modern Lady	111
What some invent, the rest enlarge;		449	Modern Lady	145
A perfect Nuissance to the rest.		455	Dean Smedley	12
Took Wing to Jove, and hop'd to rest		458	Paddy's Charac	31
But you may hook in all the rest.		465	Birthday Song	150
And Strephon bids us guess the rest;		526	Lady's Dres Rm	16
Why Strephon will you tell the rest?		527	Lady's Dres Rm	69
They pay a Trifle, and enjoy the rest.		533	To Mr. Gay	48
Behold a Foe more fierce than all the rest:		538	Mr. Pulteney	32
This Maxim more than all the rest		553	Death of Swift	5
Approves his Foresight to the rest:		557	Death of Swift	128
The rest will give a Shrug and cry,		561	Death of Swift	211
I sink from Reverie to Rest.		578	Day Judgement	2
Cry'd, Caelia! thrice, and sigh'd the rest.		595	Cassinus Peter	40
Contented rest; you have your due		608	Know Not What	6
The Rest pursue as thick as Hops:		654	On Poetry	400
But all the rest shall club it I protest:---		671	Epig Carthy 24	D 6
Some Lines, more moving than the rest,		703	Cadenus Vaness	520
Or else, comparing with the rest,		728	Stella, Poems	19
Or else, to introduce the rest		755	Stella '23	23
And please all the rest,		756	Dingley Brent	14
Be soundly mawl'd, and plagues the rest.		777	Mullinix Tim	132
A <Bishop> who rul'd all the rest of his Tribe;		803	Irish Bishops	2
He's a Christian as good as the rest of the herd.		816	Yahoo's	29
The rest, who boast they have conferr'd it,		820	Dr. Rundle	15
Near the Church--you know the rest.		829	Legion Club	8
'Till he gave me my Will, I wou'd give him no Rest:		869	Grand Question	58
Then let us rise, and rest our weary Bums.		882	Pastoral Dial	52
And my Oppression gives them Rest.		918	Riddle 4	10
Yet no Watch the rest will keep,		931	Riddle 18	D 16
One enjoys them for the Rest.		931	Riddle 18	D 20
The rest of your compliment I dare not tell her,		979	Dean to Tho: S	25
RESTING				
And find a resting Place at last.		923	Riddle 7	78
RESTLESS				
That Restless Tyrant, who of late		10	Ode to King	119
Still to unhappy restless thoughts inclin'd;		55	Temple Ill	132
With restless Beak thy blooming Fruit to spoil,		792	St. Pat's Well	46
RESTOR'D				
How soon have You restor'd her Charms!		23	Ode Athenian	228
My Pow'r shall be again restor'd,		694	Cadenus Vaness	247
To their old Posts restor'd all Three,		926	Riddle 9	23
RESTORE				
Great Jove, he cry'd, the Art restore		107	V's House	43
No Painting can restore a Nose,		229	Prog of Beauty	111
Restore the Ships by Philip taken,		468	Birthday Song	249
This Infant shall restore my Reign.		691	Cadenus Vaness	147
Which, though his Conscience forc'd him to restore,		806	Judas	5
Would soon restore our antient Reign.		887	Panegyr Dean	10
Deucalion, to restore Mankind		922	Riddle 8	45
But Jest apart, restore, you Capon ye,		1033	Ans to Crown	7
RESTRAINT				
Has fed without Restraint, or Trouble;		230	Prog of Poetry	2
RESULT				
The last Result of all Designs:		921	Riddle 7	12
RESUM'D				
Resum'd the Figure of a Stick.		132	Magician's Rod	14
RESUME				
Resume their own when e'er they please.		239	Run Bankers	8
Resume not what themselves have giv'n,		695	Cadenus Vaness	260
RESUMES				
But, with the Morning-Dawn, resumes		132	Magician's Rod	19
RETAIL				
And selling basely by Retail,		19	Ode Athenian	102
Serves by retail to furnish half mankind.		45	To Congreve	54
For nicely computing the Price by Retail,		288	Bank Down	36
RETAILING				
a Jobber of Stocks by retailing false news		540	Charac Walpole	9
RETAIN				
(Which Nature never can retain,		25	Ode Athenian	289
RETAINER				
"An old Retainer to your House,		850	Old Thorn	72
RETIR'D				
Retir'd to your Imperial Seat.		326	Pethox	90
RETIRE				
He now intended to Retire.		172	Horace 1, 7	46
And canst not easily retire,		181	Horace 2, 1	34
What could be more, but decently retire?		196	Author Himself	74
"That you wou'd with your Cubbs retire:		208	Fable Bitches	28
Made her retire, and quit her Right,		208	Fable Bitches	41
Then cunningly retire unseen,		253	Bubble	71
The Man of Bus'ness must retire.		325	Pethox	48

	PAGE	TITLE	LINE
RETIRE (CONTINUED)			
When he has Virtue to retire,	484	Libel on D- D-	117
Would grant him Licence to retire,	606	Beasts Confess	171
Retire, yet still bemoan their Country's Fate.	772	Horace 1, 14	60
Keeper, I must now retire,	839	Legion Club	231
RETIREMENT			
But forc'd from their Retirement into Day,	667	Epig Carthy 5	D 3
RETIRES			
Still blushes, and with speed retires,	178	To Lord Harley	71
RETIRING			
To Lazy-Hill retiring from his Court,	284	Elegy Boat	7
RETREAT			
Their courting a Retreat like you,	28	Ode to Temple	66
Sing (belov'd Muse) the Pleasures of Retreat,	30	Ode to Temple	135
In the divin'ty of retreat,	36	Ode Sancroft	51
Thus Sancroft, in the exaltation of retreat,	41	Ode Sancroft	211
You make to truth, retreat, and innocence;	44	To Congreve	8
Yet always wishing to retreat;	202	Horace 2, 6	107
Then, by a Soldierly Retreat,	326	Pethox	89
In Virtue's best-belov'd Retreat;	385	Manly Virtue	50
Where Devils to a vale retreat	490	Dialogue	41
To seek a more secure Retreat.	849	Old Thorn	40
RETREATED			
Wisely retreated to his heavenly rest.	40	Ode Sancroft	189
RETREATING			
Retreating silent to his Cell;	375	Apology Lady C	14
RETREATS			
The muse retreats far in yon chrystal cell;	50	To Congreve	228
Bush smiling round on all, retreats	64	Discovery	44
RETRENCH'D			
For brevity I have retrench'd,	281	Journal	67
RETRIEVE			
Born to retrieve her sex's fame.	177	To Lord Harley	38
Come here their Losses to retrieve,	254	Bubble	90
As will retrieve a lost Estate:	392	Young's Satire	44
Carthy ambitious to retrieve his name,	671	Epig Carthy 24	D 1
RETROGRADE			
You're so retrograde, sure you were born under Cancer:	1019	To Sheridan	3
RETROSPECTION			
When thy Retrospection vast	862	To Janus	15
RETURN			
Nor will her Teeth return again.	229	Prog of Beauty	112
In return to her Scorn, I send her Diseases,	266	Apollo	105
At Two or after we return all,	279	Journal	26
He'll soon return to his own Vomit.	299	Horrid Plot	36
To London strait return again,	312	To Ford	48
And then your old Argument still will return:	336	Serious Poem	63
Return Him Beggar As He Went.	456	Dean Smedley	50
Ah! never to return Home;	573	Helter Skelter	16
He gladly offers in return:	711	Cadenus Vaness	785
She must return to Ormond-Key.	746	Stel Distress	26
She must return to Ormond Key:	751	Stel Wood-Park	46
Virtue herself would now return too late.	793	St. Pat's Well	86
I return home at night,	853	Lady's Lament	53
Return with unpolluted Thumb.	894	Panegyr Dean	224
And there is no return again.	932	Riddle 19	D 22
Will you return as hard you, if I call t'ye?	989	Letter Dr Sh-n	33
If when you return, your Road you dont line	1017	Swift Ans Sher	20
RETURN'D			
Return'd a finish'd spark this summer down,	47	To Congreve	119
Return'd 'em Thanks in homely Stile;	115	Bauc & Phil 2	112
And then return'd it to your Mistress,	135	Magician's Rod	82
In State return'd the grand Parade;	586	Strephon Chloe	68
Return'd this Answer to a Tittle.	742	Stel B-day 22	36
You e're return'd, or ever went?	745	Stel Distress	22
Unhappy Ship, thou art return'd in Vain:	770	Horace 1, 14	9
Lo! Infidelity return'd again.	792	St. Pat's Well	36
RETURNING			
The fancy furnish'd by returning joy;	53	Temple Ill	68
The Turnkey now his Flock returning sees,	125	Descriptn Morn	15
Returning Home at Night, you'll find the Sink	137	City Shower	5
Returning home one Day from Court,	170	Horace 1, 7	2
My Lady now returning home	377	Apology Lady C	57
Returning sound in Limb and Wind,	398	Earl of P-b-w	23
Returning at the Midnight Hour;	581	Young Nymph	7
Returning Janus now prepares,	753	Gift for Bec	1
RETURNS			
Whatever base returns you find	755	Stella '23	29
Hath met with returns of all sorts but applause;	815	Yahoo's	17
To make you suitable Returns;	887	Panegyr Dean	30
And get the like Returns again.	890	Panegyr Dean	104
REUNITE			
(In pieces cut, the Viper still did reunite)	30	Ode to Temple	132
REV'RENCE			
You find His Rev'rence past his Prime,	293	Prog Marriage	104
Your Rev'rence, but to cut one Leg off,	366	Answer Delaney	16
His Rev'rence and her Highness walking;	410	Dial Rich Marb	60
Your Rev'rence thus, with like Success,	892	Panegyr Dean	187
Comes fill'd with Rev'rence and Devotion.)	893	Panegyr Dean	212
REV'REND			
The Rev'rend Dr. Raymond guess'd,	128	Little House	43

		PAGE	TITLE	LINE
REV'REND	**(CONTINUED)**			
Said Harley, Welcome Rev'rend Dean!	. . . .	174	Horace 1, 7	121
It falls before thy Rev'rend Years,	. . . .	340	Arch-Bish Dub	14
But, Rev'rend Doctor, you, we know,	. . . .	483	Libel on D- D-	111
A Genius in the Rev'rend Gown,	. . . .	502	Doctor Delaney	79
"The Rev'rend Author's good Intention,	. . . . . .	564	Death of Swift	289
But this I am sure, the Most Rev'rend old Dragon,		803	Irish Bishops	13
Thrice Rev'rend <Dean> for all I owe;	. . . . . .	887	Panegyr Dean	2
Nor have you grumbled, rev'rend <Dean>,	. . . . .	892	Panegyr Dean	163
REVELL				
Since he no more can build, and plant, & revell,	. . .	678	Dean and Duke	9
REVELS				
His Revels to keep,	. . . .	244	Irish-Feast	5
REVENG'D				
I am too much reveng'd already by Time;	. . . . . .	266	Apollo	104
If truly you would be reveng'd on the parson,	. . . .	818	Epigr Kite	5
And thus I am fully reveng'd for your late tricks,	. .	977	Dean to Sherid	47
REVENGE				
The muse and I no more revenge desire,	. . . .	37	Ode Sancroft	90
"And I may have Revenge to Night."	. . . .	447	Modern Lady	69
You try to take Revenge in vain.	. . . .	504	Doctor Delaney	136
But, we shall keep revenge in store	. . . .	622	Scandal Poem 1	173
He'll take his revenge on his innocent wife.	. . . .	817	Yahoo's	74
"Sworn to revenge my Thorn and me.	. . . .	851	Old Thorn	80
REVENGEFUL				
And in a shrill revengeful Tone,	. . . .	850	Old Thorn	55
Observe me with revengeful Eye:	. . . .	925	Riddle 8	18
REVENUES				
Not so a Nation's Revenues are paid:		533	To Mr. Gay	49
REVERENCE				
As strictly too; as doth his Reverence.	. . . . . .	603	Beasts Confess	72
Not that I know his Reverence was ever concern'd to my knowledge,		986	Mary to Sher	15
REVEREND SEE REVND				
Since the bright essence fled, where haunts the reverend ghost?		36	Ode Sancroft	44
Here by a mountain's side, a reverend cave	. . . . .	49	To Congreve	187
The very Reverend Dean Smedley	. . . . . .	455	Dean Smedley	1
Who are all grown reverend Preachers!	. . . . . .	838	Legion Club	204
REVERENTIAL				
Upon his reverential rump.	. . . .	822	Epigr Rundle	2
Such reverential Awe express,	. . . .	889	Panegyr Dean	79
REVERIE				
I sink from Reverie to Rest.	. . . .	578	Day Judgement	2
REVERS'D				
That the letters appear'd revers'd on the Pane,	. . .	264	Apollo	49
REVERSE				
To show the World his chief Reverse in you.	. . . .	532	To Mr. Gay	38
Nor fondly hope for some Reverse of Fate,	. . . . .	793	St. Pat's Well	85
When all the sad Reverse appears!	. . . .	921	Riddle 7	10
REVERSES				
Reverses what the Prophet did;	. . . .	132	Magician's Rod	6
REVERSION				
With promise of a mad Reversion after Death.	. . . .	32	Ode to Temple	198
REVERTED				
By dark reverted rays from its reflection made;	. . .	35	Ode Sancroft	22
REVIEW				
Judicious Rymer oft review:	. . . .	648	On Poetry	249
REVILE				
Revile His great ambassador,	. . . .	38	Ode Sancroft	131
Who dare revile the integrity of verse:	. . . . . .	53	Temple Ill	70
Who dares revile the Nation's Wisdom,	. . . . . .	515	Answer Fable	93
Revile and slander, fume and storm,	. . . .	778	Mullinix Tim	167
Revile that Nation-saving Paper,	. . . .	796	Traulus 1	11
REVILES				
Reviles all People in his Jargon,	. . . .	777	Mullinix Tim	113
REVIS'D				
Revis'd by Tibbalds, Moore, and Cibber.	. . . . .	561	Death of Swift	200
REVIVE				
On the Scene of this Land very soon to revive.	. . .	337	Serious Poem	94
The Arts revive, the Vallies sing,	. . . .	387	Manly Virtue	125
Your still-born Poems shall revive,	. . . .	394	Grub-Street	7
Revive the Libels born to dye;	. . . .	561	Death of Swift	203
Or revive at its Will,	. . . .	939	Riddle Answerd	18
And revive above Ground,	. . . .	939	Riddle Answerd	20
REVIVES				
Oft' revives my drooping head:	. . . .	937	Riddle 24	D 46
REVND				
Durst there show his right or most revnd face	. . . .	522	St. Cecilia's	10
REVOKE				
And tho' I can't my gift revoke,	. . . .	121	Apollo Outwit	51
REVOLUTION				
Blest Revolution, which creates	. . . .	96	On the Union	5
REVOLVING				
For in twice twelve revolving Moons,	. . . . . .	150	Corinna	14
REWARD				
But now Your Worth its just Reward shall have;	. .	12	Ode to William	D 13
And brings the dear Reward of Victory and Peace.	. .	16	Ode Athenian	21
Far above all Reward, yet to which all is due,	. .	21	Ode Athenian	187
Next, faithful Silence hath a sure Reward:	. . .	210	Earl of Oxford	15
A Guinea shall reward your pains.	. . . .	463	Birthday Song	94

REWARD   (CONTINUED)   PAGE   TITLE   LINE
     Let due Reward to Merit be allow'd;   . . . .   533 To Mr. Gay   57
     That Virtue, stil'd its own Reward, ...   764 Stel B-day '26   26
     Thy Vertues meet their just Reward, ... 779 Mullinix Tim   201
REWARDED
     "Hath been rewarded with a Pension: . . . .   564 Death of Swift   290
     How Genius is no more rewarded;   . . . .   652 On Poetry   350
REWARDING
     What Justice in rewarding Merit?   . . . .   655 On Poetry   415
REWARDS
     Rewards too great for your Flim-Flams, ...   478 Epist on Epist   107
RHENISH
     A long-ear'd Beast, and Rhenish Wine, ...   942 Probatur Alit   13
RHET'RIC
     His rhet'ric, bombast, silly jests, are by far . . . . 815 Yahoo's   13
RHETORIC
     If all my rhetoric must fail . . . .   899 Dean's Reasons   31
     In rhetoric, or picking straws; . . . .   901 Dean's Reasons   77
RHEUMATISM
     Of Rheumatism and Pox complain, ...   311 To Ford   25
RHIME
     To deafen 'em with Puns and Rhime.   . . . . .   75 Game Traffick   D   28
     Nay, 'twas affirm'd, he sometimes dealt in Rhime: . .   193 Author Himself   10
     We should them Quote, unless for Rhime. . . . . .   372 Letter D. S-y   28
     He told the real Truth in Rhime.   . . . .   378 Apology Lady C   90
     More beneficial Ways than Rhime;   . . . . . .   495 Panegyr Swift   67
     He takes an Hour to find a Rhime: . . . . . .   556 Death of Swift   100
     Treat me not with Doggrel Rhime.   . . . . . .   631 Epistle Lady   58
     If still you be dispos'd to rhime, ...   645 On Poetry   145
     Be my Phoebus while I rhime. .· . . . . .   862 To Janus   2
     But, squeezing out four Lines in Rhime, ...   893 Panegyr Dean   195
     But find the Rhime, and you're the Man. . . . . .   912 Aenigma   14
     And for the Rhime, to you're the Man, ...   912 Aenigma Expl   D   9
     But when I would find Rhime for Rochfort, ...   993 On Picture   7
RHIMERS
     Ye Rhimers, dead as soon as born, ...   394 Grub-Street   3
     These Rhimers abundantly show it: . . . .   401 Window Inns 3   2
RHIMES
     She seem'd to laugh and squawl in Rhimes, ...   150 Corinna   15
     My Rhimes are gone   . . . . .   442 Ballyspellin   85
     Compell'd by you to tag in Rhimes . . . .   445 Modern Lady   30
     Shreds of Wit, and senseless Rhimes, ...   523 Betty Grizette   19
     And on the Marble grave these Rhimes, ...   596 Cassinus Peter   75
RHIMING
     A lust of rhiming for a poet's vein, ...   45 To Congreve   78
     But search among the rhiming Race, ...   651 On Poetry   327
     In Creatures of the rhiming Race.   . . . . . .   653 On Poetry   386
RHINE
     And yet I must except the Rhine, ...   467 Birthday Song   219
     As much as the Liffee's outdone by the Rhine . . . .   1018 Swift Ans Sher   26
RHYME
     This every Pretender to Rhyme will admit, ...   263 Apollo   19
     When the Days are at shortest, to put it in Rhyme; . . 265 Apollo   78
     To call nothing his, but the Rhyme and the Measure. . 266 Apollo   102
     I'd tell of yours in Rhyme and Print: . . . . . .   475 Epist on Epist   11
     "And had a Kind of Knack at Rhyme: . . . . . .   563 Death of Swift   264
     To rhyme almost as ill as Duck;   . . . . . .   658 On Poetry   D 186
     Who murder'd Horace without Rhyme or Reason? . . . .   666 Epig Carthy 3   D   4
     Worn out by Wits who rhyme on Faces;   . . . . . .   730 Stella, Poems   76
     To shape it into Sense and Rhyme;   . . . . . .   741 Stel B-day 22   10
     And can no longer dance in Rhyme.   . . . . . .   756 Stel B-day '24   4
     Nor ever Nymph inspir'd to Rhyme, ...   757 Stel B-day '24   21
     When Drapier's-hill appear'd in rhyme.   . . . . . .   899 Dean's Reasons   10
     You rhyme, as folks fence, in tierce and cart. . . . . 979 Dean to Tho: S   20
     But your rhyme was not double, 'cause your sight was but 980 Tho: Sheridan   2
           single.
     Or fit more exact than one eye and one rhyme. . . . . 980 Tho: Sheridan   4
     The segment so large 'twixt your reason and rhyme is, . 1026 Sheri Circles   6
RHYMER   SEE RYMER
     No Rhymer can like Welsted sink.   . . . .   654 On Poetry   394
RHYMERS
     So, Modern Rhymers strive to blast   . . . . . .   81 Vanbrug House   89
     Well, punners and rhymers must have the last word. . . 976 Dean to Sherid   8
RHYMES
     Hail Queen of Britain, Queen of Rhymes, ...   467 Birthday Song   221
     Creech murder'd Horace in his senseless Rhymes, . . .   666 Epig Carthy 3   D   1
     So if this Pile of scatter'd Rhymes . . . .   728 Stella, Poems   5
     That Phoebus help'd me in my Rhymes, ...   741 Stel B-day 22   24
     I chose these Rhymes out, for their Difficulty. . . .   989 Letter Dr Sh-n   32
RHYMING
     Draws ev'ry rhyming, prating, dressing sot, ...   48 To Congreve   153
     Out-done by none in Rhyming well, ...   650 On Poetry   291
     From rhyming in cars you may swing in a cart. . . .   976 Dean to Sherid   36
     And now I hope you'll excuse this rhyming, which I must 1024 Nim-Dan-Dean 2   D   17
       . . .
RIB'D   SEE STEEL-RIB'D
RIBBANDS
     Quoth King Robin, our Ribbands I see are too few . .   389 Order of Bath   1
RIBBIN
     Take your blue Ribbin for a String. . . . .   190 Faggot   38

```
                                                         PAGE   TITLE              LINE
RIBBINS
    With Ribbins in Knots, at its Tail and its Ears:    . .   870 Grand Question     98
RIBBON
    His Cap had a new Cherry Ribbon to ty't.     . . . . . .  399 Tom Clinch          6
RIBBONS
    Chequer'd with Ribbons blew and green;       . . . . . .  200 Horace 2, 6        29
    On Ribbons, Fans, and Gloves and Lace;        . . . . .   698 Cadenus Vaness    377
    And coxcombs in red ribbons shine: . . . . . . . .        876 To Dean Swift      22
RICH
    Like a rich Coat with Skirts of Frize:                     96 On the Union        8
    To Pan alone rich Misers call,            . . . . . . .   157 Fable of Midas     57
    Not Rich, but ow'd no Man a Groat;        . . . . . . .   171 Horace 1, 7        34
    Love never thinks of Rich and Poor,        . . . . . . .  224 Prog of Love       61
    A rich Divine began to woo    . . . .                     289 Prog Marriage       2
    The Swain is rich, the Nymph is fair;      . . . . . .    290 Prog Marriage      28
    Yes, and a Place he will grow rich in;      . . . . . .   300 Horrid Plot        65
    To spare the Rich, and plague the Poor;      . . . . .    392 Young's Satire     46
    Himself, as rich as fifty Jews,           . . . . . . .   481 Libel on D- D-     39
    By which he grew both rich and wise.      . . . . . . .   513 Answer Fable       18
    Be rich; but of your Wealth make no Parade;   . . . .     533 To Mr. Gay         61
    Starve twenty Lords to make one Scoundrel rich:  . . .    535 To Mr. Gay        104
    Or some rich benefice provide,           . . . . . . .    676 Parson's Case      21
    That ev'ry rich and lordly Swain          . . . . . .     693 Cadenus Vaness    232
    She may be handsome, young and rich,      . . . . . . .   698 Cadenus Vaness    362
    Rich Flanders Lace, and 'Colberteen.       . . . . . .    700 Cadenus Vaness    417
    Rich Ladies will furnish their Garrets with Stuff,   .    716 Answer Rebus       15
    Yet where He's not so rich as I; . . . . . . . .          954 Authors Living      9
RICHER
    Produce a richer vein or cleaner ore;      . . . . . .     45 To Congreve        52
    The Sea is richer than the Land,          . . . . . . .   254 Bubble             97
    This Paper will soon make us richer than Crags.  . . .    287 Bank Down          18
    From growing richer with good Cheer,      . . . . . .     745 Stel Distress      15
RICHES
    Riches, the Wisest Monarch sings,         . . . . . .     239 Run Bankers        21
    Give others Riches, Power, and Station,       . . . .     555 Death of Swift     43
    From growing Riches with good Chear,      .              750 Stel Wood-Park     43
RICHEST
    Roses of richest Dye, that shone         . . . . . . .    379 Apology Lady C    113
    With richest Wines and costly Cheer:       . . . . .     745 Stel Distress       4
RICHLY
    With Coat embroider'd richly shine,       . . . . . . .   182 Horace 2, 1        74
RICHMOND-LODGE
    Of Richmond-Lodge, and Marble-Hill.       . . . . . .     408 Dial Rich Marb      4
    Kind Richmond-Lodge; the same to you.      . . . . . .    411 Dial Rich Marb    104
<RICHMOND'S>
    <Sunderland>, <Orford>, <Boyl>, and <Richmond's> Grace   165 Toland's Invit     33
RICKS
    Whole Ricks of Hay and Stacks of Corn,     . . . . .     811 Bro Protestant      3
RID
    And rid her of her Lumber and Her Books,     . . . .      23 Ode Athenian      229
    Oh! that I could but once be rid   . . . . . . .         861 Lady Acheson       43
    'Twill be our Int'rest to get rid of her:    . . . . .   886 Rev Market-Hill   106
RIDDEN
    As ridden by a midnight hag: . . . . . . . . .           434 Answer Paulus      76
RIDDLE
    When, Behold the next Morning, a wonderful Riddle,        77 Lady B- B-          8
    Your Riddle I spy.                                       938 Riddle Answerd      2
    Your damnable Riddle, my poor Brains did rack nigh.      972 S-'s Ans Sh-d       2
    And that she's a Riddle, can never be right,   . . .     972 S-'s Ans Sh-d       7
    For a Riddle is dark, but a Woman is light.              972 S-'s Ans Sh-d       8
    For a riddle and sieve, or a sieve and a riddle:   . .   976 Dean to Sherid     14
    For a riddle and sieve, or a sieve and a riddle:   . .   976 Dean to Sherid     14
    You call them a riddle, as call them a sieve.   . . .    976 Dean to Sherid     16
    As for your new rebus, or riddle, or crux,   . . . .     977 Dean to Sherid     43
RIDDLES
    Nor for his prophecies in riddles: . . . . . . .         432 Answer Paulus      20
    Epistles, Riddles, Epigrams. . . . . . . . . .          478 Epist on Epist    108
    That a sieve dissolves riddles by help of the shears;  . 976 Dean to Sherid     20
    To break open riddles with shears or with scissars.  .   976 Dean to Sherid     22
RIDE
    In Summer round the Park to ride,         . . . . . .     173 Horace 1, 7        85
    Ride o'er the Waves in spacious Hoops,      . . . . .     254 Bubble             91
    "Or, throw him overboard, he'll ride   . . . . . .       304 Storm              35
    And high in Air for ever ride;      . . . . . . .        347 Prometheus         74
    A goodly Sight to see her ride,        . . . . . .       410 Dial Rich Marb     63
    I see the ship at anchor ride,        . . . . . . .       420 Holyhead            8
    He rules the Sea, you see him ride in't;    . . . . .    463 Birthday Song      98
    To Hell on the Backs of the Clergy wou'd ride;   . . .   804 Irish Bishops      18
    On their Crosiers to ride, like a Witch on a Broom.  .   804 Irish Bishops      22
    Or else I will not ride one Inch of Ground.   . . . .    943 Probatur Alit      40
RIDERS
    The Horse and both the Riders tir'd:      . . . . . .     224 Prog of Love       78
RIDES    SEE OUT-RIDES
    Rides on a Broomstick for a Nag,         . . . . . .      132 Magician's Rod     16
    Rides Day and Night at such a Rate,       . . . . . .     174 Horace 1, 7       117
    And rides through Dover in the Morn:       . . . . .     398 Earl of P-b-w      17
    Despises rapparees, and rides           . . . . . .      435 Answer Paulus      97
    And see how he rides like a Lord of the Land,    . .     870 Grand Question     95
    Nor rides, nor walks, nor hunts, nor fowls,  . . . .     901 Dean's Reasons     87
RIDET
    That Semel'n anno ridet Apollo.       . . . . . . .       741 Stel B-day 22      22
```

RIDGE

	PAGE	TITLE	LINE
And in huge Confluent join at Snow-Hill Ridge,	139	City Shower	59

RIDICUL'D

"It must be Ridicul'd, or Lash'd.	548	Life of Swift	118

RIDICULE

For an obliging Ridicule:	216	To Mr. Delany	36
And turn it all to ridicule:	468	Birthday Song	266
Turning all to Ridicule:	631	Epistle Lady	52
Ridicule has greater Pow'r	636	Epistle Lady	199
But those who aim at Ridicule	707	Cadenus Vaness	664

RIDICULOUS

Of Comments and Disputes, ridiculous and vain,	23	Ode Athenian	226

RIDING

The Prentices procur'd a Riding	221	A Quiet Life	53
All riding on Horseback to Hell and the Bank.	287	Bank Down	25
By riding Post I lose my Health;	917	Riddle 3	17
By riding this morning too long in your car:	976	Dean to Sherid	28

RIFLE

For, as the rabble daub, and rifle	436	Answer Paulus	135

RIFLED

I'm rifled, quoth Nell,	245	Irish-Feast	21

RIG

Was call'd, to rig him out a Beau:	903	Death Daphne	20

RIGG

We'll Rigg in Meath-Street, Egypt's hauty Queen,	275	Epilogue	19
To rigg her out for Juno's mayd.	619	Scandal Poem 1	78

RIGG'D

Which just like ours, new rigg'd and man'd,	96	On the Union	17

RIGHT   SEE BIRTH-RIGHT,A-RIGHT

Which is perhaps as hard t' imagine right	21	Ode Athenian	159
Which yet whoe're examines right will find	21	Ode Athenian	184
Must needs be right, so well resembling theirs.	48	To Congreve	174
Wert thou right woman, thou shouldst scorn to look	54	Temple Ill	107
I was resolved to tell my Money, to see if it was right:	69	Mrs Harris Pet	4
By antient Right are Builders too.	81	Vanbrug House	68
You're in the right, but be'n't afraid	92	Bauc & Phil 1	84
And stood up firm for Right Divine:	115	Bauc & Phil 2	134
Speak against Peace right many a Word;	147	Windsor Proph	8
"Must I, against all Right and Law,	154	Widow and Cat	D 21
My Province is, to see that all be right,	165	Toland's Invit	27
And to be kept in my right wits.	199	Horace 2, 6	D
Made her retire, and quit her Right,	208	Fable Bitches	41
Few Hints from you will set him right,	218	To Mr. Delany	97
A golden Monument would not be Right,	234	Elegy on Demar	23
Right Trusty, and so forth; We let you to know,	263	Apollo	1
But in Stella's bright Eyes were plac'd right again;	264	Apollo	50
The Wedding-day, you take me right,	290	Prog Marriage	19
Why then the Proverb is not right,	299	Horrid Plot	39
In ev'ry Council and Debate he stands for what is Right	341	Upon His Grace	5
Both Right and Left, as Fellow-sufferers.	367	Answer Delaney	40
Which if right ta'en, and but good Luck-hold	373	Letter D. S-y	60
Now you've done right, No Knight attempting	373	Letter D. S-y	75
Where Right, and Wrong, are bought and sold,	385	Manly Virtue	67
True Virtue has a Right to rise.)	386	Manly Virtue	92
Quoth Marble-Hill, right well I ween,	408	Dial Rich Marb	9
They take the wrong Way for the right.	412	Desire Possess	18
Who's in the wrong, who in the right	421	Ireld	6
And honest Paulus judges right.	432	Answer Paulus	2
Right Indian this, right Macklin that;	447	Modern Lady	83
Right Indian this, right Macklin that;	447	Modern Lady	83
And take it right, it means no more	464	Birthday Song	139
Durst there show his right or most revnd face	522	St. Cecilia's	10
And first: To make my Observation right,	532	To Mr. Gay	31
And, should a Friend attempt to set him right,	535	To Mr. Gay	111
What right had he to hold the Whip?	548	Life of Swift	120
"And your Conjectures are not right;	550	Life of Swift	195
"Where Titles give no Right or Power,	570	Death of Swift	439
Is what our Maidens claim by Right:	588	Strephon Chloe	156
And I find it answers right:	634	Epistle Lady	145
To decide of Wrong and Right?	638	Epistle Lady	270
For ever fixt by Right Divine,	642	On Poetry	57
(A Monarch's Right) on Grubstreet Line.	642	On Poetry	58
Depend upon't their Judgment's right:	644	On Poetry	134
A thousand Bards thy Right disown:	653	On Poetry	378
To neither use thy tusks contribute right,	672	Epig Carthy 25	D 3
And on the Right Hand took their Places	689	Cadenus Vaness	95
Now wou'd vouchsafe to set them right.	699	Cadenus Vaness	407
To teach her what was Right or Wrong,	705	Cadenus Vaness	599
Regardless both of Wrong and Right.	730	Stella, Poems	94
Think Eusden's Right as good as mine.	741	Stel B-day 22	30
Unless it had the right Fumette:	746	Stel Distress	16
Unless it had the right Fumette.	750	Stel Wood-Park	14
For Nature, always in the right,	757	Stel B-day '24	43
She saved Britannia's Right, and lost her own.	771	Horace 1, 14	46
If this you consider, our Emblem is right;	805	Irish Bishops	43
A modus right fit for insulters of Deans.	817	Yahoo's	59
That the Club have Right to dwell	830	Legion Club	43
They'll come down to right themselves:	838	Legion Club	210
For, the Right holds the Sword, and the Left holds the Bridle,)	870	Grand Question	108
"To give a young Gentleman right Education,	872	Grand Question	161

		PAGE	TITLE	LINE
RIGHT	(CONTINUED)			
Attack the Foe at Left and Right;		884	Rev Market-Hill	46
Sleek, <--> claims her as his Right:		897	Panegyr Dean	344
With not one opinion right:		906	Daphne	10
And reprove her when she's right;		907	Daphne	37
And that she's a Riddle, can never be right,		972	S-'s Ans Sh-d	7
To take the right way,		1038	Sheridan Cavan	11
RIGHTEOUS				
Once on a Time, a righteous Sage,		383	Manly Virtue	1
(Happy beneath his righteous Sway)		388	Manly Virtue	138
And griev'd your righteous Soul beside,		496	Panegyr Swift	91
RIGHTFUL				
Your Arm has now Your Rightful Title show'd;		12	Ode to William	D 29
RIGHTLY				
Rightly you shew, that Wit alone		495	Panegyr Swift	72
Is rightly censur'd by the Stagirite,		988	Letter Dr Sh-n	19
RIGHTS				
Shall he upon the Ducal Rights intrench,		534	To Mr. Gay	91
His indisputed Rights extend		649	On Poetry	287
He only the rights of the clergy debates,		816	Yahoo's	31
Their rights! their importance! We'll set on new rates		816	Yahoo's	32
RILL				
Strephon who heard the fuming Rill		589	Strephon Chloe	175
RIME				
But simple Topicks told in Rime.		215	To Mr. Delany	12
To Rime all day without Offence;		219	To Mr. Delany	108
How oft' am I for Rime to seek?		502	Doctor Delaney	65
RIMERS				
So Modern Rimers wisely Blast		110	V's House	131
RIMES				
You tug for Rimes		441	Ballyspellin	23
Sweet Poet, hir'd for birth-day Rimes,		462	Birthday Song	47
Observe what Loads of stupid Rimes		503	Doctor Delaney	101
And, Praise bestow'd in Grub-Street Rimes,		505	Doctor Delaney	165
RIND				
Depriv'd of Root, and Branch, and Rind,		926	Riddle 9	1
RING SEE WEDDING-RING				
Still wear, still doat on his Invisible Ring.		21	Ode Athenian	157
The Vicar and the Ring bespoke:		223	Prog of Love	23
And ring Wood's Copper in our Ears		354	Simile Silver	27
Was that, last Sunday in the Ring?		699	Cadenus Vaness	385
I join them fairly with a Ring;		926	Riddle 9	13
They part not till the Ring is broke.		926	Riddle 9	16
As his betters are us'd, shall be lash'd round the ring,		1027	Sheri Circles	19
RING'S-END				
At his Ring's-End he founders in the Port.		284	Elegy Boat	8
RINGING				
And Patricks' bell she was ringing all in muffles;		840	Ballad	D 7
She was ringing very sorry, her tongue tied up with rag;		840	Ballad	D 8
RINGS				
While from below all Grub-street rings.		231	Prog of Poetry	46
Pray, what is this Bank of which the Town Rings?		287	Bank Down	1
But pawns her Snuff-Box, Rings, and Keys.		452	Modern Lady	235
With Rings and Hinges counterfeit		528	Lady's Dres Rm	76
And with Rings so very trim,		574	Helter Skelter	27
Of their two Fames the World enough rings;		884	Rev Market-Hill	31
RIOT				
Who, in his Satyrs running riot,		548	Life of Swift	103
And forget to broil and riot,		574	Helter Skelter	52
On Corruptions running Riot.		635	Epistle Lady	184
RIP				
But, some will cry, Turn-Coat, and rip up old Stories,		143	New Song	21
RIP'NING				
Rip'ning, and kindling like the Sun.		391	Young's Satire	26
Of rip'ning fruits, and gilding flow'rs;		432	Answer Paulus	14
RIPE				
Ripe fruit shall come, and all is wele.		103	Merlin	14
Things were not ripe for a Decree,		689	Cadenus Vaness	105
Ripe 'Sparagrass,		952	Asparagus	1
RIPEN				
I forward the Grass, and ripen the Vine:		263	Apollo	8
The Dregs will serve to ripen Ore below;		532	To Mr. Gay	24
By Time, and ripen into Love.		701	Cadenus Vaness	475
RIPEN'D				
Justling some thousand years till ripen'd by the Sun,		20	Ode Athenian	129
Finding her ripen'd Time is come,		207	Fable Bitches	3
Where never yet a Codling ripen'd:		883	Rev Market-Hill	4
RIPENS				
Ripens the Grape, the Liquor sours.		731	Stella, Poems	120
What he ripens above ground, he sours below it.		979	Dean to Tho: S	32
Air ripens not, nor Earth produces:		1035	To Quilca	6
RIPT				
Their Throats were cut, their Bellies ript,		923	Riddle 7	74
RISE				
Hence Mankind fell, and here must rise again.		32	Ode to Temple	177
From thee whatever virtue takes its rise,		55	Temple Ill	135
Whence Broods of insect Poets rise.		80	Vanbrug House	54
When Rains descend, and Tempests rise,		84	Salamander	34
Whilst You shall see your Cottage rise,		92	Bauc & Phil 1	89
How Patrige made his Opticks rise,		98	Elegy Patrige	21
A Pile shall from its Ashes rise		107	V's House	49

RISE   (CONTINUED)

	PAGE	TITLE	LINE
Whilst you shall see your Cottage rise,	112	Bauc & Phil 2	49
Yet our Stocks rise Cent. per Cent,	169	Peace Dunkirk	26
Nor higher, than our Talents, rise,	184	Horace 2, 1	108
On ev'ry Genius that attempts to rise;	193	Author Himself	4
To see her from her Pillow rise	226	Prog of Beauty	13
We rise with the Light,	245	Irish-Feast	14
They rise ready drest,	245	Irish-Feast	35
They rise from their Feast,	246	Irish-Feast	61
What Magick makes our Money rise	250	Bubble	2
Their Fall is but a Trick to rise:	253	Bubble	84
The Time it falls, or when 'twill rise.	256	Bubble	144
Nor shall the Vapour upwards rise,	271	Apollo's Edict D	36
Believe me 'tis the Way to Rise.	361	Grace's Answer	12
And they like Stars shall Rise and Set.	362	Grace's Answer	50
Nor can they from infernal Mansions rise;	363	On Dreams	4
True Virtue has a Right to rise.)	386	Manly Virtue	92
He taught, how Men to Honours rise,	386	Manly Virtue	103
Behold those Monarch-Oaks that rise,	393	Modern Poets	1
Behold a Poem rise!	406	Swift to Pope	16
Can rise upon their Master's Fall.	409	Dial Rich Marb	34
Must fall, because our Masters rise.	409	Dial Rich Marb	36
Of those who want the Pow'r to rise.	414	Censure	12
Here quiet they Lie, in hopes to rise one Day,	431	Dicky Dolly	22
And asks if it be time to rise;	446	Modern Lady	43
Now Voices over Voices rise;	450	Modern Lady	174
In hope to see Spadillo rise;	452	Modern Lady	231
If your Expences rise so high;	478	Epist on Epist	95
By which himself was taught to rise;	484	Libel on D- D-	116
Men seldom by their Good Deeds rise:	495	Panegyr Swift	75
'Tis Eminence makes Envy rise,	501	Doctor Delaney	41
Point out the surest Men to rise,	502	Doctor Delaney	84
Than suffer Men of Parts to rise:	503	Doctor Delaney	92
Be often forc'd to rise at Night,	587	Strephon Chloe	122
Would rise by Merit to Promotion;	604	Beasts Confess	111
To rise in Church, or Law, or State,	641	On Poetry	40
And as their Heels elated rise,	654	On Poetry	403
Cadenus felt within him rise	706	Cadenus Vaness	624
To which (though late) shall Stella rise.	725	To Stella	54
Yet when I find your Passions rise,	731	Stella, Poems	113
In majesty rise,	756	Dingley Brent	8
And as the Vegetables rise,	759	Receipt Youth	13
One tells the Rise of Cheese, and Oat-meal,	781	Mullinix Tim	269
Shall rise one Blade of Grass, one Ear of Corn;	793	St. Pat's Well	92
Wou'd you rise in the Church, be Stupid and Dull,	807	Advice Parson	1
Yet still has Impudence to rise,	824	Printer Newgat	13
Then let us rise, and rest our weary Bums.	882	Pastoral Dial	52
Dispatch the Rogues by whom they Rise.	886	Rev Market-Hill	110
Behold; a frothy Substance rise;	892	Panegyr Dean	183
Though, if I rise before my Time,	918	Riddle 4	41
They rise, walk round, yet never fright.	920	Riddle 6	12
These crude Materials once shall rise,	924	Riddle 7	91
Most Things by me do rise and fall,	934	Riddle 21 D	1
And future Poets, as they rise,	994	On Picture	31

RISEN

When Mother Clud had risen from Play,	86	Hist V's House	1
All risen since that flatt'ring time,	899	Dean's Reasons	9

RISES

And up he rises like a Vapour,	231	Prog of Poetry	43
It rises both in Bulk and Height,	251	Bubble	13
She rises to her Tea at noon.	291	Prog Marriage	38
He rises to the highest Stations;	386	Manly Virtue	90
Than yon tall Dock that rises to thy Nose.	881	Pastoral Dial	14

RISING

Mean while the South rising with dabbled Wings,	137	City Shower	13
So Fishes rising from the Main	254	Bubble	85
With rising or with setting Sun:	270	Apollo's Edict D	13
For Venus rising from the Ocean	293	Prog Marriage	107
To shine the more still rising higher)	385	Manly Virtue	54
Then rising with Aurora's Light,	643	On Poetry	85
But rising from her Chair of State,	714	Cadenus Vaness	887
Each Moment rising in her Airs,	751	Stel Wood-Park	51
As rising from Medea's Kettle;	759	Receipt Youth	18
The House Accounts are daily rising	860	Lady Acheson	29
Who, 'ere t' other gets up, demands the rising Blow.	967	Letter Sherid	14

RISING-SUN

Not Empire to the Rising-Sun,	641	On Poetry	25

RISK

Consider what a Risk you run.	644	On Poetry	136

RITES

Proceed we to the Marriage Rites.	585	Strephon Chloe	46
The Rites perform'd, the Parson paid,	586	Strephon Chloe	67
Of foreign Customs, Rites, and Laws;	697	Cadenus Vaness	353
For she, as Priestess, knows the Rites	743	Stel B-day 22	51
The Christian Rites I introduc'd in vain:	792	St. Pat's Well	35
Contemners of thy Rites divine.	895	Panegyr Dean	272

RIVAL

And now, inflame'd with rival Rage,	385	Manly Virtue	43
The rest condemn'd, with rival Voice,	387	Manly Virtue	133
They rival Venus to a Hair;	445	Modern Lady	10
A Rival comes, and Tom---is nick'd---.	545	Life of Swift	18

	PAGE	TITLE	LINE
RIVAL (CONTINUED)			
His Rival, for the Chiefest reckon'd, ...	546	Life of Swift	56
RIVAL'S			
He spurn'd them in his Rival's Face.	412	Desire Possess	34
Nor less that Shirt, my Rival's Gift, ...	925	Riddle 8	41
RIVALS			
He'd wish his Rivals all in Hell.	554	Death of Swift	34
And, bravely drove his Rivals down	585	Strephon Chloe	41
She need no Rivals apprehend.	702	Cadenus Vaness	507
RIVER SEE NEW-RIVER-WALK			
A River at my Garden's End, ...	198	Horace 2, 6	4
The Banks of a River I know are good Things, . . .	287	Bank Down	2
To shut out the River by raising the Bank.	287	Bank Down	5
RIVER'S			
Adorn our chrystal River's Banks:	896	Panegyr Dean	302
RIVERE			
Tamys rivere twys y-frozen, ...	102	Merlin	3
RIVERS			
And lessening rivers mourn their fountains dry	419	Shall Repine	4
Find Rivers with harmonious names, ...	468	Birthday Song	241
O'er cityes, rivers, hills, and seas, ...	621	Scandal Poem 1	126
O'er Cities, Rivers, Hills, and Seas:	627	Scandal Poem 2	120
As Rivers, tho' they bend and twine, ...	709	Cadenus Vaness	720
RIVULETS			
And falls in Rivulets of Sweat, ...	227	Prog of Beauty	38
RIXHAM			
Came to a Village hard by Rixham	90	Bauc & Phil 1	9
ROACH			
Thus, if a Gudgeon meet a Roach	824	Printer Newgat	11
ROAD			
These pad on wit's high road, and suits maintain . . .	45	To Congreve	67
Along the high celestial Road;	231	Prog of Poetry	28
Beneath thy decent Steps, the Road	324	Pethox	35
Possession kept the beaten Road;	412	Desire Possess	35
No danger dreads upon the road;	435	Answer Paulus	96
And quite mistake Preferment's Road.	480	Libel on D- D-	12
By censure frighted out of honour's road, ...	506	To a Friend	9
Tho' they gallop so fast; on the Road you may find 'em,	804	Irish Bishops	23
"So, I took to the Road, and what's very odd, . . .	873	Grand Question	169
If when you return, your Road you dont line	1017	Swift Ans Sher	20
ROADS SEE BY-ROADS			
The Roads are with his Foll'wers strown, ...	398	Earl of P-b-w	20
Crouding the roads with naked feet.	401	Window Inns 5 D	10
"And turn the Tax for publick Roads	571	Death of Swift	453
How deep and foul the Roads may grow, ...	860	Lady Acheson	19
ROAM			
For foreign Aid what need they roam, ...	272	Apollo's Edict D	62
No Thought of her's does ever roam, ...	322	First of April	39
Bridles destin'd far to roam, ...	573	Helter Skelter	15
From East to west the world we roam, ...	621	Scandal Poem 1	127
From East to West, the World we roam;	627	Scandal Poem 2	121
ROAR			
But bawl'd as loud as he could roar, ...	91	Bauc & Phil 1	35
Huzza! the school-boys roar, the play'rs are come! . .	308	Billet Players	38
First with the brazen Cannons Roar.	338	Wood's Brass	2
Where loudest winds incessant roar	420	Holyhead	30
Far less the Rabble roar and rail, ...	450	Modern Lady	186
To hear the Belgick Lyon roar.	468	Birthday Song	246
Beware, and when you hear the Surges roar, ...	772	Horace 1, 14	61
And when I roar a Plot, a Plot, ...	779	Mullinix Tim	191
Could roar as loud as Stenter.	785	Mullinex Dick	38
He began as he bragg'd, with a rant and a roar; . . .	816	Yahoo's	43
And I roar out my Joy, and in Transport expire. . . .	928	Riddle 11 D	12
Tho' ten thousand Canons roar, ...	931	Riddle 18 D	23
Then I clash and roar, and rattle, ...	933	Riddle 20 D	21
I hear with some Concern you roar, ...	1002	Reply by Dean	10
ROAR'D			
So she roar'd like a Bedlam, ...	71	Mrs Harris Pet	45
Nell roar'd incessant, Dick sate mute:	219	A Quiet Life	4
And when to the Joy of your Hearts he has Roar'd, . .	336	Serious Poem	83
Punch roaring ran, and running roar'd.	776	Mullinix Tim	112
ROARING			
Punch roaring ran, and running roar'd.	776	Mullinix Tim	112
Of Ideots roaring to the Boys.	788	Dick's Variety	8
Roaring till their Lungs were spent, ...	833	Legion Club	115
Rough Roystring Rustick Roaring Strains	958	Cantata	
ROARS			
"Or, else he raves, and roars, and swears, ...	305	Storm	65
And Thunder roars, and Light'ning flies!	578	Day Judgement	6
Pierce Aeolus in Tempests roars.	924	Riddle 7	88
ROAST			
Lost by Disuse the Art to roast	93	Bauc & Phil 1	126
Lost, by Disuse, the Art to Roast, ...	113	Bauc & Phil 2	66
With good Roast Beef his Belly full, ...	231	Prog of Poetry	21
For, rule the Rump, you rule the Roast.)	513	Answer Fable	32
Of roast or boil'd, to the Hungry is charming. . . .	941	Letter	30
Fire will not roast, nor Water boil.	1035	To Quilca	8
ROAST-MEAT			
That Roast-meat which it cannot turn.	94	Bauc & Phil 1	146
That Roast-meat which it cannot turn.	113	Bauc & Phil 2	84

	PAGE	TITLE	LINE
ROASTED			
Well roasted, with Sugar and Wine in a Cup, ...	953	Oranges	3
ROASTING			
In roasting larks, or making laws:	901	Dean's Reasons	78
ROB			
With those they rob, by what their trade does gain. . .	45	To Congreve	68
Which gave them birth, can rob the world of day. . . .	46	To Congreve	82
You look like Rogues would rob a House	91	Bauc & Phil 1	40
They Nightly slunk to rob the Fold, ...	153	Widow and Cat D	8
My Ice-house rob as heretofore, ...	409	Dial Rich Marb	45
And, as they robb'd the Father, rob the Son.	535	To Mr. Gay	118
"Corrupt the Senate, rob the Crown;	568	Death of Swift	386
"To rob the Church, their Tenants rack, ...	571	Death of Swift	448
ROB'S			
A Pamphlet in Sir Rob's Defence	646	On Poetry	187
ROBB'D			
And, as they robb'd the Father, rob the Son.	535	To Mr. Gay	118
"The first Man I robb'd was a Parson by <God>. . . .	873	Grand Question	170
I never robb'd thee with Design:	896	Panegyr Dean	316
'Ere George had robb'd it of its Mud.	1020	Nim-Dan-Dean 1 D	6
ROBBER			
A publick, or a private Robber;	645	On Poetry	161
ROBBERS			
So, Robbers (and their Ends are just the same) . . .	536	To Mr. Gay	141
ROBBING			
While He went robbing on; old Master dy'd.	536	To Mr. Gay	148
ROBE			
While others of the learned Robe	604	Beasts Confess	87
ROBERT			
Are by Robert Ballentine lately brought over; . . .	236	Excellent Song	2
Than my Friend Sir <Robert> <Brass>	637	Epistle Lady	246
All this perform'd by Robert Hewit, ...	675	Curate's Compl	16
(But first let Robert on his Knees	743	Stel B-day 22	77
Robert and Darby's Coadjutor:	888	Panegyr Dean	40
Sir <Robert> weary'd by Will. <Pulteney's> Teazings, .	537	Mr. Pulteney	1
Offend our Patriot, Great Sir <Robert>, ...	548	Life of Swift	108
ROBERT'S			
Now, Chartres at Sir Robert's Levee, ...	560	Death of Swift	189
"Next, here's Sir Robert's Vindication, ...	563	Death of Swift	277
ROBES			
And in his Robes, you must agree, ...	286	Elegy Boat	41
In Royal Robes they come by dozens	465	Birthday Song	169
Sometimes imperial Robes I wear, ...	935	Riddle 23 D	20
ROBIN			
Fair Rosamond, and Robin Hood, ...	93	Bauc & Phil 1	119
Fair Rosamond, and Robin Hood, ...	114	Bauc & Phil 2	95
Robin, and Jack, and Jack, and Dan?	314	To Ford	80
To look with Robin Grattan's Eyes:	314	To Ford	86
Robin adores that Spot of Earth, ...	314	To Ford	87
Quoth King Robin, our Ribbands I see are too few . .	389	Order of Bath	1
That Robin Walpole is Mecaenas:	462	Birthday Song	60
When both the Jacks and Robin came;	741	Stel B-day 22	18
Say, Robin, what can Traulus mean	795	Traulus 1	1
Robin, to beggars, with a curse	878	Robbin & Harry	1
Robin from noon to night will prate, ...	878	Robbin & Harry	9
Robin, who ne'r his mind could fix	878	Robbin & Harry	29
Old Robin, all his youth a sloven, ...	879	Robbin & Harry	45
So am I, when Tobacco, like Robin, I chew, sick. . .	1030	Dr. Helsham	28
And Robin at Sea had like to be cast away.	1037	Four Storyes	4
Then, honest <Robin>, of thy Corps beware:	539	Mr. Pulteney	39
ROBIN'S			
Though Robin's Honour was in Pawn;	495	Panegyr Swift	83
Of Nelly's pertness, Robin's leasings, ...	753	Gift for Bec	7
ROBUST			
With Limbs robust, and Voice that stuns;	326	Pethox	76
ROBUSTIOUS			
Be so robustious like a Man.	417	Woman's Mind	48
ROCHEFOUCAULT			
Wise Rochefoucault a Maxim writ, ...	545	Life of Swift	1
As Rochefoucault his Maxims drew	553	Death of Swift	1
ROCHET			
Wou'd you wish to be wrap'd in a Rochet--In short. . .	808	Advice Parson	9
ROCHETS			
How would it pollute their Crosiers and Rochets . . .	522	St. Cecilia's	11
ROCHFORT			
Let's quarrel no longer, since Dan and George Rochfort	979	Dean to Tho: S	35
But when I would find Rhime for Rochfort, ...	993	On Picture	7
ROCK			
Prometheus on a Rock is laid, ...	346	Prometheus	53
ROCKET			
Have you seen a Rocket fly?	638	Epistle Lady	249
Such a Rocket is my Muse, ...	638	Epistle Lady	259
ROCKS			
Nor blab it on the lonely Rocks, ...	597	Cassinus Peter	107
All beneath yon flow'ry Rocks.	660	Love Song	8
Avoid the Rocks on Britain's angry Shore:	772	Horace 1, 14	62
Or sharp pointed rocks, ...	854	Lady's Lament	81
Both Mountains, Woods, and Hills, and Rocks, . . .	934	Riddle 21 D	7
ROD			
The Rod was but a harmless Wand, ...	132	Magician's Rod	1
His Rod was honest English Wood, ...	132	Magician's Rod	7

ROD   (CONTINUED)   PAGE   TITLE   LINE

About a certain Magick Rod, ...   132 Magician's Rod   22
The Rod of Hermes was renown'd   133 Magician's Rod   35
That Rod was just a Type of Sid's,   133 Magician's Rod   39
Sid's Rod was slender, white, and tall, ...   133 Magician's Rod   43
A Circle with their Rod describe, ...   134 Magician's Rod   50
Sid's Rod was of a larger Stride, ...   134 Magician's Rod   53
But, when th' enchanted Rod was broke, ...   134 Magician's Rod   57
Could with this Rod of Sid compare.   . . . . . .   135 Magician's Rod   78
To break thy Rod like naughty Lad?   135 Magician's Rod   80
And not a Rod for thy own Breech.   135 Magician's Rod   84
His next will be a Rod in Piss.   . . . .   135 Magician's Rod   86
For none but a Dunce would come under his Rod.   335 Serious Poem   34
When We are lash'd, They kiss the Rod;   561 Death of Swift   217
Stand in Awe without a Rod: . . . .   633 Epistle Lady   104
When Hermes, waiting with his rod,   762 Bec's B-Day   58
A Rod should turn them back to Dust.   813 Bro Protestant   56
Sometimes makes the Devil his Rod;   . . . .   830 Legion Club   32
RODE
Away they rode in homely Sort   . . . .   224 Prog of Love   75
As I rode in my Chariot, a Thought to my Mind;   . . .   265 Apollo   76
How Valiant George rode o'er the Dragon,   281 Journal   70
Rode stately through Holbourn, to die in his Calling; .   399 Tom Clinch   2
I rode four more to great St. Mary;   . . . .   675 Curate's Compl   3
RODS
Rebellious Waves with Rods like Xerxes.   . . . . .   463 Birthday Song   100
For, ev'ry Coxcomb lends them Rods;   501 Doctor Delaney   48
Scorpion Rods perhaps may tame them.   . . . .   836 Legion Club   158
ROGUE
Are Cat and Dog, and Rogue and Whore.   . . . . .   225 Prog of Love   100
This wicked Rogue Waters, who always is sinning,   238 Excellent Song   26
To ship a rogue, and pay him not a groat,   308 Billet Players   28
A Foot-boy to some Rogue Director?   312 To Ford   40
That, a Rogue so Obscure should make such a Clutter, .   334 Serious Poem   6
Who d vote a Rogue into the Parliament-house,   . . .   396 Dog and Thief   19
An idle Rogue, who spends his Quartridge   . . . . .   411 Dial Rich Marb   97
Of e'ery Rogue that wears an <Arse>   . . . .   497 Panegyr Swift   121
Strephon, the Rogue, display'd it wide, ...   526 Lady's Dres Rm   13
That Rogue of genuine ministerial Kind: 534 To Mr. Gay   102
The ruling Rogue, who dreads to be cashier'd;   . . .   536 To Mr. Gay   137
Was, When will They turn out this odious Rogue?   536 To Mr. Gay   146
Pronounces you a stupid Rogue;   . . . .   644 On Poetry   120
They burnish paper, or they bite a rogue: . . . . .   672 Epig Carthy 25 D 2
How <Sheridan> the Rogue would sneer, ...   741 Stel B-day 22   20
He calls you Rogue; There's nothing in it, ...   797 Traulus 1   53
Like a Rogue that steals a Sheep: . . . .   800 Traulus 2   36
Thou I hear, a pleasant Rogue art;   . . . .   839 Legion Club   220
The Rogue must call another day.   . . . .   878 Robbin & Harry   4
For Whore and Rogue; and Dog and Bitch.   . . . . . .   949 Epigr Scolding   4
Yet I know a young Rogue, that thrown flat on the Field   967 Letter Sherid   15
By that rogue Nesbitt, ...   1037 Sheridan Cavan   10
ROGUE'S
The Rogue's too Bawdy and too Prophane is.   . . . .   988 Letter Dr Sh-n   6
ROGUERY
The Roguery of Alchymy, ...   27 Ode to Temple   25
ROGUES   SEE COME-ROGUES
You look like Rogues would rob a House . . . . . .   91 Bauc & Phil 1   40
A Wretch! whom <English> Rogues to spite her,   . . .   302 Storm   7
The Rogues must dye for Want and Spight, ...   502 Doctor Delaney   72
Or call 'em Rogues, or get 'em kickt: . . . . . .   505 Doctor Delaney   154
From Rogues who ne'er believ'd a God?   . . . .   820 Dr. Rundle   30
When the Rogues their Country fleece, ...   833 Legion Club   107
Dispatch the Rogues by whom they Rise.   . . . . . .   886 Rev Market-Hill 110
Got from his crew of <rogues> in grain;   . . . . . .   435 Answer Paulus   118
Scrambling with <rogues> to get a place: . . . . .   436 Answer Paulus   140
ROGUISH
Whom Roguish Boys in Stormy Nights   100 Elegy Patrige   91
Yet cannot leave his roguish Tricks;   . . . .   777 Mullinix Tim   118
ROLL   SEE ROUL
Would hiss, and sting, and roll, and twist, ...   132 Magician's Rod   11
The Glitt'ring Constellations Roll, ...   362 Grace's Answer   33
Styx, through Hell whose Waters roll!   . . . .   832 Legion Club   84
ROLL'D
In Fillets roll'd, or cut in Pieces, ...   344 Prometheus   7
In Fillets of Brass roll'd up to his Ears: . . . .   350 Wood Insect   8
ROLLER
Sits mounted on the Garden Roller.   . . . .   410 Dial Rich Marb   62
ROLLING
You saw th' impetuous Torrent rolling on;   . . . . .   12 Ode to William D 18
Or if thought's rolling globe her circle run,   . . .   51 Temple Ill   9
ROLLS
And rolls about her dreadful Eyes, ...   30 Ode to Temple   122
And rolls the silent year   . . . .   39 Ode Sancroft   151
Then from his Arm hoarse thunder rolls . . . .   461 Birthday Song   39
Rolls from his Mouth in plenteous Streams of Mud;   . .   532 To Mr. Gay   40
ROMAN
Extol the Greek and Roman Masters, ...   652 On Poetry   347
Every Greek and Roman Author.   . . . .   838 Legion Club   214
Like Roman Generals triumphant, ...   928 Riddle 12   D 15
ROMANCE
And what I us'd to laugh at in Romance, ...   8 Ode to King   62

ROMANCE   (CONTINUED)   PAGE   TITLE   LINE
   As fits a Princess in Romance.   . . . .   888 Panegyr Dean   54
ROMANCES
   Which we ne'er join'd before, but in Romances meet, . .   28 Ode to Temple   60
   ('Tis always done, Romances tell us, ...   223 Prog of Love   47
   To her, who durst not read Romances;   . . . .   711 Cadenus Vaness   795
ROMANS
   This made the Ancient Romans to afford   . . . . . .   7 Ode to King   27
   Upon their Shoes the Romans wore, ...   99 Elegy Patrige   36
   Those Romans were too wise to think on't, ...   190 Faggot   29
   By Greeks and Romans understood, ...   697 Cadenus Vaness   348
   Or, like the Umbo of the Romans, ...   1021 Nim-Dan-Dean 1 D 31
ROMANTICK
   And like a Bold Romantick Knight   . . . .   7 Ode to King   37
   High Raptures, and romantick Flights;   . . . . . .   590 Strephon Chloe   198
   Talks in a high Romantick Strain;   . . . .   712 Cadenus Vaness   821
ROME
   Let not old Rome boast Fabius's Fate, ...   28 Ode to Temple   70
   Take twenty Gods of Rome or Greece, ...   460 Birthday Song   2
   And Hell to be sure is at Paris or Rome, ...   576 Place Damn'd   17
   Either from Muscovy or Rome;   . . . .   696 Cadenus Vaness   323
   Who scourg'd to Death that Scourge of Rome, ...   925 Riddle 8   36
ROME'S
   Ready to fall Rome's bloody Sacrifice;   . . . .   12 Ode to William D 22
ROOD
   A Terras Walk, and half a Rood   . . . .   190 Horace 2, 6   5
   With a Rood or two of Land, ...   830 Legion Club   37
ROOF   SEE FABRICK-ROOF
   The Roof began to mount aloft   . . . .   92 Bauc & Phil 1   92
   To raise a Roof with Act the Fift.   . . . .   108 V's House   92
   The Roof began to mount aloft;   . . . .   112 Bauc & Phil 2   52
   Reckoning Roof, Weather Cock and all, ...   126 Little House   7
   Observ'd the Roof behind the Grass;   . . . . . .   127 Little House   24
   While Spouts run clatt'ring o'er the Roof by Fits;   .   139 City Shower   44
   Under one Roof, or in one Ship with me.   . . . . . .   210 Earl of Oxford   18
   She'll come no more beneath your Roof.   . . . . .   408 Dial Rich Marb   12
   While the Devil upon the Roof, ...   830 Legion Club   23
ROOFS
   And Castle roofs, and Steeple Spires.   . . . . . .   257 Bubble   172
ROOKS
   Thus when by Rooks a Lord is ply'd, ...   257 Bubble   161
   (The Ladies there must needs be Rooks, ...   905 Death Daphne   79
ROOM   SEE ELBOW-ROOM
   But give the vigorous fancy room.   . . . .   49 To Congreve   206
   For want of Room by Virgo's Side, ...   100 Elegy Patrige   85
   Were spent in Building each a Room;   . . . . . .   108 V's House   90
   He said, but that it wanted Room, ...   128 Little House   45
   Will hardly fail, and there is room for more: . . . .   166 Toland's Invit   36
   Make Room; as if a Duke were passing by.   . . . .   194 Author Himself   36
   That, Faith, I think, there scarce is Room   . . . . .   371 Letter D. S-y   7
   But, when of smoak the room is clear, ...   419 Holyhead Journ   3
   Tis pre engged and in his room   . . . .   423 Ireld   71
   To a Room full of Guests for fear of a <Rape>.   . .   517 Dean Hang Rape   12
   Strephon, who found the Room was void, ...   526 Lady's Dres Rm   5
   Which waft a Stink round every Room.   . . . . . .   529 Lady's Dres Rm   114
   We thought, there now remain'd no room to doubt: . .   536 To Mr. Gay   149
   Nor give the smallest Room to guess   . . . . . .   588 Strephon Chloe   139
   The Room with Volumes litter'd round   . . . . . .   698 Cadenus Vaness   371
   "Observe how a Parson comes into a Room, ...   872 Grand Question   155
   She, as he came into the Room, ...   904 Death Daphne   57
   The Company will fly the Room.   . . . .   917 Riddle 4   8
ROOMS   SEE RAFFLING-ROOMS
   A reall House with Rooms and Stairs, ...   87 Hist V's House   23
   Thro' all the Rooms, and Courts, and Arches;   . . . .   377 Apology Lady C   62
   The costly Boast of Regal Rooms, ...   379 Apology Lady C   110
   "Of City Fogs and crowded Rooms, ...   380 Apology Lady C   140
ROOT
   How some go downward to the Root, ...   32 Ode to Temple   172
   It feels as if 'twere taking Root.   . . . .   116 Bauc & Phil 2   162
   Carrots sown Thyn a deep root may get, ...   148 Windsor Proph   17
   Root out these Carrots, O Thou, whose Name   . . . .   148 Windsor Proph   21
   There in the Soil began to root, ...   504 Doctor Delaney   121
   Die the next Year for want of Root: . . . . . .   730 Stella, Poems   68
   But from the Root a dismal Groan   . . . .   850 Old Thorn   53
   At an old stubborn Root I chanc'd to tug, ...   881 Pastoral Dial   25
   Depriv'd of Root, and Branch, and Rind, ...   926 Riddle 9   1
ROOTED   SEE DEEP-ROOTED
   A rooted Pox to last for ever.   . . . .   295 Prog Marriage   166
   Self-Love, in Nature rooted fast, ...   708 Cadenus Vaness   684
   Love rooted out, again will never grow.   . . . . . .   881 Pastoral Dial   16
ROOTING
   As when rooting in a Bin, ...   765 Dick, Maggot   1
ROOTS
   Have large proportion'd Roots that grow   . . . . . .   393 Modern Poets   3
   While each with stubbed Knife remov'd the Roots   . . .   880 Pastoral Dial   3
ROPE
   With that, he twisted his Girdle at me like a Rope,. . .   72 Mrs Harris Pet   62
   Brisk Susan whips her Linen from the Rope, ...   137 City Shower   17
   That he might yet be lifted by a Rope.   . . . . . .   285 Elegy Boat   18
   That <Hort> was destin'd to a Rope, ...   306 Storm   74
   Very soon to see Wood Drop down from a Rope.   . . .   338 Serious Poem   116

```
ROPE              (CONTINUED)                    PAGE  TITLE           LINE
    This Brazen Chain into a Rope;        . . . . . . .   347 Prometheus         72
ROPES
    Will, or ought to end in Ropes;       . . . . . . .   168 Peace Dunkirk        9
ROSAMOND
    Fair Rosamond, and Robin Hood,        . . . . . . .    93 Bauc & Phil 1      119
    Fair Rosamond, and Robin Hood,        . . . . . . .   114 Bauc & Phil 2       95
ROSE
    As if 'twould overshade the Royal Rose,    . . . . .   37 Ode Sancroft       104
    The Royal Rose the glory of our morn,      . . . . .   37 Ode Sancroft       105
    O'er the glad scene whence first she rose a bride:  . .  51 Temple Ill         12
    Aloft rose ev'ry Beam and Rafter,          . . . . .   92 Bauc & Phil 1       93
    The Sun has rose, and gone to Bed,    . . . . . . .    98 Elegy Patrige       11
    One rose a Star, the other fell       . . . . . . .   100 Elegy Patrige       67
    Rose in proportion to his Wit:        . . . . . . . .  108 V's House           80
    Aloft rose ev'ry Beam and Rafter,     . . . . . . .   112 Bauc & Phil 2       53
    But seldom rose above a Sheet:        . . . . . . .   172 Horace 1, 7         42
    Into the Precincts of the Rose,       . . . . . . .   226 Prog of Beauty      26
    But when she rose, the black and red  . . . . . . .   226 Prog of Beauty      31
    Under the Rose since here are none but friends;  . . . 275 Epilogue           13
    The Godlike Ends for which he rose;   . . . . . . .   386 Manly Virtue        98
    And at the Rose on Sunday,            . . . . . . .   426 Five Ladies         42
    Because she rose from stinking Ooze?  . . . . . . .   530 Lady's Dres Rm     132
    A Club assembled at the Rose;         . . . . . . .   565 Death of Swift     300
    "He might have rose like other Men:   . . . . . . .   567 Death of Swift     356
    "While Numbers to Preferment rose;    . . . . . . .   569 Death of Swift     401
    None ever saw her pluck a Rose.       . . . . . . .   584 Strephon Chloe      16
    When the Defendant's Council rose,    . . . . . . .   687 Cadenus Vaness      22
    On all Emergencies that rose.         . . . . . . .   689 Cadenus Vaness      98
    (For, under the rose,  . . . . . . . .                858 Lady's Lament      213
    As who should say, to pluck a Rose.   . . . . . . .   893 Panegyr Dean       216
    From whence unsav'ry Vapours rose,    . . . . . . .   895 Panegyr Dean       285
ROSES
    Should bundle Thistles up with Roses. . . . . . .      96 On the Union        10
    To scatter Roses at her Feet;         . . . . . . .   379 Apology Lady C     112
    Roses of richest Dye, that shone      . . . . . . .   379 Apology Lady C     113
    The Roses blow, the Cowslip springs;  . . . . . . .   621 Scandal Poem 1     141
    The Roses blow, the Cowslip springs;  . . . . . . .   627 Scandal Poem 2     145
    The Roses of your Cheeks, I dare      . . . . . . .   932 Riddle 19       D   9
ROSS
    Quoth Ross, for, I'll be sworn, 'twas I.   . . . . .   67 Problem             56
ROT
    "He's dead you say; why let him rot;  . . . . . . .   559 Death of Swift     183
    And let them rot, or hang, or stink.  . . . . . . .   799 Traulus 1          102
    And on some Dunghill left to rot.     . . . . . . .   916 Riddle 1            42
ROTCHET
    To give thee Lawn-Sleeves a Mitre and Rotchet,  . .   518 Dean Hang Rape      45
ROTE
    Or crazy rules to make us wits by rote     . . . . .   47 To Congreve        129
    A Set of Phrases learn't by Rote;     . . . . . . .   415 Woman's Mind         1
    "A Verse from Horace, learn'd by Rote. . . . . . .    572 Death of Swift     474
    Learn Aristotle's Rules by Rote,      . . . . . . .   648 On Poetry          247
ROTTED
    Of Shin-Bones rotted by the Pox.      . . . . . . .   904 Death Daphne        40
ROTTEN
    That old rotten Wood will Shine in the Dark.  . . .   334 Serious Poem         8
    Or swear it rotten; and with humble Airs,  . . . .    534 To Mr. Gay          97
    Chaff, straws, or fragments of some rotten boat,  . .  672 Epig Carthy 24  D  14
    And all his Handkerchiefs are rotten; . . . . . . .   875 Drapier's Hill      16
    A rotten Cabbin, dropping Rain;       . . . . . . .  1035 To Quilca            2
ROTTING
    So rotting Celia stroles the Street   . . . . . . .   229 Prog of Beauty     103
ROTUNDIS
    That you Quadrata change Rotundis?    . . . . . . .   477 Epist on Epist      76
ROUGH
    When some rough hand breaks the assembling-glass.  . .  45 To Congreve        64
    The Captain swears the sea's too rough     . . . . .  420 Holyhead             9
    But George, and Brunswick are too rough.   . . . . .  467 Birthday Song      214
    Hesse Darmstedt makes too rough a sound,   . . . . .  467 Birthday Song      215
    Too rough to polish, and too blunt to bite.  . . . .  672 Epig Carthy 25  D   4
    Behold, it cracks by yon rough Eastern Wind.  . . .   770 Horace 1, 14        18
    Then let him use you e'er so rough,   . . . . . . .   797 Traulus 1           61
    Rough Roystring Rustick Roaring Strains    . . . . .  958 Cantata
    A Smoothing Iron, itself is rough.    . . . . . . .  1021 Nim-Dan-Dean 1  D  10
ROUGHEN
    Roughen the Nap, and leave a mingled Stain.  . . . .  138 City Shower         30
ROUL
    As if he heard Loud Thunders roul,    . . . . . . .   500 Doctor Delaney      17
ROUND
    We often search contentedly the whole World round, . .  20 Ode Athenian      142
    Round all the circles of impertinence,     . . . . .   46 To Congreve        88
    While all the rest stood gaping round . . . . . . .    63 Discovery          24
    Bush smiling round on all, retreats   . . . . . . .    64 Discovery          44
    . . .that we went and search'd the Folks round,  . . . 70 Mrs Harris Pet     22
    But scatt'ring round his Fly-blows, dyes;  . . . . .   80 Vanbrug House       53
    Spreads Leprosy and Baldness round.   . . . . . . .    84 Salamander         56
    Although the Jug had twice gone round      . . . . .   92 Bauc & Phil 1       76
    The Ballads pasted round the Wall,    . . . . . . .    93 Bauc & Phil 1      117
    Moves round but twice in twice twelve Hours  . . . .   93 Bauc & Phil 1      134
    Lookt high and low, walkt often round,     . . . . .  109 V's House           97
    And saw it fairly twice go round;     . . . . . . .   112 Bauc & Phil 2       31
```

ROUND   (CONTINUED)   PAGE   TITLE   LINE

	PAGE	TITLE	LINE
Turn'd round so quick, you scarce cou'd see't;	113	Bauc & Phil 2	72
Had par'd the Dirt, and Sprinkled round the Floor. .	124	Descriptn Morn	6
And tumbling topsi-turvy round	126	Little House	9
And you may swear the Tale went round.	150	Corinna	20
He chip't his Bread, the Pieces round	156	Fable of Midas	3
And Libell'd all the Junta round;	171	Horace 1, 7	38
In Summer round the Park to ride, ...	173	Horace 1, 7	85
Two Dozen Canons round your Stall, ...	173	Horace 1, 7	89
Round all the earth she casts her eyes;	178	To Lord Harley	61
But lashing one another round:	189	Faggot	20
Hemm'd by a triple Circle round, ...	200	Horace 2, 6	28
The Neighbors round would cry out Shame.	220	A Quiet Life	36
And round the barren Common strays, ...	230	Prog of Poetry	10
They dance in a Round, ...	245	Irish-Feast	37
My Mannors all contig'ous round, ...	251	Bubble	19
Look round about how thick it lyes:	254	Bubble	104
Goes round the House to wake the rest:	278	Journal	10
You see the Crows feet round his Eyes.	291	Prog Marriage	50
The Town has whisper'd round the Jest:	293	Prog Marriage	102
With mournful Note clocks round the Brim.	295	Horrid Plot	150
To look on Vice triumphant round, ...	312	To Ford	41
And round the Margin sindg'd his Soil, ...	323	Pethox	8
Thy Head with sparkling Rubies round;	324	Pethox	34
Out-number'd, half encompass'd round, ...	326	Pethox	87
'Tis Fifty round Millions of Love, and a Mending. .	337	Serious Poem	106
When ev'ry one turns round about, ...	341	Upon His Grace	8
To every Farmer twice a Week all round about the Yoke, .	343	Upon His Grace	39
Jove stood amaz'd, but looking round, ...	346	Prometheus	47
As round as a Ball, without Head without Tail, . . .	350	Wood Insect	5
Examines all the Servants round, ...	377	Apology Lady C	63
"In dreading this vexatious Round?	380	Apology Lady C	162
When Pope has fill'd the Margins round, ...	395	Grub-Street	17
And strangers delight to walk round 'em:	403	Window Inns 9	D 3
For, all the Courtly Madams round, ...	409	Dial Rich Marb	27
There doom'd to whirl an endless Round.	413	Desire Possess	50
To move that all the Nation round	423	Ireld	67
And thus it goes round	424	Carterets Arms	11
By Vulcan form'd so round and bright:	433	Answer Paulus	28
Round all your Ballyspellin?	442	Ballyspellin	60
"Come, let us play the t'other Round.	453	Modern Lady	285
Not long enough to reach half round, ...	458	Paddy's Charac	16
The Bullets whistling round his Ears.	500	Doctor Delaney	4
Yet, in Your self when smooth and round, ...	500	Doctor Delaney	29
Round all your Brethren cast your Eyes, ...	502	Doctor Delaney	83
Ty'd round the <Dean's> Neck, for committing a <Rape>. .	519	Dean Hang Rape	66
And turn'd it round on every Side.	526	Lady's Dres Rm	14
To pluck her Brows in Arches round, ...	527	Lady's Dres Rm	56
Which waft a Stink round every Room.	529	Lady's Dres Rm	114
Hush-money sends to all the Neighbours round: . . .	535	To Mr. Gay	108
But when they smelt such foul Corruptions round him; .	536	To Mr. Gay	159
Tom for a wealthy Wife looks round, ...	545	Life of Swift	15
In half the Time, he talks them round.	556	Death of Swift	97
Than all the Sniv'llers round my Bed.	557	Death of Swift	142
For, as he view'd his Person round, ...	586	Strephon Chloe	75
His Night-Cap border'd round with Lace	587	Strephon Chloe	93
The little Cupids hov'ring round, ...	590	Strephon Chloe	193
By Decency cemented round;	593	Strephon Chloe	308
One greasy Stocking round his Head, ...	594	Cassinus Peter	12
Attending nightly round your Bed:	597	Cassinus Peter	114
Nine Muses always waiting round him, ...	598	Problem Solved	25
Inquire through all the Parish round	602	Beasts Confess	43
(The Wig was powder'd round with Sleet, ...	625	Scandal Poem 2	67
Cocker'd by the Servants round, ...	631	Epistle Lady	37
I have laugh'd, and lash'd them round.	638	Epistle Lady	248
So large to grasp the Circle round;	641	On Poetry	30
Your Portion, taking Britain round, ...	642	On Poetry	53
Inherits ev'ry Virtue round, ...	646	On Poetry	192
The Neighbours round admire his Shrewdness, ...	650	On Poetry	289
Extoll ye Bench of Bishops round, ...	658	On Poetry	D 190
But now go search all Europe round	659	On Poetry	D 410
Swiftly purling in a Round, ...	661	Love Song	26
Thus whirling round, together draws	688	Cadenus Vaness	59
She nam'd the antient Heroes round, ...	697	Cadenus Vaness	350
From round the Purlieus of St. James, ...	698	Cadenus Vaness	365
The Room with Volumes litter'd round	698	Cadenus Vaness	371
Let her describe a Circle round	743	Stel B-day 22	55
Grows plump and round, and full of Mettle, ...	759	Receipt Youth	17
Round all your Body plump your Skin;	759	Receipt Youth	30
While all the Squires from nine Miles round, ...	760	Receipt Youth	42
Of hearty gossips prating round;	762	Bec's B-Day	52
For thee alone they lye the Island round.	772	Horace 1, 14	64
When, if you search the Kingdom round, ...	773	Mullinix Tim	5
To Prance with me the Statue round.	776	Mullinix Tim	80
Run on in a perpetual Round, ...	777	Mullinix Tim	141
And sudden spreads a numerous Offspring round; . . .	792	St. Pat's Well	62
Crouded round with antic Shapes;	832	Legion Club	88
They submissive round him wait;	836	Legion Club	166
I concluded, looking round 'em, ...	839	Legion Club	241
Has canker'd all its Branches round;	849	Old Thorn	18
The neighbourhood round, ...	858	Lady's Lament	212

ROUND   (CONTINUED)   PAGE   TITLE   LINE
    Though daggled round, I scorn to fret: . . . . .   890 Panegyr Dean   110
    Which, in its Jumblings round the Skull, ...   893 Panegyr Dean   191
    Ten Thousand Altars smoking round   . . . . . . 894 Panegyr Dean   237
    But now, let all his tenants round . . . . .   902 Dean's Reasons   103
    They rise, walk round, yet never fright.   . . . . . . 920 Riddle 6   12
    Who round the Vault luxuriant reign.   . . . . . . 923 Riddle 7   60
    My Head, with Giddiness, goes round;   . . . . . . 926 Riddle 9   7
    Ever dancing round a Pole.   . . . .   927 Riddle 10   D   6
    I'm up, and down, and round about, ...   929 Riddle 14   D   1
    Many Voices joining round me;   . . . .   ,933 Riddle 20   D   6
    by Sneaking Sniv'ling Round Delays.   958 Cantata
    Comes off by out-laughing the Company round.   . . . .   968 Letter Sherid   20
    And, before we find either, our noddles turn round. . . . 1026 Sheri Circles   8
    As his betters are us'd, shall be lash'd round the ring,   1027 Sheri Circles   19
ROUNDS
    But loves to take prodigious Rounds, ...   218 To Mr. Delany   93
ROUSE
    This wretch, to rouse my wrath, for ruin meant;   . . .   47 To Congreve   136
    To rouse and warn the Nymph within.   . . . .   849 Old Thorn   36
    And rouse up your Mettle, ...   953 Oysters   8
ROUT
    At Charing-Cross, among the Rout, ...   172 Horace 1, 7   59
    But more than that, thou'lt keep a rout   . . . . . .   180 Horace 2, 1   13
    Methinks I see a black-guard Rout   . . . . . .   183 Horace 2, 1   79
    Rais'd ever such incessant Rout: . . . .   450 Modern Lady   183
    With which he makes so foul a Rout;)   . . . . . .   530 Lady's Dres Rm   140
    They'd laugh, to see me make a rout, ...   546 Life of Swift   50
    Since Woolston gave us Arms to rout him.   . . . . . .   657 On Poetry   494
    You Wrigle, Fidge, and make a Rout   . . . .   777 Mullinix Tim   139
    And tho' perhaps among the Rout, ...   796 Traulus 1   25
    Such a Rout and such a Rabble   . . . .   830 Legion Club   17
    O'er Head and Body make a Rout, ...   920 Riddle 6   15
ROUZER
    Let fly a Rouzer in her Face.   . . . .   590 Strephon Chloe   192
ROVE
    With eager Hast he longs to rove   . . . .   251 Bubble   29
    Or, where appointing Lovers rove, ...   894 Panegyr Dean   245
ROW
    The Porrengers that in a Row   . . . .   93 Bauc & Phil 1   113
    The Porringers, that in a Row   . . . .   114 Bauc & Phil 2   89
    Twelve Commoners in Caps to Row you.   . . . . . .   476 Epist on Epist   42
    I row by, and call them Names.   . . . .   635 Epistle Lady   166
ROWES
    O'er sees the Work, or Dragon rowes, ...   279 Journal   23
ROWS
    Two Rows of Teeth arm each devouring Jaw;   . . . .   532 To Mr. Gay   35
ROWZ'D
    Till rowz'd by the Noise, ...   245 Irish-Feast   31
ROXANA
    And proud Roxana fir'd with jealous Rage, ...   275 Epilogue   25
ROYAL
    As if 'twould overshade the Royal Rose, ...   37 Ode Sancroft   104
    The Royal Rose the glory of our morn, ...   37 Ode Sancroft   105
    Attending on a Royal Dame.   . . . .   119 Apollo Outwit   4
    How, by Brave Hands, the Royal Traytor fell;   . . . .   162 Toland's Invit   10
    A Crazy Prelate, and a Royal Prude.   . . . . .   193 Author Himself   2
    And thence into the Royal Ear instills.   . . . .   195 Author Himself   56
    Ireland is now our royal Care, ...   269 Apollo's Edict D   1
    My Royal Master promis'd me   . . . .   408 Dial Rich Marb   15
    Complaints against the Royal Butter.   . . . . . .   410 Dial Rich Marb   54
    Stunning her Royal Ears with talking;   . . . . . .   410 Dial Rich Marb   59
    Your Phoebus royal, every day   . . . .   462 Birthday Song   69
    And crown a Royal Dunce with Bays: . . . . .   464 Birthday Song   120
    In Royal Robes they come by dozens   . . . . . .   465 Birthday Song   169
    What tho the royal Carcase must   . . . .   467 Birthday Song   235
    To squire a Royal Girl of two Years old!   . . . . 531 To Mr. Gay   10
    And while he poisons, wins the Royal Heart.   . . . . 534 To Mr. Gay   82
    "For railing at the Royal Martyr.   . . . . . .   549 Life of Swift   167
    And Solomon in Royal Vest;   . . . .   592 Strephon Chloe   288
    All Virtues lodge in royal Ermine.   . . . . . .   647 On Poetry   228
    The Remnant of the royal Blood, ...   655 On Poetry   437
    Let a royal Grant be pass'd, ...   830 Legion Club   42
    In Royal Garments each was drest, ...   923 Riddle 7   71
    Add another of royal Nature.   . . . .   940 Letter   6
    A Turn-spit in the <Royal> Kitchen.   . . . . .   300 Horrid Plot   66
    To <Walpole's> more than <Royal> Will.   . . . . 484 Libel on D- D-   122
ROYALS   SEE PAIR-ROYALS
ROYALTY
    Rattles for Infant Royalty to play withal, ...   6 Ode to King   13
    'Tis the best Gemm in Royalty, ...   6 Ode to King   22
ROYST'RING
    Among a Crew of royst'ring Fellows   . . . .   352 Wood Ironmongr   5
ROYSTRING
    Rough Roystring Rustick Roaring Strains   . . . . . 958 Cantata
RUB
    Both stroke her Hands, and rub her Gums, ... 150 Corinna   7
    Skilld in the Horse-laugh and dry Rub, ...   217 To Mr. Delany   57
    Rub off the Dawbs of White and Red;   . . . . . .   582 Young Nymph   34
    Could rub my own gums, ...   852 Lady's Lament   20
    I must not rub a tooth: . . . .   852 Lady's Lament   24

RUB   (CONTINUED)   PAGE TITLE   LINE
    And rub thy Teeth, and pair thy Nails.   . . . . . .   897 Panegyr Dean   334
RUBBING
    When smooth'd by rubbing them together: . . . . . .   1021 Nim-Dan-Dean 1   D 20
RUBBISH
    Upon a rubbish Heap of broken Laws   . . . .   9 Ode to King   102
    The Rubbish of an antient Pile.   . . . .   81 Vanbrug House   84
    At length they in the Rubbish spy   . . . .   109 V's House   103
    The Rubbish of an Antient Pile.   . . . .   109 V's House   126
    Now Curl his Shop from Rubbish drains;   . . . . .   560 Death of Swift   197
RUBIES
    Thy Head with sparkling Rubies round;   . . . . .   324 Pethox   34
RUBS
    That's not so bad as one that rubs   . . . .   452 Modern Lady   258
    From whom she meets with frequent Rubs;   . . . . .   583 Young Nymph   53
RUDDY
    Appearing, show'd the Ruddy Morns Approach.   . . . .   124 Descriptn Morn   2
    His ruddy, wrinckled, smirking Face, ...   290 Prog Marriage   24
    His ruddy Cheeks are no Disguise;   . . . .   291 Prog Marriage   49
RUDE
    Nor in her Presence durst be Rude, ...   121 Apollo Outwit   43
    'Twere rude to make him tell it twice;   . . . . .   376 Apology Lady C   24
    "If startled at a Scene so rude, ...   379 Apology Lady C   135
    She calls it witty to be rude;   . . . .   416 Woman's Mind   18
    Rude Laughter seeming like to burst;   . . . . . .   448 Modern Lady   128
    To be scurrilous, and rude;   . . . .   523 Betty Grizette   30
    Can you call me rude, or haughty?   . . . .   631 Epistle Lady   70
    Spightful, peevish, rude, untoward;   . . . .   799 Traulus 2   11
    As rude as a bear, no mule half so crabbed;   . . . .   955 Portrait Life   5
    For, were you a Dog, I could not be rude t'ye.   . . . 968 Letter Sherid   26
RUDELY
    "But rudely press before a Duke.   . . . .   200 Horace 2, 6   39
RUDENESS
    Rudeness, Ill-nature, Incivility, ...   27 Ode to Temple   46
    As Rudeness is to Repartee.   . . . .   217 To Mr. Delany   64
    If Rudeness be the Effect of Knowledge, ...   377 Apology Lady C   69
RUDIMENTS
    From such deep Rudiments as these   . . . .   87 Hist V's House   35
RUE
    For the Smell of them made me like Garlick and Rue sick 1029 Dr. Helsham   21
RUEFUL
    With fawning Whine, and rueful Tone, ...   208 Fable Bitches   13
RUFA
    And Rufa with her Combs of Lead, ...   450 Modern Lady   168
RUFF
    A new Commode, a Top-knot, and a Ruff, ...   23 Ode Athenian   223
RUFFIAN
    The vilest Ruffian may commit a rape, ...   506 To a Friend   3
RUFFLES
    And with Ruffles to be shewn, ...   573 Helter Skelter   19
    Cambrick Ruffles not their own;   . . . .   573 Helter Skelter   20
    Arrah! who was him reading? 'twas a jauntleman in ruffles, 840 Ballad   D   6
RUG
    A Rug was o'er his Shoulders thrown;   . . . . . .   594 Cassinus Peter   19
    A Rug; for Night-gown he had none.   . . . .   594 Cassinus Peter   20
RUIN
    You saw how near we were to Ruin brought, ...   12 Ode to William   D 17
    This wretch, to rouse my wrath, for ruin meant;   . . .   47 To Congreve   136
    'Twould ruin Undertakers quite.   . . . .   106 V's House   20
    Portending ruin to our State, ...   181 Horace 2, 1   22
    You'll ow Your Ruin to your Bulk;   . . . .   258 Bubble   197
    Is humbly pray'd to ruin Twenty more.   . . . . . .   535 To Mr. Gay   106
    "While they pursu'd each others Ruin.   . . . . . .   567 Death of Swift   368
    "To ruin, slaughter, and confound;   . . . .   568 Death of Swift   382
    "To save that helpless Land from Ruin, ...   569 Death of Swift   412
    To compleat the Publick Ruin, ...   636 Epistle Lady   190
    The Ruin of her antient Seat;   . . . .   849 Old Thorn   38
    Where all goes to ruin   . . . .   857 Lady's Lament   193
    This poor Isle's approaching Ruin?   . . . .   862 To Janus   14
    Repairs a cabin gone to ruin, ...   878 Robbin & Harry   21
    Thy Ruin, Tom, I never meant, ...   1002 Reply by Dean   13
RUIN'D
    Why should the first be ruin'd and laid waste,   . . .   40 Ode Sancroft   178
    March o'er the ruin'd plain with motion slow,   . . .   55 Temple Ill   129
    The Banker's ruin'd if he pays;   . . . .   239 Run Bankers   18
    The Ruin'd Party made his Sport, ...   498 Panegyr Swift   160
    "That Ruin'd Church and Monarch too.   . . . . . .   549 Life of Swift   157
    Three Suff'rers in a ruin'd Cause.   . . . .   883 Rev Market-Hill   6
RUINS
    They from it's Ruins build their own.   . . . . . .   81 Vanbrug House   92
    They from its Ruins build their own.   . . . . . .   110 V's House   134
    Behold the Ruins of the Night!   . . . .   583 Young Nymph   58
    Only to have the Ruins made   . . . .   727 To Stella   123
RUL'D
    Where fatal Neptune rul'd e'rewhile, ...   17 Ode Athenian   39
    What Planet rul'd when you were born;   . . . . . .   258 Bubble   191
    "Had he been rul'd, for ought appears, ...   559 Death of Swift   173
    How the Helm is rul'd by <Walpole>   . . . . . .   635 Epistle Lady   159
    A <Bishop> who rul'd all the rest of his Tribe;   . . . 803 Irish Bishops   2
    When Saturn rul'd the Skies alone, ...   894 Panegyr Dean   233

RULE

	PAGE	TITLE	LINE
Railing a Rule of Wit, and Obloquy a Trade, . .	18	Ode Athenian	84
Who fain would rule the Pulpit, as they do the Stage, .	19	Ode Athenian	104
What petty Motives rule their Fates!	30	Ode to Temple	106
Nor need I ramble far to force a rule, ...	46	To Congreve	113
In how ill season her resentments rule, ...	48	To Congreve	177
If this Rule holds in ev'ry Art, ...	87	Hist V's House	44
His Genius first found out the Rule	216	To Mr. Delany	35
Than Rule yon Isle and be a Slave.	421	Holyhead	34
But swear his Line shall rule the Nation	466	Birthday Song	197
But follow the securest rule, ...	468	Birthday Song	265
For, rule the Rump, you rule the Roast.)	513	Answer Fable	32
For, rule the Rump, you rule the Roast.)	513	Answer Fable	32
And, this he makes his constant Rule;	603	Beasts Confess	81
Drop, for once, your constant Rule, ...	631	Epistle Lady	51
Maxims wise, to rule the State.	635	Epistle Lady	174
(Late, very late, O, may he rule us.)	655	On Poetry	430
You chuse to rule the Sable-flock.	656	On Poetry	454
He shap'd a King to rule ye Race	659	On Poetry	D 410
Shou'd fix upon some certain Rule, ...	707	Cadenus Vaness	665
Let Melancholy rule supreme, ...	724	To Stella	19
All ye Gods, who rule the Soul	832	Legion Club	83
To rule the Dairy next to Kit.	888	Panegyr Dean	42
Only take this rule along,.	907	Daphne	35
For you, by this Rule, must adore all Mankind. . .	947	Mrs. Houghton	6

RULES   SEE OVER-RULES

	PAGE	TITLE	LINE
All Merit that transcends the humble Rules	18	Ode Athenian	77
With Rules to search it, yet obtain'd by none. . .	26	Ode to Temple	16
With Rules from musty Morals brought, ...	27	Ode to Temple	19
Spend all our present Stock in hopes of golden Rules. .	27	Ode to Temple	27
We scrawl all o'er with old and empty Rules, . . .	27	Ode to Temple	33
Who preach the saucy pedantry of rules;	46	To Congreve	102
Or crazy rules to make us wits by rote	47	To Congreve	129
Such were thy rules to be poetically great, ...	55	Temple Ill	137
And if I pray by Reason's rules, ...	199	Horace 2, 6	D
"'Tis a fair Trick, by ancient Rules--	322	First of April	57
He rules the Sea, you see him ride in't;	463	Birthday Song	98
And 'tis against poetic rules	488	Irish-Club	27
The rules of raillery and breeding, ...	489	Dialogue	4
For long enur'd to musty Rules, ...	493	Panegyr Swift	29
Against all Rules to be a King:	513	Answer Fable	16
But if Hell by Logical Rules be defin'd, ...	575	Place Damn'd	3
Teaching by what Golden Rules	635	Epistle Lady	157
Learn Aristotle's Rules by Rote, ...	648	On Poetry	247
Rules, like an Alderman his Ward.	649	On Poetry	286
My Actions with your Rules agree, ...	706	Cadenus Vaness	615
Nor are these Rules applyd to Her:	733	Verses Vanessa	18
I hate, who gape and sneer by Rules.	787	Dick's Variety	2
By us forms his Laws, and Rules, ...	931	Riddle 18	D 11
I'll tear all your Rules, and demolish your Pun Talk:	1019	To Sheridan	8

RULING   SEE ALL-RULING

	PAGE	TITLE	LINE
The ruling Rogue, who dreads to be cashier'd;	536	To Mr. Gay	137
From ruling there the Household singly	745	Stel Distress	9
From ruling there the Household singly, ...	750	Stel Wood-Park	33

RUMBLING

	PAGE	TITLE	LINE
Or make a rumbling o'er his Head, ...	280	Journal	47
The rumbling words march fierce along, ...	461	Birthday Song	45
Than at the Rumbling of a Cart:	674	His Deafness	6

RUMMS

	PAGE	TITLE	LINE
But a Rabble of Tenants, and rusty dull Rumms; . . .	868	Grand Question	28

RUMP

	PAGE	TITLE	LINE
Were you but plac'd on Satan's Rump;	497	Panegyr Swift	137
For, rule the Rump, you rule the Roast.)	513	Answer Fable	32
The Twist, the Squeeze, the Rump, the Fidge an'all, .	783	Tim and Fables	17
With powder'd Rump, and Back and Side, ...	785	Dick, Maggot	7
Upon his reverential rump.	822	Epigr Rundle	2
Poor rump, thou hadst been better sped, ...	822	Epigr Rundle	3
All as she scrubb'd her meazly Rump.	849	Old Thorn	44

RUN   SEE OVER-RUN, O'ER-RUN

	PAGE	TITLE	LINE
Thro' many a needless sphere to run, ...	36	Ode Sancroft	68
Mistaken Ideots! see how giddily they run, ...	39	Ode Sancroft	162
Or if thought's rolling globe her circle run, . . .	51	Temple Ill	9
There all the little School-boys run	87	Hist V's House	33
While Streams run down her oil'd Umbrella's Sides. .	138	City Shower	38
While Spouts run clatt'ring o'er the Roof by Fits; .	139	City Shower	44
Instead of paying Chair-men, run them thro'.) . . .	139	City Shower	50
<Sunderland's> run out of his Wits, ...	168	Peace Dunkirk	11
Take care betimes to run him down:	171	Horace 1, 7	30
I fancy'd ev'ry nymph would run	177	To Lord Harley	31
Now manfully thou'lt run a Tilt	183	Horace 2, 1	93
Who first Run one another down, ...	217	To Mr. Delany	55
When Daughters run away with Fellows)	223	Prog of Love	48
All Parallells exactly run;	226	Prog of Beauty	10
Into the Arms of Death would run, ...	243	Horace 4, 9	22
Run as they drink and drink and run.	257	Bubble	180
Run as they drink and drink and run.	257	Bubble	180
Till those devouring Swine run down, ...	259	Bubble	214
So when this Circle we have run, ...	280	Journal	59
Scarce run a Step before they part;	290	Prog Marriage	32
But when let out, they run and muddle	294	Prog Marriage	147
"Can creep, or run, can fly or swim, ...	304	Storm	31

RUN   (CONTINUED)   PAGE   TITLE   LINE

	PAGE	TITLE	LINE
"To run the Gauntlet of the Court;	380	Apology Lady C	150
His Course of glorious Toil shou'd run,	387	Manly Virtue	118
Thro' all the Realm his Virtues run,	391	Young's Satire	25
Into the Senate-House can run,	392	Young's Satire	42
But, like a King, to run in Debt.	409	Dial Rich Marb	42
Can, at her Morning Tea, run o'er	416	Woman's Mind	23
"But run to Tom, and bid him fix	446	Modern Lady	54
"Go run, and light the Ladies up:	451	Modern Lady	212
Again a-fresh to Cards they run,	453	Modern Lady	278
To Minheer Hendel next you run,	469	Birthday Song	276
In either Case, an equal Chance is run:	535	To Mr. Gay	125
Though your Prognosticks run too fast,	558	Death of Swift	145
"The News thro' half the Town has run.	558	Death of Swift	152
Draw their Swords and run away:	574	Helter Skelter	48
And help yourself to run it down.	644	On Poetry	126
Consider what a Risk you run.	644	On Poetry	136
To cry it up, or run it down.	649	On Poetry	270
Before one race of his was run;	675	Curate's Compl	15
Run o'er their Cant of stupid Lies,	697	Cadenus Vaness	332
She must have long ago run out.	735	Stel B-day '20	32
And yet run out by starving here:	745	Stel Distress	16
In every <Arse> you run your Snout,	774	Mullinix Tim	25
Run on in a perpetual Round,	777	Mullinix Tim	141
Not half thy Course of Misery is run,	793	St. Pat's Well	87
Run to hear Jackpudding gabble;	830	Legion Club	18
Or run helter-skelter	857	Lady's Lament	191
Kit, run to your Master, and bid him come to us.	871	Grand Question	117
No haughty Nymph has Pow'r to run	916	Riddle 2	5
Sometimes run out of all I have;	918	Riddle 4	32
Many to our Counters run,	934	Riddle 22 D	3
His blood delights in mud to run;	950	Upstart D	9
So the famous Tom Leigh, when quite run a-ground,	968	Letter Sherid	19
Well, but I must run and make the Bed, . . .	987	Mary to Sher	35
Our Boys run away,	1036	Plague Country	8

RUNDALL

	PAGE	TITLE	LINE
Friend Rundall fell with grievous bump,	822	Epigr Rundle	1

RUNDLE

	PAGE	TITLE	LINE
Make Rundle Bishop; fye for Shame!	819	Dr. Rundle	1
Rundle a Bishop! well he may;	820	Dr. Rundle	19
Say, how did Rundle undermine 'em;	820	Dr. Rundle	37

RUNG

	PAGE	TITLE	LINE
Then the Bell rung, and I went down to put my Lady to Bed,	69	Mrs Harris Pet	10
Why, what a Peal the Jade has rung,	220	A Quiet Life	11
Of Chloe all the Town has rung,	584	Strephon Chloe	1
Vanessa's Praise rung in their Ear:	694	Cadenus Vaness	241

RUNNING

	PAGE	TITLE	LINE
Who, in his Satyrs running riot,	548	Life of Swift	103
"By bravely running Priest-craft down:	564	Death of Swift	292
Her Shankers, Issues, running Sores,	582	Young Nymph	30
On Corruptions running Riot.	635	Epistle Lady	184
To running out by starving here.	750	Stel Wood-Park	44
Yet you, while Time is running fast,	764	Stel B-day '26	17
Punch roaring ran, and running roar'd.	776	Mullinix Tim	112
His Mind was running on his Match.	904	Death Daphne	52

RUNS   SEE OUT-RUNS

	PAGE	TITLE	LINE
Runs violently o'er his usual Course.)	31	Ode to Temple	149
Seeds and runs up to Poetry.	33	Ode to Temple	212
A different way their Fancy runs;	83	Salamander	16
Cuckolds, elopes, and runs in Debt	150	Corinna	27
And now he runs mad for a ba-ba-ba-Bank.	287	Bank Down	20
The busy Head with mimick Art runs o'er	363	On Dreams	9
And Travels not, but runs a Race.	398	Earl of P-b-w	9
Away he runs with zealous hotness	423	Ireld	65
He runs into a Cannon's Chops.	500	Doctor Delaney	10
Runs laughing up to tell the Queen.	559	Death of Swift	180
Or, struck with Fear, her Fancy runs	583	Young Nymph	51
Which now he runs out every Year;	606	Beasts Confess	166
Well may they boast that antient Blood, which runs	791	St. Pat's Well	17
See, where the new-devouring Vermin runs,	792	St. Pat's Well	59
What care we how high runs his passion or pride?	817	Yahoo's	71
Runs out in tongue, as in estate;	878	Robbin & Harry	10
For Pegasus runs, runs every Race	956	Cantata	
For Pegasus runs, runs every Race	956	Cantata	

<RUPERT>

	PAGE	TITLE	LINE
And set the House to <Rupert> <Barber>.	477	Epist on Epist	70

RURAL

	PAGE	TITLE	LINE
The Manners of the rural Race,	270	Apollo's Edict D	30
"On Rural Squires, that Kingdom's Bane,	571	Death of Swift	443
For he was fond of rural Strain.	848	Old Thorn	12
Than what befits a rural Dame.	897	Panegyr Dean	342
His rural walks he ne'er adorns;	901	Dean's Reasons	91

RUSH

	PAGE	TITLE	LINE
But he cares not for it a Rush,	860	Lady Acheson	15

RUSHY

	PAGE	TITLE	LINE
On their Rushy Beds and Benches,	574	Helter Skelter	46
Sharp are the Stones, take thou this rushy Matt;	881	Pastoral Dial	19

RUST

	PAGE	TITLE	LINE
That, moulders into rust,	39	Ode Sancroft	141

```
                                                      PAGE    TITLE          LINE
RUST'LING
    Starts at the Rust'ling of the Trees;    . . . . . .   379 Apology Lady C   126
RUSTICK
    Rough Roystring Rustick Roaring Strains              958 Cantata
RUSTY
    What bungling, rusty tools, are us'd by fate!         47 To Congreve       131
    In that old Wig and rusty Gown!   . . . . . . . .    175 Horace 1, 7       124
    The rusty Tongs have lost a Leg   . . . . . . . .    746 Stel Distress      40
    But when they hear his rusty Voice,                 776 Mullinix Tim        95
    But a Rabble of Tenants, and rusty dull Rumms;      868 Grand Question      28
    Conversing with that rusty <Dean>!   . . . . . .    891 Panegyr Dean       142
RYMER
    Judicious Rymer oft review:   . . . . . . . . .     648 On Poetry          249
SABLE
    And both assum'd a Sable Hue;   . . . . . . .       115 Bauc & Phil 2      122
    A Sable Cloud a-thwart the Welkin flings,           137 City Shower         14
    O'er the Moon's Face a sable Hue,                   354 Simile Silver        2
    His antient Pipe in Sable dy'd,                     594 Cassinus Peter      23
    An Adder of the sable Kind,   . . . . . . . .       903 Death Daphne        27
SABLE-FLOCK
    You chuse to rule the Sable-flock.   . . . . . .    656 On Poetry          454
SABLE-GUARD
    Attended by the Sable-guard,   . . . . . . . .      779 Mullinix Tim       202
SABLES
    And grief flung sables on each menial look;   . .    53 Temple Ill          60
SABRA'S
    Have no concern for Sabra's sake,   . . . . . .     777 Mullinix Tim       129
SABRINA
    Sabrina,Medway,and the Thames.   . . . . . . .      468 Birthday Song      242
SACK
    Come, you must take a Cup of Sack or two before you go.  342 Upon His Grace  24
    He stopt at the George for a Bottle of Sack,        399 Tom Clinch           3
    For which he sends this empty sack;   . . . . . .   753 Gift for Bec        25
SACRED
    With her World's fruitful System in her sacred Ark,  .   16 Ode Athenian   13
    Are the chief Heroes in the sacred List of Fame.   .    25 Ode Athenian   307
    Chief cherub, and chief lamp of that high sacred Seven,  34 Ode Sancroft    3
    And sheds, tho' all unseen, his sacred influence here.   39 Ode Sancroft  153
    Kind Star, still may'st thou shed thy sacred influence   39 Ode Sancroft  154
      here,
    The Mitre, which his sacred head has worn,   . . . .    40 Ode Sancroft  199
    Under those Sacred Leaves, Secure   . . . . . .     119 Apollo Outwit        9
    During Her Sacred Life, should never come over:     144 New Song            36
    Stand in your sacred Presence aw'd;   . . . . . .   243 Horace 4, 9         12
    Prize Classicks more than Sacred Writ:              392 Young's Satire      40
    Those Sacred Leaves that Lightning spares.          458 Paddy's Charac      12
    But now, by Friendship's sacred Laws,   . . . . .   596 Cassinus Peter      91
    Ye Muses guard your sacred Mount,                   671 Epig Carthy 21   D   5
    Are not so sacred as her Word:   . . . . . . .      725 To Stella           56
    Where is the sacred Well, that bore my Name?   . . . .  793 St. Pat's Well  65
    Here, by the sacred Bramble ting'd,   . . . . . .   896 Panegyr Dean       313
SACRIFIC'D
    Which worship'd cats, and sacrific'd to apes;   . . . .  46 To Congreve    106
SACRIFICE
    And keep Her for a Sacrifice,   . . . . . . .         8 Ode to King         75
    Ready to fall Rome's bloody Sacrifice;   . . . . . .    12 Ode to William  D 22
    No Sacrifice on Altars blaz'd;   . . . . . . .      346 Prometheus          44
    "Nor made a Sacrifice of those   . . . . . . .      567 Death of Swift     363
    "To sacrifice old England's Glory,   . . . . . .    568 Death of Swift     387
    A larger Sacrifice in Vain you vow;                 771 Horace 1, 14        33
    Their Sacrifice with Zeal and Haste:   . . . . .    894 Panegyr Dean       240
    Present a Sacrifice unclean;   . . . . . . . .      895 Panegyr Dean       284
SACRILEGIOUS
    Cuts down with sacrilegious Hand.   . . . . . . .   849 Old Thorn           24
SAD
    When the sad, melancholy Muse   . . . . . . . .      24 Ode Athenian       273
    Nay, said she, my Lord Collway's Folks are all very sad  70 Mrs Harris Pet  27
    For so sad a Tale is no Subject of Laughter.   . . .    430 Dicky Dolly    18
    Effects of many a sad Disaster;   . . . . . . .     582 Young Nymph         31
    Cou'd Horace give so sad a Monster Birth,           669 Epig Carthy 16   D   1
    And sad Experience taught their Use:   . . . . .    705 Cadenus Vaness     607
    Beauty and Wit, too sad a Truth,   . . . . . .      757 Stel B-day '24      15
    Sad Omens of the dire Event.   . . . . . . . .      849 Old Thorn           32
    'Twas a sad rainy Night--but the Morning is fine--   869 Grand Question     74
    When all the sad Reverse appears!   . . . . . . .   921 Riddle 7            10
    Sad Charnel-house! a dismal Dome,   . . . . . .     922 Riddle 7            51
    To you the sad Account I bring,   . . . . . .       932 Riddle 19        D  23
    Ne'er sad I mourn, ne'er glad rejoice,              936 Riddle 23        D  24
    For I write but a sad Scrawl, . . .   . . . . .     987 Mary to Sher        34
    Commonly speaking, but a sad Jade is.   . . . .     988 Letter Dr Sh-n      25
    Is grown a Sad Dame,   . . . . . . . .             1014 Swift to Sheri      34
SADDLE
    The Groom was wisht to saddle Crop,   . . . . .     223 Prog of Love        35
    The dullest Beast, and the Saddle it wears,   . . .  940 Letter             10
SADDLES
    And with Saddles eke so easy   . . . . . . .        573 Helter Skelter      12
SADLY
    Down falls the summer's pride, and sadly shews . . . .   55 Temple Ill     123
SAFE
    There (A safe way to use Perfume)   . . . . . .      60 Lady Tablebook      12
    . . . .my Money was as safe as my Maidenhead.   . . . .   69 Mrs Harris Pet 11
```

SAFE	(CONTINUED)	PAGE	TITLE	LINE
To make the Bundle strong and safe,	. . . .	191	Faggot	45
All her Complexions safe and sound,	. . . . . .	226	Prog of Beauty	30
The Moon lay safe behind the Cloud.	. . . . . .	253	Bubble	80
To see you safe in Sots-Hole,	. . . .	425	Five Ladies	6
The Parson safe at Church,	. . . .	426	Five Ladies	43
Safe through the Newry mountains sides.	. . . . . .	435	Answer Paulus	98
Take my advice; to make you safe,	. . '.	487	Irish-Club	13
If fair, it brings you safe to Port,	. . . . . .	493	Panegyr Swift	19
His Life is safe, I mean his Fame,	. . . . . .	500	Doctor Delaney	24
That safe behind the Wainscoat lyes.	. . . . .	504	Doctor Delaney	138
Yet safe from injured innocence escape:	. . . . . .	506	To a Friend	4
For while he keeps his Pen, you are not safe.	. . . . .	538	Mr. Pulteney	14
Safe within my little Wherry,	. . . .	635	Epistle Lady	163
Dennis was out, and I got hither safe;	. . . . .	881	Pastoral Dial	31
Oh, there you think you have me safe! but hold Sir,	. .	1004	Dan J's Reply	27
I wish Alexander safe at St. Catherine's To-night,	. .	1014	Swift to Sheri	9
SAFE'S				
Again you fail, yet Safe's the Word,	. . . . . .	645	On Poetry	147
SAFELY				
"How Sons may safely disobey,	. . . .	181	Horace 2, 1	45
Safely glad to sup their Porridge,	. . . . . .	574	Helter Skelter	54
Safely write a smart Lampoon,	. . . .	634	Epistle Lady	153
Your Virtues safely I commend,	. . . . . .	730	Stella, Poems	79
I now could safely swear it is hers.	. . . .	993	On Picture	15
SAFER				
Take subjects safer for your wit	. . . .	489	Dialogue	21
But, the State-Emp'ric acts a safer Part;	. . . .	534	To Mr. Gay	81
SAFETY				
Was forc'd, for Safety, to alight,	. . . . . .	127	Little House	32
On Britain Europes safety lyes	. . . . . .	140	Harlyes Surgn	1
For, who with Traytors would his Safety trust,	. . .	210	Earl of Oxford	19
But there, alas! he could no Safety find;	. . . .	538	Mr. Pulteney	21
(Fear lent him Wings) for Safety to the Skies.	. . .	538	Mr. Pulteney	30
Now, for thy Safety Cares distract my Mind,	. . . .	772	Horace 1, 14	58
The publick Safety I foresee,	. . . .	776	Mullinix Tim	81
SAGACIOUS				
Why so sagacious in your guesses?	. . . .	487	Irish-Club	11
SAGE				
But, after sage Monitions from his Friends,	. . . .	194	Author Himself	23
Cryes out a Sage among the Croud,	. . . . . .	253	Bubble	78
Once on a Time, a righteous Sage,	. . . . . .	383	Manly Virtue	1
The Sage, who said he should be proud	. . . . . .	400	Window Inns 1	1
A Moralist profoundly sage,	. . . .	412	Desire Possess	5
('Tis this the Sage of Samos means,	. . . . . .	587	Strephon Chloe	125
Like the ever-laughing Sage,	. . . .	635	Epistle Lady	167
Labours of many an ancient Sage,	. . . . . .	922	Riddle 7	41
SAGES				
More oft in Fools and Mad-mens hands than Sages	. .	23	Ode Athenian	220
What could the Sages gain but unbelieving scorn;	. . .	39	Ode Sancroft	170
For this we know, all antient Sages	. . . . . .	391	Young's Satire	23
By Sages, Priests, or Poets taught;	. . . . . .	482	Libel on D- D-	76
What Preachers talk, or Sages write,	. . . . . .	691	Cadenus Vaness	150
And by all Sages understood	. . . .	764	Stel B-day '26	27
SAGITTARIUS				
The Point of Sagittarius Dart,	. . . .	100	Elegy Patrige	81
SAID SEE SD				
In vain, said He, does Utmost Thule boast	. . . .	7	Ode to King	51
Because 'tis said (and perhaps only said)	. . . .	20	Ode Athenian	146
Because 'tis said (and perhaps only said)	. . . .	20	Ode Athenian	146
Rather forgive what my first Transport said,	. . . .	23	Ode Athenian	244
Great God! (said I) what have I seen!	. . . .	29	Ode to Temple	103
And tho' as some ('tis said) for their Defence	. .	30	Ode to Temple	125
And God himself has said, He shall not find it here.	.	35	Ode Sancroft	20
Their faith was so uncourtly when they said	. . .	39	Ode Sancroft	171
Said, how a late report your friends had vex'd,	. .	47	To Congreve	143
Of whom it may be justly said,	. . . . . .	61	Lady Tablebook	29
Lord help me, said Mary, I never stirr'd out of this Place!		70	Mrs Harris Pet	16
Nay, said I, I had it in Lady Betty's Chamber, . . .		70	Mrs Harris Pet	17
Dame, said I, as loud as I could bawl, ...		70	Mrs Harris Pet	26
Nay, said she, my Lord Collway's Folks are all very sad		70	Mrs Harris Pet	27
Pugh! said I, but that's not the Business that I ail.		70	Mrs Harris Pet	29
Mrs. Dukes, said I, here's an ugly Accident has happen'd out:		71	Mrs Harris Pet	37
The Devil take me, said she, (blessing her self,) . . .		71	Mrs Harris Pet	44
No, said I, 'tis the same Thing, ...		72	Mrs Harris Pet	49
Parson, said I, can you cast a Nativity, . . .		72	Mrs Harris Pet	53
Lord, said I, don't be angry, ...		72	Mrs Harris Pet	59
. . .Lord, said I, what shall I do?		73	Mrs Harris Pet	64
Then my Lord call'd me; Harry, said my Lord, don't cry,		73	Mrs Harris Pet	66
Oh but, said I, what if after all my Chaplain won't come to?		73	Mrs Harris Pet	68
For that, he said, (an't please your Excellencies) . . .		73	Mrs Harris Pet	69
One surly Clown lookt out, and said,	. . . . . .	91	Bauc & Phil 1	37
The Strangers overheard, and said,	. . . . .	92	Bauc & Phil 1	83
We are but Saints, the Hermits said;	. . . . .	112	Bauc & Phil 2	44
Then said; my House is grown so Fine,	. . . . .	115	Bauc & Phil 2	113
Hear my Request the Virgin said	. . . .	120	Apollo Outwit	29
He said, but that it wanted Room,	. . . . . .	128	Little House	45

SAID   (CONTINUED)   PAGE   TITLE   LINE

	PAGE	TITLE	LINE
The Clerk said to her in a Heat,	128	Little House	55
And I pronounce, (the Satyr said)	150	Corinna	11
He cock't his Hat, you would have said	156	Fable of Midas	13
Went where he pleas'd, said what he thought,	171	Horace 1, 7	33
Said Harley, I desire to know	172	Horace 1, 7	47
But coldly said, Your Servant, Sir.	172	Horace 1, 7	54
Said Harley, Welcome Rev'rend Dean!	174	Horace 1, 7	121
Then where, said I, shall Harley find	177	To Lord Harley	33
What, tho' by Enemies 'tis said,	182	Horace 2, 1	65
Dick, we agree--all's true, thou'st said,	183	Horace 2, 1	99
See, said the Sire, how soon 'tis done:	189	Faggot	9
How would they blush to hear it said,	190	Faggot	31
"My only Friend, my Dear," said she,	207	Fable Bitches	9
If what You said, I wish unspoke,	217	To Mr. Delany	65
But who believ'd him when he said it:	220	A Quiet Life	38
Exactly said what now befell her,	223	Prog of Love	52
Are said to represent the Seas,	239	Run Bankers	6
Now, whereas the said Criminal seems past Repentance,	266	Apollo	93
But now there need no more be said on't,	282	Journal	86
Minds nothing that is done or said,	291	Prog Marriage	57
Said I, from thence I nothing know;	298	Horrid Plot	5
Said he-- "Great Sovereign of the Main,	303	Storm	27
"Thalia said, 'tis somewhat odd,	321	First of April	18
And said, "His Worship might ha' told us,	322	First of April	45
"Sisters, said she, my Life I'll lay,	322	First of April	55
And said: By my Shoul he's the Son of a Beech:	334	Serious Poem	28
Then said my Lord, I'm very glad to see thee honest Friend,	342	Upon His Grace	31
Then said his Lordship with a Smile, I must have Lawful Cash,	342	Upon His Grace	35
Why Sirrah said the Noble 'Squire, how dare you see my Face,	343	Upon His Grace	43
What cou'd I've said? I'm mighty glad	377	Apology Lady C	51
Said little in his own Defence:	377	Apology Lady C	74
Said the Freeman, your Guinea To-night would be spent,	396	Dog and Thief	13
And said, lack-a-day! he's a proper young Man.	399	Tom Clinch	8
Then said, I must speak to the People a little,	399	Tom Clinch	15
The Sage, who said he should be proud	400	Window Inns 1	1
But, now I fear it will be said,	410	Dial Rich Marb	55
'Tis said, their Course continu'd long;	412	Desire Possess	13
"I said I should not win a Game.	452	Modern Lady	239
His Learning, though a Poet said it,	484	Libel on D- D-	141
'Tis said, the Gods try'd all their Art,	501	Doctor Delaney	31
The Day will come, when't shall be said,	547	Life of Swift	68
Jove, nodding, shook the Heav'ns, and said,	579	Day Judgement	10
But yet, the worst that could be said,	602	Beasts Confess	27
Who said, his Gravity was feign'd:	603	Beasts Confess	50
Said, he affected Popularity:	606	Beasts Confess	160
My Works he said, cou'd ne'er afford him Meat.	670	Epig Carthy 20	D 3
And then, said she, my Son and	689	Cadenus Vaness	85
And said she must consult her Books,	689	Cadenus Vaness	106
This said, she plucks in Heav'ns high Bow'rs	691	Cadenus Vaness	154
And said, "Vanessa be the Name,	692	Cadenus Vaness	180
But it shall ne'er be said, a Child	692	Cadenus Vaness	194
And said, she valu'd nothing less	697	Cadenus Vaness	340
I said her Face would never last.	699	Cadenus Vaness	387
A modest Youth said something new,	701	Cadenus Vaness	454
Said, she shou'd be no longer teiz'd;	704	Cadenus Vaness	574
Now, said the Nymph, I'll let you see	706	Cadenus Vaness	614
I knew by what you said and writ,	706	Cadenus Vaness	618
The Sum of what each Lawyer said;	713	Cadenus Vaness	851
Yet granting all I said were true,	748	Stel Distress	75
Whatever was said,	755	Dingley Brent	4
To have them sung, they may be said.	757	Stel B-day '24	34
While none believes that what he said he meant:	797	Traulus 1	50
But, Courage, my <Lords>, tho' it cannot be said	805	Irish Bishops	49
Said to the Pippin, plump, and prim,	811	Bro Protestant	13
May well be said Man did beget it.	812	Bro Protestant	38
Said surly Peter, Magus, prithee	821	Dr. Rundle	47
What, said I, is this the Mad-House?	833	Legion Club	99
Now, said I, we are alone,	834	Legion Club	135
Than it e'er should be said	853	Lady's Lament	56
No more need be said on't,	857	Lady's Lament	201
I said--why--Let him if he will,	859	Lady Acheson	3
I've said enough to make him blush	860	Lady Acheson	13
And, Molly, she said, I should hear some ill News.	868	Grand Question	52
Pray, Madam, be quiet; what was it I said?--	870	Grand Question	85
Accosting; said, Go shake your Cream.	897	Panegyr Dean	326
Lord! said I, who's that parson? how awkwardly dangles he	978	Dean to Tho: S	2
Mary said he, (one Day, as I was mending my Master's Stocking,)	986	Mary to Sher	28
Saunders said I, I would rather than a Quart of Ale,	987	Mary to Sher	31

SAIL

	PAGE	TITLE	LINE
"He knows to sail with ev'ry Wind;	304	Storm	34
And as they sail in Charon's Boat,	647	On Poetry	211
Betwixt a State, and Vessel under Sail;	770	Horace 1, 14	6
Torn by a sudden Tempest is thy Sail,	770	Horace 1, 14	23
The People's Voice expands his Paper Sail;	770	Horace 1, 14	28
I'm now a Sail, and now a Mast;	911	Aenigma	6

	PAGE	TITLE	LINE
SAIL'D			
What Street they sail'd from, by their Sight and Smell.	139	City Shower	56
With ev'ry Wind he sail'd, and well could tack:	285	Elegy Boat	15
Our Boat is now sail'd to the Stygian Ferry,	285	Elegy Boat	23
And sail'd with Litter Side by Side;	811	Bro Protestant	8
SAILER'S			
To bless the Primitive Sailer's weary sight,	16	Ode Athenian	7
SAILING			
Instead of boldly sailing far to buy	19	Ode Athenian	97
SAILOR			
And thus address thee in the Sailor Stile.	770	Horace 1, 14	8
In vain from me the Sailor flies,	934	Riddle 21	D 13
SAILS			
Take down thy proudly swelling Sails,	897	Panegyr Dean	333
At once so like to Masts or Sails,	912	Aenigma Expl	D 6
SAINT SEE ST			
Since, happy Saint, since it has been of late	42	Ode Sancroft	240
Here you may read (Dear Charming Saint)	60	Lady Tablebook	7
With a Saint at his Chin, and a Seal in his Fob;	147	Windsor Proph	2
A Joyner to fasten a Saint in a Nitch,	336	Serious Poem	71
He would ne'er be convinc'd it was a True Saint:	336	Serious Poem	74
Which gets the better, Saint, or Snake.	777	Mullinix Tim	130
I'll make the Dev'l a Saint this Hour,	930	Riddle 15	D 15
Next make a Devil of a Saint.	930	Riddle 15	D 16
SAINTS			
Chief of the mitred saints, and from arch-prelate here,	42	Ode Sancroft	238
The Saints would often leave their Cells	90	Bauc & Phil 1	2
Two Brother-Hermits, Saints by Trade	90	Bauc & Phil 1	7
Our wand'ring Saints in wofull State,	91	Bauc & Phil 1	47
Who kindly did the Saints invite	91	Bauc & Phil 1	53
Invited both the Saints to Drink.	92	Bauc & Phil 1	72
These Men are Saints I'll lay my Life	92	Bauc & Phil 1	82
The Saints would often leave their Cells.	111	Bauc & Phil 2	2
Two Brother Hermits, Saints by Trade,	111	Bauc & Phil 2	7
Our wand'ring Saints in woful State,	111	Bauc & Phil 2	15
Who kindly did the Saints invite	111	Bauc & Phil 2	21
We are but Saints, the Hermits said;	112	Bauc & Phil 2	44
Ye bishops far remov'd from saints;	487	Irish-Club	7
And thus Fanatic Saints, tho' neither in	812	Bro Protestant	29
A Bishop in the Isle of Saints!	819	Dr. Rundle	3
SAKE SEE NAME-SAKE			
Who I, for your Sake, have us'd better than any;	263	Apollo	26
Wish't him a Coll'nell for her Sake.	291	Prog Marriage	44
Un-man the poor Knave for sake of a Trope.	335	Serious Poem	52
They only fight for fighting sake,	421	Ireld	8
For Paulus' and for <Lyndsay's> sake	433	Answer Paulus	46
And, for her sake turn base detractor	622	Scandal Poem 1	171
For your Sake, as well as mine,	637	Epistle Lady	217
But this was for Cadenus' sake;	701	Cadenus Vaness	462
Due Vengeance, for her Patron's sake.	701	Cadenus Vaness	471
Observe them but for fashion sake.	732	Verses Vanessa	6
Nor do I ask for Stella's sake;	741	Stel B-day 22	31
Have no concern for Sabra's sake,	777	Mullinix Tim	129
For Pity's Sake it would be just,	813	Bro Protestant	55
(I spare the Thistle for Sir Arthur's sake.)	881	Pastoral Dial	18
I shall, for Method Sake, begin with the last.	967	Letter Sherid	12
For the sake of your senses wou'd lay an embargo.	976	Dean to Sherid	30
SAKES			
To live and die all strollers for your sakes;	309	Billet Players	50
SALAMANDER			
Call my Lord <Cutts> a Salamander.	83	Salamander	22
Sure that must be a Salamander!	84	Salamander	46
Whether this ben't a Salamander	85	Salamander	70
Forget he's like a Salamander.	270	Apollo's Edict	D 19
SALAMANDER'S			
As from the Salamander's Spue;	85	Salamander	66
SALE			
Forcing a wretched Trade by beating down the sale,	19	Ode Athenian	101
Nor be concern'd about the Sale,	646	On Poetry	189
(For Tonson had, to help the Sale,	782	Tim and Fables	9
To have the Spirit set to Sale.	821	Dr. Rundle	46
SALERNO			
(Salerno both together joins	589	Strephon Chloe	181
SALLIES			
A lively Maggot sallies out,	785	Dick, Maggot	3
SALLOW			
Pale Dropsy with a sallow Face,	895	Panegyr Dean	275
SALMON			
We look for a Salmon, you leave us a Stone.	287	Bank Down	8
SALMONEUS			
Salmoneus, as the Grecian Tale is,	352	Wood Ironmongr	1
SALT			
Then Reader pray shed some tears of Salt Water,	430	Dicky Dolly	17
Which tho' with Art you salt and beat,	528	Lady's Dres Rm	100
Lets fall her Knife, or spills the Salt,	694	Cadenus Vaness	243
Too sour or too salt:	853	Lady's Lament	62
It cannot bear Salt;	939	Riddle Answerd	30
SALTER			
Your Beef will on Thursday be salter than brine	1018	Swift Ans Sher	24
SALUTE			
Salute her, and she turn'd her Ear:	222	Prog of Love	4

	PAGE	TITLE	LINE
SALUTE (CONTINUED)			
The brazen Bells salute his Ears:	338	Wood's Brass	6
And, I have heard thee oft salute	594	Cassinus Peter	33
SALUTES			
Meets, and salutes her sister link again;	51	Temple Ill	4
Salutes the weary trav'ller as he walks;	55	Temple Ill	120
The Captain salutes you with Congee profound;	871	Grand Question	115
Salutes the <Dean> in diff'rent Views;	888	Panegyr Dean	38
SAME			
To Valour and to Virtue the same Word:	7	Ode to King	28
Yet the same want of Brains produces each effect;	18	Ode Athenian	85
In the same Ballance with our Tears,	24	Ode Athenian	257
Still to be of the same exalted Sex with You.	24	Ode Athenian	267
Was cast in the same Mold with mine?	32	Ode to Temple	179
The Son of God pronounc'd by the same breath	38	Ode Sancroft	119
One end in both, and the design the same;	42	Ode Sancroft	256
And the bad world may well believe the same;	49	To Congreve	198
Strange to conceive, how the same objects strike	51	Temple Ill	1
No, said I, 'tis the same Thing,	72	Mrs Harris Pet	49
But neither Bulk nor Shape the same:	81	Vanbrug House	80
She soon would find, the same Effects,	85	Salamander	64
But neither Bulk, nor Shape the same:	109	V's House	122
But repeats the same Note a whole Day, like a Finch.	143	New Song	8
But still I'm in Principle ever the same,	144	New Song	25
Is backwards and forwards always the same;	148	Windsor Proph	22
Which backwards and forwards is allmost the same.	148	Windsor Proph	24
And, since the same resemblance held	177	To Lord Harley	29
In good and evil Times the same.	243	Horace 4, 9	10
But Wit and Weaving had the same beginning,	276	Epilogue	37
Then Proteus urg'd the same Request,	303	Storm	25
"There's Berkeley in the same Condition;	304	Storm	48
So your Production was the same,	324	Pethox	31
The same thy Subjects boast of Thee.	324	Pethox	42
If you make the same Tryal, and Bore him Behind;	336	Serious Poem	78
I hope you will not pay my Rent in that same Woods's Trash.	342	Upon His Grace	36
On all the same Impression stuck.	344	Prometheus	10
The same Impression on his Mind;	345	Prometheus	20
As that same viz. St. <Patrick's> Dean.	361	Grace's Answer	6
If that same Universal Passion	392	Young's Satire	35
Kind Richmond-Lodge; the same to you.	411	Dial Rich Marb	104
But, all he took was just the same:	412	Desire Possess	32
He's just the same, his brethren are	435	Answer Paulus	108
Shew me the same numerick Flea,	504	Doctor Delaney	141
So, Robbers (and their Ends are just the same)	536	To Mr. Gay	141
The same Aversions, and Desires;	546	Life of Swift	44
"He dy'd a Year ago." The same.	563	Death of Swift	256
Would still the same Ideas give ye,	591	Strephon Chloe	247
Keep the same face an hour together,	618	Scandal Poem 1	44
Keep the same Face an Hour together;	625	Scandal Poem 2	40
That same paultry Burlesque Stile:	631	Epistle Lady	50
The Case is just the same with me:	679	From Catullus	6
Unites, and both become the same,	687	Cadenus Vaness	32
Nor Flesh nor Blood will be the same,	759	Receipt Youth	33
Who ev'ry Day and Hour the same are;	787	Dick's Variety	4
Red hat, and blue bonnet, and turbant's the same,	815	Yahoo's	23
And rather than come in the same Pair of Sheets	869	Grand Question	59
All things gone on the same dull track,	877	To Dean Swift	31
Is the same avarice of mind:	900	Dean's Reasons	38
My Constancy is still the same.	916	Riddle 2	8
All prompted by the same Desire,	922	Riddle 7	25
But you may find the same in me.	932	Riddle 19	D 6
I'm still the same --- but ever new.	935	Riddle 23	D 6
In ev'ry vile Pamphlet you'll read the same Fancies,	968	Letter Sherid	21
SAMOS			
('Tis this the Sage of Samos means,	587	Strephon Chloe	125
SANCROFT			
Ill may I live, if the good Sancroft in his holy rest,	36	Ode Sancroft	50
Thus, primitive Sancroft moves too high	39	Ode Sancroft	149
And divine Sancroft, weary with the weight	40	Ode Sancroft	185
Such were the storms good Sancroft long has borne;	40	Ode Sancroft	198
Thus Sancroft, in the exaltation of retreat,	41	Ode Sancroft	211
There some high spiritual throne to Sancroft shall be given,	42	Ode Sancroft	236
SANCROFT'S			
And holy Sancroft's motion quite irregular appears,	37	Ode Sancroft	81
SAND			
By some instructed Querist sleeping on the Sand,	22	Ode Athenian	190
While you ly helpless on the Sand:	258	Bubble	200
Yet, when his Sand was out, we find at last,	285	Elegy Boat	21
To build on Sand with Hay and Stubble?	593	Strephon Chloe	306
I March'd three miles thro' scorching sand,	675	Curate's Compl	1
SANDES			
Tho as empty as Younge and as saucy as Sandes	389	Order of Bath	10
SANDS			
Was lost among Pactolus Sands,	157	Fable of Midas	34
The Sea indeed had golden Sands.	255	Bubble	112
Would offer all the Sands of Tagus;	821	Dr. Rundle	42
SANDY			
Why, Plague confound her sandy Locks:	595	Cassinus Peter	47

	PAGE	TITLE	LINE
SANG			
Went triumphant to Church, and sang stoutly Te Deum:	967	Letter Sherid	18
SANS			
Walke sans wetynge Shoes ne hosen.	102	Merlin	4
Just as a Man sans Consequence.	707	Cadenus Vaness	659
SANTRY			
Lady Santry got out of the Church when she grew sick,	1029	Dr. Helsham	10
SAP'ENCE			
He still has Gratitude and Sap'ence,	796	Traulus 1	27
SAPHICK			
Of Dan's large Nose, in modern Saphick,	993	On Picture	3
SAPIENCE			
He can Rap his own Raps, and has the true Sapience	335	Serious Poem	47
SAPLESS			
That Scepter was a sapless Twig:	134	Magician's Rod	66
This aged, sickly, sapless Thorn	849	Old Thorn	21
SAPLING			
A Sapling with a falling Oak?	703	Cadenus Vaness	535
SAPPHO'S			
Whispers that Sappho's Hair is Red:	450	Modern Lady	169
SARTA			
Since you write in a cart, keep it tecta et sarta,	979	Dean to Tho: S	15
SASH			
She ventures now to lift the Sash,	228	Prog of Beauty	65
But as for the Poem he writ on your Sash,	265	Apollo	65
Your Ladyship lifts up the Sash to be seen,	870	Grand Question	101
SAT			
And, (like a Wag) sat down to Write,	107	V's House	61
How steady in the Sterne he sat,	281	Journal	71
Behold the awful Bench on which he sat,	285	Elegy Boat	19
She sat all Night up at Quadrill.	446	Modern Lady	41
E'en quit the House, for thou too long hast sat in't,	538	Mr. Pulteney	9
The t' other he sat down to darn	594	Cassinus Peter	13
Then pray'd an Answer and sat down.	687	Cadenus Vaness	20
With silent Scorn Vanessa sat,	697	Cadenus Vaness	334
I gravely sat me down to think:	740	Stel B-day 22	4
I well remember when I sat fort.	783	Tim and Fables	22
That one cloven Tongue, ever sat on your Head;	805	Irish Bishops	50
At Dublin's high feast sat Primate and Dean,	843	Ay and No	1
Secure from Satyrs sat and sung.	848	Old Thorn	8
I sat with delight,	852	Lady's Lament	17
You sat and lows'd him all the Sun-shine Day.	882	Pastoral Dial	34
To visit where she sat at Cards:	904	Death Daphne	56
SATAN			
From Satan for a Term of Years,	240	Run Bankers	46
By Satan taught, all Conj'rers know	401	Window Inns 2	1
But, Satan never saw	429	Beau's Reply	13
"Their Loads they all on Satan lay:	497	Panegyr Swift	134
But, see how Satan spreads his Snares;	605	Beasts Confess	117
Why truly 'tis Satan, <Arch-bishop> of Hell:	803	Irish Bishops	4
Poor Satan will think the Comparison odious;	803	Irish Bishops	11
Is it Satan? No 'tis <Waller>.	834	Legion Club	138
And give Satan his due Dan begins to refine	1017	Swift Ans Sher	10
SATAN'S			
Were you but plac'd on Satan's Rump;	497	Panegyr Swift	137
SATCHELS			
And School-Boys lag with Satchels in their Hands.	125	Descriptn Morn	18
SATE			
And for a while in heav'nly Contemplation sate	16	Ode Athenian	25
Nell roar'd incessant, Dick sate mute:	219	A Quiet Life	4
Where erst sate Cupid with his Bow;	757	Stel B-day '24	38
As at their Work they sate in counterview,	880	Pastoral Dial	5
SATINS			
They on the Gold Brocades and Satins rav'd,	771	Horace 1, 14	51
SATIRA'S			
Satira's but some pocky Quean.	530	Lady's Dres Rm	134
SATIRE			
Check in thy satire, angry muse,	42	Ode Sancroft	259
In satire, to my Congreve's praises meant;	48	To Congreve	176
My satire may offend, 'tis true:	435	Answer Paulus	101
There's too much satire in my vein,	489	Dialogue	2
To Satire, Praise, or hum'rous Lines;	643	On Poetry	82
You thought that Satire Sir,--but you are bit.	669	Epig Carthy 17	D 2
(For Satire had destroy'd his little fame,)	671	Epig Carthy 24	D 2
They are not scurrilous in Satire,	729	Stella, Poems	55
He kindled, as if the whole Satire had been	816	Yahoo's	41
SATIRE'S			
Deserves your Satire's keenest Rage;	392	Young's Satire	34
SATISFACTION			
Give future times the Satisfaction	608	Know Not What	7
SATISFIE			
Than You to please and satisfie Mankind,	22	Ode Athenian	200
SATISFIED			
Methinks I'm satisfied to guess	20	Ode Athenian	135
SATISFY			
And not to satisfy the doubt:	35	Ode Sancroft	16
SATISFY'D			
Be satisfy'd, I'll do my best:--	201	Horace 2, 6	58
SATTIN			
Became Black Sattin, Flounc'd with Lace.	116	Bauc & Phil 2	142

SATURN
 Some call their Monarchs Sons of Saturn, ...   460 Birthday Song   9
 Was able Saturn to depose;   . . . .   461 Birthday Song   24
 When Saturn rul'd the Skies alone, ...   894 Panegyr Dean   233
 Old Saturn from his Empire drove;   . . . .   894 Panegyr Dean   254
SATYR
 But Cupid with a Satyr comes;   . . . .   150 Corinna   5
 And I pronounce, (the Satyr said)   . . . .   150 Corinna   11
 A Satyr where he most commends.   . . . .   216 To Mr. Delany   40
 For Satyr now's so common grown   . . . .   371 Letter D. S-y   3
 At length, presumes to vent his Satyr on   . . . .   458 Paddy's Charac   27
 A Satyr, and the Gentry buy!   . . . .   502 Doctor Delaney   76
 "Had too much Satyr in his Vein;   . . . .   571 Death of Swift   456
 "His Satyr points at no Defect, ...   571 Death of Swift   463
SATYRE
 Against the Sex to write a Satyre, ...   445 Modern Lady   7
 Of all the Satyre shall be mine.   . . . .   445 Modern Lady   29
SATYRIC
 Ne'er did a true satyric muse   . . . .   488 Irish-Club   25
 "And shew'd by one satyric Touch, ...   572 Death of Swift   481
SATYRICK
 For dealers in Satyrick Wit: . . . .   463 Birthday Song   112
 On me, when Dunces are satyrick, ...   505 Doctor Delaney   169
SATYRS
 Who, in his Satyrs running riot, ...   548 Life of Swift   103
 In Satyrs, Libels, lying Travels!   . . . .   548 Life of Swift   112
 Satyrs and Epigrams in vain you write, ...   667 Epig Carthy 4   D 1
 Secure from Satyrs sat and sung.   . . . .   848 Old Thorn   8
SAUCE
 Come, buy my fine Oranges, Sauce for your Veal,   . .   953 Oranges   1
SAUCILY
 And then, how saucily he shows   . . . .   627 Scandal Poem 2   139
SAUCY
 Who preach the saucy pedantry of rules;   . . . . .   46 To Congreve   102
 Talk'd with that saucy and familiar ease   . . . . .   47 To Congreve   141
 And on my verse pronounce their saucy doom;   . . . .   50 To Congreve   214
 Tho as empty as Younge and as saucy as Sandes   . .   389 Order of Bath   10
SAUNDER'S
 In Saunder's Cellar on the Ground: . . . .   743 Stel B-day 22   56
SAUNDERS
 And Saunders the Man says, you are always jesting and
  mocking,   986 Mary to Sher   27
 Saunders said I, I would rather than a Quart of Ale,   987 Mary to Sher   31
 And now I must go, and get Saunders to direct this   987 Mary to Sher   33
  Letter,
 . . .for Saunders already hath got above ten Jaunts.   1013 Swift to Sheri   6
SAUNT'RING
 He's all the day saunt'ring, ...   856 Lady's Lament   159
SAUNTRING
 Sauntring in Coffee-house is Dulman seen;   . . . . .   137 City Shower   11
SAV'D
 He sav'd his Country by Delays, ...   28 Ode to Temple   71
 He caught his Fish, and sav'd his Bait.   . . . . .   134 Magician's Rod   48
 And sav'd his Oar, but lost his Hat.   . . . . . .   281 Journal   72
 And sav'd him at once from the Shrew and the Rabble;   .   327 Epigram 1   4
 My Country's sav'd, as you have shown, ...   372 Letter D. S-y   17
 Who sav'd thee from a great Disaster.   . . . . . .   373 Letter D. S-y   56
 Of him that Ireland sav'd, and Harley;   . . . . . .   494 Panegyr Swift   54
 He ravish'd her fairly, and sav'd a good Shilling;   .   519 Dean Hang Rape   57
 Forgets by whom it once was sav'd;   . . . .   875 Drapier's Hill   12
 You lost a Place, and sav'd a Bribe?   . . . . . .   884 Rev Market-Hill   36
SAV'RY
 No sav'ry Dish without an Onyon;   . . . .   952 Onyons   7
SAVAGE
 Whose harp could savage beasts enchant, ...   177 To Lord Harley   11
 A savage Race by Shipwrecks fed, ...   256 Bubble   154
 The Britons, once a savage Kind, ...   326 Pethox   73
 Among ye savage Monsters crown'd   . . . .   659 On Poetry   D 410
 Poor I, a Savage bred and born, ...   891 Panegyr Dean   131
SAVAGE-PICTURES
 With Savage-Pictures fill their Gaps;   . . . . . .   645 On Poetry   178
SAVE
 Who cou'd so well a dying Nation save, ...   12 Ode to William   D 15
 You'll spend in Coach-hire more than save in Wine.   . .   137 City Shower   8
 Forget their Fewds, and join to save their Wigs,   . .   138 City Shower   42
 Think what you save or what you kill   . . . . . .   140 Harleys Surgn   4
 When known, will save a double Sorrow.   . . . . .   204 In Sickness   28
 Consult his Peace, or Credit save?   . . . .   221 A Quiet Life   40
 His Coffers from the Coffin could not save, ...   234 Elegy on Demar   21
 Resolv'd to save the British Nation, ...   300 Horrid Plot   49
 To spare a Foe, to save a Friend: . . . .   306 Storm   76
 "'Tis all to save their Mother trouble;   . . . . .   321 First of April   24
 He would not give a Groat to save his Father from the   342 Upon His Grace   16
  Gallows.
 So, Holla Boys; God save the King.   . . . .   418 Woman's Mind   64
 And why should they save her   . . . .   424 Carterets Arms   17
 In both, yet hardly save your stake.   . . . . . .   436 Answer Paulus   130
 And make him crouch to save his bacon.   . . . . .   468 Birthday Song   250
 To save his Life he leapt into the Main.   . . . . .   538 Mr. Pulteney   20
 Thy Turns and Doublings cannot save thee long.   . . .   539 Mr. Pulteney   44
 To save the Nation ev'ry hour?   . . . .   548 Life of Swift   110

SAVE	(CONTINUED)	PAGE	TITLE	LINE
"To save their sinking Country lent,	. . . .	568	Death of Swift	375
"To save that helpless Land from Ruin,	. . . . . .	569	Death of Swift	412
"To save them from their evil Fate,	. . . .	569	Death of Swift	415
Call'd up at Mid-night, ran to save		604	Beasts Confess	115
Like stepping Stones to save a Stride,	. . . . . .	645	On Poetry	169
Come and appear, and save their Bail.		713	Cadenus Vaness	841
Your skilful Hand employ'd to save	. . . . . .	764	Stel B-day '26	37
His Pen to save a sinking Nation draws,		770	Horace 1, 14	26
While others hither sent to save us,	. . . . . .	820	Dr. Rundle	33
This Petticoat shall save thy dear Back-side;		881	Pastoral Dial	22
I give Command to kill or save.		916	Riddle 1	34
'Tis true, indeed, sometimes I save,		918	Riddle 4	31
No Scraps remain to save Board-wages.	. . . . . .	954	Authors Living	6
You save the Charge of Lime and Trowels.	. . . . .	1021	Nim-Dan-Dean 1	D 24
SAVED				
She saved Britannia's Right, and lost her own.	. . .	771	Horace 1, 14	46
SAVERS				
When Actors who at best are hardly Savers,	. . . .	274	Epilogue	3
SAVES				
And, we admire the man, who saves	. . . .	436	Answer Paulus	125
She saves Half her Victuals, by feeding your Ears.	.	580	Psyche	14
SAVING SEE NATION-SAVING				
Always for saving their own bacon:	. . . .	434	Answer Paulus	65
Than saving your Souls, by damning our own?	. . . .	805	Irish Bishops	56
SAVINGS SEE COUNTY-SAVINGS				
SAVIOUR				
That the world's Saviour had been	. . . .	40	Ode Sancroft	173
Convince us they believe a Saviour;	. . . .	488	Irish-Club	22
By reading Books against their Saviour;	. . . . .	592	Strephon Chloe	272
SAVOUR				
Ay, this has some Savour.	. . . .	245	Irish-Feast	28
SAW				
For strait I saw the Field maintain'd,	. . . . . .	8	Ode to King	61
You saw how near we were to Ruin brought,	. . . . .	12	Ode to William	D 17
You saw th' impetuous Torrent rolling on;	. . . . .	12	Ode to William	D 18
Van saw, but seemd not to regard,	. . . . . .	86	Hist V's House	3
He saw the Edifice and smil'd,	. . . . .	86	Hist V's House	9
And saw them dabling in their Clay,	. . . . . .	86	Hist V's House	14
Whoever yet a Union saw	. . . . .	96	On the Union	11
Jove saw the Cheat, but thought it best		108	V's House	67
And saw it fairly twice go round;	. . . . . .	112	Bauc & Phil 2	31
And saw the Parson creeping out;	. . . .	127	Little House	26
He call'd for Drink, you saw him Sup	. . . . .	156	Fable of Midas	7
Frequented Lords; saw those that saw the Queen;	. . .	194	Author Himself	17
Frequented Lords; saw those that saw the Queen;	. . .	194	Author Himself	17
When twenty Fools I never saw	. . . . .	200	Horace 2, 6	44
But when He saw his Friend appear	. . . . .	220	A Quiet Life	5
He saw Virago Nell belabor	. . . .	220	A Quiet Life	21
Wher'er he went he never saw his Betters,	. . . . .	234	Elegy on Demar	15
And as he saw his darling Money fail,	. . . . .	235	Elegy on Demar	33
When they saw the Dean's Book they were in a great Fury		237	Excellent Song	24
They peep'd, and saw a Lady there	. . . .	321	First of April	29
The Muses when they saw her care,	. . . . .	322	First of April	43
Jove saw that all Devotion fail'd,	. . . . .	345	Prometheus	42
And saw the treach'rous Goddess smile;	. . . . .	413	Desire Possess	46
But, Satan never saw	. . . .	429	Beau's Reply	13
I never saw you play so ill.	. . . .	452	Modern Lady	247
"I saw you touch your Wedding-Ring	. . . . .	452	Modern Lady	252
"I swear I saw you thrice renounce.	. . . . .	452	Modern Lady	263
Saw Poets at his Levee wait.	. . . .	482	Libel on D- D-	70
Though 'tis confess't that those who ever saw	. . .	521	Stephen Duck	5
"Who saw this Factious Tribe caress'd,	. . . . .	549	Life of Swift	160
"Whole Swarms of Sects, with grief, he saw	. . . .	550	Life of Swift	168
"Saw Mischief by a Faction brewing,	. . . . . .	567	Death of Swift	367
I saw the Graves give up their Dead.	. . . . . .	578	Day Judgement	4
None saw her pluck a Rose.	. . . .	584	Strephon Chloe	16
Abasht at what they saw and heard,	. . . .	590	Strephon Chloe	195
On what you saw, and what you smelt;	. . . . . .	591	Strephon Chloe	246
He saw, and he was griev'd to see't,	. . . . . .	603	Beasts Confess	53
Saw all these mighty labours done,	. . . .	675	Curate's Compl	14
Nor saw the Play-House twice a Year;		696	Cadenus Vaness	313
I saw coquetting t' other Night	. . . . .	699	Cadenus Vaness	394
For Persons whom he never saw.	. . . . .	708	Cadenus Vaness	693
"She saw her Favour was misplac'd;		714	Cadenus Vaness	868
Since first I saw her at Sixteen	. . . . .	721	Stel B-Day '18	5
And swears she saw a Thing in White.		725	To Stella	74
At going in you saw her stoop	. . . . .	746	Stel Distress	
At coming in you saw her stoop;	. . . . .	751	Stel Wood-Park	49
I grieve she ever saw the light.		754	Stella '23	6
When she saw three hundred Brutes,		833	Legion Club	113
When I saw the Keeper frown,	. . . . . .	834	Legion Club	133
Dame Nature, when she saw the Blow,	. . . . .	849	Old Thorn	25
And so we saw him at our Gate	. . . .	859	Lady Acheson	7
When I saw him so often with Darby and Wood.	. . .	868	Grand Question	48
That I saw a huge Rat: O dear, how I scream'd!	. . .	868	Grand Question	50
When you saw Tady at long-bullets play,	. . . . .	882	Pastoral Dial	33
I peept, and saw you kiss the dirty Bitch.	. . . .	882	Pastoral Dial	38
I saw thee rais'd to high Renown,	. . . . . .	919	Riddle 5	5
I saw them of their Garments stript,	. . . . . .	923	Riddle 7	73
And you durst not talk thus if I saw you at our ale-house		976	Dean to Sherid	32

		PAGE	TITLE	LINE
SAW	(CONTINUED)			
When I saw you to-day, as I went with Lord Anglesey.		978	Dean to Tho: S	1
Well; if ever I saw such another Man		985	Mary to Sher	1
Tho' I ne'er saw her hold the Scissars, ...		993	On Picture	14
SAW'D				
For I saw'd them reading upon the towlsel doore. . . .		840	Ballad	D 4
SAW'T				
. . .if I ever saw't!		71	Mrs Harris Pet	44
SAWCILY				
You see how sawcily he shews		621	Scandal Poem 1	135
SAWCY				
But in a sawcy manner He		153	Widow and Cat	D 19
You sawcy Brute, ...		440	Ballyspellin	2
SAWPIT				
Have you not o'er a Sawpit seen, ...		393	Modern Poets	10
Then in a Sawpit and wet Weather, ...		393	Modern Poets	19
SAY				
(Yet Curiosity they say, ...		18	Ode Athenian	64
'Tis but to say, that what we daily meet, . . .		19	Ode Athenian	123
Say Muse, for thou, if any, know'st		36	Ode Sancroft	43
(Say hapless Isle, altho'		37	Ode Sancroft	93
Yet pardon, native Albion, when I say		38	Ode Sancroft	128
Say, why the Church is still led blindfold by the State?		40	Ode Sancroft	177
Some angel say, what were the nation's crimes, ...		42	Ode Sancroft	245
Say what their senseless malice meant, ...		42	Ode Sancroft	247
Say, whence it comes that thou art grown of late . . .		53	Temple Ill	83
Besides, as they say, Service is no Inheritance in these Ages.		71	Mrs Harris Pet	41
So you know, what could I say to her any more, ...		71	Mrs Harris Pet	46
So the Chaplain came in; now the Servants say,. . .		72	Mrs Harris Pet	50
. . .as who should say, ...		72	Mrs Harris Pet	62
The greater half I had to say, ...		80	Vanbrug House	56
As we say, Monsieur, to an Ape		83	Salamander	5
The better Half we had to say;		106	V's House	30
Step to the Doctor straight, and say, ...		172	Horace 1, 7	49
"And Fathers never shou'd say nay, ...		181	Horace 2, 1	46
Dear Will, but, what would People say?		220	A Quiet Life	34
Because her Father us'd to say		223	Prog of Love	31
Say, which among the Heav'nly Pow'rs		227	Prog of Beauty	55
Matter, as wise Logicians say, ...		228	Prog of Beauty	81
And Form, say I, as well as They, ...		228	Prog of Beauty	83
When Mortals say she's in her Wain.		228	Prog of Beauty	88
The very Chest, in which they say		235	Elegy on Demar	47
But these, you say, are factious Lyes		256	Bubble	157
No Son of mine shall dare to say, ...		270	Apollo's Edict	D 20
This Paper they say, by the Help of a Quill, ...		287	Bank Down	12
The Dean, she heard her Uncle say		291	Prog Marriage	47
She'll say, and she may truly say't		293	Prog Marriage	97
But what of that, his friends may say, ...		296	Satiric Elegy	21
And 'twas but just; for, wise Men say, ...		299	Horrid Plot	29
For to say Truth, she did intend him, ...		303	Storm	21
"For Fear the rest shou'd say he squeeks;		305	Storm	62
"And, but for Shame, wou'd say his Pray'rs. . . .		305	Storm	66
And, whisp'ring, charg'd me not to say		311	To Ford	3
She dares not say her Life's her own.		328	Epigram 3	4
Some say he's a Birch, a Thought very odd, . . .		335	Serious Poem	33
Just as when we say, the Devil's a Tinker		335	Serious Poem	54
Perhaps you will say, 'tis the Devil that puts . . .		335	Serious Poem	61
I know you will say, this is all Heathen Greek; . . .		337	Serious Poem	89
We never say more than, your Love is a Million; . . .		337	Serious Poem	104
So Goldsmiths say, the coursest Stuff, ...		345	Prometheus	23
They say, all human Things depend:		345	Prometheus	34
Say, who is to be understood, ...		346	Prometheus	59
And, since the Alderman was mad you say, ...		350	Upright Judge 3	7
'Tis true, say they, cut off the Head, ...		366	Answer Delaney	5
What is't that you or I've to say, ...		372	Letter D. S-y	39
Science and Art you say at stand are, ...		372	Letter D. S-y	41
I ask, if what you say be true, ...		392	Young's Satire	32
And all that He or They can say;		408	Dial Rich Marb	2
Yet I may say 'twixt me and you, ...		408	Dial Rich Marb	21
On what detracting People say?		414	Censure	18
They cannot say the winds are cross		420	Holyhead	15
Our Letters say a Jesuite boasts		422	Ireld	41
The sun, you say, his face has kist:		432	Answer Paulus	9
And, though the gospel seems to say, ...		434	Answer Paulus	61
Say what you dare, ...		441	Ballyspellin	32
Some Authors say not quite so soon, ...		446	Modern Lady	39
Say, foolish Females, Old and Blind, ...		449	Modern Lady	150
Say, by what fatal Turn of Mind, ...		449	Modern Lady	151
"Nay, Madam, give me leave to say		452	Modern Lady	248
You've Cause to say he meant you well:		475	Epist on Epist	25
And go to Church, and say our Prayers.		495	Panegyr Swift	71
Is this the Art, good Doctor, say, ...		497	Panegyr Swift	142
You say, the Muse will not contain, ...		501	Doctor Delaney	51
Say, did you ever know by Sight		504	Doctor Delaney	139
The worst you can say, he committed a \<Rape\>.		516	Dean Hang Rape	6
Say, had the Court no better place to chuse		531	To Mr. Gay	7
When you are Sick, your Friends, you say, ...		546	Life of Swift	58
Say what you will about his reading, ...		548	Life of Swift	101
"Vice is a Vermin; Sportsman say		548	Life of Swift	125
I say no more---, because he's dead---.		549	Life of Swift	143

SAY	(CONTINUED)	PAGE	TITLE	LINE
"He's dead you say; why let him rot;		559	Death of Swift	183
"Six Deans they say must bear the Pall.		562	Death of Swift	231
"But dearest Friends, they say, must part.		562	Death of Swift	240
Say, fair ones, must I make a Pause?		589	Strephon Chloe	161
Say, has the small or greater Pox		595	Cassinus Peter	48
Avaunt--ye cannot say 'twas I.		596	Cassinus Peter	88
When Beasts could speak, (the Learned say		601	Beasts Confess	1
He quite forgot to say his Pray'rs.		605	Beasts Confess	118
But say, what earthly nymph do you know,		619	Scandal Poem 1	63
But say, what Earthly Nymph do you know,		625	Scandal Poem 2	59
Say Britain, cou'd you ever boast, --		640	On Poetry	5
Lie Snug, and hear what Criticks say.		644	On Poetry	118
Say, Poet, in what other Nation,		656	On Poetry	465
Perhaps you say Augustus shines		658	On Poetry	D 410
Carthy, you say, writes well--his genius true.--		668	Epig Carthy 8	D 1
'Tis what no Man alive will say of you.		670	Epig Carthy 18	D 2
There was on both Sides much to say:		690	Cadenus Vaness	116
Now, gentle Clio, sing or say,		690	Cadenus Vaness	126
As who should say--she wants it here;		698	Cadenus Vaness	361
Wou'd say, He made a treach'rous Use		707	Cadenus Vaness	644
Say, Stella, was Prometheus blind,		726	To Stella	85
She dares not say the Poet lyes.		730	Stella, Poems	82
Say, Stella, when you copy next,		732	Stella, Poems	137
I told him what the World would say		741	Stel B-day 22	15
But to say truth, such Dulness reigns		742	Stel B-day 22	41
Say, Stella, which you most repent		745	Stel Distress	21
We say, she's past her Dancing Days;		756	Stel B-day '24	2
But, Stella say, what evil Tongue		757	Stel B-day '24	35
I'll ne'er believe a Word they say.		757	Stel B-day '24	40
Say, Stella, feel you no Content,		764	Stel B-day '26	35
'Tis a true Copy, I'll say that for't,		783	Tim and Fables	21
Dammee, I say, they ought to starve.		783	Tim and Fables	34
Though Dick, I dare presume to say,		788	Dick's Variety	17
Say, Robin, what can Traulus mean		795	Traulus 1	1
To say he's mad will not avail:		797	Traulus 1	38
Before you condemn us, hear what we can say.		805	Irish Bishops	54
Say to Corruption--Thou'rt my Father.		813	Bro Protestant	62
If you say this is hard, on a man that is reckon'd		817	Yahoo's	66
And say of the man what all honest men say.		819	Archbi Cashel	10
And say of the man what all honest men say.		819	Archbi Cashel	10
Say then more than they; nay, lavishly flatter,		819	Archbi Cashel	13
Say, how did Rundle undermine 'em;		820	Dr. Rundle	37
Some they do say, 'twas the big man of straw;		841	Ballad	D 12
But others they do say, that it was Jug-Joulter,		841	Ballad	D 13
"But if I say the word--take care of Armagh!"		843	Ay and No	18
And, say what I will,		853	Lady's Lament	49
Or you may say--my Wife intends,		860	Lady Acheson	21
"Now Madam, you'll think it a strange Thing to say,		873	Grand Question	171
As, who shou'd say, Now, am I Skinny and Lean?		873	Grand Question	176
And say, there shall, for years together,		876	To Dean Swift	25
Will not have one new thing to say.		878	Robbin & Harry	12
As who should say, to pluck a Rose.		893	Panegyr Dean	216
For, none can say that ever yet		901	Dean's Reasons	73
Never hears what you can say:		906	Daphne	14
Say what I am, then if you can		912	Aenigma	13
And therefore, all that know me, say		918	Riddle 4	37
You say it is quiet,		939	Riddle Answerd	7
Which you say it can kill,		939	Riddle Answerd	17
Perhaps you will say, 'tis in Gratitude due,		947	Mrs. Houghton	3
But grant her a Sieve, I can say something archer,		972	S-'s Ans Sh-d	9
You threaten the stocks: I say you are scurrilous,		976	Dean to Sherid	31
You hit it, you say,--you're a delicate hitter.		977	Dean to Sherid	40
And I think I may say, you cou'd many good shillings get		979	Dean to Tho: S	9
You say you will eat Grass on his Grave: a Christian eat Grass!		986	Mary to Sher	17
But that's as much as to say, that my Master should die before ye,		986	Mary to Sher	19
And so say I told you so,		986	Mary to Sher	21
Whereof I cou'd say more to your Verses,		987	Mary to Sher	37
Mrs. Dingley and Mrs. Johnson say,		1013	Swift to Sheri	7
. . . for, to say it we may venture,		1023	Nim-Dan-Dean 2	D 13
I had forgot to desire you to bring down what I say you have,. . .		1023	Nim-Dan-Dean 2	D 15
. . . say is (tho' written somewhat at large) trim and clean;		1024	Nim-Dan-Dean 2	D 17

SAY'T
| My Lord, who (if a Man may say't) | | 171 | Horace 1, 7 | 13 |
| She'll say, and she may truly say't | | 293 | Prog Marriage | 97 |

SAYING
| Not saying, lest I go too far, | | 373 | Letter D. S-y | 62 |
| Wearied with saying Grace and Prayer, | | 1003 | Dan J's Reply | 1 |

SAYS
Lord! Madam, says Mary, how d'ye do?.		70	Mrs Harris Pet	14
. . .Indeed, says I, never worse;		70	Mrs Harris Pet	14
Says Cary, says he, I have been a Servant.		70	Mrs Harris Pet	30
Says Cary, says he, I have been a Servant.		70	Mrs Harris Pet	30
Yes, says the Steward,.		71	Mrs Harris Pet	32
Truly, says he, Mrs. Nab,.		72	Mrs Harris Pet	55
If your Money be gone, as a Learned Divine says, d'ye see,		72	Mrs Harris Pet	56

SAYS   (CONTINUED)   PAGE   TITLE   LINE
      . . .and says my Lady, so will I.   .   .   .   .   73 Mrs Harris Pet   67
      Says Nancy, I can make for Miss, ...   128 Little House   61
      In civil Terms,--"My Friend," says she, ...   208 Fable Bitches   25
      With Forty Things more: Now hear what the Law says,   .   236 Excellent Song   3
      My Lady says she can't afford one;   .   .   .   .   .   .   283 Journal   124
      But soft says the Herald, I cannot agree: .   .   .   .   338 Serious Poem   119
      A Bishop says the noble 'Squire, I hate the very Name,   342 Upon His Grace   17
      When my old cassock says 'a Welch divine   .   .   .   .   .   419 Shall Repine   5
      He says, his Business is to know   .   .   .   .   446 Modern Lady   57
      While crooked Cynthia swearing says, ...   449 Modern Lady   160
      (Says he) tho' swell'd like any porpus.   .   .   .   .   .   456 Dean Smedley   32
      Which says, wou'd Crows in Silence eat   .   .   .   .   .   479 Epist on Epist   121
      Whate'er the noisy Scoundrel says   .   .   .   .   505 Doctor Delaney   163
      Birds, as he says, and I allow, ...   513 Answer Fable   39
      The Proverb says; No Fence against a Flayl.   .   .   .   .   521 Stephen Duck   2
      If, what he says be not a Joke, ...   545 Life of Swift   3
      He says, "Whenever Fortune sends   .   .   .   .   545 Life of Swift   7
      He recollects not what he says;   .   .   .   .   556 Death of Swift   86
      Says Lintot, "I have heard the Name: .   .   .   .   .   .   563 Death of Swift   255
      Says Grace before, and after Meat;   .   .   .   .   .   .   605 Beasts Confess   130
      Hearken, what my Lady says---:   .   .   .   .   630 Epistle Lady   11
      I find, says he, she wants a Doctor, ...   702 Cadenus Vaness   498
      Whoever says you have them, lyes.   .   .   .   .   758 Stel B-day '24   48
      Then, who says care will kill a cat?   .   .   .   .   .   .   761 Bec's B-Day   7
      As Horace says, Optat ephippia.   .   .   .   .   779 Mullinix Tim   214
      By <God> says Tim (and let a <Fart>)   .   .   .   .   .   .   783 Tim and Fables   19
      In the House 'tis all he says;   .   .   .   .   785 Mullinex Dick   39
      An Inundation, says the Fable, ...   811 Bro Protestant   1
      Says not a Word of his Departure   .   .   .   .   860 Lady Acheson   11
      "And Madam, says he, if such Dinners you give,   .   .   .   872 Grand Question   141
      But now let us hear what the Muse from your car says.   .   976 Dean to Sherid   6
      For he says, short as 'tis, it will give you a stool.   .   980 Tho: Sheridan   8
      And Saunders the Man says, you are always jesting and   986 Mary to Sher   27
          mocking,
      He and Cratinus used, as Horace says, ...   988 Letter Dr Sh-n   11
      Who says, his numbers do not fadge a-right.   .   .   .   .   988 Letter Dr Sh-n   20
SCAB
      This vap'ring Scab must needs devise   .   .   .   .   .   .   352 Wood Ironmongr   9
SCABBY
      And Ointments good for scabby Chops.   .   .   .   .   .   .   526 Lady's Dres Rm   36
SCABS
      To cure their Scabs   .   .   .   .   440 Ballyspellin   14
SCALD
      I think the best Thing we can do is to scald him.   .   .   351 Wood Insect   34
SCALDING
      But a Kettle of scalding hot Water injected, ...   351 Wood Insect   25
      Nay, further, the Moment you're free from your scalding,   1019 To Sheridan   9
SCALE
      Blew his last Breath to sink the lighter Scale.   .   .   .   235 Elegy on Demar   34
      Her Scale to neither Side inclines, ...   391 Young's Satire   16
      Shall scale the Rampart with your Bands.   .   .   .   .   .   884 Rev Market-Hill   54
SCALES
      When Other Hands the Scales shall hold, ...   241 Run Bankers   61
      Her scales you only see her hold   .   .   .   .   433 Answer Paulus   35
SCAMANDER
      The God who made Scamander boil, ...   323 Pethox   7
SCAN
      But found him thus their Merit Scan, ...   157 Fable of Midas   53
      And, though you never learn'd to scan verse, ...   658 On Poetry   D 186
SCANDAL
      Of Scandal now a Cornucopia;   .   .   .   .   150 Corinna   30
      The Scandal of the Day before.   .   .   .   .   416 Woman's Mind   24
      And Scandal ever gaping wide, ...   448 Modern Lady   125
      Iris, for Scandal most notorious, ...   450 Modern Lady   166
      If Scandal did not find them Payment.   .   .   .   .   .   .   502 Doctor Delaney   74
      From Scandal, Politicks, and Play, ...   688 Cadenus Vaness   44
      To Scandal next-----What aukward Thing   .   .   .   .   .   .   699 Cadenus Vaness   384
      O Fortune, 'tis a Scandal for thee   .   .   .   .   884 Rev Market-Hill   25
SCANDAL-CHARGE
      Now comes the gen'ral Scandal-Charge, ...   449 Modern Lady   144
SCANDAL'S
      When you are try'd in Scandal's Court.   .   .   .   .   .   .   413 Censure   6
SCANDALL
      Pursue thy Trade of Scandall picking, ...   735 Stel B-day '20   41
SCANDALOUS
      The dullest Beast, and scandalous Vermin   .   .   .   .   .   941 Letter   29
SCANTY
      Of my own dazled, scanty Sense   .   .   .   .   18 Ode Athenian   78
      And with such Scanty Wages pay   .   .   .   .   24 Ode Athenian   258
      And catch the living landscape thro' a scanty light,   . .   35 Ode Sancroft   30
      And measuring by the scanty thread of wit   .   .   .   .   .   38 Ode Sancroft   123
      Where Phoebus pays a scanty Stipend, ...   883 Rev Market-Hill   3
'SCAP'D
      And since I 'scap'd being made a Scoff, ...   377 Apology Lady C   55
'SCAP'T
      Thrice happy you have 'scap't this gen'ral Pest;   .   .   .   28 Ode to Temple   58
      A Hare, who long had 'scap't pursuing Hounds,   .   .   .   538 Mr. Pulteney   17
'SCAPE
      Who barbarously think to 'scape reproach, ...   44 To Congreve   21
      And, though the Villain 'scape a while, he feels   .   .   .   210 Earl of Oxford   21

	PAGE	TITLE	LINE
'SCAPE (CONTINUED)			
To 'scape Enquiries, leave the House in Flame. . . .	536	To Mr. Gay	142
"Shou'd Vice expect to 'scape rebuke, ...	548	Life of Swift	123
Court, nor Parli'ment, can 'scape ye;	631	Epistle Lady	54
Yet keep their Bishopricks, and 'scape the Cord. . .	806	Judas	14
To 'scape them, Sir Arthur	854	Lady's Lament	83
'SCAPES			
Nor Chick, nor Duckling 'scapes, when Grim	153	Widow and Cat	D 14
SCAPING			
Till, scaping oft without a Wound, ...	500	Doctor Delaney	7
SCAR			
Nor has it left the usual bloody Scar, ...	28	Ode to Temple	74
Or think it seated in a Scar, ...	724	To Stella	25
SCAR'D			
Scar'd at th' unheard-of Prodigy, ...	30	Ode to Temple	110
How will the Caitiff Wretch be scar'd	241	Run Bankers	53
George is half scar'd out of his Wits, ...	283	Journal	125
But fearing Berkeley might be scar'd	306	Storm	77
The Nation scar'd, the Author doom'd to Death, . . .	771	Horace 1, 14	31
<SCARBOROUGH>			
By Force of Wine ev'n <Scarborough> is Brave, . . .	163	Toland's Invit	21
SCARCE			
Can scarce th' impression of his foot-steps find; . . .	54	Temple Ill	116
Scarce had they spoke when fair and soft	92	Bauc & Phil 1	91
Would turn so quick you scarce could see't	93	Bauc & Phil 1	132
But well perceiving Wit was scarce, ...	107	V's House	56
They scarce had Spoke; when, fair and soft, ...	112	Bauc & Phil 2	51
Turn'd round so quick, you scarce cou'd see't;	113	Bauc & Phil 2	72
When Food and Rayment now grew scarce	225	Prog of Love	95
Can scarce get o'er the Barn-Door Sill:	230	Prog of Poetry	4
If the Printer will peach him, he'll scarce come off clean.	238	Excellent Song	32
If Cudgels are scarce, ...	247	Irish-Feast	86
There's scarce one in ten, but what has my Mark; . . .	265	Apollo	62
Tho' Moneys scarce we shou'd have Trade enough; . . .	275	Epilogue	32
And scarce a Crown is left to see the Play:	275	Epilogue	34
Scarce run a Step before they part;	290	Prog Marriage	32
In threed-bare Goun, would scarce a louse hold, . . .	291	Prog Marriage	61
But now, though scarce a twelvemonth marry'd, . . .	293	Prog Marriage	99
And scarce a Day, can spare a Minute	322	First of April	41
And all the Rent I pay is scarce five Shillings in the Pound.	342	Upon His Grace	22
That, Faith, I think, there scarce is Room	371	Letter D. S-y	7
Or preach, you'd like him scarce the worse.	375	Apology Lady C	12
And scarce believes his Eyes, or Ears;	376	Apology Lady C	20
My Master assure a Fortnight since, ...	409	Dial Rich Marb	37
And vows she scarce can fetch her Breath.	417	Woman's Mind	46
As when they scarce have learn'd to spell.	463	Birthday Song	96
And, crazy Congreve scarce cou'd spare	481	Libel on D- D-	41
Mitres, and Glebes could scarce do more	493	Panegyr Swift	9
Himself could scarce forbear to kick, ...	497	Panegyr Swift	139
A Bungler thus, who scarce the Nail can hit, . . .	535	To Mr. Gay	131
For Party he would scarce have Bled---:	549	Life of Swift	142
St. John himself will scarce forbear, ...	561	Death of Swift	209
Since Beauty scarce endures a Day, ...	593	Strephon Chloe	303
All your Eloquence will scarce	636	Epistle Lady	195
From Bayliffs claws thou scarce cou'd keep thy Bum free.	678	Dean and Duke	12
Scarce list'ning to their idle Chat;	697	Cadenus Vaness	335
Scarce knows what Diff'rence is between	700	Cadenus Vaness	416
Cou'd scarce oppose Vanessa's Flame;	710	Cadenus Vaness	745
That scarce a Creature can be found, ...	776	Mullinix Tim	79
Scarce glimmers, like a dying Snuff.	787	Clad in Brown	18
Thy greatest Evils yet are scarce begun.	793	St. Pat's Well	88
She scarce recover'd in a Week.	849	Old Thorn	28
The Servants amaz'd, are scarce ever able, ...	871	Grand Question	135
Will scarce one precious word impart:	900	Dean's Reasons	44
She scarce remembers what is Trumps.	904	Death Daphne	60
SCARCELY			
A Peer, a scarcely bearded Youth, ...	386	Manly Virtue	71
SCARE			
As when to scare th' ungrateful or the proud	52	Temple Ill	23
SCARE-CROW			
Thou sorry Scare-crow of Skin and Bone, ...	1003	Dan J's Reply	17
SCARF			
And get a Hatband, Scarf, and Gloves.	547	Life of Swift	65
With swelling scarf, and glossy gown, ...	676	Parson's Case	25
SCARLET			
"By Calvin, than the Scarlet Whore:	549	Life of Swift	151
But, he by Mars, in Scarlet Vest.	586	Strephon Chloe	60
Their President, in Scarlet Gown, ...	904	Death Daphne	49
In Scarlet some, and some in White;	920	Riddle 6	11
SCARLET-COAT			
A Passion for a Scarlet-Coat;	415	Woman's Mind	2
SCARS			
And, as a Proof, shew num'rous Scars	324	Pethox	13
SCARSELY			
Can scarsely speak for want of Breath, ...	379	Apology Lady C	127
"If you, unus'd, have scarsely Strength	379	Apology Lady C	133
SCATT'RING			
Scatt'ring loose features o'er the optic vein;	54	Temple Ill	96
Still scatt'ring desolation where they go.	55	Temple Ill	130

SCATT'RING   (CONTINUED)   PAGE   TITLE   LINE
    But scatt'ring round his Fly-blows, dyes; . . . . .   80 Vanbrug House   53
SCATTER
    Could scatter Opium full as well, ...   133 Magician's Rod   41
    To scatter Roses at her Feet; . . . .   379 Apology Lady C   112
SCATTER'D
    Scatter'd with flowry Vales, with fruitful Gardens   17 Ode Athenian   40
        crown'd,
    Like the sun's scatter'd beams which loosely pass, . 45 To Congreve   63
    Which, as he scatter'd, we like Dolts, ...   353 Wood Ironmongr   33
    Where Power and Titles scatter'd lay, ...   412 Desire Possess   24
    To recollect the scatter'd Parts? . . . .   583 Young Nymph   68
    So if this Pile of scatter'd Rhymes . . . .   728 Stella, Poems   5
SCATTERS
    Scatters strange agues o'er men's sickly minds, . .   52 Temple Ill   38
    While Traulus all his Ordure scatters. . . . . . .   796 Traulus 1   31
SCAVENGER
    And Dick the Scavenger with equal Grace, ...   364 On Dreams   37
SCENE
    A three Hours Scene of empty Pride, ...   6 Ode to King   17
    That this New, Noble, and Delightful Scene . . . .   20 Ode Athenian   136
    As at the closing an unhappy Scene . . . .   24 Ode Athenian   271
    Methinks, when you expose the Scene, ...   29 Ode to Temple   97
    In this new happy Scene . . . .   31 Ode to Temple   159
    Bred in my scene, and for the poet's sins . . . .   46 To Congreve   97
    But lay the scene just here at Farnham school. . . . 46 To Congreve   114
    O'er the glad scene whence first she rose a bride: 51 Temple Ill   12
    The Scene, a Wood, produc'd no more . . . . . .   108 V's House   83
    Jove sent and found far in a Country Scene, ... 118 Biddy Floyd   3
    Who change Opinions with the changing Scene: . . .   196 Author Himself   65
    Remov'd from all th' ambitious Scene . . . . .   199 Horace 2, 6   D
    But, view him in another Scene, ...   231 Prog of Poetry   31
    In that fantastick Scene, and thinks . . . . . .   251 Bubble   30
    If this you think a pleasing Scene . . . . . .   312 To Ford   47
    On the Scene of this Land very soon to revive. . .   337 Serious Poem   94
    "If startled at a Scene so rude, ...   379 Apology Lady C   135
    "A Scene so glorious and so new? . . . .   380 Apology Lady C   164
    Now change the Scene; a nobler Care . . . . . .   387 Manly Virtue   111
    To find her in a country scene, ...   401 Window Inns 5   D 6
    But, shift him to a better scene, ...   435 Answer Paulus   117
    Now to another Scene give Place, ...   447 Modern Lady   80
    The Fortunes of his latter Scene, ...   481 Libel on D- D-   46
    To him that looks behind the Scene, ...   530 Lady's Dres Rm   133
    Here shift the Scene, to represent . . . .   561 Death of Swift   205
    One Year is past; a different Scene; . . . . . .   562 Death of Swift   245
    "Beheld the dire destructive Scene, ...   568 Death of Swift   392
    In such a Scene to interfere. . . . .   583 Young Nymph   72
    Since Husbands get behind the Scene, ...   588 Strephon Chloe   137
    Where, in this Scene of endless Woe, ...   647 On Poetry   209
    Thy busy, drudging scene of life, ...   676 Parson's Case   6
    But, now shou'd fortune shift the scene, ...   676 Parson's Case   19
    In every Scene had kept his Heart; . . . . . .   703 Cadenus Vaness   541
    She fell into her former Scene, ...   747 Stel Distress   55
    She fell into her former Scene. . . . .   751 Stel Wood-Park   71
    The Scene, the Welcome, and the Spark, ...   752 Stel Wood-Park   86
    And, when she's in another scene, ...   762 Bec's B-Day   45
    While Punch is hid behind the Scene, ...   776 Mullinix Tim   94
    Shift the Scene for half an Hour, ...   832 Legion Club   77
    Now, changing the scene, ...   654 Lady's Lament   87
    I lead you to a nobler Scene; . . . .   889 Panegyr Dean   86
    Ye who frequent this hallow'd Scene, ...   893 Panegyr Dean   217
SCENES
    And hire us out their scenes, and cloaths, and faces. . 307 Billet Players   8
    The Scenes and Actions of the Day before. . . . .   363 On Dreams   10
    He now shall shine in nobler Scenes: . . . . . .   385 Manly Virtue   52
    What Scenes of Evil he unravels, ...   548 Life of Swift   111
    In doleful Scenes, that breaks our heart, ...   777 Mullinix Tim   121
    The various Scenes of mortal Life, ...   781 Mullinix Tim   265
    To chear the solitary scenes: . . . .   901 Dean's Reasons   84
SCENT
    You find his Passion by his Scent. . . . . . .   66 Problem   18
    The Hound wou'd scent, the Wolf would prole: . . .   512 Answer Fable   8
    So keen thy Hunters, and thy Scent so strong; . . . 539 Mr. Pulteney   43
    He found her, while the Scent increas'd, ...   589 Strephon Chloe   185
    With the Noise, the Sight, the Scent. . . . . .   839 Legion Club   234
SCEPTER
    What do the Scepter, Crown and Ball, ...   6 Ode to King   12
    Achilles's Scepter was of Wood, ...   134 Magician's Rod   59
    That Scepter was a sapless Twig: . . . .   134 Magician's Rod   66
    Sid's Scepter, full of Juice, did shoot . . . . .   134 Magician's Rod   71
    A Crown and Scepter in her Hands; . . . . . .   413 Desire Possess   42
    She knock't him with the Scepter down. . . . . .   413 Desire Possess   48
    Between the Scepter and the Spade. . . . . . .   895 Panegyr Dean   290
SCEPTICK
    "It serves for Sceptick, and Free-thinker, ...   550 Life of Swift   177
SCHEME
    Are Seconds in this glorious Scheme; . . . . . .   391 Young's Satire   8
    Though by the Politicians Scheme . . . .   592 Strephon Chloe   263
    To manage thy abortive Scheme; . . . .   696 Cadenus Vaness   299
    This was a visionary Scheme, ...   705 Cadenus Vaness   584
    No fault of mine, the scheme is ended: . . . . .   899 Dean's Reasons   6

		PAGE	TITLE	LINE
SCHEME	(CONTINUED)			
No--that scheme will ne'er succeed, ...		907	Daphne	39
SCHEMES				
Approve thy Schemes, thy Wit admire, ...		182	Horace 2, 1	62
"And, oh! how short are human Schemes!		567	Death of Swift	371
Were all the Schemes he had in View;		605	Beasts Confess	147
Long Schemes of Life, as heretofore;		764	Stel B-day '26	16
In public schemes, or catching flies, . . . ˙. . .		901	Dean's Reasons	79
Project <Excise> and <South-Sea> <Schemes>: . . .		647	On Poetry	216
SCHOLAR				
But you, who are a Scholar, know		283	Journal	115
As Poet, Scholar and Divine.		455	Dean Smedley	4
A Scholar to a Courtly Dame, ...		705	Cadenus Vaness	589
Her Scholar is not apt to learn;		712	Cadenus Vaness	809
The Scholar could not shew his Reading.		916	Riddle 1	32
SCHOLARD				
"A Scholard, when just from his College broke loose, .		872	Grand Question	157
SCHOLARS				
And at once grow Scholars and Fools;		27	Ode to Temple	44
Beside all this, deep Scholars know, ...		66	Problem	21
Great scholars have in Lucian Read, ...		99	Elegy Patrige	63
And Scholars give it for the Cause, ...		158	Fable of Midas	69
So, Clowns on Scholars as on Wizards look, ...		193	Author Himself	7
And well thy Scholars are endu'd		325	Pethox	61
I hear among Scholars there is a great Doubt		334	Serious Poem	25
Were Scholars then, as we are now;		513	Answer Fable	40
Scholars, when good Sense describing, ...		633	Epistle Lady	115
Your Scholars want the whip,--I shan't demur;-- . .		671	Epig Carthy 23	D 1
That Scholars wou'd forsake their Books		694	Cadenus Vaness	234
That Scholars were like other Folks:		707	Cadenus Vaness	649
And, Scholars teach, the Soul informs;		724	To Stella	12
When, among scholars, can we find		755	Stella '23	19
SCHONBERG				
When Schonberg started at the Vast Design:		12	Ode to William	D 34
SCHOOL				
But lay the scene just here at Farnham school. . . .		46	To Congreve	114
To tell what ev'ry School Boy knows:		281	Journal	82
He goes to School! he reads! is learn'd!		384	Manly Virtue	32
For less than Charly Grattan's School:		478	Epist on Epist	111
"Or naughty Boy elopes from School, ...		497	Panegyr Swift	130
But, sure a Tell-tale out of School		592	Strephon Chloe	277
In School to hear the finest Boy.		704	Cadenus Vaness	553
Hast thou been so long at School, ...		838	Legion Club	197
"The Army's the only good School in the Nation; . .		872	Grand Question	162
"But at Cuffs I was always the Cock of the School; .		873	Grand Question	164
The lowest boy in Martin's school		899	Dean's Reasons	13
With a Boy that is only fit for School, ...		941	Letter	19
The worst Dunce in your School, 'till he's heav'd from the Ground		968	Letter Sherid	34
My Master is so fond of that Minister that keeps the School;		987	Mary to Sher	29
My school decreasing, ...		1037	Sheridan Cavan	5
SCHOOL-BOY				
A School-boy ran unto't and thought, ...		127	Little House	29
For Jove, as every School-boy knows, ...		461	Birthday Song	23
That, once he heard a School-boy tell, ...		587	Strephon Chloe	106
A school-boy knows this, for it plainly appears . .		976	Dean to Sherid	19
SCHOOL-BOYS				
There all the little School-boys run		87	Hist V's House	33
And School-Boys lag with Satchels in their Hands. .		125	Descriptn Morn	18
Huzza! the school-boys roar, the play'rs are come! . .		308	Billet Players	38
Not School-boys at a Barring-out, ...		450	Modern Lady	182
To win the Truant School-Boys Hearts!		779	Mullinix Tim	200
SCHOOL-DIN				
For scolding is just quasi diceres--school-din: . . .		979	Dean to Tho: S	8
SCHOOL-MASTER				
"My School-Master call'd me a Dunce and a Fool, . .		873	Grand Question	163
SCHOOLBOYS				
Those beds of dung, where schoolboys sprout up beaus . .		46	To Congreve	99
SCHOOLS SEE BOARDING-SCHOOLS				
And all the incohaerent Jargon of the Schools, . . .		22	Ode Athenian	205
Philosophy! the Lumber of the Schools, ...		27	Ode to Temple	24
Stale Memorandums of the Schools;		27	Ode to Temple	34
Confine her Walks to Colleges and Schools, ...		27	Ode to Temple	39
These are the lords of the poetic schools, ...		46	To Congreve	101
Forg'd up in Colleges and Schools.		483	Libel on D- D-	92
And idle Morals in the Schools		493	Panegyr Swift	30
'Tis an old Maxim in the Schools, ...		710	Cadenus Vaness	758
Yet should Swift endow the Schools		830	Legion Club	35
SCIENCE				
'Twixt Cobling and the Planet Science.		98	Elegy Patrige	30
Science and Art you say at stand are, ...		372	Letter D. S-y	41
To teach the Science to your Friend.		493	Panegyr Swift	28
First learn the Science to be dull, ...		503	Doctor Delaney	111
A Science which he never taught, ...		708	Cadenus Vaness	670
The Science she designs to teach:		712	Cadenus Vaness	811
No Merit, no Science, no Virtue is wanting		808	Advice Parson	5
SCIENCES				
Nor Skill in Sciences profound, ...		641	On Poetry	29
The Learn'd in Sciences sublime, ...		918	Riddle 4	42

	PAGE	TITLE	LINE

SCIENTIFIC
In scientific Strife engage; . . . . 385 Manly Virtue 44

SCIPIO
Call'd Pompey, Scipio and Caesar; . . . . . . 82 Salamander 2
And Scipio, trail an Irish purple Plad. . . . . . 275 Epilogue 22

SCISSARS
To break open riddles with shears or with scissars. . . 976 Dean to Sherid 22
Tho' I ne'er saw her hold the Scissars, ... 993 On Picture 14

SCOFF
And since I 'scap'd being made a Scoff, ... 377 Apology Lady C 55

SCOFFING
Pray gentle-Folks forbear your Scoffing. . . . . 286 Elegy Boat 38
"Scoffing my College Aukwardness. . . . . . . 380 Apology Lady C 148

SCOLD
To show their Parts, will scold and rail, ... 216 To Mr. Delany 49
Nor scold, nor keep a splutter. . . . . 429 Beau's Reply 10
While thus they rail, and scold, and storm, ... 453 Modern Lady 270
Can in Celestial Language scold) . . . . 695 Cadenus Vaness 287
Instructs us how to tame a Scold; . . . . 781 Mullinix Tim 272
And scold at an Election; . . . . 784 Mullinex Dick 18
If your Wife be a Scold, that will mend her. . . . . 942 Probatur Alit 8
Lord! how politely they can scold; . . . . 949 Epigr Scolding 2
Be she Slut, or be she Scold, ... 953 Oysters 14
But to scold is your trade, which I soon shou'd be foil'd in, 979 Dean to Tho: S 7
Your wife a scold. . . . . 1038 Sheridan Cavan 16

SCOLDED
Nell scolded in so loud a Din . . . . 219 A Quiet Life 1
I scolded and rated; . . . . 1014 Swift to Sheri 16

SCOLDING
Scolding moves you less than Merriment. . . . . . 636 Epistle Lady 208
Now scolding at my Lady Eustace, ... 788 Dick's Variety 29
For scolding is just quasi diceres--school-din: . . . 979 Dean to Tho: S 8

SCOLDS
Hawls him, and scolds us down to Breakfast. . . . . 279 Journal 16
The more she scolds, the more she's cloudy. . . . . 617 Scandal Poem 1 14
The more she scolds, the more she's cloudy. . . . . 624 Scandal Poem 2 14

SCOPE
Thus did the Dean: his only scope . . . . . . 548 Life of Swift 130
Gives Imagination Scope, ... 636 Epistle Lady 213

SCOR'D
Instead of Five you scor'd me Ten. . . . . . . 453 Modern Lady 265

SCORCHING
The scorching Sun, or chilling Air; . . . . . . 379 Apology Lady C 122
I March'd three miles thro' scorching sand, ... 675 Curate's Compl 1

SCORCHT
Scorcht were his Shins, his Legs were bare, ... 594 Cassinus Peter 17

SCORE
And many Score of Gudgeons took; . . . . . . 133 Magician's Rod 46
On seven Score Sheep, ... 244 Irish-Feast 7
A score of guineas, given under-hand, ... 308 Billet Players 23
And hardly half a Score. . . . . 315 To Ford 108
When you have nam'd at least a Score . . . . . . 392 Young's Satire 28
(But by his Leave he sinks a Score,) . . . . . . 456 Dean Smedley 34
A score of Goddesses beside. . . . . 460 Birthday Song 8
Condemn'd for thy Crime, at three score and ten? . . 519 Dean Hang Rape 50
And, when he gravely has undone a Score, ... 535 To Mr. Gay 105
Will more than half a Score devour. . . . . . . 642 On Poetry 64
Vanessa, not in Years a Score, ... 703 Cadenus Vaness 524
He might have found a Score of Chaps, ... 821 Dr. Rundle 50
You have hardly seen a Score, ... 839 Legion Club 237
I must now, at one Sitting, pay off my old Score: . . 967 Letter Sherid 9
And flying think to quit the Score, ... 1002 Reply by Dean 11

SCORN
And scorn it when 'tis found. . . . . 20 Ode Athenian 144
The greatest scorn of Learned Vanity, ... 21 Ode Athenian 179
May all the Blood, which shall by Womans scorn be shed 23 Ode Athenian 245
(Free from our tyrant-passions, anger, scorn, or fear) . 38 Ode Sancroft 116
What could the Sages gain but unbelieving scorn; . . . 39 Ode Sancroft 170
Nor ever maid endur'd such court-like scorn, ... 44 To Congreve 13
That looks with scorn on half mankind beside; . . . . 44 To Congreve 44
A poor amusement for my scorn and hate; . . . . . 53 Temple Ill 84
Wert thou right woman, thou shouldst scorn to look . . 54 Temple Ill 107
That scorn of fools, by fools mistook for pride; . . . 55 Temple Ill 134
If nam'd with Scorn, gives just Offence. . . . . . 217 To Mr. Delany 70
In return to her Scorn, I send her Diseases, ... 266 Apollo 105
Can you on Dublin look with Scorn? . . . . . . 314 To Ford 83
He can Lye like a Courtier, and think it no Scorn, . . 335 Serious Poem 45
Will make you scorn this World below. . . . . . 362 Grace's Answer 30
And scorn to wrap up Spice. . . . . 394 Grub-Street 8
Which breeds at once both Hate and Scorn. . . . . 413 Censure 4
Reject with scorn that stupid Notion . . . . . . 468 Birthday Song 261
I can easier scorn than hate: . . . . 634 Epistle Lady 144
Scorn torments them more than Spight. . . . . . 634 Epistle Lady 146
Can personate an awkward Scorn . . . . 652 On Poetry 353
Whose graceless Children scorn to own thee! . . . . 652 On Poetry 358
The Nymphs with Scorn beheld their Foes: . . . . . 687 Cadenus Vaness 21
And yet I scorn to interpose, ... 696 Cadenus Vaness 301
With silent Scorn Vanessa sat, ... 697 Cadenus Vaness 334
To scorn the Art of Female Tears. . . . . . . 705 Cadenus Vaness 597
Which most exposes ours to Scorn? . . . . . . 725 To Stella 68

SCORN	(CONTINUED)	PAGE	TITLE	LINE
Which you expect, but scorn to ask;		739	Stel B-day '21	4
She look'd on Partridges with scorn		746	Stel Distress	13
She look'd on Partridges with scorn,		750	Stel Wood-Park	11
The Squires in Scorn will fly the House		760	Receipt Youth	53
Who hate and scorn you, to a Man;		777	Mullinix Tim	146
We scorn, for want of talk, to jabber		781	Mullinix Tim	259
Dick would cock his Nose in scorn,		784	Mullinex Dick	9
I scorn thy spurious and degenerate Line,		794	St. Pat's Well	101
Behold! the cruel Dean in Scorn		849	Old Thorn	23
Would scorn to inhabit,		857	Lady's Lament	184
Though daggled round, I scorn to fret:		890	Panegyr Dean	110
Which, if you in scorn reject,		908	Daphne	81
For, I can break, but scorn to bend.		921	Riddle 6	38
And scorn the Pleasures of a Court;		925	Riddle 8	34
With Delany or Dan I would scorn to combine		1017	Swift Ans Sher	8
Chimnies with Scorn rejecting Smoak;		1035	To Quilca	3
SCORN'D				
Was more abhor'd, and scorn'd by those		775	Mullinix Tim	53
SCORNFUL				
Too scornful now to stop his Pace,		412	Desire Possess	33
A Nod, a Shrug, a scornful Smile,		647	On Poetry	237
When to look Scornful, when to Smile,		780	Mullinix Tim	236
So, then you look'd scornful, and snift at the Dean,		873	Grand Question	175
To show my Face with scornful Air;		887	Panegyr Dean	21
SCORNING				
Scorning to show the least Respect.		133	Magician's Rod	26
SCORNS				
While innocent, he scorns ignoble Flight;		196	Author Himself	61
And scorns the Ground, and upward springs,		230	Prog of Poetry	14
And scorns the middle Way to keep:		252	Bubble	36
He scorns to make his Art a Trade;		605	Beasts Confess	135
She'll have 'em know she scorns to stay		746	Stel Distress	42
An offer'd Fee from Radcliff scorns;		811	Bro Protestant	16
SCORPION				
Scorpion Rods perhaps may tame them.		836	Legion Club	158
SCORPION'S				
Nor dread the Adder's Tooth, nor Scorpion's Sting.		792	St. Pat's Well	42
SCORPIONS				
A Whip of Scorpions in her Hand.		596	Cassinus Peter	82
SCOT				
Leaves him a Victim to the vengeful Scot;		195	Author Himself	58
Nor Bastard of a Pedlar Scot;		641	On Poetry	34
Deny their Country like a Scot:		652	On Poetry	360
Or hardy Scot, or any Land but this;		793	St. Pat's Well	80
"Then who will own thee for a Scot?		850	Old Thorn	76
Since Lice are Brethren to a <Scot>:		813	Bro Protestant	42
SCOTCH				
She piec'd it up again with Scotch.		96	On the Union	4
Scotch, Irish, English, French unite		345	Prometheus	15
And look in English, French, and Scotch for't,		993	On Picture	8
SCOTIA				
Proud Baronet of Nova Scotia,		884	Rev Market-Hill	29
SCOTISH				
By Scotish Bards of highest Fame,		848	Old Thorn	15
SCOTS				
The Scots themselves, that Discontented Brood,		8	Ode to King	82
SCOTTISH				
In Scottish Hills found precious Ore,		133	Magician's Rod	29
The Scottish Nation, whom he durst offend,		196	Author Himself	69
The Scottish Hinds too poor to house		759	Receipt Youth	1
Their Dress, their Language, and the Scottish Name,		791	St. Pat's Well	15
But be they English, Irish, Scottish,		813	Bro Protestant	45
SCOUNDREL				
To see a Scoundrel Strut and hector,		312	To Ford	39
Whate'er the noisy Scoundrel says		505	Doctor Delaney	163
Starve twenty Lords to make one Scoundrel rich:		535	To Mr. Gay	104
Whose Scoundrel Fathers would not know 'em,		729	Stella, Poems	51
From his Father's scoundrel Race,		800	Traulus 2	24
To sit among that <scoundrel> crew,		436	Answer Paulus	132
Bow <Bettesworth>, that booby, and <Scoundrel> in grain,		814	Yahoo's	3
SCOUR				
'Twill give you a scour:		402	Window Inns 8 D	6
SCOURG'D				
Who scourg'd to Death that Scourge of Rome,		925	Riddle 8	36
SCOURGE				
Scourge the Villains with a Vengeance.		635	Epistle Lady	176
The Tories Terror, Scourge and Flail.		776	Mullinix Tim	86
Who scourg'd to Death that Scourge of Rome,		925	Riddle 8	36
SCOURGES				
The Plagues and Scourges of Mankind.		654	On Poetry	408
SCOURING				
Fowl'd with the Scouring of her Hands;		526	Lady's Dres Rm	38
SCOURS				
He scours away; and to avoid the Foe,		538	Mr. Pulteney	23
SCOW'RS				
Nor scow'rs the Streets without a Shirt;		788	Dick's Variety	16
SCOWER				
Which while the Senate strove to scower,		158	Fable of Midas	71
SCOWLING				
See the Scowling Visage drop,		835	Legion Club	143

		PAGE	TITLE	LINE
SCRAMBLES				
The fool, who scrambles for a trifle;		436	Answer Paulus	136
SCRAMBLING				
Scrambling with <rogues> to get a place:		436	Answer Paulus	140
SCRAP				
His scrap of Life is but a Heap of Miseries, . . .		9	Ode to King	107
A Scrap of Parchment hung by Geometry, ...		99	Elegy Patrige	41
With the Scrap of a Sole, and a Fig for the Bank. .		287	Bank Down	30
With a Scrap of Bank Paper the Breadth of his Nail;		288	Bank Down	38
Or give my Scrap of Life to you, ...		766	Stel B-day '26	85
SCRAPE				
And scrape her Pitchy Sides for Wax.		100	Elegy Patrige	78
His <Deanship> was now in a damnable Scrape, ...		517	Dean Hang Rape	17
SCRAPERS				
Should lend your cathedrall to players and scrapers . .		522	St. Cecilia's	4
SCRAPINGS				
The Scrapings of her Teeth and Gums, ...		527	Lady's Dres Rm	40
SCRAPS				
And fling our Scraps before our Door.		28	Ode to Temple	57
From broken scraps and filings of your brain.		45	To Congreve	58
Whole Baskets full of Bits and Scraps, ...		208	Fable Bitches	19
Or bring his Vermin in, but Scraps?		484	Libel on D- D-	130
Who fatten on poetick Scraps;		504	Doctor Delaney	125
With old Scraps from Plays exploded.		523	Betty Grizette	16
All my Fire would fall in Scraps, ...		638	Epistle Lady	263
Get Scraps of Horace from your Friends, ...		648	On Poetry	245
With Scraps and Leavings to be fed.		735	Stel B-day '20	38
No Scraps remain to save Board-wages.		954	Authors Living	6
SCRATCH				
The World shall feel her scratch and bite.		150	Corinna	12
With Teeth or with Claws it will bite or will scratch,		351	Wood Insect	19
To scratch their paultry drabs on glass;		402	Window Inns 7 D	4
To scratch our endless Itch of Pow'r.		493	Panegyr Swift	10
To scratch your Head, and bite your Nails.		643	On Poetry	90
SCRATCH'D				
He scratch'd her Maid, he stole the Cream, ...		153	Widow and Cat D	11
I bit my Nails, and scratch'd my Head, ...		740	Stel B-day 22	5
SCRATCHES				
If the Maggot cries Click when it scratches the Post.		351	Wood Insect	24
SCRATCHING				
Or scratching my nose, ...		852	Lady's Lament	21
SCRATCHT				
Such a Worm was Will. Wood when he scratcht at the Doo		351	Wood Insect	29
SCRAWL				
We scrawl all o'er with old and empty Rules, ...		27	Ode to Temple	33
And when we scrawl our Paper o'r'e, ...		463	Birthday Song	109
For I write but a sad Scrawl, ...		987	Mary to Sher	34
SCRAWL'D				
Scrawl'd o'er with Trifles thus, and quite		60	Lady Tablebook	3
His Window scrawl'd by ev'ry Rake, ...		400	Window Inns 1	5
SCREAM				
At proper Times to scream and start;		725	To Stella	72
SCREAM'D				
And Brickdust Moll had Scream'd through half the Street.		124	Descriptn Morn	14
The Mother scream'd, the Father chid, ...		223	Prog of Love	27
That I saw a huge Rat: O dear, how I scream'd! . .		868	Grand Question	50
SCREAMS				
So, sweetly screams if it comes near her, ...		416	Woman's Mind	35
And feels the Lash, and faintly screams;		582	Young Nymph	42
SCREECHT				
That ever screecht or ever flew.		515	Answer Fable	107
SCREEN				
Conceal'd behind that ample Screen, ...		354	Simile Silver	23
(Give fraudful Vice the Mask and Screen, ...		386	Manly Virtue	79
Who wisely thought my Age a Screen, ...		561	Death of Swift	221
The Screen remov'd, their Hearts are trembling, . . .		561	Death of Swift	223
SCREENS				
"If long confin'd to Fires and Screens, ...		380	Apology Lady C	137
SCREW				
Till you had got them in a Screw.		494	Panegyr Swift	44
So are Ladies in Crowds, when they squeeze and they screw, sick.		1030	Dr. Helsham	26
SCREW'D				
Thy Screw'd up front; thy State Grimace;		775	Mullinix Tim	60
SCRIBBLE				
Scribble senseless Heads of Bills;		831	Legion Club	60
SCRIBBLED				
All scribbled in the worst of times, ...		550	Life of Swift	184
SCRIBBLER				
For, should the vilest scribbler to the pit, ...		48	To Congreve	165
That Scribbler lash, who neither knows, ...		515	Answer Fable	95
SCRIBBLERS				
To scribblers, and the god of light and wit;		45	To Congreve	76
SCRIBBLES				
Is he that scribbles for the Stage;		80	Vanbrug House	40
SCRIBBLING				
A window here from scribbling free:		402	Window Inns 7 D	2
SCRIBLER				
In Scribler to have had a place.		186	Scriblerus 3	6
Why does he call him paultry Scribler, ...		795	Traulus 1	3

	PAGE	TITLE	LINE
SCRIBLERS			
These Scriblers grow so bold of late, ...	783	Tim and Fables	31
SCRIBLERUM			
Quaedam quae attinent ad Scriblerum, ...	186	Scriblerus 3	3
SCRIBLING			
The Poet's Vein, or scribling Itch?	642	On Poetry	74
SCRIPTURE			
Scripture you know exhorts us to it, ...	220	A Quiet Life	17
In Scripture, to the Dev'l assign'd:	798	Traulus 1	76
'SCRITORE			
In my 'scritore lock up my quill?	489	Dialogue	12
SCROGGS			
"As modern Scroggs, or old Tressilian;	569	Death of Swift	420
SCRUB			
Prepar'd to Scrub the Entry and the Stairs. . .	124	Descriptn Morn	8
No little scrub Joint shall come on my Board: . . .	867	Grand Question	14
If this be your practice, mean scrub, I assure Ye, . .	1019	To Sheridan	5
SCRUBB'D			
All as she scrubb'd her meazly Rump.	849	Old Thorn	44
SCRUBBY			
Than a few Scrubby Trees before.	108	V's House	84
Grew Scrubby, dy'd a-top, was stunted:	117	Bauc & Phil 2	177
SCRUBEST			
The scrubest Cur in all the Pack	798	Traulus 1	67
SCRUP'LOUS			
Should be more scrup'lous than a Heathen.	461	Birthday Song	26
SCRUPLE			
Nor makes a Scruple to expose	416	Woman's Mind	21
No Scruple came on him his Gown to expose, ...	517	Dean Hang Rape	21
SCUD			
Away you see the Varlet scud, ...	824	Printer Newgat	9
SCUDS			
Away the frighted Spectre scuds, ...	905	Death Daphne	99
SCULK'T			
And thought his Bride had sculk't for shame, ...	223	Prog of Love	30
SCULL			
Drive them down on every Scull, ...	830	Legion Club	27
SCULLER			
In short, he was an able Sculler.	286	Elegy Boat	44
SCUM			
And end as it began, in Vapour, Stink, and Scum. . .	10	Ode to King	129
SCURF			
The Golden Scurf peels off his Limbs:	157	Fable of Midas	36
SCURRILITY			
Scurrility with gibing Air;	448	Modern Lady	127
SCURRILOUS			
To be scurrilous, and rude;	523	Betty Grizette	30
They are not scurrilous in Satire, ...	729	Stella, Poems	55
You threaten the stocks: I say you are scurrilous, . .	976	Dean to Sherid	31
SCURVEY			
Your scurvey Lays, ...	440	Ballyspellin	4
SCURVY			
Impertinence, the Scurvy of Mankind, ...	18	Ode Athenian	70
To write such scurvy stuff!	428	Beau's Reply	5
You sprung an Arch, which in a Scurvy	477	Epist on Epist	71
I Shou'd make a Figure scurvy, ...	637	Epistle Lady	219
Only one scurvy thing I find, ...	983	Sher, A Goose	13
SCUT			
He left his Scut behind, and Half an Ear.	538	Mr. Pulteney	36
SCYTHE			
Sweeps the broad scythe, and tramples on his face. . .	55	Temple Ill	122
That Time sits with his Scythe to mow	757	Stel B-day '24	37
SD			
My Ld, sd Bush, a Friend and I	63	Discovery	33
He sd our Ladyes were so fair	422	Ireld	29
SE'D			
No Creature valu'd what they se'd:	90	Bauc & Phil 1	25
SEA SEE SOUTH-SEA			
Into his Native Sea, ...	22	Ode Athenian	193
O'er Sea and Land conveys the Witch;	132	Magician's Rod	18
If the Stick be taken from the dead Sea.	147	Windsor Proph	14
Thus in a Sea of Folly tost, ...	202	Horace 2, 6	105
So fares it in the Southern Sea	253	Bubble	67
Each poor Subscriber to the Sea	253	Bubble	81
Thus Venus to the Sea descends	254	Bubble	93
The Sea is richer than the Land, ...	254	Bubble	97
For by the Sea she meant the South.	254	Bubble	100
The Sea indeed had golden Sands.	255	Bubble	112
Directors thrown into the Sea	258	Bubble	185
For if the Sea should sink so low	258	Bubble	195
Quiet the Raging of the Sea, ...	258	Bubble	211
Down the black Sea, and up the Streights, ...	282	Journal	107
At Sea, or Land, if e'er you found him, ...	303	Storm	15
Some South Sea Broker from the City, ...	410	Dial Rich Marb	67
He rules the Sea, you see him ride in't;	463	Birthday Song	98
Hunted from Earth, and Sea, and Hell, he flies . .	538	Mr. Pulteney	29
Fly to the Sea, my Place of Birth;	689	Cadenus Vaness	88
Still to the Sea their Course incline;	709	Cadenus Vaness	721
Worse than the Anarchy at Sea, ...	824	Printer Newgat	3
The greatest Whale, that swims the Sea	934	Riddle 21	D 11
And Robin at Sea had like to be cast away.	1037	Four Storyes	4

	PAGE	TITLE	LINE
SEA (CONTINUED)			
No Sea overwhelms him, no Coach overturns;	1037	Four Storyes	6
SEA-GOD			
The Jugling Sea-god when by chance trepann'd	22	Ode Athenian	189
SEA-SICK			
Weary and Sea-sick when in thee confin'd,	772	Horace 1, 14	57
SEA'S			
The Captain swears the sea's too rough	420	Holyhead	9
SEAL			
With a Saint at his Chin, and a Seal in his Fob;	147	Windsor Proph	2
And under Hand and Seal the Irish Nation	234	Elegy on Demar	17
Get the Great Seal, and turn out Brod'rick.	348	Whitshed Motto	18
SEAM			
But turns at every Seam, an Inch in.	1021	Nim-Dan-Dean 1	D 16
SEAM'D			
Sunk down her Nose, or seam'd her Face?	595	Cassinus Peter	49
SEARCH			
Our shallow Search and Judgment to direct.	18	Ode Athenian	94
We often search contentedly the whole World round,	20	Ode Athenian	142
Then tell us what is Fame? where shall we search for it?	21	Ode Athenian	175
Search out this Utopian Ground,	26	Ode to Temple	11
With Rules to search it, yet obtain'd by none.	26	Ode to Temple	16
How shall we search Thee in a battle gain'd,	34	Ode Sancroft	11
A search, no doubt, as curious and as wise	46	To Congreve	93
To search the Deep for Pearl and Coral.	254	Bubble	96
While We may search all Dublin o'er	315	To Ford	107
Collects the City Filth in search of Gold.	364	On Dreams	22
And fowl his Hands in Search of Hope.	528	Lady's Dres Rm	94
And in the fruitless Search pursue	592	Strephon Chloe	269
But search among the rhiming Race,	651	On Poetry	327
But now go search all Europe round	659	On Poetry	D 410
I'll search where ev'ry Virtue dwells,	691	Cadenus Vaness	148
Was, in the very Search, betray'd	702	Cadenus Vaness	491
When, if you search the Kingdom round,	773	Mullinix Tim	5
In his Grave, and search his Trunks.	836	Legion Club	168
Here, with an easy Search we find	921	Riddle 7	15
SEARCH'D			
Search'd in the nest where every worm did lie	46	To Congreve	89
But when I search'd, and miss'd my Purse,.	69	Mrs Harris Pet	13
. . .that we went and search'd the Folks round,	70	Mrs Harris Pet	22
SEARCH'T			
They search't his Pockets on the Place,	353	Wood Ironmongr	27
SEARCHER			
The De'el take the Searcher.	245	Irish-Feast	24
Pray what is a Man? he's a fine-Linen Searcher.	972	S-'s Ans Sh-d	10
SEARCHES			
The Captain walks about, and searches	377	Apology Lady C	61
SEARCHETH			
He searcheth all his Shop in vain;	563	Death of Swift	257
SEARCHING			
Searching in Books for Wisdom's Aid,	702	Cadenus Vaness	490
SEAS			
You need but cross the Irish Seas,	173	Horace 1, 7	91
The Toil, the Danger of the Seas;	199	Horace 2, 6	17
Are said to represent the Seas,	239	Run Bankers	6
In Southern Seas he leaves his Name.	252	Bubble	48
So cast it in the Southern Seas,	255	Bubble	121
Directors build 'em in the Seas,	257	Bubble	166
In seas and woods, or low as hell	620	Scandal Poem 1	100
O'er cityes, rivers, hills, and seas,	621	Scandal Poem 1	126
In Seas and Streams, or low as Hell:	626	Scandal Poem 2	98
O'er Cities, Rivers, Hills, and Seas:	627	Scandal Poem 2	120
Who in tempestuous Seas can sport,	925	Riddle 8	33
SEASON			
In how ill season her resentments rule,	48	To Congreve	177
And, must my Lady slip her Season?	294	Prog Marriage	128
. . . yet still there comes a Season	341	Upon His Grace	7
That this Eclipse was out of Season,	354	Simile Silver	6
That Strephon chose no proper Season.	588	Strephon Chloe	160
What then must Carthy do in proper Season,	666	Epig Carthy 3	D 3
In proper Season Pallas meets	695	Cadenus Vaness	284
Her fine Panegyricks are quite out of Season,	716	Answer Rebus	21
SEASONS			
At proper Seasons to be sick;	416	Woman's Mind	40
A Cloud, in proper Seasons pours	624	Scandal Poem 2	27
A long-ear'd Beast, and what seasons your Beef,	943	Probatur Alit	45
SEAT SEE JUDGEMENT-SEAT			
Depos'd from off his Seat	26	Ode to Temple	3
Shews lustre that was shaded in his seat;	41	Ode Sancroft	212
Confessing Albion once her darling seat;	49	To Congreve	194
Comes back with joy to its own seat at night;	51	Temple Ill	6
What? sell my Master's Country Seat?	128	Little House	56
Devoutly lolling in his Seat;	174	Horace 1, 7	98
Oh, could I see my Country Seat.	202	Horace 2, 6	108
Where Jove a Seat among the Gods will give	210	Earl of Oxford	13
Retir'd to your Imperial Seat.	326	Pethox	90
In his own Church he keeps a Seat;	605	Beasts Confess	129
The Ruin of her antient Seat;	849	Old Thorn	38
And foul the green seat;	857	Lady's Lament	190
I near the Side-board take my Seat;	920	Riddle 6	26

SEATED
                                                PAGE   TITLE   LINE

Entry	PAGE	TITLE	LINE
SEATED			
But ne'er since seated in one single Breast.	26	Ode to Temple	7
Seated at Table next the Men you love.	165	Toland's Invit	32
Whilst he, tho' seated on a Throne,	387	Manly Virtue	131
Now see her seated on her Throne	465	Birthday Song	173
If not, however seated high,	503	Doctor Delaney	113
Then, seated on a three-legg'd Chair,	581	Young Nymph	9
Or think it seated in a Scar,	724	To Stella	25
By Honour seated in her Breast,	725	To Stella	59
But, seated in an easy chair,	901	Dean's Reasons	89
SEATS			
His grottos and seats;	856	Lady's Lament	178
SECOND			
At Court, Vitruvius the second,	87	Hist V's House	38
When they had took a second Draught,	92	Bauc & Phil 1	73
(As being Bricks at Second Hand,)	108	V's House	77
Alcides, one of second Rate.	160	Atlas	18
Making by second hand their Offers,	253	Bubble	70
Tho' Poets have the second Sight,	270	Apollo's Edict	D 34
To drive a second, lest the whole should break.	535	To Mr. Gay	134
Himself, pass only for the Second---?	546	Life of Swift	57
A Lye, at ev'ry second word:	550	Life of Swift	191
"And well remembers Charles the Second.	556	Death of Swift	108
Change ev'ry feature ev'ry second.	618	Scandal Poem 1	46
Change ev'ry Feature, ev'ry Second.	625	Scandal Poem 2	42
Go try your Hand a second Time.	645	On Poetry	146
To turn to Ovid, Book the Second;	690	Cadenus Vaness	109
She therefore, upon second Thought,	693	Cadenus Vaness	215
With Nonsense ev'ry second Word,	696	Cadenus Vaness	329
Might furnish a Second Rate Poet a Year:	716	Answer Rebus	18
That serjeant at law, whom we call Kite the Second,	817	Yahoo's	67
Life's Autumn has no second Spring.	932	Riddle 19	D 24
I leave it for the second head.	983	Sher, A Goose	26
SECOND-HAND			
A Virtue but at second-hand;	692	Cadenus Vaness	170
SECONDED			
Yet he was seconded by few:	605	Beasts Confess	148
SECONDLY			
And, secondly, to shew my Fury	348	Whitshed Motto	13
SECONDS			
Are Seconds in this glorious Scheme;	391	Young's Satire	8
SECRECY			
And Secrecy, the Art of Courts.	325	Pethox	64
SECRET			
Of secret Malice, or of open Force.	13	Ode to William	D 44
On his own secret regular sphere,	39	Ode Sancroft	152
Ah, should I tell a secret yet unknown,	54	Temple Ill	93
But slacken'd by some secret Power,	113	Bauc & Phil 2	73
And all its secret Causes trace,	180	Horace 2, 1	16
"'Tis now no Secret--I protest	202	Horace 2, 6	98
Within our Breast be ev'ry Secret barr'd:	210	Earl of Oxford	16
He'll find the Secret out from thence	219	To Mr. Delany	107
Tho not into the Secret let.	257	Bubble	164
But the Secret is this; I did lately intend	265	Apollo	73
And let the secret Head of Nile	270	Apollo's Edict	D 14
Before the secret wise Committee;	300	Horrid Plot	54
But I'll tell you the Secret, and pray do not Blab,	335	Serious Poem	35
Or freely tell the secret Cause.	589	Strephon Chloe	162
The Secret thou shalt ne'er impart;	596	Cassinus Peter	101
So, take my Secret, and adieu;	597	Cassinus Peter	116
Your Secret kept, your Poem sunk,	644	On Poetry	143
Mean time the Boy in secret lurks,	702	Cadenus Vaness	513
Was but the Master's secret Joy	704	Cadenus Vaness	552
Is to the World a Secret yet:	712	Cadenus Vaness	819
But the Dean, if this Secret shou'd come to his Ears,	873	Grand Question	187
From me no Secret he can hide;	915	Riddle 1	23
And seeks to learn the secret Cause,	923	Riddle 7	81
That in secret feeds her flame,	936	Riddle 24	D 24
The Secret will never be known;	952	Onyons	12
But now I'll secret keep your stuff;	1002	Reply by Dean	17
SECRET'S			
Inform the Commons, that the Secret's out:	195	Author Himself	42
SECRETARY			
Free Leave to play his Secretary,	475	Epist on Epist	9
Briareus the Secretary,	833	Legion Club	105
SECRETS			
Shews all her Secrets of House keeping,	282	Journal	87
"Those Secrets of the hoary deep!	528	Lady's Dres Rm	98
Our inmost Secrets to our Foes;	706	Cadenus Vaness	611
And have no Secrets to disguise.	706	Cadenus Vaness	617
And drive at last all Secrets out:	920	Riddle 6	16
All the secrets of her heart.	936	Riddle 24	D 26
SECT			
In me, who am of the first Sect of these,	18	Ode Athenian	76
And our good Brethren of the Surly Sect	18	Ode Athenian	81
This hopeful Sect, now it begins to see	19	Ode Athenian	111
And follow the prevailing sect,	489	Dialogue	24
SECTS			
"Whole Swarms of Sects, with grief, he saw	550	Life of Swift	168
You who in different Sects have shamm'd,	579	Day Judgement	15
Which made our Swarm of Sects determine	813	Bro Protestant	43

		PAGE	TITLE	LINE
SECTS	(CONTINUED)			
And as our Sects, by all Descriptions,	. . . . .	813	Bro Protestant	51
SECUR'D				
Secur'd by Numbers from the Lay-men's Gibes;	. . .	194	Author Himself	20
By Mortgage hath secur'd the Corps of Demar;	. . .	233	Elegy on Demar	2
You, in your Capitol secur'd,	. . . .	326	Pethox	97
SECURE				
Under those Sacred Leaves, Secure	. . . . . .	119	Apollo Outwit	9
In Church, secure behind her Fan	. . . . . .	222	Prog of Love	11
Mean time secure on Garr'way Clifts	. . . . .	256	Bubble	153
But make an act secure and full	. . . . . .	423	Ireld	57
Secure of constant peace within,	. . . . . .	434	Answer Paulus	57
While he, at ease, secure and light,	. . . . .	435	Answer Paulus	91
Nor, think your self secure in doing wrong,	. . . .	533	To Mr. Gay	59
Your Lesson learnt, you'll be secure	. . . . .	649	On Poetry	275
An Heir for Britain to secure	. . . . . .	655	On Poetry	435
Bid Povey secure him while you are haranguing.		818	Epigr Kite	8
Is more secure as well as legal.	. . . . . .	821	Dr. Rundle	58
Secure from Satyrs sat and sung.	. . . . . .	848	Old Thorn	8
To seek a more secure Retreat.	. . . .	849	Old Thorn	40
Secure the Larder, and the Vault.	. . . . .	885	Rev Market-Hill	84
SECURELY				
And that he might securely Rest,	. . . . . .	235	Elegy on Demar	45
Securely, in the Thunderer's Breast,	. . . . .	458	Paddy's Charac	32
Nor can be more securely plac't	. . . . . .	747	Stel Distress	63
Nor can be more securely plac't	. . . . . .	752	Stel Wood-Park	79
SECURER				
There's a securer Way to wreck your Spite.	. . .	667	Epig Carthy 4	D 2
SECURES				
And me my Innocence secures.	. . . . . .	445	Modern Lady	33
If, while your Tenderness secures	. . . . . .	727	To Stella	119
SECUREST				
But follow the securest rule,	. . . .	468	Birthday Song	265
SEDITIOUS				
Who daily vends seditious Trash:	. . . . . .	515	Answer Fable	92
SEDITIOUSLY				
Seditiously mean	. . . .	237	Excellent Song	6
On Tuesday the Ninth, seditiously came,	. . . .	263	Apollo	29
SEDUC'D				
Seduc'd by some deceiving Light,	. . . . . .	412	Desire Possess	17
SEDUCE				
Of Wit, to flatter and seduce:	. . . . . .	707	Cadenus Vaness	645
SEDUCER				
A Sland'rer, Traytor and Seducer;	. . . . .	798	Traulus 1	80
Footman, Traytor, vile Seducer,	. . . . .	831	Legion Club	69
SEE				
And now I in the Spirit see	. . . .	7	Ode to King	45
I see the Fatal Fight begin;	. . . .	7	Ode to King	47
And glad Ierne now may see	. . . .	9	Ode to King	99
Amaz'd Thy Action at the Boyne we see!		12	Ode to William	D 33
Who both our Follies and Impertinencies see,	. . .	18	Ode Athenian	89
This hopeful Sect, now it begins to see	. . . .	19	Ode Athenian	111
We soon shall see them to their ancient Methods fall,	.	19	Ode Athenian	119
That I believe in much, I ne're can hope to see;	. .	20	Ode Athenian	134
Look where you see	. . . .	21	Ode Athenian	178
For You (ah, did I think I e'er should live to see		23	Ode Athenian	247
Which 'tis a shame to see how much of late	. . .	24	Ode Athenian	254
And foolishly are glad to see it at it's height	. . .	25	Ode Athenian	281
Wonder to see the Motions fly)	. . . . . .	29	Ode to Temple	96
How plain I see thro' the Deceit!		29	Ode to Temple	100
See, how they tremble! how they quake!	. . .	30	Ode to Temple	113
See where she lies!	. . . .	30	Ode to Temple	120
See how she rears her Head,	. . . . . .	30	Ode to Temple	121
As loth to see the hated Court and Town,	. . .	31	Ode to Temple	157
(How that which we a Kernel see,	. . . . .	31	Ode to Temple	165
The herd beneath, who see the weathercock of state		37	Ode Sancroft	73
Nothing is fix'd that mortals see or know,	. . . .	39	Ode Sancroft	143
And which for ought I see, and much I fear,	. . .	39	Ode Sancroft	159
Mistaken Ideots! see how giddily they run,	. . . .	39	Ode Sancroft	162
Whom were my Congreve blest to see and know,		49	To Congreve	183
So men may see what once was womankind,	. . .	52	Temple Ill	49
See Muse, what havock in these looks appear		55	Temple Ill	125
Enrag'd to see the World abus'd		64	Discovery	47
I was resolved to tell my Money, to see if it was right:		69	Mrs Harris Pet	4
If your Money be gone, as a Learned Divine says, d'ye see,		72	Mrs Harris Pet	56
Envying to see themselves outdone.	. . . . .	87	Hist V's House	34
Whilst You shall see your Cottage rise,	. . . .	92	Bauc & Phil 1	89
See how the double Nation lies;	. . . . .	96	On the Union	7
To see the House of Brother <Van>:	. . . . .	108	V's House	96
Whilst you shall see your Cottage rise,	. . . .	112	Bauc & Phil 2	49
Amaz'd to see Her look so Prim,	. . . . .	116	Bauc & Phil 2	147
My Dear, I see your Forehead sprout;	. . . .	116	Bauc & Phil 2	156
Deceitful Nymph I see thy Art,	. . . . . .	121	Apollo Outwit	50
You see just by the Church-yard Stile;	. . . .	127	Little House	14
Was much surpriz'd to see a Crow	. . . . .	127	Little House	27
Shall not see one New Years-Day in that Year,	. . .	147	Windsor Proph	3
My Province is, to see that all be right,	. . . .	165	Toland's Invit	27
Methinks I see thee, spruce and fine,	. . . . .	182	Horace 2, 1	73
Methinks I see a black-guard Rout	. . . . .	183	Horace 2, 1	79
See, said the Sire, how soon 'tis done:	. . . .	189	Faggot	9

SEE (CONTINUED)

	PAGE	TITLE	LINE
'Tis (let me see) three Years and more,	201	Horace 2, 6	63
Because they see me us'd so well:	202	Horace 2, 6	82
"See but the Fortune of some Folks!	202	Horace 2, 6	88
Oh, could I see my Country Seat.	202	Horace 2, 6	108
To see my Life so fast decline?	203	In Sickness	2
"You see 'tis meer Necessity,	207	Fable Bitches	10
"Their Way--for now you see they're blind;	208	Fable Bitches	34
You wonder now to see me write	218	To Mr. Delany	87
Than let you see her dress her Head;	222	Prog of Love	8
For neighb'ring Beaux to see it bare.	222	Prog of Love	18
See then what Mortals place their Bliss in!	223	Prog of Love	25
See here again the Dev'l to do;	223	Prog of Love	39
And in a Glass had made her see	224	Prog of Love	53
To see her from her Pillow rise	226	Prog of Beauty	13
On either Side you see the Tracks,	227	Prog of Beauty	39
See but her Forehead and her Chin.	229	Prog of Beauty	100
We see the Nation's Credit crackt,	253	Bubble	59
Subscribers plainly see 'um there,	257	Bubble	167
For Fools will see as Wise men please.	257	Bubble	168
We see you never can be drown'd:	258	Bubble	192
Now you see why his Verses so seldom are shown,	264	Apollo	55
They shall not see a Trail of Light:	270	Apollo's Edict D	35
Stay--But let me see how finely will it Sound,	274	Epilogue	5
See Philip's Son amidst his Persian Guard;	275	Epilogue	24
O! Cou'd I see this Audience Clad in Stuff,	275	Epilogue	31
And scarce a Crown is left to see the Play:	275	Epilogue	34
By Christmas we shall see strange things.	282	Journal	110
'Tis happy to see the whole Kingdom in Rags,	287	Bank Down	16
Oh! then but to see how Beggars will Vapour,	287	Bank Down	21
Methinks I now see them so jovial and crank,	287	Bank Down	24
You see the Crows feet round his Eyes.	291	Prog Marriage	50
While she drives on to see the Play.	292	Prog Marriage	82
Oh, may I see her soon dispensing	295	Prog Marriage	159
"You soon shall see him soundly tost.	305	Storm	56
"Or, wou'd you see his Spirits sink,	305	Storm	67
Stay, let me see-- Three hundred pounds a year,	308	Billet Players	17
To see a Scoundrel Strut and hector,	312	To Ford	39
You see, my Arguments are Strong;	315	To Ford	109
Howe'er let us try him and see how he'll burn.	336	Serious Poem	64
Very soon to see Wood Drop down from a Rope.	338	Serious Poem	116
And once I was so bold to beg that I might see His Grace,	342	Upon His Grace	27
Then said my Lord, I'm very glad to see thee honest Friend,	342	Upon His Grace	31
. . . I'd see him hanging high'r,	343	Upon His Grace	37
Why Sirrah said the Noble 'Squire, how dare you see my Face,	343	Upon His Grace	43
To see the wicked Varlet sprawling;	353	Wood Ironmongr	26
There you shall see a Rary-Show	362	Grace's Answer	29
You see the better with the other:	366	Answer Delaney	22
You see my Learning; but to shorten it,	367	Answer Delaney	41
You hate to see ought that seems Clean	372	Letter D. S-y	44
He had not heard of him--Pray see,	377	Apology Lady C	59
My Son shall never see a College.	377	Apology Lady C	70
"To see th' important Men of Dress,	380	Apology Lady C	147
"And long-deluded Mortals see,	384	Manly Virtue	13
In manly Form to let them see	384	Manly Virtue	25
Now rais'd on high, see, Virtue shews	386	Manly Virtue	97
Quoth King Robin, our Ribbands I see are too few	389	Order of Bath	1
But I'll see you all damn'd before I will whittle.	399	Tom Clinch	16
And see her marks in ev'ry face;	401	Window Inns 5 D	8
Thanks to my Stars, I once can see	402	Window Inns 7 D	1
You see, when Folks have got their Ends,	408	Dial Rich Marb	19
A goodly Sight to see her ride,	410	Dial Rich Marb	63
But, hope to see you flourish still.	411	Dial Rich Marb	102
I see the ship at anchor ride	420	Holyhead	8
In Dublin they'd be glad to see	420	Holyhead	13
And then stand by to see fair play,	421	Ireld	10
You quickly see the gudgeon bite,	421	Ireld	23
To see you safe in Sots-Hole,	425	Five Ladies	6
Where I shall see your Faces	425	Five Ladies	13
See how Corruption grows,	426	Five Ladies	29
Nor when we see Astraea stand	433	Answer Paulus	31
Her scales you only see her hold	433	Answer Paulus	35
To see her there	442	Ballyspellin	68
You see the Booby Husband sit	448	Modern Lady	114
But see, the Female Club disbands,	451	Modern Lady	196
To see a Knave's inverted Heels:	451	Modern Lady	227
In hope to see Spadillo rise;	452	Modern Lady	231
Paddy repin'd to see him wear	458	Paddy's Charac	19
He rules the Sea, you see he ride in't;	463	Birthday Song	98
Now seer her seated on her Throne	465	Birthday Song	173
That, if we could but see his Heart,	485	Libel on D- D-	157
To see the Seeds of Vice arise,	485	Libel on D- D-	176
When first in Print, you see him dread	500	Doctor Delaney	13
He cannot see one Creature dropping:	500	Doctor Delaney	22
You see him first the Peacock bring,	513	Answer Fable	15
Did ever mortal see a Peacock	513	Answer Fable	21
I see the greatest Owls in you,	515	Answer Fable	106
And bless his ravisht Sight to see	530	Lady's Dres Rm	142

SEE	(CONTINUED)	PAGE	TITLE	LINE
We see a Comrade get a fall,	. . . .	545	Life of Swift	13
See, how behave his Friends profest,	. . . .	545	Life of Swift	19
To see him always foremost stand,	. . . .	546	Life of Swift	33
To see him mortify'd at least---.	. . . .	546	Life of Swift	40
They'd laugh, to see me make a rout,	. . . . . .	546	Life of Swift	50
What Poet would not grieve to see,	. . . .	554	Death of Swift	31
See, how the Dean begins to break:	. . . .	556	Death of Swift	80
And come to see each other damn'd;	. . . .	579	Day Judgement	16
It would do your Heart good, to see how she will cark it.		580	Psyche	12
Then, see the dire Effect of Pease,	. . . .	589	Strephon Chloe	167
Can see each other do their Need.	. . . .	590	Strephon Chloe	206
To see some radiant Nymph appear	. . . .	591	Strephon Chloe	227
I come, I come,--Medusa, see,	. . . .	596	Cassinus Peter	85
But, see how Satan spreads his Snares;	. . . . . .	605	Beasts Confess	117
You'll see a Cloud in gentle weather	. . . . . .	618	Scandal Poem 1	43
We see him from our kitchen windows,	. . . . . .	620	Scandal Poem 1	108
You see how sawcily he shews	. . . .	621	Scandal Poem 1	135
You'll see a Cloud in gentle Weather	. . . . . .	625	Scandal Poem 2	39
We see him from our Kitchen-windows:	. . . . . .	626	Scandal Poem 2	106
See, what Mirth the Sport creates;	. . . .	638	Epistle Lady	255
Are you to see it advertiz'd!	. . . .	643	On Poetry	112
See my weary Days consuming,	. . . .	660	Love Song	7
See the Bird of Juno stooping.	. . . .	661	Love Song	31
(And why they were not, I can see no Cause;)	. . . .	662	Upon Ladies	6
For here you see the Man, and there the Beast.	. . .	668	Epig Carthy 9 D	2
My proof is thus: I plainly see	. . . .	679	From Catullus	5
You hardly see the Current flow,	. . . .	688	Cadenus Vaness	52
The Goddess soon began to see	. . . .	689	Cadenus Vaness	104
To see her Empire thus declin'd,	. . . .	690	Cadenus Vaness	129
To see a lovely Infant born:	. . . .	692	Cadenus Vaness	189
To see Vanessa thus endow'd;	. . . .	693	Cadenus Vaness	229
To see a Mortal Virgin deck'd	. . . .	695	Cadenus Vaness	271
Thou hast, as thou shalt quickly see,	. . . . . .	695	Cadenus Vaness	292
To see the Girl in Deshabille.	. . . .	698	Cadenus Vaness	367
To see the Virgin mind her Book,	. . . .	704	Cadenus Vaness	551
To see her cloister'd like a Nun.	. . . .	705	Cadenus Vaness	583
Now, said the Nymph, I'll let you see	. . . . . .	706	Cadenus Vaness	614
And come in Crowds to see his Face:	. . . . . .	709	Cadenus Vaness	702
I see her taste each nauseous Draught,	. . . . . .	727	To Stella	113
In vain; for see, your Friend hath brought	. . . . .	731	Stella, Poems	101
Where'e'er they see the fairest Sign,	. . . . . .	734	Stel B-day '20	2
See, at her Levee crowding Swains	. . . .	735	Stel B-day '20	23
That, should you live to see the Day	. . . . . .	735	Stel B-day '20	47
See! as you raise it from its Tomb,	. . . .	743	Stel B-day 22	67
To see that ev'ry Glass was fine.	. . . .	746	Stel Distress	22
At entring you might see her stoop	. . . .	746	Stel Distress	29
To see that ev'ry Glass was fine.	. . . .	750	Stel Wood-Park	20
And till I see them with these Eyes,	. . . . . .	758	Stel B-day '24	47
While I can better hear than see;	. . . .	758	Stel B-day '24	52
And often see a Puppet-show.	. . . .	776	Mullinix Tim	92
And first his Bum you see him Clap,	. . . . . .	776	Mullinix Tim	109
I beg, you see the Case is Nice,	. . . .	779	Mullinix Tim	196
There's Latin too that you may see	. . . .	779	Mullinix Tim	215
The cursed Villain! now I see	. . . .	783	Tim and Fables	29
Yet when we see thee thus array'd,	. . . .	787	Clad in Brown	25
I own I see but little Wit in:	. . . .	788	Dick's Variety	10
Wretched Ierne! with what Grief I see	. . . . . .	792	St. Pat's Well	33
See, where the new-devouring Vermin runs,	. . . .	792	St. Pat's Well	59
Look on him and see their Growth.	. . . .	799	Traulus 2	6
Cou'd you see his grim Grace, for a Pound to a Penny,		803	Irish Bishops	9
So, could we see a Set of new Iscariots.	. . . .	806	Judas	19
See, Brother, how we Apples swim.	. . . .	811	Bro Protestant	14
Away you see the Varlet scud,	. . . .	824	Printer Newgat	9
Just Heaven! to see the Dunghill dastard Brood	.	826	Noisy Tom	17
When they see a Clergy-Gown.	. . . .	831	Legion Club	56
See, the Muse unbars the Gate;	. . . .	832	Legion Club	81
See the dreadful Strides she takes.	. . . . . .	832	Legion Club	92
See the Scowling Visage drop,	. . . .	835	Legion Club	143
Yet would gladly see the Hunks	. . . .	836	Legion Club	167
See they gently twitch his Coat,	. . . .	836	Legion Club	169
"Yet thou could'st tamely see me slain.	. . . . .	850	Old Thorn	68
"Since you could see me treated so,	. . . . . .	850	Old Thorn	71
Sure never did man see	. . . .	851	Lady's Lament	1
To see a wild calf	. . . .	857	Lady's Lament	188
Now, see, when they meet, how their Honour's behave;		869	Grand Question	71
See, now comes the Captain all dawb'd with gold Lace:	.	870	Grand Question	93
And see how he rides like a Lord of the Land,	. . .	870	Grand Question	95
"Whenever you see a Cassock and Gown,	. . . . .	872	Grand Question	153
A longer half-p'orth never did I see:	. . . . . .	881	Pastoral Dial	27
Him on my Lap you never more should see;	. . . .	882	Pastoral Dial	47
But see, where Norah with the Sowins comes--	. . .	882	Pastoral Dial	51
Then, (let me see) we'll make the Knight	. . . .	886	Rev Market-Hill	93
And, see, the Printer's Boy below:	. . . .	887	Panegyr Dean	32
To see thy <Deanship> thus employ'd!	. . . . . .	892	Panegyr Dean	176
Though I should see him twice a day,	. . . . . .	899	Dean's Reasons	29
And, vext to see Affairs miscarry,	. . . .	903	Death Daphne	9
I see his Vanity and Pride;	. . . .	915	Riddle 1	24
But see below me all Mankind.	. . . .	917	Riddle 3	4
I let no Creature see my Face.	. . . .	917	Riddle 4	4
Here you may see, as in a Glass,	. . . .	921	Riddle 7	5

SEE   (CONTINUED)   PAGE   TITLE   LINE
        See where those mangled Corpses lye; . . . .   923 Riddle 7   61
        Yet Standers-by may plainly see . . . .   926 Riddle 9   5
        What you see is none of mine, ...   927 Riddle 10   D 2
        Most wondrous Forms you see me wear . . . . . .   927 Riddle 10   D 13
        Yet am not one of all you see. . . . .   927 Riddle 10   D 18
        I Am jet-Black, as you may see, ...   929 Riddle 15   D 1
        T' other you may see in Tin, ...   931 Riddle 17   D 5
        In me you see them full as white, ...   932 Riddle 19   D 8
        When all we see shall disappear. . . . .   932 Riddle 19   D 16
        You'll see me stretch him to a Giant; . . . . .   934 Riddle 21   D 20
        Yet neither Smell, See, Taste, or Hear. . . . .   935 Riddle 23   D 9
        See with what consequence he stalks, ...   950 Upstart   D 13
        See how the gaping crowd admire . . . .   950 Upstart   D 15
        See, see, Celia, Celia Dies, ...   960 Cantata
        See, see, Celia, Celia Dies, ...   960 Cantata
        And I wish your few friends, when they next see your car 976 Dean to Sherid   29
           go,
        And see now, it strikes ten, and I hear him coming up 987 Mary to Sher   36
           Stairs:
        Thus you may see, dear Friend, ex pede hence . . . . 988 Letter Dr Sh-n   15
        As to your Spelling, let me see, ...   1004 Dan J's Reply   34
        . . .for you see plainly my Paper is ended. . . .   1014 Swift to Sheri   12
        But I see the Sum Total, ...   1015 Swift to Sheri   39
        You see I won't stop, ...   1015 Swift to Sheri   53
SEE'T
        'Twould grieve a Body's Heart to see't: . . . . .   90 Bauc & Phil 1   18
        Would turn so quick you scarce could see't . . . .   93 Bauc & Phil 1   132
        Turn'd round so quick, you scarce cou'd see't; . . . 113 Bauc & Phil 2   72
        And the Publick shall see't, if I live 'till to Morrow; 265 Apollo   68
        He saw, and he was griev'd to see't, ...   603 Beasts Confess   53
        I'll hold you a Groat, and I wish I cou'd see't, . .   805 Irish Bishops   51
SEED
        From strength of its own native seed, ...   41 Ode Sancroft   224
        Motly Fruit of Mungril Seed . . . .   799 Traulus 2   2
SEEDS
        Which from Eternal Seeds begun, ...   20 Ode Athenian   128
        Seeds and runs up to Poetry. . . . .   33 Ode to Temple   212
        The World from justling Seeds arose, ...   324 Pethox   28
        To see the Seeds of Vice arise, ...   485 Libel on D- D-   176
        Seeds long unknown to Womankind, ...   693 Cadenus Vaness   203
        The Seeds of Knowledge, Judgment, Wit. . . . . .   693 Cadenus Vaness   205
        Those early Seeds by Venus sown, ...   701 Cadenus Vaness   472
SEEK
        Some whom ambition drives, seek Heaven's high Son . .   39 Ode Sancroft   166
        And you that did your Fortunes seek, ...   101 Elegy Patrige   109
        Ah! where must needy Poet seek for Aid, ...   138 City Shower   27
        Here English Wits will be to seek, ...   158 Fable of Midas   59
        Bids us to seek Peace and ensue it. . . . . . .   220 A Quiet Life   18
        I'm still to seek which Dog you mean; . . . . .   298 Horrid Plot   19
        You, for the News are ne'r to seek, ...   315 To Ford   103
        I own it, and therefore I leave you to seek. . . .   337 Serious Poem   90
        Mordanto at Madrid to seek: . . . .   398 Earl of P-b-w   14
        Here wont the Dean when he's to seek, ...   409 Dial Rich Marb   51
        How oft' am I for Rime to seek? . . . .   502 Doctor Delaney   65
        Or ever went to seek my Food . . . .   602 Beasts Confess   19
        From Party-Merit seek Support; . . . .   646 On Poetry   185
        In Pleasure seek for something new: . . . . . .   728 Stella, Poems   18
        To seek an old rag in the closet. . . . .   756 Dingley Brent   18
        To seek a more secure Retreat. . . . .   849 Old Thorn   40
        None seek thee now in open Air; . . . .   895 Panegyr Dean   281
        To seek, in deserts, Fields Elysian? . . . . . .   899 Dean's Reasons   16
        In me, Detractors seek to find . . . .   918 Riddle 4   23
SEEKS
        A more inferior Station seeks . . . .   227 Prog of Beauty   34
        Or in the cross-bath seeks as Heir . . . .   294 Prog Marriage   137
        "Or, else some hiding Hole he seeks, ...   305 Storm   61
        But I sing of a Famous Lord, who seeks his Country's 341 Upon His Grace   2
           Good.
        The cringing Knave who seeks a Place . . . . .   604 Beasts Confess   93
        Softly seeks her silent Mate; . . . .   661 Love Song   30
        But blinded by Resentment, seeks . . . .   731 Stella, Poems   125
        And seeks to learn the secret Cause, ...   923 Riddle 7   81
SEEM
        And seem (almost) transform'd to Water, Flame, and Air, 22 Ode Athenian   201
        And men seem walking on their heads; . . . . . .   35 Ode Sancroft   34
        Seem to discover what they would have done . . . .   38 Ode Sancroft   132
        Might seem, when first she rais'd her eyes to mine. . .   52 Temple Ill   30
        "Since thy few ill-presented graces seem . . . . .   55 Temple Ill   145
        Filth of all Hues and Odours seem to tell . . . .   139 City Shower   55
        They seem to act an Ancient Tale, ...   239 Run Bankers   19
        Who was the Man, he wish'd to seem; . . . . . .   386 Manly Virtue   76
        To make it seem in this Disguise, ...   528 Lady's Dres Rm   77
        Yet, when you sink, I seem the higher. . . . . .   555 Death of Swift   46
        If I always seem too dull t'ye; . . . .   630 Epistle Lady   19
        The Duke and Dean seem near upon a levell. . . .   678 Dean and Duke   10
        The Glass will seem as brown as those. . . . . .   786 Clad in Brown   12
        You seem to praise to make amends, ...   1003 Dan J's Reply   20
        Seem rather to renew my Grief, ...   1005 Sheridan's Sub   30
SEEM'D
        Such seem'd her eyes, as when an evening ray . . . .   51 Temple Ill   17

SEEM'D   (CONTINUED)   PAGE   TITLE   LINE
    And seem'd to knit his Brow;   . . . .   74 Game Traffick   6
    Now seem'd to look abundance better, ...   114 Bauc & Phil 2   97
    She seem'd to laugh and squawl in Rhimes, ...   150 Corinna   15
    <Swift> seem'd to wonder what he meant,   . . .   172 Horace 1, 7   51
    Why should he sink where nothing seem'd to press? . . . 284 Elegy Boat   3
    The Death of our Nation it seem'd to foretell,   . . . 351 Wood Insect   31
    "And seem'd determin'd not to starve it, ...   571 Death of Swift   457
    He seem'd as just crept out of Bed;   . . . . . .   594 Cassinus Peter   11
    Why, hang her, though she seem'd so coy, ...   595 Cassinus Peter   61
    For tho' she seem'd to listen more . . . .   704 Cadenus Vaness   564
SEEMD
    Van saw, but seemd not to regard, ...   86 Hist V's House   3
SEEMING
    But yet, tho' seeming pleas'd, can't bear   . . . .   379 Apology Lady C   121
    Tho' seeming pleas'd at all she sees, ...   379 Apology Lady C   125
    Rude Laughter seeming like to burst;   . . . . . .   448 Modern Lady   128
SEEMINGLY
    So, bowing, seemingly comply'd;   . . . .   378 Apology Lady C   95
SEEMS
    When Treason there in Person seems to stand, ...   8 Ode to King   56
    It seems some floating piece of Paradice, ...   17 Ode Athenian   44
    And tho' the Title seems to show   . . . .   21 Ode Athenian   165
    Seems to have borrow'd some ungrateful tast   . . .   22 Ode Athenian   212
    She seems a Medly of all Ages, ...   23 Ode Athenian   221
    Woman seems now above all Vanity grown, ...   24 Ode Athenian   250
    Thus censure seems that fiery froth which breeds   . . . 45 To Congreve   69
    My Lord seems pleas'd, but still directs   . . . .   64 Discovery   41
    Love's Fire, it seems, like inward Heat, ...   65 Problem   7
    Stays till 'tis fair, yet seems to call a Coach.   .   138 City Shower   36
    But here a Grievance seems to lie, ...   198 Horace 2, 6   D
    Phillis, it seems, was fled with John.   . . . . . .   223 Prog of Love   42
    The pond'rous Metal seems to swim;   . . . . . .   251 Bubble   12
    And seems a Guinnea to your View;   . . . .   255 Bubble   116
    Now, whereas the said Criminal seems past Repentance, . 266 Apollo   93
    "Besides, to me this seems a Bubble, ...   321 First of April   23
    And seems all Feet, and Hands, and Eyes.   . . . .   322 First of April   38
    You hate to see ought that seems Clean   . . . . . .   372 Letter D. S-y   44
    Where nature hardly seems alive.   . . . .   421 Holyhead   32
    And, though the gospel seems to say, ...   434 Answer Paulus   61
    Or to Jamaica seems transported, ...   583 Young Nymph   45
    Belated, seems on watch to lye, ...   583 Young Nymph   49
    It seems, they had Religion then, ...   601 Beasts Confess   3
    Yet seems to feel my pains alone, ...   754 Stella '23   17
    Which alien seems from Nature's Laws;   . . . . . .   923 Riddle 7   82
SEEN
    Great God! (said I) what have I seen!   . . . .   29 Ode to Temple   103
    And even the sharpest eye that has the prospect seen,   41 Ode Sancroft   207
    And chuse out wits who ne'er have seen his face; . . . 48 To Congreve   170
    Shrouds her still beams; how should the stars be seen?   53 Temple Ill   58
    I've seen a Snake in human Form, ...   84 Salamander   38
    So have I seen a batter'd Beau   . . . .   84 Salamander   57
    If he has seen its gilded Spires.   . . . .   109 V's House   102
    Instead of Home-spun Coifs were seen, ...   115 Bauc & Phil 2   139
    Remembers he the Trees has seen;   . . . .   116 Bauc & Phil 2   166
    Sauntring in Coffee-house is Dulman seen;   . . . .   137 City Shower   11
    She blushes when by mortals seen;   . . . .   178 To Lord Harley   70
    When you are seen, be seen from far, ...   228 Prog of Beauty   71
    When you are seen, be seen from far, ...   228 Prog of Beauty   71
    So have I seen from Severn's Brink   . . . .   253 Bubble   53
    She can swear to the Person, whom oft she has seen,   264 Apollo   53
    And let them be seen by the World if he dare,   . . .   265 Apollo   63
    To prey on his Liver, but not to be seen: . . . .   266 Apollo   98
    Fix them on high, conspicuous to be seen, ...   285 Elegy Boat   33
    'Twas answer'd, she would not be seen.   . . . . . .   290 Prog Marriage   8
    So have I seen within a Pen   . . . .   294 Prog Marriage   145
    A Dog and <Bishop> ne'er was seen, ...   301 Horrid Plot   74
    In all the various Colours seen, ...   325 Pethox   45
    Are to the Life distinctly seen.   . . . .   325 Pethox   72
    I often have seen two Plays very Good, ...   337 Serious Poem   91
    There was no Silver to be seen.   . . . .   354 Simile Silver   24
    (Not to be seen without a Glass)   . . . .   367 Answer Delaney   35
    "Be told--You are not to be seen: . . . .   380 Apology Lady C   158
    Lovely alike, or heard or seen; . . . .   385 Manly Virtue   58
    'Tis Virtue's Int'rest to be seen:)   . . . . . .   386 Manly Virtue   80
    Have you not o'er a Sawpit seen, ...   393 Modern Poets   10
    Poor Patty Blount no more be seen   . . . .   409 Dial Rich Marb   47
    Were seen contending in a Race;   . . . .   412 Desire Possess   11
    Still seen o'r'e many an Alehouse fire.   . . . .   461 Birthday Song   38
    "Must in the Ambient Hedge be seen;   . . . . . .   476 Epist on Epist   54
    His Heart is through his Libel seen, ...   514 Answer Fable   75
    Be once in Celia's Chamber seen!   . . . .   528 Lady's Dres Rm   96
    (He had not seen a Hare the Lord knows when)   . . .   538 Mr. Pulteney   26
    "This Ode you never yet have seen, ...   563 Death of Swift   271
    "So often seen caressing Chartres: . . . . .   565 Death of Swift   324
    But, such a Sight was never seen, ...   594 Cassinus Peter   9
    Have you seen a Rocket fly?   . . . .   638 Epistle Lady   249
    So have I seen ill-coupled Hounds, ...   645 On Poetry   175
    Who, tho' too little to be seen, ...   651 On Poetry   343
    The Shepherds and the Nymphs were seen   . . . . . .   686 Cadenus Vaness   1
    The Muses oft were seen to frown;   . . . .   689 Cadenus Vaness   99

SEEN	(CONTINUED)	PAGE	TITLE	LINE
But rarely seen, and seen from far:		696	Cadenus Vaness	307
But rarely seen, and seen from far:		696	Cadenus Vaness	307
The Monkey, who had seen the World.		782	Tim and Fables	8
But Dick had seen a College.		784	Mullinex Dick	4
Seen from behind a dirty Clout:		786	Clad in Brown	10
In his Dress and Figure seen:		800	Traulus 2	32
You have hardly seen a Score,		839	Legion Club	237
Keeper, I have seen enough,		839	Legion Club	239
Here Irish wit is seen		843	Epigr Irish	2
No Fruit or Blossom to be seen,		849	Old Thorn	19
So may you be seen		858	Lady's Lament	219
I think I have seen her Picture by Jervis.--		869	Grand Question	76
Your Ladyship lifts up the Sash to be seen,		870	Grand Question	101
Is seen, as when you mount our Pulpit.		889	Panegyr Dean	66
Was never seen, except her own:		904	Death Daphne	62
And often have I seen thee grace		919	Riddle 5	7
Distinctly seen as through a Glass:		920	Riddle 6	14
Fraud, Perjury, and Guilt are seen.		922	Riddle 7	22
Oft in the Train of Venus seen,		923	Riddle 7	69
All over naked I am seen,		926	Riddle 9	9
Yet ev'ry where I may be seen;		935	Riddle 23	D 4
Clouded if my face is seen,		937	Riddle 24	D 39
Not seen by our Betters.		1036	Bless Country	3
SEES				
When strait she sees the Countrey all around,		17	Ode Athenian	38
But sees thy meteor blaze about me shine,		54	Temple Ill	91
He sees, yet hardly can believe,		115	Bauc & Phil 2	119
The Turnkey now his Flock returning sees,		125	Descriptn Morn	15
A Letter on the Toylet sees		223	Prog of Love	45
The Mariner with Rapture sees		251	Bubble	26
O'er sees the Work, or Dragon rowes,		279	Journal	23
Orphans around his Bed the Lawyer sees,		364	On Dreams	23
Tho' seeming pleas'd at all she sees,		379	Apology Lady C	125
She draws an Ace, and sees it red.		452	Modern Lady	233
And sees a Son in every God		466	Birthday Song	185
Each Dame he sees with all her Stinks:		529	Lady's Dres Rm	122
Who sees, will spew; who smells, be poison'd.		583	Young Nymph	74
Who sees the Ditch too deep and wide.		640	On Poetry	18
No matter what a Fellow sees.		699	Cadenus Vaness	403
He sees one single Tory there:		789	Dick's Variety	36
When my elbows he sees		852	Lady's Lament	25
If he sees her but once,		854	Lady's Lament	91
Sees the glorious Ages past.		862	To Janus	16
SEEST				
Thou daily seest Him face to face,		34	Ode Sancroft	6
And think thou seest my owners Heart,		60	Lady Tablebook	2
But, when thou seest me laid in Dust,		596	Cassinus Peter	100
What else are those thou seest in Bishop's Geer		792	St. Pat's Well	49
SEGMENT				
The segment so large 'twixt your reason and rhyme is,		1026	Sheri Circles	6
SEISE				
To seise you in your passing by:		257	Bubble	176
The Coasters crowd to seise the Spoyl,		258	Bubble	202
SEIZ'D				
(Which since has seiz'd on all the rest)		28	Ode to Temple	54
Madness like this no fancy ever seiz'd,		55	Temple Ill	147
He would have seiz'd the Spanish Plate,		463	Birthday Song	101
An horrid Vision seiz'd my Head,		578	Day Judgement	3
Have dropt their Arms, and seiz'd the Plunder.		775	Mullinix Tim	48
SEIZE				
And now he thought to Seize his due,		120	Apollo Outwit	37
Yet swifter Fate will seize him from behind.		210	Earl of Oxford	6
On him could ever boast a Pow'r to seize;		234	Elegy on Demar	30
Fail'd but an Inch to seize him by the Back.		538	Mr. Pulteney	34
As, if the gout should seize the head,		761	Bec's B-Day	11
The Huntsmen seize the grinning Prize.		885	Rev Market-Hill	82
Then if we once can seize the Key,		885	Rev Market-Hill	87
Nor ever fail to seize my Foe:		921	Riddle 6	32
SEIZURES				
Their Reign began with cruel Seizures;		283	Journal	120
SELDOM				
But the first Knave does seldom fail		74	Game Traffick	3
The Castle seldom frequents.		75	Game Traffick	16
But seldom rose above a Sheet:		172	Horace 1, 7	42
Soon grows Domestick, seldom fails		173	Horace 1, 7	77
Without a Pilot seldom knows		256	Bubble	143
Now you see why his Verses so seldom are shown,		264	Apollo	55
Lest my Mobb's Mouth, being seldom quiet		373	Letter D. S-y	66
I guess the Hand, it seldom fails,		453	Modern Lady	268
And after all he seldom Sped.		456	Dean Smedley	26
Men seldom by their Good Deeds rise:		495	Panegyr Swift	75
"And seldom fail'd of good Success;		566	Death of Swift	336
Could Verse inspire, but seldom writ:		597	Problem Solved	2
(Which seldom is the Dunce's Case)		647	On Poetry	234
But meddle seldom with their Match.		651	On Poetry	322
Wou'd seldom at the Park appear,		696	Cadenus Vaness	312
Your barking Curs will seldom bite:		797	Traulus 1	46
Nor seldom grace the flow'ry downs,		896	Panegyr Dean	303
Seldom by the death of time;		937	Riddle 24	D 48
Yet, Ladies are seldom at Ombre, or Lue, sick;		1029	Dr. Helsham	15

```
SELF    SEE YOUR-SELF                                            PAGE   TITLE            LINE
        That I went to warm my self in Lady Betty's Chamber,.   69 Mrs Harris Pet        1
                  . .
        . . .that I might do my self no Harm:  . . . . . . .    70 Mrs Harris Pet       19
        The Devil take me, said she, (blessing her self,) . . . 71 Mrs Harris Pet       44
        Now you may go hang your self for me, and so went away. 72 Mrs Harris Pet       63
        Consumes it self to weave a Cell.  . . . . . . .        79 Vanbrug House        32
        And turning Dung it self to Gold?  . . . . . . . .     157 Fable of Midas       48
        So much, that you neglect your Self.  . . . . . . .    175 Horace 1, 7         126
        How should I thrust my self between?  . . . . . . .    200 Horace 2, 6          30
        She knows her Early self no more,  . . . . . . .       227 Prog of Beauty       49
        His other Self, his Money lay.  . . . . . . . .        235 Elegy on Demar       48
        To that dear Self he left behind,  . . . . . . . .     235 Elegy on Demar       50
        That her Eyes were as bright as our self at Noon-Day;  264 Apollo               41
        Pray never press your self for Rent, but pay me when you 342 Upon His Grace      33
          can,
        For she her self oft falls in Pieces.  . . . . . .     362 Grace's Answer       28
        To wash her self our Well in  . . . . . . . .          441 Ballyspellin         39
        Thus every Fool her self deludes;  . . . . . . . .     449 Modern Lady         154
        The fatal Box it self display'd,  . . . . . . . .      494 Panegyr Swift        41
        Yet, in Your self when smooth and round,  . . . .      500 Doctor Delaney       29
        Then Throttle thy self with an Ell of strong Tape,     519 Dean Hang Rape       53
        Nor, think your self secure in doing wrong,  . . . .   533 To Mr. Gay           59
        "I own my self no Judge of those:  . . . . . . .       565 Death of Swift      310
        But, e'er you sell your self to Laughter,  . . . .     591 Strephon Chloe      231
        Deceiv'd thy self, instead of me;  . . . . . . .       695 Cadenus Vaness      293
        Both of her self and Sex asham'd,  . . . . . . .       699 Cadenus Vaness      405
        It shews and discovers it self through a Trifle.  . .  716 Answer Rebus         12
        While I assign my self a Task  . . . . . . . .         739 Stel B-day '21        3
        A Supper worthy of her self,  . . . . . . . .          747 Stel Distress        51
        A Supper worthy of her self,  . . . . . . . .          751 Stel Wood-Park       67
        Look to thy Self, and be no more the Sport  . . .      770 Horace 1, 14         11
        To serve my self and Common-weal,  . . . . . . .       778 Mullinix Tim        170
        I'd rather hang my self by half,  . . . . . . .        778 Mullinix Tim        177
        I give my self intire to you,  . . . . . . . .         782 Mullinix Tim        283
        I'm ev'ry one, but ne'er my self;  . . . . . . .       935 Riddle 23        D   23
        Whereby you now confess your self to be a Goose or an  986 Mary to Sher         18
          Ass:
SELF-LOVE
        Self-Love, in Nature rooted fast,  . . . . . . .       708 Cadenus Vaness      684
        Self-love, Ambition, Envy, Pride,  . . . . . . .       555 Death of Swift       41
SELL    SEE OUT-SELL
        Or sell a Goose at the next Toun  . . . . . . .         95 Bauc & Phil 1       175
        What? sell my Master's Country Seat?  . . . . . .      128 Little House         56
        He wou'd not sell it for a Crown.  . . . . . . .       128 Little House         58
        And Sell for Twenty Pence a Yard of theirs;  . . .     276 Epilogue             44
        And sell them for Gold, or he can't shew his Love else, 337 Serious Poem        98
        And sell their Votes at such a Rate,  . . . . . .      392 Young's Satire       43
        Sell them to Curl for Fifty Pound,  . . . . . .        395 Grub-Street          19
        Who, for a dinner, sell a vote;  . . . . . . . .       487 Irish-Club            4
        Nor sell what they so dearly bought,  . . . . . .      488 Irish-Club           23
        To make their Trash the better sell.  . . . . . .      505 Doctor Delaney      158
        Nor, at an under Rate his Timber sell;  . . . . .      534 To Mr. Gay           95
        "To sell him for Six Hundred Pound.  . . . . . .       567 Death of Swift      354
        "Who sell their Souls and Votes for Naught;  . . .     571 Death of Swift      446
        But, e'er you sell your self to Laughter,  . . . .     591 Strephon Chloe      231
        Or sell his Children, House, and Lands,  . . . .       821 Dr. Rundle           43
        Sell the Nation for a Pin;  . . . . . . . .            831 Legion Club          48
        And sell, to pacify his wrath,  . . . . . . .          879 Robbin & Harry       35
        Here's delicate Onyons to sell,  . . . . . . .         952 Onyons                2
SELLERS
        Both buyers and sellers,  . . . . . . . . .            403 Window Inns 9    D    5
SELLING
        And selling basely by Retail,  . . . . . . . .          19 Ode Athenian        102
        and selling his Country to purchase his peace  . . .   540 Charac Walpole        8
        Howe'er for selling Bargains fam'd,  . . . . . .       590 Strephon Chloe      216
SELLS
        Yet kindly sells himself for nought  . . . . . .       421 Ireld                 4
        And sells the King of Spain a Bargain.  . . . . .      777 Mullinix Tim        114
SELVES
        Our selves are rais'd as well as she,  . . . . .        24 Ode Athenian        264
        For next to being Great our selves  . . . . . .        493 Panegyr Swift        11
SEMEL'N
        That Semel'n anno ridet Apollo.  . . . . . . .         741 Stel B-day 22        22
SEMELE
        How Semele of mortal Race,  . . . . . . . .            587 Strephon Chloe      107
SEMPSTRESS
        The tuck'd-up Sempstress walks with hasty Strides,  . . 138 City Shower         37
SENATE
        Which while the Senate strove to scower,  . . . .      158 Fable of Midas       71
        But now the Senate (if things hit  . . . . . .        182 Horace 2, 1          59
        So steadily the Senate guides:  . . . . . . . .       391 Young's Satire        6
        O, wou'd the Senate deign to show  . . . . . .        515 Answer Fable         81
        "The Irish Senate, if you nam'd,  . . . . . . .       566 Death of Swift      345
        "Corrupt the Senate, rob the Crown;  . . . . . .      568 Death of Swift      386
        His humble Senate this professes,  . . . . . .        646 On Poetry           197
        A nauseous Brood, that fills your Senate Walls,  . .   792 St. Pat's Well       57
        If noisy <Tom> should in the <Senate> prate,  . . .   825 Noisy Tom             1
        Durst thou, ungrateful, from the <Senate> chace  . .  826 Noisy Tom            15
SENATE-HOUSE
        Into the Senate-House can run,  . . . . . . .         392 Young's Satire       42
```

SENATE-HOUSE (CONTINUED)

	PAGE	TITLE	LINE
And calls the Senate-House a Cabbin;	514	Answer Fable	70
With these, the Court and Senate-house he plies,	532	To Mr. Gay	41
Both at Senate-House, and <King>	637	Epistle Lady	222

SENATE'S

	PAGE	TITLE	LINE
Which, o'er a British Senate's Lids,	133	Magician's Rod	40
The Irish Senate's Praises sing:	501	Doctor Delaney	56

SENATES

	PAGE	TITLE	LINE
In Senates bold, and fierce in War,	398	Earl of P-b-w	32
Through Courts and Senates as he goes;	486	Libel on D- D-	190
of Juries & senates the bully & briber	540	Charac Walpole	12
"In Senates sit, at making Laws;	549	Life of Swift	163
Nor with Senates keep a Fuss,	636	Epistle Lady	187

SENATOR

	PAGE	TITLE	LINE
The hireling Senator of modern Days,	364	On Dreams	35

SENATORS

	PAGE	TITLE	LINE
But, most noble Senators, 'tis a great Shame	143	New Song	13
Damn'd Senators brib'd, Damn'd prostitute Slaves;	576	Place Damn'd	8
Ye <senators>, who love to prate;	487	Irish-Club	2

SENCE

	PAGE	TITLE	LINE
And as he hears his Wit and Sence,	463	Birthday Song	91
And as very little Sence:	574	Helter Skelter	30
Have made thy Presence in a true Sence,	775	Mullinix Tim	65

SENCELESS

	PAGE	TITLE	LINE
Though you and all your senceless Tribe	736	Stel B-day '20	51

SEND

	PAGE	TITLE	LINE
'Tis with a foul design the muse you send,	44	To Congreve	15
One swore he'd send 'em to the Stocks,	91	Bauc & Phil 1	33
If <Guernsey> calls, send word you're gone abroad;	166	Toland's Invit	41
"Send for him up, take no Excuse. '	199	Horace 2, 6	16
I'd send her far enough away--	220	A Quiet Life	33
Send us new Nymphs with each new Moon.	229	Prog of Beauty	120
In return to her Scorn, I send her Diseases,	266	Apollo	105
Was forc'd to send three Miles for Yest,	282	Journal	89
For fear my Lord should send it all into the poor Man's Box.	342	Upon His Grace	26
England will send you corn enough.	422	Ireld	52
Jove send, this Nightingal may fall,	515	Answer Fable	103
Send up an excremental Smell	529	Lady's Dres Rm	111
Suppose your Lord a trusty Servant send,	534	To Mr. Gay	85
Will send their Howd'ye's ev'ry day:	546	Life of Swift	59
They send for Manners--; not for Grief---:	546	Life of Swift	61
To all my Foes, dear Fortune, send	555	Death of Swift	67
How many a Message would he send?	557	Death of Swift	137
"To all their Boroughs send them down:	564	Death of Swift	284
Heaven send thou hast not got the Hypps.	594	Cassinus Peter	35
My latest tribute here I send	608	Know Not What	1
We onely send our Thunder out	617	Scandal Poem 1	7
(Like Courtiers, when they send a Note,	649	On Poetry	271
Or send him in a Peck of Coals;	728	Stella, Poems	34
Send the Clergy all to graze;	838	Legion Club	216
Who send my mind (as I believe) less	900	Dean's Reasons	53
Send me hence ten thousand miles,	907	Daphne	21
. . .and send your Man Alexander to buy Corks,	1013	Swift to Sheri	6
But I think it base in you to send a poor Fellow	1014	Swift to Sheri	10
And cannot send one Verse.	1014	Swift to Sheri	36

SENDERS

	PAGE	TITLE	LINE
A Pox of all Senders	186	Scriblerus 4	D 1

SENDING

	PAGE	TITLE	LINE
"In sending Bolton to Clonfert.	304	Storm	42
Truly I don't know who's bound to be sending	1013	Swift to Sheri	5

SENDS

	PAGE	TITLE	LINE
When she sends forth such a malignant Birth,	8	Ode to King	54
Bids us make Bricks, yet sends us to look out for Straw;	32	Ode to Temple	188
<Toland> to you this Invitation sends,	162	Toland's Invit	3
Jove never sends us downward from the Skies,	363	On Dreams	3
'He's so unkind, he never sends	448	Modern Lady	106
She sends us our <Bishops> and <Judges> and <Deans>,	520	Dean Hang Rape	69
Hush-money sends to all the Neighbours round:	535	To Mr. Gay	108
He says, "Whenever Fortune sends	545	Life of Swift	7
Delany sends a Silver Standish,	611	By Dr. Swift	3
The vilest Doggrel Grubstreet sends,	644	On Poetry	139
She sent for Company to sup, She sends	747	Stel Distress	46
Here in this bundle Janus sends	753	Gift for Bec	15
For which he sends this empty sack;	753	Gift for Bec	25
From distant Regions, Fortune sends	883	Rev Market-Hill	1
A complimental Message sends:	904	Death Daphne	48
Thee, for a Gift, the Courtier sends	919	Riddle 5	19

SENSE

	PAGE	TITLE	LINE
No wonder then she quits the narrow Path of Sense	18	Ode Athenian	68
Of my own dazled, scanty Sense	18	Ode Athenian	78
By the new Modish System of reducing all to sense,	19	Ode Athenian	107
Of common Breeding, common Sense,	27	Ode to Temple	43
Thro' the dark mass, the dawn of so much sense,	37	Ode Sancroft	88
Strike your offended Sense with double Stink.	137	City Shower	6
Were want of Pow'r, or want of Sense:	154	Widow and Cat	D 44
Wine can give <Portland> Wit, and <Cleveland> Sense,	164	Toland's Invit	23
His Lineage, Calling, Shape or Sense	217	To Mr. Delany	69
Was both a Boat, and in one Sense a Pilat.	285	Elegy Boat	14
Which cannot in Literal Sense be made Good,	335	Serious Poem	55
We speak it in a Happier Sense.	339	Arch-Bish Dub	4

SENSE	(CONTINUED)	PAGE	TITLE	LINE
I'm sure a Man of your fine Sense		361	Grace's Answer	21
Another Case; the Sense of Hearing:		366	Answer Delaney	28
And much good Sense, as well as Breeding:		377	Apology Lady C	72
Thro' ev'ry Sense to reach the Heart.		379	Apology Lady C	116
"For once the Theme of human Sense,		384	Manly Virtue	10
Call'd want of Shame, a want of Sense,		386	Manly Virtue	81
The copy's false, and sense is rack'd:		434	Answer Paulus	67
Of common sense without a word in!		434	Answer Paulus	85
Must deviate oft from common sense,		435	Answer Paulus	112
To keep good sense in crouds of fools;		436	Answer Paulus	124
To common honesty and sense;		436	Answer Paulus	144
Wou'd be a Rake, but wanted Sense.		455	Dean Smedley	6
And in their Sense, 'twixt me and you,		461	Birthday Song	19
The Sense can ne're be too jejune,		467	Birthday Song	211
With mean Degrees of Wit and Sense?		475	Epist on Epist	16
To warp the Sense of all Mankind:		475	Epist on Epist	22
Shew Reason, Grammer, Truth, or Sense?		503	Doctor Delaney	104
More Sense than I can do in Six:		555	Death of Swift	50
On Sense and Wit your Passion found,		593	Strephon Chloe	307
However, we have too much sense		622	Scandal Poem 1	153
But, Gods like us, have too much Sense		628	Scandal Poem 2	157
With good sense to entertain us.		633	Epistle Lady	114
Scholars, when good Sense describing,		633	Epistle Lady	115
Talk with Sense, whate'er you please on,		638	Epistle Lady	271
Now Learning, Valour, Virtue, Sense,		656	On Poetry	459
And shock our Sense, till we bestow.		667	Epig Carthy 6	D 4
Nor are the Men of Sense to blame,		688	Cadenus Vaness	63
Thy Votaries, for Want of Sense?		696	Cadenus Vaness	297
To Virtue, in the Noblest Sense,		697	Cadenus Vaness	347
"To form a Nymph of Wit and Sense,		713	Cadenus Vaness	865
Proceeds that Fund of Wit and Sense;		726	To Stella	80
To Virtue,--Honor, Sense, and Wit.		732	Verses Vanessa	8
With Breeding, Humor, Wit, and Sense,		735	Stel B-day '20	25
All Men of Sense will pass your Dore		736	Stel B-day '20	57
To shape it into Sense and Rhyme;		741	Stel B-day 22	10
Honour and Virtue, Sense and Wit,		758	Stel B-day '24	50
Made your Sons Converts both to God and Sense:		792	St. Pat's Well	30
But in no other Sense, than Nature		812	Bro Protestant	33
The Man has Learning, Sense and Morals.		820	Dr. Rundle	22
Half the Globe from Sense and Knowledge.		829	Legion Club	4
"The Irish dear joys have enough common sense,		843	Ay and No	15
Behold! a proof of Irish sense!		843	Epigr Irish	1
But sense gives a grace		854	Lady's Lament	99
He dares defy both sense and wit.		876	To Dean Swift	16
To common law, or common sense;		876	To Dean Swift	20
And soon grow pert on Men of Sense;		887	Panegyr Dean	20
My Words are few, but spoke with Sense:		917	Riddle 4	5
Who can believe with common Sense,		949	Epigr Fasting	1
Without a grain of common sense.		950	Upstart	D 12
SENSELESS				
Say what their senseless malice meant,		42	Ode Sancroft	247
That, senseless, in a Corner stood,		132	Magician's Rod	8
And senseless praise		440	Ballyspellin	5
The Sum of all their senseless Prate,		449	Modern Lady	141
What senseless Cockscomb told you so,		505	Doctor Delaney	160
Shreds of Wit, and senseless Rhimes,		523	Betty Grizette	19
"For he abhorr'd that senseless Tribe,		571	Death of Swift	465
Creech murder'd Horace in his senseless Rhymes,		666	Epig Carthy 3	D 1
"They were a senseless, stupid Race:		714	Cadenus Vaness	871
Aspiring, greedy, full of senseless Prate,		792	St. Pat's Well	51
Scribble senseless Heads of Bills;		831	Legion Club	60
SENSES				
His outward senses fast asleep;		900	Dean's Reasons	46
For the sake of your senses wou'd lay an embargo.		976	Dean to Sherid	30
SENSIBLE				
Or makes 'em sensible of Shame.		453	Modern Lady	275
SENSLESS				
Contrive to shock your Minds, with many a sensless doubt,		22	Ode Athenian	207
As hard, as sensless, and as light:		60	Lady Tablebook	4
SENT				
Sent by just Heaven to threaten Earth		10	Ode to King	133
'Twas sure this Basilisk sent Temple thence,		30	Ode to Temple	124
That sent these wild reformers to our times;		42	Ode Sancroft	246
Sent to assist an old unvanquish'd pride		44	To Congreve	43
Last year, a lad hence by his parents sent		46	To Congreve	115
When man's ill genius to my presence sent		47	To Congreve	135
Jove sent and found far in a Country Scene,		118	Biddy Floyd	3
Nor wou'd believe My Lord had sent;		172	Horace 1, 7	52
York is from Lambeth sent, to shew the Queen		195	Author Himself	47
"Hath sent me to your House to whelp,		207	Fable Bitches	11
Now, John the Butler must be sent		223	Prog of Love	33
White lead was sent us to repair		227	Prog of Beauty	62
And sent him up in Air to Hell.		257	Bubble	184
Were bid in form, but sent Excuses:		290	Prog Marriage	10
Wonder'd the God had sent them there.		322	First of April	44
That he sent to all three a Challenge next morning.		327	Epigram 1	8
Sent Mercury to get another.		346	Prometheus	52
She sent to bid him come and dine.		375	Apology Lady C	6
He should be sent for thither now.		376	Apology Lady C	18
Let them be sent to Mrs. Harding;		417	Woman's Mind	59

SENT	(CONTINUED)	PAGE	TITLE	LINE
Will back be sent		440	Ballyspellin	16
Hath sent this Letter by her Maid.		446	Modern Lady	63
"And hath she sent so soon to dun?		446	Modern Lady	65
"And was not Tom this Morning sent?		451	Modern Lady	200
"An Angel sent by Heav'n's Command,		485	Libel on D- D-	166
A Blessing upon them, have sent us this Year,		516	Dean Hang Rape	3
Some Medals sent him for his Wit;		547	Life of Swift	91
"I sent them with a Load of Books,		563	Death of Swift	259
He boldly sent his Hand in quest,		589	Strephon Chloe	188
And meekly took what Fortune sent:		602	Beasts Confess	42
A Paper Book is sent by Boyle,		611	By Dr. Swift	1
Or Prologue sent from Hand unknown.		643	On Poetry	84
And sent in Quires to line a Trunk;		644	On Poetry	144
She sent for Company to sup, She sends		747	Stel Distress	46
She sent for Company to sup;		751	Stel Wood-Park	62
Sent in a bag to Doctor Swift,		753	Gift for Bec	3
Be sent to Quilca down to graze;		759	Receipt Youth	26
My Prelates and my Students, sent from hence,		792	St. Pat's Well	29
I sent the Magpye from the British Soil,		792	St. Pat's Well	45
I sent you Millions of the croaking Race;		792	St. Pat's Well	54
Sent in my Anger from the Land of Huns;		792	St. Pat's Well	60
Sent from the Dark infernal Region		798	Traulus 1	77
While others hither sent to save us,		820	Dr. Rundle	33
In Prudence and Compassion sent		849	Old Thorn	30
Sent up to thee a grateful Steam.		894	Panegyr Dean	242
She sent her Priests in Wooden Shoes		895	Panegyr Dean	263
Are sent up Off'rings more sincere		896	Panegyr Dean	296
Thus furnish't out, he sent his Train		904	Death Daphne	45
. . .and the Boy here had not been sent . . .		1013	Swift to Sheri	4
The Verses you sent on the bottling your Wine		1017	Swift Ans Sher	1
Is sent to desire that, when your August vacation comes,		1022	Nim-Dan-Dean 2	D 2
By humble companions were sent to their betters:		1026	Sheri Circles	2
SENTENC'D				
"Is sentenc'd to the fatal Tree,		497	Panegyr Swift	129
SENTENCE				
We Phoebus think fit to proceed to his Sentence;		266	Apollo	94
He left us a Laconick Sentence,		455	Dean Smedley	18
Quotes from the Bible many a Sentence		605	Beasts Confess	121
SENTIMENTS				
The Sentiments resemble Hell.		496	Panegyr Swift	109
And, by the Sentiments of Pliny,		598	Problem Solved	29
SEP'RATE				
In sep'rate Cells the He's and She's		893	Panegyr Dean	207
SEPULCHRES				
Twice from their Sepulchres were torn;		923	Riddle 7	76
SEQUEL				
(As we shall shew you in the Sequel)		446	Modern Lady	37
SEQUENTS				
For Pair-royals and Sequents;		75	Game Traffick	14
SERAPHICK				
To like with less Seraphick Ends;		712	Cadenus Vaness	823
SERENE				
Till Peace hath made the Sky serene,		84	Salamander	43
Truth, Innocence, Good Nature, Look serene;		118	Biddy Floyd	4
And when the Sky is grown serene,		354	Simile Silver	31
SERIOUS				
She bid me with a serious Face		311	To Ford	7
As serious as a Tragick Play'r.		707	Cadenus Vaness	663
Accept for once some serious Lines.		764	Stel B-day '26	14
<Zounds> Sir. But to be short and serious		774	Mullinix Tim	33
To interrupt all serious Matter,		777	Mullinix Tim	144
And, as I am serious,		855	Lady's Lament	143
SERJEANT				
Calls Singleton his Brother Serjeant.		812	Bro Protestant	28
That serjeant at law, whom we call Kite the Second,		817	Yahoo's	67
SERMON				
Contrivd to preach his Sermon next		95	Bauc & Phil 1	177
But---not one Sermon, you may swear---.		550	Life of Swift	193
SERMONS				
Knew how to preach old Sermons next,		115	Bauc & Phil 2	127
They learnt it not at Sermons or at pray'rs.		275	Epilogue	12
I spend my Time in making Sermons,		993	On Picture	4
SERPENT				
This Reptil, of the Serpent kind,		83	Salamander	30
This Serpent is extreamly cold,		84	Salamander	48
'Twas a devouring Serpent grown.		132	Magician's Rod	4
I drove the venom'd Serpent from thy Land;		792	St. Pat's Well	40
SERPENT-KIND				
Of Serpent-Kind, and what at distance kills,		941	Letter	23
SERPENT'S				
What Serpent's that which still resorts,		30	Ode to Temple	116
SERPENTS				
Her Serpents hiss direct at me.		596	Cassinus Peter	86
SERV'D				
And serv'd up in an earthen Platter;		91	Bauc & Phil 1	62
Nell serv'd him at the usu'll Rate		221	A Quiet Life	43
A Coach and Six, and serv'd in Plate:		251	Bubble	20
That he had serv'd the Prudes a Trick.		321	First of April	16
I mean when Tyger has been serv'd,		761	Bec's B-Day	37

SERV'D   (CONTINUED)   PAGE   TITLE   LINE

With whom he serv'd, than by his Foes,   . . .   775 Mullinix Tim   54

SERVANT

Says Cary, says he, I have been a Servant. . . .   70 Mrs Harris Pet   30
But coldly said, Your Servant, Sir.   . . . .   172 Horace 1, 7   54
Suppose your Lord a trusty Servant send,   . . .   534 To Mr. Gay   85
Noble Captain, your Servant--Sir Arthur your Slave;   869 Grand Question   72
You must be obey'd--your Servant, Sir Arthur; . .   869 Grand Question   80
Which, and I am sure I have been his Servant . . .   985 Mary to Sher   13
I am but a poor Servant, ...   986 Mary to Sher   24
And so I remain in a civil way, your Servant to command. 987 Mary to Sher   38

SERVANT'S

Are ill excuses for a Servant's Crimes: . . . .   533 To Mr. Gay   68

SERVANTS

So the Chaplain came in; now the Servants say,. . .   72 Mrs Harris Pet   50
The former folks were servants to the king, . . .   308 Billet Players   13
Who ever heard of servants paying wages? . . . .   308 Billet Players   30
Examines all the Servants round, ...   377 Apology Lady C   63
The Servants Faults are on the Master laid. . . .   533 To Mr. Gay   50
With Servants, Tenants, and the neighb'ring Squires.   533 To Mr. Gay   54
And Servants answer; Worse and Worse) . . . . .   557 Death of Swift   124
Cocker'd by the Servants round, ...   631 Epistle Lady   37
Servants love you, and obey: . . . .   633 Epistle Lady   106
That she might o're the Servants hector . . . .   745 Stel Distress   7
She now can or'e the servants hector. . . . . .   745 Stel Distress
That she might o'er the Servants hector. . . . .   749 Stel Wood-Park   6
The Servants amaz'd, are scarce ever able, . . .   871 Grand Question   135
How are the Servants overjoy'd . . . .   892 Panegyr Dean   175
But this my Servants much enrages, ...   954 Authors Living   5
All Servants at play. . . . .   1036 Plague Country   9

SERVE

But serve t' adorn the Baby-dress . . . . . .   6 Ode to King   14
We can not serve You every One, ...   91 Bauc & Phil 1   31
Can't you go work, or serve the King? . . . . .   91 Bauc & Phil 1   41
Canst make it serve thee for a Tilt. . . . . .   109 V's House   114
Two Balls of Glass may serve for Eyes, ...   229 Prog of Beauty   113
And, Dawson street will serve as well . . . . .   313 To Ford   61
Will serve for Sodder well enuff. . . . . . .   345 Prometheus   24
Serve for a Motto on thy Coach? . . . .   348 Whitshed Motto   4
Your delicate Bits will not serve me a Meal, . .   395 Dog and Thief   5
Let me have but your Vote to serve for the Town, .   396 Dog and Thief   11
And serve the Times as others do. . . . . . .   410 Dial Rich Marb   80
Will serve instead of place or pension . . . .   421 Ireld   18
May serve, as arguments ad hominem. . . . . .   433 Answer Paulus   48
And serve to eccho ratling Nonsense; . . . . .   461 Birthday Song   44
Disdains to serve ignoble Ends. . . . .   503 Doctor Delaney   100
To serve a tastless <Court> twelve Years in vain? .   531 To Mr. Gay   2
The Dregs will serve to ripen Ore below; . . . .   532 To Mr. Gay   24
You serve a potent Prince, as well as He. . . .   532 To Mr. Gay   44
Presume not, Gay, unless you serve a Drone, . . .   534 To Mr. Gay   87
Thus much may serve by way of Proem, ...   555 Death of Swift   71
That serve to fill her hollow Jaws. . . . . .   582 Young Nymph   18
To serve the King, and please the Nation. . . .   606 Beasts Confess   154
Do but serve to make me Sport. . . . .   634 Epistle Lady   148
With Caution us'd, may serve a-while. . . . . .   647 On Poetry   238
To serve my self and Common-weal, ...   778 Mullinix Tim   170
May serve to wait on Mrs. Leslie: . . . . . .   886 Rev Market-Hill   100
And, what may serve a common Guest. . . . . .   889 Panegyr Dean   96
To serve a friend against his will? . . . . .   902 Dean's Reasons   114

SERVED

Which the disguise of greatness only served to hide; . .   41 Ode Sancroft   214

SERVES

Whatever serves for innocent Emblems of the Court; . .   31 Ode to Temple   164
Serves by retail to furnish half mankind. . . . .   45 To Congreve   54
As when Time serves, you more shall know. . . .   373 Letter D. S-y   78
"It serves for Sceptick, and Free-thinker, . . .   550 Life of Swift   177
"It serves for Stubble, Hay, and Wood, ...   550 Life of Swift   178

SERVICE

Besides, as they say, Service is no Inheritance in these   71 Mrs Harris Pet   41
Ages.
And had the Service all by Heart; . . . . . .   115 Bauc & Phil 2   130
'Tis for the Service of the Crown. . . . . . .   199 Horace 2, 6   14
Each strait his service offers, pays his court, . .   672 Epig Carthy 24   D 7
Some for the publick Service go, ...   781 Mullinix Tim   255
Pray, how does my Lady?--My Wife's at your Service.--   869 Grand Question   75
Condemn'd to live in Service hard; . . . . . .   883 Rev Market-Hill   11
I would present my humble Service . . . .   1014 Swift to Sheri   11
Her Service to present you, ...   1014 Swift to Sheri   31
Lady Betty presents you her service most humble, .   1027 Sheri Circles   25

SERVICES

The <Queen> incens'd, his Services forgot, . . .   195 Author Himself   57
Where are thy Services and Suff'rings? . . . . .   884 Rev Market-Hill   32

SERVILE

Rejects a servile Usher's Place, ...   482 Libel on D- D-   59
"A servile Race in Folly nurs'd, ...   568 Death of Swift   397
And guilty Shame, and servile Fear, ...   725 To Stella   48

SERVING   SEE TIME-SERVING

SERVING-MAN

A serving-Man of low Degree: . . . .   224 Prog of Love   54

SERVING-MEN

To welcome Brother Serving-men; . . . .   890 Panegyr Dean   100

SESSION   PAGE TITLE   LINE
   Tho' Foes to Love, attend the Session, ...   689 Cadenus Vaness   94
   For let him sputter thro' a <Session>, ... 798 Traulus 1   63
SESSIONS
   Is of short Sessions a long Hist'ry;   . . . . . .   493 Panegyr Swift   32
SET
   But hardly ever set my Eyes together, or slept a Wink.   70 Mrs Harris Pet   21
   And set the Planets by the Ears: . . . .   99 Elegy Patrige   58
   If so be they are in Sommer set: . . . . 148 Windsor Proph   18
   I doubt your Heart is set on Pelf   . . . .   175 Horace 1, 7   125
   Their looks are all by method set, ... 178 To Lord Harley   55
   Of Land set out to plant a Wood.   . . . . 198 Horace 2, 6   6
   Set all her Cubs at once upon her;   . . . .   208 Fable Bitches   40
   Few Hints from you will set him right, ...   218 To Mr. Delany   97
   George, Nim and Dean, set out at Four, ...   280 Journal   43
   And how his Boat was over set, ... 280 Journal   66
   And, thus set out this happy Pair, ...   290 Prog Marriage   27
   Then with his Fore-foot set his Mark.   . . . . 300 Horrid Plot   56
   Our set of strollers, wand'ring up and down, ...   307 Billet Players   1
   Can'st hourly set him on the Rack, ... 325 Pethox   54
   And Yet the Land I from him hold is set so on the Rack   343 Upon His Grace   45
   And they like Stars shall Rise and Set.   . . . . . .   362 Grace's Answer   50
   A Set of Phrases learn't by Rote;   . . . . 415 Woman's Mind   1
   Set up with greasy Linnen, ... 425 Five Ladies   7
   <Lyndsay>, 'tis you have set me on   . . . .   435 Answer Paulus   99
   They set the very Lap-Dog barking;   . . . . 450 Modern Lady   179
   The Table, Cards, and Counters set, ... 451 Modern Lady   214
   The Bank where last he set his Toe, ... 456 Dean Smedley   42
   Set out in Hyperbolick Strains, ... 463 Birthday Song   93
   And set the House to <Rupert> <Barber>.   . . . .   477 Epist on Epist   70
   And, should a Friend attempt to set him right, ...   535 To Mr. Gay   111
   "Your Honour please to buy a Set?   . . . .   564 Death of Swift   280
   "Had set a Price upon his Head;   . . . . 566 Death of Swift   352
   "Whose Owners set not up for Beaux.   . . . .   572 Death of Swift   468
   I to such Blockheads set my Wit!   . . . . 579 Day Judgement   21
   A Set of Teeth completely comes.   . . . .   582 Young Nymph   20
   Set on Reading, than on Dress: . . . . 630 Epistle Lady   18
   Set your Thoughts upon their Mettle: . . . .   636 Epistle Lady   212
   Set off with num'rous Breaks--and Dashes--   . . . .   643 On Poetry   94
   Or where we find your Fury set   . . . . 645 On Poetry   157
   To set Elysium by the Ears.   . . . . 647 On Poetry   218
   Dear Madam, Let me set your Head: . . . .   699 Cadenus Vaness   398
   Now wou'd vouchsafe to set them right.   . . . .   699 Cadenus Vaness   407
   His Similes in Order set, ... 730 Stella, Poems   73
   And to your Failing set your Hand?   . . . .   732 Stella, Poems   140
   Through the whole set of <Irish> <Deans>;   . . . . . .   742 Stel B-day 22   42
   A goodly set as can be found   . . . . 762 Bec's B-Day   51
   Tim set the Volume on a Table, ... 782 Tim and Fables   5
   Can set the Mastiffs on your Back.   . . . . 798 Traulus 1   68
   So, could we see a Set of new Iscariots, ...   806 Judas   19
   Their rights! their importance! We'll set on new rates .   816 Yahoo's   32
   To have the Spirit sent to Sale.   . . . . 821 Dr. Rundle   46
   Sir <Arthur>, since you set the Pattern, ...   888 Panegyr Dean   57
   My Trade is, Pris'ners to set free.   . . . . . .   920 Riddle 6   2
   One of us in Glass is set, ... 930 Riddle 17   D   3
   Set it always in Motion.   . . . . 939 Riddle Answerd   14
   Set hoping, hoping, hoping hearts of Lovers akeing, . .   959 Cantata
   My foot was but just set out from my cathedral,   . . .   975 Dean to Sherid   3
   Knew how to set you better Patterns;   . . . . 1033 Ans to Crown   16
SETS
   The publick Stamp Heav'n sets on all that's Great and   18 Ode Athenian   93
     Good,
   How Fortune fails him when he sets: . . . .   281 Journal   76
   And tell how little weight he sets, ...   282 Journal   99
   Sets of Phrases, cut and dry, ...   523 Betty Grizette   13
   Sets the Spirits all a working.   . . . . 636 Epistle Lady   206
   He sets the Stamp of Bad and Good, ...   649 On Poetry   273
SETT
   Sett, for a Sign of Wit Within.   . . . .   457 Paddy's Charac   6
   There must another Sett be found.   . . . . 556 Death of Swift   98
SETTING
   With rising or with setting Sun: . . . .   270 Apollo's Edict D 13
   His Policy consists in setting Traps, ...   535 To Mr. Gay   121
   To-morrow, ere the setting Sun, ...   694 Cadenus Vaness   254
SETTLE
   How best to settle their Affections;   . . . . 182 Horace 2, 1   56
   When all the Bees are gone to settle, ...   775 Mullinix Tim   45
   Your Stomach they settle, ... 953 Oysters   7
SETTLED
   And settled Europe's Grand Affairs, ...   181 Horace 2, 1   40
   This Point must needs be settled first;   . . . . . .   589 Strephon Chloe   165
SETTLEMENT
   He blew a Settlement along: . . . .   585 Strephon Chloe   40
SETTLES
   And there neglected Flora settles   . . . .   901 Dean's Reasons   93
SEV'N
   Twice sev'n long Years the Court attends, ...   481 Libel on D- D-   54
   Left all below at Six and Sev'n, ...   714 Cadenus Vaness   888
SEV'RAL
   Their sev'ral Talents to your Wit, ...   890 Panegyr Dean   126

SEVEN
 Chief cherub, and chief lamp of that high sacred Seven,   34 Ode Sancroft   3
 And I had in a Purse, seven Pound, four Shillings and.   69 Mrs Harris Pet   2
     . .
 'Tis true, seven Pound, four Shillings, and six Pence,.   71 Mrs Harris Pet   40
     . .
 Seven and Ten addyd to nyne, ...   102 Merlin   1
 On seven Score Sheep, ...   244 Irish-Feast   7
 At Seven, the Dean in Night-gown drest,   278 Journal   9
 But we can afford you Six Traytors in Seven.   . . .   804 Irish Bishops   32
 My Children are seven, ...   951 Apples   6
SEVENTEEN
 In seventeen hundred eight and twenty, ...   456 Dean Smedley   47
SEVERAL
 Were several Years this Man and Wife, ...   116 Bauc & Phil 2   150
 I might have mention'd several facts, ...   280 Journal   61
 And after several Readings over, ...   475 Epist on Epist   13
SEVERE
 Thus did the Muse severe unkindly blame . . . . . .   44 To Congreve   23
 Hypocrisy with Frown severe, ...   448 Modern Lady   126
 Are you on Vices most severe . . . .   449 Modern Lady   152
 And might perhaps be too severe: . . . . . .   602 Beasts Confess   26
 He found, his Virtues too severe . . . .   603 Beasts Confess   55
 And, though by Heaven's severe Decree . . . . .   726 To Stella   103
 You think my jesting too severe: . . . .   751 Stel Wood-Park   74
 I vow to <God> you're too severe. . . . .   775 Mullinix Tim   70
SEVERELY
 Haply you judge these lines severely writ . . . . .   46 To Congreve   109
SEVERN'S
 So have I seen from Severn's Brink . . . .   253 Bubble   53
SEWEL
 Smit with the glorious prize next struts in Sewel,   . .   672 Epig Carthy 24   D 9
SEX
 Is in her Sex a Crime needs no excuse) . . . . .   18 Ode Athenian   65
 Of that proud Tyrant Sex of Hers. . . . .   23 Ode Athenian   237
 Let the vain sex dream on, their Empire comes from Us,   24 Ode Athenian   260
 Still to be of the same exalted Sex with You. . . .   24 Ode Athenian   267
 Or more employ the Female Sex? . . . .   65 Problem   2
 Celia's the Wonder of her Sex; . . . .   227 Prog of Beauty   54
 The Ladys, or Lampoon the Sex. . . . .   281 Journal   78
 Virtue was of this Sex design'd, ...   384 Manly Virtue   23
 One Sex consenting to admire, ...   387 Manly Virtue   129
 Against the Sex to write a Satyre, ...   445 Modern Lady   7
 A Crime to all her Sex unknown1) . . . .   596 Cassinus Peter   104
 Laid all the Fault on t' other Sex. . . . . . .   687 Cadenus Vaness   26
 Of either Sex, among the Crew, ...   689 Cadenus Vaness   102
 Both of her self and Sex asham'd, ...   699 Cadenus Vaness   405
 Yet some of either Sex, endow'd . . . .   700 Cadenus Vaness   444
 Her Sex, with universal Voice, ...   702 Cadenus Vaness   508
 One of her tender Sex and Age. . . . .   705 Cadenus Vaness   579
 And that unless the Sex would mend, ...   713 Cadenus Vaness   862
 "A Model for her Sex design'd, ...   714 Cadenus Vaness   866
 Was more than for her Sex was fit; . . . . . .   723 To Stella   2
 Can Cowardice her Sex adorn, ...   725 To Stella   67
 But, the folly of her sex . . . .   906 Daphne   3
 Of Spleen you cure the Female Sex. . . . . . .   919 Riddle 5   18
 And think of the sex as you please, I'd as lieve . . .   976 Dean to Sherid   15
 To my goddess Melpomene, pride of her sex, ...   979 Dean to Tho: S   23
 I'm sure you cackle like the sex. . . . .   983 Sher, A Goose   18
SEX'S
 For such is all the sex's flight, ...   177 To Lord Harley   19
 Born to retrieve her sex's fame. . . . .   177 To Lord Harley   38
SEXES
 Both Sexes, arm'd with Guilt and Spite, ...   700 Cadenus Vaness   438
 But now in all our Sexes Name, ...   887 Panegyr Dean   5
 (For, 'tis prophane when Sexes mingle; . . . . .   893 Panegyr Dean   209
SEXTON
 The Sexton shall green Sods on thee bestow. . . . .   235 Elegy on Demar   37
 Alas the Sexton is thy Banker now! . . . . . .   235 Elegy on Demar   38
 The Sexton reason'd well, ...   406 Swift to Pope   26
SHA'N'T
 You sha'n't come here nor get a Sous . . . . . .   91 Bauc & Phil 1   39
SHABBY
 (For the Dean was so shabby and look'd like a Ninny, .   872 Grand Question   151
SHADE
 And half Your Virtues had been lost in Shade. . . .   11 Ode to William   D 12
 For this inferior world is but Heaven's dusky shade, . .   35 Ode Sancroft   21
 Phoebus now shortning every Shade, ...   119 Apollo Outwit   1
 Beneath whose ill Shade no Plant ever grew. . . . .   334 Serious Poem   32
 By gen'rous Wines beneath a Shade. . . . . . .   731 Stella, Poems   112
 And here, beneath the spreading Shade, ...   848 Old Thorn   7
 New-River-walk with friendly Shade, ...   884 Rev Market-Hill   51
 For, when by chance the meagre Shade . . . . . .   905 Death Daphne   93
SHADED
 Shews lustre that was shaded in his seat; . . . .   41 Ode Sancroft   212
SHADES
 Who, to pollute my shades, bring'st with thee down . .   44 To Congreve   9
 Rend'ring shades, things, and substances of names; . .   47 To Congreve   148
 To silent Shades repeat thy Verse, ...   121 Apollo Outwit   58
 And let me in these Shades compose . . . . . .   199 Horace 2, 6   D
 His faithful Steward, in the Shades below. . . . .   234 Elegy on Demar   8

		PAGE	TITLE	LINE
SHADES	(CONTINUED)			
And with false flitting Shades our Minds delude,		363	On Dreams	2
Descends for Shelter to the Shades below.		538	Mr. Pulteney	24
May dig in vain in Pluto's Shades.		743	Stel B-day 22	74
She fancy'd, those Elysian Shades		905	Death Daphne	85
My beauty to the Shades below.		927	Riddle 10	D 12
SHADOWING				
Crusts o'er the day, shadowing its parent beam		45	To Congreve	71
SHADOWS				
Must these like empty Shadows pass,		765	Stel B-day '26	51
These, she answer'd, are but Shadows,		833	Legion Club	100
SHADY				
She, who on shady Banks has joy'd to sleep		50	To Congreve	221
"In either Angle shady Bowers:		476	Epist on Epist	52
To silver Meads, and shady Bow'rs,		590	Strephon Chloe	201
The Shelter of a shady Grove:		894	Panegyr Dean	246
SHAFT				
In vain discharging many a Shaft,		701	Cadenus Vaness	477
SHAFTS				
The wily Shafts of State, those Juggler's Tricks		29	Ode to Temple	92
SHAKE				
How the Mouse makes the mighty Mountain shake!		30	Ode to Temple	107
Which to divulge might shake profane belief,		53	Temple Ill	77
Shake it down to the Feet,		246	Irish-Feast	50
And shake it well, and down it comes.		627	Scandal Poem 2	130
Three Morning-Hours you toss and shake		892	Panegyr Dean	179
Accosting; said, Go shake your Cream.		897	Panegyr Dean	326
SHAKES				
And shakes the atheist's knees; such ghastly fear		52	Temple Ill	39
When my Ld shakes him by the hand		421	Ireld	20
She shakes her Helm, she knits her Brows,		694	Cadenus Vaness	252
For, as he shakes his Wainscot Chops,		786	Dick, Maggot	11
SHAKING SEE ALL-SHAKING				
SHAL'T				
Thus <Bob> shal't thou be mawl'd, fly where thou wil't:		538	Mr. Pulteney	38
SHALES				
Nor is old Nanny Shales, whene'er she does brew, sick.		1029	Dr. Helsham	16
SHALL 242			OMITTED WORD	
SHALLON				
In blew shallon, shall Hanniball be Clad,		275	Epilogue	21
SHALLOW				
Our shallow Search and Judgment to direct.		18	Ode Athenian	94
How shallow! and how gross the Cheat!		29	Ode to Temple	101
SHALT 10			OMITTED WORD	
SHAM				
Not a sham Thing of Clay or Cards.		87	Hist V's House	26
(For that's but a Sham Wood they carry about)		336	Serious Poem	76
With sham Quotations Peri Hupsous:		648	On Poetry	256
But I doubt 'tis a Sham,		1015	Swift to Sheri	47
. . . depend on't, in the end, he'll sham ye.		1023	Nim-Dan-Dean 2	D 10
SHAM'D				
Sham'd and amaz'd, beholds the chatt'ring throng,		50	To Congreve	223
What! thou the Spawn of him who sham'd our Isle,		826	Noisy Tom	7
SHAMBLING				
A shambling awkward Gate he took,		95	Bauc & Phil 1	171
SHAME				
Tho' all the Fumes of Fear, Hope, Love, and Shame,		22	Ode Athenian	206
Which 'tis a shame to see how much of late		24	Ode Athenian	254
Let us (for shame) no more be fed		27	Ode to Temple	21
For shame! two sturdy Rascalls beg;		91	Bauc & Phil 1	44
But, most noble Senators, 'tis a great Shame		143	New Song	13
But Bawty, lost to Shame and Honour,		208	Fable Bitches	39
With shame, I have too lately known;		215	To Mr. Delany	2
You keep Your Countenance for shame		218	To Mr. Delany	81
The Neighbors round would cry out Shame.		220	A Quiet Life	36
And thought his Bride had sculk't for shame,		223	Prog of Love	30
Thank God, 'twas neither Shame nor Sin,		224	Prog of Love	59
"And, but for Shame, wou'd say his Pray'rs.		305	Storm	66
For your displeasure is their only shame.		309	Billet Players	52
To have two thousand Pounds a Year, O 'tis a burning Shame!		342	Upon His Grace	18
Call'd want of Shame, a want of Sense,		386	Manly Virtue	81
Or makes 'em sensible of Shame.		453	Modern Lady	275
He waded without any shame,		456	Dean Smedley	23
Begins the World with Fear and Shame,		500	Doctor Delaney	12
"The World must own it, to their Shame;		550	Life of Swift	199
"A Shame, he hath not got a Mitre!		564	Death of Swift	298
Good Father I must own with Shame,		602	Beasts Confess	13
And if it be a Sin or Shame,		602	Beasts Confess	29
Have often practis'd to their Shame.		605	Beasts Confess	140
Through Modesty, or aukward Shame,		607	Beasts Confess	181
O, what Indignity and Shame		654	On Poetry	405
A burning Shame, a crying Sin		659	On Poetry	D 410
A Shame to one so much ador'd		695	Cadenus Vaness	266
Thus, to the World's perpetual Shame,		700	Cadenus Vaness	432
Shame, Disappointment, Guilt, Surprize.		706	Cadenus Vaness	625
Cadenus, to his Grief and Shame,		710	Cadenus Vaness	744
And, full of Anger, Shame, and Grief,		713	Cadenus Vaness	846
And guilty Shame, and servile Fear,		725	To Stella	48
Nor dare distort my Face for shame.		727	To Stella	116
They think it both a Shame and Sin		734	Stel B-day '20	13

SHAME	(CONTINUED)	PAGE	TITLE	LINE
How I should hide my Head for Shame,	. . . . .	741	Stel B-day 22	17
Britain, with Shame confess, this Land of mine	. . .	791	St. Pat's Well	27
To this damnable Speaker had long ow'd a shame;	. . .	816	Yahoo's	37
Make Rundle Bishop; fye for Shame!	. . . .	819	Dr. Rundle	1
I hope to quit that awkward Shame	. . . .	887	Panegyr Dean	17
. . . Fie Mr. Sheridan, 'tis a Shame	. . . .	985	Mary to Sher	5
. . . 'tis both a Shame and a Sin,	. . . . .	985	Mary to Sher	7
Every body knows, that I love to tell Truth and shame the Devil,		986	Mary to Sher	23
The De'el too that ow'd me a Shame,		1005	Sheridan's Sub	21

SHAMEFUL

How would you blush the shameful birth to hear	. . . .	46	To Congreve	85
The dullest Beast and a shameful Jeer,	. . . . . .	941	Letter	41
A long-ear'd Beast, and shameful Vermin,	. . . . .	942	Probatur Alit	21

SHAMELESS

| With shameless Visage, and perfidious Leer, | . . . . | 532 | To Mr. Gay | 34 |
| The Ladies else might think me shameless.) | . . . . . | 586 | Strephon Chloe | 80 |

SHAMES

| It shames his Cassock and his Years | . . . . . . | 294 | Prog Marriage | 140 |

SHAMM'D

| You who in different Sects have shamm'd, | . . . . . | 579 | Day Judgement | 15 |

SHAN'T

It is a sign we shan't stay here.	. . . .	419	Holyhead Journ	4
Your Scholars want the whip,--I shan't demur;--	. . .	671	Epig Carthy 23	D 1
You shan't stir a Foot--You'll think me a Clown--	. . .	869	Grand Question	78

SHANK'D   SEE SPINDLE-SHANK'D

SHANKERS

| Her Shankers, Issues, running Sores, | . . . . . . | 582 | Young Nymph | 30 |

SHANKS

| Bring down Long Shanks Jim too, but now I think on't, . . . | | 1023 | Nim-Dan-Dean 2 | D 11 |

SHAP'D

And shap'd my passion in such words as these.	. . . .	53	Temple Ill	80
To Bus'ness shap'd the Poet's Quil,	. . . . .	482	Libel on D- D-	66
He shap'd a King to rule ye Race	. . . . . .	659	On Poetry	D 410

SHAPE

Here a pale shape with upward footstep treads,	. . . .	35	Ode Sancroft	33
But neither Bulk nor Shape the same:	. . . . . .	81	Vanbrug House	80
Without offence to Human Shape:	. . . .	83	Salamander	6
In it's old shape a Font became	. . . .	93	Bauc & Phil 1	112
But neither Bulk, nor Shape the same:	. . . . . .	109	V's House	122
From Smithfield, or St. Pulchre's shape their Course,	. . .	139	City Shower	58
For Drury-lane to shape thy Stile:	. . . .	181	Horace 2, 1	42
His Lineage, Calling, Shape or Sense	. . . . . .	217	To Mr. Delany	69
We order a Vulture, in Shape of the Spleen,	. . . .	266	Apollo	97
In whom thy Features, Shape, and Mien,	. . . . .	325	Pethox	71
"Only for want of outward Shape)	. . . .	384	Manly Virtue	8
Nor spoil your Shape, distort your Face,	. . . . .	414	Censure	23
"Or snape the Yews to Antick Figure.	. . . . . .	476	Epist on Epist	58
But I only behold thee in Atherton's Shape,	. . . .	518	Dean Hang Rape	47
Her graceful Mein, her Shape, and Face,	. . . . .	584	Strephon Chloe	7
His Shape and Beauty made him proud:	. . . . . .	602	Beasts Confess	38
Jove dresst a Cloud in Juno's shape,	. . . . . .	619	Scandal Poem 1	54
Jove drest a Cloud in Juno's Shape:	. . . . . .	625	Scandal Poem 2	50
Or some worse Brute in human Shape,	. . . . . .	687	Cadenus Vaness	40
Than Titles, Figure, Shape, and Dress;	. . . . .	697	Cadenus Vaness	341
To shape it into Sense and Rhyme;	. . . .	741	Stel B-day 22	10
For, such a Shape of Skin and Bone	. . . .	904	Death Daphne	61
Your Thing of various Shape and Hue,	. . . . . .	912	Aenigma Expl	D 7
Here, in their proper Shape and Mein,	. . . . . .	922	Riddle 7	21
Swelling be my shape or small, ...		937	Riddle 24	D 37

SHAPES

Ne'er borrow'd more variety of Shapes	. . . . . .	22	Ode Athenian	199
Whence the weak shapes wild and imperfect pass,	. . . .	35	Ode Sancroft	23
Disjointing shapes as in the fairy-land of dreams,	. . .	35	Ode Sancroft	39
Nor could the nations kneel to viler shapes,	. . . .	46	To Congreve	105
Like antic shapes in dreams, from waking eyes:	. . . .	54	Temple Ill	100
When Letters are in vulgar Shapes,	. . . .	643	On Poetry	97
Assume the Shapes of filthy Brutes.	. . . . . .	670	Epig Carthy 19	D 2
Crouded round with antic Shapes;	. . . .	832	Legion Club	88
All Shapes and Features I can boast,	. . . . . .	935	Riddle 23	D 10

SHARE

In this Your Virtue claims a double share,	. . . .	12	Ode to William	D 27
Why then does Nature so unjustly share	. . . . .	32	Ode to Temple	180
And that his subjects share his happy influence;	. . .	40	Ode Sancroft	182
Through native dross your share is hardly known,	. . .	45	To Congreve	59
Let's not fall out; We all have Share.	. . . . .	67	Problem	58
And that I may have a Share in next Sunday's Collection:		73	Mrs Harris Pet	71
Where Thou, our latest Proselyte, shalt share:	. . .	162	Toland's Invit	8
Yet to the Dean his Share allot;	. . . .	406	Swift to Pope	17
I think they justly ought to share		422	Ireld	47
Wherein yourselves have greatest Share?	. . . . .	449	Modern Lady	153
When he goes out, you share his fate,	. . . . .	468	Birthday Song	258
"In every Jobb to have a Share,	. . . . . .	571	Death of Swift	451
Thy Friend would gladly share thy Fate.	. . . . .	596	Cassinus Peter	94
Give <George> and Jove an equal Share.	. . . . .	657	On Poetry	486
In vain: her Hearers had no Share	. . . . . .	698	Cadenus Vaness	356
Who gladly would your Suff'rings share;	. . . . .	766	Stel B-day '26	84
Who in the motion have no share;	. . . .	777	Mullinix Tim	127

SHARE   (CONTINUED)

	PAGE	TITLE	LINE
This, dearest Sheelah, thou shalt share with me.	881	Pastoral Dial	28
And on her Plate a treble Share, ...	895	Panegyr Dean	260
Your Mistress a Share, ...	952	Onyons	11

SHARP

When we perform, look sharp among our crew, ...	307	Billet Players	11
But, sure the Dean deserves a sharp Rebuke	678	Dean and Duke	3
Where hot and cold, where sharp and sweet, ...	711	Cadenus Vaness	774
From stomach sharp, and hearty feeding	745	Stel Distress	7
From Stomach sharp and hearty feeding, ...	750	Stel Wood-Park	31
Or sharp pointed rocks, ...	854	Lady's Lament	81
Sharp are the Stones, take thou this rushy Matt; . .	881	Pastoral Dial	19
My Genius piercing, sharp and bright, ...	920	Riddle 6	5

SHARPER

But if a Sharper once comes in, ...	253	Bubble	63
a sharper in trifles a dupe in the main	540	Charac Walpole	4
The Sharper swore he hated Play, ...	607	Beasts Confess	187
If Chloe were a Sharper still, ...	905	Death Daphne	77

SHARPERS

While English sharpers take the pay, ...	421	Ireld	9
We lose with Sharpers at Piquet;	724	To Stella	28

SHARPEST

And even the sharpest eye that has the prospect seen, .	41	Ode Sancroft	207
And thus deceive the sharpest Eye:	607	Beasts Confess	194

SHARPING

Try'd ev'ry sharping Trick for Bread, ...	456	Dean Smedley	25

SHATTER'D

My spirit's quite shatter'd, ...	853	Lady's Lament	52

SHAVE

Nor, twice a week will shave his beard.	879	Robbin & Harry	44

SHAVER

(This Lewis is a Cunning Shaver, ...	171	Horace 1, 7	17

SHE 456		OMITTED WORD	
SHE'D 11		OMITTED WORD	
SHE'LL 18		OMITTED WORD	
SHE'S 23		OMITTED WORD	

SHEARS

Nor will be able with her shears	760	Bec's B-Day	5
While his own ass's Zaggs were more fit for the shears.	816	Yahoo's	49
That a sieve dissolves riddles by help of the shears; .	976	Dean to Sherid	20
To break open riddles with shears or with scissars. . .	976	Dean to Sherid	22

SHEATH

It melts the Sword of War, yet keeps it in the Sheath.	29	Ode to Temple	91

SHEBA'S

Shews Sheba's Queen completely drest, ...	592	Strephon Chloe	287
Upon the Queen of Sheba's lap.	776	Mullinix Tim	110

SHED

May all the Blood, which shall by Womans scorn be shed	23	Ode Athenian	245
Kind Star, still may'st thou shed thy sacred influence here,	39	Ode Sancroft	154
But do not shed thy Influence down	100	Elegy Patrige	95
Commence Acquaintance underneath a Shed.	138	City Shower	40
The Wine, his Blood, our Predecessors shed: . . .	162	Toland's Invit	12
Then Reader pray shed some tears of Salt Water, . .	430	Dicky Dolly	17

SHEDDING

A dismal shedding of her Locks	85	Salamander	67

SHEDS

And sheds, tho' all unseen, his sacred influence here. .	39	Ode Sancroft	153
Then sheds about his Spaun, and dyes.	80	Vanbrug House	38

SHEELAH

When Sheelah strip't	441	Ballyspellin	38
A Nymph and Swain, Sheelah and Dermot hight, . . .	880	Pastoral Dial	1
My Love to Sheelah is more firmly fixt	880	Pastoral Dial	9
This, dearest Sheelah, thou shalt share with me. . . .	881	Pastoral Dial	28
How could you, Sheelah, listen to his Tales, . . .	882	Pastoral Dial	35
In vain we make poor Sheelah toil, ...	1035	To Quilca	7

SHEEP

Near better animals, her father's sheep;	50	To Congreve	222
On seven Score Sheep, ...	244	Irish-Feast	7
Feed nothing in your lands but sheep	422	Ireld	56
Like a Rogue that steals a Sheep:	800	Traulus 2	36
And yet the Cow, the Sheep, the Bee, ...	936	Riddle 24 D	3
A long-ear'd Beast, and the Child of a Sheep, . . .	943	Probatur Alit	31

SHEEP'S

"You cast a Sheep's Eye on her Ladyship's Maid; . .	872	Grand Question	148

SHEEPISH

For, conscious of his Sheepish Gait, ...	376	Apology Lady C	32

SHEER

For sheer Wit, and Humour passes!	523	Betty Grizette	34

SHEERS

"No Sheers to check her sprouting Vigour, ...	476	Epist on Epist	57

SHEET   SEE WINDING-SHEET

In this descending sheet you'll haply find	50	To Congreve	231
But seldom rose above a Sheet:	172	Horace 1, 7	42
The winnowing Sheet.	246	Irish-Feast	52

SHEETS   SEE WINDING-SHEETS

And rather than come in the same Pair of Sheets . . .	869	Grand Question	59

SHELF

She threw her Law-books on the Shelf, ...	691	Cadenus Vaness	140
And from the Shelf a charming Crust I whipt: . . .	881	Pastoral Dial	30

	PAGE	TITLE	LINE
SHELLING			
Who Sowins make with Shelling	441	Ballyspellin	33
SHELLS			
When Shells and Leather shall for Money pass, . . .	793	St. Pat's Well	93
SHELTER			
There, near thy Master's Throne in Shelter plac't, .	538	Mr. Pulteney	11
Descends for Shelter to the Shades below.	538	Mr. Pulteney	24
To his arbor for shelter, ...	857	Lady's Lament	192
Just big enough to shelter two in;	878	Robbin & Harry	22
The Shelter of a shady Grove:	894	Panegyr Dean	246
SHELVES			
Let the Vessel split on Shelves, ...	635	Epistle Lady	161
Bind them fast, or from the Shelves	838	Legion Club	209
SHEPHERD			
And to the Shepherd own'd her flame.	178	To Lord Harley	76
How thy Face charms ev'ry Shepherd, ...	522	Betty Grizette	3
For whom no Shepherd sighs in vain;	581	Young Nymph	2
And ev'ry Shepherd was undone	705	Cadenus Vaness	582
The Shepherd in his Bower might sleep or sing, . .	792	St. Pat's Well	41
Why should my Shepherd take amiss	924	Riddle 8	9
SHEPHERDS			
Nor Shepherds use poetick Cant:	270	Apollo's Edict	D 28
Expiring Shepherds at their Feet;	590	Strephon Chloe	200
The Shepherds and the Nymphs were seen	686	Cadenus Vaness	1
SHERIDAN			
Not Sheridan, but friend Delany.	278	Journal	6
The Dean and Sheridan, I hope, ...	313	To Ford	73
Has this any likeness to good Madam Sheridan? . .	955	Portrait Life	10
Friend Sheridan, when will you know your own Good? . .	968	Letter Sherid	24
. . . Fie Mr. Sheridan, 'tis a Shame	985	Mary to Sher	5
Knave in your Teeth, Mr. Sheridan, ...	985	Mary to Sher	7
However, they own it is very civil in Mr. Sheridan, . .	1014	Swift to Sheri	8
Dear Sheridan; a loving Pair	1020	Nim-Dan-Dean 1	D 1
But how, Mr. Sheridan, came you to venture . . .	1027	Sheri Circles	13
while <Grattan>, <Sheridan>, and I, ...	499	Panegyr Swift	177
How <Sheridan> the Rogue would sneer, ...	741	Stel B-day 22	20
While <Sheridan> is off the hooks, ...	756	Stel B-day '24	11
SHERIDAN'S			
And Sheridan's perpetual teazings.	753	Gift for Bec	8
SHERRY			
Dan's noble Mettle, Sherry base;	1004	Dan J's Reply	31
If SHE makes sher, and RI makes ry, ...	1004	Dan J's Reply	35
Poor Sherry, inglorious, ...	1004	Sheridan's Sub	1
SHERRY'S			
For Sherry's Quibbles, and thy Skill	373	Letter D. S-y	49
SHEW			
To shew the Paths of both must be together trod, . . .	7	Ode to King	29
To shew the Flood begins to cease, ...	16	Ode Athenian	20
And to all future Mankind shew	25	Ode Athenian	304
To shew it cost its Price in War, ...	28	Ode to Temple	75
Shew the Delights thy Sister Nature yields, ...	31	Ode to Temple	137
The figures all inverted shew, ...	35	Ode Sancroft	31
Be not the brightest pattern Earth can shew . . .	36	Ode Sancroft	52
How the physicians swarm to shew their mortal skill, . .	42	Ode Sancroft	253
No wonder, since wise Authors shew, ...	87	Hist V's House	39
But with the upside doun to shew	92	Bauc & Phil 1	99
To shew his Skill, he Mars would join	99	Elegy Patrige	59
But with the Upside down, to shew	113	Bauc & Phil 2	59
And goes with Folks to shew the Sight:	116	Bauc & Phil 2	168
The Philosophic Cause will shew.	126	Little House	4
The God of Wit to shew his Grudge.	157	Fable of Midas	29
At Monarchy we nobly shew our Spight, ...	163	Toland's Invit	15
York is from Lambeth sent, to shew the Queen . .	195	Author Himself	47
And, as a Proof, shew num'rous Scars	324	Pethox	13
You may shew him about for a new Groaning Board. .	336	Serious Poem	84
And sell them for Gold, or he can't shew his Love else,	337	Serious Poem	98
And, secondly, to shew my Fury	348	Whitshed Motto	13
But first resolv'd, to shew his Taste	378	Apology Lady C	97
If Clergymen, to shew their Wit, ...	392	Young's Satire	39
(As we shall shew you in the Sequel)	446	Modern Lady	37
You pawn'd to him?-- "First shew him up.	446	Modern Lady	59
Poor Envy durst not shew her Phiz, ...	456	Dean Smedley	21
But here's enough to shew your Style.	463	Birthday Song	82
Presume to shew his mortal snout, ...	464	Birthday Song	144
With so much beauty, shew me any maid	466	Birthday Song	189
You shew you Skill in Grecian Story, ...	483	Libel on D- D-	97
To Flatter, Carve, and shew your Wit;	483	Libel on D- D-	106
And shew us, <England> is our Master:	484	Libel on D- D-	126
Would shew you many a Statesman's Face.	485	Libel on D- D-	180
Who have, to shew your great Devotion, ...	495	Panegyr Swift	60
Rightly you snew, that Wit alone	495	Panegyr Swift	72
Then shew, how Statesmen oft are stung	496	Panegyr Swift	114
Shew Reason, Grammer, Truth, or Sense?	503	Doctor Delaney	104
Shew me the same numerick Flea, ...	504	Doctor Delaney	141
Yet, come in time to shew their Loves, ...	547	Life of Swift	64
Against the Court to shew his Spight---.	550	Life of Swift	189
"Pray, do but give me leave to shew 'em;	563	Death of Swift	269
Or shew the Anguish, Toil, and Pain, ...	583	Young Nymph	69
'Tis Time to shew how Things went there.	588	Strephon Chloe	146
Some shew they never want explaining, ...	592	Strephon Chloe	275
Not all the Court of Heav'n could shew	597	Problem Solved	9

		PAGE	TITLE	LINE
SHEW	(CONTINUED)			
He'd shew his Face before the <King>:	. . . . . .	602	Beasts Confess	34
Strange pride and insolence you shew,	. . . .	617	Scandal Poem 1	3
Than to shew their Vices odious:	. . . .	637	Epistle Lady	226
She ne'er could shew her Face above.	. . . .	689	Cadenus Vaness	82
Wou'd shew the Merits of the Cause,	. . . . . .	690	Cadenus Vaness	134
For Pastime, or to shew his Wit;	. . . .	703	Cadenus Vaness	543
Nor spend their Time to shew their Reading;	. . . .	713	Cadenus Vaness	848
To shew she did not judge amiss,	. . . .	713	Cadenus Vaness	855
As Tradesmen shew their Trash at first:)	. . . . .	728	Stella, Poems	22
To shew you where your Error lies,	. . . . . .	730	Stella, Poems	90
You shew Don Carlos where to dwell,	. . . . . .	748	Stel Distress	73
And shew them his wit and his learning;	. . . . . .	756	Dingley Brent	9
Oh, ne'er may Fortune shew her Spight,	. . . . .	758	Stel B-day '24	53
Shew Fire and Faggot in the Tail on't?	. . . . .	774	Mullinix Tim	20
Uniting all, to shew their Amity,	. . . .	811	Bro Protestant	9
Keeper, shew me where to fix	. . . .	835	Legion Club	145
I can shew two hundred more.	. . . .	839	Legion Club	238
I'll shew you the way:	. . . .	855	Lady's Lament	131
The Captain, to shew he is proud of the Favour,	. . .	870	Grand Question	103
I will shew no anger needless.	. . . .	908	Daphne	60
Shew your poverty of spirit,	. . . .	908	Daphne	75
Can shew more different Hues than I;	. . . . . .	911	Aenigma	4
The Scholar could not shew his Reading.	. . . . .	916	Riddle 1	32
I'll shew the World strange Things and true;	. . . .	919	Riddle 5	14
First I shew you but a Quarter,	. . . . . .	927	Riddle 10	D 3
No Lady alive can shew such a Skin.	. . . . . .	928	Riddle 13	D 2
And fairly shew a Reason, why	. . . .	930	Riddle 15	D 19
And shew where they can best confute.	. . . . .	930	Riddle 15	D 24
Then, since I shew as fine a Face,	. . . . . .	932	Riddle 19	D 11
Can shew a Nose, Eye, Tongue, or Ear,	. . . . .	935	Riddle 23	D 8
Shew me the brightest Irish Toast,	. . . . . .	993	On Picture	22
Will shew yourself a Lion.	. . . .	1005	Sheridan's Sub	16
Or else, to shew their learned Labour, you	. . . .	1021	Nim-Dan-Dean 1	D 41
SHEW'D				
The <Duke> shew'd me all his fine House; and the		143	New Song	15
<Duchess>				
And shew'd some Humour in his Face;	. . . . .	170	Horace 1, 7	8
Shew'd her the Virtues all combin'd,	. . . . . .	178	To Lord Harley	51
Nor shew'd the Parson in his Gait or Face;	. . . .	194	Author Himself	14
It shew'd the Visage of a Gyant.	. . . . . .	527	Lady's Dres Rm	62
In vain, the Workmen shew'd his Wit	. . . . . .	528	Lady's Dres Rm	75
Refin'd it first, and shew'd its Use.	. . . . .	555	Death of Swift	58
"And shew'd by one satyric Touch,	. . . . . .	572	Death of Swift	481
And shew'd but little of their Art;	. . . . . .	692	Cadenus Vaness	173
Shew'd Patterns just from India brought,	. . . . .	698	Cadenus Vaness	378
It shew'd a true Paternal Care--	. . . . . .	707	Cadenus Vaness	653
Who shew'd a better Jus divinum?	. . . . . .	820	Dr. Rundle	38
No new-flux't Rake shew'd fairer Skin;	. . . . .	904	Death Daphne	37
SHEWING				
On whose Petition (humbly shewing	. . . . . .	713	Cadenus Vaness	860
SHEWN				
Whose name must not within my lines be shewn,	. . . .	48	To Congreve	167
Shewn through a multiplying Glass	. . . . . .	255	Bubble	119
Besides you Songsters oft have shewn,	. . . . .	465	Birthday Song	163
And with Ruffles to be shewn,	. . . . . .	573	Helter Skelter	19
How well his publick Thrift is shewn?	. . . . .	659	On Poetry	D 416
SHEWS				
The crazy composition shews,	. . . .	38	Ode Sancroft	137
Shews lustre that was shaded in his seat;	. . . .	41	Ode Sancroft	212
Shews in the front the ambition of my wit;	. . . .	44	To Congreve	36
Down falls the summer's pride, and sadly shews	. . .	55	Temple Ill	123
which plainly shews the near Alliance	. . . . .	98	Elegy Patrige	29
Shews how the Art of Cobling bears	. . . . . .	99	Elegy Patrige	39
While Partridge wisely shews the Cause	. . . . .	228	Prog of Beauty	89
For Cackling shews the Goose is poor.	. . . . .	230	Prog of Poetry	8
It shews the Queen of Love intends	. . . . . .	254	Bubble	95
Shews all her Secrets of House keeping,	. . . . .	282	Journal	87
Yet Galen most acutely shews you,	. . . . . .	367	Answer Delaney	31
Now rais'd on high, see, Virtue shews	. . . . .	386	Manly Virtue	97
Shews all the malice of a Tory,	. . . . . .	489	Dialogue	26
For Gulliver divinely shews,	. . . .	498	Panegyr Swift	167
"It clearly shews that all Reflection	. . . . .	563	Death of Swift	275
"He shews, as sure as God's in Gloc'ster,	. . . .	564	Death of Swift	293
Shews Sheba's Queen completely drest,	. . . . .	592	Strephon Chloe	287
That Phebus ever shews his face;	. . . . . .	621	Scandal Poem 1	132
You see how sawcily he shews	. . . .	621	Scandal Poem 1	135
The Hawker shews you one in Print,	. . . . . .	644	On Poetry	113
It shews and discovers it self through a Trifle.	. . .	716	Answer Rebus	12
Rebecca shews they're out in that.	. . . . . .	761	Bec's B-Day	8
If Punch, to spur their fancy, shews	. . . . .	776	Mullinix Tim	103
One shews how bravely Audoin Dy'd,	. . . . . .	781	Mullinix Tim	273
Shews a Bribe in all his Hands:	. . . . . .	833	Legion Club	104
Shews all his gew-gaws,	. . . .	857	Lady's Lament	179
SHIELD				
Broke on his everlasting Shield.	. . . . . .	8	Ode to King	71
In Vain he brings his Brazen Shield.	. . . . .	340	Arch-Bish Dub	24
To shield the infant Fruits and Flowers,	. . . .	387	Manly Virtue	109
SHIFT				
Does make a wretched Shift,	. . . .	75	Game Traffick	D 27
Thus far advanc't, he made a shift	. . . . . .	108	V's House	91

SHIFT   (CONTINUED)   PAGE   TITLE   LINE
   But, shift him to a better scene, ...   435 Answer Paulus   117
   Here shift the Scene, to represent . . . .   561 Death of Swift   205
   But, now shou'd fortune shift the scene, ...   676 Parson's Case   19
   Shift the Scene for half an Hour, ...   832 Legion Club   77
   Cut from the Piece that made her Shift, ...   925 Riddle 8   42
SHIFTING
   By often shifting into distant Grounds; . . . . . .   538 Mr. Pulteney   18
SHILLING
   Thus in a Basin drop a Shilling, ...   251 Bubble   9
   A Shilling in the Bath You fling, ...   255 Bubble   113
   And now she will not have a Shilling . . . . . .   409 Dial Rich Marb   25
   A Shilling to discharge his Chair, ...   481 Libel on D- D-   42
   He ravish'd her fairly, and sav'd a good Shilling; .   519 Dean Hang Rape   57
   To raise the Volume's Price, a Shilling.) . . . .   648 On Poetry   254
   Throws the last shilling in his purse, ...   878 Robbin & Harry   2
SHILLINGS
   And I had in a Purse, seven Pound, four Shillings and.   69 Mrs Harris Pet   2
     . .
   'Tis true, seven Pound, four Shillings, and six Pence,.   71 Mrs Harris Pet   40
     . .
   Of Value five Shillings, in English a Pencil; . . .   264 Apollo   34
   And all the Rent I pay is scarce five Shillings in the   342 Upon His Grace   22
     Pound.
   Now pay four Shillings in the Pound. . . . .   409 Dial Rich Marb   28
   And I think I may say, you cou'd many good shillings get   979 Dean to Tho: S   9
SHIN-BONES
   Of Shin-Bones rotted by the Pox. . . . .   904 Death Daphne   40
SHINE   SEE MOON-SHINE,SUN-SHINE,OUT-SHINE
   When the Bright Sun of Peace began to shine,   . . .   16 Ode Athenian   24
   But sees thy meteor blaze about me shine, ...   54 Temple Ill   91
   With Coat embroider'd richly shine, ...   182 Horace 2, 1   74
   But shall with unattainted Honour shine; . . . .   210 Earl of Oxford   8
   And chiefly chuse to shine by Night. . . . .   228 Prog of Beauty   72
   Then, it must be allow'd, whenever I shine, ...   263 Apollo   7
   And the Titles I view, when I shine on the Walls: .   263 Apollo   24
   That old rotten Wood will Shine in the Dark. . . .   334 Serious Poem   8
   He now shall shine in nobler Scenes: . . . . . .   385 Manly Virtue   52
   To shine the more still rising higher) . . . . .   385 Manly Virtue   54
   Was equally allowed to shine, ...   455 Dean Smedley   3
   For yours can shine both day and night, ...   462 Birthday Song   66
   Can shine, without him is extinct. . . . .   465 Birthday Song   178
   Your Simile may better shine . . . .   486 Libel on D- D-   193
   How to shine in Conversation, ...   630 Epistle Lady   23
   To shine, where all the gay resort, ...   677 Parson's Case   27
   How she might shine in the Grand-Monde, ...   705 Cadenus Vaness   581
   And, though in Miniature, you shine, ...   752 Stel Wood-Park   84
   To shine through Life's declining Part. . . . . .   764 Stel B-day '26   34
   When pelted all with Dirt they shine; . . . . .   787 Clad in Brown   20
   And coxcombs in red ribbons shine: . . . . . .   876 To Dean Swift   22
   And whenso're you please to shine, ...   919 Riddle 5   9
   I With borrow'd Silver shine, ...   927 Riddle 10   D   1
   I with double lustre shine. . . . .   936 Riddle 24   D 12
   Like thyself I shine in all. . . . .   937 Riddle 24   D 38
   If once in your cellar my Phoebus should shine, . . .   979 Dean to Tho: S   29
   'Tis of Shine, a Mouth Moon-full, ... 1015 Swift to Sheri   49
   And the worst of them all like a barn door did shine . 1017 Swift Ans Sher   6
SHINES
   With its own Light Your dazling Glory shines,   . . .   11 Ode to William D   7
   Thus Patrige still shines in each Art, ...   100 Elegy Patrige   69
   By Harley's Favour once again he shines; . . . . .   196 Author Himself   63
   Where Wit in all its Glory shines; . . . . . .   361 Grace's Answer   2
   He shines distinguish'd in a College; . . . . .   384 Manly Virtue   34
   Now, on the Bench fair Justice shines, ...   391 Young's Satire   15
   Shines in all Climates like a Star; . . . . . .   398 Earl of P-b-w   31
   But Carolina shines the clearer . . . .   466 Birthday Song   179
   It shines most in the Marble Cover. . . . . . .   475 Epist on Epist   14
   From Ludgate shines to Temple-bar. . . . . . .   650 On Poetry   304
   Who shines alone, without a Mate. . . . .   656 On Poetry   442
   Perhaps you say Augustus shines . . . .   658 On Poetry   D 410
   As Years increase, she brighter shines, ...   703 Cadenus Vaness   536
   Truth shines the brighter, clad in Verse; . . . .   729 Stella, Poems   58
   In you, each Virtue brighter shines, ...   739 Stel B-day '21   9
   How your superior Learning shines . . . .   888 Panegyr Dean   63
SHINING
   With gawdy Coat, and shining Train, ...   83 Salamander   31
   There shining 'midst his Train, to Grace . . . .   477 Epist on Epist   81
   From gold brocade and shining armour, ...   879 Robbin & Harry   41
SHINS
   Who gets a Cold, who break their Shins. . . . . .   280 Journal   64
   Scorcht were his Shins, his Legs were bare, . . .   594 Cassinus Peter   17
SHIP   SEE CURATE-SHIP
   A Kingdom to a Ship compare; . . . .   96 On the Union   14
   Under one Roof, or in one Ship with me. . . . . .   210 Earl of Oxford   18
   <Zounds> I would ship her for Jamaica. . . . . .   220 A Quiet Life   31
   To ship a rogue, and pay him not a groat. . . . . .   308 Billet Players   28
   I see the ship at anchor ride . . . .   420 Holyhead   8
   His Ld ship as Wharton . . . .   423 Carterets Arms   6
   'Twas Greenwich. There he took a Ship, ...   456 Dean Smedley   43
   To venture in a Ship decay'd? . . . .   703 Cadenus Vaness   533
   Let me suppose thee for a Ship a-while, ...   770 Horace 1, 14   7

		PAGE	TITLE	LINE
SHIP	(CONTINUED)			
Unhappy Ship, thou art return'd in Vain:	. . . . .	770	Horace 1, 14	9
Except when I trade with a Ship or a Town,	. . . .	927	Riddle 11	D 7
The quickest Ship I can surprize,	. . . .	934	Riddle 21	D 14
SHIPS				
Our Merchant Ships may cut the Line,	. . . . . .	168	Peace Dunkirk	21
Restore the Ships by Philip taken,	. . . . . .	468	Birthday Song	249
As Ships are toss't by Waves and Wind,	. . . . .	589	Strephon Chloe	170
In Ships decay'd no Mariner confides,	. . . . . .	771	Horace 1, 14	47
SHIPWRECKS				
A savage Race by Shipwrecks fed,	. . . .	256	Bubble	154
SHIRT				
A ragged Shirt, and tawny Hyde.	. . . . . .	594	Cassinus Peter	16
Nor scow'rs the Streets without a Shirt;	. . . .	788	Dick's Variety	16
When his envenom'd Shirt he wore,	. . . . . .	925	Riddle 8	39
Nor less that Shirt, my Rival's Gift,	. . . . . .	925	Riddle 8	41
SHIRTS				
And with Holland Shirts so white,	. . . . . .	573	Helter Skelter	21
Shirts becoming to the sight,	. . . .	573	Helter Skelter	22
Shirts be wrought with different Letters,	. . . . .	573	Helter Skelter	23
<SHIT>				
Tho' on a Throne, wou'd fall to <shit>.	. . . . . .	66	Problem	20
Not only what themselves have <shit>	. . . . . .	497	Panegyr Swift	118
SHITS				
Oh! Celia, Celia, Celia shits!	. . . . . .	529	Lady's Dres Rm	118
Oh! Caelia, Caelia Caelia <shits>.	. . . . . .	597	Cassinus Peter	118
SHIV'RING				
now trembling Shiv'ring Quiv'ring Quaking,	. . . .	959	Cantata	
SHIVER				
On Icy Caucasus to shiver,	. . . .	346	Prometheus	55
SHOALS				
Whilst thus I write, vast shoals of critics come,	. .	50	To Congreve	213
SHOCK				
Contrive to shock your Minds, with many a sensless doubt,		22	Ode Athenian	207
And thus the Steeple got a Shock;	. . . . . .	127	Little House	16
And Shock her Tresses fill'd with Fleas.	. . . . .	583	Young Nymph	64
And shock our Sense, till we bestow.	. . . . . .	667	Epig Carthy 6	D 4
SHOCKING				
"No Madam, 'tis a shocking Sight,	. . . . . .	562	Death of Swift	235
SHOCKS				
A Crime that shocks all human Kind;	. . . . . .	595	Cassinus Peter	68
SHOD				
With Brass two fiery Steeds he shod,	. . . . .	352	Wood Ironmongr	11
Or, like a Cat with Walnuts shod,	. . . . . .	885	Rev Market-Hill	73
SHOE				
From a Shoe Sole to reach the Skies;	. . . . .	98	Elegy Patrige	22
Smoother than Pegasus' old Shoe,	. . . . . .	1021	Nim-Dan-Dean 1	D 7
SHOE-BOYS				
Make all true Patriots up to Shoe-boys	. . . . .	501	Doctor Delaney	61
Thus all the Footmen, Shoe-boys, Porters,	. . . .	812	Bro Protestant	21
SHOEBOY				
Worthy Offspring of a Shoeboy,	. . . .	831	Legion Club	68
SHOEING				
And whence we claim our shoeing horns,	. . . . .	99	Elegy Patrige	38
SHOES				
On t' other side (laid out for Shoes);	. . . . .	60	Lady Tablebook	14
Upon their Shoes the Romans wore,	. . . . . .	99	Elegy Patrige	36
Either for Almanacks or Shoes.	. . . . . .	99	Elegy Patrige	46
Beneath, and mended Shoes in Hell.	. . . . . .	100	Elegy Patrige	68
His Pills, his Almanacks, or Shoes.	. . . . .	101	Elegy Patrige	108
Walke sans wetynge Shoes ne hosen.	. . . . .	102	Merlin	4
Will hardly find his Wife in Shoes.	. . . . . .	292	Prog Marriage	70
Nor unsuccessful waits for dead Mens Shoes.	. . . .	364	On Dreams	30
His Beaver brush'd, his Shoes, and Gown,	. . . .	376	Apology Lady C	27
Was easy, though they wanted Shoes;	. . . . .	481	Libel on D- D-	40
"Why, is he dead without his Shoes?	. . . . .	560	Death of Swift	191
"To talk with Wits in dirty Shoes:	. . . . .	565	Death of Swift	322
Nor Boy brought up to cleaning Shoes,	. . . . .	641	On Poetry	35
And stays at home for want of Shoes:	. . . . .	728	Stella, Poems	28
And after, me thought, I had lost my new Shoes;	. . .	868	Grand Question	51
By these embroider'd high Heel Shoes,	. . . . .	885	Rev Market-Hill	63
These gaudy Shoes must Hannah place	. . . . .	885	Rev Market-Hill	67
The Shoes put on; our faithful Portress	. . . . .	885	Rev Market-Hill	69
They place before him Gloves and Shoes;	. . . .	885	Rev Market-Hill	78
She sent her Priests in Wooden Shoes	. . . . .	895	Panegyr Dean	263
Here, when my Shoes are out of case,	. . . . .	896	Panegyr Dean	311
Strengthens the Shoes of half the Rabble.	. . . .	942	Probatur Alit	12
More than the Dirt beneath my Shoes, nor fear it.	. .	1003	Dan J's Reply	15
A great want of Shoes:	. . . .	1036	Plague Country	2
SHOLE				
A Shole of Herrings down his Maw.	. . . . . .	651	On Poetry	324
SHONE				
He that has shone with Betterton and Weeks,	. . .	308	Billet Players	44
Roses of richest Dye, that shone	. . . . .	379	Apology Lady C	113
The thousand Decencies, that shone	. . . . .	384	Manly Virtue	27
Poor Cynthia never shone so bright,	. . . . .	465	Birthday Song	175
Shone ever such a Constellation.	. . . . . .	656	On Poetry	466
The Child with native Beauty shone,	. . . . .	692	Cadenus Vaness	175
SHOOK				
Harry look'd fierce, and shook his ragged Mane:	. . .	168	Peace Dunkirk	17
"When such a Tempest shook the Land,	. . . . .	568	Death of Swift	389

SHOOK   (CONTINUED)   PAGE   TITLE   LINE
    Jove, nodding, shook the Heav'ns, and said, ...   579 Day Judgement   10
SHOOT
    Sid's Scepter, full of Juice, did shoot   . . . . .   134 Magician's Rod   71
    Not for his skill to shoot the dart;   . . . .   432 Answer Paulus   18
    And making one luxuriant Shoot   . . . .   730 Stella, Poems   67
    And strongly shoot a radiant Dart, ...   764 Stel B-day '26   33
    The Neighbours all cry, Shoot him dead, ...   797 Traulus 1   39
SHOOTING
    A coming Show'r your shooting Corns presage, ...   137 City Shower   9
    Instead of your maiming, your shooting, or banging,   . .   818 Epigr Kite   7
SHOOTS
    Shoots to the Earth and dies;   . . . .   29 Ode to Temple   84
    That rais'd between the Stones their daily Shoots;   . .   880 Pastoral Dial   4
SHOP
    The dearest in Charles Mather's Shop, ...   135 Magician's Rod   76
    Now Curl his Shop from Rubbish drains;   . . . . .   560 Death of Swift   197
    He searcheth all his Shop in vain;   . . . .   563 Death of Swift   257
    He's powd'ring in a Barber's Shop;   . . . .   788 Dick's Variety   32
SHOPKEEPERS
    And all we poor Shopkeepers must our Horns pull in.   .   237 Excellent Song   16
SHOPS
    To Shops in Crouds the dagged Females fly, ...   138 City Shower   33
    They'll cry, Ye Shops, upon us fall   . . . .   241 Run Bankers   59
    At one she rambles to the Shops   . . . .   291 Prog Marriage   51
    He shuns Apothecary's Shops;   . . . .   605 Beasts Confess   133
    First issu'd from Perfumers Shops   . . . .   696 Cadenus Vaness   316
SHORE
    A Peaceful and a Flourishing Shore: . . . . . .   17 Ode Athenian   35
    And when I almost reach the Shore   . . . .   32 Ode to Temple   194
    Nor to the Shore approach too nigh, ...   257 Bubble   174
    Cart'ret was welcom'd to the Shore   . . . .   338 Wood's Brass   1
    To let me kiss your other shore?   . . . .   403 Window Inns 10   D 8
    To reach that slavish hateful shore   . . . .   420 Holyhead   20
    Else, rather on this bleaky shore   . . . .   420 Holyhead   29
    Avoid the Rocks on Britain's angry Shore: . . . .   772 Horace 1, 14   62
SHORT
    Has finish'd its short Race of Chance, ...   10 Ode to King   137
    Of Conquest in your your short and Happy Reign;   . . .   25 Ode Athenian   303
    Short glimm'rings of the prelate glorify'd;   . . . .   41 Ode Sancroft   213
    And by short views mistook for all their own;   . . . .   45 To Congreve   60
    Stay while I tell my story, short, and true;   . . . .   46 To Congreve   111
    Should spring such short and transitory kinds,   . . .   47 To Congreve   128
    Take this short lesson from the god of bayes, ...   49 To Congreve   203
    Some short refreshment for your weary mind, ...   50 To Congreve   232
    In short, they both were turn'd to Yews.   . . . . .   116 Bauc & Phil 2   164
    In short, the Gudgeon took the Bait: . . . . . .   173 Horace 1, 7   80
    But now, to make my Story Short   . . . .   220 A Quiet Life   25
    Their Journy long, their Money short;   . . . . . .   224 Prog of Love   76
    In short our Kings and Princesses within, ...   275 Epilogue   27
    In short, he was an able Sculler.   . . . .   286 Elegy Boat   44
    In short such dire Confusions follow'd, ...   346 Prometheus   45
    For still you're short (which grieves your Spirit)   . .   475 Epist on Epist   27
    Is of short Sessions a long Hist'ry;   . . . .   493 Panegyr Swift   32
    "And, oh! how short are human Schemes!   . . . . .   567 Death of Swift   371
    Their Empire holds so short a Reign;   . . . .   591 Strephon Chloe   256
    In short; Apollo had no Beard.   . . . .   598 Problem Solved   32
    His Ears are half a Foot too short;   . . . .   602 Beasts Confess   32
    A Cripple with one Foot too short: . . . .   645 On Poetry   172
    Short by the Knees intreat for Peace.   . . . . . .   655 On Poetry   424
    If one short Volume cou'd comprise   . . . .   708 Cadenus Vaness   696
    <Zounds> Sir. But to be short and serious   . . . . .   774 Mullinix Tim   33
    Wou'd you wish to be wrap'd in a Rochet--In short.   . .   808 Advice Parson   9
    And take a short Dinner here with us to-Day: . . . .   871 Grand Question   120
    Must argue with calmness, or else will come short on't.   .   976 Dean to Sherid   12
    But now I'll write short, for fear you're short taken.   .   980 Tho: Sheridan   6
    But now I'll write short, for fear you're short taken.   .   980 Tho: Sheridan   6
    For he says, short as 'tis, it will give you a stool.   .   980 Tho: Sheridan   8
    The long and the short, ... 1015 Swift to Sheri   41
    Thy Words so closely wedg'd, and short are, ... 1021 Nim-Dan-Dean 1   D 21
    Nor can we think your Measure short, ... 1022 Nim-Dan-Dean 1   D 51
SHORT'NING
    Now stinted in the short'ning Day, ...   280 Journal   51
    The Short'ning is the nicest Part.   . . . . 1021 Nim-Dan-Dean 1   D 36
SHORTEN
    You see my Learning; but to shorten it, ...   367 Answer Delaney   41
    To shorten my Tale, (for I hate a long Story,)   . . .   871 Grand Question   129
SHORTER
    I know a shorter way by half.   . . . .   487 Irish-Club   14
    Faith, he must make his Stories shorter, ...   556 Death of Swift   95
SHORTEST
    When the Days are at shortest, to put it in Rhyme;   . .   265 Apollo   78
SHORTNING
    Phoebus now shortning every Shade, ...   119 Apollo Outwit   1
SHOT   SEE BOW-SHOT
    Like sun-beams shot at too far distance from a glass;   .   35 Ode Sancroft   24
    A sign God's dart is shot, and wrath o'erblown;   . . .   52 Temple Ill   28
    The Hand that sign'd the Mortgage paid the Shot.   . .   234 Elegy on Demar   28
    Before the Drapier shot a Letter, ...   353 Wood Ironmongr   35
    Concluding, that another Shot   . . . .   500 Doctor Delaney   19
    By Lightning shot from Chloe's Eyes?   . . . .   587 Strephon Chloe   110

		PAGE	TITLE	LINE
SHOT	(CONTINUED)			
Took Aim, and shot with all his Strength		703	Cadenus Vaness	516
He shot before your Foes were prim'd:		797	Traulus 1	58
SHOU'D	66		OMITTED WORD	
SHOUL				
And said: By my Shoul he's the Son of a Beech:		334	Serious Poem	28
SHOULD	185		OMITTED WORD	
SHOULDER				
With Head reclining on his Shoulder,		63	Discovery	13
He hated Bailiffs at his shoulder.		455	Dean Smedley	10
From shoulder to flank		853	Lady's Lament	71
Powder'd from shoulder down to flank,		879	Robbin & Harry	49
SHOULDERS				
Too long upon his single Shoulders		160	Atlas	21
His arms upon the booby's shoulders		421	Ireld	22
Upon the shoulders of their neighbour,		434	Answer Paulus	63
A Rug was o'er his Shoulders thrown;		594	Cassinus Peter	19
Her Shoulders mark'd with bloody Tracks;		729	Stella, Poems	46
That graceful on his Shoulders fell)		903	Death Daphne	26
SHOULDST	2		OMITTED WORD	
SHOUT				
Attend thy Coach, and hear them shout		183	Horace 2, 1	80
SHOVE				
"You ne'er consider whom you shove,		200	Horace 2, 6	38
SHOVELS				
These Raps he will honestly dig out with Shovels,		337	Serious Poem	97
SHOW	SEE SHEW, PUPPET-SHOW, RARY-SHOW			
And tho' the Title seems to show		21	Ode Athenian	165
Her Priests, her Train and Followers show		27	Ode to Temple	40
And those, alas, do show		39	Ode Sancroft	145
For, sure, we want some guide from Heav'n to show		39	Ode Sancroft	156
Such are the smiles where drops of chrystal show,		51	Temple Ill	21
A Fryer would needs show his Talent in Latin;		76	Lady B- B-	2
Burnish and make a gaudy show,		84	Salamander	41
Hung high and made a glitt'ring Show		93	Bauc & Phil 1	114
Triumphant Star! Some Pity show		100	Elegy Patrige	89
Hung high, and made a glitt'ring Show,		114	Bauc & Phil 2	90
Scorning to show the least Respect.		133	Magician's Rod	26
And take it kindly meant to show		200	Horace 2, 6	41
Because he fain would make a Show,		216	To Mr. Delany	42
To show their Parts, will scold and rail,		216	To Mr. Delany	49
From her pale Cheeks pretends to show		228	Prog of Beauty	94
To show, I don't flinch,		246	Irish-Feast	53
Nor let my Votaries show their Skill		271	Apollo's Edict	D 46
Or more to show the Thing I mean,		393	Modern Poets	9
Your Mistress in a Glass to show,		401	Window Inns 2	2
These Rhimers abundantly show it:		401	Window Inns 3	2
My House was built but for a Show,		409	Dial Rich Marb	23
His Hat for Show, beneath his Arm.		410	Dial Rich Marb	66
Would make at least a handsom show		422	Ireld	36
And thus by demonstration show,		434	Answer Paulus	69
Dame Nature as the Learned show,		504	Doctor Delaney	127
O, wou'd the Senate deign to show		515	Answer Fable	81
Harmonious Coffee show thy Zeal,		515	Answer Fable	87
Durst there show his right or most revnd face		522	St. Cecilia's	10
To show the World his chief Reverse in you.		532	To Mr. Gay	38
Now, let me show how <Bob> and you agree.		532	To Mr. Gay	43
Who wou'd not at a crowded Show,		554	Death of Swift	15
With which he made a tearing show:		619	Scandal Poem 1	71
Strange Pride and Insolence you show,		623	Scandal Poem 2	3
With which he made a tearing Show:		625	Scandal Poem 2	69
Where Pope will never show his Face;		650	On Poetry	308
Their Sores and putrid Ulcers show,		667	Epig Carthy 6	D 3
Believe me Stella, when you show		765	Stel B-day '26	67
But you when all the Show is past		774	Mullinix Tim	41
And leaves the Tartar Phiz, in show		786	Dick, Maggot	13
For, would'st thou make a fouler Show,		786	Clad in Brown	3
If your Stockings were off, you cou'd show cloven Feet.		805	Irish Bishops	52
That he came from the Temple, his morals do show,		815	Yahoo's	11
We'll show him the way how to crop and to slit;		816	Yahoo's	52
Resolv'd my Gratitude to show,		887	Panegyr Dean	1
To show my Face with scornful Air;		887	Panegyr Dean	21
As soon as gone, will show their Spight:		891	Panegyr Dean	140
At nicely carving show thy Wit;		897	Panegyr Dean	335
A new and wond'rous Art I show		920	Riddle 6	9
And still, the more I show my Art,		920	Riddle 6	17
I'm not asham'd to show my Face,		920	Riddle 6	24
SHOW'D	SEE SHEW'D			
Your Arm has now Your Rightful Title show'd;		12	Ode to William	D 29
Appearing, show'd the Ruddy Morns Approach.		124	Descriptn Morn	2
SHOW'R				
Or melts by the first show'r away.		39	Ode Sancroft	142
(By sure Prognosticks) when to dread a Show'r:		136	City Shower	2
A coming Show'r your shooting Corns presage,		137	City Shower	9
While the first drizzling Show'r is born aslope,		137	City Shower	18
SHOW'RS				
His Blessings down in fruitful Show'rs;		624	Scandal Poem 2	28
While we, by soft prolifick Show'rs,		628	Scandal Poem 2	151
'Till Summer Show'rs and Ev'ning Dew,		759	Receipt Youth	11
SHOWED	SEE SHEW'D			
But showed no more than half her Face		290	Prog Marriage	16

		PAGE	TITLE	LINE
SHOWERS				
And bless the Earth with genial Showers.	. . . . . .	387	Manly Virtue	110
But we by gentle April showers	. . . .	621	Scandal Poem 1	147
SHOWN				
When soon the peaceful bow unstring'd is shown,	. . .	52	Temple Ill	27
Thus oft by Mariners are shown,	. . . .	257	Bubble	169
Now you see why his Verses so seldom are shown,	. . .	264	Apollo	55
My Country's sav'd, as you have shown,	. . . . . .	372	Letter D. S-y	17
A Pigeon wou'd, if shown by Aesop,	. . . .	512	Answer Fable	9
Would ne'er have shown him so much Favour;	. . . . .	514	Answer Fable	78
What early Manhood has he shown,	. . . .	655	On Poetry	431
That Virtue, pleas'd by being shown,	. . . .	706	Cadenus Vaness	608
Constr'ing the Passion she had shown,	. . . .	711	Cadenus Vaness	764
What truer Affection cou'd ever be shown,	. . . . .	805	Irish Bishops	55
SHOWS SEE SHEWS, PUPPET-SHOWS				
The Muse, like some bright country virgin, shows,	. .	50	To Congreve	215
Till Midnight never shows her Head;	. . . . . .	229	Prog of Beauty	102
From Venus born, thy Beauty shows,	. . . .	323	Pethox	1
Whether, as Epicurus shows	. . . .	324	Pethox	27
When Celia in her Glory shows,	. . . .	530	Lady's Dres Rm	135
That Phoebus ever shows his Face:	. . . .	627	Scandal Poem 2	136
And then, how saucily he shows	. . . .	627	Scandal Poem 2	139
Balls, and Masquerades, and Shows,	. . . .	631	Epistle Lady	41
As clearly shows you bred at Court!	. . . . . .	889	Panegyr Dean	84
Still her odd perverseness shows	. . . .	906	Daphne	15
Take Courage, Dan, this plainly shows	. . . . . .	993	On Picture	19
SHREDS				
With the unravelld Shreds of which	. . . .	80	Vanbrug House	47
Shreds of Wit, and senseless Rhimes,	. . . . . .	523	Betty Grizette	19
SHREW				
And sav'd him at once from the Shrew and the Rabble;	.	327	Epigram 1	4
But, I hope I shall ne'er be, like you, of a Shrew sick	1030	Dr. Sheridan	4
SHREWD				
Which thou (such <Burnet's> shrewd Advice is)	. . .	180	Horace 2, 1	5
Shrewd Fellows, and arch Wags, a Tribe	. . . . .	216	To Mr. Delany	53
Delany reports it, and he has a shrewd Tongue,	. . .	967	Letter Sherid	1
SHREWDLY				
They shrewdly suspect it is all but a bite.	. . . . .	818	Archbi Cashel	4
SHREWDNESS				
The Neighbours round admire his Shrewdness,	. . . .	650	On Poetry	289
SHREWSBURY'S				
. . .I remember when I was at my Lady Shrewsbury's,	.	71	Mrs Harris Pet	32
Or Shrewsbury's Duke	. . . .	423	Carterets Arms	
SHRIEK				
Astonish'd gave a dreadful Shriek;	. . . .	849	Old Thorn	26
SHRIEVES				
Of Lord-May'r, Aldermen, and Shrieves,	. . . . .	494	Panegyr Swift	50
SHRILL				
By a shrill Voice at noon declares,	. . . .	94	Bauc & Phil 1	144
By a shrill Voice at Noon declares,	. . . .	113	Bauc & Phil 2	82
As Bagpipe shrill, or Oyster-Strumpet,	. . . . .	182	Horace 2, 1	72
And in a shrill revengeful Tone,	. . . .	850	Old Thorn	55
SHRILLER				
'Till drown'd in Shriller Notes of Chimney-Sweep,	.	124	Descriptn Morn	12
SHRINE				
In the fair shrine of Dorothea's mind.	. . . . . .	52	Temple Ill	50
I waited at Apollo's Shrine;	. . . .	741	Stel B-day 22	14
Receives all Off'rings at her Shrine.	. . . . . .	893	Panegyr Dean	206
All make Oblations at this Shrine.	. . . .	922	Riddle 7	30
On Thursday I'll pay my Respects at your Shrine	. .	1017	Swift Ans Sher	21
SHRINK				
Then shrink into it's Hole again.	. . . .	84	Salamander	44
SHRIVEL				
That Sound will make the Parchment shrivel,	. . . .	354	Simile Silver	29
SHRIVEL'D				
Shrivel'd with a Winter's keeping.	. . . .	523	Betty Grizette	10
SHRIVELLED				
As shrivelled and as black as thine.	. . . .	787	Clad in Brown	22
SHROUD				
And you whom Pluto's Helm does wisely shroud	. . . .	18	Ode Athenian	86
Which though her Modesty would shroud,	. . . . . .	726	To Stella	81
SHROUDS				
Shrouds her still beams; how should the stars be seen?	.	53	Temple Ill	58
SHRUB				
Grows neither Grass, nor Shrub, nor Tree;	. . . . .	324	Pethox	41
SHRUG				
But read a Nod, a Shrug, a Look,	. . . .	450	Modern Lady	190
Folks shrug, and cry, There's nothing in't.	. . . .	475	Epist on Epist	12
The rest will give a Shrug and cry,	. . . . . .	561	Death of Swift	211
A Nod, a Shrug, a scornful Smile,	. . . .	647	On Poetry	237
SHTEEPLE				
Lorsha! and out of her shteeple there was hung a black	840	Ballad	D 9
flag.				
SHUDDERS				
But, alas, the poor Dean neither Shudders nor burns,	.	1037	Four Storyes	5
SHUFFLE				
The Deal, the Shuffle, and the Cut?	. . . . . .	451	Modern Lady	223
SHUN				
Which we cou'd neither obviate, nor shun.	. . . .	12	Ode to William	D 20
The Man, who Infamy to shun,	. . . .	243	Horace 4, 9	21
Who taught by Instinct how to shun	. . . .	257	Bubble	178

		PAGE	TITLE	LINE
SHUN	(CONTINUED)			
"Do now solicitiously shun		380	Apology Lady C	141
From me; or my Embraces shun.		916	Riddle 2	6
They for that Reason shun this Way:		928	Riddle 12	D 6
SHUN'D				
Not yet, the Dust had shun'd th' unequal Strife,	. .	137	City Shower	23
SHUNNING				
For shunning those of his own Coat;		171	Horace 1, 7	28
SHUNS				
He shuns Apothecary's Shops;		605	Beasts Confess	133
SHUT				
To shut out the River by raising the Bank.		287	Bank Down	5
Or else, shut out from Heaven and Earth, ...		689	Cadenus Vaness	87
SHUTS				
Full in his Face Bob shuts the Council Door: . . .		537	Mr. Pulteney	4
SHY				
And observe while you live, that no Man is shy . . .		264	Apollo	57
SIC				
And here rest, Sic transit Gloria Mundi.		431	Dicky Dolly	24
SICK SEE HEART-SICK,CROP-SICK,SEA-SICK,LOVE-SICK,PURGE-SICK,SPEW-SICK,PEW-SICK				
Falls sick in the Posteriors of the World.		10	Ode to King	146
And sick with Dregs of Knowledge grown, ...		27	Ode to Temple	47
Call Titan sick, because their sight is so;		45	To Congreve	74
Sick lust of souls, and an abortive child;		47	To Congreve	124
That time is sick, or the world's mind is dead.-- . . .		53	Temple Ill	66
Which those who tend the Sick for pay		204	In Sickness	17
Ye formal Weepers for the Sick, ...		204	In Sickness	23
Apollo laugh'd till he was sick, ...		321	First of April	15
Or sick of Obstructions, and Pains in her Chest. . .		351	Wood Insect	16
Then Woe be to those in the House who are sick: . .		351	Wood Insect	22
The Maggot will dye, and the Sick will recover. . .		351	Wood Insect	28
Affirm'd the Moon was sick, and fell		354	Simile Silver	7
At proper Seasons to be sick;		416	Woman's Mind	40
'I'm hurry'd so, it makes me sick, ...		448	Modern Lady	98
When you are Sick, your Friends, you say, ...		546	Life of Swift	58
And hates to cram the Sick with Slops:		605	Beasts Confess	134
They give the sick man joy, and praise		761	Bec's B-Day	15
That you are sick, and I grown old, ...		763	Stel B-day '26	4
"But, the Sight of a Book makes me sick to this Day.	.	873	Grand Question	172
When I left you, I found myself of the Grape's Juice sick:		1028	Dr. Helsham	1
I'm so full of Pity, I never abuse Sick;		1028	Dr. Helsham	2
And the patientest Patient that ever you knew sick;	. .	1028	Dr. Helsham	3
I pitied my Cat, whom I knew by her Mew sick; . . .		1029	Dr. Helsham	5
She mended at first, but now she's anew sick. . . .		1029	Dr. Helsham	6
Captain Butler made some in the Church black and blue sick;		1029	Dr. Helsham	7
Are not you, in a Crowd, when you sweat and you stew, sick?		1029	Dr. Helsham	9
Lady Santry got out of the Church when she grew sick,	.	1029	Dr. Helsham	10
And, as fast as she could, to the Deanery flew sick.	.	1029	Dr. Helsham	11
Miss Morice was (I can assure you 'tis true) sick:	. .	1029	Dr. Helsham	12
For, who would not be in that numerous Crew sick?	. .	1029	Dr. Helsham	13
Such Musick would make a Fanatick or Jew sick: . . .		1029	Dr. Helsham	14
Yet, Ladies are seldom at Ombre, or Lue, sick; . . .		1029	Dr. Helsham	15
Nor is old Nanny Shales, whene'er she does brew, sick.		1029	Dr. Helsham	16
My Footman came home from the Church, of a Bruise sick,		1029	Dr. Helsham	17
And look'd like a Rake, who was made in the Stews sick;		1029	Dr. Helsham	18
But you learned Doctors can make whom you chuse sick.	.	1029	Dr. Helsham	19
Poor I myself I was, when I withdrew, sick, ...		1029	Dr. Helsham	20
For the Smell of them made me like Garlick and Rue sick		1029	Dr. Helsham	21
And I got thro' the Crowd, tho' not led by a Clew, sick		1029	Dr. Helsham	22
You hop'd to find many (for that was your Cue) sick;	.	1029	Dr. Helsham	23
But, there were not a Dozen (to give 'em their Due) sick		1029	Dr. Helsham	24
And those to be sure, stuck together like Glew, sick.		1029	Dr. Helsham	25
So are Ladies in Crowds, when they squeeze and they screw, sick.		1030	Dr. Helsham	26
You may find they are all, by their yellow pale Hue, sick		1030	Dr. Helsham	27
So am I, when Tobacco, like Robin, I chew, sick. . .		1030	Dr. Helsham	28
If I write any more, it will make my poor Muse sick.	.	1030	Dr. Sheridan	1
This Night I came home with a very cold Dew sick, . .		1030	Dr. Sheridan	2
And I wish I may soon be not of an A-gue sick; . . .		1030	Dr. Sheridan	3
But, I hope I shall ne'er be, like you, of a Shrew sick		1030	Dr. Sheridan	4
Who often has made me, by looking ascue, sick. . . .		1030	Dr. Sheridan	5
SICKENS				
Faint inspiration sickens as she flies, ...		50	To Congreve	229
Pale Envy sickens--Errour flies--		307	Manly Virtue	121
SICKLY				
Scatters strange agues o'er men's sickly minds, . . .		52	Temple Ill	38
Since one false beam of joy in sickly minds		55	Temple Ill	149
When on my sickly Couch I lay, ...		726	To Stella	97
She at your sickly Couch will wait, ...		766	Stel B-day '26	77
This aged, sickly, sapless Thorn		849	Old Thorn	21
SICKNESS				
Grief, Sickness, Poverty, and Age;		764	Stel B-day '26	32
SID				
Our great Magician, Hamet Sid, ...		132	Magician's Rod	5
As ready was the Wand of Sid		133	Magician's Rod	27
Could with this Rod of Sid compare.		135	Magician's Rod	78
Dear Sid, then why wer't thou so mad		135	Magician's Rod	79
For since old Sid has broken this, ...		135	Magician's Rod	85

SID'S

	PAGE	TITLE	LINE
That Rod was just a Type of Sid's,	133	Magician's Rod	39
Sid's Rod was slender, white, and tall,	133	Magician's Rod	43
Sid's Brethren of the conj'ring Tribe	134	Magician's Rod	49
Sid's Rod was of a larger Stride,	134	Magician's Rod	53
Like Sid's, but nothing near so good;	134	Magician's Rod	60
Sid's Scepter, full of Juice, did shoot	134	Magician's Rod	71

SIDE   SEE CHARIOT-SIDE,CUSHION-SIDE,TEMPLE-SIDE,BACK-SIDE

	PAGE	TITLE	LINE
Here by a mountain's side, a reverend cave	49	To Congreve	187
On t' other side (laid out for Shoes);	60	Lady Tablebook	14
You're on the wrong side of the Door.	91	Bauc & Phil 1	36
And freely from the fattest Side	91	Bauc & Phil 1	59
Nor ever left the Chimny side.	94	Bauc & Phil 1	138
By Change of Wind to Leeward Side	96	On the Union	19
And each Part took a diff'rent Side;	99	Elegy Patrige	66
For want of Room by Virgo's Side,	100	Elegy Patrige	85
And freely from the fattest Side	112	Bauc & Phil 2	27
Had never left each other's Side;	113	Bauc & Phil 2	76
To wait at Bright Ardelia's Side.	120	Apollo Outwit	40
Could I but live on this side Trent;	199	Horace 2, 6	10
On either Side you see the Tracks,	227	Prog of Beauty	39
By vent'ring on the cheating Side,	257	Bubble	163
But the Tapster well Cudgell'd him both Side and Flank	288	Bank Down	39
For this, or that Side of a Gutter,	314	To Ford	96
You bury, on our Side the Channell	315	To Ford	101
With pungent Pains on ev'ry Side:	325	Pethox	57
Her Scale to neither Side inclines;	391	Young's Satire	16
Like a Beau in the Box, he bow'd low on each Side;	399	Tom Clinch	10
With antient Mirmont at her Side.	410	Dial Rich Marb	64
Against the Side she would defend:	417	Woman's Mind	52
Hath mention'd arms on this side Sweden;	462	Birthday Song	52
And turn'd it round on every side.	526	Lady's Dres Rm	14
Or, with her Go-Cart amble Side by Side.	531	To Mr. Gay	12
Or, with her Go-Cart amble Side by Side.	531	To Mr. Gay	12
Unless the Odds be on our Side.	554	Death of Swift	38
Stuck on with Art on either Side.	581	Young Nymph	14
Walk Hand in Hand, and Side by Side;	585	Strephon Chloe	58
Walk Hand in Hand, and Side by Side;	585	Strephon Chloe	58
To reach the Pot on t' other Side.	589	Strephon Chloe	190
And half unsmoakt, lay by his Side,	594	Cassinus Peter	24
No Love is lost on either Side.	606	Beasts Confess	164
Be grav'd on either Side in Columns,	611	By Dr. Swift	9
Our curtains blue on either side;	621	Scandal Poem 1	134
Our Curtains blue, from Side to Side:	627	Scandal Poem 2	138
Our Curtains blue, from Side to Side:	627	Scandal Poem 2	138
Nor argue on the weaker side.	644	On Poetry	128
You cannot err on Flatt'ry's Side.	657	On Poetry	470
And do no Wrong to either side:	657	On Poetry	484
Insensibly came on her Side;	709	Cadenus Vaness	729
One Lawyer to each Side was nam'd.	713	Cadenus Vaness	843
I'll here expose your weaker Side.	730	Stella, Poems	86
To Liffy's filthy side in Dublin;	744	Stel Distress	4
This box is cramm'd on ev'ry side	753	Gift for Bec	9
Like faithful Counsellors on either Side.	770	Horace 1, 14	14
To thy own Side so Damn'd a Nuisance,	775	Mullinix Tim	66
With powder'd Rump, and Back and Side,	785	Dick, Maggot	7
View him on the Mother's side,	799	Traulus 2	7
Borrow'd from the Mason Side:	800	Traulus 2	44
That no honest Heathen would be on their Side.	805	Irish Bishops	38
And sail'd with Litter Side by Side;	811	Bro Protestant	8
And sail'd with Litter Side by Side;	811	Bro Protestant	8
Though by the Female Side you proudly bring,	826	Noisy Tom	9
Where to find on this Side Hell;	837	Legion Club	184
For the Captain's entreated to sit by your Side;	871	Grand Question	132
Her Aunt's my Gossip by my Father's Side;	882	Pastoral Dial	42
On either Side his Honour's Guard:	883	Rev Market-Hill	12
Your Altars near your Couches Side;	896	Panegyr Dean	294
On either Side with Fringes grac'd;	915	Riddle 1	6
And drag'd me from my Mother's Side:	915	Riddle 1	8
To turn the true impartial Side!	921	Riddle 7	8
Come sit by my side, while this picture I draw:	955	Portrait Life	1
To the very coach side, and threaten your letters.	978	Dean to Tho: S	4

SIDE-BOARD

	PAGE	TITLE	LINE
I near the Side-board take my Seat;	920	Riddle 6	26

SIDES

	PAGE	TITLE	LINE
And scrape her Pitchy Sides for Wax.	100	Elegy Patrige	78
Laughing as if he'd burst his Sides:	108	V's House	70
While Streams run down her oil'd Umbrella's Sides.	138	City Shower	38
Safe through the Newry mountains sides.	435	Answer Paulus	98
When on thy Breast and Sides Herculean,	656	On Poetry	463
There was on both Sides much to say:	690	Cadenus Vaness	116
'Twill not avail, when thy strong Sides are broke,	771	Horace 1, 14	37
Lur'd by the gilded Stern, and painted Sides.	771	Horace 1, 14	48
And, as your old wont is, change sides in a trice:	818	Archbi Cashel	8
Or his sides they would gore	854	Lady's Lament	85
To all their weaker Sides are blind;	887	Panegyr Dean	8

SIEGE

	PAGE	TITLE	LINE
A Siege as long as Troy endur'd.	326	Pethox	98

SIEGES

	PAGE	TITLE	LINE
Renown'd in Sieges and Campaigns,	925	Riddle 8	31

SIEVE   SEE STATE-SIEVE

	PAGE	TITLE	LINE
Like Lapland Witches in a Sieve:	254	Bubble	92
Jove <pisses> on you through a Sieve;	627	Scandal Poem 2	126
A Woman's no Sieve (for with that you begin)	972	S-'s Ans Sh-d	5
But grant her a Sieve, I can say something archer,	972	S-'s Ans Sh-d	9
For a riddle and sieve, or a sieve and a riddle:	976	Dean to Sherid	14
For a riddle and sieve, or a sieve and a riddle:	976	Dean to Sherid	14
You call them a riddle, ass, call them a sieve.	976	Dean to Sherid	16
That a sieve dissolves riddles by help of the shears;	976	Dean to Sherid	20
Think again of the sieve, and I'll hold you a wager,	976	Dean to Sherid	23
A sieve keeps half in, and therefore, no doubt,	976	Dean to Sherid	25

SIFT

	PAGE	TITLE	LINE
And quickly did the Matter sift,	171	Horace 1, 7	25
"No,no," quoth the Primate, "if causes we sift,	843	Ay and No	5

SIGH

	PAGE	TITLE	LINE
I sigh when e're I think of it	24	Ode Athenian	270
With artful Sigh and feigned Groan,	208	Fable Bitches	14
The People with a Sigh their Taxes bring;	533	To Mr. Gay	51
But with a Sigh, I wish it mine:	555	Death of Swift	48
For when you sigh to leave Woodpark,	748	Stel Distress	69
Yet, when you sigh to leave Wood-Park,	752	Stel Wood-Park	85
I sigh to think of antient Days.	894	Panegyr Dean	226

SIGH'D

	PAGE	TITLE	LINE
Dick Sigh'd for his Doll and his mournfull Arms Cross'd,	430	Dicky Dolly	7
Thus loaded with Grief, Dick Sigh'd and he cry'd,	430	Dicky Dolly	10
But, Strephon sigh'd so loud and strong,	585	Strephon Chloe	39
Cry'd, Caelia! thrice, and sigh'd the rest.	595	Cassinus Peter	40
Had sigh'd and languish'd, vow'd, and writ,	703	Cadenus Vaness	542

SIGHING

	PAGE	TITLE	LINE
What ogling, sighing, toasting, vowing!	585	Strephon Chloe	34

SIGHS

	PAGE	TITLE	LINE
Nor widow's sighs, nor orphan's tears,	296	Satiric Elegy	18
For whom no Shepherd sighs in vain;	581	Young Nymph	2

SIGHT

	PAGE	TITLE	LINE
And hid him from Poetick sight,	8	Ode to King	59
Consume, and perish from our sight,	9	Ode to King	113
To bless the Primitive Sailer's weary sight,	16	Ode Athenian	7
As to paint Eccho to the Sight:	21	Ode Athenian	160
And almost got priority of Sight,	30	Ode to Temple	130
She soars clear out of sight,	31	Ode to Temple	144
Unpierc'd by the blunt Rays of Sight)	31	Ode to Temple	167
To solve appearances of sight	35	Ode Sancroft	28
Till Honesty and Conscience are clear out of sight.	36	Ode Sancroft	58
In both, false mediums cheat our sight,	39	Ode Sancroft	147
The daz'ling glory dimms their prostituted sight,	41	Ode Sancroft	221
Call Titan sick, because their sight is so;	45	To Congreve	74
But with the odious smell and sight annoy'd,	50	To Congreve	225
Such to unhallowed sight the Muse divine	52	Temple Ill	29
Troubling the chrystal fountain of the sight,	54	Temple Ill	97
You may be sure, so strange a Sight	92	Bauc & Phil 1	79
And goes with Folks to shew the Sight:	116	Bauc & Phil 2	168
On Sight of this Celestial Prude,	121	Apollo Outwit	41
What Street they sail'd from, by their Sight and Smell.	139	City Shower	56
Was like keeping her Monument always in sight.	144	New Song	38
Had purify'd her mortal sight;	178	To Lord Harley	50
At sight of Will she bawl'd no more,	220	A Quiet Life	7
Though still in Sight, had chang'd their Ground.	226	Prog of Beauty	32
Delude at once and Bless our Sight,	228	Prog of Beauty	70
Unable to endure the Sight,	240	Run Bankers	43
And They in Men and Angels Sight	241	Run Bankers	62
Good Lord, what a Sight,	246	Irish-Feast	57
The liquid Medium cheats your Sight,	251	Bubble	15
Lock up from my Sight in Pantries and Cupboards:	263	Apollo	12
There out of my Sight, just against the North-Zone,	265	Apollo	85
Tho' Poets have the second Sight,	270	Apollo's Edict	D 34
"If such a Sight as this can please ye,	305	Storm	69
To choque your Sight, and raise your Malice)	313	To Ford	64
Dims and obscures our sight:	402	Window Inns 6	D 2
A goodly Sight to see her ride,	410	Dial Rich Marb	63
Desire had now the Goal in Sight:	413	Desire Possess	39
The Sight will put her in a Swown.	416	Woman's Mind	16
If chance a Mouse creeps in her Sight,	416	Woman's Mind	33
Ne'r came in sight	441	Ballyspellin	41
Say, did you ever know by Sight	504	Doctor Delaney	139
A Glass that can to Sight disclose,	527	Lady's Dres Rm	63
But leave it standing full in Sight	528	Lady's Dres Rm	73
And bless his ravisht Sight to see	530	Lady's Dres Rm	142
I place a <Statesman> full before my Sight.	532	To Mr. Gay	32
Or Libels yet conceal'd from sight---,	550	Life of Swift	188
"No Madam, 'tis a shocking Sight,	562	Death of Swift	235
Shirts becoming to the sight,	573	Helter Skelter	22
Corinna wakes. A dreadful Sight!	583	Young Nymph	57
But, such a Sight was never seen,	594	Cassinus Peter	9
All your Virtues to my Sight.	633	Epistle Lady	98
Make you able upon Sight,	638	Epistle Lady	269
Pil'd in a Garret charm'd the Author's Sight.	667	Epig Carthy 5	D 2
Nail'd to her Window full in Sight	735	Stel B-day '20	35
To your Decays adapts my Sight,	757	Stel B-day '24	44
To make me deaf, and mend my Sight.	758	Stel B-day '24	54
Dreadful Sight! What learned Morgan	838	Legion Club	193

SIGHT   (CONTINUED)   PAGE   TITLE   LINE
    With the Noise, the Sight, the Scent.   . . . . . .   839 Legion Club   234
    Must come in my sight; . . . .   855 Lady's Lament   146
    What imports thy forward Sight?   862 To Janus   11
    "But, the Sight of a Book makes me sick to this Day. .   873 Grand Question   172
    Who keeps his wisdom out of sight; . . . .   900 Dean's Reasons   42
    To make me glorious to the Sight   . . . .   916 Riddle 2   11
    But your rhyme was not double, 'cause your sight was but   980 Tho: Sheridan   2
        single.
SIGN
    A sign God's dart is shot, and wrath o'erblown;   . . .   52 Temple Ill   28
    Besides, that slow-pac'd Sign Bo-otes   . . . . . .   98 Elegy Patrige   31
    'Tis a sign she'll keep her folks, ...   419 Holyhead Journ   2
    It is a sign we shan't stay here.   419 Holyhead Journ   4
    Convict of lyes is every sign, ...   420 Holyhead   5
    And to each other give the Sign.   . . . .   447 Modern Lady   77
    Sett, for a Sign of Wit Within.   . . . .   457 Paddy's Charac   6
    "And that, I doubt, is no good Sign.   . . . . . .   557 Death of Swift   110
    Be told the Lodging, Lane, and Sign, ...   729 Stella, Poems   41
    Where'e'er they see the fairest Sign, ...   734 Stel B-day '20   2
    But the loss of your Cough will be the best Sign . .   1017 Swift Ans Sher   14
SIGN'D
    The Hand that sign'd the Mortgage paid the Shot.   . .   234 Elegy on Demar   28
SIGN'T
    I wish you would sign't, ' . . . .   1015 Swift to Sheri   43
SIGNED
    "To get my Warrant quickly signed: . . . .   201 Horace 2, 6   56
SIGNIFY
    "By <God> they don't signify this Pinch of Snuff. . .   872 Grand Question   160
    It would not signify a pin . . . .   899 Dean's Reasons   25
SIGNIFY'D
    What signify'd the French to beat?   . . . .   169 Peace Dunkirk   32
SIGNS
    And then the Signs will be Thirteen.   . . . . . .   100 Elegy Patrige   88
    When We, by proper Signs and Symbols tell, ...   162 Toland's Invit   9
    Writ underneath the Country Signs; ' . . . .   201 Horace 2, 6   72
    His Signs aloft no longer swing;   . . . .   875 Drapier's Hill   14
SILENCE
    Next, faithful Silence hath a sure Reward: . . . .   210 Earl of Oxford   15
    Nor shall I dull in Silence sit;   . . . .   411 Dial Rich Marb   89
    Away the God of Silence flew, ...   448 Modern Lady   121
    Talks half a Day in Praise of Silence;   . . . . .   450 Modern Lady   171
    Which says, wou'd Crows in Silence eat   . . . . .   479 Epist on Epist   121
    Him the Boar in Silence creeping, ...   660 Love Song   11
    Hardly at length he Silence broke, ...   707 Cadenus Vaness   656
    All met, and Silence thrice proclaim'd, ...   713 Cadenus Vaness   842
    In Silence, or forget with Pride.   . . . .   726 To Stella   96
    But still, whene'er you Silence break, ...   889 Panegyr Dean   71
SILENT
    And rolls the silent year   . . . .   39 Ode Sancroft   151
    And gaze in silent Wonder long, ...   109 V's House   106
    To silent Shades repeat thy Verse, ...   121 Apollo Outwit   58
    The watchful Bailiffs take their silent Stands,   . .   125 Descriptn Morn   17
    Those Dreams that on the silent Night intrude,   . .   363 On Dreams   1
    Retreating silent to his Cell; . . . .   375 Apology Lady C   14
    Be silent as a Politician, ...   644 On Poetry   123
    Softly seeks her silent Mate;   . . . .   661 Love Song   30
    Thus Lamps, which burn'd in Tombs with silent Glare,   667 Epig Carthy 5   D   5
    With silent Scorn Vanessa sat, ...   697 Cadenus Vaness   334
    The Nymph stood silent out of spight, ...   699 Cadenus Vaness   406
    Now, with a soft and silent Tread, ...   727 To Stella   111
    For I hate a silent Breath, ...   933 Riddle 20   D   29
SILK
    Than those with backs of silk and golden wings;   . .   46 To Congreve   92
    What Lining best the Silk will suit;   . . . . . .   416 Woman's Mind   30
SILKS
    We'll buy English Silks for our Wives and our   237 Excellent Song   REF
        Daughters,
    Then we'll buy English Silks for our Wives and our   237 Excellent Song   REF
        Daughters,
    They would buy English Silks for their Wives. . .   .   237 Excellent Song   REF
    Then we'll buy English Silks for our Wives and our   238 Excellent Song   REF
        Daughters,
    Enter the Folks with Silks and Lace: . . . . . .   447 Modern Lady   81
SILL
    Can scarce get o'er the Barn-Door Sill: . . . . .   230 Prog of Poetry   4
SILLIER
    Always peevisher and sillier: . . . .   906 Daphne   18
SILLY
    From London they come, silly People to chouse,   . .   396 Dog and Thief   17
    But laugh'd at their own silly joking.   . . . . .   755 Dingley Brent   6
    While all the silly Wretch can do . . . .   774 Mullinix Tim   27
    His rhet'ric, bombast, silly jests, are by far . . .   815 Yahoo's   13
    That silly old puss . . . .   855 Lady's Lament   119
SILVAN
    The Silvan Pow'rs with Fear perplex'd   . . . . . .   849 Old Thorn   29
SILVER
    But plumes her Silver Wings and flies away,   . . .   16 Ode Athenian   17
    The Silver Virge, with decent Pride, ...   174 Horace 1, 7   99
    Down from her silver chariot came, ...   178 To Lord Harley   75
    And Geese their silver Plumes supply.   . . . . . .   239 Run Bankers   24

SILVER   (CONTINUED)   PAGE   TITLE   LINE
        The Silver takes a nobler Hue, ...   255 Bubble   114
        And Silver Cynthia for a Crown;   . . . .   255 Bubble   128
        Displays her Silver Face again.   . . . .   354 Simile Silver   14
        The Moon is Silver all this while.)   . . . .   354 Simile Silver   16
        There was no Silver to be seen.   . . . .   354 Simile Silver   24
        Our Silver will appear again.   . . . .   354 Simile Silver   32
        If you'll redeem the Silver Cup   . . . .   446 Modern Lady   58
        Then Mercury with Silver Tongue, ...   585 Strephon Chloe   55
        To silver Meads, and shady Bow'rs, ...   590 Strephon Chloe   201
        Were Silver, and the Axel Gold.   . . . .   598 Problem Solved   16
        Delany sends a Silver Standish, ...   611 By Dr. Swift   3
        With Jocky Boots, and Silver Spurs;   . . . .   760 Receipt Youth   44
        Her Silver Vase in Cedar-Box.   . . . .   896 Panegyr Dean   298
        I With borrow'd Silver shine, ...   927 Riddle 10   D 1
        For Silver and Gold I don't trouble my Head,   . . .   927 Riddle 11   D 5
SILVIA
        And Silvia full of inward Guilt, ...   450 Modern Lady   172
        The charming Silvia beating Flax, ...   729 Stella, Poems   45
SIMILE
        No Simile shall be begun, ...   270 Apollo's Edict   D 12
        So, (if my Simile you minded, ...   354 Simile Silver   17
        This Simile for his Excuse.   . . . .   485 Libel on D- D-   164
        Your Simile may better shine   . . . .   486 Libel on D- D-   193
        The Simile would better jump, ...   497 Panegyr Swift   136
        And here a Simile comes Pat in: . . . .   642 On Poetry   61
SIMILES
        The Similes that nothing fit;   . . . .   645 On Poetry   152
        His Similes in Order set, ...   730 Stella, Poems   73
SIMPLE
        But simple Topicks told in Rime.   . . . .   215 To Mr. Delany   12
        And simple as I now stand here, ...   778 Mullinix Tim   157
SIMPLICITY
        Simplicity alone can grace, ...   270 Apollo's Edict   D 29
        Your guides to true Simplicity.   . . . .   270 Apollo's Edict   D 32
        Simplicity alone is rare;   . . . .   378 Apology Lady C   106
SIN
        Sin and the plague ever abound   . . . .   37 Ode Sancroft   96
        In wholly equalling our sin and theirs, ...   38 Ode Sancroft   122
        Shall on a day make sin and folly bleed; . . . . . .   47 To Congreve   134
        Whom sin and want e'er furnish'd out a wit; . . . . .   48 To Congreve   166
        <Swift> had the Sin of Wit no venial Crime; . . . . .   193 Author Himself   9
        Thank God, 'twas neither Shame nor Sin, ...   224 Prog of Love   59
        He knows no guilt, who knows no sin.   . . . .   434 Answer Paulus   58
        And if it be a Sin or Shame, ...   602 Beasts Confess   29
        Confess'd a Sin, and God forgive him: . . . .   604 Beasts Confess   114
        He owns, and hopes it is no Sin, ...   606 Beasts Confess   175
        A burning Shame, a crying Sin   . . . .   659 On Poetry   D 410
        They think it both a Shame and Sin   . . . .   734 Stel B-day '20   13
        The oppression of Virtue, not wages of Sin: . . . . .   816 Yahoo's   42
        Forgive me my sin.   . . . .   855 Lady's Lament   136
        . . . 'tis both a Shame and a Sin, ...   985 Mary to Sher   7
SINCE   114   OMITTED WORD
SINCERE
        With Just, and Generous, and Sincere.   . . . .   385 Manly Virtue   62
        Fain would I think, our Female Friend sincere, . . .   531 To Mr. Gay   3
        His Fault is to be too Sincere;   . . . .   605 Beasts Confess   142
        Or grant her Passion be sincere, ...   707 Cadenus Vaness   640
        Are sent up Off'rings more sincere   . . . .   896 Panegyr Dean   296
SINCERELY
        Who, from my Soul, sincerely hate   . . . .   485 Libel on D- D-   173
        Could make you so sincerely hate   . . . .   498 Panegyr Swift   155
        I curse her ev'ry hour sincerely;   . . . .   679 From Catullus   7
SINCERER
        Bring from his Heart sincerer Groans, ...   546 Life of Swift   29
SINDG'D
        And round the Margin sindg'd his Soil, ...   323 Pethox   8
SINDGES
        Sindges Hair, but breaks no Pates.   . . . .   638 Epistle Lady   256
SINE
        Is, causa sine qua non. . . . .   406 Swift to Pope   20
SING
        Sing (belov'd Muse) the Pleasures of Retreat,   . . .   30 Ode to Temple   135
        Sing of thy Vales, sing of thy Woods, sing of thy   31 Ode to Temple   138
             Fields;
        Sing of thy Vales, sing of thy Woods, sing of thy   31 Ode to Temple   138
             Fields;
        Sing of thy Vales, sing of thy Woods, sing of thy   31 Ode to Temple   138
             Fields;
        There to surmount what bears me up, and sing   . . . .   44 To Congreve   37
        Here would we sing--But, ah! you think I dream, . . .   49 To Congreve   197
        Listen while the muse thus teaches thee to sing: . . .   52 Temple Ill   36
        Sing Muse the House of Poet Van   . . . .   80 Vanbrug House   57
        Sing Muse the House of Poet <Van>   . . . .   106 V's House   31
        What Poet e'er could sing a Note?   . . . .   231 Prog of Poetry   26
        The horned Floud, as Poets sing: . . . .   293 Prog Marriage   110
        I Sing not of the Draper's Praise, nor yet of William   341 Upon His Grace   1
             Wood;
        But I sing of a Famous Lord, who seeks his Country's   341 Upon His Grace   2
             Good.
        The Arts revive, the Vallies sing, ...   387 Manly Virtue   125

```
SING              (CONTINUED)                          PAGE  TITLE           LINE
     If there be Truth in what you sing,      . . . . . 391  Young's Satire     1
     Sing on I must, and sing I will    . . . . . . .   408  Dial Rich Marb     3
     Sing on I must, and sing I will    . . . . . . .   408  Dial Rich Marb     3
     Their Virtues never ceased to sing,      . . . .   445  Modern Lady       11
     To sing of Wars choose peaceful times.   . . . .   462  Birthday Song     48
     Now sing his little Highness Freddy,     . . . .   466  Birthday Song    187
     Or whom you once sung up, sing down.     . . . .   468  Birthday Song    260
     And sing like one of Milton's choir,     . . . .   490  Dialogue          40
     The Irish Senate's Praises sing:    . . . . . .    501  Doctor Delaney    56
     Sing my Praise in Strain sublime:   . . . . . .    631  Epistle Lady      57
     Now sing the Minister of State,     . . . . . .    656  On Poetry        441
     Thy Praises ev'ry Muse shall sing.  . . . . . .    656  On Poetry        448
     To sing his Virtues on ye Lyre,     . . . . . .    658  On Poetry      D 410
     As what those antient Poets sing;   . . . . . .    687  Cadenus Vaness    28
     Now, gentle Clio, sing or say,  . . . . . . .      690  Cadenus Vaness   126
     You yearly sing as she grows old,   . . . . . .    742  Stel B-day 22     39
     The Shepherd in his Bower might sleep or sing,     792  St. Pat's Well    41
     Sing, och, och, hoh, hoh. . . . . . . . . . .      840  Ballad         D REF
     Sing, och, och, hoh, hoh.   . . . . . . . . .      841  Ballad         D REF
     When none the Drapier's Praise shall sing;  . .    875  Drapier's Hill    13
     Good cause have I to sing and vapour,    . . . .   876  To Dean Swift      1
     Sing heavenly Muse in sweetly flowing Strain,      880  Pastoral Dial      7
     My artless Muse shall sing your Fame.    . . . .   887  Panegyr Dean       6
     To sing your Praise. And, first as <Dean>:  . .    888  Panegyr Dean      44
     (So Poets sing, with golden Bough   . . . . . .    896  Panegyr Dean     307
     Shall sing the <Dean> in Smedly's Lines.    . .    897  Panegyr Dean     346
     I can bleat, or I can sing,   . . . . . . . .      933  Riddle 20       D 11
     Then George will rejoice, and Dan will sing high-day:  980 Dean to Tho: S  37
     Swans sing when dying, geese when blind.    . .    983  Sher, A Goose     14
SINGE
     The wretched Insects singe their Wings, and fall,   . .   9  Ode to King    117
SINGERS
     Such Singers are like Nicolini.   . . . . . . .    598  Problem Solved    30
SINGING
     To rail; she singing, still whirls on her Mop.  . . .  137  City Shower     22
     He singing flies, and flying sings,      . . .     231  Prog of Poetry    45
     And for his singing, Doctor, you know,   . . .     513  Answer Fable      23
     With trumpets and fiddles and organs and singing . . . 522  St. Cecilia's    7
     His Singing was another Fault;    . . . . . . .    598  Problem Solved    27
SINGLE
     The Battel almost by Great William's single Valour      8  Ode to King    64
         gain'd;
     But ne'er since seated in one single Breast.  . . . .  26  Ode to Temple    7
     Too long upon his single Shoulders  . . . . .     160  Atlas            21
     Upon a single Dish, and Tavern Wine,     . . .     162  Toland's Invit     2
     She'll not have left one single Prelate:    . .    303  Storm            20
     No single Tongue one Moment mute;   . . . . . .    450  Modern Lady      177
     Whole Squadrons with a single blow:      . . .     461  Birthday Song     32
     And, faultless to a single Hair.    . . . . . .    584  Strephon Chloe     6
     The single Pillar for his Country's Good,   . .    770  Horace 1, 14      16
     He sees one single Tory there:  . . . . . . .      789  Dick's Variety    36
     Yet cannot prove a single Fact.     . . . . . .    795  Traulus 1          5
     And ev'ry Nymph must enter single;  . . . . . .    893  Panegyr Dean     210
     But your rhyme was not double, 'cause your sight was but  980  Tho: Sheridan    2
         single.
     In each single verse, took up a diameter.   . . . . . 1026  Sheri Circles   12
SINGLETON
     Calls Singleton his Brother Serjeant.    . . . . .  812  Bro Protestant    28
SINGLY
     From ruling there the Household singly    . . . .   745  Stel Distress      9
     From ruling there the Household singly,   . . . .   750  Stel Wood-Park    33
     Desires me singly   . . . . . . . . . . . . .     1014  Swift to Sheri    30
SINGS
     Came an Heir-loom, as Homer sings,  . . . . . .    134  Magician's Rod    64
     Whilst an alluding Hymn some Artist sings,   . .    162  Toland's Invit    13
     He singing flies, and flying sings,      . . .     231  Prog of Poetry    45
     Riches, the Wisest Monarch sings,   . . . . . .    239  Run Bankers       21
     When rapt in Heav'nly Airs, he sings     . . .     496  Panegyr Swift    102
     With Pleasure, as the Poet sings,   . . . . . .    924  Riddle 8          15
SINISTER
     And, having no sinister Ends,   . . . . . . . .    605  Beasts Confess   143
SINK
     Or images that sink in streams;  . . . . . . .     35  Ode Sancroft      40
     Returning Home at Night, you'll find the Sink   . .    137  City Shower      5
     Should sink and fall about his Ears   . . . . .    160  Atlas            10
     He must sink down, or find Up-holders    . . . .   160  Atlas            22
     Blew his last Breath to sink the lighter Scale.  . .    235  Elegy on Demar  34
     Swim where the Bird of Jove would sink,  . . . .   253  Bubble           55
     The Moysture dry'd they sink again,      . . . .   254  Bubble           87
     Shall sink, and leave no mark behind it.    . .    255  Bubble          136
     For if the Sea should sink so low   . . . . . .    258  Bubble          195
     Why should he sink where nothing seem'd to press?  . . . 284 Elegy Boat       3
     If <Hort> must sink, she grieves to tell it,  . .    303  Storm           19
     "Or, wou'd you see his Spirits sink,     . . . .   305  Storm            67
     Nor, will you find your Fortune sink,    . . . .   414  Censure          25
     If mountains sink to vales, if cityes dye   . .    419  Shall Repine       3
     Or Hairs that sink the Forehead low,     . . . .   527  Lady's Dres Rm    57
     Should some imperious Neighbour sink the Boats,    534  To Mr. Gay        89
     May sink by premier Ministers of State.  . . . .   535  To Mr. Gay       116
     You want a Hand to clear a filthy Sink;  . . . .   535  To Mr. Gay       127
```

SINK	(CONTINUED)	PAGE	TITLE	LINE
	Yet, when you sink, I seem the higher.	555	Death of Swift	46
	I sink from Reverie to Rest.	578	Day Judgement	2
	Can raise them up, or sink them down, ...	620	Scandal Poem 1	91
	Can raise them up, or sink them down, ...	626	Scandal Poem 2	89
	No Rhymer can like Welsted sink.	654	On Poetry	394
	I sink in the spleen, ...	852	Lady's Lament	35
	I almost sink with my own Weight;	917	Riddle 3	6
	Or sink her to a pocky Whore.	929	Riddle 15	D 8
SINKING				
	"To save their sinking Country lent, ...	568	Death of Swift	375
	My sinking Spirits now supplies	727	To Stella	109
	His Pen to save a sinking Nation draws, ...	770	Horace 1, 14	26
	"That sinking the coin is a dangerous joke.	843	Ay and No	14
SINKS				
	He soars sublimest when he Sinks:	80	Vanbrug House	52
	And in he leaps, and down he sinks.	252	Bubble	32
	Sinks down at once, and there he lyes, ...	253	Bubble	82
	Who lifts the Poor, and sinks the Proud, ...	258	Bubble	210
	(But by his Leave he sinks a Score,)	456	Dean Smedley	34
	Exalts the Spirits, sinks the Lees.	731	Stella, Poems	130
SINNER				
	While each pale Sinner hangs his Head, ...	579	Day Judgement	9
	Then hear an old experienc'd Sinner	642	On Poetry	75
SINNERS				
	We Sinners are too apt to slight.	942	Probatur Alit	20
SINNING				
	This wicked Rogue Waters, who always is sinning, . .	238	Excellent Song	26
SINS				
	Ah, Britain, land of angels! which of all thy sins, . .	37	Ode Sancroft	92
	Thinks heav'n has cancel'd all our sins, ...	40	Ode Sancroft	181
	Bred in my scene, and for the poet's sins	46	To Congreve	97
	Than all the Sins he ever bore.	497	Panegyr Swift	141
	Should to the Priest confess their Sins;	601	Beasts Confess	11
	He can punish Sins enormous.	830	Legion Club	34
	To punish my sins, ...	851	Lady's Lament	5
SIR SEE SR				
	How vainly (Sir) did Your fond Enemy try	9	Ode to King	101
	Then (Sir,) accept this worthless Verse.	32	Ode to Temple	199
	But coldly said, Your Servant, Sir.	172	Horace 1, 7	54
	(Ere since Sir William <Gore> was May'r, ...	180	Horace 2, 1	9
	Faith Sir, you know as much as I.	202	Horace 2, 6	96
	Sir, you mistake me all this while:	298	Horrid Plot	16
	Now, let me tell you, plainly, Sir, ...	299	Horrid Plot	43
	Sir, to be plain, I tell you what;	300	Horrid Plot	67
	You'll pardon me Sir, your Cunning I smoak, . . .	336	Serious Poem	65
	You can't, grave Sir, believe it hard, ...	475	Epist on Epist	3
	Will you, Sir <Spencer>? or, will you, or you? . .	536	To Mr. Gay	152
	Sir <Robert> weary'd by Will. <Pulteney's> Teazings,	537	Mr. Pulteney	1
	Why Sir, I differ from you there, ...	547	Life of Swift	81
	Offend our Patriot, Great Sir <Robert>, ...	548	Life of Swift	108
	"Sir, our Accounts are diff'rent quite, ...	550	Life of Swift	194
	Now, Chartres at Sir Robert's Levee:	560	Death of Swift	189
	"Sir you may find them in Duck-lane:	563	Death of Swift	258
	"Next, here's Sir Robert's Vindication, ...	563	Death of Swift	277
	And with Hats so very big, Sir, ...	573	Helter Skelter	17
	And with powder'd Caps and Wigs, Sir;	573	Helter Skelter	18
	Than my Friend Sir <Robert> <Brass>	637	Epistle Lady	246
	A Pamphlet in Sir Rob's Defence	646	On Poetry	187
	You thought that Satire Sir,--but you are bit. . . .	669	Epig Carthy 17	D 2
	<Zounds> Sir. But to be short and serious	774	Mullinix Tim	33
	Subscribes, Dear Sir, your Brother loving.	812	Bro Protestant	20
	Sir, we the Ministers of State.	812	Bro Protestant	24
	Let Sir <Tom>, that rampant Ass, ...	831	Legion Club	63
	Jack, the Grandson of Sir Hardress?	834	Legion Club	140
	Sir Archibald that val'rite Knight, ...	848	Old Thorn	9
	(Sir Archibald whose fav'rite Name	848	Old Thorn	13
	Sir Arthur begins, ...	851	Lady's Lament	6
	To 'scape them, Sir Arthur	854	Lady's Lament	83
	And so I bid Sir <Arthur> write.	859	Lady Acheson	4
	And Sir I know you hate a Crowd.	860	Lady Acheson	24
	Sir Arthur the Malster! how fine it will sound? . . .	868	Grand Question	45
	Of this, to be sure, Sir Arthur has Warning, . . .	869	Grand Question	69
	Noble Captain, your Servant--Sir Arthur your Slave; . .	869	Grand Question	72
	You must be obey'd--your Servant, Sir Arthur; . . .	869	Grand Question	80
	No, Madam; 'tis only Sir Arthur a humming. . . .	871	Grand Question	128
	Sir Arthur too shall have his Will, ...	875	Drapier's Hill	9
	(I spare the Thistle for Sir Arthur's sake.) . . .	881	Pastoral Dial	18
	Sir <Arthur>, since you set the Pattern, . . .	888	Panegyr Dean	57
	To drink Sir <Arthur's> Health and mine: . . .	890	Panegyr Dean	102
	By clapping Billets on your Door and Posts Sir. . .	1002	Reply by Dean	12
	Oh, there you think you have me safe! but hold Sir, . .	1004	Dan J's Reply	27
	By your good Leave, my most profound and bold Sir, . .	1004	Dan J's Reply	30
	Alas, Sir, I had no Design, ...	1005	Sheridan's Sub	17
SIRE				
	And then the hospitable Sire	91	Bauc & Phil 1	55
	And then the Hospitable Sire	111	Bauc & Phil 2	23
	See, said the Sire, how soon 'tis done:	189	Faggot	9
	Since Delany has dar'd, like Prometheus his Sire, . .	266	Apollo	95
	Discovers Vulcan for thy Sire, ...	323	Pethox	6
	He must be greater than his Sire:	461	Birthday Song	22

		PAGE	TITLE	LINE
SIRE	(CONTINUED)			
As Overton has drawn his Sire	. . . .	461	Birthday Song	37
The Marks peculiar of his Sire.	. . . . . .	798	Traulus 1	82
By the Sire exhal'd from Dung:	. . . .	799	Traulus 2	4
Who could this Coxcomb be, and who his Sire?	. . . .	825	Noisy Tom	6
The vig'rous Youth, and aged Sire:	. . . . . .	922	Riddle 7	26
SIRES				
Among those venerable Sires.	. . . .	702	Cadenus Vaness	501
SIRLOIN				
A Stone and a quarter of Beef from my Sirloin.	. . .	867	Grand Question	18
SIRRAH				
Why Sirrah said the Noble 'Squire, how dare you see my Face,		343	Upon His Grace	43
Would, as he lay under, cry out, Sirrah, yield:	. . .	967	Letter Sherid	16
But coach it or cart it, I'd have you know, Sirrah,	.	979	Dean to Tho: S	11
SIRS				
I must confess that as to me, Sirs,	. . . .	993	On Picture	13
SISIPHUS				
And Sisiphus lay sleeping on his Stone.	. . . . .	9	Ode to King	97
SISTER				
Her Sister Isles are Conquered too as well as She.	.	9	Ode to King	100
Shew the Delights thy Sister Nature yields,	. . . .	31	Ode to Temple	137
Meets, and salutes her sister link again;	. . . .	51	Temple Ill	4
A walking vapor, like thy sister fame.	. . . . .	54	Temple Ill	102
Take Pattern by your Sister Star,	. . . .	228	Prog of Beauty	69
My Sister has lately depos'd upon Oath,	. . . . .	264	Apollo	37
My Sister transcrib'd it last Night, to his Sorrow,	.	265	Apollo	67
. . .but my Sister Marget she writes better.	.	987	Mary to Sher	34
SISTERS				
Where tho' her elder sisters crowding throng,	. . . .	49	To Congreve	181
"Go, Sisters Nine, into that Cabbin,	. . . . .	320	First of April	3
"Sisters, said she, my Life I'll lay,	. . . . .	322	First of April	55
SIT				
Look where exalted Vertue and Religion sit	. . .	21	Ode Athenian	176
Sit clad in lawn of purer woven day,	. . . . .	41	Ode Sancroft	235
She'll strain a Point, and sit astride,	. . . . .	100	Elegy Patrige	86
But more inclining to sit still.	. . . . . .	170	Horace 1, 7	12
Sit squeezing Images of Wax.	. . . .	240	Run Bankers	32
We sit an hour to drink and chat.	. . . . .	280	Journal	54
Would sit whole Ev'nings at the Ale-house:	. . .	352	Wood Ironmongr	6
Nor shall I dull in Silence sit;	. . . . . .	411	Dial Rich Marb	89
All others who inferior sit,	. . . . . .	414	Censure	8
Whole Hours can with a Coxcomb sit,	. . . . .	416	Woman's Mind	7
Lo here I sit at holy head	. . . .	420	Holyhead	1
Sit light upon a lawyer's mind:	. . . . .	433	Answer Paulus	52
To sit among that <scoundrel> crew,	. . . . .	436	Answer Paulus	132
You see the Booby Husband sit	. . . . . .	448	Modern Lady	114
Our Madam can sit up all Night;	. . . . . .	451	Modern Lady	217
Then make this new Apollo sit	. . . . . .	462	Birthday Song	71
Get Leave to sit whene'er you will;	. . . .	480	Libel on D- D-	4
The Council sit; approve the Doctor's Skill;	. . .	534	To Mr. Gay	79
Nor lets him sit as Justice on the Bench,	. . . .	537	Mr. Pulteney	5
"In Senates sit, at making Laws;	. . . . .	549	Life of Swift	163
How does he fancy we can sit,	. . . . .	556	Death of Swift	91
The Muse invok'd, sit down to write;	. . . .	643	On Poetry	86
Sit still, and swallow down your Spittle.	. . .	644	On Poetry	122
Put on the Critick's Brow, and sit	. . . . .	647	On Poetry	235
If, on Parnassus' Top you sit,	. . . . .	651	On Poetry	329
Appointed sov'reign Judge to sit	. . . . .	655	On Poetry	427
Whole afternoons will sit beside her,	. . .	762	Bec's B-Day	49
While they sit a picking Straws	. . . . .	831	Legion Club	49
There sit <Clements>, <Dilks>, and <Harrison>,	. .	837	Legion Club	181
I should never sit still:	. . . . . .	852	Lady's Lament	38
I'm all over dawb'd when I sit by the Dean.	. . .	868	Grand Question	30
For the Captain's entreated to sit by your Side;	.	871	Grand Question	132
And, as you in Commission sit,	. . . . . .	888	Panegyr Dean	41
How could she sit the live-long Day,	. . . . .	891	Panegyr Dean	145
With Peggy Dixon thoughtful sit,	. . . . .	897	Panegyr Dean	331
Come sit by my side, while this picture I draw:	. .	955	Portrait Life	1
. . .I came back to sit with the Ladies this Night.	.	1013	Swift to Sheri	3
SITS				
Sits with his Knees up to his Chin;	. . . . . .	127	Little House	20
Box'd in a Chair the Beau impatient sits,	. . . .	139	City Shower	43
Displays his Talent, sits till Ten,	. . . . .	173	Horace 1, 7	75
Sits on her cloudy wrinckled Face.	. . . . .	226	Prog of Beauty	4
Sits down to Dinner just at four;	. . . . .	291	Prog Marriage	56
And, when he sits to write,	. . . . .	395	Grub-Street	14
Sits up till Midnight with his Host,	. . . . .	398	Earl of P-b-w	5
The Dean sits plodding on a Book,	. . . . .	405	Swift to Pope	7
Sits mounted on the Garden Roller.	. . . . .	410	Dial Rich Marb	62
While he sits by a grinning,	. . . . . .	425	Five Ladies	5
She sits tormenting every Guest,	. . . . .	448	Modern Lady	110
Now all alone poor Madam sits,	. . . . .	451	Modern Lady	198
And, sits aloft on Pindus Head,	. . . . .	483	Libel on D- D-	87
When'er the Wind of Favour sits,	. . . . .	493	Panegyr Swift	17
On Box of Cedar sits the Wife,	. . . . .	590	Strephon Chloe	207
Where Echo sits, and list'ning mocks.	. . . .	597	Cassinus Peter	108
Now at the Table head she sits	. . . . .	745	Stel Distress	11
Now at the Table-Head she sits,	. . . . .	750	Stel Wood-Park	9
That Time sits with his Scythe to mow	. . . . .	757	Stel B-day '24	37
Here poor Pomona sits on thorns:	. . . . . .	901	Dean's Reasons	92

SITS   (CONTINUED)   PAGE   TITLE   LINE
    Sits by this, to dress her soul. . . . .   907 Daphne   48
    Sits, and takes them in the Dark. . . . .   931 Riddle 18   D 8
SITTING
    Grown fat with Corn and Sitting still, ...   230 Prog of Poetry   3
    The hardest Bum will bruise with sitting squat. . . 881 Pastoral Dial   20
    I must now, at one Sitting, pay off my old Score: . 967 Letter Sherid   9
SIX
    . . .six Pence, besides Farthings, in Money, and Gold; 69 Mrs Harris Pet   2
    'Tis true, seven Pound, four Shillings, and six Pence,. 71 Mrs Harris Pet   40
    . .
    At six Years old, the subtle Jade . . . . . .   150 Corinna   17
    Then, bids the youngest of the Six, ...   189 Faggot   3
    For Life, six hundred Pounds a Year, ...   198 Horace 2, 6   2
    To spend six Months with Statesmen here. . . . .   199 Horace 2, 6   12
    A Coach and Six, and serv'd in Plate. . . . . .   251 Bubble   20
    The public should bestow the actors six. . . . .   308 Billet Players   22
    A thousand words to stand for six! . . . . . .   434 Answer Paulus   84
    "The Ladies here to Night by Six." . . . . . .   446 Modern Lady   55
    "Past Six, and not a living Soul! . . . . . .   451 Modern Lady   202
    Six thousand years hath liv'd the Goddess, . . .   465 Birthday Song   161
    More Sense than I can do in Six: . . . .   555 Death of Swift   50
    "Six Deans they say must bear the Pall. . . . .   562 Death of Swift   231
    "To sell him for Six Hundred Pound. . . . . . .   567 Death of Swift   354
    With Coach and Six, and House in Town. . . . . .   585 Strephon Chloe   42
    Left all below at Six and Sev'n, ...   714 Cadenus Vaness   888
    How Angels look at thirty six) . . . .   735 Stel B-day '20   18
    Of thirty six, and thirty eight; . . . .   735 Stel B-day '20   40
    The Cieling hardly six Foot high . . . .   746 Stel Distress   36
    The Ceiling hardly six Foot high; . . . .   751 Stel Wood-Park   54
    With six imagin'd cares to fright you. . . . . .   753 Gift for Bec   14
    At Fifty six, if this be true, ...   757 Stel B-day '24   23
    But we can afford you Six Traytors in Seven. . .   804 Irish Bishops   32
    Read six hours a-day. . . . .   855 Lady's Lament   132
    To live without a coach and six, ...   878 Robbin & Harry   30
    To troll it in a Coach and Six! . . . .   905 Death Daphne   88
    And here six Virgins in a Tomb, ...   923 Riddle 7   67
SIX-PENCE
    But Six-pence a Letter is monstrous high Wages: .   288 Bank Down   48
    Come, Six-pence a Dozen to get me some Bread, . .   953 Herrings   8
    My twelve Thirteens and Six-pence ha'penny. . . . 1033 Ans to Crown   8
SIX-PENCES
    For so many Six-pences, so many Pages, ...   288 Bank Down   47
SIXPENCE
    For three thirteens and sixpence to the clerk. . . . 308 Billet Players   20
SIXTEEN
    For Sixteen Years the Cause was spun, ...   690 Cadenus Vaness   124
    Since first I saw Thee at Sixteen . . . .   721 Stel B-Day '18   5
    The jades of sixteen, ...   855 Lady's Lament   130
SIXTEENTH
    A long-ear'd Beast, and the sixteenth Letter, . .   943 Probatur Alit   37
SIXTHLY
    And, Sixthly; for my Soul, to barter it . . . .   349 Whitshed Motto   21
SIXTY-FIVE
    With three hundred and sixty-five poems a year? . . 979 Dean to Tho: S   34
SIZE
    As Animals of largest Size . . . .   81 Vanbrug House   81
    Enlarg'd in Picture, Size and Letter . . . . .   93 Bauc & Phil 1   121
    As Animals of largest Size . . . .   109 V's House   123
    Improv'd in Picture, Size, and Letter; . . . . .   114 Bauc & Phil 2   98
    Of Size that might a Pulpit fill, ...   170 Horace 1, 7   11
    A Parchment of prodigious Size; . . . .   354 Simile Silver   22
    A Cupid in his face and size, ...   466 Birthday Song   201
    Our Equal rais'd above our Size; . . . .   554 Death of Swift   14
    By ev'ry size of Poets sung: . . . .   584 Strephon Chloe   2
    A Whale of moderate Size will draw . . . . . .   651 On Poetry   323
    Each Poet of inferior Size . . . .   651 On Poetry   331
    Although thy Size and Years are doubled, ...   721 Stel B-Day '18   4
    Thy Beauty, Size, and Years, and Wit, ...   722 Stel B-Day '18   10
    With half thy Wit, thy Years and Size: . . . . .   722 Stel B-Day '18   14
    Of ev'ry Taste to know the Size; . . . .   890 Panegyr Dean   118
    Two Temples of magnifick Size, ...   893 Panegyr Dean   201
    Greater be my size or less, ...   937 Riddle 24   D 36
SIZES
    Of all sizes and sorts, the Fanatical crew . . .   815 Yahoo's   21
SKEAN
    Whether Curr Plunket, or Whelp Skean, ...   298 Horrid Plot   20
SKEANS
    The Length of their Skeans. . . . .   246 Irish-Feast   64
SKELETON
    A Skeleton in outward Figure, ...   398 Earl of P-b-w   25
SKELLIN
    A Stiver or a Skellin . . . .   442 Ballyspellin   75
SKELTON
    To be call'd lean by a Skelton, who'd bear it? . . 1003 Dan J's Reply   18
SKIES   SEE SKYES
    As if it meant to touch the Skies; . . . . . .   10 Ode to King   123
    Th' Artillery of the skies . . . .   29 Ode to Temple   83
    From a Shoe Sole to reach the Skies; . . . . .   98 Elegy Patrige   22
    Fit to Invade or prop the Skies. . . . .   107 V's House   50
    From common Lightning of the Skies, ...   119 Apollo Outwit   10

746

SKIES   (CONTINUED)

	PAGE	TITLE	LINE
And then, descending from the skies,	178	To Lord Harley	62
Hear Sounds harmonious from the Skies.	230	Prog of Poetry	16
Nor a new Star adorn the Skies:	271	Apollo's Edict D	37
And must exalt him to the Skies:	271	Apollo's Edict D	41
Descending lately from the Skies,	302	Storm	2
To ape the Thunder of the Skies;	352	Wood Ironmongr	10
To rend the Skies with brazen Din;	354	Simile Silver	10
When she's exalted in the Skies,	362	Grace's Answer	41
Jove never sends us downward from the Skies,	363	On Dreams	3
Like gilded Vapours to the Skies,	386	Manly Virtue	104
With lofty Branches to the Skies,	393	Modern Poets	2
(Fear lent him Wings) for Safety to the Skies.	538	Mr. Pulteney	30
Jove, arm'd with Terrors, burst the Skies,	578	Day Judgement	5
Their Heads attempt the nether Skies.	654	On Poetry	404
And finds out Pallas in the Skies:	692	Cadenus Vaness	187
She ventures now to leave the Skies,	712	Cadenus Vaness	830
Among their Brethren of the Skies,	725	To Stella	53
With Neck elated tow'rds the Skies!	743	Stel B-day 22	62
By the just Vengeance of incensed Skies,	806	Judas	1
And wing'd with fame shall reach the skies.	877	To Dean Swift	34
When Saturn rul'd the Skies alone,	894	Panegyr Dean	233
Beyond the skies transports his mind,	900	Dean's Reasons	49
To fill the Earth, and Air, and Skies:	924	Riddle 7	92

SKIFFS

Ly waiting for the foundred Skiffs,	256	Bubble	155

SKILFUL

Nor can the skilful Herald trace	323	Pethox	3
Your skilful Hand employ'd to save	764	Stel B-day '26	37
Like Hemp, which by a skilful Spinster drawn	806	Judas	15
She's too cunning, and too skilful,	907	Daphne	41

SKILFULL

A skilfull Critick justly blames	467	Birthday Song	209

SKILFULLY

How skilfully Dan mends his Nets,	281	Journal	75
Or swallow'd alive, or skilfully bruis'd.	351	Wood Insect	12

SKILL

How the physicians swarm to shew their mortal skill,	42	Ode Sancroft	253
To shew his Skill, he Mars would join	99	Elegy Patrige	59
And as a Poet, he has Skill	107	V's House	41
Harly depends upon your skill,	140	Harlyes Surgn	3
Two Gods their Skill in Musick try'd,	156	Fable of Midas	25
Yet, wanting skill and pow'r to chuse,	178	To Lord Harley	57
Renown'd for Skill in Faustus Art,	182	Horace 2, 1	50
That Flamstead can with all his Skill	229	Prog of Beauty	99
Nor let my Votaries show their Skill	271	Apollo's Edict D	46
For Sherry's Quibbles, and thy Skill	373	Letter D. S-y	49
Unto the utmost Bounds of Skill,	373	Letter D. S-y	54
Improving hourly in her Skill,	416	Woman's Mind	25
Not for his skill to shoot the dart;	432	Answer Paulus	18
You shew you Skill in Grecian Story,	483	Libel on D- D-	97
The Council sit; approve the Doctor's Skill;	534	To Mr. Gay	79
For, Vengeance more embroils, than Skill repairs.	536	To Mr. Gay	140
"What St. John's Skill in State Affairs,	567	Death of Swift	373
Which by the Operator's Skill,	582	Young Nymph	25
By want of Skill, he always lost:	607	Beasts Confess	190
Nor Skill in Sciences profound,	641	On Poetry	29
But using neither Skill, nor Force,	696	Cadenus Vaness	302
A Project far above his Skill,	705	Cadenus Vaness	586
The Skill of ev'ry common Beau;	712	Cadenus Vaness	813
But, lest you should my Skill disgrace,	760	Receipt Youth	49
Madam, whose Skill does all in Dress lye,	886	Rev Market-Hill	99
Nor is your Skill, or Labour less,	892	Panegyr Dean	188
Have taught Men to extract with Skill,	920	Riddle 6	21

SKILL'D

No wonder then, if nicely skill'd	80	Vanbrug House	61
Thought himself now exactly skill'd,	87	Hist V's House	21
No wonder then, if nicely skill'd	107	V's House	35
Well skill'd in Mid-wife Artifices;	362	Grace's Answer	27
A skill'd Mechanick that has stood,	393	Modern Poets	11
You, who are skill'd in lawyer's lore,	489	Dialogue	7
Palladio was not half so skill'd in	893	Panegyr Dean	199

SKILLD

Or if his Grace were no more skilld in	88	Hist V's House	45
Skilld in the Horse-laugh and dry Rub,	217	To Mr. Delany	57

SKILLFULL

A Skillfull Houswife thus her Thumb	227	Prog of Beauty	41

SKIN

Have worn a Casement o'er their Skin,	30	Ode to Temple	126
Nor need the lion's skin conceal the ass;	48	To Congreve	172
Which happ'ning on the Skin to light,	84	Salamander	54
From House to House, wett to the Skin	90	Bauc & Phil 1	13
And from thy painted Skin conclude.	324	Pethox	26
And, Venus-like, her fragrant Skin	586	Strephon Chloe	87
As Chloe's Skin, almost as bright.	589	Strephon Chloe	174
From whence the tender Skin assumes	691	Cadenus Vaness	160
And nothing left but Skin and Bone;	759	Receipt Youth	8
Round all your Body plump your Skin;	759	Receipt Youth	30
Brac'd like a Drum her oily Skin;	895	Panegyr Dean	258
No new-flux't Rake shew'd fairer Skin;	904	Death Daphne	37
For, such a Shape of Skin and Bone	904	Death Daphne	61

```
SKIN            (CONTINUED)                        PAGE    TITLE            LINE
    The Tyrant strip't me to the Skin:      . . . . . .    915 Riddle 1          10
    My Skin he flay'd, my Hair he cropt;    . . . . . .    915 Riddle 1          11
    And Skin and Flesh in Pieces tore.      . . . . . .    925 Riddle 8          40
    No Lady alive can shew such a Skin.     . . . . . .    928 Riddle 13      D   2
    The Lillies of thy Skin compare;        . . . . . .    932 Riddle 19      D   7
    Thou sorry Scare-crow of Skin and Bone, . . . . .     1003 Dan J's Reply      17
SKIN'S
    And Skin's yet whole, I needs must own,      . . . .   372 Letter D. S-y      18
SKINNY
    With Skinny and Snipe:       . . . . . . . .           851 Lady's Lament       8
    With skinny, boney, snip and lean, . . . . . . .       861 Lady Acheson       42
    As, who shou'd say, Now, am I Skinny and Lean? . .     873 Grand Question    176
SKINS
    To Ladies Skins there's nothing comes so near.  . . . 943 Probatur Alit      42
SKIP
    Till they wriggle, howl, and skip.      . . . . . . .  635 Epistle Lady      180
    Dick nimbly skip the Gutter;      . . . . . . . .      784 Mullinex Dick      22
    But this skip of a Lawyer, where the De'el did he grow? 814 Yahoo's           7
SKIPS
    'Tis not that I value the Money three Skips of a Louse  71 Mrs Harris Pet     38
    Out skips a Book of Miscellanies.    . . . . . . .     651 On Poetry         318
SKIRMISH
    When at a Skirmish first he hears  . . . . . . . .     500 Doctor Delaney      3
SKIRTS
    Like a rich Coat with Skirts of Frize:    . . . . .     96 On the Union        8
SKULL
    So Maevius, when he drain'd his Skull     . . . . .    730 Stella, Poems      71
    Which, in its Jumblings round the Skull,  . . . . .    893 Panegyr Dean      191
SKY    SEE WINTER-SKY
    Ready to tumble down into the sky;  . . . . . . . .     35 Ode Sancroft       36
    Till Peace hath made the Sky serene,      . . . . .     84 Salamander         43
    Without one Wonder in the Sky;      . . . . . . .       98 Elegy Patrige       6
    Some new unbeaten Passage to the Sky;     . . . . .    210 Earl of Oxford     12
    Down from her Window in the Sky,    . . . . . . .      226 Prog of Beauty      7
    And when the Sky is grown serene,   . . . . . . .      354 Simile Silver      31
    Too pond'rous is thy Bulk to mount the Sky;  . . .    539 Mr. Pulteney       41
    You think some Goddess from the Sky  . . . . . .      591 Strephon Chloe    229
    The bolt discharg'd, the sky grows clear;  . . . . .   617 Scandal Poem 1     12
    You know, a cloudy sky bespeaks . . . . . . .         618 Scandal Poem 1     29
    They must be carryed through the Sky . . . . . . .    620 Scandal Poem 1    112
    The Bolt discharg'd, the Sky grows clear:  . . . . .   624 Scandal Poem 2     12
    You know a Cloudy Sky bespeaks      . . . . . . .      624 Scandal Poem 2     23
    In Vehicles they mount the Sky:     . . . . . . .      626 Scandal Poem 2    110
    You would swear it pierc'd the Sky;  . . . . . . .     638 Epistle Lady      250
    Must strole in Air 'twixt Earth and Sky;  . . . . .    689 Cadenus Vaness     86
    Direct the Zenith of the Sky;   . . . . . . . .        780 Mullinix Tim      248
    Not Iris, when she paints the Sky,  . . . . . . .      911 Aenigma             3
    And raise a Virgin to the Sky,      . . . . . . .      929 Riddle 15      D   7
    Fly, fly, above, above the Sky Rambling, . . . . .     959 Cantata
SKYES
    He bore the Skyes upon his Back     . . . . . . .      160 Atlas               3
    Bring all the Females of the Skyes: . . . . . . .      465 Birthday Song     154
SLABB'RING
    With Tyger slabb'ring in her lap;   . . . . . . .      761 Bec's B-Day        40
SLACK
    Yet Our Devotion may Grow Slack.    . . . . . . .      346 Prometheus         70
SLACK'D
    Yet Daphne never slack'd her pace,  . . . . . . .      177 To Lord Harley     27
SLACKEN'D
    But slacken'd by some secret Power, . . . . . . .      113 Bauc & Phil 2      73
SLAIN
    The Castle of Slain,                . . . . . . .      247 Irish-Feast        75
    "Here Cassy lies, by Caelia slain,  . . . . . . .      596 Cassinus Peter     77
    Thou hast slain Horace, what shou'd hinder . . . . .   666 Epig Carthy 2  D   1
    "Yet thou could'st tamely see me slain.   . . . . .    850 Old Thorn          68
SLAND'RER
    A Sland'rer, Traytor and Seducer;   . . . . . . .      798 Traulus 1          80
SLANDER
    Till Envy, Slander, Sloth, and Doubt,     . . . . .    412 Desire Possess     15
    Revile and slander, fume and storm, . . . . . . .      778 Mullinix Tim      167
    But now I smoak where lies the slander,--  . . . . .   983 Sher, A Goose      15
SLANDERS
    The common Slanders of the Times,   . . . . . . .      445 Modern Lady        31
    Their Inuendo's, Hints, and Slanders,     . . . . .    449 Modern Lady       142
SLATE
    A Lyrick Ode would Slate; a Catch   . . . . . . .       79 Vanbrug House      11
    A Lyrick Ode would Slate; a Catch   . . . . . . .      106 V's House          11
SLATTERN
    No longer calls me Snipe and Slattern;    . . . . .    888 Panegyr Dean       58
    A house-wife in bed, at table a slattern; . . . . .    955 Portrait Life       7
SLAUGHTER
    When Foes are o'ercome, we preserve them from Slaughter, 334 Serious Poem      1
    "To ruin, slaughter, and confound;  . . . . . . .      568 Death of Swift    382
    Soon repent, or put to Slaughter    . . . . . . .      838 Legion Club       213
SLAVE
    And a Grim Slave to wait on his Triumphal Car.  . .      7 Ode to King        44
    Can he who makes himself a Slave    . . . . . . .      221 A Quiet Life       39
    Than Rule yon Isle and be a Slave.  . . . . . . .      421 Holyhead           34
    "Provoke him with a slave in Power: . . . . . . .      566 Death of Swift    344
    I a Slave in thy Dominions;         . . . . . . .      660 Love Song           3
```

SLAVE	(CONTINUED)	PAGE	TITLE	LINE
The Men should slave at Cards from Morn to Night;	.	662	Upon Ladies	7
She tends me, like an humble slave;	. . . .	754	Stella '23	9
In Flatt'ry an Artist, in Fawning a Slave,	.	807	Advice Parson	4
You mistake; for a Slave, who will coax his superiors,	.	817	Yahoo's	68
Noble Captain, your Servant--Sir Arthur your Slave;	.	869	Grand Question	72
Nay; Man, my Master, is my Slave:	. . . . . .	916	Riddle 1	33
No Slave his Lord's Commands obeys,		920	Riddle 6	3
The haughty Prince, the humble Slave,	. . . . .	922	Riddle 7	28
Slave like them to Vulcan too.	. . . .	936	Riddle 24	D 18
A dirty parasite and slave;	. . . .	951	Upstart	D 26
Your now subdu'd and suppliant Slave	. . . . .	1005	Sheridan's Sub	6
SLAVER				
Why must he sputter, spaul and slaver it	. . . . .	796	Traulus 1	9
SLAVERY				
The Bondage and the Slavery of Years.	. . . .	24	Ode Athenian	259
From thee no Mark of Slavery they felt,	. . . . .	791	St. Pat's Well	21
Who now in Vice and Slavery are drown'd.	. . . . .	792	St. Pat's Well	38
Than live in Slavery to Slaves,	. . . . .	824	Printer Newgat	2
SLAVES				
These are the slaves whom reputation chains,	. . . .	48	To Congreve	163
Slaves to their Quiet and good Name,	. . . . .	221	A Quiet Life	57
Let courtly Slaves low bend the Knee	. . . .	386	Manly Virtue	93
Remove me from this land of slaves	. . . .	421	Ireld	1
Despising Slaves that cringe for Bread.	. . . .	483	Libel on D- D-	88
To treat our Betters like our Slaves,	. . . . .	493	Panegyr Swift	5
"Far to the Land of Slaves and Fens;	. . . .	568	Death of Swift	396
Damn'd Senators brib'd, Damn'd prostitute Slaves;	. . . .	576	Place Damn'd	8
At whose Oars, like Slaves, they all pull:	. . . .	635	Epistle Lady	160
From Slaves employ'd for daily Hire	. . . . . .	726	To Stella	106
Ordain'd by Fate to be the Land of Slaves:	. . . .	770	Horace 1, 14	2
His Spirit always strives with Slaves.	. . . . . .	799	Traulus 1	100
Than live in Slavery to Slaves,	. . . . . .	824	Printer Newgat	2
To be his Slaves must pay him kent;	. . . . .	883	Rev Market-Hill	22
His Slaves have ten Times more than he.	. . . . .	884	Rev Market-Hill	26
To vilest Slaves I owe my Birth.	. . . . . .	916	Riddle 2	2
SLAVISH				
Which drags the slavish World in Chains.	. . . . .	243	Horace 4, 9	14
To reach that slavish hateful shore	. . . . .	420	Holyhead	20
Abandon'd, stupid, slavish praters!	. . . . .	436	Answer Paulus	134
Redeems us from the slavish fears	. . . . .	490	Dialogue	33
To foreign Prelates make a slavish Court,	. . . . .	793	St. Pat's Well	75
SLAY				
Whate'er you did in Battle slay,	. . . . .	154	Widow and Cat	D 33
"But, ev'ry Hand may justly slay.	. . . .	548	Life of Swift	127
SLEEK				
But when he was grown Sleek and Fat,	. . . . .	153	Widow and Cat	D 3
'Twill be so oyly, and so sleek	. . . . .	780	Mullinix Tim	223
Sleek, <--> claims her as his Right:	. . . . . .	897	Panegyr Dean	344
SLEEP				
And (I hope) an Eternal Sleep,	. . . . .	8	Ode to King	80
Lords are a footboy's cronies in his sleep.	. . . . .	48	To Congreve	150
She, who on shady banks has joy'd to sleep	. . . .	50	To Congreve	221
By lodging Folks dispos'd to sleep.	. . . . .	94	Bauc & Phil 1	152
By lodging Folks dispos'd to sleep.	. . . . .	114	Bauc & Phil 2	106
To sleep could Mortal Eye-lids fix	. . . . .	133	Magician's Rod	37
Sleep, or peruse some antient Book;	. . . . .	202	Horace 2, 6	110
Not to disturb him in his Sleep;	. . . . .	280	Journal	46
He'd wish to sleep a little longer.	. . . . . .	296	Satiric Elegy	8
He can Eat, Drink and Sleep; now and then for a Friend		335	Serious Poem	43
No Creature in the Lane could sleep.		352	Wood Ironmongr	4
The Shepherd in his Bower might sleep or sing,	. . . .	792	St. Pat's Well	41
An I were to be hang'd, I can't sleep a Wink:	. . . .	869	Grand Question	64
One of us alone can sleep,	. . . . . .	931	Riddle 18	D 15
While true Lovers Eyes Weeping Sleep,	. . . . .	960	Cantata	
Sleeping Weep, Weeping Sleep.	. . . . .	961	Cantata	
Sleep like a Dormouse;	. . . . . .	1035	Servants Maxim	2
SLEEPING				
And Sisiphus lay sleeping on his Stone.	. . . . .	9	Ode to King	97
By some instructed Querist sleeping on the Sand,	. .	22	Ode Athenian	190
And He, the Dragon never sleeping,	. . . . .	134	Magician's Rod	73
The sleeping Hangman ties the fatal Noose,	. . . .	364	On Dreams	29
Steals to her sleeping Spouse to Bed.	. . . . .	453	Modern Lady	293
But Vengeance, Goddess never sleeping	. . . . .	529	Lady's Dres Rm	119
Sleeping Weep, Weeping Sleep.	. . . . .	961	Cantata	
Nor after your Vittels ly sleeping supine	. . . . .	1017	Swift Ans Sher	16
SLEEPS				
Kindled while reason sleeps, but quickly flies,	. . . .	54	Temple Ill	99
She takes a Bolus e'er she sleeps;	. . . . .	582	Young Nymph	37
While he sleeps the whole Debate,	. . . . . .	836	Legion Club	165
SLEET				
(The Wig was powder'd round with Sleet,	. . . .	625	Scandal Poem 2	67
SLEEVE SEE PUDDING-SLEEVE				
He twitcht his sleeve, and stole a word,	. . . . .	63	Discovery	19
"We oft, are Laughing in our Sleeve.	. . . . .	545	Life of Swift	10
SLEEVELESS				
Than others do, on errands sleeveless;	. . . . .	900	Dean's Reasons	54
SLEEVES SEE LAWN-SLEEVES				
The Sleeves new border'd with a List	. . . . .	94	Bauc & Phil 1	167
Will laugh in their sleeves: I can tell you they watch for't.		979	Dean to Tho: S	36

SLEIGHT
    His watchful Friends preserve him by a Sleight. . . .   196 Author Himself   62
SLENDER
    Sid's Rod was slender, white, and tall, ...   133 Magician's Rod   43
    Appear with slender Wands at Court: . . . .   189 Faggot   18
    In vain, --- for soon the slender prop gives way; . . .   672 Epig Carthy 24 D 16
    To slender Threads, may sometimes pass for Lawn. . . .   806 Judas   16
    My Person tall, and slender Waste, ...   915 Riddle 1   5
    Taper, tall, and smooth, and slender; . . . .   937 Riddle 24 D 32
SLEPT
    But hardly ever set my Eyes together, or slept a Wink. .   70 Mrs Harris Pet   21
    But ne'er consider'd where they Slept. . . . . . .   481 Libel on D- D-   38
    Which Celia slept at least a Week in? . . . . . .   527 Lady's Dres Rm   54
    What gave me Ease, and how I slept? . . . .   557 Death of Swift   140
SLEW
    He slew my Body, but you stab my Fame. . . . . . .   668 Epig Carthy 10 D 2
SLICE   SEE BACON-SLICE
    A Slice of Bread, and Mutton-Chop, ...   728 Stella, Poems   30
SLICES
    Cutt off large Slices to be fry'd; . . . .   91 Bauc & Phil 1   60
    Cut out large Slices to be fry'd: . . . .   112 Bauc & Phil 2   28
SLIDES
    Down from Olympus Top he Slides, ...   108 V's House   69
SLIDING
    So soft, so sliding, and so sweet. . . . .   467 Birthday Song   226
SLIGHT
    And surely Writes with slight of Hand . . . . . .   373 Letter D. S-y   48
    Our Invitation was but slight . . . .   859 Lady Acheson   2
    We Sinners are too apt to slight. . . . .   942 Probatur Alit   20
SLIGHTED
    'Tis all the angry slighted Muse can do . . . . . .   38 Ode Sancroft   108
    And insolently thrice, the slighted Maid . . . . .   43 To Congreve   3
SLILY
    However, I was resolv'd to bring the Discourse slily   71 Mrs Harris Pet   36
       about,
    Her Pocket-Glass drew slily out; . . . .   904 Death Daphne   64
SLIME
    All cover'd o'er with Slime and Mud. . . . . . .   255 Bubble   132
SLIP
    And, must my Lady slip her Season? . . . .   294 Prog Marriage   128
    Nor slip this Occasion to follow your Trade. . . . .   400 Tom Clinch   20
    And gave his Creditors the Slip. . . . .   456 Dean Smedley   44
    But, if I chance to make a slip, ...   548 Life of Swift   119
    "Would rather slip aside, and chuse . . . .   565 Death of Swift   321
    To slip his Ears, yet struck his Nose: . . . . . .   589 Strephon Chloe   184
    Should slip your Time of dropping Guineas; . . . .   821 Dr. Rundle   64
SLIPP'RY
    This Surly, Slipp'ry God, when He design'd . . . .   22 Ode Athenian   197
    Through slipp'ry By-roads dark and deep, ...   412 Desire Possess   19
SLIPP'T
    Out slipp't a Mystery of State . . . .   62 Discovery   7
SLIPPERS
    Her Night-gown and her Slippers brought her, ...   446 Modern Lady   46
SLIPPS
    For instance; when the Lilly slipps . . . .   226 Prog of Beauty   25
SLIPS
    Up goes her Hand, and off she slips . . . .   582 Young Nymph   27
SLIPSHOD
    The Slipshod Prentice from his Masters Door, . . .   124 Descriptn Morn   5
SLIPT
    And, instead of putting it into my Pocket, down it slipt: 69 Mrs Harris Pet   9
    She slipt Spadillo in her Breast, ...   447 Modern Lady   74
    Since this Reflection slipt your Pen, ...   485 Libel on D- D-   161
    In at the Pantry-door this Morn I slipt, ...   881 Pastoral Dial   29
SLIT
    Damn her, why don't you Slit her Tongue? . . . . .   220 A Quiet Life   12
    We'll show him the way how to crop and to slit; . . .   816 Yahoo's   52
    To slit my Tongue, and made me speak: . . . . . .   915 Riddle 1   16
SLITT
    For many good Groats his Tongue shall slitt: . . . .   147 Windsor Proph   10
SLITTING
    And slitting of noses, and cropping of ears, ...   816 Yahoo's   48
SLOBB'RING
    You, Mullinex, and slobb'ring <Carr?> . . . . . .   787 Dick's Variety   3
SLOBBER'D
    Was kiss'd and slobber'd by a Lad: . . . .   150 Corinna   22
    But, why wou'd he, except he slobber'd, ...   548 Life of Swift   107
SLOES
    His crabs and sloes may freely pillage: . . . . .   902 Dean's Reasons   108
SLOPS
    Some with Pomatum, Paints and Slops, ...   526 Lady's Dres Rm   35
    Her Washes, Slops, and every Clout, ...   530 Lady's Dres Rm   139
    And hates to cram the Sick with Slops: . . . . . .   605 Beasts Confess   134
SLOTH
    Till Envy, Slander, Sloth, and Doubt, ...   412 Desire Possess   15
    'Tis true, he hated Sloth like Pease. . . . . . .   602 Beasts Confess   46
    Bred up in Ignorance and Sloth, ...   655 On Poetry   409
    Sloth, Folly, Rapine, Mischeif, Lust . . . . . .   659 On Poetry D 410
    First, lolling Sloth in Woollen Cap, ...   895 Panegyr Dean   273
    Sloth, Dirt, and Theft around her wait. . . . . .   1035 To Quilca   12

```
                                                              PAGE   TITLE          LINE
SLOVEN
    Thus, when a greedy Sloven once has thrown  . . . . .     536 To Mr. Gay         161
    From sloven Bernard to beau Dalacourt.  . . . . . .       672 Epig Carthy 24   D   8
    Thus to a Dean some Curate Sloven,  . . . . . . .         812 Bro Protestant     19
    Old Robin, all his youth a sloven,  . . . . . .           879 Robbin & Harry     45
    You call him a Sloven in earnest or jest.  . . . . .      943 Probatur Alit      36
SLOW
    March o'er the ruin'd plain with motion slow,  . . .       55 Temple Ill        129
    Slow Vengeance, like a Blood-hound at his Heels.         210 Earl of Oxford      22
    "Winning my Way by slow Approaches,  . . . . . .          380 Apology Lady C     151
    In a dull Stream, which moving slow  . . . . . .         688 Cadenus Vaness      51
    Her Belly burst, and slow her Pace:  . . . . . . .       895 Panegyr Dean       276
SLOW-PAC'D
    Besides, that slow-pac'd Sign Bo-otes  . . . . . .         98 Elegy Patrige      31
SLOW'R
    The Number made the Motion slow'r:  . . . . . . .        113 Bauc & Phil 2       70
SLOWER
    The Number make the Motion slower  . . . . . . .          93 Bauc & Phil 1      130
SLOWLY
    The heavy Wall climb'd slowly after.  . . . . . .        112 Bauc & Phil 2       54
    A Thought came slowly from my Brain,  . . . . . .        741 Stel B-day 22        8
    Nor slowly move your Fiddle stick,  . . . . . .          958 Cantata
SLUMBERS
    Sooth my ever-waking Slumbers:  . . . . . . . .          661 Love Song           15
SLUNK
    They Nightly slunk to rob the Fold,  . . . . . . .       153 Widow and Cat    D   8
SLUT
    At other times a very slut;  . . . . . . . . .          937 Riddle 24         D  30
    Be she Slut, or be she Scold,  . . . . . . . .          953 Oysters             14
SLUTS
    Dermot, how could you touch those nasty Sluts!  . . .    882 Pastoral Dial       39
SLY
    By vertue of some sly Petition:  . . . . . . . .        182 Horace 2, 1         68
    Mark where the Sly Directors creep,  . . . . . . .      257 Bubble             173
    That a Pack of sly Knaves should get fifty per Cent,  .  288 Bank Down           52
    While the sly Mountebank attends his Trade,  . . . .    364 On Dreams           33
    Sly Hunters thus, in Borneo's Isle,  . . . . . . .      885 Rev Market-Hill     75
    But the sly Giver better knows thee;  . . . . . .       920 Riddle 5            35
    . . . a courting Sly Nancy.  . . . . . . . . .         1023 Nim-Dan-Dean 2    D  12
SLY-BOOT
    I much suspect you mean the latter, ah Sly-boot!  . . . 1003 Dan J's Reply        6
SLYNESS
    And then, with wonted Wile and Slyness,  . . . . .      1005 Sheridan's Sub      24
SMALL
    Into small States and Principalities,  . . . . .         26 Ode to Temple        5
    So small the gain those from your wit do reap,  . . . .   45 To Congreve        61
    . . .is a very small Stock,  . . . . . . . .             69 Mrs Harris Pet       6
    And one small Chamber on a Floor.  . . . . . .           81 Vanbrug House       78
    To a small Cottage came at last  . . . . . . .          91 Bauc & Phil 1       50
    To a small Kilderkin of Beer  . . . . . . . .           92 Bauc & Phil 1       67
    Your Building shall be small enough.  . . . . . .       108 V's House           74
    Thou'rt well contriv'd, tho' thou art small;  . . .     109 V's House          116
    To a small Village down in Kent,  . . . . . . .         111 Bauc & Phil 2       10
    To a small Cottage came at last;  . . . . . . .         111 Bauc & Phil 2       18
    And with small Change, a Pulpit grew.  . . . . .        114 Bauc & Phil 2       88
    Till the small ragged Flock is met.  . . . . . .        127 Little House        22
    His Quiet small, his Credit less;  . . . . . . .        221 A Quiet Life        42
    The great ones swall'wing up the small  . . . . .       253 Bubble              66
    To turn to small Money a Bill on the Bank.  . . . .     288 Bank Down           35
    We'll make a small one here by Art:  . . . . .          313 To Ford             58
    Can do it with a Small Expence.  . . . . . . .          361 Grace's Answer      22
    A boon so small! But I may weep,  . . . . . . .         403 Window Inns 10    D   9
    Complains his Budget was too small.  . . . . . .        486 Libel on D- D-     192
    Alas! that gives you small relief---!  . . . . .        546 Life of Swift       60
    Say, has the small or greater Pox  . . . . . .          595 Cassinus Peter      48
    Poor starv'ling Bard, how small thy Gains!  . . . .     642 On Poetry           59
    Tho' small the Time thou hast to spare,  . . . . .      656 On Poetry          451
    And take some small Diversions now and then?  . . . .   662 Upon Ladies          4
    With labour small, and income great;  . . . . . .       676 Parson's Case       23
    If a small Breeze obstructs the Course,  . . . . .      688 Cadenus Vaness      53
    Some small Regard for State and Wealth:  . . . . .      693 Cadenus Vaness     217
    To find her a great Witt, but the Dean a small Man.  .  716 Answer Rebus        14
    And puts them to so small Expence.  . . . . . .         735 Stel B-day '20      26
    Small Beer, a Herring, and the Dean.  . . . . . .       747 Stel Distress       56
    Small Beer, a Herring, and the <Dean>.  . . . . .       751 Stel Wood-Park      72
    Hard is the Toil, nor small the Art,  . . . . .         892 Panegyr Dean       181
    In our Ken, both great and small;  . . . . . . .        931 Riddle 18         D  10
    And as I please they're great and small;  . . . .       934 Riddle 21         D   2
    Big like Bess, and small like Sue;  . . . . . .         936 Riddle 24         D  28
    Swelling be my shape or small,  . . . . . . .           937 Riddle 24         D  37
    And they, alas, yield small Relief,  . . . . . .       1005 Sheridan's Sub      29
    Thy Words together ty'd in small Hanks,  . . . . .     1021 Nim-Dan-Dean 1    D  29
SMALLCOAL-MAN
    The Smallcoal-Man was heard with Cadence deep,  . . .    124 Descriptn Morn     11
SMALLER
    Hath smaller Fleas that on him prey,  . . . . . .       651 On Poetry          338
    And these have smaller Fleas to bite 'em,  . . . .      651 On Poetry          339
    Still their Authority was smaller.  . . . . . .         690 Cadenus Vaness     115
SMALLEST
    If hope e'er dawns the smallest of its rays.  . . . .    54 Temple Ill        112
    The smallest Worm in Celia's Nose,  . . . . . . .       527 Lady's Dres Rm      64
```

	PAGE	TITLE	LINE
SMALLEST (CONTINUED)			
Nor give the smallest Room to guess	588	Strephon Chloe	139
The Greater for the Smallest watch,	651	On Poetry	321
SMART			
And then we'll be smart on	423	Carterets Arms	5
"You never met a Thing so smart;	564	Death of Swift	285
Safely write a smart Lampoon,	634	Epistle Lady	153
Only make it smart a while:	638	Epistle Lady	265
Smart Jemmy Moor with Vigor drops,	654	On Poetry	399
With Pains unknown increas'd her Smart.	703	Cadenus Vaness	523
When bent upon some smart Lampoon,	892	Panegyr Dean	189
Can leave a Mark and give a Smart.	942	Probatur Alit	24
But keep a good tongue, or you'll find, to your smart,	976	Dean to Sherid	35
And at each Lash I feel the Smart	1005	Sheridan's Sub	33
SMART-ONE			
The smart-one replied, "There's no wit in the case;	843	Ay and No	7
SMATTER			
Of State-Affairs you cannot smatter,	642	On Poetry	51
Nor can of metaphysics smatter;	900	Dean's Reasons	60
SMEAR'D			
When dos'd with smoak, and smear'd with snuff:	936	Riddle 24	D 10
SMED			
Dear Smed I read thy Brilliant Lines,	361	Grace's Answer	1
SMEDLEY			
The very Reverend Dean Smedley,	455	Dean Smedley	1
Smedley, thou Jonathan of Cloqher,	476	Epist on Epist	31
How different is this from Smedley?	476	Epist on Epist	47
As you Dr. <Smedley> are, being sure	372	Letter D. S-y	33
<Dean> <White>, <Dean> <Daniel>, and <Dean> <Smedley>	742	Stel B-day 22	44
SMEDLEY'S			
(To thee I apply great Smedley's Successor)	518	Dean Hang Rape	44
Forming his Muse by <Smedley's> Modell,	458	Paddy's Charac	23
SMEDLY			
And Smedly, Flow'r of all Divines,	897	Panegyr Dean	345
SMEDLY'S			
Or of his own, or Smedly's Lay,	893	Panegyr Dean	221
Shall sing the <Dean> in Smedly's Lines.	897	Panegyr Dean	346
SMELL			
But with the odious smell and sight annoy'd,	50	To Congreve	225
None but the Fav'rite Nymph can smell it.	65	Problem	12
You smell the <Stink>? by <God> you lye,	67	Problem	55
What Street they sail'd from, by their Sight and Smell.	139	City Shower	56
I smell your gown and cassock	428	Beau's Reply	2
Send up an excremental Smell	529	Lady's Dres Rm	111
Could in the Dog-Days smell her Toes.	584	Strephon Chloe	24
He'll sweat, and then the Nymph may smell it.	586	Strephon Chloe	84
Let me, tho' the Smell be Noisom,	635	Epistle Lady	177
Clio stifled with the Smell,	834	Legion Club	121
I smell when I tread on't.	857	Lady's Lament	202
There's but one of us can smell.	931	Riddle 18	D 28
Yet neither Smell, See, Taste, or Hear.	935	Riddle 23	D 9
Is a damnable Smell both Morning and Night.	942	Probatur Alit	30
Come, follow me by the Smell,	952	Onyons	1
For a Grace, if we smell it.	1015	Swift to Sheri	58
For the Smell of them made me like Garlick and Rue sick	1029	Dr. Helsham	21
SMELLING			
And cure the Rank unsav'ry Smelling.	892	Panegyr Dean	166
SMELLS			
Some Mischief is Brewing, the Project smells Rank,	287	Bank Down	4
As Tisdel smells of a sock:	428	Beau's Reply	4
Who sees, will spew; who smells, be poison'd.	583	Young Nymph	74
SMELT			
I'm sure, 'twas I that smelt the <Stink>.	67	Problem	54
For I live on a smelt.	402	Window Inns 8	D 12
When he beheld and smelt the Towels,	527	Lady's Dres Rm	44
He smelt it all the Time before.	528	Lady's Dres Rm	82
But when they smelt such foul Corruptions round him;	536	To Mr. Gay	159
But, when he smelt a noysom Steam	589	Strephon Chloe	179
On what you saw, and what you smelt;	591	Strephon Chloe	246
SMIL'D			
He saw the Edifice and smil'd,	86	Hist V's House	9
Jove Smil'd, and like a gentle God,	107	V's House	51
SMILE			
Or the vast Charges of a Smile;	24	Ode Athenian	253
Just as the Rabble please to smile or frown.	210	Earl of Oxford	10
Then said his Lordship with a Smile, I must have Lawful Cash,	342	Upon His Grace	35
And saw the treach'rous Goddess smile;	413	Desire Possess	46
As we think fit to smile or frown;	620	Scandal Poem 1	92
As we think fit to smile or frown:	626	Scandal Poem 2	90
Tho' you treat us with a Smile,	633	Epistle Lady	107
Still to lash, and lashing Smile,	634	Epistle Lady	139
On your Faults no longer smile?	637	Epistle Lady	234
Then cou'd I forbear to smile,	638	Epistle Lady	266
Will smile, and think 'em all his own:	647	On Poetry	226
A Nod, a Shrug, a scornful Smile,	647	On Poetry	237
When to look Scornful, when to Smile,	780	Mullinix Tim	236
How to cut a Throat and smile:	800	Traulus 2	38
To smile on those who are least worthy.	884	Rev Market-Hill	26
A smile still ready at command,	951	Upstart	D 29

```
SMILES                                                   PAGE   TITLE          LINE
    Such are the smiles where drops of chrystal show, . . .    51 Temple Ill         21
    Or if 'tis true, Great Phœbus smiles    . . . . . .       372 Letter D. S-y       25
    <Meath> Smiles for the Joynture, though gotten, so late,  430 Dicky Dolly        19
    The Queen of Learning gravely smiles,   . . . . . .       692 Cadenus Vaness      199
    Your Ladyship smiles, and thus you begin;   . . . . .     871 Grand Question      113
    From a face that always smiles: . . . . . . . .           907 Daphne              22
SMILING
    Bush smiling round on all, retreats   . . . . . . .        64 Discovery           44
    And smiling, whispers to the next, . . . . . . .          200 Horace 2, 6         32
    And still as he writ, stood smiling and reading;  . .     264 Apollo              40
    The Soldier smiling hears the Widows Cries,   . . . .     364 On Dreams           15
    The smiling Cyprian Goddess brings   . . . . . . .        585 Strephon Chloe      49
SMIRKING
    His ruddy, wrinckled, smirking Face,  . . . . . . .       290 Prog Marriage       24
SMIT
    Smit with the glorious prize next struts in Sewel,  . .   672 Epig Carthy 24   D  9
    With mutual Beauty smit, their Passion grew.  . . . .     880 Pastoral Dial        6
SMITH   SEE BLACK-SMITH,COPPER-SMITH
    And fill <Jack Smith> with Hopes to keep his Place;  .    163 Toland's Invit      20
SMITH'S
    Smith's Dust, and Copper, Lead and Brass,   . . . .       344 Prometheus           4
SMITHFIELD
    From Smithfield, or St. Pulchre's shape their Course,     139 City Shower         58
    For lofty Lines in Smithfield Drols.  . . . . . .         650 On Poetry          300
    And Smithfield, I'll tell you, if not told before,  . .   814 Yahoo's              2
    And Smithfield, as Rap was ne'er colted before;  . . .    817 Yahoo's             57
SMITT
    That Dido smitt, might more caress him  . . . . . .       619 Scandal Poem 1      68
SMITTEN
    Who with an English Beauty smitten   . . . . . . .        293 Prog Marriage      111
    Tim, with his likeness deeply smitten,  . . . . . .       783 Tim and Fables      25
SMOAK
    Could Smoak, and Drink, and read the News;  . . . .        95 Bauc & Phil 1      174
    Not once suspecting, Jove would Smoak,  . . . . . .       107 V's House           60
    Cou'd smoak his Pipe, and read the News;  . . . . .       115 Bauc & Phil 2      126
    They vanish'd in a stinking Smoak.  . . . . . . .         134 Magician's Rod      58
    You'll pardon me Sir, your Cunning I smoak,   . . . .     336 Serious Poem        65
    But, when of smoak the room is clear,  . . . . . .        419 Holyhead Journ       3
    But, they can smoak the deep Designs,  . . . . . .        483 Libel on D- D-     101
    To stinking Smoak it turns the Flame  . . . . . .         529 Lady's Dres Rm     105
    With Eyes in Smoak and Weeping drown'd:  . . . . .        594 Cassinus Peter      26
    That Moll the Chamber-maid can smoak,  . . . . . .        890 Panegyr Dean       127
    When dos'd with smoak, and smear'd with snuff:  . . .     936 Riddle 24        D 10
    But now I smoak where lies the slander,--  . . . . .      983 Sher, A Goose       15
    Chimnies with Scorn rejecting Smoak;   . . . . . .      1035 To Quilca            3
SMOAK'D
    And Dido quickly smoak'd the Beau.  . . . . . . .         625 Scandal Poem 2      70
SMOAK'T
    And Dido quickly smoak't the Beau.  . . . . . . .         619 Scandal Poem 1      72
SMOAKING
    Ten Thousand Altars smoaking round   . . . . . . .        894 Panegyr Dean       237
SMOAKS
    The dullest Reader smoaks the Jest:  . . . . . . .        643 On Poetry          100
SMOAKY
    The smoaky Wainscot full of cracks   . . . . . . .        746 Stel Distress       37
    . . . I mean the city so smoaky,  . . . . . . . .       1022 Nim-Dan-Dean 2    D  3
SMOCK
    I keep in a Pocket ty'd about my Middle, next my Smock.    69 Mrs Harris Pet       7
    . . .my Smock was unript,  . . . . . . . . .              69 Mrs Harris Pet       8
    And first a dirty Smock appear'd,  . . . . . . .         526 Lady's Dres Rm      11
    Her Tea-Kettle's on, and her Smock at the Fire:  . .     580 Psyche               2
    "Go, bring me my Smock, and leave off your Prate,  . .   870 Grand Question      83
SMOCKS
    Smocks hempen wear;  . . . . . . . . . . .               441 Ballyspellin        44
    Bright Phillis mending ragged Smocks,  . . . . . .       729 Stella, Poems       47
    And wear out my smocks:   . . . . . . . . .              854 Lady's Lament       82
SMOKE
    Or thro' a Chink convey their Smoke,  . . . . . .        100 Elegy Patrige       93
    Thalia now began to smoke,  . . . . . . . . .            322 First of April      53
    Keeper, yon old Dotard smoke,   . . . . . . . .          836 Legion Club        159
SMOKES
    His Altar now no longer smokes,   . . . . . . .          687 Cadenus Vaness       9
SMOKS
    When Mrs Welch's Chimny smoks,  . . . . . . . .          419 Holyhead Journ       1
SMOOTH
    Smooth as that airy nymph so subtly borne   . . . .       54 Temple Ill         117
    Smooth Bawty did so far prevail;  . . . . . . .          208 Fable Bitches       16
    His Two-Year's Coat so smooth and bare,  . . . . .       231 Prog of Poetry      35
    On the smooth Ocean's azure Bed   . . . . . . .          251 Bubble              27
    But smooth your words to fit the tune,  . . . . .        467 Birthday Song      212
    Yet, in Your self when smooth and round,  . . . .        500 Doctor Delaney      29
    To smooth the Wrinkles on her Front;   . . . . .         526 Lady's Dres Rm      26
    And smooth the Furrows in her Front;  . . . . . .        582 Young Nymph         35
    Fair Utensil, as smooth and white  . . . . . . .         589 Strephon Chloe     173
    Clear your Looks, and smooth your Stile:  . . . . .      633 Epistle Lady       108
    Some famed for Numbers soft and smooth,   . . . . .      650 On Poetry          297
    Melancholly smooth Meander,  . . . . . . . . .           661 Love Song           25
    A Duke to know a Dean! go smooth your Frown,  . . .      678 Dean and Duke       13
    Taper, tall, and smooth, and slender;  . . . . . .       937 Riddle 24        D 32
    Smooth as our Bason's gentle Flood,  . . . . . .       1020 Nim-Dan-Dean 1    D  5
```

SMOOTH   (CONTINUED)   PAGE   TITLE   LINE
    Makes thy Verse smooth, and makes them last.   . . . .   1021 Nim-Dan-Dean 1   D 14
    Will ne'er be smooth, nor hold the Stitches.   . . . .   1021 Nim-Dan-Dean 1   D 18
SMOOTH'D
    When smooth'd by rubbing them together: . . . . . .   1021 Nim-Dan-Dean 1   D 20
SMOOTHER
    Smoother than Pegasus' old Shoe, ...   1021 Nim-Dan-Dean 1   D   7
SMOOTHEST
    I told him, in the smoothest way I could, ...   308 Billet Players   41
SMOOTHING
    "In mending your Cassock, and smoothing your Band: . .   872 Grand Question   150
    A Smoothing Iron, itself is rough.   . .   1021 Nim-Dan-Dean 1   D 10
SMOOTHLY
    Then in a Play-Book smoothly lays 'em.   . . . . . .   581 Young Nymph   16
    Fair Freedom's Emblem once, which smoothly flows,   . .   793 St. Pat's Well   67
SMOOTHNESS
    Adore the Smoothness of thy Lines: . . . .   1020 Nim-Dan-Dean 1   D   4
SMOTHER
    The Ladys vanish, in the Smother, ...   66 Problem   49
    I ne'er could endure my Talent to smother, ...   336 Serious Poem   69
SMUGGLE
    To hang up all who smuggle wool.   . . . .   423 Ireld   58
SMUTTY
    The smutty Wainscot full of Cracks, ...   751 Stel Wood-Park   55
SNACKS
    "Go Snacks with Thieves and Rapparees, ...   571 Death of Swift   449
SNAIL
    Thy House about thee like a Snail;   . . . .   109 V's House   110
    Like an huge Snail along the Wall;   . . . .   113 Bauc & Phil 2   86
SNAKE
    I've seen a Snake in human Form, ...   84 Salamander   38
    With Fan-Tail and with Snake, ...   426 Five Ladies   34
    Which gets the better, Saint, or Snake.   . . . . . .   777 Mullinix Tim   130
    The figure of Toope and Snake.   . . . .   780 Mullinix Tim   226
SNAKES
    Discord periwigg'd with Snakes, ...   832 Legion Club   91
    A Perriwig of twisted Snakes;   . . . .   903 Death Daphne   22
SNAKY
    Held out Medusa's snaky locks, ...   178 To Lord Harley   45
SNAP
    And snap some Cully passing by;   . . . .   583 Young Nymph   50
SNAPS
    Agreed. And yet, when Towzer snaps   . . . .   797 Traulus 1   35
SNAPT
    And not be snapt by Privateers, ...   168 Peace Dunkirk   22
SNARES
    But, see how Satan spreads his Snares;   . . . . . .   605 Beasts Confess   117
SNARL
    How oft they squabble, snarl and Cheat: . . . . . .   453 Modern Lady   281
SNARLERS
    Below the Lash of Snarlers Jokes.   . . . .   501 Doctor Delaney   46
SNARLERUS
    Snarlerus next, I'm sure has need   . . . .   373 Letter D. S-y   68
SNARLING
    And, jealous Juno, ever snarling, ...   621 Scandal Poem 1   123
    And, jealous Juno, ever snarling, ...   627 Scandal Poem 2   117
SNATCH
    Did bravely snatch the lovely helpless Prize.   . . . .   12 Ode to William   D 24
SNEAKING
    Came sneaking to the Chariot-side, ...   172 Horace 1, 7   64
    And in the sneaking Parsons Airs   . . . .   292 Prog Marriage   68
    by Sneaking Sniv'ling Round Delays.   . . . . . .   958 Cantata
SNEER
    "The powder'd Courtier's witty Sneer;   . . . . . .   380 Apology Lady C   146
    Can sneer as learnedly as they, ...   501 Doctor Delaney   49
    Tells, with a Sneer, the Tidings heavy: . . . . . .   560 Death of Swift   190
    The Statesman tells you with a Sneer, ...   605 Beasts Confess   141
    Not by Anger, but a Sneer: . . . .   637 Epistle Lady   228
    How <Sheridan> the Rogue would sneer, ...   741 Stel B-day 22   20
    I hate, who gape and sneer by Rules.   . . . . . .   787 Dick's Variety   2
SNEEZING
    Of your Sneezing; a Yean.   . . . .   246 Irish-Feast   56
SNERES
    Thy formal Nods; important Sneres;   . . . .   775 Mullinix Tim   61
SNIFT
    So, then you look'd scornful, and snift at the Dean,   .   873 Grand Question   175
SNIP
    With skinny, boney, snip and lean, ...   861 Lady Acheson   42
SNIPE
    With Skinny and Snipe: . . . .   851 Lady's Lament   8
    No longer calls me Snipe and Slattern;   . . . . . .   888 Panegyr Dean   58
SNIV'LING
    by Sneaking Sniv'ling Round Delays.   . . . . . .   958 Cantata
SNIV'LLERS
    Than all the Sniv'llers round my Bed.   . . . . . .   557 Death of Swift   142
SNORING
    From snoring all Night.   . . . .   245 Irish-Feast   16
    Sweetly snoring in his Cloak.   . . . .   836 Legion Club   160
SNOT
    All varnish'd o'er with Snuff and Snot.   . . . . .   527 Lady's Dres Rm   50
    His Snot into the Mess; 'tis all his own.   . . . . .   536 To Mr. Gay   162

```
SNOUT                                              PAGE   TITLE            LINE
    Putts This to's Excellency's Snout,      . . . . . .   63 Discovery         39
    On Tiptoe stood and rear'd his Snout,    . . . . . .  127 Little House      25
    Presume to shew his mortal snout,        . . . . . .  464 Birthday Song    144
    When you pertly raise your Snout,        . . . . . .  523 Betty Grizette    31
    In every <Arse> you run your Snout,      . . . . . .  774 Mullinix Tim      25
    You know him by his hazel Snout:         . . . . . .  785 Dick, Maggot       4
    Or hide his coward Snout in Mud.         . . . . . .  824 Printer Newgat    10
    Charm'd with his Eyes and Chin and Snout, . . . .    904 Death Daphne      63
SNOW
    By Age and Claps grown cold as Snow,     . . . . . .   84 Salamander        58
    As White as Snow, as bright as Day;      . . . . . .  362 Grace's Answer    32
    Though born in Snow, it dy'd in Flame.   . . . . . .  470 Burning Poem      16
    With Sun-shine, rain, and hail, and snow. . . . . .  621 Scandal Poem 1   130
    With Sun-shine, Rain, and Hail, or Snow. . . . . .   627 Scandal Poem 2   124
    Like a fresh <Turd> just dropt on Snow.  . . . . .   786 Dick, Maggot      14
SNOW-BALL
    The Snow-ball destin'd at thy Chops;     . . . . . .  779 Mullinix Tim     204
SNOW-HILL
    And in huge Confluent join at Snow-Hill Ridge,  . .  139 City Shower       59
SNOWY
    Shall at their snowy feet lay down:      . . . . . .  465 Birthday Song    168
    With Constitution cold and snowy,        . . . . . .  588 Strephon Chloe   152
SNUFF
    The Remnant of a falling Snuff,          . . . . . .    9 Ode to King      108
    Takes Snuff, and holds the Stakes.       . . . . . .   75 Game Traffick     12
    He burnt his candle to the snuff;        . . . . . .  296 Satiric Elegy     14
    To snuff the Lights, and stir the Fire,  . . . . .   483 Libel on D- D-   107
    All varnish'd o'er with Snuff and Snot.  . . . . .   527 Lady's Dres Rm    50
    Scarce glimmers, like a dying Snuff.     . . . . . .  787 Clad in Brown     18
    Taking then a Pinch of Snuff;            . . . . . .  839 Legion Club      240
    "By <God> they don't signify this Pinch of Snuff.    872 Grand Question   160
    With Snuff was fill'd his Ebon Box,      . . . . .   904 Death Daphne      39
    When dos'd with smoak, and smear'd with snuff: . . . 936 Riddle 24      D 10
SNUFF-BOX
    But pawns her Snuff-Box, Rings, and Keys. . . . .    452 Modern Lady      235
SNUFFLING
    From Tubs their snuffling Nonsense utter: . . . . .  892 Panegyr Dean     171
SNUG
    To some snug Cellar let's repair         . . . . . .  184 Horace 2, 1      109
    Lie Snug, and hear what Cricks say.      . . . . . .  644 On Poetry        118
SO        623                                            OMITTED WORD
SO'ER
    But find her where so'er she fled,       . . . . . .  223 Prog of Love      37
SOALS
    Or patch his broken Stocking Soals,      . . . . . .  728 Stella, Poems     33
SOAR
    Can soar with moistned Wings on high,    . . . . . .  254 Bubble            86
    To teach the humble Wren to soar.        . . . . . .  270 Apollo's Edict  D 26
    When Poets soar in youthful Strains,     . . . . . .  271 Apollo's Edict  D 52
    Like lofty Pindar I can soar,            . . . . . .  929 Riddle 15       D  6
SOARS
    She soars clear out of sight,            . . . . . .   31 Ode to Temple    144
    He soars sublimest when he sinks:        . . . . . .   80 Vanbrug House     52
SOBER
    By sober, Philosophick Laws,             . . . . . .   65 Problem           14
    When sober Folks are all a-bed.          . . . . . .  229 Prog of Beauty   104
    Thalia, tell in sober Lays,              . . . . . .  278 Journal            1
    The sober Hen not born to swim           . . . . . .  295 Horrid Plot      149
    Then ventur'd to give him some sober Advice, . . .   327 Epigram 1          5
    He may be caught with sober Lies;        . . . . . .  707 Cadenus Vaness   669
    The Nymph in sober Words intreats        . . . . . .  711 Cadenus Vaness   792
    And he never call'd me worse than Sweet-heart drunk or
        sober:                                           985 Mary to Sher      14
SOCIETY
    Thus all Society is lost,                . . . . . .  217 To Mr. Delany     73
    Find great Society in Stinking.          . . . . . .  590 Strephon Chloe   210
SOCINIAN
    "Become an Atheist, or Socinian.         . . . . . .  550 Life of Swift    175
SOCK
    As Tisdel smells of a sock:              . . . . . .  428 Beau's Reply       4
SOCRATES
    "By Plato, and by Socrates,              . . . . . .  384 Manly Virtue       6
    Tis known, that Socrates the wise        . . . . . .  619 Scandal Poem 1    79
    'Tis known, that Socrates the wise,      . . . . . .  626 Scandal Poem 2    77
    And how would Socrates proceed?          . . . . . .  724 To Stella         42
SOCRATUS
    With Socratus and Epicurius.             . . . . . .  891 Panegyr Dean     144
SODDER
    Will serve for Sodder well enuff.        . . . . . .  345 Prometheus        24
SODOMY
    For Sodomy hang'd, as thou for a <Rape>. . . . . .   518 Dean Hang Rape    48
SODS
    The Sexton shall green Sods on thee bestow. . . . .  235 Elegy on Demar    37
SOEVER
    That, let what <Dean> soever come,       . . . . . .  742 Stel B-day 22     45
SOFT
    And treads so soft, so easy, and so light, . . . .    54 Temple Ill       114
    Scarce had they spoke when fair and soft . . . . .    92 Bauc & Phil 1     91
    They scarce had Spoke; when, fair and soft, . . . .  112 Bauc & Phil 2     51
    But soft says the Herald, I cannot agree; . . . . .  338 Serious Poem     119
```

SOFT	(CONTINUED)	PAGE	TITLE	LINE

	PAGE	TITLE	LINE
Are soft and sweet as butter.	429	Beau's Reply	12
So soft, so sliding, and so sweet.	467	Birthday Song	226
Like Iv'ry dry, and soft as Wax.	584	Strephon Chloe	26
While we, by soft prolifick Show'rs,	628	Scandal Poem 2	151
Some famed for Numbers soft and smooth,	650	On Poetry	297
Wat'ring soft Elysian Plains.	661	Love Song	20
The few soft Moments they can spare,	687	Cadenus Vaness	42
That gentle, soft, engaging Air,	692	Cadenus Vaness	178
Then soft Voice and Speech absurd,	696	Cadenus Vaness	328
Now, with a soft and silent Tread,	727	To Stella	111
She, with soft speech, my anguish chears,	754	Stella '23	13
So soft, and yet so firm a mind?	755	Stella '23	20
The soft Endearments of the Nymph and Swain.	880	Pastoral Dial	8
The Cowslip soft, and sweet Jonquil.	894	Panegyr Dean	252
Can you refuse a soft Embrace,	932	Riddle 19	D 12
Often fair, and soft, and tender,	937	Riddle 24	D 31
Their Bellies are soft, and as white as a Custard.	953	Herrings	7
. . . and the soft soul of amorous Jemmy center.	1023	Nim-Dan-Dean 2	D 14

SOFT'NING
| Soft'ning the muse's thunder into praise; | 44 | To Congreve | 42 |
| Soft'ning with Songs to Son or Daughter, | 321 | First of April | 31 |

SOFTENS
| And Winter softens into Spring: | 387 | Manly Virtue | 126 |

SOFTEST
| Her Hands the softest ever felt, | 585 | Strephon Chloe | 27 |

SOFTLY
And softly steals in many Windings down,	31	Ode to Temple	156
Then softly turn'd aside to view,	112	Bauc & Phil 2	39
And softly stole to discompose her own.	124	Descriptn Morn	4
Both softly to the Cradle creep:	150	Corinna	6
Softly seeks her silent Mate;	661	Love Song	30

SOFTNESS
| Could give no Softness to his Face. | 587 | Strephon Chloe | 94 |

SOIL   SEE SOYL
Our British soil is over-rank, and breeds	37	Ode Sancroft	101
And which (to heavenly soil transplanted) will improve,	41	Ode Sancroft	228
When e'er the Soil has Golden Mines:	133	Magician's Rod	24
His odious Goun would soil her Cloaths,	292	Prog Marriage	80
And round the Margin sindg'd his Soil,	323	Pethox	8
"In wholesome Soil and Aether Pure;	476	Epist on Epist	50
There in the Soil began to root,	504	Doctor Delaney	121
Too neatly guilt for me to soil.	611	By Dr. Swift	2
Confess the Soil from whence the Victors came.	791	St. Pat's Well	16
I sent the Magpye from the British Soil,	792	St. Pat's Well	45

SOL
| When Sol pursues her with his fires. | 178 | To Lord Harley | 72 |

SOLD
Devour'd the Lambs, the Fleeces sold,	153	Widow and Cat	D 9
By Places and Commissions sold,	157	Fable of Midas	47
He wonder'd for how much an Inch 'twould be Sold:	288	Bank Down	33
Where Right, and Wrong, are bought and sold,	385	Manly Virtue	67
I never sold so cheap a Fan.	447	Modern Lady	89
Of Bargains sold, or meanings double.	469	Birthday Song	274
How cheaply had thy Liberty been sold,	531	To Mr. Gay	9
And Kings, like private Folks, are bought and sold:	536	To Mr. Gay	136
E'er drove, before he sold his Land,	598	Problem Solved	13
By Thousands I am sold and bought,	918	Riddle 4	13
Of Traytors who their Country sold.	921	Riddle 7	18
Were you drest like a bawd, and sold oysters at Billings-gate.	979	Dean to Tho: S	10

SOLDIER
To meet him next, the Soldier comes,	338	Wood's Brass	3
The Soldier smiling hears the Widows Cries,	364	On Dreams	15
Like the soldier from the Sutler;	574	Helter Skelter	34

SOLDIERLY
| Then, by a Soldierly Retreat, | 326 | Pethox | 89 |

SOLDIERS
| As Soldiers use, for love must marry, | 878 | Robbin & Harry | 18 |

SOLE
Britannia stript from her sole Guard the Laws,	12	Ode to William	D 21
Sole Patron of the building Trade,	79	Vanbrug House	24
From a Shoe Sole to reach the Skies;	98	Elegy Patrige	22
Sole Patron of the Building Trade,	106	V's House	24
With the Scrap of a Sole, and a Fig for the Bank.	287	Bank Down	30
Sole Patron, Judge, and God of Wit.	462	Birthday Song	72
By Dint of his sole Approbation.	475	Epist on Epist	20
And disappoint the sole Design,	481	Libel om D- D-	31
In all Affairs thou sole Director,	656	On Poetry	449
To Titles give the sole Pretence.	656	On Poetry	460
Don Carlos made her sole Director.	745	Stel Distress	8
Makes her sole delight to vex.	906	Daphne	4

SOLEMN
Make up its solemn Train with Death;	29	Ode to Temple	90
And others, who in solemn Sort	189	Faggot	17
"By solemn League and Cov'nant bound,	568	Death of Swift	381
Tom could talk with solemn Face,	784	Mullinex Dick	23
Death went upon a solemn Day,	903	Death Daphne	1

SOLEMNLY
| And, though I solemnly declare, | 202 | Horace 2, 6 | 101 |
| Both Solemnly put, in this hole on a Sunday, | 431 | Dicky Dolly | 23 |

                                              PAGE   TITLE   LINE
SOLICITIOUSLY
  "Do now solicitiously shun   . . . .   380 Apology Lady C   141
SOLID
  And solid Virtue does Your Name advance.   . . . . .   11 Ode to William D   4
  For solid Work, but not for Play;   . . . .   483 Libel on D- D-   90
SOLITARY
  To chear the solitary scenes: . . . .   901 Dean's Reasons   84
SOLITUDE
  "Thro' long Disuse of Solitude;   . . . .   379 Apology Lady C   136
SOLOMON
  And Solomon in Royal Vest;   . . . .   592 Strephon Chloe   288
  Or from Solomon produce   . . . .   637 Epistle Lady   237
  Should Solomon wise   . . . .   756 Dingley Brent   7
  How Solomon decides the Cause, ...   776 Mullinix Tim   98
SOLUM
  Libertas & natale Solum;   . . . .   348 Whitshed Motto   1
  Natale Solum: My Estate: . . . .   348 Whitshed Motto   6
  Libertas & natale Solum;   . . . .   349 Whitshed Motto   25
SOLVE
  To solve appearances of sight   . . . .   35 Ode Sancroft   28
  But now, to solve the Nat'ral Cause   . . . . . .   65 Problem   13
  And thus I solve this hard Phaenomenon.   . . . .   367 Answer Delaney   44
  I can solve the Difficulty.   . . . .   630 Epistle Lady   20
SOLVING
  Of Solving all Appearances they please,   . . .   19 Ode Athenian   118
SOME
  Sure there's some Wondrous Joy in Doing Good;   . . .   6 Ode to King   1
  When some Patrician God wou'd visit the Immortal Jayl,   9 Ode to King   93
  Or has he like some fearful Star appear'd?   . . . .   10 Ode to King   130
  To which they look as to some Guardian God   . . .   12 Ode to William D 31
  It seems some floating piece of Paradice, ...   17 Ode Athenian   44
  Justling some thousand years till ripen'd by the Sun,   20 Ode Athenian   129
  Is wonderfully mov'd by some exalted Men,   . . .   20 Ode Athenian   137
  To make some great Discovery, ...   20 Ode Athenian   143
  By which some fondly boast they shall for ever live, . .   20 Ode Athenian 151
  By some instructed Querist sleeping on the Sand,   . .   22 Ode Athenian   190
  Seems to have borrow'd some ungrateful tast   . . .   22 Ode Athenian   212
  Of some great King and Conqu'rors Death, ...   24 Ode Athenian   272
  It lost some mighty Pieces thro' all hands it past   . .   25 Ode Athenian 286
  Expect some great gigantick Son of Earth;   . . . .   30 Ode to Temple   111
  And tho' as some ('tis said) for their Defence   . .   30 Ode to Temple   125
  And in some untouch'd Virgin Strain   . . . . . .   30 Ode to Temple   136
  How some go downward to the Root, ...   32 Ode to Temple   172
  Some more ambitiously upwards fly, ...   32 Ode to Temple   173
  Some she binds 'Prentice to the Spade, ...   32 Ode to Temple   185
  Some to the Drudgery of a Trade, ...   32 Ode to Temple   186
  Some she does to Egyptian Bondage draw, ...   32 Ode to Temple   187
  Some she condemns for Life to try   . . . .   32 Ode to Temple   189
  And some, to be large cyphers in a state, ...   36 Ode Sancroft   59
  And some kind pow'r for once dispense   . . . . .   37 Ode Sancroft   87
  Unless, perhaps, some stars above be so;   . . . .   39 Ode Sancroft   144
  For, sure, we want some guide from Heav'n to show   . .   39 Ode Sancroft   156
  Some whom ambition drives, seek Heaven's high Son   . .   39 Ode Sancroft   166
  There some high spiritual throne to Sancroft shall be
        given,   42 Ode Sancroft   236
  Some angel say, what were the nation's crimes, ...   42 Ode Sancroft 245
  But find some new address, some fresh deceit,   . . .   44 To Congreve   17
  But find some new address, some fresh deceit,   . . .   44 To Congreve   17
  That be my thought when some large bulky writ   . . . .   44 To Congreve   35
  When some rough hand breaks the assembling-glass. . . .   45 To Congreve   64
  This bids some curious praters here below   . . . .   45 To Congreve   73
  Here, on a better day, some druid dwelt, ...   49 To Congreve   191
  The Muse, like some bright country virgin, shows,   . .   50 To Congreve   215
  Some short refreshment for your weary mind,   . . .   50 To Congreve   232
  As some fair pile, yet spar'd by zeal and rage,   . .   52 Temple Ill   47
  Or from Whitehall some new Express, ...   63 Discovery   30
  Some ply before, and some behind.   . . . .   66 Problem   38
  Some ply before, and some behind.   . . . .   66 Problem   38
  Some bungling Partner takes, ...   75 Game Traffick   10
  And tho' some Malicious Young Spirit did do't,   . .   77 Lady B- B-   29
  Some faint Resemblance to produce, ...   81 Vanbrug House   87
  Out from some Hole obscure he flies   . . . . . .   84 Salamander   33
  And should some Nymph who ne'er was cruel, ...   85 Salamander   61
  But now stopt by some hidden Pow'rs   . . . . . .   93 Bauc & Phil 1   133
  Some Wits have wondred what Analogy   . . . . . .   98 Elegy Patrige   19
  Triumphant Star! Some Pity show   . . . .   100 Elegy Patrige   89
  Some faint Resemblance to produce, ...   109 V's House   129
  But slacken'd by some secret Power, ...   113 Bauc & Phil 2   73
  To form some Beauty by a new Receit, ...   118 Biddy Floyd   2
  He hop'd to find some lucky Hour, ...   121 Apollo Outwit   45
  Some God May-Fair invented, ...   122 Empty'ng Town   2
  Such is that Sprinkling which some careless Quean   137 City Shower   19
  But, some will cry, Turn-Coat, and rip up old Stories,   143 New Song   21
  When I and some others subscribed our Names   . . . .   144 New Song   27
  Because, fcr some Reasons, I was Not in game.   . .   144 New Song   44
  And some shall admire his conyng Witt, ...   147 Windsor Proph   9
  Desires some Friend to lend a Hand   . . . . . .   160 Atlas   8
  Whilst an alluding Hymn some Artist sings, ...   162 Toland's Invit   13
  And shew'd some Humour in his Face;   . . . . . .   170 Horace 1, 7   8
  Some few Days after Harley spies   . . . .   172 Horace 1, 7   57
  You've some good Purchase in your Eye;   . . . . .   175 Horace 1, 7   128

SOME   (CONTINUED)

	PAGE	TITLE	LINE
But some gay coxcomb, or a rake.	177	To Lord Harley	22
Her love on some bright youth below,	178	To Lord Harley	60
Some strange Arcana to unfold,	180	Horace 2, 1	2
By buxom Lasses--Some repented	182	Horace 2, 1	52
By vertue of some sly Petition:	182	Horace 2, 1	68
To some snug Cellar let's repair	184	Horace 2, 1	109
Some tender Sonnet to indite,	184	Horace 2, 1	114
Except to lash some grand Delinquent.	190	Faggot	30
Some Wag observes me thus perplext,	200	Horace 2, 6	31
About some great Affair, at Two--	200	Horace 2, 6	54
Yet some I know with Envy swell,	202	Horace 2, 6	81
"I wonder what some People mean;	202	Horace 2, 6	84
"See but the Fortune of some Folks!	202	Horace 2, 6	88
Of some Express arriv'd at Court;	202	Horace 2, 6	90
Sleep, or peruse some antient Book;	202	Horace 2, 6	110
Some formal Visits, Looks, and Words,	204	In Sickness	13
Some new unbeaten Passage to the Sky;	210	Earl of Oxford	12
Some part of what I here design	218	To Mr. Delany	89
Venture to give him some Advice.	218	To Mr. Delany	96
Ay, this has some Savour:	245	Irish-Feast	28
It must be some enchanted Grove,	252	Bubble	31
From some malicious Tory's Brain,	256	Bubble	158
Some Cully often wins a Bett	257	Bubble	162
While some build Castles in the Air,	257	Bubble	165
Oh, may some Western Tempest sweep	258	Bubble	205
'Tis the Nymph that I courted some ten Years ago;	264	Apollo	44
That some Verses were writ with felonious Intent,	264	Apollo	47
To own the truth we have some private Ends.	275	Epilogue	14
From Airy Garrets some descend.	279	Journal	29
Some from the Lakes remotest end.	279	Journal	30
Some Mischief is Brewing, the Project smells Rank,	287	Bank Down	4
Think on some Remedy in time	293	Prog Marriage	103
Till banisht by some Coxcombs Raillery;	294	Prog Marriage	142
Her Favors to some broken Ensign	295	Prog Marriage	160
And that's the reason, some folks think,	296	Satiric Elegy	15
"Or, else some hiding Hole he seeks,	305	Storm	61
A Foot-boy to some Rogue Director?	312	To Ford	40
"I'll warrant she's some flaunting Dame,	321	First of April	25
Then ventur'd to give him some sober Advice,	327	Epigram 1	5
Some call him a Thorn, the Curse of a Nation,	334	Serious Poem	29
Some think him cut out from the Poisonous Yew,	334	Serious Poem	31
Some say he's a Birch, a Thought very odd,	335	Serious Poem	33
But some will object, that the Devil oft spoke	335	Serious Poem	57
And though some think him in the Wrong,	341	Upon His Grace	7
As when of old, some Sorc'ress threw	354	Simile Silver	1
To regal Rage devotes some Patriot's Head.	364	On Dreams	12
And making -- some for Ideots pass	373	Letter D. S-y	58
To one who sway'd some time before;	375	Apology Lady C	16
And yet there must be some Mistake.	376	Apology Lady C	48
Captain, I fear you've made some Blunder;	377	Apology Lady C	66
But visit him, and eat some Fruit;	378	Apology Lady C	88
And some thought modish to despise.	384	Manly Virtue	30
(Rais'd high like some celestial Fire	385	Manly Virtue	53
Except some Leather lost behind.	398	Earl of P-b-w	24
Each Atom by some other struck,	406	Swift to Pope	13
Some South Sea Broker from the City,	410	Dial Rich Marb	67
Seduc'd by some deceiving Light,	412	Desire Possess	17
In hope to spring some nobler Game:	412	Desire Possess	31
Some augmentation Sr You know	422	Ireld	35
There are some prating folks in town,	422	Ireld	39
Of some Invasion on your coasts	422	Ireld	42
Then Reader pray shed some tears of Salt Water,	430	Dicky Dolly	17
Some Authors say not quite so soon,	446	Modern Lady	39
What some invent, the rest enlarge;	449	Modern Lady	145
Ever with some new Fancy struck,	452	Modern Lady	236
I wish some Folks would pare their Nails.	453	Modern Lady	269
Some call their Monarchs Sons of Saturn,	460	Birthday Song	9
But you some white-lead ink must get,	463	Birthday Song	113
Should some obscure inferior fellow	464	Birthday Song	141
Make some provision for the Yonker,	466	Birthday Song	203
Your words to some Italian Tune.	469	Birthday Song	278
"Who only asks some pretty Cure,	476	Epist on Epist	49
Oh! cou'd'st thou, by some Magick Spell,	478	Epist on Epist	91
In some old Greek or Latian Bard,	479	Epist on Epist	120
Or, some remote inferior Post,	484	Libel on D- D-	133
Some by philosophers misled,	490	Dialogue	49
As some raw Youth in Country bred,	500	Doctor Delaney	1
Some fill'd with Washes, some with Paste,	526	Lady's Dres Rm	34
Some fill'd with Washes, some with Paste,	526	Lady's Dres Rm	34
Some with Pomatum, Paints and Slops,	526	Lady's Dres Rm	35
Satira's but some pocky Quean.	530	Lady's Dres Rm	134
On weighty Bus'ness, to some neighb'ring Friend:	534	To Mr. Gay	86
Should some imperious Neighbour sink the Boats,	534	To Mr. Gay	89
Some, when an Heir succeeds; go boldly on,	535	To Mr. Gay	117
Some Medals sent him for his Wit;	547	Life of Swift	91
Some high-flown Pamphlets, I suppose---:	550	Life of Swift	183
"Points out some Circumstance to please us.	554	Death of Swift	10
Had some heroick Action done,	554	Death of Swift	23
That I had some repute for Prose;	555	Death of Swift	60
But there's no talking to some Men.	556	Death of Swift	104

SOME   (CONTINUED)   PAGE   TITLE   LINE
    Some great Misfortune to portend, ...   557 Death of Swift   119
    Yet shou'd some Neighbour feel a Pain, ...   557 Death of Swift   135
    Some Paragraph in ev'ry Paper, ...   558 Death of Swift   167
    Some Country Squire to Lintot goes, ...   562 Death of Swift   253
    With Favour some, and some without;   . . . . . .   565 Death of Swift   304
    With Favour some, and some without;   . . . . . .   565 Death of Swift   304
    With some Law but little Justice, ...   574 Helter Skelter   31
    Some to Cuckold Farmers Spouses, ...   574 Helter Skelter   43
    Some to tumble Country-Wenches   . . . .   574 Helter Skelter   45
    (So some Folks told you, but they knew   . . . . .   579 Day Judgement   17
    At some Hedge-Tavern lies in Pawn;   . . . . .   582 Young Nymph   44
    And snap some Cully passing by;   . . . .   583 Young Nymph   50
    Yet, some assign a diff'rent Reason;   . . . . . .   588 Strephon Chloe   159
    To see some radiant Nymph appear   . . . . . .   591 Strephon Chloe   227
    You think some Goddess from the Sky   . . . . . .   591 Strephon Chloe   229
    Some try to learn polite Behaviour, ...   592 Strephon Chloe   271
    Some call it witty to reflect   . . . .   592 Strephon Chloe   273
    Some shew they never want explaining, ...   592 Strephon Chloe   275
    To build on some Foundation sound;   . . . . . .   592 Strephon Chloe   296
    Then gave him some familiar Thumps, ...   594 Cassinus Peter   37
    His Vigilance might some displease;   . . . . . .   602 Beasts Confess   45
    Some Faults we own: But, can you guess?   . . . . . .   603 Beasts Confess   75
    Though some had spread a thousand Lyes;   . . . . . .   605 Beasts Confess   149
    Some Criticks may object perhaps, ...   618 Scandal Poem 1   21
    When Jove would some fair nymph inveigle   . . . . .   620 Scandal Poem 1   113
    Some Critick may object, perhaps, ...   624 Scandal Poem 2   15
    When Jove would some fair Nymph inveigle, ...   627 Scandal Poem 2   111
    With some Gifts, at least endow me, ...   631 Epistle Lady   63
    You, like some acute Philosopher, ...   632 Epistle Lady   95
    That they might some better Way tread, ...   637 Epistle Lady   223
    Give your Head some gentle Raps;   . . . . . .   638 Epistle Lady   264
    'Till some fresh Blockhead takes your Place. . . . .   644 On Poetry   142
    Some famed for Numbers soft and smooth, ...   650 On Poetry   297
    And some as justly Fame extols   . . . .   650 On Poetry   299
    Translate me now some Lines, if you can,` . . . . .   657 On Poetry   481
    Come out with some lampoon on D'Anvers.   . . . . .   658 On Poetry   D 186
    Some Beast of Burthen or of Prey   . . . .   659 On Poetry   D 410
    And take some small Diversions now and then? . . . .   662 Upon Ladies   4
    Pope's Essays upon some for Young's may pass, . . .   670 Epig Carthy 18   D   5
    Chaff, straws, or fragments of some rotten boat, . .   672 Epig Carthy 24   D 14
    Or some rich benefice provide, ...   676 Parson's Case   21
    Or some worse Brute in human Shape, ...   687 Cadenus Vaness   40
    Some small Regard for State and Wealth: . . . . .   693 Cadenus Vaness   217
    Yet some of either Sex, endow'd   . . . .   700 Cadenus Vaness   444
    Some Clergy too she wou'd allow, ...   701 Cadenus Vaness   460
    For placing still some Book betwixt, ...   701 Cadenus Vaness   480
    Some Lines, more moving than the rest, ...   703 Cadenus Vaness   520
    Shou'd fix upon some certain Rule, ...   707 Cadenus Vaness   665
    Some fav'rite System to their Mind, ...   709 Cadenus Vaness   723
    "Or add some Grains of Folly more   . . . . . .   714 Cadenus Vaness   874
    To celebrate some Suburb Trull;   . . . .   730 Stella, Poems   72
    I had some Anger in my Wit.   . . . . . .   747 Stel Distress   68
    Accept for once some serious Lines.   . . . . . .   764 Stel B-day '26   14
    Some lasting Pleasure in the Mind, ...   764 Stel B-day '26   30
    Of giddy Winds, but make some friendly Port. . . . .   770 Horace 1, 14   12
    Thy Mast, which like some aged Patriot stood . . . .   770 Horace 1, 14   15
    As when some Writer in a public Cause, ...   770 Horace 1, 14   25
    I'll take you to some Friends of mine;   . . . . . .   780 Mullinix Tim   244
    Some cleaning hollow Tubes, to spy   . . . . . .   780 Mullinix Tim   247
    Some have the City in their Care, ...   780 Mullinix Tim   249
    Some teach us in these dang'rous Days, ...   780 Mullinix Tim   251
    Some whose reforming Hands engage, ...   781 Mullinix Tim   253
    Some for the publick Service go, ...   781 Mullinix Tim   255
    Nor fondly hope for some Reverse of Fate, ...   793 St. Pat's Well   85
    Some perhaps may think him able   . . . .   800 Traulus 2   45
    But, some has kiss't the Gospel Fifty Times, ...   806 Judas   11
    Some who can perjure thro' a two-Inch Board; . . . .   806 Judas   13
    Thus to a Dean some Curate Sloven, ...   812 Bro Protestant   19
    Has, with noise and odd gestures, been prating some years, .   815 Yahoo's   18
    We'll teach him some better address to afford . . . .   816 Yahoo's   53
    Some fancy this Promotion odd, ...   821 Dr. Rundle   53
    Let us try some new Expedient;   . . . . . .   832 Legion Club   76
    To bespeak some Approbation, ...   833 Legion Club   111
    Some they do say, 'twas the big man of straw; . . .   841 Ballad   D 12
    This Winter to invite some Friends, ...   860 Lady Acheson   23
    And, Molly, she said, I should hear some ill News. . .   868 Grand Question   52
    "Hist, Huzzy, I think I hear some Body coming-- . .   871 Grand Question   127
    When bent upon some smart Lampoon, ...   892 Panegyr Dean   189
    Or, offer'd in some flow'ry Vale, ...   894 Panegyr Dean   247
    Yet, some Devotion still remains   . . . . . .   896 Panegyr Dean   299
    Whether some late departed Toasts   . . . . . .   905 Death Daphne   75
    Must be some painted Toy I knew;   . . . . . .   912 Aenigma Expl   D   8
    And on some Dunghill left to rot.   . . . . . .   916 Riddle 1   42
    And some give out, that I entice   . . . . . .   917 Riddle 3   13
    I'm too profuse some Cens'rers cry, ...   918 Riddle 4   25
    Yet, some who ne'er bestow'd thee, boast   . . . . .   919 Riddle 5   29
    In Scarlet some, and some in White;   . . . . . .   920 Riddle 6   11
    In Scarlet some, and some in White;   . . . . . .   920 Riddle 6   11
    Though some are of so stubborn Kind, ...   921 Riddle 6   35
    I hourly wait some fatal End;   . . . .   921 Riddle 6   37

SOME	(CONTINUED)	PAGE	TITLE	LINE
Some enter boldly, some by Stealth, ...		922	Riddle 7	31
Some enter boldly, some by Stealth, ...		922	Riddle 7	31
Some are made, and some undone.		934	Riddle 22	D 4
Some are made, and some undone.		934	Riddle 22	D 4
Come, Six-pence a Dozen to get me some Bread, ...		953	Herrings	8
I hear with some Concern you roar, ...		1002	Reply by Dean	10
Captain Butler made some in the Church black and blue sick;		1029	Dr. Helsham	7
SOMEBODY'S				
For If somebody's grace		424	Carterets Arms	9
<SOMERS>				
Hal -- grows more Pert, and <Somers> not so Grave: .		163	Toland's Invit	22
SOMETHING				
I'll give something towards thy Loss;.		73	Mrs Harris Pet	67
For something that will conquer Fire, ...		83	Salamander	18
Thrice mutter'd something to the Air.		120	Apollo Outwit	36
They tell us something strange and odd, ...		132	Magician's Rod	21
Something in Verse as true as Prose;		199	Horace 2, 6	D
To Something Nobler in thy Face.		340	Arch-Bish Dub	16
I know the Times are something hard, but hope they soon will mend,		342	Upon His Grace	32
And may be something else withall.		361	Grace's Answer	8
It might be something in your Praise:		505	Doctor Delaney	164
I fancy, there is something in it.		545	Life of Swift	12
A modest Youth said something new, ...		701	Cadenus Vaness	454
She hourly press'd for something new;		704	Cadenus Vaness	555
Her Manner now was something new;		707	Cadenus Vaness	661
In Pleasure seek for something new:		728	Stella, Poems	18
To leave something behind;		857	Lady's Lament	200
By something form'd, I nothing am, ...		935	Riddle 23	D 1
But grant her a Sieve, I can say something archer, . .		972	S-'s Ans Sh-d	9
I've something else to do than watch.		983	Sher, A Goose	24
SOMETIMES				
Nay, 'twas affirm'd, he sometimes dealt in Rhime: .		193	Author Himself	10
And sometimes walks beyond his Bounds.		218	To Mr. Delany	94
So sometimes half a Face produce, ...		326	Pethox	83
So hard sometimes		441	Ballyspellin	22
Can sometimes drop a Voter's Claim, ...		485	Libel on D- D-	149
Be sometimes to your country true, ...		487	Irish-Club	17
Sometimes his Friend he would not spare, ...		602	Beasts Confess	25
His Zeal was sometimes indiscreet:		603	Beasts Confess	54
Sometimes to act the Parson's Part:		605	Beasts Confess	120
Further than sometimes by a Frown, ...		697	Cadenus Vaness	336
To slender Threads, may sometimes pass for Lawn. . .		806	Judas	16
Sometimes makes the Devil his Rod:		830	Legion Club	32
(Though sometimes thou wer't pleas'd to wink, . . .		894	Panegyr Dean	243
I sometimes live in House of Hair, ...		912	Aenigma	9
I sometimes give Advice in Writing, ...		917	Riddle 3	9
'Tis true, indeed, sometimes I save, ...		918	Riddle 4	31
Sometimes run out of all I have;		918	Riddle 4	32
Like Daphne sometimes in a Tree, ...		927	Riddle 10	D 17
Sometimes in Panegyrick high, ...		929	Riddle 15	D 5
Sometimes imperial Robes I wear, ...		935	Riddle 23	D 20
(An Author, where I sometimes dip a Days)		988	Letter Dr Sh-n	18
SOMEWHAT				
"Thalia said, 'tis somewhat odd, ...		321	First of April	18
I Must confess,that I was somewhat warm, ...		670	Epig Carthy 20	D 1
My Eyes are somewhat dimmish grown;		757	Stel B-day '24	42
. . . say is (tho' written somewhat at large) trim and clean;		1024	Nim-Dan-Dean 2	D 17
SOMMER				
If so be they are in Sommer set:		148	Windsor Proph	18
SOMMERS				
From Sommers down to Craigs and Walpole.		191	Faggot	52
SON				
E'er flourish't under a Successor or a Son; . . .		25	Ode Athenian	285
Expect some great gigantick Son of Earth;		30	Ode to Temple	111
Truth is eternal, and the Son of Heav'n, ...		34	Ode Sancroft	1
The Son of God pronounc'd by the same breath . . .		38	Ode Sancroft	119
To his undoubted Master, Heaven's Almighty Son. . .		38	Ode Sancroft	134
Some whom ambition drives, seek Heaven's high Son .		39	Ode Sancroft	166
That Heaven's high Son was in a village born; . . .		39	Ode Sancroft	172
When a holy black Suede, the Son of Bob, ...		147	Windsor Proph	1
From you, as from Latona's son.		177	To Lord Harley	32
"The Son and Father, join to tell us, ...		181	Horace 2, 1	44
Till pious Love inspir'd her Son?		269	Apollo's Edict	D 4
No Son of mine shall dare to say, ...		270	Apollo's Edict	D 20
See Philip's Son amidst his Persian Guard;		275	Epilogue	24
Soft'ning with Songs to Son or Daughter, ...		321	First of April	31
With Hermes, Son of Pleias bright.		326	Pethox	86
And said: By my Shoul he's the Son of a Beech: . .		334	Serious Poem	28
And instead of the Devil, this Son of Perdition . .		336	Serious Poem	67
And stabs the Son before the Mother's Eyes. . . .		364	On Dreams	16
My Son shall never see a College.		377	Apology Lady C	70
Now made--ye Gods!--a Son and Heir, ...		384	Manly Virtue	18
The Son laughs that got, the hard gotten Estate, .		430	Dicky Dolly	20
Who often long'd to eat his Son:		460	Birthday Song	12
Why then appoint him Son of Jove, ...		460	Birthday Song	15
And sees a Son in every God		466	Birthday Song	185
And, as they robb'd the Father, rob the Son. . . .		535	To Mr. Gay	118

```
SON            (CONTINUED)                                    PAGE    TITLE           LINE
    And then, said she, my Son and I      . . . . . . .      689 Cadenus Vaness      85
    You'd swear it is Apollo's Son;       . . . . . . . .    692 Cadenus Vaness     193
    "She left all Business to her Son:    . . . . . . . .    714 Cadenus Vaness     881
    Son and Brother to a Queer,           . . . . . . .      837 Legion Club        175
    The Son of Pitch, and gloomy Night;   . . . . . .        929 Riddle 15        D   2
    Witness his lazy, lousy son!          . . . . . . . . .  950 Upstart          D  10
SONG
    With many a heavenly Song             . . . . . . . .     17 Ode Athenian        54
    She still is welcome with her inn'cent song;   . . . .    49 To Congreve        182
    Not dar'd to injure with our lowly song;  . . . . . .     52 Temple Ill          44
    A Song could draw a Stone or Beam,    . . . . . . .       79 Vanbrug House        3
    Can hire a Lodging for a Song,        . . . . . . . .     79 Vanbrug House       16
    Can raise a Lodging for a Song.       . . . . . . . .    106 V's House           16
    With ev'ry Muse to Grace thy Song,    . . . . . . . .    121 Apollo Outwit       55
    Or Song of feather'd Quire.           . . . . . . . .    123 Empty'ng Town       16
    She made a Song, how little Miss      . . . . . . .      150 Corinna             21
    Atlas we read in antient Song         . . . . . . . .    160 Atlas                1
    As did Methusalem of old, and so I end my Song.          343 Upon His Grace      48
    Her Learning mounts to read a Song,   . . . . . . .      416 Woman's Mind         9
    Next, as the Laws of Song require,    . . . . . . . .    461 Birthday Song       21
    Made trebly dreadfull in your Song.   . . . . . . . .    461 Birthday Song       46
    For when you bring your Song in print,   . . . . . .     463 Birthday Song       85
    For ever fair and young--in Song.     . . . . . . . .    467 Birthday Song      234
    Supposing now you Song is done,       . . . . . . . .    469 Birthday Song      275
    Did Congreve's Wit inspire my Song:   . . . . . . .      496 Panegyr Swift       99
    Not minding when the Song was done.   . . . . . . .      775 Mullinix Tim        44
    Who, while I talk, a song will hum,   . . . . . . . .    900 Dean's Reasons      47
    Above a Song or two at most:          . . . . . . . .    993 On Picture          24
SONGS
    Soft'ning with Songs to Son or Daughter,   . . . . .     321 First of April      31
    For songs of Loyalty and Lewdness.    . . . . . . . .    650 On Poetry          290
SONGSTERS
    But Songsters must omit it not.       . . . . . . . .    464 Birthday Song      130
    Besides you Songsters oft have shewn,   . . . . . .      465 Birthday Song      163
SONNET
    Some tender Sonnet to indite,         . . . . . . . .    184 Horace 2, 1        114
SONNETS
    Sonnets and Elegyes to Chloris        . . . . . . .       79 Vanbrug House        9
    Sonnets, or Elogies to Chloris        . . . . . . . .    106 V's House            9
    These Elegies and Sonnets burn,       . . . . . . . .    595 Cassinus Peter      74
SONS
    Among her Elder Sons the whole Estate?    . . . . .       32 Ode to Temple      181
    Among thy stubborn sons there haunts that spirit of Jews, 38 Ode Sancroft       129
    "How Sons may safely disobey,         . . . . . . . .    181 Horace 2, 1         45
    "Where most true Sons of Phoebus ha' bin.   . . . .      320 First of April       4
    Some call their Monarchs Sons of Saturn,   . . . .       460 Birthday Song        9
    For, Sons of Phoebus never break their Trust.  . . .     532 To Mr. Gay          18
    Call Dunces, Fools, and Sons of Whores,   . . . . .      652 On Poetry          345
    Her Sons descended from the British Line;   . . . .      771 Horace 1, 14        42
    Her matchless Sons; whose Valour still remains           771 Horace 1, 14        43
    And Sons of Whores--behind their Backs.   . . . . .      778 Mullinix Tim       164
    Thy martial Sons, whom now they dare despise,  . . .     790 St. Pat's Well      13
    Within their Veins, who are thy younger Sons,  . . .     791 St. Pat's Well      18
    Made your Sons Converts both to God and Sense: . . .     792 St. Pat's Well      30
    Freedom and Virtue in thy Sons I found,   . . . . .      792 St. Pat's Well      37
    Soon shall thy Sons, the Time is just at Hand,  . . .    793 St. Pat's Well      89
SOON
    We soon shall see them to their ancient Methods fall,  .  19 Ode Athenian       119
    How soon have You restor'd her Charms!   . . . . . .      23 Ode Athenian       228
    Shall (I foresee it) soon with Gothick Swarms come fort   25 Ode Athenian       298
    Which soon her merit forc'd her to inspire;  . . . . .    44 To Congreve         26
    When soon the peaceful bow unstring'd is shown,  . . .    52 Temple Ill          27
    The Earth would very soon be filld:   . . . . . . .       79 Vanbrug House       20
    She soon would find, the same Effects,   . . . . . .      85 Salamander          64
    Soon reard a House two Storyes high;  . . . . . . .       86 Hist V's House       6
    The gentle Pilgrims soon aware on't,  . . . . . . .      112 Bauc & Phil 2       41
    Soon knew Apollo by his looks,        . . . . . . .      120 Apollo Outwit       15
    But soon as e'er he lay'd it down,    . . . . . . .      132 Magician's Rod       3
    He soon disclos'd his Nature.         . . . . . . .      153 Widow and Cat     D   5
    Soon grows Domestick, seldom fails    . . . . . . .      173 Horace 1, 7         77
    He soon arrives at Harley's Gate;     . . . . . . .      174 Horace 1, 7        118
    The Nymph had soon been brought to yield;   . . . .      177 To Lord Harley      14
    They'll soon enable thee to spend,    . . . . . . .      183 Horace 2, 1         90
    See, said the Sire, how soon 'tis done:   . . . . .      189 Faggot               9
    If Celia should appear too soon,      . . . . . . .      226 Prog of Beauty      11
    Since mortal Beautyes drop so soon,   . . . . . . .      229 Prog of Beauty     118
    Soon make my Dame grow lank and spare:   . . . . .      230 Prog of Poetry      12
    Because Irish Linen will soon turn to Tinder;  . . .     237 Excellent Song      20
    The Day of Judgment will be soon,     . . . . . . .      253 Bubble              77
    This House will soon turn topsy turvey;   . . . . .      283 Journal            128
    This Paper will soon make us richer than Crags.  . . .   287 Bank Down           18
    Her Spouse desires his Coffee soon,   . . . . . . .      291 Prog Marriage       37
    For leaving company so soon;          . . . . . . .      292 Prog Marriage       96
    Oh, may I see her soon dispensing     . . . . . . .      295 Prog Marriage      159
    He'll soon return to his own Vomit.   . . . . . . .      299 Horrid Plot         36
    "That Ireland must be soon destroy'd,   . . . . . .      304 Storm               39
    "You soon shall see him soundly tost.   . . . . . .      305 Storm               56
    When the True Wood arrives, as he soon will no doubt,  . 336 Serious Poem        75
    On the Scene of this Land very soon to revive.  . . .    337 Serious Poem        94
    Very soon to see Wood Drop down from a Rope.  . . .      338 Serious Poem       116
```

SOON   (CONTINUED)   PAGE TITLE   LINE

    I know the Times are something hard, but hope they soon 342 Upon His Grace   32
        will mend,
    But Jove will soon convert I hope, ...   347 Prometheus   71
    While you and Spouse transform'd, shall soon   . . . . 362 Grace's Answer   51
    Here, soon for every Art renown'd, ...   385 Manly Virtue   37
    Ye Rhimers, dead as soon as born, ...   394 Grub-Street   3
    You'll find it soon by woful Proof, ...   408 Dial Rich Marb   11
    I fear I shall be soon forgot.   . . .   408 Dial Rich Marb   18
    We soon shall find him full of Spleen, ...   410 Dial Rich Marb   57
    Soon licks up all unsav'ry steams;   . . . .   432 Answer Paulus   8
    Some Authors say not quite so soon, ...   446 Modern Lady   39
    "And hath she sent so soon to dun?   . . . . . .   446 Modern Lady   65
    Will soon subdue the Realm of Lilliput. . . . . .   467 Birthday Song   208
    You soon a Remedy may find;   . . . .   501 Doctor Delaney   44
    You then may soon be of the Club.   . . . . .   502 Doctor Delaney   64
    You then may soon your Conscience lull; . . . . .   503 Doctor Delaney   112
    Soon punish'd Strephon for his Peeping; . . . . .   529 Lady's Dres Rm   120
    He soon would learn to think like me, ...   530 Lady's Dres Rm   141
    Will soon grow necessary to his Heirs.   . . . . .   535 To Mr. Gay   120
    From Dublin soon to London spread, ...   559 Death of Swift   177
    "Too soon that precious Life was ended, ...   568 Death of Swift   377
    "I wish it soon may have a Better.   . . . . .   572 Death of Swift   484
    Forbear their Tea, or drink it soon;   . . . . .   587 Strephon Chloe   118
    But, soon with like Occasions prest, ...   589 Strephon Chloe   187
    They soon from all Constraint are freed; . . . . .   590 Strephon Chloe   205
    Is after Marriage lost so soon, ...   591 Strephon Chloe   257
    Who knows how soon you will compare us   . . . . .   622 Scandal Poem 1   164
    Alas! our Thunder soon goes out;   . . . .   624 Scandal Poem 2   7
    As soon as you can hear his Knell, ...   646 On Poetry   205
    They soon betray their native Place: . . . . . .   652 On Poetry   362
    How soon thy vain Pretension drops;   . . . . .   671 Epig Carthy 22   D 3
    In vain, --- for soon the slender prop gives way; . . . 672 Epig Carthy 24   D 16
    The Goddess soon began to see   . . . .   689 Cadenus Vaness   104
    Can do as soon as she is told.   . . . . . .   700 Cadenus Vaness   425
    The Race of Lovers soon must end:)   . . . . . .   713 Cadenus Vaness   863
    And that her Beauty, soon or late, ...   723 To Stella   3
    My Harp will soon in vain be strung, ...   739 Stel B-day '21   11
    You'll find it soon if Fate consents;   . . . . .   743 Stel B-day 22   71
    Too soon arrives the dismal Day, ...   746 Stel Distress   25
    Will soon your Appetite repair.   . . . .   759 Receipt Youth   28
    Soon shall thy Sons, the Time is just at Hand,   . .   793 St. Pat's Well   89
    And soon convinc'd them by a Floud.   . . . . .   799 Traulus 1   98
    Soon repent, or put to Slaughter   . . . .   838 Legion Club   213
    And make him soon give up the Cause.   . . . .   861 Lady Acheson   40
    As soon as her Ladyship call'd to be drest, ...   868 Grand Question   43
    And soon as we have got Possession, ...   886 Rev Market-Hill   90
    Would soon restore our antient Reign.   . . . . .   887 Panegyr Dean   10
    And soon grow pert on Men of Sense; . . . . . .   887 Panegyr Dean   20
    As soon as gone, will show their Spight: . . . . .   891 Panegyr Dean   140
    Soon would their Altars Flame expire, ...   916 Riddle 2   13
    How soon all human Pleasures pass.   . . . .   921 Riddle 7   6
    But soon will come the fatal Time, ...   932 Riddle 19   D 15
    Soon or late, my date is done, ...   937 Riddle 24   D 43
    Or, like my own Herrings, I soon shall be dead.   . .   953 Herrings   9
    But to scold is your trade, which I soon shou'd be foil'd 979 Dean to Tho: S   7
        in,
    And I wish I may soon be not of an A-gue sick;   . . . 1030 Dr. Sheridan   3
SOONER
    No sooner does she land   . . . .   17 Ode Athenian   36
    Which still the sooner it arrives, ...   24 Ode Athenian   279
    Yet so much sooner comes the long and gloomy Night. . 25 Ode Athenian   282
    Far sooner than the nobler mushroom grows: . . . .   46 To Congreve   100
    And sooner than Vote for a Peace I'll be <damnd>.   143 New Song   20
    At Windsor <Swift> no sooner can appear, ...   194 Author Himself   33
    No sooner brought within the Walls, ...   209 Fable Bitches   45
    No sooner got, than with Disdain   . . . .   412 Desire Possess   27
    Sooner shall, etc.   . . . .   445 Modern Lady   19
    You think you'll sooner be a Bishop: . . . . . .   478 Epist on Epist   102
    Will sooner coyn a Thousand Lyes   . . . . . .   503 Doctor Delaney   91
    Nothing she thought could sooner gain him, ...   905 Death Daphne   71
SOOT
    The Soot or Powder which is wont   . . . . .   226 Prog of Beauty   17
    To think of Oyl and Soot, is vain, ...   229 Prog of Beauty   110
SOOTERKIN
    For after-birth a Sooterkin;   . . . .   504 Doctor Delaney   118
SOOTH
    To feed his Luxury, or sooth his Pride. . . . .   534 To Mr. Gay   94
    Sooth my ever-waking Slumbers: . . . .   661 Love Song   15
SOOTY
    His griesly Monarch's sooty Fist, ...   903 Death Daphne   4
SOP
    Behold it swelling like a Sop.   . . . .   251 Bubble   16
    To Cerberus they give a Sop, ...   647 On Poetry   213
SOPHISTRY
    Then in Spight of your Sophistry, Honest Will. Wood   335 Serious Poem   49
SOPHOCLES
    The Weight on him, they do on Sophocles.   . . . . . 988 Letter Dr Sh-n   27
SOPHS
    Two College Sophs of Cambridge Growth, ...   593 Cassinus Peter   1

```
                                                          PAGE    TITLE            LINE
SORC'RESS
     As when of old, some Sorc'ress threw  . . . . . . .   354  Simile Silver       1
SORDID
     Hence that mean and sordid Soul,  . . . . . . . .     800  Traulus 2          33
SORE
     That's but a counterfeit sore Leg;  . . . . . . .      91  Bauc & Phil 1      43
     Because, though sore against her Will,  . . . . . .   446  Modern Lady        40
     We suffer sore against his Will;  . . . . . . .       485  Libel on D- D-    156
     The Spaniard, sore against his Will,  . . . . . .     883  Rev Market-Hill    15
     Through me, though sore against my Will,  . . . . .   918  Riddle 4           11
SORELY                                          )
     But was sorely put to't in the midst of a Verse,  . . 76  Lady B- B-          3
     How sorely I lament your Loss?  . . . . . . . . .     821  Dr. Rundle         62
SORES
     Or other Lap-Dog Cures for Sores.  . . . . . . .      494  Panegyr Swift      36
     Her Shankers, Issues, running Sores,  . . . . . .     582  Young Nymph        30
     Their Sores and putrid Ulcers show,  . . . . . .      667  Epig Carthy 6   D  3
SORIE
     And no Man shall be sorie therefore.  . . . . . .     103  Merlin             18
SORROW
     Still ev'ry tree the pendent sorrow wears;  . . . .    51  Temple Ill         20
     He has vamp't an old Speech, and the Court to their   143  New Song            5
        sorrow,
     When known, will save a double Sorrow.  . . . . .     204  In Sickness        28
     My Sister transcrib'd it last Night, to his Sorrow,  . 265 Apollo             67
     As you shall to your Sorrow know;  . . . . . . .      627  Scandal Poem 2    131
     Sorrow with Joy, and Hope with Fear.  . . . . . .     711  Cadenus Vaness    777
SORROWS
     His Troubles and Sorrows now come in a Heap,  . . .   519  Dean Hang Rape     59
SORRY
     For sorry Stuff, can get a Crown a Page;  . . . . .   276  Epilogue           42
     (Cries Bob) "I'm Sorry for the News;  . . . . . .     560  Death of Swift    192
     I'm sorry; but we all must dye.  . . . . . . . .      561  Death of Swift    212
     One Fault he hath, is sorry for't,  . . . . . . .     602  Beasts Confess     31
     -----I'm sorry Mopsa breaks so fast;  . . . . . .     699  Cadenus Vaness    386
     She was ringing very sorry, her tongue tied up with rag; 840 Ballad       D   8
     Thou sorry Scare-crow of Skin and Bone,  . . . . .   1003  Dan J's Reply      17
SORT
     Thus are the lives of fools a sort of dreams,  . . .   47  To Congreve       147
     Addicted to no sort of Vice;  . . . . . . . . .       171  Horace 1, 7        32
     And others, who in solemn Sort  . . . . . . . .       189  Faggot             17
     And deal in Vices of the graver Sort,  . . . . .      194  Author Himself     21
     Away they rode in homely Sort  . . . . . . . .        224  Prog of Love       75
     In disorderly Sort,  . . . . . . . . . . .            245  Irish-Feast        15
     To other sort of Folk was due:  . . . . . . . .       478  Epist on Epist    106
     Like supple Patriots of the modern Sort,  . . . . .   771  Horace 1, 14       55
SORTS
     Hath met with returns of art but applause;  . . . .   815  Yahoo's            17
     Of all sizes and sorts, the Fanatical crew  . . . .   815  Yahoo's            21
SOSSING
     To sossing in an elbow chair:  . . . . . . . .        744  Stel Distress       6
     To sossing in an easy Chair;  . . . . . . . . .       750  Stel Wood-Park     30
SOT
     Draws ev'ry rhyming, prating, dressing sot,  . . . .   48  To Congreve       153
     My Husband's a Sot,  . . . . . . . . . . .            952  Apples              8
SOTS
     Like sots, alone I'm dull enough,  . . . . . . .      936  Riddle 24       D   9
SOTS-HOLE
     To see you safe in Sots-Hole,  . . . . . . . .        425  Five Ladies         6
SOTTISH
     What Protestant can be so sottish,  . . . . . . .     813  Bro Protestant     46
SOUCE
     We'll soundly souce your Frize Surtout.  . . . . .    627  Scandal Poem 2    134
SOUGHT
     He sought Her out in Fight,  . . . . . . . . .          7  Ode to King        36
     To be the Man I long have sought,  . . . . . . .      215  To Mr. Delany       4
     "Because he sought for no Man's Aid.  . . . . . .     565  Death of Swift    328
     "And reapt the profit, sought his Blood.  . . . .     569  Death of Swift    414
SOUL   SEE SHOUL
     Turns up old objects to the soul her sun;  . . . .     51  Temple Ill         10
     The humble tribe mourn'd for the quick'ning soul,  . . 53 Temple Ill         61
     "T' expose thy soul, clad in this poor disguise;  . .  55 Temple Ill        144
     Before one Soul would let 'em in.  . . . . . . .       90  Bauc & Phil 1      14
     His Soul and Spirit did divide,  . . . . . . . .       99  Elegy Patrige      65
     But not a Soul would let them in.  . . . . . . .      111  Bauc & Phil 2      14
     Feels not his Soul enliven'd when he's Drunk?  . . .  163  Toland's Invit     18
     They have his Soul who have his Bonds,  . . . . .     241  Run Bankers        51
     Your steady Soul preserves my Frame  . . . . . .      243  Horace 4, 9         9
     When Damon's Soul shall take its Flight,  . . . . .   270  Apollo's Edict  D 33
     And, Sixthly; for my Soul, to barter it  . . . . .    349  Whitshed Motto     21
     Because, the Soul her Power contracts,  . . . . .     366  Answer Delaney     25
     To win the Soul, and glad the Heart;  . . . . . .     385  Manly Virtue       56
     His Soul bright-beaming from his Eye,  . . . . . .    385  Manly Virtue       60
     "Past Six, and not a living Soul!  . . . . . . .      451  Modern Lady       202
     What Agony of Soul she feels  . . . . . . . . .       451  Modern Lady       226
     A Soul with ev'ry Virtue fraught  . . . . . . .       482  Libel on D- D-     75
     Who, from my Soul, sincerely hate  . . . . . . .      485  Libel on D- D-    173
     And griev'd your righteous Soul beside,  . . . . .    496  Panegyr Swift      91
     Cryes, Lord have Mercy on his Soul,  . . . . . .      500  Doctor Delaney     18
     But, not a Soul his Office durst accept:  . . . . .   536  To Mr. Gay        153
     "Then Lord have Mercy on his Soul.  . . . . . .       562  Death of Swift    229
```

```
SOUL          (CONTINUED)                              PAGE   TITLE           LINE
    Think, Peter, how my Soul is rack'd.      . . . . . .    596 Cassinus Peter    97
    (How would her Virgin Soul bemoan    . . . . . .         596 Cassinus Peter   103
    Have my Soul entirely fill'd;        . . . . . . . . .   630 Epistle Lady      32
    While not a Soul demands your Ware?  . . . . . . .       641 On Poetry         44
    Her Soul was suddenly endu'd . . . . . . . . . .         693 Cadenus Vaness   206
    --That Lady is the dullest Soul--    . . . . . .         698 Cadenus Vaness   359
    And, Scholars teach, the Soul informs;  . . . . . .      724 To Stella         12
    And is the Spirit of the Soul.       . . . . . . . .     724 To Stella         14
    The Fire that forms a manly Soul;    . . . . . . .       726 To Stella         88
    A Truth for which thy Soul should grieve,  . . . . .     735 Stel B-day '20    46
    They just keep Life and Soul together,  . . . . . .      759 Receipt Youth     10
    And when I damn my Soul to plague 'em,  . . . . .        778 Mullinix Tim     173
    Thy Body's cloathed like thy Soul.   . . . . . .         787 Clad in Brown     16
    Thy Soul, which through thy Hide of Buff,  . . . .       787 Clad in Brown     17
    Hence that mean and sordid Soul,     . . . . . . .       800 Traulus 2         33
    Tho' his soul he despises, he values his hide:  . . . .  817 Yahoo's           72
    All ye Gods, who rule the Soul       . . . . . . .       832 Legion Club       83
    All the Soul in every Face.          . . . . . . . .     839 Legion Club      230
    By my soul there's bad news, for the gold she was pulled 840 Ballad         D   2
        down,
    Tho' not a Soul would have him stay. . . . . . . .       860 Lady Acheson      12
    Sits by this, to dress her soul.     . . . . . . . .     907 Daphne            48
    The Soul of Man with Spleen you vex; . . . . . . .       919 Riddle 5          17
    There's not a Soul, that does resort here,  . . . . .    928 Riddle 12      D  19
    As a good quiet Soul, who no Mischief intends    . . .   968 Letter Sherid     27
    . . .with all my Heart and Soul, upon my Word and      1014 Swift to Sheri      9
        Honour.
    My Soul it much grated,  . . . . . . . . . . .          1014 Swift to Sheri     17
    . . . and the soft soul of amorous Jemmy center. . . .  1023 Nim-Dan-Dean 2 D  14
SOUL'S
    My Life is here no Soul's Concern.                       203 In Sickness        6
    The Moment I get one my Soul's all a-fire,  . . . .      928 Riddle 11      D  11
SOULS
    And for a while unbends their contradicting Souls:  . .    9 Ode to King       91
    Too long have our misguided Souls been taught  . . . .   27 Ode to Temple     18
    Nature's fair Table-book our tender Souls    . . . .     27 Ode to Temple     32
    This great triumvirate of Souls.     . . . . . . .       28 Ode to Temple     69
    Where high patrician souls dress'd heavenly gay,  . . .  41 Ode Sancroft     234
    Sick lust of souls, and an abortive child;   . . . . .   47 To Congreve      124
    And drive departed Souls to Styx.    . . . . . . .      133 Magician's Rod    38
    And drive as many Souls to Hell.     . . . . . . .      133 Magician's Rod    42
    Charon in him will ferry Souls to Hell;      . . . . .  285 Elegy Boat        25
    "Who sell their Souls and Votes for Naught;  . . . . .  571 Death of Swift   446
    Amount to just Nine thousand Souls.  . . . . . .        649 On Poetry        282
    And fret the Tories Souls to Death,  . . . . . .        778 Mullinix Tim     171
    Than saving your Souls, by damning our own?   . . .     805 Irish Bishops     56
    Nay give their very Souls away.      . . . . . . .      930 Riddle 15      D  28
SOUND
    In vain she catches at the empty Sound,      . . . . .   17 Ode Athenian      57
    There first the visionary sound was heard,   . . . . .   51 Temple Ill        15
    I can't but think 'twould sound more clever, . . . . .  198 Horace 2, 6    D
    All her Complexions safe and sound,  . . . . . .        226 Prog of Beauty    30
    That Swain Endymion is not sound,    . . . . . .        228 Prog of Beauty    95
    A narrow Sound, though deep as Hell, . . . . . .        256 Bubble           139
    Stay--But let me see how finely will it Sound,  . . .   274 Epilogue           5
    We sound a trumpet, or we beat a drum;   . . . . .      308 Billet Players    37
    But when Wood's Brass began to sound, . . . . .         338 Wood's Brass       7
    And the Sound of his Brass we took for our Knell.  . .  351 Wood Insect       32
    That Sound will make the Parchment shrivel,  . . . .    354 Simile Silver     29
    Returning sound in Limb and Wind,    . . . . . .        398 Earl of P-b-w     23
    Now sound in mind, and sound in corpus,  . . . . .      456 Dean Smedley      31
    Now sound in mind, and sound in corpus,  . . . . .      456 Dean Smedley      31
    Hesse Darmstedt makes too rough a sound,     . . . . .  467 Birthday Song    215
    That sound Divine the Truth has spoke all    . . . . .  469 Birthday Song    271
    Lessens the Terror of the Sound:     . . . . . . .      500 Doctor Delaney     8
    In Church and in State was of Principles sound,  . . .  518 Dean Hang Rape    32
    "That all his vital Parts were sound.   . . . . . .     559 Death of Swift   176
    Cry'd out, ye Gods, what Sound is this?  . . . . .      589 Strephon Chloe   177
    To build on some Foundation sound;   . . . . . .        592 Strephon Chloe   296
    We leave the body sweet and sound,   . . . . . .        618 Scandal Poem 1    27
    We leave the Body sweet and sound;   . . . . . .        624 Scandal Poem 2    21
    Her Foe's Conclusions were not sound, . . . . .         695 Cadenus Vaness   279
    Sir Arthur the Malster! how fine it will sound?  . . .  868 Grand Question    45
    Who regards the dreadful Sound.      . . . . . . .      931 Riddle 18      D  26
    The Dead are all sound   . . . . . . . . . . .          939 Riddle Answerd    19
SOUNDED
    Tho' now your Depth must not be Sounded,     . . . . .  478 Epist on Epist   109
SOUNDLY
    And Lady Betty soundly chides them.  . . . . . . .      279 Journal           34
    "You soon shall see him soundly tost.    . . . . .      305 Storm             56
    And if provok'd, he soundly ferks his    . . . . .      463 Birthday Song     99
    But proud Iberia soundly maul.       . . . . . . .      468 Birthday Song    248
    We'll soundly drench your frize Sur-tout,    . . . . .  622 Scandal Poem 1   176
    We'll soundly souce your Frize Surtout.  . . . . .      627 Scandal Poem 2   134
    Be soundly mawl'd, and plagues the rest. . . . . .      777 Mullinix Tim     132
    So, the French, when our Generals soundly did pay 'em, 967 Letter Sherid     17
SOUNDS
    Sounds truly good, or truly great;   . . . . . . .       36 Ode Sancroft      49
    The Leather sounds, he trembles from within. . . . .    139 City Shower       46
    Hear Sounds harmonious from the Skies.   . . . . .      230 Prog of Poetry    16
```

```
SOUNDS          (CONTINUED)                                        PAGE     TITLE                LINE
    The Cymbals rattling Sounds dispell      . . . . . . .         354  Simile Silver             11
    Of loud un-meaning Sounds, a rapid Flood     . . . . .         532  To Mr. Gay                39
    Pass only now for empty sounds?  . . . . . . . . .            779  Mullinix Tim             188
    He sounds my Praise in Verse and Prose.  . . . . .            887  Panegyr Dean              28
    And give him Words of dreadful Sounds,  . . . . . .           904  Death Daphne              43
SOUPES
    To dress their Soupes and Fricassyes;    . . . . . .          895  Panegyr Dean             266
SOUR
    And taint all their Meat, and sour all their Drink.  .        263  Apollo                    14
    The wine is so sour,  . . . . . . . . . . . . . .            402  Window Inns 8      D      5
    When drunk with sour Election Ale.   . . . . . . .            450  Modern Lady              187
    Exhal'd from sour unsavory Streams,   . . . . . . .           526  Lady's Dres Rm            28
    To. reform the World, than Sour.  . . . . . . . .            636  Epistle Lady             200
    To a sour Pint one day in twenty.   . . . . . . . .           745  Stel Distress             14
    Too sour or too salt:  . . . . . . . . . . . . .             853  Lady's Lament             62
SOURS
    Ripens the Grape, the Liquor sours.   . . . . . . .           731  Stella, Poems            120
    What he ripens above ground, he sours below it.  . . .        979  Dean to Tho: S            32
SOUS
    You sha'n't come here nor get a Sous   . . . . . . .          91   Bauc & Phil 1             39
SOUSE    SEE SOUCE
    Nor souse to death a Birthday Beau.   . . . . . . .           622  Scandal Poem 1           178
    Souse them in their own Ex-crements.   . . . . . . .          837  Legion Club              186
SOUTH
    Mean while the South rising with dabbled Wings,  . . .        137  City Shower               13
    For by the Sea she meant the South.   . . . . . . .           254  Bubble                   100
    Some South Sea Broker from the City,   . . . . . . .          410  Dial Rich Marb            67
    At North and South are posted Centry;   . . . . . .           883  Rev Market-Hill           18
    And to the South my Squadrons bend:   . . . . . . .           884  Rev Market-Hill           50
    He feels at once both North and South:   . . . . . .          923  Riddle 7                  84
SOUTH-SEA
    Driv'n from the South-Sea to the Red.   . . . . . . .         258  Bubble                   208
    South-Sea at best a mighty Bubble.   . . . . . . .            259  Bubble                   220
    Those that dropt in the South-Sea discover'd this Plank       288  Bank Down                 49
    A Statesman, or a South-Sea Jobber.   . . . . . .            645  On Poetry                162
    Project <Excise> and <South-Sea> <Schemes>:   . . .          647  On Poetry                216
SOUTHERN
    When dropt into the Southern Main,   . . . . . . . .          250  Bubble                     3
    Then plunges in the Southern Waves,   . . . . . . .           251  Bubble                    23
    In Southern Seas he leaves his Name.   . . . . . . .          252  Bubble                    48
    So fares it in the Southern Sea   . . . . . . . .            253  Bubble                    67
    So cast it in the Southern Seas,   . . . . . . . .            255  Bubble                   121
SOV'REIGN
    Whose Councils aid the Sov'reign Pow'r,   . . . . . .         548  Life of Swift            109
    As sov'reign Med'cines for the Loins)   . . . . . .          589  Strephon Chloe           182
    As Emblems of the sov'reign Pow'r,   . . . . . . .            646  On Poetry                193
    Of Wit and Humour, Judges sov'reign.   . . . . . . .         649  On Poetry                284
    Appointed sov'reign Judge to sit   . . . . . . . .           655  On Poetry                427
    Against our Sov'reign Lady's Peace,   . . . . . . .           687  Cadenus Vaness            17
    A Sov'reign Medicine for the Brains.   . . . . . .           743  Stel B-day 22             70
    And yet they have learnt the chief Art of a Sov'reign,       805  Irish Bishops             47
SOVEREIGN
    Said he-- "Great Sovereign of the Main,   . . . . .          303  Storm                     27
SOW
    In vain all wholsome Herbs I sow,   . . . . . . .            33   Ode to Temple            208
    And thought whose Sow had farrow'd last:   . . . . .         115  Bauc & Phil 2            132
    Fresh from the Mud a wallowing Sow   . . . . . . .            786  Clad in Brown              5
    She swills like a sow, and she breeds like a rabbit:  . .    955  Portrait Life              6
SOW'D
    His Money-Bags together sow'd.   . . . . . . . .             235  Elegy on Demar            44
SOW'R
    A bitter Whig, or Tory sow'r;   . . . . . . . . .            417  Woman's Mind              50
SOWER
    "And, would you make him truly sower;   . . . . . .          566  Death of Swift           343
SOWINS
    Who Sowins make with Shelling   . . . . . . . .             441  Ballyspellin              33
    But see, where Norah with the Sowins comes--   . . . .       882  Pastoral Dial             51
SOWN
    Carrots sown Thyn a deep root may get,   . . . . . .         148  Windsor Proph             17
    Those early Seeds by Venus sown,   . . . . . . . .           701  Cadenus Vaness           472
SOWRS
    And sowrs the blood  . . . . . . . . . . . .                440  Ballyspellin              11
SOWS
    This Dragon had gotten two Sows in it's Belly;   . . .       337  Serious Poem              88
    Then sows within her tender Mind   . . . . . . . .           693  Cadenus Vaness           202
SOYL
    By calling This your native Soyl;   . . . . . . . .          311  To Ford                   10
SPACE
    Make their minds travel o'er infinity of space,   . . .      36   Ode Sancroft              61
    He left a void Space,  . . . . . . . . . . . .              76   Lady B- B-                 6
SPACIOUS
    In vain I strive to cross this spacious Main,   . . .        32   Ode to Temple            192
    Leaving the Wits the Spacious Air   . . . . . . .           106  V's House                 25
    May lodge within thy Spacious Pile.   . . . . . . .          109  V's House                118
    Ride o'er the Waves in spacious Hoops,   . . . . . .         254  Bubble                    91
    It drags behind a spacious Womb,   . . . . . . . .          743  Stel B-day 22             68
    And in the spacious Womb contains   . . . . . . .           743  Stel B-day 22             69
    A spacious Thorn before the Gate.   . . . . . . .           848  Old Thorn                  4
    Wedg'd in a spacious Elbow-Chair,   . . . . . . .           895  Panegyr Dean             259
```

```
                                                                PAGE   TITLE            LINE
SPADE
    Some she binds 'Prentice to the Spade,        . . . . .      32  Ode to Temple     185
    Dan leaves the Earthly Spade and Rake,        . . . . .     279  Journal            32
    And, Madam, there's my Lady Spade             . . . . .     446  Modern Lady        62
    Calls Lady Spade a hundred Cheats:            . . . . .     447  Modern Lady        73
    They learn to call a Spade, a Spade.          . . . . . .   590  Strephon Chloe    204
    They learn to call a Spade, a Spade.          . . . . . .   590  Strephon Chloe    204
    A Spade let prudent Archy hold,        . . . . . . . .      743  Stel B-day 22      57
    Between the Scepter and the Spade.       . . . . . . .      895  Panegyr Dean      290
SPADES
    Ten thousand Archy's arm'd with Spades        . . . . . .   743  Stel B-day 22      73
SPADILLO
    She slipt Spadillo in her Breast,             . . . . . .   447  Modern Lady        74
    In hope to see Spadillo rise;          . . . . . . .        452  Modern Lady       231
    Spadillo here has got a Mark,          . . . . . . . .      453  Modern Lady       266
SPAIN
    To hear we are making a Peace without Spain;   . . . .      143  New Song           12
    And I'll Vote against Peace, with Spain, or without:       144  New Song           46
    "For Inquisitions taught by Spain,             . . . . .   183  Horace 2, 1        97
    Mordanto in a Week from Spain.        . . . . . . . .      398  Earl of P-b-w      12
    To conquer Spain, and quell the Turk.         . . . . .   466  Birthday Song     194
    T'is the Cur dog of Brittain & spaniel of Spain.   . .    540  Charac Walpole     14
    And sells the King of Spain a Bargain.        . . . . .   777  Mullinix Tim      114
SPAKE
    He spake, and a dark Cloud flung o're his light,   . . .     8  Ode to King        58
    He spake, and grudging, lent his Ayd;     . . . . . .      108  V's House          75
SPAN
    "But, spick and span I have enough.           . . . . . .  563  Death of Swift    268
    I'll squeeze him to a little Span,        . . . . . . .    934  Riddle 21       D  18
SPANGLES
    Glitter'd like Spangles on the Ground:        . . . . . .  156  Fable of Midas      4
SPANIARD
    A <Dean>, a Spaniard, and a Knight.           . . . . . .  883  Rev Market-Hill     8
    The <Dean> and Spaniard find it too well;     . . . . .   883  Rev Market-Hill    10
    The Spaniard, sore against his Will,          . . . . .   883  Rev Market-Hill    15
    The <Dean> and Spaniard must reproach ye;     . . . . .   884  Rev Market-Hill    30
    Come Spaniard, let us from our Farms          . . . . .   884  Rev Market-Hill    43
SPANIARDS
    Taught us, like Spaniards, to be proud and poor,   . .      28  Ode to Temple      56
SPANIEL
    T'is the Cur dog of Brittain & spaniel of Spain.   . .    540  Charac Walpole     14
SPANISH
    With his Spanish flyes     . . . . . . . . . .            423  Carterets Arms
    He would have seiz'd the Spanish Plate,       . . . . .   463  Birthday Song     101
'SPARAGRASS
    Ripe 'Sparagrass,     . . . . . . . . . . . . .          952  Asparagus           1
SPAR'D
    As some fair pile, yet spar'd by zeal and rage,    . .     52  Temple Ill         47
    "Had he but spar'd his Tongue and Pen,        . . . . .   567  Death of Swift    355
    "He lash'd the Vice but spar'd the Name.      . . . . .   571  Death of Swift    460
    "He spar'd a Hump or crooked Nose,        . . . . . .     572  Death of Swift    467
SPARE
    And spare the Labour of Your Conquering Hand.  . . . .     13  Ode to William  D  40
    Eat, Honest Friends, and never spare,         . . . . .    91  Bauc & Phil 1      64
    And spare my absent Friends the Grief         . . . . .   204  In Sickness        25
    Whom to be hard on, whom to spare:  . . . . . . . .       218  To Mr. Delany     100
    Soon make my Dame grow lank and spare:        . . . . .   230  Prog of Poetry     12
    I beg you'll the Camelion spare.              . . . . .   270  Apollo's Edict  D  17
    In bed, where he can spare her best.          . . . . .   292  Prog Marriage      90
    To spare a Foe, to save a Friend:             . . . . .   306  Storm              76
    "There's one for each and one to spare:       . . . . .   321  First of April      6
    And scarce a Day, can spare a Minute          . . . . .   322  First of April     41
    To spare the Rich, and plague the Poor;       . . . . .   392  Young's Satire     46
    In all employmts we can spare.   . . . . . .             422  Ireld              48
    And, crazy Congreve scarce cou'd spare        . . . . .   481  Libel on D- D-     41
    Nor cou'd his Malice spare the <Queen>;       . . . . .   514  Answer Fable       76
    Sometimes his Friend he would not spare,      . . . . .   602  Beasts Confess     25
    Preferment get, and spare his Eyes:           . . . . .   604  Beasts Confess    108
    And, if you now so little spare us,           . . . . .   622  Scandal Poem 1    163
    Tho' small the Time thou hast to spare,       . . . . .   656  On Poetry         451
    The few soft Moments they can spare,          . . . . .   687  Cadenus Vaness     42
    I have enough besides to spare,        . . . . . . .      692  Cadenus Vaness    196
    Is thirty, and a Bit to spare.   . . . . . . . .         699  Cadenus Vaness    389
    Yet still resolv'd to spare no Cost;          . . . . .   702  Cadenus Vaness    493
    Me, surely me, you ought to spare,     . . . . . .       766  Stel B-day '26     83
    To spare the Folks that gave him Ha'pence     . . . . .   796  Traulus 1          28
    'Tis Time at last to spare his Ink,     . . . . . .       799  Traulus 1         101
    (I spare the Thistle for Sir Arthur's sake.)  . . . . .   881  Pastoral Dial      18
    How far to go, and when to spare:       . . . . . .       890  Panegyr Dean      116
    Nor uses time, nor time will spare;     . . . . . .       901  Dean's Reasons     86
    Or else you may spare    . . . . . . . . . . .           952  Onyons             10
SPARES
    Those Sacred Leaves that Lightning spares.    . . . . .   458  Paddy's Charac     12
SPARING   SEE PAPER-SPARING
    And since you're sparing of your Stuff,       . . . . .   108  V's House          73
    Not sparing even men of letters,       . . . . . . .      489  Dialogue            6
    Nor, wilt thou of Gifts be sparing,     . . . . . .       523  Betty Grizette     21
    Not sparing his own Clergy-Cloth,       . . . . . .       548  Life of Swift     113
    Be not sparing,        . . . . . . . . . . . .           953  Herrings            1
SPARK
    Nature the hidden Spark did at my Birth infuse,    . .     32  Ode to Temple     202
```

SPARK   (CONTINUED)   PAGE   TITLE   LINE
   Return'd a finish'd spark this summer down, ...   47 To Congreve   119
   At length, a spark not too well bred . . . .   63 Discovery   25
   The Place, the Welcome, and the Spark, ...   748 Stel Distress   70
   The Scene, the Welcome, and the Spark, ...   752 Stel Wood-Park   86
   No Lady was ever more fond of a Spark; . . . . . .   928 Riddle 11   D 10
SPARKLES
   Thousand Sparkles falling down . . . .   638 Epistle Lady   253
SPARKLING
   Thy Head with sparkling Rubies round;   . . . . .   324 Pethox   34
   And Anger sparkling in your Eyes, ...   731 Stella, Poems   114
SPARROWS
   Of Sparrows tam'd, of Nuts innumerable, ...   283 Journal   113
   And Pigeons billing, Sparrows treading, ...   585 Strephon Chloe   51
   Behold a cage with sparrows fill'd, ...   753 Gift for Bec   11
SPARSE
   But all the Filth both Spiss, and Sparse   497 Panegyr Swift   120
SPATIOUS
   Leaving to Wits the spatious Air, ...   79 Vanbrug House   25
SPAUL
   Why must he sputter, spaul and slaver it . . . . .   796 Traulus 1   9
SPAUN
   Then sheds about his Spaun, and dyes.   . . . . .   80 Vanbrug House   38
SPAWN
   Peeps in the Ponds to look for Spawn, ...   279 Journal   22
   The Spawn of Bridewell, or the Stews;   . . . . .   641 On Poetry   36
   Emblems of Insects vile, who spread their Spawn   . . . 792 St. Pat's Well   55
   What! thou the Spawn of him who sham'd our Isle, . .   826 Noisy Tom   7
SPEAK
   Speak, for I wait thy answer, and expect   . . . . .   53 Temple Ill   73
   Speak against Peace right many a Word;   . . . . . .   147 Windsor Proph   8
   Of Love shall always speak and write;   . . . . . .   150 Corinna   10
   (Tho' this I speak but at a venture, ...   182 Horace 2, 1   77
   Observe the dying Father speak: . . . .   189 Faggot   1
   For Verse, (I speak my Judgment) Yours: . . . . .   219 To Mr. Delany   106
   "To Neptune speak, and he'll consent;   . . . . . .   306 Storm   71
   To speak to Elrington, and all the tribe, ...   307 Billet Players   6
   And speak without the Help of Lungs.   . . . . . .   326 Pethox   80
   We speak it in a Happier Sense. . . . .   339 Arch-Bish Dub   4
   Nam'd me as plain as he cou'd speak: . . . . . .   376 Apology Lady C   47
   Can scarsely speak for want of Breath, ...   379 Apology Lady C   127
   Then said, I must speak to the People a little,   . .   399 Tom Clinch   15
   Pope has the Talent well to speak, ...   405 Swift to Pope   1
   By what they speak, or what they think. . . . . .   414 Censure   26
   All mad to speak, and none to hearken;   . . . . .   450 Modern Lady   178
   To speak a Language of their own; . . . .   450 Modern Lady   189
   Most conscious that they all speak true, ...   453 Modern Lady   272
   Yet, thus methinks, I hear 'em speak;   . . . . . .   556 Death of Swift   79
   Twelve Cups of Tea, (with Grief I speak)   . . . .   589 Strephon Chloe   163
   When Beasts could speak, (the Learned say   . . . .   601 Beasts Confess   1
   My Lines to him you give--to speak your due,   . . .   670 Epig Carthy 18   D 1
   For thine, my dear Dick, give me leave to speak plain, .   819 Archbi Cashel   15
   Watch ev'ry Syllable you speak: . . . .   889 Panegyr Dean   72
   To take Offence at what you speak.   . . . .   890 Panegyr Dean   120
   Admire to hear me speak so fine.   . . . .   891 Panegyr Dean   136
   To slit my Tongue, and made me speak: . . . . . .   915 Riddle 1   16
   I speak to Eyes and not to Ears.   . . . .   915 Riddle 1   18
   Pleasing most when most I speak, ...   933 Riddle 20   D 2
   Tho' I speak without a Tongue.   . . . .   933 Riddle 20   D 4
SPEAKER
   All Pride) our Speaker for your Coxon: . . . . .   476 Epist on Epist   40
   Now has the Speaker by the Ears, ...   788 Dick's Variety   27
   To this damnable Speaker had long ow'd a shame;   . . . 816 Yahoo's   37
SPEAKING
   The Fair approach the speaking Part, ...   66 Problem   41
   This pedlar, at speaking and making of laws,   . . .   815 Yahoo's   16
   And yet my speaking gives Offence: . . . .   917 Riddle 4   6
   Never speaking, still awake, ...   933 Riddle 20   D 1
   Commonly speaking, but a sad Jade is.   . . . . . .   988 Letter Dr Sh-n   25
SPEAKS
   Then call this verse, that speaks her largest aid,   . .   44 To Congreve   27
   The Words in Wood's Mouth, or speaks from his Guts: . .   335 Serious Poem   62
   What e'er he speaks for Madness goes, ...   798 Traulus 1   65
SPEAR
   Laoco'n struck the Outside with his Spear, ...   139 City Shower   51
SPEC'ES
   Appear'd like one continu'd Spec'es, ...   344 Prometheus   8
SPECIAL
   A Clergyman of special Note, ...   171 Horace 1, 7   27
   All special Friends, and allways jarr.   . . . . . .   217 To Mr. Delany   60
   And of my meer Motion, and special good Grace,   . . .   263 Apollo   27
   And, Curl must have a special Care   . . . .   394 Grub-Street   11
   Let me suppose, two special Friends, ...   546 Life of Swift   52
   "A Protestant's a special Clinker;   . . . .   550 Life of Swift   176
   When I foresee my special Friends, ...   556 Death of Swift   75
   Both special Wits, and Lovers both, ...   593 Cassinus Peter   2
   But always take a special care   . . . .   762 Bec's B-Day   41
   And continue special friends. . . . .   908 Daphne   84
   With Pleasure to his special Friends: . . . . . .   919 Riddle 5   20

	PAGE	TITLE	LINE
SPECIES			
Thro' all the brutal Species ran,	659	On Poetry	D 410
SPECIOUS			
Inclines to aid a specious Lye:	414	Censure	14
SPECKLED			
Or, a tawny speckled Pippin,	523	Betty Grizette	9
Your Works are like old Jacob's speckled Goats,	670	Epig Carthy 18	D 3
SPECTACLES			
Put on what Spectacles You please,	255	Bubble	123
And talk of Spectacles and Pills;	763	Stel B-day '26	6
SPECTATORS			
How well are the Spectators pleas'd!	777	Mullinix Tim	126
SPECTRE			
But, if you fail, my Spectre dread	597	Cassinus Peter	113
Away the frighted Spectre scuds,	905	Death Daphne	99
To draw the Face of such a Spectre.	993	On Picture	12
SPECTRES			
As if they all were Spectres too,	27	Ode to Temple	41
SPECULATION			
To build in Speculation still.	107	V's House	42
SPECULATIONS			
Which causes many Speculations.	283	Journal	130
Still rapt in speculations deep,	900	Dean's Reasons	45
SPED			
And after all he seldom Sped.	456	Dean Smedley	26
To work her Ends; which if it sped,	690	Cadenus Vaness	133
Poor rump, thou hadst been better sped,	822	Epigr Rundle	3
SPEECH			
The Under-wits adorn their Speech.	80	Vanbrug House	48
He has vamp't an old Speech, and the Court to their sorrow,	143	New Song	5
I have heard all the Speech repeated by Hoppy.	143	New Song	9
I'll Speech against Peace while Dismal's my Name,	145	New Song	53
Teague made a good Pun by a Brogue in his Speech,	334	Serious Poem	27
And when his last Speech the loud Hawkers did cry,	399	Tom Clinch	11
This was the Speech, and here's the jest	423	Ireld	63
Less modest than the Speech of Prudes;	691	Cadenus Vaness	167
Then soft Voice and Speech absurd,	696	Cadenus Vaness	328
Love can with Speech inspire a Mute,	709	Cadenus Vaness	712
She made a Speech in open Court;	713	Cadenus Vaness	857
She, with soft speech, my anguish chears,	754	Stella '23	13
To any speech but Tyger's barking.	762	Bec's B-Day	44
When his speech came abroad, he paid him off clean,	816	Yahoo's	38
SPEECH'D			
Thus Speech'd it like a <Lechmere>.	153	Widow and Cat	D 20
SPEECHES			
In all their Speeches, Votes, Addresses.	646	On Poetry	198
Dear Tim, no more such angry Speeches,	783	Tim and Fables	35
When your speeches are absurd,	908	Daphne	61
SPEED			
Still blushes, and with speed retires,	178	To Lord Harley	71
SPELL SEE COUNTER-SPELL			
Without your Aid, to read or spell;	325	Pethox	66
As when they scarce have learn'd to spell.	463	Birthday Song	96
Oh! cou'd'st thou, by some Magick Spell,	478	Epist on Epist	91
Altho' he never learnt to spell.	650	On Poetry	292
Who, tho' he cannot spell, is wise	712	Cadenus Vaness	814
Tom cou'd write and spell his Name,	784	Mullinex Dick	3
That I have almost learn't to spell:	891	Panegyr Dean	134
SPELLING SEE BEAU-SPELLING,ILL-SPELLING			
As to your Spelling, let me see,	1004	Dan J's Reply	34
Good Spelling, Master, your Crany has Lead on't.	1004	Dan J's Reply	36
SPELLS			
By Magick Spells, the harmless Maid;	707	Cadenus Vaness	647
<SPENCER>			
Will you, Sir <Spencer>? or, will you, or you?	536	To Mr. Gay	152
SPEND			
Spend all our present Stock in hopes of golden Rules.	27	Ode to Temple	27
Spend their base coin before the bashful maid,	50	To Congreve	219
Not knowing how to spend his Time,	75	Game Traffick	D 26
You'll spend in Coach-hire more than save in Wine.	137	City Shower	8
And, since he could not spend his Fire,	172	Horace 1, 7	45
They'll soon enable thee to spend,	183	Horace 2, 1	90
To spend six Months with Statesmen here.	199	Horace 2, 6	12
Tho' in thy Walls he ne'er did Farthing spend,	234	Elegy on Demar	26
And spend her Joynture on his Whores:	295	Prog Marriage	164
In a Jest I spend my Rage:	635	Epistle Lady	168
Nor spend their Time to shew their Reading;	713	Cadenus Vaness	848
That I could spend my Life in reading.	891	Panegyr Dean	154
Your intervals of time to spend	899	Dean's Reasons	23
Computing what I get and spend,	918	Riddle 4	34
In Weather fine I nothing spend,	954	Authors Living	7
I spend my Time in making Sermons,	993	On Picture	4
SPENDS			
An idle Rogue, who spends his Quartridge	411	Dial Rich Marb	97
Who spends his Day and Night in gall.	515	Answer Fable	104
SPENT			
Perish the Muse's hour, thus vainly spent	48	To Congreve	175
Like distant echo spent, the spirit dies.	50	To Congreve	230
Materials would be quickly spent,	79	Vanbrug House	21
Were spent in Building each a Room;	108	V's House	90

SPENT	(CONTINUED)	PAGE	TITLE	LINE
We spent our Mony and our Blood,	. . . .	169	Peace Dunkirk	33
Now all the Doctor's Money's spent,	. . . . . .	174	Horace 1, 7	107
His Money spent, his Patrons fail,	. . . . . .	231	Prog of Poetry	33
His Credit sunk, his Money spent,	. . . . . .	252	Bubble	47
In Mirth the wedding-day was spent.	. . . .	290	Prog Marriage	18
But vow'd his Money all was spent;	. . . . . .	294	Prog Marriage	126
His Money spent! a clownish Reason?	. . . .	294	Prog Marriage	127
Said the Freeman, your Guinea To-night would be spent,	.	396	Dog and Thief	13
Ye Fates, when all he gets is Spent,	. . . . .	456	Dean Smedley	49
Thus, Congreve spent, in writing Plays,	. . . . . .	481	Libel on D- D-	33
By haughty Celia spent in Dressing;	. . . . . .	525	Lady's Dres Rm	2
"Spent all his Credit for his Friends:	. . . . . .	565	Death of Swift	332
"He spent his Life's declining Part;	. . . . . .	570	Death of Swift	432
Thy credit sunk, thy money spent,	. . . .	676	Parson's Case	10
I grieve those Spirits should be spent,	. . . . . .	731	Stella, Poems	115
When all her little Money spent,	. . . .	747	Stel Distress	54
Reflecting on a Life well spent?	. . . .	764	Stel B-day '26	36
Roaring till their Lungs were spent,	. . . . .	833	Legion Club	115
But I feel my Spirits spent,	. . . .	839	Legion Club	233
My money spent is,	. . . .	1037	Sheridan Cavan	3
SPEW SEE SPUE				
Who sees, will spew; who smells, be poison'd.	. . . .	583	Young Nymph	74
Between his Legs, to spew or spit in.	. . . . .	594	Cassinus Peter	22
SPEW-SICK				
Both when I am Purge-sick, and when I am Spew-sick.	.	1028	Dr. Helsham	4
SPHEAR				
The Window is her proper Sphear;	. . . .	228	Prog of Beauty	66
SPHEARS				
So Atlas, lest the pondrous Sphears	. . . . . .	160	Atlas	9
SPHERE				
Thro' many a needless sphere to run,	. . . . . .	36	Ode Sancroft	68
On his own secret regular sphere,	. . . .	39	Ode Sancroft	152
Thou, high-exalted in thy Sphere,	. . . .	100	Elegy Patrige	73
Descended from her sphere to find	. . . . . .	179	To Lord Harley	79
Demands him in an higher Sphere;	. . . .	387	Manly Virtue	112
SPHERES				
A near Resemblance to the Spheres.	. . . . . .	99	Elegy Patrige	40
Besides, he could confound the Spheres,	. . . . .	99	Elegy Patrige	57
Wrought by the Musick of the Spheres - - -	. . . .	362	Grace's Answer	36
Their Passions move in lower Spheres,	. . . . .	687	Cadenus Vaness	37
SPHINX				
Are harder than ever were put by the Sphinx.	. . . .	977	Dean to Sherid	46
SPICE				
And scorn to wrap up Spice.	. . . .	394	Grub-Street	8
SPICK				
"But, spick and span I have enough.	. . . . . .	563	Death of Swift	268
SPIES				
From our Mysterious Club to keep out Spies,	. . . .	165	Toland's Invit	29
Some few Days after Harley spies	. . . .	172	Horace 1, 7	57
Damn'd Spies and Informers, Damn'd Friends and Damn'd		576	Place Damn'd	10
Lyars;				
'SPIGHT				
And 'spight of all that They or You can do,	. . . .	24	Ode Athenian	265
SPIGHT				
Rather put on thy anger and thy spight,	. . . . .	37	Ode Sancroft	86
But spight of the Harpy that crawls on all four,	. . .	147	Windsor Proph	11
At Monarchy we nobly shew our Spight,	. . .	163	Toland's Invit	15
Spight of Dutch Friends and English Foes,	. . .	168	Peace Dunkirk	1
But as his Gold he weigh'd, grim Death in spight,	. .	234	Elegy on Demar	31
In Spight of his Deanship and Journeyman Waters.	. .	237	Excellent Song	REF
In Spight of his Deanship and Journeyman Waters.	. .	238	Excellent Song	REF
Yet, spight of Death and Fate, I here maintain	. . .	285	Elegy Boat	29
"Now, if 'twill gratify your Spight,	. . . . . .	305	Storm	53
Then in Spight of your Sophistry, Honest Will. Wood		335	Serious Poem	49
With equal Int'rest, equal Spight,	. . . . . .	345	Prometheus	16
In Spight of Pope, in Spight of Gay,	. . . . .	408	Dial Rich Marb	1
In Spight of Pope, in Spight of Gay,	. . . . .	408	Dial Rich Marb	1
The Rogues must dye for Want and Spight,	. . . .	502	Doctor Delaney	72
For you to exercise your Spight.	. . . .	528	Lady's Dres Rm	74
His Lordship would impute it all to Spight:	. . . .	535	To Mr. Gay	112
Meerly to gratify their Spight,	. . . . . .	548	Life of Swift	129
Against the Court to shew his Spight---.	. . . .	550	Life of Swift	189
And, spight of Chloe's Charms divine,	. . . . .	591	Strephon Chloe	249
After venting all my Spight,	. . . .	629	Epistle Lady	1
Scorn torments them more than Spight.	. . . . .	634	Epistle Lady	146
And since you ne'er provok'd their Spight,	. . . .	644	On Poetry	133
The Nymph stood silent out of spight,	. . . . .	699	Cadenus Vaness	406
In spight of Pallas, now were grown;	. . . . .	701	Cadenus Vaness	473
And, how would Censure glut her Spight?	. . . .	726	To Stella	94
Don Carlos in a merry Spight	. . . .	745	Stel Distress	1
Don Carlos in a merry Spight,	. . . .	749	Stel Wood-Park	1
Oh, ne'er may Fortune shew her Spight,	. . . . .	758	Stel B-day '24	53
He prates in Spight of all Impediment	. . . . .	797	Traulus 1	49
In Spight to Justice, and refuse his Bail.	. . . .	826	Noisy Tom	20
In Spight of Envy flourish still,	. . . . . .	875	Drapier's Hill	19
As soon as gone, will show their Spight:	. . . . .	891	Panegyr Dean	140
She may then grow wise for spight.	. . . . . .	907	Daphne	38
Censorious People do in spight.	. . . .	942	Probatur Alit	18
For Spight I ne'er had any.	. . . .	1005	Sheridan's Sub	19

	PAGE	TITLE	LINE
SPIGHTFUL			
Puff'd by the people's spightful blast,	41	Ode Sancroft	220
Am I spightful, proud, unjust?	631	Epistle Lady	65
Spightful, peevish, rude, untoward;	799	Traulus 2	11
SPIGHTFULLY			
The Farmers, spightfully combin'd,	174	Horace 1, 7	109
SPILLS			
Lets fall her Knife, or spills the Salt,	694	Cadenus Vaness	243
SPILT			
"On Popes, for all the Blood they've spilt,	183	Horace 2, 1	94
The Murd'rer dreams of all the Blood he spilt.	364	Dreams	14
How I tremble to think of the Blood it hath spilt!	871	Grand Question	111
By cruel Hands her Blood was spilt,	923	Riddle 7	65
SPINA			
Thus, when the gentle Spina found	850	Old Thorn	49
SPINDLE-SHANK'D			
. . . and not a spindle-shank'd hoddy doddy.	985	Mary to Sher	10
SPINE			
And then you may kiss the low end of her Spine	1018	Swift Ans Sher	33
SPINNET			
From Husband, Children, Wheel, or Spinnet.	322	First of April	42
When Miss delights in her Spinnet,	710	Cadenus Vaness	736
SPINNING			
Pallas first taught us Poetry and Spinning;	276	Epilogue	38
"Your Business is to mind your Spinning.	304	Storm	44
Next for encouragemt of spinning,	422	Ireld	49
SPINS			
With Spittle while she spins, anoints,	227	Prog of Beauty	42
SPINSTER			
Like Hemp, which by a skilful Spinster drawn	806	Judas	15
SPIRAL			
With spiral Tops, and Copple-Crowns:	896	Panegyr Dean	304
SPIRE			
Became a Steeple with a Spire:	92	Bauc & Phil 1	96
Became a Steeple with a Spire.	113	Bauc & Phil 2	56
Why yonder Steeple wants a Spire,	126	Little House	2
Before I'd touch his filthy Dross, than is Clandalkin Spire.	343	Upon His Grace	38
SPIRES			
If he has seen its gilded Spires.	109	V's House	102
And Castle roofs, and Steeple Spires.	257	Bubble	172
Make gilded spires and altars tumble.	490	Dialogue	36
SPIRIT			
And now I in the Spirit see	7	Ode to King	45
(The Spirit of Exalted Poetry)	7	Ode to King	46
Shall I believe a Spirit so divine	32	Ode to Temple	178
Among thy stubborn sons there haunts that spirit of Jews,	38	Ode Sancroft	129
Where the bless'd spirit lodges like the dove,	41	Ode Sancroft	227
Nor be thy mighty spirit rais'd,	42	Ode Sancroft	263
The subtil spirit all flies up in fume;	49	To Congreve	210
Like distant echo spent, the spirit dies.	50	To Congreve	230
That furnish'd spirit and motion through the whole;	53	Temple Ill	62
And tho' some Malicious Young Spirit did do't,	77	Lady B-	29
His Soul and Spirit did divide,	99	Elegy Patrige	65
A spirit so inform'd as yours	176	To Lord Harley	7
Now his exalted Spirit loaths	231	Prog of Poetry	41
A Dog of Spirit for his Years,	299	Horrid Plot	45
For still you're short (which grieves your Spirit)	475	Epist on Epist	27
Nor wants a nice discerning Spirit,	484	Libel on D- D-	147
But own'd, he had a stubborn Spirit	604	Beasts Confess	109
What Magnanimity of Spirit?	655	On Poetry	416
And is the Spirit of the Soul.	724	To Stella	14
What Spirit since the World began,	799	Traulus 1	95
His Spirit always strives with Slaves.	799	Traulus 1	100
Be studious to practice true Meanness of Spirit;	808	Advice Parson	7
To have the Spirit set to Sale.	821	Dr. Rundle	46
Dear Madam, had you but the Spirit to teaze,	869	Grand Question	53
His matrimonial Spirit fled;	905	Death Daphne	96
Shew your poverty of spirit,	908	Daphne	75
. . . your own spirit of pun, and own wit.	1024	Nim-Dan-Dean 2	D 16
SPIRIT'S			
My spirit's quite shatter'd,	853	Lady's Lament	52
SPIRITS			
Then with that grief we form in spirits divine,	43	To Congreve	5
But gath'ring spirits, wisely ran for't,	64	Discovery	46
To keep mischievous Spirits out:	134	Magician's Rod	52
Where Spirits throng'd with hideous Din,	134	Magician's Rod	55
"Or, wou'd you see his Spirits sink,	305	Storm	67
His Spirits of a sudden fail'd him,	376	Apology Lady C	33
My Conscience is clear, and my Spirits are calm,	400	Tom Clinch	21
"To Spirits of less gentle kind.	485	Libel on D- D-	170
Sets the Spirits all a working.	636	Epistle Lady	206
Of diff'rent Spirits to discern,	642	On Poetry	72
My sinking Spirits now supplies	727	To Stella	109
Your Spirits kindle to a Flame,	730	Stella, Poems	87
I grieve those Spirits should be spent,	731	Stella, Poems	115
Exalts the Spirits, sinks the Lees.	731	Stella, Poems	130
Howe're to keep her Spirits up Mean time to keep	747	Stel Distress	45
Howe'er, to keep her Spirits up,	751	Stel Wood-Park	61
Choice Spirits, who employ their Parts,	780	Mullinix Tim	245
But I feel my Spirits spent,	839	Legion Club	233

```
SPIRITS              (CONTINUED)                          PAGE    TITLE           LINE
    How have I felt my Spirits rais'd,          . . . . . .   887  Panegyr Dean        13
    Now raise your Spirits, Mr. <Dean>:         . . . . .     889  Panegyr Dean        85
    My spirits with my body progging,           . . . . . .  900  Dean's Reasons      57
    Nine Spirits of blaspheming Fops,           . . . . . .   904  Death Daphne        41
    All her spirits in a flame      . . . . . . . . .         906  Daphne              19
    Of raising Spirits from below;  . . . . . . . . . .       920  Riddle 6            10
    In at each Mouth the Spirits pass,          . . . . . .   920  Riddle 6            13
SPIRITUAL
    There some high spiritual throne to Sancroft shall be      42  Ode Sancroft       236
        given,
SPISS
    But all the Filth both Spiss, and Sparse    . . . . .     497  Panegyr Swift      120
SPIT    SEE TURN-SPIT
    Between his Legs, to spew or spit in.       . . . . .     594  Cassinus Peter      22
    Contriving for the Pot and Spit.    . . . . . . . .       897  Panegyr Dean       332
SPITE   SEE SPIGHT
    In spite of the Carle   . . . . . . . . . . .            186  Scriblerus 4      D  10
    A Wretch! whom <English> Rogues to spite her,   . . .    302  Storm               7
    Then gave the Subject out of Spite:         . . . . .    445  Modern Lady         23
    Pull down an Ale-house-Bush, for Spite,     . . . . .    457  Paddy's Charac       8
    So dull, that but for Spleen and Spite,     . . . . .    514  Answer Fable        71
    To burst with Envy, Spite, and Rage,        . . . . .    611  By Dr. Swift        11
    There's a securer Way to wreck your Spite.  . . . .      667  Epig Carthy 4     D   2
    Both Sexes, arm'd with Guilt and Spite,     . . . . .    700  Cadenus Vaness     438
    Truth, Judgment, Wit, give Place to Spite,  . . . . .    730  Stella, Poems       93
    Which can in spite of all Decays,   . . . . . . .        764  Stel B-day '26      11
    In spite of the Devil would still be untoward.          804  Irish Bishops       26
    And, while at good Cashel you rail with such spite,  . . 818  Archbi Cashel        3
    His spite cannot wound, who attempted the Drapier.  . .  818  Archbi Cashel        6
    I'm in spite of my heart led:   . . . . . . . .          853  Lady's Lament       48
    And fast out of spite: . . . . . . . . . . .            853  Lady's Lament       54
SPITEFUL
    The Spiteful Insect stung the God.          . . . . .    458  Paddy's Charac      34
SPITEFULLY
    At last she spitefully was bent . . . . . . . . .        697  Cadenus Vaness     338
SPITS
    Spits in his mouth and stroaks his Chaps    . . . . .    421  Ireld               14
    For here she spits, and here she spues.     . . . . .    527  Lady's Dres Rm      42
SPITTLE
    In power of Spittle and a Clout             . . . . . .   61  Lady Tablebook      21
    With Spittle while she spins, anoints,      . . . . . .  227  Prog of Beauty      42
    To lick a Rascal Statesman's Spittle.       . . . . .    482  Libel on D- D-      82
    To lick a Rascal Statesman's Spittle,       . . . . .    495  Panegyr Swift       59
    Bob's Spittle mix'd with Harry's <Turd>     . . . . .    495  Panegyr Swift       63
    Sit still, and swallow down your Spittle.   . . . . .    644  On Poetry          122
SPITTLES
    Provided a Fund for building you Spittles:  . . . .      805  Irish Bishops       59
SPLASH
    Splish, splash in their pumps.  . . . . . . . . .        245  Irish-Feast         44
SPLEEN
    He damns the Climate, and complains of Spleen.  . . .    137  City Shower         12
    Old <Goldolphin> full of Spleen,            . . . . . .  168  Peace Dunkirk       15
    A perfect Stranger to the Spleen;           . . . . . .  170  Horace 1, 7         10
    Of Spleen, of Politicks and Nonsense,       . . . . .    181  Horace 2, 1         38
    A dang'rous Treatise writ against the Spleen;   . . .    195  Author Himself      48
    Nor puff'd by Pride, nor sunk by Spleen.    . . . . .    199  Horace 2, 6      D
    We order a Vulture, in Shape of the Spleen, . . . . .    266  Apollo              97
    I thought my very Spleen would burst        . . . . .    313  To Ford             51
    "And after all, to crown my Spleen,         . . . . .    380  Apology Lady C     157
    We soon shall find him full of Spleen,      . . . . .    410  Dial Rich Marb      57
    Of Head-ach, and the Spleen complains;      . . . . .    446  Modern Lady         44
    A dreadful Interval of Spleen!  . . . . . . . .          451  Modern Lady        204
    Her Spleen and Fits recover'd quite,        . . . . .    451  Modern Lady        216
    So dull, that but for Spleen and Spite,     . . . . .    514  Answer Fable        71
    Kind Lady Suffolk in the Spleen,            . . . . . .  559  Death of Swift     179
    The Lad lay swallow'd up in Spleen;         . . . . .    594  Cassinus Peter      10
    Can teaze, and gall, and give the Spleen;   . . . . .    651  On Poetry          344
    When Peevishness and Spleen succeed.        . . . . .    731  Stella, Poems      136
    Party and Spleen have turn'd his Brain,     . . . . .    796  Traulus 1           14
    Fill'd with Falshood, Spleen and Pride;     . . . . .    799  Traulus 2            8
    Into Spleen and Vapours fell;   . . . . . . . .          834  Legion Club        122
    I sink in the spleen,           . . . . . . . . .        852  Lady's Lament       35
    And kill with the spleen        . . . . . . . . .        855  Lady's Lament      129
    No more in the spleen:  . . . . . . . . . . .            858  Lady's Lament      220
    The Soul of Man with Spleen you vex;        . . . . .    919  Riddle 5            17
    Of Spleen you cure the Female Sex.          . . . . .    919  Riddle 5            18
    I've nothing left to vent my Spleen         . . . . . . 1005  Sheridan's Sub      27
    In thee Delany's spleen, John's mirth, Helsham's jokes, 1023  Nim-Dan-Dean 2   D  14
        . . .
SPLENDOR
    Her Splendor is but borrow'd light;         . . . . . .  465  Birthday Song      176
    Though Splendor gives the fairest Mark      . . . . . .  500  Doctor Delaney      27
SPLISH
    Splish, splash in their pumps.  . . . . . . . . .        245  Irish-Feast         44
SPLIT
    With driving wrong, will make the Pannel split:  . . .   535  To Mr. Gay         132
    Let the Vessel split on Shelves,            . . . . . .  635  Epistle Lady       161
    They'll teach you how to split a Hair,      . . . . .    657  On Poetry          485
    Oh, would it please the Gods to split       . . . . .    722  Stel B-Day '18       9
    To split my Worship too in twain.           . . . . .    722  Stel B-Day '18      18
```

SPLIT (CONTINUED)

	PAGE	TITLE	LINE
Should the Bottom be split, our <Bishops> wou'd dread	805	Irish Bishops	45
"Though with your state-sieve your own notions you split,	843	Ay and No	9
And, Madam, I laugh'd till I thought I shou'd split.	873	Grand Question	174
How nice you split the hardest Text!	888	Panegyr Dean	62

SPLITTERS

Those Splitters of Parsons in sunder shou'd burst?	805	Irish Bishops	40

SPLUTTER

Nor scold, nor keep a splutter.	429	Beau's Reply	10

SPOIL   SEE SPOYL

If I come down, I'll spoil your Trick	91	Bauc & Phil 1	45
His Horse had like to spoil his Hoof.	127	Little House	34
Nor spoil your Shape, distort your Face,	414	Censure	23
In vain; even there to spoil his Nod	458	Paddy's Charac	33
Nor let her loose to spoil your Trade.	585	Strephon Chloe	30
With restless Beak thy blooming Fruit to spoil,	792	St. Pat's Well	46
To spoil his work, and work by halves:	902	Dean's Reasons	110

SPOIL'D   SEE SPOYL'D

Spoil'd of his Leaden Crown;	7	Ode to King	41
For wit and learning spoil'd his face.	177	To Lord Harley	28
So hopeful, has by me been spoil'd;	692	Cadenus Vaness	195
(For fear young Master shou'd be spoil'd,)	693	Cadenus Vaness	224
On Plutarch's Morals struck, were spoil'd.	701	Cadenus Vaness	483
Had spoil'd his fashionable Airs;	703	Cadenus Vaness	545

SPOILD   SEE SPOYLD

Onely by Affectation spoild,	216	To Mr. Delany	26

SPOILS

The Golden Spoils flew off apace,	158	Fable of Midas	75
Or spoils a Text, or mends his Hose.	279	Journal	24
Instead of Spoils of Persian Looms,	379	Apology Lady C	109
And spoils the Credit of the Function.	502	Doctor Delaney	82
Which spoils ev'ry feature	854	Lady's Lament	97
Here lye deposited the Spoils	921	Riddle 7	13

SPOKE

He <farted> first, and then he spoke.	66	Problem	48
Scarce had they spoke when fair and soft	92	Bauc & Phil 1	91
He spoke, and presently he feels	94	Bauc & Phil 1	165
They scarce had Spoke; when, fair and soft,	112	Bauc & Phil 2	51
He spoke, and presently he feels,	115	Bauc & Phil 2	117
And Guest his Business e're he Spoke.	120	Apollo Outwit	16
Then full of Rage Apollo Spoke,	121	Apollo Outwit	49
Can howl, and bark, but never spoke.	298	Horrid Plot	18
Thus to his Choir of Muses spoke;	320	First of April	2
But some will object, that the Devil oft spoke	335	Serious Poem	57
She spoke ten Thousand Times before.	416	Woman's Mind	12
"You spoke a Word began with H,	452	Modern Lady	254
That sound Divine the Truth has spoke all	469	Birthday Song	271
How many pleasant Things he spoke,	480	Libel on D- D-	7
By Lovers spoke in Punch's Booth.	650	On Poetry	298
The Pleader having spoke his best,	688	Cadenus Vaness	67
Then spoke with Censure, or Applause,	697	Cadenus Vaness	352
In all she spoke, except to stare.	698	Cadenus Vaness	357
To all he spoke, than e'er before;	704	Cadenus Vaness	565
He cou'd not hope she spoke in Jest.	706	Cadenus Vaness	629
And faulter'd ev'ry Word he spoke;	707	Cadenus Vaness	657
And what she spoke was in an Air,	707	Cadenus Vaness	662
Thus spoke to my Lady, the Knight full of Care;	866	Grand Question	1
My Words are few, but spoke with Sense:	917	Riddle 4	5
And tho' no Marriage Words are spoke,	926	Riddle 9	15

SPOKEN

I must confess you've spoken once true.	349	Whitshed Motto	24
Ne'er minded a word that was spoken;	755	Dingley Brent	3
Dear Madam, be sure he's a fine spoken Man,	872	Grand Question	139

SPOKES

The Spokes, we are by Ovid told,	598	Problem Solved	15

SPOON-FULL

You won't part with a Spoon-full,	1015	Swift to Sheri	50

SPORT

Whatever moves our Wonder or our Sport,	31	Ode to Temple	163
To give the Town and Country Sport.	62	Discovery	8
And gives the Whigs and Rabble Sport.	190	Faggot	26
O there is the Sport	245	Irish-Feast	13
"To be the strutting Cornet's Sport,	380	Apology Lady C	149
And gives the Maids of Honor Sport.	468	Birthday Song	268
And when 'tis foul, affords you Sport.	493	Panegyr Swift	20
The Ruin'd Party made his Sport,	498	Panegyr Swift	160
Do but serve to make me Sport.	634	Epistle Lady	148
See, what Mirth the Sport creates;	638	Epistle Lady	255
Look to thy Self, and be no more the Sport	770	Horace 1, 14	11
If Tories must have all the sport,	778	Mullinix Tim	153
Who in tempestuous Seas can sport,	925	Riddle 8	33
I with either sport and toy.	933	Riddle 20	D 18

SPORTED

And with the youthful Damsel sported.	372	Letter D. S-y	46

SPORTS

The Mind unburthen'd sports in various Whims,	363	On Dreams	8

SPORTSMAN

"Vice is a Vermin; Sportsman say	548	Life of Swift	125

SPOT

Was but to light Earth's inconsiderable spot.	36	Ode Sancroft	72
If once they get you on the Spot	312	To Ford	31

```
SPOT            (CONTINUED)                           PAGE   TITLE               LINE
    Robin adores that Spot of Earth,      . . . . . .   314 To Ford                87
    That litt'rall Spot which gave him Birth,  . . . . .  314 To Ford                88
    On that poor Spot, call'd Del-Ville, yonder:  . . .   476 Epist on Epist         60
    Will strike him dead upon the Spot:            . .    500 Doctor Delaney         20
    But took Memorials on the Spot:       . . . . . . .   606 Beasts Confess        158
    But tell me, Tim, upon the spot,      . . . . . .     778 Mullinix Tim          151
    'Tis best to hang her on the Spot;    . . . . . . .   886 Rev Market-Hill       108
SPOTS
    But loathsom Spots his Body stain:            . .      83 Salamander            32
    Her Spots are gone, her Visage clears.  . . . . .     226 Prog of Beauty         8
SPOTTED
    Spotted over like a Le'pard!          . . . . . . .   522 Betty Grizette         4
SPOUSE
    Chose, for her spouse, a mortal born:  . . . . . .    178 To Lord Harley        66
    What tho' her Highness and her Spouse           .     183 Horace 2, 1           87
    In kindness to maintain her Spouse;   . . . . . .     225 Prog of Love          90
    Her Spouse desires his Coffee soon,           . .     291 Prog Marriage         37
    There your Dear Spouse and you together   . . . .     361 Grace's Answer        23
    Your Spouse shall there no longer hector   . . . .    362 Grace's Answer        37
    While you and Spouse transform'd, shall soon  . . .   362 Grace's Answer        51
    Mopsa, who stinks her Spouse to Death,  . . . . .     449 Modern Lady          156
    Steals to her sleeping Spouse to Bed.  . . . . . .    453 Modern Lady          293
    With neither Spouse nor Brother near her,  . . . .    466 Birthday Song        180
    To keep her Spouse deluded still,  . . . . . . .      588 Strephon Chloe       143
    And, from the Spouse each Blemish hide   . . . . .    591 Strephon Chloe       253
    Yet, though her spouse hath often curst her,  . . .   618 Scandal Poem 1        17
    With haughty spouse in vesture fine,  . . . . . .     677 Parson's Case         33
    "Or chid the Dean, or pinch'd thy Spouse.  . . . .    850 Old Thorn             70
    And boyls Potatoes for her Spouse,    . . . . . .     878 Robbin & Harry        26
    Death must not be a Spouse for thee:  . . . . . .     905 Death Daphne          92
    You always are making a God of your Spouse,   . . .   947 Mrs. Houghton          1
    On <Swift's> Reproaches for her <murdered> <spouse>   .  195 Author Himself     54
SPOUSE'S
    'But really 'tis my Spouse's Way;     . . . . . .     448 Modern Lady          105
SPOUSES
    Some to Cuckold Farmers Spouses,            . . . .   574 Helter Skelter        43
    And may your three spouses  . . . . . . . . . .       858 Lady's Lament        225
SPOUT
    Is but a Still which wants a Spout.   . . . . . .     128 Little House          42
SPOUT'S
    The Templer spruce, while ev'ry Spout's a-broach,  . .  138 City Shower         35
SPOUTS
    While Spouts run clatt'ring o'er the Roof by Fits;  .   139 City Shower         44
SPOYL
    The Coasters crowd to seise the Spoyl,   . . . . .    258 Bubble               202
    And not my Compliment to spoyl  . . . . . . . . .     311 To Ford                9
SPOYL'D
    But lest your Kissing should be spoyl'd,  . . . . .   952 Onyons                 8
SPOYLD
    Till Swains unwholsome spoyld the Trade,  . . . . .   225 Prog of Love          91
SPRANG
    Ne'er sprang a youth from out this isle before  . . .   44 To Congreve         11
SPRATS
    Drown'd Puppies, stinking Sprats, all drench'd in Mud,  139 City Shower         62
SPRAWL'D
    There sprawl'd a while, at last got out,  . . . . .   255 Bubble               131
SPRAWLING
    To see the wicked Varlet sprawling;   . . . . . .     353 Wood Ironmongr        26
SPREAD
    Spread all their Charms to catch a <Fart>;  . . . .    66 Problem               36
    Now, through the Realm a Proclamation spread,  . . .  196 Author Himself        59
    Then over us spread,                          . .     246 Irish-Feast           51
    Thro' the Zodiack around, it shall quickly be spread,  .  265 Apollo            69
    From Dublin soon to London spread,    . . . . . .     559 Death of Swift       177
    Though some had spread a thousand Lyes;  . . . . .    605 Beasts Confess       149
    Was never known to spread so wide. . . . . . . .      640 On Poetry              4
    Spread thro' Augusta Trinobantum)     . . . . . .     649 On Poetry            280
    Flutt'ring spread thy purple Pinions,  . . . . . .    660 Love Song              1
    Emblems of Insects vile, who spread their Spawn   .   792 St. Pat's Well        55
SPREADING
    And here, beneath the spreading Shade,  . . . . . .   848 Old Thorn              7
SPREADS
    And now he spreads his little Fans,   . . . . . .      80 Vanbrug House         49
    Spreads Leprosy and Baldness round.   . . . . . .      84 Salamander            56
    Fame spreads the News, and People travel  . . . . .   157 Fable of Midas        37
    But, see how Satan spreads his Snares;  . . . . .     605 Beasts Confess       117
    And sudden spreads a numerous Offspring round;  . . .  792 St. Pat's Well       62
SPRED
    But Gold upon this Ocean spred  . . . . . . . .       255 Bubble               135
SPRIG
    A Sprig of Bays in Fifty Years:       . . . . . .     640 On Poetry              8
    A Sprig of Amaranthine Flow'rs,       . . . . . .     691 Cadenus Vaness       155
SPRIGHTLY
    And fill your Veins with sprightly Blood:  . . . . .  759 Receipt Youth         32
SPRING
    Too flourishing a spring,             . . . . . .      37 Ode Sancroft          99
    Should spring such short and transitory kinds, . . . .  47 To Congreve        128
    . . .this Five and Twenty Years, come Spring,  . . .   70 Mrs Harris Pet        30
    That <Swift> oils many a Spring which Harley moves.  .  194 Author Himself      40
    By Magick Virtue in the Spring,       . . . . . . .   255 Bubble               115
```

SPRING	(CONTINUED)		PAGE	TITLE	LINE
That mixt with Achelous Spring,	. . . .		293	Prog Marriage	109
And Winter softens into Spring:	. . . .		387	Manly Virtue	126
In hope to spring some nobler Game:	. . . .		412	Desire Possess	31
"I wish he may hold out till Spring.	. . . . . .		557	Death of Swift	114
Can ev'ry Spring produce you Flow'rs.	. . . . .		628	Scandal Poem 2	152
To spring more profitable Game.	. . . .		646	On Poetry	184
Yet guess'd not whence could spring the Change.	. .		704	Cadenus Vaness	567
Their Phoebus I, my Spring their Hippocrene.	.		793	St. Pat's Well	72
As from the trodden Dust they spring,	. . . . .		813	Bro Protestant	53
Life's Autumn has no second Spring.	. . . . . .		932	Riddle 19	D 24
Like the Warblers of the Spring.	. . . .		933	Riddle 20	D 12
SPRINGS					
And scorns the Ground, and upward springs,	. . . .		230	Prog of Poetry	14
Perhaps you wonder whence this Friendship Springs,	.		275	Epilogue	35
But a Pox o' those Banks that choak up the Springs.	.		287	Bank Down	3
With which from earth to heav'n he springs;	. . . . .		621	Scandal Poem 1	118
The Roses blow, the Cowslip springs;	. . . . . .		621	Scandal Poem 1	141
The Roses blow, the Cowslip springs;	. . . . . .		627	Scandal Poem 2	145
In Time a new Creation springs.	. . . .		924	Riddle 7	90
SPRINKLED					
Had par'd the Dirt, and Sprinkled round the Floor.	.		124	Descriptn Morn	6
SPRINKLES					
And sprinkles thrice the new-born Maid.	. . . . . .		691	Cadenus Vaness	159
SPRINKLING					
Such is that Sprinkling which some careless Quean	. .		137	City Shower	19
SPRITE					
For he wisely consider'd it must be a Sprite,	. . . .		77	Lady B- B-	13
SPROUT					
Those beds of dung, where schoolboys sprout up beaus	. .		46	To Congreve	99
My Dear, I see your Forehead sprout:	. . . . . .		116	Bauc & Phil 2	156
Sprout, quoth the Man, What's this you tell us?	. . .		116	Bauc & Phil 2	157
Cut down the Dock, 'twill sprout again: but O!	. . .		881	Pastoral Dial	15
SPROUTING					
"No Sheers to check her sprouting Vigour,	. . . . .		476	Epist on Epist	57
SPRUCE					
The Templer spruce, while ev'ry Spout's a-broach,	.		138	City Shower	35
Methinks I see thee, spruce and fine,	. . . . . .		182	Horace 2, 1	73
Cooks make their Fowl look tight and spruce.	. . . .		942	Probatur Alit	10
SPRUNG					
Sprung from a better world, and chosen then	. . . . .		52	Temple Ill	45
Turn'd to that dirt from whence he sprung.	. . . . .		297	Satiric Elegy	32
You sprung an Arch, which in a Scurvy	. . . . .		477	Epist on Epist	71
From hence the Critick Vermin sprung	. . . . .		504	Doctor Delaney	123
Such Order from Confusion sprung,	. . . .		530	Lady's Dres Rm	143
Who from thee sprung, yet on thy Vitals feed;	. . . .		794	St. Pat's Well	96
By the Dam from Lordlings sprung,	. . . .		799	Traulus 2	3
Sprung from Papists and a Regicide;	. . . .		832	Legion Club	72
This bloated Harpy sprung from Hell,	. . . .		895	Panegyr Dean	269
Sprung from her Womb that impious Line,	. . . . .		895	Panegyr Dean	271
But sprung (and I this Truth maintain)	. . . . .		927	Riddle 10	D 9
Has he forgot from whence he sprung?	. . . .		950	Upstart	D 3
SPUD					
My Spud these Nettles from the Stones can part,	. .		881	Pastoral Dial	11
I almost wisht this Spud were in your Guts.	. . . .		882	Pastoral Dial	40
SPUE					
As from the Salamander's Spue;	. . . .		85	Salamander	66
SPUES					
Beside, it Spues a filthy Froth,	. . . .		84	Salamander	51
For here she spits, and here she spues.	. . . . . .		527	Lady's Dres Rm	42
SPUN SEE ILL-SPUN,HOME-SPUN					
For Sixteen Years the Cause was spun,	. . . . . .		690	Cadenus Vaness	124
As my thread of life is spun;	. . . .		937	Riddle 24	D 44
SPUNGE					
To spunge a Breakfast once a Week;	. . . .		409	Dial Rich Marb	52
We only dip a Spunge in Water;	. . . .		627	Scandal Poem 2	128
To spunge for good cheer,	. . . .		852	Lady's Lament	16
But often spunge upon a Friend:	. . . .		954	Authors Living	8
SPUNGING-HOUSE					
What Spunging-House in dread of Jayl	. . . . .		504	Doctor Delaney	145
SPUR					
And then we cry, to spur the bumkins on,	. . . . .		308	Billet Players	39
Which hath she most need of, a Spur or a Bridle?	. .		580	Psyche	4
But then, I'm sure, friend Charles, you want the spur.			671	Epig Carthy 23	D 2
If Punch, to spur their fancy, shews	. . . . . .		776	Mullinix Tim	103
They mounted, and labour'd with Whip and with Spur,	.		804	Irish Bishops	19
SPURIOUS					
These Venus cleans'd from ev'ry spurious Grain	. . .		118	Biddy Floyd	9
To find a Verse in Virgil Spurious;	. . . . . .		483	Libel on D- D-	100
Betwixt a true and spurious Merit;	. . . .		484	Libel on D- D-	148
Nor Infants dropt, the spurious Pledges	. . . . .		641	On Poetry	37
That spurious Virtue in a Maid,	. . . .		691	Cadenus Vaness	169
I scorn thy spurious and degenerate Line,	. . . . .		794	St. Pat's Well	101
Nor have I bred a spurious Race;	. . . .		925	Riddle 8	23
SPURN'D					
He spurn'd them in his Rival's Face.	.		412	Desire Possess	34
SPURS					
And with Whips and Spurs so neat,	. . . . . .		573	Helter Skelter	9
With Jocky Boots, and Silver Spurs;	. . . . .		760	Receipt Youth	44
SPUTT'RING					
A long-ear'd Beast, and a sputt'ring old Whig,	. . .		942	Probatur Alit	27

	PAGE	TITLE	LINE
SPUTTER			
I'll Sputter, Swagger, Curse and Rail,	776	Mullinix Tim	85
Nor sputter out your Oaths so fast,	780	Mullinix Tim	237
But Dick could better sputter.	784	Mullinex Dick	24
Why must he sputter, spaul and slaver it	796	Traulus 1	9
For let him sputter thro' a <Session>,	798	Traulus 1	63
SPY			
Ere Mornings dawn stole out to spy	63	Discovery	35
At length they in the Rubbish spy	109	V's House	103
"A Rake, a Bully, Pimp, or Spy.	303	Storm	30
He chanc't to spy a Clergy Lark;	513	Answer Fable	46
Spy the strutting chatt'ring Vermin?	634	Epistle Lady	152
Began a thousand faults to spy	746	Stel Distress	35
Began a Thousand Faults to spy;	751	Stel Wood-Park	53
Will they not trust me for a Spy?	779	Mullinix Tim	194
Some cleaning hollow Tubes, to spy	780	Mullinix Tim	247
Spy a Building large and lofty,	829	Legion Club	2
Your Riddle I spy.	938	Riddle Answerd	2
SPY'D			
That since I was born, I hardly have spy'd it;	263	Apollo	6
But, as from the Windows the Ladies he spy'd,	399	Tom Clinch	9
Had you but through a Cranny spy'd	591	Strephon Chloe	237
As when you spy'd her on the Privy.	591	Strephon Chloe	248
SQUABBLE			
Tom's three dearest Friends came by in the Squabble,	327	Epigram 1	3
How oft they squabble, snarl and Cheat:	453	Modern Lady	281
SQUADRONS			
Whole Squadrons with a single blow:	461	Birthday Song	32
And to the South my Squadrons bend:	884	Rev Market-Hill	50
SQUAL			
He long'd for a Girl that would struggle and squal,	519	Dean Hang Rape	56
SQUALS			
He squals in such a hellish Noise	513	Answer Fable	25
SQUANDER			
We squander there an Hour and more,	279	Journal	17
But you forsooth, your All must squander,	476	Epist on Epist	59
SQUANDER'D			
Squander'd his noisy talents to my face;	47	To Congreve	138
SQUANDRING			
No Money left for squandring Heirs!	240	Run Bankers	25
SQUARE			
You change a Circle to a Square,	477	Epist on Epist	73
In Square or in Opposite-Circle or Trine	1018	Swift Ans Sher	23
SQUARES			
That with me shall break no squares.	908	Daphne	78
SQUASH			
Then order Squash to call a Hackney Chair.	166	Toland's Invit	46
SQUAT			
Squat on her Hams, to make Maid's Water.	584	Strephon Chloe	18
The hardest Bum will bruise with sitting squat.	881	Pastoral Dial	20
SQUAWL			
She seem'd to laugh and squawl in Rhimes,	150	Corinna	15
SQUEEKS			
"For Fear the rest shou'd say he squeeks;	305	Storm	62
SQUEEZ'D			
Squeez'd in a Coffin turn to dust;	467	Birthday Song	236
He never squeez'd a needy Clyent:	603	Beasts Confess	80
And charming when squeez'd in a Pot of brown Ale.	953	Oranges	2
SQUEEZE			
And squeeze it in, or quit your Place:	190	Faggot	40
I hug them till I squeeze their Blood.	348	Whitshed Motto	10
To squeeze it out from Head to Tail;	527	Lady's Dres Rm	66
Then, squeeze it close between our Thumbs,	627	Scandal Poem 2	129
The Twist, the Squeeze, the Rump, the Ridge an'all,	783	Tim and Fables	17
And, out you squeeze an Ounce at least.	892	Panegyr Dean	186
But heavy, and dark, when you squeeze me together.	928	Riddle 13	D 4
I'll squeeze him to a little Span,	934	Riddle 21	D 18
So are Ladies in Crowds, when they squeeze and they screw, sick.	1030	Dr. Helsham	26
SQUEEZING			
Sit squeezing Images of Wax.	240	Run Bankers	32
But, squeezing out four Lines in Rhime,	893	Panegyr Dean	195
SQUIB			
Flies like a Squib from Place to Place,	398	Earl of P-b-w	8
SQUIBBING			
But, when with squibbing, flashing, popping,	500	Doctor Delaney	21
SQUIBS			
With Squibs and Crackers arm'd, to throw	353	Wood Ironmongr	19
SQUINTING			
A squinting Monkey load with charms;	464	Birthday Song	121
SQUINTS			
But that he struts, and that he squints,	462	Birthday Song	61
But that he squints, and that he struts,	462	Birthday Song	63
'SQUIRE			
But for her 'Squire when he's from home;	322	First of April	40
First, Love In A Tub: 'Squire Wood has in Store	337	Serious Poem	95
Why, there's my Landlord now the 'Squire,	342	Upon His Grace	15
A Bishop says the noble 'Squire, I hate the very Name,	342	Upon His Grace	17
And then I went to pay the 'Squire and in the Way I found,	343	Upon His Grace	41
Why Sirrah said the Noble 'Squire, how dare you see my Face,	343	Upon His Grace	43

		PAGE	TITLE	LINE
'SQUIRE	(CONTINUED)			
	When first the 'Squire, and Tinker Wood	344	Prometheus	1
	But then the 'Squire so trim and nice,	376	Apology Lady C	23
	No 'Squire to be found	858	Lady's Lament	211
	'Twas the damn'd 'Squire with the hard Name,	1005	Sheridan's Sub	20
SQUIRE				
	But most obsequious to the Squire.	95	Bauc & Phil 1	180
	E'er he could prove the good Squire ly'd.	98	Elegy Patrige	4
	But the Squire he was cunning and found what they meant,	288	Bank Down	51
	A trav'lling Tutor to a Squire;	482	Libel on D- D-	64
	To squire a Royal Girl of two Years old!	531	To Mr. Gay	10
	Some Country Squire to Lintot goes,	562	Death of Swift	253
	Conducted by their Squire, Apollo:	585	Strephon Chloe	54
	To recommend him to the Squire;	605	Beasts Confess	138
	Yet, the plain Squire, when Dinner's done,	920	Riddle 6	27
SQUIRES				
	Lords, Knights and Squires were all his humble Debtors.	234	Elegy on Demar	16
	With Servants, Tenants, and the neighb'ring Squires.	533	To Mr. Gay	54
	"On Rural Squires, that Kingdom's Bane,	571	Death of Swift	443
	"Biennial Squires, to Market brought;	571	Death of Swift	445
	Damn'd Lawyers and Judges, Damn'd Lords and Damn'd Squires,	576	Place Damn'd	9
	While all the Squires from nine Miles round,	760	Receipt Youth	42
	The Squires in Scorn will fly the House	760	Receipt Youth	53
	By the worst of all Squires,	853	Lady's Lament	45
SR				
	Some augmentation Sr You know	422	Ireld	35
	But Sr we must support the Crown.	422	Ireld	40
ST				
	Upon St. James's End o' th' Town;	100	Elegy Patrige	96
	From Smithfield, or St. Pulchre's shape their Course,	139	City Shower	58
	But, St. John comes and whispers in his Ear;	194	Author Himself	34
	St James's Park and Stephen's Green;	313	To Ford	60
	As that same viz. St. <Patrick's> Dean.	361	Grace's Answer	6
	of St Andrew's the Green, and St George's the Blue	389	Order of Bath	2
	of St Andrew's the Green, and St George's the Blue	389	Order of Bath	2
	To Kensington, or hot St. James's;	411	Dial Rich Marb	88
	To Fort St. George a Pedlar went he.	456	Dean Smedley	48
	Hither convey St. Patrick's Well;	478	Epist on Epist	92
	And leaves St. James's in Disgrace.	482	Libel on D- D-	60
	Grave D. of st <Patrick> how comes it to pass	522	St. Cecilia's	1
	Yet still St. Stephen's Chappel open lies	538	Mr. Pulteney	7
	St. John, as well as Pultney knows,	555	Death of Swift	59
	St. John himself will scarce forbear,	561	Death of Swift	209
	"What St. John's Skill in State Affairs,	567	Death of Swift	373
	"Remote from St. John, Pope, and Gay.	570	Death of Swift	434
	Poultney deep, accomplish'd St. Johns,	635	Epistle Lady	175
	Than the Owners of St. <James>.	637	Epistle Lady	242
	As the Hirelings of St. <Stephens>.	637	Epistle Lady	244
	St. George beheld thee with Delight,	656	On Poetry	461
	I rode four more to great St. Mary;	675	Curate's Compl	3
	From round the Purlieus of St. James,	698	Cadenus Vaness	365
	St. George himself he plays the wag on,	777	Mullinix Tim	115
	About St. James's, cry, We Courtiers.	812	Bro Protestant	22
	Jolly boys of St. Kevans, St. Patrick's, Donore,	814	Yahoo's	1
	Jolly boys of St. Kevans, St. Patrick's, Donore,	814	Yahoo's	1
	We'll colt him thro' Kevan, St. Patrick's, Donore,	817	Yahoo's	56
	As well become St. <Patrick's> <Dean>;	889	Panegyr Dean	78
	Which is all at present from Dean of St. Patrick's.	977	Dean to Sherid	48
	I wish Alexander safe at St. Catherine's To-night,	1014	Swift to Sheri	9
	You would really on Thursday leave St Catharine	1017	Swift Ans Sher	12
	I thought the Lady at St. Cath'rines	1033	Ans to Crown	15
STAB				
	Each line shall stab, shall blast, like daggers and like fire;	37	Ode Sancroft	91
	He slew my Body, but you stab my Fame.	668	Epig Carthy 10 D	2
STABB'D				
	The greatest monarch may be stabb'd by night,	506	To a Friend	1
	Stabb'd to the Heart, condemn'd to Flame,	916	Riddle 2	7
STABLE				
	O'erflow'd a Farmer's Barn and Stable;	811	Bro Protestant	2
STABLE'S				
	My Stable's unslated,	1014	Swift to Sheri	24
STABS				
	What Stabs and what Cuts,	246	Irish-Feast	65
	And stabs the Son before the Mother's Eyes.	364	On Dreams	16
STACKS				
	Whole Ricks of Hay and Stacks of Corn,	811	Bro Protestant	3
STAFF				
	Lay by your White Staff & gray Habit,	187	Scriblerus 4 D	15
	In other Words, You with the Staff,	188	Scriblerus 6	3
	Or Constable with Staff of Peace,	189	Faggot	23
	Great Ormonde lend thy Gen'ral's Staff:	191	Faggot	46
	Nor stoops to take the Staff, nor lays it down,	210	Earl of Oxford	9
	With Dick's own Staff his Peacefull Neighbor,	220	A Quiet Life	22
	To lead thee, as a Staff directs the Blind,	770	Horace 1, 14	17
STAFFS	SEE QUARTER-STAFFS			
STAGE				
	Who fain would rule the Pulpit, as they do the Stage,	19	Ode Athenian	104
	By hopes my Congreve will reform the stage;	45	To Congreve	50

```
STAGE          (CONTINUED)                            PAGE    TITLE            LINE
    Is he that scribbles for the Stage;      . . . . . . .    80  Vanbrug House      40
    When Charity begins to tread the Stage:  . . . . . .     274  Epilogue            2
    With fifty Yards of Crape, shall sweep the Stage.  .     275  Epilogue           26
    Their Brother Quill-Men Workers for the Stage,     .     276  Epilogue           41
    Enter the Stage they never mind him;     . . . . . .     776  Mullinix Tim      102
    Till he appears upon the Stage.     . . . . . . .        776  Mullinix Tim      108
STAGERS
    Had you been cunning Stagers,       . . . . . . . .      426  Five Ladies        26
STAGES
    "To pass to many crowded Stages,    . . . . . . . .      380  Apology Lady C    155
STAGG
    The Stagg was swift, the Fox a Knave:    . . . . . .     512  Answer Fable        6
STAGGER
    They reel and stagger too and fro,  . . . . . . . .      256  Bubble            151
STAGIRITE
    Is rightly censur'd by the Stagirite,    . . . . . .     988  Letter Dr Sh-n     19
STAGNATES
    Corrupts and stagnates in the Veins,     . . . . . . .   239  Run Bankers        10
STAGNATING
    From stagnating preserves the Flood;     . . . . . . .   731  Stella, Poems     128
STAIN
    But loathsom Spots his Body stain:       . . . . . .      83  Salamander         32
    Roughen the Nap, and leave a mingled Stain.    . . . .   138  City Shower        30
    Her Arm-pits would not stain her Gown:   . . . . .      584  Strephon Chloe     22
    Was unsusceptible of Stain:     . . . . . . .           586  Strephon Chloe     86
    With Honour, which no Breath can Stain,    . . . . .    693  Cadenus Vaness    208
STAIN'D
    All stain'd with Infamy and Vice,   . . . . . . .        84  Salamander         39
    Your num'rous virtues foully stain'd;    . . . . . .    436  Answer Paulus     142
    Stain'd with the Marks of stinking Toes;   . . . . .    527  Lady's Dres Rm     52
STAINS
    My Lord and me as far as Stains,    . . . . . . .       201  Horace 2, 6        76
    They keep at Stains the old blue Boar,   . . . . . .    225  Prog of Love       99
    Incapable of outward Stains;    . . . . . . . .         691  Cadenus Vaness    163
STAIR
    That when I strut, and stair, and stink,    . . . . .   778  Mullinix Tim      166
STAIRS
    A reall House with Rooms and Stairs.     . . . . . .     87  Hist V's House     23
    Prepar'd to Scrub the Entry and the Stairs.    . . .    124  Descriptn Morn      8
    But if he will break in, and walk up Stairs,   . . .    166  Toland's Invit     44
    And Climb the dark Stairs to your friends who have none: 185  Scriblerus 1        4
    By Adam lighted walk up stairs:     . . . . . . .       280  Journal            56
    He enters in, and walks up Stairs,  . . . . . . .       292  Prog Marriage      87
    To raise the Stairs, or build the Cieling;     . . .    409  Dial Rich Marb     26
    They Cudgell'd, and Cuft him, and kickt him down Stairs 517  Dean Hang Rape     16
    Request it of him to compleat your Stairs      . . .    534  To Mr. Gay         98
    Grew louder, all the Way up Stairs;      . . . . .      698  Cadenus Vaness    369
    She curs'd the dark & winding Stairs     . . . . .      746  Stel Distress      33
    She curst the narrow winding Stairs:     . . . . . .    751  Stel Wood-Park     52
    And see now, it strikes ten, and I hear him coming up   987  Mary to Sher       36
        Stairs:
STAKE
    Stood without Motion, like a Stake.      . . . . .      133  Magician's Rod     34
    And when their country lyse at stake     . . . . .      421  Ireld               7
    In both, yet hardly save your stake.     . . . . .      436  Answer Paulus     130
    'Tis my own Credit lies at Stake.   . . . . . . .       741  Stel B-day 22      32
STAKES
    Takes Snuff, and holds the Stakes.       . . . . . .     75  Game Traffick      12
STALE
    Stale Memorandums of the Schools;   . . . . . . .        27  Ode to Temple      34
    Stale forms of course, all mean deceivers use,   . . .   44  To Congreve        20
    Are mingled with stale.     . . . . .                   402  Window Inns 8    D  8
    To cry the Bread was stale, and mutter   . . . . .      410  Dial Rich Marb     53
    In Phrases battered, stale, and trite,   . . . . .      448  Modern Lady       112
    Altho' the Metaphor be worn and stale    . . . . .      770  Horace 1, 14        5
    Are Stale, and Worn as Troy-Town Story.    . . . .      774  Mullinix Tim       36
STALKS
    Which bow'd by evening-breeze with bending stalks,  .    54  Temple Ill        119
    See with what consequence he stalks.     . . . . . .    950  Upstart          D 13
STALL
    He stood behind a Stall to lurk,    . . . . . . .        86  Hist V's House     15
    Unloads upon a Stall to rest    . . . . . . . .         160  Atlas               6
    Cheapning old Authors on a Stall.   . . . . . . .       170  Horace 1, 7         6
    Two Dozen Canons round your Stall,  . . . . . . .       173  Horace 1, 7        89
    I'll give thee Surplice, Verge and Stall,      . . .    361  Grace's Answer      7
STALLS
    Sweepings from Butchers Stalls, Dung, Guts, and Blood   139  City Shower        61
    They lie open on Purpose, on Counters and Stalls,   .   263  Apollo             23
STAMP    SEE PAPER-STAMP
    The publick Stamp Heav'n sets on all that's Great and    18  Ode Athenian       93
        Good,
    He sets the Stamp of Bad and Good,  . . . . . . .       649  On Poetry         273
STAMPING
    Did not burst with their stamping.  . . . . . . . .     245  Irish-Feast        40
STAMPT
    The bullion stampt in your refining mind   . . . . .     45  To Congreve        53
STANCH
    Nay, hector and swagger, you'll still find me stanch,  . 979  Dean to Tho: S     13
STAND
    When Treason there in Person seems to stand,   . . . .    8  Ode to King        56
```

STAND   (CONTINUED)

	PAGE	TITLE		LINE
But the Thing I stand upon, is the Credit of the House	71	Mrs Harris Pet		39
In making a Ballad, but was at a Stand, ...	77	Lady B- B-		23
Now move, and now in Order Stand.	108	V's House		78
Then Madam bid the Chariot stand, ...	128	Little House		50
Of this, we'll grant you stand acquit, ...	154	Widow and Cat	D	36
Or when he can no longer stand	160	Atlas		7
The Waiters stand in Ranks; the Yeomen cry, ...	194	Author Himself		35
Desiring I would stand their Friend.	200	Horace 2, 6		46
They stand amaz'd, and think me grown	202	Horace 2, 6		103
Tis but when others stand the Test, ...	218	To Mr. Delany		84
Stand in your sacred Presence aw'd;	243	Horace 4, 9		12
Your Foes already waiting stand	258	Bubble		198
"When we come there we'll stand unseen, ...	321	First of April		27
I'm sure Old <Jour--> you'd not stand by it; . . .	372	Letter D. S-y		20
Science and Art you say at stand are, ...	372	Letter D. S-y		41
"And stand the Staring of your Pages;	380	Apology Lady C		156
Stand high in Honour, Wealth, or Wit;	414	Censure		7
And then stand by to see fair play, ...	421	Ireld		10
Nor when we see Astraea stand	433	Answer Paulus		31
A thousand words to stand for six!	434	Answer Paulus		84
"Stand further Girl, or get you gone, ...	452	Modern Lady		244
Behold three beauteous Vowels stand	467	Birthday Song		229
To see him always foremost stand, ...	546	Life of Swift		33
Stand high himself, keep others low?	554	Death of Swift		16
When Death approach'd, to stand between:	561	Death of Swift		222
"How could unguarded Virtue stand?	568	Death of Swift		390
"The greatful People stand his Friends:	570	Death of Swift		426
And there--behold Alecto stand, ...	596	Cassinus Peter		81
Stand in Awe without a Rod.	633	Epistle Lady		104
But Pallas here was at a Stand;	693	Cadenus Vaness		211
The Urchin from his private Stand	702	Cadenus Vaness		515
And shou'd Want or Desert stand in need of his Aid,	717	Answer Rebus		27
Dare you let these Reproaches stand, ...	732	Stella, Poems		139
First, nine Ways looking, let her stand	743	Stel B-day 22		53
Shall moving Delos now deep-rooted stand, ...	770	Horace 1, 14		3
Resolve to it out the last;	774	Mullinix Tim		42
And simple as I now stand here, ...	778	Mullinix Tim		157
Ne're hold my peace, and ne'er stand still.	778	Mullinix Tim		160
I allow the Pile may stand.	830	Legion Club		38
Shall stand for Ages on Record, ...	848	Old Thorn		14
Which must alas no longer stand;	849	Old Thorn		22
Drawn up in our Court; when the Captain cries, Stand.	870	Grand Question		100
Thy Breeches torn behind, stand gaping wide; . . .	881	Pastoral Dial		
At first did put me to a stand;	912	Aenigma Expl	D	2
Lo, here I stand with double Face;	917	Riddle 3		2
He kindly bids me near him stand;	921	Riddle 6		29
And yet I firmly stand my Ground:	926	Riddle 9		8

STANDARD

Which could he to the Standard bring, ...	602	Beasts Confess		33

STANDER   SEE BY-STANDER
STANDER-BY

For, ev'ry Stander-by was marking	299	Horrid Plot		25
The World, a willing Stander-by, ...	414	Censure		13
Can only be a Stander-by.	741	Stel B-day 22		34

STANDERS-BY

Yes; you are all malicious standers-by, ...	49	To Congreve		199
And I'll be judg'd by standers-by.	83	Salamander		28
Yet Standers-by may plainly see	926	Riddle 9		5

STANDING

With inoffensive feet o'er standing corn;	54	Temple Ill		118
To half the world a standing jest, ...	455	Dean Smedley		11
This Peacock kept a standing Force, ...	513	Answer Fable		27
But leave it standing full in Sight	528	Lady's Dres Rm		73
Conceives a Lady standing by:	529	Lady's Dres Rm		124
That, Standing Troops were his Aversion:	606	Beasts Confess		152

STANDISH

Delany sends a Silver Standish, ...	611	By Dr. Swift		3

STANDS   SEE UNDER-STANDS

And, lo! where a Destroying Angel stands, ...	7	Ode to King		48
Stands in the gap 'twixt me and wretched men, . . .	45	To Congreve		47
Still at Whitehall it stands in view, ...	87	Hist V's House		31
The watchful Bailiffs take their silent Stands, . .	125	Descriptn Morn		17
Where there are none, it stands erect, ...	133	Magician's Rod		25
And Midas now neglected stands, ...	158	Fable of Midas		81
But fill'd with Admiration, stands, ...	227	Prog of Beauty		50
"Look, there he stands, and 'tis but just	304	Storm		49
Observe where bloody Townshend stands	312	To Ford		43
The Bus'ness of the Nation stands.	325	Pethox		52
Where Wisdom stands to keep the Field, ...	340	Arch-Bish Dub		23
In ev'ry Council and Debate he stands for what is Right	341	Upon His Grace		5
Where, on the Summit Fortune stands:	413	Desire Possess		41
The <Devil> ready stands, my <Swift>, ...	497	Panegyr Swift		124
Hard by a filthy Bason stands, ...	526	Lady's Dres Rm		37
The World stands trembling at his Throne.	579	Day Judgement		8
Confest the conqu'ring Hero stands.	655	On Poetry		420
This Atlas stands to prop the Court:	656	On Poetry		444
In the Porch Briareus stands, ...	833	Legion Club		103
While you, from where the Basin stands, ...	884	Rev Market-Hill		53
That stands 'twixt Heav'n, and Earth, and Hell, . .	928	Riddle 12	D	2

```
STANZA                                                            PAGE    TITLE          LINE
    And yet before your Stanza ends you flout me      . . . .    1003 Dan J's Reply       21
STAR
    Or has he like some fearful Star appear'd?    . . . . .        10 Ode to King        130
    Rapt in the Vortex of the Brittish Star;      . . . . .        10 Ode to King        139
    Kind Star, still may'st thou shed thy sacred influence         39 Ode Sancroft      154
      here,
    To peep upon a twinkling Star.    . . . . . . . . .            99 Elegy Patrige      56
    One rose a Star, the other fell       . . . . . . .           100 Elegy Patrige      67
    And is Install'd as good a Star,      . . . . . . .           100 Elegy Patrige      71
    Triumphant Star! Some Pity show       . . . . . . .           100 Elegy Patrige      89
    Take Pattern by your Sister Star,     . . . . . . .           228 Prog of Beauty     69
    Nor a new Star adorn the Skies:       . . . . . . .           271 Apollo's Edict  D  37
    Without a Star this may be done,      . . . . . . .           271 Apollo's Edict  D  42
    Shines in all Climates like a Star;   . . . . . . .           398 Earl of P-b-w      31
    He fixt the Star and String Cerulean.         . . . .         656 On Poetry         464
    Advanc'd like Atalanta's Star,        . . . . . . .           696 Cadenus Vaness    306
STAR-GAZING
    The Cobling and Star-gazing Part,     . . . . . . .           100 Elegy Patrige      70
STARE
    How would you stare    . . . . . . . . . . . .                442 Ballyspellin       67
    But, Lord how the Rabble will stare and will gape,    . .     520 Dean Hang Rape     71
    In all she spoke, except to stare. . . . . . . . .           698 Cadenus Vaness    357
    But purely come to hear, and stare;   . . . . . . .           777 Mullinix Tim      128
    Let them stare and storm and frown,   . . . . . . .           831 Legion Club        55
    Let them stare and stink together;   . . . . . . . .         835 Legion Club       154
STARES
    The Message told, he gapes--and stares,       . . . . .       376 Apology Lady C     19
STARING
    "And stand the Staring of your Pages;         . . . . .       380 Apology Lady C    156
    Tim with surprize and pleasure staring,       . . . . . .     783 Tim and Fables     13
STARMONGER
    A Cobler, Starmonger, and Quack,      . . . . . . .           101 Elegy Patrige     104
STARS
    Is fix't like Fate among the Stars,   . . . . . . .             6 Ode to King        20
    'Tis all the Portion of my niggard Stars;     . . . . .        32 Ode to Temple     201
    Unless, perhaps, some stars above be so;      . . . . .        39 Ode Sancroft      144
    But thanks his stars, that Phyllis has been kind;   . .        48 To Congreve       158
    Shrouds her still beams; how should the stars be seen?  .      53 Temple Ill         58
    But still, tho' fixt among the Stars,     . . . . . .          66 Problem            27
    Not one of all his Crony Stars,       . . . . . . .            98 Elegy Patrige       7
    Adorn'd with Golden Stars and Rays,   . . . . . . .            98 Elegy Patrige      28
    Can like the Stars foretel the Weather;       . . . . .        99 Elegy Patrige      43
    Consider where the Moon and Stars     . . . . . . .           100 Elegy Patrige      97
    Who to the Stars in pure Good-will,   . . . . . . .           101 Elegy Patrige     105
    The Golden Stars for Guinneas took,   . . . . . . .           255 Bubble            127
    And they like Stars shall Rise and Set.       . . . . .       362 Grace's Answer     50
    If This to Clouds and Stars will venture,     . . . . .       393 Modern Poets        7
    Thanks to my Stars, I once can see    . . . . . . .           402 Window Inns 7   D   1
    "I thank my Stars they are all light;     . . . . . .         447 Modern Lady        68
    "Despis'd the Fools with Stars and Garters,   . . . .         565 Death of Swift    323
    Above the Stars exalt your Stile,     . . . . . . .           657 On Poetry         471
    High as Longinus to the Stars ascends,    . . . . . .         669 Epig Carthy 14  D   1
    So Stars beyond a certain Height      . . . . . . .           700 Cadenus Vaness    442
    He flies, and leaves the Stars behind,    . . . . . .         728 Stella, Poems      36
    Consult the Stars, and thence foretell    . . . . . .         918 Riddle 4           43
START
    I talk'd of a Peace, and they both gave a start,      . . .   143 New Song           17
    Both from the Goal together start;    . . . . . . .           290 Prog Marriage      31
    Will duck his Head, aside will start,     . . . . . .         500 Doctor Delany       5
    At Thunder now no more I start,       . . . . . . .           674 His Deafness        5
    At proper Times to scream and start;      . . . . . .         725 To Stella          72
    Mean Time, the Wise a Question start,     . . . . . .         919 Riddle 5           31
STARTED
    When Schonberg started at the Vast Design:    . . . . .        12 Ode to William  D  34
STARTLED
    "If startled at a Scene so rude,      . . . . . . .           379 Apology Lady C    135
    Where a cow would be startled,        . . . . . . . .         853 Lady's Lament      47
STARTS
    Out starts the little Beast, and mocks their idle Fears.  . .  30 Ode to Temple     114
    Starts at the Rust'ling of the Trees;     . . . . . .         379 Apology Lady C    126
    "When up a dangerous Faction starts,      . . . . . .         568 Death of Swift    379
STARV'D
    "I shall be starv'd with Cold and Hunger."    . . . .         208 Fable Bitches      30
    Or else poor Stella may be starv'd.   . . . . .              761 Bec's B-Day        38
STARV'LING
    With pennyless and starv'ling strains;    . . . . . .         432 Answer Paulus      16
    Poor starv'ling Bard, how small thy Gains!    . . . .         642 On Poetry          59
STARVE
    Rather than starve, a better man would strole.    . . . .     308 Billet Players     16
    And when we starve for want of Corn,      . . . . . .         464 Birthday Song     125
    Was left to starve, and dye in Wales.     . . . . . .         481 Libel on D- D-     52
    Or Cellar, where they starve to Day.      . . . . . .         505 Doctor Delany     150
    There let him starve, and vent his Rage.      . . . . .       515 Answer Fable       84
    Starve twenty Lords to make one Scoundrel rich:       . .     535 To Mr. Gay        104
    "And seem'd determin'd not to starve it,      . . . . .       571 Death of Swift    457
    Let them neither starve, nor stuff:   . . . . . . .           633 Epistle Lady      130
    Dammee, I say, they ought to starve.      . . . . . .         783 Tim and Fables     34
    How to plague and starve the City;    . . . . . . .           831 Legion Club        54
STARVING
    Here we ly starving in the Street     . . . . . . .            90 Bauc & Phil 1      17
```

STARVING   (CONTINUED)   PAGE   TITLE   LINE
    By starving in the midst of Store, ...   157 Fable of Midas   49
    Carve for all, yourself is starving.   . . . .   633 Epistle Lady   124
    A Poet, starving in a Garret, ...   728 Stella, Poems   25
    And yet run out by starving here: . . . .   745 Stel Distress   16
    To running out by starving here.   . . . .   750 Stel Wood-Park   44
    In frosty Nights their starving Cows, ...   759 Receipt Youth   2
STATE   SEE MOCK-STATE,MIDDLE-STATE
    Kings would indeed be Victims of the State;   . . . .   6 Ode to King   6
    Whom all the Charms of an Usurped Wife and State,   .   20 Ode Athenian   154
    The wily Shafts of State, those Juggler's Tricks   . .   29 Ode to Temple   92
    And some, to be large cyphers in a state, ...   36 Ode Sancroft   59
    The herd beneath, who see the weathercock of state   37 Ode Sancroft   73
    Say, why the Church is still led blindfold by the State?   40 Ode Sancroft   177
    Ah, may no unkind earthquake of the State, ...   40 Ode Sancroft   190
    Out slipp't a Mystery of State   . . . .   62 Discovery   7
    Our wand'ring Saints in wofull State, ...   91 Bauc & Phil 1   47
    And mindfull of it's antient State, ...   93 Bauc & Phil 1   109
    Our wand'ring Saints in woful State, ...   111 Bauc & Phil 2   15
    The Peaceful State of common Brooms.   . . . . . .   132 Magician's Rod   20
    A Premier Minister of State   . . . .   160 Atlas   17
    Portending ruin to our State, ...   181 Horace 2, 1   22
    In Favour grows with Ministers of State;   . . . . . .   194 Author Himself   29
    "To haunt a certain Minister of State: . . . . . .   195 Author Himself   44
    My State of Health none care to learn;   . . . . . .   203 In Sickness   5
    Quakers and Aldermen, in State, ...   239 Run Bankers   14
    An Eagle's Flight and State assumes, ...   252 Bubble   35
    Who float upon the tide of state, ...   296 Satiric Elegy   27
    Inform'd a Minister of State.   . . . .   298 Horrid Plot   4
    The haughty Minister of State   . . . .   325 Pethox   49
    The Latent Wiles, and Tricks of State, ...   340 Arch-Bish Dub   11
    Both Church and State, being still dependent. . . . .   372 Letter D. S-y   22
    He trembles at the Thoughts of State;   . . . . . .   376 Apology Lady C   31
    To state the question pro and con: . . . .   435 Answer Paulus   100
    When weary'd with Intrigues of State, ...   480 Libel on D- D-   27
    And grown a Minister of State, ...   482 Libel on D- D-   69
    Both <Kings> and Ministers of State, ...   485 Libel on D- D-   174
    Ye paultry underlings of state, ...   487 Irish-Club   1
    Both <Kings> and Ministers of State.   . . . . . .   498 Panegyr Swift   156
    To be your Asses Colts of State, ...   499 Panegyr Swift   180
    In Church and in State was of Principles sound,   .   518 Dean Hang Rape   32
    Our Church and our State dear <England> maintains,   .   520 Dean Hang Rape   67
    May sink by premier Ministers of State.   . . . . .   535 To Mr. Gay   116
    I knew a brazen Minister of State, ...   536 To Mr. Gay   143
    "That Church and State had suffer'd more   . . . . .   549 Life of Swift   150
    Could maul a Minister of State.   . . . .   555 Death of Swift   62
    "What St. John's Skill in State Affairs, ...   567 Death of Swift   373
    "In him was held a Crime of State.   . . . .   569 Death of Swift   416
    In State return'd the grand Parade;   . . . . . .   586 Strephon Chloe   68
    Observe the case: I state it thus: . . . .   622 Scandal Poem 1   157
    Wicked Ministers of State   . . . .   634 Epistle Lady   143
    Maxims wise, to rule the State.   . . . .   635 Epistle Lady   174
    To rise in Church, or Law, or State, ...   641 On Poetry   40
    And lo, his Ministers of State, ...   646 On Poetry   207
    Lives in a State of War by Nature.   . . . .   651 On Poetry   320
    Now sing the Minister of State, ...   656 On Poetry   441
    With chariot less for use than state;   . . . .   676 Parson's Case   24
    Some small Regard for State and Wealth: . . . . .   693 Cadenus Vaness   217
    Caress'd by Ministers of State, ...   702 Cadenus Vaness   504
    But Time, and Books, and State Affairs   . . . . . .   703 Cadenus Vaness   544
    But rising from her Chair of State, ...   714 Cadenus Vaness   887
    The Changes which Faction has made in the State,   .   716 Answer Rebus   23
    Might breed Confusion in the State, ...   723 To Stella   4
    Base Kings and Ministers of State, ...   725 To Stella   63
    And guide you to a better State.   . . . .   766 Stel B-day '26   78
    Betwixt a State, and Vessel under Sail;   . . . . .   770 Horace 1, 14   6
    As those who long have stood the Storms of State,   .   772 Horace 1, 14   59
    Thy Screw'd up front; thy State Grimace;   . . . . .   775 Mullinix Tim   60
    Of twenty <Ministers> of State.   . . . .   781 Mullinix Tim   258
    Against us Ministers of State!   . . . .   783 Tim and Fables   32
    Devour the Church, and chatter to the State. . . . .   792 St. Pat's Well   52
    In the State to build a Babel.   . . . .   800 Traulus 2   46
    Sir, we the Ministers of State.   . . . .   812 Bro Protestant   24
    That he would answer both for Church and State;   . .   825 Noisy Tom   2
    Now, Madam, observe, how he marches in State: . . .   870 Grand Question   89
    That must attend the marry'd state;   . . . .   879 Robbin & Harry   40
    So suited to your State, and Years!   . . . .   888 Panegyr Dean   50
    When to the Vault you walk in State, ...   889 Panegyr Dean   87
    In state affairs, or planting cale;   . . . . . .   901 Dean's Reasons   76
    The poorest hither march in State, ...   928 Riddle 12   D   13
    And her chief Officers of State, ...   1035 To Quilca   11
    Nor Minister of State.   . . . .   1036 Heathen Christ   4
STATE-AFFAIRS
    But is for State-Affairs as fit, ...   183 Horace 2, 1   105
    Of State-Affairs you cannot smatter, ...   642 On Poetry   51
STATE-AIRS
    Now Enter Bush with new State-Airs, ...   62 Discovery   9
STATE-EMP'RIC
    But, the State-Emp'ric acts a safer Part;   . . . .   534 To Mr. Gay   81
STATE-OPINIONS
    In State-Opinions a-la Mode, ...   171 Horace 1, 7   35

	PAGE	TITLE	LINE

STATE-SIEVE
"Though with your state-sieve your own notions you split,   843 Ay and No   9
STATED
The Case, I have stated, ...   1014 Swift to Sheri   22
STATELY
Rode stately through Holbourn, to die in his Calling;   .   399 Tom Clinch   2
STATES
Into small States and Principalities, ...   26 Ode to Temple   5
The Thoughts of Monarchs, and Designs of States,   . .   30 Ode to Temple   105
Divided Hearts, united States.   . . . .   96 On the Union   6
For framing Laws to govern States;   . . . .   641 On Poetry   28
STATESMAN
Henceforward let no Statesman dare, ...   96 On the Union   13
Of a governing Statesman, or favorite Whore: . . . .   351 Wood Insect   30
The Statesman rakes the Town to find a Plot, ...   364 On Dreams   19
Nor less <Tom-T--d-Man> of true Statesman mold,   . . .   364 On Dreams   21
The Statesman tells you with a Sneer, ...   605 Beasts Confess   141
A Statesman, or a South-Sea Jobber.   . . . . . .   645 On Poetry   162
Did not an able Statesman   . . . .   774 Mullinix Tim   17
I place a <Statesman> full before my Sight.   . . . .   532 To Mr. Gay   32
STATESMAN'S
To lick a Rascal Statesman's Spittle, ...   482 Libel on D- D-   82
Would shew you many a Statesman's Face.   . . . . . .   485 Libel on D- D-   180
To lick a Rascal Statesman's Spittle, ...   495 Panegyr Swift   59
The Lawyer's Fees, the Statesman's Bribes.   . . . .   922 Riddle 7   20
STATESMEN
All Statesmen are in this Condition, ...   160 Atlas   15
To spend six Months with Statesmen here.   . . . . .   199 Horace 2, 6   12
For Statesmen never want Dog-tricks.   . . . .   300 Horrid Plot   60
To cry, like statesmen, quanta patimur!   . . . . . .   433 Answer Paulus   42
Detesting all the Statesmen kind, ...   482 Libel on D- D-   72
And, Statesmen by ten thousand odds   . . . . . .   486 Libel on D- D-   197
Then shew, how Statesmen oft are stung   . . . . . .   496 Panegyr Swift   114
Had Statesmen too of ev'ry Kind, ...   513 Answer Fable   29
To Statesmen wou'd you give a Wipe, ...   643 On Poetry   95
STATION
While in the Station of a Jack   . . . . . .   94 Bauc & Phil 1   135
It fell into its proper Station.   . . . .   127 Little House   12
But only what my Station fits, ...   199 Horace 2, 6   D
A more inferior Station seeks   . . . .   227 Prog of Beauty   34
While Montague, who claim'd the Station   . . . . .   481 Libel on D- D-   35
And place you in a better Station, ...   484 Libel on D- D-   119
Give others Riches, Power, and Station, ...   555 Death of Swift   43
"He never courted Men in Station, ...   565 Death of Swift   325
Damn'd Villians, Corrupted in every Station, ...   576 Place Damn'd   11
His Practice was, in ev'ry Station   . . . .   606 Beasts Confess   153
And, with Credit fill my Station;   . . . .   630 Epistle Lady   24
End, as it befits your Station, ...   636 Epistle Lady   185
Attending each his proper Station, ...   650 On Poetry   313
Cou'd we place him in a Station, ...   801 Traulus 2   47
His Station despising, unaw'd by the Place, ...   809 Epigr Prelate   3
For one of his station!   . . . .   857 Lady's Lament   182
Regardful of your Age and Station, ...   889 Panegyr Dean   68
But, duly e'er you leave your Station, ...   893 Panegyr Dean   219
Which in its proper Station plac'd, ...   1021 Nim-Dan-Dean 1   D 13
STATIONS
Have in More Fields their Stations fix, ...   101 Elegy Patrige   100
He rises to the highest Stations;   . . . .   386 Manly Virtue   90
A Genius for all Stations fit, ...   482 Libel on D- D-   79
Who owe their Virtues to their Stations, ...   484 Libel on D- D-   137
He thought it base for Men in Stations, ...   606 Beasts Confess   177
If both shou'd now their Stations change.   . . . . .   712 Cadenus Vaness   805
Let Folks in high, or holy Stations, ...   813 Bro Protestant   57
STATUE
But finding the Statue to make no Complaint, ...   336 Serious Poem   73
To Prance with me the Statue round.   . . . .   776 Mullinix Tim   80
STATURE
The dullest Beast when high in Stature, ...   940 Letter   5
STATUTE
High Treason by Statute! But here you object,   . . .   266 Apollo   89
STATUTES
Against the Statutes in that Case, ...   687 Cadenus Vaness   18
STAY
Stay but a little while and down again 'twill come,   . .   10 Ode to King   128
And the Dove-muse, will now no longer stay   . . . . .   16 Ode Athenian   16
We fondly stay at home in fear   . . . .   19 Ode Athenian   99
Fain the fair Nymph would stay, ...   31 Ode to Temple   153
Stay while I tell my story, short, and true;   . . . .   46 To Congreve   111
Why near the dregs of youth perversely wilt thou stay,   .   54 Temple Ill   105
Apollo thought it vain to stay, ...   121 Apollo Outwit   42
"I am a Cat of Honour--Stay, ...   154 Widow and Cat   D 31
Let no pretence of Bus'ness make you stay, ...   166 Toland's Invit   39
"For shou'd you stay but one Week longer, ...   208 Fable Bitches   29
"Stay till my tender Cubs can find, ...   208 Fable Bitches   33
Stay--But let me see how finely will it Sound, ...   274 Epilogue   5
She can't abide to stay out late.   . . . .   293 Prog Marriage   98
Stay, let me see-- Three hundred pounds a year,   . . .   308 Billet Players   17
Owns all your favours; here intends to stay, ...   309 Billet Players   47
Whether he ought to stay or go.   . . . .   377 Apology Lady C   82
It is a sign we shan't stay here.   . . . .   419 Holyhead Journ   4
And thus the Dean is forc't to stay   . . . .   420 Holyhead   11

STAY	(CONTINUED)	PAGE	TITLE	LINE
She'll have 'em know she scorns to stay		746	Stel Distress	42
She vows she will no longer stay,		751	Stel Wood-Park	58
For if to Michaelmas you stay,		760	Receipt Youth	51
Bravely I resolved to stay.		834	Legion Club	132
My chin will not stay,		853	Lady's Lament	75
Tho' not a Soul would have him stay.		860	Lady Acheson	12
So much his Stay do's swell the Bills;		860	Lady Acheson	30
And, Captain, you'll do us the Favour to stay,		871	Grand Question	119
A Beast long-ear'd, and till Midnight you stay,		943	Probatur Alit	33
For why should you stay in that filthy hole,		1022	Nim-Dan-Dean 2	D 3
That wrote the Prologue, and if you stay with him,		1023	Nim-Dan-Dean 2	D 10
STAY'D				
Of which, as she grew up, there stay'd		693	Cadenus Vaness	218
STAYS				
Stays but to catch his utmost breath,		24	Ode Athenian	274
Stays till 'tis fair, yet seems to call a Coach.		138	City Shower	36
Comes up with, "Madam, Dinner stays;		447	Modern Lady	93
That Florimel wears Iron Stays:		449	Modern Lady	161
"I'm so uneasy in my Stays;		452	Modern Lady	242
And stays at home for want of Shoes:		728	Stella, Poems	28
Her Stays stick to her Heart,		733	Verses Vanessa	26
Or thrashing Babby in her new Stays.		788	Dick's Variety	30
In civil Language, if he stays		860	Lady Acheson	18
STEAD				
Despair and he lodge ever in its stead;		55	Temple Ill	128
And I must be hang'd in your Stead.		395	Dog and Thief	8
STEADILY				
So steadily the Senate guides:		391	Young's Satire	6
STEADY				
Your steady Soul preserves her Frame		243	Horace 4, 9	9
How steady in the Sterne he sat,		281	Journal	71
"In Exile with a steady Heart,		570	Death of Swift	431
STEAKS				
To feast on Ales and Steaks.		425	Five Ladies	4
STEAL				
Since knaves are ne'er oblig'd for what they steal.		45	To Congreve	66
Duly let out a Nights to Steal for Fees.		125	Descriptn Morn	16
And Steal to mend your Wages?		154	Widow and Cat	D 40
Steal by the Back-door out, and leave him there;		166	Toland's Invit	45
If I light on a Thought, he will certainly steal it,		265	Apollo	59
To climb to our Region, and thence to steal Fire;		266	Apollo	96
He strove to steal that Chain of Gold,		346	Prometheus	64
You'll fly when you get what you come here to steal,		395	Dog and Thief	7
And steal my Artichokes no more;		409	Dial Rich Marb	46
"To steal a Hint was never known,		565	Death of Swift	317
Pray steal me not, I'm Mrs. Dingley's		763	Collar Lap-Dog	1
"(For thou shalt steal thy Landlord's Mare)		851	Old Thorn	87
Not you, to steal your Master's Wine;		890	Panegyr Dean	98
As you can steal one, how 'twould please ye!		1033	Ans to Crown	14
STEALING				
A Stealing Brook, and strove to creep away		22	Ode Athenian	192
Is dress'd, and stealing thro' the Crowd,		377	Apology Lady C	77
For stealing Cows, nor could he read the Psalter.		826	Noisy Tom	14
STEALS				
And softly steals in many Windings down,		31	Ode to Temple	156
Steals from her Private Cell by Night,		99	Elegy Patrige	51
Steals thence his Plot, and ev'ry Joke,		107	V's House	59
So a Thief steals my Horse, and then gets him well drest		266	Apollo	92
Steals off to dose away his Beef,		279	Journal	40
Steals to her sleeping Spouse to Bed.		453	Modern Lady	293
Steals out her Hand by Nature led,		589	Strephon Chloe	171
And yet through ev'ry Motion steals.		726	To Stella	84
Like a Rogue that steals a Sheep:		800	Traulus 2	36
Steals from the Cully when he's drunk;		1033	Ans to Crown	2
STEALTH				
That no Physician dares prescribe by Stealth:		533	To Mr. Gay	78
Infus'd, yet as it were by Stealth,		693	Cadenus Vaness	216
Infecting thus our Hearts by Stealth;		895	Panegyr Dean	280
Some enter boldly, some by Stealth,		922	Riddle 7	31
STEAM				
All reeking in a cloudy Steam,		226	Prog of Beauty	14
But, when he smelt a noysom Steam		589	Strephon Chloe	179
Sent up to thee a grateful Steam.		894	Panegyr Dean	242
STEAMS				
Vapors and Steams her Looks disgrace,		226	Prog of Beauty	2
Soon licks up all unsav'ry steams;		432	Answer Paulus	8
Here Allum Flower to stop the Steams,		526	Lady's Dros Rm	27
No Humours gross, or frowzy Steams,		584	Strephon Chloe	11
From noxious Steams to purge the Air;		780	Mullinix Tim	250
By the Stygian Steams that flew,		834	Legion Club	123
STED SEE BED-STED				
STEDDYNESS				
Who, for our Steddyness are famous		618	Scandal Poem 1	40
STEDS SEE BED-STEDS				
STEED				
So when Troy Chair-men bore the Wooden Steed,		139	City Shower	47
The mettled and the vicious Steed		217	To Mr. Delany	61
The Steed, oppress'd, would break his Girth,		231	Prog of Poetry	29
His milk-white Steed upon it's haunches,		461	Birthday Song	35
But e'er you mount his mettled Steed,		666	Epig Carthy 2	D 3

	PAGE	TITLE	LINE
STEEDS			
With Brass two fiery Steeds he shod,	352	Wood Ironmongr	11
STEEL			
Britannia long will wear like steel	468	Birthday Song	243
Thus, Steel who own'd what other writ,	481	Libel on D- D-	49
Pierce us all with wounding Steel,	931	Riddle 18	D 21
Steel affords me present aid.	937	Riddle 24	D 42
STEEL-RIB'D			
Unlaces next her Steel-Rib'd Bodice;	582	Young Nymph	24
STEELE			
Was truer than Steele to the <Hanover> Line,	518	Dean Hang Rape	33
STEEP			
O'er mountains steep, o'er dusty plains,	403	Window Inns 10	D 5
STEEPLE SEE SHTEEPLE			
Became a Steeple with a Spire:	92	Bauc & Phil 1	96
The Chimny to a Steeple grown,	94	Bauc & Phil 1	139
But up against the Steeple rear'd,	94	Bauc & Phil 1	141
Became a Steeple with a Spire.	113	Bauc & Phil 2	56
The Chimney to a Steeple grown,	113	Bauc & Phil 2	77
But up against the Steeple rear'd,	113	Bauc & Phil 2	79
Why yonder Steeple wants a Spire,	126	Little House	2
And thus the Steeple got a Shock;	127	Little House	16
The Steeple, Knock, the Vicar, Walls.	127	Little House	18
And Castle roofs, and Steeple Spires.	257	Bubble	172
STEERAGE			
"While they who at the Steerage stood,	569	Death of Swift	413
Proud to attend you at the Steerage.	656	On Poetry	456
Dear Vessel, still be to thy Steerage just,	771	Horace 1, 14	53
STEERS			
Where-e'er Caprice or Folly steers.	687	Cadenus Vaness	38
STELLA			
With a certain false Traitress, one Stella by Name,	263	Apollo	30
Whilst Stella aforesaid stood by with the Light;	264	Apollo	36
That Stella was helping, abetting and aiding,	264	Apollo	39
And lastly for Stella, just out of her Prime,	266	Apollo	103
For, Stella has betray'd her Trust,	311	To Ford	2
Stella may vye with your Mountharmar:	313	To Ford	70
Stella this Day is thirty four,	721	Stel B-Day '18	1
However Stella, be not troubled,	721	Stel B-Day '18	3
To which (though late) shall Stella rise.	725	To Stella	54
E'er Stella can deceive a Friend.	725	To Stella	58
For Stella never learn'd the Art,	725	To Stella	71
Say, Stella, was Prometheus blind,	726	To Stella	85
Then Stella ran to my Relief	726	To Stella	101
What Stella by her Friendship warm'd,	726	To Stella	107
Thou Stella, wert no longer young,	728	Stella, Poems	9
Whom Stella chuses for a Friend.	728	Stella, Poems	24
Stella, when you these Lines transcribe,	730	Stella, Poems	83
Stella, for once you reason wrong;	731	Stella, Poems	131
Say, Stella, when you copy next,	732	Stella, Poems	137
Whom Stella freely entertains	735	Stel B-day '20	24
Thy Hints that Stella is no Chickin,	735	Stel B-day '20	42
That Stella loves to talk with Fellows	735	Stel B-day '20	44
While, Stella to your lasting Praise	739	Stel B-day '21	1
If Stella were unsung to Day;	741	Stel B-day 22	16
And Stella will be sung, while I	741	Stel B-day 22	33
Let Stella look with watchful Eye,	743	Stel B-day 22	59
Poor Stella must pack off to Town.	744	Stel Distress	2
Say, Stella, which you most repent	745	Stel Distress	21
Did Stella to his House invite,	745	Stel Distress	2
Good-natur'd Stella will forgive:	747	Stel Distress	58
Did Stella to his House invite:	749	Stel Wood-Park	2
Poor Stella must pack off to Town.	750	Stel Wood-Park	26
From me, Dear Stella, still be kind.	755	Stella '23	30
That Stella may avoid Disgrace	757	Stel B-day '24	13
But, Stella say, what evil Tongue	757	Stel B-day '24	35
Why, Stella, should you knit your Brow,	759	Receipt Youth	21
Nor ought of Stella, but the Name;	759	Receipt Youth	34
Or else poor Stella may be starv'd.	761	Bec's B-Day	38
Stella long dead, but first the Dean,	762	Bec's B-Day	46
Than the Dean storm, or Stella rattle.	762	Bec's B-Day	56
Say, Stella, feel you no Content,	764	Stel B-day '26	35
Believe me Stella, when you show	765	Stel B-day '26	67
STELLA'S			
But in Stella's bright Eyes were plac'd right again;	264	Apollo	50
Pallas observing Stella's Wit	723	To Stella	1
Let Stella's fair Example preach	724	To Stella	33
If I should Stella's Kindness hide	726	To Stella	95
Now, this is Stella's Case in Fact;	734	Stel B-day '20	15
The fainting Rays of Stella's Eyes:	735	Stel B-day '20	22
When Stella's Locks must all be grey	735	Stel B-day '20	48
And crowd to Stella's at fourscore.	736	Stel B-day '20	58
They must have Stella's of their own;	739	Stel B-day '21	16
By Duty bound, on Stella's Day;	740	Stel B-day 22	2
Nor do I ask for Stella's sake;	741	Stel B-day 22	31
With Stella's Praise to crown the Year.	743	Stel B-day 22	80
Than on a Nymph of Stella's Tast.	747	Stel Distress	64
Than on a Nymph of Stella's Taste.	752	Stel Wood-Park	80
With Stella's magisterial pride.	753	Gift for Bec	10
My verse on Stella's native day:	754	Stella '23	4
To raise up Stella's virtue higher;	755	Stella '23	22

STELLA'S (CONTINUED)	PAGE	TITLE	LINE
Then, think on Stella's chicken porridge;	761	Bec's B-Day	36
STENCH			
And up exhales a greasy Stench,	529	Lady's Dres Rm	107
Not the Stench of Lake Avernus,	834	Legion Club	125
STENTER			
Could roar as loud as Stenter,	785	Mullinex Dick	38
STEP			
Step to this Grave but once a Week,	101	Elegy Patrige	110
And step in Booths for Air.	122	Empty'ng Town	12
Step to the Doctor straight, and say,	172	Horace 1, 7	49
Scarce run a Step before they part;	290	Prog Marriage	32
But just a Step below the Crown:	392	Young's Satire	38
Stumbling at ev'ry Step she trod.	885	Rev Market-Hill	74
STEP'D			
You who thro' Frailty step'd aside,	579	Day Judgement	13
STEP'T			
Step't with a Jug, and made a Vent;	92	Bauc & Phil 1	70
STEPHEN			
"By Stephen Duck, upon the Queen.	563	Death of Swift	272
STEPHEN'S			
St James's Park and Stephen's Green;	313	To Ford	60
Yet still St. Stephen's Chappel open lies	538	Mr. Pulteney	7
STEPHEN'S-GREEN			
Form'd like the Triple-Tree near Stephen's-Green;	285	Elegy Boat	34
<STEPHENS>			
As the Hirelings of St. <Stephens>.	637	Epistle Lady	244
STEPPING			
And stepping o'er the Fabrick-roof,	127	Little House	33
Like stepping Stones to save a Stride,	645	On Poetry	169
STEPS SEE FOOT-STEPS,PARTY-STEPS,INFANT-STEPS			
Beneath thy decent Steps, the Road	324	Pethox	35
The Victor, when your Steps he trac'd,	326	Pethox	91
We'll watch your Steps where-e'er you go:	627	Scandal Poem 2	132
To kiss your Steps at Quilca Gates;	760	Receipt Youth	48
Thy graceful Steps, and Coll'nell's Air	779	Mullinix Tim	205
STEPT			
You strait stept in, and from the Monster's Jaws	12	Ode to William	D 23
Then stept aside to fetch 'em Drink,	112	Bauc & Phil 2	29
In a new World with Caution stept,	696	Cadenus Vaness	308
STERLINE'S			
Wise Hawthornden and Sterline's Lord.)	848	Old Thorn	16
STERLING			
Nor can four hundred thousand sterling Pound	233	Elegy on Demar	3
STERN			
Whether from War's stern God you claim	323	Pethox	11
Lur'd by the gilded Stern, and painted Sides.	771	Horace 1, 14	48
STERNE			
How steady in the Sterne he sat,	281	Journal	71
STEW			
Are not you, in a Crowd, when you sweat and you stew, sick?	1029	Dr. Helsham	9
STEWARD			
Yes, says the Steward,. . .	71	Mrs Harris Pet	32
His faithful Steward, in the Shades below.	234	Elegy on Demar	8
Then Master Steward takes my Rent, and tells me, honest Jo.	342	Upon His Grace	23
With hasty Zeal, behold, the Steward come,	533	To Mr. Gay	71
A Dext'rous Steward, when his Tricks are found,	535	To Mr. Gay	107
STEWARDS			
To Treasurers, Controllers, Stewards,	189	Faggot	16
STEWS			
These are the beaten methods of the stews,	44	To Congreve	19
a prater at Court in the Stile of the Stews	540	Charac Walpole	10
The Spawn of Bridewell, or the Stews;	641	On Poetry	36
And look'd like a Rake, who was made in the Stews sick;	1029	Dr. Helsham	18
STICK			
And cure You both with a good Stick.	91	Bauc & Phil 1	46
Resum'd the Figure of a Stick.	132	Magician's Rod	14
If the Stick be taken from the dead Sea.	147	Windsor Proph	14
Come Courtiers: Every Man his Stick:	190	Faggot	35
And he who will leap over a Stick for the King	389	Order of Bath	11
They stick athwart my maw	429	Beau's Reply	15
And ten to one drags down his feeble stick.	672	Epig Carthy 24	D 18
Her Stays stick to her Heart.	733	Verses Vanessa	26
That the Mitre wou'd never stick fast on their Head,	805	Irish Bishops	46
Whisper'd me, let down your Stick;	833	Legion Club	98
When a paradox you stick to,	908	Daphne	57
Nor slowly move your Fiddle stick,	958	Cantata	
One word shou'd stick thus in your gizzard.	983	Sher, A Goose	10
STICKS SEE WILLOW-STICKS			
Take up a well-bound Heap of Sticks.	189	Faggot	4
Prepar'd to leap o'er Sticks, or bind 'em.	190	Faggot	44
I'd teach her how to handle Sticks:	220	A Quiet Life	30
What clatt'ring of Sticks,	246	Irish-Feast	66
The Matter now no longer sticks;	300	Horrid Plot	59
No Butter sticks upon his Bread.	410	Dial Rich Marb	56
Are ten crooked sticks:	853	Lady's Lament	78
This Hamilton's Bawn, while it sticks on my Hand,	866	Grand Question	3
STIFF			
Hard, tough, cramp, gutt'rall, harsh, stiff Names.	467	Birthday Song	210

784

```
STIFLE                                                PAGE   TITLE            LINE
    If they would but lye quiet, and stifle their Voice,    .    519 Dean Hang Rape      63
    And my few Perfections stifle.    . . . . . . . .       631 Epistle Lady        62
    But a Genius like her's no Subject can stifle,    . . .    716 Answer Rebus       11
STIFLED
    Clio stifled with the Smell,    . . . . . . . .       834 Legion Club       121
STIL'D
    As Pies and Daws are often stil'd       . . . . . .    82 Salamander          3
    Since I'm Apollo stil'd by you,    . . . . . . . .    373 Letter D. S-y      51
    That Virtue, stil'd its own Reward,    . . . . . . .    764 Stel B-day '26     26
STILE
    Return'd 'em Thanks in homely Stile;    . . . . . .    115 Bauc & Phil 2     112
    You see just by the Church-yard Stile;    . . . . . .    127 Little House       14
    For Drury-lane to shape thy Stile:    . . . . . . .    181 Horace 2, 1        42
    Which (in their Stile) is purely hung.    . . . . . .    183 Horace 2, 1        82
    The Turn of Verse, nor Stile of Prose;    . . . . . .    515 Answer Fable       96
    a prater at Court in the Stile of the Stews    . . . .    540 Charac Walpole     10
    That same paultry Burlesque Stile:    . . . . . . .    631 Epistle Lady        50
    Clear your Looks, and smooth your Stile:    . . . . .    633 Epistle Lady      108
    Ill befits a lofty Stile.    . . . . . . . . .       634 Epistle Lady      140
    I the lofty Stile decline.    . . . . . . . . .      637 Epistle Lady      218
    Wou'd you have me change my Stile,    . . . . . . .    637 Epistle Lady      233
    Treat you in a Stile sublime,    . . . . . . . . .    638 Epistle Lady      256
    Above the Stars exalt your Stile,    . . . . . . . .    657 On Poetry         471
    And thus address thee in the Sailor Stile.    . . . .    770 Horace 1, 14        8
STILL
    (As those still do wh' have none at all)    . . . . .    8 Ode to King         84
    Still murmuring in their Wilderness for Food,    . . .    9 Ode to King         87
    Tho' we be of two different Factions still,    . . . .    18 Ode Athenian       72
    Still wear, still doat on his Invisible Ring.    . . .    21 Ode Athenian      157
    Still wear, still doat on his Invisible Ring.    . . .    21 Ode Athenian      157
    Still boasting of Her Great Unknown;    . . . . . .    24 Ode Athenian      251
    Still to be of the same exalted Sex with You.    . . .    24 Ode Athenian      267
    Which still the sooner it arrives,    . . . . . . .    24 Ode Athenian      279
    And that her troubled Ghost still haunts there since she    27 Ode to Temple     38
        dy'd;
    Still cast it up and nauseate Company.    . . . . . .    27 Ode to Temple     49
    What Serpent's that which still resorts,    . . . . .    30 Ode to Temple    116
    Still lurks in Palaces and Courts,    . . . . . . .    30 Ode to Temple    117
    (In pieces cut, the Viper still did reunite)    . . . .    30 Ode to Temple    132
    But foolish Man still judges what is best    . . . . .    36 Ode Sancroft       54
    Believe it firm, because perhaps the day is mild and still    37 Ode Sancroft       75
    Kind Star, still may'st thou shed thy sacred influence    39 Ode Sancroft      154
        here,
    Say, why the Church is still led blindfold by the State?    40 Ode Sancroft      177
    She still is welcome with her inn'cent song.    . . . .    49 To Congreve      182
    Our predecessors foot-steps, still in view;    . . . .    49 To Congreve      196
    Still ev'ry tree the pendent sorrow wears;    . . . .    51 Temple Ill         20
    Shrouds her still beams; how should the stars be seen?    53 Temple Ill         58
    And passing o'er, mistakes thee still for mine:    . . .    54 Temple Ill         92
    Still scatt'ring desolation where they go.    . . . .    55 Temple Ill        130
    Still to unhappy restless thoughts inclin'd;    . . . .    55 Temple Ill        132
    Still to be cheated, never to be pleas'd;    . . . . .    55 Temple Ill        148
    My Lord seems pleas'd, but still directs    . . . . .    64 Discovery          41
    But still, tho' fixt among the Stars,    . . . . . .    66 Problem            27
    Still at Whitehall it stands in view,    . . . . . .    87 Hist V's House     31
    It still was full up to the Top    . . . . . . . .    92 Bauc & Phil 1      77
    Still Groans while tatling Gossips prate.    . . . . .    93 Bauc & Phil 1     110
    Became a Clock, and still adher'd,    . . . . . . .    94 Bauc & Phil 1     142
    And still it's Love to Houshold Cares    . . . . . .    94 Bauc & Phil 1     143
    Thus Patrige still shines in each Art,    . . . . . .    100 Elegy Patrige     69
    May'st follow still thy Calling there.    . . . . . .    100 Elegy Patrige     74
    Does to his best look upward still.    . . . . . . .    101 Elegy Patrige    106
    To build in Speculation still.    . . . . . . . .      107 V's House          42
    'Twas still replenished to the Top,    . . . . . . .    112 Bauc & Phil 2     33
    Became a Clock, and still adher'd:    . . . . . . .    113 Bauc & Phil 2     80
    And still its Love to Household Cares    . . . . . .    113 Bauc & Phil 2     81
    Which still their antient Nature keep;    . . . . . .    114 Bauc & Phil 2    105
    Methinks, I still wou'd call it mine:    . . . . . .    115 Bauc & Phil 2    114
    Is but a Still which wants a Spout.    . . . . . . .    128 Little House       42
    Yet, still so happy was his Fate,    . . . . . . .    134 Magician's Rod     47
    To rail; she singing, still whirls on her Mop.    . . .    137 City Shower        22
    But aided by the Wind, fought still for Life;    . . . .    137 City Shower        24
    But still I'm in Principle ever the same,    . . . . .    144 New Song           25
    And Englond wouldst thou be happy still,    . . . . .    148 Windsor Proph      25
    But more inclining to sit still.    . . . . . . . .    170 Horace 1, 7        12
    Still blushes, and with speed retires,    . . . . . .    178 To Lord Harley     71
    Yet Mum for that, hope still the best,    . . . . . .    182 Horace 2, 1        69
    Yet, still was at the Tables of the Great.    . . . . .    194 Author Himself     16
    Yet still you think your Friend to blame.    . . . . .    218 To Mr. Delany      82
    Though still in Sight, had chang'd their Ground.    . . .    226 Prog of Beauty     32
    Grown fat with Corn and Sitting still,    . . . . . .    230 Prog of Poetry      3
    Your Guinnea's but a Guinnea still.    . . . . . . .    255 Bubble            124
    And Still the Madness of the Crowd.    . . . . . . .    258 Bubble            212
    And still as he writ, stood smiling and reading;    . . .    264 Apollo             40
    Still brings us Hares when he can catch them:    . . . .    281 Journal            74
    The Nymph who still with Passion burnd,    . . . . . .    293 Prog Marriage     117
    I'm still to seek which Dog you mean;    . . . . . .    298 Horrid Plot        19
    If you have London still at heart    . . . . . . .    313 To Ford            57
    Still pleas'd with the good-natur'd Noise,    . . . . .    322 First of April     33
    And still the bloody Field frequent,    . . . . . . .    324 Pethox             17
```

785

STILL   (CONTINUED)   PAGE   TITLE   LINE

Line	PAGE	TITLE	LINE
And then your old Argument still will return:	336	Serious Poem	63
And still the Truth he will Maintain, whate'er he loses by't.	341	Upon His Grace	6
. . . yet still there comes a Season	341	Upon His Grace	7
To beg his Favour is the Way new Favours still to win,	341	Upon His Grace	13
Both Church and State, being still dependent.	372	Letter D. S-y	22
They are as once, and Idem still.	373	Letter D. S-y	50
To shine the more still rising higher)	385	Manly Virtue	54
And still her favourites we meet,	401	Window Inns 5	D 9
O Neptune! Neptune! must I still	403	Window Inns 10	D 1
But, hope to see you flourish still.	411	Dial Rich Marb	102
But, still at Variance with each other,	412	Desire Possess	10
Still seen o'r'e many an Alehouse fire.	461	Birthday Song	38
For thunder still his arm supplyes,	461	Birthday Song	41
Thou still with Battles stuff thy head full	462	Birthday Song	55
Yet still you must consult the Maps,	467	Birthday Song	240
For still you're short (which grieves your Spirit)	475	Epist on Epist	27
Yet still you fancy you inherit	478	Epist on Epist	97
This may be true--submitting still	484	Libel on D- D-	121
"Perhaps, may feel Compassion still,	485	Libel on D- D-	168
It still your Constitution hits.	493	Panegyr Swift	18
Then keep your Virtue still unmixt,	503	Doctor Delaney	107
He still was comforted to find	528	Lady's Dres Rm	87
And still appearing in Contrast.	529	Lady's Dres Rm	128
Yet still St. Stephen's Chappel open lies	538	Mr. Pulteney	7
Yet still I fear your Work is done but Half;	538	Mr. Pulteney	13
atchieving of nothing Still promising wonders	540	Charac Walpole	5
"But, still our Monarchy wou'd leave us---.	549	Life of Swift	155
Oh, were the Wretch but living still,	560	Death of Swift	193
"Who still were true, to please his Foes.	567	Death of Swift	364
But, still the hardest Part remains.	586	Strephon Chloe	71
To keep her Spouse deluded still,	588	Strephon Chloe	143
That Fortune still assists the bold,	588	Strephon Chloe	148
Would still the same Ideas give ye,	591	Strephon Chloe	247
They still must practise to maintain it.	592	Strephon Chloe	266
Your Friendship shall continue still:	593	Strephon Chloe	312
They still can do so every Day)	601	Beasts Confess	2
Still to lash, and lashing Smile,	634	Epistle Lady	139
Sit still, and swallow down your Spittle.	644	On Poetry	122
If still you be dispos'd to rhime,	645	On Poetry	145
Remains a Difficulty still,	652	On Poetry	367
You still are low ten thousand Mile.	657	On Poetry	472
Still their Authority was smaller.	690	Cadenus Vaness	115
But still the Work was not compleat,	692	Cadenus Vaness	184
For placing still some Book betwixt,	701	Cadenus Vaness	480
Yet still resolv'd to spare no Cost;	702	Cadenus Vaness	493
For Nature must be Nature still.	705	Cadenus Vaness	587
Wou'd still her Dignity maintain,	705	Cadenus Vaness	595
Two Maxims she could still produce,	705	Cadenus Vaness	606
Still to the Sea their Course incline;	709	Cadenus Vaness	721
She still determines what is best:	725	To Stella	60
Variety we still Pursue,	728	Stella, Poems	17
But Virtue still to Virtue tends.	733	Verses Vanessa	12
Then Cloe, still go on to prate	735	Stel B-day '20	39
And still encreasing in her Airs	746	Stel Distress	34
Still to be curious, never hearken	753	Gift for Bec	22
From me, Dear Stella, still be kind.	755	Stella '23	30
Tho' I continue still a brute.	755	Stella '23	32
But I'll be still your Friend in Prose:	757	Stel B-day '24	30
Thus you may still be young to me,	758	Stel B-day '24	51
Still be she curious, never hearken	762	Bec's B-Day	43
Shall still be kept with Joy by me:	763	Stel B-day '26	2
And, had it not been still supply'd,	765	Stel B-day '26	57
And still continued by the last:	765	Stel B-day '26	64
Her matchless Sons; whose Valour still remains	771	Horace 1, 14	43
Dear Vessel, still be to thy Steerage just,	771	Horace 1, 14	53
Retire, yet still bemoan their Country's Fate.	772	Horace 1, 14	60
You Clutter still your Brazen Kettle.	775	Mullinix Tim	46
You still divert with merry Stories;	778	Mullinix Tim	148
Ne're hold my peace, and ne'er stand still.	778	Mullinix Tim	160
To better Judgments still submitting,	788	Dick's Variety	9
Thou still with Tyrants in Succession curst,	793	St. Pat's Well	83
But still insist the Man is mad.	796	Traulus 1	22
He still has Gratitude and Sap'ence,	796	Traulus 1	27
Still swarm and buzz about his Nose?	798	Traulus 1	87
Yet still the <Dean> on Freedom raves,	799	Traulus 1	99
Changing still, and still adhering,	799	Traulus 2	10
Changing still, and still adhering,	799	Traulus 2	10
In spite of the Devil would still be untoward.	804	Irish Bishops	26
But if, still obdurate, your anger remains,	819	Archbi Cashel	11
If still your foul bosom more rancour contains;	819	Archbi Cashel	12
He's still a Christian more than they.	820	Dr. Rundle	20
There is a Reason still more weighty;	820	Dr. Rundle	23
Yet still has Impudence to rise,	824	Printer Newgat	13
Half the best are still behind:	839	Legion Club	236
I should never sit still:	852	Lady's Lament	38
He's still finding fault,	853	Lady's Lament	61
But still to the Dean:	854	Lady's Lament	88
Beg you would here continue still,	860	Lady Acheson	26
I'll have Youth and Beauty still.	863	To Janus	30

STILL	(CONTINUED)	PAGE	TITLE	LINE

STILL (CONTINUED)

	PAGE	TITLE	LINE
In Spight of Envy flourish still,	875	Drapier's Hill	19
And Drapier's-hill been still Drumlack;	877	To Dean Swift	32
And then, to mend the Matter still;	888	Panegyr Dean	35
But still, whene'er you Silence break,	889	Panegyr Dean	71
Yet, some Devotion still remains	896	Panegyr Dean	299
Still rapt in speculations deep,	900	Dean's Reasons	45
He still may keep a pack of knaves	902	Dean's Reasons	109
For, why should I continue still	902	Dean's Reasons	113
If Chloe were a Sharper still,	905	Death Daphne	77
Still her odd perverseness shows	906	Daphne	15
Or in folly still befriend her,	907	Daphne	27
My Constancy is still the same.	916	Riddle 2	8
I'm but a Meer Depender still:	918	Riddle 4	20
And still, the more I show my Art,	920	Riddle 6	17
More precious Juice than from a Still.	920	Riddle 6	22
To Strephon I have still been true,	924	Riddle 8	3
Never speaking, still awake,	933	Riddle 20	D 1
I'm still the same --- but ever new.	935	Riddle 23	D 6
Growing old, grow still the fairer.	936	Riddle 24	D 8
A smile still ready at command,	951	Upstart	D 29
Yet still are no wiser than we were at first.	967	Letter Sherid	4
Yet still you are out (tho' to vex you I'm loth),	976	Dean to Sherid	17
Are you still in your cart with convitia ex plaustro?	979	Dean to Tho: S	6
Nay, hector and swagger, you'll still find me stanch,	979	Dean to Tho: S	13
So your eternal pen is still,	983	Sher, A Goose	21
Who when I fought still cut me down,	1005	Sheridan's Sub	8
One Letter still another Locks;	1021	Nim-Dan-Dean 1	D 25
Would you get still more?	1038	Sheridan Cavan	13

STILL-BORN

	PAGE	TITLE	LINE
Your still-born Poems shall revive,	394	Grub-Street	7

STING

	PAGE	TITLE	LINE
Death's sting is swallow'd up in victory at last,	40	Ode Sancroft	201
Would hiss, and sting, and roll, and twist,	132	Magician's Rod	11
"Whose Protestation hides a Sting	550	Life of Swift	172
Nor dread the Adder's Tooth, nor Scorpion's Sting.	792	St. Pat's Well	42

STINGS

	PAGE	TITLE	LINE
She turns to Envy, Stings and Hisses:	554	Death of Swift	36
The <Dean> hath felt their Stings before;	798	Traulus 1	85

STINK

	PAGE	TITLE	LINE
And needs must stink when e're it dies;	9	Ode to King	110
And end as it began, in Vapour, Stink, and Scum.	10	Ode to King	129
Strike your offended Sense with double Stink.	137	City Shower	6
And honest Harry is too apt to stink.	166	Toland's Invit	38
All Christian vittals stink of fish	420	Holyhead	3
Which waft a Stink round every Room.	529	Lady's Dres Rm	114
No cleanly Workman can endure the Stink.	535	To Mr. Gay	128
But Nonsense wrapt up in a Stink)	775	Mullinix Tim	64
That when I strut, and stair, and stink,	778	Mullinix Tim	166
And let them rot, or hang, or stink.	799	Traulus 1	102
Let them stare and stink together;	835	Legion Club	154
Jove ever form'd to make a <Stink>?	65	Problem	4
Which brings a <Stink> from ev'ry Pore,	65	Problem	9
I'm sure, 'twas I that smelt the <Stink>.	67	Problem	54
You smell the <Stink>? by <God> you lye,	67	Problem	55
"Relaxing downwards in a <Stink>?	305	Storm	68
He left behind so great a <stink>.	296	Satiric Elegy	16

STINKING

	PAGE	TITLE	LINE
And ev'ry stinking weed so lofty grows,	37	Ode Sancroft	103
They vanish'd in a stinking Smoak.	134	Magician's Rod	58
Drown'd Puppies, stinking Sprats, all drench'd in Mud,	139	City Shower	62
The stinking Load of all the Crimes,	497	Panegyr Swift	116
Stain'd with the Marks of stinking Toes;	527	Lady's Dres Rm	52
To stinking Smoak it turns the Flame	529	Lady's Dres Rm	105
Because she rose from stinking Ooze?	530	Lady's Dres Rm	132
Thorow stinking Lanes and Allies;	574	Helter Skelter	42
Find great Society in Stinking.	590	Strephon Chloe	210
To Liffy's stinking Tide in Dublin:	750	Stel Wood-Park	28

STINKS

	PAGE	TITLE	LINE
Mopsa, who stinks her Spouse to Death,	449	Modern Lady	156
Each Dame he sees with all her Stinks:	529	Lady's Dres Rm	122
Surrounded with a Hundred Stinks,	583	Young Nymph	48
Foulest Brute that stinks below,	786	Clad in Brown	1

STINT

	PAGE	TITLE	LINE
To stint me at Night to one Bottle of Wine;	867	Grand Question	16

STINTED

	PAGE	TITLE	LINE
Now stinted in the short'ning Day,	280	Journal	51

STIPEND

	PAGE	TITLE	LINE
Where Phoebus pays a scanty Stipend,	883	Rev Market-Hill	3

STIR

	PAGE	TITLE	LINE
Nay, --now I cannot stir my Foot:	116	Bauc & Phil 2	161
All that you make this Stir about,	128	Little House	41
So never offer'd once to stir,	172	Horace 1, 7	53
To snuff the Lights, and stir the Fire,	483	Libel on D- D-	107
Tim thour't the Punch to stir up trouble in;	777	Mullinix Tim	138
In vain--for the Devil a Parson wou'd stir.	804	Irish Bishops	20
You shan't stir a Foot--You'll think me a Clown--	869	Grand Question	78
She'll not have Pow'r to stir an Inch;	885	Rev Market-Hill	66
And, wheezing Asthma, loth to stir:	895	Panegyr Dean	276
Teach Dennis how to stir the Guile:	897	Panegyr Dean	330

		PAGE	TITLE	LINE
STIR'D				
You ne'er was known, by Passion stir'd,		889	Panegyr Dean	69
STIRR'D				
Lord help me, said Mary, I never stirr'd out of this Place!		70	Mrs Harris Pet	16
So when our passions Love hath stirr'd,		402	Window Inns 6	D 3
Hum--excellent good--your anger was stirr'd:		976	Dean to Sherid	7
STIRRING				
Without stirring out,		939	Riddle Answerd	10
STIRS				
Apollo stirs not out of dore		621	Scandal Poem 1	121
Apollo stirs not out of Door,		627	Scandal Poem 2	115
STITCHES				
Will ne'er be smooth, nor hold the Stitches.		1021	Nim-Dan-Dean 1	D 18
STIVER				
A Stiver or a Skellin		442	Ballyspellin	75
STOCK				
A Stock of Wisdom and Philosophy,		19	Ode Athenian	98
Spend all our present Stock in hopes of golden Rules.		27	Ode to Temple	27
By vile pretenders, who a stock maintain		45	To Congreve	57
. . .is a very small Stock,		69	Mrs Harris Pet	6
A Stock of tawdry Stuff besides,		80	Vanbrug House	46
In Stock three hundred thousand Pounds;		251	Bubble	17
When Stock is high they come between,		253	Bubble	69
And from my own Stock, provided with Topicks,		265	Apollo	83
Could change the Stock, or cog a Dye,		607	Beasts Confess	193
To earn a Stock of Pence and Praise,		642	On Poetry	66
Of pious Prelates what a Stock		656	On Poetry	453
'Twere grafting on an annual Stock		729	Stella, Poems	65
And, had her Stock been less, no doubt		735	Stel B-day '20	31
And thus, my Stock of Wit decay'd;		740	Stel B-day '21	17
The Magpye, lighting on the Stock,		849	Old Thorn	33
With Colonies might stock around		903	Death Daphne	17
STOCK-JOBBER				
The Stock-jobber thus, from Change-Alley goes down,		396	Dog and Thief	9
STOCK'D				
Stock'd with the freshest gibberish of the town;		47	To Congreve	120
STOCK'T				
Stock't with Repartees and Jokes,		523	Betty Grizette	17
STOCKBRIDGE				
And thou at Stockbridge wert not bit)		182	Horace 2, 1	60
STOCKING				
One greasy Stocking round his head,		594	Cassinus Peter	12
Or patch his broken Stocking Soals,		728	Stella, Poems	33
Mary said he, (one Day, as I was mending my Master's Stocking,)		986	Mary to Sher	28
STOCKINGS				
His Waistcoat and Stockings, and Breeches were white,		399	Tom Clinch	5
The Stockings, why shou'd I expose,		527	Lady's Dres Rm	51
If your Stockings were off, you cou'd show cloven Feet.		805	Irish Bishops	52
STOCKS				
One swore he'd send 'em to the Stocks,		91	Bauc & Phil 1	33
Yet our Stocks rise Cent. per Cent,		169	Peace Dunkirk	26
What! I suppose now Stocks are high,		175	Horace 1, 7	127
Which stupify'd them all to stocks.		178	To Lord Harley	46
a Jobber of Stocks by retailing false news		540	Charac Walpole	9
Since all he got by Fraud, is lost by Stocks,		678	Dean and Duke	6
You threaten the stocks: I say you are scurrilous,		976	Dean to Sherid	31
STOFFE				
From Toune of Stoffe to fattyn Londe		102	Merlin	6
STOIC				
And is a Stoic in her own.		754	Stella '23	18
STOICK				
That you, friend Marcus, like a stoick		676	Parson's Case	1
STOICK'S				
Might well excuse a Stoick's Rage.		603	Beasts Confess	58
STOICKS				
What Stoicks call without our Power,		729	Stella, Poems	63
Where stubborn Stoicks would complain.		765	Stel B-day '26	50
STOL'N				
I'll make it appear that they're all stol'n Ware:		265	Apollo	64
STOLE				
Before this Milk-white Heifer can be stole away,		8	Ode to King	77
He twitcht his sleeve, and stole a word,		63	Discovery	19
Ere Mornings dawn stole out to spy		63	Discovery	35
However, she stole away my Garters, . .		70	Mrs Harris Pet	19
And softly stole to discompose her own.		124	Descriptn Morn	4
Stole to the Pantry-Door, and found		150	Corinna	18
He scratch'd her Maid, he stole the Cream,		153	Widow and Cat	D 11
He only stole Hints; the Verse is correct;		266	Apollo	90
She stole away with much ado,		292	Prog Marriage	94
Fine Words; I wonder where you stole 'um.		348	Whitshed Motto	2
You had good Reason when you stole 'um.		349	Whitshed Motto	26
Stole in, and took a strict Survey,		526	Lady's Dres Rm	7
Disgusted Strephon stole away		529	Lady's Dres Rm	116
A wicked Rat her Plaister stole,		583	Young Nymph	59
When Chloe stole your Heart away,		591	Strephon Chloe	236
No: 'Twas for you alone he stole		726	To Stella	87
STOLEN				
In Physick, Stolen Goods, or Love,		101	Elegy Patrige	115
Having stolen from mine Hostess,		574	Helter Skelter	32

STOMACH	PAGE	TITLE	LINE
Is maukish, and his Stomach gone;	291	Prog Marriage	60
"His Stomach too begins to fail:	557	Death of Swift	111
From stomach sharp, and hearty feeding	745	Stel Distress	7
And pull your haughty Stomach down,	748	Stel Distress	72
From Stomach sharp and hearty feeding,	750	Stel Wood-Park	31
And pull your haughty Stomach down;	752	Stel Wood-Park	88
'Til coffee has her stomach lin'd;	761	Bec's B-Day	34
In stomach or limb.	853	Lady's Lament	58
Your Stomach they settle;	953	Oysters	7
With me you'll no more have a Stomach to Dine	1017	Swift Ans Sher	15

STOMACHS

	PAGE	TITLE	LINE
To Stomachs clog'd with costly Fare,	378	Apology Lady C	105

STONE

	PAGE	TITLE	LINE
And Sisiphus lay sleeping on his Stone.	9	Ode to King	97
Like the Philosopher's Stone,	26	Ode to Temple	15
A Song could draw a Stone or Beam,	79	Vanbrug House	3
A Verse could draw a Stone or Beam	106	V's House	3
We look for a Salmon, you leave us a Stone.	287	Bank Down	8
To keep out of Danger, a Doublet of Stone.	351	Wood Insect	10
Under this Stone, lies Dicky and Dolly	430	Dicky Dolly	1
Half convert me to a Stone.	838	Legion Club	196
A Stone and a quarter of Beef from my Sirloin.	867	Grand Question	18
And then, with Heart more hard than Stone,	915	Riddle 1	13

STONES

	PAGE	TITLE	LINE
Without, they pelted him with Stones,	221	A Quiet Life	52
Like stepping Stones to save a Stride,	645	On Poetry	169
Who bring the Lime, or place the Stones;	727	Stella, Poems	3
Crack the Stones, and melt the Lead;	830	Legion Club	26
That rais'd between the Stones their daily Shoots;	880	Pastoral Dial	4
Than strongest Weeds that grow these Stones betwixt:	880	Pastoral Dial	10
My Spud these Nettles from the Stones can part,	881	Pastoral Dial	11
Sharp are the Stones, take thou this rushy Matt;	881	Pastoral Dial	19
Was bid to throw the Stones behind;	922	Riddle 7	46
Though his Claret is bad, and he foots it on Stones,	1037	Four Storyes	7

STONY

	PAGE	TITLE	LINE
For how can stony Bowels melt,	561	Death of Swift	215

STOOD

	PAGE	TITLE	LINE
And stood 'twixt Him and every Fate:	8	Ode to King	66
While all the rest stood gaping round	63	Discovery	24
Our Listner stood a while confus'd,	64	Discovery	45
He stood behind a Stall to lurk,	86	Hist V's House	15
And there stood fastned to a Joyst,	92	Bauc & Phil 1	98
And there stood fast'ned to a Joist,	113	Bauc & Phil 2	58
And stood up firm for Right Divine:	115	Bauc & Phil 2	134
On Tiptoe stood and rear'd his Snout,	127	Little House	25
That, senseless, in a Corner stood,	132	Magician's Rod	8
Stood without Motion, like a Stake.	133	Magician's Rod	34
And he stood there to take them in.	134	Magician's Rod	56
I had my Advantage, and stood at Defiance,	144	New Song	31
That Her <Majesty> stood in great need of a Tutor,	144	New Song	41
Whilst Stella aforesaid stood by with the Light;	264	Apollo	36
And still as he writ, stood smiling and reading;	264	Apollo	40
Now hear an old Tale. There antiently stood	334	Serious Poem	17
Jove stood amaz'd, but looking round,	346	Prometheus	47
The Doctor stood not to debate,	378	Apology Lady C	93
A skill'd Mechanick that has stood,	393	Modern Poets	11
But the Company stood in Defence of the Dame,	517	Dean Hang Rape	15
"But never stood in Awe before 'em:	566	Death of Swift	340
"For her she prepar'd to die;	566	Death of Swift	348
"For her he boldly stood alone;	566	Death of Swift	349
"While they who at the Steerage stood,	569	Death of Swift	413
Stood Hymen with a flaming Torch.	585	Strephon Chloe	48
His Jordan stood in Manner fitting	594	Cassinus Peter	21
And then stood where it first begun.	690	Cadenus Vaness	125
The Nymph stood silent out of spight,	699	Cadenus Vaness	406
Thy Mast, which like some aged Patriot stood	770	Horace 1, 14	15
As those who long have stood the Storms of State,	772	Horace 1, 14	59
There stood for many a hundred Years	848	Old Thorn	3
Stood chatt'ring with incessant Din;	849	Old Thorn	34
When you with Oonah stood behind a Ditch,	882	Pastoral Dial	37

STOOL   SEE DUCKING-STOOL

	PAGE	TITLE	LINE
For he says, short as 'tis, it will give you a stool.	980	Tho: Sheridan	8
Works in my Lord by <Stool> and Sweat,	65	Problem	8

STOOLS

	PAGE	TITLE	LINE
Stools, Tables, Chairs, and Bed-steds broke:	1035	To Quilca	4

STOOP

	PAGE	TITLE	LINE
Of those you so ignobly stoop to fear;	46	To Congreve	86
"Stoop not to int'rest, flattery, or deceit;	55	Temple Ill	138
If e'er I stoop beneath a crown'd Head:	410	Dial Rich Marb	74
Sure, you are not asham'd to stoop;	699	Cadenus Vaness	401
At entring you might see her stoop	746	Stel Distress	29
At going in you saw her stoop	746	Stel Distress	
At coming in you saw her stoop;	751	Stel Wood-Park	49

STOOPING

	PAGE	TITLE	LINE
See the Bird of Juno stooping.	661	Love Song	31

STOOPS

	PAGE	TITLE	LINE
Nor stoops to take the Staff, nor lays it down,	210	Earl of Oxford	9
"How from his Altitude he stoops,	462	Birthday Song	73

STOP

	PAGE	TITLE	LINE
You fly, invoke the Gods; then turning, stop	137	City Shower	21

STOP	(CONTINUED)	PAGE	TITLE	LINE
For John must neither light nor stop;		223	Prog of Love	36
Hear one Story more and then I will stop.		337	Serious Poem	109
Too scornful now to stop his Pace,		412	Desire Possess	33
He knew to stop a quater trois.		456	Dean Smedley	30
Here Allum Flower to stop the Steams,		526	Lady's Dres Rm	27
If Strephon would but stop his Nose;		530	Lady's Dres Rm	136
But would not have him stop my View;		554	Death of Swift	18
His triple-barking Mouth to Stop:		647	On Poetry	214
Or stop and light at Cloe's Head		735	Stel B-day '20	37
But, stop ambitious Muse, in time;		896	Panegyr Dean	319
...for Corks to stop your Bottles, with a Vengeance.		1013	Swift to Sheri	5
You see I won't stop,		1015	Swift to Sheri	53

STOP'D
| He stop'd, and cou'd not tell what ail'd him. | | 376 | Apology Lady C | 34 |

STOPP'D
| As the Coach stopp'd, she look'd & swore | | 746 | Stel Distress | 27 |
| As the Coach stopp'd, she look'd & swore | | 746 | Stel Distress | |

STOPPING
| In finding Ways and Means, and stopping Gaps: | | 535 | To Mr. Gay | 122 |

STOPS
Whene'er I mourn, stops my complaining Breath,		32	Ode to Temple	197
Apply'd at Bottom stops it's Course,		93	Bauc & Phil 1	102
Apply'd at Bottom, stops its Course,		113	Bauc & Phil 2	62
"And feel my Pulse, I know it stops:		451	Modern Lady	207
Stops thus, and turns with ev'ry Wind;		688	Cadenus Vaness	58
The Dean never stops,		852	Lady's Lament	11

STOPT
But now stopt by some hidden Pow'rs		93	Bauc & Phil 1	133
He pull'd the String, and stopt his Coach,		172	Horace 1, 7	61
I'm stopt by all the Fools I meet,		202	Horace 2, 6	91
A Cloud arose and stopt the Light,		253	Bubble	75
That she stopt in her Course to look on them both;		264	Apollo	38
He stopt at the George for a Bottle of Sack,		399	Tom Clinch	3
The Coachman stopt, she lookt, and swore		751	Stel Wood-Park	47

STOR'D
And then get off with Money stor'd,		253	Bubble	62
"The Garden stor'd with artless Flowers,		476	Epist on Epist	51
With a Dozen large Vessels my Vault shall be stor'd,		867	Grand Question	13

STORE
By starving in the midst of Store,		157	Fable of Midas	49
I ask not to increase my Store,		198	Horace 2, 6	8
Then if cutting down Wood brings Money good Store,		334	Serious Poem	15
First, Love In A Tub: 'Squire Wood has in Store		337	Serious Poem	95
Has ev'ry Repartee in Store,		416	Woman's Mind	11
But, we shall keep revenge in store		622	Scandal Poem 1	173
Two Bottles call'd for, (half her Store,		747	Stel Distress	49
Two Bottles call'd for, (half her Store;		751	Stel Wood-Park	65
And then supporting with your Store,		764	Stel B-day '26	39
And from his endless hoarded Store,		875	Drapier's Hill	7
Preserve his health, his store increase;		902	Dean's Reasons	101

STORES
| Or, whether op'ning all his Stores, | | 924 | Riddle 7 | 87 |

STORIES
Once on a time, as old Stories reherse,		76	Lady B- B-	1
Might raise a House about two Stories;		106	V's House	10
Discoursing on old Stories past,		116	Bauc & Phil 2	152
But, some will cry, Turn-Coat, and rip up old Stories,		143	New Song	21
Their ups and downs, with fifty Stories		181	Horace 2, 1	18
Who tell us these troublesome stories,		186	Scriblerus 4	D 3
These Stories were, of old, design'd		478	Epist on Epist	83
Plyes you with Stories o'er and o'er,		556	Death of Swift	89
Faith, he must make his Stories shorter,		556	Death of Swift	95
"He knew an hundred pleasant Stories,		572	Death of Swift	475
Four Stories climbing to her Bow'r;		581	Young Nymph	8
You still divert with merry Stories;		778	Mullinix Tim	148

STORM
The first of Plants after the Thunder, Storm, and Rain		16	Ode Athenian	28
Disturb the present Mitre, as that fearful storm of late,		40	Ode Sancroft	192
So when the War has rais'd a Storm		84	Salamander	37
He'd give his Orders for a Storm;		302	Storm	4
A Storm, to drown that Rascal <Hort>,		302	Storm	5
While thus they rail, and scold, and storm,		453	Modern Lady	270
Not to direct a Plague, or Storm,		496	Panegyr Swift	93
Wou'd make him rage, and storm, and fret,		546	Life of Swift	28
Foretell a storm to last till night.		618	Scandal Poem 1	32
Foretel a Storm to last till Night.		624	Scandal Poem 2	26
I may storm and rage in vain;		636	Epistle Lady	209
Than the Dean storm, or Stella rattle.		762	Bec's B-Day	56
Revile and slander, fume and storm,		778	Mullinix Tim	167
He now began to storm and rave;		783	Tim and Fables	28
Let them stare and storm and frown,		831	Legion Club	55
Admits us in, to storm the Fortress;		885	Rev Market-Hill	70

STORMING
| Is by Laughing, not by Storming. | | 637 | Epistle Lady | 230 |

STORMS
| Such were the storms good Sancroft long has borne; | | 40 | Ode Sancroft | 198 |
| As those who long have stood the Storms of State, | | 772 | Horace 1, 14 | 59 |

STORMY
| Whom Roguish Boys in Stormy Nights | | 100 | Elegy Patrige | 91 |
| 'Till Pow'r, discharging all her stormy Bags, | | 771 | Horace 1, 14 | 29 |

STORY

	PAGE	TITLE	LINE
Stay while I tell my story, short, and true;	46	To Congreve	111
One Story high, one postern Door,	81	Vanbrug House	77
In antient Time, as Story tells	90	Bauc & Phil 1	1
In antient Times, as Story tells,	111	Bauc & Phil 2	1
Midas, we are in Story told,	156	Fable of Midas	1
If possible, to learn his Story,	171	Horace 1, 7	21
"At last--and so the Story ends.	181	Horace 2, 1	48
But now, to make my Story Short	220	A Quiet Life	25
Hear one Story more and then I will stop.	337	Serious Poem	109
Whatever Grecian Story tells:	482	Libel on D- D-	78
You shew you Skill in Grecian Story,	483	Libel on D- D-	97
Assert that Hyde in writing story	489	Dialogue	25
And 'tis as true, or Story lies,	495	Panegyr Swift	74
For, I have heard another Story,	547	Life of Swift	82
"And make her infamous in Story.	568	Death of Swift	388
Are Stale, and Worn as Troy-Town Story.	774	Mullinix Tim	36
To shorten my Tale, (for I hate a long Story,)	871	Grand Question	129
He need not tell a Story twice,	878	Robbin & Harry	14
Not a jest, or hum'rous story,	908	Daphne	65
. . . and I don't believe that's a true Story,	986	Mary to Sher	20

STORYES

	PAGE	TITLE	LINE
Would raise a House about two Storyes;	79	Vanbrug House	10
Soon reard a House two Storyes high;	86	Hist V's House	6

STOUT

	PAGE	TITLE	LINE
Who'll write my Panegyrick?---come, be stout:	671	Epig Carthy 24	D 4
Surprize him with a Pint of Stout,	728	Stella, Poems	32
For Liberty a Champion stout,	820	Dr. Rundle	31
And, Madam, I always believ'd you so stout,	869	Grand Question	55
Tho' a Lady, I am stout,	933	Riddle 20	D 19

STOUTLY

	PAGE	TITLE	LINE
Went triumphant to Church, and sang stoutly Te Deum:	967	Letter Sherid	18

STRAIGHT

	PAGE	TITLE	LINE
And straight deny you to be Men, or any thing at all;	19	Ode Athenian	120
Impatient of all Answers, straight became	22	Ode Athenian	191
Step to the Doctor straight, and say,	172	Horace 1, 7	49
Yet, why should we be lac'd so straight;	657	On Poetry	487

STRAIN

	PAGE	TITLE	LINE
And in some untouch'd Virgin Strain	30	Ode to Temple	136
In higher Strain than we began.	80	Vanbrug House	58
She'll strain a Point, and sit astride,	100	Elegy Patrige	86
Where, in the Strolers Canting Strain,	111	Bauc & Phil 2	11
Sing my Praise in Strain sublime:	631	Epistle Lady	57
Treat you in Heroick Strain.	634	Epistle Lady	136
Can wish to die, in strain heroick,	676	Parson's Case	2
But in a mild dejected Strain,	704	Cadenus Vaness	572
Talks in a high Romantick Strain;	712	Cadenus Vaness	821
We may, while they strain their Throats,	831	Legion Club	61
For he was fond of rural Strain.	848	Old Thorn	12
Strain their Necks with looking back:	863	To Janus	22
Sing heavenly Muse in sweetly flowing Strain,	880	Pastoral Dial	7
Let Lawyers bawl and strain their Throats,	930	Riddle 15	D 25

STRAINED

	PAGE	TITLE	LINE
Phil wish't, that she had strain'd a Limb	224	Prog of Love	81
Is strained thro' Glasses.	938	Riddle Answerd	6

STRAININGS

	PAGE	TITLE	LINE
Distortions, Groanings, Strainings, Heavings;	591	Strephon Chloe	241

STRAINS

	PAGE	TITLE	LINE
Heroick Strains could build a Tower;	79	Vanbrug House	8
Heroick Strains could build a Tow'r;	106	V's House	8
In higher Strains than we began.	106	V's House	32
When Poets soar in youthful Strains,	271	Apollo's Edict	D 52
To put the question strains his throat.	421	Ireld	16
With pennyless and starv'ling strains;	432	Answer Paulus	16
Set out in Hyperbolick Strains,	463	Birthday Song	93
"Not Strains of Law, nor Judges Frown,	570	Death of Swift	427
What Sword-knots! What Poetic Strains!	585	Strephon Chloe	37
His Chloe in the homeli'st Strains;	590	Strephon Chloe	212
The Court with annual Birth-day Strains;	650	On Poetry	306
Vanessa in exalted Strains,	711	Cadenus Vaness	791
Lamenting in unmanly Strains,	726	To Stella	99
Can I devise poetic strains?	754	Stella '23	2
Tho' he cring'd to his Deanship in very low strains,	816	Yahoo's	46
And grace my villa with his strains;	876	To Dean Swift	5
--Let indignation fire my strains,	950	Upstart	D 21
Rough Roystring Rustick Roaring Strains	958	Cantata	

STRAIT

	PAGE	TITLE	LINE
For strait I saw the Field maintain'd,	8	Ode to King	61
You strait stept in, and from the Monster's Jaws	12	Ode to William	D 23
When strait she sees the Countrey all around,	17	Ode Athenian	38
Strait turns the Muse turns the Helm, and I launch out again;	32	Ode to Temple	195
Which strait pronounc'd his death;	38	Ode Sancroft	120
Would strait become a Golden Pippin:	156	Fable of Midas	6
To London strait return again,	312	To Ford	48
Each strait his service offers, pays his court,	672	Epig Carthy 24	D 7
A Giant now, and strait an Elf,	935	Riddle 23	D 22

STRAND

	PAGE	TITLE	LINE
On the delightful Strand,	17	Ode Athenian	37
Turns all again to barren Strand.	239	Run Bankers	4
So fine a Coach along the Strand;	598	Problem Solved	14
Down in the Strand just where the new Pole is,	988	Letter Dr Sh-n	8

791

STRANGE

	PAGE	TITLE	LINE
How strange a Paradox is true, ...	25	Ode Athenian	305
Tho' in strange uncouth postures, and uncomely dress; .	35	Ode Sancroft	26
Strange to conceive, how the same objects strike . . .	51	Temple Ill	1
Scatters strange agues o'er men's sickly minds, . .	52	Temple Ill	38
You may be sure, so strange a Sight	92	Bauc & Phil 1	79
Strange, an Astrologer should Die, ...	98	Elegy Patrige	5
They tell us something strange and odd, ...	132	Magician's Rod	21
Some strange Arcana to unfold, ...	180	Horace 2, 1	2
There flies about a strange Report	202	Horace 2, 6	89
He who so long was Currant 'twould be strange . .	235	Elegy on Demar	35
By Christmas we shall see strange things.	282	Journal	110
A strange Event! whom Gold incites, ...	345	Prometheus	21
"Can it be strange if I eschew	380	Apology Lady C	163
'Tis strange, what diff'rent Thoughts inspire . . .	411	Desire Possess	1
The strange Stupidity of Birds.	514	Answer Fable	60
We Mortals are strange kind of Folk.	545	Life of Swift	4
Strange pride and insolence you shew, ...	617	Scandal Poem 1	3
Strange Pride and Insolence you show, ...	623	Scandal Poem 2	3
And hopes he will not think it strange	712	Cadenus Vaness	804
What is there in it strange or new?	820	Dr. Rundle	10
"Now Madam, you'll think it a strange Thing to say, . .	873	Grand Question	171
I'll shew the World strange Things and true;	919	Riddle 5	14
I, a virtue strange and rare, ...	936	Riddle 24	D 5

STRANGELY

He found it was strangely fill'd in the Middle. . . .	77	Lady B- B-	9
But, Jacobites are strangely dull.	299	Horrid Plot	42
"Now strangely pleads in my Excuse:	379	Apology Lady C	132
But Things are strangely chang'd since then, . . .	498	Panegyr Swift	163

STRANGER

A perfect Stranger to the Spleen;	170	Horace 1, 7	10
An Heir? and Stranger yet to hear, ...	384	Manly Virtue	19
"I find you're but a Stranger here.	563	Death of Swift	262

STRANGERS

The Strangers overheard, and said, ...	92	Bauc & Phil 1	83
And strangers delight to walk round 'em:	403	Window Inns 9	D 3
"So ready to do Strangers good, ...	558	Death of Swift	163
In hopes that Strangers may mistake it, ...	734	Stel B-day '20	12

STRATAGEM

| I have a Stratagem contriv'd; . . . . | 885 | Rev Market-Hill | 62 |

STRAW

Bids us make Bricks, yet sends us to look out for Straw;	32	Ode to Temple	188
Give us but Straw, and let us Ly	90	Bauc & Phil 1	21
Bring Straw for our Bed, ...	246	Irish-Feast	49
His Poems, think them all not worth a Straw. . . .	521	Stephen Duck	6
Some they do say, 'twas the big man of straw; . . .	841	Ballad	D 12
I then shall not value his Deanship a Straw, ...	868	Grand Question	33
No Straw, Oats, or Hay;	1036	Plague Country	6

STRAWS

Chaff, straws, or fragments of some rotten boat, . .	672	Epig Carthy 24	D 14
Nothing but Chaff, and Straws, and Feathers: . . .	688	Cadenus Vaness	56
Fools, Fops, and Rakes, for Chaff and Straws. . . .	688	Cadenus Vaness	60
And then they value not two Straws, ...	776	Mullinix Tim	97
While they sit a picking Straws	831	Legion Club	49
In rhetoric, or picking straws;	901	Dean's Reasons	77

STRAYS

| And round the barren Common strays, ... | 230 | Prog of Poetry | 10 |

STREAM

That feeds the huge unequal stream.	20	Ode Athenian	148
Vext at their Follies, murmur'd in his Stream; . . .	22	Ode Athenian	194
Be what it will; late near yon whisp'ring stream, . . .	51	Temple Ill	13
An Ass was drinking at a Stream, ...	253	Bubble	74
Here may it re-assume its Stream, ...	478	Epist on Epist	93
Which oft attends that luke-warm Stream;	589	Strephon Chloe	180
In a dull Stream, which moving slow	688	Cadenus Vaness	51
The Margin of a purling Stream, ...	894	Panegyr Dean	241

STREAMING

| 'Tis the world's wat'ry hour-glass streaming fast, . . | 49 | To Congreve | 189 |

STREAMS

Come from thy dear-lov'd Streams, ...	31	Ode to Temple	151
Or images that sink in streams;	35	Ode Sancroft	40
While Streams run down her oil'd Umbrella's Sides. . .	138	City Shower	38
"For Lands enrich'd by crimson Streams, ...	183	Horace 2, 1	96
In trickling Streams betwixt her Joynts.	227	Prog of Beauty	44
"From both your Streams in George's Reign! . . .	462	Birthday Song	80
To real Muses, Gods, and Streams, ...	478	Epist on Epist	86
Exhal'd from sour unsavory Streams, ...	526	Lady's Dres Rm	28
Rolls from his Mouth in plenteous Streams of Mud; . .	532	To Mr. Gay	40
No noisom Whiffs, or sweaty Streams, ...	584	Strephon Chloe	12
In Seas, and Streams, or low as Hell:	626	Scandal Poem 2	98
From purling Streams & Fountains bubbling	744	Stel Distress	3
From purling Streams and Fountains bubbling, ...	750	Stel Wood-Park	27
Yet endless Tears flow down in Streams.	932	Riddle 19	D 4

STREET   SEE GRUB-STREET,CAVAN-STREET,MEATH-STREET

Here we ly starving in the Street	90	Bauc & Phil 1	17
And Brickdust Moll had Scream'd through half the Street.	124	Descriptn Morn	14
What Street they sail'd from, by their Sight and Smell.	139	City Shower	56
His Works were hawk'd in ev'ry Street, ...	172	Horace 1, 7	41
And catechis'd in ev'ry Street.	202	Horace 2, 6	92
So rotting Celia stroles the Street	229	Prog of Beauty	103

STREET	(CONTINUED)	PAGE	TITLE	LINE
And, Dawson street will serve as well	. . . . . .	313	To Ford	61
A hundred Whores in ev'ry Street,	. . . .	315	To Ford	106
He took to the Street, and fled for his Life,	.	327	Epigram 1	2
In ev'ry Street a City-bard	. . . .	649	On Poetry	285
Like Milk 'tis cry'd about the Street,	. . . . .	929	Riddle 15	D 11
STREETS				
He walk'd the Streets, and wore a Thread-bare Cloak;	.	234	Elegy on Demar	9
In Streets where Kennels are too wide:	. . . . .	645	On Poetry	170
When thro' the streets I cry holloo?	. . . . . .	779	Mullinix Tim	186
And in the Streets divert the City	. . . . . .	780	Mullinix Tim	240
Nor scow'rs the Streets without a Shirt;	. . . . .	788	Dick's Variety	16
With such a cross Man, I wou'd lye in the Streets.	.	869	Grand Question	60
STREIGHTS				
Down the black Sea, and up the Streights,	. . . .	282	Journal	107
STRENGTH				
From strength of its own native seed,	. . . . . .	41	Ode Sancroft	224
T' express their Valor, Strength or Wit.	. . . .	83	Salamander	12
While He his utmost Strength apply'd,	. . . . .	158	Fable of Midas	73
Though with united Strength they all pull,	. . . .	191	Faggot	51
"But when we've gather'd Strength, I swear,	. . . .	208	Fable Bitches	35
Recover Strength whene'er he fell,	. . . . .	257	Bubble	182
Recover Strength and Vigor there,	. . . . .	258	Bubble	186
Since t' other will in Strength be double;	. . . .	366	Answer Delaney	12
"If you, unus'd, have scarsely Strength	. . . .	379	Apology Lady C	133
But, little could their Strength avail,	. . . . .	501	Doctor Delaney	33
Took Aim, and shot with all his Strength	. . . .	703	Cadenus Vaness	516
And doubly twisted it for strength;	. . . . . .	760	Bec's B-Day	4
STRENGTHENS				
Strengthens the Shoes of half the Rabble.	. . . .	942	Probatur Alit	12
STREPHON				
Poor Strephon, how would he blaspheme!	. . . . .	226	Prog of Beauty	16
Strephon, who found the Room was void,	. . . . .	526	Lady's Dres Rm	5
Strephon, the Rogue, display'd it wide,	. . . . .	526	Lady's Dres Rm	13
And Strephon bids us guess the rest;	. . . . . .	526	Lady's Dres Rm	16
When frighted Strephon cast his Eye on't	. . . .	527	Lady's Dres Rm	61
Why Strephon will you tell the rest?	. . . . . .	527	Lady's Dres Rm	69
For Strephon ventur'd to look in,	. . . . . .	528	Lady's Dres Rm	79
So Strephon lifting up the Lid,	. . . .	528	Lady's Dres Rm	89
But Strephon cautious never meant	. . . . . .	528	Lady's Dres Rm	92
Disgusted Strephon stole away	. . . . . .	529	Lady's Dres Rm	116
Soon punish'd Strephon for his Peeping;	. . . . .	529	Lady's Dres Rm	120
I pity wretched Strephon blind	. . . . . .	530	Lady's Dres Rm	129
If Strephon would but stop his Nose;	. . . . .	530	Lady's Dres Rm	136
But, Strephon sigh'd so loud and strong,	. . . .	585	Strephon Chloe	39
Strephon had long perplex'd his Brains,	. . . .	586	Strephon Chloe	72
For Strephon could remember well,	. . . . . .	587	Strephon Chloe	105
And what if daring Strephon dies	. . . . . .	587	Strephon Chloe	109
Strephon, who had been often told,	. . . . . .	588	Strephon Chloe	147
That Strephon chose no proper Season.	. . . . .	588	Strephon Chloe	160
Strephon who heard the fuming Rill	. . . . . .	589	Strephon Chloe	175
Now Strephon daily entertains	. . . .	590	Strephon Chloe	211
O Strephon, e'er that fatal Day	. . . . . .	591	Strephon Chloe	235
Ah, Strephon, how can you despise	. . . . . .	924	Riddle 8	1
To Strephon I have still been true,	. . . . .	924	Riddle 8	3
Consider, Strephon, what you do;	. . . . .	925	Riddle 8	25
STREPHON'S				
But oh! it turn'd poor Strephon's Bowels,	. . . .	527	Lady's Dres Rm	43
No Object Strephon's Eye escapes,	. . . . .	527	Lady's Dres Rm	47
STRETCH				
Conclude Love's Bow-String at full Stretch;	. . .	66	Problem	30
You'll see me stretch him to a Giant;	. . . . .	934	Riddle 21	D 20
STRETCHED				
But, since the truth must needs be stretched	. . .	433	Answer Paulus	43
STRETCHES				
She stretches, gapes, unglues her Eyes,	. . . . .	446	Modern Lady	42
STRETCHING				
Numberless Nations, stretching far and wide,	. . .	25	Ode Athenian	297
STRICT				
And join in friendship, with a strict tye,	. . . .	436	Answer Paulus	145
Stole in, and took a strict Survey,	. . . . .	526	Lady's Dres Rm	7
With Ladies what a strict Decorum!	. . . . .	888	Panegyr Dean	51
STRICTER				
Who look on Courts with stricter Eyes,	. . . . .	485	Libel on D- D-	175
STRICTEST				
Whose Virtues bear the strictest Test;	. . . . .	655	On Poetry	412
In vain you make ye strictest View	. . . . . .	659	On Poetry	D 410
STRICTLY				
Wou'd strictly after Truth enquire	. . . . .	455	Dean Smedley	7
Allow your hatred strictly just;	. . . .	498	Panegyr Swift	170
The Law so strictly guards the Monarch's Health,	.	533	To Mr. Gay	77
As strictly too; as doth his Reverence.	. . . .	603	Beasts Confess	72
Will you keep strictly to the Text?	. . . . .	732	Stella, Poems	138
STRICTNESS				
Indeed, the Strictness of his Morals	. . . .	603	Beasts Confess	51
STRIDE				
Sid's Rod was of a larger Stride,	. . . . . .	134	Magician's Rod	53
Like stepping Stones to save a Stride,	. . . .	645	On Poetry	169
STRIDES				
The tuck'd-up Sempstress walks with hasty Strides,	. .	138	City Shower	37
See the dreadful Strides she takes.	. . . . . .	832	Legion Club	92

STRIFE

	PAGE	TITLE	LINE
Approaching joy at strife with parting woe.	51	Temple Ill	22
Not yet, the Dust had shun'd th' unequal Strife, . .	137	City Shower	23
Which mingling with prolifick Strife	324	Pethox	29
In scientific Strife engage;	385	Manly Virtue	44
Engage, and in the glorious Strife, ...	385	Manly Virtue	45
To kindle strife Dame Nature taught her, ...	618	Scandal Poem 1	37
To kindle Strife, Dame-Nature taught her:	624	Scandal Poem 2	35

STRIKE

Strange to conceive, how the same objects strike . . .	51	Temple Ill	1
Strike your offended Sense with double Stink.	137	City Shower	6
Come, Harper, strike up, ...	245	Irish-Feast	25
Shall strike him dumb, and quell their Noise.	340	Arch-Bish Dub	28
Will strike him dead upon the Spot:	500	Doctor Delaney	20
As how to strike the Muses Lyre.	641	On Poetry	32
"This might their mutual Fancy strike, ...	714	Cadenus Vaness	878
To strike him for a pot of ale?	899	Dean's Reasons	32

STRIKES

Explaining strikes opposers Dumb;	281	Journal	84
Love or Contempt, her Fancy strikes.	708	Cadenus Vaness	683
And see now, it strikes ten, and I hear him coming up Stairs:	987	Mary to Sher	36

STRING   SEE BOW-STRING

That the main String of Cupid's Bow, ...	66	Problem	22
We have got it in a String, ...	168	Peace Dunkirk	5
He pull'd the String, and stopt his Coach, ...	172	Horace 1, 7	61
Take your blue Ribbin for a String.	190	Faggot	38
And change it for a Brazen String.	346	Prometheus	66
Is qualified best for a Dog in a String.	389	Order of Bath	12
Since first I learn'd to tune a String.	445	Modern Lady	12
He fixt the Star and String Cerulean.	656	On Poetry	464
Fair Discretion string the Lyre.	661	Love Song	14
Oh! would His Majesty but add a String.	678	Dean and Duke	16
Who o'er each String and Wire preside, ...	798	Traulus 1	73
Three fellows with whips, and the Dean holds the string.	1027	Sheri Circles	20

STRINGS

Whole Crouds about its Brazen Strings.	345	Prometheus	30
In Leading strings her Infant-Steps to guide; . . .	531	To Mr. Gay	11

STRIP

Strip her of ev'ry ornament and grace, ...	42	Ode Sancroft	249
The Birds are met to strip the Jays.	239	Run Bankers	20
And strip the Bodyes of the Dead.	256	Bubble	156
And strip the Bones, and melt the Oyl.	258	Bubble	204
Then come the Poor and strip him so, they leave him not a Cross,	341	Upon His Grace	11
And strip his Hyde, and pick his Bones, ...	413	Desire Possess	57
Strip their Bums; let Caleb hoyse 'em;	635	Epistle Lady	178
And strip their Clients to their Coats;	930	Riddle 15	D 27

STRIP'T

When Sheelah strip't	441	Ballyspellin	38
The Tyrant strip't me to the Skin:	915	Riddle 1	10

STRIPS

But strips himself to pay the Porter.	928	Riddle 12	D 20

STRIPT

Britannia stript from her sole Guard the Laws, . . .	12	Ode to William	D 21
"The Nation stript go joyful back, ...	571	Death of Swift	447
He follow'd, stript, and in he crept, ...	587	Strephon Chloe	113
I saw them of their Garments stript, ...	923	Riddle 7	73

STRIVE

In vain I strive to cross this spacious Main, . . .	32	Ode to Temple	192
To thee, what oft I vainly strive to hide, ...	55	Temple Ill	133
So, Modern Rhymers strive to blast	81	Vanbrug House	89
And strive, and strive, your Wife to please. . . .	362	Grace's Answer	46
And strive, and strive, your Wife to please. . . .	362	Grace's Answer	46
Nor shall you strive your Horns to hide, ...	362	Grace's Answer	53
And strive to pass, in publick view, ...	546	Life of Swift	35
Let Prudence with Good Nature strive, ...	593	Strephon Chloe	309
And strive to tear you Limb from Limb, ...	651	On Poetry	333
How all wou'd for his Friendship strive;	709	Cadenus Vaness	701
Could always bear to Strive with Man?	799	Traulus 1	96

STRIVES

His Spirit always strives with Slaves.	799	Traulus 1	100

STRIVING

In striving to wash off th' imaginary paint: . . .	42	Ode Sancroft	250

STROAK'D

There to be stroak'd and fed with Pap;	607	Beasts Confess	210

STROAKS

Spits in his mouth and stroaks his Chaps	421	Ireld	14

STROKE

Both stroke her Hands, and rub her Gums, ...	150	Corinna	7
Or how the Bulley at a stroke	781	Mullinix Tim	267
For ev'ry Stroke goes to my Heart, ...	1005	Sheridan's Sub	32

STROKES

What Strokes on Guts, ...	246	Irish-Feast	67

STROLE

And strole about, but hide their Quality, ...	90	Bauc & Phil 1	3
And strole about, but hide their Quality, ...	111	Bauc & Phil 2	3
Rather than starve, a better man would strole. . .	308	Billet Players	16
Must strole in Air 'twixt Earth and Sky;	689	Cadenus Vaness	86
As I strole the City, oft I	829	Legion Club	1

	PAGE	TITLE	LINE
STROLERS			
Thus in the Strolers usuall Cant	90	Bauc & Phil 1	23
Where, in the Strolers Canting Strain, ...	111	Bauc & Phil 2	11
STROLES			
So rotting Celia stroles the Street	229	Prog of Beauty	103
STROLING			
Of Stroling God's, whose usual Trade is, ...	120	Apollo Outwit	22
STROLLER			
I told him what it was to be a stroller, ...	308	Billet Players	33
And, as a stroller, act in ev'ry play:	309	Billet Players	48
Whilst Lady Charlotte, like a Stroller, ...	410	Dial Rich Marb	61
STROLLERS			
Our set of strollers, wand'ring up and down, ...	307	Billet Players	1
We, humble strollers, always on the wing.	308	Billet Players	14
To live and die all strollers for your sakes;	309	Billet Players	50
STROLLING			
So bright a batter'd, strolling Toast;	581	Young Nymph	4
STRONG			
Thus fools, for being strong and num'rous known, . . .	37	Ode Sancroft	79
Was so exceeding tall and Strong, ...	160	Atlas	2
Yet Hercules was not so strong, ...	160	Atlas	13
Were much too strong for all their Hands.	189	Faggot	8
So strong you'll be, in Friendship ty'd;	189	Faggot	11
To make the Bundle strong and safe, ...	191	Faggot	45
Infus'd a strong prolifick Potion, ...	293	Prog Marriage	108
Strong Arguments to keep You here, ...	311	To Ford	14
You see, my Arguments are Strong;	315	To Ford	109
Strong Tubs for his Raps, Two thousand and more; . . .	337	Serious Poem	96
So strong, that from the lower End, ...	345	Prometheus	33
Inclos'd Cap-a-pee in a strong Coat of Mail.	350	Wood Insect	6
For, This was active, That was strong:	412	Desire Possess	14
Though strong in Limbs, he lagg'd behind.	412	Desire Possess	38
But, all Appearances are strong.	414	Censure	16
As strong upon your back	428	Beau's Reply	3
Thus your Encomiums, to be strong, ...	464	Birthday Song	117
Then Throttle thy self with an Ell of strong Tape, . .	519	Dean Hang Rape	53
Nor would there be need of a strong Hempen Cape, . .	519	Dean Hang Rape	65
By telling Noses with a Party strong.	533	To Mr. Gay	60
A strong Dilemma in a desp'rate Case!	535	To Mr. Gay	129
So keen thy Hunters, and thy Scent so strong;	539	Mr. Pulteney	43
"Yet here we had a strong report, ...	547	Life of Swift	84
"Last Year we thought him strong and hale;	557	Death of Swift	112
But, Strephon sigh'd so loud and strong, ...	585	Strephon Chloe	39
Appearances were all so strong, ...	707	Cadenus Vaness	642
But tho' her Arguments were strong, ...	710	Cadenus Vaness	746
Pour'd in a strong inspiring Juice;	743	Stel B-day 22	66
When the strong Cords of Union once are Broke. . . .	770	Horace 1, 14	22
'Twill not avail, when thy strong Sides are broke, . .	771	Horace 1, 14	37
Judgement weak, and Passion strong, ...	800	Traulus 2	17
STRONGER			
But always with a stronger relish of the Last. . . .	22	Ode Athenian	215
The common Death of many a stronger Boat.	284	Elegy Boat	10
And, trust me, as the noise grows stronger, ...	296	Satiric Elegy	7
The t' other will be stronger twice;	366	Answer Delaney	18
Are stronger, and almost as good.	367	Answer Delaney	50
Oft' swallow'd down a stronger Potion, ...	495	Panegyr Swift	61
Must yield her Foe the stronger Cause;	695	Cadenus Vaness	265
STRONGEST			
You'll then defy the strongest Whig, ...	191	Faggot	49
Take the three strongest of his broken Planks, . . .	285	Elegy Boat	32
And Guelph the strongest ear will wound.	467	Birthday Song	216
The strongest Friendship yields to Pride, ...	554	Death of Swift	37
Placing in the strongest Light, ...	633	Epistle Lady	97
She plac'd it in the strongest View.	701	Cadenus Vaness	455
The strongest Reason will submit	732	Verses Vanessa	7
Than strongest Weeds that grow these Stones betwixt: .	880	Pastoral Dial	10
I'm chiefly unruly, when strongest confin'd.	927	Riddle 11 D	4
STRONGLY			
And strongly shoot a radiant Dart, ...	764	Stel B-day '26	33
STROVE			
A Stealing Brook, and strove to creep away	22	Ode Athenian	192
You strove to cultivate a barren Court in vain, . . .	32	Ode to Temple	175
Which while the Senate strove to scower, ...	158	Fable of Midas	71
And strove by Turns to break the Faggot:	189	Faggot	6
You strove for ev'ry Inch of Ground;	326	Pethox	88
He strove to steal that Chain of Gold, ...	346	Prometheus	64
He strove to pick up all he found, ...	412	Desire Possess	25
All humble Worth she strove to raise;	701	Cadenus Vaness	456
She did her best to ape Woodpark. She strove in vain to ape	747	Stel Distress	48
She strove in vain to ape Wood-Park.	751	Stel Wood-Park	64
With Omens oft I strove to warn thy Swains, ...	792	St. Pat's Well	43
And Lemnian God consulting strove, ...	916	Riddle 2	10
STROW			
And tune your Harps, and strow your Bays.	656	On Poetry	468
STROW'D			
Is all with precious Jewels strow'd.	324	Pethox	36
And, gather'd all his Brother strow'd;	412	Desire Possess	36
STROWN			
The Roads are with his Foll'wers strown, ...	398	Earl of P-b-w	20

		PAGE	TITLE	LINE
STROWS				
Which with unsparing Hand, he strows	. . . . . .	486	Libel on D- D-	189
STRUCK				
Laoco'n struck the Outside with his Spear,	. . .	139	City Shower	51
Struck with Endymion's graceful mien,	. . . . .	178	To Lord Harley	74
An hundred struck lame.	. . .	246	Irish-Feast	72
Struck all his Rage and Malice down;	. . .	340	Arch-Bish Dub	20
And by the forming Engine struck,	. . . . . .	344	Prometheus	9
Each Atom by scme other struck,	. . .	406	Swift to Pope	13
Ever with some new Fancy struck,	. . . . . .	452	Modern Lady	236
Or, struck with Fear, her Fancy runs	. . . . .	583	Young Nymph	51
To slip his Ears, yet struck his Nose:	. . . . .	589	Strephon Chloe	184
On Plutarch's Morals struck, were spoil'd.	. . . .	701	Cadenus Vaness	483
Was struck with Love, Esteem, and Awe,	. . . .	708	Cadenus Vaness	692
First issuing, struck the Murd'rer's Ears;	. . .	850	Old Thorn	54
STRUCTURE				
The glorious Structure of Your Fame to raise;	. . .	11	Ode to William	D 6
STRUGGLE				
He long'd for a Girl that would struggle and squal,	. .	519	Dean Hang Rape	56
Why are they so willful to struggle with Men?	. . . .	519	Dean Hang Rape	62
And should he struggle; I know what--	. . .	586	Strephon Chloe	82
STRUGLED				
She bustled and strugled, and made her Escape,	. . .	517	Dean Hang Rape	11
STRUGLING				
When now the flood invades his strugling breath,	. . .	672	Epig Carthy 24	D 12
STRUMPET SEE OYSTER-STRUMPET				
STRUNG				
Or strung on Pegs behind the Door;	. . . . . .	592	Strephon Chloe	290
When first for thee my Harp I strung:	. . . . . .	728	Stella, Poems	10
My Harp will soon in vain be strung,	. . . . . .	739	Stel B-day '21	11
STRUT				
Whilst Patr'ot-like thou'lt strut and frown.	. . .	182	Horace 2, 1	64
To see a Scoundrel Strut and hector,	. . . . . .	312	To Ford	39
That when I strut, and stair, and stink,	. . . . .	778	Mullinix Tim	166
STRUTS				
But that he struts, and that he squints,	. . . . .	462	Birthday Song	61
But that he squints, and that he struts,	. . . . .	462	Birthday Song	63
Who struts like any King already.	. . . . . .	466	Birthday Song	188
And, when Apollo struts on Pindus,	. . . . . .	620	Scandal Poem 1	107
And when Apollo struts on Pindus,	. . . . . .	626	Scandal Poem 2	105
Smit with the glorious prize next struts in Sewel,	. .	672	Epig Carthy 24	D 9
STRUTTING				
This is the little strutting Pile,	. . . . . .	127	Little House	13
And strutting Hal-- is off the Hooks;	. . . . .	168	Peace Dunkirk	14
"To be the strutting Cornet's Sport,	. . . . . .	380	Apology Lady C	149
Spy the strutting chatt'ring Vermin?	. . . . . .	634	Epistle Lady	152
STUB'D				
So, the next Parson stub'd and burnt it.	. . . . .	117	Bauc & Phil 2	178
STUBBED				
While each with stubbed Knife remov'd the Roots	. . .	880	Pastoral Dial	3
STUBBLE				
The Farmer's Goose, who in the Stubble,	. . .	230	Prog of Poetry	1
Thrice happy Duck, employ'd in threshing Stubble!	. .	521	Stephen Duck	7
"It serves for Stubble, Hay, and Wood,	. . . .	550	Life of Swift	178
To build on Sand with Hay and Stubble?	. . . . .	593	Strephon Chloe	306
STUBBORN				
Among thy stubborn sons there haunts that spirit of Jews,		38	Ode Sancroft	129
Let Stubborn Pride Possess thee long,	. . .	121	Apollo Outwit	53
But own'd, he had a stubborn Spirit	. . . . . .	604	Beasts Confess	109
The Triumphs of that stubborn Dame,	. . . . . .	702	Cadenus Vaness	495
Where stubborn Stoicks would complain.	. . . .	765	Stel B-day '26	50
At an old stubborn Root I chanc'd to tug,	. . . .	881	Pastoral Dial	25
Though some are of so stubborn Kind,	. . . . . .	921	Riddle 6	35
STUBBORNESS				
Your Presence all their Native Stubborness controuls,		9	Ode to King	90
STUCK				
There stuck, and to a Pulpitt grew,	. . . . . .	93	Bauc & Phil 1	107
There stuck aloft, in Publick View,	. . . . . .	114	Bauc & Phil 2	87
Stuck underneath his Cushion-side:	. . . . . .	174	Horace 1, 7	100
On all the same Impression stuck.	. . . . .	344	Prometheus	10
Till in a Lump together stuck,	. . . . . .	406	Swift to Pope	15
"This odious Chair how came I stuck in't,	. . . .	452	Modern Lady	240
Stuck in an Irish Cabbin's Brow,	. . . . .	457	Paddy's Charac	2
Stuck on with Art on either Side,	. . . . . .	581	Young Nymph	14
With greasy Paper stuck upon't.	. . . . . .	582	Young Nymph	36
Stuck to the Point that pierc'd her Breast;	. . . .	703	Cadenus Vaness	521
Stuck artfully a Parchment Case.	. . . . .	904	Death Daphne	36
With a quill stuck across his nose.	. . . . .	983	Sher, A Goose	20
And those to be sure, stuck together like Glew, sick.	.	1029	Dr. Helsham	25
STUDENTS				
My Prelates and my Students, sent from hence,	. . .	792	St. Pat's Well	29
The Students drinking, rais'd their Wit and Parts;	.	793	St. Pat's Well	70
STUDIED				
Who have well studied in the Worlds Disease,	. . . .	20	Ode Athenian	138
And studied Affection came,	. . . .	449	Modern Lady	132
STUDIES				
Then diff'rent Studies chuse,	. . . . . .	405	Swift to Pope	6
But lest he shou'd neglect his Studies	. . . . .	693	Cadenus Vaness	222
And in dull Studies to engage	. . . . . .	705	Cadenus Vaness	578
STUDIOUS				
Be studious well to imitate	. . . .	780	Mullinix Tim	233

		PAGE	TITLE	LINE
STUDIOUS	(CONTINUED)			
Nor are we studious to enquire, ...		781	Mullinix Tim	261
Be studious to practice true Meanness of Spirit;	. .	808	Advice Parson	7
STUDY				
To study the obliging Jest, ...		219	To Mr. Delany	103
Then study to correct your Taste, ...		270	Apollo's Edict D	10
The Wife should study to be clean;		588	Strephon Chloe	138
To study bright Vanessa's Looks:		694	Cadenus Vaness	235
"She'd study to reform the Men;		714	Cadenus Vaness	873
Is at study or pray'r.		856	Lady's Lament	158
STUDY'D				
I study'd a Fortnight, before I could find, ...		265	Apollo	75
She study'd well the Point, and found		695	Cadenus Vaness	278
STUFF				
With a huge Fardingal to swell her Fustian Stuff,	. .	23	Ode Athenian	222
A Stock of tawdry Stuff besides, ...		80	Vanbrug House	46
And since you're sparing of your Stuff, ...		108	V's House	73
O! Cou'd I see this Audience Clad in Stuff, ...		275	Epilogue	31
For sorry Stuff, can get a Crown a Page;		276	Epilogue	42
What Stuff he is made on you quickly may find, . . .		336	Serious Poem	77
So Goldsmiths say, the coursest Stuff, ...		345	Prometheus	23
To write such scurvy stuff!		428	Beau's Reply	5
Observe this Pattern; there's a Stuff, ...		447	Modern Lady	84
And while, with all this paultry Stuff, ...		448	Modern Lady	109
Thou still with Battles stuff thy head full		462	Birthday Song	55
Live on, and Stuff, to Boot, their Maws.		479	Epist on Epist	126
That Human Friendship is but Stuff.		545	Life of Swift	24
"I keep no antiquated Stuff;		563	Death of Swift	267
How long the Stuff is like to last;		592	Strephon Chloe	294
Let them neither starve, nor stuff:		633	Epistle Lady	130
I own, that out-of-fashion Stuff		700	Cadenus Vaness	426
Rich Ladies will furnish their Garrets with Stuff,	.	716	Answer Rebus	15
To hear such mortifying Stuff.		763	Stel B-day '26	8
Stuff his Guts with Flax and Grass;		831	Legion Club	64
What he means by this stuff:		854	Lady's Lament	108
His Brace of Puppies how they stuff, ...		861	Lady Acheson	33
"Your Noveds, and Blutraks, and Omurs and Stuff, . .		872	Grand Question	159
Taught harmless Man to cram and stuff.		895	Panegyr Dean	262
We comb the Wool, refine the Stuff, ...		948	Jason Hassard	3
But now I'll secret keep your stuff;		1002	Reply by Dean	17
And all that stuff of Toylet, Glass, and Box-comb?	.	1003	Dan J's Reply	9
STUFF-HER-EARS				
Which made my Grand-Dame always stuff-her-Ears,	. .	367	Answer Delaney	39
STUFF'D				
Or stuff'd with Phlegm up to the Throat		231	Prog of Poetry	25
Long Bills, and Answers, stuff'd with Lies, . . .		690	Cadenus Vaness	121
'Tis a vast Subject stuff'd with Matter, ...		993	On Picture	17
STUMBLE				
Should stumble once into the Fount, ...		671	Epig Carthy 21 D	7
STUMBLING				
Stumbling at ev'ry Step she trod.		885	Rev Market-Hill	74
STUMM				
Demand a Croun a Quart for Stumm.		313	To Ford	68
STUMP				
He is an old Stump cut out of a Crab, ...		335	Serious Poem	36
To ease his Itch against the Stump, ...		849	Old Thorn	42
STUMPS				
The Youth with Broomy Stumps began to trace . . .		124	Descriptn Morn	9
STUN'D				
She stun'd, and then she broke his Pate.		221	A Quiet Life	44
STUNG				
The Spiteful Insect stung the God.		458	Paddy's Charac	34
Then shew, how Statesmen oft are stung		496	Panegyr Swift	114
STUNN'D				
I'm daily stunn'd with such a Medley, ...		742	Stel B-day 22	43
STUNNING				
Stunning her Royal Ears with talking;		410	Dial Rich Marb	59
STUNS				
With Limbs robust, and Voice that stuns;		326	Pethox	76
STUNTED				
Grew Scrubby, dy'd a-top, was stunted:		117	Bauc & Phil 2	177
STUPID				
For when like stupid alchymists you try		49	To Congreve	207
Abandon'd, stupid, slavish praters!		436	Answer Paulus	134
Reject with scorn that stupid Notion		468	Birthday Song	261
Such stupid blasphemy and nonsense?		490	Dialogue	38
Shou'd stupid Libels grieve your Mind, ...		501	Doctor Delaney	43
Observe what Loads of stupid Rimes		503	Doctor Delaney	101
The Ass was never known so stupid		607	Beasts Confess	207
Pronounces you a stupid Rogue;		644	On Poetry	120
Run o'er their Cant of stupid Lies, ...		697	Cadenus Vaness	332
"They were a senseless, stupid Race:		714	Cadenus Vaness	871
With such a stupid vicious Age,)		723	To Stella	8
Wou'd you rise in the Church, be Stupid and Dull,		807	Advice Parson	1
The stupid blockhead and the liar.		950	Upstart D	16
STUPIDITY				
The strange Stupidity of Birds.		514	Answer Fable	60
STUPIFIES				
It but stupifies your Brain.		636	Epistle Lady	210
STUPIFY'D				
Which stupify'd them all to stocks.		178	To Lord Harley	46

	PAGE	TITLE	LINE
STUPIFYING			
Went down like stupifying Draughts:	470	Burning Poem	8
STURDY			
For shame! two sturdy Rascalls beg;	91	Bauc & Phil 1	44
STUT-TUT-TUT-TER			
And, though you hear him Stut-tut-tut-ter,	797	Traulus 1	47
STYES			
To make for Pigs convenient Styes:	892	Panegyr Dean	160
STYGIAN			
Our Boat is now sail'd to the Stygian Ferry,	285	Elegy Boat	23
By the Stygian Steams that flew,	834	Legion Club	123
STYL'D			
His Conduct might have made him styl'd	704	Cadenus Vaness	548
STYLE			
A Type of Modern Witt and Style,	81	Vanbrug House	83
Reply'd in complementall Style:	94	Bauc & Phil 1	158
Then, from the motly mingled Style	108	V's House	63
A Type of Modern Wit and Style,	109	V's House	125
Which by the Style, the Matter, and the Drift,	195	Author Himself	49
We style him by no other Phrase;	298	Horrid Plot	8
Come, help your lame Dog o'er the Style.	298	Horrid Plot	15
(Note here, that in the Chymick Style,	354	Simile Silver	15
She answers in her usual Style,	447	Modern Lady	94
But here's enough to shew your Style.	463	Birthday Song	82
Such Language, with her usual Style:	706	Cadenus Vaness	627
In lofty Style to make Replies,	711	Cadenus Vaness	796
Mark my Address, and learn my Style,	780	Mullinix Tim	235
In courtly style addresses Franck;	879	Robbin & Harry	50
Your style so clear, and so concise,	889	Panegyr Dean	73
Permit me then to raise my Style,	894	Panegyr Dean	227
Thee best befits a lowly Style:	897	Panegyr Dean	329
To answer your style without circumlocution.	1027	Sheri Circles	24
STYX			
Confest his Flame, and swore by Styx,	120	Apollo Outwit	18
And drive departed Souls to Styx.	133	Magician's Rod	38
Styx, through Hell whose Waters roll!	832	Legion Club	84
How pleasant on the Banks of Styx,	905	Death Daphne	87
SUAE			
Aetatis suae fifty two	289	Prog Marriage	1
SUBDU'D			
Because he had the world subdu'd:	464	Birthday Song	146
A Nymph so hard to be subdu'd,	702	Cadenus Vaness	496
Your now subdu'd and suppliant Slave	1005	Sheridan's Sub	6
SUBDUE			
'Tis you who must this Land subdue,	26	Ode to Temple	8
Will soon subdue the Realm of Lilliput.	467	Birthday Song	208
Did once their Land subdue and civilize:	790	St. Pat's Well	14
Metals I like them subdue,	936	Riddle 24	D 17
SUBJECT			
Or a more worthy subject chuse:	42	Ode Sancroft	260
Subject or Patron of his Muse,	157	Fable of Midas	52
Which links the Subject to the King:	346	Prometheus	65
For so sad a Tale is no Subject of Laughter.	430	Dicky Dolly	18
No Subject fit	441	Ballyspellin	25
Then gave the Subject out of Spite:	445	Modern Lady	23
And fit your present Subject best.	460	Birthday Song	4
To such a subject tune my lyre	490	Dialogue	39
Shall a Subject so Loyal be hang'd by the Nape,	518	Dean Hang Rape	35
I grow the Subject of their Chat:	565	Death of Swift	302
That ev'ry Subject in the Land	601	Beasts Confess	10
What Subject you can manage best;	642	On Poetry	80
And gracefully her Subject chang'd:	698	Cadenus Vaness	355
Cadenus is a Subject fit,	702	Cadenus Vaness	502
On so mean a Design, and a Subject so low.	716	Answer Rebus	4
For mean's her Design, and her Subject as mean,	716	Answer Rebus	5
But a Genius like her's no Subject can stifle,	716	Answer Rebus	11
Are you a Subject fit for me?	757	Stel B-day '24	26
We know the Subject of their Quarrels;	820	Dr. Rundle	21
A subject for their genius fit;	876	To Dean Swift	15
Me for the Subject of his Muse.	887	Panegyr Dean	26
Domestick Subject for Disputes,	919	Riddle 5	2
For we who debate on a subject important,	976	Dean to Sherid	11
'Tis a vast Subject stuff'd with Matter,	993	On Picture	17
And, as to the subject, our judgment mehercle	1026	Sheri Circles	3
SUBJECT'S			
So gravely, where the Subject's light.	218	To Mr. Delany	88
SUBJECTION			
And held them in subjection.	784	Mullinex Dick	20
SUBJECTS			
Are nobler Subjects for your learned Pen;	31	Ode to Temple	160
And that his subjects share his happy influence;	40	Ode Sancroft	182
All Subjects like Dan Jackson's Nose.	218	To Mr. Delany	102
And we order our Subjects, of every Degree,	266	Apollo	99
Let his Success our Subjects sway	270	Apollo's Edict	D 7
And you, our Subjects, when you here resort,	275	Epilogue	29
The same thy Subjects boast of Thee.	324	Pethox	42
Beware of Subjects you call Trite,	371	Letter D. S-y	2
That will make all my Subjects with pride to obey.	389	Order of Bath	4
Thus my Subjects with pleasure will obey my Commands	389	Order of Bath	9
Take subjects safer for your wit	489	Dialogue	21
Nor dwell on Subjects too sublime.	896	Panegyr Dean	320

		PAGE	TITLE	LINE
SUBLIME				
	No Thought, no Fancy, no Sublime,	215	To Mr. Delany	11
	Sing my Praise in Strain sublime:	631	Epistle Lady	57
	Treat you in a Stile sublime,	638	Epistle Lady	258
	How few have reach'd the low Sublime?	652	On Poetry	370
	A Truce with all sublime Conceits.	711	Cadenus Vaness	793
	Nor dwell on Subjects too sublime.	896	Panegyr Dean	320
	Betwixt the Knight sublime and me?	901	Dean's Reasons	66
	The Learn'd in Sciences sublime,	918	Riddle 4	42
SUBLIMEST				
	He soars sublimest when he Sinks:	,80	Vanbrug House	52
SUBLUNARY				
	Two foolish guides in ev'ry sublunary dance:	34	Ode Sancroft	9
	To pick up Sublunary Ladies.	120	Apollo Outwit	24
	But, ev'ry sublunary dowdy	617	Scandal Poem 1	13
	But, ev'ry sublunary Dowdy,	624	Scandal Poem 2	13
SUBMISSION				
	With those two pow'rful swords, Submission and Humility,	36	Ode Sancroft	48
	Thy just submission for this bold neglect.	53	Temple Ill	74
	"With due Submission to the God,	321	First of April	17
SUBMISSIONS				
	Or vile Submissions, when in Place;	494	Panegyr Swift	34
SUBMISSIVE				
	In manner submissive most humbly do pray,	185	Scriblerus 1	2
	They submissive round him wait;	836	Legion Club	166
SUBMIT				
	To better Judgments willing to submit,	194	Author Himself	25
	We gladly hear you, and submit:	314	To Ford	94
	My Word is past, I must submit,	445	Modern Lady	26
	I submit; and answer thus.	636	Epistle Lady	188
	Will force all Nature to submit.	709	Cadenus Vaness	725
	The strongest Reason will submit	732	Verses Vanessa	7
SUBMITS				
	As to an Oracle submits.	649	On Poetry	268
SUBMITTING				
	This may be true--submitting still	484	Libel on D- D-	121
	To better Judgments still submitting,	788	Dick's Variety	9
SUBORDINATION				
	And all in due Subordination;	650	On Poetry	314
SUBORN				
	When Gold's to be got, to Forswear and Suborn.	335	Serious Poem	46
SUBSCRIBED				
	When I and some others subscribed our Names	144	New Song	27
SUBSCRIBER				
	Each poor Subscriber to the Sea	253	Bubble	81
SUBSCRIBERS				
	Subscribers here by thousands float,	256	Bubble	145
	Subscribers plainly see 'um there,	257	Bubble	167
SUBSCRIBES				
	Subscribes, Dear Sir, your Brother loving.	812	Bro Protestant	20
SUBSCRIPTION				
	I withdrew my Subscription by help of a Blot,	144	New Song	29
SUBSIDING				
	By Time subsiding, you may find	731	Stella, Poems	133
SUBSIST				
	Cannot without a Form subsist,	228	Prog of Beauty	82
SUBSTANCE				
	To a less noble Substance chang'd	93	Bauc & Phil 1	115
	To a less Noble Substance chang'd,	114	Bauc & Phil 2	91
	Behold; a frothy Substance rise;	892	Panegyr Dean	183
SUBSTANCES				
	Rend'ring shades, things, and substances of names;	47	To Congreve	148
SUBSTANTIAL				
	But for a more substantial cause:	433	Answer Paulus	21
SUBTERRANEOUS				
	Who hir'd a subterraneous Friend,	393	Modern Poets	13
SUBTIL				
	The subtil spirit all flies up in fume;	49	To Congreve	210
SUBTLE				
	At six Years old, the subtle Jade	150	Corinna	17
	When that subtle Companion, in hopes to surpass us,	265	Apollo	80
	The subtle Knave had all the Plunder swept.	536	To Mr. Gay	154
SUBTLY				
	Smooth as that airy nymph so subtly borne	54	Temple Ill	117
SUBURB				
	To punish Thieves, or lash a Suburb Wench.	537	Mr. Pulteney	6
	To celebrate some Suburb Trull;	730	Stella, Poems	72
SUBURB-WENCH				
	A Duchess, or a Suburb-Wench.	645	On Poetry	166
SUCCEED				
	Intended in Time to succeed to your Place;	263	Apollo	28
	Of Prayers, that he might well succeed,	373	Letter D. S-y	69
	When Peevishness and Spleen succeed.	731	Stella, Poems	136
	No--that scheme will ne'er succeed,	907	Daphne	39
SUCCEEDING				
	And Day succeeding after Day,	860	Lady Acheson	10
SUCCEEDS				
	Some, when an Heir succeeds; go boldly on,	535	To Mr. Gay	117
SUCCESS				
	That you should meet, in love, success?	177	To Lord Harley	24
	Dick found it by his ill Success	221	A Quiet Life	41

	PAGE	TITLE	LINE

SUCCESS   (CONTINUED)

Let his Success our Subjects sway   270 Apollo's Edict   D 7
Her last Night's ill Success repeats,   447 Modern Lady   72
"And seldom fail'd of good Success;   566 Death of Swift   336
Without Success; thus tells his Case: 604 Beasts Confess   94
But what Success Vanessa met,   712 Cadenus Vaness   818
Your Rev'rence thus, with like Success,   892 Panegyr Dean   187

SUCCESSION

Had You by dull Succession gain'd Your Crown, 11 Ode to William   D 9
Thou still with Tyrants in Succession curst, 793 St. Pat's Well   83

SUCCESSOR

E'er flourish't under a Successor or a Son;   25 Ode Athenian   285
(To thee I apply great Smedley's Successor) 518 Dean Hang Rape   44

SUCCESSOR'S

And bear the new Successor's frown;   468 Birthday Song   259

SUCCESSORS

To be Successors to these Great Unknown,   25 Ode Athenian   294

SUCCINCT

Thy Muse is tuck'd up, and succinct;   1021 Nim-Dan-Dean 1   D 27

SUCCOUR'D

"But succour'd Virtue in Distress,   566 Death of Swift   335

SUCH   201   OMITTED WORD

SUCK

For want of Milk, wou'd suck her Blood.   208 Fable Bitches   22
Lice from your Body suck their Food;   812 Bro Protestant   35

SUCK'T

He suck't his Vittels thro' a Quill;   156 Fable of Midas   10

SUDDEN

A sudden Alteration feels,   93 Bauc & Phil 1   127
A sudden Alteration feels,   113 Bauc & Phil 2   67
His Spirits of a sudden fail'd him,   376 Apology Lady C   33
A sudden universal Crew   528 Lady's Dres Rm   85
"Poor Man! he went, all on a sudden---!   547 Life of Swift   70
But now a sudden Change was wrought,   704 Cadenus Vaness   560
Because she heard a sudden Drum,   726 To Stella   77
Torn by a sudden Tempest is thy Sail,   770 Horace 1, 14   23
Nor, change thy Course with ev'ry sudden Gust: 771 Horace 1, 14   54
Then sudden draws it back again,   776 Mullinix Tim   105
And sudden spreads a numerous Offspring round; 792 St. Pat's Well   62
Were down the sudden Current born;   811 Bro Protestant   4

SUDDENLY

Her Soul was suddenly endu'd   693 Cadenus Vaness   206

SUDS

And leaves my Lady in the Suds.   905 Death Daphne   100

SUE

Big like Bess, and small like Sue;   936 Riddle 24   D 28

SUEDE

When a holy black Suede, the Son of Bob,   147 Windsor Proph   1

SUES

He sues for Pardon, and repents too late.   195 Author Himself   52
Most humbly sues for Pardon,   1005 Sheridan's Sub   7

SUFF'RERS

Three Suff'rers in a ruin'd Cause,   883 Rev Market-Hill   6

SUFF'RINGS

Who gladly would your Suff'rings share;   766 Stel B-day '26   84
Where are thy Services and Suff'rings?   884 Rev Market-Hill   32

SUFFER

Dear Will, I suffer this for Peace;   220 A Quiet Life   14
Or suffer Envy to conceal   243 Horace 4, 9   5
Can suffer Want, and not repine.   243 Horace 4, 9   20
We suffer sore against his Will;   485 Libel on D- D-   156
Than suffer Men of Parts to rise: 503 Doctor Delaney   92
From Phoebus Rays they suffer Pain,   731 Stella, Poems   110

SUFFER'D

Just so the Mighty Nile has suffer'd in it's Fame, 20 Ode Athenian 145
Dick suffer'd for his Peace and Credit,   220 A Quiet Life   37
"That Church and State had suffer'd more   549 Life of Swift   150

SUFFERERS   SEE FELLOW-SUFFERERS

SUFFERS

Immortal Joy, that suffers no Allay from Fears, 6 Ode to King   2
And suffers numberless Fatigues.   174 Horace 1, 7   96
She suffers hourly more than me,   726 To Stella   104

SUFFICE

'Twill not suffice, it was a Joke.   217 To Mr. Delany   66

SUFFICIENT

Sufficient it were, one would think, in your mad rant, 1026 Sheri Circles 9

SUFFOLK

As bad as Suffolk cheese.   429 Beau's Reply   16
Kind Lady Suffolk in the Spleen,   559 Death of Swift   179

SUFFRAGAN

Has got on the Bench many <Bishops> suffragan: 803 Irish Bishops   14

SUGAR

Well roasted, with Sugar and Wine in a Cup, 953 Oranges   3

SUIT

Names that would best their Natures suit: 83 Salamander   8
And wou'd not only grant his Suit.   378 Apology Lady C   87
And this will suit Men of more Money than Wit. 389 Order of Bath   8
What Lining best the Silk will suit;   416 Woman's Mind   30
Their Tales wou'd always justly suit   512 Answer Fable   3
"Ill suit with those profess'd of late: 549 Life of Swift   147
That best ye regal Nature suit,   659 On Poetry   D 410

```
SUIT            (CONTINUED)                                PAGE    TITLE        LINE
    Suit your Words to your Musick well,    . . . . . .    956 Cantata
    Suit your Words to your Musick well,    . . . . . .    956 Cantata
    Suit your Words to your Musick well,    . . . . . .    956 Cantata
SUITABLE
    To make you suitable Returns;           . . . . . . . .  887 Panegyr Dean      30
SUITED
    Suited to all Christian Fokes:          . . . . . . . .  523 Betty Grizette     18
    So suited to your State, and Years!     . . . . . . .    888 Panegyr Dean       50
SUITOR
    I now become your humble Suitor,        . . . . . . .    891 Panegyr Dean      129
SUITS
    These pad on wit's high road, and suits maintain  . . .   45 To Congreve        67
    How just it suits with human Kind.      . . . . . . .    603 Beasts Confess     74
    Whene'er it suits her private ends;     . . . . . . .    761 Bec's B-Day        32
SULLEN
    Our Wives they grow sullen              . . . . . . . . .  237 Excellent Song    14
SULPHUR
    Surrounded with Jewels of Sulphur and Nitre.      . . .   803 Irish Bishops      6
    (With Flow'r of Sulphur powder'd well,  . . . . . . .    903 Death Daphne       25
SULTAN
    Of Guardian Eunuchs to the Sultan Dames,          . . . .  532 To Mr. Gay        20
SULTAN'S
    Where once their Sultan's Horse hath trod,        . . . .  324 Pethox           40
SUM
    In sum, a glitt'ring voice, a painted name,  . . . . . .   54 Temple Ill       101
    The Sum of all their senseless Prate,   . . . . . . .    449 Modern Lady       141
    By his own Credit to advance the Sum;   . . . . . . .    533 To Mr. Gay         72
    The Sum of what each Lawyer said;       . . . . . . .    713 Cadenus Vaness    851
    But I see the Sum Total,    . . . . . . . . .            1015 Swift to Sheri     39
SUMM'D
    One Argument she summ'd up all in,      . . . . . . .    224 Prog of Love       67
SUMMARY
    She'd have a summary Proceeding.        . . . . . . . .   713 Cadenus Vaness    849
SUMMER
    Return'd a finish'd spark this summer'down,       . . .    47 To Congreve      119
    In Summer round the Park to ride,       . . . . . . .    173 Horace 1, 7        85
    In Summer, on my verdant Lap:           . . . . . . .    410 Dial Rich Marb     86
    In Summer had she walkt the Town,       . . . . . . .    584 Strephon Chloe     21
    'Till Summer Show'rs and Ev'ning Dew,   . . . . . . .    759 Receipt Youth      11
    In Summer is very pleasant and cool.    . . . . . . .    941 Letter             20
SUMMER'S
    Down falls the summer's pride, and sadly shews  . . . .   55 Temple Ill        123
    Just Fifteen, coming Summer's Grass:    . . . . . . .    760 Receipt Youth      40
SUMMERS
    And too warm summers bring:             . . . . . . . . .   37 Ode Sancroft     100
SUMMIT
    Where, on the Summit Fortune stands:    . . . . . . .    413 Desire Possess     41
    The Heat that makes the Summit glow,    . . . . . . .    731 Stella, Poems     107
SUMMON'D
    For which he summon'd you to Dine.      . . . . . . .    481 Libel on D- D-     32
SUMMONING
    This summoning of blackguard boys?      . . . . . . . .   487 Irish-Club        10
SUMMONS
    The Doctor now obeys the Summons,       . . . . . . .    173 Horace 1, 7        73
SUN    SEE WINTER-SUN,RISING-SUN
    Just as the Sun puts out a Fire;        . . . . . . .      9 Ode to King      114
    When the Bright Sun of Peace began to shine,      . . .   16 Ode Athenian      24
    Justling some thousand years till ripen'd by the Sun,  .  20 Ode Athenian     129
    Or from the Sun, or from the Air, or from the Earth,   .  31 Ode to Temple    170
    Who, like hard masters, taught the Sun  . . . . . .       36 Ode Sancroft      67
    Why should the Sun, alas, be proud      . . . . . . .     41 Ode Sancroft     215
    Turns up old objects to the soul her sun;  . . . . . .    51 Temple Ill        10
    Till the blest sun to give kind dawn of grace     . . .   52 Temple Ill        25
    Till the Sun clears the Air; and then   . . . . . . .     84 Salamander        35
    The Sun has rose, and gone to Bed,      . . . . . . .     98 Elegy Patrige     11
    With rising or with setting Sun:        . . . . . . .    270 Apollo's Edict  D 13
    But when the Sun goes to the Deep,      . . . . . . .    280 Journal           45
    Be a New Sun, and a New Moon.           . . . . . . .    362 Grace's Answer    52
    By the horned Sun, he sure meant <Cuckold>,       . . .  373 Letter D. S-y     61
    The scorching Sun, or chilling Air;     . . . . . . .    379 Apology Lady C   122
    "The cooler Air, and dazzling Sun;      . . . . . . .    380 Apology Lady C   142
    And Manly Virtue, like the Sun,         . . . . . . .    387 Manly Virtue     117
    Rip'ning, and kindling like the Sun.    . . . . . . .    391 Young's Satire    26
    Then, why these quarrels to the sun,    . . . . . . .    432 Answer Paulus      3
    Did Paulus e'er the sun forget?         . . . . . . .    432 Answer Paulus      6
    The sun, you say, his face has kist:    . . . . . . .    432 Answer Paulus      9
    At which the Sun should hide his Face.  . . . . . . .    595 Cassinus Peter    70
    As long as Sun and Moon endure.         . . . . . . .    655 On Poetry        436
    My Emblem, the laborious sun,           . . . . . . .    675 Curate's Compl    13
    To-morrow, ere the setting Sun,         . . . . . . .    694 Cadenus Vaness   254
    Breaks like the Sun behind a Cloud,     . . . . . . .    726 To Stella         82
    Not one Jot better looks the Sun        . . . . . . .    786 Clad in Brown      9
SUN-BEAMS
    Like sun-beams shot at too far distance from a glass;  .   35 Ode Sancroft      24
SUN-SHINE
    With Sun-shine, rain, and hail, and snow.         . . .  621 Scandal Poem 1   130
    With Sun-shine, Rain, and Hail, or Snow.          . . .  627 Scandal Poem 2   124
    You sat and lows'd him all the Sun-shine Day.     . . .  882 Pastoral Dial     34
SUN'S
    Like the sun's scatter'd beams which loosely pass,  . .   45 To Congreve        63
```

```
SUN'S              (CONTINUED)                              PAGE    TITLE        LINE
    O'er the sun's face, and from his heat proceeds,  . . .   45 To Congreve        70
    So the Sun's Heat, with different Powers,      . . . .   731 Stella, Poems      119
SUNDAY
    And at the Rose on Sunday,  . . . . . . . . . . .        426 Five Ladies         42
    Both Solemnly put, in this hole on a Sunday,  . . . .    431 Dicky Dolly         23
    Was that, last Sunday in the Ring?  . . . . . . .        699 Cadenus Vaness     385
SUNDAY'S
    And that I may have a Share in next Sunday's             73 Mrs Harris Pet       71
        Collection:
SUNDAYS
    On Sundays to be fine in,  . . . . . . . . . .           75 Game Traffick        22
    On Sundays, after Ev'ning Prayer.  . . . . . . .        116 Bauc & Phil 2       169
SUNDER
    Those Splitters of Parsons in sunder shou'd burst?  . .  805 Irish Bishops       40
<SUNDERLAND>
    <Sunderland>, <Orford>, <Boyl>, and <Richmond's> Grace  165 Toland's Invit      33
<SUNDERLAND'S>
    <Sunderland's> run out of his Wits,  . . . . . . .      168 Peace Dunkirk       11
SUNG    SEE OUT-SUNG
    And must be sung, like Argus, into ease                   8 Ode to King         76
    And Poets their own Verses sung,  . . . . . . . .        79 Vanbrug House        2
    And Poets their own Verses Sung,  . . . . . . . .       106 V's House            2
    Be sung ten hundred thousand times.  . . . . . .        467 Birthday Song      222
    Or whom you once sung up, sing down.  . . . . . .       468 Birthday Song      260
    By ev'ry size of Poets sung:  . . . . . . . . .         584 Strephon Chloe       2
    And Phoebus sung th' Epithalamium.  . . . . . .         586 Strephon Chloe      62
    Tis sung; wherever Celia treads,  . . . . . . .         621 Scandal Poem 1     139
    Tis sung. But we know better things.  . . . . .         621 Scandal Poem 1     142
    'Tis sung, where-ever Celia treads,  . . . . . .        627 Scandal Poem 2     143
    'Tis sung, but we know better Things.  . . . . .        627 Scandal Poem 2     146
    Tis sung Prometheus forming Man                         659 On Poetry      D 410
    And Stella will be sung, while I  . . . . . . .         741 Stel B-day 22       33
    No Poet ever sweetly sung,  . . . . . . . . . .         757 Stel B-day '24      19
    To have them sung, they may be said.  . . . . .         757 Stel B-day '24      34
    Secure from Satyrs sat and sung.  . . . . . . .         848 Old Thorn            8
    Of Brazen Knight they vainly sung:  . . . . . .         876 To Dean Swift       14
    And thence, as fam'd John Bunyan sung,  . . . . .       983 Sher, A Goose        6
SUNK
    . . . Lord! I thought I should have sunk outright:  . .   69 Mrs Harris Pet      13
    By their own Weight sunk to the Bottom;  . . . . .      158 Fable of Midas      79
    Who, by Disgraces or ill Fortune sunk,  . . . . .       163 Toland's Invit      17
    Nor puff'd by Pride, nor sunk by Spleen.  . . . .       199 Horace 2, 6     D
    Deep sunk in Plenty, and Delight,  . . . . . . .        231 Prog of Poetry      23
    His Credit sunk, his Money spent,  . . . . . . .        252 Bubble              47
    Ten thousand sunk by leaping in.  . . . . . . . .       254 Bubble             108
    Since cruel Fate hath sunk our Justice Boat;  . . .     284 Elegy Boat           2
    He sunk beneath the cumbrous Weight:  . . . . . .       413 Desire Possess      52
    Half sunk beneath his brief and bag,  . . . . . .       434 Answer Paulus       75
    His Fancy sunk, his Muse a Jade.  . . . . . . . .       556 Death of Swift     102
    Sunk down her Nose, or seam'd her Face?  . . . . .      595 Cassinus Peter      49
    No Wonder how his Fortune sunk,  . . . . . . . .        607 Beasts Confess     195
    Your Secret kept, your Poem sunk,  . . . . . . .        644 On Poetry          143
    He sunk at length to wasting Age a Prey,  . . . .       669 Epig Carthy 13  D   3
    Thy credit sunk, thy money spent,  . . . . . . .        676 Parson's Case       10
    I'd rather the Bawn were sunk under Ground.  . . .      868 Grand Question      46
    Sunk over head and ears in matter,  . . . . . . .       900 Dean's Reasons      59
SUNNY
    His Wig was made of sunny Rays,  . . . . . . . .        597 Problem Solved       7
    Or gilding in a sunny Morn  . . . . . . . . . .         896 Panegyr Dean       305
SUP
    He call'd for Drink, you saw him Sup  . . . . .         156 Fable of Midas       7
    We sup and we dine,  . . . . . . . . . . . . .          244 Irish-Feast          6
    "It must be One before we Sup.'  . . . . . . . .        451 Modern Lady        213
    Safely glad to sup their Porridge,  . . . . . .         574 Helter Skelter      54
    No Cellar where on Tick to sup;  . . . . . . . .        581 Young Nymph          6
    They may discharge it ev'ry Sup;  . . . . . . .         587 Strephon Chloe     120
    She sent for Company to sup, She sends  . . . . .       747 Stel Distress       46
    She sent for Company to sup;  . . . . . . . . .         751 Stel Wood-Park      62
    They'll make a sweet Bishop when Gentlefolks sup.  . .  953 Oranges              4
SUP'D
    He Din'd and Sup'd at Charge of other Folk,  . . .      234 Elegy on Demar      10
SUPERFICIAL
    Not for his superficial powers  . . . . . . . .         432 Answer Paulus       13
SUPERFLUOUS
    Remov'd the tough superfluous Flesh,  . . . . . .       326 Pethox              78
    All the Superfluous Whims relate,  . . . . . . .        451 Modern Lady        224
SUPERIOR
    In vain; for a superior Force  . . . . . . . .          93 Bauc & Phil 1      101
    In vain; for a Superior Force  . . . . . . . . .       113 Bauc & Phil 2       61
    A virgin of superior mind,  . . . . . . . . . .        177 To Lord Harley      34
    A Mortal of superior kind.  . . . . . . . . . .        179 To Lord Harley      80
    The Force of thy superior Voice  . . . . . . . .       340 Arch-Bish Dub       27
    A Fund of such Superior Merit,  . . . . . . . .        478 Epist on Epist      98
    Their Foes superior by an Inch.  . . . . . . . .       651 On Poetry          336
    With Gifts superior to the Crowd,  . . . . . . .       700 Cadenus Vaness     445
    His Genius of superior Kind;  . . . . . . . . .        788 Dick's Variety      14
    Not by thy Valour, but superior Guile:  . . . . .      791 St. Pat's Well      26
    How your superior Learning shines  . . . . . . .       888 Panegyr Dean        63
    Superior none on Earth I find;  . . . . . . . .        917 Riddle 3             3
```

	PAGE	TITLE	LINE

SUPERIORS
Admitted private, when Superiors wait: . . . . — 194 Author Himself — 30
You mistake; for a Slave, who will coax his superiors, . — 817 Yahoo's — 68

SUPERNACULUM
Is a poor Supernaculum; . . . . — 1015 Swift to Sheri — 56

SUPINE
Nor after your Vittels ly sleeping supine . . . . . — 1017 Swift Ans Sher — 16

SUPPER
Till Supper comes, and after that, ... — 280 Journal — 53
And Supper gobbled up in haste, ... — 453 Modern Lady — 277
A Supper worthy of her self, ... — 747 Stel Distress — 51
A Supper worthy of her self, ... — 751 Stel Wood-Park — 67

SUPPLE
Like supple Patriots of the modern Sort, ... — 771 Horace 1, 14 — 55

SUPPLIANT
Your now subdu'd and suppliant Slave . . . . — 1005 Sheridan's Sub — 6

SUPPLICATE
And prostrate, supplicate pour ma vie. . . . . . . — 1005 Sheridan's Sub — 12

SUPPLIES
With Cunning that Defect supplies, ... — 107 V's House — 57
'Tis true, a Glass will bring supplies . . . . . . — 367 Answer Delaney — 45
Which only Winter's Rain supplies. . . . . — 478 Epist on Epist — 90
All Fortitude of Mind supplies: . . . . — 561 Death of Swift — 214
If Decency brings no Supplies, ... — 591 Strephon Chloe — 225
My sinking Spirits now supplies . . . . — 727 To Stella — 109
Once more the <Dean> supplies their Place. . . . . — 757 Stel B-day '24 — 14
The famish't Cow her Want supplies; . . . . — 759 Receipt Youth — 14
And all her bustling but supplies . . . . — 761 Bec's B-Day — 27

SUPPLY
And Geese their silver Plumes supply. . . . . . . — 239 Run Bankers — 24
The Dean must with his Quilt supply, ... — 283 Journal — 121
There to supply old Charon's leaky Wherry: . . . . — 285 Elegy Boat — 24
To let our company supply their places, ... — 307 Billet Players — 7
Will half supply a Gay and Pope, ... — 313 To Ford — 74
Can ready Compliments supply . . . . — 416 Woman's Mind — 13
What Income can your Wants supply? . . . . — 478 Epist on Epist — 96
Evermore thy Tongue supply. . . . . — 523 Betty Grizette — 14
No Loss more easy to supply. . . . . — 562 Death of Swift — 244
The Bolsters that supply her Hips. . . . . — 582 Young Nymph — 28
For Bec, a new supply of cares, ... — 753 Gift for Bec — 2
Where each Supply of Dead, renews . . . . — 923 Riddle 7 — 55

SUPPLY'D
If you would have us well supply'd, ... — 229 Prog of Beauty — 119
The Master's pressing Wants must be supply'd; . . . — 533 To Mr. Gay — 70
Blackmore alone his Place supply'd: . . . . — 652 On Poetry — 372
And, had it not been still supply'd, ... — 765 Stel B-day '26 — 57

SUPPLYES
But these alas, are poor Supplyes . . . . — 229 Prog of Beauty — 115
For thunder still his arm supplyes, ... — 461 Birthday Song — 41
And ev'ry Virtue now supplyes . . . . — 735 Stel B-day '20 — 21

SUPPLYING
Supplying those defects by dress . . . . — 879 Robbin & Harry — 53

SUPPORT
Harley, the Nation's great Support, ... — 170 Horace 1, 7 — 1
And now, the publick Int'rest to support, ... — 194 Author Himself — 27
Bare Innocence is no Support, ... — 413 Censure — 5
But Sr we must support the Crown. . . . . — 422 Ireld — 40
Or like a Heel-piece to support . . . . — 645 On Poetry — 171
From Party-Merit seek Support; . . . . — 646 On Poetry — 185
By Charity a mean Support, ... — 667 Epig Carthy 6 — D 2
Support a few remaining Days: . . . . — 764 Stel B-day '26 — 12
Whose able Heads support the Weight, ... — 781 Mullinix Tim — 257
And by their Sweat procure a mean Support; . . . . — 793 St. Pat's Well — 76
Precedence, and support your Grandeur: . . . . . — 888 Panegyr Dean — 46
Vow'd, he no longer could support . . . . — 903 Death Daphne — 11

SUPPORTED
Supported high on Wings of Paper; . . . . — 231 Prog of Poetry — 44
Is best supported by Opinion; . . . . — 590 Strephon Chloe — 224

SUPPORTING
And then supporting with your Store, ... — 764 Stel B-day '26 — 39
Supporting my chops, ... — 852 Lady's Lament — 28
Supporting half the British Crown; . . . . — 919 Riddle 5 — 6

SUPPORTS
With Patience, which all Ills supports, ... — 325 Pethox — 63
Supports their Minds with heav'nly Food. . . . . . — 605 Beasts Confess — 124

SUPPOS'D
That the Captain suppos'd he was Curate to Jenny.) . — 872 Grand Question — 152

SUPPOSE
Suppose the truth, like all the world, their own; . . — 37 Ode Sancroft — 80
Suppose then Atlas ne'er so wise, ... — 160 Atlas — 19
Suppose him, now, a Dean compleat, ... — 174 Horace 1, 7 — 97
Suppose him gone through all Vexations, ... — 174 Horace 1, 7 — 101
What! I suppose now Stocks are high, ... — 175 Horace 1, 7 — 127
Nor indiscreetly to suppose . . . . — 218 To Mr. Delany — 101
Suppose all Partyes now agreed, ... — 222 Prog of Love — 21
Must we suppose she has in view, ... — 433 Answer Paulus — 33
Suppose my Lord and you alone; . . . . — 480 Libel on D- D- — 13
Suppose you had them all trepann'd . . . . — 505 Doctor Delaney — 151
Suppose your Lord a trusty Servant send, ... — 534 To Mr. Gay — 85
Suppose your Friend and You, were Equal, ... — 546 Life of Swift — 32
Let me suppose, two special Friends, ... — 546 Life of Swift — 52

	PAGE	TITLE	LINE
SUPPOSE (CONTINUED)			
Let me suppose the Case my own.	547	Life of Swift	67
Some high-flown Pamphlets, I suppose---:	550	Life of Swift	183
Suppose me dead; and then suppose	565	Death of Swift	299
Suppose me dead; and then suppose	565	Death of Swift	299
And, though contriv'd, we may suppose	589	Strephon Chloe	183
Suppose Cadenus flourish'd then,	708	Cadenus Vaness	694
Suppose the Question not your own:	724	To Stella	38
Let me suppose thee for a Ship a-while,	770	Horace 1, 14	7
Thus Tim, Philosophers suppose,	777	Mullinix Tim	133
I suppose meaning mine.)	854	Lady's Lament	104
First, let me suppose I make it a Malt-House:	867	Grand Question	7
Never more will I suppose	908	Daphne	69
Suppose I call'd you goose, it is hard	983	Sher, A Goose	9
SUPPOSING			
Supposing thou hast Tick with Hunter)	182	Horace 2, 1	78
Supposing now you Song is done,	469	Birthday Song	275
"Supposing these Reflections just;	549	Life of Swift	158
SUPREME			
For, Beauty, like supreme Dominion,	590	Strephon Chloe	223
Whoe'er arrives at Pow'r supreme,	592	Strephon Chloe	264
Let Melancholy rule supreme,	724	To Stella	19
Condemn'd by Fate's supreme Decree,	849	Old Thorn	47
SUR-TOUT			
We'll soundly drench your frize Sur-tout,	622	Scandal Poem 1	176
SURE			
Sure there's some Wondrous Joy in Doing Good;	6	Ode to King	1
'Twas sure this Basilisk sent Temple thence,	30	Ode to Temple	124
For, sure, we want some guide from Heav'n to show	39	Ode Sancroft	156
Follow the model close, for so I'm sure they should,	40	Ode Sancroft	183
I'm sure I found them other kind of things	46	To Congreve	91
"Be this thy sure defence, thy brazen wall,	55	Temple Ill	141
For sure (thought He) it can't be less.	63	Discovery	32
I'm sure, 'twas I that smelt the <Stink>.	67	Problem	54
. . .I'm sure I never thought you so;	72	Mrs Harris Pet	59
Sure that must be a Salamander.	84	Salamander	46
You may be sure, so strange a Sight	92	Bauc & Phil 1	79
(By sure Prognosticks) when to dread a Show'r:	136	City Shower	2
I'm sure I never shou'd neglect--	173	Horace 1, 7	69
If you'll be sure to come at Four.	173	Horace 1, 7	72
Why sure you won't appear in Town,	175	Horace 1, 7	123
Next, faithful Silence hath a sure Reward:	210	Earl of Oxford	15
For, sure, by Wit is onely meant	215	To Mr. Delany	17
For sure if this be Luna's Fate,	229	Prog of Beauty	105
Sure such Intelligence between	301	Horrid Plot	73
Be sure conceal the Time and Place,	311	To Ford	8
You, happy Folks, are sure to meet	315	To Ford	105
But sure if nothing else must pass,	346	Prometheus	67
For, as sure as a Gun they will give up the Ghost	351	Wood Insect	23
I'm sure a Man of your fine Sense	361	Grace's Answer	21
I'm sure Old <Jour--> you'd not stand by it;	372	Letter D. S-y	20
As you Dr. <Smedley> are, being sure	372	Letter D. S-y	33
By the horned Sun, he sure meant <Cuckold>,	373	Letter D. S-y	61
Snarlerus next, I'm sure has need	373	Letter D. S-y	68
I'm sure he call'd me by my Name;	376	Apology Lady C	46
She gets a Cold as sure as Death;	417	Woman's Mind	45
'My Dear, for sure if I had known	448	Modern Lady	103
And sure no Christian Poet breathing	461	Birthday Song	25
Will sure the Pretendr and Popery bring in.	522	St. Cecilia's	8
"And, sure he must be deeply learn'd---!	547	Life of Swift	76
"He shews, as sure as God's in Gloc'ster,	564	Death of Swift	293
And Hell to be sure is at Paris or Rome,	576	Place Damn'd	17
Whose Favour she is sure to find,	583	Young Nymph	55
And, last to make the Matter sure,	586	Strephon Chloe	63
But, sure a Tell-tale out of School	592	Strephon Chloe	277
Be sure at Will's the following Day,	644	On Poetry	
But then, I'm sure, friend Charles, you want the spur.	671	Epig Carthy 23	D 2
But, sure the Dean deserves a sharp Rebuke	678	Dean and Duke	3
Sure, you are not asham'd to stoop;	699	Cadenus Vaness	401
But, sure, she never talk'd so well.	710	Cadenus Vaness	749
Grant this the Case, yet sure 'tis hard,	764	Stel B-day '26	25
But this I am sure, the Most Rev'rend old Dragon,	803	Irish Bishops	13
The gold she was pull'd down, of that I'm very sure,	840	Ballad	D 3
Sure never did man see	851	Lady's Lament	1
The Captain, I'm sure, will always come here;	868	Grand Question	32
Of this, to be sure, Sir Arthur has Warning,	869	Grand Question	69
Next Day, to be sure, the Captain will come,	870	Grand Question	87
(For sure, I had dizen'd you out like a Queen:)	870	Grand Question	102
I'm sure he'll be proud of the Honour you do us;	871	Grand Question	118
Lord! Madam! your Ladyship sure is in jest;	871	Grand Question	124
Dear Madam, be sure he's a fine spoken Man,	872	Grand Question	139
Cry'd, Huzzy, why sure the Wench is gone mad:	873	Grand Question	184
And sure, as monument of brass,	876	To Dean Swift	11
And, sure as they're alive, at Night;	891	Panegyr Dean	139
And ev'ry Guest be sure to ply:	897	Panegyr Dean	338
Why sure, Mr. Poet, your head got a jar	976	Dean to Sherid	27
But thanks to the lady: I'm sure she's too good to ye;	976	Dean to Sherid	38
I'm sure you cackle like the sex.	983	Sher, A Goose	18
I am sure such Words does not become a Man of your Cloth,	985	Mary to Sher	3
Which, and I am sure I have been his Servant . . .	985	Mary to Sher	13

		PAGE	TITLE		LINE
SURE	(CONTINUED)				
You're so retrograde, sure you were born under Cancer:	.	1019	To Sheridan		3
Or, else be sure, your Broad-cloath Breeches,	. .	1021	Nim-Dan-Dean 1	D	17
For, as for honest John, tho' I'm not sure on't,	. . .	1022	Nim-Dan-Dean 2	D	5
. . .and you'll believe me as sure as a gun, and own it;	.	1023	Nim-Dan-Dean 2	D	15
And those to be sure, stuck together like Glew, sick.	.	1029	Dr. Helsham		25
SURELY					
(But, surely such whom God did never for his People chuse)		8	Ode to King		86
And surely Writes with slight of Hand	. . . . . .	373	Letter D. S-y		48
Me, surely me, you ought to spare,	. . . . . .	766	Stel B-day '26		83
Cry'd, Madam, why surely my Master's possest;	. . .	868	Grand Question		44
SURER					
Surer ways to be despis'd:	. . . .	906	Daphne		6
SUREST					
Of Innocence, the surest Guard,	. . . .	386	Manly Virtue		73
Point out the surest Men to rise,	. . . .	502	Doctor Delaney		84
"In surest way to be preferr'd---;	. . . .	549	Life of Swift		165
SURFACE					
Yet He that on the Surface lyes	. . . .	256	Bubble		142
If haply on the liquid surface float,	. . . . . .	672	Epig Carthy 24	D	13
SURGEON					
For now the Surgeon must be paid;	. . . .	225	Prog of Love		92
SURGES					
Beware, and when you hear the Surges roar,	. . . .	772	Horace 1, 14		61
SURLY					
And our good Brethren of the Surly Sect	. . . .	18	Ode Athenian		81
This Surly, Slipp'ry God, when He design'd	. . . .	22	Ode Athenian		197
One surly Clown lookt out, and said,	. . . .	91	Bauc & Phil 1		37
Another in a surly Fit,	. . . .	200	Horace 2, 6		35
Said surly Peter, Magus, prithee	. . . .	821	Dr. Rundle		47
And, then in surly Mode come here	. . . .	884	Rev Market-Hill		37
SURMOUNT					
There to surmount what bears me up, and sing	. . . .	44	To Congreve		37
SURPASS					
When that subtle Companion, in hopes to surpass us,	. .	265	Apollo		80
SURPLICE					
I'll give thee Surplice, Verge and Stall,	. . . .	361	Grace's Answer		7
SURPRISE					
That gives Surprise, and this Delight:	. . . . .	215	To Mr. Delany		24
Morgan! Would it not surprise one?	. . . .	838	Legion Club		205
SURPRISES					
That what surprises us can only please:	. . . . . .	20	Ode Athenian		141
SURPRIZ'D					
Was much surpriz'd to see a Crow	. . . .	127	Little House		27
And, how agreeably surpriz'd	. . . .	643	On Poetry		111
Surpriz'd with ev'ry day a hot meal	. . . . . .	745	Stel Distress		5
Dear Tom, I'm surpriz'd that your verse did not jingle;	.	980	Tho: Sheridan		1
SURPRIZE					
Philemon was in great Surprize,	. . . .	116	Bauc & Phil 2		145
Shame, Disappointment, Guilt, Surprize.	. . . . . .	706	Cadenus Vaness		625
Surprize him with a Pint of Stout,	. . . .	728	Stella, Poems		32
Tim with surprize and pleasure staring,	. . . . . .	783	Tim and Fables		13
When they surprize me at my Book!	. . . .	891	Panegyr Dean		138
I feel not the least Love Surprize,	. . . .	932	Riddle 19	D	3
The quickest Ship I can surprize,	. . . .	934	Riddle 21	D	14
Shall read with Envy and Surprize,	. . . . . .	994	On Picture		32
SURPRIZING					
Which made it more surprizing how	. . . .	376	Apology Lady C		17
My dearest Life it is surprizing,	. . . .	860	Lady Acheson		31
SURRENDER					
They must surrender at Discretion:	. . . .	885	Rev Market-Hill		89
SURROUNDED					
Surrounded with companions, fit	. . . .	435	Answer Paulus		119
Surrounded with her Noisy Clans	. . . .	448	Modern Lady		118
Surrounded with a Hundred Stinks,	. . . .	583	Young Nymph		48
Surrounded with Jewels of Sulphur and Nitre.	. . .	803	Irish Bishops		6
SURTOUT					
We'll soundly souce your Frize Surtout.	. . . . .	627	Scandal Poem 2		134
SURVEY					
Henceforth expect a different survey,	. . . .	283	Journal		127
But let me now a while survey	. . . .	448	Modern Lady		116
Stole in, and took a strict Survey,	. . . .	526	Lady's Dres Rm		7
Thus finishing his grand Survey,	. . . .	529	Lady's Dres Rm		115
SURVIVE					
Survive in thee, and make the Proverb good	. . . . .	826	Noisy Tom		18
SURVIVING					
The Limb surviving, you may swear,	. . . .	366	Answer Delaney		13
SUSAN					
Brisk Susan whips her Linen from the Rope,	. . . .	137	City Shower		17
Whilst Mrs. Susan comb'd her Head:	. . . . . .	698	Cadenus Vaness		373
SUSPECT					
Cadenus, who cou'd ne'er suspect	. . . .	709	Cadenus Vaness		726
They shrewdly suspect it is all but a bite.	. . . .	818	Archbi Cashel		4
I much suspect you mean the latter, ah Sly-boot!	.	1003	Dan J's Reply		6
SUSPECTED					
So I went to the Party suspected,...	. . . . .	71	Mrs Harris Pet		34
Suspected for the Love he bore	. . . .	375	Apology Lady C		15
SUSPECTING					
Not once suspecting, Jove would Smoak,	. . . . .	107	V's House		60
Wisdom's above suspecting Wiles:	. . . .	692	Cadenus Vaness		198

	PAGE	TITLE	LINE
SUSPENCE			
Dame Floyd looks out in grave Suspence	75	Game Traffick	13
Doom'd ever in Suspence to dwell,	113	Bauc & Phil 2	63
Are tortur'd with Suspence and Fear.	561	Death of Swift	220
SUSPEND			
Dar'd to suspend her unregarded aid;	43	To Congreve	4
Should heaven suspend to act but for a day;	53	Temple Ill	64
Suspend a while your vain ambitious Hopes,	162	Toland's Invit	5
But, I beg, suspend a While,	631	Epistle Lady	49
SUSPENDED			
Suspended every Horror of the Place,	9	Ode to King	95
There whole herds suspended lie	35	Ode Sancroft	35
Suspended for a while in Air.	258	Bubble	188
Your Virtues, all suspended, wait	730	Stella, Poems	95
"When thou, suspended high in Air,	851	Old Thorn	85
SUSPENDS			
A pride that well suspends poor mortals fate,	45	To Congreve	45
SUSPENSE			
Doom'd ever in suspense to dwell,	93	Bauc & Phil 1	103
SUSPICION			
When you have not the least Suspicion,	398	Earl of P-b-w	29
For talking may beget Suspicion:	644	On Poetry	124
To live in fear, suspicion, variance,	899	Dean's Reasons	17
SUSPICIOUS			
Hence that wild suspicious Peep,	800	Traulus 2	35
SUSTAIN'D			
That all the Loss your Purse sustain'd	496	Panegyr Swift	88
SUTLER			
Like the soldier from the Sutler;	574	Helter Skelter	34
SWAGGER			
First; how to swagger in a Court;	348	Whitshed Motto	12
I'll Sputter, Swagger, Curse and Rail,	776	Mullinix Tim	85
And swagger while the Coast is clear:	824	Printer Newgat	7
How they swagger from their Garrison.	837	Legion Club	182
Nay, hector and swagger, you'll still find me stanch,	979	Dean to Tho: S	13
SWAIN			
That Swain Endymion is not sound,	228	Prog of Beauty	95
The Swain is rich, the Nymph is fair;	290	Prog Marriage	28
The Swain is old, the Nymph Coquette.	290	Prog Marriage	30
While she engrosseth ev'ry Swain,	585	Strephon Chloe	31
How did the humbled Swain detest	586	Strephon Chloe	91
The Swain at last, with Grief opprest,	595	Cassinus Peter	39
She loves a more deserving Swain.	595	Cassinus Peter	66
That ev'ry rich and lordly Swain	693	Cadenus Vaness	232
Whether the Nymph, to please her Swain,	712	Cadenus Vaness	820
(That either Nymph might have her Swain,)	722	Stel B-Day '18	17
A Nymph and Swain, Sheelah and Dermot hight,	880	Pastoral Dial	1
The soft Endearments of the Nymph and Swain.	880	Pastoral Dial	8
She doubted not to win the Swain.	905	Death Daphne	70
Let the happy Swain rejoice,	933	Riddle 20	D 15
SWAINS			
Till Swains unwholsome spoyld the Trade,	225	Prog of Love	91
Thus by the Nymphs and Swains ador'd,	694	Cadenus Vaness	246
Her Virtues fewer Swains admir'd:	700	Cadenus Vaness	441
"How she was cheated by the Swains:	713	Cadenus Vaness	859
See, at her Levee crowding Swains	735	Stel B-day '20	23
With Omens oft I strove to warn thy Swains,	792	St. Pat's Well	43
Among our harmless Northern Swains;	896	Panegyr Dean	300
And lowing Herds, and piping Swains,	934	Riddle 21	D 9
SWALL'WING			
The great ones swall'wing up the small	253	Bubble	66
SWALLOW			
Which greedily they swallow down,	27	Ode to Temple	48
And you like a Booby, the Bubble can swallow;	265	Apollo	87
To swallow Will. Wood either bruis'd or alive.	351	Wood Insect	14
And <Wood's> ditto Pills do Swallow,	372	Letter D. S-y	30
Sit still, and swallow down your Spittle.	644	On Poetry	122
I swallow with pleasure.	853	Lady's Lament	66
SWALLOW'D			
And swallow'd them at last, or flung them down.	40	Ode Sancroft	197
Death's sting is swallow'd up in victory at last,	40	Ode Sancroft	201
An Ass hath swallow'd up the Moon,	253	Bubble	79
Earth must have been in Chaos swallow'd.	346	Prometheus	46
Or swallow'd alive, or skilfully bruis'd.	351	Wood Insect	12
Oft' swallow'd down a stronger Potion,	495	Panegyr Swift	61
The Lad lay swallow'd up in Spleen;	594	Cassinus Peter	10
Are swallow'd o'er a Dish of Tea;	642	On Poetry	68
SWAN			
He was transform'd into a Swan,	666	Epig Carthy 1	D 2
SWANS			
(For all the Muses Geese are Swans)	80	Vanbrug House	50
And you know all my geese are swans:	983	Sher, A Goose	12
Swans sing when dying, geese when blind.	983	Sher, A Goose	14
SWARM			
How the physicians swarm to shew their mortal skill,	42	Ode Sancroft	253
The Bees are gather'd to a Swarm:	345	Prometheus	26
Still swarm and buzz about his Nose?	798	Traulus 1	87
Which made our Swarm of Sects determine	813	Bro Protestant	43
To call a Swarm of Lice his Brethren?	813	Bro Protestant	48
SWARMS			
Shall (I foresee it) soon with Gothick Swarms come fort	25	Ode Athenian	298

```
SWARMS          (CONTINUED)                              PAGE   TITLE          LINE
    Than swarms of gnats, that wanton in a ray  . . . . .   46 To Congreve       81
    New Lovers now will come in Swarms.   . . . . . . .    295 Prog Marriage    158
    Are swarms of Bugs and Hanoverians.   . . . . . . .    313 To Ford           50
    "Whole Swarms of Sects, with grief, he saw  . . . .    550 Life of Swift    168
SWAY
    Let his Success our Subjects sway     . . . . . . .    270 Apollo's Edict  D  7
    (Happy beneath his righteous Sway)    . . . . . . .    388 Manly Virtue     138
    Let all Domesticks feel' your gentle Sway;   . . . .   533 To Mr. Gay        55
    "Where, Folly, Pride, and Faction sway,   . . . . .    570 Death of Swift   433
    While We, whom Reason ought to sway,    . . . . . .    607 Beasts Confess   205
    Tho' by your obliging Sway  . . . . . . . . . . .      633 Epistle Lady     105
    You, next to Dennis bear the Sway:    . . . . . . .    889 Panegyr Dean      89
SWAY'D
    To one who sway'd some time before;   . . . . . . .    375 Apology Lady C    16
SWEAR
    The Ladys vow, and swear they'll try,   . . . . . .     65 Problem            5
    And you may swear the Tale went round.    . . . . .    150 Corinna           20
    <Wharton> can only Swear by Fits,     . . . . . . .    168 Peace Dunkirk     13
    "But when we've gather'd Strength, I swear,  . . . .   208 Fable Bitches     35
    She can swear to the Person, whom oft she has seen,  . .  264 Apollo         53
    "You'll find him swear, blaspheme, and damn,   . . . .  305 Storm           57
    Hear him Blaspheme; and Swear, and Rayl,   . . . . .   312 To Ford           45
    They swear I am so kind and good,   . . . . . . . .    348 Whitshed Motto     9
    The Limb surviving, you may swear,    . . . . . . .    366 Answer Delaney    13
    Minerva ne'er an Oath did Swear   . . . . . . . .     372 Letter D. S-y     12
    And swear they are your own.    . . . . . . . . .      395 Grub-Street       20
    And thine I swear are such.   . . . . . . . . . .      401 Window Inns 2      6
    They swear that they all by Love are inspir'd,   . .   401 Window Inns 3      3
    You'd swear, he never took a fee,   . . . . . . . .    436 Answer Paulus    121
    "I swear I saw you thrice renounce.   . . . . . . .    452 Modern Lady      263
    But swear his Line shall rule the Nation    . . . .    466 Birthday Song    197
    Who wou'd not swear, when you contrive thus,   . . .   478 Epist on Epist    87
    Swear, he's a most facetious Man,   . . . . . . . .    480 Libel on D- D-     9
    Shou'd swear he never meant us ill;   . . . . . . .    485 Libel on D- D-   155
    Or swear it rotten; and with humble Airs,    . . . .   534 To Mr. Gay        97
    "He was an honest man I'll swear---:    . . . . . .    547 Life of Swift     80
    But---not one Sermon, you may swear---.   . . . . .    550 Life of Swift    193
    You'd swear, that so divine a Creature    . . . . .    584 Strephon Chloe    19
    You would swear it pierc'd the Sky;   . . . . . . .    638 Epistle Lady     250
    You'd swear it is Apollo's Son;   . . . . . . . .     692 Cadenus Vaness   193
    The Town wou'd swear he had betray'd,   . . . . . .    707 Cadenus Vaness   646
    And swear it does not always follow,    . . . . . .    741 Stel B-day 22     21
    Although I swear them Disaffected?    . . . . . . .    779 Mullinix Tim     190
    So qualify'd to Swear and Lye,    . . . . . . . .     779 Mullinix Tim     193
    Swear they were with the Swedes at Bender,   . . . .   788 Dick's Variety    23
    You'd swear it must be the Baboon of <Kilkenny>:   .   803 Irish Bishops     10
    Such Assemblies, you might swear,     . . . . . . .    829 Legion Club       13
    You might swear they both are Brethren:   . . . . .    835 Legion Club      148
    He'll swear she's a dunce;    . . . . . . . . . .      854 Lady's Lament     92
    The Dean, you will swear,   . . . . . . . . . . .      856 Lady's Lament    157
    Dermot, I swear, tho' Tady's Locks could hold    . .   882 Pastoral Dial     45
    Is that by which all Irishmen swear.    . . . . . .    940 Letter            15
    I swear from henceforward you shall be my Phoebus. .   973 S-'s Ans Sh-d     14
    I now could safely swear it is hers.    . . . . . .    993 On Picture        15
    And swear by each Fate, and your new friends, each Fury, 1019 To Sheridan     6
SWEARING
    So next Morning we told Whittle, and he fell a Swearing  70 Mrs Harris Pet   24
    And, if Swearing can do't, shall be swingingly mawl'd:  238 Excellent Song   29
    While crooked Cynthia swearing says,    . . . . . .    449 Modern Lady      160
    But keep your Swearing to the last.   . . . . . . .    780 Mullinix Tim     238
    Ever dearest Friendship swearing;     . . . . . . .    800 Traulus 2         16
    Leave off swearing  . . . . . . . . . . . . . .       953 Herrings           2
SWEARS
    But the Lord of Oxford Swears,    . . . . . . . .     169 Peace Dunkirk     35
    "Or, else he raves, and roars, and swears,   . . . .   305 Storm             65
    And swears, Cushogue is to his Tast,    . . . . . .    314 To Ford           89
    Wood swears he will do it for Ireland's Good,   . .    337 Serious Poem      99
    The Captain swears the sea's too rough    . . . . .    420 Holyhead           9
    For want of matter swears and fretts,   . . . . . .    420 Holyhead          17
    Swears you have a World of Wit.   . . . . . . . .     523 Betty Grizette    36
    But swears how damnably the Men lie,    . . . . . .    526 Lady's Dres Rm    17
    The Lawyer swears, you may rely on't,   . . . . . .    603 Beasts Confess    79
    Or that on which his Lordship swears,   . . . . . .    724 To Stella         31
    And swears she saw a Thing in White.    . . . . . .    725 To Stella         74
    He swears my elbows  . . . . . . . . . . . . .        853 Lady's Lament     79
    Swears, he could get her in an hour     . . . . . .    879 Robbin & Harry    33
    So much, he swears the very best Piece is    . . . .   988 Letter Dr Sh-n    22
SWEAT
    Works in my Lord by <Stool> and Sweat,    . . . . .     65 Problem            8
    A mingled Mass of Dirt and Sweat.     . . . . . . .    226 Prog of Beauty    20
    And falls in Rivulets of Sweat,   . . . . . . . .     227 Prog of Beauty    38
    While the Water and Sweat,  . . . . . . . . . . .     245 Irish-Feast       43
    Did Paulus e'er complain of sweat?    . . . . . . .    432 Answer Paulus      5
    Hircina rank with Sweat, presumes     . . . . . . .    449 Modern Lady      158
    Sweat, Dandriff, Powder, Lead and Hair.   . . . . .    526 Lady's Dres Rm    24
    With Dirt, and Sweat, and Ear-Wax grim'd.    . . . .   527 Lady's Dres Rm    46
    He'll sweat, and then the Nymph may smell it.   . .    586 Strephon Chloe    84
    A Haunch of Ven'son made her sweat    . . . . . . .    746 Stel Distress     15
    A Haunch of Ven'son made her sweat,     . . . . . .    750 Stel Wood-Park    13
    And by their Sweat procure a mean Support;   . . . .   793 St. Pat's Well    76
```

	PAGE	TITLE	LINE
SWEAT (CONTINUED)			
Tho' born of human Filth and Sweat, it	812	Bro Protestant	37
Dermot, I vow, 'tis nothing else but Sweat.	881	Pastoral Dial	24
Are not you, in a Crowd, when you sweat and you stew, sick?	1029	Dr. Helsham	9
SWEAT'S			
Tho' Half a Crown o'er-pays his Sweat's Worth; . .	812	Bro Protestant	26
SWEATING			
The Product of your Toil and Sweating;	644	On Poetry	115
SWEATY			
Poor sweaty Paulus, who'd believe us ?	433	Answer Paulus	38
No noisom Whiffs, or sweaty Streams, ...	584	Strephon Chloe	12
SWEDEN			
And since he owns the King of Sweden	282	Journal	103
But by his Name-sake Charles of Sweden.	398	Earl of P-b-w	36
Hath mention'd arms on this side Sweden;	462	Birthday Song	52
SWEDES			
Swear they were with the Swedes at Bender, . . .	788	Dick's Variety	23
SWEEP SEE CHIMNEY-SWEEP			
'Till Neptune with a Gen'ral Sweep	239	Run Bankers	3
Oh, may some Western Tempest sweep	258	Bubble	205
With fifty Yards of Crape, shall sweep the Stage. . .	275	Epilogue	26
To sweep the Mansion-house they dwell in;	892	Panegyr Dean	165
At Whist they will make a desperate Sweep.	943	Probatur Alit	32
Now Creep, Sweep, Sweep, Sweep the Deep, ...	960	Cantata	
Now Creep, Sweep, Sweep, Sweep the Deep, ...	960	Cantata	
Now Creep, Sweep, Sweep, Sweep the Deep, ...	960	Cantata	
SWEEPING			
With a long sweeping Train	23	Ode Athenian	225
SWEEPINGS			
Sweepings from Butchers Stalls, Dung, Guts, and Blood	139	City Shower	61
SWEEPS			
Yet at the last the Box sweeps all away.	29	Ode to Temple	80
Sweeps the broad scythe, and tramples on his face. . .	55	Temple Ill	122
He throws at all, and sweeps the Board.	253	Bubble	64
SWEET			
So sweet a Passion who cou'd think, ...	65	Problem	3
And there in sweet Oblivion drown	202	Horace 2, 6	111
Are soft and sweet as butter.	429	Beau's Reply	12
A Lass so sweet	442	Ballyspellin	59
Sweet Poet, hir'd for birth-day Rimes, ...	462	Birthday Song	47
So soft, so sliding, and so sweet.	467	Birthday Song	226
In calling Celia sweet and cleanly.	526	Lady's Dres Rm	18
Were duly washt to keep 'em sweet;	586	Strephon Chloe	78
To Goddesses so heav'nly sweet, ...	590	Strephon Chloe	199
On Love and Books in Rapture sweet;	593	Cassinus Peter	4
Sweet Five and Twenty was his Age.	597	Problem Solved	6
We leave the body sweet and sound, ...	618	Scandal Poem 1	27
We leave the Body sweet and sound;	624	Scandal Poem 2	21
Which form'd into a Garland sweet, ...	647	On Poetry	223
Where hot and cold, where sharp and sweet, ...	711	Cadenus Vaness	774
His own sweet Figure with the Print, ...	783	Tim and Fables	15
I cannot be sweet	852	Lady's Lament	41
O law! the sweet Gentleman! look in his Face; . . .	870	Grand Question	94
To keep our Poultry sweet and clean;	892	Panegyr Dean	164
The Cowslip soft, and sweet Jonquil.	894	Panegyr Dean	252
My Blood this Day is very sweet, ...	929	Riddle 15	D 9
But think it as sweet as her own.	952	Onyons	15
So sweet is their Flesh, ...	952	Oysters	4
They'll make a sweet Bishop when Gentlefolks sup. . .	953	Oranges	4
or Ambling or Sweet Canterbury, ...	957	Cantata	
SWEET-HEART			
. . .he is my Sweet-heart, ...	72	Mrs Harris Pet	50
And he never call'd me worse than Sweet-heart drunk or sober:	985	Mary to Sher	14
SWEET'NER			
Must be a Sweet'ner by your Trade, ...	485	Libel on D- D-	154
SWEET'NING			
I must take up the sweet'ning Trade.	496	Panegyr Swift	97
The true, the genuine sweet'ning Lay?	497	Panegyr Swift	143
SWEETEN			
Sweeten your Tea, and watch your Toast.	897	Panegyr Dean	328
SWEETER			
Is sweeter and moyster, ...	953	Oysters	6
SWEETEST			
Produce in May the sweetest flowrs.	621	Scandal Poem 1	148
Duke William, sweetest Prince alive.	656	On Poetry	440
The sweetest Place for Masquerades:	905	Death Daphne	86
SWEETLY			
So, sweetly screams if it comes near her, ...	416	Woman's Mind	35
Nor yet, because he sweetly fiddles;	432	Answer Paulus	19
No Poet ever sweetly sung, ...	757	Stel B-day '24	19
Sweetly snoring in his Cloak.	836	Legion Club	160
Sing heavenly Muse in sweetly flowing Strain, . . .	880	Pastoral Dial	7
And sweetly moralize a while.	894	Panegyr Dean	228
SWEETNESS			
Where Majesty with Sweetness vyes, ...	466	Birthday Song	191
A Sweetness above all Perfumes;	691	Cadenus Vaness	161
SWELL			
With a huge Fardingal to swell her Fustian Stuff, . .	23	Ode Athenian	222
Yet some I know with Envy swell, ...	202	Horace 2, 6	81

808

		PAGE	TITLE	LINE
SWELL	(CONTINUED)			
So much his Stay do's swell the Bills;		860	Lady Acheson	30
SWELL'D				
(Says he) tho' swell'd like any porpus.		456	Dean Smedley	32
And as he pass'd, so swell'd the Dee		476	Epist on Epist	45
SWELLING				
Pleas'd with an empty swelling to be counted great; . .		36	Ode Sancroft	60
Now from all Parts the swelling Kennels flow, . .		139	City Shower	53
Behold it swelling like a Sop.		251	Bubble	16
With swelling scarf, and glossy gown, ...		676	Parson's Case	25
Take down thy proudly swelling Sails, ...		897	Panegyr Dean	333
Swelling be my shape or small, ...		937	Riddle 24 D	37
SWEPT				
Swept up whole churches as it list, ...		40	Ode Sancroft	194
The subtle Knave had all the Plunder swept.		536	To Mr. Gay	154
If Nayads swept them from the Brink)		894	Panegyr Dean	244
SWIFT				
Time o'er the happy takes so swift a flight, ...		54	Temple Ill	113
With these is Parson Swift, ...		75	Game Traffick D	25
The Stagg was swift, the Fox a Knave:		512	Answer Fable	6
Enquires for Swift in Verse and Prose:		562	Death of Swift	254
Bestow my next I pray, to Pope or Swift.		669	Epig Carthy 17 D	4
Sent in a bag to Doctor Swift, ...		753	Gift for Bec	3
Yet should Swift endow the Schools		830	Legion Club	35
"This mischief arises from witty Dean Swift."		843	Ay and No	6
Make up a Bird very swift of Flight, ...		940	Letter	4
No Bird in Air so swift can fly.		942	Probatur Alit	26
Then Good Dr. <Swift>		77	Lady B- B-	26
Found out that it was Dr. <Swift>:		171	Horace 1, 7	26
<Swift> seem'd to wonder what he meant, ...		172	Horace 1, 7	51
<Swift>, who could neither fly nor hide, ...		172	Horace 1, 7	63
<Swift> much admires the Place and Air, ...		173	Horace 1, 7	83
Poor <Swift> departs, and, what is worse, ...		173	Horace 1, 7	93
Poor <Swift>, with all his Losses vext, ...		174	Horace 1, 7	113
<Swift> had the Sin of Wit no venial Crime;		193	Author Himself	9
By Harley <Swift> invited comes to Court.		194	Author Himself	28
At Windsor <Swift> no sooner can appear, ...		194	Author Himself	33
That <Swift> oils many a Spring which Harley moves. .		194	Author Himself	40
'Tis thought could be the Work of none but <Swift> . .		195	Author Himself	50
Again apply that <Swift> would be their Friend. . .		196	Author Himself	70
Of our Metropolis to <Swift>;		494	Panegyr Swift	48
The <Devil> ready stands, my <Swift>, ...		497	Panegyr Swift	124
To oblige your Crony <Swift>, ...		862	To Janus	3
A Panegyrick on <Dean> <Swift>.		887	Panegyr Dean	34
SWIFT'S				
Three genuine Tomes of Swift's Remains.		560	Death of Swift	198
On <Swift's> Reproaches for her <murdered> <spouse> .		195	Author Himself	54
And, in <Swift's> Ear thrusts half his powder'd Nose.		196	Author Himself	68
SWIFTER				
Yet swifter Fate will seize him from behind.		210	Earl of Oxford	6
Desire, the swifter of the two, ...		412	Desire Possess	21
SWIFTEST				
Syrius, the swiftest of the heavn'ly Pack, ...		538	Mr. Pulteney	33
SWIFTLY				
And Youth so swiftly glides away;		593	Strephon Chloe	304
Swiftly purling in a Round, ...		661	Love Song	26
Swiftly I come, and enter there, ...		935	Riddle 23 D	14
SWIFTNESS				
Away the Hare with double Swiftness fled.		538	Mr. Pulteney	28
SWILL				
His Morning-Draughts 'till Noon can swill, ...		231	Prog of Poetry	19
SWILL'D				
That swill'd more Liquor than it could contain, . . .		137	City Shower	15
SWILLD				
I hope you have swilld with new milk from the Kine . .		1018	Swift Ans Sher	25
SWILLS				
How much he eats, how much he swills, ...		860	Lady Acheson	32
She swills like a sow, and she breeds like a rabbit: . .		955	Portrait Life	6
SWIM				
To Swim against this Pop'lar Tide, ...		158	Fable of Midas	74
The pond'rous Metal seems to swim;		251	Bubble	12
Swim where the Bird of Jove would sink, ...		253	Bubble	55
The sober Hen not born to swim		295	Horrid Plot	149
"Can creep, or run, can fly or swim, ...		304	Storm	31
I found my Head began to swim, ...		470	Burning Poem	9
Resolv'd for a Fortnight to Swim in Delight, . . .		517	Dean Hang Rape	26
See, Brother, how we Apples swim.		811	Bro Protestant	14
SWIMMING				
And swimming never wet a Feather.		253	Bubble	56
SWIMMINGLY				
By which they might Swimmingly land on a Bank. . . .		288	Bank Down	50
SWIMS				
Against whose Torrent while he Swims, ...		157	Fable of Midas	35
"This Head of mine, Lord, how it Swims!		451	Modern Lady	208
The greatest Whale, that swims the Sea		934	Riddle 21 D	11
SWINE				
Fat Bullocks and Swine.		244	Irish-Feast	8
Till those devouring Swine run down, ...		259	Bubble	214
The Swine with contrite Heart allow'd, ...		602	Beasts Confess	37
Och ma ceade millia mollighart, on the feeders of swine!		841	Ballad D	19
Last trolled forth a gentle Swine		849	Old Thorn	41

		PAGE	TITLE	LINE
SWINE	**(CONTINUED)**			
	His meadows may be dug by swine,	902	Dean's Reasons	111
	Where I hear you are cramm'd evry day like a Swine	1017	Swift Ans Sher	13
SWINE'S				
	The dullest Beast, and Swine's Delight	940	Letter	3
SWING				
	And the Whigs may all go Swing,	168	Peace Dunkirk	6
	If once we let you have your Swing.	622	Scandal Poem 1	166
	Tom had the genteeler Swing,	785	Mullinex Dick	29
	Dick knew better how to swing	785	Mullinex Dick	31
	His Signs aloft no longer swing;	875	Drapier's Hill	14
	From rhyming in cars you may swing in a cart.	976	Dean to Sherid	36
SWINGINGLY				
	And, if Swearing can do't, shall be swingingly mawl'd:	238	Excellent Song	29
SWISS				
	The Swiss and Dutch whole Millions drain.	256	Bubble	160
	O! had I been Apostle to the Swiss,	793	St. Pat's Well	79
SWITCH				
	Or made it a Newmarket Switch,	135	Magician's Rod	83
SWITCHES				
	Switches better guide than Cudgels.	636	Epistle Lady	202
SWOON'D				
	Well; I thought I should have swoon'd;.	73	Mrs Harris Pet	64
SWORD				
	It melts the Sword of War, yet keeps it in the Sheath.	29	Ode to Temple	91
	Had drawn his Sword for Marius' Fall,	340	Arch-Bish Dub	18
	The Duke of Lorrain drew his Sword,	776	Mullinix Tim	111
	To the Dean of all Deans, tho' he wears not a sword.	816	Yahoo's	54
	Then fear not his tongue, his sword, or his knife;	817	Yahoo's	73
	With the fine flaming Sword that he holds in his Hand;	870	Grand Question	96
	For, the Right holds the Sword, and the Left holds the Bridle,)	870	Grand Question	108
	Then flourishes thrice his Sword in the Air,	870	Grand Question	109
SWORD-KNOTS				
	What Sword-knots! What Poetic Strains!	585	Strephon Chloe	37
SWORDS				
	(For swords are madmen's tongues, and tongues are mad-men's swords)	35	Ode Sancroft	14
	(For swords are madmen's tongues, and tongues are mad-men's swords)	35	Ode Sancroft	14
	With those two pow'rful swords, Submission and Humility,	36	Ode Sancroft	48
	Draw their Swords and run away:	574	Helter Skelter	48
SWORE				
	Swore all the wits were his peculiar friends;	47	To Congreve	140
	One swore he'd send 'em to the Stocks,	91	Bauc & Phil 1	33
	Confest his Flame, and swore by Styx,	120	Apollo Outwit	18
	His <Grace> swore by <God>, and her <Grace> let a <Fart>:	143	New Song	18
	I swore to the <Queen> that the <Prince> of <Hanover>	144	New Song	35
	Swore he'd rather lose a Crown,	168	Peace Dunkirk	19
	But the Cobler was angry, and swore he had rather	287	Bank Down	26
	His Firmness to the publick Good, as one that knows it Swore,	341	Upon His Grace	9
	He swore from his Cart, it was all a damn'd Lye.	399	Tom Clinch	12
	The Sharper swore he hated Play,	607	Beasts Confess	187
	Which when he had enjoy'd, he swore,	619	Scandal Poem 1	55
	Which when he had enjoy'd, he swore	625	Scandal Poem 2	51
	And swore the fawning Rascals ly'd:	657	On Poetry	476
	As the Coach stopp'd, she look'd & swore	746	Stel Distress	27
	As the Coach stopp'd, she look'd & swore	746	Stel Distress	
	The Coachman stopt, she lookt, and swore	751	Stel Wood-Park	47
	He bragg'd how he bounc'd, and he swore how he swore.	816	Yahoo's	44
	He bragg'd how he bounc'd, and he swore how he swore.	816	Yahoo's	44
SWORN				
	Quoth Ross, for, I'll be sworn, 'twas I.	67	Problem	56
	"Sworn to revenge my Thorn and me.	851	Old Thorn	80
SWOWN				
	The Sight will put her in a Swown.	416	Woman's Mind	16
SYGNE				
	Of Fraunce hir woe thys is the sygne,	102	Merlin	2
SYLLA				
	From whom great Sylla found his Doom;	925	Riddle 8	35
SYLLABLE				
	Pretend to answer one Syl--lable,	183	Horace 2, 1	85
	Thinks ev'ry Syllable is true;	282	Journal	102
	Watch ev'ry Syllable you speak:	889	Panegyr Dean	72
SYLLABLES				
	Three Syllables did never meet	467	Birthday Song	225
	In Chains, thy Syllables are link'd.	1021	Nim-Dan-Dean 1	D 28
SYLVAN				
	For, while the bashful Sylvan Maid,	922	Riddle 7	33
SYLVIA				
	For Chloe, Sylvia, Phillis, Iris;	729	Stella, Poems	40
SYMBOLS				
	When We, by proper Signs and Symbols tell,	162	Toland's Invit	9
SYMNELE				
	Yonge Symnele shall agayne miscarrye:	103	Merlin	11
SYMPATHETICK				
	Will damp all Passion Sympathetick;	588	Strephon Chloe	134
SYMPATHIZE				
	Does sympathize with Human <Arse>.	66	Problem	28

```
                                                    PAGE   TITLE            LINE
SYRIUS
     Syrius, the swiftest of the heavn'ly Pack,  . . . . .   538 Mr. Pulteney       33
     When Syrius o'er the welkin rages,       . . . . . . .   618 Scandal Poem 1     33
     When Syrius o'er the Welkin rages        . . . . . . .   624 Scandal Poem 2     31
SYSTEM
     With her World's fruitful System in her sacred Ark,      16 Ode Athenian       13
     By the new Modish System of reducing all to sense,   .  .  19 Ode Athenian     107
     Found his Head fill'd with many a System,  . . . . . .  115 Bauc & Phil 2     135
     His Converse is a System, fit              . . . . . .  709 Cadenus Vaness    708
     Some fav'rite System to their Mind,        . . . . . .  709 Cadenus Vaness    723
'T        3                                               ,      OMITTED WORD
T'        29                                                     OMITTED WORD
T'OTHER   1                                                      OMITTED WORD
T'US
     Here I have computed the Profit will fall t'us.  . . .   867 Grand Question     8
     Come back t'us well freighted;  . . . . . . . . .      1014 Swift to Sheri     25
T'YE
     If I always seem too dull t'ye;            . . . . . .   630 Epistle Lady       19
     For, were you a Dog, I could not be rude t'ye.   . . .   968 Letter Sherid      26
     Will you return as hard ones, if I call t'ye?  . . . .   989 Letter Dr Sh-n     33
TA'EN
     Which if right ta'en, and but good Luck-hold   . . . .   373 Letter D. S-y      60
TA'NE
     And now the Duke has wisely ta'ne him      . . . . . .    87 Hist V's House     41
TABBIES
     Brocado's, and Damasks, and Tabbies, and Gawses,   . .   236 Excellent Song      1
TABLE
     Seated at Table next the Men you love.     . . . . . .   165 Toland's Invit     32
     At Table now she acts her Part,            . . . . . .   448 Modern Lady       100
     The Table, Cards, and Counters set,        . . . . . .   451 Modern Lady       214
     For Poets open Table kept, .  . . . . . . . . .         481 Libel on D- D-     37
     At Table you can Horace quote;             . . . . . .   483 Libel on D- D-     95
     Now at the Table head she sits             . . . . . .   745 Stel Distress      11
     Your Table neat, your Linnen fine;         . . . . . .   752 Stel Wood-Park     83
     Tim set the Volume on a Table,             . . . . . .   782 Tim and Fables      5
     To keep off their Eyes, as they wait at the Table;  . .   871 Grand Question   136
     A house-wife in bed, at table a slattern;  . . . . . .   955 Portrait Life       7
TABLE-BOOK
     Nature's fair Table-book our tender Souls   . . . . .    27 Ode to Temple      32
     The Model in his Table-book;               . . . . . .    87 Hist V's House     20
TABLE-HEAD
     Where Battus from the Table-head,          . . . . . .   649 On Poetry         264
     Now at the Table-Head she sits,            . . . . . .   750 Stel Wood-Park      9
TABLES
     Yet, still was at the Tables of the Great.  . . . . .   194 Author Himself     16
     Though at the Tables of the Great,         . . . . . .   920 Riddle 6           25
     Stools, Tables, Chairs, and Bed-steds broke:  . . . .  1035 To Quilca           4
TACK
     With ev'ry Wind he sail'd, and well could tack:  . . .   285 Elegy Boat         15
     Prudes decay'd about may tack,  . . . . . . . . .        863 To Janus           21
TADY
     When you saw Tady at long-bullets play,   . . . . . .   882 Pastoral Dial      33
TADY'S
     Dermot, I swear, tho' Tady's Locks could hold   . . .   882 Pastoral Dial      45
TAG
     Compell'd by you to tag in Rhimes  . . . . . . .        445 Modern Lady        30
TAGUS
     Would offer all the Sands of Tagus;  . . . . . . .      821 Dr. Rundle         42
TAIL    SEE TAYL, FAN-TAIL
     Long dreaded for his Bloody Tail and Fiery Beard,   .    10 Ode to King       131
     Her Frolicks, and pursues her Tail no more.  . . . .   136 City Shower         4
     As round as a Ball, without Head without Tail,   . .   350 Wood Insect         5
     That in his Tail he wore his Eyes,         . . . . . .   513 Answer Fable       17
     To squeeze it out from Head to Tail;       . . . . . .   527 Lady's Dres Rm     66
     Shew Fire and Faggot in the Tail on't?     . . . . . .   774 Mullinix Tim       20
     All powder'd o'er from Tail to Chin;       . . . . . .   785 Dick, Maggot        2
     Hang's down his Head, and drops his Tail,  . . . . . .   797 Traulus 1          37
     With Ribbins in Knots, at its Tail and its Ears:   . .   870 Grand Question     98
     . . .and I would pin a Dish-clout to his Tail.  . . .   987 Mary to Sher       32
TAIL'D   SEE DOVE-TAIL'D
TAINT
     And taint all their Meat, and sour all their Drink.  .   263 Apollo            14
     To taint the Parts from whence they fell.  . . . . .   529 Lady's Dres Rm    112
TAINTED
     Her tainted Carcase to pursue,             . . . . . .    85 Salamander         65
     Accuses Chloe's tainted Breath;            . . . . . .   449 Modern Lady       157
     Will in your tainted Heart preside.        . . . . . .   725 To Stella          50
     And make thee tear thy tainted Hyde.       . . . . . .   925 Riddle 8           44
TAINTLESS
     Could from her taintless Body flow.        . . . . . .   584 Strephon Chloe     14
TAKE
     Will quickly take another course           . . . . . .    19 Ode Athenian      116
     Take thy unwonted Flight,                  . . . . . .    30 Ode to Temple     118
     Take up at best with Lumber and the Leavings of a Fate:    32 Ode to Temple    184
     And thousand incoherent journies take,     . . . . . .    36 Ode Sancroft       70
     Take this short lesson from the god of bayes,  . . .    49 To Congreve       203
     Take, youth, these thoughts, large matter to employ  . .    53 Temple Ill       67
     The Devil take me, said she, (blessing her self,) . . .    71 Mrs Harris Pet    44
     . . .and I always take his Part;           . . . . . .    72 Mrs Harris Pet    51
     You are no Text for my Handling, so take that from me:    72 Mrs Harris Pet    57
     Then curious Hands this Texture take,      . . . . . .    79 Vanbrug House      33
```

TAKE   (CONTINUED)

		PAGE	TITLE	LINE
And call'd to take the Cards away,	. . . . . .	86	Hist V's House	2
Pray take your Answer and be gone.	. . . . . .	91	Bauc & Phil 1	32
Makes you take all things in good Part:	. . . . .	94	Bauc & Phil 1	160
To take thee kindly in between,	. . . .	100	Elegy Patrige	87
Take Journies in it like a Chaise;	. . . . . .	109	V's House	112
To the Church-yard, to take a walk;	. . . . .	116	Bauc & Phil 2	154
May you Descend to take Renown,	. . . . .	121	Apollo Outwit	62
The watchful Bailiffs take their silent Stands,	. .	125	Descriptn Morn	17
And he stood there to take them in.	. . . . .	134	Magician's Rod	56
That he might take his Rest awhile	. . . . .	160	Atlas	12
Yet take one Word of Counsel by the way:	. . .	166	Toland's Invit	40
Take care betimes to run him down:	. . . . .	171	Horace 1, 7	30
Force him to take his Tythes in kind;	. . . .	174	Horace 1, 7	110
Give us our earl, the devil take their duke.	. .	186	Scriblerus 3	2
Come then, my lord, and take your part in	. .	186	Scriblerus 3	7
And the Devil may take their Duke.	. . . .	186	Scriblerus 4	D 12
Then come and take part in	. . . . .	186	Scriblerus 4	D 13
Take up a well-bound Heap of Sticks.	. . . .	189	Faggot	4
Take your blue Ribbin for a String.	. . . . .	190	Faggot	38
And take a Folio for a conj'ring Book.	. . . .	193	Author Himself	8
"Send for him up, take no Excuse.	. . . . .	199	Horace 2, 6	16
And take it kindly meant to show	. . . .	200	Horace 2, 6	41
Would take me in his Coach to chat,	. . . .	201	Horace 2, 6	67
Nor stoops to take the Staff, nor lays it down,	.	210	Earl of Oxford	9
But loves to take prodigious Rounds,	. . . .	210	To Mr. Delany	93
Will drew out Dick to take a Quart,	. . . . .	220	A Quiet Life	26
She'd rather take you to her Bed	. . . . .	222	Prog of Love	7
Take Pattern by your Sister Star,	. . . . .	228	Prog of Beauty	69
What Poet e'er could take his Flight?	. . . .	231	Prog of Poetry	24
The De'el take the Searcher.	. . . . .	245	Irish-Feast	24
When Damon's Soul shall take its Flight,	. . .	270	Apollo's Edict	D 33
Take Qualities from Donegal.	. . . . .	272	Apollo's Edict	D 75
But Chints, Brocades, and Lace take all away,	. .	275	Epilogue	33
Take the three strongest of his broken Planks,	. .	285	Elegy Boat	32
The Wedding-day, you take me right,	. . . . .	290	Prog Marriage	19
Then goes alone to take his Rest	. . . . .	292	Prog Marriage	89
"And ev'ry Moment take a Dram,	. . . . .	305	Storm	58
For, take it kindly, or amiss,	. . . . .	315	To Ford	99
"Each take a Child into her Care,	. . . . .	321	First of April	5
"Divide the rest, but then take care,	. . . .	321	First of April	11
Too wise to take Council, too proud to take Warning,	.	327	Epigram 1	7
Too wise to take Council, too proud to take Warning,	.	327	Epigram 1	7
Come, you must take a Cup of Sack or two before you go.	.	342	Upon His Grace	24
To take the Noise of Brass for Thunder!	. . . .	353	Wood Ironmongr	30
Or take it in a diff'rent View:	. . . . . .	392	Young's Satire	31
To take his Iron by the End;	. . . . . .	393	Modern Poets	14
Take Courage, dear Comrades, and be not afraid,	.	400	Tom Clinch	19
And fairly bid the <Devil> take	. . . . .	400	Window Inns 1	7
Then, let him come and take a Nap,	. . . . .	410	Dial Rich Marb	85
They take the wrong Way for the right.	. . . .	412	Desire Possess	18
And take his Nonsense all for Wit:	. . . .	416	Woman's Mind	8
Take Notice, she has my Commission	. . . .	418	Woman's Mind	61
While English sharpers take the pay,	. . . . .	421	Ireld	9
And we shall take you there	. . . . .	426	Five Ladies	17
<Lyndsay>, you know, what pains you take	. . . .	436	Answer Paulus	129
To take, for Interest Cent. per Cent.	. . . .	446	Modern Lady	61
"Here Betty, let me take my Drops,	. . . .	451	Modern Lady	206
Dear Madam, try to take a Nap--	. . . . .	451	Modern Lady	210
Take twenty Gods of Rome or Greece,	. . . .	460	Birthday Song	2
He'll get it read, and take the hint,	. . . .	463	Birthday Song	86
And take it right, it means no more	. . . .	464	Birthday Song	139
And take a Guinea for your Fee.	. . . . .	469	Birthday Song	282
And take a Greater Patrick's Name.	. . . .	478	Epist on Epist	94
Take this Advice then from your Friend,	. . . .	478	Epist on Epist	113
(Take Notice, to avoid Offence	. . . . .	486	Libel on D- D-	183
Take my advice; to make you safe,	. . . . .	487	Irish-Club	13
Take subjects safer for your wit	. . . . .	489	Dialogue	21
I must take up the sweet'ning Trade.	. . . .	496	Panegyr Swift	97
You try to take Revenge in vain.	. . . . .	504	Doctor Delaney	136
I take it for a Panegyrick.	. . . . .	505	Doctor Delaney	170
If Fortune should please to take such a Crotchet,	.	518	Dean Hang Rape	43
Come, tell me truly, wou'd you take well,	. . .	546	Life of Swift	31
Affect to take the upper hand,	. . . . .	546	Life of Swift	34
Wou'd either Poet take it well,	. . . . .	546	Life of Swift	54
I cry, Pox take him, and his Wit.	. . . . .	555	Death of Swift	52
"But he would never take Advice:	. . . . .	558	Death of Swift	172
"My Lady Club wou'd take it ill,	. . . .	562	Death of Swift	237
And to take a double Fee;	. . . .	574	Helter Skelter	50
They take Possession of the Crown,	. . . . .	592	Strephon Chloe	261
What various Ways our Females take,	. . . .	592	Strephon Chloe	267
Rash Mortals, e'er you take a Wife,	. . . . .	593	Strephon Chloe	301
So, take my Secret, and adieu.	. . . . .	597	Cassinus Peter	116
At Poets flights to take offence:	. . . . .	622	Scandal Poem 1	154
At Poet's Flights to take Offence.	. . . . .	628	Scandal Poem 2	158
Tho' Chickens take a Month to fatten,	. . . .	642	On Poetry	62
Take Courage, and attempt a Third.	. . . .	645	On Poetry	148
To take, his mornings Cup of Gin.	. . . .	659	On Poetry	D 410
And take some small Diversions now and then?	. .	662	Upon Ladies	4
But what's dy'd black will take no other hue.	. .	670	Epig Carthy 18	D 8
She thought it best to take Advice.	. . . . .	689	Cadenus Vaness	92

TAKE   (CONTINUED)   PAGE   TITLE   LINE

Vows, on Vanessa's Heart to take . . . .   701 Cadenus Vaness   470
He came to take his last Adieu. . . . . . .   705 Cadenus Vaness   593
For, take it in its proper Light, ...   708 Cadenus Vaness   672
Will condescend to take a Bit. . . . .   710 Cadenus Vaness   761
She vows to take him at his Word, ...   712 Cadenus Vaness   803
But, lest we should for Honour take . . . . .   724 To Stella   23
Take Comfort, that our own is best: . . . .   728 Stella, Poems   20
Lest you should take them for a Bribe, ... 730 Stella, Poems   84
And tho you must the Fashions take, ...   732 Verses Vanessa   5
And so take all upon your back. . . . .   753 Gift for Bec   26
But always take a special care . . . .   762 Bec's B-Day   41
Take Pity on your pitying Friends; . . . . . .   766 Stel B-day '26   80
I take thee under my Protection. . . . . . .   779 Mullinix Tim   208
You'll find it well prepar'd to take . . . . . .   780 Mullinix Tim   225
I'll take you to some Friends of mine; . . . . .   780 Mullinix Tim   244
That thou shouldst take an honest Trade, ... 787 Clad in Brown   27
And the Clergy, forsooth, must take up with their   804 Irish Bishops   34
     Leavings.
First take you our Tyths, and give us your Lands. . 805 Irish Bishops   62
And let his Bishoprick another take. . . .   806 Judas   26
Must take no Fee of one another. . . . .   812 Bro Protestant   18
He'll take his revenge on his innocent Wife. . . . 817 Yahoo's   74
Then, prithee reflect, take a word of advice; . . . 818 Archbi Cashel   7
His Brethren find to take Offence: . . . . . .   820 Dr. Rundle   12
Would take the Kingdom into his Protection: . . . . 825 Noisy Tom   4
The devil he may take her into hell and Boult-her! 841 Ballad   D   14
"But if I say the word--take care of Armagh!" . . . 843 Ay and No   18
Nor for my Life will take the Hint. . . . . . .   860 Lady Acheson   16
Or Mr. <Moor> will take it ill. . . . .   860 Lady Acheson   28
Can you take Delight in viewing . . . .   862 To Janus   13
And take a short Dinner here with us to-Day: . . . 871 Grand Question   120
"I never cou'd take to my Book for the Blood o'me, 873 Grand Question   165
Come hither, and take this old Gown for your Pains. 873 Grand Question   186
Sharp are the Stones, take thou this rushy Matt; . 881 Pastoral Dial   19
We'll take her Heels five Inches lower. . . . . .   886 Rev Market-Hill   104
To take Offence at what you speak. . . . . .   890 Panegyr Dean   120
And Gaghagan take ev'ry Joke. . . . .   890 Panegyr Dean   128
Take down thy proudly swelling Sails, ...   897 Panegyr Dean   333
I use to take in friends affairs, ...   901 Dean's Reasons   96
To take a House in Warwick Lane: . . . . . .   904 Death Daphne   46
Never take it in your thought, ...   907 Daphne   31
Only take this rule along, ...   907 Daphne   35
On Airy Wings you take your Flight, ...   919 Riddle 5   25
I near the Side-board take my Seat; . . . .   920 Riddle 6   26
Take wise Advice, and look behind, ...   921 Riddle 7   3
Why should my Shepherd take amiss . . . .   924 Riddle 8   9
Shall on thee take a Vengeance dire; . . . . 925 Riddle 8   37
What other Way they take to go, ...   928 Riddle 12   D   9
And then they take a Turn and jump on't. . . . . . 928 Riddle 12   D   16
The foulest Impressions I easily take. . . . . .   929 Riddle 13   D   8
Is useful in Journies, take Notice of that. . . .   943 Probatur Alit   44
I'll first take you up, and then take you down: . . 968 Letter Sherid   32
I'll first take you up, and then take you down: . . 968 Letter Sherid   32
To take his greatest Grandees for Asses. . . . .   988 Letter Dr Sh-n   12
Take Courage, Dan, this plainly shows . . . . .   993 On Picture   19
To take the right way, ...   1038 Sheridan Cavan   11
TAKEN   SEE TA'NE
I was never taken for a Conjurer before,. . . . . . 72 Mrs Harris Pet   58
If the Stick be taken from the dead Sea. . . . .   147 Windsor Proph   14
Restore the Ships by Philip taken, ...   468 Birthday Song   249
Was taken with his Person outward, ...   514 Answer Fable   47
Lately taken out of Lim-- . . . .   574 Helter Skelter   28
But now I'll write short, for fear you're short taken. 980 Tho: Sheridan   6
And has taken just now a firm resolution . . . . . 1027 Sheri Circles   23
TAKES
The Rebel Muse, alas, takes part . . . .   23 Ode Athenian   238
Whene'er she takes this Flight . . . .   31 Ode to Temple   143
Whence takes it its Increase, and whence its Birth, 31 Ode to Temple   169
Time o'er the happy takes so swift a flight, . . .   54 Temple Ill   113
From thee whatever virtue takes its rise, ...   55 Temple Ill   135
Some bungling Partner takes, ...   75 Game Traffick   10
Takes Snuff, and holds the Stakes. . . . . . .   75 Game Traffick   12
Takes a French Play as lawful Prize, ...   107 V's House   58
Here conns his Notes, and takes a Whet, ...   127 Little House   21
And down to Windsor takes his Guest. . . . . .   173 Horace 1, 7   82
Takes Horse, and in a mighty Fret . . . . . .   174 Horace 1, 7   116
Takes him to Windsor in his Coach, alone. . . . .   194 Author Himself   32
Takes up with Copper in the Place; . . . . . .   216 To Mr. Delany   44
And takes Possession of the Lips, ...   226 Prog of Beauty   27
As when a Conj'rer takes a Lease . . . .   240 Run Bankers   45
And Wool it is greasy, and quickly takes Fire. . . 237 Excellent Song   21
On Paper Wings he takes his Flight, ...   252 Bubble   37
The Silver takes a nobler Hue, ...   255 Bubble   114
And the whole crew this resolution takes, ...   309 Billet Players   49
Then Master Steward takes my Rent, and tells me, honest 342 Upon His Grace 23
     Jo.
And takes the Plaintiff's and Defendant's Fees. .   364 On Dreams   24
The Doctor takes his hint from hence, ...   379 Apology Lady C   129
What pains he takes to be prolix! . . . .   434 Answer Paulus   83
Takes a large Dram of Citron Water. . . . . . .   446 Modern Lady   47

TAKES	(CONTINUED)	PAGE	TITLE	LINE
'No woman breathing takes up less;	. . . .	447	Modern Lady	97
Thus Berecynthia takes her place,	. . . .	466	Birthday Song	183
"But Nature freely takes her Course,	. . . . .	476	Epist on Epist	55
The Danger past, takes Heart of Grace,	. . . . .	500	Doctor Delaney	25
The Bason takes whatever comes	. . . .	527	Lady's Dres Rm	39
But he takes up with younger Pokes,	. . . . .	556	Death of Swift	93
He takes an Hour to find a Rhime:	. . . . .	556	Death of Swift	100
But ever with Prudence takes Care of the Main.	. .	580	Psyche	8
Takes off her artificial Hair:	. . . .	581	Young Nymph	10
She takes a Bolus e'er she sleeps;	. . . . .	582	Young Nymph	37
'Till some fresh Blockhead takes your Place.	. . . .	644	On Poetry	142
And this she takes to be her Case.	. . . . . .	709	Cadenus Vaness	703
See the dreadful Strides she takes.	. . . . .	832	Legion Club	92
He takes me to pieces.	. . . .	853	Lady's Lament	70
For, a Captain of Horse never takes off his Hat;	.	870	Grand Question	106
From her own Head, Megaera takes	. . . . . .	903	Death Daphne	21
And often takes me by the Hand.	. . . . . .	921	Riddle 6	30
Sits, and takes them in the Dark.	. . . . . .	931	Riddle 18	D 8
Because she let's out more, than e'er she takes in.	. .	972	S-'s Ans Sh-d	6
TAKING				
Taking their Tour in Masquerade	. . . . . .	90	Bauc & Phil 1	8
Taking their Tour in Masquerade;	. . . . . .	111	Bauc & Phil 2	8
It feels as if 'twere taking Root.	. . . . .	116	Bauc & Phil 2	162
Under pretence of Taking Air,	. . . .	120	Apollo Outwit	23
By taking Fits whene'er she please:	. . . . .	416	Woman's Mind	38
Your Portion, taking Britain round,	. . . . .	642	On Poetry	53
Taking then a Pinch of Snuff,	. . . . . .	839	Legion Club	240
Taking her After-dinner Nap:	. . . .	895	Panegyr Dean	274
TALE SEE TELL-TALE				
And you may swear the Tale went round.	. . . . .	150	Corinna	20
This Tale inclines the gentle Reader,	. . . . .	157	Fable of Midas	41
This Tale may be apply'd in few Words	. . . .	189	Faggot	15
With couchant Cringe, and flattering Tale,	. . .	208	Fable Bitches	15
They seem to act an Ancient Tale,	. . . . .	239	Run Bankers	19
Now hear an old Tale. There antiently stood	. . .	334	Serious Poem	17
My Tale is a wise one if well understood,	. . . .	334	Serious Poem	23
I told you one Tale, I will tell you another.	. . .	336	Serious Poem	70
Salmoneus, as the Grecian Tale is,	. . . . .	352	Wood Ironmongr	1
The Moral of this Tale is proper,	. . . . .	353	Wood Ironmongr	31
Related thus the following Tale.	. . . . .	412	Desire Possess	8
For so sad a Tale is no Subject of Laughter.	. . .	430	Dicky Dolly	18
Through ev'ry Game pursues her Tale,	. . . . .	447	Modern Lady	78
"You have the Tale as cheap as I:	. . . . .	449	Modern Lady	147
The Eagle in the Tale, ye know,	. . . . . .	458	Paddy's Charac	29
The Moral of the Tale is pleasant,	. . . . .	514	Answer Fable	51
Through Cambridge waft the direful Tale.	. . . .	597	Cassinus Peter	110
Apply the Tale, and you shall find	. . . . .	603	Beasts Confess	73
Besides, the Tale is false in Fact;	. . . . .	607	Beasts Confess	198
An idle Tale, 'tis no such Matter;	. . . . .	627	Scandal Poem 2	127
Prefixt a Cut to ev'ry Tale.)	. . . . . .	782	Tim and Fables	10
The merry Tale with moral Grave.	. . . . .	783	Tim and Fables	27
Tare out the Tale, and wipe your <Arse>	. . . .	783	Tim and Fables	37
To shorten my Tale, (for I hate a long Story,)	. .	871	Grand Question	129
Can listen to a tale humdrum,	. . . .	900	Dean's Reasons	55
TALENT				
A Fryer would needs show his Talent in Latin;	. .	76	Lady B- B-	2
Told <Van> he knew his Talent best,	. . . . .	107	V's House	53
Her Talent she display'd betimes;	. . . . .	150	Corinna	13
Displays his Talent, sits till Ten,	. . . . .	173	Horace 1, 7	75
With ev'ry Talent of a Prude,	. . . . . .	222	Prog of Love	2
I ne'er could endure my Talent to smother,	. . .	336	Serious Poem	69
Pope has the Talent well to speak,	. . . . .	405	Swift to Pope	1
Whose meanest Talent is his Wit:	. . . . .	482	Libel on D- D-	80
That vulgar Talent I despise	. . . . . .	787	Dick's Variety	5
Oh that Jove would give me such a talent as thine	. .	1017	Swift Ans Sher	7
TALENTS				
Squander'd his noisy talents to my face;	. . . . .	47	To Congreve	138
Nor higher, than our Talents, rise,	. . . . .	184	Horace 2, 1	108
His Talents to employ for nobler Ends;	. . . .	194	Author Himself	24
Whom, when I with the best of my Talents endu'd,	. .	264	Apollo	45
An Office for your Talents fit,	. . . . . .	483	Libel on D- D-	105
Thus, with Talents well endu'd	. . . . . .	523	Betty Grizette	29
If with such Talents Heav'n hath blest 'em	. . .	555	Death of Swift	65
Mistake our Talents ev'ry Day:	. . . . . .	607	Beasts Confess	206
Brutes find out where their Talents lie:	. . . .	640	On Poetry	13
A Project for thy Talents fit,	. . . . . .	695	Cadenus Vaness	290
Mens Talents to their proper Use;	. . . . .	700	Cadenus Vaness	449
Use all the Talents of your mind.	. . . . .	780	Mullinix Tim	232
Their sev'ral Talents to your Wit,	. . . . .	890	Panegyr Dean	126
Conceal their talents from our eyes,	. . . . .	900	Dean's Reasons	34
TALES				
For, if those antient Tales be true,	. . . . .	177	To Lord Harley	25
Tales here forgot, or yet unheard;	. . . . .	386	Manly Virtue	74
Who, under Tales conveying Truth,	. . . . .	482	Libel on D- D-	55
Their Tales wou'd always justly suit	. . . . .	512	Answer Fable	3
How could you, Sheelah, listen to his Tales,	. . .	882	Pastoral Dial	35
TALK				
No wonder, then, we talk amiss	. . . .	35	Ode Sancroft	41
(Methods in talk whereof our pride and ignorance make use)		38	Ode Sancroft	125
Cordials are in their talk, whilst all they mean	. . .	42	Ode Sancroft	257

```
TALK              (CONTINUED)                              PAGE  TITLE          LINE
    His Talk was now of Tythes and Dues,        . . . . .  115 Bauc & Phil 2    125
    They went by chance, amidst their Talk,     . . . . .  116 Bauc & Phil 2    153
    He'll talk of them from Noon till Night,    . .        116 Bauc & Pail 2    167
    And talk what Fools call Treason all the Night.  . .   163 Toland's Invit    16
    But, if I may with freedom talk,    . . . . . . .      183 Horace 2, 1      101
    They talk of further Alterations,    . . . . .         283 Journal          129
    To cheapen Tea, and talk with Fops.    . . . . . .     291 Prog Marriage     52
    Talk not of making of thy Nest,    . . . . . . .       361 Grace's Answer    13
    This Couple met to talk of News.    . . . . . . .      408 Dial Rich Marb     6
    Their Malice, is--to let them talk.    . .            414 Censure           30
    Admires how Girls can talk with Fellows,    . . . .    449 Modern Lady      163
    Nor shall we think you talk at random,    . . . . .    465 Birthday Song    159
    He cannot talk of Bus'ness now:    . . . . . . .       460 Libel on D- D-    16
    Loll out their Tongues, and thus they talk,   . . .    545 Life of Swift     21
    'Tis true, we talk of Friendship much,    . . . .      546 Life of Swift     41
    In such a Case they talk in Tropes,    . . . . . .     557 Death of Swift   117
    "To talk with Wits in dirty Shoes:    . . . . . .      565 Death of Swift   322
    Talk with Sense, whate'er you please on,    . . . .    638 Epistle Lady     271
    Then talk with more authentick Face,    . . . . .      648 On Poetry        243
    To talk on me she never fails:    . . . . . . .        679 From Catullus      2
    Desir'd them not to talk so loud,    . . . . . . .     689 Cadenus Vaness    77
    What Preachers talk, or Sages write,    . . . . .      691 Cadenus Vaness   150
    And since his Talk offensive grew,    . . . . . .      705 Cadenus Vaness   592
    That Stella loves to talk with Fellows    . . . .      735 Stel B-day '20    44
    And talk of Spectacles and Pills,    . . . . . .       763 Stel B-day '26     6
    We scorn, for want of talk, to jabber    . . . . .     781 Mullinix Tim     259
    Tom could talk with solemn Face,    . . . . . . .      784 Mullinex Dick     23
    Thus merciless Hannah ran on in her Talk,   . . . .    873 Grand Question   179
    Talk of their Milk for Babes of Grace;    . . . .      892 Panegyr Dean     170
    Who, while I talk, a song will hum,    . . . . . .     900 Dean's Reasons    47
    If when I talk, as talk I must,    . . . . . . .       901 Dean's Reasons    67
    If when I talk, as talk I must,    . . . . . . .       901 Dean's Reasons    67
    When I talk, and you are heedless,    . . . . . .      908 Daphne            59
    And you durst not talk thus if I saw you at our ale-house  976 Dean to Sherid   32
    I'll tear all your Rules, and demolish your Pun Talk: 1019 To Sheridan       8
TALK'D
    Talk'd with that saucy and familiar ease   . . . .     47 To Congreve      141
    I talk'd of a Peace, and they both gave a start,  . .  143 New Song          17
    Who talk'd of Justice, and of Truth,    . . . . .      386 Manly Virtue      72
    For since they talk'd with Doctor Clark,    . . . .    468 Birthday Song    269
    But, sure, she never talk'd so well.    . . . . .      710 Cadenus Vaness   749
TALK'T
    He mov'd, and bow'd and talk't with too much Grace;  . .  194 Author Himself  13
TALKING
    In talking ore a moderate Glass.    . . . . . . .      279 Journal           38
    Stunning her Royal Ears with talking;    . . . . .     410 Dial Rich Marb    59
    But there's no talking to some Men.    . . . . . .     556 Death of Swift   104
    For talking may beget Suspicion:    . . . . . . .      644 On Poetry        124
    Then fell to talking of the Weather:    . . . . . .    696 Cadenus Vaness   325
    No reading, nor talking?    . . . . . . . . .          854 Lady's Lament    112
    Much talking is not Harry's vice,    . . . . . . .     878 Robbin & Harry    13
TALKS
    Who by that, vainly talks of bafling Death,   . . .    21 Ode Athenian     182
    Talks Politicks, and gives the Toast.    . . . . .     398 Earl of P-b-w      6
    Talks half a Day in Praise of Silence;    . . . .      450 Modern Lady      171
    In half the Time, he talks them round;    . . . .      556 Death of Swift    97
    Talks in a high Romantick Strain;    . . . . . .       712 Cadenus Vaness   821
    Talks whate'er comes in his Head,    . . . . . .       800 Traulus 2         21
    How proudly he talks    . . . . . . . . . .            856 Lady's Lament    173
    With what pomposity he talks;    . . . . . . . .       950 Upstart        D  14
TALKT    SEE MUCH-TALKT
    Talkt of his Off'rings, Tyths, and Dues,    . . . .    95 Bauc & Phil 1    173
TALL
    Sid's Rod was slender, white, and tall,    . . . .     133 Magician's Rod    43
    Then shall the tall black Daventry Bird    . . . .     147 Windsor Proph      7
    Was so exceeding tall and Strong,    . . . . . .       160 Atlas              2
    Than yon tall Dock that rises to thy Nose.   . . .     881 Pastoral Dial     14
    My Person tall, and slender Waste,    . . . . . .      915 Riddle 1           5
    Taper, tall, and smooth, and slender;    . . . . .     937 Riddle 24      D  32
TALLER
    Taller than Misse's by two yards,    . . . . . . .     87 Hist V's House    25
TALLEST
    Nay, bring me here the tallest Man,    . . . . . .     934 Riddle 21      D  17
TALLOW
    Like a fly blown Cake of Tallow,    . . . . . . .      523 Betty Grizette     7
    His Tallow Face and Wainscot Paws,    . . . . . .      861 Lady Acheson      38
TAM
    Qui nil moliris tam inepte?    . . . . . . . .         476 Epist on Epist    30
    That she makes of your verses a hoop for Miss Tam,  . . 1027 Sheri Circles   27
TAM'D
    But may be tam'd another way,    . . . . . . . .       258 Bubble           187
    Of Sparrows tam'd, of Nuts innumerable,    . . . .     283 Journal          113
TAME
    No parish ducking-stool can tame her,    . . . . .     618 Scandal Poem 1    36
    No Parish Ducking-Stool can tame her:    . . . . .     624 Scandal Poem 2    34
    Instructs us how to tame a Scold;    . . . . . .       781 Mullinix Tim     272
    Scorpion Rods perhaps may tame them.    . . . . .      836 Legion Club      158
    Oh! could we tame yon watchful Dragon,    . . . . .    948 Jason Hassard      5
TAMELY
    I tamely can endure the first,    . . . . . . . .      555 Death of Swift    69
```

	PAGE	TITLE	LINE
TAMELY (CONTINUED)			
"Yet thou could'st tamely see me slain.	850	Old Thorn	68
TAMER			
Know all Men by these Presents, Death the Tamer . .	233	Elegy on Demar	1
TAMYS			
Tamys rivere twys y-frozen, ...	102	Merlin	3
TAN-TAN-TAN-TAN-TAN-TI-VI			
Now, tan-tan-tan-tan-tan-ti-vi	958	Cantata	
Now, tan-tan-tan-tan-tan-ti-vi quick quick, ...	958	Cantata	
TANKARDS			
He found he could purchase Two Tankards of Ale . .	288	Bank Down	37
TANN'D			
By Phoebus newly Tann'd and Dry'd.	100	Elegy Patrige	76
TANTARA			
Tantara, tantara, while all the Boys hollow.	870	Grand Question	92
Tantara, tantara, while all the Boys hollow.	870	Grand Question	92
TAPE			
Then Throttle thy self with an Ell of strong Tape, .	519	Dean Hang Rape	53
TAPER			
Taper, tail, and smooth, and slender;	937	Riddle 24	D 32
TAPSTER			
But the Tapster well Cudgell'd him both Side and Flank	288	Bank Down	39
TARE			
Tare out the Tale, and wipe your <Arse>	783	Tim and Fables	37
TARNISH			
Which Time and Accidents will tarnish:	595	Cassinus Peter	52
TARNISH'D			
In her tarnish'd brocade?	855	Lady's Lament	122
Unweeting gild the tarnish'd Lace:	896	Panegyr Dean	312
TARNISH'T			
And only Coat of tarnish't Lace;	295	Prog Marriage	162
TARR			
A Land-Commander, and a Tarr.	398	Earl of P-b-w	33
TARRY			
No longer will tarry, ...	245	Irish-Feast	34
TARRY'D			
To do the Jobb too long he tarry'd, ...	349	Upright Judge 2	2
TARTAR			
From him the Tartar, and Chinese, ...	655	On Poetry	423
And leaves the Tartar Phiz, in show	786	Dick, Maggot	13
Like the Bow that guards the Tartar, ...	927	Riddle 10	D 4
TASK			
My very good Lord, it's a very hard task	368	Verses Window	1
The Task is Arduous, Patrons find, ...	475	Epist on Epist	21
"And wish the Task had been assign'd	485	Libel on D- D-	169
While I assign my self a Task	739	Stel B-day '21	3
If I perform this Task with Pain	739	Stel B-day '21	5
An account of my task.	855	Lady's Lament	138
TAST			
Seems to have borrow'd some ungrateful tast	22	Ode Athenian	212
But not the Virtue Tast nor Juyce.	81	Vanbrug House	88
But not the Virtue, Tast or Juice.	109	V's House	130
What a corrupted Tast is ours	122	Empty'ng Town	5
And swears, Cushogue is to his Tast, ...	314	To Ford	89
Than on a Nymph of Stella's Tast.	747	Stel Distress	64
TASTE			
Then study to correct your Taste, ...	270	Apollo's Edict	D 10
So methought, he resolv'd no Liquor to taste, . . .	337	Serious Poem	111
But first resolv'd, to shew his Taste	378	Apology Lady C	97
To fit them to his Vulgar Taste.	410	Dial Rich Marb	70
To taste his humour, and his wit;	435	Answer Paulus	120
How cou'd so fine a Taste dispense	475	Epist on Epist	15
Appealing to the Nation's Taste, ...	483	Libel on D- D-	83
Must taste your irony and wit, ...	491	Dialogue	52
Our Thoughts, to hit your nicer Taste, ...	496	Panegyr Swift	106
Our Ministers are void of Taste, ...	497	Panegyr Swift	145
"The Town hath got a better Taste:	563	Death of Swift	266
For her Taste is almost as refin'd as her Wit. . . .	580	Psyche	10
Nor let them taste what causes Wind;	587	Strephon Chloe	124
How wrong a Taste prevails among us;	652	On Poetry	351
Grown so corrupted in their Taste.	688	Cadenus Vaness	66
In Judgment, Knowledge, Wit, and Taste;	697	Cadenus Vaness	343
With Virtue, Knowledge, Taste and Wit, ...	700	Cadenus Vaness	446
In her, a most judicious Taste.	711	Cadenus Vaness	767
"The Fellows had a wretched Taste;	714	Cadenus Vaness	869
I see her taste each nauseous Draught, ...	727	To Stella	113
Than on a Nymph of Stella's Taste.	752	Stel Wood-Park	80
Why, Tim, you have a Taste I know, ...	776	Mullinix Tim	91
Such Pastimes, when our Taste is nice, ...	788	Dick's Variety	11
And could not endure so vulgar a Taste, ...	868	Grand Question	42
That court and courtiers have no taste:	877	To Dean Swift	28
Of ev'ry Taste to know the Size;	890	Panegyr Dean	118
Whom you allow a man of taste, ...	899	Dean's Reasons	22
You can taste my verse or prose:	908	Daphne	70
Yet neither Smell, See, Taste, or Hear.	935	Riddle 23	D 9
TASTED			
Except they tasted of the Corn:	746	Stel Distress	14
Except they tasted of the Corn:	750	Stel Wood-Park	12
TASTER			
Who's but my Caterer and Taster?	918	Riddle 4	18

	PAGE	TITLE	LINE

TASTING
Call it Tasting, and Imbibing: . . . . 633 Epistle Lady 116
TASTLESS
To serve a tastless <Court> twelve Years in vain? . . 531 To Mr. Gay 2
TATLING
Still Groans while tatling Gossips prate. . . . . . 93 Bauc & Phil 1 110
TATTER'D
Disguis'd in tatter'd Habits, went . . . . 111 Bauc & Phil 2 9
'Till, daggled and tatter'd, ... 853 Lady's Lament 51
TATTLE
Such Tattle often entertains . . . . 291 Horace 2, 6 75
Then told the Tattle of the Day, ... 696 Cadenus Vaness 319
And please her more to hear them tattle . . . . . 762 Bec's B-Day 55
TATTLING
For want of tattling to the Queen; . . . . 410 Dial Rich Marb 58
Nor whisper to the tattling Reeds, ... 596 Cassinus Peter 105
My children tattling. . . . . 1037 Sheridan Cavan 2
TAUDRY
Without his taudry coach and four: . . . . 621 Scandal Poem 1 122
TAUGHT
You've taught the Cov'tous Wretches to o're-rate, . . 24 Ode Athenian 255
Too long have our misguided Souls been taught . . . . 27 Ode to Temple 18
Taught us, like Spaniards, to be proud and poor, . . . 28 Ode to Temple 56
Who, like hard masters, taught the Sun . . . . . . 36 Ode Sancroft 67
(By frequent observation taught) . . . . 176 To Lord Harley 6
"For Inquisitions taught by Spain, ... 183 Horace 2, 1 97
To you, by Art and Nature taught . . . . 215 To Mr. Delany 3
When first she taught them where to find . . . . . 227 Prog of Beauty 59
Pallas first taught us Poetry and Spinning; . . . . 257 Bubble 178
Let pride be taught by this rebuke, ... 276 Epilogue 38
Taught them to modulate their Tongues, ... 297 Satiric Elegy 29
Thus, acting what he taught so well, ... 326 Pethox 79
He taught, how Men to Honours rise, ... 386 Manly Virtue 83
By Satan taught, all Conj'rers know . . . . . . 386 Manly Virtue 103
Have taught him his poetick Words. . . . . . . 401 Window Inns 2 1
Well taught by practice to imbibe . . . . 411 Dial Rich Marb 92
Till Prudence taught him to appeal . . . . 435 Answer Paulus 109
By Sages, Priests, or Poets taught; . . . . . . 481 Libel on D- D- 43
By Homer dead was taught to thrive, ... 482 Libel on D- D- 76
By which himself was taught to rise: . . . . . . 483 Libel on D- D- 85
And in his Palace fed and taught him. . . . . . . 484 Libel on D- D- 116
"Are taught to use them for their Creed. . . . . . 514 Answer Fable 50
"Taught Fools their Int'rest how to know; . . . . . 564 Death of Swift 288
To kindle strife Dame Nature taught her, ... 569 Death of Swift 409
To kindle Strife, Dame-Nature taught her: . . . . . 618 Scandal Poem 1 37
Vanessa, tho' by Pallas taught, ... 624 Scandal Poem 2 35
She minds no longer what he taught. . . . . . . 702 Cadenus Vaness 488
And sad Experience taught their Use: . . . . . . 704 Cadenus Vaness 561
A Science which he never taught, ... 705 Cadenus Vaness 607
And taught Vanessa to dispute. . . . . 708 Cadenus Vaness 670
Each Girl when pleas'd with what is taught, ... 709 Cadenus Vaness 713
Which he had taught her to despise. . . . . . . 710 Cadenus Vaness 734
Have taught you from the World to hide: . . . . . 711 Cadenus Vaness 797
First taught thee human Knowledge and divine; . . . 730 Stella, Poems 100
As Machiavel taught 'em; divide and ye govern. . . . 791 St. Pat's Well 28
Taught harmless Man to cram and stuff. . . . . . 805 Irish Bishops 48
Have taught Men to extract with Skill, ... 895 Panegyr Dean 262
Whate'er your Predecessors taught us, ... 920 Riddle 6 21
988 Letter Dr Sh-n 1
TAVERN   SEE HEDGE-TAVERN
Upon a single Dish, and Tavern Wine, ... 162 Toland's Invit 2
Oh London Tavern! Thou hast lost a Friend, . . . 234 Elegy on Demar 25
TAWDRY
A Stock of tawdry Stuff besides, ... 80 Vanbrug House 46
TAWNY
Or, a tawny speckled Pippin, ... 523 Betty Grizette 9
A ragged Shirt, and tawny Hyde. . . . . 594 Cassinus Peter 16
You cannot blanch his tawny Hide; . . . . 785 Dick, Maggot 8
TAX
Nor tax the goddess of a mean design . . . . . . 44 To Congreve 33
For thee they Argo's Hulk will Tax, ... 100 Elegy Patrige 77
And hardly pay Eighteenpence Tax in the Pound: . . . 144 New Song 50
"And turn the Tax for publick Roads . . . . . . 571 Death of Swift 453
Nor can you tax me as unsteady, ... 899 Dean's Reasons 7
TAXES
By Bills for Taxes and Repairs. . . . . 174 Horace 1, 7 112
The People with a Sigh their Taxes bring; . . . . 533 To Mr. Gay 51
TAYL
Both are fastned by the Tayl. . . . . 501 Doctor Delaney 34
TAYLOR
From the Vintner and the Taylor, ... 574 Helter Skelter 35
And Muggleton, Toland, and Bradley the taylor, . . . 815 Yahoo's 27
Thus a wise Taylor is not pinching, ... 1021 Nim-Dan-Dean 1 D 15
TE
Went triumphant to Church, and sang stoutly Te Deum: . 967 Letter Sherid 18
TEA
She rises to her Tea at noon. . . . . 291 Prog Marriage 38
To cheapen Tea, and talk with Fops. . . . . . . 291 Prog Marriage 52
Can, at her Morning Tea, run o'er . . . . 416 Woman's Mind 23
Now, loit'ring o'er her Tea and Cream, ... 447 Modern Lady 70
Our Madam o'er her Ev'ning Tea; . . . . 448 Modern Lady 117

```
TEA          (CONTINUED)                                 PAGE   TITLE              LINE
    Like Females o'er their Morning Tea.        . . . . . .   501 Doctor Delaney        50
    Forbear their Tea, or drink it soon;  . . . . . .   .     587 Strephon Chloe       118
    Twelve Cups of Tea, (with Grief I speak)      . . . .     589 Strephon Chloe       163
    Are swallow'd o'er a Dish of Tea;     . . . . . .   .     642 On Poetry             68
    They call'd for Tea and Chocolate,    . . . . . .   .     698 Cadenus Vaness       374
    And Chest, that keeps my Lady's Tea,  . . . . . .   .     885 Rev Market-Hill       88
    Sweeten your Tea, and watch your Toast.   . . . . .       897 Panegyr Dean         328
TEA-KETTLE'S
    Her Tea-Kettle's on, and her Smock at the Fire:   . .     580 Psyche                 2
TEACH
    And teach him how to be polite. . . . . . . . .          218 To Mr. Delany         98
    By reading those who teach it best.   . . . . . . .      219 To Mr. Delany        104
    I'd teach her how to handle Sticks;   . . . . . . .      220 A Quiet Life          30
    And teach her Cheeks again to blush.  . . . . . . .      227 Prog of Beauty        48
    To teach the humble Wren to soar.     . . . . . . .      270 Apollo's Edict    D  26
    And teach her to despise thee more    . . . . . . .      292 Prog Marriage         76
    Since you can teach dead Dogs to bite. . . . . . .       299 Horrid Plot           40
    "And I know whom you mean to teach,   . . . . . . .      452 Modern Lady          255
    To teach the Science to your Friend.  . . . . . . .      493 Panegyr Swift         28
    Oh, could'st thou teach us how to zest  . . . . . .      495 Panegyr Swift         64
    You wou'd teach me to be wise;  . . . . . . . .          630 Epistle Lady          21
    They'll teach you how to split a Hair,  . . . . . .      657 On Poetry            485
    With underlings thy flock to teach,   . . . . . . .      677 Parson's Case         31
    To teach her what was Right or Wrong,     . . . . .      705 Cadenus Vaness       599
    Is but to learn what he can teach,  . . . . . . .        709 Cadenus Vaness       707
    The Science she designs to teach:     . . . . . . .      712 Cadenus Vaness       811
    And, Scholars teach, the Soul informs;    . . . . .      724 To Stella             12
    A Lesson she alone can teach.   . . . . . . . .          724 To Stella             34
    To teach her ears the art of list'ning,   . . . . .      762 Bec's B-Day           54
    Some teach us in these dang'rous Days,    . . . . .      780 Mullinix Tim         251
    We'll teach him some better address to afford  . . .     816 Yahoo's               53
    Teach Dennis how to stir the Guile:   . . . . . . .      897 Panegyr Dean         330
    While I teach, and you forget;  . . . . . . . .          908 Daphne                72
    'Twas to teach you in modester Language your Duty;  . .   968 Letter Sherid         25
TEACHER
    Will have the Teacher in her Thought.     . . . . . .    710 Cadenus Vaness       735
TEACHERS
    Thou, ungrateful to thy Teachers,   . . . . . . . .      838 Legion Club          203
TEACHES
    Listen while the muse thus teaches thee to sing:   . . .  52 Temple Ill            36
TEACHING
    Teaching others how to ape ye;  . . . . . . . .          631 Epistle Lady          53
    Teaching by what Golden Rules   . . . . . . . .          635 Epistle Lady         157
    Maxims teaching Wisdom's Use.   . . . . . . . .          637 Epistle Lady         238
TEAGUE
    To be cloath'd like a Carcass would make a Teague mad,   237 Excellent Song        12
    Teague made a good Pun by a Brogue in his Speech,  . .   334 Serious Poem          27
    With Teague O'Murphy, or an Earl;   . . . . . . .        890 Panegyr Dean         123
TEAGUES
    'Twixt Jades and Teagues    . . . . . . . . .            441 Ballyspellin          29
    "Pigs and Fanaticks, Cows, and Teagues    . . . . .      851 Old Thorn             77
    A parcel of Teagues,    . . . . . . . . . .              856 Lady's Lament        162
    The dullest Beast and fam'd College for Teagues   . . .  940 Letter                16
TEAM
    That now would overload a Team,     . . . . . . . .       79 Vanbrug House          4
    That now would overload a Team;     . . . . . . . .      106 V's House              4
TEAR
    To tear Religion's lovely face;     . . . . . . . .       42 Ode Sancroft         248
    Without a Tear will tend my Herse.  . . . . . . .        203 In Sickness            8
    To tear you like a foundred Hulk.   . . . . . . .        258 Bubble               199
    To bite his Pen, and drop a Tear.   . . . . . . .        561 Death of Swift       210
    And strive to tear you Limb from Limb,    . . . . .      651 On Poetry            333
    Tear the Bible all to Pieces.   . . . . . . . .          831 Legion Club           66
    "To tear thy Hedges join in Leagues,  . . . . . .        851 Old Thorn             79
    She'll tear me with her desp'rate Nails;  . . . . .      925 Riddle 8              20
    And make thee tear thy tainted Hyde.  . . . . . .        925 Riddle 8              44
    I'll tear all your Rules, and demolish your Pun Talk:    1019 To Sheridan           8
TEARING
    With which he made a tearing show:  . . . . . . .        619 Scandal Poem 1        71
    With which he made a tearing Show:  . . . . . . .        625 Scandal Poem 2        69
    Reputation ever tearing,    . . . . . . . . .            800 Traulus 2             15
TEARS
    In the same Ballance with our Tears,  . . . . . .         24 Ode Athenian         257
    Nor dipt in Blood, nor Widow's Tears, nor Orphan's        29 Ode to Temple         86
        Cries:
    Pity a miserable Church's tears,    . . . . . . .         42 Ode Sancroft         243
    Weak is the beam to dry up nature's tears,  . . . .       51 Temple Ill            19
    Nor widow's sighs, nor orphan's tears,    . . . . .      296 Satiric Elegy         18
    But Elrington, tears falling from his cheeks,  . . .     308 Billet Players        43
    Then Reader pray shed some tears of Salt Water,  . .     430 Dicky Dolly           17
    No more let fall those precious Tears.    . . . . .      445 Modern Lady           18
    Unlucky Madam left in Tears,    . . . . . . . .          453 Modern Lady          290
    Envy, a Canker-worm which tears     . . . . . . .        458 Paddy's Charac        11
    To scorn the Art of Female Tears.   . . . . . . .        705 Cadenus Vaness       597
    Or melts my passions down with tears;     . . . . .      754 Stella '23            14
    How will your Eyes contain their Tears,   . . . . .      921 Riddle 7               9
    Yet endless Tears flow down in Streams.   . . . . .      932 Riddle 19         D   4
TEASE
    All people tease me,    . . . . . . . . . . .           1037 Sheridan Cavan         7
```

```
                                              PAGE   TITLE            LINE
TEAZ'D
    Teaz'd by a Buzzing Wasp, Below,         458 Paddy's Charac       30
    So teaz'd day and night                  851 Lady's Lament         3
TEAZD
    And half the Company is teazd            217 To Mr. Delany        75
TEAZE
    He'll teaze you with King Charles and Bishop Laud,  166 Toland's Invit  42
    To a good honest Junta that never will teaze you.   185 Scriblerus 1     6
    The Vermin only teaze and pinch          651 On Poetry           335
    Can teaze, and gall, and give the Spleen; 651 On Poetry          344
    Dear Madam, had you but the Spirit to teaze,  869 Grand Question  53
TEAZING
    For teazing me.                         1014 Swift to Sheri      28
TEAZINGS
    Sir <Robert> weary'd by Will. <Pulteney's> Teazings,  537 Mr. Pulteney  1
    And Sheridan's perpetual teazings,       753 Gift for Bec         8
TECTA
    Since you write in a cart, keep it tecta et sarta,  979 Dean to Tho: S  15
TEDIOUS
    Finch, fam'd for tedious Elocution, proves  194 Author Himself   39
    Descriptions tedious, flat and dry,      645 On Poetry          155
    Of tedious Moralists describe,           724 To Stella           16
TEEMING
    Her Litter teeming from her Womb,        207 Fable Bitches        4
    When Jove was, from his teeming Head,    504 Doctor Delaney     115
TEES
    Your effs and tees, and arrs, and esses? 487 Irish-Club          12
TEETH
    Crackt Lips, foul Teeth, and gummy Eyes,  226 Prog of Beauty      15
    Nor will her Teeth return again.         229 Prog of Beauty     112
    No Lips of Coral Teeth of Pearl.         272 Apollo's Edict   D  55
    With Teeth or with Claws it will bite or will scratch,  351 Wood Insect  19
    Is by the Teeth of Envy torn,            458 Paddy's Charac      10
    The Scrapings of her Teeth and Gums,     527 Lady's Dres Rm      40
    Two Rows of Teeth arm each devouring Jaw; 532 To Mr. Gay         35
    A Set of Teeth completely comes.         582 Young Nymph         20
    I broke his Teeth, but where's the mighty harm?  670 Epig Carthy 20  D  2
    And Teeth are useless, where there's nought to eat.  670 Epig Carthy 20  D  4
    A Mastiff's teeth are justly held in vogue,  672 Epig Carthy 25  D  1
    But Time with Iron Teeth I ween          849 Old Thorn           17
    And rub thy Teeth, and pair thy Nails.   897 Panegyr Dean       334
    Knave in your Teeth, Mr. Sheridan,       985 Mary to Sher         7
TEIZ'D
    Have teiz'd, by calling to their Aid     371 Letter D. S-y         5
    Said, she shou'd be no longer teiz'd;    704 Cadenus Vaness     574
    While teizing all, by all he's teiz'd,   777 Mullinix Tim       125
TEIZE
    Then presently he falls to teize,        201 Horace 2, 6         59
    Can dext'rously her Husband teize,       416 Woman's Mind        37
    To Teize, Perplex, Disturb, Confound,    777 Mullinix Tim       142
TEIZING
    Thy peevish, and perpetual teizing,      775 Mullinix Tim        57
    While teizing all, by all he's teiz'd,   777 Mullinix Tim       125
TEL
    Here in Beau-spelling (tru tel deth)      60 Lady Tablebook       9
TELL
    Then tell us what is Fame? where shall we search for it?  21 Ode Athenian  175
    Like a just Map to tell the vast Extent   25 Ode Athenian       302
    Then tell (dear fav'rite Muse)            30 Ode to Temple      115
    Stay while I tell my story, short, and true;  46 To Congreve    111
    And tell the irreligion of my grief;      53 Temple Ill          78
    Ah, should I tell a secret yet unknown,   54 Temple Ill          93
    Yet, what is wonderful to tell it,        65 Problem             11
    I was resolved to tell my Money, to see if it was right:  69 Mrs Harris Pet  4
    But pray, Mary, can you tell what I have done with my
       Purse!                                 70 Mrs Harris Pet      15
    That I durst Pawn my Ears, 'twill tell   101 Elegy Patrige      113
    Sprout, quoth the Man, What's this you tell us?  116 Bauc & Phil 2  157
    They tell us something strange and odd,  132 Magician's Rod      21
    Filth of all Hues and Odours seem to tell  139 City Shower       55
    This Day, (the Year I dare not tell,)    149 Corinna              1
    Tell me, Perfidious! Was it fit          154 Widow and Cat    D 38
    When We, by proper Signs and Symbols tell,  162 Toland's Invit   9
    Thou'lt tell of Leagues among the Great  181 Horace 2, 1         21
    "The Son and Father, join to tell us,    181 Horace 2, 1         44
    Who tell us these troublesome stories,   186 Scriblerus 4     D  3
    'Tis one to me.--"Then, tell us, pray    202 Horace 2, 6         99
    ('Tis always done, Romances tell us,     223 Prog of Love        47
    The Muse has now not time to tell 'um.   224 Prog of Love        86
    She'll tell you who's who,               247 Irish-Feast         82
    Inform us, You that best can tell,       252 Bubble              49
    Thalia, tell in sober Lays,              278 Journal              1
    And tell who loses, and who wins,        280 Journal             63
    To tell what ev'ry School Boy knows:     281 Journal             82
    And tell how little weight he sets,      282 Journal             99
    Why shou'd I tell of Ponds and Drains,   283 Journal            111
    Then pray be free, and tell me which:    299 Horrid Plot         24
    Now, let me tell you, plainly, Sir,      299 Horrid Plot         43
    Sir, to be plain, I tell you what;       300 Horrid Plot         67
    If <Hort> must sink, she grieves to tell it,  303 Storm          19
    The glitt'ring Beau could hardly tell,   325 Pethox              65
```

TELL	(CONTINUED)	PAGE	TITLE	LINE
But I'll tell you the Secret, and pray do not Blab,	.	335	Serious Poem	35
I told you one Tale, I will tell you another.	. . .	336	Serious Poem	70
This Brass was a Dragon (observe what I tell ye)	. .	337	Serious Poem	87
This, when my Grandsire knew; they tell us he,	. . .	350	Upright Judge 3	5
'Twere rude to make him tell it twice;	. . . . .	376	Apology Lady C	24
He stop'd, and cou'd not tell what ail'd him.	. . . .	376	Apology Lady C	34
Yet cannot tell the Reason why:	. . . .	415	Woman's Mind	4
Will tell aloud your greatest Failing;	. . . . . .	416	Woman's Mind	20
To morrow I shall tell you more,	. . . .	423	Ireld	61
'To tell, when he invites his Friends:	. . . . . .	448	Modern Lady	107
"Be witness if I tell a Flam:	. . . .	462	Birthday Song	78
Or name him, but to tell his Faults.	. . . . . .	465	Birthday Song	148
I'd tell of yours in Rhyme and Print:	. . . . .	475	Epist on Epist	11
That you are thankful who can tell?	. . . . . .	475	Epist on Epist	26
Then, boasting tell us where you din'd,	. . . . .	480	Libel on D- D-	5
You tell me, till my Fortune's made,	. . . . . .	496	Panegyr Swift	96
Themselves would be the first to tell,	. . . . .	505	Doctor Delaney	157
Why Strephon will you tell the rest?	. . . . . .	527	Lady's Dres Rm	69
Come, tell me truly, wou'd you take well,	. . . .	546	Life of Swift	31
Wou'd please 'em better than to tell,	. . . . . .	557	Death of Swift	125
Runs laughing up to tell the Queen.	. . . . . .	559	Death of Swift	180
"Nor, can I tell what Criticks thought 'em;	. . . .	565	Death of Swift	311
The Place of the Damn'd,--I'll tell you my Mind.	. .	575	Place Damn'd	4
Why let it go, if I must tell it--	. . . . . .	586	Strephon Chloe	83
That, once he heard a School-boy tell,	. . . . .	587	Strephon Chloe	106
Or freely tell the secret Cause.	. . . .	589	Strephon Chloe	162
Come, tell us, has she play'd the Whore?	. . . .	595	Cassinus Peter	45
I here conjure thee, tell the Cause;	. . . . . .	596	Cassinus Peter	92
Tell me, what have I to write?	. . . .	629	Epistle Lady	2
And tell the Murders of her Eyes.	. . . . . .	697	Cadenus Vaness	333
Howe'er it came, he cou'd not tell,	. . . . . .	710	Cadenus Vaness	748
"She needs must tell them to their Face,	. . . .	714	Cadenus Vaness	870
Your Innuendo's when you tell us	. . . . . .	735	Stel B-day '20	43
You tell a good jest,	. . . .	756	Dingley Brent	13
That I'm alive to tell you so.	. . . .	766	Stel B-day '26	88
But tell me, Tim, upon the spot,	. . . . . .	778	Mullinix Tim	151
Am, as you tell me, but their may-game,	. . . .	778	Mullinix Tim	174
Again he'll tell him, and again on't.	. . . . .	789	Dick's Variety	38
In him, tell me which prevail,	. . . .	801	Traulus 2	53
What produc'd them, can you tell?	. . . . . .	801	Traulus 2	55
(And, Parsons tell us, no Man can do more)	. . .	806	Judas	6
And Smithfield, I'll tell you, if not told before,	. .	814	Yahoo's	2
Dear Dick, prithee tell by what passion you move?	.	818	Archbi Cashel	1
Tell us, what this Pile contains?	. . . . . .	829	Legion Club	9
Let me be allow'd to tell	. . . .	832	Legion Club	85
Such a Triplet could you tell	. . . .	837	Legion Club	183
"go tell your friend Bob and the other great folk,	.	843	Ay and No	13
(For none could tell whose Turn was next)	. . .	849	Old Thorn	31
Can tell by her looks	. . . .	854	Lady's Lament	93
Will tell him that Chaplains should not be so pert;	.	868	Grand Question	36
"Can hardly tell how to cry Bo to a Goose;	. . .	872	Grand Question	158
He need not tell a Story twice,	. . . .	878	Robbin & Harry	14
But, must not think, I tell him that,	. . . . .	886	Rev Market-Hill	95
Will I ever tell before ye:	. . . .	908	Daphne	66
And makes me tell a Thousand Lyes:	. . . . .	915	Riddle 1	20
Do what is not fit to tell,	. . . .	931	Riddle 18	D 27
Then prythee tell me what am I.	. . . .	936	Riddle 23	D 27
Now tell me, friend Thomas, Ford, Grattan, and merry Dan,		955	Portrait Life	9
Pudet haec opprobria, I freely must tell ye,	. . . .	967	Letter Sherid	5
Now tell me a Thing that wants Interpretation,	. .	973	S-'s Ans Sh-d	11
The rest of your compliment I dare not tell her,	. .	979	Dean to Tho: S	25
I tell you I'd not give a fig for your wine;	. . . .	979	Dean to Tho: S	30
Will laugh in their sleeves; I can tell you they watch for't.		979	Dean to Tho: S	36
. . . and you may go tell my Master; what care I?	.	986	Mary to Sher	21
Every body knows, that I love to tell Truth and shame the Devil,		986	Mary to Sher	23
For I can tell you one Thing, that I can,	. . . .	988	Letter Dr Sh-n	9
And tell who was it could direct her	. . . . . .	993	On Picture	11
. . .in plain English tell us so?	. . . . . .	1013	Swift to Sheri	2
Tho' perhaps you may tell it	. . . .	1015	Swift to Sheri	57
I wish you would tell me which way you incline	. .	1017	Swift Ans Sher	19
But now for your verses; we tell you, imprimis,	. .	1026	Sheri Circles	5
TELL-TALE				
But, sure a Tell-tale out of School	. . . . . .	592	Strephon Chloe	277
TELLER SEE FORTUNE-TELLER				
TELLING				
By telling Noses with a Party strong.	. . . . .	533	To Mr. Gay	60
TELLS				
In antient Time, as Story tells	. . . .	90	Bauc & Phil 1	1
In antient Times, as Story tells,	. . . .	111	Bauc & Phil 2	1
As Homer tells us o'er and o'er,	. . . .	134	Magician's Rod	69
Tells me i have more Zeal than Wit,	. . . . . .	200	Horace 2, 6	36
Tells ev'ry thing that you can think of,	. . . . .	282	Journal	91
Then Master Steward takes my Rent, and tells me, honest Jo.		342	Upon His Grace	23
He tells his brothr fools at night	. . . .	421	Ireld	24
Whatever Grecian Story tells:	. . . .	482	Libel on D- D-	78
Tells, with a Sneer, the Tidings heavy:	. . . . .	560	Death of Swift	190

		PAGE	TITLE	LINE

TELLS (CONTINUED)
Without Success; thus tells his Case: . . . . . . 604 Beasts Confess 94
The Statesman tells you with a Sneer, ... 605 Beasts Confess 141
One tells the Rise of Cheese, and Oat-meal, ... 781 Mullinix Tim 269

TELLUS
And Mother Tellus trembled so . . . . 849 Old Thorn 27

TEMP'RANCE
With Temp'rance, and with Fortitude; . . . . . . 325 Pethox 62

TEMPER
Whether thy Temper, full of Fire, ... 323 Pethox 5
And, such was then the Temper of the Times, ... 536 To Mr. Gay 155
They temper Love and Books together; . . . . . . 712 Cadenus Vaness 825
A temper the Devil himself could not bridle, . . . 955 Portrait Life 3

TEMPEST
Like that prophetic tempest in the virgin reign, . . . 40 Ode Sancroft 196
Oh, may some Western Tempest sweep . . . . 258 Bubble 205
"When such a Tempest shook the Land, ... 568 Death of Swift 389
Torn by a sudden Tempest is thy Sail, ... 770 Horace 1, 14 23

TEMPESTS
Tempests long frown, and thunder threatens loud, . . . 52 Temple Ill 24
When Rains descend, and Tempests rise, ... 84 Salamander 34
Fierce Aeolus in Tempests roars. . . . . 924 Riddle 7 88

TEMPESTUOUS
Gives glad farewell to a tempestuous day; . . . . . 51 Temple Ill 18
Tost in the Waves of this tempestuous World, ... 284 Elegy Boat 5
Who in tempestuous Seas can sport, ... 925 Riddle 8 33

TEMPLE
'Twas sure this Basilisk sent Temple thence, ... 30 Ode to Temple 124
Where her own Temple was her darling theme; . . . . 51 Temple Ill 14
The Couple to the Temple went: . . . . 290 Prog Marriage 6
No Temple, to his Godship rais'd, ... 346 Prometheus 43
To Fame a Temple you Erect, ... 477 Epist on Epist 77
Imprimis, at the Temple Porch . . . . 585 Strephon Chloe 47
That he came from the Temple, his morals do show, . . 815 Yahoo's 11

TEMPLE-BAR
From Ludgate shines to Temple-bar. . . . . . . 650 On Poetry 304

TEMPLE-DOOR
Janus hath lock'd his Temple-door? . . . . . . 462 Birthday Song 50

TEMPLE-SIDE
A Trophy, on his Temple-side.) . . . . 458 Paddy's Charac 18

TEMPLER
The Templer spruce, while ev'ry Spout's a-broach, . . 138 City Shower 35

TEMPLES
A List the Coblers Temples ties, ... 98 Elegy Patrige 23
Wou'd his own Temples better fit, ... 458 Paddy's Charac 22
Two Temples of magnifick Size, ... 893 Panegyr Dean 201
To Temples why do we confine? . . . . 894 Panegyr Dean 230

TEMPORA
O tempora, O mores! as 'tis in the adage. . . . . 975 Dean to Sherid 2

TEMPT
With nothing to tempt ye: . . . . 402 Window Inns 8 D 4
In vain I tempt too high a Flight. . . . . . . 897 Panegyr Dean 324

TEMPTATIONS
Thus young, thus proof to all Temptations, ... 386 Manly Virtue 89

TEMPTED
They tempted me t' attack your Highness, ... 1005 Sheridan's Sub 23

TEMPTS
This tempts Free-thinkers to refine, ... 687 Cadenus Vaness 11

TEN
Seven and Ten addyd to nyne, ... 102 Merlin 1
A finer House ten times than this, ... 128 Little House 62
Displays his Talent, sits till Ten, ... 173 Horace 1, 7 75
Ten thousand footsteps, full in view, ... 177 To Lord Harley 17
There are ten thousand Dicks beside; . . . . . . 221 A Quiet Life 56
Here's ev'ry Piece as big as ten. . . . . . . 251 Bubble 8
Ten thousand sunk by leaping in. . . . . . . 254 Bubble 108
'Tis the Nymph that I courted some ten Years ago; . . 264 Apollo 44
There's scarce one in ten, but what has my Mark; . . . 265 Apollo 62
At Ten, my Lady comes and Hectors, ... 278 Journal 13
But use You ten times worse than Pri'r. . . . . . 312 To Ford 34
Has lost His Grace for Ten Years past . . . . . . 341 Upon His Grace 10
. . . Ten thousand Pounds and more: . . . . . . 341 Upon His Grace 10
For he regards Ten thousand Pounds no more than Woods's Dross. 341 Upon His Grace 12
He makes no more to give ten Pounds than I to give a Pin. 341 Upon His Grace 14
Ten Thousand Cymbals now begin . . . . 354 Simile Silver 9
And get Ten thousand Girls and Boys. . . . . . . 362 Grace's Answer 48
Ten thousand Girls and Boys you'll get . . . . . 362 Grace's Answer 49
But pray. To morrow go at Ten, ... 377 Apology Lady C 67
Nor can ten Hundred Thousand Lyes, ... 414 Censure 27
She spoke ten Thousand Times before. . . . . . . 416 Woman's Mind 12
The clamours of ten thousand tongues . . . . . . 433 Answer Paulus 53
And all for ten poor moidores fee! . . . . . . 434 Answer Paulus 80
"Here, carry down those ten Pistoles . . . . . . 447 Modern Lady 66
Instead of Five you scor'd me Ten. . . . . . . 453 Modern Lady 265
Be sung ten hundred thousand times. . . . . . . 467 Birthday Song 222
And, Statesmen by ten thousand odds . . . . . . 486 Libel on D- D- 197
Condemn'd for thy Crime, at three score and ten? . . . 519 Dean Hang Rape 50
Who bore for twice ten Years the publick Hate. . . . 536 To Mr. Gay 144
A Nymph, that brings ten thousand Pound: . . . . . 545 Life of Swift 16

	PAGE	TITLE	LINE
TEN (CONTINUED)			
Enough to win ten Thousand Hearts;	598	Problem Solved	20
He's poorer by ten thousand Pound.	606	Beasts Confess	174
'Tis ten to one the Wit escapes;	643	On Poetry	98
You still are low ten thousand Mile.	657	On Poetry	472
'Tis ten to one, he breaks your Neck.	666	Epig Carthy 2 D	8
And ten to one drags down his feeble stick. . .	672	Epig Carthy 24 D	18
Ten thousand Oaths upon Record.	725	To Stella	55
Ten thousand Archy's arm'd with Spades . . .	743	Stel B-day 22	73
Who held a Cabbin for ten Groats a Year; . .	826	Noisy Tom	12
Are ten crooked sticks:	853	Lady's Lament	78
'Till threescore and ten, ...	855	Lady's Lament	128
Twice ten years older than his wife	879	Robbin & Harry	51
Ten thousand Lice, and ev'ry Louse was gold, . .	882	Pastoral Dial	46
His Slaves have ten Times more than he.	884	Rev Market-Hill	28
Ten Thousand Altars smoaking round	894	Panegyr Dean	237
Send me hence ten thousand miles, ...	907	Daphne	21
Give yourself ten thousand airs	908	Daphne	77
Can grant ten Thousand Pounds a Year, ...	916	Riddle 1	35
Tho' ten thousand Canons roar, ...	931	Riddle 18 D	23
Add to them ten thousand more, ...	931	Riddle 18 D	24
And see now, it strikes ten, and I hear him coming up Stairs:	987	Mary to Sher	36
An Ounce of Gold's worth ten of Brass, dull Pedant. .	1004	Dan J's Reply	33
. . .for Saunders already hath got above ten Jaunts.	1013	Swift to Sheri	6
TENANT			
And under him no Tenant yet was ever known to thrive. .	342	Upon His Grace	20
If I make it a Barrack, the Crown is my Tenant. . .	867	Grand Question	19
TENANT'S			
The Tenant's in a Dismal Case	240	Run Bankers	47
TENANTS			
His Tenants wrong him in his Rent;	174	Horace 1, 7	108
While his Tenants in Paper must pay him his Rent: . .	288	Bank Down	53
My Tenants, if you doubt, will prove it: . . .	348	Whitshed Motto	8
With Servants, Tenants, and the neighb'ring Squires. .	533	To Mr. Gay	54
The Tenants poor, the Hardness of the Times, . .	533	To Mr. Gay	67
"To rob the Church, their Tenants rack, ...	571	Death of Swift	448
From his Tenants vital Blood.	800	Traulus 2	42
But a Rabble of Tenants, and rusty dull Rumms; . .	868	Grand Question	28
But now, let all his tenants round	902	Dean's Reasons	103
TENARIFFA			
While we, o'er Tenariffa plac't, ...	620	Scandal Poem 1	105
While we, o'er Tenariffa plac't, ...	626	Scandal Poem 2	103
TENCH			
Because he brib'd you with a Brace of Tench?	534	To Mr. Gay	92
TEND			
Without a Tear will tend my Herse.	203	In Sickness	8
Which those who tend the Sick for pay	204	In Sickness	17
Her Arguments directly tend	417	Woman's Mind	51
TENDER			
Nature's fair Table-book our tender Souls	27	Ode to Temple	32
Some tender Sonnet to indite, ...	184	Horace 2, 1	114
But, no obliging, tender Friend	204	In Sickness	19
"Stay till my tender Cubs can find, ...	208	Fable Bitches	33
Dick lost in Doll, a Wife Tender and Dear, . . .	430	Dicky Dolly	4
"And crack'd her tender Maidenhead	497	Panegyr Swift	132
The Doctors tender of their Fame, ...	558	Death of Swift	169
My female Friends, whose tender Hearts	562	Death of Swift	225
She by the tender Graces drest, ...	586	Strephon Chloe	59
The Tender Embryos half unknown decay, ...	667	Epig Carthy 5 D	4
From whence the tender Skin assumes	691	Cadenus Vaness	160
Then sows within her tender Mind	693	Cadenus Vaness	202
One of her tender Sex and Age.	705	Cadenus Vaness	579
So tender of the Young and Fair?	707	Cadenus Vaness	652
No more that Bry'r thy tender Leg shall rake: . .	881	Pastoral Dial	17
The tender Pledges of our Joy.	925	Riddle 8	22
Yet so tender is my Ear, ...	933	Riddle 20 D	25
Or bring a tender Child and pliant, ...	934	Riddle 21 D	19
Often fair, and soft, and tender, ...	937	Riddle 24 D	31
With a tender Chicken.	952	Asparagus	5
TENDERLY			
The Premises tenderly consider'd,.	73	Mrs Harris Pet	70
TENDERNESS			
And, then their Tenderness appears, ...	556	Death of Swift	105
Tenderness my greatest Fault.)	637	Epistle Lady	232
If, while your Tenderness secures	727	To Stella	119
TENDS			
Or if to Blasphemy it tends, ...	461	Birthday Song	27
So deeply Carthy to the Center tends.	669	Epig Carthy 14 D	2
But Virtue still to Virtue tends.	733	Verses Vanessa	12
She tends me, like an humble slave;	754	Stella '23	9
TENNIS-BALL			
That Tennis-Ball of Fate;	10	Ode to King	121
TENOR			
"But, kept the Tenor of his Mind, ...	567	Death of Swift	361
TENT			
Familiar in each Leader's Tent.	324	Pethox	18
TENTHS			
First-Fruits and Tenths, and Chapter-Treats, . .	174	Horace 1, 7	103
TERENCE			
More Wit and Humour than from Terence.	988	Letter Dr Sh-n	4

```
                                                        PAGE    TITLE            LINE
TERM
    Who may object against the Term,        . . . . . . .  83 Salamander         25
    From Satan for a Term of Years,         . . . . . . . 240 Run Bankers        46
    When term is ended, leaves the town,    . . . . . . . 435 Answer Paulus      93
    A hundred Fees last Easter Term.                      604 Beasts Confess     86
    Above a Term or two at most.            . . . . . . . 604 Beasts Confess     92
TERMS
    In civil Terms,--"My Friend," says she, . . . . . . . 208 Fable Bitches      25
    With periods long, in terms abstruse!   . . . . . . . 434 Answer Paulus      82
    Unskill'd in all the Terms of Art?      . . . . . . . 451 Modern Lady       221
    Then, if you find the Terms too hard,   . . . . . . . 50? Doctor Delaney     53
    In proper Terms to write a Fable;       . . . . . . . 512 Answer Fable        2
    Before you learn the Terms of Art:      . . . . . . . 647 On Poetry         240
TERRA
    Virtue's Terra Incognita,               . . . . . . . .  26 Ode to Temple     12
TERRAS
    And on the Terras light. . . . . . . . . .            30 Ode to Temple      119
    A Terras Walk, and half a Rood          . . . . . . . 198 Horace 2, 6         5
TERRESTRIAL
    Terrestrial nymphs, by formal arts,     . . . . . . . 178 To Lord Harley     53
TERRIFY'D
    She was so terrify'd at his. . . . . . . . . . .      456 Dean Smedley       22
TERROR
    With trembling Knees, and Terror at his Back;  . . .  210 Earl of Oxford      4
    Lessens the Terror of the Sound:  . . . . . . .       500 Doctor Delaney      8
    The Tories Terror, Scourge and Flail.   . . . . . .   776 Mullinix Tim       86
    The Terror of Women, and Pleasure of Boys,  . . . .   927 Riddle 11       D   2
TERRORS
    With equal Terrors, not with equal Guilt,  . . . . .  364 On Dreams          13
    Jove, arm'd with Terrors, burst the Skies, . . . . .  578 Day Judgement       5
    Gloomy Pluto, King of Terrors,          . . . . . . . 661 Love Song          17
    His Majesty of Terrors came,            . . . . . . . 904 Death Daphne       54
TEST
    Tis but when others stand the Test,     . . . . . . . 218 To Mr. Delany      84
    Whose Virtues bear the strictest Test;  . . . . . . . 655 On Poetry         412
TETE
    "Always together, tete a tete:          . . . . . . . 202 Horace 2, 6        86
    "Always together, tete a tete:          . . . . . . . 202 Horace 2, 6        86
    Chuse for Companions tete a tete,       . . . . . . . 480 Libel on D- D-      2
    Chuse for Companions tete a tete,       . . . . . . . 480 Libel on D- D-      2
    And when we can't be tete a tete        . . . . . . . 493 Panegyr Swift      13
    And when we can't be tete a tete        . . . . . . . 493 Panegyr Swift      13
TETHER
    Thus, Fame and Censure with a Tether    . . . . . . . 501 Doctor Delaney     35
    Tye them Keeper in a Tether,            . . . . . . . 835 Legion Club       153
    By which your jade Pegasus fixt in a tether,  . . . . 1027 Sheri Circles     18
TEXT
    You are no Text for my Handling, so take that from me:  72 Mrs Harris Pet    57
    Chang'd in the Preface and the Text:    . . . . . . .  95 Bauc & Phil 1     178
    Vampt in the Preface and the Text;      . . . . . . . 115 Bauc & Phil 2     128
    Or spoils a Text, or mends his Hose.    . . . . . . . 279 Journal            24
    As if he was awake, nods o'er his Text: . . . . . . . 364 On Dreams          32
    Wou'd have the Text as well as Comment; . . . . . . . 375 Apology Lady C      4
    No doubt the text is here mistaken:     . . . . . . . 434 Answer Paulus      66
    And plainly prove by dint of Text,      . . . . . . . 456 Dean Smedley       39
    Where the Nymph has entirely forsaken her Text:       716 Answer Rebus       20
    Will you keep strictly to the Text?     . . . . . . . 732 Stella, Poems     138
    Who knows in Law, nor Text, nor Margent, . . . . . .  812 Bro Protestant     27
    How nice you split the hardest Text!    . . . . . . . 888 Panegyr Dean       62
TEXTS
    Quote you Texts from Plutarch's Morals; . . . . . . . 637 Epistle Lady      236
TEXTURE
    Then curious Hands this Texture take,   . . . . . . .  79 Vanbrug House      33
TEXTURES
    The various Textures of their Minds,    . . . . . . . 291 Prog Marriage      34
TH'         45                                               OMITTED WORD
TH'ROUGHLY
    Your Onyons must be th'roughly boyl'd;  . . . . . . . 952 Onyons              9
THALIA
    Thalia heard the Call and Flew          . . . . . . . 120 Apollo Outwit      39
    Thalia, tell in sober Lays,  . . . . . . . . .        278 Journal             1
    "Thalia said, 'tis somewhat odd,        . . . . . . . 321 First of April     18
    Thalia now began to smoke,   . . . . . . . . .        322 First of April     53
THAMES    SEE TAMYS
    The crooked Paths of wandering Thames.  . . . . . . .  31 Ode to Temple     152
    No longer shall forsaken Thames         . . . . . . . 107 V's House          47
    Another, of the Thames enquires,        . . . . . . . 109 V's House         101
    In my own Thames may I be drownded,     . . . . . . . 410 Dial Rich Marb     73
    Prefer our Villaes where the Thames is, . . . . . . . 411 Dial Rich Marb     87
    Sabrina, Medway, and the Thames.        . . . . . . . 468 Birthday Song     242
    Like the Watermen of Thames,            . . . . . . . 635 Epistle Lady      165
THAN        221                                              OMITTED WORD
THANK
    Thank God, 'twas neither Shame nor Sin, . . . . . . . 224 Prog of Love       59
    So for their Quack-Bills he knows whom to thank,  . . 288 Bank Down          54
    And she wou'd kindly thank him for't. . . . . . . .   302 Storm               6
    "I thank my Stars they are all light;   . . . . . .   447 Modern Lady        68
    "I answer, they may thank themselves;   . . . . . . . 548 Life of Swift     116
    Tho' he does not, I thank you for your Gift;          669 Epig Carthy 17  D  3
    To half a Joint, and God be thank it:   . . . . . . . 750 Stel Wood-Park     36
    They've done it, we thank 'em, but not as they meant;  . 804 Irish Bishops   36
```

		PAGE	TITLE	LINE
THANKED				
To half a Joynt, & God be thanked:	. . . . . .	745	Stel Distress	12
THANKFUL				
So bow'd, was thankful for the Honour:	. . . . . .	376	Apology Lady C	25
That you are thankful who can tell?	. . . . . .	475	Epist on Epist	26
And then, how thankful to the Town,	. . . . . .	502	Doctor Delaney	67
THANKLESS				
Like thee, to please this thankless Town!	. . . . .	779	Mullinix Tim	198
Those thankless and officious cares	. . . . . .	901	Dean's Reasons	95
THANKS				
But thanks his stars, that Phyllis has been kind;	. .	48	To Congreve	158
Pay Thanks for the Gift,	. . . . . .	77	Lady B- B-	27
Return'd 'em Thanks in homely Stile;	. . . . . .	115	Bauc & Phil 2	112
The Way is thus; and well deserves your Thanks:	. . .	285	Elegy Boat	31
But Thanks to the House, the Projectors look blank,	.	287	Bank Down	9
And Thanks to the Members that Kickt down the Bank.	.	287	Bank Down	10
Thanks to my Stars, I once can see	. . . . . .	402	Window Inns 7	D 1
"Thy Thanks and Verse, devoid of Art:	. . . . . .	476	Epist on Epist	34
And well deserves the Nation's Thanks.	. . . . . .	515	Answer Fable	80
Pays all the Cost, and gives the Villain Thanks.	. .	535	To Mr. Gay	110
Too long I have my Thanks delay'd;	. . . . . .	887	Panegyr Dean	3
But thanks to the lady: I'm sure she's too good to ye;	.	976	Dean to Sherid	38
THAT 856			OMITTED WORD	
THAT'S 26			OMITTED WORD	
THATCH				
Would Tile; an Epigram would Thatch.	. . . . . .	79	Vanbrug House	12
Would Tile; an Epigram would Thatch.	. . . . . .	106	V's House	12
THATCHER				
Our Thatcher, Ditcher, Gard'ner, Baily.	. . . . .	891	Panegyr Dean	156
THATCHT				
(Under Correction) with the thatcht,	. . . . . .	313	To Ford	66
THE 5351			OMITTED WORD	
THEATRE				
(As in a Theatre the Ignorant Fry,	. . . . . .	29	Ode to Temple	94
THEE 125			OMITTED WORD	
THEFT				
By Rapine, Theft, or Thirst of Blood.	. . . . .	602	Beasts Confess	20
Sloth, Dirt, and Theft around her wait.	. . . . .	1035	To Quilca	12
THEIR 590			OMITTED WORD	
THEIRS 12			OMITTED WORD	
THEM 190			OMITTED WORD	
THEME				
Where her own Temple was her darling theme;	. .	51	Temple Ill	14
"For once the Theme of human Sense.	. . . . . .	384	Manly Virtue	10
If Others, whom you make your Theme,	. . . . . .	391	Young's Satire	7
She enters on her usual Theme;	. . . . . .	447	Modern Lady	71
Nor on a Theme like this repine,	. . . . . .	515	Answer Fable	89
Nor shall Vanessa be the Theme	. . . . . .	696	Cadenus Vaness	298
THEMSELVES 17			OMITTED WORD	
THEN 367			OMITTED WORD	
THENCE				
And thence with joyful, nimble Wing	. . . . . .	16	Ode Athenian	29
'Twas sure this Basilisk sent Temple thence,	. . . .	30	Ode to Temple	124
To lodge in Garrats comes from thence.	. . . . . .	79	Vanbrug House	28
To lodge in Garrats, comes from thence.	. . . . . .	106	V's House	28
Steals thence his Plot, and ev'ry Joke,	. . . . . .	107	V's House	59
And thence Beheld a Lovely Maid	. . . . . .	119	Apollo Outwit	3
Thence, thro' a long Descent of Kings,	. . . . . .	134	Magician's Rod	63
And thence into the Royal Ear instills.	. . . . . .	195	Author Himself	56
He'll find the Secret out from thence	. . . . . .	219	To Mr. Delany	107
To climb to our Region, and thence to steal Fire;	. .	266	Apollo	96
Said I, from thence I nothing know;	. . . . . .	298	Horrid Plot	5
Thence to the Neck; and moving thorow there;	. . . .	367	Answer Delaney	37
From thence a plenteous Draught infuse,	. . . . . .	743	Stel B-day 22	75
Consult the Stars, and thence foretell	. . . . . .	918	Riddle 4	43
And thence, as fam'd John Bunyan sung,	. . . . . .	983	Sher, A Goose	6
THEOCRITUS				
Theocritus and Philips be,	. . . . . .	270	Apollo's Edict	D 31
THEOLOGIC				
For, whate'er theologic lev'llers dream,	. . . . . .	41	Ode Sancroft	230
THERE 180			OMITTED WORD	
THERE-HENCE				
And think your Boys may gather there-hence	. .	988	Letter Dr Sh-n	3
THERE'S 45			OMITTED WORD	
THEREABOUTS				
Call'd thereabouts Goodman Philemon;	. . . . .	91	Bauc & Phil 1	52
THEREFORE 18			OMITTED WORD	
THERSITES				
Thersites (he was your Relation)	. . . . . .	775	Mullinix Tim	52
THESE 117			OMITTED WORD	
THESPIS'S				
For ought he knows, as bad as Thespis's.	. . . . .	988	Letter Dr Sh-n	23
THEY 511			OMITTED WORD	
THEY'D 3			OMITTED WORD	
THEY'LL 13			OMITTED WORD	
THEY'RE 10			OMITTED WORD	
THEY'VE 4			OMITTED WORD	
THICK				
When Folks came thick to make their Court	. . . . .	62	Discovery	6
. . .and she, you know, is thick of Hearing;	. . . .	70	Mrs Harris Pet	25
Look round about how thick it lyes:	. . . . . .	254	Bubble	104

		PAGE	TITLE	LINE
THICK	**(CONTINUED)**			
Thro' thick and thin, to get a name.		456	Dean Smedley	24
Fly Bullets now as thick as Hops,		500	Doctor Delaney	9
Resolv'd to go thro' thick and thin;		528	Lady's Dres Rm	80
The Rest pursue as thick as Hops:		654	On Poetry	400
Thick her arguments she lays on,		906	Daphne	11
THICKET				
Hemm'd in by a Thicket,		938	Riddle Answerd	4
THIEF				
. . .I hate a Thief.)		71	Mrs Harris Pet	35
So a Thief steals my Horse, and then gets him well drest		266	Apollo	92
Dan growing drowsy like a Thief,		279	Journal	39
And, when we view it thus, with Thief at End on't,		285	Elegy Boat	35
By that old Thief Prometheus? Wood		346	Prometheus	60
This Thief and Black-Smith was so bold,		346	Prometheus	63
Quoth the Thief to the Dog; let me into your Door,		395	Dog and Thief	1
The Daw a Thief, the Ape a Drole,		512	Answer Fable	7
When a Brother Thief is hanging.		830	Legion Club	16
THIEVES				
The Gift (good Heav'ns preserve 't from Thieves)		494	Panegyr Swift	49
To punish Thieves, or lash a Suburb Wench.		537	Mr. Pulteney	6
"Go Snacks with Thieves and Rapparees,		571	Death of Swift	449
A <Parliament>, or Den of Thieves.		645	On Poetry	164
While the Den of Thieves is full,		830	Legion Club	28
With Thieves, Fanatics, and Barbarians?		899	Dean's Reasons	18
THIMBLE				
If I can fill my Thimble,		1015	Swift to Sheri	52
THIN SEE THYN				
But was so dirty, pale and thin,		174	Horace 1, 7	119
In half a Month she looks so thin		229	Prog of Beauty	98
Thro' thick and thin, to get a name.		456	Dean Smedley	24
Resolv'd to go thro' thick and thin;		528	Lady's Dres Rm	80
My nose, long and thin,		853	Lady's Lament	73
No Wonder now I look so thin;		915	Riddle 1	9
THINE 12				
THING			OMITTED WORD	
And straight deny you to be Men, or any thing at all;		19	Ode Athenian	120
Is but one thing under two different names;		41	Ode Sancroft	206
And in all the Places I liv'd, I never heard of such a Thing.		70	Mrs Harris Pet	31
Such a thing as this happen'd, just about the time of Goosberries.		71	Mrs Harris Pet	33
But the Thing I stand upon, is the Credit of the House		71	Mrs Harris Pet	39
No, said I, 'tis the same Thing,..		72	Mrs Harris Pet	49
Not a sham Thing of Clay or Cards.		87	Hist V's House	26
You blind and lame! tis no such Thing		91	Bauc & Phil 1	42
A Thing resembling a Goose Py,		109	V's House	104
Prevail'd on by the Thing you name,		121	Apollo Outwit	63
Pray reach that Thing here to the Child,		128	Little House	52
That Thing, I mean, among the Kale,		128	Little House	53
Turn'd ev'ry thing he touch't to Gold:		156	Fable of Midas	2
The Thing was done and past recalling:		224	Prog of Love	68
Tells ev'ry thing that you can think of,		282	Journal	91
To cut down fine Wood is a very bad Thing,		334	Serious Poem	13
I think the best Thing we can do is to scald him.		351	Wood Insect	34
Like'd ev'ry Thing - - - at least thought fit		379	Apology Lady C	119
Or more to show the Thing I mean,		393	Modern Poets	9
That, without which a Thing is not		406	Swift to Pope	19
But now it will be no such thing,		409	Dial Rich Marb	39
They may out-sell a better Thing;		418	Woman's Mind	63
One thing he did before he went hence,		455	Dean Smedley	17
Yet many a foolish thing he writ---;		547	Life of Swift	75
"For ev'ry thing---, but what it should.		550	Life of Swift	179
"But now, he's quite another Thing;		557	Death of Swift	113
"You know 'tis quite a different Thing.		560	Death of Swift	188
"You never met a Thing so smart;		564	Death of Swift	285
This is not the Thing we wish.		633	Epistle Lady	110
That modern Love is no such Thing		687	Cadenus Vaness	27
To Scandal next-----What aukward Thing		699	Cadenus Vaness	384
A Thing never known to the Muses or Phoebus:		716	Answer Rebus	8
And swears she saw a Thing in White.		725	To Stella	74
Perhaps you're quite another Thing.		730	Stella, Poems	70
Whose Heart in this Four-footed Thing lies.		763	Collar Lap-Dog	2
"Now Madam, you'll think it a strange Thing to say,		873	Grand Question	171
Will not have one new thing to say.		878	Robbin & Harry	12
Your Thing of various Shape and Hue,		912	Aenigma Expl	D 7
Nor can our Parson blame the Thing:		926	Riddle 9	14
Nought but one Thing can confound me,		933	Riddle 20	D 5
Yet ev'ry Thing that you can name;		935	Riddle 23	D 2
A long-ear'd Beast, a Thing that Force must drive in,		943	Probatur Alit	47
Now tell me a Thing that wants Interpretation,		973	S-'s Ans Sh-d	11
Only one scurvy thing I find,		983	Sher, A Goose	13
For I can tell you one Thing, that I can,		988	Letter Dr Sh-n	9
Yet one thing vexes me, I own,		1003	Dan J's Reply	16
THING'S				
How very mean a thing's a Duke;		297	Satiric Elegy	30
THINGS				
To judge of things above by things below.		35	Ode Sancroft	38
To judge of things above by things below.		35	Ode Sancroft	38
I'm sure I found them other kind of things		46	To Congreve	91
Rend'ring shades, things, and substances of names;		47	To Congreve	148

825

THINGS	(CONTINUED)	PAGE	TITLE	LINE
So because I had been buying things for my Lady last Night,		69	Mrs Harris Pet	3
(Now you must know, of all Things in the World,. .		71	Mrs Harris Pet	35
Mean time a Pair of awkward Things		80	Vanbrug House	35
Makes you take all things in good Part:		94	Bauc & Phil 1	160
But now the Senate (if things hit		182	Horace 2, 1	59
Two brightest, brittlest earthly Things		227	Prog of Beauty	63
With Forty Things more: Now hear what the Law says,		236	Excellent Song	3
Of all the fine Things he keeps in the Dark,		265	Apollo	61
By Christmas we shall see strange things.		282	Journal	110
How transient all things are below:		283	Journal	116
The Banks of a River I know are good Things,		287	Bank Down	2
Come hither, all ye empty things,		296	Satiric Elegy	25
They say, all human Things depend:		345	Prometheus	34
He whisprd publick things at last,		422	Ireld	33
When Things of more Importance press:		475	Epist on Epist	2
How many pleasant Things he spoke,		480	Libel on D- D-	7
For, no imaginable things		486	Libel on D- D-	195
But Things are strangely chang'd since then,		498	Panegyr Swift	163
So Things, which must not be exprest,		529	Lady's Dres Rm	109
Would so discreetly Things dispose,		584	Strephon Chloe	15
'Tis Time to shew how Things went there.		588	Strephon Chloe	146
We govern all things there below.		620	Scandal Poem 1	88
Tis sung. But we know better things.		621	Scandal Poem 1	142
We govern all Things there below.		626	Scandal Poem 2	86
'Tis sung, but we know better Things.		627	Scandal Poem 2	146
Things were not ripe for a Decree,		689	Cadenus Vaness	105
Leave all Things to their Nat'ral Course.		696	Cadenus Vaness	303
Cadenus many things had writ;		702	Cadenus Vaness	510
How dang'rous Things were Men of Wit,		706	Cadenus Vaness	619
But not to dwell on Things minute,		708	Cadenus Vaness	674
Things took a Turn he never meant.		709	Cadenus Vaness	731
It answers Faith in Things divine.		723	To Stella	10
Got all things at the highest Price.		745	Stel Distress	10
Got all things at the highest Price.		749	Stel Wood-Park	8
That true Contempt for Things below,		765	Stel B-day '26	68
While Things of heterogeneous Kind,		811	Bro Protestant	5
All things gone on the same dull track,		877	To Dean Swift	31
I'll shew the World strange Things and true;		919	Riddle 5	14
Yet from this mingled Mass of Things,		924	Riddle 7	89
And our Marks of Things declare,		931	Riddle 18	D 6
Most Things by me do rise and fall,		934	Riddle 21	D 1
In all Things false, yet always true,		935	Riddle 23	D 5
All Things on Earth I imitate,		935	Riddle 23	D 18
For a Parson, who shou'd know better Things, . . .		985	Mary to Sher	6

THINK				
And one would think 'twere past Omnipotence to please;		9	Ode to King	89
And think, alas, to be by mortals writ,		20	Ode Athenian	126
For You (ah, did I think I e'er should live to see		23	Ode Athenian	247
I sigh when e're I think of it		24	Ode Athenian	270
Think she there does all her Treasures hide,		27	Ode to Temple	37
And think the Church itself does so;		37	Ode Sancroft	78
Who barbarously think to 'scape reproach,		44	To Congreve	21
For, could you think? the fiercest foes you dread,		46	To Congreve	95
And can you think the wise forbear to laugh		46	To Congreve	107
Here would we sing--But, ah! you think I dream,		49	To Congreve	197
To think what cattle she has got among;		50	To Congreve	224
And thou seest my owners Heart,		60	Lady Tablebook	2
To think that your Brains Issue is		61	Lady Tablebook	19
So sweet a Passion who cou'd think,		65	Problem	3
Quoth Neal, whate'er the rest may think,		67	Problem	53
. . .as you may very well think,		70	Mrs Harris Pet	20
Let Censuring Criticks then think what they list on't,		77	Lady B- B-	REF
Think of a Bucket or a Pump.		83	Salamander	20
Then pray think this a lucky Hitt,		123	Empty'ng Town	21
Think what you save or what you kill		140	Harlyes Surgn	4
To think upon a certain Leader,		157	Fable of Midas	42
Well, I shall think of that no more,		173	Horace 1, 7	71
While, wise Men think they ought to fight		189	Faggot	21
Those Romans were too wise to think on't,		190	Faggot	29
I can't but think 'twould sound more clever,		198	Horace 2, 6	D
Great Ministers ne'er think of these;		199	Horace 2, 6	18
"How think you of our Friend the Dean?		202	Horace 2, 6	83
They stand amaz'd, and think me grown		202	Horace 2, 6	103
Yet still you think your Friend to blame.		218	To Mr. Delany	82
To think of Oyl and Soot, is vain,		229	Prog of Beauty	110
Will think his better Half alive.		235	Elegy on Demar	52
That I have an ill Eye, they wickedly think,		263	Apollo	13
I think I have now got him under my Lash;		265	Apollo	66
For I think in my Conscience he deals with Old Nick;		265	Apollo	82
We Phoebus think fit to proceed to his Sentence;		266	Apollo	94
Tells ev'ry thing that you can think of,		282	Journal	91
Think on some Remedy in time		293	Prog Marriage	103
Threescore, I think, is pretty high;		296	Satiric Elegy	11
And that's the reason, some folks think,		296	Satiric Elegy	15
Now, for my part, I think upon the whole,		308	Billet Players	15
We think, though You judge hardly of it,		311	To Ford	15
If this you think a pleasing Scene		312	To Ford	47
What think you of my fav'rite Clan,		314	To Ford	79
We cannot think it worth your while.		315	To Ford	98

THINK   (CONTINUED)   PAGE TITLE   LINE

	PAGE	TITLE	LINE
Some think him cut out from the Poisonous Yew,	334	Serious Poem	31
He can Lye like a Courtier, and think it no Scorn,	335	Serious Poem	45
And though some think him in the Wrong, ...	341	Upon His Grace	7
I think the best Thing we can do is to scald him.	351	Wood Insect	34
Nor shall she think that she is un-done	362	Grace's Answer	39
She'll never think of Mutton Pies.	362	Grace's Answer	42
You'll never think of Goody Griz.	362	Grace's Answer	44
That, Faith, I think, there scarce is Room	371	Letter D. S-y	7
I think I'm very fairly off.	377	Apology Lady C	56
Think what they wish so great a Blessing,	411	Desire Possess	3
By what they speak, or what they think.	414	Censure	26
I think they justly ought to share	422	Ireld	47
To think such Ladies fine,	426	Five Ladies	22
And think there's no refelling	440	Ballyspellin	3
On me, who think them all so fair,	445	Modern Lady	9
"I think I never had good Luck in't.	452	Modern Lady	241
But this I think will not go down,	460	Birthday Song	13
I think this Practice only fit	463	Birthday Song	111
Nor shall we think you talk at random,	465	Birthday Song	159
When, who could think, tho' cold as Ice,	470	Burning Poem	13
Who think your Muse must first aspire;	475	Epist on Epist	23
Think this Wall low, and that Wall bevel.	477	Epist on Epist	66
You think you'll sooner be a Bishop:	478	Epist on Epist	102
Most think what has been heap'd on You,	478	Epist on Epist	105
Your case consider'd, I must think	489	Dialogue	15
It is to think all great Ones Elves,	493	Panegyr Swift	12
No Wonder you should think it little	495	Panegyr Swift	58
His Poems, think them all not worth a Straw.	521	Stephen Duck	6
He soon would learn to think like me,	530	Lady's Dres Rm	141
Fain would I think, our Female Friend sincere,	531	To Mr. Gay	3
Nor, think your self secure in doing wrong,	533	To Mr. Gay	59
And, when I think upon't, this minute,	545	Life of Swift	11
"And yet, I think, for all your Jokes,	547	Life of Swift	93
Think what a Case all Men are now in,	585	Strephon Chloe	33
The Ladies else might think me shameless.)	586	Strephon Chloe	80
O, think what Evils must ensue;	588	Strephon Chloe	127
Think what can give the Colick Ease,	589	Strephon Chloe	168
You think some Goddess from the Sky	591	Strephon Chloe	229
You'd think she utter'd from behind,	592	Strephon Chloe	281
Think, Peter, how my Soul is rack'd.	596	Cassinus Peter	97
As we think fit to smile or frown;	620	Scandal Poem 1	92
(Who makes you think the Clouds he pierces:	620	Scandal Poem 1	103
But think how damnably you err	622	Scandal Poem 1	159
As we think fit to smile or frown:	626	Scandal Poem 2	90
(Who makes you think, the Clouds he pierces:	626	Scandal Poem 2	101
If you think me too conceited,	630	Epistle Lady	15
Think it Wit to fleer, and gibe?	632	Epistle Lady	78
Think not Cards my chief Diversion,	632	Epistle Lady	81
I shall read and think with Pleasure:	632	Epistle Lady	88
Is to understand, and think:	633	Epistle Lady	118
Will smile, and think 'em all his own:	647	On Poetry	226
But if you think this Trade too base,	647	On Poetry	233
For Instance: When you rashly think,	654	On Poetry	393
Then think, what Wonders will be done	655	On Poetry	433
Thus think on Kings, ye Name denotes	659	On Poetry	D 410
The World must think him in the Wrong,	707	Cadenus Vaness	643
And hopes he will not think it strange	712	Cadenus Vaness	804
Which others for Mantuas wou'd think fine enough;	716	Answer Rebus	16
Or think it seated in a Scar,	724	To Stella	25
Ask no Advice, but think alone,	724	To Stella	37
You think this Turbulence of Blood	731	Stella, Poems	127
They think it both a Shame and Sin	734	Stel B-day '20	13
Then, who can think we'll quit the Place	735	Stel B-day '20	33
I gravely sat me down to think:	740	Stel B-day 22	4
Think Eusden's Right as good as mine.	741	Stel B-day 22	30
You think my jesting too severe:	751	Stel Wood-Park	74
We think you quite mistake the Case;	752	Stel Wood-Park	89
Then, think on Stella's chicken porridge;	761	Bec's B-Day	36
Nor think on our approaching Ills,	763	Stel B-day '26	5
And think it far beneath your Due;	766	Stel B-day '26	86
(Which are, whatever you may think,	775	Mullinix Tim	63
You e'ry moment think an Age,	776	Mullinix Tim	107
But cou'd you bring me once to think,	778	Mullinix Tim	165
The Neighbours think it is but just	787	Clad in Brown	26
Why Tom, I think the Case is plain,	796	Traulus 1	13
Think on ev'ry Vice in both,	799	Traulus 2	5
Some perhaps may think him able	800	Traulus 2	45
Poor Satan will think the Comparison odious;	803	Irish Bishops	11
Lord Pam in the Church (cou'd you think it) kneel'd down	809	Epigr Prelate	1
For who would not think it a much better choice,	818	Epigr Kite	3
"Then bloody Caitiff think on me.	851	Old Thorn	88
And think you but twenty.	855	Lady's Lament	134
Least we should think ourselves neglected,	859	Lady Acheson	6
Yet never think they get enough;	861	Lady Acheson	35
Dear Madam, whene'er of a Barrack I think,	869	Grand Question	63
I think I have seen her Picture by Jervis.--	869	Grand Question	76
You shan't stir a Foot--You'll think me a Clown--	869	Grand Question	78
How I tremble to think of the Blood it hath spilt!	871	Grand Question	111
"Hist, Huzzy, I think I hear some Body coming--	871	Grand Question	127
"Now Madam, you'll think it a strange Thing to say,	873	Grand Question	171

THINK   (CONTINUED)   PAGE   TITLE   LINE

	PAGE	TITLE	LINE
But, must not think, I tell him that,	886	Rev Market-Hill	95
You think your giddy Head will burst:	893	Panegyr Dean	194
I sigh to think of antient Days.	894	Panegyr Dean	226
And think all notions too abstracted	900	Dean's Reasons	63
And after all you'll think it odd,	930	Riddle 15	D 21
But think it as sweet as her own.	952	Onyons	15
I Cannot but think that we live in a bad age,	975	Dean to Sherid	1
And think of the sex as you please, I'd as lieve	976	Dean to Sherid	15
Think again of the sieve, and I'll hold you a wager,	976	Dean to Sherid	23
And I think I may say, you cou'd many good shillings get	979	Dean to Tho: S	9
. . . but I think Gentle folks should be civil.	986	Mary to Sher	24
And think your Boys may gather there-hence	988	Letter Dr Sh-n	3
And flying think to quit the Score,	1002	Reply by Dean	11
Oh, there you think you have me safe! but hold Sir,	1004	Dan J's Reply	27
But I think it base in you to send a poor Fellow . . .	1014	Swift to Sheri	10
I think you are fated,	1014	Swift to Sheri	19
I think you inspird by the Muses all nine	1017	Swift Ans Sher	4
I hope you will not think this a Pasquine	1018	Swift Ans Sher	34
Nor can we think your Measure short,	1022	Nim-Dan-Dean 2	D 51
Bring down Long Shanks Jim too, but now I think on't,	1023	Nim-Dan-Dean 2	D 11
. . .			
Sufficient it were, one would think, in your mad rant,	1026	Sheri Circles	9

THINKER   SEE FREE-THINKER

	PAGE	TITLE	LINE
'Tis a Metaphor known to ev'ry plain Thinker.	335	Serious Poem	53

THINKERS   SEE FREE-THINKERS
THINKING   SEE LONG-THINKING

	PAGE	TITLE	LINE
Not thinking it is Levee-Day;	200	Horace 2, 6	26
And thinking this Cockade of Wit	458	Paddy's Charac	21
And, by the beastly way of Thinking,	590	Strephon Chloe	209
Pass our Nights, to drive out thinking.	632	Epistle Lady	86

THINKS   SEE ME-THINKS

	PAGE	TITLE	LINE
Thinks heav'n has cancel'd all our sins,	40	Ode Sancroft	181
But H' thinks upon Jack How.	74	Game Traffick	8
He flutters when he Thinks he flyes,	80	Vanbrug House	37
And borne on fancy's Pinions, thinks,	80	Vanbrug House	51
Love never thinks of Rich and Poor,	224	Prog of Love	61
In that fantastick Scene, and thinks	251	Bubble	30
Thinks ev'ry Syllable is true;	282	Journal	102
Thinks nothing gives one Airs so pretty;	417	Woman's Mind	41
Who thinks the Nation always err'd,	514	Answer Fable	73
If Lintot thinks 'twill quit the Cost,	643	On Poetry	109
Nor further looks, but thinks him young.	703	Cadenus Vaness	531
She thinks that Nature ne'er design'd	725	To Stella	65
From Ford who thinks of nothing mean	745	Stel Distress	17
From Ford, who thinks of nothing mean,	750	Stel Wood-Park	41

THIRD

	PAGE	TITLE	LINE
And could pick up a Third.	75	Game Traffick	20
A third could not forbear his Mocks,	91	Bauc & Phil 1	34
A Third, who lost his Way by Night,	127	Little House	31
(The third Night's Profits of his Play;)	230	Prog of Poetry	18
The Third is an Insect we call a Wood-Worm,	351	Wood Insect	17
Perhaps, his Travels, Part the Third;	550	Life of Swift	190
Take Courage, and attempt a Third.	645	On Poetry	148
But tho' you miss your third Essay,	646	On Poetry	181
And so she did, and then a Third,	690	Cadenus Vaness	118

THIRDLY

	PAGE	TITLE	LINE
But thirdly and lastly, it must be allow'd,	263	Apollo	15
And, Thirdly; 'tis a new Invention	348	Whitshed Motto	15

THIRST

	PAGE	TITLE	LINE
To Arms by Thirst of Honour led,	500	Doctor Delaney	2
By Rapine, Theft, or Thirst of Blood.	602	Beasts Confess	20

THIRTEEN

	PAGE	TITLE	LINE
And then the Signs will be Thirteen.	100	Elegy Patrige	88
In Drugget drest of Thirteen Pence a Yard,	275	Epilogue	23

THIRTEENS

	PAGE	TITLE	LINE
For three thirteens and sixpence to the clerk.	308	Billet Players	20
My twelve Thirteens and Six-pence ha'penny.	1033	Ans to Crown	8

THIRTY

	PAGE	TITLE	LINE
Is thirty, and a Bit to spare.	699	Cadenus Vaness	389
Stella this Day is thirty four,	721	Stel B-day '18	1
How Angels look at thirty six)	735	Stel B-day '20	18
Of thirty six, and thirty eight;	735	Stel B-day '20	40
Of thirty six, and thirty eight;	735	Stel B-day '20	40
Where thirty weigh, as much as eighty.	1022	Nim-Dan-Dean 1	D 48

THIS   479   OMITTED WORD
THISTLE

	PAGE	TITLE	LINE
"Not leave a Thistle on the Land;	850	Old Thorn	75
(I spare the Thistle for Sir Arthur's sake.)	881	Pastoral Dial	18

THISTLES

	PAGE	TITLE	LINE
Should bundle Thistles up with Roses.	96	On the Union	10
But, carries Loads, and feeds on Thistles;	607	Beasts Confess	214

THITHER

	PAGE	TITLE	LINE
To lead you thither, as Pell-mell,	313	To Ford	62
He should be sent for thither now.	376	Apology Lady C	18
You thither are compelling	440	Ballyspellin	15
Thither, gentle Muse, conduct me,	832	Legion Club	79

THO   14   OMITTED WORD
THO'   136   OMITTED WORD
THO'T

	PAGE	TITLE	LINE
The Flyer, tho't had Leaden Feet,	113	Bauc & Phil 2	71

THOMAS   PAGE   TITLE   LINE

	PAGE	TITLE	LINE
THOMAS			
As Thomas was cudgelld one day by his Wife,	327	Epigram 1	1
Nay, though the treach'rous Rascal Thomas	734	Stel B-day '20	9
Now tell me, friend Thomas, Ford, Grattan, and merry Dan,	955	Portrait Life	9
THORN			
But, ah, too much without a thorn.	37	Ode Sancroft	106
Was, like his Master's Crown, inwreath'd with thorn.	40	Ode Sancroft	200
Some call him a Thorn, the Curse of a Nation,	334	Serious Poem	29
A spacious Thorn before the Gate.	848	Old Thorn	4
This aged, sickly, sapless Thorn	849	Old Thorn	21
The Thorn committed to her Care,	850	Old Thorn	50
"Sworn to revenge my Thorn and me.	851	Old Thorn	80
The humble Branches of a Thorn.	896	Panegyr Dean	306
THORN-BUSH			
As a Thorn-bush, or Oaken-bough,	457	Paddy's Charac	1
THORNS			
As Thorns were design'd to be from the Creation.	334	Serious Poem	30
And thorns, to make fires;	857	Lady's Lament	198
Here poor Pomona sits on thorns:	901	Dean's Reasons	92
THOROUGH			
Thorough Town and thorough Village,	574	Helter Skelter	39
Thorough Town and thorough Village,	574	Helter Skelter	39
THOROW			
Thence to the Neck; and moving thorow there;	367	Answer Delaney	37
Thorow Mountains thorow Vallies;	574	Helter Skelter	41
Thorow Mountains thorow Vallies;	574	Helter Skelter	41
Thorow stinking Lanes and Allies;	574	Helter Skelter	42
THOSE 114		OMITTED WORD	
THOU 128		OMITTED WORD	
THOU'LT 7		OMITTED WORD	
THOU'RT 5		OMITTED WORD	
THOU'ST 3		OMITTED WORD	
THOUGH 87		OMITTED WORD	
THOUGHT			
And thought too great ev'n for effects of Chance,	8	Ode to King	63
And timely on the coming Danger thought,	12	Ode to William D	19
Were I to form a regular Thought of Fame,	21	Ode Athenian	158
Rapp'd through the wide expanse of thought,	36	Ode Sancroft	62
That be my thought when some large bulky writ	44	To Congreve	35
Nor thought to find so great a Peer	62	Discovery	3
For sure (thought He) it can't be less.	63	Discovery	32
Whom each one thought the happy Dame:	67	Problem	52
And, God knows, I thought. . .	69	Mrs Harris Pet	11
. . . Lord! I thought I should have sunk outright:	69	Mrs Harris Pet	13
. . .I'm sure I never thought you so;	72	Mrs Harris Pet	59
Well; I thought I should have swoon'd;. .	73	Mrs Harris Pet	64
Van's Genius without Thought or Lecture	86	Hist V's House	7
Thought himself now exactly skill'd,	87	Hist V's House	21
Jove saw the Cheat, but thought it best	108	V's House	67
Ay, thought the God, are these your Tricks?	108	V's House	71
And thought whose Sow had farrow'd last:	115	Bauc & Phil 2	132
He fondly thought he might endure	119	Apollo Outwit	11
And now he thought to Seize his due,	120	Apollo Outwit	37
Apollo thought it vain to stay,	121	Apollo Outwit	42
A School-boy ran unto't and thought,	127	Little House	29
But when I thought proper, I alter'd my Note;	144	New Song	39
Went where he pleas'd, said what he thought,	171	Horace 1, 7	33
Forgive me, when I fondly thought	176	To Lord Harley	5
They thought it was an old Man's Maggot:	189	Faggot	5
'Tis thought could be the Work of none but <Swift>	195	Author Himself	50
"I thought the <Dean> had been too proud,	200	Horace 2, 6	33
But when she thought her Pains were done,	208	Fable Bitches	23
No Thought, no Fancy, no Sublime;	215	To Mr. Delany	11
Whene're they would be thought refin'd	216	To Mr. Delany	46
And what he thought the hardest Case,	221	A Quiet Life	45
And thought his Bride had sculk't for shame,	223	Prog of Love	30
She valued not what others thought her;	224	Prog of Love	71
He might be thought an Object fit for Alms.	234	Elegy on Demar	12
If I light on a Thought, he will certainly steal it,	265	Apollo	59
As I rode in my Chariot, a Thought to my Mind;	265	Apollo	76
Tho' the Thought be Apollo's, 'tis finely express'd;	266	Apollo	91
Then Plodding, he thought on a whimsical Prank	288	Bank Down	34
I thought it was a Dog in Doublet:	300	Horrid Plot	58
And, in a crew, 'tis no injustice thought	308	Billet Players	27
I thought my very Spleen would burst	313	To Ford	51
No Thought of her's does ever roam,	322	First of April	39
Some say he's a Birch, a Thought very odd,	335	Serious Poem	33
That writes without the Toil of Thought.	361	Grace's Answer	16
Thought human Learning wou'd not lessen	375	Apology Lady C	9
She went Abroad - - - She'd thought me mad.	377	Apology Lady C	52
Told him, she thought she might believe him;	378	Apology Lady C	86
Thought it more courtly and discreet,	379	Apology Lady C	111
Like'd ev'ry Thing - - - at least thought fit	379	Apology Lady C	119
And some thought modish to despise.	384	Manly Virtue	30
Because he ne'er one Thought allow'd	400	Window Inns 1	3
'Tis come to what I always thought;	409	Dial Rich Marb	29
Alas! I never thought	425	Five Ladies	9
For Dick without Doll thought Living a Folly.	430	Dicky Dolly	3
'A Loss that Dick thought, no Mortal cou'd bear.	430	Dicky Dolly	6
Thought much of his Doll, and the Jointure he lost,	430	Dicky Dolly	8

	PAGE	TITLE	LINE

THOUGHT   (CONTINUED)

Then thought to turn it to a Jest.	447	Modern Lady	75
'I thought we were to Dine alone,	448	Modern Lady	102
(I freely grant the Thought is old)	464	Birthday Song	131
Nor entertain a thought so odd,	468	Birthday Song	263
To dress a Thought, may toyl a Week;	502	Doctor Delaney	66
Were by the Vulgar thought Magicians;	503	Doctor Delaney	96
(And this was thought the highest Post;	513	Answer Fable	31
Who never had one publick Thought,	515	Answer Fable	99
His meanest Work: For, had he thought it fit,	532	To Mr. Gay	25
We thought, there now remain'd no room to doubt:	536	To Mr. Gay	149
"And thought they Both were equal Foes:	549	Life of Swift	149
"Thought Popish and Fanatick Zeal,	549	Life of Swift	152
"Thought Protestant too Good a Name	550	Life of Swift	170
Is thought too base for human Breast;	553	Death of Swift	6
"Last Year we thought him strong and hale;	557	Death of Swift	112
Who wisely thought my Age a Screen,	561	Death of Swift	221
"Nor, can I tell what Criticks thought 'em;	565	Death of Swift	311
"He never thought an Honour done him,	565	Death of Swift	319
"But, Power was never in his Thought;	567	Death of Swift	357
With a Whirl of Thought oppress'd,	578	Day Judgement	1
Was Maid in Thought, and Word, and Deed,	588	Strephon Chloe	158
He thought it base for Men in Stations,	606	Beasts Confess	177
Thought the Life of ev'ry Lady	631	Epistle Lady	39
Thought no Method more commodious,	637	Epistle Lady	225
(For my Friends have always thought	637	Epistle Lady	231
You thought that Satire Sir,--but you are bit.	669	Epig Carthy 17	D 2
She thought it best to take Advice.	689	Cadenus Vaness	92
Where not one careless Thought intrudes,	691	Cadenus Vaness	166
When Venus thought on a Deceit:	692	Cadenus Vaness	185
She therefore, upon second Thought,	693	Cadenus Vaness	215
And gravely ask'd her what she thought,	698	Cadenus Vaness	379
By Love invulnerable thought,	702	Cadenus Vaness	489
She thought he had himself describ'd,	708	Cadenus Vaness	678
Will have the Teacher in her Thought.	710	Cadenus Vaness	735
'Tis all her Thought and Art,	733	Verses Vanessa	24
A Thought came slowly from my Brain,	741	Stel B-day 22	8
Apollo having thought a little,	742	Stel B-day 22	35
She thought that all the world was Oatmeal:	745	Stel Distress	6
A better and more pleasing Thought,	764	Stel B-day '26	10
Dick was thought the brighter Wit,	785	Mullinex Dick	35
And be thought a near Relation;	833	Legion Club	112
And after, me thought, I had lost my new Shoes;	868	Grand Question	51
And, Madam, I laugh'd till I thought I shou'd split.	873	Grand Question	174
Or, ponder long with anxious Thought,	892	Panegyr Dean	161
Thought him Adonis in his Bloom.	904	Death Daphne	58
Nothing she thought could sooner gain him,	905	Death Daphne	71
Never take it in your thought,	907	Daphne	31
Like Thought I'm in a Moment gone,	935	Riddle 23	D 16
Is by all pious Christians thought,	942	Probatur Alit	5
I thought my Master a wise Man,	987	Mary to Sher	30
I thought an Ace you'd ne'er have bated,	1002	Reply by Dean	2
. . .to my Lady Mountcashell: but, truly, I thought .	1014	Swift to Sheri	11
I thought the Lady at St. Cath'rines	1033	Ans to Crown	15

THOUGHT'S

Or if thought's rolling globe her circle run,	51	Temple Ill	9

THOUGHTFUL

Thoughtful upon a Point of Moment:	375	Apology Lady C	3
With Peggy Dixon thoughtful sit,	897	Panegyr Dean	331

THOUGHTLESS

From us the Blind and thoughtless Croud,	18	Ode Athenian	87

THOUGHTS

And ev'n my very Thoughts transfers	23	Ode Athenian	235
The Thoughts of Monarchs, and Designs of States,	30	Ode to Temple	105
Take, youth, these thoughts, large matter to employ	53	Temple Ill	67
A female pow'r, loose-govern'd thoughts create;	54	Temple Ill	104
Still to unhappy restless thoughts inclin'd;	55	Temple Ill	132
"Nor with hir'd thoughts be thy devotion paid;	55	Temple Ill	139
Their Thoughts, and Actions, Hopes, and Fears,	291	Prog Marriage	35
He trembles at the Thoughts of State;	376	Apology Lady C	31
'Tis strange, what diff'rent Thoughts inspire	411	Desire Possess	1
Oh! let him not debase your Thoughts,	465	Birthday Song	147
The cold Conceits, the chilling Thoughts,	470	Burning Poem	7
Whose Thoughts are of a diff'rent Mold,	485	Libel on D- D-	172
Commend the times, your thoughts correct	489	Dialogue	23
Our Thoughts, to hit your nicer Taste,	496	Panegyr Swift	106
Set your Thoughts upon their Mettle:	636	Epistle Lady	212
Damns all your Thoughts as low and little,	644	On Poetry	121
But first with Care imploy your Thoughts,	645	On Poetry	149
Lay now aside all Thoughts of Fame,	646	On Poetry	183
He found her Thoughts would absent range,	704	Cadenus Vaness	566
She own'd the wand'ring of her Thoughts,	705	Cadenus Vaness	602
His Thoughts had wholly been confin'd	706	Cadenus Vaness	630
Vanessa's earliest Thoughts engage.	706	Cadenus Vaness	637

THOUR'T   3   OMITTED WORD

THOUSAND

Justling some thousand years till ripen'd by the Sun,	20	Ode Athenian	129
And thousand incoherent journies take,	36	Ode Sancroft	70
Among the noblest flow'rs a thousand pois'nous weeds,	37	Ode Sancroft	102
And whispers in a thousand Lies;	158	Fable of Midas	64
Above a Thousand Pounds in Debt,	174	Horace 1, 7	115

THOUSAND	(CONTINUED)	PAGE	TITLE	LINE
Ten thousand footsteps, full in view, ...		177	To Lord Harley	17
There are ten thousand Dicks beside;		221	A Quiet Life	56
Nor can four hundred thousand sterling Pound		233	Elegy on Demar	3
In Stock three hundred thousand Pounds;		251	Bubble	17
Each Knave hath made a thousand Fools.		253	Bubble	60
Ten thousand sunk by leaping in.		254	Bubble	108
And has a thousand times her Wit.		313	To Ford	72
Strong Tubs for his Raps, Two thousand and more; . .		337	Serious Poem	96
. . . Ten thousand Pounds and more:		341	Upon His Grace	10
For he regards Ten thousand Pounds no more than Woods's Dross.		341	Upon His Grace	12
To have two thousand Pounds a Year, O 'tis a burning Shame!		342	Upon His Grace	18
Two thousand Pounds a Year, Good Lord!		342	Upon His Grace	19
Ten Thousand Cymbals now begin		354	Simile Silver	9
And get Ten thousand Girls and Boys.		362	Grace's Answer	48
Ten thousand Girls and Boys you'll get		362	Grace's Answer	49
The thousand Decencies, that shone		384	Manly Virtue	27
Nor can ten Hundred Thousand Lyes, ...		414	Censure	27
She spoke ten Thousand Times before.		416	Woman's Mind	12
The clamours of ten thousand tongues		433	Answer Paulus	53
A thousand words to stand for six!		434	Answer Paulus	84
An Hundred Thousand were too few!		449	Modern Lady	139
Six thousand years hath liv'd: the Goddess, ...		465	Birthday Song	161
Tho George is gone a thousand miles.		466	Birthday Song	182
Be sung ten hundred thousand times.		467	Birthday Song	222
And, Statesmen by ten thousand odds		486	Libel on D- D-	197
Which lasted near two thousand years, ...		490	Dialogue	34
Will sooner coyn a Thousand Lyes		503	Doctor Delaney	91
Would vex one more a thousand Times.		505	Doctor Delaney	166
Blunder'd out a Thousand Times.		523	Betty Grizette	20
He knows a Thousand Tricks, whene'er he please, . . .		535	To Mr. Gay	123
A Nymph, that brings ten thousand Pound:		545	Life of Swift	16
"I hear about two thousand Pound---		547	Life of Swift	73
But once in Twenty Thousand Years.		584	Strephon Chloe	4
With Twenty Thousand Pounds a Year Rents, ...		598	Problem Solved	12
Enough to win ten Thousand Hearts;		598	Problem Solved	20
Though some had spread a thousand Lyes;		605	Beasts Confess	149
He's poorer by ten thousand Pound.		606	Beasts Confess	174
Who had contriv'd a thousand Feats;		607	Beasts Confess	192
Fam'd for a thousand bold adventures		619	Scandal Poem 1	60
Fam'd for a thousand bold Adventures;		625	Scandal Poem 2	56
Thousand Sparkles falling down		638	Epistle Lady	253
Amount to just Nine thousand Souls.		649	On Poetry	282
A Wolf destroys a thousand Lambs.		651	On Poetry	326
A thousand Bards thy Right disown:		653	On Poetry	378
You still are low ten thousand Mile.		657	On Poetry	472
Of Incense many a thousand Load;		657	On Poetry	474
'Tis fifty thousand Times below it.		657	On Poetry	480
From all the thousand Female Toys, ...		688	Cadenus Vaness	47
'Twou'd come to just Five Thousand Pound.		693	Cadenus Vaness	227
Five thousand Guineas in her Purse?		707	Cadenus Vaness	654
Ten thousand Oaths upon Record, ...		725	To Stella	55
If not, a thousand Mrs. Brents, ...		743	Stel B-day 22	72
Ten thousand Archy's arm'd with Spades		743	Stel B-day 22	73
Began a thousand faults to spy		746	Stel Distress	35
Began a Thousand Faults to spy;		751	Stel Wood-Park	53
It must a thousand Times have dy'd.		765	Stel B-day '26	58
He gets a thousand Thumps and Kicks		777	Mullinix Tim	117
Jason arriv'd two thousand Years before.		790	St. Pat's Well	8
Incarnate with a thousand Imps, ...		798	Traulus 1	71
In Rents three thousand Pounds a Year.		821	Dr. Rundle	52
A Mistress worth five thousand pound;		879	Robbin & Harry	32
Ten thousand Lice, and ev'ry Louse was gold, . . .		882	Pastoral Dial	46
Ten Thousand Altars smoaking round		894	Panegyr Dean	237
Send me hence ten thousand miles, ...		907	Daphne	21
Give yourself ten thousand airs		908	Daphne	77
And makes me tell a Thousand Lyes:		915	Riddle 1	20
Can grant ten Thousand Pounds a Year, ...		916	Riddle 1	35
Tho' ten thousand Canons roar, ...		931	Riddle 18	D 23
Add to them ten thousand more, ...		931	Riddle 18	D 24
THOUSANDS				
Where hundreds and where thousands fell, ...		252	Bubble	51
There is a Gulph where thousands fell, ...		256	Bubble	137
Subscribers here by thousands float, ...		256	Bubble	145
"Where Thousands equally were meant.		571	Death of Swift	462
Concerns by thousands for your friends:		753	Gift for Bec	16
By Thousands I am sold and bought, ...		918	Riddle 4	13
THOUSANDTH				
But these are not a thousandth Part		650	On Poetry	311
THRASHING				
Or thrashing Babby in her new Stays.		788	Dick's Variety	30
THREAD				
And measuring by the scanty thread of wit		38	Ode Sancroft	123
Through ev'ry Thread it lets in Air;		231	Prog of Poetry	36
She chose a thread of greatest length		760	Bec's B-Day	3
As my thread of life is spun;		937	Riddle 24	D 44
Yet to cut the fatal thread		937	Riddle 24	D 45
THREAD-BARE				
As Thread-bare, and as full of Dust.		115	Bauc & Phil 2	124

THREAD-BARE   (CONTINUED)   PAGE   TITLE   LINE
    He walk'd the Streets, and wore a Thread-bare Cloak;   .   234 Elegy on Demar   9
    Thy thread-bare gown, thy cassock rent, ...   676 Parson's Case   9
THREADBARE
    As threadbare, and as full of Dust.   . . . .   94 Bauc & Phil 1   170
THREADS
    With Threads of diff'rent colour'd Yarn.   . . . . .   594 Cassinus Peter   14
    To slender Threads, may sometimes pass for Lawn.   . .   806 Judas   16
THREAT'NING
    Threat'ning with Deluge this Devoted Town.   . . . .   138 City Shower   32
THREATEN
    Sent by just Heaven to threaten Earth   . . . . . .   10 Ode to King   133
    You threaten the stocks: I say you are scurrilous,   . .   976 Dean to Sherid   31
    To the very coach side, and threaten your letters.   . .   978 Dean to Tho: S   4
THREATEN'D
    While Jonathan's threaten'd with loss of his ears;   . .   818 Epigr Kite   2
THREATENS
    Tempests long frown, and thunder threatens loud,   . .   52 Temple Ill   24
THREATNED
    How Jonny wheadled, threatned, fawnd, ...   224 Prog of Love   87
THREATNING
    Threatning the Pillory and Jayl.   . . . .   312 To Ford   46
THREATS
    But as for your threats, you may do what you can,   . . .   976 Dean to Sherid   33
THREDDARE
    Disguis'd in two old thredbare Coats   . . . .   63 Discovery   34
THREE
    A three Hours Scene of empty Pride, ...   6 Ode to King   17
    'Tis not that I value the Money three Skips of a Louse   71 Mrs Harris Pet   38
    Geryon shall have three Hedes agayne   . . . .   103 Merlin   19
    By Pensions, Bribes, and three per Cent?   . . . . .   157 Fable of Midas   46
    'Tis (let me see) three Years and more, ...   201 Horace 2, 6   63
    I meet perhaps from three or four, ...   204 In Sickness   15
    Three Gifts for Conversation fit   . . . .   215 To Mr. Delany   13
    Three Colours, Black, and Red, and White, ...   226 Prog of Beauty   21
    Cast in his Dart which made three Moydores Light.   . .   234 Elegy on Demar   32
    In Stock three hundred thousand Pounds;   . . . . . .   251 Bubble   17
    Was forc'd to send three Miles for Yest, ...   282 Journal   89
    Take the three strongest of his broken Planks,   . .   285 Elegy Boat   32
    Stay, let me see-- Three hundred pounds a year,   . . .   308 Billet Players   17
    For three thirteens and sixpence to the clerk.   . . . .   308 Billet Players   20
    Three hundred pounds! Were I the price to fix,   . . .   308 Billet Players   21
    Tom's three dearest Friends came by in the Squabble,   .   327 Epigram 1   3
    That he sent to all three a Challenge next morning.   .   327 Epigram 1   8
    Three Duels he fought, thrice ventur'd his Life   . . .   327 Epigram 1   9
    That three little Vermin are kin to Will. Wood: . . .   350 Wood Insect   2
    To dine with Her! and come at Three!   . . . . . .   376 Apology Lady C   37
    'Tis now a Quarter after three   . . . .   377 Apology Lady C   60
    There hang three crosses at thy door: . . . . . .   404 Window Inns 11   D   1
    'There are Three Crosses at your door--   . . . . .   404 Window Inns 11   D   5
    Three times a Week to brush my Gown.   . . . .   411 Dial Rich Marb   100
    To live without both full three Months he try'd,   . .   430 Dicky Dolly   11
    And Latin, vilest of the three: . . . .   434 Answer Paulus   79
    Three Graces by Lucina brought her, ...   465 Birthday Song   165
    Just three; and every Grace a Daughter.   . . . . . .   465 Birthday Song   166
    Three Syllables did never meet   . . . .   467 Birthday Song   225
    Behold three beauteous Vowels stand   . . . .   467 Birthday Song   229
    Condemn'd for thy Crime, at three score and ten?   . . .   519 Dean Hang Rape   50
    Three genuine Tomes of Swift's Remains.   . . . . . .   560 Death of Swift   198
    Three weighty Causes were assign'd, ...   598 Problem Solved   23
    Three Poets in an Age at most?   . . . .   640 On Poetry   6
    I March'd three miles thro' scorching sand, ...   675 Curate's Compl   1
    To three fair virgins I did tie men   . . . .   675 Curate's Compl   5
    I preached three congregations deaf, ...   675 Curate's Compl   10
    Three times refin'd in Titan's Rays: . . . .   691 Cadenus Vaness   157
    Yet lik'd three Footmen to her Chair.   . . . . . .   693 Cadenus Vaness   221
    Or at the Age of Forty three, ...   757 Stel B-day '24   25
    And have left us but Three out of Twenty behind 'em.   .   804 Irish Bishops   24
    So God bless the Church, and three of our Mitres;   . .   805 Irish Bishops   63
    In Rents three thousand Pounds a Year.   . . . . . .   821 Dr. Rundle   52
    When she saw three hundred Brutes, ...   833 Legion Club   113
    And may your three spouses   . . . .   858 Lady's Lament   225
    Three Days before he was expected.   . . . .   859 Lady Acheson   8
    And they must have three Meals a Day, ...   861 Lady Acheson   34
    I increase it to Twelve, so three Hundred remain: . .   867 Grand Question   10
    Three Dishes a Day, and three Hogsheads a Year.   . .   867 Grand Question   12
    Three Dishes a Day, and three Hogsheads a Year.   . .   867 Grand Question   12
    Three Suff'rers in a ruin'd Cause.   . . . .   883 Rev Market-Hill   6
    Weigh but the Merits of the three, ...   884 Rev Market-Hill   27
    Three Morning-Hours you toss and shake   . . . . . .   892 Panegyr Dean   179
    To their old Posts restor'd all Three, ...   926 Riddle 9   23
    How many to answer? One, two, three, four.   . . . .   967 Letter Sherid   10
    But because the three former are long ago past,   . . .   967 Letter Sherid   11
    With three hundred and sixty-five poems a year?   . . .   979 Dean to Tho: S   34
    Whilst you three merry Poets traffick   . . . . . .   993 On Picture   1
    For thee three Poets now are drudging all, ...   993 On Picture   25
    Three days for Answer I have waited, ...   1002 Reply by Dean   1
    Three fellows with whips, and the Dean holds the string.   1027 Sheri Circles   20
THREE-LEGG'D
    Then, seated on a three-legg'd Chair, ...   581 Young Nymph   9

```
                                                          PAGE    TITLE           LINE
THREED-BARE
     In threed-bare Goun, would scarce a louse hold,  . . .  291 Prog Marriage      61
THREESCORE
     Threescore, I think, is pretty high;  . . . . . . .    296 Satiric Elegy       11
     You come to threescore,  . . . . . . . . . .          854 Lady's Lament       116
     'Till threescore and ten,  . . . . . . . . . .        855 Lady's Lament       128
THRESH
     From threshing Corn, he turns to thresh his Brains;  .  521 Stephen Duck        3
THRESHER
     The Thresher Duck, could o'er the <Queen> prevail.  .   521 Stephen Duck        1
THRESHING
     From threshing Corn, he turns to thresh his Brains;  .  521 Stephen Duck        3
     Thrice happy Duck, employ'd in threshing Stubble!  . .  521 Stephen Duck        7
THREW
     As when of old, some Sorc'ress threw  . . . . . . .   354 Simile Silver        1
     He threw them on the Ground again;  . . . . . . .     412 Desire Possess       28
     "Twas you that threw the Game away;  . . . . . . .    452 Modern Lady         249
     I threw the Volume in the Fire:  . . . . . . . . .    470 Burning Poem         12
     She threw her Law-books on the Shelf,  . . . . . .    691 Cadenus Vaness      140
     When the Dean threw me this Tobacco-plug.  . . . . .  881 Pastoral Dial        26
THRICE
     Thrice happy you have 'scap't this gen'ral Pest;  . .   28 Ode to Temple       58
     Thrice, with a prophet's voice and prophet's pow'r,  .  43 To Congreve          1
     And insolently thrice, the slighted Maid  . . . .     43 To Congreve          3
     Thrice happy Poet, who may trail  . . . . . . .      109 V's House          109
     He wav'd his Wreath Thrice o'er her Head,  . . . .   120 Apollo Outwit       35
     Thrice mutter'd something to the Air.  . . . . . .   120 Apollo Outwit       36
     And made a Circle thrice as wide.  . . . . . . .    134 Magician's Rod      54
     Three Duels he fought, thrice ventur'd his Life  . .  327 Epigram 1            9
     "I swear I saw you thrice renounce.  . . . . . .    452 Modern Lady         263
     Thrice happy Duck, employ'd in threshing Stubble!  .   521 Stephen Duck        7
     Cry'd, Caelia!  thrice, and sigh'd the rest.  . . .  595 Cassinus Peter       40
     We hardly thunder thrice a year:  . . . . . . .     617 Scandal Poem 1       11
     We hardly Thunder thrice a Year;  . . . . . . .     624 Scandal Poem 2       11
     In Nectar thrice infuses Bays,  . . . . . . . .     691 Cadenus Vaness      156
     And sprinkles thrice the new-born Maid.  . . . . .   691 Cadenus Vaness      159
     Each breathing on her thrice, inspir'd  . . . . .    692 Cadenus Vaness      177
     All met, and Silence thrice proclaim'd,  . . . . .   713 Cadenus Vaness      842
     But thrice refus'd Episcopari.  . . . . . . . .     821 Dr. Rundle          40
     Then flourishes thrice his Sword in the Air,  . . .  870 Grand Question     109
     Thrice Rev'rend <Dean> for all I owe;  . . . . .     887 Panegyr Dean         2
     Till you please to ask me thrice;  . . . . . . .     908 Daphne              80
THRIFT
     How well his publick Thrift is shewn?  . . . . .     659 On Poetry        D 416
THRIFTY
     Like a young Heir, the thrifty Goddess  . . . . .    693 Cadenus Vaness      223
     And, if he always be so thrifty,  . . . . . . .     878 Robbin & Harry       15
THRIVE
     And under him no Tenant yet was ever known to thrive.  . 342 Upon His Grace     20
     He gave it me, and ever since I find I thrive amain.  .  342 Upon His Grace     30
     I know a Trick to make you thrive,  . . . . . .     394 Grub-Street          5
     Where neither herb nor tree will thrive,  . . . . .  421 Holyhead            31
     Took proper Principles to thrive;  . . . . . . .    481 Libel on D- D-      47
     By Homer dead was taught to thrive,  . . . . . .    483 Libel on D- D-      85
     Then Poet, if you mean to thrive,  . . . . . . .    647 On Poetry          219
     Does not the Body thrive and grow  . . . . . . .    765 Stel B-day '26      55
THRIVES
     The nettle never thrives the better.  . . . . . .   621 Scandal Poem 1      146
     The Nettle never thrives the better;  . . . . . .   628 Scandal Poem 2      150
     The vilest Verse thrives best at Court.  . . . . .   646 On Poetry          186
THRIVING
     To hinder Clergymen from thriving;  . . . . . . .   174 Horace 1, 7        106
     Our thriving <Dean> has purchas'd Land;  . . . . .   875 Drapier's Hill       2
THRO       6                                                         OMITTED WORD
THRO'     53                                                         OMITTED WORD
THROAT
     Or stuff'd with Phlegm up to the Throat  . . . .     231 Prog of Poetry      25
     In Church your Grandsire cut his Throat;  . . . .    349 Upright Judge 2      1
     To cut his Throat before he marry'd.  . . . . .     349 Upright Judge 2      4
     In Christ-Church cut his Throat for Jealousy.  . .   350 Upright Judge 3      6
     To put the question strains his throat.  . . . .     421 Ireld               16
     To bring in (I could Cut his Throat)  . . . . .     773 Mullinix Tim        14
     How to cut a Throat and smile:  . . . . . . .      800 Traulus 2            38
THROATS
     We may, while they strain their Throats,  . . . .   831 Legion Club         61
     Their Throats were cut, their Bellies ript,  . . .   923 Riddle 7            74
     Let Lawyers bawl and strain their Throats,  . . .   930 Riddle 15         D 25
THROB
     Old Aches throb, your hollow Tooth will rage.  . . .  137 City Shower         10
THRONE
     On Learning's high-establish't Throne.  . . . . .    25 Ode Athenian       295
     Which guard the throne by night, and are its light by day:  34 Ode Sancroft   4
     There some high spiritual throne to Sancroft shall be
       given,                                              42 Ode Sancroft       236
     Tho' on a Throne, wou'd fall to <shit>.  . . . . .   66 Problem             20
     When <Ann> for Heav'n resigns Her Throne.  . . . .  180 Horace 2, 1         12
     But fasten'd to his Throne above;  . . . . . . .    345 Prometheus          32
     Whilst he, tho' seated on a Throne,  . . . . . .    387 Manly Virtue       131
     And Mercy here exalts her Throne;  . . . . . . .    391 Young's Satire      18
     Then offer'd at the throne of justice,  . . . . .    433 Answer Paulus       29
     Now see her seated on her Throne  . . . . . . .     465 Birthday Song      173
```

THRONE   (CONTINUED)   PAGE   TITLE   LINE

		PAGE	TITLE	LINE
There, near thy Master's Throne in Shelter plac't,	.	538	Mr. Pulteney	11
The World stands trembling at his Throne.	. . . . .	579	Day Judgement	8
Who, as the Odours reach his Throne,	. . . . . .	647	On Poetry	225
But, oh, how unsecure thy Throne!	. . . . . .	653	On Poetry	377
The Consort of his Throne and Bed,	. . . . . .	655	On Poetry	425
With Vice polluting every Throne	. . . . . .	659	On Poetry	D 410
He fairly abdicates his Throne,	. . . . .	712	Cadenus Vaness	800
She declares from her throne you must learn better manners		979	Dean to Tho: S	28

THRONG

		PAGE	TITLE	LINE
Where tho' her elder sisters crowding throng,	. .	49	To Congreve	181
Sham'd and amaz'd, beholds the chatt'ring throng,	. . .	50	To Congreve	223
Not one of all the tunefull Throng	. . . . . .	79	Vanbrug House	15
Not one of all our tuneful Throng	. . . . . .	106	V's House	15
Farther in haste the Poets throng,	. . . . . .	109	V's House	105
Mingling with Apples in the Throng,	. . . . . .	811	Bro Protestant	12

THRONG'D

		PAGE	TITLE	LINE
Where Spirits throng'd with hideous Din,	. . . . .	134	Magician's Rod	55

<THROP>

		PAGE	TITLE	LINE
Just as when he murther'd <Throp>.	. . . . . .	835	Legion Club	144

THROTTLE

		PAGE	TITLE	LINE
Then Throttle thy self with an Ell of strong Tape,	.	519	Dean Hang Rape	53

THROUGH   46   OMITTED WORD

THROUGHOUT

		PAGE	TITLE	LINE
Throughout two Realms nineteen in twenty.	. . . . .	549	Life of Swift	135

THROVE

		PAGE	TITLE	LINE
Your Industry no better throve,	. . . .	495	Panegyr Swift	81

THROW

		PAGE	TITLE	LINE
"Or, throw him overboard, he'll ride	. . . . .	304	Storm	35
I throw into the Bargain, Jim:	. . . .	314	To Ford	77
With Squibs and Crackers arm'd, to throw	. . . . .	353	Wood Ironmongr	19
And made me throw my Pen aside;	. . . . . .	555	Death of Swift	64
I'd have him throw away his Pen;	. . . . . .	556	Death of Swift	103
And then throw all their Weapons down;	. . . .	592	Strephon Chloe	262
Or may we never thunder throw,	. . . . . .	622	Scandal Poem 1	177
You need not throw your Pen away.	. . . . . .	646	On Poetry	182
Which thus she will Venture profusely to throw,	. . .	716	Answer Rebus	3
Or throw cold Water in her Face,	. . . . .	725	To Stella	76
Was bid to throw the Stones behind;	. . . . . .	922	Riddle 7	46

THROWN

		PAGE	TITLE	LINE
And then the Toys are thrown aside.	. . . . . .	6	Ode to King	18
Directors thrown into the Sea	. . . . . .	258	Bubble	185
As if he had thrown down a Dish.	. . . . . .	299	Horrid Plot	34
And, over these Fillets he wisely has thrown,	. . . .	351	Wood Insect	9
Thus, when a greedy Sloven once has thrown	. . . .	536	To Mr. Gay	161
A Rug was o'er his Shoulders thrown;	. . . . .	594	Cassinus Peter	19
So the Wit that is lavishly thrown away here,	. . . .	716	Answer Rebus	17
Yet I know a young Rogue, that thrown flat on the Field		967	Letter Sherid	15

THROWS

		PAGE	TITLE	LINE
Throws all his Witt and Hours away	. . . . . .	80	Vanbrug House	43
After hard Throws of many a Day	. . . . . .	81	Vanbrug House	73
He throws at all, and sweeps the Board.	. . . . .	253	Bubble	64
Such a Croud their Ordure throws	. . . . . .	830	Legion Club	19
Throws the last shilling in his purse,	. . . . .	878	Robbin & Harry	2
That she throws away as foul;	. . . . . .	907	Daphne	47

THRUSH

		PAGE	TITLE	LINE
The Finch, the Linnet and the Thrush,	. . . . . .	594	Cassinus Peter	31

THRUST

		PAGE	TITLE	LINE
How should I thrust my self between?	. . . . . .	200	Horace 2, 6	30
And, Molly and I have thrust in our Nose,	. . . .	872	Grand Question	137

THRUSTING

		PAGE	TITLE	LINE
Now at the Anti-Chamber thrusting	. . . . . .	788	Dick's Variety	33

THRUSTS

		PAGE	TITLE	LINE
And, in <Swift's> Ear thrusts half his powder'd Nose.		196	Author Himself	68
In every Action thrusts his Nose	. . . . . .	777	Mullinix Tim	119

THULE

		PAGE	TITLE	LINE
In vain, said He, does Utmost Thule boast	. . . .	7	Ode to King	51

THUMB

		PAGE	TITLE	LINE
A Skillfull Houswife thus her Thumb	. . . . .	227	Prog of Beauty	41
And with his Finger on his Thumb,	. . . . .	281	Journal	83
Puts in his Finger and his Thumb,	. . . . .	797	Traulus	51
Return with unpolluted Thumb.	. . . . . .	894	Panegyr Dean	224
And, with attention, read Tom Thumb;	. . . . .	900	Dean's Reasons	56

THUMBS

		PAGE	TITLE	LINE
Then, squeeze it close between our Thumbs,	. . . .	627	Scandal Poem 2	129
With two bony thumbs	. . . .	852	Lady's Lament	19

THUMPS

		PAGE	TITLE	LINE
Then gave him some familiar Thumps,	. . . . . .	594	Cassinus Peter	37
He gets a thousand Thumps and Kicks	. . . . . .	777	Mullinix Tim	117

THUNDER

		PAGE	TITLE	LINE
With Lightning in his Eyes, and Thunder in his Hands;		7	Ode to King	50
The first of Plants after the Thunder, Storm, and Rain		16	Ode Athenian	28
No Thunder e'er can blast,	. . . . . .	29	Ode to Temple	82
Soft'ning the muse's thunder into praise;	. . . . .	44	To Congreve	42
Tempest long frown, and thunder threatens loud,	. . .	52	Temple Ill	24
To ape the Thunder of the Skies;	. . . . .	352	Wood Ironmongr	10
And He must thunder, with a Pox.	. . . . .	352	Wood Ironmongr	16
With real Thunder knock't him down.	. . . . .	353	Wood Ironmongr	24
To take the Noise of Brass for Thunder!	. . . .	353	Wood Ironmongr	30
Like real Thunder knock't him down.	. . . . .	353	Wood Ironmongr	38
Then from his Arm hoarse thunder rolls	. . . . .	461	Birthday Song	39

834

THUNDER	(CONTINUED)	PAGE	TITLE	LINE
For thunder still his arm supplyes,		461	Birthday Song	41
Let Will. unheard by thee, his Thunder waste.		538	Mr. Pulteney	12
And Thunder roars, and Light'ning flies!		578	Day Judgement	6
By Thunder dy'd in Jove's Embrace;		587	Strephon Chloe	108
And is our thunder in your ears		617	Scandal Poem 1	5
We onely send our Thunder out		617	Scandal Poem 1	7
We hardly thunder thrice a year:		617	Scandal Poem 1	11
How usefull were a womans thunder		617	Scandal Poem 1	15
Or may we never thunder throw,		622	Scandal Poem 1	177
And, is our Thunder in your Ears		624	Scandal Poem 2	5
Alas! our Thunder soon goes out;		624	Scandal Poem 2	7
We hardly Thunder thrice a Year;		624	Scandal Poem 2	11
At Thunder now no more I start,		674	His Deafness	5
Hear the rattling Thunder drop,		830	Legion Club	22
If the Devil be Thunder Proof,		830	Legion Club	24
You shall never hear me thunder,		908	Daphne	73
Jove, with all his loudest Thunder,		933	Riddle 20	D 23
THUNDER-BOLTS				
Mistook at first for Thunder-Bolts;		353	Wood Ironmongr	34
THUNDERER'S				
Securely, in the Thunderer's Breast,		458	Paddy's Charac	32
THUNDERS				
As if he heard Loud Thunders roul,		500	Doctor Delaney	17
THUNDRING				
For hourly thundring in his face,		618	Scandal Poem 1	19
Which, thundring out with lungs long-winded,		675	Curate's Compl	11
THURSDAY				
Gallants, next Thursday night will be our last,		309	Billet Players	55
You would really on Thursday leave St Catharine		1017	Swift Ans Sher	12
On Thursday I'll pay my Respects at your Shrine		1017	Swift Ans Sher	21
Your Beef will on Thursday be salter than brine		1018	Swift Ans Sher	24
THUS 213				
THWART SEE A-THWART			OMITTED WORD	
THY 335				
THYN			OMITTED WORD	
Carrots sown Thyn a deep root may get,		148	Windsor Proph	17
THYS				
Of Fraunce hir woe thys is the sygne,		102	Merlin	2
THYSELF				
Like thyself I shine in all.		937	Riddle 24	D 38
TIBBALDS				
Revis'd by Tibbalds, Moore, and Cibber.		561	Death of Swift	200
TIBULLUS'S				
As for Tibullus's Reports,		690	Cadenus Vaness	112
TICK				
Supposing thou hast Tick with Hunter)		182	Horace 2, 1	78
No Cellar where on Tick to sup;		581	Young Nymph	6
TICKELL				
So Tickell mourn'd his Addison.		271	Apollo's Edict	D 43
TIDDEST				
Devour the Church's tiddest Bits,		498	Panegyr Swift	150
TIDE SEE NOON-TIDE				
To Swim against this Pop'lar Tide,		158	Fable of Midas	74
Thus when a Whale hath lost the Tide		258	Bubble	201
Who float upon the tide of state,		296	Satiric Elegy	27
"As well against, as with the Tide,		304	Storm	36
I'm fasnd both by wind and tide		420	Holyhead	7
To Liffy's stinking Tide in Dublin:		750	Stel Wood-Park	28
Collect Excise, or wait upon the Tide.		793	St. Pat's Well	78
Together float with Tide and Wind;		811	Bro Protestant	6
TIDINGS				
Unworthy the glad tidings which I bring,		52	Temple Ill	35
Tells, with a Sneer, the Tidings heavy:		560	Death of Swift	190
First, this large parcel brings you tidings		753	Gift for Bec	5
TIE SEE TYE				
To three fair virgins I did tie men		675	Curate's Compl	5
TIED SEE TY'D				
She was ringing very sorry, her tongue tied up with rag;		840	Ballad	D 8
TIERCE				
You rhyme, as folks fence, in tierce and cart.		979	Dean to Tho: S	20
TIES				
A List the Coblers Temples ties,		98	Elegy Patrige	23
The sleeping Hangman ties the fatal Noose,		364	On Dreams	29
TIGELLIUS				
Tigellius plac'd in Phoebus' Car,		650	On Poetry	303
<TIGHE>				
To <Marshall>, <Conolly>, and <Dick> <Tighe>.		436	Answer Paulus	146
TIGHT				
Cooks make their Fowl look tight and spruce.		942	Probatur Alit	10
TILE				
Would Tile; an Epigram would Thatch.		79	Vanbrug House	12
Would Tile; an Epigram would Thatch.		106	V's House	12
TILL ('TIL, 'TILL)				
98			OMITTED WORDS	
TILLS				
They break up Counters, Doors, and Tills,		240	Run Bankers	39
TILT				
Canst make it serve thee for a Tilt.		109	V's House	114
Now manfully thou'lt run a Tilt		183	Horace 2, 1	93
TILTERS				
With their Tilters at their Arses,		573	Helter Skelter	6

TIM

	PAGE	TITLE	LINE
But prithee Tim, why all this Clutter?	773	Mullinix Tim	2
But Tim Convinc't by your Perswasion,	774	Mullinix Tim	29
Tim, you mistake the matter quite,	776	Mullinix Tim	87
Why, Tim, you have a Taste I know,	776	Mullinix Tim	91
Thus Tim, Philosophers suppose,	777	Mullinix Tim	133
Tim thour't the Punch to stir up trouble in;	777	Mullinix Tim	138
But tell me, Tim, upon the spot,	778	Mullinix Tim	151
There's Nimble Tim a passing by.	778	Mullinix Tim	182
When I premise, that Tim has Travell'd.	782	Tim and Fables	2
Tim set the Volume on a Table,	782	Tim and Fables	5
Tim with surprize and pleasure staring,	783	Tim and Fables	13
By <God> says Tim (and let a <Fart>)	783	Tim and Fables	19
Tim, with his likeness deeply smitten,	783	Tim and Fables	25
Dear Tim, no more such angry Speeches,	783	Tim and Fables	35

TIM'D

| His Friendship was exactly tim'd, | 797 | Traulus 1 | 57 |

TIMBER

Compos'd of Timber many a Load;	94	Bauc & Phil 1	148
Compact of Timber many a Load,	114	Bauc & Phil 2	102
Infallibly cures the Timber affected;	351	Wood Insect	26
Nor, at an under Rate his Timber sell;	534	To Mr. Gay	95
"To hack my hallow'd Timber down;	851	Old Thorn	84

TIME

The fatal Time when that cou'd be)	23	Ode Athenian	248
Till at last tir'd with loss of Time and Ease,	30	Ode Lo Temple	133
Of time or place,	34	Ode Sancroft	8
Time is no more when th' utmost drop is past;	49	To Congreve	190
'Tis time to bid my friend a long farewell,	50	To Congreve	227
Whether in time, deduction's broken chain	51	Temple Ill	3
That time is sick, or the world's mind is dead.--	53	Temple Ill	66
Time o'er the happy takes so swift a flight,	54	Temple Ill	113
Once on a Time, was an <Arse> Gut,	66	Problem	23
Such a thing as this happen'd, just about the time of Goosberries.	71	Mrs Harris Pet	33
Not knowing how to spend his Time,	75	Game Traffick	D 26
Once on a time, as old Stories reherse,	76	Lady B- B-	1
In times of old, when Time was young,	79	Vanbrug House	1
Mean time a Pair of awkward Things	80	Vanbrug House	35
Which in due time brought forth a House;	81	Vanbrug House	75
In antient Time, as Story tells	90	Bauc & Phil 1	1
Brew'd for the good time of the Year	92	Bauc & Phil 1	68
In Times of Old, when Time was Young,	106	V's House	1
Once, on a Time a Western Blast,	126	Little House	5
Then let us both in time grow wise,	184	Horace 2, 1	107
Finding that ripen'd Time was come,	207	Fable Bitches	3
And now 'twas high Time to be gone;	208	Fable Bitches	24
The Time pass'd on, and Musick came,	208	Fable Bitches	37
She'll never do't another Time,	224	Prog of Love	64
The Muse has now not time to tell 'um.	224	Prog of Love	86
The Time it falls, or when 'twill rise.	256	Bubble	144
Mean time secure on Garr'way Clifts	256	Bubble	153
Intended in Time to succeed to your Place;	263	Apollo	28
And resolv'd the next Winter, for that is the Time,	265	Apollo	77
I am too much reveng'd already by Time;	266	Apollo	104
Who neither time nor order kept.	279	Journal	20
Think on some Remedy in time	293	Prog Marriage	103
His Money and her Time employs	294	Prog Marriage	135
'Twas time in conscience he should die.	296	Satiric Elegy	12
Lose not your Time, nor our diversion miss,	309	Billet Players	57
Be sure conceal the Time and Place,	311	To Ford	8
I know no Reason at this Time	372	Letter D. S-y	27
As when Time serves, you more shall know.	373	Letter D. S-y	78
To one who sway'd some time before;	375	Apology Lady C	16
Nay then 'tis time for me to go.	376	Apology Lady C	44
Provided, at a proper Time;	378	Apology Lady C	89
Once on a Time, a righteous Sage,	383	Manly Virtue	1
Mean time the whig is always winner	421	Ireld	11
And asks if it be time to rise;	446	Modern Lady	43
'I never can have Time to Dress,	447	Modern Lady	96
How shall we pass the Time between?	451	Modern Lady	205
The Time too precious now to waste,	453	Modern Lady	276
The Time was, when you'd have compounded	478	Epist on Epist	110
Then we might also have in Time	495	Panegyr Swift	66
For once there was a Time, God wot,	498	Panegyr Swift	157
And this was no Time for committing a <Rape>.	517	Dean Hang Rape	18
He smelt it all the Time before.	528	Lady's Dres Rm	82
Yet, come in time to shew their Loves,	547	Life of Swift	64
The Time is not remote, when I	556	Death of Swift	73
In half the Time, he talks them round;	556	Death of Swift	97
Cries, "Is he gone? 'Tis time he shou'd.	559	Death of Swift	182
"His Time was come, he ran his Race;	562	Death of Swift	241
"The Dean was famous in his Time;	563	Death of Swift	263
Her Time was not till Nine Months hence.	586	Strephon Chloe	66
The Time when Wants of Nature press;	588	Strephon Chloe	140
'Tis Time to shew how Things went there.	588	Strephon Chloe	146
Which Time and Accidents will tarnish:	595	Cassinus Peter	52
And, but little at a Time.	633	Epistle Lady	128
Go try your Hand a second Time.	645	On Poetry	146
Of Unities, in Time and Place.	648	On Poetry	244
From Flecknoe down to Howard's Time,	652	On Poetry	369

```
TIME          (CONTINUED)                               PAGE   TITLE             LINE
     Tho' small the Time thou hast to spare,     . . . . . .    656  On Poetry          451
     For when in time the Martial Maid     . . . . . . .    694  Cadenus Vaness     250
     A wholesome Law, Time out of mind,     . . . . . . .    694  Cadenus Vaness     257
     By Time, and ripen into Love.     . . . . . . . . .    701  Cadenus Vaness     475
     Mean time the Boy in secret lurks,     . . . . . . .    702  Cadenus Vaness     513
     And he must fall a Prey to Time,     . . . . . . . .    703  Cadenus Vaness     538
     But Time, and Books, and State Affairs     . . . . .    703  Cadenus Vaness     544
     Had he employ'd his Time so long,     . . . . . . .    705  Cadenus Vaness     598
     Mean time the mournful Queen of Love     . . . . . .    712  Cadenus Vaness     828
     Nor spend their Time to shew their Reading;     . . .    713  Cadenus Vaness     848
     Till Time hath open'd Reason's Gate:     . . . . . .    730  Stella, Poems       96
     By Time subsiding, you may find     . . . . . . . .    731  Stella, Poems      133
     Could Art or Time or Nature bribe     . . . . . . .    736  Stel B-day '20      52
     It cost me Lord knows how much Time     . . . . . . .   741  Stel B-day 22        9
     Howe're to keep her Spirits up Mean time to keep     . .  747  Stel Distress       45
     Time was, when I could yearly pay     . . . . . . .    754  Stella '23           3
     So, Poets lose their Feet by Time,     . . . . . . .    756  Stel B-day '24       3
     That Time sits with his Scythe to mow     . . . . . .    757  Stel B-day '24      37
     No Length of Time can make you quit     . . . . . . .    758  Stel B-day '24      49
     To morrow will be Time enough     . . . . . . . . .    763  Stel B-day '26       7
     Yet you, while Time is running fast,     . . . . . . .   764  Stel B-day '26      17
     Expect in time, to be a <Peer>     . . . . . . . . .    778  Mullinix Tim       158
     My precious Time, so long mispent,     . . . . . . .    781  Mullinix Tim       278
     What Time the Goth, the Vandal, and the Hun,     . . .   789  St. Pat's Well       3
     The fatal Changes Time hath made in thee.     . . . .    792  St. Pat's Well      34
     Soon shall thy Sons, the Time is just at Hand,     . .   793  St. Pat's Well      89
     'Tis Time at last to spare his Ink,     . . . . . . .   799  Traulus 1          101
     Should slip your Time of dropping Guineas;     . . . .   821  Dr. Rundle          64
     Time and Place are in thy Power.     . . . . . . . .    832  Legion Club         78
     But Time with Iron Teeth I ween     . . . . . . . .    849  Old Thorn           17
     Make use of your time.     . . . . . . . . . . . .    854  Lady's Lament      114
     Two-fac'd Janus, God of Time,     . . . . . . . . .    862  To Janus             1
     God of Time, if you be wise,     . . . . . . . . . .    862  To Janus             9
     Give me Time when coming on:     . . . . . . . . . .    863  To Janus            23
     You come in the very worst Time of the Year;     . . .   871  Grand Question     122
     Are largely paid for all your time.     . . . . . . .   893  Panegyr Dean       196
     But, stop ambitious Muse, in time;     . . . . . . .    896  Panegyr Dean       319
     All risen since that flatt'ring time,     . . . . . .    899  Dean's Reasons       9
     Your intervals of time to spend     . . . . . . . .    899  Dean's Reasons      23
     Nor uses time, nor time will spare;     . . . . . . .   901  Dean's Reasons      86
     Nor uses time, nor time will spare;     . . . . . . .   901  Dean's Reasons      86
     Lose not time to contradict her,     . . . . . . . .    907  Daphne              29
     Though, if I rise before my Time,     . . . . . . .    918  Riddle 4            41
     Mean Time, the Wise a Question start,     . . . . . .    919  Riddle 5            31
     In Time a new Creation springs.     . . . . . . . .    924  Riddle 7            90
     Another Time I'll let you know.     . . . . . . . .    928  Riddle 12        D  10
     But soon will come the fatal Time,     . . . . . . .    932  Riddle 19        D  15
     For Time with Beauty flies away,     . . . . . . . .    932  Riddle 19        D  21
     Seldom by the death of time;     . . . . . . . . .    937  Riddle 24        D  48
     I spend my Time in making Sermons,     . . . . . . .    993  On Picture           4
     . . .out so late at this Time of Year, . . . . . . .   1014  Swift to Sheri      10
     Oh! but I forgot, perhaps, by this time, you may have one  1023  Nim-Dan-Dean 2   D   7
       . . .
TIME-SERVING
     Damn'd Time-Serving Priests all over the Nation;     . .   576  Place Damn'd        12
TIME'S
     The mortal force of Time's dystructive hand     . . . .   419  Shall Repine         2
TIMELY
     And timely on the coming Danger thought,     . . . . .    12  Ode to William    D  19
     For, had We made him timely Offers,     . . . . . . .   549  Life of Swift      138
     Adores her for the timely Aid. . . . . . . . . . .    729  Stella, Poems       38
TIMES     SEE AFTER-TIMES
     That sent these wild reformers to our times;     . . .    42  Ode Sancroft       246
     In times of old, when Time was young,     . . . . . .    79  Vanbrug House        1
     Five times at least as big as theirs,     . . . . . .    87  Hist V's House      24
     In Times of Old, when Time was Young,     . . . . . .   106  V's House            1
     In antient Times, as Story tells,     . . . . . . .    111  Bauc & Phil 2        1
     A finer House ten times than this,     . . . . . . .    128  Little House        62
     In good and evil Times the same.     . . . . . . . .    243  Horace 4, 9         10
     Nine times a day it ebbs and flows,     . . . . . . .   256  Bubble             141
     As they did in old Times, make Money of Leather,     . .  287  Bank Down           27
     His Lady has twelve times miscarry'd,     . . . . . .   293  Prog Marriage      100
     Wont at such times each heart to pierce,     . . . . .   296  Satiric Elegy       19
     But use You ten times worse than Pri'r.     . . . . .    312  To Ford             34
     And has a thousand times her Wit.     . . . . . . .    313  To Ford             72
     In Heathenish Times from the Trunk of an Oak:     . . .  335  Serious Poem        58
     More Heathenish Times than those of our own;     . . .   335  Serious Poem        60
     I know the Times are something hard, but hope they soon   342  Upon His Grace      32
          will mend,
     For Fifty Times its Worth, to Carteret,     . . . . .    349  Whitshed Motto      22
     And serve the Times as others do.     . . . . . . .    410  Dial Rich Marb      80
     Three times a Week to brush my Gown.     . . . . . .    411  Dial Rich Marb     100
     She spoke ten Thousand Times before.     . . . . . .    416  Woman's Mind        12
     The common Slanders of the Times,     . . . . . . .    445  Modern Lady         31
     Of modern Times, the Guilt is yours,     . . . . . .    445  Modern Lady         32
     To sing of Wars choose peaceful times.     . . . . . .   462  Birthday Song       48
     And golden Times, and Halcyon days,     . . . . . . .   466  Birthday Song      196
     Be sung ten hundred thousand times.     . . . . . . .   467  Birthday Song      222
     Commend the times, your thoughts correct     . . . . .   489  Dialogue            23
     And Nastiness of modern Times,     . . . . . . . . .    497  Panegyr Swift      117
```

TIMES	(CONTINUED)	PAGE	TITLE	LINE
Oppress us in corrupted Times:		503	Doctor Delaney	102
On Poets in all times abusive,		504	Doctor Delaney	133
Would vex one more a thousand Times.		505	Doctor Delaney	166
In antient Times the Wise were able,		512	Answer Fable	1
Blunder'd out a Thousand Times.		523	Betty Grizette	20
The Tenants poor, the Hardness of the Times,		533	To Mr. Gay	67
And, such was then the Temper of the Times,		536	To Mr. Gay	155
But, Discontent against the Times;		549	Life of Swift	137
All scribbled in the worst of times,		550	Life of Swift	184
He told them fifty Times before.		556	Death of Swift	90
For our corrupted Times to bear;		603	Beasts Confess	56
Give future times the Satisfaction		608	Know Not What	7
'Tis fifty thousand Times below it.		657	On Poetry	480
Three times refin'd in Titan's Rays:		691	Cadenus Vaness	157
Which in old Times adorn'd the Fair;		692	Cadenus Vaness	179
That, present Times have no Pretence		697	Cadenus Vaness	346
At proper Times to scream and start;		725	To Stella	72
I have assur'd them twenty times,		741	Stel B-day 22	23
It must a thousand Times have dy'd.		765	Stel B-day '26	58
Perversely comes in evil Times,		798	Traulus 1	91
But, some have kiss't the Gospel Fifty Times,		806	Judas	11
Their fame to future times shall pass,		876	To Dean Swift	12
His Slaves have ten Times more than he.		884	Rev Market-Hill	28
At other times a very slut;		937	Riddle 24	D 30
TIN				
T' other you may see in Tin,		931	Riddle 17	D 5
TINCTURE				
A Tincture in the prudent Maid:		693	Cadenus Vaness	219
Which gave a Tincture o'er the Mass:		709	Cadenus Vaness	719
TINDAL				
Hobbes, Tindal, and Woolston, and Collins, and Nayler,		815	Yahoo's	26
TINDER				
Because Irish Linen will soon turn to Tinder;		237	Excellent Song	20
TING'D				
Here, by the sacred Bramble ting'd,		896	Panegyr Dean	313
TINGLING				
The lovely tingling in your Ears,		362	Grace's Answer	35
When I found the tingling Pain,		638	Epistle Lady	267
TINKER				
Just as when we say, the Devil's a Tinker		335	Serious Poem	54
When first the 'Squire, and Tinker Wood		344	Prometheus	1
TINSEL				
Or glitt'ring Tinsel of May-Fair,		135	Magician's Rod	77
TINSEL'D				
With their pretty tinsel'd Boxes,		573	Helter Skelter	25
TIPLING				
In tipling at the Dog and Partridge;		411	Dial Rich Marb	98
TIPPING				
Tipping him with Half a Crown;		834	Legion Club	134
TIPPLING				
With Footmen tippling under Ground,		729	Stella, Poems	44
TIPS				
And tips you the Freeman a Wink;		396	Dog and Thief	10
TIPT				
He's a Gold Pencil tipt with Lead.		61	Lady Tablebook	30
Then tipt their Forehead in a Jeer,		698	Cadenus Vaness	360
And Flatt'ry tipt with nauseous Fleer,		725	To Stella	47
His tongue with oily accents tipt,		951	Upstart	D 28
TIPTOE				
Advanc't on tiptoe, lean'd his Head		63	Discovery	27
On Tiptoe stood and rear'd his Snout,		127	Little House	25
TIR'D				
Till at last tir'd with loss of Time and Ease,		30	Ode to Temple	133
By Faction tir'd, with Grief he waits a while,		196	Author Himself	71
The Horse and both the Riders tir'd:		224	Prog of Love	78
His Pupil might be tir'd with Lectures;		704	Cadenus Vaness	569
TIRE				
Contriv'd to tire all patience out,		35	Ode Sancroft	15
Description would but tire my Muse:		116	Bauc & Phil 2	163
TIRES				
He tires me to death.		852	Lady's Lament	44
TIS	('TIS, T'IS)			
	232		OMITTED WORDS	
<TISDALL>				
Is Dr. <Tisdall> to my Knowledge.		942	Probatur Alit	16
TISDEL				
As Tisdel smells of a sock:		428	Beau's Reply	4
TISSUES				
Array'd in Lace, Brocades and Tissues.		525	Lady's Dres Rm	4
TITAN				
Call Titan sick, because their sight is so;		45	To Congreve	74
TITAN'S				
Three times refin'd in Titan's Rays:		691	Cadenus Vaness	157
TITE				
And rather Tite than Great,		23	Ode Athenian	231
TITLE				
(Cowards are Monarchs by that Title made)		11	Ode to William	D 10
Your Arm has now Your Rightful Title show'd;		12	Ode to William	D 29
And tho' the Title seems to show		21	Ode Athenian	165
And vanish to an empty Title in the Last.		25	Ode Athenian	287
That Title by anothers Pains.		293	Prog Marriage	122

TITLE   (CONTINUED)   PAGE   TITLE   LINE
    That with no Title to inherit, ...   464 Birthday Song   135
    I have no Title to aspire;   . . . .   555 Death of Swift   45
    Your Title had been so much better.   . . . .   821 Dr. Rundle   66
TITLES
    Who claim so many Titles to be Jews, ...   8 Ode to King   85
    If all that our weak knowledge titles virtue, be   . . .   36 Ode Sancroft   45
    Were Hero's Titles heretofore,   .   83 Salamander   10
    Of titles, birth, and fortune proud,   .   177 To Lord Harley   40
    And the Titles I view, when I shine on the Walls: .   263 Apollo   24
    Where Power and Titles scatter'd lay, ...   412 Desire Possess   24
    These Titles and Arms   .   424 Carterets Arms   7
    Who in his Titles always lyes?   . . . .   505 Doctor Delaney   162
    "Where Titles give no Right or Power, ...   570 Death of Swift   439
    To Titles give the sole Pretence.   . . . .   656 On Poetry   460
    Than Titles, Figure, Shape, and Dress;   . . . . .   697 Cadenus Vaness   341
    And by such various Titles call, ...   724 To Stella   17
TITTLE
    Return'd this Answer to a Tittle.   . . . .   742 Stel B-day 22   36
    Knows one Tittle of the other;   . . . .   931 Riddle 18   D   4
TO   3436   OMITTED WORD
TO-DAY
    That those forsaken wretches who to-day   . . . . . .   38 Ode Sancroft   130
    Expir'd To-day, entomb'd To-morrow, ...   204 In Sickness   27
    And take a short Dinner here with us to-Day: . .   871 Grand Question   120
    When I saw you to-day, as I went with Lord Anglesey.   978 Dean to Tho: S   1
TO-MORROW
    Expir'd To-day, entomb'd To-morrow, ...   204 In Sickness   27
    The Company to-morrow Night.   . . . .   453 Modern Lady   289
    "And he's engag'd To-morrow Night!   . . . .   562 Death of Swift   236
    To-morrow, ere the setting Sun, ...   694 Cadenus Vaness   254
    To-morrow of a bitter Juice, ...   929 Riddle 15   D   10
    . . .whether the Wine is to be bottled To-morrow, or no. 1013 Swift to Sheri   1
TO-NIGHT
    Said the Freeman, your Guinea To-night would be spent,   396 Dog and Thief   13
    I wish Alexander safe at St. Catherine's To-night, . .   1014 Swift to Sheri   9

TO'S
    Putts This to's Excellency's Snout, ...   63 Discovery   39
TO'T
    But was sorely put to't in the midst of a Verse,   . . .   76 Lady B- B-   3
    To read your Answer, and prepare Reply to't.   . . . .   1003 Dan J's Reply   3
TOAD
    He hated <Wharton> like a Toad;   . . . .   171 Horace 1, 7   36
TOAST
    We toast Confusion to the Race of Kings: .   162 Toland's Invit   14
    If to <Maccartney> thou wilt toast, ...   183 Horace 2, 1   91
    Talks Politicks, and gives the Toast.   . . . . .   398 Earl of P-b-w   6
    He calld my Dol a perfect toast.   . . . . . .   422 Ireld   32
    He'll turn it off with; Name your Toast.   . . . .   480 Libel on D- D-   18
    And toast them at the clearest Fire;   . . . . . .   529 Lady's Dres Rm   102
    So bright a batter'd, strolling Toast;   . . . . .   581 Young Nymph   4
    But why proclaim her for a Toast?   . . . .   699 Cadenus Vaness   413
    Toast old Glorious in your Piss.   . . . .   835 Legion Club   152
    Sweeten your Tea, and watch your Toast.   . . . . .   897 Panegyr Dean   328
    Shew me the brightest Irish Toast, ...   993 On Picture   22
TOASTED
    With whom you toasted half the Night, ...   311 To Ford   24
TOASTING
    What ogling, sighing, toasting, vowing!   . . . . . .   585 Strephon Chloe   34
TOASTS
    Of Belles and Toasts   . . . .   442 Ballyspellin   83
    Whether some late departed Toasts   . . . .   905 Death Daphne   75
TOBACCA
    And truck the Carrion for Tobacca, ...   220 A Quiet Life   32
TOBACCO
    Tobacco, Censure, Coffee, Pride, and Port.   . . . .   194 Author Himself   22
    So am I, when Tobacco, like Robin, I chew, sick.   . . 1030 Dr. Helsham   28
TOBACCO-PLUG
    When the Dean threw me this Tobacco-plug: . . . . . 881 Pastoral Dial   26
TOE
    The Bank where last he set his Toe, ...   456 Dean Smedley   42
    Climbs from the Toe to touch the Heart.   . . . . .   710 Cadenus Vaness   741
    Thus drest alike from Top to Toe, ...   780 Mullinix Tim   227
TOES
    Like that fantastic medley in the idol's toes, ... 38 Ode Sancroft   138
    Whose Wideness kept their Toes from Corns, ...   99 Elegy Patrige   37
    Who, wanting both, have us'd their Toes.   . . . . .   367 Answer Delaney   52
    Stain'd with the Marks of stinking Toes;   . . . . .   527 Lady's Dres Rm   52
    Could in the Dog-Days smell her Toes.   . . . . .   584 Strephon Chloe   24
    And jogging my toes;   . . . .   852 Lady's Lament   22
    So well contriv'd her Toes to pinch, ...   885 Rev Market-Hill   65
TOGETHER
    To shew the Paths of both must be together trod,   . . .   7 Ode to King   29
    But hardly ever set my Eyes together, or slept a Wink.   70 Mrs Harris Pet   21
    Joyned together in the Low-Countree.   . . . . . .   147 Windsor Proph   6
    "Always together, tete a tete: . . . .   202 Horace 2, 6   86
    Always together by the Ears;   . . . .   216 To Mr. Delany   52
    That came together to be pleasd: . . . .   217 To Mr. Delany   76
    His Money-Bags together sow'd.   . . . .   235 Elegy on Demar   44
    A Flock of Geese jump down together, ...   253 Bubble   54

TOGETHER   (CONTINUED)   PAGE TITLE   LINE
    For then he could Coyn and could Cobble together; . . 287 Bank Down   28
    Both from the Goal together start; . . . . 290 Prog Marriage   31
    Together mingl'd in a Mass . . . . 344 Prometheus   3
    Together mingled in a Lump, ... 345 Prometheus   17
    There your Dear Spouse and you together . . . . 361 Grace's Answer   23
    Shou'd Young and Phillips drudge together. . . 393 Modern Poets   20
    Till in a Lump together stuck, ... 406 Swift to Pope   15
    Of Witches met together, ... 426 Five Ladies   19
    By Fate are always link'd together. . . . . 501 Doctor Delaney   36
    He jumbles Men and Birds together, ... 513 Answer Fable   13
    (Salerno both together joins . . . . 589 Strephon Chloe 181
    Keep the same face an hour together, ... 618 Scandal Poem 1   44
    Keep the same Face an Hour together: . . . . 625 Scandal Poem 2   40
    In different Breasts together burn, ... 687 Cadenus Vaness   33
    Together both to Ashes turn. . . . . . . 687 Cadenus Vaness   34
    Thus whirling round, together draws . . . . 688 Cadenus Vaness   59
    Gave Hints of who and who's together, . . . 696 Cadenus Vaness 324
    They temper Love and Books together; . . . . 712 Cadenus Vaness 825
    They just keep Life and Soul together, . . . 759 Receipt Youth   10
    Together float with Tide and Wind; . . . . 811 Bro Protestant   6
    Let them stare and stink together; . . . . 835 Legion Club   154
    And say, there shall, for years together, . . . 876 To Dean Swift   25
    Both hand in hand together jogging; . . . . 900 Dean's Reasons   58
    But heavy, and dark, when you squeeze me together. . . 928 Riddle 13   4
    When smooth'd by rubbing them together: . . . . 1021 Nim-Dan-Dean 1 D 20
    Thy Words together ty'd in small Hanks, . . . 1021 Nim-Dan-Dean 1 D 29
    And those to be sure, stuck together like Glew, sick. . 1029 Dr. Helsham   25
TOIL   SEE TOYL
    The Toil, the Danger of the Seas; . . . . . 199 Horace 2, 6   17
    The Bird of Jove shall toil no more, ... 270 Apollo's Edict D 25
    That writes without the Toil of Thought. . . . 361 Grace's Answer   16
    His Course of glorious Toil shou'd run, . . . 387 Manly Virtue   118
    Thy Toil is lessen'd, and thy Profits double. . . . 521 Stephen Duck   8
    Or shew the Anguish, Toil, and Pain, ... 583 Young Nymph   69
    The Product of your Toil and Sweating; . . . 644 On Poetry   115
    Hard is the Toil, nor small the Art, ... 892 Panegyr Dean   181
    In vain we make poor Sheelah toil, ... 1035 To Quilca   7
TOILING
    So, after toiling twenty Days, ... 642 On Poetry   65
TOILS
    Of busy Mortals endless Toils: . . . . . 921 Riddle 7   14
TOLAND
    And Muggleton, Toland, and Bradley the taylor, . . 815 Yahoo's   27
    <Toland> to you this Invitation sends, ... 162 Toland's Invit   3
TOLD
    Long wandring thro the Deep, as we are told . . . 17   Ode Athenian   46
    (The goddess Muse herself has told me so) . . . 41   Ode Sancroft   233
    And told you so at Will's but t' other night. . . . 47   To Congreve   146
    So next Morning we told Whittle, and he fell a Swearing 70   Mrs Harris Pet   24
    Farther, we are by Pliny told 84   Salamander   47
    Told <Van> he knew his Talent best, ... 107 V's House   53
    Told 'em their Calling, and their Errant: . . . 112 Bauc & Phil 2   42
    Their Conyngs mark thou, for I have been told, . . 148 Windsor Proph   19
    Midas, we are in Story told, ... 156 Fable of Midas   1
    Hence we are by wise Farmers told, ... 156 Fable of Midas   19
    Dick, thou'rt resolv'd, as I am told, ... 180 Horace 2, 1   1
    But simple Topicks told in Rime. . . . . . 215 To Mr. Delany   12
    Put in Your Money fairly told; . . . . ._ . 251 Bubble   5
    Thus by Directors we are told, ... 254 Bubble   101
    For, first, I have often by Chymists been told, . . 263 Apollo   3
    I might have told how oft Dean <Percival> . . . 281 Journal   79
    By a Parliament Man when the Farmer was told, . . 288 Bank Down   31
    As by the news-papers we're told? . . . . . 296 Satiric Elegy   10
    I told him what it was to be a stroller, . . . 308 Billet Players   33
    I told him, in the smoothest way I could, . . . 308 Billet Players   41
    Where you have told us from Experience, ... 313 To Ford   49
    And said, "His Worship might ha' told us, . . . 322 First of April   45
    I told you one Tale, I will tell you another. . . . 336 Serious Poem   70
    I dream't Wood was told he should Dye by a Drop   337 Serious Poem   110
    The Message told, he gapes--and stares, . . . 376 Apology Lady C   19
    And fain wou'd hear it told again; . . . . . 376 Apology Lady C   22
    Told him, she thought she might believe him; . . . 378 Apology Lady C   86
    He told the real Truth in Rhime. . . . . . 378 Apology Lady C   90
    "Be told--You are not to be seen: . . . . . 380 Apology Lady C 158
    Why then, your Hero must be told, ... 464 Birthday Song   132
    What senseless Cockscomb told you so, ... 505 Doctor Delaney 160
    A noble Lord hath told his Pranks, ... 515 Answer Fable   79
    He told them fifty Times before. . . . . . 556 Death of Swift   90
    "And often told you so at first:" . . . . . 557 Death of Swift 130
    'Tis told at Court, tne Dean is dead. . . . . 559 Death of Swift 178
    (So some Folks told you, but they knew . . . . 579 Day Judgement   17
    Strephon, who had been often told, ... 588 Strephon Chloe 147
    "And dying, never told his Pain. . . . . . 596 Cassinus Peter   78
    The Spokes, we are by Ovid told, ... 598 Problem Solved   15
    I have often told before. . . . . 630 Epistle Lady   10
    "Her Name on Earth ----shall not be told. . . 692 Cadenus Vaness 183
    (For Gods, we are by Homer told, ... 695 Cadenus Vaness 286
    Then told the Tattle of the Day, ... 696 Cadenus Vaness 319
    Can do as soon as she is told. . . . . . . 700 Cadenus Vaness 425
    He hardly knew, Till he was told, ... 706 Cadenus Vaness 632

TOLD	(CONTINUED)	PAGE	TITLE	LINE
Must never to Mankind be told,	. . . .	712	Cadenus Vaness	826
Be told the Lodging, Lane, and Sign,	. . . . . .	729	Stella, Poems	41
I told him what the World would say	. . . . .	741	Stel B-day 22	15
This Day then, let us not be told,	. . . . . .	763	Stel B-day '26	3
'Tis true, nor need I to be told,	. . . .	776	Mullinix Tim	77
When told the Lieutenant was just come to Town,	. . .	809	Epigr Prelate	2
And Smithfield, I'll tell you, if not told before,	. .	814	Yahoo's	2
By the <Dean> though gravely told,	. . . . . .	863	To Janus	25
And I love you so well, as I told you long ago,	. . .	979	Dean to Tho: S	17
And so say I told you so, ...	986	Mary to Sher	21
And, if they had not told me there was a Letter from you,		1013	Swift to Sheri	4
. . .				
TOM				
And with Tom <D'urfey>, <Phillips>, <Dennis>,	. . .	184	Horace 2, 1	115
Nay, Voiture is as like Tom Lee,	. . . .	217	To Mr. Delany	63
But Tom is a Person of Honor so nice,	. . . . . .	327	Epigram 1	6
As clever Tom Clinch, while the Rabble was bawling,	.	399	Tom Clinch	1
Tom gave him a Kick in the Guts for his Fee.	. . .	399	Tom Clinch	14
Then follow the Practice of clever Tom Clinch,	. . .	400	Tom Clinch	23
With little Tom contrive	425	Five Ladies	3
But, Tom will prate	. . . .	441	Ballyspellin	49
"But run to Tom, and bid him fix	. . . . . .	446	Modern Lady	54
"And was not Tom this Morning sent?	. . . . . .	451	Modern Lady	200
Tom having earn'd a Twig of Lawrel,	. . . . . .	458	Paddy's Charac	14
Tom for a wealthy Wife looks round,	. . . . . .	545	Life of Swift	15
A Rival comes, and Tom---is nick'd---.	. . . .	545	Life of Swift	18
Poor Tom has got a plaguy baulk---!	. . . . . .	545	Life of Swift	22
As pitiful as Tom MacLobe.	. . . .	670	Epig Carthy 21	D 4
Tom and Dick had equal Fame,	. . . .	784	Mullinex Dick	1
Tom cou'd write and spell his Name,	. . . . . .	784	Mullinex Dick	3
Dick a Coxcomb, Tom was mad,	. . . .	784	Mullinex Dick	5
Tom was held the merrier Lad,	. . . .	784	Mullinex Dick	7
But Tom was kind and loving;	. . . .	784	Mullinex Dick	10
Tom a Foot-Boy bred and born,	. . . .	784	Mullinex Dick	11
But Tom was best at Borees;	. . . .	784	Mullinex Dick	14
Tom would pray for ev'ry Whig,	. . . .	784	Mullinex Dick	15
Tom huzza'd the black-guard Boys,	. . . . . .	784	Mullinex Dick	19
Tom could move with lordly Grace,	. . . . . .	784	Mullinex Dick	21
Tom could talk with solemn Face,	. . . . . .	784	Mullinex Dick	23
Tom was held by all the Town	. . . .	785	Mullinex Dick	27
Tom had the genteeler Swing,	. . . .	785	Mullinex Dick	29
And Tom for deep discerning;	. . . .	785	Mullinex Dick	34
But Tom had better Learning.	. . . .	785	Mullinex Dick	36
But Tom is eloquenter.	. . . .	785	Mullinex Dick	40
Forgive him, Tom, his Head is crackt.	. . . . .	795	Traulus 1	6
Why Tom, I think the Case is plain,	. . . . . .	796	Traulus 1	13
Why Tom, the Man has lost his Wits!	. . . . . .	797	Traulus 1	34
Tom, you mistake the Matter quite;	. . . . . .	797	Traulus 1	45
At the Parsons, Tom, Halloo Boy,	. . . . . .	831	Legion Club	67
And, with attention, read Tom Thumb;	. . . . .	900	Dean's Reasons	56
So the famous Tom Leigh, when quite run a-ground,	.	968	Letter Sherid	19
Dear Tom, I'm surpriz'd that your verse did not jingle;		980	Tho: Sheridan	1
Tom, for a goose you keep but base quills,	. . . .	982	Sher, A Goose	1
For that, dear Tom, ne'er fret and vex,	. . . . .	983	Sher, A Goose	17
Thy Ruin, Tom, I never meant,	. . . .	1002	Reply by Dean	13
Poor Tom, wilt thou never accept a Defiance,	. . .	1019	To Sheridan	1
Dear Tom, this verse, which however the beginning may		1022	Nim-Dan-Dean 2	D 1
appear,. . .				
If noisy <Tom> should in the <Senate> prate,	. . . .	825	Noisy Tom	1
Let Sir <Tom>, that rampant Ass,	. . . . . .	831	Legion Club	63
TOM'S				
Tom's three dearest Friends came by in the Squabble,	.	327	Epigram 1	3
Lets drive at Tom's devoted Noddle,	.	458	Paddy's Charac	24
The Dean, Tom's honour'd Friend and Patron.	.	458	Paddy's Charac	28
TOMB				
It might have been a Pigmy's Tomb.	. . . . . .	128	Little House	46
Let both around my Tomb be plac'd,	. . . . . .	611	By Dr. Swift	5
But once you fix him in a Tomb,	. . . .	646	On Poetry	199
See! as you raise it from its Tomb,	. . . . . .	743	Stel B-day 22	67
And here six Virgins in a Tomb,	. . . .	923	Riddle 7	67
TOMBS				
Thus Lamps, which burn'd in Tombs with silent Glare,	.	667	Epig Carthy 5	D 5
TOMES				
Three genuine Tomes of Swift's Remains.	. . . . .	560	Death of Swift	198
TONE				
Try'd ev'ry Tone might Pity win,	. . . .	111	Bauc & Phil 2	13
With fawning Whine, and rueful Tone,	. . . . . .	208	Fable Bitches	13
A pox on Elrington's majestic tone!	. . . . . .	309	Billet Players	53
To Elegies in mournful Tone,	. . . .	643	On Poetry	83
And in a shrill revengeful Tone,	. . . .	850	Old Thorn	55
But, while in an ill tone,	. . . .	856	Lady's Lament	155
TONGS				
The rusty Tongs have lost a Leg	. . . .	746	Stel Distress	40
TONGUE				
Whilst Angels tune the Voice, and God inspires the		17	Ode Athenian	56
Tongue.				
Detractors with an evil Tongue,	. . . . . .	83	Salamander	24
For many good Groats his Tongue shall slitt:	. . . .	147	Windsor Proph	10
In Approbation of thy Tongue,	. . . .	183	Horace 2, 1	81
Damn her, why don't you Slit her Tongue?	. . . . .	220	A Quiet Life	12

```
TONGUE          (CONTINUED)                              PAGE    TITLE           LINE
    He bids me then to hold my Tongue, and up the Money  342 Upon His Grace       25
        locks,
    The bashful Dame, and loose'd her Tongue;     . . . . .   386 Manly Virtue     86
    Never to hold her Tongue a Minute;    . . . . . . .   415 Woman's Mind          5
    Nor gives her Tongue one Moment's Rest,   . . . . .   448 Modern Lady         111
    Aura, whose Tongue you hear a Mile hence,   . . . .   450 Modern Lady         170
    No single Tongue one Moment mute;   . . . . . . .   450 Modern Lady         177
    Nor do they trust their Tongue alone,   . . . . . .   450 Modern Lady         188
    With Harpy Claws, and Pois'nous Tongue,   . . . . .   504 Doctor Delaney      124
    Evermore thy Tongue supply. . . . . . . . . .   523 Betty Grizette        14
    "Had he but spar'd his Tongue and Pen,   . . . . .   567 Death of Swift      355
    Then Mercury with Silver Tongue,    . . . . . . .   585 Strephon Chloe       55
    But, I defy the basest Tongue   . . . . . . .   602 Beasts Confess        17
    She fancies Musick in his Tongue,   . . . . . . .   703 Cadenus Vaness      530
    But, Stella say, what evil Tongue   . . . . . . .   757 Stel B-day '24       35
    Fierce in Tongue, in Heart a Coward:   . . . . . .   799 Traulus 2            12
    That one cloven Tongue, ever sat on your Head;   . . .   805 Irish Bishops     50
    Then fear not his tongue, his sword, or his knife;   . .   817 Yahoo's         73
    While they never hold their Tongue,   . . . . . .   831 Legion Club          51
    She was ringing very sorry, her tongue tied up with rag;   840 Ballad       D   8
    Do but hear on the Clergy how glib his Tongue ran;   . .   872 Grand Question   140
    How, with a weakly warbling tongue,   . . . . . . .   876 To Dean Swift       13
    Runs out in tongue, as in estate;   . . . . . . . .   878 Robbin & Harry      10
    Transform'd by your convincing Tongue   . . . . . .   887 Panegyr Dean        15
    I will grieve, and hold my tongue. . . . . . . . .   908 Daphne               64
    To slit my Tongue, and made me speak:   . . . . . .   915 Riddle 1             16
    My Tongue is black, my Mouth is furr'd,   . . . . .   916 Riddle 1             39
    Tho' I speak without a Tongue.   . . .. . . . . .   933 Riddle 20         D   4
    Can shew a Nose, Eye, Tongue, or Ear,   . . . . .   935 Riddle 23         D   8
    While a coarse English Tongue will itch,   . . . . .   949 Epigr Scolding       3
    His tongue with oily accents tipt,   . . . . . . . .   951 Upstart           D  28
    Delany reports it, and he has a shrewd Tongue,   . . .   967 Letter Sherid      1
    But keep a good tongue, or you'll find, to your smart,   .   976 Dean to Sherid  35
    Will quickly fall upon the tongue,   . . . . . . . .   983 Sher, A Goose        5
TONGUES
    Of glorious Deeds, that must all Tongues Employ:   . .    13 Ode to William   D  46
    (For swords are madmen's tongues, and tongues are         35 Ode Sancroft        14
        mad-men's swords)
    (For swords are madmen's tongues, and tongues are         35 Ode Sancroft        14
        mad-men's swords)
    Build Babel with their Tongues confounded.   . . . . .   108 V's House           66
    Their tongues and pens to give you joy,   . . . . . .   176 To Lord Harley       2
    Taught them to modulate their Tongues,   . . . . . .   326 Pethox              79
    Troops of all Tongues and Nations Muster:   . . . . .   345 Prometheus          28
    That Walls have Tongues, and Hedges, Ears.   . . . .   408 Dial Rich Marb       8
    For, let Mankind discharge their Tongues   . . . . .   414 Censure             19
    The clamours of ten thousand tongues   . . . . . .   433 Answer Paulus        53
    An Hundred Tongues, as Poets use,   . . . . . . .   449 Modern Lady        137
    Loll out their Tongues, and thus they talk,   . . . . .   545 Life of Swift       21
    How evil Tongues his Life bespatter:   . . . . . .   602 Beasts Confess       48
    Which evil Tongues might else report,   . . . . . .   713 Cadenus Vaness     856
TONSON
    (For Tonson had, to help the Sale,   . . . . . . .   782 Tim and Fables        9
TOO          173                                             OMITTED WORD
TOOK
    Took its first Growth and Birth   . . . . . . . .    10 Ode to King        126
    The eager Muse took wing upon the Waves decline,   . .    16 Ode Athenian      22
    I never took one in Your Coat.  . . . . . . . . .    72 Mrs Harris Pet      61
    The Plan he much admir'd, and took   . . . . . . .    87 Hist V's House      19
    Whilst he from out the Chimny took   . . . . . . .    91 Bauc & Phil 1        57
    When they had took a second Draught,   . . . . . .    92 Bauc & Phil 1        73
    A shambling awkward Gate he took,   . . . . . . .    95 Bauc & Phil 1       171
    Tho' we all took it for a Jest:   . . . . . . . .    98 Elegy Patrige         2
    And each Part took a diff'rent Side;   . . . . . . .    99 Elegy Patrige        66
    While He from out of Chimney took   . . . . . . .   112 Bauc & Phil 2        25
    Warburton took it in his Noddle,   . . . . . . . .   127 Little House         35
    And many Score of Gudgeons took;   . . . . . . .   133 Magician's Rod       46
    The Towns we took ne'er did us good,   . . . . . .   169 Peace Dunkirk        31
    In short, the Gudgeon took the Bait:   . . . . . .   173 Horace 1, 7          80
    Then, took and broke them one by one.  . . . . . .   189 Faggot               10
    The Golden Stars for Guinneas took,   . . . . . .   255 Bubble              127
    Then Hebe came and took her Place   . . . . . . .   290 Prog Marriage        15
    And took their Progress tow'rds <Loughall>.   . . . .   321 First of April     14
    He took to the Street, and fled for his Life,   . . . .   327 Epigram 1            2
    And the Sound of his Brass we took for our Knell.   . .   351 Wood Insect       32
    But, all he took was just the same:   . . . . . . .   412 Desire Possess       32
    You'd swear, he never took a fee,   . . . . . . .   436 Answer Paulus      121
    "You took it with a Matadore,   . . . . . . . . .   452 Modern Lady        251
    'Twas Greenwich. There he took a Ship,   . . . . .   456 Dean Smedley        43
    Took Wing to Jove, and hop'd to rest   . . . . . .   458 Paddy's Charac      31
    Then Built, then took up with your Arbour,   . . . .   477 Epist on Epist      69
    Took proper Principles to thrive;   . . . . . . . .   481 Libel on D- D-      47
    Took up himself the Courtier's Trade,   . . . . . .   482 Libel on D- D-      68
    Stole in, and took a strict Survey,   . . . . . . .   526 Lady's Dres Rm        7
    Attacking, when he took the Whim,   . . . . . . .   548 Life of Swift      105
    Took Col'nel Peleus to her Bed,   . . . . . . . .   587 Strephon Chloe     102
    And meekly took what Fortune sent:   . . . . . . .   602 Beasts Confess       42
    But took Memorials on the Spot:   . . . . . . . .   606 Beasts Confess      158
    From Jupiter took all dominion,   . . . . . . . .   620 Scandal Poem 1       83
    From Jupiter took all Dominion,   . . . . . . . .   626 Scandal Poem 2       81
```

TOOK	(CONTINUED)	PAGE	TITLE	LINE
And on the Right Hand took their Places	. . . . .	689	Cadenus Vaness	95
Took Aim, and shot with all his Strength	. . . . .	703	Cadenus Vaness	516
That innocent Delight he took	. . . .	704	Cadenus Vaness	550
Things took a Turn he never meant.	. . . . . .	709	Cadenus Vaness	731
I took Advice except my own,		775	Mullinix Tim	72
"So, I took to the Road, and what's very odd,		873	Grand Question	169
Nature to form me took Delight,	. . . .	915	Riddle 1	3
To vex me more, he took a Freak,		915	Riddle 1	15
If you had not took physick, I'd pay off your bacon,	.	980	Tho: Sheridan	5
But we took our dividers, and found your <damn'd> metre,		1026	Sheri Circles	11
In each single verse, took up a diameter.	. . . . .	1026	Sheri Circles	12
TOOL				
Is in all Points the fittest Tool,		61	Lady Tablebook	28
Poor York! the harmless Tool of others Hate;		195	Author Himself	51
Now to turn a Factious Tool!	. . . . .	838	Legion Club	198
The dullest Beast and a Cobler's Tool,	. . . . .	941	Letter	18
TOOLS				
What bungling, rusty tools, are us'd by fate!	. . . .	47	To Congreve	131
Shou'd never meddle with Edg'd Tools.	. . . . .	181	Horace 2, 1	32
Directors better know their Tools,	. . . . . .	253	Bubble	58
Nor ever chuse to Work with Tools	. . . . . .	483	Libel on D- D-	91
The fittest Tools to work for Bobb.	. . . . .	503	Doctor Delaney	90
You should try your graving Tools	. . . . . .	839	Legion Club	223
He's our Master, we his Tools;	. . . . . .	931	Riddle 18	D 12
TOOPE				
The figure of Toope and Snake.	. . . .	780	Mullinix Tim	226
TOOTH				
Old Aches throb, your hollow Tooth will rage.	. . .	137	City Shower	10
"I! who so long with Tooth and Claw	. . . . .	154	Widow and Cat	D 23
Your Head, or Tooth, or Finger ake:	. . . . .	414	Censure	22
Gor'd with unrelenting Tooth.	. . . . . .	660	Love Song	12
Nor dread the Adder's Tooth, nor Scorpion's Sting.	. .	792	St. Pat's Well	42
I must not rub a tooth:	. . . .	852	Lady's Lament	24
TOOTHLESS				
So I wish you were toothless like Lord Masserine	. .	1017	Swift Ans Sher	17
TOP SEE A-TOP				
On the high Top of peaceful Ararat;	. . . . . .	16	Ode Athenian	26
It still was full up to the Top	. . . . . .	92	Bauc & Phil 1	77
The Kettle to the Top was hoist	. . . . . .	92	Bauc & Phil 1	97
Down from Olympus Top he Slides,	. . . . . .	108	V's House	69
'Twas still replenished to the Top,	. . . . .	112	Bauc & Phil 2	33
The Kettle to the Top was hoist,	. . . . . .	113	Bauc & Phil 2	57
That, bending down it's Top, divines	. . . . .	133	Magician's Rod	23
No Hobby-horse, with gorgeous Top,	. . . . .	135	Magician's Rod	75
Behold it mounting to the Top,	. . . . . .	251	Bubble	14
E'er I reach'd Parnassus Top	. . . .	638	Epistle Lady	261
If, on Parnassus' Top you sit,	. . . . . .	651	On Poetry	329
Thus drest alike from Top to Toe,	. . . . .	780	Mullinix Tim	227
Could I from the Building's Top	. . . . . .	830	Legion Club	21
Had she flown but o'er the Top,	. . . . . .	834	Legion Club	127
TOP-KNOT				
A new Commode, a Top-knot, and a Ruff,	. . . . .	23	Ode Athenian	223
TOPICK				
This Topick, never touch'd before,	. . . . . .	709	Cadenus Vaness	714
TOPICKS				
But simple Topicks told in Rime.	. . . .	215	To Mr. Delany	12
And from my own Stock, provided with Topicks,	. . .	265	Apollo	83
But if these Topicks should appear	. . . . . .	311	To Ford	13
Her Topicks from the Tories draws.	. . . . . .	417	Woman's Mind	56
By topicks, which tho' I abomine 'em,	. . . . .	433	Answer Paulus	47
"Nor Topicks brought to please the Crown,	. . . . .	570	Death of Swift	428
Conning old Topicks like a Parrot,	. . . . . .	728	Stella, Poems	26
TOPPING				
Render'd the topping beauty of the town,	. . . . . .	48	To Congreve	152
TOPS SEE TURNIP-TOPS				
Adjourn'd from tops and grammar to the inns;		46	To Congreve	98
Parnassus' Hill has but two Tops,	. . . . .	671	Epig Carthy 22	D 4
With spiral Tops, and Copple-Crowns:	. . . . .	896	Panegyr Dean	304
TOPSI-TURVY				
And tumbling topsi-turvy round	. . . .	126	Little House	9
TOPSY				
This House will soon turn topsy turvey;	. . . . .	283	Journal	128
Humour, you tumbled Topsy Turvy.	. . . .	477	Epist on Epist	72
TOPSY-TURVY				
And your Head turn Topsy-turvy.	. . . . . .	637	Epistle Lady	220
TOPT SEE OVER-TOPT				
TORCH				
Blew out Love's Torch or chill'd the Flame:	. . . .	85	Salamander	60
With farthing Candle for a Torch,	. . . . .	290	Prog Marriage	12
Stood Hymen with a flaming Torch.	. . . . . .	585	Strephon Chloe	48
TORE				
He tore her best lac'd Pinner;	. . . .	153	Widow and Cat	D 12
"I tore in Frolick; to your Eyes	. . . . . .	154	Widow and Cat	D 29
And Skin and Flesh in Pieces tore.	. . . . .	925	Riddle 8	40
TORIES				
Triumphant Tories, and desponding Whigs,	. . . .	138	City Shower	41
How I always pretended to be for the Tories:	. . .	143	New Song	22
I answer; the Tories were in my good Graces,	. . .	144	New Song	23
Since the Tories have thus disappointed my Hopes,	. .	145	New Song	51
And Tories (dress'd like Waiters) in Disguise.	. . .	165	Toland's Invit	30

TORIES	(CONTINUED)	PAGE	TITLE	LINE
The Bucket-play 'twixt Whigs and Tories,	. . . . .	181	Horace 2, 1	17
Whigs, Tories, Trimmers, Hannoverians,	. . . . .	345	Prometheus	13
Her Topicks from the Tories draws.	. . . . .	417	Woman's Mind	56
"With all the Turns of Whigs and Tories:	. . . . .	572	Death of Swift	476
The Tories are gone ev'ry Man over	. . . . .	773	Mullinix Tim	9
The Tories Terror, Scourge and Flail.	. . . . .	776	Mullinix Tim	86
The Tories! you are their Delight.	. . . . .	776	Mullinix Tim	88
But then the Lookers on, the Tories	. . . . .	778	Mullinix Tim	147
If Tories must have all the sport,	. . . . .	778	Mullinix Tim	153
I bravely call the Tories Jacks,	. . . . .	778	Mullinix Tim	163
And fret the Tories Souls to Death,	. . . . .	778	Mullinix Tim	171
<God> <damn> the Whigs and Tories too.	. . . . .	782	Mullinix Tim	284
And Dick curse all the Tories.	. . . . .	784	Mullinex Dick	16
TORMENT				
So, when a Weasel you torment,	. . . . .	66	Problem	17
Torment, by pissing out their Lights;	. . . . .	100	Elegy Patrige	92
TORMENTED				
With Pains of Love tormented lies;	. . . . .	582	Young Nymph	39
Tormented with incessant pains,	. . . . .	754	Stella '23	1
TORMENTING				
Tormenting Fools behind their Backs;	. . . . .	240	Run Bankers	30
She sits tormenting every Guest,	. . . . .	448	Modern Lady	110
TORMENTS				
So Regulus in Torments dy'd.	. . . . .	325	Pethox	58
Scorn torments them more than Spight.	. . . . .	634	Epistle Lady	146
TORN				
Is by the Teeth of Envy torn,	. . . . .	458	Paddy's Charac	10
His Breeches torn exposing wide	. . . . .	594	Cassinus Peter	15
Torn by a sudden Tempest is thy Sail,	. . . . .	770	Horace 1, 14	23
"Thy Gown and Cassock oft be torn:	. . . . .	850	Old Thorn	60
Thy Breeches torn behind, stand gaping wide;	. . . . .	881	Pastoral Dial	21
Twice from their Sepulchres were torn;	. . . . .	923	Riddle 7	76
TORRENT				
You saw th' impetuous Torrent rolling on;	. . . . .	12	Ode to William	D 18
They, as each Torrent drives, with rapid Force	. . . . .	139	City Shower	57
Against whose Torrent while he Swims,	. . . . .	157	Fable of Midas	35
The Torrent, merciless, imbibes	. . . . .	158	Fable of Midas	77
TORT'RING				
That Patience under tort'ring Pain,	. . . . .	765	Stel B-day '26	49
TORTUR'D				
And, were I tortur'd with the Gout,	. . . . .	546	Life of Swift	49
Are tortur'd with Suspence and Fear.	. . . . .	561	Death of Swift	220
While tortur'd Madam bound remains,	. . . . .	885	Rev Market-Hill	71
TORTURE				
Where <Young> must torture his Invention,	. . . . .	650	On Poetry	309
Had this been your method to torture him, long since,	.	818	Epigr Kite	9
TORY				
And whether he were Whig or Tory?	. . . . .	171	Horace 1, 7	22
Nor dares one Jacobite or Tory	. . . . .	183	Horace 2, 1	84
Let not the whigs our tory club rebuke;	. . . . .	186	Scriblerus 3	1
A bitter Whig, or Tory sow'r;	. . . . .	417	Woman's Mind	50
Will prove herself a Tory plain,	. . . . .	417	Woman's Mind	53
Where Whig and Tory fiercely fight	. . . . .	421	Ireld	5
But, they can manage Whig and Tory:	. . . . .	483	Libel on D- D-	98
Shews all the malice of a Tory,	. . . . .	489	Dialogue	26
And griev'd that a Tory should live above Ground.	. . . . .	518	Dean Hang Rape	34
He was a most confounded Tory---!	. . . . .	547	Life of Swift	83
Without Regard to Whig or Tory,	. . . . .	605	Beasts Confess	146
If I laugh at Whig and Tory;	. . . . .	636	Epistle Lady	193
And one is Whig, and one is Tory.	. . . . .	650	On Poetry	294
These brangling jars of Whig and Tory,	. . . . .	774	Mullinix Tim	35
Will none the Tory Dogs pursue,	. . . . .	779	Mullinix Tim	185
Shall Tory Rascals be Elected,	. . . . .	779	Mullinix Tim	189
He sees one single Tory there:	. . . . .	789	Dick's Variety	36
TORY'S				
From some malicious Tory's Brain,	. . . . .	256	Bubble	158
TOSS				
And, while they toss my Name about,	. . . . .	565	Death of Swift	303
Three Morning-Hours you toss and shake	. . . . .	892	Panegyr Dean	179
You toss and turn your Brain till Noon;	. . . . .	892	Panegyr Dean	190
TOSS'D				
So I tumbl'd and toss'd all Night,. . .	. . . . .	70	Mrs Harris Pet	20
TOSS'T				
As Ships are toss't by Waves and Wind,	. . . . .	589	Strephon Chloe	170
TOSSING				
So tossing Faction will o'erwhelm	. . . . .	96	On the Union	21
Or by the tossing of the Fan,	. . . . .	450	Modern Lady	194
TOSST				
Which tosst up in a Pan with Batter,	. . . . .	91	Bauc & Phil 1	61
TOST				
Thus in a Sea of Folly tost,	. . . . .	202	Horace 2, 6	105
Tost in the Waves of this tempestuous World,	. . . . .	284	Elegy Boat	5
"You soon shall see him soundly tost.	. . . . .	305	Storm	56
Poor floating Isle, tost on ill Fortune's Waves,	. .	770	Horace 1, 14	1
TOTAL				
But I see the Sum Total,	. . . . .	1015	Swift to Sheri	39
TOTNESS				
Exceeding all the fools of Totness.	. . . . .	423	Ireld	66
TOUCH				
As if it meant to touch the Skies;	. . . . .	10	Ode to King	123

TOUCH   (CONTINUED)   PAGE   TITLE   LINE
    Whose Breath or Touch, where e'er he came,   85   Salamander   59
    But Gold defiles with frequent Touch,   158   Fable of Midas   67
    Before I'd touch his filthy Dross, than is Clandalkin 343   Upon His Grace   38
      Spire.
    "Well, if I ever touch a Card: 446   Modern Lady   51
    "I saw you touch your Wedding-Ring   452   Modern Lady   252
    But, who are they that can keep touch---?   546   Life of Swift   42
    "And shew'd by one satyric Touch,   572   Death of Swift 481
    With gentlest Touch, she next explores   582   Young Nymph   29
    A mortal human Touch impure?   586   Strephon Chloe   90
    Permit a brutish Man to touch her?   588   Strephon Chloe 153
    Was too good to touch the Ground: 631   Epistle Lady   36
    Climbs from the Toe to touch the Heart.   710   Cadenus Vaness 741
    Mov'd with the lightest Touch of Blame,   730   Stella, Poems   88
    To make Her only touch a Quail: 746   Stel Distress   20
    To make her only touch a Quail.   750   Stel Wood-Park   18
    Dermot, how could you touch those nasty Sluts!   882   Pastoral Dial   39
    But, if I ever touch her Lips again,   882   Pastoral Dial   43
    It cries at a Touch,   939   Riddle Answerd   26
TOUCH'D
    He touch'd the Pence when others touch'd the Pot;   234   Elegy on Demar   27
    He touch'd the Pence when others touch'd the Pot;   234   Elegy on Demar   27
    What Midas touch'd, became true Gold; but then,   668   Epig Carthy 12 D 1
    Gold becomes Lead, touch'd lightly by thy Pen.   668   Epig Carthy 12 D 2
    This Topick, never touch'd before,   709   Cadenus Vaness 714
TOUCH'T
    Turn'd ev'ry thing he touch't to Gold: 156   Fable of Midas   2
TOUCHES
    Whose moving Touches, when they please, kill us.   988   Letter Dr Sh-n   29
TOUCHT
    As if they ne'er had toucht a Drop.   112   Bauc & Phil 2   34
TOUGH
    Remov'd the tough superfluous Flesh,   326   Pethox   78
    Hard, tough, cramp, gutt'rall, harsh, stiff Names.   467   Birthday Song   210
TOUN
    Or sell a Goose at the next Toun   95   Bauc & Phil 1   175
TOUNE
    From Toune of Stoffe to fattyn Londe   102   Merlin   6
TOUPETS
    Like Toupets of this upper World;   903   Death Daphne   24
TOUR
    Taking their Tour in Masquerade   90   Bauc & Phil 1   8
    Taking their Tour in Masquerade;   111   Bauc & Phil 2   8
TOW'R
    This could I do, and proudly o'er him tow'r,   44   To Congreve   39
    Heroick Strains could build a Tow'r;   106   V's House   8
    Inclose him in a wooden Tow'r,   325   Pethox   56
    It was a Tow'r of monstrous Height,   413   Desire Possess   40
    Like other Bawbles of the Tow'r.   646   On Poetry   194
TOW'RDS
    And took their Progress tow'rds <Loughall>.   321   First of April   14
    With Neck elated tow'rds the Skies!   743   Stel B-day 22   62
    Its Head reclining tow'rds the Ground.   849   Old Thorn   20
TOWARDS
    I'll give something towards thy Loss;   73   Mrs Harris Pet   67
TOWELS
    When he beheld and smelt the Towels,   527   Lady's Dres Rm   44
TOWER
    Heroick Strains could build a Tower;   79   Vanbrug House   8
    Are now in Exil, or the Tower,   311   To Ford   28
    "His Friends in Exile, or the Tower,   568   Death of Swift 393
TOWLSEL
    For I saw'd them reading upon the towlsel doore.   840   Ballad   D 4
TOWN   SEE GALLS-TOWN,KENTISH-TOWN,TROY-TCWN
    As loth to see the hated Court and Town,   31   Ode to Temple   157
    The most ungen'rous vices of the town;   44   To Congreve   10
    Stock'd with the freshest gibberish of the town;   47   To Congreve   120
    Render'd the topping beauty of the town,   48   To Congreve   152
    To ev'ry lew'd pretender of the town.   48   To Congreve   160
    To give the Town and Country Sport.   62   Discovery   8
    Upon St. James's End o' th' Town;   100   Elegy Patrige   96
    Till once, a Parson of our Town,   117   Bauc & Phil 2   173
    In pity to the empty'ng Town   122   Empty'ng Town   1
    Where he comes ev'ry Week from Town;   128   Little House   57
    Threat'ning with Deluge this Devoted Town.   138   City Shower   32
    Why sure you won't appear in Town,   175   Horace 1, 7   123
    Where Town and Country Vicars flock in Tribes,   194   Author Himself   19
    I must by all means come to Town,   199   Horace 2, 6   13
    "Let my Lord know you're come to Town.   200   Horace 2, 6   24
    To Windsor, and again to Town,   201   Horace 2, 6   78
    Those Cares that haunt the Court and Town.   202   Horace 2, 6   112
    By all the Dogs and Curs in Town;   207   Fable Bitches   2
    And then fall foul on all the Town;   217   To Mr. Delany   56
    Pray, what is this Bank of which the Town Rings?   287   Bank Down   1
    The Town has whisper'd round the Jest: 293   Prog Marriage   102
    Hearing the House was empty, came to town;   307   Billet Players   2
    For leave to act in town? 'Tis plaguy dear.   308   Billet Players   18
    In ev'ry town we wait on Mr. May'r,   308   Billet Players   35
    Approaching near the Town, he hears   338   Wood's Brass   5
    Lord William's Grace of Dublin Town,   341   Upon His Grace   3

```
TOWN            (CONTINUED)                                    PAGE    TITLE              LINE
     When Jove, in pity to the Town,        . . . . . . . .    353  Wood Ironmongr      23
     The Statesman rakes the Town to find a Plot,      . . .   364  On Dreams           19
     That ev'ry <S--th>, and Type in Town    . . . . . . .     371  Letter D. S-y        4
     But as to Ditto 't thro the Town,       . . . . . .       372  Letter D. S-y       15
     Away he trudges into Town;     . . . . . . . . .          376  Apology Lady C      28
     Let me have but your Vote to serve for the Town,    . .   396  Dog and Thief       11
     He left the Town above a Week.      . . . . . . .         398  Earl of P-b-w       15
     The walls of this Town     . . . . . . . . . .            403  Window Inns 9   D    1
     There are some prating folks in town,     . . . . . .     422  Ireld               39
     When term is ended, leaves the town,      . . . . . .     435  Answer Paulus       93
     And then, how thankful to the Town,       . . . . . .     502  Doctor Delaney      67
     "The News thro' half the Town has run.     . . . . .      558  Death of Swift     152
     With Elegies, the Town is cloy'd:      . . . . . . .      558  Death of Swift     166
     "The Town hath got a better Taste:     . . . . . . .      563  Death of Swift     266
     "The Country Members, when in Town,    . . . . . . .      564  Death of Swift     283
     Thorough Town and thorough Village,    . . . . . . .      574  Helter Skelter      39
     Hey for Dublin Town agen!    . . . . . . . . . .          574  Helter Skelter      56
     Of Chloe all the Town has rung;    . . . . . . . .        584  Strephon Chloe       1
     In Summer had she walkt the Town,     . . . . . . .       584  Strephon Chloe      21
     With Coach and Six, and House in Town.    . . . . .       585  Strephon Chloe      42
     Or praise the Judgment of the Town,    . . . . . . .      644  On Poetry          125
     The Town will mark you for a Dunce:    . . . . . . .      644  On Poetry          138
     He gives Directions to the Town,      . . . . . . .       649  On Poetry          269
     And license to reside in town;     . . . . . . . .        676  Parson's Case       26
     The Town wou'd swear he had betray'd,     . . . . . .     707  Cadenus Vaness     646
     Poor Stella must pack off to Town.     . . . . . . .      744  Stel Distress        2
     To languish in this odious Town,      . . . . . . .       748  Stel Distress       71
     Poor Stella must pack off to Town.     . . . . . . .      750  Stel Wood-Park      26
     To languish in this odious Town.      . . . . . . .       752  Stel Wood-Park      87
     Lest you the town may have less trouble in,     . . . .   753  Gift for Bec        23
     Like thee, to please this thankless Town!     . . . .     779  Mullinix Tim       198
     Tom was held by all the Town     . . . . . . . .          785  Mullinex Dick       27
     When told the Lieutenant was just come to Town,    . .    809  Epigr Prelate        2
     Patrick astore, what news upon the town?    . . . . .     840  Ballad          D    1
     Harangu'd, and welcom'd him to Town.      . . . . . .     904  Death Daphne        50
     And once a Weaver in our Town,     . . . . . . . .        926  Riddle 9            19
     Except when I trade with a Ship or a Town,      . . . .   927  Riddle 11       D    7
     And when I, vanquish'd, fled the Town,    . . . . . .    1005  Sheridan's Sub       9
     When you have not one friend left in town, . . . . . .   1022  Nim-Dan-Dean 2  D    4
     . . . come to town, but I don't know whether he be friend 1023 Nim-Dan-Dean 2  D    7
       . . .
TOWN-JESTS
     Town-Jests, and Coffee-house Conceits;     . . . . .      645  On Poetry          154
TOWNS
     Holland got Towns, and we got Blows,      . . . . . .     168  Peace Dunkirk        3
     The Towns we took ne'er did us good,      . . . . . .     169  Peace Dunkirk       31
     Place Elephants for want of Towns.     . . . . . . .      646  On Poetry          180
TOWNSHEND
     Observe where bloody Townshend stands     . . . . . .     312  To Ford             43
TOWNSHENDS
     Townshends cast Page or Walpole's groom     . . . . .     423  Ireld               72
TOWRING
     And down the towring Boy is cast:     . . . . . . . .     252  Bubble              40
TOWSE
     To towse and kiss     . . . . . . . . . . . .            442  Ballyspellin        76
TOWZER
     Here, Towzer!--Do Him Justice.     . . . . . . . .        154  Widow and Cat   D   45
     Agreed. And yet, when Towzer snaps     . . . . . . .      797  Traulus 1           35
     Than the barking of Towzer, or leap of a louse?    . . .  814  Yahoo's              9
TOWZER'S
     Towzer's the less offensive Brute.     . . . . . . .      797  Traulus 1           44
TOY
     Must be some painted Toy I knew;      . . . . . . . .     912  Aenigma Expl    D    8
     I with either sport and toy.    . . . . . . . . .        933  Riddle 20       D   18
TOYL
     To dress a Thought, may toyl a Week;      . . . . . .     502  Doctor Delaney      66
     Be put to the Peril, and Toyl of a <Rape>?     . . . .    518  Dean Hang Rape      42
TOYLET
     A Letter on the Toylet sees     . . . . . . . .           223  Prog of Love        45
     And all that stuff of Toylet, Glass, and Box-comb?    .  1003  Dan J's Reply        9
TOYLETS
     Between their Toylets and their Beds.     . . . . . .     688  Cadenus Vaness      50
TOYS
     And then the Toys are thrown aside.    . . . . . . .        6  Ode to King         18
     In musick, Raffling-rooms, and Toys,      . . . . . .     294  Prog Marriage      136
     From all the thousand Female Toys,     . . . . . . .      688  Cadenus Vaness      47
TRAC'D
     Nor beaten Paths be longer trac'd.     . . . . . . .      270  Apollo's Edict  D   11
     The Victor, when your Steps he trac'd,    . . . . . .     326  Pethox              91
TRACE
     You that would grief describe, come here and trace   . .   52  Temple Ill          51
     The Youth with Broomy Stumps began to trace     . . .    124  Descriptn Morn       9
     And all its secret Causes trace,      . . . . . . .       180  Horace 2, 1         16
     Nor can the skilful Herald trace     . . . . . . . .      323  Pethox               3
     With what Delight, methinks, I trace     . . . . . . .    325  Pethox              69
     And ev'ry where her footsteps trace,      . . . . . .     401  Window Inns 5   D    7
     Thy various Follies, who can trace?    . . . . . . .      555  Death of Swift      40
     To oblige a good Friend, she will trace ev'ry Market,    .  580  Psyche             11
     Than what a curious Eye may trace     . . . . . . . .     653  On Poetry          385
     What Lineaments divine we trace     . . . . . . . .       655  On Poetry          417
```

		PAGE	TITLE	LINE
TRACE	(CONTINUED)			
When Age must print a furrow'd Trace	. . . . . .	735	Stel B-day '20	49
From thee, with Pride, the Caledonians trace	. . . .	790	St. Pat's Well	11
Let me now the Vices trace,	. . . .	800	Traulus 2	23
Draw them so that we may trace	. . . .	839	Legion Club	229
Her folly can trace;	. . . .	854	Lady's Lament	96
TRACES				
Yet shall these Traces of your Wit remain	. . . . .	25	Ode Athenian	301
TRACK				
At trudging in a beaten Track,	. . . .	183	Horace 2, 1	104
All things gone on the same dull track,	. . . . .	877	To Dean Swift	31
TRACKS				
On either Side you see the Tracks,	. . . . . .	227	Prog of Beauty	39
Her Shoulders mark'd with bloody Tracks;	. . . .	729	Stella, Poems	46
TRACTS				
Gain by Degrees huge Tracts of Land,	. . . . .	239	Run Bankers	2
"Here's Wolston's Tracts, the twelfth Edition;	. . .	564	Death of Swift	281
TRADE				
Railing a Rule of Wit, and Obloquy a Trade,	. . .	18	Ode Athenian	84
Our Wit and Learning, narrow as our Trade;	. . .	19	Ode Athenian	96
Forcing a wretched Trade by beating down the sale,	. .	19	Ode Athenian	101
Some to the Drudgery of a Trade,	. . . .	32	Ode to Temple	186
With those they rob, by what their trade does gain.	. .	45	To Congreve	68
Or the Chaplain, (for 'tis his Trade). . . .		73	Mrs Harris Pet	75
Sole Patron of the building Trade,	. . . .	79	Vanbrug House	24
Two Brother-Hermits, Saints by Trade	. . . . .	90	Bauc & Phil 1	7
He knew his Trade, and call'd it Boots.	. . . . .	99	Elegy Patrige	34
Sole Patron of the Building Trade,	. . . . . .	106	V's House	24
Th' experienc't Bricks that knew their Trade,	. . .	108	V's House	76
Two Brother Hermits, Saints by Trade,	. . . . .	111	Bauc & Phil 2	7
Of Stroling God's, whose usual Trade is,	. . . . .	120	Apollo Outwit	22
Who knows his Art but not his Trade;	. . . . . .	204	In Sickness	10
Till Swains unwholsome spoyld the Trade,	. . . .	225	Prog of Love	91
Tho' Moneys scarce we shou'd have Trade enough;	. .	275	Epilogue	32
A Trade, our Boat had practic'd here so well.	. . .	285	Elegy Boat	26
With like Remorse his Brother of the Trade,	. . . .	364	On Dreams	17
While the sly Mountebank attends his Trade,	. . . .	364	On Dreams	33
Nor slip this Occasion to follow your Trade.	. . . .	400	Tom Clinch	20
Took up himself the Courtier's Trade,	. . . . . .	482	Libel on D- D-	68
Must be a Sweet'ner by your Trade,	. . . .	485	Libel on D- D-	154
I must take up the sweet'ning Trade.	. . . . . .	496	Panegyr Swift	97
For why, they had both been brought up to the Trade	. .	517	Dean Hang Rape	27
Nor let her loose to spoil your Trade.	. . . . . .	585	Strephon Chloe	30
He scorns to make his Art a Trade;	. . . .	605	Beasts Confess	135
He better understands his Trade:	. . . .	607	Beasts Confess	212
But if you think this Trade too base,	. . . . . .	647	On Poetry	233
The House will never loose it's Trade;	. . . . . .	734	Stel B-day '20	8
Pursue thy Trade of Scandall picking,	. . . . .	735	Stel B-day '20	41
That thou shouldst take an honest Trade,	. . . . .	787	Clad in Brown	27
Proficient in their Father's Trade,	. . . . . .	903	Death Daphne	16
My Trade is, Pris'ners to set free.	. . . .	920	Riddle 6	2
Except when I trade with a Ship or a Town,	. . . . .	927	Riddle 11	D 7
But to scold is your trade, which I soon shou'd be foil'd in,	. . .	979	Dean to Tho: S	7
TRADERS				
The Traders now no longer cheat;	. . . .	391	Young's Satire	13
TRADESMEN				
And Tradesmen, to compare Brocades.	. . . . . .	291	Prog Marriage	54
As Tradesmen shew their Trash at first:)	. . . . .	728	Stella, Poems	22
TRADING				
Whoever our Trading with England would hinder,	. . .	237	Excellent Song	18
TRADUCE				
Then, I must be so too, ex traduce.	. . . .	350	Upright Judge 3	8
TRAFFICK				
Whilst you three merry Poets traffick	. . . . . .	993	On Picture	1
TRAGEDIES				
And that a Woman, in those Tragedies	. . . . . .	988	Letter Dr Sh-n	24
TRAGEDY				
For, tragedy, he knew, would lose you quite,	. . . .	47	To Congreve	145
TRAGICK				
Your tragick Heroes shall not rant,	. . . .	270	Apollo's Edict	D 27
As serious as a Tragick Play'r.	. . . .	707	Cadenus Vaness	663
And as for the Tragick	. . . .	939	Riddle Answerd	15
TRAGICKS				
Proceed to Tragicks, first Euripides	. . . . . .	988	Letter Dr Sh-n	17
TRAIL				
Thrice happy Poet, who may trail	. . . .	109	V's House	109
They shall not see a Trail of Light:	. . . . . .	270	Apollo's Edict	D 35
And Scipio, trail an Irish purple Plad.	. . . . .	275	Epilogue	22
TRAIN SEE TREYN				
With a long sweeping Train	. . . .	23	Ode Athenian	225
Her Priests, her Train and Followers show	. . . .	27	Ode to Temple	40
Make up its solemn Train with Death;	. . . . . .	29	Ode to Temple	90
With gawdy Coat, and shining Train,	. . . . . .	83	Salamander	31
While Mistress Iris held her Train,	. . . . . .	290	Prog Marriage	13
This Day arriv'd without his Train,	. . . .	398	Earl of P-b-w	11
There shining 'midst his Train, to Grace	. . . . .	477	Epist on Epist	81
How could you, Gay, disgrace the Muses Train,	. . .	531	To Mr. Gay	1
Thus furnish't out, he sent his Train	. . . . . .	904	Death Daphne	45
Oft in the Train of Venus seen,	. . . .	923	Riddle 7	69

	PAGE	TITLE	LINE
TRAINS			
Where Whigs their cursed Trains had laid;	494	Panegyr Swift	42
TRAITEROUSLY			
Did maliciously, falsly, and traiterously write, . . .	264	Apollo	35
TRAITOR SEE TRAYTOR			
That Traitor, Assassin, Informer vile.	826	Noisy Tom	8
TRAITRESS			
With a certain false Traitress, one Stella by Name, .	263	Apollo	30
TRAMPLED			
He trampled on this Haughty Bajazet, ...	7	Ode to King	42
And Virtue trampled on the Ground:	312	To Ford	42
TRAMPLES			
Sweeps the broad scythe, and tramples on his face. . .	55	Temple Ill	122
TRAMPLING			
The last Invaders trampling on the first:	793	St. Pat's Well	84
TRANSCENDENT			
Like all transcendent excellence below;	39	Ode Sancroft	146
TRANSCENDING			
Transcending Nature's ordinary Laws, ...	10	Ode to King	132
TRANSCENDS			
All Merit that transcends the humble Rules	18	Ode Athenian	77
TRANSCRIB'D			
My Sister transcrib'd it last Night, to his Sorrow, .	265	Apollo	67
TRANSCRIBE			
I but transcribe, for not a Line	445	Modern Lady	28
Is needful, to transcribe it fair.	643	On Poetry	92
Stella, when you these Lines transcribe, ...	730	Stella, Poems	83
TRANSFERS			
And ev'n my very Thoughts transfers	23	Ode Athenian	235
TRANSFIX'D			
And deep transfix'd her Bosom too.	703	Cadenus Vaness	519
TRANSFORM'D			
And seem (almost) transform'd to Water, Flame, and Air,	22	Ode Athenian	201
Her Petticoat transform'd apace, ...	116	Bauc & Phil 2	141
While you and Spouse transform'd, shall soon	362	Grace's Answer	51
Transform'd to Imps, his Levee wait.	646	On Poetry	208
He was transform'd into a Swan, ...	666	Epig Carthy 1	D 2
Transform'd by your convincing Tongue	887	Panegyr Dean	15
TRANSFUSION			
And hopes to lengthen Life by a Transfusion of Breath,	21	Ode Athenian	183
TRANSGRESSION			
As antient Judas by Transgression fell, ...	806	Judas	17
TRANSIENT			
How transient all things are below:	283	Journal	116
Love, hitherto a transient Guest, ...	711	Cadenus Vaness	768
TRANSIT			
And here rest, Sic transit Gloria Mundi.	431	Dicky Dolly	24
TRANSITORY			
Less should I dawb it o're with transitory Praise, . .	21	Ode Athenian	169
Should spring such short and transitory kinds, ...	47	To Congreve	128
TRANSLATE			
But, let me now the Words translate:	348	Whitshed Motto	5
Translate me now some Lines, if you can, ...	657	On Poetry	481
Dunkin has been for Latin fam'd--translate. . . .	667	Epig Carthy 4	D 4
TRANSLATED			
Translated to arch-angel there.	42	Ode Sancroft	239
Was all decypher'd, and translated.	300	Horrid Plot	52
Translated from Boileau's Translation, ...	649	On Poetry	261
And wish you Translated, ...	1014	Swift to Sheri	27
TRANSLATION			
Translated from Boileau's Translation, ...	649	On Poetry	261
TRANSMITTED			
Transmitted to the Heroes Line, ...	134	Magician's Rod	62
TRANSPARENT			
Made up of Virtue and transparent Innocence:	30	Ode to Temple	128
TRANSPLANTED			
Transplanted to the Hero's Brow)	6	Ode to King	10
And which (to heavenly soil transplanted) will improve, .	41	Ode Sancroft	228
TRANSPORT			
Rather forgive what my first Transport said, ...	23	Ode Athenian	244
And I roar out my Joy, and in Transport expire. . .	928	Riddle 11	D 12
TRANSPORTED			
And the transported Muse imagin'd it	17	Ode Athenian	48
Then each transported Fop will cry, ...	228	Prog of Beauty	75
Or to Jamaica seems transported, ...	583	Young Nymph	45
TRANSPORTS			
Beyond the skies transports his mind, ...	900	Dean's Reasons	49
TRAPPINGS			
In the gay Trappings of a Birth-Day Night:	771	Horace 1, 14	50
TRAPPS			
Too cunning to be caught in Trapps.	504	Doctor Delaney	126
TRAPS			
What has he else to bait his Traps, ...	484	Libel on D- D-	129
His Policy consists in setting Traps, ...	535	To Mr. Gay	121
TRASH			
I hope you will not pay my Rent in that same Woods's Trash.	342	Upon His Grace	36
To make their Trash the better sell.	505	Doctor Delaney	158
Who daily vends seditious Trash:	515	Answer Fable	92
In modern Wit all printed Trash, is	643	On Poetry	93
Who crowd the Press with hourly Trash.	652	On Poetry	356

TRASH   (CONTINUED)   PAGE   TITLE   LINE
    As Tradesmen shew their Trash at first:)   . . . . . .   728 Stella, Poems   22
    But trash without measure . . . .   853 Lady's Lament   65
TRAULUS
    Say, Robin, what can Traulus mean   . . . .   795 Traulus 1   1
    That Traulus calls for Vengeance on him?   . . . . . .   796 Traulus 1   8
    For Traulus long his Rancour nurst, ...   796 Traulus 1   17
    While Traulus all his Ordure scatters.   . . . . . .   796 Traulus 1   31
    So, Traulus when he first harangu'd, ...   797 Traulus 1   41
    Traulus of amphibious Breed, ...   799 Traulus 2   1
TRAV'LLER
    Salutes the weary trav'ller as he walks;   . . . . . .   55 Temple Ill   120
    Here, oft the Curious Trav'ller finds, ...   923 Riddle 7   79
TRAV'LLERS
    Attract the curious Trav'llers Eyes, ...   893 Panegyr Dean   202
TRAV'LLING
    A trav'lling Tutor to a Squire;   . . . .   482 Libel on D- D-   64
TRAVEL
    Make their minds travel o'er infinity of space,   . . .   36 Ode Sancroft   61
    Fame spreads the News, and People travel   . . . . .   157 Fable of Midas   37
    As once a week we travel down . . . .   201 Horace 2, 6   77
    You Travel with a heavy Load, ...   480 Libel on D- D-   11
    Briskly travel on their Journies, ...   573 Helter Skelter   2
TRAVELL'D
    For, ill to them, long have I travell'd since . . . .   46 To Congreve   87
    When I premise, that Tim has Travell'd.   . . . . .   782 Tim and Fables   2
TRAVELLER
    A Traveller, who by did pass, ...   127 Little House   23
TRAVELLERS
    All Travellers at first incline   . . . .   734 Stel B-day '20   1
TRAVELS
    Travels at least a Hundred Leagues, ...   174 Horace 1, 7   95
    And Travels not, but runs a Race.   . . . .   398 Earl of P-b-w   9
    In Satyrs, Libels, lying Travels!   . . . .   548 Life of Swift   112
    Perhaps, his Travels, Part the Third;   . . . .   550 Life of Swift   190
TRAY
    To act the Part of Tray, or Cupid;   . . . .   607 Beasts Confess   208
TRAYTOR
    How, by Brave Hands, the Royal Traytor fell;   . . .   162 Toland's Invit   10
    But a Comrade of yours, that Traytor Delany,   . . .   263 Apollo   25
    "But, not a Traytor cou'd be found, ...   567 Death of Swift   353
    A Sland'rer, Traytor and Seducer;   . . . .   798 Traulus 1   80
    A Traytor to the Vices regnant.   . . . .   798 Traulus 1   94
    In a Dozen Apostles but one prov'd a Traytor!   . .   804 Irish Bishops   30
    One Traytor alone, and faithful Eleven;   . . . . .   804 Irish Bishops   31
    Footman, Traytor, vile Seducer, ...   831 Legion Club   69
TRAYTORS
    For, who with Traytors would his Safety trust,   . .   210 Earl of Oxford   19
    But we can afford you Six Traytors in Seven.   . .   804 Irish Bishops   32
    Of Traytors who their Country sold.   . . . .   921 Riddle 7   18
TREACH'ROUS
    And saw the treach'rous Goddess smile;   . . . . . .   413 Desire Possess   46
    Nor let the Zephyr's treach'rous Gale   . . . . . .   597 Cassinus Peter   109
    To what her treach'rous Foe expects.   . . . .   695 Cadenus Vaness   283
    Wou'd say, He made a treach'rous Use   . . . .   707 Cadenus Vaness   644
    Nay, though the treach'rous Rascal Thomas   . . . .   734 Stel B-day '20   9
TREACHEROUS
    With eager hand he grasps the treacherous prey,   . . .   672 Epig Carthy 24   D 15
TREAD
    When Charity begins to tread the Stage: . . . . . .   274 Epilogue   2
    That they might some better Way tread, ...   637 Epistle Lady   223
    What dangerous Paths young Virgins tread;   . . . . .   696 Cadenus Vaness   311
    Now, with a soft and silent Tread, ...   727 To Stella   111
    No more my dear Delightful way tread, ...   779 Mullinix Tim   183
    I smell when I tread on't.   . . . .   857 Lady's Lament   202
    The crude Consistence oft I tread.   . . . .   896 Panegyr Dean   310
    In vain on lofty Heels I tread, ...   897 Panegyr Dean   321
    But whether you can tread or hatch, ...   983 Sher, A Goose   23
TREADING
    And Pigeons billing, Sparrows treading, ...   585 Strephon Chloe   51
TREADS   SEE TREEDS
    Here a pale shape with upward footstep treads,   . . .   35 Ode Sancroft   33
    And treads so soft, so easy, and so light, ...   54 Temple Ill   114
    'Tis sung, where-ever Celia treads, ...   627 Scandal Poem 2   143
TREAS'RER
    A faithful Treas'rer! What could he do more?   . . . .   533 To Mr. Gay   75
TREASON
    When Treason there in Person seems to stand,   . . .   8 Ode to King   56
    And talk what Fools call Treason all the Night.   . .   163 Toland's Invit   16
    High Treason by Statute! But here you object,   . . .   266 Apollo   89
    And dreams of Forfeitures by Treason got.   . . . .   364 On Dreams   20
    And what She describes to be Merit is Treason: . .   716 Answer Rebus   22
    With Plots; and Jacobites and Treason;   . . . . .   775 Mullinix Tim   58
TREASURE
    Remembrance is our Treasure and our Food;   . . . . .   27 Ode to Temple   31
    "Direct my Plow to find a Treasure:"   . . . .   199 Horace 2, 6   D
    When o'er your Patron's Treasure you preside,   . . .   532 To Mr. Gay   16
    A Treasure here of Learning lurks, ...   922 Riddle 7   39
TREASURER   SEE LORD-TREASURER
TREASURERS
    To Treasurers, Controllers, Stewards, ...   189 Faggot   16

		PAGE	TITLE	LINE
TREASURES				
For Learning's mighty Treasures look	. . . . .	27	Ode to Temple	35
Think she there does all her Treasures hide,	. . . .	27	Ode to Temple	37
Who to yon rav'nous Isle thy Treasures bear,	. . . .	794	St. Pat's Well	97
TREAT				
"Inform us, will the Emp'ror treat?	. . . .	202	Horace 2, 6	94
He'd treat with nothing that was Rare,	. . . . . .	378	Apology Lady C	99
To treat a dull Divine:	. . . .	426	Five Ladies	24
I'll treat you with Burgundy.	. . . .	426	Five Ladies	44
With too much freedom treat my betters,	. . . . . .	489	Dialogue	5
To treat our Betters like our Slaves,	. . . . . .	493	Panegyr Swift	5
Presume to treat him at his own Expence.	. . . . .	533	To Mr. Gay	64
He'll treat me as he does my Betters.	. . . . . .	561	Death of Swift	201
Treat the Publick, and your Friends,	. . . . . .	631	Epistle Lady	55
Treat me not with Doggrel Rhime.	. . . .	631	Epistle Lady	58
Tho' you treat us with a Smile,	. . . .	633	Epistle Lady	107
Treat you in Heroick Strain.	. . . .	634	Epistle Lady	136
If I treat you like <a> <crown'd> <Head>	. . . . .	637	Epistle Lady	239
Treat you in a Stile sublime,	. . . .	638	Epistle Lady	258
With ale and chops I'll treat who writes the best,	. .	671	Epig Carthy 24	D 5
Thus Tutors often treat their Betters.	. . . . . .	705	Cadenus Vaness	591
Treat thy Mother like a Harlot!	. . . .	838	Legion Club	202
"To treat gold reduc'd like Wood's copper pence.	. . .	843	Ay and No	16
How dare you treat your Betters thus?	. . . . . .	884	Rev Market-Hill	41
Treat me with so much Complaisance,	. . . .	888	Panegyr Dean	53
Treat not your Lovers with Disdain;	. . . .	932	Riddle 19	D 20
You treat me like a Boy that knocks down his Foe,	. .	967	Letter Sherid	13
Nor is contented with a Treat,	. . . .	1033	Ans to Crown	3
TREATED				
Treated at this ungodly Rate	. . . .	91	Bauc & Phil 1	48
Treated at this ungodly Rate,	. . . .	111	Bauc & Phil 2	16
"Like Pole-Cat vile be treated?	. . . .	154	Widow and Cat	D 22
You might yourselves be treated	. . . .	426	Five Ladies	27
"Who truckle most, when treated worst.	. . . . . .	568	Death of Swift	398
I am not to be treated so,	. . . .	778	Mullinix Tim	176
"Since you could see me treated so,	. . . .	850	Old Thorn	71
TREATISE				
A dang'rous Treatise writ against the Spleen;	. . .	195	Author Himself	48
TREATMENT				
With feeding high, & Treatment civil,	. . . . . .	746	Stel Distress	24
With feeding high, and Treatment civil,	. . . . . .	750	Stel Wood-Park	22
TREATS SEE CHAPTER-TREATS				
Are really but Vulgar Treats:	. . . .	378	Apology Lady C	108
TREBLE				
And on her Plate a treble Share,	. . . .	895	Panegyr Dean	260
TREBLY				
Made trebly dreadfull in your Song.	. . . . . .	461	Birthday Song	46
TREE SEE TRIPLE-TREE,HOLLOW-TREE				
Shall e'er long grow into a Tree,	. . . . . .	31	Ode to Temple	168
Still ev'ry tree the pendent sorrow wears;	. . .	51	Temple Ill	20
And from the Tree where Blosums fele,	. . .	103	Merlin	13
How much the other Tree was griev'd,	. . . . .	117	Bauc & Phil 2	176
Grows neither Grass, nor Shrub, nor Tree;	. . . .	324	Pethox	41
From what Kind of Tree this Wood was Hewn out.	. . .	334	Serious Poem	26
Where neither herb nor tree will thrive,	. . . . .	421	Holyhead	31
"Is sentenc'd to the fatal Tree,	. . . . . .	497	Panegyr Swift	129
Drop from the Tree with all his Bowels burst;	. . .	806	Judas	22
The Nymph who dwells in every Tree,	. . . . . .	849	Old Thorn	45
"Dy'st on a more ignoble Tree,	. . . .	851	Old Thorn	86
Like Daphne sometimes in a Tree,	. . . . . .	927	Riddle 10	D 17
TREEDS				
Tis sung; wherever Celia treeds,	. . . .	621	Scandal Poem 1	139
TREES				
Than a few Scrubby Trees before.	. . . .	108	V's House	84
Remembers he the Trees has seen;	. . . .	116	Bauc & Phil 2	166
Enamell'd Fields, and verdant Trees;	. . . . . .	251	Bubble	28
Starts at the Rust'ling of the Trees,	. . . . . .	379	Apology Lady C	126
Which is; Our Trees are felling;	. . . .	443	Ballyspellin	87
TREMBLE				
See, how they tremble! how they quake!	. . . . .	30	Ode to Temple	113
Must I tremble at his Frown?	. . . .	634	Epistle Lady	150
How I tremble to think of the Blood it hath spilt!	.	871	Grand Question	111
TREMBLED				
She trembled when a Man drew near;	. . . .	222	Prog of Love	3
And Mother Tellus trembled so	. . . .	849	Old Thorn	27
TREMBLES				
The Leather sounds, he trembles from within.	. . . .	139	City Shower	46
He trembles at the Thoughts of State;	. . . . . .	376	Apology Lady C	31
But his has the Odds, who believes and who trembles.	.	803	Irish Bishops	8
TREMBLING				
Trembling beheld the doubtful hand of fate;	. . . . .	52	Temple Ill	42
Which darts on poets eyes a trembling light;	. . . .	54	Temple Ill	98
With trembling Knees, and Terror at his Back;	. . . .	210	Earl of Oxford	4
Warn'd by the Bell, all Flocks come trembling,	. . .	279	Journal	28
With Trembling must thy Leisure wait;	. . . . . .	325	Pethox	50
Among the trembling Croud below.	. . . .	353	Wood Ironmongr	20
And feel a trembling at his Heart:	. . . . . .	500	Doctor Delaney	6
The Screen remov'd, their Hearts are trembling,	. . .	561	Death of Swift	223
The World stands trembling at his Throne.	. . . . .	579	Day Judgement	8
Which, tho' with Trembling, all admire;	. . . . . .	731	Stella, Poems	106
This Prophecy he trembling hears.	. . . .	850	Old Thorn	56

		PAGE	TITLE	LINE
TREMBLING	(CONTINUED)			
Olympus trembling as he nods.		924	Riddle 7	96
now trembling Shiv'ring Quiv'ring Quaking, ...		959	Cantata	
TREMENDOUS				
Why at this Cave's tremendous Mouth, ...		923	Riddle 7	83
TRENT				
Could I but live on this side Trent;		199	Horace 2, 6	10
TREPAN'D				
When to the window he's trepan'd		421	Ireld	19
TREPANING				
A fawning, base, trepaning Lyar, ...		798	Traulus 1	81
TREPANN'D				
The Jugling Sea-god when by chance trepann'd . . .		22	Ode Athenian	189
Suppose you had them all trepann'd		505	Doctor Delaney	151
'Twill appear, to your cost, you are fairly trepann'd,		1027	Sheri Circles	15
TRESSES				
Falls from her Tresses on her Front		226	Prog of Beauty	19
When Mercury her Tresses mows		229	Prog of Beauty	109
And Shock her Tresses fill'd with Fleas.		583	Young Nymph	64
And oft in Celia's Tresses play.		919	Riddle 5	12
TRESSILIAN				
"As modern Scroggs, or old Tressilian;		569	Death of Swift	420
TREYN				
With Bands of Fidlers to extend his Treyn. . . .		678	Dean and Duke	8
TRIBE				
The humble tribe mourn'd for the quick'ning soul, . .		53	Temple Ill	61
Of a Churchwarden or a Tribe.		93	Bauc & Phil 1	124
The Heraldry of ev'ry Tribe.		114	Bauc & Phil 2	100
Sid's Brethren of the conj'ring Tribe		134	Magician's Rod	49
What Humor is, not all the Tribe		215	To Mr. Delany	19
Shrewd Fellows, and arch Wags, a Tribe		216	To Mr. Delany	53
To speak to Elrington, and all the tribe, ...		307	Billet Players	6
"Quite thro' the Tribe of waiting Gentry;		380	Apology Lady C	154
The fundamentals of this tribe;		435	Answer Paulus	110
"Who saw this Factious Tribe caress'd, ...		549	Life of Swift	160
"For he abhorr'd that senseless Tribe, ...		571	Death of Swift	465
Do I, like the Female Tribe, ...		632	Epistle Lady	77
To whom the Tribe of circling Wits, ...		649	On Poetry	267
Those num'rous Virtues which the Tribe		724	To Stella	15
Though you and all your senceless Tribe		736	Stel B-day '20	51
A <Bishop> who rul'd all the rest of his Tribe; . .		803	Irish Bishops	2
Amounting hardly to a Crown a Tribe;		806	Judas	4
There observe the Tribe of <Bingham>, ...		836	Legion Club	163
What, if among the courtly Tribe, ...		884	Rev Market-Hill	35
TRIBES				
Where Town and Country Vicars flock in Tribes, . .		194	Author Himself	19
TRIBUTE				
The Tribute of an humble Muse, ...		32	Ode to Temple	200
Grief that excus'd the tribute of my knees, ...		53	Temple Ill	79
On thee to wreak the tribute when I rail;		53	Temple Ill	86
My latest tribute here I send		608	Know Not What	1
The Muse her am'nall Tribute pays, ...		739	Stel B-day '21	2
To pay your Tribute on the Plain?		896	Panegyr Dean	292
TRICE				
Erect a new one in a Trice;		80	Vanbrug House	66
Leap from the Dunghill in a trice, ...		84	Salamander	40
Erect a new one in a trice.		107	V's House	40
It burnt to Ashes in a Trice.		470	Burning Poem	14
And, as your old wont is, change sides in a trice: . .		818	Archbi Cashel	8
TRICK				
If I come down, I'll spoil your Trick		91	Bauc & Phil 1	45
By any Trick, or any Fault;		199	Horace 2, 6	D
Their Fall is but a Trick to rise:		253	Bubble	84
Conveys out my Paper of Hints by a Trick, ...		265	Apollo	81
That he had serv'd the Prudes a Trick.		321	First of April	16
"'Tis a fair Trick, by ancient Rules--		322	First of April	57
And, Fourthly; 'tis to play an odd Trick, ...		348	Whitshed Motto	17
I know a Trick to make you thrive;		394	Grub-Street	5
By frequent Practice learns the Trick		416	Woman's Mind	39
Try'd ev'ry sharping Trick for Bread, ...		456	Dean Smedley	25
Found out the Trick that Venus play'd, ...		694	Cadenus Vaness	251
For you can't but have heard of a trick among wizards, .		976	Dean to Sherid	21
TRICK'T				
O how was I trick't, ...		245	Irish-Feast	17
TRICKLING				
In trickling Streams betwixt her Joynts.		227	Prog of Beauty	44
TRICKS SEE DOG-TRICKS				
The wily Shafts of State, those Juggler's Tricks . .		29	Ode to Temple	92
Ay, thought the God, are these your Tricks?		108	V's House	71
But Wise Ardelia knew his Tricks.		120	Apollo Outwit	20
Of Tricks, the Lord of <Oxford> knows, ...		181	Horace 2, 1	19
If she were Mine, and had such Tricks, ...		220	A Quiet Life	29
The Latent Wiles, and Tricks of State, ...		340	Arch-Bish Dub	11
The deepest Tricks of Courtiers knew.		494	Panegyr Swift	38
A Dext'rous Steward, when his Tricks are found, . .		535	To Mr. Gay	107
He knows a Thousand Tricks, whene'er he please, . .		535	To Mr. Gay	123
Yet cannot leave his roguish Tricks;		777	Mullinix Tim	118
Conceal your Form with various Tricks;		919	Riddle 5	27
Tho' we play them Tricks for ever, ...		934	Riddle 22	D 7
And thus I am fully reveng'd for your late tricks, . .		977	Dean to Sherid	47

TRICKSY

	PAGE	TITLE	LINE
"When Lady Tricksy play'd a Four, ...	452	Modern Lady	250

TRIDENT

| Next call him Neptune with his Trident, ... | 463 | Birthday Song | 97 |

TRIES   SEE TRYES

Her Body light, she tries her Wings, ...	230	Prog of Poetry	13
All Turns and Motion tries;	406	Swift to Pope	14
Tries twenty Charms to mend her Luck.	452	Modern Lady	237
Before he tries a five-barr'd Gate:	640	On Poetry	16
And human Caution tries in vain	702	Cadenus Vaness	486
And when a Friend in Kindness tries	730	Stella, Poems	89
In vain to frisk or climb he tries;	885	Rev Market-Hill	81
Tries who shall have it by the End.	993	On Picture	30

TRIFLE

The fool, who scrambles for a trifle;	436	Answer Paulus	136
That's but a trifle among Friends.	461	Birthday Song	28
They pay a Trifle, and enjoy the rest.	533	To Mr. Gay	48
Not to publish ev'ry Trifle, ...	631	Epistle Lady	61
From every Trifle that employs	688	Cadenus Vaness	48
It shews and discovers it self through a Trifle. . .	716	Answer Rebus	12
By reading this Trifle, I quickly began	716	Answer Rebus	13

TRIFLES

| Scrawl'd o'er with Trifles thus, and quite . . . . | 60 | Lady Tablebook | 3 |
| a sharper in trifles a dupe in the main . . . . . | 540 | Charac Walpole | 4 |

TRIM

But then the 'Squire so trim and nice, ...	376	Apology Lady C	23
And with Rings so very trim, ...	574	Helter Skelter	27
. . . say is (tho' written somewhat at large) trim and clean:	1024	Nim-Dan-Dean 2	D 17

TRIMMERS

| Whigs, Tories, Trimmers, Hannoverians, ... | 345 | Prometheus | 13 |

TRIMMING

| Come trimming Harcourt; bring your Mace; . . . . . | 190 | Faggot | 39 |
| By cutting of his Phrase, and trimming, ... | 455 | Dean Smedley | 19 |

TRINE

| In Square or in Opposite-Circle or Trine . . . . | 1018 | Swift Ans Sher | 23 |

TRINKETS

| Till Phillis all her Trinkets pawn'd: . . . . . | 224 | Prog of Love | 88 |

TRINOBANTUM

| Spread thro' Augusta Trinobantum) . . . . | 649 | On Poetry | 280 |

TRIPLE

| Hemm'd by a triple Circle round, ... | 200 | Horace 2, 6 | 28 |
| Out bounc't the Mastiff of the triple Head; . . . | 538 | Mr. Pulteney | 27 |

TRIPLE-BARKING

| His triple-barking Mouth to Stop: . . . . . . | 647 | On Poetry | 214 |

TRIPLE-TREE

| Form'd like the Triple-Tree near Stephen's-Green; . | 285 | Elegy Boat | 34 |

TRIPLET

| Such a Triplet could you tell . . . . | 837 | Legion Club | 183 |

TRIPOD

| Fresh from the Tripod of Apollo, ... | 485 | Libel on D- D- | 181 |
| As from the tripod of Apollo . . . . | 490 | Dialogue | 47 |

TRIPPLE

| The loud Cerberian tripple Bark. . . . . | 596 | Cassinus Peter | 80 |

TRIPS

| He trips up my props, ... | 852 | Lady's Lament | 31 |

TRIPSY

| Bequeath'd by Tripsy when she dy'd, ... | 526 | Lady's Dres Rm | 30 |

TRIPSY'S

| There Night-gloves made of Tripsy's Hide, ... | 526 | Lady's Dres Rm | 29 |
| Distill'd from Tripsy's darling Whelp; . . . . . | 526 | Lady's Dres Rm | 32 |

TRITE

| Beware of Subjects you call Trite, ... | 371 | Letter D. S-y | 2 |
| In Phrases battered, stale, and trite, ... | 448 | Modern Lady | 112 |

TRIUMPH

| The Goddess Want in Triumph reigns; . . . . . . | 1035 | To Quilca | 10 |

TRIUMPHAL

And a Grim Slave to wait on his Triumphal Car. . .	7	Ode to King	44
Nor its triumphal Cavalcade to grace	29	Ode to Temple	89
You, o'er the high Triumphal Arch	326	Pethox	93
Or on a proud triumphal Car, ...	724	To Stella	26

TRIUMPHANT

Triumphant Star! Some Pity show	100	Elegy Patrige	89
Triumphant Tories, and desponding Whigs, ...	138	City Shower	41
Your Foes, triumphant o'er the Laws, ...	312	To Ford	29
To look on Vice triumphant round, ...	312	To Ford	41
From Fleets triumphant o'er the Gallick Coast. . .	771	Horace 1, 14	40
The Knight triumphant reigns betwixt:	883	Rev Market-Hill	20
Like Roman Generals triumphant, ...	928	Riddle 12	D 15
How long shall vice triumphant reign?	950	Upstart	D 17
Went triumphant to Church, and sang stoutly Te Deum:	967	Letter Sherid	18

TRIUMPHS

| What Trophies and what Triumphs are Your Due! . . | 12 | Ode to William | D 14 |
| The Triumphs of that stubborn Dame, ... | 702 | Cadenus Vaness | 495 |

TRIUMVIRATE

| This great triumvirate of Souls. . . . . | 28 | Ode to Temple | 69 |
| An odd Triumvirate of Friends; . . . . | 883 | Rev Market-Hill | 2 |

TRIVIAL

| The trivial Turns, the borrow'd Wit, ... | 645 | On Poetry | 151 |

TROD

| To shew the Paths of both must be together trod, . . | 7 | Ode to King | 29 |

```
TROD                (CONTINUED)                          PAGE    TITLE           LINE
    Beat not the dirty paths where vulgar feet have trod,    .    49 To Congreve       205
    Where once their Sultan's Horse hath trod,       .  .  .  .  324 Pethox            40
    To make a Clatt'ring as they trod.       .  .  .  .  .  .  352 Wood Ironmongr     12
    Unless you other Ways had trod  .  .  .  .  .  .  .  .  495 Panegyr Swift      78
    For their Ancestor trod Mortar,   .  .  .  .  .  .  .  837 Legion Club       178
    Stumbling at ev'ry Step she trod.   .  .  .  .  .  .  885 Rev Market-Hill    74
TRODDEN
    As from the trodden Dust they spring,   .  .  .  .  .  .  813 Bro Protestant     53
TROIS
    He knew to stop a quater trois.   .  .  .  .  .  .  .  .  456 Dean Smedley       30
TROJAN
    The Trojan Heroe paid his Vow.)   .  .  .  .  .  .  .  896 Panegyr Dean      308
TROLL
    To troll it in a Coach and Six!   .  .  .  .  .  .  .  905 Death Daphne       88
TROLLED
    Last trolled forth a gentle Swine   .  .  .  .  .  .  .  849 Old Thorn          41
TROLLOP
    Lolloping, Galloping, Trollop,   .  .  .  .  .  .  .  .  960 Cantata
TROLLOPING
    Trolloping, Lolloping, Galloping, Trolloping    .  .  .  960 Cantata
    Trolloping, Lolloping, Galloping, Trolloping    .  .  .  960 Cantata
    Lolloping, Trolloping, Galloping, Lolloping,    .  .  .  960 Cantata
    Trolloping, Galloping, Lollop,   .  .  .  .  .  .  .  960 Cantata
TROOP
    At Hamilton's Bawn, and the Troop is arriv'd.   .  .  .  869 Grand Question     68
    At the Head of his Troop, with Trumpet and Drum:   .  .  870 Grand Question     88
    At last comes the Troop, by the Word of Command   .  .  870 Grand Question     99
TROOPS
    "When are the Troops to have their Pay?   .  .  .  .  .  202 Horace 2, 6       100
    Undone at Play, the Femal Troops   .  .  .  .  .  .  .  254 Bubble             89
    Troops of all Tongues and Nations Muster:   .  .  .  .  345 Prometheus         28
    That, Standing Troops were his Aversion:   .  .  .  .  606 Beasts Confess    152
    And listing Troops for the Pretender.   .  .  .  .  .  788 Dick's Variety     24
    Full Northward, let your Troops be led:   .  .  .  .  884 Rev Market-Hill    48
TROPE
    I made use of a Trope; that an Heir to invite,   .  .  .  144 New Song           37
    Un-man the poor Knave for sake of a Trope.   .  .  .  .  335 Serious Poem       52
TROPES
    And will neither regard my Figures nor Tropes;   .  .  .  145 New Song           52
    Leave hunting after Bribes, forget your Tropes:   .  .  162 Toland's Invit      6
    In such a Case they talk in Tropes,   .  .  .  .  .  557 Death of Swift    117
TROPHIES
    What Trophies and what Triumphs are Your Due!   .  .  .   12 Ode to William   D 14
    These are the tyrant's trophies of a year;   .  .  .  .   55 Temple Ill        126
    And bear their Trophies with them as they go:   .  .  .  139 City Shower        54
    As Trophies of a Muse deceas'd;   .  .  .  .  .  .  .  611 By Dr. Swift        6
TROPHY
    A Trophy, on his Temple-side.)   .  .  .  .  .  .  .  458 Paddy's Charac     18
    A Champion kill'd, or Trophy won;   .  .  .  .  .  .  554 Death of Swift     24
TROPICK
    Up to the Northern Tropick came,   .  .  .  .  .  .  .  119 Apollo Outwit       2
TROPICKS
    He gets to a Window beyond both the Tropicks;   .  .  .  265 Apollo             84
TROT
    by Jogling, Jogling, Jogling trot,   .  .  .  .  .  .  957 Cantata
    When whip you trot up, without minding your betters,  .  .  978 Dean to Tho: S      3
'TROTH
    'Troth I could pity you; but this is it,   .  .  .  .  .   48 To Congreve       161
TROTH
    I would not give such Language to a Dog, faith and troth    985 Mary to Sher        4
TROTS
    Trots to his country mansion down;   .  .  .  .  .  .  435 Answer Paulus      94
TROUBLE
    Has fed without Restraint, or Trouble;   .  .  .  .  .  230 Prog of Poetry      2
    Computing all their Cost and Trouble,   .  .  .  .  .  259 Bubble            218
    "'Tis all to save their Mother trouble;   .  .  .  .  .  321 First of April     24
    The Loss of one is no such Trouble,   .  .  .  .  .  366 Answer Delaney     11
    This will not give them half the trouble   .  .  .  .  469 Birthday Song     273
    Lest you the town may have less trouble in,   .  .  .  .  753 Gift for Bec       23
    Tim thour't the Punch to stir up trouble in;   .  .  .  777 Mullinix Tim      138
    For Silver and Gold I don't trouble my Head,   .  .  .  927 Riddle 11        D  5
TROUBLED
    And that her troubled Ghost still haunts there since she     27 Ode to Temple      38
        dy'd;
    However Stella, be not troubled,   .  .  .  .  .  .  721 Stel B-Day '18      3
    They ne'er troubled their head,   .  .  .  .  .  .  .  755 Dingley Brent       5
    "And nothing of that ever troubled your Grace.   .  .  .  843 Ay and No           8
TROUBLES
    His Troubles and Sorrows now come in a Heap,   .  .  .  519 Dean Hang Rape     59
    A peck of troubles for a coach.   .  .  .  .  .  .  .  753 Gift for Bec       20
TROUBLESOME
    Who tell us these troublesome stories,   .  .  .  .  .  186 Scriblerus 4     D  3
TROUBLING
    Troubling the chrystal fountain of the sight,   .  .  .   54 Temple Ill         97
    Without troubling his Head about Judgment or Wit:   .  .  263 Apollo             20
TROUT
    Where ev'ry Trout can make as high Rants   .  .  .  .  824 Printer Newgat      5
TROW
    Is the poison and dagger you boast in your jaws, trow?  .  979 Dean to Tho: S      5
```

		PAGE	TITLE	LINE
TROWEL				
This was dext'rous at his Trowel, ...		800	Traulus 2	29
TROWELS				
You save the Charge of Lime and Trowels.		1021	Nim-Dan-Dean 1	D 24
TROY				
So when Troy Chair-men bore the Wooden Steed, .		139	City Shower	47
A Siege as long as Troy endur'd.		326	Pethox	98
Which might alone have conquer'd Troy;		731	Stella, Poems	124
TROY-TOWN				
Are Stale, and Worn as Troy-Town Story.		774	Mullinix Tim	36
TRU				
Here in Beau-spelling (tru tel deth)		60	Lady Tablebook	9
TRUANT				
To win the Truant School-Boys Hearts!		779	Mullinix Tim	200
TRUBY'S				
At Child's or Truby's never once had been; . .		194	Author Himself	18
TRUCE				
Truce, good My Lord, I beg a Truce!		175	Horace 1, 7	130
Truce, good My Lord, I beg a Truce!		175	Horace 1, 7	130
A Truce with all sublime Conceits.		711	Cadenus Vaness	793
TRUCK				
And truck the Carrion for Tobacca, ...		220	A Quiet Life	32
TRUCKLE				
"Who truckle most, when treated worst.		568	Death of Swift	398
TRUCKLED				
Perhaps he might have truckled down, ...		549	Life of Swift	140
I despise any poet that truckled to Dan.		976	Dean to Sherid	34
TRUCKS				
For Candles, how she trucks her Driping; · . .		282	Journal	88
I will either explain, or repay it by trucks; . . .		977	Dean to Sherid	44
TRUDGES				
Away he trudges into Town;		376	Apology Lady C	28
TRUDGING				
At trudging in a beaten Track, ...		183	Horace 2, 1	104
TRUE				
And when you find out these, believe true Fame is there.		21	Ode Athenian	186
How strange a Paradox is true, ...		25	Ode Athenian	305
Stay while I tell my story, short, and true;		46	To Congreve	111
'Tis true, seven Pound, four Shillings, and six Pence,.		71	Mrs Harris Pet	40
With true Delight observed them all		87	Hist V's House	17
But yet, methinks, I feel it true;		116	Bauc & Phil 2	159
And be a true Whig, while I am Not in game. .		145	New Song	54
"'Tis true, the Pinner which you prize		154	Widow and Cat	D 28
But true English Men will fill, ...		169	Peace Dunkirk	38
For, if those antient Tales be true, ...		177	To Lord Harley	25
Dick, we agree--all's true, thou'st said, ...		183	Horace 2, 1	99
Something in Verse as true as Prose;		199	Horace 2, 6	D
'Tis true,--then why should I repine, ...		203	In Sickness	1
True Humor must with Wit combine:		216	To Mr. Delany	30
Our true Irish Hearts from old England to wean; .		237	Excellent Song	7
She knows it is true, ...		247	Irish-Feast	84
Your guides to true Simplicity.		270	Apollo's Edict	D 32
Thinks ev'ry Syllable is true;		282	Journal	102
True to his profit and his pride, ...		296	Satiric Elegy	23
For, true or false, they'll ne'r enquire, ...		312	To Ford	33
"Where most true Sons of Phoebus ha' bin. .		320	First of April	4
He can Rap his own Raps, and has the true Sapience .		335	Serious Poem	47
Is a Man of this World all true Flesh and Blood; .		335	Serious Poem	50
He would ne'er be convinc'd it was a True Saint: .		336	Serious Poem	74
When the True Wood arrives, as he soon will no doubt, .		336	Serious Poem	75
Why that may be true, yet Wood upon Wood, . .		338	Serious Poem	121
I must confess you've spoken once true.		349	Whitshed Motto	24
Nor less <Tom-T--d-Man> of true Statesman mold, .		364	On Dreams	21
'Tis true, say they, cut off the Head, ...		366	Answer Delaney	5
'Tis true, a Glass will bring supplies		367	Answer Delaney	45
The Weather's Fair, nay, that is true, ...		372	Letter D. S-y	23
Or if 'tis true, Great Phabus smiles		372	Letter D. S-y	25
True Virtue has a Right to rise.)		386	Manly Virtue	92
If this be true, then how much more, ...		392	Young's Satire	27
I ask, if what you say be true, ...		392	Young's Satire	32
Pray God they now may find as true.		408	Dial Rich Marb	22
True lawyers, for the wisest ends, ...		432	Answer Paulus	11
'Tis very true, and none denies, ...		433	Answer Paulus	39
My satire may offend, 'tis true:		435	Answer Paulus	101
Most conscious that they all speak true, ...		453	Modern Lady	272
It may be literally true.		461	Birthday Song	20
'Tis partly false, and partly true, ...		464	Birthday Song	138
True Politicians only Pay		483	Libel on D- D-	89
This may be true--submitting still		484	Libel on D- D-	121
Betwixt a true and spurious Merit;		484	Libel on D- D-	148
Be sometimes to your country true, ...		487	Irish-Club	17
Ne'er did a true satyric muse		488	Irish-Club	25
And 'tis as true, or Story lies, ...		495	Panegyr Swift	74
The true, the genuine sweet'ning Lay?		497	Panegyr Swift	143
Make all true Patriots up to Shoe-boys		501	Doctor Delany	61
For the Good of our Church a true <English> <Dean>. .		516	Dean Hang Rape	4
For which all true Protestant Hearts should be glad; .		520	Dean Hang Rape	68
Is offensive to every true Protestant ear		522	St. Cecilia's	6
oppressing true merit exalting the base		540	Charac Walpole	7
'Tis true, we talk of Friendship much, ...		546	Life of Swift	41

TRUE	(CONTINUED)	PAGE	TITLE	LINE
True Friendship in two breasts requires		546	Life of Swift	43
From Nature, I believe 'em true:		553	Death of Swift	2
"Who still were true, to please his Foes.		567	Death of Swift	364
"True genuine Dulness mov'd his Pity,		572	Death of Swift	469
All other Methods but the true.		592	Strephon Chloe	270
'Tis true, he hated Sloth like Pease.		602	Beasts Confess	46
'Tis true, he was not much inclin'd		603	Beasts Confess	63
'Tis true, the People understood,		606	Beasts Confess	161
And, if the whole may pass for true,		608	Know Not What	5
Tis true; a Woman on her mettle		621	Scandal Poem 1	143
We kill, 'tis true, but never wound;		624	Scandal Poem 2	22
'Tis true; a Woman on her Mettle,		628	Scandal Poem 2	147
Madam, I allow 'tis true;		632	Epistle Lady	93
Apply'd to <George> exactly true is:		657	On Poetry	478
Exactly true! Invidious Poet!		657	On Poetry	479
Without reproach of flattery true.		658	On Poetry	D 410
Carthy, you say, writes well--his genius true.--		668	Epig Carthy 8	D 1
What Midas touch'd, became true Gold; but then,		668	Epig Carthy 12	D 1
That ev'ry Article was true;		688	Cadenus Vaness	71
It shew'd a true Paternal Care--		707	Cadenus Vaness	653
True Honour comprehends them all.		724	To Stella	18
Best Pattern of true Friends, beware;		727	To Stella	117
True Poets can depress and raise;		729	Stella, Poems	53
Do but insinuate what is true.		729	Stella, Poems	60
And when your Lover is not true,		733	Verses Vanessa	13
To quit the true old Angel-Inn.		734	Stel B-day '20	14
Regard not what is false or true,		747	Stel Distress	60
Yet granting all I said were true,		748	Stel Distress	75
Regard not whether false or true:		751	Stel Wood-Park	76
For though my Raillery were true,		752	Stel Wood-Park	91
At Fifty six, if this be true,		757	Stel B-day '24	23
'Tis true, but let it not be known,		757	Stel B-day '24	41
That true Contempt for Things below,		765	Stel B-day '26	68
Have made thy Presence in a true Sence,		775	Mullinix Tim	65
'Tis true, nor need I to be told,		776	Mullinix Tim	77
Which the true Mother, which Pretender,		776	Mullinix Tim	99
No more--In mark of true Affection		779	Mullinix Tim	207
'Tis a true Copy, I'll say that for't,		783	Tim and Fables	21
True indeed, I should be gladder,		801	Traulus 2	49
Be studious to practice true Meanness of Spirit;		808	Advice Parson	7
Are his Brother Protestants, good men and true;		815	Yahoo's	22
Causeless Joy, and true Despair;		832	Legion Club	90
(If all be true that Poets chant)		849	Old Thorn	46
True, Lady Anne no Danger fears,		885	Rev Market-Hill	57
'Tis true, but what advantage comes		899	Dean's Reasons	27
'Tis true, indeed, sometimes I save,		918	Riddle 4	31
I'll shew the World strange Things and true;		919	Riddle 5	14
Who feels true Joys when he bestows thee.		920	Riddle 5	36
To turn the tune impartial Side!		921	Riddle 7	8
To Strephon I have still been true,		924	Riddle 8	3
In all Things false, yet always true,		935	Riddle 23	D 5
While true Lovers Eyes Weeping Sleep,		960	Cantata	
. . . and I don't believe that's a true Story,		986	Mary to Sher	20
'Tis true no Nose could come in better,		993	On Picture	16
'Tis true indeed, to curry Friends,		1003	Dan J's Reply	19
Miss Morice was (I can assure you 'tis true) sick:		1029	Dr. Helsham	12
TRUE-LOVE				
I have lost my Money, and shall lose my True-Love too.		73	Mrs Harris Pet	65
TRUER				
Was truer than Steele to the <Hanover> Line,		518	Dean Hang Rape	33
What truer Affection cou'd ever be shown,		805	Irish Bishops	55
TRUEST				
Or else the truest Maxim lyes:		391	Young's Satire	22
To use them as his truest friends		422	Ireld	46
TRULL				
You may compare your Trull to us;		622	Scandal Poem 1	158
To celebrate some Suburb Trull;		730	Stella, Poems	72
TRULY				
Sounds truly good, or truly great;		36	Ode Sancroft	49
Sounds truly good, or truly great;		36	Ode Sancroft	49
Truly, says he, Mrs. Nab,. . .		72	Mrs Harris Pet	55
For truly John was missing too:		223	Prog of Love	40
She'll say, and she may truly say't		293	Prog Marriage	97
<Helsham> does truly Wit command		373	Letter D. S-y	47
Contented to be truly great,		385	Manly Virtue	49
To bless, is truly to be great!		386	Manly Virtue	102
And truly, Madam, I know when		453	Modern Lady	264
But hark'ee, is it truly so,		493	Panegyr Swift	23
Then must it truly be confest;		497	Panegyr Swift	144
Come, tell me truly, wou'd you take well,		546	Life of Swift	31
But, truly there the Dean was bit---.		547	Life of Swift	92
"And, would you make him truly sower;		566	Death of Swift	343
Why truly 'tis Satan, <Arch-bishop> of Hell:		803	Irish Bishops	4
If truly you would be reveng'd on the parson,		818	Epigr Kite	5
Truly I don't know who's bound to be sending . . .		1013	Swift to Sheri	5
. . .truly they don't care for your Wife's Company, . . .		1013	Swift to Sheri	7
. . .to my Lady Mountcashell: but, truly, I thought .		1014	Swift to Sheri	11
TRUMP				
Would you describe Turenne or Trump		83	Salamander	19
The last loud trump must wake him now:		296	Satiric Elegy	6

TRUMP	(CONTINUED)	PAGE	TITLE	LINE
Mordanto fills the Trump of Fame, ...		397	Earl of P-b-w	1

TRUMPET
Methinks I hear thee loud, as Trumpet, ...		182	Horace 2, 1	71
At the last Trumpet, unprepar'd, ...		241	Run Bankers	55
We sound a trumpet, or we beat a drum;		308	Billet Players	37
At the Head of his Troop, with Trumpet and Drum: . .		870	Grand Question	88

TRUMPETERS
| Dub, dub, a-dub, dub. The Trumpeters follow, ... | | 870 | Grand Question | 91 |

TRUMPETS
Guns, Trumpets, Drums, and Bells were drown'd.		338	Wood's Brass	8
So by the Brazen Trumpets Bluster, ...		345	Prometheus	27
With trumpets and fiddles and organs and singing . .		522	St. Cecilia's	7
Drums and Trumpets bring me out;		933	Riddle 20	D 20

TRUMPS
With brazen Trumps and brazen Drums.		338	Wood's Brass	4
"The Dean is dead, (and what is Trumps?)		562	Death of Swift	228
She scarce remembers what is Trumps.		904	Death Daphne	60

TRUNK
Now you must know, because my Trunk has a very bad Lock,		69	Mrs Harris Pet	5
In Heathenish Times from the Trunk of an Oak: . . .		335	Serious Poem	58
And sent in Quires to line a Trunk;		644	On Poetry	144

TRUNKS
| In his Grave, and search his Trunks. . . . . . . | | 836 | Legion Club | 168 |

TRUST
So vile Thy Breach of Trust is;		154	Widow and Cat	D 42
For trust us, friend Mortimer		187	Scriblerus 4	D 16
For, who with Traytors would his Safety trust, . .		210	Earl of Oxford	19
And, trust me, as the noise grows stronger, ...		296	Satiric Elegy	7
For, Stella has betray'd her Trust, ...		311	To Ford	2
In thy great Care we place our Trust, ...		339	Arch-Bish Dub	7
That we should put no Trust in Princes;		408	Dial Rich Marb	14
Nor do they trust their Tongue alone, ...		450	Modern Lady	188
Than those of Wit, or Trust in God.		495	Panegyr Swift	79
For, Sons of Phoebus never break their Trust. . . .		532	To Mr. Gay	18
And trust his Honesty just so much more.		535	To Mr. Gay	114
"In Princes never put thy Trust.		566	Death of Swift	342
That made him trust alone in Merit:		604	Beasts Confess	110
Did I ever break my Trust?		631	Epistle Lady	66
And factious Rage, and Breach of Trust, ...		725	To Stella	46
Who fondly put his Trust in pop'lar Breath.		771	Horace 1, 14	32
Will they not trust me for a Spy?		779	Mullinix Tim	194
To you we often trust the Key:		889	Panegyr Dean	90
To me he chiefly gives in Trust		915	Riddle 1	21
There's nobody but a Fool that would trust. . . .		941	Letter	32

TRUSTED
| The Ducal Coffers, trusted to your Charge, ... | | 533 | To Mr. Gay | 45 |
| "Though trusted long in great Affairs, ... | | 565 | Death of Swift | 329 |

TRUSTEES
| By clients to her priests and trustees. . . . . . | | 433 | Answer Paulus | 30 |

TRUSTY
To eat the Calves-Head with your trusty Friends. . .		162	Toland's Invit	4
Right Trusty, and so forth; We let you to know, . .		263	Apollo	1
Suppose your Lord a trusty Servant send, ...		534	To Mr. Gay	85

TRUTH
Truth is eternal, and the Son of Heav'n, ...		34	Ode Sancroft	1
Of truth, and what, or where it is:		35	Ode Sancroft	42
(High Truth) the best resemblance of exalted Thee, . .		36	Ode Sancroft	46
Of heav'n-born Truth below:		36	Ode Sancroft	53
Suppose the truth, like all the world, their own; . .		37	Ode Sancroft	80
You make to truth, retreat, and innocence;		44	To Congreve	8
Whether it be a Truth, or Lye.		65	Problem	6
Truth, Innocence, Good Nature, Look serene; . . .		118	Biddy Floyd	4
Performs just Friendship, Justice, Truth require: . .		196	Author Himself	73
And from a Fable form a Truth:		252	Bubble	44
To own the truth we have some private Ends.		275	Epilogue	14
For to say Truth, she did intend him, ...		303	Storm	21
Is not the truth the truth? Look full on me; . . .		307	Billet Players	9
Is not the truth the truth? Look full on me; . . .		307	Billet Players	9
And still the Truth he will Maintain, whate'er he loses by't.		341	Upon His Grace	6
He told the real Truth in Rhime.		378	Apology Lady C	90
Who talk'd of Justice, and of Truth, ...		386	Manly Virtue	72
If there be Truth in what you sing, ...		391	Young's Satire	1
If this be Truth, as you attest, ...		391	Young's Satire	11
The truth will be got out		423	Carterets Arms	4
But, since the truth must needs be stretched . . .		433	Answer Paulus	43
Madam, if there be Truth in Man, ...		447	Modern Lady	80
Wou'd strictly after Truth enquire		455	Dean Smedley	7
That sound Divine the Truth has spoke all		469	Birthday Song	271
Who, under Tales conveying Truth, ...		482	Libel on D- D-	55
In Verse; but there is Truth in mine.		486	Libel on D- D-	194
For learning, probity and truth, ...		490	Dialogue	30
Shew Reason, Grammer, Truth, or Sense?		503	Doctor Delaney	104
Made up of Malice, Truth, and Wit:		545	Life of Swift	2
Truth and Honour how to prize;		630	Epistle Lady	22
Learn to relish Truth and Reason.		638	Epistle Lady	272
With Justice, Truth and Fortitude;		693	Cadenus Vaness	207
Truth shines the brighter, clad in Verse;		729	Stella, Poems	58
Now should my Praises owe their Truth		729	Stella, Poems	61
Truth, Judgment, Wit, give Place to Spite, ...		730	Stella, Poems	93

TRUTH	(CONTINUED)	PAGE	TITLE	LINE
A Truth for which thy Soul should grieve,		735	Stel B-day '20	46
But to say truth, such Dulness reigns		742	Stel B-day 22	41
Where Truth has not the least Pretence;		747	Stel Distress	62
Where Truth has not the least Pretence;		752	Stel Wood-Park	78
Beauty and Wit, too sad a Truth,		757	Stel B-day '24	15
One for truth, and one for errors:		907	Daphne	44
But sprung (and I this Truth maintain)		927	Riddle 10	D 9
Tho' Candor and Truth in my Aspect I bear,		929	Riddle 13	D 5
Every body knows, that I love to tell Truth and shame the Devil,		986	Mary to Sher	23

TRUTHS

And to mistaken man these truths rehearse,		53	Temple Ill	69
To make these Truths the better known,		547	Life of Swift	66

TRY

How vainly (Sir) did Your fond Enemy try		9	Ode to King	101
Some she condemns for Life to try		32	Ode to Temple	189
In vain to quench this foolish Fire I try		33	Ode to Temple	206
So when Cartesian artists try		35	Ode Sancroft	27
For when like stupid alchymists you try		49	To Congreve	207
The Ladys vow, and swear they'll try,		65	Problem	5
To try the great Experiment;		66	Problem	34
To try the Back-way to his Heart;		66	Problem	42
To try the People's Hospitality.		90	Bauc & Phil 1	4
To try good People's Hospitality.		111	Bauc & Phil 2	4
Try Lads, can you this Bundle break;		189	Faggot	2
Or gravely try to read the Lines		201	Horace 2, 6	71
Virtue, to crown her Fav'rites, loves to try		210	Earl of Oxford	11
No other way but try the Bath:		293	Prog Marriage	106
Howe'er let us try him and see how he'll burn.		336	Serious Poem	64
I'll Try his Manners once again;		377	Apology Lady C	68
To try your Wit		441	Ballyspellin	26
Dear Madam, try to take a Nap--		451	Modern Lady	210
You try to take Revenge in vain.		504	Doctor Delaney	136
Will try to find their private Ends:		556	Death of Swift	76
Some try to learn polite Behaviour,		592	Strephon Chloe	271
Are awkward when you try to flatter.		642	On Poetry	52
Go try your Hand a second Time.		645	On Poetry	146
To try a new Experiment:		691	Cadenus Vaness	139
To try their Wisdom's full Extent;		697	Cadenus Vaness	339
Dear Madam try this Pigeon's leg:		746	Stel Distress	18
Dear Madam, try this Pigeon's Leg;		750	Stel Wood-Park	16
I have a Coat at home, that you may try,		780	Mullinix Tim	217
Let us try some new Expedient;		832	Legion Club	76
You should try your graving Tools		839	Legion Club	223

TRY'D

A Friend in Turns and Windings try'd		94	Bauc & Phil 1	137
Try'd ev'ry Tone might Pity win,		111	Bauc & Phil 2	13
But she the Charm already try'd,		120	Apollo Outwit	38
Two Gods their Skill in Musick try'd,		156	Fable of Midas	25
When you are try'd in Scandal's Court.		413	Censure	6
To live without both full three Months he try'd,		430	Dicky Dolly	11
Try'd ev'ry sharping Trick for Bread,		456	Dean Smedley	25
'Tis said, the Gods try'd all their Art,		501	Doctor Delaney	31
These they have often try'd before;		505	Doctor Delaney	155
Their kind Affections he has try'd;		606	Beasts Confess	163
And all their Conduct wou'd be try'd		694	Cadenus Vaness	238
And, by the Project vainly try'd,		713	Cadenus Vaness	836
In Points of Honour to be try'd,		724	To Stella	35
He'd have 'em try'd at the Assizes		788	Dick's Variety	21
Lastly, let his Gifts be try'd,		800	Traulus 2	43
Better ne'er was try'd.		953	Herrings	5

TRYAL

And was resolv'd upon a Tryal,		120	Apollo Outwit	27
If you make the same Tryal, and Bore him Behind;		336	Serious Poem	78
And there can be no Harm in making a Tryal;		336	Serious Poem	82
Thus, for a Tryal, let me beg of		366	Answer Delaney	15

TRYES

His wings are clipp't; he tryes no more in vain		678	Dean and Duke	7

TRYSYLLABLE

To hold out longer in Trysyllable.		989	Letter Dr Sh-n	31

TU

Ah! Quanto rectius, Tu Adepte,		476	Epist on Epist	29

TUB

Call'd, Love In A Tub, and Love In A Wood.		337	Serious Poem	92
First, Love In A Tub: 'Squire Wood has in Store		337	Serious Poem	95
He'll mount his Tub, and preach his best,		456	Dean Smedley	38

TUBES

Some cleaning hollow Tubes, to spy		780	Mullinix Tim	247

TUBS

Strong Tubs for his Raps, Two thousand and more;		337	Serious Poem	96
From Tubs their snuffling Nonsense utter:		892	Panegyr Dean	171
Thy Milk shall make us Tubs of Butter.		892	Panegyr Dean	172

TUCK'D

Thy Muse is tuck'd up, and succinct;		1021	Nim-Dan-Dean 1	D 27

TUCK'D-UP

The tuck'd-up Sempstress walks with hasty Strides,		138	City Shower	37

TUESDAY

For my Lord Dromedary comes a Tuesday without fail;		70	Mrs Harris Pet	28
On Tuesday the Ninth, seditiously came,		263	Apollo	29
Gallants, by Tuesday next we must be gone.		308	Billet Players	40

		PAGE	TITLE	LINE
TUESDAY	(CONTINUED)			
I remember it was upon a Tuesday, of all Days in the Year.		986	Mary to Sher	26
TUG				
In vain I tug and pull the Oar,	. . . .	32	Ode to Temple	193
You tug for Rimes	. . . .	441	Ballyspellin	23
At an old stubborn Root I chanc'd to tug,	. . . . .	881	Pastoral Dial	25
TULIPS				
Such gaudy Tulips rais'd from Dung.	. . . .	530	Lady's Dres Rm	144
TUMBL'D				
So I tumbl'd and toss'd all Night,. . .	. . . .	70	Mrs Harris Pet	20
TUMBLE				
Ready to tumble down into the sky;	. . . .	35	Ode Sancroft	36
Make gilded spires and altars tumble.	. . . . . .	490	Dialogue	36
Some to tumble Country-Wenches	. . . . . .	574	Helter Skelter	45
Must not inevitably tumble?	. . . .	593	Strephon Chloe	298
TUMBLED				
He tumbled in the Gulph profound;	. . . .	413	Desire Possess	49
Humour, you tumbled Topsy Turvy.	. . . .	477	Epist on Epist	72
TUMBLING				
And tumbling topsi-turvy round	. . . .	126	Little House	9
The Walls in tumbling gave a Knock;	. . . . . .	127	Little House	15
Dead Cats and Turnip-Tops come tumbling down the Flood		139	City Shower	63
Come headlong tumbling from their mitred Chariots,	. .	806	Judas	20
TUNBRIDGE				
Was marry'd to the Tunbridge Beau,	. . . . . .	699	Cadenus Vaness	393
TUNE				
Whilst Angels tune the Voice, and God inspires the Tongue.		17	Ode Athenian	56
Since first I learn'd to tune a String.	. . . . .	445	Modern Lady	12
But smooth your words to fit the tune,	. . . . . .	467	Birthday Song	212
Your words to some Italian Tune.	. . . . . .	469	Birthday Song	278
To such a subject tune my lyre	. . . .	490	Dialogue	39
And tune your Harps, and strow your Bays.	. . . . .	656	On Poetry	468
Cynthia, tune harmonious Numbers;	. . . .	661	Love Song	13
TUNEFUL				
Not one of all our tuneful Throng	. . . .	106	V's House	15
Nine other tuneful words like that	. . . .	467	Birthday Song	227
TUNEFULL				
Not one of all the tunefull Throng	. . . .	79	Vanbrug House	15
And Horace brought ye tunefull Choir	. . . . . .	658	On Poetry	D 410
TURBANT'S				
Red hat, and blue bonnet, and turbant's the same,	. . .	815	Yahoo's	23
TURBULENCE				
You think this Turbulence of Blood	. . . . . .	731	Stella, Poems	127
TURBULENT				
Though very turbulent and very loud;	. . . .	38	Ode Sancroft	136
TURD SEE COW-TURD				
From giving Passage to a <Turd>.	. . . .	66	Problem	26
Bob's Spittle mix'd with Harry's <Turd>	. . . . .	495	Panegyr Swift	63
Like a fresh <Turd> just dropt on Snow.	. . . .	786	Dick, Maggot	14
<TURDS>				
So <Turds> within a Glass inclose,	. . . . . .	786	Clad in Brown	11
TURENNE				
Would you describe Turenne or Trump	. . . .	83	Salamander	19
TURK				
To conquer Spain, and quell the Turk.	. . . . . .	466	Birthday Song	194
Yet, were he Heathen, Turk or Jew,	. . . .	820	Dr. Rundle	9
Eat like a Turk,	. . . .	1035	Servants Maxim	1
TURN				
But when they find it turn with the first blast of fate,		37	Ode Sancroft	76
So would earth's face turn pale, and life decay,	. . .	53	Temple Ill	63
"Know no base action, at no guilt turn pale;	. . . .	55	Temple Ill	142
No Christian would turn out a Beast	. . . . . .	90	Bauc & Phil 1	19
Would turn so quick you scarce could see't	. . . . .	93	Bauc & Phil 1	132
'Twas never known to turn its back	. . . . . .	94	Bauc & Phil 1	136
That Roast-meat which it cannot turn.	. . . . . .	94	Bauc & Phil 1	146
To turn the Hatter to a Jest;	. . . .	108	V's House	68
That Roast-meat which it cannot turn.	. . . . . .	113	Bauc & Phil 2	84
Not knowing where to turn him next;	. . . . . .	174	Horace 1, 7	114
Bills turn the Lenders into Debters,	. . . . . .	240	Run Bankers	26
Because Irish Linen will soon turn to Tinder,	. . . .	237	Excellent Song	20
This House will soon turn topsy turvey;	. . . . . .	283	Journal	128
To turn to small Money a Bill on the Bank.	. . . .	288	Bank Down	35
To turn her Naked out of Doors,	. . . . . .	295	Prog Marriage	163
"Turn him adrift, and you shall find	. . . . . .	304	Storm	33
To turn a Good Penny to Twenty Bad Ha'pence.	. . .	335	Serious Poem	48
Get the Great Seal, and turn out Brod'rick.	. . . .	348	Whitshed Motto	18
And never turn upon thy Master	. . . . . .	373	Letter D. S-y	55
That would turn a Man out of his own?	. . . . . .	396	Dog and Thief	20
I then will turn a Courtier too,	. . . .	410	Dial Rich Marb	79
Than I turn Rebel to the Fair.	. . . . . .	445	Modern Lady	21
Then thought to turn it to a Jest.	. . . . . .	447	Modern Lady	75
Say, by what fatal Turn of Mind,	. . . .	449	Modern Lady	151
Makes mighty Armys turn their Arses.	. . . . . .	461	Birthday Song	30
Squeez'd in a Coffin turn to dust;	. . . .	467	Birthday Song	236
And turn it all to ridicule:	. . . .	468	Birthday Song	266
He'll turn it off with; Name your Toast.	. . . . .	480	Libel on D- D-	18
For keep him in, or turn him out,	. . . .	484	Libel on D- D-	139
Their Fellows, turn their Dread and Hate.	. . . . .	493	Panegyr Swift	14
Can turn their Hands to ev'ry Jobb,	. . . .	503	Doctor Delaney	89

	PAGE	TITLE	LINE

TURN (CONTINUED)

The Turn of Verse, nor Stile of Prose;	. . . . .	515	Answer Fable	96
For, keep, or turn him out, my Lord's undone.	. . . . .	535	To Mr. Gay	126
Was, When will They turn out this odious Rogue?	. . . . .	536	To Mr. Gay	146
They turn the Matter to a Jest;	. . . .	545	Life of Swift	20
"To turn Religion to a Fable,	. . . .	568	Death of Swift	383
"And turn the Tax for publick Roads	. . . . . .	571	Death of Swift	453
In ev'ry Turn of Life content,	. . . .	602	Beasts Confess	41
He had not learn'd to turn his Coat,	. . . . . .	604	Beasts Confess	97
And, for her sake turn base detractor	. . . . . .	622	Scandal Poem 1	171
Into Knaves they turn their Fools:	. . . .	635	Epistle Lady	158
And your Head turn Topsy-turvy.	. . . .	637	Epistle Lady	220
They plot to turn in factious Zeal,	. . . . . .	653	On Poetry	379
What Herds of Kings would turn to Grazers.	. . . . .	659	On Poetry	D 410
High up in Air he'll turn your Brains;	. . . . .	666	Epig Carthy 2	D 6
Together both to Ashes turn.	. . . .	687	Cadenus Vaness	34
To turn to Ovid, Book the Second;	. . . . .	690	Cadenus Vaness	109
Things took a Turn he never meant.	. . . . .	709	Cadenus Vaness	731
The Nymph will have her Turn, to be	. . . . .	712	Cadenus Vaness	806
One Passion, with a diff'rent Turn,	. . . . .	731	Stella, Poems	117
But turn the deaf ear,	. . . .	756	Dingley Brent	11
Who turn with ev'ry Gale that blows from Court.	. . .	771	Horace 1, 14	56
But all turn Leasers to that Mongril Breed,	. . . .	794	St. Pat's Well	95
A Rod should turn them back to Dust.	. . . . . .	813	Bro Protestant	56
Now to turn a Factious Tool!	. . . .	838	Legion Club	198
Turn thy Nourishment to Poison!	. . . .	838	Legion Club	206
(For none could tell whose Turn was next)	. . . . .	849	Old Thorn	31
You toss and turn your Brain till Noon;	. . . .	892	Panegyr Dean	190
Turn ev'ry Way thy watchful Eye;	. . . . .	897	Panegyr Dean	337
May turn and wind me like a fool.	. . . . .	899	Dean's Reasons	14
And turn and wind me as they please.	. . . . .	920	Riddle 6	8
To turn the true impartial Side!	. . . . .	921	Riddle 7	8
And then they take a Turn and jump on't.	. . . . .	928	Riddle 12	D 16
Turn and wind him where we please.	. . . . . .	931	Riddle 18	D 14
And turn it as I have a Mind,	. . . . . .	934	Riddle 21	D 15
. . .when one would not turn out a Dog that one valued;	.	1014	Swift to Sheri	10
And, before we find either, our noddles turn round.	. .	1026	Sheri Circles	8

TURN-COAT

But, some will cry, Turn-Coat, and rip up old Stories,		143	New Song	21

TURN-SPIT

A Turn-spit in the <Royal> Kitchen.	. . . . .	300	Horrid Plot	66

TURN'D

Then softly turn'd aside to view,	. . . .	112	Bauc & Phil 2	39
Turn'd round so quick, you scarce cou'd see't;	. . . .	113	Bauc & Phil 2	72
In short, they both were turn'd to Yews.	. . . . .	116	Bauc & Phil 2	164
Turn'd ev'ry thing he touch't to Gold:	. . . . .	156	Fable of Midas	2
Salute her, and she turn'd her Ear:	. . . . . .	222	Prog of Love	4
But when she must be turn'd to graze,	. . . . .	230	Prog of Poetry	9
Was to a boiling Fountain turn'd.	. . . .	293	Prog Marriage	118
Turn'd to that dirt from whence he sprung.	. . . .	297	Satiric Elegy	32
By Nature turn'd to play the Rake-well,	. . . . .	446	Modern Lady	36
But if she against his play,	. . . .	456	Dean Smedley	29
Or, on Parchment, Ink turn'd yellow:	. . . . .	523	Betty Grizette	8
And turn'd it round on every Side.	. . . . .	526	Lady's Dres Rm	14
But oh! it turn'd poor Strephon's Bowels,	. . . .	527	Lady's Dres Rm	43
The Tutor turn'd a mortal Lover.	. . . . . .	707	Cadenus Vaness	651
That half your Locks are turn'd to Grey;	. . . .	757	Stel B-day '24	39
Party and Spleen have turn'd his Brain,	. . . .	796	Traulus 1	14
In Egypt turn'd the Dust to Lice:	. . . . . .	813	Bro Protestant	50
And, turn'd to Lice, infest the King:	. . . . .	813	Bro Protestant	54

TURND

Is hugely turnd to Architecture,	. . . .	86	Hist V's House	8

TURNING

You fly, invoke the Gods; then turning, stop	. . .	137	City Shower	21
And turning Dung it self to Gold?	. . . . . .	157	Fable of Midas	48
That you are turning fourty two.	. . . .	311	To Ford	12
Turning all to Ridicule:	. . . .	631	Epistle Lady	52
Then, turning to Hannah, and forcing a Frown,	. . . .	873	Grand Question	182

TURNIP-TOPS

Dead Cats and Turnip-Tops come tumbling down the Flood		139	City Shower	63

TURNKEY

The Turnkey now his Flock returning sees,	. . . . .	125	Descriptn Morn	15

TURNS

And into Adoration turns our Praise.	. . . .	11	Ode to William	D 8
Strait the Muse turns the Helm, and I launch out again;		32	Ode to Temple	195
The giddy turns of pop'lar rage,	. . . . .	38	Ode Sancroft	117
Turns up old objects to the soul her sun;	. . . . .	51	Temple Ill	10
A Friend in Turns and Windings try'd	. . . . .	94	Bauc & Phil 1	137
Turns to an Awl by Heav'nly Art;	. . . . . .	100	Elegy Patrige	82
Turns Auth'ress, and is Curll's for Life.	. . . . .	150	Corinna	28
And strove by Turns to break the Faggot:	. . . . .	189	Faggot	6
He turns to Politicks his dang'rous Wit,	. . . . .	194	Author Himself	26
That Irony which turns to Praise.	. . . . . .	216	To Mr. Delany	34
Turns all again to barren Strand.	. . . . . .	239	Run Bankers	4
When ev'ry one turns round about,	. . . .	341	Upon His Grace	8
All Turns and Motion tries;	. . . .	406	Swift to Pope	14
Pelts him by Turns with Verse and Prose,	. . . . .	458	Paddy's Charac	25
From threshing Corn, he turns to thresh his Brains;	. .	521	Stephen Duck	3
To stinking Smoak it turns the Flame	. . . . .	529	Lady's Dres Rm	105
Thy Turns and Doublings cannot save thee long.	. . .	539	Mr. Pulteney	44

TURNS   (CONTINUED)   PAGE   TITLE   LINE
 She turns to Envy, Stings and Hisses: . . . . . . 554 Death of Swift 36
 "With all the Turns of Whigs and Tories: . . . . 572 Death of Swift 476
 A Dog by Instinct turns aside, ... 640 On Poetry 17
 The trivial Turns, the borrow'd Wit, ... 645 On Poetry 151
 This God on Earth turns Devil in Hell. . . . . 646 On Poetry 206
 Stops thus, and turns with ev'ry Wind; . . . . 688 Cadenus Vaness 58
 And gave, by turns, their Censures Vent. . . . 699 Cadenus Vaness 409
 But turns aside like mad Ulysses: . . . . . 796 Traulus 1 30
 To give them by Turns an invisible Jog. . . . 804 Irish Bishops 16
 But turns at every Seam, an Inch in. . . . . 1021 Nim-Dan-Dean 1 D 16
TURVEY
 This House will soon turn topsy turvey; . . . 283 Journal 128
TURVY SEE TOPSI-TURVY,TOPSY-TURVY
 Humour, you tumbled Topsy Turvy. . . . . . . 477 Epist on Epist 72
TUSK
 Like the tusk of a boar. . . . . 854 Lady's Lament 86
TUSKS
 To neither use thy tusks contribute right, . . . 672 Epig Carthy 25 D 3
TUTOR
 That Her <Majesty> stood in great need of a Tutor, . 144 New Song 41
 A trav'lling Tutor to a Squire; . . . . . . 482 Libel on D- D- 64
 Whom Pallas, once Vanessa's Tutor, ... 701 Cadenus Vaness 464
 The Tutor turn'd a mortal Lover. . . . . . . 707 Cadenus Vaness 651
 How was her Tutor wont to praise . . . . . 708 Cadenus Vaness 688
 But when her Tutor will affect . . . . . 711 Cadenus Vaness 798
 The Tutor; and the Pupil, he: . . . . . . 712 Cadenus Vaness 807
 <Dean>, Butler, Usher, Jester, Tutor; . . . 888 Panegyr Dean 39
 To let me praise you as my Tutor. . ; . . . . 891 Panegyr Dean 130
TUTORS
 Thus Tutors often treat their Betters. . . . . 705 Cadenus Vaness 591
TWAIN
 These Comedies twain Friend Wood will contrive . . 337 Serious Poem 93
 That, where we find the Members twain, . . . 366 Answer Delaney 10
 To split my Worship too in twain. . . . . . 722 Stel B-Day '18 18
 We are little Brethren twain, ... 934 Riddle 22 D 1
TWAS ('TWAS)
  41   OMITTED WORDS
TWATTLING
 You keep such a twattling . . . . 1015 Swift to Sheri 37
TWAYNE
 Till Hapsburge makyth them but twayne. . . . 103 Merlin 20
TWEAK
 But gives it a Tweak; . . . . 939 Riddle Answerd 12
TWEEZERS
 A Pair of Tweezers next he found . . . . . 527 Lady's Dres Rm 55
TWELFTH
 "Here's Wolston's Tracts, the twelfth Edition; . . . 564 Death of Swift 281
TWELVE
 Moves round but twice in twice twelve Hours . . . 93 Bauc & Phil 1 134
 At least twelve Inches overcast, ... 126 Little House 6
 For in twice twelve revolving Moons, ... 150 Corinna 14
 At twelve, a Wit and a Coquette; . . . . . . 150 Corinna 25
 Twelve Coronets, without thy leave! . . . . . 181 Horace 2, 1 26
 His Lady has twelve times miscarry'd, ... 293 Prog Marriage 100
 But Dick lost by Doll, twelve hundred a Year, . . 430 Dicky Dolly 5
 This Lace is worth twelve Pounds a Yard: . . . 447 Modern Lady 87
 Twelve Commoners in Caps to Row you. . . . . 476 Epist on Epist 42
 To serve a tastless <Court> twelve Years in vain? . 531 To Mr. Gay 2
 Twelve Cups of Tea, (with Grief I speak) . . . 589 Strephon Chloe 163
 I increase it to Twelve, so three Hundred remain: . 867 Grand Question 10
 So about twelve at Night, the Punk . . . . . 1033 Ans to Crown 1
 My twelve Thirteens and Six-pence ha'penny. . . 1033 Ans to Crown 8
TWELVEMONTH
 But now, though scarce a twelvemonth marry'd, . . 293 Prog Marriage 99
 And e'er a twelvemonth and a day . . . . . 878 Robbin & Harry 11
TWELVEPENCE
 Twelvepence a Corner, if you dare. . . . . . 315 To Ford 114
TWENTIES
 My Grand-dame had Gallants by Twenties, . . . 350 Upright Judge 3 3
TWENTY
 . . .this Five and Twenty Years, come Spring, . . 70 Mrs Harris Pet 30
 When twenty Fools I never saw . . . . . . 200 Horace 2, 6 44
 And Sell for Twenty Pence a Yard of theirs; . . . 276 Epilogue 44
 To turn a Good Penny to Twenty Bad Ha'pence. . . 335 Serious Poem 48
 Each twenty visits on her Hands. . . . . . . 451 Modern Lady 197
 Tries twenty Charms to mend her Luck. . . . . 452 Modern Lady 237
 In seventeen hundred eight and twenty, ... 456 Dean Smedley 47
 Take twenty Gods of Rome or Greece, ... 460 Birthday Song 2
 Starve twenty Lords to make one Scoundrel rich: . 535 To Mr. Gay 104
 Is humbly pray'd to ruin Twenty more. . . . . 535 To Mr. Gay 106
 Throughout two Realms nineteen in twenty. . . . 549 Life of Swift 135
 "He might have liv'd these Twenty Years: . . . 559 Death of Swift 174
 But once in Twenty Thousand Years. . . . . . 584 Strephon Chloe 4
 Sweet Five and Twenty was his Age. . . . . . 597 Problem Solved 6
 With Twenty Thousand Pounds a Year Rents, . . . 598 Problem Solved 12
 Those, and twenty Follies more, ... 630 Epistle Lady 9
 So, after toiling twenty Days, ... 642 On Poetry 65
 I have assur'd them twenty times, ... 741 Stel B-day 22 23
 To a sour Pint one day in twenty. . . . . . 745 Stel Distress 14
 To half a Pint one Day in twenty. . . . . . 750 Stel Wood-Park 38
 He Twenty one, and She Fifteen: . . . . . . 757 Stel B-day '24 18

```
TWENTY           (CONTINUED)                           PAGE    TITLE           LINE
    By Food of twenty Years ago?         . . . . . .    765  Stel B-day '26      56
    On French Records for twenty long Campains;  . . . . .  771  Horace 1, 14       44
    There's hardly twenty to be found;   . . . . . . . .   773  Mullinix Tim        6
    I <Part> with twenty Ladies by;      . . . . . . . .   778  Mullinix Tim      161
    Of twenty <Ministers> of State.      . . . . . . . .   781  Mullinix Tim      258
    And have left us but Three out of Twenty behind 'em.  .  804  Irish Bishops      24
    Now twenty Years from Court exploded?  . . . . . .     820  Dr. Rundle         28
    And think you but twenty.  . . . . . . . . . .         855  Lady's Lament     134
    That for twenty Denials you would not give out.  . . .  869  Grand Question     56
    Rais'd up by you in twenty Weeks;    . . . . . . . .   893  Panegyr Dean      204
    I lay a Prisoner twenty Years;       . . . . . . . .   926  Riddle 9           21
'TWERE)    7                                            OMITTED WORD
TWICE
    Although the Jug had twice gone round  . . . . . .      92  Bauc & Phil 1      76
    Moves round but twice in twice twelve Hours   . . . .   93  Bauc & Phil 1     134
    Moves round but twice in twice twelve Hours   . . . .   93  Bauc & Phil 1     134
    And 'twice a Year he'll cut th' Aequator,   . . . . .   98  Elegy Patrige      17
    And saw it fairly twice go round;    . . . . . . . .   112  Bauc & Phil 2      31
    For in twice twelve revolving Moons,  . . . . . . .    150  Corinna            14
    Nor cross the Channel twice a Year,   . . . . . . .    199  Horace 2, 6        11
    Has twice two Legs, two hanging Ears; . . . . . . .    299  Horrid Plot        46
    To every Farmer twice a Week all round about the Yoke, 343  Upon His Grace     39
    The t' other will be stronger twice;  . . . . . . .    366  Answer Delaney     18
    'Twere rude to make him tell it twice;  . . . . . .    376  Apology Lady C     24
    Him twice a Week I here expect,      . . . . . . . .   411  Dial Rich Marb     95
    Twice sev'n long Years the Court attends,  . . . . .   481  Libel on D- D-     54
    who bore for twice ten Years the publick Hate.  . . .   536  To Mr. Gay        144
    His Household twice a Day to Pray'rs. . . . . . . .    605  Beasts Confess    132
    Nor saw the Play-House twice a Year;  . . . . . . .    696  Cadenus Vaness    313
    Can please at most but once or twice. . . . . . . .    788  Dick's Variety     12
    He need not tell a Story twice,      . . . . . . . .   878  Robbin & Harry     14
    Nor, twice a week will shave his beard.  . . . . . .   879  Robbin & Harry     44
    Twice ten years older than his wife   . . . . . . .    879  Robbin & Harry     51
    We never ask to hear you twice.  . . . . . . . . .     889  Panegyr Dean       74
    Though I should see him twice a day, . . . . . . . .    899  Dean's Reasons     29
    I twice a Day a hunting go;          . . . . . . . .   921  Riddle 6           31
    Twice were they bury'd, twice were born,  . . . . . .   923  Riddle 7           75
    Twice were they bury'd, twice were born,  . . . . . .   923  Riddle 7           75
    Twice from their Sepulchres were torn;  . . . . . . .   923  Riddle 7           76
TWIG
    That Scepter was a sapless Twig:     . . . . . . . .   134  Magician's Rod     66
    With both his Hands to bend a Twig;   . . . . . . .    191  Faggot             50
    Tom having earn'd a Twig of Lawrel,   . . . . . . .    458  Paddy's Charac     14
'TWILL
           21                                           OMITTED WORD
TWINE
    As Rivers, tho' they bend and twine,  . . . . . . .    709  Cadenus Vaness    720
    nor shall you twine the Crackling,Crackling Bays  . .   958  Cantata
    Wherever you bend, wherever you twine . . . . . . .   1017  Swift Ans Sher     22
TWINKLING
    To peep upon a twinkling Star.       . . . . . . . .    99  Elegy Patrige      56
TWIRL'D
    And found, as he the pages twirl'd,  . . . . . . .     782  Tim and Fables      7
TWIST
    Would hiss, and sting, and roll, and twist,  . . . .   132  Magician's Rod     11
    The Twist, the Squeeze, the Rump, the Fidge an'all,  .  783  Tim and Fables     17
TWISTED
    With that, he twisted his Girdle at me like a Rope,. . .  72  Mrs Harris Pet     62
    And doubly twisted it for strength;   . . . . . . .    760  Bec's B-Day         4
    A Perriwig of twisted Snakes;        . . . . . . . .   903  Death Daphne       22
TWISTING
    In twisting up an ill-spun Play:     . . . . . . . .    80  Vanbrug House      44
TWITCH
    See they gently twitch his Coat,     . . . . . . . .   836  Legion Club       169
TWITCHT
    He twitcht his sleeve, and stole a word,  . . . . . .   63  Discovery          19
TWITTER
    Till she lent you her help, you were in a fine twitter: .  977  Dean to Sherid     39
'TWIXT
    'Twixt Cobling and the Planet Science.  . . . . . .    98  Elegy Patrige      30
    'Twixt Raillery and gross Abuse,     . . . . . . . .   216  To Mr. Delany      48
    'Twixt earthly Femals and the Moon   . . . . . . . .   226  Prog of Beauty      9
    'Twixt Jades and Teagues             . . . . . . . .   441  Ballyspellin       29
    'Twixt you and me <God> Damn the Lyers.  . . . . . .   773  Mullinix Tim        8
    And stood 'twixt Him and every Fate:  . . . . . . .     8  Ode to King        66
    Stands in the gap 'twixt me and wretched men,  . . .    45  To Congreve        47
    There is 'twixt Cobling and Astrology:  . . . . . . .   98  Elegy Patrige      20
    The Bucket-play 'twixt Whigs and Tories,  . . . . . .  181  Horace 2, 1        17
    Yet I may say 'twixt me and you,     . . . . . . . .   408  Dial Rich Marb     21
    And in their Sense, 'twixt me and you,  . . . . . . .  461  Birthday Song      19
    Must strole in Air 'twixt Earth and Sky;  . . . . . .  689  Cadenus Vaness     86
    A middle-state 'twixt peace and war;  . . . . . . .    876  To Dean Swift      24
    Daphne, 'twixt the Dean and you,     . . . . . . . .   907  Daphne             50
    That stands 'twixt Heav'n, and Earth, and Hell,  . . .  928  Riddle 12       D  2
    The segment so large 'twixt your reason and rhyme is, . 1026  Sheri Circles       6
TWO
    Tho' we be of two different Factions still,  . . . .    18  Ode Athenian       72
    Two foolish guides in ev'ry sublunary dance:  . . . .   34  Ode Sancroft        9
    With those two pow'rful swords, Submission and Humility,  36  Ode Sancroft       48
    Is but one thing under two different names;  . . . .    41  Ode Sancroft      206
    While two fond lovers prate, the Muse and I.  . . . .   49  To Congreve       200
```

TWO   (CONTINUED)

	PAGE	TITLE		LINE
Disguis'd in two old thredbare Coats	63	Discovery		34
With that he draws two Handfulls out,	63	Discovery		37
By two such whisp'ring Kings of Branford.	64	Discovery		48
Would raise a House about two Storyes;	79	Vanbrug House		10
Soon reard a House two Storyes high;	86	Hist V's House		6
Taller than Misse's by two yards,	87	Hist V's House		25
That no two Chairmen could be found	87	Hist V's House		29
Two Brother-Hermits, Saints by Trade	90	Bauc & Phil 1		7
For shame! two sturdy Rascalls beg;	91	Bauc & Phil 1		44
Might raise a House about two Stories;	106	V's House		10
Two Acts it cost him under Ground.	108	V's House		88
Two other Acts we may presume	108	V's House		89
Two Brother Hermits, Saints by Trade,	111	Bauc & Phil 2		7
Two Gods their Skill in Musick try'd,	156	Fable of Midas		25
Two Dozen Canons round your Stall,	173	Horace 1, 7		89
About some great Affair, at Two--	200	Horace 2, 6		54
Receiv'd a brace or two of Blows.	220	A Quiet Life		24
Two brightest, brittlest earthly Things	227	Prog of Beauty		63
Two Balls of Glass may serve for Eyes,	229	Prog of Beauty		113
At Two or after we return all,	279	Journal		26
A word or two of Lord Chief Baron;	282	Journal		98
He found he could purchase Two Tankards of Ale	288	Bank Down		37
Aetatis suae fifty two	289	Prog Marriage		1
The Masquerade began at two,	292	Prog Marriage		93
Has twice two Legs, two hanging Ears;	299	Horrid Plot		46
Has twice two Legs, two hanging Ears;	299	Horrid Plot		46
That you are turning fourty two.	311	To Ford		12
Hath joyn'd with himself two Hags in Commission:	336	Serious Poem		68
This Dragon had gotten two Sows in it's Belly;	337	Serious Poem		88
I often have seen two Plays very Good,	337	Serious Poem		91
Strong Tubs for his Raps, Two thousand and more;	337	Serious Poem		96
To have two thousand Pounds a Year, O 'tis a burning Shame!	342	Upon His Grace		18
Two thousand Pounds a Year, Good Lord!	342	Upon His Grace		19
Come, you must take a Cup of Sack or two before you go.	342	Upon His Grace		24
With Brass two fiery Steeds he shod,	352	Wood Ironmongr		11
Why are we then so fond of two?	366	Answer Delaney		3
With t' other Hand the Work of two:	366	Answer Delaney		24
There creeps two Auditory Nerves,	367	Answer Delaney		34
Without your Legs, two Legs of Wood	367	Answer Delaney		49
Two Bards that now in fashion reign,	393	Modern Poets		5
Above two hundred miles from home?	403	Window Inns 10	D	4
Desire, the swifter of the two,	412	Desire Possess		21
Which lasted near two thousand years,	490	Dialogue		34
To squire of two Years old!	531	To Mr. Gay		10
Two Rows of Teeth arm each devouring Jaw;	532	To Mr. Gay		35
The Court invited more than One, or Two;	536	To Mr. Gay		151
True Friendship in two breasts requires	546	Life of Swift		43
Let me suppose, two special Friends,	546	Life of Swift		52
"I hear about two thousand Pound---	547	Life of Swift		73
Throughout two Realms nineteen in twenty.	549	Life of Swift		135
"Two Kingdoms, just as Faction led,	566	Death of Swift		351
At two Afternoon for our Psyche inquire,	580	Psyche		1
And then between two Blankets creeps.	582	Young Nymph		38
Two College Sophs of Cambridge Growth,	593	Cassinus Peter		1
Above a Term or two at most.	604	Beasts Confess		92
Two bordering Wits contend for Glory;	650	On Poetry		293
So two poor Knaves, who find their Credit fail,	668	Epig Carthy 8	D	3
Parnassus' Hill has but two Tops,	671	Epig Carthy 22	D	4
Using four legs when two were weary.	675	Curate's Compl		4
I dipp'd two babes in holy-water,	675	Curate's Compl		7
A Duel fought last Night at Two,	696	Cadenus Vaness		320
Two Maxims she could still produce,	705	Cadenus Vaness		606
Hangs a new Angel two doors from us	734	Stel B-day '20		10
Two Bottles call'd for, (half her Store,	747	Stel Distress		49
Two Bottles call'd for, (half her Store;	751	Stel Wood-Park		65
And then they value not two Straws,	776	Mullinix Tim		97
Jason arriv'd two thousand Years before.	790	St. Pat's Well		8
For of the two, without Dispute,	797	Traulus 1		43
With a Rood or two of Land,	830	Legion Club		37
I can shew two hundred more.	839	Legion Club		238
With two bony thumbs	852	Lady's Lament		19
My arms, like two props,	852	Lady's Lament		27
Are two iron crows,	853	Lady's Lament		80
He will but add two Hundred Pound,	875	Drapier's Hill		6
With two pence left, walks home in rain.	878	Robbin & Harry		8
Just big enough to shelter two in;	878	Robbin & Harry		22
At fifty two, when he grew loving,	879	Robbin & Harry		46
Of their two Fames the World enough rings;	884	Rev Market-Hill		31
Divide the Realm between us two.	886	Rev Market-Hill		92
Two Temples of magnifick Size,	893	Panegyr Dean		201
Nature holds her forth two mirrors,	907	Daphne		43
Two Vices of a diff'rent Kind:	918	Riddle 4		24
How many to answer? One, two, three, four.	967	Letter Sherid		10
Above a Song or two at most:	993	On Picture		24
Then which of us two is the quaint-er Coxcomb?	1003	Dan J's Reply		12

TWO-FAC'D

	PAGE	TITLE		LINE
Two-fac'd Janus, God of Time,	862	To Janus		1

TWO-INCH

	PAGE	TITLE		LINE
Some who can perjure thro' a two-Inch Board;	806	Judas		13

```
TWO-YEAR'S                                           PAGE   TITLE           LINE
      His Two-Year's Coat so smooth and bare,   . . . . .  231 Prog of Poetry    35
'TWOULD    ('TWOU'D)
      12                                                   OMITTED WORDS
TWYS
      Tamys rivere twys y-frozen,   . . . . . . . . . .    102 Merlin            3
TY'D
      Look where the Pully's ty'd above!   . . . . . .      29 Ode to Temple   102
      Me she has to the Muse's Gallies ty'd,   . . . . .    32 Ode to Temple   191
      I keep in a Pocket ty'd about my Middle, next my Smock.  69 Mrs Harris Pet   7
      . . .ty'd in a Rag, the Money was found.   . . . .    70 Mrs Harris Pet   23
      So strong you'll be, in Friendship ty'd;   . . . .   189 Faggot           11
      Ty'd with the Chain himself had made;   . . . . .    346 Prometheus       54
      With which Prometheus shall be ty'd,   . . . . .     347 Prometheus       73
      But like a Girl's Cockade, was ty'd   . . . . . .    458 Paddy's Charac   17
      Ty'd round the <Dean's> Neck, for committing a <Rape>.  519 Dean Hang Rape  66
      Thy Words together ty'd in small Hanks,   . . . . . 1021 Nim-Dan-Dean 1  D 29
TY'T
      His Cap had a new Cherry Ribbon to ty't.   . . . .   399 Tom Clinch        6
TYDE
      And move it against Tyde and Wind.   . . . . . . .   934 Riddle 21       D 16
TYE
      And join in friendship, with a strict tye,   . . .  436 Answer Paulus   145
      He comes to tye our Chains on faster,   . . . . .    484 Libel on D- D-  125
      And, e'er he flyes is forc'd to tye em.   . . . . .  621 Scandal Poem 1  120
      Tye them Keeper in a Tether,   . . . . . . . . .     835 Legion Club     153
TYGER
      I mean when Tyger has been serv'd,   . . . . . . .   761 Bec's B-Day      37
      With Tyger slabb'ring in her lap;   . . . . . . .    761 Bec's B-Day      40
TYGER'S
      To any speech but Tyger's barking.   . . . . . . .   762 Bec's B-Day      44
TYPE
      A Type of Modern Witt and Style,   . . . . . . .      81 Vanbrug House    83
      A Type of Modern Wit and Style,   . . . . . . . .    109 V's House       125
      That Rod was just a Type of Sid's,   . . . . . . .   133 Magician's Rod   39
      That ev'ry <S--th>, and Type in Town   . . . . .     371 Letter D. S-y     4
      You print it in Italick Type.   . . . . . . . . .    643 On Poetry        96
TYPES
      Omens, the Types of thy impending Chains.   . . . .  792 St. Pat's Well   44
TYRANNY
      Nor dreads the Tyranny of Years,   . . . . . . . .     6 Ode to King      3
TYRANT
      The Tyrant Death lay crouching down,   . . . . . .     7 Ode to King     39
      That Restless Tyrant, who of late   . . . . . . .     10 Ode to King    119
      Her Tyrant too an unexpected Wound shall feel   . .   10 Ode to King    140
      Of that proud Tyrant Sex of Hers.   . . . . . . .     23 Ode Athenian   237
      Necessity, thou tyrant conscience of the great,   .   40 Ode Sancroft   176
      At least confine the tyrant to his cell.   . . . .    53 Temple Ill      56
      And you the Tyrant o'er them all:   . . . . . . .    173 Horace 1, 7     90
      The drowsy Tyrant by his Minions led,   . . . . .    364 On Dreams       11
      A Tyrant for his Mercy praise,   . . . . . . . .     464 Birthday Song  119
      He grows a tyrant, dunce, or beast.   . . . . . .    658 On Poetry     D 204
      Th' amphibious Tyrant, with his rav'nous Band,   .   793 St. Pat's Well   63
      Of that insulting Tyrant Dean.   . . . . . . . .     861 Lady Acheson     44
      Till me that Tyrant Man espy'd,   . . . . . . . .    915 Riddle 1          7
      The Tyrant strip't me to the Skin:   . . . . . .     915 Riddle 1         10
      All-ruling Tyrant of the Earth,   . . . . . . . .    916 Riddle 2          1
TYRANT-GUARD
      That Tyrant-Guard on Peace,   . . . . . . . . .        8 Ode to King     73
TYRANT-PASSIONS
      (Free from our tyrant-passions, anger, scorn, or fear)  .  38 Ode Sancroft  116
TYRANT'S
      These are the tyrant's trophies of a year;   . . . .  55 Temple Ill     126
      The Meat shall represent the Tyrant's Head,   . . .  162 Toland's Invit   11
      Necessity, the Tyrant's Law,   . . . . . . . . .     922 Riddle 7         23
TYRANTS
      The Bed in which these Tyrants lie:   . . . . . .    283 Journal         122
      Thou still with Tyrants in Succession curst,   . . . 793 St. Pat's Well   83
      O'er his Inferiors as our Tyrants;   . . . . . . .   824 Printer Newgat    6
TYRE
      To court her Majesty of Tyre   . . . . . . . . .     619 Scandal Poem 1   66
      To court her Majesty of Tyre,   . . . . . . . . .    625 Scandal Poem 2   62
TYTH
      With the Tyth of the Tyth of the Tyth to maintain you;  805 Irish Bishops  58
      With the Tyth of the Tyth of the Tyth to maintain you;  805 Irish Bishops  58
      With the Tyth of the Tyth of the Tyth to maintain you;  805 Irish Bishops  58
TYTHES
      His Talk was now of Tythes and Dues,   . . . . .     115 Bauc & Phil 2   125
      Force him to take his Tythes in kind;   . . . . .    174 Horace 1, 7     110
      On their tythes at half-nothing, their priesthood at less:  816 Yahoo's  33
TYTHS
      Talkt of his Off'rings, Tyths, and Dues,   . . . . .  95 Bauc & Phil 1   173
      First take you our Tyths, and give us your Lands.   . .  805 Irish Bishops  62
UGLY
      Mrs. Dukes, said I, here's an ugly Accident has        71 Mrs Harris Pet   37
        happen'd out;
ULCERS
      Can Clouds give buboes, ulcers, blotches?   . . . .  618 Scandal Poem 1   25
      Can Clouds give Bubo's, Ulcers, Blotches,   . . . .  624 Scandal Poem 2   19
      Their Sores and putrid Ulcers show,   . . . . . .    667 Epig Carthy 6   D  3
ULYSSES
      But turns aside like mad Ulysses:   . . . . . . .    796 Traulus 1        30
```

'UM   PAGE   TITLE   LINE
      Much good may do 'em that have caught 'um. . . . . .   158 Fable of Midas   80
      But what Adventures more befell 'um . . . .   224 Prog of Love   85
      The Muse has now not time to tell 'um. . . . . . .   224 Prog of Love   86
      Subscribers plainly see 'um there, ...   257 Bubble   167
      Fine Words; I wonder where you stole 'um.   348 Whitshed Motto   2
      You had good Reason when you stole 'um.   349 Whitshed Motto   26
      Never know I any Good in 'um, ...   632 Epistle Lady   83
      Their Cow-boys bearing Cloaks before 'um,   760 Receipt Youth   46
      With what Devotion you adore 'um! . . . . . .   888 Panegyr Dean   52
UMBO
      Or, like the Umbo of the Romans, ...   1021 Nim-Dan-Dean 1 D 31
UMBRELLA'S
      While Streams run down her oil'd Umbrella's Sides. . 138 City Shower   38
UN-DONE
      Nor shall she think that she is un-done . . . . .   362 Grace's Answer   39
UN-MAN
      Un-man the poor Knave for sake of a Trope. . . .   335 Serious Poem   52
UN-MEANING
      Of loud un-meaning Sounds, a rapid Flood . . . .   532 To Mr. Gay   39
UNABLE
      Unable to endure the Sight, ...   240 Run Bankers   43
      But now, unable grown to write, ...   754 Stella '23   5
UNANSWER'D
      Unanswer'd at your Patron's Gate; . . . . . .   475 Epist on Epist   6
UNATTAINTED
      But shall with unattainted Honour shine; . . . .   210 Earl of Oxford   8
UNAW'D
      Unaw'd by Jove's all-shaking Nod. . . . . . .   466 Birthday Song   186
      His Station despising, unaw'd by the Place, ... 809 Epigr Prelate   3
UNAWARE
      And heave her Bosom unaware . . . .   222 Prog of Love   17
UNBARS
      See, the Muse unbars the Gate; . . . .   832 Legion Club   81
UNBEATEN
      Some new unbeaten Passage to the Sky; . . . . .   210 Earl of Oxford   12
UNBELIEVING
      What could the Sages gain but unbelieving scorn; . . . 39 Ode Sancroft   170
UNBENDS
      And for a while unbends their contradicting Souls: . .   9 Ode to King   91
UNBINDS
      That noble genius, who unbinds . . . .   490 Dialogue   31
UNBISHOPRICK'D
      So long unbishoprick'd lie by, ...   497 Panegyr Swift   147
UNBOUND
      The Consul's Fasces were unbound; . . . .   190 Faggot   28
UNBURTHEN'D
      The Mind unburthen'd sports in various Whims, . . .   363 On Dreams   8
UNBUTTON
      Unbutton and let down your Breeches, ...   783 Tim and Fables   36
UNCLE
      The Dean, she heard her Uncle say . . . .   291 Prog Marriage   47
UNCLE'S
      She could not doubt her Uncle's Favour. . . . . .   303 Storm   24
UNCLEAN
      Nought it contains is common or unclean, ...   50 To Congreve   233
      Present a Sacrifice unclean; . . . .   895 Panegyr Dean   284
UNCLUB'D
      And crop-sick with unclub'd for wine, ...   434 Answer Paulus   73
UNCOMELY
      Tho' in strange uncouth postures, and uncomely dress; . 35 Ode Sancroft   26
UNCOMMUNICATIVE
      Whose uncommunicative heart, ...   900 Dean's Reasons   43
UNCOMPLYING
      Against an uncomplying Jury: . . . .   348 Whitshed Motto   14
UNCONSCIOUS
      Thy grate unconscious of a blaze, ...   676 Parson's Case   12
UNCORRUPT
      For ever, uncorrupt and pure; . . . .   691 Cadenus Vaness   145
UNCOURTLY
      For Man to dress and polish his Uncourtly Mind, . .   22 Ode Athenian   218
      Their faith was so uncourtly when they said . . . . .   39 Ode Sancroft   171
UNCOUTH
      Has forc't to grope her uncouth way . . . . . .   18 Ode Athenian   66
      Tho' in strange uncouth postures, and uncomely dress; . 35 Ode Sancroft   26
UNDECENT
      With how undecent clouds are overcast . . . . . .   52 Temple Ill   33
UNDER
      The Gyants under Aetna ceas'd to groan, ...   9 Ode to King   96
      E'er flourish't under a Successor or a Son; . . . .   25 Ode Athenian   285
      Is but one thing under two different names; . . . .   41 Ode Sancroft   206
      Two Acts it cost him under Ground. . . . . . .   108 V's House   88
      Under those Sacred Leaves, Secure . . . .   119 Apollo Outwit   9
      Under pretence of Taking Air, ...   120 Apollo Outwit   23
      For Charms above and under Ground; . . . . . .   133 Magician's Rod   36
      Bury those Carrots under a Hill. . . . .   148 Windsor Proph   26
      Under one Roof, or in one Ship with me. . . . . .   210 Earl of Oxford   18
      Redeem him from his Prison under Ground. . . . . .   233 Elegy on Demar   4
      And under Hand and Seal the Irish Nation . . . . .   234 Elegy on Demar   17
      I think I have now got him under my Lash; . . . .   265 Apollo   66
      And under the Pain of our highest Displeasure, . . . 266 Apollo   101

864

UNDER	(CONTINUED)	PAGE	TITLE	LINE
Under the Rose since here are none but friends;		275	Epilogue	13
Ran under Ground from Greece to Brittain,		293	Prog Marriage	112
(Under Correction) with the thatcht,		313	To Ford	66
For none but a Dunce would come under his Rod.		335	Serious Poem	34
And under him no Tenant yet was ever known to thrive.		342	Upon His Grace	20
The Man above, or under Ground.		393	Modern Poets	16
Under this Stone, lies Dicky and Dolly		430	Dicky Dolly	1
Who, under Tales conveying Truth,		482	Libel on D- D-	55
And calumny, by working under ground,		506	To a Friend	5
Nor, at an under Rate his Timber sell;		534	To Mr. Gay	95
Of Gipsies littering under Hedges,		641	On Poetry	38
In Garrets high, or under Ground:		651	On Poetry	316
She gather'd, under ev'ry Head,		713	Cadenus Vaness	850
With Footmen tippling under Ground,		729	Stella, Poems	44
That Patience under tort'ring Pain,		765	Stel B-day '26	49
Betwixt a State, and Vessel under Sail;		770	Horace 1, 14	6
The Leaders whom you listed under,		775	Mullinix Tim	47
I take thee under my Protection.		779	Mullinix Tim	208
By leaving him under the pen of the Dean.		816	Yahoo's	39
(For, under the rose,		858	Lady's Lament	213
I'd rather the Bawn were sunk under Ground.		868	Grand Question	46
Under whose wise and careful Guardship,		890	Panegyr Dean	107
His large Dominions under Ground.		903	Death Daphne	18
When I'm vext, can't keep me under;		933	Riddle 20	D 24
Would, as he lay under, cry out, Sirrah, yield:		967	Letter Sherid	16
But before you can put yourself under her banners,		979	Dean to Tho: S	27
You're so retrograde, sure you were born under Cancer:		1019	To Sheridan	3
UNDER-HAND				
A score of guineas, given under-hand,		308	Billet Players	23
UNDER-STANDS				
Now, Mrs. Dukes, you know, and every Body under-stands,		71	Mrs Harris Pet	42
UNDER-WITS				
The Under-wits adorn their Speech.		80	Vanbrug House	48
UNDERGO				
What burthens lawyers undergo.		434	Answer Paulus	70
Must undergo the common Fate;		562	Death of Swift	251
That I these pains can undergo.		754	Stella '23	8
UNDERLINGS				
Ye paultry underlings of state,		487	Irish-Club	1
With underlings thy flock to teach,		677	Parson's Case	31
UNDERMINE				
Say, how did Rundle undermine 'em;		820	Dr. Rundle	37
Those rascally paviours who did us undermine,		841	Ballad	D 18
UNDERMINES				
With harpy Claws it undermines the Ground,		792	St. Pat's Well	61
UNDERNEATH				
Commence Acquaintance underneath a Shed.		138	City Shower	40
Stuck underneath his Cushion-side:		174	Horace 1, 7	100
Writ underneath the Country Signs;		201	Horace 2, 6	72
Wou'd read what underneath was written,		783	Tim and Fables	26
UNDERSTAND				
To make them understand, and feel me when I write;		37	Ode Sancroft	89
Which now I clearly understand,		254	Bubble	99
For a good word or so, we understand.		308	Billet Players	24
And makes her Part'ner understand		452	Modern Lady	260
Is to understand, and think:		633	Epistle Lady	118
They blush because they understand.		692	Cadenus Vaness	171
We give the World to understand,		875	Drapier's Hill	1
Envy must own, you understand your		888	Panegyr Dean	45
To understand Malebranche or Cambray;		900	Dean's Reasons	52
Yet not a Word I understand.		915	Riddle 1	28
UNDERSTANDS				
He better understands his Trade:		607	Beasts Confess	212
UNDERSTOND				
And dear Englond, if ought I understond,		148	Windsor Proph	15
UNDERSTONDE				
Then comyth foorthe, Ich understonde,		102	Merlin	5
UNDERSTOOD				
By none but its Possessors to be understood:		6	Ode to King	4
But Censure's to be understood		18	Ode Athenian	91
And tho' I should but ill be understood		38	Ode Sancroft	121
For, what is understood by Fame		83	Salamander	13
My Tale is a wise one if well understood,		334	Serious Poem	23
Say, who is to be understood,		346	Prometheus	59
By long Observation I have understood,		350	Wood Insect	1
Tho' it is hardly understood,		556	Death of Swift	77
His Crime he quickly understood;		604	Beasts Confess	99
'Tis true, the People understood,		606	Beasts Confess	161
(Tho' it must be understood,		635	Epistle Lady	169
Tho' not a Word be understood.		649	On Poetry	274
By Greeks and Romans understood,		697	Cadenus Vaness	348
Too late with Grief she understood,		700	Cadenus Vaness	434
But understood not what was Love.		703	Cadenus Vaness	547
For, what was ever understood		759	Receipt Youth	35
And by all Sages understood		764	Stel B-day '26	27
This Graver understood his Art.		783	Tim and Fables	20
My Offers of Peace you ill understood.		968	Letter Sherid	23
UNDERTAKE				
Will undertake to do it for thee:		190	Faggot	42
This parodox I'll undertake		433	Answer Paulus	45

UNDERTAKE   (CONTINUED)   PAGE   TITLE   LINE
  Nor, dares an abler Workman undertake . . . . . .   535 To Mr. Gay   133
  I'll undertake my little Nancy . . . . . , . . .   700 Cadenus Vaness   418
UNDERTAKEN
  Believe me, what thou'st undertaken . . . .   181 Horace 2, 1   29
UNDERTAKERS
  'Twould ruin Undertakers quite. . . . .   106 V's House   20
UNDERTOOK
  At every Motion undertook, ...   917 Riddle 3   7
UNDISTINGUISH'D
  And Wrinkles undistinguish'd pass, ...   758 Stel B-day '24   45
  And lye an undistinguish'd Mass. . . . .   922 Riddle 7   44
UNDO
  She'd all undo, that she had done. . . . .   694 Cadenus Vaness   255
UNDOING
  To make them work their own undoing. . . . . .   484 Libel on D- D-   128
UNDONE   SEE UN-DONE
  Alas, the Nymph would be undone. . . . .   226 Prog of Beauty   12
  Undone at Play, the Femal Troops . . . . . .   254 Bubble   89
  How near was she to be undone, ...   269 Apollo's Edict   D 3
  If Bankrupts, when they are undone, ...   392 Young's Satire   41
  Without whose aid you're all undone? . . . . .   432 Answer Paulus   4
  And, when he gravely has undone a Score, . . .   535 To Mr. Gay   105
  For, keep, or turn him out, my Lord's undone. . . .   535 To Mr. Gay   126
  Inevitably be undone. . . . .   606 Beasts Confess   168
  But if you blab, you are undone; . . . .   644 On Poetry   135
  And ev'ry Shepherd was undone . . . .   705 Cadenus Vaness   582
  Some are made, and some undone. . . . .   934 Riddle 22   D 4
UNDOUBTED
  To his undoubted Master, Heaven's Almighty Son. . .   38 Ode Sancroft   134
UNDOUBTEDLY
  And thus undoubtedly 'twill fare, ...   25 Ode Athenian   292
UNEASY
  "I'm so uneasy in my Stays; . . . .   452 Modern Lady   242
UNENDOW'D
  With Grace and Learning unendow'd, ...   503 Doctor Delaney   88
UNEQUAL
  That feeds the huge unequal stream. . . . . . .   20 Ode Athenian   148
  Not yet, the Dust had shun'd th' unequal Strife, . .   137 City Shower   23
UNERRING
  Unerring Heav'n, with bounteous Hand, ...   272 Apollo's Edict   D 64
  By her, as an unerring Guide. . . . .   694 Cadenus Vaness   239
UNEXPECTED
  Her Tyrant too an unexpected Wound shall feel . . .   10 Ode to King   140
UNEXPERIENC'T
  Did with new, unexperienc't Glories wait, ...   21 Ode Athenian   156
UNFELT
  With all that Power unfelt, courts Mankind to be Great, .   21 Ode Athenian   155
UNFIT
  Is a Person very unfit for Intrigues. . . . . . .   940 Letter   17
UNFOLD
  Some strange Arcana to unfold, ...   180 Horace 2, 1   2
  Nor shall the conscious Muse unfold. . . . . . .   712 Cadenus Vaness   827
UNFORESEEN
  It was an unforeseen Event, ...   709 Cadenus Vaness   730
UNFORTUNATE
  Was an unfortunate gallant. . . . .   177 To Lord Harley   12
  Was so unfortunate in Love. . . . .   598 Problem Solved   22
UNFRIENDLY
  It was a most unfriendly Part . . . .   444 Modern Lady   1
UNGEN'ROUS
  The most ungen'rous vices of the town; . . . . .   44 To Congreve   10
UNGLUES
  She stretches, gapes, unglues her Eyes, ...   446 Modern Lady   42
UNGODLY
  Treated at this ungodly Rate . . . .   91 Bauc & Phil 1   48
  Treated at this ungodly Rate, ...   111 Bauc & Phil 2   16
UNGRATEFUL
  Seems to have borrow'd some ungrateful tast . . . .   22 Ode Athenian   212
  As when to scare th' ungrateful or the proud . . . .   52 Temple Ill   23
  "Nor fears from him ungrateful Force: . . . . .   476 Epist on Epist   56
  How that ungrateful charming Maid, ...   595 Cassinus Peter   57
  Ungrateful; since to her I owe . . . .   754 Stella '23   7
  Britain, by thee we fell, ungrateful Isle! . . . .   791 St. Pat's Well   25
  Durst thou, ungrateful, from the <Senate> chace . . .   826 Noisy Tom   15
  Thou, ungrateful to thy Teachers, ...   838 Legion Club   203
  Be not ungrateful to the <Dean>; . . . .   893 Panegyr Dean   218
UNGRATEFULLY
  How could you forget so ungratefully a lass? . . .   977 Dean to Sherid   41
UNGUARDED
  "How could unguarded Virtue stand? . . . . . .   568 Death of Swift   390
UNHABITABLE
  And o'er unhabitable Downs . . . .   646 On Poetry   179
UNHALLOWED
  Such to unhallowed sight the Muse divine . . . . .   52 Temple Ill   29
UNHAND
  Begone; unhand me, hellish Fry; . . . .   596 Cassinus Peter   87
UNHAPPY
  To fann th' unhappy Fire: . . . .   23 Ode Athenian   241
  As at the closing an unhappy Scene . . . . . .   24 Ode Athenian   271
  With what unhappy Men shall dare, ...   25 Ode Athenian   293

	PAGE	TITLE	LINE
UNHAPPY (CONTINUED)			
Still to unhappy restless thoughts inclin'd;	55	Temple Ill	132
"And since unhappy distance thus denies	55	Temple Ill	143
What must the unhappy Doctor do?	376	Apology Lady C	42
Unhappy Ship, thou art return'd in Vain:	770	Horace 1, 14	9
Unhappy Wretch! for now, I ween,	1005	Sheridan's Sub	26
UNHARMONIOUS			
By loud and unharmonious Croaking:	479	Epist on Epist	124
To din thine Ears with unharmonious Clack,	792	St. Pat's Well	47
UNHEARD			
Tales here forgot, or yet unheard;	386	Manly Virtue	74
Let Will. unheard by thee, his Thunder waste.	538	Mr. Pulteney	12
Unheard she moves about my Bed.	727	To Stella	112
UNHEARD-OF			
Scar'd at th' unheard-of Prodigy,	30	Ode to Temple	110
UNHELPT			
Unhelpt by Practice, Books, or Art.	215	To Mr. Delany	22
UNHORS'D			
So the Commons unhors'd them, and this was their Doom,	804	Irish Bishops	21
UNHURT			
They might, unhurt by Envy's Claws,	479	Epist on Epist	125
UNIFORMITY			
Dull Uniformity in Fools	787	Dick's Variety	1
UNION			
Whoever yet a Union saw	96	On the Union	11
When the strong Cords of Union once are Broke.	770	Horace 1, 14	22
It forms an union in the mind:	901	Dean's Reasons	70
UNITE			
Scotch, Irish, English, French unite	345	Prometheus	15
Must ev'ry Morn her Limbs unite.	583	Young Nymph	66
These I will gather and unite,	691	Cadenus Vaness	151
Against Vanessa's Pow'r unite;	700	Cadenus Vaness	439
The <Bishops> divide, but the Clergy unite.	805	Irish Bishops	44
By Faction banish't here unite,	883	Rev Market-Hill	7
Unite; but on Conditions cruel;	883	Rev Market-Hill	9
Our Forces let us both unite,	884	Rev Market-Hill	45
UNITED			
We find in you at last united grown.	28	Ode to Temple	61
Divided Hearts, united States.	96	On the Union	6
Though with united Strength they all pull,	191	Faggot	51
United close in ev'ry Part.	344	Prometheus	6
Is divided above, but united below.	805	Irish Bishops	42
UNITES			
To Blood and Quarrels, Brass unites:	345	Prometheus	22
The charming Couple now unites;	585	Strephon Chloe	45
Unites, and both become the same,	687	Cadenus Vaness	32
UNITIES			
Of Unities, in Time and Place.	648	On Poetry	244
UNITING			
Uniting all, to shew their Amity,	811	Bro Protestant	9
UNIVERSAL			
Appear'd, above the Universal Main,	16	Ode Athenian	6
As if the Universal Nile	17	Ode Athenian	42
From Ignorance's Universal North,	25	Ode Athenian	299
Thou universal cause of all my woes;	53	Temple Ill	82
My Lord's an universal Lover.	67	Problem	60
If that same Universal Passion	392	Young's Satire	35
A sudden universal Crew	528	Lady's Dres Rm	85
Young's universal Passion, Pride,	640	On Poetry	3
Her Sex, with universal Voice,	702	Cadenus Vaness	508
UNIVERSALL			
For in that Universall Call	241	Run Bankers	57
UNIVERSE			
I mean, what no other mortal in the universe can boast of,	1024	Nim-Dan-Dean 2	D 16
UNJUST			
For that were not unjust a Bit,	497	Panegyr Swift	119
Am I spightful, proud, unjust?	631	Epistle Lady	65
'Tis a wrong, unjust Aspersion:	632	Epistle Lady	82
UNJUSTLY			
Why then does Nature so unjustly share	32	Ode to Temple	180
Unjustly all our Nymphs complain,	591	Strephon Chloe	255
Unjustly Poets we asperse;	729	Stella, Poems	57
UNKIND			
Ah, may no unkind earthquake of the State,	40	Ode Sancroft	190
'He's so unkind, he never sends	448	Modern Lady	106
That mov'd the Nymphs to be unkind.	598	Problem Solved	24
To fancy they can be unkind.	766	Stel B-day '26	82
UNKINDLY			
Thus did the Muse severe unkindly blame	44	To Congreve	23
UNKNOWN			
An unknown Musick all around,	17	Ode Athenian	52
Pardon Ye great Unknown, and far-exalted Men,	17	Ode Athenian	60
And this Ye great Unknown, is only known in You.	21	Ode Athenian	188
Cruel Unknown! what is it You intend!	23	Ode Athenian	242
Still boasting of Her Great Unknown;	24	Ode Athenian	251
To be Successors to these Great Unknown,	25	Ode Athenian	294
Unknown the forms we the high-priesthood use	53	Temple Ill	75
Ah, should I tell a secret yet unknown,	54	Temple Ill	93
Their Lands and their Faces unknown;	396	Dog and Thief	18
"Who, but for him, had been unknown.	566	Death of Swift	338

		PAGE	TITLE	LINE	
UNKNOWN	(CONTINUED)				
Amaz'd, confus'd, its Fate unknown,		579	Day Judgement	7	
A Deed unknown to Female Race,		595	Cassinus Peter	69	
A Crime to all her Sex unknown!)		596	Cassinus Peter	104	
Or Prologue sent from Hand unknown.		643	On Poetry	84	
The Tender Embryos half unknown decay,		667	Epig Carthy 5	D	4
Seeds long unknown to Womankind,		693	Cadenus Vaness	203	
With Graces, hitherto unknown		695	Cadenus Vaness	272	
With Pains unknown increas'd her Smart.		703	Cadenus Vaness	523	
Your Worth will be to them unknown,		739	Stel B-day '21	15	
When haughty Britain was a Land unknown.		790	St. Pat's Well	10	
The Jest of Wits, and to the Court unknown.		794	St. Pat's Well	100	
My humble Respects to my Lady unknown.--		869	Grand Question	81	
That golden Age, to Gold unknown;		894	Panegyr Dean	234	
Where, to us unknown, a Clerk		931	Riddle 18	D	7
UNLACES					
Unlaces next her Steel-Rib'd Bodice;		582	Young Nymph	24	
UNLAMENTED					
Unpitied, unlamented too,		937	Riddle 24	D	53
UNLESS 21			OMITTED WORD		
UNLOADS					
Unloads upon a Stall to rest		160	Atlas	6	
UNLUCKY					
But, we unlucky and unwise,		409	Dial Rich Marb	35	
Unlucky Madam left in Tears,		453	Modern Lady	290	
UNMANLY					
Call'd it unmanly and unwise		306	Manly Virtue	77	
Lamenting in unmanly Strains,		726	To Stella	99	
UNMATCHT					
Let me praise thy Wit unmatcht.		523	Betty Grizette	12	
UNMERCIFUL					
Displays his Pedantry unmerciful,		281	Journal	80	
UNMERITED					
of favour & fortune unmerited vain		540	Charac Walpole	3	
UNMIXT					
Then keep your Virtue still unmixt,		503	Doctor Delaney	107	
UNMOV'D					
The courtly Dame, unmov'd by Fear,		922	Riddle 7	37	
UNNATURAL					
'Tis an unnatural Conjunction,		502	Doctor Delaney	81	
UNOBSERV'D					
Here unobserv'd, she boldly goes,		893	Panegyr Dean	215	
UNPASSABLE					
A mighty gulph unpassable betwixt.		44	To Congreve	32	
UNPAY'D					
I dying leave the Debt unpay'd,		740	Stel B-day '21	18	
Your Favours left too long unpay'd;		887	Panegyr Dean	4	
UNPIERC'D					
Unpierc'd by the blunt Rays of Sight)		31	Ode to Temple	167	
UNPITIED					
Pine unpitied to my urn,		937	Riddle 24	D	51
Unpitied, unlamented too,		937	Riddle 24	D	53
UNPITY'D					
I dye unpity'd and forgot;		916	Riddle 1	41	
UNPOETIC					
First chid the zeal as unpoetic fire,		44	To Congreve	25	
UNPOLITE					
So grave, as to be unpolite;		375	Apology Lady C	8	
UNPOLLUTED					
Return with unpolluted Thumb.		894	Panegyr Dean	224	
UNPREPAR'D					
At the last Trumpet, unprepar'd,		241	Run Bankers	55	
UNPROPORTION'D					
How unproportion'd to thy Pains!		642	On Poetry	60	
UNPROVIDED					
Which unprovided where to dwell,		79	Vanbrug House	31	
UNPUNISH'D					
To rail, and go unpunish'd too;		492	Panegyr Swift	4	
UNRAVELL'D					
My meaning will be best unravell'd,		782	Tim and Fables	1	
UNRAVELLD					
With the unravelld Shreds of which		80	Vanbrug House	47	
UNRAVELS					
What Scenes of Evil he unravels,		548	Life of Swift	111	
UNREGARDED					
Dar'd to suspend her unregarded aid;		43	To Congreve	4	
UNRELENTING					
Gor'd with unrelenting Tooth.		660	Love Song	12	
UNREMITTING					
Assign'd for life to unremitting grief;		54	Temple Ill	110	
UNREVENG'D					
Can, unreveng'd, the greatest merit wound.		506	To a Friend	6	
UNRIGHTEOUS					
Who, while th' unrighteous Mammon is his Friend,		533	To Mr. Gay	73	
UNRIPT					
...my Smock was unript,		69	Mrs Harris Pet	8	
UNRULY					
(The Pegasus, like an unruly Horse		31	Ode to Temple	146	
Both are apt to be unruly,		835	Legion Club	155	
I'm chiefly unruly, when strongest confin'd.		927	Riddle 11	D	4

		PAGE	TITLE	LINE
UNSAID				
Wishes it were all unsaid.	. . . .	800	Traulus 2	22
UNSAV'RY				
Watching the first unsav'ry Wind,	. . . .	66	Problem	37
Soon licks up all unsav'ry steams;	. . . .	432	Answer Paulus	8
And, if unsav'ry Odours fly,	. . . .	529	Lady's Dres Rm	123
And cure the Rank unsav'ry Smelling.	. . . . . .	892	Panegyr Dean	166
From whence unsav'ry Vapours rose,	. . . . . .	895	Panegyr Dean	285
UNSAVORY				
Exhal'd from sour unsavory Streams,	. . . .	526	Lady's Dres Rm	28
UNSECURE				
Rais'd on a Basis unsecure?	. . . .	593	Strephon Chloe	300
But, oh, how unsecure thy Throne!	. . . .	653	On Poetry	377
UNSEEN				
(By all but Heaven and Me unseen,)	. . . .	7	Ode to King	49
And sheds, tho' all unseen, his sacred influence here.	.	39	Ode Sancroft	153
For, youth, believe, to you unseen, is fix'd	. . . .	44	To Congreve	31
Then cunningly retire unseen,	. . . .	253	Bubble	71
"When we come there we'll stand unseen,	. . . . . .	321	First of April	27
To drive unseen her magick Chair,	. . . .	354	Simile Silver	3
Contemning Courts, at Courts unseen,	. . . .	482	Libel on D- D-	73
And fly unseen both Day and Night;	. . . .	919	Riddle 5	26
UNSHAKEN				
Thy Breast unshaken can oppose	. . . .	339	Arch-Bish Dub	9
UNSKILL'D				
Unskill'd in all the Terms of Art?	. . . .	451	Modern Lady	221
UNSLATED				
My Stable's unslated,	. . . .	1014	Swift to Sheri	24
UNSMOAKT				
And half unsmoakt, lay by his Side,	. . . .	594	Cassinus Peter	24
UNSOLD				
Unsold upon the Printer's Lines.	. . . .	502	Doctor Delaney	78
UNSOUGHT				
So bright a Nymph to come unsought,	. . . .	710	Cadenus Vaness	752
UNSOUND				
The dullest Beast and Eggs unsound,	. . . .	941	Letter	25
A long-ear'd Beast give me, and Eggs unsound,	. . .	943	Probatur Alit	39
UNSPARING				
Which with unsparing Hand, he strows	. . . .	486	Libel on D- D-	189
UNSPOKE				
If what You said, I wish unspoke,	. . . .	217	To Mr. Delany	65
UNSPOTTED				
A Goddess of unspotted Fame:	. . . .	695	Cadenus Vaness	275
UNSTEADY				
Nor can you tax me as unsteady,	. . . .	899	Dean's Reasons	7
When soon the peaceful bow unstring'd is shown,	. . .	52	Temple Ill	27
UNSTRUNG				
Oh, wond'rous Box! my Lyre unstrung	. . . .	494	Panegyr Swift	45
UNSUCCESSFUL				
Nor unsuccessful waits for dead Mens Shoes.	. . . .	364	On Dreams	30
UNSUNG				
Shall be, when thou art left unsung;	. . . .	494	Panegyr Swift	46
And all Your Virtues left unsung:	. . . .	739	Stel B-day '21	12
If Stella were unsung to Day;	. . . .	741	Stel B-day 22	16
UNSUSCEPTIBLE				
Was unsusceptible of Stain:	. . . .	586	Strephon Chloe	86
UNSUSPICIOUS				
His Master, unsuspicious of his Pranks,	. . . . .	535	To Mr. Gay	109
UNTHINKING				
So, at a Ball, unthinking Fools delight	. . . . .	771	Horace 1, 14	49
UNTHRIFTY				
Many an eccentric and unthrifty motion make,	. . . .	36	Ode Sancroft	69
UNTILL				
Untill thou shalt have eas'd thy Conscience,	. . . .	181	Horace 2, 1	37
UNTO				
Unto the utmost Bounds of Skill,	. . . .	373	Letter D. S-y	54
UNTO'T				
A School-boy ran unto't and thought,	. . . .	127	Little House	29
UNTOLD				
You'd leave her Virtues half untold.	. . . .	742	Stel B-day 22	40
UNTOUCH'D				
And in some untouch'd Virgin Strain	. . . .	30	Ode to Temple	136
UNTOUCH'T				
Untouch't it pass't between his Grinders,	. . . . .	156	Fable of Midas	11
UNTOWARD				
"To move this Walk's untoward Length	. . . .	379	Apology Lady C	134
Spightful, peevish, rude, untoward;	. . . .	799	Traulus 2	11
In spite of the Devil would still be untoward.	. . .	804	Irish Bishops	26
UNTWISTS				
Untwists a Wire; and from her Gums	. . . .	582	Young Nymph	19
UNUS'D				
"If you, unus'd, have scarsely Strength	. . . . .	379	Apology Lady C	133
UNVANQUISH'D				
Sent to assist an old unvanquish'd pride	. . . . .	44	To Congreve	43
UNWARILY				
But was unwarily drawn in;	. . . .	1005	Sheridan's Sub	18
UNWEETING				
Unweeting gild the tarnish'd Lace:	. . . .	896	Panegyr Dean	312
UNWHOLSOME				
Till Swains unwholsome spoyld the Trade,	. . . . .	225	Prog of Love	91

		PAGE	TITLE	LINE
UNWHOLSOME	(CONTINUED)			
Unwholsome Damps, offensive Dews:	. . . .	923 Riddle 7		56
UNWILLING				
Unwilling Muse begin thy Lay,	. . . .	445 Modern Lady		34
UNWISE				
Call'd it unmanly and unwise	. . . .	386 Manly Virtue		77
But, we unlucky and unwise,	. . . .	409 Dial Rich Marb		35
UNWONTED				
Take thy unwonted Flight,	. . . .	30 Ode to Temple		118
UNWORTHY				
Unworthy the glad tidings which I bring,	. . . . .	52 Temple Ill		35
UP SEE TUCK'D-UP				
Like Love, wrapt up in Fire;	. . . .	8 Ode to King		69
To be an Art as vain, as Bottling up of Wind:)	. . .	21 Ode Athenian		185
Still cast it up and nauseate Company.	. . .	27 Ode to Temple		49
Make up its solemn Train with Death;	. . . .	29 Ode to Temple		90
Made up of Virtue and transparent Innocence:	. . .	30 Ode to Temple		128
Take up at best with Lumber and the Leavings of a Fate:	. .	32 Ode to Temple		184
Seeds and runs up to Poetry.	. . . .	33 Ode to Temple		212
Has given thee up a dwelling-place to fiends?	. . . . .	37 Ode Sancroft		95
Made up of iron mixt with clay,	. . . .	39 Ode Sancroft		139
Swept up whole churches as it list,	. . . .	40 Ode Sancroft		194
Death's sting is swallow'd up in victory at last,	. . .	40 Ode Sancroft		201
There to surmount what bears me up, and sing	. . . .	44 To Congreve		37
Those beds of dung, where schoolboys sprout up beaus	. . .	46 To Congreve		99
The subtil spirit all flies up in fume;	. . . . . .	49 To Congreve		210
And once drawn up, is ne'er let down again.	. . . . .	50 To Congreve		234
Turns up old objects to the soul her sun;	. . . . .	51 Temple Ill		10
Weak is the beam to dry up nature's tears,	. . . . . .	51 Temple Ill		19
With this He putt up to My <Lord>	. . . . . .	63 Discovery		17
So when I went to put up my Purse, as God would have it,. . .		69 Mrs Harris Pet		8
So when I came up again, I found my Pocket feel very light,		69 Mrs Harris Pet		12
So Mary got me to Bed, and cover'd me up warm,	. . .	70 Mrs Harris Pet		18
And could pick up a Third.	. . . .	75 Game Traffick		20
In twisting up an ill-spun Play:	. . . .	80 Vanbrug House		44
Raking up Mud to build a Wall;	. . . .	87 Hist V's House		18
He built up such a monstrous Pile,	. . . .	87 Hist V's House		28
Which tosst up in a Pan with Batter,	. . . .	91 Bauc & Phil 1		61
And serv'd up in an earthen Platter;	. . . .	91 Bauc & Phil 1		62
It still was full up to the Top	. . . .	92 Bauc & Phil 1		77
Like a huge Insect up the Wall,	. . . .	93 Bauc & Phil 1		106
But up against the Steeple rear'd,	. . . .	94 Bauc & Phil 1		141
She piec'd it up again with Scotch.	. . . .	96 On the Union		4
Should bundle Thistles up with Roses.	. . . . . .	96 On the Union		10
Nor shall grin Berris make up the Losse.	. . . . .	103 Merlin		10
Fill'd a large Jug up to the Brink;	. . . .	112 Bauc & Phil 2		30
But up against the Steeple rear'd,	. . . .	113 Bauc & Phil 2		79
And stood up firm for Right Divine:	. . . .	115 Bauc & Phil 2		134
Thus having furbish'd up a Parson,	. . . .	115 Bauc & Phil 2		137
Jove mix'd up all, and his best Clay imploy'd;	. . . .	118 Biddy Floyd		11
Up to the Northern Tropick came,	. . . .	119 Apollo Outwit		2
To pick up Sublunary Ladies.	. . . .	120 Apollo Outwit		24
Sits with his Knees up to his Chin,	. . . .	127 Little House		20
And like a Drunkard gives it up again.	. . . . . .	137 City Shower		16
Is come up, vi & armis, to break the <Queen's> Peace.	. .	142 New Song		4
But, some will cry, Turn-Coat, and rip up old Stories,		143 New Song		21
Wine can clear up <Godolphin's> cloudy Face,	. . .	163 Toland's Invit		19
But if he will break in, and walk up Stairs,	. . . .	166 Toland's Invit		44
Must furbish up and Nickname Crisis.	. . . . . .	180 Horace 2, 1		6
Take up a well-bound Heap of Sticks.	. . . . . .	189 Faggot		4
Came up, and knock't the Praetor down.	. . . . .	190 Faggot		34
"Send for him up, take no Excuse.	. . . .	199 Horace 2, 6		16
Takes up with Copper in the Place;	. . . .	216 To Mr. Delany		44
Would lift her Eyes up to the Ceeling,	. . . . . .	222 Prog of Love		16
Old Madam who went up to find	. . . .	223 Prog of Love		43
One Argument she summ'd up all in,	. . . .	224 Prog of Love		67
Keep up the Glasses of your Chair,	. . . .	228 Prog of Beauty		74
White Lead can plaister up a Cleft,	. . . .	229 Prog of Beauty		114
Or stuff'd with Phlegm up to the Throat	. . . . .	231 Prog of Poetry		25
And up he rises like a Vapour,	. . . .	231 Prog of Poetry		43
They break up Counters, Doors, and Tills,	. . . .	240 Run Bankers		39
In Pails was brought up,	. . . .	244 Irish-Feast		10
Come, Harper, strike up,	. . . .	245 Irish-Feast		25
Fill the Bowl up again,	. . . .	246 Irish-Feast		54
As far up as Adam,	. . . .	247 Irish-Feast		83
Rais'd up on Hope's aspiring Plumes,	. . . . . .	252 Bubble		33
The great ones swall'wing up the small	. . . . .	253 Bubble		66
But Whale Directors eat up all.	. . . .	253 Bubble		68
An Ass hath swallow'd up the Moon,	. . . . . .	253 Bubble		79
Now mounted up to Heav'n again,	. . . .	256 Bubble		150
And sent him up in Air to Hell.	. . . .	257 Bubble		184
Lock up from my Sight in Pantries and Cupboards:	. .	263 Apollo		12
Hold up the prices of their Old Brocades.	. . .	275 Epilogue		16
By Adam lighted walk up stairs:	. . . .	280 Journal		56
Down the black Sea, and up the Streights,	. . .	282 Journal		107
Both Pitch and Brimstone to fill up his Flaws;	. . .	285 Elegy Boat		28
But a Pox o' those Banks that choak up the Springs.	.	287 Bank Down		3
He enters in, and walks up Stairs,	. . . .	292 Prog Marriage		87
Our set of strollers, wand'ring up and down,	. . . .	307 Billet Players		1

UP (CONTINUED)   PAGE TITLE LINE

	PAGE	TITLE		LINE
Then, without fail, we pack up for Belfast.	309	Billet Players		56
'Tis Kindness to hold a Friend up by the Chin;	338	Serious Poem		118
He bids me then to hold my Tongue, and up the Money locks,	342	Upon His Grace		25
That folds up itself in itself for a House:	350	Wood Insect		4
In Fillets of Brass roll'd up to his Ears:	350	Wood Insect		8
For, as sure as a Gun they will give up the Ghost	351	Wood Insect		23
Up at his Forge by Morning-peep,	352	Wood Ironmongr		3
And up he mounts into the Box,	352	Wood Ironmongr		15
With new Delight looks up and loves;	387	Manly Virtue		128
And scorn to wrap up Spice.	394	Grub-Street		8
Sits up till Midnight with his Host,	398	Earl of P-b-w		5
Hang up thy wife, and she'll make four.	404	Window Inns 11	D	2
'Fool, to put up four Crosses at your door,	404	Window Inns 11	D	3
Put up your Wife, she's crosser than all four',	404	Window Inns 11	D	4
Hang up your Wife, and you'l count Four',	404	Window Inns 11	D	6
He strove to pick up all he found,	412	Desire Possess		25
To hang up all who smuggle wool.	423	Ireld		58
Set up with greasy Linnen,	425	Five Ladies		7
Soon licks up all unsav'ry steams;	432	Answer Paulus		8
Nor yields up virtue, at discretion,	436	Answer Paulus		127
She sat all Night up at Quadrill.	446	Modern Lady		41
You pawn'd to him?-- "First shew him up.	446	Modern Lady		59
Comes up with, "Madam, Dinner stays;	447	Modern Lady		93
'No woman breathing takes up less;	447	Modern Lady		97
"Go run, and light the Ladies up:	451	Modern Lady		212
Our Madam can sit up all Night;	451	Modern Lady		217
She draws up Card by Card, to find	452	Modern Lady		228
And Supper gobbled up in haste,	453	Modern Lady		277
"To raise up Virtue when she droops,	462	Birthday Song		74
Give up the phrase of haughty Gaul,	468	Birthday Song		247
Or whom you once sung up, sing down.	468	Birthday Song		260
(His Name is up, he may in Bed lye)	476	Epist on Epist		48
Then Built, then took up with your Arbour,	477	Epist on Epist		69
For the more Livings you can fish up,	478	Epist on Epist		101
Took up himself the Courtier's Trade,	482	Libel on D- D-		68
Forg'd up in Colleges and Schools.	483	Libel on D- D-		92
And give up Party to his Fame.	485	Libel on D- D-		150
In my 'scritore lock up my quill?	489	Dialogue		12
I must take up the sweet'ning Trade.	496	Panegyr Swift		97
Make all true Patriots up to Shoe-boys	501	Doctor Delaney		61
Fly from the Hawk, or pick his Pease up.	512	Answer Fable		10
Could read all Volumes up to Folio's,	513	Answer Fable		41
A holier Priest ne'er was wrapt up in Crape,	516	Dean Hang Rape		5
For why, they had both been brought up to the Trade	517	Dean Hang Rape		27
When the good <English> <Dean> is hang'd up for a <Rape>.	520	Dean Hang Rape		72
Fill'd up with Dirt so closely fixt,	526	Lady's Dres Rm		21
So Strephon lifting up the Lid,	528	Lady's Dres Rm		89
And up exhales a greasy Stench,	529	Lady's Dres Rm		107
Send up an excremental Smell	529	Lady's Dres Rm		111
Made up of Noise, and Impudence, and Lies.	532	To Mr. Gay		42
Made up of Malice, Truth, and Wit:	545	Life of Swift		2
But he takes up with younger Fokes,	556	Death of Swift		93
Runs laughing up to tell the Queen.	559	Death of Swift		180
"When up a dangerous Faction starts,	568	Death of Swift		379
"Against him lifting up their Heels.	569	Death of Swift		406
"And, keep the Peace, to pick up Fees:	571	Death of Swift		450
"Whose Owners set not up for Beaux.	572	Death of Swift		468
I saw the Graves give up their Dead.	578	Day Judgement		4
No drunken Rake to pick her up,	581	Young Nymph		5
Up goes her Hand, and off she slips	582	Young Nymph		27
Of gath'ring up herself again?	583	Young Nymph		70
That, e'er to Bed they venture up,	587	Strephon Chloe		119
Drest up with Amaranthine Flow'rs.	590	Strephon Chloe		202
The Lad lay swallow'd up in Spleen;	594	Cassinus Peter		10
Call'd up at Mid-night, ran to save	604	Beasts Confess		115
And, so absurd, that could I raise up	607	Beasts Confess		199
Can raise them up, or sink them down,	620	Scandal Poem 1		91
Can raise them up, or sink them down,	626	Scandal Poem 2		89
But, to patch up all our Quarrels,	637	Epistle Lady		235
Nor Boy brought up to cleaning Shoes,	641	On Poetry		35
Give up your fond paternal Grin,	644	On Poetry		127
With Prudence gath'ring up a Cluster	647	On Poetry		221
To cry it up, or run it down.	649	On Poetry		270
Bred up in Ignorance and Sloth,	655	On Poetry		409
High up in Air he'll turn your Brains;	666	Epig Carthy 2	D	6
Thy week made up of fasting days,	676	Parson's Case		11
Of which, as she grew up, there stay'd	693	Cadenus Vaness		218
Grew louder, all the Way up Stairs;	698	Cadenus Vaness		369
Alone to fill up all her Wit;	709	Cadenus Vaness		709
Made up so largly in thy Mind.	722	Stel B-Day '18		8
Nor calls up all the House at Night,	725	To Stella		73
Howe're to keep her Spirits up Mean time to keep	747	Stel Distress		45
Howe'er, to keep her Spirits up,	751	Stel Wood-Park		61
To raise up Stella's virtue higher;	755	Stella '23		22
This dang'rous horrid motion Dish up?	774	Mullinix Tim		18
Thy Screw'd up front; thy State Grimace;	775	Mullinix Tim		60
But Nonsense wrapt up in a Stink)	775	Mullinix Tim		64
Tim thour't the Punch to stir up trouble in;	777	Mullinix Tim		138

```
UP          (CONTINUED)                              PAGE    TITLE            LINE
    Of keeping up a party hatred.   . . . . . . . . .   779  Mullinix Tim      184
    Our <Bishops> puft up with Wealth and with Pride.   . .  804  Irish Bishops    17
    And the Clergy, forsooth, must take up with their        804  Irish Bishops    34
       Leavings.
    She was ringing very sorry, her tongue tied up with rag;  840  Ballad        D   8
    Held up by my knees,   . . . . . . . . . . . . . .  852  Lady's Lament     26
    He trips up my props,   . . . . . . . . . . . .  852  Lady's Lament     31
    Haul'd up every hill;   . . . . . . . . . . . .  853  Lady's Lament     50
    And make him soon give up the Cause.   . . . . . .  861  Lady Acheson      40
    Drawn up in our Court; when the Captain cries, Stand.  870  Grand Question   100
    Your Ladyship lifts up the Sash to be seen,   . . .  870  Grand Question   101
    Looks up to your Window, and cocks up her Beaver.  . .  870  Grand Question   104
    Looks up to your Window, and cocks up your Beaver.  . .  870  Grand Question   104
    While Harry's fencing up his ditches.   . . . . . .  878  Robbin & Harry    28
    Rais'd up by you in twenty Weeks;   . . . . . . . .  893  Panegyr Dean     204
    Sent up to thee a grateful Steam.   . . . . . . . .  894  Panegyr Dean     242
    Her Napkin pinn'd up to her Jaws,   . . . . . . . .  894  Panegyr Dean     256
    And, lordly Gout wrapt up in Furr:   . . . . . . .  895  Panegyr Dean     277
    Are sent up Off'rings more sincere   . . . . . . .  896  Panegyr Dean     296
    I last get up, am first a-bed;   . . . . . . . . .  918  Riddle 4          40
    I'm up, and down, and round about,   . . . . . . .  929  Riddle 14     D   1
    Make up a Bird very swift of Flight.   . . . . . .  940  Letter            4
    Bears up his House, that's of his own contriving.  . .  943  Probatur Alit    48
    Wrapt up in Majesty divine,   . . . . . . . . . . .  949  Epigr Fasting     5
    Puff'd up with pride and insolence,   . . . . . . .  950  Upstart       D  11
    And rouse up your Mettle,   . . . . . . . . . . . .  953  Oysters           8
    Who, 'ere t' other gets up, demands the rising Blow.  967  Letter Sherid    14
    I'll first take you up, and then take you down:  . . .  968  Letter Sherid    32
    When whip you trot up, without minding your betters,  . .  978  Dean to Tho: S   3
    You a Gentleman! marry come up, . . .   . . . . . .  985  Mary to Sher      2
    And see now, it strikes ten, and I hear him coming up   987  Mary to Sher     36
       Stairs:
    Thy Muse is tuck'd up, and succinct;   . . . . . . .  1021 Nim-Dan-Dean 1 D  27
    In each single verse, took up a diameter.   . . . . .  1026 Sheri Circles    12
UP-HOLDERS
    He must sink down, or find Up-holders   . . . . . .   160  Atlas            22
UPBRAID
    Besides; your Patron may upbraid ye,   . . . . . . .   483  Libel on D- D-   103
UPHELD
    Upheld by each good Action past,   . . . . . . . .   765  Stel B-day '26   63
UPON      103                                               OMITTED WORD
UPON'T
    "Depend upon't, I never will.   . . . . . . . . . .   446  Modern Lady      53
    A Forehead Cloth with Oyl upon't   . . . . . . . .   526  Lady's Dres Rm   25
    And, when I think upon't, this minute,   . . . . . .   545  Life of Swift    11
    With greasy Paper stuck upon't.   . . . . . . . . .   582  Young Nymph      36
    Depend upon't their Judgment's right:   . . . . . .   644  On Poetry       134
UPPER
    In the Play-House upper Regions;   . . . . . . . .   523  Betty Grizette   24
    Affect to take the upper hand,   . . . . . . . . .   546  Life of Swift    34
    Like Toupets of this upper World;   . . . . . . . .   903  Death Daphne     24
UPRIGHT
    How to walk upright in our ways;   . . . . . . . .   780  Mullinix Tim    252
UPS
    Their ups and downs, with fifty Stories   . . . . .   181  Horace 2, 1      18
UPSIDE
    But with the upside doun to shew   . . . . . . . .    92  Bauc & Phil 1    99
    But with the Upside down, to shew   . . . . . . . .   113  Bauc & Phil 2    59
UPSTART
    For, none among the upstart Race   . . . . . . . .   739  Stel B-day '21   13
UPTON
    Brave as the Upton Fan she wears:   . . . . . . . .   885  Rev Market-Hill  58
UPWARD
    Here a pale shape with upward footstep treads,   . . . .   35  Ode Sancroft     33
    Does to his best look upward still.   . . . . . . .   101  Elegy Patrige   106
    And scorns the Ground, and upward springs,   . . . .   230  Prog of Poetry   14
UPWARDS
    Some more ambitiously upwards fly,   . . . . . . .    32  Ode to Temple   173
    By gazing upwards giddy grow,   . . . . . . . . . .    37  Ode Sancroft     77
    Nor shall the Vapour upwards rise,   . . . . . . .   271  Apollo's Edict D  36
    Of humane Evils upwards flew;   . . . . . . . . . .   528  Lady's Dres Rm   86
    I drag him upwards from his Hole.   . . . . . . . .   921  Riddle 6         34
URCHIN
    The Urchin from his private Stand   . . . . . . . .   702  Cadenus Vaness  515
URG'D
    Then Proteus urg'd the same Request,   . . . . . .   303  Storm            25
URGE
    'Twas in an evil hour to urge my hate,   . . . . .    47  To Congreve     132
    A powerful Impulse urge your Mind,   . . . . . . .   642  On Poetry        78
URN
    Yet, kind Arcadians, on my Urn   . . . . . . . . .   595  Cassinus Peter   73
    Pine unpitied to my urn,   . . . . . . . . . . . .   937  Riddle 24     D  51
US        201                                               OMITTED WORD
US'D
    And what I us'd to laugh at in Romance,   . . . . .     8  Ode to King      62
    To the lov'd Pasture where he us'd to feed,   . . . .    31  Ode to Temple   148
    What bungling, rusty tools, are us'd by fate!   . . . .    47  To Congreve     131
    Which oft he us'd to fish withal:   . . . . . . . .   133  Magician's Rod   44
    Because they see me us'd so well:   . . . . . . . .   202  Horace 2, 6      82
    Are us'd like Dick, and bear the Blame.   . . . . .   221  A Quiet Life     58
```

US'D   (CONTINUED)   PAGE   TITLE   LINE
      Because her Father us'd to say . . . .   223 Prog of Love   31
      By others us'd in the like Cases. . . . .   223 Prog of Love   50
      He us'd 'em full as kindly as himself. . . . . .   234 Elegy on Demar   14
      We are very ill us'd by you Mortals below; . . .   263 Apollo   2
      Who I, for your Sake, have us'd better than any;   263 Apollo   26
      The Dean, who us'd to dine at one, ...   291 Prog Marriage   59
      The Louse of the Wood for a Med'cine is us'd, . .   351 Wood Insect   11
      Who, wanting both, have us'd their Toes. . . . .   367 Answer Delaney   52
      Confering as they us'd to meet, ...   593 Cassinus Peter   3
      With Caution us'd, may serve a-while. . . . . . .   647 On Poetry   238
      (The only Logick us'd by Us) . . . .   658 On Poetry   D 190
      Lost are thy Oars that us'd thy Course to guide,   770 Horace 1, 14   13
      Poets, in those Days, us'd to venture high, . . .   988 Letter Dr Sh-n   13
      As his betters are us'd, shall be lash'd round the ring, 1027 Sheri Circles 19
US'RER'S
      To me from all a us'rer's plumbs; . . . .   899 Dean's Reasons   28
      His Coat, an Us'rer's Velvet Pall, ...   904 Death Daphne   31
USE
      They would not use Us thus. . . . .   24 Ode Athenian   262
      (Methods in talk whereof our pride and ignorance make use) 38 Ode Sancroft 125
      Stale forms of course, all mean deceivers use, . .   44 To Congreve   20
      Unknown the forms we the high-priesthood use . . .   53 Temple Ill   75
      There (A safe way to use Perfume) . . . .   60 Lady Tablebook   12
      Such as our Grandfathers did use, ...   94 Bauc & Phil 1   149
      Which an Astrologer might use, ...   99 Elegy Patrige   45
      Weep all you Customers that use . . . .   101 Elegy Patrige   107
      Such as our Ancestors did use, ...   114 Bauc & Phil 2   103
      I made use of a Trope; that an Heir to invite, . .   144 New Song   37
      Or is your Money out at use?-- . . . .   175 Horace 1, 7   129
      "Lewis; the Dean will be of Use, ...   199 Horace 2, 6   15
      What Use in Life, to make Men frett? . . . . . .   217 To Mr. Delany   71
      Each Colour to it's Place and Use, ...   227 Prog of Beauty   47
      To use the Gifts, that Heav'n bestows; . . . . .   243 Horace 4, 9   18
      These Gentlemen use me with Kindness and.Freedom,   263 Apollo   21
      Nor Shepherds use poetick Cant: . . . .   270 Apollo's Edict   D   28
      But use You ten times worse than Pri'r. . . . . .   312 To Ford   34
      Keep t' other Half for private Use. . . . .   326 Pethox   84
      And England has put this Crab to hard Use, . . .   335 Serious Poem   37
      "Madam, the mighty Pow'r of Use . . . .   379 Apology Lady C   131
      Their noblest Use is to abate . . . .   387 Manly Virtue   107
      Last Friday Night, as Neighbours use, ...   408 Dial Rich Marb   5
      To use them as his truest friends . . . .   422 Ireld   46
      Made use of by detracting foes. . . . .   433 Answer Paulus   50
      An Hundred Tongues, as Poets use, ...   449 Modern Lady   137
      Nor dare to use the gifts by heav'n bestow'd; . .   506 To a Friend   10
      Refin'd it first, and shew'd its Use. . . . . . .   555 Death of Swift   58
      "To publick Use! A perfect Whim! . . . .   558 Death of Swift   157
      "Are taught to use them for their Creed. . . . .   564 Death of Swift   288
      Though Mercury makes use of Wings . . . .   621 Scandal Poem 1   117
      Come to use, and Application: . . . .   636 Epistle Lady   186
      Maxims teaching Wisdom's Use. . . . .   637 Epistle Lady   238
      For private Life, or publick Use? . . . .   641 On Poetry   46
      He only publish'd for my private Use. . . . . . .   668 Epig Carthy 11   D   2
      To neither use thy tusks contribute right, . . .   672 Epig Carthy 25   D   3
      With chariot less for use than state; . . . . . .   676 Parson's Case   24
      Wou'd use him like a younger Child; . . . .   693 Cadenus Vaness   225
      Mens Talents to their proper Use; . . . .   700 Cadenus Vaness   449
      The Boy made use of all his Craft, ...   701 Cadenus Vaness   476
      And sad Experience taught their Use: . . . . . .   705 Cadenus Vaness   607
      Wou'd say, He made a treach'rous Use . . . . . .   707 Cadenus Vaness   644
      "And let him use it at Discretion. . . . .   714 Cadenus Vaness   883
      I furnish Hints, and you should use all 'em, . .   742 Stel B-day 22   38
      And Bacchus for the Poet's Use . . . .   743 Stel B-day 22   65
      For I'm asham'd to use a Glass; . . . .   758 Stel B-day '24   46
      Use all the Talents of your mind. . . . .   780 Mullinix Tim   232
      When, for the Use of no Hibernian born, ...   793 St. Pat's Well   91
      Then let him use you e'er so rough, ...   797 Traulus 1   61
      Make use of your time. . . . .   854 Lady's Lament   114
      I hope you will use my House as your own. . . . .   869 Grand Question   82
      As Soldiers use, for love must marry, ...   878 Robbin & Harry   18
      I use to take in friends affairs, ...   901 Dean's Reasons   96
      And so apply'd to diff'rent use. . . . .   929 Riddle 15   D   12
      With a long-ear'd Beast, and Med'cines Use, . . .   942 Probatur Alit   9
      I promise to use you well. . . . .   952 Onyons   3
      And I'll use you as he did that overgrown Clown,   968 Letter Sherid   31
USED
      He and Cratinus used, as Horace says, ...   988 Letter Dr Sh-n   11
USEFUL
      To mend the World by useful Arts. . . . .   780 Mullinix Tim   246
      Less useful is her Light than thine; . . . . . .   919 Riddle 5   10
      For breeding is a useful Creature. . . . .   940 Letter   7
      Is useful in Journies, take Notice of that. . . .   943 Probatur Alit   44
USEFULL
      How usefull were a womans thunder . . . .   617 Scandal Poem 1   15
USELESS
      And Teeth are useless, where there's nought to eat. . . 670 Epig Carthy 20 D 4
      An useless machine. . . . .   852 Lady's Lament   36
USES
      The various Combs for various Uses, ...   526 Lady's Dres Rm   20
      "'Tis all bequeath'd to publick Uses. . . . . . .   558 Death of Swift   156

USES   (CONTINUED)   PAGE   TITLE   LINE
    Nor uses time, nor time will spare;   . . . .   901 Dean's Reasons   86
    Here Elements have lost their Uses, ...   1035 To Quilca   5
USH
    Like good King Phys: and good King Ush: . . . . .   63 Discovery   23
USHER
    <Dean>, Butler, Usher, Jester, Tutor;   . . . . . .   888 Panegyr Dean   39
USHER'D
    Aurora usher'd in the Day, ...   270 Apollo's Edict   D 21
USHER'S
    Rejects a servile Usher's Place, ...   482 Libel on D- D-   59
    Your Usher's Post must next be handled: . . . . .   890 Panegyr Dean   105
USING
    Using four legs when two were weary.   . . . .   675 Curate's Compl   4
    But using neither Skill, nor Force, ...   696 Cadenus Vaness   302
    Without using my feet: . . . .   852 Lady's Lament   42
USQUEBAGH
    Usquebagh to our Feast   . . . .   244 Irish-Feast   9
USU
    (Consult his Book de Partium usu)   . . . .   367 Answer Delaney   32
USU'LL
    Nell serv'd him at the usu'll Rate   . . . .   221 A Quiet Life   43
USUAL
    Nor has it left the usual bloody Scar, ...   28 Ode to Temple   74
    Runs violently o'er his usual Course.)   . . . . .   31 Ode to Temple   149
    Consenting with the usual Nod, ...   107 V's House   52
    Of Stroling God's, whose usual Trade is, ...   120 Apollo Outwit   22
    When he ask'd for my Aid, in the Forms that are usual: 265 Apollo   72
    She enters on her usual Theme;   . . . .   447 Modern Lady   71
    The Footman in his usual Phrase, ...   447 Modern Lady   92
    She answers in her usual Style, ...   447 Modern Lady   94
    And fell into their usual Chat, ...   698 Cadenus Vaness   375
    Such Language, with her usual Style: . . . . . .   706 Cadenus Vaness   627
    Or, if with more than usual Pain, ...   741 Stel B-day 22   7
    And so I conclude, with humble respects as usual, . . 1024 Nim-Dan-Dean 2   D 18
USUALL
    Consented with the usuall Nod.   . . . .   81 Vanbrug House   72
    Thus in the Strolers usuall Cant   . . . .   90 Bauc & Phil 1   23
    According to my usuall habit, ...   311 To Ford   6
USURP
    Should such a wretch usurp my Congreve's place,   .   48 To Congreve   169
    An Arrian to usurp the Name!   . . . .   819 Dr. Rundle   2
    Thy Founder's Grandson and usurp his Place.   . . .   826 Noisy Tom   16
USURPATION
    'Tis all on me an Usurpation.   . . . .   555 Death of Swift   44
USURPED
    Whom all the Charms of an Usurped Wife and State,   . 20 Ode Athenian   154
USURPERS
    Against the proud usurpers of the pit;   . . . . .   46 To Congreve   110
USURPING
    But, when at last usurping Jove   . . . .   894 Panegyr Dean   253
UTENSIL
    Then and there, Vi & Armis, with a certain Utensil,   264 Apollo   33
    Fair Utensil, as smooth and white   . . . .   589 Strephon Chloe   173
UTMOST
    In vain, said He, does Utmost Thule boast   . . . .   7 Ode to King   51
    Stays but to catch his utmost breath, ...   24 Ode Athenian   274
    Time is no more when th' utmost drop is past;   . .   49 To Congreve   190
    While He his utmost Strength apply'd, ...   158 Fable of Midas   73
    Unto the utmost Bounds of Skill, ...   373 Letter D. S-y   54
    Their utmost Malice cannot make   . . . .   414 Censure   21
    A Rat your utmost Rage defyes   . . . .   504 Doctor Delaney   137
    Wou'd you at once display your utmost Hate,   . . .   667 Epig Carthy 4   D 3
    The utmost her Desires will reach, ...   709 Cadenus Vaness   706
    In utmost Cleanlyness excell   . . . .   732 Verses Vanessa   4
UTOPIA
    Or Memoirs of the New Utopia.   . . . .   150 Corinna   32
UTOPIAN
    Search out this Utopian Ground, ...   26 Ode to Temple   11
UTTER
    He barks as fast as he can utter.   . . . .   797 Traulus 1   48
    From Tubs their snuffling Nonsense utter: . . . .   892 Panegyr Dean   171
UTTER'D
    You'd think she utter'd from behind, ...   592 Strephon Chloe   281
UTTERS
    Now no one regards what he Utters with freedom,   . . 717 Answer Rebus   25
VACANT
    Or, mention but a vacant Post, ...   480 Libel on D- D-   17
VACATION
    Is sent to desire that, when your August vacation comes, 1022 Nim-Dan-Dean 2   D 2
VACATION'S
    And Vacation's over--then   . . . .   574 Helter Skelter   55
VAGRANT
    That vagrant leader of the mind, ...   36 Ode Sancroft   57
    Thus vagrant Beggars, to extort   . . . .   667 Epig Carthy 6   D 1
VAIN
    In vain, said He, does Utmost Thule boast   . . . .   7 Ode to King   51
    France do's in vain her feeble Arts apply   . . . .   13 Ode to William   D 41
    Your Influence do's the vain Attacks defy   . . . .   13 Ode to William   D 43
    In vain she catches at the empty Sound, ...   17 Ode Athenian   57

874

VAIN   (CONTINUED)   PAGE   TITLE   LINE

In vain pursues the Musick with her longing Eye,   . .   17 Ode Athenian   58
To be an Art as vain, as Bottling up of Wind:)   . . .   21 Ode Athenian   185
Of Comments and Disputes, ridiculous and vain,   . . .   23 Ode Athenian   226
Let the vain sex dream on, their Empire comes from Us,   24 Ode Athenian   260
Alas, how fleeting, and how vain, ...   24 Ode Athenian   268
Oft she looks back in vain, ...   31 Ode to Temple   154
You strove to cultivate a barren Court in vain,   . . .   32 Ode to Temple   175
In vain I strive to cross this spacious Main,   . . .   32 Ode to Temple   192
In vain I tug and pull the Oar, ...   32 Ode to Temple   193
In vain to quench this foolish Fire I try   . . .   33 Ode to Temple   206
In vain all wholsome Herbs I sow, ...   33 Ode to Temple   208
In vain then would the Muse the multitude advise,   . . .   37 Ode Sancroft   83
In vain; for a superior Force   . . .   93 Bauc & Phil 1   101
They beg'd from Door to Door in vain;   . . .   111 Bauc & Phil 2   12
In vain; for a Superior Force . . . .   113 Bauc & Phil 2   61
Of Nice, Coquet, Affected, Pert, and Vain.   . . .   118 Biddy Floyd   10
Apollo thought it vain to stay,   . . .   121 Apollo Outwit   42
Suspend a while your vain ambitious Hopes, ...   162 Toland's Invit   5
(As fools are insolent and vain) . . . .   177 To Lord Harley   41
In vain: The complicated Wands . . . .   189 Faggot   7
The Youth, in vain, would fly from Fate's Attack,   . . .   210 Earl of Oxford   3
In vain expects a longer Date . . . .   229 Prog of Beauty   107
To think of Oyl and Soot, is vain, ...   229 Prog of Beauty   110
But never asks, or asks in vain; . . . .   292 Prog Marriage   66
"To drown him all Attempts are vain, ...   303 Storm   28
In Vain he brings his Brazen Shield. . . . . . .   340 Arch-Bish Dub   24
And Fools consult Interpreters in vain.   . . .   363 On Dreams   6
In vain - - - no Doctor's to be found   . . .   377 Apology Lady C   64
Or Pride, or vain Magnificence; . . . .   378 Apology Lady C   102
Pursue the Goddess Health in vain, ...   401 Window Inns 5   D   5
Thus, Pope, in vain you boast your Wit;   . . .   406 Swift to Pope   21
In vain, alas! her Hope is fed; . . . .   452 Modern Lady   232
In vain; even there to spoil his Nod . . . . . .   458 Paddy's Charac   33
In vain are all attempts from Germany   . . .   467 Birthday Song   217
With Begging, Vain, Familiar Letters.   . . .   479 Epist on Epist   118
You try to take Revenge in vain. . . . .   504 Doctor Delaney   136
In vain, the Workmen shew'd his Wit   . . .   528 Lady's Dres Rm   75
To serve a tastless <Court> twelve Years in vain?   . . .   531 To Mr. Gay   2
But, finding all his Artifices vain; . . . . . .   538 Mr. Pulteney   19
of favour & fortune unmerited vain . . . .   540 Charac Walpole   3
Vain human Kind! Fantastick Race!   . . .   555 Death of Swift   39
He searcheth all his Shop in vain; . . . .   563 Death of Swift   257
"But, finding vain was all his Care, ...   567 Death of Swift   369
"He vented oft his Wrath in vain: . . . . . .   571 Death of Swift   444
For whom no Shepherd sighs in vain; . . . . . .   581 Young Nymph   2
Advice in vain you would apply-- . . . . . .   595 Cassinus Peter   71
Vain empty World farewel. But hark, ...   596 Cassinus Peter   79
You worship other Gods in vain . . . . . .   620 Scandal Poem 1   86
You worship other Gods in vain: . . . . . .   626 Scandal Poem 2   84
I may storm and rage in vain; . . . .   636 Epistle Lady   209
In vain you make ye strictest View . . . .   659 On Poetry   D 410
Satyrs and Epigrams in vain you write,   . . .   667 Epig Carthy 4   D   1
Why then in vain he would excite our Mirth.   . . .   669 Epig Carthy 16   D   2
How scorn thy vain Pretension drops; . . . . . .   671 Epig Carthy 22   D   3
In vain, --- for soon the slender prop gives way;   . . .   672 Epig Carthy 24   D 16
His wings are clipp't; he tryes no more in vain   . . .   678 Dean and Duke   7
Which Malice must attack in vain; . . . .   693 Cadenus Vaness   209
So Venus hop'd, but hop'd in vain. . . . .   694 Cadenus Vaness   249
Perfidious Goddess! but in vain . . . .   695 Cadenus Vaness   288
In vain: her Hearers had no Share . . . .   698 Cadenus Vaness   356
For great Examples are but vain, ...   700 Cadenus Vaness   436
On Pallas all Attempts are vain; . . . .   701 Cadenus Vaness   468
In vain discharging many a Shaft, ...   701 Cadenus Vaness   477
And human Caution tries in vain . . . .   702 Cadenus Vaness   486
That all his Lectures were in vain? . . . .   705 Cadenus Vaness   601
In vain; for see, your Friend hath brought . . . . .   731 Stella, Poems   101
My Harp will soon in vain be strung, ...   739 Stel B-day '21   11
May dig in vain in Pluto's Shades. . . . . . .   743 Stel B-day 22   74
She did her best to ape Woodpark. She strove in vain to   747 Stel Distress   48
  ape
She strove in vain to ape Wood-Park. . . . . . .   751 Stel Wood-Park   64
Our Fate in vain we would oppose, ...   757 Stel B-day '24   29
Must let their Cattle range in vain . . . . . .   759 Receipt Youth   5
Unhappy Ship, thou art return'd in Vain: . . . . .   770 Horace 1, 14   9
A larger Sacrifice in Vain you vow; . . . . . .   771 Horace 1, 14   33
In Vain from injur'd Heav'n Relief expects.   . . .   771 Horace 1, 14   36
And you who ever <Fart> in vain, ...   774 Mullinix Tim   31
The Christian Rites I introduc'd in vain: . . . . .   792 St. Pat's Well   35
In vain, against the People's Fav'rite?   . . .   796 Traulus 1   10
In vain--for the Devil a Parson wou'd stir.   . . .   804 Irish Bishops   20
Phantoms, bodiless and vain, ...   833 Legion Club   101
"To thee I often call'd in vain, ...   850 Old Thorn   66
Thus argu'd my Lady, but argu'd in vain;   . . .   868 Grand Question   39
In vain to frisk or climb he tries; . . . . . .   885 Rev Market-Hill   81
In vain on lofty Heels I tread, ...   897 Panegyr Dean   321
In vain I tempt too high a Flight. . . . . . .   897 Panegyr Dean   324
And have been often chid in vain: . . . . . .   901 Dean's Reasons   98
Was of her Beauty grown so vain, ...   905 Death Daphne   69
Vain Man, of all thy vain Pursuits. . . . . . .   921 Riddle 7   2
Vain Man, of all thy vain Pursuits. . . . . . .   921 Riddle 7   2

VAIN	(CONTINUED)	PAGE	TITLE	LINE
In vain from me the Sailor flies, ...		934	Riddle 21	D 13
I went in vain to look for Eupolis, ...		988	Letter Dr Sh-n	7
In vain we make poor Sheelah toil, ...		1035	To Quilca	7

VAINLY

How vainly (Sir) did Your fond Enemy try		9	Ode to King	101
Who by that, vainly talks of bafling Death, ...		21	Ode Athenian	182
Perish the Muse's hour, thus vainly spent		48	To Congreve	175
To thee, what oft I vainly strive to hide, ...		55	Temple Ill	133
And, by the Project vainly try'd, ...		713	Cadenus Vaness	836
Of Brazen Knight they vainly sung:		876	To Dean Swift	14

VAL'ROUS

| Sir Archibald that val'rous Knight, ... | | 848 | Old Thorn | 9 |

VALE

| Where Devils to a vale retreat . . . . | | 490 | Dialogue | 41 |
| Or, offer'd in some flow'ry Vale, ... | | 894 | Panegyr Dean | 247 |

VALES

Scatter'd with flowry Vales, with fruitful Gardens crown'd,		17	Ode Athenian	40
Sing of thy Vales, sing of thy Woods, sing of thy Fields;		31	Ode to Temple	138
If mountains sink to vales, if cityes dye		419	Shall Repine	3
Enriching all the Vales below.		731	Stella, Poems	108

VALIANT

How Valiant George rode o'er the Dragon;		281	Journal	70
Into whose pocket valiant Willy put, ...		467	Birthday Song	207
Is gen'rous, valiant, just and wise, ...		646	On Poetry	195
Her valiant Arm should force us back, ...		885	Rev Market-Hill	60
The valiant Dennis you must fix on, ...		885	Rev Market-Hill	85
Jason, the valiant Prince of Greece, ...		948	Jason Hassard	1

VALLIES

The Arts revive, the Vallies sing, ...		387	Manly Virtue	125
Thorow Mountains thorow Vallies;		574	Helter Skelter	41
Thro' all the Vallies, Hills, and Plains, ...		1035	To Quilca	9

VALOR

| T' express their Valor, Strength or Wit. . . . . | | 83 | Salamander | 12 |

VALOUR

Parent of Valour and of Fame, ...		7	Ode to King	24
To Valour and to Virtue the same Word:		7	Ode to King	28
The Battel almost by Great William's single Valour gain'd;		8	Ode to King	64
"What Ormond's Valour, Oxford's Cares, ...		567	Death of Swift	374
By Valour, Conduct, Fortune won;		641	On Poetry	26
Now Learning, Valour, Virtue, Sense, ...		656	On Poetry	459
His Valour would no more employ;		731	Stella, Poems	123
Her matchless Sons; whose Valour still remains . .		771	Horace 1, 14	43
Renown'd for Valour, Policy and Arts.		789	St. Pat's Well	6
Not by thy Valour, but superior Guile:		791	St. Pat's Well	26

VALU'D

No Creature valu'd what they se'd:		90	Bauc & Phil 1	25
But she valu'd her Honour much more than her Life. . .		517	Dean Hang Rape	10
"And, Wealth he valu'd not a Groat:		567	Death of Swift	358
And said, she valu'd nothing less		697	Cadenus Vaness	340

VALUE

'Tis not that I value the Money three Skips of a Louse		71	Mrs Harris Pet	38
Of Value five Shillings, in English a Pencil; . . .		264	Apollo	34
And whilst he made her Value known, ...		386	Manly Virtue	87
To value that which Men despise.		689	Cadenus Vaness	84
(The best we value by the worst, ...		728	Stella, Poems	21
And then they value not two Straws, ...		776	Mullinix Tim	97
I then shall not value his Deanship a Straw, . . .		868	Grand Question	33
I value not your Jokes of Noose, ...		1003	Dan J's Reply	13

VALUED

| She valued not what others thought her; . . . . . | | 224 | Prog of Love | 71 |
| . . .when one would not turn out a Dog that one valued; . | | 1014 | Swift to Sheri | 10 |

VALUES

| He values not the Poet's Praise, ... | | 157 | Fable of Midas | 55 |
| Tho' his soul he despises, he values his hide: . . . | | 817 | Yahoo's | 72 |

VAMP

| To vamp the good Old Cause again, ... | | 180 | Horace 2, 1 | 4 |

VAMP'T

| He has vamp't an old Speech, and the Court to their sorrow, | | 143 | New Song | 5 |

VAMPT

| Vampt in the Preface and the Text; . . . . . . | | 115 | Bauc & Phil 2 | 128 |

VAN

Sing Muse the House of Poet Van		80	Vanbrug House	57
Van, (for 'tis fit the Reader know it)		80	Vanbrug House	59
Van was deliver'd of a Play, ...		81	Vanbrug House	74
Van saw, but seemd not to regard, ...		86	Hist V's House	3
Van is become by due Degrees		87	Hist V's House	36
I'll lead the Van, keep you the Rear.		780	Mullinix Tim	230
Sing Muse the House of Poet <Van>		106	V's House	31
<Van> (for 'tis fit the Reader know it)		107	V's House	33
Told <Van> he knew his Talent best, ...		107	V's House	53
So <Van> resolv'd to write a Farce, ...		107	V's House	55
To see the House of Brother <Van>:		108	V's House	96
To praise the Pile, and Builder <Van>.		109	V's House	108

VAN'S

| Van's Genius without Thought or Lecture . . . . . | | 86 | Hist V's House | 7 |

		PAGE	TITLE	LINE
VANDAL				
What Time the Goth, the Vandal, and the Hun,		789	St. Pat's Well	3
VANDALS				
The Vandals of the present Age.		611	By Dr. Swift	12
VANESSA				
And said, "Vanessa be the Name,		692	Cadenus Vaness	180
"Vanessa, by the Gods enroll'd:		692	Cadenus Vaness	182
Mistakes Vanessa for a Boy;		693	Cadenus Vaness	201
To see Vanessa thus endow'd;		693	Cadenus Vaness	229
"'Tis what Vanessa never did.		694	Cadenus Vaness	245
Nor shall Vanessa be the Theme		696	Cadenus Vaness	298
When, lo! Vanessa in her Bloom,		696	Cadenus Vaness	305
With silent Scorn Vanessa sat,		697	Cadenus Vaness	334
Vanessa held Montaigne, and read,		698	Cadenus Vaness	372
And what they cost? Vanessa guess'd,		698	Cadenus Vaness	381
Vanessa, tho' by Pallas taught,		702	Cadenus Vaness	488
Vanessa much esteem'd his Wit,		702	Cadenus Vaness	511
Vanessa, not in Years a Score,		703	Cadenus Vaness	524
Vanessa, fill'd with just Disdain,		705	Cadenus Vaness	594
Vanessa finish'd the Dispute,		708	Cadenus Vaness	675
And taught Vanessa to dispute.		709	Cadenus Vaness	713
Vanessa in exalted Strains,		711	Cadenus Vaness	791
But what Success Vanessa met,		712	Cadenus Vaness	818
But here Vanessa cannot err,		733	Verses Vanessa	17
VANESSA'S				
To study bright Vanessa's Looks:		694	Cadenus Vaness	235
Vanessa's Praise rung in their Ear:		694	Cadenus Vaness	241
They railly'd next Vanessa's Dress;		699	Cadenus Vaness	396
Against Vanessa's Pow'r unite;		700	Cadenus Vaness	439
Whom Pallas, once Vanessa's Tutor,		701	Cadenus Vaness	464
Vows, on Vanessa's Heart to take		701	Cadenus Vaness	470
Vanessa's earliest Thoughts engage.		706	Cadenus Vaness	637
Cou'd scarce oppose Vanessa's Flame;		710	Cadenus Vaness	745
Grown by Vanessa's Conduct wise.		712	Cadenus Vaness	831
VANISH				
Would vanish in a Pyramid of Fire.		22	Ode Athenian	196
The Ladys vanish, in the Smother,		66	Problem	49
For fine Ideas vanish fast,		591	Strephon Chloe	233
VANISH'D				
They vanish'd in a stinking Smoak.		134	Magician's Rod	58
She fled and vanish'd into Air.		850	Old Thorn	52
VANISHT				
And vanisht to an empty Title in the Last.		25	Ode Athenian	287
VANITY				
The greatest scorn of Learned Vanity,		21	Ode Athenian	179
Woman seems now above all Vanity grown,		24	Ode Athenian	250
And Vanity with Pocket-Glass;		448	Modern Lady	130
Wherewith our Vanity endows us,		603	Beasts Confess	77
I see his Vanity and Pride:		915	Riddle 1	24
VANITY'S				
That Vanity's the Food of Fools;		710	Cadenus Vaness	759
VANQUISH'D				
And when I, vanquish'd, fled the Town,		1005	Sheridan's Sub	9
VAP'RING				
This vap'ring Scab must needs devise		352	Wood Ironmongr	9
VAPOR				
'Tis but a low-born vapor kindled by a ray;		41	Ode Sancroft	218
A walking vapor, like thy sister fame.		54	Temple Ill	102
VAPORS				
Vapors and Steams her Looks disgrace,		226	Prog of Beauty	2
VAPOUR				
And end as it began, in Vapour, Stink, and Scum.		10	Ode to King	129
And up he rises like a Vapour,		231	Prog of Poetry	43
Nor shall the Vapour upwards rise,		271	Apollo's Edict	D 36
Oh! then but to see how Beggars will Vapour,		287	Bank Down	21
You certainly know, tho' so loudly you vapour,		818	Archbi Cashel	5
Good cause have I to sing and vapour,		876	To Dean Swift	1
VAPOURS				
Like gilded Vapours to the Skies,		386	Manly Virtue	104
In Vapours and Hysterick Fits:		451	Modern Lady	199
The Vapours flew from out the Vent,		528	Lady's Dres Rm	91
Into Spleen and Vapours fell;		834	Legion Club	122
From whence unsav'ry Vapours rose,		895	Panegyr Dean	285
VARIANCE				
But, still at Variance with each other,		412	Desire Possess	10
In Mother Church to breed a Variance,		820	Dr. Rundle	7
To live in fear, suspicion, variance,		899	Dean's Reasons	17
VARIES				
Howe'er our Earthly Motion varies,		98	Elegy Patrige	16
VARIETY				
Ne'er borrow'd more variety of Shapes		22	Ode Athenian	199
Variety we still Pursue,		728	Stella, Poems	17
VARIOUS				
Here various Kinds by various Fortunes led,		138	City Shower	39
Here various Kinds by various Fortunes led,		138	City Shower	39
Display their various nets for hearts;		178	To Lord Harley	54
Voiture in various Lights displays		216	To Mr. Delany	33
The various Textures of their Minds,		291	Prog Marriage	34
In all the various Colours seen,		325	Pethox	45
The Mind unburthen'd sports in various Whims,		363	On Dreams	8
The various Combs for various Uses,		526	Lady's Dres Rm	20

877

VARIOUS (CONTINUED)	PAGE	TITLE	LINE
The various Combs for various Uses, ...	526	Lady's Dres Rm	20
Thy various Follies, who can trace?	555	Death of Swift	40
What various Ways our Females take, ...	592	Strephon Chloe	267
And by such various Titles call, ...	724	To Stella	17
The various Scenes of mortal Life, ...	781	Mullinix Tim	265
Always various, always wrong:	800	Traulus 2	18
Your Thing of various Shape and Hue, ·	912	Aenigma Expl	D 7
Conceal your Form with various Tricks;	919	Riddle 5	27
In various Forms appear agen	924	Riddle 7	93
Various is my bulk and hue, ...	936	Riddle 24	D 27
VARLET			
To see the wicked Varlet sprawling;	353	Wood Ironmongr	26
Away you see the Varlet scud, ...	824	Printer Newgat	9
Thou a disobedient Varlet, ...	838	Legion Club	201
VARNISH			
Oh Peter! Beauty's but a Varnish, ...	595	Cassinus Peter	51
VARNISH'D			
All varnish'd o'er with Snuff and Snot.	527	Lady's Dres Rm	50
VARY			
But lest Chronology should vary, ...	456	Dean Smedley	45
From antient Canons would not vary, ...	821	Dr. Rundle	39
VASE			
And as he fill'd the reeking Vase, ...	590	Strephon Chloe	191
Her Silver Vase in Cedar-Box.	896	Panegyr Dean	298
VASSALS			
His Vassals easy, and the Owner blest;	533	To Mr. Gay	47
VAST			
When Schonberg started at the Vast Design: . . .	12	Ode to William	D 34
Or the vast Charges of a Smile;	24	Ode Athenian	253
Like a just Map to tell the vast Extent	25	Ode Athenian	302
Whilst thus I write, vast shoals of critics come, . .	50	To Congreve	213
And when you've been at vast Expences	477	Epist on Epist	61
Beneath the vast abyss he plunges quick, ...	672	Epig Carthy 24	D 17
When thy Retrospection vast	862	To Janus	15
'Tis a vast Subject stuff'd with Matter, ...	993	On Picture	17
VATICAN			
You will not find it in the Vatican.	988	Letter Dr Sh-n	10
VAULT			
With a Dozen large Vessels my Vault shall be stor'd, .	867	Grand Question	13
Secure the Larder, and the Vault.	885	Rev Market-Hill	84
When to the Vault you walk in State, ...	889	Panegyr Dean	87
To banish Rats that haunt our Vault.	892	Panegyr Dean	162
Who round the Vault luxuriant reign.	923	Riddle 7	60
VAULTS			
But, in their Cells and Vaults obscene	895	Panegyr Dean	283
VEAL			
The veal is such carrion, ...	402	Window Inns 8	D 9
Come, buy my fine Oranges, Sauce for your Veal, . .	953	Oranges	1
VEGETABLES			
And as the Vegetables rise, ...	759	Receipt Youth	13
Of Vegetables, Brutes, and Men.	924	Riddle 7	94
VEHICLES			
In Vehicles they mount the Sky:	626	Scandal Poem 2	110
VEIN			
Produce a richer vein or cleaner ore;	45	To Congreve	52
A lust of rhiming for a poet's vein, ...	45	To Congreve	78
Scatt'ring loose features o'er the optic vein;	54	Temple Ill	96
Not owing to his happy Vein	481	Libel on D- D-	45
There's too much satire in my vein, ...	489	Dialogue	2
And write you must, or break a Vein:	501	Doctor Delaney	52
"His Vein, ironically grave, ...	565	Death of Swift	315
"Had too much Satyr in his Vein;	571	Death of Swift	456
Nor, against my nat'ral Vein, ...	634	Epistle Lady	135
The Poet's Vein, or scribling Itch?	642	On Poetry	74
But my Poetick Vein declines.	739	Stel B-day '21	10
Here, for an Age and more, improv'd their Vein, . . .	793	St. Pat's Well	71
VEINS			
Corrupts and stagnates in the Veins, ...	239	Run Bankers	10
And fill your Veins with sprightly Blood:	759	Receipt Youth	32
Within their Veins, who are thy younger Sons, . . .	791	St. Pat's Well	18
VELIT			
Hoc Ithacus velit, et magni mercentur Atridae. . . .	980	Dean to Tho: S	38
VELVET			
In Velvet Cap his Head lies warm;	410	Dial Rich Marb	65
Give me Velvet and Quadrille, ...	863	To Janus	29
His Coat, an Us'rer's Velvet Pall, ...	904	Death Daphne	31
VEN'SON			
A Haunch of Ven'son made her sweat	746	Stel Distress	15
A Haunch of Ven'son made her sweat, ...	750	Stel Wood-Park	13
VENDS			
Who daily vends seditious Trash:	515	Answer Fable	92
VENERABLE			
Among those venerable Sires.	702	Cadenus Vaness	501
VENEREAL			
Compar'd for mischief, to Venereal?	618	Scandal Poem 1	24
Compar'd for Mischief, to Venereal?	624	Scandal Poem 2	18
VENGEANCE			
And last, my Vengeance to Compleat, ...	121	Apollo Outwit	61
Now, <Madam Coningsmark> her Vengeance vows . . .	195	Author Himself	53
Slow Vengeance, like a Blood-hound at his Heels. . .	210	Earl of Oxford	22

```
VENGEANCE        (CONTINUED)                          PAGE   TITLE            LINE
    But Vengeance, Goddess never sleeping      . . . . .   529 Lady's Dres Rm    119
    For, Vengeance more embroils, than Skill repairs.  . .  536 To Mr. Gay       140
    "With Wrath and Vengeance in their Hearts:     . . . .  568 Death of Swift   380
    Scourge the Villains with a Vengeance.    . . . . . .   635 Epistle Lady     176
    Due Vengeance, for her Patron's sake.    . . . . . .    701 Cadenus Vaness   471
    For Vengeance on his Friends the Greeks.     . . .     731 Stella, Poems    126
    That Traulus calls for Vengeance on him?     . . . .   796 Traulus 1          8
    By the just Vengeance of incensed Skies,    . . . .    806 Judas              1
    Shall on thee take a Vengeance dire;  . . . . . . .    925 Riddle 8          37
    . . .for Corks to stop your Bottles, with a Vengeance. 1013 Swift to Sheri    5
'VENGEFUL
    Invited here to 'vengeful Morrough's Aid,    . . . . . 791 St. Pat's Well    23
VENGEFUL
    Leaves him a Victim to the vengeful Scot;    . . . . . 195 Author Himself    58
VENIAL
    <Swift> had the Sin of Wit no venial Crime;    . . . . 193 Author Himself     9
VENOM
    From her red Locks her Mouth with Venom fills:   . . . 195 Author Himself    55
    In Venom, till they burst their Lungs,    . . . . . .  414 Censure           20
VENOM'D
    I drove the venom'd Serpent from thy Land;   . . . . . 792 St. Pat's Well    40
VENT
    Step't with a Jug, and made a Vent;    . . . . . . .    92 Bauc & Phil 1     70
    At length, presumes to vent his Satyr on    . . . . .  458 Paddy's Charac    27
    There let him starve, and vent his Rage.    . . . . .  515 Answer Fable      84
    The Vapours flew from out the Vent,    . . . . . . .   528 Lady's Dres Rm    91
    "Vow'd on the Dean his Rage to vent,    . . . . . .    570 Death of Swift   423
    An A's and B's your Malice vent,    . . . . . . . .    645 On Poetry        159
    And gave, by turns, their Censures Vent.   . . . . .   699 Cadenus Vaness   409
    Through Clefts oppugnant force a Vent;    . . . . . .  923 Riddle 7          86
    I've nothing left to vent my Spleen   . . . . . . .   1005 Sheridan's Sub    27
VENT'RING
    By vent'ring on the cheating Side,     . . . . . .     257 Bubble           163
    By vent'ring on his heav'nly Wife?     . . . . . .     587 Strephon Chloe   104
VENTED
    "He vented oft his Wrath in vain:    . . . . . . . .   571 Death of Swift   444
VENTING
    After venting all my Spight,    . . . . . . . .        629 Epistle Lady       1
VENTUR'D
    When first she ventur'd out with him. . . . . . . .    224 Prog of Love      82
    Then ventur'd to give him some sober Advice,   . . . . 327 Epigram 1          5
    Three Duels he fought, thrice ventur'd his Life  . . . 327 Epigram 1          9
    For Strephon ventur'd to look in,    . . . . . . .     528 Lady's Dres Rm    79
    At last he ventur'd to complain:    . . . . . . . .    704 Cadenus Vaness   573
    You never ventur'd to be hang'd.    . . . . . . . .    884 Rev Market-Hill   40
VENTURE
    Venture to build his Nest so low.    . . . . . . . .   127 Little House      28
    (Tho' this I speak but at a venture,    . . . . . .    182 Horace 2, 1       77
    Now venture at a Pint of Port,    . . . . . . . .      184 Horace 2, 1      112
    Venture to give him some Advice.    . . . . . . . .    218 To Mr. Delany     96
    That Will durst hardly venture in;    . . . . . . .    219 A Quiet Life       2
    If Virtue dares not venture down,    . . . . . . .     392 Young's Satire    37
    If This to Clouds and Stars will venture,    . . . .   393 Modern Poets       7
    And will you venture both a-new?    . . . . . . . .    436 Answer Paulus    131
    Must venture down to entertain us.    . . . . . . .    465 Birthday Song    156
    They now can venture in the dark.    . . . . . . .     468 Birthday Song    270
    "(Ladies I'll venture for the Vole.)    . . . . . .    562 Death of Swift   230
    That, e'er to Bed they venture up,    . . . . . . .    587 Strephon Chloe   119
    To venture in a Ship decay'd?    . . . . . . . .       703 Cadenus Vaness   533
    Which thus she will Venture profusely to throw,  . . . 716 Answer Rebus       3
    Dick I could venture every where,    . . . . . . .     788 Dick's Variety    19
    He dare not venture to approach;    . . . . . . . .    824 Printer Newgat    12
    Where many for a Passage venture,    . . . . . . .     928 Riddle 12       D  3
    Poets, in those Days, us'd to venture high,    . . . . 988 Letter Dr Sh-n    13
    . . . for, to say it we may venture,    . . . . . .   1023 Nim-Dan-Dean 2  D 13
    But how, Mr. Sheridan, came you to venture    . . . . 1027 Sheri Circles     13
VENTURES
    She ventures now to lift the Sash,    . . . . . . .    228 Prog of Beauty    65
    When my Muse officious ventures    . . . . . . . .     635 Epistle Lady     155
    She ventures now to leave the Skies,    . . . . . .    712 Cadenus Vaness   830
VENUS
    To Venus in Aspect Mali'n,    . . . . . . . . .         99 Elegy Patrige     60
    And Cure the Wounds that Venus made.    . . . . . .     99 Elegy Patrige     62
    These Venus cleans'd from ev'ry spurious Grain   . . . 118 Biddy Floyd        9
    Venus, indulgent to her Kind    . . . . . . . .        227 Prog of Beauty    57
    Thus Venus to the Sea descends    . . . . . . . .      254 Bubble            93
    For Venus rising from the Ocean    . . . . . . . .     293 Prog Marriage    107
    But Venus had been there before    . . . . . . . .     302 Storm             11
    From Venus born, thy Beauty shows,    . . . . . . .    323 Pethox             1
    (Venus was Brib'd to let it pass.)    . . . . . . .    345 Prometheus        40
    Than Venus like an Owl.  . . . . . . . . .             425 Five Ladies       16
    They rival Venus to a Hair;    . . . . . . . . .       445 Modern Lady       10
    The Graces and their Mistress Venus    . . . . . .     465 Birthday Song    155
    For Venus might be her great Grandam.    . . . . . .   465 Birthday Song    160
    Dear Venus, hide this wond'rous Maid,    . . . . . .   585 Strephon Chloe    29
    Though Venus be as light as air,    . . . . . . .      621 Scandal Poem 1   115
    What Drabs have been compar'd to Venus?    . . . . .   622 Scandal Poem 1   156
    Though Venus be as light as Air,    . . . . . . .      627 Scandal Poem 2   113
    Each Drab has been compar'd to Venus:    . . . . . .   628 Scandal Poem 2   160
    That Venus, from the Judgement-Seat,    . . . . . .    688 Cadenus Vaness    76
```

VENUS	(CONTINUED)	PAGE	TITLE	LINE
What Venus meant by this Delay.		690	Cadenus Vaness	127
When Venus thought on a Deceit.		692	Cadenus Vaness	185
So Venus hop'd, but hop'd in vain.		694	Cadenus Vaness	249
Found out the Trick that Venus play'd,		694	Cadenus Vaness	251
Venus wou'd fail in her Design:		695	Cadenus Vaness	277
Those early Seeds by Venus sown,		701	Cadenus Vaness	472
Unless, like Venus, in her Prime.		757	Stel B-day '24	22
Oft in the Train of Venus seen,		923	Riddle 7	69

VENUS-LIKE
| And, Venus-like, her fragrant Skin | | 586 | Strephon Chloe | 87 |

VENUS'
| I must, like him that painted Venus' Face, | | 28 | Ode to Temple | 63 |

VERDANT
Beneath this verdant Hillock lies		235	Elegy on Demar	41
Enamell'd Fields, and verdant Trees;		251	Bubble	28
In Summer, on my verdant Lap:		410	Dial Rich Marb	86
Mournful Cypress, verdant Willow,		661	Love Song	21
Again the verdant Glebe renew;		759	Receipt Youth	12
To thee no verdant Altars rear;		895	Panegyr Dean	282

VERDICT
| Then Mrs. Johnson gave her Verdict, | | 128 | Little House | 39 |

VERGE
| I'll give thee Surplice, Verge and Stall, | | 361 | Grace's Answer | 7 |

VERIFY'D
| They must be verify'd at last. | | 558 | Death of Swift | 146 |

VERJUICE
| To Cudgel our Bones, and for Drink give us Verjuice; | | 335 | Serious Poem | 38 |

VERMIN
When Man himself's the Vermin of Her Earth;		8	Ode to King	55
Work out, as Anger does in Vermin?		66	Problem	16
That three little Vermin are kin to Will. Wood:		350	Wood Insect	2
Or bring his Vermin in, but Scraps?		484	Libel on D- D-	130
From hence the Critick Vermin sprung		504	Doctor Delaney	123
"Vice is a Vermin; Sportsman say		548	Life of Swift	125
"No Vermin can demand fair Play,		548	Life of Swift	126
Spy the strutting chatt'ring Vermin?		634	Epistle Lady	152
The Vermin only teaze and pinch		651	On Poetry	335
See, where the new-devouring Vermin runs,		792	St. Pat's Well	59
Employments for their Brother Vermin.		813	Bro Protestant	44
To nourish Vermin, may be bit.		813	Bro Protestant	64
The dullest Beast, and scandalous Vermin		941	Letter	29
A long-ear'd Beast, and shameful Vermin,		942	Probatur Alit	21

VERSE
And Deifi'd in Verse;		6	Ode to King	21
Then (Sir,) accept this worthless Verse,		32	Ode to Temple	199
Then call this verse, that speaks her largest aid,		44	To Congreve	27
And on my verse pronounce their saucy doom;		50	To Congreve	214
Who dare revile the integrity of verse:		53	Temple Ill	70
But was sorely put to't in the midst of a Verse,		76	Lady B- B-	3
A Verse could draw a Stone or Beam		106	V's House	3
To build by Verse as heretofore,		107	V's House	44
To silent Shades repeat thy Verse,		121	Apollo Outwit	58
Howe'er such Verse as yours, I grant		123	Empty'ng Town	17
Nor pump to cobble wicked Verse;		181	Horace 2, 1	36
Something in Verse as true as Prose;		199	Horace 2, 6	D
To you the Muse this Verse bestows;		215	To Mr. Delany	1
For Verse, (I speak my Judgment) Yours:		219	To Mr. Delany	106
He only stole Hints; the Verse is correct;		266	Apollo	90
Pelts him by Turns with Verse and Prose,		458	Paddy's Charac	25
"Thy Thanks and Verse, devoid of Art:		476	Epist on Epist	34
To find a Verse in Virgil Spurious:		483	Libel on D- D-	100
In Verse; but there is Truth in mine.		486	Libel on D- D-	194
Either in verse or hum'rous prose,		489	Dialogue	10
The Turn of Verse, nor Stile of Prose;		515	Answer Fable	96
"A few, in Verse; but most, in Prose---.		550	Life of Swift	182
Enquires for Swift in Verse and Prose:		562	Death of Swift	254
"As for his Works in Verse and Prose,		565	Death of Swift	309
"A Verse from Horace, learn'd by Rote.		572	Death of Swift	474
Could Verse inspire, but seldom writ:		597	Problem Solved	2
The vilest Verse thrives best at Court.		646	On Poetry	186
And, though you never learn'd to scan verse,		658	On Poetry	D 186
Known by the Verse, yet better by the Notes.		670	Epig Carthy 18	D 4
The Corruption of Verse, for when all is done,		716	Answer Rebus	9
Thus much for the Verse, we proceed to the next,		716	Answer Rebus	19
Truth shines in the bright, clad in Verse;		729	Stella, Poems	58
Resolv'd my annual Verse to pay		740	Stel B-day 22	1
My verse on Stella's native day:		754	Stella '23	4
He sounds my Praise in Verse and Prose.		887	Panegyr Dean	28
You can taste my verse or prose:		908	Daphne	70
Dear Tom, I'm surpriz'd that your verse did not jingle;		980	Tho: Sheridan	1
And cannot send one Verse.		1014	Swift to Sheri	36
Makes thy Verse smooth, and makes them last.		1021	Nim-Dan-Dean 1	D 14
Thy Verse like Bricks, defy the Weather,		1021	Nim-Dan-Dean 1	D 19
Dear Tom, this verse, which however the beginning may appear,. . .		1022	Nim-Dan-Dean 2	D 1
In each single verse, took up a diameter.		1026	Sheri Circles	12

VERSES
Who would not Write Verses with such an assistant.		77	Lady B- B-	REF
And Poets their own Verses sung,		79	Vanbrug House	2
And Poets their own Verses Sung,		106	V's House	2

VERSES   (CONTINUED)   PAGE   TITLE   LINE
   That some Verses were writ with felonious Intent,   . .   264 Apollo   47
   Now you see why his Verses so seldom are shown, . . .   264 Apollo   55
   To write a few Verses on you as my Friend;   . . . .   265 Apollo   74
   To believe all his Verses were written by me; . . .   266 Apollo   100
   Get all your Verses printed fair, ...   394 Grub-Street   9
   None e'er made Verses worse than he, ...   401 Window Inns 2   5
   Their verses give delight . . . .   429 Beau's Reply   11
   We own, Your Verses are melodious, ...   622 Scandal Poem 1 179
   We own, your Verses are melodious; . . . . . .   628 Scandal Poem 2 161
   Before I could my Verses bring, ...   730 Stella, Poems   69
   I can't pray in quiet for you and your verses,-- . . .   976 Dean to Sherid   5
   Whereof I cou'd say more to your Verses, . . .   987 Mary to Sher   37
   The Verses you sent on the bottling your Wine . . . 1017 Swift Ans Sher   1
   But now for your verses; we tell you, imprimis, . . . 1026 Sheri Circles   5
   That she makes of your verses a hoop for Miss Tam, . . 1027 Sheri Circles 27
VERTIGO
   That old Vertigo in his Head, ...   556 Death of Swift   83
VERTUE
   Look where exalted Vertue and Religion sit   . . .   21 Ode Athenian 176
   By vertue of some sly Petition: . . . . . .   182 Horace 2, 1   68
VERTUES
   Thy Vertues meet their just Reward, ...   779 Mullinix Tim 201
VERY
   The very Brightness of His Face . . . .   9 Ode to King   94
   How little, very little do prevail . . . .   19 Ode Athenian 112
   Whether that very Name was He, or You, or I? . . .   21 Ode Athenian 168
   And ev'n my very Thoughts transfers . . . . . .   23 Ode Athenian 235
   Though very turbulent and very loud; . . . . . .   38 Ode Sancroft 136
   Though very turbulent and very loud; . . . . . .   38 Ode Sancroft 136
   So much in mode, so very city-born; . . . . . .   44 To Congreve   14
   Now you must know, because my Trunk has a very bad Lock,   69 Mrs Harris Pet   5
   . . .is a very small Stock, ...   69 Mrs Harris Pet   6
   So when I came up again, I found my Pocket feel very
      light,   69 Mrs Harris Pet   12
   . . .as you may very well think,   70 Mrs Harris Pet   20
   Nay, said she, my Lord Collway's Folks are all very sad   70 Mrs Harris Pet   27
   The Earth would very soon be filld: . . . . . .   79 Vanbrug House   20
   'Twill make the very Flames expire, ...   84 Salamander   50
   And very much in Harley's Favour) . . . . . .   171 Horace 1, 7   18
   Did very much his Genius cramp; . . . .   172 Horace 1, 7   44
   And entring in the very nick, ...   220 A Quiet Life   20
   The very Chest, in which they say . . . . . .   235 Elegy on Demar   47
   We are very ill us'd by you Mortals below; . . . .   263 Apollo   2
   He knows very well I ne'er gave a Refusal, . . .   265 Apollo   71
   How very mean a thing's a Duke; . . . . . .   297 Satiric Elegy   30
   I thought my very Spleen would burst . . . . . .   313 To Ford   51
   Now, although to Draw Water is not very good,   . .   334 Serious Poem   3
   To cut down fine Wood is a very bad Thing,   . .   334 Serious Poem   13
   Some say he's a Birch, a Thought very odd,   . .   335 Serious Poem   33
   I often have seen two Plays very Good,   . . .   337 Serious Poem   91
   On the Scene of this Land very soon to revive.   . .   337 Serious Poem   94
   Very soon to see Wood Drop down from a Rope.   . .   338 Serious Poem 116
   A Bishop says the noble 'Squire, I hate the very Name,   342 Upon His Grace   17
   Then said my Lord, I'm very glad to see thee honest
      Friend,   342 Upon His Grace   31
   My very good Lord, it's a very hard task   . . . .   368 Verses Window   1
   My very good Lord, it's a very hard task   . . . .   368 Verses Window   1
   I think I'm very fairly off. . . . .   377 Apology Lady C   56
   Are very near a-kin; . . . .   401 Window Inns 4   2
   'Tis very true, and none denies, ...   433 Answer Paulus   39
   They set the very Lap-Dog barking; . . . . . .   450 Modern Lady 179
   The very Reverend Dean Smedley, ...   455 Dean Smedley   1
   And in their very Ports besiege, ...   463 Birthday Song 103
   And with Boots so very grazy . . . .   573 Helter Skelter   11
   And with Hats so very big, Sir, ...   573 Helter Skelter   17
   And with Rings so very trim, ...   574 Helter Skelter   27
   And with very little Pence, ...   574 Helter Skelter   29
   And as very little Sence: . . . .   574 Helter Skelter   30
   Which my very Foes allow me. . . . .   631 Epistle Lady   64
   (Late, very late, O, may he rule us.) . . . . .   655 On Poetry 430
   Was, in the very Search, betray'd . . . . . .   702 Cadenus Vaness 491
   My very Face, at first I knew it, ...   783 Tim and Fables   23
   Tho' he cring'd to his Deanship in very low strains; .   816 Yahoo's   46
   On his virtues hold forth; 'tis the very best way; .   819 Archbi Cashel   9
   Like a very foul mop, dirty more than they clean. . .   819 Archbi Cashel   16
   The gold she was pull'd down, of that I'm very sure, .   840 Ballad   D   3
   She was ringing very sorry, her tongue tied up with rag;   840 Ballad   D   8
   Is very imperious. . . . .   855 Lady's Lament 144
   You come in the very worst Time of the Year; . . . .   871 Grand Question 122
   "So, I took to the Road, and what's very odd, . .   873 Grand Question 169
   But very few are found to enter; . . . . . .   928 Riddle 12   D   4
   My Blood this Day is very sweet, ...   929 Riddle 15   D   9
   Nay give their very Souls away. . . . . . .   930 Riddle 15   D 28
   At other times a very slut; . . . .   937 Riddle 24   D 30
   Make up a Bird very swift of Flight. . . . . .   940 Letter   4
   Is a Person very unfit for Intrigues. . . . .   940 Letter   17
   In Summer is very pleasant and cool. . . . . .   941 Letter   20
   You found out my rebus with very much modesty; . . .   976 Dean to Sherid   37
   To the very coach side, and threaten your letters. . .   978 Dean to Tho: S   4
   So much, he swears the very best Piece is . . . .   988 Letter Dr Sh-n   22

VERY   (CONTINUED)   PAGE   TITLE   LINE
   However, they own it is very civil in Mr. Sheridan, . . 1014 Swift to Sheri   8
   This Night I came home with a very cold Dew sick,   . . 1030 Dr. Sheridan   2
VESPUTIO'S
   From Realms that bear Vesputio's Name: . . . . .   324 Pethox   24
VESSEL
   A Vessel with a double Keel: . . . .   96 On the Union   16
   Then fill the Vessel to the Brim, ...   251 Bubble   10
   No Vessel but an Ass's Head, ...   469 Burning Poem   4
   And brings a Vessel into Bed: . . . .   589 Strephon Chloe   172
   Let the Vessel split on Shelves, ...   635 Epistle Lady   161
   Betwixt a State, and Vessel under Sail;   . . . . .   770 Horace 1, 14   6
   Dear Vessel, still be to thy Steerage just, ... 771 Horace 1, 14   53
   Dilates, and makes the Vessel full: . . . . . .   893 Panegyr Dean   192
VESSELS
   With a Dozen large Vessels my Vault shall be stor'd,   . 867 Grand Question   13
VEST
   But, he by Mars, in Scarlet Vest.   . . . .   586 Strephon Chloe   60
   And Solomon in Royal Vest;   . . . .   592 Strephon Chloe   288
   Each with a Gold and Purple Vest;   . . . .   923 Riddle 7   72
VESTURE
   With haughty spouse in vesture fine, ... 677 Parson's Case   33
VEX
   Or how the Dean delights to vex   . . . .   281 Journal   77
   Or vex the Ladyes, when they knew   . . . .   311 To Ford   11
   Would vex one more a thousand Times.   . . . .   505 Doctor Delaney   166
   But, what the gentlest Heart would vex, ...   687 Cadenus Vaness   25
   How to vex and how to please;   . . . .   906 Daphne   2
   Makes her sole delight to vex.   . . . .   906 Daphne   4
   To vex me more, he took a Freak, ...   915 Riddle 1   15
   The Soul of Man with Spleen you vex;   . . . . 919 Riddle 5   17
   Yet still you are out (tho' to vex you I'm loth),   . . 976 Dean to Sherid   17
   For that, dear Tom, ne'er fret and vex, ...   983 Sher, A Goose   17
VEX'D
   Said, how a late report your friends had vex'd,   . . . 47 To Congreve   143
   The first vex'd him much, but the other vex'd most. . . 430 Dicky Dolly   9
   The first vex'd him much, but the other vex'd most. . . 430 Dicky Dolly   9
VEXATIONS
   Suppose him gone through all Vexations, ...   174 Horace 1, 7   101
   Whate'er Vexations Love attend, ...   702 Cadenus Vaness   506
VEXATIOUS
   To humble that vexatious Dean.   . . . .   348 Whitshed Motto   20
   "In dreading this vexatious Round?   . . . .   380 Apology Lady C   162
VEXES
   Yet one thing vexes me, I own, ... 1003 Dan J's Reply   16
VEXING
   To please themselves by vexing You   . . . .   217 To Mr. Delany   78
VEXT
   Vext at their Follies, murmur'd in his Stream;   . . . 22 Ode Athenian   194
   Poor <Swift>, with all his Losses vext, ...   174 Horace 1, 7   113
   And yet, grow mortify'd and vext   . . . .   501 Doctor Delaney   39
   The <Dean> he was vext that his Whores were so willing, 519 Dean Hang Rape   55
   And, vext to see Affairs miscarry, ...   903 Death Daphne   9
   When I'm vext, can't keep me under;   . . . .   933 Riddle 20   D   24
VI
   Is come up, vi & armis, to break the <Queen's> Peace. . 142 New Song   4
   Then and there, Vi & Armis, with a certain Utensil,   . 264 Apollo   33
VI'LETS
   The Vi'lets ope their purple heads, ...   621 Scandal Poem 1   140
   The Vi'lets ope their Purple Heads;   . . . .   627 Scandal Poem 2   144
VIALS
   Here Gallypots and Vials plac'd, ...   526 Lady's Dres Rm   33
VICAR
   The Steeple, Knock, the Vicar, Walls.   . . . . .   127 Little House   18
   The Vicar once a Week creeps in, ...   127 Little House   19
   The Vicar and the Ring bespoke: . . . .   223 Prog of Love   23
   Thy insolent illit'rate vicar, ...   676 Parson's Case   7
   When young is often due to the Vicar.   . . . . .   940 Letter   2
VICARAGE
   A hungry Vicarage at best;   . . . .   484 Libel on D- D-   132
VICARS
   Where Town and Country Vicars flock in Tribes,   . . . 194 Author Himself   19
VICE
   Grows a misfortune, or becomes a vice;   . . . . . .   55 Temple Ill   136
   All stain'd with Infamy and Vice, ...   84 Salamander   39
   Addicted to no sort of Vice;   . . . .   171 Horace 1, 7   32
   To look on Vice triumphant round, ...   312 To Ford   41
   (Give fraudful Vice the Mask and Screen, ...   386 Manly Virtue   79
   To Wealth and Vice, in high Degree, ...   386 Manly Virtue   94
   With ev'ry Vice hath fill'd the Nation;   . . . . .   392 Young's Satire   36
   To see the Seeds of Vice arise, ...   485 Libel on D- D-   176
   "If Vice can ever be abash'd, ...   548 Life of Swift   117
   "Shou'd Vice expect to 'scape rebuke, ...   548 Life of Swift   123
   "Vice is a Vermin; Sportsman say   . . . .   548 Life of Swift   125
   "He lash'd the Vice but spar'd the Name.   . . . . .   571 Death of Swift   460
   But Gluttony was ne'er his Vice: . . . .   602 Beasts Confess   40
   I encounter Vice with Mirth.   . . . .   634 Epistle Lady   142
   And ev'ry Vice that nurses both.   . . . .   655 On Poetry   410
   With Vice polluting every Throne   . . . .   659 On Poetry   D   410
   And fit their Proselytes for Vice;   . . . .   764 Stel B-day '26   22
   For Vice in all its glitt'ring Dress: . . . . . .   765 Stel B-day '26   48

		PAGE	TITLE	LINE

VICE   (CONTINUED)

Who now in Vice and Slavery are drown'd. . . . . . . 792 St. Pat's Well 38
Directing ev'ry Vice we find . . . . 798 Traulus 1 75
Think on ev'ry Vice in both, ... 799 Traulus 2 5
Much talking is not Harry's vice, ... 878 Robbin & Harry 13
How long shall vice triumphant reign? . . . . . . 950 Upstart D 17

VICE-ROY

The Vice-Roy, whom you now attend, ... 483 Libel on D- D- 113
I hate the Vice-Roy, love the Man. . . . . . . 485 Libel on D- D- 152

VICEGERENT

What cannot our Vicegerent do, ... 270 Apollo's Edict D 5
To qualify him God's Vicegerent, ... 464 Birthday Song 134
Thou great Vicegerent of the King, ... 656 On Poetry 447

VICEROY

We lately fix'd our Viceroy there: . . . . . 269 Apollo's Edict D 2
When e'er my Viceroy is address'd, ... 271 Apollo's Edict D 50
Was Viceroy of a neighbouring Hill: . . . . . 513 Answer Fable 44
And in the Chambers of your Viceroy crawls. . . . . 792 St. Pat's Well 58
From Hell a <Viceroy> Dev'l ascends, ... 486 Libel on D- D- 186

VICES

The most ungen'rous vices of the town; . . . . . . 44 To Congreve 10
And deal in Vices of the graver Sort, ... 194 Author Himself 21
Griev'd at the Vices of the Age, ... 383 Manly Virtue 2
Are you on Vices most severe . . . . 449 Modern Lady 152
"To cure the Vices of Mankind: . . . . 565 Death of Swift 314
All the Vices of a Court, ... 634 Epistle Lady 147
Than to shew their Vices odious: . . . . 637 Epistle Lady 226
His Virtues fade, his Vices bloom; . . . . 646 On Poetry 200
For Vices all have diff'rent Ends, ... 733 Verses Vanessa 11
A Traytor to the Vices regnant. . . . . . . 798 Traulus 1 94
Let me now the Vices trace, ... 800 Traulus 2 23
Female Vices most, or Male, ... 801 Traulus 2 54
Two Vices of a diff'rent Kind: . . . . 918 Riddle 4 24

VICIOUS

The mettled and the vicious Steed . . . . 217 To Mr. Delany 61
Of Pandars to a vicious Mind, ... 480 Libel on D- D- 24
By vicious Fancy coupled fast, ... 529 Lady's Dres Rm 127
With such a stupid vicious Age,) . . . . 723 To Stella 8

VICTIM

Leaves him a Victim to the vengeful Scot; . . . . . 195 Author Himself 58
A Victim to the last Essays . . . . 295 Horrid Plot 153
Points out where each new Victim falls; . . . . . . 923 Riddle 7 58

VICTIMS

Kings would indeed be Victims of the State; . . . . 6 Ode to King 6

VICTOR

The Victor, when your Steps he trac'd, ... 326 Pethox 91

VICTOR'S

Add to the Victor's Happiness? . . . . 6 Ode to King 11

VICTORIOUS

Whilst at Your Victorious Light . . . . 9 Ode to King 111
Like the victorious wren perch'd on the eagle's wing; . 44 To Congreve 38
Because he never was victorious, ... 468 Birthday Song 252
To Dan the victorious, ... 1004 Sheridan's Sub 2
To you victorious and brave, ... 1005 Sheridan's Sub 5

VICTORS

Confess the Soil from whence the Victors came. . . . 791 St. Pat's Well 16
From Victors o'er the Memphian King; . . . . . . 925 Riddle 8 30

VICTORY

Thus has our Prince compleated every Victory, . . . 9 Ode to King 98
To climb at Victory . . . . 9 Ode to King 103
And His best Victory a Noble Death; . . . . . . 9 Ode to King 106
And brings the dear Reward of Victory and Peace. . . 16 Ode Athenian 21
(Glad of the Victory, yet frighted at the War) . . 17 Ode Athenian 33
For though with Loss or Victory awhile . . . . 29 Ode to Temple 78
Death's sting is swallow'd up in victory at last, . . 40 Ode Sancroft 201
While Victory, with Wings outspread, ... 461 Birthday Song 33
No, no Victory, Victory he ever got, ... 957 Cantata
No, no Victory, Victory he ever got, ... 957 Cantata

VICTUALS

Yet their Wine and their Victuals, those curmudgeon 263 Apollo 11
   Lubbards
She saves Half her Victuals, by feeding your Ears. . 580 Psyche 14
If Wine's bought, or Victuals drest . . . . . 931 Riddle 18 D 19
And for his Victuals let a Ragman dish'em. . . . 1033 Ans to Crown 18
At Victuals foremost. . . . . 1035 Servants Maxim 4

VIDE

In Virgil (vide Dido's Case:) . . . . 690 Cadenus Vaness 111

VIE   SEE VYE

His outward Form, and Inward, vie, ... 385 Manly Virtue 59
And prostrate, supplicate pour ma vie. . . . . . 1005 Sheridan's Sub 12

VIES   SEE VYES

While each to be the loudest vies, ... 450 Modern Lady 175
But now your name with Penshurst vies, ... 877 To Dean Swift 33

VIEW

Our predecessors foot-steps, still in view; . . . . 49 To Congreve 196
When to poetic view the Muse appear'd. . . . . 51 Temple Ill 16
Still at Whitehall it stands in view, ... 87 Hist V's House 31
Then softly turn'd aside to view, ... 112 Bauc & Phil 2 39
There stuck aloft, in Publick View, ... 114 Bauc & Phil 2 87
Ten thousand footsteps, full in view, ... 177 To Lord Harley 17
For all Buffoons have most in View . . . . . . 217 To Mr. Delany 77

VIEW	(CONTINUED)	PAGE	TITLE	LINE
But, view him in another Scene,		231	Prog of Poetry	31
And leave his emty Chests in View.		240	Run Bankers	40
I have in view a Lord's Estate,		251	Bubble	18
And seems a Guinnea to your View:		255	Bubble	116
And view it through a Jobber's Bill,		255	Bubble	122
And the Titles I view, when I shine on the Walls:		263	Apollo	24
And, when we view it thus, with Thief at End on't,		285	Elegy Boat	35
Or take it in a diff'rent View;		392	Young's Satire	31
We ne'er can have her full in view.		401	Window Inns 5	D 12
Fresh Objects fairer to his View;		412	Desire Possess	30
Must we suppose she has in view,		433	Answer Paulus	33
Have once the public good in view:		487	Irish-Club	18
To view what in the Chest was hid.		528	Lady's Dres Rm	90
My Fancy drags this Monster to my View,		532	To Mr. Gay	37
And strive to pass, in publick view,		546	Life of Swift	35
But would not have him stop my View;		554	Death of Swift	134
"As with a moral View design'd		565	Death of Swift	313
But, view them litter'd on the Floor,		592	Strephon Chloe	289
Were all the Schemes he had in View;		605	Beasts Confess	147
As learned Commentators view		643	On Poetry	103
In vain you make ye strictest View		659	On Poetry	D 410
She plac'd it in the strongest View.		701	Cadenus Vaness	455
View him on the Mother's Side,		799	Traulus 2	7
Thus you have the case in view,		907	Daphne	49
To place thee in another View,		919	Riddle 5	13
VIEW'D				
The Nymph, with indignation, view'd		178	To Lord Harley	47
For, as he view'd his Person round,		586	Strephon Chloe	75
Thro candle-light she view'd the Wine		746	Stel Distress	21
Through Candle-Light she view'd the Wine,		750	Stel Wood-Park	19
Who could forbear, that view'd each guilty Face,		806	Judas	23
VIEWING				
Can you take Delight in viewing		862	To Janus	13
VIEWS				
And by short views mistook for all their own;		45	To Congreve	60
How far their Hearts from private Views,		501	Doctor Delaney	60
Nor ever acts on private Views,		607	Beasts Confess	185
And Criticks have no partial Views,		644	On Poetry	131
Salutes the <Dean> in diff'rent Views;		888	Panegyr Dean	38
VIG'ROUS				
The vig'rous Youth, and aged Sire:		922	Riddle 7	26
VIGILANCE				
His Vigilance might some displease;		602	Beasts Confess	45
VIGOR				
Recover Strength and Vigor there,		258	Bubble	186
Assumes an artificiall Vigor;		290	Prog Marriage	22
Of Vigor in declining Days.		295	Horrid Plot	154
Smart Jemmy Moor with Vigor drops,		654	On Poetry	399
VIGOROUS				
But give the vigorous fancy room.		49	To Congreve	206
VIGOUR				
New Vigour to the Leg remaining.		366	Answer Delaney	20
His meagre Corps, though full of Vigour,		398	Earl of P-b-w	26
"No Sheers to check her sprouting Vigour,		476	Epist on Epist	57
With Vigour and Delight perform'd.		726	To Stella	106
VILE				
And as a Mortal to his Vile Disease,		10	Ode to King	145
In a vile manger laid,		40	Ode Sancroft	174
By vile pretenders, who a stock maintain		45	To Congreve	57
Who in his idiom vile, with Gray's-inn grace,		47	To Congreve	137
"Like Pole-Cat vile be treated?		154	Widow and Cat	D 22
So vile Thy Breach of Trust is;		154	Widow and Cat	D 42
In English vile, and viler French,		434	Answer Paulus	78
Or vile Submissions, when in Place;		494	Panegyr Swift	34
Who, had she known his vile Behaviour,		514	Answer Fable	77
O never may such vile Machine		528	Lady's Dres Rm	95
"Not so, the vile Fanatick Crew;		549	Life of Swift	156
"As vile and profligate a Villain,		569	Death of Swift	419
Dare you, vile Murderer of Flaccus,		671	Epig Carthy 22	D 1
Emblems of Insects vile, who spread their Spawn		792	St. Pat's Well	55
That Traitor, Assassin, Informer vile.		826	Noisy Tom	8
Footman, Traytor, vile Seducer,		831	Legion Club	69
In ev'ry vile Pamphlet you'll read the same Fancies,		968	Letter Sherid	21
VILER				
Nor could the nations kneel to viler shapes,		46	To Congreve	105
In English vile, and viler French,		434	Answer Paulus	78
VILEST				
For, should the vilest scribbler to the pit,		48	To Congreve	165
And Latin, vilest of the three:		434	Answer Paulus	79
The vilest Ruffian may commit a rape,		506	To a Friend	3
The vilest Doggrel Grubstreet sends,		644	On Poetry	139
The vilest Verse thrives best at Court.		646	On Poetry	186
To vilest Slaves I owe my Birth.		916	Riddle 2	2
VILLA				
And grace my villa with his strains;		876	To Dean Swift	5
VILLAES				
Prefer our Villaes where the Thames is,		411	Dial Rich Marb	87
VILLAGE				
That Heaven's high Son was in a village born;		39	Ode Sancroft	172

VILLAGE   (CONTINUED)   PAGE   TITLE   LINE

Came to a Village hard by Rixham . . . .   90 Bauc & Phil 1   9
Having thro all the Village pass't, ...   91 Bauc & Phil 1   49
They and their Village shall be droun'd, ...   92 Bauc & Phil 1   88
To a small Village down in Kent; . . . .   111 Bauc & Phil 2   10
Having thro' all the Village pass'd, ...   111 Bauc & Phil 2   17
It frightens all the Village Boys. . . . .   513 Answer Fable   26
Thorough Town and thorough Village, ...   574 Helter Skelter   39
Hither came every Village Maid . . . .   848 Old Thorn   5
The girls of the village . . . .   857 Lady's Lament   195
The naughty boys about the village . . . .   902 Dean's Reasons   107
VILLAIN
And, though the Villain 'scape a while, he feels . .   210 Earl of Oxford   21
A Villain, who his Friend betrays, ...   298 Horrid Plot   7
Quoth the Dog, I should then be more Villain than
you're,   396 Dog and Thief   3
Pays all the Cost, and gives the Villain Thanks. . .   535 To Mr. Gay   110
"As vile and profligate a Villain, ...   569 Death of Swift   419
The cursed Villain! now I see . . . .   783 Tim and Fables   29
Another villain yet remains-- . . . .   950 Upstart   D   22
VILLAIN'S
On a far less Villain's Nose. . . . .   830 Legion Club   20
VILLAINS
To villains of his own profession. . . . .   436 Answer Paulus   128
Damn'd Villains, Corrupted in every Station, . . .   576 Place Damn'd   11
Scourge the Villains with a Vengeance. . . . . .   635 Epistle Lady   176
VINDICATE
To vindicate his late Offence: . . . .   379 Apology Lady C   130
To vindicate his Mother's Wrongs. . . . .   701 Cadenus Vaness   467
VINDICATION
"Next, here's Sir Robert's Vindication, ...   563 Death of Swift   277
VINE
I forward the Grass, and ripen the Vine: . . . .   263 Apollo   8
VINTNER
From the Vintner and the Taylor, ...   574 Helter Skelter   35
VIOLENT
And wafted with its Foe by violent Gust, ...   137 City Shower   25
VIOLENTLY
Runs violently o'er his usual Course.) . . . . .   31 Ode to Temple   149
VIPER
(In pieces cut, the Viper still did reunite) . . .   30 Ode to Temple   132
VIRAGO
He saw Virago Nell belabor . . . .   220 A Quiet Life   21
VIRGE
The Silver Virge, with decent Pride, ...   174 Horace 1, 7   99
VIRGIL
Virgil and Epicurus will not do, ...   28 Ode to Temple   65
To find a Verse in Virgil Spurious; . . . . . .   483 Libel on D- D-   100
From Virgil, Martial, Ovid, Lucan; . . . . . .   657 On Poetry   482
In Virgil (vide Dido's Case:) . . . .   690 Cadenus Vaness   111
Homer, Plutarch, Virgil, Flaccus, ...   838 Legion Club   211
VIRGIL'S
Immortal made in Virgil's Lines, ...   658 On Poetry   D 410
VIRGIN
And in some untouch'd Virgin Strain . . . . . .   30 Ode to Temple   136
Like that prophetic tempest in the virgin reign, . .   40 Ode Sancroft   196
The Muse, like some bright country virgin, shows, . .   50 To Congreve   215
Hear my Request the Virgin said . . . .   120 Apollo Outwit   29
A virgin of superior mind, ...   177 To Lord Harley   34
Tho', like a virgin of fifteen, ...   178 To Lord Harley   69
(How would her Virgin Soul bemoan . . . . . .   596 Cassinus Peter   103
To see a Mortal Virgin deck'd . . . .   695 Cadenus Vaness   271
To see the Virgin mind her Book, ...   704 Cadenus Vaness   551
The brightest Virgin of the Green, ...   721 Stel B-Day '18   6
A Virgin in thy Bosom bred; . . . .   924 Riddle 8   6
And raise a Virgin to the Sky, ...   929 Riddle 15   D   7
VIRGIN-MUSE
Forgive a young and (almost) Virgin-muse, ...   18 Ode Athenian   62
VIRGINS
He left them Virgins as he found 'em. . . . . .   598 Problem Solved   26
To three fair virgins I did tie men . . . . . .   675 Curate's Compl   5
What dangerous Paths young Virgins tread; . . . .   696 Cadenus Vaness   311
And here six Virgins in a Tomb, ...   923 Riddle 7   67
VIRGO'S
For want of Room by Virgo's Side, ...   100 Elegy Patrige   85
VIRTOUS
Make you less virtous, learn'd, or wise. . . . .   414 Censure   28
VIRTUE
To Valour and to Virtue the same Word: . . . .   7 Ode to King   28
And solid Virtue does Your Name advance. . . . .   11 Ode to William   D   4
In this Your Virtue claims a double share, . . .   12 Ode to William   D   27
Virtue, the greatest of all Monarchies, ...   26 Ode to Temple   1
To drive all Virtue out, or look it dead! . . . .   30 Ode to Temple   123
Made up of Virtue and transparent Innocence: . . .   30 Ode to Temple   128
If all that our weak knowledge titles virtue, be . .   36 Ode Sancroft   45
From thee whatever virtue takes its rise, ...   55 Temple Ill   135
But not the Virtue Tast nor Juyce. . . . . . .   81 Vanbrug House   88
Which yet their former Virtue keep, ...   94 Bauc & Phil 1   151
You'll find has so much Virtue in't, ...   101 Elegy Patrige   112
But not the Virtue, Tast or Juice. . . . . . .   109 V's House   130

VIRTUE   (CONTINUED)   PAGE   TITLE   LINE
By the meer Virtue of his Fist: . . . .   132 Magician's Rod   12
And now the Virtue of his Hands, ...   157 Fable of Midas   33
That Virtue in the Fingers ends: . . . .   157 Fable of Midas   44
With wit and virtue to discover, ...   177 To Lord Harley   35
Virtue repuls't, yet knows not to repine;   . . . . . .   210 Earl of Oxford   7
Virtue, to crown her Fav'rites, loves to try . . . .   210 Earl of Oxford   11
Virtue conceal'd within our Breast   . . . .   242 Horace 4, 9   1
By Magick Virtue in the Spring, ...   255 Bubble   115
The genial Virtue with him brought, ...   293 Prog Marriage   113
She left him Virtue for a Guard.   . . . .   306 Storm   78
And Virtue trampled on the Ground: . . . .   312 To Ford   42
"With Virtue, Prudence, Wit besides;   . . . .   322 First of April   48
"O Jove, if Virtue be so fair   . . . . . .   383 Manly Virtue   4
Jove grants the Prayer, gives Virtue Birth, ...   384 Manly Virtue   15
Virtue was of this Sex design'd, ...   384 Manly Virtue   23
Where Virtue is in least Repute, ...   385 Manly Virtue   65
Yet Manly Virtue even here   . . . .   385 Manly Virtue   69
True Virtue has a Right to rise.)   . . . . . .   386 Manly Virtue   92
Now rais'd on high, see, Virtue shews . . . . .   386 Manly Virtue   97
And Manly Virtue, like the Sun, ...   387 Manly Virtue   117
If Virtue dares not venture down, ...   392 Young's Satire   37
Nor yields up virtue, at discretion, ...   436 Answer Paulus   127
"To raise up Virtue when she droops, ...   462 Birthday Song   74
To Virtue form'd a Princely Youth, ...   482 Libel on D- D-   56
A Soul with ev'ry Virtue fraught   . . . . . .   482 Libel on D- D-   75
When he has Virtue to retire, ...   484 Libel on D- D-   117
Virtue or innocence abuse;   . . . . . .   488 Irish-Club   26
That force free virtue shou'd enthrall?   . . . . .   490 Dialogue   44
By that rebuff your Virtue gain'd.   . . . . . .   496 Panegyr Swift   89
Then keep your Virtue still unmixt, ...   503 Doctor Delaney   107
But in the Praise of Virtue is dumb: . . . . . .   515 Answer Fable   94
Did Female Virtue e'er so high ascend, ...   531 To Mr. Gay   5
of Virtue & worth by profession a giber   . . . . .   540 Charac Walpole   11
"But succour'd Virtue in Distress, ...   566 Death of Swift   335
"How could unguarded Virtue stand?   . . . . . .   568 Death of Swift   390
Inherits ev'ry Virtue round, ...   646 On Poetry   192
Now Learning, Valour, Virtue, Sense, ...   656 On Poetry   459
And, O what virtue you express   . . . . . .   676 Parson's Case   17
Are won by Virtue, Wit, and Parts;   . . . . .   688 Cadenus Vaness   62
I'll search where ev'ry Virtue dwells, ...   691 Cadenus Vaness   148
That spurious Virtue in a Maid, ...   691 Cadenus Vaness   169
A Virtue but at second-hand;   . . . .   692 Cadenus Vaness   170
Bare Virtue could not live on Praise, ...   693 Cadenus Vaness   213
To Virtue, in the Noblest Sense, ...   697 Cadenus Vaness   347
With Virtue, Knowledge, Taste and Wit, ...   700 Cadenus Vaness   446
That Virtue, pleas'd by being shown, ...   706 Cadenus Vaness   608
To Virtue,--Honor, Sense, and Wit.   . . . . . .   732 Verses Vanessa   8
But Virtue still to Virtue tends.   . . . . . .   733 Verses Vanessa   12
But Virtue still to Virtue tends.   . . . . . .   733 Verses Vanessa   12
Tis Virtue fails in Him or You: . . . . . .   733 Verses Vanessa   14
Except where Wit and Virtue grew   . . . . . .   733 Verses Vanessa   22
And ev'ry Virtue now supplyes   . . . . . .   735 Stel B-day '20   21
In you, each Virtue brighter shines, ...   739 Stel B-day '21   9
The Virtue lies not in the Place: . . . .   752 Stel Wood-Park   90
To raise up Stella's virtue higher;   . . . . . .   755 Stella '23   22
Honour and Virtue, Sense and Wit, ...   758 Stel B-day '24   50
That Virtue, stil'd its own Reward, ...   764 Stel B-day '26   26
And, is not Virtue in Mankind   . . . .   765 Stel B-day '26   61
That all Effects of Virtue end?   . . . . . .   765 Stel B-day '26   66
For Virtue in her daily Race, ...   765 Stel B-day '26   73
Freedom and Virtue in thy Sons I found, ...   792 St. Pat's Well   37
Virtue herself would now return too late. . . . . .   793 St. Pat's Well   86
No Merit, no Science, no Virtue is wanting   . . . .   808 Advice Parson   5
The oppression of Virtue, not wages of Sin: . . . .   816 Yahoo's   42
I, a virtue strange and rare, ...   936 Riddle 24   D   5
How long shall virtue hide her face, ...   950 Upstart   D 19
VIRTUE'S
Virtue's Terra Incognita, ...   26 Ode to Temple   12
In Virtue's best-belov'd Retreat;   . . . .   385 Manly Virtue   50
'Tis Virtue's Int'rest to be seen:)   . . . .   386 Manly Virtue   80
Or fearless enter in thro' virtue's gate, ...   506 To a Friend   11
On Virtue's Basis fix'd to last, ...   711 Cadenus Vaness   782
VIRTUES
And half Your Virtues had been lost in Shade.   . . .   11 Ode to William D 12
Shew'd her the Virtues all combin'd, ...   178 To Lord Harley   51
To You, whose Virtues I must own   . . . . . .   215 To Mr. Delany   1
To let your Virtues lye obscure, ...   242 Horace 4, 9   4
From thee our Youth all Virtues learn, ...   325 Pethox   59
Such Godlike Virtues in the King, ...   391 Young's Satire   2
Thro' all the Realm his Virtues run, ...   391 Young's Satire   25
More virtues in a Woman's Mind, ...   417 Woman's Mind   58
Your num'rous virtues foully stain'd; . . . . . .   436 Answer Paulus   142
Their Virtues never ceased to sing, ...   445 Modern Lady   11
On Virtues which they know they want. . . . . . .   464 Birthday Song   128
In such Virtues lye inherent, ...   464 Birthday Song   133
Who owe their Virtues to their Stations, ...   484 Libel on D- D-   137
His Virtues battling with his Place;   . . . . . .   484 Libel on D- D-   146
Most of his Virtues, all my Brains.   . . . . . .   494 Panegyr Swift   57
And with the Virtues pant to wear   . . . .   498 Panegyr Swift   173
The Virtues we must not let pass, ...   527 Lady's Dres Rm   59

886

VIRTUES   (CONTINUED)   PAGE   TITLE   LINE
    He found, his Virtues too severe   . . . .   603 Beasts Confess   55
    Why?--Virtues carry'd to Excess;   . . . .   603 Beasts Confess   76
    All your Virtues to my Sight.   . . . .   633 Epistle Lady   98
    His Virtues fade, his Vices bloom;   646 On Poetry   200
    Of all the Virtues you can muster: . . . . . .   647 On Poetry   222
    All Virtues lodge in royal Ermine.   . . . . . .   647 On Poetry   228
    Whose Virtues bear the strictest Test;   . . . .   655 On Poetry   412
    To sing his Virtues on ye Lyre, ...   658 On Poetry   D 410
    Her Virtues fewer Swains admir'd: 700 Cadenus Vaness   441
    His Virtues she might call her own;   . . . . . .   708 Cadenus Vaness   681
    Those num'rous Virtues which the Tribe   724 To Stella   15
    Your Virtues safely I commend, ...   730 Stella, Poems   79
    Your Virtues, all suspended, wait   . . . . . .   730 Stella, Poems   95
    And all Your Virtues left unsung: . . . . . .   739 Stel B-day '21   12
    You'd leave her Virtues half untold.   . . . .   742 Stel B-day 22   40
    Where Virtues are imputed Crimes, ...   798 Traulus 1   92
    On his virtues hold forth; 'tis the very best way;   . .   819 Archbi Cashel   9
VIRTUES'S
    Wit, as the chief of Virtues's Friends, ...   503 Doctor Delaney   99
VIRTUOSO
    Nor shall the bubbl'd virtuoso find   . . . .   50 To Congreve   211
VIRTUOSOES'
    As virtuosoes' in dissecting flies;   . . . .   46 To Congreve   94
VIRTUOUS
    And ev'ry virtuous Man his Brother: . . . .   606 Beasts Confess   180
VIRUMQUE
    Of Arma Virumque   . . . .   186 Scriblerus 4   D   5
VISAGE
    Nature's bare visage furrowed as he mows: . . . . .   55 Temple Ill   124
    Her Spots are gone, her Visage clears.   . . . . . .   226 Prog of Beauty   8
    "His ghostly Visage with an Air   . . . . . .   305 Storm   59
    To change your Visage like the Moon,   326 Pethox   82
    His Visage drops, he knits his Brow,   480 Libel on D- D-   15
    It shew'd the Visage of a Gyant.   . . . . . .   527 Lady's Dres Rm   62
    With shameless Visage, and perfidious Leer, ...   532 To Mr. Gay   34
    Observe our visage in a morning;   . . . . . .   619 Scandal Poem 1   47
    The Gypsey Visage to conceal: . . . .   786 Dick, Maggot   10
    See the Scowling Visage drop, ...   835 Legion Club   143
VISION
    An horrid Vision seiz'd my Head, ...   578 Day Judgement   3
    How could I form so wild a vision, ...   899 Dean's Reasons   15
VISIONARY
    There first the visionary sound was heard, ...   51 Temple Ill   15
    I here renounce thy visionary pow'r;   . . . .   55 Temple Ill   152
    This was a visionary Scheme, ...   705 Cadenus Vaness   584
VISIONS
    Empty Visions of the Brain.   . . . .   833 Legion Club   102
VISIT
    When some Patrician God wou'd visit the Immortal Jayl,   9 Ode to King   93
    Will went again to visit Dick   . . . .   220 A Quiet Life   19
    But visit him, and eat some Fruit;   . . . . . .   378 Apology Lady C   88
    Come down to visit mortal Men;   . . . .   587 Strephon Chloe   98
    To visit and to court them too;   . . . .   587 Strephon Chloe   99
    The Dean wou'd visit Market-hill, ...   859 Lady Acheson   1
    To visit where she sat at Cards: . . . .   904 Death Daphne   56
VISITS
    Some formal Visits, Looks, and Words, ...   204 In Sickness   13
    Each twenty visits on her Hands.   . . . . . .   451 Modern Lady   197
    Refus'd the Visits of a Queen;   . . . .   482 Libel on D- D-   74
    Visits, Plays, and Powder'd Beaux.   . . . . . .   631 Epistle Lady   42
    With visits, or to beg a place;   . . . .   677 Parson's Case   30
    From Visits to receive and pay, ...   688 Cadenus Vaness   43
    For Visits, Ombre, Balls and Plays.)   . . . . .   700 Cadenus Vaness   431
    To Visits of Archdeacon Wall.   . . . .   745 Stel Distress   20
    To visits of <Archdeacon> <Wall>   . . . . . .   750 Stel Wood-Park   40
    His guests are few, his visits rare, ...   901 Dean's Reasons   85
VISTOS
    Your Vistos, Barges, and (A Pox on   . . . . . .   476 Epist on Epist   39
VITAL
    It quite o'recame the vital Heat,)   . . . .   16 Ode Athenian   4
    "That all his vital Parts were sound.   559 Death of Swift   176
    And while this Vital Breath I blow,   776 Mullinix Tim   83
    From his Tenants vital Blood.   . . . .   800 Traulus 2   42
VITALS
    Consume my Vitals they shall know,   778 Mullinix Tim   175
    Who from thee sprung, yet on thy Vitals feed;   . .   794 St. Pat's Well   96
VITRUVIUS
    At Court, Vitruvius the second, ...   87 Hist V's House   38
VITTALS
    All Christian vittals stink of fish   . . . . . .   420 Holyhead   3
VITTELLS
    Their Vittells bad, their Lodging worse, ...   224 Prog of Love   79
VITTELS
    And if we find our Vittels fail   . . . .   92 Bauc & Phil 1   65
    He suck't his Vittels thro' a Quill;   . . . . . .   156 Fable of Midas   10
    Nor after your Vittels ly sleeping supine   . . . . .   1017 Swift Ans Sher   16
VITTLE
    I must confess your Wine and Vittle   . . . . . .   747 Stel Distress   65
    I must confess, your Wine and Vittle   . . . . . .   752 Stel Wood-Park   81

887

		PAGE	TITLE	LINE
VITTLES				
You are only to live four Years without Vittles!	. .	805	Irish Bishops	60
Besides, you found fault with our Vittles		986	Mary to Sher	25
VIZ				
As that same viz. St. <Patrick's> Dean.	. . . . .	361	Grace's Answer	6
When you're advanc'd above Dean Viz.	. . . . . .	362	Grace's Answer	43
But now observe my Counsel (viz)		779	Mullinix Tim	211
VIZARDS				
Off fly the Vizards and discover all,	. . . . . .	29	Ode to Temple	99
VOCATION				
Or, when a Whore in her Vocation,	. . . . . .	724	To Stella	29
Always firm in his Vocation, ...		836	Legion Club	171
VOGUE				
For tho' possess'd of present Vogue they've made	. .	18	Ode Athenian	83
In every Mouth the Question most in Vogue	. . . .	536	To Mr. Gay	145
And if you find the general Vogue		644	On Poetry	119
A Mastiff's teeth are justly held in vogue,	. . . .	672	Epig Carthy 25	D 1
VOICE				
Whilst Angels tune the Voice, and God inspires the Tongue.		17	Ode Athenian	56
Thrice, with a prophet's voice and prophet's pow'r,	. .	43	To Congreve	1
Yes, that beau's look, that voice, those critic ears,	.	48	To Congreve	173
In sum, a glitt'ring voice, a painted name,	. . . .	54	Temple Ill	101
By a shrill Voice at noon declares,	. . . . . .	94	Bauc & Phil 1	144
By a shrill Voice at Noon declares,	. . . . . .	113	Bauc & Phil 2	82
With Limbs robust, and Voice that stuns;	. . . . .	326	Pethox	76
The Force of thy superior Voice	. . . .	340	Arch-Bish Dub	27
The powerful Voice, the graceful Mien,	. . . . .	385	Manly Virtue	57
The rest condemn'd, with rival Voice,	. . . . .	387	Manly Virtue	133
His loudest Voice is low and weak,	. . . . . .	405	Swift to Pope	3
A Peacock chose for Flight and Voice:	. . . . .	513	Answer Fable	20
If they would but lye quiet, and stifle their Voice,	.	519	Dean Hang Rape	63
Then, for his Voice, there's none disputes	. . . .	602	Beasts Confess	35
Then soft Voice and Speech absurd,	. . . . . .	696	Cadenus Vaness	328
Her Sex, with universal Voice,	. . . . . .	702	Cadenus Vaness	508
A Blockhead with melodious Voice	. . . . . .	710	Cadenus Vaness	738
And if your Voice had not been loud,	. . . . .	742	Stel B-day 22	47
The People's Voice expands his Paper Sail;	. . .	770	Horace 1, 14	28
But when they hear his rusty Voice,	. . . . . .	776	Mullinix Tim	95
Charm'd by thy voice the 'Prentice drops	. . . .	779	Mullinix Tim	203
By your knife to be mangled than rack'd with your voice.		818	Epigr Kite	4
All of diff'rent Voice and Features,	. . . . .	930	Riddle 17	D 2
And I join my helping Voice;	. . . . . .	933	Riddle 20	D 16
That the lowest Voice I fear;	. . . . . .	933	Riddle 20	D 26
I move my Lips, but want a Voice;	. . . . .	936	Riddle 23	D 25
The dullest Beast and kind Voice of a Cat,	. . .	940	Letter	12
VOICES				
Now Voices over Voices rise;	. . . .	450	Modern Lady	174
Now Voices over Voices rise;	. . . .	450	Modern Lady	174
Ye Hawkers all, your Voices lift;	. . . .	887	Panegyr Dean	33
Many Voices joining round me;		933	Riddle 20	D 6
VOID				
He left a void Space,	. . . .	76	Lady B- B-	6
Our Ministers are void of Taste,	. . . . . .	497	Panegyr Swift	145
Strephon, who found the Room was void,	. . . .	526	Lady's Dres Rm	5
The Bride must either void or burst.		589	Strephon Chloe	166
VOITURE				
Voiture in various Lights displays	. . . . . .	216	To Mr. Delany	33
Nay, Voiture is as like Tom Lee,	. . . . . .	217	To Mr. Delany	63
VOITURE'S				
For Prose, I recommend Voiture's,	. . . . . .	219	To Mr. Delany	105
VOLATILE				
This volatile mercury, ...		49	To Congreve	209
VOLE				
"I might by this have won a Vole."	. . . . . .	451	Modern Lady	203
"(Ladies I'll venture for the Vole.)	. . . . .	562	Death of Swift	230
VOLUME				
I threw the Volume in the Fire:	. . . .	470	Burning Poem	12
It pierc'd the feeble Volume thro',	. . . . . .	703	Cadenus Vaness	518
If one short Volume cou'd comprise	. . . . . .	708	Cadenus Vaness	696
Tim set the Volume on a Table, ...		782	Tim and Fables	5
VOLUME'S				
To raise the Volume's Price, a Shilling.)		648	On Poetry	254
VOLUMES				
Could read all Volumes up to Folio's,	. . . . .	513	Answer Fable	41
More to my Praise than all my Volumes;	. . . .	611	By Dr. Swift	10
The Room with Volumes litter'd round	. . . . .	698	Cadenus Vaness	371
VOLUPTUOUS				
Voluptuous Ease, the Child of Wealth,	. . . . .	895	Panegyr Dean	279
VOMIT				
He'll soon return to his own Vomit.		299	Horrid Plot	36
VORTEX				
Rapt in the Vortex of the Brittish Star;	. . . .	10	Ode to King	139
And oft in contradiction's vortex caught,	. . . .	36	Ode Sancroft	63
VOT'RIES				
But if thou be'st what thy mad vot'ries prate,	. . . .	54	Temple Ill	103
Where numberless thy Vot'ries crowd:		324	Pethox	22
And here thy daily Vot'ries plac't		894	Panegyr Dean	239
VOTARIES				
Nor let my Votaries show their Skill	. . . . .	271	Apollo's Edict	D 46
Thy Votaries, for Want of Sense?		696	Cadenus Vaness	297

	PAGE	TITLE	LINE
VOTARIES (CONTINUED)			
And leave her votaries in disgrace?	950	Upstart	D 20
VOTE			
And sooner than Vote for a Peace I'll be <damnd>. . .	143	New Song	20
And in Her own hearing I boldly did Vote, ...	144	New Song	40
And I'll Vote against Peace, with Spain, or without:	144	New Song	46
He should have had my hearty Vote, ...	349	Upright Judge 2	3
Let me have but your Vote to serve for the Town, . . .	396	Dog and Thief	11
I'll vote for my Landlord to whom I pay Rent, . . .	396	Dog and Thief	15
Who d vote a Rogue into the Parliament-house, . . .	396	Dog and Thief	19
The humble whelp gives ev'ry vote.	421	Ireld	15
They at a Pinch can bribe a Vote:	483	Libel on D- D-	96
Who, for a dinner, sell a vote;	487	Irish-Club	4
Nor for a Party give his Vote:	604	Beasts Confess	98
Contrive to bribe the Judge's Vote.	647	On Poetry	212
Instructing Members how to Vote.)	649	On Poetry	272
Did not an Earl but lately Vote	773	Mullinix Tim	13
Then vote a worthy Citizen to Jail, ...	826	Noisy Tom	19
Just to yawn, and give his Vote;	836	Legion Club	170
That I'll ne'er give my vote for Delenda Cart-ago. .	979	Dean to Tho: S	18
VOTED			
What's next to be voted with ease you may guess. . . .	816	Yahoo's	34
VOTER'S			
Can sometimes drop a Voter's Claim, ...	485	Libel on D- D-	149
VOTES			
And sell their Votes at such a Rate, ...	392	Young's Satire	43
"Who sell their Souls and Votes for Naught;	571	Death of Swift	446
In all their Speeches, Votes, Addresses.	646	On Poetry	198
Who votes for Mannors, who for Hire.	781	Mullinix Tim	262
Wipe our <Arses> with their <Votes>.	831	Legion Club	62
VOUCH			
First, of the first. To vouch your Lyes	465	Birthday Song	153
You pawn your Word for him--who'll vouch for you? . .	668	Epig Carthy 8	D 2
VOUCHSAFE			
As thus, "Vouchsafe, Oh gracious Maker!	199	Horace 2, 6	D
And wou'd my Lord vouchsafe to grant	475	Epist on Epist	7
Vouchsafe to be an azure Knight, ...	656	On Poetry	462
Now wou'd vouchsafe to set them right.	699	Cadenus Vaness	407
VOW			
The Ladys vow, and swear they'll try, ...	65	Problem	5
By Vow Oblig'd, By Passion led, ...	120	Apollo Outwit	33
For, he had made a holy Vow	603	Beasts Confess	69
A larger Sacrifice in Vain you vow;	771	Horace 1, 14	33
I vow to <God> you're too severe.	775	Mullinix Tim	70
Dermot, I vow, 'tis nothing else but Sweat. . . .	881	Pastoral Dial	24
The Trojan Heroe paid his Vow.)	896	Panegyr Dean	308
VOW'D			
Vow'd it was pretty for a Child;	86	Hist V's House	10
But vow'd his Money all was spent;	294	Prog Marriage	126
"Vow'd on the Dean his Rage to vent, ...	570	Death of Swift	423
Had sigh'd and languish'd, vow'd, and writ, ...	703	Cadenus Vaness	542
Vow'd, he no longer could support	903	Death Daphne	11
VOWELS			
Behold three beauteous Vowels stand	467	Birthday Song	229
By leaving out the needless Vowels, ...	1021	Nim-Dan-Dean 1	D 23
VOWING			
What ogling, sighing, toasting, vowing!	585	Strephon Chloe	34
VOWS			
For Vows Divine are kept by Fate.	121	Apollo Outwit	48
Now, <Madam Coningsmark> her Vengeance vows . . .	195	Author Himself	53
How oft she broke her marriage Vows	225	Prog of Love	89
And vows she scarce can fetch her Breath.	417	Woman's Mind	46
The Chaplain vows, he cannot fawn, ...	604	Beasts Confess	103
Hear me pay my dying Vows.	661	Love Song	24
And fir'd with Indignation vows, ...	694	Cadenus Vaness	253
Vows, on Vanessa's Heart to take	701	Cadenus Vaness	470
She vows to take him at his Word, ...	712	Cadenus Vaness	803
She vows she will no longer stay, ...	751	Stel Wood-Park	58
Here pay their Vows with bended Knees:	893	Panegyr Dean	208
VULCAN			
And Vulcan wheeled by his Wife, ...	100	Elegy Patrige	83
Discovers Vulcan for thy Sire, ...	323	Pethox	6
By Vulcan form'd so round and bright:	433	Answer Paulus	28
Slave like them to Vulcan too.	936	Riddle 24	D 18
'Ere Vulcan comes to make him new.	1021	Nim-Dan-Dean 1	D 8
VULGAR			
To be observ'd by vulgar eye, ...	39	Ode Sancroft	150
Beat not the dirty paths where vulgar feet have trod, .	49	To Congreve	205
Old as he was, no vulgar known Disease	234	Elegy on Demar	29
Are really but Vulgar Treats:	378	Apology Lady C	108
To fit them to his Vulgar Taste;	410	Dial Rich Marb	70
Were by the Vulgar thought Magicians;	503	Doctor Delaney	96
A Cabinet to vulgar Eyes;	528	Lady's Dres Rm	78
No Vulgar Deity above	598	Problem Solved	21
When Letters are in vulgar Shapes, ...	643	On Poetry	97
That I can vulgar Forms despise, ...	706	Cadenus Vaness	616
When vulgar Knaves would lose their Ears:	724	To Stella	32
That vulgar Talent I despise	787	Dick's Variety	5
And could not endure so vulgar a Taste, ...	868	Grand Question	42
Affected by each vulgar Dame;	887	Panegyr Dean	18
The Vulgar all consult my Look.	917	Riddle 3	8

```
                                                            PAGE    TITLE       LINE
VULTURE
     We order a Vulture, in Shape of the Spleen,     . . . .   266 Apollo           97
     The Raven, Vulture, Owl, and Kite,        . . . . . .     413 Desire Possess   55
VULTURES
     While Vultures eat his growing Liver:     . . . . . .     346 Prometheus       56
     For want of Vultures, we have Crows.      . . . . . .     347 Prometheus       76
VYE
     Stella may vye with your Mountharmar:     . . . . . .     313 To Ford          70
     And Drapier's vye with Cooper's Hill.     . . . . . .     875 Drapier's Hill   20
VYES
     Where Majesty with Sweetness vyes,        . . . . . . .   466 Birthday Song   191
W'YE
     . . . or at least not one that's witty, to joke w'ye? . . 1022 Nim-Dan-Dean 2  D  4
WADDLES
     And hardly waddles forth, to cool   . . . . . . . .       230 Prog of Poetry    5
WADED
     He waded without any shame,     . . . . . . . . . .       456 Dean Smedley     23
WADGAR
     Then my Dame Wadgar came,. . .      . . . . . . . .        70 Mrs Harris Pet   25
WAFT
     Prepare a Fleet to waft him o'r'e,      . . . . . .       466 Birthday Song   205
     Which waft a Stink round every Room.    . . . . . .       529 Lady's Dres Rm  114
     Beck'ning to waft me o'er the Ferry.    . . . . . .       596 Cassinus Peter   84
     Through Cambridge waft the direful Tale.    . . . . .     597 Cassinus Peter  110
WAFTED
     And wafted with its Foe by violent Gust,    . . . . .     137 City Shower      25
     Were wafted by a gentle Gale.   . . . . . . . . .         894 Panegyr Dean    248
WAG
     And, (like a Wag) sat down to Write,    . . . . . .       107 V's House        61
     Some Wag observes me thus perplext,     : . . . . . .     200 Horace 2, 6      31
     A Wag he was, he needs must own,   . . . . . . .          602 Beasts Confess   23
     St. George himself he plays the wag on,    . . . . .      777 Mullinix Tim    115
WAGER
     Think again of the sieve, and I'll hold you a wager,   .  976 Dean to Sherid   23
WAGES     SEE BOARD-WAGES
     And with such Scanty Wages pay     . . . . . . .           24 Ode Athenian    258
     . . .makes a great Hole in my Wages,    . . . . . . .      71 Mrs Harris Pet   40
     And Steal to mend your Wages?   . . . . . . . .           154 Widow and Cat   D 40
     But Six-pence a Letter is monstrous high Wages:     . .   288 Bank Down        48
     Who ever heard of servants paying wages?   . . . . . .    308 Billet Players   30
     The oppression of Virtue, not wages of Sin:     . . . .   816 Yahoo's          42
WAGGING
     With watry Chaps, and wagging Chin,     . . . . . . .     895 Panegyr Dean    257
WAGS
     Shrewd Fellows, and arch Wags, a Tribe     . . . . .      216 To Mr. Delany    53
WAIN
     When Mortals say she's in her Wain.     . . . . . . .     228 Prog of Beauty   88
WAINSCOAT
     That safe behind the Wainscoat lyes.    . . . . . . .     504 Doctor Delaney  138
WAINSCOT
     The smoaky Wainscot full of cracks      . . . . . . .     746 Stel Distress    37
     The smutty Wainscot full of Cracks,     . . . . . . .     751 Stel Wood-Park   55
     For, as he shakes his Wainscot Chops,   . . . . . .       786 Dick, Maggot     11
     His Tallow Face and Wainscot Paws,      . . . . . .       861 Lady Acheson     38
WAISTCOAT     SEE WAST-COAT,WASTCOAT
     His Waistcoat and Stockings, and Breeches were white,     399 Tom Clinch        5
WAIT
     And a Grim Slave to wait on his Triumphal Car.    . .       7 Ode to King      44
     Did with new, unexperienc't Glories wait,    . . . . .    21 Ode Athenian    156
     Speak, for I wait thy answer, and expect    . . . . .     53 Temple Ill       73
     To wait at Bright Ardelia's Side.       . . . . . . .    120 Apollo Outwit    40
     When on their Queen the Muses wait;     . . . . . . .    121 Apollo Outwit    46
     Admitted private, when Superiors wait:     . . . . . .   194 Author Himself   30
     In ev'ry town we wait on Mr. May'r,     . . . . . . .    308 Billet Players   35
     While We perhaps must wait a Week:       . . . . . . .   315 To Ford         104
     With Trembling must thy Leisure wait;    . . . . . . .   325 Pethox           50
     To wait so long and have nothing to ask. . . . . . . .   368 Verses Window     2
     And wou'd not fail to wait upon her.    . . . . . . .    376 Apology Lady C   26
     With rage impatient makes me wait    . . . . . . .       420 Holyhead         27
     Shou'd cool your Heels a while, and wait    . . . . .    475 Epist on Epist    5
     Saw Poets at his Levee wait.    . . . . . . . .          482 Libel on D- D-   70
     Could all we little Folks that wait,    . . . . . .      492 Panegyr Swift     1
     An humbler Prospect only wait,      . . . . . . .        499 Panegyr Swift   179
     Receives them while they wait for Bayl?     . . . . .    504 Doctor Delaney  146
     Transform'd to Imps, his Levee wait.    . . . . . . .    646 On Poetry       208
     The Goddess wou'd no longer wait;       . . . . . . .    714 Cadenus Vaness  886
     Your Virtues, all suspended, wait       . . . . . . .    730 Stella, Poems    95
     She at your sickly Couch will wait,     . . . . . . .    766 Stel B-day '26   11
     Collect Excise, or wait upon the Tide.      . . . . .    793 St. Pat's Well   78
     They submissive round him wait;     . . . . . . .        836 Legion Club     166
     His Manners would not let him wait,     . . . . . . .    859 Lady Acheson      5
     Good Morrow, good Captain,--I'll wait on you down,--  .  869 Grand Question   77
     To keep off their Eyes, as they wait at the Table;    .  871 Grand Question  136
     May serve to wait on Mrs. Leslie:       . . . . . . .    886 Rev Market-Hill 100
     I hourly wait some fatal End;       . . . . . . . .      921 Riddle 6         37
     Sloth, Dirt, and Theft around her wait.     . . . . .   1035 To Quilca        12
WAITED
     Who waited on his Eyes behind.      . . . . . . . .      513 Answer Fable     30
     I waited at Apollo's Shrine;        . . . . . . .        741 Stel B-day 22    14
     Three days for Answer I have waited,    . . . . . .     1002 Reply by Dean     1
     For your Man, I long waited.    . . . . . . . . .       1014 Swift to Sheri   18
```

		PAGE	TITLE	LINE
WAITERS				
And Tories (dress'd like Waiters) in Disguise.	. . .	165	Toland's Invit	30
The Waiters stand in Ranks; the Yeomen cry,	. . . .	194	Author Himself	35
WAITING				
Waiting for Orders at his Feet,	. . . .	7	Ode to King	40
Ly waiting for the foundred Skiffs,	. . . .	256	Bubble	155
Your Foes already waiting stand	. . . .	258	Bubble	198
Since Waiting Women like Exacting Jades,	. . . . .	275	Epilogue	15
"Quite thro' the Tribe of waiting Gentry;	. . . . .	380	Apology Lady C	154
Nine Muses always waiting round him,	. . . .	598	Problem Solved	25
When Hermes, waiting with his rod,	. . . .	762	Bec's B-Day	58
WAITS				
By Faction tir'd, with Grief he waits a while,	. . .	196	Author Himself	71
Nor unsuccessful waits for dead Mens Shoes.	. . .	364	On Dreams	30
Madam, the Goldsmith waits below,	. . . .	446	Modern Lady	56
(So Providence on Mortals waits,	. . . .	764	Stel B-day '26	41
Provocation never waits,	. . . .	800	Traulus 2	19
And waits on the Captain betimes the next Morning.	. .	869	Grand Question	70
WAK'D				
I wak'd with Delight, and not without Hope,	. . . .	338	Serious Poem	115
The modern Dame is wak'd by Noon,	. . . .	446	Modern Lady	38
He wak'd, and found it but a Dream;	. . . .	705	Cadenus Vaness	585
WAKE				
Wake from thy wanton Dreams,	. . . .	31	Ode to Temple	150
Goes round the House to wake the rest:	. . . . . .	278	Journal	10
The last loud trump must wake him now:	. . . . . .	296	Satiric Elegy	6
That oft I wake thee with a Kiss?	. . . .	924	Riddle 8	10
WAKES				
Corinna wakes. A dreadful Sight!	. . . .	583	Young Nymph	57
WAKING SEE EVER-WAKING				
Like antic shapes in dreams, from waking eyes:	. . . .	54	Temple Ill	100
WALES				
To place me with the Prince of Wales.	. . . . .	410	Dial Rich Marb	76
Was left to starve, and dye in Wales.	. . . . . .	481	Libel on D- D-	52
But on the highest mount in Wales . .	. . . . . .	733	Verses Vanessa	29
WALK SEE NEW-RIVER-WALK				
Or loves the muse to walk with conscious pride	. . . .	51	Temple Ill	11
Yet they were forc't to walk an Hour	. . . .	90	Bauc & Phil 1	12
To the Church-yard, to take a walk;	. . . .	116	Bauc & Phil 2	154
But if he will break in, and walk up Stairs,	. . . .	166	Toland's Invit	44
All this is foreign to thy Walk:	. . . .	183	Horace 2, 1	102
A Terras Walk, and half a Rood	. . . .	198	Horace 2, 6	5
By Adam lighted walk up stairs:	. . . .	280	Journal	56
In half a Walk fatigu'd to Death.	. . . .	379	Apology Lady C	128
And strangers delight to walk round 'em:	. . . . .	403	Window Inns 9	D 3
Glad, that themselves cou'd walk about.	. . . . . .	546	Life of Swift	51
Walk Hand in Hand, and Side by Side;	. . . . . .	585	Strephon Chloe	58
For since we knew you walk a-foot,	. . . .	622	Scandal Poem 1	175
And since we find, you walk a-foot	. . . .	627	Scandal Poem 2	133
Walk by my place, before my Betters,	. . . . . .	778	Mullinix Tim	156
Be careful, as you walk behind,	. . . .	780	Mullinix Tim	231
How to walk upright in our ways;	. . . .	780	Mullinix Tim	252
When you walk among your Books,	. . . .	838	Legion Club	207
Pray, Captain, be pleas'd to light, and walk in:	. . .	871	Grand Question	114
Till she heard the Dean call, Will your Ladyship walk?	.	873	Grand Question	180
When to the Vault you walk in State,	. . . . . .	889	Panegyr Dean	87
I wisely chuse to walk behind:	. . . .	917	Riddle 4	2
They rise, walk round, yet never fright.	. . . . . .	920	Riddle 6	12
Without it I rather would walk on the Ground.	. . . .	941	Letter	26
That we walk all about, like a horse in a pound,	. . .	1026	Sheri Circles	7
WALK'D				
He walk'd the Streets, and wore a Thread-bare Cloak;	.	234	Elegy on Demar	9
The Ladies walk'd till after Nine.	. . . .	696	Cadenus Vaness	327
WALK'S				
"To move this Walk's untoward Length	. . . . . .	379	Apology Lady C	134
WALKE				
Walke sans wetynge Shoes ne hosen.	. . . . . .	102	Merlin	4
WALKING				
And men seem walking on their heads;	. . . .	35	Ode Sancroft	34
A walking vapor, like thy sister fame.	. . . . . .	54	Temple Ill	102
His Rev'rence and her Highness walking:	. . . . .	410	Dial Rich Marb	60
What, Madam? No walking,	. . . .	854	Lady's Lament	111
WALKS				
Confine her Walks to Colleges and Schools,	. . . . .	27	Ode to Temple	39
Salutes the weary trav'ller as he walks;	. . . . . .	55	Temple Ill	120
He at fit Periods walks through Aries,	. . . . . .	98	Elegy Patrige	15
The tuck'd-up Sempstress walks with hasty Strides,	. .	138	City Shower	37
And sometimes walks beyond his Bounds.	. . . . . .	218	To Mr. Delany	94
He enters in, and walks up Stairs,	. . . .	292	Prog Marriage	87
The Captain walks about, and searches	. . . . . .	377	Apology Lady C	61
But winding Walks and purer Air;	. . . .	378	Apology Lady C	100
Pope walks, and courts the Muse.	. . . .	405	Swift to Pope	8
Bedraggled in my Walks so green;	. . . .	409	Dial Rich Marb	48
Walks boldly home at dead of night;	. . . . . .	435	Answer Paulus	92
Mounts, Walks, on high; and in a Hollow	. . . . .	477	Epist on Epist	79
Of zigzacks and walks;	. . . .	856	Lady's Lament	174
With two pence left, walks home in rain.	. . . . . .	878	Robbin & Harry	8
Nor rides, nor walks, nor hunts, nor fowls,	. . . .	901	Dean's Reasons	87
His rural walks he ne'er adorns;	. . . .	901	Dean's Reasons	91
WALKT				
Lookt high and low, walkt often round,	. . . . . .	109	V's House	97

```
WALKT            (CONTINUED)                          PAGE    TITLE           LINE
    In Summer had she walkt the Town,      . . . . . .   584 Strephon Chloe     21
WALL
    "Be this thy sure defence, thy brazen wall,  . . . . .    55 Temple Ill       141
    Raking up Mud to build a Wall;        . . . . . . .     87 Hist V's House     18
    The heavy Wall went clamb'ring after.    . . . . . .    92 Bauc & Phil 1      94
    Like a huge Insect up the Wall,       . . . . . . .     93 Bauc & Phil 1     106
    The Ballads pasted round the Wall,    . . . . . . .     93 Bauc & Phil 1     117
    And first the Prologue built a Wall   . . . . . . .    108 V's House          81
    The heavy Wall climb'd slowly after.     . . . . . .   112 Bauc & Phil 2      54
    Like an huge Snail along the Wall;    . . . . . . .    113 Bauc & Phil 2      86
    The Ballads pasted on the Wall,       . . . . . . .    114 Bauc & Phil 2      93
    'Tis like the Writing on the Wall.    . . . . . . .    241 Run Bankers        52
    Her Chairmen push him from the Wall:     . . . . . .   292 Prog Marriage      86
    Think this Wall low, and that Wall bevel.   . . . .   477 Epist on Epist     66
    Think this Wall low, and that Wall bevel.   . . . .   477 Epist on Epist     66
    To Visits of Archdeacon Wall.         . . . . . . .    745 Stel Distress      20
    His Beetle-brows and Eyes of Wall,    . . . . . . .    861 Lady Acheson       39
    To visits of <Archdeacon> <Wall>      . . . . . . .    750 Stel Wood-Park     40
WALLER
    For Cowley's Briefs, and Pleas of Waller,    . . . .  690 Cadenus Vaness    114
    Is it Satan? No 'tis <Waller>.        . . . . . . .    834 Legion Club       138
WALLOW
    In Gold, Perhaps, my Friend you Wallow      . . . .   372 Letter D. S-y      29
WALLOWING
    Fresh from the Mud a wallowing Sow       . . . . . .   786 Clad in Brown       5
WALLOWS
    . . . who all in Money wallows,       . . . . . . .    342 Upon His Grace     15
WALLS
    The Art of battring Walls, than building,    . . . .   88 Hist V's House     46
    The Walls in tumbling gave a Knock;      . . . . . .   127 Little House        15
    The Steeple, Knock, the Vicar, Walls.    . . . . . .  127 Little House        18
    No sooner brought within the Walls,      . . . . . .  209 Fable Bitches      45
    Tho' in thy Walls he ne'er did Farthing spend,  . .   234 Elegy on Demar     26
    And the Titles I view, when I shine on the Walls:   .  263 Apollo             24
    The walls of this Town                . . . . . . .    403 Window Inns 9   D  19
    That Walls have Tongues, and Hedges, Ears.   . . . .  408 Dial Rich Marb      8
    And haunt thy holy Walls in white and black.   . . .  792 St. Pat's Well     48
    A nauseous Brood, that fills your Senate Walls,  . .  792 St. Pat's Well     57
    And lo! the Writing on the Walls      . . . . . . .    923 Riddle 7           57
    Like Walls, more lasting without Mortar:   . . . . . 1021 Nim-Dan-Dean 1  D  22
WALMSLEY
    Or Walmsley or Whaley,                . . . . . . .    857 Lady's Lament     205
    May Walmsley give wine,               . . . . . . .    858 Lady's Lament     221
WALNUTS
    Or, like a Cat with Walnuts shod,     . . . . . . .    885 Rev Market-Hill    73
WALPOLE
    From Sommers down to Craigs and Walpole.    . . . .   191 Faggot             52
    That Robin Walpole is Mecaenas:       . . . . . . .    462 Birthday Song      60
    To Walpole you might lend a Line,     . . . . . . .    468 Birthday Song     255
    To Chatres, Walpole, or a King,       . . . . . . .    622 Scandal Poem 1    165
    <Walpole> and Ayslaby, to clear the Doubt,   . . . .  195 Author Himself     41
    Dog <Walpole> laid a Quart of Nog on't,      . . . .  299 Horrid Plot        31
    How the Helm is rul'd by <Walpole>    . . . . . . .    635 Epistle Lady      159
WALPOLE'S
    Townshends cast Page or Walpole's groom     . . . .   423 Ireld              72
    Will come; and <Hampden> shall have <Walpole's> Place.  165 Toland's Invit   34
    Flirts from his Cart the Mud in <Walpole's> Face.   .  364 On Dreams          38
    To <Walpole's> more than <Royal> Will.     . . . . .  484 Libel on D- D-    122
WAN
    My complexion wan and green,          . . . . . . .    937 Riddle 24       D  40
WAND
    The Rod was but a harmless Wand,      . . . . . . .    132 Magician's Rod      1
    As ready was the Wand of Sid          . . . . . . .    133 Magician's Rod     27
    <Cholmondeley>, when Drunk, can never lose his Wand,  .  164 Toland's Invit   25
WAND'RING
    The way which ev'ry wand'ring fool below    . . . .    39 Ode Sancroft      157
    Our wand'ring Saints in wofull State,    . . . . . .   91 Bauc & Phil 1      47
    Our wand'ring Saints in wofull State,    . . . . . .  111 Bauc & Phil 2      15
    Our set of strollers, wand'ring up and down,   . . .  307 Billet Players      1
    If my wand'ring Head be less          . . . . . . .    630 Epistle Lady       17
    She own'd the wand'ring of her Thoughts,     . . . .  705 Cadenus Vaness    602
WANDER
    Since thus I wander from my first intent,    . . . .   49 To Congreve       201
    On thy Margin Lovers wander,          . . . . . . .    661 Love Song          27
    Her hands may meddle, feet may wander,      . . . .   761 Bec's B-Day        25
WANDERING
    The crooked Paths of wandering Thames.      . . . .    31 Ode to Temple     152
WANDERS
    It wanders about,                     . . . . . . .    939 Riddle Answerd      9
WANDRED
    And as he wandred in his Park,        . . . . . . .    513 Answer Fable       45
WANDRING
    Long wandring thro the Deep, as we are told    . . .   17 Ode Athenian       46
    After a mighty Light that leads her wandring Eye;  .   18 Ode Athenian       67
    Who now the wandring Pair pursues:       . . . . . .  224 Prog of Love       74
    "Direct, and fix the wandring Mind,      . . . . . .  384 Manly Virtue       12
WANDS
    In vain: The complicated Wands        . . . . . . .    189 Faggot              7
    Appear with slender Wands at Court:      . . . . . .  189 Faggot             18
```

WANT

	PAGE	TITLE	LINE
Yet the same want of Brains produces each effect;	18	Ode Athenian	85
Would want a God Himself to help him out.	22	Ode Athenian	210
For, sure, we want some guide from Heav'n to show	39	Ode Sancroft	156
Yet want your critics no just cause to rail,	45	To Congreve	65
Whom sin and want e'er furnish'd out a wit;	48	To Congreve	166
For want of which by way of Botch,	96	On the Union	3
For want of Room by Virgo's Side,	100	Elegy Patrige	85
Attend when e'er I want their Aid,	120	Apollo Outwit	31
Out of Zeal for his Country, and want of a Place,	142	New Song	3
Were want of Pow'r, or want of Sense:	154	Widow and Cat	D 44
Were want of Pow'r, or want of Sense:	154	Widow and Cat	D 44
Want your assistance now to clear 'em.	186	Scriblerus 3	4
For want of Milk, wou'd suck her Blood.	208	Fable Bitches	22
We want our Money on the Nail;	239	Run Bankers	17
Can suffer Want, and not repine.	243	Horace 4, 9	20
For Statesmen never want Dog-tricks.	300	Horrid Plot	60
"This House don't want, nor will it hold us.	322	First of April	46
For want of Vultures, we have Crows.	347	Prometheus	76
Can scarsely speak for want of Breath,	379	Apology Lady C	127
"Only for want of outward Shape)	384	Manly Virtue	8
Call'd want of Shame, a want of Sense,	386	Manly Virtue	81
Call'd want of Shame, a want of Sense,	386	Manly Virtue	81
For want of tattling to the Queen;	410	Dial Rich Marb	58
Of those who want the Pow'r to rise.	414	Censure	12
For want of matter swears and fretts,	420	Holyhead	17
And when we starve for want of Corn,	464	Birthday Song	125
On Virtues which they know they want.	464	Birthday Song	128
And only wants to want his eyes.	466	Birthday Song	202
This one, poor, humble Boon I want,	475	Epist on Epist	8
Above the Reach of Want is plac't:	483	Libel on D- D-	84
Would much compensate all we want.	493	Panegyr Swift	8
The Rogues must dye for Want and Spight,	502	Doctor Delaney	72
Must dye for Want of Food and Rayment,	502	Doctor Delaney	73
You want a Hand to clear a filthy Sink;	535	To Mr. Gay	127
Some shew they never want explaining,	592	Strephon Chloe	275
His Enemies, for want of Charity,	606	Beasts Confess	159
By want of Skill, he always lost:	607	Beasts Confess	190
Court, City, Country want you not;	641	On Poetry	47
Place Elephants for want of Towns.	646	On Poetry	180
Our Poets (you can never want 'em,	649	On Poetry	279
Why should they want the Privilege of Men,	662	Upon Ladies	3
Your Scholars want the whip,--I shan't demur;--	671	Epig Carthy 23	D 1
But then, I'm sure, friend Charles, you want the spur.	671	Epig Carthy 23	D 2
Thy want of all-consoling liquor,	676	Parson's Case	8
It whirls about for Want of Force,	688	Cadenus Vaness	54
Thy Votaries, for Want of Sense?	696	Cadenus Vaness	297
His Want of Passion will redeem,	711	Cadenus Vaness	786
And shou'd Want or Desert stand in need of his Aid,	717	Answer Rebus	27
And stays at home for want of Shoes:	728	Stella, Poems	28
Die the next Year for want of Root:	730	Stella, Poems	68
Yet, merry Folks who want by chance	756	Stel B-day '24	7
To fill a Place, for want of better:	756	Stel B-day '24	10
Expos'd to Want, and Wind, and Weather,	759	Receipt Youth	9
The famish't Cow her Want supplies;	759	Receipt Youth	14
Might want such noisy Fools as you;	774	Mullinix Tim	40
We scorn, for want of talk, to jabber	781	Mullinix Tim	259
If they fail 'tis Want of Parts.	837	Legion Club	188
How I want thee, humorous Hogart?	839	Legion Club	219
"You'll never want Parsons as long as you live;	872	Grand Question	142
I move my Lips, but want a Voice;	936	Riddle 23	D 25
For want of your Converse,	1014	Swift to Sheri	35
The Goddess Want in Triumph reigns;	1035	To Quilca	10
A great want of Shoes;	1036	Plague Country	2

WANTED

	PAGE	TITLE	LINE
He said, but that it wanted Room,	128	Little House	45
His Wife and Children wanted Bread,	352	Wood Ironmongr	7
Wou'd be a Rake, but wanted Sense.	455	Dean Smedley	6
Was easy, though they wanted Shoes;	481	Libel on D- D-	40
"No Nation wanted it so much:	572	Death of Swift	482
But Ireland's Friends ne'er wanted Foes.	798	Traulus 1	88
When wanted by his Country most;	798	Traulus 1	90

WANTING

	PAGE	TITLE	LINE
Yet, wanting skill and pow'r to chuse,	178	To Lord Harley	57
Who, wanting both, have us'd their Toes.	367	Answer Delaney	52
Your Assets fail, and Cash is wanting	477	Epist on Epist	63
No Merit, no Science, no Virtue is wanting	808	Advice Parson	5

WANTON

	PAGE	TITLE	LINE
And Courts the wanton Echoes as they fly.	17	Ode Athenian	59
Wake from thy wanton Dreams,	31	Ode to Temple	150
Than swarms of gnats, that wanton in a ray	46	To Congreve	81

WANTS

	PAGE	TITLE	LINE
Which hardly wants another puff,	9	Ode to King	109
Why yonder Steeple wants a Spire,	126	Little House	2
Is but a Still which wants a Spout.	128	Little House	42
Hath she no other wants beside?	292	Prog Marriage	73
And only wants to want his eyes.	466	Birthday Song	202
What Income can your Wants supply?	478	Epist on Epist	96
Nor wants a nice discerning Spirit,	484	Libel on D- D-	147
The Master's pressing Wants must be supply'd;	533	To Mr. Gay	70
The Time when Wants of Nature press;	588	Strephon Chloe	140

WANTS   (CONTINUED)   PAGE   TITLE   LINE
    As who should say--she wants it here;   . . . .   698 Cadenus Vaness   361
    I find, says he, she wants a Doctor, ...   702 Cadenus Vaness   498
    Or wants Capacity to reach   . . . .   712 Cadenus Vaness   810
    She wants assistance more than I;   . . . .   754 Stella '23   16
    No Lady who wants them   . . . .   854 Lady's Lament   105
    Now tell me a Thing that wants Interpretation,   . . . 973 S-'s Ans Sh-d   11
WAPPING
    Bavius in Wapping gains Renown, ... 650 On Poetry   301
WAR
    Made him his Footstool in the War, ...   7 Ode to King   43
    With War, and Pestilence, and Dearth, ...   10 Ode to King   134
    So after th' Inundation of a War   . . . .   16 Ode Athenian   11
    When War her cloudy aspect just withdrew, ...   16 Ode Athenian   23
    (Glad of the Victory, yet frighted at the War)   . . . 17 Ode Athenian   33
    The War methinks has made   . . . .   19 Ode Athenian   95
    To shew it cost its Price in War, ...   28 Ode to Temple   75
    War! that mad Game, the World so loves to play,   . .   28 Ode to Temple   76
    It melts the Sword of War, yet keeps it in the Sheath.   29 Ode to Temple   91
    So when the War has rais'd a Storm   . . . .   84 Salamander   37
    There shall be Peace, pardie, and War no more.   . . . 147 Windsor Proph   12
    And the loud Laugh proclaims the War;   . . . . . .   218 To Mr. Delany   80
    In Senates bold, and fierce in War, ...   398 Earl of P-b-w   32
    Lives in a State of War by Nature.   . . . .   651 On Poetry   320
    And when the War is past you come   . . . .   775 Mullinix Tim   49
    A middle-state 'twixt peace and war;   . . . .   876 To Dean Swift   24
    Be peace and war, and both, and neither.   . . . . . . 876 To Dean Swift   26
WAR'S
    Whether from War's stern God you claim   . . . . 323 Pethox   11
    Then as to War's Alarms I pray   . . . .   372 Letter D. S-y   38
WARBLED
    (It must be read before 'tis warbled   . . . .   463 Birthday Song   87
WARBLERS
    Like the Warblers of the Spring.   . . . .   933 Riddle 20   D   12
WARBLING
    How, with a weakly warbling tongue, ...   876 To Dean Swift   13
WARBURTON
    Warburton took it in his Noddle, ...   127 Little House   35
WARD   SEE GOSPEL-WARD
    "And gave them Arms to ward the Blow.   . . . .   569 Death of Swift   410
    Rules, like an Alderman his Ward.   . . . .   649 On Poetry   286
WARDED
    Cadenus warded off the Blows: . . . .   701 Cadenus Vaness   479
WARE
    A Lady's Face, and China ware.   . . . .   227 Prog of Beauty   64
    Expos'd with all their Magick Ware.   . . . .   240 Run Bankers   36
    I'll make it appear that they're all stol'n Ware: . 265 Apollo   64
    First get a licence, then produce our ware: . . . . 308 Billet Players   36
    While not a Soul demands your Ware?   . . . .   641 On Poetry   44
    When from the homeliest Earthen Ware   . . . .   896 Panegyr Dean   295
WARES
    Come buy my fine Wares, ... 951 Apples   1
WARLIKE
    Tho fond of warlike Lyes as most men;   . . . .   462 Birthday Song   54
WARM   SEE LUKE-WARM
    And too warm summers bring: . . . .   37 Ode Sancroft   100
    At the warm zeal that breeds this golden calf?   . . . 46 To Congreve   108
    That I went to warm my self in Lady Betty's Chamber,.   69 Mrs Harris Pet   1

    So Mary got me to Bed, and cover'd me up warm,   . . . 70 Mrs Harris Pet   18
    In Velvet Cap his Head lies warm;   . . . .   410 Dial Rich Marb   65
    And but neglects to warm her Hair-Lace, ...   417 Woman's Mind   44
    Yet would rather be hang'd than he'd leave a warm Place. 580 Psyche   6
    And makes it warm for Dearest Life.   . . . .   590 Strephon Chloe   208
    To chat a while, and warm his Nose: . . . .   594 Cassinus Peter   8
    Entring warm your frigid Brain   . . . .   638 Epistle Lady   268
    I Must confess,that I was somewhat warm, ...   670 Epig Carthy 20 D   18
    Into contradiction warm her, ...   907 Daphne   33
    Nor warm the fair for whom I burn;   . . . .   937 Riddle 24   D   52
WARM'D
    What Stella by her Friendship warm'd, ...   726 To Stella   107
WARMER
    Those who in warmer Climes complain   . . . .   731 Stella, Poems   109
    And must against the warmer Days   . . . .   759 Receipt Youth   25
    They make the Blood warmer, ...   952 Onyons   4
WARMS
    Which gently warms, but cannot burn;   . . . .   711 Cadenus Vaness   784
    As nat'ral Life the Body warms, ...   724 To Stella   11
WARN
    Directors; for tis you I warn, ...   258 Bubble   189
    That careless Wench! no Creature warn her   . . . . . 528 Lady's Dres Rm   71
    But let me warn thee to believe   . . . .   735 Stel B-day '20   45
    With Omens oft I strove to warn thy Swains, ... 792 St. Pat's Well   43
    To rouse and warn the Nymph within.   . . . .   849 Old Thorn   36
WARN'D
    Ovid had warn'd her to beware, ...   120 Apollo Outwit   21
    Warn'd by the Bell, all Flocks come trembling,   . . . 279 Journal   28
WARNING
    Warning the Cook-maid not to burn   . . . .   94 Bauc & Phil 1   145
    Warning the Cook-maid, not to burn   . . . .   113 Bauc & Phil 2   83
    Too wise to take Council, too proud to take Warning,   . 327 Epigram 1   7

WARNING   (CONTINUED)   PAGE   TITLE   LINE
   Of foul and fair we give you warning; . . . .   619 Scandal Poem 1   48
   Of Foul or Fair we give you warning; . . . . . .   625 Scandal Poem 2   44
   Of this, to be sure, Sir Arthur has Warning,   . . .   869 Grand Question   69
WARP
   To warp the Sense of all Mankind: . . . .   475 Epist on Epist   22
WARRANT
   "To get my Warrant quickly signed: . . . .   201 Horace 2, 6   56
   Now, here's a warrant; Gallants please to mark, . . . 308 Billet Players   19
   "I'll warrant she's some flaunting Dame, ...   321 First of April   25
   For the Captain, I warrant, will keep him in Awe; . . 868 Grand Question   34
WARRIOR
   And could that Mighty Warrior fall? . . . .   296 Satiric Elegy   3
WARS
   By fierce Encounters made in Wars; . . . .   324 Pethox   14
   To sing of Wars choose peaceful times. . . . . . .   462 Birthday Song   48
WARWICK
   To take a House in Warwick Lane: . . . .   904 Death Daphne   46
WAS   535   OMITTED WORD
WASH
   In striving to wash off th' imaginary paint: . . . .   42 Ode Sancroft   250
   Here in the Deep to wash their Hands, ...   255 Bubble   110
   To wash her self our Well in . . . .   441 Ballyspellin   39
   To wash thy injur'd Off'rings out. . . . .   896 Panegyr Dean   318
WASHES
   Some fill'd with Washes, some with Paste, ...   526 Lady's Dres Rm   34
   Her Washes, Slops, and every Clout, ...   530 Lady's Dres Rm   139
WASHT
   They washt away the Chymick Power. . . . . . .   158 Fable of Midas   72
   Were duly washt to keep 'em sweet; . . . .   586 Strephon Chloe   78
WASP
   Teaz'd by a Buzzing Wasp, Below, ...   458 Paddy's Charac   30
WASPS
   We join like Flyes, and Wasps, in buzzing about Wit. . 18 Ode Athenian   75
WAST
   She durst not look above your Wast; . . . .   222 Prog of Love   6
WAST-COAT
   A flaxen wig, and wast-coat gay, ...   879 Robbin & Harry   48
WASTCOAT
   His Wastcoat to a Cassock grew, ...   115 Bauc & Phil 2   121
WASTE
   Why should the first be ruin'd and laid waste, ... 40 Ode Sancroft   178
   Pound all the Realms before him waste; . . . . . .   326 Pethox   92
   Lay all my fine Plantations waste, ...   410 Dial Rich Marb   69
   The Time too precious now to waste, ...   453 Modern Lady   276
   Let Will. unheard by thee, his Thunder waste. . . . 538 Mr. Pulteney   12
   And waste in Luxury thy Harvests there; . . . . .   794 St. Pat's Well   98
   His famous Letters made waste Paper; . . . . . .   875 Drapier's Hill   17
   My Person tall, and slender Waste, ...   915 Riddle 1   5
WASTED
   So long till all your Flesh is wasted, ...   759 Receipt Youth   24
   Wasted he appears, and pale, ...   936 Riddle 24   D   21
WASTING
   He sunk at length to wasting Age a Prey, ...   669 Epig Carthy 13 D   3
WASTS
   Yet as she wasts, she grows discreet, ... 229 Prog of Beauty   101
WAT'RING
   Wat'ring soft Elysian Plains. . . . .   661 Love Song   20
WAT'RY
   'Tis the world's wat'ry hour-glass streaming fast, . . 49 To Congreve   189
   Darts weeping beams across heaven's wat'ry face; . . . 52 Temple Ill   26
WATCH   SEE DEATH-WATCH
   Who watch Her like a Prey, ...   8 Ode to King   74
   We watch his Motions to a Minute, ...   280 Journal   49
   Because like a Watch it always cries Click: . . . . 351 Wood Insect   21
   Belated, seems on watch to lye, ...   583 Young Nymph   49
   We'll watch your Steps where-e'er you go: . . . .   627 Scandal Poem 2   132
   The Greater for the Smallest watch, ...   651 On Poetry   321
   Watch ev'ry Syllable you speak: . . . .   889 Panegyr Dean   72
   Sweeten your Tea, and watch your Toast. . . . .   897 Panegyr Dean   328
   Yet no Watch the rest will keep, ...   931 Riddle 18   D   16
   Will laugh in their sleeves: I can tell you they watch 979 Dean to Tho: S   36
     for't.
   I've something else to do than watch. . . . . . .   983 Sher, A Goose   24
WATCH'D
   Watch'd all the Company she kept, ...   696 Cadenus Vaness   309
WATCHFUL
   The watchful Bailiffs take their silent Stands, . . . 125 Descriptn Morn   17
   His watchful Friends preserve him by a Sleight. . . . 196 Author Himself   62
   Let Stella look with watchful Eye, ...   743 Stel B-day 22   59
   Turn ev'ry Way thy watchful Eye; . . . .   897 Panegyr Dean   337
   Oh! could we tame yon watchful Dragon, ...   948 Jason Hassard   5
WATCHING
   Watching the first unsav'ry Wind, ...   66 Problem   37
   His Fellow Pick-Purse, watching for a job, ...   364 On Dreams   25
   There Cerberus lay watching in his Den, ...   538 Mr. Pulteney   25
   Watching for the public weal. . . . .   936 Riddle 24   D   22
WATCHMAN
   At last they hear the Watchman knock, ...   453 Modern Lady   282
WATCHMEN
   On Watchmen, Constables and Duns, ...   583 Young Nymph   52

WATER SEE HOLY-WATER

	PAGE	TITLE	LINE
And seem (almost) transform'd to Water, Flame, and Air,	22	Ode Athenian	201
While the Water and Sweat,	245	Irish-Feast	43
Upon the Water cast thy Bread	255	Bubble	133
With Water fill'd he could no longer float,	284	Elegy Boat	9
The persecution of cold Water.	321	First of April	32
To be Hewers of Wood and Drawers of Water,	334	Serious Poem	2
Now, although to Draw Water is not very good,	334	Serious Poem	3
But a Kettle of scalding hot Water injected,	351	Wood Insect	25
Then Reader pray shed some tears of Salt Water,	430	Dicky Dolly	17
Takes a large Dram of Citron Water.	446	Modern Lady	47
With Puppy Water, Beauty's Help	526	Lady's Dres Rm	31
Squat on her Hams, to make Maid's Water.	584	Strephon Chloe	18
Like fire-works, she can burn in water.	618	Scandal Poem 1	38
Like Fire-works, she can burn in Water.	624	Scandal Poem 2	36
We only dip a Spunge in Water;	627	Scandal Poem 2	128
Or throw cold Water in her Face,	725	To Stella	76
To make their Water pass;	952	Asparagus	3
Fire will not roast, nor Water boil.	1035	To Quilca	8

WATER-COLOURS

| And water-colours of these Days, | 21 | Ode Athenian | 170 |

WATER-GRUEL

| Whose Phiz bespeaks his diet water-gruel. | 672 | Epig Carthy 24 | D 10 |

WATER'D

| Had rather water'd it, than drown'd: | 17 | Ode Athenian | 43 |

WATER'S

| Now Water's brought, and Dinner done, | 279 | Journal | 35 |
| Your water's mud, | 440 | Ballyspellin | 10 |

WATERMEN

| One asks the Watermen hard by, | 109 | V's House | 99 |
| Like the Watermen of Thames, | 635 | Epistle Lady | 165 |

WATERS

In Spight of his Deanship and Journeyman Waters.	237	Excellent Song	REF
This wicked Rogue Waters, who always is sinning,	238	Excellent Song	26
In Spight of his Deanship and Journeyman Waters.	238	Excellent Song	REF
And headlong in the Waters drown.	259	Bubble	216
Have Peter Waters always in your Mind;	534	To Mr. Gay	101
Styx, through Hell whose Waters roll!	832	Legion Club	84
Or bathing in the Waters fair;	915	Riddle 1	2

WATERY

| It's watery footsteps in Dorinda's face; | 52 | Temple Ill | 52 |

WATRY

| With watry Chaps, and wagging Chin, | 895 | Panegyr Dean | 257 |

WAV'D

| He wav'd his Wreath Thrice o'er her Head, | 120 | Apollo Outwit | 35 |

WAVE

| Gives murmuring passage to a lasting wave; | 49 | To Congreve | 188 |

WAVES

The eager Muse took wing upon the Waves decline,	16	Ode Athenian	22
Then plunges in the Southern Waves,	251	Bubble	23
Ride o'er the Waves in spacious Hoops,	254	Bubble	91
Tost in the Waves of this tempestuous World,	284	Elegy Boat	5
Rebellious Waves with rods like Xerxes.	463	Birthday Song	100
As Ships are toss't by Waves and Wind,	589	Strephon Chloe	170
Poor floating Isle, tost on ill Fortune's Waves,	770	Horace 1, 14	1
New Waves shall drive thee to the Deep again.	770	Horace 1, 14	10
The Waves impetuous entring at your Keel.	770	Horace 1, 14	20

WAVING

| "You dread the waving of these Greens; | 380 | Apology Lady C | 138 |

WAX SEE EAR-WAX

And scrape her Pitchy Sides for Wax.	100	Elegy Patrige	78
Sit squeezing Images of Wax.	240	Run Bankers	32
With Wax the Father bound them fast,	252	Bubble	38
The Wax is melted by the Height,	252	Bubble	39
He melts his Wax at ev'ry Flame,	252	Bubble	46
Like Iv'ry dry, and soft as Wax.	584	Strephon Chloe	26
This ball of wax your ears will darken,	753	Gift for Bec	21

WAY SEE BACK-WAY,HIGH-WAY

Has forc't to grope her uncouth way	18	Ode Athenian	66
And which they've now Conscience to way	24	Ode Athenian	256
Where none ever led the Way,	26	Ode to Temple	13
'Tis you must put us in the Way;	27	Ode to Temple	20
The way which ev'ry wand'ring fool below	39	Ode Sancroft	157
I mean, the way which leads to Christ:	39	Ode Sancroft	161
There (A safe way to use Perfume)	60	Lady Tablebook	12
Premising thus in Modern way	80	Vanbrug House	55
For Leave to build the Poet's Way.	81	Vanbrug House	70
A different way their Fancy runs;	83	Salamander	16
So many Beggers pass this way,	90	Bauc & Phil 1	29
For want of which by way of Botch,	96	On the Union	3
Premising thus in Modern way	106	V's House	29
A Third, who lost his Way by Night,	127	Little House	31
Yet take one Word of Counsel by the way:	166	Ioland's Invit	40
Mark out the way where Daphne flew	177	To Lord Harley	18
"Their Way--for now you see they're blind;	208	Fable Bitches	34
The Girl had such a Bashfull way.	223	Prog of Love	32
To learn the Way that Phillis went;	223	Prog of Love	34
Attacks her in the milky Way:	228	Prog of Beauty	92
And scorns the middle Way to keep:	252	Bubble	36
But may be tam'd another way,	258	Bubble	187
And follow where he leads the Way:	270	Apollo's Edict	D 9

WAY	(CONTINUED)	PAGE	TITLE	LINE
Or ever name the milky Way.		270	Apollo's Edict	D 22
Here (by the Way) by Gallus mean I,		278	Journal	5
The Way is thus; and well deserves your Thanks:		285	Elegy Boat	31
No other way but try the Bath:		293	Prog Marriage	106
I told him, in the smoothest way I could,		308	Billet Players	41
To beg his Favour is the Way new Favours still to win,		341	Upon His Grace	13
And then I went to pay the 'Squire and in the Way I found,		343	Upon His Grace	41
Believe me 'tis the Way to Rise.		361	Grace's Answer	12
When you behold the milky Way		362	Grace's Answer	31
"Winning my Way by slow Approaches,		380	Apology Lady C	151
They take the wrong Way for the right.		412	Desire Possess	18
The most effectual Way to baulk		414	Censure	29
'But really 'tis my Spouse's Way;		448	Modern Lady	105
I know a shorter way by half.		487	Irish-Club	14
No Brush could force a way betwixt.		526	Lady's Dres Rm	22
"In surest way to be preferr'd---;		549	Life of Swift	165
In my own hum'rous biting Way?		555	Death of Swift	54
Thus much may serve by way of Proem,		555	Death of Swift	71
Which way my Death can do them good;		556	Death of Swift	78
"His way of Writing now is past;		563	Death of Swift	265
"And Friends would let him have his Way.		572	Death of Swift	478
And, by the beastly way of Thinking,		590	Strephon Chloe	209
That they might some better Way tread,		637	Epistle Lady	223
Nature must give Way to Art.		660	Love Song	4
There's a securer Way to wreck your Spite.		667	Epig Carthy 4	D 2
In vain, --- for soon the slender prop gives way;		672	Epig Carthy 24	D 16
Grew louder, all the Way up Stairs;		698	Cadenus Vaness	369
One way he knows to give her Pain:		701	Cadenus Vaness	469
Then to compleat it ev'ry way,		726	To Stella	89
No more my dear Delightful way tread,		779	Mullinix Tim	183
We'll show him the way how to crop and to slit;		816	Yahoo's	52
On his virtues hold forth; 'tis the very best way;		819	Archbi Cashel	9
But meets it half way;		853	Lady's Lament	76
I'll shew you the way:		855	Lady's Lament	131
And your Ladyship curchyes half way to the Ground!		871	Grand Question	116
Turn ev'ry Way thy watchful Eye;		897	Panegyr Dean	337
And am his neighbour cross the way;		899	Dean's Reasons	30
Answers in decisive way,		906	Daphne	13
I am a Courtier in my Way;		917	Riddle 3	11
I justly keep the middle Way.		918	Riddle 4	38
Thy num'rous Fingers know their Way,		919	Riddle 5	11
Are forc't to look another Way;		922	Riddle 7	48
They for that Reason shun this Way:		928	Riddle 12	D 6
What other way they take to go,		928	Riddle 12	D 9
And so I remain in a civil way, your Servant to command.		987	Mary to Sher	38
I wish you would tell me which way you incline		1017	Swift Ans Sher	19
To take the right way,		1038	Sheridan Cavan	11
WAYS				
These are the Ways		7	Ode to King	31
And by their never-failing ways		19	Ode Athenian	117
Thus the deluding Muse oft leads me to her Ways,		23	Ode Athenian	234
Such are the ways ill-guided mortals go		35	Ode Sancroft	37
And when he has got it, finds Ways to conceal it;		265	Apollo	60
More beneficial Ways than Rhime;		495	Panegyr Swift	67
Unless you owner Ways had trod		495	Panegyr Swift	78
In finding Ways and Means, and stopping Gaps:		535	To Mr. Gay	122
What various Ways our Females take,		592	Strephon Chloe	267
Drag diff'rent Ways in miry Grounds.		645	On Poetry	176
First, nine Ways looking, let her stand		743	Stel B-day 22	53
How to walk upright in our ways;		780	Mullinix Tim	252
Surer ways to be despis'd:		906	Daphne	6
With such insinuating Ways.		920	Riddle 6	4
WE	454		OMITTED WORD	
WE'D	1		OMITTED WORD	
WE'LL	34		OMITTED WORD	
WE'RE	1		OMITTED WORD	
WE'VE	2		OMITTED WORD	
WEAK				
Or a weak argument by force maintain'd?		34	Ode Sancroft	12
Whence the weak shapes wild and imperfect pass,		35	Ode Sancroft	23
If all that our weak knowledge titles virtue, be		36	Ode Sancroft	45
But zeal is weak and ignorant, tho' wond'rous proud,		38	Ode Sancroft	135
Form'd by diseas'd conceptions, weak, and wild,		47	To Congreve	123
Weak is the beam to dry up nature's tears,		51	Temple Ill	19
Fools common-place thou art, their weak ensconcing fort,		53	Temple Ill	87
To weak, or old, or clouded Eyes.		367	Answer Delaney	46
His loudest Voice is low and weak,		405	Swift to Pope	3
Judgement weak, and Passion strong,		800	Traulus 2	17
For, let us hear the weak Pretence,		820	Dr. Rundle	11
To Modesty a weak Pretence;		887	Panegyr Dean	19
There's none so ignorant or weak		890	Panegyr Dean	119
No Passions so weak		939	Riddle Answerd	11
Your Argument's weak, and so you will find,		947	Mrs. Houghton	5
WEAKER				
Nor argue on the weaker Side;		644	On Poetry	128
I'll here expose your weaker Side.		730	Stella, Poems	86
To all their weaker Sides are blind;		887	Panegyr Dean	8
WEAKEST				
Your Lessons found the weakest Part,		706	Cadenus Vaness	622

897

WEAKLY   PAGE   TITLE   LINE
    How, with a weakly warbling tongue, ...   876 To Dean Swift   13
    Paradoxes weakly wielding, ...   906 Daphne   7
WEAKNESS
    Who must my Weakness and my Ignorance confess,   . . .   20 Ode Athenian   133
WEAL   SEE COMMON-WEAL
    Your Labours for the Publick Weal.   . . . . . .   243 Horace 4, 9   6
    "Both bitter Foes to Britain's Weal.   . . . . .   549 Life of Swift   153
    "On which alone, our Weal depended.   . . . . . .   568 Death of Swift   378
    Watching for the public weal.   . . . .   936 Riddle 24   D   22
WEALTH
    The God of Wealth was therefore made   . . . . .   79 Vanbrug House   23
    On Earth, the God of Wealth was made   . . . . .   106 V's House   23
    His Heirs might well of all his Wealth possest,   .   233 Elegy on Demar   5
    Pluto the god of Wealth, will joy to know   . . .   234 Elegy on Demar   7
    And to the God of Wealth his Brother, ...   346 Prometheus   51
    To Wealth and Vice, in high Degree, ...   386 Manly Virtue   94
    We fly from luxury and wealth, ...   401 Window Inns 5   D   1
    Stand high in Honour, Wealth, or Wit;   . . . . .   414 Censure   7
    Or, shall the charms of wealth and power   . . . .   490 Dialogue   45
    That, Wealth should be the Appenage of Wit,   . . .   532 To Mr. Gay   26
    Be rich; but of your Wealth make no Parade;   . . .   533 To Mr. Gay   61
    "And, Wealth he valu'd not a Groat: . . . . .   567 Death of Swift   358
    "He gave the little Wealth he had, ...   572 Death of Swift   479
    Yet, with his Beauty, Wealth, and Parts, ...   598 Problem Solved   19
    Some small Regard for State and Wealth: . . . .   693 Cadenus Vaness   217
    Our <Bishops> puft up with Wealth and with Pride.   .   804 Irish Bishops   17
    Voluptuous Ease, the Child of Wealth, ...   895 Panegyr Dean   279
    And only to get others Wealth.   . . . .   917 Riddle 3   18
    And leave behind their fruitless Wealth.   . . . .   922 Riddle 7   32
    And yet her Wealth was all her Guilt.   . . . . .   923 Riddle 7   66
WEALTHY
    If he be Wealthy and a Fool   . . . .   61 Lady Tablebook   27
    Demar the Wealthy, and the Wise.   . . . .   235 Elegy on Demar   42
    Was grown as wealthy as a Prince;   . . . .   409 Dial Rich Marb   38
    Tom for a wealthy Wife looks round, ...   545 Life of Swift   15
    The Wealthy have you in Derision.   . . . . . .   641 On Poetry   50
    That such a pair of wealthy Ninnies   . . . . . .   821 Dr. Rundle   63
WEAM
    A Blow on the Weam, ...   247 Irish-Feast   87
WEAN
    Our true Irish Hearts from old England to wean;   . . 237 Excellent Song   7
WEAPONS
    And then throw all their Weapons down;   . . . . .   592 Strephon Chloe   262
WEAR
    Still wear, still doat on his Invisible Ring.   . . . 21 Ode Athenian   157
    That Princes wear derives from them;   . . . . . .   98 Elegy Patrige   26
    Madly aspir'd to wear her chain: . . . .   177 To Lord Harley   42
    Lord, what a Dress these Parsons wear, ...   291 Prog Marriage   42
    Will deign your Livery to wear, ...   325 Pethox   44
    If we who wear our Wigs   . . . .   426 Five Ladies   33
    I'gad I'd wear a Gown.   . . . .   426 Five Ladies   40
    Smocks hempen wear;   . . . .   441 Ballyspellin   44
    Paddy repin'd to see him wear   . . . .   458 Paddy's Charac   19
    Britannia long will wear like steel   . . . . . .   468 Birthday Song   243
    And with the Virtues pant to wear   . . . .   498 Panegyr Swift   173
    Shou'd a Monkey wear a Crown, ...   634 Epistle Lady   149
    Old carted Bawds such Garments wear, ...   787 Clad in Brown   19
    In his Mouth to wear his Knife.   . . . .   800 Traulus 2   40
    And wear out my smocks;   . . . .   854 Lady's Lament   82
    Like Lorimer, to wear his Hat.   . . . .   886 Rev Market-Hill   96
    Most wondrous Forms you see me wear   . . . . . .   927 Riddle 10   D   13
    Lifeless, Life's perfect Form I wear, ...   935 Riddle 23   D   7
    Sometimes imperial Robes I wear, ...   935 Riddle 23   D   20
WEARIED
    Wearied with saying Grace and Prayer, ...   1003 Dan J's Reply   1
WEARING
    At wearing of Woollen, ...   237 Excellent Song   15
    Which can ne'er be worse for wearing.   . . . . .   523 Betty Grizette   22
WEARS
    Still ev'ry tree the pendent sorrow wears;   . . .   51 Temple Ill   20
    A <Whig> and one that wears a Gown.   . . . . . .   121 Apollo Outwit   64
    That Florimel wears Iron Stays;   . . . .   449 Modern Lady   161
    Of e'ery Rogue that wears an <Arse>   . . . . . .   497 Panegyr Swift   121
    To the Dean of all Deans, tho' he wears not a sword.   . 816 Yahoo's   54
    Brave as the Upton Fan she wears: . . . .   885 Rev Market-Hill   58
    The dullest Beast, and the Saddle it wears,   . . .   940 Letter   10
WEARY
    To bless the Primitive Sailer's weary sight,   . . .   16 Ode Athenian   7
    And divine Sancroft, weary with the weight   . . .   40 Ode Sancroft   185
    Some short refreshment for your weary mind,   . . .   50 To Congreve   232
    For, let heaven's wrath enlarge these weary days,   . 54 Temple Ill   111
    Salutes the weary trav'ller as he walks;   . . . .   55 Temple Ill   120
    The weary Dean goes to his Chamber, ...   280 Journal   57
    For, when in Bed we rest our weary Limbs, ...   363 On Dreams   7
    Weary the Gods with ceaseless Prayer, ...   388 Manly Virtue   139
    A dog would be weary on.   . . . .   402 Window Inns 8   D   10
    See my weary Days consuming, ...   660 Love Song   7
    Using four legs when two were weary.   . . . . .   675 Curate's Compl   4
    Led but a weary Life above.   . . . .   712 Cadenus Vaness   829
    Weary and Sea-sick when in thee confin'd, ...   772 Horace 1, 14   57

```
WEARY              (CONTINUED)                              PAGE    TITLE              LINE
    For long disputes will only weary us. . . . . . . .    774 Mullinix Tim           34
    Then let us rise, and rest our weary Bums.  . . . . .  882 Pastoral Dial          52
WEARY'D
    When weary'd with Intrigues of State,  . . . . . . .   480 Libel on D- D-         27
    Sir <Robert> weary'd by Will. <Pulteney's> Teazings,   537 Mr. Pulteney            1
WEASEL
    So, when a Weasel you torment, . . . . . . . . .        66 Problem                17
WEATHER
    Can like the Stars foretel the Weather;    . . . . .    99 Elegy Patrige          43
    Reckoning Roof, Weather Cock and all,    . . . . . .   126 Little House            7
    Then in a Sawpit and wet Weather,      . . . . . .     393 Modern Poets           19
    The Weather and his Love were hot;     . . . . . .     586 Strephon Chloe         81
    Fair weather when the morning breaks,  . . . . . .     618 Scandal Poem 1         30
    You'll see a Cloud in gentle weather   . . . . . .     618 Scandal Poem 1         43
    As if he made the weather fair. . . . . . . . . .      621 Scandal Poem 1        138
    Fair Weather, when the Morning breaks;  . . . . . .    624 Scandal Poem 2         24
    You'll see a Cloud in gentle Weather   . . . . . .     625 Scandal Poem 2         39
    As if He made the Weather fair.  . . . . . . .         627 Scandal Poem 2        142
    Then fell to talking of the Weather:  . . . . . .      696 Cadenus Vaness        325
    Expos'd to Want, and Wind, and Weather,  . . . . .     759 Receipt Youth           9
    In Weather fine I nothing spend,   . . . . . . .       954 Authors Living          7
    Thy Verse like Bricks, defy the Weather,   . . . .   1021 Nim-Dan-Dean 1      D  19
WEATHER-BEATEN
    Both, weather-beaten are without;  . . . . . . .       401 Window Inns 4           3
WEATHER'S
    The Weather's Fair, nay, that is true,  . . . . .      372 Letter D. S-y          23
WEATHERCOCK
    The herd beneath, who see the weathercock of state . . 37 Ode Sancroft           73
WEAVE
    Consumes it self to weave a Cell. . . . . . . .        79 Vanbrug House          32
WEAVER
    And once a Weaver in our Town,   . . . . . . . .       926 Riddle 9               19
WEAVERS
    Will give a Night of Benefit to Weavers. . . . . .     274 Epilogue                4
    Between the Weavers and us Play-House Kings.  . . .    275 Epilogue               36
    For Weavers now are just as poor as Wits;  . . . .     276 Epilogue               40
    But Weavers will be Kinder to the Players,  . . . .    276 Epilogue               43
WEAVING
    But Wit and Weaving had the same beginning,  . . . .   276 Epilogue               37
WEAZON
    For, there my Grandsire cut his Weazon:  . . . . .     349 Upright Judge 1         2
    He cut his Weazon at the Altar;  . . . . . . . .       349 Upright Judge 1         3
WEDDING
    Fair Emblems of a fruitful Wedding.  . . . . . .       585 Strephon Chloe         52
    Fresh from a wedding, or a christ'ning,  . . . . .     762 Bec's B-Day            53
WEDDING-DAY
    In Mirth the wedding-day was spent.   . . . . . .      290 Prog Marriage          18
    The Wedding-day, you take me right,   . . . . . .      290 Prog Marriage          19
WEDDING-NIGHT
    Demean himself the Wedding-Night:   . . . . . . .      586 Strephon Chloe         74
    Resistance on the Wedding-Night  . . . . . . . .       588 Strephon Chloe        155
WEDDING-RING
    "I saw you touch your Wedding-Ring   . . . . . . .     452 Modern Lady           252
WEDDING-SHEETS
    Her Bridegroom in the Wedding-Sheets.   . . . . . .    588 Strephon Chloe        132
WEDG'D
    And wedg'd in Corner of a Chair   . . . . . . .        75 Game Traffick          11
    Wedg'd in a spacious Elbow-Chair,   . . . . . . .      895 Panegyr Dean          259
    Thy Words so closely wedg'd, and short are,  . . . .  1021 Nim-Dan-Dean 1      D  21
WEED
    Or no Infectious Weed,   . . . . . . . . . .            7 Ode to King            53
    And ev'ry stinking weed so lofty grows,  . . . . .     37 Ode Sancroft          103
    And, for Corruptions, how they weed 'em.   . . . .     501 Doctor Delaney         58
    Who wont to weed the Court of Gosford Knight,  . . .   880 Pastoral Dial           2
    No Knife so keen to weed thee from my Heart.  . . .    881 Pastoral Dial          12
    May I be doom'd for Life to weed in Rain.   . . . .    882 Pastoral Dial          44
WEEDING-KNIFE
    Or may I loose my Weeding-knife--and Thee.   . . . .   882 Pastoral Dial          48
WEEDS
    Where nought but Weeds will grow.  . . . . . . .       33 Ode to Temple         209
    Among the noblest flow'rs a thousand pois'nous weeds, . 37 Ode Sancroft          102
    Than strongest Weeds that grow these Stones betwixt: . 880 Pastoral Dial          10
WEEK
    E'er a week pas't committing Blunders:   . . . . .     62 Discovery               4
    Step to this Grave but once a Week,  . . . . . .       101 Elegy Patrige         110
    The Vicar once a Week creeps in,   . . . . . . .       127 Little House           19
    Where he comes ev'ry Week from Town;   . . . . .       128 Little House           57
    As once a week we travel down  . . . . . . . .         201 Horace 2, 6            77
    "For shou'd you stay but one Week longer,  . . . .     208 Fable Bitches          29
    While We perhaps must wait a Week:   . . . . . .       315 To Ford               104
    To every Farmer twice a Week all round about the Yoke, 343 Upon His Grace         39
    Your Rent is due almost a Week beside the Days of      343 Upon His Grace         44
        Grace.
    Mordanto in a Week from Spain.  . . . . . . .          398 Earl of P-b-w          12
    He left the Town above a Week.  . . . . . . . .        398 Earl of P-b-w          15
    To spunge a Breakfast once a Week;   . . . . . .       409 Dial Rich Marb         52
    Him twice a Week I here expect,  . . . . . . .         411 Dial Rich Marb         95
    Three times a Week to brush my Gown.   . . . . . .     411 Dial Rich Marb        100
    To dress a Thought, may toyl a Week;   . . . . .       502 Doctor Delaney         66
    Which Celia slept at least a Week in?   . . . . .      527 Lady's Dres Rm         54
```

WEEK	(CONTINUED)	PAGE	TITLE	LINE
A Week; and Arbuthnott a Day.		561	Death of Swift	208
Thy week made up of fasting days,		676	Parson's Case	11
In half a week the Dame grew nice,		745	Stel Distress	9
Thus for a week the Farce went on		747	Stel Distress	
In half a Week the Dame grew nice,		749	Stel Wood-Park	7
Thus, for a Week the Farce went on;		751	Stel Wood-Park	69
When I have lain in it a Week!		780	Mullinix Tim	224
She scarce recover'd in a Week.		849	Old Thorn	28
After a Week, a Month, a Quarter,		860	Lady Acheson	9
Nor, twice a week will shave his beard.		879	Robbin & Harry	44
How oft a Week was kept a Ball		905	Death Daphne	83

WEEKLY

And weekly persecute his grace		677	Parson's Case	29
And weekly carry out our Dust.		787	Clad in Brown	28
Presented him the weekly Bills		903	Death Daphne	5

WEEKS

He that has shone with Betterton and Weeks,		308	Billet Players	44
Rais'd up by you in twenty Weeks:		893	Panegyr Dean	204

WEEN

Quoth Marble-Hill, right well I ween,		408	Dial Rich Marb	9
But Time with Iron Teeth I ween		849	Old Thorn	17
Unhappy Wretch! for now, I ween,		1005	Sheridan's Sub	26

WEENING   SEE OVER-WEENING

WEEP

Weep all you Customers that use		101	Elegy Patrige	107
He made them weep before he dy'd.		296	Satiric Elegy	24
A boon so small! But I may weep,		403	Window Inns 10	D 9
Sleeping Weep, Weeping Sleep.		961	Cantata	
If you do not come back we shall weep out our eyn		1018	Swift Ans Sher	28

WEEPERS

Ye formal Weepers for the Sick,		204	In Sickness	23

WEEPING

Darts weeping beams across heaven's wat'ry face;		52	Temple Ill	26
With Eyes in Smoak and Weeping drown'd:		594	Cassinus Peter	26
Thus the Cyprian Goddess weeping,		660	Love Song	9
While true Lovers Eyes Weeping Sleep,		960	Cantata	
Sleeping Weep, Weeping Sleep.		961	Cantata	

WEEZLES

And how her Doves were kill'd by Weezles:		282	Journal	94

WEIGH

And begs, He would the other weigh.		63	Discovery	40
We learn't to weigh our Gold by Grains.		156	Fable of Midas	22
To weigh her priests, the lawyers, gold.		433	Answer Paulus	36
Weigh but the Merits of the three,		884	Rev Market-Hill	27
Where thirty weigh, as much as eighty.		1022	Nim-Dan-Dean 1	D 48

WEIGH'D

Whose Reason is weigh'd down by Popular air,		21	Ode Athenian	181
But as his Gold he weigh'd, grim Death in spight,		234	Elegy on Demar	31
Weigh'd in the Ballance, and found Light.		241	Run Bankers	64

WEIGHT   SEE BUTTER-WEIGHT

It fell, and broke with its own Weight		26	Ode to Temple	4
And divine Sancroft, weary with the weight		40	Ode Sancroft	185
Gets between them and my resentment's weight,		45	To Congreve	46
By their own Weight sunk to the Bottom;		159	Fable of Midas	79
Yet when the Weight of Kingdoms lyes		160	Atlas	20
And tell how little weight he sets,		282	Journal	99
He sunk beneath the cumbrous Weight:		413	Desire Possess	52
Yet, whence proceeds this Weight we lay		414	Censure	17
No less than Reasons of such Weight,		498	Panegyr Swift	154
And press you down with all their Weight.		503	Doctor Delaney	94
The Cause appear'd of so much Weight,		688	Cadenus Vaness	75
Whose able Heads support the Weight,		781	Mullinix Tim	257
"it's matter of weight, and a mere money-job;		843	Ay and No	11
I almost sink with my own Weight;		917	Riddle 3	6
The Weight on him, they do on Sophocles.		988	Letter Dr Sh-n	27
Number, and Weight, and Measure join.		1022	Nim-Dan-Dean 1	D 46

WEIGHTY

Her weighty Morning Bus'ness o'er		291	Prog Marriage	55
A weighty Argument indeed;		298	Horrid Plot	13
On weighty Bus'ness, to some neighb'ring Friend:		534	To Mr. Gay	86
Three weighty Causes were assign'd,		598	Problem Solved	23
The Brief with weighty Crimes was charg'd,		686	Cadenus Vaness	5
Brought weighty Arguments to prove		708	Cadenus Vaness	676
But, in a weighty Case like this,		713	Cadenus Vaness	854
There is a Reason still more weighty;		820	Dr. Rundle	23
An head so weighty and profound,		822	Epigr Rundle	5
Let me have your Advice in a weighty Affair.		866	Grand Question	2
Then all must grant, your Lines are weighty,		1022	Nim-Dan-Dean 1	D 47

WEIRS

The Dams and the Weirs must all be your own,		287	Bank Down	6

WELCH

When my old cassock says a Welch divine		419	Shall Repine	5

WELCH'S

When Mrs Welch's Chimny smoks,		419	Holyhead Journ	1

WELCOM'D

Cart'ret was welcom'd to the Shore		338	Wood's Brass	1
Harangu'd, and welcom'd him to Town.		904	Death Daphne	50

WELCOME

She still is welcome with her inn'cent song;		49	To Congreve	182
Said Harley, Welcome Rev'rend Dean!		174	Horace 1, 7	121

WELCOME   (CONTINUED)
                                             PAGE   TITLE   LINE

Entry	PAGE	TITLE		LINE
The Place, the Welcome, and the Spark,	748	Stel Distress		70
The Scene, the Welcome, and the Spark,	752	Stel Wood-Park		86
You're heartily welcome: But as for good Chear,	871	Grand Question		121
"But the Devil's as welcome wherever he goes:	872	Grand Question		144
Will make them welcome to his modicum:	878	Robbin & Harry		24
To welcome Brother Serving-men;	890	Panegyr Dean		100
Both are welcome, Grief or Joy,	933	Riddle 20	D	17
WELE				
Ripe fruit shall come, and all is wele.	103	Merlin		14
WELKIN				
A Sable Cloud a-thwart the Welkin flings,	137	City Shower		14
When Syrius o'er the welkin rages,	618	Scandal Poem 1		33
When Syrius o'er the Welkin rages	624	Scandal Poem 2		31
WELL SEE RAKE-WELL				
Her Sister Isles are Conquered too as well as She.	9	Ode to King		100
Who cou'd so well a dying Nation save,	12	Ode to William	D	15
Which, what it bravely Won, do's well Maintain.	12	Ode to William	D	28
Who have well studied in the Worlds Disease,	20	Ode Athenian		138
So well You answer all Phaenomenaes there;	22	Ode Athenian		202
Well--tho' you've rais'd Her to this high Degree,	24	Ode Athenian		263
Our selves are rais'd as she,	24	Ode Athenian		264
Resolv'd to give himself, as well as Country Peace.	30	Ode to Temple		134
Since Heaven will claim its residence as well as birth,	35	Ode Sancroft		19
Yet does this high perfection well proceed	41	Ode Sancroft		223
As well as here below,	41	Ode Sancroft		232
A pride that well suspends poor mortals fate,	45	To Congreve		45
And well, methinks, does this allusion fit	45	To Congreve		75
Where having cast his coat, and well pursu'd	46	To Congreve		117
Must needs be right, so well resembling theirs.	48	To Congreve		174
And the bad world may well believe the same;	49	To Congreve		198
At length, a spark not too well bred	63	Discovery		25
. . .as you may very well think,	70	Mrs Harris Pet		20
Well: But then they would have had me gone.	72	Mrs Harris Pet		48
Well; I thought I should have swoon'd;	73	Mrs Harris Pet		64
For he ne're could have fill'd it so well of himself.	77	Lady B- B-		20
For Jove consider'd well the Case,	79	Vanbrug House		17
'Tis well.--But since we live among	83	Salamander		23
Well, 'tis as Bickerstaff has guest,	98	Elegy Patrige		1
So Learned Patrige could as well	99	Elegy Patrige		53
Whate'er concerns you full as well,	101	Elegy Patrige		114
For, Jove consider'd well the Case,	106	V's House		17
But well perceiving Wit was scarce,	107	V's House		56
Thou'rt well contriv'd, tho' thou art small;	109	V's House		116
At Christnings well could act his Part,	115	Bauc & Phil 2		129
How well a Cully's Purse was lin'd;	133	Magician's Rod		32
Could scatter Opium full as well,	133	Magician's Rod		41
But Englond must cry well and well a day,	147	Windsor Proph		13
Will drink it now as well as Peers:	169	Peace Dunkirk		24
The Priest was pretty well in case,	170	Horace 1, 7		7
Well, I shall think of that no more,	173	Horace 1, 7		71
Well, now I have all this and more,	198	Horace 2, 6		7
Because they see me us'd so well:	202	Horace 2, 6		82
For well she knew her num'rus Brood,	208	Fable Bitches		21
Which might as well have been in Prose;	215	To Mr. Delany		10
Is well conceiv'd tho not defin'd;	215	To Mr. Delany		16
From both, we learn to Railly well;	216	To Mr. Delany		31
The loving Couple well bemir'd,	224	Prog of Love		77
And Form, say I, as well as They,	228	Prog of Beauty		83
If you would have us well supply'd,	229	Prog of Beauty		119
His Heirs might well of all his Wealth possest,	233	Elegy on Demar		5
Why then fare them well,	245	Irish-Feast		23
Well harden'd in Flame,	246	Irish-Feast		70
Directors fall as well as they,	253	Bubble		83
He knows very well I ne'er gave a Refusal,	265	Apollo		71
So a Thief steals my Horse, and then gets him well drest	266	Apollo		92
With ev'ry Wind he sail'd, and well could tack:	285	Elegy Boat		15
A Trade, our Boat had practic'd here so well.	285	Elegy Boat		26
The Way is thus; and well deserves your Thanks:	285	Elegy Boat		31
But the Tapster well Cudgell'd him both Side and Flank	288	Bank Down		39
You raise Desire as well as Pride,	292	Prog Marriage		74
Well, since he's gone, no matter how,	296	Satiric Elegy		5
You pay them well; the Dogs have got	299	Horrid Plot		27
"As well against, as with the Tide,	304	Storm		36
And, Dawson street will serve as well	313	To Ford		61
The Deanry-house may well be match't	313	To Ford		65
And well thy Scholars are endu'd	325	Pethox		61
My Tale is a wise one if well understood,	334	Serious Poem		23
For fear the First Drop might as well be his Last:	337	Serious Poem		112
Will serve for Sodder well enuff.	345	Prometheus		24
My dear Estate, how well I love it;	348	Whitshed Motto		7
That Head so well by Wisdom fraught!	361	Grace's Answer		15
Well skill'd in Mid-wife Artifices,	362	Grace's Answer		27
As well as you, for a Midas:	372	Letter D. S-y		37
Of Prayers, that he might well succeed,	373	Letter D. S-y		69
A Lady, Wise as well Fair,	375	Apology Lady C		1
Wou'd have the Text as well as Comment;	375	Apology Lady C		4
Well then, I'll e'en go home, and fast;	377	Apology Lady C		54
And much good Sense, as well as Breeding:	377	Apology Lady C		72
For well he knew, to such a Guest,	378	Apology Lady C		103
The gracious Dame, tho' well she knew	379	Apology Lady C		117

Thus, acting what he taught so well, ...   386 Manly Virtue   83
Then, let them well be dry'd;   . . . .   394 Grub-Street   10
Pope has the Talent well to speak, ...   405 Swift to Pope   1
The Sexton reason'd well, ...   406 Swift to Pope   26
Quoth Marble-Hill, right well I ween, ...   408 Dial Rich Marb   9
The Kingly Prophet well evinces, ...   408 Dial Rich Marb   13
For Conversation well endu'd;   . . . .   416 Woman's Mind   17
How well the Governor's inclin'd.   . . . .   422 Ireld   25
I know you well enough, ...   428 Beau's Reply   7
Yet well they merit be pitied, ...   434 Answer Paulus   59
Well taught by practice to imbibe   . . . .   435 Answer Paulus   109
As well may I   . . . .   440 Ballyspellin   20
To wash her self our Well in   . . . .   441 Ballyspellin   39
So well acquainted with my Zeal   . . . .   444 Modern Lady   3
"Well, if I ever touch a Card: . . . .   446 Modern Lady   51
"Well, I remember what she won;   . . . . . .   446 Modern Lady   64
With Godliness cou'd well dispense, ...   455 Dean Smedley   5
Well knowing what the Poets meant: . . . . . .   461 Birthday Song   18
If well apply'd, can hardly miss: . . . .   463 Birthday Song   84
For Patrons never pay so well, ...   463 Birthday Song   95
Hanover may do well enough;   . . . .   467 Birthday Song   213
You've Cause to say he meant you well: . . . . .   475 Epist on Epist   25
Hither convey St. Patrick's Well;   . . . .   478 Epist on Epist   92
And well deserves the Nation's Thanks.   . . . . .   515 Answer Fable   80
Thus, with Talents well endu'd   . . . .   523 Betty Grizette   29
Beneath the Arm pits well besmear'd.   . . . . .   526 Lady's Dres Rm   12
But let me now, for I can do it well, ...   532 To Mr. Gay   29
You serve a potent Prince, as well as He.   . . . .   532 To Mr. Gay   44
May well conclude his Pow'r will never end.   . . .   533 To Mr. Gay   74
And, with an Oath, assure him; all is well.   . . .   534 To Mr. Gay   96
Come, tell me truly, wou'd you take well, ...   546 Life of Swift   31
Wou'd either Poet take it well, ...   546 Life of Swift   54
"Which might as well, in his opinion, ...   550 Life of Swift   174
I love my Friend as well as you, ...   554 Death of Swift   17
His Brethren write as well as he?   . . . . . .   554 Death of Swift   32
St. John, as well as Pultney knows, ...   555 Death of Swift   59
"And well remembers Charles the Second.   . . . . .   556 Death of Swift   108
That, God be prais'd, the Dean is well.   . . . . .   557 Death of Swift   126
Which Pope must bear, as well as I.   . . . . . .   561 Death of Swift   204
"To merit well of human Kind: . . . .   567 Death of Swift   362
For Strephon could remember well, ...   587 Strephon Chloe   105
Now, Ponder well ye Parents dear;   . . . . . .   587 Strephon Chloe   115
Consider well what may come after;   . . . . . .   591 Strephon Chloe   232
But, well embrown'd with Dirt and Hair.   . . . .   594 Cassinus Peter   18
As well as Chymists by their Books: . . . . .   597 Problem Solved   4
Might well excuse a Stoick's Rage.   . . . . . .   603 Beasts Confess   58
Ne'er kept a Cause, he well may boast, ...   604 Beasts Confess   91
At which, however well intended, ...   605 Beasts Confess   125
And, well he might; for to his Cost, ...   607 Beasts Confess   189
Well comprehend their nat'ral Powers;   . . . . .   607 Beasts Confess   204
And shake it well, and down it comes.   . . . . .   627 Scandal Poem 2   130
Well I know, you can discern, ...   630 Epistle Lady   29
It is well observ'd by Horace, ...   636 Epistle Lady   198
For your Sake, as well as mine, ...   637 Epistle Lady   217
Out-done by none in Rhyming well, ...   650 On Poetry   291
How well his publick Thrift is shewn?   . . . . .   659 On Poetry   D 416
Carthy, you say, writes well--his genius true.--   .   668 Epig Carthy 8   D 1
His Humour might our Laughter well command,   . . .   669 Epig Carthy 16   D 3
Well: but a Duke thou art; so pleasd the King   678 Dean and Duke   15
She study'd well the Point, and found   . . . . .   695 Cadenus Vaness   278
Well knowing from the Books she read   . . . . .   696 Cadenus Vaness   310
Becomes the Creature well enough.   . . . . . .   700 Cadenus Vaness   427
She well remember'd to her Cost, ...   705 Cadenus Vaness   604
She railly'd well, he always knew, ...   707 Cadenus Vaness   660
But, sure, she never talk'd so well.   . . . . .   710 Cadenus Vaness   749
First, to adorn your Person well, ...   732 Verses Vanessa   3
Reflecting on a Life well spent?   . . . . . .   764 Stel B-day '26   36
How well are the Spectators pleas'd!   . . . . . .   777 Mullinix Tim   126
I wish they had been well apply'd.   . . . . . .   779 Mullinix Tim   210
You'll find it well prepar'd to take   . . . . . .   780 Mullinix Tim   225
Be studious well to imitate   . . . .   780 Mullinix Tim   233
I well remember when I sat fort.   . . . . . .   783 Tim and Fables   22
Could do such Feats as well as they.   . . . . .   788 Dick's Variety   18
Well may they boast that antient Blood, which runs   791 St. Pat's Well   17
Where is the sacred Well, that bore my Name?   . . .   793 St. Pat's Well   65
That was bred to kill a Cow well: . . . . . .   800 Traulus 2   30
May well be said Man did beget it.   . . . . . .   812 Bro Protestant   38
As well may claim you for their Kin.   . . . . .   813 Bro Protestant   40
And, when they gave it, well 'tis known, ...   820 Dr. Rundle   17
Rundle a Bishop! well he may;   . . . . . .   820 Dr. Rundle   19
And well we know, The Congee Regal   . . . . .   821 Dr. Rundle   57
Is more secure as well as legal.   . . . . . .   821 Dr. Rundle   58
At Market Hill, as well appears   . . . . . .   848 Old Thorn   1
I guess well enough   . . . .   854 Lady's Lament   107
Hail fellow, well met, ...   856 Lady's Lament   165
Well, if you could lose it quite.   . . . . . .   862 To Janus   12
All for Love, or the World well lost.   . . . . .   878 Robbin & Harry   20
The <Dean> and Spaniard find it too well;   . . . .   883 Rev Market-Hill   10
So well contriv'd her Toes to pinch, ...   885 Rev Market-Hill   65
How well to win the Ladies Hearts, ...   887 Panegyr Dean   11

```
WELL            (CONTINUED)                          PAGE    TITLE           LINE
   As well become St. <Patrick's> <Dean>;      . . . . .   889 Panegyr Dean       78
   So well, what Bottle holds a Quart:     . . . . . .     889 Panegyr Dean       92
   Already have improv'd so well,          . . . . . .     891 Panegyr Dean      133
   (With Flow'r of Sulphur powder'd well,      . . . .     903 Death Daphne       25
   There is a Gate, we know full well,     . . . . . .     928 Riddle 12      D    1
   I promise to use you well.      . . . . . . . .         952 Onyons              3
   Well roasted, with Sugar and Wine in a Cup,    . . . .  953 Oranges             3
   Suit your Words to your Musick well,        . . . . .   956 Cantata
   Musick well, Musick well;       . . . . . . . .         956 Cantata
   Musick well, Musick well,       . . . . . . . .         956 Cantata
   Suit your Words to your Musick well,        . . . . .   956 Cantata
   Suit your Words to your Musick well,        . . . . .   956 Cantata
   Well, punners and rhymers must have the last word. . .  976 Dean to Sherid      8
   And I love you so well, as I told you long ago,   . . . 979 Dean to Tho: S     17
   Well; if ever I saw such another Man . . .             985 Mary to Sher        1
   Well, well, that's as God pleaseś, . . .    . . . .     986 Mary to Sher       20
   Well, well, that's as God pleases, . . .    . . . .     986 Mary to Sher       20
   Well, but I must run and make the Bed, . . .    . . .   987 Mary to Sher       35
   At least, I'm well assured, that no Folk lays          988 Letter Dr Sh-n     26
   Come back t'us well freighted;` . . . . . . . .        1014 Swift to Sheri     25
WELL-BOUND
   Take up a well-bound Heap of Sticks.    . . . . . .     189 Faggot              4
WELL-COMPACTED
   Whose well-compacted Forms escape the Light,   . . . .   31 Ode to Temple     166
WELL-RECEIV'D
   "That he was well-receiv'd at Court---.    . . . . .    547 Life of Swift      85
WELSTED
   No Rhymer can like Welsted sink.    . . . . . . .       654 On Poetry         394
WENCH    SEE SUBURB-WENCH
   Where can this idle Wench be hid?   . . . . . . .       223 Prog of Love       28
   'Till <Hort> arriv'd ne'er kept a Wench;    . . . .     303 Storm              18
   Nor Cindercola, charming Wench!     . . . . . . .       373 Letter D. S-y      65
   Lords keep a Pimp to bring a Wench;     . . . . . .     480 Libel on D- D-     22
   That careless Wench! no Creature warn her   . . . .     528 Lady's Dres Rm     71
   For which you curse the careless Wench; . . . . . .     529 Lady's Dres Rm    108
   To punish Thieves, or lash a Suburb Wench.  . . . .     537 Mr. Pulteney        6
   Cry'd, Huzzy, why sure the Wench is gone mad:  . . .    873 Grand Question    184
WENCHES   SEE COUNTRY-WENCHES
WENT
   With other cattle to the city went;    . . . . . .      46 To Congreve       116
   How Markets went for Hey and Oats.  . . . . . . .       63 Discovery          36
   That I went to warm my self in Lady Betty's Chamber,.   69 Mrs Harris Pet      1
        . .
   So when I went to put up my Purse, as God would have    69 Mrs Harris Pet      8
        it,. . .
   Then the Bell rung, and I went down to put my Lady to   69 Mrs Harris Pet     10
        Bed,
   . . .that we went and search'd the Folks round,   . .   70 Mrs Harris Pet     22
   So I went to the Party suspected,. . . . . . . .        71 Mrs Harris Pet     34
   Now you may go hang your self for me, and so went away. .72 Mrs Harris Pet     63
   And so went to Bed in a desperate Case.    . . . . .    77 Lady B- B-          7
   The heavy Wall went clamb'ring after.   . . . . . .     92 Bauc & Phil 1      94
   Disguis'd in tatter'd Habits, went  . . . . . . .      111 Bauc & Phil 2       9
   They went by chance, amidst their Talk, . . . . . .    116 Bauc & Phil 2     153
   But made his Leg and went away.     . . . . . . .      121 Apollo Outwit      44
   And you may swear the Tale went round.  . . . . . .    150 Corinna            20
   And how, when Master went to <piss>,    . . . . . .    150 Corinna            23
   A Codling e'er it went his Lip in,  . . . . . . .      156 Fable of Midas      5
   Went where he pleas'd, said what he thought,   . . .   171 Horace 1, 7        33
   Went here and there, and ev'ry where,   . . . . . .    207 Fable Bitches       5
   Will went again to visit Dick   . . . . . . . .        220 A Quiet Life       19
   To learn the Way that Phillis went;     . . . . . .    223 Prog of Love       34
   Old Madam who went up to find   . . . . . . . .        223 Prog of Love       43
   So Celia went entire to bed,    . . . . . . . .        226 Prog of Beauty     29
   Wher'er he went he never saw his Betters,   . . . .    234 Elegy on Demar     15
   Direct to the North, where I never yet went;   . . .   264 Apollo             48
   The Couple to the Temple went:  . . . . . . . .        290 Prog Marriage       6
   To Neptune went, and begg'd in Form     . . . . . .    302 Storm               3
   "But he'll come back the Knave he went."   . . . .     306 Storm              72
   Went to one Griffith, formerly a play'r:    . . . .    307 Billet Players      4
   Went home, and was cudgell'd again by his Wife.    . . 327 Epigram 1          10
   Concerning this Image there went a Prediction,  . . .  334 Serious Poem       19
   Then down I went upon my Knees, his Blessing to obtain, 342 Upon His Grace     29
   And then I went to pay the 'Squire and in the Way I    343 Upon His Grace     41
        found,
   While he went always drunk to Bed.  . . . . . . .      352 Wood Ironmongr      8
   She went Abroad - - - She'd thought me mad.    . . .   377 Apology Lady C     52
   Worse than they went    . . . . . . . . . . .          440 Ballyspellin       17
   When you went Colonelling    . . . . . . . . .         441 Ballyspellin       27
   "I'd lay my Life he never went:     . . . . . . .      451 Modern Lady       201
   One thing he did before he went hence,  . . . . . .    455 Dean Smedley       17
   To Fort St. George a Pedlar went he.    . . . . . .    456 Dean Smedley       48
   Return Him Beggar As He Went.   . . . . . . . .        456 Dean Smedley       50
   Went down like stupifying Draughts: . . . . . . .      470 Burning Poem        8
   While He went robbing on; old Master dy'd.  . . . .    536 To Mr. Gay        148
   "Poor Man! he went, all on a sudden---!    . . . .     547 Life of Swift      70
   'Tis Time to shew how Things went there.    . . . .    588 Strephon Chloe    146
   Or ever went to seek my Food    . . . . . . . .        602 Beasts Confess     19
   Gone, where the Chickens went before.   . . . . . .    642 On Poetry          70
   Away the fair Detractors went,  . . . . . . . .        699 Cadenus Vaness    408
```

WENT	(CONTINUED)	PAGE	TITLE	LINE
You e're return'd, or ever went?		745	Stel Distress	22
And thus the Farce a fortnight went		747	Stel Distress	53
Thus for a week the Farce went on		747	Stel Distress	
Thus, for a Week the Farce went on;		751	Stel Wood-Park	69
Wherever they went,		755	Dingley Brent	2
And burst asunder e'er he went to Hell;		806	Judas	18
Death went upon a solemn Day,		903	Death Daphne	1
Went triumphant to Church, and sang stoutly Te Deum:		967	Letter Sherid	18
When I saw you to-day, as I went with Lord Anglesey.		978	Dean to Tho: S	1
I went in vain to look for Eupolis,		988	Letter Dr Sh-n	7
WEPT				
Thus, when Dorinda wept, joy ev'ry face forsook,		53	Temple Ill	59
WER'T	4		OMITTED WORD	
WERE	208		OMITTED WORD	
WERT	4		OMITTED WORD	
WEST				
From East to west the world we roam,		621	Scandal Poem 1	127
From East to West, the World we roam;		627	Scandal Poem 2	121
WESTERN				
Once, on a Time a Western Blast,		126	Little House	5
Oh, may some Western Tempest sweep		258	Bubble	205
Fame now reports, the western Isle		387	Manly Virtue	135
WESTON				
But Weston has a new-cast Gown		75	Game Traffick	21
WET				
The Floor is all wet		245	Irish-Feast	41
And swimming never wet a Feather.		253	Bubble	56
Then in a Sawpit and wet Weather,		393	Modern Poets	19
For once to wet thy Pen Divine:		515	Answer Fable	90
All dirty and wet:		856	Lady's Lament	166
Nor need I blush, although you feel it wet;		881	Pastoral Dial	23
Familiar grown to Dirt and Wet,		890	Panegyr Dean	109
WETT				
From House to House, wett to the Skin		90	Bauc & Phil 1	13
WETTER				
Yet, though we grant she makes it wetter		621	Scandal Poem 1	145
But, though we own, she makes it wetter,		628	Scandal Poem 2	149
WETYNGE				
Walke sans wetynge Shoes ne hosen.		102	Merlin	4
WEXFORD				
Be gone down to the county of Wexford		1022	Nim-Dan-Dean 2	D 6
WHALE				
But Whale Directors eat up all.		253	Bubble	68
Thus when a Whale hath lost the Tide		258	Bubble	201
A Whale of moderate Size will draw		651	On Poetry	323
The greatest Whale, that swims the Sea		934	Riddle 21	D 11
WHALEY				
Or Walmsley or Whaley,		857	Lady's Lament	205
May Whaley disgrace		858	Lady's Lament	223
WHARTON				
His Ld ship as Wharton		423	Carterets Arms	6
<Wharton>, unless prevented by a Whore,		166	Toland's Invit	35
<Wharton> can only Swear by Fits,		168	Peace Dunkirk	13
He hated <Wharton> like a Toad;		171	Horace 1, 7	36
WHAT	463		OMITTED WORD	
WHAT'S	12		OMITTED WORD	
WHATE'ER				
Whate'er I plant (like Corn on barren Earth)		33	Ode to Temple	210
For, whate'er theologic lev'llers dream,		41	Ode Sancroft	230
Quoth Neal, whate'er the rest may think,		67	Problem	53
Whate'er concerns you full as well,		101	Elegy Patrige	114
Whate'er you did in Battle slay,		154	Widow and Cat	D 33
Whate'er these dire fore-bodings meant,		290	Prog Marriage	17
And still the Truth he will Maintain, whate'er he loses by't.		341	Upon His Grace	6
Whate'er you brag,		441	Ballyspellin	47
Whate'er the noisy Scoundrel says		505	Doctor Delaney	163
Talk with Sense, whate'er you please on,		638	Epistle Lady	271
Whate'er Vexations Love attend,		702	Cadenus Vaness	506
Whate'er she gains is young and fresh;		759	Receipt Youth	16
This Day, whate'er the Fates decree,		763	Stel B-day '26	1
Talks whate'er comes in his Head,		800	Traulus 2	21
Whate'er I promised or intended,		899	Dean's Reasons	5
Whate'er your Predecessors taught us,		988	Letter Dr Sh-n	1
WHATEVER				
Whatever moves our Wonder or our Sport,		31	Ode to Temple	163
Whatever serves for innocent Emblems of the Court;		31	Ode to Temple	164
From thee whatever virtue takes its rise,		55	Temple Ill	135
Whatever Grecian Story tells:		482	Libel on D- D-	78
The Bason takes whatever comes		527	Lady's Dres Rm	39
Whatever base returns you find		755	Stella '23	29
Whatever was said,		755	Dingley Brent	4
O then, whatever Heav'n intends,		766	Stel B-day '26	79
(Which are, whatever you may think,		775	Mullinix Tim	63
Whatever they give me I must be content,		867	Grand Question	22
Whatever climate you were in.		899	Dean's Reasons	26
But, whatever be my dress,		937	Riddle 24	D 35
And whatever passes		938	Riddle Answerd	5
WHATSO'ER				
That Gods, of whatso'er Degree,		694	Cadenus Vaness	259

WHEADLED

		PAGE	TITLE	LINE
How Jonny wheadled, threatned, fawnd,	. . . . . .	224	Prog of Love	87

WHEAT

| The generous Wheat forgot its Pride, | . . . . . . | 811 | Bro Protestant | 7 |

WHEEDLED

| And Vulcan wheedled by his Wife, | . . . . | 100 | Elegy Patrige | 83 |

WHEEL

| From Husband, Children, Wheel, or Spinnet. | . . . . | 322 | First of April | 42 |

WHEELBARROW

| I'll write, tho' I'm forc'd to write in a wheelbarrow: | . | 979 | Dean to Tho: S | 12 |

WHEELS

Encreas't by new intestin Wheels	. . . .	93	Bauc & Phil 1	128
Increas'd by new Intestine Wheels:	. . . . . .	113	Bauc & Phil 2	68
The Kennel-Edge, where Wheels had worn the Place.	.	124	Descriptn Morn	10
Like a clock without wheels;	. . . .	852	Lady's Lament	34

WHEEZING

| And, wheezing Asthma, loth to stir: | . . . . . | 895 | Panegyr Dean | 278 |

WHELP

"Hath sent me to your House to whelp,	. . . . . .	207	Fable Bitches	11
Whether Curr Plunket, or Whelp Skean,	. . . . .	298	Horrid Plot	20
The humble whelp gives ev'ry vote.	. . . .	421	Ireld	15
Distill'd from Tripsy's darling Whelp;	. . . . .	526	Lady's Dres Rm	32

WHEN   635

OMITTED WORD

WHEN'T

| The Day will come, when't shall be said, | . . . . . | 547 | Life of Swift | 68 |

WHENCE

Whence takes it its Increase, and whence its Birth,	.	31	Ode to Temple	169
Whence takes it its Increase, and whence its Birth,	.	31	Ode to Temple	169
Whence the weak shapes wild and imperfect pass,	. .	35	Ode Sancroft	23
Whence came these Goths to overrun the pit?	. . .	46	To Congreve	84
O'er the glad scene whence first she rose a bride:	.	51	Temple Ill	12
Say, whence it comes that thou art grown of late	. .	53	Temple Ill	83
Whence Broods of insect Poets rise.	. . . . . .	80	Vanbrug House	54
From whence 'tis plain the Diadem	. . . .	98	Elegy Patrige	25
And whence we claim our shoeing horns,	. . . .	99	Elegy Patrige	38
From whence the neighbouring Farmer calls	. . . .	127	Little House	17
"From whence, with half an Eye we may discover,	. .	195	Author Himself	45
But whence this Wonderous Charity, in Play'rs,	. .	275	Epilogue	11
Perhaps you wonder whence this Friendship Springs,	.	275	Epilogue	35
Turn'd to that dirt from whence he sprung.	. . . .	297	Satiric Elegy	32
(From whence Philosophers agree,	. . . .	323	Pethox	9
The high Descent from whence you came,	. . . .	323	Pethox	12
Yet, whence proceeds this Weight we lay	. . . .	414	Censure	17
Who can imagine whence the Fund is,	. . . . . .	477	Epist on Epist	75
From whence the Consquence is plain,	. . . . .	495	Panegyr Swift	76
From whence 'tis plain, they quite have lost	. . .	498	Panegyr Swift	165
Pois'ning the Flesh from whence it came;	. . . .	529	Lady's Dres Rm	106
To taint the Parts from whence they fell.	. . . .	529	Lady's Dres Rm	112
From whence you draw such bold conclusions;	. . .	622	Scandal Poem 1	161
Whence Gay was banish'd in Disgrace,	. . . . .	650	On Poetry	307
From whence the tender Skin assumes	. . . . .	691	Cadenus Vaness	160
From whence a Cleanliness remains,	. . . . . .	691	Cadenus Vaness	162
From whence that Decency of Mind,	. . . . . .	691	Cadenus Vaness	164
Yet guess'd not whence could spring the Change.	. .	704	Cadenus Vaness	567
Her Hearers are amaz'd from whence	. . . . . .	726	To Stella	79
I bless the Hand from whence they came,	. . . .	727	To Stella	115
Confess the Soil from whence the Victors came.	. .	791	St. Pat's Well	16
Fled to the Fountain back, from whence it came!	. .	793	St. Pat's Well	66
Whence come these inconsistent Fits?	. . . . .	796	Traulus 1	33
What the De'el is't to him whence the Devil they came?		815	Yahoo's	24
From whence unsav'ry Vapours rose,	. . . . . .	895	Panegyr Dean	285
Does he forget from whence he came?	. . . . .	950	Upstart	D 2
Has he forgot from whence he sprung?	. . . . .	950	Upstart	D 3

WHENE'ER   (WHEN'ER,WHENE'RE,WHEN'RE)
       22

OMITTED WORDS

WHENEVER   5

OMITTED WORD

WHENSO'RE

| And whenso're you please to shine, | . . . . | 919 | Riddle 5 | 9 |

WHERE   225

OMITTED WORD

WHERE'S

Else where's the Gain in being Great?	. . . . .	6	Ode to King	5
As Poets fein; but where's the Moral?	. . . . .	254	Bubble	94
A Boat a Judge! yes, where's the Blunder?	. . . .	286	Elegy Boat	39
Where's now this Fav'rite of Apollo?	. . . . .	562	Death of Swift	249
I broke his Teeth, but where's the mighty harm?	. .	670	Epig Carthy 20	D 2

WHEREAS

| Whereas, Notwithstanding, I am in great Pain, | . . | 143 | New Song | 11 |
| Now, whereas the said Criminal seems past Repentance, | . | 266 | Apollo | 93 |

WHEREBY

And now whereby I find you would fain make an Excuse,	.	985	Mary to Sher	11
Whereby you now confess your self to be a Goose or an		986	Mary to Sher	18
Ass:				

WHEREIN

In gifts, wherein you both excell'd,	. . . . .	177	To Lord Harley	30
wherein French Writers most excell:	. . . . .	216	To Mr. Delany	32
Wherein she distinctly could read ev'ry Line,	. .	264	Apollo	51
Wherein yourselves have greatest Share?	. . . .	449	Modern Lady	153
wherein the Moralist design'd	. . . .	608	Beasts Confess	217
To that wherein it most excell'd;	. . . . . .	701	Cadenus Vaness	451
Wherein his Dignity and Age	. . . .	711	Cadenus Vaness	778
Wherein his Genius was below	. . . .	712	Cadenus Vaness	812
Wherein she grievously complains,	. . . . . .	713	Cadenus Vaness	858
Wherein the God of Earth delights.	. . . . .	743	Stel B-day 22	52

	PAGE	TITLE	LINE
WHEREIN (CONTINUED)			
Wherein the Men of Wit delight.	920	Riddle 6	6
Wherein they need not lose a Bit, ...	1022	Nim-Dan-Dean 1	D 43
WHEREOF			
(Methods in talk whereof our pride and ignorance make use)	38	Ode Sancroft	125
Whereof, to make the Matter clear, ...	526	Lady's Dres Rm	9
Whereof I cou'd say more to your Verses, ...	987	Mary to Sher	37
WHERESOE'RE			
Yet wheresoe're you look you'll always find	18	Ode Athenian	74
WHEREVER (WHERE-E'ER,WHERE-EVER,WHERE'E'ER,WHERE'ER,WHER'ER)			
15		OMITTED WORDS	
WHEREWITH			
Wherewith our Vanity endows us, ...	603	Beasts Confess	77
WHERRY			
There to supply old Charon's leaky Wherry:	285	Elegy Boat	24
Lo, Charon from his leaky Wherry, ...	596	Cassinus Peter	83
Safe within my little Wherry, ...	635	Epistle Lady	163
WHET			
Here conns his Notes, and takes a Whet, ...	127	Little House	21
WHETHER 38		OMITTED WORD	
WHEY			
The Butter from the Whey to part:	892	Panegyr Dean	182
WHEY-FACE			
Dull Daniel's whey-face;	858	Lady's Lament	224
WHICH 328		OMITTED WORD·	
WHIFFS			
No noisom Whiffs, or sweaty Streams, ...	584	Strephon Chloe	12
WHIG			
And be a true Whig, while I am Not in game.	145	New Song	54
And whether he were Whig or Tory?	171	Horace 1, 7	22
You'll then defy the strongest Whig, ...	191	Faggot	49
On all Whig Papers, and Gazets:	282	Journal	100
I Ask'd a Whig the other Night, ...	298	Horrid Plot	1
A bitter Whig, or Tory sow'r;	417	Woman's Mind	50
Where Whig and Tory fiercely fight	421	Ireld	5
Mean time the whig is always winner	421	Ireld	11
But, they can manage Whig and Tory:	483	Libel on D- D-	98
Without Regard to Whig or Tory, ...	605	Beasts Confess	146
If I laugh at Whig and Tory;	636	Epistle Lady	193
And one is Whig, and one is Tory.	650	On Poetry	294
These brangling jars of Whig and Tory, ...	774	Mullinix Tim	35
Tom would pray for ev'ry Whig, ...	784	Mullinex Dick	15
A long-ear'd Beast, and a sputt'ring old Whig, . . .	942	Probatur Alit	27
A <Whig> and one that wears a Gown.	121	Apollo Outwit	64
WHIGGISH			
And, to defend the Whiggish Cause, ...	417	Woman's Mind	55
WHIGS			
Triumphant Tories, and desponding Whigs, ...	138	City Shower	41
And the whigs may all go Swing, ...	168	Peace Dunkirk	6
The Dutch-hearted Whigs may rail and complain; . . .	169	Peace Dunkirk	37
The Bucket-play 'twixt Whigs and Tories, ...	181	Horace 2, 1	17
Let not the whigs our tory club rebuke;	186	Scriblerus 3	1
And gives the Whigs and Rabble Sport.	190	Faggot	26
Whigs, Tories, Trimmers, Hannoverians, ...	345	Prometheus	13
From Principles the Whigs maintain;	417	Woman's Mind	54
Lampoons on Whigs, when in Disgrace;	494	Panegyr Swift	33
Where Whigs their cursed Trains had laid;	494	Panegyr Swift	42
"With all the Turns of Whigs and Tories:	572	Death of Swift	476
<God> <damn> the Whigs and Tories too.	782	Mullinix Tim	284
And fierce against the Whigs harangu'd?	884	Rev Market-Hill	39
Or murmuring at Whigs Preferments.	993	On Picture	6
WHILE SEE A-WHILE			
And for a while unbends their contradicting Souls: . .	9	Ode to King	91
Stay but a little while and down again 'twill come, . .	10	Ode to King	128
And for a while in heav'nly Contemplation sate . . .	16	Ode Athenian	25
Stay while I tell my story, short, and true;	46	To Congreve	111
While two fond lovers prate, the Muse and I.	49	To Congreve	200
Listen while the muse thus teaches thee to sing: . . .	52	Temple Ill	36
Kindled while reason sleeps, but quickly flies, . . .	54	Temple Ill	99
While every ignorant Beholder	63	Discovery	15
While all the rest stood gaping round	63	Discovery	24
Our Listner stood a while confus'd, ...	64	Discovery	45
And so he did; for in a while	87	Hist V's House	27
Still Groans while tatling Gossips prate.	93	Bauc & Phil 1	110
While in the Station of a Jack	94	Bauc & Phil 1	135
Philemon having paus'd a while	94	Bauc & Phil 1	157
While He from out of Chimney took	112	Bauc & Phil 2	25
Philemon, having paus'd a while, ...	115	Bauc & Phil 2	111
While Moses held it in his Hand, ...	132	Magician's Rod	2
While Rain depends, the pensive Cat gives o'er . .	136	City Shower	3
Mean while the South rising with dabbled Wings, . .	137	City Shower	13
While the first drizzling Show'r is born aslope, . .	137	City Shower	18
The Templer spruce, while ev'ry Spout's a-broach, . .	138	City Shower	35
While Streams run down her oil'd Umbrella's Sides. . .	138	City Shower	38
While Spouts run clatt'ring o'er the Roof by Fits; .	139	City Shower	44
There should be a Peace, while I'm Not in game. . .	143	New Song	14
And will quit my best Riendds, while I'm Not in game.	144	New Song	26
I'll Speech against Peace while Dismal's my Name, .	145	New Song	53
And be a true Whig, while I am Not in game. . . .	145	New Song	54
While the poor Child lay fast asleep.	150	Corinna	8

WHILE   (CONTINUED)   PAGE   TITLE   LINE

Against whose Torrent while he Swims, ...   157 Fable of Midas   35
Which while the Senate strove to scower, ...   158 Fable of Midas   71
While He his utmost Strength apply'd, ...   158 Fable of Midas   73
Suspend a while your vain ambitious Hopes, ...   162 Toland's Invit   5
'Twill then, perhaps, be worth thy while . . . . . .   181 Horace 2, 1   41
While, wise Men think they ought to fight   . . . .   189 Faggot   21
While innocent, he scorns ignoble Flight;   . . . . .   196 Author Himself   61
By Faction tir'd, with Grief he waits a while,   196 Author Himself   71
And, though the Villain 'scape a while, he feels   .   210 Earl of Oxford   21
While at her Chin the Conflu'ents met.   . . . . . .   227 Prog of Beauty   40
With Spittle while she spins, anoints, ...   227 Prog of Beauty   42
While Partridge wisely shews the Cause   . . . . . .   228 Prog of Beauty   89
While all the Parish, as she flies, ...   230 Prog of Poetry   15
While from below all Grub-street rings.   . . . . . .   231 Prog of Poetry   46
While the Water and Sweat, ...   245 Irish-Feast   43
There sprawl'd a while, at last got out, ...   255 Bubble   131
While some build Castles in the Air, ...   257 Bubble   165
Suspended for a while in Air. . . . .   258 Bubble   188
While you ly helpless on the Sand: . . . . . .   258 Bubble   200
And observe while you live, that no Man is shy   . . .   264 Apollo   57
While George, and Dean, go back to Gammon.   . . . .   280 Journal   42
While his Tenants in Paper must pay him his Rent: . .   288 Bank Down   53
While Mistress Iris held her Train, ...   290 Prog Marriage   13
While He goes out to cheapen Books, ...   291 Prog Marriage   39
While Betty's buzzing at her Ear, ...   291 Prog Marriage   41
While she drives on to see the Play.   . . . . . .   292 Prog Marriage   82
He for a while would not consent, ...   294 Prog Marriage   125
Sir, you mistake me all this while: . . . . . .   298 Horrid Plot   16
Then all this while have I been bubbled;   . . . .   300 Horrid Plot   57
We cannot think it worth your while.   . . . . . .   315 To Ford   98
While We perhaps must wait a Week: . . . . . .   315 To Ford   104
While We may search all Dublin o'er   . . . . . .   315 To Ford   107
And while his Fate is in thy Hands, ...   325 Pethox   51
Now while this Brazen Chain prevail'd, ...   345 Prometheus   41
While Vultures eat his growing Liver: . . . . . .   346 Prometheus   56
While he went always drunk to Bed.   . . . . . .   352 Wood Ironmongr   8
The Moon is Silver all this while.)   . . . . . .   354 Simile Silver   16
While others wrack their busy Brains, ...   361 Grace's Answer   17
While you and Spouse transform'd, shall soon   . . . .   362 Grace's Answer   51
While the sly Mountebank attends his Trade, ...   364 On Dreams   33
Is made his Mansion for a while;   . . . .   387 Manly Virtue   136
As clever Tom Clinch, while the Rabble was bawling,   .   399 Tom Clinch   1
A while they on each other look, ...   405 Swift to Pope   5
Desire, in Rapture gaz'd a while, ...   413 Desire Possess   45
While all she prates has nothing in it.   . . . .   415 Woman's Mind   6
While English sharpers take the pay, ...   421 Ireld   9
While he sits by a grinning, ...   425 Five Ladies   5
While Mothers, Daughters, Aunts, ...   426 Five Ladies   30
One Bed while alive held both Doll and Dick   . . . .   430 Dicky Dolly   13
While he, at ease, secure and light, ...   435 Answer Paulus   91
'The Cook must keep it back a while;   . . . . . .   447 Modern Lady   95
And while, with all this paultry Stuff, ...   448 Modern Lady   109
But let me now a while survey   . . . .   448 Modern Lady   116
While Ignorance, with Brain of Lead, ...   449 Modern Lady   134
While crooked Cynthia swearing says, ...   449 Modern Lady   160
While each to be the loudest vies, ...   450 Modern Lady   175
While thus they rail, and scold, and storm, ...   453 Modern Lady   270
While Victory, with Wings outspread, ...   461 Birthday Song   33
Shou'd cool your Heels a while, and wait   . . . .   475 Epist on Epist   5
While Montague, who claim'd the Station   . . .   481 Libel on D- D-   35
"While he obeys Almighty Will, ...   485 Libel on D- D-   167
While Burnet in his deathless page   . . . . . .   490 Dialogue   27
While most that are or would be great, ...   491 Dialogue   53
While Dunces of the coarsest Clay, ...   497 Panegyr Swift   148
While <Grattan>, <Sheridan>, and I, ...   499 Panegyr Swift   177
While my hard-labour'd Poem pines   . . . . . .   502 Doctor Delaney   77
Receives them while they wait for Bayl?   . . . . . .   504 Doctor Delaney   146
Now listen while he next produces, ...   526 Lady's Dres Rm   19
Who, while th' unrighteous Mammon is his Friend,   . .   533 To Mr. Gay   73
And while he poisons, wins the Royal Heart.   . . .   534 To Mr. Gay   82
And drain the Fish-ponds; while your Master doats;   .   534 To Mr. Gay   90
While He went robbing on; old Master dy'd.   . . .   536 To Mr. Gay   148
For while he keeps his Pen, you are not safe.   . . . .   538 Mr. Pulteney   14
"While Nature kindly bent to ease us, ...   554 Death of Swift   9
And, while they toss my Name about, ...   565 Death of Swift   303
"While they pursu'd each others Ruin.   . . . . . .   567 Death of Swift   368
"While Numbers to Preferment rose;   . . . . . .   569 Death of Swift   401
"While they who at the Steerage stood, ...   569 Death of Swift   413
While each pale Sinner hangs his Head, ...   579 Day Judgement   9
While she engrosseth ev'ry Swain, ...   585 Strephon Chloe   31
While she a Goddess dy'd in Grain.   . . . . . .   586 Strephon Chloe   85
While these Reflections fill'd his Head, ...   587 Strephon Chloe   111
He found her, while the Scent increas'd, ...   589 Strephon Chloe   185
While all the gross and filthy last.   . . . . . .   591 Strephon Chloe   234
To chat a while, and warm his Nose: . . . . . .   594 Cassinus Peter   8
While others of the learned Robe   . . . . . .   604 Beasts Confess   87
While We, whom Reason ought to sway, ...   607 Beasts Confess   205
While Women, if it could be reckon'd   . . . . . .   618 Scandal Poem 1   45
While we, o'er Tenariffa plac't, ...   620 Scandal Poem 1   105
While Women, if it could be reckon'd, ...   625 Scandal Poem 2   41

WHILE	(CONTINUED)	PAGE	TITLE	LINE
While we, o'er Tenariffa plac't,		626	Scandal Poem 2	103
While we, by soft prolifick Show'rs,		628	Scandal Poem 2	151
But, I beg, suspend a While,		631	Epistle Lady	49
Both alike; while neither mends.		631	Epistle Lady	56
While a little gentle Jerking		636	Epistle Lady	205
Only make it smart a while:		638	Epistle Lady	265
While ev'ry Fool his Claim alledges,		640	On Poetry	9
While not a Soul demands your Ware?		641	On Poetry	44
While Readers wonder whom you meant.		645	On Poetry	160
While others do as much for him.		651	On Poetry	334
While with the Fustian of thy Book		670	Epig Carthy 21	D 1
And while the Book was in her Hand,		702	Cadenus Vaness	514
While she continues in her Prime.		703	Cadenus Vaness	539
While ev'ry Passion of her Mind		709	Cadenus Vaness	710
While thus Cadenus entertains		711	Cadenus Vaness	790
While Gracefulness its Art conceals,		726	To Stella	83
If, while your Tenderness secures		727	To Stella	119
While, Stella to your lasting Praise		739	Stel B-day '21	1
While I assign my self a Task		739	Stel B-day '21	3
And Stella will be sung, while I		741	Stel B-day 22	33
(While there are Houses to be let)		746	Stel Distress	43
When all the while you might remark Where all		747	Stel Distress	47
While there are Lodgings to be lett.		751	Stel Wood-Park	60
When all the while you might remark,		751	Stel Wood-Park	63
While <Sheridan> is off the hooks,		756	Stel B-day '24	11
While I can better hear than see;		758	Stel B-day '24	52
While not a Blade of Grass, or Hay,		759	Receipt Youth	3
While all the Squires from nine Miles round,		760	Receipt Youth	42
Yet you, while Time is running fast,		764	Stel B-day '26	17
While all is Calm, his Arguments prevail,		770	Horace 1, 14	27
While all the silly Wretch can do		774	Mullinix Tim	27
And while this Vital Breath I blow,		776	Mullinix Tim	83
While Punch is hid behind the Scene,		776	Mullinix Tim	94
While teizing all, by all he's teiz'd,		777	Mullinix Tim	125
While Traulus all his Ordure scatters.		796	Traulus 1	31
While none believes that what he said he meant:		797	Traulus 1	50
While Things of heterogeneous Kind,		811	Bro Protestant	5
While o'er the Church these Clouds are gathering,		813	Bro Protestant	47
While I, with humble Job, had rather,		813	Bro Protestant	61
While his own ass's Zaggs were more fit for the shears.		816	Yahoo's	49
While Jonathan's threaten'd with loss of his ears;		818	Epigr Kite	2
Command his attendance while you act your farce on,		818	Epigr Kite	6
Bid Povey secure him while you are haranguing,		818	Epigr Kite	8
And, while at good Cashel you rail with such spite,		818	Archbi Cashel	3
While others hither sent to save us,		820	Dr. Rundle	33
And swagger while the Coast is clear:		824	Printer Newgat	7
While the Devil upon the Roof,		830	Legion Club	23
While the Den of Thieves is full,		830	Legion Club	28
While they sit a picking Straws		831	Legion Club	49
While they never hold their Tongue,		831	Legion Club	51
We may, while they strain their Throats,		831	Legion Club	61
While he sleeps the whole Debate,		836	Legion Club	165
While you in your Faction's Phrase		838	Legion Club	215
Form their Features, while I gibe them;		839	Legion Club	226
But, while in an ill tone,		856	Lady's Lament	155
Be my Phoebus while I rhime.		862	To Janus	2
This Hamilton's Bawn, while it sticks on my Hand,		866	Grand Question	3
Tantara, tantara, while all the Boys hollow.		870	Grand Question	92
While Harry's fencing up his ditches.		878	Robbin & Harry	28
While each with stubbed Knife remov'd the Roots		880	Pastoral Dial	3
While in his lordly Castle fixt,		883	Rev Market-Hill	19
While I from Drapier's-Mount descend,		884	Rev Market-Hill	49
While you, from where the Basin stands,		884	Rev Market-Hill	53
While tortur'd Madam bound remains,		885	Rev Market-Hill	71
While nothing comes but Froth at first,		893	Panegyr Dean	193
And sweetly moralize a while.		894	Panegyr Dean	228
Who, while I talk, a song will hum,		900	Dean's Reasons	47
While I teach, and you forget;		908	Daphne	72
But, while I thus my Life relate,		916	Riddle 1	37
While others give me many a Curse,		918	Riddle 4	27
For, while the bashful Sylvan Maid,		922	Riddle 7	33
Then catch Admirers while you may;		932	Riddle 19	D 19
While a coarse English Tongue will itch,		949	Epigr Scolding	3
Come sit by my side, while this picture I draw:		955	Portrait Life	1
While true Lovers Eyes Weeping Sleep,		960	Cantata	
WHILST				
Whilst at Your Victorious Light		9	Ode to King	111
Whilst Angels tune the Voice, and God inspires the Tongue.		17	Ode Athenian	56
Whilst all th' advantage by it got,		36	Ode Sancroft	71
Cordials are in their talk, whilst all they mean		42	Ode Sancroft	257
Whilst thus I write, vast shoals of criticks come,		50	To Congreve	213
Whilst he from out the Chimny took		91	Bauc & Phil 1	57
Whilst You shall see your Cottage rise,		92	Bauc & Phil 1	89
Whilst you shall see your Cottage rise,		112	Bauc & Phil 2	49
Whilst an alluding Hymn some Artist sings,		162	Toland's Invit	13
Whilst Patr'ot-like thou'lt strut and frown.		182	Horace 2, 1	64
Whilst Stella aforesaid stood by with the Light;		264	Apollo	36
Whilst high, and nice, and curious Meats,		378	Apology Lady C	107
And whilst he made her Value known,		386	Manly Virtue	87

WHILST	(CONTINUED)	PAGE	TITLE	LINE
Whilst he, tho' seated on a Throne,		387	Manly Virtue	131
Whilst you're, like Baal, fast asleep.		403	Window Inns 10	D 10
Whilst Lady Charlotte, like a Stroller,		410	Dial Rich Marb	61
Whilst, ev'ry Critick can devour		502	Doctor Delaney	69
Whilst Mrs. Susan comb'd her Head:		698	Cadenus Vaness	373
And so am I whilst thou art here;		932	Riddle 19	D 14
Whilst you three merry Poets traffick		993	On Picture	1
That you're a Dawb, whilst I but paint,		1003	Dan J's Reply	11

WHIM
| Attacking, when he took the Whim, | | 548 | Life of Swift | 105 |
| "To publick Use! A perfect Whim! | | 558 | Death of Swift | 157 |

WHIMS
Why Dick, thy Wife has dev'lish Whims:		220	A Quiet Life	27
The Mind unburthen'd sports in various Whims,		363	On Dreams	8
All the Superfluous Whims relate,		451	Modern Lady	224
In Whims, Parterres, Canals and Fences:		477	Epist on Epist	62
He comes with his whims,		852	Lady's Lament	39

WHIMSEYS
| But by peculiar Whimseys drawn, | | 279 | Journal | 21 |

WHIMSICAL
| Then Plodding, he thought on a whimsical Prank | | 288 | Bank Down | 34 |
| Your Whimsical, Poetick Place. | | 477 | Epist on Epist | 82 |

WHIMSYES
| Men's Folly, Whimsyes, and Inconstancy, | | 21 | Ode Athenian | 173 |

WHINE
With fawning Whine, and rueful Tone,		208	Fable Bitches	13
And dismally was heard to whine		849	Old Thorn	43
But if too many come your Madam will whine		1018	Swift Ans Sher	31

WHIP
What right had he to hold the Whip?		548	Life of Swift	120
A Whip of Scorpions in her Hand.		596	Cassinus Peter	82
Then, apply Alecto's Whip,		635	Epistle Lady	179
Your Scholars want the whip,--I shan't demur;--		671	Epig Carthy 23	D 1
They mounted, and labour'd with Whip and with Spur,		804	Irish Bishops	19
When whip you trot up, without minding your betters,		978	Dean to Tho: S	3

WHIPS
Brisk Susan whips her Linen from the Rope,		137	City Shower	17
Then whips me on a Chain of Brass,		345	Prometheus	39
And with Whips and Spurs so neat,		573	Helter Skelter	9
Three fellows with whips, and the Dean holds the string.		1027	Sheri Circles	20

WHIPT
| Would I was whipt | | 441 | Ballyspellin | 37 |
| And from the Shelf a charming Crust I whipt: | | 881 | Pastoral Dial | 30 |

WHIRL
| There doom'd to whirl an endless Round. | | 413 | Desire Possess | 50 |
| With a Whirl of Thought oppress'd, | | 578 | Day Judgement | 1 |

WHIRL'D
| Now Moll had whirl'd her Mop with dext'rous Airs, | | 124 | Descriptn Morn | 7 |

WHIRLING
| Thus whirling round, together draws | | 688 | Cadenus Vaness | 59 |

WHIRLS
| To rail; she singing, still whirls on her Mop. | | 137 | City Shower | 22 |
| It whirls about for Want of Force, | | 688 | Cadenus Vaness | 54 |

WHIRLWIND
| Wrapp'd in a whirlwind and a mist; | | 40 | Ode Sancroft | 195 |

WHISK
| So--let us now for Whisk prepare; | | 315 | To Ford | 113 |

WHISP'RING
Be what it will; late near yon whisp'ring stream,		51	Temple Ill	13
Whisp'ring in Junto most profound,		63	Discovery	22
By two such whisp'ring Kings of Branford.		64	Discovery	48
And, whisp'ring, charg'd me not to say		311	To Ford	3
And, whisp'ring wisht, the Devil burst her		618	Scandal Poem 1	18

WHISP'RINGS
| Thy Whisp'rings foisted in all Ears; | | 775 | Mullinix Tim | 62 |

WHISPER
Would whisper to himself; A Bite,		107	V's House	62
I get a Whisper, and withdraw,		200	Horace 2, 6	43
Nor whisper to the tattling Reeds,		596	Cassinus Peter	105
Or, if to whisper I presume,		917	Riddle 1	7
And a Whisper is my Death.		933	Riddle 20	D 30

WHISPER'D
Philemon whisper'd to his Wife,		92	Bauc & Phil 1	81
The Town has whisper'd round the Jest:		293	Prog Marriage	102
Whisper'd me, let down your Stick;		833	Legion Club	98

WHISPERS
And whispers in a thousand Lies;		158	Fable of Midas	64
But, St. John comes and whispers in his Ear;		194	Author Himself	34
And smiling, whispers to the next,		200	Horace 2, 6	32
Whispers that Sappho's Hair is Red:		450	Modern Lady	169

WHISPRD
| He whisprd publick things at last, | | 422 | Ireld | 33 |

WHIST
| At Whist they will make a desperate Sweep. | | 943 | Probatur Alit | 32 |

WHISTLES
| Nor comes whene'er his Lady whistles; | | 607 | Beasts Confess | 213 |

WHISTLING
| The Bullets whistling round his Ears, | | 500 | Doctor Delaney | 4 |

WHITE   SEE MILK-WHITE
| Of Matter purulent and white | | 84 | Salamander | 53 |

WHITE	(CONTINUED)	PAGE	TITLE	LINE
Sid's Rod was slender, white, and tall,		133	Magician's Rod	43
Lay by your White Staff & gray Habit,		187	Scriblerus 4	D 15
With Quarter-staffs instead of White;		189	Faggot	22
Three Colours, Black, and Red, and White,		226	Prog of Beauty	21
White Lead, and Lusitanian Dish.		227	Prog of Beauty	60
Love with White lead cements his Wings,		227	Prog of Beauty	61
White lead was sent us to repair		227	Prog of Beauty	62
White Lead can plaister up a Cleft,		229	Prog of Beauty	114
As White as Snow, as bright as Day;		362	Grace's Answer	32
His Waistcoat and Stockings, and Breeches were white,		399	Tom Clinch	5
A Bum so white		441	Ballyspellin	40
Our Ink is black, our Paper white;		463	Birthday Song	108
We blacken what was white before.		463	Birthday Song	110
And with Holland Shirts so white,		573	Helter Skelter	21
Rub off the Dawbs of White and Red;		582	Young Nymph	34
Fair Utensil, as smooth and white		589	Strephon Chloe	173
And swears she saw a Rise in White.		725	To Stella	74
And haunt thy holy Walls in white and black.		792	St. Pat's Well	48
"I wish she wou'd lend you her pretty white Hand,		872	Grand Question	149
In every point, like black and white:		901	Dean's Reasons	72
And clad my Body all in White:		915	Riddle 1	4
In Scarlet some, and some in White;		920	Riddle 6	11
A comely Dame once clad in white,		923	Riddle 7	63
In me you see them full as white,		932	Riddle 19	D 8
Their Bellies are soft, and as white as a Custard.		953	Herrings	7
<Dean> <White>, <Dean> <Daniel>, and <Dean> <Smedley>		742	Stel B-day 22	44
WHITE-LEAD				
But you some white-lead ink must get,		463	Birthday Song	113
WHITEHALL				
Or from Whitehall some new Express,		63	Discovery	30
Still at Whitehall it stands in view,		87	Hist V's House	31
Lament his old Whitehall in Flames,		107	V's House	48
Observ'd a Parson near Whitehall,		170	Horace 1, 7	5
WHITENING				
Of whitening what before was black.		464	Birthday Song	116
WHITEWAY				
Consult friend Whiteway.		1038	Sheridan Cavan	12
WHITTLE				
So next Morning we told Whittle, and he fell a Swearing		70	Mrs Harris Pet	24
But I'll see you all damn'd before I will whittle.		399	Tom Clinch	16
WHO 423			OMITTED WORD	
WHO'D 2			OMITTED WORD	
WHO'LL 2			OMITTED WORD	
WHO'S 8			OMITTED WORD	
WHOEVER (WHOE'ER,WHOE'RE)				
12			OMITTED WORD	
WHOLE				
We often search contentedly the whole World round,		20	Ode Athenian	142
Among her Elder Sons the whole Estate?		32	Ode to Temple	181
There whole herds suspended lie		35	Ode Sancroft	35
Swept up whole churches as it list,		40	Ode Sancroft	194
That furnish'd spirit and motion through the whole;		53	Temple Ill	62
Thus with a puff the whole delusion ends.		55	Temple Ill	154
But repeats the same Note a whole Day, like a Finch.		143	New Song	8
And all my whole Family, Places by Dozens;		144	New Song	48
Whole Baskets full of Bits and Scraps,		208	Fable Bitches	19
Conceive the whole Enchantment broke,		240	Run Bankers	33
The Swiss and Dutch whole Millions drain.		256	Bubble	160
The whole Nations Pockets with Money will fill.		287	Bank Down	13
'Tis happy to see the whole Kingdom in Rags,		287	Bank Down	16
(What could he less,) his whole Estate.		295	Prog Marriage	156
Now, for my part, I think upon the whole,		308	Billet Players	15
And the whole crew this resolution takes,		309	Billet Players	49
It would Burn a whole Forest; nor was it a Fiction;		334	Serious Poem	20
Whole Crouds about its Brazen Strings.		345	Prometheus	30
Would sit whole Ev'nings at the Ale-house:		352	Wood Ironmongr	6
And Skin's yet whole, I needs must own,		372	Letter D. S-y	18
He lengthen'd my Life with a whole Year of Grace.		399	Tom Clinch	18
Whole Hours can with a Coxcomb sit,		416	Woman's Mind	7
And neither Muggs nor Pots whole.		425	Five Ladies	8
Whole Squadrons with a single blow:		461	Birthday Song	32
To drive a second, lest the whole should break.		535	To Mr. Gay	134
"Whole Swarms of Sects, with grief, he saw		550	Life of Swift	168
Thus, a Greyhound out-runs the whole Pack in a Race,		580	Psyche	5
Your Heart had been as whole as mine.		591	Strephon Chloe	250
And, if the whole may pass for true,		608	Know Not What	5
Absurdly bends his Whole Designs.		641	On Poetry	24
And you must bear the whole Disgrace,		644	On Poetry	141
And praise the whole Administration,		658	On Poetry	D 190
Their Judgment was upon the Whole,		698	Cadenus Vaness	358
So Honour animates the Whole,		724	To Stella	13
Perverseness is your whole Defence:		730	Stella, Poems	92
Will answer for the whole Arrear.		740	Stel B-day '21	20
Through the whole set of <Irish> <Deans>;		742	Stel B-day 22	42
When the whole month's Allowance gone		747	Stel Distress	
Whole afternoons will sit beside her,		762	Bec's B-Day	49
Our whole Accounts of publick Debts.		774	Mullinix Tim	15
Whole Ricks of Hay and Stacks of Corn,		811	Bro Protestant	3
He kindled, as if the whole Satire had been		816	Yahoo's	41
While he sleeps the whole Debate,		836	Legion Club	165
So gentle in your whole Proceeding,		891	Panegyr Dean	153

```
WHOLE            (CONTINUED)                           PAGE    TITLE           LINE
   Then the Half, and then the Whole,         . . . . . . .    927 Riddle 10         D   5
   . . . than you have in your whole Body,     . . . . . .    985 Mary to Sher          9
   Yet he gets home at night with Health and whole Bones.    1037 Four Storyes          8
WHOLESOM
   From wholesom Exercise and Air             . . . . . . .    744 Stel Distress        5
WHOLESOME
   "In wholesome Soil and Aether Pure;         . . . . . .    476 Epist on Epist       50
   A wholesome Law, Time out of mind,          . . . . . . .   694 Cadenus Vaness      257
   The part of wholesome exercise: .           . . . . . .    761 Bec's B-Day          28
   Instead of wholesome Bread and Cheese,      . . . . . .    895 Panegyr Dean        265
WHOLLY
   Th' Impulse, the Fight, th' Event, were wholly Thine.       12 Ode to William     D  36
   In wholly equalling our sin and theirs,     . . . . . .     38 Ode Sancroft        122
   The world has wholly miss'd; .  . . . . . . . . .           39 Ode Sancroft        160
   And give him wholly to your Care.           . . . . . . .   692 Cadenus Vaness      197
   His Thoughts had wholly been confin'd       . . . . . .    706 Cadenus Vaness      630
WHOLSOM
   Quoth Baucis, this is wholsom Fare,         . . . . . . .    91 Bauc & Phil 1        63
WHOLSOME
   In vain all wholsome Herbs I sow,           . . . . . . .    33 Ode to Temple       208
   Keep them to wholsome Food confin'd,        . . . . . . .   587 Strephon Chloe      123
   From wholsome Exercise and Air              . . . . . . .   750 Stel Wood-Park       29
WHOM       96                                                     OMITTED WORD
WHORE
   Marries for Love, half Whore, half Wife;    . . . . .      150 Corinna              26
   <Wharton>, unless prevented by a Whore,     . . . . . .    166 Toland's Invit       35
   Are Cat and Dog, and Rogue and Whore.       . . . . . .    225 Prog of Love        100
   Of a governing Statesman, or favorite Whore:  . . . .      351 Wood Insect          30
   If Law be such a partial Whore,             . . . . . . .   392 Young's Satire       45
   And orders the Landlord to bring him a Whore;  . . . .      517 Dean Hang Rape       20
   "By Calvin, than the Scarlet Whore:         . . . . . .    549 Life of Swift       151
   Come, tell us, has she play'd the Whore?    . . . . .      595 Cassinus Peter       45
   Or, when a Whore in her Vocation,           . . . . . .    724 To Stella            29
   Or sink her to a pocky Whore. .  . . . . . . . .           929 Riddle 15          D   8
   For Whore and Rogue; and Dog and Bitch.     . . . . . .    949 Epigr Scolding        4
   Pleaded the <Bishop> lov'd a <Whore>,       . . . . . .    302 Storm                12
   "Resolve to perish with his <Whore>;        . . . . . . .   305 Storm                64
WHORES
   Born between whores and fops, by lewd compacts,   . . .     47 To Congreve         125
   And spend her Joynture on his Whores:       . . . . . .    295 Prog Marriage       164
   A hundred Whores in ev'ry Street,           . . . . . . .   315 To Ford             106
   Poems address'd to great Men's Whores;      . . . . . .    494 Panegyr Swift        35
   Then, why should the <Dean>, when Whores are so cheap,     518 Dean Hang Rape       41
   The <Dean> he was vext that his Whores were so willing,    519 Dean Hang Rape       55
   Call Dunces, Fools, and Sons of Whores,     . . . . .      652 On Poetry           345
   And Sons of Whores--behind their Backs.     . . . . . .    778 Mullinix Tim        164
WHORING
   Of drinking all Day, and whoring all Night.  . . . .       517 Dean Hang Rape       28
WHOSE      70                                                     OMITTED WORD
WHY       114                                                     OMITTED WORD
WICKED
   But wicked kings draw more examples than the good;  . .     40 Ode Sancroft        184
   Like a cast mistress to your wicked friend; . . . . .       44 To Congreve          16
   (The wicked Laity's contriving,            . . . . . . .   174 Horace 1, 7         105
   Nor pump to cobble wicked Verse;            . . . . . .    181 Horace 2, 1          36
   Lest with the Wicked, Heaven involve the Just?   . . .     210 Earl of Oxford       20
   This wicked Rogue Waters, who always is sinning,   . .     238 Excellent Song       26
   How came this wicked Plot to Light:         . . . . . .    298 Horrid Plot           2
   To see the wicked Varlet sprawling;         . . . . . .    353 Wood Ironmongr       26
   And curse his wicked Burthen more           . . . . . . .   497 Panegyr Swift       140
   "A wicked Monster on the Bench,             . . . . . . .   569 Death of Swift      417
   A wicked Rat her Plaister stole,            . . . . . . .   583 Young Nymph          59
   Such wicked insolence appears               . . . . . . .   622 Scandal Poem 1      167
   Wicked Ministers of State                   . . . . . . .   634 Epistle Lady        143
   First in every wicked Jobb,  . . . . . . . . . . .         836 Legion Club         174
   I know they have many a wicked Design       . . . . .     1017 Swift Ans Sher        9
   But were you as wicked as lewd Aretine      . . . . .     1017 Swift Ans Sher       18
WICKEDLY
   That I have an ill Eye, they wickedly think,  . . . .      263 Apollo               13
WICKEDNESS
   Than Pimps to Wickedness in Pow'r?          . . . . . . .   493 Panegyr Swift        26
WICKET
   I observe your Wicket  . . . . . . . . . . . . .           938 Riddle Answerd        3
WIDE
   Numberless Nations, stretching far and wide,   . . . .      25 Ode Athenian        297
   Rapp'd through the wide expanse of thought,  . . . . .      36 Ode Sancroft         62
   So wide as to encompass all. . . . . . . . . .            108 V's House            82
   And made a Circle thrice as wide,           . . . . . . .   134 Magician's Rod       54
   A goodly pair, erect and wide,              . . . . . . .   157 Fable of Midas       31
   And had enlarg'd her Empire wide,           . . . . . . .   303 Storm                13
   To leave the Margin wide.                   . . . . . . .   394 Grub-Street          12
   And Scandal ever gaping wide,  . . . . . . . . .           448 Modern Lady         125
   Strephon, the Rogue, display'd it wide,     . . . . . .    526 Lady's Dres Rm       13
   His Breeches torn exposing wide             . . . . . . .   594 Cassinus Peter       15
   For when we please, we open wide            . . . . . . .   621 Scandal Poem 1      133
   For, when we please, we open wide           . . . . . . .   627 Scandal Poem 2      137
   Was never known to spread so wide.          . . . . . . .   640 On Poetry             4
   Who sees the Ditch too deep and wide.       . . . . . .    640 On Poetry            18
   In Streets where Kennels are too wide:      . . . . . .    645 On Poetry           170
   Thy Breeches torn behind, stand gaping wide;  . . . .      881 Pastoral Dial        21
```

		PAGE	TITLE	LINE
WIDE (CONTINUED)				
With Hoop expanded wide and light, ...		897	Panegyr Dean	323
WIDEN'D				
The Chimny widen'd and grew high'r, ...		92	Bauc & Phil 1	95
The Chimney widen'd, and grew higher, ...		113	Bauc & Phil 2	55
WIDENESS				
Whose Wideness kept their Toes from Corns, . . .		99	Elegy Patrige	37
WIDN'D				
Widn'd and gatherd at his Wrist;		94	Bauc & Phil 1	168
WIDOW				
A Widow kept a Favourite Cat, ...		153	Widow and Cat	D 1
The Widow goes through all her Forms;		295	Prog Marriage	157
WIDOW'S				
Nor dipt in Blood, nor Widow's Tears, nor Orphan's Cries:		29	Ode to Temple	86
Nor widow's sighs, nor orphan's tears, ...		296	Satiric Elegy	18
WIDOWS				
The Soldier smiling hears the Widows Cries, . . .		364	On Dreams	15
WIELDING				
Paradoxes weakly wielding, ...		906	Daphne	7
WIFE SEE MID-WIFE,HOUSE-WIFE				
Whom all the Charms of an Usurped Wife and State, .		20	Ode Athenian	154
. . .I design to be a Parson's Wife, ...		72	Mrs Harris Pet	60
Philemon whisper'd to his Wife, ...		92	Bauc & Phil 1	81
And Vulcan wheedled by his Wife, ...		100	Elegy Patrige	83
Were several Years this Man and Wife, ...		116	Bauc & Phil 2	150
Marries for Love, half Whore, half Wife;		150	Corinna	26
I never quarrell with my Wife, ...		220	A Quiet Life	15
Why Dick, thy Wife has dev'lish Whims:		220	A Quiet Life	27
Within, his wife would break his Bones, ...		221	A Quiet Life	51
Once disobey'd him, Maid nor Wife.		224	Prog of Love	66
And how his Wife that Female Pedant, ...		282	Journal	85
Last Night arriv'd Clem and his Wife.		283	Journal	118
Will hardly find his Wife in Shoes.		292	Prog Marriage	70
"A Wife as good as Heart cou'd wish one, ...		322	First of April	49
As Thomas was cudgelld one day by his Wife, . . .		327	Epigram 1	1
Went home, and was cudgell'd again by his Wife. .		327	Epigram 1	10
A Kinder Wife was never born, ...		328	Epigram 2	3
His Wife and Children wanted Bread, ...		352	Wood Ironmongr	7
She'll help your Wife when she's in Labour. . .		362	Grace's Answer	26
And strive, and strive, your Wife to please. . .		362	Grace's Answer	46
Hang up thy wife, and she'll make four.		404	Window Inns 11	D 2
Put up your Wife, she's crosser than all four', .		404	Window Inns 11	D 4
Hang up your Wife, and you'l count Four', . . .		404	Window Inns 11	D 6
Dick lost in Doll, a Wife Tender and Dear, . . .		430	Dicky Dolly	4
And there he grew fond of another Man's Wife, . .		517	Dean Hang Rape	8
Tom for a wealthy Wife looks round, ...		545	Life of Swift	15
By vent'ring on his heav'nly Wife?		587	Strephon Chloe	104
The Wife should study to be clean;		588	Strephon Chloe	138
On Box of Cedar sits the Wife, ...		590	Strephon Chloe	207
Why is a handsome Wife ador'd		592	Strephon Chloe	283
Rash Mortals, e'er you take a Wife, ...		593	Strephon Chloe	301
Are an humble, prudent Wife;		633	Epistle Lady	100
Thy curate's place, thy fruitful wife, ...		676	Parson's Case	5
The Friend, the Mistress, and the Wife, ...		728	Stella, Poems	16
Who beats her Husband, who his Wife;		781	Mullinix Tim	266
He'll take his revenge on his innocent wife. . .		817	Yahoo's	74
Or you may say--my Wife intends, ...		860	Lady Acheson	21
Thus ended the Knight: Thus began his meek Wife: .		867	Grand Question	25
"He caught me one Morning coquetting his Wife, .		873	Grand Question	167
Twice ten years older than his wife		879	Robbin & Harry	51
Embrac'd thee closer than a Wife;		924	Riddle 8	7
If your Wife be a Scold, that will mend her. . .		942	Probatur Alit	8
And, Madam your Wife		953	Oysters	11
My wife a rattling, ...		1037	Sheridan Cavan	1
Your wife a scold.		1038	Sheridan Cavan	16
WIFE'S				
Philemon by his Wife's consent		92	Bauc & Phil 1	69
Pray, how does my Lady?--My Wife's at your Service.--		869	Grand Question	75
. . .truly they don't care for your Wife's Company, . . .		1013	Swift to Sheri	7
WIG				
In that old Wig and rusty Gown!		175	Horace 1, 7	124
His Wig was made of sunny Rays, ...		597	Problem Solved	7
A flaxen wig, and clouded cane, ...		619	Scandal Poem 1	70
A Flaxen Wig, and Clouded Cane.		625	Scandal Poem 2	66
(The Wig was powder'd round with Sleet, ...		625	Scandal Poem 2	67
That Wig, I wou'd not for the world		780	Mullinix Tim	221
A flaxen wig, and wast-coat gay, ...		879	Robbin & Harry	48
WIG-BLOCK				
Nim lost his Wig-block, Dan his Jordan, ...		283	Journal	123
WIGS				
Forget their Fewds, and join to save their Wigs, .		138	City Shower	42
If we who wear our Wigs		426	Five Ladies	33
And with powder'd Caps and Wigs, Sir;		573	Helter Skelter	18
What powder'd Wigs! What Flames and Darts! . .		585	Strephon Chloe	35
WIL'T				
Thus <Bob> shal't thou be mawl'd, fly where thou wil't:		538	Mr. Pulteney	38
WILD				
The wild excursions of a youthful pen;		17	Ode Athenian	61
Whence the weak shapes wild and imperfect pass, . .		35	Ode Sancroft	23
And which our wild ambition foolishly compares . . .		38	Ode Sancroft	126

912

```
WILD       (CONTINUED)                                   PAGE    TITLE           LINE
    That sent these wild reformers to our times;     . . . .    42 Ode Sancroft      246
    Those who by wild delusions entertain . . . . . . .       45 To Congreve        77
    Form'd by diseas'd conceptions, weak, and wild,   .   .   . 47 To Congreve       123
    But a wild form dependent on the brain,  . . . . . .       54 Temple Ill         95
    Humor is odd, grotesque, and wild,  . . . . . . . .      216 To Mr. Delany       25
    My honest Friend Wild, may he long hold his Place,  .    399 Tom Clinch          17
    Hence that wild suspicious Peep,  . . . . . . . .        800 Traulus 2           35
    All involv'd in wild Disputes;  . . . . . . . . .        833 Legion Club        114
    To see a wild calf  . . . . . . . . .                    857 Lady's Lament      188
    How could I form so wild a vision,  . . . . . . .        899 Dean's Reasons      15
WILDERNESS
    Still murmuring in their Wilderness for Food,  . . .       9 Ode to King        87
    This wilderness the world, like that poetic wood of old, 41 Ode Sancroft       225
    O'er Nile, with all its wilderness of gods;  . . . . .   46 To Congreve        104
WILDERNESSES
    We Gardens, and you Wildernesses,  . . . . . . .        411 Dial Rich Marb      93
WILDLY
    He wildly flings his Filth about,  . . . . . . . .      796 Traulus 1           26
WILE
    Platonick Champions, gain'd without one Female Wile,  .  24 Ode Athenian       252
    To catch a Monkey by a Wile;  . . . . . . . . .         885 Rev Market-Hill     76
    And then, with wonted Wile and Slyness,  . . . . .     1005 Sheridan's Sub      24
WILES
    The Latent Wiles, and Tricks of State,  . . . . . .     340 Arch-Bish Dub       11
    Wisdom's above suspecting Wiles:  . . . . . . .         692 Cadenus Vaness     198
WILL       (AS A VERB)
    416                                                          OMITTED WORD
WILL       (AS A NOUN; SEE GOOD-WILL)
    "Or if it be thy Will and Pleasure  . . . . . . .       199 Horace 2, 6       D
    At sight of Will she bawl'd no more,  . . . . . .       220 A Quiet Life        7
    Quoth Will; thy House is worse than Hell:  . . . .      220 A Quiet Life       10
    Dear Will, I suffer this for Peace;  . . . . . .        220 A Quiet Life       14
    Will went again to visit Dick  . . . . . . .           220 A Quiet Life       19
    Poor Will, who needs must interpose,  . . . . . .      220 A Quiet Life       23
    Will drew out Dick to take a Quart,  . . . . . .       220 A Quiet Life       26
    Dear Will, but, what would People say?  . . . . .      220 A Quiet Life       34
    Will cudgell's Bess, yet Will's a Cully  . . . . .     328 Epigram 3           2
    Dye Ned and Bess; give Will to Joan,  . . . . . .      328 Epigram 3           3
    Dye Joan and Will; give Bess to Ned,  . . . . . .      328 Epigram 3           5
    Then in Spight of your Sophistry, Honest Will. Wood     335 Serious Poem       49
    That three little Vermin are kin to Will. Wood:  .      350 Wood Insect         2
    Such a Worm was Will. Wood when he scratcht at the Doo  351 Wood Insect        29
    Be here detained against my will?  . . . . . . . .      403 Window Inns 10    D  2
    Because, though sore against her Will,  . . . . .       446 Modern Lady        40
    To <Walpole's> more than <Royal> Will.  . . . . .       484 Libel on D- D-    122
    We suffer sore against his Will;  . . . . . . .         485 Libel on D- D-    156
    "While he obeys Almighty Will,  . . . . . . .           485 Libel on D- D-    167
    This Pheasant by the Peacock's Will,  . . . . . .       513 Answer Fable       43
    Sir <Robert> weary'd by Will. <Pulteney's> Teazings,   537 Mr. Pulteney        1
    Resolv'd that Will. and he should meet no more;  . . .  537 Mr. Pulteney        3
    For Will. to enter.--What shall I advise?  . . . .      538 Mr. Pulteney        8
    Let Will. unheard by thee, his Thunder waste.  . . .    538 Mr. Pulteney       12
    And in his Place my good Friend Will;  . . . . .        560 Death of Swift    194
    Publish my Will, my Life, my Letters.  . . . . .        561 Death of Swift    202
    Resigning to the Will of God.  . . . . . . . .          561 Death of Swift    218
    Got? <Damn> me, why I got my will!  . . . . . .         778 Mullinix Tim      159
    If he had his will,  . . . . . . . . .                  852 Lady's Lament      37
    'Till he gave me my Will, I wou'd give him no Rest:     869 Grand Question     58
    Sir Arthur too shall have his Will,  . . . . . .        875 Drapier's Hill      9
    The Spaniard, sore against his Will,  . . . . . .       883 Rev Market-Hill    15
    To serve a friend against his will?  . . . . . .        902 Dean's Reasons    114
    Through me, though sore against my Will,  . . . .       918 Riddle 4           11
    Yet, though I always have my Will,  . . . . . . .       918 Riddle 4           19
    Or revive at its Will,  . . . . . . . . .               939 Riddle Answerd     18
    Will Hancock declares you are out of your compass,  . . 1027 Sheri Circles     21
WILL'S
    And told you so at Will's but t' other night.  . . . .   47 To Congreve       146
    Will cudgell's Bess, yet Will's a Cully  . . . . .      328 Epigram 3           2
    Be sure at Will's the following Day,  . . . . . .       644 On Poetry         117
WILLFUL
    Why are they so willful to struggle with Men?  . . . .  519 Dean Hang Rape     62
    When to yield, and when be willful.  . . . . . . .      907 Daphne             42
WILLIAM
    (Ere since Sir William <Gore> was May'r,  . . . .       180 Horace 2, 1         9
    Then how can we dread William Wood,  . . . . . .        340 Arch-Bish Dub      21
    I Sing not of the Draper's Praise, nor yet of William   341 Upon His Grace      1
        Wood;
    And thus William Wood to my Fancy appears  . . . .      350 Wood Insect         7
    Than George and William claim'd before.  . . . .       464 Birthday Song     140
    Duke William, sweetest Prince alive.  . . . . . .       656 On Poetry         440
WILLIAM'S
    The Battel almost by Great William's single Valour        8 Ode to King        64
        gain'd,
    William's the Pledge and Earnest given by Fate  . . .    13 Ode to William   D 47
    Lord William's Grace of Dublin Town, . . .   . . . .    341 Upon His Grace      3
WILLING
    To better Judgments willing to submit,  . . . . . .     194 Author Himself     25
    For when you express a Friend's Love we are willing,  . 337 Serious Poem      103
    The World, a willing Stander-by,  . . . . . . .         414 Censure            13
    The <Dean> he was vext that his Whores were so willing, 519 Dean Hang Rape     55
```

```
                                                          PAGE    TITLE        LINE
WILLINGLY
  And willingly resigns its Place    . . . . . . . .      340  Arch-Bish Dub     15
WILLOW
  Mournful Cypress, verdant Willow,    . . . . . . .      661  Love Song         21
WILLOW-STICKS
  The Dean will give me Willow-Sticks,    . . . . . .     128  Little House      63
WILLS
  At Wills the puny Judge of Wit.    . . . . . . . .      647  On Poetry        236
  At Wills you hear a Poem read,    . . . . . . . .       649  On Poetry        263
WILLY
  Into whose pocket valiant Willy put,    . . . . . .     467  Birthday Song    207
WILT
  Why near the dregs of youth perversely wilt thou stay,  .   54  Temple Ill   105
  Or in a Boat when e're thou wilt    . . . . . . . .     109  V's House        113
  Thou pompously wilt let us know  .    . . . . . .       180  Horace 2, 1        7
  If to <Maccartney> thou wilt toast,    . . . . . . .    183  Horace 2, 1       91
  Nor, wilt thou of Gifts be sparing,    . . . . . . .    523  Betty Grizette    21
  Why, Cassy, thou wilt doze thy Pate:    . . . . .       594  Cassinus Peter    29
  I fear thou wilt be mad indeed. . . . . . . . .         596  Cassinus Peter    90
  Poor Tom, wilt thou never accept a Defiance,    . . . . 1019  To Sheridan       1
WILY
  The wily Shafts of State, those Juggler's Tricks    . .  29  Ode to Temple     92
  Hounds hunt the Hare, the wily Fox    . . . . . .       504  Doctor Delaney   129
WIMBLE
  I'll hold you a Groat, when you wimble his Bumm,    . .  336  Serious Poem     79
WIN
  And if she can but win a Crown,    . . . . . . . .       75  Game Traffick     23
  Try'd ev'ry Tone might Pity win,    . . . . . . . .     111  Bauc & Phil 2     13
  One Fool may from another win,  . . . . . . . .         253  Bubble            61
  To beg his Favour is the Way new Favours still to win,  341  Upon His Grace    13
  To win the Soul, and glad the Heart;    . . . . . .     385  Manly Virtue      56
  "I said I should not win a Game.    . . . . . . . .     452  Modern Lady      239
  Enough to win ten Thousand Hearts;    . . . . . . .     598  Problem Solved    20
  To win the Truant School-Boys Hearts!    . . . . . .    779  Mullinix Tim     200
  If I could but win ye,    . . . . . . . . . .           857  Lady's Lament    204
  Nor need we doubt the Fort to win;    . . . . . . .     885  Rev Market-Hill   55
  How well to win the Ladies Hearts,    . . . . . . .     887  Panegyr Dean      11
  She doubted not to win the Swain.    . . . . . . .      905  Death Daphne      70
  I cannot find I lose or win,    . . . . . . . . .       918  Riddle 4          36
WIND
  To be an Art as vain, as Bottling up of Wind:)    . .    21  Ode Athenian     185
  Watching the first unsav'ry Wind,    . . . . . . .       66  Problem           37
  By Change of Wind to Leeward Side    . . . . . . .       96  On the Union      19
  But aided by the Wind, fought still for Life;    . . .  137  City Shower       24
  As, "what's a-Clock?" And, "How's the Wind?    . . .    201  Horace 2, 6       69
  Though Fear should lend him Pinions like the Wind,    . 210  Earl of Oxford     5
  The last, as boundless as the Wind;    . . . . . .      215  To Mr. Delany     15
  His Guts and Belly full of Wind;    . . . . . . .       231  Prog of Poetry    38
  Directors Promises but Wind,  . . . . . . . . .        259  Bubble           219
  With ev'ry Wind he sail'd, and well could tack:    . .  285  Elegy Boat        15
  "He knows to sail with ev'ry Wind;    . . . . . .       304  Storm             34
  Returning sound in Limb and Wind,    . . . . . . .      398  Earl of P-b-w     23
  But overcharg'd, and out of Wind,    . . . . . . .      412  Desire Possess    37
  I'm fasnd both by wind and tide  . . . . . . . .       420  Holyhead           7
  Before, I always found the Wind    . . . . . . . .      420  Holyhead          21
  When'er the Wind of Favour sits,    . . . . . . .       493  Panegyr Swift     17
  A Pack of Dog-fish had him in the Wind:    . . . . .    538  Mr. Pulteney      22
  Nor let them taste what causes Wind;    . . . . . .     587  Strephon Chloe   124
  As Ships are toss't by Waves and Wind,    . . . . .     589  Strephon Chloe   170
  Or when a-bed, to let out Wind.    . . . . . . . .      590  Strephon Chloe   218
  Or at her Mouth was breaking Wind.    . . . . . . .     592  Strephon Chloe   282
  Stops thus, and turns with ev'ry Wind;    . . . . .     688  Cadenus Vaness    58
  Expos'd to Want, and Wind, and Weather,    . . . . .    759  Receipt Youth      9
  Behold, it cracks by yon rough Eastern Wind.    . . .   770  Horace 1, 14      18
  Together float with Tide and Wind;    . . . . . . .     811  Bro Protestant     6
  May turn and wind me like a fool.    . . . . . . .      899  Dean's Reasons    14
  And turn and wind 'me as they please.    . . . . .      920  Riddle 6           8
  Like the Fiction of Poets concerning the Wind,    . .   927  Riddle 11     D    3
  Turn and wind him where we please.    . . . . . . .     931  Riddle 18     D   14
  And move it against Tyde and Wind.    . . . . . .       934  Riddle 21     D   16
WINDED    SEE LONG-WINDED
  Which, I confess, is too long winded)    . . . . .      354  Simile Silver     18
WINDING
  But winding Walks and purer Air;    . . . . . . .       378  Apology Lady C   100
  She curs'd the dark & winding Stairs    . . . . . .     746  Stel Distress     33
  She curst the narrow winding Stairs:    . . . . . .     751  Stel Wood-Park    52
WINDING-SHEET
  His Heirs for Winding-Sheet bestow'd    . . . . . .     235  Elegy on Demar    43
WINDINGS
  And softly steals in many Windings down,    . . . .      31  Ode to Temple    156
  A Friend in Turns and Windings try'd    . . . . .        94  Bauc & Phil 1    137
WINDOW
  Down from her Window in the Sky,    . . . . . . .       226  Prog of Beauty     7
  The Window is her proper Sphear;    . . . . . . .       228  Prog of Beauty    66
  He gets to a Window beyond both the Tropicks;    . .    265  Apollo            84
  His Window scrawl'd by ev'ry Rake,    . . . . . .       400  Window Inns 1      5
  A window here from scribbling free:    . . . . . .      402  Window Inns 7  D   2
  When to the window he's trepan'd    . . . . . . .       421  Ireld             19
  Nail'd to her Window full in Sight    . . . . . . .     735  Stel B-day '20    35
  Looks up to your Window, and cocks up his Beaver.   . . 870  Grand Question   104

                              914
```

		PAGE	TITLE	LINE
WINDOWS	SEE KITCHEN-WINDOWS			
	But, as from the Windows the Ladies he spy'd,	399	Tom Clinch	9
	Of Windows in his Breast;	400	Window Inns 1	2
	We see him from our kitchen windows,	620	Scandal Poem 1	108
	The Ladies from the Windows gaping:	780	Mullinix Tim	241
WINDS				
	Tho' blasts from contrariety of winds,	41	Ode Sancroft	204
	As parent earth, burst by imprison'd winds,	52	Temple Ill	37
	Next Day the Post-boy winds his Horn,	398	Earl of P-b-w	16
	They cannot say the winds are cross	420	Holyhead	15
	Where loudest winds incessant roar	420	Holyhead	30
	The God of Winds and God of Fire	743	Stel B-day 22	63
	Of giddy Winds, but make some friendly Port.	770	Horace 1, 14	12
	The Combat of opposing Winds:	923	Riddle 7	80
	Whether the Winds in Caverns pent	923	Riddle 7	85
WINDSOR				
	Windsor and Bristow then shall be	147	Windsor Proph	5
	And down to Windsor takes his Guest.	173	Horace 1, 7	82
	Takes him to Windsor in his Coach, alone.	194	Author Himself	32
	At Windsor <Swift> no sooner can appear,	194	Author Himself	33
	To Windsor, and again to Town,	201	Horace 2, 6	78
WINE				
	You'll spend in Coach-hire more than save in Wine.	137	City Shower	8
	Upon a single Dish, and Tavern Wine,	162	Toland's Invit	2
	The Wine, his Blood, our Predecessors shed:	162	Toland's Invit	12
	Wine can clear up <Godolphin's> cloudy Face,	163	Toland's Invit	19
	By Force of Wine ev'n <Scarborough> is Brave,	163	Toland's Invit	21
	Wine can give <Portland> Wit, and <Cleveland> Sense,	164	Toland's Invit	23
	And Commoners who love good Wine,	169	Peace Dunkirk	23
	Yet their Wine and their Victuals, those curmudgeon Lubbards	263	Apollo	11
	The wine is so sour,	402	Window Inns 8	D 5
	Shall keep the Key of my (no) Wine;	409	Dial Rich Marb	44
	The Inn has not one drop of wine	420	Holyhead	6
	And crop-sick with unclub'd for wine,	434	Answer Paulus	73
	Pish at his Cook'ry, damn his Wine;	495	Panegyr Swift	69
	Who for his Wine will bear his Jokes:'	556	Death of Swift	94
	"He hardly drinks a Pint of Wine."	557	Death of Swift	109
	With plenteous meals, and gen'rous wine;	677	Parson's Case	34
	Thro candle-light she view'd the Wine	746	Stel Distress	21
	I must confess your Wine and Vittle	747	Stel Distress	65
	Through Candle-Light she view'd the Wine,	750	Stel Wood-Park	19
	I must confess, your Wine and Vittle	752	Stel Wood-Park	81
	May Walmsley give wine,	858	Lady's Lament	221
	A handsome Addition for Wine and good Chear,	867	Grand Question	11
	To stint me at Night to one Bottle of Wine;	867	Grand Question	16
	Decant his Wine, and carve his Beef.	883	Rev Market-Hill	24
	Not you, to steal your Master's Wine;	890	Panegyr Dean	98
	But, in the midst of mirth and wine,	936	Riddle 24	D 11
	A long-ear'd Beast, and Rhenish Wine,	942	Probatur Alit	13
	Well roasted, with Sugar and Wine in a Cup,	953	Oranges	3
	Upon a Chick, and Pint of Wine.	954	Authors Living	2
	I tell you I'd not give a fig for your wine;	979	Dean to: S	30
	. . .whether the Wine is to be bottled To-morrow, or no.	1013	Swift to Sheri	1
	. . .although they like your Wine; but they had rather	1013	Swift to Sheri	7
	The Verses you sent on the bottling your Wine	1017	Swift Ans Sher	1
WINE'S				
	If Wine's bought, or Victuals drest	931	Riddle 18	D 19
WINES				
	Despis'd luxurious Wines, and costly Meat;	194	Author Himself	15
	From gen'rous wines and costly fare,	401	Window Inns 5	D 3
	By gen'rous Wines beneath a Shade,	731	Stella, Poems	112
	With richest Wines and costly Cheer:	745	Stel Distress	4
	With gen'rous Wines and costly Chear.	749	Stel Wood-Park	4
WING				
	The eager Muse took wing upon the Waves decline,	16	Ode Athenian	22
	And thence with joyful, nimble Wing	16	Ode Athenian	29
	Like the victorious wren perch'd on the eagle's wing;	44	To Congreve	38
	We, humble strollers, always on the wing.	308	Billet Players	14
	Took Wing to Jove, and hop'd to rest	458	Paddy's Charac	31
	But raise your Fancy on the Wing;	501	Doctor Delaney	55
	The wing of a chick	853	Lady's Lament	63
WING'D				
	And wing'd with fame shall reach the skies.	877	To Dean Swift	34
WINGED				
	And boldly Force the winged Quill	373	Letter D. S-y	53
WINGS				
	The wretched Insects singe their Wings, and fall,	9	Ode to King	117
	But plumes her Silver Wings and flies away,	16	Ode Athenian	17
	Than those with backs of silk and golden wings;	46	To Congreve	92
	Grew to his Back instead of Wings;	80	Vanbrug House	36
	The Bat, because her Wings are Leather,	99	Elegy Patrige	50
	Mean while the South rising with dabbled Wings,	137	City Shower	13
	Love with White lead cements his Wings,	227	Prog of Beauty	61
	Her Body light, she tries her Wings,	230	Prog of Poetry	13
	Supported high on Wings of Paper;	231	Prog of Poetry	44
	They fly like Bats, on Parchment Wings,	239	Run Bankers	23
	On Paper Wings he takes his Flight,	252	Bubble	37
	His Wings are his Paternall Rent,	252	Bubble	45
	Can soar with moistned Wings on high,	254	Bubble	86

WINGS	(CONTINUED)	PAGE	TITLE	LINE
	while Victory, with Wings outspread,	461	Birthday Song	33
	(Fear lent him Wings) for Safety to the Skies.	538	Mr. Pulteney	30
	Her infant Loves with purple Wings;	585	Strephon Chloe	50
	Though Mercury makes use of Wings	621	Scandal Poem 1	117
	His wings are clipp't; he tryes no more in vain	678	Dean and Duke	7
	On Airy Wings you take your Flight,	919	Riddle 5	25
	Provide me but with Paper Wings,	930	Riddle 15	D 18
WINK				
	But hardly ever set my Eyes together, or slept a Wink.	70	Mrs Harris Pet	21
	And tips you the Freeman a Wink;	396	Dog and Thief	10
	And wink a Reputation down;	450	Modern Lady	193
	An I were to be hang'd, I can't sleep a Wink:	869	Grand Question	64
	(Though sometimes thou wer't pleas'd to wink,	894	Panegyr Dean	243
WINNER				
	Mean time the whig is always winner	421	Ireld	11
	But first, the Winner must invite	453	Modern Lady	288
WINNING				
	"Winning my Way by slow Approaches,	380	Apology Lady C	151
WINNOWING				
	The winnowing Sheet.	246	Irish-Feast	52
WINS				
	Some Cully often wins a Bett	257	Bubble	162
	And tell who loses, and who wins,	280	Journal	63
	And while he poisons, wins the Royal Heart.	534	To Mr. Gay	82
WINTER				
	It happen'd on a Winter Night,	111	Bauc & Phil 2	5
	In Winter--never to reside.	173	Horace 1, 7	86
	And resolv'd the next Winter, for that is the Time,	265	Apollo	77
	And Winter softens into Spring:	387	Manly Virtue	126
	The Winter now begins to frown;	744	Stel Distress	1
	This Winter to invite some Friends,	860	Lady Acheson	23
WINTER-SKY				
	The Winter-Sky began to frown,	750	Stel Wood-Park	25
WINTER-SUN				
	Altho' we boast our Winter-Sun looks bright,	25	Ode Athenian	280
WINTER'S				
	It happen'd on a Winter's night,	90	Bauc & Phil 1	5
	Which only Winter's Rain supplies.	478	Epist on Epist	90
	Shrivel'd with a Winter's keeping.	523	Betty Grizette	10
WINTERS				
	Half wither'd by a Winters keeping	290	Prog Marriage	26
WIPE				
	To Statesmen wou'd you give a Wipe,	643	On Poetry	95
	Tare out the Tale, and wipe your <Arse>	783	Tim and Fables	37
	Wipe our <Arses> with their <Votes>.	831	Legion Club	62
	And gives me a wipe	851	Lady's Lament	7
WIPES				
	She wipes it clean, and lays it by.	581	Young Nymph	12
WIRE				
	And Puppets mov'd by Wire	123	Empty'ng Town	14
	Untwists a Wire; and from her Gums	582	Young Nymph	19
	Who wisely hides his Wood and Wire;	592	Strephon Chloe	286
	Who o'er each String and Wire preside,	798	Traulus 1	73
WISDOM				
	A Stock of Wisdom and Philosophy,	19	Ode Athenian	98
	In Wisdom and Philosophy;	33	Ode to Temple	207
	Within your Breast all Wisdom lyes,	243	Horace 4, 9	7
	Your Wisdom can with Ease Defeat.	340	Arch-Bish Dub	12
	Where Wisdom stands to keep the Field,	340	Arch-Bish Dub	23
	Whose Wisdom and whose Piety, do far exceed his Years.	341	Upon His Grace	4
	That Head so well by Wisdom fraught!	361	Grace's answer	15
	And Wisdom for the Common-Weal.	391	Young's Satire	4
	And call the laws of wisdom fate,	490	Dialogue	42
	Who dares revile the Nation's Wisdom,	515	Answer Fable	93
	Nor highest Wisdom in Debates	641	On Poetry	27
	Above her Wisdom to compose,	690	Cadenus Vaness	131
	For Wisdom, at Jove's Council-Board.	695	Cadenus Vaness	267
	For how can Heav'nly Wisdom prove	695	Cadenus Vaness	294
	Thus making others Wisdom known,	701	Cadenus Vaness	452
	The Queen of Wisdom cou'd foresee	701	Cadenus Vaness	484
	For Learning, Wit, and Wisdom fam'd;)	708	Cadenus Vaness	691
	Who keeps his wisdom out of sight;	900	Dean's Reasons	42
WISDOM'S				
	Indifference clad in Wisdom's Guise,	561	Death of Swift	213
	Maxims teaching Wisdom's Use.	637	Epistle Lady	238
	Wisdom's above suspecting Wiles:	692	Cadenus Vaness	198
	To try their Wisdom's full Extent;	697	Cadenus Vaness	339
	Searching in Books for Wisdom's Aid,	702	Cadenus Vaness	490
WISE SEE WORLDLY-WISE				
	In gath'ring follies from the wise;	37	Ode Sancroft	85
	Others, ignorantly wise,	39	Ode Sancroft	168
	A search, no doubt, as curious and as wise	46	To Congreve	93
	And can you think the wise forbear to laugh	46	To Congreve	107
	Mild Dorothea, peaceful, wise and great,	52	Temple Ill	41
	But hid with Caution from the Wise.	60	Lady Tablebook	6
	When wise Ld <Berkeley> first came here,	62	Discovery	1
	I e'en left her, and came away as wise as I was before.	71	Mrs Harris Pet	47
	No wonder, since wise Authors shew,	87	Hist V's House	39
	But Wise Ardelia knew his Tricks.	120	Apollo Outwit	20
	If you be wise, then go not far to Dine,	137	City Shower	7

WISE   (CONTINUED)   PAGE TITLE   LINE

Hence we are by wise Farmers told, ...   156 Fable of Midas   19
Suppose then Atlas ne'er so wise, ...   160 Atlas   19
"By which wise Conduct they grow Friends   . . . .   181 Horace 2, 1   47
Then let us both in time grow wise, ...   184 Horace 2, 1   107
While, wise Men think they ought to fight   . . . . . .   189 Faggot   21
Those Romans were too wise to think on't, ...   190 Faggot   29
Matter, as wise Logicians say, ...   228 Prog of Beauty   81
Demar the Wealthy, and the Wise.   . . . .   235 Elegy on Demar   42
Ye wise Philosophers explain   . . . . . .   250 Bubble   1
Fools chiefly float, the Wise are drown'd. . . . . . .   252 Bubble   52
For Fools will see as Wise men please.   . . . . . .   257 Bubble   168
Then, like the Dogs of Nile be wise, ...   257 Bubble   177
And 'twas but just; for, wise Men say, ...   299 Horrid Plot   29
Before the secret wise Committee;   . . . .   300 Horrid Plot   54
Pallas, a Goddess chaste and wise;   . . . . . .   302 Storm   1
Oh, were but You and I so wise   . . . . . .   314 To Ford   85
Too wise to take Council, too proud to take Warning, . .   327 Epigram 1   7
My Tale is a wise one if well understood, ...   334 Serious Poem   23
Wise People, who believ'd with Reason   . . . . .   354 Simile Silver   5
Write worse then if you can - - - - be wise - - - -   361 Grace's Answer   11
The Wise pretend to make it clear, ...   366 Answer Delaney   1
A Lady, Wise as well Fair, ...   375 Apology Lady C   1
Where Governors are good and wise;   . . . . . .   391 Young's Satire   21
Ye Wise, instruct me to endure   . . . . . .   413 Censure   1
Make you less virtous, learn'd, or wise.   . . . . . .   414 Censure   28
Or Bolton the wise   . . . . .   423 Carterets Arms
At least, that such complaints are wise: . . . . . .   433 Answer Paulus   40
'Tis wise, no doubt, as clients fat ye more, ...   433 Answer Paulus   41
And like his Father early wise.   . . . . . .   466 Birthday Song   192
The Wise and Learned of our Isle;   . . . . .   475 Epist on Epist   18
In antient Times the Wise were able, ...   512 Answer Fable   1
By which he grew both rich and wise.   . . . . .   513 Answer Fable   18
By old Popish Cannons, as wise Men have Penn'd'em, . .   518 Dean Hang Rape   37
The World shall own, his Choice was wise and just, . .   532 To Mr. Gay   17
Wise Rochefoucault a Maxim writ, ...   545 Life of Swift   1
"And only chose the Wise and Good;   . . . . . .   566 Death of Swift   333
Tis known, that Socrates the wise   . . . . . .   619 Scandal Poem 1   79
'Tis known, that Socrates the wise, ...   626 Scandal Poem 2   77
You wou'd teach me to be wise;   . . . . . .   630 Epistle Lady   21
Maxims wise, to rule the State.   . . . . . .   635 Epistle Lady   174
I to laugh, and you grow wise.   . . . . . .   638 Epistle Lady   274
Is gen'rous, valiant, just and wise, ...   646 On Poetry   195
Wise Dennis, and profound Bossu.   . . . . . .   648 On Poetry   250
Yet, all must own, thy wish is wise.   . . . . . .   676 Parson's Case   4
For Gods, their Betters, are too wise   . . . . . .   689 Cadenus Vaness   83
For, let a Man be ne'er so wise, ...   707 Cadenus Vaness   668
All that was witty, learn'd, and wise, ...   708 Cadenus Vaness   697
Who, tho' he cannot spell, is wise   . . . . . .   712 Cadenus Vaness   814
Grown by Vanessa's Conduct wise.   . . . . . .   712 Cadenus Vaness   831
Of Nymphs so gracefull, Wise and fair   . . . . . .   722 Stel B-Day '18   12
To such a Nymph the Wise and Good   . . . . . .   733 Verses Vanessa   9
Should Solomon wise   . . . . .   756 Dingley Brent   7
You must be grave, and I be wise.   . . . . . .   757 Stel B-day '24   28
Be grave and wise, 'twou'd break their Heart. . . . .   776 Mullinix Tim   90
Clio, who had been so wise   . . . . .   833 Legion Club   109
Wise Hawthornden and Sterline's Lord.)   . . . . . .   848 Old Thorn   16
Wise books and reflection   . . . . . .   854 Lady's Lament   101
God of Time, if you be wise, ...   862 To Janus   9
As all your Politicians wise   . . . . . .   886 Rev Market-Hill 109
Under whose wise and careful Guardship, ...   890 Panegyr Dean   107
By long Experience grown so wise, ...   890 Panegyr Dean   117
Thus, when the learned and the wise   . . . . . .   900 Dean's Reasons   33
She may then grow wise for spight.   . . . . . .   907 Daphne   38
Mean Time, the Wise a Question start, ...   919 Riddle 5   31
Take wise Advice, and look behind, ...   921 Riddle 7   3
Wise and glorious to behold;   . . . . . .   936 Riddle 24   D 20
I've often heard it from the wise, ...   982 Sher, A Goose   3
I thought my Master a wise Man, ...   987 Mary to Sher   30
Thus a wise Taylor is not pinching, ...   1021 Nim-Dan-Dean 1 D 15
WISELY
And you whom Pluto's Helm does wisely shroud . . . .   18 Ode Athenian   86
Wisely retreated to his heavenly rest.   . . . . . .   40 Ode Sancroft   189
And wisely judge, no pow'r beneath divine   . . . . . .   44 To Congreve   29
But gath'ring spirits, wisely ran for't, ...   64 Discovery   46
But wisely cautious of her Pence, ...   75 Game Traffick   15
For he wisely consider'd it must be a Sprite, ...   77 Lady B- B-   13
Which having wisely overthrown, ...   81 Vanbrug House   91
And now the Duke has wisely ta'ne him   . . . . . .   87 Hist V's House   41
He wisely chang'd their Element: . . . . . .   106 V's House   22
So Modern Rimers wisely Blast   . . . . . .   110 V's House   131
The Dame full wisely did Decree, ...   153 Widow and Cat D 16
While Partridge wisely shews the Cause   . . . . . .   228 Prog of Beauty   89
And, happy he, who wisely knows   . . . . . .   243 Horace 4, 9   17
But antient Philosophers wisely Remark, ...   334 Serious Poem   7
And, over these Fillets he wisely has thrown, ...   351 Wood Insect   9
And wisely do as other men do.   . . . . . .   435 Answer Paulus   116
But, wisely left the Muses Hill, ...   482 Libel on D- D-   65
Wisely on me lay all the Blame: . . . . . .   558 Death of Swift   170
Who wisely thought my Age a Screen, ...   561 Death of Swift   221
Who wisely hides his Wood and Wire;   . . . . . .   592 Strephon Chloe   286

917

	PAGE	TITLE	LINE
WISELY (CONTINUED)			
Are ills you wisely wish to leave, ...	676	Parson's Case	15
I wisely chuse to walk behind;	917	Riddle 4	2
WISER			
Yet still are no wiser than we were at first.	967	Letter Sherid	4
WISEST			
Riches, the Wisest Monarch sings, ...	239	Run Bankers	21
True lawyers, for the wisest ends, ...	432	Answer Paulus	11
He found the wisest Men he could, ...	607	Beasts Confess	183
That not the wisest Mortal knows	993	On Picture	20
WISH			
If what You said, I wish unspoke, ...	217	To Mr. Delany	65
Gave Women all their Hearts could wish	227	Prog of Beauty	58
Because we wish the Earth upon him Light, ...	234	Elegy on Demar	24
The Wish of Nero now is Theirs, ...	240	Run Bankers	27
He'd wish to sleep a little longer.	296	Satiric Elegy	8
And look't since he has got his Wish, ...	299	Horrid Plot	33
"A Wife as good as Heart cou'd wish one, ...	322	First of April	49
Think what they wish so great a Blessing, ...	411	Desire Possess	3
I'm where my enemyes would wish	420	Holyhead	4
'I wish the Dinner at Old Nick."	448	Modern Lady	99
'I wish ye may but have enough.'	448	Modern Lady	108
I wish some Folks would pare their Nails.	453	Modern Lady	269
"And wish the Task had been assign'd	485	Libel on D- D-	169
Would you not wish his Lawrels cropt?	554	Death of Swift	26
He'd wish his Rivals all in Hell.	554	Death of Swift	34
But with a Sigh, I wish it mine:	555	Death of Swift	48
"I wish he may hold out till Spring.	557	Death of Swift	114
"(I wish I knew what King to call.)	562	Death of Swift	232
"I wish it soon may have a Better.	572	Death of Swift	484
This is not the Thing we wish.	633	Epistle Lady	110
Can wish to die, in strain heroick, ...	676	Parson's Case	2
Yet, all must own, thy wish is wise.	676	Parson's Case	4
Are ills you wisely wish to leave, ...	676	Parson's Case	15
Wou'dst thou not wish, in so much ease, ...	677	Parson's Case	35
At least, cou'd hardly wish them wrong.	710	Cadenus Vaness	747
I wish they had been well apply'd.	779	Mullinix Tim	210
I wish I could find him out one more commodious. . . .	803	Irish Bishops	12
I'll hold you a Groat, and I wish I cou'd see't, . . .	805	Irish Bishops	51
Wou'd you wish to be wrap'd in a Rochet--In short. . .	808	Advice Parson	9
"I wish she wou'd lend you her pretty white Hand, . .	872	Grand Question	149
I wish he were in it a dancing a Jig.	942	Probatur Alit	28
I wish them in Heaven, ...	951	Apples	7
And I wish your few friends, when they next see your car go,	976	Dean to Sherid	29
I wish Alexander safe at St. Catherine's To-night, . .	1014	Swift to Sheri	9
I wish when you prated, ...	1014	Swift to Sheri	13
And wish you Translated, ...	1014	Swift to Sheri	27
I wish you would sign't, ...	1015	Swift to Sheri	43
However I wish, honest Comrade of mine	1017	Swift Ans Sher	11
So I wish you were toothless like Lord Masserine . .	1017	Swift Ans Sher	17
I wish you would tell me which way you incline	1017	Swift Ans Sher	19
And I wish I may soon be not of an A-gue sick; . . .	1030	Dr. Sheridan	3
WISH'D			
Wish'd Women might have Children fast, ...	115	Bauc & Phil 2	131
I Often wish'd, that I had clear	198	Horace 2, 6	1
Who was the Man, he wish'd to seem;	386	Manly Virtue	76
WISH'T			
Phil wish't, that she had strained a Limb	224	Prog of Love	81
John wish't, that he had broke a Leg	224	Prog of Love	83
Wish't him a Coll'nell for her Sake.	291	Prog Marriage	44
WISHES			
Had the best wishes they cou'd give him.	455	Dean Smedley	14
Wishes it were all unsaid.	800	Traulus 2	22
WISHING			
Yet always wishing to retreat;	202	Horace 2, 6	107
In wishing such afflictions less!	676	Parson's Case	18
WISHT			
The Groom was wisht to saddle Crop, ...	223	Prog of Love	35
And, whisp'ring wisht, the Devil burst her	618	Scandal Poem 1	18
I almost wisht this Spud were in your Guts.	882	Pastoral Dial	40
WIT SEE WITT			
To be a fitter Birth-place for the God of Wit; . . .	17	Ode Athenian	49
We join like Flyes, and Wasps, in buzzing about Wit. .	18	Ode Athenian	75
Railing a Rule of Wit, and Obloquy a Trade, ...	18	Ode Athenian	84
Our Wit and Learning, narrow as our Trade;	19	Ode Athenian	96
Perhaps imagine to be wondrous Wit	20	Ode Athenian	125
Although they praise the Learning and the Wit, . . .	21	Ode Athenian	164
Enthron'd with Heav'nly Wit, ...	21	Ode Athenian	177
And You with fatal and Immortal Wit conspire . . .	23	Ode Athenian	240
Is even the nobler Man, our Learning and our Wit, . .	24	Ode Athenian	269
Yet shall these Traces of your Wit remain	25	Ode Athenian	301
And measuring by the scanty thread of wit	38	Ode Sancroft	123
Shews in the front the ambition of my wit;	44	To Congreve	36
With indignation I behold your wit	45	To Congreve	55
So small the gain those from your wit do reap, . . .	45	To Congreve	61
To scribblers, and the god of light and wit;	45	To Congreve	76
What northern hive pour'd out these foes to wit? . . .	46	To Congreve	83
A jargon form'd from the lost language, wit, ...	47	To Congreve	121
You find, to be the fashionable wit;	48	To Congreve	162

918

WIT   (CONTINUED)   PAGE   TITLE   LINE

Line	Page	Title	Line
Whom sin and want e'er furnish'd out a wit;	48	To Congreve	166
Who that had Wit would place it here,	60	Lady Tablebook	17
He had mixt little Wit with a great deal of Pains,	77	Lady B- B-	24
T' express their Valor, Strength or Wit.	83	Salamander	12
Thus Patrige, by his Wit and Parts,	99	Elegy Patrige	47
But well perceiving Wit was scarce,	107	V's House	56
Rose in proportion to his Wit:	108	V's House	80
For ev'ry Wit in Britain's Isle	109	V's House	117
A Type of Modern Wit and Style,	109	V's House	125
Breeding, and Wit, and Air, and decent Pride;	1,18	Biddy Floyd	8
At twelve, a Wit and a Coquette;	150	Corinna	25
And People fancy'd he had Wit.	156	Fable of Midas	24
The God of Wit to shew his Grudge.	157	Fable of Midas	29
Wine can give <Portland> Wit, and <Cleveland> Sense,	164	Toland's Invit	23
Kept Company with Men of Wit,	171	Horace 1, 7	39
What friendship dicates more than wit.	176	To Lord Harley	4
The God of Wit, and Light, and Arts,	176	To Lord Harley	9
They fly from learning, wit, and light:	177	To Lord Harley	20
For wit and learning spoil'd his face.	177	To Lord Harley	28
With wit and virtue to discover,	177	To Lord Harley	35
Approve thy Schemes, thy Wit admire,	182	Horace 2, 1	62
As mine for Politicks and Wit.	183	Horace 2, 1	106
<Swift> had the Sin of Wit no venial Crime;	193	Author Himself	9
He reconcil'd Divinity and Wit.	194	Author Himself	12
He turns to Politicks his dang'rous Wit,	194	Author Himself	26
Tells me i have more Zeal than Wit,	200	Horace 2, 6	36
For, sure, by Wit is onely meant	215	To Mr. Delany	17
For Wit and Humor differ quite,	215	To Mr. Delany	23
True Humor must with Wit combine:	216	To Mr. Delany	30
Who full of Humor, Fire and Wit,	218	To Mr. Delany	91
Without troubling his Head about Judgment or Wit:	263	Apollo	20
But Wit and Weaving had the same beginning,	276	Epilogue	37
And shou'd our Galls-town Wit grow fallow,	278	Journal	3
And has a thousand times her Wit.	313	To Ford	72
For Grandeur, Elegance and Wit,	314	To Ford	93
This morn the God of Wit and Joke,	320	First of April	1
"With Virtue, Prudence, Wit besides;	322	First of April	48
Where Wit in all its Glory shines;	361	Grace's Answer	2
<Helsham> does truly Wit command	373	Letter D. S-y	47
Men of more Wit than Money, our Pensions will fit	389	Order of Bath	7
And this will suit Men of more Money than Wit.	389	Order of Bath	8
If Clergymen, to shew their Wit,	392	Young's Satire	39
That had I been the God of Wit,	393	Modern Poets	18
Thus, Pope, in vain you boast your Wit;	406	Swift to Pope	21
For, 'tis to me he owes his Wit;	411	Dial Rich Marb	90
Stand high in Honour, Wealth, or Wit;	414	Censure	7
And take his Nonsense all for Wit!	416	Woman's Mind	8
To taste his humour, and his wit;	435	Answer Paulus	120
To try your Wit	441	Ballyspellin	26
In Admiration at her Wit!	448	Modern Lady	115
Sett, for a Sign of Wit Within.	457	Paddy's Charac	6
And thinking this Cockade of Wit	458	Paddy's Charac	21
Sole Patron, Judge, and God of Wit.	462	Birthday Song	72
And as he hears his Wit and Sence,	463	Birthday Song	91
For dealers in Satyrick Wit:	463	Birthday Song	112
'Tis grown the choicest Wit at Court,	468	Birthday Song	267
With mean Degrees of Wit and Sense?	475	Epist on Epist	16
So, Men of Wit are but a kind	480	Libel on D- D-	23
And flourish'd by imputed Wit,	481	Libel on D- D-	50
Whose meanest Talent is his Wit:	482	Libel on D- D-	80
To Flatter, Carve, and shew your Wit;	483	Libel on D- D-	106
Nor Pope wou'd dare deny him Wit,	484	Libel on D- D-	143
Take subjects safer for your wit	489	Dialogue	21
Must taste your irony and wit,	491	Dialogue	52
That Men of Wit can be no more	493	Panegyr Swift	25
Rightly you shew, that Wit alone	495	Panegyr Swift	72
Than those of Wit, or Trust in God.	495	Panegyr Swift	79
Did Congreve's Wit inspire my Song;	496	Panegyr Swift	99
In wit before the common Herd?	501	Doctor Delaney	38
Pronounce all Men of Wit, Free-thinkers.	503	Doctor Delaney	98
Wit, as the chief of Virtues's Friends,	503	Doctor Delaney	99
What's to be done? shall wit and learning chuse,	506	To a Friend	7
This Pheasant was a Man of Wit,	513	Answer Fable	35
Whose Wit at best was next to none,	514	Answer Fable	67
Queen of Wit and Beauty, Betty,	522	Betty Grizette	1
Let me praise thy Wit unmatcht.	523	Betty Grizette	12
Shreds of Wit, and senseless Rhimes,	523	Betty Grizette	19
Picking Wit among Collegions,	523	Betty Grizette	23
For sheer Wit, and Humour passes!	523	Betty Grizette	34
Swears you have a World of Wit.	523	Betty Grizette	36
In vain, the Workmen shew'd his Wit	528	Lady's Dres Rm	75
That, Wealth should be the Appenage of Wit,	532	To Mr. Gay	26
Made up of Malice, Truth, and Wit:	545	Life of Swift	2
"'tis own'd he was a Man of Wit---,	547	Life of Swift	74
Some Medals sent him for his Wit;	547	Life of Swift	91
I cry, Pox take him, and his Wit.	555	Death of Swift	52
To hear his out-of-fashion'd Wit?	556	Death of Swift	92
His Fire is out, his Wit decay'd,	556	Death of Swift	101
His Kind of Wit is out of Date.	562	Death of Swift	252
I to such Blockheads set my Wit!	579	Day Judgement	21

WIT   (CONTINUED)   PAGE   TITLE   LINE

For her Taste is almost as refin'd as her Wit.   . . .   580 Psyche   10
On Sense and Wit your Passion found, ...   593 Strephon Chloe   307
Apollo, God of Light and Wit, ...   597 Problem Solved   1
He was a Wit both born and bred;   . . . .   602 Beasts Confess   28
In praise of long departed Wit, ...   611 By Dr. Swift   8
Due Regard for Men of Wit?   . . . .   632 Epistle Lady   74
Think it Wit to fleer, and gibe?   . . . .   632 Epistle Lady   78
In modern Wit all printed Trash, is   . . . .   643 On Poetry   93
'Tis ten to one the Wit escapes;   . . . .   643 On Poetry   98
The trivial Turns, the borrow'd Wit, ...   645 On Poetry   151
At Wills the puny Judge of Wit.   . . . .   647 On Poetry   236
Of Wit and Humour, Judges sov'reign.   . . . . . .   649 On Poetry   284
On Learning, Eloquence and Wit.   . . . .   655 On Poetry   428
Of Wit and Learning chief Protector;   . . . . . .   656 On Poetry   450
Presume to borrow Wit from Bacchus?   . . . . . .   671 Epig Carthy 22   D 2
Are won by Virtue, Wit, and Parts;   . . . . . .   688 Cadenus Vaness   62
The Seeds of Knowledge, Judgment, Wit.   . . . . .   693 Cadenus Vaness   205
With much Deceit and little Wit;   . . . . . .   695 Cadenus Vaness   291
In Judgment, Knowledge, Wit, and Taste;   . . . . .   697 Cadenus Vaness   343
For Wit, I wonder where it lies.   . . . . . .   699 Cadenus Vaness   411
With all her Wit, I wou'd not ask   . . . . . .   700 Cadenus Vaness   420
With Virtue, Knowledge, Taste and Wit, ...   700 Cadenus Vaness   446
Grown old in Politicks and Wit;   . . . . . .   702 Cadenus Vaness   503
Vanessa much esteem'd his Wit, ...   702 Cadenus Vaness   511
For Pastime, or to shew his Wit;   . . . .   703 Cadenus Vaness   543
How dang'rous Things were Men of Wit, ...   706 Cadenus Vaness   619
Of Wit, to flatter and seduce: . . . .   707 Cadenus Vaness   645
For Learning, Wit, and Wisdom fam'd;)   . . . . . .   708 Cadenus Vaness   691
Alone to fill up all her Wit   . . . .   709 Cadenus Vaness   709
Yet now and then your Men of Wit   . . . . . .   710 Cadenus Vaness   760
"To form a Nymph of Wit and Sense;   . . . . . .   713 Cadenus Vaness   865
I cannot but Envy the Pride of her Wit.   . . . . .   716 Answer Rebus   2
So the Wit that is lavishly thrown away here, ...   716 Answer Rebus   17
Thy Beauty, Size, and Years, and Wit, ...   722 Stel B-Day '18   10
With half thy Wit, thy Years and Size: . . . . .   722 Stel B-Day '18   14
Pallas observing Stella's Wit   . . . .   723 To Stella   1
Proceeds that Fund of Wit and Sense;   . . . . . .   726 To Stella   80
Truth, Judgment, Wit, give Place to Spite, ...   730 Stella, Poems   93
Makes Wit inflame, or Anger burn;   . . . . .   731 Stella, Poems   118
To Virtue,--Honor, Sense, and Wit.   . . . . . .   732 Verses Vanessa   8
Except where Wit and Virtue grew   . . . .   733 Verses Vanessa   22
With Breeding, Humor, Wit, and Sense, ...   735 Stel B-day '20   25
And thus, my Stock of Wit decay'd;   . . . . . .   740 Stel B-day '21   17
But found my Wit and Fancy fled: . . . . . .   740 Stel B-day 22   6
I had some Anger in my Wit.   . . . .   747 Stel Distress   68
And shew them his wit and his learning;   . . . . .   756 Dingley Brent   9
Beauty and Wit, too sad a Truth, ...   757 Stel B-Day '24   15
The God of Wit, and Beauty's Queen, ...   757 Stel B-day '24   17
Adieu bright Wit, and radiant Eyes;   . . . . .   757 Stel B-day '24   27
Honour and Virtue, Sense and Wit, ...   758 Stel B-day '24   50
Dick was thought the brighter Wit, ...   785 Mullinex Dick   35
I own I see but little Wit in: . . . .   788 Dick's Variety   10
The Students drinking, rais'd their Wit and Parts;   . .   793 St. Pat's Well   70
For he that has so little Wit, ...   813 Bro Protestant   63
The smart-one replied, "There's no wit in the case;   .   843 Ay and No   7
"A Boulter by name is no bolter of wit.   . . . . .   843 Ay and No   10
Here Irish wit is seen   . . . .   843 Epigr Irish   2
Never since I was born did I hear so much Wit,   . . .   873 Grand Question   173
He dares defy both sense and wit.   . . . . . .   876 To Dean Swift   16
You celebrate their Wit and Parts!   . . . . . .   887 Panegyr Dean   12
Their sev'ral Talents to your Wit, ...   890 Panegyr Dean   126
At nicely carving show thy Wit;   . . . . . .   897 Panegyr Dean   335
Than with her Wit to entertain him.   . . . . . .   905 Death Daphne   72
Wherein the Men of Wit delight.   . . . . . .   920 Riddle 6   6
It cannot be Wit.   . . . .   939 Riddle Answerd   22
More Wit and Humour than from Terence.   . . . . .   988 Letter Dr Sh-n   4
Or, of thy Harmony, or Wit.   . . . . . .   1022 Nim-Dan-Dean 1   D 44
. . . your own spirit of pun, and own wit.   . . . . .   1024 Nim-Dan-Dean 2   D 16
WIT'S
These pad on wit's high road, and suits maintain   . . .   45 To Congreve   67
Of Wit's fair Goddess brought to Bed, ...   504 Doctor Delaney   116
WITCH
O'er Sea and Land conveys the Witch;   . . . . . .   132 Magician's Rod   18
But none will burn her for a Witch.   . . . . . .   698 Cadenus Vaness   363
Nor listen to the Witch of Endor;   . . . . . .   776 Mullinix Tim   100
On their Crosiers to ride, like a Witch on a Broom.   .   804 Irish Bishops   22
WITCHES
The Witches left in open Air, ...   240 Run Bankers   34
Like Lapland Witches in a Sieve: . . . . . .   254 Bubble   92
Of Witches met together, ...   426 Five Ladies   19
So Witches bent on bad Pursuits, ...   670 Epig Carthy 19   D 1
WITH   1232   OMITTED WORD
WITH-HOLD   SEE WITHOLD
And, from deserving friends, with-hold   . . . . . .   900 Dean's Reasons   35
WITHAL
Rattles for Infant Royalty to play withal, ...   6 Ode to King   13
Which oft he us'd to fish withal: . . . .   133 Magician's Rod   44
WITHALL
And may be something else withall.   . . . .   361 Grace's Answer   8

		PAGE	TITLE	LINE
WITHDRAW				
I get a Whisper, and withdraw,		200	Horace 2, 6	43
You shou'd withdraw from pen and ink,		489	Dialogue	16
WITHDREW				
When War her cloudy aspect just withdrew,		16	Ode Athenian	23
Then to a Corner both withdrew.		63	Discovery	20
I withdrew my Subscription by help of a Blot,		144	New Song	29
Poor I myself I was, when I withdrew, sick,		1029	Dr. Helsham	20
WITHER'D				
Half wither'd by a Winters keeping		290	Prog Marriage	26
"And Peerage is a wither'd Flower,		570	Death of Swift	440
WITHIN				
So he wore his within,		30	Ode to Temple	127
Whose name must not within my lines be shewn,		48	To Congreve	167
May lodge within thy Spacious Pile.		109	V's House	118
The Leather sounds, he trembles from within.		139	City Shower	46
No sooner brought within the Walls,		209	Fable Bitches	45
Within our Breast be ev'ry Secret barr'd:		210	Earl of Oxford	16
Within, his wife would break his Bones,		221	A Quiet Life	51
He hides within his darkest Tail.		240	Run Bankers	44
Virtue conceal'd within our Breast		242	Horace 4, 9	1
Within your Breast all Wisdom lyes,		243	Horace 4, 9	7
Nor come within your Cullyes Reach,		258	Bubble	194
In short our Kings and Princesses within,		275	Epilogue	27
Here lies Judge Boat within a Coffin.		286	Elegy Boat	37
So have I seen within a Pen,		294	Prog Marriage	145
"T' observe her Management within.		321	First of April	28
Had now my Lady been within.		377	Apology Lady C	50
And empty both within.		401	Window Inns 4	4
Secure of constant peace within,		434	Answer Paulus	57
"Whoever comes, I'm not within--		451	Modern Lady	218
Sett, for a Sign of Wit Within.		457	Paddy's Charac	6
As from within Pandora's Box,		528	Lady's Dres Rm	83
"Himself within the Frown of Power;		568	Death of Swift	394
Exhal'd Ambrosia from within:		586	Strephon Chloe	88
Safe within my little Wherry,		635	Epistle Lady	163
Impartial judge within your Breast		642	On Poetry	79
Within an hour, and eke a half,		675	Curate's Compl	9
Then sows within her tender Mind		693	Cadenus Vaness	202
Cadenus felt within him rise		706	Cadenus Vaness	624
Her Lace hath got within her Head		733	Verses Vanessa	25
The Nutriment will from within		759	Receipt Youth	29
So <Turds> within a Glass inclose,		786	Clad in Brown	11
All outward and within is foul;		787	Clad in Brown	14
Within their Veins, who are thy younger Sons,		791	St. Pat's Well	18
Each within his proper Cell;		830	Legion Club	44
To rouse and warn the Nymph within.		849	Old Thorn	36
I hold Intelligence within.		885	Rev Market-Hill	56
This Cave within its Womb confines		921	Riddle 7	11
And the fourth a Box within,		931	Riddle 17	D 6
WITHOLD				
Did I e'er my Mite withold		632	Epistle Lady	71
WITHOUT				
Without the Footing of a Cause;		9	Ode to King	104
Platonick Champions, gain'd without one Female Wile,		24	Ode Athenian	252
That Men, who liv'd and dy'd without a Name,		25	Ode Athenian	306
But, ah, too much without a thorn.		37	Ode Sancroft	106
(Madam, I dye without your Grace)		60	Lady Tablebook	15
For my Lord Dromedary comes a Tuesday without fail;		70	Mrs Harris Pet	28
That tho' 'tis hard to judge, yet Money can't go without Hands.		71	Mrs Harris Pet	43
Without offence to Human Shape:		83	Salamander	6
Van's Genius without Thought or Lecture		86	Hist V's House	7
Of Kingdoms, without Faith or Law.		96	On the Union	12
Without one Wonder in the Sky;		98	Elegy Patrige	6
Stood without Motion, like a Stake.		133	Magician's Rod	34
To hear we are making a Peace without Spain;		143	New Song	12
I came in without Danger; and was I to blame?		144	New Song	33
And I'll Vote against Peace, with Spain, or without:		144	New Song	46
Twelve Coronets, without thy leave!		181	Horace 2, 1	26
"Without your Help the Cause is gone--		200	Horace 2, 6	52
Without a Tear will tend my Herse.		203	In Sickness	8
To Rime all day without Offence:		219	To Mr. Delany	108
Without, they pelted him with Stones,		221	A Quiet Life	52
Cannot without a Form subsist,		228	Prog of Beauty	82
Has fed without Restraint, or Trouble;		230	Prog of Poetry	2
Without one Ave Mary.		245	Irish-Feast	36
Without a Pilot seldom knows		256	Bubble	143
Without whom they could get neither Claret nor Beef;		263	Apollo	10
Without troubling his Head about Judgment or Wit:		263	Apollo	20
Without a Star this may be done,		271	Apollo's Edict	D 42
Is dead at last without evading.		282	Journal	104
I mean a Dog, without a Joke,		298	Horrid Plot	17
Without a Mistress, hang or drown him.		303	Storm	16
Then, without fail, we pack up for Belfast.		309	Billet Players	56
(Without your passing thro the Palace		313	To Ford	63
Without your Aid, to read or spell)		325	Pethox	66
And speak without the Help of Lungs.		326	Pethox	80
I wak'd with Delight, and not without Hope,		338	Serious Poem	115
As round as a Ball, without Head without Tail,		350	Wood Insect	5
As round as a Ball, without Head without Tail,		350	Wood Insect	5

WITHOUT   (CONTINUED)   PAGE   TITLE   LINE
      That writes without the Toil of Thought.   . . . .   361 Grace's Answer   16
      (Not to be seen without a Glass)   . . . .   367 Answer Delaney   35
      Without your Legs, two Legs of Wood   . . .   .   .   .   367 Answer Delaney   49
      Wou'd entertain without Expence, ...   378 Apology Lady C   101
      This Day arriv'd without his Train, ...   398 Earl of P-b-w   11
      And thus I go off without Pray'r-Book or Psalm.   .   .   400 Tom Clinch   22
      Both, weather-beaten are without;   . . . .   401 Window Inns 4   3
      That, without which a Thing is not   . . . .   406 Swift to Pope   19
      For Dick without Doll thought Living a Folly.   .   .   .   430 Dicky Dolly   3
      To live without both full three Months he try'd,   .   .   430 Dicky Dolly   11
      Without whose aid you're all undone?   . . . .   .   .   432 Answer Paulus   4
      Of common sense without a word in!   . . . .   434 Answer Paulus   85
      He waded without any shame, ...   456 Dean Smedley   23
      Can shine, without him is extinct.   . . . .   465 Birthday Song   178
      I mean the Head without the Brain.   . . . .   469 Burning Poem   6
      Discovers freedom without rage;   . . . .   490 Dialogue   28
      And there without a mitre dye.   . . . .   491 Dialogue   56
      Till, scaping oft without a Wound, ...   500 Doctor Delaney   7
      They glance aside without a Wound.   . . . .   500 Doctor Delaney   30
      For who wou'd have <Ferns> without a Commendum?   .   518 Dean Hang Rape   39
      Lies rackt with Pain, and you without: . . .   .   .   .   554 Death of Swift   28
      "Why, is he dead without his Shoes?   . . . .   560 Death of Swift   191
      They mourn for me without dissembling.   . . .   .   .   561 Death of Swift   224
      With Favour some, and some without;   . . . .   .   .   565 Death of Swift   304
      "Without regarding private Ends, ...   565 Death of Swift   331
      ('Twas Nature's Fault) without a Beard.   . . .   .   .   603 Beasts Confess   62
      Without Success; thus tells his Case: . . . .   604 Beasts Confess   94
      And calls, without affecting Airs, ...   605 Beasts Confess   131
      Without Regard to Whig or Tory, ...   605 Beasts Confess   146
      Without Respect to Friends, or Blood, ...   607 Beasts Confess   184
      Without his taudry Coach and four: . . . .   621 Scandal Poem 1   122
      Without his lacker'd Coach and Four, ...   627 Scandal Poem 2   116
      Stand in Awe without a Rod.   . . . .   633 Epistle Lady   104
      For Poems read without a Name   . . . .   644 On Poetry   129
      Who shines alone, without a Mate.   . . . .   656 On Poetry   442
      We now can better do without him, ...   657 On Poetry   493
      Without reproach of flattery true   . . . .   658 On Poetry   D 410
      Who murder'd Horace without Rhyme or Reason?   .   .   666 Epig Carthy 3   D   4
      So like my own, without his Bow, ...   692 Cadenus Vaness   191
      A Pettycoat without a Hoop!   . . . .   699 Cadenus Vaness   400
      She reason'd, without plodding long, ...   704 Cadenus Vaness   558
      Can make us without Fear disclose   . . . .   706 Cadenus Vaness   610
      Without distinguishing her Face.   . . . .   706 Cadenus Vaness   635
      Should at their Peril without fail   . . . .   713 Cadenus Vaness   840
      Without one Word of Cupid's Darts, ...   728 Stella, Poems   11
      What Stoicks call without our Power, ...   729 Stella, Poems   63
      Or You without a Cause complain.   . . . .   733 Verses Vanessa   16
      Without an Ounce of last Year's Flesh, ...   759 Receipt Youth   15
      Nor scow'rs the Streets without a Shirt;   . . .   .   .   788 Dick's Variety   16
      For of the two, without Dispute, ...   797 Traulus 1   43
      You are only to live four Years without Vittles!   .   .   805 Irish Bishops   60
      A face for to kiss, without eyes, ears, or nose.   . .   817 Yahoo's   64
      "It's a pity a Prelate should die without law;   . . .   843 Ay and No   17
      Like a clock without wheels;   . . . .   852 Lady's Lament   34
      Without using my feet;   . . . .   852 Lady's Lament   42
      But trash without measure   . . . .   853 Lady's Lament   65
      "I ne'er knew a Parson without a good Nose,   .   .   .   872 Grand Question   143
      A judge, without the least pretence   . . . .   876 To Dean Swift   19
      To live without a coach and six, ...   878 Robbin & Harry   30
      Yet, when we dine without a Friend, ...   886 Rev Market-Hill   97
      Without my Aid, the best Divine   . . . .   915 Riddle 1   29
      Her, who, without thy Pity, dies?   . . . .   924 Riddle 8   2
      Tho' I speak without a Tongue.   . . . .   933 Riddle 20   D   4
      Invading Foes, without Resistance, ...   934 Riddle 21   D   3
      All Colours, without Paint, put on, ...   935 Riddle 23   D 12
      Without stirring out, ...   939 Riddle Answerd   10
      Without it I rather would walk on the Ground.   .   .   941 Letter   26
      Without it a Writer is not worth a Louse.   . . .   .   .   941 Letter   28
      Without it a Lady should never appear.   . . .   .   .   941 Letter   42
      Without a grain of common sense, ...   950 Upstart   D 12
      No sav'ry Dish without an Onyon;   . . . .   952 Onyons   7
      When whip you trot up, without minding your betters,   . .   978 Dean to Tho: S   3
      Like Walls, more lasting without Mortar: . . .   .   .   1021 Nim-Dan-Dean 1   D 22
      To answer your style without circumlocution.   .   .   1027 Sheri Circles   24
      Without her Privilege to cheat.   . . . .   1033 Ans to Crown   4
      A Church without Pews.   . . . .   1036 Plague Country   4
WITHSTAND
      If neither brass nor marble can withstand   . . . .   .   419 Shall Repine   1
WITHSTANDS
      The bashful Nymph no more withstands, ...   585 Strephon Chloe   43
WITHSTOOD
      If by thy Presence he's withstood?   . . . .   340 Arch-Bish Dub   22
WITLINGS
      For none but witlings there resort, ...   876 To Dean Swift   8
WITNESS
      Lives pious witness of a better age;   . . . .   52 Temple Ill   48
      Our Witness is a real Curr, ...   299 Horrid Plot   44
      "Be witness if I tell a Flam: . . . .   462 Birthday Song   78
      "Nor Witness hir'd, nor Jury pick'd, ...   570 Death of Swift   429
      Had Witness ready to attest, ...   688 Cadenus Vaness   68

	PAGE	TITLE	LINE
WITNESS (CONTINUED)			
Be Witness for me, Nymph divine,	896	Panegyr Dean	315
Witness his lazy, lousy son!	950	Upstart	D 10
WITNESSES			
And therefore his Witnesses justly may boast	335	Serious Poem	39
WITS SEE UNDER-WITS			
The Wits, I mean the Atheists of the Age,	19	Ode Athenian	103
Tho' Madmen and the Wits, Philosophers and Fools,	22	Ode Athenian	203
Or crazy rules to make us wits by rote	47	To Congreve	129
Swore all the wits were his peculiar friends;	47	To Congreve	140
And chuse out wits who ne'er have seen his face;	48	To Congreve	170
Leaving to Wits the spatious Air,	79	Vanbrug House	25
Some Wits have wondred what Analogy	98	Elegy Patrige	19
Leaving the Wits the Spacious Air	106	V's House	25
Here English Wits will be to seek,	158	Fable of Midas	59
<Sunderland's> run out of his Wits,	168	Peace Dunkirk	11
For Madmen, Children, Wits and Fools	181	Horace 2, 1	31
And to be kept in my right wits.	199	Horace 2, 6	D
At their Wits end like drunken Men.	256	Bubble	152
For Weavers now are just as poor as Wits;	276	Epilogue	40
The Poets Wits, than in the Players Dressing.	276	Epilogue	46
George is half scar'd out of his Wits,	283	Journal	125
And besides must be out of my Wits:	395	Dog and Thief	4
The Perquisites of Pimps and Wits.	498	Panegyr Swift	151
And both Idea's jump like Wits:	529	Lady's Dres Rm	126
I envy not the Wits who write	548	Life of Swift	128
Now Grub-Street Wits are all employ'd;	558	Death of Swift	165
"To talk with Wits in dirty Shoes:	565	Death of Swift	322
To pass for wits before a Rake!	592	Strephon Chloe	268
Is of all Wits the greatest Fool;	592	Strephon Chloe	278
Both special Wits, and Lovers both,	593	Cassinus Peter	2
Nor wonder how I lost my Wits;	597	Cassinus Peter	117
All Human Race wou'd fain be Wits,	640	On Poetry	1
To whom the Tribe of circling Wits,	649	On Poetry	267
Two bordering Wits contend for Glory;	650	On Poetry	293
Worn out by Wits who rhyme on Faces;	730	Stella, Poems	76
The Jest of the Court, and to the Courts unknown.	794	St. Pat's Well	100
Why Tom, the Man has lost his Wits!	797	Traulus 1	34
The wits will frequent ye,	855	Lady's Lament	133
WITT			
Throws all his Witt and Hours away	80	Vanbrug House	43
A Type of Modern Witt and Style,	81	Vanbrug House	83
For honest Harry is no Witt,	123	Empty'ng Town	23
And some shall admire his conyng Witt,	147	Windsor Proph	9
Are Humor, Raillery and Witt:	215	To Mr. Delany	14
To find her a great Witt, but the Dean a small Man.	716	Answer Rebus	14
WITTY			
The Brave, the Witty, and the Fair;	216	To Mr. Delany	38
"The powder'd Courtier's witty Sneer;	380	Apology Lady C	146
She calls it witty to be rude;	416	Woman's Mind	18
"Unless it offer'd to be witty.	572	Death of Swift	470
Some call it witty to reflect	592	Strephon Chloe	273
Are witty, dull, rejoyce, complain.	620	Scandal Poem 1	94
Are witty, dull, rejoyce, complain.	626	Scandal Poem 2	92
Ill it fits you to be witty,	630	Epistle Lady	13
The witty Ancient you enrobe,	670	Epig Carthy 21	D 2
All that was witty, learn'd, and wise,	708	Cadenus Vaness	697
Then at your leisure we'll be witty,	780	Mullinix Tim	239
Dear Baldwin chaste, and witty Crosse,	821	Dr. Rundle	61
"This mischief arises from witty Dean Swift."	843	Ay and No	6
To witty, beautiful, and young.	887	Panegyr Dean	16
. . . or at least not one that's witty, to joke w'ye?	1022	Nim-Dan-Dean 2	D 4
WIVES SEE FISH-WIVES			
We'll buy English Silks for our Wives and our Daughters,	237	Excellent Song	REF
Our Wives they grow sullen	237	Excellent Song	14
Then we'll buy English Silks for our Wives and our Daughters,	237	Excellent Song	REF
They would buy English Silks for their Wives. . .	237	Excellent Song	REF
Then we'll buy English Silks for our Wives and our Daughters,	238	Excellent Song	REF
Where Childless wives crowd ev'ry morn	293	Prog Marriage	119
That all our wives should go in Chints.	423	Ireld	60
If your wives will permit ye,	858	Lady's Lament	215
WIZARDS			
So, Clowns on Scholars as on Wizards look,	193	Author Himself	7
For you can't but have heard of a trick among wizards,	976	Dean to Sherid	21
WO			
Then, wo be to my Lord Lieutenant,	789	Dick's Variety	37
WOE			
Approaching joy at strife with parting woe.	51	Temple Ill	22
Of Fraunce hir woe thys is the sygne,	102	Merlin	2
An herdie Chiftan, woe the morne	103	Merlin	7
Then Woe be to those in the House who are sick:	351	Wood Insect	22
It fills my Heart with Woe,	426	Five Ladies	21
Where, in this Scene of endless Woe,	647	On Poetry	209
WOES			
Thou universal cause of all my woes;	53	Temple Ill	82
To have Companions in their Woes.)	764	Stel B-day '26	24
WOFUL			
Our wand'ring Saints in woful State,	111	Bauc & Phil 2	15

		PAGE	TITLE	LINE
WOFUL	**(CONTINUED)**			
You'll find it soon by woful Proof,	. . . .	408	Dial Rich Marb	11
Dick would make a woful Noise,	. . . .	784	Mullinex Dick	17
WOFULL				
Our wand'ring Saints in wofull State,	. . . . .	91	Bauc & Phil 1	47
You men would be in wofull pickle	. . . .	618	Scandal Poem 1	41
WOLF				
Devours your Geese, the Wolf your Flocks:	. . .	504	Doctor Delaney	130
The Hound wou'd scent, the Wolf would prole:	. . .	512	Answer Fable	8
And, thus the pious Wolf begins:	. . . . . .	601	Beasts Confess	12
A Wolf destroys a thousand Lambs.	. . . . . .	651	On Poetry	326
WOLSTON'S				
"Here's Wolston's Tracts, the twelfth Edition;	. . .	564	Death of Swift	281
WOLVES				
Hogs, Asses, Wolves, Baboons, & Goats	. . . . .	659	On Poetry	D 410
WOMAN				
Woman seems now above all Vanity grown,	. . . . . .	24	Ode Athenian	250
Wert thou right woman, thou shouldst scorn to look	. .	54	Temple Ill	107
'No woman breathing takes up less;	. . . . . .	447	Modern Lady	97
A Cloud with Woman kind compare?	. . . .	617	Scandal Poem 1	2
But, Woman is a curst inflamer;	. . . . . .	618	Scandal Poem 1	35
Tis true; a Woman on her mettle	. . . . . .	621	Scandal Poem 1	143
To flatter Woman by a Metaphor!	. . . . .	622	Scandal Poem 1	169
A Woman with a Cloud compare?	. . . .	623	Scandal Poem 2	2
But, Woman was by Fate design'd	. . . . . .	624	Scandal Poem 2	29
But Woman is a curst Inflamer,	. . . . . .	624	Scandal Poem 2	33
'Tis true; a Woman on her Mettle,	. . . . .	628	Scandal Poem 2	147
Never woman more devis'd	. . . .	906	Daphne	5
A Man, a Woman, Lion, Bear,	. . . . .	927	Riddle 10	D 14
A long-ear'd Beast, and Woman of Endor,	. . . .	942	Probatur Alit	7
For a Riddle is dark, but a Woman is light.	. . .	972	S-'s Ans Sh-d	8
Like a woman it keeps in less than it lets out.	. .	976	Dean to Sherid	26
And that a Woman, in those Tragedies	. . . .	988	Letter Dr Sh-n	24
WOMAN-HATER				
And brand me for a Woman-Hater?	. . . .	445	Modern Lady	8
WOMAN-KIND				
In mild Reproof to Woman-kind;	. . . .	384	Manly Virtue	24
WOMAN'S				
More virtues in a Woman's Mind,	. . . . . .	417	Woman's Mind	58
But, can you guess from Woman's Air,	. . . . .	625	Scandal Poem 2	45
I hardly hear a Woman's Clack.	. . . . . .	674	His Deafness	8
A Woman's no Sieve (for with that you begin)	. .	972	S-'s Ans Sh-d	5
WOMANKIND				
So men may see what once was womankind,	. . . .	52	Temple Ill	49
Seeds long unknown to Womankind,	. . . . .	693	Cadenus Vaness	203
As she advanc'd, that Womankind	. . . . .	694	Cadenus Vaness	236
WOMANS				
May all the Blood, which shall by Womans scorn be shed		23	Ode Athenian	245
How usefull were a womans thunder	. . . .	617	Scandal Poem 1	15
WOMB				
As from the Womb of Earth a field of Corn.	. . . .	20	Ode Athenian	131
Her Litter teeming from her Womb,	. . . . . .	207	Fable Bitches	4
It drags behind a spacious Womb,	. . . . . .	743	Stel B-day 22	68
And in the spacious Womb contains	. . . . .	743	Stel B-day 22	69
Sprung from her Womb that impious Line,	. . . .	895	Panegyr Dean	271
This Cave within its Womb confines	. . . . .	921	Riddle 7	11
All beauteous Offspring of one Womb,	. . . . .	923	Riddle 7	68
WOMEN				
Wish'd Women might have Children fast,	. . . . .	115	Bauc & Phil 2	131
Gave Women all their Hearts could wish	. . . .	227	Prog of Beauty	58
With Women Compounds I am cloy'd,	. . . . .	272	Apollo's Edict	D 60
Since Waiting Women like Exacting Jades,	. . . .	275	Epilogue	15
Admires how modest Women can	. . . . .	417	Woman's Mind	47
That Women should be such Coquets:	. . . . .	450	Modern Lady	165
To prove that Bishops were old Women.	. . . . .	455	Dean Smedley	20
All Women his Description fits,	. . . . . .	529	Lady's Dres Rm	125
Direct that Women must be decent;	. . . . .	591	Strephon Chloe	252
But, women in a cloudy plight	. . . . . .	618	Scandal Poem 1	31
While Women, if it could be reckon'd	. . . . .	618	Scandal Poem 1	45
But, Women in a Cloudy Plight,	. . . . .	624	Scandal Poem 2	25
While Women, if it could be reckon'd,	. . . . .	625	Scandal Poem 2	41
Had Women been the Makers of our Laws;	. . . .	662	Upon Ladies	5
But Women now feel no such Fire,	. . . . . .	687	Cadenus Vaness	35
That Women were not worth the wooing,	. . . .	713	Cadenus Vaness	861
"To Women than they had before,	. . . . .	714	Cadenus Vaness	875
The Terror of Women, and Pleasure of Boys,	. . .	927	Riddle 11	D 2
WOMEN'S				
Hence we conclude, no Women's Hearts	. . . . .	688	Cadenus Vaness	61
WOMENS				
But, can you guess from womens air	. . . .	619	Scandal Poem 1	49
WON				
Which, what it bravely Won, do's well Maintain.	. . .	12	Ode to William	D 28
I'd won it on my Word,	. . . .	75	Game Traffick	18
I hope you won it fairly.	. . . .	154	Widow and Cat	D 35
Behold the Glory he has won,	. . . .	385	Manly Virtue	41
"Well, I remember what she won;	. . . . . .	446	Modern Lady	64
"I might by this have won a Vole."	. . . . . .	451	Modern Lady	203
A Champion kill'd, or Trophy won;	. . . . . .	554	Death of Swift	24
By Valour, Conduct, Fortune won;	. . . . . .	641	On Poetry	26
Are won by Virtue, Wit, and Parts;	. . . . . .	688	Cadenus Vaness	62
By Beauty cou'd your Heart be won,	. . . . . .	692	Cadenus Vaness	192

924

```
WON'T                                                          PAGE    TITLE            LINE
    Won't pay th' Impertinence of being known;    . . . . .     20   Ode Athenian       152
    Oh but, said I, what if after all my Chaplain won't come    73   Mrs Harris Pet      68
       to?
    Why sure you won't appear in Town,      . . . . . . .      175   Horace 1, 7        123
    (We won't dispute a Year or more)       . . . . . . .      721   Stel B-Day '18       2
    You won't give us a Dram.       . . . . . . .            1015   Swift to Sheri      48
    You won't part with a Spoon-full,    . . . . . . .       1015   Swift to Sheri      50
    You see I won't stop,     . . . . . . . .               1015   Swift to Sheri      53
WOND'ROUS
    But zeal is weak and ignorant, tho' wond'rous proud,  . .    38   Ode Sancroft       135
    The wond'rous Arch behind you fell,    . . . . . .         326   Pethox              95
    Oh, wond'rous Box! my Lyre unstrung    . . . . . .         494   Panegyr Swift       45
    Dear Venus, hide this wond'rous Maid,    . . . . . .       585   Strephon Chloe      29
    Produc'd on Earth a wond'rous Maid,    . . . . . .         690   Cadenus Vaness     137
    Did to it's wond'rous Birth conspire;    . . . . . .       743   Stel B-day 22       64
    A new and wond'rous Art I show      . . . . . . .         920   Riddle 6             9
    Most wond'rous is my Magick Power;    . . . . . . .        930   Riddle 15        D  13
    Brethren of a wond'rous Kind,      . . . . . . . .         931   Riddle 18        D   2
WONDER
    Preserv'd by wonder from the Flood,    . . . . . .          17   Ode Athenian        45
    No wonder then she quits the narrow Path of Sense  . .      18   Ode Athenian        68
    Wonder to see the Motions fly     . . . . . . . .          29   Ode to Temple       96
    Whatever moves our Wonder or our Sport,    . . . . .        31   Ode to Temple      163
    No wonder, then, we talk amiss      . . . . . . .          35   Ode Sancroft        41
    Nor wonder, if from such polluted minds    . . . . .        47   To Congreve        127
    No wonder then, if nicely skill'd    . . . . . . .          80   Vanbrug House       61
    No wonder, since wise Authors shew,    . . . . . .          87   Hist V's House      39
    But what adds to the Wonder more,    . . . . . . .          93   Bauc & Phil 1      129
    Without one Wonder in the Sky;      . . . . . . .          98   Elegy Patrige        6
    No wonder then, if nicely skill'd    . . . . . . .         107   V's House           35
    And gaze in silent Wonder long,      . . . . . . .        109   V's House          106
    And, what exalts the Wonder more,    . . . . . . .        113   Bauc & Phil 2       69
    <Swift> seem'd to wonder what he meant,    . . . . .      172   Horace 1, 7         51
    "I wonder what some People mean;    . . . . . . .         202   Horace 2, 6         84
    You wonder now to see me write      . . . . . . .        218   To Mr. Delany       87
    Celia's the Wonder of her Sex;      . . . . . . .         227   Prog of Beauty      54
    Perhaps you wonder whence this Friendship Springs,  . .   275   Epilogue           35
    A wooden Judge is no such Wonder.    . . . . . . .        286   Elegy Boat         40
    I wonder you held out so long,      . . . . . . .        315   To Ford           110
    Fine Words; I wonder where you stole 'um.    . . . .      348   Whitshed Motto      2
    My Lady could not chuse but wonder:    . . . . . .       377   Apology Lady C      65
    No wonder when you raise and level,    . . . . . .       477   Epist on Epist      65
    No Wonder you should think it little    . . . . . .      495   Panegyr Swift       58
    Nor wonder how I lost my Wits;      . . . . . . .        597   Cassinus Peter     117
    No Wonder how his Fortune sunk,      . . . . . . .       607   Beasts Confess     195
    While Readers wonder whom you meant.    . . . . . .      645   On Poetry          160
    For Wit, I wonder where it lies.      . . . . . . .       699   Cadenus Vaness     411
    Such Wonder by his Merit wrought;    . . . . . . .       710   Cadenus Vaness     753
    We really wonder how she lives;      . . . . . . .       735   Stel B-day '20      30
    I wonder why he was not hang'd;      . . . . . . .       797   Traulus 1           42
    The neighbours wonder why the Knight    . . . . . .      901   Dean's Reasons      81
    No Wonder now I look so thin;      . . . . . . . .        915   Riddle 1             9
    . . . I wonder where you were bred?    . . . . . .       985   Mary to Sher         2
WONDER'D
    He wonder'd for how much an Inch 'twould be Sold:  . .    288   Bank Down          33
    His Debtors they wonder'd to find him so frank,  . .      288   Bank Down          44
    Wonder'd the God had sent them there.    . . . . .       322   First of April     44
WONDERFUL
    Yet, what is wonderful to tell it,    . . . . . . .        65   Problem            11
    When, Behold the next Morning, a wonderful Riddle,  . .    77   Lady B- B-          8
    Yet (what is wonderful) they found,    . . . . . .       112   Bauc & Phil 2       32
    So wonderful his Expedition,      . . . . . . . .        398   Earl of P-b-w       28
    But, that which wonderful appears,    . . . . . . .      915   Riddle 1            17
WONDERFULL
    Could cause such wonderfull Effects.    . . . . . .      227   Prog of Beauty      56
WONDERFULLY
    Is wonderfully mov'd by some exalted Men,    . . . .      20   Ode Athenian       137
    So quickly, and so wonderfully carried on,    . . . .     24   Ode Athenian       276
WONDEROUS
    But whence this Wonderous Charity, in Play'rs,    . . .  275   Epilogue           11
WONDERS
    We Irish Folks expected wonders,      . . . . . . .       62   Discovery           2
    He wonders what employs her Brain;    . . . . . . .      292   Prog Marriage      65
    atchieving of nothing Still promising wonders    . . .   540   Charac Walpole      5
    Then think, what Wonders will be done    . . . . .       655   On Poetry         433
    She wonders where the Charm appears    . . . . . .       725   To Stella          69
WONDRED
    Some Wits have wondred what Analogy    . . . . . . .      98   Elegy Patrige       19
    Good Lord! I wondred how I dar'd to look him in the     342   Upon His Grace      28
       Face.
WONDRING
    The wondring World, where'er he moves,    . . . . .      387   Manly Virtue      127
WONDROUS
    Sure there's some Wondrous Joy in Doing Good;    . .       6   Ode to King         1
    Wondrous Refiners of Philosophy,      . . . . . . .       19   Ode Athenian      105
    Perhaps imagine to be wondrous Wit      . . . . . .       20   Ode Athenian      125
    <God> <damn> me Jack, she's wondrous fair.    . . .     228   Prog of Beauty     76
    Most wondrous Forms you see me wear    . . . . . .       927   Riddle 10        D 13
WONT
    The Soot or Powder which was wont      . . . . . . .     226   Prog of Beauty     17
```

WONT   (CONTINUED)   PAGE   TITLE   LINE
    Wont at such times each heart to pierce, ...   296 Satiric Elegy   19
    "With Rapture, what they wont to flee.   . . . . . .   384 Manly Virtue   14
    Here wont the Dean when he's to seek, ...   409 Dial Rich Marb   51
    How was her Tutor wont to praise . . . .   708 Cadenus Vaness   688
    And, as your old wont is, change sides in a trice: . . .   818 Archbi Cashel   8
    Who wont to weed the Court of Gosford Knight,   . . .   880 Pastoral Dial   2
WONTED
    And then, with wonted Wile and Slyness, ...   1005 Sheridan's Sub   24
WOO
    A rich Divine began to woo . . . .   289 Prog Marriage   2
WOOD
    And many a pleasant Wood, ...   17 Ode Athenian   41
    This wilderness the world, like that poetic wood of old,   41 Ode Sancroft   225
    The little Children in the Wood, ...   93 Bauc & Phil 1   120
    The Scene, a Wood, produc'd no more   . . . . . .   108 V's House   83
    The Little Children in the Wood: . . . . . .   114 Bauc & Phil 2   96
    His Rod was honest English Wood, ...   132 Magician's Rod   7
    Achilles's Scepter was of Wood, ...   134 Magician's Rod   59
    Of Land set out to plant a Wood.   . . . . . .   198 Horace 2, 6   6
    He was as hard, and pond'rous Wood at that: . . . .   285 Elegy Boat   20
    To be Hewers of Wood and Drawers of Water,   . . .   334 Serious Poem   2
    Yet we all should Rejoyce to be Hewers of Wood.   . .   334 Serious Poem   4
    That old rotten Wood will Shine in the Dark.   . . .   334 Serious Poem   8
    The Heathens, we Read, had Gods made of Wood,   . .   334 Serious Poem   9
    But this Idol Wood may do us great Evil,   . . .   334 Serious Poem   11
    Their Gods were of Wood, but our Wood is the Devil;   . .   334 Serious Poem   12
    Their Gods were of Wood, but our Wood is the Devil: 334 Serious Poem   12
    To cut down fine Wood is a very bad Thing',   . . .   334 Serious Poem   13
    Then if cutting down Wood brings Money good Store,   . .   334 Serious Poem   15
    (I forget in what Church) an Image of Wood;   . .   334 Serious Poem   18
    Find you but the Fryer, and I'll find the Wood.   . .   334 Serious Poem   24
    From what Kind of Tree this Wood was Hewn out.   . .   334 Serious Poem   26
    But here Mr. Wood complains that We Mock, ...   335 Serious Poem   41
    Then in Spight of your Sophistry, Honest Will. Wood   335 Serious Poem   49
    Unless by the Devil we mean Mr. Wood.   . . . . .   335 Serious Poem   56
    But Wood I assure you is no Heart of Oak;   . . .   336 Serious Poem   66
    When the True Wood arrives, as he soon will no doubt,   .   336 Serious Poem   75
    (For that's but a Sham Wood they carry about)   . .   336 Serious Poem   76
    Wood got so much Copper? He got it by Brass;   . .   336 Serious Poem   86
    Call'd, Love In A Tub, and Love In A Wood.   . . .   337 Serious Poem   92
    These Comedies twain Friend Wood will contrive   . .   337 Serious Poem   93
    First, Love In A Tub: 'Squire Wood has in Store   337 Serious Poem   95
    Wood swears he will do it for Ireland's Good,   . . .   337 Serious Poem   99
    Then can you deny it is Love in a Wood?   . . .   337 Serious Poem   100
    I dream't Wood was told he should Dye by a Drop   337 Serious Poem   110
    Very soon to see Wood Drop down from a Rope.   . .   338 Serious Poem   116
    Why that may be true, yet Wood upon Wood, ...   338 Serious Poem   121
    Why that may be true, yet Wood upon Wood, ...   338 Serious Poem   121
    Then how can we dread William Wood, ...   340 Arch-Bish Dub   21
    I Sing not of the Draper's Praise, nor yet of William   341 Upon His Grace   1
        Wood;
    When first the 'Squire, and Tinker Wood   . . . . .   344 Prometheus   1
    By that old Thief Prometheus? Wood   . . . . . .   346 Prometheus   60
    To favour Wood and keep my Pension: . . . . .   348 Whitshed Motto   16
    That three little Vermin are kin to Will. Wood: . .   350 Wood Insect   2
    And thus William Wood to my Fancy appears   . . .   350 Wood Insect   7
    The Louse of the Wood for a Med'cine is us'd,   . .   351 Wood Insect   11
    To swallow Will. Wood either bruis'd or alive.   . .   351 Wood Insect   14
    That lies in old Wood like a Hare in her Form;   . . .   351 Wood Insect   18
    Such a Worm was Will. Wood when he scratcht at the Doo   351 Wood Insect   29
    Without your Legs, two Legs of Wood   . . . . . .   367 Answer Delaney   49
    High on a Length of prostrate Wood, ...   393 Modern Poets   12
    This Lark was hated in the Wood, ...   514 Answer Fable   61
    "It serves for Stubble, Hay, and Wood, ...   550 Life of Swift   178
    Who wisely hides his .Wood and Wire;   . . . . .   592 Strephon Chloe   286
    There's not a Puppet made of Wood, ...   777 Mullinix Tim   123
    When I saw him so often with Darby and Wood.   . .   868 Grand Question   48
    Both Dukes and Lords abhor its Wood, ...   928 Riddle 12   D   7
WOOD-LOUSE
    The first is an Insect they call a Wood-Louse,   . . .   350 Wood Insect   3
WOOD-PARK
    She strove in vain to ape Wood-Park.   . . . . .   751 Stel Wood-Park   64
    Yet, when you sigh to leave Wood-Park, ...   752 Stel Wood-Park   85
    A Cottage is Wood-Park with you.   . . . . . .   752 Stel Wood-Park   92
WOOD-WORM
    The Third is an Insect we call a Wood-Worm,   . . .   351 Wood Insect   17
WOOD'S
    The Words in Wood's Mouth, or speaks from his Guts: .   335 Serious Poem   62
    But with honest Wood's Love there is no contending,   .   337 Serious Poem   105
    But when Wood's Brass began to sound, ...   338 Wood's Brass   7
    Apply'd to Wood's adult'rate Copper;   . . . . .   353 Wood Ironmongr   32
    And ring Wood's Copper in our Ears   . . . . . .   354 Simile Silver   27
    If Wood's Coin should 'mongst Us pass   . . . . .   372 Letter D. S-y   35
    "To treat gold reduc'd like Wood's copper pence.   . . .   843 Ay and No   16
    And <Wood's> ditto Pills do Swallow, ...   372 Letter D. S-y   30
WOODEN
    The wooden Jack which had almost   . . . .   93 Bauc & Phil 1   125
    A wooden Jack, which had almost   . . . .   113 Bauc & Phil 2   65
    So when Troy Chair-men bore the Wooden Steed,   . .   139 City Shower   47
    Thus did the Grecian Wooden Horse, ...   209 Fable Bitches   43

                                         926

WOODEN	(CONTINUED)	PAGE	TITLE	LINE
A wooden Judge is no such Wonder.	. . . .	286	Elegy Boat	40
Inclose him in a wooden Tow'r,	. . . .	325	Pethox	56
She sent her Priests in Wooden Shoes	. . . . . .	895	Panegyr Dean	263

WOODPARK

She did her best to ape Woodpark. She strove in vain to ape		747	Stel Distress	48
For when you sigh to leave Woodpark,	. . . .	748	Stel Distress	69
A Cottage is Woodpark with You.		748	Stel Distress	76

WOODS

Sing of thy Vales, sing of thy Woods, sing of thy Fields;		31	Ode to Temple	138
In seas and woods, or low as hell		620	Scandal Poem 1	100
Both Mountains, Woods, and Hills, and Rocks,	. . .	934	Riddle 21	D 7

WOODS'S

For he regards Ten thousand Pounds no more than Woods's Dross.		341	Upon His Grace	12
I hope you will not pay my Rent in that same Woods's Trash.		342	Upon His Grace	36

WOOING

Caressing Knaves and Dunces wooing,	. . . . . .	484	Libel on D- D-	127
That Women were not worth the wooing,	. . . . . .	713	Cadenus Vaness	861

WOOL

And Wool it is greasy, and quickly takes Fire.	. . .	237	Excellent Song	21
To hang up all who smuggle wool.	. . . .	423	Ireld	58
We comb the Wool, refine the Stuff,	. . . .	948	Jason Hassard	3

WOOLLEN

In England the Dead in Woollen are clad,	. . . . .	237	Excellent Song	10
At wearing of Woollen,	. . . .	237	Excellent Song	15
First, lolling Sloth in Woollen Cap,	. . . . . .	895	Panegyr Dean	273

WOOLSTON

To Woolston recommend our youth	. . . .	490	Dialogue	29
Since Woolston gave us Arms to rout him.	. . . . .	657	On Poetry	494
Hobbes, Tindal, and Woolston, and Collins, and Nayler,		815	Yahoo's	26

WORD

To Valour and to Virtue the same Word:	·	7	Ode to King	28
He twitcht his sleeve, and stole a word,	. . . . . .	63	Discovery	19
I'd won it on my Word,	. . . .	75	Game Traffick	18
Because he could find no Word to come pat in.	. . . .	76	Lady B- B-	4
Speak against Peace right many a Word;	. . . . . .	147	Windsor Proph	8
Yet take one Word of Counsel by the way:	. . . . . .	166	Toland's Invit	40
If <Guernsey> calls, send word you're gone abroad;	. .	166	Toland's Invit	41
"And Mr. Dean, one Word from you--	. . . .	201	Horace 2, 6	62
Pray not a word of Halcyon Days.	. . . .	271	Apollo's Edict	D 45
A word or two of Lord Chief Baron;	. . . .	282	Journal	98
For a good word or so, we understand.	. . . . . .	308	Billet Players	24
Now to a word of bus'ness in our own.	. . . . . .	309	Billet Players	54
With half a Word, when you require,	. . . .	325	Pethox	47
Or may be I mistook the Word;	. . . .	376	Apology Lady C	39
Of common sense without a word in!	. . . .	434	Answer Paulus	85
My Word is past, I must submit,	. . . .	445	Modern Lady	26
Quadrill's the Word, and so begin.	. . . .	451	Modern Lady	219
"You spoke a Word began with W,	. . . .	452	Modern Lady	254
And pawn'd his word Hell is not local.	. . . . . .	469	Birthday Song	272
A Lye, at ev'ry second word:	. . . .	550	Life of Swift	191
Was Maid in Thought, and Word, and Deed,	. . . . .	588	Strephon Chloe	158
How? Not a Word come from thy lips?	. . . .	594	Cassinus Peter	36
Again you fail, yet Safe's the Word,	. . . .	645	On Poetry	147
Tho' not a Word be understood.	. . . .	649	On Poetry	274
You pawn your Word for him--who'll vouch for you?	. .	668	Epig Carthy 8	D 2
She heard it--there she kept her Word;	. . . . . .	690	Cadenus Vaness	119
With Nonsense ev'ry second Word,	. . . .	696	Cadenus Vaness	329
And faulter'd ev'ry Word he spoke;	. . . .	707	Cadenus Vaness	657
She vows to take him at his Word,	. . . .	712	Cadenus Vaness	803
Are not so sacred as her Word:	. . . .	725	To Stella	56
Without one Word of Cupid's Darts,	. . . .	728	Stella, Poems	11
With gall in ev'ry word I speak,	. . . .	754	Stella '23	12
Ne'er minded a word that was spoken;	. . . . . .	755	Dingley Brent	3
I'll ne'er believe a Word they say.	. . . .	757	Stel B-day '24	40
Then, prithee reflect, take a word of advice;	. . . .	818	Archbi Cashel	7
"But if I say the word--take care of Armagh!"	. . . .	843	Ay and No	18
Put a word out of joint,	. . . .	855	Lady's Lament	139
Says not a Word of his Departure	. . . .	860	Lady Acheson	11
At last comes the Troop, by the Word of Command	. .	870	Grand Question	99
For your Life, not a Word of the Matter, I charge ye:		873	Grand Question	189
To give the least offensive Word;	. . . .	889	Panegyr Dean	70
Nor can the plainest Word pronounce,	. . . . . .	891	Panegyr Dean	149
Will scarce one precious word impart:	. . . . . .	900	Dean's Reasons	44
I will ne'er object a word.	. . . .	908	Daphne	62
Yet not a Word I understand.	. . . .	915	Riddle 1	28
I hardly now can force a Word.	. . . .	916	Riddle 1	40
That I shou'd point the Word of God,	. . . . . .	930	Riddle 15	D 23
Well, punners and rhymers must have the last word.	. .	976	Dean to Sherid	8
One word shou'd stick thus in your gizzard.	. . . . .	983	Sher, A Goose	10
. . .with all my Heart and Soul, upon my Word and Honour.		1014	Swift to Sheri	9

WORDS

In dagger-contests, and th' artillery of words,	. . .	35	Ode Sancroft	13
And shap'd my passion in such words as these.	. . . .	53	Temple Ill	80
In other Words, You with the Staff,	. . . . .	188	Scriblerus 6	3
This Tale may be apply'd in few Words	. . . . . .	189	Faggot	15

927

WORDS	(CONTINUED)	PAGE	TITLE	LINE
Some formal Visits, Looks, and Words,		204	In Sickness	13
The Words in Wood's Mouth, or speaks from his Guts:		335	Serious Poem	62
Fine Words; I wonder where you stole 'um.		348	Whitshed Motto	2
But, let me now the Words translate:		348	Whitshed Motto	5
Have taught him his poetick Words.		411	Dial Rich Marb	92
But, half the Words pronouncing wrong;		416	Woman's Mind	10
A thousand words to stand for six!		434	Answer Paulus	84
The rumbling words march fierce along,		461	Birthday Song	45
But smooth your words to fit the tune,		467	Birthday Song	212
To find out proper words for Harmony:		467	Birthday Song	218
Nine other tuneful words like that		467	Birthday Song	227
Your words to some Italian Tune.		469	Birthday Song	278
I had it in the Words that follow.		485	Libel on D- D-	182
Hear from my desk the words that follow;		490	Dialogue	48
Yet how shall I express in Words,		514	Answer Fable	59
On such a Point few Words are best,		526	Lady's Dres Rm	15
And yet her Words were so exprest,		706	Cadenus Vaness	628
The Nymph in sober Words intreats		711	Cadenus Vaness	792
To grope for Words, and out they come.		797	Traulus 1	52
And give him Words of dreadful Sounds,		904	Death Daphne	43
My Words are few, but spoke with Sense:		917	Riddle 4	5
And tho' no Marriage Words are spoke,		926	Riddle 9	15
Suit your Words to your Musick well,		956	Cantata	
Suit your Words to your Musick well,		956	Cantata	
Suit your Words to your Musick well,		956	Cantata	
I am sure such Words does not become a Man of your Cloth.		985	Mary to Sher	3
Thy Words so closely wedg'd, and short are,		1021	Nim-Dan-Dean 1	D 21
Thy Words together ty'd in small Hanks,		1021	Nim-Dan-Dean 1	D 29
WORE				
So he wore his within,		30	Ode to Temple	127
Upon their Shoes the Romans wore,		99	Elegy Patrige	36
Those Men who wore the Breeches least		221	A Quiet Life	47
He walk'd the Streets, and wore a Thread-bare Cloak;		234	Elegy on Demar	9
That in his Tail he wore his Eyes,		513	Answer Fable	17
Thy Brother (far thy Betters) wore a Gown.		678	Dean and Duke	14
And He was a Primate, and He wore a Mitre,		803	Irish Bishops	5
When his envenom'd Shirt he wore,		925	Riddle 8	39
WORK SEE HANDY-WORK				
Your Name shall the remaining Work perform,		13	Ode to William	D 39
I grieve, this Noble Work so happily begun,		24	Ode Athenian	275
Work out, as Anger does in Vermin?		66	Problem	16
And mark the Progress of their Work,		86	Hist V's House	16
Can't you go work, or serve the King?		91	Bauc & Phil 1	41
But this a Work so hard was found,		108	V's House	87
'Tis thought could be the Work of none but <Swift>		195	Author Himself	50
Where Nothing's left to work upon.		228	Prog of Beauty	80
O'er sees the Work, or Dragon rowes,		279	Journal	23
Her ev'ning Work so fills her Head;		291	Prog Marriage	58
With t' other Hand the Work of two:		366	Answer Delaney	24
Then cut him out a world of work,		466	Birthday Song	193
For solid Work, but not for Play;		483	Libel on D- D-	90
Nor ever chuse to Work with Tools		483	Libel on D- D-	91
To make them work their own undoing.		484	Libel on D- D-	128
My Work and me in half an Hour.		502	Doctor Delaney	70
The fittest Tools to work for Bobb.		503	Doctor Delaney	90
His meanest Work: For, had he thought it fit,		532	To Mr. Gay	25
His Work is done, the Minister must out.		536	To Mr. Gay	150
Yet still I fear your Work is done but Half;		538	Mr. Pulteney	13
To work her Ends; which if it sped,		690	Cadenus Vaness	133
Their Work was half already done,		692	Cadenus Vaness	174
But still the Work was not compleat,		692	Cadenus Vaness	184
His Med'cine work as he design'd		746	Stel Distress	32
His Malice work as he design'd:		750	Stel Wood-Park	24
To work whose Ends, his Madness pimps.		798	Traulus 1	72
As at their Work they sate in counterview,		880	Pastoral Dial	5
No Work is grievous or offensive.		891	Panegyr Dean	158
To spoil his work, and work by halves:		902	Dean's Reasons	110
To spoil his work, and work by halves:		902	Dean's Reasons	110
To make a Work compleatly fine,		1022	Nim-Dan-Dean 1	D 45
Be last at Work,		1035	Servants Maxim	3
WORKERS				
Their Brother Quill-Men Workers for the Stage,		276	Epilogue	41
WORKING				
And calumny, by working under ground,		506	To a Friend	5
Sets the Spirits all a working.		636	Epistle Lady	206
Fall a Working like a Mole,		832	Legion Club	73
WORKMAN				
No cleanly Workman can endure the Stink.		535	To Mr. Gay	128
Nor, dares an abler Workman undertake		535	To Mr. Gay	133
WORKMANSHIP				
The Workmanship of their own Hands.		227	Prog of Beauty	52
WORKMEN				
In vain, the Workmen shew'd his Wit		528	Lady's Dres Rm	75
He pays his Workmen on the Nail.		646	On Poetry	190
We never hear the Workmen prais'd,		727	Stella, Poems	2
WORKS SEE FIRE-WORKS				
Works in my Lord by <Stool> and Sweat,		65	Problem	8
His Works were hawk'd in ev'ry Street,		172	Horace 1, 7	41
Conceive the Works of Midnight Hags,		240	Run Bankers	29

WORKS	(CONTINUED)	PAGE	TITLE	LINE
And as for their Works, when I please I may read 'em;		263	Apollo	22
Departed; and his Works must follow:		562	Death of Swift	250
"As for his Works in Verse and Prose,		565	Death of Swift	309
Your Works are like old Jacob's speckled Goats,		670	Epig Carthy 18	D 3
My Works he said, cou'd ne'er afford him Meat,		670	Epig Carthy 20	D 3
And call'd for his Poetick Works;		702	Cadenus Vaness	512
Whose names and works (tho' dead) are made		876	To Dean Swift	9
To Works of more exalted Kind.		893	Panegyr Dean	198
Huge Heaps of never-dying Works;		922	Riddle 7	40
WORLD				
Falls sick in the Posteriors of the World.		10	Ode to King	146
We often search contentedly the whole World round,		20	Ode Athenian	142
War! that mad Game, the World so loves to play,		28	Ode to Temple	76
For this inferior World is but Heaven's dusky shade,		35	Ode Sancroft	21
Suppose the truth, like all the world, their own;		37	Ode Sancroft	80
The world has wholly miss'd;		39	Ode Sancroft	160
And yet the world, whose eyes are on our mighty Prince,		40	Ode Sancroft	180
This wilderness the world, like that poetic wood of old,		41	Ode Sancroft	225
Could leap the bounds which part your world and mine;		44	To Congreve	30
Which gave them birth, can rob the world of day.		46	To Congreve	82
And the bad world may well believe the same;		49	To Congreve	198
Sprung from a better world, and chosen then		52	Temple Ill	45
Enrag'd to see the world abus'd		64	Discovery	47
(Now you must know, of all Things in the World,. .		71	Mrs Harris Pet	35
Into the World Corinna fell,		149	Corinna	3
The World shall feel her scratch and bite.		150	Corinna	12
What all the World knew long ago,		180	Horace 2, 1	8
"Of which the Christian World complain.		183	Horace 2, 1	98
What I desire the World should know.		200	Horace 2, 6	42
Which drags the slavish World in Chains.		243	Horace 4, 9	14
And let them be seen by the World if he dare,		265	Apollo	63
Tost in the Waves of this tempestuous World,		284	Elegy Boat	5
This world he cumber'd long enough;		296	Satiric Elegy	13
The World from justling Seeds arose,		324	Pethox	28
Is a Man of this World all true Flesh and Blood;		335	Serious Poem	50
The World in any Chain but Gold;		346	Prometheus	50
Will make you scorn this World below.		362	Grace's Answer	30
The wondring World, where'er he moves,		387	Manly Virtue	127
The Christian World his Deeds proclaim,		397	Earl of P-b-w	2
The World, a willing Stander-by,		414	Censure	13
Fresh Matter for a World of Chat,		447	Modern Lady	82
Cries, "Lord, the World is so censorious!		450	Modern Lady	167
To half the world a standing jest.		455	Dean Smedley	11
This World is his, and theirs the next.		456	Dean Smedley	40
Because he had the world subdu'd:		464	Birthday Song	146
Then cut him out a world of work,		466	Birthday Song	193
Begins the World with Fear and Shame,		500	Doctor Delaney	12
Swears you have a World of Wit.		523	Betty Grizette	36
The World shall own, his Choice was wise and just,		532	To Mr. Gay	17
To show the World his chief Reverse in you.		532	To Mr. Gay	38
Cou'd never leave the World in quiet---;		548	Life of Swift	104
"The World must own it, to their Shame;		550	Life of Swift	199
The World stands trembling at his Throne.		579	Day Judgement	8
You but o'er half the World can reign.		585	Strephon Chloe	32
More than from all the World beside.		591	Strephon Chloe	254
Vain empty World farewel. But hark,		596	Cassinus Peter	79
Much of the cens'ring World complain'd,		603	Beasts Confess	49
As Esop would the World perswade;		607	Beasts Confess	211
From East to West the world we roam,		621	Scandal Poem 1	127
From East to West, the World we roam;		627	Scandal Poem 2	121
Must, that all the World may know 'em,		631	Epistle Lady	47
To reform the World, than Sour.		636	Epistle Lady	200
Yet what the World refus'd to Lewis,		657	On Poetry	477
To cheat the World, become each other's Bail.		668	Epig Carthy 8	D 4
In a new World with Caution stept,		696	Cadenus Vaness	308
To know the World a little better.		700	Cadenus Vaness	429
(To know the World! a modern Phrase,		700	Cadenus Vaness	430
To hide her from the World so long;		705	Cadenus Vaness	577
The World must think him in the Wrong;		707	Cadenus Vaness	643
Is to the World a Secret yet;		712	Cadenus Vaness	819
"She puts the World in his Possession,		714	Cadenus Vaness	882
The World shall in its Atoms end,		725	To Stella	57
Have taught you from the World to hide:		730	Stella, Poems	100
I told him what the World would say		741	Stel B-day 22	15
She thought that all the world was Oatmeal:		745	Stel Distress	6
The World consists of Puppet-shows;		777	Mullinix Tim	134
That Wig, I wou'd not for the world		780	Mullinix Tim	221
To mend the World by useful Arts.		780	Mullinix Tim	246
The Monkey, who had seen the World.		782	Tim and Fables	8
What Spirit since the World began,		799	Traulus 1	95
Not for the World--we Doctors, Brother,		812	Bro Protestant	17
The World is in doubt, whether hatred or love;		818	Archbi Cashel	2
Let all the world judge.		856	Lady's Lament	152
For all the World, Captain, not half an Inch farther--		869	Grand Question	79
We give the world to understand,		875	Drapier's Hill	1
All for Love, or the World well lost.		878	Robbin & Harry	20
Which I must leave the world to guess.		879	Robbin & Harry	54
Of their two Fames the World enough rings;		884	Rev Market-Hill	31
My Gratitude the World shall know:		887	Panegyr Dean	31
Like Toupets of this upper World;		903	Death Daphne	24

```
WORLD            (CONTINUED)                              PAGE    TITLE           LINE
   By all the World I am oppress't,       . . . . . . . .  918 Riddle 4            9
   I'll shew the World strange Things and true;  . . . .   919 Riddle 5           14
   Yet all the World can't find me out,   . . . . . . .    929 Riddle 14         D  2
   Till I eat the World at last.  . . . . . . . . .        930 Riddle 16         D  4
WORLD'S
   With her World's fruitful System in her sacred Ark,  .   16 Ode Athenian       13
   That the world's Saviour had been  . . . . . . . .  .    40 Ode Sancroft      173
   'Tis the World's wat'ry hour-glass streaming fast,  .    49 To Congreve       189
   That time is sick, or the world's mind is dead.--  . .   53 Temple Ill         66
   The World's mad Business now is o'er,  . . . . . .      579 Day Judgement      19
   Thus, to the World's perpetual Shame,  . . . . . .      700 Cadenus Vaness    432
   Ierne, to the World's remotest Parts,  . . . . . . .    789 St. Pat's Well      5
WORLDLY-WISE
   He might, if he were worldly-wise, . . . . . . . .      604 Beasts Confess    107
WORLDS
   Who have well studied in the Worlds Disease,  . . . .    20 Ode Athenian      138
   Than dreams of worlds intelligible;  . . . . . . . .    900 Dean's Reasons     62
WORM   SEE CANKER-WORM,WOOD-WORM
   Search'd in the nest where every worm did lie . . . .    46 To Congreve        89
   There is a Worm by Phoebus bred,  . . . . . . . .       79 Vanbrug House       29
   And Chambermaids christen this Worm a Death-Watch:  .   351 Wood Insect        20
   Such a Worm was Will. Wood when he scratch't at the Doo 351 Wood Insect        29
   The smallest Worm in Celia's Nose,  . . . . . . . .     527 Lady's Dres Rm     64
WORMS
   Corrupt to Maggots Worms and Flyes.  . . . . . . .      81 Vanbrug House       82
   Corrupt to Maggots, Worms and Flyes.  . . . . . . .    109 V's House         124
   The Food of Worms, and Beasts obscene,  . . . . .      923 Riddle 7           59
WORN
   Have worn a Casement o'er their Skin,  . . . . . .      30 Ode to Temple     126
   The Mitre, which his sacred head has worn,  . . . . .   40 Ode Sancroft      199
   The Kennel-Edge, where Wheels had worn the Place.  .   124 Descriptn Morn     10
   Elijah's Mantle's worn out.  . . . . . . . . . .       270 Apollo's Edict    D 24
   The Lawrel so, by Poets worn,  . . . . . . . .         458 Paddy's Charac      9
   Worn out by Wits who rhyme on Faces;  . . . . . .      730 Stella, Poems      76
   Altho' the Metaphor be worn and stale  . . . . . .     770 Horace 1, 14        5
   Are Stale, and Worn as Troy-Town Story.  . . . . .     774 Mullinix Tim       36
WORRIED
   The Brave are worried by the Base.  . . . . . . .      651 On Poetry         328
WORRIER
   On this Worrier of Deans whene'er we can hit,  . . .   816 Yahoo's            51
WORRY
   And worry him out, 'till he gives his Consent.  . . .  869 Grand Question     62
WORRY'D
   That the false Wretch shou'd worry'd be:  . . . . .    153 Widow and Cat     D 18
WORSE
   Of a declining Church, by Faction her worse foe opprest, 40 Ode Sancroft     186
   . . .Indeed, says I, never worse;  . . . . . . . .      70 Mrs Harris Pet     14
   Poor <Swift> departs, and, what is worse,  . . . . .   173 Horace 1, 7        93
   Part in worse humor than they met?  . . . . . . .      217 To Mr. Delany      72
   Quoth Will; thy House is worse than Hell.  . . . .     220 A Quiet Life       10
   Their Vittells bad, their Lodging worse,  . . . . .    224 Prog of Love       79
   But use You ten times worse than Pri'r.  . . . . .     312 To Ford            34
   Worse than a Pun, or Irish Phrase,  . . . . . . .      312 To Ford            38
   Write worse then if you can - - - - be wise - - - -    361 Grace's Answer     11
   Or preach, you'd like him scarce the worse.  . . .     375 Apology Lady C     12
   None e'er made Verses worse than he,  . . . . . .      401 Window Inns 2       5
   Chang'd for the worse in ev'ry Part,  . . . . . .      410 Dial Rich Marb     71
   Who kindly would leave thee no worse nor no better.  . 424 Carterets Arms     20
   Worse than they went  . . . . . . . . . . .           440 Ballyspellin       17
   And what Condition can be worse?  . . . . . . . .      484 Libel on D- D-    123
   Which can ne'er be worse for wearing.  . . . . . .     523 Betty Grizette     22
   And Servants answer; Worse and Worse)  . . . . .      557 Death of Swift    124
   And Servants answer; Worse and Worse)  . . . . .      557 Death of Swift    124
   And is not femal clattring worse,  . . . . . . . .     617 Scandal Poem 1      9
   Then, is not Female Clatter worse,  . . . . . . .      624 Scandal Poem 2      9
   From bad to worse, and worse they fall,  . . . . .     653 On Poetry         387
   From bad to worse, and worse they fall,  . . . . .     653 On Poetry         387
   Or some worse Brute in human Shape,  . . . . . .       687 Cadenus Vaness     40
   The Doctor might have fancy'd worse.--  . . . . .      707 Cadenus Vaness    655
   And what is worse, your Passion bends  . . . . . .     730 Stella, Poems      97
   Long-thinking made my Fancy worse.  . . . . . .        741 Stel B-day 22      12
   Thou would'st be pelted worse than they're.  . . .     787 Clad in Brown      24
   Worse than the Anarchy at Sea,  . . . . . . . .        824 Printer Newgat      3
   And he never call'd me worse than Sweet-heart drunk or 985 Mary to Sher       14
      sober:
WORSHIP
   What makes your Worship look so lean?  . . . . . .     174 Horace 1, 7       122
   As thro' the Hall thy Worship paces:  . . . . . .      182 Horace 2, 1        76
   And said, "His Worship might ha' told us,  . . . .     322 First of April     45
   You worship other Gods in vain  . . . . . . . .        620 Scandal Poem 1     86
   You worsnip other Gods in vain:  . . . . . . . .       626 Scandal Poem 2     84
   To split my Worship too in twain.  . . . . . . .       722 Stel B-Day '18     18
   If your Worship will please to explain me this Rebus,  973 S-'s Ans Sh-d     13
   And is not afraid your Worsnip will grumble,  . . .   1027 Sheri Circles      26
   My worship is bit,  . . . . . . . . . . . .           1037 Sheridan Cavan      9
WORSHIP'D
   Which worship'd cats, and sacrific'd to apes;  . . .    46 To Congreve       106
WORSHIPPERS
   Have their devoutest Worshippers,  . . . . . . . .     100 Elegy Patrige      98
```

WORSLY'S

	PAGE	TITLE	LINE
Or were it Worsly's writing.	123	Empty'ng Town	20

WORST

	PAGE	TITLE	LINE
From the worst Excrements of Earth;	10	Ode to King	127
Then since you now have done your worst,	175	Horace 1, 7	137
If these be of all Crimes the worst,	392	Young's Satire	47
With whom I'm happy in the worst	420	Holyhead	26
And Malice always judging worst;	448	Modern Lady	129
The Worst of disaffected Deans:	514	Answer Fable	66
Whose Malice, for the Worst of Ends,	515	Answer Fable	97
The worst you can say, he committed a <Rape>.	516	Dean Hang Rape	6
To deal it to the worst of Human-kind.	532	To Mr. Gay	28
All scribbled in the worst of times,	550	Life of Swift	184
"You know, I always fear'd the worst,	557	Death of Swift	129
"Who truckle most, when treated worst.	568	Death of Swift	398
How happy I, were that the worst?	595	Cassinus Peter	43
But yet, the worst that could be said,	602	Beasts Confess	27
But, who can reach the Worst of all?	653	On Poetry	388
The worst & best that could be had	659	On Poetry	D 410
Nam'd half the Rates, and lik'd the worst.	698	Cadenus Vaness	383
(The best we value by the worst,	728	Stella, Poems	21
By the worst of all Squires,	853	Lady's Lament	45
You come in the very worst Time of the Year;	871	Grand Question	122
The worst Dunce in your School, 'till he's heav'd from the Ground	968	Letter Sherid	34
And the worst of them all like a barn door did shine	017	Swift Ans Sher	6

WORTH

	PAGE	TITLE	LINE
But now Your Worth its just Reward shall have;	12	Ode to William	D 13
Your Garden's better worth your noble Pain,	32	Ode to Temple	176
Poor we Cadets of Heav'n, not worth her Care,	32	Ode to Temple	183
You know I am not worth a Groat:	175	Horace 1, 7	134
'Twill then, perhaps, be worth thy while	181	Horace 2, 1	41
In half a Minute is not worth one Groat;	234	Elegy on Demar	20
"Although 'tis hardly worth the Cost,	305	Storm	55
Corbet, though yet I know his Worth not,	314	To Ford	75
Fellows of modest Worth and Parts,	314	To Ford	81
We cannot think it worth your while.	315	To Ford	98
For Fifty Times its Worth, to Carteret.	349	Whitshed Motto	22
Exalted Worth disdains to owe	386	Manly Virtue	95
To Worth and Learning is a Friend.	391	Young's Satire	10
My Dame is hardly worth a Groat.	409	Dial Rich Marb	30
This Lace is worth twelve Pounds a Yard:	447	Modern Lady	87
His Poems, think them all not worth a Straw.	521	Stephen Duck	6
of Virtue & worth by profession a giber	540	Charac Walpole	11
All humble Worth she strove to raise;	701	Cadenus Vaness	456
That Women were not worth the wooing,	713	Cadenus Vaness	861
Your Worth will be to them unknown,	739	Stel B-day '21	15
Tho' Half a Crown o'er-pays his Sweat's Worth;	812	Bro Protestant	26
When nothing's left, that's worth defence,	843	Epigr Irish	3
A Mistress worth five thousand pound;	879	Robbin & Harry	32
Without it a Writer is not worth a Louse.	941	Letter	28
Will dress a Dinner worth five Pound.	941	Letter	36
An Ounce of Gold's worth ten of Brass, dull Pedant.	1004	Dan J's Reply	33

WORTHLESS

	PAGE	TITLE	LINE
Then (Sir,) accept this worthless Verse,	32	Ode to Temple	199
To keep that worthless clod, the body, in one place:	36	Ode Sancroft	64

WORTHY

	PAGE	TITLE	LINE
Or a more worthy subject chuse:	42	Ode Sancroft	260
"No worthy Friend, no poor Relation?	558	Death of Swift	162
To keep a worthy Lover's heart	732	Verses Vanessa	2
A Supper worthy of her self,	747	Stel Distress	51
A Supper worthy of her self,	751	Stel Wood-Park	67
Then vote a worthy Citizen to Jail,	826	Noisy Tom	19
Worthy Offspring of a Shoeboy,	831	Legion Club	68
If I had expected so worthy a Guest:--	871	Grand Question	123
To smile on those who are least worthy.	884	Rev Market-Hill	26

WOT

	PAGE	TITLE	LINE
His Name is Harlequin, I wot,	300	Horrid Plot	47
But now He's grown a King, God wot,	408	Dial Rich Marb	17
For once there was a Time, God wot,	498	Panegyr Swift	157

WOU'D   108

OMITTED WORD

WOU'DST

	PAGE	TITLE	LINE
Wou'dst thou not wish, in so much ease,	677	Parson's Case	35

WOULD   303

OMITTED WORD

WOULD'ST

	PAGE	TITLE	LINE
Whom would'st thou resemble? I leave thee a Guesser;	518	Dean Hang Rape	46
For, would'st thou make a fouler Show,	786	Clad in Brown	3
Thou would'st be pelted worse than they're.	787	Clad in Brown	24

WOULDN'T

	PAGE	TITLE	LINE
Musha! Why Parliament wouldn't you maul,	841	Ballad	D 16

WOULDST

	PAGE	TITLE	LINE
And Englond wouldst thou be happy still,	148	Windsor Proph	25
Poor Kingdom thou wouldst be that Governor's debtor,	424	Carterets Arms	19

WOUND

	PAGE	TITLE	LINE
Her Tyrant too an unexpected Wound shall feel	10	Ode to King	140
And there corrupting to a Wound	84	Salamander	55
Had giv'n the Faction many a Wound,	171	Horace 1, 7	37
And Guelph the strongest ear will wound.	467	Birthday Song	216
Till, scaping oft without a Wound,	500	Doctor Delaney	7
They glance aside without a Wound.	500	Doctor Delaney	30
Can, unreveng'd, the greatest merit wound.	506	To a Friend	6

WOUND	(CONTINUED)	PAGE	TITLE	LINE
"And pity'd those who meant the Wound:	. . . . . .	567	Death of Swift	360
May kill perhaps, but never wound.		618	Scandal Poem 1	28
We kill, 'tis true, but never wound;	. . . . . .	624	Scandal Poem 2	22
His spite cannot wound, who attempted the Drapier.	. .	818	Archbi Cashel	6
Receive its last and deadly Wound,	. . . . . .	850	Old Thorn	51
"And wound her Legs with ev'ry Bry'r.		850	Old Thorn	64
And, 'tis your own Case, for you never can wound	. . .	968	Letter Sherid	33

WOUNDING

| Pierce us all with wounding Steel, | . . . . | 931 | Riddle 18 | D 21 |

WOUNDS

And Cure the Wounds that Venus made.		99	Elegy Patrige	62
(Those honourable Wounds you bore	. . . .	324	Pethox	15
My Wounds Bleed all anew:	. . . .	1005	Sheridan's Sub	31
Must all my <Dammee's>, <Bloods> and <Wounds>		779	Mullinix Tim	187
<God> <damn> his Blood, and <Blood> and <Wounds>.	. .	904	Death Daphne	44

WOVEN

| Sit clad in lawn of purer woven day, | . . . . . . | 41 | Ode Sancroft | 235 |

WRACK

| While others wrack their busy Brains, | . . . . . | 361 | Grace's Answer | 17 |

WRANGLE

| To cheat and wrangle at Quadrille. | . . . . . . | 416 | Woman's Mind | 26 |

WRANGLINGS

| But, (not in Wranglings to engage | . . . . | 723 | To Stella | 7 |

WRAP

| And scorn to wrap up Spice. | . . . . | 394 | Grub-Street | 8 |

WRAP'D

| Wou'd you wish to be wrap'd in a Rochet--In short. | . . | 808 | Advice Parson | 9 |

WRAPP'D

| Wrapp'd in a whirlwind and a mist; . . : . . . . . | | 40 | Ode Sancroft | 195 |

WRAPT

Like Love, wrapt up in Fire;	. . . .	8	Ode to King	69
A holier Priest ne'er was wrapt up in Crape,	. . . .	516	Dean Hang Rape	5
But Nonsense wrapt up in a Stink)	. . . . . .	775	Mullinix Tim	64
And, lordly Gout wrapt up in Furr:	. . . . . .	895	Panegyr Dean	277
Wrapt up in Majesty divine, ...		949	Epigr Fasting	5

WRATH

This wretch, to rouse my wrath, for ruin meant;	. . .	47	To Congreve	136
A sign God's dart is shot, and wrath o'erblown;	. . .	52	Temple Ill	28
For, let heav'n's wrath enlarge these weary days,	. . .	54	Temple Ill	111
"With Wrath and Vengeance in their Hearts:	. . .	568	Death of Swift	380
"He vented oft his Wrath in vain:	. . . . . .	571	Death of Swift	444
And sell, to pacify his wrath, ...		879	Robbin & Harry	35

WREAK

| On thee to wreak the tribute when I rail; | . . . . . | 53 | Temple Ill | 86 |

WREATH

His Lawrel now must only be a Cypress Wreath,		9	Ode to King	105
And now a Laurel wreath she brings from far,	. . . .	16	Ode Athenian	18
He wav'd his Wreath Thrice o'er her Head,	. . . .	120	Apollo Outwit	35

WRECK

| There's a securer Way to wreck your Spite. | . . . . | 667 | Epig Carthy 4 | D 2 |

WREN

| Like the victorious wren perch'd on the eagle's wing; | . | 44 | To Congreve | 38 |
| To teach the humble Wren to soar. . . . . | | 270 | Apollo's Edict | D 26 |

WRETCH

Curst be the Wretch, nay doubly curst,	. . . . .	28	Ode to Temple	50
This wretch, to rouse my wrath, for ruin meant;	. . .	47	To Congreve	136
Should such a wretch usurp my Congreve's place,	. . .	48	To Congreve	169
On an abandon'd wretch by hopes forsook;	. . . . .	54	Temple Ill	108
That the false Wretch shou'd worry'd be:	. . . . .	153	Widow and Cat	D 18
How will the Caitiff Wretch be scar'd	. . . . .	241	Run Bankers	53
A Wretch! whom <English> Rogues to spite her,	. . .	302	Storm	7
The wretch must be at court by nine:	. . . . . .	434	Answer Paulus	74
Tho I name not the wretch you know who I mean	. . .	540	Charac Walpole	13
Oh, were the Wretch but living still,	. . . . .	560	Death of Swift	193
"If such a Wretch had known his Face.	. . . . .	571	Death of Swift	442
Wretch that I was, I broke my Fast:	. . . . .	602	Beasts Confess	16
So a poor wretch upon the brink of death,	. . . . .	672	Epig Carthy 24	D 11
While all the silly Wretch can do		774	Mullinix Tim	27
Yet many a Wretch in Bedlam, knows,	. . . . .	796	Traulus 1	23
"And thou, the Wretch ordain'd by Fate,	. . . . .	851	Old Thorn	81
A wretch like poor Nancy, ...		851	Lady's Lament	2
Unhappy Wretch! for now, I ween, ...		1005	Sheridan's Sub	26

WRETCHED

The wretched Insects singe their Wings, and fall,		9	Ode to King	117
In the last wretched Remnant of his Days;		10	Ode to King	141
Forcing a wretched Trade by beating down the sale,	. .	19	Ode Athenian	101
And foster'd in a wretched inn.		40	Ode Sancroft	175
Stands in the gap 'twixt me and wretched men,	. . .	45	To Congreve	47
That we the wretched, creeping far behind,	. . .	54	Temple Ill	115
Does make a wretched Shift, ...		75	Game Traffick	D 27
When wretched Lovers live on Air,	. . . . .	270	Apollo's Edict	D 16
To prove, that lawyers are so wretched;		433	Answer Paulus	44
I pity wretched Strephon blind		530	Lady's Dres Rm	129
"The Fellows had a wretched Taste;	. . . . .	714	Cadenus Vaness	869
Wretched Ierne! with what Grief I see	. . . .	792	St. Pat's Well	33
The wretched Purchase here behold		921	Riddle 7	17

WRETCHES

You've taught the Cov'tous Wretches to o're-rate,	. .	24	Ode Athenian	255
That those forsaken wretches who to-day		38	Ode Sancroft	130
Despairing Wretches from the Grave;		764	Stel B-day '26	38

```
WRETCHES      (CONTINUED)                                    PAGE   TITLE          LINE
    And, what the Wretches most resent,      . . . . . . .  883 Rev Market-Hill    21
WRIGGLE
    Till they wriggle, howl, and skip.  . . . . . . . . .   635 Epistle Lady      180
WRIGGLING
    Forth issues wriggling Dick Drawcensir,  . . . . . . .  785 Dick, Maggot        6
WRIGLE
    You Wrigle, Fidge, and make a Rout     . . . . . . .    777 Mullinix Tim      139
WRINCKLED
    Sits on her cloudy wrinckled Face.     . . . . . . .    226 Prog of Beauty      4
    His ruddy, wrinckled, smirking Face,   . . . . . . .    290 Prog Marriage      24
WRINCKLES
    The Cracks and Wrinckles of your Mind,   . . . . . .    736 Stel B-day '20     56
WRINKLES
    To smooth the Wrinkles on her Front;    . . . . . . .   526 Lady's Dres Rm     26
    And Wrinkles undistinguish'd pass,     . . . . . . .    758 Stel B-day '24     45
WRIST
    Widn'd and gatherd at his Wrist;    . . . . . . . .     94 Bauc & Phil 1      168
WRIT
    And think, alas, to be by mortals writ,  . . . . . .    20 Ode Athenian      126
    The Name and Man, by whom the Book was writ,   . . .    21 Ode Athenian      166
    That be my thought when some large bulky writ   . .     44 To Congreve        35
    Haply you judge these lines severely writ   . . . .     46 To Congreve       109
    The Building, as the Poet Writ,    . . . . . . . .     108 V's House          79
    Who often father'd what he writ;    . . . . . . .      171 Horace 1, 7        40
    Humour, and Mirth, had Place in all he writ:    . .    194 Author Himself     11
    A dang'rous Treatise writ against the Spleen;   . .    195 Author Himself     48
    Writ underneath the Country Signs;     . . . . . .     201 Horace 2, 6        72
    And still as he writ, stood smiling and reading;  .    264 Apollo             40
    That some Verses were writ with felonious Intent,  .   264 Apollo             47
    But as for the Poem he writ on your Sash,   . . .      265 Apollo             65
    Prize Classicks more than Sacred Writ:   . . . . .     392 Young's Satire     40
    You had not writ a Line.   . . . . . . . . . .         406 Swift to Pope      24
    Thus, Steel who own'd what other writ,   . . . . .     481 Libel on D- D-     49
    Although to Praise it Philips Writ.   . . . . . .      484 Libel on D- D-    144
    Than those on which you lately writ,   .. . . . .      489 Dialogue           22
    And such as know what Greece has writ   . . . . .      491 Dialogue           51
    Cou'd read all Books were ever writ;   . . . . . .     513 Answer Fable       36
    Wise Rochefoucault a Maxim writ,   . . . . . . .       545 Life of Swift       1
    Yet many a foolish thing he writ---;    . . . . .      547 Life of Swift      75
    "Twas he that writ the Drapier's Letters---!  . .      548 Life of Swift      97
    "But what he writ was all his own.   . . . . . .       565 Death of Swift    318
    Could Verse inspire, but seldom writ:   . . . . .      597 Problem Solved      2
    To give him but a Writ of Ease,     . . . . . . .      606 Beasts Confess    170
    And let the friendly Lines they writ    . . . . .      611 By Dr. Swift        7
    (Tho' meerly writ at first for filling   . . . . .     648 On Poetry         253
    To Dunkin you attribute what I writ,   . . . . . .     669 Epig Carthy 17   D  1
    Cadenus many things had writ;    . . . . . . . .       702 Cadenus Vaness    510
    Had sigh'd and languish'd, vow'd, and writ,   . . .    703 Cadenus Vaness    542
    I knew by what you said and writ,    . . . . . . .     706 Cadenus Vaness    618
    And you must know in what I writ    . . . . . . .      747 Stel Distress      67
    The Fables writ by Mr. Gay,    . . . . . . . . .       782 Tim and Fables      4
    After all you have writ,  . . . . . . . . . . .        939 Riddle Answerd     21
WRITE
    To make them understand, and feel me when I write;  . .  37 Ode Sancroft      89
    Who heard you meant to write heroics next;   . . . .    47 To Congreve       144
    Whilst thus I write, vast shoals of critics come,  . .  50 To Congreve       213
    Who would not Write Verses with such an assistant.  . .  77 Lady B- B-       REF
    And it needs must be one that could both Read and Write:  77 Lady B- B-       15
    As Authors of the Legend write     . . . . . . . .      90 Bauc & Phil 1       6
    And should they Build as fast as Write,   . . . . .    106 V's House          19
    So <Van> resolv'd to write a Farce,    . . . . . .     107 V's House          55
    And, (like a Wag) sat down to Write,   . . . . . .     107 V's House          61
    As Authors of the Legend write;    . . . . . . .       111 Bauc & Phil 2       6
    Of Love shall always speak and write;   . . . . .      150 Corinna            10
    You wonder now to see me write     . . . . . . .       218 To Mr. Delany      87
    Did maliciously, falsly, and traiterously write,  . .  264 Apollo             35
    To write a few Verses on you as my Friend;   . . .     265 Apollo             74
    Now who but Delany can write like Apollo?   . . .      265 Apollo             88
    Knows how to write a Billet-doux.     . . . . . .      325 Pethox             68
    Write worse then if you can - - - - be wise - - - -    361 Grace's Answer     11
    Dear Dean, if e're again you Write,    . . . . . .     371 Letter D. S-y       1
    And, when he sits to write,   . . . . . . . . .        395 Grub-Street        14
    Or could I read and write,    . . . . . . . . .        426 Five Ladies        39
    To write such scurvy stuff!    . . . . . . . . .       428 Beau's Reply        5
    Fine Ladyes when they write,    . . . . . . . .        429 Beau's Reply        9
    As those you write   . . . . . . . . . . . . .         443 Ballyspellin       89
    Against the Sex to write a Satyre,    . . . . . .      445 Modern Lady         7
    'Twas you engag'd me first to write,   . . . . . .     445 Modern Lady        22
    'Tis not deny'd that when we write,    . . . . . .     463 Birthday Song     107
    And write on paper black as Jet:    . . . . . . .      463 Birthday Song     114
    Insert it when you write agen:    . . . . . . .        485 Libel on D- D-    162
    And write you must, or break a Vein:   . . . . . .     501 Doctor Delaney     52
    Would Men of Genius cease to write,    . . . . . .     502 Doctor Delaney     71
    In proper Terms to write a Fable;    . . . . . . .     512 Answer Fable        2
    We ne'er shou'd know that he could write:   . . . .    514 Answer Fable       72
    I envy not the Wits who write     . . . . . . .        548 Life of Swift     128
    His Brethren write as well as he?    . . . . . . .     554 Death of Swift     32
    Tell me, what have I to write?    . . . . . . .        629 Epistle Lady        2
    Safely write a smart Lampoon,    . . . . . . . .       634 Epistle Lady      153
    The Muse invok'd, sit down to write;   . . . . . .     643 On Poetry          86

                              933
```

WRITE (CONTINUED)	PAGE	TITLE		LINE
And Female Pleasures be to read and write.	662	Upon Ladies		8
Satyrs and Epigrams in vain you write,	667	Epig Carthy 4	D	1
Who'll write my Panegyrick?---come, be stout:	671	Epig Carthy 24	D	4
What Preachers talk, or Sages write,	691	Cadenus Vaness		150
And shou'd he write Pamphlets, no Great Man wou'd read 'em:	717	Answer Rebus		26
But now, unable grown to write,	754	Stella '23		5
Tom cou'd write and spell his Name,	784	Mullinex Dick		3
And so I bid Sir <Arthur> write.	859	Lady Acheson		4
Our Clerk, for he can read and write;	886	Rev Market-Hill		94
A long-ear'd Beast, and Liquor to write,	942	Probatur Alit		29
The oft'ner you fall, the oft'ner you write;	968	Letter Sherid		30
I'll write, tho' I'm forc'd to write in a wheelbarrow:	979	Dean to Tho: S		12
I'll write, tho' I'm forc'd to write in a wheelbarrow:	979	Dean to Tho: S		12
Since you write in a cart, keep it tecta et sarta,	979	Dean to Tho: S		15
Now you write from your cellar,--I find out your art,	979	Dean to Tho: S		19
But now I'll write short, for fear you're short taken.	980	Tho: Sheridan		6
For I write but a sad Scrawl,	987	Mary to Sher		34
. . .if I could write written hand,	987	Mary to Sher		37
But now I can write no more,	1014	Swift to Sheri		12
If I write any more, it will make my poor Muse sick.	1030	Dr. Sheridan		1

WRITER

	PAGE	TITLE		LINE
And were you not so good a Writer	361	Grace's Answer		9
"The Church had never such a Writer:	564	Death of Swift		297
Altho' the Writer long were dead?	708	Cadenus Vaness		699
As when some Writer in a public Cause,	770	Horace 1, 14		25
Without it a Writer is not worth a Louse.	941	Letter		28

WRITERS

	PAGE	TITLE		LINE
Wherein French Writers most excell:	216	To Mr. Delany		32

WRITES

	PAGE	TITLE		LINE
Writes down my Conceits, and then calls them his own:	265	Apollo		86
That writes without the Toil of Thought.	361	Grace's Answer		16
And surely Writes with slight of Hand	373	Letter D. S-y		48
Carthy, you say, writes well--his genius true.--	668	Epig Carthy 8	D	1
With ale and chops I'll treat who writes the best,	671	Epig Carthy 24	D	5
. . .but my Sister Marget she writes better.	987	Mary to Sher		34

WRITING

	PAGE	TITLE		LINE
Or were it Worsly's writing.	123	Empty'ng Town		20
'Tis like the Writing on the Wall.	241	Run Bankers		52
Thus, Congreve spent, in writing Plays,	481	Libel on D- D-		33
Assert that Hyde in writing story	489	Dialogue		25
That you who was found writing of Drapiers	522	St. Cecilia's		3
"His way of Writing now is past;	563	Death of Swift		265
To purchase Fame by writing ill:	652	On Poetry		368
I sometimes give Advice in Writing,	917	Riddle 3		9
And lo! the Writing on the Walls	923	Riddle 7		57
As for you're writing I am dead,	983	Sher, A Goose		25
Or writing Libels on the <Germans>,	993	On Picture		5
To encroach on his art by writing of bombas';	1027	Sheri Circles		22

WRITINGS

	PAGE	TITLE		LINE
The Writings drawn, the Lawyer fee'd,	222	Prog of Love		22
What Writings had he left behind---?	550	Life of Swift		180
"Tis plain, his Writings were design'd	550	Life of Swift		196

WRITTEN

	PAGE	TITLE		LINE
To believe all his Verses were written by me;	266	Apollo		100
Wou'd read what underneath was written,	783	Tim and Fables		26
. . .if I could write written hand,	987	Mary to Sher		37
. . . say is (tho' written somewhat at large) trim and clean;	1024	Nim-Dan-Dean 2	D	17

WROGHT

	PAGE	TITLE		LINE
Behold, a Miracle was wroght	92	Bauc & Phil 1		74

WRONG

	PAGE	TITLE		LINE
You're on the wrong side of the Door.	91	Bauc & Phil 1		36
His Tenants wrong him in his Rent;	174	Horace 1, 7		108
Our Country then can dread no Wrong:	339	Arch-Bish Dub		6
And though some think him in the Wrong,	341	Upon His Grace		7
Where Right, and Wrong, are bought and sold,	385	Manly Virtue		67
They take the wrong Way for the right.	412	Desire Possess		18
Alas; they would not do you wrong;	414	Censure		15
But, half the Words pronouncing wrong;	416	Woman's Mind		10
Who's in the wrong, who in the right	421	Ireld		6
Must be apply'd directly wrong:	464	Birthday Song		118
I own, the Counsel were not wrong,	496	Panegyr Swift		98
Nor, think your self secure in doing wrong,	533	To Mr. Gay		59
With driving wrong, will make the Pannel split:	535	To Mr. Gay		132
To prove I did my Neighbour wrong;	602	Beasts Confess		18
'Tis a wrong, unjust Aspersion:	632	Epistle Lady		82
To decide of Wrong and Right?	638	Epistle Lady		270
And each Perfection wrong imputed	646	On Poetry		201
How wrong a Taste prevails among us;	652	On Poetry		351
And do no Wrong to either Side:	657	On Poetry		484
Nor ever gave her Judgment wrong.	704	Cadenus Vaness		559
Was now convinc'd he acted wrong,	705	Cadenus Vaness		576
To teach her what was Right or Wrong,	705	Cadenus Vaness		599
The World must think him in the Wrong;	707	Cadenus Vaness		643
At least, cou'd hardly wish them wrong.	710	Cadenus Vaness		747
Regardless both of Wrong and Right.	730	Stella, Poems		94
Stella, for once you reason wrong;	731	Stella, Poems		131
The Wrong is certain you were both in,	774	Mullinix Tim		37
Always various, always wrong:	800	Traulus 2		18

		PAGE	TITLE	LINE
WRONG	(CONTINUED)			
Always to advise her wrong;		907	Daphne	36
When you furious argue wrong,		908	Daphne	63
WRONGS				
To vindicate his Mother's Wrongs.		701	Cadenus Vaness	467
WROTE				
The Nymph who wrote this in an Amorous Fit,		716	Answer Rebus	1
That wrote the Prologue, and if you stay with him,		1023	Nim-Dan-Dean 2	D 10
WROUGHT				
Wrought by the Musick of the Spheres - - -		362	Grace's Answer	36
But Prodigies are wrought to prove		384	Manly Virtue	21
Shirts be wrought with different Letters,		573	Helter Skelter	23
But now a sudden Change was wrought,		704	Cadenus Vaness	560
Such Wonder by his Merit wrought;		710	Cadenus Vaness	753
WYCHERLY				
Of Wycherly, and you, and Mr. Bays;		47	To Congreve	142
\<WYNNE\>				
Who is he? 'Tis hum-drum \<Wynne\>,		836	Legion Club	161
XERXES				
Rebellious Waves with rods like Xerxes.		463	Birthday Song	100
Y-FROZEN				
Tamys rivere twys y-frozen,		102	Merlin	3
YAHOOS				
That Humankind are all Yahoos.		498	Panegyr Swift	168
YARD SEE CHURCH-YARD				
(Item, for half a Yard of Lace.)		60	Lady Tablebook	16
In Drugget drest of Thirteen Pence a Yard,		275	Epilogue	23
And Sell for Twenty Pence a Yard of theirs;		276	Epilogue	44
Passes the Lower Castle Yard,		376	Apology Lady C	29
This Lace is worth twelve Pounds a Yard:		447	Modern Lady	87
Climbs downwards, deeper by a Yard:		654	On Poetry	398
YARDS				
Taller than Misse's by two yards,		87	Hist V's House	25
With fifty Yards of Crape, shall sweep the Stage.		275	Epilogue	26
YARN				
With Threads of diff'rent colour'd Yarn.		594	Cassinus Peter	14
YAWN				
Just to yawn, and give his Vote;		836	Legion Club	170
'YE				
You must no longer thus equip 'ye		779	Mullinix Tim	213
YE				
Pardon Ye great Unknown, and far-exalted Men,		17	Ode Athenian	60
And this Ye great Unknown, is only known in You.		21	Ode Athenian	188
Now, now you carry all before ye,		183	Horace 2, 1	83
Ye formal Weepers for the Sick,		204	In Sickness	23
Ye Pow'rs who over Love preside,		229	Prog of Beauty	117
They'll cry, Ye Shops, upon us fall		241	Run Bankers	59
Conceal, and cover us, Ye Counters.		241	Run Bankers	60
Therefore I assure ye,		237	Excellent Song	22
Ye wise Philosophers explain		250	Bubble	1
Come hither, all ye empty things,		296	Satiric Elegy	25
Ye bubbles rais'd by breath of Kings;		296	Satiric Elegy	26
"If such a Sight as this can please ye,		305	Storm	69
"Ye don't fall out about the Heir.		321	First of April	12
"Ye have forgot this Month and Day.--		322	First of April	56
This Brass was a Dragon (observe what I tell ye)		337	Serious Poem	87
Ye Pow'rs of Grub-street make me able,		346	Prometheus	57
Now made--ye Gods!--a Son and Heir,		384	Manly Virtue	18
Ye Poets ragged and forlorn,		394	Grub-Street	1
Ye Rhimers, dead as soon as born,		394	Grub-Street	2
With nothing to tempt ye:		402	Window Inns 8	D 4
Ye wise, instruct me to endure		413	Censure	1
'Tis wise, no doubt, as clients fat ye more,		433	Answer Paulus	41
'I wish ye may but have enough.'		448	Modern Lady	108
Ye Fates, when all he gets is Spent,		456	Dean Smedley	49
The Eagle in the Tale, ye know,		458	Paddy's Charac	29
"Fair Isis, and ye Banks of Cam,		462	Birthday Song	77
Besides; your Patron may upbraid ye,		483	Libel on D- D-	103
Ye paultry underlings of state,		487	Irish-Club	1
Ye \<senators\>, who love to prate;		487	Irish-Club	2
Ye \<rascals\> of inferior note,		487	Irish-Club	3
Ye pack of pensionary \<Peers\>,		487	Irish-Club	5
Ye bishops far remov'd from saints;		487	Irish-Club	7
And Precedents we can produce, if it please ye,		518	Dean Hang Rape	40
Never may the Muse forget ye:		522	Betty Grizette	2
Now, Ponder well ye Parents dear;		587	Strephon Chloe	115
Cry'd out, ye Gods, what Sound is this?		589	Strephon Chloe	177
Would still the same Ideas give ye,		591	Strephon Chloe	247
Avaunt--ye cannot say 'twas I.		596	Cassinus Peter	88
Teaching others how to ape ye;		631	Epistle Lady	53
Court, nor Parli'ment, can 'scape ye;		631	Epistle Lady	54
Then, lest with Greek he over-run ye,		648	On Poetry	259
attend ye Popes, and Youngs, and Gays,		656	On Poetry	467
Extoll ye Bench of Bishops round,		658	On Poetry	D 190
And Horace brought ye tunefull Choir		658	On Poetry	D 410
To sing his Virtues on ye Lyre,		658	On Poetry	D 410
Among ye savage Monsters crown'd		659	On Poetry	D 410
In vain you make ye strictest View		659	On Poetry	D 410
To find a King in all ye Crew,		659	On Poetry	D 410
He shap'd a King to rule ye Race		659	On Poetry	D 410
That best ye regal Nature suit,		659	On Poetry	D 410

```
YE          (CONTINUED)                                        PAGE    TITLE          LINE
    Thus think on Kings, ye Name denotes        . . . . .      659  On Poetry       D 410
    Ye Muses guard your sacred Mount,            . . . . . .   671  Epig Carthy 21  D  5
    Ye Daintyes, I know nothing of ye,           . . . . . .   733  Verses Vanessa    28
    Ye Daintyes, I know nothing of ye,           . . . . . .   733  Verses Vanessa    28
    Had fate a lucky'r one, she'd give it ye:    . . . . .     760  Bec's B-Day        2
    As Machiavel taught 'em; divide and ye govern. . . . .     805  Irish Bishops     48
    All ye Gods, who rule the Soul                             832  Legion Club       83
    The wits will frequent ye,                   . . . . . . . 855  Lady's Lament    133
    If I could but win ye,         . . . . .                   857  Lady's Lament    204
    If your wives will permit ye,                . . . . . .   858  Lady's Lament    215
    For your Life, not a Word of the Matter, I charge ye:      873  Grand Question   189
    The <Dean> and Spaniard must reproach ye;    . . . . .     884  Rev Market-Hill   30
    Ye Hawkers all, your Voices lift;            . . . . . .   887  Panegyr Dean      33
    Ye who frequent this hallow'd Scene,         . . . . . .   893  Panegyr Dean     217
    Ye Great ones, why will ye disdain           . . . . . .   896  Panegyr Dean     291
    Ye Great ones, why will ye disdain           . . . . . .   896  Panegyr Dean     291
    Ye who hate such inconsistence,              . . . . . .   907  Daphne            25
    Will I ever tell before ye:    . . . . . .                908  Daphne            66
    Pudet haec opprobria, I freely must tell ye, . . . . .     967  Letter Sherid      5
    But thanks to the lady: I'm sure she's too good to ye;     976  Dean to Sherid    38
    But that's as much as to say, that my Master should die    986  Mary to Sher      19
      before ye,
    If this be your practice, mean scrub, I assure Ye,  . .   1019  To Sheridan        5
    . . .for I know there's no delaying ye. . . . . . . .      1023  Nim-Dan-Dean 2  D  8
    . . . depend on't, in the end, he'll sham ye. . . . .     1023  Nim-Dan-Dean 2  D 10
    But Jest apart, restore, you Capon ye,                    1033  Ans to Crown       7
    As you can steal one, how 'twould please ye! . . . .     1033  Ans to Crown      14
YEAN
    Of your Sneezing; a Yean.      . . . . . . . . .           246  Irish-Feast       56
YEAR
    And rolls the silent year . . . . . . . .                  39  Ode Sancroft     151
    Last year, a lad hence by his parents sent   . . . . .     46  To Congreve      115
    These are the tyrant's trophies of a year;   . . . . .     55  Temple Ill       126
    We might expect to find next Year . . . . . . . .          88  Hist V's House    47
    Brew'd for the good time of the Year         . . . . .     92  Bauc & Phil 1     68
    And 'twice a Year he'll cut th' Aequator,    . . . . .     98  Elegy Patrige     17
    Shall not see one New Years-Day in that Year,            147  Windsor Proph      3
    This Day, (the Year I dare not tell,)        . . . . .    149  Corinna            1
    For Life, six hundred Pounds a Year,         . . . . .    198  Horace 2, 6        2
    Nor cross the Channel twice a Year,          . . . . .    199  Horace 2, 6       11
    Stay, let me see-- Three hundred pounds a year, . . .    308  Billet Players    17
    To have two thousand Pounds a Year, O 'tis a burning     342  Upon His Grace    18
      Shame!
    Two thousand Pounds a Year, Good Lord! . .  . . . .      342  Upon His Grace    19
    He lengthen'd my Life with a whole Year of Grace. . .    399  Tom Clinch        18
    But Dick lost by Doll, twelve hundred a Year,  . . .     430  Dicky Dolly        5
    With forty Pounds a Year at most.            . . . . .   484  Libel on D- D-   134
    A Blessing upon them, have sent us this Year, . . .      516  Dean Hang Rape     3
    To act such an opera once in a year          . . . . .   522  St. Cecilia's      5
    "Last Year we thought him strong and hale;   . . . . .   557  Death of Swift   112
    For though you may mistake a Year;           . . . . .   558  Death of Swift   144
    The Fools, my Juniors by a Year,             . . . . .   561  Death of Swift   219
    One Year is past; a different Scene;         . . . . .   562  Death of Swift   245
    "He dy'd a Year ago." The same.              . . . . .   563  Death of Swift   256
    "To fancy they cou'd live a Year!   . . . . . . .        563  Death of Swift   261
    With Twenty Thousand Pounds a Year Rents,                598  Problem Solved    12
    Which now he runs out every Year . . . . . . . .         606  Beasts Confess   166
    We hardly thunder thrice a year:             . . . . .   617  Scandal Poem 1    11
    We hardly Thunder thrice a Year.             . . . . .   624  Scandal Poem 2    11
    And Reason good; for many a Year             . . . . .   657  On Poetry        489
    Nor saw the Play-House twice a Year.         . . . . .   696  Cadenus Vaness   313
    Might furnish a Second Rate Poet a Year:     . . . . .   716  Answer Rebus      18
    (We won't dispute a Year or more)            . . . . .   721  Stel B-Day '18     2
    Die the next Year for want of Root.          . . . . .   730  Stella, Poems     68
    You, every Year the Debt enlarge,            . . . . .   739  Stel B-day '21     7
    With Stella's Praise to crown the Year.      . . . . .   743  Stel B-day 22     80
    He entertain'd her half a year  . . . . . . . .          745  Stel Distress      3
    He entertain'd her half a year  . . . . . . . .          749  Stel Wood-Park     3
    That Herrings will be cheap this Year.       . . . . .   781  Mullinix Tim     276
    Thou must go naked all the Year.             . . . . .   786  Clad in Brown      4
    In Rents three thousand Pounds a Year.       . . . . .   821  Dr. Rundle        52
    Who held a Cabbin for ten Groats a Year;     . . . . .   826  Noisy Tom         12
    Three Dishes a Day, and three Hogsheads a Year.  . .     867  Grand Question    12
    You come in the very worst Time of the Year; . . . .     871  Grand Question   122
    Above his Rent four Pounds a Year;           . . . . .   875  Drapier's Hill     4
    To Fifteen Hundred Pounds a Year,            . . . . .   884  Rev Market-Hill   38
    Can grant ten Thousand Pounds a Year,        . . . . .   916  Riddle 1          35
    But when the Year is at an End,              . . . . .   918  Riddle 4          33
    With three hundred and sixty-five poems a year?  . .     979  Dean to Tho: S    34
    I remember it was upon a Tuesday, of all Days in the     986  Mary to Sher      26
      Year.
    . . .out so late at this Time of Year, . . . . . . .    1014  Swift to Sheri    10
YEAR'S   SEE NEW-YEAR'S-GIFT,NEW-YEAR'S,TWO-YEAR'S
    Five hundred Pound a Year's no Fool.         . . . . .   478  Epist on Epist   112
    Without an Ounce of last Year's Flesh,       . . . . .   759  Receipt Youth     15
    Burnishes an old Year's Face.                . . . . .   863  To Janus          28
YEARLY
    For those affronts they give him yearly. . . . . . .    463  Birthday Song    106
    You yearly sing as she grows old,  . . . . . . . .      742  Stel B-day 22     39
    Time was, when I could yearly pay  . . . . . . .        754  Stella '23         3
```

```
YEARS   SEE NEW-YEARS                                          PAGE    TITLE            LINE
    Nor dreads the Tyranny of Years,        . . . . . . .        6  Ode to King          3
    Justling some thousand years till ripen'd by the Sun,  .    20  Ode Athenian       129
    The Bondage and the Slavery of Years.     . . . . . .       24  Ode Athenian       259
    . . .this Five and Twenty Years, come Spring,     . . .     70  Mrs Harris Pet      30
    Were several Years this Man and Wife,     . . . . . .      116  Bauc & Phil 2      150
    Who has forty Years let out his Conscience to hire,        142  New Song             2
    At six Years old, the subtle Jade     . . . . . .          150  Corinna             17
    Should you live years forty more      . . . . . .          187  Scriblerus 4    D   17
    'Tis (let me see) three Years and more,     . . . . .      201  Horace 2, 6         63
    From Satan for a Term of Years,        . . . . . . .       240  Run Bankers         46
    'Tis the Nymph that I courted some ten Years ago;         264  Apollo              44
    Less corresponding than their Years.      . . . . . .      291  Prog Marriage       36
    It shames his Cassock and his Years       . . . . . .      294  Prog Marriage      140
    A Dog of Spirit for his Years,        . . . . . . .        299  Horrid Plot         45
    It falls before thy Rev'rend Years,      . . . . .         340  Arch-Bish Dub       14
    Whose Wisdom and whose Piety, do far exceed his Years.     341  Upon His Grace       4
    Has lost His Grace for Ten Years past . . .               341  Upon His Grace      10
    For, he'll be Prince these fifty Years.      . . . .       410  Dial Rich Marb      78
    What tho for fifteen years and more      . . . . .         462  Birthday Song       49
    Six thousand years hath liv'd the Goddess,     . . . .     465  Birthday Song      161
    That five years hence will both be Hebes.      . . . .     465  Birthday Song      172
    Twice sev'n long Years the Court attends,     . . . .      481  Libel on D- D-      54
    Which lasted near two thousand years,     . . . . . .      490  Dialogue            34
    To serve a tastless <Court> twelve Years in vain?    . .   531  To Mr. Gay           2
    To squire a Royal Girl of two Years old!      . . . .      531  To Mr. Gay          10
    Who bore for twice ten Years the publick Hate.     . .     536  To Mr. Gay         144
    By adding largely to my Years:        . . . . . . . .      556  Death of Swift     106
    "He might have liv'd these Twenty Years:      . . . .      559  Death of Swift     174
    But once in Twenty Thousand Years.       . . . . . .       584  Strephon Chloe       4
    A Sprig of Bays in Fifty Years:        . . . . . . .       640  On Poetry            8
    Thy years as num'rous as thy days?    . . . . . . .        677  Parson's Case       36
    For Sixteen Years the Cause was spun,     . . . . . .      690  Cadenus Vaness     124
    Which every Girl at five Years old       . . . . . .       700  Cadenus Vaness     424
    Vanessa, not in Years a Score,        . . . . . . .        703  Cadenus Vaness     524
    Declin'd in Health, advanc'd in Years.     . . . . .       703  Cadenus Vaness     529
    As Years increase, she brighter shines,     . . . . .      703  Cadenus Vaness     536
    Instructed from her early Years       . . . . . .          705  Cadenus Vaness     596
    Although thy Size and Years are doubled,      . . . .      721  Stel B-Day '18       4
    Thy Beauty, Size, and Years, and Wit,     . . . . . .      722  Stel B-Day '18      10
    With half thy Wit, thy Years and Size:      . . . . .      722  Stel B-Day '18      14
    To cut it off these forty years.       . . . . . . .       760  Bec's B-Day          6
    By Food of twenty Years ago?     . . . . . . . .           765  Stel B-day '26      56
    Jason arriv'd two thousand Years before.      . . . .      790  St. Pat's Well       8
    You are only to live four Years without Vittles!    . .    805  Irish Bishops       60
    Has, with noise and odd gestures, been prating some years, 815  Yahoo's             18
    Now twenty Years from Court exploded?     . . . . . .      820  Dr. Rundle          28
    There stood for many a hundred Years     . . . . . .       848  Old Thorn            3
    New Years help to make me old;    . . . . . . . .          863  To Janus            26
    And say, there shall, for years together,     . . . .      876  To Dean Swift       25
    Twice ten years older than his wife      . . . . . .       879  Robbin & Harry      51
    So suited to your State, and Years!      . . . . . .       888  Panegyr Dean        50
    I lay a Prisoner twenty Years;        . . . . . . .        926  Riddle 9            21
    . . . four Years since October,      . . . . . . .         985  Mary to Sher        13
YEARS-DAY
    Shall not see one New Years-Day in that Year,     . . .    147  Windsor Proph        3
YELLOW
    Of Red, and Yellow, Blue, and Green.      . . . . . .      325  Pethox              46
    Or, on Parchment, Ink turn'd yellow:      . . . . . .      523  Betty Grizette       8
    Thy fav'rite Flow'rs of yellow Hue      . . . . . . .      894  Panegyr Dean       250
    You may find they are all, by their yellow pale Hue, sick 1030  Dr. Helsham         27
YEMAN
    Where dwelt a poor old honest Yeman    . . . . . . .        91  Bauc & Phil 1       51
YEOMAN
    Where dwelt a good old honest Yeoman,     . . . . . .      111  Bauc & Phil 2       19
YEOMEN
    The Waiters stand in Ranks; the Yeomen cry,     . . .      194  Author Himself      35
YES
    Yes, that beau's look, that voice, those critic ears,  .    48  To Congreve        173
    Yes; you are all malicious standers-by,     . . . . .       49  To Congreve        199
    Yes, says the Steward, . . . . . . . . . .                  71  Mrs Harris Pet      32
    A Boat a Judge! yes, where's the Blunder?     . . . .      286  Elegy Boat          39
    Yes, and a Place he will grow rich in;     . . . . .       300  Horrid Plot         65
    O yes! If any Man can find     . . . . . . . .             417  Woman's Mind        57
    The Court, so made his last O yes!       . . . . . .       714  Cadenus Vaness     885
    Yes; you call'd my Master a Knave: . .                     985  Mary to Sher         5
YEST
    Was forc'd to send three Miles for Yest,      . . . . .    282  Journal             89
YESTERDAY
    That bit your Neck but Yesterday,      . . . . . .         504  Doctor Delaney     142
YET     276                                                        OMITTED WORD
YEW
    Points out the Place of either Yew;      . . . . .         116  Bauc & Phil 2      171
    Some think him cut out from the Poisonous Yew,     . . .   334  Serious Poem        31
YEWS
    In short, they both were turn'd to Yews.      . . . . .    116  Bauc & Phil 2      164
    "Or shape the Yews to Antick Figure.      . . . . . .      476  Epist on Epist      58
YIELD
    The Nymph had soon been brought to yield;     . . . .      177  To Lord Harley      14
    Must yield her Foe the stronger Cause;     . . . . .       695  Cadenus Vaness     265
    I yield there might be an Invasion,      . . . . . .       774  Mullinix Tim        30
```

937

	PAGE	TITLE	LINE
YIELD (CONTINUED)			
When to yield, and when be willful.	907	Daphne	42
All Figures Heav'n or Earth can yield, ...	927	Riddle 10	D 16
Would, as he lay under, cry out, Sirrah, yield: . .	967	Letter Sherid	16
And art thou forc'd to yield, ill-fated Poetaster? . .	1002	Reply by Dean	3
And they, alas, yield small Relief, ...	1005	Sheridan's Sub	29
YIELDING			
On her Promise of yielding, she acted the Prude; . .	264	Apollo	46
Always conquer'd, never yielding.	906	Daphne	8
YIELDS			
Shew the Delights thy Sister Nature yields, ...	31	Ode to Temple	137
So are the Joys which Nature yields	122	Empty'ng Town	9
Nor yields up virtue, at discretion, ...	436	Answer Paulus	127
The strongest Friendship yields to Pride, ...	554	Death of Swift	37
YOKE			
To every Farmer twice a Week all round about the Yoke,	343	Upon His Grace	39
What Planter will attempt to yoke	703	Cadenus Vaness	534
Thus, Commonwealths receive a foreign Yoke, ...	770	Horace 1, 14	21
YON			
The muse retreats far in yon chrystal cell; . . .	50	To Congreve	228
Be what it will; late near yon whisp'ring stream, . .	51	Temple Ill	13
Why in yon dang'rous Gulph profound	252	Bubble	50
Than Rule yon Isle and be a Slave.	421	Holyhead	34
The Lead yon Critick's Quill contains, ...	500	Doctor Delaney	15
All beneath yon flow'ry Rocks.	660	Love Song	8
Behold, it cracks by yon rough Eastern Wind. . . .	770	Horace 1, 14	18
Who to yon rav'nous Isle thy Treasures bear, . . .	794	St. Pat's Well	97
Keeper, yon old Dotard smoke, ...	836	Legion Club	159
Chairman to yon damn'd Committee! . . . , . .	838	Legion Club	191
Than yon tall Dock that rises to thy Nose. . . .	881	Pastoral Dial	14
Oh! could we tame yon watchful Dragon, ...	948	Jason Hassard	5
YONDER			
All this we grant--why, then look yonder	84	Salamander	45
In yonder Barn to keep us dry.	90	Bauc & Phil 1	22
Why yonder Steeple wants a Spire, ...	126	Little House	2
In yonder lane	442	Ballyspellin	56
On that poor Spot, call'd Del-Ville, yonder: . . .	476	Epist on Epist	60
To move it out from yonder Corner;	528	Lady's Dres Rm	72
From yonder Puppet-Man inquire, ...	592	Strephon Chloe	285
A Boy in yonder Isle below, ...	692	Cadenus Vaness	190
What I heard in yonder Hell.	832	Legion Club	86
I will not build on yonder mount:	899	Dean's Reasons	1
YONGE			
Yonge Symnele shall agayne miscarrye:	103	Merlin	11
YONKER			
Make some provision for the Yonker, ...	466	Birthday Song	203
YORE			
Thus Edgar proud, in Days of Yore, ...	476	Epist on Epist	43
YORK			
York is from Lambeth sent, to shew the Queen . . .	195	Author Himself	47
Poor York! the harmless Tool of others Hate; . . .	195	Author Himself	51
YOU 1429		OMITTED WORD	
YOU'D			
And when you'd make an Herbe grander, ...	270	Apollo's Edict	D 18
Yet if his Name you'd eternize	271	Apollo's Edict	D 40
Whom you'd consigne to endless Fame?	272	Apollo's Edict	D 71
I'm sure Old <Jour--> you'd not stand by it; . .	372	Letter D. S-y	20
Or preach, you'd like him scarce the worse. . . .	375	Apology Lady C	12
You'd swear, he never took a fee, ...	436	Answer Paulus	121
You'd know him by Apollo's Prints	462	Birthday Song	62
You'd know him by Apollo's Cuts.	462	Birthday Song	64
The Time was, when you'd have compounded	478	Epist on Epist	110
You'd swear, that so divine a Creature	584	Strephon Chloe	19
You'd think she utter'd from behind, ...	592	Strephon Chloe	281
You'd swear it is Apollo's Son;	692	Cadenus Vaness	193
You'd leave her Virtues half untold.	742	Stel B-day 22	40
You'd swear it must be the Baboon of <Kilkenny>: . .	803	Irish Bishops	10
I thought an Ace you'd ne'er have bated, ...	1002	Reply by Dean	2
Your Letter you'd dated, ...	1014	Swift to Sheri	14
. . . your friends you'd meet here.	1022	Nim-Dan-Dean 2	D 2
YOU'L			
Hang up your wife, and you'l count Four', . . .	404	Window Inns 11	D 6
But then, consider Dick, you'l find	788	Dick's Variety	13
YOU'LL			
Yet wheresoe're you look you'll always find	18	Ode Athenian	74
Consider Humane Folly, and you'll quickly own, . .	20	Ode Athenian	149
In this descending sheet you'll haply find . . .	50	To Congreve	231
You'll find has so much Virtue in't, ...	101	Elegy Partige	112
Returning Home at Night, you'll find the Sink . .	137	City Shower	5
You'll spend in Coach-hire more than save in Wine. . .	137	City Shower	8
If you'll be sure to come at Four.	173	Horace 1, 7	72
So strong you'll be, in Friendship ty'd;	189	Faggot	11
You'll then defy the strongest Whig, ...	191	Faggot	49
You'll ow Your Ruin to your Bulk;	258	Bubble	197
I beg you'll the Camelion spare.	270	Apollo's Edict	D 17
"But, if you'll leave us <Bishop> Judas, ...	305	Storm	51
"You'll find him swear, blaspheme, and damn, . . .	305	Storm	57
You'll pardon me Sir, your Cunning I smoak, . . .	336	Serious Poem	65
You'll never think of Goody Griz.	362	Grace's Answer	44
In her you'll center all your Joys, ...	362	Grace's Answer	47
Ten thousand Girls and Boys you'll get	362	Grace's Answer	49

	PAGE	TITLE		LINE
YOU'LL (CONTINUED)				
But, Yet, you'll find by what will follow,	371	Letter D. S-y		9
You'll fly when you get what you come here to steal,	395	Dog and Thief		7
You'll find it soon by woful Proof,	408	Dial Rich Marb		11
If you'll redeem the Silver Cup	446	Modern Lady		58
You think you'll sooner be a Bishop:	478	Epist on Epist		102
You'll see a Cloud in gentle weather	618	Scandal Poem 1		43
You'll see a Cloud in gentle Weather	625	Scandal Poem 2		39
Mention Courts, you'll ne'er be quiet;	635	Epistle Lady		183
Your Lesson learnt, you'll be secure	649	On Poetry		275
You'll find it soon if Fate consents;	743	Stel B-day 22		71
In your own heart you'll reap the fruit,	755	Stella '23		31
You'll be no more your former You;	760	Receipt Youth		38
I feel you'll be disgrac'd at Court.	778	Mullinix Tim		154
You'll find it well prepar'd to take	780	Mullinix Tim		225
You shan't stir a Foot--You'll think me a Clown--	869	Grand Question		78
And, Captain, you'll do us the Favour to stay,	871	Grand Question		119
"You'll never want Parsons as long as you live;	872	Grand Question		142
"Now Madam, you'll think it a strange Thing to say,	873	Grand Question		171
And after all you'll think it odd,	930	Riddle 15	D	21
One of us you'll find in Jet,	930	Riddle 17	D	4
All of us in one you'll find,	931	Riddle 18	D	1
You'll see me stretch him to a Giant;	934	Riddle 21	D	20
May give you a Blow you'll for ever repent.	941	Letter		40
You'll feed like a Farmer:	952	Onyons		5
In ev'ry vile Pamphlet you'll read the same Fancies,	968	Letter Sherid		21
You'll dare not to question my minor or major.	976	Dean to Sherid		24
But keep a good tongue, or you'll find, to your smart,	976	Dean to Sherid		35
Nay, hector and swagger, you'll still find me stanch,	979	Dean to Tho: S		13
With me you'll no more have a Stomach to Dine	1017	Swift Ans Sher		15
. . .and you'll believe me as sure as a gun, and own it;	1023	Nim-Dan-Dean 2	D	15
And now I hope you'll excuse this rhyming, which I must . . .	1024	Nim-Dan-Dean 2	D	17
YOU'RE				
You're on the wrong side of the Door.	91	Bauc & Phil 1		36
You're in the right, but be'n't afraid	92	Bauc & Phil 1		84
And since you're sparing of your Stuff,	108	V's House		73
If <Guernsey> calls, send word you're gone abroad;	166	Toland's Invit		41
"Let my Lord know you're come to Town.	200	Horace 2, 6		24
When you're advanc'd above Dean Viz.	362	Grace's Answer		43
Quoth the Dog, I should then be more Villain than you're,	395	Dog and Thief		3
Whilst you're, like Baal, fast asleep.	403	Window Inns 10	D	10
Without whose aid you're all undone?	432	Answer Paulus		4
For still you're short (which grieves your Spirit)	475	Epist on Epist		27
That you're Don Quixote Redivivus?	478	Epist on Epist		88
And now you're out, enjoy your Grin.	493	Panegyr Swift		22
"I find you're but a Stranger here.	563	Death of Swift		262
I damn such Fools!--Go, go, you're bit."	579	Day Judgement		22
Perhaps you're quite another Thing.	730	Stella, Poems		70
Come back before you're out of Case;	760	Receipt Youth		50
I vow to <God> you're too severe.	775	Mullinix Tim		70
You're now in your prime;	854	Lady's Lament		113
You're heartily welcome: But as for good Chear,	871	Grand Question		121
But find the Rhime, and you're the Man,	912	Aenigma		14
And for the Rhime, to you're the Man,	912	Aenigma Expl	D	9
You're reported to dwell	939	Riddle Answerd	D	
You hit it, you say,--you're a delicate hitter.	977	Dean to Sherid		40
But now I'll write short, for fear you're short taken.	980	Tho: Sheridan		6
You're my goose, and no other man's;	983	Sher, A Goose		11
As for you're writing I am dead,	983	Sher, A Goose		25
That you're a Dawb, whilst I but paint,	1003	Dan J's Reply		11
You're so retrograde, sure you were born under Cancer:	1019	To Sheridan		3
Nay, further, the Moment you're free from your scalding,	1019	To Sheridan		9
YOU'VE				
You've taught the Cov'tous Wretches to o're-rate,	24	Ode Athenian		255
Well--tho' you've rais'd Her to this high Degree,	24	Ode Athenian		263
You've rais'd a Church here in a Minute,	94	Bauc & Phil 1		161
You've some good Purchase in your Eye;	175	Horace 1, 7		128
"My House you've had on Courtesy;	208	Fable Bitches		26
"But, Pallas, you've apply'd too late,	304	Storm		37
I must confess you've spoken once true.	349	Whitshed Motto		24
Now you've done right, No Knight attempting	373	Letter D. S-y		75
Captain, I fear you've made some Blunder;	377	Apology Lady C		66
You've Cause to say he meant you well:	475	Epist on Epist		25
And when you've been at vast Expences	477	Epist on Epist		61
YOUNG SEE YONGE				
Forgive a young and (almost) Virgin-muse,	18	Ode Athenian		62
Godlike the force of my young Congreve's bays,	44	To Congreve		41
And the young Muse's early favour felt;	49	To Congreve		192
And tho' some Malicious Young Spirit did do't,	77	Lady B- B-		29
In times of old, when Time was young,	79	Vanbrug House		1
In Times of Old, when Time was Young,	106	V's House		1
And must have an old, or a young Coadjutor:	144	New Song		42
They Assassine when young, and Poison when old.	148	Windsor Proph		20
Fresh blooming, in young Harley's mind.	178	To Lord Harley		52
The young Advent'rer o'er the Deep	252	Bubble		34
A handsome young imperious Girl	289	Prog Marriage		3
Young Ducklings, fostered by a Hen;	294	Prog Marriage		146
When Jove was Young, was made of Gold.	345	Prometheus		36
Thus young, thus proof to all Temptations,	386	Manly Virtue		89

YOUNG   (CONTINUED)   PAGE   TITLE   LINE
   Shou'd Young and Phillips drudge together.   . . . . .   393 Modern Poets   20
   And said, lack-a-day! he's a proper young Man. . .   399 Tom Clinch   8
   So fair so young, ...   442 Ballyspellin   64
   For ever fair and young--in Song. . . . . . .   467 Birthday Song   234
   Now the active young Attornies . . . . . .   573 Helter Skelter   1
   And Hebe, Goddess ever young. . . . .   585 Strephon Chloe   56
   Instructing thus a young Beginner. . . . . .   642 On Poetry   76
   Like a young Heir, the thrifty Goddess . . .   693 Cadenus Vaness   223
   (For fear young Master shou'd be spoil'd,) . .   693 Cadenus Vaness   224
   What dangerous Paths young Virgins tread; . .   696 Cadenus Vaness   311
   She may be handsome, young and rich, . . .   698 Cadenus Vaness   362
   Nor further looks, but thinks him young. . .   703 Cadenus Vaness   531
   Whether the Nymph were Young or Old; . . .   706 Cadenus Vaness   633
   So tender of the Young and Fair? . . . .   707 Cadenus Vaness   652
   Thou Stella, wert no longer young, . . .   728 Stella, Poems   9
   Unless he were like Phoebus, young; . . .   757 Stel B-day '24   20
   Reports you are no longer young? . . . .   757 Stel B-day '24   36
   Thus you may still be young to me, . . .   758 Stel B-day '24   51
   Whate'er she gains is young and fresh; . .   759 Receipt Youth   16
   Every young Divine thy Brother. . . . .   838 Legion Club   200
   "To give a young Gentleman right Education, .   872 Grand Question   161
   Young Harry, as all Europe knows, . . .   879 Robbin & Harry   37
   To witty, beautiful, and young. . . . .   887 Panegyr Dean   16
   Young Deathlings, who, by Practice made .   903 Death Daphne   15
   I please the Young, I grace the Old, . .   912 Aenigma   11
   The Young, the Beautiful, and Brave, . .   923 Riddle 7   53
   The Delight of old and young, ...   933 Riddle 20   D 3
   When young is often due to the Vicar. . .   940 Letter   2
   Yet I know a young Rogue, that thrown flat on the Field   967 Letter Sherid   15
   Where <Young> must torture his Invention, . .   650 On Poetry   309
YOUNG'S
   Young's universal Passion, Pride, . . .   640 On Poetry   3
   Pope's Essays upon some for Young's may pass, .   670 Epig Carthy 18   D 5
YOUNGE
   Tho as empty as Younge and as saucy as Sandes . .   389 Order of Bath   10
YOUNGER
   Tho' he's a younger Brother. . . . . .   123 Empty'ng Town   24
   'Tis late, the old and younger Pairs, . .   280 Journal   55
   But he takes up with younger Fokes, . . .   556 Death of Swift   93
   Wou'd use him like a younger Child; . . .   693 Cadenus Vaness   225
   Within their Veins, who are thy younger Sons, . .   791 St. Pat's Well   18
YOUNGEST
   Then, bids the youngest of the Six, . . .   189 Faggot   3
YOUNGS
   Attend ye Popes, and Youngs, and Gays, . .   656 On Poetry   467
YOUR   934   OMITTED WORD
YOUR-SELF   1   OMITTED WORD
YOURS   18   OMITTED WORD
YOURSELF   10   OMITTED WORD
YOURSELVES   2   OMITTED WORD
YOUTH
   Ne'er sprang a youth from out this isle before . . .   44 To Congreve   11
   For, youth, believe, to you unseen, is fix'd . . .   44 To Congreve   31
   Lost youth, she cry'd, since first I met thee here! . .   52 Temple Ill   32
   Take, youth, these thoughts, large matter to employ . .   53 Temple Ill   67
   Ah fav'rite youth, how happy is thy lot!-- . . .   53 Temple Ill   71
   Why near the dregs of youth perversely wilt thou stay, .   54 Temple Ill   105
   The Youth with Broomy Stumps began to trace . . .   124 Descriptn Morn   9
   Dear Harley, gen'rous Youth, admit . . . .   176 To Lord Harley   3
   Her love on some bright youth below, . . .   178 To Lord Harley   60
   And bids the ravish'd youth be bless'd. . .   178 To Lord Harley   64
   The Youth, in vain, would fly from Fate's Attack, . .   210 Earl of Oxford   3
   The Rashness of the Cretan Youth, ...   252 Bubble   42
   For Husbands past their Youth to find; . .   293 Prog Marriage   116
   From thee our Youth all Virtues learn, . .   325 Pethox   59
   Th' inferiour Youth, to Learning led . .   385 Manly Virtue   39
   A Peer, a scarcely bearded Youth, . . .   336 Manly Virtue   71
   As Julius, or the Youth of Pella, . . .   464 Birthday Song   142
   To Virtue form'd a Princely Youth, . . .   482 Libel on D- D-   56
   To Woolston recommend our youth . . . .   490 Dialogue   29
   As some raw Youth in Country bred, . . .   500 Doctor Delaney   1
   And Youth so swiftly glides away; . . .   593 Strephon Chloe   304
   Follies, from my Youth instill'd, . . .   630 Epistle Lady   31
   Mourn'd Adonis, darling Youth: . . . .   660 Love Song   10
   His Mother's Aid no Youth invokes: . . .   687 Cadenus Vaness   10
   A modest Youth said something new, . . .   701 Cadenus Vaness   454
   And if her Youth Indifference met, . . .   706 Cadenus Vaness   638
   To Beauty, Dress, or Paint, or Youth, . .   729 Stella, Poems   62
   No Bloom of Youth can ever blind . . .   736 Stel B-day '20   55
   Have always been confin'd to Youth; . . .   757 Stel B-day '24   16
   With Youth and Beauty to enchant . . .   759 Receipt Youth   19
   I'll have Youth and Beauty still. . . .   863 To Janus   30
   Old Robin, all his youth a sloven, . . .   879 Robbin & Harry   45
   In Youth exalted high in Air, ...   915 Riddle 1   1
   The vig'rous Youth, and aged Sire: . . .   922 Riddle 7   26
YOUTHFUL
   The wild excursions of a youthful pen; . .   17 Ode Athenian   61
   When Poets soar in youthful Strains, . .   271 Apollo's Edict   D 52
   And with the youthful Damsel sported. . .   372 Letter D. S-y   46
   He crown'd his youthful Head with Bays: . .   597 Problem Solved   8

```
YOUTHFUL          (CONTINUED)                              PAGE    TITLE            LINE
    And, first excus'd his youthful Face;     . . . . . .   603  Beasts Confess      60
    Corinna with that youthful Air,   . . . . . . . . .     699  Cadenus Vaness     388
YOUTHS
    Discourag'd Youths, now all their Hopes must fail,  . .  793  St. Pat's Well      73
ZAGGS
    while his own ass's Zaggs were more fit for the shears.  816  Yahoo's             49
ZEAL
    Forgive (Original Mildness) this ill-govern'd zeal,   .   38  Ode Sancroft       107
    But zeal is weak and ignorant, tho' wond'rous proud,  .   38  Ode Sancroft       135
    First chid the zeal as unpoetic fire,  . . . . . . .      44  To Congreve         25
    At the warm zeal that breeds this golden calf?  . . . .   46  To Congreve        108
    As some fair pile, yet spar'd by zeal and rage,   . . .   52  Temple Ill          47
    Out of Zeal for his Country, and want of a Place,   . .  142  New Song             3
    Tells me i have more Zeal than Wit,   . . . . . . .      200  Horace 2, 6         36
    A Minister so filled with Zeal,   . . . . . . . . .      391  Young's Satire       3
    So well acquainted with my Zeal   . . . . . . . .        444  Modern Lady          3
    From Paean's Fire to Party Zeal;  . . . . . . . .        481  Libel on D- D-      44
    Harmonious Coffee show thy Zeal,   . . . . . . . .       515  Answer Fable        87
    With hasty Zeal, behold, the Steward come,  . . . .      533  To Mr. Gay          71
    His Zeal was not to lash our Crimes,   . . . . . .       549  Life of Swift      136
    "Thought Popish and Fanatick Zeal,   . . . . . .        549  Life of Swift      152
    "And make him of his Zeal repent:  . . . . . . . .       570  Death of Swift     424
    His Zeal was sometimes indiscreet:   . . . . . . .       603  Beasts Confess      54
    They plot to turn in factious Zeal,   . . . . . . .      653  On Poetry          379
    With zeal in heart, and notes in hand;   . . . . .       675  Curate's Compl       2
    With such a constant, Loyal Zeal,   . . . . . . .        778  Mullinix Tim       169
    By holy Zeal inspir'd, and led by Fame,   . . . .        789  St. Pat's Well       1
    Their Sacrifice with Zeal and Haste:   . . . . . .       894  Panegyr Dean       240
ZEALOT
    This Protestant Zealot, this <English> Divine    . . .   518  Dean Hang Rape      31
ZEALOUS
    Away he runs with zealous hotness   . . . . . . . .      423  Ireld               65
    Too zealous for the Nation's Good:   . . . . . . .       604  Beasts Confess     100
    Dick with zealous No's and Ay's,   . . . . . . . .       785  Mullinex Dick       37
    Nor, will zealous Hannah pout   . . . . . . . . .        896  Panegyr Dean       317
ZENITH
    Direct the Zenith of the Sky;   . . . . . . . . .        780  Mullinix Tim       248
ZEPHIRS
    With cooling Gales, like Zephirs fraught;   . . . . .    911  Aenigma              2
ZEPHYR'S
    Nor let the Zephyr's treach'rous Gale   . . . . . .      597  Cassinus Peter     109
ZEST
    Oh, could'st thou teach us how to zest   . . . . .       495  Panegyr Swift       64
ZIGZACKS
    Of zigzacks and walks;  . . . . . . . . . . . .          856  Lady's Lament      174
ZODIACK
    Thro' the Zodiack around, it shall quickly be spread,  .  265  Apollo             69
ZONE    SEE NORTH-ZONE
<ZOUNDS>
    <Zounds> I would ship her for Jamaica    . . . . . .     220  A Quiet Life        31
    <Zounds> who wou'd be a Rake?  . . . . . . . . .         426  Five Ladies         36
    <Zounds> Sir. But to be short and serious   . . . . .    774  Mullinix Tim        33
    "But, <Zounds>, by their Looks, they never keep Lent:    872  Grand Question     146
```

APPENDIX

Index Words
in Order of Frequency

5351 THE	704 OR	398 CAN	236 COULD	170 KNOW
4424 AND	657 FROM	384 ME	232 TIS	169 OLD
3436 TO	635 WHEN	377 OUR	226 MAKE	164 DEAN
3397 A	632 AT	367 THEN	225 WHERE	162 COME
2230 IN	623 SO	358 HOW	221 EV'RY THAN	159 FIRST GIVE
2150 OF	592 ON	351 LIKE	213 THUS	155 TAKE THINK
1604 HIS	590 THEIR	343 MUST	208 WERE	144 SAY
1503 I	585 NOT	335 THY	202 DOWN	138 MADE
1429 YOU	535 WAS	328 WHICH	201 SUCH US	136 THO'
1258 FOR	518 NO	326 NOR	200 LET	132 BEFORE
1232 WITH	511 THEY	305 AN	197 OWN UP	131 BOTH
1123 BUT	479 THIS	303 WOULD	195 HERE	128 PLACE THOU
1119 HE	463 WHAT	289 MORE	193 WHILE	126 EVER
934 HER YOUR	456 SHE	286 HAD	190 GOOD THEM	125 THEE
908 ALL	454 WE	276 YET	186 WELL	124 FACE
879 BY	446 ARE	271 MAY	185 SHOULD	122 DAY MAN
859 MY	436 HIM	266 OUT	183 FIND	120 DO
856 THAT	425 HAVE	264 ONE	180 STILL THERE	118 GREAT TIME
844 AS	423 WHO	262 NEVER	176 WIT	117 HALF HEAD THESE
793 BE	416 WILL (VERB)	251 SOME	173 TOO	116 ROUND
770 IS	411 IF	243 SEE	172 HAS	
729 IT	409 NOW	242 SHALL		

115	91	74	60	50 (CONT.)
DID	HEART	COU'D	E'ER	WORD
JUST		DEAR	FATE	YEAR
	90	EVERY	RISE	
114		STATE		49
	TWO	THOUSAND	59	
FOUND				DICK
FRIEND	89	73	KNOWS	GIVES
LONG			MEAN	HARD
SINCE	INTO	COMES	PASS	KNEW
THOSE	NAME	KIND		RACE
WHY			58	SOUL
	88	72		
113			DOES	48
	ITS	PLEASE	GRACE	
ONCE	LORD		NATURE	AFTER
WITHOUT	MEN	71	NOTHING	CHURCH
	SOON			EARS
111		LEFT	57	HARDLY
	87	NYMPH		STAND
TRUE			FAR	THINGS
	EYES	70	HE'S	YOU'LL
110	MUSE		LESS	
	THOUGH	GO	PART	47
GOD		LOOK	USE	
MUCH	86	ONLY	WENT	ANOTHER
		WAY	WRITE	BLOOD
109	I'M	WHOSE		CANNOT
	NIGHT		56	CAUSE
LAST		69		CROWN
THOUGHT	85		MADAM	FLY
		SURE	OFT	LIVE
108	ART		PAY	NOSE
	FAIR	68	RUN	PRAY
SAID			TOLD	SIR
WOU'D	84	AGAINST	WOOD	WHOLE
		BECAUSE		
107	WORLD	GOT	55	46
		LIGHT		
EACH	82	SEEN	BELOW	CARE
			CASE	LATE
105	BEEN	67	FIT	LOOKS
	COURT		OFTEN	THING
LOVE	HEAR	GET		THROUGH
TELL	HIGH	LADY	54	TOM
		RIGHT		TOOK
103	81	TURN	DEAD	
		VERY	GONE	45
O'ER	BEST		KING	
UPON	LEAVE	66	PUT	ELSE
			SAME	FINE
102	80	POETS		GROUND
		SHOU'D	53	HANDS
BETTER	WISE	TOWN		HOPE
			ABOVE	MONEY
101	79	65	ALONE	TH'
			QUEEN	THERE'S
NE'ER	LIFE	LITTLE	REST	WIFE
	PRIDE		SET	
98		64	TEN	44
	78		THRO'	
OTHER		GROWN	YEARS	CALL'D
TILL	ALWAYS	PRAISE		EARTH
	MOST	SIDE	52	HUNDRED
97	NEW			TRUTH
	SHEW	63	NONE	YOUNG
MIGHT	VIRTUE		SENT	
		AIR		43
96	77	FULL	51	
		LOST		BEGAN
FRIENDS	BEHIND	SIGHT	DIVINE	DEATH
VAIN	CALL	WANT	FAME	HOLD
WHOM	CAME		FIRE	KNOWN
	HOUSE	62	FOOLS	PERHAPS
95			GAVE	SCARCE
	76	AMONG	GOLD	SCORN
MIND		READ	JOVE	SHAME
	AGAIN		MAKES	SING
93	I'LL	61	TIMES	TAKES
	YE			
POOR		ABOUT	50	42
	75	AM		
92		SAW	AWAY	BACK
	'EM	SENSE	BEAST	FEAR
KEEP	HAND	THREE	BRING	HIMSELF
	MANY		HATH	LAND
	NEXT		LEAST	SAYS
			SHOW	SCENE
			SICK	STELLA

42 (CONT.)

VERSE

41

BED
CUT
GODDESS
LONGER
OFF
POET
POW'R
TWAS
WISH

40

BEAR
BORN
FALL
FOUR
HAPPY
HONOUR
O
PEACE
RAISE
SWEAR
UNDER

39

COUNTRY
CRY
FANCY
LAY
MASTER
OTHERS
TAUGHT

38

AGE
BELIEVE
DAME
DAYS
DEEP
END
ENOUGH
HEARD
JEST
PLAIN
REASON
SMALL
TALK
TONGUE
WHETHER
WITHIN

37

DARE
DELIGHT
GREW
HELL
MANKIND
NATION
NEITHER
PLAY
QUITE
SIT
WHENCE
WILL

36

DEVIL
DUE
ENDS
HOUR
ILL
MERIT
MINE
OH

35

BEAUTY
BEHOLD
FEMALE

35 (CONT.)

FEW
FOLKS
GODS
HUMAN
LEARNING
LOSE
MAID
MATTER
PROUD
SPIGHT
TOGETHER
TRADE

34

DOCTOR
DONE
DULL
EYE
FORTUNE
HELP
NEAR
PAST
PUBLICK
SELF
SHORT
VIRTUES
WE'LL
WONDER
WRIT
YOUTH

33

AID
APPEARS
EITHER
FORM
GRAVE
GROW
HUMBLE
MEANT
NEED
PROPER
ST
STOOD
WINE
WITS

32

ANY
APPEAR
BRIGHT
COMMON
FOES
KEPT
SAVE
TWENTY
VIEW
WORDS
WORK

31

ALAS
BREAK
BROTHER
BROUGHT
BUILD
CHANGE
DOUBT
DRESS
GENTLE
GOWN
HONEST
JOY
LEARN
LYE
PAPER
PASSION
RATHER
SON
SPEAK
STRONG

30

ANTIENT
BROKE
DOG
FAST
GOES
GREATEST
HATE
HE'LL
HIDE
IT'S
LIES
MODERN
RAGE
TRY
WIND
WRONG

29

ACT
BOAST
DAMN'D
DOOR
FELL
FIVE
HOME
PAIN
SEND
SPARE
STAY
T'
TASTE
WAIT
WORSE
YOU'RE

28

BENEATH
CHUSE
CLOUD
DY'D
EASE
ENVY
FILL
FORCE
GOLDEN
GRIEF
HEAV'N
KINGS
LYES
MIGHTY
MORTAL
PHOEBUS
SERVE
SHINE
SIX
SKIES
SPLEEN
THUNDER

27

BIRTH
BOOK
BURST
DYE
FILL'D
FLIES
GLASS
LOUD
LOW
OVER
PARTS
RAIS'D
SKILL
SOUND
SPIRIT
STUFF
SUN
SWIFT
TURNS
VENUS
VOICE
WEEK
WHITE

26

APOLLO
BETWEEN
COACH
DIFF'RENT
ENGLISH
EXCEPT
FLAME
HEARTS
LADIES
LAWS
MORTALS
PARSON
POUND
PROVE
QUICKLY
SECRET
SEX
SHEWS
SINK
SUPPOSE
THAT'S
TWICE
WORTH

25

ANSWER
BLACK
BOOKS
CAN'T
CAPTAIN
EQUAL
FAIL
GAY
HELD
HENCE
LAW
LINES
OBSERVE
PEN
RESOLV'D
ROYAL
SEEMS
SHAPE
SPIRITS
SPOKE
STREPHON
SUBJECT
SWEET
TALE

24

ALIVE
BLIND
BODY
BOYS
COMPLAIN
DRINK
DURST
EAR
FEEL
FOOL
JUDGE
LEAD
LED
MEET
MR
PALLAS
PLEAS'D
POPE
ROSE
RULE
RULES
SEA
SHOES
SPENT
TEACH
UNKNOWN
WALK

23

ARMS
ASK
BREAST
CLEAR
COAT

23 (CONT.)

DAN
DESIRE
DROP
FAULT
FOE
FOUL
GENIUS
GROWS
HOPES
I'D
IRISH
LINE
LONG-EAR'D
NAY
ON'T
PAINS
PITY
POWER
SHE'S
STRANGE
TREAT
VICE

22

ADVICE
AH
BIT
BOY
BRETHREN
CHAIR
COLD
DUKE
FALSE
FEET
FRIENDSHIP
GEORGE
GRANT
MALICE
MOTHER
PEOPLE
ROGUE
SITS
SOFT
STARS
THOUGHTS
WHENE'ER
WISELY
WORST

21

'TWILL
BAD
BRAIN
BREATH
CHIEF
CLAIM
COURSE
CROWD
DULLEST
EAT
EMPTY
FOLLOW
FROWN
GAIN
KNIGHT
KNOWLEDGE
LARGE
LAUGH
LETTER
MEND
MUSES
NICE
NOBLE
READY
SOMETIMES
SONG
STANDS
THRICE
UNLESS
WHILST
ZEAL

20

ALMOST
ARTS

20 (CONT.)

BASE
BEG
BESIDES
BETTERS
BID
BLAME
BRAZEN
CALLS
CARES
COST
DESIGN'D
DRAW
DREAD
FAVOUR
GLAD
HAIR
INSTEAD
MAINTAIN
MET
MISS
MORNING
NEEDS
PAIR
POINT
PRIVATE
SECOND
SHARE
SKY
STORY
TENDER
TRUST
US'D
VENTURE
WEALTH
WINGS

19

BAYS
BLESS
BRINGS
DIE
DINE
DISGRACE
FIFTY
FLED
FORGOT
GATE
HITHER
LACE
LEARNED
MAD
MARK
MOTION
NINE
NOISE
PRESENT
PRINCE
ROD
SEARCH
SEEK
SEES
SELDOM
SILVER
SKIN
SPOUSE
STATION
TOUCH
TRIBE
TRULY
UNDERSTOOD
VANESSA
WEAR

18

ALE
BEAU
BRAINS
BRASS
BURN
BUY
CHANCE
CONSCIENCE
CREATURE
CREW
CURSE
DARK

18 (CONT.)

DIES
DON'T
DRY
DUST
EASY
FATHER
FLIGHT
FOLLY
FOOT
GLORIOUS
GUESS
HANG
HAVING
HEAVEN
HIGHER
ISLE
LEAVES
LEST
LORDS
MAKING
PLOT
POUNDS
RAIL
REACH
RICH
ROOM
RUNS
SAFE
SELL
SHE'LL
SOMETHING
STELLA'S
STRAINS
STYLE
SUNG
SUNK
SWORE
THEREFORE
THRONE
TORIES
TURN'D
VARIOUS
VERSES
WATER
WISDOM
WOMEN
WRETCH
YOURS

17

ALTHOUGH
ATTEND
BISHOP
CLOUDS
COMPANY
COMPARE
CREDIT
DAILY
DESCRIBE
DESIGN
DOUBLE
DREAMS
DREST
DRIVE
EXALTED
FAIRLY
FATAL
FIX
FORMS
FRESH
GETS
GRACES
HAST
HAUGHTY
JOHN
LENGTH
LETTERS
LOVERS
MOUTH
NOBLER
OPEN
PACK
PILE
POST
PRODUCE
PROSE
QUIET

17 (CONT.)

READING
RED
RENT
RETURN
SIZE
SLEEP
SMELL
SMOOTH
STINK
THEMSELVES
TORY
VILE
VOTE
WAR
WIDE
WOMAN
YOU'D

16

'TWIXT
BANISHT
BEING
BITE
BOAT
BOLD
BRED
CAST
CELIA
CHARMS
CHILD
CHIN
CHRISTIAN
CLEAN
CONFIN'D
CRY'D
DAMN
DIRECT
ENTER
FACTION
FAM'D
FLESH
FOOD
FORGET
FORM'D
GIFTS
GROAT
HERO
HORSE
HOWEVER
JOIN
JUDGMENT
JUSTICE
KINDLY
LAID
LASH
LOSS
LOVELY
LOVES
MRS
NEWS
NYMPHS
OUGHT
PRATE
PURSE
RAN
RHYME
ROBIN
SACRED
SAD
SAKE
SAT
SENDS
SERVANTS
SHINES
SLAVE
SLAVES
SMILE
SPEND
SPRING
STOCK
STOLE
STORM
TRY'D
WALKS
WALL
WEIGHT
WHATE'ER

16 (CONT.)

WHIG
WICKED

15

AIRS
ANGER
APPLY'D
BOX
BREED
CADENUS
CHEAT
CHLOE
COURTS
DEAREST
DIFFERENT
DIRTY
DRAWN
DWELL
ENDURE
EVIL
FAV'RITE
FORC'D
FREE
GAME
GLORY
GREEN
HORACE
KISS
KNOCK
LEND
METHINKS
MINISTERS
MOUNT
MOVE
MUSICK
NUMBERS
ODD
PAID
PERSON
PLAC'D
PLAINLY
PLEASURE
PRETENCE
PROCEED
PURSUE
QUOTH
RAPE
REIGN
RUIN
SAINTS
SCHOOL
SCORE
SEEM
SIN
SONS
SPITE
SWEAT
THENCE
TRACE
TYRANT
VULGAR
WANTS
WEAK
WEARY
WHEREVER
WITTY

14

APPEAR'D
ASIDE
BALLYSPELLIN
BECOME
BEGIN
BESIDE
BOLDLY
BREAD
CHAIN
CLUB
CONFESS
CONSIDER
CRIES
DESPISE
DIRT
EXCUSE
EXPECT
EXPRESS

14 (CONT.)

FEARS
FEELS
FELLOWS
FIGHT
FIGURE
FITS
FLEW
FORMER
FREELY
GREATER
HARLEY
HE'D
HEAV'NLY
HEIR
INDEED
JACK
JUSTLY
KNAVE
KNAVES
LEARN'D
LIE
LOCKS
MINDS
MINISTER
PARTY
PRIZE
RAKE
ROAR
SCHOLARS
SECURE
SINGLE
SOULS
SPEECH
SPORT
STEAL
STILE
STRAIN
STREAMS
SWAIN
SWEARS
TALENTS
TEARS
TEETH
THINKS
THO
TIM
TONGUES
TOP
TWELVE
VERMIN
WAYS
WEATHER
WHIGS
WOUND

13

ABLE
AGREE
ALLOW
BARD
BEGINS
BETWIXT
BISHOPS
BORE
BROKEN
BUILDING
BUS'NESS
CAUGHT
CELL
CERTAIN
CHILDREN
CHOICE
CHOSE
CIRCLE
CLERGY
COMMAND
CROWN'D
CURE
CURIOUS
DARES
DEVOTION
DISPUTE
DROPS
DUBLIN
EV'N
EXPERIENCE
FAIN

13 (CONT.)	12 (CONT.)	11 (CONT.)	10	10 (CONT.)
FELT	ESTATE	BRUTE	'SQUIRE	PETER
FIERCE	FAITH	CIVIL	ACTS	PHILOSOPHY
FLATTER	FALLS	COLLEGE	ADORE	PRACTICE
FOND	FLOOD	CONCEAL	AGES	PRECIOUS
FORBEAR	GLITT'RING	CONSULT	AGO	PRESUME
FURTHER	GOOSE	COURTIERS	ALLOW'D	PRETTY
GIFT	GUILT	COXCOMB	ALONG	PRIESTS
GIRL	HANG'D	DANCE	ALTHO'	PRIME
GRAND	HEELS	DEBT	AMAZ'D	PRINT
GRIEVE	HOLE	DENY	APE	PROJECT
GUEST	HOURS	DINNER	BEAM	PULL
GUIDE	HUMBLY	DREADFUL	BEARS	PURCHASE
HEIGHT	HUMOUR	DROWN	BEAUX	PURSU'D
HERE'S	INCH	DYING	BEND	QUICK
HILL	INT'REST	E'RE	BLAST	REAL
HOLY	JOKE	ENDLESS	BLOODY	REFIN'D
INVITE	KILL	EXPOSE	BLOW	RETREAT
KEEPS	LOAD	FEE	BLUSH	RIDE
LADY'S	LOFTY	FIXT	BREAKS	ROAD
LATELY	LOOK'D	FORGIVE	BREEDING	RUDE
MAJESTY	MAGICK	FORTH	BRIBE	SAV'D
MASTER'S	MEER	FORTY	BUSINESS	SCRAPS
MEAT	MISTRESS	FREEDOM	BUSY	SENATE
MISTAKE	MITRE	FRENCH	BUTTER	SERVICE
MOMENT	MUD	HEADS	CARDS	SHADES
MOON	NATIVE	HEARS	CARLOS	SHALT
MORN	OPINION	HIGHEST	CHARGE	SHOWN
NAMES	OWE	HINTS	CHIEFLY	SIEVE
NATION'S	PALE	HOLDS	CLOUDY	SILENCE
ODIOUS	PENCE	HOMER	COMPANIONS	SMART
OFFENCE	POET'S	HUNG	COMPLEAT	SNUFF
OWN'D	POETICK	INNOCENCE	CONDEMN'D	SOIL
PAINT	POETRY	KNEES	CONDUCT	SPREAD
POEM	POT	LANGUAGE	CONVERSATION	STARVE
RAILLERY	POX	LAWYER	CREEP	STEALS
RATE	PREY	LIMB	CRUEL	STEEPLE
RHIME	PROFOUND	LIVES	CURST	STINKING
SEAT	RABBLE	LOVER	DANGER	STIR
SHEW'D	RAIN	MAIN	DART	STOMACH
SILENT	SHERIDAN	MIDAS	DEFENCE	STONE
SMOAK	SHIP	MILD	DIN	STONES
STAIRS	SOLD	MISCHIEF	DISDAIN	SUIT
STAR	SOLE	OBJECT	DISMAL	TABLE
STICK	SOONER	ORDER	DIVIDE	TAIL
STOP	SPRUNG	PAINTED	EMPLOY'D	TALENT
STUCK	STORIES	PARSONS	ESTEEM	TEAR
STUPID	STRENGTH	PASSIONS	FACT	THEY'RE
THEY'LL	STRING	PATIENCE	FARCE	TRAIN
TREMBLING	STROVE	PAYS	FAT	TY'D
TRICKS	STRUCK	PIECES	FED	UNDERSTAND
VENGEANCE	SUBJECTS	PLAC'T	FINGERS	UTMOST
VICES	SUDDEN	PLAGUE	FISH	VALOUR
WARM	SUPERIOR	PLAYS	FIX'D	VEX
WHATEVER	SUPPLY	POLITICKS	FLYES	VICTORY
WHORE	SUPPORT	POWDER'D	FREQUENT	VISAGE
WILD	TEA	QUIT	FRUITFUL	VISITS
WIN	TELLS	REGARD	GEN'ROUS	WON
WRETCHED	TEXT	RELIEF	GHOST	YONDER
	THANKS	RETIRE	GRAIN	YOURSELF
12	THEIRS	RISING	GRASS	
	THINE	ROUT	GUARD	**9**
'TWOULD	TITLES	SCOLD	HASTE	
ADMIRE	TREE	SEAS	HAY	'UM
AFFAIRS	TRICK	SEEM'D	HEALTH	AFRAID
BECAME	USUAL	SENSELESS	HEAT	AIM
BILLS	VAN	SHE'D	HIT	ANCIENT
BLEST	VEIN	SHOWS	HOWE'ER	ANSWERS
BOUGHT	VIRGIN	SIDES	HUE	APPROACH
BRAVE	WALLS	SIGN	HUGE	ARGUMENTS
CART	WHAT'S	SIRE	IDLE	ASHAM'D
CHARMING	WHOEVER	SPECIAL	IGNORANCE	ATTEMPT
CITY	WORKS	SPY	INSPIRE	AUTHORS
CLAD	WRITING	STORE	LEARNT	BACKS
CLOSE	YON	STREET	LEG	BARRACK
CONTENT		STRIVE	LIPS	BEEF
CORN	**11**	THROW	LO	BEGUN
COURAGE		TOAST	MERRY	BELL
CRIMES	ALREADY	UNDONE	MIDNIGHT	BENCH
CRITICKS	APPLY	VILLAGE	MINUTE	BESTOW'D
CUP	ARTHUR	VOWS	MORAL	BETTY
CUPID	ASS	WATCH	MOVES	BEWARE
DELANY	BESTOW	WEIGHTY	NATURE'S	BIDS
DIRECTORS	BIRD	WHEREIN	NOTE	BOB
DON	BLUE	YOU'VE	NUM'ROUS	CALLING
DRAWS	BOW		OFFENSIVE	CARTHY
DROWN'D	BRAVELY		PARDON	CAT
DRUNK	BRITAIN		PARISH	CATCH
EARLY	BRITISH		PEER	CELLAR

CENSURE	ORDERS	CHEAP	PATRON'S	TRIES
CHANG'D	PEEP	CHEEKS	PATTERN	TROUBLE
CHAT	PERFECT	CLAY	PEACEFUL	UNHAPPY
CHEST	PHRASE	CONCEIVE	PECULIAR	UNITE
CHOPS	PICK	CONTRIVE	PHILEMON	UNSEEN
CLIMB	PIOUS	COTTAGE	PHILLIS	VALUE
COMING	POINTS	CROSS	PHILOSOPHERS	VAST
CONCLUDE	PRAY'RS	CROUD	PIECE	VESSEL
CONFOUND	PRESS	CUNNING	PISS	WASTE
CONTINUE	PRETEND	DAUGHTERS	PLEASING	WENCH
CONTRIV'D	PREVAIL	DEAF	PLENTY	WHO'S
COPPER	PRICE	DEANSHIP	POETIC	WHORES
COUNCIL	PRIEST	DEBATE	PORT	WILT
CRIME	PROVIDE	DESCEND	POSSESSION	WINDOW
CRITICK	QUOTE	DISH	PRAISES	WIVES
DANG'ROUS	RASCAL	DOCTORS	PRAYER	WOOD'S
DARTS	RAYS	DOGS	PREACH	WORE
DATE	REMAINS	DRAGON	PRESENCE	WORN
DECREE	RENOWN	DREAM	PROVIDED	YES
DEFEND	REV'REND	DRIVES	PRUDENCE	YIELD
DEGREE	RIDDLE	DROVE	PURPLE	
DEGREES	ROGUES	EARL	PURSUES	7
DEPEND	ROOF	EARTHLY	PUTS	
DIFF'RENCE	ROOT	EMBLEM	QUARRELS	'SCAPE
DIRE	ROUGH	ENGAGE	QUART	ABUSE
DISCOVER	SATAN	ENTERTAINS	QUARTER	ACTIONS
DISGUISE	SATIRE	EVENT	QUESTION	ADDRESS
DISTANCE	SCHOOLS	FAMILIAR	RAGS	ADORN
DIVINES	SEATED	FAULTS	REBUKE	ADVISE
DOLL	SHAPES	FEED	REFUSE	AFFORD
DREW	SPLIT	FELLOW	RENOWN'D	ALOFT
DUNCE	SPOT	FOLK	REPAIR	ALTARS
DUNG	SQUEEZE	FOLLIES	RESTORE	ANGRY
EMPIRE	SQUIRE	FOR'T	RETURN'D	APPROACHING
EMPLOY	STATESMEN	FORD	RETURNING	ASKS
ENGLAND	STAYS	GAIN'D	REWARD	ASSES
EXPIRE	STRAIT	GEESE	ROB	ATTENDING
EXPOS'D	STRONGEST	GIDDY	RUNNING	AWE
FABLE	SUP	GRACEFUL	SACRIFICE	BALL
FILTHY	SUPPLIES	GRAVELY	SAGE	BANKS
FINDING	TENANTS	GROSS	SAINT	BARE
FRET	THIEF	GUTS	SATYR	BARREN
FRIGHT	THIRD	HEAVEN'S	SCANDAL	BASHFUL
FRIGHTED	TOIL	HERSELF	SEASON	BEAMS
FRUIT	TREAD	HID	SEEKS	BEARD
FUTURE	TRIUMPHANT	HUMOR	SEIZE	BEGG'D
GOD'S	TUTOR	I'VE	SERVANT	BELIEV'D
HANDSOME	UNGRATEFUL	IMMORTAL	SEVEN	BIRDS
HARE	UNIVERSAL	IN'T	SEVERE	BITS
HARRY	VANESSA'S	INFLUENCE	SHADE	BLESSING
HAT	VENT	INK	SHARP	BO
HATED	WAVES	INTENT	SHORE	BONES
HEAVENLY	WELCOME	JUDGES	SHOT	BOTTOM
HEAVY	WINDS	JUICE	SISTER	BRACE
HIRE	WOND'ROUS	JUNO	SLEEPING	BREECHES
HOP'D	WORSHIP	KETTLE	SNOUT	BROCADES
HOT	WORTHY	LABOURS	SOBER	BRUTES
INFERIOR		LAD	SORT	CAELIA
INSPIR'D	8	LANDLORD	SOUNDLY	CARELESS
IRON		LANDS	SOUNDS	CARRY
JOKES	<FART>	LAWYERS	SOV'REIGN	CASTLE
KINGDOM	ADD	LEAVING	SPACIOUS	CERTAINLY
LABOUR	ADIEU	LENT	SPADE	CHAPLAIN
LADYSHIP	ALIKE	LETS	SQUIRES	CHEAR
LAYS	AMBITION	LEWD	STAGE	CHID
LIGHTNING	ANGEL	LIBERTY	STATESMAN	CHLOE'S
LIMBS	APOLLO'S	LODGE	STICKS	COMPAR'D
LIQUOR	ARM	LODGING	STREAM	COMPLIMENT
LIST	AROUND	LORD'S	STRIKE	CONCERN
LISTEN	ATTACK	LORDLY	STRIP	CONGREVE'S
LONDON	AUTHOR	LOUSE	SUBLIME	CONSENT
LOOKING	AVOID	LOWER	SUCCESS	CONSIDER'D
MAN'S	BAUCIS	LUST	SURPRIZE	CONTAINS
MANNERS	BEHELD	MARY	SWAINS	CONVEY
MASS	BENT	MATCH	SWALLOW'D	CORNER
MEANS	BIG	MERCURY	SWEEP	COSTLY
MERCY	BORROW'D	MINGLED	SWIM	COURTLY
MONARCH	BOTTLE	MIRTH	SWORD	DARLING
MORALS	BOUND	MISTOOK	TAKING	DEANS
NAM'D	BRIDE	MODEL	TALKS	DEARLY
NECK	BUILT	MONTH	THANK	DELIGHTS
NEIGHBOURS	BULK	MORROW	THICK	DENNIS
NICELY	CAR	OBSCURE	THORN	DESCRIPTION
NOD	CARVE	OFF'RINGS	THRIVE	DESERVES
NOON	CASSOCK	OPPOSE	THROWN	DESPAIR
NOUGHT	CELESTIAL	OUTWARD	TIDE	DISEASE
OBEY	CHAINS	PAGE	TITLE	DISPLAYS
OBSERV'D	CHAMBER	PARCHMENT	TRAYTOR	DISPUTES

7 (CONT.)	7 (CONT.)	7 (CONT.)	6 (CONT.)	6 (CONT.)
DR.	NUMBER	TOPICKS	CONSTANT	IMPERTINENCE
DRAPIER	OBJECTS	TRASH	CONTAIN	IMPORTANT
DRAPIER'S	OFFER'D	TREATED	CORRUPTED	IMPROVE
DRESS'D	OFFERS	TRIFLE	COUNTERS	INCLIN'D
DRUM	ONES	TROD	COVER	INDIGNATION
EFFECTS	OWNS	TUNE	COW	INDULGENT
ELOQUENCE	PACE	TWERE	COWS	INSECT
ENDED	PALACE	VISIT	COXCOMBS	INTERPOSE
ENDOW'D	PASS'D	VOW	DAMNABLE	JANUS
ENQUIRE	PASSAGE	WAITING	DAPHNE	JOVE'S
ENTERTAIN	PASSING	WALPOLE	DEAL	JUMP
ERECT	PATRICK'S	WANTED	DEAN'S	KINDLED
ETERNAL	PATRIGE	WATERS	DECAY'D	KNIFE
EVEN	PATRON	WAX	DECENT	KNOWING
EXACTLY	PAULTRY	WEARS	DECLARES	LAP
EXERCISE	PERISH	WET	DEITY	LARK
EXPLAIN	PERT	WIG	DERMOT	LASH'D
FACTIOUS	PINCH	WING	DESIGNS	LAUGH'D
FAILS	PINT	WITNESS	DESIRES	LAUREL
FAN	PLACES	WOMB	DESTIN'D	LAWREL
FARE	PLATE	WON'T	DIFFER	LEADEN
FARMER	PLEASANT	WONT	DIG	LEAN
FARTHER	POCKET	WOODEN	DIGNITY	LEAP
FEAST	PRAYERS	WORLD'S	DINGLEY	LEATHER
FEATURE	PRELATE		DISCRETION	LET'S
FEES	PRESERVE	6	DISPLAY'D	LEWIS
FIELD	PRESIDE		DISTANT	LIFT
FIELDS	PRETENDER	<ARSE>	DO'T	LINNEN
FILLS	PRODUC'D	<HORT>	DOOM'D	LORDSHIP
FILTH	PROMETHEUS	'ERE	DRAIN	LOUDEST
FINDS	PRONOUNCE	ABROAD	DULY	LUCKY
FIRM	PROOF	ABSENT	DUNCES	LUSTRE
FLOW'RS	PRUDE	ACTION	DUTY	LY
FOREIGN	PUNCH	ADOR'D	EFFECT	MADNESS
FURNISH	PURE	ADVANC'D	ENDU'D	MAGGOT
FURY	QUILL	ADVANCE	ESCAPE	MARRIAGE
GAPING	RANK	AFFIRM	ET	MATE
GLADLY	REFINE	AGEN	EV'NING	MATERIALS
GOVERN	REGARDS	AIRY	EXPENCE	MAXIM
GRANDSIRE	REPINE	ANGELS	FAITHFUL	MEAL
GREASY	REPORT	APPEAL	FAMOUS	MEANING
GUILTY	REQUIRE	ARGUE	FANCIES	MEETS
GULPH	RING	ARRIV'D	FANCY'D	MERE
HARMLESS	ROBERT	ARRIVES	FARTHING	MERITS
HEAP	RUMP	ASHES	FATES	METHODS
HEIRS	SAFETY	ASPIRING	FEATS	METTLE
HERALD	SCENES	ASSIGN'D	FEATURES	MIEN
HINT	SCEPTER	ASSURE	FEMALES	MILE
HOOP	SCIENCE	AVARICE	FIERY	MILES
HOURLY	SCOUNDREL	AWKWARD	FIFTEEN	MILK
HUSBAND	SEEDS	BACON	FIG	MILLIONS
IGNORANT	SHIFT	BAR	FINGER	MISTAKEN
IMPATIENT	SHILLING	BARDS	FINISH'D	MODESTY
INFANT	SIGH	BEASTS	FLAMES	MONARCH'S
INNOCENT	SINS	BEAT	FLOAT	MOTHER'S
INSOLENCE	SKILL'D	BEAUTEOUS	FLOCKS	MOV'D
INTENDS	SLIP	BEAUTIFUL	FONDLY	MYSELF
IRIS	SLY	BEAUTY'S	FOOLISH	NAILS
JADE	SMELT	BEER	FOREHEAD	NAKED
JAMES	SNEER	BELLY	FORMAL	NARROW
JEALOUS	SORRY	BESS	FORT	NATIONS
JUDAS	SOUR	BETRAY'D	FORTNIGHT	NELL
KEEPER	SPAIN	BEYOND	FORWARD	NICK
KIN	SPELL	BILL	FOX	NILE
KINDNESS	SPOIL	BIRTH-DAY	FRONT	NOISY
LAME	SPRINGS	BITTER	FRUITS	OATH
LAMENT	SPURIOUS	BONE	FURNISH'D	ODDS
LEGS	STAFF	BOSOM	GALLANTS	OFFER
LICE	STALE	BREEDS	GIRLS	OFT'
LIVING	STARVING	BRIBES	GRANDEUR	ONELY
LOV'D	STATIONS	BRICKS	GREECE	ORE
MARCH	STOCKS	BROOD	GREEK	PATCH
MARKS	STOOP	BROW	GRIEV'D	PEERS
MASTERS	STOPT	BROWN	HANNAH	PENSION
MODEST	STRAW	BUSH	HAPPEN'D	PEOPLE'S
MONKEY	STRIFE	CAUSES	HARM	PERFORM
MONSTER	STRONGER	CEASE	HARMONIOUS	PERPETUAL
MOVING	STUBBORN	CENT	HEARING	PICKING
MUSE'S	SWAY	CHEESE	HEARTY	PIPE
NAT'RAL	SWINE	CLAWS	HECTOR	PLAINS
NEGLECT	TAKEN	CLERK	HERD	PLANT
NEIGHB'RING	TALKING	CLIENTS	HEROES	PLAY'D
NEIGHBOUR	TEMPLE	CLOWN	HEROICK	POCKETS
NEPTUNE	THAMES	COFFEE	HIDES	POEMS
NEST	THOU'LT	COIN	HONOURS	PORTER
NEW-FLUX'T	THROAT	COMMITTING	HOST	POW'RS
NIM	TOES	CONCEIV'D	HOUSES	PREPARE
NONSENSE	TOOLS	CONDESCEND	IMAGINE	PRESENTLY

6 (CONT.)	6 (CONT.)	5 (CONT.)	5 (CONT.)	5 (CONT.)
PRINCES	SWING	BRIDEGROOM	DROPT	JOIN'D
PROMISE	TALL	BRIGHTEST	DUCK	JOYS
PROTESTANT	TASK	BRINK	DWELT	KEEPING
PRUDENT	TAST	BRISK	EAGER	KEY
PRUDES	TERMS	BROWS	EAGLE	KINDRED
PUN	TETE	BULLY	EARNEST	LADYES
RADIANT	THEME	BUM	ENJOY	LADYS
RAGGED	THIEVES	BUTLER	ENLARGE	LANE
RASCALS	THIN	CANT	ENROLL'D	LASS
READER	THIRTY	CAUTION	ENTRING	LASTING
REALM	THOUSANDS	CELIA'S	EVILS	LAWFUL
REBUS	THREW	CELLS	EXCEEDING	LAWN
RECOVER	THRO	CENTER	EXCELLENCE	LEADS
REFORM	THRONG	CHARACTER	EXPECTED	LEATHERN
RELIGION	THROWS	CHARIOT	EXPECTS	LEAVINGS
REMAIN	TO-MORROW	CHARLES	FAIL'D	LESSONS
REMEMBER	TONE	CHASTE	FAINT	LIBELS
REMOV'D	TOOTH	CHATT'RING	FAIREST	LICENCE
REPENT	TORN	CHEATS	FALLING	LIFE'S
REPROACH	TRANSFORM'D	CHIMNEY	FAMILY	LIGHTS
REQUEST	TRAULUS	CHIMNY	FASHION	LIK'D
RESORT	TREASON	CHRYSTAL	FATHER'S	LOOSE
REVENGE	TRIBUTE	CLAIMS	FEEBLE	LOTH
REVIVE	TROOPS	CLAPS	FEEDING	LOVING
RIDES	VAINLY	CLIO	FEEDS	LUNGS
RINGS	VALIANT	CLOUDED	FLATT'RING	LUXURY
RITES	VAPOUR	CLUTTER	FLEER	LYRE
ROAST	VENTUR'D	COFFERS	FLIGHTS	MANLY
ROPE	VERDANT	COLOURS	FLOCK	MANNER
ROSES	VEXT	COMBINE	FLOW	MARS
RUB	VILEST	COMMONS	FLOW'R	MEASURE
RUIN'D	WAGES	COMPLAINS	FOLLOW'D	MELT
RUL'D	WAITS	COMPUTING	FOOTMEN	MENDING
RUSTY	WAND'RING	COMRADES	FOPS	MESSAGE
SAGES	WARE	CONFOUNDED	FORBID	METHOD
SAIL	WARNING	CONGREVE	FORESEE	MIDDLE
SANCROFT	WEALTHY	CONSPIRE	FORETEL	MODE
SCATTER'D	WEED	CONTENTED	FORTITUDE	MOLD
SCHEME	WHIP	COPY	FOUGHT	MOLL
SCHEMES	WILLIAM	CORINNA	FOUNTAIN	MONSTROUS
SCORNS	WINTER	CORRECT	FRANCE	MOUNTAINS
SCOT	WITT	CORRUPTIONS	FUND	MOUNTS
SECRETS	WOE	COUNTERFEIT	GAINS	MOURN
SEE'T	WRATH	COUNTRY'S	GALL	MOURNFUL
SERIOUS	WRITES	COUPLE	GALLOPING	NAIL
SERV'D	YARD	COURTED	GEN'RAL	NAP
SETS	YOUTHFUL	COURTIER	GENEROUS	NE'R
SHAKE		COWARD	GILDED	NE'RE
SHED	5	CRACK	GODDESSES	NED
SHEELAH		CRACKS	GOODLY	NETTLE
SHEEP	ACCOUNTS	CRACKT	GOODY	NICEST
SHEPHERD	ADMIRATION	CRAZY	GOTTEN	NIGHTINGAL
SHILLINGS	ADMIT	CREEPS	GOUT	NIMBLE
SHONE	AFFECT	CROOKED	GRATITUDE	NORTH
SHOULDERS	AFFECTED	CROWS	GRECIAN	NOTES
SHUN	ALMIGHTY	CULLY	GREEKS	O'RE
SID'S	AMBITIOUS	DAMES	GROWING	OAK
SIMILE	ANNUAL	DANCING	GRUB-STREET	OAR
SINGS	APPEARANCES	DAUGHTER	GUINEA	OCCASION
SINKS	APT	DEBTOR	HAIL	OCH
SLENDER	ARCH	DEBTS	HARP	OFFICE
SLOTH	ARM'D	DECAY	HATRED	OURS
SMILES	AROSE	DECEIT	HAUNT	OWL
SNOW	ARSES	DECENCY	HEARKEN	PAN
SORROW	ASLEEP	DECLINING	HEATHEN	PARENT
SOUTH	ATLAS	DECREED	HEDGES	PARNASSUS
SPARK	ATOMS	DEFY	HEEL	PASSES
SPITTLE	ATTENDS	DEMANDS	HELM	PATE
SPOIL'D	BABEL	DEN	HERETOFORE	PATHS
SPOILS	BARKING	DEPARTED	HILLS	PAULUS
STANDING	BARN	DESCENDED	HOLLOW	PAWS
STARE	BEGGAR'S	DESCENDING	HONOUR'S	PEDANTRY
START	BELIEVES	DESCENDS	HORN	PERQUISITES
STEAMS	BESTOWS	DESERVE	HORRID	PETITION
STEP	BETRAY	DEV'L	HOUSEHOLD	PHEASANT
STOPS	BIND	DEVICE	HYDE	PHIZ
STRAWS	BISHOP'S	DEVIL'S	IMPOSSIBLE	PICTURE
STREETS	BLEW	DEXT'ROUS	INCESSANT	PIERCE
STRUTS	BLOCKHEAD	DIRECTOR	INCLINES	PINIONS
STUDY	BLOOM	DISPATCH	INCREASE	PIPPIN
SUBMIT	BLOOMING	DISPOS'D	INFORM	PIT
SUFFER	BLOWS	DO'S	INTENDED	PLEASURES
SUMMER	BLUNDER	DOCTOR'S	INVENTION	PLUMP
SURLY	BOARD	DOING	INVITED	PLUNDER
SWALLOW	BORNE	DOOM	INWARD	PLUTO'S
SWEARING	BOW'D	DOORS	ITCH	POISON
SWEETLY	BREECH	DOVES	JAMES'S	POLITICIAN
SWELLING	BRIB'D	DOZEN	JAWS	POWERS

Column 1 — 5 (CONT.)

PRATING
PREFERR'D
PRELATES
PROFIT
PRONOUNC'D
PROTEST
PROUDLY
PROV'D
PROVIDENCE
PUBLIC
PUPPY
RAPS
RARE
RAT
RATTLE
REAR
RECEIV'D
RECEIVE
RECKON'D
REFLECTION
REFUS'D
REGIONS
REJOICE
REPEAT
REPRESENT
RESEMBLANCE
RESENT
RESPECT
REV'RENCE
REVILE
RHIMES
RHYMES
RIDICULE
RISES
RIVAL
RIVERS
ROAM
ROCKS
RODE
ROMANS
ROME
ROTTEN
RUBBISH
RURAL
SABLE
SAFELY
SALT
SAND
SAVAGE
SCANTY
SCAR'D
SCENT
SCHOLAR
SCHOOL-BOYS
SCORNFUL
SCOTTISH
SCRAP
SCRATCH
SCURVY
SEIZ'D
SENATES
SERVES
SHAM
SHELTER
SHEWN
SHOOT
SHOPS
SHRINE
SICKLY
SID
SIGH'D
SILKS
SILLY
SINCERE
SINGING
SLAVISH
SLOVEN
SLOW
SMEDLEY
SMILING
SMOCK
SOFTLY
SOLEMN
SORE
SOUTH-SEA
SOUTHERN
SPANIARD
SPARING

Column 2 — 5 (CONT.)

SPEAKING
SPHERE
SPREADS
SPUR
SPUTTER
STAIN
STALL
STEED
STEPS
STEWARD
STOUT
STRICTLY
STROLE
SUM
SUSPENDED
SWAGGER
SWARM
SWARMS
SYSTEM
TALES
TALK'D
TAME
TAX
TEAZE
TERM
THOU'RT
THREAD
THUMB
TIMBER
TOMB
TOUCH'D
TOW'R
TRAVEL
TREACH'ROUS
TREES
TRICE
TURNING
TYPE
UNITED
UNSAV'RY
UPON'T
UPWARDS
VANITY
VAPOURS
VAULT
VICAR
VICEROY
VICTORIOUS
VICTUALS
VIEW'D
VIEWS
VILLAIN
VIRGIL
VIRTUE'S
VOTES
VOW'D
VULCAN
WARN
WATCHFUL
WEEP
WEEPING
WEIGH
WHENEVER
WHERE'S
WHIMS
WHISP'RING
WHISPER
WHOLLY
WINDSOR
WINES
WINK
WISDOM'S
WONDERFUL
WONDERS
WONDROUS
WORM
WOUNDS
WRAPT
WRITER
WROUGHT
YOUNGER

4

<LYNDSAY>
<ZOUNDS>
A-BED
ABSURD

Column 3 — 4 (CONT.)

ACCEPT
ACCOUNT
ACTED
ACTIVE
ACTORS
AD
ADMIRES
ADORN'D
ADVANCES
AFFECTION
ALEXANDER
ALLOWS
ALLUSION
AMIDST
AMISS
ANIMALS
APPROVE
ARGUMENT
ASK'D
ASPECT
ASPIRE
ASSUME
ATTEMPTS
ATTENDED
AUKWARD
AURORA
AUTHOR'S
AVAIL
AWAKE
AY
BACCHUS
BAIT
BAND
BANKER
BARK
BATTLE
BAWL
BEATEN
BECOMES
BEFITS
BEGET
BEGGARS
BEGS
BERKELEY
BESPATTER
BETIMES
BITCH
BLAB
BLADE
BLEED
BLOT
BOASTED
BODY'S
BOLTON
BOOBY
BOON
BOTTLES
BRAG
BRANCHES
BREAKFAST
BREASTS
BRIGHTER
BRITAIN'S
BROCADE
BUBBLE
BUNDLE
BURNING
BURNT
BURTHEN
BURY
CABBIN
CAELIA'S
CARCASE
CARD
CARROTS
CASSY
CASTLES
CATTLE
CAUTIOUS
CELEBRATE
CHAIRS
CHAMPION
CHANGES
CHAPS
CHARITY
CHARM
CHARM'D
CHEATED

Column 4 — 4 (CONT.)

CHEER
CHOICEST
CHOIR
CHRIST
CHRISTIANS
CHURCH'S
CHYMISTS
CLAN
CLAP
CLATT'RING
CLATTER
CLEARLY
CLOATHS
CLOTH
CLOVEN
COALS
COBLING
COMBS
COMMEND
COMMISSION
COMMON-WEAL
COMPLAINTS
COMPLEXION
COMPOSITION
COMPOUND
COMRADE
CONCEAL'D
CONCEITS
CONCERNS
CONDITION
CONFESS'D
CONFEST
CONQUER
CONQUEST
CONSCIOUS
CONSULTING
CONTEMPT
CONTENDING
CONTINU'D
CONVERSE
COOL
COQUETTE
CORPS
COVER'D
CRAMM'D
CREAM
CREATURES
CREPT
CROUDS
CROWDED
CRYES
CURRENT
CUTTING
CYNTHIA
CYPRIAN
DAN'S
DANGEROUS
DAR'D
DE'EL
DEALS
DEBTORS
DECAYS
DECLINE
DEEDS
DEEPLY
DEFECT
DELICATE
DELIGHTFUL
DELUDED
DEPENDS
DESERT
DESPIS'D
DESPISES
DESTROY
DEVOUR
DEVOURING
DEVOUT
DIDO
DIN'D
DISAPPOINT
DISAPPOINTED
DISCERN
DISCHARGE
DISCOURSE
DISCOVERS
DISPENSE
DISPLAY
DISPOSE

Column 5 — 4 (CONT.)

DISTRESS
DOMESTICK
DORE
DOTH
DOUBTFUL
DRAG
DRAGS
DRAUGHT
DREADFULL
DRINKING
DRUMS
DUB
DUES
DUKES
DULNESS
DUMB
DUNGHILL
DUTCH
DYES
E'EN
EKE
ELRINGTON
ELYSIAN
EMBLEMS
EMPLOYS
ENEMIES
ENEMY
ENGAG'D
ENGLOND
ENTERS
ENUFF
EQUALLY
ERROR
EUROPE'S
EXACT
EXPREST
FACES
FANATICK
FASHIONABLE
FAVOUR'D
FAVOURS
FAWNING
FEAR'D
FEATHER
FIGURES
FINCH
FINELY
FIRES
FIRMLY
FIST
FLAMING
FLAT
FLEECE
FLING
FLOOR
FLOW'RY
FLUNG
FOOTMAN
FORC'T
FORMING
FORSAKE
FORSAKEN
FORSOOTH
FORTUNE'S
FORTUNES
FRAME
FRAUGHT
FURIOUS
FUSTIAN
GALE
GAPES
GARDEN
GARMENTS
GARRETS
GARTERS
GATH'RING
GATHER'D
GAUDY
GAUL
GENERAL
GENTLEMAN
GENTLEMEN
GENTRY
GENUINE
GIBE
GIVEN
GLOBE
GODLIKE

GOODNESS
GOSPEL
GRAINS
GRANDSON
GRATIFY
GREY
GRIEVOUS
GRIM
GRIN
GROAN
GROPE
GROVE
GROWTH
GRUBSTREET
GUARDIAN
GUESS'D
GUINEAS
GUINNEA
GUMS
HAG
HANDLE
HANGS
HANOVER
HAPPINESS
HARDEST
HARLEY'S
HARPY
HATES
HAWKERS
HEAV'NS
HELPLESS
HERALDRY
HERRING
HIBERNIAN
HIDEOUS
HIGHNESS
HINDER
HIR'D
HOH
HONESTY
HOOK
HORNS
HORSES
HOUNDS
HUG
HUM'ROUS
HUMBLED
HUNGRY
ILLS
IMAGE
IMAGINATION
IMPART
IMPARTIAL
IMPRESSION
IMPROV'D
IMPUDENCE
INCOME
INFAMY
INSTINCT
INTEND
INTEREST
INVENT
INVOKE
IRELAND
ISSUE
ITSELF
JARGON
JAYL
JEWS
JOAN
JOBB
JOLLY
JOURNIES
JUNO'S
KINDLE
KINGDOMS
KNOCK'T
LAMBS
LAMPOON
LANK
LARGER
LARGEST
LATIN
LAUGHING
LAUGHTER
LAZY
LD
LEISURE

LESSON
LEVEE
LIBEL
LIFTS
LIGHT'NING
LINTOT
LITTER
LIV'D
LOADS
LOCK
LOLLOPING
LORDSHIP'S
LOUDLY
LOVE'S
LUCK
LUMBER
LY'D
LYON
MAIDS
MALICIOUS
MARGIN
MARKET
MARKET-HILL
MARRY
MARRY'D
MATCHLESS
MAUL
MAUL'D
MAXIMS
MAY'ST
MEAGRE
MEALS
MELTS
MEMBERS
MEN'S
MENDS
METAMORPHOS'D
METAPHOR
MIDST
MIMICK
MINDED
MISS'D
MISSING
MISTAKES
MITRED
MIX'D
MIXT
MIXTURE
MOCKS
MONARCHS
MONUMENT
MOP
MORDANTO
MORTIFY
MORTIFY'D
MOTIONS
MOUNTAIN
MOUNTED
MOUSE
NANCY
NASTY
NAUSEOUS
NEAT
NEEDLESS
NEGLECTED
NIGHTS
NODS
NORTHERN
NOSES
NOTICE
NOTIONS
OBLIGE
OBLIGING
OCEAN
OFFEND
OFFENDED
OFFSPRING
ORIGINAL
OVID
OW'D
OYL
PAGES
PAMPHLETS
PANEGYRICK
PAPERS
PARENTS
PARK
PARLIAMENT

PARTIES
PASTE
PATRIOT
PATRONS
PAWN
PEACOCK
PEEPING
PEGASUS
PENNY
PER
PERFORM'D
PERMIT
PERSONS
PHEBUS
PHIL
PHYSICIAN
PICK'D
PICK'T
PILLS
PIMP
PIN
PITCH
PLANET
PLENTEOUS
PLIGHT
PLINY
PLUTO
POIS'NOUS
POLE
POLITE
POLITICIANS
POSSESS'T
POW'RFUL
PRAIS'D
PRANKS
PRATES
PREPAR'D
PREVENT
PRIMATE
PRINCIPLES
PRINTS
PRITHEE
PRIVILEGE
PRODIGIOUS
PROGRESS
PROMIS'D
PROP
PROVERB
PULPIT
PURLING
QUALITY
QUEST
RACK
RAG
RAILING
RAPTURE
RAPTURES
RATTLING
RAV'NOUS
RAVE
RAVES
RAY
REACH'D
REALLY
REALMS
REBEL
REBELLIOUS
RECOMMEND
RECONCILE
REEKING
REGAL
REIGNS
RELATE
RELISH
REMARK
REMOVE
REPORTS
REQUIRES
RESOLUTION
RESPECTS
RETRIEVE
RETURNS
REVEREND
RHYMING
RICHER
RIDDLES
RIDING
RIGHTS

RIMES
ROADS
ROAR'D
ROARING
ROBB'D
ROLLS
ROOMS
ROTE
ROW
RUINS
RUNG
SAIL'D
SALAMANDER
SALE
SALUTES
SATE
SATURN
SATYRS
SAUCY
SAUNDERS
SCARLET
SCHOOL-BOY
SCREEN
SECT
SECTS
SECURELY
SEEST
SENATE-HOUSE
SERPENT
SHADY
SHAKES
SHARPER
SHEARS
SHIPS
SHIRT
SHOCK
SHOP
SHOULDER
SHOW'R
SHRILL
SHRUG
SIGNS
SINKING
SKILFUL
SLAIN
SLAVERY
SLEPT
SLIPT
SMALLEST
SMITHFIELD
SNAKE
SOAR
SOCRATES
SOLOMON
SOLVE
SOMEWHAT
SOUGHT
SOW
SPAR'D
SPAWN
SPHERES
SPILT
SPIRE
SPROUT
SPUNGE
SPY'D
STAKE
STATES
STATESMAN'S
STEALTH
STEEL
STEWS
STING
STINKS
STRAIGHT
STRAND
STRANGELY
STRANGERS
STRIPT
STRUTTING
STUBBLE
STYX
SUBDUE
SUBLUNARY
SUCCEED
SUPPER
SUPPLY'D
SUPREME

SURELY
SURPRIZ'D
SURROUNDED
SURVEY
SUSPEND
SWORDS
TAINTED
TEAGUES
TEMPER
TEMPEST
TEMPLES
TENDS
TERROR
TERRORS
THALIA
THEY'VE
THINKING
THITHER
THOROW
THURSDAY
TIPT
TIR'D
TO-DAY
TOOL
TORRENT
TOST
TRANSLATED
TRAVELS
TREASURE
TRESSES
TRIUMPHAL
TROLLOPING
TROPHIES
TROUBLED
TRUMPET
TRUMPETS
TRYAL
TUESDAY
TUMBLE
TUMBLING
TWAIN
TYE
UNDERNEATH
UNDERTAKE
UNKIND
USEFUL
USES
VALES
VALU'D
VICIOUS
VIGOR
VIGOUR
VIRGINS
VITAL
VOGUE
VOICES
VOID
VOLUME
VOUCHSAFE
WAFT
WAG
WAINSCOT
WAITED
WAKE
WALKING
WALPOLE'S
WANDRING
WANTING
WARRANT
WASH
WATCHING
WEAL
WEAVERS
WER'T
WERT
WHALE
WHARTON
WHEELS
WHELP
WHIPS
WHISPERS
WHITEHALL
WHOLESOME
WIGS
WILLING
WINDOWS
WIPE
WIRE

WISEST	BLESSINGS	COMMENCE	DEVOUTLY	FARMERS
WITCH	BLUNDERS	COMMITTED	DICE	FASTEN'D
WITCHES	BLUSHES	COMMITTEE	DIET	FASTER
WITHDREW	BOAR	COMMODIOUS	DIFFICULTY	FASTNED
WOLF	BOASTS	COMMONERS	DINT	FATE'S
WOMAN'S	BOATS	COMPANION	DIP	FEARFUL
WRETCHES	BOLINGBROKE	COMPLEATLY	DIPT	FEMAL
WRITTEN	BOOTS	COMPOSE	DIRECTED	FEMALS
YELLOW	BORROW	CONCEITED	DIRECTLY	FERRY
YIELDS	BOTTLING	CONCLUSIONS	DISARM	FICTION
ZEALOUS	BOUNDS	CONFESS'T	DISCERNING	FILLETS
	BOUNTEOUS	CONFINE	DISCLOSE	FISHES
3	BOUNTY	CONFUS'D	DISTINCTLY	FITTER
	BOW'RS	CONFUSION	DISTINGUISH	FITTEST
'T	BOWELS	CONGEE	DISTINGUISH'D	FLACCUS
AB	BRANCH	CONSORT	DISTURBS	FLANDERS
ABANDON'D	BRAT	CONSTITUTION	DISUSE	FLANK
ACCIDENTS	BREACH	CONSUME	DIVERSION	FLAXEN
ACCOMPLISH'D	BREATHING	CONTINUES	DOMINION	FLEAS
ACE	BREWING	CONTRADICT	DOST	FLEET
ACQUAINTANCE	BRIDLE	CONTRIVANCE	DOUBLY	FLINCH
ACQUAINTED	BRIDLES	CONTRIVING	DOUBTS	FLIRTS
ADAM	BRIEF	CONVICT	DOWNS	FLORA
ADMIR'D	BROAD	CONVINC'D	DRABS	FLOUNCE
ADORES	BROOK	CONVINC'T	DRAINS	FLOURISH
ADVANTAGE	BRUSH	COOK—MAID	DRAM	FLOURISHING
ADVENTURES	BUBBLED	COQUETS	DREADS	FLOWERS
AFFORDS	BULLETS	CORD	DREGS	FLOWN
AFORESAID	BURNISH'D	CORNS	DRESSING	FLOWS
AFTERNOON	BURY'D	CORRUPT	DRESST	FLOYD
AGAYNE	BUTCHER	CORRUPTION	DRIVING	FLYING
AGED	BUTCHERS	COUNSEL	DRONE	FOKES
AGREED	BUZZING	COUNTENANCE	DROOPING	FOLLOWING
ALCIDES	CANDLE	COURTIER'S	DROPPING	FOOTSTEPS
ALLIANCE	CANDLE—LIGHT	COWSLIP	DROSS	FOP
ALLWAYS	CANE	CRAPE	DRUDGE	FORETEL
AMENDS	CANON	CRAVE	DRUNKEN	FORGE
AMOROUS	CANONS	CRAWLS	DRY'D	FORGETS
AMPLY	CANST	CREATES	DUCAL	FORLORN
ANCESTORS	CANTING	CREATION	DUG	FORSOOK
ANIMAL	CAP	CREEPING	DUNS	FOUNTAINS
ANNE	CAPACITY	CRINGING	EARN	FOWL
ANON	CAREFUL	CRITICK'S	EARNESTLY	FRAUD
ANTIQUE	CARESS	CROP	EAST	FREED
APACE	CAREST	CROSSES	ECCHO	FRETS
APART	CAROLINE	CROWDS	ELBOWS	FRIENDLY
APPLAUSE	CARRIED	CROWNS	ELEGIES	FRIGID
APPLES	CARRY'D	CRUELTY	ELEMENTS	FRISK
APPROBATION	CASH	CUCKOLD	EMBRACE	FRIZE
ARCHITECT	CAVAN	CUDGELL'D	EMBROIDER'D	FROTH
ARISTOPHANES	CERBERUS	CUDGELS	EMPRESS	FROTHY
ARTFULLY	CHAFF	CUPID'S	ENDEAVOUR	FRUITLESS
ARTIST	CHAIR—MEN	CURATE	ENDOW	FRYER
ASS'S	CHANC'D	CURL	ENGLAND'S	FUME
ASSIST	CHANGING	CURR	ENLARG'D	GAIT
ASSISTANCE	CHAOS	CURS	ENTIRELY	GALLANT
ASSUMES	CHASM	CURSES	ENTRANCE	GALLOP
ASSUR'D	CHEAPEN	CUTS	ENTRY	GAPS
AUTHORITY	CHECK	D'YE	ERE	GARLAND
BAIL	CHICK	DAMNS	ERR	GARLANDS
BALLS	CHICKEN	DANIEL	ERRORS	GARRET
BANDS	CHIDE	DAWN	ESCAPES	GATES
BANKERS	CHILLING	DEANERY	ESSAYS	GATHER
BARGAIN	CHINK	DECENTLY	ESSENCE	GENIAL
BATH	CHYMICK	DECIDE	ESTEEM'D	GENTEEL
BATTER'D	CIBBER	DECLARE	EUROPE	GENTLY
BAWL'D	CIRCUMSTANCE	DECLIN'D	EVENING	GERMAN
BAWN	CLAIM'D	DECLINES	EX	GIBES
BEAUS	CLARET	DECORUM	EXALT	GILDING
BEAUTIES	CLEANLY	DEED	EXALTS	GIV'N
BEAVER	CLERGYMEN	DEFIN'D	EXAMPLE	GIVING
BEC	CLEVER	DEGEN'RATE	EXCEED	GLANCE
BEDS	CLIMATE	DEGENERATE	EXCEL	GLASSES
BEES	CLOAK	DELUSION	EXCELL'D	GLOOMY
BEG'D	CLOCK	DEMAND	EXCELLENCIES	GLOVES
BEGGAR	CLOSET	DEMEAN	EXCISE	GLOW
BEHAVIOUR	CLOUT	DEMURE	EXHAL'D	GOATS
BELLES	CLOY'D	DENY'D	EXPERIMENT	GOOD—NATUR'D
BELLIES	CLUBS	DEPOSE	EXPIRING	GOODS
BEMOAN	COADJUTOR	DEPTH	EXPLAINING	GOUN
BENCHES	COCK	DESCENT	EXPLODED	GOVERNMENT
BESPEAKS	COFFEE—HOUSE	DESERVING	EXTEND	GRACIOUS
BETTY'S	COFFIN	DESIR'D	FABLES	GRASP
BILLET—DOUX	COIFS	DESP'RATE	FADE	GRATEFUL
BIN	COL'NEL	DESTROY'D	FAGGOT	GRAZE
BIRCH	COLOUR	DESTRUCTIVE	FAILING	GRAZIER'S
BLASPHEME	COMBIN'D	DETRACTORS	FAIRER	GREEDY
BLESS'D	COMMANDS	DEVOTED	FANS	GRINNING

GROANING	JACOBITES	MENTION	PEDANT	PROPHET
GROANS	JADES	MENTION'D	PEDLAR	PROSTITUTE
GROOM	JASON	METAL	PEERAGE	PROTECTION
GROUNDS	JEER	METEOR	PEEVISH	PROTESTANTS
GUARDS	JET	METHOUGHT	PELL-MELL	PROVES
GUDGEON	JEW	METRE	PELTED	PROVISION
GUESTS	JEWELS	MILK-WHITE	PENCIL	PROVOK'D
GUIDES	JIM	MILKY	PENS	PROVOKE
GUILE	JOB	MINDING	PERFIDIOUS	PUBLISH
GUN	JOGLING	MINES	PERPLEX'D	PUFF
HABIT	JOHNSON	MISFORTUNE	PERVERSELY	PUFF'D
HAEC	JOINS	MISLED	PERVERSENESS	PULL'D
HALL	JOINT	MOB	PETTICOAT	PUNISH
HALTER	JUDGEMENT	MODISH	PEWS	PURSUITS
HANGING	JUDGMENTS	MOLLY	PHOENIX	PUSS
HAPLY	JUG	MONSTERS	PHRASES	QUADRILL
HARANGU'D	JUPITER	MONTHS	PHYLLIS	QUADRILLE
HARMONY	JURY	MORALIST	PICKT	QUENCH
HARRY'S	JUSTLING	MORGAN	PIERC'D	QUILCA
HAUNTS	KICK	MORTAR	PIES	RACK'D
HELSHAM	KICKT	MORTGAGE	PIETY	RAGES
HENCEFORTH	KILL'D	MOTHERS	PIGS	RAINS
HENCEFORWARD	KINDER	MOTTO	PILLAGE	RAINY
HERCULES	KISS'D	MOURN'D	PIMPS	RANDOM
HERDS	KISS'T	MUDDY	PINDUS	RANG'D
HERMES	KITCHEN	MULLINIX	PLACING	RANT
HERMITS	KNACK	MURMURING	PLAGUES	RAP
HERO'S	KNEE	MUTE	PLAGUY	RAPT
HERRINGS	KNELL	MUTUAL	PLAISTER	RARELY
HIGH'R	LAKE	NATALE	PLATES	RATES
HIGHLY	LANDLORD'S	NAUGHTY	PLAY-HOUSE	REAR'D
HOARSE	LARGELY	NECESSITY	PLAYER	REARS
HOIST	LASTLY	NEGLECTS	PLAYERS	REASON'S
HOLLAND	LATENT	NEIGHBOURHOOD	PLEADER	REASONS
HONESTLY	LATTER	NEIGHBOURING	PLEADING	REBECCA
HONOR	LAWYER'S	NICER	PLEADS	RECLINING
HONOUR'D	LEAGUE	NIGH	PLEAS'D	RECOLLECT
HOPEFUL	LEAGUES	NIGHT-GOWN	PLEASES	RECOVER'D
HOPING	LEAKY	NIGHT'S	PLEDGES	REDEEM
HORNED	LEAPS	NIGHTLY	PLODDING	REDUC'D
HOSE	LEARN'T	NOBLEST	PLUCK	REFLECT
HOUND	LEASE	NOODLE	PLUMBS	REGARDLESS
HOV'RING	LECTURES	NON	PLUMES	REJOYCE
HOWARD	LENDS	NONSENCE	PLY	RELATION
HUES	LIBERTAS	NOOSE	POCKY	RELATIONS
HUMANITY	LIGHTED	NOTION	POISON'D	REMAINING
HUNTED	LINK	NUMBERLESS	POLISH	REMEMBERS
HUNTERS	LION	NUMEROUS	POLLUTE	REMEMBRANCE
HURT	LIST'NING	O'	POND'ROUS	REMNANT
HUSBANDS	LITTER'D	O'R'E	POP'LAR	REMOTE
IDEAS	LIVER	OATS	POPISH	REPAIRS
IDEOTS	LOADED	OBEDIENT	PORCH	REPARTEE
IERNE	LODGINGS	OBEYS	PORE	REPEATS
IGNOBLE	LONGS	OBSERVATION	POSSESS'D	REPLY
IMAGIN'D	LOVER'S	OBSERVES	POSSESST	REPLY'D
IMAGINARY	LOWEST	OBTAIN'D	POSSEST	REPROACHES
IMITATE	LOWLY	OCCASIONS	POUR	REPUTATION
IMPENDING	LOYAL	ODE	POURS	RESEMBLING
IMPERIAL	LUMP	ODOURS	POVERTY	RESIGNS
IMPERIOUS	LURKS	OFFALS	PRACTIS'D	RESTLESS
IMPORTANCE	LUXURIANT	OLYMPUS	PRACTISE	RESTOR'D
IMPRIMIS	MAGGOTS	OMENS	PRAETOR	RETAIL
IMPS	MAIDENS	OPPRESSION	PRAY'R	REVENG'D
IMPUTED	MAINTAINS	OPPREST	PREACHERS	REVERSE
INCENSE	MAJESTICK	OR'E	PREACHING	RHIMING
INCLINE	MALIGNANT	ORIGINE	PREDECESSORS	RIBBONS
INCREAS'D	MANAGE	OUNCE	PREGNANT	RICHES
INFERNAL	MANGLED	OUTDONE	PREMIER	RID
INFINITE	MANSION	OVER-RUN	PRESENTED	RIGHTEOUS
INJUR'D	MARBLE	OVERTHROWN	PRESENTS	RIME
INN	MARBLE-HILL	OWNER	PRESERV'D	RIOT
INQUIRE	MARINER	OWNERS	PRESIDES	RIPE
INSIST	MARTIAL	OYSTERS	PRETENDS	RIPEN
INSOLENT	MARTIN	PAINTS	PREVAILS	RIPEN'D
INSPIRING	MASQUERADE	PAMPHLET	PRIMITIVE	RIPENS
INSTANCE	MAW	PARADOX	PRINCELY	RIVALS
INSTRUCT	MAWL'D	PARNASSUS'	PRINTED	RIVER
INSTRUCTED	MAY-FAIR	PARSON'S	PRINTER	ROARS
INTERRUPT	MAY'R	PARTIAL	PRIVY	ROBES
INTRODUCE	MEANEST	PARTRIDGE	PROCEEDING	RODS
INTRUDE	MED'CINE	PARTRIDGES	PROCEEDS	ROLL
INVERTED	MED'CINES	PASS'T	PROCURE	ROMAN
INVISIBLE	MEDALS	PATES	PRODUCES	ROMANCES
IRELAND'S	MEDDLE	PATIENT	PROFANE	ROMANTICK
IRONY	MEDLEY	PATRICK	PROFESSION	ROOTED
ISLES	MELODIOUS	PATRIOTS	PROLIFICK	ROT
ISSUES	MEMORY	PAWN'D	PROLOGUE	ROUSE
ITEM	MENS	PEASE	PROMOTION	RUDDY

3 (CONT.)	3 (CONT.)	3 (CONT.)	3 (CONT.)	2 (CONT.)
RUDENESS	SPRUCE	TIMELY	WEIGH'D	AKE
RUFFLES	SQUEEZ'D	TOE	WELKIN	ALACK
RULING	STAIN'D	TOPS	WESTERN	ALARMS
RUMBLING	STAINS	TOM'S	WHEREOF	ALBION
RUNDLE	STANDER-BY	TORCH	WHERRY	ALDERMAN
SACK	STANDERS-BY	TORE	WHINE	ALDERMEN
SALUTE	STARTS	TORTUR'D	WHISPER'D	ALE-HOUSE
SANDS	STEADY	TOSS	WHOLSOME	ALLEGIANCE
SASH	STEALING	TOW'RDS	WIFE'S	ALLIES
SAVIOUR	STEAM	TOWER	WILDERNESS	ALMANACKS
SCALE	STEERAGE	TOWNS	WILE	ALTAR
SCATT'RING	STEPT	TOWZER	WILL'S	ALTERATION
SCOLDING	STIFLE	TOYS	WILLIAM'S	ALTITUDE
SCOLDS	STIL'D	TRAGICK	WINDING	AMARANTHINE
SCOTCH	STIRR'D	TRAIL	WINS	AMAZEMENT
SCOURGE	STOCKING	TRANSCRIBE	WINTER'S	AMAZING
SCRAWL	STOCKINGS	TRANSLATE	WISH'D	AMOUNT
SCREAM'D	STOR'D	TRANSPORTED	WISH'T	AMOUNTS
SCRUB	STRANGER	TRAYTORS	WISHT	AMPHIBIOUS
SCURRILOUS	STRICT	TREADS	WOFUL	ANCHOR
SEAL	STRIKES	TREASURES	WOMANKIND	ANEW
SEARCH'D	STROKE	TREMBLE	WONDER'D	ANGEL-INN
SEASONS	STROLLER	TREMBLES	WOOD-PARK	ANGEL'S
SECUR'D	STROLLERS	TREPANN'D	WOODPARK	ANGLESEY
SEEMING	STRUGGLE	TRIM	WOODS	ANGUISH
SELLING	STRUNG	TROOP	WOOL	ANSWER'D
SENATORS	STRUT	TROPES	WOOLLEN	ANTAEUS
SENCE	STUDIES	TROY	WOOLSTON	ANTIC
SENTENCE	STUDIOUS	TRUCE	WORKING	ANTIQUATED
SERENE	STUFF'D	TRUMP	WORKMEN	ANXIOUS
SERMONS	SUBDU'D	TRUMPS	WORMS	APPEARANCE
SERVILE	SUBMISSION	TRUNK	WOT	APPEARING
SETTING	SUBSTANCE	TRUSTY	WOULD'ST	APPLIES
SETTLE	SUBTLE	TUB	WREATH	APPROVES
SEVERAL	SUFFER'D	TUBS	WRITINGS	ARBUTHNOT
SEXES	SUFFERS	TUG	YEAR'S	ARCADIANS
SEXTON	SUITS	TURD	YEARLY	ARCHDEACON
SHAMEFUL	SUN-SHINE	TURK	YOKE	ARCHES
SHAN'T	SUN'S	TWIG		ARCHIBALD
SHAP'D	SUNDAY	TWINE	2	ARDELIA
SHEET	SUPPLYES	TWISTED		ARDELIA'S
SHEPHERDS	SUPPORTING	TYRANT'S	<BURNET'S>	ARGU'D
SHERRY	SUPPOSING	TYRANTS	<CARR>	ARK
SHIELD	SUREST	TYTH	<CLEMENTS>	ARM-PITS
SHINING	SUSPECT	TYTHES	<DILKS>	ARMAGH
SHIRTS	SUSPENCE	ULCERS	<FARTS>	ARMIS
SHOOK	SUSPICION	UNDERGO	<HARRISON>	ARMOUR
SHOW'RS	SWANS	UNHEARD	<SHIT>	ARRAY'D
SHREWD	SWEDEN	UNION	'GAINST	ARTHUR'S
SIMPLICITY	SWEEPS	UNITES	'PRENTICE	ARTICLE
SINCERELY	SWEETEST	UNJUST	'SCAP'T	ARTIFICES
SINGLY	SWELL	UNJUSTLY	A-CLOCK	ARTIFICIAL
SIRRAH	SWEPT	UNRULY	A-DREAM'D	ARTIFICIALL
SISTERS	SWIFT'S	UNSUNG	A-FOOT	ARTILLERY
SITTING	SWIFTLY	UNTOWARD	A-WHILE	ARTLESS
SIX-PENCE	SWIMS	UPPER	ABHOR'D	ASCENDS
SIXTEEN	SYLLABLE	UPWARD	ABLER	ASPERSION
SKINNY	SYRIUS	USING	ABORTIVE	ASPIR'D
SKIP	T'YE	USUALL	ABOUND	ASSASSIN
SLANDER	TABLES	USURP	ABSTRUSE	ASSERT
SLAUGHTER	TARTAR	VALLIES	ABUNDANCE	ASSIGN
SLEEK	TATTLE	VANISH	ACCUSE	ASTORE
SLEEPS	TATTLING	VARIANCE	ACCUSER	ASTRAY
SLIGHT	TAWNY	VARLET	ACQUIR'D	ASTRIDE
SLIT	TAYLOR	VEINS	ACROSS	ASTROLOGER
SLOPS	TEACHING	VELVET	ACTING	ASTROLOGERS
SLOWLY	TEAGUE	VENTURES	ACUTE	ASUNDER
SMALLER	TEARING	VEST	ADAMANTINE	ATHEISTS
SMELLS	TEDIOUS	VEX'D	ADDISON	ATOM
SMOCKS	TEIZ'D	VICEGERENT	ADDRESS'D	ATTACKS
SMOKE	TEIZE	VICTIM	ADDRESSES	ATTENDANCE
SNEAKING	TEMPESTS	VISIONARY	ADHER'D	ATTEST
SOLDIER	TEMPESTUOUS	VITTELS	ADMITS	ATTRACT
SOLUM	TEND	VIZ	ADMITTED	AUDIENCE
SONNETS	TENDERNESS	VOLUMES	ADO	AUTHENTICK
SORES	TETHER	VOT'RIES	ADONIS	AWARE
SPADILLO	THANKFUL	VOTARIES	ADORNS	AWFUL
SPARROWS	THEY'D	WAK'D	ADVANC'T	AWHILE
SPEAKER	THOMAS	WALES	ADVENT'RER	AZURE
SPEAKS	THORNS	WAND	AENEAS	B
SPECTRE	THOU'ST	WANDER	AETHER	BABES
SPED	THOUR'T	WANTON	AETHERIAL	BABOON
SPEECHES	THREAD-BARE	WARMER	AFFAIR	BACKWARDS
SPIES	THREATEN	WEAKER	AFFECTIONS	BAG
SPIGHTFUL	THREESCORE	WEDG'D	AFFIRM'D	BAGS
SPINNING	THRIVES	WEEDS	AFTER-TIMES	BAILIFFS
SPIRES	THROATS	WEEKLY	AIDING	BAILY
SPOKEN	TIDINGS	WEEN	AIM'D	BAITED

BALANCE
BALDWIN
BALLAD
BALLADS
BALLANCE
BANE
BANISH'D
BANKER'S
BANKRUPTS
BANQUET
BARBER
BARBER'S
BARGAINS
BASIN
BASIS
BASON
BASTARD
BASTINGS
BAT
BAULK
BAWTY
BEAK
BEATING
BECK'NING
BEDLAM
BEFELL
BEGETS
BEGINNING
BEGOT
BEGUILE
BEHAVE
BEHOLDS
BELATED
BELLS
BENDED
BENDING
BENDS
BENEFACTORS
BEQUEATH'D
BERLIN
BESMEAR'D
BETRAYS
BETT
BETTESWORTH
BIBLE
BIGGER
BINDS
BISHOPRICK
BISHOPRICKS
BITING
BLACK-GUARD
BLAM'D
BLASPHEMY
BLAZE
BLEEDING
BLINDLY
BLOATED
BLOCK
BLOCK-HEADS
BLOSSOM
BLOTCHES
BLUNDER'D
BLUNT
BLUSH'D
BOASTING
BODIES
BOIL
BOLDER
BOLT
BONDAGE
BONY
BOORS
BOOTH
BORDER'D
BOTCH
BOUGHS
BOUNDLESS
BOW'R
BOWER
BOWERS
BOWLS
BOYL
BRAGG'D
BRANGLING
BREAKING
BREATH'D
BRENT
BREW

BRIAREUS
BRIDEWELL
BRIDGE
BRIERS
BRIM
BRITANNIA
BRITTAIN
BRITTISH
BROTH
BROTHERS
BRUIS'D
BRUISE
BRUTISH
BRY'R
BUBBLING
BUCKETS
BUDGET
BUILDER
BUMS
BUNGLING
BURNISH
BURNS
BURSTING
BURTHENS
BUZZ
BY-STANDER
BY'T
CA'NDISH
CAESAR'S
CAGE
CAITIFF
CAKE
CALF
CALLD
CALM
CALVIN
CAMBRIDGE
CANAL
CANCER
CANDIDATES
CANNONS
CAPITALS
CAPRICIOUS
CAPS
CARCASS
CAREFULLY
CARESS'D
CARESSING
CARRION
CARTERET
CARVING
CARY
CASEMENT
CASES
CASSINUS
CATCHES
CATO
CATS
CAVE
CEAS'D
CEASED
CENSORIOUS
CENSURES
CENSURING
CENTAURS
CENTRE
CENTRY
CHAIRMAN
CHAIRMEN
CHAISE
CHALLENGE
CHAMBERS
CHAMPIONS
CHANT
CHARACTERS
CHARG'D
CHARGES
CHARING-CROSS
CHARMER
CHARON
CHARON'S
CHARTRES
CHATRES
CHATTER
CHEAPER
CHEARFUL
CHEW
CHICKENS

CHIEFEST
CHINTS
CHLORIS
CHOAK
CHOSEN
CHURCH-YARD
CHURLISH
CHUSES
CIELING
CINDERCOLA
CIRCLING
CITYES
CLACK
CLAMBER
CLASSICKS
CLAW
CLEANING
CLEANLINESS
CLEARS
CLEM
CLICK
CLIENT'S
CLIMATES
CLIMB'D
CLIMBS
CLIME
CLINCH
CLOACINE
CLOAKS
CLOD
CLOSELY
CLOSER
CLUMSY
COARSE
COAST
COATS
COBBLE
COBLER
COBLERS
COCKADE
CODILL
CODLING
COG
COIN'D
COLBERTEEN
COLCHOS
COLLECTION
COLLEGES
COLOUR'D
COMB
COMBAT
COMBING
COMFORT
COMMENC'D
COMMISSIONS
COMMON-PLACES
COMMONWEAL
COMPARING
COMPARISONS
COMPASS
COMPASSION
COMPLAIN'D
COMPLAISANCE
COMPLETELY
COMPLIMENTS
COMPOUNDED
COMPREHEND
CONCEIT
CONCERN'D
CONCERNING
CONCLUDING
CONDEMN
CONDESCENSION
CONFER
CONFIDE
CONFINES
CONJ'RERS
CONJ'RING
CONJECTURES
CONJURER
CONQU'RORS
CONQUER'D
CONSENTING
CONSEQUENCE
CONSIGN'D
CONSISTS
CONSTANCY
CONSTRAINT

CONSUL'S
CONSUMING
CONTEND
CONTINUED
CONTRARY
CONTRIVER
CONTRIVES
CONTROULS
CONVENIENT
CONVERT
CONVEYS
CONVICTION
CONVINCE
COOK
COOLING
COOPER'S
COQUETTING
CORAL
CORDIALS
CORDS
CORKS
COUCH
COULD'ST
COUNCILS
COUNT
COUNTS
COUNTY
COUPLED
COURTING
COUSINS
COVERS
COW-BOYS
COWARDICE
COXCOMB'S
COY
COYN
CRAB
CRACH'RODE
CRACK'D
CRACKLING
CRAFT
CRAM
CRAMP
CRAWL
CREATE
CREDITORS
CREED
CRIMINAL
CRING'D
CRINGE
CRITIC
CRITICS
CROAKING
CRONY
CROPT
CROSIER
CROSIERS
CROSS'D
CROTCHET
CROW
CROWDING
CRUDE
CRUST
CRYSTAL
CUBS
CUDGELL'S
CULLY'S
CULTIVATE
CUR
CURES
CURIOSITY
CURL'D
CURLL'S
CURRANT
CURS'D
CURSED
CURTAIN
CURTAINS
CUSTOMERS
CYMBALS
CYPRESS
D'ANVERS
DAGGLED
DAINTY
DAIRY
DAMNABLY
DAMNING
DAMP

DAPPER
DATED
DAWB
DAWB'D
DAWSON
DEADLY
DEALT
DEATHS
DEBATES
DEBAUCH
DECAYD
DECEIV'D
DECEIVE
DECISIVE
DECK'D
DEEPER
DEFEAT
DEFEATED
DEFECTS
DEFENDANT'S
DEFENDING
DEFIANCE
DEIGN
DEJECTED
DELAY
DELAYS
DELIVER'D
DELOS
DELUDE
DELUGE
DELUSIONS
DEMAR
DEMUR
DENIAL
DENIES
DENOTES
DEPENDENT
DEPOS'D
DEPRIV'D
DESCRIPTIONS
DESPERATE
DESPISING
DESPONDING
DESTROYING
DETERMINE
DETEST
DETESTATION
DETRACTING
DEVILS
DEVISE
DEW
DIANA
DIANA'S
DICKS
DIGEST
DINNERS
DIRECTIONS
DIRECTS
DISAFFECTED
DISASTER
DISCERN'D
DISCHARG'D
DISCHARGING
DISCIPLES
DISCLAIM
DISCORD
DISCOURSING
DISCOVER'D
DISCOVERY
DISCREET
DISCREETLY
DISDAINS
DISGUIS'D
DISOBEY
DISOBLIGE
DISPLEASURE
DISPUTING
DISSEMBLING
DISSENTERS
DISTORT
DISTRESS'D
DISTRESS'T
DISTRESSES
DISTREST
DISTURB
DITCH
DITTO
DIVERSIONS

DIVERT	ENDOR	FINEST	GETTING	HEWERS
DIVIDED	ENDUR'D	FIR'D	GIANT	HEY
DIVIN'D	ENDURES	FIRE-WORKS	GIGANTICK	HIDDEN
DIVINITY	ENGAGING	FIRMNESS	GILD	HILLOCK
DIXON	ENGINE	FITTING	GIN	HIPPOCRENE
DIZEN'D	ENGINES	FIX'T	GIRTH	HIPS
DOCK	ENJOY'D	FLASHES	GLIDES	HISS
DOGGREL	ENJOYS	FLATT'RY	GLUTTONY	HISTORY
DOINGS	ENQUIRES	FLATTERS	GNATS	HITHERTO
DOLEFUL	ENQUIRIES	FLATTERY	GOAL	HITS
DOME	ENSLAV'D	FLAX	GOD-LIKE	HOBBES
DOMINIONS	ENSUE	FLEA	GODSHIP	HOMELIEST
DONORE	ENTERTAIN'D	FLEE	GOING	HOMELY
DORINDA	ENTICE	FLEECES	GOLD'S	HONDE
DORINDA'S	ENTREATED	FLEECY	GOOD-WILL	HONESTER
DOROTHEA	ENVENOM'D	FLINGS	GORE	HOOD
DOUBLET	ENVIOUS	FLITCH	GOSFORD	HOOF
DOUBTED	ENVY'S	FLOATING	GOSSIPS	HOOKS
DOVE	EPICURUS	FLORIMEL	GOVERNOR'S	HOPS
DOVE-MUSE	EPIGRAM	FLOUD	GOWNS	HORROR
DOWDY	EPIGRAMS	FLOUNCES	GRACEFULL	HORSE'S
DOWNWARD	EPITHETS	FLOURISH'D	GRAFTON	HOSPITABLE
DOWNWARDS	EQUALL	FLOUT	GRAND-DAME	HOSPITALITY
DOZE	EQUIP	FLOWER	GRANDER	HOSTESS
DOZENS	ERMIN	FLOWRS	GRANTED	HOUSHOLD
DRAGG'D	ESOP	FLOWRY	GRANTS	HOWE'RE
DRANK	ESSAY	FLUTTERS	GRAPE	HOWL
DRAPER	EVERMORE	FLYE	GRATTAN	HULK
DRAPER'S	EVRY	FOB	GRATTAN'S	HUM
DRAUGHTS	EXAMINES	FOGGY	GRAVER	HUM-DRUM
DREADED	EXAMPLES	FONDNESS	GRAVES	HUMAN-KIND
DREADING	EXCELL	FOOLISHLY	GRAVEST	HUMANE
DREAM'T	EXCELLENCY'S	FOOT-BOY	GRAY	HUMBLER
DRENCH'D	EXCELS	FOOT-STEPS	GREATNESS	HUMMING
DROOPS	EXCESS	FORCING	GRIEVANCE	HUNDREDS
DROWSY	EXCURSIONS	FOREMOST	GRIEVES	HUNS
DRUDGING	EXCUS'D	FOREST	GRIFFITH	HUNT
DRUID	EXCUSES	FORFEIT	GRIMACE	HUNTER
DRUMLACK	EXILE	FORGETFUL	GRIZ	HUNTING
DRURY-LANE	EXPANDED	FORWARDS	GROATS	HURRY
DUCHESS	EXPELLING	FOULEST	GULLIVER	HURRY'D
DUCKING-STOOL	EXPENCES	FOULNESS	GUNS	HUSBAND'S
DULLNESS	EXPERIENC'D	FOUNDATION	GUST	HUZZA
DUMPS	EXPRESS'D	FOUNDER	GUTTER	HUZZY
DUN	EXTENT	FOUNDER'D	GYANTS	HYMEN
DUNKIN	EXTOL	FOUNDRED	HA'	IDIOM
DUSKY	EXTREMELY	FOURSCORE	HA'PENCE	IDOL
DUTCHESS	EXTREMES	FOURTY	HADST	IMAGES
DWELLS	FACETIOUS	FRANK	HAGS	IMBIBES
DWINDLED	FADED	FRAUNCE	HAIRY	IMPATIENCE
E'RY	FAINTLY	FREE-THINKERS	HAL	IMPETUOUS
EAGLE'S	FAITHLESS	FREEMAN	HALCYON	IMPOTENT
EARTH'S	FALSHOOD	FREQUENTED	HALLOW'D	IMPRISON'D
EARTHEN	FALSLY	FRIDAY	HAMILTON'S	IMPROVING
EARTHQUAKE	FANATICAL	FRIGHTFUL	HANDKERCHIEFS	IMPULSE
EASILY	FANATICKS	FRING'D	HANDSOM	INCAPABLE
EATING	FANTASTICK	FRO	HANGMAN	INCHES
EATS	FAREWELL	FROLICKS	HAPLESS	INCLOS'D
EBB	FARMER'S	FROSTY	HARANGUES	INCLOSE
ECHO	FARTHINGS	FROWZY	HARANGUING	INCLUSIVE
ECLIPSE	FASTING	FRUGAL	HARDEN'D	INCONSIDERABLE
EDG'D	FATED	FRY	HARDER	INDIAN
EDGE	FATHERS	FRY'D	HARES	INDIFFERENCE
EDIFICE	FATTEN	FULLY	HARK	INDIVIDUAL
EDITION	FATTEST	FUMES	HARLY	INEVITABLY
EDUCATION	FAULTY	FUMETTE	HARNESS'D	INFAMOUS
EELS	FAUSTUS	FUNERAL	HASTY	INFECTIOUS
EGGS	FAVOR	FYE	HATEFUL	INFLAME
EIGHT	FAVOURITE	GABBLE	HAUNCH	INFLAMER
ELATED	FAVOURITES	GALES	HEADLONG	INFLICT
ELBOW-CHAIR	FAYL	GALLOWS	HEAPS	INFORM'D
ELDER	FEATHER'D	GAMBLING	HEARERS	INFORMER
ELECT	FEAVER	GAMESTER	HEARTILY	INFORMERS
ELECTION	FEEDERS	GAMING	HEATED	INFUS'D
ELEPHANTS	FENCE	GANDER	HEATHENISH	INFUSE
ELF	FERMENT	GAPE	HEAV'N'S	INGLONDE
ELL	FETCH	GARDEN'S	HEBE	INGLORIOUS
ELOPE	FETTERS	GARDENS	HEEDLESS	INGRATITUDE
ELOPES	FICKLENESS	GARRATS	HELLISH	INHERIT
ELVES	FIDDLE	GATHERS	HELP'D	INJURE
EMBROILS	FIDDLES	GAZ'D	HELPING	INSECTS
EMPLOYMENTS	FIDGE	GAZE	HEMM'D	INSERT
EMULATION	FIE	GEER	HEMPEN	INSPIRES
ENCHANT	FIERCELY	GENERALS	HEN	INSTRUCTING
ENCHANTED	FIERCEST	GENTLEST	HER'S	INSULT
ENCHANTMENT	FILIAL	GEOMETRY	HEROE	INSULTING
ENCOMPASS'D	FILLING	GEORGE'S	HERS	INTELLIGENCE
ENCREAS'T	FINER	GESTURES	HERSE	INTREAT

INTRIGUES	LEGION	METROPOLIS	OILY	PERPLEX
INTRODUC'D	LENGTHEN	METTLED	OINTMENTS	PERPLEXT
INUNDATION	LEPROSY	MICHAELMAS	OLDE	PERSECUTE
INVADE	LESSEN	MILDER	OLDER	PERSECUTION
INVADERS	LESSEN'D	MILL	OLYMP	PERSIAN
INVASION	LEVEL	MILLION	OMBRE	PERUSE
INVEIGLE	LEWDNESS	MINGLING	OMIT	PERVERSE
INVENTED	LIBELL'D	MIRRORS	ONYONS	PETTY
INVITATION	LICENSE	MISAPPLY'D	OONAH	PETTYCOATS
INVITES	LICK	MISERS	OPE	PHILIP
INVOKES	LID	MIST	OPEN'D	PHILIPS
IS'T	LIEUTENANT	MITE	OPPOSITE	PHILLIPS
ISLAND	LIFELESS	MITRES	OPPRESS'D	PHLEGM
ITALIAN	LIFFY'S	MOCK	OPPRESSING	PHYSICIANS
ITALY	LIFTING	MODERATE	ORACLES	PHYSICK
IV'RY	LIGHTING	MOLDED	ORDAIN'D	PICK-PURSE
IXION'S	LIKENESS	MONARCHY	ORDURE	PIDDLE
JACKS	LIKES	MONEY'S	ORMONDE	PIERCES
JACOBITE	LIME	MONTAGUE	ORPHAN'S	PIGEON
JAMAICA	LIN'D	MOON'S	OTHER'S	PIGEON'S
JANE	LINEAGE	MOOR	OTHERWISE	PILLOW
JEMMY	LINEN	MOORE	OURSELVES	PILOT
JENNY	LINING	MOPSA	OUT-DONE	PINDAR
JESTER	LINK'D	MORNINGS	OUTRIGHT	PINE
JESTING	LINKS	MORTAL'S	OUTSIDE	PINNER
JESTS	LINKT	MOSES	OVEN	PINNERS
JESUS	LIQUID	MOTLY	OVERCAST	PISSES
JIG	LOCK'D	MOW	OVERGROWN	PISSING
JOBBER	LOGICK	MOWS	OVERLOAD	PITIED
JOE	LOLLING	MUNGRIL	OVERSET	PITYING
JOGGING	LONELY	MURD'RER	OXFORD	PLAINEST
JOHN'S	LONG'D	MURDER	OXFORD'S	PLANTER
JONATHAN	LONGINUS	MURDER'D	PACIFY	PLANTING
JORDAN	LOOK'T	MURDERER	PACKET	PLATONICK
JOURNAL	LOOSELY	MUSCOVY	PACTOLUS	PLAY-DAY
JOURNEYMAN	LOSES	MUSHROOM	PAEAN'S	PLAY'R
JOVIAL	LOSSES	MUSTARD	PAILS	PLAY'RS
JOYFUL	LOT	MUSTER	PAINTERS	PLIANT
JOYNTURE	LOUDER	MUSTY	PAINTING	PLUMPERS
JUDICIOUS	LOVE-SICK	MUTTER	PALACES	PLUNGES
JUGLERS	LOYALTY	MUTTON	PALATE	PLUTARCH'S
JUMPS	LUCKLESS	MYSTERIOUS	PALL	POCKET-GLASS
JUNTA	LUNA	NAG	PALLIATE	POINTED
JUSTLE	LURK	NATIVITY	PALMS	POKER
KEEL	LURKING	NATURAL	PALTRY	POLICY
KEEN	LYARS	NAUGHT	PANEGYRICKS	PONDER
KENNEL	LYING	NEAL	PANEGYRICS	PONDS
KENNELS	LYING-IN	NEAREST	PANTING	PONTACK
KENT	LYRICK	NEARLY	PANTRY-DOOR	POPES
KICKS	MA	NEATLY	PAPISTS	PORRIDGE
KILLS	MACHINE	NEEDY	PARADE	PORTERS
KINDS	MADMEN	NEIGHBOR	PARCEL	PORTION
KING'S	MAEVIUS	NET	PARE	POSITIVE
KINGLY	MAGICIAN	NETS	PARIS	POSSIBLE
KISSES	MAGPYE	NETTLES	PARROT	POSTERIORS
KIT	MAGUS	NEW-BORN	PARTING	POSTS
KITCHIN	MAIDENHEAD	NIGHT-CAP	PARTLY	POSTURES
KITE	MAINTAIN'D	NITCH	PARTNER	POTION
KNIGHTS	MALE	NODDING	PASTED	POTUISSE
KNIT	MALT-HOUSE	NOISOM	PAT	POUR'D
KNITS	MAMMON	NOTCHES	PATERNAL	POWDER
KNOW'ST	MANNORS	NOTHING'S	PATIENTLY	POWERFUL
LABOUR'D	MARGERY	NOTHINGS	PATRICIAN	POYS'NOUS
LABOURERS	MARK'D	NOTORIOUS	PATTERNS	PRACTIC'D
LAC'D	MARKET-HILL'S	NOURISHMENT	PAUS'D	PRATERS
LADS	MASK	NUBIGENAE	PAVIOURS	PRAY'D
LAGG'D	MASON	NUISSANCE	PAYING	PREDECESSOR
LAIN	MASQUERADES	NURS'D	PAYMENT	PREDICTION
LAKES	MAST	NURSE	PEACOCKS	PREFACE
LAMB	MATADORE	NURSES	PEARL	PREFER
LAMP	MATCH'T	NURST	PECK	PREFERMENT
LAMPOONS	MATERIALLS	NUTRIMENT	PEEP'D	PREFERMENT'S
LANGUISH	MATT	O'ME	PEG	PREMISING
LANTHORN	MEANINGS	O'ROURK'S	PEGGY	PRENTICE
LAP-DOG	MEASURES	OARS	PELF	PREPARES
LASHING	MECHANICK	OATHS	PENDENT	PRESERVES
LASSES	MEERLY	OBLIG'D	PENN'U	PRESSING
LATEST	MEIN	OBSCENE	PENSIONS	PRESTO
LAVISHLY	MELANCHOLLY	OBSCURELY	PENSIVE	PRESUMES
LAY'D	MELANCHOLY	OBSERVING	PENT	PRESUMPTUOUS
LEADER	MELTED	OBTAIN	PERFECTION	PRETENDED
LEAPT	MEMOIRS	OCEAN'S	PERFECTLY	PRETENDERS
LEARNING'S	MENDED	OCTOBER	PERFUME	PREVAIL'D
LEASINGS	MERCILESS	OFF'RING	PERFUMES	PREVENTED
LECHMERE	MERELY	OFFENDING	PERIL	PRIESTHOOD
LEER	MESS	OFFICERS	PERIODS	PRIM
LEES	MESSENGER	OFFICIOUS	PERISH'D	PRINCESS
LEGEND	METHUSALEM	OFT'NER	PERJUR'D	PRINTER'S

PRIS'NERS	REGION	SCIPIO	SLEEVES	STEAD
PROCLAIM	REGULAR	SCISSARS	SLICES	STENCH
PROCLAIM'D	REHEARSE	SCOFFING	SLIGHTED	STEPHEN'S
PROCLAMATION	REINS	SCOLDED	SLILY	STEPPING
PROFEST	REJECT	SCOPE	SLIPP'RY	STERN
PROFITS	RELATED	SCORCHING	SLOBBER'D	STINGS
PROFUSE	RELENTLESS	SCRAPE	SLUT	STIRS
PROFUSELY	RELY	SCRATCH'D	SMATTER	STOICKS
PROGNOSTICKS	REMAIN'D	SCRAWL'D	SMEDLEY'S	STOLEN
PROLIX	REMEDY	SCREAMS	SMEDLY'S	STOOL
PROLONG	REMOTEST	SCREW	SMIL'D	STOOPS
PROMISES	REND	SCRIBBLER	SMIT	STOPP'D
PRONE	RENEW	SCRIBLER	SMITTEN	STORMS
PROPHANE	RENOUNCE	SCRIPTURE	SMOAKY	STORMY
PROPHET'S	RENTS	SCRUBBY	SMOOTHING	STORYES
PROPOSE	REPENTANCE	SCRUPLE	SMOOTHLY	STRAINED
PROPS	REPENTING	SCYTHE	SMOTHER	STREPHON'S
PROSELYTE	REPLIES	SD	SNAIL	STRETCH
PROSPECT	REPUTE	SEARCHER	SNAKES	STRICTEST
PROSTRATE	REQUIR'D	SECRETARY	SNARLING	STRIDE
PROTEUS	RESEMBLE	SECURES	SNIPE	STRIDES
PROUDER	RESENTMENT	SEDITIOUSLY	SNORING	STRINGS
PROVERBS	RESENTMENTS	SEDUCER	SNOT	STRIP'T
PROVIDES	RESIDE	SEED	SNOWY	STROLERS
PROVINCE	RESISTANCE	SEISE	SNUG	STROW'D
PUBLISH'D	RESOLVE	SELF-LOVE	SOARS	STUDENTS
PUBLISHING	RESOLVED	SELLS	SOCIETY	STUDIED
PULLS	RESUME	SELVES	SOFT'NING	STUDY'D
PUMP	RETREATS	SENATE'S	SOLEMNLY	STUMP
PUPIL	REVENGEFUL	SENDING	SOLID	STUNG
PUPPET-SHOW---	REVERENCE	SENSES	SONGS	STYGIAN
PUPPETS	REVERENTIAL	SENSLESS	SONGSTERS	SUBMISSIVE
PUPPIES	REWARDED	SENTIMENTS	SOOT	SUBMITTING
PURELY	RHETORIC	SERJEANT	SOOTH	SUBSCRIBERS
PURER	RHIMERS	SERMON	SOP	SUBURB
PUREST	RHINE	SERVICES	SORELY	SUCCESSION
PURGE	RHYMERS	SESSION	SORTS	SUCCESSOR
PURIFY'D	RICHEST	SETT	SOSSING	SUCK
PURPOSE	RICHMOND-LODGE	SETTLED	SOT	SUES
PURSUING	RIGG	SEV'N	SOUL'S	SUFF'RINGS
PURSUIT	RIGHTLY	SEX'S	SOURS	SUFFOLK
PUTTING	RINGING	SHADOWS	SOUSE	SUITED
QUACK	RIP'NING	SHALLOW	SOWINS	SULPHUR
QUAIL	RISEN	SHAM'D	SOWN	SUMMER'S
QUAINT	RIVAL'S	SHAMELESS	SOWS	SUMMIT
QUAKE	ROAST-MEAT	SHARPERS	SPACE	SUNDAYS
QUAKERS	ROBERT'S	SHARPEST	SPAKE	SUNNY
QUARREL	ROBIN'S	SHEBA'S	SPAN	SUPERFLUOUS
QUARTER'S	ROCHEFOUCAULT	SHEDS	SPANISH	SUPERIORS
QUEAN	ROCHFORT	SHELF	SPARKLING	SUPPORTED
QUELL	ROCKET	SHELVES	SPECKLED	SUPPORTS
QUI	ROGUISH	SHINS	SPECTACLES	SURFACE
QUILLS	ROLL'D	SHITS	SPECULATIONS	SURPRISE
QUOTATION	ROLLING	SHOD	SPELLING	SURPRIZING
RABBIT	ROMANCE	SHOE	SPENDS	SUSAN
RAFTER	ROOD	SHOE-BOYS	SPEW	SUSPECTED
RAGING	ROOKS	SHOOTING	SPINNET	SUSPECTING
RAILLY'D	ROOTS	SHOOTS	SPIT	SWEATY
RAILS	ROSAMOND	SHORT'NING	SPITS	SWEET-HEART
RAISING	ROVE	SHORTEN	SPLENDOR	SWEET'NING
RAKES	ROYALTY	SHORTER	SPOTS	SWEETNESS
RAMBLE	RUBS	SHOULDST	SPOUSES	SWELL'D
RAMBLING	RUG	SHOW'D	SPOYL	SWIFTER
RANCOUR	RUSHY	SHOWERS	SPRIG	SWILLS
RANG	SADDLE	SHREDS	SPUD	SWISS
RANGE	SAFER	SHREW	SPUES	SWORN
RANKS	SAILOR	SHREWSBURY'S	SPUN	SYLLABLES
RAPID	SAILS	SHROUD	SPURS	T'US
RAPINE	SANS	SHUT	SQUABBLE	TABLE-BOOK
RAPPAREES	SAPLESS	SICKENS	SQUADRONS	TABLE-HEAD
RASH	SATYRE	SIFT	SQUANDER	TACK
RAV'D	SATYRIC	SIGHS	SQUARE	TAINT
RAVEN	SATYRICK	SIGNIFY	SQUAT	TALLOW
RAVISH	SAVES	SILK	SQUEEZING	TAM
RAVISH'D	SAVING	SILVIA	SQUINTS	TAM'D
RAYMENT	SAWCY	SIMILES	SR	TAMELY
REAP	SAWPIT	SIMPLE	STAB	TAN-TAN-TAN-TAN-TA
REASON'D	SAY'T	SINNER	STABB'D	TANTARA
RECEIT	SAYING	SKILFULLY	STABS	TARNISH'D
RECEIVES	SCALDING	SKILLD	STALKS	TASTED
RECKONING	SCALES	SKIPS	STALLS	TATTER'D
RECORD	SCAN	SKULL	STAMP	TAVERN
REDUCE	SCAR	SKYES	STARING	TAXES
REEL	SCARF	SLANDERS	STARTLED	TEAM
REFLECTIONS	SCARSELY	SLATE	STARV'D	TEAZ'D
REFORMERS	SCATTER	SLATTERN	STARV'LING	TEAZINGS
REFORMING	SCATTERS	SLAY	STATE-AFFAIRS	TEEMING
REGARDING	SCIENCES	SLEEVE	STATUE	TEIZING

2 (CONT.)	2 (CONT.)	2 (CONT.)	1 (CONT.)	1 (CONT.)
TEMPT	TUMBLED	WARMS	\<D'URFEY>	ABSTAINS
TENANT	TUNEFUL	WARN'D	\<DAMER>	ABSTERSIVE
TENARIFFA	TUNEFULL	WARS	\<DAMMEE'S>	ABSTRACTED
TERRAS	TWELVEMONTH	WASHES	\<DAMND>	ABSURDLY
TEST	TWIST	WASHT	\<FARTED>	ABUNDANTLY
THANKLESS	TYGER	WASTED	\<FERNS>	ABUS'D
THATCH	TYRE	WAT'RY	\<GERMANS>	ABUSIVE
THEFT	TYTHS	WATER'S	\<GODOLPHIN>	ABYSS
THIRDLY	UNABLE	WATERMEN	\<GODOLPHIN'S>	ACADEMICK
THIRST	UNAW'D	WE'VE	\<GRAFTON'S>	ACCENTS
THIRTEEN	UNCLEAN	WEAKLY	\<GUERNSEY>	ACCIDENT
THIRTEENS	UNCOURTLY	WEARING	\<HAMPDEN>	ACCIDENTAL
THISTLE	UNCOUTH	WEARY'D	\<HANMER>	ACCORDING
THISTLES	UNDERLINGS	WEAZON	\<KILKENNY>	ACCOST
THOROUGH	UNDERMINE	WEDDING	\<LEGISLATORS>	ACCOSTING
THOUGHTFUL	UNDISTINGUISH'D	WEDDING-DAY	\<LINCOLN>	ACCOUTRED
THREADS	UNEQUAL	WEDDING-NIGHT	\<LOOSENESS>	ACCURST
THRESHING	UNERRING	WEEKS	\<LOUGHALL>	ACCUSATION
THRIFTY	UNFOLD	WELCOM'D	\<LYNDSAY'S>	ACCUSES
THRIVING	UNFORTUNATE	WEST	\<MACCARTNEY>	ACCUSING
THRUST	UNGODLY	WETTER	\<MARSHALL>	ACES
THRUSTS	UNHARMONIOUS	WHALEY	\<MEATH>	ACHELOUS
THUMBS	UNLUCKY	WHEREAS	\<MURD'RING>	ACHES
THUMPS	UNMANLY	WHEREBY	\<MURDERED>	ACHILLES
THUNDRING	UNPAY'D	WHIM	\<ORFORD>	ACHILLES'S
TICK	UNPITIED	WHIMSICAL	\<PERCIVAL>	ACHILOUS'
TIES	UNSECURE	WHIPT	\<PISSPOT>	ACHING
TILE	UNSOUND	WHIRL	\<PISST>	ACID
TILT	UNWHOLSOME	WHIRLS	\<PORTLAND>	ACKNOWLEDGE
TINCTURE	UNWISE	WHITTLE	\<PULTENEY'S>	ACONITE
TINGLING	UPSIDE	WHO'D	\<QUEEN'S>	ACQUIT
TINKER	URGE	WHO'LL	\<REDHAIR'D>	ACRE
TIPTOE	URN	WIDEN'D	\<RICHMOND'S>	ACTAEON
TIRE	US'RER'S	WIDOW	\<RUPERT>	ACUTELY
TITTLE	USELESS	WIDOW'S	\<SCARBOROUGH>	ADAGE
TO-NIGHT	USHER'S	WILES	\<SOMERS>	ADAPT
TO'T	UTENSIL	WILLFUL	\<SPENCER>	ADAPTED
TOASTS	UTTER	WILLS	\<STEPHENS>	ADAPTS
TOBACCO	VAGRANT	WILY	\<SUNDERLAND>	ADDER
TOLAND	VALE	WINDINGS	\<SUNDERLAND'S>	ADDER'S
TOPSY	VALUED	WINNER	\<THROP>	ADDICTED
TORMENT	VALUES	WISHES	\<TIGHE>	ADDING
TORMENTED	VANISH'D	WISHING	\<TISDALL>	ADDISON'S
TORMENTING	VAPOR	WIT'S	\<TURDS>	ADDITION
TORMENTS	VARIETY	WITHAL	\<WYNNE>	ADDS
TORTURE	VARY	WITHDRAW	'BOUT	ADDYD
TOSSING	VASE	WITHER'D	'ENTENDRES	ADEPTE
TOUGH	VEAL	WIZARDS	'GIN	ADEPTS
TOUR	VEGETABLES	WOES	'LIGHTING	ADHERING
TOY	VEN'SON	WOFULL	'MIDST	ADJOURN'D
TOYL	VENEREAL	WOMANS	'MONGST	ADMINISTRATION
TOYLET	VENOM	WONDERFULLY	'SCAP'D	ADMIRERS
TRAC'D	VENT'RING	WONDRED	'SCAPES	ADMIRING
TRACK	VERTUE	WOODS'S	'SCRITORE	ADMITTANCE
TRACKS	VEXATIONS	WOOING	'SPARAGRASS	ADORATION
TRACTS	VEXATIOUS	WORKMAN	'SPIGHT	ADORING
TRADESMEN	VI	WORLDS	'TROTH	ADOWN
TRAMPLED	VI'LETS	WORTHLESS	'VENGEFUL	ADRIFT
TRANSIENT	VICE-ROY	WOULDST	'YE	ADULT'RATE
TRANSITORY	VICTORS	WREN	A-BROACH	ADVANCING
TRANSPLANTED	VIE	WRINCKLED	A-DAY	ADVENT'RERS
TRANSPORT	VIES	WRINKLES	A-FAR	ADVERTIZ'D
TRAPS	VILER	WROTE	A-FIRE	ADVIS'D
TRAV'LLER	VILLAINS	YARDS	A-FRESH	ADVISER
TRAVELL'D	VINDICATE	YEW	A-GROUND	AEOLUS
TREATMENT	VISION	YEWS	A-GUE	AEQUATOR
TREMBLED	VITALS	YIELDING	A-KIN	AESCHYLUS
TRIFLES	VITTLE	YORK	A-LA-MAIN	AESOP
TRIMMING	VITTLES	YOU'L	A-NEW	AETATIS
TRIPLE	VOCATION	YOUNG'S	A-REEK	AETNA
TRIPLE-BARKING	VOITURE	YOURSELVES	A-RIGHT	AETNA'S
TRIPOD	VOLE		A-THWART	AFAR
TRIPSY'S	VORTEX	1	A-TOP	AFFECTATION
TRITE	VOUCH		A'S	AFFECTING
TRIUMPHS	VOWELS	\<ALLENS>	ABASH'D	AFFLICTED
TRIUMVIRATE	VULTURE	\<ANN>	ABASHT	AFFLICTIONS
TROPE	VULTURES	\<ANTWERP>	ABATE	AFFORDED
TROPHY	VYE	\<ARCH-BISHOP>	ABDICATES	AFFRONTS
TROT	WAFTED	\<BINGHAM>	ABEL	AFRESH
TROUBLES	WAITERS	\<BLOODS>	ABETTING	AFRIC-MAPS
TROUBLING	WALK'D	\<BOLTON'S>	ABHOR	AFTER-BIRTH
TRUCKLED	WALKT	\<CHESTER>	ABHORR'D	AFTER-DINNER
TRUCKS	WALLER	\<CHOLMONDELEY>	ABIDE	AFTERNOONS
TRUER	WALMSLEY	\<CLEVELAND>	ABJURATIONS	AG'EN
TRUEST	WANDS	\<CONINGSMARK>	ABODES	AGHNACLOY
TRULL	WAR'S	\<CONOLLY>	ABOMINE	AGILITY
TRUSTED	WARD	\<CUFFE>	ABSENTEES	AGITATE
TRUTHS		\<CUTTS>	ABSOLUTION	AGMONDISHAM

AGONY	ANNA'S	ASCEND	AW'D	BAYL
AGREEABLY	ANNALS	ASCENDING	AWFULLY	BAYLIFFS
AGUE	ANNEXT	ASCUE	AWKWARDLY	BE-DUK'D
AGUES	ANNO	ASK'T	AWL	BE'N'T
AIDED	ANNOY'D	ASKT	AXEL	BE'ST
AIL	ANOINT	ASLOPE	AY'S	BE'T
AIL'D	ANOINTED	ASP	AYD	BEACH
AILMENTS	ANOINTS	ASPERSE	AYRS	BEANS
AIMS	ANOTHER'S	ASQUINT	AYSLABY	BEARDED
AJAX	ANOTHERS	ASSASSINE	B'S	BEARING
AKEING	ANOTHR	ASSAULT	B'Y'	BEASTLY
ALASS	ANSWERD	ASSEMBLED	BA-BA-BA-BANK	BEATS
ALBION'S	ANTHONY	ASSEMBLIES	BAAL	BEAU-SPELLING
ALCHYMISTS	ANTI-CHAMBER	ASSEMBLING	BABBY	BEAU'S
ALCHYMY	ANTICK	ASSEMBLING-GLASS	BABOONS	BEAUTIFULL
ALE-DRINKERS	ANTIENTLY	ASSESSORS	BABY	BEAUTYES
ALE-HOUSE-BUSH	APEING	ASSETS	BABY-DRESS	BECKON'D
ALECTO	APES	ASSIGNATION	BABYES	BECOMING
ALECTO'S	APING	ASSISTANT	BACK-DOOR	BED-STED
ALEHOUSE	APOSTLE	ASSISTERS	BACK-SIDE	BED-STEDS
ALERT	APOSTLES	ASSISTS	BACK-WAY	BEDAUBS
ALES	APOTHECARY'S	ASSIZES	BACKWARD	BEDRAGGLED
ALEXANDRIAN	APPARITION	ASSUAGE	BACON-SLICE	BEDSTEAD
ALEXANDRINE	APPEALING	ASSUAGES	BACON'S	BEE
ALICANT	APPENAGE	ASSUM'D	BADE	BEECH
ALIEN	APPETITE	ASSURED	BADGE	BEELZEBUB'S
ALIGHT	APPETITES	ASSWAGES	BADGER	BEETLE-BROWS
ALIIS	APPLAUD	ASTHMA	BAFLING	BEFALL
ALL-CONSOLING	APPLICATION	ASTONISH'D	BAGNIO	BEFITTING
ALL-DEVOURING	APPLYD	ASTRAEA	BAGPIPE	BEFRIEND
ALL-DIGESTING	APPLYING	ASTROLOGY	BAJAZET	BEFRIENDED
ALL-RULING	APPOINT	ASTRONOMERS	BAKE	BEGETTING
ALL-SHAKING	APPOINTED	ATALANTA'S	BALCONIES	BEGGAR'S-OP'RA
ALL'S	APPOINTING	ATAVUS	BALDNESS	BEGGERS
ALLARM	APPOLLO	ATCHIEVE	BALLANC'D	BEGGING
ALLAY	APPREHEND	ATCHIEVING	BALLAST	BEGINNER
ALLEDGE	APPROACH'D	ATCHIEVMENTS	BALLENTINE	BEGONE
ALLEDGES	APPROACHES	ATCHIVEMENT	BALLYSPELLING	BEGOTTEN
ALLEY	APPROV'D	ATHEIST	BANDY	BEGUMM'D
ALLMOST	APRIL	ATHEIST'S	BANGING	BEHOLDER
ALLOT	APRIL-FOOLS	ATHERTON'S	BANGOR	BEHOLDERS
ALLOWANCE	APRON	ATHWART	BANISH	BELABOR
ALLOWED	APTLY	ATLANTIS	BANISH'T	BELFAST
ALLUDING	AQUILINE	ATRIDAE	BANISHMENT	BELGICK
ALLUM	AR'T	ATROPHY	BANKRUPT	BELIEF
ALLURE	ARARAT	ATTACKING	BANNERS	BELINDA'S
ALLUREMENTS	ARBITERS	ATTAIN'D	BANT'RING	BELL'WING
ALLUSIONS	ARBITRARY	ATTAINDER	BANTER	BELLE
ALLY	ARBOR	ATTEMPTED	BARBARIANS	BELLOW
ALLY'D	ARBOUR	ATTEMPTER	BARBAROUS	BELONGING
ALMA	ARBUTHNOT'S	ATTEMPTING	BARBAROUSLY	BELONGS
ALMANACK	ARBUTHNOTT	ATTENTION	BARGES	BELOV'D
ALMIGHTY'S	ARCANA	ATTINENT	BARKS	BELOVED
ALMS	ARCH-ANGEL	ATTON'D	BARN-DOOR	BELYE
ALOUD	ARCH-PRELATE	ATTONE	BAROMETRY	BELZEBUB
ALPHABET	ARCHER	ATTORNEY	BARON	BEMATTER'D
ALSO	ARCHITECTURE	ATTORNEY'S	BARONET	BEMIR'D
ALT	ARCHY	ATTORNIES	BARR'D	BEN'T
ALTER'D	ARCHY'S	ATTRIBUTE	BARREL	BENDER
ALTERATIONS	ARDELIAH'S	ATTRIBUTES	BARRING-OUT	BENEFACTOR
AMAIN	ARDUOUS	AUDITORY	BARTER	BENEFICE
AMALTHEA'S	ARETINE	AUDOIN	BARTER'D	BENEFICIAL
AMBASSADOR	ARGO'S	AUGMENTATION	BASELY	BENEFIT
AMBIENT	ARGUMENT'S	AUGRE-HOLE	BASER	BEQUEATHED
AMBITION'S	ARGUS	AUGURY	BASEST	BEREAVE
AMBITIOUSLY	ARIADNE	AUGUST	BASHFULL	BERECYNTHIA
AMBLE	ARIES	AUGUSTA	BASILISK	BERMUDAS
AMBLING	ARISE	AUGUSTUS	BASKETS	BERNARD
AMBROSIA	ARISES	AUKWARDNESS	BASON'S	BERRIS
AMBUSCADE	ARISTOTLE'S	AUNT	BATCHELORS	BESET
AMITY	ARMA	AUNT'S	BATE	BESIEGE
AMONGST	ARMED	AUNTS	BATED	BESLIM'D
AMORET	ARMY'S	AURA	BATHING	BESPEAK
AMOUNTING	ARMYS	AURELIA'S	BATS	BESPOKE
AMOURS	ARRAH	AURELIAN'S	BATTEL	BEST-BELOV'D
AMPLE	ARRANT	AURORA'S	BATTER	BESTRODE
AMUSE	ARREAR	AUTH'RESS	BATTERED	BETOKENS
AMUSEMENT	ARREARS	AUTHORITIES	BATTLES	BETRAYED
AN'ALL	ARRIAN	AUTUMN	BATTLING	BETTERTON
AN'T	ARRIANS	AVAILS	BATTRING	BEVEL
ANALOGY	ARRIVE	AVAUNT	BATTUS	BEWEYLE
ANARCHY	ARROWS	AVE	BAVIUS	BEWITCH
ANCESTOR	ARRS	AVERNUS	BAWBLES	BICKERSTAFF
ANDREW'S	ARTFUL	AVERR'D	BAWD	BIDDER
ANGLE	ARTICHOKES	AVERSION	BAWDS	BIDDY
ANIMATES	ARTICK	AVERSIONS	BAWDY	BIENNIAL
ANIMATING	ARTIFICERS	AVERT	BAWLING	BILLET
ANN'ALL	ARTISTS	AVIGNION	BAYES	BILLETS

BILLING
BILLINGS-GATE
BILLINGSGATE
BIPES
BIRTH-PLACE
BIRTH-RIGHT
BIRTHDAY
BISHOP-HATERS
BITERS
BLABBING
BLACK-HALL
BLACK-SMITH
BLACKBIRD
BLACKEN
BLACKEST
BLACKGUARD
BLACKMORE
BLACKMORE'S
BLAMELESS
BLAMES
BLANCH
BLANCHE
BLAND
BLANK
BLANKETS
BLASPHEMES
BLASPHEMING
BLASTED
BLASTS
BLAZ'D
BLEAKY
BLEAT
BLED
BLEMISH
BLEND
BLENHEIM
BLES'T
BLEW-EY'D
BLINDED
BLINDFOLD
BLINDNESS
BLINDS
BLISS
BLOCK-HEAD
BLOCKHEADS
BLOOD-HOUND
BLOODLESS
BLOOM'D
BLOSUMS
BLOUNT
BLOWN
BLOWSE
BLUE-BOYS
BLUFF
BLUNTED
BLUNTER
BLUNTS
BLURR'D
BLUSHING
BLUSTER
BLUTRAKS
BO-OTES
BOARD-WAGES
BOARDING-SCHOOLS
BOASTER
BOB'S
BOBB
BODICE
BODILESS
BODING
BODYES
BOG
BOGS
BOIL'D
BOILEAU'S
BOILING
BOIST'ROUS
BOLDNESS
BOLSTERS
BOLTER
BOLUS
BOMBAS'
BOMBAST
BOND
BONDS
BONEY
BONNET
BONNY-CLABBER

BOOBY'S
BOOT
BOOTHS
BOR'D
BORDERING
BOREES
BORNEO'S
BOROUGHS
BOSOMS
BOSSE
BOSSU
BOTARGO
BOTTLED
BOUGH
BOULT-HER
BOULTER
BOULTER'S
BOUNC'D
BOUNC'T
BOUNCE
BOW-SHOT
BOW-STRING
BOWING
BOWL
BOX-COMB
BOX'D
BOXES
BOYL'D
BOYLE
BOYLS
BOYNE
BRAC'D
BRAC'T
BRACTONS
BRADLEY
BRAGS
BRAIDED
BRAINSICK
BRAMBLE
BRAND
BRANDISH
BRANFORD
BRATS
BRAWLER
BREADTH
BREATHES
BREEZE
BRENTS
BRETH
BREVITY
BREW'D
BRIBER
BRIBERY
BRICKDUST
BRIDEGROOM'S
BRIEFS
BRIGHT-BEAMING
BRIGHTEN'D
BRIGHTNESS
BRILLIANT
BRIMSTONE
BRINE
BRING'ST
BRINKS
BRISKLY
BRISTLES
BRISTOW
BRITANNIA'S
BRITONS
BRITTLEST
BROACH
BROAD-CLOATH
BROCADO'S
BROD'RICK
BROGUE
BROGUES
BROIL
BROKER
BROODS
BROOM
BROOMS
BROOMSTICK
BROOMY
BROTHER-GOD
BROTHER-HERMITS
BROTHER'S
BROTHR
BRUGES

BRUNSWICK
BRUSH'D
BRUSHT
BRUTAL
BRUTUS
BUBBL'D
BUBBLES
BUBO'S
BUBOES
BUCKET
BUCKET-PLAY
BUCKLEY'S
BUCKS
BUDDING
BUDS
BUFF
BUFFOONS
BUGS
BUILDERS
BUILDING'S
BUILDINGS
BULKY
BULL
BULLEY
BULLION
BULLOCKS
BUMKINS
BUMM
BUMP
BUNGLER
BUNYAN
BURDEN
BURGUNDY
BURIAL
BURLESQUE
BURN'D
BURND
BURNET
BURNISHES
BUST
BUSTLED
BUSTLING
BUTCHER'S
BUTLER'S
BUTTER-WEIGHT
BUTTERFLY
BUTTON
BUXOM
BUYERS
BUYING
BY-ROADS
C
CABBIN'S
CABIN
CABINET
CABLE'S
CACKLE
CACKLES
CACKLING
CADENCE
CADENUS'
CADETS
CAESAR
CAESARS
CAINS
CALAMITY
CALE
CALEB
CALEDONIANS
CALENTURE
CALMNESS
CALUMNY
CALVES-HEAD
CAM
CAMBRAY
CAMBRICK
CAMELEON
CAMELION
CAMP
CAMPAIGNS
CAMPAINS
CAN'ST
CANALS
CANCEL'D
CANDIDATE
CANDLES
CANDOR

CANKER-WORM
CANKER'D
CANN
CANNON'S
CANTERBURY
CANVAS
CAP-A-PEE
CAPACIOUS
CAPACITIES
CAPE
CAPERS
CAPITOL
CAPON
CAPRICE
CAPT
CAPTAIN'S
CAPTAINS
CAPTIVE
CAPTIVES
CAR'CATURA
CAREFULL
CARESS'T
CARK
CARLE
CARLETON
CARMINA
CARMINATIVE
CAROLINA
CARPS
CARRICKDRUMRUSK
CARRIES
CARROT
CARRYD
CARRYED
CARS
CART-AGO
CART'RET
CARTA
CARTE
CARTED
CARTERS
CARTESIAN
CARVES
CASCADES
CASHEL
CASHIER'D
CASTS
CAT'S
CATCHING
CATECHIS'D
CATERER
CATH'RINES
CATHARINE
CATHEDRAL
CATHEDRALL
CATHERINE'S
CATSUP
CAUCASUS
CAULDRON
CAUSA
CAUSELESS
CAUTION'D
CAVALCADE
CAVALIERS
CAVAN-STREET
CAVE'S
CAVEER
CAVERNS
CAVES
CAVILS
CEADE
CEAS'T
CEASELESS
CEASING
CEDAR
CEDAR-BOX
CEELING
CEILING
CEMENTED
CEMENTS
CENS'RERS
CENS'RING
CENSUR'D
CENSURE'S
CENTER'D
CENTURY
CERBERIAN
CERULEAN

CHACE
CHAMBER-DAMSELS
CHAMBER-MAID
CHAMBERMAIDS
CHAMPAGNE
CHAMPAIN
CHANC'T
CHANCERY
CHANGE-ALLEY
CHANGE-ALLY
CHANNEL
CHANNELL
CHANTICLEER
CHAPLAIN'S
CHAPLAINS
CHAPLET
CHAPLETS
CHAPOON
CHAPPEL
CHAPTER-TREATS
CHARGE'S
CHARIOT-SIDE
CHARIOT'S
CHARIOTS
CHARLEY
CHARLOTTE
CHARLY
CHARNEL-HOUSE
CHASTER
CHASTEST
CHASTISES
CHASTITY
CHATTERING
CHEAPLY
CHEAPNING
CHEARFULL
CHEARFULLY
CHEARS
CHEATING
CHEQUER'D
CHERRY
CHERUB
CHESTS
CHICKIN
CHIDDEN
CHIDES
CHIDING
CHIDINGS
CHIFTAN
CHILD'S
CHILDLESS
CHILDRENS
CHILL'D
CHIMAERA'S
CHIME
CHIMERAES
CHIMNEY-SWEEP
CHIMNIES
CHINA
CHINCOUGH
CHINE
CHINESE
CHIP'T
CHIVY-CHASE
CHOAK'D
CHOCOLATE
CHOKE
CHOLER
CHOOSE
CHOPP'D
CHOQUE
CHOUSE
CHRIST-CHURCH
CHRIST'NING
CHRISTEN
CHRISTMAS
CHRISTNINGS
CHRONICAL
CHRONICLE
CHRONICLES
CHRONOLOGY
CHURCHES
CHURCHWARDEN
CHURLE
CHURN
CHUSING
CHYMERICK
CHYMIST

CIBBER'S	COBLER'S	COMRADE'S	CONTRADICTING	COW-<TURD>
CICERO	COCK'D	COMYTH	CONTRADICTION	COW-DUNG
CINDER	COCK'T	CON	CONTRADICTION'S	COW'D
CINDER-PICKING	COCKADED	CONCANNEN	CONTRADICTIONS	COWARDS
CIRCLES	COCKER'D	CONCEALS	CONTRARIETY	COWLEY'S
CIRCULAR	COCKS	CONCEIVES	CONTRAST	COXON
CIRCULATION	COCKSCOMB	CONCEPTIONS	CONTRIBUTE	COYL
CIRCUMCISION	COELESTIAL	CONCISE	CONTRIBUTIONS	COYN'S
CIRCUMFLEX	COFFEEHOUSE	CONCLUDED	CONTRITE	COYNER
CIRCUMLOCUTION	COKES	CONCLUSION	CONTRIVD	CRABBED
CITHEREA'S	COL'NELS	CONCORD	CONTROLLER	CRABS
CITIES	COLCHESTER	CONCUBINE	CONTROLLERS	CRACK'T
CITIZEN	COLDLY	CONDEMNS	CONVERS'D	CRACKERS
CITRON	COLICK	CONDENSED	CONVERSIBLE	CRACKING
CITY-BARD	COLL'NELL	CONDESCENDED	CONVERSING	CRADLE
CITY-BORN	COLL'NELL'S	CONDESCENDS	CONVERTS	CRADLES
CIVILIZE	COLLEAGUES	CONDITIONS	CONVEYING	CRAFTSMAN
CLAM'ROUS	COLLECT	CONDUCTED	CONVINCING	CRAGS
CLAMB'RING	COLLECTED	CONDUIT	CONVITIA	CRAIGS
CLAMOUR	COLLECTIONS	CONFED'RATE	CONVULSIONS	CRAMBO
CLAMOURS	COLLECTS	CONFERR'D	CONYNG	CRAMMD
CLANDALKIN	COLLEDGE	CONFERRING	CONYNGS	CRAMMING
CLANS	COLLEGE-ARTS	CONFESSES	COOK'D	CRAMS
CLAP'T	COLLEGE-GREEN	CONFESSING	COOK'RY	CRANK
CLAPP'T	COLLEGIONS	CONFIDENCE	COOK'S	CRANNY
CLAPPING	COLLEY	CONFIDENTLY	COOKERY	CRANY
CLARK	COLLINS	CONFIDES	COOKS	CRATINUS
CLASH	COLLOGUING	CONFIRM'D	COOLER	CRAWLL
CLASS	COLLWAY'S	CONFLAGRATION	COPPER-SMITH	CRAZ'D
CLASSICK	COLONEL	CONFLU'ENTS	COPPLE-CROWNS	CREAMS
CLATTRING	COLONELLING	CONFLUENT	COPY'S	CREATED
CLEANER	COLONIES	CONFORMISTS	COQUET	CREATING
CLEANLYNESS	COLONY	CONFOUNDS	CORAM	CREDIT'S
CLEANS'D	COLT	CONFUSIONS	CORBET	CREECH
CLEAR'D	COLTED	CONFUSSION	CORNET'S	CREEPLE
CLEARER	COLTS	CONFUTE	CORNUCOPIA	CRETAN
CLEAREST	COLUMNS	CONFUTED	CORONATION-DAY	CRETER
CLEAVINGS	COMB'D	CONGENIAL	CORONETS	CRIB
CLEFT	COMBATS	CONGREGATIONS	CORPSE	CRIMSON
CLEFTS	COME-ROGUES	CONJ'RER	CORPSES	CRIPPLE
CLERGY-CLOTH	COMEDIANS	CONJECTORS	CORPUS	CRISIS
CLERGY-GOWN	COMEDIES	CONJECTURE	CORRECTION	CRITICIZE
CLERGYMAN	COMELY	CONJUGALL	CORRECTLY	CROCHETS
CLEW	COMET	CONJUNCTION	CORRESPONDENCE	CROCODILE
CLIFF	COMFORTED	CONJUR'D	CORRESPONDING	CROCUS
CLIFFS	COMIC	CONJURE	CORRUPTING	CROMWELLIAN
CLIFTS	COMINGS	CONNA	CORRUPTS	CRONIES
CLIMBING	COMMENCEMENT	CONNING	CORUM	CROP-SICK
CLIMES	COMMENDAM	CONNS	COSTS	CROPPING
CLINCHER	COMMENDS	CONOISSEUR	COTEMPORARY	CROSS-BATH
CLING	COMMENDUM	CONQ'ROR	COTTAGER	CROSSE
CLINKER	COMMENT	CONQU'RER	COTTAGERS	CROSSER
CLINKS	COMMENTATORS	CONQU'RING	COTTAGES	CROSST
CLIPP'D	COMMENTS	CONQUERED	COU'D'ST	CROST
CLIPP'T	COMMIT	CONQUERING	COUCHANT	CROUCH
CLIPPINGS	COMMODE	CONQUEROUR	COUCHES	CROUCH'D
CLO'ES	COMMODORE	CONQUEST'S	COUGH	CROUCHING
CLOACINA	COMMON-PLACE	CONQUESTS	COUNCEL	CROUDED
CLOATH'D	COMMON-PLACE-BOOK	CONSENTED	COUNCELLORS	CROUDING
CLOATHED	COMMONLY	CONSENTS	COUNCIL-BOARD	CROUN
CLOCKS	COMMONWEALTHS	CONSIDERS	COUNSELLORS	CRUMBLE
CLOE	COMPACT	CONSIGN	COUNTED	CRUMBLES
CLOE'S	COMPACTS	CONSIGNE	COUNTER-CHARM	CRUSHD
CLOG'D	COMPAIR	CONSISTENCE	COUNTER-SPELL	CRUSTS
CLOGHER	COMPARES	CONSONANT	COUNTERMAND	CRUX
CLOISTER'D	COMPARISON	CONSPICUOUS	COUNTERPART	CRY'R
CLONFERT	COMPELL'D	CONSQUENCE	COUNTERVIEW	CRYING
CLOSES	COMPELLING	CONSTABLE	COUNTREY	CUBBARD
CLOSEST	COMPENSATE	CONSTABLES	COUNTRY-BRED	CUBBS
CLOSING	COMPETENCE	CONSTELLATION	COUNTRY-FAIR	CUBIT
CLOWNISH	COMPETITION	CONSTELLATIONS	COUNTRY-WENCHES	CUCKOLDS
CLOWNS	COMPLAINING	CONSTR'ING	COUNTY-SAVINGS	CUCKOW'S
CLOYING	COMPLAINT	CONSTRAIN'D	COUP	CUD-GELLING
CLUB'D	COMPLAISANT	CONSTRUE	COUPLE-BEGGAR	CUDGEL
CLUD	COMPLEATED	CONSUL	COUPLET	CUDGELLD
CLUSTER	COMPLEMENTALL	CONSULTS	COUPLING	CUE
CLUTCHES	COMPLEXIONS	CONSUMES	COURSEST	CUFF'D
CLYENT	COMPLICATED	CONTEMNERS	COURT-BREEDING	CUFFS
CLYMATES	COMPLIMENTAL	CONTEMNING	COURT-LIKE	CUFT
CLYMES	COMPLY'D	CONTEMPLATION	COURT'S	CULLING
COACH-HIRE	COMPLYES	CONTEMPORARY	COURT'SIES	CULLYES
COACH-MAN	COMPOS'D	CONTENTEDLY	COURTESY	CUM
COACHES	COMPOUNDS	CONTENTION	COURTOWN	CUMBER'D
COACHMAN	COMPREHENDS	CONTEST	COURTSHIP	CUMBROUS
COARSEST	COMPRISE	CONTIG'OUS	COV'NANT	CUNNINGLY
COASTERS	COMPTER	CONTIGUOUS	COV'TOUS	CUPBOARD
COASTS	COMPUTED	CONTINUAL	COVENT	CUPBOARDS
COAX	COMPUTES	CONTRACTS	COVERD	CUPIDS

CUPS	DEAFEN	DEPRESS	DISASTERS	DOMITIAN
CUR'D	DEALERS	DERISION	DISBANDS	DONEGAL
CURATE-SHIP	DEALING	DERIVES	DISCARDED	DONOURS
CURATE'S	DEAN'RY	DERN	DISCERNED	DOOMD
CURCHYES	DEANRY	DERRY	DISCIPLINE	DOORE
CURMUDGEON	DEANRY-HOUSE	DESCANT	DISCLOS'D	DORMANT
CURRY	DEAR-LOV'D	DESCENDENTS	DISCOMPOSE	DORMOUSE
CURSING	DEARER	DESCRIB'D	DISCONTENT	DOROTHEA'S
CURTAIN-LECTURE	DEARTH	DESCRIBES	DISCONTENTED	DOS'D
CUSHION-SIDE	DEATH-BED	DESCRIBING	DISCOUNTS	DOSE
CUSHOGUE	DEATH-WATCH	DESCRY	DISCOURAG'D	DOTARD
CUSTARD	DEATH'S	DESERTS	DISDAIN'D	DOTARDS
CUSTOM	DEATH'S-HEAD	DESERV'D	DISEAS'D	DOTING
CUSTOMS	DEATHLESS	DESHABILLE	DISEASES	DOUBLE-BOTTOM'D
CUTLER	DEATHLINGS	DESIGNED	DISENCUMBERED	DOUBLE-DISMAL
CUTLETS	DEBAS'D	DESIGNING	DISGRAC'D	DOUBLED
CUTT	DEBASE	DESIRING	DISGRACES	DOUBLINGS
CYBEL'S	DEBATED	DESK	DISGUISES	DOUBTLESS
CYCLOPS'	DEBAUCH'D	DESOLATION	DISGUST	DOUGLAS
CYPHERS	DEBTER	DESPAIRING	DISGUSTED	DOUN
CYPRUS	DEBTERS	DESPONDS	DISH-CLOUT	DOUX
CZAR	DECANT	DESPOTICK	DISHES	DOVE-TAIL'D
D	DECEAS'D	DESTROYS	DISJOINTING	DOVER
D'ACQUIT	DECEITFUL	DETAINED	DISLIKES	DOWDYS
D'ECLAT	DECEIVERS	DETERMIN'D	DISMAL'S	DOWNY
DABBLE	DECEIVING	DETERMINES	DISMALLY	DOXIES
DABBLED	DECEMBER	DETESTING	DISMEMBER'D	DRAB
DABLING	DECENCIES	DETH	DISMISS	DRAG'D
DAD	DECENDS	DETRACTION	DISMISSING	DRAIN'D
DAFFODIL	DECIDES	DETRACTOR	DISMIST	DRAINED
DAGGED	DECIDING	DEUCALION	DISOBEDIENT	DRAPIER'S-MOUNT
DAGGER	DECISION	DEUCE	DISOBEY'D	DRAPIERS
DAGGER-CONTESTS	DECKT	DEUM	DISORDERLY	DRAWBACKS
DAGGERS	DECLAIM'D	DEV'LISH	DISOWN	DRAWCENSIR
DAGGL'D	DECLAR'D	DEVIATE	DISPATCHT	DRAWERS
DAINTILY	DECREASE	DEVIS'D	DISPELL	DREAM'S
DAINTYES	DECREASING	DEVOID	DISPELLING	DRENCH
DALACOURT	DECYPHER'D	DEVOLV'D	DISPENSING	DRESSING-PLATE
DAM	DEDICATIONS	DEVOTES	DISPLEASE	DRIBBLE
DAMASKS	DEDUCTION'S	DEVOUR'D	DISQUALIFIED	DRIFT
DAME-NATURE	DEDUCTIONS	DEVOURS	DISSECTING	DRINKS
DAMMEE	DEE	DEVOUTEST	DISSOLV'D	DRIPING
DAMNATION	DEE'L	DEWS	DISSOLVES	DRIV'N
DAMON'S	DEEM'D	DEXT'ROUSLY	DISTANTLY	DRIVEN
DAMPS	DEEP-ROOTED	DEXTERITY	DISTILL	DRIZZLING
DAMS	DEEPEST	DEXTROUSLY	DISTILL'D	DROLE
DAMSEL	DEFAMES	DI'MOND	DISTILLING	DROLL
DANCES	DEFENDED	DIADEM	DISTILLS	DROLS
DANCING-MASTER'S	DEFENDS	DIAMETER	DISTINCTION	DROMEDARY
DANDRIFF	DEFILES	DICATES	DISTINGUISHER	DROP'D
DANGERS	DEFINE	DICERES	DISTINGUISHING	DROPP'D
DANGLE	DEFLOWER'D	DICK'S	DISTORTIONS	DROPSY
DANGLES	DEFY'D	DICKY	DISTRACT	DROUN'D
DANIEL'S	DEFYES	DICTATES	DISTRACTED	DROWNDED
DAPHNE'S	DEIFI'D	DIDO'S	DISTRICTS	DRUDGERY
DAR'ST	DEIGNS	DIDST	DITCHER	DRUGGET
DARBY	DEITIES	DIED	DITCHES	DRUNKARD
DARBY'S	DEITYES	DIFFER'D	DITTIES	DRYDEN
DARING	DEL-VILLE	DIFFICULT	DIU	DUBLIN'S
DARK'NED	DELANY'S	DIFFUS'D	DIURETICK	DUCK-LANE
DARKEN	DELAWERE	DIFFUSING	DIVERTED	DUCKLING
DARKENS	DELAY'D	DIGGER	DIVERTING	DUCKLINGS
DARKEST	DELAYING	DIGNIFY	DIVIDERS	DUEL
DARMSTEDT	DELENDA	DIGNIFY'D	DIVIDINGS	DUELS
DARN	DELF	DIGNITARY'S	DIVIN'TY	DUGS
DARNS	DELINQUENT	DILAPIDATIONS	DIVINELY	DUKES'S
DARTED	DELIVERS	DILATES	DIVINUM	DULLER
DASHES	DELPH	DILEMMA	DIVISIONS	DULMAN
DASTARD	DELPHICK	DILIGENCE	DIVULGE	DUNCE'S
DAUB	DELUDES	DIMENSIONS	DO'ST	DUNCENIA
DAUB'D	DELUDING	DIMINISH	DOAT	DUNCIAD
DAUBS	DEMANDING	DIMMISH	DOATS	DUNDALK
DAUNCE	DEMOLISH	DIMMS	DOBSON	DUNKIN'S
DAVENTRY	DEMOLISH'D	DIMS	DOCTRINE	DUNKIRK
DAVID'S	DEMONIACS	DINES	DOCTRINES	DUNKIRK'S
DAW	DEMONSTRATE	DINGLEY'S	DODDY	DUNNS
DAWBERS	DEMONSTRATION	DINGLY	DOG-DAYS	DUPE
DAWBS	DENIALS	DINING	DOG-FISH	DUPES
DAWNS	DENIED	DINNER-CANT	DOG-LOGICK	DURING
DAWS	DEPART	DINNER'S	DOG-TRICKS	DURUEL
DAYLY	DEPARTING	DIPP'D	DOGS-HEADS	DUSTY
DAZ'LING	DEPARTS	DIRECTING	DOL	DUTCH-HEARTED
DAZLED	DEPARTURE	DIRECTION	DOLLS	DUTCH-MEN
DAZLING	DEPENDED	DIREFUL	DOLLY	DUTIFUL
DAZZLE	DEPENDER	DISAFFECTION	DOLTS	DUTIFULLY
DAZZLED	DEPONENTS	DISAPPEAR	DOMES	DWELLERS
DAZZLING	DEPOSITED	DISAPPOINTMENT	DOMESTIC	DWELLING-PLACE
DE	DEPRAVITY	DISARM'D	DOMESTICKS	DY'ST

DYET	ENDANGER	EUSDEN'S	FAMISH'T	FILLD
DYSTRUCTIVE	ENDEARMENTS	EUSTACE	FAN-TAIL	FILLED
E'ERY	ENDOWS	EV'NINGS	FANATIC	FINE-LINEN
E'REWHILE	ENDYMION	EVADING	FANATICS	FINISHING
EAR-WAX	ENDYMION'S	EVENING-BREEZE	FANCIED	FINS
EAR'S	ENEMYES	EVER-LAUGHING	FANCY'S	FIRST-FRUITS
EARLD	ENFLAMES	EVER-WAKING	FANN	FISH-PONDS
EARLE	ENGAGES	EVERE	FANTASTIC	FISH-WIVES
EARLIEST	ENGGED	EVERLASTING	FAR-EXALTED	FITT
EARN'D	ENGINEER	EVIDENCE	FARDINGAL	FITTED
EARWIG	ENGLANDS	EVINCES	FARES	FITZ-BAKER
EAS'D	ENGRAV'D	EX-CREMENTS	FAREWEL	FITZPATRICK
EASIE	ENGROSS	EXACTING	FARMS	FIVE-BARR'D
EASIER	ENGROSSETH	EXALTATION	FARNHAM	FIXES
EASTER	ENHANCE	EXALTER	FARROW'D	FLABBY
EASTERN	ENHAUNCE	EXALTING	FARWEL	FLAG
EBBS	ENISKELLIN	EXAMIND	FASCES	FLAGRANT
EBON	ENLIVEN'D	EXAMPLE'S	FASHIONS	FLAIL
ECCENTRIC	ENNOBLING	EXCEEDINGLY	FASND	FLAM
ECCHOES	ENORMOUS	EXCELLENCY	FAST'NED	FLAM'D
ECCLESIAE	ENRAG'D	EXCELLENT	FASTED	FLAMMEUM
ECHOES	ENRAGES	EXCHANGE	FASTEN	FLAMSTEAD
EDGAR	ENRICH	EXCHEQUER	FASTIDIOUSLY	FLANNELL
EFFECTUAL	ENRICH'D	EXCITE	FATHER'D	FLASHING
EFFICIENT	ENRICHES	EXCREMENT	FATIGU'D	FLATLY
EFFLUENCE	ENRICHING	EXCREMENTAL	FATIGUE	FLATT'RERS
EFFS	ENROBE	EXCREMENTS	FATIGUES	FLATT'RY'S
EGYPT	ENSCONCING	EXECUTE	FATTYN	FLATTERING
EGYPT'S	ENSIGN	EXEMPLIFIE	FAU'T	FLAUNTING
EGYPTIAN	ENSLAVE	EXEMPLUM	FAULCHION	FLAWS
EGYPTIANS	ENSLAVERS	EXEMPT	FAULT'S	FLAY'D
EIGHTEEN-PENNY	ENSNARE	EXEMPTING	FAULTER'D	FLAYL
EIGHTEENPENCE	ENTER'D	EXERT	FAULTLESS	FLECKNOE
EIGHTY	ENTERTAINMENT	EXHALATIONS	FAULTING	FLEET-DITCH'S
EJECT	ENTHRALL	EXHALES	FAV'RING	FLEETING
EJECTS	ENTHRON'D	EXHAUSTED	FAV'RITES	FLEETS
EL	ENTHUSIASTICK	EXHORTS	FAVORITE	FLETA'S
ELBOW	ENTICING	EXIL	FAVORS	FLIM-FLAMS
ELBOW-ROOM	ENTIRE	EXIST	FAWN	FLITTING
ELDEST	ENTIRELY-ENGLISH	EXPANDS	FAWND	FLOCKING
ELECTED	ENTOMB'D	EXPANSE	FAWNS	FLORIMEL'S
ELECTIONS	ENTRENCHES	EXPECTATION	FEAR'S	FLORINDA
ELEGANCE	ENUR'D	EXPEDIENT	FEARING	FLOUNC'D
ELEGIACK	ENVELOPE	EXPEDITION	FEARLESS	FLOURISH'T
ELEGYES	ENVIOUSLY	EXPEL	FEASTS	FLOURISHES
ELEMENT	ENVOYS	EXPERIENC'T	FEATHERS	FLOURISHT
ELEVEN	ENVY'D	EXPIATE	FEBRUARY	FLOWING
ELIJAH'S	ENVYING	EXPIR'D	FEE'D	FLUTE
ELIS	EPHESIANS	EXPLAIN'D	FEIGN	FLUTT'RING
ELISION	EPHIPPIA	EXPLOIT	FEIGN'D	FLY-BLOWS
ELOCUTION	EPICKS	EXPLORES	FEIGNED	FLY'R
ELOGIES	EPICURIUS	EXPOSES	FEILDING	FLYER
ELOQUENTER	EPIDEMICK	EXPOSING	FEIN	FLYING-CASE
ELRINGTON'S	EPILOGUE	EXTENSIVE	FELE	FOE'S
ELYSIUM	EPIMETHEUS	EXTINCT	FELLING	FOGS
ELYZIAN	EPISCOPARI	EXTINGUISH'T	FELLOW-CREATURE	FOIL'D
EMBARGO	EPISODES	EXTOLL	FELLOW-FEELING	FOISTED
EMBARK	EPISTLES	EXTOLS	FELLOW-SUFFERERS	FOKE
EMBARKING	EPITHALAMIUM	EXTORT	FELLS	FOLD
EMBELLISH	EQUALLING	EXTRACT	FELON	FOLDS
EMBERS	EQUALLS	EXTRAVAGANCE	FELONIOUS	FOLIO
EMBRAC'D	EQUIPAGE	EXTREAMEST	FEMININE	FOLIO'S
EMBRACES	EQUIPAGES	EXTREAMLY	FENC'D	FOLL'WERS
EMBROWN'D	EQUITY	EYE-BROWS	FENCES	FOLL'WING
EMBRYOS	EQUIVOCAL	EYE-LIDS	FENCING	FOLLOWERS
EMERGENCIES	ERMINE	EYN	FENS	FOLLOWS
EMINENCE	ERN	FABIUS	FERKS	FOLLY'S
EMITS	ERR'D	FABIUS'S	FERMENTING	FONDLED
EMP'ROR	ERRAND	FABLING	FERULA	FONDLING
EMPEROR	ERRANDS	FABRICK-ROOF	FERVENT	FONT
EMPLOYMENT	ERRANT	FABULOUS	FETTER	FOOL'S
EMPLOYMTS	ERRING	FACTION'S	FEVER	FOORTHE
EMPTY'NG	ERRONEOUS	FACTIONS	FEVERS	FOOT-MAN'S
EMTY	ERROUR	FACTS	FEWDS	FOOTBOY'S
EN	ERST	FACULTY	FEWER	FOOTING
ENABLE	ESCHEW	FADGE	FICKLE	FOOTS
ENAGIN	ESPOUS'D	FAGGOTS	FICTIONS	FOOTSTEP
ENAMELL'D	ESPY'D	FAINTING	FIDLER	FOOTSTOOL
ENAMOUR'D	ESSES	FAIRS	FIDLERS	FORBIDDING
ENCOMIUMS	ESSOIGN	FAIRY-LAND	FIELD-HOUSE	FORBIDS
ENCOMPASS	ETC	FAITHFULLY	FIENDS	FORCED
ENCOUNTER	ETERNITY	FALL'N	FIERY-RED	FORCES
ENCOUNTERS	ETERNIZE	FALLOW	FIFT	FORE-BODINGS
ENCOURAGEMT	EUNUCHS	FALSTAFF	FIFTH	FORE-FOOT
ENCREASING	EUPOLIS	FAMED	FIFTHLY	FORECAST
ENCROACH	EURIPIDES	FAMES	FIGHTING	FOREFATHERS
ENCROACHERS	EUROPA'S	FAMILIES	FIGHTS	FORESAW
END'S	EUROPES	FAMILLE	FILINGS	FORESEES

FORESIGHT	FURR'D	GLITTER'D	GRIM'D	HANOVERIANS
FORETELS	FURROW'D	GLOC'STER	GRINAGIN	HAPP'NING
FOREVER	FURROWED	GLORIA	GRINDERS	HAPPENS
FORFEITS	FURROWS	GLORIES	GRINDING	HAPPIER
FORFEITURE	FUSS	GLORIFY'D	GRINS	HAPPILY
FORFEITURES	FYSHE	GLOSS	GRIPING	HAPPYNESS
FORG'D	GADBURY	GLOSSY	GRISETTE	HAPSBURGE
FORGETTING	GAFFER	GLOVE	GRISETTS	HARANGUE
FORGIVEN	GAGHAGAN	GLUT	GRIST	HARCOURT
FORGIVENESS	GAHAGAN	GLYSTER	GRIZETTE	HARD-BOUND
FORGOTTEN	GAILY	GO-CART	GROANINGS	HARD-LABOUR'D
FORMED	GAINING	GO'ST	GROGRAM	HARDING
FORMERLY	GALEN	GOAT	GROOV'D	HARDNESS
FORREST	GALL'RY	GOBBLED	GROSSLY	HARDRESS
FORSWEAR	GALLERY	GODHEAD	GROTESQUE	HARDSHIP
FORSWEARS	GALLICK	GODLINESS	GROTTOS	HARDSHIPS
FORTEL	GALLIES	GODSHIPS	GROUP	HARDY
FORTIFY	GALLO	GODWIN'S	GROUSE	HARK'EE
FORTIORI	GALLOPS	GODZOOKS	GROVES	HARLEQUIN
FORTRESS	GALLS-TOWN	GOINGS	GRUB	HARLOT
FORTUNE-TELLER	GALLUS	GOLD-FINDERS	GRUDGE	HARMONIUS
FORTY-FOUR	GALLYPOTS	GOLDSMITH	GRUDGING	HARNESS-BUCKLES
FOSTER'D	GALSTOWN	GOLDSMITHS	GRUMBLE	HARPER
FOSTERED	GAMESTER'S	GOOD-MAN	GRUMBLED	HARPIES
FOULER	GAMESTERS	GOODMAN	GUARDED	HARPS
FOULLY	GAMMON	GOODNES	GUARDSHIP	HARRIDAN
FOULS	GANGES	GOOSBERRIES	GUDGEONS	HARRIDANS
FOUNDATIONS	GANYMEDE	GOR'D	GUELPH	HARSH
FOUNDER'S	GAP	GORGAN	GUESS'T	HARVESTS
FOUNDERS	GARBAGE	GORGEOUS	GUESSER	HASTED
FOUNT	GARD'NER	GOSFORD'S	GUESSES	HASTEN
FOUR-FOOT	GARLICK	GOSLING	GUESST	HASTEN'D
FOUR-FOOTED	GARR'WAY	GOSPEL-WARD	GUIDED	HASTILY
FOURTH	GARRAT	GOSSIP	GUINNEA'S	HASTING
FOURTHLY	GARRISON	GOTH	GUINNEAS	HATBAND
FOWL'D	GATHERD	GOTHICK	GUISE	HATCH
FOWLS	GATHERING	GOTHS	GULLET	HATCHET
FRAGMENTS	GAUNTLET	GOVERNING	GUMMY	HATER
FRAGRANT	GAWDY	GOVERNMENTS	GUT	HATS
FRAILER	GAWSES	GOVERNORS	GUTT'RALL	HAUGHTILY
FRAILTY	GAYS	GOWN'D	GUZZLING	HAUL'D
FRAMING	GAZETS	GOWNMAN	GYANT	HAUNCHES
FRANCK	GAZETTE	GRAC'D	GYPSEY	HAUNTED
FRANTICK	GAZETTES	GRACEFULLY	H	HAUTY
FRAUDFUL	GAZETTS	GRACEFULNESS	H'	HAVOCK
FRAY	GAZING	GRACELESS	H'AS	HAWK
FREAK	GEAR	GRAFTING	HA'D	HAWK'D
FREAKS	GEMM	GRAMMAR	HA'PENNY	HAWKER
FRECKLED	GEN'RAL'S	GRAMMER	HABITATION	HAWKER'S
FREDDY	GENERALLS	GRANARD	HABITS	HAWLS
FREE-BORN	GENEROSITY	GRAND-MONDE	HABITUDES	HAWS
FREE-THINKER	GENIUS'S	GRANDAM	HACK	HAWTHORNDEN
FREEDOM'S	GENTEELER	GRANDAME	HACKNEY	HAYCOCK
FREIGHT	GENTLE-FOLKS	GRANDAMES	HACKNEY-COACH	HAZARDS
FREIGHTED	GENTLEFOLKS	GRANDEES	HACKNY	HAZEL
FREQUENTS	GENTLEMAN'S	GRANDFATHERS	HAGGARD	HEAD-ACH
FRESHEST	GENUIN	GRANNAM'S	HAIR-LACE	HEALING
FRETFUL	GEOGRAPHERS	GRANTING	HAIRS	HEALTHY
FRETT	GERMANY	GRAPE'S	HALE	HEAP'D
FRETTS	GERYON	GRAPHICK	HALF-NOTHING	HEARSE
FRICASSEES	GEW-GAWS	GRASPS	HALF-P'ORTH	HEART-SICK
FRICASSYES	GHASTLY	GRATE	HALLOO	HEATHENS
FRIEND'S	GHOSTLY	GRATED	HALLOOING	HEAV'D
FRIENDSHIP'S	GHOSTS	GRATEFULLY	HALT	HEAV'N-BORN
FRIENDSHP	GIANT'S	GRATING	HALVES	HEAVE
FRIGHTEN'D	GIBBERISH	GRATTONS	HAMBDEN	HEAVINGS
FRIGHTENS	GIBER	GRAV'D	HAMET	HEAVN'LY
FRIGHTFULL	GIBING	GRAVEL	HAMMOND	HEBES
FRIGHTFULLY	GIDDILY	GRAVING	HAMMS	HEBREW
FRINGES	GIDDINESS	GRAVITATION	HAMPER	HEBREWS
FRISKING	GILT	GRAVITY	HAMPERS	HECTORS
FROLICK	GINN	GRAY'S-INN	HAMPTON-COURT	HEDES
FROST	GIPSIES	GRAZERS	HAMS	HEDGE
FROUZY	GIRDLE	GRAZY	HANCOCK	HEDGE-TAVERN
FROWNS	GIRL'S	GREAS'D	HAND-MAID	HEEL-PIECE
FRYAR	GIVER	GREATER'S	HANDFULLS	HEIFER
FRYERS	GIZZARD	GREATFUL	HANDLED	HEIGHT'NING
FULLER	GLADDER	GREAZY	HANDLING	HEIGHTEN
FUMING	GLARE	GREEDILY	HANDY-WORK	HEIGHTEN'D
FUNCTION	GLEANINGS	GREENS	HANG'S	HEIGHTNING
FUNDAMENTALS	GLEBE	GREENWICH	HANGED	HEIR-LOOM
FUNERAL-BLAZE	GLEBES	GREET	HANGER	HEIRESS
FUR	GLEW	GREETING	HANGER-ON	HELICON
FURBISH	GLIB	GREETS	HANK	HELL-FEATUR'D
FURBISH'D	GLIBBER	GREYHOUND	HANKS	HELSHAM'S
FURL'D	GLIMM'RINGS	GRIESLY	HANNIBALL	HELTER-SKELTER
FURNISH'T	GLIMMERS	GRIEVOUSLY	HANNONIAE	HEMP
FURR	GLISTERS		HANNOVERIANS	HENDEL

HENLY'S	HOUSE-WIFE	IMAGINABLE	INFLUENCES	INVULNERABLE
HERB	HOUSEKEEPER	IMAGINATION'S	INFORMATIONS	INWREATH'D
HERBAGE	HOUSWIFE	IMAGINES	INFORMS	IRE
HERBS	HOVERS	IMBIB'D	INFUSES	IRISHMEN
HERCULEAN	HOW'S	IMBIBE	INGREDIENTS	IRONICALLY
HERDIE	HOWARD'S	IMBIBING	INHABIT	IRREGULAR
HERESY	HOWD'Y'S	IMMENSE	INHABITANTS	IRRELIGION
HEROICS	HOWD'YE'S	IMMORAL	INHERENT	ISCARIOTS
HEROINE	HOWL'D	IMMORTALIZE	INHERITANCE	ISIS
HEROINS	HOWSOEVER	IMPARLANCE	INHERITS	ISLE'S
HERRIES	HOYSE	IMPEACH	INIGO	ISSU'D
HESPERIAN	HUDDLE	IMPEDIMENT	INJECTED	ISSUE-PEAS
HESSE	HUGELY	IMPERFECT	INJURED	ISSUING
HETEROCLIT	HUGH	IMPERIALL	INJUSTICE	ITALICK
HETEROGENEOUS	HUMANKIND	IMPERTINENCIES	INMOST	ITHACUS
HEWIT	HUMDRUM	IMPERTINENT	INN'CENT	IULUS
HEWN	HUMILITY	IMPIOUS	INNS	JABBER
HEYS	HUMM'D	IMPIOUSLY	INNUENDO'S	JACKDAW
HI'ROGLYPHICKS	HUMMS	IMPLIES	INNUENDOS	JACKPUDDING
HIBERNIA	HUMOROUS	IMPLORE	INNUMERABLE	JACKSON'S
HIC	HUMOURS	IMPLOY	INOFFENSIVE	JACOB'S
HIDING	HUMP	IMPLOY'D	INQUIRIES	JACOBITS
HIGH-BORN	HUMPHRY	IMPLUMIS	INQUIRYES	JAIL
HIGH-DAY	HUMS	IMPORT	INQUISITIONS	JAILER
HIGH-ESTABLISH'T	HUN	IMPORTS	INRAG'D	JAR
HIGH-EXALTED	HUNGER	IMPOSTOR	INSATIABLE	JARR
HIGH-FLOWN	HUNKS	IMPOSTOR'S	INSCRIPTION	JARRING
HIGH-PRIESTHOOD	HUNTS	IMPRECATIONS	INSENSIBLY	JARS
HIGH-WAY	HUNTSMEN	IMPRESSIONS	INSIDE	JASONS
HIGHT	HUPSOUS	IMPUDENTLY	INSINUATE	JAUNDICE
HIGHWAYS	HURL'D	IMPURE	INSINUATING	JAUNTLEMAN
HILT	HURRICANO	IMPUTE	INSIPID	JAUNTS
HILTED	HUSH-MONEY	INACTIVITY	INSOLENTLY	JAW
HIMSELF'S	HUSSIES	INCARNATE	INSPIR'ST	JAYLS
HINDS	HUT	INCENS'D	INSPIRATION	JAYS
HINGES	HUZZA'D	INCENSED	INSPIRATIONS	JEALOUSY
HIR	HUZZA'S	INCESTUOUS	INSPIRD	JEAR
HIRCINA	HYDASPES	INCITES	INSTALL'D	JEAR'D
HIRELING	HYMN	INCIVILITY	INSTALMENTS	JEARS
HIRELINGS	HYPERBOLE'S	INCLINATION	INSTANCES	JEERS
HISSES	HYPERBOLES	INCLINATIONS	INSTILL	JEJUNE
HIST	HYPERBOLICK	INCLIND	INSTILL'D	JENNEYS
HIST'RY	HYPOCRISY	INCLINING	INSTILLS	JEOPARDY
HITT	HYPOCRITE	INCOG	INSTRUCTORS	JERKING
HITTER	HYPOCRITES	INCOGNITA	INSTRUCTS	JERUSALEM
HIVE	HYPPS	INCOHAERENT	INSTRUMENT	JERVIS
HOADLY	HYPROCRITE	INCOHERENT	INSULTED	JESUITE
HOARDED	HYSTERICK	INCONSISTENCE	INSULTERS	JESUITS
HOARY	I'GAD	INCONSISTENT	INSUR'D	JET-BLACK
HOATH	I'TH'	INCONSTANCY	INTEGRITY	JETTY
HOBBLES	IBERIA	INCREDIBLE	INTELLIGIBLE	JIBE
HOBBY-HORSE	ICE	INCUMBRANCES	INTENTION	JILT
HOC	ICE-HOUSE	INCURABLE	INTER	JINGLE
HODDY	ICH	INCURIOUS	INTERCEPTING	JO
HOG	ICY	INCURR'D	INTERCOURSE	JOBBER'S
HOGART	IDEA	INDECENTLY	INTERFERE	JOBBERS
HOGS	IDEA'S	INDENTURES	INTERLIN'D	JOCKEY
HOGSHEADS	IDEM	INDIA	INTERLINE	JOCKEY-COATS
HOLBORN-BRIDGE	IDES	INDIA'S	INTERMEDDL'D	JOCKEYS
HOLBOURN	IDIOT	INDIES	INTERPRET	JOCKY
HOLIER	IDOL-FACES	INDIFF'RENT	INTERPRETATION	JOG
HOLLA	IDOL'S	INDIGINATION	INTERPRETERS	JOHNNY
HOLLOO	IERNA'S	INDIGNITY	INTERPRETING	JOHNS
HOLLOW-TREE	IERNE'S	INDISCREET	INTERRUPTED	JOINING
HOLLOWS	IGN'RANCE	INDISCREETLY	INTERRUPTS	JOINTS
HOLY-WATER	IGNOBLY	INDISPUTED	INTERVAL	JOINTURE
HOME-BRED	IGNOMINIOUS	INDITE	INTERVALS	JOIST
HOME-SPUN	IGNORANCE'S	INDITING	INTERVENE	JOKER
HUMELI'ST	IGNORANTLY	INDOLENCE	INTESTIN	JOKING
HOMER'S	ILL-COUPLED	INDULGE	INTESTINE	JONATHAN'S
HOMINEM	ILL-FATED	INDUS	INTIRE	JONES
HONEY-MOON	ILL-GOT	INDUSTRY	INTO'T	JONNY
HONOR'D	ILL-GOVERN'D	INEPTE	INTREATS	JONQUIL
HONORS	ILL-GUIDED	INFALLIBLY	INTREGUES	JOT
HONOURABLE	ILL-LINES	INFANT-STEPS	INTRENCH	JOURNALS
HOODS	ILL-MANNER'D	INFANT'S	INTRIGUE	JOURNEY
HOOPS	ILL-MANNERD	INFANTS	INTRUDES	JOURNEY-MEN
HOP	ILL-NATURE	INFECTING	INUENDO'S	JOURNEYS
HOPE'S	ILL-ORGAN'D	INFERIORS	INVADES	JOURNY
HOPELESS	ILL-PRESENTED	INFERIOUR	INVADING	JOWLER
HOPPY	ILL-SPELLING	INFEST	INVENOM'D	JOY'D
HORNET	ILL-SPUN	INFIDELITY	INVENTORY	JOYN
HORNET'S	ILLIT'RATE	INFINITUM	INVIDIOUS	JOYN'D
HORSE-LAUGH	ILLITERATE	INFINITY	INVITING	JOYNED
HORSEBACK	ILLIUM'S	INFLAM'D	INVOCATION	JOYNER
HOSEN	ILLUSTRATE	INFLAME'D	INVOK'D	JOYNT
HOTNESS	ILLUSTRIOUS	INFLAMES	INVOLV'D	JOYNTS
HOUR-GLASS	IMAGE'S	INFLAMMATIONS	INVOLVE	JOYST

JUDG'D	LANDSCAPE	LIFE-BLOOD	LUCASS'S	MANSIONS
JUDGE'S	LANES	LIFFEE'S	LUCENDO	MANTLE
JUDGEMENT-SEAT	LANGUAGES	LIFTED	LUCIAN	MANTLE'S
JUDGING	LANGUID	LIGAMENT	LUCINA	MANTUAS
JUDGMENT'S	LANGUISH'D	LIGHTER	LUCINA'S	MANUFACTURE
JUG-JOULTER	LAOCO'N	LIGHTEST	LUCK-HOLD	MANUFACTURES
JUGGLER'S	LAPLAND	LIGHTLY	LUCKY'R	MAP
JUGLING	LARDER	LIKE'D	LUCRETIUS	MAPS
JULIA	LARGLY	LILLIES	LUCUS	MARBLED
JULIUS	LARKS	LILLIPUT	LUDGATE'	MARCH'D
JUMBLES	LASHES	LILLY	LUE	MARCHES
JUMBLING	LASTED	LINEAMENTS	LUKE-WARM	MARCUS
JUMBLINGS	LATE-HEAD	LINNET	LULL	MARE
JUNCTURE	LATH	LION-HEARTED	LULL'D	MARGENT
JUNIORS	LATIAN	LION'S	LUMPS	MARGET
JUNTO	LATIMER	LIONS	LUNA'S	MARGINS
JURE	LATONA'S	LIP	LUNATICKS	MARINERS
JURIES	LAUD	LIQUIDS	LUNATICS	MARISH
JUS	LAUGHLIN	LISTED	LUR'D	MARIUS'
JUSTER	LAUGHS	LISTEN'D	LURCH	MARK'T
JUSTICES	LAUGHT	LISTING	LUSITANIAN	MARKETS
JUSTIFY	LAUNCH	LISTNER	LUSK	MARKING
JUVABIT	LAUREAT	LITERAL	LUSTURE	MARR
JUYCE	LAW-BOOKS	LITERALLY	LUTHERINE	MARRALL
K	LAWN-SLEEVES	LITT'RALL	LUXURIOUS	MARREYE
KALE	LAWREL'S	LITTERING	LY'RS	MARRIAGES
KECK	LAWRELS	LIV'RY	LY'ST	MARRIED
KEENEST	LAY-HER	LIVE-LONG	LYAR	MARRIES
KEN	LAY-MEN'S	LIVELY	LYDIAN	MARROW
KENNEL-EDGE	LAYD	LIVERY	LYERS	MARS'S
KENSINGTON	LAYING	LIVINGS	LYSE	MARTIN'S
KENTISH-TOWN	LAYN	LIVY	MACE	MARTIS
KERCHER	LAZY-HILL	LOAF	MACEDONIAN	MARTYR
KERNEL	LDSHP	LOAN	MACHI'VILLIAN	MASONS
KETTLE-DRUM	LE'PARD	LOATHS	MACHIAVEL	MASSACRES
KETTLES	LEADER'S	LOATHSOM	MACHINATIONS	MASSERINE
KEVAN	LEADERS	LOCAL	MACKLIN	MASTIFF
KEVANS	LEADING	LOCUSTS	MACLOBE	MASTIFF'S
KEY-HOLE	LEAF	LODANUM	MAD-HOUSE	MASTIFFS
KEYS	LEAK	LODGES	MAD-MEN'S	MASTIVE
KICK'D	LEAKS	LOFTIER	MAD-MENS	MASTS
KILDARE	LEAN'D	LOFTY'R	MADAMS	MATER
KILDERKIN	LEANING	LOG	MADDER	MATES
KILLING	LEAPING	LOGICAL	MADLY	MATHEMATICIANS
KILLMAINHAM	LEARNEDLY	LOGICIANS	MADMEN'S	MATHER'S
KILMORE	LEARNEST	LOGICK-MONGERS	MADRID	MATRIMONIAL
KINDLIER	LEARNINGS	LOINS	MAECENAS	MATTADORES
KINDLING	LEARNS	LOIT'RING	MAGAZEEN	MATTERS
KINDLLY	LEASERS	LOITRING	MAGAZINE	MATTINS
KINE	LECTURE	LOLL	MAGAZINES	MAUKINS
KINGDOMS	LEE	LOLLOP	MAGICAL	MAUKISH
KISSING	LEEWARD	LONDE	MAGICIANS	MAWS
KIST	LEGAL	LONG-BULLETS	MAGISTERIAL	MAY-GAME
KITCHEN-WINDOWS	LEGHORN	LONG-DELUDED	MAGISTERIALLY	MAY'RESS
KNAVE'S	LEIGH	LONG-EXPECTING	MAGNA	MAYD
KNEEL	LEMNIAN	LONG-THINKING	MAGNANIMITY	MAYOR
KNEEL'D	LENDERS	LONG-WINDED	MAGNI	MAZE
KNEELING	LENGTHEN'D	LONGD	MAGNIFICENCE	MAZES
KNOCK'D	LENTEN	LONGING	MAGNIFICK	ME-THINKS
KNOCKING	LESBIA	LONGITUDE	MAGNIFYING	MEADOWS
KNOCKS	LESLIE	LOOBY	MAGPIE	MEADS
KNOCKT	LESSENING	LOOKERS	MAID'S	MEAGER
KNOGGING	LESSENS	LOOMS	MAIL	MEALY
KNOT	LESSER	LOOSE-GOVERN'D	MAILS	MEAN'S
KNOTS	LETT	LOOSE'D	MAIMING	MEANDER
KNOTTY	LEV'LLERS	LOPT	MAINTENANCE	MEANDERS
LABORIOUS	LEVEE-DAY	LORD-MAY'R	MAJESTIC	MEANNESS
LABOURING	LEVEES	LORD-TREASURER	MAJOR	MEANTIME
LACK-A-DAY	LEVELL	LORDLINGS	MAJORS	MEASUR'D
LACK'D	LEVELL'D	LORDSHIPS	MAKER	MEASURING
LACKER'D	LEVENS	LORE	MAKERS	MEATH-STREET
LACKS	LEVITY	LORIMER	MAKYTH	MEATS
LACONICK	LEW'D	LORRAIN	MALAHIDE	MEAZLES
LADDER	LEWELLIN	LORRAINE'S	MALEBRANCHE	MEAZLY
LADING	LIAR	LORSHA	MALI'N	MECAENAS
LADY-DAY	LIB'LLER	LOSING	MALICIOUSLY	MEDEA'S
LADYSHIP'S	LIBATION	LOSSE	MALL	MEDICINE
LAG	LIBELLER	LOUSY	MALSTER	MEDIUM
LAITY	LIBELLING	LOVELINESS	MAMBRINO'S	MEDIUMS
LAITY'S	LIBERTIES	LOW-BORN	MAN'D	MEDLICOT
LAMBENT	LIBERTINE	LOW-COUNTREE	MANAG'D	MEDLY
LAMBETH	LICENCES	LOW'RS	MANAGEMENT	MEDUSA
LAMENTING	LICENTIOUS	LOWING	MANE	MEDUSA'S
LAMPOONING	LICKING	LOWS'D	MANFULLY	MEDWAY
LAMPS	LICKS	LOWSY	MANGER	MEEK
LAND-COMMANDER	LICKT	LOYT'RES	MANHOOD	MEEKLY
LANDED	LIDS	LUBBARDS	MANIERE	MEGAERA
LANDED-MEN	LIEVE	LUCAN	MANSION-HOUSE	MEHERCLE

MELODY
MELPOMENE
MEMINISSE
MEMORANDUMS
MEMORIALS
MEMPHIAN
MENIAL
MERCENARY
MERCENTUR
MERCHANT
MERCURY'S
MERIT'S
MERITING
MERMAIDS
MERRIER
MERRIMENT
MERYE
METALS
METAMORPHOS'T
METAPHORICK
METAPHYSICS
METHODICALLY
METTAL
METTALS
MEW
MICE
MID-NIGHT
MID-WIFE
MIDDLE-AGED
MIDDLE-STATE
MIDLING
MIDWIFE'S
MILDNESS
MILITANT
MILK-MAIDS
MILKS
MILKSOP
MILLIA
MILTON
MILTON'S
MIMIC
MIMICKRY
MINCE
MINDFUL
MINDFULL
MINERVA
MINGL'D
MINGLE
MINGLES
MINHEER
MINIATURE
MINIMMS
MINIONS
MINISTERIAL
MINISTRE
MINOR
MINT
MIRACLE
MIRACLES
MIRMONT
MIRY
MISANTHROPE
MISCALL'D
MISCARRY
MISCARRY'D
MISCARRYE
MISCELLANIES
MISCHANCES
MISCHEIF
MISCHIEVOUS
MISERABLE
MISERIES
MISERY
MISFORTUNES
MISGUIDE
MISGUIDED
MISHAP
MISPENT
MISPLAC'D
MISS'T
MISSE'S
MISSED
MISSES
MISTER
MISTS
MITES
MOBB'S
MOCK-HABITS

MOCK-STATE
MOCKING
MOD'RATE
MODELL
MODELS
MODERATION
MODERNS
MODESTER
MODESTLY
MODICUM
MODULATE
MODUS
MOIDORES
MOISTNED
MOISTURE
MOLE
MOLIRIS
MOLLIGHART
MOMENT'S
MOMENTS
MONARCH-OAKS
MONARCHIES
MONDAY
MONEY-BAGS
MONEY-JOB
MONEY-LEAGUE
MONEYS
MONGRIL
MONITIONS
MONK
MONKEYS
MONKS
MONSIEUR
MONSTER'S
MONTAIGNE
MONTEZUME
MONTH'S
MONY
MOOD
MOODY
MOON-FULL
MOON-SHINE
MOONS
MOORLANDS
MOPUS
MORALISTS
MORALIZE
MORDANTO'S
MORE'S
MORES
MORICE
MORNE
MORNING-DAWN
MORNING-DRAUGHTS
MORNING-HOURS
MORNING-PEEP
MORNS
MORPHEUS
MORROUGH'S
MORTALITY
MORTALL
MORTIFYING
MORTIMER
MOSSY
MOTH
MOTHER-KINGDOM
MOTIVES
MOULD
MOULDERS
MOULDY
MOUNTAGUE
MOUNTAIN'S
MOUNTAINEER
MOUNTCASHELL
MOUNTEBANK
MOUNTERS
MOUNTHARMAR
MOUNTING
MOURNFULL
MOURNING
MOUSE'S
MOUSETRAP-MAN
MOYDORES
MOYNALTA
MOYSTER
MOYSTURE
MUCH-TALKT
MUDDLE

MUDDLES
MUFF
MUFFLES
MUGGLETON
MUGGS
MULBERRY
MULE
MULLINEX
MULTIPLYING
MULTIS
MULTITUDE
MULTITUDE'S
MUM
MUNDI
MUNDUNGUS
MURD'RER'S
MURDERS
MURMUR'D
MURMURS
MURTHER
MURTHER'D
MUSES'
MUSHA
MUSICAL
MUSICK'S
MUTTER'D
MUTTON-CHOP
MUZZLE
MYST'RY
MYSTERIES
MYSTERY
MYSTICK
MYTHOLOGICK
NAB
NAIL'D
NAME-SAKE
NAMELESS
NANNY
NAPE
NAPKIN
NASSAU
NASTINESS
NAT'RALISTS
NATAL
NATION-SAVING
NATIVES
NATURALLY
NATURES
NAUSEATE
NAVY
NAYADS
NAYLER
NE
NEBUCHADNAZZARS
NECESSARY
NECESSITIES
NECKS
NECTAR
NED'S
NEEDFUL
NEEDFULL
NEGATIVES
NEGET
NEGLIGENT
NEIGHBORS
NELLY'S
NENO
NEPHEWS
NERO
NERVES
NESBITT
NESTLE
NESTLED
NETHER
NEVER-DYING
NEVER-FAILING
NEVER-MEANING
NEW-CAST
NEW-DEVOURING
NEW-DROPT
NEW-RIVER-WALK
NEW-YEAR'S
NEW-YEAR'S-GIFT
NEW-YEARS
NEWER
NEWLY
NEWMARKET
NEWRY

NEWS-PAPERS
NICETIES
NICETY
NICK-NAMES
NICK'D
NICKNAME
NICOLINI
NIGGARD
NIGH'R
NIGHT-GLOVES
NIL
NIM-DAN-DEAN
NIMBLY
NINETEEN
NINNIES
NINNY
NINTH
NITRE
NO'S
NOAH'S
NOBLY
NOBODY
NOBUS
NODDLES
NOE
NOG
NOON-DAY
NOON-TIDE
NORAH
NORTH-ZONE
NORTHEY
NORTHUMBERLOND
NORTHWARD
NORWAYS
NOS
NOSE'S
NOTED
NOTTINGHAMSHIRE
NOTWITHSTANDING
NOURISH
NOVA
NOVEDS
NOW-A-DAYS
NOW'S
NOXIOUS
NOYSOM
NUISANCE
NUM'RUS
NUMBNESS
NUMERICK
NUN
NURS'RY
NURSE-KEEPERS
NURSERIES
NURSERY
NUT
NUTS
NYNE
O'ER-PAYS
O'ER-RUN
O'ERBLOWN
O'ERCOME
O'ERFLOW'D
O'ERWHELM
O'MURPHY
O'RE-RATE
O'RECAME
OAKEN-BOUGH
OAT-MEAL
OATEN
OATES
OATMEAL
OBDURATE
OBEY'D
OBJECTION
OBJECTIONS
OBLATIONS
OBLIGATION
OBLIGINGLY
OBLIVION
OBLOQUY
OBSCURES
OBSEQUIOUS
OBSERVED
OBSERVERS
OBSTINACY
OBSTRUCTIONS
OBSTRUCTS

OBTRUDE
OBTUSE
OBVIATE
OCCUPATION
ODIUM
ODLY
ODS
OFFENDER
OFFENDS
OFFICES
OFTNER
OGLING
OIL
OIL'D
OILS
OLD-FASHION'D
OLIM
OLIO'S
OLIVE
OMEN
OMINOUS
OMNIPOTENCE
OMURS
ONYON
OOZE
OOZY
OP'D
OP'NING
OPENS
OPERA
OPERATION
OPERATOR'S
OPINIONS
OPIUM
OPPOSERS
OPPOSING
OPPOSITE-CIRCLE
OPPRESS
OPPRESS'T
OPPROBRIA
OPPUGNANT
OPTAT
OPTIC
OPTICKS
OR'T
ORACLE
ORACULAR
ORACULUM
ORANGES
ORATION
ORATOR
ORB
ORDAIN
ORDAINS
ORDER'D
ORDERLY
ORDINARY
ORGANS
ORIS
ORMOND
ORMOND-KEY
ORMOND'S
ORNAMENT
ORPHAN
ORPHANS
ORTHODOX
OS
OSTRICH-LIKE
OUT-LAUGHING
OUT-NUMBER'D
OUT-OF-FASHION
OUT-OF-FASHION'D
OUT-RIDES
OUT-RUNS
OUT-SELL
OUT-SHINE
OUT-SUNG
OUTCAST
OUTCASTS
OUTRAGES
OUTSHINING
OUTSPREAD
OUTWARDLY
OVER-BEARING
OVER-BLOWN
OVER-BULKY
OVER-NICE
OVER-RANK

OVER-RULES
OVER-TOPT
OVER-WEENING
OVERBOARD
OVERCHARG'D
OVERCOME
OVERFLOWN
OVERHEARD
OVERHEARE
OVERJOY'D
OVERPAYS
OVERPRESST
OVERRUN
OVERSHADE
OVERTAKE
OVERTON
OVERTOP
OVERTURND
OVERTURNS
OVERWHELMS
OVERWITTED
OW
OWES
OWING
OWLS
OWNING
OYLY
OYSTER
OYSTER-STRUMPET
PACES
PAD
PADDY
PADLING
PAGEANT
PAINTER
PAINTER'S
PAIR-ROYALS
PAIRS
PALLADIO
PAM
PAMPER
PAN'S
PANDARS
PANDORA'S
PANE
PANNEL
PANT
PANTHEON
PANTRIES
PANTS
PANYGYRICK
PAP
PAPA
PAPER-SPARING
PAPER-STAMP
PAPIST
PAPS
PAR
PAR'D
PARADICE
PARADISES
PARADOXES
PARAGRAPH
PARALLEL
PARALLELLS
PARAPHRASE
PARASITE
PARD'NING
PARDIE
PARENT'S
PARING-KNIFE
PARK-PARADES
PARLI'MENT
PARLIAMENT-HOUSE
PARLIAMENTS
PARLOUR
PARLY
PARNEL
PARNELL
PARODOX
PARSONABLE
PART'NER
PARTED
PARTERRE
PARTERRES
PARTHENOPE
PARTIALL
PARTICLES

PARTIUM
PARTY-FOOL
PARTY-MERIT
PARTY-PAMPHLETEER
PARTY-STEPS
PARTYES
PARVISOL
PAS'T
PASQUILS
PASQUIN
PASQUINE
PASSENGERS
PASSING-BELL
PASSION'S
PASTIME
PASTIMES
PASTORS
PASTRY-COOKS
PASTURE
PATCH'T
PATENT
PATENTS
PATERNALL
PATH
PATIENT'S
PATIENTEST
PATIENTS
PATIMUR
PATR'OT-LIKE
PATRICKS'
PATRIOT'S
PATRONAGE
PATT
PATTY
PAUL'S
PAULUS'
PAUNCH
PAUNCHES
PAUSE
PAUSING
PAWING
PAWNS
PAY'D
PAYD
PAYMENTS
PEACEFULL
PEACH
PEACOCK'S
PEAL
PEARS
PEASANTS
PECCAVI
PECKS
PEDE
PEELS
PEEPS
PEEPT
PEEVISHER
PEEVISHNESS
PEGASUS'
PEGS
PELEUS
PELLA
PELLING
PELT
PELTS
PEN'D
PENALTY
PENDENTS
PENDULUM
PENNY-POST
PENNYLESS
PENSHURST
PENSIONARY
PENURIOUS
PENY
PERCEIVING
PERCH'D
PERDITION
PERFECTIONS
PERFORMS
PERFUMERS
PERI
PERICRANIES
PERIOD
PERIWIGG'D
PERJURE
PERJURY

PERJURY'S
PERKIN
PERMISSION
PERMITTED
PERPENDICULAR
PERPLEXES
PERQUISITE
PERRIWIG
PERSONATE
PERSPIRATION
PERSUADED
PERSWADE
PERSWASION
PERTLY
PERTNESS
PERUS'D
PERVERT
PEST
PESTER'D
PESTILENCE
PETITIONER
PETITIONS
PETROSUM
PETTICOATS
PETTYCOAT
PETULANT
PEW-SICK
PEWTER
PHABUS
PHAENOMENAES
PHAENOMENON
PHAETON
PHALANX
PHANTOM
PHANTOMS
PHARISEES
PHILIP'S
PHILISTINES
PHILOLOGERS
PHILOMELA
PHILOSOPHER
PHILOSOPHER'S
PHILOSOPHIC
PHILOSOPHICK
PHILOSOPHY'S
PHOEBUS'
PHYS
PICKLE
PICQUET
PICTURES
PIEC'D
PIERCING
PIGEON-HOUSE
PIGEONS
PIGMY'S
PIKE
PIL'D
PILAT
PILATE
PILGRIMS
PILL
PILLAR
PILLION
PILLORY
PIN'D
PINCH'D
PINCHING
PINES
PINN'D
PINNACLE
PINNING
PINTS
PIPING
PIPPINS
PIQUET
PISH
PISTOLES
PITCHY
PITIFUL
PITTYING
PITY'D
PITY'S
PLAD
PLAGIARY
PLAGUILY
PLAINTIFF'S
PLAN
PLANETS

PLANK
PLANKS
PLANNING
PLANTATIONS
PLANTED
PLANTS
PLATO
PLATO'S
PLATTER
PLAUSTRO
PLAUTUS
PLAY-BOOK
PLEADED
PLEADINGS
PLEAS
PLEASED
PLEASETH
PLEDGE
PLEIAS
PLENIPOES
PLENTIFULLY
PLIES
PLOTS
PLOUGH
PLOW
PLUCKS
PLUCKT
PLUM
PLUMPT
PLUNDER'D
PLUNKET
PLUTARCH
PLY'D
PLYES
PODESWAY
POETASTER
POETASTERS
POETICAL
POETICALLY
POH
POIS'NING
POISONOUS
POISONS
POKES
POLE-CAT
POLISH'D
POLISH'T
POLITELY
POLLUTED
POLLUTING
POLLUTION
POMATUM
POMONA
POMP
POMPEY
POMPOSITY
POMPOUSLY
PONDER'D
PONDROUS
PONTIFICK
POOL
POORER
POOREST
POP-RY
POPE'S
POPERY
POPPING
POPULACE
POPULAR
POPULARITY
PORING
PORPUS
PORRENGERS
PORRIDGE-POT
PORRINGERS
PORTEND
PORTENDING
PORTLY
PORTRESS
PORTS
POSIES
POSSESS
POSSESSING
POSSESSION'S
POSSESSORS
POSSITIVE
POST-BOY
POST-MEN

POSTED
POSTERITY
POSTERN
POT-GUN
POTABLE
POTATOES
POTENT
POTHER
POTS
POULTNEY
POULTRY
POUNDAGE
POURING
POUT
POVEY
POWD'R
POWD'RING
POX'D
PRAEMIUM
PRANCE
PRANCES
PRANK
PRATED
PRATER
PRAY'R-BOOK
PRAYRS
PRE
PREACH'D
PREACHED
PRECEDENCE
PRECEDENTS
PRECINCTS
PRECOX
PREFACES
PREFERMENTS
PREFERRING
PREFIXT
PREMISE
PREMISES
PREMISSES
PRENDERGAST
PRENTICES
PRESAGE
PRESBYTERIANS
PRESCRIBE
PRESERVATION
PRESERVING
PRESIDENT
PRESS'D
PREST
PRETENDING
PRETENDR
PRETENSION
PRETTILY
PREVAILING
PREVAYL
PRI'R
PRIAM
PRICES
PRICKLED
PRIEST-CRAFT
PRIESTESS
PRIGS
PRIM'D
PRIMUS
PRINCESSES
PRINCIPALITIES
PRINCIPLE
PRINTERS
PRIOR
PRIORITY
PRIS'NER
PRISON
PRISONER
PRIV'LEGE
PRIVATEER
PRIVATEERS
PRIVILEDGE
PRO
PROBABLY
PROBITY
PROBLEM
PROCEEDED
PROCLAIMS
PROCUR'D
PRODIGAL
PRODIGIES
PRODIGY

PRODIGYS	PUPPET	RAKE-WELL	REGIMENTS	REVOKE
PRODUCT	PUPPET-MAN	RAKING	REGINA	REVOLUTION
PRODUCTION	PUPPET-SHOWS	RALLY	REGIS	REVOLVING
PRODUCTIONS	PURCHAS'D	RAMBLES	REGISTER	REWARDING
PROEM	PURGE-SICK	RAMINES	REGNANT	REWARDS
PROFESS	PURLIEUS	RAMPANT	REGULUS	RHENISH
PROFESS'D	PURLOIN	RAMPART	REHERSE	RHET'RIC
PROFESSES	PURLOIN'D	RAMPING	REJECTING	RHEUMATISM
PROFICIENT	PURSE-PROUD	RANTS	REJECTS	RHYMER
PROFITABLE	PURSES	RAPP'D	REJOIN	RIBBANDS
PROFLIGATE	PURTEST	RAPPAREE	REJOINDERS	RIBBIN
PROFOUNDLY	PURULENT	RARER	RELAPSE	RIBBINS
PROGGING	PUSH	RARY-SHOW	RELAX'D	RIBBON
PROJECTORS	PUTRID	RASCALLS	RELAXING	RICHLY
PROLE	PUTT	RASCALLY	RELENT	RICKS
PROLIFIC	PUTTS	RASHLY	RELIEVE	RIDDEN
PROLOGUES	PUZZLED	RASHNESS	RELIGION'S	RIDERS
PROMISED	PY	RATED	RELIGIONS	RIDET
PROMISING	PYRAMID	RATIONAL	RELIGIOUS	RIDGE
PROMPTED	QUA	RATLING	RELIQUES	RIDICUL'D
PROMPTS	QUACK-BILLS	RATS	REMAINDER	RIDICULOUS
PRONOUNCES	QUACKS	RATTEEN	REMEMBER'D	RIFLE
PRONOUNCING	QUADRANT	RATTLES	REMORSE	RIFLED
PROOFS	QUADRATA	RAVINGS	REND'RING	RIG
PROPERLY	QUADRILL'S	RAVISH'T	RENDER'D	RIGG'D
PROPERTIES	QUADRUPEDS	RAVISHES	RENEGADOES	RIGHTFUL
PROPERTY	QUADRUPLE	RAVISHING	RENEW'D	RILL
PROPHECIES	QUAE	RAVISHT	RENEWS	RIMERS
PROPHECY	QUAEDAM	RAW	REPARTEES	RIND
PROPHECY'D	QUAFF	RAYL	REPAST	RING'S-END
PROPHETIC	QUAILS	RAYMOND	REPAY	RIP
PROPORTION	QUAINT-ER	RE-ACTS	REPEATED	RIPT
PROPORTION'D	QUAK'D	RE-ASSUME	REPEATING	RISING-SUN
PROPOSITION	QUAKING	RE'LY	REPELLING	RISK
PROSELYTES	QUALIFIED	READERS	REPENTED	RIVER'S
PROSERPINE	QUALIFY	READILY	REPENTS	RIVERE
PROSPER	QUALIFY'D	READINGS	REPIN'D	RIVULETS
PROSTITUTED	QUALITIES	READS	REPINING	RIXHAM
PROSTITUTING	QUANTA	REALL	REPLENISHED	ROACH
PROSTRATION	QUANTO	REAPT	REPLIED	ROASTED
PROTECT	QUARRELL	REARD	REPORTED	ROASTING
PROTECTOR	QUARRELL'D	REASONABLE	REPOSE	ROB'S
PROTECTORS	QUARRELSOME	REASONING	REPOSES	ROBBER
PROTESTANT'S	QUARTER-STAFFS	REATED	REPRESENTERS	ROBBERS
PROTESTATION	QUARTERLY	REAUMS	REPRISAL	ROBBING
PROVENDER	QUARTERS	REBECCA'S	REPROBATION	ROBE
PROVIDING	QUARTRIDGE	REBUFF	REPROOF	ROBUST
PROVING	QUASI	RECAL	REPROVE	ROBUSTIOUS
PROVISO	QUATER	RECALLING	REPTIL	ROCHET
PROVOCATION	QUAVERS	RECALS	REPULS'T	ROCHETS
PROVOKING	QUEER	RECEIVER	RESCU'D	ROCK
PROX'	QUERIST	RECENT	RESEMBLES	ROGUE'S
PRUNE	QUESTIONS	RECEPTION	RESENTMENT'S	ROGUERY
PRYD	QUIBBLE	RECKOND	RESIDENCE	ROLLER
PRYTHEE	QUIBBLES	RECLAIM	RESIGN	ROME'S
PSALM	QUICK'NING	RECOIL'D	RESIGNING	ROOFS
PSALTER	QUICKEST	RECOLLECTS	RESORTS	ROOTING
PSYCHE	QUIETLY	RECOMMENDATION	RESTING	ROPES
PUDDEN	QUIL	RECONCIL'D	RESTRAINT	ROSS
PUDDING-PIES	QUILL-MEN	RECORDS	RESULT	ROTCHET
PUDDING-SLEEVE	QUILT	RECTIUS	RESUM'D	ROTTED
PUDDLE	QUIN	REDEEM'D	RESUMES	ROTTING
PUDET	QUINTESSENCE	REDEEMS	RETAILING	ROTUNDIS
PUE	QUIRE	REDIVIVUS	RETAIN	ROUGHEN
PUFT	QUIRES	REDOUBT	RETAINER	ROUL
PUGH	QUIS	REDOUNDS	RETIR'D	ROUNDS
PULCHRE'S	QUITS	REDUCING	RETIREMENT	ROUZER
PULLED	QUITTED	REED	RETIRES	ROWES
PULLY'S	QUITTING	REEDS	RETIRING	ROWS
PULPITS	QUIV'RING	REEL'D	RETREATED	ROWZ'D
PULPITT	QUIXOTE	REFELLI	RETREATING	ROXANA
PULSE	QUO'	REFELLING	RETRENCH'D	ROYST'RING
PULT'NEY	QUONDAM	REFERR'D	RETROGRADE	ROYSTRING
PULTNEY	QUORUM	REFINEMENT	RETROSPECTION	RUBBING
PUMPS	QUOTATIONS	REFINERS	REUNITE	RUBIES
PUNCH'S	QUOTES	REFINING	REVELL	RUDELY
PUNCHINELLOES	RABBLE'S	REFLECTED	REVELS	RUDIMENTS
PUNCTUAL	RACER	REFLECTING	REVENUES	RUE
PUNGENT	RACKS	REFRAIN	REVERIE	RUEFUL
PUNISH'D	RACKT	REFRESHMENT	REVERS'D	RUFA
PUNISHING	RADCLIFF	REFUGE	REVERSES	RUFF
PUNISHMENT	RADIENT	REFUSAL	REVERSION	RUFFIAN
PUNISHMENTS	RADIUS	REGARD'ST	REVERTED	RUMMS
PUNK	RAFFLING-ROOMS	REGARDED	REVIEW	RUNDALL
PUNN	RAGMAN	REGARDFUL	REVILES	RUSH
PUNNERS	RAGOUS	REGENT'S	REVIS'D	RUST
PUNS	RAILLY	REGICIDE	REVIVES	RUST'LING
PUNY	RAIN'D	REGIMEN	REVND	RUSTICK

RYMER	SCORPION'S	SERPENTS	SIGN'T	SMOOTHNESS
SABLE-FLOCK	SCORPIONS	SERVANT'S	SIGNED	SMUGGLE
SABLE-GUARD	SCOTIA	SERVED	SIGNIFY'D	SMUTTY
SABLES	SCOTISH	SERVING-MAN	SILL	SNACKS
SABRA'S	SCOTS	SERVING-MEN	SILLIER	SNAKY
SABRINA	SCOUR	SESSIONS	SILVAN	SNAP
SACRIFIC'D	SCOURG'D	SETTLEMENT	SINCERER	SNAPS
SACRILEGIOUS	SCOURGES	SETTLES	SINDG'D	SNAPT
SADDLES	SCOURING	SEV'RAL	SINDGES	SNARES
SADLY	SCOURS	SEVENTEEN	SINE	SNARL
SAFE'S	SCOW'RS	SEVERELY	SINGE	SNARLERS
SAGACIOUS	SCOWER	SEVERN'S	SINGERS	SNARLERUS
SAGITTARIUS	SCOWLING	SEWEL	SINGLETON	SNATCH
SAILER'S	SCRAMBLES	SHA'N'T	SINISTER	SNEEZING
SAILING	SCRAMBLING	SHABBY	SINNERS	SNERES
SAKES	SCRAPERS	SHADED	SINNING	SNIFT
SALAMANDER'S	SCRAPINGS	SHADOWING	SIRES	SNIP
SALERNO	SCRATCHES	SHAFT	SIRLOIN	SNIV'LING
SALLIES	SCRATCHING	SHAFTS	SIRS	SNIV'LLERS
SALLOW	SCRATCHT	SHAL'T	SISIPHUS	SNOW-BALL
SALMON	SCREAM	SHALES	SIX-PENCES	SNOW-HILL
SALMONEUS	SCREECHT	SHALLON	SIXPENCE	SNUFF-BOX
SALTER	SCREENS	SHAMBLING	SIXTEENTH	SNUFFLING
SAMOS	SCREW'D	SHAMES	SIXTHLY	SO'ER
SANCROFT'S	SCRIBBLE	SHAMM'D	SIXTY-FIVE	SOALS
SANDES	SCRIBBLED	SHANKERS	SIZES	SOCINIAN
SANDY	SCRIBBLERS	SHANKS	SKEAN	SOCK
SANG	SCRIBBLES	SHARPING	SKEANS	SOCRATUS
SANTRY	SCRIBBLING	SHATTER'D	SKELETON	SODDER
SAP'ENCE	SCRIBLERS	SHAVE	SKELLIN	SODOMY
SAPHICK	SCRIBLERUM	SHAVER	SKELTON	SODS
SAPIENCE	SCRIBLING	SHEATH	SKIFFS	SOEVER
SAPLING	SCROGGS	SHEDDING	SKILFULL	SOFTENS
SAPPHO'S	SCRUBB'D	SHEEP'S	SKILLFULL	SOFTEST
SARTA	SCRUBEST	SHEEPISH	SKIN'S	SOFTNESS
SATAN'S	SCRUP'LOUS	SHEER	SKINS	SOL
SATCHELS	SCUD	SHEERS	SKIRMISH	SOLDIERLY
SATINS	SCUDS	SHEETS	SKIRTS	SOLDIERS
SATIRA'S	SCULK'T	SHELLING	SLABB'R ING	SOLICITIOUSLY
SATIRE'S	SCULL	SHELLS	SLACK	SOLITARY
SATISFACTION	SCULLER	SHERIDAN'S	SLACK'D	SOLITUDE
SATISFIE	SCUM	SHERRY'S	SLACKEN'D	SOLVING
SATISFIED	SCURF	SHEWING	SLAND'RER	SOMEBODY'S
SATISFY	SCURRILITY	SHIFTING	SLAVER	SOMMER
SATISFY'D	SCURVEY	SHIN-BONES	SLEET	SOMMERS
SATTIN	SCUT	SHIPWRECKS	SLEEVELESS	SONNET
SAUCE	SE'D	SHIV'RING	SLEIGHT	SOOTERKIN
SAUCILY	SEA-GOD	SHIVER	SLEW	SOOTY
SAUNDER'S	SEA-SICK	SHOALS	SLICE	SOPHISTRY
SAUNT'RING	SEA'S	SHOCKING	SLIDES	SOPHOCLES
SAUNTRING	SEAM	SHOCKS	SLIDING	SOPHS
SAV'RY	SEAM'D	SHOEBOY	SLIME	SORC'RESS
SAVAGE-PICTURES	SEARCH'T	SHOEING	SLIPP'T	SORDID
SAVED	SEARCHES	SHOLE	SLIPPERS	SORIE
SAVERS	SEARCHETH	SHOPKEEPERS	SLIPPS	SORROWS
SAVOUR	SEARCHING	SHORTEST	SLIPS	SOTS
SAW'D	SEATS	SHORTNING	SLIPSHOD	SOTS-HOLE
SAW'T	SECOND-HAND	SHOUL	SLITT	SOTTISH
SAWCILY	SECONDED	SHOUT	SLITTING	SOUCE
SCAB	SECONDLY	SHOVE	SLOBB'R ING	SOUNDED
SCABBY	SECONDS	SHOVELS	SLOES	SOUPES
SCABS	SECRECY	SHOWED	SLOW-PAC'D	SOUS
SCALD	SECRET'S	SHREWDLY	SLOW'R	SOVEREIGN
SCAMANDER	SECURER	SHREWDNESS	SLOWER	SOW'D
SCANDAL-CHARGE	SECUREST	SHRIEK	SLUMBERS	SOW'R
SCANDAL'S	SEDITIOUS	SHRIEVES	SLUNK	SOWER
SCANDALL	SEDUC'D	SHRILLER	SLUTS	SOWRS
SCANDALOUS	SEDUCE	SHRINK	SLY-BOOT	SOYL
SCAPING	SEEMD	SHRIVEL	SLYNESS	SPADES
SCARCELY	SEEMINGLY	SHRIVEL'D	SMALLCOAL-MAN	SPANGLES
SCARE	SEGMENT	SHRIVELLED	SMART-ONE	SPANIARDS
SCARE-CROW	SEIZURES	SHROUDS	SMEAR'D	SPANIEL
SCARLET-COAT	SELLERS	SHRUB	SMED	SPARES
SCARS	SEMEL'N	SHTEEPLE	SMEDLY	SPARKLES
SCAVENGER	SEMELE	SHUDDERS	SMELLING	SPARSE
SCEPTICK	SEMPSTRESS	SHUFFLE	SMIRKING	SPATIOUS
SCHOLARD	SENATOR	SHUN'D	SMITH	SPAUL
SCHONBERG	SENCELESS	SHUNNING	SMITH'S	SPAUN
SCHOOL-DIN	SENDERS	SHUNS	SMITT	SPEAR
SCHOOL-MASTER	SENSIBLE	SHUTS	SMOAK'D	SPEC'ES
SCHOOLBOYS	SENTENC'D	SHY	SMOAK'T	SPECIES
SCIENTIFIC	SEP'RATE	SIC	SMOAKING	SPECIOUS
SCOFF	SEPULCHRES	SICKNESS	SMOAKS	SPECTATORS
SCOR'D	SEQUEL	SIDE-BOARD	SMOKES	SPECTRES
SCORCHT	SEQUENTS	SIEGE	SMOKS	SPECULATION
SCORN'D	SERAPHICK	SIEGES	SMOOTH'D	SPEECH'D
SCORNING	SERPENT-KIND	SIGHING	SMOOTHER	SPEED
SCORPION	SERPENT'S	SIGN'D	SMOOTHEST	SPELLS

SPEW-SICK	STATE-EMP'RIC	STUMM	SUSPICIOUS	TEMPORA
SPHEAR	STATE-OPINIONS	STUMPS	SUSTAIN'D	TEMPTATIONS
SPHEARS	STATE-SIEVE	STUN'D	SUTLER	TEMPTED
SPHINX	STATED	STUNN'D	SWALL'WING	TEMPTS
SPICE	STATELY	STUNNING	SWAN	TENANT'S
SPICK	STATURE	STUNS	SWAY'D	TENCH
SPIGHTFULLY	STATUTE	STUNTED	SWEAT'S	TENDERLY
SPILLS	STATUTES	STUPIDITY	SWEATING	TENNIS-BALL
SPINA	STAY'D	STUPIFIES	SWEDES	TENOR
SPINDLE-SHANK'D	STEADILY	STUPIFY'D	SWEEPING	TENT
SPINE	STEAKS	STUPIFYING	SWEEPINGS	TENTHS
SPINS	STEDDYNESS	STURDY	SWEET'NER	TERENCE
SPINSTER	STEEDS	STUT-TUT-TUT-TER	SWEETEN	TERRA
SPIRAL	STEEL-RIB'D	STYES	SWEETER	TERRESTRIAL
SPIRIT'S	STEELE	STYL'D	SWIFTEST	TERRIFY'D
SPIRITUAL	STEEP	SUAE	SWIFTNESS	TEXTS
SPISS	STEERS	SUBJECT'S	SWILL	TEXTURE
SPITEFUL	STENTER	SUBJECTION	SWILL'D	TEXTURES
SPITEFULLY	STEP'D	SUBLIMEST	SWILLD	TH'ROUGHLY
SPITTLES	STEP'T	SUBMISSIONS	SWIMMING	THANKED
SPLASH	STEPHEN	SUBMITS	SWIMMINGLY	THATCHER
SPLISH	STEPHEN'S-GREEN	SUBORDINATION	SWINE'S	THATCHT
SPLITTERS	STERLINE'S	SUBORN	SWINGINGLY	THEATRE
SPLUTTER	STERLING	SUBSCRIBED	SWITCH	THEOCRITUS
SPOILD	STERNE	SUBSCRIBER	SWITCHES	THEOLOGIC
SPOKES	STEW	SUBSCRIBES	SWOON'D	THERE-HENCE
SPOON-FULL	STEWARDS	SUBSCRIPTION	SWORD-KNOTS	THEREABOUTS
SPORTED	STIFF	SUBSIDING	SWOWN	THERSITES
SPORTS	STIFLED	SUBSIST	SYGNE	THESPIS'S
SPORTSMAN	STILL-BORN	SUBSTANCES	SYLLA	THICKET
SPOTTED	STINT	SUBSTANTIAL	SYLVAN	THIMBLE
SPOUSE'S	STINTED	SUBTERRANEOUS	SYLVIA	THING'S
SPOUT	STIPEND	SUBTIL	SYMBOLS	THINKER
SPOUT'S	STIR'D	SUBTLY	SYMNELE	THO'T
SPOUTS	STIRRING	SUBURB-WENCH	SYMPATHETICK	THORN-BUSH
SPOYL'D	STITCHES	SUCCEEDING	SYMPATHIZE	THOUGHT'S
SPOYLD	STIVER	SUCCEEDS	T'OTHER	THOUGHTLESS
SPRANG	STOCK-JOBBER	SUCCESSOR'S	TA'EN	THOUSANDTH
SPRATS	STOCK'D	SUCCESSORS	TA'NE	THRASHING
SPRAWL'D	STOCK'T	SUCCINCT	TABBIES	THREADBARE
SPRAWLING	STOCKBRIDGE	SUCCOUR'D	TADY	THREAT'NING
SPREADING	STOFFE	SUCK'T	TADY'S	THREATEN'D
SPRED	STOIC	SUDDENLY	TAG	THREATENS
SPRIGHTLY	STOICK	SUDS	TAGUS	THREATNED
SPRINKLED	STOICK'S	SUE	TAINTLESS	THREATNING
SPRINKLES	STOL'N	SUEDE	TALK'T	THREATS
SPRINKLING	STOMACHS	SUFF'RERS·	TALKT	THREDBARE
SPRITE	STONY	SUFFICE	TALLER	THREE-LEGG'D
SPROUTING	STOOLS	SUFFICIENT	TALLEST	THREED-BARE
SPUE	STOOPING	SUFFRAGAN	TAMER	THRESH
SPUNGING-HOUSE	STOP'D	SUGAR	TAMYS	THRESHER
SPURN'D	STOPPING	SUITABLE	TANKARDS	THRIFT
SPUTT'RING	STORES	SUITOR	TANN'D	THROB
SQUAL	STORMING	SULLEN	TAPE	THRONG'D
SQUALS	STOUTLY	SULTAN	TAPER	THROTTLE
SQUANDER'D	STRAININGS	SULTAN'S	TAPSTER	THROUGHOUT
SQUANDRING	STRATAGEM	SUMM'D	TARE	THROVE
SQUARES	STRAYS	SUMMARY	TARNISH	THRUSH
SQUASH	STREAMING	SUMMERS	TARNISH'T	THRUSTING
SQUAWL	STREIGHTS	SUMMON'D	TARR	THULE
SQUEEKS	STRENGTHENS	SUMMONING	TARRY	THUNDER-BOLTS
SQUIB	STRETCHED	SUMMONS	TARRY'D	THUNDERER'S
SQUIBBING	STRETCHES	SUN-BEAMS	TASTER	THUNDERS
SQUIBS	STRETCHING	SUNDAY'S	TASTING	THYN
SQUINTING	STRICTER	SUNDER	TASTLESS	THYS
STABLE	STRICTNESS	SUP'D	TATLING	THYSELF
STABLE'S	STRIPS	SUPERFICIAL	TAUDRY	TIBBALDS
STACKS	STRIVES	SUPERNACULUM	TAWDRY	TIBULLUS'S
STAGERS	STRIVING	SUPINE	TAYL	TICKELL
STAGES	STROAK'D	SUPPLE	TE	TIDDEST
STAGG	STROAKS	SUPPLIANT	TEA-KETTLE'S	TIE
STAGGER	STROKES	SUPPLICATE	TEACHER	TIED
STAGIRITE	STROLES	SUPPLYING	TEACHERS	TIERCE
STAGNATES	STROLING	SUPPOS'D	TEACHES	TIGELLIUS
STAGNATING	STROLLING	SUR-TOUT	TEASE	TIGHT
STAIR	STRONGLY	SURER	TEAZD	TILLS
STAKES	STROW	SURGEON	TEAZING	TILTERS
STAMPING	STROWN	SURGES	TECTA	TIM'D
STAMPT	STROWS	SURMOUNT	TEES	TIME-SERVING
STANCH	STRUCTURE	SURPASS	TEL	TIME'S
STANDARD	STRUGLED	SURPLICE	TELL-TALE	TIN
STANDISH	STRUGLING	SURPRISES	TELLING	TINDAL
STANZA	STUB'D	SURRENDER	TELLUS	TINDER
STAR-GAZING	STUBBED	SURTOUT	TEMP'RANCE	TING'D
STARES	STUBBORNESS	SURVIVE	TEMPLE-BAR	TINSEL
STARMONGER	STUFF-HER-EARS	SURVIVING	TEMPLE-DOOR	TINSEL'D
STARTED	STUMBLE	SUSPENDS	TEMPLE-SIDE	TIPLING
STATE-AIRS	STUMBLING	SUSPENSE	TEMPLER	TIPPING

TIPPLING	TREATISE	TWITTER	UNOBSERV'D	VANDALS
TIPS	TREATS	TWO-FAC'D	UNPASSABLE	VANISHT
TIRES	TREBLE	TWO-INCH	UNPIERC'D	VANITY'S
TISDEL	TREBLY	TWO-YEAR'S	UNPITY'D	VANQUISH'D
TISSUES	TREEDS	TWYS	UNPOETIC	VAP'RING
TITAN	TREMENDOUS	TY'T	UNPOLITE	VAPORS
TITAN'S	TRENT	TYDE	UNPOLLUTED	VARIES
TITE	TREPAN'D	TYGER'S	UNPREPAR'D	VARNISH
TO'S	TREPANING	TYPES	UNPROPORTION'D	VARNISH'D
TOAD	TRESSILIAN	TYRANNY	UNPROVIDED	VASSALS
TOASTED	TREYN	TYRANT-GUARD	UNPUNISH'D	VATICAN
TOASTING	TRIBES	TYRANT-PASSIONS	UNRAVELL'D	VAULTS
TOBACCA	TRICK'T	UGLY	UNRAVELLD	VEHICLES
TOBACCO-PLUG	TRICKLING	ULYSSES	UNRAVELS	VELIT
TOILING	TRICKSY	UMBO	UNREGARDED	VENDS
TOILS	TRIDENT	UMBRELLA'S	UNRELENTING	VENERABLE
TOMBS	TRIMMERS	UN-DONE	UNREMITTING	VENGEFUL
TOMES	TRINE	UN-MAN	UNREVENG'D	VENIAL
TONGS	TRINKETS	UN-MEANING	UNRIGHTEOUS	VENOM'D
TONSON	TRINOBANTUM	UNANSWER'D	UNRIPT	VENTED
TOOPE	TRIPLET	UNATTAINTED	UNSAID	VENTING
TOOTHLESS	TRIPPLE	UNAWARE	UNSAVORY	VENUS-LIKE
TOP-KNOT	TRIPS	UNBARS	UNSHAKEN	VENUS'
TOPICK	TRIPSY	UNBEATEN	UNSKILL'D	VERDICT
TOPPING	TRIUMPH	UNBELIEVING	UNSLATED	VERGE
TOPSI-TURVY	TRIVIAL	UNBENDS	UNSMOAKT	VERIFY'D
TOPSY-TURVY	TRODDEN	UNBINDS	UNSOLD	VERJUICE
TORT'RING	TROIS	UNBISHOPRICK'D	UNSOUGHT	VERTIGO
TORY'S	TROJAN	UNBOUND	UNSPARING	VERTUES
TOSS'D	TROLL	UNBURTHEN'D	UNSPOKE	VESPUTIO'S
TOSS'T	TROLLED	UNBUTTON	UNSPOTTED	VESSELS
TOSST	TROLLOP	UNCLE	UNSTEADY	VESTURE
TOTAL	TROPICK	UNCLE'S	UNSTRING'D	VEXES
TOTNESS	TROPICKS	UNCLUB'D	UNSTRUNG	VEXING
TOUCH'T	TROTH	UNCOMELY	UNSUCCESSFUL	VIALS
TOUCHES	TROTS	UNCOMMUNICATIVE	UNSUSCEPTIBLE	VICARAGE
TOUCHT	TROUBLESOME	UNCOMPLYING	UNSUSPICIOUS	VICARS
TOUN	TROUT	UNCONSCIOUS	UNTHINKING	VICTIMS
TOUNE	TROW	UNCORRUPT	UNTHRIFTY	VICTOR
TOUPETS	TROWEL	UNDECENT	UNTILL	VICTOR'S
TOWARDS	TROWELS	UNDER-HAND	UNTO	VIDE
TOWELS	TROY-TOWN	UNDER-STANDS	UNTO'T	VIEWING
TOWLSEL	TRU	UNDER-WITS	UNTOLD	VIG'ROUS
TOWN-JESTS	TRUANT	UNDERMINES	UNTOUCH'D	VIGILANCE
TOWNSHEND	TRUBY'S	UNDERSTANDS	UNTOUCH'T	VIGOROUS
TOWNSHENDS	TRUCK	UNDERSTOOD	UNTWISTS	VILLA
TOWRING	TRUCKLE	UNDERSTONDE	UNUS'D	VILLAES
TOWSE	TRUDGES	UNDERTAKEN	UNVANQUISH'D	VILLAIN'S
TOWZER'S	TRUDGING	UNDERTAKERS	UNWARILY	VINDICATION
TOYLETS	TRUE-LOVE	UNDERTOOK	UNWEETING	VINE
TRACES	TRUMPETERS	UNDO	UNWILLING	VINTNER
TRADERS	TRUNKS	UNDOING	UNWONTED	VIOLENT
TRADING	TRUSTEES	UNDOUBTED	UNWORTHY	VIOLENTLY
TRADUCE	TRYES	UNDOUBTEDLY	UP-HOLDERS	VIPER
TRAFFICK	TRYSYLLABLE	UNEASY	UPBRAID	VIRAGO
TRAGEDIES	TU	UNENDOW'D	UPHELD	VIRGE
TRAGEDY	TUBES	UNEXPECTED	UPRIGHT	VIRGIL'S
TRAGICKS	TUCK'D	UNEXPERIENC'T	UPS	VIRGIN-MUSE
TRAINS	TUCK'D-UP	UNFELT	UPSTART	VIRGO'S
TRAITEROUSLY	TULIPS	UNFIT	UPTON	VIRTOUS
TRAITOR	TUMBL'D	UNFORESEEN	URCHIN	VIRTUES'S
TRAITRESS	TUNBRIDGE	UNFRIENDLY	URG'D	VIRTUOSO
TRAMPLES	TURBANT'S	UNGEN'ROUS	USED	VIRTUOSOES'
TRAMPLING	TURBULENCE	UNGLUES	USEFULL	VIRTUOUS
TRANSCENDENT	TURBULENT	UNGRATEFULLY	USH	VIRUMQUE
TRANSCENDING	TURENNE	UNGUARDED	USHER	VISIONS
TRANSCENDS	TURN-COAT	UNHABITABLE	USHER'D	VISTOS
TRANSCRIB'D	TURN-SPIT	UNHALLOWED	USQUEBAGH	VITRUVIUS
TRANSFERS	TURND	UNHAND	USU	VITTALS
TRANSFIX'D	TURNIP-TOPS	UNHEARD-OF	USU'LL	VITTELLS
TRANSFUSION	TURNKEY	UNHELPT	USURPATION	VIZARDS
TRANSGRESSION	TURVEY	UNHORS'D	USURPED	VOITURE'S
TRANSIT	TURVY	UNHURT	USURPERS	VOLATILE
TRANSLATION	TUSK	UNIFORMITY	USURPING	VOLUME'S
TRANSMITTED	TUSKS	UNITIES	UTOPIA	VOLUPTUOUS
TRANSPARENT	TUTORS	UNITING	UTOPIAN	VOMIT
TRANSPORTS	TWATTLING	UNIVERSALL	UTTER'D	VOTED
TRAPPINGS	TWAYNE	UNIVERSE	UTTERS	VOTER'S
TRAPPS	TWEAK	UNKINDLY	VACANT	VOWING
TRAV'LLERS	TWEEZERS	UNLACES	VACATION	VYES
TRAV'LLING	TWELFTH	UNLAMENTED	VACATION'S	W'YE
TRAVELLER	TWELVEPENCE	UNLOADS	VAL'ROUS	WADDLES
TRAVELLERS	TWENTIES	UNMATCHT	VALOR	WADED
TRAY	TWINKLING	UNMERCIFUL	VAMP	WADGAR
TREACHEROUS	TWIRL'D	UNMERITED	VAMP'T	WAGER
TREADING	TWISTING	UNMIXT	VAMPT	WAGGING
TREAS'RER	TWITCH	UNMOV'D	VAN'S	WAGS
TREASURERS	TWITCHT	UNNATURAL	VANDAL	

WAIN
WAINSCOAT
WAISTCOAT
WAKES
WAKING
WALK'S
WALKE
WALLOW
WALLOWING
WALLOWS
WALNUTS
WAN
WANDERING
WANDERS
WANDRED
WAPPING
WARBLED
WARBLERS
WARBLING
WARBURTON
WARDED
WARES
WARLIKE
WARM'D
WARP
WARRIOR
WARWICK
WASP
WASPS
WAST
WAST-COAT
WASTCOAT
WASTING
WASTS
WAT'RING
WATCH'D
WATCHMAN
WATCHMEN
WATER-COLOURS
WATER-GRUEL
WATER'D
WATERY
WATRY
WAV'D
WAVE
WAVING
WE'D
WE'RE
WEAKEST
WEAKNESS
WEAM
WEAN
WEAPONS
WEARIED
WEASEL
WEATHER-BEATEN
WEATHER'S
WEATHERCOCK
WEAVE
WEAVER
WEAVING
WEDDING-RING
WEDDING-SHEETS
WEEDING-KNIFE
WEEPERS
WEEZLES
WEIRS
WELCH
WELCH'S
WELE
WELL-BOUND
WELL-COMPACTED
WELL-RECEIV'D
WELSTED
WEPT
WESTON
WETT
WETYNGE
WEXFORD
WHATSO'ER
WHEADLED
WHEAT
WHEEDLED
WHEEL
WHEELBARROW
WHEEZING
WHEN'T
WHENSO'RE

WHERESOE'RE
WHEREWITH
WHET
WHEY
WHEY-FACE
WHIFFS
WHIGGISH
WHIMSEYS
WHIMSYES
WHIRL'D
WHIRLING
WHIRLWIND
WHISK
WHISP'RINGS
WHISPRD
WHIST
WHISTLES
WHISTLING
WHITE-LEAD
WHITENING
WHITEWAY
WHOLESOM
WHOLSOM
WHORING
WICKEDLY
WICKEDNESS
WICKET
WIDENESS
WIDN'D
WIDOWS
WIELDING
WIG-BLOCK
WIL'T
WILDERNESSES
WILDLY
WILLINGLY
WILLOW
WILLOW-STICKS
WILLY
WIMBLE
WINDED
WINDING-SHEET
WINE'S
WING'D
WINGED
WINNING
WINNOWING
WINTER-SKY
WINTER-SUN
WINTERS
WIPES
WISER
WITH-HOLD
WITHALL
WITHOLD
WITHSTAND
WITHSTANDS
WITHSTOOD
WITLINGS
WITNESSES
WO
WOLSTON'S
WOLVES
WOMAN-HATER
WOMAN-KIND
WOMEN'S
WOMENS
WONDERFULL
WONDEROUS
WONDRING
WONTED
WOO
WOOD-LOUSE
WOOD-WORM
WORKERS
WORKMANSHIP
WORLDLY-WISE
WORRIED
WORRIER
WORRY
WORRY'D
WORSHIP'D
WORSHIPPERS
WORSLY'S
WOU'DST
WOULDN'T
WOUNDING

WOVEN
WRACK
WRANGLE
WRANGLINGS
WRAP
WRAP'D
WRAPP'D
WREAK
WRECK
WRIGGLE
WRIGGLING
WRIGLE
WRINCKLES
WRIST
WRITERS
WROGHT
WRONGS
WYCHERLY
XERXES
Y-FROZEN
YAHOOS
YARN
YAWN
YEAN
YEARS-DAY
YEMAN
YEOMAN
YEOMEN
YEST
YESTERDAY
YONGE
YONKER
YORE
YOUNGE
YOUNGEST
YOUNGS
YOUR-SELF
YOUTHS
ZAGGS
ZEALOT
ZENITH
ZEPHIRS
ZEPHYR'S
ZEST
ZIGZACKS
ZODIACK

Library of Congress Cataloging in Publication Data
(For library cataloging purposes only)

Shinagel, Michael.
  A concordance to the poems of Jonathan Swift.

  (The Cornell concordances)
  "Based on . . . The poems of Jonathan Swift, second
edition, prepared by the late Sir Harold Williams."
    1. Swift, Jonathan, 1667–1745—Concordances.
I. Swift, Jonathan, 1667–1745. Poems. II. Title.
III. Series.
PR3726.S45 1972   821'.5   72-4870
ISBN 0-8014-0747-8